RAND McNALLY
WORLD
ATLAS

RAND McNALLY

CONTENTS

USING THE ATLAS .... I·3 – I·4

WORLD PATTERNS .... I·5 – I·16
World Terrain .... I·6 – I·7
World Climate .... I·8 – I·9
World Vegetation .... I·10 – I·11
World Population .... I·12 – I·13
World Environments .... I·14 – I·15
World Time Zones .... I·16

REFERENCE MAPS .... 1 – 128
Map Symbols and Index Map 1
World .... 2 – 3
Europe .... 4 – 5
Scandinavia 6
British Isles 7
Central Europe .... 8 – 9
France and the Alps .... 10 – 11
Spain and Portugal .... 12 – 13
Italy .... 14 – 15
Southeastern Europe .... 16 – 17
Baltic and Moscow Regions .... 18 – 19
Asia .... 20 – 21
Northwest
    Asia .... 22 – 23
Northeast
    Asia .... 24 – 25
China, Japan, and Korea .... 26 – 27
Eastern and Southeastern China .. 28 – 29
Japan .... 30 – 31
Southeastern Asia .... 32 – 33
Myanmar, Thailand, and Indochina 34 – 35
India and Pakistan 36
Southern India and Sri Lanka 37
Northern India and Pakistan .... 38 – 39
Eastern Mediterranean Lands 40
Africa 41
Northern Africa .... 42 – 43
Southern Africa .... 44 – 45
Eastern Africa and Middle East 46
Antarctica 47
Pacific Ocean .... 48 – 49
Australia .... 50 – 51
New Zealand 52
South America 53
Northern South America .... 54 – 55
Southern South America 56
Southeastern Brazil 57
Colombia, Ecuador, Venezuela,
    and Guyana .... 58 – 59
Atlantic Ocean 60

North America 61
Mexico .... 62 – 63
Central America
    and the Caribbean .... 64 – 65
Canada .... 66 – 67
Alberta 68
British Columbia 69
Manitoba 70
New Brunswick, Nova Scotia,
    and Prince Edward Island 71
Newfoundland 72
Ontario 73
Quebec 74
Saskatchewan 75
United States of America .... 76 – 77
Alabama 78
Alaska 79
Arizona 80
Arkansas 81
California 82
Colorado 83
Connecticut 84
Delaware 85
Florida 86
Georgia 87
Hawaii 88
Idaho 89
Illinois 90
Indiana 91
Iowa 92
Kansas 93
Kentucky 94
Louisiana 95
Maine 96
Maryland 97
Massachusetts 98
Michigan 99
Minnesota 100
Mississippi 101
Missouri 102
Montana 103
Nebraska 104
Nevada 105
New Hampshire 106
New Jersey 107
New Mexico 108
New York 109
North Carolina 110
North Dakota 111
Ohio 112
Oklahoma 113
Oregon 114
Pennsylvania 115

Rhode Island 116
South Carolina 117
South Dakota 118
Tennessee 119
Texas 120
Utah 121
Vermont 122
Virginia 123
Washington 124
West Virginia 125
Wisconsin 126
Wyoming 127
North Polar Regions 128

INDEX TO
    REFERENCE MAPS .... 129 – 192

WORLD GEOGRAPHICAL
    TABLES .... 193 – 215
World Political Information ...... 193 – 196
General Information 197
Principal Mountains 198
World Oceans, Seas, Gulfs, Lakes,
    Rivers, and Islands 199
World Populations .... 200 – 215

UNITED STATES
GEOGRAPHICAL
    TABLES .... 216 – 240
United States General Information ... 216

United States Populations
    and Zip Codes .... 217 – 240
Latest 1990 Census Information

Copyright © 1994 by Rand McNally & Company
1995 Revised Printing

All rights reserved. No part of this publication may be
reproduced, stored in a retrieval system, or transmitted,
in any form or by any means – electronic, mechanical,
photocopied, recorded, or other – without the prior written
permission of Rand McNally.

Library of Congress Cataloging-in-Publication Data

Rand McNally and Company.
    World Atlas.
        p.   cm.
    Includes index.
    1. Atlases.   I. Title.
G1021.R21   1991 <G&M>   91-16938
912—dc20   CIP
                                                  MAP

USING
THE ATLAS

Maps and Atlases

Satellite images of the world (figure 1) constantly give us views of the shape and size of the earth. It is hard, therefore, to imagine how difficult it once was to ascertain the look of our planet. Yet from early history we have evidence of humans trying to work out what the world actually looked like.

Twenty-five hundred years ago, on a tiny clay tablet the size of a hand, the Babylonians inscribed the earth as a flat disk (figure 2) with Babylon at the center. The section of the Cantino map of 1502 (figure 3) is an example of a *portolan* chart used to chart the newly discovered Americas. The maps in this atlas show the detail and accuracy that cartographers are now able to achieve.

In 1589 Gerardus Mercator used the word "atlas" to describe a collection of maps. Atlases now bring together not only a variety of maps, but an assortment of tables and other reference material as well. They have become a unique and indispensable reference for graphically defining the world and answering the question, "Where?" With them, routes between places can be traced, trips planned, distances measured, places imagined, and our earth visualized.

FIGURE 1

FIGURE 2

FIGURE 3

Sequence of the Maps

The world is made up of seven major landmasses: the continents of Europe, Asia, Africa, Antarctica, Australia, South America, and North America. The maps in this atlas follow this continental sequence. To allow for the inclusion of detail, each continent is broken down into a series of maps, and this grouping is arranged so that as consecutive pages are turned, a successive part of the continent is shown. Larger-scale maps are used for regions of greater detail or for areas of global significance.

Getting the Information

To realize the potential of an atlas the user must be able to:

1. Find places on the maps
2. Measure distances
3. Determine directions
4. Understand map symbols

Finding Places

One of the most common and important tasks facilitated by an atlas is finding the location of a place in the world. A river's name in a book, a city mentioned in the news, or a vacation spot may prompt your need to know where the place is located. The illustrations and text below explain how to find Yangon (Rangoon), Myanmar (Burma).

Yancheng, China	B9	28
Yandoon, Mya.	F3	34
Yangjiang, China	G9	26
Yangon (Rangoon), Mya.	B2	32
Yangquan, China	D9	26
Yangtze see Chang, stm., China	E10	26
Yangzhou, China	C8	28

FIGURE 4

1. Look up the place-name in the index at the back of the atlas. Yangon, Myanmar can be found on the map on page 32, and it can be located on the map by the letter-number key *B2* (figure 4). If you know the general area in which a place is found, you may turn directly to the appropriate map and use the special marginal index.

2. Turn to the map of Southeastern Asia found on page 32. Note that the letters *A* through *H* and the numbers *1* through *11* appear in the margins of the map.

3. To find Yangon on the map, place your left index finger on *B* and your right index finger on *2*. Move your left finger across the map and your right finger down the map. Your fingers will meet in the area in which Yangon is located (figure 5).

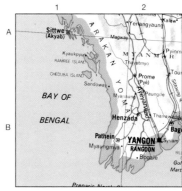

FIGURE 5

Measuring Distances

When planning trips, determining the distance between two places is essential, and an atlas can help in travel preparation. For instance, to determine the approximate distance between Paris and Rouen, France, follow these three steps:

1. Lay a slip of paper on the map on page 10 so that its edge touches the two cities. Adjust the paper so one corner touches Rouen. Mark the paper directly at the spot where Paris is located (figure 6).

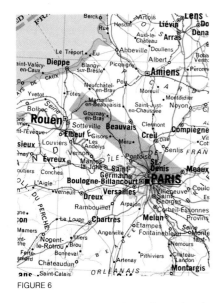

FIGURE 6

2. Place the paper along the scale of miles beneath the map. Position the corner at 0 and line up the edge of the paper along the scale. The pencil mark on the paper indicates Rouen is between 50 and 100 miles from Paris (figure 7).

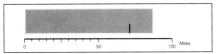

FIGURE 7

3. To find the exact distance, move the paper to the left so that the pencil mark is at 100 on the scale. The corner of the paper stands on the fourth 5-mile unit on the scale. This means that the two towns are 50 plus 20, or 70 miles apart (figure 8).

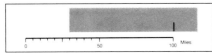

FIGURE 8

Determining Directions

Most of the maps in the atlas are drawn so that when oriented for normal reading, north is at the top of the map, south is at the bottom, west is at the left, and east is at the right. Most maps have a series of lines drawn across them—the lines of *latitude* and *longitude*. Lines of latitude, or *parallels* of latitude, are drawn east and west. Lines of longitude, or *meridians* of longitude, are drawn north and south (figure 9).

Parallels and meridians appear as either curved or straight lines. For example, in the section of the map of Europe (figure 10) the parallels of latitude appear as curved lines. The meridians of longitude are straight lines that come together toward the top of the map. Latitude and longitude lines help locate places on maps. Parallels of latitude are numbered in degrees north and south of the *Equator*. Meridians of longitude are numbered in degrees east and west of a line called the *Prime Meridian*, running through Greenwich, England, near London. Any place on earth can be located by the latitude and longitude lines running through it.

To determine directions or locations on the map, you must use the parallels and meridians. For example, suppose you want to know which is farther north, Bergen, Norway, or Norrköping, Sweden. The map (figure 10) shows that Norrköping is south of the 60° parallel of latitude and Bergen is north of it. Bergen is farther north than Norrköping. By looking at the meridians of longitude, you can determine which city is farther east. Bergen is approximately 5° east of the 0° meridian (Prime Meridian), and Norrköping is more than 15° east of it. Norrköping is farther east than Bergen.

FIGURE 10

Understanding Map Symbols

In a very real sense, the whole map is a symbol, representing the world or a part of it. It is a reduced representation of the earth; each of the world's features—cities, rivers, etc.—is represented on the map by a symbol. Map symbols may take the form of points, such as dots or squares (often used for cities, capital cities, or points of interest), or lines (roads, railroads, rivers). Symbols may also occupy an area, showing extent of coverage (terrain, forests, deserts). They seldom look like the feature they represent and therefore must be identified and interpreted. For instance, the maps in this atlas define political units by a colored line depicting their boundaries. Neither the colors nor the boundary lines are actually found on the surface of the earth, but because countries and states are such important political components of the world, strong symbols are used to represent them. The Map Symbols page in this atlas identifies the symbols used on the maps.

FIGURE 9

WORLD PATTERNS

The five world maps in this section portray the distribution of major natural and human elements that describe the world's fundamental geographic character. The lines and colors show basic patterns caused by the movement and interaction of land, air, water, and human activity.

The world terrain map on pages I·6 and I·7 portrays the surface of the uppermost layer of the earth's crust. The crust, broken into six gigantic and several smaller plates, floats on denser rock. Constant movement of the plates in the geologic past helped create the terrain features we see today. Motion of the plates along with the erosive force of water, wind, and human development continues to reshape the earth's terrain.

The earth's oceans are in constant motion. Water near the surface and in the deeps flows in well established currents that are like rivers within the ocean. The earth's atmosphere is an ocean of gases with currents that span the globe. The sun drives these moving currents of water and air. The average of the widely varying weather phenomena caused by these movements establishes the patterns of global climate shown on pages I·8 and I·9.

Climate is the single most important factor determining where plants can grow. And vegetation is the major factor determining where animals–including humans–can live. The map on pages I·10 and I·11 shows the distribution of vegetation types that might exist if humans did not intervene. Notice how similar the patterns of vegetation and climate are. Tundra vegetation is associated with polar climates. The rain forests of South America, Africa, and Asia grow in hot, wet climates near the Equator. The steppes of Central Asia and the short-grass prairies of North America grow in cool climates with dry summers. The evergreen forests of northern Eurasia and North America coincide with moist climates with cold winters and cool summers.

The population density map on pages I·12 and I·13 indicates that almost all areas of the earth are inhabited by humankind, from the Poles to the Equator. Humanity's densest settlement has been in the most fertile regions of the earth. These areas combine adequate rainfall and growing season with terrain that is neither too rough nor mountainous. A comparison of the terrain and climate maps with the population map shows this relationship. Abundant mineral deposits as well as people's ability to develop natural resources also explain settlement preferences. Densely settled areas in Southwest Asia, Southeast Asia, and China are rural-agricultural populations. In western Europe,

the northeastern United States, and parts of Japan, high-density regions are urban-industrial in character.

The environment map on pages I·14 and I·15 indicates how human habitation has impacted our planet. Compare this map with the vegetation map that shows what the world might be like if humankind had played a less dominant role. Millions of square miles of land that were once forests or grasslands are now plowed fields and pastures. Much of North America, Europe, and Southeast Asia has been almost completely remade by farmers. Though the urban areas occupy a small percentage of the land area in the world, their impact on the environment is extensive.

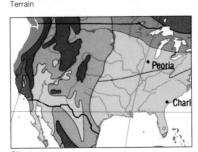
Terrain

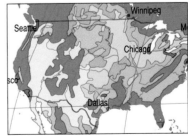
Population

Climate

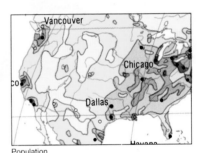
Environments

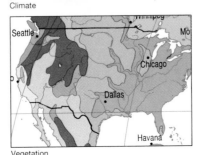
Vegetation

The distribution, relationship, and interaction of the major elements shown on the maps establish fundamental world patterns that distinguish one area from another. Upon the differences and similarities indicated by these patterns the world builds its intriguing variety of cultures and histories.

WORLD TERRAIN

Terrain

Land Elevations in Profile

Ocean Depths in Profile

Elevations and depressions

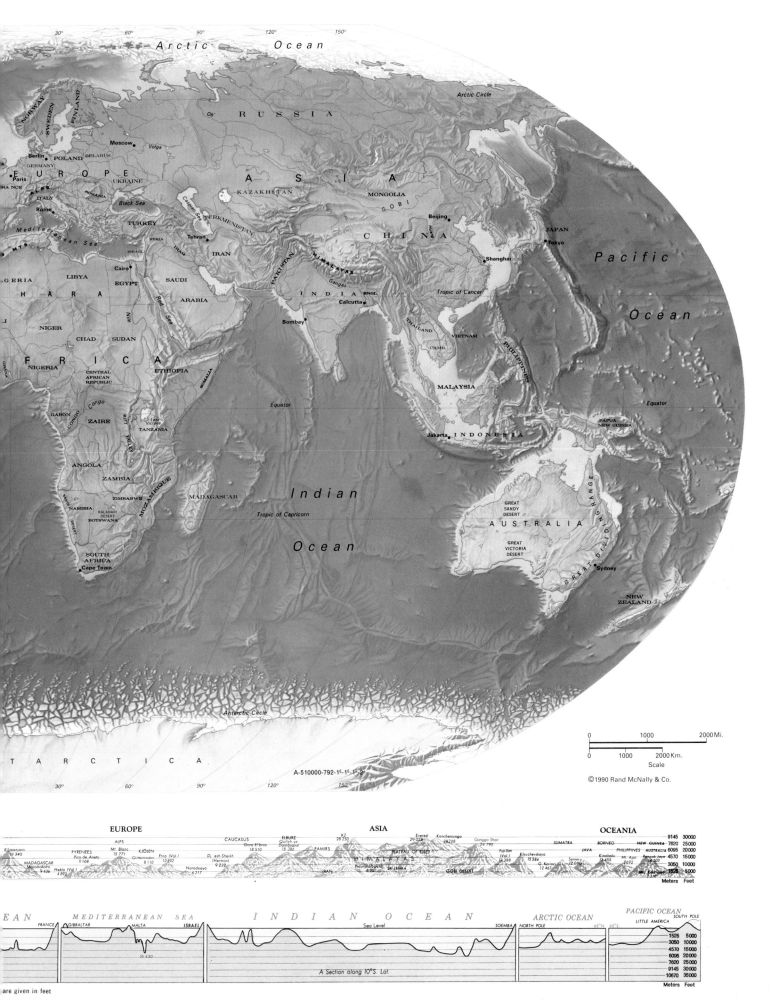

Arctic Ocean

30° 60° 90° 120° 150°

Arctic Circle

NORWAY SWEDEN FINLAND
Moscow *R U S S I A*
Volga Ob'
Berlin POLAND BELARUS
GERMANY *A S I A*
E U R O P E UKRAINE KAZAKHSTAN MONGOLIA
FRANCE ALPS ROMANIA GOBI
ITALY Black Sea TURKMENISTAN
Rome Caspian Sea CHINA Beijing JAPAN
Mediterranean Sea TURKEY SYRIA IRAQ Tehran IRAN PAKISTAN Tokyo
ISRAEL HIMALAYAS Shanghai *Pacific*
Cairo SAUDI Ganges BANG. Tropic of Cancer *Ocean*
ALGERIA LIBYA EGYPT ARABIA INDIA Calcutta
SAHARA Red Sea Bombay THAILAND VIETNAM PHILIPPINES
NIGER CHAD SUDAN CAMB.
AFRICA NIGERIA ETHIOPIA MALAYSIA
GHANA CENTRAL AFRICAN REPUBLIC SOMALIA Equator Equator
GABON Congo Lake Victoria PAPUA NEW GUINEA
Congo ZAIRE TANZANIA Jakarta I N D O N E S I A
ANGOLA RIFT VALLEY *Indian*
ZAMBIA GREAT SANDY DESERT
NAMIBIA ZIMBABWE MADAGASCAR Tropic of Capricorn *Ocean*
KALAHARI DESERT MOZAMBIQUE AUSTRALIA GREAT DIVIDING RANGE
BOTSWANA GREAT VICTORIA DESERT
SOUTH AFRICA *Ocean* Sydney
Cape Town NEW ZEALAND

Antarctic Circle

ANTARCTICA

A-510000-792-1ᴱ-1ᴱ-1ᴱ-2
©1990 Rand McNally & Co.

0   1000   2000 Mi.
0   1000   2000 Km.
Scale

30° 60° 90° 120° 150°

EUROPE   ASIA   OCEANIA

ALPS CAUCASUS ELBURZ K2 28,250 Everest Kanchenjunga 9145 30000
Mt. Blanc Gora El'brus Qolleh-ye 29,028 28,208 Gongga Shan SUMATRA NEW GUINEA 7620 25000
PYRENEES 15,771 18,510 Damāvand PAMIRS 24,790 BORNEO AUSTRALIA 6095 20000
Kilimanjaro Pico de Aneto KJØLEN Glittertinden Etna (Vol.) Dj. esh-Sheikh JAVA PHILIPPINES Puncak Jaya 4570 15000
19,340 11,168 8110 10,902 (Hermon) Fuji-San Klyuchevskaya 16,503 3050 10000
MADAGASCAR Hekla (Vol.) Narodnaya 9232 12,388 15,584 Semeru Mt. Apo Kinabalu 1525 5000
Maromokotro 4,892 6,217 IRAN Pidurutalagala PLATEAU OF TIBET 12,060 9692 13,455 Mt. Kosciusko Meters Feet
9,436 8,297 SRI LANKA GOBI DESERT G. Kerinci 7,310
HIMALAYAS 12,467

OCEAN M E D I T E R R A N E A N   S E A I N D I A N   O C E A N ARCTIC OCEAN PACIFIC OCEAN SOUTH POLE
FRANCE GIBRALTAR MALTA ISRAEL SOEMBA NORTH POLE LITTLE AMERICA 1525 5000
Sea Level 65°N 65°S 3050 10000
16,420 4570 15000
6095 20000
7620 25000
A Section along 10°S. Lat. 9145 30000
10670 35000
Meters Feet

are given in feet

I·7

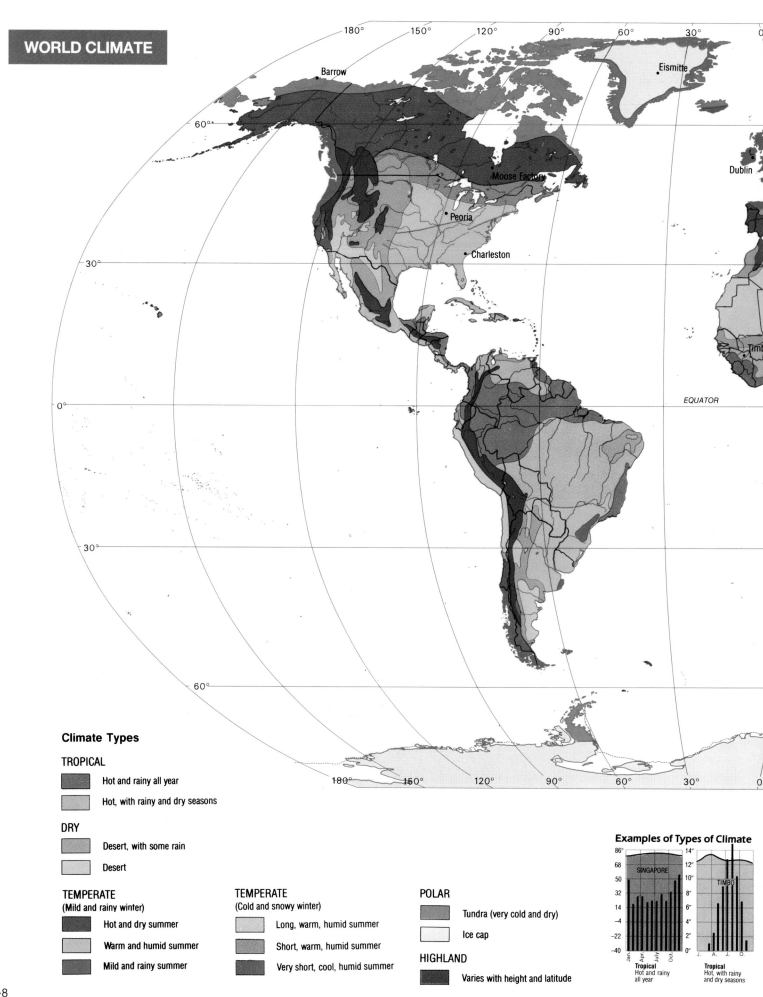

WORLD CLIMATE

Climate Types

TROPICAL

Hot and rainy all year

Hot, with rainy and dry seasons

DRY

Desert, with some rain

Desert

TEMPERATE
(Mild and rainy winter)

Hot and dry summer

Warm and humid summer

Mild and rainy summer

TEMPERATE
(Cold and snowy winter)

Long, warm, humid summer

Short, warm, humid summer

Very short, cool, humid summer

POLAR

Tundra (very cold and dry)

Ice cap

HIGHLAND

Varies with height and latitude

Examples of Types of Climate

SINGAPORE

TIMBO

Tropical
Hot and rainy
all year

Tropical
Hot, with rainy
and dry seasons

I·8

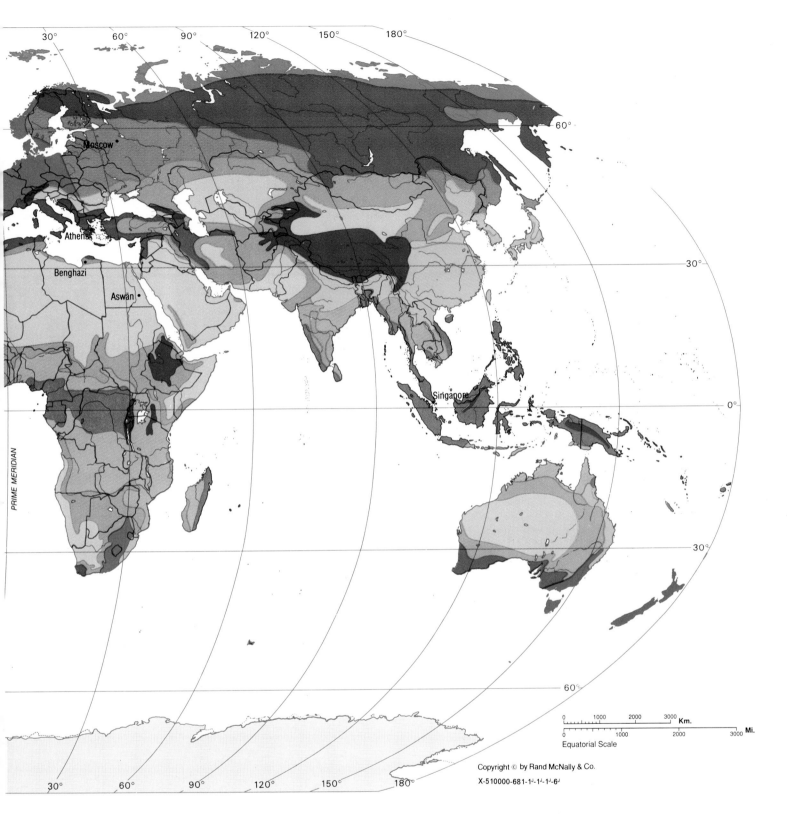

30° 60° 90° 120° 150° 180°

60°

Moscow

Athens

30°

Benghazi

Aswān

PRIME MERIDIAN

0°

Singapore

30°

60°

0 1000 2000 3000 Km.

0 1000 2000 3000 Mi.

Equatorial Scale

Copyright © by Rand McNally & Co.

X-510000-681-1ᴶ-1ᴶ-1ᴶ-6ᴶ

30° 60° 90° 120° 150° 180°

The curved lines on the graphs below show fahrenheit temperatures. The vertical bars show rainfall in inches.

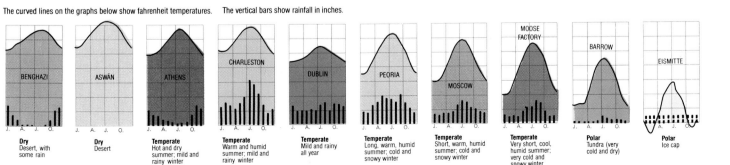

BENGHAZI
J. A. J. O.
Dry
Desert, with
some rain

ASWĀN
J. A. J. O.
Dry
Desert

ATHENS
J. A. J. O.
Temperate
Hot and dry
summer; mild and
rainy winter

CHARLESTON
J. A. J. O.
Temperate
Warm and humid
summer; mild and
rainy winter

DUBLIN
J. A. J. O.
Temperate
Mild and rainy
all year

PEORIA
J. A. J. O.
Temperate
Long, warm, humid
summer; cold and
snowy winter

MOSCOW
J. A. J. O.
Temperate
Short, warm, humid
summer; cold and
snowy winter

MOOSE FACTORY
J. A. J. O.
Temperate
Very short, cool,
humid summer;
very cold and
snowy winter

BARROW
J. A. J. O.
Polar
Tundra (very
cold and dry)

EISMITTE
J. A. J. O.
Polar
Ice cap

I·9

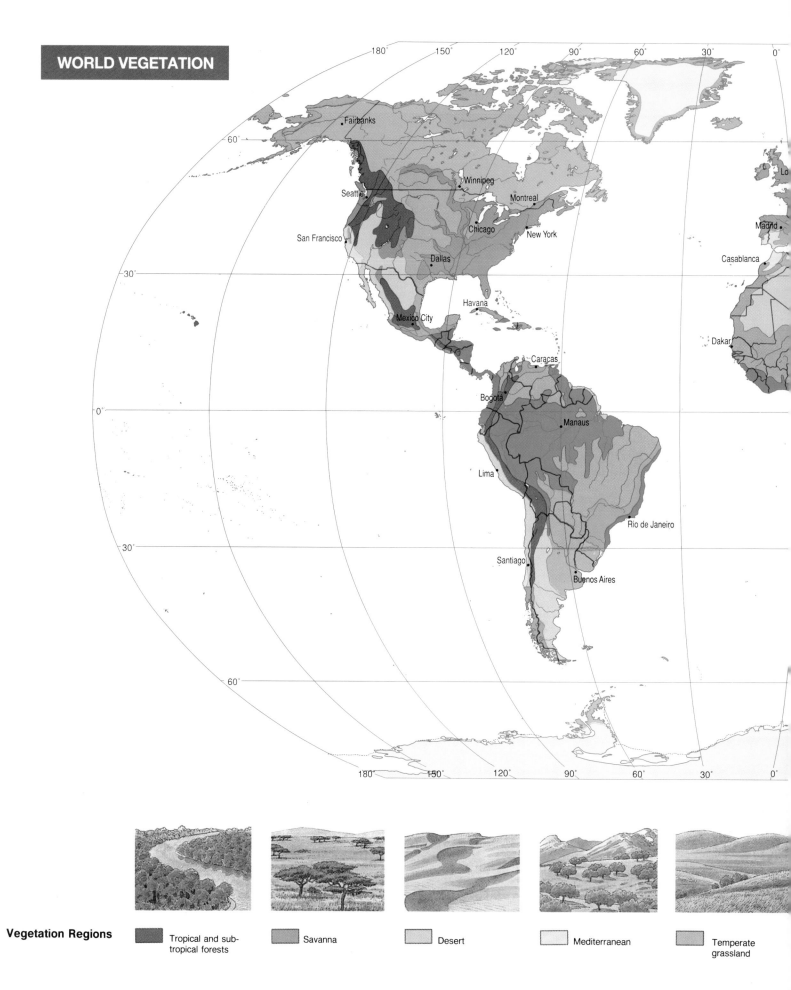

Vegetation Regions

Tropical and sub-tropical forests

Savanna

Desert

Mediterranean

Temperate grassland

Stockholm

Moscow · Novosibirsk

Berlin ·
Volgograd

Tashkent
Rome ·
Beijing

Tehrân
Damascus ·
Tōkyô

Cairo ·
30°
Chongqing
Shanghai
New Delhi

Calcutta
Hong Kong
Bombay ·

Khartoum
Bangkok ·

Lagos
0°
Nairobi ·

Kinshasa ·
Jakarta ·

Darwin ·

Johannesburg ·
30°
Perth
Cape Town ·
Sydney

60°

| 0 | 1000 | 2000 | 3000 | Km. |

| 0 | 1000 | 2000 | 3000 | Mi. |

Equatorial Scale

Copyright © 1991 by Rand McNally & Co.

Temperate forest   Taiga (northern forests)   Tundra (lichen and moss)   Mountain   Polar and high mountain

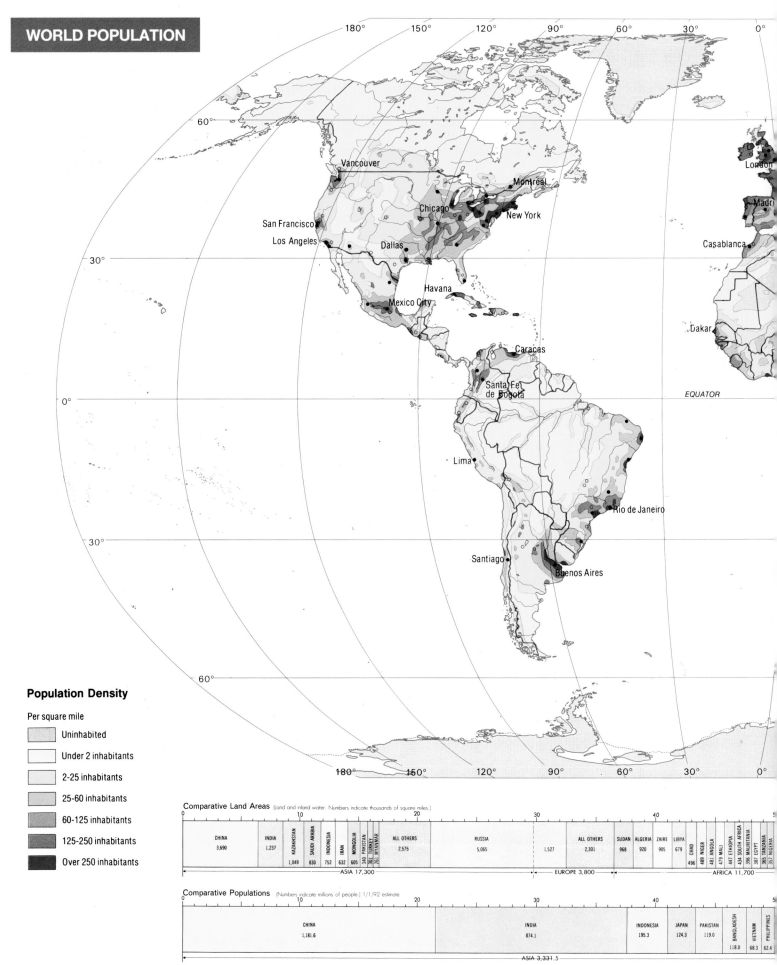

180° 150° 120° 90° 60° 30° 0°

60°

Vancouver
Montréal
Chicago
New York
San Francisco
Los Angeles
Dallas
30°

London
Madrid
Casablanca

Havana
Mexico City

Dakar

0° EQUATOR

Caracas

Santa Fe
de Bogota

Lima

Rio de Janeiro

30°

Santiago
Buenos Aires

60°

180° 150° 120° 90° 60° 30° 0°

Population Density

Per square mile

	Uninhabited
	Under 2 inhabitants
	2-25 inhabitants
	25-60 inhabitants
	60-125 inhabitants
	125-250 inhabitants
	Over 250 inhabitants

Comparative Land Areas (Land and inland water. Numbers indicate thousands of square miles.)

0 10 20 30 40 5

CHINA 3,690	INDIA 1,237	KAZAKHSTAN 1,049	SAUDI ARABIA 830	INDONESIA 752	IRAN 632	MONGOLIA 605	PAKISTAN 340	TURKEY 301	MYANMAR 261	ALL OTHERS 2,575	RUSSIA 5,065	1,527	ALL OTHERS 2,301	SUDAN 968	ALGERIA 920	ZAIRE 905	LIBYA 679	CHAD 496	NIGER 489	ANGOLA 481	MALI 479	ETHIOPIA 447	SOUTH AFRICA 434	MAURITANIA 396	EGYPT 387	TANZANIA 365	NIGERIA 357

◄———— ASIA 17,300 ————► ◄—— EUROPE 3,800 ——► ◄—— AFRICA 11,700

Comparative Populations (Numbers indicate millions of people.) 1/1/92 estimate

0 10 20 30 40 5

CHINA 1,181.6	INDIA 874.1	INDONESIA 195.3	JAPAN 124.3	PAKISTAN 119.0	BANGLADESH 118.0	VIETNAM 68.3	PHILIPPINES 62.4

◄———— ASIA 3,331.5 ————►

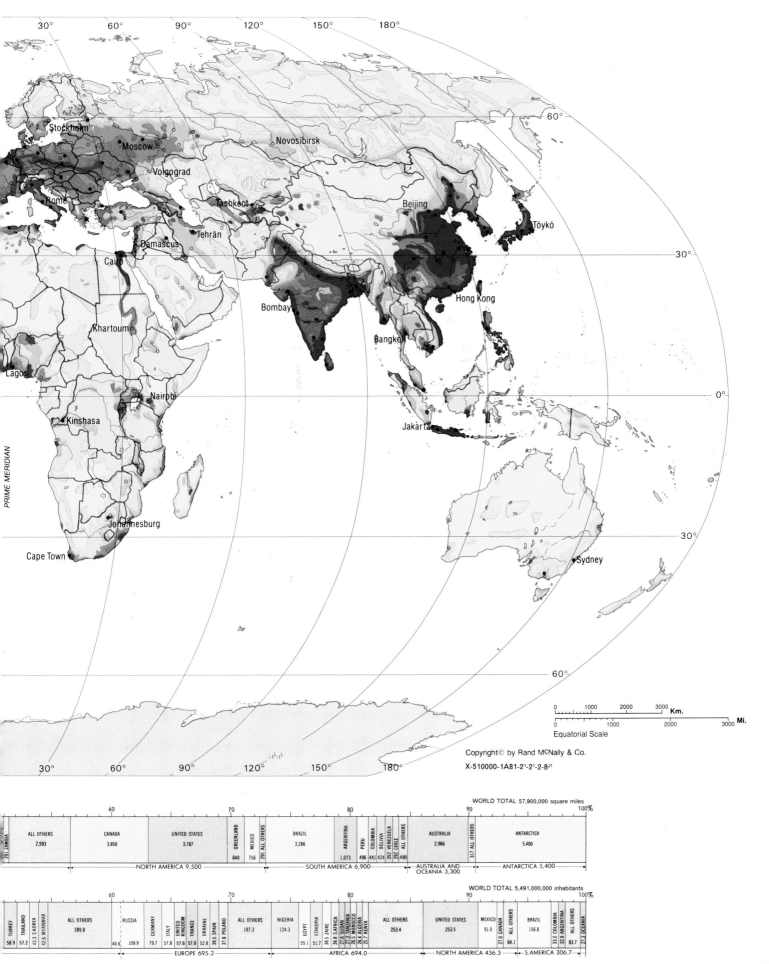

WORLD ENVIRONMENTS

Fairbanks
Seattle
Winnipeg
Montreal
Chicago
New York
San Francisco
Dallas
Havana
Mexico City
Caracas
Manaus
Lima
Rio de Janeiro
Santiago
Buenos Aires
Casablanca
Dakar

Environments   Urban   Cropland   Cropland and Woodland   Cropland and Grazing Land   Grassland, Grazing Land

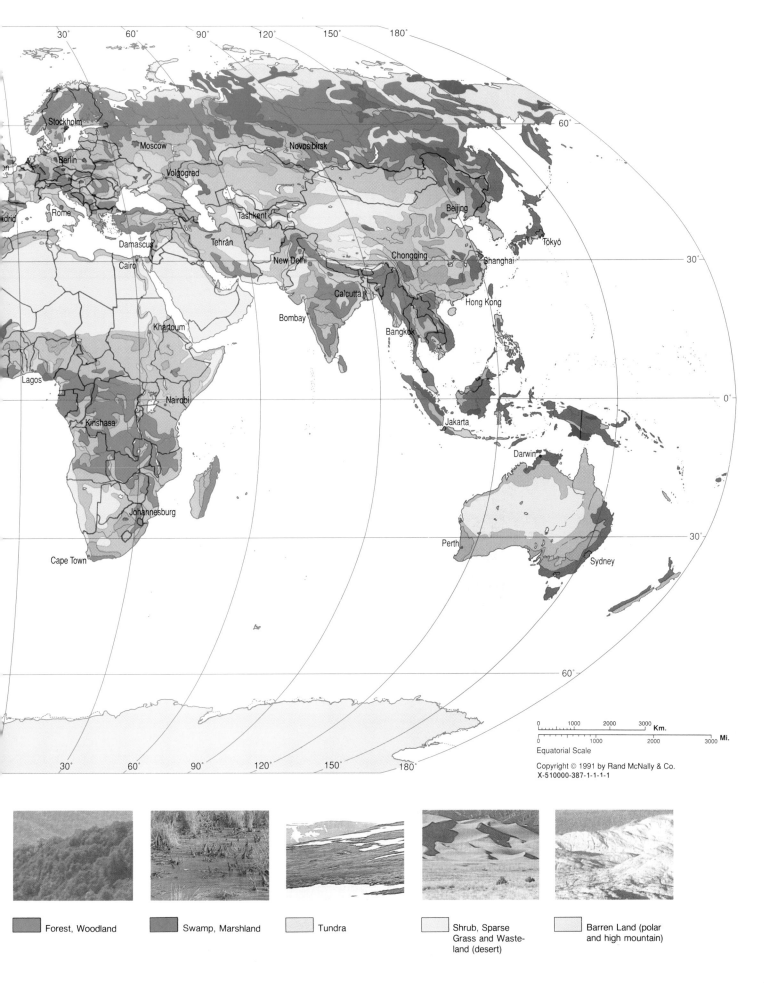

30° 60° 90° 120° 150° 180°

60°

Stockholm
Moscow
Berlin
Novosibirsk
Volgograd
Tashkent
Beijing
Rome
Madrid
Damascus
Tehrān
Chongqing
Tōkyō
Cairo
New Delhi
Shanghai
Calcutta
Hong Kong
Khartoum
Bombay
Bangkok
Lagos
Nairobi
Kinshasa
Jakarta
Darwin
Johannesburg
Perth
Sydney
Cape Town

60°

30°

0°

30°

60°

| 0 | 1000 | 2000 | 3000 | **Km.** |

| 0 | 1000 | 2000 | 3000 | **Mi.** |

Equatorial Scale

Copyright © 1991 by Rand McNally & Co.
X-510000-387-1-1-1-1

30° 60° 90° 120° 150° 180°

Forest, Woodland   Swamp, Marshland   Tundra   Shrub, Sparse Grass and Wasteland (desert)   Barren Land (polar and high mountain)

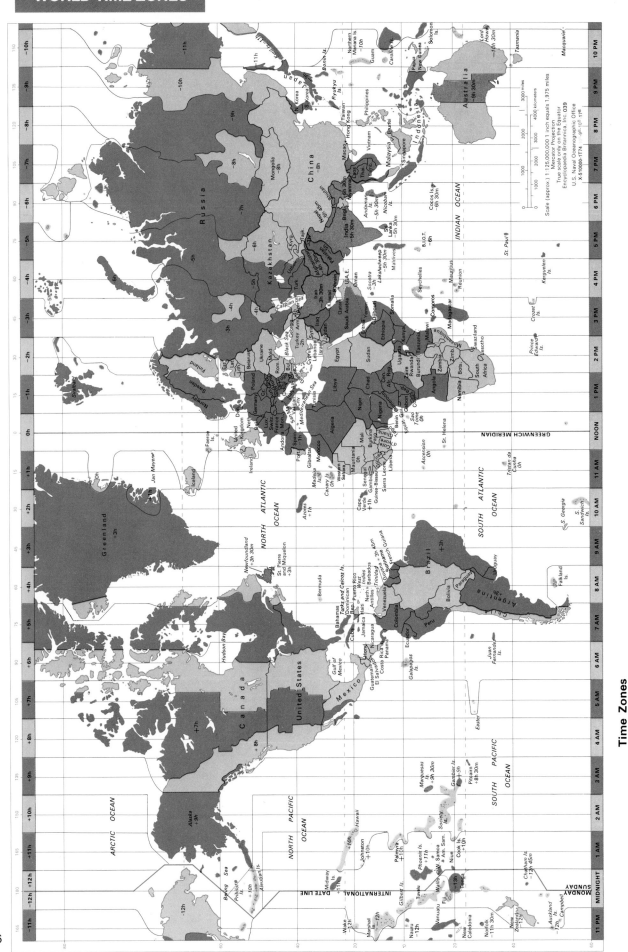

The standard time zone system, fixed by international agreement and by law in each country, is based on a theoretical division of the globe into 24 zones of 15° longitude each. The mid-meridian of each zone fixes the hour for the entire zone. The zero time zone extends 7½° east and 7½° west of the Greenwich meridian, 0° longitude. Since the earth rotates toward the east, time zones to the west of Greenwich are earlier, to the east, later.

Plus and minus hours at the top of the map are added to or subtracted from local time to find Greenwich time. Local standard time can be determined for any area in the world by adding one hour for each time zone counted in an easterly direction from

one's own, or by subtracting one hour for each zone counted in a westerly direction. To separate one day from the next, the 180th meridian has been designated as the international date line. On both sides of the line the time of day is the same, but west of the line it is one day later than it is to the east. Countries that adhere to the international zone system adopt the zone applicable to their location. Some countries, however, establish time zones based on political boundaries, or adopt the time zone of a neighboring unit. For all or part of the year some countries also advance their time by one hour, thereby utilizing more daylight hours each day.

Time Zones

Standard time zone of even-numbered hours from Greenwich time

Standard time zone of odd-numbered hours from Greenwich time

Time varies from the standard time zone by half an hour

Time varies from the standard time zone by other than half an hour

h m hours, minutes

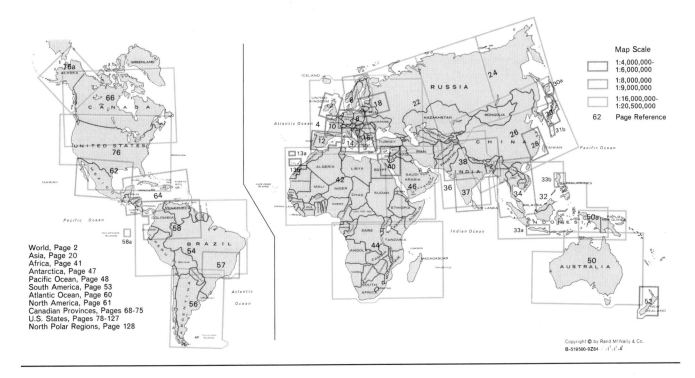

Map Scale

▭	1:4,000,000- 1:6,000,000
▭	1:8,000,000 1:9,000,000
▭	1:16,000,000- 1:20,500,000
62	Page Reference

World, Page 2
Asia, Page 20
Africa, Page 41
Antarctica, Page 47
Pacific Ocean, Page 48
South America, Page 53
Atlantic Ocean, Page 60
North America, Page 61
Canadian Provinces, Pages 68-75
U.S. States, Pages 78-127
North Polar Regions, Page 128

World Maps Symbols

Inhabited Localities

The size of type indicates the relative economic and political importance of the locality

Écommoy	Lisieux	**Rouen**
Trouville	**Orléans**	**PARIS**
Bi'r Safâjah °	Oasis	

Alternate Names

MOSKVA
MOSCOW — English or second official language names are shown in reduced size lettering

Basel
Bâle

Volgograd
(Stalingrad) — Historical or other alternates in the local language are shown in parentheses

▭ Urban Area (Area of continuous industrial, commercial, and residential development)

Capitals of Political Units

BUDAPEST Independent Nation

Cayenne Dependency (Colony, protectorate, etc.)

Recife State, Province, County, Oblast, etc.

Political Boundaries

International (First-order political unit)

▬▬▬	Demarcated and Undemarcated
– · – · –	Disputed de jure
▬▬▬	Indefinite or Undefined
– – – – –	Demarcation Line

Internal

▬▬▬	State, Province, etc. (Second-order political unit)
MURCIA	Historical Region (No boundaries indicated)
GALAPAGOS (Ecuador)	Administering Country

Transportation

▬▬▬	Primary Road
───	Secondary Road
- - - -	Minor Road, Trail
─┼─┼─	Railway
Canal du Midi	Navigable Canal
══╪══	Bridge
─┤- - -├─	Tunnel
TO MALMÖ	Ferry

Hydrographic Features

	Shoreline
	Undefined or Fluctuating Shoreline
Amur	River, Stream
	Intermittent Stream
	Rapids, Falls
	Irrigation or Drainage Canal
	Reef
The Everglades	Swamp
RIMO GLACIER	Glacier
L. Victoria	Lake, Reservoir
Tuz Gölü	Salt Lake
	Intermittent Lake, Reservoir
	Dry Lake Bed
(395)	Lake Surface Elevation

Topographic Features

Matterhorn △ 4478	Elevation Above Sea Level
76 ▽	Elevation Below Sea Level
Mount Cook ▲ 3764	Highest Elevation in Country
133 ▼	Lowest Elevation in Country
Khyber Pass ≍ 1067	Mountain Pass

Elevations are given in meters.
The highest and lowest elevations in a continent are underlined

	Sand Area
	Lava
	Salt Flat

State, Province Maps Symbols

✪	Capital
⊙	County Seat
▲	Military Installation
△	Point of Interest
+	Mountain Peak

– · – · –	International Boundary
– ·· – ·· –	State, Province Boundary
– – – –	County Boundary
───	Railroad
───	Road
	Urban Area

Europe

ALBANIA................G11
Amsterdam, 6,965,000
  ('89) (1,860,000★) ....E 8
ANDORRA................G 8
Antwerpen, 497,748 ('87)
  (1,100,000★) ....E 8
Athínai (Athens), 885,737
  ('81) (3,027,331★) ...H12
AUSTRIA................F10
Barcelona, 1,714,355 ('88)
  (4,040,000★) ....G 8
BELARUS................E13
Belfast, 303,800 ('87)
  (685,000★) ....E 8
BELGIUM................E 8
Beograd (Belgrade),
  1,130,000 ('87)
  (1,400,000★) G12
Berlin, 3,352,848 ('89)
  (3,825,000★) E10
Bern, 134,393 ('90)
  (298,800★) ....F 9
Birmingham, 1,013,995
  ('81) (2,675,000★) ....E 7
Bonn, 282,190 ('89)
  (570,000★) ....E 9
BOSNIA AND
  HERZEGOVINA........G11
Bratislava, 444,482
  ('91)..................F11
Bremen, 535,058 ('89)
  (800,000★) ....E 9
Bruxelles, 136,920 ('87)
  (2,385,000★) ....E 8
Bucureşti, 1,989,823 ('86)
  (2,275,000★) G13
Budapest, 2,016,132 ('90)
  (2,565,000★) F11
BULGARIA................G12
Cardiff, 262,313 ('81)
  (625,000★) ....E 7
CROATIA................F11
CZECH REPUBLIC.....F11
DENMARK................D 9
Dnipropetrovsk, 1,179,000
  ('89) (1,600,000★) F14
Donets'k, 1,110,000 ('89)
  (2,200,000★) F15
Dresden, 518,057 ('89)
  (670,000★) E10
Dublin, 502,749 ('86)
  (1,140,000★) ....E 6
Düsseldorf, 569,641 ('89)
  (1,190,000★) ....E 9
Edinburgh, 433,200 ('89)
  (630,000★) ....D 7
Essen, 620,594 ('89)
  (4,950,000★) ....E 9
ESTONIA................D12
FAEROE ISLANDS.......C 6
FINLAND................C13
Firenze, 425,835 ('87)
  (640,000★) G10
FRANCE................F 8
Frankfurt, 625,258 ('89)
  (1,855,000★) ....E 9
Gdańsk, 461,500 ('89)
  (909,000★) E11
Genève (Geneva), 165,404
  ('90) (460,000★) ....F 9
Genova, 727,427 ('87)
  (805,000★) ....G 9
GERMANY................E10
Gibraltar, 30,077 ('88).H 6
Glasgow, 695,630 ('89)
  (1,800,000★) ....D 7
GREECE................H12
GUERNSEY................F 7
Hamburg, 1,603,070 ('89)
  (2,225,000★) ....E 9
Helsinki, 490,034 ('88)
  (1,040,000★) C12
HUNGARY................F11
ICELAND................B 4
IRELAND................E 6
ISLE OF MAN..........E 7
İstanbul, 6,748,435 ('90)
  (7,000,000★) G13
ITALY................G10
JERSEY................F 7
Katowice, 365,800 ('89)
  (2,778,000★) E11
Kazan', 1,094,000 ('89)
  (1,140,000★) D17
Kharkiv, 1,611,000 ('89)
  (1,940,000★) F15
København, 466,723 ('90)
  (1,685,000★) D10
Köln, 937,482 ('89)
  (1,760,000★) ....E 9
Kraków, 743,700 ('89)
  (828,000★) E11
Kyyiv (Kiev), 2,587,000
  ('89) (2,900,000★) E14
LATVIA................D12
Leipzig, 545,307 ('89)
  (700,000★) E10
Leningrad see Sankt-
  Peterburg...............D14
LIECHTENSTEIN........F 9
Ljubljana, 233,200 ('87)
  (316,607▲) F10
Lisboa, 807,167 ('81)
  (2,250,000★) ....H 6

★ Population of metropolitan
area, including suburbs.

4

LITHUANIA................D12
Liverpool, 538,809 ('81)
  (1,525,000★) ....E 7
Łódź, 851,500 ('89)
  (1,061,000★) E11
London, 6,574,009 ('81)
  (11,100,000★) ....E 7
LUXEMBOURG.............F 9
Lyon, 413,095 ('82)
  (1,275,000★) ....F 8
MACEDONIA................G12
Madrid, 3,102,846 ('88)
  (4,650,000★) ....G 7
MALTA........................H10
Manchester, 437,612 ('81)
  (2,775,000★) ....E 7
Marseille, 874,436 ('82)
  (1,225,000★) ....G 9
Milano, 1,495,260 ('87)
  (3,750,000★) ....F 9
Minsk, 1,589,000 ('89)
  (1,650,000★) E13
MOLDOVA....................F13
MONACO.....................G 9
Moskva (Moscow),
  8,769,000 ('89)
  (13,100,000★) D15
München, 1,211,617 ('89)
  (1,955,000★) F10
Napoli, 1,204,211 ('87)
  (2,875,000★) G10
NETHERLANDS............E 9
Nižnij Novgorod (Gor'kij),
  1,438,000 ('89)
  (2,025,000★) D16
NORWAY......................C 9
Nürnberg, 480,078 ('89)
  (1,030,000★) F10
Odesa, 1,115,000 ('89)
  (1,185,000★) F14
Oslo, 452,415 ('87)
  (720,000★) D10
Paris, 2,078,900 ('87)
  (9,775,000★) ....F 8
POLAND......................E11
Porto, 327,368 ('81)
  (1,225,000★) ....G 6
PORTUGAL..................G 6
Praha, 1,215,656 ('90)
  (1,325,000★) E10
Reykjavík, 93,425 ('87)
  (137,941★) ....C 3
Rīga, 915,000 ('89)
  (1,005,000★) D12
Roma, 2,815,457 ('87)
  (3,175,000★) G10
ROMANIA....................F12
Rostov-na-Donu,
  1,020,000 ('89)
  (1,165,000★) F15
Rotterdam, 576,300 ('89)
  (1,110,000★) ....E 8
RUSSIA.......................D16
Samara, 1,257,000 ('89)
  (1,505,000★) E18
Sankt-Peterburg,
  4,456,000 ('89)
  (5,825,000★) D14
SAN MARINO..............G10
Sarajevo, 341,200 ('87)
  (479,688★) G11
Saratov, 905,000 ('89)
  (1,155,000★) E17
Sevilla, 663,132 ('88)
  (945,000★) ....H 6
's-Gravenhage (The
  Hague), 443,900 ('89)
  (770,000★) ....E 8
Skopje, 444,900 ('87)
  (547,214★) G12
SLOVAKIA...................F11
SLOVENIA...................F10
Sofija, 1,119,152 ('86)
  (1,205,000★) G12
SPAIN..........................H 7
Stockholm, 672,187 ('90)
  (1,449,972★) D11
SWEDEN......................C11
SWITZERLAND............F 9
Tallinn, 482,000 ('89)..D12
Thessaloníki, 406,413 ('81)
  (706,180★) G12
Tiranë, 255,700 ('87)...G11
Torino, 1,035,565 ('87)
  (1,550,000★) ....F 9
UKRAINE.....................F14
UNITED KINGDOM.....E 7
Valencia, 743,933 ('88)
  (1,270,000★) ....H 7
Valletta, 9,210 ('89)
  (215,000★) H10
Vilnius, 582,000 ('89)...E12
Warszawa, 1,651,200
  ('89) (2,323,000★) ... E12
Wien (Vienna), 1,482,800
  ('88) (1,875,000★) F11
YUGOSLAVIA...............F11
Zagreb, 697,925 ('87)..F11
Zürich, 342,861 ('90)
  (860,000★) ....F 9

Scandinavia

Denmark
1990 ESTIMATE
Ålborg, 114,000
 (155,019▲) . . . . H 7
Århus, 202,300
 (261,437▲) . . . . H 8
Copenhagen *see*
Købenavn . . . . I 9
Købenavn (Copenhagen),
 466,723
 (1,685,000▲) . . . . . . I 9
Odense, 140,100
 (176,133▲) . . . . I 8

Finland
1988 ESTIMATE
Helsinki (Helsingfors),
 490,034
 (1,040,000★) F15
Lahti, 74,300
 (108,000★) F15
Oulu, 98,582
 (121,000★) D15
Tampere, 170,533
 (241,000★) F14
Turku (Åbo), 160,456
 (228,000★) F14

Norway
1987 ESTIMATE
Bergen, 209,320
 (239,000★) . . . . F 5
Hammerfest,
 7,208('83) A14
Oslo, 452,415
 (720,000★) . . . . G 8
Stavanger, 94,200
 (132,000★)('85) . . . G 5
Trondheim, 135,010 . . E 8

Sweden
1990 ESTIMATE
Göteborg (Gothenburg),
 431,840 (710,894★) H 8
Helsingborg, 108,359 H 9
Jönköping, 110,860 . . H10
Linköping, 120,562 . . G10

Malmö, 232,908
 (445,000★) . . . . I 9
Norrköping, 119,921 G11
Örebro, 120,353 . . . . G10
Stockholm, 672,187
 (1,449,972★) G12
Uppsala, 164,754 . . . . G11
Västerås, 118,386 . . . G11

★ Population of metropolitan area, including suburbs.
▲ Population of entire district, including rural area.

6

British Isles

Ireland
1986 CENSUS

Cork, 133,271
(173,694★) . . . . J 4
Dublin (Baile Átha Cliath),
502,749
(1,140,000★) . . . . . . H 6
Galway, 47,104 . . . . . H 3
Limerick, 56,279
(76,557★) . . . . I 4
Waterford, 39,529
(41,054★) . . . . I 5

Isle of Man
1986 CENSUS

Douglas, 20,368
(28,500★) . . . . . . G 8

United Kingdom

England
1981 CENSUS

Birmingham, 1,013,995
(2,675,000★) I11
Blackpool, 146,297
(280,000★) . . . . . H 9
Bournemouth, 142,829
(315,000★) K11
Bradford, 293,336 . . H11
Brighton, 134,581
(420,000★) K12
Bristol, 413,861
(630,000★) J10
Coventry, 318,718
(645,000★) I11
Derby, 218,026
(275,000★) I11
Kingston upon Hull,
322,144 (350,000★) H12
Leeds, 445,242
(1,540,000★) H11
Leicester, 324,394
(495,000★) I11
Liverpool, 538,809
(1,525,000★) H10
London, 6,574,009
(11,100,000★) . . . J12
Manchester, 437,612
(2,775,000★) H10
Newcastle upon Tyne,
199,064
(1,300,000★) G11
Nottingham, 273,300
(655,000★) I11
Oxford, 113,847
(230,000★) J11
Plymouth, 238,583
(290,000★) . . . . . K 8
Portsmouth, 174,218
(485,000★) K11
Preston, 166,675
(250,000★) H10
Reading, 194,727
(200,000★) J12
Sheffield, 470,685
(710,000★) H11
Southampton, 211,321
(415,000★) K11
Southend-on-Sea,
155,720 . . . . J13
Stoke-on-Trent, 272,446
(440,000★) H10
Sunderland, 195,064 G11
Teesside, 158,516
(580,000★) G11
Wolverhampton,
263,501 . . . . I10

Northern Ireland
1987 ESTIMATE

Bangor, 70,700 . . . . G 7
Belfast, 303,800
(685,000★) . . . . . G 7
Londonderry, 97,500
(97,200★) . . . . . G 5
Newtownabbey,
72,300 . . . . G 7

Scotland
1989 ESTIMATE

Aberdeen, 210,700 . . D10
Dundee, 172,540 . . E 9
Edinburgh, 433,200
(630,000★) . . . . . F 9
Glasgow, 695,630
(1,800,000★) . . . . F 8
Greenock, 58,436
(101,000★)('81) . . F 8
Inverness, 38,204('81) D 9
Paisley, 84,330('81) . F 8

Wales
1981 CENSUS

Cardiff, 262,313
(625,000★) . . . . . J 9
Newport, 115,896
(310,000★) . . . . . J 9
Swansea, 172,433
(275,000★) . . . . . J 9

★ Population of metropolitan
area, including suburbs.

7

Central Europe

Austria
1981 CENSUS

Graz, 243,166
  (325,000★)........H15
Innsbruck, 117,287
  (185,000★)........H11
Linz, 199,910
  (335,000★)........G14
Salzburg, 139,426
  (220,000★)........H13
Villach, 52,692
  (65,000★)........I13
Vienna see Wien....G16
Wien (Vienna), 1,482,800
  (1,875,000★)('88).G16

Belgium
1987 ESTIMATE

Antwerpen (Antwerp),
  479,748
  (1,100,000★)......D 4
Brugge, 117,755
  (223,000★)......D 3
Bruxelles (Brussel),
  136,920
  (2,385,000★)......E 4
Charleroi, 209,395
  (480,000★)......E 4
Gent (Gand), 233,856
  (465,000★)......D 3
Hasselt, 65,563
  (290,000★)......E 5
Liège, 200,891
  (750,000★)......E 5
Mons, 89,697
  (242,000★)......E 3

Czech Republic
1990 ESTIMATE

Brno, 392,285
  (450,000★)......F16
Hradec Králové, 101,302
  (113,000★)......E15
Liberec, 104,256
  (175,000★)......E15
Olomouc, 107,044
  (126,000★)......F17
Ostrava, 331,557
  (760,000★)......F18
Plzeň, 175,038
  (210,000★)......F13
Praha (Prague), 1,215,656
  (1,325,000★)......E14
Ústí nad Labem, 106,499
  (115,000★)......E14

Germany
1989 ESTIMATE

Aachen, 233,255
  (535,000★)........E 6
Augsburg, 247,731
  (405,000★)........G10
Berlin, 3,352,848
  (3,825,000★)......C13
Bielefeld, 311,946
  (515,000★)........C 8
Bochum, 389,087....D 7
Bonn, 282,190
  (570,000★)........E 7
Braunschweig, 253,794
  (330,000★)........C10
Bremen, 535,058
  (800,000★)........B 8
Bremerhaven, 126,934
  (190,000★)........B 8
Chemnitz, 311,765
  (450,000★)........E12
Cologne see Köln..E 6
Dortmund, 587,328..D 7
Dresden, 518,057
  (670,000★)........D13
Duisburg, 527,447..D 6
Düsseldorf, 569,641
  (1,190,000★)......D 6
Erfurt, 220,016
  (425,000★)......E11
Essen, 620,594
  (4,950,000★)......D 7
Frankfurt am Main,
  625,258
  (1,855,000★)......E 8
Gelsenkirchen,
  287,255........D 7
Hagen, 210,640....D 7
Halle, 236,044
  (475,000★)........D11
Hamburg, 1,603,070
  (2,225,000★)......B 9
Hannover, 498,495
  (1,000,000★)......C 9
Karlsruhe, 265,100
  (485,000★)........F 8
Kiel, 240,675
  (335,000★)........A10
Köln (Cologne), 937,482
  (1,760,000★)......E 6
Leipzig, 545,307
  (700,000★)........D12
Lübeck, 210,681
  (260,000★)........B10
Magdeburg, 290,579
  (400,000★)........C11

★ Population of metropolitan
area, including suburbs.

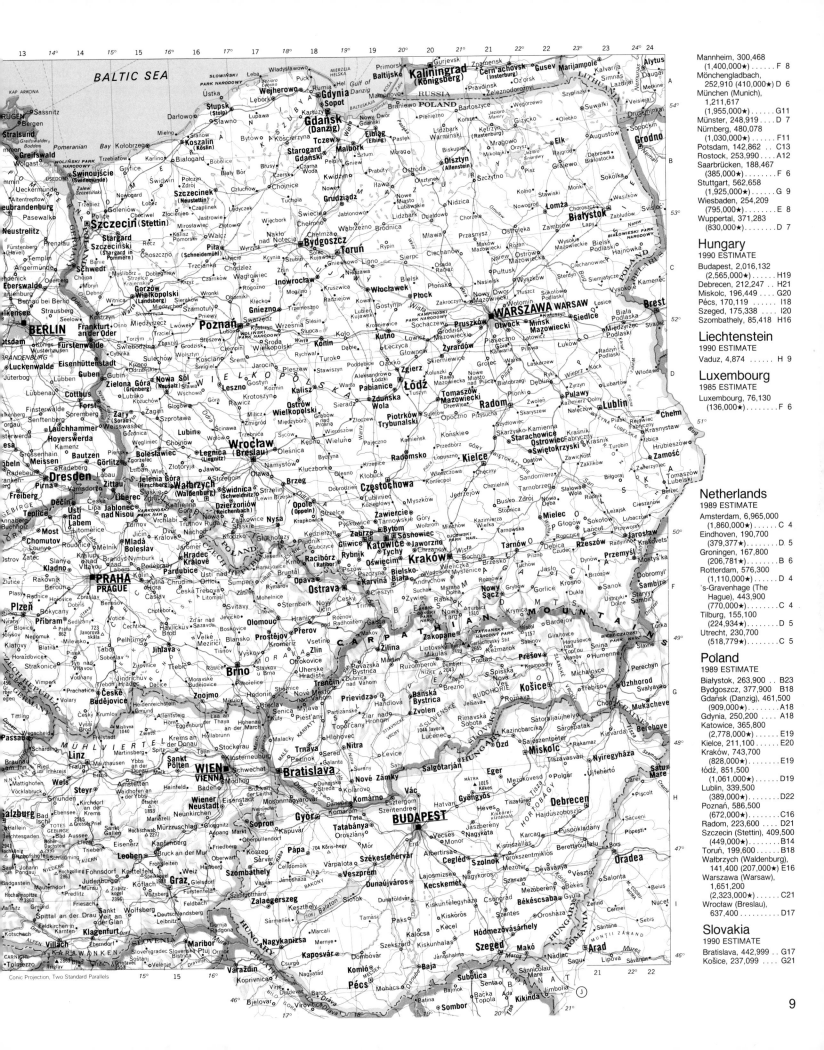

Mannheim, 300,468
(1,400,000★) ..... F 8
Mönchengladbach,
252,910 (410,000★) D 6
München (Munich),
1,211,617
(1,955,000★) G11
Münster, 248,919 .... D 7
Nürnberg, 480,078
(1,030,000★) F11
Potsdam, 142,862 .. C13
Rostock, 253,990 .... A12
Saarbrücken, 188,467
(385,000★) ...... F 6
Stuttgart, 562,658
(1,925,000★) ...... G 9
Wiesbaden, 254,209
(795,000★) ...... E 8
Wuppertal, 371,283
(830,000★) ...... D 7

Hungary
1990 ESTIMATE
Budapest, 2,016,132
(2,565,000★) H19
Debrecen, 212,247 .. H21
Miskolc, 196,449 .... G20
Pécs, 170,119 ...... I18
Szeged, 175,338 .... I20
Szombathely, 85,418 H16

Liechtenstein
1990 ESTIMATE
Vaduz, 4,874 ...... H 9

Luxembourg
1985 ESTIMATE
Luxembourg, 76,130
(136,000★) .... F 6

Netherlands
1989 ESTIMATE
Amsterdam, 6,965,000
(1,860,000★) ...... C 4
Eindhoven, 190,700
(379,377★) ...... D 5
Groningen, 167,800
(206,781★) ...... B 6
Rotterdam, 576,300
(1,110,000★) ...... D 4
's-Gravenhage (The
Hague), 443,900
(770,000★) ...... C 4
Tilburg, 155,100
(224,934★) .... D 5
Utrecht, 230,700
(518,779★) ...... C 5

Poland
1989 ESTIMATE
Białystok, 263,900 .. B23
Bydgoszcz, 377,900 B18
Gdańsk (Danzig), 461,500
(909,000★) A18
Gdynia, 250,200 .. A18
Katowice, 365,800
(2,778,000★) E19
Kielce, 211,100 .... E20
Kraków, 743,700
(828,000★) E19
łódź, 851,500
(1,061,000★) D19
Lublin, 339,500
(389,000★) D22
Poznań, 586,500
(672,000★) C16
Radom, 223,600 .. D21
Szczecin (Stettin), 409,500
(449,000★) B14
Toruń, 199,600 .... B18
Wałbrzych (Waldenburg),
141,400 (207,000★) E16
Warszawa (Warsaw),
1,651,000
(2,323,000★) C21
Wrocław (Breslau),
637,400 ....D17

Slovakia
1990 ESTIMATE
Bratislava, 442,999 .. G17
Košice, 237,099 .... G21

9

France and the Alps

France
1982 CENSUS

Aix-en-Provence, 121,327
(126,552★) I12
Alès, 43,268
(70,180★) H11
Amiens, 131,332
(154,498★) .... C 9
Angers, 136,038
(195,859★) .... E 6
Angoulême, 46,197
(103,552★) .... G 7
Bayonne, 41,381
(127,477★) .... I 5
Belfort, 51,206
(76,221★) E13
Besançon, 113,283
(120,772★) E13
Béziers, 76,647
(81,347★) I10
Bordeaux, 208,159
(640,012★) .... H 6
Boulogne-Billancourt,
102,582 .... D 9
Boulogne-sur-Mer, 47,653
(98,566★) .... B 8
Brest, 156,060
(201,145★) .... D 2
Brive-la-Gaillarde, 51,511
(64,301★) .... G 8
Caen, 114,068
(183,526★) .... C 6
Calais, 76,527
(100,823★) .... B 8
Cannes, 72,259
(295,525★) I14
Chalon-sur-Saône, 56,194
(78,064★) F11
Chambéry, 53,427
(96,163★) G12
Cherbourg, 28,442
(85,485★) .... C 5
Cholet, 55,524
(55,984★) .... E 6
Clermont-Ferrand,
147,361 (256,189★) G10
Compiègne, 40,384
(62,778★) .... C 9
Creil, 34,709
(82,505★) .... C 9
Dieppe, 35,957
(41,812★) .... C 8
Dijon, 140,942
(215,865★) E12
Douai, 42,576
(202,366★) B10
Dunkerque, 73,120
(195,705★) .... A 9
Fontainebleau, 15,679
(35,629★) .... D 9
Grenoble, 156,637
(392,021★) G12
La Rochelle, 75,840
(102,143★) .... F 5
Laval, 50,360
(55,984★) .... D 6
Le Havre, 199,388
(254,595★) .... C 7
Le Mans, 147,697
(191,080★) .... D 7
Lens, 38,244
(327,383★) .... B 9
Lille, 168,424
(1,020,000★) B10
Limoges, 140,400
(171,689★) .... G 8
Lorient, 62,554
(104,025★) .... E 3
Lourdes, 17,425
(17,425★) .... I 6
Lyon, 413,095
(1,275,000★) G11
Mâcon, 38,404
(47,274★) F11
Marseille, 874,436
(1,225,000★) J12
Maubeuge, 36,061
(105,714★) B10
Meaux, 45,005
(55,797★) .... D 9
Melun, 35,005
(82,479★) .... D 9
Metz, 114,232
(186,437★) C13
Montbéliard, 31,836
(128,194★) E13
Montluçon, 49,912
(67,963★) .... F 9
Montpellier, 197,231
(221,307★) I10
Mulhouse, 112,157
(220,613★) E14
Nancy, 96,317
(306,982★) D13
Nantes, 240,539
(464,857★) .... E 5
Nevers, 43,013
(59,274★) E10
Nice, 337,085
(449,496★) I14
Nîmes, 124,220
(132,343★) I11
Niort, 58,203
(61,959★) .... F 6

ATLANTIC OCEAN

Bay of Biscay

Kilometers 0 50 100 150 Km.

Miles 0 50 100 150 Mi.

1 : 4 000 000

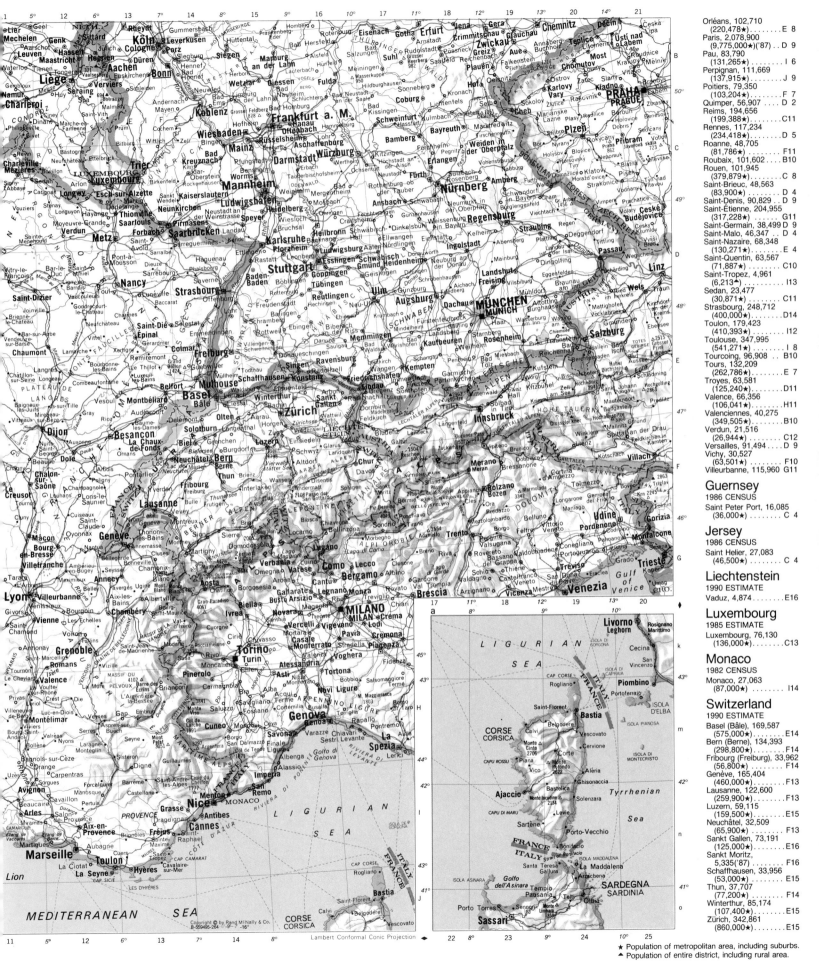

Orléans, 102,710
(220,478★).......E 8
Paris, 2,078,900
(9,775,000★)('87) .. D 9
Pau, 83,790
(131,265★).......I 6
Perpignan, 111,669
(137,915★).......J 9
Poitiers, 79,350
(103,204★).......F 7
Quimper, 56,907 ... D 2
Reims, 194,656
(199,388★).......C11
Rennes, 117,234
(234,418★).......D 5
Roanne, 48,705
(81,786★) F11
Roubaix, 101,602 .. B10
Rouen, 101,945
(379,879★) .... C 8
Saint-Brieuc, 48,563
(83,900★) .... D 4
Saint-Denis, 90,829 .. D 9
Saint-Étienne, 204,955
(317,228★) G11
Saint-Germain, 38,499 D 9
Saint-Malo, 46,347 .. D 4
Saint-Nazaire, 68,348
(130,271★).......E 4
Saint-Quentin, 63,567
(71,887★) C10
Saint-Tropez, 4,961
(6,213▲) I13
Sedan, 23,477
(30,871★) C11
Strasbourg, 248,712
(400,000★).......D14
Toulon, 179,423
(410,393★) I12
Toulouse, 347,995
(541,271★) .... I 8
Tourcoing, 96,908 .. B10
Tours, 132,209
(262,786★).......E 7
Troyes, 63,581
(125,240★).......D11
Valence, 66,356
(106,041★).......H11
Valenciennes, 40,275
(349,505★) .. B10
Verdun, 21,516
(26,944▲) C12
Versailles, 91,494 .... D 9
Vichy, 30,527
(63,501★) F10
Villeurbanne, 115,960 G11

Guernsey
1986 CENSUS
Saint Peter Port, 16,085
(36,000★) .... C 4

Jersey
1986 CENSUS
Saint Helier, 27,083
(46,500★) .... C 4

Liechtenstein
1990 ESTIMATE
Vaduz, 4,874........E16

Luxembourg
1985 ESTIMATE
Luxembourg, 76,130
(136,000★)........C13

Monaco
1982 CENSUS
Monaco, 27,063
(87,000★) I14

Switzerland
1990 ESTIMATE
Basel (Bâle), 169,587
(575,000★).......E14
Bern (Berne), 134,393
(298,800★).......F14
Fribourg (Freiburg), 33,962
(56,800★) F14
Genève, 165,404
(460,000★).......F13
Lausanne, 122,600
(259,900★).......F13
Luzern, 59,115
(159,500★).......E15
Neuchâtel, 32,509
(65,900★) F13
Sankt Gallen, 73,191
(125,000★).......E16
Sankt Moritz,
5,335('87) F16
Schaffhausen, 33,956
(53,000★) E15
Thun, 37,707
(77,200★) F14
Winterthur, 85,174
(107,400★).......E15
Zürich, 342,861
(860,000★).......E15

★ Population of metropolitan area, including suburbs.
▲ Population of entire district, including rural area.

11

Spain and Portugal

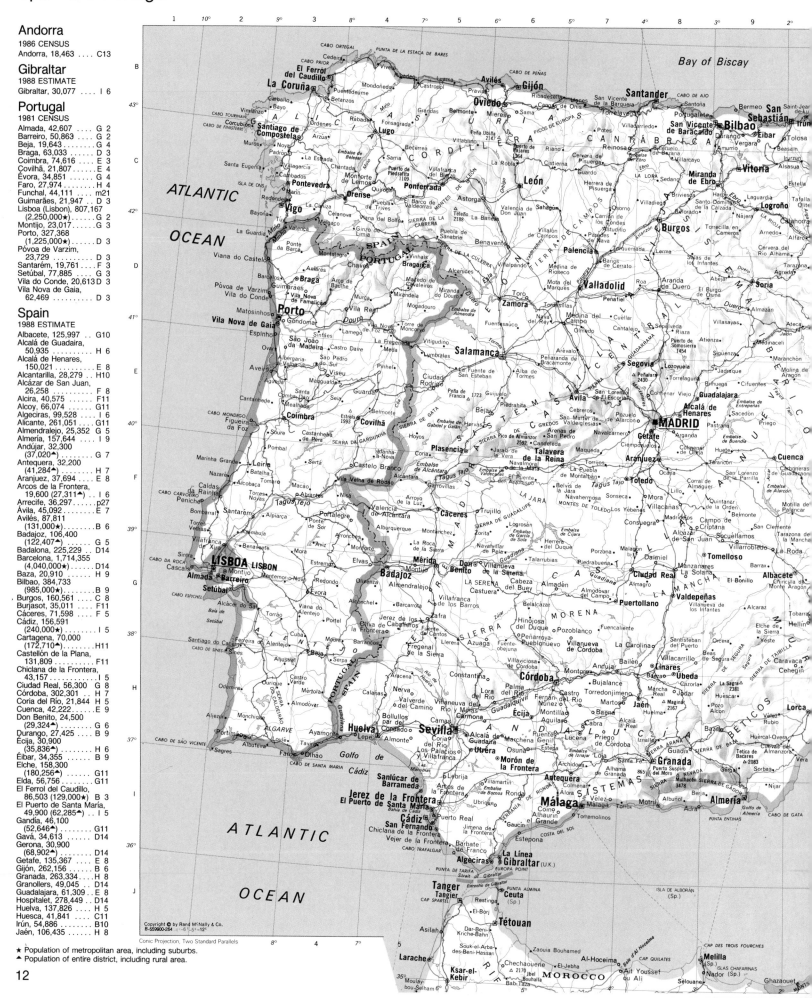

Andorra
1986 CENSUS
Andorra, 18,463 .... C13

Gibraltar
1988 ESTIMATE
Gibraltar, 30,077 .... I 6

Portugal
1981 CENSUS
Almada, 42,607 ...... G 2
Barreiro, 50,863 ..... G 2
Beja, 19,643 .... G 4
Braga, 63,033 ...... D 3
Coimbra, 74,616 .... E 3
Covilhã, 21,807 ..... E 4
Évora, 34,851 ...... G 4
Faro, 27,974 .... H 4
Funchal, 44,111 .... m21
Guimarães, 21,947 .. D 3
Lisboa (Lisbon), 807,167
  (2,250,000★) .... G 2
Montijo, 23,017 ..... G 3
Porto, 327,368
  (1,225,000★) .... D 3
Póvoa de Varzim,
  23,729 .... D 3
Santarém, 19,761 .... F 3
Setúbal, 77,885 ..... G 3
Vila do Conde, 20,613 D 3
Vila Nova de Gaia,
  62,469 .... D 3

Spain
1988 ESTIMATE
Albacete, 125,997 .. G10
Alcalá de Guadaira,
  50,935 .... H 6
Alcalá de Henares,
  150,021 .... E 8
Alcantarilla, 28,279 . H10
Alcázar de San Juan,
  26,258 .... F 8
Alcira, 40,575 ...... F11
Alcoy, 66,074 ...... G11
Algeciras, 99,528 ... I 6
Alicante, 261,051 ... G11
Almendralejo, 25,352 G 5
Almería, 157,644 ... I 9
Andújar, 32,300
  (37,020▲) ...... G 7
Antequera, 32,200
  (41,284▲) ...... H 7
Aranjuez, 37,694 ... E 8
Arcos de la Frontera,
  19,600 (27,311▲) . I 6
Arrecife, 36,297 .... p27
Ávila, 45,092 ...... E 7
Avilés, 87,811
  (131,000★) ..... B 6
Badajoz, 106,400
  (122,407▲) ..... G 5
Badalona, 225,229 . D14
Barcelona, 1,714,355
  (4,040,000★) ... D14
Baza, 20,910 ...... H 9
Bilbao, 384,733
  (985,000★) ..... B 9
Burgos, 160,561 ... C 8
Burjasot, 35,011 ... F11
Cáceres, 71,598 .... F 5
Cádiz, 156,591
  (240,000★) ..... I 5
Cartagena, 70,000
  (172,710▲) H11
Castellón de la Plana,
  131,809 .... F11
Chiclana de la Frontera,
  43,157 .... I 5
Ciudad Real, 56,300 G 8
Córdoba, 302,301 .. H 7
Coria del Río, 21,844 H 5
Cuenca, 42,222 .... E 9
Don Benito, 24,500
  (29,324▲) ...... G 6
Durango, 27,425 ... B 9
Écija, 30,900
  (35,836▲) ...... H 6
Éibar, 34,355 ...... B 9
Elche, 158,300
  (180,256▲) G11
Elda, 56,756 .... G11
El Ferrol del Caudillo,
  86,503 (129,000★) B 3
El Puerto de Santa María,
  49,900 (62,285▲) . I 5
Gandía, 46,100
  (52,646▲) G11
Gavá, 34,613 ...... D14
Gerona, 30,900
  (68,902▲) D14
Getafe, 135,367 .... E 8
Gijón, 262,156 ..... B 6
Granada, 263,334 .. H 8
Granollers, 49,045 . D14
Guadalajara, 61,309 . E 8
Hospitalet, 278,449 . D14
Huelva, 137,826 ... H 5
Huesca, 41,841 .... C11
Irún, 54,886 .... B10
Jaén, 106,435 ..... H 8

★ Population of metropolitan area, including suburbs.
▲ Population of entire district, including rural area.

12

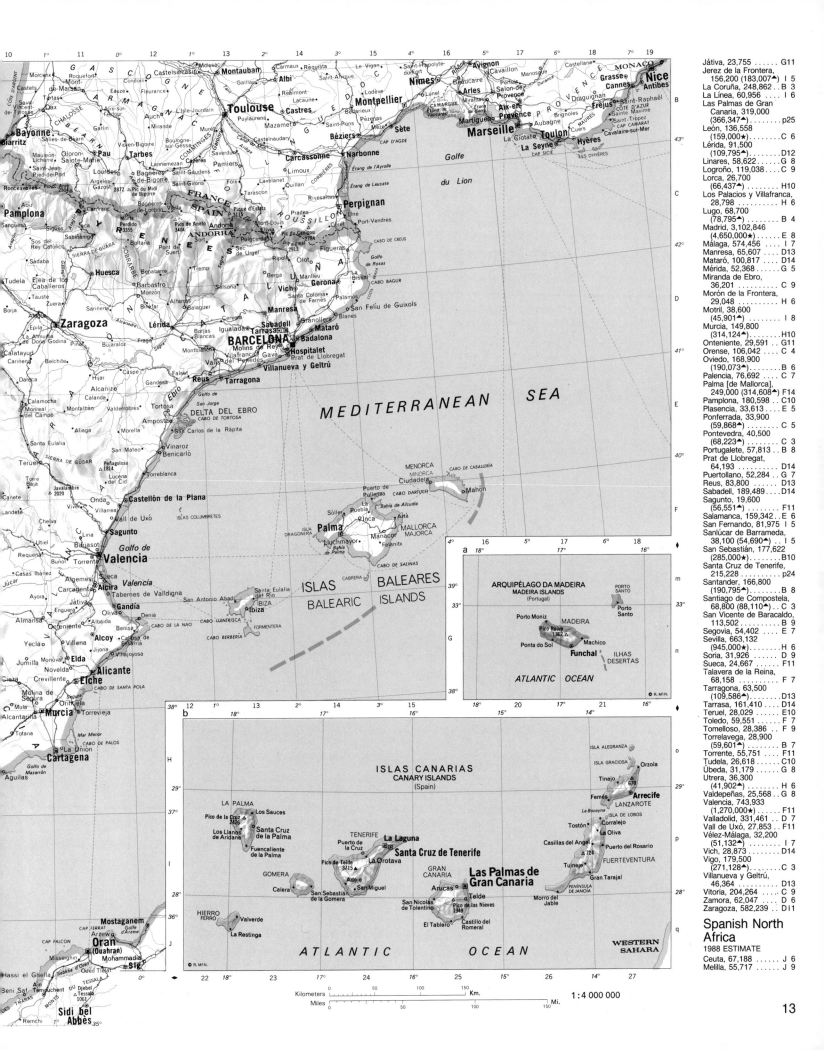

Játiva, 23,755 . . . . . . G11
Jerez de la Frontera,
  156,200 (183,007▲) I 5
La Coruña, 248,862 . . B 3
La Línea, 60,956 . . . . I 6
Las Palmas de Gran
  Canaria, 319,000
  (366,347▲) p25
León, 136,558
  (159,000★) . . . . C 6
Lérida, 91,500
  (109,795▲) D12
Linares, 58,622 . . . . . G 8
Logroño, 119,038 . . . C 9
Lorca, 26,700
  (66,467▲) H10
Los Palacios y Villafranca,
  28,798 . . . . H 6
Lugo, 68,700
  (78,795▲) . . . . B 4
Madrid, 3,102,846
  (4,650,000★) . . . . . E 8
Málaga, 574,456 . . . . I 7
Manresa, 65,607 . . . . D13
Mataró, 100,817 . . . . D14
Mérida, 52,368 . . . . . G 5
Miranda de Ebro,
  36,201 . . . . C 9
Morón de la Frontera,
  29,048 . . . . H 6
Motril, 38,600
  (45,901▲) . . . . I 8
Murcia, 149,800
  (314,124▲) H10
Onteniente, 29,591 . . G11
Orense, 106,042 . . . . C 4
Oviedo, 168,900
  (190,073▲) . . . . . . .B 6
Palencia, 76,692 . . . . C 7
Palma [de Mallorca],
  249,000 (314,608▲) F14
Pamplona, 180,598 . . C10
Plasencia, 33,613 . . . E 5
Ponferrada, 33,900
  (59,868▲) . . . . C 5
Pontevedra, 40,500
  (68,223▲) . . . . C 3
Portugalete, 57,813 . . B 8
Prat de Llobregat,
  64,193 . . . . D14
Puertollano, 52,284 . . G 7
Reus, 83,800 . . . . . . D13
Sabadell, 189,489 . . .D14
Sagunto, 19,600
  (56,551▲) F11
Salamanca, 159,342 . .E 6
San Fernando, 81,975 I 5
Sanlúcar de Barrameda,
  38,100 (54,690▲) . . I 5
San Sebastián, 177,622
  (285,000★) B10
Santa Cruz de Tenerife,
  215,228 . . . . p24
Santander, 166,800
  (190,795▲) . . . . . . B 8
Santiago de Compostela,
  68,800 (88,110▲) . . C 3
San Vicente de Baracaldo,
  113,502 . . . . B 9
Segovia, 54,402 . . . . E 7
Sevilla, 663,132
  (945,000★) . . . . . . H 6
Soria, 31,926 . . . . . . D 9
Sueca, 24,667 . . . . . F11
Talavera de la Reina,
  68,158 . . . . F 7
Tarragona, 63,500
  (109,586▲) D13
Tarrasa, 161,410 . . . .D14
Teruel, 28,029 . . . . . E10
Toledo, 59,551 . . . . . F 7
Tomelloso, 28,386 . . . F 9
Torrelavega, 28,900
  (59,601▲) . . . . B 7
Torrente, 55,751 . . . . F11
Tudela, 26,618 . . . . . C10
Úbeda, 31,179 . . . . . G 8
Utrera, 36,300
  (41,902▲) . . . . H 6
Valdepeñas, 25,568 . . G 8
Valencia, 743,933
  (1,270,000★) F11
Valladolid, 331,461 . . D 7
Vall de Uxó, 27,853 . . F11
Vélez-Málaga, 32,200
  (51,132▲) . . . . I 7
Vich, 28,873 . . . . D14
Vigo, 179,500
  (271,128▲) . . . . . . .C 3
Villanueva y Geltrú,
  46,364 . . . . D13
Vitoria, 204,264 . . . . C 9
Zamora, 62,047 . . . . D 6
Zaragoza, 582,239 . . Di1

Spanish North Africa

1988 ESTIMATE

Ceuta, 67,188 . . . . . . J 6
Melilla, 55,717 . . . . . J 9

1:4 000 000

Italy

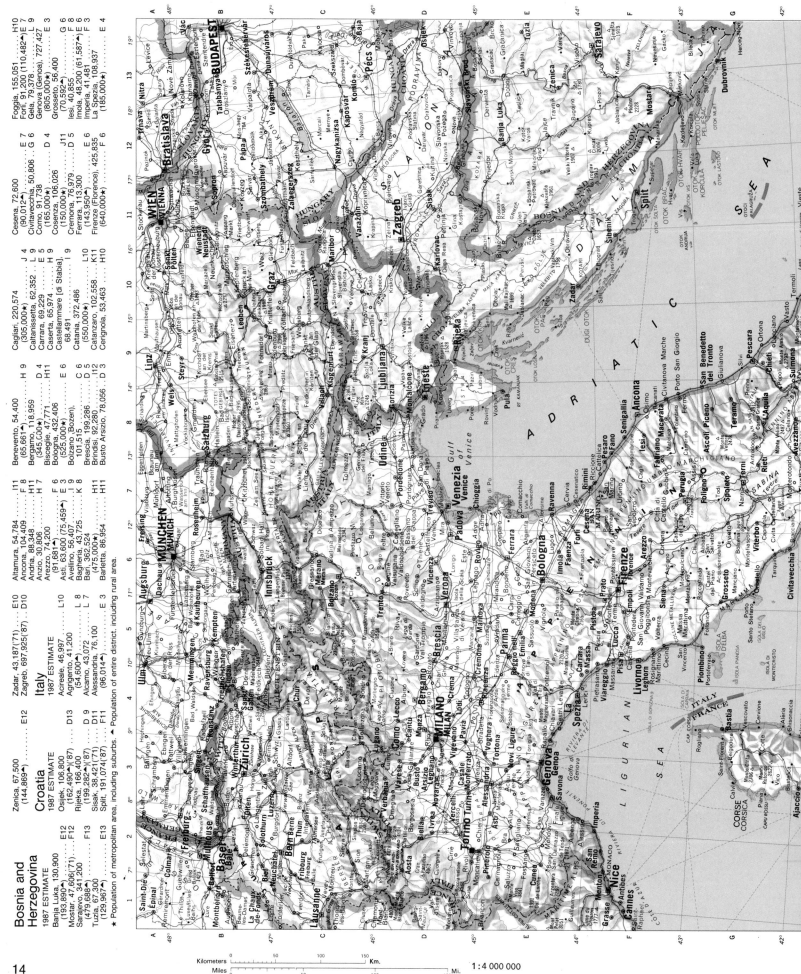

Foglia, 155,051	H10
Forlì, 91,200 (110,482▲)	E 7
Gela, 79,378	L 9
Genoa (Genova), 727,427	
(805,000▲)	E 3
Grosseto, 56,400	
(70,592▲)	G 6
Iesi, 40,855	F 8
Imola, 48,200 (61,587▲)	F 6
Imperia, 41,481	F 3
La Spezia, 108,937	
(185,000▲)	E 4

Cesena, 72,600	
(90,012▲)	E 7
Civitavecchia, 50,806	G 6
Como, 91,738	D 4
Cosenza, 106,026	
(165,000▲)	J11
Caserta, 65,974	
(150,000▲)	D 5
Castellammare [di Stabia],	
68,491	I 9
Catania, 372,486	
(550,000▲)	L10
Catanzaro, 102,558	K11
Cerignola, 53,463	H10

Cagliari, 220,574	
(305,000▲)	J 4
Caltanissetta, 62,352	L 9
Carrara, 69,229	E 5
Como, 91,738	D 4
Cosenza, 65,974	H 9

Benevento, 54,400	H 9
(65,661▲)	D 4
Bergamo, 118,959	
(345,000▲)	D 4
Bisceglie, 47,771	H11
Bologna, 432,406	
(525,000▲)	E 6
Bolzano (Bozen),	
101,515	C 6
Brescia, 199,286	D 5
Brindisi, 92,280	I12
Busto Arsizio, 78,056	D 3

Altamura, 54,784	I11
Ancona, 104,409	F 8
Andria, 88,348	H11
Anzio, 30,806	H 7
Arezzo, 46,997	F 6
Asti, 63,600 (75,459▲)	E 3
Agrigento, 41,200	I 9
Avellino, 56,407	I 9
Bagheria, 43,725	K 8
Bari, 362,524	H11
(475,000▲)	H11
Barletta, 86,954	H11

Bosnia and Herzegovina

1987 ESTIMATE

Banja Luka, 130,900	
(193,890▲)	E12
Mostar, 47,606('71)	F12
Sarajevo, 341,200	
(479,688▲)	F13
Tuzla, 67,300	
(129,967▲)	E13

Zadar, 43,187('71)	E12
Zagreb, 697,925('87)	

Croatia

1987 ESTIMATE

Osijek, 106,800	
(162,490▲'87)	E12
Rijeka, 166,400	
(199,282▲'87)	D 9
Sisak, 38,421('71)	D11
Split, 191,074('87)	F11

Italy

1987 ESTIMATE

Acireale, 46,997	L10
Agrigento, 41,200	
(54,600▲)	L 8
Alcamo, 43,072	L 7
Alessandria, 76,100	E 3

★ Population of metropolitan area, including suburbs. ▲ Population of entire district, including rural area.

Kilometers 0   50   100   150   Km.

Miles 0   50   100   150   Mi.

1 : 4 000 000

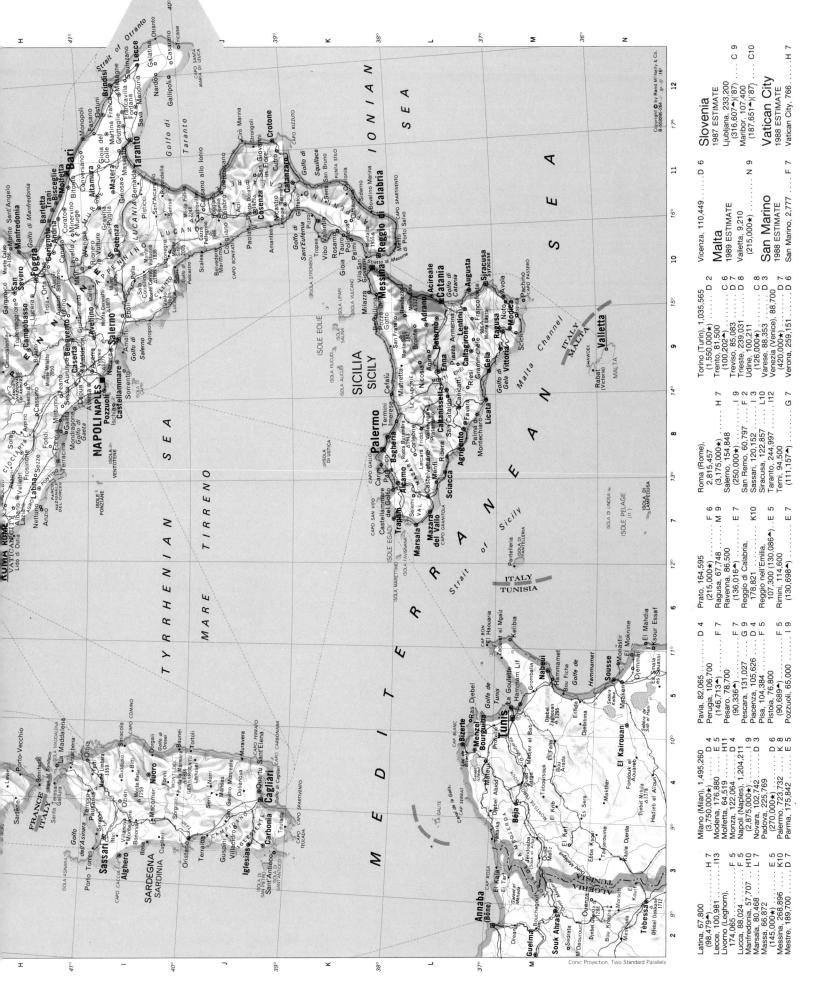

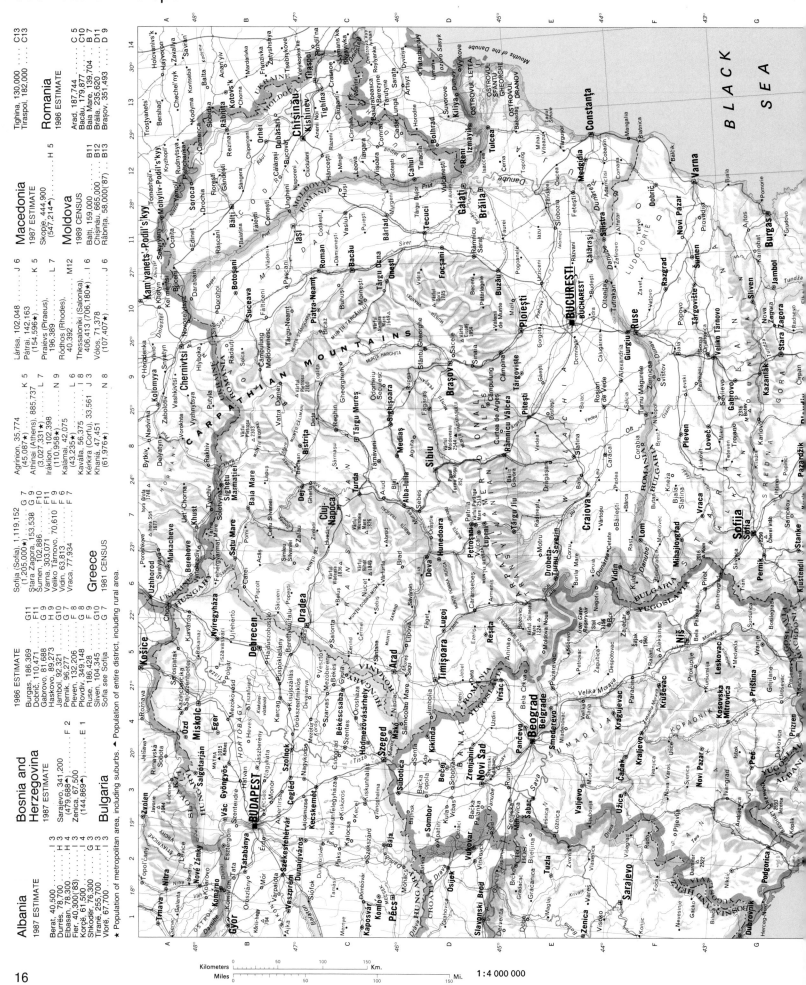

Albania
1987 ESTIMATE

Berat, 40,500 ..... I 3
Durrës, 78,700 ..... H 3
Elbasan, 78,300 ..... H 4
Fier, 40,300(83) ..... I 4
Korçë, 61,500 ..... I 4
Shkodër, 76,300 ..... G 3
Tiranë, 255,700 ..... H 3
Vlorë, 67,700 ..... I 3

Bosnia and Herzegovina
1987 ESTIMATE

Sarajevo, 341,200
(479,688▲) ..... F 2
Zenica, 67,500
(144,869▲) ..... E 1

Bulgaria
1986 ESTIMATE

Burgas, 186,369 ..... G11
Dobrič, 110,471 ..... F11
Gabrovo, 81,688 ..... G 9
Haskovo, 89,273 ..... H10
Jambol, 92,321 ..... G 7
Pernik, 96,277 ..... F 8
Pleven, 132,206 ..... F 8
Plovdiv, 349,148 ..... F 9
Ruse, 186,428 ..... F 9
Sliven, 104,345 ..... G10
Sofia see Sofija ..... G 7

Sofija (Sofia), 1,119,152
(1,205,000▲) ..... G 7
Štara Zagora, 153,538 ..... G 9
Šumen, 102,886 ..... F10
Varna, 303,071 ..... F11
Veliko Tărnovo, 70,610 ..... F 9
Vidin, 63,813 ..... F 7
Vraca, 77,934 ..... F 7

Greece
1981 CENSUS

Agrínion, 35,774
(45,087★) ..... K 5
Athínai (Athens), 885,737
(3,027,331★) ..... L 7
Iráklion, 102,398
(110,958★) ..... N 9
Kalámai, 42,075
(43,235★) ..... L 6
Kérkira (Corfu), 33,561 ..... K 4
Khaniá, 47,451
(61,976★) ..... N 8

Lárisa, 102,048 ..... K 6
Pátrai, 142,163
(154,596★) ..... L 5
Piraiévs (Piraeus),
196,389 ..... L 7
Ródhos (Rhodes),
40,392 ..... M12
Thessaloníki (Saloníki),
406,413 (706,180★) ..... I 6
Vólos, 71,378
(107,407★) ..... J 6

Macedonia
1987 ESTIMATE

Skopje, 444,900
(547,214▲) ..... H 5

Moldova
1989 CENSUS

Chisinău, 665,000 ..... B12
Răbnita, 58,000('87) B11
Tighina, 130,000 ..... C13
Tiraspol, 182,000 ..... C13

Romania
1986 ESTIMATE

Arad, 187,744 ..... C 5
Bacău, 179,877 ..... C10
Baia Mare, 139,704 ..... B 7
Brăila, 235,620 ..... D11
Brașov, 351,493 ..... D 9

★ Population of metropolitan area, including suburbs. ▲ Population of entire district, including rural area.

Kilometers 0 50 100 150 Km.
Miles 0 50 100 150 Mi.
1:4 000 000

BLACK SEA

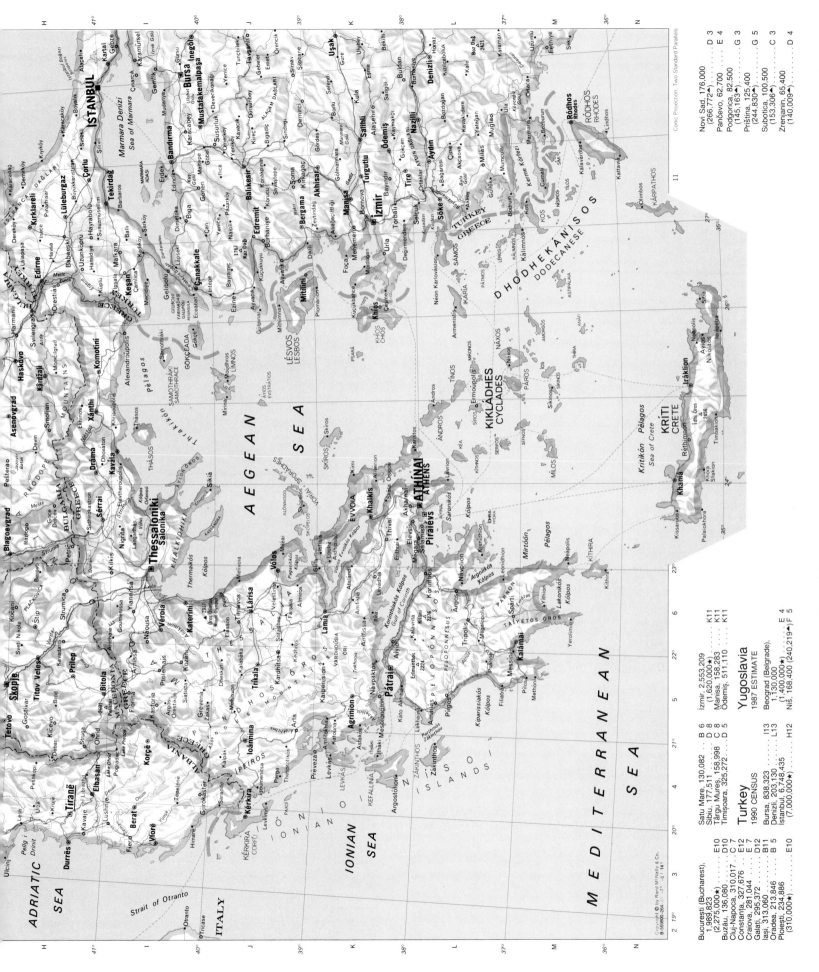

Baltic and Moscow Regions

Belarus
1989 CENSUS

Baranoviči, 159,000 . . H 9
Bobrujsk, 223,000 . . H12
Borisov, 144,000 . . . . G11
Brest, 258,000 . . . . . . I 6
Gomel', 500,000 . . . . .I14
Grodno, 270,000 . . . H 6
Lida, 81,000('87) . . . H 8
Minsk, 1,589,000
  (1,650,000★) H10
Mogil'ov, 356,000 . . .H13
Molodečno,
  87,000('87) . . . . . . G 9
Novopolock,
  90,000('87) F11
Orša, 123,000 . . . . . G13
Pinsk, 119,000 . . . . . I 9
Polock, 80,000('87) . . F11
Rečica, 71,000('87) . . I13
Sluck, 55,000('87) . . H10
Svetlogorsk,
  68,000('87) . . . . . . G 3
Vitebsk, 350,000 . . . F13
Žlobin, 52,000('87) I13

Estonia
1989 CENSUS

Kohtla-Järve,
  78,000('87) B10
Narva, 81,000('87) . . B11
Pärnu, 53,000('87) . . C 7
Tallinn, 482,000 . . . . B 7
Tartu, 114,000 . . . . . . C 9

Latvia
1989 CENSUS

Daugavpils, 127,000 . .F 9
Jelgava, 72,000('87) . . E 6
Jūrmala, 65,000('87) . . E 6
Liepāja, 114,000 . . . . E 4
Rēzekne, 35,620('79) E10
Rīga, 915,000
  (1,005,000★) . . . . . . E 7
Ventspils, 52,000('87) . D 4

Lithuania
1989 CENSUS

Kaunas, 423,000 . . . . G 6
Klaipėda (Memel),
  204,000 . . . . F 4
Panevėžys, 126,000 . . F 7
Šiauliai, 145,000 . . . . F 6
Vilnius, 582,000 . . . . G 8

Russia
1989 CENSUS

Aleksandrov,
  66,000('87) E21
Aleksin, 72,000('87) . .G20
Balachna, 35,359('79) E26
Balašicha, 136,000 . . F20
Bežeck, 30,711('79) . .D19
Bor, 65,000('87) E27
Boroviči, 64,000('87) . C16
Br'ansk, 452,000 . . . .H17
Čechov, 57,000('87) . .F20
Čerepovec, 310,000 . .B20
Čern'achovsk,
  36,361('79) . . . . . . G 4
Chimki, 133,000 . . . . F20
Dmitrov, 64,000('87) . .E20
Domodedovo,
  51,000('87) F20
Dubna, 64,000('87) . . E20
Dzeržinsk, 285,000 . . E26
Elektrostal', 153,000 . F21
Furmanov, 44,430('79)D24
Gatčina, 81,000('87) . .B13
Gorki see Nižnij
  Novgorod E27
Gr'azi, 41,082('87) . . .I22
Gus'-Chrustal'nyj,
  75,000('87) F23
Ivanovo, 481,000 . . . D23
Jarcevo, 40,908('79) . F15
Jaroslavl', 633,000 . . D22
Jefremov, 58,000('87) H21
Jegorjevsk,
  73,000('87) F22

★ Population of metropolitan
  area, including suburbs.

18

Copyright by Rand McNally & Co.
B-570495-264

Kilometers
Miles

1 : 4 000 000

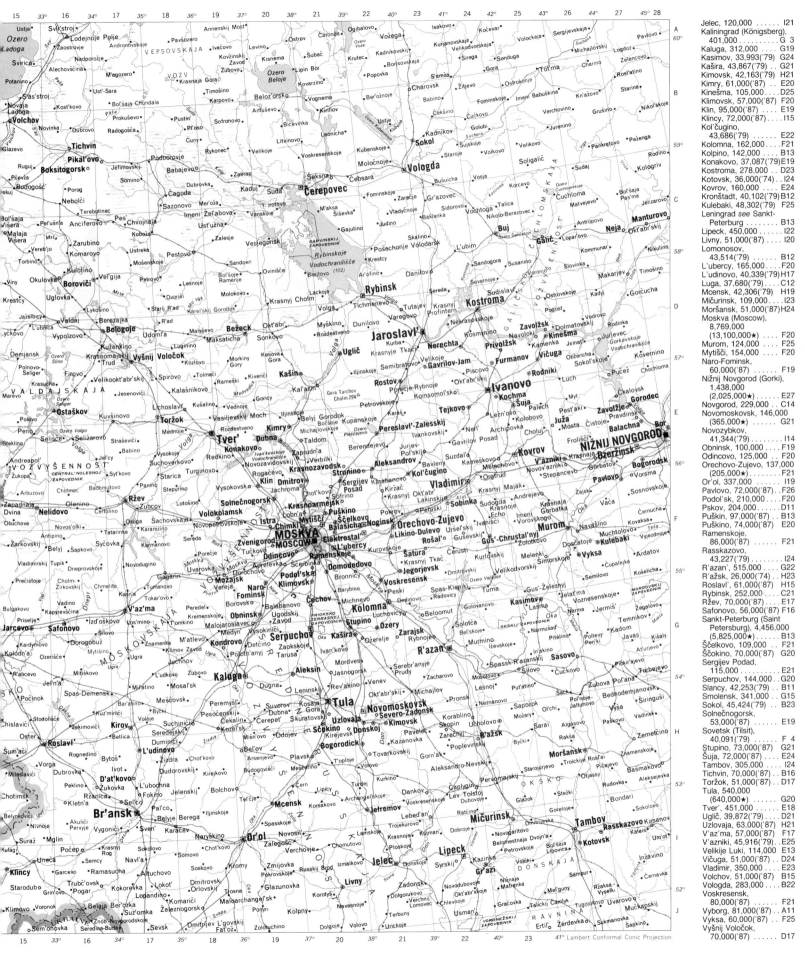

Jelec, 120,000 . . . . . . I21
Kaliningrad (Königsberg),
  401,000 . . . . G 3
Kaluga, 312,000 . . . . . G19
Kasimov, 33,993('79) G24
Kašira, 43,867('79) . . G21
Kimovsk, 42,163('79) H21
Kimry, 61,000('87) . . E20
Kinešma, 105,000 . . . . D25
Klimovsk, 57,000('87) F20
Klin, 95,000('87) E19
Klincy, 72,000('87) . . . I15
Kol'čugino,
  43,686('79) E22
Kolomna, 162,000 . . . . F21
Kolpino, 142,000 . . . . B13
Konakovo, 37,087('79)E19
Kostroma, 278,000 . . . D23
Kotovsk, 36,000('74) . . I24
Kovrov, 160,000 . . . . E24
Kronštadt, 40,102('79)B12
Kulebaki, 48,302('79) F25
Leningrad see Sankt-
  Peterburg B13
Lipeck, 450,000 . . . . I22
Livny, 51,000('87) . . . I20
Lomonosov,
  43,514('79) B12
L'ubercy, 165,000 . . . . F20
L'udinovo, 40,339('79) H17
Luga, 37,680('79) C12
Mcensk, 42,306('79) H19
Mičurinsk, 109,000 . . . I23
Moršansk, 51,000('87) H24
Moskva (Moscow),
  8,769,000
  (13,100,000★) F20
Murom, 124,000 . . . . F25
Mytišči, 154,000 . . . . F20
Naro-Fominsk,
  60,000('87) F19
Nižnij Novgorod (Gorki),
  1,438,000
  (2,025,000★) E27
Novgorod, 229,000 . . . C14
Novomoskovsk, 146,000
  (365,000★) G21
Novozybkov,
  41,344('79) I14
Obninsk, 100,000 . . . . F19
Odincovo, 125,000 . . . F20
Orechovo-Zujevo, 137,000
  (205,000★) F21
Or'ol, 337,000 . . . . . I19
Pavlovo, 72,000('87) . . F26
Podol'sk, 210,000 . . . . F20
Pskov, 204,000 . . . . D11
Puškin, 97,000('87) . . B13
Puškino, 74,000('87) E20
Ramenskoje,
  86,000('87) F21
Rasskazovo,
  43,227('79) I24
R'azan', 515,000 . . . . G22
R'ažsk, 26,000('74) . . H23
Roslavl', 61,000('87) H15
Rybinsk, 252,000 . . . . C21
Ržev, 70,000('87) . . . E17
Safonovo, 56,000('87) F16
Sankt-Peterburg (Saint
  Petersburg), 4,456,000
  (5,825,000★) B13
Ščelkovo, 109,000 . . . F21
Ščokino, 70,000('87) G20
Sergijev Posad,
  115,000 . . . . E21
Serpuchov, 144,000 . . G20
Slancy, 42,253('79) . . B11
Smolensk, 341,000 . . . G15
Sokol, 45,424('79) . . . B23
Solnečnogorsk,
  53,000('87) E19
Sovetsk (Tilsit),
  40,091('79) . . . . . F 4
Stupino, 73,000('87) G21
Šuja, 72,000('87) E24
Tambov, 305,000 . . . . I24
Tichvin, 70,000('87) . . B16
Toržok, 51,000('87) . . D17
Tula, 540,000
  (640,000★) G20
Tver', 451,000 . . . . . E18
Uglič, 39,872('79) D21
Uzlovaja, 63,000('87) H21
V'az'ma, 57,000('87) F16
V'azniki, 45,916('79) . E25
Velikije Luki, 114,000 E13
Vičuga, 51,000('87) . . D24
Vladimir, 350,000 . . . E23
Volchov, 51,000('87) B15
Vologda, 283,000 . . . B22
Voskresensk,
  80,000('87) F21
Vyborg, 81,000('87) . . A11
Vyksa, 60,000('87) . . F25
Vyšnij Voloček,
  70,000('87) D17

19

Asia

'Adan, 176,100 ('84)
  (318,000★) ....H 7
AFGHANISTAN..........F 9
Ahmadābād, 2,059,725
  ('81) (2,400,000★) ..G10
Al Baṣrah, 616,700
  ('85)..........................F 7
Al-Kuwayt, 44.335 ('85)
  (1,375,000★) ....G 7
Alma-Ata,
  1,128,000 ('89)
  (1,190,000★) E10
Al-Madīnah, 290,000
  ('80).........................G 6
'Ammān, 936,300 ('89)
  (1,450,000★) ....F 6
Ankara, 2,553,209 ('90)
  (2,670,000★) ....F 6
ARMENIA ....F 7
Ar-Riyād, 1,250,000
  ('80).........................G 7
Aschabad, 398,000
  ('89).........................F 8
AZERBAIJAN..........E 7
Baghdād, 3,841,268
  ('87).........................F 7
Baku, 1,150,000 ('89)
  (2,020,000★) ....E 7
Bangalore,
  2,476,355 ('81)
  (2,950,000★) H10
Bangkok see Krung
  Thep H13
BANGLADESH........G12
Batumi, 136,000 ('89)..E 7
Bayrūt, 509,000 ('82)
  (1,675,000★) ....F 6
Beijing (Peking),
  6,710,000 ('88)
  (6,450,000★) F14
BHUTAN..................G12
Biškek, 616,000 ('89)..E10
Bombay, 8,243,405 ('81)
  (9,950,000★) H10
BRUNEI.....................I14
Calcutta, 3,305,006 ('81)
  (11,100,000★) H11
CAMBODIA..............H13
Canton see
  Guangzhou G14
Celinograd, 277,000
  ('89)........................D10
Chabarovsk, 601,000
  ('89)........................E16
Changchun, 1,822,000
  ('88) (2,000,000▲) ...E15
Changsha, 1,230,000
  ('88)........................G14
Chengdu, 1,884,000 ('88)
  (2,960,000▲) F13
CHINA......................F12
Chongqing (Chungking),
  2,502,000 ('88)
  (2,890,000▲) G13
Čita, 366,000 ('89)......D14
Colombo, 683,000 ('86)
  (2,050,000★) I10
CYPRUS....................F 6
CYPRUS, NORTH.......F 6
Dacca see Dhaka G12
Dalian, 2,280,000 ('88) F15
Damascus see
  Dimashq ....F 6
Da Nang, 318,653
  ('79).........................H13
Delhi, 4,884,234 ('81)
  (7,200,000★) G10
Dhaka (Dacca), 2,365,695
  ('81) (3,430,312★) ..G12

Dimashq (Damascus),
  1,326,000 ('88)
  (1,950,000★) ....F 6
Dušanbe, 595,000
  ('89)..........................F 9
Esfahān, 986,753 ('86)
  (1,175,000★) ....F 8
Frunze see Biškek E10
Fukuoka, 1,160,440 ('85)
  (1,750,000★) F16
Fuzhou, 910,000 ('88)
  (1,240,000▲) G14
George Town, 248,241
  ('80) (495,000★) I13
GEORGIA ....E 7
Guangzhou (Canton),
  3,100,000 ('88)
  (3,420,000★) G14
Hakodate, 319,194
  ('85)........................E17
Ha Noi, 1,089,000 ('89)
  (1,500,000★) G13
Harbin, 2,710,000
  ('88)........................E15
Herāt, 177,300 ('88)....F 9
Hiroshima,
  1,044,118 ('85)
  (1,575,000★) F16
HONG KONG............G14
Hyderābād, 2,187,262
  ('81) (2,750,000★) ..H10
INDIA.......................G10
INDONESIA...............I13
IRAN..........................F 8
IRAQ..........................F 7
Irkutsk, 626,000 ('89)..D13
Islāmābād, 204,364
  ('81)........................F10
ISRAEL......................F 6
izmir, 2,553,209 ('90)
  (1,620,000★) ....F 5
Jakutsk,
  187,000 ('89)...........C15
JAPAN......................F16
Jekateringbug,
  1,367,000 ('89)
  (1,620,000★) ....D 9
Jerevan, 1,199,000 ('89)
  (1,315,000★) ....E 7
Jerusalem see
  Yerushalayim ....F 6
Jiddah, 1,300,000
  ('80).........................G 6
Jinan, 1,546,000 ('88)
  (2,140,000▲) F14
JORDAN....................F 6
Kābol (Kabul), 1,424,400
  ('88)..........................F 9
Kānpur, 1,481,789 ('81)
  (1,875,000★) G11
Karāchi, 4,901,627 ('81)
  (5,300,000★) ....G 9
Kashi, 146,300 ('86)
  (194,500▲) F10
Kathmāndū, 235,160
  ('81) (320,000★) G11
KAZAKHSTAN...........E 9
Kermān,
  257,284 ('86)...........F 8
Konsomol'sk-na-Amure,
  315,000 ('89)..........D16
KOREA, NORTH........E15
KOREA, SOUTH........F15
Krasnojarsk, 912,000
  ('89)........................D12
Krung Thep (Bangkok),
  5,716,779 ('88)
  (6,450,000★) H13
Kuala Lumpur, 919,610
  ('80) (1,475,000★) ...I13
Kuching, 72,555 ('80)...I14

Kunming, 1,310,000 ('88)
(1,550,000▲) G13
KUWAIT.................... G 7
Kyōto,
1,479,218 ('85).........F16
KYRGYZSTAN............. E10
Kyzyl, 80,000 ('87)......D12
Lahore, 2,707,215 ('81)
(3,025,000★) F10
Lanzhou, 1,297,000 ('88)
(1,420,000▲) F13
LAOS......................... H13
LEBANON.................... F 6
Lhasa, 84,400 ('86)
(107,700▲) G12
MACAU....................... G14
Madras, 3,276,622 ('81)
(4,475,000★) H11
Makkah,
550,000 ('80).......... G 6
MALAYSIA................... I13
MALDIVES.................. I10
Mandalay, 532,949
('83).................... G12
Manila, 1,587,000 ('90)
(6,800,000★) H15
Mashhad, 1,463,508
('86).................... F 8
Masqaṭ, 50,000 ('81)...G 8
Mawlamyine, 219,961
('83).................... H12
MONGOLIA.................. E13
MYANMAR.................G12
Nāgpur, 1,219,461 ('81)
(1,302,066★) G10
Nanjing, 2,390,000
('88).................... F14
NEPAL...................... G11
New Delhi, 273,036
('81).................... G10
Novosibirsk, 1,436,000
('89) (1,600,000★) .. D11
Ochotsk, 9,000.......... D17
OMAN....................... G 8
Omsk, 1,148,000 ('89)
(1,175,000★) D10
Ōsaka, 2,636,249 ('85)
(1,645,000★) F16
PAKISTAN................... G 9
Patna, 776,371 ('81)
(1,025,000★) G11
Peking see Beijing F14
Peshāwar, 506,896 ('81)
(566,248★) F10
Petropavlovsk-Kamčatskij,
269,000 ('89)..........D18
PHILIPPINES...............H15
Phnum Penh, 700,000
('86)...................... H13
Pyŏngyang, 1,283,000
('81) (1,600,000★) ...F15
QATAR......................G 8
Qingdao (Tsingtao),
1,300,000 ('88).........F15
Quetta, 244,842 ('81)
(285,719★) .... F 9
Quezon City, 1,632,000
('90)..................... H15
Rangoon see
Yangon H12
Rāwalpindi, 457,091 ('81)
(1,040,000★) F10
RUSSIA......................D10
Saigon see Thanh Pho Ho
Chi Minh H13
Samarkand, 366,000
('89)..........................F 9
San'ā', 427,150 ('86)...H 7
SAUDI ARABIA..........G 7
Semipalatinsk, 334,000
('89)..........................D11

Sendai, 700,254 ('85)
(1,175,000★) F17
Shanghai,
7,220,000 ('88)
(9,300,000★) F15
Shenyang (Mukden),
3,910,000 ('88)
(4,370,000▲) E15
Shīrāz, 848,289 ('86)...G 8
SINGAPORE.................I13
Sŏul, 10,522,000 ('89)
(15,850,000★) F15
SRI LANKA...................I11
Srīnagar, 594,775 ('81)
(606,002★) F10
SYRIA........................F 6
Tabrīz, 971,482 ('86)... F 7
T'aipei, 2,637,100 ('88)
(6,130,000★) G15
TAIWAN.....................G15
Taiyuan, 1,700,000 ('88)
(1,980,000▲) F14
TAJIKISTAN.................F10
Taškent, 2,073,000 ('89)
(2,325,000★) .... E 9
Tbilisi, 1,260,000 ('89)
(1,460,000★) .... E 7
Tehrān, 6,042,584 ('86)
(7,500,000★) .... F 8
THAILAND.................. H13
Thanh Pho Ho Chi Minh
(Saigon), 3,169,000 ('89)
(3,100,000★) H13
Tianjin (Tientsin),
4,950,000 ('88)
(5,540,000▲) F14
Tobol'sk,
82,000 ('87)........... D 9
Tōkyō, 8,354,615 ('85)
(27,700,000★) F16
Tomsk, 502,000 ('89)..D11
TURKEY......................F 6
TURKMENISTAN.......... F 9
Ulaanbaatar, 548,400
('89)....................E13
**UNITED ARAB
EMIRATES**............. G 8
Ürümqi, 1,060,000
('88)....................E11
UZBEKISTAN.............. E 9
Vārānasi, 708,647 ('81)
(925,000★) G11
Verchojansk, 1,400..... C16
Viangchan, 377,409
('85)....................H13
VIETNAM....................H13
Vladivostok, 648,000
('89)....................E16
Wuhan, 3,570,000
('88)....................F14
Xiamen, 343,700 ('86)
(546,400▲) G14
Xi'an, 2,210,000 ('88)
(2,580,000▲) F13
Yangon (Rangoon),
2,705,039 ('83)
(2,800,000▲) H12
YEMEN.......................H 7
Yerevan see Jerevan ..E 7
Yerushalayim (Jerusalem),
493,500 ('89)
(530,000★) .... F 6
Yokohama, 2,992,926
('85)....................F16
Zhangjiakou,
500,000 ('88)
(640,000▲) E14

★ Population of metropolitan area, including suburbs.
▲ Population of entire district, including rural area.

21

Northwest Asia

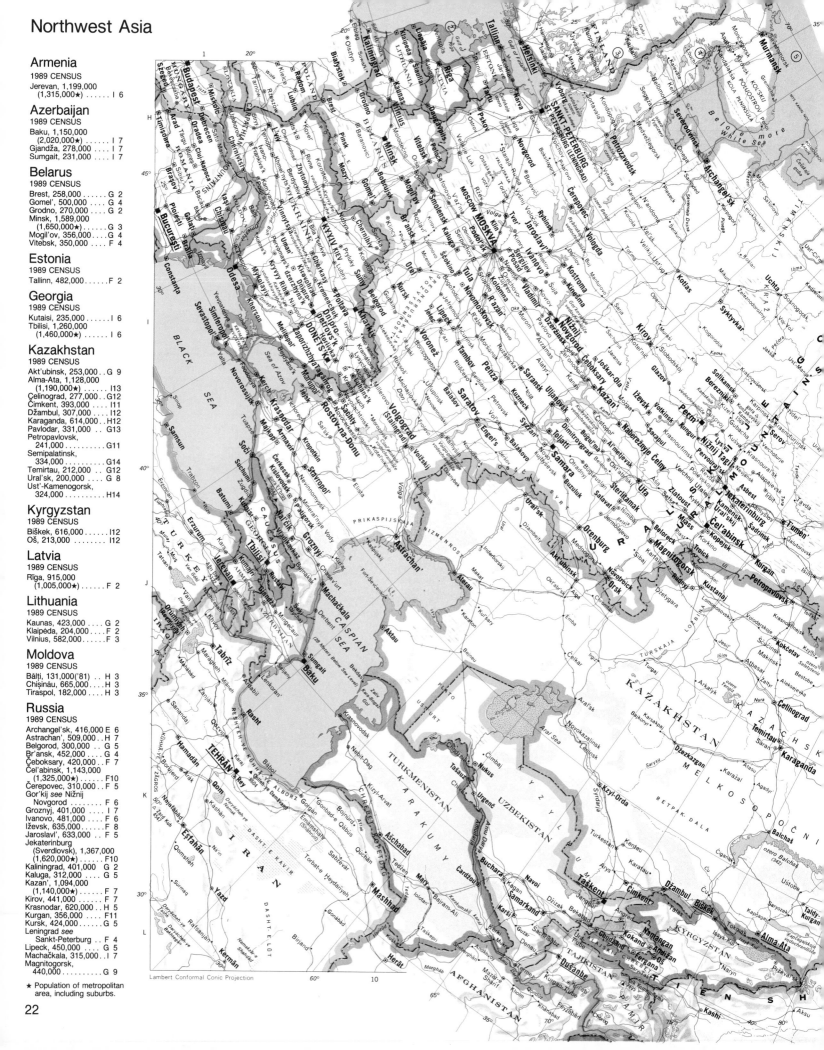

Armenia
1989 CENSUS
Jerevan, 1,199,000
(1,315,000★) ...... I 6

Azerbaijan
1989 CENSUS
Baku, 1,150,000
(2,020,000★) .... I 7
Gjandža, 278,000 .... I 7
Sumgait, 231,000 .... I 7

Belarus
1989 CENSUS
Brest, 258,000 ..... G 2
Gomel', 500,000 ... G 4
Grodno, 270,000 ... G 2
Minsk, 1,589,000
(1,650,000★) ... G 3
Mogil'ov, 356,000 ... G 4
Vitebsk, 350,000 ... F 4

Estonia
1989 CENSUS
Tallinn, 482,000 ..... F 2

Georgia
1989 CENSUS
Kutaisi, 235,000 ..... I 6
Tbilisi, 1,260,000
(1,460,000★) ...... I 6

Kazakhstan
1989 CENSUS
Akt'ubinsk, 253,000 .. G 9
Alma-Ata, 1,128,000
(1,190,000★) I13
Čelinograd, 277,000 ..G12
Čimkent, 393,000 ..I11
Džambul, 307,000 ..I12
Karaganda, 614,000 ..H12
Pavlodar, 331,000 ..G13
Petropavlovsk,
241,000 .. G11
Semipalatinsk,
334,000, ..G14
Temirtau, 212,000 .. G12
Ural'sk, 200,000 .. G 8
Ust'-Kamenogorsk,
324,000 .... H14

Kyrgyzstan
1989 CENSUS
Biškek, 616,000 ......I12
Oš, 213,000 .... I12

Latvia
1989 CENSUS
Rīga, 915,000
(1,005,000★) ..... F 2

Lithuania
1989 CENSUS
Kaunas, 423,000 ... G 2
Klaipėda, 204,000 ... F 2
Vilnius, 582,000 .... F 3

Moldova
1989 CENSUS
Bălți, 131,000('81) .. H 3
Chişinău, 665,000 ... H 3
Tiraspol, 182,000 .... H 3

Russia
1989 CENSUS
Archangel'sk, 416,000 E 6
Astrachan', 509,000 ..H 7
Belgorod, 300,000 ... G 5
Br'ansk, 452,000 .... G 4
Čeboksary, 420,000 .. F 7
Čel'abinsk, 1,143,000
(1,325,000★) F10
Čerepovec, 310,000 .. F 5
Gor'kij see Nižnij
Novgorod .... F 6
Groznyj, 401,000 .... I 7
Ivanovo, 481,000 ... F 6
Iževsk, 635,000 .... F 8
Jaroslavl', 633,000 ... F 5
Jekaterinburg
(Sverdlovsk), 1,367,000
(1,620,000★) F10
Kaliningrad, 401,000 . G 2
Kaluga, 312,000 .... G 5
Kazan', 1,094,000
(1,140,000★) ...... F 7
Kirov, 441,000 ...... F 7
Krasnodar, 620,000 .. H 5
Kurgan, 356,000 ... F11
Kursk, 424,000 ..... G 5
Leningrad see
Sankt-Peterburg .. F 4
Lipeck, 450,000 ..... G 5
Machačkala, 315,000 . I 7
Magnitogorsk,
440,000 .... G 9

★ Population of metropolitan area, including suburbs.

22

Lambert Conformal Conic Projection

Moskva (Moscow),
8,769,000
(13,100,000★) .... F 5
Murmansk, 468,000 . . D 4
Naberežnyje Čelny,
501,000 .... F 8
Nižnij Novgorod (Gor'kij),
1,438,000
(2,025,000★) ...... F 6
Nižnij Tagil, 440,000 . . F 9
Orel, 337,000 ...... G 5
Orenburg, 547,000 . . G 9
Orsk, 271,000 ..... G 9
Penza, 543,000 .... G 7
Perm', 1,091,000
(1,160,000★) ...... F 9
Petrozavodsk,
270,000 .... E 4
R'azan', 515,000 ... G 5
Rostov-na-Donu,
1,020,000
(1,165,000★) ...... H 5
Samara, 1,257,000
(1,505,000★) ...... G 8
Sankt-Peterburg (St.
Petersburg), 4,456,000
(5,825,000★) ...... F 4
Saransk, 312,000 ... G 7
Saratov, 905,000
(1,155,000★) ...... G 7
Smolensk, 341,000 . . G 4
Soči, 337,000 ...... I 5
Stalingrad see
Volgograd .... H 6
Stavropol', 318,000 . . H 6
Sverdlovsk see
Jekaterinburg F10
Syktyvkar, 233,000 . . E 8
Taganrog, 291,000 . . H 5
Tambov, 305,000 ... G 6
Toljatti, 630,000 ... G 7
Tula, 540,000
(640,000★) .... G 5
Tver' (Kalinin),
451,000 .... F 5
Ufa, 1,083,000
(1,100,000★) ...... G 9
Uljanovsk, 625,000 . . G 7
Vladikavkaz, 300,000 . I 6
Vladimir, 350,000 ... F 6
Volgograd (Stalingrad),
999,000
(1,360,000★) ...... H 6
Vologda, 283,000 ... F 5
Volžskij, 269,000 ... H 6
Voronež, 887,000 . . . G 5

Tajikistan
1989 CENSUS
Dušanbe, 595,000 .... J11

Turkmenistan
1989 CENSUS
Aschabad, 398,000 . . J 9

Ukraine
1989 CENSUS
Cherkasy, 290,000 . . H 4
Chernihiv, 296,000 . . G 4
Dniprodzerzhynsk,
282,000 .... H 4
Dnipropetrovsk, 1,179,000
(1,600,000★) ...... H 4
Donets'k, 1,110,000
(2,200,000★) ...... H 5
Horlivka, 337,000
(710,000★) .... H 5
Kharkiv, 1,611,000
(1,940,000★) ...... G 5
Kherson, 355,000 . . H 4
Kryvyy Rih, 713,000 . . H 4
Kyyiv (Kiev), 2,587,000
(2,900,000★) ...... G 4
Luhansk, 497,000 . . H 5
L'viv, 790,000 ..... H 2
Mariupol' (Ždanov),
517,000 .... H 4
Mykolayiv, 503,000 . . H 4
Odesa, 1,115,000
(1,185,000★) ...... H 4
Poltava, 315,000 .... H 4
Sevastopol', 356,000 . I 4
Simferopol', 344,000 . I 4
Sumy, 291,000 .... G 4
Vinnytsya, 374,000 . . H 3
Yalta, 89,000('87) .... I 4
Zaporizhzhya,
884,000,
.... H 5
Zhytomyr, 292,000 . . G 3

Uzbekistan
1989 CENSUS
Andižan, 293,000 .... I12
Buchara, 224,000 . . J10
Fergana, 200,000 ... I12
Namangan, 308,000 . . I12
Samarkand, 366,000 . . J11
Taškent, 2,073,000
(2,325,000★) I11

23

Northeast Asia

Russia

1989 CENSUS

Abakan, 154,000 .... G12
Ačinsk, 122,000 .... F12
Alapajevsk,
  51,000('87) .... F 6
Aldan, 20,000('74) .. F19
Alejsk, 31,390('79) .. G10
Aleksandrovsk-
  Sachalinskij,
  20,000('74) G22
Angarsk, 266,000 .... G14
Anžero-Sudžensk,
  108,000 .... F11
Arsenjev, 67,000('87) .. I20
Art'om, 73,000('87) .. I20
Art'omovsk,
  17,000('79) G12
Asbest, 83,000('87) .. F 6
Asino, 31,329('79) F11
Balej, 25,000('79) G17
Barabinsk, 35,035('79) F 9
Barnaul, 602,000
  (665,000★) G10
Belogorsk,
  71,000('87) G19
Belovo, 118,000('87) .. G11
Berdsk, 77,000('87) .. G10
Berezniki, 201,000 .. F 5
Bijsk, 233,000 ...... G11
Bikin, 18,000('79) .. H20
Birobidžan,
  82,000('87) H20
Blagoveščensk,
  206,000 .... G19
Bogotol, 29,000('79). F11
Bolotnoje, 20,000('79) F10
Bratsk, 255,000 ...... F14
Čel'abinsk, 1,143,000
  (1,325,000★) ...... F 6

Čeremchovo,
  73,000('87) G14
Černogorsk,
  80,000('87) G12
Chabarovsk, 601,000 H21
Chanty-Mansijsk,
  27,961('79) ...... E 7
Cholmsk, 50,000('87) H22
Čita, 366,000 ...... G16
Čusovoj, 59,000('79) F 5
Dudinka, 23,000('74) D11
Gorno-Altajsk,
  39,917('79) G11
Gubacha, 32,461('79) F 5
Gusinoozersk,
  18,000('79) G15
Igarka, 16,918('79) .. D11
Inta, 58,000('87) .... D 6
Irbit, 53,000('87) .... F 6
Irkutsk, 626,000 .... G14
Iskitim, 69,000('87) .. G10
Issyk-Kul', 64,000('87) I 9
Jakutsk, 187,000 .... E19
Jekaterinburg, 1,367,000
  (1,620,000★) ...... F 6
Jenisejsk, 22,000('79) F12
Jurga, 92,000('87) .. F10
Južno-Sachalinsk,
  157,000 .... H22
Kamen'-na-Obi,
  40,684('79) G10
Kamensk-Ural'skij,
  209,000 .... F 6
Kansk, 110,000 .... F13
Karpinsk, 36,569('79) F 6
Kemerovo, 520,000 .. F11
Kirensk, 16,000('74) .. F15
Kisel'ovsk, 128,000 .. G11
Kizel, 40,157('79) .. F 5
Kolpaševo,
  27,000('79) F10
Komsomol'sk-na-Amure,
  315,000 .... G21
Kopejsk, 99,000('87) F 6
Korkino, 63,000('81) G 6
Korsakov, 43,348('79) H22
Krasnojarsk, 912,000 F12

★ Population of metropolitan
  area, including suburbs.

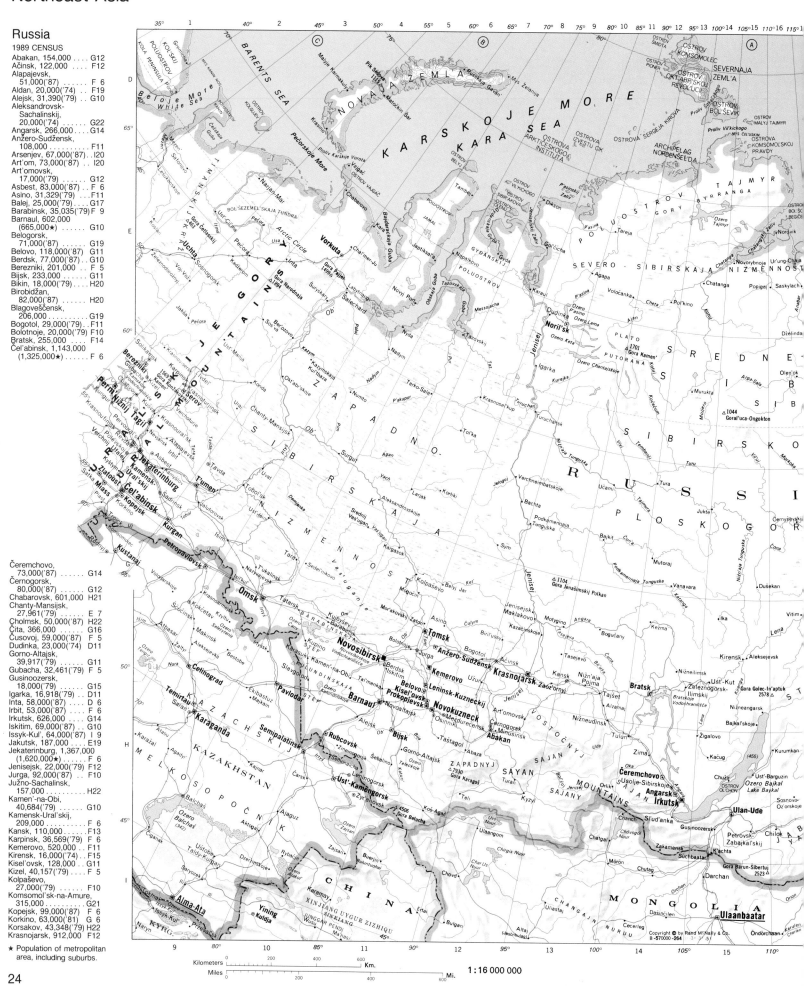

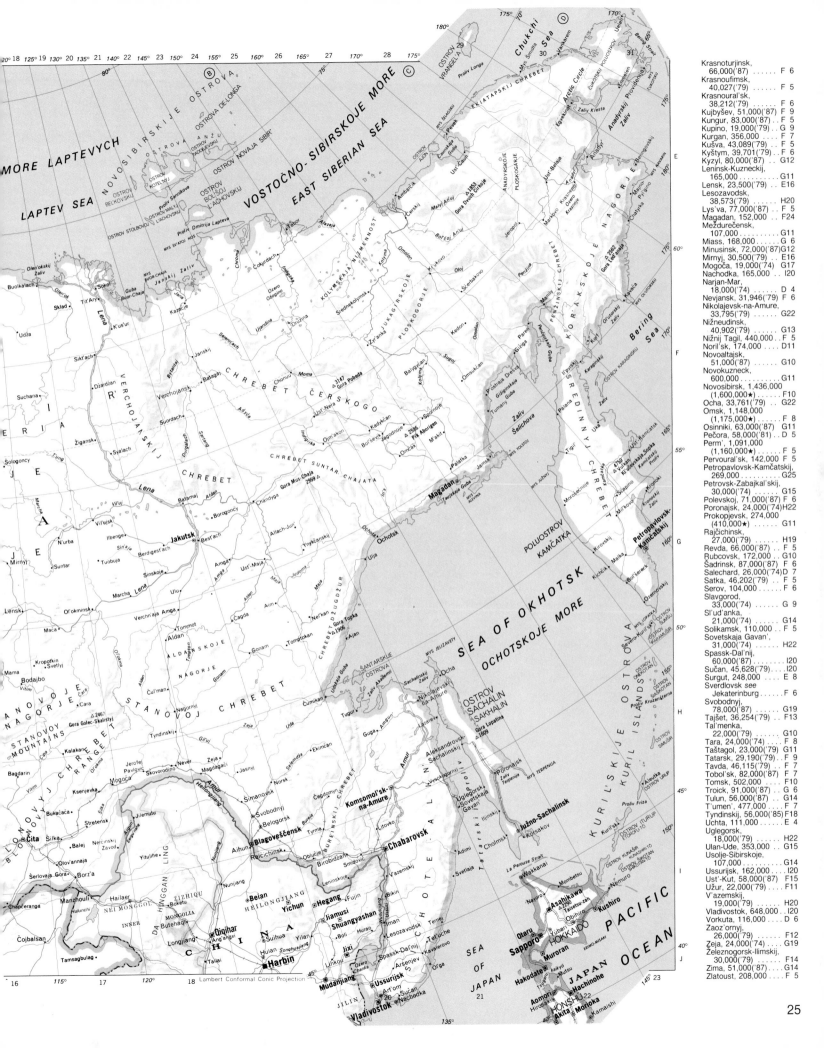

Krasnoturjinsk,
  66,000('87) . . . . . F 6
Krasnoufimsk,
  40,027('79) . . . . . F 5
Krasnoural'sk,
  38,212('79) . . . . . F 6
Kujbyšev, 51,000('87) F 9
Kungur, 83,000('87) . . F 5
Kupino, 19,000('79) . . G 9
Kurgan, 356,000 . . . . . F 7
Kušva, 43,089('79) . . . F 5
Kyštym, 39,701('79) . . F 6
Kyzyl, 80,000('87) . . G12
Leninsk-Kuzneckij,
  165,000 . . . . G11
Lensk, 23,000('79) . . E16
Lesozavodsk,
  38,573('79) H20
Lys'va, 77,000('87) . . . F 5
Magadan, 152,000 . . F24
Meždurečensk,
  107,000 . . . . G11
Miass, 168,000 . . . . . G 6
Minusinsk, 72,000('87)G12
Mirnyj, 30,500('79) . . E16
Mogoča, 19,000('74) . G17
Nachodka, 165,000 . . I20
Narjan-Mar,
  18,000('74) . . . . . . D 4
Nevjansk, 31,946('79) F 6
Nikolajevsk-na-Amure,
  33,795('79) G22
Nižneudinsk,
  40,902('79) G13
Nižnij Tagil, 440,000 . . F 5
Noril'sk, 174,000 . . . . D11
Novoaltajsk,
  51,000('87) G10
Novokuzneck,
  600,000 . . . . G11
Novosibirsk, 1,436,000
  (1,600,000★) F10
Ocha, 33,761('79) . . G22
Omsk, 1,148,000
  (1,175,000★) . . . . F 8
Osinniki, 63,000('87) G11
Pečora, 58,000('81) . . D 5
Perm', 1,091,000
  (1,160,000★) . . . . F 5
Pervoural'sk, 142,000 F 5
Petropavlovsk-Kamčatskij,
  269,000 . . . . G25
Petrovsk-Zabajkal'skij,
  30,000('74) G15
Polevskoj, 71,000('87) F 6
Poronajsk, 24,000('74)H22
Prokopjevsk, 274,000
  (410,000★) G11
Rajčichinsk,
  27,000('79) H19
Revda, 66,000('87) . . F 5
Rubcovsk, 172,000 . . G10
Šadrinsk, 87,000('87) F 6
Salechard, 26,000('74)D 7
Satka, 46,202('79) . . . F 5
Serov, 104,000 . . . . . F 6
Slavgorod,
  33,000('74) . . . . . . G 9
Sl'ud'anka,
  21,000('74) G14
Solikamsk, 110,000 . . F 5
Sovetskaja Gavan',
  31,000('74) H22
Spassk-Dal'nij,
  60,000('87) I20
Sučan, 45,628('79) . . . I20
Surgut, 248,000 . . . . E 8
Sverdlovsk see
  Jekaterinburg . . . . F 6
Svobodnyj,
  78,000('87) G19
Tajšet, 36,254('79) . . F13
Tal'menka,
  22,000('79) G10
Tara, 24,000('74) . . . . F 8
Taštagol, 23,000('79) G11
Tatarsk, 29,190('79) . . F 9
Tavda, 46,115('79) . . . F 7
Tobol'sk, 82,000('87) F 7
Tomsk, 502,000 . . . . F10
Troick, 91,000('87) . . G 6
Tulun, 56,000('87) . . G14
T'umen', 477,000 . . . . F 7
Tyndinskij, 56,000('85) F18
Uchta, 111,000 . . . . E 4
Uglegorsk,
  18,000('79) H22
Ulan-Ude, 353,000 . . G15
Usolje-Sibirskoje,
  107,000 . . . . G14
Ussurijsk, 162,000 . . I20
Ust'-Kut, 58,000('87) F15
Užur, 22,000('79) F11
V'azemskij,
  19,000('79) H20
Vladivostok, 648,000 . I20
Vorkuta, 116,000 . . . . D 6
Zaoz'ornyj,
  26,000('79) F12
Zeja, 24,000('74) . . . G19
Železnogorsk-Ilimskij,
  30,000('79) F14
Zima, 51,000('87) . . G14
Zlatoust, 208,000 . . . . F 5

25

Bhutan

1982 ESTIMATE
Thimphu, 12,000 .... F 4

China

1988 ESTIMATE
Andong, 579,800('86) C11
Anshan, 1,330,000 .. C11
Bangbu, 403,900
  (612,600▲)('86) E10
Baoding, 423,200
  (535,100▲)('86) D10
Baotou, 1,130,000 .. C 8
Beijing (Peking), 6,710,000
  (6,450,000★) D10
Benxi, 860,000 ...... C11
Canton see
  Guangzhou ...... G 9
Changchun, 1,822,000
  (2,000,000▲) C12
Changsha, 1,230,000 F 9
Changzhou,
  522,700('86) E10
Chengdu, 1,884,000
  (2,960,000▲) ...... E 7
Chongqing, 2,502,000
  (2,890,000▲) ...... F 8
Dalian, 2,280,000 .. D11
Datong, 810,000
  (1,040,000▲) ...... C 9
Fushun, 1,290,000 .. C11
Fuzhou, 910,000
  (1,240,000▲) F10
Guangzhou (Canton),
  3,100,000
  (3,420,000▲) ...... G 9
Guiyang, 1,030,000
  (1,430,000▲) ...... F 8
Handan, 870,000
  (1,030,000▲) ...... D 9
Hanzhou, 1,290,000 E 11
Harbin, 2,710,000 .. B12
Hefei, 740,000
  (930,000▲) E10
Hegang, 588,300('86) B13
Hengyang, 419,200
  (601,300▲)('86) .... F 9
Hohhot, 670,000
  (830,000▲) ...... C 9
Huainan, 700,000
  (1,110,000▲) E10
Huangshi,
  451,900('86) E10
Jilin, 1,200,000 ...... C12
Jinan (Tsinan), 1,546,000
  (2,140,000▲) D10
Jinzhou, 710,000
  (810,000▲) C11
Jixi, 700,000
  (820,000▲) B13
Kaifeng, 458,800
  (629,100▲)('86) .... E 9
Kunming, 1,310,000
  (1,550,000▲) ...... F 7
Lanzhou, 1,297,000
  (1,420,000▲) ...... D 7
Lasa (Lhasa), 84,400
  (107,700▲)('86) .... F 5
Liuzhou, 680,000 .... G 8
Luoyang, 760,000
  (1,090,000▲) ...... E 9
Mudanjiang, 650,000 C12
Nanchang, 1,090,000
  (1,260,000▲) F10
Nanjing, 2,390,000 .. E10
Nanning, 720,000
  (1,000,000▲) ...... G 8
Ningbo, 570,000
  (1,050,000▲) F11
Peking see Beijing .. D10
Qingdao (Tsingtao),
  1,300,000 ...... D11
Shanghai, 7,220,000
  (9,300,000★) E11
Shantou (Swatow),
  560,000 (790,000▲) G10
Shenyang (Mukden),
  3,910,000
  (4,370,000▲) C11
Shijiazhuang,
  1,220,000 ...... D 9
Suzhou, 740,000 .... E11
Taiyuan, 1,700,000
  (1,980,000▲) ...... D 9
Tangshan, 1,080,000
  (1,440,000▲) D10
Tianjin (Tientsin),
  4,950,000
  (5,540,000▲) D10
Ürümqi, 1,060,000 .. C 4
Wenzhou, 372,200
  (530,600▲)('86) F11
Wuhan, 3,570,000 .. E 9
Wuhu, 396,000
  (502,200▲)('86) E10
Wuxi, 880,000 ...... E11
Xi'an (Sian), 2,210,000
  (2,580,000▲) ...... E 8
Xining, 620,000 ...... D 7
Xuzhou, 860,000 .... E10
Zhangjiakou (Kalgan),
  500,000 (640,000▲) C 9

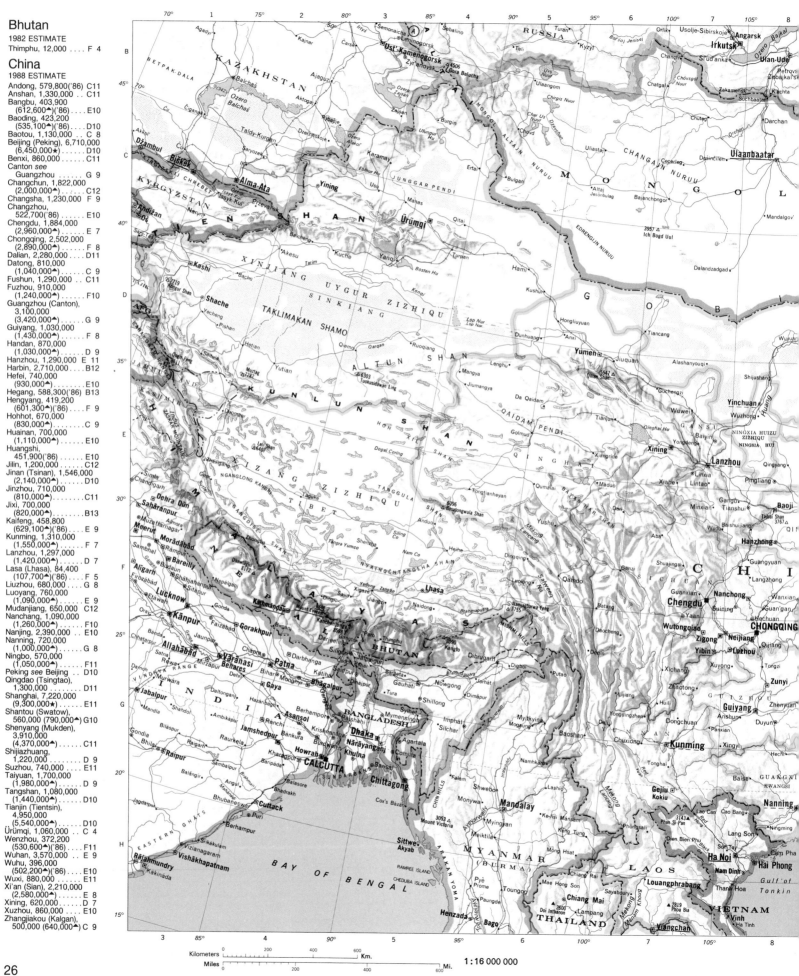

Zhengzhou, 1,150,000
 (1,580,000▲) . . . . . E 9
Zibo, 840,000
 (2,370,000▲) D10

Hong Kong
1986 CENSUS

Kowloon (Jiulong),
 774,781 . . . . . . G 9
Victoria (Xianggang),
 1,175,860
 (4,770,000★) . . . . . G 9

Japan
1985 CENSUS

Asahikawa, 363,631 . . C15
Chiba, 788,930 . . . . D15
Fukuoka, 1,160,440
 (1,750,000★) E13
Hakodate, 319,194 . . C15
Hamamatsu, 514,118 E14
Himeji, 452,917
 (660,000★) E13
Hiroshima, 1,044,118
 (1,575,000★) E13
Kagoshima, 530,502 . E13
Kanazawa, 430,481 . . D14
Kitakyūshū, 1,056,402
 (1,525,000★) E13
Kōbe, 1,410,834 . . . . E14
Kumamoto, 555,719 . . E13
Kurashiki, 413,632 . . E13
Kyōto, 1,479,218 . . . D14
Matsuyama, 426,658 E13
Nagasaki, 449,382 . . E12
Nagoya, 2,116,381
 (4,800,000★) D14
Niigata, 475,630 . . . . D14
Okayama, 572,479 . . E13
Ōsaka, 2,636,249
 (16,450,000★) E14
Sapporo, 1,542,979
 (1,900,000★) C15
Sendai, 700,254
 (1,175,000★) D15
Shizuoka, 468,362
 (975,000★) E14
Tōkyō, 8,354,615
 (27,700,000★) D14
Utsunomiya, 405,375 D14
Yokohama, 2,992,926 D14

Korea, North
1981 ESTIMATE

Ch'ŏngjin, 490,000 . . C12
Kaesŏng, 259,000 . . D12
Namp'o, 241,000 . . . D12
P'yŏngyang, 1,283,000
 (1,600,000★) D12
Sinŭiju, 305,000 . . . . C11
Wŏnsan, 398,000 . . . . D12

Korea, South
1989 ESTIMATE

Chŏnju, 426,473('85) D12
Inch'ŏn, 1,628,000 . . D12
Kwangju, 1,165,000 . . D12
Masan, 448,746
 (625,000★)('85) D12
Pusan, 3,773,000
 (3,800,000★) D12
Sŏul (Seoul), 10,522,000
 (15,850,000★) D12
Taegu, 2,207,000 . . . . D12
Taejŏn, 1,041,000 . . D12

Macau
1987 ESTIMATE

Macau (Aomen),
 429,000 . . . . G 9

Mongolia
1989 ESTIMATE

Ulaanbaatar (Ulan Bator),
 548,400 . . . . B 8

Nepal
1981 CENSUS

Kāthmāndāū
 (Kathmandu), 235,160
 (320,000★) . . . . F 4

Taiwan
1988 ESTIMATE

Kaohsiung, 1,342,797
 (1,845,000★) G11
T'aichung, 715,107 . . G11
T'ainan, 656,927 . . . G11
T'aipei, 2,637,100
 (6,130,000★) F11

★ Population of metropolitan area, including suburbs.
▲ Population of entire district, including rural area.

Eastern and Southeastern China

China

1986 ESTIMATE

Anlu, 35,199('85)	D 2
Anqing, 213,200	E 6
(433,900▲)	B 8
Baoying, 50,479('85)	B 8
Bengbu, 403,900	C 6
(612,600▲)	A 8
Binhai (Dongkan),	
37,565('85)	

Boxian, 63,222('85)	B 4
Canton see Guangzhou	L 2
Changsha,	
1,230,000('88)	G 1
Changshu, 281,300	D 9
Changzhou (Changchow),	
522,700	D 8
Chaoan, 265,400	L 5
(1,214,500▲)	D 6
Chaoxian, 116,800	

Chezhou, 143,500	C 4
(191,900▲)	
Chuxian, 113,300	C 7
(365,000▲)	E11
Dinghai, 50,161('85)	D 8
Dingshan, 46,253('85)	C 6
Dongguan, 254,900	L 2
(1,208,500▲)	B 8
Echeng, 217,400	C 8
(938,000▲)	E 3
Foshan, 243,500	L 2

Fuyang, 143,400	C 4
(195,200▲)	G 5
Fuzhou, 106,700	I 8
(171,800▲)	
Fuzhou (Foochow), 910,000	
(1,240,000▲)('88)	J 3
Ganzhou, 191,600	
(346,000▲)	C 8
Gaoyou, 57,844('82)	E 3
Guangzhou (Canton),	
3,100,000	L 2
(3,420,000▲)('88)	

Huzhou, 208,500	E 9
(964,400▲)	H 3
Jian, 132,200	M 2
(184,300▲)	D 9
Jiangmen, 168,800	E 9
(231,700▲)	L 5
Jiangyin, 66,476('85)	E 4
(1,110,000▲)('88)	F 6
Jiaxing, 201,700	
(382,500▲)	
Jieyang, 65,961('82)	
Jingdezhen (Kingtechen),	
304,000 (569,700▲)	

Jinhua, 147,800	F 8
(799,900▲)	F 4
Jiujiang, 248,500	F 8
(382,300▲)	J 2
Lanxi, 70,500	
(606,800▲)	H 2
Lechang, 56,913	
Liling, 107,100	G 4
(856,700▲)	D 5
Linhai, 52,653('85)	
Liuan, 122,600	
(163,400▲)	

Longyan, 114,500	J 6
(378,400▲)	B 3
Luohe, 102,300	D 7
(159,100▲)	
Maanshan, 258,900	K 5
(367,000▲)	G 4
Meixian, 169,100	C 7
(740,600▲)	
Nanchang, 1,090,000	
(1,260,000▲)('88)	
Nanjing (Nanking),	
2,390,000('88)	

★ Population of metropolitan area, including suburbs. ▲ Population of entire district, including rural area.

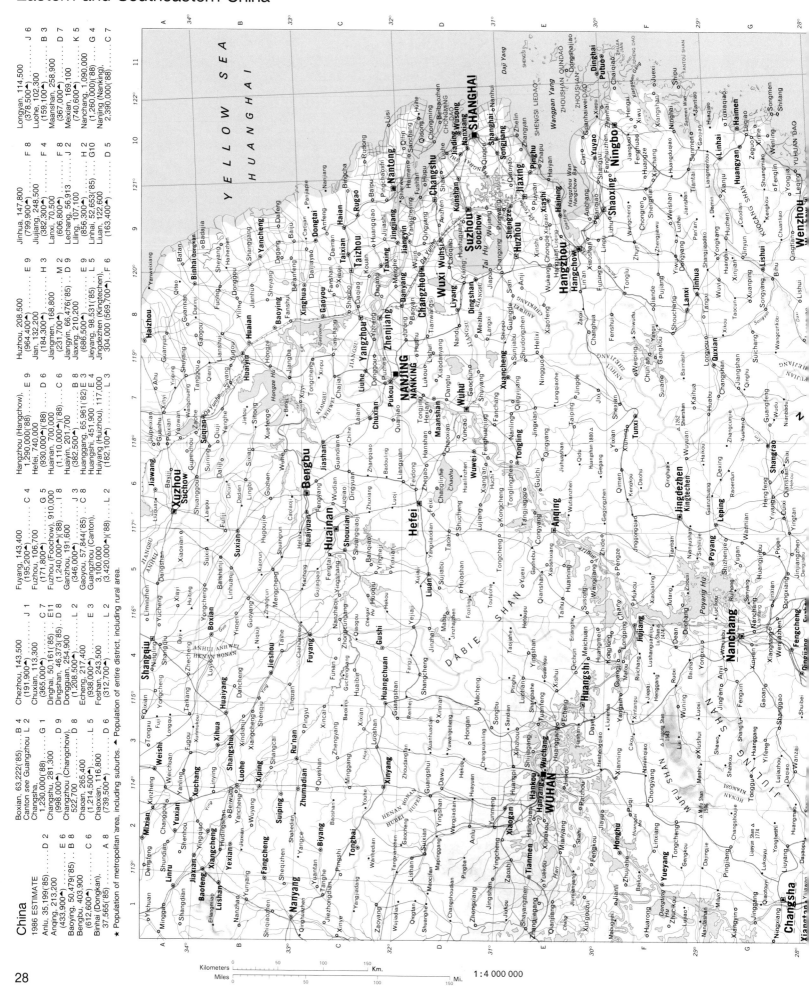

Kilometers 0 · 50 · 100 · 150 · Km.

Miles 0 · 50 · 100 · 150 · Mi.

1 : 4 000 000

28

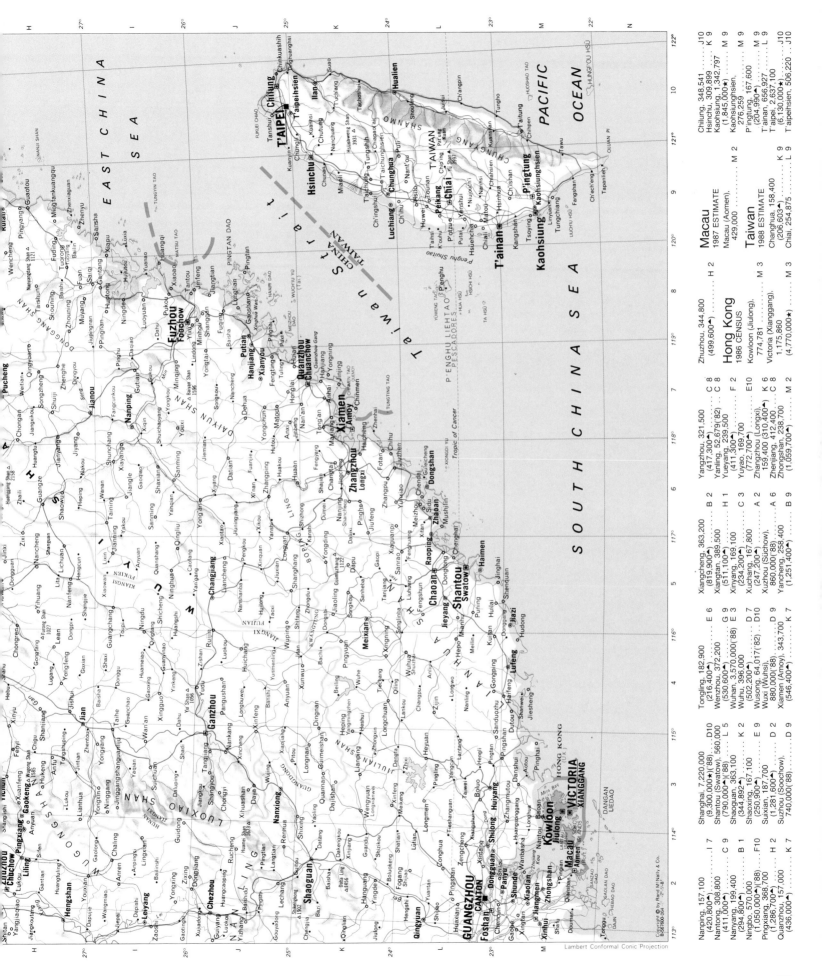

Japan

1985 CENSUS

Aizu-wakamatsu, 118,140 ... E12
Akita, 296,400 ... C13
Amagasaki, 509,115 ... H8
Aomori, 294,045 ... B13
Asahikawa, 363,631 ... p20
Ashikaga, 167,656 ... F12

Beppu, 134,775 ... I4
Chiba, 788,930 ... G13
Chigasaki, 185,030 ... G12
Chōshi, 87,883 ... G13
Fuji, 214,448 (370,000★) ... G11

Fukuyama, 360,261 ... F12
Funabashi, 506,966 ... G13
Gifu, 411,743 ... G9
Hachinohe, 241,430 ... B14
Hachiōji, 426,654 ... G12
Hakodate, 319,194 ... r18
Hamamatsu, 514,118 ... H10
Handa, 92,883 ... H9
Higashiōsaka, 522,805 ... H8
Hikone, 94,204 ... G9
Himeji, 452,917 (660,000★) ... H7

Hiratsuka, 229,990 ... G12
Hirosaki, 134,800 (176,082▲) ... B13
Hiroshima, 1,044,118 (1,575,000★) ... H5
Hitachi, 206,074 ... F13
Hōfu, 118,067 ... H4
Ichinomiya, 257,388 ... G9
Iizuka, 81,868 ... I3
Imabari, 125,115 ... I6
Ise, 105,455 ... H9

Isesaki, 112,459 ... G12
Ishinomaki, 122,674 ... E13
Iwaki (Taira), 350,569 ... F12
Iwakuni, 111,833 ... H5
Kagoshima, 530,502 ... K3
Kakogawa, 227,311 ... H7
Kamaishi, 60,007 ... C14
Kamakura, 175,495 ... G12
Kanazawa, 430,481 ... F9
Kariya, 112,403 ... H9
Kashiwa, 273,128 ... G12
Kasugai, 256,990 ... G9

Kawagoe, 285,437 ... G12
Kawaguchi, 403,015 ... G12
Kawasaki, 1,088,624 ... E13
Kiryū, 131,267 ... F12
Kishiwada, 185,731 ... H8
Kitakyūshū, 1,056,402 (1,525,000★) ... I3
Kitami, 107,281 ... p21
Kōbe, 1,410,834 ... H8
Kōchi, 312,241 ... I6
Kōfu, 202,405 ... G11
Komatsu, 106,041 ... F9

Kōriyama, 301,673 ... F12
Kumagaya, 143,496 ... F12
Kumamoto, 555,719 ... J3
Kurashiki, 413,632 ... H6
Kure, 226,488 ... H5
Kurume, 222,847 ... I3
Kushiro, 214,541 (195,000★) ... q22
Kyōto, 1,479,218 ... G8
Maebashi, 277,319 ... F12
Maizuru, 98,775 ... G8
Matsudo, 427,473 ... G12
Matsue, 140,005 ... G6

Matsumoto, 197,340 ... F10
Matsusaka, 116,886 ... H9
Matsuyama, 426,658 ... I5
Mito, 228,985 ... F13
Miyazaki, 279,114 ... K4
Morioka, 235,469 ... C14
Muroran, 136,208 (195,000★) ... q18
Nagahama, 55,531 ... G9
Nagano, 336,973 ... F11
Nagaoka, 183,756 ... E11
Nagasaki, 449,382 ... J2

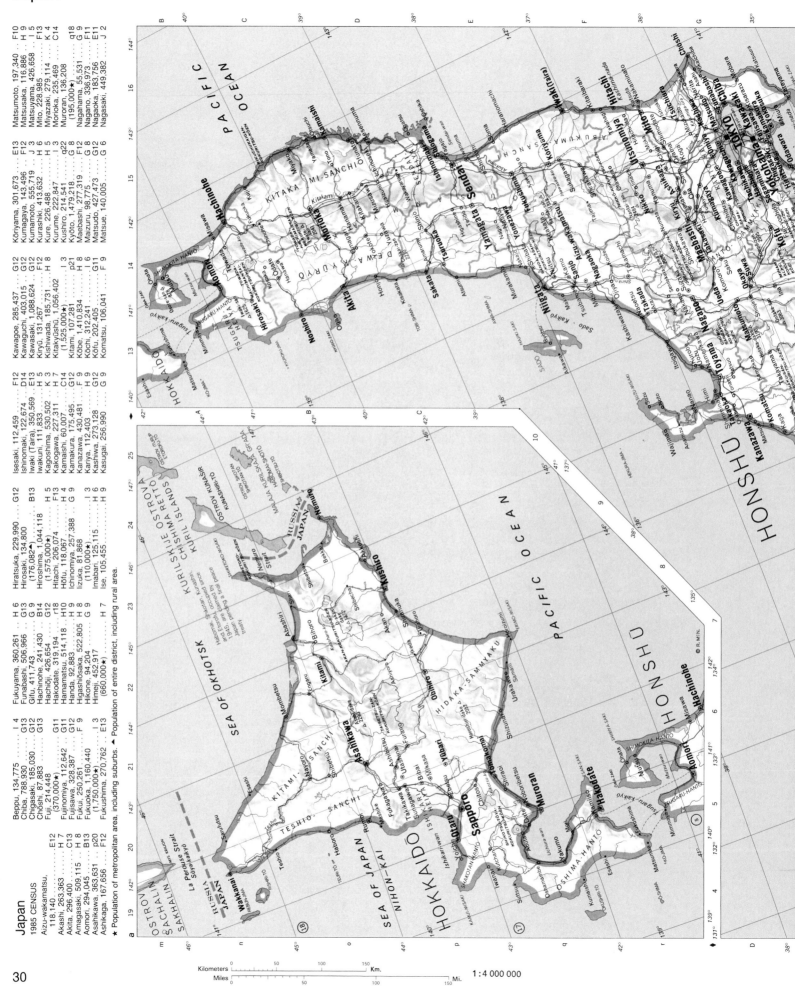

★ Population of metropolitan area, including suburbs. ▲ Population of entire district, including rural area.

Kilometers 0 50 100 150 Km.

Miles 0 50 100 150 Mi.

1 : 4 000 000

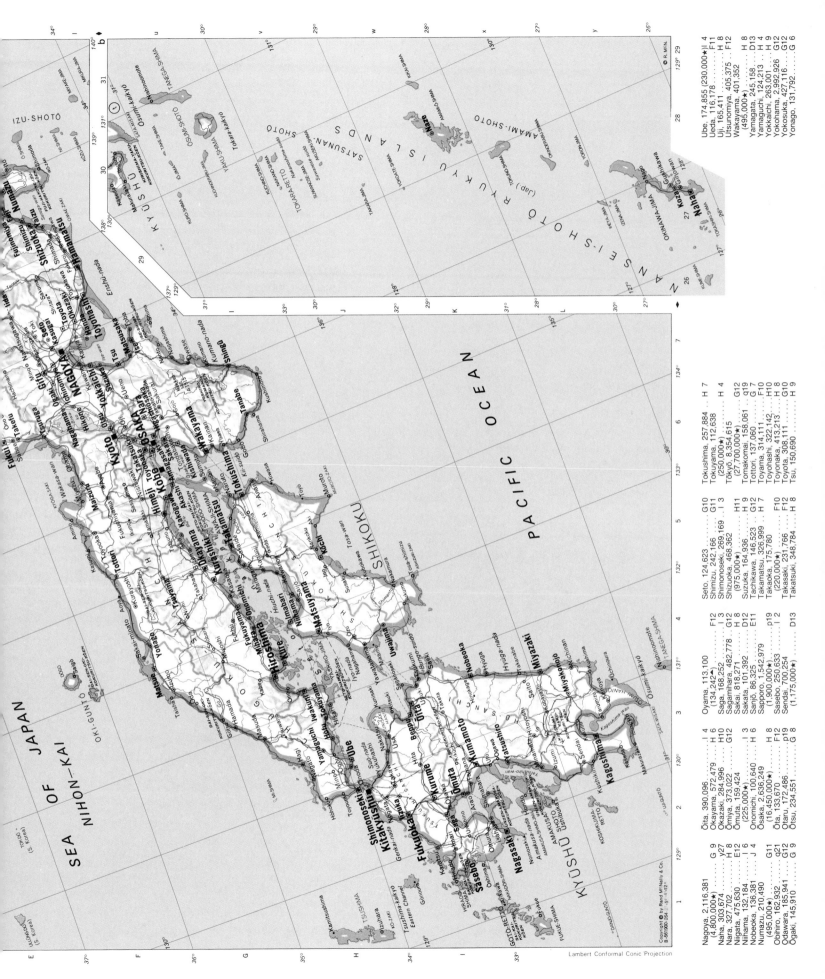

Southeastern Asia

Brunei
1981 CENSUS
Bandar Seri Begawan,
22,777 (64,000★) . . E 5

Cambodia
1986 ESTIMATE
Phnum Pénh, 700,000 C 3

Indonesia
1980 CENSUS
Ambon, 111,914
 (207,702▲) . . . . F 8
Balikpapan, 208,040
 (279,852▲) . . . . F 6
Bandung, 1,633,000
 (1,800,000★)('85) . . m13
Banjarmasin,
 424,000('83) . . . . F 5
Banjuwangi, 90,378 . . n17
Blitar, 78,503
 (100,000★) n16
Bogor, 246,946
 (560,000★) m13
Cilacap, 127,017 . . . . m14
Cirebon, 223,504
 (275,000★) m14
Denpasar, 159,233 . . G 6
Dili, 6,890 (67,039▲) . . G 8
Garut, 145,624 . . . . . m13
Jakarta, 9,200,000
 (10,000,000★)('89) m13
Jambi, 155,761
 (230,046▲) . . . . F 3
Jember, 171,284 . . . . n16
Kediri, 176,261
 (221,830▲) m16
Kudus, 154,478 . . . . m15
Kupang, 84,587 . . . . H 7
Madiun, 150,562
 (180,000★) m15
Magelang, 123,358
 (160,000★) m15
Malang, 547,000('83) m16
Manado, 217,091 . . . E 7
Medan, 2,110,000('85)E 2
Padang, 405,600
 (657,000★)('83) . . . . F 3
Pakanbaru, 186,199 . . E 3
Palembang,
 874,000('83) . . . . . F 3
Pangkalpinang, 90,078 F 4
Pasuruan, 95,864
 (125,000★) n16
Pekalongan, 132,413
 (260,000★) m14
Pemalang, 72,663 . . m14
Pematangsiantar, 150,296
 (175,000★) . . . . . . E 2
Pontianak,
 343,000('83) . . . . F 4
Probolinggo, 100,296 m16
Purwokerto, 143,787 m14
Salatiga, 85,740 . . . m15
Samarinda, 182,473
 (264,012▲) . . . . . . F 6
Semarang,
 1,206,000('83) . . m15
Sukabumi, 109,898
 (225,000★) m13
Surabaya,
 2,345,000('85) . . m16
Surakarta, 491,000
 (575,000★)('83) m15
Tanjungkarang-
 Telukbetung, 284,167
 (375,000★) k12
Tasikmalaya, 192,267 m14
Tegal, 131,440
 (340,000★) m14
Tual, 7,833 . . . . G 9
Tulungagung, 91,585 n15
Ujungpandang,
 841,000('83) . . . . G 6
Yogyakarta, 421,000
 (510,000★)('83) m15

Laos
1975 ESTIMATE
Louangphrabang,
 46,000 . . . . B 3
Paksé, 47,000 . . . . . B 4
Savannakhet, 53,000 B 3
Viangchan,
 377,409('85) . . . . . . B 3

Malaysia
1980 CENSUS
Alor Setar, 69,435 . . D 3
George Town (Pinang),
 248,241 (495,000★) D 3
Ipoh, 293,849 . . . . . E 3
Johor Baharu,
 246,395 . . . . E 3
Kelang, 192,080 . . . . E 3
Kota Baharu, 167,872 D 3
Kuala Lumpur, 919,610
 (1,475,000★) . . . . . . E 3
Kuala Terengganu,
 180,296 . . . . D 3
Kuantan, 131,547 . . . E 3

1:16 000 000

Kuching, 72,555 .... E 5
Melaka, 87,494 ...... E 3
Sandakan, 70,420 .. D 6
Seremban, 132,911 .. E 3
Sibu, 85,231 .... E 5

Myanmar
1983 CENSUS

Bago, 150,528 ..... B 2
Henzada, 82,005 ... B 2
Mandalay, 532,949 . A 2
Mawlamyine, 219,961 B 2
Monywa, 106,843 ... A 2
Pathein, 144,096 ... B 1
Pyè (Prome), 83,332 .. B 2
Sittwe (Akyab),
  107,621 .... A 1
Yangon (Rangoon),
  2,705,039
  (2,800,000★) ...... B 2

Philippines
1990 CENSUS

Angeles, 236,000 .... q19
Bacolod, 364,000 ... C 7
Baguio, 183,000 .... p19
Batangas, 31,600
  (184,000▲) r19
Cabanatuan, 75,700
  (173,000) q19
Cavite, 92,000
  (175,000★) q19
Cebu, 610,000
  (720,000★) .... C 7
Cotabato, 127,000 .. D 7
Dagupan, 122,000 .. p19
Davao, 569,300
  (850,000★) .... D 8
Dumaguete, 80,000 .. D 7
Iloilo, 311,000 .... C 7
Legaspi, 63,000
  (121,000▲) r20
Lipa, 30,000
  (160,000▲) r19
Lucena, 151,000 ... r19
Malalos, 95,699('80) .. q19
Manila, 1,587,000
  (6,800,000★) q19
Naga, 115,000 ..... r20
Pasig, 318,853('84) .. q19
Puerto Princesa, 52,000
  (92,000▲) .... D 6
Quezon City,
  1,632,000 .... q19
San Fernando,
  110,891('80) q19
San Pablo, 83,900
  (161,000▲) q19
Tarlac, 38,205
  (175,691▲)('80) ... q19
Zamboanga, 107,000
  (444,000▲) .... D 7

Singapore
1989 ESTIMATE

Singapore, 2,685,400
  (3,025,000★) ...... E 3

Thailand
1988 ESTIMATE

Bangkok see Krung
  Thep .... C 3
Chiang Mai, 164,030 . B 2
Hat Yai, 138,046 ... D 3
Khon Kaen, 131,340 . B 3
Krung Thep (Bangkok),
  5,716,779
  (6,450,000★) ...... C 3
Nakhon Ratchasima,
  204,982 .... C 3
Nakhon Sawan,
  105,220 .... B 3
Nakhon Si Thammarat,
  72,407 .... D 2
Phitsanulok, 77,675 . B 3
Songkhla, 84,433 ... D 3
Ubon Ratchathani,
  100,374 .... B 3
Udon Thani, 81,202 . B 3

Vietnam
1979 CENSUS

Can Tho, 182,856 .. C 4
Da Nang, 318,653 .. B 4
Hai Phong, 456,000
  (1,279,067▲)('89) . A 4
Ha Noi, 1,089,000
  (1,500,000★)('89) . A 4
Hue, 165,710 ..... B 4
My Tho, 101,493 ... C 4
Nam Dinh, 160,179 .. A 4
Nha Trang, 172,663 .. C 4
Phan Thiet, 75,241 . C 4
Qui Nhon, 127,211 .. C 4
Rach Gia, 81,075 ... C 4
Saigon see Thanh Pho Ho
  Chi Minh .... C 4
Thanh Pho Ho Chi Minh
  (Saigon), 3,169,000
  (3,300,000★)('89) . C 4
Vinh, 159,753 ..... B 4

★ Population of metropolitan area, including suburbs.
▲ Population of entire district, including rural area.

33

Myanmar, Thailand, and Indochina

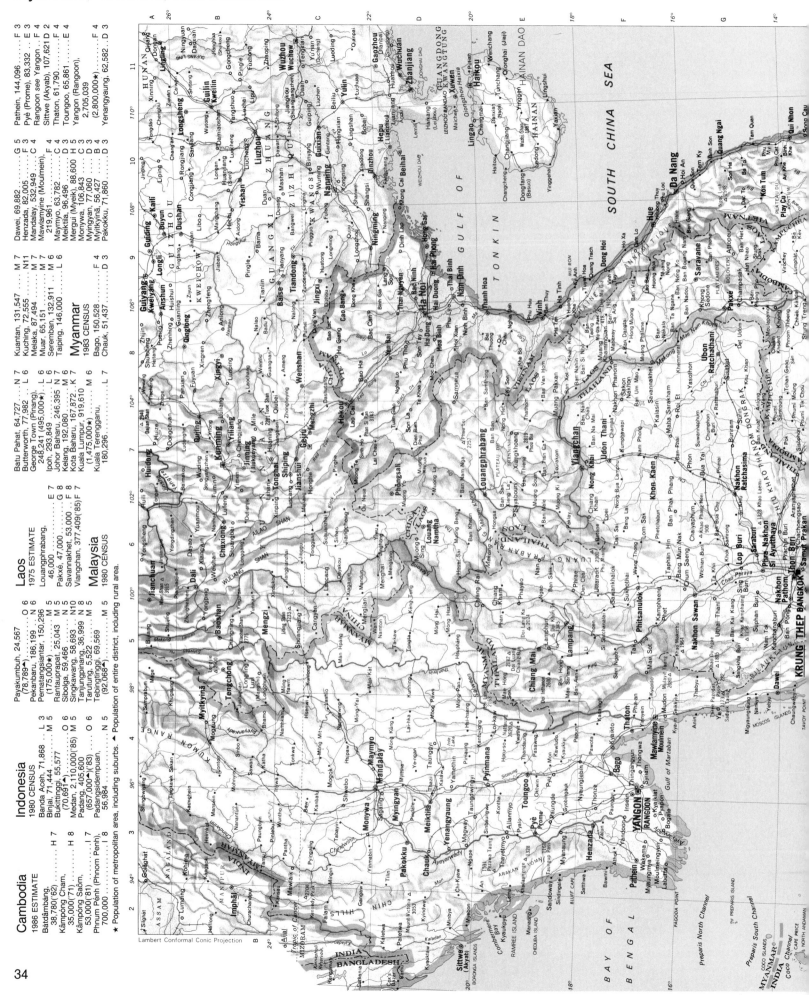

Cambodia

1986 ESTIMATE

Bătdâmbâng,
38,780('62) .... H 7
Kâmpóng Cham,
35,000('71) .... H 8
Kâmpóng Saôm,
53,000('81) .... I 7
Phnom Pénh (Phnom Penh),
700,000 .... I 8

Indonesia

1980 CENSUS

Banda Aceh, 71,868 ..... L 3
Binjai, 71,444 .... M 5
Bukittinggi, 55,577
(70,691)▲ .... O 6
Medan, 2,110,000('85) .. M 5
Padang, 405,600 .... O 6
Padangsidempuan,
56,984 .... N 5

Payakumbuh, 24,567
(78,789▲) .... O 6
Pekanbaru, 186,199 ..... N 6
Pematangsiantar, 150,296
(175,000★) .... M 5
Rantauprapat, 25,043 ... M 5
Sibolga, 59,466
(70,691)▲ .... M 5
Singkawang, 58,693 .... N10
Tanjungpinang, 36,999 .. M 5
Tarutung, 5,522 .... M 5
Tebingtinggi, 69,569
(92,068▲) .... N 5

Laos

1975 ESTIMATE

Louangphrabang,
46,000 .... E 7
Pakxé, 47,000 .... G 8
Savannakhét, 53,000 ... F 8
Viangchan, 377,409('85) F 7

Malaysia

1980 CENSUS

Batu Pahat, 64,727 ..... N 7
Butterworth, 77,982 .... L 6
George Town (Pinang),
248,241 (495,000★) .. L 6
Ipoh, 293,849 .... L 6
Johor Baharu, 246,395 .. N 7
Kelang, 192,080 .... M 6
Kota Baharu, 167,872 ... K 7
Kuala Lumpur, 919,610
(1,475,000★) .... M 7
Kuala Terengganu,
180,296 .... L 7

Myanmar

1983 CENSUS

Bago, 150,528 .... F 4
Chauk, 51,437 .... D 3

Dawei, 69,882 .... G 5
Henzada, 82,005 .... F 4
Mandalay, 532,949 ..... C 4
Mawlamyine (Moulmein),
219,961 .... F 4
Maymyo, 63,782 .... C 4
Meiktila, 96,496 .... D 3
Mergui (Myeik), 88,600 . H 5
Monywa, 106,843 ...... C 3
Myingyan, 77,060 ...... D 3
Myitkyina, 56,427 ...... B 4
Pakokku, 71,860 .... D 3

Pathein, 144,096 .... F 3
Pyè (Prome), 83,332 .... E 3
Rangoon see Yangon
Sittwe (Akyab), 107,621 D 2
Thaton, 61,790 .... F 4
Toungoo, 65,861 .... E 4
Yangon (Rangoon),
2,705,039
(2,800,000★) .... F 4
Yenangyaung, 62,582 .. D 3

★ Population of metropolitan area, including suburbs. ▲ Population of entire district, including rural area.

Lambert Conformal Conic Projection

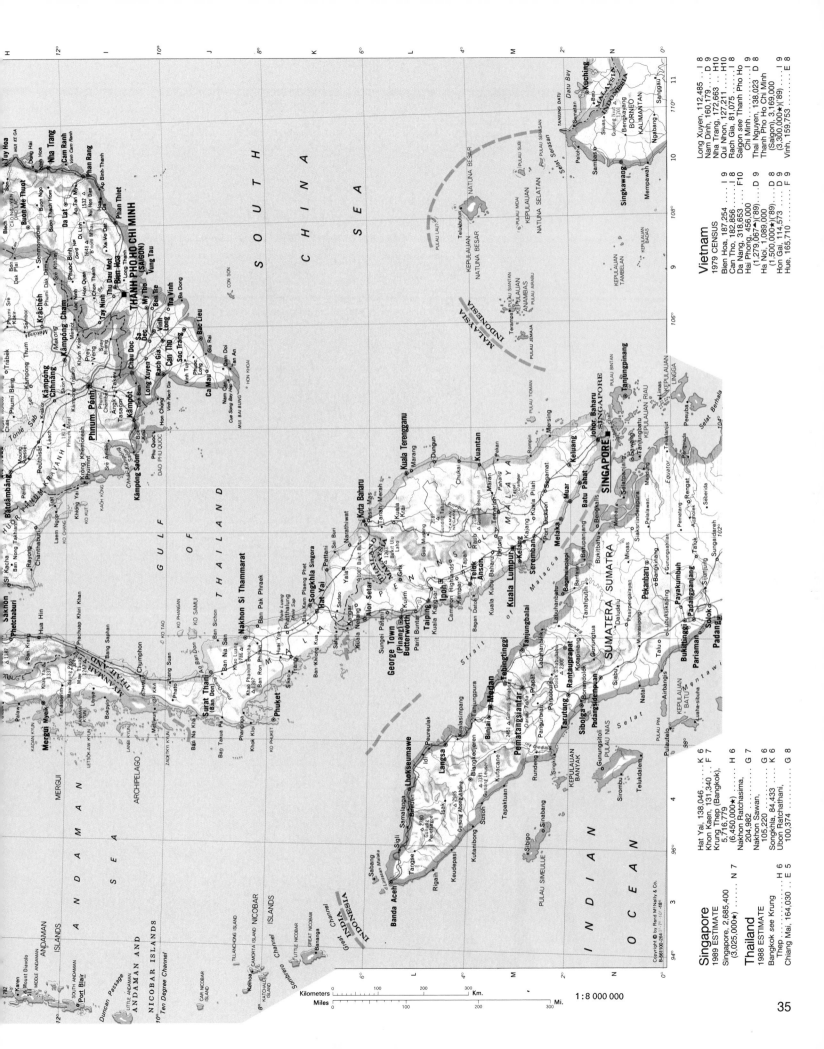

Long Xuyen, 112,485 .... I 8
Nam Dinh, 160,179 .... D 9
Nha Trang, 172,663 .... H10
Qui Nhon, 127,211 .... H10
Rach Gia, 81,075 .... I 8
Saigon see Thanh Pho Ho Chi Minh
Thai Nguyen, 138,023 .... D 8
Thanh Pho Ho Chi Minh (Saigon), 3,169,000 (3,300,000★)('89) .... I 9
Vinh, 159,753 .... E 8

Vietnam
1979 CENSUS
Bien Hoa, 187,254 .... I 9
Can Tho, 182,856 .... I 8
Da Nang, 318,653 .... F10
Hai Phong, 456,000 Chi Minh 9
(1,279,067★)('89) .... D 9
Ha Noi, 1,089,000 (1,500,000★)('89) .... D 8
Hon Gai, 114,573 .... D 9
Hue, 165,710 .... F 9

Singapore
1989 ESTIMATE
Singapore, 2,685,400 (3,025,000★) .... N 7

Thailand
1988 ESTIMATE
Bangkok see Krung Thep .... H 6
Chiang Mai, 164,030 .... E 5

Hat Yai, 138,046 .... K 6
Khon Kaen, 131,340 .... F 7
Krung Thep (Bangkok), 5,716,779 (6,450,000★) .... H 6
Nakhon Ratchasima, 204,982 .... G 7
Nakhon Sawan, 105,220 .... G 6
Songkhla, 84,433 .... K 6
Ubon Ratchathani, 100,374 .... G 8

1:8 000 000

Kilometers 0 100 200 300 Km.
Miles 0 100 200 300 Mi.

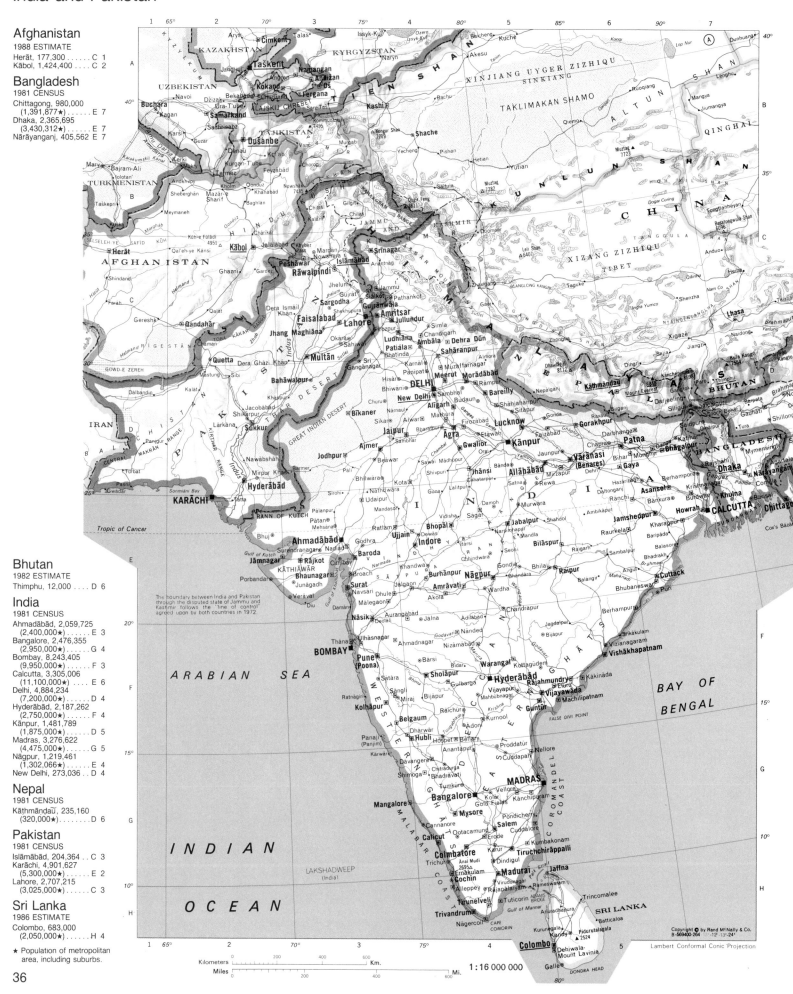

India and Pakistan

Afghanistan
1988 ESTIMATE
Herāt, 177,300 . . . . . . C 1
Kābol, 1,424,400 . . . . C 2

Bangladesh
1981 CENSUS
Chittagong, 980,000
(1,391,877★) . . . . . . E 7
Dhaka, 2,365,695
(3,430,312★) . . . . . . E 7
Nārāyanganj, 405,562 E 7

Bhutan
1982 ESTIMATE
Thimphu, 12,000 . . . . D 6

India
1981 CENSUS
Ahmadābād, 2,059,725
(2,400,000★) . . . . . . E 3
Bangalore, 2,476,355
(2,950,000★) . . . . . . G 4
Bombay, 8,243,405
(9,950,000★) . . . . . . F 3
Calcutta, 3,305,006
(11,100,000★) . . . . . E 6
Delhi, 4,884,234
(7,200,000★) . . . . . . D 4
Hyderābād, 2,187,262
(2,750,000★) . . . . . . F 4
Kānpur, 1,481,789
(1,875,000★) . . . . . . D 5
Madras, 3,276,622
(4,475,000★) . . . . . . G 5
Nāgpur, 1,219,461
(1,302,066★) . . . . . . E 4
New Delhi, 273,036 . . D 4

Nepal
1981 CENSUS
Kāthmāndaŭ, 235,160
(320,000★) . . . . D 6

Pakistan
1981 CENSUS
Islāmābād, 204,364 . . C 3
Karāchi, 4,901,627
(5,300,000★) . . . . . . E 2
Lahore, 2,707,215
(3,025,000★) . . . . . . C 3

Sri Lanka
1986 ESTIMATE
Colombo, 683,000
(2,050,000★) . . . . . . H 4

★ Population of metropolitan
   area, including suburbs.

36

The boundary between India and Pakistan
through the disputed state of Jammu and
Kashmir follows the "line of control"
agreed upon by both countries in 1972.

Copyright © by Rand McNally & Co.
B-569400-264

Lambert Conformal Conic Projection

Kilometers
Km.
Miles
Mi.

1 : 16 000 000

India

1981 CENSUS

Akola, 225,412 . . . . . . B 4	
Amrāvati, 261,404 . . B 4	
Aurangābād, 284,607	
(316,421★) . . . . . . C 3	
Bangalore, 2,476,355	
(2,950,000★) . . . . F 4	
Baroda, 734,473	
(744,881★) . . . . . . A 2	
Belgaum, 274,430	
(300,372★) . . . . . . E 3	
Bhāvnagar, 307,121	
(308,642★) . . . . . . B 2	
Bhilai, 290,090	
(490,214★) . . . . . . B 6	
Bhubaneswar,	
219,211 . . . . B 8	
Bombay, 8,243,405	
(9,950,000★) . . . . C 2	
Calicut, 394,447	
(546,058★) . . . . . . G 3	
Cochin, 513,249	
(685,836★) . . . . . . H 4	
Coimbatore, 704,514	
(965,000★) . . . . . . G 4	
Cuttack, 269,950	
(327,412★) . . . . . . B 8	
Dhule, 210,759 . . . . B 3	
Gulbarga, 221,325 . . . D 4	
Guntūr, 367,699 . . . . D 6	
Hubli, 527,108 . . . . . E 3	
Hyderābād, 2,187,262	
(2,750,000★) . . . . D 5	
Indore, 829,327	
(850,000★) . . . . . . A 3	
Kolhāpur, 340,625	
(351,392★) . . . . . . D 3	
Madras, 3,276,622	
(4,475,000★) . . . . F 6	
Madurai, 820,891	
(960,000★) . . . . . . H 5	
Mālegaon, 245,883 . . . B 3	
Mysore, 441,754	
(479,081★) . . . . . . F 4	
Nāgpur, 1,219,461	
(1,302,066★) . . . . B 5	
Nāsik, 262,428	
(429,034★) . . . . . . C 2	
Nellore, 237,065 . . . . E 5	
Pondicherry, 162,636	
(251,420★) . . . . . . G 5	
Pune (Poona), 1,203,351	
(1,775,000★) . . . . C 2	
Raipur, 338,245 . . . . B 6	
Salem, 361,394	
(518,615★) . . . . . . G 5	
Sholāpur, 511,103	
(514,860★) . . . . . . D 3	
Surat, 776,583	
(913,806★) . . . . . . B 2	
Thāna, 309,897 . . . . C 2	
Tiruchchirāppalli, 362,045	
(609,548★) . . . . . . G 5	
Trivandrum, 483,086	
(520,125★) . . . . . . H 4	
Ulhāsnagar, 273,668 . C 2	
Vijayawāda, 454,577	
(543,008★) . . . . . . D 6	
Vishākhapatnam, 565,321	
(603,630★) . . . . . . D 7	
Warangal, 335,150 . . C 5	

Sri Lanka

1986 ESTIMATE

Colombo, 683,000	
(2,050,000★) . . . . . I 5	
Dehiwala-Mount Lavinia,	
191,000 . . . . I 5	
Kandy, 130,000 . . . . I 6	
Kotte, 104,000 . . . . I 5	

★ Population of metropolitan
area, including suburbs.

37

Northern India and Pakistan

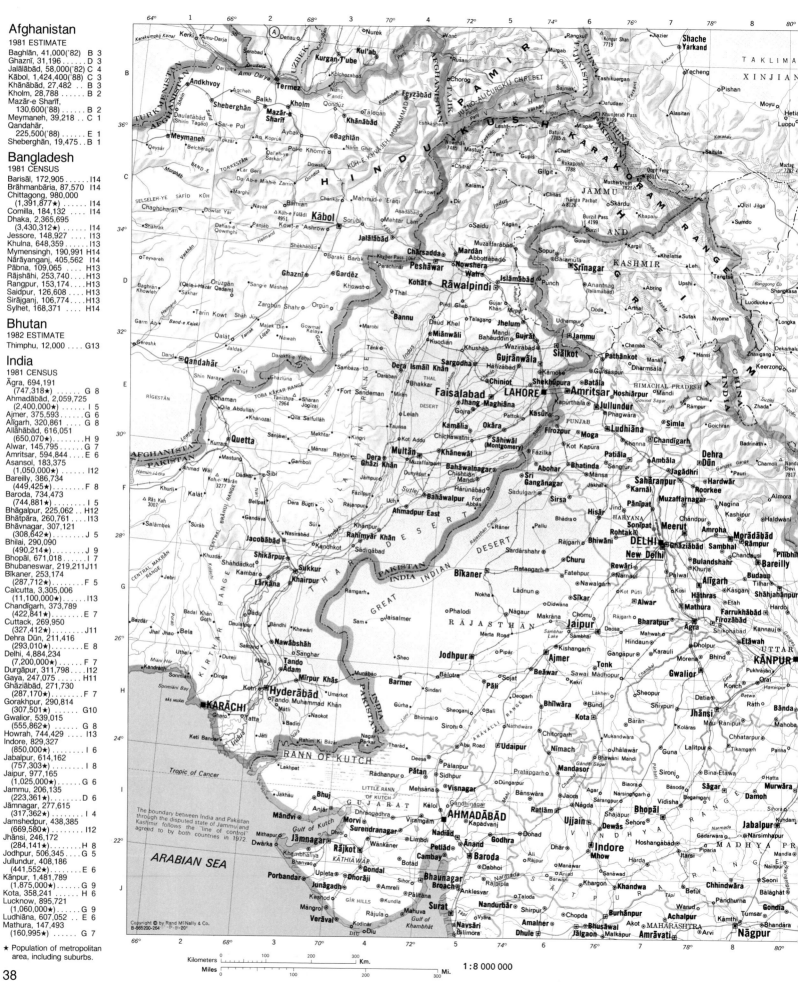

Afghanistan
1981 ESTIMATE
Baghlān, 41,000('82) . . . . B 3
Ghaznī, 31,196 . . . . D 3
Jalālābād, 58,000('82) . C 4
Kābol, 1,424,400('88) . C 3
Khānābād, 27,482 . . . . . B 3
Kholm, 28,788 . . . . . B 2
Mazār-e Sharīf,
  130,600('88) . . . . . . B 2
Meymaneh, 39,218 . . C 1
Qandahār,
  225,500('88) . . . . . . E 1
Sheberghān, 19,475 . . B 1

Bangladesh
1981 CENSUS
Barisāl, 172,905 . . . . I14
Brāhmanbāria, 87,570 I14
Chittagong, 980,000
  (1,391,877★) I14
Comilla, 184,132 . . . . I14
Dhaka, 2,365,695
  (3,430,312★) I14
Jessore, 148,927 . . . . I13
Khulna, 648,359 . . . . I14
Mymensingh, 190,991 H14
Nārāyanganj, 405,562 I14
Pābna, 109,065 . . . . . H13
Rājshāhi, 253,740 . . . H13
Rangpur, 153,174 . . . . H13
Saidpur, 126,608 . . . . H13
Sirājganj, 106,774 . . . H13
Sylhet, 168,371 . . . . . H14

Bhutan
1982 ESTIMATE
Thimphu, 12,000 . . . . G13

India
1981 CENSUS
Āgra, 694,191
  (747,318★) . . . . . . G 8
Ahmadābād, 2,059,725
  (2,400,000★) . . . . . I 5
Ajmer, 375,593 . . . . . G 6
Alīgarh, 320,861 . . . . G 8
Allāhābād, 616,051
  (650,070★) . . . . . . H 9
Alwar, 145,795 . . . . . . G 7
Amritsar, 594,844 . . . E 6
Asansol, 183,375
  (1,050,000★) I12
Bareilly, 386,734
  (449,425★) . . . . . . F 8
Baroda, 734,473
  (744,881★) . . . . . . I 5
Bhāgalpur, 225,062 . . H12
Bhātpāra, 260,761 . . . I13
Bhāvnagar, 307,121
  (308,642★) . . . . . . J 5
Bhilai, 290,090
  (490,214★) . . . . . . J 9
Bhopāl, 671,018 . . . . . I 7
Bhubaneswar, 219,211 J11
Bīkaner, 253,174
  (287,712★) . . . . . . F 5
Calcutta, 3,305,006
  (11,100,000★) I13
Chandīgarh, 373,789
  (422,841★) . . . . . . E 7
Cuttack, 269,950
  (327,412★) J11
Dehra Dūn, 211,416
  (293,010★) . . . . . . E 8
Delhi, 4,884,234
  (7,200,000★) . . . . . F 7
Durgāpur, 311,798 . . . I12
Gaya, 247,075 . . . . . . H11
Ghāziābād, 271,730
  (287,170★) . . . . . . F 7
Gorakhpur, 290,814
  (307,501★) G10
Gwalior, 539,015
  (555,862★) . . . . . . G 8
Howrah, 744,429 . . . . I13
Indore, 829,327
  (850,000★) . . . . . . I 6
Jabalpur, 614,162
  (757,303★) . . . . . . I 8
Jaipur, 977,165
  (1,025,000★) . . . . . G 6
Jammu, 206,135
  (223,361★) . . . . . . D 6
Jāmnagar, 277,615
  (317,362★) . . . . . . I 4
Jamshedpur, 438,385
  (669,580★) I12
Jhānsi, 246,172
  (284,141★) . . . . . . H 8
Jodhpur, 506,345 . . . . G 5
Jullundur, 408,186
  (441,552★) . . . . . . E 6
Kānpur, 1,481,789
  (1,875,000★) . . . . . G 9
Kota, 358,241 . . . . . . H 6
Lucknow, 895,721
  (1,060,000★) . . . . . G 9
Ludhiāna, 607,052 . . . E 6
Mathura, 147,493
  (160,995★) . . . . . . G 7

★ Population of metropolitan
  area, including suburbs.

38

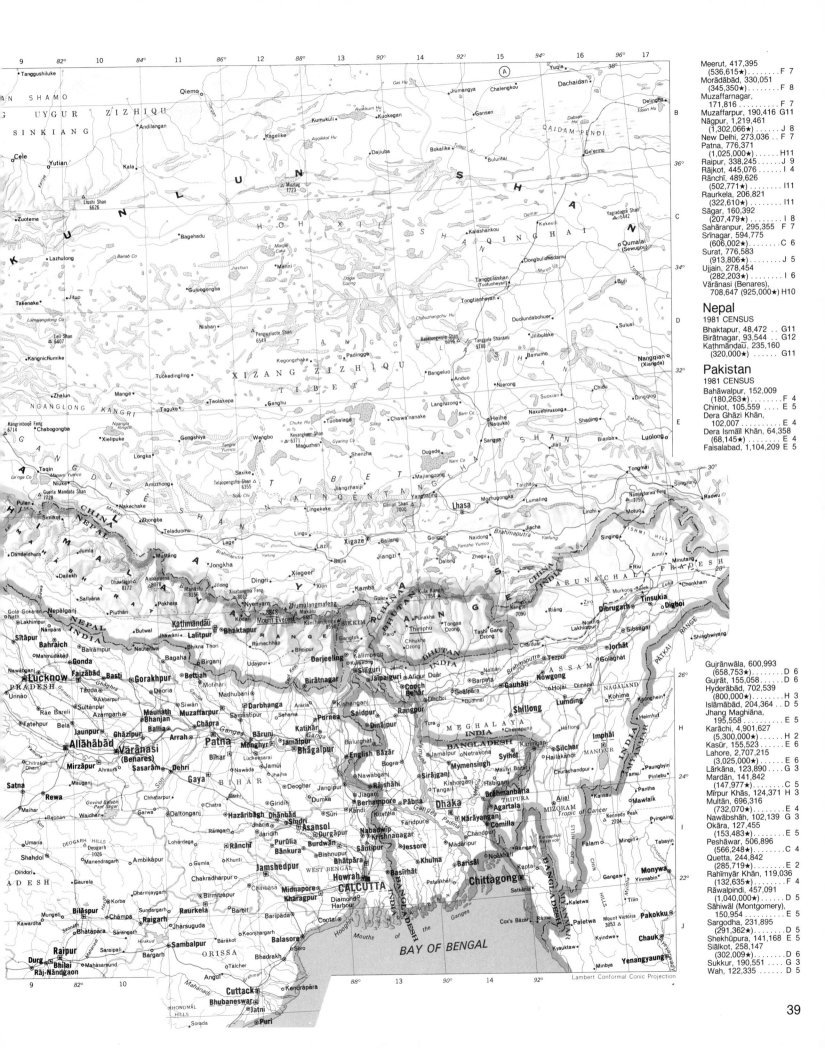

Meerut, 417,395
  (536,615★)........ F 7
Morādābād, 330,051
  (345,350★)........ F 8
Muzaffarnagar,
  171,816 .... F 7
Muzaffarpur, 190,416 G11
Nāgpur, 1,219,461
  (1,302,066★)..... J 8
New Delhi, 273,036 .. F 7
Patna, 776,371
  (1,025,000★)..... H11
Raipur, 338,245..... J 9
Rājkot, 445,076..... I 4
Rānchī, 489,626
  (502,771★)....... I11
Raurkela, 206,821
  (322,610★)....... I11
Sāgar, 160,392
  (207,479★)....... I 8
Sahāranpur, 295,355.. F 7
Srīnagar, 594,775
  (606,002★)....... C 6
Surat, 776,583
  (913,806★)....... J 5
Ujjain, 278,454
  (282,203★)....... I 6
Vārānasi (Benares),
  708,647 (925,000★) H10

Nepal
1981 CENSUS

Bhaktapur, 48,472 .. G11
Birātnagar, 93,544 .. G12
Kathmāndaū, 235,160
  (320,000★) G11

Pakistan
1981 CENSUS

Bahāwalpur, 152,009
  (180,263★)....... F 4
Chiniot, 105,559 .... E 5
Dera Ghāzi Khān,
  102,007 .... E 4
Dera Ismāīl Khān, 64,358
  (68,145★) .... E 4
Faisalabad, 1,104,209 E 5

Gujrānwāla, 600,993
  (658,753★)....... D 6
Gujrāt, 155,058 ....D 6
Hyderābād, 702,539
  (800,000★)....... H 3
Islāmābād, 204,364 .. D 5
Jhang Maghiāna,
  195,558 .... E 5
Karāchi, 4,901,627
  (5,300,000★)..... H 2
Kasūr, 155,523 ..... E 6
Lahore, 2,707,215
  (3,025,000★)..... E 6
Lārkāna, 123,890 ... G 3
Mardān, 141,842
  (147,977★)....... C 5
Mīrpur Khās, 124,371 H 3
Multān, 696,316
  (732,070★)....... E 4
Nawābshāh, 102,139 G 3
Okāra, 127,455
  (153,483★)....... E 5
Peshāwar, 506,896
  (566,248★)....... C 4
Quetta, 244,842
  (285,719★)....... E 2
Rahīmyār Khān, 119,036
  (132,635★)....... F 4
Rāwalpindi, 457,091
  (1,040,000★)..... D 5
Sāhiwāl (Montgomery),
  150,954 .... E 5
Sargodha, 231,895
  (291,362★)....... D 5
Shekhūpura, 141,168 E 5
Siālkot, 258,147
  (302,009★)....... D 6
Sukkur, 190,551 ... G 3
Wah, 122,335 ...... D 5

39

Eastern Mediterranean Lands

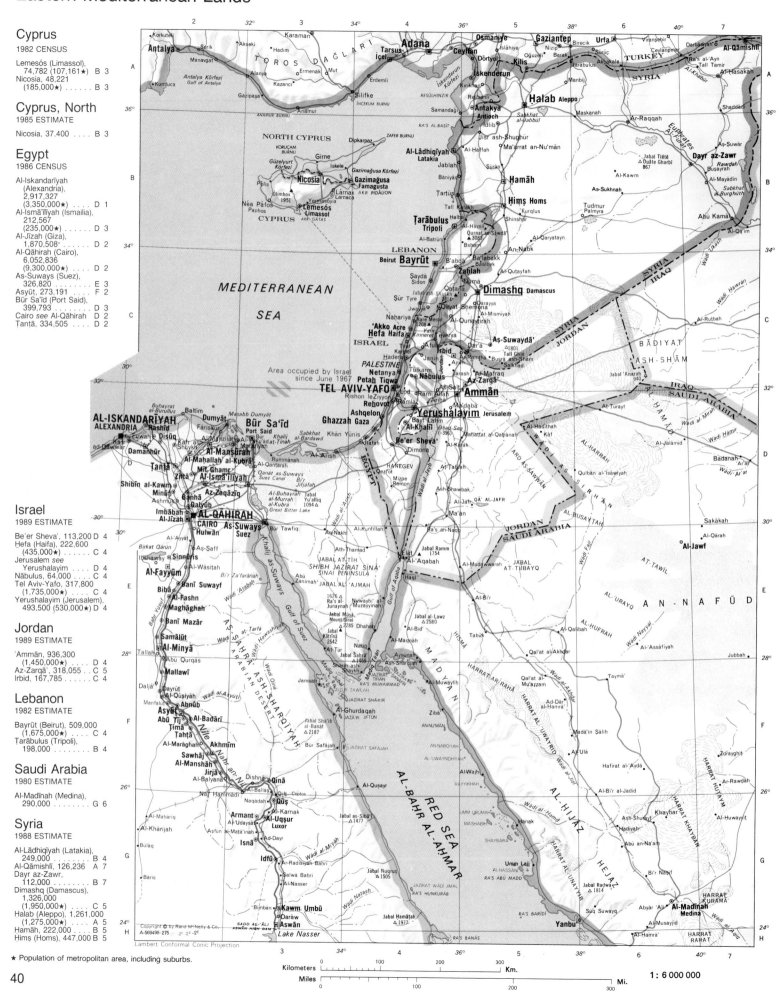

Cyprus
1982 CENSUS

Lemesós (Limassol),
74,782 (107,161★) . B 3
Nicosia, 48,221
(185,000★) . . . . . B 3

Cyprus, North
1985 ESTIMATE

Nicosia, 37,400 . . . . B 3

Egypt
1986 CENSUS

Al-Iskandarīyah
(Alexandria),
2,917,327
(3,350,000★) . . . . D 1
Al-Ismāʿīlīyah (Ismailia),
212,567
(235,000★) . . . . . D 3
Al-Jīzah (Giza),
1,870,508* . . . . . D 2
Al-Qāhirah (Cairo),
6,052,836
(9,300,000★) . . . . D 2
As-Suways (Suez),
326,820 . . . . E 3
Asyūṭ, 273,191 . . . . F 2
Būr Saʿīd (Port Said),
399,793 . . . . D 3
Cairo see Al-Qāhirah . D 2
Ṭanṭā, 334,505 . . . . D 2

Israel
1989 ESTIMATE

Beʾer Shevaʾ, 113,200 D 4
Ḥefa (Haifa), 222,600
(435,000★) . . . . . . C 4
Jerusalem see
Yerushalayim . . . . D 4
Nābulus, 64,000 . . . . C 4
Tel Aviv-Yafo, 317,800
(1,735,000★) . . . . D 4
Yerushalayim (Jerusalem),
493,500 (530,000★) D 4

Jordan
1989 ESTIMATE

ʿAmmān, 936,300
(1,450,000★) . . . . D 4
Az-Zarqāʾ, 318,055 . . C 5
Irbid, 167,785 . . . . . C 4

Lebanon
1982 ESTIMATE

Bayrūt (Beirut), 509,000
(1,675,000★) . . . . C 4
Ṭarābulus (Tripoli),
198,000 . . . . B 4

Saudi Arabia
1980 ESTIMATE

Al-Madīnah (Medina),
290,000 . . . . G 6

Syria
1988 ESTIMATE

Al-Lādhiqīyah (Latakia),
249,000 . . . . B 4
Al-Qāmishlī, 126,236 . A 7
Dayr az-Zawr,
112,000 . . . . B 7
Dimashq (Damascus),
1,326,000
(1,950,000★) . . . . C 5
Halab (Aleppo), 1,261,000
(1,275,000★) . . . . A 5
Hamāh, 222,000 . . . . B 5
Hims (Homs), 447,000 B 5

★ Population of metropolitan area, including suburbs.

40

Lambert Conformal Conic Projection

Africa

Abidjan, 1,950,000 ('83) .... E 3
Accra, 859,640 ('84) (1,250,000★) .... E 3
Adis Abeba (Addis Ababa), 1,686,300 ('88) (1,500,000★) .... E 7
Alger (Algiers), 1,507,241 ('87) (2,547,983★) ...B 4
ALGERIA .... C 4
Al-Iskandarīyah (Alexandria), 2,917,327 ('86) (3,350,000★) ...B 6
Al-Khartūm (Khartoum), 476,218 ('83) (1,450,000★) ...D 7
Al-Qāhirah (Cairo), 6,052,836 ('86) (9,300,000★) ...B 7
ANGOLA .... G 5
BENIN .... E 4
BOTSWANA .... H 6
Brazzaville, 585,812 ('84) .... F 5
BURKINA FASO .... D 3
BURUNDI .... F 6
CAMEROON .... E 4
Cape Town, 776,617 ('85) (1,790,000★) .... I 5
Casablanca, 2,139,204 ('82) (2,475,000★) ...B 3
CENTRAL AFRICAN REPUBLIC .... E 5
CHAD .... D 5
COMOROS .... G 8
CONGO .... F 5
COTE D'IVOIRE .... E 3
Dakar, 1,447,642 ('88) ...D 2
Dar es Salaam, 1,300,000 ('84) .... F 7
DJIBOUTI .... D 8
EGYPT .... C 6
EQUATORIAL GUINEA .... E 4
ERITREA .... D 7

ETHIOPIA .... E 7
GABON .... F 5
GAMBIA .... D 2
GHANA .... E 3
GUINEA .... D 2
GUINEA-BISSAU .... D 2
Johannesburg, 632,369 ('85) (3,650,000★) .... H 6
Kampala, 1,008,707 ('90) .... E 7
KENYA .... E 7
Kinshasa (Léopoldville), 3,000,000 ('86) (3,800,000★) .... F 5
Lagos, 1,213,000 ('87) (3,800,000★) .... E 4
LESOTHO .... H 6
LIBERIA .... E 3
LIBYA .... C 5
MADAGASCAR .... G 8
MALAWI .... G 7
MALI .... D 3
Maputo (Lourenço Marques), 1,069,727 ('89) .... H 7
MAURITANIA .... D 2
MOROCCO .... B 3
MOZAMBIQUE .... G 7
Nairobi, 1,505,000 ('90) .... E 7
NAMIBIA .... H 5
NIGER .... D 4
NIGERIA .... E 4
RWANDA .... F 6
SAO TOME AND PRINCIPE .... E 4
SENEGAL .... D 2
SIERRA LEONE .... E 2
SOMALIA .... E 8
SOUTH AFRICA ....I 6
SUDAN .... D 6
SWAZILAND .... H 7
TANZANIA .... F 7
Tarābulus (Tripoli), 990,697 ('84) .... B 5
TOGO .... E 4
Tunis, 596,654 ('84) (1,225,000★) .... B 5
TUNISIA .... B 4
UGANDA .... E 7
WESTERN SAHARA ....C 2
ZAIRE .... F 6
ZAMBIA .... G 6
ZIMBABWE .... G 6

★ Population of metropolitan area, including suburbs.

41

Copyright © by Rand McNally & Co.
A-580000-286   -3 -2 -4ᴱ

Lambert Azimuthal Equal Area Projection

Miles   0   200   400   600   800   1000 Mi.
Kilometers   0   400   800   1200   1600 Km.

1:40 000 000

Northern Africa

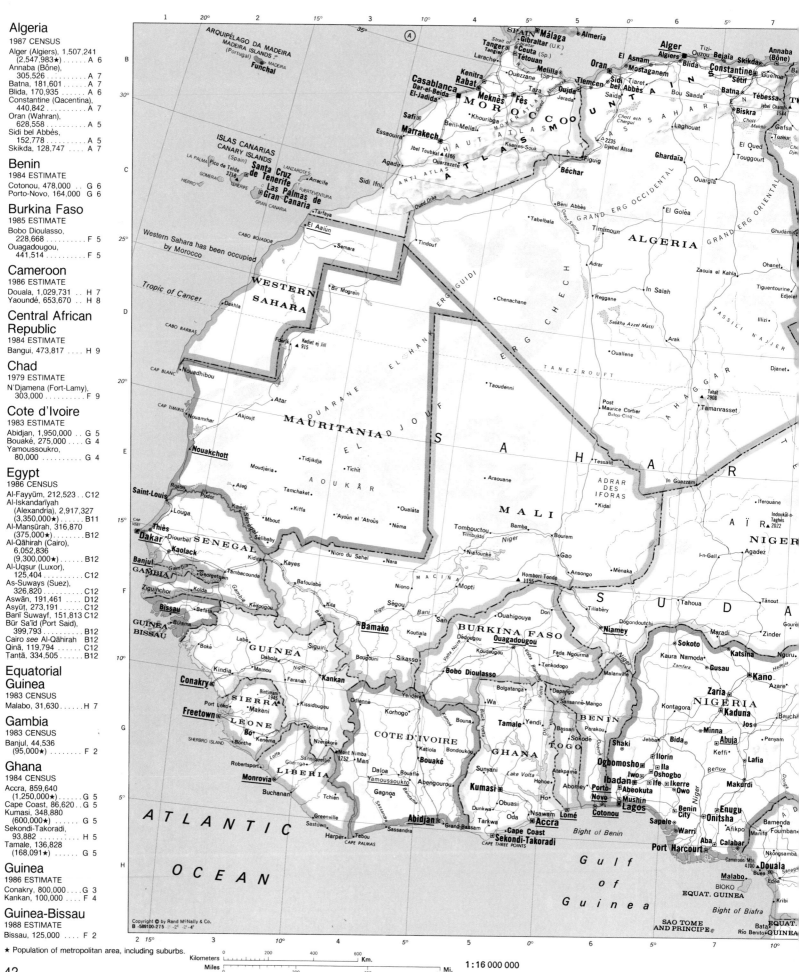

Algeria
1987 CENSUS
Alger (Algiers), 1,507,241
(2,547,983★) . . . . . . A 6
Annaba (Bône),
305,526 . . . . . A 7
Batna, 181,601 . . . . . A 7
Blida, 170,935 . . . . . A 6
Constantine (Qacentina),
440,842 . . . . A 7
Oran (Wahran),
628,558 . . . . A 5
Sidi bel Abbès,
152,778 . . . . . . A 5
Skikda, 128,747 . . . . A 7

Benin
1984 ESTIMATE
Cotonou, 478,000 . . G 6
Porto-Novo, 164,000 G 6

Burkina Faso
1985 ESTIMATE
Bobo Dioulasso,
228,668 . . . . F 5
Ouagadougou,
441,514 . . . . F 5

Cameroon
1986 ESTIMATE
Douala, 1,029,731 . . H 7
Yaoundé, 653,670 . . H 8

Central African Republic
1984 ESTIMATE
Bangui, 473,817 . . . . H 9

Chad
1979 ESTIMATE
N'Djamena (Fort-Lamy),
303,000 . . . . F 9

Cote d'Ivoire
1983 ESTIMATE
Abidjan, 1,950,000 . . G 5
Bouaké, 275,000 . . . . G 4
Yamoussoukro,
80,000 . . . . G 4

Egypt
1986 CENSUS
Al-Fayyūm, 212,523 . . C 12
Al-Iskandarīyah
(Alexandria), 2,917,327
(3,350,000★) . . . . . . B 11
Al-Manṣūrah, 316,870
(375,000★) . . . . . . B 12
Al-Qāhirah (Cairo),
6,052,836
(9,300,000★) . . . . . . B 12
Al-Uqṣur (Luxor),
125,404 . . . . C 12
As-Suways (Suez),
326,820 . . . . C 12
Aswān, 191,461 . . . . D 12
Asyūṭ, 273,191 . . . . C 12
Banī Suwayf, 151,813 C 12
Būr Saʿīd (Port Said),
399,793 . . . . B 12
Cairo see Al-Qāhirah B 12
Qinā, 119,794 . . . . . C 12
Ṭanṭā, 334,505 . . . . B 12

Equatorial Guinea
1983 CENSUS
Malabo, 31,630 . . . . . H 7

Gambia
1983 CENSUS
Banjul, 44,536
(95,000★) . . . . F 2

Ghana
1984 CENSUS
Accra, 859,640
(1,250,000★) . . . . . . G 5
Cape Coast, 86,620 . . G 5
Kumasi, 348,880
(600,000★) . . . . G 5
Sekondi-Takoradi,
93,882 . . . . H 5
Tamale, 136,828
(168,091★) . . . . . . G 5

Guinea
1986 ESTIMATE
Conakry, 800,000 . . . . G 3
Kankan, 100,000 . . . . F 4

Guinea-Bissau
1988 ESTIMATE
Bissau, 125,000 . . . . F 2

★ Population of metropolitan area, including suburbs.

42

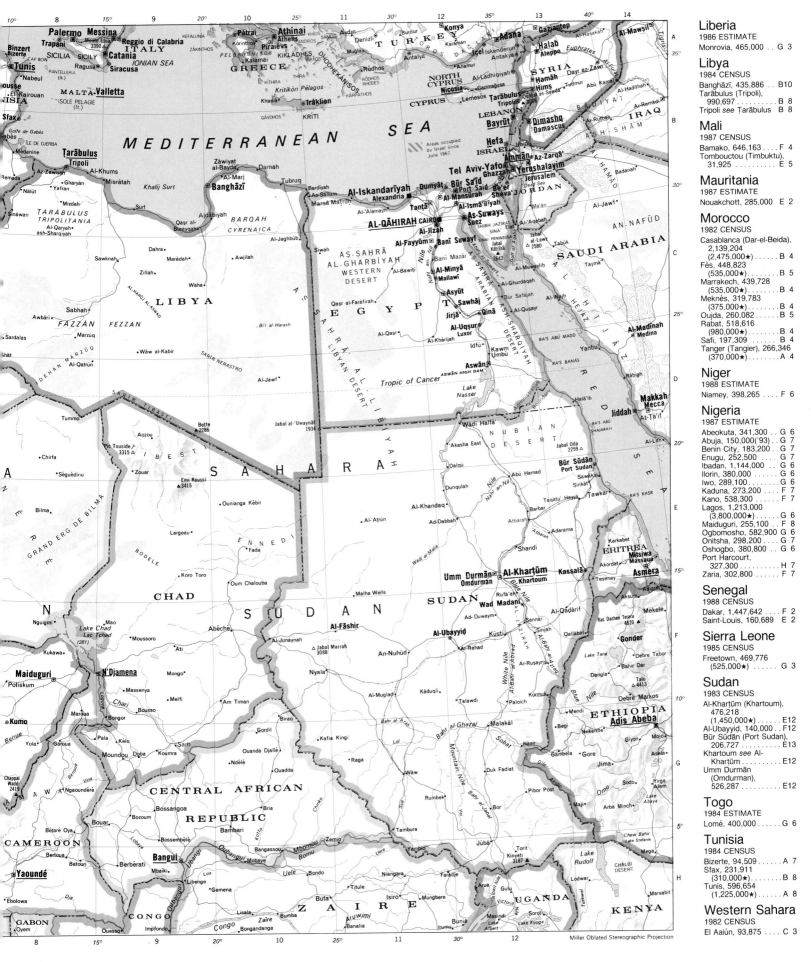

Liberia
1986 ESTIMATE
Monrovia, 465,000 . . G 3

Libya
1984 CENSUS
Banghāzī, 435,886 . . B10
Tarābulus (Tripoli),
   990,697 . . . . B 8
Tripoli see Tarābulus B 8

Mali
1987 CENSUS
Bamako, 646,163 . . . . F 4
Tombouctou (Timbuktu),
   31,925 . . . . E 5

Mauritania
1987 ESTIMATE
Nouakchott, 285,000 E 2

Morocco
1982 CENSUS
Casablanca (Dar-el-Beida),
   2,139,204
   (2,475,000★) . . . . . B 4
Fès, 448,823
   (535,000★) . . . . . . B 5
Marrakech, 439,728
   (535,000★) . . . . . . B 4
Meknès, 319,783
   (375,000★) . . . . . . B 4
Oujda, 260,082 . . . . . B 5
Rabat, 518,616
   (980,000★) . . . . . . B 4
Safi, 197,309 . . . . . . B 4
Tanger (Tangier), 266,346
   (370,000★) . . . . . . A 4

Niger
1988 ESTIMATE
Niamey, 398,265 . . . . F 6

Nigeria
1987 ESTIMATE
Abeokuta, 341,300 . . G 6
Abuja, 150,000('93) . . G 7
Benin City, 183,200 . . G 7
Enugu, 252,500 . . . . . G 7
Ibadan, 1,144,000 . . . G 6
Ilorin, 380,000 . . . . . . G 6
Iwo, 289,100 . . . . G 6
Kaduna, 273,200 . . . . F 7
Kano, 538,300 . . . . . F 7
Lagos, 1,213,000
   (3,800,000★) . . . . . G 6
Maiduguri, 255,100 . . F 8
Ogbomosho, 582,900 G 6
Onitsha, 298,200 . . . . G 7
Oshogbo, 380,800 . . . G 6
Port Harcourt,
   327,300 . . . . H 7
Zaria, 302,800 . . . . . F 7

Senegal
1988 CENSUS
Dakar, 1,447,642 . . . . F 2
Saint-Louis, 160,689 . E 2

Sierra Leone
1985 CENSUS
Freetown, 469,776
   (525,000★) . . . . . . G 3

Sudan
1983 CENSUS
Al-Khartūm (Khartoum),
   476,218
   (1,450,000★) E12
Al-Ubayyid, 140,000 . . F12
Būr Sūdān (Port Sudan),
   206,727 . . . . E13
Khartoum see Al-
   Khartūm E12
Umm Durmān
   (Omdurman),
   526,287 . . . . E12

Togo
1984 ESTIMATE
Lomé, 400,000 . . . . . G 6

Tunisia
1984 CENSUS
Bizerte, 94,509 . . . . . A 7
Sfax, 231,911
   (310,000★) . . . . . . B 8
Tunis, 596,654
   (1,225,000★) . . . . . A 8

Western Sahara
1982 CENSUS
El Aaiún, 93,875 . . . . C 3

Miller Oblated Stereographic Projection

43

Southern Africa

Angola
1983 ESTIMATE
Benguela, 155,000 . . D 2
Huambo, 203,000 . . . D 3
Lobito, 150,000 . . . . D 2
Luanda,
  1,459,900('89) . . . . C 2
Namibe, 100,000('81) E 2

Botswana
1987 ESTIMATE
Gaborone, 107,677 . . F 5

Burundi
1986 ESTIMATE
Bujumbura, 273,000 . B 5

Comoros
1990 ESTIMATE
Moroni, 23,432 . . . . D 8

Congo
1984 CENSUS
Brazzaville, 585,812 B 3
Pointe-Noire, 294,203 B 2

Gabon
1985 ESTIMATE
Libreville, 235,700 . A 1
Port-Gentil, 124,400 . . B 1

Kenya
1990 ESTIMATE
Mombasa, 537,000 . . B 7
Nairobi, 1,505,000 . . B 7
Nakuru, 101,700('84) B 7

Lesotho
1986 CENSUS
Maseru, 109,382 . . . . G 5

Madagascar
1984 ESTIMATE
Antananarivo,
  663,000('85) . . . . E 9
Antsiranana, 100,000 D 9
Fianarantsoa, 130,000 F 9
Mahajanga, 85,000 . . E 9
Toamasina, 100,000 . E 9

Malawi
1987 CENSUS
Blantyre, 331,588 . . E 7
Lilongwe, 233,973 . . D 6
Zomba, 42,878 . . . . E 7

Mauritius
1987 ESTIMATE
Port Louis, 139,730
  (420,000★) F11

Mayotte
1985 ESTIMATE
Dzaoudzi, 5,865
  (6,979★) . . . . D 9

Mozambique
1989 ESTIMATE
Beira, 291,604 . . . . . E 6
Maputo (Lourenço
  Marques),
  1,069,727 . . . . . . G 6
Xai-Xai, 51,620('86) . . G 6

Namibia
1988 ESTIMATE
Windhoek, 114,500 . . F 3

Reunion
1982 CENSUS
Saint-Denis, 84,400
  (109,072▲) F11

Rwanda
1983 ESTIMATE
Kigali, 181,600 . . . . B 6

Sao Tome and Principe
1970 CENSUS
São Tomé, 17,380 . . . A 1

Seychelles
1984 ESTIMATE
Victoria, 23,000 . . . . B11

★ Population of metropolitan area, including suburbs.
▲ Population of entire district, including rural area.

44

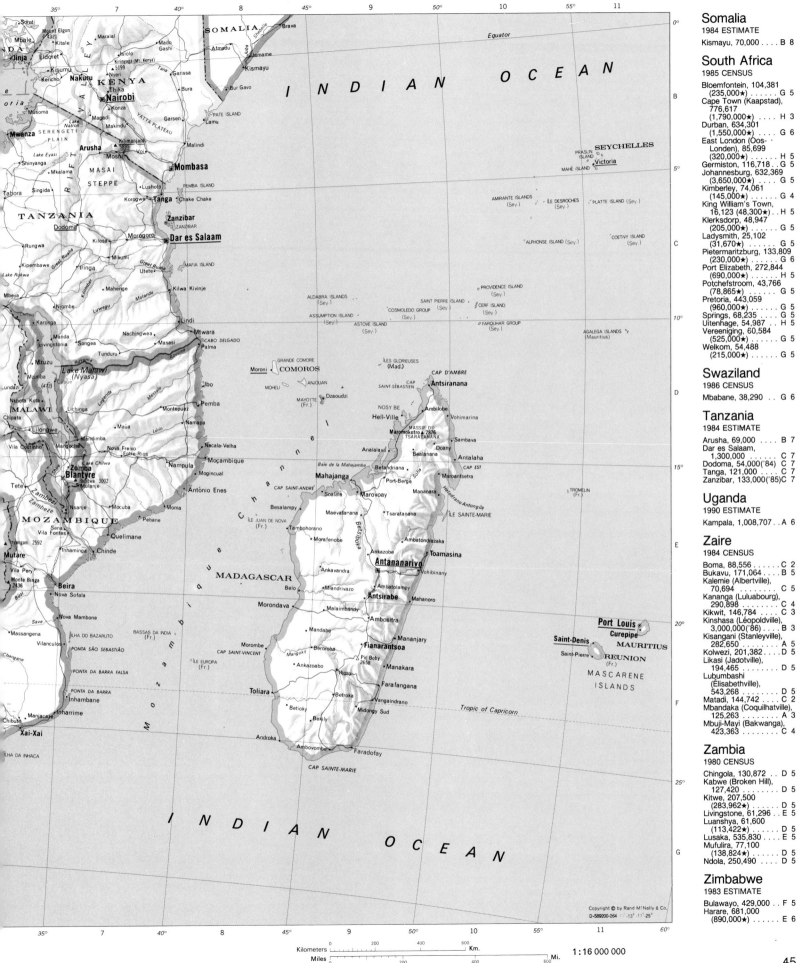

Somalia
1984 ESTIMATE

Kismayu, 70,000 . . . . B 8

South Africa
1985 CENSUS

Bloemfontein, 104,381
(235,000★) . . . . . . G 5
Cape Town (Kaapstad),
776,617
(1,790,000★) . . . . H 3
Durban, 634,301
(1,550,000★) . . . . G 6
East London (Oos-
Londen), 85,699
(320,000★) . . . . . H 5
Germiston, 116,718 . . G 5
Johannesburg, 632,369
(3,650,000★) . . . . G 5
Kimberley, 74,061
(145,000★) . . . . . G 4
King William's Town,
16,123 (48,300★) . . H 5
Klerksdorp, 48,947
(205,000★) . . . . . G 5
Ladysmith, 25,102
(31,670★) . . . . . . G 5
Pietermaritzburg, 133,809
(230,000★) . . . . . G 6
Port Elizabeth, 272,844
(690,000★) . . . . . H 5
Potchefstroom, 43,766
(78,865★) . . . . . . G 5
Pretoria, 443,059
(960,000★) . . . . . G 5
Springs, 68,235 . . . . G 5
Uitenhage, 54,987 . . . H 5
Vereeniging, 60,584
(525,000★) . . . . . G 5
Welkom, 54,488
(215,000★) . . . . . G 5

Swaziland
1986 CENSUS

Mbabane, 38,290 . . . . G 6

Tanzania
1984 ESTIMATE

Arusha, 69,000 . . . . B 7
Dar es Salaam,
1,300,000 . . . . . . C 7
Dodoma, 54,000('84) C 7
Tanga, 121,000 . . . . C 7
Zanzibar, 133,000('85)C 7

Uganda
1990 ESTIMATE

Kampala, 1,008,707 . . A 6

Zaire
1984 CENSUS

Boma, 88,556 . . . . . . C 2
Bukavu, 171,064 . . . . B 5
Kalemie (Albertville),
70,694 . . . . C 5
Kananga (Luluabourg),
290,898 . . . . C 4
Kikwit, 146,784 . . . . C 3
Kinshasa (Léopoldville),
3,000,000('86) . . . B 3
Kisangani (Stanleyville),
282,650 . . . . A 5
Kolwezi, 201,382 . . . . D 5
Likasi (Jadotville),
194,465 . . . . D 5
Lubumbashi
(Élisabethville),
543,268 . . . . D 5
Matadi, 144,742 . . . . C 2
Mbandaka (Coquilhatville),
125,263 . . . . A 3
Mbuji-Mayi (Bakwanga),
423,363 . . . . C 4

Zambia
1980 CENSUS

Chingola, 130,872 . . D 5
Kabwe (Broken Hill),
127,420 . . . . D 5
Kitwe, 207,500
(283,962★) . . . . . D 5
Livingstone, 61,296 . . E 5
Luanshya, 61,600
(113,422★) . . . . . D 5
Lusaka, 535,830 . . . . E 5
Mufulira, 77,100
(138,824★) . . . . . D 5
Ndola, 250,490 . . . . D 5

Zimbabwe
1983 ESTIMATE

Bulawayo, 429,000 . . F 5
Harare, 681,000
(890,000★) . . . . . E 6

45

Eastern Africa and Middle East

Bahrain
1981 CENSUS
Al-Manāmah, 115.054
(224.643★) . . . . C 5

Djibouti
1976 ESTIMATE
Djibouti, 120,000 . . . . F 3

Eritrea
1988 ESTIMATE
Asmara, 319.353 . . . . E 2

Ethiopia
1988 ESTIMATE
Adis Abeba, 1,686.300
(1.500.000★) . . . . . G 2
Asmera, 319.353 . . . . E 2

Iran
1986 CENSUS
Esfahān, 986,753
(1.175.000★) . . . . . B 5
Shīrāz, 848,289 . . . . C 5

Iraq
1985 ESTIMATE
Al-Basrah, 616,700 . . B 4
Baghdād,
3,841,268('87) . . . B 3

Kuwait
1985 ESTIMATE
Al-Kuwayt, 44,335
(1.375.000★) . . . . C 4

Oman
1981 ESTIMATE
Masqat (Muscat),
50,000 . . . . D 6

Qatar
1986 CENSUS
Ad-Dawhah (Doha),
217.294 (310.000★) C 5

Saudi Arabia
1980 ESTIMATE
Al-Madīnah (Medina),
290,000 . . . . D 2
Ar-Riyād (Riyadh),
1,250,000 . . . . . D 4
Jiddah, 1,300,000 . . . D 2
Makkah (Mecca),
550,000 . . . . D 2

Somalia
1984 ESTIMATE
Muqdisho, 600,000 . . H 4

United Arab Emirates
1980 CENSUS
Abū Zaby, 242,975 . . D 5
Dubayy (Dubai),
265,702 . . . . C 6

Yemen
1984 ESTIMATE
'Adan (Aden), 176,100
(318,000★) . . . . . F 4
San'ā', 427,150('86) . E 3

★ Population of metropolitan
area, including suburbs.

46

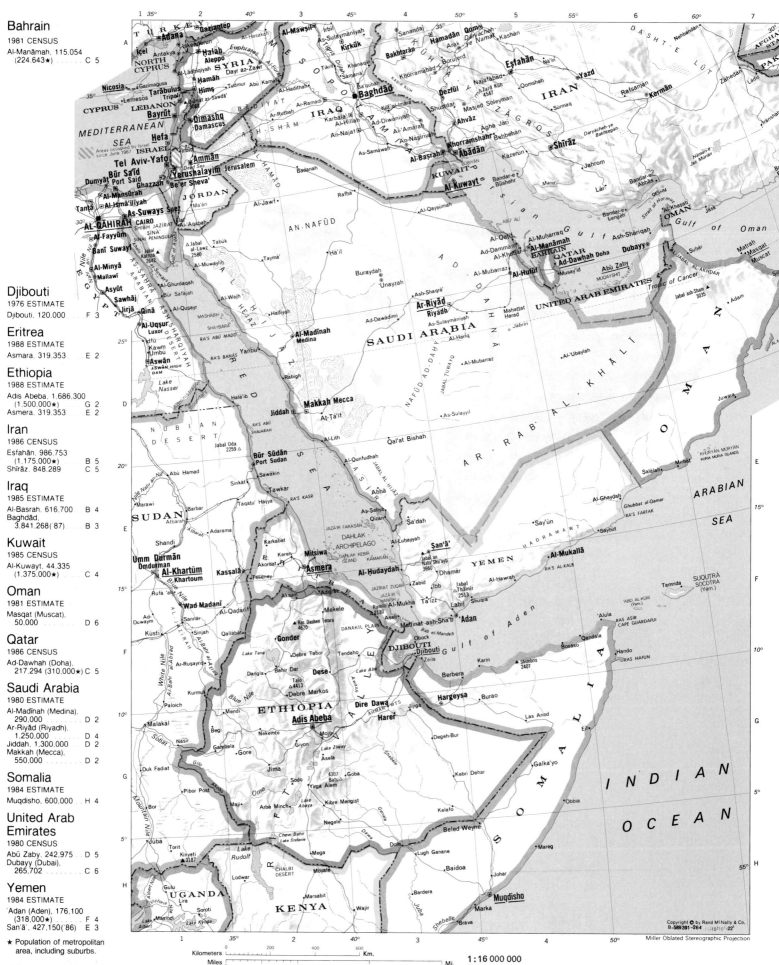

Antarctica

Adelaide Island . . . . C 5
Albert Markham, Mount A29
Alexander Island . . . . B 5
American Highland . . B21
Amery Ice Shelf C20
Amsterdam, Île (island) F20
Amundsen Sea . . . . B 1
Antarctic Circle C34
Antarctic Peninsula . . B 6
Auckland Islands D29
Balleny Islands C29
Belgica Mountains . . B16
Bellingshausen Sea . . C 3
Berkner Island . . . . . . B 8
Bounty Islands D30
Bouvetøya (island) . . D13
Campbell Islands D29
Coats Land (region) . . B10
Crozet, Îles (islands) . . E18
Dibble Iceberg Tongue C26
Drake Passage . . . . D 5
Ellsworth Mountains . B 3
Enderby Land (region) B18
Erebus, Mount B29
Executive Committee Range B35
Filchner Ice Shelf . . . . B 9
Heard Island D20
Horlick Mountains . . A35
Kerguélen, Îles (islands) E19
Lambert Glacier B20
Macquarie Islands . . D28
Markham, Mount . . A29
McClintock, Mount . . A28
Mühlighofmann Mountains B13
Napier Mountains . . C18
Pensacola Mountains A 7
Prince Edward Islands E16
Queen Fabiola Mountains B16
Queen Maud Land (region) B14
Queen Maud Mountains A33
Rex, Mount . . . . . . B 5
Rockefeller Plateau . . A35
Ronne Ice Shelf . . . . B 7
Roosevelt Island B32
Ross Ice Shelf A30
Ross Island B29
Ross Sea B31
Sabine, Mount B29
Saint Paul, Île (island) F21
Shackleton Ice Shelf C22
Sidley, Mount B36
Siple, Mount B36
Sør Rondane Mountains B15
South Georgia (island) . . . . D 9
South Magnetic Pole C26
South Orkney Islands . . . . D 8
South Pole . . . . . . A 1
South Sandwich Islands D10
South Shetland Islands . . . . C 5
Thiel Mountains . . . . A 3
Thurston Island . . . . B 2
Ulmer, Mount . . . . B 4
Victoria Land (region) B28
Vinson Massif (mountain) . . . . . . B 4
Weddell Sea . . . . . . B 8
West Ice Shelf C21
Whitmore Mountains A 2
Wilkes Land (region) B25

Pacific Ocean

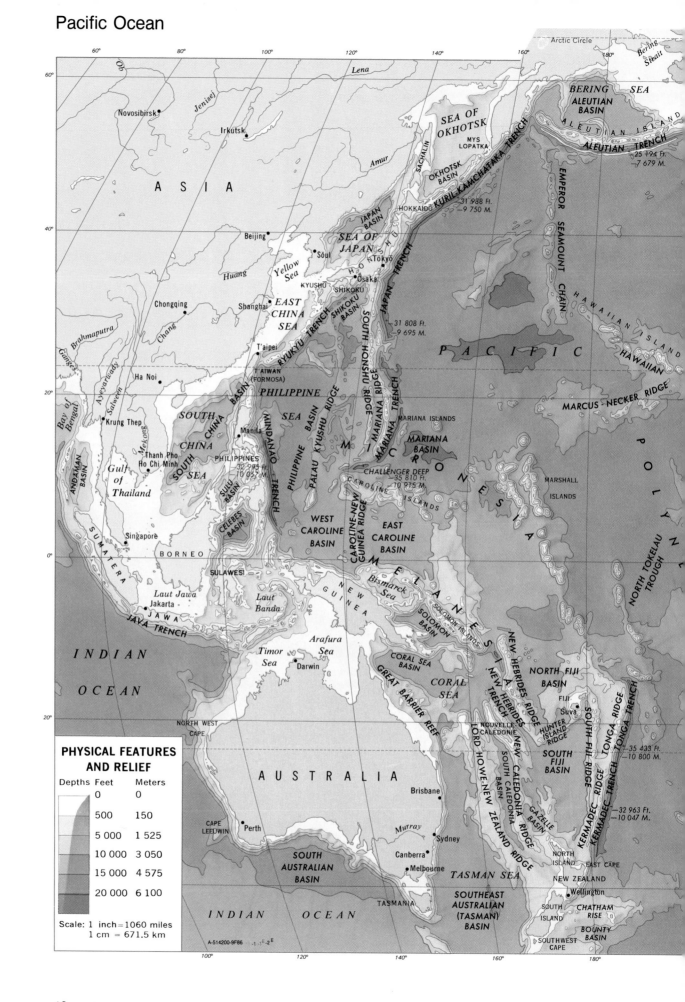

PHYSICAL FEATURES AND RELIEF

Depths	Feet	Meters
	0	0
	500	150
	5 000	1 525
	10 000	3 050
	15 000	4 575
	20 000	6 100

Scale: 1 inch = 1060 miles
1 cm = 671.5 km

A-514200-9/86   -1 -1^E -2^E

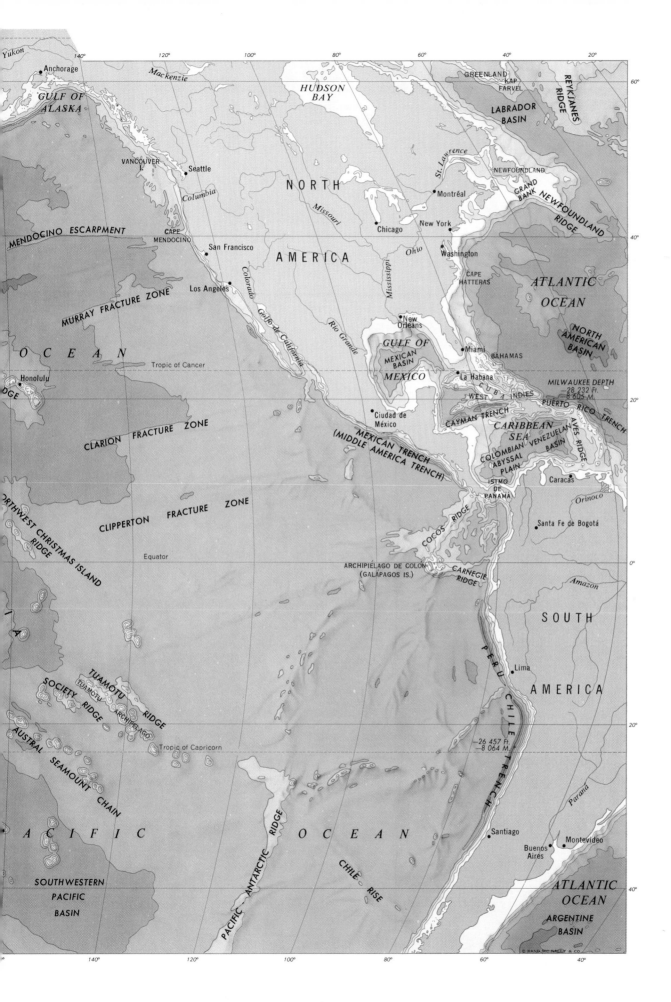

Yukon

Anchorage

Mackenzie

GREENLAND
KAP
FARVEL

REYKJANES RIDGE

GULF OF
ALASKA

HUDSON
BAY

LABRADOR
BASIN

VANCOUVER
I.

Seattle

NORTH

St. Lawrence

NEWFOUNDLAND

Columbia

Montréal

GRAND
BANK

NEWFOUNDLAND
RIDGE

MENDOCINO ESCARPMENT

CAPE
MENDOCINO

San Francisco

AMERICA

Missouri

Chicago

New York

Ohio

Washington

ATLANTIC
OCEAN

Los Angeles

Colorado

MURRAY FRACTURE ZONE

CAPE
HATTERAS

NORTH
AMERICAN
BASIN

O C E A N

Golfo de California

Rio Grande

GULF OF

New
Orleans

MEXICAN
BASIN

Honolulu

Tropic of Cancer

MEXICO

Miami

BAHAMAS

MILWAUKEE DEPTH
-28 232 Ft.
-8 605 M.

La Habana

CUBA

WEST

INDIES

20°

DGE

CLARION FRACTURE ZONE

Ciudad de
México

MEXICAN TRENCH
(MIDDLE AMERICA TRENCH)

CAYMAN TRENCH

CARIBBEAN
SEA

PUERTO RICO TRENCH

AVES RIDGE

COLOMBIAN VENEZUELAN
ABYSSAL BASIN
PLAIN

Caracas

ORTHWEST CHRISTMAS ISLAND
RIDGE

CLIPPERTON FRACTURE ZONE

ISTMO
DE
PANAMA

COCOS RIDGE

Orinoco

Santa Fe de Bogotá

Equator

ARCHIPIÉLAGO DE COLON
(GALÁPAGOS IS.)

CARNEGIE
RIDGE

Amazon

SOUTH

I
A

TUAMOTU
RIDGE

SOCIETY RIDGE

TUAMOTU
ARCHIPIÉLAGO

AMERICA

PERU

Lima

CHILE TRENCH

AUSTRAL SEAMOUNT CHAIN

Tropic of Capricorn

-26 457 Ft.
-8 064 M.

20°

Paraná

ACIFIC

O C E A N

Santiago

Montevideo

PACIFIC ANTARCTIC RIDGE

CHILE RISE

Buenos
Aires

ATLANTIC
OCEAN

SOUTHWESTERN
PACIFIC
BASIN

ARGENTINE
BASIN

40°

© RAND MC NALLY & CO.

Australia

Australia

1989 ESTIMATE
Adelaide, 12,340
  (1,036,747★) ..... F 7
Albany, 14,958 ...... G 3
Albury, 40,730
  (66,530★) .... G 9
Alice Springs,
  23,600 .... D 6
Ararat, 8,015('86) .. G 8
Armidale, 21,600 ... F10
Augusta, 933('86) ... F 3
Ballarat, 36,680
  (80,090★) .... G 8
Barcaldine,
  1,427('86) ...... D 9
Bendigo, 32,050
  (67,920★) .... G 8
Blackall, 1,497('86) . D 9
Bombala, 1,458('86) . G 9
Bordertown,
  2,318('86) ...... G 8
Bourke, 3,018('86) .. F 9
Bowen, 7,705('86) .. C 9
Brisbane, 744,828
  (1,273,511★) E10
Broken Hill, 22,550 .. F 8
Broome, 5,778('86) .. C 4
Bunbury, 26,398 .... F 3
Bundaberg, 33,024
  (45,161★) D10
Burketown,
  232('86) .... C 7
Burnie, 20,665('86) .. H 9
Busselton,
  7,784('86) ...... F 3
Cairns, 42,839
  (80,875★) .... C 9
Camooweal,
  315('86) .... C 7
Canberra, 247,194
  (271,362★)('86) ... G 9
Carnarvon,
  6,847('86) ...... D 2
Ceduna, 2,877('86) .. F 6
Cessnock, 43,870 ... F10
Charleville,
  3,588('86) ...... E 9
Charters Towers,
  7,208('86) ...... D 9
Cloncurry,
  2,297('86) ...... D 8
Coffs Harbour,
  47,890 .... F10
Cooktown, 964('86) .. C 9
Coolgardie, 989('86) . F 4
Cooma, 7,406('86) .. G 9
Croydon, 229('86) ... C 8
Cunnamulla,
  1,697('86) ...... E 9
Dampier, 2,201('86) .. D 3
Darwin, 63,900
  (72,937★) .... B 6
Derby, 3,258('86) ... C 4
Devonport, 25,370 .. H 9
Dongara, 1,496('86) .. E 2
Dubbo, 32,230 ..... F 9
Elizabeth, 29,998 ... F 7
Emerald, 5,982('86) . D 9
Esperance,
  6,440('86) ...... F 4
Geelong, 13,190
  (148,980★) ...... G 8
Geraldton, 20,968 ... E 2
Gladstone,
  22,033('86) D10
Glen Innes,
  5,971('86) E10
Goondiwindi,
  4,103('86) E10
Goulburn, 21,580 ... F 9
Grafton, 15,890 .... E10
Griffith, 13,630('86) . F 9
Gympie, 10,772('86) . E10
Halls Creek,
  1,182('86) ...... C 5
Hay, 2,961('86) ..... F 8
Hobart, 47,280
  (181,210★) ...... H 9
Home Hill,
  3,286('86) ...... C 9
Horsham, 12,850 ... G 8
Hughenden,
  1,791('86) ...... D 8
Ingham, 5,202('86) .. C 9
Inverell, 9,693('86) .. E10
Ipswich, 75,283 .... E10
Kalgoorlie, 26,813 ... F 4
Kingaroy, 6,362('86) . E10
Launceston, 32,150
  (92,350★) .... H 9
Leonora, 1,004('86) .. E 4
Lismore, 39,450 .... E10
Longreach,
  3,159('86) ...... D 8
Mackay, 22,583
  (50,885★) .... D 9
Maitland, 47,280 ... F10
Marble Bar, 332('86) . D 3
Mareeba, 6,614('86) . C 9
Marree, 300('76) .... E 7
Meekatharra,
  1,018('86) ...... E 3

★ Population of metropolitan
  area, including suburbs.

Melbourne, 55,300
  (3,039,100★) ...... G 8
Mildura, 20,512('86) .. F 8
Mitchell, 1,212('86) .. E 9
Moora, 1,469('86) .... F 3
Moree, 10,215('86) ... E 9
Morwell, 16,880 ...... G 9
Mount Gambier, 22,194
  (27,228★) .... G 8
Mount Isa, 24,023 .... D 7
Mount Magnet,
  1,000('86) .... E 3
Mullewa, 758('86) .... E 3
Murwillumbah,
  7,678('86) E10
Nambour, 9,579('86) .. E10
Naracoorte,
  4,636('86) .... G 8
Newcastle, 130,940
  (425,610★) F10
New Norfolk,
  6,152('86) .... H 9
Normanton,
  1,109('86) .... C 8
Norseman,
  1,775('86) .... F 4
Northam, 6,377('86) .. F 3
Nyngan, 2,502('86) ... F 9
Onslow, 750('86) ..... D 3
Oodnadatta, 200('76) . E 7
Orange, 32,980 ...... F 9
Pemberton, 802('86) .. F 3
Perth, 82,413
  (1,158,387★) ..... F 3
Peterborough,
  2,239('86) .... F 7
Port Augusta,
  15,752 .... F 7
Port Hedland,
  13,069('86) .... D 3
Port Lincoln, 12,941 .. F 7
Port Macquarie,
  22,884('86) F10
Port Pirie, 15,210 .... F 7
Quilpie, 780('86) .... E 8
Ravensthorpe,
  299('86) .... F 3
Richmond, 704('86) .. D 8
Rockhampton, 58,890
  (61,694★) D10
Roebourne,
  1,269('86) .... D 3
Roma, 6,069('86) .... E 9
Saint George,
  2,323('86) .... E 9
Sale, 13,800 .... G 9
Shepparton, 26,420
  (39,700★) .... G 9
Smithton, 3,414('86) .. H 9
Southern Cross,
  898('86) .... F 3
Swan Hill,
  8,831('86) .... G 8
Sydney, 9,800
  (3,623,550★) F10
Tamworth, 34,430 ... F10
Taree, 38,760 ...... F10
Tennant Creek,
  3,503('86) .... C 6
Tenterfield,
  3,370('86) E10
Theodore, 576('86) .. D10
Toowoomba,
  81,071 .... E10
Townsville, 83,339
  (111,972★) .... C 9
Wagga Wagga,
  52,180 .... G 9
Walgett, 2,151('86) .. E 9
Wangaratta, 16,320 .. G 9
Warrnambool,
  24,480 .... G 8
Weipa, 2,406('86) ... B 8
Whyalla, 26,706 .... F 7
Wilcannia, 1,048('86) . F 8
Wiluna, 279('86) .... E 4
Winton, 1,281('86) .. D 8
Wollongong, 174,770
  (236,690★) F10
Woomera,
  1,805('86) .... F 7
Wyndham,
  1,329('86) .... C 5

Indonesia
1980 CENSUS

Jayapura, 60,641 .... k15
Kupang, 84,587 .... B 4
Sorong, 52,041 ...... k13

Papua New Guinea
1987 ESTIMATE

Lae, 79,600 .... m16
Madang, 24,700 .... m16
Port Moresby,
  152,100 .... m16
Rabaul, 14,954('80) .. k17
Wewak, 23,200 ...... k15

51

New Zealand

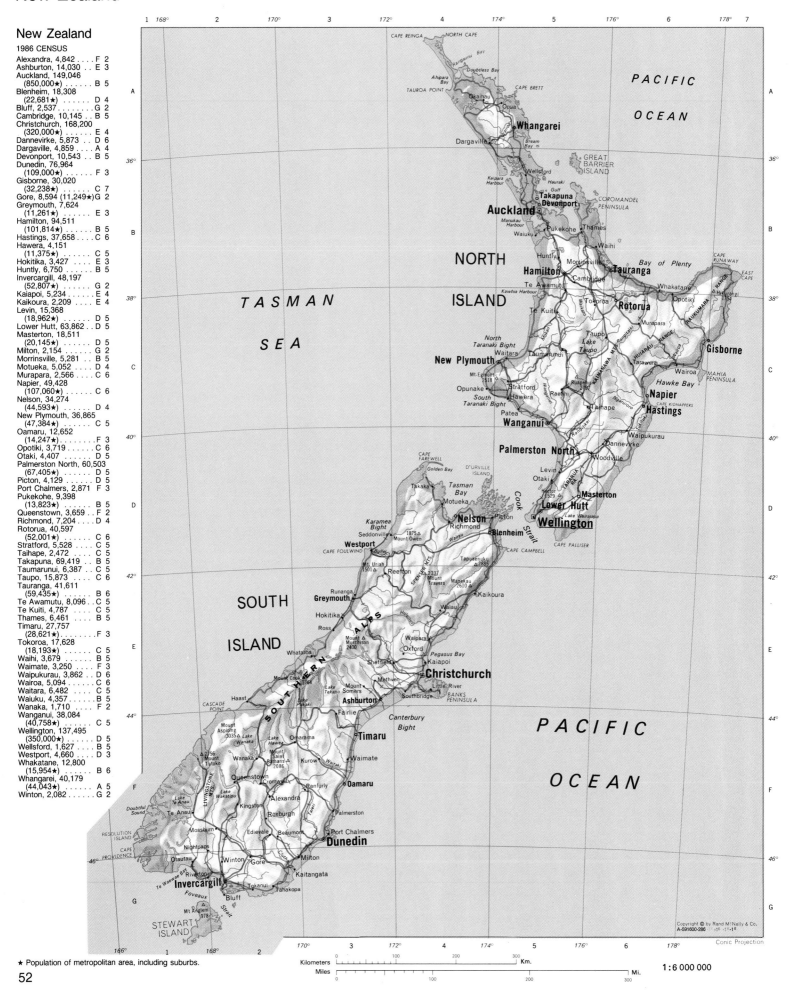

New Zealand
1986 CENSUS

Alexandra, 4,842 . . . . F 2
Ashburton, 14,030 . . . E 3
Auckland, 149,046
  (850,000★) . . . . . . B 5
Blenheim, 18,308
  (22,681★) . . . . . . D 4
Bluff, 2,537 . . . . G 2
Cambridge, 10,145 . . B 5
Christchurch, 168,200
  (320,000★) . . . . . . E 4
Dannevirke, 5,873 . . D 6
Dargaville, 4,859 . . . A 4
Devonport, 10,543 . . B 5
Dunedin, 76,964
  (109,000★) . . . . . . F 3
Gisborne, 30,020
  (32,238★) . . . . . . C 7
Gore, 8,594 (11,249★)G 2
Greymouth, 7,624
  (11,261★) . . . . . . E 3
Hamilton, 94,511
  (101,814★) . . . . . . B 5
Hastings, 37,658 . . . C 6
Hawera, 4,151
  (11,375★) . . . . . . C 5
Hokitika, 3,427 . . . . E 3
Huntly, 6,750 . . . . . B 5
Invercargill, 48,197
  (52,807★) . . . . . . G 2
Kaiapoi, 5,234 . . . . E 4
Kaikoura, 2,209 . . . E 4
Levin, 15,368
  (18,962★) . . . . . . D 5
Lower Hutt, 63,862 . . D 5
Masterton, 18,511
  (20,145★) . . . . . . D 5
Milton, 2,154 . . . . . G 2
Morrinsville, 5,281 . . B 5
Motueka, 5,052 . . . . D 4
Murapara, 2,566 . . . C 6
Napier, 49,428
  (107,060★) . . . . . . C 6
Nelson, 34,274
  (44,593★) . . . . . . D 4
New Plymouth, 36,865
  (47,384★) . . . . . . C 5
Oamaru, 12,652
  (14,247★) . . . . . . F 3
Opotiki, 3,719 . . . . C 6
Otaki, 4,407 . . . . . . D 5
Palmerston North, 60,503
  (67,405★) . . . . . . D 5
Picton, 4,129 . . . . . D 5
Port Chalmers, 2,871 F 3
Pukekohe, 9,398
  (13,823★) . . . . . . B 5
Queenstown, 3,659 . F 2
Richmond, 7,204 . . . D 4
Rotorua, 40,597
  (52,001★) . . . . . . C 6
Stratford, 5,528 . . . C 5
Taihape, 2,472 . . . . C 5
Takapuna, 69,419 . . B 5
Taumarunui, 6,387 . . C 5
Taupo, 15,873 . . . . C 6
Tauranga, 41,611
  (59,435★) . . . . . . B 6
Te Awamutu, 8,096 . . C 5
Te Kuiti, 4,787 . . . . C 5
Thames, 6,461 . . . . B 5
Timaru, 27,757
  (28,621★) . . . . . . F 3
Tokoroa, 17,628
  (18,193★) . . . . . . C 5
Waihi, 3,679 . . . . . B 5
Waimate, 3,250 . . . . F 3
Waipukurau, 3,862 . . D 6
Wairoa, 5,094 . . . . C 6
Waitara, 6,482 . . . . C 5
Waiuku, 4,357 . . . . B 5
Wanaka, 1,710 . . . . F 2
Wanganui, 38,084
  (40,758★) . . . . . . C 5
Wellington, 137,495
  (350,000★) . . . . . . D 5
Wellsford, 1,627 . . . B 5
Westport, 4,660 . . . D 3
Whakatane, 12,800
  (15,954★) . . . . . . B 6
Whangarei, 40,179
  (44,043★) . . . . . . A 5
Winton, 2,082 . . . . . G 2

★ Population of metropolitan area, including suburbs.

52

Copyright © by Rand McNally & Co.
A-591600-266

Conic Projection

Kilometers

Km.

Miles

Mi.

1:6 000 000

South America

Antofagasta, 185,486
('82)....................F 3
Arequipa, 108,023 ('81)
(446,942★) ....E 3
ARGENTINA..............G 4
Asunción, 477,100 ('85)
(700,000★) ....F 5
Barranquilla, 899,781 ('85)
(1,140,000★) ....B 3
Belém, 1,116,578 ('85)
(1,200,000★) ....D 6
Belo Horizonte, 2,114,429
('85) (2,950,000★) ...E 6
Bogotá see Santa Fe de
Bogotá...................C 3
BOLIVIA..................E 4
Brasília, 1,567,709
('85)......................E 6
BRAZIL....................E 5
Buenos Aires, 2,922,829
('80) (10,750,000★) G 5
Caracas, 1,816,901 ('81)
(3,600,000★) ....B 4
Cartagena, 531,426
('85)......................B 3
Cayenne, 38,091 ('82)..C 5
Chiclayo, 213,095 ('81)
(279,527★) ....D 3
CHILE......................G 3
Ciudad Bolívar, 182,941
('81)......................C 4
COLOMBIA.................C 3
Concepción, 267,891 ('82)
(675,000★) ....G 3
Cuzco, 89,563 ('81)
(184,550★) ....E 3
ECUADOR..................D 3
FALKLAND ISLANDS...I 5
Fortaleza, 1,582,414 ('85)
(1,825,000★) ....D 7
FRENCH GUIANA.......C 5
Georgetown, 78,500 ('83)
(188,000★) ....C 5
Guayaquil, 1,572,615 ('87)
(1,580,000★) ....D 3
GUYANA...................C 5
Iquitos, 178,738 ('81)...D 3
João Pessoa, 348,500
('85) (550,000★) .....D 7
La Paz, 992,592 ('85)..E 4
La Plata, 477,175
('80).....................G 5
Lima, 371,122 ('81)
(4,608,010★) ....E 3
Maceió, 482,195 ('85) D 7
Manaus, 809,914 ('85)D 5
Maracaibo, 890,643
('81)......................B 3
Medellín, 1,468,089 ('85)
(2,095,000★) ....C 3
Mendoza, 119,088 ('80)
(650,000★) ....G 4
Montevideo, 1,251,647
('85) (1,550,000★) .. G 5
Natal, 510,106 ('85).....D 7
PARAGUAY................F 5
Paramaribo, 241,000 ('88)
(296,000★) ....C 5
PERU......................E 3
Porto Alegre, 1,272,121
('85) (2,600,000★) .. G 5
Quito, 1,137,705 ('87)
(1,300,000★) ....D 3
Recife, 1,287,623 ('85)
(2,625,000★) ....D 7
Rio Branco, 109,800 ('85)
(145,486▲) ....D 4
Rio de Janeiro, 5,603,388
('85) (10,150,000★) .F 6
Rosario, 938,120 ('80)
(1,045,000★) ....G 4
Salta, 260,744 ('80).....F 4
Salvador, 1,804,438 ('85)
(2,050,000★) ....E 7
San Miguel de Tucumán,
392,888 ('80)
(525,000★) ....F 4
Santa Fe, 292,165
('80)......................G 4
Santa Fe de Bogotá,
3,982,941 ('85)
(4,260,000★) ....C 3
Santiago, 232,667 ('82)
(4,100,000★) ....G 3
Santos, 460,100 ('85)
(1,065,000★) ....F 6
São Luís, 227,900 ('85)
(600,000★) ....D 6
São Paulo, 10,063,110
('85) (15,175,000★) .F 6
Stanley, 1,200 ('86)......I 5
Sucre, 86,609 ('85).....E 4
SURINAME.................C 5
Teresina, 425,300 ('85)
(525,000★) ....D 6
Trujillo, 202,469 ('81)
(354,301★) ....D 3
URUGUAY..................G 5
Valparaíso, 265,355 ('82)
(675,000★) ....G 3
VENEZUELA...............C 4
Vitória, 201,500 ('85)
(735,000★) ....F 6

★ Population of metropolitan area, including suburbs.
▲ Population of entire district, including rural area.

1:40 000 000

53

Northern South America

Bolivia
1985 ESTIMATE
Cochabamba, 317,251.G 5
La Paz, 992,592 . . . . G 5
Oruro, 178,393 . . . . . G 5
Potosí, 113,380 . . . . . G 5
Santa Cruz, 441,717 . G 6
Sucre, 86,609 . . . . . . G 5

Brazil
1985 ESTIMATE
Anápolis, 225,840 . . G 9
Aracaju, 360,013 . . . . F11
Araçatuba, 129,304 . . H 8
Bauru, 220,105 . . . . . H 9
Belém, 1,116,578
  (1,200,000) . . . . D 9
Belo Horizonte, 2,114,429
  (2,950,000) G10
Brasília, 1,567,709 . G 9
Campina Grande,
  279,929 . . . . E11
Campinas, 841,016
  (1,125,000) . . . . H 9
Campo Grande,
  384,398 . . . . H 8
Campos, 187,900
  (366,716▲) H10
Caruaru, 152,100
  (190,794) E11
Cuiabá, 220,400
  (279,651▲) . . . . . G 7
Feira de Santana, 278,600
  (355,201▲) F11
Fortaleza, 1,582,414
  (1,825,000★) D11
Goiânia, 923,333
  (990,000★) . . . . . G 9
Governador Valadares,
  192,300 (216,957▲) G10
João Pessoa, 348,500
  (550,000★) E12
Juàzeiro do Norte,
  159,806 . . . . E11
Juiz de Fora, 349,720 H10
Jundiaí, 268,900
  (313,652▲) . . . . . H 9
Maceió, 482,195 . . . E11
Manaus, 809,914 . . . D 6
Montes Claros, 183,500
  (214,472▲) G10
Natal, 510,106 . . . . E11
Niterói, 441,684 . . . H10
Petrolina, 92,100
  (225,000★) E10
Petrópolis, 170,300 . H10
Piracicaba, 211,000
  (252,079★) . . . . . H 9
Porto Velho, 152,700
  (202,011▲) . . . . . E 6
Presidente Prudente,
  155,883 . . . . H 8
Recife, 1,287,623
  (2,625,000★) E12
Ribeirão Prêto,
  383,125 . . . . H 9
Rio de Janeiro, 5,603,388
  (10,150,000★) H10
Salvador, 1,804,438
  (2,050,000★) F11
Santarém, 120,800
  (226,618▲) . . . . . D 8
Santos, 460,100
  (1,065,000★) . . . . H 9
São Carlos, 140,383 . H 9
São José do Rio Prêto,
  229,221 . . . . H 9
São Luís, 227,900
  (600,000★) D10
São Paulo, 10,063,110
  (15,175,000★) . . . . H 9
Sorocaba, 327,468 . . H 9
Teresina, 425,300
  (525,000★) E10
Uberaba, 244,875 . . . G 9
Uberlândia, 312,024 . G 9
Vitória, 201,500
  (735,000★) H10
Vitória da Conquista,
  145,800 (198,150▲) F10
Volta Redonda, 219,267
  (375,000★) H10

Colombia
1985 CENSUS
Armenia, 187,130 . . . . C 3
Barrancabermeja,
  137,406 . . . . B 4
Barranquilla, 899,781
  (1,140,000★) . . . . A 4
Bogotá see Santa Fe de
  Bogotá . . . . C 4
Bucaramanga, 352,326
  (550,000★) . . . . . B 4
Buenaventura,
  160,342 . . . . C 3
Buga, 82,992 . . . . . C 3
Cali, 1,350,565
  (1,400,000★) . . . . C 3
Cartagena, 531,426 . . A 3
Cúcuta, 379,478
  (445,000★) . . . . . B 4

54

Ibagué, 292,965 . . . . C 3
Manizales, 299,352
 (330,000★) . . . . B 3
Medellín, 1,468,089
 (2,095,000★) . . . . . . B 3
Montería, 157,466 . . B 3
Neiva, 194,556 . . . . . C 3
Palmira, 175,186 . . . C 3
Pasto, 197,407 . . . . C 3
Pereira, 233,271
 (390,000★) . . . . C 3
Popayán, 141,964 . . C 3
Santa Fe de Bogotá,
 3,982,941
 (4,260,000★) . . . . . . C 4
Santa Marta, 177,922 A 4
Tuluá, 99,721 . . . . . . C 3
Valledupar, 142,771 . A 4
Villavicencio, 178,685 C 4

Ecuador
1987 ESTIMATE
Ambato, 126,067 . . . . D 3
Cuenca, 201,490 . . . . D 3
Guayaquil, 1,572,615
 (1,580,000★) . . . . . . D 3
Machala, 144,396 . . . D 3
Manta, 135,990 . . . . D 2
Portoviejo, 141,568 . . D 2
Quito, 1,137,705
 (1,300,000★) . . . . . . D 3

French Guiana
1982 CENSUS
Cayenne, 38,091 . . . . C 8

Guyana
1983 ESTIMATE
Georgetown, 78,500
 (188,000★) . . . . B 7

Peru
1981 CENSUS
Arequipa, 108,023
 (446,942★) . . . . . . G 4
Ayacucho, 57,432
 (69,533★) . . . . F 4
Cajamarca, 62,259 . . E 3
Callao, 264,133 . . . . F 3
Cerro de Pasco, 55,597
 (66,373★) . . . . F 3

Chiclayo, 213,095
 (279,527★) . . . . E 3
Chimbote, 223,341 . . E 3
Cuzco, 89,563
 (184,550★) . . . . F 4
Huancayo, 84,845
 (164,954★) . . . . F 3
Huánuco, 61,812 . . . E 3
Ica, 114,786 . . . . . . F 3
Iquitos, 178,738 . . . . D 4
Lima, 371,122
 (4,608,010★) . . . . . . F 3
Piura, 144,609
 (207,934★) . . . . E 2
Sullana, 89,037 . . . . D 2
Tacna, 97,173 . . . . . G 4
Trujillo, 202,469
 (354,301★) . . . . E 3
Tumbes, 47,936 . . . . D 2
Vitarte, 145,504 . . . . F 3

Suriname
1988 ESTIMATE
Paramaribo, 241,000
 (296,000★) . . . . B 7

Venezuela
1981 CENSUS
Acarigua, 91,662 . . . B 5
Barinas, 110,462 . . . B 4
Barquisimeto, 497,635 A 5
Cabimas, 140,435 . . A 4
Calabozo, 61,995 . . . B 5
Caracas, 1,816,901
 (3,600,000★) . . . . . . A 5
Ciudad Bolívar,
 182,941 . . . . B 6
Ciudad Guayana,
 314,497 . . . . B 6
Ciudad Ojeda, 83,565 A 4
Cumaná, 179,814 . . A 6
El Tigre, 73,595 . . . . B 6
Maracaibo, 890,643 . A 4
Maracay, 322,560 . . A 5
Maturín, 154,976 . . . B 6
Mérida, 143,209 . . . B 4
Puerto Cabello,
 71,759 . . . . A 5
Punto Fijo, 71,114 . . A 4
San Cristóbal,
 198,793 . . . . B 4
Valencia, 616,224 . . A 5
Valera, 102,068 . . . . B 4

★ Population of metropolitan area, including suburbs.
▲ Population of entire district, including rural area.

Southern South America

Argentina
1980 CENSUS
Avellaneda, 334,145 . . C 5
Bahía Blanca, 223,818 D 4
Buenos Aires, 2,922,829
(10,750,000★) . . . . . . C 5
Catamarca, 78,799
(90,000★) . . . . B 3
Comodoro Rivadavia,
96,817 . . . . F 3
Concordia, 94,222 . . C 5
Córdoba, 993,055
(1,070,000★) . . . . . . C 4
Corrientes, 180,612 . . B 5
La Plata, 477,175 . . . . C 5
Mar del Plata,
414,696 . . . . D 5
Mendoza, 119,088
(650,000★) . . . . C 3
Paraná, 161,638 . . . . C 4
Posadas, 143,889 . . . . B 5
Río Cuarto, 110,254 . . C 4
Rosario, 938,120
(1,045,000★) . . . . . . C 4
Salta, 260,744 . . . . . A 3
San Isidro, 289,170 . . C 5
San Juan, 118,046
(300,000★) . . . . C 3
San Miguel de Tucumán,
392,888 (525,000★) B 3
Santa Fe, 292,165 . . C 4
Santiago del Estero,
148,758 (200,000★) B 4

Brazil
1985 ESTIMATE
Bauru, 220,105 . . . A 7
Blumenau, 192,074 . . B 7
Campinas, 841,016
(1,125,000★) . . . . . A 7
Caxias do Sul,
266,809 . . . . B 6
Curitiba, 1,279,205
(1,700,000★) . . . . . B 7
Florianópolis, 178,400
(365,000★) . . . . . . B 7
Joinvile, 302,877 . . B 7
Jundiaí, 268,900
(313,652▲) . . . . . . A 7
Londrina, 296,400
(346,676▲) . . . . . . A 6
Maringá, 196,871 . . A 6
Pelotas, 210,300
(277,730▲) . . . . . . C 6
Piracicaba, 211,000
(252,079▲) . . . . . . A 7
Ponta Grossa,
223,154 . . . . B 6
Porto Alegre, 1,272,121
(2,600,000★) . . . . . C 6
Presidente Prudente,
155,883 . . . . A 6
Ribeirão Prêto,
383,125 . . . . A 7
Rio Grande, 164,221 C 6
Santa Maria, 163,900
(196,827▲) . . . . . . B 6
Santos, 460,100
(1,065,000★) . . . . . A 7
São Carlos, 140,383 A 7
São Paulo, 10,063,110
(15,175,000★) . . . . A 7
Sorocaba, 327,468 . . A 7

Chile
1982 CENSUS
Antofagasta, 185,486 A 2
Chillán, 118,163 . . . D 2
Concepción, 267,891
(675,000★) . . . . . . D 2
Osorno, 95,286 . . . . . E 2
Punta Arenas, 95,332 G 2
Rancagua, 139,925 . . C 2
Santiago, 232,667
(4,100,000★) . . . . . C 2
Talca, 128,544 . . . . D 2
Talcahuano, 202,368 D 2
Temuco, 157,297 . . D 2
Valdivia, 100,046 . . D 2
Valparaíso, 265,355
(675,000★) . . . . . . C 2
Viña del Mar, 244,899 C 2

Falkland Islands
1986 ESTIMATE
Stanley, 1,200 . . . . . . G 5

Paraguay
1985 ESTIMATE
Asunción, 477,100
(700,000★) . . . . B 5

Uruguay
1985 CENSUS
Montevideo, 1,251,647
(1,550,000★) . . . . . C 5
Paysandú, 76,191 . . . C 5
Salto, 80,823 . . . . . . C 5

★ Population of metropolitan area, including suburbs.
▲ Population of entire district, including rural area.

56

Copyright © by Rand McNally & Co.
B-549200-264

Oblique Conic Conformal Projection

Kilometers
Km.
Miles
Mi.

1 : 16 000 000

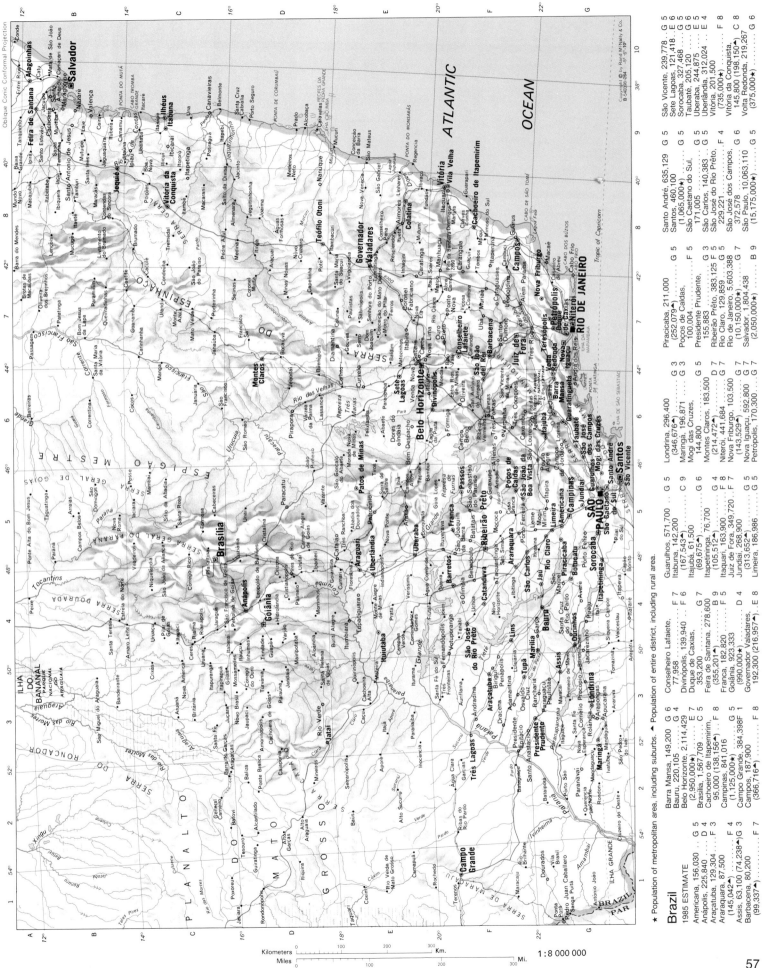

★ Population of metropolitan area, including suburbs. ▲ Population of entire district, including rural area.

Brazil

1985 ESTIMATE

Americana, 156,030	G 5	
Anápolis, 225,840	D 4	
Araçatuba, 129,304	F 3	
Araraquara, 87,500	F 4	
Assis, 63,100 (74,238▲)	G 3	
Barbacena, 80,200	F 7	

Barra Mansa, 149,200	G 6	
Bauru, 220,105	G 4	
Belo Horizonte, 2,114,429	E 7	
(2,950,000★)		
Brasília, 1,567,709	C 5	
Cachoeiro de Itapemirim,	F 8	
95,000 (138,156▲)		
Campinas, 841,016	F 4	
(1,125,000★)		
Campo Grande, 384,398	F 1	
Campos, 187,900	F 7	
(366,716▲)		

Conselheiro Lafaiete,	F 7	
77,958		
Divinópolis, 139,940	F 6	
Duque de Caxias,	G 7	
353,200		
Feira de Santana, 278,600	B 9	
(355,201▲)		
Franca, 182,820	F 5	
Goiânia, 923,333	D 4	
(990,000★)		
Governador Valadares,	E 8	
192,300 (216,957▲)		

Guarulhos, 571,700	G 5	
Itabuna, 142,200	C 9	
Itajaí, 61,500	G 6	
(69,675▲)		
Itapetininga, 76,700	G 4	
(105,512▲)		
Itaquari, 163,900	F 8	
Juiz de Fora, 349,720	F 7	
(143,529▲)		
Limeira, 186,986	G 5	

Londrina, 296,400	G 3	
Maringá, 196,871	G 3	
Mogi das Cruzes,	G 5	
144,800		
Montes Claros, 183,500	D 7	
(214,472▲)		
Niterói, 441,684	G 7	
Nova Friburgo, 103,500	F 7	
(143,529▲)		
Nova Iguaçu, 592,800	G 7	
(313,652▲)		
Petrópolis, 170,300	G 5	

Piracicaba, 211,000	G 5	
(252,079▲)		
Poços de Caldas,	F 5	
100,004		
Presidente Prudente,	G 3	
155,883		
Ribeirão Prêto, 383,125	F 5	
Rio Claro, 129,859	G 5	
229,221		
Rio de Janeiro, 5,603,388	G 7	
(10,150,000★)		
Salvador, 1,804,438	B 9	
(2,050,000★)		

Santo André, 635,129	G 5	
Santos, 460,100	G 5	
(1,065,000★)		
São Caetano do Sul,	G 5	
171,005		
São Carlos, 140,383	G 5	
São José do Rio Prêto,	F 4	
(735,000▲)		
São Paulo,	F 5	
São Vicente, 239,778	G 5	
Sete Lagoas, 121,418	E 6	
Sorocaba, 327,468	G 5	
Taubaté, 205,120	G 5	
Uberaba, 244,875	E 5	
Uberlândia, 312,024	E 4	
Vitória, 201,500	F 8	
(735,000★)		
Vitória da Conquista,	C 8	
145,800 (198,150▲)		
Volta Redonda, 219,267	G 6	
(375,000★)		

57

Colombia, Ecuador, Venezuela, and Guyana

Aruba
1987 ESTIMATE
Oranjestad, 19,800 . . A 7

Colombia
1985 CENSUS
Armenia, 187,130 . . . . E 5
Barrancabermeja,
  137,406 . . . . D 6
Barranquilla, 899,781
  (1,140,000★) . . . . . B 5
Bello, 212,861 . . . . . D 5
Bogotá see Santa Fe de
  Bogotá . . . . E 5
Bucaramanga, 352,326
  (550,000★) . . . . . . D 6
Buenaventura,
  160,342 . . . . F 4
Buga, 82,992 . . . . . . F 4
Cali, 1,350,565
  (1,400,000★) . . . . . F 4
Cartagena, 531,426 . . B 5
Cartago, 97,791 . . . . E 5
Ciénaga, 56,860 . . . . B 5
Cúcuta, 379,478
  (445,000★) . . . . . . D 6
Duitama, 56,390 . . . . E 6
Envigado, 91,391 . . . D 5
Espinal, 37,563 . . . . E 5
Facatativá, 44,331 . . . E 5
Florencia, 66,430 . . . G 5
Florida, 30,040 . . . . F 4
Floridablanca,
  143,824 . . . . D 6
Girardot, 70,078 . . . . E 5
Ibagué, 292,965 . . . . E 5
Ipiales, 45,419 . . . . . G 4
Itagüí, 137,623 . . . . . D 5
La Dorada, 48,572 . . . E 5
Magangué, 49,160 . . . C 5
Manizales, 299,352
  (330,000★) . . . . . . E 5
Medellín, 1,468,089
  (2,095,000★) . . . . . D 5
Montería, 157,466 . . . C 5
Neiva, 194,556 . . . . . F 5
Ocaña, 51,443 . . . . . C 6
Palmira, 175,186 . . . . F 4
Pamplona, 34,213 . . . D 6
Pasto, 197,407 . . . . . G 4
Pereira, 233,271
  (390,000★) . . . . . . E 5
Planeta Rica, 24,238 . C 5
Popayán, 141,964 . . . F 4
Puerto Berrío, 21,414 . D 5
Quibdó, 47,950 . . . . . E 4
Ríohacha, 46,667 . . . B 6
Santa Fe de Bogotá,
  3,982,941
  (4,260,000★) . . . . . E 5
Santa Marta,
  177,922 . . . . B 5
Santa Rosa de Cabal,
  37,112 . . . . E 5
Sincelejo, 120,537 . . . C 5
Sogamoso, 64,437 . . . E 6
Soledad, 165,791 . . . B 5
Tuluá, 99,721 . . . . . . E 4
Tumaco, 45,456 . . . . G 3
Tunja, 93,792 . . . . . . E 6
Valledupar, 142,771 . . B 6
Villavicencio, 178,685 E 6
Zipaquirá, 45,676 . . . E 5

Ecuador
1987 ESTIMATE
Alfaro, 51,023('82) . . . . I 3
Ambato, 126,067 . . . . H 3
Babahoyo,
  42,266('82) . . . . . . H 3
Chone, 33,839('82) . . H 2
Cuenca, 201,490 . . . . I 3
Esmeraldas, 120,387 G 3
Guayaquil, 1,572,615
  (1,580,000★) . . . . . I 3
Ibarra, 53,428('82) . . G 3
Jipijapa, 27,146('82) . . H 2
Latacunga,
  28,764('82) . . . . . . H 3
Loja, 71,652('82) . . . . J 3
Machala, 144,396 . . . I 3
Manta, 135,990 . . . . H 2
Milagro, 102,884 . . . . I 3
Portoviejo, 141,568 . . H 2
Quevedo,
  67,023('82) . . . . . . H 3
Quito, 1,137,705
  (1,300,000★) . . . . . H 3
Riobamba,
  75,455('82) . . . . . . H 3
Santo Domingo de los
  Colorados, 104,059 H 3
Tulcán, 30,985('82) . . G 4

Guyana
1983 ESTIMATE
Georgetown, 78,500
  (188,000★) D13
New Amsterdam,
  20,000('82) D14

★ Population of metropolitan
  area, including suburbs.

58

Netherlands Antilles
1981 CENSUS

Willemstad, 31,883
(130,000★) . . . . A 8

Panama
1990 CENSUS

Colón, 54,469
(96,000★) . . . . C 3
David, 65,635 . . . . . . C 1
La Chorrera, 44,110 . . C 3
Panamá, 411,549
(770,000★) . . . . C 3
Puerto Armuelles,
12,562('80) . . . . . . C 1
Santiago, 43,678 . . . . C 2

Trinidad and Tobago
1990 CENSUS

Arima, 29,695 . . . . . . B12
Point Fortin,
6,538('80) B12
Port of Spain, 50,878
(370,000★) B12
San Fernando, 30,092
(75,000★) B12
Scarborough,
6,089('80) B12

Venezuela
1981 CENSUS

Acarigua, 91,662 . . . . C 8
Altagracia de Orituco,
31,582 . . . . C 9
Anaco, 43,607 . . . . . . C10
Araure, 41,747 . . . . . C 8
Barcelona, 156,461 . . B10
Barinas, 110,462 . . . . C 7
Barquisimeto,
497,635 . . . . B 8
Cabimas, 140,435 . . . B 7
Calabozo, 61,995 . . . . C 9
Cantaura, 21,236 . . . . C10
Caracas, 1,816,901
(3,600,000★) . . . . . . B 9
Caripito, 18,172 . . . . B11
Carora, 58,694 . . . . . B 7
Carúpano, 64,579 . . . B11
Ciudad Bolívar,
182,941 . . . . C11
Ciudad Guayana,
314,497 . . . . C11
Ciudad Ojeda (Lagunillas),
83,565 . . . . B 7
Coro, 96,339 . . . . B 8
Cumaná, 179,814 . . . . B10
El Tigre, 73,595 . . . . . C10
El Tocuyo, 22,854 . . . . C 8
Guanare, 64,025 . . . . C 8
La Guaira, 21,815 . . . . B 9
Los Teques, 112,857 B 9
Machiques, 27,242 . . . B 6
Maiquetía, 66,056 . . . B 9
Maracaibo, 890,643 . . B 7
Maracay, 322,560 . . . . B 9
Maturín, 154,976 . . . . C11
Mérida, 143,209 . . . . C 7
Ocumare del Tuy,
40,666 . . . . B 9
Porlamar, 51,079 . . . . B11
Puerto Ayacucho,
28,248 . . . . E 9
Puerto Cabello,
71,759 . . . . B 8
Puerto la Cruz,
53,881 . . . . B10
Punto Fijo, 71,114 . . B 7
Rosario, 23,914 . . . . . B 6
San Carlos, 37,892 . . C 8
San Carlos del Zulia,
31,437 . . . . C 7
San Cristóbal,
198,793 . . . . D 6
San Felipe, 57,526 . . B 8
San Fernando de Apure,
57,308 . . . . D 9
San José de Guanipa,
35,689 . . . . C10
San Juan de Colón,
23,447 . . . . C 6
San Juan de los Morros,
57,219 . . . . C 9
Tinaquillo, 28,168 . . . C 8
Trujillo, 31,774 . . . . . C 7
Tucupita, 27,299 . . . . C11
Upata, 33,238 . . . . . . C11
Valencia, 616,224 . . . C 8
Valera, 102,068 . . . . C 7
Valle de la Pascua,
55,761 . . . . C 9
Yaritagua, 31,936 . . . . B 8
Zaraza, 24,562 . . . . . . C10

Atlantic Ocean

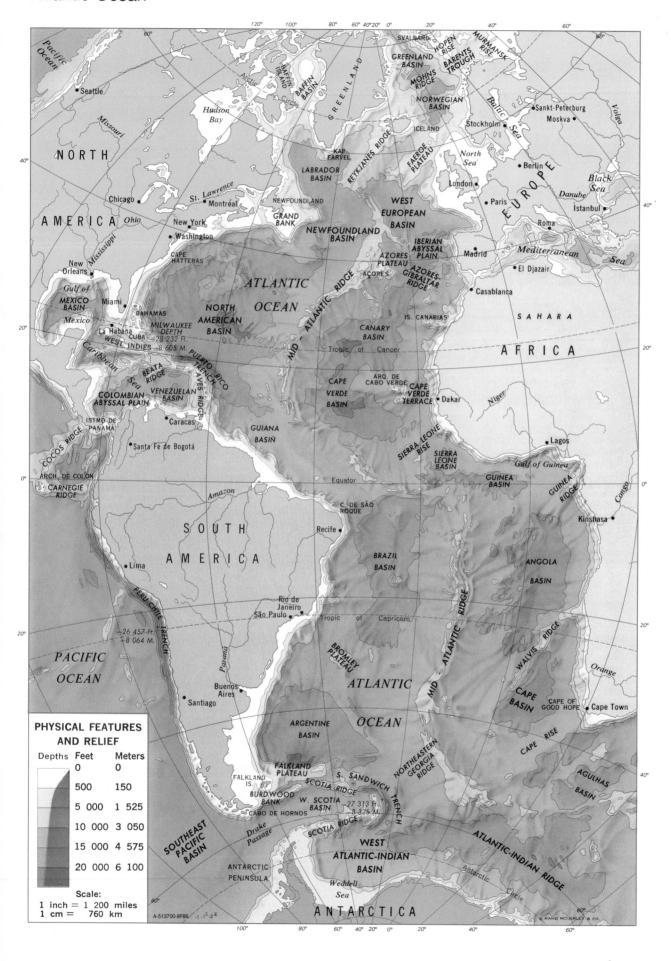

PHYSICAL FEATURES AND RELIEF

Depths	Feet	Meters
	0	0
	500	150
	5 000	1 525
	10 000	3 050
	15 000	4 575
	20 000	6 100

Scale:
1 inch = 1 200 miles
1 cm = 760 km

A-513700-9F86   -1 -1^E -2^E E   © RAND M?NALLY & CO.

60

North America

Atlanta, 394,017 ('90)..F12
BAHAMAS............G13
Baltimore, 736,014
  ('90)............F13
BARBADOS............H14
BELIZE............H12
Boston, 574,283 ('90) E13
Calgary, 636,104 ('86)
  (671,326★)............D 9
CANADA............D11
Chicago, 2,783,726
  ('90)............E12
Ciudad de México (Mexico
  City), 8,831,079 ('80)
  (14,100,000★)........H11
COSTA RICA............H12
CUBA............G13
Dallas, 1,006,877 ('90) F11
Denver, 467,610 ('90)..F10
Detroit, 1,027,974
  ('90)............E12
DOMINICAN
  REPUBLIC............H13
EL SALVADOR............H12
GREENLAND............B16
Guadalajara, 1,626,152
  ('80) (2,325,000★) ..H10
GUATEMALA............H11
HAITI............H13
HONDURAS............H12
Houston, 1,630,553
  ('90)............G11
JAMAICA............H13
Kansas City, 435,146
  ('90)............F11
La Habana (Havana),
  2,036,800 ('87)
  (2,125,000★)........G12
Los Angeles, 3,485,398
  ('90)............F 9
Memphis, 610,337
  ('90)............F11
MEXICO............G10
Miami, 358,548 ('90)...G12
Milwaukee, 628,088
  ('90)............E12
Minneapolis, 368,383
  ('90)............E11
Montréal, 1,015,420 ('86)
  (2,921,357★)........E13
New Orleans, 496,938
  ('90)............G11
New York, 7,322,564
  ('90)............E13
NICARAGUA............H12
Ottawa, 300,763 ('86)
  (819,263★)............E13
PANAMA............I13
Philadelphia, 1,585,577
  ('90)............F13
Phoenix, 900,013 ('90) F 9
PUERTO RICO............H14
San Antonio, 935,933
  ('90)............G11
San Francisco, 723,959
  ('90)............F 8
Santo Domingo, 1,313,172
  ('81)............H13
Seattle, 516,259 ('90)..E 8
Toronto, 612,289 ('86)
  (3,427,168★)........E13
TRINIDAD AND
  TOBAGO............H14
UNITED STATES........F11
Washington, 606,900
  ('90)............F13

★ Population of metropolitan
  area, including suburbs.

61

Copyright © by Rand McNally & Co.
A-520000-286
Lambert Azimuthal Equal Area Projection

Miles 0   200 400 600 800 1000 Mi.
Kilometers 0   400   800   1200 1600 Km.
1:40 000 000

Mexico

Mexico

1980 CENSUS

Acámbaro, 38,224 . . . G 9
Acapulco [de Juárez],
301,902 . . . . I10
Aguascalientes,
293,152 . . . . G 8
Ameca, 25,946 . . . G 7
Apatzingán [de la
Constitución],
55,522 . . . . H 8
Apizaco, 30,498 . . . H10
Caborca, 33,696 . . . B 3
Campeche, 128,434 . H14
Celaya, 141,675 . . . G 9
Chihuahua, 385,603 . C 6
Chilpancingo [de los
Bravos], 67,498 . . . I10
Ciudad Acuña, 38,898 C 9
Ciudad Chetumal,
56,709 . . . . H15
Ciudad del Carmen,
72,489 . . . . H14
Ciudad de México (Mexico
City), 8,831,079
(14,100,000★) H10
Ciudad de Valles,
65,609 . . . . G10
Ciudad Guzmán,
60,938 . . . . H 8
Ciudad Hidalgo,
32,311 . . . . H 9
Ciudad Juárez,
544,496 . . . . B 6
Ciudad Madero,
132,444 . . . . F11
Ciudad Mante, 70,647 F10
Ciudad Obregón,
165,572 . . . . D 5
Ciudad Victoria,
140,161 . . . . F10
Coatzacoalcos,
127,170 . . . . H12
Colima, 86,044 . . . . H 8
Córdoba, 99,972 . . . H11
Cuernavaca, 192,770 H10
Culiacán, 304,826 . . E 6
Delicias, 65,504 . . . C 7
Durango, 257,915 . . E 7
Empalme, 31,555 . . D 4
Ensenada, 120,483 . B 1
Fresnillo, 56,066 . . . F 8
Gómez Palacio,
116,967 . . . . E 8
Guadalajara, 1,626,152
(2,325,000★) . . . . G 8
Guadalupe, 370,524 . E 9
Guanajuato, 48,981 . G 9
Guaymas, 54,826 . . D 4
Hermosillo, 297,175 . C 4
Hidalgo del Parral,
75,590 . . . . D 7
Iguala, 66,005 . . . . H10
Irapuato, 170,138 . . G 9
Jalapa Enríquez,
204,594 . . . . H11
Juchitán [de Zaragoza],
38,801 . . . . I12
La Barca, 20,889 . . . G 8
Lagos de Moreno,
44,223 . . . . G 9
La Paz, 91,453 . . . . E 4
La Piedad [Cavadas],
47,441 . . . . G 8
León [de los Aldamas],
593,002 . . . . G 9
Los Mochis, 122,531 . E 5
Manzanillo, 39,088 . . H 7
Matamoros, 188,745 . E11
Matehuala, 41,550 . . F 9
Mazatlán, 199,830 . . F 6
Mérida, 400,142 . . . G15
Mexicali, 341,559
(365,000★) . . . . . . A 2
Mexico City see Ciudad
de México H10
Minatitlán, 106,765 . . I12
Monclova, 115,786 . . D 9
Montemorelos, 28,342 E10
Monterrey, 1,090,009
(2,015,000★) . . . . E 9
Morelia, 297,544 . . . H 9
Navojoa, 62,901 . . . D 5
Nogales, 65,603 . . . B 4
Nueva Casas Grandes,
28,514 . . . . B 6
Nueva Rosita, 33,121 D 9
Nuevo Laredo,
201,731 . . . . D10
Oaxaca [de Juárez],
154,223 . . . . I11
Ocotlán, 48,931 . . . G 8
Orizaba, 114,848
(215,000★) H11
Pachuca [de Soto],
110,351 . . . . G10
Papantla [de Olarte],
43,935 . . . . G11
Pátzcuaro, 32,902 . . H 9
Piedras Negras,
67,455 . . . . C 9
Poza Rica de Hidalgo,
166,799 . . . . G11

★ Population of metropolitan
area, including suburbs.

Progreso, 24,257 . . G15
Puebla [de Zaragoza],
    835,759
    (1,055,000★) H10
Puerto Vallarta,
    38,645 . . . . G 7
Querétaro, 215,976 . . G 9
Reynosa, 194,693 . . D10
Sabinas, 27,413 . . . . D 9
Sabinas Hidalgo,
    23,187 . . . . D 9
Sahuayo, 43,258 . . . G 8
Salamanca, 96,703 . . G 9
Salina Cruz, 40,010 . . I12
Saltillo, 284,937 . . . E 9
Salvatierra, 28,878 . . G 9
San Andrés Tuxtla,
    40,412 . . . . H12
San Cristóbal las Casas,
    42,026 . . . . I13
San Francisco del Rincón,
    40,943 . . . . G 9
San Luis Potosí, 362,371
    (470,000★) . . . . . F 9
San Luis Río Colorado,
    76,684 . . . . A 2
San Pedro de las
    Colonias, 35,879 . . E 8
Santa Bárbara, 14,894 D 7
Tampico, 267,957
    (435,000★) F11
Tapachula, 85,766 . . J13
Tecomán, 46,371 . . . H 8
Tehuacán, 79,547 . . H11
Tehuantepec, 22,019 . I12
Teocaltiche, 16,559 . . G 8
Tepatitlán [de Morelos],
    41,813 . . . . G 8
Tepic, 145,741 . . . . G 7
Ticul, 18,255 . . . . . G15
Tierra Blanca, 31,653 H11
Tijuana, 429,500 . . . . A 1
Tizimin, 26,305 . . . . G15
Toluca [de Lerdo],
    199,778 . . . . H10
Torreón, 328,086
    (575,000★) . . . . . E 8
Tulancingo, 53,400 . . G10
Tuxpan de Rodríguez
    Cano, 56,037 . . . . G11
Tuxtla Gutiérrez,
    131,096 . . . . I13
Uruapan [del Progreso],
    122,828 . . . . H 8
Valle de Santiago,
    37,645 . . . . G 9
Valle Hermoso, 27,966 E11
Veracruz [Llave], 284,822
    (385,000★) H11
Villa Frontera, 32,568 D 9
Villahermosa, 158,216 I13
Zacapu, 39,570 . . . . H 9
Zacatecas, 80,088 . . F 8
Zamora de Hidalgo,
    86,998 . . . . H 8
Zitácuaro, 47,520 . . . H 9

63

Central America and the Caribbean

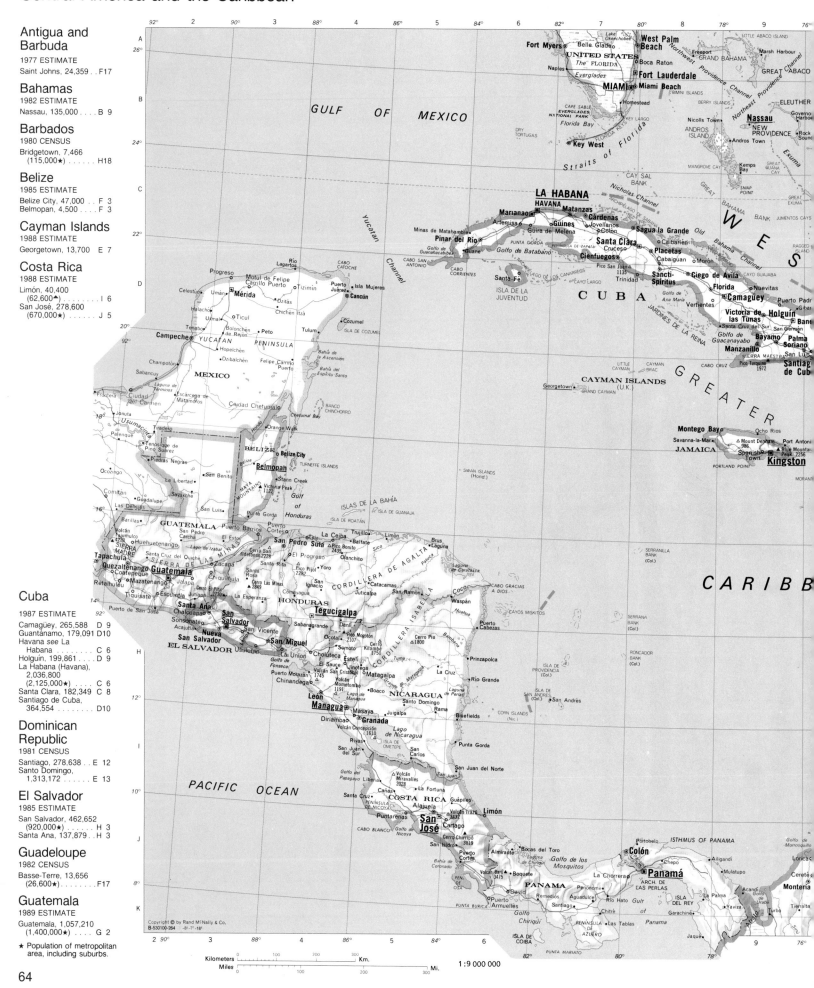

Antigua and Barbuda
1977 ESTIMATE
Saint Johns, 24,359 . . F17

Bahamas
1982 ESTIMATE
Nassau, 135,000 . . . . B 9

Barbados
1980 CENSUS
Bridgetown, 7,466
(115,000★) H18

Belize
1985 ESTIMATE
Belize City, 47,000 . . F 3
Belmopan, 4,500 . . . F 3

Cayman Islands
1988 ESTIMATE
Georgetown, 13,700 E 7

Costa Rica
1988 ESTIMATE
Limón, 40,400
(62,600▲) . . . . . . I 6
San José, 278,600
(670,000★) . . . . . . J 5

Cuba
1987 ESTIMATE
Camagüey, 265,588 . D 9
Guantánamo, 179,091 D10
Havana see La
Habana . . . . C 6
Holguín, 199,861 . . . D 9
La Habana (Havana),
2,036,800
(2,125,000★) . . . . C 6
Santa Clara, 182,349 C 8
Santiago de Cuba,
364,554 . . . . D10

Dominican Republic
1981 CENSUS
Santiago, 278,638 . . E 12
Santo Domingo,
1,313,172 . . . . . . E 13

El Salvador
1985 ESTIMATE
San Salvador, 462,652
(920,000★) . . . . . H 3
Santa Ana, 137,879 . H 3

Guadeloupe
1982 CENSUS
Basse-Terre, 13,656
(26,600★) F17

Guatemala
1989 ESTIMATE
Guatemala, 1,057,210
(1,400,000★) . . . . G 2

★ Population of metropolitan
area, including suburbs.

64

Scale 1 : 9 000 000

ATLANTIC OCEAN

BAHAMAS

Tropic of Cancer

TURKS AND CAICOS ISLANDS
(U.K.)

SILVER BANK

W E S T

I N D I E S

HISPANIOLA

HAITI

Port-au-Prince

Santo Domingo

DOMINICAN REPUBLIC

PUERTO RICO
(U.S.)

San Juan

VIRGIN ISLANDS
(U.S.) (U.K.)

Charlotte Amalie

Ponce

A N T I L L E S

SAINT KITTS
AND NEVIS

Basseterre

Saint Johns

ANTIGUA AND
BARBUDA

MONTSERRAT
(U.K.) Plymouth

ANGUILLA
(U.K.)

Pointe-à-Pitre

GUADELOUPE

BASSE-TERRE

DOMINICA

Roseau

C A R I B B E A N   S E A

Fort-de-France
MARTINIQUE
(Fr.)

Castries

SAINT LUCIA

Kingstown

SAINT VINCENT
AND THE
GRENADINES

Saint George's GRENADA

Bridgetown

BARBADOS

ARUBA
(Neth.)

Oranjestad

NETHERLANDS ANTILLES

BONAIRE

CURAÇAO Willemstad

TOBAGO

Scarborough

TRINIDAD

Port of Spain

TRINIDAD
AND
TOBAGO

Barranquilla

Maracaibo

CARACAS

VENEZUELA

COLOMBIA

Ciudad Guayana

Ciudad Bolívar

Haiti
1987 ESTIMATE
Port-au-Prince, 797,000
(880,000★) E11

Honduras
1988 CENSUS
San Pedro Sula,
279,356 . . . . G 4
Tegucigalpa, 551,606 G 4

Jamaica
1987 ESTIMATE
Kingston, 646,400
(770,000★) . . . . . E 9
Montego Bay,
70,265('82) . . . . . . E 9

Martinique
1982 CENSUS
Fort-de-France, 99,844
(116,017★) G17

Netherlands Antilles
1981 CENSUS
Willemstad, 31,883
(130,000★) . . . . . . H 13

Nicaragua
1985 ESTIMATE
León, 101,000 . . . . . H 4
Managua, 682,000 . . H 4

Panama
1990 CENSUS
Colón, 54,469
(96,000★) . . . . J 8
Panamá, 411,549
(770,000★) . . . . . . J 8

Puerto Rico
1980 CENSUS
Ponce, 161,739
(232,551★) E14
San Juan, 424,600
(1,775,260★) E14

Saint Lucia
1987 ESTIMATE
Castries, 53,933 . . . . G17

Saint Vincent and the Grenadines
1987 ESTIMATE
Kingstown, 19,028
(28,936★) H17

Trinidad and Tobago
1988 ESTIMATE
Port of Spain, 59,200
(370,000★) I17

Lambert Conformal Conic Projection

65

Canada

ALBERTA...............F10
Alma, 25,923 ('86)
   (29,977★)..............G18
Baie-Comeau, 26,244 ('86)
   (33,047★)..............G19
Banff, 4,208 ('81).......F 9
Barrie, 48,287 ('86)
   (67,703★)..............H17
Bathurst, 14,683 ('86)
   (34,895★)..............G19
Belleville, 36,041 ('86)
   (87,530★)..............H17
Brandon, 38,708 ('86).G13
BRITISH COLUMBIA... F 8
Brockville, 20,880 ('86)
   (37,115★)..............H17
Calgary, 636,104 ('86)
   (671,326★)............F10
Cambridge, 79,920
   ('86)...................H16
Campbell River, 15,370
   ('81)...................F 7
Campbellton, 9,077 ('86)
   (17,418★)..............G19
CANADA...............D13
Charlottetown, 15,776
   ('86) (53,868★) G20
Chatham, 42,211 ('86).H16
Chicoutimi, 61,083 ('86)
   (158,468★)............G18
Chilliwack, 41,337 ('86)
   (50,288★)..............G 8
Churchill, 1,186 ('81)..E14
Corner Brook, 22,719
   ('86) (33,730★)........G21
Cornwall, 46,425 ('86)
   (51,719★)..............G18
Dartmouth, 65,243
   ('86)...................H20
Dawson Creek, 10,544
   ('86)...................E 8
Dolbeau, 8,554 ('86)
   (15,288★)..............G18
Drummondville, 36,020
   ('86) (56,283★)........G18
Edmonton, 573,982 ('86)
   (785,465★)............F10
Edmundston, 11,497 ('86)
   (22,614★)..............G19
Eskimo Point, 1,189
   ('86)...................D14
Flin Flon, 7,591 ('86)
   (9,211★) F12
Fort McMurray, 34,949
   ('86) (48,497★) E10
Fort Saint John, 13,355
   ('86)...................E 8
Fredericton, 44,352 ('86)
   (65,768★)..............G19
Gander, 10,207 ('86)
   (10,899★)..............G22
Gaspé, 17,350 ('86)....G20
Granby, 38,508 ('86)
   (51,176★)..............G18
Grande-Prairie, 26,471
   ('86)...................E 9
Grand Falls, 9,121 ('86)
   (25,612★)..............G21
Guelph, 78,235 ('86)
   (85,962★)..............H16
Halifax, 113,577 ('86)
   (295,990★)............H20
Hamilton, 306,728 ('86)
   (557,029★) H17
Happy Valley-Goose Bay,
   7,248 ('86)............F20
Hull, 58,722 ('86).......G17
Inuvik, 3,389 ('86)......C 6
Jasper, 3,269 ('81)......F 9
Joliette, 16,845 ('86)
   (34,897★)..............G18
Jonquière, 58,467
   ('86)...................G18
Kamloops, 61,773
   ('86)...................F 8
Kelowna, 61,213 ('86)
   (89,730★)..............G 9
Kenora, 9,621 ('86)
   (15,456★)..............G14
Kirkland Lake, 11,604
   ('86)...................G16
Kitchener, 150,604 ('86)
   (311,195★)............H17
Kitimat, 11,196 ('86)....F 7
Labrador City, 8,664 ('86)
   (11,301★)..............F19
La Tuque, 10,723 ('86)
   (13,468★)..............G18
Laval, 284,164 ('86)..G18
Lethbridge, 58,841
   ('86)...................G10
Lloydminster, 17,356
   ('86)...................F11
London, 269,140 ('86)
   (342,302★)............H16
MANITOBA..............F13
Matane, 13,243 ('86)
   (15,361★)..............G19
Medicine Hat, 41,804 ('86)
   (50,734★)..............F10
Midland, 12,092 ('86)
   (35,003★)..............H17
Moncton, 55,468 ('86)
   (102,084★) G20

★ Population of metropolitan
   area, including suburbs.

Montréal, 1,015,420 ('86)
  (2,921,357★) G18
Moose Jaw, 35,073 ('86)
  (37,219★) F11
Nanaimo, 49,029 ('86)
  (60,420★) .... G 8
NEW BRUNSWICK..... G19
NEWFOUNDLAND.......F21
New Glasgow, 10,022
  ('86) (38,737★) G20
Niagara Falls, 72,107
  ('86) H17
North Bay, 50,623 ('86)
  (57,422★) G17
NORTHWEST
  TERRITORIES.........C13
NOVA SCOTIA........... G20
ONTARIO................. G16
Orillia, 24,077 ('86)
  (31,252★) H17
Oshawa, 123,651 ('86)
  (203,543★) H17
Ottawa, 300,763 ('86)
  (819,263★) G17
Owen Sound, 19,804 ('86)
  (27,364★) H16
Pembroke, 14,131 ('86)
  (22,560★) G17
Penticton, 23,588 ('86)
  (38,966★) .... G 9
Peterborough, 61,049
  ('86) (87,083★) H17
Portage-la-Prairie, 13,198
  ('86) G13
Port Alberni, 18,241
  ('86) .... G 8
Prince Albert, 33,686 ('86)
  (40,841★) F11
PRINCE EDWARD
  ISLAND................. G20
Prince George, 67,621
  ('86) .... F 8
Prince Rupert, 15,755
  ('86) (17,581★) .... F 6
QUÉBEC.................. F18
Québec, 164,580 ('86)
  (603,267★) G18
Rankin Inlet, 1,374
  ('86)....................... D14
Red Deer, 54,425 ('86)F10
Regina, 175,064 ('86)
  (186,521★) F12
Saint-Hyacinthe, 38,603
  ('86) (48,303★) G18
Saint-Jérôme, 23,316 ('86)
  (44,048★) G18
Saint John, 76,831 ('86)
  (121,265★) G19
Saint John's, 96,216 ('86)
  (161,901★) G22
Sarnia, 49,033 ('86)
  (85,700★) H16
SASKATCHEWAN.......F11
Saskatoon, 177,641 ('86)
  (200,665★) F11
Sault Sainte Marie, 80,905
  ('86) (84,617★) G16
Selkirk, 10,013 ('86)... F13
Sept-Îles (Seven Islands),
  25,637 ('86)
  (28,050★) F19
Shawinigan, 21,470 ('86)
  (61,965★) G18
Sherbrooke, 74,438 ('86)
  (129,960★) G18
Sorel, 19,522 ('86)
  (46,096★) G18
Sudbury, 88,717 ('86)
  (148,877★) G16
Summerside, 8,020 ('86)
  (15,614★) G20
Swift Current, 15,666
  ('86)....................... F11
Sydney Mines, 8,063
  ('86)....................... G20
Thetford Mines, 18,561
  ('86) (31,940★) G18
Thunder Bay, 112,272
  ('86) (122,217★) G15
Timmins, 46,657 ('86). G16
Toronto, 612,289 ('86)
  (3,427,168★) H17
Trail, 7,948 ('86)
  (20,257★) .... G 9
Trois-Rivières, 50,122
  ('86) (128,888★) G18
Truro, 12,124 ('86)
  (41,516★) G20
Val-d'Or, 22,252 ('86)
  (27,178★) G17
Vancouver, 431,147 ('86)
  (1,380,729★) .... G 8
Victoria, 66,303 ('86)
  (255,547★) .... G 8
Whitehorse, 15,199
  ('86)....................... D 5
Windsor, 193,111 ('86)
  (253,988★) H16
Winnipeg, 594,551 ('86)
  (625,304★) G13
Yellowknife, 11,753
  ('86)....................... D10
YUKON...................... D 5

Lambert Conformal Conic Projection

Alberta

Alberta
1986 CENSUS

Airdrie, 10,390 . . . . . . D 3
Athabasca, 1,970 . . . . B 4
Banff . . . . D 3
Barrhead, 3,991 . . . . . B 3
Beaumont, 3,944 . . . . C 4
Beaverlodge, 1,808 . . B 1
Blackfalds, 1,688 . . . . C 4
Bonnyville, 5,470 . . . . B 5
Bow Island, 1,650 . . E 5
Brooks, 9,464 . . . . . . D 5
Calgary, 636,104
  (671,326★) . . . . . . D 3
Camrose, 12,968 . . . . C 4
Canmore, 4,182 . . . . D 3
Cardston, 3,497 . . . . E 4
Carstairs, 1,629 . . . . D 3
Claresholm, 3,382 . . D 4
Coaldale, 4,796 . . . . E 4
Cochrane, 4,190 . . . . D 3
Cold Lake, 3,195 . . . B 5
Coronation, 1,310 . . C 5
Crowsnest Pass,
  6,912 . . . . E 3
Devon, 3,691 . . . . . C 4
Didsbury, 3,184 . . . . D 3
Drayton Valley, 5,290 C 3
Drumheller, 6,366 . . D 4
Edmonton, 573,982
  (785,465★) . . . . . C 4
Edson, 7,323 . . . . . C 2
Fairview, 2,998 . . . . A 1
Fort Chipewyan, 922 . f 8
Fort Macleod, 3,123 . E 4
Fort McMurray, 34,949
  (48,497★) . . . . . . A 5
Fort Saskatchewan,
  11,983 . . . . C 4
Fox Creek, 2,068 . . . B 2
Gibbons, 2,335 . . . . C 4
Grand Centre, 3,655 B 5
Grande Cache, 3,646 C 1
Grande Prairie,
  26,471 . . . . B 1
Grimshaw, 2,579 . . . A 2
Hanna, 3,017 . . . . . D 5
High Level, 3,004 . . F 7
High Prairie, 2,817 . B 2
High River, 5,096 . . D 4
Hinton, 8,629 . . . . . C 2
Innisfail, 5,535 . . . . C 4
Jasper . . . . C 1
Lac La Biche, 2,553 . B 5
Lacombe, 6,080 . . . . C 4
La Crete, 689 . . . . . f 7
Lake Louise, 688 . . . D 2
Lamont, 1,576 . . . . . C 4
Leduc, 13,126 . . . . . C 4
Lethbridge, 58,841 . . E 4
Lloydminster, 17,354 C 5
Magrath, 1,637 . . . . E 4
Medicine Hat, 41,804
  (50,734★) . . . . . . D 5
Morinville, 5,364 . . . C 4
Nordegg, 53 . . . . . . C 2
Okotoks, 5,214 . . . . D 4
Olds, 4,871 . . . . D 3
Peace River, 6,288 . . A 2
Penhold, 1,580 . . . . C 4
Picture Butte, 1,576 . E 4
Pincher Creek, 3,800 E 4
Ponoka, 5,473 . . . . . C 4
Provost, 1,725 . . . . . C 5
Raymond, 2,957 . . . E 4
Redcliff, 3,834 . . . . D 5
Red Deer, 54,425 . . C 4
Redwater, 1,982 . . . C 4
Rimbey, 1,786 . . . . . C 3
Rocky Mountain House,
  5,182 . . . . C 3
Saint Albert, 36,710 . C 4
Saint Paul, 5,030 . . . B 5
Sherwood Park . . . . C 4
Slave Lake, 5,429 . . B 3
Smith, 251 . . . . B 3
Spruce Grove, 11,918 C 4
Stettler, 5,147 . . . . . C 4
Stony Plain, 5,802 . . C 4
Strathmore, 3,544 . . D 4
Sundre, 1,712 . . . . . D 3
Swan Hills, 2,403 . . . B 3
Sylvan Lake, 3,937 . . C 3
Taber, 6,382 . . . . . . E 4
Three Hills, 2,528 . . D 4
Valleyview, 1,987 . . . B 2
Vegreville, 5,276 . . . C 4
Vermilion, 3,879 . . . C 5
Vulcan, 1,420 . . . . . D 4
Wainwright, 4,665 . . C 5
Westlock, 4,532 . . . . B 4
Wetaskiwin, 10,071 . . C 4
Whitecourt, 5,737 . . B 3

★ Population of metropolitan
  area, including suburbs.

68

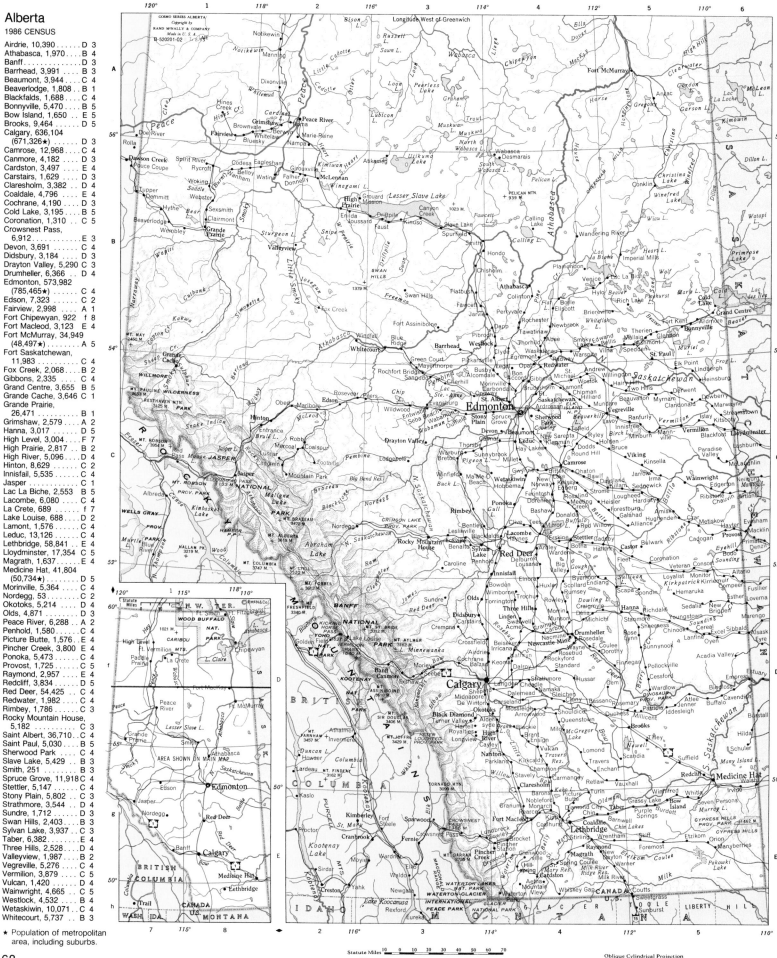

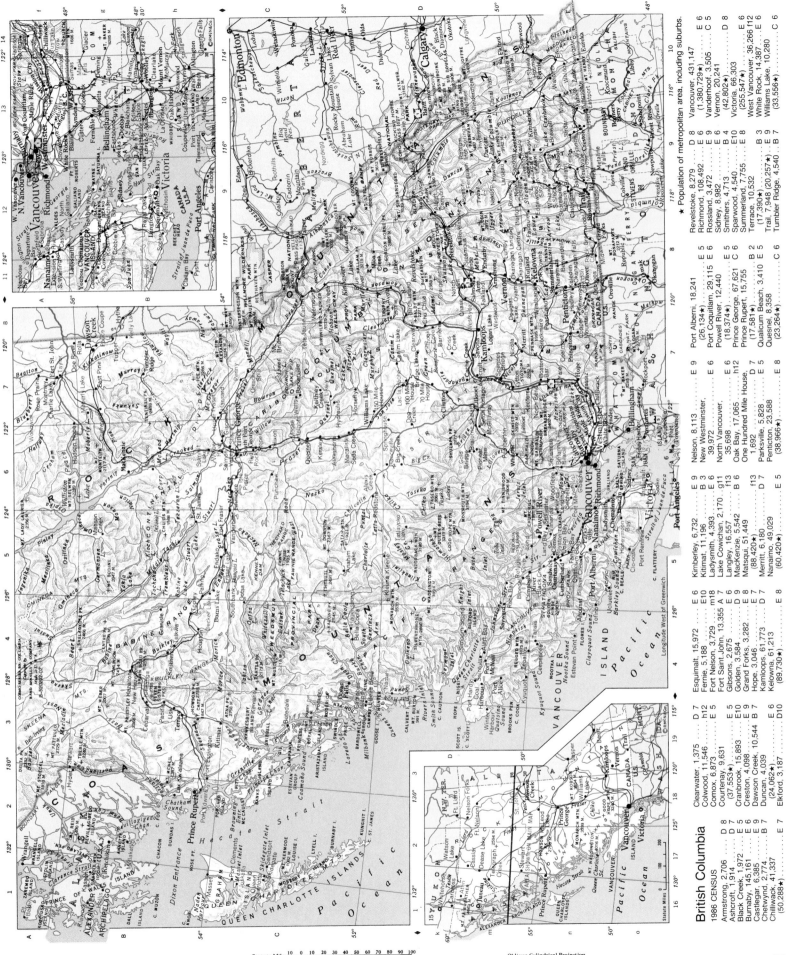

British Columbia

1986 CENSUS

Armstrong, 2,706	D 8	
Ashcroft, 1,914	D 7	
Black Creek, 1,972	E 6	
Burnaby, 145,161	E 9	
Castlegar, 6,385	E 6	
Chetwynd, 2,774	B 7	
Chilliwack, 41,337 (50,288★)	E 7	
Clearwater, 1,375	D 7	
Colwood, 11,546	h12	
Comox, 6,873	E 5	
Courtenay, 9,631 (37,553★)	E 5	
Cranbrook, 15,893	E 10	
Creston, 4,098	E 9	
Dawson Creek, 10,544	B 7	
Duncan, 4,039 (24,062★)	E 6	
Elkford, 3,187	D 10	
Esquimalt, 15,972	D 7	
Fernie, 5,188	E 10	
Fort Nelson, 3,729	m18	
Fort Saint John, 13,355	A 7	
Gibsons, 2,675	E 6	
Golden, 3,584	D 9	
Grand Forks, 3,282	E 8	
Hope, 3,046	E 7	
Kamloops, 61,773 (88,420★)	D 7	
Kelowna, 61,213 (89,730★)	E 8	
Kimberley, 6,732	E 6	
Kitimat, 11,196	B 3	
Ladysmith, 4,393	E 6	
Lake Cowichan, 2,170	g11	
Langley, 16,557	f13	
MacKenzie, 5,542	B 6	
Matsqui, 51,449	E 6	
Merritt, 6,180	D 7	
Nanaimo, 49,029 (60,420★)	E 5	
Nelson, 8,113	E 9	
New Westminster, 39,972	E 6	
North Vancouver, 35,698	E 6	
Oak Bay, 17,065	h12	
One Hundred Mile House, 1,692	D 7	
Parksville, 5,828	E 5	
Penticton, 23,588 (38,966★)	E 8	
Port Alberni, 18,241 (26,134★)	E 5	
Port Coquitlam, 29,115 (18,374★)	E 6	
Powell River, 12,440	E 5	
Prince George, 67,621	C 6	
Prince Rupert, 15,755	B 2	
Quesnel, 8,358 (23,264★)	C 6	
Revelstoke, 8,279	D 8	
Richmond, 108,492	E 6	
Rossland, 3,472	E 9	
Sidney, 8,982	B 4	
Smithers, 4,713	E 10	
Sparwood, 4,540	E 8	
Summerland, 7,755	E 8	
Terrace, 10,532 (17,390★)	B 3	
Trail, 7,948 (20,257★)	E 6	
Tumbler Ridge, 4,540	B 7	
Vancouver, 431,147 (1,380,729★)	D 8	
Vanderhoof, 3,505 (42,802★)	E 6	
Vernon, 20,241	C 5	
Victoria, 66,303 (255,547★)	D 8	
West Vancouver, 36,266 (12 (17,581★)	E 6	
White Rock, 14,387	E 6	
Williams Lake, 10,280 (33,556★)	B 6	
		C 6

★ Population of metropolitan area, including suburbs.

Statute Miles 10 0 10 20 30 40 50 60 70 80 90 100

Kilometers 10 0 10 20 40 60 80 100 120 140

Oblique Cylindrical Projection

Manitoba

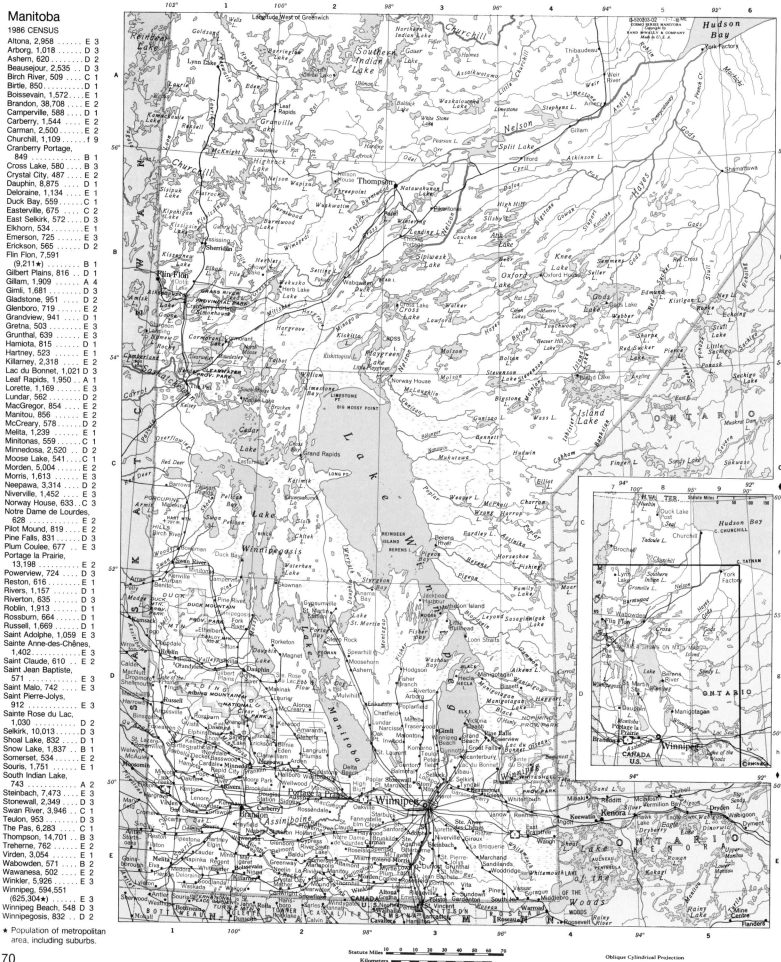

Manitoba
1986 CENSUS

Altona, 2,958 ..... E 3
Arborg, 1,018 .... D 3
Ashern, 620 .... D 2
Beausejour, 2,535 .. D 3
Birch River, 509 .... C 1
Birtle, 850 .... D 1
Boissevain, 1,572 ... E 1
Brandon, 38,708 .... E 2
Camperville, 588 ... D 1
Carberry, 1,544 .... E 2
Carman, 2,500 ..... E 2
Churchill, 1,109 .... f 9
Cranberry Portage,
    849 .... B 1
Cross Lake, 580 .... B 3
Crystal City, 487 ... E 2
Dauphin, 8,875 .... D 1
Deloraine, 1,134 ... E 1
Duck Bay, 559 ..... C 1
Easterville, 675 .... C 2
East Selkirk, 572 ... D 3
Elkhorn, 534 ...... E 1
Emerson, 725 ...... E 3
Erickson, 565 ..... D 2
Flin Flon, 7,591
    (9,211★) .... B 1
Gilbert Plains, 816 .. D 1
Gillam, 1,909 ...... A 4
Gimli, 1,681 ...... D 3
Gladstone, 951 .... E 2
Glenboro, 719 ..... E 2
Grandview, 941 .... D 1
Gretna, 503 ...... E 3
Grunthal, 639 ..... E 3
Hamiota, 815 ..... D 1
Hartney, 523 ..... E 1
Killarney, 2,318 ... E 2
Lac du Bonnet, 1,021 D 3
Leaf Rapids, 1,950 . A 1
Lorette, 1,169 ..... E 3
Lundar, 562 ...... D 2
MacGregor, 854 ... E 2
Manitou, 856 ..... E 2
McCreary, 578 .... D 2
Melita, 1,239 ..... E 1
Minitonas, 559 .... C 1
Minnedosa, 2,520 .. D 2
Moose Lake, 541 ... C 1
Morden, 5,004 .... E 3
Morris, 1,613 ..... E 3
Neepawa, 3,314 ... D 2
Niverville, 1,452 ... E 3
Norway House, 633 .C 3
Notre Dame de Lourdes,
    628 .... E 2
Pilot Mound, 819 ... E 2
Pine Falls, 831 .... D 3
Plum Coulee, 677 .. E 3
Portage la Prairie,
    13,198 .... E 2
Powerview, 724 .... D 3
Reston, 616 ...... E 1
Rivers, 1,157 ..... D 1
Riverton, 635 ..... D 3
Roblin, 1,913 ..... D 1
Rossburn, 664 .... D 1
Russell, 1,669 .... D 1
Saint Adolphe, 1,059 E 3
Sainte Anne-des-Chênes,
    1,402 .... E 3
Saint Claude, 610 .. E 2
Saint Jean Baptiste,
    571 .... E 3
Saint Malo, 742 ... E 3
Saint Pierre-Jolys,
    912 .... E 3
Sainte Rose du Lac,
    1,030 .... D 2
Selkirk, 10,013 .... D 3
Shoal Lake, 832 ... D 1
Snow Lake, 1,837 .. B 1
Somerset, 534 .... E 2
Souris, 1,751 ..... E 1
South Indian Lake,
    743 .... A 2
Steinbach, 7,473 ... E 3
Stonewall, 2,349 ... D 3
Swan River, 3,946 .. C 1
Teulon, 953 ...... D 3
The Pas, 6,283 .... C 1
Thompson, 14,701 .. B 3
Treherne, 762 ..... E 2
Virden, 3,054 ..... E 1
Wabowden, 571 ... B 2
Wawanesa, 502 ... E 2
Winkler, 5,926 .... E 3
Winnipeg, 594,551
    (625,304★) ..... E 3
Winnipeg Beach, 548 D 3
Winnipegosis, 832 .. D 2

★ Population of metropolitan
  area, including suburbs.

70

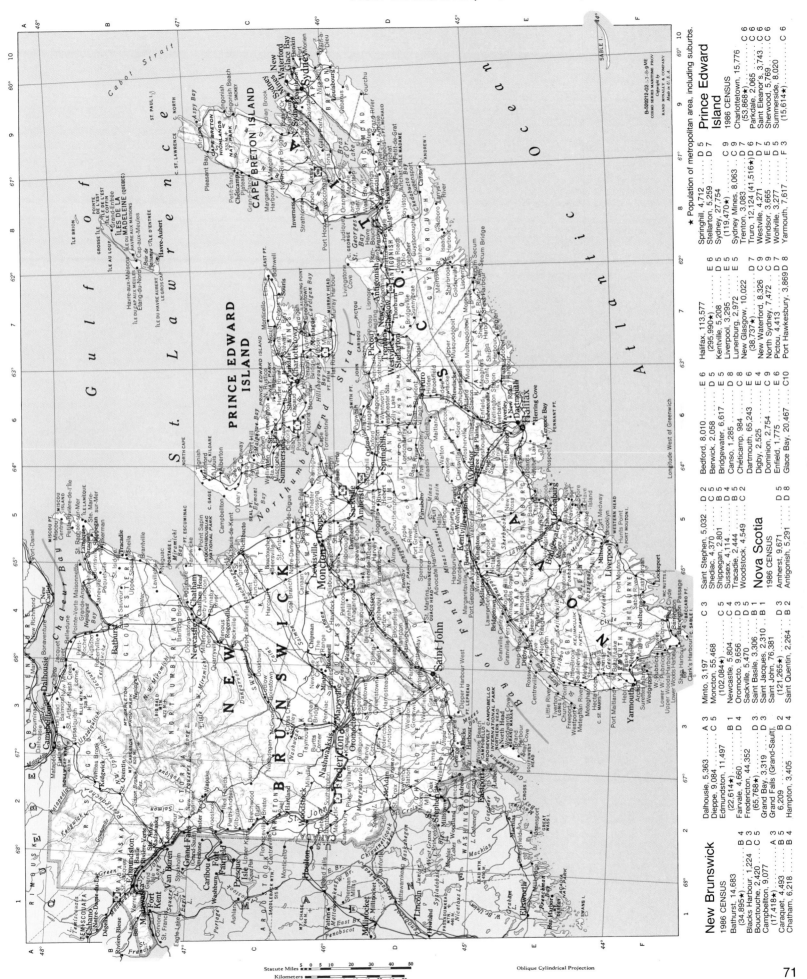

Newfoundland

Newfoundland and Labrador

1986 CENSUS

Arnold's Cove, 1,117 . . . E 4
Badger, 1,151 . . . . . . D 3
Baie Verte, 2,049 . . . . D 3
Bay Bulls, 1,114 . . . . . E 5
Bay Roberts, 4,446 . . E 5
Bishop's Falls, 4,213 D 4
Bonavista, 4,605 . . . . D 5
Botwood, 3,916 . . . . D 4
Buchans, 1,281 . . . . D 3
Burgeo, 2,582 . . . . E 3
Burin, 2,892 . . . . . E 4
Burnt Islands, 1,042 . E 2
Carbonear, 5,337
  (13,082★) . . . . . . E 5
Carmanville, 987 . . . D 4
Cartwright, 674 . . . . B 3
Catalina, 1,211 . . . . . D 5
Channel-Port-aux-
  Basques, 5,901 . . . E 2
Clarenville, 2,967 . . . D 5
Conception Bay South,
  15,531 . . . . E 5
Corner Brook, 22,719
  (33,730★) . . . . . . D 3
Cox's Cove, 999 . . . . D 2
Deer Lake, 4,233 . . . . D 3
Dunville, 1,833 . . . . . E 5
Durrell, 1,060 . . . . . D 4
Englee, 1,012 . . . . . C 3
Fogo, 1,153 . . . . . . D 4
Fortune, 2,370 . . . . . E 4
Gambo, 2,723 . . . . . D 4
Gander, 10,207 . . . . D 4
Glenwood, 1,038 . . . . D 4
Glovertown, 2,184 . . . D 4
Grand Bank, 3,732 . . E 4
Grand Falls, 9,121
  (25,612★) . . . . . . D 4
Hampden, 875 . . . . . . D 3
Happy Valley-Goose Bay,
  7,248 . . . . B 1
Harbour Breton,
  2,432 . . . . E 4
Harbour Grace, 3,053 E 5
Hare Bay, 1,436 . . . . D 4
Hermitage, 831 . . . . E 4
Isle-aux-Morts, 1,203 E 2
Joe Batt's Arm [-Barr'd
  Islands-Shoal Bay],
  1,232 . . . . D 4
King's Point, 923 . . . D 3
Labrador City, 8,664
  (11,301★) . . . . . . h 8
Lark Harbour, 829 . . . D 2
La Scie, 1,429 . . . . . D 4
Lawn, 1,015 . . . . . . E 4
Lewisporte, 3,978 . . . D 4
Lourdes, 937 . . . . . . D 2
Marystown, 6,660 . . . E 4
Milltown [-Head of Bay
  d'Espoir], 1,276 . . . E 4
Mount Pearl, 20,293 E 5
Musgrave Harbour,
  1,527 . . . . D 5
Nain, 1,018 . . . . g 9
New Harbour, 957 . . . E 5
Norris Arm, 1,127 . . . D 4
Norris Point, 1,010 . . D 3
Pasadena, 3,268 . . . . D 3
Placentia, 2,016 . . . . E 5
Point Leamington,
  850 . . . . D 4
Port au Port [West-
  Aguathuna-Felix Cove],
  842 . . . . D 2
Pouch Cove, 1,576 . . E 5
Ramea, 1,380 . . . . . E 3
Robert's Arm, 1,111 . D 4
Rocky Harbour, 1,268 D 3
Roddickton, 1,223 . . . C 3
Rose-Blanche [-Harbour le
  Cou], 967 . . . . E 2
Saint Alban's, 1,780 . E 4
Saint Anthony, 3,182 . C 4
Saint George's, 1,852 D 2
Saint John's, 96,216
  (161,901★) . . . . . . E 5
Saint Lawrence,
  1,841 . . . . E 4
Shoal Harbour, 1,049 D 4
Spaniard's Bay, 2,190 E 5
Springdale, 3,555 . . . D 3
Stephenville, 7,994 . . D 2
Stephenville Crossing,
  2,252 . . . . D 2
Summerford, 1,169 . . D 4
Torbay, 3,730 . . . . . E 5
Trepassey, 1,460 . . . E 4
Twillingate, 1,506 . . . D 4
Upper Island Cove,
  2,055 . . . . E 5
Victoria, 1,895 . . . . E 5
Wabana (Bell Island),
  4,057 . . . . E 5
Wabush, 2,637 . . . . . h 8
Wesleyville, 1,208 . . D 5
Whitbourne, 1,151 . . E 5
Windsor, -5,545 . . . . D 4
Witless Bay, 1,022 . . E 5

★ Population of metropolitan
  area, including suburbs.

72

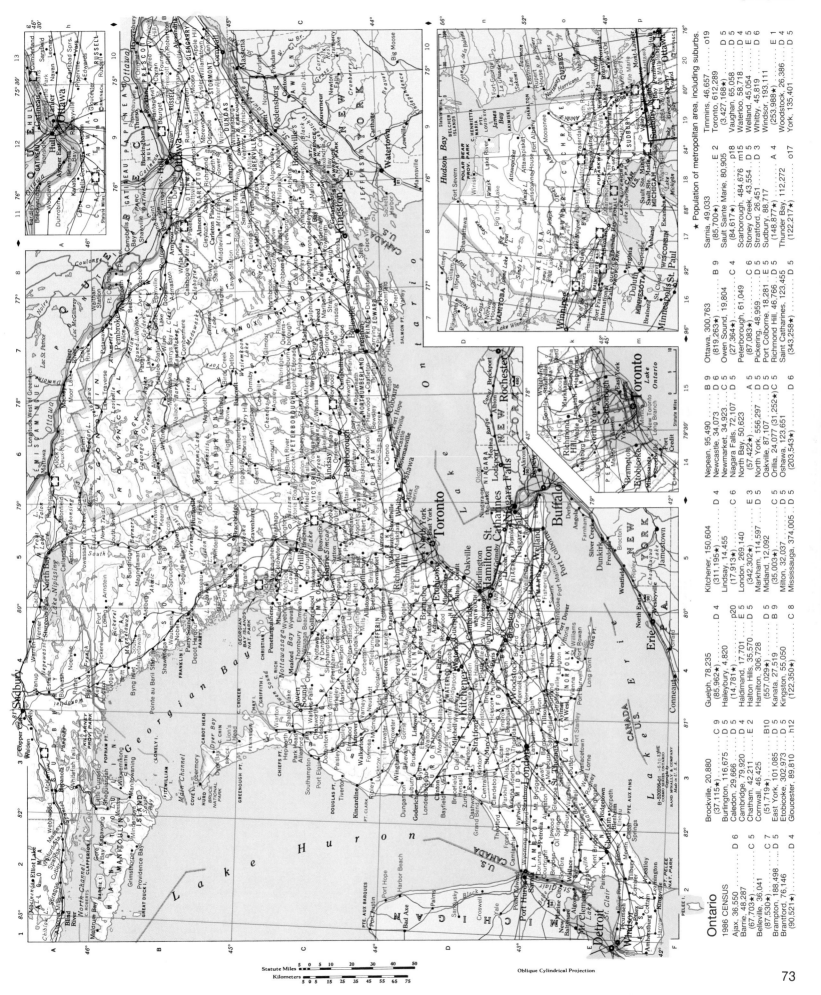

Oblique Cylindrical Projection

Statute Miles
Kilometers

Ontario

1986 CENSUS

★ Population of metropolitan area, including suburbs.

Place	Population	Ref.
Ajax, 36,550		D 6
Barrie, 48,287	(67,703★)	C 5
Belleville, 37,243	(87,530★)	C 7
Brampton, 188,498		D 5
Brantford, 76,146	(90,521★)	D 4
Brockville, 20,880	(37,115★)	D 4
Burlington, 116,675		D 5
Caledon, 29,666		D 5
Cambridge, 79,920		D 4
Chatham, 42,211	(51,719★)	E 2
Cornwall, 46,425		D 5
East York, 101,085		D 5
Etobicoke, 302,973		D 5
Gloucester, 89,810		D 4
Guelph, 78,235	(85,962★)	C 9
Haileybury, 4,820		D 5
Haldimand, 17,701		D 4
Halton Hills, 35,570		E 2
Hamilton, 306,728	(557,029★)	D 5
Kanata, 27,519		B 9
Kingston, 55,050		C 8
Kitchener, 150,604	(311,195★)	D 4
Lindsay, 14,455	(17,913★)	C 6
London, 269,140	(342,302★)	E 3
Markham, 114,597	(35,003★)	D 5
Midland, 12,092		D 5
Milton, 32,037		B 9
Mississauga, 374,005	(122,350★)	C 8
Nepean, 95,490		B 9
Newcastle, 34,073		D 6
Newmarket, 34,923		D 5
Niagara Falls, 72,107	(57,422★)	A 5
North Bay, 50,623	(87,083★)	C 6
North York, 556,297		D 5
Oakville, 87,107		D 5
Orillia, 24,077 (31,252★)		C 5
Oshawa, 123,651	(203,543★)	D 5
Ottawa, 300,763	(819,263★)	B 9
Owen Sound, 19,804		C 4
Peterborough, 61,049	(87,083★)	C 6
Pickering, 48,959		D 5
Port Colborne, 18,281		E 5
Port Hope, 11,505		
Richmond Hill, 46,766		D 5
Saint Catharines, 123,455	(343,258★)	D 5
Sarnia, 49,033	(85,700★)	E 2
Sault Sainte Marie, 80,905	(84,617★)	p18
Scarborough, 484,676		m15
Stoney Creek, 43,554		D 5
Stratford, 26,451		D 3
Sudbury, 88,717	(148,877★)	A 4
Thunder Bay, 112,272	(122,217★)	o17
Timmins, 46,657		o19
Toronto, 612,289	(3,427,168★)	D 5
Vaughan, 65,058		D 5
Waterloo, 58,718		E 5
Welland, 45,054		E 5
Whitby, 45,819		D 6
Windsor, 193,111	(253,988★)	E 1
Woodstock, 26,386		D 5
York, 135,401	(122,217★)	D 5

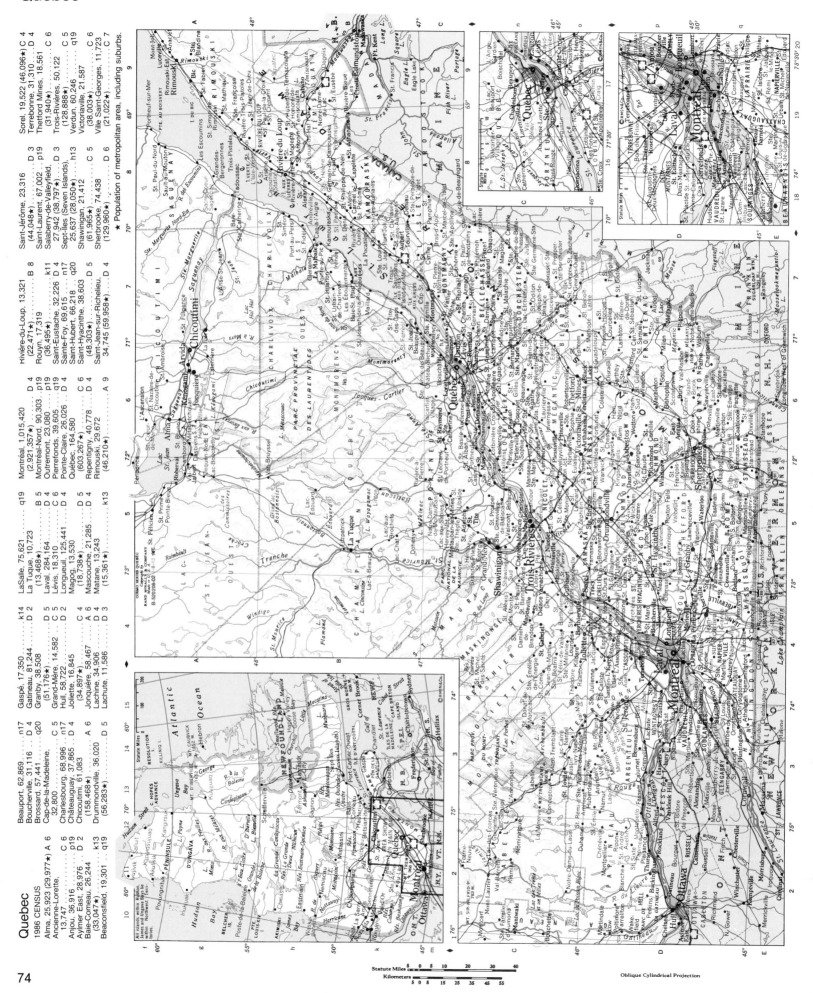

Saskatchewan

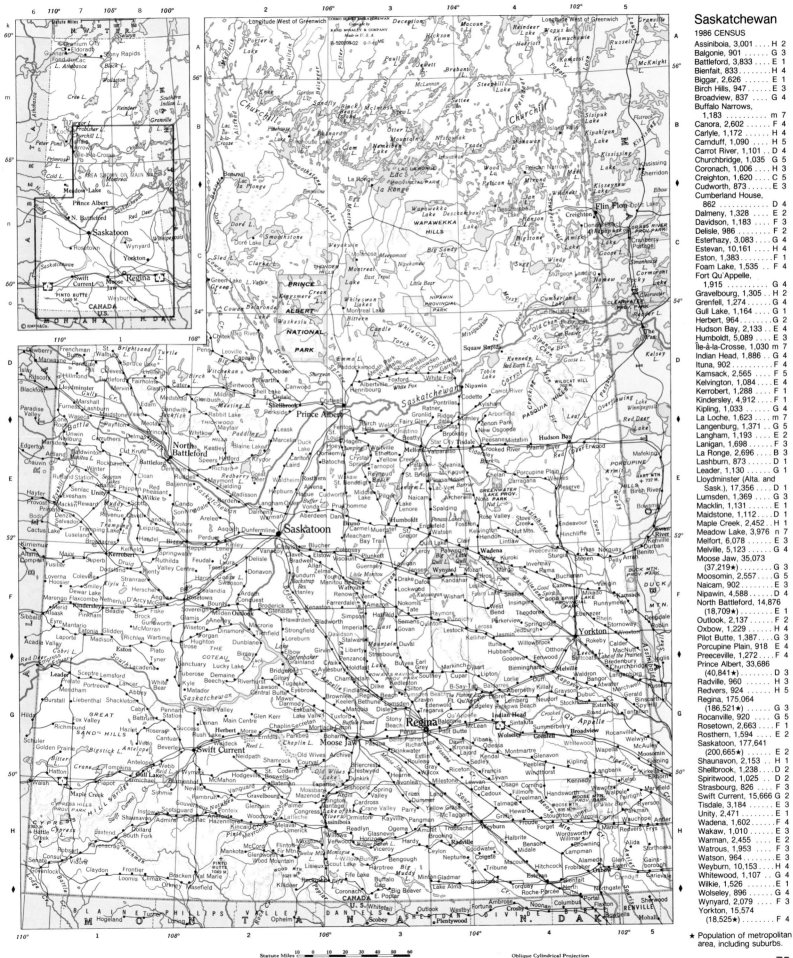

Saskatchewan

1986 CENSUS

Assiniboia, 3,001 . . . . H 2
Balgonie, 901 . . . . . . G 3
Battleford, 3,833 . . . . . E 1
Bienfait, 833 . . . . . . H 4
Biggar, 2,626 . . . . . . E 1
Birch Hills, 947 . . . . . E 3
Broadview, 837 . . . . . G 4
Buffalo Narrows,
 1,183 . . . . m 7
Canora, 2,602 . . . . . F 4
Carlyle, 1,172 . . . . . H 4
Carnduff, 1,090 . . . . . H 5
Carrot River, 1,101 . . D 4
Churchbridge, 1,035 . G 5
Coronach, 1,006 . . . . H 3
Creighton, 1,620 . . . . C 5
Cudworth, 873 . . . . . . E 3
Cumberland House,
 862 . . . . D 4
Dalmeny, 1,328 . . . . . E 2
Davidson, 1,183 . . . . F 3
Delisle, 986 . . . . F 2
Esterhazy, 3,083 . . . . G 4
Estevan, 10,161 . . . . H 4
Eston, 1,383 . . . . . . F 1
Foam Lake, 1,535 . . . F 4
Fort Qu'Appelle,
 1,915 . . . . G 4
Gravelbourg, 1,305 . . H 2
Grenfell, 1,274 . . . . . G 4
Gull Lake, 1,164 . . . . G 1
Herbert, 964 . . . . G 2
Hudson Bay, 2,133 . . E 4
Humboldt, 5,089 . . . . E 3
Île-à-la-Crosse, 1,030 m 7
Indian Head, 1,886 . . G 4
Ituna, 902 . . . . F 4
Kamsack, 2,565 . . . . F 5
Kelvington, 1,084 . . . E 4
Kerrobert, 1,288 . . . . F 1
Kindersley, 4,912 . . . F 1
Kipling, 1,033 . . . . . . G 4
La Loche, 1,623 . . . . m 7
Langenburg, 1,371 . . G 5
Langham, 1,193 . . . . E 2
Lanigan, 1,698 . . . . . F 3
La Ronge, 2,696 . . . . B 3
Lashburn, 873 . . . . . D 1
Leader, 1,130 . . . . . . G 1
Lloydminster (Alta. and
 Sask.), 17,356 . . . . D 1
Lumsden, 1,369 . . . . G 3
Macklin, 1,131 . . . . . E 1
Maidstone, 1,112 . . . D 1
Maple Creek, 2,452 . . H 1
Meadow Lake, 3,976 . n 7
Melfort, 6,078 . . . . . . E 3
Melville, 5,123 . . . . . G 4
Moose Jaw, 35,073
 (37,219★) . . . . G 3
Moosomin, 2,557 . . . G 5
Naicam, 902 . . . . . . E 3
Nipawin, 4,588 . . . . . D 4
North Battleford, 14,876
 (18,709★) . . . . E 2
Outlook, 2,137 . . . . . F 2
Oxbow, 1,229 . . . . . . H 4
Pilot Butte, 1,387 . . . G 3
Porcupine Plain, 918 . E 4
Preeceville, 1,272 . . . F 4
Prince Albert, 33,686
 (40,841★) . . . . D 3
Radville, 960 . . . . . . H 3
Redvers, 924 . . . . . . H 5
Regina, 175,064
 (186,521★) . . . . . . G 3
Rocanville, 920 . . . . G 5
Rosetown, 2,663 . . . . F 1
Rosthern, 1,594 . . . . E 2
Saskatoon, 177,641
 (200,665★) . . . . . . E 2
Shaunavon, 2,153 . . . H 1
Shellbrook, 1,238 . . . D 2
Spiritwood, 1,025 . . . D 2
Strasbourg, 826 . . . . F 3
Swift Current, 15,666 G 2
Tisdale, 3,184 . . . . . E 4
Unity, 2,471 . . . . E 1
Wadena, 1,602 . . . . . F 4
Wakaw, 1,010 . . . . . E 3
Warman, 2,455 . . . . . E 2
Watrous, 1,953 . . . . . F 3
Watson, 964 . . . . E 3
Weyburn, 10,153 . . . . H 4
Whitewood, 1,107 . . . G 4
Wilkie, 1,526 . . . . . . E 1
Wolseley, 896 . . . . . G 4
Wynyard, 2,079 . . . . F 3
Yorkton, 15,574
 (18,525★) . . . . F 4

★ Population of metropolitan
 area, including suburbs.

75

United States of America

Akron, 223,019 ('90)...C10
ALABAMA..................E 9
ALASKA......................M19
Albany, 101,082 ('90)..C12
Albuquerque, 384,736
  ('90).....................D 5
Amarillo, 157,615 ('90)D 6
Anchorage, 226,338
  ('90).....................M20
Annapolis, 33,187
  ('90).....................D11
ARIZONA...................E 4
ARKANSAS................E 8
Atlanta, 394,017 ('90)..E10
Augusta, 21,325 ('90)..C13
Austin, 465,622 ('90)...E 7
Baltimore, 736,014
  ('90).....................D11
Baton Rouge, 219,531
  ('90).....................E 8
Billings, 81,151 ('90)...B 5
Birmingham, 265,968
  ('90).....................E 9
Bismarck, 49,256 ('90)B 6
Boise, 125,738 ('90)....C 3
Boston, 574,283 ('90). C12
Buffalo, 328,123 ('90). C11
CALIFORNIA...............D 2
Carson City, 40,443
  ('90).....................D 3
Charleston, 57,287
  ('90).....................D10
Charleston, 80,414
  ('90).....................E11
Charlotte, 395,934
  ('90).....................D10
Chattanooga, 152,466
  ('90).....................D 9
Cheyenne, 50,008
  ('90).....................C 6
Chicago, 2,783,726
  ('90).....................C 9
Cincinnati, 364,040
  ('90).....................D10
Cleveland, 505,616
  ('90).....................C10
COLORADO.................D 5
Colorado Springs, 281,140
  ('90).....................D 6
Columbia, 98,052 ('90)E10
Columbus, 178,681
  ('90).....................E10
Columbus, 632,910
  ('90).....................D10
Concord, 36,006 ('90).C12
CONNECTICUT............C12
Dallas, 1,006,877 ('90) E 7
DELAWARE...............D11
Denver, 467,610 ('90). D 6
Des Moines, 193,187
  ('90).....................C 8
Detroit, 1,027,974
  ('90).....................C10
Dover, 27,630 ('90)....D11
El Paso, 515,342 ('90).E 5
FLORIDA...................F10
Fort Wayne, 173,072
  ('90).....................C 9
Fort Worth, 447,619
  ('90).....................E 7
Frankfort, 25,968 ('90)D10
Fresno, 354,202 ('90)..D 3
GEORGIA...................E10
Grand Rapids, 189,126
  ('90).....................C 9
Harrisburg, 52,376
  ('90).....................C11
Hartford, 139,739
  ('90).....................C12
Helena, 24,569 ('90)...B 4
Houston, 1,630,553
  ('90).....................F 7
IDAHO......................C 4
ILLINOIS....................C 9
INDIANA....................C 9
Indianapolis, 731,327
  ('90).....................D 9
IOWA........................C 8
Jackson, 196,637 ('90)E 8
Jacksonville, 635,230
  ('90).....................E10
Jefferson City, 35,481
  ('90).....................D 8
Juneau, 26,751 ('90)...N21
KANSAS.....................D 7
Kansas City, 435,146
  ('90).....................D 8
KENTUCKY.................D 9
Knoxville, 165,121
  ('90).....................D10
Las Vegas, 258,295
  ('90).....................D 3
Lincoln, 191,972 ('90).C 7
Little Rock, 175,795
  ('90).....................E 8
Los Angeles, 3,485,398
  ('90).....................E 3
LOUISIANA.................E 8
Louisville, 269,063
  ('90).....................D 9
Madison, 191,262
  ('90).....................C 9
MAINE......................B13
MARYLAND................D11

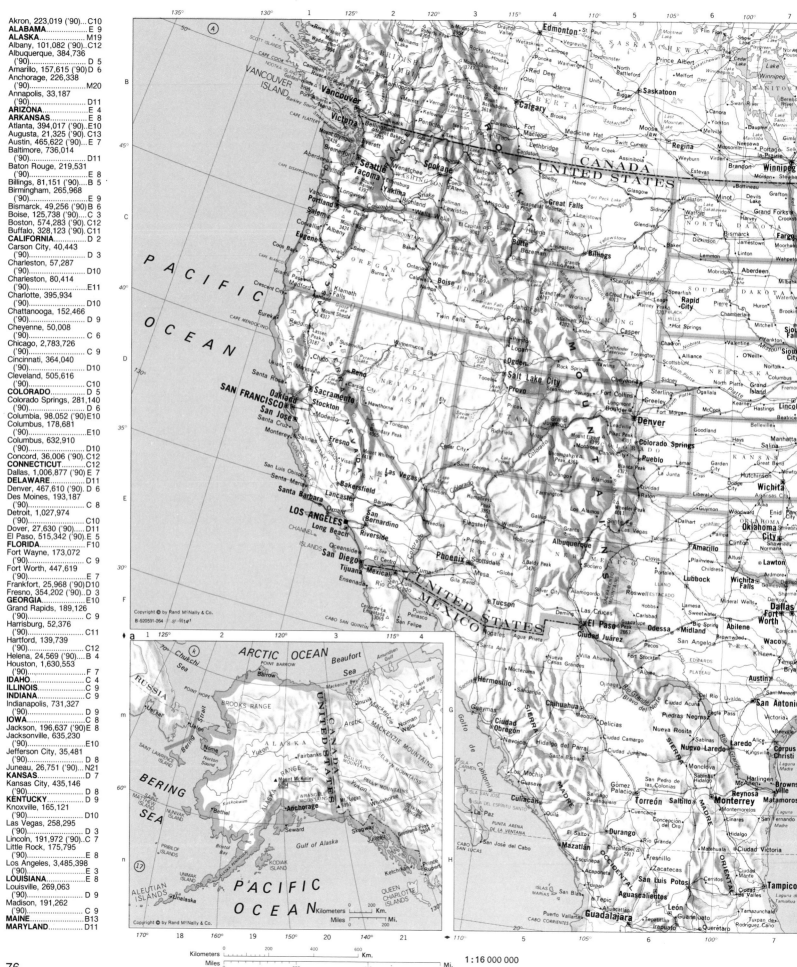

1:16 000 000

MASSACHUSETTS.....C12
Memphis, 610,337
 ('90).................... D 8
Miami, 358,548 ('90)...F10
MICHIGAN.................C10
Milwaukee, 628,088
 ('90).................... C 9
Minneapolis, 368,383
 ('90).................... C 8
MINNESOTA.............B 8
MISSISSIPPI.............E 9
MISSOURI..................D 8
Mobile, 196,278 ('90)...E 9
MONTANA..................B 5
Montgomery, 187,106
 ('90).................... E 9
Montpelier, 8,247 ('90)C12
Nashville, 487,969
 ('90).................... D 9
NEBRASKA................C 7
NEVADA....................D 3
Newark, 275,221 ('90)C12
NEW HAMPSHIRE....C12
NEW JERSEY...........C12
NEW MEXICO...........E 5
New Orleans, 496,938
 ('90).................... F 8
NEW YORK...............C11
New York, 7,322,564
 ('90).................... C12
Norfolk, 261,229 ('90).D11
NORTH CAROLINA....D11
NORTH DAKOTA.......B 6
Oakland, 372,242 ('90)D 2
OHIO.........................C10
OKLAHOMA...............D 7
Oklahoma City, 444,719
 ('90).................... D 7
Olympia, 33,840 ('90)..B 2
Omaha, 335,795 ('90).C 7
OREGON....................C 2
PENNSYLVANIA.......C11
Philadelphia, 1,585,577
 ('90).................... D11
Phoenix, 900,013 ('90) E 4
Pierre, 12,906 ('90)......C 6
Pittsburgh, 369,879
 ('90).................... C11
Portland, 64,358 ('90). C12
Providence, 160,728
 ('90).................... C12
Raleigh, 207,951 ('90).D11
Rapid City, 54,523
 ('90).................... C 6
Reno, 133,850 ('90)...D 3
RHODE ISLAND.......C12
Richmond, 203,056
 ('90).................... D11
Rochester, 231,636
 ('90).................... C11
Sacramento, 369,365
 ('90).................... D 2
Saint Louis, 396,685
 ('90).................... D 8
Saint Paul, 272,235
 ('90).................... C 8
Saint Petersburg, 238,629
 ('90).................... F10
Salem, 107,786 ('90).. C 2
Salt Lake City, 159,936
 ('90).................... C 4
San Antonio, 935,933
 ('90).................... F 7
San Diego, 1,110,549
 ('90).................... E 3
San Francisco, 723,959
 ('90).................... D 2
San Jose, 782,248
 ('90).................... D 2
Santa Fe, 55,859 ('90) D 5
Savannah, 137,560
 ('90).................... E10
Seattle, 516,259 ('90)..B 2
Shreveport, 198,525
 ('90).................... E 8
SOUTH CAROLINA....E10
SOUTH DAKOTA.......C 7
Spokane, 177,196
 ('90).................... B 3
Springfield, 105,227
 ('90).................... D 9
Syracuse, 163,860
 ('90).................... C11
Tacoma, 176,664 ('90)B 2
Tallahassee, 124,773
 ('90).................... E10
Tampa, 280,015 ('90). F10
TENNESSEE..............D 9
TEXAS......................E 7
Toledo, 332,943 ('90)..C10
Topeka, 119,883 ('90). D 7
Trenton, 88,675 ('90).. C12
Tulsa, 367,302 ('90)...D 7
UNITED STATES........D 7
UTAH........................D 4
VERMONT.................C12
VIRGINIA..................D11
WASHINGTON...........B 2
Washington, 606,900
 ('90).................... D11
WEST VIRGINIA........D10
Wichita, 304,011 ('90).D 7
WISCONSIN...............C 9
WYOMING..................C 5

Alabama

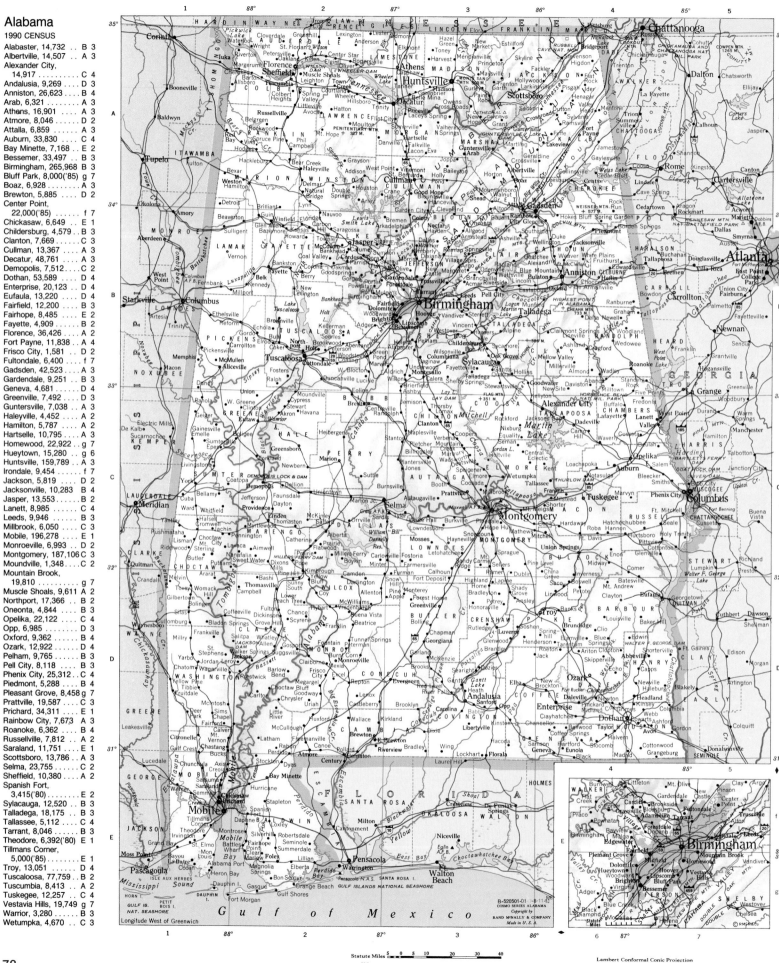

Alabama
1990 CENSUS

Alabaster, 14,732 . . . B 3
Albertville, 14,507 . . . A 3
Alexander City,
  14,917 . . . . C 4
Andalusia, 9,269 . . . D 3
Anniston, 26,623 . . . B 4
Arab, 6,321 . . . . . . A 3
Athens, 16,901 . . . . A 3
Atmore, 8,046 . . . . . D 2
Attalla, 6,859 . . . . . A 3
Auburn, 33,830 . . . . C 4
Bay Minette, 7,168 . E 2
Bessemer, 33,497 . . B 3
Birmingham, 265,968 . B 3
Bluff Park, 8,000('85) g 7
Boaz, 6,928 . . . . . . A 3
Brewton, 5,885 . . . . D 2
Center Point,
  22,000('85) . . . . f 7
Chickasaw, 6,649 . . E 1
Childersburg, 4,579 . B 3
Clanton, 7,669 . . . . C 3
Cullman, 13,367 . . . A 3
Decatur, 48,761 . . . A 3
Demopolis, 7,512 . . . C 2
Dothan, 53,589 . . . . D 4
Enterprise, 20,123 . . D 4
Eufaula, 13,220 . . . D 4
Fairfield, 12,200 . . . B 3
Fairhope, 8,485 . . . E 2
Fayette, 4,909 . . . . B 2
Florence, 36,426 . . . A 2
Fort Payne, 11,838 . . A 4
Frisco City, 1,581 . . D 2
Fultondale, 6,400 . . f 7
Gadsden, 42,523 . . . A 3
Gardendale, 9,251 . . B 3
Geneva, 4,681 . . . . D 4
Greenville, 7,492 . . . D 3
Guntersville, 7,038 . . A 3
Haleyville, 4,452 . . . A 2
Hamilton, 5,787 . . . A 2
Hartselle, 10,795 . . . A 3
Homewood, 22,922 . . g 7
Hueytown, 15,280 . . g 6
Huntsville, 159,789 . . A 3
Irondale, 9,454 . . . . f 7
Jackson, 5,819 . . . . D 2
Jacksonville, 10,283 . B 4
Jasper, 13,553 . . . . B 2
Lanett, 8,985 . . . . . C 4
Leeds, 9,946 . . . . . B 3
Millbrook, 6,050 . . . C 3
Mobile, 196,278 . . . E 1
Monroeville, 6,993 . . D 2
Montgomery, 187,106 C 3
Moundville, 1,348 . . . C 2
Mountain Brook,
  19,810 . . . . g 7
Muscle Shoals, 9,611 A 2
Northport, 17,366 . . B 2
Oneonta, 4,844 . . . . B 3
Opelika, 22,122 . . . . C 4
Opp, 6,985 . . . . . . D 3
Oxford, 9,362 . . . . . B 4
Ozark, 12,922 . . . . D 4
Pelham, 9,765 . . . . B 3
Pell City, 8,118 . . . B 3
Phenix City, 25,312 . C 4
Piedmont, 5,288 . . . B 4
Pleasant Grove, 8,458 g 7
Prattville, 19,587 . . . C 3
Prichard, 34,311 . . . E 1
Rainbow City, 7,673 . A 3
Roanoke, 6,362 . . . . B 4
Russellville, 7,812 . . A 2
Saraland, 11,751 . . . E 1
Scottsboro, 13,786 . . A 3
Selma, 23,755 . . . . C 2
Sheffield, 10,380 . . . A 2
Spanish Fort,
  3,415('80) . . . . . . E 2
Sylacauga, 12,520 . . B 3
Talladega, 18,175 . . B 3
Tallassee, 5,112 . . . C 4
Tarrant, 8,046 . . . . B 3
Theodore, 6,392('80) E 1
Tillmans Corner,
  5,000('85) . . . . . . E 1
Troy, 13,051 . . . . . D 4
Tuscaloosa, 77,759 . B 2
Tuscumbia, 8,413 . . A 2
Tuskegee, 12,257 . . C 4
Vestavia Hills, 19,749 g 7
Warrior, 3,280 . . . . B 3
Wetumpka, 4,670 . . C 3

78

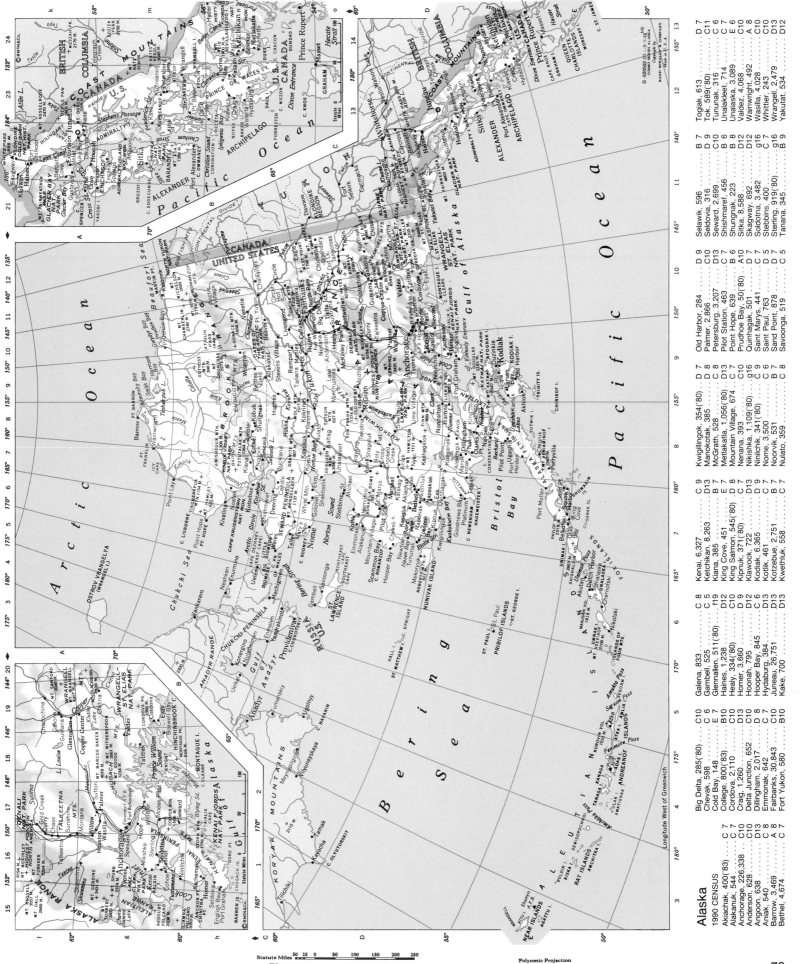

Statute Miles 50 25 0 50 100 150 200 250
Kilometers 50 0 100 200 300

Polyconic Projection

Alaska

1990 CENSUS

Akiachak, 400('83)	C 7	
Alakanuk, 544	C 7	
Anchorage, 226,338	C10	
Anderson, 628	C10	
Angoon, 638	D13	
Aniak, 540	C 8	
Barrow, 3,469	A 8	
Bethel, 4,674	C 7	
Big Delta, 285('80)	C10	
Chevak, 598	C 8	
Cold Bay, 148	E 7	
College, 800('83)	B10	
Cordova, 2,110	C10	
Craig, 1,260	D13	
Delta Junction, 652	C10	
Dillingham, 2,017	D 8	
Emmonak, 642	C 7	
Fairbanks, 30,843	C10	
Fort Yukon, 580	B10	
Galena, 833	C 8	
Gambell, 525	C 5	
Glennallen, 511('80)	C10	
Haines, 1,238	C12	
Healy, 334('80)	C10	
Homer, 3,660	D 9	
Hoonah, 795	D12	
Hooper Bay, 845	C 7	
Hydaburg, 384	D13	
Juneau, 26,751	C12	
Kake, 700	D13	
Kenai, 6,327	C 9	
Ketchikan, 8,263	D13	
Kiana, 385	B 7	
King Cove, 451	E 7	
King Salmon, 545('80)	D 8	
Kipnuk, 371('80)	C 7	
Klawock, 722	D13	
Kodiak, 6,365	D 9	
Kotlik, 461	C 7	
Kotzebue, 2,751	B 7	
Kwethluk, 558	C 8	
Kwigillingok, 354('80)	C 9	
Manokotak, 385	D13	
McGrath, 528	B 7	
Metlakatla, 1,056('80)	D13	
Mountain Village, 674	B 6	
Nenana, 393	C10	
Nikiski, 1,109('80)	g16	
Ninilchik, 341('80)	g16	
Nome, 3,500	C 6	
Noorvik, 531	B 7	
Nulato, 359	C 7	
Old Harbor, 284	D 7	
Palmer, 2,866	C10	
Petersburg, 3,207	D13	
Pilot Station, 463	C 8	
Point Hope, 639	B 6	
Prudhoe Bay, 50('80)	A10	
Quinhagak, 501	C 7	
Saint Marys, 441	C 9	
Saint Paul, 763	C 6	
Sand Point, 878	D 7	
Savoonga, 519	C 5	
Selawik, 596	B 7	
Seldovia, 316	D 9	
Seward, 2,699	C10	
Shishmaref, 456	B 6	
Shungnak, 223	B 8	
Sitka, 8,588	D12	
Skagway, 692	C12	
Soldotna, 3,482	g16	
Stebbins, 400	C 7	
Sterling, 919('80)	g16	
Tanana, 345	C 7	
Togiak, 613	B 7	
Tok, 589('80)	D 9	
Tununak, 316	C10	
Unalakleet, 714	C 7	
Unalaska, 3,089	E 6	
Valdez, 4,068	C10	
Wainwright, 492	A 8	
Wasilla, 4,028	C10	
Whittier, 243	C 7	
Wrangell, 2,479	D13	
Yakutat, 534	D12	

Arizona

Arizona

1990 CENSUS

Ajo, 5,189('80) . . . . . . E 3
Apache Junction,
 18,100 . . . . m 9
Avondale, 16,169 . . . . D 3
Bagdad, 2,331('80) . . . C 2
Benson, 3,824 . . . . . . F 5
Bisbee, 6,288 . . . . . . F 6
Black Canyon City,
 850('86) . . . . C 3
Buckeye, 5,038 . . . . . D 3
Bullhead City, 21,951 B 1
Camp Verde, 6,243 . . C 4
Casa Grande, 19,082 E 4
Casas Adobes,
 12,155('86) . . . . . E 5
Cashion, 3,014('80) . . m 8
Cave Creek, 2,925 . . . D 4
Chandler, 90,533 . . . . D 4
Chinle, 2,815('80) . . . . A 6
Chino Valley, 4,837 . . C 3
Claypool, 2,362('80) . . D 5
Clifton, 2,840 . . . . . . D 6
Coolidge, 6,927 . . . . . E 4
Cottonwood, 5,918 . . C 3
Crane, 2,650('86) . . . . E 1
Douglas, 12,822 . . . . . F 6
Eagar, 4,025 . . . . C 6
El Mirage, 5,001 . . . . k 8
Eloy, 7,211 . . . . E 4
Flagstaff, 45,857 . . . . B 4
Florence, 7,510 . . . . . D 4
Fort Defiance,
 3,431('80) . . . . . . B 6
Ganado, 3,400('86) . . B 6
Gila Bend, 1,747 . . . . E 3
Gilbert, 29,188 . . . . . D 4
Glendale, 148,134 . . . D 3
Globe, 6,062 . . . . D 5
Goodyear, 6,258 . . . . D 3
Grand Canyon,
 1,348('80) . . . . . . A 3
Green Valley,
 7,999('80) . . . . . . F 5
Guadalupe, 5,458 . . . m 9
Holbrook, 4,686 . . . . C 5
Huachuca City, 1,782 F 5
Kayenta, 3,343('80) . . A 5
Kearny, 2,262 . . . . . . D 5
Kingman, 12,722 . . . . B 1
Lake Havasu City,
 24,363 . . . . C 1
Lakeside-Pinetop,
 2,422 . . . . C 6
Litchfield Park, 3,303 m 8
Mammoth, 1,845 . . . . E 5
Mesa, 288,091 . . . . . D 4
Miami, 2,018 . . . . . . D 5
Nogales, 19,489 . . . . F 5
Oracle, 2,484('80) . . . E 5
Page, 6,598 . . . . A 4
Paradise Valley,
 11,671 . . . . k 9
Parker, 2,897 . . . . . . C 1
Payson, 8,377 . . . . . . C 4
Peoria, 50,618 . . . . . D 3
Phoenix, 900,013 . . . . D 3
Prescott, 26,455 . . . . C 3
Sacaton, 1,951('80) . . D 4
Safford, 7,359 . . . . . . E 6
Saint Johns, 3,294 . . C 6
San Carlos,
 2,668('80) . . . . . . D 5
San Luis, 70('86) . . . . E 3
San Manuel,
 5,443('80) . . . . . . E 5
Scottsdale, 130,069 . . D 4
Sedona, 7,720 . . . . . . C 4
Sells, 1,864('80) . . . . F 4
Show Low, 5,019 . . . . C 5
Sierra Vista, 32,983 . . F 5
Snowflake, 3,679 . . . . C 5
Somerton, 5,282 . . . . E 1
South Tucson, 5,093 . E 5
Sun City, 57,000 . . . . k 8
Superior, 3,468 . . . . . D 4
Surprise, 7,122 . . . . . k 8
Taylor, 2,418 . . . . . . C 5
Tempe, 141,865 . . . . D 4
Thatcher, 3,763 . . . . . E 6
Tolleson, 4,434 . . . . . m 8
Tombstone, 1,220 . . . F 5
Tuba City, 5,045('80) A 4
Tucson, 405,390 . . . . E 5
Twin Knolls,
 5,210('86) . . . . . . m 9
Wickenburg, 4,515 . . D 3
Willcox, 3,122 . . . . . . E 6
Williams, 2,532 . . . . . C 4
Window Rock,
 2,230('80) . . . . . . B 6
Winslow, 8,190 . . . . . C 5
Youngtown, 2,542 . . . k 8
Yuma, 54,923 . . . . . . E 1

80

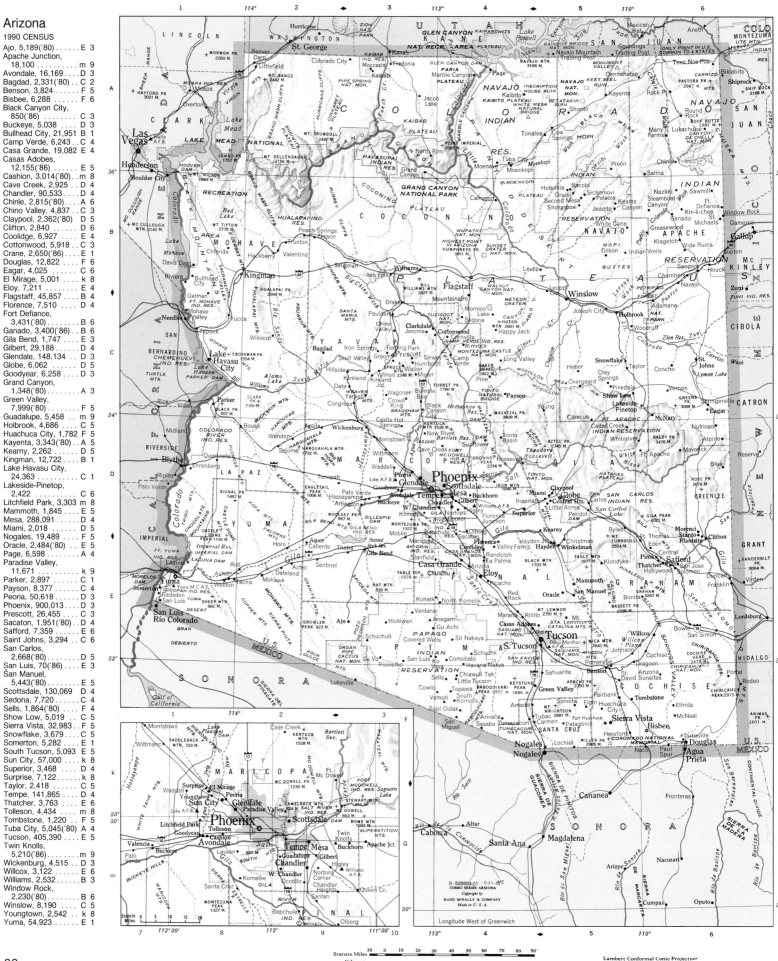

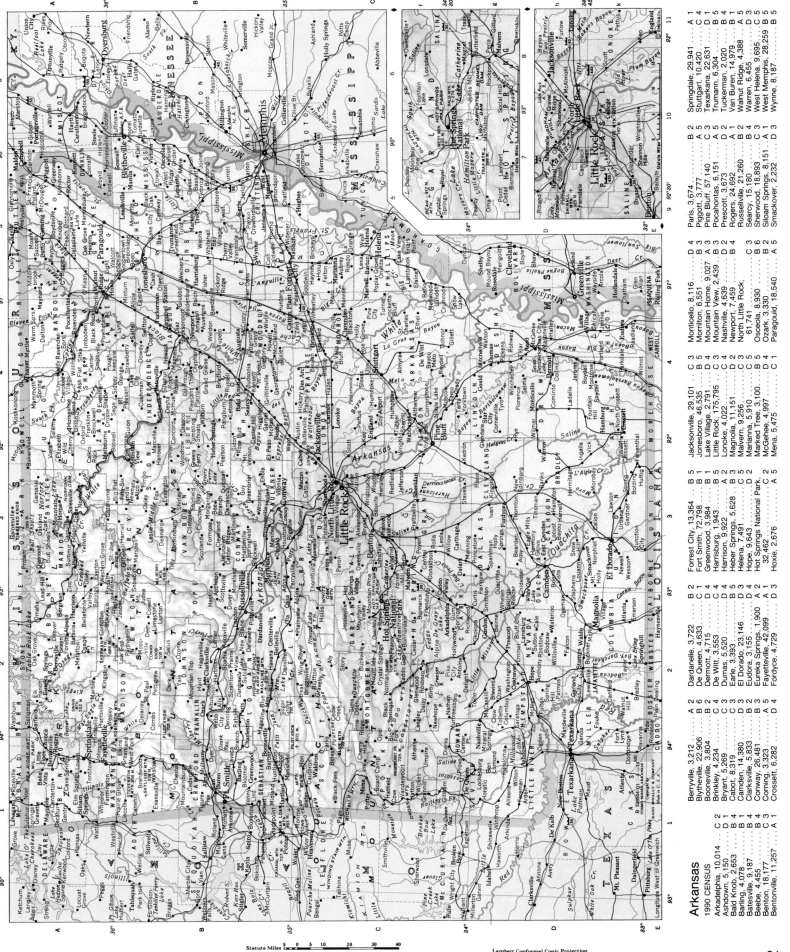

Lambert Conformal Conic Projection

Statute Miles
Kilometers

Arkansas

1990 CENSUS

City	Pop.	Grid
Arkadelphia	10,014	C 2
Ashdown	5,150	D 1
Bald Knob	2,653	B 4
Barling	4,078	B 1
Batesville	9,187	B 4
Beebe	4,455	B 4
Benton	18,177	C 3
Bentonville	11,257	A 1
Berryville	3,212	A 2
Blytheville	22,906	B 6
Booneville	3,804	B 2
Brinkley	4,234	C 4
Bryant	5,269	C 3
Cabot	8,319	B 4
Camden	14,380	D 3
Clarksville	5,833	B 2
Conway	26,481	B 3
Corning	3,323	A 5
Crossett	6,282	D 4
Dardanelle	3,722	B 2
De Queen	4,633	C 1
Dermott	4,715	D 4
De Witt	3,553	C 4
Dumas	5,520	D 4
Earle	3,393	B 5
El Dorado	23,146	D 3
Eudora	3,155	D 4
Eureka Springs	1,900	A 2
Fayetteville	42,099	A 1
Fordyce	4,729	D 3
Forrest City	13,364	B 5
Fort Smith	72,798	B 1
Greenwood	3,984	B 1
Harrisburg	1,943	B 5
Harrison	9,922	A 2
Heber Springs	5,628	B 3
Helena	7,491	C 5
Hope	9,643	D 2
Hot Springs National Park	32,462	C 2
Hoxie	2,676	A 5
Jacksonville	29,101	C 3
Jonesboro	46,535	B 5
Lake Village	2,791	D 4
Little Rock	175,795	C 3
Lonoke	4,022	C 4
Magnolia	11,151	D 2
Malvern	9,256	C 3
Marianna	5,910	C 5
Marked Tree	3,100	B 5
McGehee	4,997	D 4
Mena	5,475	C 1
Monticello	6,551	D 4
Morrilton	6,551	B 3
Mountain Home	9,027	A 3
Mountain View	2,439	B 3
Nashville	4,639	D 2
Newport	7,459	B 4
North Little Rock	61,741	C 3
Osceola	8,930	B 6
Ozark	3,330	B 2
Paragould	18,540	A 5
Paris	3,674	B 3
Piggott	3,777	A 5
Pine Bluff	57,140	C 3
Pocahontas	6,151	A 5
Prescott	3,673	D 2
Rogers	24,692	A 1
Russellville	21,260	B 2
Searcy	15,180	B 4
Sherwood	18,893	C 3
Siloam Springs	8,151	A 1
Smackover	2,232	D 3
Springdale	29,941	A 1
Stuttgart	10,420	C 4
Texarkana	22,631	D 1
Trumann	6,304	B 5
Tuckerman	2,020	B 5
Van Buren	14,979	B 1
Walnut Ridge	4,388	A 5
Warren	6,455	D 3
West Helena	9,695	C 5
West Memphis	28,259	B 5
Wynne	8,187	B 5

© RMcN&Co.

California

California
1990 CENSUS

Alameda, 76,459 .... h 8
Alhambra, 82,106 .... m12
Anaheim, 266,406 .... F 5
Antioch, 62,195 .... h 9
Bakersfield, 174,820 E 4
Berkeley, 102,724 .. D 2
Beverly Hills, 31,971 m12
Burbank, 93,643 .... E 4
Calexico, 18,633 .... F 6
Chico, 40,079 .... C 3
Chula Vista, 135,163 .. F 5
Compton, 90,454 .... n12
Concord, 111,348 .. h 8
Costa Mesa, 96,357 .n13
Daly City, 92,311 .. h 8
Davis, 46,209 .... C 3
Downey, 91,444 .... n12
East Los Angeles,
 126,379 .... m12
El Cajon, 88,693 .... F 5
El Centro, 31,384 .... F 6
Escondido, 108,635 .. F 5
Eureka, 27,025 .... B 1
Fairfield, 77,211 .. C 2
Fremont, 173,339 .. D 2
Fresno, 354,202 .... D 4
Fullerton, 114,144 ..n13
Garden Grove,
 143,050 ....n13
Glendale, 180,038 .. m12
Hayward, 111,498 .. h 8
Huntington Beach,
 181,519 .... F 4
Indio, 36,793 .... F 5
Inglewood, 109,602 ..n12
Irvine, 110,330 .....n13
Lancaster, 97,291 .. E 4
Lompoc, 37,649 .... E 3
Long Beach, 429,433 F 4
Los Angeles,
 3,485,398 .... E 4
Marysville, 12,324 .. C 3
Menlo Park, 28,040 .. k 8
Merced, 56,216 .... D 3
Modesto, 164,730 .. D 3
Monterey, 31,954 .. D 3
Napa, 61,842 .... C 2
Newport Beach,
 66,643 ....n13
Norwalk, 94,279 ....n12
Oakland, 372,242 .. D 2
Oceanside, 128,398 . F 5
Ontario, 133,179 .. E 5
Orange, 110,658 ....n13
Oxnard, 142,216 .... E 4
Palm Springs, 40,181 F 5
Palo Alto, 55,900 .. D 2
Pasadena, 131,591 .. E 4
Pomona, 131,723 .. E 5
Redding, 66,462 .. B 2
Redwood City,
 66,072 ....D 2
Richmond, 87,425 .. D 2
Riverside, 226,505 .. F 5
Sacramento, 369,365 C 3
Salinas, 108,777 .. D 3
San Bernardino,
 164,164 ....E 5
San Clemente, 41,100 F 5
San Diego, 1,110,549 F 5
San Francisco,
 723,959 ....D 2
San Jose, 782,248 .. D 3
San Juan Capistrano,
 26,183 ....F 5
San Luis Obispo,
 41,958 ....E 3
San Mateo, 85,486 .. D 2
Santa Ana, 293,742 . F 5
Santa Barbara,
 85,571 ....E 4
Santa Clara, 93,613 .. D 2
Santa Cruz, 49,040 .. D 2
Santa Maria, 61,284 E 3
Santa Monica, 86,905 m12
Santa Rosa, 113,313 . C 2
Simi Valley, 100,217 . E 4
South Gate, 86,284 ..n12
South Lake Tahoe,
 21,586 ....C 4
Stockton, 210,943 .. D 3
Sunnyvale, 117,229 .. k 8
Torrance, 133,107 ..n12
Tulare, 33,249 .... D 4
Turlock, 42,198 .. D 3
Vallejo, 109,199 .... C 2
Ventura (San
 Buenaventura),
 92,575 ....E 4
Visalia, 75,636 .... D 4
West Covina, 96,086 m13
Westminster, 78,118 n12
Whittier, 77,671 .... F 4
Yuba City, 27,437 .. C 3

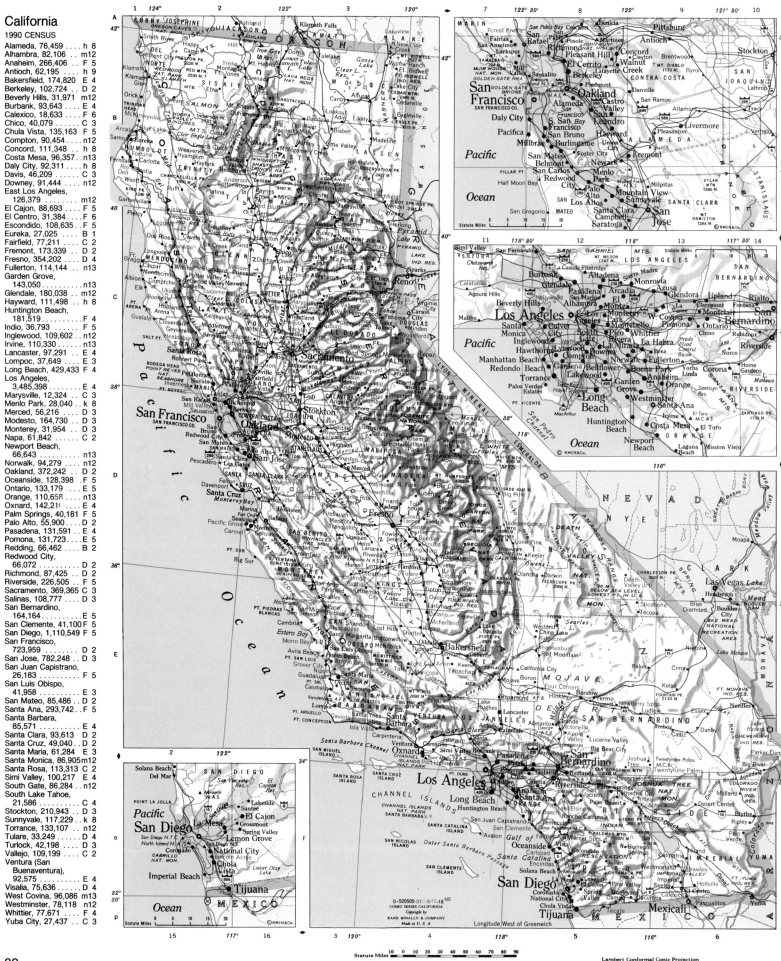

B-520505-01-9-42-16
COSMO SERIES CALIFORNIA
Copyright by
RAND McNALLY & COMPANY
Made in U.S.A.

Longitude West of Greenwich

Lambert Conformal Conic Projection

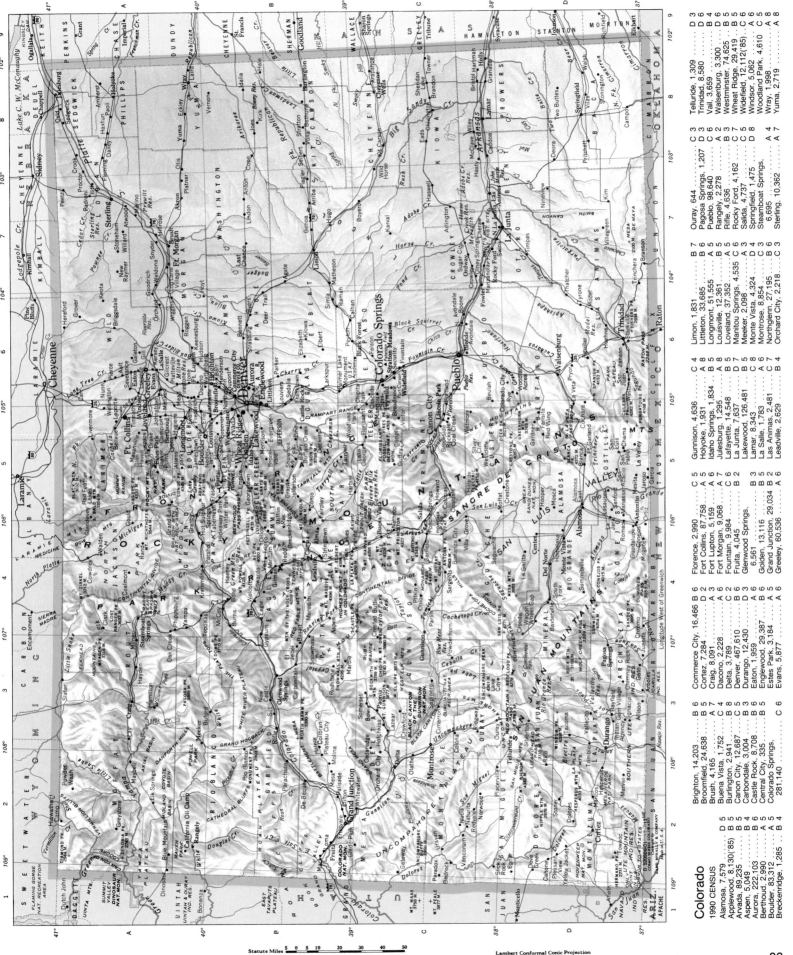

Colorado

1990 CENSUS

Alamosa, 7,579	D 5
Applewood, 8,130('85)	B 5
Arvada, 89,235	B 5
Aspen, 5,049	B 4
Aurora, 222,103	B 6
Berthoud, 2,990	A 5
Boulder, 83,312	A 5
Breckenridge, 1,285	B 4

Brighton, 14,203	B 6
Broomfield, 24,638	A 7
Brush, 4,165	C 4
Buena Vista, 1,752	B 8
Burlington, 2,941	C 2
Canon City, 12,687	B 6
Carbondale, 3,004	D 3
Castle Rock, 8,708	B 4
Central City, 335	A 6
Colorado Springs, 281,140	C 6

Commerce City, 16,466	B 6
Cortez, 8,091	D 2
Craig, 8,091	A 3
Dacono, 2,228	A 6
Delta, 3,789	C 2
Denver, 467,610	B 6
Durango, 12,430	D 3
Eaton, 1,959	A 6
Englewood, 29,387	B 6
Estes Park, 3,184	A 5
Evans, 5,877	A 6

Florence, 2,990	B 6
Fort Collins, 87,758	A 5
Fort Lupton, 5,159	A 6
Fort Morgan, 9,068	C 5
Fountain, 8,961	C 6
Fruita, 4,045	B 2
Glenwood Springs, 6,561	B 3
Golden, 13,116	B 5
Grand Junction, 29,034	B 2
Greeley, 60,536	A 6

Gunnison, 4,636	C 4
Holyoke, 1,931	A 8
Idaho Springs, 1,834	A 8
Julesburg, 1,295	B 5
Lafayette, 14,548	D 7
La Junta, 7,637	B 5
Lakewood, 126,481	D 4
Lamar, 8,343	A 6
La Salle, 1,783	B 5
Las Animas, 2,481	C 7
Leadville, 2,629	B 4

Limon, 1,831	C 4
Littleton, 33,685	A 8
Longmont, 51,555	A 5
Louisville, 12,361	B 5
Loveland, 37,352	C 6
Manitou Springs, 4,535	C 6
Meeker, 2,098	A 3
Monte Vista, 4,324	D 4
Montrose, 8,854	A 6
Northglenn, 27,195	B 6
Orchard City, 2,218	C 3

Ouray, 644	B 7
Pagosa Springs, 1,207	B 6
Pueblo, 98,640	A 5
Rangely, 2,278	A 2
Rifle, 4,636	B 3
Rocky Ford, 4,162	C 6
Salida, 4,737	A 3
Springfield, 1,475	C 6
Steamboat Springs, 6,695	B 6
Sterling, 10,362	C 3

Telluride, 1,309	D 3
Trinidad, 8,580	B 4
Vail, 3,659	D 6
Walsenburg, 3,300	B 5
Westminster, 74,625	B 5
Wheat Ridge, 29,419	C 7
Widefield, 12,112('85)	C 5
Windsor, 5,062	D 8
Woodland Park, 4,610	A 6
Wray, 1,998	C 5
Yuma, 2,719	A 8

Statute Miles 5 0 5 10 20 30 40 50

Kilometers 5 0 5 15 25 35 45 55 65 75

Lambert Conformal Conic Projection

83

Connecticut

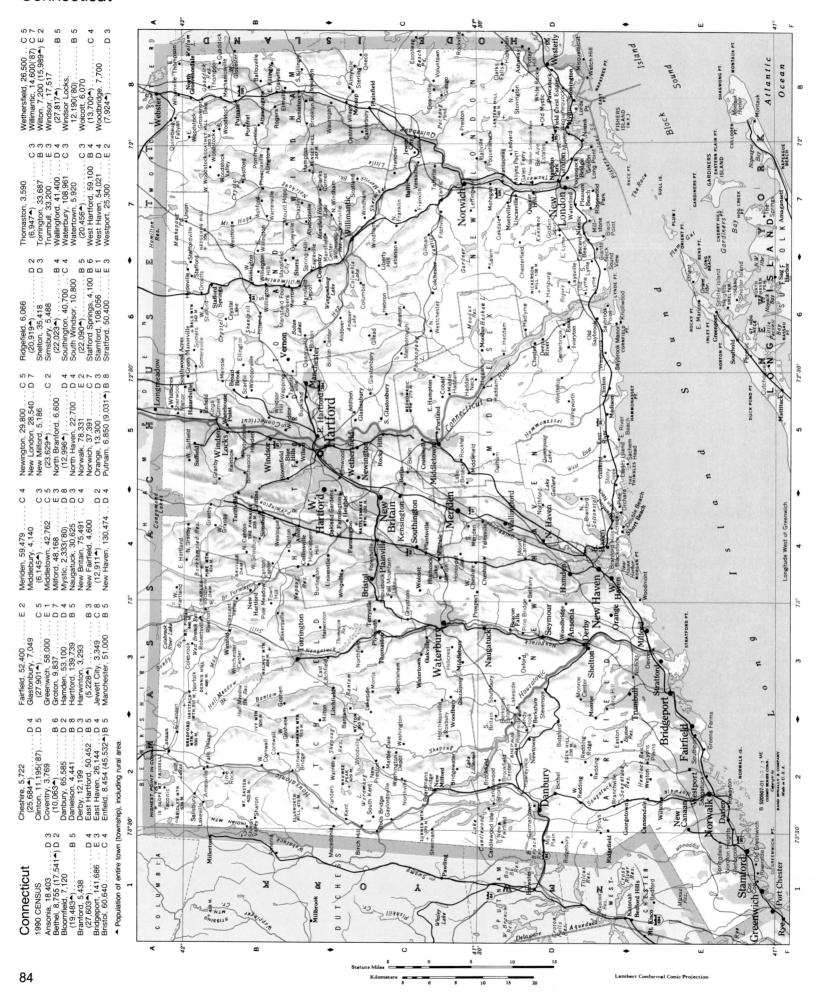

Connecticut
1990 CENSUS

Ansonia, 18,403 .... D 4
Bethel, 8,755 (17,541▲) D 2
Bloomfield, (19,483▲) ..... B 5
Branford, 7,120 .... B 5
Branford, 5,438 ....
(27,603▲) .... D 4
Bridgeport, 141,686 ..... E 3
Bristol, 60,640 .... C 4

Cheshire, 5,722 .... D 4
(25,684▲) ....
Clinton, 11,195('87) ..... D 5
Coventry, 3,769 .... D 2
(10,063▲) ....
Danbury, 65,585 .... D 2
Danielson, 4,441 .... B 8
Derby, 12,199 .... D 3
East Hartford, 50,452 ..... C 5
East Haven, 26,144 .... D 4
Enfield, 8,454 (45,532▲) B 5

Fairfield, 52,400 .... E 2
Glastonbury, 7,049 .... C 5
(27,901▲) ....
Greenwich, 58,000 .... E 1
Groton, 9,837 .... D 7
Hamden, 52,585 .... D 4
Hartford, 139,739 .... C 5
Harwinton, 3,293 .... C 4
Jewett City, 3,349 .... C 7
Manchester, 51,000 .... C 5

Meriden, 59,479 .... D 4
Middlebury, 4,140 ....
(6,145▲) .... D 3
Middletown, 42,762 .... C 5
(42,023▲) ....
Milford, 48,168 .... E 1
Mystic, 2,333('80) .... D 8
Naugatuck, 30,625 .... D 3
New Britain, 75,491 .... C 4
New Fairfield, 4,600 .... E 2
New Haven, 130,474 .... D 4

Newington, 29,800 .... C 5
New London, 28,540 .... D 7
New Milford, 5,186 .... C 2
North Branford, 6,600 .... D 4
North Haven, 22,700 .... D 4
Norwalk, 78,331 .... E 2
Norwich, 37,391 .... C 7
Orange, 13,300 .... D 4
Putnam, 6,850 (9,031▲) B 8

Ridgefield, 6,066 .... D 2
(20,919▲) ....
Shelton, 35,418 .... D 3
Simsbury, 5,488 .... B 4
(22,023▲) ....
Southington, 40,700 .... C 4
South Windsor, 10,800 .... B 5
(22,090▲) ....
Stafford Springs, 4,100 .... C 7
Stamford, 108,056 .... E 1
Stratford, 50,400 .... E 3

Thomaston, 3,590 .... C 3
Torrington, 33,687 .... B 3
Trumbull, 33,200 .... E 3
Wallingford, 41,400 .... D 4
Waterbury, 108,961 .... C 3
Watertown, 5,920 .... C 3
(20,456▲) .... C 4
West Hartford, 59,100 .... C 5
West Haven, 54,021 .... D 4
Westport, 25,300 .... E 2

Wethersfield, 26,500 .... C 5
Willimantic, 14,600('87) ..... C 7
(6,947) .... C 7
Wilton, 7,200 (15,989▲) ..... E 2
Windsor, 17,517 .... B 5
Windsor Locks, ... B 5
(27,817) ....
Wolcott, 6,070 .... C 4
(13,700▲) ....
Woodbridge, 7,700 .... D 3
(7,924) .... D 3

▲ Population of entire town (township), including rural area.

Statute Miles

Kilometers

Lambert Conformal Conic Projection

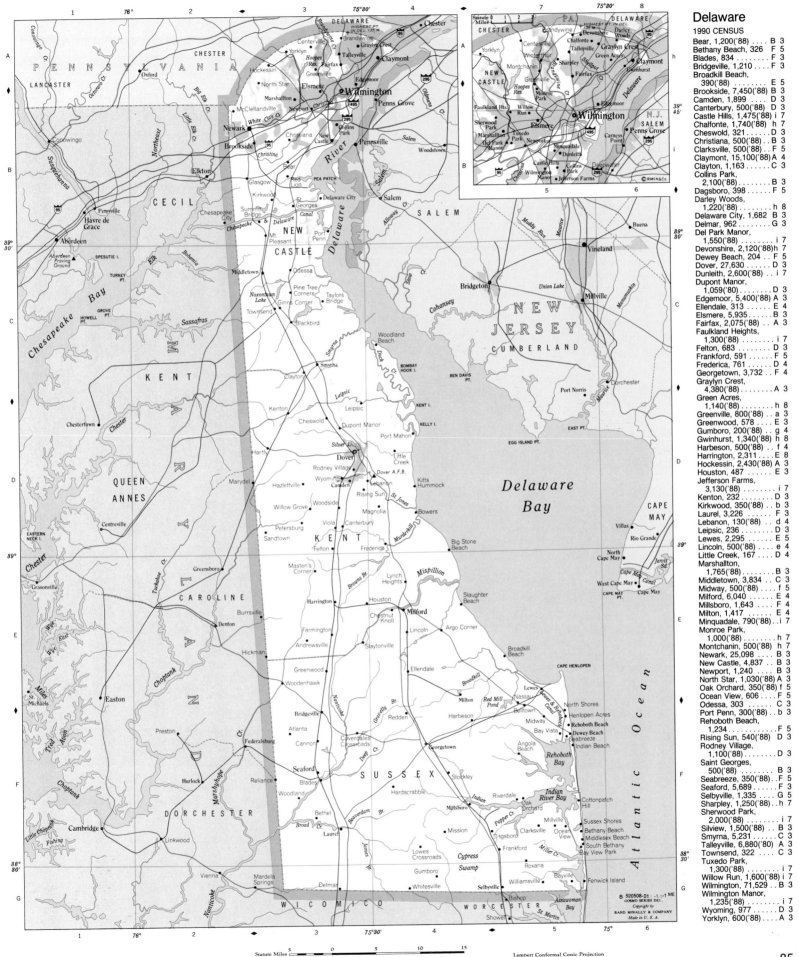

1990 CENSUS

Bear, 1,200('88) . . . . B 3
Bethany Beach, 326 . . F 5
Blades, 834 . . . . F 3
Bridgeville, 1,210 . . . . F 3
Broadkill Beach,
 390('88) . . . . E 5
Brookside, 7,450('88) . B 3
Camden, 1,899 . . . . . D 3
Canterbury, 500('88) . D 3
Castle Hills, 1,475('88) i 7
Chalfonte, 1,740('88) . h 7
Cheswold, 321 . . . . . D 3
Christiana, 500('88) . . B 3
Clarksville, 500('88) . . F 5
Claymont, 15,100('88) A 4
Clayton, 1,163 . . . . . . C 3
Collins Park,
 2,100('88) . . . . B 3
Dagsboro, 398 . . . . . F 5
Darley Woods,
 1,220('88) . . . . h 8
Delaware City, 1,682 . B 3
Delmar, 962 . . . . G 3
Del Park Manor,
 1,550('88) . . . . i 7
Devonshire, 2,120('88)h 7
Dewey Beach, 204 . . F 5
Dover, 27,630 . . . . . . D 3
Dunleith, 2,600('88) . . i 7
Dupont Manor,
 1,059('80) . . . . D 3
Edgemoor, 5,400('88) A 3
Ellendale, 313 . . . . . . E 4
Elsmere, 5,935 . . . . . B 3
Fairfax, 2,075('88) . . A 3
Faulkland Heights,
 1,300('88) . . . . i 7
Felton, 683 . . . . D 3
Frankford, 591 . . . . . F 5
Frederica, 761 . . . . . D 4
Georgetown, 3,732 . . F 4
Graylyn Crest,
 4,380('88) . . . . A 3
Green Acres,
 1,140('88) . . . . h 8
Greenville, 800('88) . . a 3
Greenwood, 578 . . . . E 3
Gumboro, 200('88) . . g 4
Gwinhurst, 1,340('88) h 8
Harbeson, 500('88) . . f 4
Harrington, 2,311 . . . . E 8
Hockessin, 2,430('88) A 3
Houston, 487 . . . . . . E 3
Jefferson Farms,
 3,130('88) . . . . i 7
Kenton, 232 . . . . D 3
Kirkwood, 350('88) . . b 3
Laurel, 3,226 . . . . . . F 3
Lebanon, 130('88) . . d 4
Leipsic, 236 . . . . D 3
Lewes, 2,295 . . . . . . E 5
Lincoln, 500('88) . . . . e 4
Little Creek, 167 . . . . D 4
Marshallton,
 1,765('88) . . . . B 3
Middletown, 3,834 . . C 3
Midway, 500('88) . . . f 5
Milford, 6,040 . . . . . . E 4
Millsboro, 1,643 . . . . F 4
Milton, 1,417 . . . . . . E 4
Minquadale, 790('88) . i 7
Monroe Park,
 1,000('88) . . . . h 7
Montchanin, 500('88) . h 7
Newark, 25,098 . . . . . B 3
New Castle, 4,837 . . . B 3
Newport, 1,240 . . . . . B 3
North Star, 1,030('88) A 3
Oak Orchard, 350('88) f 5
Ocean View, 606 . . . . F 5
Odessa, 303 . . . . . . C 3
Port Penn, 300('88) . . b 3
Rehoboth Beach,
 1,234 . . . . F 5
Rising Sun, 540('88) . D 3
Rodney Village,
 1,100('88) . . . . D 3
Saint Georges,
 500('88) . . . . B 3
Seabreeze, 350('88). . F 5
Seaford, 5,689 . . . . . F 3
Selbyville, 1,335 . . . . G 5
Sharpley, 1,250('88) . h 7
Sherwood Park,
 2,000('88) . . . . i 7
Silview, 1,500('88) . . B 3
Smyrna, 5,231 . . . . . C 3
Talleyville, 6,880('80) A 3
Townsend, 322 . . . . . C 3
Tuxedo Park,
 1,300('88) . . . . i 7
Willow Run, 1,600('88) i 7
Wilmington, 71,529 . . B 3
Wilmington Manor,
 1,235('88) . . . . i 7
Wyoming, 977 . . . . . D 3
Yorklyn, 600('88) . . . . A 3

Florida

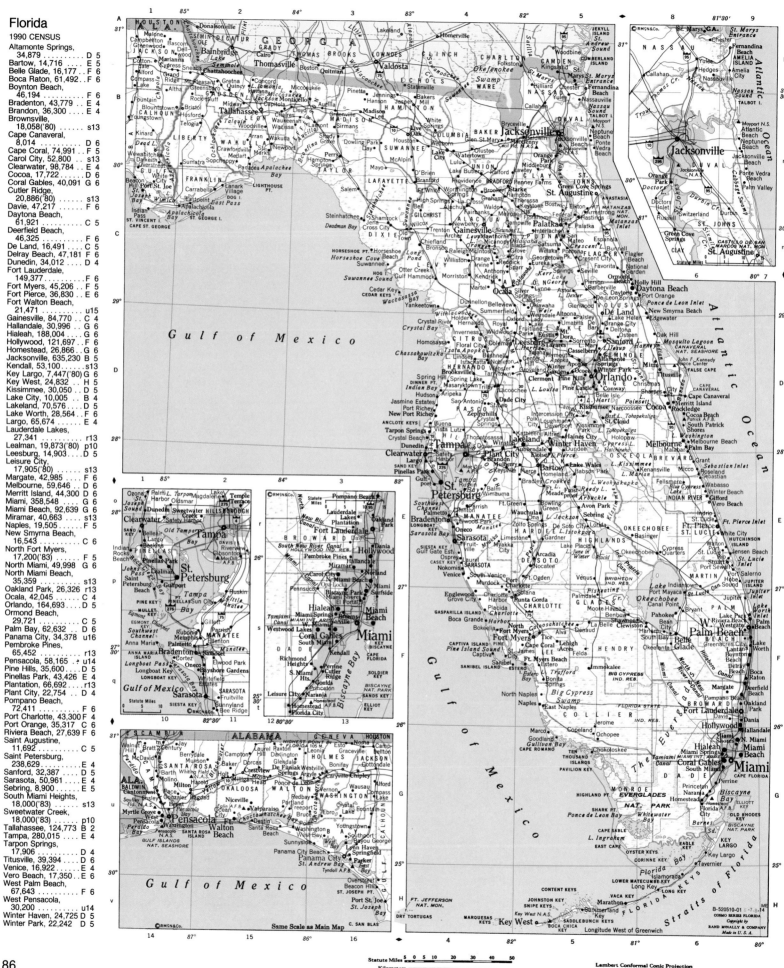

Florida

1990 CENSUS

Altamonte Springs,
34,879 . . . . . D 5
Bartow, 14,716 . . . . E 5
Belle Glade, 16,177 . . F 6
Boca Raton, 61,492 . . F 6
Boynton Beach,
46,194 . . . . F 6
Bradenton, 43,779 . . . E 4
Brandon, 36,300 . . . . E 4
Brownsville,
18,058('80) s13
Cape Canaveral,
8,014 . . . . D 6
Cape Coral, 74,991 . . F 5
Carol City, 52,802 . . . s13
Clearwater, 98,784 . . E 4
Cocoa, 17,722 . . . . . . D 6
Coral Gables, 40,091 G 6
Cutler Ridge,
20,886('80) s13
Davie, 47,217 . . . . . . F 6
Daytona Beach,
61,921 . . . . C 5
Deerfield Beach,
46,325 . . . . F 6
De Land, 16,491 . . . . C 5
Delray Beach, 47,181 F 6
Dunedin, 34,012 . . . . D 4
Fort Lauderdale,
149,377 . . . . F 6
Fort Myers, 45,206 . . F 5
Fort Pierce, 36,830 . . E 6
Fort Walton Beach,
21,471 . . . . u15
Gainesville, 84,770 . . C 4
Hallandale, 30,996 . . . G 6
Hialeah, 188,004 . . . . G 6
Hollywood, 121,697 . . F 6
Homestead, 26,866 . . G 6
Jacksonville, 635,230 B 5
Kendall, 53,100 . . . . . s13
Key Largo, 7,447('80) G 6
Key West, 24,832 . . . H 5
Kissimmee, 30,050 . . D 5
Lake City, 10,005 . . . B 4
Lakeland, 70,576 . . . . D 5
Lake Worth, 28,564 . . F 6
Largo, 65,674 . . . . . . E 4
Lauderdale Lakes,
27,341 . . . . r13
Lealman, 19,873('80) p10
Leesburg, 14,903 . . . D 5
Leisure City,
17,905('80) s13
Margate, 42,985 . . . . F 6
Melbourne, 59,646 . . D 6
Merritt Island, 44,300 D 6
Miami, 358,548 . . . . G 6
Miami Beach, 92,639 G 6
Miramar, 40,663 . . . . s13
Naples, 19,505 . . . . . F 5
New Smyrna Beach,
16,543 . . . . C 6
North Fort Myers,
17,200('83) . . . . F 5
North Miami, 49,998 G 6
North Miami Beach,
35,359 . . . . s13
Oakland Park, 26,326 r13
Ocala, 42,045 . . . . . C 4
Orlando, 164,693 . . . D 5
Ormond Beach,
29,721 . . . . C 5
Palm Bay, 62,632 . . . D 6
Panama City, 34,378 u16
Pembroke Pines,
65,452 . . . . r13
Pensacola, 58,165 . . u14
Pine Hills, 35,600 . . . D 5
Pinellas Park, 43,426 E 4
Plantation, 66,692 . . r13
Plant City, 22,754 . . . D 4
Pompano Beach,
72,411 . . . . F 6
Port Charlotte, 43,300 F 4
Port Orange, 35,317 . C 6
Riviera Beach, 27,639 F 6
Saint Augustine,
11,692 . . . . C 5
Saint Petersburg,
238,629 . . . . . . E 4
Sanford, 32,387 . . . . D 5
Sarasota, 50,961 . . . E 4
Sebring, 8,900 . . . . . E 5
South Miami Heights,
18,000('83) s13
Sweetwater Creek,
18,000('83) p10
Tallahassee, 124,773 B 2
Tampa, 280,015 . . . . E 4
Tarpon Springs,
17,906 . . . . D 4
Titusville, 39,394 . . . D 6
Venice, 16,922 . . . . . E 4
Vero Beach, 17,350 . . E 6
West Palm Beach,
67,643 . . . . F 6
West Pensacola,
30,200 . . . . u14
Winter Haven, 24,725 D 5
Winter Park, 22,242 . D 5

Georgia

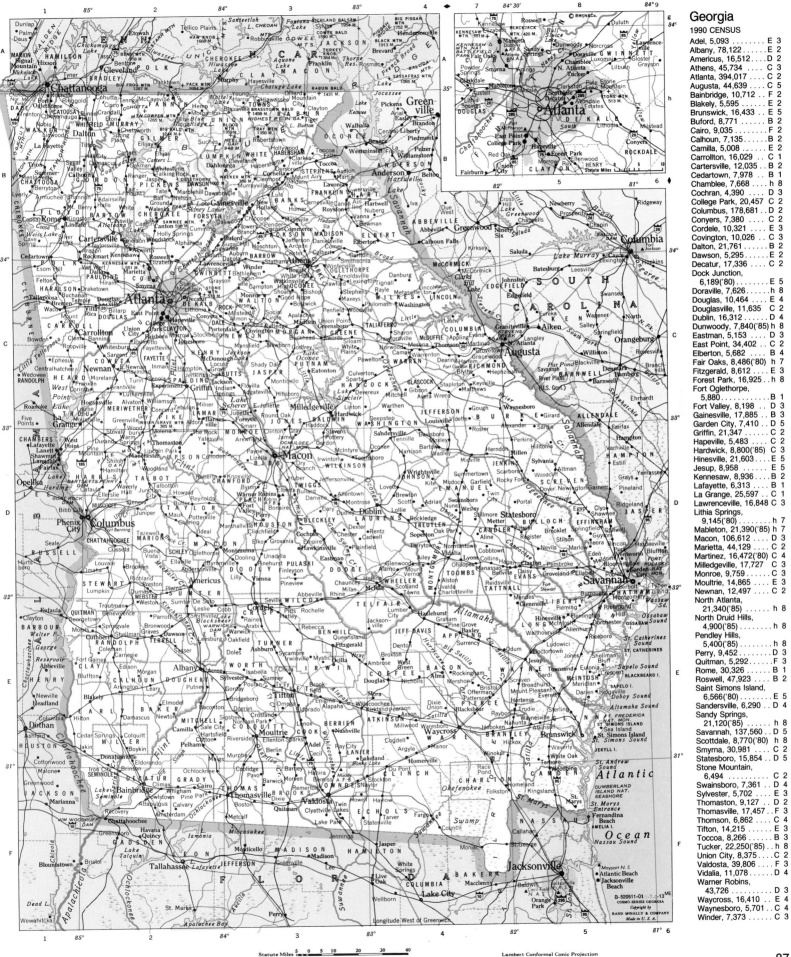

Georgia
1990 CENSUS

Adel, 5,093 . . . . E 3
Albany, 78,122 . . . . . . D 2
Americus, 16,512 . . . . D 2
Athens, 45,734 . . . . . . C 3
Atlanta, 394,017 . . . . C 2
Augusta, 44,639 . . . . C 5
Bainbridge, 10,712 . . F 2
Blakely, 5,595 . . . . . . E 2
Brunswick, 16,433 . . E 5
Buford, 8,771 . . . . B 2
Cairo, 9,035 . . . . F 2
Calhoun, 7,135 . . . . . B 2
Camilla, 5,008 . . . . . . F 2
Carrollton, 16,029 . . C 1
Cartersville, 12,035 . B 2
Cedartown, 7,978 . . B 1
Chamblee, 7,668 . . . . h 8
Cochran, 4,390 . . . . . D 3
College Park, 20,457 . C 2
Columbus, 178,681 . . D 2
Conyers, 7,380 . . . . . C 2
Cordele, 10,321 . . . . E 3
Covington, 10,026 . . C 3
Dalton, 21,761 . . . . . . B 2
Dawson, 5,295 . . . . . E 2
Decatur, 17,336 . . . . C 2
Dock Junction,
6,189('80) . . . . E 5
Doraville, 7,626 . . . . h 8
Douglas, 10,464 . . . . E 4
Douglasville, 11,635 . C 2
Dublin, 16,312 . . . . . D 4
Dunwoody, 7,840('85) h 8
Eastman, 5,153 . . . . . D 3
East Point, 34,402 . . C 2
Elberton, 5,682 . . . . . B 4
Fair Oaks, 8,486('80) h 7
Fitzgerald, 8,612 . . . E 3
Forest Park, 16,925 . . h 8
Fort Oglethorpe,
5,880 . . . . B 1
Fort Valley, 8,198 . . D 3
Gainesville, 17,885 . . B 3
Garden City, 7,410 . . D 5
Griffin, 21,347 . . . . . C 2
Hapeville, 5,483 . . . . C 2
Hardwick, 8,800('85) C 3
Hinesville, 21,603 . . E 5
Jesup, 8,958 . . . . E 5
Kennesaw, 8,936 . . . B 2
Lafayette, 6,313 . . . . B 1
La Grange, 25,597 . . C 1
Lawrenceville, 16,848 C 3
Lithia Springs,
9,145('80) . . . . h 7
Mableton, 21,390('85) h 7
Macon, 106,612 . . . . D 3
Marietta, 44,129 . . . . C 2
Martinez, 16,472('80) C 4
Milledgeville, 17,727 . C 3
Monroe, 9,759 . . . . . C 3
Moultrie, 14,865 . . . . E 3
Newnan, 12,497 . . . . C 2
North Atlanta,
21,340('85) . . . . . . h 8
North Druid Hills,
4,900('85) . . . . h 8
Pendley Hills,
5,400('85) . . . . h 8
Perry, 9,452 . . . . D 3
Quitman, 5,292 . . . . F 3
Rome, 30,326 . . . . . . B 1
Roswell, 47,923 . . . . B 2
Saint Simons Island,
6,566('80) . . . . E 5
Sandersville, 6,290 . . D 4
Sandy Springs,
21,120('85) . . . . . . h 8
Savannah, 137,560 . . D 5
Scottdale, 8,770('80) . C 2
Smyrna, 30,981 . . . . C 2
Statesboro, 15,854 . . D 5
Stone Mountain,
6,494 . . . . C 2
Swainsboro, 7,361 . . D 4
Sylvester, 5,702 . . . . E 3
Thomaston, 9,127 . . D 2
Thomasville, 17,457 . F 3
Thomson, 6,862 . . . . C 4
Tifton, 14,215 . . . . . . E 3
Toccoa, 8,266 . . . . . . B 3
Tucker, 22,250('85) . . h 8
Union City, 8,375 . . . C 2
Valdosta, 39,806 . . . . F 3
Vidalia, 11,078 . . . . . D 4
Warner Robins,
43,726 . . . . D 3
Waycross, 16,410 . . E 4
Waynesboro, 5,701 . . C 4
Winder, 7,373 . . . . . . C 3

87

Hawaii

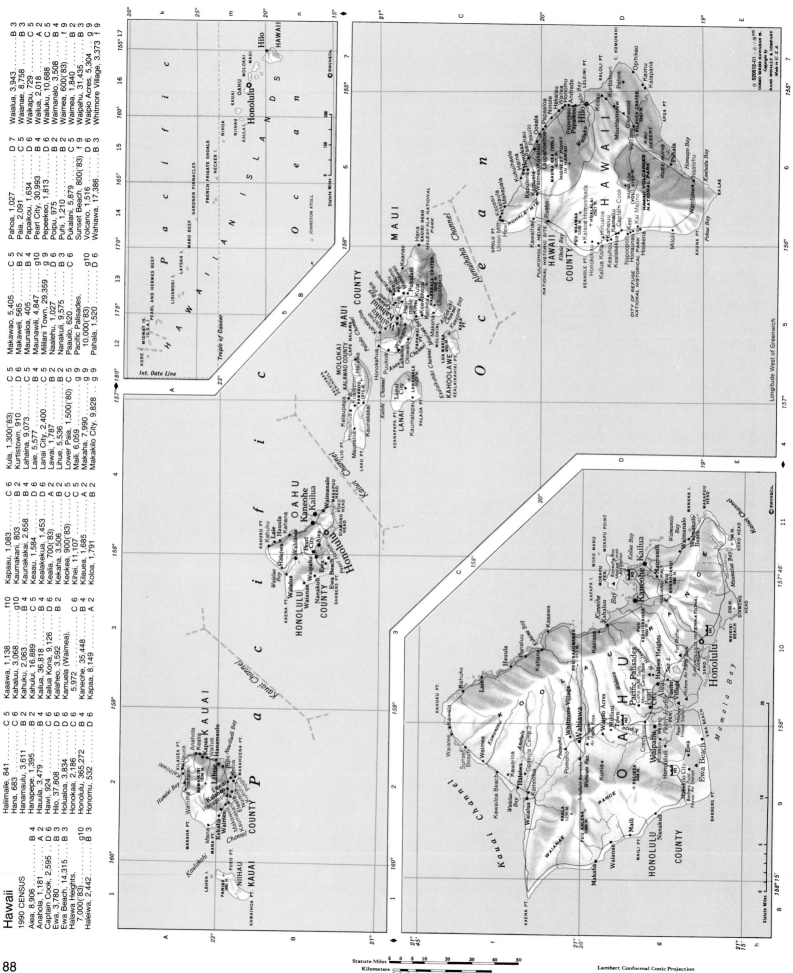

Hawaii
1990 CENSUS

Place	Pop.	Ref.
Aiea, 8,906		B 4
Anahola, 1,181		A 2
Captain Cook, 2,595		D 6
Ewa, 3,780		B 3
Ewa Beach, 14,315		B 3
Halawa Heights, 7,000('83)		g10
Haleiwa, 2,442		B 3
Haliimaile, 841		C 6
Hana, 683		C 6
Hanamaulu, 3,611		B 2
Hanapepe, 1,395		B 4
Hauula, 3,479		B 4
Hawi, 924		D 6
Hilo, 37,808		D 6
Holualoa, 3,834		D 6
Honokaa, 2,186		C 6
Honolulu, 365,272		B 4
Honomu, 532		D 6
Kaaawa, 1,138		C 6
Kahaluu, 3,068		B 2
Kahuku, 2,063		B 2
Kahului, 16,889		C 5
Kailua, 36,818		B 4
Kailua Kona, 9,126		D 6
Kalaheo, 3,592		B 2
Kamuela (Waimea), 5,972		C 6
Kaneohe, 35,448		B 4
Kapaa, 8,149		A 2
Kapaau, 1,083		C 6
Kaumakani, 803		B 2
Kaunakakai, 2,658		B 4
Keaau, 1,584		D 6
Kealakekua, 1,453		D 6
Kealia, 700('83)		A 2
Kekaha, 3,506		B 2
Keokea, 900('83)		C 5
Kihei, 11,107		C 6
Kilauea, 1,685		A 2
Koloa, 1,791		B 2
Kula, 1,300('83)		C 6
Kurtistown, 910		B 2
Lahaina, 9,073		B 4
Laie, 5,577		B 4
Lanai City, 2,400		C 5
Lawai, 1,787		B 2
Lihue, 5,536		B 3
Lower Paia, 1,500('80)		C 5
Maili, 6,059		B 3
Makaha, 7,990		B 4
Makakilo City, 9,828		B 2
Makawao, 5,405		C 5
Makaweli, 565		B 2
Maunaloa, 405		B 4
Maunawili, 4,847		g10
Mililani Town, 29,359		B 4
Naalehu, 1,027		D 6
Nanakuli, 9,575		B 3
Paauilo, 620		C 6
Pacific Palisades, 10,000('83)		g10
Pahala, 1,520		D 6
Pahoa, 1,027		D 7
Paia, 2,091		C 5
Papaikou, 1,634		D 6
Pearl City, 30,993		B 4
Pepeekeo, 1,813		D 6
Poipu, 975		B 2
Puhi, 1,210		B 2
Pukalani, 5,879		C 5
Waialua, 3,943		B 3
Waianae, 8,758		B 3
Waikapu, 729		C 5
Wailua, 2,018		A 2
Wailuku, 10,688		C 5
Waimanalo, 3,508		B 2
Waimea, 600('83)		f 9
Waimea, 1,840		B 2
Waipahu, 31,435		B 3
Waipio Acres, 5,304		B 3
Whitmore Village, 3,373		f 9
Volcano, 1,516		D 6
Wahiawa, 17,386		B 3

Lambert Conformal Conic Projection

Illinois
1990 CENSUS

Addison, 32,058 . . . . k 8
Alton, 32,905 . . . . . E 3
Arlington Heights, 75,460 . . . . . A 5
Aurora, 99,581 . . . . B 5
Belleville, 42,785 . . . E 4
Berwyn, 45,426 . . . . k 9
Bloomington, 51,972 C 4
Bolingbrook, 40,843 . k 8
Bourbonnais, 13,934 B 6
Brookfield, 18,876 . . k 9
Burbank, 27,600 . . . . k 9
Cahokia, 17,550 . . . . E 3
Cairo, 4,846 . . . . F 4
Calumet City, 37,840 B 6
Canton, 13,922 . . . . C 3
Carbondale, 27,033 . F 4
Centralia, 14,274 . . . E 4
Champaign, 63,502 . . C 5
Charleston, 20,398 . . D 5
Chicago, 2,783,726 . . B 6
Chicago Heights, 33,072 . . . . B 6
Cicero, 67,436 . . . . . B 6
Danville, 33,828 . . . . C 6
Decatur, 83,885 . . . . D 5
De Kalb, 34,925 . . . . B 5
Des Plaines, 53,223 . A 6
Dixon, 15,144 . . . . . B 4
Downers Grove, 46,858 . . . . B 5
East Saint Louis, 40,944 . . . . E 3
Elgin, 77,010 . . . . . . A 5
Elk Grove Village, 33,429 . . . . h 9
Elmhurst, 42,029 . . . B 6
Evanston, 73,233 . . . A 6
Freeport, 25,840 . . . A 4
Galena, 3,647 . . . . . A 3
Galesburg, 33,530 . . C 3
Glenview, 37,093 . . . h 9
Granite City, 32,862 . E 3
Gurnee, 13,701 . . . . h 9
Hanover Park, 32,895 k 8
Harvey, 29,771 . . . . B 6
Highland Park, 30,575 A 6
Hoffman Estates, 46,561 . . . . h 8
Jacksonville, 19,324 D 3
Joliet, 76,836 . . . . . B 5
Kankakee, 27,575 . . B 6
Kewanee, 12,969 . . . B 4
Lake Forest, 17,836 . A 6
Lansing, 28,086 . . . . B 6
La Salle, 9,717 . . . . B 5
Lincoln, 15,418 . . . . C 4
Lombard, 39,408 . . . k 8
Macomb, 19,952 . . . C 3
Marion, 14,545 . . . . F 5
Mattoon, 18,441 . . . D 5
Moline, 43,202 . . . . B 3
Monmouth, 9,489 . . . C 3
Mount Prospect, 53,170 . . . . A 6
Mount Vernon, 16,988 E 5
Naperville, 85,351 . . B 5
Nauvoo, 1,108 . . . . . C 2
Niles, 28,284 . . . . . . h 9
Normal, 40,023 . . . . C 5
Northbrook, 32,308 . h 9
North Chicago, 34,978 . . . . A 6
Oak Lawn, 56,182 . . B 6
Oak Park, 53,648 . . . B 6
Ottawa, 17,451 . . . . B 5
Palatine, 39,253 . . . A 5
Park Ridge, 36,175 . B 6
Pekin, 32,254 . . . . . C 4
Peoria, 113,504 . . . . C 4
Peru, 9,302 . . . . B 5
Pontiac, 11,428 . . . . C 5
Quincy, 39,681 . . . . D 2
Rockford, 139,426 . . A 4
Rock Island, 40,552 . B 3
Salem, 7,470 . . . . . E 5
Schaumburg, 68,586 h 8
Skokie, 59,432 . . . . B 6
Springfield, 105,227 . D 4
Sterling, 15,132 . . . B 4
Streator, 14,121 . . . C 5
Taylorville, 11,133 . D 4
Tinley Park, 37,121 . k 9
Urbana, 36,344 . . . . C 5
Vandalia, 6,114 . . . . E 4
Waukegan, 69,392 . . A 6
Wheaton, 51,464 . . . B 5
Zion, 19,775 . . . . . . A 6

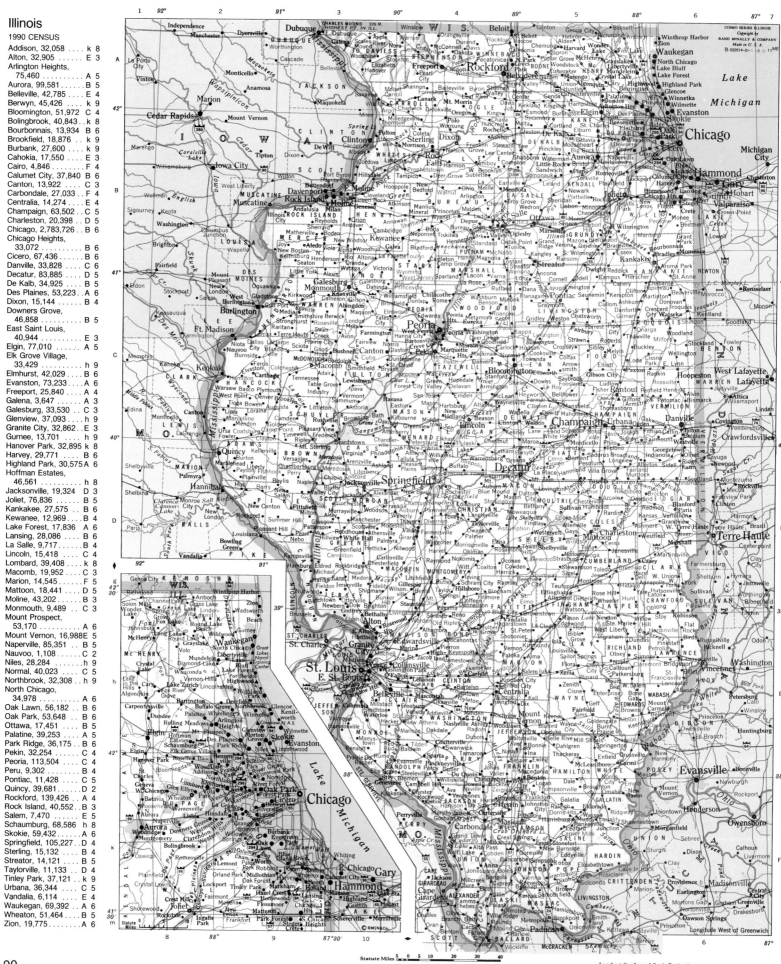

90

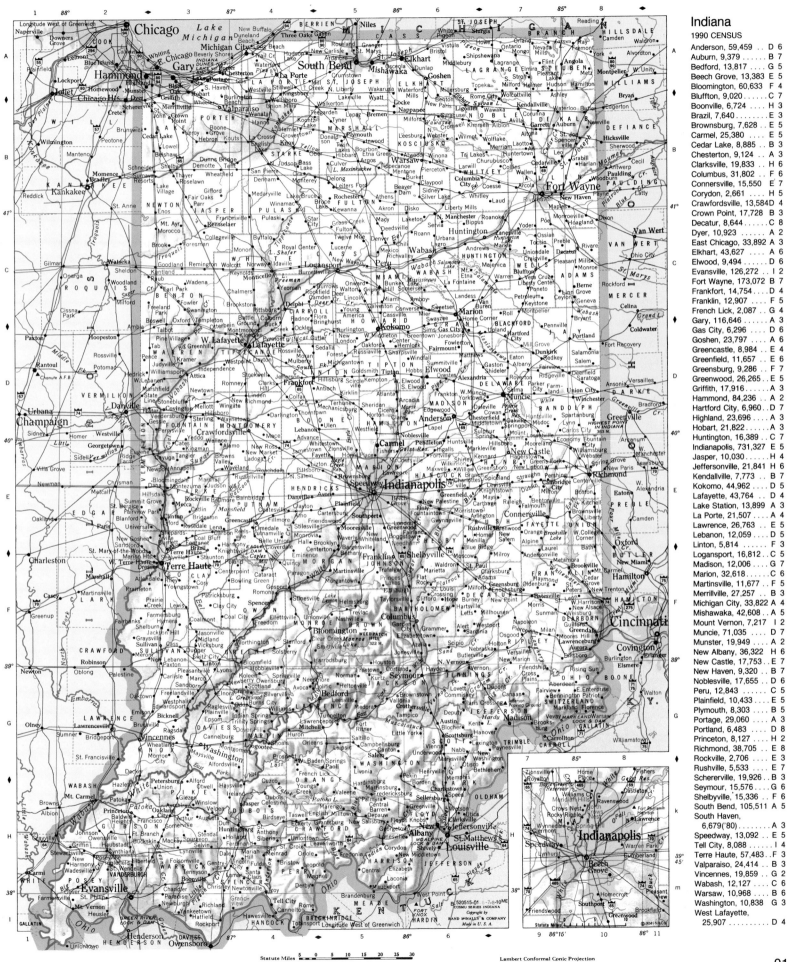

Indiana

1990 CENSUS

Anderson, 59,459 . . D 6
Auburn, 9,379 . . . . . B 7
Bedford, 13,817 . . G 5
Beech Grove, 13,383 E 5
Bloomington, 60,633 . F 4
Bluffton, 9,020 . . . . C 7
Boonville, 6,724 . . . H 3
Brazil, 7,640 . . . . . . E 3
Brownsburg, 7,628 . . E 5
Carmel, 25,380 . . . . E 5
Cedar Lake, 8,885 . . B 3
Chesterton, 9,124 . . A 3
Clarksville, 19,833 . . H 6
Columbus, 31,802 . . F 6
Connersville, 15,550 . E 7
Corydon, 2,661 . . . H 5
Crawfordsville, 13,584 D 4
Crown Point, 17,728 . B 3
Decatur, 8,644 . . . C 8
Dyer, 10,923 . . . . . A 2
East Chicago, 33,892 A 3
Elkhart, 43,627 . . . A 6
Elwood, 9,494 . . . . D 6
Evansville, 126,272 . . I 2
Fort Wayne, 173,072 B 7
Frankfort, 14,754 . . D 4
Franklin, 12,907 . . . F 5
French Lick, 2,087 . . G 4
Gary, 116,646 . . . . A 3
Gas City, 6,296 . . . D 6
Goshen, 23,797 . . . . A 6
Greencastle, 8,984 . E 4
Greenfield, 11,657 . . E 6
Greensburg, 9,286 . . F 7
Greenwood, 26,265 . E 5
Griffith, 17,916 . . . A 3
Hammond, 84,236 . . A 2
Hartford City, 6,960 . D 7
Highland, 23,696 . . A 3
Hobart, 21,822 . . . . A 3
Huntington, 16,389 . C 7
Indianapolis, 731,327 E 5
Jasper, 10,030 . . . . H 4
Jeffersonville, 21,841 H 6
Kendallville, 7,773 . B 7
Kokomo, 44,962 . . D 5
Lafayette, 43,764 . . D 4
Lake Station, 13,899 A 3
La Porte, 21,507 . . . A 4
Lawrence, 26,763 . . E 5
Lebanon, 12,059 . . . D 5
Linton, 5,814 . . . . . F 3
Logansport, 16,812 . C 5
Madison, 12,006 . . . G 7
Marion, 32,618 . . . . D 6
Martinsville, 11,677 . F 5
Merrillville, 27,257 . . B 3
Michigan City, 33,822 A 4
Mishawaka, 42,608 . A 5
Mount Vernon, 7,217 I 2
Muncie, 71,035 . . . D 7
Munster, 19,949 . . . A 2
New Albany, 36,322 . H 6
New Castle, 17,753 . E 7
New Haven, 9,320 . . B 7
Noblesville, 17,655 . D 6
Peru, 12,843 . . . . . C 5
Plainfield, 10,433 . . E 5
Plymouth, 8,303 . . . B 5
Portage, 29,060 . . . A 3
Portland, 6,483 . . . D 8
Princeton, 8,127 . . . H 2
Richmond, 38,705 . . E 8
Rockville, 2,706 . . . E 3
Rushville, 5,533 . . . E 7
Schererville, 19,926 . B 3
Seymour, 15,576 . . . G 6
Shelbyville, 15,336 . . F 6
South Bend, 105,511 A 5
South Haven,
　6,679 ('80) . . . . . A 3
Speedway, 13,092 . E 5
Tell City, 8,088 . . . . . I 4
Terre Haute, 57,483 . F 3
Valparaiso, 24,414 . . A 3
Vincennes, 19,859 . . G 2
Wabash, 12,127 . . . C 6
Warsaw, 10,968 . . . C 6
Washington, 10,838 . G 3
West Lafayette,
　25,907 . . . . D 4

Iowa

Iowa

1990 CENSUS

Algona, 6,015	A 3
Altoona, 7,191	C 4
Amana, 540('87)	C 6
Ames, 47,198	B 6
Anamosa, 5,100	B 6
Ankeny, 18,482	C 2
Atlantic, 7,432	C 2
Bettendorf, 28,132	C 7

Boone, 12,392	B 4
Burlington, 27,208	D 6
Camanche, 4,436	C 7
Carroll, 9,579	B 3
Cedar Falls, 34,298	B 5
Cedar Rapids, 108,751	C 6
Centerville, 5,936	C 5
Chariton, 4,616	C 4
Charles City, 7,878	A 5
Cherokee, 6,026	B 2
Clarinda, 5,104	C 2

Clear Lake, 8,183	B 4
Clinton, 29,201	C 7
Clive, 7,462	C 7
Coralville, 10,347	C 6
Council Bluffs, 54,315	C 2
Creston, 7,911	C 3
Davenport, 95,333	C 7
Decorah, 4,616	A 5
Denison, 6,604	B 2
Des Moines, 193,187	C 4
Dubuque, 57,546	B 6

Estherville, 6,720	A 3
Evansdale, 4,638	B 5
Fairfield, 9,768	C 6
Forest City, 4,430	A 4
Fort Dodge, 25,894	B 3
Fort Madison, 11,618	D 6
Glenwood, 4,571	C 2
Grinnell, 8,902	C 5
Hampton, 4,133	B 4
Harlan, 5,148	C 2
Hiawatha, 4,986	B 6

Humboldt, 4,438	B 3
Independence, 5,972	B 6
Indianola, 11,340	C 4
Iowa City, 59,738	C 6
Iowa Falls, 5,424	B 4
Jefferson, 4,292	B 3
Keokuk, 12,451	D 6
Knoxville, 8,232	C 4
Le Mars, 8,454	B 2
Manchester, 5,137	B 6
Maquoketa, 6,111	B 7

Marion, 20,403	B 6
Marshalltown, 25,178	B 5
Mason City, 29,040	A 4
Mount Pleasant, 8,027	D 6
Muscatine, 22,881	C 6
Nevada, 6,009	B 4
Newton, 14,789	C 4
Oelwein, 6,493	B 6
Orange City, 4,940	B 1
Oskaloosa, 10,632	C 5

Ottumwa, 24,488	C 4
Pella, 9,270	B 5
Perry, 6,652	C 3
Red Oak, 6,264	D 2
Sheldon, 4,937	A 2
Shenandoah, 5,572	D 2
Sioux Center, 5,074	A 1
Sioux City, 80,505	B 1
Spencer, 11,066	A 2
Spirit Lake, 3,871	A 2
Storm Lake, 8,769	B 2

Urbandale, 23,500	C 4
Vinton, 5,103	B 5
Washington, 7,074	C 3
Waterloo, 66,467	D 2
Waukon, 4,019	A 2
Waverly, 8,539	B 5
Webster City, 7,894	B 4
West Branch, 1,908	C 6
West Des Moines, 31,702	C 4
Windsor Heights, 5,190	e 8

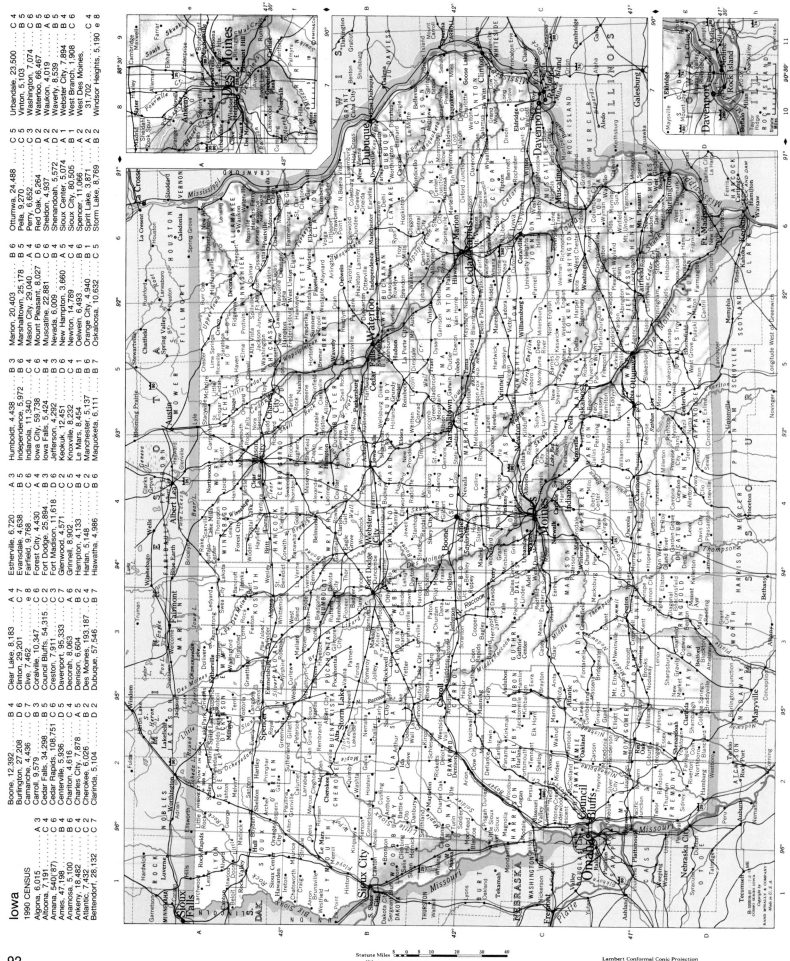

92

Statute Miles

Kilometers

Lambert Conformal Conic Projection

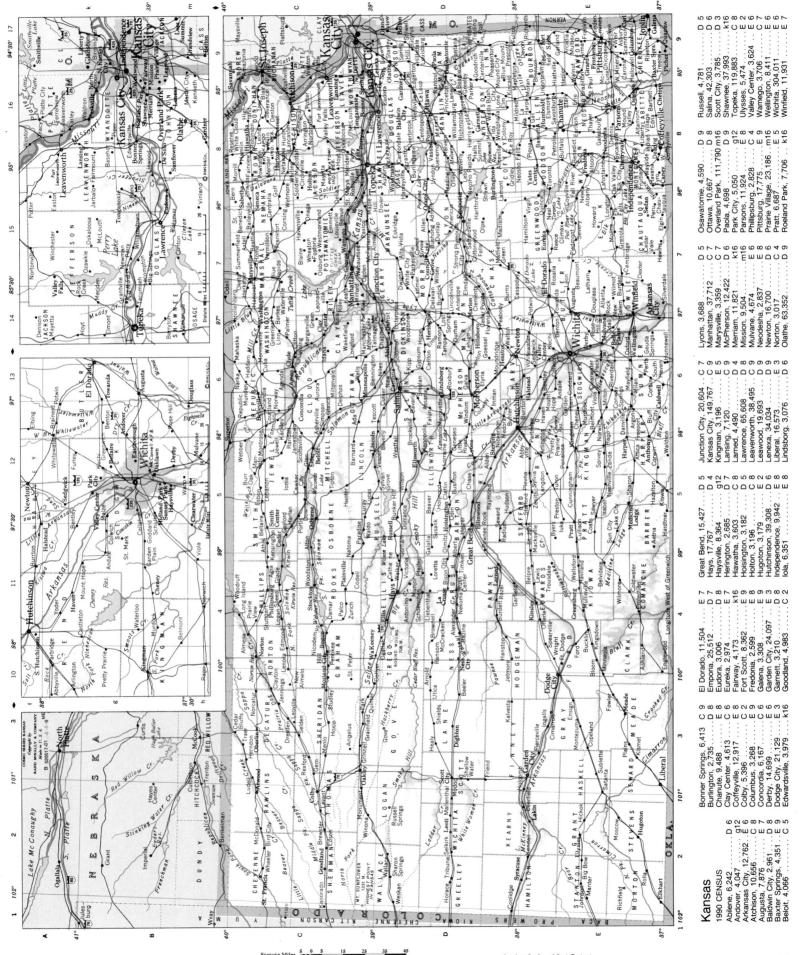

Statute Miles

Kilometers

Lambert Conformal Conic Projection

Kansas

1990 CENSUS

Abilene, 6,242	D 6	
Andover, 4,047	g12	
Arkansas City, 12,762	E 7	
Atchison, 10,656	C 8	
Augusta, 7,876	E 7	
Baldwin City, 2,961	D 8	
Baxter Springs, 4,351	E 9	
Beloit, 4,066	C 5	

Bonner Springs, 6,413	C 9	
Burlington, 2,735	D 8	
Chanute, 9,488	E 8	
Clay Center, 4,613	C 6	
Coffeyville, 12,917	E 8	
Colby, 5,396	C 2	
Columbus, 3,268	E 9	
Concordia, 6,167	C 6	
Derby, 14,699	E 7	
Dodge City, 21,129	D 3	
Edwardsville, 3,979	k16	

El Dorado, 11,504	D 7	
Emporia, 25,512	D 7	
Eudora, 3,006	D 8	
Eureka, 2,974	D 7	
Fairway, 4,173	k16	
Fort Scott, 8,362	E 9	
Fredonia, 2,599	E 8	
Galena, 3,308	E 9	
Garden City, 24,097	D 3	
Garnett, 3,210	D 8	
Goodland, 4,983	D 6	

Great Bend, 15,427	D 5	
Hays, 17,767	D 4	
Haysville, 8,364	g12	
Herington, 2,685	D 7	
Hiawatha, 3,603	C 8	
Hoisington, 3,182	D 5	
Holton, 3,196	C 8	
Hugoton, 3,179	E 2	
Hutchinson, 39,308	D 6	
Independence, 9,942	E 8	
Iola, 6,351	D 8	

Junction City, 20,604	C 7	
Kansas City, 149,767	C 9	
Kingman, 3,196	E 5	
Larned, 4,490	D 4	
Lawrence, 65,608	D 8	
Leavenworth, 38,495	C 8	
Leawood, 19,693	m16	
Lenexa, 34,034	E 9	
Liberal, 16,573	E 2	
Lindsborg, 3,076	D 6	

Lyons, 3,688	C 7	
Manhattan, 37,712	C 7	
Marysville, 3,359	C 7	
McPherson, 12,422	D 6	
Merriam, 11,821	k16	
Mission, 9,504	k16	
Mulvane, 4,674	E 6	
Neodesha, 2,837	E 8	
Newton, 16,700	D 6	
Norton, 3,017	C 4	
Olathe, 63,352	D 9	

Osawatomie, 4,590	D 5	
Ottawa, 10,667	D 8	
Overland Park, 111,790	m16	
Paola, 4,698	g12	
Park City, 5,050	g12	
Parsons, 11,924	E 4	
Phillipsburg, 2,828	C 4	
Pittsburg, 17,775	E 9	
Prairie Village, 23,186	m16	
Pratt, 6,687	D 4	
Roeland Park, 7,706	k16	

Russell, 4,781	D 5	
Salina, 42,303	D 6	
Scott City, 3,785	D 3	
Shawnee, 37,993	k16	
Topeka, 119,883	C 8	
Ulysses, 5,474	E 2	
Valley Center, 3,624	g12	
Wamego, 3,706	C 7	
Wellington, 8,411	E 6	
Wichita, 304,011	E 6	
Winfield, 11,931	E 7	

Kentucky

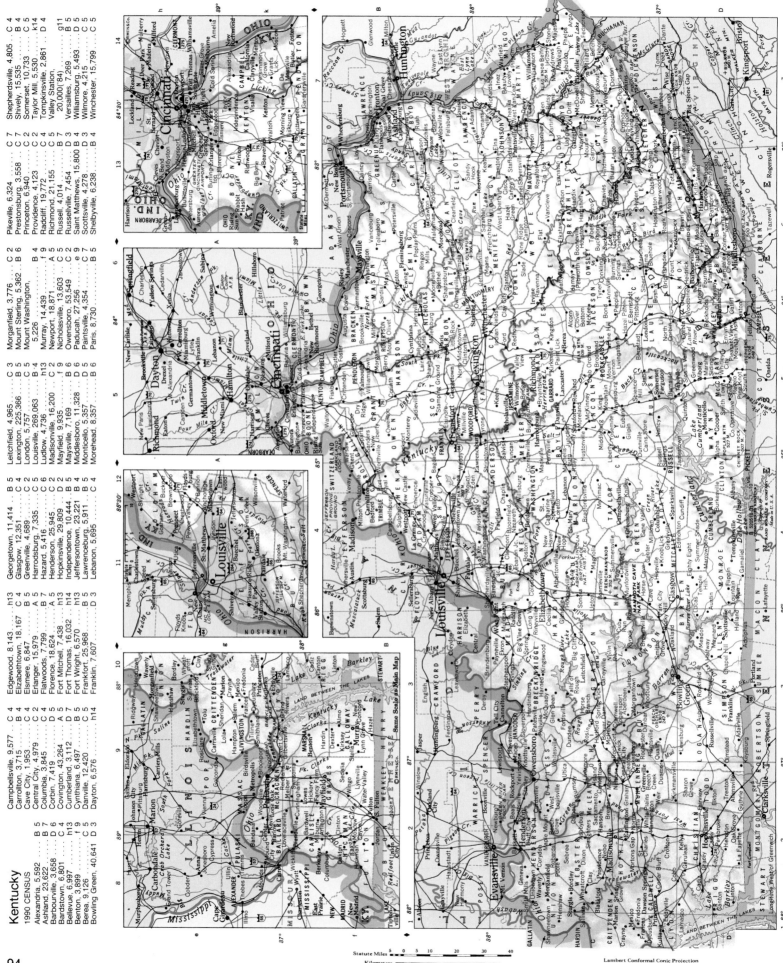

Kentucky
1990 CENSUS

Alexandria, 5,592	B 5	
Ashland, 23,622	B 7	
Barbourville, 3,658	D 6	
Bardstown, 6,801	C 4	
Bellevue, 6,997	f 9	
Benton, 3,899	C 5	
Berea, 9,126	C 5	
Bowling Green, 40,641	D 3	

Campbellsville, 9,577	C 4	
Carrollton, 3,715	B 4	
Cave City, 1,953	C 4	
Central City, 4,979	C 2	
Columbia, 3,845	D 5	
Corbin, 7,419	C 6	
Covington, 43,264	A 5	
Cumberland, 3,112	D 7	
Cynthiana, 6,497	B 5	
Danville, 12,420	C 5	
Dayton, 6,576	D 3	

Edgewood, 8,143	h13	
Elizabethtown, 18,167	C 4	
Elsmere, 6,847	C 2	
Erlanger, 15,979	B 4	
Flatwoods, 7,799	B 7	
Florence, 18,624	A 5	
Fort Mitchell, 7,438	h13	
Fort Thomas, 16,032	h14	
Fort Wright, 6,570	h13	
Frankfort, 25,968	B 5	
Franklin, 7,607	D 3	

Georgetown, 11,414	B 5	
Glasgow, 12,351	C 4	
Greenville, 4,689	C 2	
Harrodsburg, 7,335	C 5	
Hazard, 5,416	C 6	
Henderson, 25,945	A 2	
Hopkinsville, 29,809	D 2	
Independence, 10,444	B 5	
Jeffersontown, 23,221	B 4	
Lawrenceburg, 5,911	C 5	
Lebanon, 5,695	C 4	

Leitchfield, 4,965	C 3	
Lexington, 225,366	B 5	
London, 5,757	C 6	
Louisville, 269,063	B 4	
Ludlow, 4,736	h13	
Madisonville, 16,200	C 2	
Mayfield, 9,935	f 9	
Maysville, 7,169	B 6	
Middlesboro, 11,328	D 6	
Monticello, 5,911	D 5	
Morehead, 8,357	B 6	

Morganfield, 3,776	C 2	
Mount Sterling, 5,362	B 6	
Mount Washington, 5,226	B 4	
Murray, 14,439	f 9	
Newport, 18,871	A 5	
Nicholasville, 13,603	C 5	
Owensboro, 53,549	C 2	
Paducah, 27,256	e 9	
Paintsville, 4,354	C 7	
Paris, 8,730	B 5	

Pikeville, 6,324	C 7	
Prestonsburg, 3,558	C 7	
Princeton, 6,940	C 2	
Providence, 4,123	C 2	
Radcliff, 19,772	C 4	
Richmond, 21,155	B 5	
Russell, 4,014	B 7	
Russellville, 7,454	D 3	
Saint Matthews, 15,800	B 4	
Scottsville, 4,278	D 3	
Shelbyville, 6,238	B 4	

Shepherdsville, 4,805	C 4	
Shively, 15,535	B 4	
Somerset, 10,733	k14	
Taylor Mill, 5,530	C 2	
Tompkinsville, 2,861	D 4	
Valley Station, 20,000('84)	g11	
Versailles, 7,269	B 5	
Williamsburg, 5,493	D 5	
Wilmore, 4,215	C 5	
Winchester, 15,799	C 5	

Statute Miles
Kilometers

Lambert Conformal Conic Projection

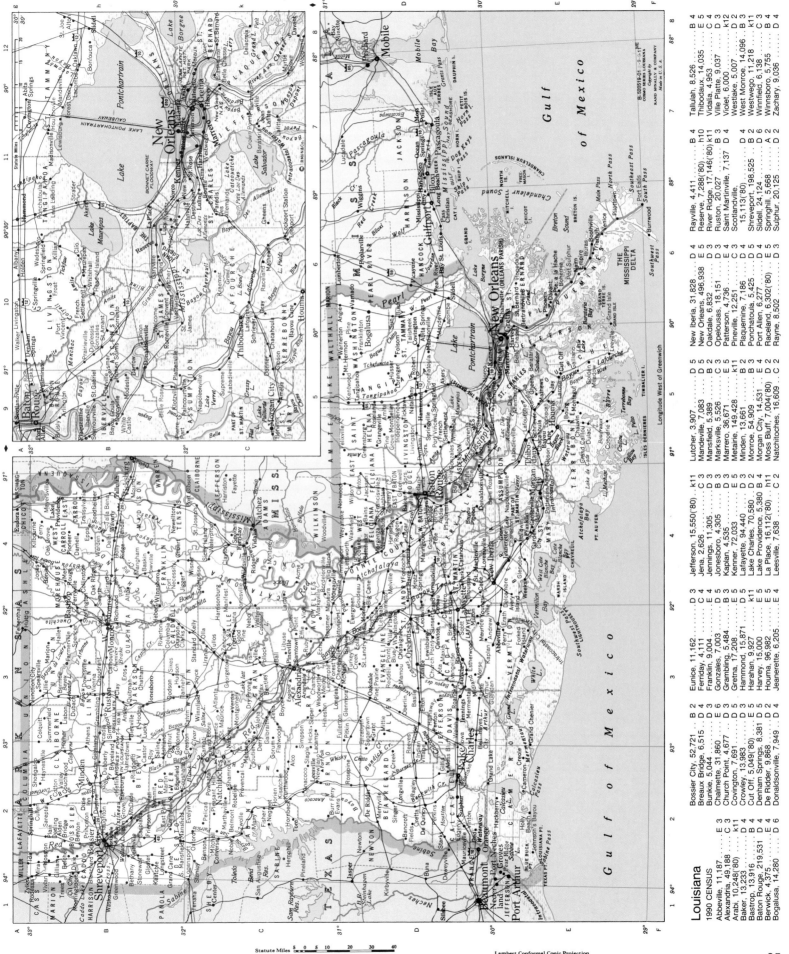

Statute Miles 5 0 5 10 20 30 40
Kilometers 5 0 5 10 15 25 35 45 55

Lambert Conformal Conic Projection

Louisiana

1990 CENSUS

Place	Grid
Abbeville, 11,187	E 3
Alexandria, 49,188	C 3
Arabi, 10,248('80)	k11
Baker, 13,233	D 4
Bastrop, 13,916	B 4
Baton Rouge, 219,531	D 4
Berwick, 4,375	E 4
Bogalusa, 14,280	D 6
Bossier City, 52,721	B 2
Breaux Bridge, 6,515	D 4
Bunkie, 5,044	D 4
Chalmette, 31,860	E 6
Church Point, 4,677	D 3
Covington, 7,691	D 5
Crowley, 13,983	D 3
Cut Off, 5,049('80)	E 5
Denham Springs, 8,381	D 4
De Ridder, 9,868	D 3
Donaldsonville, 7,949	D 4
Eunice, 11,162	D 3
Ferriday, 4,111	C 4
Franklin, 9,004	E 4
Gonzales, 7,003	D 5
Grambling, 4,305	B 3
Gretna, 17,208	E 5
Hammond, 15,871	D 5
Harahan, 9,927	k11
Harvey, 15,000	k11
Houma, 96,982	E 5
Jeanerette, 6,205	D 4
Jefferson, 15,550('80)	k11
Jena, 2,626	C 3
Jennings, 11,305	D 3
Jonesboro, 4,305	B 3
Kaplan, 4,535	E 3
Kenner, 72,033	E 5
Lafayette, 94,440	D 3
Lake Charles, 70,580	D 2
Lake Providence, 5,380	B 4
La Place, 16,112('80)	h11
Leesville, 7,638	C 2
Lutcher, 3,907	D 5
Mandeville, 7,083	D 5
Mansfield, 5,389	B 2
Marksville, 5,526	C 3
Marrero, 36,671	E 5
Metairie, 149,428	E 5
Minden, 13,661	B 2
Monroe, 54,909	B 3
Morgan City, 14,531	E 4
Moss Bluff, 7,004('80)	h1
Natchitoches, 16,609	C 2
New Iberia, 31,828	D 4
New Orleans, 496,938	E 5
Oakdale, 6,832	D 3
Opelousas, 18,151	D 3
Patterson, 4,736	E 4
Pineville, 12,251	C 3
Plaquemine, 7,186	D 4
Ponchatoula, 5,425	D 5
Port Allen, 6,277	D 4
Raceland, 6,302('80)	E 5
Rayne, 8,502	D 3
Rayville, 4,411	B 4
Reserve, 7,288('80)	h10
River Ridge, 17,146('80)	k11
Ruston, 20,027	B 3
Saint Martinville, 7,137	D 4
Scotlandville, 15,113('80)	D 4
Shreveport, 198,525	B 2
Slidell, 24,124	D 6
Springhill, 5,668	A 2
Sulphur, 20,125	D 2
Tallulah, 8,526	B 4
Thibodaux, 14,035	E 5
Vidalia, 4,953	C 4
Ville Platte, 9,037	k12
Violet, 5,007	D 4
Westlake, 5,007	D 4
West Monroe, 14,096	B 3
Westwego, 11,218	k11
Winnfield, 6,138	C 3
Winnsboro, 5,755	B 4
Zachary, 9,036	D 4

B-500519-01 0-4-1 ME
COSMO/PREMIER — MARK III LOUISIANA
RAND M*NALLY & COMPANY
Copyright by
Made in U.S.A.

95

Maine

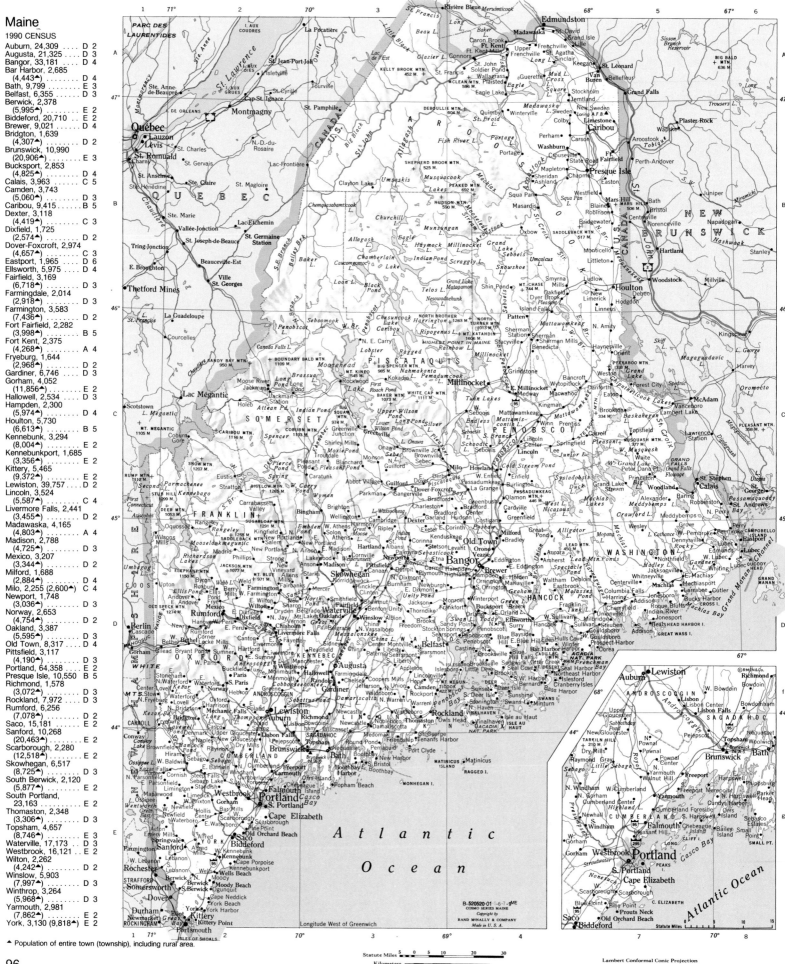

Maine
1990 CENSUS

Auburn, 24,309	. . . .	D 2
Augusta, 21,325	. . . .	D 3
Bangor, 33,181	. . . .	D 4
Bar Harbor, 2,685		D 4
(4,443▲)		D 4
Bath, 9,799	. . . .	E 3
Belfast, 6,355	. . . .	D 4
Berwick, 2,378		E 2
(5,995▲)		E 2
Biddeford, 20,710		E 2
Brewer, 9,021	. . . .	D 4
Bridgton, 1,639		D 2
(4,307▲)		D 2
Brunswick, 10,990		E 3
(20,906▲)		E 3
Bucksport, 2,853		D 4
(4,825▲)		D 4
Calais, 3,963	. . . .	C 5
Camden, 3,743		D 4
(5,060▲)		D 4
Caribou, 9,415	. . . .	B 5
Dexter, 3,118		C 3
(4,419▲)		C 3
Dixfield, 1,725		D 2
(2,574▲)		D 2
Dover-Foxcroft, 2,974		C 3
(4,657▲)		C 3
Eastport, 1,965		D 6
Ellsworth, 5,975	. . . .	D 4
Fairfield, 3,169		D 3
(6,718▲)		D 3
Farmingdale, 2,014		D 3
(2,918▲)		D 3
Farmington, 3,583		D 2
(7,436▲)		D 2
Fort Fairfield, 2,282		B 5
(3,998▲)		B 5
Fort Kent, 2,375		A 4
(4,268▲)		A 4
Fryeburg, 1,644		D 2
(2,968▲)		D 2
Gardiner, 6,746		D 3
Gorham, 4,052		E 2
(11,856▲)		E 2
Hallowell, 2,534		D 3
Hampden, 2,300		D 4
(5,974▲)		D 4
Houlton, 5,730		B 5
(6,613▲)		B 5
Kennebunk, 3,294		E 2
(8,004▲)		E 2
Kennebunkport, 1,685		E 2
(3,356▲)		E 2
Kittery, 5,465		E 2
(9,372▲)		E 2
Lewiston, 39,757	. . . .	D 2
Lincoln, 3,524		C 4
(5,587▲)		C 4
Livermore Falls, 2,441		D 2
(3,455▲)		D 2
Madawaska, 4,165		A 4
(4,803▲)		A 4
Madison, 2,788		D 3
(4,725▲)		D 3
Mexico, 3,207		D 2
(3,344▲)		D 2
Milford, 1,688		D 4
(2,884▲)		D 4
Milo, 2,255 (2,600▲)		C 4
Newport, 1,748		D 3
(3,036▲)		D 3
Norway, 2,653		D 2
(4,754▲)		D 2
Oakland, 3,387		D 3
(5,595▲)		D 3
Old Town, 8,317	. . . .	D 4
Pittsfield, 3,117		D 3
(4,190▲)		D 3
Portland, 64,358	. . . .	E 2
Presque Isle, 10,550		B 5
Richmond, 1,578		D 3
(3,072▲)		D 3
Rockland, 7,972	. . . .	D 3
Rumford, 6,256		D 2
(7,078▲)		D 2
Saco, 15,181	. . . .	E 2
Sanford, 10,268		E 2
(20,463▲)		E 2
Scarborough, 2,280		E 2
(12,518▲)		E 2
Skowhegan, 6,517		D 3
(8,725▲)		D 3
South Berwick, 2,120		E 2
(5,877▲)		E 2
South Portland, 23,163		E 2
Thomaston, 2,348		D 3
(3,306▲)		D 3
Topsham, 4,657		E 3
(8,746▲)		E 3
Waterville, 17,173		D 3
Westbrook, 16,121		E 2
Wilton, 2,262		D 2
(4,242▲)		D 2
Winslow, 5,903		D 3
(7,997▲)		D 3
Winthrop, 3,264		D 3
(5,968▲)		D 3
Yarmouth, 2,981		E 2
(7,862▲)		E 2
York, 3,130 (9,818▲)		E 2

▲ Population of entire town (township), including rural area.

96

Statute Miles

Kilometers

Longitude West of Greenwich

B-520520-01 —6-7-8ME
COSMO SERIES MAINE
Copyright by
RAND McNALLY & COMPANY
Made in U.S.A.

Lambert Conformal Conic Projection

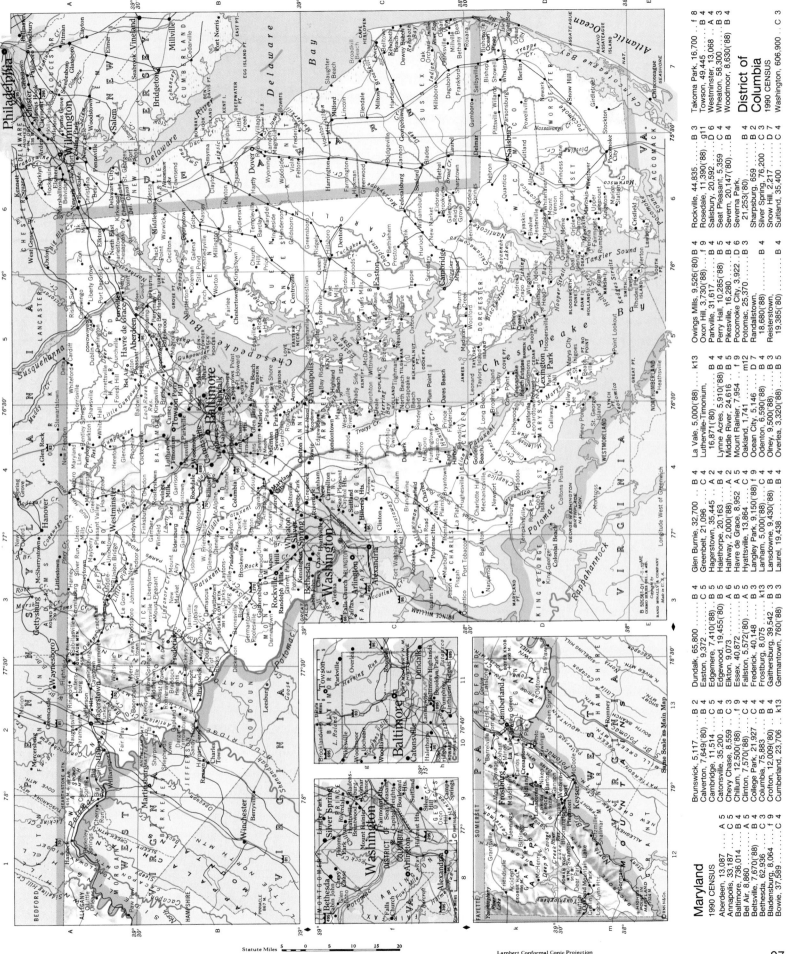

Statute Miles

Kilometers

Lambert Conformal Conic Projection

Maryland
1990 CENSUS

Aberdeen, 13,087	A	5
Annapolis, 33,187	C	4
Baltimore, 736,014	B	4
Bel Air, 8,860	A	5
Beltsville, 7,670(88)	B	4
Bethesda, 62,936	B	4
Bladensburg, 8,064	f	9
Bowie, 37,589	C	4
Brunswick, 5,117	B	3
Calverton, 7,649('80)	B	4
Cambridge, 11,514	C	5
Catonsville, 35,200	g	9
Chevy Chase, 8,559	C	3
Chillum, 12,500(88)	f	9
Clinton, 7,570('80)	C	4
College Park, 21,927	C	4
Columbia, 75,883	B	4
Crofton, 12,009('80)	f	9
Cumberland, 23,706	k13	
Dundalk, 65,800	B	4
Easton, 9,372	C	5
Edgemere, 7,410('88)	C	5
Edgewood, 19,455('80)	B	5
Elkton, 9,073	A	6
Essex, 40,872	B	4
Fallston, 5,572('80)	A	5
Frederick, 40,148	B	4
Frostburg, 8,075	k13	
Gaithersburg, 39,542	B	3
Germantown, 23,706	B	3
Glen Burnie, 32,700	B	4
Greenbelt, 21,096	C	4
Halethorpe, 20,163	g	9
Halfway, 2,000('88)	A	2
Havre de Grace, 8,952	A	5
Hyattsville, 13,864	C	4
La Vale, 5,000('88)	k13	
Lutherville-Timonium, 16,871(80)	B	4
Langley Park, 9,150(88)	f	9
Lanham, 5,000('88)	C	4
Lansdowne, 9,430(88)	B	4
Laurel, 19,438	B	4
Lynne Acres, 5,910('88)	B	4
Middle River, 24,616	B	5
Mount Rainier, 7,954	f	9
Oakland, 1,741	m12	
Ocean City, 5,146	D	7
Odenton, 6,590(88)	B	4
Olney, 9,500(88)	B	3
Overlea, 3,320(88)	B	4
Owings Mills, 9,526(80)	B	4
Oxon Hill, 3,730(88)	B	4
Parkville, 31,617	B	4
Perry Hall, 10,285('88)	B	5
Pikesville, 16,280	B	4
Pocomoke City, 3,922	D	6
Potomac, 25,370	B	3
Randallstown, 18,680(88)	B	4
Reisterstown, 19,385('80)	B	4
Rockville, 44,835	B	4
Rosedale, 11,390(88)	B	4
Salisbury, 20,592	D	6
Seat Pleasant, 5,359	C	4
Severn, 20,147(80)	B	4
Severna Park, 21,253('80)	B	3
Sharpsburg, 659	B	2
Silver Spring, 76,200	C	3
Snow Hill, 2,217	D	7
Suitland, 35,400	C	4
Takoma Park, 16,700	f	8
Towson, 49,445	B	4
Westminster, 13,068	B	3
Woodmoor, 8,630(88)	B	4

District of Columbia
1990 CENSUS

Washington, 606,900	C	3

Massachusetts

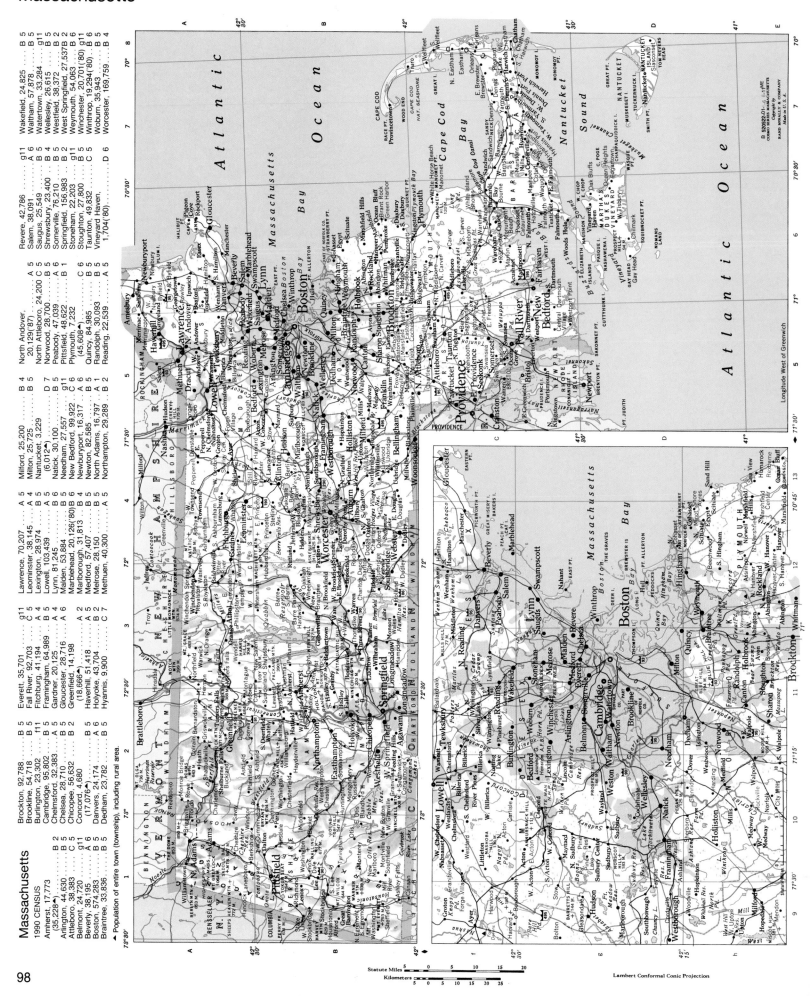

Massachusetts
1990 CENSUS

Amherst, 17,773 .... (35,228▲) .... B 5
Arlington, 44,630 .... B 5
Attleboro, 38,383 .... B 5
Belmont, 24,720 .... B 5
Beverly, 38,195 .... A 6
Boston, 574,283 .... B 5
Braintree, 33,836 .... B 5

Brockton, 92,788 .... B 5
Brookline, 54,718 .... B 5
Burlington, 23,302 .... f11
Cambridge, 95,802 .... B 5
Chelmsford, 32,383 .... A 5
Chelsea, 28,710 .... B 5
Chicopee, 56,632 .... B 2
Concord, 4,680 .... (17,076▲) .... B 5
Danvers, 24,174 .... A 6
Dedham, 33,782 .... B 5

Everett, 35,701 .... B 5
Fall River, 92,703 .... B 5
Fitchburg, 41,194 .... A 4
Framingham, 64,989 .... B 5
Gardner, 20,125 .... A 4
Gloucester, 28,716 .... A 6
Greenfield, 14,198 .... (18,666▲) .... A 2

Haverhill, 51,418 .... A 5
Holyoke, 43,704 .... B 2
Hyannis, 9,900 .... C 7

Lawrence, 70,207 .... A 5
Leominster, 38,145 .... A 4
Lexington, 28,974 .... A 4
Lowell, 103,439 .... A 5
Lynn, 81,245 .... A 6
Malden, 53,884 .... B 5
Marblehead, 20,126(80) .... B 6
New Bedford, 99,922 .... B 5
Newburyport, 16,317 .... A 2
Newton, 82,585 .... A 5
North Adams, 16,797 .... A 1
Northampton, 29,289 .... B 2

North Andover, 20,129('87) .... A 6
North Attleboro, 24,200 .... C 5
Norwood, 28,700 .... B 4
Peabody, 47,039 .... B 5
Pittsfield, 48,622 .... B 1
Plymouth, 7,232 .... (45,608▲) .... C 6
Quincy, 84,985 .... B 5
Randolph, 30,093 .... B 5
Reading, 22,539 .... A 5

Revere, 42,786 .... g11
Salem, 38,091 .... A 6
Saugus, 25,549 .... B 5
Shrewsbury, 23,400 .... B 4
Somerville, 76,210 .... B 5
Springfield, 156,983 .... B 2
Stoneham, 22,203 .... g11
Stoughton, 26,777 .... B 5
Taunton, 49,832 .... B 5

Wakefield, 24,825 .... B 5
Waltham, 57,878 .... B 5
Watertown, 33,284 .... g11
Wellesley, 26,615 .... B 5
Westfield, 38,372 .... B 2
West Springfield, 27,537 .... B 2
Weymouth, 54,063 .... B 6
Winchester, 20,701('80) g11
Winthrop, 19,294('80) .... B 6
Woburn, 35,943 .... B 5
Worcester, 169,759 .... B 4

▲ Population of entire town (township), including rural area.

98

Statute Miles

Kilometers

Lambert Conformal Conic Projection

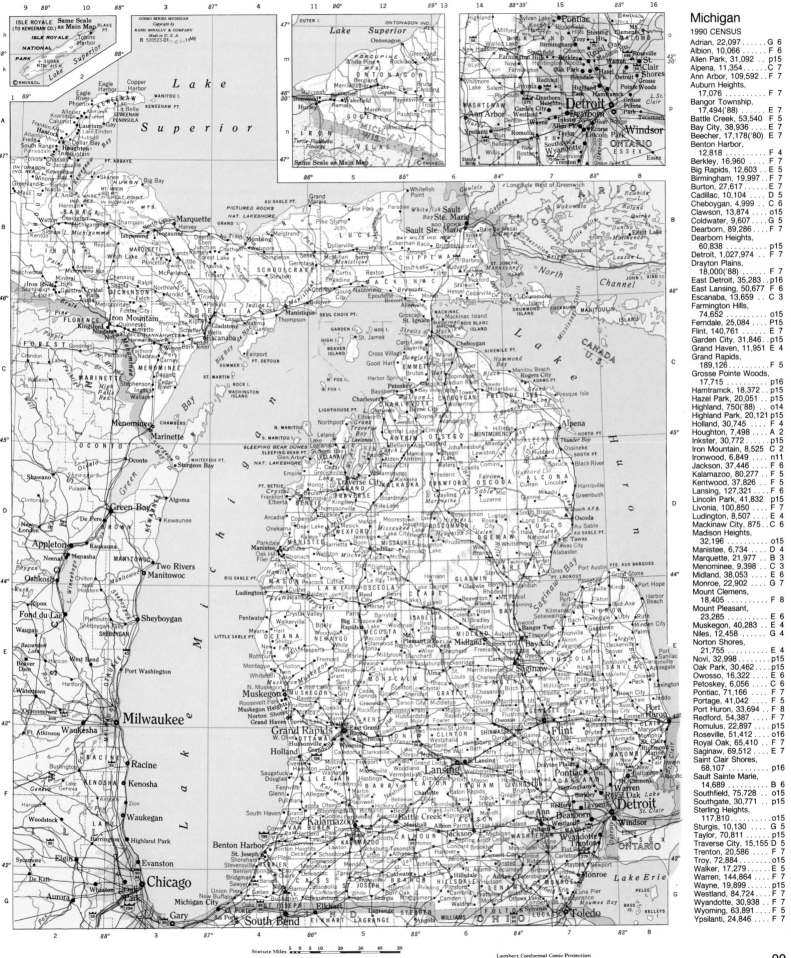

Michigan
1990 CENSUS

Adrian, 22,097 . . . . . . G 6
Albion, 10,066 . . . . F 6
Allen Park, 31,092 . . . p15
Alpena, 11,354 . . . . C 7
Ann Arbor, 109,592 . . F 7
Auburn Heights,
17,076 . . . . F 7
Bangor Township,
17,494('88) . . . . E 7
Battle Creek, 53,540 . . F 5
Bay City, 38,936 . . . . . E 7
Beecher, 17,178('80) . . E 7
Benton Harbor,
12,818 . . . . F 4
Berkley, 16,960 . . . . . F 7
Big Rapids, 12,603 . . E 5
Birmingham, 19,997 . . F 7
Burton, 27,617 . . . . . . E 7
Cadillac, 10,104 . . . . . D 5
Cheboygan, 4,999 . . . . C 6
Clawson, 13,874 . . . . o15
Coldwater, 9,607 . . . . G 5
Dearborn, 89,286 . . . . F 7
Dearborn Heights,
60,838 . . . . p15
Detroit, 1,027,974 . . . . F 7
Drayton Plains,
18,000('88) . . . . . . F 7
East Detroit, 35,283 . . p16
East Lansing, 50,677 . . F 6
Escanaba, 13,659 . . . . C 3
Farmington Hills,
74,652 . . . . o15
Ferndale, 25,084 . . . P15
Flint, 140,761 . . . . . . E 7
Garden City, 31,846 . . p15
Grand Haven, 11,951 E 4
Grand Rapids,
189,126 . . . . F 5
Grosse Pointe Woods,
17,715 . . . . p16
Hamtramck, 18,372 . . p15
Hazel Park, 20,051 . . p15
Highland, 750('88) . . o14
Highland Park, 20,121 p15
Holland, 30,745 . . . . F 4
Houghton, 7,498 . . . . A 2
Inkster, 30,772 . . . . . p15
Iron Mountain, 8,525 C 2
Ironwood, 6,849 . . . . n11
Jackson, 37,446 . . . . . F 6
Kalamazoo, 80,277 . . F 5
Kentwood, 37,826 . . . F 5
Lansing, 127,321 . . . . F 6
Lincoln Park, 41,832 p15
Livonia, 100,850 . . . . F 7
Ludington, 8,507 . . . . D 4
Mackinaw City, 875 . . C 6
Madison Heights,
32,196 . . . . o15
Manistee, 6,734 . . . . D 4
Marquette, 21,977 . . B 3
Menominee, 9,398 . . C 3
Midland, 38,053 . . . . E 6
Monroe, 22,902 . . . . G 7
Mount Clemens,
18,405 . . . . F 8
Mount Pleasant,
23,285 . . . . E 6
Muskegon, 40,283 . . E 4
Niles, 12,458 . . . . . . G 4
Norton Shores,
21,755 . . . . E 4
Novi, 32,998 . . . . p15
Oak Park, 30,462 . . . p15
Owosso, 16,322 . . . . E 6
Petoskey, 6,056 . . . . C 6
Pontiac, 71,166 . . . . F 7
Portage, 41,042 . . . . F 5
Port Huron, 33,694 . . F 8
Redford, 54,387 . . . . F 7
Romulus, 22,897 . . . p15
Roseville, 51,412 . . . o16
Royal Oak, 65,410 . . F 7
Saginaw, 69,512 . . . E 7
Saint Clair Shores,
68,107 . . . . p16
Sault Sainte Marie,
14,689 . . . . B 6
Southfield, 75,728 . . o15
Southgate, 30,771 . . p15
Sterling Heights,
117,810 . . . . o15
Sturgis, 10,130 . . . . G 5
Taylor, 70,811 . . . . . p15
Traverse City, 15,155 D 5
Trenton, 20,586 . . . . F 7
Troy, 72,884 . . . . . . o15
Walker, 17,279 . . . . E 5
Warren, 144,864 . . . F 7
Wayne, 19,899 . . . . p15
Westland, 84,724 . . . F 7
Wyandotte, 30,938 . . F 7
Wyoming, 63,891 . . . F 5
Ypsilanti, 24,846 . . . . F 7

Minnesota

1990 CENSUS

Albert Lea, 18,310 .. G 5
Alexandria, 7,838 .... E 3
Andover, 15,216 .... m12
Anoka, 17,192 ...... E 5
Apple Valley, 34,598 n12
Austin, 21,907 ...... G 6
Bemidji, 11,245 .... C 4
Blaine, 38,975 ...... m12
Bloomington, 86,335 F 5
Brainerd, 12,353 .... D 4
Brooklyn Center, 28,887 .... E 5
Brooklyn Park, 56,381 .... m12
Burnsville, 51,288 .... F 5
Champlin, 16,849 .. m12
Chisholm, 5,290 ... C 6
Cloquet, 10,885 .... D 6
Columbia Heights, 18,910 .... m12
Coon Rapids, 52,978 E 5
Cottage Grove, 22,935 .... n13
Crookston, 8,119 .... C 2
Crystal, 23,788 .... m12
Detroit Lakes, 6,635 D 3
Duluth, 85,493 ...... D 6
Eagan, 47,409 ...... n12
East Bethel, 8,050 .. E 5
East Grand Forks, 8,658 .... C 2
Eden Prairie, 39,311 .. n12
Edina, 46,070 ...... F 5
Ely, 3,968 .... C 7
Fairmont, 11,265 .... G 4
Faribault, 17,085 .... F 5
Fergus Falls, 12,362 D 2
Fridley, 28,335 ...... m12
Golden Valley, 20,971 n12
Grand Marais, 1,171 k 9
Grand Rapids, 7,976 C 5
Hastings, 15,445 .... F 6
Hibbing, 18,046 .... C 6
Hopkins, 16,534 .... n12
Hutchinson, 11,523 .. F 4
International Falls, 8,325 .... B 5
Inver Grove Heights, 22,477 .... n12
Lakeville, 24,854 .... F 5
Litchfield, 6,041 .... E 4
Little Falls, 7,232 .... E 4
Mankato, 31,477 .... F 5
Maple Grove, 38,736 m12
Maplewood, 30,954 .. n12
Marshall, 12,023 .... F 3
Minneapolis, 368,383 F 5
Minnetonka, 48,370 .. n12
Montevideo, 5,499 .. F 3
Moorhead, 32,295 .. D 2
Morris, 5,613 ...... E 3
Mound, 9,634 ...... n11
Mounds View, 12,541 m12
New Brighton, 22,207 m12
New Hope, 21,853 .. m12
New Ulm, 13,132 .... F 4
Northfield, 14,684 .. F 5
North Mankato, 10,164 .... F 4
North St. Paul, 12,376 .... m13
Owatonna, 19,386 .. F 5
Pipestone, 4,554 .... G 2
Plymouth, 50,889 .. m12
Prior Lake, 11,482 .. F 5
Ramsey, 12,408 .... E 5
Red Wing, 15,134 .. F 6
Redwood Falls, 4,859 F 3
Richfield, 35,710 .... F 5
Robbinsdale, 14,396 m12
Rochester, 70,745 .. F 6
Roseville, 33,485 .... m12
Saint Cloud, 48,812 .. E 4
Saint Louis Park, 43,787 .... n12
Saint Paul, 272,235 .. F 5
Saint Peter, 9,421 .. F 5
Shakopee, 11,739 .. F 5
Shoreview, 24,587 .. m12
South St. Paul, 20,197 .... n12
Stillwater, 13,882 .. E 6
Thief River Falls, 8,010 .... B 2
Virginia, 9,410 ...... C 6
Waseca, 8,385 ...... F 5
West Saint Paul, 19,248 .... n12
White Bear Lake, 24,704 .... E 5
Willmar, 17,531 .... E 3
Winona, 25,399 .... F 7
Woodbury, 20,075 .. F 6
Worthington, 9,977 .. G 3

Statute Miles 5 0 5 10 20 30 40 50

Kilometers 5 0 5 15 25 35 45 55 65

Lambert Conformal Conic Projection

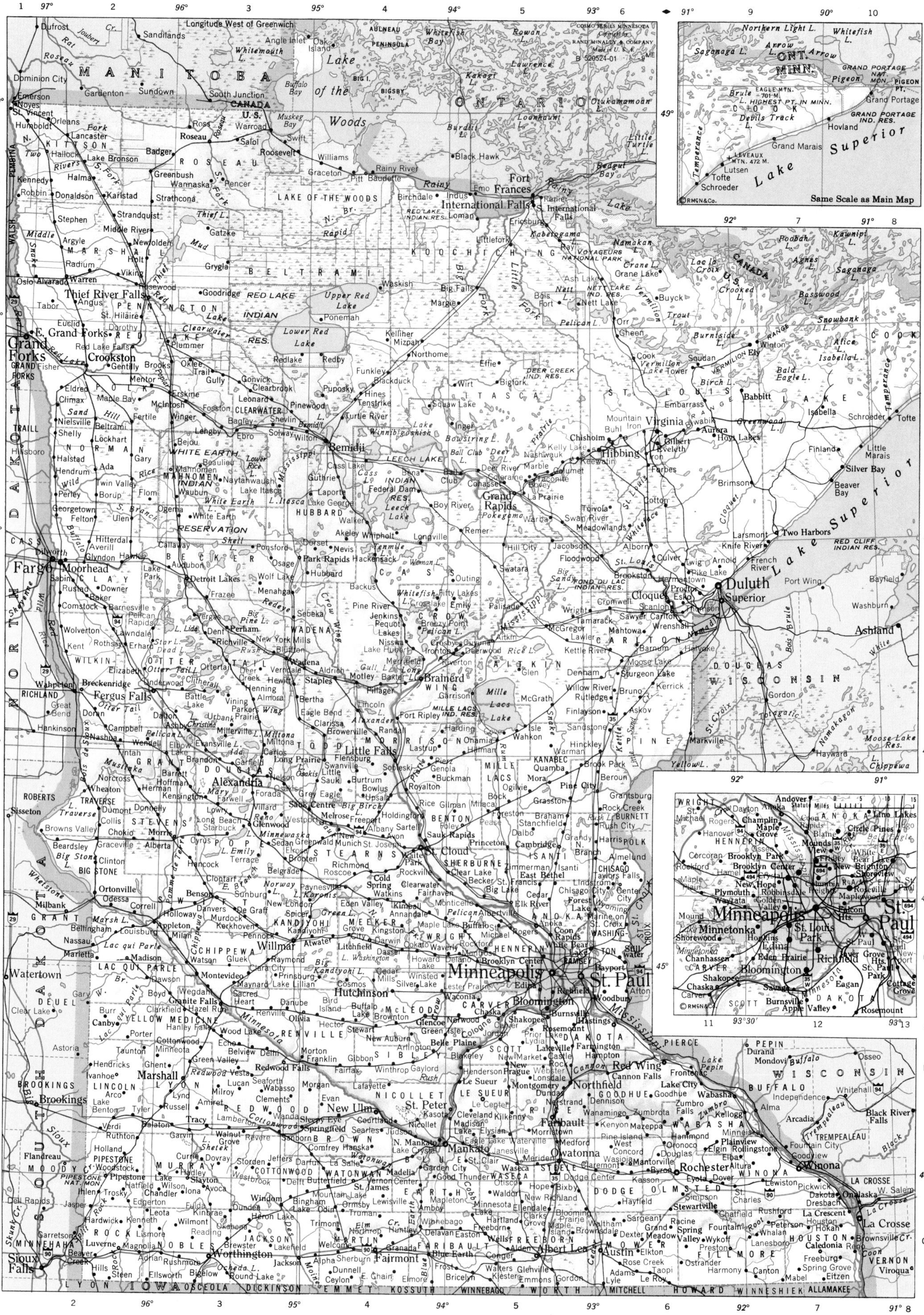

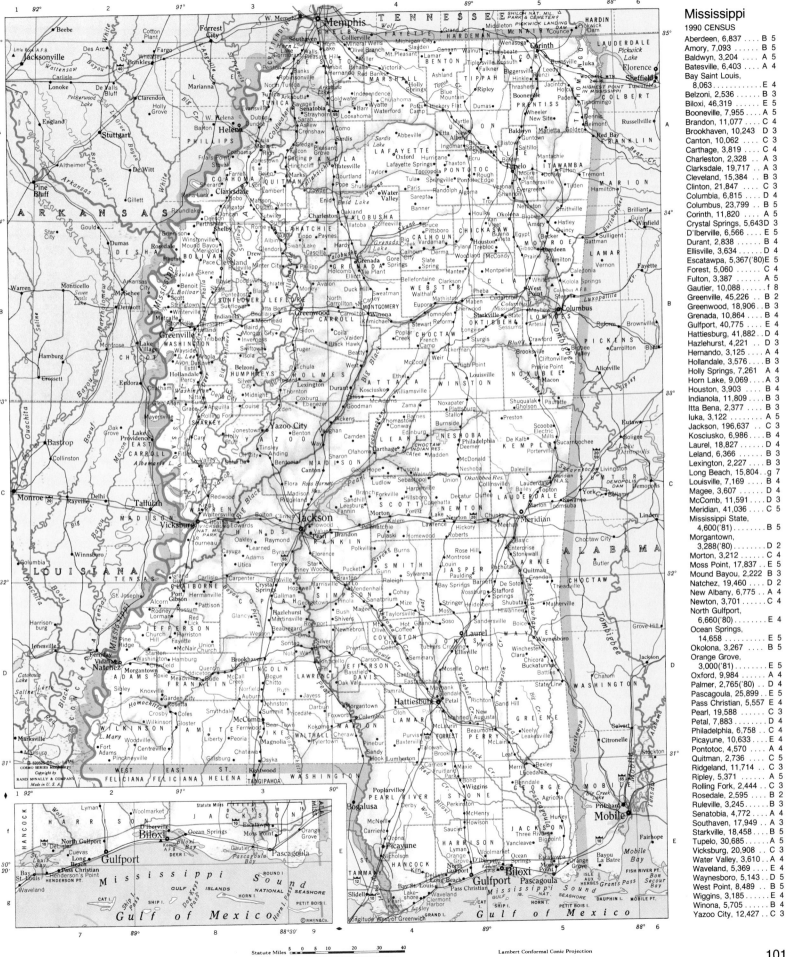

Mississippi

1990 CENSUS

Aberdeen, 6,837 .... B 5
Amory, 7,093 ...... A 5
Baldwyn, 3,204 .... A 5
Batesville, 6,403 .... A 4
Bay Saint Louis,
  8,063 .... E 4
Belzoni, 2,536 ...... B 3
Biloxi, 46,319 ...... E 5
Booneville, 7,955 ... A 5
Brandon, 11,077 .... C 4
Brookhaven, 10,243 D 3
Canton, 10,062 .... C 3
Carthage, 3,819 .... C 4
Charleston, 2,328 ... A 3
Clarksdale, 19,717 .. A 3
Cleveland, 15,384 .. B 3
Clinton, 21,847 ..... C 3
Columbia, 6,815 .... D 4
Columbus, 23,799 .. B 5
Corinth, 11,820 .... A 5
Crystal Springs, 5,643 D 3
D'Iberville, 6,566 ... E 5
Durant, 2,838 ...... B 4
Ellisville, 3,634 ...... D 4
Escatawpa, 5,367('80)E 5
Forest, 5,060 ...... C 4
Fulton, 3,387 ...... A 5
Gautier, 10,088 ...... f 8
Greenville, 45,226 ... B 2
Greenwood, 18,906 . B 3
Grenada, 10,864 .... B 4
Gulfport, 40,775 .... E 4
Hattiesburg, 41,882 . D 4
Hazlehurst, 4,221 ... D 3
Hernando, 3,125 .... A 4
Hollandale, 3,576 ... B 3
Holly Springs, 7,261 . A 4
Horn Lake, 9,069 .... A 3
Houston, 3,903 .... B 4
Indianola, 11,809 ... B 3
Itta Bena, 2,377 .... B 3
Iuka, 3,122 .... A 5
Jackson, 196,637 ... C 3
Kosciusko, 6,986 ... B 4
Laurel, 18,827 ...... D 4
Leland, 6,366 ...... B 3
Lexington, 2,227 ... B 3
Long Beach, 15,804 .. g 7
Louisville, 7,169 .... B 4
Magee, 3,607 ...... D 4
McComb, 11,591 .... D 3
Meridian, 41,036 ... C 5
Mississippi State,
  4,600('81) ...... B 5
Morgantown,
  3,288('80) .... D 2
Morton, 3,212 ...... C 4
Moss Point, 17,837 .. E 5
Mound Bayou, 2,222 B 3
Natchez, 19,460 ... D 2
New Albany, 6,775 .. A 4
Newton, 3,701 ...... C 4
North Gulfport,
  6,660('80) ...... E 4
Ocean Springs,
  14,658 .... E 5
Okolona, 3,267 ... B 5
Orange Grove,
  3,000('81) ...... E 5
Oxford, 9,984 ...... A 4
Palmer, 2,765('80) .. D 4
Pascagoula, 25,899 . E 5
Pass Christian, 5,557 E 4
Pearl, 19,588 ...... C 3
Petal, 7,883 ...... D 4
Philadelphia, 6,758 . C 4
Picayune, 10,633 .... E 4
Pontotoc, 4,570 .... A 4
Quitman, 2,736 .... C 5
Ridgeland, 11,714 .. C 3
Ripley, 5,371 ...... A 4
Rolling Fork, 2,444 .. C 3
Rosedale, 2,595 .... B 2
Ruleville, 3,245 .... B 3
Senatobia, 4,772 .... A 4
Southaven, 17,949 .. A 3
Starkville, 18,458 ... B 5
Tupelo, 30,685 ...... A 5
Vicksburg, 20,908 .. C 3
Water Valley, 3,610 .. A 4
Waveland, 5,369 .... E 4
Waynesboro, 5,143 .. D 5
West Point, 8,489 ... B 5
Wiggins, 3,185 ...... E 4
Winona, 5,705 ...... B 4
Yazoo City, 12,427 .. C 3

Missouri

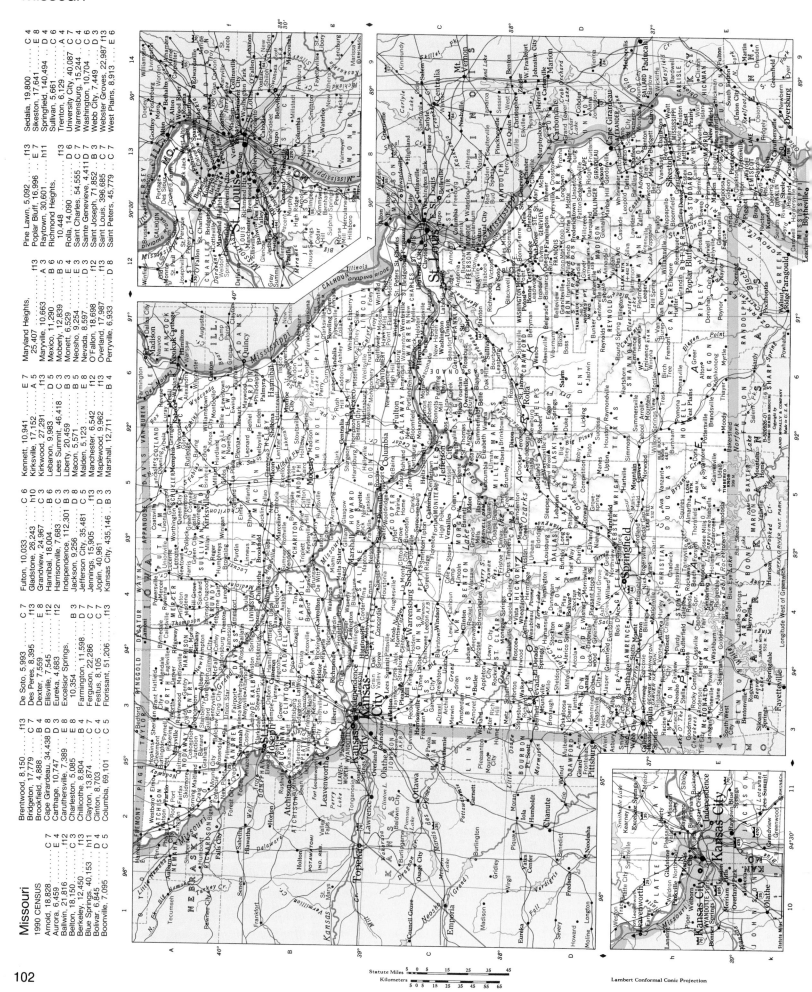

Missouri
1990 CENSUS

Arnold, 18,828	C 7	Sedalia, 19,800	C 4
Aurora, 6,459	E 4	Sikeston, 17,641	E 8
Ballwin, 21,816	f12	Springfield, 140,494	D 4
Belton, 18,150	C 3	Sullivan, 5,661	C 6
Berkeley, 12,450	f13	Trenton, 6,129	A 4
Blue Springs, 40,153	B 3	University City, 40,087	C 7
Bolivar, 6,845	D 4	Warrensburg, 15,244	C 4
Boonville, 7,095	C 5	Washington, 10,704	C 6
		Webb City, 7,449	D 3
Brentwood, 8,150	C 7	Webster Groves, 22,987	f13
Bridgeton, 17,779	B 4	West Plains, 8,913	E 6
Brookfield, 4,888	B 4		
Cape Girardeau, 34,438	D 8	Pine Lawn, 5,092	C 7
Carthage, 10,747	E 3	Poplar Bluff, 16,996	E 7
Caruthersville, 7,389	E 8	Raytown, 30,601	h11
Charleston, 5,085	E 8	Richmond Heights,	
Chillicothe, 8,804	B 4	10,448	f13
Clayton, 13,874	C 7	Rolla, 14,090	D 6
Clinton, 8,703	C 4	Saint Charles, 54,555	C 7
Columbia, 69,101	C 5	Sainte Genevieve, 4,411	D 7
		Saint Joseph, 71,852	B 3
De Soto, 5,993	C 7	Saint Peters, 45,779	C 7
Des Peres, 8,395	f13	Saint Louis, 396,685	C 7
Dexter, 7,559	E 8	O'Fallon, 18,698	f12
Ellisville, 7,545	f12	Overland, 17,987	D 3
Eureka, 4,683	f12	Perryville, 6,933	D 8
Excelsior Springs,			
10,354	B 3	Maryland Heights,	
Farmington, 11,598	D 7	25,407	E 7
Ferguson, 22,286	C 7	Maryville, 10,663	A 3
Festus, 8,105	C 7	Mexico, 11,290	B 6
Florissant, 51,206	f13	Moberly, 12,839	B 5
		Monett, 6,529	E 4
Fulton, 10,033	C 6	Neosho, 9,254	E 3
Gladstone, 26,243	h10	Nevada, 8,597	D 3
Grandview, 24,967	B 6		
Hannibal, 18,004	B 6	Jackson, 9,256	D 8
Harrisonville, 7,683	B 3	Jefferson City, 35,481	C 5
Independence, 112,301	B 3	Jennings, 15,905	f13
Liberty, 20,459	B 3	Joplin, 40,961	D 3
Macon, 5,571	B 5	Kansas City, 435,146	B 3
Malden, 5,123	E 8		
Manchester, 6,542	f13		
Maplewood, 9,962	C 7		
Marshall, 12,711	B 4		
Kennett, 10,941	E 7		
Kirksville, 17,152	f13		
Kirkwood, 27,291	f13		
Lebanon, 9,983	D 5		
Lees Summit, 46,418	C 3		

Statute Miles

Kilometers

Lambert Conformal Conic Projection

Montana

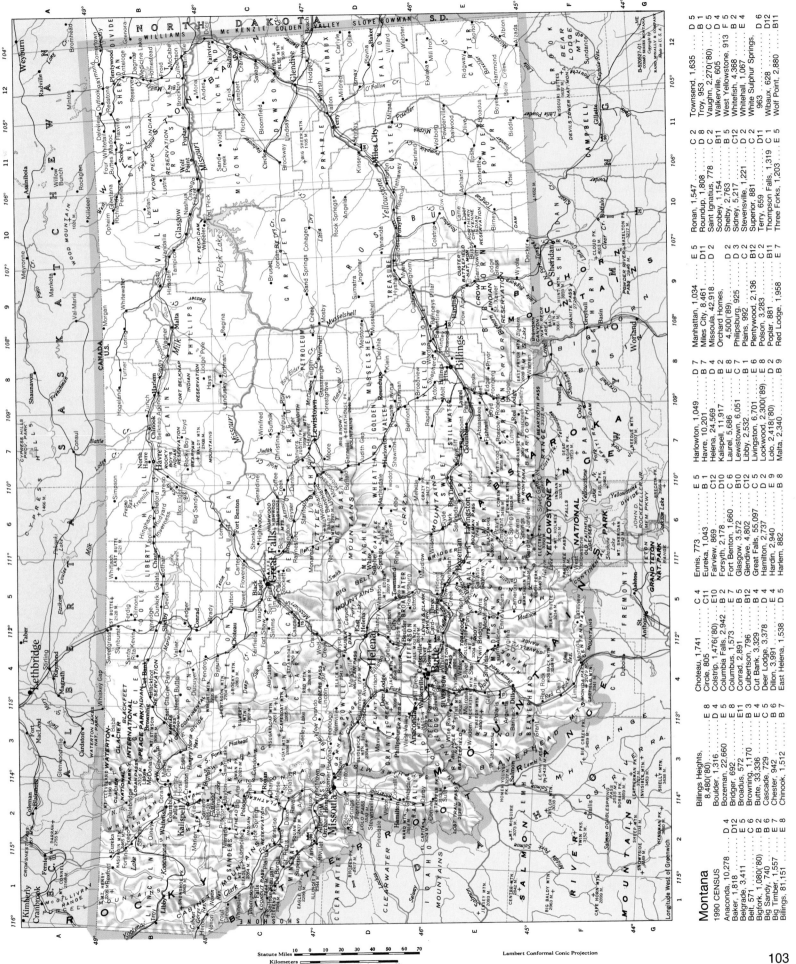

Lambert Conformal Conic Projection

Statute Miles 10 0 10 20 30 40 50 60 70

Kilometers 10 0 10 20 30 40 50 60 70 80 90

Longitude West of Greenwich

Montana

1990 CENSUS

Anaconda, 10,278	D 4	
Baker, 1,818	D12	
Belgrade, 3,411	C 6	
Belt, 571	C 6	
Bigfork, 1,080('80)	B 2	
Big Sandy, 740	B 6	
Big Timber, 1,557	D 7	
Billings, 81,151	E 8	

Billings Heights,		
8,480('80).	E 8	
Boulder, 1,316.	D 5	
Bozeman, 22,660	E 5	
Bridger, 692	E11	
Broadus, 572	E11	
Browning, 1,170	B 3	
Butte, 33,336	D 4	
Cascade, 729	C 5	
Chester, 942	B 6	
Chinook, 1,512	B 7	

Choteau, 1,741	C 4	
Circle, 805	C11	
Columbia Falls, 2,942.	B 2	
Columbus, 1,573	D10	
Conrad, 2,891	C 6	
Culbertson, 796	B12	
Cut Bank, 3,329	B 4	
Deer Lodge, 3,378	D 4	
Dillon, 3,991	E 4	
East Helena, 1,538	D 5	

Ennis, 773	E 5	
Eureka, 1,043	B 1	
Fairview, 869	C12	
Forsyth, 2,178	D10	
Fort Benton, 1,660	C 6	
Glasgow, 3,572	B 10	
Glendive, 4,802	C12	
Great Falls, 55,097	C 5	
Hamilton, 2,737	D 4	
Hardin, 2,940	E 9	
Harlem, 882	B 8	

Harlowton, 1,049	D 7	
Havre, 10,201	B 4	
Helena, 24,569	D 4	
Kalispell, 11,917	B 2	
Laurel, 5,686	C 7	
Lewistown, 6,051	C 7	
Libby, 2,532	B 1	
Livingston, 6,701	E 6	
Lockwood, 2,300('89)	E 8	
Lolo, 2,418('80)	B 2	
Malta, 2,340	B 8	

Manhattan, 1,034	D 7	
Miles City, 8,461	D11	
Missoula, 42,918	D 2	
Orchard Homes,		
4,500('89)	D 2	
Philipsburg, 925	D 3	
Plains, 992	C 2	
Plentywood, 2,136	B12	
Polson, 3,283	C 2	
Poplar, 881	B11	
Red Lodge, 1,958	E 7	

Ronan, 1,547	C 2	
Roundup, 1,808	D 8	
Saint Ignatius, 778	C 2	
Scobey, 1,154	B11	
Shelby, 2,763	B 5	
Sidney, 5,217	C12	
Stevensville, 1,221	D 2	
Superior, 881	C 2	
Terry, 659	D11	
Thompson Falls, 1,319	C 1	
Three Forks, 1,203	E 5	

Townsend, 1,635	D 5	
Troy, 953.	B 1	
Vaughn, 2,270('80)	C 5	
Walkerville, 605	D 4	
West Yellowstone, 913	F 5	
Whitefish, 4,368	B 2	
Whitehall, 1,067	E 4	
White Sulphur Springs,		
963	D 6	
Wibaux, 628	D12	
Wolf Point, 2,880	B11	

103

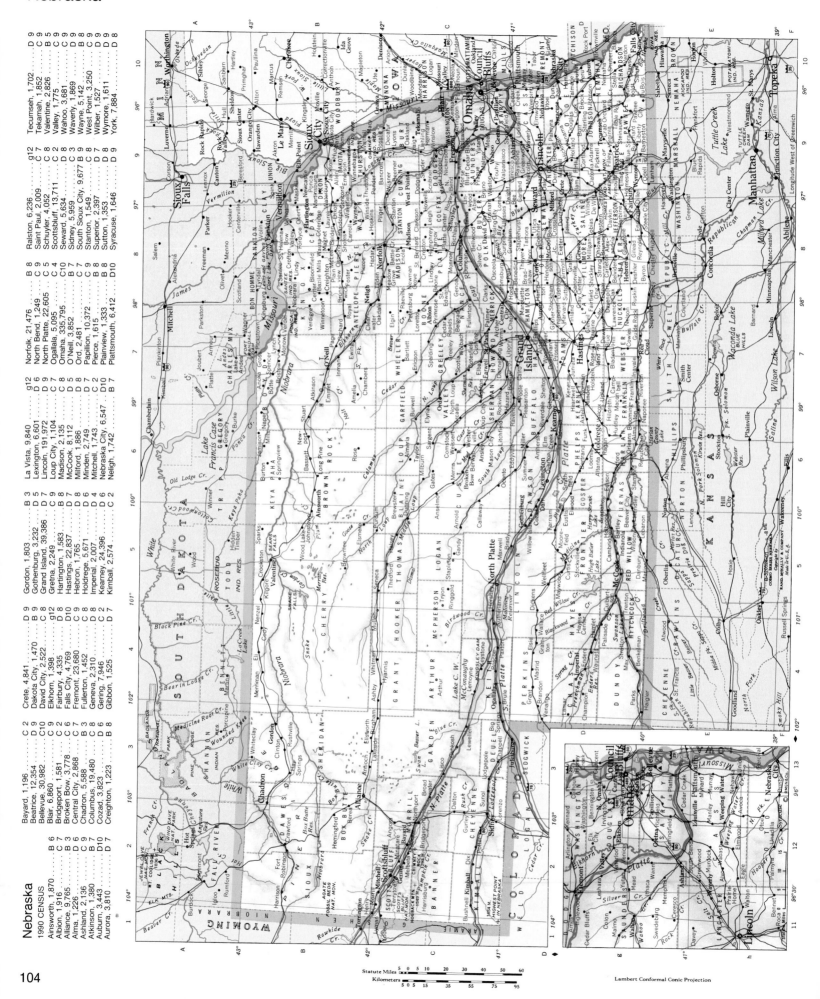

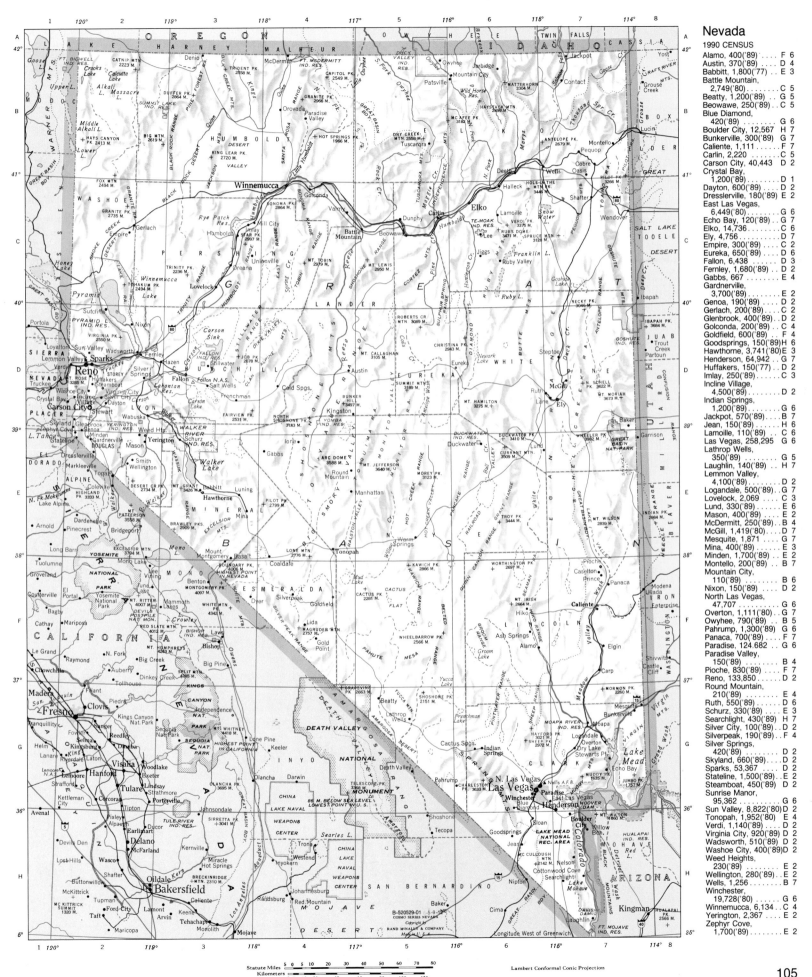

Nevada

1990 CENSUS

Alamo, 400('89) . . . . . . F 6
Austin, 370('89) . . . . . . D 4
Babbitt, 1,800('77) . . . . E 3
Battle Mountain,
    2,749('80) . . . . . . C 5
Beatty, 1,200('89) . . . . G 5
Beowawe, 250('89) . . . . C 5
Blue Diamond,
    420('89) . . . . G 6
Boulder City, 12,567 . . H 7
Bunkerville, 300('89) . . G 7
Caliente, 1,111 . . . . . . F 7
Carlin, 2,220 . . . . C 5
Carson City, 40,443 . . D 2
Crystal Bay,
    1,200('89) . . . . . . D 1
Dayton, 600('89) . . . . D 2
Dresslerville, 180('89) . E 2
East Las Vegas,
    6,449('80) . . . . . . G 6
Echo Bay, 120('89) . . . G 7
Elko, 14,736 . . . . C 6
Ely, 4,756 . . . . D 7
Empire, 300('89) . . . . C 2
Eureka, 650('89) . . . . D 6
Fallon, 6,438 . . . . D 3
Fernley, 1,680('89) . . . D 2
Gabbs, 667 . . . . E 4
Gardnerville,
    3,700('89) . . . . . . E 2
Genoa, 190('89) . . . . . D 2
Gerlach, 200('89) . . . . C 2
Glenbrook, 400('89) . . D 2
Golconda, 200('89) . . . C 4
Goldfield, 600('89) . . . F 4
Goodsprings, 150('89)H 6
Hawthorne, 3,741('80)E 3
Henderson, 64,942 . . G 7
Huffakers, 150('77) . . . D 2
Imlay, 250('89) . . . . . . C 3
Incline Village,
    4,500('89) . . . . . . D 2
Indian Springs,
    1,200('89) . . . . . . G 6
Jackpot, 570('89) . . . . B 7
Jean, 150('89) . . . . . . H 6
Lamoille, 110('89) . . . . C 6
Las Vegas, 258,295 . . G 6
Lathrop Wells,
    350('89) . . . . G 5
Laughlin, 140('89) . . . . H 7
Lemmon Valley,
    4,100('89) . . . . . . D 2
Logandale, 500('89) . . G 7
Lovelock, 2,069 . . . . . C 3
Lund, 330('89) . . . . . . E 6
Mason, 400('89) . . . . . E 2
McDermitt, 250('89) . . B 4
McGill, 1,419('80) . . . . D 7
Mesquite, 1,871 . . . . . G 7
Mina, 400('89) . . . . . . E 3
Minden, 1,700('89) . . . D 2
Montello, 200('89) . . . B 7
Mountain City,
    110('89) . . . . B 6
Nixon, 150('89) . . . . . D 2
North Las Vegas,
    47,707 . . . . G 6
Overton, 1,111('80) . . . G 7
Owyhee, 790('89) . . . . B 5
Pahrump, 1,300('89) . . G 6
Panaca, 700('89) . . . . F 7
Paradise, 124.682 . . . G 6
Paradise Valley,
    150('89) . . . . B 4
Pioche, 830('89) . . . . . F 7
Reno, 133,850 . . . . . . D 2
Round Mountain,
    210('89) . . . . E 4
Ruth, 550('89) . . . . . . D 7
Schurz, 330('89) . . . . E 2
Searchlight, 430('89) . . H 7
Silver City, 100('89) . . D 2
Silverpeak, 190('89) . . F 4
Silver Springs,
    420('89) . . . . D 2
Skyland, 660('89) . . . . D 2
Sparks, 53,367 . . . . . . D 2
Stateline, 1,500('89) . . D 2
Steamboat, 450('89) . . D 2
Sunrise Manor,
    95,362 . . . . G 6
Sun Valley, 8,822('80)D 2
Tonopah, 1,952('80) . . E 4
Verdi, 1,140('89) . . . . D 2
Virginia City, 920('89) D 2
Wadsworth, 510('89) . . D 2
Washoe City, 400('89)D 2
Weed Heights,
    230('89) . . . . E 2
Wellington, 280('89) . . E 2
Wells, 1,256 . . . . B 7
Winchester,
    19,728('80) . . . . . G 6
Winnemucca, 6,134 . . C 4
Yerington, 2,367 . . . . E 2
Zephyr Cove,
    1,700('89) . . . . . . E 2

New Hampshire

New Hampshire
1990 CENSUS

Alton, 975 (3,286▲)..D 4
Amherst, 850
 (9,068▲) ...... E 3
Antrim, 1,142
 (2,360▲) ...... D 3
Ashland, 1,479
 (1,915▲) ...... C 3
Bedford, 1,400
 (12,563▲) ..... E 3
Berlin, 11,824 ... B 4
Bristol, 1,258
 (2,537▲) ...... C 3
Charlestown, 1,294
 (4,630▲) ...... D 2
Claremont, 13,902 . D 2
Colebrook, 1,131
 (2,444▲) ...... g 7
Concord, 36,006 .. D 3
Conway, 1,781
 (7,940▲) ...... C 4
Derry, 12,248
 (29,603▲) ..... E 4
Dover, 25,042 .... D 5
Durham, 8,448
 (11,818▲) ..... D 5
Enfield, 1,581
 (3,979▲) ...... C 2
Epping, 1,384
 (5,162▲) ...... D 4
Exeter, 8,947
 (12,481▲) ..... E 5
Farmington, 3,284
 (5,739▲) ...... D 4
Franklin, 8,304 ... D 3
Goffstown, 2,700
 (14,621▲) ..... E 4
Gorham, 2,180
 (3,173▲) ...... B 4
Greenville, 1,447
 (2,231▲) ...... E 3
Hampton, 6,779
 (12,278▲) ..... E 5
Hanover, 6,861
 (9,212▲) ...... C 2
Henniker, 1,538
 (4,151▲) ...... D 3
Hinsdale, 1,546
 (3,936▲) ...... E 2
Hooksett, 1,868
 (8,767▲) ...... D 4
Hudson, 6,248
 (19,530▲) ..... E 4
Jaffrey, 2,684
 (5,361▲) ...... E 2
Keene, 22,430 .... E 2
Laconia, 15,743 ... C 4
Lancaster, 2,134
 (3,522▲) ...... B 3
Lebanon, 12,183 .. C 2
Lisbon, 1,151
 (1,664▲) ...... B 3
Littleton, 4,480
 (5,827▲) ...... B 3
Manchester, 99,567 . E 4
Marlborough, 1,184
 (1,927▲) ...... E 2
Meredith, 1,202
 (4,837▲) ...... C 3
Merrimack, 1,300
 (22,156▲) ..... E 4
Milford, 6,269
 (11,795▲) ..... E 3
Milton, 1,000 (3,691▲)D 5
Nashua, 79,662 ... E 4
New London, 1,335
 (3,180▲) ...... D 3
Newmarket, 3,749
 (7,157▲) ...... D 5
Newport, 4,388
 (6,110▲) ...... D 2
Northfield, 1,375
 (4,263▲) ...... D 3
North Hampton, 1,000
 (3,637▲) ...... E 5
Peterborough, 2,100
 (5,239▲) ...... E 3
Pittsfield, 1,584
 (3,701▲) ...... D 4
Plaistow, 1,850
 (7,316▲) ...... E 4
Plymouth, 3,628
 (5,811▲) ...... C 3
Portsmouth, 25,925 . D 5
Raymond, 1,192
 (8,713▲) ...... D 4
Rochester, 26,630 . D 5
Rollinsford, 1,173
 (2,645▲) ...... D 5
Rye, 835 (4,612▲) . D 5
Salem, 12,000
 (25,746▲) ..... E 4
Somersworth, 11,249 D 5
Tilton, 1,380 (3,240▲) D 3
Troy, 1,318 (2,097▲) . E 2
Whitefield, 1,005
 (1,909▲) ...... B 3
Winchester, 1,732
 (4,038▲) ...... E 2
Wolfeboro, 2,000
 (4,807▲) ...... C 4

▲ Population of entire town (township), including rural area.

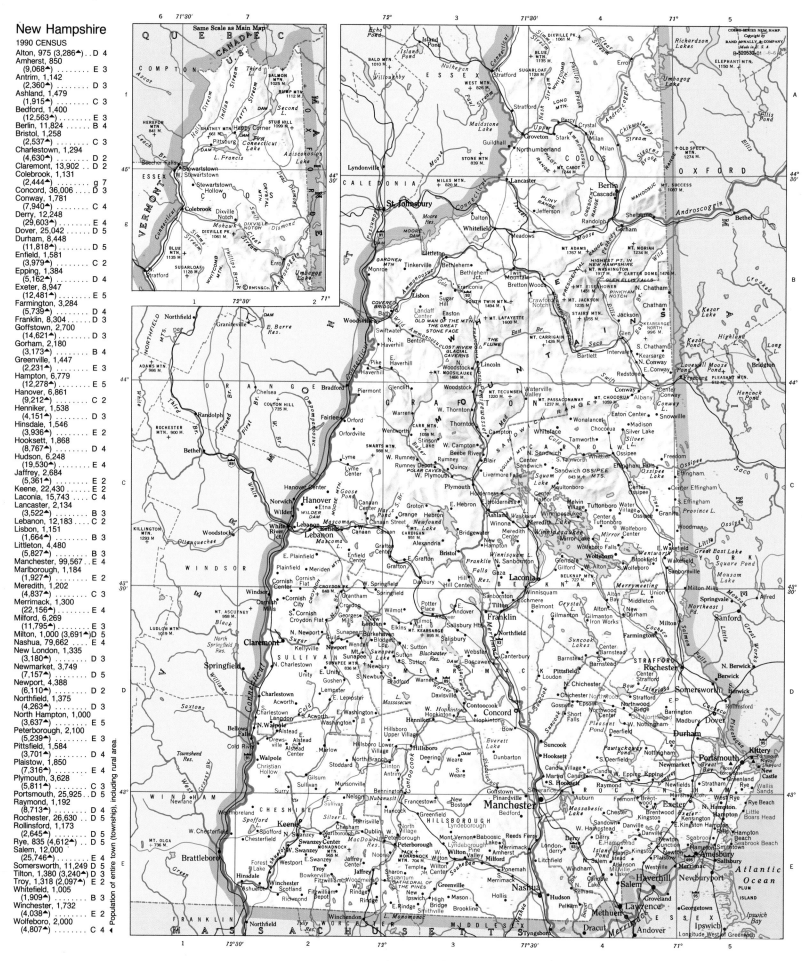

Statute Miles

Kilometers

Lambert Conformal Conic Projection

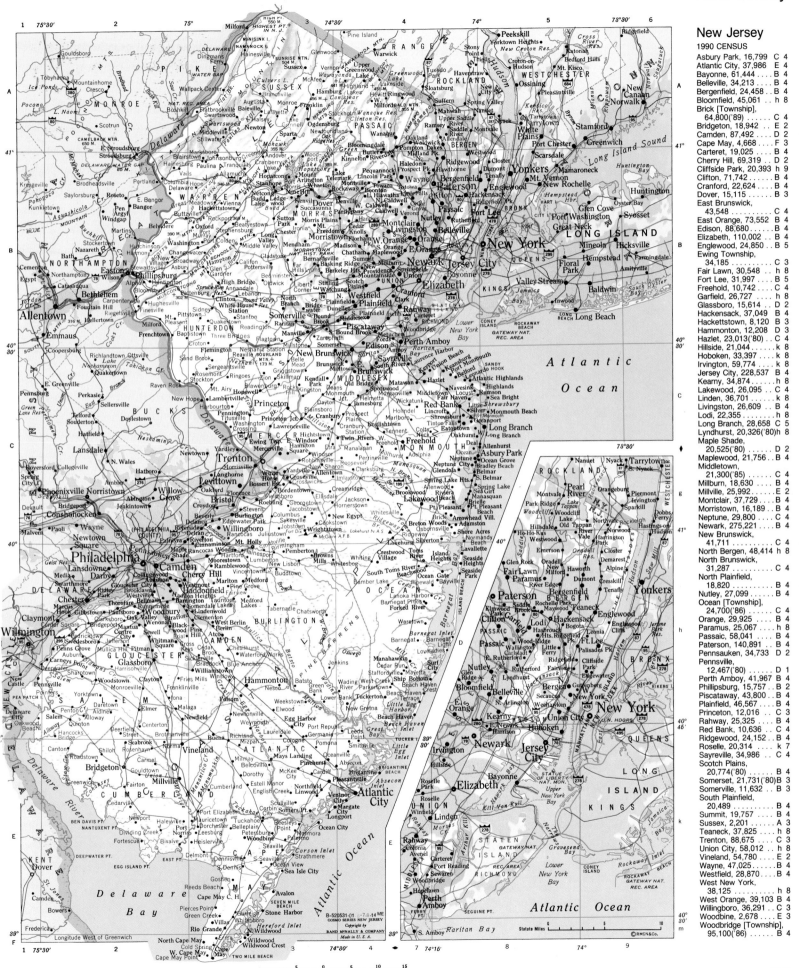

Asbury Park, 16,799 . . C 4
Atlantic City, 37,986 . . E 4
Bayonne, 61,444 . . . . B 4
Belleville, 34,213 . . . B 4
Bergenfield, 24,458 . . B 4
Bloomfield, 45,061 . . h 8
Brick [Township],
  64,800('89) . . . . . . C 4
Bridgeton, 18,942 . . E 2
Camden, 87,492 . . . . D 2
Cape May, 4,668 . . . . F 3
Carteret, 19,025 . . . . B 4
Cherry Hill, 69,319 . . D 2
Cliffside Park, 20,393 h 9
Clifton, 71,742 . . . . B 4
Cranford, 22,624 . . . . B 4
Dover, 15,115 . . . . . B 3
East Brunswick,
  43,548 . . . . C 4
East Orange, 73,552 B 4
Edison, 88,680 . . . . B 4
Elizabeth, 110,002 . . B 4
Englewood, 24,850 . . B 5
Ewing Township,
  34,185 . . . . C 3
Fair Lawn, 30,548 . . h 8
Fort Lee, 31,997 . . . B 5
Freehold, 10,742 . . . C 4
Garfield, 26,727 . . . . h 8
Glassboro, 15,614 . . D 2
Hackensack, 37,049 . . B 4
Hackettstown, 8,120 . . B 3
Hammonton, 12,208 . . D 3
Hazlet, 23,013('80) . . C 4
Hillside, 21,044 . . . . k 8
Hoboken, 33,397 . . . k 8
Irvington, 59,774 . . . . k 8
Jersey City, 228,537 B 4
Kearny, 34,874 . . . . h 8
Lakewood, 26,095 . . C 4
Linden, 36,701 . . . . k 8
Livingston, 26,609 . . h 8
Lodi, 22,355 . . . . . . h 8
Long Branch, 28,658 C 5
Lyndhurst, 20,326('80)h 8
Maple Shade,
  20,525('80) . . . . D 2
Maplewood, 21,756 . . B 4
Middletown,
  21,300('85) . . . . C 4
Millburn, 18,630 . . . B 4
Millville, 25,992 . . . . E 2
Montclair, 37,729 . . . B 4
Morristown, 16,189 . . B 4
Neptune, 29,800 . . . . C 4
Newark, 275,221 . . . . B 4
New Brunswick,
  41,711 . . . . C 4
North Bergen, 48,414 h 8
North Brunswick,
  31,287 . . . . C 4
North Plainfield,
  18,820 . . . . B 4
Nutley, 27,099 . . . . B 4
Ocean [Township],
  24,700('85) . . . . C 4
Orange, 29,925 . . . . B 4
Paramus, 25,067 . . . h 8
Passaic, 58,041 . . . . B 4
Paterson, 140,891 . . B 4
Pennsauken, 34,733 . D 2
Pennsville,
  12,467('80) . . . . D 1
Perth Amboy, 41,967 B 4
Phillipsburg, 15,757 . . B 2
Piscataway, 43,800 . . B 4
Plainfield, 46,567 . . . B 4
Princeton, 12,016 . . C 3
Rahway, 25,325 . . . . B 4
Red Bank, 10,636 . . C 4
Ridgewood, 24,152 . . B 4
Roselle, 20,314 . . . . k 7
Sayreville, 34,986 . . C 4
Scotch Plains,
  20,774('80) . . . . . . B 4
Somerset, 21,731('80)B 3
Somerville, 11,632 . . B 3
South Plainfield,
  20,489 . . . . B 4
Summit, 19,757 . . . . B 4
Sussex, 2,201 . . . . . A 3
Teaneck, 37,825 . . . h 8
Trenton, 88,675 . . . . C 3
Union City, 58,012 . . h 8
Vineland, 54,780 . . . E 2
Wayne, 47,025 . . . . B 4
Westfield, 28,870 . . . B 4
West New York,
  38,125 . . . . h 8
West Orange, 39,103 B 4
Willingboro, 36,291 . . C 3
Woodbine, 2,678 . . . E 3
Woodbridge [Township],
  95,100('86) . . . . . . B 4

107

New Mexico

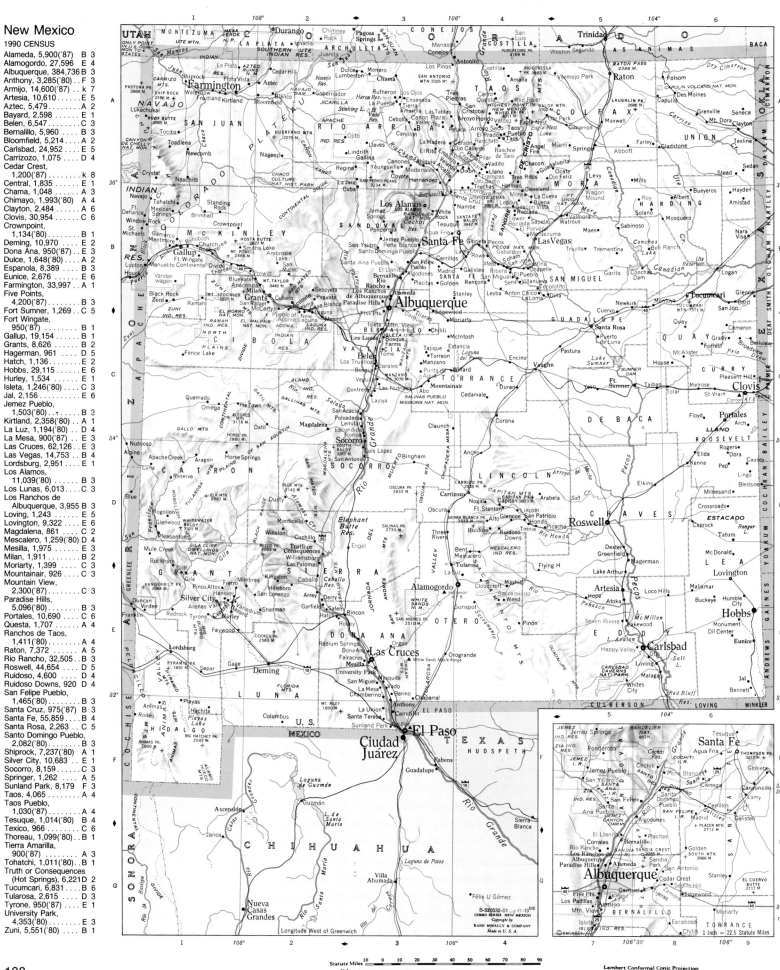

New Mexico
1990 CENSUS

Alameda, 5,900('87) . . . . B 3
Alamogordo, 27,596 . . . E 4
Albuquerque, 384,736 B 3
Anthony, 3,285('80) . . F 3
Armijo, 14,600('87) . . k 7
Artesia, 10,610 . . . . . E 5
Aztec, 5,479 . . . . A 2
Bayard, 2,598 . . . . . . E 1
Belen, 6,547 . . . . C 3
Bernalillo, 5,960 . . . . B 3
Bloomfield, 5,214 . . . A 2
Carlsbad, 24,952 . . . . E 5
Carrizozo, 1,075 . . . . D 4
Cedar Crest,
 1,200('87) . . . . . . k 8
Central, 1,835 . . . . . E 1
Chama, 1,048 . . . . . . A 3
Chimayo, 1,993('80) . A 4
Clayton, 2,484 . . . . . A 6
Clovis, 30,954 . . . . . C 6
Crownpoint,
 1,134('80) . . . . . . B 1
Deming, 10,970 . . . . . E 2
Dona Ana, 950('87) . . E 3
Dulce, 1,648('80) . . . A 2
Espanola, 8,389 . . . . B 3
Eunice, 2,676 . . . . . . E 6
Farmington, 33,997 . . A 1
Five Points,
 4,200('87) . . . . . . B 3
Fort Sumner, 1,269 . . C 5
Fort Wingate,
 950('87) . . . . B 1
Gallup, 19,154 . . . . . B 1
Grants, 8,626 . . . . . . C 2
Hagerman, 961 . . . . . D 5
Hatch, 1,136 . . . . . . E 2
Hobbs, 29,115 . . . . . E 6
Hurley, 1,534 . . . . . . E 1
Isleta, 1,246('80) . . . C 3
Jal, 2,156 . . . . E 6
Jemez Pueblo,
 1,503('80) . . . . . . B 3
Kirtland, 2,358('80) . . A 1
La Luz, 1,194('80) . . . D 4
La Mesa, 900('87) . . . E 3
Las Cruces, 62,126 . . E 3
Las Vegas, 14,753 . . . B 4
Lordsburg, 2,951 . . . . E 1
Los Alamos,
 11,039('80) . . . . . B 3
Loving, 1,243 . . . . . . E 5
Lovington, 9,322 . . . . E 6
Magdalena, 861 . . . . . C 2
Mescalero, 1,259('80) D 4
Mesilla, 1,975 . . . . . E 3
Milan, 1,911 . . . . . . C 2
Moriarty, 1,399 . . . . C 3
Mountainair, 926 . . . . C 3
Mountain View,
 2,300('87) . . . . . . C 3
Paradise Hills,
 5,096('80) . . . . . . B 3
Portales, 10,690 . . . . C 6
Questa, 1,707 . . . . . . A 4
Ranchos de Taos,
 1,411('80) . . . . . . A 4
Raton, 7,372 . . . . . . A 5
Rio Rancho, 32,505 . . B 3
Roswell, 44,654 . . . . D 5
Ruidoso, 4,600 . . . . . D 4
Ruidoso Downs, 920 . . D 4
San Felipe Pueblo,
 1,465('80) . . . . . . B 3
Santa Cruz, 975('87) . B 3
Santa Fe, 55,859 . . . B 4
Santa Rosa, 2,263 . . . C 5
Santo Domingo Pueblo,
 2,082('80) . . . . . . B 3
Shiprock, 7,237('80) . A 1
Silver City, 10,683 . . E 1
Socorro, 8,159 . . . . . C 3
Springer, 1,262 . . . . A 5
Sunland Park, 8,179 . F 3
Taos, 4,065 . . . . A 4
Taos Pueblo,
 1,030('87) . . . . . . A 4
Tesuque, 1,014('80) . B 4
Texico, 966 . . . . C 6
Thoreau, 1,099('80) . B 1
Tierra Amarilla,
 900('87) . . . . A 3
Tohatchi, 1,011('80) . B 1
Truth or Consequences
 (Hot Springs), 6,221 D 2
Tucumcari, 6,831 . . . C 6
Tularosa, 2,615 . . . . D 4
Tyrone, 950('87) . . . E 1
University Park,
 4,353('80) . . . . . . E 3
Zuni, 5,551('80) . . . . B 1

108

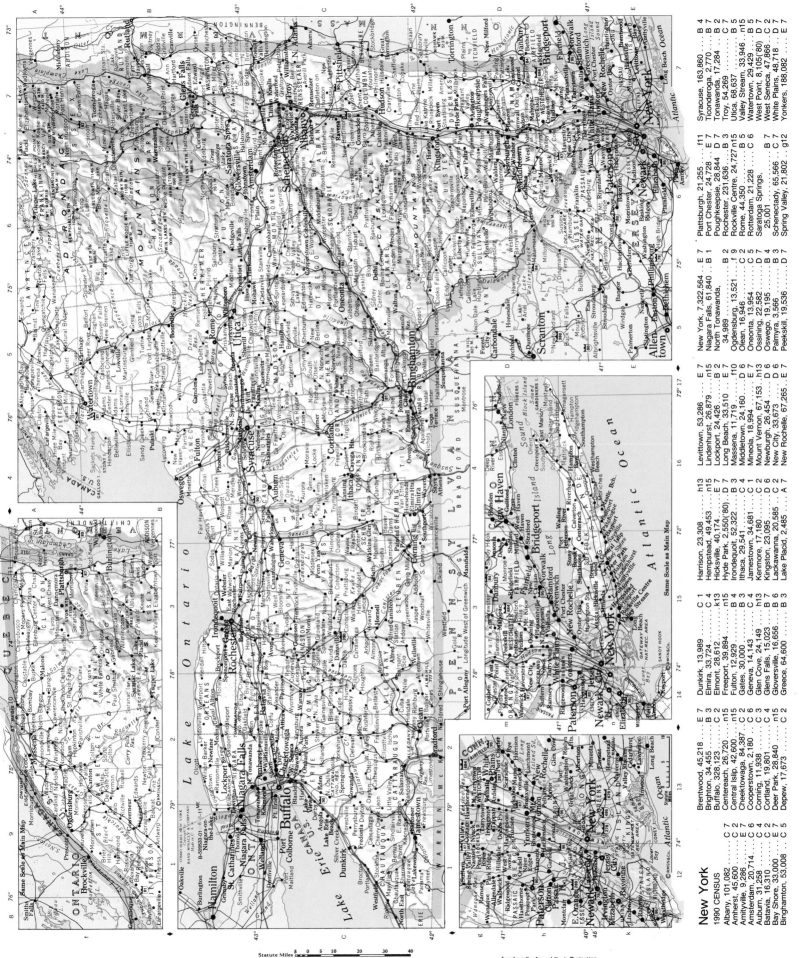

North Carolina

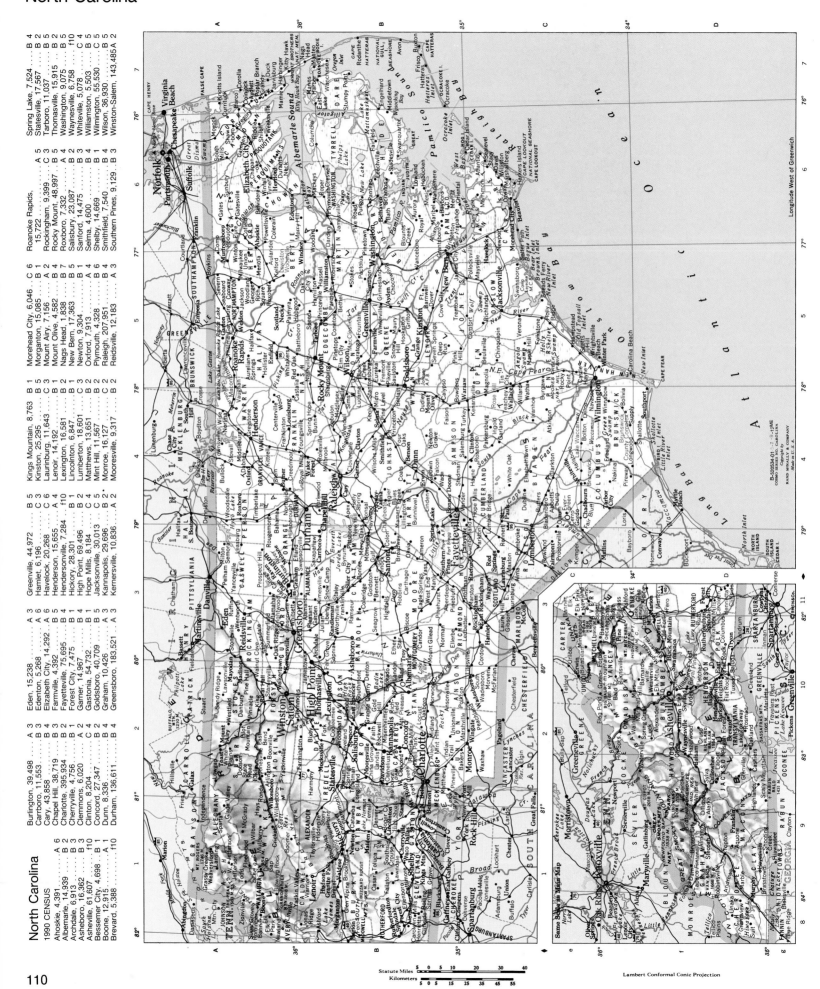

North Carolina

1990 CENSUS

Ahoskie, 4,391	A 6	
Albemarle, 14,939	B 3	
Archdale, 6,913	B 3	
Asheboro, 16,362	B 3	
Asheville, 61,607	f10	
Bessemer City, 4,698	B 1	
Boone, 12,915	A 2	
Brevard, 5,388	f10	

Burlington, 39,498	B 4	
Carrboro, 11,553	B 4	
Cary, 43,858	B 4	
Chapel Hill, 38,719	B 3	
Charlotte, 395,934	B 2	
Cherryville, 4,756	B 1	
Clemmons, 6,020	A 2	
Clinton, 8,204	C 4	
Concord, 27,347	B 2	
Dunn, 8,336	B 4	
Durham, 136,611	B 4	

Eden, 15,238	A 3	
Edenton, 5,268	A 6	
Elizabeth City, 14,292	A 6	
Farmville, 4,392	B 5	
Fayetteville, 75,695	B 4	
Forest City, 7,475	B 1	
Garner, 14,967	B 4	
Gastonia, 54,732	B 1	
Goldsboro, 40,709	B 5	
Kannapolis, 29,696	B 2	
Kernersville, 10,836	A 2	

Greenville, 44,972	B 5	
Hamlet, 6,196	C 3	
Havelock, 20,268	C 6	
Henderson, 15,655	A 4	
Hendersonville, 7,284	f10	
Hickory, 28,301	B 1	
High Point, 69,496	B 2	
Hope Mills, 8,184	C 4	
Jacksonville, 30,013	C 5	
Kings Mountain, 8,763	B 1	
Kinston, 25,295	B 5	
Laurinburg, 11,643	C 3	
Lenoir, 14,192	B 1	
Lexington, 16,581	B 2	
Lincolnton, 6,847	B 1	
Lumberton, 18,601	C 4	
Matthews, 13,651	B 2	
Mint Hill, 11,567	C 2	
Monroe, 16,127	C 2	
Mooresville, 9,317	B 2	

Morehead City, 6,046	C 6	
Morganton, 15,085	B 1	
Mount Airy, 7,156	A 2	
Mount Olive, 4,582	B 5	
Nags Head, 1,838	B 7	
New Bern, 17,363	B 5	
Newton, 9,304	B 1	
Oxford, 7,913	A 4	
Plymouth, 4,328	B 6	
Raleigh, 207,951	B 4	
Reidsville, 12,183	B 2	

Roanoke Rapids, 15,722	A 5	
Rockingham, 9,399	C 3	
Roxboro, 7,332	A 4	
Salisbury, 23,087	B 2	
Sanford, 14,475	B 3	
Selma, 4,600	B 4	
Shelby, 14,669	B 1	
Smithfield, 7,540	B 4	
Southern Pines, 9,129	B 3	

Spring Lake, 7,524	B 4	
Statesville, 17,567	B 2	
Tarboro, 11,037	B 5	
Thomasville, 15,915	B 2	
Washington, 9,075	B 5	
Waynesville, 6,758	f10	
Whiteville, 5,078	C 4	
Williamston, 5,503	B 5	
Wilmington, 55,530	C 5	
Wilson, 36,930	B 4	
Winston-Salem, 143,485	A 2	

Statute Miles

Kilometers

Lambert Conformal Conic Projection

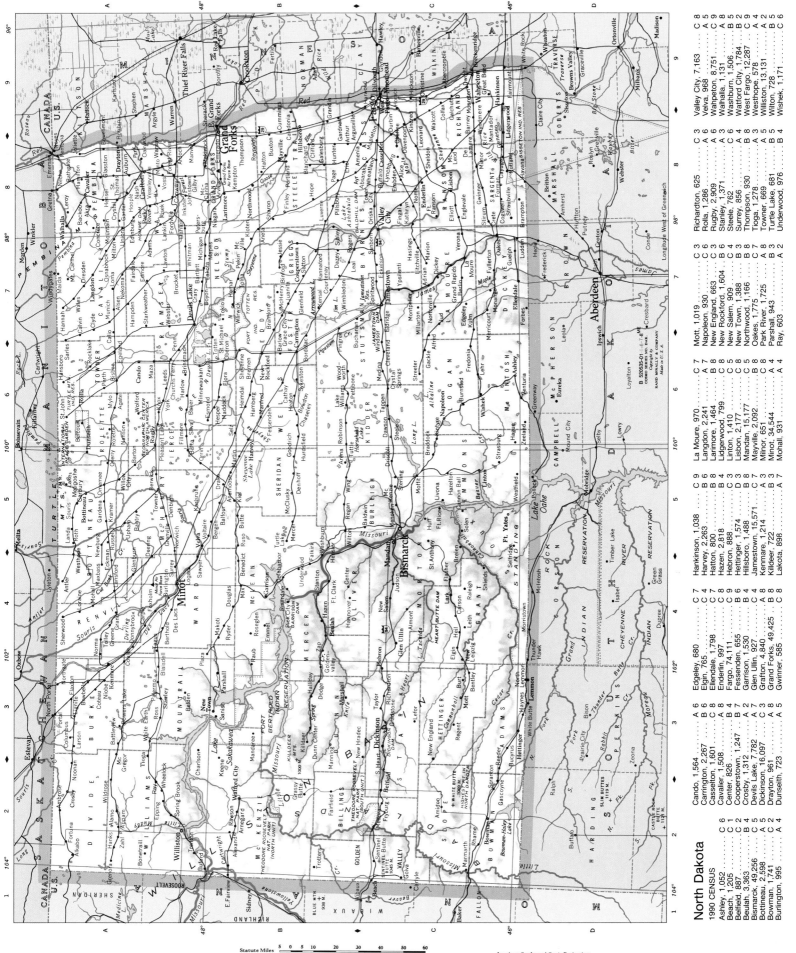

North Dakota

1990 CENSUS

Ashley, 1,052	C 6	
Beach, 1,205	C 1	
Belfield, 887	C 2	
Beulah, 3,363	B 4	
Bismarck, 49,256	C 5	
Bottineau, 2,598	A 5	
Bowman, 1,741	C 2	
Burlington, 995	A 4	

Cando, 1,564	A 6	
Carrington, 2,267	B 6	
Casselton, 1,601	C 8	
Cavalier, 1,508	A 8	
Center, 826	B 4	
Cooperstown, 1,247	B 7	
Crosby, 1,312	A 2	
Devils Lake, 7,782	A 7	
Dickinson, 16,097	C 3	
Drayton, 961	A 8	
Dunseith, 723	A 5	

Edgeley, 680	C 7	
Elgin, 765	C 4	
Ellendale, 1,798	C 7	
Enderlin, 997	C 8	
Fargo, 74,111	C 9	
Fessenden, 655	B 6	
Garrison, 1,530	B 4	
Glen Ullin, 927	C 4	
Grafton, 4,840	A 8	
Grand Forks, 49,425	B 8	
Gwinner, 585	C 8	

Hankinson, 1,038	C 9	
Harvey, 2,263	B 6	
Hatton, 800	B 8	
Hazen, 2,818	B 4	
Hebron, 888	C 4	
Hettinger, 1,574	D 3	
Hillsboro, 1,488	B 8	
Jamestown, 15,571	C 7	
Kenmare, 1,214	A 4	
Killdeer, 722	B 3	
Lakota, 898	A 7	

La Moure, 970	C 7	
Langdon, 2,241	A 7	
Larimore, 1,464	B 8	
Lidgerwood, 799	C 8	
Linton, 1,410	C 5	
Lisbon, 2,177	C 8	
Mandan, 15,177	C 5	
Mayville, 2,092	B 8	
Milnor, 651	C 8	
Minot, 34,544	A 4	
Parshall, 943	B 3	
Ray, 603	A 2	

Mott, 1,019	C 3	
Napoleon, 930	C 6	
New England, 663	C 3	
New Rockford, 1,604	B 6	
New Salem, 909	C 4	
New Town, 1,388	B 3	
Northwood, 1,166	B 8	
Oakes, 1,775	C 7	
Park River, 1,725	A 8	
Towner, 669	A 5	
Turtle Lake, 681	B 5	
Underwood, 976	B 4	

Richardton, 625	C 3	
Rolla, 1,286	A 6	
Rugby, 2,909	A 6	
Stanley, 1,371	A 3	
Steele, 762	C 6	
Surrey, 856	A 4	
Thompson, 930	B 8	
Tioga, 1,278	A 3	
Westhope, 578	A 4	
Williston, 13,131	A 2	
Wilton, 728	B 5	
Wishek, 1,171	C 6	

Valley City, 7,163	C 8	
Velva, 968	A 5	
Wahpeton, 8,751	C 9	
Walhalla, 1,131	A 8	
Washburn, 1,506	B 5	
Watford City, 1,784	B 2	
West Fargo, 12,287	C 9	
Wyndmere, 533	A 4	

B 520535-01—6-7-8 WE
COSMO SERIES NO. DAK.
Copyright by
RAND McNALLY & COMPANY
Made in U.S.A.

Statute Miles 5 0 10   20   30   40   50   60
Kilometers 5 0   5   15   25   35   45   55   65   75

Lambert Conformal Conic Projection

111

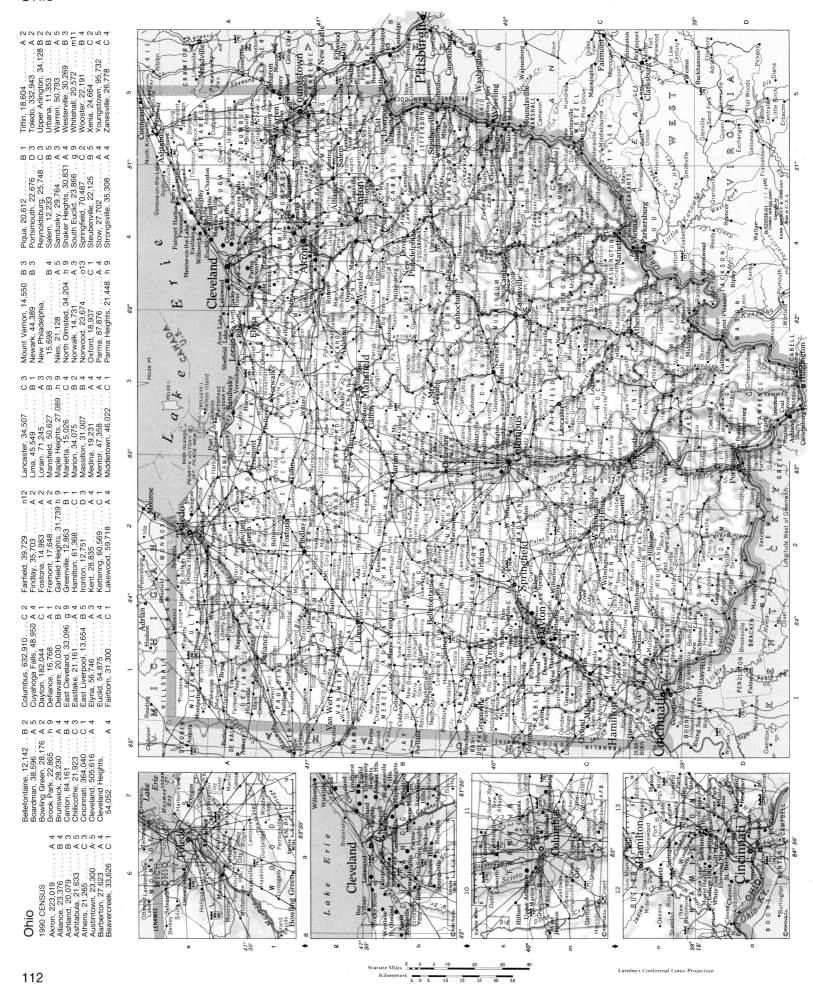

Ohio

Ohio

1990 CENSUS

Akron, 223,019	A 4	
Alliance, 23,376	B 3	
Ashland, 20,079	B 3	
Ashtabula, 21,633	A 5	
Athens, 21,265	C 3	
Austintown, 23,300	A 5	
Barberton, 27,623	A 4	
Beavercreek, 33,626	C 1	

Bellefontaine, 12,142	C 2	
Boardman, 38,596	A 5	
Bowling Green, 28,176	A 2	
Brook Park, 22,865	h 9	
Brunswick, 28,230	B 4	
Canton, 84,161	B 4	
Chillicothe, 21,923	C 3	
Cincinnati, 364,040	C 1	
Cleveland, 505,616	A 4	
Cleveland Heights, 54,052	h 9	

Columbus, 632,910	C 2	
Cuyahoga Falls, 48,950	A 4	
Dayton, 182,044	C 1	
Defiance, 16,768	A 1	
Delaware, 20,030	B 2	
East Cleveland, 33,096	h 9	
Eastlake, 21,161	A 4	
East Liverpool, 13,654	B 5	
Elyria, 56,746	A 4	
Euclid, 54,875	A 4	
Fairborn, 31,300	C 1	

Fairfield, 39,729	C 1	
Findlay, 35,703	B 2	
Fostoria, 14,983	A 2	
Fremont, 17,648	A 2	
Garfield Heights, 31,739	h 9	
Greenville, 12,863	B 1	
Hamilton, 61,368	C 1	
Ironton, 12,751	D 3	
Kent, 28,835	A 4	
Kettering, 60,569	C 1	
Lakewood, 59,718	A 4	

Lancaster, 34,507	C 3	
Lima, 45,549	B 1	
Lorain, 71,245	A 3	
Mansfield, 50,627	B 3	
Maple Heights, 27,089	h 9	
Marietta, 15,026	C 4	
Marion, 34,075	B 2	
Massillon, 31,007	B 4	
Medina, 19,231	A 4	
Mentor, 47,358	A 4	
Middletown, 46,022	C 1	

Mount Vernon, 14,550	B 3	
New Philadelphia, 15,698	B 4	
Niles, 21,128	A 5	
North Olmsted, 34,204	h 9	
Norwalk, 14,731	A 3	
Norwood, 23,674	o13	
Oxford, 18,937	C 1	
Parma, 87,876	h 9	
Parma Heights, 21,448	h 9	

Piqua, 20,612	B 1	
Portsmouth, 22,676	D 3	
Reynoldsburg, 25,748	C 3	
Salem, 12,233	B 5	
Sandusky, 29,764	A 3	
Shaker Heights, 30,831	h 9	
South Euclid, 23,866	g 9	
Springfield, 70,487	C 1	
Steubenville, 22,125	B 5	
Stow, 27,702	A 4	
Strongsville, 35,308	A 4	

Tiffin, 18,604	A 2	
Toledo, 332,943	A 2	
Upper Arlington, 34,128	B 2	
Urbana, 11,353	B 2	
Warren, 50,793	A 5	
Westerville, 30,269	B 3	
Whitehall, 20,572	m11	
Wooster, 22,191	B 4	
Xenia, 24,664	C 2	
Youngstown, 95,732	A 5	
Zanesville, 26,778	C 4	

Lambert Conformal Conic Projection

Oklahoma

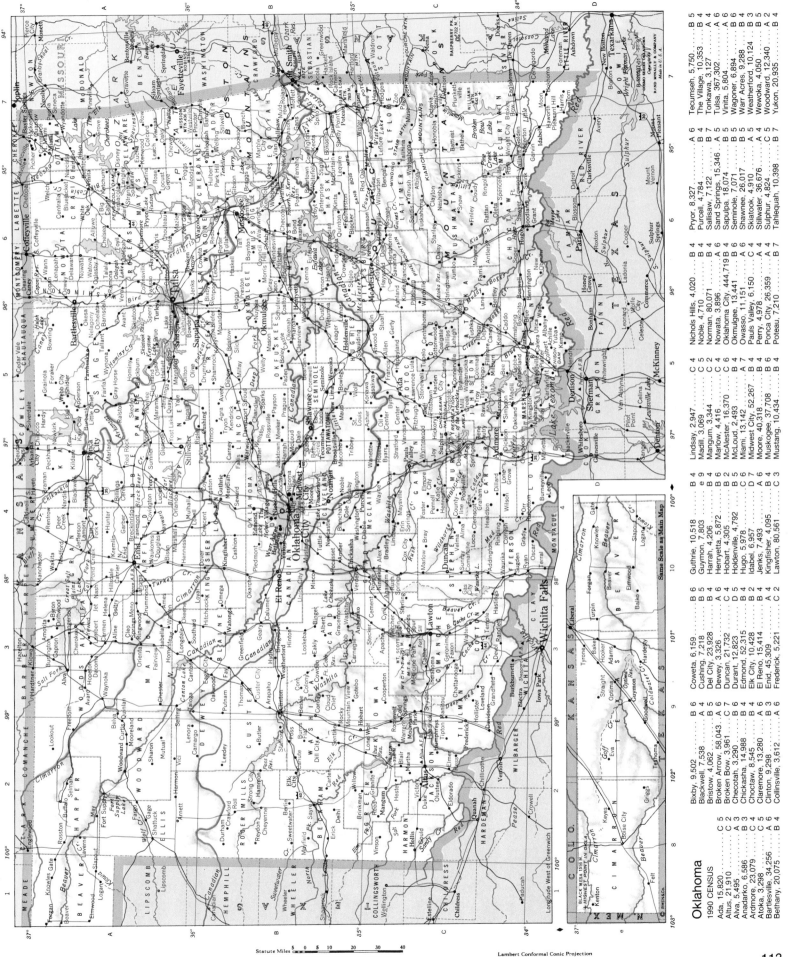

Oklahoma

1990 CENSUS

Ada, 15,820	C 5	
Altus, 21,910	C 2	
Alva, 5,495	A 3	
Anadarko, 6,586	B 3	
Ardmore, 23,079	C 5	
Atoka, 3,298	B 6	
Bartlesville, 34,256	A 6	
Bethany, 20,075	B 4	

Bixby, 9,502	B 6	
Blackwell, 7,538	A 4	
Bristow, 4,062	B 5	
Broken Arrow, 58,043	A 6	
Broken Bow, 3,961	C 4	
Checotah, 3,290	B 6	
Chickasha, 14,988	B 4	
Choctaw, 8,545	B 4	
Claremore, 13,280	A 6	
Clinton, 9,298	B 3	
Collinsville, 3,612	B 4	

Coweta, 6,159	B 6	
Cushing, 7,218	B 4	
Del City, 23,928	B 4	
Dewey, 3,326	A 6	
Duncan, 21,732	C 4	
Durant, 12,823	D 5	
Edmond, 52,315	B 4	
Elk City, 10,428	B 2	
El Reno, 15,414	B 4	
Enid, 45,309	A 4	
Frederick, 5,221	C 3	

Guthrie, 10,518	B 4	
Guymon, 7,803	e 9	
Harrah, 4,206	B 4	
Henryetta, 5,872	B 6	
Hobart, 4,305	B 3	
Holdenville, 4,792	B 5	
Hugo, 5,978	C 6	
Idabel, 6,957	C 7	
Jenks, 7,493	B 6	
Kingfisher, 4,095	B 4	
Lawton, 80,561	C 3	

Lindsay, 2,947	B 4	
Madill, 3,069	C 5	
Mangum, 3,344	C 2	
Marlow, 4,416	C 4	
McAlester, 16,370	B 6	
McLoud, 2,493	B 4	
Miami, 13,142	A 7	
Midwest City, 52,267	B 4	
Moore, 40,318	B 4	
Muskogee, 37,708	B 6	
Mustang, 10,434	B 4	

Nichols Hills, 4,020	B 4	
Noble, 4,710	B 4	
Nowata, 3,896	A 6	
Oklahoma City, 444,719	B 4	
Okmulgee, 13,441	B 6	
Owasso, 11,151	A 6	
Pauls Valley, 6,150	C 4	
Perry, 4,978	A 4	
Ponca City, 26,359	A 4	
Poteau, 7,210	B 7	

Pryor, 8,327	B 6	
Purcell, 4,784	B 4	
Sallisaw, 7,122	B 7	
Sand Springs, 15,346	A 6	
Sapulpa, 18,074	B 6	
Seminole, 7,071	B 5	
Shawnee, 26,017	B 5	
Skiatook, 4,910	A 6	
Stillwater, 36,676	A 4	
Sulphur, 4,824	C 5	
Tahlequah, 10,398	B 7	

Tecumseh, 5,750	B 5	
The Village, 10,353	B 4	
Tonkawa, 3,127	A 4	
Tulsa, 367,302	A 6	
Vinita, 5,804	A 6	
Wagoner, 6,894	B 6	
Warr Acres, 9,288	B 4	
Weatherford, 10,124	B 3	
Wewoka, 4,050	B 5	
Woodward, 12,340	A 2	
Yukon, 20,935	B 4	

Statute Miles 5 0 5 10 20 30 40

Kilometers 5 0 5 15 30 45 55

Lambert Conformal Conic Projection

113

Oregon

1990 CENSUS

Albany, 29,462	C 4	
Aloha, 10,000('82)	h12	
Altamont, 19,805('80)	E 5	
Ashland, 16,234	E 4	
Astoria, 10,069	A 3	
Baker, 9,140	C 9	
Beaverton, 53,310	B 4	
Bend, 20,469	C 5	

Brookings, 4,400	E 2	
Burns, 2,913	D 7	
Canby, 8,983	B 4	
Central Point, 7,509	E 4	
Coos Bay, 15,076	D 2	
Coquille, 4,121	D 2	
Cornelius, 6,148	g11	
Corvallis, 44,757	C 3	
Cottage Grove, 7,402	D 3	
Dallas, 9,422	C 3	
Eugene, 112,669	C 3	

Florence, 5,162	D 2	
Forest Grove, 13,559	B 3	
Gladstone, 10,152	B 4	
Grants Pass, 17,488	E 3	
Green, 3,897('80)	D 3	
Gresham, 68,235	B 4	
Hermiston, 10,040	B 7	
Hillsboro, 37,520	B 3	
Hood River, 4,632	B 5	
Independence, 4,425	C 3	
John Day, 1,836	C 8	

Junction City, 3,670	C 3	
Keizer, 21,884	C 3	
Klamath Falls, 17,737	E 5	
La Grande, 11,766	B 8	
Lake Oswego, 30,576	B 4	
Lakeview, 2,526	E 6	
Lebanon, 10,950	C 4	
Lincoln City, 5,892	C 3	
McMinnville, 17,894	B 3	
Medford, 46,951	E 4	
Metzger, 5,544('80)	h12	

Milton-Freewater, 5,533	B 8	
Milwaukie, 18,692	B 4	
Molalla, 3,651	C 3	
Monmouth, 6,288	C 3	
Mount Angel, 2,778	C 4	
Myrtle Creek, 3,063	D 3	
Myrtle Point, 2,712	D 2	
Newberg, 13,086	B 8	
Newport, 8,437	C 2	
North Albany, 4,499('80)	k11	
North Bend, 9,614	D 2	

Nyssa, 2,629	D 9	
Oak Grove, 11,640('80)	B 4	
Ontario, 9,392	C10	
Oregon City, 14,698	B 4	
Parkrose, 21,108('80)	B 4	
Pendleton, 15,126	B 8	
Portland, 437,319	B 4	
Prineville, 5,355	C 6	
Redmond, 7,163	C 5	
Reedsport, 4,796	D 2	

River Road, 10,370('80)	C 3	
Roseburg, 17,032	D 3	
Saint Helens, 7,535	B 4	
Salem, 107,786	C 3	
Sandy, 4,152	B 4	
Scappoose, 3,529	B 3	
Seaside, 5,359	A 3	
Silverton, 5,635	C 4	
Springfield, 44,683	C 4	
Stayton, 5,011	C 4	
Sutherlin, 5,020	D 3	

Sweet Home, 6,850	C 4	
The Dalles, 11,060	B 5	
Tigard, 29,344	h12	
Tillamook, 4,001	B 3	
Toledo, 3,174	C 3	
Tri City, 3,439('80)	E 3	
Umatilla, 3,046	B 7	
West Linn, 16,367	B 4	
Wilsonville, 7,106	h12	
Winston, 3,773	D 3	
Woodburn, 13,404	B 4	

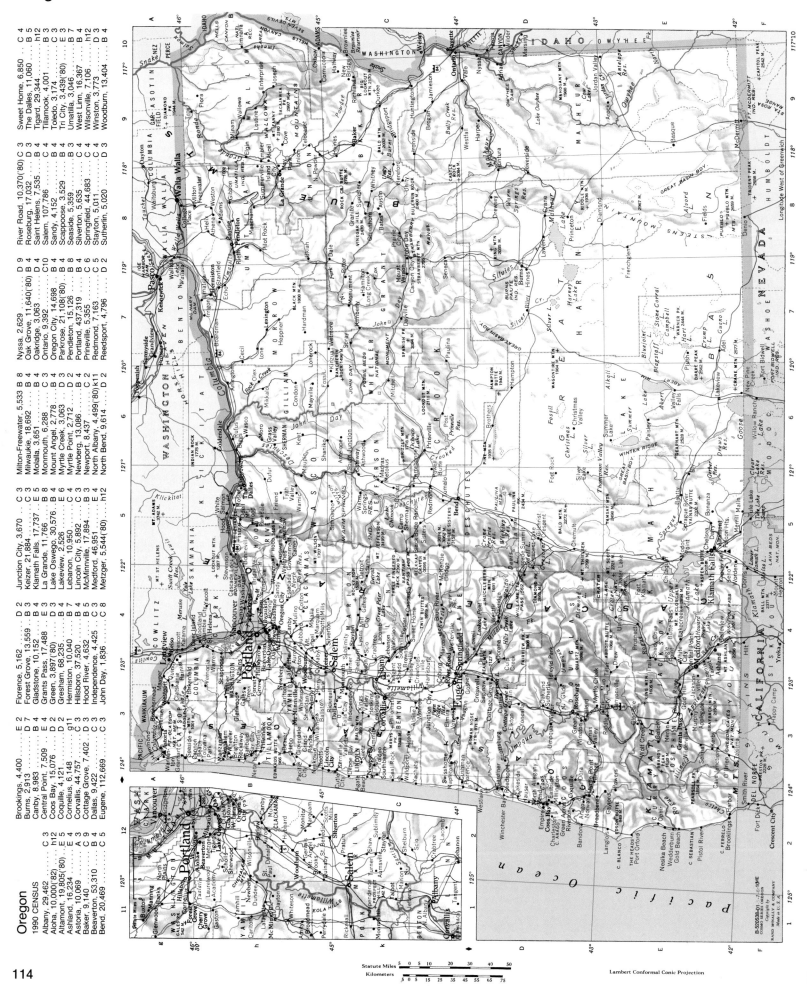

Statute Miles

Kilometers

Lambert Conformal Conic Projection

114

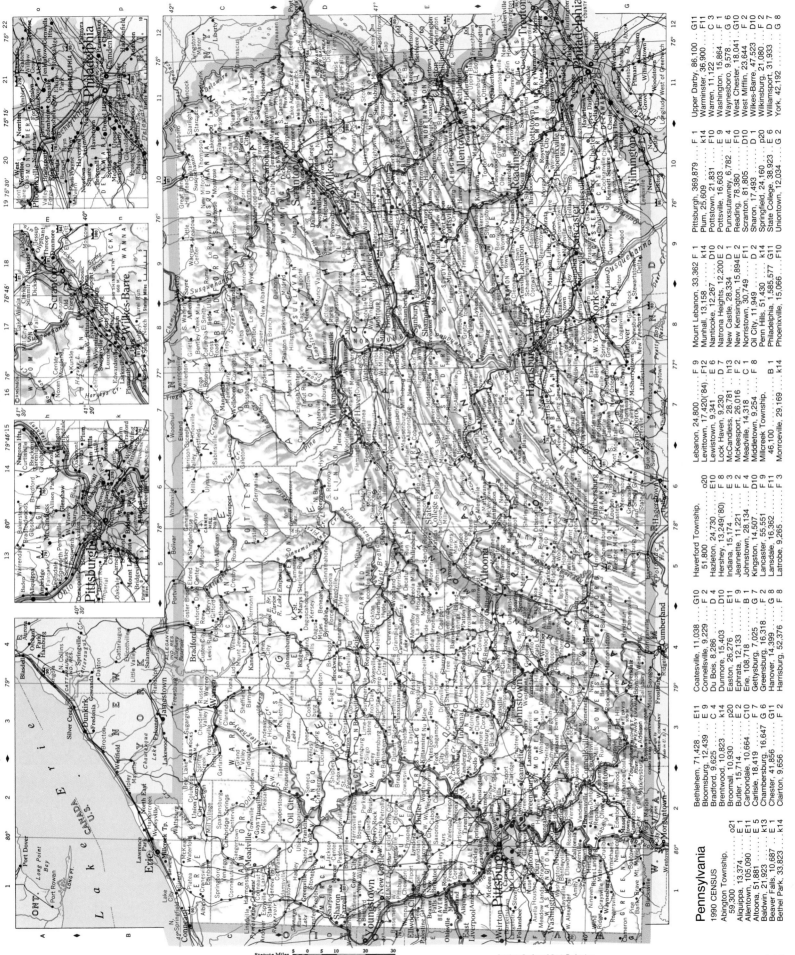

Pennsylvania
Statute Miles
Kilometers
Lambert Conformal Conic Projection

Pennsylvania

1990 CENSUS

Abington Township, 59,300	o21	
Aliquippa, 13,374	E 1	
Allentown, 105,090	E11	
Altoona, 51,881	E 5	
Baldwin, 21,923	k13	
Beaver Falls, 10,687	E 1	
Bethel Park, 33,823	k14	
Bethlehem, 71,428	E11	
Bloomsburg, 12,439	E 9	
Bradford, 9,625	C 4	
Brentwood, 10,823	k14	
Broomall, 10,930	o20	
Butler, 15,714	E 2	
Carbondale, 10,664	C10	
Carlisle, 18,419	F 7	
Chambersburg, 16,647	G 6	
Chester, 41,856	G11	
Clairton, 9,656	F 2	
Coatesville, 11,038	G10	
Connellsville, 9,229	F 2	
Du Bois, 8,286	D 4	
Dunmore, 15,403	D10	
Easton, 26,276	E11	
Ephrata, 12,133	F 9	
Erie, 108,718	B 1	
Gettysburg, 7,025	G 7	
Greensburg, 16,318	F 2	
Hanover, 14,399	G 7	
Harrisburg, 52,376	F 8	
Haverford Township, 51,800	o20	
Hazleton, 24,730	E10	
Hershey, 13,249(80)	F 8	
Indiana, 15,174	E 3	
Jeannette, 11,221	F 2	
Johnstown, 28,134	F 4	
Kingston, 14,507	D10	
Lancaster, 55,551	F 9	
Lansdale, 16,362	F11	
Latrobe, 9,265	F 3	
Lebanon, 24,800	F 9	
Levittown, 17,420('84)	F12	
Lewistown, 9,341	E 6	
Lock Haven, 9,230	D 7	
McCandless, 28,334	E 2	
McKeesport, 26,016	F 2	
Meadville, 14,318	C 1	
Middletown, 9,254	F 8	
Millcreek Township, 46,100	B 1	
Monroeville, 29,169	k14	
Mount Lebanon, 33,362	F 1	
Munhall, 13,158	k14	
Nanticoke, 12,267	D10	
Natrona Heights, 12,200	E 2	
New Castle, 28,334	E 1	
New Kensington, 15,894	E 2	
Norristown, 30,749	F10	
Oil City, 11,949	D 2	
Penn Hills, 51,430	k14	
Philadelphia, 1,585,577	G11	
Phoenixville, 15,066	F10	
Pittsburgh, 369,879	F 1	
Plum, 25,609	F11	
Pottstown, 21,831	F10	
Pottsville, 16,603	E 9	
Punxsutawney, 6,782	E 4	
Reading, 78,380	F10	
Scranton, 81,805	D10	
Sharon, 17,493	D 1	
Springfield, 24,160	p20	
State College, 38,923	E 6	
Uniontown, 12,034	G 2	
Upper Darby, 86,100	G11	
Warminster, 36,900	F11	
Warren, 11,122	C 3	
Washington, 15,864	G 6	
Waynesboro, 9,578	G 6	
West Chester, 18,041	G10	
West Mifflin, 23,644	F10	
Wilkes-Barre, 47,523	D10	
Wilkinsburg, 21,080	D 1	
Williamsport, 31,933	D 7	
York, 42,192	G 8	

Rhode Island

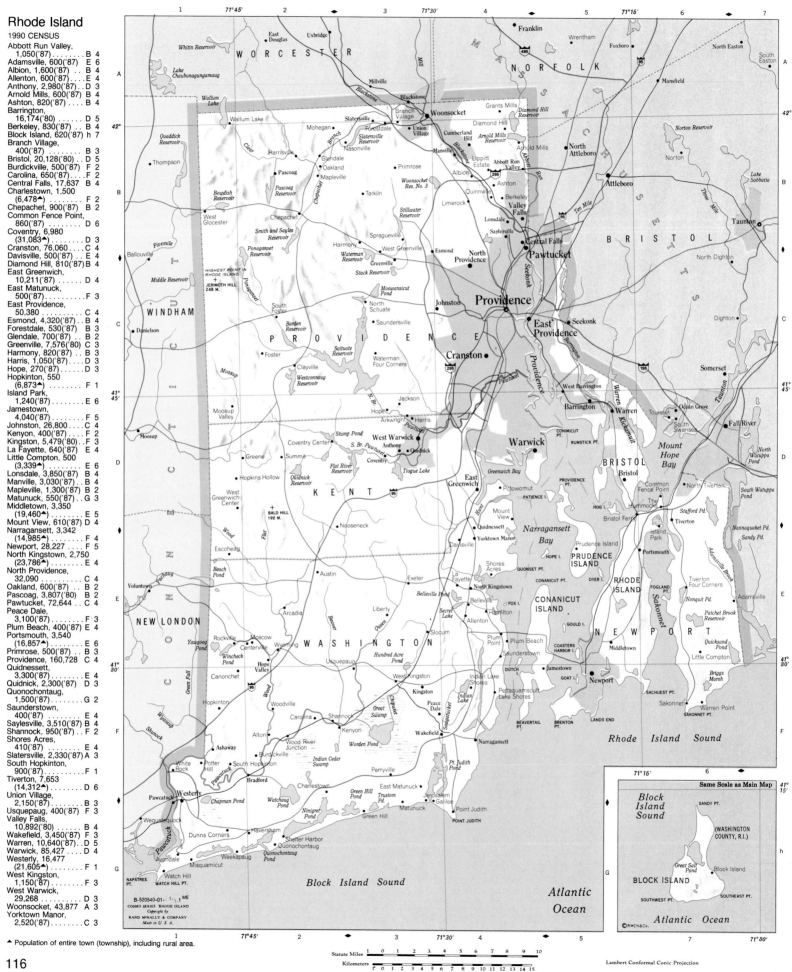

Rhode Island

1990 CENSUS

Abbott Run Valley,
  1,050('87) . . . . B 4
Adamsville, 600('87) . . . E 6
Albion, 1,600('87) . . . . B 4
Allenton, 600('87) . . . . . E 4
Anthony, 2,980('87) . . . . D 3
Arnold Mills, 600('87) . . B 4
Ashton, 820('87) . . . . B 4
Barrington,
  16,174('80) . . . . D 5
Berkeley, 830('87) . . . . B 4
Block Island, 620('87) h 7
Branch Village,
  400('87) . . . . B 3
Bristol, 20,128('80) . . D 5
Burdickville, 500('87) . . F 2
Carolina, 650('87) . . . . F 2
Central Falls, 17,637 . . B 4
Charlestown, 1,500
  (6,478▲) . . . . G 2
Chepachet, 900('87) . . B 2
Common Fence Point,
  860('87) . . . . D 6
Coventry, 6,980
  (31,083▲) . . . . D 3
Cranston, 76,060 . . . . C 4
Davisville, 500('87) . . . D 5
Diamond Hill, 810('87) B 4
East Greenwich,
  10,211('87) . . . . D 4
East Matunuck,
  500('87) . . . . F 3
East Providence,
  50,380 . . . . C 4
Esmond, 4,320('87) . . B 4
Forestdale, 530('87) . . B 3
Glendale, 700('87) . . . B 2
Greenville, 7,576('80) C 3
Harmony, 820('87) . . . D 3
Harris, 1,050('87) . . . . D 3
Hope, 270('87) . . . . . . D 3
Hopkinton, 550
  (6,873▲) . . . . F 1
Island Park,
  1,240('87) . . . . E 6
Jamestown,
  4,040('87) . . . . F 5
Johnston, 26,800 . . . . C 4
Kenyon, 400('87) . . . . F 2
Kingston, 5,479('80) . . F 3
La Fayette, 640('87) . . E 4
Little Compton, 500
  (3,339▲) . . . . E 6
Lonsdale, 3,850('87) . . B 4
Manville, 3,030('87) . . B 4
Mapleville, 1,300('87) B 3
Matunuck, 550('87) . . G 3
Middletown, 3,350
  (19,460▲) . . . . E 5
Mount View, 610('87) D 4
Narragansett, 3,342
  (14,985▲) . . . . F 4
Newport, 28,227 . . . . F 5
North Kingstown, 2,750
  (23,786▲) . . . . E 4
North Providence,
  32,090 . . . . C 4
Oakland, 600('87) . . . B 2
Pascoag, 3,807('80) . . B 2
Pawtucket, 72,644 . . . C 4
Peace Dale,
  3,100('87) . . . . F 3
Plum Beach, 400('87) E 4
Portsmouth, 3,540
  (16,857▲) . . . . E 6
Primrose, 500('87) . . B 3
Providence, 160,728 . . C 4
Quidnessett,
  3,300('87) . . . . E 4
Quidnick, 2,300('87) . . D 3
Quonochontaug,
  1,500('87) . . . . G 2
Saunderstown,
  400('87) . . . . E 4
Saylesville, 3,510('87) B 4
Shannock, 950('87) . . F 2
Shores Acres,
  410('87) . . . . E 4
Slatersville, 2,330('87) A 3
South Hopkinton,
  900('87) . . . . F 1
Tiverton, 7,653
  (14,312▲) . . . . D 6
Union Village,
  2,150('87) . . . . B 4
Usquepaug, 400('87) F 3
Valley Falls,
  10,892('80) . . . . B 4
Wakefield, 3,450('87) F 3
Warren, 10,640('87) . . D 5
Warwick, 85,427 . . . . D 4
Westerly, 16,477
  (21,605▲) . . . . F 1
West Kingston,
  1,150('87) . . . . F 3
West Warwick,
  29,268 . . . . D 3
Woonsocket, 43,877 . . A 3
Yorktown Manor,
  2,520('87) . . . . C 3

▲ Population of entire town (township), including rural area.

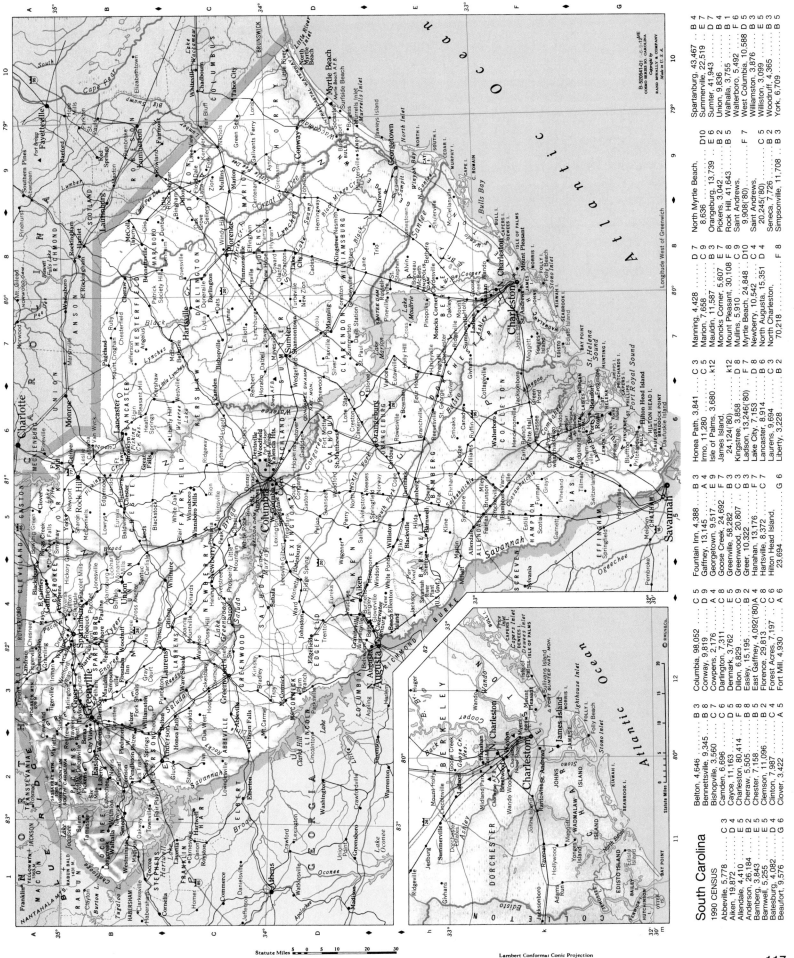

South Dakota

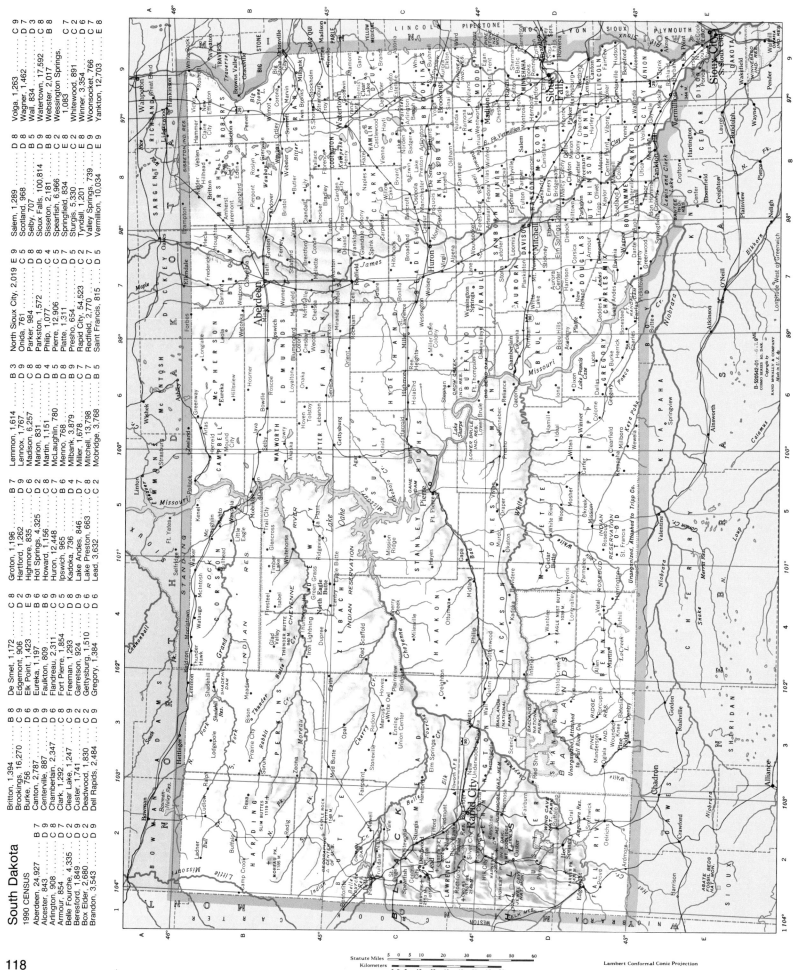

Volga, 1,263 .... C 9
Wagner, 1,462 .... D 7
Wall, 834 .... D 4
Watertown, 17,592 .... C 8
Webster, 2,017 .... B 8
Wessington Springs, ... C 7
1,083 .... C 9
Whitewood, 891 .... C 2
Winner, 3,354 .... D 6
Woonsocket, 766 .... C 7
Yankton, 12,703 .... E 8

Salem, 1,289 .... D 8
Scotland, 968 .... D 8
Selby, 707 .... B 5
Sioux Falls, 100,814 .... D 9
Sisseton, 2,181 .... B 8
Spearfish, 6,966 .... C 2
Springfield, 834 .... E 8
Sturgis, 5,330 .... C 2
Tyndall, 1,201 .... E 8
Valley Springs, 739 .... C 9
Vermillion, 10,034 .... E 9

North Sioux City, 2,019 .... E 9
Onida, 761 .... D 8
Parker, 984 .... D 8
Parkston, 1,572 .... D 8
Philip, 1,077 .... C 4
Pierre, 12,906 .... C 5
Platte, 1,311 .... D 7
Presho, 654 .... D 5
Rapid City, 54,523 .... C 2
Redfield, 2,770 .... C 7
Saint Francis, 815 .... D 5

Lemmon, 1,614 .... B 3
Lennox, 1,767 .... D 9
Madison, 6,257 .... C 8
Marion, 831 .... D 9
Martin, 1,151 .... D 4
McLaughlin, 780 .... B 5
Menno, 768 .... D 8
Milbank, 3,879 .... B 9
Miller, 1,678 .... C 6
Mitchell, 13,798 .... C 8
Mobridge, 3,768 .... C 2

Groton, 1,196 .... C 8
Hartford, 1,262 .... D 9
Highmore, 835 .... C 6
Hot Springs, 4,325 .... D 2
Howard, 1,156 .... B 6
Huron, 12,448 .... C 7
Ipswich, 965 .... C 9
Kadoka, 736 .... D 8
Lake Andes, 846 .... D 8
Lake Preston, 663 .... C 8
Lead, 3,632 .... D 6

De Smet, 1,172 .... B 8
Edgemont, 906 .... C 9
Elk Point, 1,423 .... E 9
Eureka, 1,197 .... B 6
Faulkton, 809 .... D 9
Flandreau, 2,311 .... D 6
Fort Pierre, 1,854 .... C 5
Freeman, 1,293 .... D 8
Garretson, 924 .... C 9
Gettysburg, 1,510 .... C 2
Gregory, 1,384 .... D 9

South Dakota

1990 CENSUS

Aberdeen, 24,927 .... B 7
Alcester, 843 .... D 9
Arlington, 908 .... C 8
Armour, 854 .... D 7
Belle Fourche, 4,335 .... C 2
Beresford, 1,849 .... D 9
Box Elder, 2,680 .... C 2
Brandon, 3,543 .... D 9

Britton, 1,394 .... B 8
Brookings, 16,270 .... C 9
Burke, 756 .... D 6
Canton, 2,787 .... D 9
Centerville, 887 .... D 9
Chamberlain, 2,347 .... D 6
Clark, 1,292 .... C 7
Clear Lake, 1,247 .... C 9
Custer, 1,741 .... D 2
Deadwood, 1,830 .... C 2
Dell Rapids, 2,484 .... D 9

Statute Miles 5 0 5 10 20 30 40 50 60
Kilometers 5 0 5 15 25 35 45 55 65 75

Lambert Conformal Conic Projection

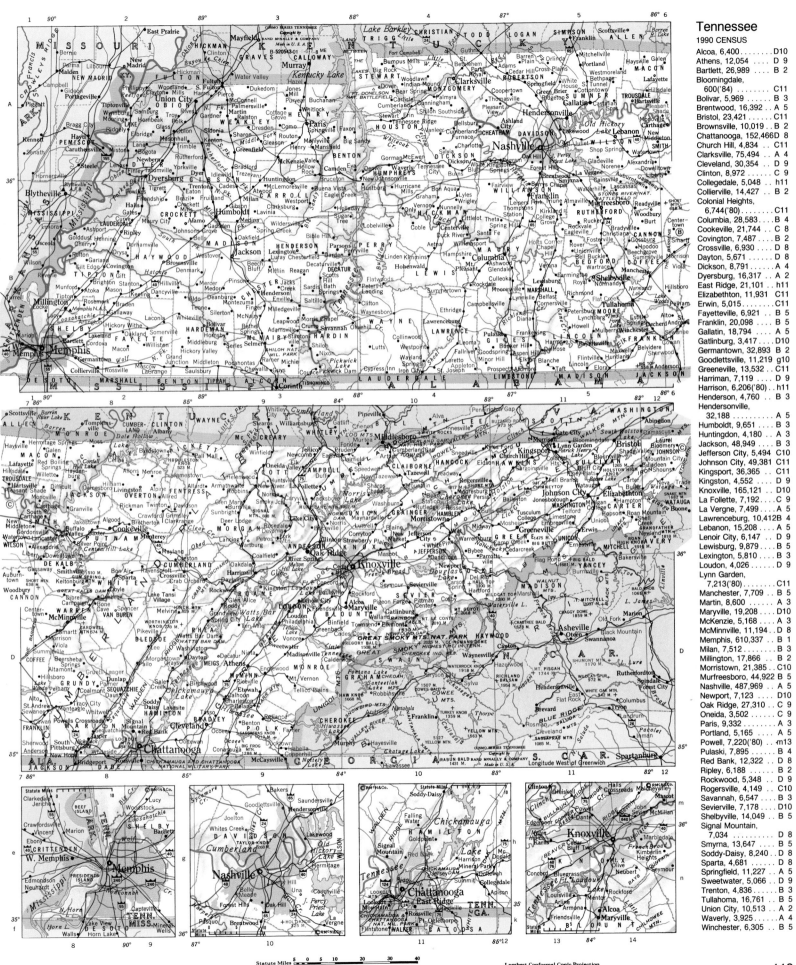

1990 CENSUS

Alcoa, 6,400		D10
Athens, 12,054		D 9
Bartlett, 26,989		B 2
Bloomingdale, 600('84)		C11
Bolivar, 5,969		B 3
Brentwood, 16,392		A 5
Bristol, 23,421		C11
Brownsville, 10,019		B 2
Chattanooga, 152,466		D 8
Church Hill, 4,834		C11
Clarksville, 75,494		A 4
Cleveland, 30,354		D 9
Clinton, 8,972		C 9
Collegedale, 5,048		h11
Collierville, 14,427		B 2
Colonial Heights, 6,744('80)		C11
Columbia, 28,583		B 4
Cookeville, 21,744		C 8
Covington, 7,487		B 2
Crossville, 6,930		D 8
Dayton, 5,671		D 8
Dickson, 8,791		A 4
Dyersburg, 16,317		A 2
East Ridge, 21,101		h11
Elizabethton, 11,931		C11
Erwin, 5,015		C11
Fayetteville, 6,921		B 5
Franklin, 20,098		B 5
Gallatin, 18,794		A 5
Gatlinburg, 3,417		D10
Germantown, 32,893		B 2
Goodlettsville, 11,219		g10
Greeneville, 13,532		C11
Harriman, 7,119		D 9
Harrison, 6,206('80)		h11
Henderson, 4,760		B 3
Hendersonville, 32,188		A 5
Humboldt, 9,651		B 3
Huntingdon, 4,180		A 3
Jackson, 48,949		B 3
Jefferson City, 5,494		C10
Johnson City, 49,381		C11
Kingsport, 36,365		C11
Kingston, 4,552		D 9
Knoxville, 165,121		D10
La Follette, 7,192		C 9
La Vergne, 7,499		A 5
Lawrenceburg, 10,412		B 4
Lebanon, 15,208		A 5
Lenoir City, 6,147		D 9
Lewisburg, 9,879		B 5
Lexington, 5,810		B 3
Loudon, 4,026		D 9
Lynn Garden, 7,213('80)		C11
Manchester, 7,709		B 5
Martin, 8,600		A 3
Maryville, 19,208		D10
McKenzie, 5,168		A 3
McMinnville, 11,194		D 8
Memphis, 610,337		B 1
Milan, 7,512		B 3
Millington, 17,866		B 2
Morristown, 21,385		C10
Murfreesboro, 44,922		B 5
Nashville, 487,969		A 5
Newport, 7,123		D10
Oak Ridge, 27,310		C 9
Oneida, 3,502		C 9
Paris, 9,332		A 3
Portland, 5,165		A 5
Powell, 7,220('80)		m13
Pulaski, 7,895		B 4
Red Bank, 12,322		D 8
Ripley, 6,188		B 2
Rockwood, 5,348		D 9
Rogersville, 4,149		C10
Savannah, 6,547		B 3
Sevierville, 7,178		D10
Shelbyville, 14,049		B 5
Signal Mountain, 7,034		D 8
Smyrna, 13,647		B 5
Soddy-Daisy, 8,240		D 8
Sparta, 4,681		C 8
Springfield, 11,227		A 5
Sweetwater, 5,066		D 9
Trenton, 4,836		B 3
Tullahoma, 16,761		B 5
Union City, 10,513		A 2
Waverly, 3,925		A 4
Winchester, 6,305		B 5

Texas

Texas

1990 CENSUS

Abilene, 106,654 . . . C 3
Alice, 19,788 . . . . . . F 3
Alvin, 19,220 . . . . . E 5
Amarillo, 157,615 . . . B 2
Arlington, 261,721 . . n 9
Austin, 465,622 . . . . D 4
Bay City, 18,170 . . . E 5
Baytown, 63,850 . . . D 5
Beaumont, 114,323 . . D 5
Beeville, 13,547 . . . . E 4
Big Spring, 23,093 . . C 2
Borger, 15,675 . . . . . B 2
Brownsville, 98,962 . . G 4
Brownwood, 18,387 . . D 3
Bryan, 55,002 . . . . . D 4
Cleburne, 22,205 . . . C 4
College Station,
    52,456 . . . . D 4
Conroe, 27,610 . . . . D 5
Copperas Cove,
    24,079 . . . . D 4
Corpus Christi,
    257,453 . . . . F 4
Corsicana, 22,911 . . . C 4
Dallas, 1,006,877 . . . C 4
Del Rio, 30,705 . . . . E 2
Denison, 21,505 . . . . C 4
Denton, 66,270 . . . . C 4
Duncanville, 35,748 . . n10
Eagle Pass, 20,651 . . E 2
Edinburg, 29,885 . . . F 3
El Paso, 515,342 . . . o11
Farmers Branch,
    24,250 . . . . n10
Fort Worth, 447,619 . C 4
Galveston, 59,070 . . . E 5
Garland, 180,650 . . . n10
Grand Prairie, 99,616 n10
Greenville, 23,071 . . . C 4
Harlingen, 48,735 . . . F 4
Hereford, 14,745 . . . . B 1
Houston, 1,630,553 . . E 5
Huntsville, 27,925 . . . D 5
Irving, 155,037 . . . . n10
Kerrville, 17,384 . . . D 3
Killeen, 63,535 . . . . D 4
Kingsville, 25,276 . . . F 4
Lake Jackson, 22,776 E 5
La Porte, 27,910 . . . r14
Laredo, 122,899 . . . . F 3
Lewisville, 46,521 . . . C 4
Longview, 70,311 . . . C 5
Lubbock, 186,206 . . . C 2
Lufkin, 30,206 . . . . . D 5
Marshall, 23,682 . . . C 5
McAllen, 84,021 . . . . F 3
Mesquite, 101,484 . . n10
Midland, 89,443 . . . . D 1
Mineral Wells, 14,870 C 3
Mission, 28,653 . . . . F 3
Missouri City, 36,176 r14
Nacogdoches, 30,872 D 5
New Braunfels,
    27,334 . . . . E 3
North Richland Hills,
    45,895 . . . . n 9
Odessa, 89,699 . . . . D 1
Orange, 19,381 . . . . D 6
Palestine, 18,042 . . . D 5
Pampa, 19,959 . . . . . B 2
Paris, 24,699 . . . . . . C 4
Pasadena, 119,363 . . r14
Pecos, 12,069 . . . . . D 1
Pharr, 32,921 . . . . . F 3
Plainview, 21,700 . . . B 2
Plano, 128,713 . . . . C 4
Port Arthur, 58,724 . E 6
Richardson, 74,840 . . n10
Rosenberg, 20,183 . . E 5
San Angelo, 84,474 . . D 2
San Antonio, 935,933 E 3
San Benito, 20,125 . . F 4
San Marcos, 28,743 . E 4
Seguin, 18,853 . . . . . E 4
Sherman, 31,601 . . . . C 4
Temple, 46,109 . . . . D 4
Texarkana, 31,656 . . . C 5
Texas City, 40,822 . . E 5
Tyler, 75,450 . . . . . . C 5
University Park,
    22,259 . . . . n10
Uvalde, 14,729 . . . . . E 3
Victoria, 55,076 . . . . E 4
Waco, 103,590 . . . . . D 4
Waxahachie, 18,168 . C 4
Weslaco, 21,877 . . . . F 4
Wichita Falls, 96,259 C 3

120

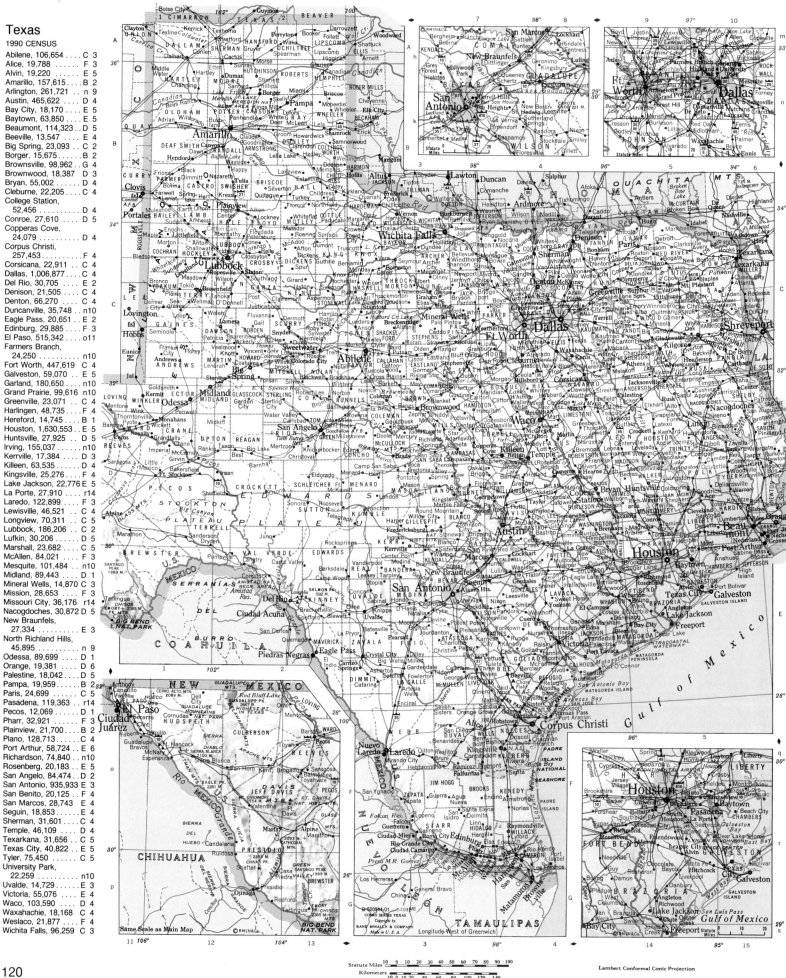

Statute Miles
Kilometers

Lambert Conformal Conic Projection

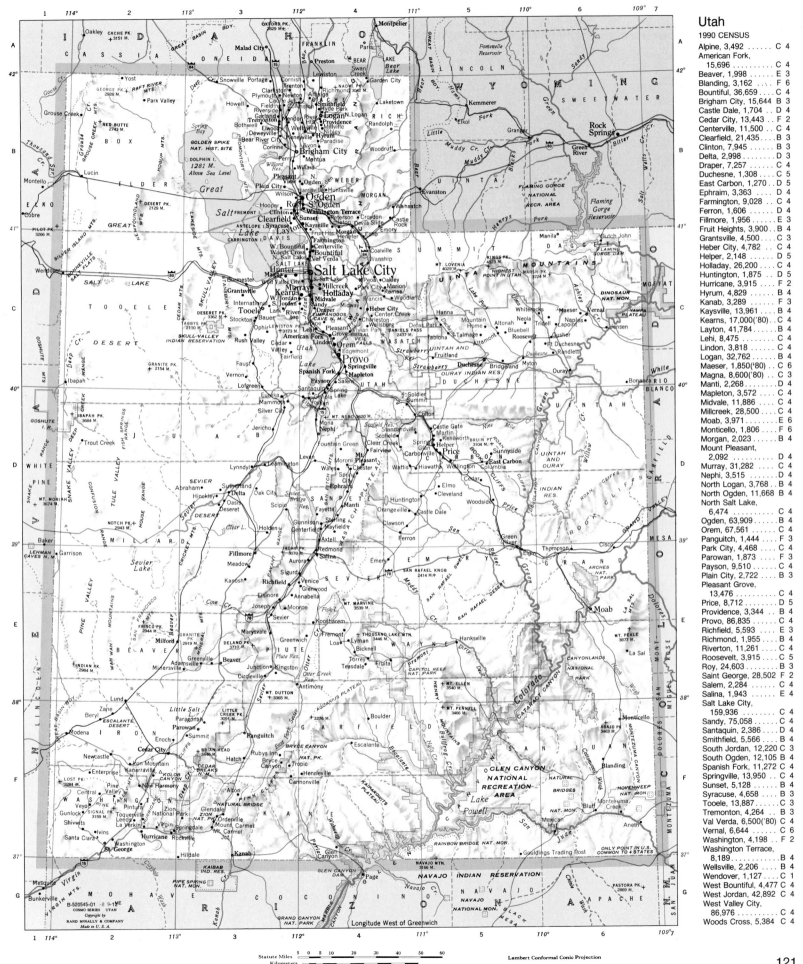

Utah

1990 CENSUS

Alpine, 3,492 ...... C 4
American Fork,
  15,696 .... C 4
Beaver, 1,998 ...... E 3
Blanding, 3,162 .... F 6
Bountiful, 36,659 ... C 4
Brigham City, 15,644 B 3
Castle Dale, 1,704 .. D 4
Cedar City, 13,443 . F 2
Centerville, 11,500 . C 4
Clearfield, 21,435 .. B 3
Clinton, 7,945 ...... B 3
Delta, 2,998 .... D 3
Draper, 7,257 ...... C 4
Duchesne, 1,308 ... C 5
East Carbon, 1,270 . D 5
Ephraim, 3,363 .... D 4
Farmington, 9,028 .. C 4
Ferron, 1,606 ...... D 4
Fillmore, 1,956 .... E 3
Fruit Heights, 3,900 . C 4
Grantsville, 4,500 .. C 3
Heber City, 4,782 .. C 4
Helper, 2,148 ...... D 5
Holladay, 26,200 ... C 4
Huntington, 1,875 .. D 5
Hurricane, 3,915 ... F 2
Hyrum, 4,829 ...... B 4
Kanab, 3,289 ...... F 3
Kaysville, 13,961 .. B 4
Kearns, 17,000('80) . C 4
Layton, 41,784 ..... B 4
Lehi, 8,475 .... C 4
Lindon, 3,818 ...... C 4
Logan, 32,762 ('80) . B 4
Maeser, 1,850('80) .. C 6
Magna, 8,600('80) .. C 3
Manti, 2,268 .... D 4
Mapleton, 3,572 .... C 4
Midvale, 11,886 .... C 4
Millcreek, 28,500 ... C 4
Moab, 3,971 .... E 6
Monticello, 1,806 .. F 6
Morgan, 2,023 ..... B 4
Mount Pleasant,
  2,092 .... D 4
Murray, 31,282 ..... C 4
Nephi, 3,515 .... D 4
North Logan, 3,768 . B 4
North Ogden, 11,668 B 4
North Salt Lake,
  6,474 .... C 4
Ogden, 63,909 ..... B 4
Orem, 67,561 ...... C 4
Panguitch, 1,444 ... F 3
Park City, 4,468 .... C 4
Parowan, 1,873 .... F 3
Payson, 9,510 ...... C 4
Plain City, 2,722 ... B 3
Pleasant Grove,
  13,476 .... C 4
Price, 8,712 .... D 5
Providence, 3,344 .. B 4
Provo, 86,835 ...... C 4
Richfield, 5,593 .... E 3
Richmond, 1,955 ... B 4
Riverton, 11,261 ... C 4
Roosevelt, 3,915 ... C 5
Roy, 24,603 .... B 3
Saint George, 28,502 F 2
Salem, 2,284 ...... C 4
Salina, 1,943 ...... E 4
Salt Lake City,
  159,936 .... C 4
Sandy, 75,058 ...... C 4
Santaquin, 2,386 ... D 4
Smithfield, 5,566 ... B 4
South Jordan, 12,220 C 3
South Ogden, 12,105 B 4
Spanish Fork, 11,272 C 4
Springville, 13,950 . C 4
Sunset, 5,128 ...... B 4
Syracuse, 4,658 .... B 3
Tooele, 13,887 ..... C 3
Tremonton, 4,264 .. B 3
Val Verda, 6,500('80) C 4
Vernal, 6,644 ...... C 6
Washington, 4,198 . F 2
Washington Terrace,
  8,189 .... B 4
Wellsville, 2,206 ... B 4
Wendover, 1,127 ... C 1
West Bountiful, 4,477 C 4
West Jordan, 42,892 . C 4
West Valley City,
  86,976 .... C 4
Woods Cross, 5,384 C 4

Vermont

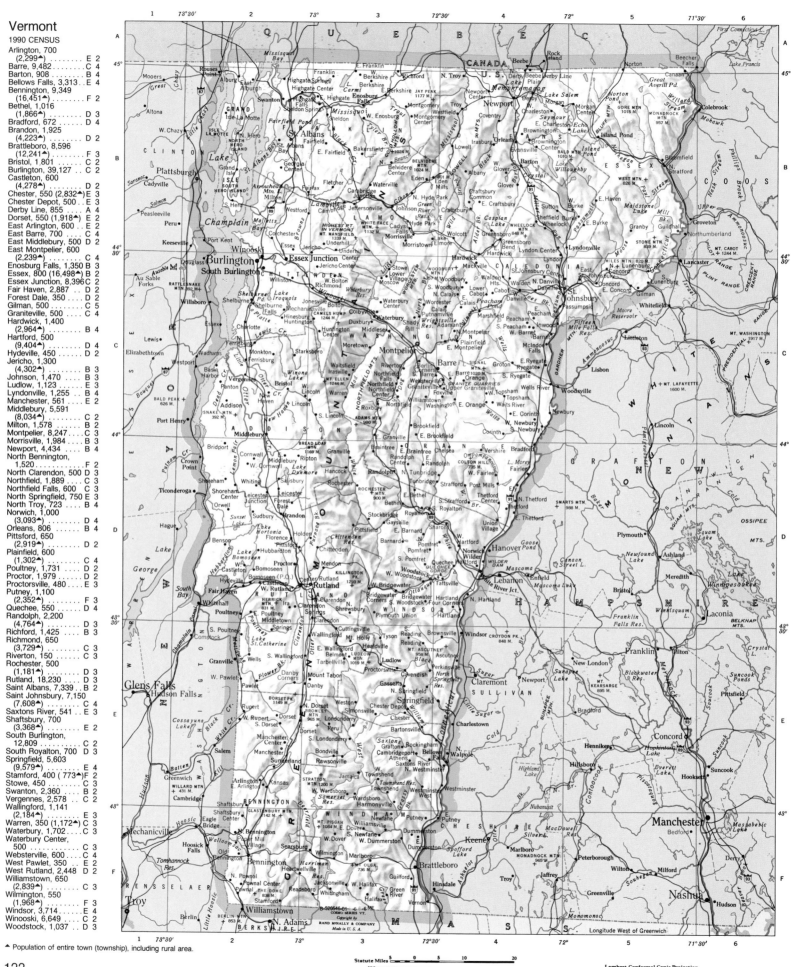

Vermont

1990 CENSUS

Arlington, 700
  (2,299▲) . . . . E 2
Barre, 9,482 . . . . C 4
Barton, 908 . . . . B 4
Bellows Falls, 3,313 . . E 4
Bennington, 9,349
  (16,451▲) . . . . F 2
Bethel, 1,016
  (1,866▲) . . . . D 3
Bradford, 672 . . . . . D 4
Brandon, 1,925
  (4,223▲) . . . . D 2
Brattleboro, 8,596
  (12,241▲) . . . . F 3
Bristol, 1,801 . . . . . C 2
Burlington, 39,127 . . C 2
Castleton, 600
  (4,278▲) . . . . E 3
Chester, 550 (2,832▲) E 3
Chester Depot, 500 . . E 3
Derby Line, 855 . . . A 4
Dorset, 550 (1,918▲) E 2
East Arlington, 600 . . E 2
East Barre, 700 . . . . C 4
East Middlebury, 500 D 2
East Montpelier, 600
  (2,239▲) . . . . C 3
Enosburg Falls, 1,350 B 3
Essex, 800 (16,498▲) B 2
Essex Junction, 8,396 C 2
Fair Haven, 2,887 . . D 2
Forest Dale, 350 . . . D 2
Gilman, 500 . . . . . . C 5
Graniteville, 500 . . . C 4
Hardwick, 1,400
  (2,964▲) . . . . B 4
Hartford, 500
  (9,404▲) . . . . D 4
Hyde Park, 450 . . . . C 2
Jericho, 1,300
  (4,302▲) . . . . B 3
Johnson, 1,470 . . . . B 3
Ludlow, 1,123 . . . . . E 3
Lyndonville, 1,255 . . B 4
Manchester, 561 . . . E 2
Middlebury, 5,591
  (8,034▲) . . . . C 2
Milton, 1,578 . . . . . B 2
Montpelier, 8,247 . . C 3
Morrisville, 1,984 . . B 3
Newport, 4,434 . . . . B 4
North Bennington,
  1,520 . . . . F 2
North Clarendon, 500 D 3
Northfield, 1,889 . . . C 3
Northfield Falls, 600 C 3
North Springfield, 750 E 3
North Troy, 723 . . . B 4
Norwich, 1,000
  (3,093▲) . . . . D 4
Orleans, 806 . . . . . . B 4
Pittsford, 650
  (2,919▲) . . . . D 2
Plainfield, 600
  (1,302▲) . . . . C 4
Poultney, 1,731 . . . . D 2
Proctor, 1,979 . . . . . D 2
Proctorsville, 480 . . E 3
Putney, 1,100
  (2,352▲) . . . . F 3
Quechee, 550 . . . . . D 4
Randolph, 2,200
  (4,764▲) . . . . D 3
Richford, 1,425 . . . . B 3
Richmond, 650
  (3,729▲) . . . . C 2
Riverton, 150 . . . . . C 3
Rochester, 500
  (1,181▲) . . . . D 3
Rutland, 18,230 . . . . D 2
Saint Albans, 7,339 . . B 2
Saint Johnsbury, 7,150
  (7,608▲) . . . . C 4
Saxtons River, 541 . . E 3
Shaftsbury, 700
  (3,368▲) . . . . E 2
South Burlington,
  12,809 . . . . C 2
South Royalton, 700 D 3
Springfield, 5,603
  (9,579▲) . . . . E 4
Stamford, 400 (773▲) F 2
Stowe, 450 . . . . B 2
Swanton, 2,360 . . . . B 2
Vergennes, 2,578 . . . C 2
Wallingford, 1,141
  (2,184▲) . . . . E 3
Warren, 350 (1,172▲) C 3
Waterbury, 1,702 . . . C 3
Waterbury Center,
  500 . . . . C 3
Websterville, 600 . . . C 4
West Pawlet, 350 . . E 2
West Rutland, 2,448 D 2
Williamstown, 650
  (2,839▲) . . . . C 3
Wilmington, 550
  (1,968▲) . . . . F 3
Windsor, 3,714 . . . . E 4
Winooski, 6,649 . . . C 2
Woodstock, 1,037 . . D 3

▲ Population of entire town (township), including rural area.

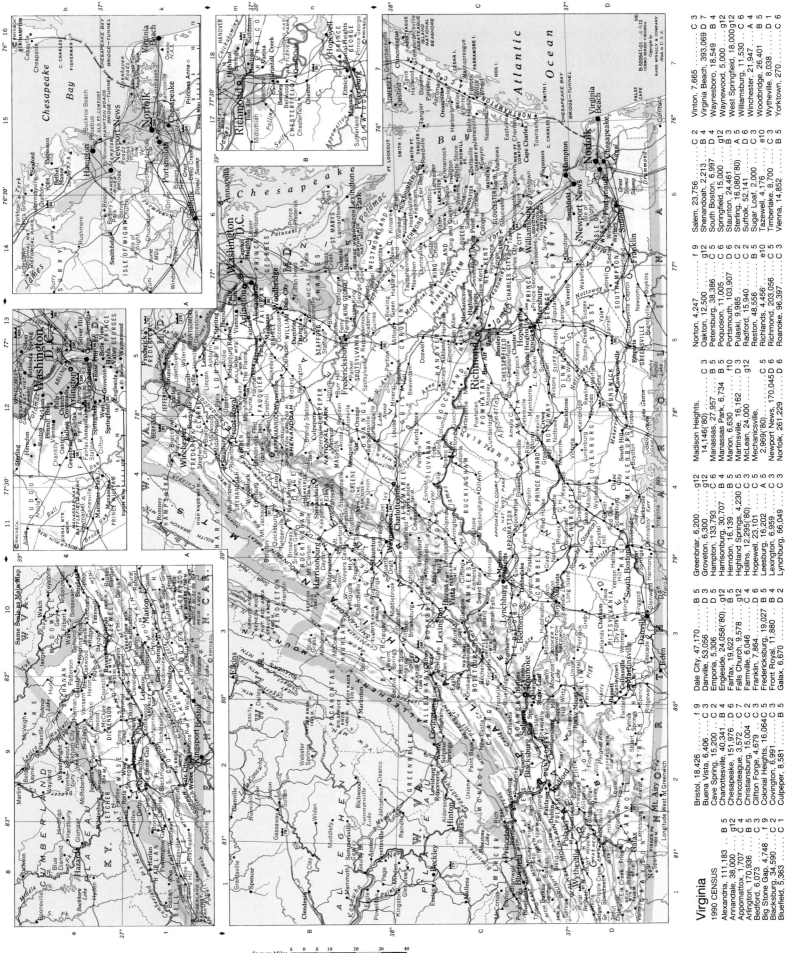

Lambert Conformal Conic Projection

Statute Miles
Kilometers

Virginia

1990 CENSUS

Alexandria, 111,183	B 5
Annandale, 38,000	g12
Appomattox, 1,707	C 3
Arlington, 170,936	B 5
Bedford, 6,073	C 3
Big Stone Gap, 4,748	f 9
Blacksburg, 34,590	C 1
Bluefield, 5,363	D 2
Bristol, 18,426	f 9
Buena Vista, 6,406	C 3
Cave Spring, 15,200	C 2
Charlottesville, 40,341	B 4
Chesapeake, 151,976	D 6
Chincoteague, 3,572	C 7
Christiansburg, 15,004	C 2
Clifton Forge, 4,679	C 3
Colonial Heights, 16,064	C 5
Covington, 6,991	C 3
Culpeper, 8,581	B 4
Dale City, 47,170	f 9
Danville, 53,056	D 3
Emporia, 5,306	D 5
Engleside, 24,058('80)	g12
Fairfax, 19,622	B 5
Falls Church, 9,578	g12
Farmville, 6,046	C 4
Franklin, 7,864	D 6
Fredericksburg, 19,027	B 5
Front Royal, 11,880	B 4
Galax, 6,670	D 2
Greenbriar, 6,200	g12
Groveton, 15,000	g12
Hampton, 133,793	C 6
Harrisonburg, 30,707	B 4
Herndon, 16,139	B 5
Highland Springs, 4,230	g12
Hollins, 12,295('80)	C 2
Hopewell, 23,101	C 5
Leesburg, 16,202	A 5
Lexington, 6,959	C 3
Lynchburg, 66,049	C 3
Madison Heights, 14,146('80)	C 3
Manassas, 27,957	B 5
Manassas Park, 6,734	B 5
Marion, 6,630	D 1
Martinsville, 16,162	D 2
McLean, 24,000	g12
Mechanicsville, 2,969('80)	C 5
Newport News, 170,045	C 6
Norfolk, 261,229	D 6
Norton, 4,247	f 9
Oakton, 12,500	g12
Petersburg, 38,386	C 5
Poquoson, 11,005	C 6
Portsmouth, 103,907	D 6
Pulaski, 9,985	C 1
Radford, 15,940	C 1
Reston, 48,556	B 5
Richlands, 4,456	D 1
Richmond, 203,056	C 5
Roanoke, 96,397	C 3
Salem, 23,756	C 2
Shenandoah, 2,213	B 4
South Boston, 6,997	D 2
Springfield, 15,000	g12
Staunton, 24,461	B 3
Sterling, 16,080('80)	A 5
Suffolk, 52,141	D 6
Sugar Loaf, 2,000	C 3
Tazewell, 4,176	D 1
Timberlake, 8,700	C 3
Vienna, 14,852	B 5
Vinton, 7,665	C 3
Virginia Beach, 393,069	D 7
Waynesboro, 18,549	B 4
Waynewood, 5,000	g12
West Springfield, 18,000	g12
Williamsburg, 11,530	C 6
Winchester, 21,947	A 4
Woodbridge, 26,401	B 5
Wytheville, 8,038	D 1
Yorktown, 270	C 6

Washington

Washington
1990 CENSUS

Aberdeen, 16,565 .... C 2
Anacortes, 11,451 .... A 3
Auburn, 33,102 .... B 3
Bellevue, 86,874 .... e11
Bellingham, 52,179 .... A 3
Bonney Lake, 7,494 .... B 3
Bothell, 12,345 .... B 3
Bremerton, 38,142 .... B 3

Camas, 6,442 .... B 4
Centralia, 12,101 .... C 3
Chehalis, 6,527 .... B 8
Cheney, 7,723 .... B 8
Clarkston, 6,753 .... C 8
College Place, 6,308 .... C 8
Colville, 4,360 .... A 8
Coulee Dam, 1,087 .... B 7
Des Moines, 17,283 .... B 3
Edmonds, 30,744 .... B 3
Ellensburg, 12,361 .... B 3

Enumclaw, 7,227 .... B 4
Ephrata, 5,349 .... B 6
Everett, 69,961 .... B 3
Ferndale, 5,398 .... f10
Fircrest, 5,258 .... A 3
Goldendale, 3,319 .... D 5
Grandview, 7,169 .... C 6
Hoquiam, 8,972 .... B 7
Issaquah, 7,786 .... B 3
Kelso, 11,820 .... C 2
Kennewick, 42,155 .... C 6

Kent, 37,960 .... B 3
Kirkland, 40,052 .... B 6
Lacey, 19,279 .... B 3
Lakewood Center, 62,000 .... B 3
Longview, 31,499 .... C 2
Lynden, 5,709 .... A 3
Lynnwood, 28,695 .... B 3
Marysville, 10,328 .... A 3
Medical Lake, 3,664 .... B 8
Mercer Island, 20,816 .... B 3

Montesano, 3,064 .... C 2
Moses Lake, 11,235 .... B 6
Mount Vernon, 17,647 .... A 3
Oak Harbor, 17,176 .... A 3
Olympia, 33,840 .... B 3
Omak, 4,117 .... A 6
Othello, 4,638 .... C 6
Parkland, 27,300 .... f11
Parkwater, 4,300('91) g14
Pasco, 20,337 .... C 6
Port Angeles, 17,710 .... A 2

Port Orchard, 4,984 .... C 2
Port Townsend, 7,001 .... A 3
Prosser, 4,476 .... C 6
Pullman, 23,478 .... B 8
Puyallup, 23,875 .... B 3
Quincy, 3,738 .... B 6
Redmond, 35,800 .... e11
Renton, 41,688 .... B 3
Richland, 32,315 .... C 6
Richmond Beach, 6,700('91) .... B 3

Richmond Highlands, 27,900 .... B 3
Riverton Heights, 14,182 .... f11
Seattle, 516,259 .... B 3
Sedro Woolley, 6,031 .... A 3
Selah, 5,113 .... C 5
Shelton, 7,241 .... B 3
Snohomish, 6,499 .... B 3
Spokane, 177,196 .... B 8
Steilacoom, 5,728 .... f10
Sumner, 6,281 .... B 3

Sunnyside, 11,238 .... C 5
Tacoma, 176,664 .... B 3
Toppenish, 7,419 .... C 5
Tukwila, 11,874 .... f11
Tumwater, 9,976 .... B 3
Vancouver, 46,380 .... D 3
Walla Walla, 26,478 .... C 7
Wenatchee, 21,756 .... B 5
White Center, 18,000('91) e11
Yakima, 54,827 .... C 5

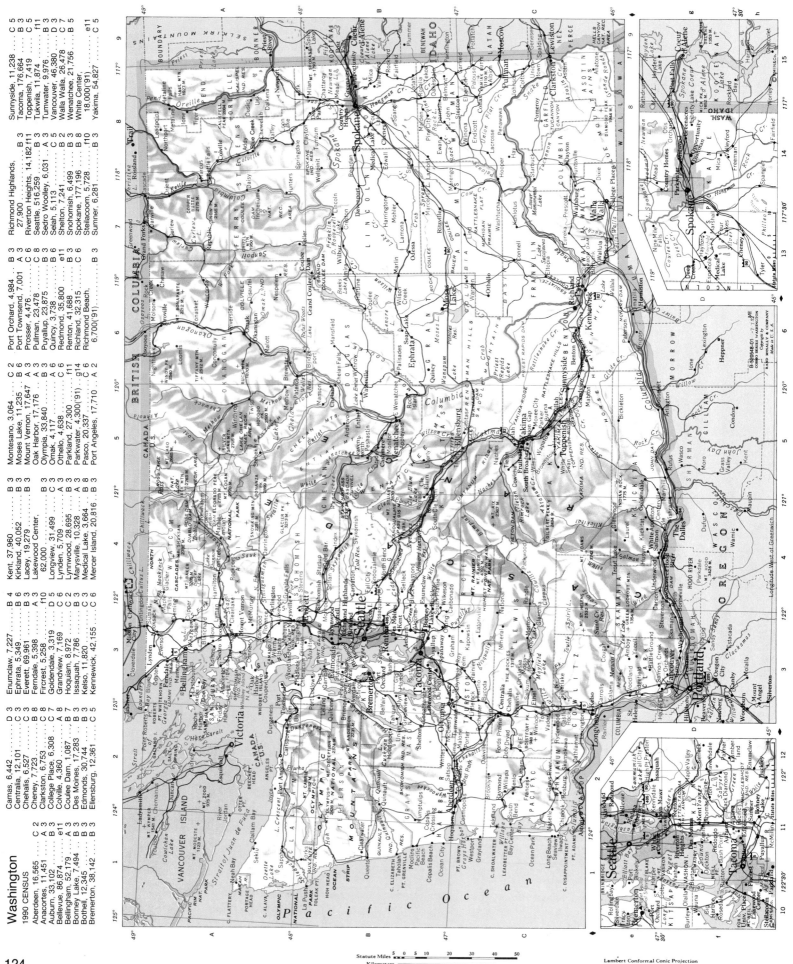

Statute Miles
Kilometers

Lambert Conformal Conic Projection

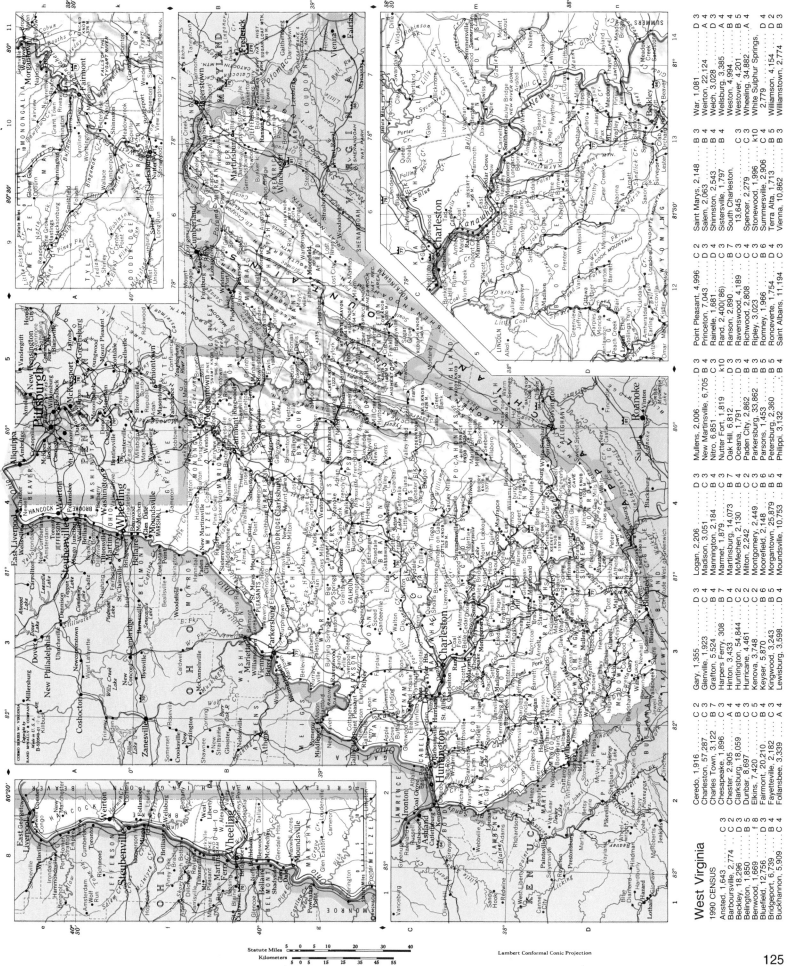

West Virginia

West Virginia

1990 CENSUS

Ansted, 1,643	C 3	
Barboursville, 2,774	C 2	
Beckley, 18,296	D 3	
Belington, 1,850	C 4	
Benwood, 1,669	f 8	
Bluefield, 12,756	D 4	
Bridgeport, 6,739	B 4	
Buckhannon, 5,909	C 4	

Ceredo, 1,916	C 2	
Charleston, 57,287	C 3	
Charles Town, 3,122	B 7	
Chesapeake, 1,896	C 3	
Chester, 2,905	A 4	
Clarksburg, 18,059	B 4	
Dunbar, 8,697	C 3	
Elkins, 7,420	C 5	
Fairmont, 20,210	B 4	
Fayetteville, 2,182	C 3	
Follansbee, 3,339	A 4	

Gary, 1,355	D 3	
Glenville, 1,923	C 4	
Grafton, 5,524	B 4	
Harpers Ferry, 308	B 7	
Hinton, 3,433	D 4	
Huntington, 54,844	C 2	
Hurricane, 4,461	C 2	
Kenova, 3,748	C 2	
Keyser, 5,870	B 6	
Kingwood, 3,243	B 5	
Lewisburg, 3,598	D 4	

Logan, 2,206	D 3	
Madison, 3,051	C 3	
Mannington, 2,184	B 4	
Marmet, 1,879	k 10	
Martinsburg, 14,073	B 7	
McMechen, 2,130	f 8	
Milton, 2,242	C 2	
Montgomery, 2,449	C 3	
Moorefield, 2,148	C 6	
Morgantown, 25,879	B 5	
Moundsville, 10,753	B 4	

Mullens, 2,006	D 3	
New Martinsville, 6,705	B 4	
Nitro, 6,851	C 3	
Nutter Fort, 1,819	k 10	
Oak Hill, 6,812	D 3	
Oceana, 1,791	D 3	
Paden City, 2,862	B 4	
Parkersburg, 33,862	C 3	
Parsons, 1,453	B 5	
Petersburg, 2,360	C 6	
Philippi, 3,132	B 4	

Point Pleasant, 4,996	C 2	
Princeton, 7,043	D 4	
Rainelle, 1,681	D 4	
Rand, 2,400(86)	C 3	
Ravenswood, 4,189	B 7	
Richwood, 2,808	C 4	
Ripley, 3,023	C 3	
Romney, 1,966	B 6	
Ronceverte, 1,754	D 4	
Saint Albans, 11,194	C 3	

Saint Marys, 2,148	D 3	
Salem, 2,063	B 4	
Shinnston, 2,543	B 4	
Sistersville, 1,797	B 4	
South Charleston, 13,645	C 3	
Spencer, 2,279	C 3	
Stonewood, 1,996	k10	
Summersville, 2,906	C 4	
Terra Alta, 1,713	B 5	
Vienna, 10,862	B 3	

War, 1,081	D 3	
Weirton, 22,124	A 4	
Welch, 3,028	D 4	
Wellsburg, 3,385	A 4	
Weston, 4,994	B 4	
Westover, 4,201	B 5	
Wheeling, 34,882	A 4	
White Sulphur Springs, 2,779	D 4	
Williamson, 4,154	D 2	
Williamstown, 2,774	B 3	

Statute Miles

Kilometers

Lambert Conformal Conic Projection

125

Wisconsin

Wisconsin
1990 CENSUS

Allouez, 14,431 .... h 9
Antigo, 8,276 ..... C 4
Appleton, 65,695 ... D 5
Ashland, 8,695 ..... B 3
Ashwaubenon, 16,376 D 5
Baraboo, 9,203 ..... E 4
Beaver Dam, 14,196 . E 5
Beloit, 35,573 ..... F 4
Brookfield, 35,184 . m11
Brown Deer, 12,236 . m12
Burlington, 8,855 ... F 5
Cedarburg, 9,895 ... E 6
Chippewa Falls,
12,727 .... D 2
Cudahy, 18,659 .... F 6
De Pere, 16,569 .... D 5
Eau Claire, 56,856 .. D 2
Fond du Lac, 37,757 . E 5
Fort Atkinson, 10,227 F 5
Franklin, 21,855 ... n11
Germantown, 13,658 . E 5
Glendale, 14,088 ... m12
Grafton, 9,340 ..... E 6
Green Bay, 96,466 .. D 6
Greendale, 15,128 .. F 6
Greenfield, 33,403 . n11
Hayward, 1,897 .... B 2
Howard, 9,874 ..... D 5
Hudson, 6,378 ..... D 1
Janesville, 52,133 .. F 4
Kaukauna, 11,982 .. D 5
Kenosha, 80,352 ... F 6
La Crosse, 51,003 .. E 2
Lake Geneva, 5,979 . F 5
Little Chute, 9,207 . D 5
Madison, 191,262 .. E 4
Manitowoc, 32,520 . D 6
Marinette, 11,843 .. C 6
Marshfield, 19,291 . D 3
Menasha, 14,711 ... D 5
Menomonee Falls,
26,840 .... E 5
Menomonie, 13,547 . D 2
Mequon, 18,885 ... E 6
Merrill, 9,860 ..... C 4
Middleton, 13,289 . E 4
Milwaukee, 628,088 . E 6
Monona, 8,637 ..... E 4
Monroe, 10,241 .... F 4
Muskego, 16,813 ... F 5
Neenah, 23,219 .... D 5
New Berlin, 33,592 . n11
New London, 6,658 . D 5
Oak Creek, 19,513 . n12
Oconomowoc, 10,993 E 5
Oconto, 4,474 ..... D 6
Onalaska, 11,284 .. E 2
Oshkosh, 55,006 ... D 5
Park Falls, 3,104 ... C 3
Platteville, 9,708 .. F 3
Portage, 8,640 ..... E 4
Port Washington,
9,338 .... E 6
Prairie du Chien,
5,659 .... E 2
Racine, 84,298 .... F 6
Reedsburg, 5,834 .. E 3
Rhinelander, 7,427 . C 4
Rice Lake, 7,998 ... C 2
River Falls, 10,610 . D 1
Saint Francis, 9,245 . n12
Shawano, 7,598 .... D 5
Sheboygan, 49,676 . E 6
Shorewood, 14,116 . E 6
South Milwaukee,
20,958 .... F 6
Stevens Point, 23,006 D 4
Stoughton, 8,786 ... F 4
Sturgeon Bay, 9,176 . D 6
Sun Prairie, 15,333 . E 4
Superior, 27,134 ... B 1
Tomah, 7,570 ..... E 3
Two Rivers, 13,030 . D 6
Watertown, 19,142 . E 5
Waukesha, 56,958 .. F 5
Waupun, 8,207 .... E 5
Wausau, 37,060 ... D 4
Wauwatosa, 49,366 . m11
West Allis, 63,221 . m11
West Bend, 23,916 . E 5
Weston, 8,775('80) . D 4
Whitefish Bay, 14,272 m12
Whitewater, 12,636 . F 5
Wisconsin Dells,
2,393 .... E 4
Wisconsin Rapids,
18,245 .... D 4

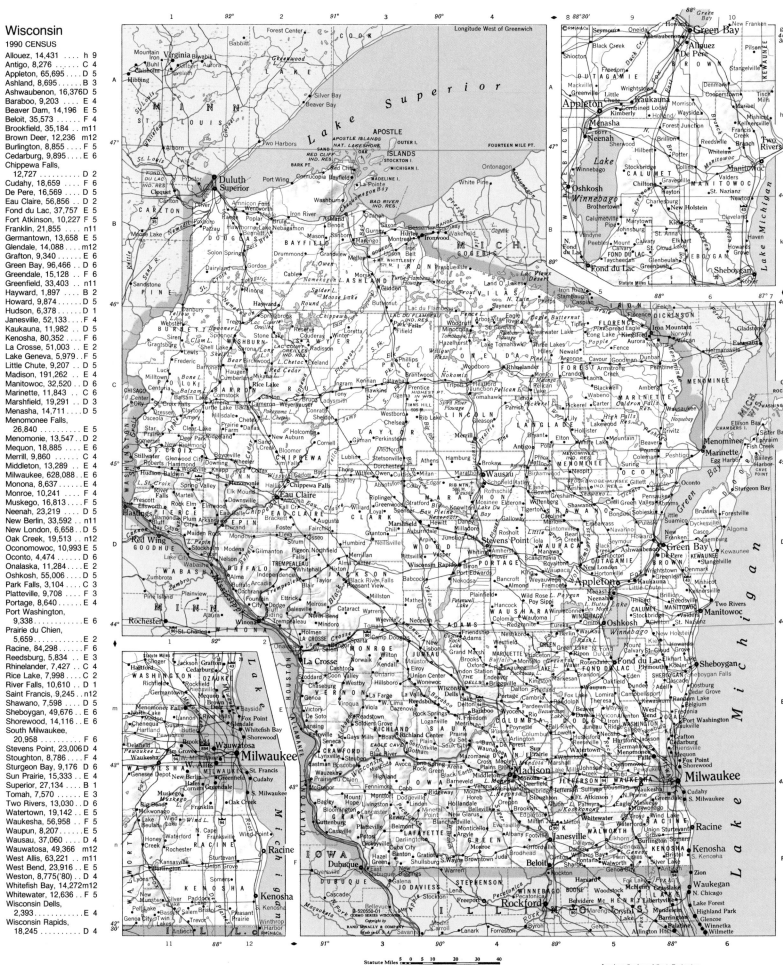

Wyoming

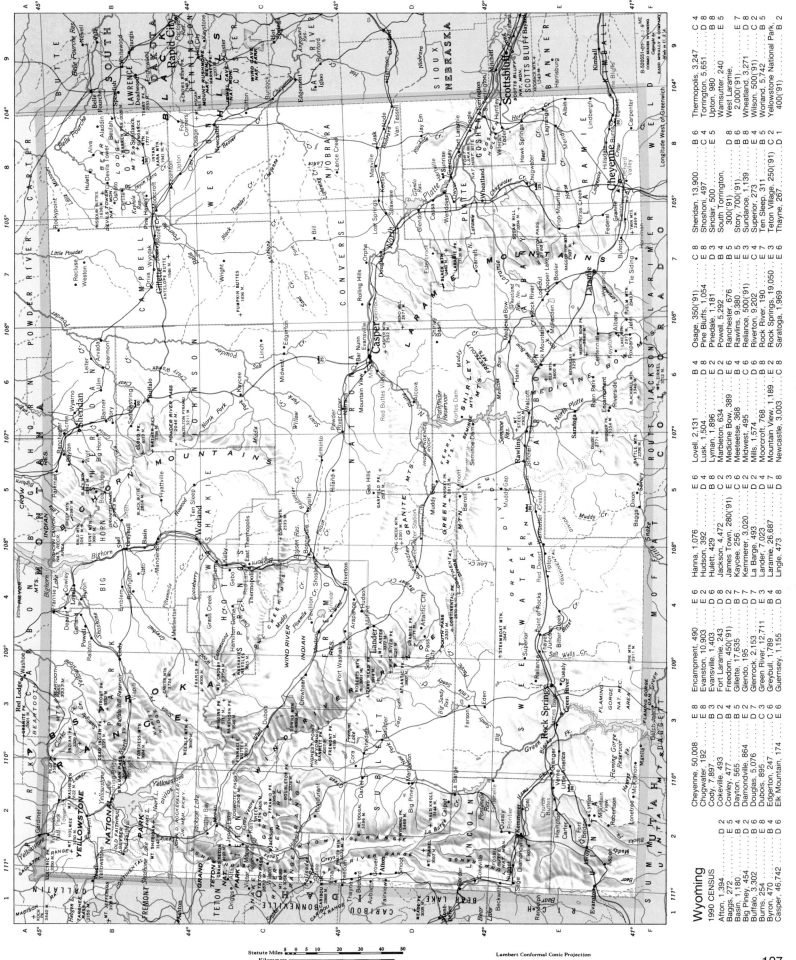

Wyoming

1990 CENSUS

Afton, 1,394	D 2		
Baggs, 272	E 5		
Basin, 1,180	B 4		
Big Piney, 454	D 3		
Buffalo, 3,302	B 6		
Byron, 470	B 4		
Casper, 46,742	D 6		

Cheyenne, 50,008	E 8	Encampment, 490	E 6
Chugwater, 192	E 8	Evanston, 10,903	E 2
Cody, 7,897	B 3	Evansville, 1,403	D 6
Cokeville, 493	D 2	Fort Laramie, 243	D 2
Cowley, 477	B 4	Freedom, 450(91)	C 2
Dayton, 565	B 5	Gillette, 17,635	B 7
Diamondville, 864	E 2	Glendo, 195	D 7
Douglas, 5,076	D 7	Glenrock, 2,153	D 7
Dubois, 895	C 3	Green River, 12,711	E 3
Edgerton, 247	D 6	Greybull, 1,789	B 4
Elk Mountain, 174	E 6	Guernsey, 1,155	D 8

Hanna, 1,076	E 6	Lovell, 2,131	B 4
Hudson, 392	C 4	Lusk, 1,504	D 8
Hulett, 429	B 8	Lyman, 1,896	E 2
Jackson, 4,472	C 2	Marbleton, 634	D 3
James Town, 280(91)	E 3	Medicine Bow, 389	E 6
Kaycee, 256	C 6	Meeteetse, 368	B 4
Kemmerer, 3,020	E 2	Midwest, 495	D 6
La Barge, 493	D 2	Mills, 1,574	D 6
Lander, 7,023	C 4	Moorcroft, 768	B 8
Laramie, 26,687	E 7	Mountain View, 1,189	E 2
Lingle, 473	D 8	Newcastle, 3,003	C 8

Osage, 350(91)	C 8	Sheridan, 13,900	B 6
Pine Bluffs, 1,054	E 8	Shoshoni, 497	C 4
Pinedale, 1,181	D 3	Sinclair, 500	E 5
Powell, 5,292	B 4	South Torrington,	
Ranchester, 676	B 5	300(91)	D 8
Rawlins, 9,380	E 5	Story, 700(91)	B 6
Reliance, 500(91)	E 3	Sundance, 1,139	B 8
Riverton, 9,202	C 4	Superior, 273	E 4
Rock River, 190	E 7	Ten Sleep, 311	B 5
Rock Springs, 19,050	E 3	Teton Village, 250(91)	C 2
Saratoga, 1,969	E 6	Thayne, 267	D 1

Thermopolis, 3,247	C 4	
Torrington, 5,651	D 8	
Upton, 980	B 8	
Wamsutter, 240	E 5	
West Laramie,		
2,000(91)	E 7	
Wheatland, 3,271	D 8	
Wilson, 500(91)	C 2	
Worland, 5,742	B 5	
Yellowstone National Park,		
400(91)	B 2	

Statute Miles

Kilometers

Lambert Conformal Conic Projection

127

North Polar Regions

Anchorage, 226,338
('90)................C27
Archangel'sk, 416,000
('89)..................C 8
BELGIUM..................D12
Berlin, 3,352,848 ('89)
(3,825,000★).........D11
CANADA..................D22
Chicago, 2,783,726
('90)..................E21
CHINA....................F 2
Churchill, 1,186 ('81)..D22
DENMARK.................D11
Dublin, 502,749 ('86)
(1,140,000★)........D13
Dutch Harbor, 20 ('81)D29
Edmonton, 573,982 ('86)
(785,465★)..........D24
ESTONIA..................C10
FAEROE ISLANDS.....C13
Fairbanks, 30,843
('90)..................C27
FINLAND..................C10
FRANCE..................E12
Gander, 10,207 ('86)
(10,899★)...........E18
GERMANY................D11
Godthåb, 12,217 ('90).C18
GREENLAND............B17
Hammerfest, 7,208
('83)..................B10
Happy Valley-Goose Bay,
7,248 ('86)..........D19
Helsinki, 490,034 ('88)
(1,040,000★)........C10
ICELAND.................C14
Igarka, 16,918 ('79)....C 4
IRELAND.................D13
JAPAN....................F35
Jekaterinburg, 1,367,000
('89) (1,620,000★) .. D 6
Juneau, 26,751 ('90)..D26
Kijev (Kiev), 2,587,000
('89) (2,900,000★) .. D 9
KOREA, NORTH........E36
KOREA, SOUTH........F36
LATVIA...................C10
LITHUANIA..............C10
Leningrad, 4,456,000 ('89)
(5,825,000★)........D 9
LUXEMBOURG.........E12
Magadan, 152,000
('89)..................D33
MONGOLIA...............E 2
Moskva (Moscow),
8,769,000 ('89)
(13,100,000★)......D 9
Murmansk, 468,000
('89)..................C 9
NETHERLANDS.........D12
New York, 7,322,564
('90)..................E20
Nižnij Novgorod (Gorky),
1,438,000 ('89)
(2,025,000★)........D 8
Nome, 3,500 ('90)......C29
Noril'sk, 174,000 ('89).C 4
NORWAY.................C12
Novosibirsk, 1,436,000
('89) (1,600,000★) .. D 4
Ōsaka, 2,636,249 ('85)
(16,450,000★).......F35
Oslo, 452,415 ('87)
(720,000★)..........D11
Ottawa, 300,763 ('86)
(819,263★)..........E20
Paris, 2,078,900 ('87)
(9,775,000★)........E12
POLAND..................D11
Québec, 164,580 ('86)
(603,267★)..........E20
Reykjavík, 93,425 ('87)
(137,941★)..........C15
RUSSIA...................C 4
Saint John's, 96,216 ('86)
(161,901★)..........E18
Sankt-Peterburg,
4,456,000 ('89)
(5,825,000★)..........D 9
Seattle, 516,259 ('90)..E25
Shenyang (Mukden),
3,910,000 ('88)
(4,370,000▲)........E36
Sŏul (Seoul), 10,522,000
('89) (15,850,000★)..F36
Stockholm, 672,187 ('90)
(1,449,972★)........D11
SWEDEN.................C11
Thule, 551 ('90)........B19
Tōkyō, 8,354,615 ('85)
(27,700,000★)......F35
UKRAINE.................E 9
Ulaanbaatar (Ulan Bator),
548,400 ('89)........E 2
UNITED KINGDOM.....D13
UNITED STATES.......F22
Vancouver, 431,147 ('86)
(1,380,729★)........E25
Vladivostok, 648,000
('89)..................E35
Vorkuta, 116,000 ('89)C 6
Warszawa, 1,651,200
('89) (2,323,000★)..D10
Winnipeg, 594,551 ('86)
(625,304★)..........E22

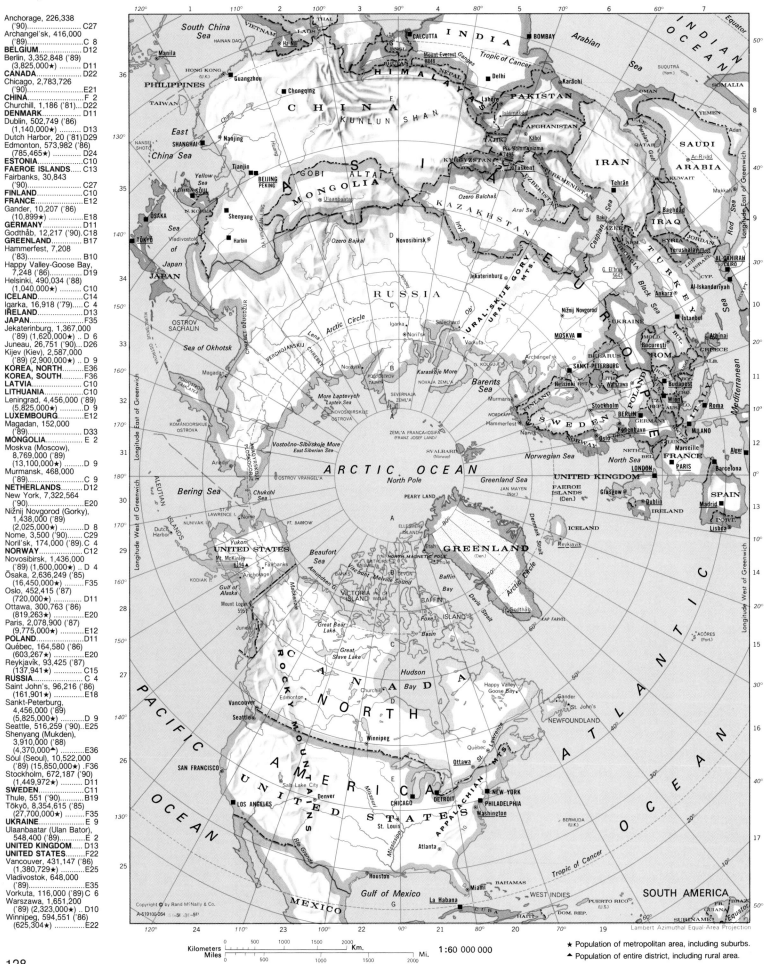

128

★ Population of metropolitan area, including suburbs.

▲ Population of entire district, including rural area.

Index to World Reference Maps

Introduction to the Index

This universal index includes in a single alphabetical list approximately 38,000 names of features that appear on the reference maps. Each name is followed by the name of the country or continent in which it is located, a map-reference key and a page reference.

Names The names of cities appear in the index in regular type. The names of all other features appear in *italics*, followed by descriptive terms (hill, mtn., state) to indicate their nature.

Names that appear in shortened versions on the maps due to space limitations are spelled out in full in the index. The portions of these names omitted from the maps are enclosed in brackets — for example, Acapulco [de Juárez].

Abbreviations of names on the maps have been standardized as much as possible. Names that are abbreviated on the maps are generally spelled out in full in the index.

Country names and names of features that extend beyond the boundaries of one country are followed by the name of the continent in which each is located. Country designations follow the names of all other places in the index. The locations of places in the United States, Canada, and the United Kingdom are further defined by abbreviations that indicate the state, province, or political division in which each is located.

All abbreviations used in the index are defined in the List of Abbreviations below.

Alphabetization Names are alphabetized in the order of the letters of the English alphabet. Spanish *ll* and *ch*, for example, are not treated as distinct letters. Furthermore, diacritical marks are disregarded in alphabetization — German or Scandinavian ä or ö are treated as a or o.

The names of physical features may appear inverted, since they are always alphabetized under the proper, not the generic, part of the name, thus: 'Gibraltar, Strait of'. Otherwise every entry, whether consisting of one word or more, is alphabetized as a single continuous entity. 'Lakeland', for example, appears after 'La Crosse' and before 'La Salle'. Names beginning with articles (Le Havre, Den Helder, Al Manşūrah) are not inverted. Names beginning 'St.', 'Ste.' and 'Sainte' are alphabetized as though spelled 'Saint'.

In the case of identical names, towns are listed first, then political divisions, then physical features. Entries that are completely identical are listed alphabetically by country name.

Map-Reference Keys and Page References The map-reference keys and page references are found in the last two columns of each entry.

Each map-reference key consists of a letter and number. The letters appear along the sides of the maps. Lowercase letters indicate reference to inset maps. Numbers appear across the tops and bottoms of the maps.

Map reference keys for point features, such as cities and mountain peaks, indicate the locations of the symbols. For extensive areal features, such as countries or mountain ranges, locations are given for the approximate centers of the features. Those for linear features, such as canals and rivers, are given for the locations of the names.

Names of some important places or features that are omitted from the maps due to space limitations are included in the index. Each of these places is identified by an asterisk (*) preceding the map-reference key.

The page number generally refers to the main map for the country in which the feature is located. Page references to two-page maps always refer to the left-hand page.

List of Abbreviations

Afg.	Afghanistan	*ctry.*	country	*is.*	islands	Nic.	Nicaragua	Sp. N. Afr.	Spanish North Africa
Afr.	Africa	C.V.	Cape Verde	Isr.	Israel	Nig.	Nigeria	Sri L.	Sri Lanka
Ak., U.S.	Alaska, U.S.	Cyp.	Cyprus	Jam.	Jamaica	N. Ire., U.K.	Northern Ireland, U.K.	*state*	state, republic, canton
Al., U.S.	Alabama, U.S.	Czech.	Czech Republic	Jord.	Jordan	N.J., U.S.	New Jersey, U.S.	St. Hel.	St. Helena
Alb.	Albania	D.C., U.S.	District of Columbia,	Kaz.	Kazakhstan	N. Kor.	North Korea	St. K./N	St. Kitts and Nevis
Alg.	Algeria		U.S.	Kir.	Kiribati	N.M., U.S.	New Mexico, U.S.	St. Luc.	St. Lucia
Alta., Can.	Alberta, Can.	De., U.S.	Delaware, U.S.	Ks., U.S.	Kansas, U.S.	N. Mar. Is.	Northern Mariana	*stm.*	stream (river, creek)
Am. Sam.	American Samoa	Den.	Denmark	Kuw.	Kuwait		Islands	S. Tom./P.	Sao Tome and
anch.	anchorage	*dep.*	dependency, colony	Ky., U.S.	Kentucky, U.S.	Nmb.	Namibia		Principe
And.	Andorra	*depr.*	depression	Kyrg.	Kyrgyzstan	Nor.	Norway	St. P./M.	St. Pierre and
Ang.	Angola	*dept.*	department, district	*l.*	lake, pond	Norf. I.	Norfolk Island		Miquelon
Ant.	Antarctica	*des.*	desert	Lat.	Latvia	N.S., Can.	Nova Scotia, Can.	*strt.*	strait, channel, sound
Antig.	Antigua and Barbuda	Dji.	Djibouti	Leb.	Lebanon	Nv., U.S.	Nevada, U.S.	St. Vin.	St. Vincent and the
Ar., U.S.	Arkansas, U.S.	Dom.	Dominica	Leso.	Lesotho	N.W. Ter.,	Northwest Territories,		Grenadines
Arg.	Argentina	Dom. Rep.	Dominican Republic	Lib.	Liberia	Can.	Can.	Sud.	Sudan
Arm.	Armenia	Ec.	Ecuador	Liech.	Liechtenstein	N.Y., U.S.	New York, U.S.	Sur.	Suriname
Aus.	Austria	El Sal.	El Salvador	Lith.	Lithuania	N.Z.	New Zealand	*sw.*	swamp, marsh
Austl.	Australia	Eng., U.K.	England, U.K.	Lux.	Luxembourg	Oc.	Oceania	Swaz.	Swaziland
Az., U.S.	Arizona, U.S.	Eq. Gui.	Equatorial Guinea	Ma., U.S.	Massachusetts, U.S.	Oh., U.S.	Ohio, U.S.	Swe.	Sweden
Azer.	Azerbaijan	Erit.	Eritrea	Mac.	Macedonia	Ok., U.S.	Oklahoma, U.S.	Switz.	Switzerland
b.	bay, gulf, inlet, lagoon	*est.*	estuary	Madag.	Madagascar	Or., U.S.	Oregon, U.S.	Tai.	Taiwan
Bah.	Bahamas	Est.	Estonia	Malay.	Malaysia	Pa., U.S.	Pennsylvania, U.S.	Taj.	Tajikistan
Bahr.	Bahrain	Eth.	Ethiopia	Mald.	Maldives	Pak.	Pakistan	Tan.	Tanzania
Barb.	Barbados	Eur.	Europe	Man., Can.	Manitoba, Can.	Pan.	Panama	T./C. Is.	Turks and Caicos
B.A.T.	British Antarctic	Faer. Is.	Faeroe Islands	Marsh. Is.	Marshall Islands	Pap. N. Gui.	Papua New Guinea		Islands
	Territory	Falk. Is.	Falkland Islands	Mart.	Martinique	Para.	Paraguay	*ter.*	territory
B.C., Can.	British Columbia, Can.	Fin.	Finland	Maur.	Mauritania	P.E.I., Can.	Prince Edward Island,	Thai.	Thailand
Bdi.	Burundi	Fl., U.S.	Florida, U.S.	May.	Mayotte		Can.	Tn., U.S.	Tennessee, U.S.
Bel.	Belgium	*for.*	forest, moor	Md., U.S.	Maryland, U.S.	*pen.*	peninsula	Tok.	Tokelau
Bela.	Belarus	Fr.	France	Me., U.S.	Maine, U.S.	Phil.	Philippines	Trin.	Trinidad and Tobago
Ber.	Bermuda	Fr. Gu.	French Guiana	Mex.	Mexico	Pit.	Pitcairn	Tun.	Tunisia
Bhu.	Bhutan	Fr. Poly.	French Polynesia	Mi., U.S.	Michigan, U.S.	*pl.*	plain, flat	Tur.	Turkey
B.I.O.T.	British Indian Ocean	F.S.A.T.	French Southern and	Micron.	Federated States of	*plat.*	plateau, highland	Turk.	Turkmenistan
	Territory		Antarctic Territory		Micronesia	Pol.	Poland	Tx., U.S.	Texas, U.S.
Bngl.	Bangladesh	Ga., U.S.	Georgia, U.S.	Mid. Is.	Midway Islands	Port.	Portugal	U.A.E.	United Arab Emirates
Bol.	Bolivia	Gam.	Gambia	*mil.*	military installation	P.R.	Puerto Rico	Ug.	Uganda
Bos.	Bosnia and	Geor.	Georgia	Mn., U.S.	Minnesota, U.S.	*prov.*	province, region	U.K.	United Kingdom
	Herzegovina	Ger.	Germany	Mo., U.S.	Missouri, U.S.	Que., Can.	Quebec, Can.	Ukr.	Ukraine
Bots.	Botswana	Gib.	Gibraltar	Mol.	Moldova	*reg.*	physical region	Ur.	Uruguay
Braz.	Brazil	Golan Hts.	Golan Heights	Mon.	Monaco	*res.*	reservoir	U.S.	United States
Bru.	Brunei	Grc.	Greece	Mong.	Mongolia	Reu.	Reunion	Ut., U.S.	Utah, U.S.
Br. Vir. Is.	British Virgin Islands	Gren.	Grenada	Monts.	Montserrat	*rf.*	reef, shoal	Uzb.	Uzbekistan
Bul.	Bulgaria	Grnld.	Greenland	Mor.	Morocco	R.I., U.S.	Rhode Island, U.S.	Va., U.S.	Virginia, U.S.
Burkina	Burkina Faso	Guad.	Guadeloupe	Moz.	Mozambique	Rom.	Romania	*val.*	valley, watercourse
c.	cape, point	Guat.	Guatemala	Mrts.	Mauritius	Rw.	Rwanda	Vat.	Vatican City
Ca., U.S.	California, U.S.	Gui.	Guinea	Ms., U.S.	Mississippi, U.S.	S.A.	South America	Ven.	Venezuela
Cam.	Cameroon	Gui.-B.	Guinea-Bissau	Mt., U.S.	Montana, U.S.	S. Afr.	South Africa	Viet.	Vietnam
Camb.	Cambodia	Guy.	Guyana	*mth.*	river mouth or channel	Sask., Can.	Saskatchewan, Can.	V.I.U.S.	Virgin Islands (U.S.)
Can.	Canada	Hi., U.S.	Hawaii, U.S.	*mtn.*	mountain	Sau. Ar.	Saudi Arabia	*vol.*	volcano
Cay. Is.	Cayman Islands	*hist.*	historic site, ruins	*mts.*	mountains	S.C., U.S.	South Carolina, U.S.	Vt., U.S.	Vermont, U.S.
Cen. Afr.	Central African	*hist. reg.*	historic region	Mwi.	Malawi	*sci.*	scientific station	Wa., U.S.	Washington, U.S.
Rep.	Republic	H.K.	Hong Kong	Mya.	Myanmar	Scot., U.K.	Scotland, U.K.	Wal./F.	Wallis and Futuna
Christ. I.	Christmas Island	Hond.	Honduras	N.A.	North America	S.D., U.S.	South Dakota, U.S.	W. Bank	West Bank
C. Iv.	Cote d'Ivoire	Hung.	Hungary	N.B., Can.	New Brunswick, Can.	Sen.	Senegal	Wi., U.S.	Wisconsin, U.S.
clf.	cliff, escarpment	*i.*	island	N.C., U.S.	North Carolina, U.S.	Sey.	Seychelles	W. Sah.	Western Sahara
co.	county, parish	Ia., U.S.	Iowa, U.S.	N. Cal.	New Caledonia	Sing.	Singapore	W. Sam.	Western Samoa
Co., U.S.	Colorado, U.S.	Ice.	Iceland	N. Cyp.	North Cyprus	S. Kor.	South Korea	*wtfl.*	waterfall
Col.	Colombia	*ice*	ice feature, glacier	N.D., U.S.	North Dakota, U.S.	S.L.	Sierra Leone	W.V., U.S.	West Virginia, U.S.
Com.	Comoros	Id., U.S.	Idaho, U.S.	Ne., U.S.	Nebraska, U.S.	Slo.	Slovenia	Wy., U.S.	Wyoming, U.S.
cont.	continent	Il., U.S.	Illinois, U.S.	Neth.	Netherlands	Slov.	Slovakia	Yugo.	Yugoslavia
C.R.	Costa Rica	In., U.S.	Indiana, U.S.	Neth. Ant.	Netherlands Antilles	S. Mar.	San Marino	Yukon, Can.	Yukon Territory, Can.
crat.	crater	Indon.	Indonesia	Newf., Can.	Newfoundland, Can.	Sol. Is.	Solomon Islands	Zam.	Zambia
Cro.	Croatia	I. of Man	Isle of Man	N.H., U.S.	New Hampshire; U.S.	Som.	Somalia	Zimb.	Zimbabwe
Ct., U.S.	Connecticut, U.S.	Ire.	Ireland						

Index

A

Name — Map Ref — Page

Aachen, Ger. E6 8
Aalen, Ger. G10 8
Aalst, Bel. E4 8
Äänekoski, Fin. E15 6
Aarau, Switz. E15 10
Aarschot, Bel. E4 8
Aba, China E7 26
Aba, Nig. G7 42
Ābādān, Iran B4 46
Abaeté, Braz. E6 57
Abajo Peak, mtn., Ut., U.S. F6 121
Abakan, Russia G12 24
Abancay, Peru F4 54
Abashiri, Japan o22 30a
Abasolo, Mex. E7 62
Abaya, Lake, l., Eth. G2 46
Abaza, Russia G12 24
Abbadia San Salvatore, Italy G6 14
Abbaye, Point, c., Mi., U.S. B2 99
Abbeville, Fr. B8 10
Abbeville, Al., U.S. D4 78
Abbeville, Ga., U.S. E3 87
Abbeville, La., U.S. E3 95
Abbeville, S.C., U.S. C3 117
Abbeville, co., S.C., U.S. C2 117
Abbotsford, Wi., U.S. D3 126
Abbottābād, Pak. C5 38
Abbott Butte, mtn., Or., U.S. E4 114
Abbott Run, stm., U.S. B4 116
Abbott Run Valley, R.I., U.S. B4 116
ʿAbd al-Kūrī, i., Yemen F5 46
Abe, Lake, l., Afr. F3 46
Abéché, Chad F10 42
Abéjar, Spain D9 12
Abengourou, C. Iv. G5 42
Abeokuta, Nig. G6 42
Aberayron, Wales, U.K. I8 7
Aberdeen, Scot., U.K. D10 7
Aberdeen, Id., U.S. G6 89
Aberdeen, Md., U.S. A5 97
Aberdeen, Ms., U.S. B5 101
Aberdeen, N.C., U.S. B3 110
Aberdeen, Oh., U.S. D2 112
Aberdeen, S.D., U.S. B7 118
Aberdeen, Wa., U.S. C2 124
Aberdeen Lake, l., N.W. Ter., Can. D13 66
Aberdeen Proving Ground, mil., Md., U.S. A5 97
Abernathy, Tx., U.S. C2 120
Abert, Lake, l., Or., U.S. E6 114
Abert Rim, clf, Or., U.S. E6 114
Aberystwyth, Wales, U.K. I8 7
Abhā, Sau. Ar. E3 46
Abidjan, C. Iv. G5 42
Abilene, Ks., U.S. D6 93
Abilene, Tx., U.S. C3 120
Abingdon, Il., U.S. C3 90
Abingdon, Md., U.S. B5 97
Abingdon, Va., U.S. f10 123
Abington, Ma., U.S. B6 98
Abington [Township], Pa., U.S. o21 115
Abisko, Swe. B12 6
Abita Springs, La., U.S. D5 95
Abitibi, stm., Ont., Can. o19 73
Abitibi, Lake, l., Can. G17 66
Abohar, India E6 38
Abomey, Benin G6 42
Aborigen, Pik, mtn., Russia E23 24
Abraham Lake, res., Alta., Can. C2 68
Abraham Lincoln Birthplace National Historic Site, hist., Ky., U.S. C4 94
Abrantes, Port. F3 12
Absaroka Range, mts., U.S. F7 127
Absarokee, Mt., U.S. E7 103
Absecon, N.J., U.S. E4 107
Absecon Inlet, b., N.J., U.S. E4 107
Abū ʿAlī, i., Sau. Ar. C4 46
Abu Dhabi see Abū Ẓaby, U.A.E. D5 46
Abū Ḥamad, Sudan E12 42
Abuja, Nig. G7 42
Abū Kamāl, Syria B7 40
Abukuma-sanchi, mts., Japan E13 30
Abū Madd, Ra's, c., Sau. Ar. D2 46
Abunã, Braz. E5 54
Abū Shajarah, Ra's, c., Sudan D13 42
Abū Ẓaby, U.A.E. D5 46
Academia, Oh., U.S. B3 112
Acadia, co., La., U.S. D3 95
Acadia National Park, Me., U.S. D4 96
Acajutla, El Sal. H3 64
Acámbaro, Mex. G9 62
Acaponeta, Mex. F7 62
Acapulco [de Juárez], Mex. I10 62
Acarai Mountains, mts., S.A. C7 54
Acaraú, Braz. D10 54
Acarigua, Ven. C8 58
Acatlán [de Osorio], Mex. H10 62
Acayucan, Mex. I12 62
Accomack, co., Va., U.S. C7 123
Accoville, W.V., U.S. D3 125
Accra, Ghana G5 42
Acerra, Italy I9 14
Achaguas, Ven. D8 58
Achalpur, India B4 37
Acheng, China B12 26
Achí, Col. C5 58
Achill Island, i., Ire. H2 7
Achtubinsk, Russia H7 22
Ačinsk, Russia F12 24
Acireale, Italy L10 14
Ackerman, Ms., U.S. B4 101
Ackley, Ia., U.S. B4 92
Acklins Island, i., Bah. C10 64
Acoma Indian Reservation, N.M., U.S. C2 108
Aconcagua, Cerro, mtn., Arg. C2 56
Açores (Azores), is., Port. D11 2
Acquapendente, Italy G6 14
Acqui Terme, Italy E3 14
Acre, stm., S.A. E5 54
Acri, Italy J11 14
Acton, Ma., U.S. B5 98
Acton Vale, Que., Can. D5 74
Acushnet, Ma., U.S. C6 98
Acworth, Ga., U.S. B2 87
Ada, Mn., U.S. C2 100
Ada, Oh., U.S. B2 112
Ada, Ok., U.S. C5 113
Ada, co., Id., U.S. F2 89
Ada, Mount, mtn., Ak., U.S. m22 79
Adair, Ia., U.S. C3 92
Adair, Ok., U.S. A6 113
Adair, co., Ia., U.S. C3 92
Adair, co., Ky., U.S. C4 94
Adair, co., Mo., U.S. A5 102
Adair, co., Ok., U.S. B7 113
Adair, Cape, c., N.W. Ter., Can. B18 66
Adairsville, Ga., U.S. B2 87
Adairville, Ky., U.S. D3 94
Adak Island, i., Ak., U.S. E4 79
Adak Naval Station, mil., Ak., U.S. E4 79
Ādam, Oman D6 46
Adamantina, Braz. F3 57
Adamawa, mts., Afr. G8 42
Adam Island, i., Md., U.S. D5 97
Adams, Ma., U.S. A1 98
Adams, Mn., U.S. G6 100
Adams, N.Y., U.S. B4 109
Adams, Wi., U.S. E4 126
Adams, co., Co., U.S. B6 83
Adams, co., Id., U.S. E2 89
Adams, co., Il., U.S. D2 90
Adams, co., In., U.S. C8 91
Adams, co., Ia., U.S. C3 92
Adams, co., Ms., U.S. D2 101
Adams, co., Ne., U.S. D7 104
Adams, co., N.D., U.S. C3 111
Adams, co., Oh., U.S. D2 112
Adams, co., Pa., U.S. G7 115
Adams, co., Wa., U.S. B7 124
Adams, co., Wi., U.S. D4 126
Adams, Mount, mtn., N.H., U.S. B4 106
Adams, Mount, mtn., Wa., U.S. C4 124
Adams Bridge, rf., Asia H5 37
Adams Point, c., Mi., U.S. C7 99
Adams Run, S.C., U.S. k11 117
Adamstown, Pa., U.S. F9 115
Adamsville, Al., U.S. f7 78
Adamsville, R.I., U.S. E6 116
Adamsville, Tn., U.S. B3 119
Adamsville Brook, stm., R.I., U.S. E6 116
ʿAdan (Aden), Yemen F4 46
Adana, Tur. H15 4
Adapazarı, Tur. G14 4
Adarama, Sudan E12 42
Ad-Dabbah, Sudan E12 42
Ad-Dahnā, des., Sau. Ar. D4 46
Ad-Dammām, Sau. Ar. C5 46
Ad-Dawādimī, Sau. Ar. D3 46
Ad-Dawḥah (Doha), Qatar C5 46
Addis, La., U.S. D4 95
Addis Ababa see Adis Abeba, Eth. G2 46
Addison, Al., U.S. A2 78
Addison, Ct., U.S. C5 84
Addison, Il., U.S. k8 90
Addison, N.Y., U.S. C3 109
Addison, co., Vt., U.S. C2 122
Ad-Dīwānīyah, Iraq B3 46
Ad-Duwaym, Sudan F12 42
Addyston, Oh., U.S. o12 112
Adel, Ga., U.S. E3 87
Adel, Ia., U.S. C3 92
Adelaide, Austl. F7 50
Adelaide Peninsula, pen., N.W. Ter., Can. C13 66
Adelanto, Ca., U.S. E5 82
Aden, Gulf of, b. F4 46
Aden see ʿAdan, Yemen F4 46
Adieu, Cape, c., Austl. F6 50
Adige, stm., Italy D7 14
Adigrat, Eth. F2 46
Ādilābād, India C5 37
Adimi, Russia H21 24
Adirondack Mountains, mts., N.Y., U.S. A6 109
Adis Abeba, Eth. G2 46
Admiralty Bay, b., Ak., U.S. A9 79
Admiralty Inlet, b., N.W. Ter., Can. B15 66
Admiralty Island, i., Ak., U.S. m22 79
Admiralty Islands, is., Pap. N. Gui. k16 50a
Adobe Acres, N.M., U.S. *B3 108
Adobe Creek Reservoir, res., Co., U.S. C7 83
Adolfo López Mateos, Presa, res., Mex. E6 62
Ādoni, India E4 37
Adour, stm., Fr. I7 10
Adra, Spain I8 12
Adrano, Italy L9 14
Adrar, Alg. C5 42
Adria, Italy D7 14
Adrian, Ga., U.S. D4 87
Adrian, Mi., U.S. G6 99
Adrian, Mn., U.S. G3 100
Adrian, Mo., U.S. C3 102
Adriatic Sea, Eur. G11 4
Advance, Mo., U.S. D8 102
Adyča, stm., Russia D21 24
Aegean Sea J8 16
Afars and Issas see Djibouti, ctry., Afr. F3 46
Afghanistan, ctry., Asia C1 36
Afikpo, Nig. G7 42
Åfjord, Nor. E8 6
Afmadu, Som. A8 44
Afognak Island, i., Ak., U.S. D9 79
Africa D6 41
Afton, Ia., U.S. C3 92
Afton, Mn., U.S. F6 100
Afton, Ok., U.S. A7 113
Afton, Wy., U.S. D2 127
ʿAfula, Isr. C4 40
Afyon, Tur. H14 4
Agadez, Niger E7 42
Agadir, Mor. B4 42
Agalega Islands, is., Mrts. D11 44
Agalta, Cordillera de, mts., Hond. G5 64
Agapa, Russia C11 24
Agartala, India I14 38
Agate Fossil Beds National Monument, Ne., U.S. B2 104
Agattu Island, i., Ak., U.S. E2 79
Agawam, Ma., U.S. B2 98
Agen, Fr. H7 10
Agency, Ia., U.S. D5 92
Agency, Mo., U.S. B3 102
Āghā Jārī, Iran B4 46
Agira, Italy L9 14
Agnone, Italy H9 14
Agoura Hills, Ca., U.S. m11 82
Āgra, India G8 38
Ágreda, Spain D10 12
Ağrı Dağı (Mount Ararat), mtn., Tur. H16 4
Agrigento, Italy L8 14
Agrinion, Grc. K5 16
Agropoli, Italy I9 14
Agua Caliente, Mex. F7 62
Agua Caliente Grande, Mex. D5 62
Aguachica, Col. C6 58
Água Clara, Braz. F2 57
Agua Fria, N.M., U.S. B3 108
Agua Fria, stm., Az., U.S. D3 80
Agua Prieta, Mex. B5 62
Aguascalientes, Mex. G8 62
Águas Formosas, Braz. D8 57
Águeda, Port. E3 12
Aguila, Az., U.S. D2 80
Aguilar, Spain H7 12
Águilas, Spain H10 12
Agulhas, Cape, c., S. Afr. H3 44
Agustín Codazzi, Col. B6 58
Agustín Codazzi, Col. I11 64
Ahaggar, mts., Alg. D7 42
Ahipara Bay, b., N.Z. A4 52
Ahklun Mountains, mts., Ak., U.S. D7 79
Ahlen, Ger. D7 8
Ahmadābād, India I5 38
Ahmadnagar, India C3 37
Ahmadpur East, Pak. F4 38
Ahmar Mountains, mts., Eth. G3 46
Ahoskie, N.C., U.S. A6 110
Ahtanum Creek, stm., Wa., U.S. C5 124
Ahu, China A7 28
Ahuacatlán, Mex. G7 62
Ahvāz, Iran B4 46
Ahvenanmaa (Åland), is., Fin. F12 6
Aialik, Cape, c., Ak., U.S. D10 79
Aichach, Ger. G11 8
Aiea, Hi., U.S. B4 88
Aihun, China A12 26
Aijal, India I15 38
Aiken, S.C., U.S. D4 117
Aiken, co., S.C., U.S. D4 117
Ailsa Craig, Ont., Can. D3 73
Aim, Russia F20 24
Aimorés, Braz. E8 57
Ainslie Lake, l., N.S., Can. C8 71
Ainsworth, Ne., U.S. B6 104
Aipe, Col. F5 58
Aïr, mts., Niger E7 42
Airdrie, Alta., Can. D3 68
Aire-sur-l'Adour, Fr. I6 10
Air Force Island, i., N.W. Ter., Can. C18 66
Air Park West, Ne., U.S. *D9 104
Aisne, stm., Fr. C10 10
Aïssa, Djebel, mtn., Alg. B5 42
Aitape, Pap. N. Gui. k15 50a
Aitkin, Mn., U.S. D5 100
Aitkin, co., Mn., U.S. D5 100
Aix, Mount, mtn., Wa., U.S. C4 124
Aix-en-Provence, Fr. I12 10
Aix-la-Chapelle see Aachen, Ger. E6 8
Aix-les-Bains, Fr. G12 10
Aizu-wakamatsu, Japan E12 30
Ajaccio, Fr. n23 11a
Ajaguz, Kaz. H10 24
Ajan, Russia F21 24
Ajan, stm., Russia C13 24
Ajax, Ont., Can. D6 73
Ajdābiyah, Libya B10 42
Ajjer, Tassili n', plat., Alg. C7 42
ʿAjlūn, Jord. C4 40
Ajmer, India G6 38
Ajo, Az., U.S. E3 80
Ajo, Cabo de, c., Spain B8 12
Ajon, Ostrov, i., Russia D27 24
Ajtos, Bul. G11 16
Akademii, Zaliv, b., Russia G21 24
Akaltara, India A7 37
Akan, Japan p22 30a
ʿAkasha East, Sudan D12 42
Akashi, Japan H7 30
Akçakale, Tur. A6 40
Ak-Chin Indian Reservation, Az., U.S. E3 80
Akesu, China C3 26
Akharnaí, Grc. K7 16
Akhisar, Tur. H13 4
Akiachak, Ak., U.S. C7 79
Akimiski Island, i., N.W. Ter., Can. F16 66
Akita, Japan C13 30
Akjoujt, Maur. E3 42
ʿAkko (Acre), Isr. C4 40
Aklavik, N.W. Ter., Can. C6 66
Akō, Japan H7 30
Akobo, stm., Afr. G12 42
Akola, India B4 37
Akordat, Erit. E2 46
Akot, India B4 37
Akpatok Island, i., N.W. Ter., Can. D19 66
Akron, Co., U.S. A7 83
Akron, In., U.S. B5 91
Akron, Ia., U.S. B1 92
Akron, N.Y., U.S. B2 109
Akron, Oh., U.S. A4 112
Akron, Pa., U.S. F9 115
Aksaray, Tur. H14 4
Akşehir, Tur. H14 4
Aksum, Eth. F2 46
Aktau, Kaz. I8 22
Akt'ubinsk, Kaz. G9 22
Akureyri, Ice. B4 4
Ål, Nor. F7 6
Alabama, state, U.S. C3 78
Alabama, stm., Al., U.S. D2 78
Alabaster, Al., U.S. B3 78
Alachua, Fl., U.S. C4 86
Alachua, co., Fl., U.S. C4 86
Alagoinhas, Braz. B9 57
Alagón, Spain D10 12
Alajuela, C.R. I5 64
Alakanuk, Ak., U.S. C7 79
Alalakeiki Channel, strt., Hi., U.S. C5 88
Al-ʿAlamayn, Egypt B11 42
Alamance, co., N.C., U.S. B3 110
Al-ʿAmārah, Iraq B4 46
Alameda, Ca., U.S. h8 82
Alameda, N.M., U.S. B3 108
Alameda, co., Ca., U.S. D3 82
Alameda Naval Air Station, mil., Ca., U.S. h8 82
Alamito Creek, stm., Tx., U.S. p12 120
Alamo, Ga., U.S. D4 87
Alamo, Nv., U.S. F6 105
Alamo, Tn., U.S. B2 119
Alamo, Tx., U.S. F3 120
Alamogordo, N.M., U.S. E4 108
Alamo Heights, Tx., U.S. E3 120
Alamo Hueco Mountains, mts., N.M., U.S. F1 108
Alamo Indian Reservation, N.M., U.S. C2 108
Alamo Lake, res., Az., U.S. C2 80
Alamosa, Co., U.S. D5 83
Alamosa, co., Co., U.S. D5 83
Alamosa, stm., Co., U.S. D4 83
Alamosa Creek, stm., N.M., U.S. D2 108
Alamosa East, Co., U.S. D5 83
Alanäs, Swe. D10 6
Alanya, Tur. A3 40
Alapaha, Ga., U.S. E3 87
Alapaha, stm., U.S. E3 87
Al-ʿAqabah, Jord. E4 40
Alaşehir, Tur. K12 16
Alashanyouqi, China C7 26
Alaska, state, U.S. C9 79
Alaska, Gulf of, b., Ak., U.S. D10 79
Alaska Peninsula, pen., Ak., U.S. D8 79
Alaska Range, mts., Ak., U.S. C9 79
Alassio, Italy E3 14
Alatna, stm., Ak., U.S. B9 79
Al-ʿAṭrūn, Sudan E11 42
Alava, Cape, c., Wa., U.S. A1 124
Alazeja, stm., Russia C24 24
Alba, Italy E3 14
Albacete, Spain G10 12
Alba de Tormes, Spain E6 12
Albaida, Spain G11 12
Albanel, Lac, l., Que., Can. F18 66
Albania, ctry., Eur. G11 4
Albano Laziale, Italy H7 14
Albany, Austl. G3 50
Albany, Ga., U.S. E2 87
Albany, Il., U.S. B3 90
Albany, In., U.S. D7 91
Albany, Ky., U.S. D4 94
Albany, La., U.S. g10 95
Albany, Mn., U.S. E4 100
Albany, Mo., U.S. A3 102
Albany, N.Y., U.S. C7 109
Albany, Or., U.S. C3 114
Albany, Tx., U.S. C3 120
Albany, Wi., U.S. F4 126
Albany, co., N.Y., U.S. C6 109
Albany, co., Wy., U.S. E7 127
Albany, stm., Ont., Can. o18 73
Al-Baṣrah, Iraq B4 46
Albatross Bay, b., Austl. B8 50
Al-Batrūn, Leb. B4 40
Al-Bawīṭī, Egypt C11 42
Albemarle, N.C., U.S. B2 110
Albemarle, co., Va., U.S. C4 123
Albemarle Lake, l., Ms., U.S. C2 101
Albemarle Sound, strt., N.C., U.S. A6 110
Albenga, Italy E3 14
Albergaria-a-Velha, Port. E3 12
Albert, Fr. B9 10
Albert, Lake, l., Afr. A6 44
Alberta, prov., Can. C4 68
Alberta, Mount, mtn., Alta., Can. C2 68
Albert City, Ia., U.S. B3 92
Albert Lea, Mn., U.S. G5 100
Albert Nile, stm., Ug. H12 42
Alberton, P.E.I., Can. C5 71
Albertson, N.Y., U.S. k13 109
Albertville, Fr. G13 10
Albertville, Al., U.S. A3 78
Albertville, Mn., U.S. E5 100
Albertville see Kalemie, Zaire C5 44
Albi, Fr. I9 10
Albia, Ia., U.S. C5 92
Albino, Italy D4 14
Albion, Il., U.S. E5 90
Albion, In., U.S. B7 91
Albion, Mi., U.S. F6 99
Albion, Ne., U.S. C7 104
Albion, N.Y., U.S. B2 109
Albion, Pa., U.S. C1 115
Albion, R.I., U.S. B4 116
Albion, Wa., U.S. C8 124
Alborán, Isla de, i., Spain J8 12
Ålborg, Den. H7 6
Alborz, Reshteh-ye Kūhhā-ye, mts., Iran J8 22
Albufeira, Port. H3 12
Albuñol, Spain I8 12
Albuquerque, N.M., U.S. B3 108
Alburquerque, Spain F4 12
Alburtis, Pa., U.S. F10 115
Albury, Austl. G9 50
Alcácer do Sal, Port. G3 12
Alcalá de Guadaira, Spain H6 12
Alcalá de Henares, Spain E8 12
Alcalá la Real, Spain H8 12
Alcalde, N.M., U.S. A3 108
Alcamo, Italy L7 14
Alcañices, Spain D5 12
Alcañiz, Spain D11 12
Alcântara, Braz. D10 54
Alcántara, Spain F5 12
Alcantarilla, Spain H10 12
Alcaraz, Spain G9 12
Alcázar de San Juan, Spain F8 12
Alcester, S.D., U.S. D9 118
Alcira, Spain F11 12
Alcoa, Tn., U.S. D10 119
Alcobaça, Braz. D9 57
Alcobaça, Port. F3 12
Alcolu, S.C., U.S. D7 117
Alcona, co., Mi., U.S. D7 99
Alconchel, Spain G4 12
Alcorn, co., Ms., U.S. A5 101
Alcoy, Spain G11 12
Aldabra Islands, atoll, Sey. C9 44
Aldan, Russia F19 24
Aldan, stm., Russia E20 24
Aldanskoje Nagorje, plat., Russia F19 24
Alden, Ia., U.S. B4 92
Alden, Mn., U.S. G5 100
Alden, N.Y., U.S. C2 109
Alder Brook, stm., Vt., U.S. B4 122
Aldershot, Eng., U.K. J12 7
Alderson, W.V., U.S. D4 125
Aldrich, Al., U.S. B3 78
Aledo, Il., U.S. B3 90
Aleg, Maur. E3 42
Alegres Mountain, mtn., N.M., U.S. C2 108
Alegrete, Braz. B5 56
Alejsk, Russia G10 24
Aleksandrov, Russia E21 18
Aleksandrovsk-Sachalinskij, Russia G22 24
Aleksejevsk, Russia F15 24
Aleksin, Russia G20 18
Além Paraíba, Braz. F7 57
Alençon, Fr. D7 10
Alenuihaha Channel, strt., Hi., U.S. C5 88
Aleppo see Ḥalab, Syria A5 40
Alert Bay, B.C., Can. D4 69
Alès, Fr. H11 10
Alessandria, Italy E3 14
Alessano, Italy J13 14
Ålesund, Nor. E6 6
Aleutian Islands, is., Ak., U.S. E3 79
Aleutian Range, mts., Ak., U.S. D9 79
Aleutka, Russia H24 24
Alevina, Mys, c., Russia F24 24
Alex, Ok., U.S. C4 113
Alexander, co., Il., U.S. F4 90
Alexander, co., N.C., U.S. B1 110
Alexander, Lake, l., Mn., U.S. D4 100
Alexander Archipelago, is., Ak., U.S. D12 79
Alexander Bay, S. Afr. G3 44
Alexander City, Al., U.S. C4 78
Alexander Island, i., Ant. B6 47
Alexandra, N.Z. F2 52
Alexandretta, Gulf of see İskenderun Körfezi, b., Tur. A4 40
Alexandria, Ont., Can. B10 73
Alexandria, In., U.S. D6 91
Alexandria, Ky., U.S. B5 94
Alexandria, La., U.S. C3 95
Alexandria, Mn., U.S. E3 100
Alexandria, Tn., U.S. A5 119
Alexandria, Va., U.S. B5 123
Alexandria see Al-Iskandarīyah, Egypt B11 42
Alexandroúpolis, Grc. I9 16
Alexis, Il., U.S. B3 90
Alfalfa, co., Ok., U.S. A3 113
Alfaro, Ec. I3 58
Alfaro, Spain C10 12
Alfarrás, Spain D12 12
Al-Fāshir, Sudan F11 42
Al-Fayyūm, Egypt C12 42
Alfeld, Ger. D9 8
Alfenas, Braz. F6 57
Alfred, Ont., Can. B10 73
Alfred, N.Y., U.S. C3 109
Algarve, hist. reg., Port. H3 12
Algeciras, Spain I6 12
Algemesí, Spain F11 12
Alger (Algiers), Alg. A6 42
Alger, Oh., U.S. B2 112
Alger, co., Mi., U.S. B4 99
Algeria, ctry., Afr. C6 42
Al-Ghayḍah, Yemen E5 46
Alghero, Italy I3 14
Al-Ghurdaqah, Egypt C12 42
Algiers see Alger, Alg. A6 42
Algoma, Wi., U.S. D6 126
Algona, Ia., U.S. A3 92
Algona, Wa., U.S. B3 124
Algonac, Mi., U.S. F8 99
Algonquin, Il., U.S. A5 90
Algonquin Provincial Park, Ont., Can. B6 73
Algood, Tn., U.S. C8 119
Algorta, Ur. C5 56
Al-Ḥadīthah, Iraq B3 46
Al-Ḥaffah, Syria B5 40
Al-Hamād, pl., Sau. Ar. B2 46
Alhama de Granada, Spain H8 12
Alhambra, Ca., U.S. m12 82
Al-Ḥarīq, Sau. Ar. D4 46
Al-Ḥarūj al-Aswad, hills, Libya C9 42
Al-Ḥasakah, Syria A7 40
Alhaurín el Grande, Spain I7 12
Al-Ḥawrah, Yemen F4 46
Al-Ḥijāz (Hejaz), reg., Sau. Ar. C2 46
Al-Ḥillah, Iraq B3 46
Al-Hirmil, Leb. B5 40
Al-Ḥudaydah, Yemen F3 46
Al-Hufūf, Sau. Ar. C4 46
Aliaga, Spain E11 12
Alicante, Spain G11 12
Alice, Tx., U.S. F3 120
Alice Lake, l., Mn., U.S. C7 100
Alice Springs, Austl. D6 50
Aliceville, Al., U.S. B1 78
Alīgarh, India G8 38
Alijos, Escollos, Mex. E2 62
Alingsås, Swe. H9 6
Alīpur Duār, India G13 38
Aliquippa, Pa., U.S. E1 115
Al-Iskandarīyah (Alexandria), Egypt B11 42
Al-Ismāʿīlīyah, Egypt B12 42
Aliwal North, S. Afr. H5 44
Alix, Alta., Can. C4 68
Al-Jabal al-Akhḍar, mts., Oman D6 46
Al-Jafr, Jord. D5 40
Al-Jaghbūb, Libya C10 42

Name	Map Ref	Page
Al-Jawf, Libya	D10	42
Al-Jawf, Sau. Ar.	C2	46
Al-Jazīrah, reg., Sudan	F12	42
Aljezur, Port.	H3	12
Al-Jīzah, Egypt	B12	42
Al-Junaynah, Sudan	F10	42
Aljustrel, Port.	H3	12
Alkali Lake, l., Nv., U.S.	B2	105
Alkali Lake, l., Or., U.S.	E6	114
Alkaline Lake, l., N.D., U.S.	C6	111
Al-Karak, Jord.	D4	40
Al-Kawm, Syria	B6	40
Al-Khābūr, stm., Syria	A7	40
Al-Khalīl, W. Bank	D4	40
Al-Khandaq, Sudan	E12	42
Al-Khārijah, Egypt	C12	42
Al-Kharṭūm (Khartoum), Sudan	E12	42
Al-Khaṣab, Oman	C6	46
Al-Khubar, Sau. Ar.	C5	46
Al-Khums, Libya	B8	42
Alkmaar, Neth.	C4	8
Al-Kuwayt, Kuw.	C4	46
Allach-Jun', Russia	E21	24
Al-Lādhiqīyah (Latakia), Syria	B4	40
Allagash, stm., Me., U.S.	B3	96
Allagash Lake, l., Me., U.S.	B3	96
Allāhābād, India	H9	38
Allamakee, co., Ia., U.S.	A6	92
Allan, Sask., Can.	F2	75
Allanche, Fr.	G9	10
Allanmyo, Mya.	E3	34
Allardt, Tn., U.S.	C9	119
Allatoona Lake, res., Ga., U.S.	B2	87
Allegan, Mi., U.S.	F5	99
Allegan, co., Mi., U.S.	F5	99
Allegany, N.Y., U.S.	C2	109
Allegany, co., Md., U.S.	k13	97
Allegany, co., N.Y., U.S.	C2	109
Allegany Indian Reservation, N.Y., U.S.	C2	109
Alleghany, co., N.C., U.S.	A1	110
Alleghany, co., Va., U.S.	C2	123
Allegheny, co., Pa., U.S.	E2	115
Allegheny, stm., U.S.	E2	115
Allegheny Reservoir, res., U.S.	B4	115
Allemands, Lac Des, l., La., U.S.	E5	95
Allen, Ok., U.S.	C5	113
Allen, co., In., U.S.	B7	91
Allen, co., Ks., U.S.	E8	93
Allen, co., Ky., U.S.	D3	94
Allen, co., La., U.S.	D3	95
Allen, co., Oh., U.S.	B1	112
Allen, Mount, mtn., Ak., U.S.	C11	79
Allendale, N.J., U.S.	A4	107
Allendale, S.C., U.S.	E5	117
Allendale, co., S.C., U.S.	F5	117
Allen Park, Mi., U.S.	p15	99
Allenton, R.I., U.S.	E4	116
Allenton, Wi., U.S.	E5	126
Allentown, Pa., U.S.	E11	115
Allentsteig, Aus.	G15	8
Alleppey, India	H4	37
Aller, stm., Ger.	C9	8
Allerton, Point, c., Ma., U.S.	B6	98
Allgäuer Alpen, mts., Eur.	H10	8
Alliance, Ne., U.S.	B3	104
Alliance, Oh., U.S.	B4	112
Alligator, stm., N.C., U.S.	B6	110
Alligator Lake, l., Me., U.S.	D4	96
Allison, Ia., U.S.	B5	92
Allison, Pa., U.S.	G2	115
Allison Park, Pa., U.S.	h14	115
Alliston [Beeton Tecumseth and Tottenham], Ont., Can.	C5	73
Al-Līth, Sau. Ar.	D3	46
Allouez, Wi., U.S.	h9	126
Alloway Creek, stm., N.J., U.S.	D2	107
Al-Luḥayyah, Yemen	E3	46
Allumette Lake, l., Can.	B7	73
Allyn, Wa., U.S.	B3	124
Alma, Que., Can.	A6	74
Alma, Ar., U.S.	B1	81
Alma, Ga., U.S.	E4	87
Alma, Ks., U.S.	C7	93
Alma, Mi., U.S.	E6	99
Alma, Ne., U.S.	D6	104
Alma, Wi., U.S.	D2	126
Alma-Ata, Kaz.	I9	24
Almada, Port.	G2	12
Al-Madīnah (Medina), Sau. Ar.	D2	46
Al-Mafraq, Jord.	C5	40
Almagro, Spain	G8	12
Al-Manāmah, Bahr.	C5	46
Almanor, Lake, l., Ca., U.S.	B3	82
Almansa, Spain	G10	12
Al-Manṣūrah, Egypt	B12	42
Al-Marj, Libya	B10	42
Almas, Pico das, mtn., Braz.	F10	54
Al-Maṣīrah, i., Oman	D6	46
Al-Mawṣil, Iraq	A3	46
Al-Mayādīn, Syria	B7	40
Almazán, Spain	D9	12
Almelo, Neth.	C6	8
Almenara, Braz.	D8	57
Almendralejo, Spain	G5	12
Almería, Spain	I9	12
Al'metjevsk, Russia	G8	22
Al-Minyā, Egypt	C12	42
Almirante, Pan.	J6	64
Al-Mismīyah, Syria	C5	40
Almodôvar, Port.	H3	12
Almodóvar del Campo, Spain	G7	12
Almont, Mi., U.S.	F7	99
Almonte, Ont., Can.	B8	73
Almonte, Spain	H5	12
Almora, India	F8	38
Al-Mubarraz, Sau. Ar.	C4	46
Al-Mubarraz, Sau. Ar.	D4	46
Al-Muglad, Sudan	F11	42
Al-Muḥarraq, Bahr.	C5	46
Al-Mukallā, Yemen	F4	46
Al-Mukhā, Yemen	F3	46
Al-Muwayliḥ, Sau. Ar.	C2	46
Alnwick, Eng., U.K.	F11	7
Aloândia, Braz.	D4	57
Aloha, Or., U.S.	h12	114
Alor, Pulau, i., Indon.	G7	32
Álora, Spain	I7	12
Alor Setar, Malay.	K6	34
Aloysius, Mount, mtn., Austl.	E5	50
Alpena, Mi., U.S.	C7	99
Alpena, co., Mi., U.S.	D7	99
Alpharetta, Ga., U.S.	B2	87
Alphonse Island, i., Sey.	C10	44
Alpiarça, Port.	F3	12
Alpine, Az., U.S.	D6	80
Alpine, Tx., U.S.	D1	120
Alpine, Ut., U.S.	C4	121
Alpine, co., Ca., U.S.	C4	82
Alps, mts., Eur.	F9	4
Al-Qaḍārif, Sudan	F13	42
Al-Qāhirah (Cairo), Egypt	B12	42
Al-Qāmishlī, Syria	A7	40
Al-Qaryah ash-Sharqīyah, Libya	B8	42
Al-Qaryatayn, Syria	B5	40
Al-Qaṣr, Egypt	C11	42
Al-Qaṭīf, Sau. Ar.	C4	46
Al-Qaṭrūn, Libya	D8	42
Al-Qayṣūmah, Sau. Ar.	C4	46
Al-Qunayṭirah, Golan Hts.	C4	40
Al-Qunfudhah, Sau. Ar.	E3	46
Al-Quṣayr, Egypt	C12	42
Al-Quṭayfah, Syria	C5	40
Alsace, hist. reg., Fr.	E14	10
Alsasua, Spain	C9	12
Alsfeld, Ger.	E9	8
Alta, Nor.	B14	6
Alta, Ia., U.S.	B2	92
Altadena, Ca., U.S.	m12	82
Altagracia, Ven.	B7	58
Altagracia de Orituco, Ven.	C9	58
Altai, mts., Asia	B4	26
Altaj (Jesönbulag), Mong.	B6	26
Altamaha, stm., Ga., U.S.	E4	87
Altamira, Braz.	D8	54
Altamont, Il., U.S.	D5	90
Altamont, Ks., U.S.	E8	93
Altamont, Or., U.S.	E5	114
Altamont, Tn., U.S.	D8	119
Altamonte Springs, Fl., U.S.	D5	86
Altamura, Italy	I11	14
Altar, Mex.	B4	62
Altar, Desierto de, des., Mex.	B3	62
Altata, Mex.	E6	62
Altavista, Va., U.S.	C3	123
Altdorf, Switz.	F15	10
Altenburg, Ger.	E12	8
Altheimer, Ar., U.S.	C4	81
Altiplano, plat., S.A.	G5	54
Alto, Ga., U.S.	B3	87
Alto, N.M., U.S.	D4	108
Alto Araguaia, Braz.	D2	57
Alton, Il., U.S.	E3	90
Alton, Ia., U.S.	B2	92
Alton, Mo., U.S.	E6	102
Alton, N.H., U.S.	D4	106
Altona, Man., Can.	E3	70
Alton Bay, N.H., U.S.	D4	106
Altoona, Al., U.S.	A3	78
Altoona, Fl., U.S.	D5	86
Altoona, Ia., U.S.	C4	92
Altoona, Pa., U.S.	E5	115
Altoona, Wi., U.S.	D2	126
Alto Parnaíba, Braz.	E9	54
Altötting, Ger.	G12	8
Altun Shan, mts., China	D4	26
Alturas, Ca., U.S.	B3	82
Altus, Ok., U.S.	C2	113
Altus Air Force Base, mil., Ok., U.S.	C2	113
Altus Reservoir, res., Ok., U.S.	C2	113
Al-'Ubaylah, Sau. Ar.	D5	46
Al-Ubayyiḍ, Sudan	F12	42
'Alula, Som.	F5	46
Alum Bank, Pa., U.S.	F4	115
Alum Creek, stm., Oh., U.S.	k11	112
Al-Uqṣur (Luxor), Egypt	C12	42
Alva, Fl., U.S.	F5	86
Alva, Ok., U.S.	A3	113
Alvarado, Mex.	H12	62
Alvarado, Tx., U.S.	C4	120
Álvaro Obregón, Presa, res., Mex.	D5	62
Älvdalen, Swe.	F10	6
Alvin, Tx., U.S.	E5	120
Alvinston, Ont., Can.	E3	73
Älvkarleby, Swe.	F11	6
Alvord Lake, l., Or., U.S.	E8	114
Älvsbyn, Swe.	D13	6
Al-Wajh, Sau. Ar.	C2	46
Alwar, India	G7	38
Alzamaj, Russia	F13	24
Ama, La., U.S.	k11	95
Amadeus, Lake, l., Austl.	D6	50
Amadjuak Lake, l., N.W. Ter., Can.	C18	66
Amador, co., Ca., U.S.	C3	82
Amagansett, N.Y., U.S.	n16	109
Amagasaki, Japan	H8	30
Amakusa-nada, Japan	J2	30
Amakusa-shotō, is., Japan	J3	30
Åmål, Swe.	G9	6
Amalāpuram, India	D7	37
Amalfi, Italy	I9	14
Amalner, India	J6	38
Amambaí, stm., Braz.	G1	57
Amambaí, Serra de, mts., S.A.	H7	54
Amami-Ō-shima, i., Japan	w29	31b
Amami-shotō, is., Japan	x29	31b
Amana, Ia., U.S.	C6	92
Amantea, Italy	J11	14
Amares, Port.	D3	12
Amargosa, stm., U.S.	D5	82
Amargosa Desert, des., U.S.	G5	105
Amargosa Range, mts., U.S.	G5	105
Amarillo, Tx., U.S.	B2	120
Amatignak Island, i., Ak., U.S.	E4	79
Amazon (Solimões) (Amazonas), stm., S.A.	D7	54
Ambāla, India	E7	38
Ambarčik, Russia	D26	24
Ambāsamudram, India	H4	37
Ambato, Ec.	H3	58
Ambatolampy, Madag.	E9	44
Ambatondrazaka, Madag.	E9	44
Amberg, Ger.	F11	8
Ambérieu-en-Bugey, Fr.	G1	10
Ambert, Fr.	G10	10
Ambikāpur, India	I10	38
Ambilobe, Madag.	D9	44
Amble, Eng., U.K.	F11	7
Ambler, Pa., U.S.	F11	115
Amboise, Fr.	E7	10
Ambon, Indon.	F8	32
Ambositra, Madag.	F9	44
Ambovombe, Madag.	G9	44
Amboy, Il., U.S.	B4	90
Ambre, Cap d', c., Madag.	D9	44
Ambridge, Pa., U.S.	E1	115
Ambrières, Fr.	D6	10
Ambriz, Ang.	C2	44
Āmbūr, India	F5	37
Amchitka Island, i., Ak., U.S.	E3	79
Amchitka Pass, strt., Ak., U.S.	E4	79
Ameca, Mex.	G7	62
Amecameca [de Juárez], Mex.	H10	62
Amelia, La., U.S.	E4	95
Amelia, Oh., U.S.	C1	112
Amelia, co., Va., U.S.	C4	123
Amelia Court House, Va., U.S.	C5	123
Amelia Island, i., Fl., U.S.	k9	86
American, stm., Ca., U.S.	C3	82
Americana, Braz.	G5	57
American Falls, Id., U.S.	G6	89
American Falls Dam, Id., U.S.	G6	89
American Falls Reservoir, res., Id., U.S.	F5	89
American Fork, Ut., U.S.	C4	121
American Highland, plat., Ant.	B20	47
American Samoa, dep., Oc.	G1	2
Americus, Ga., U.S.	D2	87
Americus, Ks., U.S.	D7	93
Amersfoort, Neth.	C5	8
Amery, Wi., U.S.	C1	126
Ames, Ia., U.S.	B4	92
Amesbury, Ma., U.S.	A6	98
Amfilokhía, Grc.	K5	16
Ámfissa, Grc.	K6	16
Amga, Russia	E20	24
Amga, stm., Russia	E20	24
Amgun', stm., Russia	G21	24
Amherst, Ma., U.S.	B2	98
Amherst, N.H., U.S.	E3	106
Amherst, N.Y., U.S.	C2	109
Amherst, Oh., U.S.	A3	112
Amherst, Va., U.S.	C3	123
Amherst, Wi., U.S.	D4	126
Amherst, co., Va., U.S.	C3	123
Amherstburg, Ont., Can.	E1	73
Amherstdale, W.V., U.S.	n12	125
Amiens, Fr.	C9	10
Amīndīvi Islands, is., India	G2	37
Amirante Islands, is., Sey.	C10	44
Amisk Lake, l., Sask., Can.	C4	75
Amistad National Recreation Area, Tx., U.S.	E2	120
Amistad Reservoir, res., N.A.	C9	62
Amite, La., U.S.	D5	95
Amite, co., Ms., U.S.	D3	101
Amite, stm., La., U.S.	D5	95
Amity, Or., U.S.	B3	114
Amityville, N.Y., U.S.	E7	109
Amlia Island, i., Ak., U.S.	E5	79
'Ammān, Jord.	D4	40
Ämmänsaari, Fin.	D17	6
Ammon, Id., U.S.	F7	89
Ammonoosuc, stm., N.H., U.S.	B3	106
Amo, stm., Asia	G13	38
Amory, Ms., U.S.	B5	101
Amos, Que., Can.	k11	74
Åmot, Nor.	G6	6
Amoy see Xiamen, China	K7	28
Amposta, Spain	E12	12
Amrāvati, India	B4	37
Amreli, India	J4	38
Amritsar, India	E6	38
Amroha, India	F8	38
Amsterdam, Neth.	C4	8
Amsterdam, N.Y., U.S.	C6	109
Amstetten, Aus.	G14	8
Am Timan, Chad	F10	42
Amu Darya (Amudarja), stm., Asia	I10	22
Amukta Pass, strt., Ak., U.S.	E5	79
Amundsen Gulf, b., N.W. Ter., Can.	B8	66
Amundsen Sea, Ant.	B1	47
Amuntai, Indon.	F6	32
Amur (Heilongjiang), stm., Asia	G21	24
An, Mya.	E3	34
Anabar, stm., Russia	C16	24
Anaco, Ven.	C10	58
Anacoco, La., U.S.	C2	95
Anaconda, Mt., U.S.	D4	103
Anaconda Range, mts., Mt., U.S.	E3	103
Anacortes, Wa., U.S.	A3	124
Anacostia, stm., U.S.	C4	97
Anacostia, Northwest Branch, stm., Md., U.S.	B3	97
Anadarko, Ok., U.S.	B3	113
Anadyr', Russia	E29	24
Anadyr', stm., Russia	E29	24
Anadyrskij Zaliv, b., Russia	E30	24
Anagni, Italy	H8	14
Anaheim, Ca., U.S.	F5	82
Anahola, Hi., U.S.	A2	88
Anahuac, Tx., U.S.	E5	120
Ānai Mudi, mtn., India	G4	37
Anakāpalle, India	D7	37
Analalava, Madag.	D9	44
Ana María, Golfo de, b., Cuba	D8	64
Anambas, Kepulauan, is., Indon.	M9	34
Anamosa, Ia., U.S.	B6	92
Anamur, Tur.	H14	4
Anamur Burnu, c., Tur.	A3	40
Anan, Japan	I7	30
Ānand, India	I5	38
Anantapur, India	E4	37
Anantnāg (Islāmābād), India	D6	38
Anápolis, Braz.	D4	57
Anastasia Island, i., Fl., U.S.	C5	86
Añatuya, Arg.	B4	56
'Anazah, Jabal, mtn., Asia	C6	40
Ancaster, Ont., Can.	D4	73
Ancha, Sierra, mts., Az., U.S.	D4	80
Anchang, China	E9	28
Anchorage, Ak., U.S.	C10	79
Anchorage, Ky., U.S.	g11	94
Anchor Point, Ak., U.S.	D9	79
Anchor Point, c., Ak., U.S.	h15	79
Ancienne-Lorette, Que., Can.	C6	74
Anclote Keys, is., Fl., U.S.	D4	86
Ancona, Italy	F8	14
Ancud, Chile	E2	56
Ancud, Golfo de, b., Chile	E2	56
Andalucía, hist. reg., Spain	H7	12
Andalusia, Al., U.S.	D3	78
Andalusia, Il., U.S.	B3	90
Andaman Islands, is., India	H2	34
Andaman Sea, Asia	I3	34
Andermatt, Switz.	F15	10
Andernach, Ger.	E7	8
Anderson, Ak., U.S.	C10	79
Anderson, Ca., U.S.	B2	82
Anderson, In., U.S.	D6	91
Anderson, Mo., U.S.	E3	102
Anderson, S.C., U.S.	B2	117
Anderson, co., Ks., U.S.	D8	93
Anderson, co., Ky., U.S.	C4	94
Anderson, co., S.C., U.S.	B2	117
Anderson, co., Tn., U.S.	C9	119
Anderson, co., Tx., U.S.	D5	120
Anderson, stm., N.W. Ter., Can.	C7	66
Anderson, stm., In., U.S.	H4	91
Anderson, Mount, mtn., Wa., U.S.	B2	124
Anderson Ranch Reservoir, res., Id., U.S.	F3	89
Andes, mts., S.A.	F4	53
Andes, Lake, l., S.D., U.S.	D7	118
Andhra Pradesh, state, India	D5	37
Andižan, Uzb.	I12	22
Andkhvoy, Afg.	B1	38
Andong, China	C11	26
Andong, S. Kor.	D12	26
Andorra, And.	C13	12
Andorra, ctry., Eur.	G8	4
Andover, Ks., U.S.	g12	93
Andover, Ma., U.S.	A5	98
Andover, Mn., U.S.	m12	100
Andover, Oh., U.S.	A5	112
Andover Lake, res., Ct., U.S.	C6	84
Andradina, Braz.	F3	57
Andreanof Islands, is., Ak., U.S.	E4	79
Andrew, co., Mo., U.S.	B3	102
Andrew Island, i., N.S., Can.	D9	71
Andrews, In., U.S.	C6	91
Andrews, N.C., U.S.	f9	110
Andrews, S.C., U.S.	E8	117
Andrews, Tx., U.S.	C1	120
Andrews, co., Tx., U.S.	C1	120
Andrews Air Force Base, mil., Md., U.S.	C4	97
Andria, Italy	H11	14
Androka, Madag.	G8	44
Ándros, i., Grc.	L8	16
Androscoggin, co., Me., U.S.	D2	96
Androscoggin, stm., Me., U.S.	D2	96
Androscoggin Lake, l., Me., U.S.	D2	96
Andros Island, i., Bah.	B8	64
Andros Town, Bah.	B9	64
Andújar, Spain	G7	12
Anduo, China	D14	38
Anegada Passage, strt., N.A.	E16	64
Anfeng, China	C9	28
Anfu, China	H3	28
Ang'angxi, China	B11	26
Angara, stm., Russia	F13	24
Angarsk, Russia	G14	24
Ånge, Swe.	E10	6
Ángel, Salto (Angel Falls), wtfl, Ven.	E11	58
Ángel de la Guarda, Isla, i., Mex.	C3	62
Angeles, Phil.	q19	32
Angeles Point, c., Wa., U.S.	A2	124
Angel Falls see Ángel, Salto, wtfl, Ven.	E11	58
Ängelholm, Swe.	H9	6
Angelina, co., Tx., U.S.	D5	120
Angels Camp, Ca., U.S.	C3	82
Angermünde, Ger.	B13	8
Angers, Fr.	E6	10
Angerville, Fr.	D8	10
Angicos, Braz.	E11	54
Angier, N.C., U.S.	B4	110
Ângk Tasaôm, Camb.	I8	34
Angleton, Tx., U.S.	E5	120
Angmagssalik, Grnld.	C25	66
Angol, Chile	D2	56
Angola, In., U.S.	A8	91
Angola, N.Y., U.S.	C1	109
Angola, ctry., Afr.	D3	44
Angola Swamp, sw., N.C., U.S.	C5	110
Angoon, Ak., U.S.	D13	79
Angostura Reservoir, res., S.D., U.S.	D2	118
Angoulême, Fr.	G7	10
Angra dos Reis, Braz.	G6	57
Anguilla, Ms., U.S.	C3	101
Anguilla, dep., N.A.	E16	64
Anguille, Cape, c., Newf., Can.	E2	72
Angul, India	J11	38
Anhai, China	K7	28
Anhui, prov., China	E10	26
Aniak, Ak., U.S.	C8	79
Animas, stm., U.S.	D3	83
Animas Mountains, mts., N.M., U.S.	F1	108
Animas Peak, mtn., N.M., U.S.	F2	108
Animas Valley, val., N.M., U.S.	F1	108
Anita, Ia., U.S.	C3	92
Anjār, India	I4	38
Anji, China	E8	28
Anjiang, China	F9	26
Anjou, Que., Can.	p19	74
Anjouan, i., Com.	D8	44
Ankang, China	E8	26
Ankara, Tur.	H14	4
Ankavandra, Madag.	E9	44
Ankazoabo, Madag.	F8	44
Ankazobe, Madag.	E9	44
Ankeny, Ia., U.S.	C4	92
Anklesvar, India	B2	37
Anlong, China	B8	34
Anlu, China	D2	28
Ann, Cape, c., Ma., U.S.	A6	98
Anna, Il., U.S.	F4	90
Anna, Oh., U.S.	B1	112
Anna, Lake, res., Va., U.S.	B5	123
Annaba (Bône), Alg.	A7	42
Annaberg-Buchholz, Ger.	E12	8
An-Nabk, Syria	B5	40
An-Nafūd, des., Sau. Ar.	C3	46
An-Najaf, Iraq	B3	46
Anna Maria, Fl., U.S.	p10	86
Anna Maria Island, i., Fl., U.S.	q10	86
Annandale, Mn., U.S.	E4	100
Annandale, Va., U.S.	g12	123
Annapolis, Md., U.S.	C5	97
Annapolis, stm., N.S., Can.	E4	71
Annapolis Junction, Md., U.S.	B4	97
Annapolis Royal, N.S., Can.	E4	71
Annapurna, mtn., Nepal	F10	38
Ann Arbor, Mi., U.S.	F7	99
Anna Regina, Guy.	D13	58
An-Nāṣirīyah, Iraq	B4	46
Annawan, Il., U.S.	B4	90
Anne Arundel, co., Md., U.S.	B4	97
Annecy, Fr.	G13	10
Annemasse, Fr.	F13	10
Annette, Ak., U.S.	n24	79
Anniston, Al., U.S.	B4	78
Annobón, i., Eq. Gui.	B1	44
Annonay, Fr.	G11	10
An-Nuhūd, Sudan	F11	42
Annville, Pa., U.S.	F8	115
Anoka, Mn., U.S.	E5	100
Anoka, co., Mn., U.S.	E5	100
Anqing, China	E6	28
Anren, China	I2	28
Ansbach, Ger.	F10	8
Anshan, China	C11	26
Anshun, China	A8	34
Anson, Me., U.S.	D3	96
Anson, Tx., U.S.	C3	120
Anson, co., N.C., U.S.	B2	110
Ansonia, Ct., U.S.	D3	84
Ansonia, Oh., U.S.	B1	112
Ansted, W.V., U.S.	C3	125
Antakya, Tur.	H15	4
Antalaha, Madag.	D10	44
Antalya, Tur.	H14	4
Antalya, Gulf of see Antalya Körfezi, b., Tur.	A2	40
Antalya Körfezi, b., Tur.	A2	40
Antananarivo, Madag.	E9	44
Antarctica	A18	47
Antarctic Peninsula, pen., Ant.	C6	47
Antelope, co., Ne., U.S.	B7	104
Antelope Creek, stm., Wy., U.S.	C7	127
Antelope Island, i., Ut., U.S.	B3	121
Antelope Peak, mtn., Nv., U.S.	B7	105
Antelope Range, mts., Nv., U.S.	D7	105
Antelope Reservoir, res., Or., U.S.	E9	114
Antelope Wash, val., Nv., U.S.	D5	105
Antequera, Spain	H7	12
Antero, Mount, mtn., Co., U.S.	C4	83
Antero Reservoir, res., Co., U.S.	C5	83
Anthon, Ia., U.S.	B2	92
Anthony, Fl., U.S.	C4	86
Anthony, Ks., U.S.	E5	93
Anthony, N.M., U.S.	F3	108
Anthony, R.I., U.S.	D3	116
Anthony, Tx., U.S.	o11	120
Anthony Creek, stm., W.V., U.S.	D4	125
Anti Atlas, mts., Mor.	B4	42
Antibes, Fr.	I14	10
Anticosti, Île d', i., Que., Can.	k14	74
Antietam National Battlefield, hist., Md., U.S.	B2	97
Antigo, Wi., U.S.	C4	126
Antigua and Barbuda, ctry., N.A.	F17	64
Antioch, Ca., U.S.	h9	82
Antioch, Il., U.S.	A5	90
Antioch see Antakya, Tur.	H15	4
Antisana, vol., Ec.	H3	58
Antlers, Ok., U.S.	C6	113
Antofagasta, Chile	A2	56
Antofalla, Salar de, pl., Arg.	B3	56
Anton, Tx., U.S.	C1	120
Antongila, Helodrano, b., Madag.	E9	44
António Enes, Moz.	E7	44
Antônio João, Braz.	G1	57
Antonito, Co., U.S.	D5	83
Antora Peak, mtn., Co., U.S.	C4	83
Antrim, N.H., U.S.	D3	106
Antrim, co., Mi., U.S.	C5	99
Antrodoco, Italy	G8	14
Antsirabe, Madag.	E9	44
Antsiranana, Madag.	D9	44
Antwerp, Oh., U.S.	A1	112
Antwerp see Antwerpen, Bel.	D4	8
Antwerpen (Antwerp), Bel.	D4	8
Anuradhapura, Sri L.	H6	37
Anxi, China	C6	26
Anxi, China	J7	28
Anyang, China	D9	26
Anyi, China	G4	28
Anyuan, China	H2	28
Anyuan, China	J4	28
Anžero-Sudžensk, Russia	F11	24
Anzio, Italy	H7	14
Anžu, Ostrova, is., Russia	B23	24
Aoiz, Spain	C10	12
Aomori, Japan	B13	30
Aóös (Vijosë), stm., Eur.	J4	16
Aôral, Phnum, mtn., Camb.	H8	34
Aosta, Italy	D2	14
Aoukâr, reg., Maur.	E4	42
Aozou, Chad	D9	42
Apache, Ok., U.S.	C3	113
Apache, co., Az., U.S.	B6	80
Apache Junction, Az., U.S.	m9	80
Apache Peak, mtn., Az., U.S.	F5	80
Apalachee Bay, b., Fl., U.S.	B2	86
Apalachicola, Fl., U.S.	C2	86
Apalachicola, stm., Fl., U.S.	B1	86
Apalachicola Bay, b., Fl., U.S.	C2	86
Apaporis, stm., S.A.	H7	58
Aparri, Phil.	B7	32
Apatzingán [de la Constitución], Mex.	H8	62
Apeldoorn, Neth.	C5	8
Apennines see Appennino, mts., Italy	F7	14

Name — Map Ref — Page

Apex, N.C., U.S. B4 110
Apishapa, stm., Co., U.S. D6 83
Apizaco, Mex. H10 62
Aplington, Ia., U.S. B5 92
Apo, Mount, mtn., Phil. D8 32
Apolda, Ger. D11 8
Apollo, Pa., U.S. E2 115
Apopka, Fl., U.S. D5 86
Apopka, Lake, l., Fl., U.S. D5 86
Aporé, Braz. E2 57
Apostle Islands, is., Wi., U.S. A3 126
Apostle Islands National Lakeshore, Wi., U.S. A3 126
Appalachia, Va., U.S. f9 123
Appalachian Mountains, mts., N.A. D10 76
Appanoose, co., Ia., U.S. D5 92
Appennino (Apennines), mts., Italy F7 14
Appiano, Italy C6 14
Apple, stm., Wi., U.S. C1 126
Apple Creek, Oh., U.S. B4 112
Applegate, Or., U.S. E3 114
Applegate, stm., Or., U.S. E3 114
Appleton, Mn., U.S. E2 100
Appleton, Wi., U.S. D5 126
Appleton City, Mo., U.S. C3 102
Apple Valley, Ca., U.S. E5 82
Apple Valley, Mn., U.S. n12 100
Applewood, Co., U.S. *B5 83
Appleyard, Wa., U.S. B5 124
Appling, co., Ga., U.S. E4 87
Appomattox, Va., U.S. C4 123
Appomattox, co., Va., U.S. C4 123
Appomattox, stm., Va., U.S. C4 123
Appomattox Court House National Historical Park, Va., U.S. C4 123
Apua Point, c., Hi., U.S. D6 88
Apucarana, Braz. G3 57
Apure, stm., Ven. D9 58
Apurímac, stm., Peru F4 54
Aqaba, Gulf of, b. E4 40
Āqcheh, Afg. B2 38
Āq Koprūk, Afg. B2 38
Aquarius Mountains, mts., Az., U.S. C2 80
Aquidauana, Braz. H7 54
Arab, Al., U.S. A3 78
'Arab, Bahr al-, stm., Sudan G11 42
Arabelo, Ven. E10 58
Arabi, La., U.S. k11 95
Arabian Desert see Sharqīyah, Aṣ-Ṣaḥrā' al-, des., Egypt C12 42
Arabian Sea E17 2
Aracaju, Braz. F11 54
Aracati, Braz. D11 54
Araçatuba, Braz. F3 57
Aracena, Spain H5 12
Araçuaí, Braz. D7 57
Arad, Rom. C5 16
Arafura Sea G9 32
Arago, Cape, c., Or., U.S. D2 114
Aragon, Ga., U.S. B1 87
Aragón, hist. reg., Spain D11 12
Araguacema, Braz. E9 54
Aragua de Barcelona, Ven. C10 58
Araguari, Braz. E4 57
Arak, Alg. C6 42
Arāk, Iran B4 46
Arakan Yoma, mts., Mya. E3 34
Aral Sea, Asia H10 22
Arambaza, Col. I6 58
Aranda de Duero, Spain D8 12
Arandas, Mex. G8 62
Ārani, India F5 37
Aran Island, i., Ire. G4 7
Aran Islands, is., Ire. H3 7
Aranjuez, Spain E8 12
Aransas, co., Tx., U.S. E4 120
Aransas Bay, b., Tx., U.S. E4 120
Aransas Pass, Tx., U.S. F4 120
Aranyaprathet, Thai. H7 34
Arao, Japan I3 30
Arapaho, Ok., U.S. B3 113
Arapahoe, Ne., U.S. D6 104
Arapahoe, co., Co., U.S. B6 83
Arapiraca, Braz. E11 54
Arapongas, Braz. G3 57
Araraquara, Braz. F4 57
Ararat, Austl. G8 50
Ararat, Mount see Ağrı Dağı, mtn., Tur. H16 4
Arauca, Col. D7 58
Araure, Ven. C8 58
Arāvalli Range, mts., India H5 38
Araxá, Braz. E5 57
Araya, Punta de, c., Ven. B10 58
Arba Minch, Eth. G2 46
Arbois, Fr. F12 10
Arbon, Switz. E16 10
Arborg, Man., Can. D3 70
Arbroath, Scot., U.K. E10 7
Arbuckle, Lake, l., Fl., U.S. E5 86
Arbuckle Mountains, mts., Ok., U.S. C4 113
Arbuckles, Lake of the, res., Ok., U.S. C5 113
Arcachon, Fr. H5 10
Arcade, Ca., U.S. *C3 82
Arcade, Ga., U.S. B3 87
Arcade, N.Y., U.S. C2 109
Arcadia, Ca., U.S. m12 82
Arcadia, Fl., U.S. E5 86
Arcadia, In., U.S. D5 91
Arcadia, La., U.S. B3 95
Arcadia, Mo., U.S. D7 102
Arcadia, S.C., U.S. B4 117
Arcadia, Wi., U.S. D2 126
Arcanum, Oh., U.S. C1 112
Arcata, Ca., U.S. B1 82
Arc Dome, mtn., Nv., U.S. E4 105
Archangel'sk, Russia E6 22
Archbald, Pa., U.S. m18 115
Archbold, Oh., U.S. A1 112
Archdale, N.C., U.S. B3 110
Archer, Fl., U.S. C4 86
Archer, co., Tx., U.S. C3 120
Archer City, Tx., U.S. C3 120
Arches National Park, Ut., U.S. E6 121
Archidona, Spain H7 12
Archie, Mo., U.S. C3 102
Archuleta, co., Co., U.S. D3 83
Arcis-sur-Aube, Fr. D11 10
Arco, Id., U.S. F5 89
Arco de Baúlhe, Port. D4 12
Arcola, Il., U.S. D5 90
Arcos de la Frontera, Spain I6 12
Arctic Bay, N.W. Ter., Can. B15 66
Arctic Ocean A32 128
Arda, stm., Eur. H9 16
Ardabīl, Iran J7 22
Årdalstangen, Nor. F6 6
Ardennes, reg., Eur. E5 8
Ardlussa, Scot., U.K. E7 7
Ardmore, Al., U.S. A3 78
Ardmore, In., U.S. A5 91
Ardmore, Ok., U.S. C4 113
Ardmore, Tn., U.S. B5 119
Ardsley, N.Y., U.S. g13 109
Åre, Swe. E9 6
Arecibo, P.R. E14 64
Arena, Point, c., Ca., U.S. C2 82
Arena, Punta, c., Mex. F5 62
Arenac, co., Mi., U.S. D7 99
Arenas de San Pedro, Spain E6 12
Arendal, Nor. G7 6
Arequipa, Peru G4 54
Arès, Fr. H5 10
Arévalo, Spain D7 12
Arezzo, Italy F6 14
Arganda, Spain E8 12
Arga-Sala, stm., Russia D15 24
Argelès-Gazost, Fr. I7 10
Argenta, Italy E6 14
Argenta, Il., U.S. D5 90
Argentan, Fr. D6 10
Argentat, Fr. G8 10
Argentera, mtn., Italy E2 14
Argentina, ctry., S.A. C4 56
Argentino, Lago, l., Arg. G2 56
Argenton-sur-Creuse, Fr. F8 10
Argonne, reg., Fr. C12 10
Árgos, Grc. L6 16
Argos, In., U.S. B5 91
Argostólion, Grc. K4 16
Argun' (Ergun), stm., Asia A11 26
Argyle, Mn., U.S. B2 100
Argyle, Wi., U.S. F4 126
Århus, Den. H8 6
Ariano Irpino, Italy H10 14
Arica, Chile G4 54
Arica, Col. I7 58
Arichat, N.S., Can. D8 71
Arid, Cape, c., Austl. F4 50
Arīḥā (Jericho), W. Bank D4 40
Arikaree, stm., U.S. B8 83
Arima, Trin. I17 64
Arinos, stm., Braz. F7 54
Aripuanã, stm., Braz. E7 54
Ariquemes, Braz. E6 54
Arismendi, Ven. C8 58
Aristazabal Island, i., B.C., Can. C3 69
Ariton, Al., U.S. D4 78
Arizona, state, U.S. C4 80
Arizona Sunsites, Az., U.S. F6 80
Arizpe, Mex. B4 62
Arjay, Ky., U.S. D6 94
Arjeplog, Swe. C11 6
Arjona, Col. B5 58
Arkabutla Lake, res., Ms., U.S. A4 101
Arkadelphia, Ar., U.S. C2 81
Arkansas, co., Ar., U.S. C4 81
Arkansas, state, U.S. C3 81
Arkansas, stm., U.S. D8 76
Arkansas City, Ks., U.S. E6 93
Arklow, Ire. I6 7
Arkoma, Ok., U.S. B7 113
Arkonam, India F5 37
Arktičeskogo Instituta, Ostrova, is., Russia B10 24
Arles, Fr. I11 10
Arlington, Ga., U.S. E2 87
Arlington, Ma., U.S. B5 98
Arlington, Mn., U.S. F4 100
Arlington, Ne., U.S. C9 104
Arlington, N.Y., U.S. D7 109
Arlington, N.C., U.S. A2 110
Arlington, Oh., U.S. B2 112
Arlington, S.C., U.S. B3 117
Arlington, S.D., U.S. C8 118
Arlington, Tn., U.S. B2 119
Arlington, Tx., U.S. n9 120
Arlington, Vt., U.S. E2 122
Arlington, Va., U.S. B5 123
Arlington, Wa., U.S. A3 124
Arlington, co., Va., U.S. g12 123
Arlington, Lake, res., Tx., U.S. n9 120
Arlington Heights, Il., U.S. A5 90
Arma, Ks., U.S. E9 93
Armada, Mi., U.S. F8 99
Armagh, Que., Can. C7 74
Armavir, Russia H6 22
Armenia, Col. E5 58
Armenia, ctry., Asia I6 22
Armentières, Fr. B9 10
Armidale, Austl. F10 50
Armijo, N.M., U.S. k7 108
Armour, S.D., U.S. D7 118
Armstrong, B.C., Can. D8 69
Armstrong, Ia., U.S. A3 92
Armstrong, co., Pa., U.S. E2 115
Armstrong, co., Tx., U.S. B2 120
Armstrong, Mount, mtn., Yukon, Can. D6 66
Armstrong Creek, stm., W.V., U.S. m13 125
Arnaudville, La., U.S. D4 95
Arnedo, Spain C9 12
Arnett, W.V., U.S. D3 125
Arnhem, Neth. D5 8
Arnhem, Cape, c., Austl. B7 50
Arnhem Land, reg., Austl. B6 50
Arnissa, Grc. I5 16
Arno, stm., Italy F5 14
Arnold, Mn., U.S. D6 100
Arnold, Mo., U.S. C7 102
Arnold, Ne., U.S. C5 104
Arnold, Pa., U.S. h14 115
Arnold Mills, R.I., U.S. B4 116
Arnold Mills Reservoir, res., R.I., U.S. B4 116
Arnold's Cove, Newf., Can. E4 72
Arnolds Park, Ia., U.S. A2 92
Arnprior, Ont., Can. B8 73
Arnsberg, Ger. D8 8
Arnstadt, Ger. E10 8
Arona, Italy D3 14
Aroostook, co., Me., U.S. B4 96
Arpajon, Fr. D9 10
Ar-Rab' al-Khālī, des., Asia D5 46
Arrah, India H11 38
Ar-Rahad, Sudan F12 42
Ar-Ramadi, Iraq B3 46
Ar-Ramthā, Jord. C4 40
Arran, Island of, i., Scot., U.K. F7 7
Ar-Raqqah, Syria B6 40
Arras, Fr. B9 10
Arrecife, Spain C3 42
Arriaga, Mex. I13 62
Ar-Riyāḍ (Riyadh), Sau. Ar. D4 46
Arronches, Port. F4 12
Arrowhead Mountain Lake, res., Vt., U.S. B2 122
Arrowrock Reservoir, res., Id., U.S. F3 89
Arrowwood Lake, res., N.D., U.S. B7 111
Arroyo de la Luz, Spain F5 12
Arroyo Grande, Ca., U.S. E3 82
Ar-Ruṣayriṣ, Sudan F12 42
Ar-Ruṭbah, Iraq C7 40
Arsenjev, Russia I20 24
Árta, Grc. J4 16
Artá, Spain F15 12
Artemisa, Cuba C6 64
Artemus, Ky., U.S. D6 94
Artenay, Fr. D8 10
Arter, Mount, mtn., Wy., U.S. D4 127
Artesia, N.M., U.S. E5 108
Arthabaska, Que., Can. C6 74
Arthur, Ont., Can. D4 73
Arthur, Il., U.S. D5 90
Arthur, co., Ne., U.S. C4 104
Arthur, Lake, l., La., U.S. D3 95
Arthur, Lake, res., Pa., U.S. E1 115
Arthur Kill, stm., N.J., U.S. k8 107
Arthurs Town, Bah. B10 64
Artigas, Ur. C5 56
Art'om, Russia I20 24
Art'omovsk, Russia G12 24
Artvin, Tur. G16 4
Aru, Kepulauan, is., Indon. G9 32
Arua, Ug. H12 42
Aruanã, Braz. C3 57
Aruba, dep., N.A. H13 64
Arunachal Pradesh, ter., India F16 38
Aruppukkottai, India H5 37
Arusha, Tan. B7 44
Aruwimi, stm., Zaire A5 44
Arvada, Co., U.S. B5 83
Arvi, India B5 37
Arvidsjaur, Swe. D12 6
Arvika, Swe. G9 6
Arvin, Ca., U.S. E4 82
Arvon, Mount, mtn., Mi., U.S. B2 99
Arvonia, Va., U.S. C4 123
Arzachena, Italy H4 14
Arzignano, Italy D6 14
Arzúa, Spain C3 12
Asadābād, Afg. C4 38
Asahi-dake, mtn., Japan p20 30a
Asahikawa, Japan p20 30a
Asansol, India I12 38
Asbestos, Que., Can. D6 74
Asbury Park, N.J., U.S. C4 107
Ascensión, Mex. E10 62
Ascension, co., La., U.S. D5 95
Ascensión, Bahía de la, b., Mex. H16 62
Aščhabad, Turk. J9 22
Aschaffenburg, Ger. F9 8
Aschersleben, Ger. D11 8
Asciano, Italy F6 14
Ascoli Piceno, Italy G8 14
Ascoli Satriano, Italy H10 14
Aseb, Erit. F3 46
Asela, Eth. G2 46
Åsele, Swe. D11 6
Åsen, Nor. E8 6
Asenovgrad, Bul. G8 16
Ashaway, R.I., U.S. F1 116
Ashburn, Ga., U.S. E3 87
Ashburton, N.Z. E3 52
Ashcroft, B.C., Can. D7 69
Ashdown, Ar., U.S. D1 81
Ashe, co., N.C., U.S. A1 110
Asheboro, N.C., U.S. B3 110
Ashepoo, stm., S.C., U.S. F6 117
Ashern, Man., Can. D2 70
Asherton, Tx., U.S. E3 120
Asheville, N.C., U.S. f10 110
Ash Flat, Ar., U.S. A4 81
Ashford, Eng., U.K. J13 7
Ashford, Al., U.S. D4 78
Ashford, W.V., U.S. m12 125
Ash Grove, Mo., U.S. D4 102
Ashibetsu, Japan p20 30a
Ashikaga, Japan F12 30
Ashizuri-zaki, c., Japan J6 30
Ashkhabad see Aščhabad, Turk. J9 22
Ashland, Al., U.S. B4 78
Ashland, Il., U.S. D3 90
Ashland, Ks., U.S. E4 93
Ashland, Ky., U.S. B7 94
Ashland, Me., U.S. B4 96
Ashland, Ma., U.S. g10 98
Ashland, Mo., U.S. C5 102
Ashland, Ne., U.S. C9 104
Ashland, N.H., U.S. C3 106
Ashland, Oh., U.S. B3 112
Ashland, Or., U.S. E4 114
Ashland, Pa., U.S. E9 115
Ashland, Va., U.S. C5 123
Ashland, Wi., U.S. B3 126
Ashland, co., Oh., U.S. B3 112
Ashland, co., Wi., U.S. B3 126
Ashland, Mount, mtn., Or., U.S. E4 114
Ashland City, Tn., U.S. A4 119
Ashland Reservoir, res., Ma., U.S. h10 98
Ashley, In., U.S. A7 91
Ashley, N.D., U.S. C6 111
Ashley, Oh., U.S. B3 112
Ashley, Pa., U.S. n17 115
Ashley, co., Ar., U.S. D4 81
Ashley, stm., S.C., U.S. F7 117
Ashley Creek, stm., Ut., U.S. C6 121
Ashmore, Il., U.S. D5 90
Ashokan Reservoir, res., N.Y., U.S. D6 109
Ashqelon, Isr. D4 40
Ash-Shaqrā', Sau. Ar. C4 46
Ash-Shāriqah, U.A.E. C6 46
Ash-Shawbak, Jord. D4 40
Ashtabula, Oh., U.S. A5 112
Ashtabula, co., Oh., U.S. A5 112
Ashtabula, Lake, res., N.D., U.S. B8 111
Ashton, Id., U.S. E7 89
Ashton, Il., U.S. B4 90
Ashton, Md., U.S. B3 97
Ashton, R.I., U.S. B4 116
Ashuanipi Lake, l., Newf., Can. h8 72
Ashuelot, stm., N.H., U.S. E2 106
Ashville, Al., U.S. B3 78
Ashville, Oh., U.S. C3 112
Ashwaubenon, Wi., U.S. D5 126
Asia D12 20
Asia, Kepulauan, is., Indon. E9 32
Asia Minor, reg., Tur. H14 4
Asino, Russia F11 24
'Asīr, reg., Sau. Ar. E3 46
Asir, Ras, c., Som. F5 46
Askham, S. Afr. G4 44
Askvoll, Nor. F5 6
Asmara see Asmera, Erit. E2 46
Asmera, Erit. E2 46
Asotin, Wa., U.S. C8 124
Asotin, co., Wa., U.S. C8 124
Asotin Creek, stm., Wa., U.S. C8 124
Aspang Markt, Aus. H16 8
Aspen, Co., U.S. B4 83
Aspen Butte, mtn., Or., U.S. E4 114
Aspermont, Tx., U.S. C2 120
Aspinwall, Pa., U.S. k14 115
Aspiring, Mount, mtn., N.Z. F2 52
Aspres-sur-Buëch, Fr. H12 10
Aspy Bay, b., N.S., Can. C9 71
Assabet, stm., Ma., U.S. g9 98
Aṣ-Ṣabyā, Sau. Ar. E3 46
As-Sallūm, Egypt B11 42
As-Salṭ, Jord. C4 40
Assam, state, India G15 38
As-Samāwah, Iraq B4 46
Assateague Island, i., U.S. D7 97
Assateague Island National Seashore, U.S. D7 97
Assawoman Bay, b., Md., U.S. D7 97
Assen, Neth. C6 8
Assiniboine, stm., Can. E2 70
Assiniboine, Mount, mtn., Can. D3 68
Assis, Braz. G3 57
Assisi, Italy F7 14
As-Sulaymānīyah, Iraq A4 46
As-Sulaymānīyah, Sau. Ar. D4 46
As-Sulayyil, Sau. Ar. D4 46
Assumption, Il., U.S. D4 90
Assumption, co., La., U.S. E4 95
Assumption Island, i., Sey. C9 44
Aṣ-Ṣuwār, Syria B7 40
As-Suwaydā', Syria C5 40
As-Suways (Suez), Egypt C12 42
Asti, Italy E3 14
Astorga, Spain C5 12
Astoria, Il., U.S. C3 90
Astoria, Or., U.S. A3 114
Astove Island, i., Sey. D9 44
Astrachan', Russia H7 22
Astrakhan see Astrachan', Russia H7 22
Astudillo, Spain C7 12
Asunción, Para. B5 56
Aswān, Egypt D12 42
Aswān High Dam, Egypt D12 42
Asyūṭ, Egypt C12 42
Atacama, Desierto de, des., Chile A3 56
Atacama, Puna de, plat., S.A. A3 56
Atacama, Salar de, pl., Chile A3 56
Ataco, Col. F5 58
Atakpamé, Togo G6 42
Atami, Japan G12 30
Atar, Maur. D3 42
Atascadero, Ca., U.S. E3 82
Atascosa, co., Tx., U.S. E3 120
'Aṭbarah, Sudan E12 42
'Aṭbarah (Atbara), stm., Afr. E12 42
Atchafalaya, stm., La., U.S. D4 95
Atchafalaya Bay, b., La., U.S. E4 95
Atchison, Ks., U.S. C8 93
Atchison, co., Ks., U.S. C8 93
Atchison, co., Mo., U.S. A2 102
Ateca, Spain D10 12
Aterau, Kaz. H8 22
Athabasca, Alta., Can. B4 68
Athabasca, stm., Alta., Can. f8 68
Athabasca, Lake, l., Can. m7 75
Athena, Or., U.S. B8 114
Athenry, Ire. H4 7
Athens, Ont., Can. C9 73
Athens, Al., U.S. A3 78
Athens, Ga., U.S. C3 87
Athens, Il., U.S. D4 90
Athens, Mi., U.S. F5 99
Athens, N.Y., U.S. C7 109
Athens, Oh., U.S. C3 112
Athens, Pa., U.S. C8 115
Athens, Tn., U.S. D9 119
Athens, Tx., U.S. C5 120
Athens, W.V., U.S. D3 125
Athens, Wi., U.S. C3 126
Athens, co., Oh., U.S. C3 112
Athens see Athínai, Grc. L7 16
Athínai (Athens), Grc. L7 16
Athlone, Ire. H5 7
Athol, Ma., U.S. A3 98
Ati, Chad F9 42
Atienza, Spain D9 12
Atik Lake, l., Man., Can. B4 70
Atikonak Lake, l., Newf., Can. h8 72
Atka Island, i., Ak., U.S. E5 79
Atkins, Ar., U.S. B3 81
Atkins, Va., U.S. D1 123
Atkinson, Il., U.S. B3 90
Atkinson, Ne., U.S. B7 104
Atkinson, N.H., U.S. E4 106
Atkinson, co., Ga., U.S. E4 87
Atlanta, Ga., U.S. C2 87
Atlanta, Il., U.S. C4 90
Atlanta, In., U.S. D5 91
Atlanta, Mi., U.S. C6 99
Atlanta, Tx., U.S. C5 120
Atlantic, Ia., U.S. C2 92
Atlantic, N.C., U.S. C6 110
Atlantic, co., N.J., U.S. E3 107
Atlantic Beach, Fl., U.S. m9 86
Atlantic City, N.J., U.S. E4 107
Atlantic Highlands, N.J., U.S. C4 107
Atlantic Ocean G11 2
Atlantic Peak, mtn., Wy., U.S. D3 127
Atlas Mountains, mts., Afr. B5 42
Atlas Saharien, mts., Alg. B6 42
Atmore, Al., U.S. D2 78
Atna Peak, mtn., B.C., Can. C3 69
Atoka, Ok., U.S. C5 113
Atoka, Tn., U.S. B2 119
Atoka, co., Ok., U.S. C5 113
Atoka Reservoir, res., Ok., U.S. C5 113
Atotonilco el Alto, Mex. G8 62
Atrato, stm., Col. D4 58
Aṭ-Ṭafīlah, Jord. D4 40
Aṭ-Ṭā'if, Sau. Ar. D3 46
Attala, co., Ms., U.S. B4 101
Attalla, Al., U.S. A3 78
Attawapiskat, stm., Ont., Can. n18 73
Attica, In., U.S. D3 91
Attica, Ks., U.S. E5 93
Attica, N.Y., U.S. C2 109
Attica, Oh., U.S. A3 112
Attleboro, Ma., U.S. C5 98
Attopeu, Laos G9 34
Attow, Ben, mtn., Scot., U.K. D7 7
Attu Island, i., Ak., U.S. E2 79
Āttūr, India G5 37
Atwater, Ca., U.S. D3 82
Atwater, Mn., U.S. E4 100
Atwood, Ont., Can. D3 73
Atwood, Il., U.S. D5 90
Atwood, Ks., U.S. C2 93
Atwood, Tn., U.S. B3 119
Atwood Lake, res., Oh., U.S. B4 112
Auau Channel, strt., Hi., U.S. C5 88
Aubagne, Fr. I12 10
Aube, stm., Fr. D11 10
Auberry, Ca., U.S. D4 82
Aubigny-sur-Nère, Fr. E9 10
Aubin, Fr. H9 10
Auburn, Al., U.S. C4 78
Auburn, Ca., U.S. C3 82
Auburn, Ga., U.S. B3 87
Auburn, Il., U.S. D4 90
Auburn, In., U.S. B7 91
Auburn, Ks., U.S. D8 93
Auburn, Ky., U.S. D3 94
Auburn, Me., U.S. D2 96
Auburn, Ma., U.S. B4 98
Auburn, Mi., U.S. E6 99
Auburn, Ne., U.S. D10 104
Auburn, N.Y., U.S. C4 109
Auburn, Wa., U.S. B3 124
Auburndale, Fl., U.S. D5 86
Auburn Heights, Mi., U.S. F7 99
Aubusson, Fr. G9 10
Auch, Fr. I7 10
Aucilla, stm., Fl., U.S. B3 86
Auckland, N.Z. B5 52
Audincourt, Fr. E13 10
Audrain, co., Mo., U.S. B6 102
Audubon, Ia., U.S. C3 92
Audubon, N.J., U.S. D2 107
Audubon, co., Ia., U.S. C2 92
Aue, Ger. E12 8
Auglaize, co., Oh., U.S. B1 112
Auglaize, stm., Oh., U.S. A1 112
Au Gres, Mi., U.S. D7 99
Augsburg, Ger. G10 8
Augusta, Italy L10 14
Augusta, Ar., U.S. B4 81
Augusta, Ga., U.S. C5 87
Augusta, Ks., U.S. E7 93
Augusta, Ky., U.S. B6 94
Augusta, Me., U.S. D3 96
Augusta, Mi., U.S. F5 99
Augusta, Wi., U.S. D2 126
Augusta, co., Va., U.S. B3 123
Augustus, Mount, mtn., Austl. D3 50
Aulander, N.C., U.S. A5 110
Auld, Lake, l., Austl. D4 50
Aulneau Peninsula, pen., Ont., Can. E4 70
Ault, Co., U.S. A6 83
Aumont-Aubrac, Fr. H10 10
Aumsville, Or., U.S. k12 114
Aurangābād, India C3 37
Auray, Fr. E4 10
Aurelia, Ia., U.S. B2 92
Aurich, Ger. B7 8
Auriflama, Braz. F3 57
Aurillac, Fr. H9 10
Aurora, Ont., Can. C5 73
Aurora, Co., U.S. B6 83
Aurora, Il., U.S. B5 90
Aurora, In., U.S. F8 91
Aurora, Mn., U.S. C6 100
Aurora, Mo., U.S. E4 102
Aurora, Ne., U.S. D7 104
Aurora, Oh., U.S. A4 112
Aurora, S.D., U.S. C9 118
Aurora, Ut., U.S. E4 121
Aurora, co., S.D., U.S. D7 118
Aus, Nmb. G3 44
Au Sable, Mi., U.S. D7 99
Au Sable, stm., Mi., U.S. D6 99
Ausable, stm., N.Y., U.S. f11 109
Au Sable Forks, N.Y., U.S. f11 109
Au Sable Point, c., Mi., U.S. D7 99
Au Sable Point, c., Mi., U.S. B4 99
Auschwitz see Oświęcim, Pol. E19 8
Austell, Ga., U.S. h7 87
Austin, In., U.S. G6 91

Name | Map Ref | Page

Austin, Mn., U.S. G6 100
Austin, Nv., U.S. D4 105
Austin, Tx., U.S. D4 120
Austin, co., Tx., U.S. E4 120
Austin, Lake, l., Austl. E3 50
Austin Channel, strt., N.W. Ter., Can. A12 66
Austintown, Oh., U.S. A5 112
Austinville, Va., U.S. D2 123
Australia, ctry., Oc. D6 50
Australian Capital Territory, ter., Austl. G9 50
Austria, ctry., Eur. F10 4
Autauga, co., Al., U.S. C3 78
Autaugaville, Al., U.S. C3 78
Autlán de Navarro, Mex. H7 62
Autun, Fr. F11 10
Auxerre, Fr. E10 10
Auxier, Ky., U.S. C7 94
Auxi-le-Château, Fr. B9 10
Auxonne, Fr. E12 10
Auxvasse, Mo., U.S. B6 102
Auyán Tepuy, mtn., Ven. E11 58
Auzances, Fr. F9 10
Ava, Mo., U.S. E5 102
Avallon, Fr. E10 10
Avalon, Ca., U.S. F4 82
Avalon, Pa., U.S. h13 115
Avalon, Lake, res., N.M., U.S. E5 108
Avalon Peninsula, pen., Newf., Can. E5 72
Avaré, Braz. G4 57
Aveiro, Port. E3 12
Avella, Pa., U.S. F1 115
Avellaneda, Arg. C5 56
Avellino, Italy I9 14
Avenal, Ca., U.S. E3 82
Avery, co., N.C., U.S. e11 110
Aves, Islas de, is., Ven. A9 58
Avesnes, Fr. B10 10
Avesta, Swe. F11 6
Avezzano, Italy G8 14
Aviemore, Scot., U.K. D9 7
Avignon, Fr. I11 10
Ávila, Spain E7 12
Avilés, Spain B6 12
Avilla, In., U.S. B7 91
Avis, Pa., U.S. D7 115
Avispa, Cerro, mtn., Ven. G10 58
Aviston, Il., U.S. E4 90
Aviz, Port. F4 12
Avoca, Ia., U.S. C2 92
Avoca, Pa., U.S. m18 115
Avola, Italy M10 14
Avon, Ct., U.S. B4 84
Avon, Il., U.S. C3 90
Avon, Ma., U.S. B5 98
Avon, Mn., U.S. E4 100
Avon, N.Y., U.S. C3 109
Avon, Oh., U.S. A3 112
Avondale, Az., U.S. D3 80
Avondale, Co., U.S. C6 83
Avondale, Pa., U.S. G10 115
Avondale Estates, Ga., U.S. h8 87
Avon Lake, Ia., U.S. e8 92
Avon Lake, Oh., U.S. A3 112
Avonmore, Pa., U.S. E3 115
Avon Park, Fl., U.S. E5 86
Avoyelles, co., La., U.S. C3 95
Avranches, Fr. D5 10
Awaji-shima, i., Japan H7 30
Awash, stm., Eth. F3 46
Awbārī, Libya C8 42
Awe, Loch, l., Scot., U.K. E7 7
Awjilah, Libya C10 42
Axiós (Vardar), stm., Eur. I6 16
Axis, Al., U.S. E1 78
Axtell, Ne., U.S. D6 104
Ayabe, Japan G8 30
Ayacucho, Peru F4 54
Ayamonte, Spain H4 12
Ayapel, Col. C5 58
Ayaviri, Peru F4 54
Aybak, Afg. B3 38
Ayden, N.C., U.S. B5 110
Aydın, Tur. H13 4
Ayer, Ma., U.S. A4 98
Ayers Cliff, Que., Can. D5 74
Ayeyarwady (Irrawaddy), stm., Mya. G3 34
Áyion Óros, pen., Grc. I8 16
Áyios Nikólaos, Grc. N9 16
Aylesbury, Eng., U.K. J12 7
Aylesford, N.S., Can. D5 71
Aylmer, Mount, mtn., Alta., Can. D3 68
Aylmer East, Que., Can. D2 74
Aylmer Lake, l., N.W. Ter., Can. D11 66
Aylmer West, Ont., Can. E4 73
Ayora, Spain F10 12
'Ayoûn el 'Atroûs, Maur. E4 42
Ayr, Scot., U.K. F8 7
Ayre, Point of, c., I. of Man G8 7
Ayu, Kepulauan, is., Indon. E9 32
Ayvalık, Tur. J10 16
Azambuja, Port. F3 12
Azamgarh, India G10 38
Azare, Nig. F8 42
Azerbaijan, ctry., Asia I7 22
Aziscohos Lake, l., Me., U.S. C1 96
Azle, Tx., U.S. n9 120
Azogues, Ec. I3 58
Azores see Açores, is., Port. D11 2
Azov, Sea of, Eur. H5 22
Aztec, N.M., U.S. A2 108
Aztec Peak, mtn., Az., U.S. D5 80
Aztec Ruins National Monument, N.M., U.S. A1 108
Azua, Dom. Rep. E12 64
Azuaga, Spain G6 12
Azuero, Península de, pen., Pan. K7 64
Azul, Arg. D5 56
Azur, Côte d', Fr. I14 10
Azusa, Ca., U.S. m13 82
Az-Zaqāzīq, Egypt D2 40
Az-Zarqā', Jord. C5 40
Az-Zāwiyah, Libya B8 42
Azzel Matti, Sebkha, pl., Alg. C6 42

B

Ba, stm., Viet. H10 34
Babaeski, Tur. H11 16
Babahoyo, Ec. H3 58
Babar, Kepulauan, is., Indon. G8 32
Babb Creek, stm., Pa., U.S. C7 115
Babbitt, Mn., U.S. C7 100
Babbitt, Nv., U.S. E3 105
B'abdā, Leb. C4 40
Bāb el-Mandeb see Mandeb, Bāb el-, strt. F3 46
Babine, stm., B.C., Can. B4 69
Babine Lake, l., B.C., Can. B5 69
Babine Range, mts., B.C., Can. B4 69
Bābol, Iran J8 22
Baboquivari Mountains, mts., Az., U.S. F4 80
Baboquivari Peak, mtn., Az., U.S. F4 80
Babuyan Islands, is., Phil. B7 32
Babylon, N.Y., U.S. n15 109
Baca, co., Co., U.S. D8 83
Bacabal, Braz. D10 54
Bacan, Pulau, i., Indon. F8 32
Bacău, Rom. C10 16
Bac Can, Viet. C8 34
Bacerac, Mex. B5 62
Bachaquero, Ven. C7 58
Bachta, Russia E11 24
Bachu, China D2 26
Back, stm., N.W. Ter., Can. C13 66
Back, stm., S.C., U.S. h12 117
Backbone Mountain, mtn., U.S. m12 97
Backnang, Ger. G9 8
Bac Lieu, Viet. J8 34
Bac Ninh, Viet. D9 34
Bacolod, Phil. C7 32
Bacon, co., Ga., U.S. E4 87
Baconton, Ga., U.S. E2 87
Bacoor, Phil. q19 33b
Bad, stm., S.D., U.S. C5 118
Bad, stm., Wi., U.S. B3 126
Badagara, India G3 37
Badajia, China B9 28
Badajoz, Spain G5 12
Badalona, Spain D14 12
Badanah, Sau. Ar. B3 46
Bad Aussee, Aus. H13 8
Bad Axe, Mi., U.S. E8 99
Baddeck, N.S., Can. C9 71
Bad Doberan, Ger. A11 8
Bad Ems, Ger. E7 8
Baden, Aus. G16 8
Baden, Ont., Can. D4 73
Baden, Switz. E15 10
Baden, Pa., U.S. E1 115
Baden-Baden, Ger. G8 8
Badgastein, Aus. H13 8
Badger, Newf., Can. D3 72
Bad Hersfeld, Ger. E9 8
Bad Homburg [vor der Höhe], Ger. E8 8
Bad Honnef, Ger. E7 8
Badin, N.C., U.S. B2 110
Badin Lake, res., N.C., U.S. B2 110
Bad Ischl, Aus. H13 8
Bad Kissingen, Ger. E10 8
Bad Kreuznach, Ger. F7 8
Badlands, hills, S.D., U.S. D3 118
Badlands, reg., U.S. C2 111
Badlands National Park, S.D., U.S. D3 118
Bad Lauterberg, Ger. D10 8
Bad Nauheim, Ger. E8 8
Bad Neustadt an der Saale, Ger. E10 8
Bad Oldesloe, Ger. B10 8
Bad Reichenhall, Ger. H12 8
Bad River Indian Reservation, Wi., U.S. B3 126
Bad Salzungen, Ger. E10 8
Bad Schwartau, Ger. B10 8
Bad Segeberg, Ger. B10 8
Bad Tölz, Ger. H11 8
Badulla, Sri L. I6 37
Badwater Creek, stm., Wy., U.S. C5 127
Bad Wildungen, Ger. D9 8
Bad Wörishofen, Ger. G10 8
Baena, Spain H7 12
Baeza, Spain H8 12
Bafatá, Gui.-B. F3 42
Baffin Bay, b., N.A. B14 61
Baffin Bay, b., Tx., U.S. E4 120
Baffin Island, i., N.W. Ter., Can. C18 66
Bafwasende, Zaire A5 44
Bāgaha, India G11 38
Bāgalkot, India D3 37
Bagansiapiapi, Indon. M6 34
Bağarası, Tur. L11 16
Bagdad, Az., U.S. C2 80
Bagdad, Fl., U.S. u14 86
Bagdad see Baghdād, Iraq B3 46
Bagdarin, Russia G16 24
Bagé, Braz. C6 56
Baggs, Wy., U.S. E5 127
Baghdād, Iraq B3 46
Bagheria, Italy K8 14
Baghlān, Afg. B3 38
Baghrān Khowleh, Afg. D1 38
Bagley, Mn., U.S. C3 100
Bagnères-de-Bigorre, Fr. I7 10
Bagnères-de-Luchon, Fr. J7 10
Bagnols-sur-Cèze, Fr. H11 10
Bago, Mya. F4 34
Baguio, Phil. p19 32
Bahamas, ctry., N.A. B9 64
Bahāwalnagar, Pak. F5 38
Bahāwalpur, Pak. F4 38
Bahía, Islas de la, is., Hond. F4 64
Bahía Blanca, Arg. D4 56
Bahía de Caráquez, Ec. H2 58
Bahía Kino, Mex. C4 62
Bahir Dar, Eth. F2 46
Bahraich, India G9 38
Bahrain, ctry., Asia C5 46
Baia-Mare, Rom. B7 16
Bai Bung, Mui, c., Viet. J8 34
Baicheng, China B11 26
Baicheng, China C3 26
Baidoa, Som. H3 46
Baie-Comeau, Que., Can. k13 74
Baie-d'Urfé, Que., Can. q19 74
Baie-Saint-Paul, Que., Can. B7 74
Baie Verte, Newf., Can. D3 72
Baigneux-les-Juifs, Fr. E11 10
Baiju, China B9 28
Bailén, Spain G8 12
Bailey, co., Tx., U.S. B1 120
Bailey Island, Me., U.S. g8 96
Bailey Island, i., S.C., U.S. k11 117
Baileys Crossroads, Va., U.S. g12 123
Bainbridge, Ga., U.S. F2 87
Bainbridge, In., U.S. E4 91
Bainbridge, Oh., U.S. C2 112
Bainbridge Island, i., Wa., U.S. e10 124
Bain-de-Bretagne, Fr. E5 10
Baing, Indon. H7 32
Baird, Tx., U.S. C3 120
Bairdford, Pa., U.S. h14 115
Baird Inlet, b., Ak., U.S. C7 79
Baird Mountains, mts., Ak., U.S. B7 79
Bais, Fr. D6 10
Baise, China C9 34
Baishuijiang, China E8 26
Baiyin, China D7 26
Baiyunebo, China C9 26
Baja, Hung. I18 8
Baja, Punta, c., Mex. C4 62
Baja California, pen., Mex. D3 62
Bajanchongor, Mong. B7 26
Bajkal, Ozero (Lake Baykal), l., Russia G15 24
Bajkal'skoje, Russia F15 24
Bajkit, Russia E13 24
Bajkonyr, Kaz. H11 22
Bajo Baudó, Col. E4 58
Baker, La., U.S. D4 95
Baker, Mt., U.S. D12 103
Baker, Or., U.S. C9 114
Baker, co., Fl., U.S. B4 86
Baker, co., Ga., U.S. E2 87
Baker, co., Or., U.S. C9 114
Baker, stm., N.H., U.S. C3 106
Baker, Mount, mtn., Wa., U.S. A4 124
Baker Air Force Base, mil., Ar., U.S. B6 81
Baker Butte, mtn., Az., U.S. C4 80
Baker Island, i., Ak., U.S. n22 79
Baker Lake, N.W. Ter., Can. D13 66
Baker Lake, l., Me., U.S. B3 96
Baker Lake, res., Wa., U.S. A4 124
Bakersfield, Ca., U.S. E4 82
Bakers Island, i., Ma., U.S. f12 98
Bakerstown, Pa., U.S. h14 115
Bakhtarān, Iran B4 46
Bakhtegān, Daryācheh-ye, l., Iran C5 46
Bakır, stm., Tur. J11 16
Bakoye, stm., Afr. F4 42
Baku, Azer. I7 22
Balabac Island, i., Phil. D6 32
Balabac Strait, strt., Asia D6 32
Ba'labakk (Baalbek), Leb. B5 40
Balachna, Russia E26 18
Bālāghāt, India J9 38
Bālāghāt Range, mts., India C4 37
Balaguer, Spain D12 12
Balakovo, Russia G7 22
Balallan, Scot., U.K. C6 7
Balāngīr, India B7 37
Balašicha, Russia F20 18
Balasore, India J12 38
Balašov, Russia G6 22
Balaton, Mn., U.S. F3 100
Balaton, l., Hung. I17 8
Balbriggan, Ire. H6 7
Balcarres, Sask., Can. G4 75
Balchaš, Ozero, l., Kaz. H9 24
Bald Eagle Lake, l., Mn., U.S. m12 100
Bald Eagle Lake, l., Mn., U.S. C7 100
Baldhill Dam, N.D., U.S. B7 111
Bald Knob, Ar., U.S. B4 81
Bald Knoll, mtn., Wy., U.S. D2 127
Bald Mountain, mtn., Or., U.S. D5 114
Bald Mountain, mtn., Or., U.S. C9 114
Bald Mountain, mtn., Wy., U.S. B5 127
Bald Mountains, mts., N.C., U.S. f10 110
Baldwin, Fl., U.S. B5 86
Baldwin, Ga., U.S. B3 87
Baldwin, La., U.S. E4 95
Baldwin, Mi., U.S. E5 99
Baldwin, Pa., U.S. k14 115
Baldwin, S.C., U.S. B5 117
Baldwin, Wi., U.S. D1 126
Baldwin, co., Al., U.S. E2 78
Baldwin, co., Ga., U.S. C3 87
Baldwin City, Ks., U.S. D8 93
Baldwinsville, N.Y., U.S. B4 109
Baldwinville, Ma., U.S. A3 98
Baldwyn, Ms., U.S. A5 101
Baldy Mountain, mtn., B.C., Can. D7 69
Baldy Mountain, mtn., Man., Can. D1 70
Baldy Mountain, mtn., Mt., U.S. B7 103
Baldy Mountain, mtn., N.M., U.S. A4 108
Baldy Peak, mtn., Az., U.S. D6 80
Baleares, Islas (Balearic Islands), is., Spain F14 12
Balearic Islands see Baleares, Islas, is., Spain E15 12
Baleine, Rivière à la, stm., Que., Can. g13 74
Balej, Russia G17 24
Balfate, Hond. G4 64
Balfour, N.C., U.S. f10 110
Bali, i., Indon. G5 32
Bali, Laut (Bali Sea), Indon. G6 32
Balıkesir, Tur. H13 4
Balikpapan, Indon. F6 32
Balimo, Pap. N. Gui. G11 32
Balingen, Ger. G8 8
Balintang Channel, strt., Phil. B7 32
Baliza, Braz. D2 57
Balkan Mountains see Stara Planina, mts., Eur. G8 16
Balkh, Afg. B2 38
Balkhash, Lake see Balchaš, Ozero, l., Kaz. H9 24
Ball, La., U.S. C3 95
Ballachulish, Scot., U.K. E7 7
Ballālpur, India C5 37
Ballarat, Austl. G8 50
Ballard, co., Ky., U.S. e8 94
Ball Club Lake, l., Mn., U.S. C5 100
Ballenas, Canal de, strt., Mex. C3 62
Ball Ground, Ga., U.S. B2 87
Ballia, India H11 38
Ballina, Ire. G3 7
Ballinger, Tx., U.S. D3 120
Ballinrobe, Ire. H3 7
Ball Mountain Lake, res., Vt., U.S. E3 122
Ballston Spa, N.Y., U.S. B7 109
Ballwin, Mo., U.S. f12 102
Bally, Pa., U.S. F10 115
Ballycastle, N. Ire., U.K. F6 7
Ballymena, N. Ire., U.K. G6 7
Ballyshannon, Ire. G4 7
Balmoral, N.B., Can. B3 71
Balmoral, Scot., U.K. D9 7
Balmville, N.Y., U.S. D6 109
Balovale, Zam. D4 44
Balrāmpur, India G10 38
Balsam Lake, Wi., U.S. C1 126
Balsam Lake, l., Wi., U.S. C1 126
Balsas, Braz. E9 54
Baltasar Brum, Ur. C5 56
Baltic, Ct., U.S. C7 84
Baltic, S.D., U.S. D9 118
Baltic Sea, Eur. H12 6
Baltijsk, Russia G2 18
Baltijskaja Kosa, spit, Eur. A19 8
Baltimore, Ire. J3 7
Baltimore, Md., U.S. B4 97
Baltimore, Oh., U.S. C3 112
Baltimore, co., Md., U.S. B4 97
Baltimore Highlands, Md., U.S. h11 97
Baluchistan, hist. reg., Asia D1 36
Bālurghāt, India H13 38
Balygyčan, Russia E24 24
Balzar, Ec. H3 58
Bamako, Mali F4 42
Bambana, stm., Nic. H6 64
Bambari, Cen. Afr. Rep. G10 42
Bamberg, Ger. F10 8
Bamberg, S.C., U.S. E5 117
Bamberg, co., S.C., U.S. E5 117
Bamenda, Cam. G8 42
Bāmīān, Afg. C2 38
Banalia, Zaire A5 44
Banana, Zaire C2 44
Bananal, Ilha do, i., Braz. F8 54
Banana River, b., Fl., U.S. D6 86
Banās, Ra's, c., Egypt D13 42
Banbridge, N. Ire., U.K. G6 7
Banbury, Eng., U.K. I11 7
Bancroft, Ont., Can. B7 73
Bancroft, Ia., U.S. A3 92
Bānda, India H9 38
Banda, Kepulauan, is., Indon. F8 32
Banda, Laut (Banda Sea), Indon. G8 32
Banda Aceh, Indon. D2 32
Bandama, stm., C. Iv. G4 42
Bandar Beheshtī, Iran C7 46
Bandar-e 'Abbās, Iran C6 46
Bandar-e Būshehr, Iran C5 46
Bandar-e Lengeh, Iran C5 46
Bandar Seri Begawan, Bru. E5 32
Banded Peak, mtn., Co., U.S. D4 83
Bandeira, Pico da, mtn., Braz. F8 57
Bandelier National Monument, N.M., U.S. B3 108
Bandera, co., Tx., U.S. E3 120
Banderas, Bahía de, b., Mex. G7 62
Bandırma, Tur. G13 4
Bandon, Ire. J4 7
Bandon, Or., U.S. D2 114
Bandundu, Zaire B3 44
Bandung, Indon. m13 32
Banes, Cuba D10 64
Banff, Scot., U.K. D10 7
Banff National Park, Alta., Can. D2 68
Bangalore, India F4 37
Bangassou, Cen. Afr. Rep. H10 42
Banggai, Kepulauan, is., Indon. F7 32
Banggi, Pulau, i., Malay. D6 32
Banghāzī, Libya B10 42
Bangil, Indon. m16 33a
Bangka, i., Indon. F4 32
Bangkalan, Indon. m16 33a
Bangkinang, Indon. N6 34
Bangkok see Krung Thep, Thai. H6 34
Bangladesh, ctry., Asia E6 36
Bangor, N. Ire., U.K. G7 7
Bangor, Wales, U.K. H8 7
Bangor, Me., U.S. D4 96
Bangor, Mi., U.S. F4 99
Bangor, Pa., U.S. E11 115
Bangor, Wi., U.S. E3 126
Bangor Township, Mi., U.S. E7 99
Bangs, Tx., U.S. D3 120
Bangs, Mount, mtn., Az., U.S. A2 80
Bangui, Cen. Afr. Rep. H9 42
Bangweulu, Lake, l., Zam. D5 44
Baní, Dom. Rep. E12 64
Banī Mazār, Egypt C12 42
Banister, stm., Va., U.S. D4 123
Banī Suwayf, Egypt C12 42
Bāniyās, Syria B4 40
Banja Luka, Bos. E12 14
Banjarmasin, Indon. F5 32
Banjul, Gam. F2 42
Bankhead Lake, res., Al., U.S. B2 78
Banks, co., Ga., U.S. B3 87
Banks Island, i., B.C., Can. C2 69
Banks Island, i., N.W. Ter., Can. B8 66
Banks Lake, res., Wa., U.S. B6 124
Banks Strait, strt., Austl. H9 50
Bānkura, India I12 38
Bann, stm., N. Ire., U.K. G6 7
Banner, co., Ne., U.S. C2 104
Banner Elk, N.C., U.S. A1 110
Banning, Ca., U.S. F5 82
Bannock, co., Id., U.S. G6 89
Bannock Peak, mtn., Id., U.S. F6 89
Bannock Range, mts., Id., U.S. G6 89
Bannu, Pak. D4 38
Baños de Cerrato, Spain D7 12
Ban Pak Phraek, Thai. J6 34
Ban Phak Phang, Thai. F6 34
Ban Pong, Thai. H5 34
Banská Bystrica, Slov. G19 8
Bānswāra, India I6 38
Bantam, stm., Ct., U.S. B3 84
Bantam Lake, l., Ct., U.S. C3 84
Bantry, Ire. J3 7
Banyak, Kepulauan, is., Indon. M4 34
Banyuwangi, Indon. n17 33a
Baoding, China D10 26
Baofeng, China B2 28
Bao Ha, Viet. C8 34
Baoji, China E8 26
Baoshan, China B5 34
Baotou, China C8 26
Baoying, China B8 28
Ba'qūbah, Iraq B3 46
Baquedano, Chile A3 56
Baraboo, Wi., U.S. E4 126
Baraboo, stm., Wi., U.S. E3 126
Baracoa, Cuba D10 64
Baraga, Mi., U.S. B2 99
Baraga, co., Mi., U.S. B2 99
Barakī Barak, Afg. D3 38
Baram, stm., Malay. E5 32
Bārāmati, India C3 37
Bārāmūla, India C6 38
Bārān, India H7 38
Baranagar, India I13 38
Baranoa, Col. B5 58
Baranof Island, i., Ak., U.S. m22 79
Baranoviči, Bela. H9 18
Barataria, La., U.S. E5 95
Barataria Bay, b., La., U.S. E6 95
Barat Daya, Kepulauan, is., Indon. G8 32
Barbacena, Braz. F7 57
Barbados, ctry., N.A. H18 64
Barbar, Sudan E12 42
Barbas, Cabo, c., W. Sah. D2 42
Barbastro, Spain C12 12
Barbate de Franco, Spain I6 12
Barber, co., Ks., U.S. E5 93
Barbers Point, c., Hi., U.S. B3 88
Barbers Point Naval Air Station, mil., Hi., U.S. g9 88
Barberton, Oh., U.S. A4 112
Barbezieux, Fr. G6 10
Barbosa, Col. E6 58
Barbour, co., Al., U.S. D4 78
Barbour, co., W.V., U.S. B4 125
Barboursville, W.V., U.S. C2 125
Barbourville, Ky., U.S. D6 94
Barbuda, i., Antig. F17 64
Barcaldine, Austl. D9 50
Barcellona Pozzo di Gotto, Italy K10 14
Barcelona, Spain D14 12
Barcelona, Ven. B10 58
Barcelos, Braz. D6 54
Barcelos, Port. D3 12
Barcroft, Lake, res., Va., U.S. g12 123
Barden Reservoir, res., R.I., U.S. C2 116
Bardera, Som. H3 46
Bardīyah, Libya B11 42
Bardstown, Ky., U.S. C4 94
Bardufoss, Nor. B12 6
Bardwell, Ky., U.S. f9 94
Bardwell Lake, res., Tx., U.S. C4 120
Bareilly, India F8 38
Barents Sea, Eur. B8 128
Barfleur, Fr. C5 10
Bargersville, In., U.S. E5 91
Bar Harbor, Me., U.S. D4 96
Bari, Italy H11 14
Barīkowṭ, Afg. C4 38
Barillas, Guat. G2 64
Barinas, Ven. C7 58
Barinitas, Ven. C7 58
Baripāda, India J12 38
Barisāl, Bngl. I14 38
Barisan, Pegunungan, mts., Indon. F3 32
Barito, stm., Indon. F5 32
Barker Heights, N.C., U.S. f10 110
Barkhamsted Reservoir, res., Ct., U.S. B3 84
Barkley, Lake, res., U.S. f10 94
Barkley Sound, strt., B.C., Can. E5 69
Barkly Tableland, plat., Austl. C7 50
Bark Point, c., Wi., U.S. B2 126
Barksdale Air Force Base, mil., La., U.S. B2 95
Bar-le-Duc, Fr. D12 10
Barlee, Lake, l., Austl. E3 50
Barletta, Italy H11 14
Barling, Ar., U.S. B1 81
Barlow, Ky., U.S. e8 94
Barmer, India H4 38
Barmouth, Wales, U.K. I8 7
Barnaul, Russia G10 24
Barnegat Bay, b., N.J., U.S. D4 107
Barnegat Inlet, b., N.J., U.S. D4 107
Barnes, co., N.D., U.S. B7 111
Barnesboro, Pa., U.S. E4 115
Barnes Sound, strt., Fl., U.S. G6 86
Barnesville, Ga., U.S. C2 87
Barnesville, Mn., U.S. D2 100
Barnesville, Oh., U.S. C4 112
Barneville-Carteret, Fr. C5 10
Barnhart, Mo., U.S. C7 102
Barnsdall, Ok., U.S. A5 113
Barnsley, Eng., U.K. H11 7
Barnstable, Ma., U.S. C7 98
Barnstable, co., Ma., U.S. C7 98
Barnstaple, Eng., U.K. J8 7
Barnwell, S.C., U.S. E5 117
Barnwell, co., S.C., U.S. E5 117
Baroda, India I5 38
Barpeta, India G14 38
Barqah (Cyrenaica), reg., Libya B10 42
Barques, Pointe aux, c., Mi., U.S. D8 99
Barquisimeto, Ven. B8 58
Barra, Braz. F10 54
Barra, Ponta da, c., Moz. F7 44
Barrackville, W.V., U.S. B4 125
Barra do Corda, Braz. E9 54
Barra Falsa, Ponta da, c., Moz. F7 44
Barra Mansa, Braz. G6 57

Name	Map Ref	Page
Barrancabermeja, Col.	D6	58
Barranca del Cobre, Parque Nacional, Mex.	D6	62
Barrancas, Ven.	C11	58
Barrancos, Port.	G5	12
Barranquilla, Col.	B5	58
Barras, Braz.	D10	54
Barrax, Spain	F9	12
Barre, Vt., U.S.	C4	122
Barre, Lake, l., La., U.S.	E5	95
Barre Falls Reservoir, res., Ma., U.S.	B4	98
Barreiras, Braz.	B6	57
Barreiro, Port.	G2	12
Barreiros, Braz.	E11	54
Barrême, Fr.	I13	10
Barren, co., Ky., U.S.	D4	94
Barren, stm., Ky., U.S.	C3	94
Barren Island, i., Md., U.S.	D5	97
Barren Islands, is., Ak., U.S.	h15	79
Barren River Lake, res., Ky., U.S.	D3	94
Barretos, Braz.	F4	57
Barrett, W.V., U.S.	D3	125
Barrhead, Alta., Can.	B3	68
Barrie, Ont., Can.	C5	73
Barrie Island, i., Ont., Can.	B2	73
Barrière, B.C., Can.	D7	69
Barrington, Il., U.S.	A5	90
Barrington, N.J., U.S.	D2	107
Barrington, R.I., U.S.	D5	116
Barrington, stm., R.I., U.S.	C5	116
Barron, Wi., U.S.	C2	126
Barron, co., Wi., U.S.	C2	126
Barron Lake, Mi., U.S.	G4	99
Barrow, Ak., U.S.	A8	79
Barrow, co., Ga., U.S.	B3	87
Barrow, Point, c., Ak., U.S.	A8	79
Barrow Creek, Austl.	D6	50
Barrow-in-Furness, Eng., U.K.	G9	7
Barrow Island, i., Austl.	D3	50
Barrow Strait, strt., N.W. Ter., Can.	B14	66
Barry, Il., U.S.	D2	90
Barry, co., Mi., U.S.	F5	99
Barry, co., Mo., U.S.	E4	102
Barrys Bay, Ont., Can.	B7	73
Bārsi, India	C3	37
Barstow, Ca., U.S.	E5	82
Bar-sur-Aube, Fr.	D11	10
Barth, Ger.	A12	8
Bartholomew, co., In., U.S.	F6	91
Bartholomew, Bayou, stm., U.S.	D4	81
Bartica, Guy.	D13	58
Bartlesville, Ok., U.S.	A6	113
Bartlett, N.H., U.S.	B4	106
Bartlett, Tn., U.S.	B2	119
Bartlett, Tx., U.S.	D4	120
Bartlett Reservoir, res., Az., U.S.	D4	80
Bartletts Ferry Dam, U.S.	C4	78
Barton, Oh., U.S.	B5	112
Barton, Vt., U.S.	B4	122
Barton, co., Ks., U.S.	D5	93
Barton, co., Mo., U.S.	D3	102
Barton, stm., Vt., U.S.	B4	122
Bartonville, Il., U.S.	C4	90
Bartow, Fl., U.S.	E5	86
Bartow, co., Ga., U.S.	B2	87
Barú, Volcán, vol., Pan.	J6	64
Bāruni, India	H11	38
Baruun Urt, Mong.	B9	26
Barvas, Scot., U.K.	C6	7
Basalt, Co., U.S.	B3	83
Basankusu, Zaire	A3	44
Basatongwula Shan, mtn., China	D14	38
Bascuñán, Cabo, c., Chile	B2	56
Basehor, Ks., U.S.	k16	93
Basel (Bâle), Switz.	E14	10
Bashan Lake, l., Ct., U.S.	D6	84
Bashaw, Alta., Can.	C4	68
Bashi Channel, strt., Asia	G11	26
Basilan Island, i., Phil.	D7	32
Basildon, Eng., U.K.	J13	7
Basile, La., U.S.	D3	95
Basin, Wy., U.S.	B4	127
Basingstoke, Eng., U.K.	J11	7
Basīrhāt, India	I13	38
Basīt, Ra's al-, c., Syria	B4	40
Baskahegan Lake, l., Me., U.S.	C5	96
Baskatong, Réservoir, res., Que., Can.	G17	66
Basking Ridge, N.J., U.S.	B3	107
Basoko, Zaire	A4	44
Basra see Al-Başrah, Iraq	B4	46
Bassano, Alta., Can.	D4	68
Bassano del Grappa, Italy	D6	14
Bassari, Togo	G6	42
Bassas da India, rf., Reu.	F7	44
Basse-Terre, Guad.	F17	64
Basseterre, St. K./N.	F16	64
Basse-Terre, i., Guad.	F17	64
Bassett, Ne., U.S.	B6	104
Bassett, Va., U.S.	D3	123
Bassett Peak, mtn., Az., U.S.	E5	80
Bass Islands, is., Oh., U.S.	A3	112
Bass Lake, In., U.S.	B4	91
Bass Strait, strt., Austl.	G9	50
Basswood Lake, l., Mn., U.S.	B7	100
Basti, India	G10	38
Bastogne, Bel.	E5	8
Bastrop, La., U.S.	B4	95
Bastrop, Tx., U.S.	D4	120
Bastrop, co., Tx., U.S.	D4	120
Bastuträsk, Swe.	D13	6
Bata, Eq. Gui.	H7	42
Bataan Peninsula, pen., Phil.	q19	33b
Batabanó, Golfo de, b., Cuba	C6	64
Batagaj, Russia	D20	24
Bataguaçu, Braz.	F2	57
Bataiporã, Braz.	G2	57
Batāla, India	E6	38
Batalha, Port.	F3	12
Batamaj, Russia	E19	24
Batang, China	E6	26
Batangas, Phil.	r19	33b
Batan Islands, is., Phil.	A7	32
Batanta, Pulau, i., Indon.	F9	32
Batatais, Braz.	F5	57
Batavia, Il., U.S.	B5	90
Batavia, N.Y., U.S.	C2	109
Batavia, Oh., U.S.	C1	112
Batchelor Bay, b., N.C., U.S.	B6	110
Bātdâmbâng, Camb.	H7	34
Batepito, Mex.	B5	62
Bates, co., Mo., U.S.	C3	102
Batesburg, S.C., U.S.	D4	117
Batesville, Ar., U.S.	B4	81
Batesville, In., U.S.	F7	91
Batesville, Ms., U.S.	A4	101
Bath, N.B., Can.	C2	71
Bath, Ont., Can.	C8	73
Bath, Eng., U.K.	J10	7
Bath, Me., U.S.	E3	96
Bath, N.Y., U.S.	C3	109
Bath, Pa., U.S.	E11	115
Bath, S.C., U.S.	D4	117
Bath, co., Ky., U.S.	B6	94
Bath, co., Va., U.S.	B3	123
Bathurst, N.B., Can.	B4	71
Bathurst, Cape, c., N.W. Ter., Can.	B7	66
Bathurst Inlet, N.W. Ter., Can.	C11	66
Bathurst Inlet, b., N.W. Ter., Can.	C11	66
Bathurst Island, i., Austl.	B6	50
Bathurst Island, i., N.W. Ter., Can.	A12	66
Batiscan, stm., Que., Can.	B5	74
Batna, Alg.	A7	42
Baton Rouge, La., U.S.	D4	95
Batouri, Cam.	H8	42
Batsto, stm., N.J., U.S.	D3	107
Batten Kill, stm., U.S.	E2	122
Batticaloa, Sri L.	I6	37
Battle, stm., Can.	F10	66
Battle Creek, Ia., U.S.	B2	92
Battle Creek, Mi., U.S.	F5	99
Battle Creek, Ne., U.S.	C8	104
Battle Ground, In., U.S.	C4	91
Battle Ground, Wa., U.S.	D3	124
Battle Lake, Mn., U.S.	D3	100
Battle Mountain, Nv., U.S.	C5	105
Battle Mountain, mtn., Wy., U.S.	E5	127
Batu, mtn., Eth.	G2	46
Batu, Kepulauan, is., Indon.	O5	34
Batumi, Geor.	I6	22
Batu Pahat, Malay.	N7	34
Baturité, Braz.	D11	54
Baubau, Indon.	G7	32
Bauchi, Nig.	F7	42
Baud, Fr.	E3	10
Baudette, Mn., U.S.	B4	100
Bauld, Cape, c., Newf., Can.	C4	72
Baume-les-Dames, Fr.	E13	10
Baunei, Italy	I4	14
Bauru, Braz.	G4	57
Baús, Braz.	E2	57
Bautzen, Ger.	D14	8
Bawean, Pulau, i., Indon.	G5	32
Baxley, Ga., U.S.	E4	87
Baxter, Ia., U.S.	C4	92
Baxter, Mn., U.S.	D4	100
Baxter, Tn., U.S.	C8	119
Baxter, co., Ar., U.S.	A3	81
Baxter Springs, Ks., U.S.	E9	93
Bay, Ar., U.S.	B5	81
Bay, co., Fl., U.S.	u16	86
Bay, co., Mi., U.S.	E6	99
Bay, Laguna de, l., Phil.	q19	33b
Bayamo, Cuba	D9	64
Bayan Har Shan, mts., China	E6	26
Bayard, Ne., U.S.	C2	104
Bayard, N.M., U.S.	E1	108
Bayberry, N.Y., U.S.	*B4	109
Bayboro, N.C., U.S.	B6	110
Bay Bulls, Newf., Can.	E5	72
Bay City, Mi., U.S.	E7	99
Bay City, Or., U.S.	B3	114
Bay City, Tx., U.S.	E5	120
Bay de Verde, Newf., Can.	D5	72
Bayerische Alpen, mts., Eur.	H11	8
Bayeux, Fr.	C6	10
Bayfield, Ont., Can.	D3	73
Bayfield, Co., U.S.	D3	83
Bayfield, Wi., U.S.	B3	126
Bayfield, co., Wi., U.S.	B2	126
Bayındır, Tur.	K11	16
Baykonur see Bajkonyr, Kaz.	H11	22
Baylor, co., Tx., U.S.	C3	120
Bay Mills Indian Reservation, Mi., U.S.	B6	99
Bay Minette, Al., U.S.	E2	78
Bayo, Spain	B3	12
Bayona, Spain	C3	12
Bayonne, Fr.	I5	10
Bayonne, N.J., U.S.	B4	107
Bayou Bodcau Reservoir, res., La., U.S.	B2	95
Bayou D'Arbonne Lake, res., La., U.S.	B3	95
Bayou George, Fl., U.S.	u16	86
Bayou Goula, La., U.S.	D4	95
Bayou La Batre, Al., U.S.	E1	78
Bay Point, c., S.C., U.S.	G7	117
Bayport, Mn., U.S.	E6	100
Bayport, N.Y., U.S.	n15	109
Bayramıç, Tur.	J10	16
Bayreuth, Ger.	F11	8
Bay Ridge, Md., U.S.	C5	97
Bay Roberts, Newf., Can.	E5	72
Bayrūt (Beirut), Leb.	C4	40
Bays, Lake of, l., Ont., Can.	B5	73
Bay Saint Louis, Ms., U.S.	E4	101
Bay Shore, N.Y., U.S.	E7	109
Bayshore Gardens, Fl., U.S.	q10	86
Bayside, Wi., U.S.	m12	126
Bay Springs, Ms., U.S.	D4	101
Bayt Laḥm, W. Bank	D4	40
Baytown, Tx., U.S.	E5	120
Bayview, Al., U.S.	f7	78
Bay Village, Oh., U.S.	h9	112
Baza, Spain	H9	12
Bazaruto, Ilha do, i., Moz.	F7	44
Bazas, Fr.	H6	10
Be, Nosy, i., Madag.	D9	44
Beach, Il., U.S.	h9	90
Beach, N.D., U.S.	C1	111
Beachburg, Ont., Can.	B8	73
Beach City, Oh., U.S.	B4	112
Beach Haven Inlet, b., N.J., U.S.	D4	107
Beach Pond, res., U.S.	C8	84
Beachville, Ont., Can.	D4	73
Beachwood, N.J., U.S.	D4	107
Beachy Head, c., Eng., U.K.	K13	7
Beacon, N.Y., U.S.	D7	109
Beacon Falls, Ct., U.S.	D3	84
Beaconsfield, Que., Can.	q19	74
Beadle, co., S.D., U.S.	C7	118
Beagle Gulf, b., Austl.	B6	50
Bealanana, Madag.	D9	44
Beale, Cape, c., B.C., Can.	E5	69
Beale Air Force Base, mil., Ca., U.S.	C3	82
Bear, De., U.S.	B3	85
Bear, stm., U.S.	B3	121
Bear Creek, Al., U.S.	A2	78
Bear Creek, stm., U.S.	E2	93
Bear Creek, stm., Or., U.S.	E4	114
Bear Creek, stm., Wy., U.S.	E8	127
Bearden, Ar., U.S.	D3	81
Beardstown, Il., U.S.	C3	90
Bear Inlet, b., N.C., U.S.	C5	110
Bear Lake, co., Id., U.S.	G7	89
Bear Lake, l., U.S.	A4	121
Bear Lake, l., Wi., U.S.	C2	126
Bear Lodge Mountains, mts., Wy., U.S.	B8	127
Bear Mountain, mtn., Or., U.S.	D4	114
Bearpaw Mountains, mts., Mt., U.S.	B7	103
Bear River, N.S., Can.	E4	71
Bear River City, Ut., U.S.	B3	121
Beartooth Pass, Wy., U.S.	B3	127
Beartooth Range, mts., U.S.	E7	103
Bear Town, Ms., U.S.	D3	101
Beasain, Spain	B9	12
Beas de Segura, Spain	G9	12
Beata, Isla, i., Dom. Rep.	F12	64
Beatrice, Ne., U.S.	D9	104
Beatton, stm., B.C., Can.	E8	66
Beatty, Nv., U.S.	G5	105
Beattyville, Ky., U.S.	C6	94
Beaucaire, Fr.	I11	10
Beaufort, N.C., U.S.	C6	110
Beaufort, S.C., U.S.	G6	117
Beaufort, co., N.C., U.S.	B5	110
Beaufort, co., S.C., U.S.	G6	117
Beaufort Marine Corps Air Station, mil., S.C., U.S.	F6	117
Beaufort Sea, N.A.	B7	61
Beaufort West, S. Afr.	H4	44
Beaugency, Fr.	E8	10
Beauharnois, Que., Can.	D4	74
Beau Lake, l., Me., U.S.	A3	96
Beauly, Scot., U.K.	D8	7
Beaumont, Alta., Can.	C4	68
Beaumont, Ms., U.S.	D5	101
Beaumont, Tx., U.S.	D5	120
Beaumont-sur-Sarthe, Fr.	D7	10
Beaune, Fr.	E11	10
Beauport, Que., Can.	n17	74
Beaupré, Que., Can.	B7	74
Beaupréau, Fr.	E5	10
Beauregard, co., La., U.S.	D2	95
Beausejour, Man., Can.	D3	70
Beauvais, Fr.	C9	10
Beauval, Sask., Can.	B2	75
Beauvoir-sur-Niort, Fr.	F6	10
Beaver, Ok., U.S.	A1	113
Beaver, Pa., U.S.	E1	115
Beaver, Ut., U.S.	E3	121
Beaver, W.V., U.S.	D3	125
Beaver, co., Ok., U.S.	e10	113
Beaver, co., Pa., U.S.	E1	115
Beaver, co., Ut., U.S.	E2	121
Beaver, stm., Can.	D7	66
Beaver, stm., Can.	B2	75
Beaver, stm., U.S.	A2	113
Beaver, stm., N.Y., U.S.	B6	109
Beaver, stm., R.I., U.S.	E2	116
Beaver, stm., Ut., U.S.	E2	121
Beaverbank, N.S., Can.	E6	71
Beaver Brook, stm., U.S.	E4	106
Beaver City, Ne., U.S.	D6	104
Beavercreek, Oh., U.S.	C1	112
Beaver Creek, stm., U.S.	E4	104
Beaver Creek, stm., U.S.	C8	127
Beaver Creek, stm., N.D., U.S.	C5	111
Beaver Creek, stm., N.D., U.S.	C1	111
Beaver Creek, stm., Ok., U.S.	C3	113
Beaver Creek, stm., Tn., U.S.	m13	119
Beaver Creek, stm., Wy., U.S.	D4	127
Beaverdale, Pa., U.S.	F4	115
Beaver Dam, Ky., U.S.	C3	94
Beaver Dam, Wi., U.S.	E5	126
Beaverdam Branch, stm., De., U.S.	F3	85
Beaverdam Lake, res., Wi., U.S.	E5	126
Beaver Falls, Pa., U.S.	E1	115
Beaverhead, co., Mt., U.S.	E3	103
Beaverhead, stm., Mt., U.S.	E4	103
Beaverhead Mountains, mts., U.S.	D5	89
Beaverhill Lake, l., Alta., Can.	C4	68
Beaver Island, i., Mi., U.S.	C5	99
Beaver Lake, res., Ar., U.S.	A2	81
Beaverlodge, Alta., Can.	B1	68
Beaver Meadows, Pa., U.S.	E10	115
Beaver Run Reservoir, res., Pa., U.S.	F2	115
Beavertail Point, c., R.I., U.S.	F4	116
Beaverton, Mi., U.S.	E6	99
Beaverton, Or., U.S.	B4	114
Beāwar, India	G6	38
Bebedouro, Braz.	F4	57
Bécancour, Que., Can.	C5	74
Bečej, Yugo.	D4	16
Becerreá, Spain	C4	12
Béchar, Alg.	B5	42
Becharof Lake, l., Ak., U.S.	D8	79
Beckemeyer, Il., U.S.	E4	90
Becker, Mn., U.S.	E5	100
Becker, co., Mn., U.S.	D3	100
Beckham, co., Ok., U.S.	B2	113
Beckley, W.V., U.S.	D3	125
Beckum, Ger.	D8	8
Becky Peak, mtn., Nv., U.S.	D7	105
Bédarieux, Fr.	I10	10
Bedford, Que., Can.	D5	74
Bedford, Eng., U.K.	I12	7
Bedford, In., U.S.	G5	91
Bedford, Ia., U.S.	D3	92
Bedford, Ky., U.S.	B4	94
Bedford, Ma., U.S.	B5	98
Bedford, N.H., U.S.	E3	106
Bedford, Oh., U.S.	A4	112
Bedford, Pa., U.S.	F4	115
Bedford, Va., U.S.	C3	123
Bedford, co., Pa., U.S.	G4	115
Bedford, co., Tn., U.S.	B5	119
Bedford, co., Va., U.S.	C3	123
Bedford Hills, N.Y., U.S.	D7	109
Bee, co., Tx., U.S.	E4	120
Beebe, Que., Can.	D5	74
Beebe, Ar., U.S.	B4	81
Beecher, Il., U.S.	B6	90
Beecher, Mi., U.S.	*E7	99
Beech Fork, stm., Ky., U.S.	C4	94
Beech Grove, In., U.S.	E5	91
Beech Island, S.C., U.S.	E4	117
Beemer, Ne., U.S.	C9	104
Bee Ridge, Fl., U.S.	q11	86
Beersheba see Be'er Sheva', Isr.	D4	40
Be'er Sheva', Isr.	D4	40
Beeton (part of Alliston Beeton Tecumseth and Tottenham), Ont., Can.	C5	73
Beeville, Tx., U.S.	E4	120
Befale, Zaire	A4	44
Befandriana, Madag.	E9	44
Beggs, Ok., U.S.	B5	113
Begi, Eth.	G1	46
Behbehān, Iran	B5	46
Behm Canal, strt., Ak., U.S.	n24	79
Bei, stm., China	G9	26
Bei'an, China	B12	26
Beihai, China	D10	34
Beijing (Peking), China	D10	26
Beijing Shih, China	C10	26
Beipiao, China	C11	26
Beira, Moz.	E6	44
Beirut see Bayrūt, Leb.	C4	40
Beja, Port.	G4	12
Béja, Tun.	M4	14
Bejaïa, Alg.	A7	42
Béjar, Spain	E6	12
Békéscsaba, Hung.	I21	8
Bekily, Madag.	F9	44
Bela, India	H9	38
Bel Air, Md., U.S.	A5	97
Belalcázar, Spain	G6	12
Bel Alton, Md., U.S.	D4	97
Belampalli, India	C5	37
Belarus, ctry., Eur.	G3	22
Bela Vista, Braz.	A5	56
Belcamp, Md., U.S.	B5	97
Belcherāgh, Afg.	C1	38
Belcher Islands, is., N.W. Ter., Can.	E17	66
Belchertown, Ma., U.S.	B3	98
Belchite, Spain	D11	12
Belcourt, N.D., U.S.	A6	111
Belden, Ms., U.S.	A5	101
Belding, Mi., U.S.	E5	99
Beled Weyne, Som.	H4	46
Belém, Braz.	D9	54
Belén, Para.	A5	56
Belen, N.M., U.S.	C3	108
Belfair, Wa., U.S.	B3	124
Belfast, N. Ire., U.K.	G7	7
Belfast, Me., U.S.	D3	96
Belfield, N.D., U.S.	C2	111
Belford, N.J., U.S.	C4	107
Belfort, Fr.	E13	10
Belfry, Ky., U.S.	C7	94
Belgaum, India	E3	37
Belgium, Wi., U.S.	E6	126
Belgium, ctry., Eur.	E8	4
Belgorod, Russia	G5	22
Belgrade, Mn., U.S.	E3	100
Belgrade, Mt., U.S.	E5	103
Belgrade see Beograd, Yugo.	E4	16
Belhaven, N.C., U.S.	B6	110
Belin, Fr.	H6	10
Belington, W.V., U.S.	B5	125
Belitung, i., Indon.	F4	32
Belize, ctry., N.A.	F3	64
Belize City, Belize	F3	64
Belknap, co., N.H., U.S.	C3	106
Belknap Crater, crat., Or., U.S.	C5	114
Bell, co., Ky., U.S.	D6	94
Bell, co., Tx., U.S.	D4	120
Bellac, Fr.	F8	10
Bella Coola, stm., B.C., Can.	C4	69
Bellaire, Ks., U.S.	g12	93
Bellaire, Mi., U.S.	D5	99
Bellaire, Oh., U.S.	C5	112
Bellaire, Tx., U.S.	r14	120
Bellamy, Al., U.S.	C1	78
Bellary, India	E4	37
Bellavista, Peru	E3	54
Bella Vista, Ar., U.S.	A1	81
Bellbrook, Oh., U.S.	C1	112
Belle, Mo., U.S.	C6	102
Belle, W.V., U.S.	C3	125
Belle, stm., La., U.S.	k9	95
Belleair, Fl., U.S.	p10	86
Belle Bay, b., Newf., Can.	E4	72
Belle Chasse, La., U.S.	E5	95
Bellefontaine, Oh., U.S.	B2	112
Bellefonte, Pa., U.S.	E6	115
Belle Fourche, S.D., U.S.	C2	118
Belle Fourche, stm., U.S.	C3	118
Belle Fourche Reservoir, res., S.D., U.S.	C2	118
Bellegarde, Fr.	F12	10
Belle Glade, Fl., U.S.	F6	86
Belle Isle, Fl., U.S.	D5	86
Belle Isle, i., Newf., Can.	C4	72
Belle Isle, Strait of, strt., Newf., Can.	C3	72
Belle Meade, Tn., U.S.	g10	119
Belle Plaine, Ia., U.S.	C5	92
Belle Plaine, Ks., U.S.	E6	93
Belle Plaine, Mn., U.S.	F5	100
Belle River, Ont., Can.	E2	73
Belle Rose, La., U.S.	D4	95
Belle Vernon, Pa., U.S.	F2	115
Belleview, Fl., U.S.	C4	86
Belle View, Va., U.S.	g12	123
Belleville, Ont., Can.	C7	73
Belleville, Il., U.S.	E4	90
Belleville, Ks., U.S.	C6	93
Belleville, Mi., U.S.	p15	99
Belleville, N.J., U.S.	B4	107
Belleville, Pa., U.S.	E6	115
Belleville, Wi., U.S.	F4	126
Belleville Pond, l., R.I., U.S.	E4	116
Bellevue, Id., U.S.	F4	89
Bellevue, Ia., U.S.	B7	92
Bellevue, Ky., U.S.	h13	94
Bellevue, Mi., U.S.	F5	99
Bellevue, Ne., U.S.	C10	104
Bellevue, Oh., U.S.	A3	112
Bellevue, Pa., U.S.	F1	115
Bellevue, Wa., U.S.	e11	124
Belley, Fr.	G12	10
Bellflower, Ca., U.S.	n12	82
Bellingham, Ma., U.S.	B5	98
Bellingham, Wa., U.S.	A3	124
Bellingshausen Sea, Ant.	B4	47
Bellinzona, Switz.	F16	10
Bell Island, i., Newf., Can.	C4	72
Bellmawr, N.J., U.S.	D2	107
Bello, Col.	D5	58
Bellows Falls, Vt., U.S.	E4	122
Bell Peninsula, pen., N.W. Ter., Can.	D16	66
Bellport, N.Y., U.S.	n16	109
Bells, Tn., U.S.	B2	119
Bells Creek, stm., W.V., U.S.	m13	125
Belluno, Italy	C7	14
Bell Ville, Arg.	C4	56
Bellville, Oh., U.S.	B3	112
Bellville, Tx., U.S.	E4	120
Bellwood, Il., U.S.	k9	90
Bellwood, Pa., U.S.	E5	115
Bellwood, Va., U.S.	n18	123
Belmar, N.J., U.S.	C4	107
Belmond, Ia., U.S.	B4	92
Belmont, Ont., Can.	E3	73
Belmont, Ca., U.S.	h8	82
Belmont, Ma., U.S.	g11	98
Belmont, Ms., U.S.	A5	101
Belmont, N.H., U.S.	D4	106
Belmont, N.C., U.S.	B1	110
Belmont, W.V., U.S.	B3	125
Belmont, Wi., U.S.	F3	126
Belmont, co., Oh., U.S.	C4	112
Belmonte, Braz.	C9	57
Belmonte, Port.	E4	12
Belmonte, Spain	B5	12
Belmonte, Spain	F9	12
Belmopan, Belize	F3	64
Belmullet, Ire.	G2	7
Bel-Nor, Mo., U.S.	f13	102
Belo, Madag.	E8	44
Beloeil, Que., Can.	D4	74
Belogorsk, Russia	G19	24
Belo Horizonte, Braz.	E7	57
Beloit, Ks., U.S.	C5	93
Beloit, Oh., U.S.	B5	112
Beloit, Wi., U.S.	F4	126
Beloit North, Wi., U.S.	*F4	126
Beloje, Ozero, l., Russia	A20	18
Beloje more (White Sea), Russia	D5	22
Belorado, Spain	C8	12
Beloreck, Russia	G9	22
Belorussia see Belarus, ctry., Eur.	G3	22
Belovo, Russia	G11	24
Belpre, Oh., U.S.	C4	112
Belt, Mt., U.S.	C6	103
Belted Range, mts., Nv., U.S.	F5	105
Belton, Mo., U.S.	C3	102
Belton, S.C., U.S.	B3	117
Belton, Tx., U.S.	D4	120
Belton Lake, res., Tx., U.S.	D4	120
Beltrami, co., Mn., U.S.	B3	100
Beltsville, Md., U.S.	B4	97
Belucha, Gora, mtn., Asia	H11	24
Belvedere, S.C., U.S.	D4	117
Belvedere Marittimo, Italy	J10	14
Belvidere, Il., U.S.	A5	90
Belvidere, N.J., U.S.	B2	107
Belyj, Ostrov, i., Russia	C8	24
Belyj Jar, Russia	F11	24
Belzoni, Ms., U.S.	B3	101
Bement, Il., U.S.	D5	90
Bemidji, Mn., U.S.	C4	100
Bemidji, Lake, l., Mn., U.S.	C4	100
Benabarre, Spain	C12	12
Bena-Dibele, Zaire	B4	44
Benavente, Port.	G3	12
Benavente, Spain	C6	12
Benavides, Tx., U.S.	F3	120
Benbrook Lake, res., Tx., U.S.	n9	120
Bend, Or., U.S.	C5	114
Ben Davis Point, c., N.J., U.S.	E2	107
Bendeleben, Mount, mtn., Ak., U.S.	B7	79
Bendigo, Austl.	G8	50
Benedict, Md., U.S.	C4	97
Benedito Leite, Braz.	E10	54
Benevento, Italy	H9	14
Benewah, co., Id., U.S.	B2	89
Bengal, Bay of, b., Asia	F6	36
Bengbu, China	C6	28
Benghazi see Banghāzī, Libya	B10	42
Bengkalis, Indon.	N7	34
Bengkulu, Indon.	F3	32
Benguela, Ang.	D2	44
Benham, Ky., U.S.	D7	94
Ben Hill, co., Ga., U.S.	E3	87
Beni, stm., Bol.	F5	54
Béni Abbès, Alg.	B5	42
Benicarló, Spain	E12	12
Benicia, Ca., U.S.	C2	82
Beni-Mellal, Mor.	B4	42
Benin, ctry., Afr.	G6	42
Benin, Bight of, Afr.	G6	42
Benin City, Nig.	G7	42
Benisa, Spain	G12	12
Benito Juárez, Presa, res., Mex.	I12	62
Benjamin Constant, Braz.	D4	54
Benjamín Hill, Mex.	B4	62

Name	Map Ref	Page
Benkelman, Ne., U.S.	D4	104
Benld, Il., U.S.	D4	90
Bennett, Co., U.S.	B6	83
Bennett, co., S.D., U.S.	D4	118
Bennettsville, S.C., U.S.	B8	117
Bennington, Ne., U.S.	g12	104
Bennington, N.H., U.S.	D3	106
Bennington, Vt., U.S.	F2	122
Bennington, co., Vt., U.S.	E2	122
Benoit, Ms., U.S.	B2	101
Bénoué (Benue), stm., Afr.	G8	42
Bensenville, Il., U.S.	B6	90
Bensheim, Ger.	F8	8
Bensley, Va., U.S.	C5	123
Benson, Az., U.S.	F5	80
Benson, Mn., U.S.	E3	100
Benson, N.C., U.S.	B4	110
Benson, co., N.D., U.S.	A6	111
Bent, co., Co., U.S.	D7	83
Bentley, Alta., Can.	C3	68
Bentleyville, Pa., U.S.	F1	115
Benton, Ar., U.S.	C3	81
Benton, Il., U.S.	E5	90
Benton, Ks., U.S.	E6	93
Benton, Ky., U.S.	f9	94
Benton, La., U.S.	B2	95
Benton, Pa., U.S.	D9	115
Benton, Tn., U.S.	B7	119
Benton, Wi., U.S.	F3	126
Benton, co., Ar., U.S.	A1	81
Benton, co., In., U.S.	C3	91
Benton, co., Ia., U.S.	B5	92
Benton, co., Mn., U.S.	E4	100
Benton, co., Ms., U.S.	A4	101
Benton, co., Mo., U.S.	C4	102
Benton, co., Or., U.S.	C3	114
Benton, co., Tn., U.S.	A3	119
Benton, co., Wa., U.S.	C6	124
Benton City, Wa., U.S.	C6	124
Benton Harbor, Mi., U.S.	F4	99
Benton Heights, Mi., U.S.	F4	99
Bentonville, Ar., U.S.	A1	81
Ben Treang, Viet.	I9	34
Bent's Old Fort National Historic Site, hist., Co., U.S.	C7	83
Benue (Bénoué), stm., Afr.	G7	42
Benwood, W.V., U.S.	f8	125
Benxi, China	C11	26
Benzie, co., Mi., U.S.	D4	99
Beograd (Belgrade), Yugo.	E4	16
Beowawe, Nv., U.S.	C5	105
Beppu, Japan	I4	30
Berau, Teluk, b., Indon.	F9	32
Berbera, Som.	F4	46
Berbérati, Cen. Afr. Rep.	H9	42
Berchtesgaden, Ger.	H13	8
Berck, Fr.	B8	10
Berdigest'ach, Russia	E19	24
Berdsk, Russia	G10	24
Berea, Ky., U.S.	C5	94
Berea, Oh., U.S.	A4	112
Berea, S.C., U.S.	B3	117
Berens, stm., Can.	F13	66
Berens, stm., Can.	C3	70
Beresford, S.D., U.S.	D9	118
Berg, Nor.	B11	6
Berga, Spain	C13	12
Bergama, Tur.	J11	16
Bergamo, Italy	D4	14
Bergen, Nor.	F5	6
Bergen, co., N.J., U.S.	A4	107
Bergen [auf Rügen], Ger.	A13	8
Bergenfield, N.J., U.S.	B4	107
Bergen op Zoom, Neth.	D4	8
Bergerac, Fr.	H7	10
Bergland, Mi., U.S.	m12	99
Bergstrom Air Force Base, mil., Tx., U.S.	D4	120
Berhampore, India	H13	38
Berhampur, India	C8	37
Beringovskij, Russia	E29	24
Bering Sea	D30	128
Bering Strait, strt.	m18	76a
Berja, Spain	I9	12
Berkåk, Nor.	E7	6
Berkeley, Ca., U.S.	D2	82
Berkeley, Mo., U.S.	f13	102
Berkeley, R.I., U.S.	B4	116
Berkeley, co., S.C., U.S.	E8	117
Berkeley, co., W.V., U.S.	B6	125
Berkeley Heights, N.J., U.S.	B4	107
Berkeley Springs, W.V., U.S.	B6	125
Berkley, Mi., U.S.	F7	99
Berkner Island, i., Ant.	B8	47
Berks, co., Pa., U.S.	F9	115
Berkshire, co., Ma., U.S.	B1	98
Berkshire Hills, hills, Ma., U.S.	B1	98
Berlin, Ger.	C13	8
Berlin, Ct., U.S.	C5	84
Berlin, Md., U.S.	D7	97
Berlin, N.H., U.S.	B4	106
Berlin, N.J., U.S.	D3	107
Berlin, Pa., U.S.	G4	115
Berlin, Wi., U.S.	E5	126
Berlin Lake, res., Oh., U.S.	A4	112
Bermeo, Spain	B9	12
Bermuda, dep., N.A.	E14	76
Bern (Berne), Switz.	F14	10
Bernalillo, N.M., U.S.	B3	108
Bernalillo, co., N.M., U.S.	C3	108
Bernardsville, N.J., U.S.	B3	107
Bernasconi, Arg.	D4	56
Bernau bei Berlin, Ger.	C13	8
Bernay, Fr.	C7	10
Bernburg, Ger.	D11	8
Berne, In., U.S.	C8	91
Bernice, La., U.S.	B3	95
Bernie, Mo., U.S.	E8	102
Bernier Island, i., Austl.	D2	50
Bernina, Piz, mtn., Eur.	F16	10
Beroroha, Madag.	F9	44
Berre, Étang de, b., Fr.	I12	10
Berrien, co., Ga., U.S.	E3	87
Berrien, co., Mi., U.S.	F4	99
Berrien Springs, Mi., U.S.	G4	99
Berry, Al., U.S.	B2	78
Berryessa, Lake, res., Ca., U.S.	C2	82
Berry Hill, Tn., U.S.	g10	119
Berry Islands, is., Bah.	B9	64
Berryville, Ar., U.S.	A2	81
Berryville, Va., U.S.	A5	123
Berthierville, Que., Can.	C4	74
Berthoud, Co., U.S.	A5	83
Berthoud Pass, Co., U.S.	B5	83
Bertie, co., N.C., U.S.	A5	110
Bertoua, Cam.	H8	42
Bertrand, Mo., U.S.	E8	102
Bertrand, Ne., U.S.	D6	104
Berwick, Ia., U.S.	e8	92
Berwick, La., U.S.	E4	95
Berwick, Me., U.S.	E2	96
Berwick, Pa., U.S.	D9	115
Berwick-upon-Tweed, Eng., U.K.	F10	7
Berwyn, Alta., Can.	A2	68
Berwyn, Il., U.S.	k9	90
Berwyn, Pa., U.S.	o20	115
Besalampy, Madag.	E8	44
Besançon, Fr.	E13	10
Beskid Mountains, mts., Eur.	F19	8
Bessemer, Al., U.S.	B3	78
Bessemer, Mi., U.S.	n11	99
Bessemer, Pa., U.S.	E1	115
Bessemer City, N.C., U.S.	B1	110
Best'ach, Russia	E19	24
Betanzos, Spain	B3	12
Bétaré Oya, Cam.	G8	42
Betatakin Ruin, hist., Az., U.S.	A5	80
Bethalto, Il., U.S.	E3	90
Bethany, Ct., U.S.	D4	84
Bethany, Il., U.S.	D5	90
Bethany, Mo., U.S.	A3	102
Bethany, Ok., U.S.	B4	113
Bethany, W.V., U.S.	A4	125
Bethany Beach, De., U.S.	F5	85
Bethel, Ak., U.S.	C7	79
Bethel, Ct., U.S.	D2	84
Bethel, Me., U.S.	D2	96
Bethel, N.C., U.S.	B5	110
Bethel, Oh., U.S.	D1	112
Bethel, Vt., U.S.	D3	122
Bethel Park, Pa., U.S.	k14	115
Bethel Springs, Tn., U.S.	B3	119
Bethesda, Md., U.S.	C3	97
Bethesda, Oh., U.S.	B4	112
Bethlehem, S. Afr.	G5	44
Bethlehem, Ct., U.S.	C3	84
Bethlehem, N.H., U.S.	B3	106
Bethlehem, Pa., U.S.	E11	115
Bethlehem see Bayt Lahm, W. Bank	D4	40
Béthune, Fr.	B9	10
Beticos, Sistemas, mts., Spain	H9	12
Betioky, Madag.	F8	44
Betong, Malay.	M6	34
Betroka, Madag.	F9	44
Betsiboka, stm., Madag.	E9	44
Betsie, Point, c., Mi., U.S.	D4	99
Betsy Layne, Ky., U.S.	C7	94
Bette, mtn., Libya	D9	42
Bettendorf, Ia., U.S.	C7	92
Bettiah, India	G11	38
Betūl, India	B4	37
Betzdorf, Ger.	E7	8
Beulah, Co., U.S.	C6	83
Beulah, N.D., U.S.	B4	111
Beulah, Lake, l., Ms., U.S.	B3	101
Beulaville, N.C., U.S.	C5	110
B. Everett Jordan Lake, res., N.C., U.S.	B3	110
Beverley, Austl.	F3	50
Beverley, Eng., U.K.	H12	7
Beverley Head, c., Newf., Can.	D2	72
Beverly, Ma., U.S.	A6	98
Beverly, N.J., U.S.	C3	107
Beverly, Oh., U.S.	C4	112
Beverly, W.V., U.S.	C5	125
Beverly Hills, Ca., U.S.	m12	82
Beverly Shores, In., U.S.	A4	91
Bexar, co., Tx., U.S.	E3	120
Bexley, Oh., U.S.	m11	112
Beypore, India	G3	37
Bežeck, Russia	D19	18
Béziers, Fr.	I10	10
Bhadrakh, India	J12	38
Bhadrāvati, India	F3	37
Bhāgalpur, India	H12	38
Bhakkar, Pak.	E4	38
Bhaktapur, Nepal	G11	38
Bhandāra, India	B5	37
Bharatpur, India	G7	38
Bhatinda, India	E6	38
Bhātpāra, India	I13	38
Bhāvnagar, India	J5	38
Bhilai, India	B6	37
Bhīlwāra, India	H6	38
Bhīma, stm., India	D4	37
Bhīmavaram, India	D6	37
Bhind, India	G8	38
Bhiwandi, India	C2	37
Bhiwāni, India	F7	38
Bhopāl, India	I7	38
Bhubaneswar, India	J11	38
Bhuj, India	I3	38
Bhusāwal, India	B3	37
Bhutan, ctry., Asia	D7	36
Bia, Phou, mtn., Laos	E7	34
Biafra, Bight of, Afr.	H7	42
Biak, i., Indon.	F10	32
Biała Podlaska, Pol.	C23	8
Białystok, Pol.	B23	8
Biarritz, Fr.	I5	10
Biasca, Switz.	F15	10
Bibai, Japan	p19	30a
Bibb, co., Al., U.S.	C2	78
Bibb, co., Ga., U.S.	D3	87
Biberach an der Riss, Ger.	G9	8
Bic, Que., Can.	A9	74
Bic, Île du, i., Que., Can.	A9	74
Biche, Lac la, l., Alta., Can.	B4	68
Bicknell, In., U.S.	G3	91
Bida, Nig.	G7	42
Bīdar, India	D4	37
Biddeford, Me., U.S.	E2	96
Bideford, Eng., U.K.	J8	7
Bidwell, Mount, mtn., Ca., U.S.	B3	82
Biel [Bienne], Switz.	E14	10
Bielefeld, Ger.	C8	8
Bieler Lake, l., N.W. Ter., Can.	B18	66
Bielersee, l., Switz.	E14	10
Biella, Italy	D3	14
Bielsko-Biała, Pol.	F19	8
Bien Hoa, Viet.	I9	34
Bienville, co., La., U.S.	B2	95
Bienville, Lac, l., Que., Can.	g12	74
Big, stm., Mo., U.S.	c7	102
Biga, Tur.	I11	16
Bigadiç, Tur.	J12	16
Big Bald, mtn., Ga., U.S.	B2	87
Big Bald Mountain, mtn., N.B., Can.	B3	71
Big Baldy, mtn., Id., U.S.	E3	89
Big Baldy Mountain, mtn., Mt., U.S.	D6	103
Big Bay De Noc, b., Mi., U.S.	C4	99
Big Bear City, Ca., U.S.	E5	82
Big Belt Mountains, mts., Mt., U.S.	D5	103
Big Bend, Wi., U.S.	n11	126
Big Bend Dam, S.D., U.S.	C6	118
Big Bend National Park, Tx., U.S.	E1	120
Big Birch Lake, l., Mn., U.S.	E4	100
Big Black, stm., Me., U.S.	B3	96
Big Black, stm., Ms., U.S.	C3	101
Big Blue, stm., In., U.S.	E6	91
Big Burro Mountains, mts., N.M., U.S.	E1	108
Big Cabin Creek, stm., Ok., U.S.	A6	113
Big Coal, stm., W.V., U.S.	C3	125
Big Costilla Peak, mtn., N.M., U.S.	A4	108
Big Creek, stm., Tn., U.S.	e8	119
Big Creek Lake, res., Al., U.S.	E1	78
Big Creek Peak, mtn., Id., U.S.	E5	89
Big Cypress Indian Reservation, Fl., U.S.	F5	86
Big Cypress Swamp, sw., Fl., U.S.	F5	86
Big Darby Creek, stm., Oh., U.S.	C2	112
Big Delta, Ak., U.S.	C10	79
Big Duke Dam, N.C., U.S.	B2	110
Big Eau Pleine, stm., Wi., U.S.	D3	126
Big Eau Pleine Reservoir, res., Wi., U.S.	D4	126
Big Escambia Creek, stm., U.S.	D2	78
Big Flats, N.Y., U.S.	C4	109
Bigfork, Mt., U.S.	B2	103
Big Fork, stm., Mn., U.S.	B5	100
Biggs, Ca., U.S.	C3	82
Big Hatchet Peak, mtn., N.M., U.S.	F1	108
Big Hole, stm., Mt., U.S.	E4	103
Big Hole National Battlefield, hist., Mt., U.S.	E3	103
Big Horn, co., Mt., U.S.	E9	103
Big Horn, co., Wy., U.S.	B4	127
Bighorn Canyon National Recreation Area, U.S.	F8	103
Bighorn Lake, res., U.S.	E8	103
Bighorn Mountains, mts., U.S.	B5	127
Big Horn Mountains, mts., Az., U.S.	D2	80
Big Kandiyohi Lake, l., Mn., U.S.	F4	100
Big Lake, Mn., U.S.	E5	100
Big Lake, Tx., U.S.	D2	120
Big Lake, l., Me., U.S.	C5	96
Biglerville, Pa., U.S.	G7	115
Big Lookout Mountain, mtn., Or., U.S.	C9	114
Big Lost, stm., Id., U.S.	F5	89
Big Mossy Point, c., Man., Can.	C2	70
Big Mountain, mtn., Nv., U.S.	B2	105
Big Muddy, stm., Il., U.S.	F4	90
Big Nemaha, stm., Ne., U.S.	D10	104
Big Otter, stm., Va., U.S.	C3	123
Big Pine Lake, l., Mn., U.S.	D3	100
Big Pine Mountain, mtn., Ca., U.S.	E4	82
Big Piney, Wy., U.S.	D2	127
Big Piney, stm., Mo., U.S.	D5	102
Bigpoint, Ms., U.S.	E5	101
Big Rapids, Mi., U.S.	E5	99
Big Rib, stm., Wi., U.S.	C3	126
Big River, Sask., Can.	D2	75
Big Sable Point, c., Mi., U.S.	D4	99
Big Sandy, Mt., U.S.	B6	103
Big Sandy, Tx., U.S.	C5	120
Big Sandy, stm., U.S.	C2	125
Big Sandy, stm., Az., U.S.	C2	80
Big Sandy, stm., Tn., U.S.	B3	119
Big Sandy, stm., Wy., U.S.	D3	127
Big Sandy Creek, stm., W.V., U.S.	C3	125
Big Sandy Lake, l., Mn., U.S.	D5	100
Big Sandy Reservoir, res., Wy., U.S.	D3	127
Big Sheep Mountain, mtn., Mt., U.S.	C11	103
Big Sioux, stm., U.S.	E9	118
Big Smoky Valley, val., Nv., U.S.	E4	105
Big Snowy Mountains, mts., Mt., U.S.	D7	103
Big Southern Butte, mtn., Id., U.S.	F5	89
Big South Fork, stm., Ky., U.S.	k13	94
Big Spring, Tx., U.S.	C2	120
Big Stone, co., Mn., U.S.	E2	100
Big Stone City, S.D., U.S.	B9	118
Big Stone Gap, Va., U.S.	f9	123
Big Stone Lake, l., U.S.	E2	100
Big Sunflower, stm., Ms., U.S.	B3	101
Big Thompson, stm., Co., U.S.	A5	83
Big Timber, Mt., U.S.	E7	103
Big Trout Lake, l., Ont., Can.	n17	73
Big Walnut Creek, stm., Oh., U.S.	m11	112
Big Wood, stm., Id., U.S.	F4	89
Bihać, Bos.	E10	14
Bihār, India	H11	38
Bihār, state, India	H11	38
Biharamulo, Tan.	B6	44
Bihoro, Japan	p22	30a
Bija, stm., Russia	G11	24
Bijāpur, India	D3	37
Bījāpur, India	C6	37
Bijsk, Russia	G11	24
Bīkaner, India	F5	38
Bikin, Russia	H20	24
Bikoro, Zaire	B3	44
Bilāspur, India	I10	38
Bila Tserkva, Ukr.	H4	22
Bilauktaung Range, mts., Asia	G5	34
Bilbao, Spain	B9	12
Bilimora, India	B2	37
Bilk Creek Mountains, mts., Nv., U.S.	B3	105
Billerica, Ma., U.S.	A5	98
Billings, Mo., U.S.	D4	102
Billings, Mt., U.S.	E8	103
Billings, co., N.D., U.S.	B2	111
Billings Heights, Mt., U.S.	E8	103
Bill Williams, stm., Az., U.S.	C1	80
Bill Williams Mountain, mtn., Az., U.S.	B3	80
Bilma, Niger	E8	42
Biloxi, Ms., U.S.	E5	101
Biloxi, stm., Ms., U.S.	E4	101
Biloxi Bay, b., Ms., U.S.	f8	101
Biltmore Forest, N.C., U.S.	f10	110
Bimini Islands, is., Bah.	B8	64
Bīna-Etāwa, India	H8	38
Bindura, Zimb.	E6	44
Binéfar, Spain	D12	12
Binga, Monte, mtn., Afr.	E6	44
Bingamon Creek, stm., W.V., U.S.	k10	125
Bingen, Ger.	F7	8
Bingen, Wa., U.S.	D4	124
Binger, Ok., U.S.	B3	113
Bingham, Me., U.S.	C3	96
Bingham, co., Id., U.S.	F6	89
Binghamton, N.Y., U.S.	C5	109
Binhai (Dongkan), China	A8	28
Binjai, Indon.	M5	34
Bintimani, mtn., S.L.	G3	42
Biograd, Cro.	F10	14
Bioko, i., Eq. Gui.	H7	42
Bīr, India	C3	37
Birao, Cen. Afr. Rep.	F10	42
Birātnagar, Nepal	G12	38
Birch, stm., W.V., U.S.	C4	125
Birch Island, i., Man., Can.	C2	70
Birch Lake, l., Mn., U.S.	C7	100
Birch River, Man., Can.	C1	70
Birch Run, Mi., U.S.	E7	99
Birchwood City, Md., U.S.	*f9	97
Birchy Bay, Newf., Can.	D4	72
Bird Creek, stm., Ok., U.S.	A6	113
Bird Island, Mn., U.S.	F4	100
Bird Island, i., N.C., U.S.	D4	110
Birdsboro, Pa., U.S.	F10	115
Birdum, Austl.	C6	50
Birecik, Tur.	A5	40
Bīrganj, Nepal	G11	38
Birigui, Braz.	F3	57
Biril'ussy, Russia	F12	24
Bīrjand, Iran	K9	22
Birkenfeld, Ger.	F7	8
Birkenhead, Eng., U.K.	H9	7
Bîrlad, Rom.	C11	16
Birmingham, Eng., U.K.	I11	7
Birmingham, Al., U.S.	B3	78
Birmingham, Mi., U.S.	F7	99
Birmitrapur, India	I11	38
Bir Mogreïn, Maur.	C3	42
Birobidžan, Russia	H20	24
Biron, Wi., U.S.	D4	126
Birr, Ire.	H5	7
Bi'r Safājah, Egypt	C12	42
Birtle, Man., Can.	D1	70
Bisbee, Az., U.S.	F6	80
Biscarrosse, Fr.	H5	10
Biscay, Bay of, b., Eur.	G7	4
Biscayne, Key, i., Fl., U.S.	s13	86
Biscayne Bay, b., Fl., U.S.	G6	86
Biscayne National Monument, Fl., U.S.	G6	86
Biscayne Park, Fl., U.S.	s13	86
Bisceglie, Italy	H11	14
Bischofshofen, Aus.	H13	8
Biscoe, N.C., U.S.	B3	110
Bishnupur, India	I12	38
Bishop, Ca., U.S.	D4	82
Bishop, Tx., U.S.	F4	120
Bishop Auckland, Eng., U.K.	G11	7
Bishop's Falls, Newf., Can.	D4	72
Bishopville, S.C., U.S.	C7	117
Biškek (Bishkek), Kyrg.	I12	22
Biskra, Alg.	B7	42
Bismarck, Il., U.S.	C6	90
Bismarck, Mo., U.S.	D7	102
Bismarck, N.D., U.S.	C5	111
Bismarck Archipelago, is., Pap. N. Gui.	m16	50a
Bismarck Range, mts., Pap. N. Gui.	m15	50a
Bison Peak, mtn., Co., U.S.	B5	83
Bissau, Gui.-B.	F2	42
Bistineau, Lake, res., La., U.S.	B2	95
Bistrița, Rom.	B8	16
Bitola, Mac.	H5	16
Bitonto, Italy	H11	14
Bitter Creek, stm., Wy., U.S.	E4	127
Bitterfeld, Ger.	D12	8
Bitterfontein, S. Afr.	H3	44
Bitter Lake, l., S.D., U.S.	B8	118
Bitterroot, stm., Mt., U.S.	D2	103
Bitterroot Range, mts., U.S.	B3	89
Bitti, Italy	I4	14
Biwabik, Mn., U.S.	C6	100
Biwa-ko, l., Japan	G9	30
Bixby, Ok., U.S.	B6	113
Biyang, China	C2	28
Bizen, Japan	H7	30
Bizerte, Tun.	L4	14
Bjelovar, Cro.	D11	14
Black (Lixian) (Da), stm., Asia	D8	34
Black, stm., Az., U.S.	D5	80
Black, stm., Ar., U.S.	B4	81
Black, stm., La., U.S.	C4	95
Black, stm., Mi., U.S.	E8	99
Black, stm., N.Y., U.S.	B4	109
Black, stm., N.C., U.S.	C4	110
Black, stm., S.C., U.S.	D8	117
Black, stm., Vt., U.S.	B4	122
Black, stm., Vt., U.S.	E3	122
Black, stm., Wi., U.S.	D3	126
Blackall, Austl.	D9	50
Black Bear Creek, stm., Ok., U.S.	A4	113
Blackbeard Island, i., Ga., U.S.	E5	87
Blackburn, Eng., U.K.	H10	7
Blackburn, Mount, mtn., Ak., U.S.	C11	79
Black Butte, mtn., Mt., U.S.	F5	103
Black Butte Lake, res., Ca., U.S.	C2	82
Black Canyon, val., Co., U.S.	C3	83
Black Canyon City, Az., U.S.	C3	80
Black Canyon of the Gunnison National Monument, Co., U.S.	C3	83
Black Creek, B.C., Can.	E5	69
Black Creek, Wi., U.S.	D5	126
Black Creek, stm., U.S.	B1	108
Black Creek, stm., S.C., U.S.	B7	117
Black Diamond, Alta., Can.	D3	68
Black Diamond, Wa., U.S.	B4	124
Blackduck, Mn., U.S.	C4	100
Black Eagle, Mt., U.S.	C5	103
Black Earth, Wi., U.S.	E4	126
Blackfalds, Alta., Can.	C4	68
Blackfeet Indian Reservation, Mt., U.S.	B4	103
Blackfoot, Id., U.S.	F6	89
Blackfoot, stm., Mt., U.S.	C3	103
Blackfoot Mountains, mts., Id., U.S.	F7	89
Blackfoot Reservoir, res., Id., U.S.	G7	89
Blackford, co., In., U.S.	D7	91
Black Forest, Co., U.S.	C6	83
Black Forest see Schwarzwald, mts., Ger.	G8	8
Blackhall Mountain, mtn., Wy., U.S.	E6	127
Black Hawk, S.D., U.S.	C2	118
Black Hawk, co., Ia., U.S.	B5	92
Black Hills, mts., U.S.	C2	118
Blackjack Mountain, mtn., Ga., U.S.	h8	87
Black Lake, Que., Can.	C6	74
Black Lake, l., Mi., U.S.	C6	99
Black Lake, l., N.Y., U.S.	f9	109
Black Lick, Pa., U.S.	F3	115
Blacklick Estates, Oh., U.S.	*m11	112
Black Mesa, mtn., Ok., U.S.	e8	113
Black Mingo Creek, stm., S.C., U.S.	D9	117
Blackmore, Mount, mtn., Mt., U.S.	E6	103
Black Mountain, N.C., U.S.	f10	110
Black Mountain, mtn., U.S.	D7	94
Black Mountain, mtn., Az., U.S.	E4	80
Black Mountain, mtn., Co., U.S.	A5	83
Black Mountain, mtn., Id., U.S.	C3	89
Black Mountain, mtn., Mt., U.S.	D4	103
Black Mountain, mtn., Or., U.S.	B7	114
Black Mountain, mtn., Wy., U.S.	B5	127
Black Mountains, mts., Az., U.S.	B1	80
Black Peak, mtn., Az., U.S.	C1	80
Black Pine Peak, mtn., Id., U.S.	G5	89
Blackpool, Eng., U.K.	H9	7
Black Range, mts., N.M., U.S.	D2	108
Black River Falls, Wi., U.S.	D3	126
Black Rock, Ar., U.S.	A4	81
Black Rock, N.M., U.S.	B1	108
Black Rock Desert, des., Nv., U.S.	B3	105
Black Rock Range, mts., Nv., U.S.	B3	105
Blacksburg, S.C., U.S.	A4	117
Blacksburg, Va., U.S.	C2	123
Black Sea	G14	4
Blacks Fork, stm., U.S.	E3	127
Blacks Harbour, N.B., Can.	D3	71
Blackshear, Ga., U.S.	E4	87
Blackstone, Ma., U.S.	B4	98
Blackstone, Va., U.S.	C5	123
Blackstone, stm., R.I., U.S.	B4	116
Black Thunder Creek, stm., Wy., U.S.	C8	127
Blackville, N.B., Can.	C4	71
Blackville, S.C., U.S.	E5	117
Black Volta (Volta Noire), stm., Afr.	G5	42
Blackwalnut Point, c., Md., U.S.	C5	97
Black Warrior, stm., Al., U.S.	C2	78
Blackwater, stm., Fl., U.S.	u15	86
Blackwater, stm., Md., U.S.	D5	97
Blackwater, stm., N.H., U.S.	D3	106
Blackwater, stm., Va., U.S.	D6	123
Blackwater Reservoir, res., N.H., U.S.	D3	106
Blackwell, Ok., U.S.	A4	113
Blackwood, N.J., U.S.	D2	107
Bladen, co., N.C., U.S.	C4	110
Bladenboro, N.C., U.S.	C4	110
Bladensburg, Md., U.S.	f9	97
Blades, De., U.S.	F3	85
Blagoevgrad, Bul.	G7	16
Blagoveščensk, Russia	G19	24
Blaine, Me., U.S.	B5	96
Blaine, Mn., U.S.	m12	100
Blaine, Tn., U.S.	C10	119
Blaine, Wa., U.S.	A3	124
Blaine, co., Id., U.S.	F4	89
Blaine, co., Mt., U.S.	B7	103
Blaine, co., Ne., U.S.	C6	104
Blaine, co., Ok., U.S.	B3	113
Blaine Lake, Sask., Can.	E2	75
Blair, Ne., U.S.	C9	104
Blair, Ok., U.S.	C2	113
Blair, W.V., U.S.	n12	125
Blair, Wi., U.S.	D2	126
Blair, co., Pa., U.S.	E5	115
Blair Athol, Austl.	D9	50
Blairstown, Ia., U.S.	C5	92
Blairsville, Pa., U.S.	F3	115
Blake Island, i., Wa., U.S.	e11	124
Blakely, Ga., U.S.	E2	87
Blakely, Pa., U.S.	m18	115
Blake Point, c., Mi., U.S.	h10	99
Blanc, Cap, c., Afr.	D2	42
Blanc, Mont (Monte Bianco), mtn., Eur.	G13	10
Blanca Peak, mtn., Co., U.S.	D5	83
Blanchard, La., U.S.	B2	95
Blanchard, Ok., U.S.	B4	113
Blanchard, stm., Oh., U.S.	A1	112
Blanchardville, Wi., U.S.	F4	126
Blanchester, Oh., U.S.	C2	112
Blanco, Tx., U.S.	D3	120

Name	Map Ref	Page
Blanco, co., Tx., U.S.	D3	120
Blanco, Cape, c., Or., U.S.	E2	114
Bland, Mo., U.S.	C6	102
Bland, co., Va., U.S.	C1	123
Blanding, Ut., U.S.	F6	121
Blandinsville, Il., U.S.	C3	90
Blanes, Spain	D14	12
Blangkedjeren, Indon.	M4	34
Blangy-sur-Bresle, Fr.	C8	10
Blanquilla, Isla, i., Ven.	B10	58
Blantyre, Mwi.	E7	44
Blasdell, N.Y., U.S.	C2	109
Blawnox, Pa., U.S.	k14	115
Blaye-et-Sainte-Luce, Fr.	G6	10
Bleckley, co., Ga., U.S.	D3	87
Bled, Slo.	C9	14
Bledsoe, co., Tn., U.S.	D8	119
Blende, Co., U.S.	C6	83
Blenheim, Ont., Can.	E3	73
Blenheim, N.Z.	D4	52
Blennerhassett, W.V., U.S.	B3	125
Bléré, Fr.	E7	10
Blida, Alg.	A6	42
Blind, stm., La., U.S.	h10	95
Blind River, Ont., Can.	A2	73
Blissfield, Mi., U.S.	G7	99
Blitar, Indon.	n16	32
Block Island, R.I., U.S.	h7	116
Block Island, i., R.I., U.S.	h7	116
Block Island Sound, strt., U.S.	G2	116
Bloemfontein, S. Afr.	G5	44
Bloemhof, S. Afr.	G5	44
Blois, Fr.	E8	10
Blood Mountain, mtn., Ga., U.S.	B3	87
Bloodsworth Island, i., Md., U.S.	D5	97
Bloodvein, stm., Can.	D3	70
Bloody Foreland, c., Ire.	F4	7
Bloomer, Wi., U.S.	C2	126
Bloomfield, Ont., Can.	D7	73
Bloomfield, Ct., U.S.	B5	84
Bloomfield, In., U.S.	F4	91
Bloomfield, Ia., U.S.	D5	92
Bloomfield, Ky., U.S.	C4	94
Bloomfield, Mo., U.S.	E8	102
Bloomfield, Ne., U.S.	B8	104
Bloomfield, N.J., U.S.	h8	107
Bloomfield, N.M., U.S.	A2	108
Bloomfield Hills, Mi., U.S.	o15	99
Bloomingdale, Ga., U.S.	D5	87
Bloomingdale, Il., U.S.	k8	90
Bloomingdale, N.J., U.S.	A4	107
Bloomingdale, Tn., U.S.	C11	119
Blooming Prairie, Mn., U.S.	G5	100
Bloomington, Il., U.S.	C4	90
Bloomington, In., U.S.	F4	91
Bloomington, Mn., U.S.	F5	100
Bloomington, Tx., U.S.	E4	120
Bloomington, Wi., U.S.	F3	126
Bloomington, Lake, res., Il., U.S.	C5	90
Bloomsburg, Pa., U.S.	E9	115
Bloomville, Oh., U.S.	A2	112
Blora, Indon.	m15	33a
Blossburg, Pa., U.S.	C7	115
Blossom, Tx., U.S.	C5	120
Blount, co., Al., U.S.	B3	78
Blount, co., Tn., U.S.	D10	119
Blountstown, Fl., U.S.	B1	86
Blountsville, Al., U.S.	A3	78
Blountville, Tn., U.S.	C11	119
Blowing Rock, N.C., U.S.	A1	110
Bludenz, Aus.	H9	8
Blue, stm., Co., U.S.	B4	83
Blue, stm., In., U.S.	H5	91
Blue, stm., Mo., U.S.	k10	102
Blue, stm., Ok., U.S.	C5	113
Blue Ash, Oh., U.S.	o13	112
Blue Buck Point, c., La., U.S.	E2	95
Blue Creek, W.V., U.S.	m13	125
Blue Creek, stm., W.V., U.S.	m13	125
Blue Cypress Lake, l., Fl., U.S.	E6	86
Blue Diamond, Nv., U.S.	G6	105
Blue Earth, Mn., U.S.	G4	100
Blue Earth, co., Mn., U.S.	G4	100
Blue Earth, stm., Mn., U.S.	G4	100
Bluefield, Va., U.S.	C1	123
Bluefield, W.V., U.S.	D3	125
Bluefields, Nic.	H6	64
Blue Grass, Ia., U.S.	C7	92
Blue Hill, Me., U.S.	D4	96
Blue Hill, Ne., U.S.	D7	104
Blue Hill Range, hills, Ma., U.S.	h11	98
Blue Hills, Ct., U.S.	B5	84
Blue Island, Il., U.S.	B6	90
Bluejoint Lake, l., Or., U.S.	E7	114
Blue Lake, Ca., U.S.	B2	82
Blue Mesa Reservoir, res., Co., U.S.	C3	83
Blue Mound, Il., U.S.	D4	90
Blue Mountain, Ms., U.S.	A4	101
Blue Mountain, mtn., Mt., U.S.	C12	103
Blue Mountain, mtn., N.M., U.S.	D2	108
Blue Mountain, mtn., Pa., U.S.	F6	115
Blue Mountain Lake, res., Ar., U.S.	B2	81
Blue Mountain Peak, mtn., Jam.	E9	64
Blue Nile (Al-Bahr al-Azraq), stm., Afr.	F12	42
Blue Point, Me., U.S.	g7	96
Blue Rapids, Ks., U.S.	C7	93
Blue Ridge, Ga., U.S.	B2	87
Blue Ridge, Va., U.S.	C3	123
Blue Ridge, mtn., U.S.	E10	76
Blue Ridge Summit, Pa., U.S.	G7	115
Blue Springs, Mo., U.S.	h11	102
Bluestone, stm., W.V., U.S.	D3	125
Bluestone Lake, res., U.S.	D4	125
Bluewell, W.V., U.S.	D3	125
Bluff City, Tn., U.S.	C11	119
Bluff Creek, stm., Ok., U.S.	A4	113
Bluff Lake, res., Ms., U.S.	B5	101
Bluff Park, Al., U.S.	g7	78
Bluffs, Il., U.S.	D3	90
Bluffton, In., U.S.	C7	91
Bluffton, Oh., U.S.	B2	112
Bluffton, S.C., U.S.	G6	117
Blumenau, Braz.	B7	56
Bly, Or., U.S.	E5	114
Blying Sound, strt., Ak., U.S.	h17	79
Blyth, Ont., Can.	D3	73
Blyth, Eng., U.K.	F11	7
Blythe, Ca., U.S.	F6	82
Blytheville, Ar., U.S.	B6	81
Bø, Nor.	B10	6
Bø, Nor.	G7	6
Bo, S.L.	G3	42
Boaco, Nic.	H5	64
Boalsburg, Pa., U.S.	E6	115
Boa Nova, Braz.	C8	57
Boardman, Oh., U.S.	A5	112
Boardman, Or., U.S.	B7	114
Boa Vista, Braz.	C6	54
Boavita, Col.	D6	58
Boaz, Al., U.S.	A3	78
Bobbili, India	C7	37
Bobbio, Italy	E4	14
Bobcaygeon, Ont., Can.	C6	73
Böblingen, Ger.	G9	8
Bobo Dioulasso, Burkina	F5	42
Bobrujsk, Bela.	H12	18
Bobtown, Pa., U.S.	G2	115
Bobures, Ven.	C7	58
Boby, Pic, mtn., Madag.	F9	44
Boca Chica Key, i., Fl., U.S.	H5	86
Boca Ciega Bay, b., Fl., U.S.	p10	86
Bôca do Acre, Braz.	E5	54
Boca Grande, Fl., U.S.	F4	86
Boca Raton, Fl., U.S.	F6	86
Bocas del Toro, Pan.	J6	64
Bocholt, Ger.	D6	8
Bochum, Ger.	D7	8
Bodajbo, Russia	F16	24
Bodega Head, c., Ca., U.S.	C2	82
Bodele, reg., Chad	E9	42
Boden, Swe.	D13	6
Bodensee, l., Eur.	H9	8
Bodhan, India	C4	37
Bodie Island, i., N.C., U.S.	B7	110
Bodināyakkanūr, India	G4	37
Bodkin Point, c., Md., U.S.	B5	97
Bodø, Nor.	C10	6
Boende, Zaire	B4	44
Boën-sur-Lignon, Fr.	G10	10
Boerne, Tx., U.S.	E3	120
Boeuf, stm., La., U.S.	C4	95
Boeuf, Lake, l., La., U.S.	k10	95
Bogale, Mya.	F3	34
Bogalusa, La., U.S.	D6	95
Bogart, Ga., U.S.	C3	87
Bogata, Tx., U.S.	C5	120
Bogenfels, Nmb.	G3	44
Boger City, N.C., U.S.	B1	110
Bognes, Nor.	B10	6
Bogor, Indon.	m13	32
Bogorodick, Russia	H21	18
Bogorodsk, Russia	E26	18
Bogota, N.J., U.S.	h8	107
Bogotá see Santa Fe de Bogotá, Col.	E5	58
Bogotol, Russia	F11	24
Bogra, Bngl.	H13	38
Bogučany, Russia	F13	24
Bogue Chitto, Ms., U.S.	D3	101
Bogue Chitto, stm., U.S.	D5	95
Bogue Inlet, b., N.C., U.S.	C5	110
Bogue Phalia, stm., Ms., U.S.	B3	101
Bo Hai, b., China	D10	26
Bohain-en-Vermandois, Fr.	C10	10
Bohemia see Čechy, hist. reg., Czech.	F14	8
Bohemian Forest, mts., Eur.	F12	8
Bohol, i., Phil.	D7	32
Boiano, Italy	H9	14
Boigu, i., Austl.	A8	50
Boiling Springs, N.C., U.S.	B1	110
Boiling Springs, Pa., U.S.	F7	115
Bois Blanc Island, i., Mi., U.S.	C6	99
Bois Brule, stm., Wi., U.S.	B2	126
Boischâtel, Que., Can.	C6	74
Bois-des-Filion, Que., Can.	p19	74
Bois de Sioux, stm., Mn., U.S.	E2	100
Boise, Id., U.S.	F2	89
Boise, co., Id., U.S.	F3	89
Boise City, Ok., U.S.	e8	113
Boissevain, Man., Can.	E1	70
Boissevain, Va., U.S.	e10	123
Boistfort Peak, mtn., Wa., U.S.	C2	124
Boizenburg, Ger.	B10	8
Bojador, Cabo, c., W. Sah.	C3	42
Bojeador, Cape, c., Phil.	B7	32
Bojnūrd, Iran	J9	22
Bojonegoro, Indon.	m15	33a
Boké, Gui.	F3	42
Boketu, China	B11	26
Boknafjorden, Nor.	G5	6
Boksitogorsk, Russia	B16	18
Bokungu, Zaire	B4	44
Bolama, Gui.-B.	F2	42
Bolbec, Fr.	C7	10
Bolesławiec, Pol.	D15	8
Boley, Ok., U.S.	B5	113
Bolgatanga, Ghana	F5	42
Boli, China	B13	26
Bolingbrook, Il., U.S.	k8	90
Bolívar, Arg.	D4	56
Bolivar, Mo., U.S.	D4	102
Bolivar, Oh., U.S.	B4	112
Bolivar, Tn., U.S.	B3	119
Bolivar, W.V., U.S.	B7	125
Bolivar, co., Ms., U.S.	B3	101
Bolívar, Cerro, mtn., Ven.	D11	58
Bolivar, Lake, l., Ms., U.S.	B3	101
Bolívar, Pico, mtn., Ven.	C7	58
Bolivia, ctry., S.A.	G5	54
Bollène, Fr.	H11	10
Bollinger, co., Mo., U.S.	D7	102
Bollnäs, Swe.	F11	6
Bollullos par del Condado, Spain	H5	12
Bolobo, Zaire	B3	44
Bologna, Italy	E6	14
Bologoje, Russia	D17	18
Bolotnoje, Russia	F10	24
Bolsena, Italy	G6	14
Bol'šereck, Russia	G25	24
Bol'ševik, Russia	E23	24
Bol'ševik, Ostrov, i., Russia	B14	24
Bol'šoj An'uj, stm., Russia	D26	24
Bol'šoj Begičev, Ostrov, i., Russia	C16	24
Bol'šoj L'achovskij, Ostrov, i., Russia	C22	24
Bolton, Eng., U.K.	H10	7
Bolton, Ms., U.S.	C3	101
Bolton Lakes, l., Ct., U.S.	B6	84
Bolton Landing, N.Y., U.S.	B7	109
Bolzano (Bozen), Italy	C6	14
Boma, Zaire	C2	44
Bombala, Austl.	G9	50
Bombarral, Port.	F2	12
Bombay, India	C2	37
Bombay Hook Island, i., De., U.S.	C4	85
Bom Despacho, Braz.	E6	57
Bom Jesus da Lapa, Braz.	B7	57
Bomoseen, Lake, l., Vt., U.S.	D2	122
Bomu (Mbomou), stm., Afr.	H10	42
Bon, Cap, c., Tun.	A8	42
Bon Accord, Alta., Can.	C4	68
Bon Air, Va., U.S.	C5	123
Bonaire, Ga., U.S.	D3	87
Bonaire, i., Neth. Ant.	H13	64
Bonanza Peak, mtn., Wa., U.S.	A5	124
Bonao, Dom. Rep.	E12	64
Bonaparte, Mount, mtn., Wa., U.S.	A6	124
Bonaparte Archipelago, is., Austl.	B5	50
Bonarbridge, Scot., U.K.	D8	7
Bonasila Dome, mtn., Ak., U.S.	C7	79
Bonaventure, Que., Can.	A4	71
Bonavista, Newf., Can.	D5	72
Bonavista, Cape, c., Newf., Can.	D5	72
Bonavista Bay, b., Newf., Can.	G22	66
Bonavista Bay, b., Newf., Can.	D5	72
Bond, co., Il., U.S.	E4	90
Bondeno, Italy	E6	14
Bondo, Zaire	H10	42
Bondoukou, C. Iv.	G5	42
Bondowoso, Indon.	m16	33a
Bondsville, Ma., U.S.	B3	98
Bonduel, Wi., U.S.	D5	126
Bondurant, Ia., U.S.	C4	92
Bone, Teluk, b., Indon.	F7	32
Bone Lake, l., Wi., U.S.	C1	126
Bongandanga, Zaire	A4	44
Bongor, Chad	F9	42
Bonham, Tx., U.S.	C4	120
Bon Homme, co., S.D., U.S.	D8	118
Bonifati, Capo, c., Italy	J10	14
Bonifay, Fl., U.S.	u16	86
Bonita Springs, Fl., U.S.	F5	86
Bonn, Ger.	E7	8
Bonneauville, Pa., U.S.	G7	115
Bonne Bay, b., Newf., Can.	D3	72
Bonner, co., Id., U.S.	A2	89
Bonners Ferry, Id., U.S.	A2	89
Bonner Springs, Ks., U.S.	C9	93
Bonnet Carre Floodway, La., U.S.	h11	95
Bonne Terre, Mo., U.S.	D7	102
Bonneval, Fr.	D8	10
Bonneville, Fr.	F13	10
Bonneville, co., Id., U.S.	F7	89
Bonneville Dam, U.S.	B4	114
Bonneville Peak, mtn., Id., U.S.	F6	89
Bonneville Salt Flats, pl., Ut., U.S.	C2	121
Bonney Lake, Wa., U.S.	B3	124
Bonnie Doone, N.C., U.S.	B4	110
Bonny Reservoir, res., Co., U.S.	B8	83
Bonnyville, Alta., Can.	B5	68
Bono, Ar., U.S.	B5	81
Bonorva, Italy	I3	14
Bon Secour, Al., U.S.	E2	78
Bonthe, S.L.	G3	42
Booker, Tx., U.S.	A2	120
Booker T. Washington National Monument, Va., U.S.	C3	123
Boomer, W.V., U.S.	C3	125
Boone, Ia., U.S.	B4	92
Boone, N.C., U.S.	A1	110
Boone, co., Ar., U.S.	A2	81
Boone, co., Il., U.S.	A5	90
Boone, co., In., U.S.	D4	91
Boone, co., Ia., U.S.	B3	92
Boone, co., Ky., U.S.	B5	94
Boone, co., Mo., U.S.	B5	102
Boone, co., Ne., U.S.	C7	104
Boone, co., W.V., U.S.	C3	125
Boone, stm., Ia., U.S.	B4	92
Boone Lake, res., Tn., U.S.	C11	119
Booneville, Ar., U.S.	B2	81
Booneville, Ms., U.S.	A5	101
Boonsboro, Md., U.S.	A2	97
Boonton, N.J., U.S.	B4	107
Boonville, In., U.S.	H3	91
Boonville, Mo., U.S.	C5	102
Boonville, N.Y., U.S.	B5	109
Boonville, N.C., U.S.	A2	110
Boothbay Harbor, Me., U.S.	E3	96
Boothia, Gulf of, b., N.W. Ter., Can.	B14	66
Boothia Peninsula, pen., N.W. Ter., Can.	B14	66
Booths Creek, stm., W.V., U.S.	h11	125
Boothville, La., U.S.	E6	95
Booué, Gabon	B2	44
Boquete, Pan.	J6	64
Boquillas del Carmen, Mex.	C8	62
Bor, Russia	E27	18
Bor, Sudan	G12	42
Boraha, Nosy, i., Madag.	E9	44
Borah Peak, mtn., Id., U.S.	E5	89
Borås, Swe.	H9	6
Bordeaux, Fr.	H6	10
Borden, co., Tx., U.S.	C2	120
Borden Peninsula, pen., N.W. Ter., Can.	B16	66
Bordentown, N.J., U.S.	C3	107
Bordertown, Austl.	G8	50
Borgå (Porvoo), Fin.	F15	6
Borgarnes, Ice.	C3	4
Borger, Tx., U.S.	B2	120
Borgne, Lake, b., La., U.S.	D6	95
Borgo, Italy	C6	14
Borgo San Dalmazzo, Italy	E2	14
Borgosesia, Italy	D3	14
Borgo Val di Taro, Italy	E4	14
Borisov, Bela.	G11	18
Borja, Spain	D10	12
Borjas Blancas, Spain	D12	12
Borken, Ger.	D6	8
Borlänge, Swe.	F10	6
Borlu, Tur.	K12	16
Borneo (Kalimantan), i., Asia	E5	32
Bornholm, i., Den.	I10	6
Bornova, Tur.	K11	16
Borogoncy, Russia	E20	24
Boron, Ca., U.S.	E5	82
Boronga Islands, is., Mya.	E2	34
Borovići, Russia	C16	18
Borrego Springs, Ca., U.S.	F5	82
Bort-les-Orgues, Fr.	G9	10
Borūjerd, Iran	B4	46
Borz'a, Russia	G17	24
Bosa, Italy	I3	14
Bosanska Gradiška, Bos.	D12	14
Bosanska Krupa, Bos.	E11	14
Bosanski Novi, Bos.	D11	14
Bosanski Petrovac, Bos.	E11	14
Bosaso, Som.	F4	46
Boscobel, Wi., U.S.	E3	126
Boshan, China	D10	26
Bosnia and Herzegovina, ctry., Eur.	E12	14
Bosporus see İstanbul Boğazı, strt., Tur.	H13	16
Bosque, co., Tx., U.S.	D4	120
Bossangoa, Cen. Afr. Rep.	G9	42
Bossembélé, Cen. Afr. Rep.	G9	42
Bossier, co., La., U.S.	B2	95
Bossier City, La., U.S.	B2	95
Bosten Hu, l., China	C4	26
Boston, Eng., U.K.	I12	7
Boston, Ga., U.S.	F3	87
Boston, Ma., U.S.	B5	98
Boston Bay, b., Ma., U.S.	B6	98
Boston Mountains, mts., Ar., U.S.	B2	81
Boswell, In., U.S.	C3	91
Boswell, Ok., U.S.	C6	113
Boswell, Pa., U.S.	F3	115
Botād, India	I4	38
Boteti, stm., Bots.	F4	44
Botetourt, co., Va., U.S.	C3	123
Bothell, Wa., U.S.	B3	124
Bothnia, Gulf of, b., Eur.	E12	6
Bothwell, Ont., Can.	E3	73
Botkins, Oh., U.S.	B1	112
Botoşani, Rom.	B10	16
Botswana, ctry., Afr.	F4	44
Bottenhavet (Selkämeri), b., Eur.	F12	6
Bottenviken (Perämeri), b., Eur.	D14	6
Bottineau, N.D., U.S.	A5	111
Bottineau, co., N.D., U.S.	A4	111
Botucatu, Braz.	G4	57
Botwood, Newf., Can.	D4	72
Bouaflé, C. Iv.	G4	42
Bouaké, C. Iv.	G4	42
Bouar, Cen. Afr. Rep.	G9	42
Bou Arada, Tun.	M4	14
Boucherville, Que., Can.	D4	74
Bouctouche, N.B., Can.	C5	71
Boudreaux, Lake, l., La., U.S.	E5	95
Bou Ficha, Tun.	M5	14
Bougainville Reef, rf., Austl.	C9	50
Bougouni, Mali	F4	42
Bouillon, Bel.	F5	8
Boulder, Co., U.S.	A5	83
Boulder, Mt., U.S.	D4	103
Boulder, co., Co., U.S.	A5	83
Boulder City, Nv., U.S.	H7	105
Boulevard Heights, Md., U.S.	f9	97
Boulogne-Billancourt, Fr.	D9	10
Boulogne-sur-Gesse, Fr.	I7	10
Boulogne-sur-Mer, Fr.	B8	10
Bouna, C. Iv.	G5	42
Boundary, co., Id., U.S.	A2	89
Boundary Bay, b., Wa., U.S.	A3	124
Boundary Peak, mtn., Nv., U.S.	F3	105
Bound Brook, N.J., U.S.	B3	107
Bountiful, Ut., U.S.	C4	121
Bourbeuse, stm., Mo., U.S.	C6	102
Bourbon, In., U.S.	B5	91
Bourbon, Mo., U.S.	C6	102
Bourbon, co., Ks., U.S.	E9	93
Bourbon, co., Ky., U.S.	B5	94
Bourbonnais, Il., U.S.	B6	90
Bourbonnais, hist. reg., Fr.	F9	10
Bourbonne-les-Bains, Fr.	E12	10
Bourem, Mali	E5	42
Bourg, La., U.S.	E5	95
Bourganeuf, Fr.	G8	10
Bourg-en-Bresse, Fr.	F12	10
Bourges, Fr.	E9	10
Bourg-Lastic, Fr.	G9	10
Bourgogne, hist. reg., Fr.	E11	10
Bourgoin, Fr.	G12	10
Bourg-Saint-Andéol, Fr.	H11	10
Bourg-Saint-Maurice, Fr.	G13	10
Bourke, Austl.	F9	50
Bournemouth, Eng., U.K.	K11	7
Bou Saâda, Alg.	A6	42
Bouse, Az., U.S.	D2	80
Boussac, Fr.	F9	10
Bousso, Chad	F9	42
Boutte, La., U.S.	k11	95
Bøvågen, Nor.	F5	6
Bovalino Marina, Italy	K11	14
Bovec, Slo.	C8	14
Bøverdal, Nor.	F7	6
Bovey, Mn., U.S.	C5	100
Bovina, Tx., U.S.	B1	120
Bow, N.H., U.S.	D3	106
Bow, stm., Alta., Can.	D4	68
Bowden, Alta., Can.	D4	68
Bowdish Reservoir, res., R.I., U.S.	B1	116
Bowdon, Ga., U.S.	C1	87
Bowen, Austl.	C9	50
Bowie, Az., U.S.	E6	80
Bowie, Md., U.S.	C4	97
Bowie, Tx., U.S.	C4	120
Bowie, co., Tx., U.S.	C5	120
Bow Island, Alta., Can.	E5	68
Bow Lake, l., N.H., U.S.	D4	106
Bowling Green, Fl., U.S.	E5	86
Bowling Green, Ky., U.S.	D3	94
Bowling Green, Mo., U.S.	B6	102
Bowling Green, Oh., U.S.	A2	112
Bowling Green, S.C., U.S.	A5	117
Bowling Green, Va., U.S.	B5	123
Bowman, Ga., U.S.	B3	87
Bowman, N.D., U.S.	C2	111
Bowman, S.C., U.S.	E6	117
Bowman, co., N.D., U.S.	C2	111
Bowman Creek, stm., Pa., U.S.	m16	115
Bowman-Haley Lake, res., N.D., U.S.	C2	111
Bowron, stm., B.C., Can.	C7	69
Bowstring Lake, l., Mn., U.S.	C5	100
Box Butte, co., Ne., U.S.	B2	104
Box Butte Reservoir, res., Ne., U.S.	B2	104
Box Elder, S.D., U.S.	C2	118
Box Elder, co., Ut., U.S.	B2	121
Boxford, Ma., U.S.	A6	98
Boxian, China	B4	28
Boyce, La., U.S.	C3	95
Boyceville, Wi., U.S.	C1	126
Boyd, Tx., U.S.	C4	120
Boyd, co., Ky., U.S.	B7	94
Boyd, co., Ne., U.S.	B7	104
Boyden, Ia., U.S.	A2	92
Boyd Lake, l., Me., U.S.	C4	96
Boyer, stm., Ia., U.S.	C2	92
Boyertown, Pa., U.S.	F10	115
Boykins, Va., U.S.	D5	123
Boyle, Alta., Can.	B4	68
Boyle, Ire.	H4	7
Boyle, Ms., U.S.	B3	101
Boyle, co., Ky., U.S.	C5	94
Boyne City, Mi., U.S.	C6	99
Boynton Beach, Fl., U.S.	F6	86
Boysen Reservoir, res., Wy., U.S.	C4	127
Boys Town, Ne., U.S.	g12	104
Bozburun, Tur.	M12	16
Boz Dağ, mtn., Tur.	L13	16
Bozeman, Mt., U.S.	E5	103
Bozeman Pass, Mt., U.S.	E6	103
Bozoum, Cen. Afr. Rep.	G9	42
Bra, Italy	E2	14
Bracciano, Italy	G7	14
Bracebridge, Ont., Can.	B5	73
Bräcke, Swe.	E10	6
Bracken, co., Ky., U.S.	B5	94
Brackenridge, Pa., U.S.	h15	115
Brackettville, Tx., U.S.	E2	120
Braddock, Pa., U.S.	k14	115
Braddock Heights, Md., U.S.	B2	97
Braddock Point, c., S.C., U.S.	G6	117
Bradenton, Fl., U.S.	E4	86
Bradenville, Pa., U.S.	F3	115
Bradford, Eng., U.K.	H11	7
Bradford, Ar., U.S.	B4	81
Bradford, Oh., U.S.	B1	112
Bradford, Pa., U.S.	C4	115
Bradford, R.I., U.S.	F2	116
Bradford, Tn., U.S.	A3	119
Bradford, Vt., U.S.	D4	122
Bradford, co., Fl., U.S.	C4	86
Bradford, co., Pa., U.S.	C8	115
Bradford [West Gwillimbury], Ont., Can.	C5	73
Bradfordwoods, Pa., U.S.	h13	115
Bradley, Il., U.S.	B6	90
Bradley, Me., U.S.	D4	96
Bradley, W.V., U.S.	D3	125
Bradley, co., Ar., U.S.	D3	81
Bradley, co., Tn., U.S.	D9	119
Bradley Beach, N.J., U.S.	C4	107
Bradner, Oh., U.S.	A2	112
Bradshaw, Md., U.S.	B5	97
Bradshaw Mountains, mts., Az., U.S.	C3	80
Brady, Tx., U.S.	D3	120
Braga, Port.	D3	12
Bragado, Arg.	D4	56
Bragança, Port.	D5	12
Braham, Mn., U.S.	E5	100
Brāhmanbāria, Bngl.	I14	38
Brāhmani, stm., India	J11	38
Brahmaputra (Yarlung), stm., Asia	G15	38
Braich y Pwll, c., Wales, U.K.	I8	7
Braidwood, Il., U.S.	B5	90
Brăila, Rom.	D11	16
Brainerd, Mn., U.S.	D4	100
Braintree, Ma., U.S.	B5	98
Brake, Ger.	B8	8
Brampton, Ont., Can.	D5	73
Bramsche, Ger.	C7	8
Bramwell, W.V., U.S.	D3	125
Branch, co., Mi., U.S.	G5	99
Branch, stm., R.I., U.S.	B3	116
Branch, stm., Wi., U.S.	h10	126
Branch Lake, l., Me., U.S.	D4	96
Branch Village, R.I., U.S.	B3	116
Branchville, S.C., U.S.	E6	117
Branco, stm., Braz.	C6	54
Brandberg, mtn., Nmb.	F2	44
Brandbu, Nor.	F8	6
Brandenburg, Ger.	C12	8
Brandenburg, Ky., U.S.	C3	94
Brandon, Man., Can.	E2	70
Brandon, Fl., U.S.	E4	86
Brandon, Ms., U.S.	C4	101
Brandon, S.C., U.S.	B3	117
Brandon, S.D., U.S.	D9	118
Brandon, Vt., U.S.	D2	122
Brandon, Wi., U.S.	E5	126
Brandvlei, S. Afr.	H4	44
Brandy Peak, mtn., Or., U.S.	E3	114
Brandywine, Md., U.S.	C4	97
Brandywine Creek, stm., U.S.	A3	85
Branford, Ct., U.S.	D4	84
Branford Hills, Ct., U.S.	D4	84
Br'ansk, Russia	H17	18
Branson, Mo., U.S.	E4	102
Brantford, Ont., Can.	D4	73
Brantley, Al., U.S.	D3	78
Brantley, co., Ga., U.S.	E4	87
Brantôme, Fr.	G7	10
Brant Rock, Ma., U.S.	B6	98
Brantville, N.B., Can.	B5	71
Bras d'Or Lake, l., N.S., Can.	D9	71
Brasília, Braz.	C5	57
Braşov, Rom.	D9	16
Brasstown Bald, mtn., Ga., U.S.	B3	87
Brassua Lake, res., Me., U.S.	C3	96
Bratenahl, Oh., U.S.	g9	112

Name	Map Ref	Page
Bratislava, Slov.	G17	8
Bratsk, Russia	F14	24
Bratskoje Vodochranilišče, res., Russia	F14	24
Brattleboro, Vt., U.S.	F3	122
Braunau [am Inn], Aus.	G13	8
Braunschweig, Ger.	C10	8
Brava, Som.	H3	46
Brava, Costa, Spain	D15	12
Bravo del Norte (Rio Grande), stm., N.A.	F6	76
Brawley, Ca., U.S.	F6	82
Brawley Peaks, mts., Nv., U.S.	E3	105
Braxton, co., W.V., U.S.	C4	125
Bray, Ire.	H6	7
Bray, Ok., U.S.	C4	113
Bray Island, i., N.W. Ter., Can.	C17	66
Braymer, Mo., U.S.	B4	102
Brazeau, stm., Alta., Can.	C2	68
Brazil, In., U.S.	E3	91
Brazil, ctry., S.A.	E7	54
Brazoria, Tx., U.S.	r14	120
Brazoria, co., Tx., U.S.	E5	120
Brazos, co., Tx., U.S.	D4	120
Brazos, stm., Tx., U.S.	D4	120
Brazzaville, Congo	B3	44
Brčko, Bos.	E2	16
Brea, Ca., U.S.	n13	82
Breakenridge, Mount, mtn., B.C., Can.	E7	69
Breathitt, co., Ky., U.S.	C6	94
Breaux Bridge, La., U.S.	D4	95
Brebes, Indon.	m14	33a
Breckenridge, Co., U.S.	B4	83
Breckenridge, Mi., U.S.	E6	99
Breckenridge, Mn., U.S.	D2	100
Breckenridge, Tx., U.S.	C3	120
Breckinridge, co., Ky., U.S.	C3	94
Brecksville, Oh., U.S.	A4	112
Brecon Beacons National Park, Wales, U.K.	J9	7
Breda, Neth.	D4	8
Bredstedt, Ger.	A8	8
Breese, Il., U.S.	E4	90
Bréhal, Fr.	D5	10
Brekstad, Nor.	E7	6
Bremen, Ger.	B8	8
Bremen, Ga., U.S.	C1	87
Bremen, In., U.S.	B5	91
Bremen, Oh., U.S.	C3	112
Bremer, co., Ia., U.S.	B5	92
Bremerhaven, Ger.	B8	8
Bremerton, Wa., U.S.	B3	124
Bremond, Tx., U.S.	D4	120
Brenham, Tx., U.S.	D4	120
Brenner Pass, Eur.	B6	14
Breno, Italy	D5	14
Brent, Al., U.S.	C2	78
Brent, Fl., U.S.	u14	86
Brenton Point, c., R.I., U.S.	F5	116
Brentwood, Ca., U.S.	h9	82
Brentwood, Md., U.S.	f9	97
Brentwood, Mo., U.S.	f13	102
Brentwood, N.Y., U.S.	E7	109
Brentwood, Pa., U.S.	k14	115
Brentwood, S.C., U.S.	k11	117
Brentwood, Tn., U.S.	A5	119
Brescia, Italy	D5	14
Breslau see Wrocław, Pol.	D17	8
Bressanone, Italy	C6	14
Bressuire, Fr.	F6	10
Brest, Bela.	I6	18
Brest, Fr.	D2	10
Bretagne, hist. reg., Fr.	D3	10
Breton Islands, is., La., U.S.	E6	95
Breton Sound, strt., La., U.S.	E6	95
Brevard, N.C., U.S.	f10	110
Brevard, co., Fl., U.S.	E6	86
Brevoort Lake, l., Mi., U.S.	B6	99
Brewer, Me., U.S.	D4	96
Brewster, Ma., U.S.	C7	98
Brewster, N.Y., U.S.	D7	109
Brewster, Oh., U.S.	B4	112
Brewster, Wa., U.S.	A6	124
Brewster, co., Tx., U.S.	E1	120
Brewster Islands, is., Ma., U.S.	g12	98
Brewton, Al., U.S.	D2	78
Brežice, Slo.	D10	14
Bria, Cen. Afr. Rep.	G10	42
Brian Boru Peak, mtn., B.C., Can.	B4	69
Briançon, Fr.	H13	10
Brian Head, mtn., Ut., U.S.	F3	121
Briare, Fr.	E9	10
Briceville, Tn., U.S.	C9	119
Brick [Township], N.J., U.S.	C4	107
Bricquebec, Fr.	C5	10
Bridal Veil Falls, wtfl, Ut., U.S.	C4	121
Bridgehampton, N.Y., U.S.	n16	109
Bridgeport, Al., U.S.	A4	78
Bridgeport, Ct., U.S.	E3	84
Bridgeport, Il., U.S.	E6	90
Bridgeport, Mi., U.S.	E7	99
Bridgeport, Ne., U.S.	C2	104
Bridgeport, Oh., U.S.	B5	112
Bridgeport, Pa., U.S.	o20	115
Bridgeport, Tx., U.S.	C4	120
Bridgeport, Wa., U.S.	B6	124
Bridgeport, W.V., U.S.	B4	125
Bridger, Mt., U.S.	E8	103
Bridger Peak, mtn., Wy., U.S.	E5	127
Bridger Range, mts., Mt., U.S.	E6	103
Bridgeton, Mo., U.S.	C7	102
Bridgeton, N.J., U.S.	E2	107
Bridgetown, Barb.	H18	64
Bridgetown, N.S., Can.	E4	71
Bridgeville, De., U.S.	F3	85
Bridgeville, Pa., U.S.	k13	115
Bridgewater, Ma., U.S.	C6	98
Bridgewater, N.J., U.S.	B3	107
Bridgewater, Va., U.S.	B4	123
Bridgman, Mi., U.S.	G4	99
Bridgton, Me., U.S.	D2	96
Bridgwater, Eng., U.K.	J9	7
Bridlington, Eng., U.K.	G12	7
Briec, Fr.	D2	10
Brielle, N.J., U.S.	C4	107
Brienne-le-Château, Fr.	D11	10
Brienz, Switz.	F15	10
Brig, Switz.	F14	10
Brigantine, N.J., U.S.	E4	107
Brigantine Beach, N.J., U.S.	E4	107
Brigden, Ont., Can.	E2	73
Briggs Marsh, sw., R.I., U.S.	F6	116
Brigham City, Ut., U.S.	B3	121
Brighton, Ont., Can.	C7	73
Brighton, Eng., U.K.	K12	7
Brighton, Al., U.S.	B3	78
Brighton, Co., U.S.	B6	83
Brighton, Il., U.S.	D3	90
Brighton, Ia., U.S.	C6	92
Brighton, Mi., U.S.	F7	99
Brighton, N.Y., U.S.	B3	109
Brighton, Tn., U.S.	B2	119
Brighton Indian Reservation, Fl., U.S.	E5	86
Brihuega, Spain	E9	12
Brilliant, Al., U.S.	A2	78
Brilliant, Oh., U.S.	B5	112
Brillion, Wi., U.S.	D5	126
Brilon, Ger.	D8	8
Brimfield, Il., U.S.	C4	90
Brindisi, Italy	I12	14
Brinkley, Ar., U.S.	C4	81
Brinnon, Wa., U.S.	B3	124
Brioude, Fr.	G10	10
Brisbane, Austl.	E10	50
Briscoe, co., Tx., U.S.	B2	120
Bristol, N.B., Can.	C2	71
Bristol, Eng., U.K.	J10	7
Bristol, Ct., U.S.	C4	84
Bristol, In., U.S.	A6	91
Bristol, N.H., U.S.	C3	106
Bristol, R.I., U.S.	D5	116
Bristol, Tn., U.S.	C11	119
Bristol, Vt., U.S.	C2	122
Bristol, Va., U.S.	f9	123
Bristol, co., Ma., U.S.	C5	98
Bristol, co., R.I., U.S.	D5	116
Bristol Bay, b., Ak., U.S.	D7	79
Bristol Channel, strt., U.K.	J8	7
Bristol [Township], Pa., U.S.	F12	115
Bristow, Ok., U.S.	B5	113
British Columbia, prov., Can.	C6	69
British Honduras see Belize, ctry., N.A.	F3	64
British Indian Ocean Territory, dep., Afr.	G17	2
British Mountains, mts., N.A.	C5	66
British Solomon Islands see Solomon Islands, ctry., Oc.	G23	2
Britstown, S. Afr.	H4	44
Britt, Ia., U.S.	A4	92
Brittany see Bretagne, hist. reg., Fr.	D3	10
Britton, S.D., U.S.	B8	118
Brive-la-Gaillarde, Fr.	G8	10
Briviesca, Spain	C8	12
Brno, Czech.	F16	8
Broach, India	B2	37
Broad, stm., S.C., U.S.	C5	117
Broad Brook, Ct., U.S.	B5	84
Broadford, Scot., U.K.	D7	7
Broadkill, stm., De., U.S.	E4	85
Broadkill Beach, De., U.S.	E5	85
Broad Law, mtn., Scot., U.K.	F9	7
Broad Run, stm., Va., U.S.	g11	123
Broadus, Mt., U.S.	E11	103
Broadview Heights, Oh., U.S.	h9	112
Broadwater, co., Mt., U.S.	D5	103
Broadway, N.C., U.S.	B3	110
Broadway, Va., U.S.	B4	123
Brockport, N.Y., U.S.	B3	109
Brockton, Ma., U.S.	B5	98
Brockton Reservoir, res., Ma., U.S.	h11	98
Brockville, Ont., Can.	C9	73
Brockway, Pa., U.S.	D4	115
Brodeur Peninsula, pen., N.W. Ter., Can.	B15	66
Brodhead, Ky., U.S.	C5	94
Brodhead, Wi., U.S.	F4	126
Brodheadsville, Pa., U.S.	E11	115
Broken Arrow, Ok., U.S.	A6	113
Broken Bow, Ne., U.S.	C6	104
Broken Bow, Ok., U.S.	C7	113
Broken Bow Lake, res., Ok., U.S.	C7	113
Broken Hill, Austl.	F8	50
Brokopondo, Sur.	B8	54
Brome, Lac, l., Que., Can.	D5	74
Bromptonville, Que., Can.	D6	74
Bromsgrove, Eng., U.K.	I10	7
Bronlund Peak, mtn., B.C., Can.	E7	66
Brønnøysund, Nor.	D9	6
Bronson, Mi., U.S.	G5	99
Bronte, Italy	L9	14
Bronx, co., N.Y., U.S.	E7	109
Bronxville, N.Y., U.S.	h13	109
Brook, In., U.S.	C3	91
Brooke, co., W.V., U.S.	A4	125
Brookfield, N.S., Can.	D6	71
Brookfield, Ct., U.S.	D2	84
Brookfield, Il., U.S.	k9	90
Brookfield, Mo., U.S.	B4	102
Brookfield, Va., U.S.	*B5	123
Brookfield, Wi., U.S.	m11	126
Brookfield Center, Ct., U.S.	D2	84
Brookhaven, Ms., U.S.	D3	101
Brookhaven, W.V., U.S.	h11	125
Brookings, Or., U.S.	E2	114
Brookings, S.D., U.S.	C9	118
Brookings, co., S.D., U.S.	C9	118
Brookland, Ar., U.S.	B5	81
Brooklandville, Md., U.S.	g10	97
Brooklet, Ga., U.S.	D5	87
Brookline, Ma., U.S.	B5	98
Brooklyn, N.S., Can.	E5	71
Brooklyn, Ct., U.S.	B8	84
Brooklyn, In., U.S.	E5	91
Brooklyn, Ia., U.S.	C5	92
Brooklyn, Mi., U.S.	F6	99
Brooklyn, Ms., U.S.	D4	101
Brooklyn, Oh., U.S.	h9	112
Brooklyn, S.C., U.S.	B6	117
Brooklyn, Wi., U.S.	F4	126
Brooklyn Center, Mn., U.S.	E5	100
Brooklyn Park, Md., U.S.	h11	97
Brooklyn Park, Mn., U.S.	m12	100
Brookneal, Va., U.S.	C4	123
Brook Park, Oh., U.S.	h9	112
Brookport, Il., U.S.	F5	90
Brooks, Alta., Can.	D5	68
Brooks, Ky., U.S.	g11	94
Brooks, co., Ga., U.S.	F3	87
Brooks, co., Tx., U.S.	F3	120
Brooks Air Force Base, mil., Tx., U.S.	k7	120
Brookshire, Tx., U.S.	E5	120
Brookside, Al., U.S.	f7	78
Brookside, De., U.S.	B3	85
Brooks Range, mts., Ak., U.S.	B9	79
Brookston, In., U.S.	C4	91
Brooksville, Fl., U.S.	D4	86
Brooksville, Ky., U.S.	B5	94
Brooksville, Ms., U.S.	B5	101
Brookville, In., U.S.	F8	91
Brookville, Oh., U.S.	C1	112
Brookville, Pa., U.S.	D3	115
Brookville Lake, res., In., U.S.	E7	91
Brookwood, Al., U.S.	B2	78
Brookwood, N.J., U.S.	C4	107
Broomall, Pa., U.S.	p20	115
Broome, Austl.	C4	50
Broome, co., N.Y., U.S.	C5	109
Broomfield, Co., U.S.	B5	83
Broons, Fr.	D4	10
Brossard, Que., Can.	q20	74
Brou, Fr.	D8	10
Broussard, La., U.S.	D4	95
Broward, co., Fl., U.S.	F6	86
Browerville, Mn., U.S.	D4	100
Brown, co., Il., U.S.	D3	90
Brown, co., In., U.S.	F5	91
Brown, co., Ks., U.S.	C8	93
Brown, co., Mn., U.S.	F4	100
Brown, co., Ne., U.S.	B6	104
Brown, co., Oh., U.S.	D2	112
Brown, co., S.D., U.S.	B7	118
Brown, co., Tx., U.S.	D3	120
Brown, co., Wi., U.S.	D6	126
Brown, Point, c., Wa., U.S.	C1	124
Brown City, Mi., U.S.	E8	99
Brown Deer, Wi., U.S.	m12	126
Brownfield, Tx., U.S.	C1	120
Browning, Mt., U.S.	B3	103
Brownlee Dam, U.S.	E2	89
Brownlee Reservoir, res., U.S.	C10	114
Browns, stm., Vt., U.S.	B2	122
Browns Branch, stm., De., U.S.	E3	85
Brownsburg, Que., Can.	D3	74
Brownsburg, In., U.S.	E5	91
Brownsdale, Mn., U.S.	G6	100
Browns Inlet, b., N.C., U.S.	C5	110
Browns Mills, N.J., U.S.	D3	107
Browns Peak, mtn., Az., U.S.	D4	80
Brownstown, In., U.S.	G5	91
Browns Valley, Mn., U.S.	E2	100
Brownsville, Fl., U.S.	s13	86
Brownsville, Ky., U.S.	C3	94
Brownsville, Or., U.S.	C4	114
Brownsville, Pa., U.S.	F2	115
Brownsville, Tn., U.S.	B2	119
Brownsville, Tx., U.S.	G4	120
Brownton, Mn., U.S.	F4	100
Brownville Junction, Me., U.S.	C3	96
Brownwood, Tx., U.S.	D3	120
Brownwood, Lake, res., Tx., U.S.	D3	120
Broxton, Ga., U.S.	E4	87
Bruay-en-Artois, Fr.	B9	10
Bruce, Ms., U.S.	B4	101
Bruce, Wi., U.S.	C2	126
Bruce, Mount, mtn., Austl.	D3	50
Bruce National Park, Ont., Can.	B3	73
Bruce Peninsula, pen., Ont., Can.	B3	73
Bruceton, Tn., U.S.	A3	119
Bruchsal, Ger.	F8	8
Bruck an der Leitha, Aus.	H16	8
Bruck an der Mur, Aus.	H15	8
Bruderheim, Alta., Can.	C4	68
Brugge, Bel.	D3	8
Bruin Point, mtn., Ut., U.S.	D5	121
Brule, co., S.D., U.S.	D6	118
Brule, stm., U.S.	C5	126
Brule Lake, l., Mn., U.S.	k9	100
Brundidge, Al., U.S.	D4	78
Bruneau, stm., U.S.	G3	89
Brunei, ctry., Asia	E5	32
Brunico, Italy	C6	14
Brunkeberg, Nor.	G7	6
Bruno, Sask., Can.	E3	75
Brunsbüttel, Ger.	B9	8
Brunswick, Ga., U.S.	E5	87
Brunswick, Me., U.S.	E3	96
Brunswick, Md., U.S.	B2	97
Brunswick, Mo., U.S.	B4	102
Brunswick, Oh., U.S.	A4	112
Brunswick, co., N.C., U.S.	C4	110
Brunswick, co., Va., U.S.	D5	123
Brunswick Naval Air Station, mil., Me., U.S.	E3	96
Brush, Co., U.S.	A7	83
Brushy Mountains, mts., N.C., U.S.	B1	110
Brus Laguna, Hond.	G5	64
Brusly, La., U.S.	D4	95
Brussels, Ont., Can.	D3	73
Brussels see Bruxelles, Bel.	E4	8
Bruxelles (Brussel), Bel.	E4	8
Bryan, Oh., U.S.	A1	112
Bryan, Tx., U.S.	D4	120
Bryan, co., Ga., U.S.	D5	87
Bryan, co., Ok., U.S.	D5	113
Bryans Road, Md., U.S.	C3	97
Bryant, Ar., U.S.	C3	81
Bryantville, Ma., U.S.	B6	98
Bryce Canyon National Park, Ut., U.S.	F3	121
Bryn Mawr, Wa., U.S.	e11	124
Bryson City, N.C., U.S.	f9	110
Brzeg, Pol.	E17	8
Bsharrī, Leb.	B5	40
Būbiyān, i., Kuw.	C4	46
Bucaramanga, Col.	D6	58
Buccaneer Archipelago, is., Austl.	C4	50
Buchanan, Lib.	G3	42
Buchanan, Ga., U.S.	C1	87
Buchanan, Mi., U.S.	G4	99
Buchanan, Va., U.S.	C3	123
Buchanan, co., Ia., U.S.	B6	92
Buchanan, co., Mo., U.S.	B3	102
Buchanan, co., Va., U.S.	e9	123
Buchan Gulf, b., N.W. Ter., Can.	B18	66
Buchans, Newf., Can.	D3	72
Buchara, Uzb.	J10	22
Bucharest see Bucureşti, Rom.	E10	16
Buchholz, Ger.	B9	8
Buckatunna, Ms., U.S.	D5	101
Bückeburg, Ger.	C9	8
Buckeye, Az., U.S.	D3	80
Buckeye Lake, Oh., U.S.	C3	112
Buckhannon, W.V., U.S.	C4	125
Buck Hill Falls, Pa., U.S.	D11	115
Buckhorn Lake, res., Ky., U.S.	C6	94
Buckingham, Que., Can.	D2	74
Buckingham, co., Va., U.S.	C4	123
Buckley, Wa., U.S.	B3	124
Bucklin, Ks., U.S.	E4	93
Bucklin, Mo., U.S.	B5	102
Buck Mountain, mtn., Wa., U.S.	A6	124
Buckner, Mo., U.S.	h11	102
Bucks, co., Pa., U.S.	F11	115
Buckskin Mountains, mts., Az., U.S.	C2	80
Bucksport, Me., U.S.	D4	96
Bucksport, S.C., U.S.	D9	117
Bucureşti (Bucharest), Rom.	E10	16
Bucyrus, Oh., U.S.	B3	112
Buda, Tx., U.S.	D4	120
Budapest, Hung.	H19	8
Budaun, India	F8	38
Budd Lake, l., N.J., U.S.	B3	107
Buddusò, Italy	I4	14
Bude, Eng., U.K.	K8	7
Bude, Ms., U.S.	D3	101
Buea, Cam.	H7	42
Buechel, Ky., U.S.	B4	94
Buena, N.J., U.S.	D3	107
Buena, Wa., U.S.	C5	124
Buena Park, Ca., U.S.	n12	82
Buena Vista, Bol.	G6	54
Buena Vista, Co., U.S.	C4	83
Buena Vista, Fl., U.S.	D4	86
Buena Vista, Ga., U.S.	D2	87
Buena Vista, Va., U.S.	C3	123
Buena Vista, co., Ia., U.S.	B2	92
Buenópolis, Braz.	D6	57
Buenos Aires, Arg.	C5	56
Buffalo, Ia., U.S.	C7	92
Buffalo, Mn., U.S.	E5	100
Buffalo, Mo., U.S.	D4	102
Buffalo, N.Y., U.S.	C2	109
Buffalo, Ok., U.S.	A2	113
Buffalo, S.C., U.S.	B4	117
Buffalo, Tx., U.S.	D5	120
Buffalo, W.V., U.S.	C3	125
Buffalo, Wi., U.S.	D2	126
Buffalo, Wy., U.S.	B6	127
Buffalo, co., Ne., U.S.	D6	104
Buffalo, co., S.D., U.S.	C6	118
Buffalo, co., Wi., U.S.	D2	126
Buffalo, stm., Ar., U.S.	B3	81
Buffalo, stm., Mn., U.S.	D2	100
Buffalo, stm., Tn., U.S.	B4	119
Buffalo, stm., Wi., U.S.	D2	126
Buffalo Bill Reservoir, res., Wy., U.S.	B3	127
Buffalo Center, Ia., U.S.	A4	92
Buffalo Creek, stm., U.S.	f8	125
Buffalo Creek, stm., W.V., U.S.	h10	125
Buffalo Creek, stm., W.V., U.S.	n12	125
Buffalo Grove, Il., U.S.	h9	90
Buffalo Lake, Mn., U.S.	F4	100
Buffalo Lake, l., Alta., Can.	C4	68
Buffalo Lake, l., N.W. Ter., Can.	D9	66
Buffalo Lake, res., Tx., U.S.	B1	120
Buffalo Lake, res., Wi., U.S.	E4	126
Buffumville Lake, res., Ma., U.S.	B4	98
Buford, Ga., U.S.	B2	87
Bug, stm., Eur.	E12	4
Buga, Col.	F4	58
Bugøynes, Nor.	B17	6
Bugsuk Island, i., Phil.	D6	32
Bugul'ma, Russia	G8	22
Buhl, Id., U.S.	G4	89
Buhl, Mn., U.S.	C6	100
Buhler, Ks., U.S.	D6	93
Buies Creek, N.C., U.S.	B4	110
Buj, Russia	C24	18
Bujalance, Spain	H7	12
Bujaraloz, Spain	D11	12
Bujumbura, Bdi.	B5	44
Bukačača, Russia	G17	24
Bukama, Zaire	C5	44
Bukavu, Zaire	B5	44
Bukittinggi, Indon.	F3	32
Bukoba, Tan.	B6	44
Bukovina, hist. reg., Eur.	B9	16
Bula, Indon.	F9	32
Bulan, Ky., U.S.	C6	94
Bulandshahr, India	F7	38
Bulawayo, Zimb.	F5	44
Buldan, Tur.	K12	16
Buldāna, India	B4	37
Bulgan, Mong.	B5	26
Bulgaria, ctry., Eur.	G12	4
Bulkley, stm., B.C., Can.	B4	69
Bull Creek, stm., S.D., U.S.	B2	118
Bulle, Switz.	F14	10
Bullfinch, Austl.	F3	50
Bullfrog Creek, stm., Ut., U.S.	F5	121
Bullhead City, Az., U.S.	B1	80
Bull Island, i., S.C., U.S.	G6	117
Bull Island, i., S.C., U.S.	D9	117
Bull Island, i., S.C., U.S.	F8	117
Bullitt, co., Ky., U.S.	C4	94
Bull Mountain, mtn., Mt., U.S.	D4	103
Bulloch, co., Ga., U.S.	D5	87
Bullock, co., Al., U.S.	C4	78
Bullock Creek, Mi., U.S.	E6	99
Bull Run, stm., Va., U.S.	g11	123
Bullrun Rock, mtn., Or., U.S.	C8	114
Bulls Bay, b., S.C., U.S.	F8	117
Bulls Gap, Tn., U.S.	C10	119
Bull Shoals, Ar., U.S.	A3	81
Bull Shoals Lake, res., U.S.	A3	81
Bully Creek Reservoir, res., Or., U.S.	C9	114
Bulsār, India	B2	37
Bulukumba, Indon.	G7	32
Bumba, Zaire	A4	44
Bumping, stm., Wa., U.S.	C4	124
Buna, Tx., U.S.	D6	120
Bunbury, Austl.	F3	50
Buncombe, co., N.C., U.S.	f10	110
Buncrana, Ire.	F5	7
Bundaberg, Austl.	D10	50
Būndi, India	H6	38
Bundoran, Ire.	G4	7
Bungo-suidō, strt., Japan	I5	30
Bunia, Zaire	A6	44
Bunker Hill, Il., U.S.	D4	90
Bunker Hill, In., U.S.	C5	91
Bunker Hill, W.V., U.S.	B6	125
Bunker Hill, W.V., U.S.	m12	125
Bunker Hill, mtn., Nv., U.S.	D4	105
Bunkerville, Nv., U.S.	G7	105
Bunkie, La., U.S.	D3	95
Bunnell, Fl., U.S.	C5	86
Buñol, Spain	F11	12
Buntok, Indon.	F5	32
Buolkalach, Russia	C17	24
Buon Me Thuot, Viet.	H10	34
Buor-Chaja, Guba, b., Russia	C20	24
Buor-Chaja, Mys, c., Russia	C20	24
Bura, Kenya	B7	44
Burao, Som.	G4	46
Buras, La., U.S.	E6	95
Buraydah, Sau. Ar.	C3	46
Burbank, Ca., U.S.	E4	82
Burbank, Il., U.S.	k9	90
Burbank, Wa., U.S.	C7	124
Burdickville, R.I., U.S.	F2	116
Burdur, Tur.	H14	4
Burdwān, India	I12	38
Bureau, co., Il., U.S.	B4	90
Burejnskij Chrebet, mts., Russia	G20	24
Bureja, stm., Russia	G20	24
Burfjord, Nor.	B13	6
Burgas, Bul.	G11	16
Bur Gavo, Som.	B8	44
Burgaw, N.C., U.S.	C5	110
Burg [bei Magdeburg], Ger.	C11	8
Burgdorf, Switz.	E14	10
Burgeo, Newf., Can.	E3	72
Burgettstown, Pa., U.S.	F1	115
Burghausen, Ger.	G12	8
Burghūth, Sabkhat al-, l., Syria	B7	40
Burgin, China	B4	26
Burgin, Ky., U.S.	C5	94
Burglengenfeld, Ger.	F12	8
Burgos, Spain	C8	12
Burgsteinfurt, Ger.	C7	8
Burgundy see Bourgogne, hist. reg., Fr.	E11	10
Burhaniye, Tur.	J10	16
Burhānpur, India	B4	37
Burica, Punta, c., N.A.	J6	64
Burin, Newf., Can.	E4	72
Burin Peninsula, pen., Newf., Can.	E4	72
Buriram, Thai.	G7	34
Burjasot, Spain	F11	12
Burkburnett, Tx., U.S.	B3	120
Burke, S.D., U.S.	D6	118
Burke, co., Ga., U.S.	C4	87
Burke, co., N.C., U.S.	B1	110
Burke, co., N.D., U.S.	A3	111
Burke Channel, strt., B.C., Can.	C4	69
Burkesville, Ky., U.S.	D4	94
Burketown, Austl.	C7	50
Burkina Faso, ctry., Afr.	F5	42
Burk's Falls, Ont., Can.	B5	73
Burleigh, co., N.D., U.S.	C5	111
Burleson, Tx., U.S.	n9	120
Burleson, co., Tx., U.S.	D4	120
Burley, Id., U.S.	G5	89
Burlingame, Ca., U.S.	h8	82
Burlingame, Ks., U.S.	D8	93
Burlington, Ont., Can.	D5	73
Burlington, Co., U.S.	B8	83
Burlington, Ia., U.S.	D6	92
Burlington, Ks., U.S.	D8	93
Burlington, Ky., U.S.	A5	94
Burlington, Ma., U.S.	f11	98
Burlington, N.J., U.S.	C3	107
Burlington, N.C., U.S.	A3	110
Burlington, N.D., U.S.	A4	111
Burlington, Vt., U.S.	C2	122
Burlington, Wa., U.S.	A3	124
Burlington, Wi., U.S.	F5	126
Burlington, co., N.J., U.S.	D3	107
Burlington Beach, In., U.S.	B3	91
Burlington Junction, Mo., U.S.	A2	102
Burma, ctry., Asia	A2	32
Burnaby, B.C., Can.	E6	69
Burnet, Tx., U.S.	D3	120
Burnet, co., Tx., U.S.	D3	120
Burnett, co., Wi., U.S.	C1	126
Burney, Ca., U.S.	B3	82
Burnham, Pa., U.S.	E6	115
Burnie, Austl.	H9	50
Burns, Or., U.S.	D7	114
Burns, Tn., U.S.	A4	119
Burns, Wy., U.S.	E8	127
Burns Flat, Ok., U.S.	B2	113
Burnside, Ky., U.S.	D5	94
Burns Lake, B.C., Can.	B5	69
Burns Paiute Indian Reservation, Or., U.S.	D7	114
Burnsville, Mn., U.S.	F5	100
Burnsville, Ms., U.S.	A5	101
Burnsville, N.C., U.S.	f10	110
Burnsville Lake, res., W.V., U.S.	C4	125
Burnt Islands, Newf., Can.	E2	72
Burnt Mills, Lake, l., Va., U.S.	k14	123
Burntside Lake, l., Mn., U.S.	C6	100
Burntwood, stm., Man., Can.	B2	70
Burravoe, Scot., U.K.	A11	7
Burr Oak, Mi., U.S.	G5	99
Burr Oak Reservoir, res., Oh., U.S.	C3	112
Burrton, Ks., U.S.	D6	93
Bursa, Tur.	G13	4
Būr Sa'īd (Port Said), Egypt	B12	42

Name — Map Ref — Page

Būr Sūdān (Port Sudan), Sudan E13 42
Burt, co., Ne., U.S. C9 104
Burt Lake, l., Mi., U.S. C6 99
Burton, Mi., U.S. F7 99
Burton, Oh., U.S. A4 112
Burton upon Trent, Eng., U.K. I11 7
Burtts Corner, N.B., Can. C3 71
Buru, i., Indon. F8 32
Burundi, ctry., Afr. B5 44
Burwell, Ne., U.S. C6 104
Burwick, Scot., U.K. C10 7
Bury Saint Edmunds, Eng., U.K. I13 7
Busalla, Italy E3 14
Buşayrah, Syria B7 40
Bushnell, Fl., U.S. D4 86
Bushnell, Il., U.S. C3 90
Bush River, b., Md., U.S. B5 97
Buşrá ash-Shām, Syria C5 40
Busselton, Austl. F3 50
Busto Arsizio, Italy D3 14
Busuanga Island, i., Phil. C7 32
Buta, Zaire H10 42
Butare, Rw. B5 44
Butehaqi, China B11 26
Bute Inlet, b., B.C., Can. D5 69
Butler, Al., U.S. C1 78
Butler, Ga., U.S. D2 87
Butler, In., U.S. B8 91
Butler, Ky., U.S. B5 94
Butler, Mo., U.S. C3 102
Butler, N.J., U.S. B4 107
Butler, Oh., U.S. B3 112
Butler, Pa., U.S. E2 115
Butler, Wi., U.S. m11 126
Butler, co., Al., U.S. D3 78
Butler, co., Ia., U.S. B5 92
Butler, co., Ks., U.S. E7 93
Butler, co., Ky., U.S. C3 94
Butler, co., Mo., U.S. E7 102
Butler, co., Ne., U.S. C8 104
Butler, co., Oh., U.S. C1 112
Butler, co., Pa., U.S. E2 115
Butner, N.C., U.S. A4 110
Buttahatchee, stm., U.S. B5 101
Butte, Mt., U.S. E4 103
Butte, co., Ca., U.S. C3 82
Butte, co., Id., U.S. F5 89
Butte, co., S.D., U.S. C2 118
Butte des Morts, Lake, l., Wi., U.S. D5 126
Butte Mountains, mts., Nv., U.S. D6 105
Butternut Lake, l., Wi., U.S. C5 126
Butterworth, Malay. L6 34
Butt of Lewis, c., Scot., U.K. C6 7
Buttonwillow, Ca., U.S. E4 82
Butts, co., Ga., U.S. C3 87
Butuan, Phil. D8 32
Butung, Pulau, i., Indon. F7 32
Bützow, Ger. B11 8
Buxtehude, Ger. B9 8
Buxton, N.C., U.S. B7 110
Büyükmenderes, stm., Tur. L11 16
Buzançais, Fr. F8 10
Buzău, Rom. D10 16
Búzi, stm., Moz. F6 44
Buzuluk, Russia G8 22
Buzzards Bay, Ma., U.S. C6 98
Buzzards Bay, b., Ma., U.S. C6 98
Byam Channel, strt., N.W. Ter., Can. A11 66
Byam Martin Island, i., N.W. Ter., Can. A12 66
Bydgoszcz, Pol. B18 8
Byers, Co., U.S. B6 83
Byesville, Oh., U.S. C4 112
Byhalia, Ms., U.S. A4 101
Bylas, Az., U.S. D5 80
Bylot Island, i., N.W. Ter., Can. B17 66
Byng, Ok., U.S. C5 113
Byrdstown, Tn., U.S. C8 119
Byron, Ga., U.S. D3 87
Byron, Il., U.S. A4 90
Byron, Mn., U.S. F6 100
Byron, Wy., U.S. B4 127
Byrranga, Gory, mts., Russia B14 24
Bytantaj, stm., Russia D20 24
Bytom (Beuthen), Pol. E18 8
Byxelkrok, Swe. H11 6

C

Caacupé, Para. B5 56
Cabaiguán, Cuba C8 64
Caballo Mountains, mts., N.M., U.S. E2 108
Caballo Reservoir, res., N.M., U.S. E2 108
Cabanatuan, Phil. q19 32
Cabano, Que., Can. B9 74
Cabarrus, co., N.C., U.S. B2 110
Cabbage Swamp, sw., Fl., U.S. m9 86
Cabell, co., W.V., U.S. C2 125
Cabeza del Buey, Spain G6 12
Cabimas, Ven. B7 58
Cabin Creek, W.V., U.S. m13 125
Cabin Creek, stm., W.V., U.S. m13 125
Cabinda, Ang. C2 44
Cabinda, dept., Ang. C2 44
Cabinet Gorge Reservoir, res., U.S. B1 103
Cabinet Mountains, mts., Mt., U.S. B1 103
Cabin John, Md., U.S. C3 97
Cabo Frio, Braz. G7 57
Cabonga, Réservoir, res., Que., Can. k11 74
Cabool, Mo., U.S. D5 102
Caborca, Mex. B3 62
Cabot, Ar., U.S. C3 81
Cabot, Mount, mtn., N.H., U.S. A4 106
Cabot Head, c., Ont., Can. B3 73
Cabot Strait, strt., Can. G21 66
Cabra, Spain H7 12
Cabri, Sask., Can. G1 75
Cabrillo National Monument, Ca., U.S. o15 82
Cabrobó, Braz. E11 54
Cabruta, Ven. D9 58
Çaçador, Braz. B6 56
Čačak, Yugo. F4 16
Cacapon, stm., W.V., U.S. B6 125
Cáceres, Braz. G7 54
Cáceres, Col. D5 58
Cáceres, Spain F5 12
Cache, Ok., U.S. C3 113
Cache, co., Ut., U.S. B4 121
Cache, stm., Ar., U.S. C4 81
Cache, stm., Il., U.S. F4 90
Cache Bay, Ont., Can. A5 73
Cache Creek, B.C., Can. D7 69
Cache la Poudre, stm., Co., U.S. A5 83
Cache Mountain, mtn., Ak., U.S. B10 79
Cache Peak, mtn., Id., U.S. G5 89
Cachimbo, Serra do, mts., Braz. E7 54
Cachoeira, Braz. B9 57
Cachoeira do Sul, Braz. C6 56
Cachoeiro de Itapemirim, Braz. F8 57
Cacólo, Ang. D3 44
Caconda, Ang. D3 44
Cactus Flat, pl., Nv., U.S. F5 105
Cactus Peak, mtn., Nv., U.S. F5 105
Caddo, Ok., U.S. C5 113
Caddo, co., La., U.S. B2 95
Caddo, co., Ok., U.S. B3 113
Caddo, stm., Ar., U.S. C2 81
Caddo Creek, stm., Ok., U.S. C4 113
Caddo Lake, res., U.S. B2 95
Cader Idris, mtn., Wales, U.K. I9 7
Cadillac, Fr. H6 10
Cadillac, Mi., U.S. D5 99
Cadillac Mountain, mtn., Me., U.S. D4 96
Cádiz, Spain I5 12
Cadiz, Ky., U.S. D2 94
Cadiz, Oh., U.S. B4 112
Cádiz, Golfo de, b., Eur. I4 12
Cadott, Wi., U.S. D2 126
Caen, Fr. C6 10
Caernarvon, Wales, U.K. H8 7
Caesar Creek Lake, res., Oh., U.S. C2 112
Caeté, Braz. E7 57
Cagayan de Oro, Phil. D7 32
Cagayan Islands, is., Phil. D7 32
Čagda, Russia F20 24
Cagles Mill Lake, res., In., U.S. F4 91
Cagli, Italy F7 14
Cagliari, Italy J4 14
Caguas, P.R. E14 64
Cahaba, stm., Al., U.S. C2 78
Caha Mountains, mts., Ire. J3 7
Cahirciveen, Ire. J2 7
Cahokia, Il., U.S. E3 90
Cahore Point, c., Ire. I6 7
Cahors, Fr. H8 10
Caiapó, Serra, mts., Braz. D2 57
Caibarién, Cuba C8 64
Caicara, Ven. D9 58
Caicos Islands, is., T./C. Is. D12 64
Caicos Passage, strt., N.A. C11 64
Caillou Bay, b., La., U.S. E5 95
Caillou Lake, l., La., U.S. E5 95
Cairnbrook, Pa., U.S. F4 115
Cairngorm Mountains, mts., Scot., U.K. D9 7
Cairns, Austl. C9 50
Cairo, Ga., U.S. F2 87
Cairo, Il., U.S. F4 90
Cairo, Ne., U.S. D7 104
Cairo see Al-Qāhirah, Egypt B12 42
Caiundo, Ang. E3 44
Cajamarca, Peru E3 54
Cajàzeiras, Braz. E11 54
Čakovec, Cro. C11 14
Calabar, Nig. H7 42
Calabozo, Ven. C9 58
Calahorra, Spain C10 12
Calais, Fr. B8 10
Calais, Me., U.S. C5 96
Calais, Pas de (Strait of Dover), strt., Eur. K14 7
Calamar, Col. B5 58
Calamian Group, is., Phil. C6 32
Calamocha, Spain E10 12
Calamus, stm., Ne., U.S. B6 104
Calanda, Spain E11 12
Calapan, Phil. r19 33b
Călăraşi, Rom. E11 16
Calatayud, Spain D10 12
Calaveras, co., Ca., U.S. C3 82
Calcasieu, co., La., U.S. D2 95
Calcasieu, stm., La., U.S. D2 95
Calcasieu Lake, l., La., U.S. E2 95
Calcasieu Pass, strt., La., U.S. E2 95
Calçoene, Braz. C8 54
Calcutta, India I13 38
Calcutta, Oh., U.S. B5 112
Calcutta Lake, l., Nv., U.S. B2 105
Caldas da Rainha, Port. F2 12
Calderwood, Tn., U.S. D10 119
Caldron Falls Reservoir, res., Wi., U.S. C5 126
Caldwell, Id., U.S. F2 89
Caldwell, Ks., U.S. E6 93
Caldwell, N.J., U.S. B4 107
Caldwell, Oh., U.S. C4 112
Caldwell, Tx., U.S. D4 120
Caldwell, co., Ky., U.S. C2 94
Caldwell, co., La., U.S. B3 95
Caldwell, co., Mo., U.S. B3 102
Caldwell, co., N.C., U.S. B1 110
Caldwell, co., Tx., U.S. E4 120
Caledon, Ont., Can. D5 73
Caledonia, Mi., U.S. F5 99
Caledonia, Mn., U.S. G7 100
Caledonia, Ms., U.S. B5 101
Caledonia, N.Y., U.S. C3 109
Caledonia, co., Vt., U.S. C4 122
Calera, Al., U.S. B3 78
Calera, Ok., U.S. D5 113
Calexico, Ca., U.S. F6 82
Calgary, Alta., Can. D3 68
Calhoun, Ga., U.S. B2 87
Calhoun, Ky., U.S. C2 94
Calhoun, co., Al., U.S. B4 78
Calhoun, co., Ar., U.S. D3 81
Calhoun, co., Fl., U.S. B1 86
Calhoun, co., Ga., U.S. E2 87
Calhoun, co., Il., U.S. D3 90
Calhoun, co., Ia., U.S. B3 92
Calhoun, co., Mi., U.S. F5 99
Calhoun, co., Ms., U.S. B4 101
Calhoun, co., S.C., U.S. D6 117
Calhoun, co., Tx., U.S. E4 120
Calhoun, co., W.V., U.S. C3 125
Calhoun City, Ms., U.S. B4 101
Calhoun Falls, S.C., U.S. C2 117
Cali, Col. F4 58
Calico Rock, Ar., U.S. A3 81
Calicut, India G3 37
Caliente, Nv., U.S. F7 105
California, Mo., U.S. C5 102
California, Pa., U.S. F2 115
California, state, U.S. D4 82
California, Golfo de, b., Mex. D4 62
California Aqueduct, Ca., U.S. E4 82
Calimere, Point, c., India G5 37
Calipatria, Ca., U.S. F6 82
Calispell Peak, mtn., Wa., U.S. A8 124
Calistoga, Ca., U.S. C2 82
Calitri, Italy I10 14
Callac, Fr. D3 10
Callaghan, Mount, mtn., Nv., U.S. D5 105
Callahan, co., Tx., U.S. C3 120
Callao, Peru F3 54
Callaway, co., Mo., U.S. C6 102
Calling Lake, l., Alta., Can. B4 68
Callosa de Ensarriá, Spain G11 12
Calloway, co., Ky., U.S. f9 94
Calmar, Alta., Can. C4 68
Calmar, Ia., U.S. A6 92
Caloosahatchee, stm., Fl., U.S. F5 86
Caltagirone, Italy L9 14
Caltanissetta, Italy L9 14
Calumet, Que., Can. D3 74
Calumet, Mi., U.S. A2 99
Calumet, co., Wi., U.S. D5 126
Calumet, Lake, l., Il., U.S. k9 90
Calumet City, Il., U.S. B6 90
Calunda, Ang. D4 44
Calvert, Tx., U.S. D4 120
Calvert, co., Md., U.S. C4 97
Calvert City, Ky., U.S. e9 94
Calverton, Md., U.S. *B4 97
Calverton Park, Mo., U.S. f13 102
Calvinia, S. Afr. H3 44
Camacho, Mex. E8 62
Camacupa, Ang. D3 44
Camaguán, Ven. C9 58
Camagüey, Cuba D9 64
Camaná, Peru G4 54
Camanche, Ia., U.S. C7 92
Camano Island, i., Wa., U.S. A3 124
Camapuã, Braz. E1 57
Camaquã, Braz. C6 56
Camas, Spain H5 12
Camas, Wa., U.S. D3 124
Camas, co., Id., U.S. F4 89
Ca Mau, Viet. J8 34
Cambados, Spain C3 12
Cambay, India I5 38
Cambodia (Kampuchea), ctry., Asia C3 32
Cambrai, Fr. B10 10
Cambria, Ca., U.S. E3 82
Cambria, Wi., U.S. E4 126
Cambria, co., Pa., U.S. E4 115
Cambrian Mountains, mts., Wales, U.K. I9 7
Cambridge, Ont., Can. D4 73
Cambridge, Eng., U.K. I13 7
Cambridge, Il., U.S. B3 90
Cambridge, Ia., U.S. C4 92
Cambridge, Md., U.S. C5 97
Cambridge, Ma., U.S. B5 98
Cambridge, Mn., U.S. E5 100
Cambridge, Ne., U.S. D5 104
Cambridge, N.Y., U.S. B7 109
Cambridge, Oh., U.S. B4 112
Cambridge, Wi., U.S. F4 126
Cambridge Bay, N.W. Ter., Can. C11 66
Cambridge City, In., U.S. E7 91
Cambridge Reservoir, res., Ma., U.S. g10 98
Cambridge Springs, Pa., U.S. C1 115
Cambuci, Braz. F8 57
Camden, Al., U.S. D2 78
Camden, Ar., U.S. D3 81
Camden, De., U.S. D3 85
Camden, In., U.S. C4 91
Camden, Me., U.S. D3 96
Camden, N.J., U.S. D2 107
Camden, N.Y., U.S. B5 109
Camden, Oh., U.S. C1 112
Camden, S.C., U.S. C6 117
Camden, Tn., U.S. A3 119
Camden, co., Ga., U.S. F5 87
Camden, co., Mo., U.S. C5 102
Camden, co., N.J., U.S. D3 107
Camden, co., N.C., U.S. A6 110
Camdenton, Mo., U.S. D5 102
Camelback Mountain, mtn., Az., U.S. k9 80
Cameron, Az., U.S. B4 80
Cameron, La., U.S. E2 95
Cameron, Mo., U.S. B3 102
Cameron, Tx., U.S. D4 120
Cameron, W.V., U.S. B4 125
Cameron, Wi., U.S. C2 126
Cameron, co., La., U.S. E2 95
Cameron, co., Pa., U.S. D5 115
Cameron, co., Tx., U.S. F4 120
Cameron Highlands, Malay. L6 34
Cameron Hills, hills, Can. E9 66
Cameroon, ctry., Afr. G8 42
Cameroon Mountain, mtn., Cam. H7 42
Cametá, Braz. D9 54
Camilla, Ga., U.S. E2 87
Camino, Ca., U.S. C3 82
Camiranga, Braz. D9 54
Camissombo, Ang. C4 44
Cam Lo, Viet. F9 34
Cammack Village, Ar., U.S. C3 81
Camooweal, Austl. C7 50
Camorta Island, i., India J2 34
Camp, co., Tx., U.S. C5 120
Campana, Isla, i., Chile F1 56
Campanero, Cerro, mtn., Ven. E10 58
Campbell, Ca., U.S. k8 82
Campbell, Fl., U.S. D5 86
Campbell, Mo., U.S. E7 102
Campbell, Oh., U.S. A5 112
Campbell, co., Ky., U.S. B5 94
Campbell, co., S.D., U.S. B5 118
Campbell, co., Tn., U.S. C9 119
Campbell, co., Va., U.S. C3 123
Campbell, co., Wy., U.S. B7 127
Campbellford, Ont., Can. C7 73
Campbell Hill, hill, Oh., U.S. B2 112
Campbell Lake, l., Or., U.S. E7 114
Campbellsburg, In., U.S. G5 91
Campbellsburg, Ky., U.S. B4 94
Campbells Creek, stm., W.V., U.S. m13 125
Campbellsport, Wi., U.S. E5 126
Campbellsville, Ky., U.S. C4 94
Campbellton, N.B., Can. A3 71
Campbellton, Newf., Can. D4 72
Campbeltown, Scot., U.K. F7 7
Campeche, Mex. H14 62
Campeche, Bahía de, b., Mex. H13 62
Camperville, Man., Can. D1 70
Camp Hill, Al., U.S. C4 78
Camp Hill, Pa., U.S. F8 115
Camp H. M. Smith Marine Corps Base, mil., Hi., U.S. g10 88
Camp Howard Ridge, mtn., Id., U.S. D2 89
Campina Grande, Braz. E11 54
Campinas, Braz. G5 57
Camp Lejeune Marine Corps Base, mil., N.C., U.S. C5 110
Campoalegre, Col. F5 58
Campo Alegre de Goiás, Braz. D5 57
Campobasso, Italy H9 14
Campobello Island, i., N.B., Can. E3 71
Campo Belo, Braz. F6 57
Campo de Criptana, Spain F8 12
Campo de la Cruz, Col. B5 58
Campo Grande, Braz. F1 57
Campo Maior, Braz. D10 54
Campos, Braz. F8 57
Campos do Jordão, Braz. G6 57
Camp Pendleton Marine Corps Base, mil., Ca., U.S. F5 82
Camp Point, Il., U.S. C2 90
Camp Springs, Md., U.S. f9 97
Campti, La., U.S. C2 95
Campton, N.H., U.S. C3 106
Camp Verde, Az., U.S. C4 80
Camp Verde Indian Reservation, Az., U.S. C4 80
Cam Ranh, Viet. I10 34
Camrose, Alta., Can. C4 68
Canaan, Ct., U.S. A2 84
Canaan, N.H., U.S. C2 106
Canaan, stm., N.B., Can. C4 71
Canada, ctry., N.A. D14 66
Canada Bay, b., Newf., Can. C3 72
Canada Falls Lake, res., Me., U.S. C2 96
Canadensis, Pa., U.S. D11 115
Canadian, Tx., U.S. B2 120
Canadian, co., Ok., U.S. B3 113
Canadian, stm., U.S. D6 76
Canajoharie, N.Y., U.S. C6 109
Çanakkale, Tur. G13 4
Çanakkale Boğazı (Dardanelles), strt., Tur. I10 16
Canal Flats, B.C., Can. D10 69
Canal Fulton, Oh., U.S. B4 112
Canal Winchester, Oh., U.S. C3 112
Canandaigua, N.Y., U.S. C3 109
Canandaigua Lake, l., N.Y., U.S. C3 109
Cananea, Mex. B4 62
Cañar, Ec. I3 58
Canarias, Islas (Canary Islands), is., Spain p24 136
Canary Islands see Canarias, Islas, is., Spain p24 136
Cañas, C.R. I5 64
Canastota, N.Y., U.S. B5 109
Canaveral, Cape, c., Fl., U.S. D6 86
Canaveral National Seashore, Fl., U.S. D6 86
Canavieiras, Braz. C9 57
Canberra, Austl. G9 50
Canby, Mn., U.S. F2 100
Canby, Or., U.S. B4 114
Cancale, Fr. D5 10
Cancon, Fr. H7 10
Cancún, Mex. G16 62
Candeleda, Spain E6 12
Candiac, Que., Can. q19 74
Candle Lake, l., Sask., Can. D3 75
Candler, co., Ga., U.S. D4 87
Candlewood, Lake, l., Ct., U.S. D1 84
Candlewood Isle, Ct., U.S. D2 84
Candlewood Shores, Ct., U.S. D2 84
Cando, N.D., U.S. A6 111
Candor, N.C., U.S. B3 110
Cane, stm., La., U.S. C2 95
Cañete, Spain E10 12
Caney, Ks., U.S. E8 93
Caney, stm., Ok., U.S. A5 113
Caney Creek, stm., Tx., U.S. r14 120
Caney Fork, stm., Tn., U.S. C8 119
Canfield, Oh., U.S. A5 112
Canfranc, Spain C11 12
Cangas de Onís, Spain B6 12
Cangombe, Ang. D3 44
Canguçu, Braz. C6 56
Cangzhou, China D10 26
Caniapiscau, stm., Que., Can. g13 74
Caniapiscau, Lac, l., Que., Can. F19 66
Canicattì, Italy L8 14
Canisteer Reservoir, res., N.J., U.S. A4 107
Canisteo, N.Y., U.S. C3 109
Canisteo, stm., N.Y., U.S. C3 109
Canistota, S.D., U.S. D8 118
Cañitas, Mex. F8 62
Çankırı, Tur. G14 4
Canmore, Alta., Can. D3 68
Cannanore, India G3 37
Cannelton, In., U.S. I4 91
Cannes, Fr. I14 10
Canning, N.S., Can. D5 71
Cannon, co., Tn., U.S. B5 119
Cannon, stm., Mn., U.S. F5 100
Cannon Air Force Base, mil., N.M., U.S. C6 108
Cannonball, stm., N.D., U.S. C5 111
Cannon Beach, Or., U.S. B3 114
Cannondale, Ct., U.S. E2 84
Cannon Falls, Mn., U.S. F6 100
Cannonsburg, Ky., U.S. B7 94
Cannonsville Reservoir, res., N.Y., U.S. C5 109
Canon, Ga., U.S. B3 87
Canon City, Co., U.S. C5 83
Canonsburg, Pa., U.S. F1 115
Canosa [di Puglia], Italy H11 14
Cantábrica, Cordillera, mts., Spain B7 12
Cantalejo, Spain D8 12
Cantanhede, Port. E3 12
Cantaura, Ven. C10 58
Canterbury, Eng., U.K. J14 7
Canterbury, De., U.S. D3 85
Canterbury Bight, N.Z. F3 52
Can Tho, Viet. I8 34
Canton, Ct., U.S. B4 84
Canton, Ga., U.S. B2 87
Canton, Il., U.S. C3 90
Canton, Ks., U.S. D6 93
Canton, Ma., U.S. B5 98
Canton, Ms., U.S. C3 101
Canton, Mo., U.S. A6 102
Canton, N.Y., U.S. f9 109
Canton, N.C., U.S. f10 110
Canton, Oh., U.S. B4 112
Canton, Ok., U.S. A3 113
Canton, Pa., U.S. C8 115
Canton, S.D., U.S. D9 118
Canton, Tx., U.S. C5 120
Canton see Guangzhou, China L2 28
Canton Lake, res., Ok., U.S. A3 113
Cantonment, Fl., U.S. u14 86
Cantù, Italy D4 14
Canutillo, Tx., U.S. o11 120
Canyon, Tx., U.S. B2 120
Canyon, co., Id., U.S. F2 89
Canyon City, Or., U.S. C8 114
Canyon de Chelly National Monument, Az., U.S. A6 80
Canyon Ferry Lake, res., Mt., U.S. D5 103
Canyon Lake, Tx., U.S. E3 120
Canyon Lake, res., Tx., U.S. E3 120
Canyonlands National Park, Ut., U.S. E6 121
Canyonville, Or., U.S. E3 114
Cao Bang, Viet. C9 34
Capac, Mi., U.S. F8 99
Cap-à-l'Aigle, Que., Can. B7 74
Cap-aux-Meules, Que., Can. B8 71
Cap-de-la-Madeleine, Que., Can. C5 74
Cape Breton Highlands National Park, N.S., Can. C9 71
Cape Breton Island, i., N.S., Can. C9 71
Cape Broyle, Newf., Can. E5 72
Cape Canaveral, Fl., U.S. D6 86
Cape Charles, Va., U.S. C6 123
Cape Coast, Ghana G5 42
Cape Cod Bay, b., Ma., U.S. C7 98
Cape Cod Canal, Ma., U.S. C6 98
Cape Cod National Seashore, Ma., U.S. C7 98
Cape Coral, Fl., U.S. F5 86
Cape Dorset, N.W. Ter., Can. D17 66
Cape Elizabeth, Me., U.S. E2 96
Cape Fear, stm., N.C., U.S. C4 110
Cape Girardeau, Mo., U.S. D8 102
Cape Girardeau, co., Mo., U.S. D8 102
Cape Hatteras National Seashore, N.C., U.S. B7 110
Cape Horn Mountain, mtn., Id., U.S. E3 89
Cape Island, i., S.C., U.S. E9 117
Cape Lookout National Seashore, N.C., U.S. C6 110
Cape May, N.J., U.S. F3 107
Cape May, co., N.J., U.S. E3 107
Cape May Court House, N.J., U.S. E3 107
Capers Inlet, b., S.C., U.S. k12 117
Capers Island, i., S.C., U.S. G6 117
Capers Island, i., S.C., U.S. F8 117
Cape Sable Island, i., N.S., Can. F4 71
Cape Town (Kaapstad), S. Afr. H3 44
Cape Verde, ctry., Afr. E11 2
Cape York Peninsula, pen., Austl. B8 50
Cap-Haïtien, Haiti E11 64
Capim, stm., Braz. D9 54
Capitan, N.M., U.S. D4 108
Capitan Mountains, mts., N.M., U.S. D4 108
Capitan Peak, mtn., N.M., U.S. D4 108
Capitol Heights, Ia., U.S. e8 92
Capitol Heights, Md., U.S. C4 97
Capitol Peak, mtn., Nv., U.S. B4 105
Capitol Reef National Park, Ut., U.S. E4 121
Čapljina, Bos. F12 14
Cap-Pelé, N.B., Can. C5 71
Capreol, Ont., Can. p19 73
Capri, Italy I9 14
Caprivi Strip, hist. reg., Nmb. E4 44
Cap-Rouge, Que., Can. n17 74
Cap-Saint-Ignace, Que., Can. B7 74
Captain Cook, Hi., U.S. D6 88
Captieux, Fr. H6 10
Captiva, Fl., U.S. F4 86
Captiva Island, i., Fl., U.S. F4 86
Capua, Italy H9 14
Capulin Volcano National Monument, N.M., U.S. A6 108
Caquetá (Japurá), stm., S.A. D5 54
Čara, Russia F17 24
Čara, stm., Russia F17 24
Caracaraí, Braz. C6 54
Caracas, Ven. B9 58
Carajás, Serra dos, mts., Braz. E8 54

Name	Map Ref	Page
Carangola, Braz.	F7	57
Caraquet, N.B., Can.	B5	71
Caratasca, Laguna de, b., Hond.	G6	64
Caratinga, Braz.	E7	57
Carauari, Braz.	D5	54
Caravaca, Spain	G10	12
Caravelas, Braz.	D9	57
Caraway, Ar., U.S.	B5	81
Carballo, Spain	B3	12
Carberry, Man., Can.	E2	70
Carbon, co., Mt., U.S.	E7	103
Carbon, co., Pa., U.S.	E10	115
Carbon, co., Ut., U.S.	D5	121
Carbon, co., Wy., U.S.	E5	127
Carbondale, Co., U.S.	B3	83
Carbondale, Il., U.S.	F4	90
Carbondale, Ks., U.S.	D8	93
Carbondale, Pa., U.S.	C10	115
Carbonear, Newf., Can.	E5	72
Carboneras de Guadazaon, Spain	F10	12
Carbon Hill, Al., U.S.	B2	78
Carbonia, Italy	J3	14
Carcagente, Spain	F11	12
Carcassonne, Fr.	I9	10
Carcross, Yukon, Can.	D6	66
Cárdenas, Cuba	C7	64
Cárdenas, Mex.	F10	62
Cardiff, Wales, U.K.	J9	7
Cardigan, Wales, U.K.	I8	7
Cardigan Bay, b., P.E.I., Can.	C7	71
Cardigan Bay, b., Wales, U.K.	I8	7
Cardinal, Ont., Can.	C9	73
Cardington, Oh., U.S.	B3	112
Cardston, Alta., Can.	E4	68
Cardwell, Mo., U.S.	E7	102
Čardžou, Turk.	J10	22
Carencro, La., U.S.	D3	95
Carentan, Fr.	C5	10
Caretta, W.V., U.S.	D3	125
Carey, Id., U.S.	F5	89
Carey, Oh., U.S.	B2	112
Carey, Lake, l., Austl.	E4	50
Caribbean Sea	G10	64
Cariboo Mountains, mts., B.C., Can.	C7	69
Caribou, Me., U.S.	B5	96
Caribou, co., Id., U.S.	G7	89
Caribou Island, i., N.S., Can.	D7	71
Caribou Lake, l., Me., U.S.	C3	96
Caribou Mountain, mtn., Id., U.S.	F7	89
Caribou Mountains, mts., Alta., Can.	f7	68
Caribou Range, mts., Id., U.S.	F7	89
Carignan, Fr.	C12	10
Cariñena, Spain	D10	12
Carinhanha, Braz.	C7	57
Carini, Italy	K8	14
Caripito, Ven.	B11	58
Carl Blackwell, Lake, res., Ok., U.S.	A4	113
Carleton, Mi., U.S.	F7	99
Carleton, Mount, mtn., N.B., Can.	B3	71
Carleton Place, Ont., Can.	B8	73
Carlin, Nv., U.S.	C5	105
Carlinville, Il., U.S.	D4	90
Carlisle, Eng., U.K.	G10	7
Carlisle, Ar., U.S.	C4	81
Carlisle, In., U.S.	G3	91
Carlisle, Ia., U.S.	C4	92
Carlisle, Ky., U.S.	B5	94
Carlisle, Oh., U.S.	C1	112
Carlisle, Pa., U.S.	F7	115
Carlisle, co., Ky., U.S.	f8	94
Carl Junction, Mo., U.S.	D3	102
Carlow, Ire.	I6	7
Carlsbad, Ca., U.S.	F5	82
Carlsbad, N.M., U.S.	E5	108
Carlsbad Caverns National Park, N.M., U.S.	E5	108
Carlstadt, N.J., U.S.	h8	107
Carlton, Mn., U.S.	D6	100
Carlton, Or., U.S.	B3	114
Carlton, co., Mn., U.S.	D6	100
Carlyle, Il., U.S.	E4	90
Carlyle Lake, res., Il., U.S.	E4	90
Carmacks, Yukon, Can.	D5	66
Carmagnola, Italy	E2	14
Carman, Man., Can.	E2	70
Carmanville, Newf., Can.	D4	72
Carmarthen, Wales, U.K.	J8	7
Carmaux, Fr.	H9	10
Carmel, Ca., U.S.	D3	82
Carmel, In., U.S.	E5	91
Carmel, N.Y., U.S.	D7	109
Carmel Head, c., Wales, U.K.	H8	7
Carmen, Isla, i., Mex.	E4	62
Carmen, Isla del, i., Mex.	H14	62
Carmen de Patagones, Arg.	E4	56
Carmi, Il., U.S.	E5	90
Carmi, Lake, l., Vt., U.S.	B3	122
Carmona, Spain	H6	12
Carnarvon, Austl.	D2	50
Carnarvon, S. Afr.	H4	44
Carnation, Wa., U.S.	B4	124
Carndonagh, Ire.	F5	7
Carnegie, Ok., U.S.	B3	113
Carnegie, Pa., U.S.	F1	115
Carnegie, Lake, l., Austl.	E4	50
Carneys Point, N.J., U.S.	D2	107
Carniche, Alpi, mts., Eur.	C8	14
Car Nicobar Island, i., India	J2	34
Carnsore Point, c., Ire.	I6	7
Caro, Mi., U.S.	E7	99
Carol City, Fl., U.S.	s13	86
Caroleen, N.C., U.S.	B1	110
Carolina, Braz.	E9	54
Carolina, Col.	D5	58
Carolina, R.I., U.S.	F2	116
Carolina, W.V., U.S.	k10	125
Carolina Beach, N.C., U.S.	C5	110
Caroline, co., Md., U.S.	C6	97
Caroline, co., Va., U.S.	C5	123
Caroní, stm., Ven.	D11	58
Carora, Ven.	B7	58
Carpathian Mountains, mts., Eur.	F12	4
Carpații Meridionali, mts., Rom.	D8	16
Carpentaria, Gulf of, b., Austl.	B7	50
Carpenter Dam, Ar., U.S.	g7	81
Carpentersville, Il., U.S.	A5	90
Carpentras, Fr.	H12	10
Carpi, Italy	E5	14
Carpinteria, Ca., U.S.	E4	82
Carquefou, Fr.	E5	10
Carrabelle, Fl., U.S.	C2	86
Carrara, Italy	E5	14
Carrauntoohill, mtn., Ire.	I3	7
Carrboro, N.C., U.S.	B3	110
Carreta, Punta, c., Peru	F3	54
Carrickfergus, N. Ire., U.K.	G7	7
Carrickmacross, Ire.	H6	7
Carrie, Mount, mtn., Wa., U.S.	B2	124
Carriere, Ms., U.S.	E4	101
Carrier Mills, Il., U.S.	F5	90
Carrillo, Mex.	D8	62
Carrington, N.D., U.S.	B6	111
Carrington Island, i., Ut., U.S.	C3	121
Carrión de los Condes, Spain	C7	12
Carrizo Creek, stm., U.S.	A1	120
Carrizo Mountain, mtn., N.M., U.S.	D4	108
Carrizo Mountains, mts., U.S.	A6	80
Carrizo Springs, Tx., U.S.	*E3	120
Carrizozo, N.M., U.S.	D4	108
Carroll, Ia., U.S.	B3	92
Carroll, co., Ar., U.S.	A2	81
Carroll, co., Ga., U.S.	C1	87
Carroll, co., Il., U.S.	A4	90
Carroll, co., In., U.S.	C4	91
Carroll, co., Ia., U.S.	B3	92
Carroll, co., Ky., U.S.	B4	94
Carroll, co., Md., U.S.	A3	97
Carroll, co., Ms., U.S.	B4	101
Carroll, co., Mo., U.S.	B4	102
Carroll, co., N.H., U.S.	C4	106
Carroll, co., Oh., U.S.	B4	112
Carroll, co., Tn., U.S.	B3	119
Carroll, co., Va., U.S.	D2	123
Carrollton, Al., U.S.	B1	78
Carrollton, Ga., U.S.	C1	87
Carrollton, Il., U.S.	D3	90
Carrollton, Ky., U.S.	B4	94
Carrollton, Mi., U.S.	E7	99
Carrollton, Mo., U.S.	B4	102
Carrollton, Oh., U.S.	B4	112
Carrolltown, Pa., U.S.	E4	115
Carrot, stm., Can.	D4	75
Carry Falls Reservoir, res., N.Y., U.S.	f10	109
Čarsk, Kaz.	H10	24
Carson, Ia., U.S.	C2	92
Carson, Wa., U.S.	D4	124
Carson, co., Tx., U.S.	B2	120
Carson, stm., Nv., U.S.	D2	105
Carson City, Mi., U.S.	E6	99
Carson City, Nv., U.S.	D2	105
Carson Lake, l., Nv., U.S.	D3	105
Carson Sink, l., Nv., U.S.	D3	105
Carson Spring, Tn., U.S.	D10	119
Carstairs, Alta., Can.	D3	68
Carswell Air Force Base, mil., Tx., U.S.	n9	120
Cartagena, Col.	B5	58
Cartagena, Spain	H11	12
Cartago, Col.	E5	58
Cartago, C.R.	J6	64
Carter, co., Ky., U.S.	B6	94
Carter, co., Mo., U.S.	E7	102
Carter, co., Mt., U.S.	E12	103
Carter, co., Ok., U.S.	C4	113
Carter, co., Tn., U.S.	C11	119
Carteret, N.J., U.S.	B4	107
Carteret, co., N.C., U.S.	C6	110
Carter Lake, Ia., U.S.	C2	92
Carter Mountain, mtn., Wy., U.S.	B3	127
Carters Lake, res., Ga., U.S.	B2	87
Cartersville, Ga., U.S.	B2	87
Carterville, Il., U.S.	F4	90
Carterville, Mo., U.S.	D3	102
Carthage, Il., U.S.	C2	90
Carthage, In., U.S.	E6	91
Carthage, Ms., U.S.	C4	101
Carthage, Mo., U.S.	D3	102
Carthage, N.Y., U.S.	B5	109
Carthage, N.C., U.S.	B3	110
Carthage, Tn., U.S.	C8	119
Carthage, Tx., U.S.	C5	120
Cartier Island, i., Austl.	B4	50
Cartwright, Newf., Can.	B3	72
Cartwright, Ok., U.S.	D5	113
Caruaru, Braz.	E11	54
Carúpano, Ven.	B11	58
Caruthersville, Mo., U.S.	E8	102
Carver, Ma., U.S.	C6	98
Carver, Mn., U.S.	F5	100
Carver, co., Mn., U.S.	F5	100
Carville, La., U.S.	h9	95
Cary, Il., U.S.	h8	90
Cary, N.C., U.S.	B4	110
Caryville, Tn., U.S.	C9	119
Casablanca (Dar-el-Beida), Mor.	B4	42
Casacalenda, Italy	H9	14
Casa Grande, Az., U.S.	E4	80
Casa Grande National Monument, Az., U.S.	E4	80
Casale Monferrato, Italy	D3	14
Casarano, Italy	I13	14
Casas Adobes, Az., U.S.	E5	80
Casas Ibáñez, Spain	F10	12
Cascade, Co., U.S.	C6	83
Cascade, Id., U.S.	E2	89
Cascade, Ia., U.S.	B6	92
Cascade, Mt., U.S.	C5	103
Cascade, co., Mt., U.S.	C5	103
Cascade Locks, Or., U.S.	B5	114
Cascade Range, mts., N.A.	C2	76
Cascade Reservoir, res., Id., U.S.	E3	89
Cascade Tunnel, Wa., U.S.	B4	124
Cascais, Port.	G2	12
Cascina, Italy	F5	14
Casco Bay, b., Me., U.S.	E3	96
Caserta, Italy	H9	14
Caseville, Mi., U.S.	E7	99
Casey, Il., U.S.	D6	90
Casey, co., Ky., U.S.	C5	94
Casey, Mount, mtn., Id., U.S.	A2	89
Casey Key, i., Fl., U.S.	E4	86
Cashion, Az., U.S.	m8	80
Cashmere, Wa., U.S.	B5	124
Cashton, Wi., U.S.	E3	126
Casigua, Ven.	C6	58
Caspe, Spain	D11	12
Casper, Wy., U.S.	D6	127
Casper Mountain, mtn., Wy., U.S.	D6	127
Caspian, Mi., U.S.	B2	99
Caspian Lake, l., Vt., U.S.	B4	122
Caspian Sea	G17	4
Cass, co., Il., U.S.	D3	90
Cass, co., In., U.S.	C5	91
Cass, co., Ia., U.S.	C3	92
Cass, co., Mi., U.S.	G4	99
Cass, co., Mn., U.S.	D4	100
Cass, co., Mo., U.S.	C3	102
Cass, co., Ne., U.S.	D9	104
Cass, co., N.D., U.S.	C8	111
Cass, co., Tx., U.S.	C5	120
Cass, stm., Mi., U.S.	E7	99
Cassai (Kasai), stm., Afr.	C4	44
Cassano allo Ionio, Italy	J11	14
Cass City, Mi., U.S.	E7	99
Casselberry, Fl., U.S.	D5	86
Casselman, Ont., Can.	B9	73
Casselman, stm., U.S.	k12	97
Casselton, N.D., U.S.	C8	111
Cassia, co., Id., U.S.	G5	89
Cassiar, B.C., Can.	m17	69
Cassinga, Ang.	E3	44
Cassino, Italy	H8	14
Cass Lake, Mn., U.S.	C4	100
Cass Lake, l., Mn., U.S.	C4	100
Cassopolis, Mi., U.S.	G4	99
Cassville, Ga., U.S.	B2	87
Cassville, Mo., U.S.	E4	102
Cassville, Wi., U.S.	F3	126
Castalia, Oh., U.S.	A3	112
Castanea, Pa., U.S.	D7	115
Castanheira de Pêra, Port.	E3	12
Castel del Piano, Italy	G6	14
Castelfranco Veneto, Italy	D6	14
Castellamare del Golfo, Italy	K7	14
Castellammare [di Stabia], Italy	I9	14
Castellane, Fr.	I13	10
Castellón de la Plana, Spain	F11	12
Castelnaudary, Fr.	I8	10
Castelo Branco, Port.	F4	12
Castelsarrasin, Fr.	H8	10
Castelvetrano, Italy	L7	14
Castets, Fr.	I5	10
Castiglione del Lago, Italy	F7	14
Castilla, Peru	E2	54
Castilla la Nueva, hist. reg., Spain	F8	12
Castillo de San Marcos National Monument, Fl., U.S.	n9	86
Castine, Me., U.S.	D4	96
Castle Air Force Base, mil., Ca., U.S.	D3	82
Castlebar, Ire.	H3	7
Castleberry, Al., U.S.	D2	78
Castle Dale, Ut., U.S.	D4	121
Castle Dome Mountains, mts., Az., U.S.	D1	80
Castle Dome Peak, mtn., Az., U.S.	D1	80
Castlegar, B.C., Can.	E9	69
Castle Hayne, N.C., U.S.	C5	110
Castle Hills, De., U.S.	i7	85
Castle Mountain, mtn., Yukon, Can.	D5	66
Castle Mountains, mts., Mt., U.S.	D6	103
Castle Peak, mtn., Co., U.S.	B4	83
Castle Peak, mtn., Id., U.S.	E4	89
Castle Point, Mo., U.S.	f13	102
Castle Rock, Co., U.S.	B6	83
Castle Rock, Wa., U.S.	C3	124
Castle Rock, mtn., Or., U.S.	C8	114
Castle Rock Lake, res., Wi., U.S.	E4	126
Castleton, Vt., U.S.	D2	122
Castletown, I. of Man	G8	7
Castletown Berehaven, Ire.	J3	7
Castlewood, Va., U.S.	f9	123
Castor, Alta., Can.	C5	68
Castor, stm., Mo., U.S.	D7	102
Castres, Fr.	I9	10
Castries, St. Luc.	G17	64
Castro, co., Tx., U.S.	B1	120
Castro Daire, Port.	E4	12
Castro del Río, Spain	H7	12
Castropol, Spain	B4	12
Castro Valley, Ca., U.S.	h8	82
Castrovillari, Italy	J11	14
Castroville, Tx., U.S.	E3	120
Castuera, Spain	G6	12
Caswell, co., N.C., U.S.	A3	110
Catacamas, Hond.	G5	64
Cataguases, Braz.	F7	57
Catahoula, co., La., U.S.	C4	95
Catahoula Lake, l., La., U.S.	C3	95
Catalão, Braz.	E5	57
Catalina, Newf., Can.	D5	72
Catalina, Chile	B3	56
Catamarca, Arg.	B3	56
Catamayo, Ec.	I3	58
Catanduanes Island, i., Phil.	C7	32
Catanduva, Braz.	F4	57
Catania, Italy	L10	14
Catanzaro, Italy	K11	14
Cataouatche, Lake, l., La., U.S.	k11	95
Catarman, Phil.	C7	32
Catasauqua, Pa., U.S.	E11	115
Catastrophe, Cape, c., Austl.	F7	50
Cataumet, Ma., U.S.	C6	98
Catawba, co., N.C., U.S.	B1	110
Catawba, stm., S.C., U.S.	B6	117
Catawba, South Fork, stm., N.C., U.S.	B1	110
Catawissa, Pa., U.S.	E9	115
Catete, Ang.	C2	44
Cathance, Lake, l., Me., U.S.	D5	96
Cathcart, S. Afr.	H5	44
Cathedral City, Ca., U.S.	F5	82
Cathedral of the Pines, N.H., U.S.	E3	106
Catherine, Lake, res., Ar., U.S.	C3	81
Cat Island, i., Bah.	B10	64
Cat Island, i., Ma., U.S.	f12	98
Cat Island, i., Ms., U.S.	E4	101
Cat Island, i., S.C., U.S.	E9	117
Catlettsburg, Ky., U.S.	B7	94
Catlin, Il., U.S.	C6	90
Catnip Mountain, mtn., Nv., U.S.	B2	105
Catoche, Cabo, c., Mex.	G16	62
Cato Island, i., Austl.	D11	50
Catonsville, Md., U.S.	B4	97
Catoosa, Ok., U.S.	A6	113
Catoosa, co., Ga., U.S.	B1	87
Catorce, Mex.	F9	62
Catron, co., N.M., U.S.	D1	108
Catskill, N.Y., U.S.	C7	109
Catskill Mountains, mts., N.Y., U.S.	C6	109
Catt, Mount, mtn., B.C., Can.	B3	69
Cattaraugus, co., N.Y., U.S.	C2	109
Cattaraugus Creek, stm., N.Y., U.S.	C2	109
Cattaraugus Indian Reservation, N.Y., U.S.	C2	109
Cattolica, Italy	F7	14
Catus, Fr.	H8	10
Caubvick, Mount (Mont d'Iberville), mtn., Can.	f9	72
Cauca, stm., Col.	D5	58
Caucasia, Col.	C5	58
Caucasus, mts., Eur.	I6	22
Caucomgomoc Lake, l., Me., U.S.	B3	96
Caudry, Fr.	B10	10
Caulonia, Italy	K11	14
Caúngula, Ang.	C3	44
Čaunskaja Guba, b., Russia	D27	24
Cauquenes, Chile	D2	56
Caura, stm., Ven.	D10	58
Caussade, Fr.	H8	10
Cauvery, stm., India	G5	37
Cavalaire-sur-Mer, Fr.	I13	10
Cavalier, N.D., U.S.	A8	111
Cavalier, co., N.D., U.S.	A7	111
Cavan, Ire.	G5	7
Cave City, Ar., U.S.	B4	81
Cave City, Ky., U.S.	C4	94
Cave Creek, Az., U.S.	D4	80
Cave Junction, Or., U.S.	E3	114
Cave Point, c., Wi., U.S.	D6	126
Cave Run Lake, res., Ky., U.S.	B6	94
Cave Spring, Ga., U.S.	B1	87
Cave Spring, Va., U.S.	C2	123
Cavetown, Md., U.S.	A2	97
Caviana, Ilha, i., Braz.	C8	54
Cavite, Phil.	q19	33b
Cawood, Ky., U.S.	D6	94
Cawston, B.C., Can.	E8	69
Caxambu, Braz.	F6	57
Caxias, Braz.	D10	54
Caxias do Sul, Braz.	B6	56
Caxito, Ang.	C2	44
Cayambe, Ec.	G3	58
Cayambe, vol., Ec.	H4	58
Cayce, S.C., U.S.	D5	117
Cayenne, Fr. Gu.	C8	54
Cayman Brac, i., Cay. Is.	E8	64
Cayman Islands, dep., N.A.	E7	64
Cayuga, In., U.S.	E3	91
Cayuga, co., N.Y., U.S.	C4	109
Cayuga Heights, N.Y., U.S.	C4	109
Cayuga Lake, l., N.Y., U.S.	C4	109
Cazenovia, N.Y., U.S.	C5	109
Cazères, Fr.	I8	10
Cazin, Bos.	E10	14
Cazorla, Spain	H8	12
Čeboksary, Russia	F7	22
Cebollar, Arg.	B3	56
Cebreros, Spain	E7	12
Cebu, Phil.	C7	32
Cebu, i., Phil.	C7	32
Čecerleg, Mong.	B7	26
Čechov, Russia	F20	18
Čechy, hist. reg., Czech.	F14	8
Cecil, co., Md., U.S.	A6	97
Cecil Field Naval Air Station, mil., Fl., U.S.	B5	86
Cecilia, Ky., U.S.	C4	94
Cecina, Italy	F5	14
Cedar, co., Ia., U.S.	C6	92
Cedar, co., Mo., U.S.	D4	102
Cedar, co., Ne., U.S.	B8	104
Cedar, stm., U.S.	C6	92
Cedar, stm., Ne., U.S.	B7	104
Cedar, stm., Wa., U.S.	B4	124
Cedar Bluff, Al., U.S.	A4	78
Cedar Bluff Reservoir, res., Ks., U.S.	D4	93
Cedar Bluff Two, Tn., U.S.	D9	119
Cedar Breaks National Monument, Ut., U.S.	F3	121
Cedarburg, Wi., U.S.	E6	126
Cedar City, Ut., U.S.	F2	121
Cedar Creek, stm., N.J., U.S.	D4	107
Cedar Creek, stm., N.D., U.S.	C3	111
Cedar Creek, stm., Oh., U.S.	e7	112
Cedar Creek Lake, res., Tx., U.S.	C4	120
Cedar Crest, N.M., U.S.	k8	108
Cedaredge, Co., U.S.	C3	83
Cedar Falls, Ia., U.S.	B5	92
Cedar Grove, N.J., U.S.	B4	107
Cedar Grove, W.V., U.S.	C3	125
Cedar Grove, Wi., U.S.	E6	126
Cedar Hill, Mo., U.S.	g12	102
Cedar Hill, Tx., U.S.	n10	120
Cedarhurst, N.Y., U.S.	k13	109
Cedar Island, i., N.C., U.S.	C6	110
Cedar Island, i., S.C., U.S.	E9	117
Cedar Island, i., Va., U.S.	C7	123
Cedar Key, Fl., U.S.	C3	86
Cedar Keys, is., Fl., U.S.	C3	86
Cedar Lake, In., U.S.	B3	91
Cedar Lake, res., Man., Can.	C1	70
Cedar Lake, res., Il., U.S.	F4	90
Cedar Mountain, mtn., Ca., U.S.	B3	82
Cedar Point, c., Md., U.S.	D5	97
Cedar Point, c., Oh., U.S.	A3	112
Cedar Point, c., Oh., U.S.	e7	112
Cedar Rapids, Ia., U.S.	C6	92
Cedar Springs, Mi., U.S.	E5	99
Cedartown, Ga., U.S.	B1	87
Cedar Vale, Ks., U.S.	E7	93
Cedarville, Oh., U.S.	C2	112
Cedros, Isla, i., Mex.	C2	62
Ceduna, Austl.	F6	50
Cefalù, Italy	K9	14
Čegdomyn, Russia	G20	24
Cegléd, Hung.	H19	8
Cehegín, Spain	G10	12
Cela, Ang.	D3	44
Čel'abinsk, Russia	F10	22
Celano, Italy	G8	14
Celanova, Spain	C4	12
Celaya, Mex.	G9	62
Cele, China	B9	38
Celebes Sea, Asia	E7	32
Celebes see Sulawesi, i., Indon.	F7	32
Celina, Oh., U.S.	B1	112
Celina, Tn., U.S.	C8	119
Celina, Tx., U.S.	C4	120
Celinograd, Kaz.	G8	24
Celje, Slo.	C10	14
Celle, Ger.	C10	8
Cement, Ok., U.S.	C3	113
Cementon, Pa., U.S.	E10	115
Centennial Mountains, mts., Id., U.S.	E7	89
Center, Co., U.S.	D4	83
Center, N.D., U.S.	B4	111
Center, Tx., U.S.	D5	120
Centerbrook, Ct., U.S.	D6	84
Centerburg, Oh., U.S.	B3	112
Centereach, N.Y., U.S.	n15	109
Centerfield, Ut., U.S.	D4	121
Center Hill Lake, res., Tn., U.S.	C8	119
Center Moriches, N.Y., U.S.	n16	109
Center Mountain, mtn., Id., U.S.	D3	89
Center Point, Al., U.S.	f7	78
Center Point, Ia., U.S.	B6	92
Centerville, In., U.S.	E8	91
Centerville, Ia., U.S.	D5	92
Centerville, La., U.S.	E4	95
Centerville, Ma., U.S.	C7	98
Centerville, Oh., U.S.	C1	112
Centerville, Pa., U.S.	F2	115
Centerville, S.D., U.S.	D9	118
Centerville, Tn., U.S.	B4	119
Centerville, Ut., U.S.	C4	121
Cento, Italy	E6	14
Central, N.M., U.S.	E1	108
Central, S.C., U.S.	B2	117
Central, Cordillera, mts., Bol.	G6	54
Central, Cordillera, mts., Col.	E5	58
Central, Cordillera, mts., Peru	E3	54
Central, Massif, mts., Fr.	G10	10
Central, Planalto, plat., Braz.	G9	54
Central, Sistema, mts., Spain	E6	12
Central African Republic, ctry., Afr.	G10	42
Central City, Co., U.S.	B5	83
Central City, Il., U.S.	E4	90
Central City, Ia., U.S.	B6	92
Central City, Ky., U.S.	C2	94
Central City, Ne., U.S.	C7	104
Central City, Pa., U.S.	F4	115
Central Falls, R.I., U.S.	B4	116
Central Heights, Az., U.S.	D5	80
Centralia, Il., U.S.	E4	90
Centralia, Mo., U.S.	B5	102
Centralia, Wa., U.S.	C3	124
Central Islip, N.Y., U.S.	n15	109
Central Lake, Mi., U.S.	C5	99
Central Makrān Range, mts., Pak.	D1	36
Central Park, Wa., U.S.	C2	124
Central Point, Or., U.S.	E4	114
Central Square, N.Y., U.S.	B4	109
Central Valley, Ca., U.S.	B2	82
Central Valley, N.Y., U.S.	D6	109
Central Village, Ct., U.S.	C8	84
Centre, Al., U.S.	A4	78
Centre, co., Pa., U.S.	E6	115
Centre Hall, Pa., U.S.	E6	115
Centreville, Al., U.S.	C2	78
Centreville, Il., U.S.	E3	90
Centreville, Md., U.S.	B5	97
Centreville, Mi., U.S.	G5	99
Centreville, Ms., U.S.	D2	101
Centuria, Wi., U.S.	C1	126
Century, Fl., U.S.	u14	86
Cepu, Indon.	m15	33a
Ceram Sea see Seram, Laut, Indon.	F8	32
Cerbat Mountains, mts., Az., U.S.	B1	80
Ceredo, W.V., U.S.	C2	125
Čeremchovo, Russia	G14	24
Čerepovec, Russia	B20	18
Ceres, Ca., U.S.	D3	82
Ceresco, Ne., U.S.	C9	104
Céret, Fr.	J9	10
Cereté, Col.	C5	58
Cerf Island, i., Sey.	C10	44
Cerignola, Italy	H10	14
Cérilly, Fr.	F9	10
Čerkassy, Ukr.	H4	22
Čerkessk, Russia	I6	22
Čern'achovsk, Russia	G4	18
Černigov, Ukr.	G4	22
Černogorsk, Russia	G12	24
Černyševskij, Russia	E16	24
Cerralvo, Isla, i., Mex.	E5	62
Cerritos, Mex.	F9	62
Cerro de Pasco, Peru	F3	54
Cerro Gordo, Il., U.S.	D5	90
Cerro Gordo, co., Ia., U.S.	A4	92
Čerskij, Russia	D26	24
Čerskogo, Chrebet, mts., Russia	E23	24
Cervera del Río Alhama, Spain	C10	12
Cervera de Pisuerga, Spain	C7	12
Cervia, Italy	E7	14
Cesena, Italy	E7	14
Cesenatico, Italy	E7	14
České Budějovice, Czech.	G14	8
Cessnock, Austl.	F10	50
Ceuta, Sp. N. Afr.	A4	42
Ceyhan, Tur.	A4	40
Ceylânpınar, Tur.	A7	40
Ceylon see Sri Lanka, ctry., Asia	H5	36
Chabanais, Fr.	G7	10
Chabarovsk, Russia	H21	24
Chachoengsao, Thai.	H6	34
Chaco, stm., N.M., U.S.	A1	108
Chaco Culture National Historic Park, N.M., U.S.	A2	108

Name	Map Ref	Page
Chacon, Cape, c., Ak., U.S.	**n24**	79
Chad, ctry., Afr.	**E9**	42
Chad, Lake (Lac Tchad), l., Afr.	**F8**	42
Chadbourn, N.C., U.S.	**C4**	110
Chadds Ford, Pa., U.S.	**G10**	115
Chadileuvú, stm., Arg.	**D3**	56
Chadron, Ne., U.S.	**B3**	104
Chadwicks, N.Y., U.S.	**B5**	109
Chaffee, Mo., U.S.	**D8**	102
Chaffee, co., Co., U.S.	**C4**	83
Chaffin, Ma., U.S.	**B4**	98
Chaghcharān, Afg.	**C1**	38
Chagny, Fr.	**F11**	10
Chagos Archipelago, is., B.I.O.T.	**G17**	2
Chagrin Falls, Oh., U.S.	**A4**	112
Chaibāsā, India	**I11**	38
Chaîne Annamitique, mts., Asia	**F9**	34
Chakachamna Lake, l., Ak., U.S.	**g15**	79
Chake Chake, Tan.	**C7**	44
Chalais, Fr.	**G7**	10
Chalbi Desert, des., Kenya	**H2**	46
Chalcuapa, El Sal.	**H3**	64
Chaleur Bay, b., Can.	**B4**	71
Chalfonte, De., U.S.	**h7**	85
Chālisgaon, India	**B3**	37
Chalk River, Ont., Can.	**A7**	73
Challans, Fr.	**F5**	10
Challis, Id., U.S.	**E4**	89
Chalmette, La., U.S.	**E6**	95
Chalonnes-sur-Loire, Fr.	**E6**	10
Châlons-sur-Marne, Fr.	**D11**	10
Chalon-sur-Saône, Fr.	**F11**	10
Châlus, Fr.	**G7**	10
Cham, Ger.	**F12**	8
Chama, N.M., U.S.	**A3**	108
Chama, Rio, stm., N.M., U.S.	**A3**	108
Chaman, Pak.	**E2**	38
Chambal, stm., India	**G7**	38
Chamberlain, S.D., U.S.	**D6**	118
Chamberlain Lake, l., Me., U.S.	**B3**	96
Chamberlin, Mount, mtn., Ak., U.S.	**B10**	79
Chambers, co., Al., U.S.	**C4**	78
Chambers, co., Tx., U.S.	**E5**	120
Chambersburg, Pa., U.S.	**G6**	115
Chambers Island, i., Wi., U.S.	**C6**	126
Chambéry, Fr.	**G12**	10
Chambi, Jebel, mtn., Tun.	**A7**	42
Chamblee, Ga., U.S.	**h8**	87
Chambly, Que., Can.	**D4**	74
Chambon-sur-Voueize, Fr.	**F9**	10
Chamisal, N.M., U.S.	**A4**	108
Chamonix-Mont-Blanc, Fr.	**G13**	10
Champagne, hist. reg., Fr.	**D11**	10
Champagnole, Fr.	**F12**	10
Champaign, Il., U.S.	**C5**	90
Champaign, co., Il., U.S.	**C5**	90
Champaign, co., Oh., U.S.	**B2**	112
Champassak, Laos	**G8**	34
Champion, Oh., U.S.	**A5**	112
Champlain, Lake, l., N.A.	**C12**	76
Champlin, Mn., U.S.	**m12**	100
Chāmrājnagar Rāmasamudram, India	**G4**	37
Chañaral, Chile	**B2**	56
Chance, Md., U.S.	**D6**	97
Chanch, Mong.	**A7**	26
Chanchelulla Peak, mtn., Ca., U.S.	**B2**	82
Chandalar, stm., Ak., U.S.	**B10**	79
Chandausi, India	**F8**	38
Chandeleur Islands, is., La., U.S.	**E7**	95
Chandeleur Sound, strt., La., U.S.	**E6**	95
Chandīgarh, India	**E7**	38
Chandler, Que., Can.	**k14**	74
Chandler, Az., U.S.	**D4**	80
Chandler, In., U.S.	**H3**	91
Chandler, Ok., U.S.	**B5**	113
Chandler, Tx., U.S.	**C5**	120
Chandler Heights, Az., U.S.	**m9**	80
Chāndpur, Bngl.	**I14**	38
Chāndpur, India	**F8**	38
Chandrapur, India	**C5**	37
Chandyga, Russia	**E21**	24
Chang (Yangtze), stm., China	**E10**	26
Changajn Nuruu, mts., Mong.	**B6**	26
Changchun, China	**C12**	26
Changde, China	**F9**	26
Changhua, Tai.	**K9**	28
Changjiang, China	**J5**	28
Changli, China	**D10**	26
Changsha, China	**G1**	28
Changshu, China	**D9**	28
Changzhi, China	**D9**	26
Changzhou (Changchow), China	**D8**	28
Chanhassen, Mn., U.S.	**n11**	100
Chanka, Ozero (Xingkathu), l., Asia	**I20**	24
Channahon, Il., U.S.	**B5**	90
Channapatna, India	**F4**	37
Channel Islands, is., Eur.	**C4**	10
Channel Islands National Park, Ca., U.S.	**F4**	82
Channel Lake, Il., U.S.	**H8**	90
Channel-Port-aux-Basques, Newf., Can.	**E2**	72
Channelview, Tx., U.S.	**r14**	120
Chantada, Spain	**C4**	12
Chantajskoje, Ozero, l., Russia	**D12**	24
Chanthaburi, Thai.	**H7**	34
Chantilly, Va., U.S.	**g12**	123
Chantrey Inlet, b., N.W. Ter., Can.	**C13**	66
Chanute, Ks., U.S.	**E8**	93
Chanute Air Force Base, mil., Il., U.S.	**C5**	90
Chaoan, China	**L5**	28
Chao Phraya, stm., Thai.	**G6**	34
Chapala, Lago de, l., Mex.	**G8**	62
Chaparral, Col.	**F5**	58
Chapčeranga, Russia	**H16**	24
Chapel Hill, N.C., U.S.	**B3**	110
Chapel Hill, Tn., U.S.	**B5**	119
Chaplin, stm., Ky., U.S.	**C4**	94
Chaplin Lake, l., Sask., Can.	**G2**	75
Chapman, Ks., U.S.	**D6**	93
Chapman Pond, l., R.I., U.S.	**F1**	116
Chapmanville, W.V., U.S.	**D2**	125
Chappaquiddick Island, i., Ma., U.S.	**D7**	98
Chappell, Ne., U.S.	**C3**	104
Chāpra, India	**H11**	38
Chapultepec, mtn., Mex.	**F8**	62
Charadai, Arg.	**B5**	56
Charcas, Mex.	**F9**	62
Chardon, Oh., U.S.	**A4**	112
Chardzhou see Čardžou, Turk.	**J10**	22
Charenton, La., U.S.	**E4**	95
Chari, stm., Afr.	**F9**	42
Chārīkār, Afg.	**C3**	38
Chariton, Ia., U.S.	**C4**	92
Chariton, co., Mo., U.S.	**B4**	102
Chariton, stm., U.S.	**A5**	102
Charity, Guy.	**D13**	58
Charleroi, Bel.	**E4**	8
Charleroi, Pa., U.S.	**F2**	115
Charles, co., Md., U.S.	**C3**	97
Charles, stm., Ma., U.S.	**B5**	98
Charles, Cape, c., Va., U.S.	**C6**	123
Charles A. Goodwin Dam, Ct., U.S.	**B3**	84
Charlesbourg, Que., Can.	**n17**	74
Charles City, Ia., U.S.	**A5**	92
Charles City, co., Va., U.S.	**C5**	123
Charles Island, i., N.W. Ter., Can.	**D18**	66
Charles Mill Lake, res., Oh., U.S.	**B3**	112
Charles Mix, co., S.D., U.S.	**D7**	118
Charles Mound, hill, Il., U.S.	**A3**	90
Charleston, Ar., U.S.	**B1**	81
Charleston, Il., U.S.	**D5**	90
Charleston, Ms., U.S.	**A3**	101
Charleston, Mo., U.S.	**E8**	102
Charleston, Or., U.S.	**D2**	114
Charleston, S.C., U.S.	**F8**	117
Charleston, Tn., U.S.	**D9**	119
Charleston, W.V., U.S.	**C3**	125
Charleston, co., S.C., U.S.	**F8**	117
Charleston Air Force Base, mil., S.C., U.S.	**k11**	117
Charleston Naval Shipyard, mil., S.C., U.S.	**k12**	117
Charleston Peak, mtn., Nv., U.S.	**G6**	105
Charlestown, In., U.S.	**H6**	91
Charlestown, N.H., U.S.	**D2**	106
Charlestown, R.I., U.S.	**F2**	116
Charles Town, W.V., U.S.	**B7**	125
Charleville, Austl.	**E9**	50
Charleville-Mézières, Fr.	**C11**	10
Charlevoix, Mi., U.S.	**C5**	99
Charlevoix, co., Mi., U.S.	**C5**	99
Charlevoix, Lake, l., Mi., U.S.	**C5**	99
Charlo, N.B., Can.	**B3**	71
Charlotte, Mi., U.S.	**F6**	99
Charlotte, N.C., U.S.	**B2**	110
Charlotte, Tn., U.S.	**A4**	119
Charlotte, Tx., U.S.	**E3**	120
Charlotte, co., Fl., U.S.	**F5**	86
Charlotte, co., Va., U.S.	**C4**	123
Charlotte Amalie, V.I.U.S.	**E15**	64
Charlotte Hall, Md., U.S.	**D4**	97
Charlotte Harbor, Fl., U.S.	**F4**	86
Charlotte Harbor, b., Fl., U.S.	**F4**	86
Charlottenberg, Swe.	**G9**	6
Charlottesville, Va., U.S.	**B4**	123
Charlottetown, P.E.I., Can.	**C6**	71
Charlton, co., Ga., U.S.	**F4**	87
Charmco, W.V., U.S.	**C4**	125
Charmes, Fr.	**D13**	10
Charny, Que., Can.	**C6**	74
Charolles, Fr.	**F11**	10
Chārsadda, Pak.	**C4**	38
Charters Towers, Austl.	**D9**	50
Chartres, Fr.	**D8**	10
Char Us Nuur, l., Mong.	**B5**	26
Chascomús, Arg.	**D5**	56
Chase, B.C., Can.	**D8**	69
Chase, Md., U.S.	**B5**	97
Chase, co., Ks., U.S.	**D7**	93
Chase, co., Ne., U.S.	**D4**	104
Chase City, Va., U.S.	**D4**	123
Chase Field Naval Air Station, mil., Tx., U.S.	**E4**	120
Chaska, Mn., U.S.	**F5**	100
Chassahowitzka Bay, b., Fl., U.S.	**D4**	86
Chassell, Mi., U.S.	**B2**	99
Chatanbulag, Mong.	**C8**	26
Chatanga, Russia	**C14**	24
Chatanga, stm., Russia	**C14**	24
Chatangskij Zaliv, b., Russia	**C15**	24
Châteaubriant, Fr.	**E5**	10
Château-du-Loir, Fr.	**E7**	10
Châteaudun, Fr.	**D8**	10
Château-Gontier, Fr.	**E6**	10
Châteauguay, Que., Can.	**D4**	74
Château-Landon, Fr.	**D9**	10
Châteaulin, Fr.	**D2**	10
Châteaumeillant, Fr.	**F9**	10
Châteauneuf-sur-Charente, Fr.	**G6**	10
Châteauneuf-sur-Loire, Fr.	**E9**	10
Château-Renault, Fr.	**E7**	10
Château-Richer, Que., Can.	**C6**	74
Châteauroux, Fr.	**F8**	10
Château-Thierry, Fr.	**C10**	10
Châtellerault, Fr.	**F7**	10
Chatfield, Mn., U.S.	**G6**	100
Chatgal, Mong.	**A7**	26
Chatham, N.B., Can.	**B4**	71
Chatham, Ont., Can.	**E2**	73
Chatham, Eng., U.K.	**J13**	7
Chatham, Il., U.S.	**D4**	90
Chatham, La., U.S.	**B3**	95
Chatham, Ma., U.S.	**C8**	98
Chatham, N.J., U.S.	**B4**	107
Chatham, N.Y., U.S.	**C7**	109
Chatham, Va., U.S.	**D3**	123
Chatham, co., Ga., U.S.	**E5**	87
Chatham, co., N.C., U.S.	**B3**	110
Chatham Strait, strt., Ak., U.S.	**m22**	79
Châtillon, Italy	**D2**	14
Châtillon-Coligny, Fr.	**E9**	10
Châtillon-sur-Indre, Fr.	**F8**	10
Châtillon-sur-Seine, Fr.	**E11**	10
Chatom, Al., U.S.	**D1**	78
Chatsworth, Ga., U.S.	**B2**	87
Chatsworth, Il., U.S.	**C5**	90
Chatsworth Reservoir, res., Ca., U.S.	**m11**	82
Chattahoochee, Fl., U.S.	**B2**	86
Chattahoochee, co., Ga., U.S.	**D2**	87
Chattahoochee, stm., U.S.	**E1**	87
Chattanooga, Tn., U.S.	**D8**	119
Chattaroy, W.V., U.S.	**D2**	125
Chattooga, co., Ga., U.S.	**B1**	87
Chattooga, stm., U.S.	**B1**	117
Chatuge Lake, res., U.S.	**g9**	110
Chatyrka, Russia	**E29**	24
Chaudière, stm., Que., Can.	**C7**	74
Chau Doc, Viet.	**I8**	34
Chauk, Mya.	**D3**	34
Chaumont, Fr.	**D12**	10
Chauncey, Oh., U.S.	**C3**	112
Chauny, Fr.	**C10**	10
Chautauqua, co., Ks., U.S.	**E7**	93
Chautauqua, co., N.Y., U.S.	**C1**	109
Chautauqua Lake, l., N.Y., U.S.	**C1**	109
Chauvigny, Fr.	**F7**	10
Chauvin, La., U.S.	**E5**	95
Chavakkad, India	**G4**	37
Chaves, Port.	**D4**	12
Chaves, co., N.M., U.S.	**D5**	108
Cháviva, Col.	**E6**	58
Chbukha Dzong, Bhu.	**G13**	38
Cheaha Mountain, mtn., Al., U.S.	**B4**	78
Cheat, Shavers Fork, stm., W.V., U.S.	**B5**	125
Cheatham, co., Tn., U.S.	**A4**	119
Chebanse, Il., U.S.	**C6**	90
Cheboygan, Mi., U.S.	**C6**	99
Cheboygan, co., Mi., U.S.	**C6**	99
Chech, Erg, des., Afr.	**C5**	42
Checotah, Ok., U.S.	**B6**	113
Chedabucto Bay, b., N.S., Can.	**D8**	71
Cheduba Island, i., Mya.	**E2**	34
Cheektowaga, N.Y., U.S.	**C2**	109
Cheeseman Lake, res., Co., U.S.	**B5**	83
Chehalem Mountains, mts., Or., U.S.	**h12**	114
Chehalis, Wa., U.S.	**C3**	124
Chehalis, stm., Wa., U.S.	**C2**	124
Cheju-do, i., S. Kor.	**E12**	26
Chelan, Wa., U.S.	**B5**	124
Chelan, co., Wa., U.S.	**B4**	124
Chelan, Lake, l., Wa., U.S.	**A5**	124
Chelan Mountains, mts., Wa., U.S.	**A5**	124
Chełm, Pol.	**D23**	8
Chełmno, Pol.	**B18**	8
Chelmsford, Eng., U.K.	**J13**	7
Chelmsford, Ma., U.S.	**A5**	98
Chelsea, Que., Can.	**D2**	74
Chelsea, Al., U.S.	**g7**	78
Chelsea, Ma., U.S.	**B5**	98
Chelsea, Mi., U.S.	**F6**	99
Chelsea, Ok., U.S.	**A6**	113
Cheltenham, Eng., U.K.	**J10**	7
Cheltenham, Md., U.S.	**C4**	97
Chelva, Spain	**F11**	12
Chelyabinsk see Čel'abinsk, Russia	**F10**	22
Chelyan, W.V., U.S.	**C3**	125
Chemehuevi Indian Reservation, Ca., U.S.	**E6**	82
Chemnitz, Ger.	**E12**	8
Chemquasabamticook Lake (Ross Lake), l., Me., U.S.	**B3**	96
Chemung, co., N.Y., U.S.	**C4**	109
Chemung, stm., Pa., U.S.	**C8**	115
Chemung Lake, l., Ont., Can.	**C6**	73
Chenāb, stm., Asia	**E5**	38
Chenachane, Alg.	**C6**	42
Chenango, co., N.Y., U.S.	**C5**	109
Chenango, stm., N.Y., U.S.	**C5**	109
Chenango Bridge, N.Y., U.S.	**C5**	109
Chenes, River Aux, b., La., U.S.	**k12**	95
Chénéville, Que., Can.	**D2**	74
Cheney, Ks., U.S.	**E6**	93
Cheney, Wa., U.S.	**B8**	124
Cheney Reservoir, res., Ks., U.S.	**E6**	93
Cheneyville, La., U.S.	**C3**	95
Chengde, China	**C10**	26
Chengdu, China	**E7**	26
Chengutu, Zimb.	**E6**	44
Chenoa, Il., U.S.	**C5**	90
Chenoweth, Or., U.S.	**B5**	114
Chepachet, R.I., U.S.	**B2**	116
Chepachet, stm., R.I., U.S.	**B2**	116
Chepo, Pan.	**J8**	64
Chequamegon Bay, b., Wi., U.S.	**B3**	126
Cheraw, S.C., U.S.	**B8**	117
Cherbourg, Fr.	**C5**	10
Chergui, Chott ech, l., Alg.	**B6**	42
Cherkasy, Ukr.	**H4**	22
Chernihiv, Ukr.	**G4**	22
Chernivtsi, Ukr.	**H3**	22
Cherokee, Al., U.S.	**A2**	78
Cherokee, Ia., U.S.	**B2**	92
Cherokee, Ks., U.S.	**E9**	93
Cherokee, Ok., U.S.	**A3**	113
Cherokee, co., Al., U.S.	**A4**	78
Cherokee, co., Ga., U.S.	**B2**	87
Cherokee, co., Ia., U.S.	**B2**	92
Cherokee, co., Ks., U.S.	**E9**	93
Cherokee, co., N.C., U.S.	**f8**	110
Cherokee, co., Ok., U.S.	**B6**	113
Cherokee, co., S.C., U.S.	**A4**	117
Cherokee, co., Tx., U.S.	**D5**	120
Cherokee Indian Reservation, N.C., U.S.	**f9**	110
Cherokee Lake, res., Tn., U.S.	**C10**	119
Cherokees, Lake O' The, res., Ok., U.S.	**A7**	113
Cherokee Village, Ar., U.S.	**A4**	81
Cherry, co., Ne., U.S.	**B4**	104
Cherry Creek, stm., S.D., U.S.	**C3**	118
Cherry Hill, N.J., U.S.	**D2**	107
Cherry Point, c., Va., U.S.	**C6**	123
Cherry Point Marine Corps Air Station, mil., N.C., U.S.	**C6**	110
Cherryvale, Ks., U.S.	**E8**	93
Cherry Valley, Ar., U.S.	**B5**	81
Cherry Valley, Il., U.S.	**A5**	90
Cherryville, N.C., U.S.	**B1**	110
Chesaning, Mi., U.S.	**E6**	99
Chesapeake, Oh., U.S.	**D3**	112
Chesapeake, Va., U.S.	**D6**	123
Chesapeake, W.V., U.S.	**C3**	125
Chesapeake and Delaware Canal, U.S.	**B3**	85
Chesapeake Bay, b., U.S.	**D11**	76
Chesapeake Bay Bridge-Tunnel, Va., U.S.	**D7**	123
Chesapeake Beach, Md., U.S.	**C4**	97
Chesapeake City, Md., U.S.	**A6**	97
Chesdin, Lake, res., Va., U.S.	**C5**	123
Cheshire, Ct., U.S.	**D4**	84
Cheshire, co., N.H., U.S.	**E2**	106
Cheshire Reservoir, res., Ma., U.S.	**A1**	98
Chesley, Ont., Can.	**C3**	73
Chesnee, S.C., U.S.	**A4**	117
Chester, Eng., U.K.	**H10**	7
Chester, Ca., U.S.	**B3**	82
Chester, Ct., U.S.	**D6**	84
Chester, Ga., U.S.	**D3**	87
Chester, Il., U.S.	**F4**	90
Chester, Md., U.S.	**C5**	97
Chester, Mt., U.S.	**B6**	103
Chester, N.H., U.S.	**E4**	106
Chester, N.Y., U.S.	**D6**	109
Chester, Pa., U.S.	**G11**	115
Chester, S.C., U.S.	**B5**	117
Chester, Vt., U.S.	**E3**	122
Chester, Va., U.S.	**C5**	123
Chester, W.V., U.S.	**A4**	125
Chester, co., Pa., U.S.	**G10**	115
Chester, co., S.C., U.S.	**B5**	117
Chester, co., Tn., U.S.	**B3**	119
Chester, stm., Md., U.S.	**B5**	97
Chester Basin, N.S., Can.	**E5**	71
Chester Depot, Vt., U.S.	**E3**	122
Chesterfield, In., U.S.	**D6**	91
Chesterfield, S.C., U.S.	**B7**	117
Chesterfield, co., S.C., U.S.	**B7**	117
Chesterfield, co., Va., U.S.	**C5**	123
Chesterfield, Îles, is., N. Cal.	**C11**	50
Chesterfield Inlet, N.W. Ter., Can.	**D14**	66
Chesterfield Inlet, b., N.W. Ter., Can.	**D14**	66
Chesterton, In., U.S.	**A3**	91
Chestertown, Md., U.S.	**B5**	97
Chesterville, Ont., Can.	**B9**	73
Chesuncook Lake, l., Me., U.S.	**C3**	96
Cheswick, Pa., U.S.	**h14**	115
Cheswold, De., U.S.	**D3**	85
Cheta, stm., Russia	**C13**	24
Chetac, Lake, l., Wi., U.S.	**C2**	126
Chetco, stm., Or., U.S.	**E2**	114
Chetek, Wi., U.S.	**C2**	126
Chetek, Lake, l., Wi., U.S.	**C2**	126
Chetopa, Ks., U.S.	**E8**	93
Chetumal Bay, b., N.A.	**H15**	62
Chetwynd, B.C., Can.	**B7**	69
Chevak, Ak., U.S.	**C6**	79
Cheval Blanc, Pointe du, c., Haiti	**E11**	64
Cheviot, Oh., U.S.	**C1**	112
Chevreuil, Point, c., La., U.S.	**E4**	95
Chevy Chase, Md., U.S.	**C3**	97
Chewack, stm., Wa., U.S.	**A5**	124
Chew Bahir (Lake Stefanie), l., Afr.	**H2**	46
Chewelah, Wa., U.S.	**A8**	124
Cheyenne, Ok., U.S.	**B2**	113
Cheyenne, Wy., U.S.	**E8**	127
Cheyenne, co., Co., U.S.	**C8**	83
Cheyenne, co., Ks., U.S.	**C2**	93
Cheyenne, co., Ne., U.S.	**C2**	104
Cheyenne, stm., U.S.	**C4**	118
Cheyenne, Dry Fork, stm., Wy., U.S.	**C7**	127
Cheyenne River Indian Reservation, S.D., U.S.	**B4**	118
Cheyenne Wells, Co., U.S.	**C8**	83
Chezhou, China	**J1**	28
Chhatarpur, India	**H8**	38
Chhindwāra, India	**I8**	38
Chi, stm., Thai.	**G8**	34
Chiai, Tai.	**L9**	28
Chiali, Tai.	**L9**	28
Chiang Khan, Thai.	**F6**	34
Chiang Mai, Thai.	**E5**	34
Chiang Rai, Thai.	**E5**	34
Chiari, Italy	**D4**	14
Chiavari, Italy	**E4**	14
Chiavenna, Italy	**C4**	14
Chiba, Japan	**G13**	30
Chiblow Lake, l., Ont., Can.	**A1**	73
Chibougamau, Que., Can.	**k12**	74
Chibuto, Moz.	**F6**	44
Chicago, Il., U.S.	**B6**	90
Chicago Heights, Il., U.S.	**B6**	90
Chicago Sanitary and Ship Canal, Il., U.S.	**k8**	90
Chicamacomico, stm., Md., U.S.	**D6**	97
Chicapa, stm., Afr.	**C4**	44
Chichagof Island, i., Ak., U.S.	**m22**	79
Chīchāwatni, Pak.	**E5**	38
Chichén Itzá, Mex.	**G15**	62
Chichibu, Japan	**G12**	30
Chickahominy, stm., Va., U.S.	**C5**	123
Chickamauga, Ga., U.S.	**B1**	87
Chickamauga and Chattanooga National Military Park, U.S.	**k11**	119
Chickamauga Dam, Tn., U.S.	**h11**	119
Chickamauga Lake, res., Tn., U.S.	**D8**	119
Chickasaw, Al., U.S.	**E1**	78
Chickasaw, co., Ia., U.S.	**A5**	92
Chickasaw, co., Ms., U.S.	**B5**	101
Chickasawhay, stm., Ms., U.S.	**D5**	101
Chickasaw National Recreation Area, Ok., U.S.	**C5**	113
Chickasha, Ok., U.S.	**B4**	113
Chickasha, Lake, res., Ok., U.S.	**B3**	113
Chickwolnepy Stream, stm., N.H., U.S.	**A4**	106
Chiclana de la Frontera, Spain	**I5**	12
Chiclayo, Peru	**E3**	54
Chico, Ca., U.S.	**C3**	82
Chicoa, Moz.	**E6**	44
Chicopee, Ga., U.S.	**B3**	87
Chicopee, Ma., U.S.	**B2**	98
Chicora, Pa., U.S.	**E2**	115
Chicot, Lake, l., Ar., U.S.	**D4**	81
Chicot Island, i., La., U.S.	**E6**	95
Chicoutimi, Que., Can.	**A6**	74
Chicoutimi, stm., Que., Can.	**A6**	74
Chidambaram, India	**G5**	37
Chidley, Cape, c., Can.	**D20**	66
Chiefland, Fl., U.S.	**C4**	86
Chieri, Italy	**D2**	14
Chieti, Italy	**G9**	14
Chifeng, China	**C10**	26
Chigasaki, Japan	**G12**	30
Chignecto, Cape, c., N.S., Can.	**D5**	71
Chignecto Bay, b., Can.	**D5**	71
Ch'ihu, Tai.	**L9**	28
Chihuahua, Mex.	**C6**	62
Chikaskia, stm., U.S.	**A4**	113
Chik Ballāpur, India	**F4**	37
Chikmagalūr, India	**F3**	37
Chilakalūrupet, India	**D6**	37
Chilapa de Alvarez, Mex.	**I10**	62
Chilās, Pak.	**C6**	38
Childersburg, Al., U.S.	**B3**	78
Childress, Tx., U.S.	**B2**	120
Childress, co., Tx., U.S.	**B2**	120
Chile, ctry., S.A.	**C2**	56
Chilete, Peru	**E3**	54
Chilhowie, Va., U.S.	**f10**	123
Chililabombwe (Bancroft), Zam.	**D5**	44
Chilka Lake, l., India	**C8**	37
Chilko, stm., B.C., Can.	**D6**	69
Chilko Lake, l., B.C., Can.	**D5**	69
Chillán, Chile	**D2**	56
Chillicothe, Il., U.S.	**C4**	90
Chillicothe, Mo., U.S.	**B4**	102
Chillicothe, Oh., U.S.	**C3**	112
Chilliwack, B.C., Can.	**E7**	69
Chillum, Md., U.S.	**f9**	97
Chiloé, Isla de, i., Chile	**E2**	56
Chilok, Russia	**G16**	24
Chiloquin, Or., U.S.	**E5**	114
Chilpancingo [de los Bravos], Mex.	**I10**	62
Chilton, Wi., U.S.	**D5**	126
Chilton, co., Al., U.S.	**C3**	78
Chilung, Tai.	**J10**	28
Chilwa, Lake, l., Afr.	**E7**	44
Chimacum, Wa., U.S.	**A3**	124
Chimayo, N.M., U.S.	**A4**	108
Chimborazo, vol., Ec.	**H3**	58
Chimbote, Peru	**E3**	54
Chimkent see Čimkent, Kaz.	**I11**	22
Chimki, Russia	**F20**	18
Chimney Rock, mtn., Ne., U.S.	**C2**	104
China, ctry., Asia	**D7**	26
China Grove, N.C., U.S.	**B2**	110
China Lake, l., Me., U.S.	**D3**	96
Chinandega, Nic.	**H4**	64
Chincha Alta, Peru	**F3**	54
Chincilla de Monte Aragón, Spain	**G10**	12
Chincoteague, Va., U.S.	**C7**	123
Chincoteague Bay, b., U.S.	**D7**	97
Chinde, Moz.	**E7**	44
Chindwinn, stm., Mya.	**C3**	34
Chingleput, India	**F5**	37
Chingola, Zam.	**D5**	44
Ch'ingshui, Tai.	**K9**	28
Chin Hills, hills, Mya.	**D2**	34
Chinhoyi, Zimb.	**E6**	44
Chiniot, Pak.	**E5**	38
Chinitna Point, c., Ak., U.S.	**h15**	79
Chinju, S. Kor.	**D12**	26
Chinko, stm., Cen. Afr. Rep.	**G10**	42
Chinkuashih, Tai.	**J10**	28
Chinle, Az., U.S.	**A6**	80
Chinmen Tao, i., Tai.	**K7**	28
Chino, Ca., U.S.	**F5**	82
Chinon, Fr.	**E7**	10
Chinook, Mt., U.S.	**B7**	103
Chinook, Wa., U.S.	**C2**	124
Chinook, Lake, res., Or., U.S.	**C5**	114
Chino Valley, Az., U.S.	**C3**	80
Chinshan, Tai.	**J10**	28
Chioggia, Italy	**D7**	14
Chipata, Zam.	**D6**	44
Chipita Park, Co., U.S.	**C6**	83
Chipley, Fl., U.S.	**u16**	86
Chipman, N.B., Can.	**C4**	71
Chipola, stm., Fl., U.S.	**B1**	86
Chippewa, co., Mi., U.S.	**B6**	99
Chippewa, co., Mn., U.S.	**E3**	100
Chippewa, co., Wi., U.S.	**C2**	126
Chippewa, stm., Mn., U.S.	**E3**	100
Chippewa, stm., Wi., U.S.	**D2**	126
Chippewa, Lake, l., Wi., U.S.	**C2**	126
Chippewa Falls, Wi., U.S.	**D2**	126
Chipuxet, stm., R.I., U.S.	**F3**	116
Chiquimula, Guat.	**G3**	64
Chiquinquirá, Col.	**E6**	58
Chīrāla, India	**E6**	37
Chirfa, Niger	**D8**	42
Chirgis Nuur, l., Mong.	**B5**	26
Chiricahua Mountains, mts., Az., U.S.	**E6**	80
Chiricahua National Monument, Az., U.S.	**F6**	80
Chiricahua Peak, mtn., Az., U.S.	**F6**	80
Chiriguaná, Col.	**C6**	58
Chirikof Island, i., Ak., U.S.	**D8**	79
Chiriquí, Golfo, b., Pan.	**K6**	64
Chiriquí, Laguna de, b., Pan.	**J7**	64
Chirripó, Cerro, mtn., C.R.	**J6**	64
Chisago, co., Mn., U.S.	**E6**	100
Chisago City, Mn., U.S.	**E6**	100
Chisholm, Me., U.S.	**D2**	96
Chisholm, Mn., U.S.	**C6**	100
Chishtiān Mandi, Pak.	**F5**	38
Chişinău, Mol.	**H3**	22
Chisos Mountains, mts., Tx., U.S.	**E1**	120
Chitato, Ang.	**C4**	44
Chitembo, Ang.	**D3**	44
Chitina, stm., Ak., U.S.	**g19**	79
Chitipa, Mwi.	**C6**	44
Chitorgarh, India	**H6**	38
Chitose, Japan	**q19**	30a
Chitradurga, India	**E4**	37
Chitrāl, Pak.	**C4**	38
Chitré, Pan.	**K7**	64
Chittagong, Bngl.	**I14**	38
Chittenango, N.Y., U.S.	**B5**	109
Chittenden, co., Vt., U.S.	**C2**	122
Chittenden Reservoir, res., Vt., U.S.	**D3**	122
Chittoor, India	**F5**	37

Name	Map Ref	Page
Chiusi, Italy	F6	14
Chivasso, Italy	D2	14
Choapan, Mex.	I12	62
Chocolate Mountains, mts., U.S.	F6	82
Chocontá, Col.	E6	58
Choctaw, Ok., U.S.	B4	113
Choctaw, co., Al., U.S.	C1	78
Choctaw, co., Ms., U.S.	B4	101
Choctaw, co., Ok., U.S.	C6	113
Choctawhatchee Bay, b., Fl., U.S.	u15	86
Choctaw Indian Reservation, Ms., U.S.	C4	101
Choele-Choel, Arg.	D3	56
Cholet, Fr.	E6	10
Cholmsk, Russia	H22	24
Choluteca, Hond.	H4	64
Choma, Zam.	E5	44
Chomutov, Czech.	E13	8
Chon Buri, Thai.	H6	34
Chone, Ec.	H2	58
Ch'ŏngjin, N. Kor.	C12	26
Ch'ŏngju, S. Kor.	D12	26
Chongmingdao, i., China	D10	28
Chongqing, China	F8	26
Chŏnju, S. Kor.	D12	26
Chonos, Archipiélago de los, is., Chile	F2	56
Chonuu, Russia	D22	24
Choptank, stm., Md., U.S.	C6	97
Chōshi, Japan	G13	30
Chos Malal, Arg.	D2	56
Choteau, Mt., U.S.	C4	103
Chouteau, Ok., U.S.	A6	113
Chouteau, co., Mt., U.S.	C6	103
Chovd, Mong.	B5	26
Chövsgöl Nuur, l., Mong.	A7	26
Chowan, co., N.C., U.S.	A6	110
Chowan, stm., N.C., U.S.	A6	110
Chowchilla, Ca., U.S.	D3	82
Chrisman, Il., U.S.	D6	90
Christanshåb, Grnld.	C22	66
Christchurch, N.Z.	E4	52
Christian, co., Il., U.S.	D4	90
Christian, co., Ky., U.S.	D2	94
Christian, co., Mo., U.S.	E4	102
Christian, Cape, c., N.W. Ter., Can.	B19	66
Christiana, De., U.S.	B3	85
Christiana, Pa., U.S.	G9	115
Christiansburg, Va., U.S.	C2	123
Christian Sound, strt., Ak., U.S.	n22	79
Christiansted, V.I.U.S.	F15	64
Christina, stm., Alta., Can.	A5	68
Christina, stm., De., U.S.	B3	85
Christina, Lake, l., Mn., U.S.	D3	100
Christina Peak, mtn., Nv., U.S.	D6	105
Christmas, Fl., U.S.	D5	86
Christmas Island, dep., Oc.	H4	32
Christmas Lake, l., Or., U.S.	D6	114
Christopher, Il., U.S.	F4	90
Chroma, stm., Russia	C22	24
Chrzanów, Pol.	E19	8
Chubbuck, Id., U.S.	G6	89
Chugach Islands, is., Ak., U.S.	h16	79
Chugach Mountains, mts., Ak., U.S.	g18	79
Chūgoku-sanchi, mts., Japan	H5	30
Chugwater, Wy., U.S.	E8	127
Chugwater Creek, stm., Wy., U.S.	E8	127
Chukai, Malay.	L7	34
Chukchi Sea	C30	128
Chula Vista, Ca., U.S.	F5	82
Chulucanas, Peru	E2	54
Chumphon, Thai.	I5	34
Chum Saeng, Thai.	G6	34
Chunchi, Ec.	I3	58
Ch'unch'ŏn, S. Kor.	D12	26
Chunchula, Al., U.S.	E1	78
Ch'ungju, S. Kor.	D12	26
Chungking see Chongqing, China	F8	26
Chungli, Tai.	K10	28
Chungyang Shanmo, mts., Tai.	L10	28
Chuŏr Phnum Krâvanh, mts., Asia	H7	34
Chupadera Mesa, mtn., N.M., U.S.	D3	108
Chupaderos, Mex.	F8	62
Chuquicamata, Chile	A3	56
Chur, Switz.	F16	10
Church Hill, Tn., U.S.	C11	119
Churchill, Man., Can.	f9	70
Churchill, co., Nv., U.S.	D3	105
Churchill, stm., Can.	E13	66
Churchill, stm., Newf., Can.	h9	72
Churchill, Cape, c., Man., Can.	f9	70
Churchill, Mount, mtn., B.C., Can.	E6	69
Churchill Falls, wtfl, Newf., Can.	h8	72
Churchill Lake, l., Sask., Can.	m7	75
Churchill Lake, l., Me., U.S.	B3	96
Church Point, La., U.S.	D3	95
Church Rock, N.M., U.S.	B1	108
Churchton, Md., U.S.	C4	97
Churchville, N.Y., U.S.	B3	109
Churu, India	F6	38
Churubusco, In., U.S.	B7	91
Churuguara, Ven.	B8	58
Chuska Mountains, mts., Az., U.S.	A6	80
Chutag, Mong.	B7	26
Chuxian, China	C7	28
Chuxiong, China	B6	34
Chužir, Russia	G15	24
Cianjur, Indon.	G4	32
Cibecue, Az., U.S.	C5	80
Cibinong, Indon.	m13	33a
Cibola, co., N.M., U.S.	C1	108
Cibolo Creek, stm., Tx., U.S.	h7	120
Cicero, Il., U.S.	B6	90
Cicero, In., U.S.	D5	91
Ciechanów, Pol.	C20	8
Ciego de Avila, Cuba	D8	64
Ciempozuelos, Spain	E8	12
Ciénaga, Col.	B5	58
Cienfuegos, Cuba	C7	64
Cieszyn, Pol.	F18	8
Cieza, Spain	G10	12
Cifuentes, Spain	E9	12
Cikampek, Indon.	m13	33a
Cilacap, Indon.	m14	33a
Cilleruelo de Bezana, Spain	C8	12
Cimarron, Ks., U.S.	E3	93
Cimarron, N.M., U.S.	A5	108
Cimarron, co., Ok., U.S.	e8	113
Čimkent, Kaz.	I11	22
Çınarcık, Tur.	I13	16
Cincinnati, Oh., U.S.	C1	112
Çine, Tur.	L12	16
Ciney, Bel.	E5	8
Cinnaminson, N.J., U.S.	D3	107
Cipa, stm., Russia	F17	24
Cipolletti, Arg.	D3	56
Circle, Ak., U.S.	B11	79
Circle, Mt., U.S.	C11	103
Circle Pines, Mn., U.S.	m12	100
Circleville, Oh., U.S.	C3	112
Cirebon, Indon.	m14	32
Cirencester, Eng., U.K.	J11	7
Ciriè, Italy	D2	14
Cirò Marina, Italy	J12	14
Cisco, Tx., U.S.	C3	120
Cispus, stm., Wa., U.S.	C4	124
Cissna Park, Il., U.S.	C6	90
Cistierna, Spain	C6	12
Čita, Russia	G16	24
Citra, Fl., U.S.	C4	86
Citronelle, Al., U.S.	D1	78
Citrus, co., Fl., U.S.	D4	86
Città di Castello, Italy	F7	14
City of Refuge National Historical Park, Hi., U.S.	D5	88
City View, S.C., U.S.	B3	117
Ciudad, Mex.	F7	62
Ciudad Acuña, Mex.	C9	62
Ciudad Altamirano, Mex.	H9	62
Ciudad Bolívar, Ven.	C11	58
Ciudad Bolivia, Ven.	C7	58
Ciudad Camargo, Mex.	D7	62
Ciudad Chetumal, Mex.	H15	62
Ciudad del Carmen, Mex.	H14	62
Ciudad del Maíz, Mex.	F10	62
Ciudad de México (Mexico City), Mex.	H10	62
Ciudad de Nutrias, Ven.	C8	58
Ciudad de Valles, Mex.	G10	62
Ciudadela, Spain	E15	12
Ciudad Guayana, Ven.	C11	58
Ciudad Guzmán, Mex.	H8	62
Ciudad Hidalgo, Mex.	H9	62
Ciudad Ixtepec, Mex.	I12	62
Ciudad Jiménez, Mex.	D7	62
Ciudad Juárez, Mex.	B6	62
Ciudad Madero, Mex.	F11	62
Ciudad Mante, Mex.	F10	62
Ciudad Melchor Múzquiz, Mex.	D9	62
Ciudad Obregón, Mex.	D5	62
Ciudad Ojeda (Lagunillas), Ven.	B7	58
Ciudad Piar, Ven.	D11	58
Ciudad Real, Spain	G8	12
Ciudad Rodrigo, Spain	E5	12
Ciudad Victoria, Mex.	F10	62
Civita Castellana, Italy	G7	14
Civitanova Marche, Italy	F8	14
Civitavecchia, Italy	G6	14
Civray, Fr.	F7	10
C.J. Strike Reservoir, res., Id., U.S.	G3	89
Clackamas, Or., U.S.	h12	114
Clackamas, co., Or., U.S.	B4	114
Clacton-on-Sea, Eng., U.K.	J14	7
Claflin, Ks., U.S.	D5	93
Claiborne, co., La., U.S.	B2	95
Claiborne, co., Ms., U.S.	D3	101
Claiborne, co., Tn., U.S.	C10	119
Claiborne, Lake, res., La., U.S.	B3	95
Clair, N.B., Can.	B1	71
Claire, Lake, l., Alta., Can.	f8	68
Clair Engle Lake, res., Ca., U.S.	B2	82
Clairton, Pa., U.S.	F2	115
Clallam, co., Wa., U.S.	B1	124
Clallam Bay, Wa., U.S.	A1	124
Clamecy, Fr.	E10	10
Clam Lake, l., Wi., U.S.	C1	126
Clan Alpine Mountains, mts., Nv., U.S.	D4	105
Clanton, Al., U.S.	C3	78
Clanwilliam, S. Afr.	H3	44
Clara City, Mn., U.S.	F3	100
Clara Peak, mtn., Az., U.S.	C2	80
Clare, Mi., U.S.	E6	99
Clare, co., Mi., U.S.	E6	99
Claremont, Ca., U.S.	m13	82
Claremont, N.H., U.S.	D2	106
Claremont, N.C., U.S.	B1	110
Claremont, mtn., Ca., U.S.	C3	82
Claremore, Ok., U.S.	A6	113
Claremorris, Ire.	H3	7
Clarence, Ia., U.S.	C6	92
Clarence, Mo., U.S.	B5	102
Clarence Strait, strt., Ak., U.S.	n23	79
Clarendon, Ar., U.S.	C4	81
Clarendon, Tx., U.S.	B2	120
Clarendon, co., S.C., U.S.	D7	117
Clarendon, stm., Vt., U.S.	E2	122
Clarendon Hills, Il., U.S.	k9	90
Clarenville, Newf., Can.	D4	72
Claresholm, Alta., Can.	D4	68
Claridge, Pa., U.S.	F2	115
Clarinda, Ia., U.S.	D2	92
Clarines, Ven.	C10	58
Clarion, Ia., U.S.	B4	92
Clarion, Pa., U.S.	D3	115
Clarion, co., Pa., U.S.	D3	115
Clarion, stm., Pa., U.S.	D3	115
Clarión, Isla, i., Mex.	H2	62
Clarissa, Mn., U.S.	D4	100
Clark, N.J., U.S.	B4	107
Clark, S.D., U.S.	C8	118
Clark, co., Ar., U.S.	C2	81
Clark, co., Id., U.S.	E6	89
Clark, co., Il., U.S.	D6	90
Clark, co., In., U.S.	H6	91
Clark, co., Ks., U.S.	E4	93
Clark, co., Ky., U.S.	C5	94
Clark, co., Mo., U.S.	A6	102
Clark, co., Nv., U.S.	G6	105
Clark, co., Oh., U.S.	C2	112
Clark, co., S.D., U.S.	C8	118
Clark, co., Wa., U.S.	D3	124
Clark, co., Wi., U.S.	D3	126
Clark, Lake, l., Ak., U.S.	C9	79
Clark, Point, c., Ont., Can.	C3	73
Clarkdale, Az., U.S.	C3	80
Clarkdale, Ga., U.S.	h7	87
Clarke, co., Al., U.S.	D2	78
Clarke, co., Ga., U.S.	C3	87
Clarke, co., Ia., U.S.	D4	92
Clarke, co., Ms., U.S.	C5	101
Clarke, co., Va., U.S.	A4	123
Clarkesville, Ga., U.S.	B3	87
Clarkfield, Mn., U.S.	F3	100
Clark Fork, stm., U.S.	C1	103
Clarks, La., U.S.	B3	95
Clarks, stm., Ky., U.S.	f9	94
Clarksburg, Md., U.S.	B3	97
Clarksburg, W.V., U.S.	B4	125
Clarksdale, Ms., U.S.	A3	101
Clarks Grove, Mn., U.S.	G5	100
Clark's Harbour, N.S., Can.	F4	71
Clarks Hill, In., U.S.	D4	91
Clarkson, Ky., U.S.	C3	94
Clarkson, Ne., U.S.	C8	104
Clarks Summit, Pa., U.S.	m18	115
Clarkston, Ga., U.S.	h8	87
Clarkston, Mi., U.S.	F7	99
Clarkston, Ut., U.S.	B3	121
Clarkston, Wa., U.S.	C8	124
Clarksville, Ar., U.S.	B2	81
Clarksville, De., U.S.	F5	85
Clarksville, In., U.S.	H6	91
Clarksville, Ia., U.S.	B5	92
Clarksville, Tn., U.S.	A4	119
Clarksville, Tx., U.S.	C5	120
Clarksville, Va., U.S.	D4	123
Clarkton, Mo., U.S.	E8	102
Clarkton, N.C., U.S.	C4	110
Clatskanie, Or., U.S.	A3	114
Clatsop, co., Or., U.S.	A3	114
Claude, Tx., U.S.	B2	120
Clausthal-Zellerfeld, Ger.	D10	8
Clawson, Mi., U.S.	o15	99
Claxton, Ga., U.S.	D5	87
Clay, Ky., U.S.	C2	94
Clay, co., Al., U.S.	B4	78
Clay, co., Ar., U.S.	A5	81
Clay, co., Fl., U.S.	B5	86
Clay, co., Ga., U.S.	E2	87
Clay, co., Il., U.S.	E5	90
Clay, co., In., U.S.	F3	91
Clay, co., Ia., U.S.	A2	92
Clay, co., Ks., U.S.	C6	93
Clay, co., Ky., U.S.	C6	94
Clay, co., Mn., U.S.	D2	100
Clay, co., Ms., U.S.	B5	101
Clay, co., Mo., U.S.	B3	102
Clay, co., Ne., U.S.	D7	104
Clay, co., N.C., U.S.	f9	110
Clay, co., S.D., U.S.	E8	118
Clay, co., Tn., U.S.	C8	119
Clay, co., Tx., U.S.	C3	120
Clay, co., W.V., U.S.	C3	125
Clay Center, Ks., U.S.	C6	93
Clay Center, Ne., U.S.	D7	104
Clay City, Il., U.S.	E5	90
Clay City, In., U.S.	F3	91
Clay City, Ky., U.S.	C6	94
Clay Creek, stm., S.D., U.S.	D8	118
Claymont, De., U.S.	A4	85
Clayoquot Sound, strt., B.C., Can.	E4	69
Claypool, Az., U.S.	D5	80
Claysburg, Pa., U.S.	F5	115
Claysville, Pa., U.S.	F1	115
Clayton, Al., U.S.	D4	78
Clayton, De., U.S.	C3	85
Clayton, Ga., U.S.	B3	87
Clayton, In., U.S.	E4	91
Clayton, La., U.S.	C4	95
Clayton, Mo., U.S.	f13	102
Clayton, N.J., U.S.	D2	107
Clayton, N.M., U.S.	A6	108
Clayton, N.Y., U.S.	A4	109
Clayton, N.C., U.S.	B4	110
Clayton, Ok., U.S.	C6	113
Clayton, co., Ga., U.S.	C2	87
Clayton, co., Ia., U.S.	B6	92
Claytor Lake, res., Va., U.S.	C2	123
Clear, stm., R.I., U.S.	B2	116
Clear Boggy Creek, stm., Ok., U.S.	C5	113
Clear Creek, co., Co., U.S.	B5	83
Clear Creek, stm., Tn., U.S.	C9	119
Clear Creek, stm., Wy., U.S.	B6	127
Cleare, Cape, c., Ak., U.S.	D10	79
Clearfield, Ky., U.S.	B6	94
Clearfield, Pa., U.S.	D5	115
Clearfield, Ut., U.S.	B3	121
Clearfield, co., Pa., U.S.	D5	115
Clear Fork, stm., W.V., U.S.	D3	125
Clear Fork, stm., W.V., U.S.	n13	125
Clearlake, Ca., U.S.	C2	82
Clear Lake, Ia., U.S.	A4	92
Clear Lake, S.D., U.S.	C9	118
Clearlake, Wa., U.S.	A3	124
Clear Lake, Wi., U.S.	C1	126
Clear Lake, l., Ia., U.S.	A4	92
Clear Lake, l., Ut., U.S.	D3	121
Clear Lake, res., Ca., U.S.	C2	82
Clear Lake Reservoir, res., Ca., U.S.	B3	82
Clear Lake Shores, Tx., U.S.	r15	120
Clear Stream, stm., N.H., U.S.	g7	106
Clearwater, B.C., Can.	D7	69
Clearwater, Fl., U.S.	E4	86
Clearwater, Ks., U.S.	E6	93
Clearwater, S.C., U.S.	E4	117
Clearwater, co., Id., U.S.	C3	89
Clearwater, co., Mn., U.S.	C3	100
Clearwater, stm., Can.	A5	68
Clearwater, stm., Id., U.S.	C2	89
Clearwater, stm., Mn., U.S.	C3	100
Clearwater Lake, res., Mo., U.S.	D7	102
Clearwater Mountains, mts., Id., U.S.	C2	89
Cleburne, Tx., U.S.	C4	120
Cleburne, co., Al., U.S.	B4	78
Cleburne, co., Ar., U.S.	B3	81
Cle Elum, Wa., U.S.	B5	124
Cle Elum, stm., Wa., U.S.	B4	124
Cle Elum Lake, res., Wa., U.S.	B4	124
Clementon, N.J., U.S.	D3	107
Clemmons, N.C., U.S.	A2	110
Clemson, S.C., U.S.	B2	117
Clendenin, W.V., U.S.	C3	125
Clendening Lake, res., Oh., U.S.	B4	112
Cleona, Pa., U.S.	F9	115
Clermont, Que., Can.	B7	74
Clermont, Fr.	C9	10
Clermont, Fl., U.S.	D5	86
Clermont, co., Oh., U.S.	C1	112
Clermont-Ferrand, Fr.	G10	10
Cles, Italy	C6	14
Cleveland, Al., U.S.	A3	78
Cleveland, Ga., U.S.	B3	87
Cleveland, Mn., U.S.	F5	100
Cleveland, Ms., U.S.	B3	101
Cleveland, N.C., U.S.	B2	110
Cleveland, Oh., U.S.	A4	112
Cleveland, Ok., U.S.	A5	113
Cleveland, Tn., U.S.	D9	119
Cleveland, Tx., U.S.	D5	120
Cleveland, Wi., U.S.	k10	126
Cleveland, co., Ar., U.S.	D3	81
Cleveland, co., N.C., U.S.	B1	110
Cleveland, co., Ok., U.S.	B4	113
Cleveland, Mount, mtn., Mt., U.S.	B3	103
Cleveland Heights, Oh., U.S.	A4	112
Cleves, Oh., U.S.	o12	112
Clewiston, Fl., U.S.	F6	86
Clifden, Ire.	H2	7
Cliff Island, i., Me., U.S.	g7	96
Clifford, Ont., Can.	D4	73
Cliffside, N.C., U.S.	B1	110
Cliffside Park, N.J., U.S.	h9	107
Clifton, Az., U.S.	D6	80
Clifton, Co., U.S.	B2	83
Clifton, Il., U.S.	C6	90
Clifton, N.J., U.S.	B4	107
Clifton, S.C., U.S.	B4	117
Clifton, Tn., U.S.	B4	119
Clifton, Tx., U.S.	D4	120
Clifton Forge, Va., U.S.	C3	123
Clifton Knolls, N.Y., U.S.	C7	109
Clifton Springs, N.Y., U.S.	C3	109
Clinch, co., Ga., U.S.	F4	87
Clinch, stm., U.S.	D9	119
Clinchco, Va., U.S.	e9	123
Clinch Mountain, mtn., U.S.	C10	119
Clingmans Dome, mtn., U.S.	D10	119
Clinton, B.C., Can.	D7	69
Clinton, Ont., Can.	D3	73
Clinton, Ar., U.S.	B3	81
Clinton, Ct., U.S.	D5	84
Clinton, Il., U.S.	C5	90
Clinton, In., U.S.	E3	91
Clinton, Ia., U.S.	C7	92
Clinton, Ky., U.S.	f9	94
Clinton, La., U.S.	D4	95
Clinton, Me., U.S.	D3	96
Clinton, Md., U.S.	C4	97
Clinton, Ma., U.S.	B4	98
Clinton, Mi., U.S.	F7	99
Clinton, Ms., U.S.	C3	101
Clinton, Mo., U.S.	C4	102
Clinton, N.Y., U.S.	B5	109
Clinton, N.C., U.S.	C4	110
Clinton, Ok., U.S.	B3	113
Clinton, S.C., U.S.	C4	117
Clinton, Tn., U.S.	C9	119
Clinton, Ut., U.S.	B3	121
Clinton, Wa., U.S.	B3	124
Clinton, Wi., U.S.	F5	126
Clinton, co., Il., U.S.	E4	90
Clinton, co., In., U.S.	D4	91
Clinton, co., Ia., U.S.	C7	92
Clinton, co., Ky., U.S.	D4	94
Clinton, co., Mi., U.S.	F6	99
Clinton, co., Mo., U.S.	B3	102
Clinton, co., N.Y., U.S.	f11	109
Clinton, co., Oh., U.S.	C2	112
Clinton, co., Pa., U.S.	D6	115
Clinton, Lake, res., Il., U.S.	C5	90
Clinton-Colden Lake, l., N.W. Ter., Can.	D11	66
Clinton Lake, res., Ks., U.S.	m15	93
Clinton Reservoir, res., N.J., U.S.	A4	107
Clintonville, Wi., U.S.	D5	126
Clintwood, Va., U.S.	e9	123
Clio, Al., U.S.	D4	78
Clio, Mi., U.S.	E7	99
Clio, S.C., U.S.	B8	117
Clive, Ia., U.S.	e8	92
Clogher Head, c., Ire.	H6	7
Cloncurry, Austl.	D8	50
Clonmel, Ire.	I5	7
Cloppenburg, Ger.	C8	8
Cloquet, Mn., U.S.	D6	100
Cloquet, stm., Mn., U.S.	C6	100
Closter, N.J., U.S.	B5	107
Clothier, W.V., U.S.	n12	125
Cloud, co., Ks., U.S.	C6	93
Cloudcroft, N.M., U.S.	E4	108
Cloud Peak, mtn., Wy., U.S.	B5	127
Clover, S.C., U.S.	A5	117
Cloverdale, Al., U.S.	A2	78
Cloverdale, Ca., U.S.	C2	82
Cloverdale, In., U.S.	E4	91
Cloverport, Ky., U.S.	C3	94
Clovis, Ca., U.S.	D4	82
Clovis, N.M., U.S.	C6	108
Cluj-Napoca, Rom.	C7	16
Cluny, Fr.	F11	10
Cluses, Fr.	F13	10
Clusone, Italy	D4	14
Clute, Tx., U.S.	r14	120
Clutha, stm., N.Z.	G2	52
Clyde, N.W. Ter., Can.	B19	66
Clyde, Ks., U.S.	C6	93
Clyde, N.Y., U.S.	B4	109
Clyde, N.C., U.S.	f10	110
Clyde, Oh., U.S.	A3	112
Clyde, Tx., U.S.	C3	120
Clyde, stm., Scot., U.K.	F9	7
Clyde, Firth of, est., Scot., U.K.	F7	7
Clymer, Pa., U.S.	E3	115
Coachella, Ca., U.S.	F5	82
Coachella Canal, Ca., U.S.	F6	82
Coacoyole, Mex.	E6	62
Coahoma, Tx., U.S.	C2	120
Coahoma, co., Ms., U.S.	A3	101
Coal, co., Ok., U.S.	C5	113
Coal, stm., W.V., U.S.	C3	125
Coal Branch, N.B., Can.	C4	71
Coal City, Il., U.S.	B5	90
Coalcomán de Matamoros, Mex.	H8	62
Coal Creek, stm., Ok., U.S.	B6	113
Coaldale, Alta., Can.	E4	68
Coal Fork, W.V., U.S.	C3	125
Coal Fork, stm., W.V., U.S.	m13	125
Coalgate, Ok., U.S.	C5	113
Coal Grove, Oh., U.S.	D3	112
Coal Hill, Ar., U.S.	B2	81
Coalhurst, Alta., Can.	E4	68
Coalinga, Ca., U.S.	D3	82
Coalmont, Tn., U.S.	D8	119
Coalville, Ut., U.S.	C4	121
Coalwood, W.V., U.S.	D3	125
Coari, Braz.	D6	54
Coasters Harbor Island, i., R.I., U.S.	E5	116
Coast Mountains, mts., N.A.	E6	66
Coast Ranges, mts., U.S.	C2	76
Coatepeque, Guat.	G2	64
Coatesville, Pa., U.S.	G10	115
Coaticook, Que., Can.	D6	74
Coats, N.C., U.S.	B4	110
Coats Island, i., N.W. Ter., Can.	D16	66
Coats Land, reg., Ant.	B10	47
Coatzacoalcos, Mex.	H12	62
Cobalt, Ont., Can.	p19	73
Cobb, co., Ga., U.S.	C2	87
Cobb, stm., Mn., U.S.	G5	100
Cobble Mountain Reservoir, res., Ma., U.S.	B2	98
Cobbosseecontee Lake, l., Me., U.S.	D3	96
Cobden, Ont., Can.	B8	73
Cobden, Il., U.S.	F4	90
Cobequid Mountains, mts., N.S., Can.	D5	71
Cobham, stm., Can.	C4	70
Cobija, Bol.	F5	54
Cobleskill, N.Y., U.S.	C6	109
Cobourg, Ont., Can.	D6	73
Cóbuè, Moz.	D6	44
Cobun Creek, stm., W.V., U.S.	h11	125
Coburg, Ger.	E10	8
Coburg, Or., U.S.	C3	114
Coburg Island, i., N.W. Ter., Can.	A17	66
Cochabamba, Bol.	G5	54
Cocheco, stm., N.H., U.S.	D5	106
Cochin, India	H4	37
Cochise, co., Az., U.S.	F5	80
Cochise Head, mtn., Az., U.S.	E6	80
Cochiti Indian Reservation, N.M., U.S.	h8	108
Cochiti Reservoir, res., N.M., U.S.	B3	108
Cochituate, Ma., U.S.	g10	98
Cochituate, Lake, l., Ma., U.S.	g10	98
Cochran, Ga., U.S.	D3	87
Cochran, co., Tx., U.S.	C1	120
Cochrane, Alta., Can.	D3	68
Cochrane, Ont., Can.	o19	73
Cochranton, Pa., U.S.	C1	115
Cocke, co., Tn., U.S.	D10	119
Cockeysville, Md., U.S.	B4	97
Cockrell Hill, Tx., U.S.	n10	120
Coco, stm., N.A.	G6	64
Coco, Isla del, i., C.R.	B1	54
Cocoa, Fl., U.S.	D6	86
Cocoa Beach, Fl., U.S.	D6	86
Coco Channel, strt., Asia	H2	34
Coco Islands, is., Mya.	G2	34
Coconino, co., Az., U.S.	B3	80
Cocopah Indian Reservation, Az., U.S.	E1	80
Côcos, Braz.	C6	57
Cocula, Mex.	G8	62
Cod, Cape, c., Ma., U.S.	C7	98
Codajás, Braz.	D6	54
Coden, Al., U.S.	E1	78
Codigoro, Italy	E7	14
Codington, co., S.D., U.S.	C8	118
Codogno, Italy	D4	14
Codroipo, Italy	D7	14
Cody, Wy., U.S.	B3	127
Coeburn, Va., U.S.	f9	123
Coen, Austl.	B8	50
Coëtivy Island, i., Sey.	C11	44
Coeur d'Alene, Id., U.S.	B2	89
Coeur d'Alene, stm., Id., U.S.	B2	89
Coeur d'Alene Indian Reservation, Id., U.S.	B2	89
Coeur d'Alene Lake, res., Id., U.S.	B2	89
Coeur d'Alene Mountains, mts., Id., U.S.	B2	89
Coffee, co., Al., U.S.	D3	78
Coffee, co., Ga., U.S.	E4	87
Coffee, co., Tn., U.S.	B5	119
Coffeeville, Ms., U.S.	B4	101
Coffey, co., Ks., U.S.	D8	93
Coffeyville, Ks., U.S.	E8	93
Coffs Harbour, Austl.	F10	50
Coggon, Ia., U.S.	B6	92
Cognac, Fr.	G6	10
Cohansey, stm., N.J., U.S.	E2	107
Cohasset, Ma., U.S.	B6	98
Cohasset, Mn., U.S.	C5	100
Cohocton, stm., N.Y., U.S.	C3	109
Cohoes, N.Y., U.S.	C7	109
Cohoon, Lake, res., Va., U.S.	k14	123
Cohutta Mountain, mtn., Ga., U.S.	B2	87
Coiba, Isla de, i., Pan.	K7	64
Coimbatore, India	G4	37
Coimbra, Braz.	F7	57
Coimbra, Port.	E3	12
Coín, Spain	I7	12
Cojbalsan, Mong.	B9	26
Cokato, Mn., U.S.	E4	100
Coke, co., Tx., U.S.	D2	120
Cokeville, Wy., U.S.	D2	127
Čokurdach, Russia	C23	24
Colatina, Braz.	E8	57
Colbert, Ok., U.S.	D5	113
Colbert, co., Al., U.S.	A2	78

Name — Map Ref — Page

Colborne, Ont., Can. C7 73
Colby, Ks., U.S. C2 93
Colby, Wi., U.S. D3 126
Colchester, Eng., U.K. J13 7
Colchester, Ct., U.S. C6 84
Colchester, Il., U.S. C3 90
Colcord, Ok., U.S. A7 113
Cold, stm., N.H., U.S. C4 106
Cold, stm., N.H., U.S. D2 106
Cold Bay, Ak., U.S. E7 79
Cold Lake, Alta., Can. B5 68
Cold Spring, Ky., U.S. A5 94
Cold Spring, Mn., U.S. E4 100
Coldwater, Ont., Can. C5 73
Coldwater, Ks., U.S. E4 93
Coldwater, Mi., U.S. G5 99
Coldwater, Ms., U.S. A4 101
Coldwater, Oh., U.S. B1 112
Coldwater, stm., Ms., U.S. A3 101
Coldwater Creek, stm., U.S. e9 113
Cole, co., Mo., U.S. C5 102
Colebrook, N.H., U.S. g7 106
Colebrook River Lake, res., Ct., U.S. A3 84
Cole Camp, Mo., U.S. C4 102
Coleen, stm., Ak., U.S. B11 79
Coleman, Mi., U.S. E6 99
Coleman, Tx., U.S. D3 120
Coleman, Wi., U.S. C5 126
Coleman, co., Tx., U.S. D3 120
Coleraine, N. Ire., U.K. F6 7
Coleraine, Mn., U.S. C5 100
Coles, co., Il., U.S. D5 90
Colesberg, S. Afr. H5 44
Colfax, Ca., U.S. C3 82
Colfax, Il., U.S. C5 90
Colfax, In., U.S. D4 91
Colfax, Ia., U.S. C4 92
Colfax, La., U.S. C3 95
Colfax, Wa., U.S. C8 124
Colfax, Wi., U.S. D2 126
Colfax, co., Ne., U.S. C8 104
Colfax, co., N.M., U.S. A5 108
Colhué Huapi, Lago, l., Arg. F3 56
Colima, Mex. H8 62
Colima, Nevado de, mtn., Mex. H8 62
Colinas, Braz. E10 54
Coll, i., Scot., U.K. E6 7
College, Ak., U.S. B10 79
Collegedale, Tn., U.S. h11 119
College Park, Ga., U.S. C2 87
College Park, Md., U.S. C4 97
College Place, Wa., U.S. C7 124
College Station, Ar., U.S. C3 81
College Station, Tx., U.S. D4 120
Collegeville, In., U.S. C3 91
Collegeville, Pa., U.S. F11 115
Colleton, co., S.C., U.S. F6 117
Collier, co., Fl., U.S. F5 86
Collier Bay, b., Austl. C4 50
Colliers, W.V., U.S. f8 125
Collierville, Tn., U.S. B2 119
Collin, co., Tx., U.S. C4 120
Collingdale, Pa., U.S. p20 115
Collingswood, N.J., U.S. D2 107
Collingsworth, co., Tx., U.S. B2 120
Collingwood, Ont., Can. C4 73
Collins, Ms., U.S. D4 101
Collins Park, De., U.S. B3 85
Collinsville, Al., U.S. A4 78
Collinsville, Ct., U.S. B4 84
Collinsville, Il., U.S. E4 90
Collinsville, Ms., U.S. C5 101
Collinsville, Ok., U.S. A6 113
Collinsville, Va., U.S. D3 123
Collinwood, Tn., U.S. B4 119
Collooney, Ire. G4 7
Colmar, Fr. D14 10
Colmar Manor, Md., U.S. f9 97
Colmenar, Spain I7 12
Colmenar de Oreja, Spain E8 12
Colmenar Viejo, Spain E8 12
Colo, Ia., U.S. B4 92
Cologne see Köln, Ger. E6 8
Coloma, Mi., U.S. F4 99
Colomb-Béchar see Béchar, Alg. B5 42
Colombia, ctry., S.A. C4 54
Colombo, Sri L. I5 37
Colón, Cuba C7 64
Colón, Pan. J8 64
Colon, Mi., U.S. G5 99
Colon, Archipiélago de (Galapagos Islands), is., Ec. m15 58a
Colonia Dora, Arg. B4 56
Colonia Las Heras, Arg. F3 56
Colonial Beach, Va., U.S. B6 123
Colonial Heights, Tn., U.S. C11 119
Colonial Heights, Va., U.S. C5 123
Colonial National Historical Park, Va., U.S. C6 123
Colonia Vicente Guerrero, Mex. B1 62
Colonie, N.Y., U.S. C7 109
Coloradas, Lomas, hills, Arg. E3 56
Colorado, co., Tx., U.S. E4 120
Colorado, state, U.S. B5 83
Colorado, stm., Arg. D4 56
Colorado, stm., N.A. E4 76
Colorado, stm., Tx., U.S. D3 120
Colorado City, Az., U.S. A3 80
Colorado City, Co., U.S. D6 83
Colorado City, Tx., U.S. C2 120
Colorado City, Lake, res., Tx., U.S. C2 120
Colorado National Monument, Co., U.S. B2 83
Colorado River Aqueduct, Ca., U.S. F6 82
Colorado River Indian Reservation, U.S. D1 80
Colorado Springs, Co., U.S. C6 83
Colotlán, Mex. F8 62
Colquitt, Ga., U.S. E2 87
Colquitt, co., Ga., U.S. E3 87
Colstrip, Mt., U.S. E10 103
Colton, S.D., U.S. D9 118
Coltons Point, Md., U.S. D4 97
Columbia, Al., U.S. D4 78
Columbia, Il., U.S. E3 90
Columbia, Ky., U.S. C4 94
Columbia, Md., U.S. B4 97
Columbia, Ms., U.S. D4 101
Columbia, Mo., U.S. C5 102
Columbia, N.C., U.S. B6 110
Columbia, Pa., U.S. F9 115
Columbia, S.C., U.S. C5 117
Columbia, Tn., U.S. B4 119
Columbia, co., Ar., U.S. D2 81
Columbia, co., Fl., U.S. B4 86
Columbia, co., Ga., U.S. C4 87
Columbia, co., N.Y., U.S. C7 109
Columbia, co., Or., U.S. B3 114
Columbia, co., Pa., U.S. D9 115
Columbia, co., Wa., U.S. C7 124
Columbia, co., Wi., U.S. E4 126
Columbia, stm., N.A. G8 66
Columbia, Mount, mtn., Can. C2 68
Columbia City, In., U.S. B7 91
Columbia City, Or., U.S. B4 114
Columbia Falls, Mt., U.S. B2 103
Columbia Heights, Mn., U.S. m12 100
Columbia Lake, res., Ct., U.S. C6 84
Columbia Mountains, mts., B.C., Can. C7 69
Columbiana, Al., U.S. B3 78
Columbiana, Oh., U.S. B5 112
Columbiana, co., Oh., U.S. B5 112
Columbiaville, Mi., U.S. E7 99
Columbus, Ga., U.S. D2 87
Columbus, In., U.S. F6 91
Columbus, Ks., U.S. E9 93
Columbus, Ms., U.S. B5 101
Columbus, Mt., U.S. E7 103
Columbus, Ne., U.S. C8 104
Columbus, N.M., U.S. F2 108
Columbus, N.C., U.S. f10 110
Columbus, Oh., U.S. C2 112
Columbus, Tx., U.S. E4 120
Columbus, Wi., U.S. E4 126
Columbus, co., N.C., U.S. C4 110
Columbus Air Force Base, mil., Ms., U.S. B5 101
Columbus Grove, Oh., U.S. B1 112
Columbus Junction, Ia., U.S. C6 92
Columbus Lake, res., Ms., U.S. B5 101
Colusa, Ca., U.S. C2 82
Colusa, co., Ca., U.S. C2 82
Colver, Pa., U.S. E4 115
Colville, Wa., U.S. A8 124
Colville, stm., Ak., U.S. B9 79
Colville, stm., Wa., U.S. A8 124
Colville Indian Reservation, Wa., U.S. A6 124
Colvos Passage, strt., Wa., U.S. f10 124
Colwich, Ks., U.S. E6 93
Colwood, B.C., Can. h12 69
Comacchio, Italy E7 14
Comal, co., Tx., U.S. E3 120
Comanche, Ok., U.S. C4 113
Comanche, Tx., U.S. D3 120
Comanche, co., Ks., U.S. E4 93
Comanche, co., Ok., U.S. C3 113
Comanche, co., Tx., U.S. D3 120
Comandante Fontana, Arg. B5 56
Comayagua, Hond. G4 64
Combahee, stm., S.C., U.S. F6 117
Combarbalá, Chile C2 56
Combeaufontaine, Fr. E12 10
Comber, Ont., Can. E2 73
Combermere Bay, b., Mya. E2 34
Combined Locks, Wi., U.S. h9 126
Combourg, Fr. D5 10
Combs, Ky., U.S. C6 94
Comer, Ga., U.S. B3 87
Comfort, Tx., U.S. E3 120
Comilla, Bngl. I14 38
Comitán [de Domínguez], Mex. I13 62
Comite, stm., La., U.S. D4 95
Commentry, Fr. F9 10
Commerce, Ga., U.S. B3 87
Commerce, Ok., U.S. A7 113
Commerce, Tx., U.S. C5 120
Commerce City, Co., U.S. B6 83
Committee Bay, b., N.W. Ter., Can. C15 66
Common Fence Point, R.I., U.S. D6 116
Como, Italy D4 14
Como, Ms., U.S. A4 101
Como, Lago di, l., Italy C4 14
Comodoro Rivadavia, Arg. F3 56
Comorin, Cape, c., India H4 37
Comoros, ctry., Afr. D8 44
Comox, B.C., Can. E5 69
Compiègne, Fr. C9 10
Compton, Que., Can. D6 74
Compton, Ca., U.S. n12 82
Comstock, Mi., U.S. F5 99
Con, stm., Viet. E8 34
Cona, stm., Russia E16 24
Conakry, Gui. G3 42
Conanicut Island, i., R.I., U.S. E5 116
Conanicut Point, c., R.I., U.S. E5 116
Concarneau, Fr. E3 10
Conceição do Araguaia, Braz. E9 54
Concepción, Arg. B3 56
Concepción, Bol. G6 54
Concepción, Chile D2 56
Concepción, Para. A5 56
Concepción, Laguna, l., Bol. G6 54
Concepción, Volcán, vol., Nic. I5 64
Concepcion del Oro, Mex. E9 62
Concepción del Uruguay, Arg. C5 56
Conception, Point, c., Ca., U.S. E3 82
Conception Bay, b., Newf., Can. E5 72
Conception Bay South, Newf., Can. E5 72
Conchas Lake, res., N.M., U.S. B5 108
Conches, Fr. D7 10
Concho, co., Tx., U.S. D3 120
Concho, stm., Tx., U.S. D2 120
Conchos, stm., Mex. C7 62
Concord, Ca., U.S. h8 82
Concord, Ma., U.S. B5 98
Concord, Mi., U.S. F6 99
Concord, Mo., U.S. g13 102
Concord, N.H., U.S. D3 106
Concord, N.C., U.S. B2 110
Concord, stm., Ma., U.S. A5 98
Concordia, Arg. C5 56
Concordia, Mex. F6 62
Concordia, Ks., U.S. C6 93
Concordia, Mo., U.S. C4 102
Concordia, co., La., U.S. C4 95
Concrete, Wa., U.S. A4 124
Condé, Fr. D6 10
Condom, Fr. I7 10
Condon, Or., U.S. B6 114
Condoto, Col. E4 58
Conecuh, co., Al., U.S. D2 78
Conecuh, stm., U.S. D3 78
Conegliano, Italy D7 14
Conejos, co., Co., U.S. D4 83
Conejos, stm., Co., U.S. D4 83
Conejos Peak, mtn., Co., U.S. D4 83
Conemaugh, Pa., U.S. F4 115
Conemaugh River Lake, res., Pa., U.S. F3 115
Confolens, Fr. F7 10
Congamond Lakes, l., U.S. A4 84
Congaree, stm., S.C., U.S. D6 117
Congaree Swamp National Monument, S.C., U.S. D6 117
Congo, ctry., Afr. B2 44
Congo (Zaire), stm., Afr. C2 44
Congress, Az., U.S. C3 80
Conimicut Point, c., R.I., U.S. D5 116
Conitaca, Mex. E6 62
Conklin, N.Y., U.S. C5 109
Conn, Lough, l., Ire. G3 7
Connaught, hist. reg., Ire. H3 7
Conneaut, Oh., U.S. A5 112
Conneaut Creek, stm., Oh., U.S. A5 112
Conneaut Lake, l., Pa., U.S. C1 115
Connecticut, state, U.S. C5 84
Connecticut, stm., U.S. C12 76
Connell, Wa., U.S. C7 124
Connellsville, Pa., U.S. F2 115
Connemara, reg., Ire. H3 7
Connersville, In., U.S. E7 91
Conover, N.C., U.S. B1 110
Conowingo, Md., U.S. A5 97
Conrad, Ia., U.S. B5 92
Conrad, Mt., U.S. B5 103
Conroe, Tx., U.S. D5 120
Conselheiro Lafaiete, Braz. F7 57
Conshohocken, Pa., U.S. F11 115
Con Son, is., Viet. J9 34
Consort, Alta., Can. C5 68
Constance, Lake see Bodensee, l., Eur. H9 8
Constanța, Rom. E12 16
Constantina, Spain H6 12
Constantine (Qacentina), Alg. A7 42
Constantine, Mi., U.S. G5 99
Constantine, Cape, c., Ak., U.S. D8 79
Consuegra, Spain F8 12
Contai, India J12 38
Contas, Rio de, stm., Braz. C9 57
Content Keys, is., Fl., U.S. H5 86
Continental, Oh., U.S. A1 112
Continental Peak, mtn., Wy., U.S. D4 127
Continental Reservoir, res., Co., U.S. D3 83
Contoocook, N.H., U.S. D3 106
Contoocook, stm., N.H., U.S. D3 106
Contra Costa, co., Ca., U.S. D3 82
Contrecoeur, Que., Can. D4 74
Contres, Fr. E8 10
Contwoyto Lake, l., N.W. Ter., Can. C10 66
Convención, Col. C6 58
Conversano, Italy I12 14
Converse, In., U.S. C6 91
Converse, S.C., U.S. B4 117
Converse, co., Wy., U.S. C7 127
Convoy, Oh., U.S. B1 112
Conway, Ar., U.S. B3 81
Conway, Fl., U.S. D5 86
Conway, Mo., U.S. D5 102
Conway, N.H., U.S. C4 106
Conway, N.C., U.S. A5 110
Conway, Pa., U.S. E1 115
Conway, S.C., U.S. D9 117
Conway, co., Ar., U.S. B3 81
Conway, Lake, res., Ar., U.S. B3 81
Conway Lake, l., N.H., U.S. C4 106
Conway Springs, Ks., U.S. E6 93
Conyers, Ga., U.S. C2 87
Cooch Behār, India G13 38
Cook, Mn., U.S. C6 100
Cook, co., Ga., U.S. E3 87
Cook, co., Il., U.S. B6 90
Cook, co., Mn., U.S. k9 100
Cook, Cape, c., B.C., Can. D4 69
Cook, Mount, mtn., N.Z. E3 52
Cooke, co., Tx., U.S. C4 120
Cookes Peak, mtn., N.M., U.S. E2 108
Cookeville, Tn., U.S. C8 119
Cook Inlet, b., Ak., U.S. D9 79
Cook Islands, dep., Oc. H2 2
Cook Point, c., Md., U.S. C5 97
Cookshire, Que., Can. D6 74
Cookson, Ok., U.S. B7 113
Cookstown, N. Ire., U.K. G6 7
Cook Strait, strt., N.Z. D5 52
Cooktown, Austl. C9 50
Cooleemee, N.C., U.S. B2 110
Coolgardie, Austl. F4 50
Coolidge, Az., U.S. E4 80
Coolidge, Ga., U.S. E3 87
Cooma, Austl. G9 50
Coonoor, India G4 37
Coon Rapids, Ia., U.S. C3 92
Coon Rapids, Mn., U.S. E5 100
Coon Valley, Wi., U.S. E2 126
Cooper, Tx., U.S. C5 120
Cooper, co., Mo., U.S. C5 102
Cooper, stm., S.C., U.S. F8 117
Cooper Mountain, mtn., Ak., U.S. g17 79
Coopersburg, Pa., U.S. F11 115
Cooperstown, N.Y., U.S. C6 109
Cooperstown, N.D., U.S. B7 111
Coopersville, Mi., U.S. E5 99
Coos, co., N.H., U.S. A4 106
Coos, co., Or., U.S. D2 114
Coos, stm., Or., U.S. D2 114
Coosa, co., Al., U.S. C3 78
Coosa, stm., U.S. C3 78
Coosada, Al., U.S. C3 78
Coosawhatchie, stm., S.C., U.S. F5 117
Coos Bay, Or., U.S. D2 114
Copalis Beach, Wa., U.S. B1 124
Copan, Ok., U.S. A6 113
Copan Reservoir, res., Ok., U.S. A6 113
Copenhagen see København, Den. I9 6
Copiah, co., Ms., U.S. D3 101
Copiapó, Chile B2 56
Coplay, Pa., U.S. E10 115
Copparo, Italy E6 14
Copper, stm., Ak., U.S. C11 79
Copperas Cove, Tx., U.S. D4 120
Copper Butte, mtn., Wa., U.S. A7 124
Coppermine, N.W. Ter., Can. C9 66
Coppermine, stm., N.W. Ter., Can. C10 66
Copper Mountain, mtn., Wy., U.S. C5 127
Copper Mountains, mts., Az., U.S. E2 80
Coquille, Or., U.S. D2 114
Coquimbo, Chile B2 56
Coral Gables, Fl., U.S. G6 86
Coral Harbour, N.W. Ter., Can. D16 66
Coral Sea, Oc. B10 50
Coralville, Ia., U.S. C6 92
Coralville Lake, res., Ia., U.S. C5 92
Corantijn (Corentyne), stm., S.A. E14 58
Coraopolis, Pa., U.S. E1 115
Corato, Italy H11 14
Corbeil-Essonnes, Fr. D9 10
Corbigny, Fr. E10 10
Corbin, Ky., U.S. D5 94
Corcoran, Ca., U.S. D4 82
Corcoran, Mn., U.S. m11 100
Corcovado, Golfo, b., Chile E2 56
Corcovado, Volcán, vol., Chile E2 56
Corcubión, Spain C2 12
Cordele, Ga., U.S. E3 87
Cordell, Ok., U.S. B3 113
Cordell Hull Lake, res., Tn., U.S. C8 119
Cordes, Fr. H8 10
Córdoba, Arg. C4 56
Córdoba, Mex. H11 62
Córdoba, Spain H7 12
Cordova, Al., U.S. B2 78
Cordova, Ak., U.S. C10 79
Cordova, N.M., U.S. A4 108
Cordova, N.C., U.S. C3 110
Cordova Peak, mtn., Ak., U.S. C10 79
Corentyne (Corantijn), stm., S.A. E14 58
Corfu see Kérkira, Grc. J3 16
Coria, Spain F5 12
Coria del Río, Spain H5 12
Corigliano Calabro, Italy J11 14
Coringa Islets, is., Austl. C9 50
Corinna, Me., U.S. D3 96
Corinne, Ut., U.S. B3 121
Corinne Key, i., Fl., U.S. G6 86
Corinth, Ms., U.S. A5 101
Corinth, N.Y., U.S. B7 109
Corinth see Kórinthos, Grc. L6 16
Corinto, Braz. E6 57
Cork, Ire. J4 7
Corlay, Fr. D3 10
Corleone, Italy L8 14
Corleto Perticara, Italy I11 14
Çorlu, Tur. H11 16
Cormorant Lake, l., Man., Can. B1 70
Cornelia, Ga., U.S. B3 87
Cornélio Procópio, Braz. G3 57
Cornelius, N.C., U.S. B2 110
Cornelius, Or., U.S. g11 114
Cornell, Wi., U.S. C2 126
Corner Brook, Newf., Can. D3 72
Cornersville, Tn., U.S. B5 119
Cornfield Point, c., Ct., U.S. D6 84
Cornie Bayou, stm., U.S. D3 81
Corning, Ar., U.S. A5 81
Corning, Ca., U.S. C2 82
Corning, Ia., U.S. D3 92
Corning, N.Y., U.S. C3 109
Cornish, Me., U.S. E2 96
Corn Islands, is., Nic. H6 64
Corno Grande, mtn., Italy G8 14
Cornville, Az., U.S. C4 80
Cornwall, Ont., Can. B10 73
Cornwall, Pa., U.S. F9 115
Cornwallis Island, i., N.W. Ter., Can. A14 66
Cornwall on Hudson, N.Y., U.S. D6 109
Coro, Ven. B8 58
Corocoro, Bol. G5 54
Coroico, Bol. G5 54
Coromandel Coast, India F6 37
Coromandel Peninsula, pen., N.Z. B5 52
Corona, Ca., U.S. F5 82
Coronado, Ca., U.S. F5 82
Coronado National Memorial, Az., U.S. F5 80
Coronation, Alta., Can. C5 68
Coronation Gulf, b., N.W. Ter., Can. C10 66
Coronation Island, i., Ak., U.S. n22 79
Coronel Dorrego, Arg. D4 56
Coronel Fabriciano, Braz. E7 57
Coronel Pringles, Arg. D4 56
Coronel Suárez, Arg. D4 56
Coropuna, Nevado, mtn., Peru G4 54
Corpus Christi, Tx., U.S. F4 120
Corpus Christi Naval Air Station, mil., Tx., U.S. F4 120
Corral de Almaguer, Spain F8 12
Correctionville, Ia., U.S. B2 92
Correggio, Italy E5 14
Corrente, stm., Braz. B7 57
Corrib, Lough, l., Ire. H3 7
Corrientes, Arg. B5 56
Corrientes, Cabo, c., Col. E4 58
Corrientes, Cabo, c., Cuba D5 64
Corrientes, Cabo, c., Mex. G7 62
Corrigan, Tx., U.S. D5 120
Corriganville, Md., U.S. k13 97
Corry, Pa., U.S. C2 115
Corse (Corsica), i., Fr. m19 11a
Corsica, S.D., U.S. D7 118
Corsica see Corse, i., Fr. m19 11a
Corsicana, Tx., U.S. C4 120
Corson, co., S.D., U.S. B4 118
Corson Inlet, b., N.J., U.S. E3 107
Cortemilia, Italy E3 14
Cortez, Co., U.S. D2 83
Cortez, Fl., U.S. q10 86
Cortez Mountains, mts., Nv., U.S. C5 105
Cortina d'Ampezzo, Italy C7 14
Cortland, Il., U.S. B5 90
Cortland, N.Y., U.S. C4 109
Cortland, Oh., U.S. A5 112
Cortland, co., N.Y., U.S. C4 109
Çorum, Tur. G14 4
Corumbá, Braz. G7 54
Corumbá, stm., Braz. E4 57
Corunna, Mi., U.S. F6 99
Corvallis, Or., U.S. C3 114
Corydon, In., U.S. H5 91
Corydon, Ia., U.S. D4 92
Corydon, Ky., U.S. C2 94
Coryell, co., Tx., U.S. D4 120
Cosamaloapan [de Carpio], Mex. H12 62
Cosenza, Italy J11 14
Coshocton, Oh., U.S. B4 112
Coshocton, co., Oh., U.S. B4 112
Cosmoledo Group, is., Sey. C9 44
Cosmopolis, Wa., U.S. C2 124
Cosmos, Mn., U.S. F4 100
Cosne-sur-Loire, Fr. E9 10
Cossatot, stm., Ar., U.S. C1 81
Costa Mesa, Ca., U.S. n13 82
Costa Rica, Mex. C4 62
Costa Rica, ctry., N.A. I5 64
Costilla, co., Co., U.S. D5 83
Cotabato, Phil. D7 32
Coteau-Landing, Que., Can. D3 74
Cotentin, pen., Fr. C5 10
Cotonou, Benin G6 42
Cotopaxi, vol., Ec. H3 58
Cottage Grove, Mn., U.S. n13 100
Cottage Grove, Or., U.S. D3 114
Cottage Grove Reservoir, res., Or., U.S. D3 114
Cottam, Ont., Can. E2 73
Cottbus, Ger. D14 8
Cotter, Ar., U.S. A3 81
Cottiennes, Alpes (Alpi Cozie), mts., Eur. H13 10
Cottle, co., Tx., U.S. B2 120
Cottleville, Mo., U.S. f12 102
Cotton, co., Ok., U.S. C3 113
Cottondale, Al., U.S. B2 78
Cotton Plant, Ar., U.S. B4 81
Cottonport, La., U.S. C3 95
Cotton Valley, La., U.S. B2 95
Cottonwood, Al., U.S. D4 78
Cottonwood, Az., U.S. C3 80
Cottonwood, Ca., U.S. B2 82
Cottonwood, Id., U.S. C2 89
Cottonwood, Mn., U.S. F3 100
Cottonwood, co., Mn., U.S. F3 100
Cottonwood, stm., Ks., U.S. D7 93
Cottonwood, stm., Mn., U.S. F3 100
Cottonwood Creek, stm., Wy., U.S. C4 127
Cottonwood Falls, Ks., U.S. D7 93
Cotuit, Ma., U.S. C7 98
Cotulla, Tx., U.S. E3 120
Coudersport, Pa., U.S. C5 115
Cougar Reservoir, res., Or., U.S. C4 114
Couhé, Fr. F7 10
Coulee Creek, stm., Wa., U.S. g13 124
Coulee Dam, Wa., U.S. B7 124
Coulee Dam National Recreation Area, Wa., U.S. A7 124
Coulommiers, Fr. D10 10
Coulterville, Il., U.S. E4 90
Counce, Tn., U.S. B3 119
Council, Id., U.S. E2 89
Council Bluffs, Ia., U.S. C2 92
Council Grove, Ks., U.S. D7 93
Council Grove Lake, res., Ks., U.S. D7 93
Council Mountain, mtn., Id., U.S. E2 89
Country Homes, Wa., U.S. B8 124
Coupeville, Wa., U.S. A3 124
Courtenay, B.C., Can. E5 69
Courte Oreilles, Lac, l., Wi., U.S. C2 126
Courtland, Ont., Can. E4 73
Courtland, Al., U.S. A2 78
Courtland, Va., U.S. D5 123
Coushatta, La., U.S. B2 95
Coutances, Fr. C5 10
Coutras, Fr. G6 10
Cove Creek, stm., Ut., U.S. E3 121
Covedale, Oh., U.S. o12 112
Coventry, Eng., U.K. I11 7
Coventry, Ct., U.S. B6 84
Coventry, R.I., U.S. D3 116
Cove Point, c., Md., U.S. D5 97
Covilhã, Port. E4 12
Covina, Ca., U.S. m13 82
Covington, Ga., U.S. C3 87
Covington, In., U.S. D3 91
Covington, Ky., U.S. A5 94
Covington, La., U.S. D5 95
Covington, Oh., U.S. B1 112
Covington, Tn., U.S. B2 119
Covington, Va., U.S. C3 123
Covington, co., Al., U.S. D3 78
Covington, co., Ms., U.S. D4 101
Cowan, Tn., U.S. B5 119
Cowan, Lake, l., Austl. F4 50
Cowansville, Que., Can. D5 74
Cowarts, Al., U.S. D4 78
Cow Creek, stm., Wa., U.S. C7 124
Cowee Mountains, mts., N.C., U.S. f9 110
Cowen, Mount, mtn., Mt., U.S. E6 103
Coweta, Ok., U.S. B6 113
Coweta, co., Ga., U.S. C2 87
Cow Head, Newf., Can. D3 72
Cowichan Bay, B.C., Can. g12 69
Cow Lakes, l., Or., U.S. D9 114
Cowley, Wy., U.S. B4 127
Cowley, co., Ks., U.S. E7 93
Cowlington, Ok., U.S. B7 113
Cowlitz, co., Wa., U.S. C2 124

Name	Map Ref	Page
Cowlitz, stm., Wa., U.S.	C3	124
Cowpasture, stm., Va., U.S.	B3	123
Cowpen Mountain, mtn., Ga., U.S.	B2	87
Cowpens, S.C., U.S.	A4	117
Coxim, Braz.	E1	57
Coxsackie, N.Y., U.S.	C7	109
Cox's Bāzār, Bngl.	J14	38
Cox's Cove, Newf., Can.	D2	72
Coyhaique, Chile	F2	56
Cozad, Ne., U.S.	D6	104
Cozumel, Isla de, i., Mex.	G16	62
Crab Creek, stm., Wa., U.S.	C6	124
Crab Creek, stm., Wa., U.S.	B7	124
Crab Orchard, Ky., U.S.	C5	94
Crab Orchard, Tn., U.S.	D9	119
Crab Orchard, W.V., U.S.	n13	125
Crab Orchard Lake, res., Il., U.S.	F4	90
Crabtree, Pa., U.S.	F3	115
Crabtree Mills, Que., Can.	D4	74
Cradock, S. Afr.	H5	44
Crafton, Pa., U.S.	k13	115
Craig, Ak., U.S.	D13	79
Craig, Co., U.S.	A3	83
Craig, co., Ok., U.S.	A6	113
Craig, co., Va., U.S.	C2	123
Craig Air Force Base, mil., Al., U.S.	C3	78
Craig Creek, stm., Va., U.S.	C2	123
Craighead, co., Ar., U.S.	B5	81
Craigsville, Va., U.S.	B3	123
Craigsville, W.V., U.S.	C4	125
Crailsheim, Ger.	F10	8
Craiova, Rom.	E7	16
Cramerton, N.C., U.S.	B1	110
Cranberry Lake, l., N.Y., U.S.	A6	109
Cranberry Portage, Man., Can.	B1	70
Cranbrook, B.C., Can.	E10	69
Crandall, Tx., U.S.	n10	120
Crandon, Wi., U.S.	C5	126
Crane, Az., U.S.	*E1	80
Crane, Mo., U.S.	E4	102
Crane, Tx., U.S.	D1	120
Crane, co., Tx., U.S.	D1	120
Crane Creek, stm., Oh., U.S.	e7	112
Crane Creek Reservoir, res., Id., U.S.	E2	89
Crane Lake, l., Il., U.S.	C3	90
Crane Lake, l., Mn., U.S.	B6	100
Crane Mountain, mtn., Or., U.S.	E6	114
Crane Prairie Reservoir, res., Or., U.S.	D5	114
Cranford, N.J., U.S.	B4	107
Cranston, R.I., U.S.	C4	116
Craon, Fr.	E6	10
Craponne, Fr.	G10	10
Crater Lake, l., Or., U.S.	E4	114
Crater Lake National Park, Or., U.S.	E4	114
Craters of the Moon National Monument, Id., U.S.	F5	89
Cratéus, Braz.	E10	54
Crato, Braz.	E11	54
Crauford, Cape, c., N.W. Ter., Can.	B16	66
Craven, co., N.C., U.S.	B5	110
Crawford, Ga., U.S.	C3	87
Crawford, Ms., U.S.	B5	101
Crawford, Ne., U.S.	B2	104
Crawford, co., Ar., U.S.	B1	81
Crawford, co., Ga., U.S.	D3	87
Crawford, co., Il., U.S.	D6	90
Crawford, co., In., U.S.	H4	91
Crawford, co., Ia., U.S.	B2	92
Crawford, co., Ks., U.S.	E9	93
Crawford, co., Mi., U.S.	D6	99
Crawford, co., Mo., U.S.	D6	102
Crawford, co., Oh., U.S.	B3	112
Crawford, co., Pa., U.S.	C1	115
Crawford, co., Wi., U.S.	E3	126
Crawford Lake, l., Me., U.S.	C5	96
Crawford Notch State Park, N.H., U.S.	B4	106
Crawfordsville, Ar., U.S.	B5	81
Crawfordsville, In., U.S.	D4	91
Crawfordville, Fl., U.S.	B2	86
Crazy Mountains, mts., Mt., U.S.	D6	103
Crazy Peak, mtn., Mt., U.S.	D6	103
Crazy Woman Creek, stm., Wy., U.S.	B6	127
Creal Springs, Il., U.S.	F5	90
Cree, stm., Sask., Can.	E11	66
Creedmoor, N.C., U.S.	A4	110
Creek, co., Ok., U.S.	B5	113
Cree Lake, l., Sask., Can.	m7	75
Creemore, Ont., Can.	C4	73
Creighton, Ne., U.S.	B8	104
Creighton, Pa., U.S.	h14	115
Creil, Fr.	C9	10
Crema, Italy	D4	14
Cremona, Italy	D5	14
Crenshaw, Ms., U.S.	A3	101
Crenshaw, co., Al., U.S.	D3	78
Creola, Al., U.S.	E1	78
Cres, Cro.	E9	14
Cresaptown, Md., U.S.	k13	97
Crescent, Ok., U.S.	B4	113
Crescent, Or., U.S.	D5	114
Crescent, Lake, l., Wa., U.S.	A2	124
Crescent City, Ca., U.S.	B1	82
Crescent City, Fl., U.S.	C5	86
Crescent Lake, l., Fl., U.S.	C5	86
Crescent Lake, l., Or., U.S.	D5	114
Crescent Springs, Ky., U.S.	h13	94
Cresco, Ia., U.S.	A5	92
Cresskill, N.J., U.S.	h9	107
Cresson, Pa., U.S.	F4	115
Cressona, Pa., U.S.	E9	115
Crest, Fr.	H12	10
Crested Butte, Co., U.S.	C4	83
Crest Hill, Il., U.S.	k8	90
Crestline, Oh., U.S.	B3	112
Creston, B.C., Can.	E9	69
Creston, Ia., U.S.	C3	92
Creston, Oh., U.S.	B4	112
Crestone Peak, mtn., Co., U.S.	D5	83
Crestview, Fl., U.S.	u15	86
Crestview, Hi., U.S.	g10	88
Crestwood, Ky., U.S.	B4	94
Crestwood Village, N.J., U.S.	D4	107
Creswell, Or., U.S.	D3	114
Crete, Il., U.S.	B6	90
Crete, Ne., U.S.	D9	104
Crete see Kríti, i., Grc.	N8	16
Creve Coeur, Il., U.S.	C4	90
Crevillente, Spain	G11	12
Crewe, Eng., U.K.	H10	7
Crewe, Va., U.S.	C4	123
Criciúma, Braz.	B7	56
Cricket, N.C., U.S.	A1	110
Cridersville, Oh., U.S.	B1	112
Crikvenica, Cro.	D9	14
Crimea see Kryms'kyy pivostriv, pen., Ukr.	H4	22
Crimmitschau, Ger.	E12	8
Crisfield, Md., U.S.	E6	97
Crisp, co., Ga., U.S.	E3	87
Cristalândia, Braz.	F9	54
Cristalina, Braz.	D5	57
Cristianópolis, Braz.	D4	57
Cristóbal Colón, Pico, mtn., Col.	B6	58
Crittenden, Ky., U.S.	B5	94
Crittenden, co., Ar., U.S.	B5	81
Crittenden, co., Ky., U.S.	e9	94
Crivitz, Wi., U.S.	C6	126
Črnomelj, Slo.	D10	14
Croatia, ctry., Eur.	D10	14
Crocker, Mo., U.S.	D5	102
Crockett, Ca., U.S.	g8	82
Crockett, Tx., U.S.	D5	120
Crockett, co., Tn., U.S.	B2	119
Crockett, co., Tx., U.S.	D2	120
Crofton, Ky., U.S.	C2	94
Crofton, Md., U.S.	B4	97
Crofton, Ne., U.S.	B8	104
Croix, Lac la, l., Mn., U.S.	B6	100
Croker, Cape, c., Ont., Can.	C4	73
Croker Island, i., Austl.	B6	50
Cromarty, Scot., U.K.	D8	7
Cromona, Ky., U.S.	C7	94
Cromwell, Ct., U.S.	C5	84
Crook, co., Or., U.S.	C6	114
Crook, co., Wy., U.S.	B8	127
Crooked, stm., Or., U.S.	C6	114
Crooked Creek, stm., U.S.	E3	93
Crooked Creek, stm., Pa., U.S.	C7	115
Crooked Creek Lake, res., Pa., U.S.	E3	115
Crooked Island, i., Bah.	C10	64
Crooked Island Passage, strt., Bah.	C10	64
Crooked Lake, l., Fl., U.S.	E5	86
Crooked Lake, l., Mn., U.S.	B7	100
Crooks, S.D., U.S.	D9	118
Crooks Lake, l., Nv., U.S.	B2	105
Crookston, Mn., U.S.	C2	100
Crooksville, Oh., U.S.	C3	112
Crosby, Mn., U.S.	D5	100
Crosby, N.D., U.S.	A2	111
Crosby, Tx., U.S.	r14	120
Crosby, co., Tx., U.S.	C2	120
Crosby, Mount, mtn., Wy., U.S.	C3	127
Crosbyton, Tx., U.S.	C2	120
Cross, co., Ar., U.S.	B5	81
Cross Bay, b., Man., Can.	C2	70
Cross City, Fl., U.S.	C3	86
Cross Creek, stm., W.V., U.S.	f8	125
Crossett, Ar., U.S.	D4	81
Crossfield, Alta., Can.	D3	68
Cross Island, i., Me., U.S.	D5	96
Cross Lake, Man., Can.	B3	70
Crosslake, Mn., U.S.	D4	100
Cross Lake, l., Me., U.S.	A4	96
Cross Lake, res., La., U.S.	B2	95
Cross Lanes, W.V., U.S.	C3	125
Crossman Peak, mtn., Az., U.S.	C1	80
Cross Plains, Tn., U.S.	A5	119
Cross Plains, Tx., U.S.	C3	120
Cross Plains, Wi., U.S.	E4	126
Cross Sound, strt., Ak., U.S.	k21	79
Crossville, Al., U.S.	A4	78
Crossville, Il., U.S.	E5	90
Crossville, Tn., U.S.	D8	119
Croswell, Mi., U.S.	E8	99
Crothersville, In., U.S.	G6	91
Crotone, Italy	J12	14
Croton-on-Hudson, N.Y., U.S.	D7	109
Crouse, N.C., U.S.	B1	110
Crow, stm., Mn., U.S.	F4	100
Crow Agency, Mt., U.S.	E9	103
Crow Creek, stm., U.S.	A6	83
Crow Creek Indian Reservation, S.D., U.S.	C6	118
Crowder, Ms., U.S.	A3	101
Crowell, Tx., U.S.	C3	120
Crow Indian Reservation, Mt., U.S.	E9	103
Crowley, La., U.S.	D3	95
Crowley, Tx., U.S.	n9	120
Crowley, co., Co., U.S.	C7	83
Crowley, Lake, res., Ca., U.S.	D4	82
Crowleys Ridge, mtn., U.S.	B5	81
Crown Point, In., U.S.	B3	91
Crown Point, La., U.S.	k11	95
Crownpoint, N.M., U.S.	B1	108
Crown Prince Frederick Island, i., N.W. Ter., Can.	B15	66
Crow Peak, mtn., Mt., U.S.	D5	103
Crowsnest Pass, Alta., Can.	E3	68
Crowsnest Pass, Can.	E3	68
Crow Wing, co., Mn., U.S.	D4	100
Crow Wing, stm., Mn., U.S.	D4	100
Croydon, Austl.	C8	50
Crozet, Va., U.S.	B4	123
Crozon, Fr.	D2	10
Cruces, Cuba	C7	64
Crump Lake, l., Or., U.S.	E7	114
Cruz Alta, Braz.	B6	56
Cruz del Eje, Arg.	C4	56
Cruzeiro do Sul, Braz.	E4	54
Crystal, Mn., U.S.	m12	100
Crystal, stm., Co., U.S.	B3	83
Crystal Bay, Nv., U.S.	D1	105
Crystal Bay, b., Fl., U.S.	D4	86
Crystal Beach, Fl., U.S.	D4	86
Crystal City, Man., Can.	E2	70
Crystal City, Mo., U.S.	C7	102
Crystal City, Tx., U.S.	E3	120
Crystal Falls, Mi., U.S.	B2	99
Crystal Lake, Ct., U.S.	B6	84
Crystal Lake, Fl., U.S.	u16	86
Crystal Lake, Il., U.S.	A5	90
Crystal Lake, l., Ct., U.S.	B6	84
Crystal Lake, l., Mi., U.S.	D4	99
Crystal Lake, l., N.H., U.S.	D4	106
Crystal Lake, l., Vt., U.S.	B4	122
Crystal Lawns, Il., U.S.	k8	90
Crystal Pond, res., Ct., U.S.	B7	84
Crystal River, Fl., U.S.	D4	86
Crystal Springs, Ms., U.S.	D3	101
Cuando (Kwando), stm., Afr.	E4	44
Cuangar, Ang.	E3	44
Cuango, Ang.	C3	44
Cuango (Kwango), stm., Afr.	C3	44
Cuanza, stm., Ang.	C3	44
Cuauhtémoc, Mex.	C6	62
Cuautla, Mex.	H10	62
Cuba, Port.	G4	12
Cuba, Il., U.S.	C3	90
Cuba, Mo., U.S.	C6	102
Cuba, N.M., U.S.	A3	108
Cuba, N.Y., U.S.	C2	109
Cuba, ctry., N.A.	D8	64
Cuba City, Wi., U.S.	F3	126
Cubango (Okavango), stm., Afr.	E3	44
Cubero, N.M., U.S.	B2	108
Cucharas, Mex.	F7	62
Cucharas, stm., Co., U.S.	D6	83
Cudahy, Wi., U.S.	F6	126
Cuddalore, India	G5	37
Cuddapah, India	E5	37
Cuddy Mountain, mtn., Id., U.S.	E2	89
Čudskoje Ozero (Peipsi Järv), l., Eur.	C10	18
Cuéllar, Spain	D7	12
Cuenca, Ec.	I3	58
Cuenca, Spain	E9	12
Cuencamé [de Ceniceros], Mex.	E8	62
Cuernavaca, Mex.	H10	62
Cuero, Tx., U.S.	E4	120
Cuers, Fr.	I13	10
Cuervos, Mex.	A2	62
Cuevas del Almanzora, Spain	H10	12
Cuglieri, Italy	I3	14
Cuiabá, Braz.	G7	54
Cuiseaux, Fr.	F12	10
Cuíto, stm., Ang.	E3	44
Cuíto-Cuanavale, Ang.	E3	44
Cuivre, West Fork, stm., Mo., U.S.	B6	102
Čukotskij, Mys, c., Russia	E31	24
Čukotskij Poluostrov, pen., Russia	D30	24
Culberson, co., Tx., U.S.	o12	120
Culbertson, Mt., U.S.	B12	103
Culbertson, Ne., U.S.	D5	104
Culebra Peak, mtn., Co., U.S.	D5	83
Culiacán, Mex.	E6	62
Cullen, La., U.S.	B2	95
Cullman, Al., U.S.	A3	78
Cullman, co., Al., U.S.	A3	78
Culloden, W.V., U.S.	C2	125
Cullowhee, N.C., U.S.	f9	110
Cul'man, Russia	F18	24
Culpeper, Va., U.S.	B4	123
Culpeper, co., Va., U.S.	B5	123
Culver, In., U.S.	B5	91
Culver City, Ca., U.S.	m12	82
Culvers Lake, l., N.J., U.S.	A3	107
Culym, Russia	F10	24
Cumalı, Tur.	M11	16
Cumaná, Ven.	B10	58
Cumanacoa, Ven.	B11	58
Cumbal, Nevado de, mtn., Col.	G4	58
Cumberland, B.C., Can.	E5	69
Cumberland, Ky., U.S.	D7	94
Cumberland, Md., U.S.	k13	97
Cumberland, Wi., U.S.	C2	126
Cumberland, co., Il., U.S.	D5	90
Cumberland, co., Ky., U.S.	D4	94
Cumberland, co., Me., U.S.	E2	96
Cumberland, co., N.J., U.S.	E2	107
Cumberland, co., N.C., U.S.	C4	110
Cumberland, co., Pa., U.S.	F7	115
Cumberland, co., Tn., U.S.	D8	119
Cumberland, co., Va., U.S.	C4	123
Cumberland, stm., U.S.	D4	94
Cumberland, Lake, res., Ky., U.S.	D5	94
Cumberland Center, Me., U.S.	g7	96
Cumberland Foreside, Me., U.S.	E2	96
Cumberland Gap, U.S.	D6	94
Cumberland Gap National Historical Park, U.S.	D6	94
Cumberland Hill, R.I., U.S.	B4	116
Cumberland Island National Seashore, Ga., U.S.	F5	87
Cumberland Islands, is., Austl.	D9	50
Cumberland Lake, l., Sask., Can.	C4	75
Cumberland Peninsula, pen., N.W. Ter., Can.	C19	66
Cumberland Sound, strt., N.W. Ter., Can.	C19	66
Cumbres Pass, Co., U.S.	D4	83
Čumikan, Russia	G21	24
Cuming, co., Ne., U.S.	C9	104
Cumming, Ga., U.S.	B2	87
Cumnock, Scot., U.K.	F8	7
Čuna, stm., Russia	F13	24
Čun'a, stm., Russia	E13	24
Cunani, Braz.	C8	54
Cunene, stm., Afr.	E2	44
Cuneo, Italy	E2	14
Cunnamulla, Austl.	E9	50
Cunningham, Ky., U.S.	f9	94
Cupar, Sask., Can.	G3	75
Curaçao, i., Neth. Ant.	H13	64
Curecanti National Recreation Area, Co., U.S.	C3	83
Curepipe, Mrts.	F11	44
Curiapo, Ven.	C12	58
Curicó, Chile	C2	56
Curitiba, Braz.	B7	56
Curlew Creek, stm., Wa., U.S.	A7	124
Curlew Lake, l., Wa., U.S.	A7	124
Curralinho, Braz.	D9	54
Currant Mountain, mtn., Nv., U.S.	E6	105
Current, stm., U.S.	A5	81
Currituck, co., N.C., U.S.	A6	110
Curry, co., N.M., U.S.	C6	108
Curry, co., Or., U.S.	E2	114
Curtis, Ne., U.S.	D5	104
Curtisville, Pa., U.S.	E2	115
Curvelo, Braz.	E6	57
Curwensville, Pa., U.S.	E4	115
Curwensville Lake, res., Pa., U.S.	E4	115
Curwood, Mount, mtn., Mi., U.S.	B2	99
Cushing, Ok., U.S.	B5	113
Cushman, Lake, res., Wa., U.S.	B2	124
Cusseta, Ga., U.S.	D2	87
Custer, S.D., U.S.	D2	118
Custer, co., Co., U.S.	C5	83
Custer, co., Id., U.S.	E4	89
Custer, co., Mt., U.S.	D11	103
Custer, co., Ne., U.S.	C6	104
Custer, co., Ok., U.S.	B2	113
Custer, co., S.D., U.S.	D2	118
Custer Battlefield National Monument, Mt., U.S.	E9	103
Cut Bank, Mt., U.S.	B4	103
Cut Bank Creek, stm., N.D., U.S.	A4	111
Cutchogue, N.Y., U.S.	m16	109
Cuthbert, Ga., U.S.	E2	87
Cutler Ridge, Fl., U.S.	s13	86
Cut Off, La., U.S.	E5	95
Cutro, Italy	J11	14
Cuttack, India	J11	38
Cuttyhunk Island, i., Ma., U.S.	D6	98
Cuxhaven, Ger.	B8	8
Cuyahoga, co., Oh., U.S.	A4	112
Cuyahoga, stm., Oh., U.S.	A4	112
Cuyahoga Falls, Oh., U.S.	A4	112
Cuyama, stm., Ca., U.S.	E4	82
Cuyamaca Peak, mtn., Ca., U.S.	F5	82
Cuyo Islands, is., Phil.	C7	32
Cuyuni, stm., S.A.	D13	58
Cuzco, Peru	F4	54
C.W. McConaughy, Lake, res., Ne., U.S.	C4	104
Cyclades see Kikládhes, is., Grc.	L8	16
Cynthiana, In., U.S.	H2	91
Cynthiana, Ky., U.S.	B5	94
Cypress Creek, stm., Tx., U.S.	r14	120
Cypress Hills Provincial Park, Sask., Can.	H1	75
Cypress Lake, l., Fl., U.S.	D5	86
Cypress Quarters, Fl., U.S.	E6	86
Cypress Swamp, sw., U.S.	F4	85
Cyprus, ctry., Asia	B3	40
Cyril, Ok., U.S.	C3	113
Czech Republic, ctry., Eur.	F11	4
Częstochowa, Pol.	E19	8

D

Name	Map Ref	Page
Dabeiba, Col.	D4	58
Dabhoi, India	I5	38
Dabie Shan, mts., China	D4	28
Dabola, Gui.	F3	42
Dacca see Dhaka, Bngl.	I14	38
Dachaidan, China	B16	38
Dachau, Ger.	G11	8
Dacono, Co., U.S.	A6	83
Dacula, Ga., U.S.	C3	87
Dadanawa, Guy.	F13	58
Dade, co., Fl., U.S.	G6	86
Dade, co., Ga., U.S.	B1	87
Dade, co., Mo., U.S.	D4	102
Dade City, Fl., U.S.	D4	86
Dadeville, Al., U.S.	C4	78
Dādra and Nagar Haveli, ter., India	B2	37
Dādu, Pak.	G2	38
Daet, Phil.	q20	33b
Daggett, co., Ut., U.S.	C6	121
Dagsboro, De., U.S.	F5	85
Dagupan, Phil.	p19	33b
Dahan-e Qowmghī, Afg.	C2	38
Da Hinggan Ling, mts., China	C11	26
Dahlak Archipelago, is., Erit.	E3	46
Dahlak Kebir Island, i., Erit.	E3	46
Dahlonega, Ga., U.S.	B3	87
Dahomey see Benin, ctry., Afr.	G6	42
Dahra, Libya	C9	42
Dahy, Nafūd ad-, des., Sau. Ar.	D4	46
Daimiel, Spain	F8	12
Daingerfield, Tx., U.S.	C5	120
Dairen see Dalian, China	D11	26
Dakar, Sen.	F2	42
Dakhla, W. Sah.	D2	42
Dakota, co., Mn., U.S.	F5	100
Dakota, co., Ne., U.S.	B9	104
Dakota City, Ia., U.S.	B3	92
Dakota City, Ne., U.S.	B9	104
Dalandzadgad, Mong.	C7	26
Da Lat, Viet.	I10	34
Dālbandin, Pak.	D1	36
Dalby, Austl.	E10	50
Dale, In., U.S.	H4	91
Dale, co., Al., U.S.	D4	78
Dale City, Va., U.S.	B5	123
Dale Hollow Lake, res., U.S.	C8	119
Daleville, Al., U.S.	D4	78
Daleville, In., U.S.	D6	91
Dalhart, Tx., U.S.	A1	120
Dalhousie, N.B., Can.	A3	71
Dalhousie, Cape, c., N.W. Ter., Can.	B7	66
Dali, China	B6	34
Dalian, China	D11	26
Dall, Mount, mtn., Ak., U.S.	f15	79
Dallam, co., Tx., U.S.	A1	120
Dallas, Ga., U.S.	C2	87
Dallas (part of Melcher), Ia., U.S.	C4	92
Dallas, N.C., U.S.	B1	110
Dallas, Or., U.S.	C3	114
Dallas, Pa., U.S.	D10	115
Dallas, Tx., U.S.	C4	120
Dallas, co., Al., U.S.	C2	78
Dallas, co., Ar., U.S.	D3	81
Dallas, co., Ia., U.S.	C3	92
Dallas, co., Mo., U.S.	D4	102
Dallas, co., Tx., U.S.	C4	120
Dallas Center, Ia., U.S.	C4	92
Dallas City, Il., U.S.	C2	90
Dallas Naval Air Station, mil., Tx., U.S.	n9	120
Dallastown, Pa., U.S.	G8	115
Dall Island, i., Ak., U.S.	n23	79
Dalmacija, hist. reg., Eur.	F11	14
Dalmatia see Dalmacija, hist. reg., Eur.	F11	14
Daloa, C. Iv.	G4	42
Dalqū, Sudan	D12	42
Dalton, Ga., U.S.	B2	87
Dalton, Ma., U.S.	B1	98
Dalton, Oh., U.S.	B4	112
Dalton, Pa., U.S.	C10	115
Daltonganj, India	H11	38
Dalton Gardens, Id., U.S.	B2	89
Dalwallinu, Austl.	F3	50
Daly City, Ca., U.S.	h8	82
Damān, India	B2	37
Damān, ter., India	B2	37
Damar, Pulau, i., Indon.	G8	32
Damariscotta, Me., U.S.	D3	96
Damariscotta Lake, l., Me., U.S.	D3	96
Damascus, Md., U.S.	B3	97
Damascus, Va., U.S.	f10	123
Damascus see Dimashq, Syria	C5	40
Damāvand, Qolleh-ye, mtn., Iran	J8	22
Damba, Ang.	C3	44
Damoh, India	I8	38
Dampar, Tasek, l., Malay.	M7	34
Dampier, Austl.	D3	50
Dampier, Selat, strt., Indon.	F9	32
Dampier Archipelago, is., Austl.	D3	50
Dan, stm., U.S.	D3	123
Dana, In., U.S.	E3	91
Danakil Plain, pl., Erit.	F3	46
Da Nang, Viet.	F10	34
Danbury, Ct., U.S.	D2	84
Danbury, Tx., U.S.	r14	120
Dand, Afg.	E1	38
Dandridge, Tn., U.S.	C10	119
Dane, co., Wi., U.S.	E4	126
Dangila, Eth.	F2	46
Dania, Fl., U.S.	F6	86
Daniels, co., Mt., U.S.	B11	103
Danielson, Ct., U.S.	B8	84
Daniels Pass, Ut., U.S.	C4	121
Danilov, Russia	C23	18
Danlí, Hond.	G4	64
Dannemora, N.Y., U.S.	f11	109
Dansville, N.Y., U.S.	C3	109
Dante, Va., U.S.	f9	123
Danube, stm., Eur.	G13	4
Danube, Mouths of the, mth., Eur.	D13	16
Danvers, Il., U.S.	C4	90
Danvers, Ma., U.S.	A6	98
Danville, Que., Can.	D5	74
Danville, Ar., U.S.	B2	81
Danville, Ca., U.S.	h9	82
Danville, Il., U.S.	C6	90
Danville, In., U.S.	E4	91
Danville, Ia., U.S.	D6	92
Danville, Ky., U.S.	C5	94
Danville, Oh., U.S.	B3	112
Danville, Pa., U.S.	E8	115
Danville, Va., U.S.	D3	123
Danyang, China	C8	28
Danzig, Gulf of, b., Eur.	A19	8
Danzig see Gdańsk, Pol.	A18	8
Daocheng, China	F7	26
Dapango, Togo	F6	42
Daphne, Al., U.S.	E2	78
Dar'ā, Syria	C5	40
Darakht-e Yahyá, Afg.	E3	38
Dārayyā, Syria	C5	40
Darbāsīyah, Syria	A7	40
Darbhanga, India	G11	38
Darby, Mt., U.S.	D2	103
Darby, Pa., U.S.	G11	115
Darchan, Mong.	B8	26
Dardanelle, Ar., U.S.	B2	81
Dardanelle Lake, res., Ar., U.S.	B2	81
Dardanelles see Çanakkale Boğazı, strt., Tur.	I10	16
Dare, co., N.C., U.S.	B7	110
Dar es Salaam, Tan.	C7	44
Dargaville, N.Z.	A4	52
Dari, China	E6	26
Darien, Ct., U.S.	E2	84
Darien, Ga., U.S.	E5	87
Darien, Wi., U.S.	F5	126
Dariganga, Mong.	B9	26
Darjeeling, India	G13	38
Darke, co., Oh., U.S.	B1	112
Darley Woods, De., U.S.	h8	85
Darling, stm., Austl.	F9	50
Darling, Lake, res., N.D., U.S.	A4	111
Darling Range, mts., Austl.	F3	50
Darlington, Eng., U.K.	G11	7
Darlington, In., U.S.	D4	91
Darlington, Md., U.S.	A5	97
Darlington, S.C., U.S.	C8	117
Darlington, Wi., U.S.	F3	126
Darlington, co., S.C., U.S.	C8	117
Darmstadt, Ger.	F8	8
Darnah, Libya	B10	42
Daroca, Spain	D10	12
Darrah, Mount, mtn., Can.	E3	68
Darrington, Wa., U.S.	A4	124
Dartmoor National Park, Eng., U.K.	K9	7
Dartmouth, Eng., U.K.	K9	7
Daru, Pap. N. Gui.	G11	32
Darwin, Austl.	B6	50
Dašinčilen, Mong.	B7	26
Dassel, Mn., U.S.	E4	100
Datia, India	H8	38
Datil Mountains, mts., N.M., U.S.	C2	108
D'at'kovo, Russia	H17	18
Datong, China	C9	26
Datu, Tanjung, c., Asia	M10	34
Dāūd Khel, Pak.	D4	38
Daufuskie Island, i., S.C., U.S.	G6	117
Daugavpils, Lat.	F9	18
Daulatābād (Shirin Tagāo), Afg.	B1	38
Daule, Ec.	I3	58
Dauphin, Man., Can.	D1	70
Dauphin, co., Pa., U.S.	F8	115
Dauphin, stm., Man., Can.	D2	70

Name	Map Ref	Page
Dauphin Island, Al., U.S.	E1	78
Dauphin Island, i., Al., U.S.	E1	78
Dauphin Lake, l., Man., Can.	D2	70
Dāvangere, India	E3	37
Davao, Phil.	D8	32
Davao Gulf, b., Phil.	D8	32
Daveluyville, Que., Can.	C5	74
Davenport, Fl., U.S.	D5	86
Davenport, Ia., U.S.	C7	92
Davenport, Ok., U.S.	B5	113
Davenport, Wa., U.S.	B7	124
David, Pan.	J6	64
David City, Ne., U.S.	C8	104
Davidson, N.C., U.S.	B2	110
Davidson, co., N.C., U.S.	B2	110
Davidson, co., Tn., U.S.	A5	119
Davidsville, Pa., U.S.	F4	115
Davie, Fl., U.S.	F6	86
Davie, co., N.C., U.S.	B2	110
Daviess, co., In., U.S.	G3	91
Daviess, co., Ky., U.S.	C2	94
Daviess, co., Mo., U.S.	B3	102
Davis, Ca., U.S.	C3	82
Davis, Ok., U.S.	C4	113
Davis, W.V., U.S.	B5	125
Davis, co., Ia., U.S.	D5	92
Davis, co., Ut., U.S.	C3	121
Davis, Mount, mtn., Pa., U.S.	G3	115
Davis Creek, stm., W.V., U.S.	m12	125
Davis Dam, U.S.	H7	105
Davis Islands, is., Fl., U.S.	p11	86
Davis Lake, l., Or., U.S.	E5	114
Davis-Monthan Air Force Base, mil., Az., U.S.	E5	80
Davison, Mi., U.S.	E7	99
Davison, co., S.D., U.S.	D7	118
Davis Strait, strt., N.A.	C21	66
Davisville, R.I., U.S.	E4	116
Davos, Switz.	F16	10
Dawa (Daua), stm., Afr.	H3	46
Dawei, Mya.	G5	34
Dawes, co., Ne., U.S.	B2	104
Daws Island, i., S.C., U.S.	G6	117
Dawson, Ga., U.S.	E2	87
Dawson, Mn., U.S.	F2	100
Dawson, co., Ga., U.S.	B2	87
Dawson, co., Mt., U.S.	C11	103
Dawson, co., Ne., U.S.	D6	104
Dawson, co., Tx., U.S.	C1	120
Dawson, Mount, mtn., B.C., Can.	D9	69
Dawson Creek, B.C., Can.	B7	69
Dawson Springs, Ky., U.S.	C2	94
Dax, Fr.	I5	10
Day, co., S.D., U.S.	B8	118
Dayr az-Zawr, Syria	B7	40
Daysland, Alta., Can.	C4	68
Dayton, In., U.S.	D4	91
Dayton, Ia., U.S.	B3	92
Dayton, Ky., U.S.	h14	94
Dayton, Md., U.S.	B4	97
Dayton, Mn., U.S.	m12	100
Dayton, Nv., U.S.	D2	105
Dayton, Oh., U.S.	C1	112
Dayton, Or., U.S.	B3	114
Dayton, Tn., U.S.	D8	119
Dayton, Tx., U.S.	D5	120
Dayton, Va., U.S.	B4	123
Dayton, Wa., U.S.	C8	124
Dayton, Wy., U.S.	B5	127
Daytona Beach, Fl., U.S.	C5	86
Da Yunhe, China	E10	26
Dayville, Ct., U.S.	B8	84
De Aar, S. Afr.	H4	44
Dead, North Branch, stm., Me., U.S.	C2	96
Dead, South Branch, stm., Me., U.S.	C2	96
Dead Creek, stm., Vt., U.S.	C2	122
Dead Diamond, stm., N.H., U.S.	g7	106
Dead Indian Peak, mtn., Wy., U.S.	B3	127
Dead Lake, l., Mn., U.S.	D3	100
Dead Lakes, l., Fl., U.S.	B1	86
Deadman Bay, b., Fl., U.S.	C3	86
Deadman Creek, stm., Wa., U.S.	g14	124
Deadmans Cay, Bah.	C10	64
Dead Sea, l., Asia	D4	40
Deadwood, S.D., U.S.	C2	118
Deadwood Reservoir, res., Id., U.S.	E3	89
Deaf Smith, co., Tx., U.S.	B1	120
Deale, Md., U.S.	C4	97
Deal Island, Md., U.S.	D6	97
Deal Island, i., Md., U.S.	D6	97
Dean, stm., B.C., Can.	C4	69
Dean Channel, strt., B.C., Can.	C4	69
Deán Funes, Arg.	C4	56
Dearborn, Mi., U.S.	F7	99
Dearborn, co., In., U.S.	F7	91
Dearborn Heights, Mi., U.S.	p15	99
Dearg, Beinn, mtn., Scot., U.K.	D8	7
Dease Strait, strt., N.W. Ter., Can.	C11	66
Death Valley, val., Ca., U.S.	D5	82
Death Valley National Monument, U.S.	D5	82
Deauville, Fr.	C7	10
De Baca, co., N.M., U.S.	C5	108
De Bary, Fl., U.S.	D5	86
Debauch Mountain, mtn., Ak., U.S.	C8	79
Dębica, Pol.	E21	8
Debrecen, Hung.	H21	8
Debre Markos, Eth.	F2	46
Debre Tabor, Eth.	F2	46
De Cade, Lake, l., La., U.S.	E5	95
Decatur, Al., U.S.	A3	78
Decatur, Ar., U.S.	A1	81
Decatur, Ga., U.S.	C2	87
Decatur, Il., U.S.	D5	90
Decatur, In., U.S.	C8	91
Decatur, Mi., U.S.	F5	99
Decatur, Ms., U.S.	C4	101
Decatur, Ne., U.S.	B9	104
Decatur, Tn., U.S.	D9	119
Decatur, Tx., U.S.	C4	120
Decatur, co., Ga., U.S.	F2	87
Decatur, co., In., U.S.	F6	91
Decatur, co., Ia., U.S.	D4	92
Decatur, co., Ks., U.S.	C3	93
Decatur, co., Tn., U.S.	B3	119
Decatur, Lake, res., Il., U.S.	D5	90
Decaturville, Tn., U.S.	B3	119
Decazeville, Fr.	H9	10
Deccan, plat., India	E4	37
Deception, Mount, mtn., Wa., U.S.	B2	124
Decherd, Tn., U.S.	B5	119
Děčín, Czech.	E14	8
Decize, Fr.	F10	10
Deckerville, Mi., U.S.	E8	99
Decorah, Ia., U.S.	A6	92
Dedham, Ma., U.S.	B5	98
Dédougou, Burkina	F5	42
Dedovsk, Russia	F20	18
Deep, stm., N.C., U.S.	B3	110
Deep Creek, stm., Ut., U.S.	C2	121
Deep Creek, stm., Ut., U.S.	B3	121
Deep Creek, stm., Ut., U.S.	F3	121
Deep Creek, stm., Wa., U.S.	g13	124
Deep Creek Lake, res., Md., U.S.	K12	97
Deep Creek Mountains, mts., Id., U.S.	G6	89
Deep Fork, stm., Ok., U.S.	B5	113
Deep Inlet, b., Newf., Can.	g10	72
Deep Red Creek, stm., Ok., U.S.	C3	113
Deep River, Ont., Can.	A7	73
Deep River, Ct., U.S.	D6	84
Deer Creek, stm., Oh., U.S.	C2	112
Deer Creek Indian Reservation, Mn., U.S.	C5	100
Deerfield, Il., U.S.	h9	90
Deerfield, Ks., U.S.	E2	93
Deerfield, Ma., U.S.	A2	98
Deerfield, Mi., U.S.	G7	99
Deerfield, Wi., U.S.	E4	126
Deerfield, stm., U.S.	A2	98
Deerfield Beach, Fl., U.S.	F6	86
Deer Island, pen., Ma., U.S.	g12	98
Deer Island, i., Ms., U.S.	f8	101
Deer Isle, i., Me., U.S.	D4	96
Deer Lake, Newf., Can.	D3	72
Deer Lake, l., Newf., Can.	D3	72
Deer Lake, l., Mn., U.S.	C5	100
Deer Lodge, Mt., U.S.	D4	103
Deer Lodge, co., Mt., U.S.	E3	103
Deer Park, N.Y., U.S.	n15	109
Deer Park, Oh., U.S.	o13	112
Deer Park, Wa., U.S.	B8	124
Deer Peak, mtn., Co., U.S.	C5	83
Deer River, Mn., U.S.	C5	100
Deesa, India	H5	38
Defiance, Oh., U.S.	A1	112
Defiance, co., Oh., U.S.	A1	112
Defiance, Mount, mtn., Or., U.S.	B5	114
De Forest, Wi., U.S.	E4	126
De Funiak Springs, Fl., U.S.	u15	86
Degeh-Bur, Eth.	G3	46
Dégelis, Que., Can.	B9	74
Deggendorf, Ger.	G12	8
De Graff, Oh., U.S.	B2	112
De Gray Lake, res., Ar., U.S.	C2	81
Dehiwala-Mount Lavinia, Sri L.	I5	37
Dehra Dūn, India	E8	38
Dehri, India	H11	38
Dehu, India	C2	37
Dehui, China	C12	26
Dej, Rom.	B7	16
Deje, Swe.	G9	6
De Kalb, Il., U.S.	B5	90
De Kalb, Ms., U.S.	C5	101
De Kalb, Tx., U.S.	C5	120
De Kalb, co., Al., U.S.	A4	78
De Kalb, co., Ga., U.S.	C2	87
De Kalb, co., Il., U.S.	B5	90
De Kalb, co., In., U.S.	B7	91
De Kalb, co., Mo., U.S.	B3	102
De Kalb, co., Tn., U.S.	D8	119
Dekese, Zaire	B4	44
Delafield, Wi., U.S.	m11	126
Delanco, N.J., U.S.	C3	107
De Land, Fl., U.S.	C5	86
Delano, Ca., U.S.	E4	82
Delano, Mn., U.S.	E5	100
Delano Peak, mtn., Ut., U.S.	E3	121
Delaronde Lake, l., Sask., Can.	C2	75
Delavan, Il., U.S.	C4	90
Delavan, Wi., U.S.	F5	126
Delaware, Oh., U.S.	B2	112
Delaware, co., In., U.S.	D7	91
Delaware, co., Ia., U.S.	B6	92
Delaware, co., N.Y., U.S.	C5	109
Delaware, co., Oh., U.S.	B2	112
Delaware, co., Ok., U.S.	A7	113
Delaware, co., Pa., U.S.	G11	115
Delaware, state, U.S.	D3	85
Delaware, stm., U.S.	G11	115
Delaware, stm., Ks., U.S.	C8	93
Delaware, East Branch, stm., N.Y., U.S.	C5	109
Delaware Bay, b., U.S.	D11	76
Delaware City, De., U.S.	B3	85
Delaware Lake, res., Oh., U.S.	B3	112
Delaware Water Gap, N.J., U.S.	B2	107
Delaware Water Gap National Recreation Area, U.S.	B2	107
Delbarton, W.V., U.S.	D2	125
Delcambre, La., U.S.	E4	95
Del City, Ok., U.S.	B4	113
Delémont, Switz.	E14	10
De Leon, Tx., U.S.	C3	120
De Leon Springs, Fl., U.S.	C5	86
Delft, Neth.	C4	8
Delfzijl, Neth.	B6	8
Delgado, Cabo, c., Moz.	D8	44
Delhi, India	F7	38
Delhi, La., U.S.	B4	95
Delhi, N.Y., U.S.	C6	109
Delicias, Mex.	C7	62
De Lisle, Ms., U.S.	E4	101
Delitzsch, Ger.	D12	8
Dellenbaugh, Mount, mtn., Az., U.S.	A2	80
Dell Rapids, S.D., U.S.	D9	118
Del Mar, Ca., U.S.	o15	82
Delmar, De., U.S.	G3	85
Delmar, Md., U.S.	D6	97
Delmar, N.Y., U.S.	C7	109
Delmenhorst, Ger.	B8	8
Delnice, Cro.	D9	14
Del Norte, Co., U.S.	D4	83
Del Norte, co., Ca., U.S.	B2	82
De-Longa, Ostrova, is., Russia	B23	24
Deloraine, Man., Can.	E1	70
Del Park Manor, De., U.S.	i7	85
Delphi, In., U.S.	C4	91
Delphos, Oh., U.S.	B1	112
Delran, N.J., U.S.	C3	107
Delray Beach, Fl., U.S.	F6	86
Del Rio, Tx., U.S.	E2	120
Delson, Que., Can.	q19	74
Delta, Co., U.S.	C2	83
Delta, Oh., U.S.	A2	112
Delta, Ut., U.S.	D3	121
Delta, co., Co., U.S.	C3	83
Delta, co., Mi., U.S.	C3	99
Delta, co., Tx., U.S.	C5	120
Delta, reg., Ms., U.S.	B3	101
Delta Junction, Ak., U.S.	C10	79
Delta Peak, mtn., B.C., Can.	A3	69
Delta Reservoir, res., N.Y., U.S.	B5	109
Deltaville, Va., U.S.	C6	123
Deltona, Fl., U.S.	D5	86
Demarest, N.J., U.S.	h9	107
Deming, N.M., U.S.	E2	108
Demirci, Tur.	J12	16
Demirköy, Tur.	H11	16
Demmin, Ger.	B13	8
Demopolis, Al., U.S.	C2	78
Demorest, Ga., U.S.	B3	87
Demotte, In., U.S.	B3	91
Denain, Fr.	B10	10
Denali National Park, Ak., U.S.	C9	79
Denare Beach, Sask., Can.	C4	75
Denham Springs, La., U.S.	D5	95
Den Helder, Neth.	C4	8
Denia, Spain	G12	12
Denison, Ia., U.S.	B2	92
Denison, Tx., U.S.	C4	120
Denison Dam, U.S.	D5	113
Denizli, Tur.	H13	4
Denmark, S.C., U.S.	E5	117
Denmark, Wi., U.S.	D6	126
Denmark, ctry., Eur.	D9	4
Denmark Strait, strt.	C15	128
Dennehotso, Az., U.S.	A6	80
Dennis, Ma., U.S.	C7	98
Dennison, Oh., U.S.	B4	112
Dennis Port, Ma., U.S.	C7	98
Denny Terrace, S.C., U.S.	C5	117
Denpasar, Indon.	G6	32
Dent, co., Mo., U.S.	D6	102
Denton, Md., U.S.	C6	97
Denton, N.C., U.S.	B2	110
Denton, Tx., U.S.	C4	120
Denton, co., Tx., U.S.	C4	120
D'Entrecasteaux Islands, is., Pap. N. Gui.	m17	50a
Dentsville, S.C., U.S.	C6	117
Denver, Co., U.S.	B6	83
Denver, Ia., U.S.	B5	92
Denver, Pa., U.S.	F9	115
Denver, co., Co., U.S.	B6	83
Denver City, Tx., U.S.	C1	120
Denville, N.J., U.S.	B4	107
Deoghar, India	H12	38
Deolāli, India	C2	37
Deoria, India	G10	38
De Pere, Wi., U.S.	D5	126
Depew, N.Y., U.S.	C2	109
Depoe Bay, Or., U.S.	C2	114
Depok, Indon.	m13	33a
Deposit, N.Y., U.S.	C5	109
Depue, Il., U.S.	B4	90
Deqin, China	F6	26
De Queen, Ar., U.S.	C1	81
De Queen Reservoir, res., Ar., U.S.	C1	81
De Quincy, La., U.S.	D2	95
Dera Ghāzi Khān, Pak.	E4	38
Dera Ismāīl Khān, Pak.	E4	38
Derby, Austl.	C4	50
Derby, Eng., U.K.	I11	7
Derby, Ct., U.S.	D3	84
Derby, Ks., U.S.	E6	93
Derby, Vt., U.S.	B4	122
Derby Line, Vt., U.S.	A4	122
Derg, Lough, l., Ire.	I4	7
De Ridder, La., U.S.	D2	95
Derma, Ms., U.S.	B4	101
Dermott, Ar., U.S.	D4	81
Dernieres, Isles, is., La., U.S.	E5	95
Derry, N.H., U.S.	E4	106
Derry, Pa., U.S.	F3	115
Derval, Fr.	E5	10
Derventa, Bos.	E12	14
Derwood, Md., U.S.	B3	97
Desaguadero, stm., Arg.	C3	56
Des Allemands, La., U.S.	E5	95
Des Arc, Ar., U.S.	C4	81
Desbiens, Que., Can.	A6	74
Descartes, Fr.	F7	10
Deschaillons [-sur-Saint-Laurent], Que., Can.	C5	74
Deschambault, Que., Can.	C6	74
Deschambault Lake, l., Sask., Can.	C4	75
Deschutes, co., Or., U.S.	D5	114
Deschutes, stm., Or., U.S.	B6	114
Dese, Eth.	F2	46
Deseado, stm., Arg.	F3	56
Deseret Peak, mtn., Ut., U.S.	C3	121
Deseronto, Ont., Can.	C7	73
Desert Creek Peak, mtn., Nv., U.S.	E2	105
Desert Hot Springs, Ca., U.S.	F5	82
Desert Peak, mtn., Ut., U.S.	B2	121
Desert Valley, val., Nv., U.S.	B3	105
Desha, Ar., U.S.	B4	81
Desha, co., Ar., U.S.	D4	81
Deshler, Ne., U.S.	D8	104
Deshler, Oh., U.S.	A2	112
Des Lacs, stm., N.D., U.S.	A4	111
Desloge, Mo., U.S.	D7	102
De Smet, S.D., U.S.	C8	118
Des Moines, Ia., U.S.	C4	92
Des Moines, Wa., U.S.	B3	124
Des Moines, co., Ia., U.S.	D6	92
Des Moines, stm., U.S.	D5	92
Desolación, Isla, i., Chile	G2	56
De Soto, Il., U.S.	F4	90
De Soto, Ia., U.S.	C3	92
De Soto, Ks., U.S.	D9	93
De Soto, Mo., U.S.	C7	102
De Soto, co., Fl., U.S.	E5	86
De Soto, co., La., U.S.	B2	95
De Soto, co., Ms., U.S.	A3	101
Despard, W.V., U.S.	k10	125
Des Peres, Mo., U.S.	f13	102
Des Plaines, Il., U.S.	A6	90
Des Plaines, stm., U.S.	k8	90
Desroches, Île, i., Sey.	C10	44
Dessau, Ger.	D12	8
Destin, Fl., U.S.	u15	86
Destrehan, La., U.S.	E5	95
Desvres, Fr.	B8	10
Detmold, Ger.	D8	8
Detour, Point, c., Mi., U.S.	C4	99
Detroit, Mi., U.S.	F7	99
Detroit Lake, res., Or., U.S.	C4	114
Detroit Lakes, Mn., U.S.	D3	100
Deuel, co., Ne., U.S.	C3	104
Deuel, co., S.D., U.S.	C9	118
Deutsche Bucht, b., Ger.	A7	8
Deutschlandsberg, Aus.	I15	8
Deux-Montagnes, Que., Can.	p19	74
Deux Montagnes, Lac des, l., Que., Can.	q19	74
Deva, Rom.	D6	16
Devakottai, India	H5	37
De Valls Bluff, Ar., U.S.	C4	81
Deventer, Neth.	C6	8
DeView, Bayou, stm., Ar., U.S.	B4	81
Devil's Island see Diable, Île du, i., Fr. Gu.	B8	54
Devils Lake, N.D., U.S.	A7	111
Devils Lake, l., N.D., U.S.	A6	111
Devils Paw, mtn., Ak., U.S.	k23	79
Devils Postpile National Monument, Ca., U.S.	D4	82
Devils Tower National Monument, Wy., U.S.	B8	127
Devil Track Lake, l., Mn., U.S.	k9	100
Devine, Tx., U.S.	E3	120
DeVola, Oh., U.S.	C4	112
Devon, Alta., Can.	C4	68
Devon Island, i., N.W. Ter., Can.	A15	66
Devonport, Austl.	H9	50
Devonport, N.Z.	B5	52
Devonshire, De., U.S.	h7	85
Dewa-kyūryō, hills, Japan	C13	30
Dewar, Ok., U.S.	B6	113
Dewās, India	I7	38
Dewees Inlet, b., S.C., U.S.	k12	117
Dewees Island, i., S.C., U.S.	F8	117
Dewey, Az., U.S.	C3	80
Dewey, Ok., U.S.	A6	113
Dewey, co., Ok., U.S.	B2	113
Dewey, co., S.D., U.S.	B4	118
Dewey Beach, De., U.S.	F5	85
Dewey Lake, res., Ky., U.S.	C7	94
Deweyville, Tx., U.S.	D6	120
De Witt, Ar., U.S.	C4	81
De Witt, Ia., U.S.	C7	92
De Witt, Mi., U.S.	F6	99
De Witt, N.Y., U.S.	B4	109
De Witt, co., Il., U.S.	C4	90
De Witt, co., Tx., U.S.	E4	120
Dexter, Ia., U.S.	C3	92
Dexter, Me., U.S.	C3	96
Dexter, Mi., U.S.	F7	99
Dexter, Mo., U.S.	E8	102
Dexter, N.M., U.S.	D5	108
Dexter, Lake, l., Fl., U.S.	C5	86
Dezfūl, Iran	B4	46
Dezhou, China	D10	26
Dhaka, Bngl.	I14	38
Dhamār, Yemen	F3	46
Dhamtari, India	B6	37
Dhānbād, India	I12	38
Dhār, India	I6	38
Dharmapuri, India	F5	37
Dharmavaram, India	E4	37
Dhārwār, India	E3	37
Dhawlāgiri, mtn., Nepal	F10	38
Dhodhekánisos (Dodecanese), is., Grc.	M10	16
Dholpur, India	G7	38
Dhorāji, India	J4	38
Dhrol, India	I4	38
Dhubri, India	G13	38
Dhule, India	B3	37
Diable, Île du, i., Fr. Gu.	B8	54
Diablo, Canyon, val., Az., U.S.	C4	80
Diablo, Mount, mtn., Ca., U.S.	h9	82
Diablo Dam, Wa., U.S.	A4	124
Diablo Lake, res., Wa., U.S.	A4	124
Diablo Range, mts., Ca., U.S.	D3	82
Diamante, Arg.	C4	56
Diamantina, Braz.	E7	57
Diamantino, Braz.	F7	54
Diamond Head, crat., Hi., U.S.	B4	88
Diamond Hill, R.I., U.S.	B4	116
Diamond Hill Reservoir, res., R.I., U.S.	A4	116
Diamond Lake, Il., U.S.	h9	90
Diamond Lake, l., Or., U.S.	D4	114
Diamond Mountains, mts., Nv., U.S.	D6	105
Diamond Peak, mtn., Co., U.S.	A2	83
Diamond Peak, mtn., Id., U.S.	E5	89
Diamond Peak, mtn., Or., U.S.	D4	114
Diamond Peak, mtn., Wa., U.S.	C8	124
Diamondville, Wy., U.S.	E2	127
Diaz, Ar., U.S.	B4	81
Dibaya, Zaire	C4	44
D'Iberville, Ms., U.S.	E5	101
Diboll, Tx., U.S.	D5	120
Dibrugarh, India	G16	38
Dickens, co., Tx., U.S.	C2	120
Dickenson, co., Va., U.S.	e9	123
Dickerson, Md., U.S.	B3	97
Dickey, co., N.D., U.S.	C7	111
Dickeyville, Wi., U.S.	F3	126
Dickinson, N.D., U.S.	C3	111
Dickinson, co., Ia., U.S.	A2	92
Dickinson, co., Ks., U.S.	D6	93
Dickinson, co., Mi., U.S.	B3	99
Dickinson Dam, N.D., U.S.	C3	111
Dickson, Ok., U.S.	C5	113
Dickson, Tn., U.S.	A4	119
Dickson, co., Tn., U.S.	A4	119
Dickson City, Pa., U.S.	D10	115
Didsbury, Alta., Can.	D3	68
Die, Fr.	H12	10
Dieburg, Ger.	F8	8
Dieciocho de Marzo, Mex.	E11	62
Diefenbaker, Lake, res., Sask., Can.	F2	75
Diégo-Suarez see Antsiranana, Madag.	D9	44
Dien Bien Phu, Viet.	D7	34
Diepholz, Ger.	C8	8
Dieppe, N.B., Can.	C5	71
Dieppe, Fr.	C8	10
Dierks, Ar., U.S.	C1	81
Dieuze, Fr.	D13	10
Digboi, India	G16	38
Dighton, Ks., U.S.	D3	93
Digne, Fr.	H13	10
Digoin, Fr.	F10	10
Dijon, Fr.	E12	10
Dike, Ia., U.S.	B5	92
Dikson, Russia	C10	24
Dili, Indon.	G8	32
Dillard, Or., U.S.	D3	114
Dill City, Ok., U.S.	B2	113
Dilley, Tx., U.S.	E3	120
Dillingen [an der Donau], Ger.	G10	8
Dillingham, Ak., U.S.	D8	79
Dillon, Mt., U.S.	E4	103
Dillon, S.C., U.S.	C9	117
Dillon, co., S.C., U.S.	C9	117
Dillon Lake, res., Oh., U.S.	B3	112
Dillon Reservoir, res., Co., U.S.	B4	83
Dillonvale, Oh., U.S.	B5	112
Dillsboro, In., U.S.	F7	91
Dillsburg, Pa., U.S.	F7	115
Dilolo, Zaire	D4	44
Dilworth, Mn., U.S.	D2	100
Dimāpur, India	H15	38
Dimashq (Damascus), Syria	C5	40
Dimitrovgrad, Bul.	G9	16
Dimitrovgrad, Russia	G7	22
Dimmit, co., Tx., U.S.	E3	120
Dimmitt, Tx., U.S.	B1	120
Dimona, Isr.	D4	40
Dimondale, Mi., U.S.	F6	99
Dinagat Island, i., Phil.	C8	32
Dinājpur, Bngl.	H13	38
Dinan, Fr.	D4	10
Dinant, Bel.	E4	8
Dinara, mts., Eur.	F11	14
Dinard, Fr.	D4	10
Dinaric Alps see Dinara, mts., Eur.	F11	14
Dindigul, India	G4	37
Dinghai, China	E11	28
Dingle, Ire.	I2	7
Dingmans Ferry, Pa., U.S.	D12	115
Dingolfing, Ger.	G12	8
Dingqing, China	E16	38
Dingri, China	F12	38
Dingshan, China	D8	28
Dingwall, Scot., U.K.	D8	7
Dinh Lap, Viet.	D9	34
Dinner Point, c., Fl., U.S.	D4	86
Dinosaur National Monument, U.S.	C6	121
Dinuba, Ca., U.S.	D4	82
Dinwiddie, co., Va., U.S.	C5	123
Diourbel, Sen.	F2	42
Dipkarpaz, N. Cyp.	B4	40
Dipolog, Phil.	D7	32
Dire Dawa, Eth.	G3	46
Diriamba, Nic.	I4	64
Dirico, Ang.	E4	44
Dirk Hartog Island, i., Austl.	E2	50
Dirty Devil, stm., Ut., U.S.	E5	121
Disappointment, Cape, c., Falk. Is.	G9	56
Disappointment, Cape, c., Wa., U.S.	C1	124
Disappointment, Lake, l., Austl.	D4	50
Disentis, Switz.	F15	10
Dishman, Wa., U.S.	g14	124
Disko, i., Grnld.	C22	66
Disko Bugt, b., Grnld.	C22	66
Dismal, stm., Ne., U.S.	C5	104
Disraëli, Que., Can.	D6	74
District of Columbia, dept., U.S.	f8	97
Diu, India	J4	38
Diu, ter., India	J4	38
Divernon, Il., U.S.	D4	90
Divide, co., N.D., U.S.	A2	111
Divide Peak, mtn., Wy., U.S.	E5	127
Divinópolis, Braz.	F6	57
Divisor, Serra do, plat., S.A.	E4	54
Dix, stm., Ky., U.S.	C5	94
Dixfield, Me., U.S.	D2	96
Dixie, co., Fl., U.S.	C3	86
Dixie Valley, val., Nv., U.S.	D4	105
Dixon, Ca., U.S.	C3	82
Dixon, Il., U.S.	B4	90
Dixon, Mo., U.S.	D5	102
Dixon, N.M., U.S.	A4	108
Dixon, co., Ne., U.S.	B9	104
Dixon Entrance, strt., N.A.	F6	66
Dixonville, Pa., U.S.	E3	115
Diyarbakır, Tur.	H16	4
Dja, stm., Afr.	H8	42
Djakarta see Jakarta, Indon.	m13	32
Djambala, Congo	B2	44
Djanet, Alg.	D7	42
Djebel Abiod, Tun.	M4	14
Djebibina, Tun.	M5	14
Djemmal, Tun.	N5	14
Djerba, Île de, i., Tun.	B8	42
Djerid, Chott, sw., Tun.	B7	42
Djibouti, Dji.	F3	46
Djibouti, ctry., Afr.	F3	46
Dmitrija Lapteva, Proliv, strt., Russia	C22	24
Dmitrov, Russia	E20	18
Dnieper, stm., Eur.	H4	22
Dniester, stm., Eur.	H3	22

Name	Map Ref	Page
Dniprodzerzhyns'k, Ukr.	H4	22
Dnipropetrovs'k, Ukr.	H4	22
Dno, Russia	D12	18
Do Āb-e Mīkh-e Zarrīn, Afg.	C2	38
Doaktown, N.B., Can.	C3	71
Doany, Madag.	D9	44
Doba, Chad	E9	42
Dobbiaco, Italy	C7	14
Dobbs Ferry, N.Y., U.S.	g13	109
Döbeln, Ger.	D13	8
Doberai, Jazirah, pen., Indon.	F9	32
Dobo, Indon.	G9	32
Doboj, Bos.	E2	16
Dobrič, Bul.	F11	16
Dobruš, Bela.	I14	18
Dobson, N.C., U.S.	A2	110
Doce, stm., Braz.	E8	57
Docena, Al., U.S.	f7	78
Dock Junction, Ga., U.S.	*E5	87
Doctors Lake, l., Fl., U.S.	m8	86
Doddridge, co., W.V., U.S.	B4	125
Dodecanese see Dhodhekánisos, is., Grc.	M10	16
Dodge, Ne., U.S.	C9	104
Dodge, co., Ga., U.S.	D3	87
Dodge, co., Mn., U.S.	G6	100
Dodge, co., Ne., U.S.	C9	104
Dodge, co., Wi., U.S.	E5	126
Dodge Center, Mn., U.S.	F6	100
Dodge City, Ks., U.S.	E3	93
Dodgeville, Wi., U.S.	F3	126
Dodoma, Tan.	C7	44
Doerun, Ga., U.S.	E3	87
Doe Run, Mo., U.S.	D7	102
Doetinchem, Neth.	D6	8
Dog, stm., Vt., U.S.	C3	122
Dogai Coring, l., China	C13	38
Dog Island, i., Fl., U.S.	C2	86
Dog Keys Pass, strt., Ms., U.S.	g8	101
Dog Lake, l., Man., Can.	D2	70
Dogondoutchi, Niger	F6	42
Doha see Ad-Dawḩah, Qatar	C5	46
Dohad, India	I6	38
Doiran, Lake, l., Eur.	H6	16
Dokka, Nor.	F8	6
Dokkum, Neth.	B5	8
Dolak, Pulau, i., Indon.	G10	32
Dolbeau, Que., Can.	k12	74
Dol-de-Bretagne, Fr.	D5	10
Dolgeville, N.Y., U.S.	B6	109
Dolianova, Italy	J4	14
Dolisie, Congo	B2	44
Dollar Bay, Mi., U.S.	A2	99
Dolo, Som.	H3	46
Dolomite, Al., U.S.	B3	78
Dolomites see Dolomiti, mts., Italy	C6	14
Dolomiti, mts., Italy	C6	14
Dolores, Arg.	D5	56
Dolores, Col.	F5	58
Dolores, Co., U.S.	D2	83
Dolores, co., Co., U.S.	D2	83
Dolores, stm., U.S.	E7	121
Dolores Hidalgo, Mex.	G9	62
Dolphin and Union Strait, strt., N.W. Ter., Can.	C9	66
Dolphin Island, i., Ut., U.S.	B3	121
Dolton, Il., U.S.	k9	90
Dombås, Nor.	E7	6
Dome Mountain, mtn., Az., U.S.	k9	80
Dome Peak, mtn., Co., U.S.	B3	83
Domeyko, Chile	B2	56
Domeyko, Cordillera, mts., Chile	A3	56
Domfront, Fr.	D6	10
Dominica, ctry., N.A.	G17	64
Dominica Channel, strt., N.A.	G17	64
Dominican Republic, ctry., N.A.	E12	64
Dominion, Cape, c., N.W. Ter., Can.	C18	66
Domodedovo, Russia	F20	18
Domodossola, Italy	C3	14
Domžale, Slo.	C9	14
Don, stm., Russia	H6	22
Dona Ana, N.M., U.S.	E3	108
Dona Ana, co., N.M., U.S.	E2	108
Donaldsonville, La., U.S.	D4	95
Donalsonville, Ga., U.S.	E2	87
Donaueschingen, Ger.	H8	8
Donauwörth, Ger.	G10	8
Don Benito, Spain	G6	12
Doncaster, Eng., U.K.	H11	7
Dondo, Ang.	C2	44
Dondra Head, c., Sri L.	J6	37
Donegal Bay, b., Ire.	G4	7
Doneraile, S.C., U.S.	C8	117
Donetsk, Ukr.	H5	22
Donga, stm., Nig.	G8	42
Dongara, Austl.	E2	50
Dongchuan, China	A7	34
Dongfang, China	H8	26
Dongfang (Basuo), China	E10	34
Dongguan, China	L2	28
Donghai Dao, i., China	D11	34
Dong Hoi, Viet.	F9	34
Dongshan, China	L6	28
Dongtai, China	C9	28
Dongting Hu, l., China	F1	28
Doniphan, Mo., U.S.	E7	102
Doniphan, Ne., U.S.	D7	104
Doniphan, co., Ks., U.S.	C8	93
Donkey Creek, stm., Wy., U.S.	B7	127
Donkin, N.S., Can.	C10	71
Donley, co., Tx., U.S.	B2	120
Donna, Tx., U.S.	F3	120
Donnacona, Que., Can.	C6	74
Donnellson, Ia., U.S.	D6	92
Donner Pass, Ca., U.S.	C3	82
Donora, Pa., U.S.	F2	115
Donskoj, Russia	H21	18
Dooly, co., Ga., U.S.	D3	87
Doonerak, Mount, mtn., Ak., U.S.	B9	79
Door, co., Wi., U.S.	D6	126
Dora, Al., U.S.	B2	78
Doraville, Ga., U.S.	h8	87
Dorcheat, Bayou, stm., U.S.	B2	95
Dorchester, N.B., Can.	D5	71
Dorchester, Eng., U.K.	K10	7
Dorchester, Ne., U.S.	D8	104
Dorchester, co., Md., U.S.	D5	97
Dorchester, co., S.C., U.S.	E7	117
Dorchester, Cape, c., N.W. Ter., Can.	C17	66
Dordogne, stm., Fr.	H8	10
Dordrecht, Neth.	D4	8
Doré Lake, l., Sask., Can.	C2	75
Dorena Lake, res., Or., U.S.	D3	114
Dores do Indaiá, Braz.	E6	57
Dorgali, Italy	I4	14
Dori, Burkina	F5	42
Dorion-Vaudreuil, Que., Can.	q18	74
Dormont, Pa., U.S.	k13	115
Dornbirn, Aus.	H9	8
Dorothy Pond, Ma., U.S.	B4	98
Dorr, Mi., U.S.	F5	99
Dorset, Vt., U.S.	E2	122
Dorsey, Md., U.S.	B4	97
Dortmund, Ger.	D7	8
Dorton, Ky., U.S.	C7	94
Dorval, Que., Can.	q19	74
Dos Bahías, Cabo, c., Arg.	E3	56
Dothan, Al., U.S.	D4	78
Douai, Fr.	B10	10
Douala, Cam.	H7	42
Douarnenez, Fr.	D2	10
Double Beach, Ct., U.S.	D4	84
Doublespring Pass, Id., U.S.	E5	89
Double Springs, Al., U.S.	A2	78
Doubletop Peak, mtn., Wy., U.S.	C2	127
Doubs, stm., Eur.	E12	10
Dougherty, co., Ga., U.S.	E2	87
Douglas, I. of Man	G8	7
Douglas, Az., U.S.	F6	80
Douglas, Ga., U.S.	E4	87
Douglas, Mi., U.S.	F4	99
Douglas, Wy., U.S.	D7	127
Douglas, co., Co., U.S.	B6	83
Douglas, co., Ga., U.S.	C2	87
Douglas, co., Il., U.S.	D5	90
Douglas, co., Ks., U.S.	D8	93
Douglas, co., Mn., U.S.	E3	100
Douglas, co., Mo., U.S.	E5	102
Douglas, co., Ne., U.S.	C9	104
Douglas, co., Nv., U.S.	E2	105
Douglas, co., Or., U.S.	D3	114
Douglas, co., S.D., U.S.	D7	118
Douglas, co., Wa., U.S.	B6	124
Douglas, co., Wi., U.S.	B2	126
Douglas, Mount, mtn., Ak., U.S.	D9	79
Douglas Channel, strt., B.C., Can.	C3	69
Douglas Lake, l., Mi., U.S.	C6	99
Douglas Lake, res., Tn., U.S.	D10	119
Douglass, Ks., U.S.	E7	93
Douglastown, N.B., Can.	B4	71
Douglasville, Ga., U.S.	C2	87
Dourada, Serra, plat., Braz.	B4	57
Dourados, Braz.	G1	57
Douro (Duero), stm., Eur.	D4	12
Dousman, Wi., U.S.	E5	126
Dove Creek, Co., U.S.	D2	83
Dover, Eng., U.K.	J14	7
Dover, Ar., U.S.	B2	81
Dover, De., U.S.	D3	85
Dover, Fl., U.S.	D4	86
Dover, Ma., U.S.	h10	98
Dover, N.H., U.S.	D5	106
Dover, N.J., U.S.	B3	107
Dover, Oh., U.S.	B4	112
Dover, Pa., U.S.	F8	115
Dover, Tn., U.S.	A4	119
Dover, Strait of (Pas de Calais), strt., Eur.	J14	7
Dover Air Force Base, mil., De., U.S.	D4	85
Dover-Foxcroft, Me., U.S.	C3	96
Dover Plains, N.Y., U.S.	D7	109
Dowagiac, Mi., U.S.	G4	99
Dowlat Yār, Afg.	C1	38
Downers Grove, Il., U.S.	B5	90
Downey, Ca., U.S.	n12	82
Downey, Id., U.S.	G6	89
Downingtown, Pa., U.S.	F10	115
Downpatrick, N. Ire., U.K.	G7	7
Downpatrick Head, c., Ire.	G3	7
Downs, Ks., U.S.	C5	93
Downs Mountain, mtn., Wy., U.S.	C3	127
Downton, Mount, mtn., B.C., Can.	C5	69
Dows, Ia., U.S.	B4	92
Dowshī, Afg.	C3	38
Doylestown, Oh., U.S.	B4	112
Doylestown, Pa., U.S.	F11	115
Doyline, La., U.S.	B2	95
Drâa, Oued, val., Afr.	C4	42
Dracena, Braz.	F3	57
Drachten, Neth.	B6	8
Dracut, Ma., U.S.	A5	98
Draguignan, Fr.	I13	10
Drain, Or., U.S.	D3	114
Drake Passage, strt.	D6	47
Drake Peak, mtn., Or., U.S.	E6	114
Dráma, Grc.	H8	16
Drammen, Nor.	G8	6
Draper, Ut., U.S.	C4	121
Drau (Drava), stm., Eur.	C8	14
Drava (Drau), stm., Eur.	D13	14
Drayton, Ont., Can.	D4	73
Drayton, N.D., U.S.	A8	111
Drayton, S.C., U.S.	B4	117
Drayton Plains, Mi., U.S.	F7	99
Drayton Valley, Alta., Can.	C3	68
Dresden, Ont., Can.	E2	73
Dresden, Ger.	D13	8
Dresden, Oh., U.S.	B3	112
Dresden, Tn., U.S.	A3	119
Dresslerville, Nv., U.S.	E2	105
Dreux, Fr.	D8	10
Drew, Ms., U.S.	B3	101
Drew, co., Ar., U.S.	D4	81
Drews Reservoir, res., Or., U.S.	E6	114
Drexel, Mo., U.S.	C3	102
Drexel, N.C., U.S.	B1	110
Drexel, Oh., U.S.	C1	112
Drift, Ky., U.S.	C7	94
Driggs, Id., U.S.	F7	89
Driskill Mountain, hill, La., U.S.	B3	95
Drogheda, Ire.	H6	7
Drumheller, Alta., Can.	D4	68
Drum Island, i., S.C., U.S.	k12	117
Drummond, Lake, l., Va., U.S.	D6	123
Drummond Island, i., Mi., U.S.	C7	99
Drummondville, Que., Can.	D5	74
Drumright, Ok., U.S.	B5	113
Družina, Russia	D23	24
Drybranch, W.V., U.S.	m13	125
Dry Cimarron, stm., U.S.	A6	108
Dry Creek Mountain, mtn., Nv., U.S.	B5	105
Dryden, Ont., Can.	o16	73
Dryden, N.Y., U.S.	C4	109
Dry Fork, stm., Mo., U.S.	D6	102
Dry Fork, stm., W.V., U.S.	D3	125
Dry Fork, stm., W.V., U.S.	B5	125
Dry Ridge, Ky., U.S.	B5	94
Dry Tortugas, is., Fl., U.S.	H5	86
Duarte, Pico, mtn., Dom. Rep.	E12	64
Dubach, La., U.S.	B3	95
Dubai see Dubayy, U.A.E.	C6	46
Dubawnt, stm., N.W. Ter., Can.	D12	66
Dubawnt Lake, l., N.W. Ter., Can.	D12	66
Du Bay, Lake, res., Wi., U.S.	D4	126
Dubayy (Dubai), U.A.E.	C6	46
Dubbo, Austl.	F9	50
Dublin (Baile Átha Cliath), Ire.	H6	7
Dublin, Ga., U.S.	D4	87
Dublin, In., U.S.	E7	91
Dublin, N.H., U.S.	E2	106
Dublin, Oh., U.S.	k10	112
Dublin, Pa., U.S.	F11	115
Dublin, Tx., U.S.	C3	120
Dublin, Va., U.S.	C2	123
Dubna, Russia	E20	18
Dubois, In., U.S.	H4	91
Du Bois, Pa., U.S.	D4	115
Dubois, Wy., U.S.	C3	127
Dubois, co., In., U.S.	H4	91
Duboistown, Pa., U.S.	D7	115
Dubrovnik, Cro.	G13	14
Dubuque, Ia., U.S.	B7	92
Dubuque, co., Ia., U.S.	B7	92
Duchesne, Ut., U.S.	C5	121
Duchesne, co., Ut., U.S.	C5	121
Duchesne, stm., Ut., U.S.	C5	121
Duchess, Austl.	D7	50
Duck, stm., Tn., U.S.	B4	119
Duck Bay, Man., Can.	C1	70
Duck Creek, stm., Oh., U.S.	C4	112
Duck Creek, stm., Wi., U.S.	h9	126
Duck Lake, Sask., Can.	E2	75
Duck Lake, l., Me., U.S.	C4	96
Duck Mountain Provincial Park, Sask., Can.	F5	75
Duck Valley Indian Reservation, U.S.	B5	105
Duckwater Indian Reservation, Nv., U.S.	E6	105
Duckwater Peak, mtn., Nv., U.S.	E6	105
Dudelange, Lux.	F6	8
Dudinka, Russia	D11	24
Dudley, Ma., U.S.	B4	98
Duenweg, Mo., U.S.	D3	102
Duero (Douro), stm., Eur.	D5	12
Due West, S.C., U.S.	C3	117
Duffer Peak, mtn., Nv., U.S.	B3	105
Dufour Spitze, mtn., Eur.	G14	10
Duga Resa, Cro.	D10	14
Dugdemona, stm., La., U.S.	B3	95
Dugger, In., U.S.	F3	91
Duida, Cerro, mtn., Ven.	F10	58
Duifken Point, c., Austl.	B8	50
Duisburg, Ger.	D6	8
Duke Island, i., Ak., U.S.	n24	79
Dukes, co., Ma., U.S.	D6	98
Duk Fadiat, Sudan	G12	42
Dulce, N.M., U.S.	A2	108
Dulgalach, stm., Russia	D20	24
Duluth, Ga., U.S.	B2	87
Duluth, Mn., U.S.	D6	100
Dūmā, Syria	C5	40
Dumaguete, Phil.	D7	32
Dumaran Island, i., Phil.	C6	32
Dumaring, Indon.	E6	32
Dumas, Ar., U.S.	D4	81
Dumas, Tx., U.S.	B2	120
Dumbarton, Scot., U.K.	F8	7
Dumfries, Scot., U.K.	F9	7
Dumfries, Va., U.S.	B5	123
Dumont, Ia., U.S.	B5	92
Dumont, N.J., U.S.	B5	107
Dumyāṭ, Egypt	B12	42
Dunaújváros, Hung.	I18	8
Dunbar, Pa., U.S.	G2	115
Dunbar, W.V., U.S.	C3	125
Duncan, B.C., Can.	E6	69
Duncan, Az., U.S.	E6	80
Duncan, Ok., U.S.	C4	113
Duncan, S.C., U.S.	B3	117
Duncan Falls, Oh., U.S.	C4	112
Duncan Lake, res., B.C., Can.	D9	69
Duncannon, Pa., U.S.	F7	115
Duncansville, Pa., U.S.	F5	115
Duncanville, Tx., U.S.	n10	120
Dundalk, Ont., Can.	C4	73
Dundalk, Ire.	G6	7
Dundalk, Md., U.S.	B4	97
Dundas, Ont., Can.	D5	73
Dundas Peninsula, pen., N.W. Ter., Can.	B10	66
Dundee, S. Afr.	G6	44
Dundee, Scot., U.K.	E9	7
Dundee, Fl., U.S.	D5	86
Dundee, Il., U.S.	A5	90
Dundee, Mi., U.S.	G7	99
Dundee, N.Y., U.S.	C4	109
Dundee, Or., U.S.	h11	114
Dundy, co., Ne., U.S.	D4	104
Dunedin, N.Z.	F3	52
Dunedin, Fl., U.S.	D4	86
Dunellen, N.J., U.S.	B4	107
Dunfermline, Scot., U.K.	E9	7
Dungarvan, Ire.	I5	7
Dungeness, stm., Wa., U.S.	A2	124
Dungun, Malay.	L7	34
Dunham, Que., Can.	D5	74
Dunhua, China	C12	26
Dunhuang, China	C5	26
Dunkard Creek, stm., U.S.	B4	125
Dunkerque, Fr.	A9	10
Dunkerton, Ia., U.S.	B5	92
Dunkirk, In., U.S.	D7	91
Dunkirk, N.Y., U.S.	C1	109
Dunkirk, Oh., U.S.	B2	112
Dunklin, co., Mo., U.S.	E7	102
Dunkwa, Ghana	G5	42
Dún Laoghaire, Ire.	H6	7
Dunlap, Il., U.S.	C4	90
Dunlap, In., U.S.	A6	91
Dunlap, Ia., U.S.	C2	92
Dunlap, Tn., U.S.	D8	119
Dunleith, De., U.S.	i7	85
Dunloup Creek, stm., W.V., U.S.	n13	125
Dunmore, Pa., U.S.	D10	115
Dunmore, Lake, l., Vt., U.S.	D2	122
Dunn, N.C., U.S.	B4	110
Dunn, co., N.D., U.S.	B3	111
Dunn, co., Wi., U.S.	D2	126
Dunnellon, Fl., U.S.	C4	86
Dunnville, Ont., Can.	E5	73
Dunqulah, Sudan	E12	42
Duns, Scot., U.K.	F10	7
Dunseith, N.D., U.S.	A5	111
Dunsmuir, Ca., U.S.	B2	82
Duntou, China	F8	28
Dunville, Newf., Can.	E5	72
Dunwoody, Ga., U.S.	h8	87
Duomaer, China	E2	26
Du Page, co., Il., U.S.	B5	90
Du Page, stm., Il., U.S.	k8	90
Duplin, co., N.C., U.S.	C5	110
Dupont, Co., U.S.	B6	83
Dupont, Pa., U.S.	n18	115
Dupont City, W.V., U.S.	m12	125
Dupont Manor, De., U.S.	B1	41
Dupont Manor, De., U.S.	D3	85
Duque de Caxias, Braz.	G7	57
Duque de York, Isla, i., Chile	G1	56
Duquesne, Pa., U.S.	F2	115
Du Quoin, Il., U.S.	E4	90
Durand, Il., U.S.	A4	90
Durand, Mi., U.S.	F6	99
Durand, Wi., U.S.	D2	126
Durango, Mex.	E7	62
Durango, Spain	B9	12
Durango, Co., U.S.	D3	83
Durant, Ia., U.S.	C7	92
Durant, Ms., U.S.	B4	101
Durant, Ok., U.S.	D5	113
Durazno, Ur.	C5	56
Durban, S. Afr.	G6	44
Đurđevac, Cro.	C12	14
Düren, Ger.	E6	8
Durg, India	B6	37
Durgāpur, India	I12	38
Durham, Ont., Can.	C4	73
Durham, Eng., U.K.	G11	7
Durham, Ca., U.S.	C3	82
Durham, Ct., U.S.	D5	84
Durham, N.H., U.S.	D5	106
Durham, N.C., U.S.	B4	110
Durham, co., N.C., U.S.	A4	110
Durness, Scot., U.K.	C8	7
Durrell, Newf., Can.	D4	72
Durrës, Alb.	H3	16
Dursunbey, Tur.	J12	16
D'Urville, Tanjung, c., Indon.	F10	32
Duryea, Pa., U.S.	D10	115
Dušanbe, Taj.	J11	22
Dušekan, Russia	E15	24
Dushan, China	B9	34
Dushanbe see Dušanbe, Taj.	J11	22
Duson, La., U.S.	D3	95
Düsseldorf, Ger.	D6	8
Dutchess, co., N.Y., U.S.	D7	109
Dutch Island, i., R.I., U.S.	F4	116
Dutton, Ont., Can.	E3	73
Dutton, Mount, mtn., Ut., U.S.	E3	121
Duval, co., Fl., U.S.	B5	86
Duval, co., Tx., U.S.	F3	120
Duxbury, Ma., U.S.	B6	98
Duyun, China	A9	34
Dwight, Il., U.S.	B5	90
Dwight D. Eisenhower Lock, N.Y., U.S.	f9	109
Dworshak Reservoir, res., Id., U.S.	C3	89
Dyer, In., U.S.	A2	91
Dyer, Tn., U.S.	A3	119
Dyer, co., Tn., U.S.	A2	119
Dyer, Cape, c., N.W. Ter., Can.	C20	66
Dyer Island, i., R.I., U.S.	E5	116
Dyersburg, Tn., U.S.	A2	119
Dyersville, Ia., U.S.	B6	92
Dyess Air Force Base, mil., Tx., U.S.	C3	120
Dysart, Ia., U.S.	B5	92
Džalinda, Russia	G18	24
Džambul, Kaz.	I12	22
Dzaoudzi, May.	D9	44
Džardžan, Russia	D18	24
Dzavchan, stm., Mong.	B5	26
Dzeržinsk, Russia	E26	18
Dzeržinskoje, Kaz.	H10	24
Džezkazgan, Kaz.	H11	22
Dzhambul see Džambul, Kaz.	I12	22
Dzierżoniów (Reichenbach), Pol.	E16	8
Džugdžur, Chrebet, mts., Russia	F21	24

E

Name	Map Ref	Page
Eads, Co., U.S.	C8	83
Eagan, Mn., U.S.	n12	100
Eagar, Az., U.S.	C6	80
Eagle, Co., U.S.	B4	83
Eagle, Id., U.S.	F2	89
Eagle, Ne., U.S.	h12	104
Eagle, Wi., U.S.	F5	126
Eagle, co., Co., U.S.	B4	83
Eagle, stm., Newf., Can.	B2	72
Eagle Creek Reservoir, res., In., U.S.	E5	91
Eagle Grove, Ia., U.S.	B4	92
Eagle Key, i., Fl., U.S.	G6	86
Eagle Lake, Me., U.S.	A4	96
Eagle Lake, Mn., U.S.	F5	100
Eagle Lake, Tx., U.S.	E4	120
Eagle Lake, l., Ca., U.S.	B3	82
Eagle Lake, l., Me., U.S.	A4	96
Eagle Lake, l., Me., U.S.	B3	96
Eagle Lake, l., Ms., U.S.	C3	101
Eagle Lake, l., Wi., U.S.	C4	126
Eagle Mountain, mtn., Mn., U.S.	k9	100
Eagle Mountain Lake, res., Tx., U.S.	m9	120
Eagle Nest Lake, l., N.M., U.S.	A4	108
Eagle Pass, Tx., U.S.	E2	120
Eagle Peak, mtn., Ca., U.S.	B3	82
Eagle Point, Or., U.S.	E4	114
Eagle River, Wi., U.S.	C4	126
Eagletail Mountains, mts., Az., U.S.	D2	80
Eagletail Peak, mtn., Az., U.S.	D2	80
Eagletown, Ok., U.S.	C7	113
Earle, Ar., U.S.	B5	81
Earlham, Ia., U.S.	C3	92
Earlimart, Ca., U.S.	E4	82
Earlington, Ky., U.S.	C2	94
Earlville, Il., U.S.	B5	90
Earlville, Ia., U.S.	B6	92
Early, Ia., U.S.	B2	92
Early, co., Ga., U.S.	E2	87
Earth, Tx., U.S.	B1	120
Easley, S.C., U.S.	B2	117
East, stm., Ct., U.S.	D5	84
East, stm., N.Y., U.S.	k13	109
East, stm., Wi., U.S.	h9	126
East Alton, Il., U.S.	E3	90
East Angus, Que., Can.	D6	74
East Arlington, Vt., U.S.	E2	122
East Aurora, N.Y., U.S.	C2	109
East Bangor, Pa., U.S.	E11	115
East Bank, W.V., U.S.	m13	125
East Barre, Vt., U.S.	C4	122
East Baton Rouge, co., La., U.S.	D4	95
East Bay, b., Fl., U.S.	u16	86
East Bay, b., Tx., U.S.	R15	120
East Beckwith Mountain, mtn., Co., U.S.	C3	83
East Berlin, Ct., U.S.	C5	84
East Berlin, Pa., U.S.	G8	115
East Bernard, Tx., U.S.	E4	120
East Bernstadt, Ky., U.S.	C5	94
East Bethel, Mn., U.S.	E5	100
East Billerica, Ma., U.S.	f11	98
Eastborough, Ks., U.S.	g12	93
Eastbourne, Eng., U.K.	K13	7
East Brady, Pa., U.S.	E2	115
East Branch Clarion River Lake, res., Pa., U.S.	C4	115
East Brewton, Al., U.S.	D2	78
East Bridgewater, Ma., U.S.	B6	98
East Brimfield Lake, res., Ma., U.S.	B3	98
East Brooklyn, Ct., U.S.	B8	84
East Broughton, Que., Can.	C6	74
East Brunswick, N.J., U.S.	C4	107
East Butte, mtn., Mt., U.S.	B5	103
East Cache Creek, stm., Ok., U.S.	C3	113
East Cape, c., Fl., U.S.	G5	86
East Carbon, Ut., U.S.	D5	121
East Carroll, co., La., U.S.	B4	95
East Chicago, In., U.S.	A3	91
East China Sea, Asia	E12	26
East Chop, c., Ma., U.S.	D6	98
East Cleveland, Oh., U.S.	g9	112
East Cote Blanche Bay, b., La., U.S.	E4	95
East Dennis, Ma., U.S.	C7	98
East Derry, N.H., U.S.	E4	106
East Detroit, Mi., U.S.	p16	99
East Douglas, Ma., U.S.	B4	98
East Dubuque, Il., U.S.	A3	90
Eastend, Sask., Can.	H1	75
Easter Island see Pascua, Isla de, i., Chile	H5	2
Eastern Bay, b., Md., U.S.	C5	97
Eastern Channel see Tsushima-kaikyō, strt., Japan	I2	30
Eastern Ghāts, mts., India	F5	37
Eastern Neck Island, i., Md., U.S.	B5	97
Eastern Point, c., Ma., U.S.	f13	98
Easterville, Man., Can.	C2	70
East Falkland, i., Falk. Is.	G5	56
East Falmouth, Ma., U.S.	C6	98
East Feliciana, co., La., U.S.	D4	95
East Flat Rock, N.C., U.S.	f10	110
East Fork, stm., Wy., U.S.	D3	127
East Fork Lake, res., Oh., U.S.	C1	112
East Gaffney, S.C., U.S.	A4	117
East Galesburg, Il., U.S.	C3	90
East Granby, Ct., U.S.	B5	84
East Grand Forks, Mn., U.S.	C2	100
East Grand Rapids, Mi., U.S.	F5	99
East Greenville, Pa., U.S.	F10	115
East Greenwich, R.I., U.S.	D4	116
East Gwillimbury, Ont., Can.	C5	73
East Hampstead, N.H., U.S.	E4	106
East Hampton, Ct., U.S.	C5	84
Easthampton, Ma., U.S.	B2	98
East Hanover, N.J., U.S.	*B4	107
East Hartford, Ct., U.S.	B5	84
East Hartland, Ct., U.S.	B4	84
East Haven, Ct., U.S.	D4	84
East Helena, Mt., U.S.	D5	103
East Jordan, Mi., U.S.	C5	99
Eastlake, Oh., U.S.	A4	112
East Lake Tohopekaliga, l., Fl., U.S.	D5	86
Eastland, Tx., U.S.	C3	120
Eastland, co., Tx., U.S.	C3	120
East Lansing, Mi., U.S.	F6	99
East Las Vegas, Nv., U.S.	G6	105
East Liverpool, Oh., U.S.	B5	112
East London (Oos-Londen), S. Afr.	H5	44
East Longmeadow, Ma., U.S.	B2	98
East Los Angeles, Ca., U.S.	m12	82
East Lyme, Ct., U.S.	D7	84
East Lynn Lake, res., W.V., U.S.	C2	125
Eastmain, stm., Que., Can.	F17	66
Eastmain-Opinaca, Réservoir, res., Que., Can.	h11	74
Eastman, Que., Can.	D5	74
Eastman, Ga., U.S.	D3	87

Name | Map Ref | Page

East Matunuck, R.I., U.S. F3 116
East Middlebury, Vt., U.S. D2 122
East Millinocket, Me., U.S. C4 96
East Moline, Il., U.S. B3 90
East Montpelier, Vt., U.S. C4 122
East Naples, Fl., U.S. F5 86
East Newnan, Ga., U.S. C2 87
East Nishnabotna, stm., Ia., U.S. C2 92
East Norriton, Pa., U.S. o20 115
East Olympia, Wa., U.S. C3 124
Easton, Md., U.S. C5 97
Easton, Pa., U.S. E11 115
Easton Reservoir, res., Ct., U.S. E2 84
East Orange, N.J., U.S. B4 107
East Orleans, Ma., U.S. C8 98
Eastover, S.C., U.S. D6 117
East Palatka, Fl., U.S. C5 86
East Palestine, Oh., U.S. B5 112
East Pass, strt., Fl., U.S. C2 86
East Pea Ridge, W.V., U.S. C2 125
East Peoria, Il., U.S. C4 90
East Pepperell, Ma., U.S. A4 98
East Petersburg, Pa., U.S. F9 115
East Pittsburgh, Pa., U.S. k14 115
Eastpoint, Fl., U.S. C2 86
East Point, Ga., U.S. C2 87
East Point, c., P.E.I., Can. C8 71
East Point, c., Ma., U.S. B6 98
East Point, c., N.J., U.S. E2 107
Eastport, Newf., Can. D5 72
Eastport, Me., U.S. D6 96
East Prairie, Mo., U.S. E8 102
East Providence, R.I., U.S. C4 116
East Pryor Mountain, mtn., Mt., U.S. E8 103
East Quogue, N.Y., U.S. n16 109
East Range, mts., Nv., U.S. C4 105
East Ridge, Tn., U.S. h11 119
East River, Ct., U.S. D5 84
East Rochester, N.Y., U.S. B3 109
East Rockingham, N.C., U.S. C3 110
East Rutherford, N.J., U.S. h8 107
East Saint Louis, Il., U.S. E3 90
East Selkirk, Man., Can. D3 70
Eastsound, Wa., U.S. A3 124
East Spencer, N.C., U.S. B2 110
East Stroudsburg, Pa., U.S. D11 115
East Tawas, Mi., U.S. D7 99
East Troy, Wi., U.S. F5 126
East Vestal, N.Y., U.S. C4 109
East View, W.V., U.S. k10 125
East Walker, stm., U.S. E2 105
East Walpole, Ma., U.S. h11 98
East Wareham, Ma., U.S. C6 98
East Washington, Pa., U.S. F1 115
East Wenatchee, Wa., U.S. B5 124
East Windsor, N.J., U.S. C3 107
East York, Ont., Can. D5 73
Eaton, Co., U.S. A6 83
Eaton, In., U.S. D7 91
Eaton, Oh., U.S. C1 112
Eaton, co., Mi., U.S. F6 99
Eaton Rapids, Mi., U.S. F6 99
Eatonton, Ga., U.S. C3 87
Eatontown, N.J., U.S. C4 107
Eatonville, Wa., U.S. C3 124
Eau Claire, Wi., U.S. D2 126
Eau Claire, co., Wi., U.S. D2 126
Eau Claire, stm., Wi., U.S. D2 126
Eau Claire, Lac à l', l., Que., Can. g11 74
Eauze, Fr. I7 10
Ebano, Mex. F10 62
Ebba Ksour, Tun. N3 14
Ebbw Vale, Wales, U.K. J9 7
Ebensburg, Pa., U.S. F4 115
Eberndorf, Aus. I14 8
Eberswalde, Ger. C13 8
Ebetsu, Japan p19 30a
Ebingen, Ger. G9 8
Ebinur Hu, l., China B3 26
Eboli, Italy I10 14
Ebolowa, Cam. H8 42
Ebro, stm., Spain E12 12
Ebro, Delta del, Spain E12 12
Eccles, W.V., U.S. n13 125
Echo Bay, Nv., U.S. G7 105
Echo Lake, l., Me., U.S. D3 96
Echo Lake, l., Vt., U.S. B5 122
Echols, co., Ga., U.S. F4 87
Écija, Spain H6 12
Eckernförde, Ger. A9 8
Eckhart Mines, Md., U.S. k13 97
Eckville, Alta., Can. C3 68
Eclectic, Al., U.S. C3 78
Eclipse Sound, strt., N.W. Ter., Can. B17 66
Écommoy, Fr. E7 10
Econfina, stm., Fl., U.S. B3 86
Economy, Pa., U.S. *h13 115
Écorces, Rivière aux, stm., Que., Can. A6 74
Ecorse, Mi., U.S. p15 99
Ecru, Ms., U.S. A4 101
Ector, co., Tx., U.S. D1 120
Ecuador, ctry., S.A. D3 54
Ed, Swe. G8 6
Edcouch, Tx., U.S. F4 120
Eddy, co., N.M., U.S. E5 108
Eddy, co., N.D., U.S. B7 111
Eddystone, Pa., U.S. p20 115
Eddyville, Ia., U.S. C5 92
Eddyville, Ky., U.S. e9 94
Ede, Neth. C5 8
Edéa, Cam. H8 42
Eden, Ga., U.S. D5 87
Eden, Md., U.S. D6 97
Eden, N.Y., U.S. C2 109
Eden, N.C., U.S. A3 110
Eden, Tx., U.S. D3 120
Edenderry, Ire. H5 7
Eden Prairie, Mn., U.S. n12 100
Edenton, N.C., U.S. A6 110
Eden Valley, Mn., U.S. E4 100
Edgar, Ne., U.S. D8 104
Edgar, Wi., U.S. D4 126
Edgar, co., Il., U.S. D6 90
Edgard, La., U.S. D5 95
Edgartown, Ma., U.S. D6 98
Edgecombe, co., N.C., U.S. B5 110
Edgecumbe, Cape, c., Ak., U.S. m21 79
Edgefield, S.C., U.S. D4 117
Edgefield, co., S.C., U.S. D4 117
Edgeley, N.D., U.S. C7 111
Edgemere, Md., U.S. B5 97
Edgemont, S.D., U.S. D2 118
Edgemoor, De., U.S. A3 85
Edgerton, Ks., U.S. D8 93
Edgerton, Mn., U.S. G2 100
Edgerton, Oh., U.S. A1 112
Edgerton, Wi., U.S. F4 126
Edgerton, Wy., U.S. C6 127
Edgewater, Al., U.S. f7 78
Edgewater, Fl., U.S. D6 86
Edgewater, Md., U.S. C4 97
Edgewater, N.J., U.S. h9 107
Edgewater Park, N.J., U.S. C3 107
Edgewood, In., U.S. D6 91
Edgewood, Ia., U.S. B6 92
Edgewood, Ky., U.S. h13 94
Edgewood, Md., U.S. B5 97
Edgewood, N.M., U.S. B3 108
Edgewood, Oh., U.S. A5 112
Edgewood, Pa., U.S. k14 115
Edgewood, Wa., U.S. f11 124
Edgeworth, Pa., U.S. h13 115
Edina, Mn., U.S. F5 100
Edina, Mo., U.S. A5 102
Edinboro, Pa., U.S. C1 115
Edinburg, Il., U.S. D4 90
Edinburg, Tx., U.S. F3 120
Edinburg, Va., U.S. B4 123
Edinburgh, Scot., U.K. F9 7
Edinburgh, In., U.S. F6 91
Edirne, Tur. G13 4
Edison, Ga., U.S. E2 87
Edison, N.J., U.S. B4 107
Edisto, stm., S.C., U.S. E6 117
Edisto Island, i., S.C., U.S. F7 117
Edith, Mount, mtn., Mt., U.S. D5 103
Edjeleh, Alg. C7 42
Edmond, Ok., U.S. B4 113
Edmonds, Wa., U.S. B3 124
Edmondson Heights, Md., U.S. *g10 97
Edmonson, co., Ky., U.S. C3 94
Edmonton, Alta., Can. C4 68
Edmonton, Ky., U.S. D4 94
Edmore, Mi., U.S. E5 99
Edmunds, co., S.D., U.S. B6 118
Edmundston, N.B., Can. B1 71
Edna, Tx., U.S. E4 120
Edon, Oh., U.S. A1 112
Édouard, Lac, l., Que., Can. B5 74
Edremit, Tur. J11 16
Edrengijn Nuruu, mts., Mong. C6 26
Edsbyn, Swe. F10 6
Edson, Alta., Can. C2 68
Edson Butte, mtn., Or., U.S. E2 114
Eduardo Castex, Arg. D4 56
Edward, Lake, l., Afr. B5 44
Edwards, Ms., U.S. C3 101
Edwards, co., Il., U.S. E5 90
Edwards, co., Ks., U.S. E4 93
Edwards, co., Tx., U.S. E2 120
Edwards Air Force Base, mil., Ca., U.S. E5 82
Edwardsburg, Mi., U.S. G4 99
Edwards Butte, mtn., Or., U.S. B3 114
Edwardsville, Il., U.S. E4 90
Edwardsville, Ks., U.S. k16 93
Edwardsville, Pa., U.S. n17 115
Eel, stm., Ca., U.S. B2 82
Eel, stm., In., U.S. F3 91
Eel, stm., In., U.S. C6 91
Effigy Mounds National Monument, Ia., U.S. A6 92
Effingham, Il., U.S. D5 90
Effingham, co., Ga., U.S. D5 87
Effingham, co., Il., U.S. D5 90
Efland, N.C., U.S. A3 110
Egan Range, mts., Nv., U.S. E7 105
Eganville, Ont., Can. B7 73
Egede og Rothes Fjord, Grnld. C25 66
Egedesminde, Grnld. C22 66
Eger, Hung. H20 8
Egersund, Nor. G5 6
Eggenfelden, Ger. G12 8
Egg Harbor City, N.J., U.S. D3 107
Egg Island Point, c., N.J., U.S. E2 107
Égletons, Fr. G9 10
Eglin Air Force Base, mil., Fl., U.S. u15 86
Egmont, Mount, mtn., N.Z. C5 52
Egmont Bay, b., P.E.I., Can. C5 71
Egmont Channel, strt., Fl., U.S. p10 86
Egmont Key, i., Fl., U.S. p10 86
Egvekinot, Russia D29 24
Egypt, ctry., Afr. C11 42
Egypt, Lake of, res., Il., U.S. F5 90
Ehingen, Ger. G9 8
Ehrenberg, Az., U.S. D1 80
Éibar, Spain B9 12
Eichstätt, Ger. G11 8
Eidsvoll, Nor. F8 6
Eielson Air Force Base, mil., Ak., U.S. C10 79
Eifel, mts., Ger. E6 8
Eighty Mile Beach, Austl. C4 50
Eil, Som. G4 46
Eilenburg, Ger. D12 8
Eindhoven, Neth. D5 8
Einsiedeln, Switz. E15 10
Eirunepé, Braz. E5 54
Eisenach, Ger. E10 8
Eisenberg, Ger. E11 8
Eisenerz, Aus. H14 8
Eisenhower, Mount, mtn., N.H., U.S. B4 106
Eisenhüttenstadt, Ger. C14 8
Eisenstadt, Aus. H16 8
Eisleben, Ger. D11 8
Ejea de los Caballeros, Spain C10 12
Ekiatapskij Chrebet, mts., Russia D29 24
Ekimčan, Russia G20 24
Ekwan, stm., Ont., Can. F16 66
El Aaiún, W. Sah. C3 42
Elaine, Ar., U.S. C5 81
El Asnam, Alg. A6 42
Elat, Isr. E4 40
El Avión, Mex. E6 62
Elâzığ, Tur. H15 4
Elba, Al., U.S. D3 78
Elba, Isola d', i., Italy G5 14
El Banco, Col. C6 58
El Barco de Valdeorras, Spain C5 12
Elbasan, Alb. H4 16
El Baúl, Ven. C8 58
Elbe (Labe), stm., Eur. B9 8
Elberfeld, In., U.S. H3 91
Elbert, co., Co., U.S. B6 83
Elbert, co., Ga., U.S. B4 87
Elbert, Mount, mtn., Co., U.S. B4 83
Elberta, Ga., U.S. D3 87
Elberton, Ga., U.S. B4 87
Elbeuf, Fr. C8 10
Elbląg (Elbing), Pol. A19 8
El Bonillo, Spain G9 12
El Bordo, Col. F4 58
Elbow, stm., Alta., Can. D3 68
Elbow Lake, Mn., U.S. E3 100
El'brus, gora (Mount Elbrus), mtn., Russia I6 22
El Burgo de Osma, Spain D8 12
Elburn, Il., U.S. B5 90
Elburz Mountains see Alborz, Reshteh-ye Kūhhā-ye, mts., Iran J8 22
El Cajon, Ca., U.S. F5 82
El Callao, Ven. D12 58
El Campo, Tx., U.S. E4 120
El Capitan, mtn., Mt., U.S. D2 103
El Capitan Reservoir, res., Ca., U.S. o16 82
El Carmen, Arg. A3 56
El Carmen de Bolívar, Col. C5 58
El Centro, Ca., U.S. F6 82
El Cerrito, Col. F4 58
El Cerrito, Ca., U.S. h8 82
Elche, Spain G11 12
Elche de la Sierra, Spain G9 12
El Cozón, Mex. B3 62
El Cuervo Butte, mtn., N.M., U.S. k9 108
Elda, Spain G11 12
El Desemboque, Mex. C3 62
El Diviso, Col. G3 58
El Djouf, des., Afr. D4 42
Eldon, Ia., U.S. D5 92
Eldon, Mo., U.S. C5 102
Eldora, Ia., U.S. B4 92
Eldorado, Mex. E6 62
Eldorado, Ar., U.S. D3 81
Eldorado, Il., U.S. F5 90
El Dorado, Ks., U.S. E7 93
Eldorado, Tx., U.S. D2 120
El Dorado, co., Ca., U.S. C3 82
Eldorado Peak, mtn., Wa., U.S. A4 124
Eldorado Springs, Co., U.S. B5 83
El Dorado Springs, Mo., U.S. D3 102
Eldoret, Kenya A7 44
Eldridge, Ia., U.S. C7 92
Eleanor, W.V., U.S. C3 125
Electra, Tx., U.S. C3 120
Electra Lake, res., Co., U.S. D3 83
Electric Peak, mtn., Co., U.S. C5 83
Electric Peak, mtn., Mt., U.S. E6 103
Elektrostal', Russia F21 18
El Encanto, Col. H6 58
Elephant Butte Reservoir, res., N.M., U.S. D2 108
El Estor, Guat. G3 64
Eleuthera, i., Bah. B9 64
Eleven Mile Canyon Reservoir, res., Co., U.S. C5 83
Eleven Point, stm., U.S. A4 81
Elevsís, Grc. K7 16
El Fahs, Tun. M4 14
El Ferrol del Caudillo, Spain B3 12
El Galpón, Arg. B4 56
Elgin, Scot., U.K. D9 7
Elgin, Il., U.S. A5 90
Elgin, Ia., U.S. B6 92
Elgin, Mn., U.S. F6 100
Elgin, Ne., U.S. C7 104
Elgin, N.D., U.S. C4 111
Elgin, Ok., U.S. C3 113
Elgin, Or., U.S. B9 114
Elgin, S.C., U.S. B6 117
Elgin, Tx., U.S. D4 120
El Goléa, Alg. B6 42
El Golfo de Santa Clara, Mex. B2 62
Elgon, Mount, mtn., Afr. A6 44
El Hank, clf, Afr. D4 42
El Haouaria, Tun. L6 14
Elida, Oh., U.S. B1 112
Élisabethville see Lubumbashi, Zaire D5 44
Elizabeth, Austl. F7 50
Elizabeth, Co., U.S. B6 83
Elizabeth, N.J., U.S. B4 107
Elizabeth, W.V., U.S. B3 125
Elizabeth, Cape, c., Wa., U.S. B1 124
Elizabeth City, N.C., U.S. A6 110
Elizabeth Islands, is., Ma., U.S. D6 98
Elizabeth Reef, atoll, Austl. E11 50
Elizabethton, Tn., U.S. C11 119
Elizabethtown, Ky., U.S. C4 94
Elizabethtown, N.C., U.S. C4 110
Elizabethtown, Pa., U.S. F8 115
Elizabethville, Pa., U.S. E8 115
El-Jadida, Mor. B4 42
El Jebel, Co., U.S. B3 83
Ełk, Pol. B22 8
Elk, co., Ks., U.S. E7 93
Elk, co., Pa., U.S. D4 115
Elk, stm., U.S. A2 78
Elk, stm., Co., U.S. A4 83
Elk, stm., Ks., U.S. E7 93
Elk, stm., W.V., U.S. C3 125
Elk, stm., Wi., U.S. C3 126
Elkader, Ia., U.S. B6 92
El Kairouan, Tun. N5 14
Elk City, Id., U.S. D3 89
Elk City, Ok., U.S. B2 113
Elk City Lake, res., Ks., U.S. E7 93
Elk Creek, stm., Ok., U.S. B2 113
Elk Creek, stm., S.D., U.S. C3 118
El Kef, Tun. M3 14
Elkford, B.C., Can. D10 69
Elk Grove, Ca., U.S. C3 82
Elk Grove Village, Il., U.S. h9 90
Elkhart, In., U.S. A6 91
Elkhart, Ks., U.S. E2 93
Elkhart, Tx., U.S. D5 120
Elkhart, co., In., U.S. A6 91
Elkhart, stm., In., U.S. B6 91
Elkhart Lake, Wi., U.S. E5 126
Elkhead Mountains, mts., Co., U.S. A3 83
Elkhorn, Man., Can. E1 70
Elk Horn, Ia., U.S. C2 92
Elkhorn, Ne., U.S. g12 104
Elkhorn, Wi., U.S. F5 126
Elkhorn, stm., Ne., U.S. B7 104
Elkhorn City, Ky., U.S. C7 94
Elkhorn Peaks, mts., Id., U.S. F7 89
Elkin, N.C., U.S. A2 110
Elkins, Ar., U.S. A1 81
Elkins, W.V., U.S. C5 125
Elkland, Pa., U.S. C7 115
Elk Mills, Md., U.S. A6 97
Elk Mound, Wi., U.S. D2 126
Elk Mountain, Wy., U.S. E6 127
Elk Mountain, mtn., N.M., U.S. D1 108
Elk Mountain, mtn., Wy., U.S. E6 127
Elk Mountains, mts., U.S. D1 118
Elk Mountains, mts., Co., U.S. B3 83
Elko, Nv., U.S. C6 105
Elko, co., Nv., U.S. B6 105
Elk Peak, mtn., Mt., U.S. D6 103
Elk Point, Alta., Can. C5 68
Elk Point, S.D., U.S. E9 118
Elk Rapids, Mi., U.S. D5 99
El Krib, Tun. M4 14
Elkridge, Md., U.S. B4 97
Elk River, Mn., U.S. E5 100
Elkton, Ky., U.S. D2 94
Elkton, Md., U.S. A6 97
Elkton, Mi., U.S. E7 99
Elkton, S.D., U.S. C9 118
Elkton, Va., U.S. B4 123
Elkview, W.V., U.S. m13 125
Elkville, Il., U.S. F4 90
Ellaville, Ga., U.S. D2 87
Ellen, Mount, mtn., Ut., U.S. E5 121
Ellendale, De., U.S. E4 85
Ellendale, N.D., U.S. C7 111
Ellensburg, Wa., U.S. C5 124
Ellenton, Fl., U.S. E4 86
Ellenville, N.Y., U.S. D6 109
Ellerbe, N.C., U.S. B3 110
Ellerslie, Md., U.S. k13 97
Ellesmere Island, i., N.W. Ter., Can. A21 128
Ellettsville, In., U.S. F4 91
Ellice Islands see Tuvalu, ctry., Oc. G24 2
Ellicott City, Md., U.S. B4 97
Ellijay, Ga., U.S. B2 87
Ellington, Ct., U.S. B6 84
Ellington, Mo., U.S. D7 102
Ellinwood, Ks., U.S. D5 93
Elliot Lake, Ont., Can. A2 73
Elliott, Ms., U.S. B4 101
Elliott, co., Ky., U.S. B6 94
Elliott Bay, b., Wa., U.S. e11 124
Elliott Key, i., Fl., U.S. G6 86
Ellis, Ks., U.S. D4 93
Ellis, co., Ks., U.S. D4 93
Ellis, co., Ok., U.S. A2 113
Ellis, co., Tx., U.S. C4 120
Ellis, stm., N.H., U.S. B4 106
Elliston, Va., U.S. C2 123
Ellisville, Ms., U.S. D4 101
Ellisville, Mo., U.S. f12 102
Ellon, Scot., U.K. D10 7
Elloree, S.C., U.S. D6 117
Ellport, Pa., U.S. E1 115
Ellsworth, Ks., U.S. D5 93
Ellsworth, Me., U.S. D4 96
Ellsworth, Pa., U.S. F1 115
Ellsworth, Wi., U.S. D1 126
Ellsworth, co., Ks., U.S. D5 93
Ellsworth Air Force Base, mil., S.D., U.S. C2 118
Ellwangen, Ger. G10 8
Ellwood City, Pa., U.S. E1 115
Elm, stm., N.D., U.S. B8 111
Elma, Ia., U.S. A5 92
Elma, Wa., U.S. C2 124
El Mahdia, Tun. N6 14
El Manteco, Ven. D11 58
Elm City, N.C., U.S. B5 110
Elm Creek, Ne., U.S. D6 104
El Médano, Mex. E4 62
Elmendorf Air Force Base, mil., Ak., U.S. C10 79
Elm Grove, Wi., U.S. m11 126
Elmhurst, Il., U.S. B6 90
Elmhurst, Pa., U.S. D10 115
Elmira, N.Y., U.S. C4 109
El Mirage, Az., U.S. k8 80
Elmira Heights, N.Y., U.S. C4 109
El Moknine, Tun. N5 14
Elmont, N.Y., U.S. k13 109
Elmora, Pa., U.S. E4 115
Elmore, Mn., U.S. G4 100
Elmore, Oh., U.S. A2 112
Elmore, co., Al., U.S. C3 78
Elmore, co., Id., U.S. F3 89
El Morro National Monument, N.M., U.S. B1 108
Elmsdale, N.S., Can. E6 71
Elmshorn, Ger. B9 8
Elm Springs, Ar., U.S. A1 81
Elmvale, Ont., Can. C5 73
Elmwood, Il., U.S. C3 90
Elmwood, Wi., U.S. D1 126
Elmwood Park, Il., U.S. k9 90
Elmwood Park, N.J., U.S. h8 107
Elmwood Place, Oh., U.S. o13 112
Elne, Fr. J9 10
Elnora, In., U.S. G3 91
Eloise, Fl., U.S. E5 86
Elon College, N.C., U.S. A3 110
Elora, Ont., Can. D4 73
Elorza, Ven. D8 58
El Oued, Alg. B7 42
Eloy, Az., U.S. E4 80
El Palmar, Ven. D12 58
El Paso, Il., U.S. C4 90
El Paso, Tx., U.S. o11 120
El Paso, co., Co., U.S. C6 83
El Paso, co., Tx., U.S. o11 120
El Pilar, Ven. B11 58
El Pital, Cerro, mtn., N.A. G3 64
El Portal, Fl., U.S. s13 86
El Prado, N.M., U.S. A4 108
El Progreso, Hond. G4 64
El Puente del Arzobispo, Spain F6 12
El Puerto de Santa María, Spain I5 12
El Quelite, Mex. F6 62
El Reno, Ok., U.S. B4 113
Elrose, Sask., Can. F1 75
Elroy, Wi., U.S. E3 126
Elsa, Yukon, Can. D5 66
Elsa, Tx., U.S. F3 120
Elsah, Il., U.S. E3 90
El Salto, Mex. F7 62
El Salvador, ctry., N.A. H3 64
El Sauce, Nic. H4 64
El Sauzal, Mex. B1 62
Elsberry, Mo., U.S. B7 102
Elsie, Mi., U.S. E6 99
Elsinore, Ut., U.S. E3 121
Elsmere, De., U.S. B3 85
Elsmere, Ky., U.S. B5 94
El Socorro, Ven. C10 58
El Sombrero, Ven. C9 58
Elspe, Ger. D8 8
Elsterwerda, Ger. D13 8
El Tigre, Col. F8 58
El Tigre, Ven. C10 58
El Tocuyo, Ven. C8 58
Elton, La., U.S. D3 95
El Toro Marine Corps Air Station, mil., Ca., U.S. n13 82
El Trapiche, Col. F4 58
El Triunfo, Mex. F4 62
El Turbio, Arg. G2 56
Elūru, India D6 37
El Vado Reservoir, res., N.M., U.S. A3 108
Elvas, Port. G4 12
Elverum, Nor. F8 6
El Vigía, Ven. C7 58
Elvins, Mo., U.S. D7 102
Elwell, Lake, res., Mt., U.S. B5 103
Elwha, stm., Wa., U.S. A2 124
Elwood, In., U.S. D6 91
Elwood, Ks., U.S. C9 93
Elwood, Ne., U.S. D6 104
Ely, Eng., U.K. I13 7
Ely, Mn., U.S. C7 100
Ely, Nv., U.S. D7 105
Elyria, Oh., U.S. A3 112
Elysburg, Pa., U.S. E8 115
Emanuel, co., Ga., U.S. D4 87
Embarcación, Arg. A4 56
Embarras, stm., Il., U.S. E6 90
Embarrass, stm., Wi., U.S. D5 126
Embro, Ont., Can. D4 73
Embrun, Fr. H13 10
Emden, Ger. B7 8
Emerald, Austl. D9 50
Emerson, Man., Can. E3 70
Emerson, Ga., U.S. B2 87
Emerson, Ne., U.S. B9 104
Emerson, N.J., U.S. h8 107
Emery, co., Ut., U.S. E5 121
Emet, Tur. J13 16
Emily, Mn., U.S. D5 100
Emily, Lake, l., Mn., U.S. E3 100
Eminence, Ky., U.S. B4 94
Emmaus, Pa., U.S. E11 115
Emmen, Neth. C6 8
Emmendingen, Ger. G7 8
Emmet, co., Ia., U.S. A3 92
Emmet, co., Mi., U.S. C6 99
Emmetsburg, Ia., U.S. A3 92
Emmett, Id., U.S. F2 89
Emmiganūru, India E4 37
Emmitsburg, Md., U.S. A3 97
Emmonak, Ak., U.S. C7 79
Emmons, co., N.D., U.S. C5 111
Emory Peak, mtn., Tx., U.S. E1 120
Empalme, Mex. D4 62
Empangeni, S. Afr. G6 44
Empedrado, Arg. B5 56
Empire, La., U.S. E6 95
Empire, Nv., U.S. C2 105
Empoli, Italy F5 14
Emporia, Ks., U.S. D7 93
Emporia, Va., U.S. D5 123
Emporium, Pa., U.S. D5 115
Empty Quarter see Ar-Rab' al-Khālī, des., Asia D5 46
Emsdetten, Ger. C7 8
Emsworth, Pa., U.S. h13 115
Encampment, Wy., U.S. E6 127
Encarnación, Para. B5 56
Encinitas, Ca., U.S. F5 82
Encontrados, Ven. C6 58
Ende, Indon. G7 32
Enderby, B.C., Can. D8 69
Enderby Land, reg., Ant. C18 47
Enderlin, N.D., U.S. C8 111
Enders Reservoir, res., Ne., U.S. D4 104
Endicott, N.Y., U.S. C4 109
Endicott Mountains, mts., Ak., U.S. B9 79
Endless Lake, l., Me., U.S. C4 96
Endwell, N.Y., U.S. C4 109
Enfida, Tun. M5 14
Enfield (Thompsonville), Ct., U.S. B5 84
Enfield, N.H., U.S. C2 106
Enfield, N.C., U.S. A5 110
Engel's, Russia G7 22
Enggano, Pulau, i., Indon. G3 32
England, Ar., U.S. C4 81
England, ter., U.K. I11 7
England Air Force Base, mil., La., U.S. C3 95
Englee, Newf., Can. C3 72
Engleside, Va., U.S. g12 123

Name | Map Ref | Page

Englewood, Co., U.S. **B6** 83
Englewood, Fl., U.S. **F4** 86
Englewood, N.J., U.S. **B5** 107
Englewood, Oh., U.S. **C1** 112
Englewood, Tn., U.S. **D9** 119
Englewood Cliffs, N.J., U.S. **h9** 107
English, In., U.S. **H5** 91
English Bāzār, India **H13** 38
English Channel (La Manche), strt., Eur. **B5** 10
Enguera, Spain **G11** 12
Enid, Ok., U.S. **A4** 113
Enid Lake, res., Ms., U.S. **A4** 101
Enigma, Ga., U.S. **E3** 87
Enka, N.C., U.S. **f10** 110
Enkhuizen, Neth. **C5** 8
Enköping, Swe. **G11** 6
Enmelen, Russia **D30** 24
Enna, Italy **L9** 14
Ennadai Lake, l., N.W. Ter., Can. **D12** 66
Ennedi, plat., Chad **E10** 42
Ennis, Ire. **I4** 7
Ennis, Mt., U.S. **E5** 103
Ennis, Tx., U.S. **C4** 120
Enniskillen, N. Ire., U.K. **G5** 7
Enoch, Ut., U.S. **F2** 121
Enola, Pa., U.S. **F8** 115
Enon, Oh., U.S. ***C2** 112
Enoree, S.C., U.S. **B4** 117
Enoree, stm., S.C., U.S. **B3** 117
Enosburg Falls, Vt., U.S. **B3** 122
Enriquillo, Dom. Rep. **F12** 64
Enschede, Neth. **C6** 8
Ensenada, Mex. **B1** 62
Enshi, China **E8** 26
Enshū-nada, Japan **H10** 30
Ensley, Fl., U.S. **u14** 86
Entebbe, Ug. **A6** 44
Enterprise, Al., U.S. **D4** 78
Enterprise, Ks., U.S. **D6** 93
Enterprise, Or., U.S. **B9** 114
Enterprise, Ut., U.S. **F2** 121
Enterprise, W.V., U.S. **B4** 125
Entiat, stm., Wa., U.S. **B5** 124
Entiat, Lake, l., Wa., U.S. **B5** 124
Entiat Mountains, mts., Wa., U.S. **B5** 124
Entraygues, Fr. **H9** 10
Entre-Rios, Moz. **D7** 44
Enugu, Nig. **G7** 42
Enumclaw, Wa., U.S. **B4** 124
Envigado, Col. **D5** 58
Eola Hills, hills, Or., U.S. **h11** 114
Épernay, Fr. **C10** 10
Ephraim, Ut., U.S. **D4** 121
Ephrata, Pa., U.S. **F9** 115
Ephrata, Wa., U.S. **B6** 124
Épila, Spain **D10** 12
Épinal, Fr. **D13** 10
Epping, N.H., U.S. **D4** 106
Epworth, Ia., U.S. **B7** 92
Equatorial Guinea, ctry., Afr. **H7** 42
Eraclea, Italy **D7** 14
Erath, La., U.S. **E3** 95
Erath, co., Tx., U.S. **C3** 120
Erdek, Tur. **I11** 16
Erdemli, Tur. **A4** 40
Erebus, Mount, mtn., Ant. **B29** 47
Erechim, Braz. **B6** 56
Erfurt, Ger. **E11** 8
Erichsen Lake, l., N.W. Ter., Can. **B16** 66
Erick, Ok., U.S. **B2** 113
Erickson, Man., Can. **D2** 70
Erie, Co., U.S. **A5** 83
Erie, Il., U.S. **B3** 90
Erie, Ks., U.S. **E8** 93
Erie, Mi., U.S. **G7** 99
Erie, Pa., U.S. **B1** 115
Erie, co., N.Y., U.S. **C2** 109
Erie, co., Oh., U.S. **A3** 112
Erie, co., Pa., U.S. **C1** 115
Erie, Lake, l., N.A. **C10** 76
Erie Canal, N.Y., U.S. **B5** 109
Erimo-misaki, c., Japan **r21** 30a
Erin, Ont., Can. **D4** 73
Erin, Tn., U.S. **A4** 119
Eritrea, ctry., Afr. **E2** 46
Erlangen, Ger. **F11** 8
Erlanger, Ky., U.S. **A5** 94
Erlian, China **C9** 26
Erling, Lake, res., Ar., U.S. **D2** 81
Ermelo, S. Afr. **G5** 44
Ermenak, Tur. **A3** 40
Ernākulam, India **H4** 37
Erne, Lower Lough, l., N. Ire., U.K. **G5** 7
Ernée, Fr. **D6** 10
Erode, India **G4** 37
Errigal, mtn., Ire. **F4** 7
Ertai, China **B5** 26
Erwin, N.C., U.S. **B4** 110
Erwin, Tn., U.S. **C11** 119
Erzgebirge (Krušné hory), mts., Eur. **E12** 8
Erzincan, Tur. **H15** 4
Erzurum, Tur. **H16** 4
Esashi, Japan **A13** 30
Esbjerg, Den. **I7** 6
Escalante, Ut., U.S. **F4** 121
Escalante, stm., Ut., U.S. **F4** 121
Escalón, Mex. **D7** 62
Escalon, Ca., U.S. **D3** 82
Escambia, co., Al., U.S. **D2** 78
Escambia, co., Fl., U.S. **u14** 86
Escambia, stm., Fl., U.S. **u14** 86
Escanaba, Mi., U.S. **C3** 99
Escanaba, stm., Mi., U.S. **B3** 99
Escarpada Point, c., Phil. **B7** 32
Escatawpa, Ms., U.S. **E5** 101
Escatawpa, stm., U.S. **D5** 101
Esch-sur-Alzette, Lux. **F5** 8
Eschwege, Ger. **D10** 8
Escondido, Ca., U.S. **F5** 82
Escoumins, Rivière des, stm., Que., Can. **A8** 74
Escuinapa [de Hidalgo], Mex. **F7** 62
Escuintla, Guat. **G2** 64
Escuintla, Mex. **J13** 62
Escuminac, Point, c., N.B., Can. **B5** 71
Eşfahān, Iran **B5** 46
Eshkāshem, Afg. **B4** 38
Eskilstuna, Swe. **G11** 6
Eskimo Lakes, l., N.W. Ter., Can. **C6** 66
Eskimo Point, N.W. Ter., Can. **D14** 66
Eskişehir, Tur. **H14** 4
Eşme, Tur. **K12** 16
Esmeralda, co., Nv., U.S. **F4** 105
Esmeraldas, Ec. **G3** 58
Esmond, R.I., U.S. **B4** 116
Espalion, Fr. **H9** 10
Espanola, Ont., Can. **A3** 73
Espanola, N.M., U.S. **B3** 108
Esparto, Ca., U.S. **C2** 82
Espelkamp, Ger. **C8** 8
Esperance, Austl. **F4** 50
Espinal, Col. **E5** 58
Espinhaço, Serra do, mts., Braz. **C7** 57
Espinho, Port. **D3** 12
Espíritu Santo, Bahía del, b., Mex. **H16** 62
Espíritu Santo, Isla del, i., Mex. **E4** 62
Espoo (Esbo), Fin. **F15** 6
Espy, Pa., U.S. **D9** 115
Esquel, Arg. **E2** 56
Esquimalt, B.C., Can. **E6** 69
Esquina, Arg. **B5** 56
Essaouira, Mor. **B4** 42
Essen, Ger. **D7** 8
Essendon, Mount, mtn., Austl. **D4** 50
Essequibo, stm., Guy. **E13** 58
Es Sers, Tun. **M4** 14
Essex, Ont., Can. **E2** 73
Essex, Ct., U.S. **D6** 84
Essex, Ia., U.S. **D2** 92
Essex, Md., U.S. **B5** 97
Essex, Ma., U.S. **A6** 98
Essex, Vt., U.S. **B2** 122
Essex, co., Ma., U.S. **A5** 98
Essex, co., N.J., U.S. **B4** 107
Essex, co., N.Y., U.S. **B7** 109
Essex, co., Vt., U.S. **B5** 122
Essex, co., Va., U.S. **C6** 123
Essex Junction, Vt., U.S. **C2** 122
Essexville, Mi., U.S. **E7** 99
Esslingen, Ger. **G9** 8
Es Smala es Souassi, Tun. **N5** 14
Est, Cap, c., Madag. **E10** 44
Est, Pointe de l', c., Que., Can. **G20** 66
Estacada, Or., U.S. **B4** 114
Estaca de Bares, Punta de la, c., Spain **B4** 12
Estacado, Llano, pl., U.S. **C1** 120
Estados, Isla de los, i., Arg. **G4** 56
Estancia, N.M., U.S. **C3** 108
Estcourt, S. Afr. **G5** 44
Este, Italy **D6** 14
Estelí, Nic. **H4** 64
Estella, Spain **C9** 12
Estelline, S.D., U.S. **C9** 118
Estepona, Spain **I6** 12
Esternay, Fr. **D10** 10
Estero Bay, b., Ca., U.S. **E3** 82
Estero Bay, b., Fl., U.S. **F5** 86
Estero Island, i., Fl., U.S. **F5** 86
Estes Park, Co., U.S. **A5** 83
Estherville, Ia., U.S. **A3** 92
Estherwood, La., U.S. **D3** 95
Estill, S.C., U.S. **F5** 117
Estill, co., Ky., U.S. **C6** 94
Estill Springs, Tn., U.S. **B5** 119
Estonia, ctry., Eur. **C9** 18
Estremoz, Port. **G4** 12
Esztergom, Hung. **H18** 8
Etah, Grnld. **B20** 128
Etah, India **G8** 38
Étampes, Fr. **D9** 10
Étang-du-Nord, Que., Can. **B8** 71
Étaples, Fr. **B8** 10
Etāwah, India **G8** 38
Ethel, W.V., U.S. **n12** 125
Ethiopia, ctry., Afr. **G2** 46
Etna, Pa., U.S. **k14** 115
Etna, Monte, vol., Italy **L9** 14
Etobicoke, Ont., Can. **D5** 73
Etolin Island, i., Ak., U.S. **m23** 79
Etolin Strait, strt., Ak., U.S. **C6** 79
Etoshapan, pl., Nmb. **E3** 44
Etowah, Tn., U.S. **D9** 119
Etowah, co., Al., U.S. **A3** 78
Etowah, stm., Ga., U.S. **B2** 87
Ettelbruck, Lux. **F6** 8
Ettlingen, Ger. **G8** 8
Ettrick, Va., U.S. **C5** 123
Eu, Fr. **B8** 10
Eucla, Austl. **F5** 50
Euclid, Oh., U.S. **A4** 112
Eudora, Ar., U.S. **D4** 81
Eudora, Ks., U.S. **D8** 93
Eufaula, Al., U.S. **D4** 78
Eufaula, Ok., U.S. **B6** 113
Eufaula Lake, res., Ok., U.S. **B6** 113
Eugene, Or., U.S. **C3** 114
Eugenia, Punta, c., Mex. **D2** 62
Eunice, La., U.S. **D3** 95
Eunice, N.M., U.S. **E6** 108
Euphrates (Al-Furāt), stm., Asia **A2** 46
Eupora, Ms., U.S. **B4** 101
Eureka, Ca., U.S. **B1** 82
Eureka, Il., U.S. **C4** 90
Eureka, Ks., U.S. **E7** 93
Eureka, Mo., U.S. **f12** 102
Eureka, Mt., U.S. **B1** 103
Eureka, Nv., U.S. **D6** 105
Eureka, S.C., U.S. **B5** 117
Eureka, S.D., U.S. **B6** 118
Eureka, co., Nv., U.S. **D5** 105
Eureka Springs, Ar., U.S. **A2** 81
Europa, Île, i., Reu. **F8** 44
Europa Point, c., Gib. **I6** 12
Europe **E11** 4
Euskirchen, Ger. **E6** 8
Eustis, Fl., U.S. **D5** 86
Eutaw, Al., U.S. **C2** 78
Eutin, Ger. **A10** 8
Eutsuk Lake, l., B.C., Can. **C4** 69
Evangeline, co., La., U.S. **D3** 95
Evans, Co., U.S. **A6** 83
Evans, Ga., U.S. **C4** 87
Evans, W.V., U.S. **C3** 125
Evans, co., Ga., U.S. **D5** 87
Evans, Lac, l., Que., Can. **F17** 66
Evans, Mount, mtn., Co., U.S. **B5** 83
Evansburg, Alta., Can. **C3** 68
Evans City, Pa., U.S. **E1** 115
Evansdale, Ia., U.S. **B5** 92
Evans Strait, strt., N.W. Ter., Can. **D16** 66
Evanston, Il., U.S. **A6** 90
Evanston, Wy., U.S. **E2** 127
Evansville, Il., U.S. **E4** 90
Evansville, In., U.S. **I2** 91
Evansville, Wi., U.S. **F4** 126
Evansville, Wy., U.S. **D6** 127
Evart, Mi., U.S. **E5** 99
Evarts, Ky., U.S. **D6** 94
Eveleth, Mn., U.S. **C6** 100
Everard, Lake, l., Austl. **F7** 50
Everest, Mount, mtn., Asia **G12** 38
Everett, Ma., U.S. **g11** 98
Everett, Pa., U.S. **F5** 115
Everett, Wa., U.S. **B3** 124
Everett Lake, res., N.H., U.S. **D3** 106
Everglades National Park, Fl., U.S. **G5** 86
Evergreen, Al., U.S. **D3** 78
Evergreen, Co., U.S. **B5** 83
Evergreen Park, Il., U.S. **k9** 90
Everly, Ia., U.S. **A2** 92
Everson, Wa., U.S. **A3** 124
Evesham, Eng., U.K. **I11** 7
Evje, Nor. **G6** 6
Évora, Port. **G4** 12
Évreux, Fr. **C8** 10
Évros (Marica) (Meriç), stm., Eur. **H10** 16
E.V. Spence Reservoir, res., Tx., U.S. **D2** 120
Évvoia, i., Grc. **K7** 16
Ewa, Hi., U.S. **B3** 88
Ewa Beach, Hi., U.S. **B3** 88
Ewa Beach, Hi., U.S. **g9** 88
Ewing Township, N.J., U.S. **C3** 107
Ewo, Congo **B2** 44
Excelsior Mountain, mtn., Ca., U.S. **C4** 82
Excelsior Mountains, mts., Nv., U.S. **E3** 105
Excelsior Springs, Mo., U.S. **B3** 102
Executive Committee Range, mts., Ant. **B36** 47
Exeter, Ont., Can. **D3** 73
Exeter, Eng., U.K. **K9** 7
Exeter, Ca., U.S. **D4** 82
Exeter, Ne., U.S. **D8** 104
Exeter, N.H., U.S. **E5** 106
Exeter, Pa., U.S. **D10** 115
Exeter, stm., N.H., U.S. **E5** 106
Exeter Sound, strt., N.W. Ter., Can. **C20** 66
Exira, Ia., U.S. **C3** 92
Exmore, Va., U.S. **C7** 123
Exmouth, Eng., U.K. **K9** 7
Exmouth Gulf, b., Austl. **D2** 50
Experiment, Ga., U.S. **C2** 87
Exploits, stm., Newf., Can. **D3** 72
Exploits, Bay of, b., Newf., Can. **D4** 72
Export, Pa., U.S. **F2** 115
Exuma Sound, strt., Bah. **B9** 64
Eyasi, Lake, l., Tan. **B6** 44
Eylar Mountain, mtn., Ca., U.S. **D3** 82
Eymoutiers, Fr. **G8** 10
Eyota, Mn., U.S. **G6** 100
Eyre (North), Lake, l., Austl. **E7** 50
Eyre (South), Lake, l., Austl. **E7** 50
Eyre Peninsula, pen., Austl. **F7** 50

F

Fabens, Tx., U.S. **o11** 120
Fabius, stm., Mo., U.S. **A6** 102
Fabriano, Italy **F7** 14
Facatativá, Col. **E5** 58
Factoryville, Pa., U.S. **C10** 115
Fada, Chad **E10** 42
Fada Ngourma, Burkina **F6** 42
Faddejevskij, Ostrov, i., Russia **B22** 24
Faenza, Italy **E6** 14
Faeroe Islands, dep., Eur. **C6** 4
Fagernes, Nor. **F7** 6
Fagersta, Swe. **F10** 6
Fairacres, N.M., U.S. **E3** 108
Fairbank, Ia., U.S. **B5** 92
Fairbanks, Ak., U.S. **C10** 79
Fair Bluff, N.C., U.S. **C3** 110
Fairborn, Oh., U.S. **C1** 112
Fairburn, Ga., U.S. **C2** 87
Fairbury, Il., U.S. **C5** 90
Fairbury, Ne., U.S. **D8** 104
Fairchance, Pa., U.S. **G2** 115
Fairchild Air Force Base, mil., Wa., U.S. **g13** 124
Fairdale, Ky., U.S. **B4** 94
Fairfax, Ca., U.S. **C2** 82
Fairfax, De., U.S. **A3** 85
Fairfax, Ia., U.S. **C6** 92
Fairfax, Mn., U.S. **F4** 100
Fairfax, Mo., U.S. **A2** 102
Fairfax, Ok., U.S. **A5** 113
Fairfax, S.C., U.S. **F5** 117
Fairfax, Va., U.S. **B5** 123
Fairfax, co., Va., U.S. **B5** 123
Fairfield, Al., U.S. **B3** 78
Fairfield, Ca., U.S. **C2** 82
Fairfield, Ct., U.S. **E2** 84
Fairfield, Il., U.S. **E5** 90
Fairfield, Ia., U.S. **C6** 92
Fairfield, Me., U.S. **D3** 96
Fairfield, Mt., U.S. **C5** 103
Fairfield, Oh., U.S. **n12** 112
Fairfield, Tx., U.S. **D4** 120
Fairfield, co., Ct., U.S. **D2** 84
Fairfield, co., Oh., U.S. **C3** 112
Fairfield, co., S.C., U.S. **C5** 117
Fairfield Bay, Ar., U.S. **B3** 81
Fairfield Pond, l., Vt., U.S. **B3** 122
Fair Grove, Mo., U.S. **D4** 102
Fair Grove, N.C., U.S. **B2** 110
Fairhaven, Ma., U.S. **C6** 98
Fair Haven, Mi., U.S. **F8** 99
Fair Haven, N.J., U.S. **C4** 107
Fair Haven, Vt., U.S. **D2** 122
Fairhope, Al., U.S. **E2** 78
Fair Isle, i., Scot., U.K. **B11** 7
Fairland, In., U.S. **E6** 91
Fairland, Ok., U.S. **A7** 113
Fair Lawn, N.J., U.S. **h8** 107
Fairlawn, Va., U.S. **C2** 123
Fairlea, W.V., U.S. **D4** 125
Fairmont, Il., U.S. **C6** 90
Fairmont, Mn., U.S. **G4** 100
Fairmont, Ne., U.S. **D8** 104
Fairmont, N.C., U.S. **C3** 110
Fairmont, W.V., U.S. **B4** 125
Fairmount, Ga., U.S. **B2** 87
Fairmount, In., U.S. **D6** 91
Fairmount Heights, Md., U.S. **f9** 97
Fair Oaks, Ga., U.S. **h7** 87
Fairoaks, Pa., U.S. **h13** 115
Fair Plain, Mi., U.S. **F4** 99
Fairport, N.Y., U.S. **B3** 109
Fairport Harbor, Oh., U.S. **A4** 112
Fairvale, N.B., Can. **D4** 71
Fairview, Alta., Can. **A1** 68
Fairview, Mt., U.S. **C12** 103
Fairview, N.J., U.S. **h8** 107
Fairview, Ok., U.S. **A3** 113
Fairview, Pa., U.S. **B1** 115
Fairview, Tn., U.S. **B4** 119
Fairview, Ut., U.S. **D4** 121
Fairview Heights, Il., U.S. **E3** 90
Fairview Park, In., U.S. **E3** 91
Fairview Park, Oh., U.S. **g9** 112
Fairview Peak, mtn., Nv., U.S. **D3** 105
Fairview Peak, mtn., Or., U.S. **D4** 114
Fairway, Ks., U.S. **k16** 93
Fairweather, Mount, mtn., N.A. **E5** 66
Faisalabad, Pak. **E5** 38
Faison, N.C., U.S. **B4** 110
Faizābād, India **G10** 38
Fakenham, Eng., U.K. **I13** 7
Fakfak, Indon. **F9** 32
Falaise, Fr. **D6** 10
Falam, Mya. **C2** 34
Falconer, N.Y., U.S. **C1** 109
Falcon Heights, Mn., U.S. **n12** 100
Falcon Heights, Or., U.S. **E5** 114
Falcon Reservoir, res., N.A. **D10** 62
Falfurrias, Tx., U.S. **F3** 120
Falher, Alta., Can. **B2** 68
Falkenberg, Swe. **H9** 6
Falkensee, Ger. **C13** 8
Falkenstein, Ger. **E12** 8
Falkland Islands (Islas Malvinas), dep., S.A. **G5** 56
Falköping, Swe. **G9** 6
Falkville, Al., U.S. **A3** 78
Fall, stm., Ks., U.S. **E7** 93
Fall Branch, Tn., U.S. **C11** 119
Fallbrook, Ca., U.S. **F5** 82
Fall City, Wa., U.S. **B4** 124
Fall Creek, Wi., U.S. **D2** 126
Falling Creek, stm., Va., U.S. **n17** 123
Falling Rock Creek, stm., W.V., U.S. **m13** 125
Fall Mountain Lake, Ct., U.S. **C4** 84
Fallon, Nv., U.S. **D3** 105
Fallon, co., Mt., U.S. **D12** 103
Fallon Indian Reservation, Nv., U.S. **D3** 105
Fallon Naval Air Station, mil., Nv., U.S. **D3** 105
Fall River, Ma., U.S. **C5** 98
Fall River, Wi., U.S. **E4** 126
Fall River, co., S.D., U.S. **D2** 118
Fall River Lake, res., Ks., U.S. **E7** 93
Falls, co., Tx., U.S. **D4** 120
Falls Church, Va., U.S. **g12** 123
Falls City, Ne., U.S. **D10** 104
Falls City, Or., U.S. **C3** 114
Falls Creek, Pa., U.S. **D4** 115
Fallston, Md., U.S. **A5** 97
Falmouth, N.S., Can. **E5** 71
Falmouth, Eng., U.K. **K7** 7
Falmouth, Ky., U.S. **B5** 94
Falmouth, Me., U.S. **E2** 96
Falmouth, Ma., U.S. **C6** 98
Falmouth, Va., U.S. **B5** 123
False Cape, c., Fl., U.S. **D6** 86
False Cape, c., Va., U.S. **D7** 123
False Divi Point, c., India **E6** 37
Falset, Spain **D12** 12
Falun, Swe. **F10** 6
Famagusta see Gazimağusa, N. Cyp. **B3** 40
Famatina, Nevado de, mts., Arg. **B3** 56
Fancy Farm, Ky., U.S. **f9** 94
Fangcheng, China **B1** 28
Fannin, co., Ga., U.S. **B2** 87
Fannin, co., Tx., U.S. **C4** 120
Fanny, Mount, mtn., Or., U.S. **B9** 114
Fano, Italy **F8** 14
Faradje, Zaire **H11** 42
Faradofay, Madag. **G9** 44
Farafangana, Madag. **F9** 44
Farāh, Afg. **C1** 36
Faranah, Gui. **F3** 42
Farasān, Jazā'ir, is., Sau. Ar. **E3** 46
Farewell, Cape, c., N.Z. **D4** 52
Fargo, Ga., U.S. **F4** 87
Fargo, N.D., U.S. **C9** 111
Faribault, Mn., U.S. **F5** 100
Faribault, co., Mn., U.S. **G4** 100
Farīdpur, Bngl. **I13** 38
Färjestaden, Swe. **H11** 6
Farley, Ia., U.S. **B6** 92
Farmer City, Il., U.S. **C5** 90
Farmers Branch, Tx., U.S. **n10** 120
Farmersburg, In., U.S. **F3** 91
Farmerville, La., U.S. **B3** 95
Farmingdale, Me., U.S. **D3** 96
Farmington, Ar., U.S. **A1** 81
Farmington, Ct., U.S. **C4** 84
Farmington, Il., U.S. **C3** 90
Farmington, Ia., U.S. **D6** 92
Farmington, Me., U.S. **D2** 96
Farmington, Mi., U.S. **p15** 99
Farmington, Mn., U.S. **F5** 100
Farmington, Mo., U.S. **D7** 102
Farmington, N.H., U.S. **D4** 106
Farmington, N.M., U.S. **A1** 108
Farmington, Ut., U.S. **C4** 121
Farmington, stm., Ct., U.S. **B4** 84
Farmington Hills, Mi., U.S. **o15** 99
Farmland, In., U.S. **D7** 91
Farmville, N.C., U.S. **B5** 110
Farmville, Va., U.S. **C4** 123
Farnham, Que., Can. **D5** 74
Faro, Braz. **D7** 54
Faro, Port. **H4** 12
Faro, Punta del, c., Italy **K10** 14
Fårösund, Swe. **H12** 6
Farquhar Group, is., Sey. **D10** 44
Farrell, Pa., U.S. **D1** 115
Farrukhābād, India **G8** 38
Fartak, Ra's, c., Yemen **E5** 46
Farvel, Kap, c., Grnld. **E24** 66
Farwell, Mi., U.S. **E6** 99
Farwell, Tx., U.S. **B1** 120
Fasano, Italy **I12** 14
Fatehpur, India **H9** 38
Fatehpur, India **G6** 38
Faulk, co., S.D., U.S. **B6** 118
Faulkland Heights, De., U.S. **i7** 85
Faulkner, co., Ar., U.S. **B3** 81
Faulkton, S.D., U.S. **B6** 118
Fauquier, co., Va., U.S. **B5** 123
Fauske, Nor. **C10** 6
Favara, Italy **L8** 14
Faverges, Fr. **G13** 10
Fawnie Nose, mtn., B.C., Can. **C5** 69
Fayette, Al., U.S. **B2** 78
Fayette, Ia., U.S. **B6** 92
Fayette, Ms., U.S. **D2** 101
Fayette, Mo., U.S. **B5** 102
Fayette, Oh., U.S. **A1** 112
Fayette, co., Al., U.S. **B3** 78
Fayette, co., Ga., U.S. **C2** 87
Fayette, co., Il., U.S. **D5** 90
Fayette, co., In., U.S. **E7** 91
Fayette, co., Ia., U.S. **B6** 92
Fayette, co., Ky., U.S. **B5** 94
Fayette, co., Oh., U.S. **C2** 112
Fayette, co., Pa., U.S. **G2** 115
Fayette, co., Tn., U.S. **B2** 119
Fayette, co., Tx., U.S. **E4** 120
Fayette, co., W.V., U.S. **C3** 125
Fayetteville, Ar., U.S. **A1** 81
Fayetteville, Ga., U.S. **C2** 87
Fayetteville, N.C., U.S. **B4** 110
Fayetteville, Pa., U.S. **G6** 115
Fayetteville, Tn., U.S. **B5** 119
Fayetteville, W.V., U.S. **C3** 125
Fāzilka, India **E6** 38
Fazzān (Fezzan), reg., Libya **C8** 42
Fdérik, Maur. **D3** 42
Fear, Cape, c., N.C., U.S. **D5** 110
Feather, stm., Ca., U.S. **C3** 82
Fécamp, Fr. **C7** 10
Federalsburg, Md., U.S. **C6** 97
Feeding Hills, Ma., U.S. **B2** 98
Fehmarn Belt, strt., Eur. **A11** 8
Feijó, Braz. **E4** 54
Feira de Santana, Braz. **B9** 57
Felanitx, Spain **F15** 12
Feldbach, Aus. **I15** 8
Feldkirch, Aus. **H9** 8
Feldkirchen in Kärnten, Aus. **I14** 8
Félix Gómez, Mex. **C4** 62
Felletin, Fr. **G9** 10
Fellsmere, Fl., U.S. **E6** 86
Felton, Ca., U.S. **D2** 82
Felton, De., U.S. **D3** 85
Feltre, Italy **C6** 14
Femundsenden, Nor. **F8** 6
Fence, stm., Mi., U.S. **B2** 99
Fence Lake, l., Wi., U.S. **C4** 126
Fenelon Falls, Ont., Can. **C6** 73
Fengcheng, China **G4** 28
Fengzhen, China **C9** 26
Fenimore Pass, strt., Ak., U.S. **E4** 79
Fennimore, Wi., U.S. **F3** 126
Fennville, Mi., U.S. **F4** 99
Fenton, Mi., U.S. **F7** 99
Fentress, co., Tn., U.S. **C9** 119
Fenwick Island, i., S.C., U.S. **k11** 117
Fenyang, China **D9** 26
Feodosiya, Ukr. **H5** 22
Fer, Point au, c., La., U.S. **E4** 95
Ferdinand, In., U.S. **H4** 91
Fergana, Uzb. **I12** 22
Fergus, Ont., Can. **D4** 73
Fergus, co., Mt., U.S. **C7** 103
Fergus Falls, Mn., U.S. **D2** 100
Ferguson, Ky., U.S. **C5** 94
Ferguson, Mo., U.S. **C7** 102
Ferme-Neuve, Que., Can. **C2** 74
Fermo, Italy **F8** 14
Fermont, Que., Can. **h13** 74
Fermoy, Ire. **I4** 7
Fernandina Beach, Fl., U.S. **B5** 86
Fernando de Noronha, Ilha, i., Braz. **D12** 54
Fernandópolis, Braz. **F3** 57
Fernando Póo see Bioko, i., Eq. Gui. **H7** 42
Fernán-Núñez, Spain **H7** 12
Fern Creek, Ky., U.S. **g11** 94
Ferndale, Ca., U.S. **B1** 82
Ferndale, Md., U.S. **B4** 97
Ferndale, Mi., U.S. **P15** 99
Ferndale, Pa., U.S. **F4** 115
Ferndale, Wa., U.S. **A3** 124
Fernie, B.C., Can. **E10** 69
Fernley, Nv., U.S. **D2** 105
Fern Ridge Lake, res., Or., U.S. **C3** 114
Fernwood, Id., U.S. **B2** 89
Fernwood, Ms., U.S. **D3** 101
Ferrara, Italy **E6** 14
Ferreira do Alentejo, Port. **G3** 12
Ferrelo, Cape, c., Or., U.S. **E2** 114
Ferriday, La., U.S. **C4** 95
Ferris, Tx., U.S. **C4** 120
Ferris Mountains, mts., Wy., U.S. **D5** 127
Ferron, Ut., U.S. **D4** 121

Index

Name	Map Ref	Page
Ferrum, Va., U.S.	D2	123
Ferry, co., Wa., U.S.	A7	124
Ferry Farms, Va., U.S.	B5	123
Ferryland, Newf., Can.	E5	72
Ferry Point, c., N.J., U.S.	k7	107
Fertile, Mn., U.S.	C2	100
Fès, Mor.	B5	42
Feshi, Zaire	C3	44
Fessenden, N.D., U.S.	B6	111
Festus, Mo., U.S.	C7	102
Fethiye, Tur.	M13	16
Feuilles, Rivière aux, stm., Que., Can.	g12	74
Feurs, Fr.	G11	10
Feyẕābād, Afg.	B4	38
Fez see Fès, Mor.	B5	42
Fianarantsoa, Madag.	F9	44
Ficksburg, S. Afr.	G5	44
Fidalgo Island, i., Wa., U.S.	A3	124
Fidenza, Italy	E5	14
Fieldale, Va., U.S.	D3	123
Fields, Lake, l., Fl., U.S.	B3	86
Fields, Lake, l., La., U.S.	k10	95
Fier, Alb.	I3	16
Fifteenmile Creek, stm., Wy., U.S.	B4	127
Fifteen Mile Falls Reservoir, res., U.S.	C5	122
Figeac, Fr.	H9	10
Figueira da Foz, Port.	E3	12
Figueras, Spain	C14	12
Figuig, Mor.	B5	42
Fiji, ctry., Oc.	H1	2
Filchner Ice Shelf, Ant.	B9	47
Filer, Id., U.S.	G4	89
Fillmore, Ca., U.S.	E4	82
Fillmore, Ut., U.S.	E3	121
Fillmore, co., Mn., U.S.	G6	100
Fillmore, co., Ne., U.S.	D8	104
Finale Ligure, Italy	E3	14
Findlay, Il., U.S.	D5	90
Findlay, Oh., U.S.	A2	112
Finisterre, Cabo de, c., Spain	C2	12
Finland, ctry., Eur.	C13	4
Finland, Gulf of, b., Eur.	G16	6
Finlay, stm., B.C., Can.	E7	66
Finley, Tn., U.S.	A2	119
Finney, co., Ks., U.S.	D3	93
Finn Mountain, mtn., Ak., U.S.	C8	79
Finse, Nor.	F6	6
Finspång, Swe.	G10	6
Finsterwalde, Ger.	D13	8
Fiorenzuola d'Arda, Italy	E4	14
Fircrest, Wa., U.S.	f10	124
Firebaugh, Ca., U.S.	D3	82
Firenze (Florence), Italy	F6	14
Firenzuola, Italy	E6	14
Firestone, Co., U.S.	A6	83
Firminy, Fr.	G11	10
Fīrozābād, India	G8	38
Fīrozpur, India	E6	38
First Connecticut Lake, l., N.H., U.S.	f7	106
Fish, stm., Al., U.S.	E2	78
Fish, stm., Me., U.S.	A4	96
Fish Creek, stm., W.V., U.S.	g8	125
Fisher, Il., U.S.	C5	90
Fisher, co., Tx., U.S.	C2	120
Fisher Bay, b., Man., Can.	D3	70
Fishermans Island, i., Va., U.S.	h15	123
Fishers, In., U.S.	E5	91
Fishers Island, i., N.Y., U.S.	m16	109
Fishers Peak, mtn., Co., U.S.	D6	83
Fisher Strait, strt., N.W. Ter., Can.	D16	66
Fishersville, Va., U.S.	B4	123
Fishing Bay, b., Md., U.S.	D5	97
Fishing Creek, Md., U.S.	D5	97
Fishing Creek, stm., N.C., U.S.	A5	110
Fishing Creek, stm., S.C., U.S.	B5	117
Fishing Creek, stm., W.V., U.S.	B4	125
Fishing Creek Reservoir, res., S.C., U.S.	B6	117
Fishkill, N.Y., U.S.	D7	109
Fish Lake, l., Ut., U.S.	E4	121
Fish River Lake, l., Me., U.S.	B4	96
Fishtrap Lake, res., Ky., U.S.	C7	94
Fiskdale, Ma., U.S.	B3	98
Fitchburg, Ma., U.S.	A4	98
Fitzgerald, Ga., U.S.	E3	87
Fitz Roy, Arg.	F3	56
Fitzroy, stm., Austl.	C4	50
Fitzroy, Monte (Cerro Chaltel), mtn., S.A.	F2	56
Fitzroy Crossing, Austl.	C5	50
Fitzwilliam, N.H., U.S.	E2	106
Fitzwilliam Island, i., Ont., Can.	B3	73
Five Island Lake, l., Ia., U.S.	A3	92
Fivemile Creek, stm., Wy., U.S.	C4	127
Five Points, N.M., U.S.	B3	108
Flagler, co., Fl., U.S.	C5	86
Flagler Beach, Fl., U.S.	C5	86
Flagstaff, Az., U.S.	B4	80
Flagstaff Lake, l., Or., U.S.	E7	114
Flambeau, stm., Wi., U.S.	C3	126
Flamborough Head, c., Eng., U.K.	G12	7
Flaming Gorge Dam, Ut., U.S.	C6	121
Flaming Gorge National Recreation Area, U.S.	E3	127
Flaming Gorge Reservoir, res., U.S.	E3	127
Flanagan, Il., U.S.	C5	90
Flandreau, S.D., U.S.	C9	118
Flandreau Indian Reservation, S.D., U.S.	C9	118
Flat, stm., Mi., U.S.	E5	99
Flat, stm., N.C., U.S.	A4	110
Flat, stm., R.I., U.S.	E2	116
Flat Brook, stm., N.J., U.S.	A3	107
Flathead, co., Mt., U.S.	B2	103
Flathead, South Fork, stm., Mt., U.S.	C3	103
Flathead Indian Reservation, Mt., U.S.	C2	103
Flathead Lake, l., Mt., U.S.	C2	103
Flathead Valley, val., Mt., U.S.	C2	103
Flat Lake, l., La., U.S.	k9	95
Flat Lick, Ky., U.S.	D6	94
Flatonia, Tx., U.S.	E4	120
Flat River, Mo., U.S.	D7	102
Flat River Reservoir, res., R.I., U.S.	D3	116
Flat Rock, Mi., U.S.	F7	99
Flat Rock, N.C., U.S.	f10	110
Flatrock, stm., In., U.S.	F6	91
Flattery, Cape, c., Wa., U.S.	A1	124
Flatwoods, Ky., U.S.	B7	94
Fleetwood, Eng., U.K.	H9	7
Fleetwood, Pa., U.S.	F10	115
Flekkefjord, Nor.	G6	6
Fleming, co., Ky., U.S.	B6	94
Fleming-Neon, Ky., U.S.	C7	94
Flemingsburg, Ky., U.S.	B6	94
Flemington, N.J., U.S.	B3	107
Flemington, Pa., U.S.	D7	115
Flensburg, Ger.	A9	8
Flers, Fr.	D6	10
Fletcher, N.C., U.S.	f10	110
Fletcher, Ok., U.S.	C3	113
Fleurance, Fr.	I7	10
Flinders, stm., Austl.	C8	50
Flinders Island, i., Austl.	G9	50
Flin Flon, Man., Can.	B1	70
Flint, Wales, U.K.	H9	7
Flint, Mi., U.S.	E7	99
Flint, stm., Ga., U.S.	E2	87
Flint City, Al., U.S.	A3	78
Flint Creek Range, mts., Mt., U.S.	D3	103
Flint Run, stm., W.V., U.S.	k9	125
Flippin, Ar., U.S.	A3	81
Flomaton, Al., U.S.	D2	78
Flora, Il., U.S.	E5	90
Flora, In., U.S.	C4	91
Flora, Ms., U.S.	C3	101
Florac, Fr.	H10	10
Florala, Al., U.S.	D3	78
Floral City, Fl., U.S.	D4	86
Florence, Al., U.S.	A2	78
Florence, Az., U.S.	D4	80
Florence, Co., U.S.	C5	83
Florence, Ks., U.S.	D7	93
Florence, Ky., U.S.	A5	94
Florence, Ms., U.S.	C3	101
Florence, N.J., U.S.	C3	107
Florence, Or., U.S.	D2	114
Florence, S.C., U.S.	C8	117
Florence, co., S.C., U.S.	C8	117
Florence, co., Wi., U.S.	C5	126
Florence see Firenze, Italy	F6	14
Florenceville, N.B., Can.	C2	71
Florencia, Col.	G5	58
Flores, i., Indon.	G7	32
Flores, Laut (Flores Sea), Indon.	G6	32
Floresville, Tx., U.S.	E3	120
Florham Park, N.J., U.S.	B4	107
Floriano, Braz.	E10	54
Florianópolis, Braz.	B7	56
Florida, Col.	F4	58
Florida, Cuba	D8	64
Florida, N.Y., U.S.	D6	109
Florida, state, U.S.	E5	86
Florida, Cape, c., Fl., U.S.	G6	86
Florida, Straits of, strt., N.A.	B7	64
Florida Bay, b., Fl., U.S.	H6	86
Floridablanca, Col.	D6	58
Florida City, Fl., U.S.	G6	86
Florida Keys, is., Fl., U.S.	H6	86
Florida Mountains, mts., N.M., U.S.	E2	108
Florida State Indian Reservation, Fl., U.S.	F5	86
Florien, La., U.S.	C2	95
Florissant, Mo., U.S.	f13	102
Florissant Fossil Beds National Monument, Co., U.S.	C5	83
Florø, Nor.	F5	6
Flossmoor, Il., U.S.	k9	90
Flovilla, Ga., U.S.	C3	87
Flower Brook, stm., Vt., U.S.	E2	122
Flowery Branch, Ga., U.S.	B3	87
Flowood, Ms., U.S.	C3	101
Floyd, co., Ga., U.S.	B1	87
Floyd, co., In., U.S.	H6	91
Floyd, co., Ia., U.S.	A5	92
Floyd, co., Ky., U.S.	C7	94
Floyd, co., Tx., U.S.	B2	120
Floyd, co., Va., U.S.	D2	123
Floyd, stm., Ia., U.S.	B1	92
Floydada, Tx., U.S.	C2	120
Floyds Fork, stm., Ky., U.S.	B4	94
Floyds Knobs, In., U.S.	H6	91
Flushing, Mi., U.S.	E7	99
Flushing, Oh., U.S.	B4	112
Flushing see Vlissingen, Neth.	D3	8
Fluvanna, co., Va., U.S.	C4	123
Fly, stm.	m15	50a
Foard, co., Tx., U.S.	B3	120
Foça, Tur.	K10	16
Focșani, Rom.	D11	16
Fogang (Shijiao), China	L2	28
Foggia, Italy	H10	14
Fogland Point, c., R.I., U.S.	E6	116
Fogo, Newf., Can.	D4	72
Fogo, Cape, c., Newf., Can.	D5	72
Fogo Island, i., Newf., Can.	D4	72
Fohnsdorf, Aus.	H14	8
Foix, Fr.	J8	10
Foley, Al., U.S.	E2	78
Foley, Mn., U.S.	E5	100
Foley Island, i., N.W. Ter., Can.	C17	66
Foligno, Italy	G7	14
Folkestone, Eng., U.K.	J14	7
Folkston, Ga., U.S.	F4	87
Follansbee, W.V., U.S.	A4	125
Follonica, Italy	G5	14
Folly Beach, S.C., U.S.	F8	117
Folly Island, i., S.C., U.S.	F8	117
Folsom, Ca., U.S.	C3	82
Fonda, Ia., U.S.	B3	92
Fond du Lac, Wi., U.S.	E5	126
Fond du Lac, co., Wi., U.S.	E5	126
Fond du Lac Indian Reservation, Mn., U.S.	D6	100
Fondi, Italy	H8	14
Fondouk el Aouareb, Tun.	N4	14
Fonni, Italy	I4	14
Fonseca, Col.	B6	58
Fonseca, Golfo de, b., N.A.	H4	64
Fontainebleau, Fr.	D9	10
Fontana, Ca., U.S.	m14	82
Fontana, Wi., U.S.	F5	126
Fontana Lake, res., N.C., U.S.	f9	110
Fontanelle, Ia., U.S.	C3	92
Fonte Boa, Braz.	D5	54
Fontenay-le-Comte, Fr.	F6	10
Fontenelle Reservoir, res., Wy., U.S.	D2	127
Fontur, c., Ice.	B5	4
Foochow see Fuzhou, China	I8	28
Footville, Wi., U.S.	F4	126
Foraker, Mount, mtn., Ak., U.S.	f16	79
Forbach, Fr.	C13	10
Forbach, Ger.	G8	8
Forbes, Mount, mtn., Alta., Can.	D2	68
Forcalquier, Fr.	I12	10
Forchheim, Ger.	F11	8
Ford, co., Il., U.S.	C5	90
Ford, co., Ks., U.S.	E4	93
Ford, stm., Mi., U.S.	C3	99
Ford City, Ca., U.S.	E4	82
Ford City, Pa., U.S.	E2	115
Førde, Nor.	F5	6
Fordoche, La., U.S.	D4	95
Fords Prairie, Wa., U.S.	C2	124
Fordyce, Ar., U.S.	D3	81
Forel, Mont, mtn., Grnld.	C25	66
Foreman, Ar., U.S.	D1	81
Forest, Ont., Can.	D2	73
Forest, Ms., U.S.	C4	101
Forest, Oh., U.S.	B2	112
Forest, co., Pa., U.S.	C3	115
Forest, co., Wi., U.S.	C5	126
Forest, stm., N.D., U.S.	A8	111
Forest Acres, S.C., U.S.	C6	117
Forestburg, Alta., Can.	C4	68
Forest City, Ia., U.S.	A4	92
Forest City, N.C., U.S.	B1	110
Forest City, Pa., U.S.	C11	115
Forestdale, R.I., U.S.	B3	116
Forest Dale, Vt., U.S.	D2	122
Forest Glen, La., U.S.	h12	95
Forest Grove, Or., U.S.	B3	114
Forest Hill, Md., U.S.	A5	97
Forest Hills, Pa., U.S.	k14	115
Forest Knolls, Ca., U.S.	g7	82
Forest Lake, Mn., U.S.	E6	100
Forest Park, Ga., U.S.	h8	87
Forest Park, Il., U.S.	k9	90
Forest Park, La., U.S.	*B3	95
Forest Park, Oh., U.S.	*n12	112
Forfar, Scot., U.K.	E10	7
Forillon, Parc National de, Que., Can.	k14	74
Fork Creek, stm., W.V., U.S.	m12	125
Forked Deer, stm., Tn., U.S.	B2	119
Forkland, Al., U.S.	C2	78
Forks, Wa., U.S.	B1	124
Forlì, Italy	E7	14
Formia, Italy	H8	14
Formiga, Braz.	F6	57
Formosa, Arg.	B5	56
Formosa, Braz.	C5	57
Formosa, Serra, plat., Braz.	F8	54
Formosa see Taiwan, i., Asia	L9	28
Forney, Tx., U.S.	C4	120
Fornovo di Taro, Italy	E5	14
Forrest, Austl.	F5	50
Forrest, Il., U.S.	C5	90
Forrest, co., Ms., U.S.	D4	101
Forrest City, Ar., U.S.	B5	81
Forrester Island, i., Ak., U.S.	n23	79
Forreston, Il., U.S.	A4	90
Forsayth, Austl.	C8	50
Forst, Ger.	D14	8
Forsyth, Ga., U.S.	C3	87
Forsyth, Il., U.S.	D5	90
Forsyth, Mo., U.S.	E4	102
Forsyth, Mt., U.S.	D10	103
Forsyth, co., Ga., U.S.	B2	87
Forsyth, co., N.C., U.S.	A2	110
Fortaleza, Braz.	D11	54
Fort Apache Indian Reservation, Az., U.S.	D5	80
Fort-Archambault see Sarh, Chad	G9	42
Fort Ashby, W.V., U.S.	B6	125
Fort Atkinson, Wi., U.S.	F5	126
Fort Augustus, Scot., U.K.	D8	7
Fort Beaufort, S. Afr.	H5	44
Fort Belknap Indian Reservation, Mt., U.S.	B8	103
Fort Belvoir, mil., Va., U.S.	g12	123
Fort Bend, co., Tx., U.S.	E5	120
Fort Benjamin Harrison, mil., In., U.S.	k10	91
Fort Benning, mil., Ga., U.S.	D2	87
Fort Benton, Mt., U.S.	C6	103
Fort Berthold Indian Reservation, N.D., U.S.	B3	111
Fort Bidwell Indian Reservation, Ca., U.S.	B3	82
Fort Bliss, mil., Tx., U.S.	o11	120
Fort Bragg, Ca., U.S.	C2	82
Fort Bragg, mil., N.C., U.S.	B3	110
Fort Branch, In., U.S.	H2	91
Fort Calhoun, Ne., U.S.	C9	104
Fort Campbell, mil., U.S.	A4	119
Fort Carson, mil., Co., U.S.	C6	83
Fort Chipewyan, Alta., Can.	f8	68
Fort Clatsop National Memorial, hist., Or., U.S.	A3	114
Fort Cobb, Ok., U.S.	B3	113
Fort Cobb Reservoir, res., Ok., U.S.	B3	113
Fort Collins, Co., U.S.	A5	83
Fort Coulonge, Que., Can.	B8	73
Fort Davis, Tx., U.S.	o13	120
Fort Davis National Historic Site, hist., Tx., U.S.	o13	120
Fort Defiance, Az., U.S.	B6	80
Fort-de-France, Mart.	G17	64
Fort Deposit, Al., U.S.	D3	78
Fort Detrick, mil., Md., U.S.	B3	97
Fort Devens, mil., Ma., U.S.	f9	98
Fort Dix, mil., N.J., U.S.	C3	107
Fort Dodge, Ia., U.S.	B3	92
Fort Donelson National Battlefield, Tn., U.S.	A4	119
Fort Edward, N.Y., U.S.	B7	109
Fort Erie, Ont., Can.	E6	73
Fortescue, stm., Austl.	D3	50
Fort Eustis, mil., Va., U.S.	h14	123
Fort Fairfield, Me., U.S.	B5	96
Fort Frances, Ont., Can.	o16	73
Fort Franklin, N.W. Ter., Can.	C8	66
Fort Gaines, Ga., U.S.	E1	87
Fort Gay, W.V., U.S.	C2	125
Fort Gibson, Ok., U.S.	B6	113
Fort Gibson Lake, res., Ok., U.S.	A6	113
Fort Good Hope, N.W. Ter., Can.	C7	66
Fort Gordon, mil., Ga., U.S.	C4	87
Fort Greely, mil., Ak., U.S.	C10	79
Forth, Firth of, est., Scot., U.K.	E10	7
Fort Hall, Id., U.S.	F6	89
Fort Hall Indian Reservation, Id., U.S.	F6	89
Fort Hood, mil., Tx., U.S.	D4	120
Fort Howard, Md., U.S.	B5	97
Fort Huachuca, mil., Az., U.S.	F5	80
Fortín Coronel Eugenio Garay, Para.	H6	54
Fort Jackson, mil., S.C., U.S.	C6	117
Fort Jefferson National Monument, Fl., U.S.	H4	86
Fort Kent, Me., U.S.	A4	96
Fort Knox, mil., Ky., U.S.	B4	94
Fort-Lamy see N'Djamena, Chad	F9	42
Fort Laramie, Wy., U.S.	D8	127
Fort Laramie National Historic Site, hist., Wy., U.S.	D8	127
Fort Lauderdale, Fl., U.S.	F6	86
Fort Lawn, S.C., U.S.	B6	117
Fort Leavenworth, mil., Ks., U.S.	C9	93
Fort Lee, N.J., U.S.	B5	107
Fort Lee, mil., Va., U.S.	C5	123
Fort Leonard Wood, mil., Mo., U.S.	D5	102
Fort Lewis, mil., Wa., U.S.	B3	124
Fort Liard, N.W. Ter., Can.	D8	66
Fort Loramie, Oh., U.S.	B1	112
Fort Loudon, Pa., U.S.	G6	115
Fort Loudoun Lake, res., Tn., U.S.	D9	119
Fort Lupton, Co., U.S.	A6	83
Fort MacArthur, mil., Ca., U.S.	n12	82
Fort Macleod, Alta., Can.	E4	68
Fort Madison, Ia., U.S.	D6	92
Fort Matanzas National Monument, Fl., U.S.	C5	86
Fort McClellan, mil., Al., U.S.	B4	78
Fort McDermitt Indian Reservation, U.S.	B4	105
Fort McDowell Indian Reservation, Az., U.S.	D4	80
Fort McHenry National Monument And Historic Shrine, Md., U.S.	g11	97
Fort McMurray, Alta., Can.	A5	68
Fort Meade, Fl., U.S.	E5	86
Fort Meade, mil., Md., U.S.	B4	97
Fort Meadow Reservoir, res., Ma., U.S.	g9	98
Fort Mill, S.C., U.S.	A6	117
Fort Mitchell, Al., U.S.	C4	78
Fort Mitchell, Ky., U.S.	h13	94
Fort Mojave Indian Reservation, U.S.	C1	80
Fort Monmouth, mil., N.J., U.S.	C4	107
Fort Monroe, mil., Va., U.S.	h15	123
Fort Morgan, Co., U.S.	A7	83
Fort Myer, mil., Va., U.S.	g12	123
Fort Myers, Fl., U.S.	F5	86
Fort Myers Beach, Fl., U.S.	F5	86
Fort Nelson, B.C., Can.	m18	69
Fort Norman, N.W. Ter., Can.	D7	66
Fort Oglethorpe, Ga., U.S.	B1	87
Fort Ord, mil., Ca., U.S.	D3	82
Fort Payne, Al., U.S.	A4	78
Fort Peck Indian Reservation, Mt., U.S.	B11	103
Fort Peck Lake, res., Mt., U.S.	C9	103
Fort Pierce, Fl., U.S.	E6	86
Fort Pierce Inlet, b., Fl., U.S.	E6	86
Fort Pierre, S.D., U.S.	C5	118
Fort Plain, N.Y., U.S.	C6	109
Fort Polk, mil., La., U.S.	C2	95
Fort Portal, Ug.	A6	44
Fort Providence, N.W. Ter., Can.	D9	66
Fort Randall Dam, S.D., U.S.	D7	118
Fort Recovery, Oh., U.S.	B1	112
Fort Reliance, N.W. Ter., Can.	D11	66
Fort Resolution, N.W. Ter., Can.	D10	66
Fortress Mountain, mtn., Wy., U.S.	B3	127
Fort Richardson, mil., Ak., U.S.	C10	79
Fort Riley, mil., Ks., U.S.	C7	93
Fort Ritchie, mil., Md., U.S.	A3	97
Fort Rucker, mil., Al., U.S.	D4	78
Fort Saint James, B.C., Can.	B5	69
Fort Saint John, B.C., Can.	A7	69
Fort Sam Houston, mil., Tx., U.S.	k7	120
Fort Sandeman, Pak.	E3	38
Fort Saskatchewan, Alta., Can.	C4	68
Fort Scott, Ks., U.S.	E9	93
Fort Shafter, mil., Hi., U.S.	g10	88
Fort Shawnee, Oh., U.S.	B1	112
Fort Sheridan, mil., Il., U.S.	h9	90
Fort Sill, mil., Ok., U.S.	C3	113
Fort Simpson, N.W. Ter., Can.	D8	66
Fort Smith, N.W. Ter., Can.	D10	66
Fort Smith, Ar., U.S.	B1	81
Fort Stewart, mil., Ga., U.S.	D5	87
Fort Stockton, Tx., U.S.	D1	120
Fort Sumner, N.M., U.S.	C5	108
Fort Sumter National Monument, S.C., U.S.	k12	117
Fort Supply Lake, res., Ok., U.S.	A2	113
Fort Thomas, Ky., U.S.	h14	94
Fort Totten, N.D., U.S.	B7	111
Fort Totten Indian Reservation, N.D., U.S.	B7	111
Fortuna, Ca., U.S.	B1	82
Fortune, Newf., Can.	E4	72
Fortune Bay, b., Newf., Can.	E4	72
Fort Union National Monument, N.M., U.S.	B5	108
Fort Valley, Ga., U.S.	D3	87
Fort Vermilion, Alta., Can.	f7	68
Fortville, In., U.S.	E6	91
Fort Wainwright, mil., Ak., U.S.	C10	79
Fort Walton Beach, Fl., U.S.	u15	86
Fort Washington Forest, Md., U.S.	C4	97
Fort Wayne, In., U.S.	B7	91
Fort William, Scot., U.K.	E7	7
Fort Wingate, N.M., U.S.	B1	108
Fort Worth, Tx., U.S.	C4	120
Fort Wright, Ky., U.S.	h13	94
Forty Fort, Pa., U.S.	D10	115
Fort Yukon, Ak., U.S.	B10	79
Fort Yuma Indian Reservation, Ca., U.S.	F6	82
Foshan, China	L2	28
Fossano, Italy	E2	14
Fossil Butte National Monument, Wy., U.S.	E2	127
Fossil Lake, l., Or., U.S.	D6	114
Fossombrone, Italy	F7	14
Foss Reservoir, res., Ok., U.S.	B2	113
Fosston, Mn., U.S.	C3	100
Foster, Or., U.S.	C4	114
Foster, co., N.D., U.S.	B6	111
Foster Village, Hi., U.S.	g10	88
Fostoria, Oh., U.S.	A2	112
Fougamou, Gabon	B2	44
Fougères, Fr.	D5	10
Fouke, Ar., U.S.	D2	81
Foula, i., Scot., U.K.	A10	7
Foumban, Cam.	G8	42
Fountain, Co., U.S.	C6	83
Fountain, co., In., U.S.	D3	91
Fountain City, In., U.S.	E8	91
Fountain City, Wi., U.S.	D2	126
Fountain Hill, Pa., U.S.	E11	115
Fountain Inn, S.C., U.S.	B3	117
Fountain Peak, mtn., Ca., U.S.	E6	82
Fountain Place, La., U.S.	*D4	95
Fourche LaFave, stm., Ar., U.S.	C2	81
Fourche Maline, stm., Ok., U.S.	C6	113
Fourmies, Fr.	B11	10
Four Mountains, Islands of, is., Ak., U.S.	E6	79
Four Oaks, N.C., U.S.	B4	110
Fowler, Ca., U.S.	D4	82
Fowler, Co., U.S.	C6	83
Fowler, In., U.S.	C3	91
Fowler, Mi., U.S.	E6	99
Fowlerville, Mi., U.S.	F6	99
Fox, stm., Man., Can.	B4	70
Fox, stm., U.S.	B5	90
Fox, stm., U.S.	A6	102
Fox, stm., Mi., U.S.	B4	99
Fox, stm., Wi., U.S.	D5	126
Foxboro, Ont., Can.	C7	73
Foxboro, Ma., U.S.	B5	98
Fox Creek, Alta., Can.	B2	68
Foxe Basin, b., N.W. Ter., Can.	C17	66
Foxe Channel, strt., N.W. Ter., Can.	D16	66
Foxe Peninsula, pen., N.W. Ter., Can.	D17	66
Fox Island, i., R.I., U.S.	E4	116
Fox Island, i., Wa., U.S.	f10	124
Fox Islands, is., Ak., U.S.	E6	79
Fox Lake, Il., U.S.	A5	90
Fox Lake, Wi., U.S.	E5	126
Fox Lake, l., Il., U.S.	h8	90
Fox Mountain, mtn., Nv., U.S.	B2	105
Fox Point, Wi., U.S.	E6	126
Fox River Grove, Il., U.S.	h8	90
Foxworth, Ms., U.S.	D4	101
Foz do Cunene, Ang.	E2	44
Foz do Iguaçu, Braz.	B6	56
Frackville, Pa., U.S.	E9	115
Fraga, Spain	D12	12
Framingham, Ma., U.S.	B5	98
Franca, Braz.	F5	57
Francavilla Fontana, Italy	I12	14
France, ctry., Eur.	F8	4
Francesville, In., U.S.	C4	91
Franceville, Gabon	B2	44
Francis, Lake, l., N.H., U.S.	f7	106
Francis Case, Lake, res., S.D., U.S.	D6	118
Francistown, Bots.	F5	44
Francofonte, Italy	L9	14
Franconia, N.H., U.S.	B3	106
Franconia Notch, N.H., U.S.	B3	106
Francs Peak, mtn., Wy., U.S.	C3	127
Frankenberg, Ger.	E13	8
Frankenberg-Eder, Ger.	D8	8
Frankenmuth, Mi., U.S.	E7	99
Frankford, Ont., Can.	C7	73
Frankford, De., U.S.	F5	85
Frankfort, Il., U.S.	m9	90
Frankfort, In., U.S.	D4	91
Frankfort, Ks., U.S.	C7	93
Frankfort, Ky., U.S.	B5	94
Frankfort, Mi., U.S.	D4	99
Frankfort, N.Y., U.S.	B5	109
Frankfort, Oh., U.S.	C2	112
Frankfurt am Main, Ger.	E8	8
Frankfurt an der Oder, Ger.	C14	8
Franklin, Ga., U.S.	C1	87
Franklin, In., U.S.	F5	91
Franklin, Ky., U.S.	D3	94
Franklin, La., U.S.	E4	95
Franklin, Ma., U.S.	B5	98
Franklin, Ne., U.S.	D7	104
Franklin, N.H., U.S.	D3	106
Franklin, N.J., U.S.	A3	107
Franklin, N.C., U.S.	f9	110
Franklin, Oh., U.S.	C1	112
Franklin, Pa., U.S.	D2	115
Franklin, Tn., U.S.	B5	119
Franklin, Tx., U.S.	D4	120
Franklin, Va., U.S.	D6	123
Franklin, W.V., U.S.	C5	125
Franklin, Wi., U.S.	n11	126
Franklin, co., Al., U.S.	A2	78
Franklin, co., Ar., U.S.	B2	81
Franklin, co., Fl., U.S.	C2	86
Franklin, co., Ga., U.S.	B3	87
Franklin, co., Id., U.S.	G7	89
Franklin, co., Il., U.S.	E4	90
Franklin, co., In., U.S.	F7	91
Franklin, co., Ia., U.S.	B4	92

Name — Map Ref — Page

Franklin, co., Ks., U.S. D8 93
Franklin, co., Ky., U.S. B5 94
Franklin, co., La., U.S. B4 95
Franklin, co., Me., U.S. C2 96
Franklin, co., Ma., U.S. A2 98
Franklin, co., Ms., U.S. D3 101
Franklin, co., Mo., U.S. C6 102
Franklin, co., Ne., U.S. D7 104
Franklin, co., N.Y., U.S. f10 109
Franklin, co., N.C., U.S. A4 110
Franklin, co., Oh., U.S. B2 112
Franklin, co., Pa., U.S. G6 115
Franklin, co., Tn., U.S. B5 119
Franklin, co., Tx., U.S. C5 120
Franklin, co., Vt., U.S. B2 122
Franklin, co., Va., U.S. D3 123
Franklin, co., Wa., U.S. C6 124
Franklin, Point, c., Ak., U.S. A8 79
Franklin Bay, b., N.W. Ter., Can. C7 66
Franklin D. Roosevelt Lake, res., Wa., U.S. B7 124
Franklin Falls Reservoir, res., N.H., U.S. C3 106
Franklin Grove, Il., U.S. B4 90
Franklin Lake, l., N.W. Ter., Can. C13 66
Franklin Lake, l., Nv., U.S. C6 105
Franklin Mountains, mts., N.W. Ter., Can. D8 66
Franklin Park, Il., U.S. k9 90
Franklin Park, Pa., U.S. *h13 115
Franklin Strait, strt., N.W. Ter., Can. B13 66
Franklinton, La., U.S. D5 95
Franklinton, N.C., U.S. A4 110
Franklinville, N.Y., U.S. C2 109
Frankston, Tx., U.S. C5 120
Frankton, In., U.S. D6 91
Frascati, Italy H7 14
Fraser, stm., B.C., Can. E7 69
Fraser, stm., Newf., Can. g9 72
Fraser, Mount, mtn., Can. C8 69
Fraserburgh, Scot., U.K. D10 7
Fraser Lake, B.C., Can. B5 69
Fraser Plateau, plat., B.C., Can. D6 69
Frauenfeld, Switz. E15 10
Frazee, Mn., U.S. D3 100
Frazeysburg, Oh., U.S. B3 112
Frazier Park, Ca., U.S. E4 82
Fr'azino, Russia F21 18
Frederic, Wi., U.S. C1 126
Frederica, De., U.S. D4 85
Fredericia, Den. I7 6
Frederick, Co., U.S. A6 83
Frederick, Md., U.S. B3 97
Frederick, Ok., U.S. C2 113
Frederick, co., Md., U.S. B3 97
Frederick, co., Va., U.S. A4 123
Fredericksburg, Ia., U.S. B5 92
Fredericksburg, Tx., U.S. D3 120
Fredericksburg, Va., U.S. B5 123
Frederick Sound, strt., Ak., U.S. m23 79
Fredericktown, Mo., U.S. D7 102
Fredericktown, Oh., U.S. B3 112
Fredericktown, Pa., U.S. F1 115
Fredericton, N.B., Can. D3 71
Fredericton Junction, N.B., Can. D3 71
Frederikshåb, Grnld. D23 66
Frederikshavn, Den. H8 6
Fredonia, Az., U.S. A3 80
Fredonia, Ks., U.S. E8 93
Fredonia, N.Y., U.S. C1 109
Fredonia, Wi., U.S. E6 126
Fredrikstad, Nor. G8 6
Freeborn, co., Mn., U.S. G5 100
Freeburg, Il., U.S. E4 90
Freedom, Pa., U.S. E1 115
Freedom, Wy., U.S. D2 127
Freehold, N.J., U.S. C4 107
Freeland, Mi., U.S. E6 99
Freeland, Pa., U.S. D10 115
Freelandville, In., U.S. G3 91
Freel Peak, mtn., Ca., U.S. C4 82
Freels, Cape, c., Newf., Can. D5 72
Freels, Cape, c., Newf., Can. E5 72
Freeman, S.D., U.S. D8 118
Freeman, Lake, l., In., U.S. C4 91
Freemansburg, Pa., U.S. E11 115
Freemason Island, i., La., U.S. E7 95
Freeport, Bah. A8 64
Freeport, Il., U.S. A4 90
Freeport, Me., U.S. E2 96
Freeport, N.Y., U.S. n15 109
Freeport, Pa., U.S. E2 115
Freeport, Tx., U.S. E5 120
Freer, Tx., U.S. F3 120
Freestone, co., Tx., U.S. D4 120
Freetown, S.L. G3 42
Freetown, In., U.S. G5 91
Freezeout Mountains, mts., Wy., U.S. D6 127
Fregenal de la Sierra, Spain G5 12
Freiberg, Ger. E13 8
Freiburg [im Breisgau], Ger. H7 8
Freising, Ger. G11 8
Freistadt, Aus. G14 8
Freital, Ger. D13 8
Fréjus, Fr. I13 10
Fremont, Ca., U.S. D2 82
Fremont, In., U.S. A8 91
Fremont, Ia., U.S. C5 92
Fremont, Mi., U.S. E5 99
Fremont, Ne., U.S. C9 104
Fremont, N.C., U.S. B5 110
Fremont, Oh., U.S. A2 112
Fremont, co., Co., U.S. C5 83
Fremont, co., Id., U.S. E7 89
Fremont, co., Ia., U.S. D2 92
Fremont, co., Wy., U.S. C4 127
Fremont, stm., Ut., U.S. E4 121
Fremont Island, i., Ut., U.S. B3 121
Fremont Lake, l., Wy., U.S. D3 127
Fremont Peak, mtn., Wy., U.S. C3 127
French Broad, stm., U.S. D10 119
Frenchburg, Ky., U.S. C6 94
French Creek, stm., Pa., U.S. C2 115
French Frigate Shoals, rf., Hi., U.S. m14 88
French Guiana, dep., S.A. C8 54
French Lick, In., U.S. G4 91
Frenchman Bay, b., Me., U.S. D4 96
Frenchman Creek, stm., U.S. D4 104
Frenchman Hills, hills, Wa., U.S. C6 124
Frenchman Lake, l., Nv., U.S. G6 105
French Polynesia, dep., Oc. G3 2
French Settlement, La., U.S. D5 95
Freshfield, Mount, mtn., Can. D2 68
Fresnillo, Mex. F8 62
Fresno, Ca., U.S. D4 82
Fresno, co., Ca., U.S. D4 82
Fresno Reservoir, res., Mt., U.S. B6 103
Freudenstadt, Ger. G8 8
Frewsburg, N.Y., U.S. C1 109
Fria, Cape, c., Nmb. E2 44
Friars Point, Ms., U.S. A3 101
Frías, Arg. B3 56
Fribourg (Freiburg), Switz. F14 10
Friday Harbor, Wa., U.S. A2 124
Fridley, Mn., U.S. m12 100
Friedberg, Aus. H16 8
Friedrichshafen, Ger. H9 8
Friend, Ne., U.S. D8 104
Friendsville, Tn., U.S. D9 119
Fries, Va., U.S. D2 123
Friesland, hist. reg., Neth. B5 8
Frio, co., Tx., U.S. E3 120
Frio, stm., Tx., U.S. E3 120
Frio, Cabo, c., Braz. G7 57
Friona, Tx., U.S. B1 120
Fripps Island, i., S.C., U.S. G7 117
Frisco, Co., U.S. B4 83
Frisco City, Al., U.S. D2 78
Frisco Peak, mtn., Ut., U.S. E2 121
Frissell, Mount, mtn., U.S. A2 84
Fritch, Tx., U.S. B2 120
Fritzlar, Ger. D9 8
Friza, Proliv, strt., Russia H23 24
Frobisher Bay, b., N.W. Ter., Can. D19 66
Frobisher Lake, l., Sask., Can. m7 75
Frohnleiten, Aus. H15 8
Frontenac, Ks., U.S. E9 93
Frontier, co., Ne., U.S. D5 104
Front Range, mts., Co., U.S. A5 83
Front Royal, Va., U.S. B4 123
Frosinone, Italy H8 14
Frostburg, Md., U.S. k13 97
Frostproof, Fl., U.S. E5 86
Fruita, Co., U.S. B2 83
Fruit Heights, Ut., U.S. B4 121
Fruitland, Id., U.S. F2 89
Fruitland, Md., U.S. D6 97
Fruitland, N.M., U.S. A1 108
Fruitland Park, Fl., U.S. D5 86
Fruitport, Mi., U.S. E4 99
Fruitvale, B.C., Can. E9 69
Fruitvale, Co., U.S. B2 83
Fruitvale, Wa., U.S. C5 124
Fruitville, Fl., U.S. E4 86
Frunze see Biškek, Kyrg. I12 22
Frutigen, Switz. F14 10
Fryeburg, Me., U.S. D2 96
Fuchū, Japan H6 30
Fuencaliente, Spain G7 12
Fuente de Cantos, Spain G5 12
Fuente-obejuna, Spain G6 12
Fuerteventura, i., Spain p27 13b
Fuji, Japan G11 30
Fuji, Mount see Fuji-san, vol., Japan G11 30
Fujian, prov., China F10 26
Fujin, China B13 26
Fujinomiya, Japan G11 30
Fuji-san (Fujiyama), vol., Japan G11 30
Fujisawa, Japan G12 30
Fujiyama see Fuji-san, vol., Japan G11 30
Fuji-yoshida, Japan G11 30
Fukagawa, Japan p20 30a
Fukaya, Japan F12 30
Fukuchiyama, Japan G8 30
Fukue, Japan J1 30
Fukui, Japan F9 30
Fukuoka, Japan I3 30
Fukushima, Japan E13 30
Fukushima, Japan r18 30a
Fukuyama, Japan H6 30
Fūlādī, Kūh-e, mtn., Afg. C2 38
Fulda, Ger. E9 8
Fulda, Mn., U.S. G3 100
Fullerton, Ca., U.S. n13 82
Fullerton, Ne., U.S. C8 104
Fulton, Il., U.S. B3 90
Fulton, Ky., U.S. f9 94
Fulton, Md., U.S. B4 97
Fulton, Ms., U.S. A5 101
Fulton, Mo., U.S. C6 102
Fulton, N.Y., U.S. B4 109
Fulton, co., Ar., U.S. A4 81
Fulton, co., Ga., U.S. C2 87
Fulton, co., Il., U.S. C3 90
Fulton, co., In., U.S. B5 91
Fulton, co., Ky., U.S. f8 94
Fulton, co., N.Y., U.S. B6 109
Fulton, co., Oh., U.S. A1 112
Fulton, co., Pa., U.S. G5 115
Fultondale, Al., U.S. f7 78
Funabashi, Japan G13 30
Funchal, Port. n21 13a
Fundación, Col. B5 58
Fundy, Bay of, b., Can. D4 71
Fundy National Park, N.B., Can. D4 71
Funkstown, Md., U.S. A2 97
Fuquay-Varina, N.C., U.S. B4 110
Furano, Japan p20 30a
Furmanov, Russia D24 18
Furnace Brook, stm., Vt., U.S. D3 122
Furnas, co., Ne., U.S. D6 104
Furnas, Reprêsa de, res., Braz. F5 57
Furneaux Group, is., Austl. H9 50
Furqlus, Syria B5 40
Fürstenfeld, Aus. H16 8
Fürstenfeldbruck, Ger. G11 8
Fürstenwalde, Ger. C14 8
Fürth, Ger. F10 8
Fürth im Wald, Ger. F12 8
Furudal, Swe. F10 6
Fushun, China C11 26
Füssen, Ger. H10 8
Fuxian, China D11 26
Fuxian, China D8 26
Fuxinshi, China C11 26
Fuyang, China C4 28
Fuzhou, China G5 28
Fuzhou (Foochow), China I8 28
Fyffe, Al., U.S. A4 78

G

Gabbs, Nv., U.S. E4 105
Gabès, Tun. B8 42
Gabès, Golfe de, b., Tun. B8 42
Gabon, ctry., Afr. B2 44
Gaborone, Bots. F5 44
Gabriel Strait, strt., N.W. Ter., Can. D19 66
Gabriola, B.C., Can. f12 69
Gabrovo, Bul. G9 16
Gadag, India E3 37
Gäddede, Swe. D10 6
Gadsden, Al., U.S. A3 78
Gadsden, co., Fl., U.S. B2 86
Gaeta, Italy H8 14
Gaffney, S.C., U.S. A4 117
Gafsa, Tun. B7 42
Gage, co., Ne., U.S. D9 104
Gagetown, N.B., Can. D3 71
Gagliano del Capo, Italy J13 14
Gagnoa, C. Iv. G4 42
Gahanna, Oh., U.S. k11 112
Gaillac, Fr. I8 10
Gaillard, Lake, l., Ct., U.S. D5 84
Gaines, co., Tx., U.S. C1 120
Gainesboro, Tn., U.S. C8 119
Gaines Creek, stm., Ok., U.S. C6 113
Gainesville, Fl., U.S. C4 86
Gainesville, Ga., U.S. B3 87
Gainesville, Mo., U.S. E5 102
Gainesville, Tx., U.S. C4 120
Gainesville, Va., U.S. g11 123
Gairdner, Lake, l., Austl. F7 50
Gaithersburg, Md., U.S. B3 97
Galán, Cerro, mtn., Arg. B3 56
Galapagos Islands see Colón, Archipiélago de, is., Ec. m15 58a
Galashiels, Scot., U.K. F10 7
Galați, Rom. D12 16
Galatia, Il., U.S. F5 90
Galatina, Italy I13 14
Galax, Va., U.S. D2 123
Galena, Ak., U.S. C8 79
Galena, Il., U.S. A3 90
Galena, Ks., U.S. E9 93
Galeota Point, c., Trin. I17 64
Galera, Punta, c., Chile D2 56
Galera, Punta, c., Ec. G2 58
Galesburg, Il., U.S. C3 90
Galesburg, Mi., U.S. F5 99
Gales Ferry, Ct., U.S. D7 84
Galesville, Md., U.S. C4 97
Galesville, Wi., U.S. D2 126
Galeton, Pa., U.S. C6 115
Galič, Russia C25 18
Galicia, hist. reg., Eur. F21 8
Galicia, hist. reg., Spain B3 12
Galilee, Sea of see Kinneret, Yam, l., Isr. C4 40
Galion, Oh., U.S. B3 112
Galisteo Creek, stm., N.M., U.S. k8 108
Galiuro Mountains, mts., Az., U.S. E5 80
Galka'yo, Som. G4 46
Gallant, Al., U.S. B3 78
Gallarate, Italy D3 14
Gallatin, Mo., U.S. B4 102
Gallatin, Tn., U.S. A5 119
Gallatin, co., Il., U.S. F5 90
Gallatin, co., Ky., U.S. B5 94
Gallatin, co., Mt., U.S. E5 103
Gallatin, stm., Mt., U.S. E5 103
Gallatin Range, mts., Mt., U.S. E5 103
Gallaway, Tn., U.S. B2 119
Galle, Sri L. I6 37
Gallia, co., Oh., U.S. D3 112
Galliano, La., U.S. E5 95
Gallinas, Punta, c., Col. A7 58
Gallinas Mountains, mts., N.M., U.S. C2 108
Gallipoli, Italy I12 14
Gallipoli see Gelibolu, Tur. I10 16
Gallipolis, Oh., U.S. D3 112
Gallitzin, Pa., U.S. F4 115
Gällivare, Swe. C13 6
Gallo Mountains, mts., N.M., U.S. C1 108
Galloo Island, i., N.Y., U.S. B4 109
Galloway, Mull of, c., Scot., U.K. G8 7
Gallup, N.M., U.S. B1 108
Galt, Ca., U.S. C3 82
Galtür, Aus. I10 8
Galty Mountains, mts., Ire. I4 7
Galva, Il., U.S. B3 90
Galva, Ks., U.S. D6 93
Galveston, In., U.S. C5 91
Galveston, Tx., U.S. E5 120
Galveston, co., Tx., U.S. E5 120
Galveston Bay, b., Tx., U.S. E5 120
Galveston Island, i., Tx., U.S. E5 120
Gálvez, Arg. C4 56
Galway, Ire. H3 7
Gambela, Eth. G1 46
Gambell, Ak., U.S. C5 79
Gambia, ctry., Afr. F2 42
Gambia (Gambie), stm., Afr. F2 42
Gambier, Oh., U.S. B3 112
Gambo, Newf., Can. D4 72
Gambrills, Md., U.S. B4 97
Gamleby, Swe. H11 6
Ganado, Az., U.S. B6 80
Ganado, Tx., U.S. E4 120
Gananoque, Ont., Can. C8 73
Ganda, Ang. D2 44
Gandak, stm., Asia G11 38
Gander, Newf., Can. D4 72
Gander, stm., Newf., Can. D4 72
Ganderkesee, Ger. B8 8
Gander Lake, l., Newf., Can. D4 72
Gandesa, Spain D12 12
Gāndhinagar, India I5 38
Gāndhi Sāgar, res., India H6 38
Gandía, Spain G11 12
Gangāpur, India G7 38
Gangāwati, India E4 37
Gangdisê Shan, mts., China E10 38
Ganges, B.C., Can. g12 69
Ganges (Ganga) (Padma), stm., Asia I13 38
Ganges, Mouths of the, mth., Asia J13 38
Gang Mills, N.Y., U.S. C3 109
Gangtok, India G13 38
Gangu, China E8 26
Gannat, Fr. F10 10
Gannett Peak, mtn., Wy., U.S. C3 127
Gansu, prov., China D7 26
Gantt, S.C., U.S. B3 117
Gantt Lake, res., Al., U.S. D3 78
Ganzhou, China J3 28
Ganzi, China E7 26
Gao, Mali E5 42
Gaokeng, China H2 28
Gaoyou, China C8 28
Gaozhou, China D11 34
Gap, Fr. H13 10
Gap, Pa., U.S. G9 115
Gar, China E9 38
Garanhuns, Braz. E11 54
Garber, Ok., U.S. A4 113
Garberville, Ca., U.S. B2 82
Garça, Braz. G4 57
Garda, Lago di, l., Italy D5 14
Gardelegen, Ger. C11 8
Garden, co., Ne., U.S. C3 104
Gardena, Ca., U.S. n12 82
Garden City, Ga., U.S. D5 87
Garden City, Id., U.S. F2 89
Garden City, Ks., U.S. E3 93
Garden City, Mi., U.S. p15 99
Garden City, Mo., U.S. C3 102
Gardendale, Al., U.S. B3 78
Garden Grove, Ca., U.S. n13 82
Garden Island, i., Mi., U.S. C5 99
Garden Plain, Ks., U.S. E6 93
Garden Reach, India I13 38
Gardēz, Afg. D3 38
Gardiner, Me., U.S. D3 96
Gardiner, Mt., U.S. E6 103
Gardiner, Or., U.S. D2 114
Gardiners Island, i., N.Y., U.S. m16 109
Gardner, Il., U.S. B5 90
Gardner, Ks., U.S. D9 93
Gardner, Ma., U.S. A4 98
Gardner Canal, strt., B.C., Can. C3 69
Gardner Lake, l., Ct., U.S. C6 84
Gardner Lake, l., Me., U.S. D5 96
Gardner Pinnacles, Hi., U.S. k14 88
Gardnerville, Nv., U.S. E2 105
Gardone Val Trompia, Italy D5 14
Garfield, N.J., U.S. h8 107
Garfield, co., Co., U.S. B2 83
Garfield, co., Mt., U.S. C9 103
Garfield, co., Ne., U.S. C6 104
Garfield, co., Ok., U.S. A4 113
Garfield, co., Ut., U.S. F4 121
Garfield, co., Wa., U.S. C8 124
Garfield Heights, Oh., U.S. h9 112
Garfield Mountain, mtn., Mt., U.S. F4 103
Garfield Peak, mtn., Wy., U.S. D5 127
Garibaldi, Or., U.S. B3 114
Garibaldi, Mount, mtn., B.C., Can. E6 69
Garies, S. Afr. H3 44
Garissa, Kenya B7 44
Garland, N.C., U.S. C4 110
Garland, Tx., U.S. n10 120
Garland, Ut., U.S. B3 121
Garland, co., Ar., U.S. C2 81
Garlin, Fr. I6 10
Garm Āb, Afg. D1 38
Garmisch-Partenkirchen, Ger. H11 8
Garnavillo, Ia., U.S. B6 92
Garner, Ia., U.S. A4 92
Garner, N.C., U.S. B4 110
Garnet Range, mts., Mt., U.S. D3 103
Garnett, Ks., U.S. D8 93
Garnish, Newf., Can. E4 72
Garonne, stm., Eur. H6 10
Garoua, Cam. G8 42
Garrard, co., Ky., U.S. C5 94
Garretson, S.D., U.S. D9 118
Garrett, In., U.S. B7 91
Garrett, co., Md., U.S. k12 97
Garrett Park, Md., U.S. B3 97
Garrettsville, Oh., U.S. A4 112
Garrison, Ky., U.S. B6 94
Garrison, Md., U.S. B4 97
Garrison, N.D., U.S. B4 111
Garrison Dam, N.D., U.S. B4 111
Garrovillas, Spain F5 12
Garry Lake, l., N.W. Ter., Can. C12 66
Garsen, Kenya B8 44
Garut, Indon. m13 33a
Garvin, co., Ok., U.S. C4 113
Gary, In., U.S. A3 91
Gary, W.V., U.S. D3 125
Garysburg, N.C., U.S. A5 110
Garyville, La., U.S. D5 95
Garza, co., Tx., U.S. C2 120
Garza-Little Elm Reservoir, res., Tx., U.S. C4 120
Garzón, Col. F5 58
Gas City, In., U.S. D6 91
Gasconade, co., Mo., U.S. C6 102
Gasconade, stm., Mo., U.S. C6 102
Gascoyne, stm., Austl. E3 50
Gasparilla Island, i., Fl., U.S. F4 86
Gaspé, Que., Can. k14 74
Gaspésie, Péninsule de la, pen., Que., Can. k13 74
Gassaway, W.V., U.S. C4 125
Gassville, Ar., U.S. A3 81
Gaston, In., U.S. D7 91
Gaston, N.C., U.S. A5 110
Gaston, S.C., U.S. D5 117
Gaston, co., N.C., U.S. B1 110
Gaston, Lake, res., U.S. A5 110
Gaston Dam, N.C., U.S. A5 110
Gastonia, N.C., U.S. B1 110
Gátas, Akrotírion, c., Cyp. B3 40
Gatčina, Russia B13 18
Gate City, Va., U.S. f9 123
Gates, N.Y., U.S. *B3 109
Gates, Tn., U.S. B2 119
Gates, co., N.C., U.S. A6 110
Gateshead, Eng., U.K. G11 7
Gateshead Island, i., N.W. Ter., Can. B12 66
Gates of the Arctic National Park, Ak., U.S. B9 79
Gatesville, Tx., U.S. D4 120
Gatineau, Que., Can. D2 74
Gatineau, stm., Que., Can. D2 74
Gatineau, Parc de la, Que., Can. D2 74
Gatlinburg, Tn., U.S. D10 119
Gaucín, Spain I6 12
Gauhāti, India G14 38
Gauley, stm., W.V., U.S. C3 125
Gauley Bridge, W.V., U.S. C3 125
Gautier, Ms., U.S. f8 101
Gauting, Ger. G11 8
Gavá, Spain D14 12
Gavins Point Dam, U.S. B8 104
Gävle, Swe. F11 6
Gavrilov-Jam, Russia D22 18
Gawler Ranges, mts., Austl. F7 50
Gaya, India H11 38
Gay Head, c., Ma., U.S. D6 98
Gaylord, Mi., U.S. C6 99
Gaylord, Mn., U.S. F4 100
Gayndah, Austl. E10 50
Gaza see Ghazzah, Isr. Occ. D4 40
Gaziantep, Tur. H15 4
Gazimağusa, N. Cyp. B3 40
Gazimağusa Körfezi, b., N. Cyp. B4 40
Gbarnga, Lib. G4 42
Gdańsk (Danzig), Pol. A18 8
Gdynia, Pol. A18 8
Gearhart, Or., U.S. A3 114
Gearhart Mountain, mtn., Or., U.S. E6 114
Geary, N.B., Can. D3 71
Geary, Ok., U.S. B3 113
Geary, co., Ks., U.S. D7 93
Geauga, co., Oh., U.S. A4 112
Gebze, Tur. I13 16
Gediz, stm., Tur. K11 16
Geel, Bel. D4 8
Geelong, Austl. G8 50
Ge'ermu, China B16 38
Geesthacht, Ger. B10 8
Geilo, Nor. F7 6
Geislingen, Ger. G9 8
Geistown, Pa., U.S. F4 115
Geist Reservoir, res., In., U.S. E6 91
Gejiu (Kokiu), China C7 34
Gela, Italy L9 14
Gelibolu, Tur. I10 16
Gelibolu Yarımadası (Gallipoli Peninsula), pen., Tur. I10 16
Gelsenkirchen, Ger. D7 8
Gem, co., Id., U.S. E2 89
Gembloux, Bel. E4 8
Gemena, Zaire H9 42
Gemlik, Tur. I13 16
Gemona del Friuli, Italy C8 14
Genale (Juba), stm., Afr. G3 46
General Alvear, Arg. C3 56
General Bravo, Mex. E10 62
General Carneiro, Braz. C2 57
General Levalle, Arg. C4 56
General Pico, Arg. D4 56
General Pinedo, Arg. B4 56
General Roca, Arg. D3 56
General Villegas, Arg. D4 56
Genesee, Id., U.S. C2 89
Genesee, Mi., U.S. E7 99
Genesee, co., Mi., U.S. E7 99
Genesee, co., N.Y., U.S. B2 109
Genesee, stm., N.Y., U.S. C2 109
Geneseo, Il., U.S. B3 90
Geneseo, N.Y., U.S. C3 109
Geneva, Al., U.S. D4 78
Geneva, Il., U.S. B5 90
Geneva, In., U.S. C8 91
Geneva, Ne., U.S. D8 104
Geneva, N.Y., U.S. C4 109
Geneva, Oh., U.S. A5 112
Geneva, co., Al., U.S. D4 78
Geneva, Lake, l., Eur. F13 10
Geneva, Lake, l., Wi., U.S. F5 126
Geneva see Genève, Switz. F13 10
Geneva-on-the-Lake, Oh., U.S. A5 112
Genève, Switz. F13 10
Genk, Bel. E5 8
Genkai-nada, Japan I3 30
Genoa, Il., U.S. A5 90
Genoa, Ne., U.S. C8 104
Genoa, Nv., U.S. D2 105
Genoa, Oh., U.S. A2 112
Genoa City, Wi., U.S. F5 126
Genoa see Genova, Italy E3 14
Genola, Ut., U.S. D4 121
Genova (Genoa), Italy E3 14
Genova, Golfo di, b., Italy E3 14
Gent (Gand), Bel. D3 8
Genteng, Indon. n17 33a
Genthin, Ger. C12 8
Gentry, Ar., U.S. A1 81
Gentry, co., Mo., U.S. A3 102
Geographe Bay, b., Austl. F3 50
George, S. Afr. H4 44
George, Ia., U.S. A2 92
George, co., Ms., U.S. E5 101
George, stm., Que., Can. g13 74
George, Cape, c., N.S., Can. D8 71
George, Lake, l., Ug. B6 44
George, Lake, l., Fl., U.S. C5 86
George, Lake, l., N.Y., U.S. B7 109
George Air Force Base, mil., Ca., U.S. E5 82
George B. Stevenson Reservoir, res., Pa., U.S. D6 115
George Peak, mtn., Ut., U.S. B2 121
Georgetown, P.E.I., Can. C7 71
Georgetown, Cay. Is. E7 64

Name	Map Ref	Page
Georgetown, Gam.	F3	42
Georgetown, Guy.	D13	58
George Town (Pinang), Malay.	L6	34
Georgetown, Ca., U.S.	C3	82
Georgetown, Co., U.S.	B5	83
Georgetown, Ct., U.S.	D2	84
Georgetown, De., U.S.	F4	85
Georgetown, Ga., U.S.	E1	87
Georgetown, Il., U.S.	D6	90
Georgetown, In., U.S.	H6	91
Georgetown, Ky., U.S.	B5	94
Georgetown, Ma., U.S.	A6	98
Georgetown, Oh., U.S.	D2	112
Georgetown, S.C., U.S.	E9	117
Georgetown, Tx., U.S.	D4	120
Georgetown, co., S.C., U.S.	E9	117
George Washington Birthplace National Monument, Va., U.S.	B6	123
George Washington Carver National Monument, Mo., U.S.	E3	102
George West, Tx., U.S.	E3	120
Georgia, ctry., Asia	I6	22
Georgia, state, U.S.	D3	87
Georgia, Strait of, strt., N.A.	B2	76
Georgiana, Al., U.S.	D3	78
Georgian Bay, b., Ont., Can.	B3	73
Georgina, stm., Austl.	D7	50
Gera, Ger.	E12	8
Gerald, Mo., U.S.	C6	102
Geraldine, Al., U.S.	A4	78
Geral do Paranã, Serra, hills, Braz.	C5	57
Geraldton, Austl.	E2	50
Geraldton, Ont., Can.	o18	73
Gérardmer, Fr.	D13	10
Gerber Reservoir, res., Or., U.S.	E5	114
Gerdine, Mount, mtn., Ak., U.S.	C9	79
Gereshk, Afg.	E1	38
Gérgal, Spain	H9	12
Gering, Ne., U.S.	C2	104
Gerlach, Nv., U.S.	C2	105
Germantown, Il., U.S.	E4	90
Germantown, Md., U.S.	B3	97
Germantown, Oh., U.S.	C1	112
Germantown, Tn., U.S.	B2	119
Germantown, Wi., U.S.	E5	126
Germany, ctry., Eur.	E10	4
Germiston, S. Afr.	G5	44
Gerona, Spain	D14	12
Geronimo, Ok., U.S.	C3	113
Gervais, Or., U.S.	B4	114
Geseke, Ger.	D8	8
Getafe, Spain	E8	12
Gettysburg, Pa., U.S.	G7	115
Gettysburg, S.D., U.S.	C6	118
Ghāghra, stm., Asia	G10	38
Ghana, ctry., Afr.	G5	42
Ghanzi, Bots.	F4	44
Gharbīyah, Aṣ-Ṣaḥrā' al- (Western Desert), des., Egypt	C11	42
Ghardaïa, Alg.	B6	42
Gharyān, Libya	B8	42
Ghāt, Libya	D8	42
Għawdex, i., Malta	M9	14
Ghazāl, Baḥr al-, stm., Sudan	G12	42
Ghāziābād, India	F7	38
Ghāzīpur, India	H10	38
Ghaznī, Afg.	D3	38
Ghazzah (Gaza), Gaza Strip	D4	40
Ghedi, Italy	D5	14
Gheen, Mn., U.S.	C6	100
Ghent see Gent, Bel.	D3	8
Ghīn, Tall, mtn., Syria	C5	40
Ghudāmis, Libya	B7	42
Giants Neck, Ct., U.S.	D7	84
Gibbon, Mn., U.S.	F4	100
Gibbon, Ne., U.S.	D7	104
Gibbons, Alta., Can.	C4	68
Gibbstown, N.J., U.S.	D2	107
Gibeon, Nmb.	G3	44
Gibraltar, Gib.	I6	12
Gibraltar, dep., Eur.	H6	4
Gibraltar, Strait of (Estrecho de Gibraltar), strt.	J6	12
Gibraltar Point, c., Eng., U.K.	H13	7
Gibsland, La., U.S.	B2	95
Gibson, Ga., U.S.	C4	87
Gibson, co., In., U.S.	H2	91
Gibson, co., Tn., U.S.	A3	119
Gibsonburg, Oh., U.S.	A2	112
Gibson City, Il., U.S.	C5	90
Gibson Desert, des., Austl.	D4	50
Gibsonia, Pa., U.S.	h14	115
Gibson Island, i., Md., U.S.	B5	97
Gibsons, B.C., Can.	E6	69
Gibsonton, Fl., U.S.	p11	86
Gibsonville, N.C., U.S.	A3	110
Giddings, Tx., U.S.	D4	120
Gideon, Mo., U.S.	E8	102
Gien, Fr.	E9	10
Giessen, Ger.	E8	8
Gifford, Fl., U.S.	E6	86
Gifford, Il., U.S.	C5	90
Gifu, Japan	G9	30
Gig Harbor, Wa., U.S.	B3	124
Gihon, stm., Vt., U.S.	B3	122
Gijón, Spain	B6	12
Gila, co., Az., U.S.	D5	80
Gila, stm., U.S.	E4	76
Gila Bend, Az., U.S.	E3	80
Gila Bend Indian Reservation, Az., U.S.	D3	80
Gila Bend Mountains, mts., Az., U.S.	D2	80
Gila Cliff Dwellings National Monument, N.M., U.S.	D1	108
Gila Mountains, mts., Az., U.S.	D6	80
Gila Peak, mtn., Az., U.S.	D6	80
Gila River Indian Reservation, Az., U.S.	D4	80
Gilbert, Az., U.S.	D4	80
Gilbert, Ia., U.S.	B4	92
Gilbert, La., U.S.	B4	95
Gilbert, Mn., U.S.	C6	100
Gilbert Islands see Kiribati, ctry., Oc.	G24	2
Gilbert Peak, mtn., Wa., U.S.	C4	124
Gilbert Plains, Man., Can.	D1	70
Gilbertsville, Ky., U.S.	f9	94
Gilbertsville, Pa., U.S.	F10	115
Gilbertville, Ia., U.S.	B5	92
Gilbués, Braz.	E9	54
Gilchrist, Or., U.S.	D5	114
Gilchrist, co., Fl., U.S.	C4	86
Gilcrest, Co., U.S.	A6	83
Giles, co., Tn., U.S.	B4	119
Giles, co., Va., U.S.	C2	123
Gilford Island, i., B.C., Can.	D4	69
Gilgit, Pak.	C6	38
Gillam, Man., Can.	A4	70
Gillespie, Il., U.S.	D4	90
Gillespie, co., Tx., U.S.	D3	120
Gillespie Dam, Az., U.S.	D3	80
Gillett, Ar., U.S.	C4	81
Gillett, Wi., U.S.	D5	126
Gillette, Wy., U.S.	B7	127
Gilliam, co., Or., U.S.	B6	114
Gilman, Il., U.S.	C5	90
Gilman, Vt., U.S.	C5	122
Gilmanton, N.H., U.S.	D4	106
Gilmer, Tx., U.S.	C5	120
Gilmer, co., Ga., U.S.	B2	87
Gilmer, co., W.V., U.S.	C4	125
Gilo, stm., Eth.	G1	46
Gilpin, co., Co., U.S.	B5	83
Gilroy, Ca., U.S.	D3	82
Gil'uj, stm., Russia	G19	24
Giluwe, Mount, mtn., Pap. N. Gui.	m15	50a
Gimli, Man., Can.	D3	70
Ginosa, Italy	I11	14
Ginowan, Japan	y27	31b
Gioia del Colle, Italy	I11	14
Gioia Tauro, Italy	K10	14
Girard, Il., U.S.	D4	90
Girard, Ks., U.S.	E9	93
Girard, Oh., U.S.	A5	112
Girard, Pa., U.S.	B1	115
Girardot, Col.	E5	58
Girardville, Pa., U.S.	E9	115
Girīdīh, India	H12	38
Girifalco, Italy	K11	14
Girne, N. Cyp.	B3	40
Girwa, stm., Asia	F9	38
Gisborne, N.Z.	C7	52
Gisenyi, Rw.	B5	44
Gisors, Fr.	C8	10
Giugliano [in Campania], Italy	I9	14
Giulianova, Italy	G8	14
Giurgiu, Rom.	F9	16
Givet, Fr.	B11	10
Givors, Fr.	G11	10
Giyon, Eth.	G2	46
Giza see Al-Jīzah, Egypt	B12	42
Gižiga, Russia	E26	24
Gižiginskaja Guba, b., Russia	E25	24
Gjandža, Azer.	I7	22
Gjirokastër, Alb.	I4	16
Gjoa Haven, N.W. Ter., Can.	C13	66
Glacier, co., Mt., U.S.	B3	103
Glacier Bay, b., Ak., U.S.	k21	79
Glacier Bay National Park, Ak., U.S.	D12	79
Glacier National Park, B.C., Can.	D9	69
Glacier National Park, Mt., U.S.	B2	103
Glacier Peak, mtn., Wa., U.S.	A4	124
Gladbrook, Ia., U.S.	B5	92
Glade Creek, stm., Wa., U.S.	C6	124
Glade Creek, stm., W.V., U.S.	n13	125
Glade Creek, stm., W.V., U.S.	n14	125
Glades, co., Fl., U.S.	F5	86
Glade Spring, Va., U.S.	f10	123
Gladewater, Tx., U.S.	C5	120
Gladstone, Austl.	D10	50
Gladstone, Man., Can.	D2	70
Gladstone, Mi., U.S.	C4	99
Gladstone, Mo., U.S.	h10	102
Gladstone, Or., U.S.	B4	114
Gladwin, Mi., U.S.	E6	99
Gladwin, co., Mi., U.S.	D6	99
Glåma, stm., Nor.	F8	6
Glarner Alpen, mts., Switz.	F15	10
Glarus, Switz.	E16	10
Glascock, co., Ga., U.S.	C4	87
Glasford, Il., U.S.	C4	90
Glasgow, Scot., U.K.	F8	7
Glasgow, Ky., U.S.	C4	94
Glasgow, Mo., U.S.	B5	102
Glasgow, Mt., U.S.	B10	103
Glasgow, Va., U.S.	C3	123
Glasgow, W.V., U.S.	m13	125
Glassboro, N.J., U.S.	D2	107
Glasscock, co., Tx., U.S.	D2	120
Glassport, Pa., U.S.	F2	115
Glastonbury, Ct., U.S.	C5	84
Glauchau, Ger.	E12	8
Glazier Lake, l., Me., U.S.	A3	96
Glazov, Russia	F8	22
Gleason, Tn., U.S.	A3	119
Gleisdorf, Aus.	H15	8
Glen Allan, Ms., U.S.	B2	101
Glen Allen, Va., U.S.	C5	123
Glenboro, Man., Can.	E2	70
Glenbrook, Nv., U.S.	D2	105
Glen Burnie, Md., U.S.	B4	97
Glen Canyon Dam, Az., U.S.	A4	80
Glen Canyon National Recreation Area, U.S.	F5	121
Glencoe, Ont., Can.	E3	73
Glencoe, Al., U.S.	B4	78
Glencoe, Il., U.S.	A6	90
Glencoe, Mn., U.S.	F4	100
Glen Cove, N.Y., U.S.	h13	109
Glendale, Az., U.S.	D3	80
Glendale, Ca., U.S.	m12	82
Glendale, Ms., U.S.	D4	101
Glendale, Oh., U.S.	C1	112
Glendale, Or., U.S.	E3	114
Glendale, R.I., U.S.	B2	116
Glendale, S.C., U.S.	B4	117
Glen Dale, W.V., U.S.	B4	125
Glendale, Wi., U.S.	m12	126
Glendale Heights, W.V., U.S.	g8	125
Glendive, Mt., U.S.	C12	103
Glendo, Wy., U.S.	D7	127
Glendora, Ca., U.S.	m13	82
Glendo Reservoir, res., Wy., U.S.	D8	127
Glenelg, Md., U.S.	B4	97
Glen Ellis Falls, wtfl, N.H., U.S.	B4	106
Glen Ellyn, Il., U.S.	k8	90
Glenham, N.Y., U.S.	D7	109
Glen Innes, Austl.	E10	50
Glen Jean, W.V., U.S.	D3	125
Glen Lake, l., Mi., U.S.	D5	99
Glen Lyon, Pa., U.S.	D9	115
Glenmora, La., U.S.	D3	95
Glenn, co., Ca., U.S.	C2	82
Glennallen, Ak., U.S.	f19	79
Glenns Ferry, Id., U.S.	G3	89
Glennville, Ga., U.S.	E5	87
Glenolden, Pa., U.S.	p20	115
Glenpool, Ok., U.S.	B5	113
Glen Raven, N.C., U.S.	A3	110
Glen Ridge, N.J., U.S.	h8	107
Glen Rock, N.J., U.S.	h8	107
Glen Rock, Pa., U.S.	G8	115
Glenrock, Wy., U.S.	D7	127
Glen Rose, Tx., U.S.	C4	120
Glens Falls, N.Y., U.S.	B7	109
Glen Ullin, N.D., U.S.	C4	111
Glenview, Il., U.S.	h9	90
Glenview Naval Air Station, mil., Il., U.S.	h9	90
Glenville, Mn., U.S.	G5	100
Glenville, W.V., U.S.	C4	125
Glenwood, Newf., Can.	D4	72
Glenwood, Ar., U.S.	C2	81
Glenwood, Ga., U.S.	D4	87
Glenwood, Ia., U.S.	C2	92
Glenwood, Mn., U.S.	E3	100
Glenwood, Va., U.S.	D3	123
Glenwood City, Wi., U.S.	C1	126
Glenwood Springs, Co., U.S.	B3	83
Glidden, Ia., U.S.	B3	92
Glide, Or., U.S.	D3	114
Glina, Cro.	D11	14
Glittertinden, mtn., Nor.	F7	6
Gliwice (Gleiwitz), Pol.	E18	8
Globe, Az., U.S.	D5	80
Gloggnitz, Aus.	H15	8
Gloster, Ms., U.S.	D2	101
Gloucester, Ont., Can.	h12	73
Gloucester, Eng., U.K.	J10	7
Gloucester, Ma., U.S.	A6	98
Gloucester, Va., U.S.	C6	123
Gloucester, co., N.J., U.S.	D2	107
Gloucester, co., Va., U.S.	C6	123
Gloucester City, N.J., U.S.	D2	107
Gloucester Point, Va., U.S.	C6	123
Glouster, Oh., U.S.	C3	112
Glover Island, i., Newf., Can.	D3	72
Gloversville, N.Y., U.S.	B6	109
Glovertown, Newf., Can.	D4	72
Gloverville, S.C., U.S.	E4	117
Gluck, S.C., U.S.	C2	117
Glücksburg, Ger.	A9	8
Glückstadt, Ger.	B9	8
Glyndon, Md., U.S.	B4	97
Glyndon, Mn., U.S.	D2	100
Glynn, co., Ga., U.S.	E5	87
Gmünd, Aus.	G14	8
Gmunden, Aus.	H13	8
Gnadenhutten, Oh., U.S.	B4	112
Gnarp, Swe.	E11	6
Gniezno, Pol.	C17	8
Gnjilane, Yugo.	G5	16
Gō, stm., Japan	H5	30
Goa, ter., India	E2	37
Goat Island, i., R.I., U.S.	F5	116
Goat Mountain, mtn., Mt., U.S.	C3	103
Goat Rock Dam, U.S.	C4	78
Goba, Eth.	G3	46
Gobabis, Nmb.	F3	44
Gobi, des., Asia	C7	26
Gobles, Mi., U.S.	F5	99
Godāvari, stm., India	D6	37
Goddard, Ks., U.S.	E6	93
Goderich, Ont., Can.	D3	73
Godfrey, Il., U.S.	E3	90
Godhavn, Grnld.	C22	66
Godhra, India	I5	38
Godoy Cruz, Arg.	C3	56
Gods, stm., Man., Can.	A5	70
Gods Lake, l., Man., Can.	B4	70
Godthåb, Grnld.	D22	66
Godwin Austen see K2, mtn., Asia	C7	38
Goéland, Lac au, l., Que., Can.	G17	66
Goélands, Lac aux, l., Que., Can.	E20	66
Goff Creek, stm., Ok., U.S.	e9	113
Goffstown, N.H., U.S.	D3	106
Gogebic, co., Mi., U.S.	n12	99
Gogebic, Lake, l., Mi., U.S.	m12	99
Goiana, Braz.	G9	54
Goiânia, Braz.	D4	57
Goiás, Braz.	C3	57
Gojra, Pak.	E5	38
Gokāk, India	D3	37
Gökçeada, i., Tur.	I9	16
Gol'čicha, Russia	C10	24
Golconda, Il., U.S.	F5	90
Golconda, Nv., U.S.	C4	105
Gold Bar, Wa., U.S.	B4	124
Gold Beach, Or., U.S.	E2	114
Golden, B.C., Can.	D9	69
Golden, Co., U.S.	B5	83
Golden City, Mo., U.S.	D3	102
Goldendale, Wa., U.S.	D5	124
Golden Gate Bridge, Ca., U.S.	h7	82
Golden Gate National Recreation Area, Ca., U.S.	h7	82
Golden Hinde, mtn., B.C., Can.	E5	69
Golden Meadow, La., U.S.	E5	95
Golden Spike National Historic Site, hist., Ut., U.S.	B3	121
Golden Valley, Mn., U.S.	n12	100
Golden Valley, co., Mt., U.S.	D7	103
Golden Valley, co., N.D., U.S.	B2	111
Goldfield, Ia., U.S.	B4	92
Goldfield, Nv., U.S.	F4	105
Gold Hill, Or., U.S.	E3	114
Goldsboro, N.C., U.S.	B5	110
Goldsby, Ok., U.S.	B4	113
Goldthwaite, Tx., U.S.	D3	120
Goleta, Ca., U.S.	E4	82
Golf Manor, Oh., U.S.	o13	112
Goliad, Tx., U.S.	E4	120
Goliad, co., Tx., U.S.	E4	120
Golspie, Scot., U.K.	D9	7
Gomati, stm., India	G9	38
Gombe, stm., Tan.	B6	44
Gomel', Bela.	I14	18
Gomera, i., Spain	C2	42
Gómez Palacio, Mex.	E8	62
Gonābād, Iran	K9	22
Gonaïves, Haiti	E11	64
Gonam, Russia	F20	24
Gonam, stm., Russia	F28	24
Gonâve, Golfe de la, b., Haiti	E11	64
Gonâve, Île de la, i., Haiti	E11	64
Gonda, India	G9	38
Gondal, India	J4	38
Gonder, Eth.	F2	46
Gondia, India	B6	37
Gondomar, Port.	D3	12
Gondrecourt-le-Château, Fr.	D12	10
Gönen, Tur.	I11	16
Gōnoura, Japan	I2	30
Gonzales, Ca., U.S.	D3	82
Gonzales, La., U.S.	D5	95
Gonzales, Tx., U.S.	E4	120
Gonzales, co., Tx., U.S.	E4	120
Gonzalez, Fl., U.S.	u14	86
Goochland, co., Va., U.S.	C5	123
Goode, Mount, mtn., Ak., U.S.	g18	79
Goodfellow Air Force Base, mil., Tx., U.S.	D2	120
Good Hope, Cape of, c., S. Afr.	H3	44
Good Hope Mountain, mtn., B.C., Can.	D5	69
Goodhue, co., Mn., U.S.	F6	100
Gooding, Id., U.S.	G4	89
Gooding, co., Id., U.S.	F4	89
Goodland, In., U.S.	C3	91
Goodland, Ks., U.S.	C2	93
Goodlettsville, Tn., U.S.	g10	119
Goodman, Ms., U.S.	C4	101
Goodman, Mo., U.S.	E3	102
Good Pine, La., U.S.	C3	95
Goodsprings, Nv., U.S.	H6	105
Goodview, Mn., U.S.	F7	100
Goodwater, Al., U.S.	B3	78
Goodwell, Ok., U.S.	e9	113
Goodyear, Az., U.S.	D3	80
Goole, Eng., U.K.	H12	7
Goondiwindi, Austl.	E10	50
Goose, stm., N.D., U.S.	B8	111
Goose Bay, b., Newf., Can.	B1	72
Gooseberry Creek, stm., Wy., U.S.	B4	127
Goose Creek, S.C., U.S.	F7	117
Goose Creek, stm., U.S.	G5	89
Goose Creek, stm., Va., U.S.	C3	123
Goose Creek Reservoir, res., S.C., U.S.	k11	117
Goose Lake, l., U.S.	B3	82
Goose Pond, l., N.H., U.S.	C2	106
Göppingen, Ger.	G9	8
Gorakhpur, India	G10	38
Gorda, Punta, c., Cuba	C6	64
Gordil, Cen. Afr. Rep.	G10	42
Gordo, Al., U.S.	B2	78
Gordon, Ga., U.S.	D3	87
Gordon, Ne., U.S.	B3	104
Gordon, co., Ga., U.S.	B2	87
Gordonsville, Tn., U.S.	C8	119
Gordonsville, Va., U.S.	B4	123
Gore, Eth.	G2	46
Gore, N.Z.	G2	52
Gore, Ok., U.S.	B6	113
Gore Bay, Ont., Can.	B2	73
Gore Point, c., Ak., U.S.	h16	79
Gore Range, mts., Co., U.S.	B4	83
Goreville, Il., U.S.	F5	90
Gorey, Ire.	I6	7
Gorgān, Iran	J8	22
Gorge High Dam, Wa., U.S.	A4	124
Gorham, Me., U.S.	E2	96
Gorham, N.H., U.S.	B4	106
Gorinchem, Neth.	D4	8
Gorizia, Italy	D8	14
Gorki, Bela.	G13	18
Gorki see Nižnij Novgorod, Russia	E27	18
Gorkovskoje Vodochranilišče, res., Russia	D26	18
Görlitz, Ger.	B13	8
Gorman, Tx., U.S.	C3	120
Gornja Radgona, Slo.	C10	14
Gorno-Altajsk, Russia	G11	24
Gorodec, Russia	E26	18
Gorontalo, Indon.	E7	32
Gort, Ire.	H4	7
Gorzów Wielkopolski (Landsberg an der Warthe), Pol.	C15	8
Goshen, In., U.S.	A6	91
Goshen, N.Y., U.S.	D6	109
Goshen, Oh., U.S.	C1	112
Goshen, co., Wy., U.S.	D8	127
Goshute Indian Reservation, U.S.	D7	105
Goshute Lake, l., Nv., U.S.	C7	105
Goshute Mountains, mts., Nv., U.S.	C7	105
Goslar, Ger.	D10	8
Gosper, co., Ne., U.S.	D6	104
Gosport, In., U.S.	F4	91
Göteborg (Gothenburg), Swe.	H8	6
Gotemba, Japan	G11	30
Gotha, Ger.	E10	8
Gothenburg, Ne., U.S.	D5	104
Gothenburg see Göteborg, Swe.	H8	6
Gotland, i., Swe.	H12	6
Gotō-rettō, is., Japan	J1	30
Göttingen, Ger.	D9	8
Gouda, Neth.	C4	8
Gouin, Réservoir, res., Que., Can.	k12	74
Goulburn, Austl.	F9	50
Goulburn Islands, is., Austl.	B6	50
Gould, Ar., U.S.	D4	81
Goulding, Fl., U.S.	u14	86
Gould Island, i., R.I., U.S.	E5	116
Goulds, Fl., U.S.	s13	86
Gourdon, Fr.	H8	10
Gouré, Niger	F8	42
Gourin, Fr.	D3	10
Gournay-en-Bray, Fr.	C8	10
Gouverneur, N.Y., U.S.	f9	109
Gove, co., Ks., U.S.	D3	93
Governador Valadares, Braz.	E8	57
Governors Harbour, Bah.	B9	64
Govind Balabh Pant Sāgar, res., India	H10	38
Govind Sāgar, res., India	E7	38
Gowanda, N.Y., U.S.	C2	109
Gower, Mo., U.S.	B3	102
Gowmal (Gumal), stm., Asia	D3	38
Gowmal Kalay, Afg.	D3	38
Gowrie, Ia., U.S.	B3	92
Goya, Arg.	B5	56
Gozo see Għawdex, i., Malta	M9	14
Graaff-Reinet, S. Afr.	H4	44
Grabill, In., U.S.	B8	91
Grace, Id., U.S.	G7	89
Graceville, Fl., U.S.	u16	86
Graceville, Mn., U.S.	E2	100
Gracewood, Ga., U.S.	C4	87
Gracias a Dios, Cabo, c., N.A.	G6	64
Gradaús, Braz.	E8	54
Gradaús, Serra dos, plat., Braz.	E8	54
Grado, Italy	D8	14
Grady, co., Ga., U.S.	F2	87
Grady, co., Ok., U.S.	C4	113
Graettinger, Ia., U.S.	A3	92
Grafton, Austl.	E10	50
Grafton, Il., U.S.	E3	90
Grafton, Ma., U.S.	B4	98
Grafton, N.D., U.S.	A8	111
Grafton, Oh., U.S.	A3	112
Grafton, Va., U.S.	h15	123
Grafton, W.V., U.S.	B4	125
Grafton, Wi., U.S.	E6	126
Grafton, co., N.H., U.S.	C3	106
Grafton, Cape, c., Austl.	C9	50
Graham, N.C., U.S.	A3	110
Graham, Tx., U.S.	C3	120
Graham, co., Az., U.S.	E5	80
Graham, co., Ks., U.S.	C4	93
Graham, co., N.C., U.S.	f9	110
Graham, Lake, res., Tx., U.S.	C3	120
Graham, Mount, mtn., Az., U.S.	E6	80
Graham Island, i., B.C., Can.	C1	69
Graham Lake, l., Me., U.S.	D4	96
Graham Moore, Cape, c., N.W. Ter., Can.	B17	66
Grahamstown, S. Afr.	H5	44
Grahn, Ky., U.S.	B6	94
Grainger, co., Tn., U.S.	C10	119
Grain Valley, Mo., U.S.	B3	102
Grajaú, Braz.	E9	54
Gramat, Fr.	H8	10
Grambling, La., U.S.	B3	95
Gramercy, La., U.S.	h10	95
Grammichele, Italy	L9	14
Grampian Mountains, mts., Scot., U.K.	E8	7
Granada, Col.	F6	58
Granada, Nic.	I5	64
Granada, Spain	H8	12
Granard, Ire.	H5	7
Granbury, Tx., U.S.	C4	120
Granby, Que., Can.	D5	74
Granby, Co., U.S.	A5	83
Granby, Ct., U.S.	B4	84
Granby, Mo., U.S.	E3	102
Granby, Lake, res., Co., U.S.	A5	83
Gran Canaria, i., Spain	p25	13a
Gran Chaco, pl., S.A.	A4	56
Grand, co., Co., U.S.	A4	83
Grand, co., Ut., U.S.	E6	121
Grand, stm., Ont., Can.	D4	73
Grand, stm., Mi., U.S.	E5	99
Grand, stm., Mo., U.S.	A3	102
Grand, stm., Oh., U.S.	A4	112
Grand, stm., S.D., U.S.	B4	118
Grandas, Spain	B5	12
Grand Bahama, i., Bah.	A8	64
Grand Bank, Newf., Can.	E4	72
Grand-Bassam, C. Iv.	G5	42
Grand Bay, N.B., Can.	D3	71
Grand Bay, Al., U.S.	E1	78
Grand Bend, Ont., Can.	D3	73
Grand Blanc, Mi., U.S.	F7	99
Grand Caillou, La., U.S.	E5	95
Grand Canal, Ire.	H5	7
Grand Canal see Da Yunhe, China	E10	26
Grand Canyon, Az., U.S.	A3	80
Grand Canyon, val., Az., U.S.	A3	80
Grand Canyon National Park, Az., U.S.	B3	80
Grand Cayman, i., Cay. Is.	E7	64
Grand Centre, Alta., Can.	B5	68
Grand Coteau, La., U.S.	D3	95
Grand Coulee, Wa., U.S.	B6	124
Grand Coulee Dam, Wa., U.S.	B6	124
Grande, stm., Bol.	G6	54
Grande, stm., Braz.	E3	57
Grande, Bahía, b., Arg.	G3	56
Grande, Boca, mth., Ven.	C12	58
Grande, Ilha, i., Braz.	G6	57
Grande, Ilha, i., Braz.	G1	57
Grande, Rio (Bravo del Norte), stm., N.A.	F7	76
Grande-Anse, N.B., Can.	B4	71
Grande Cache, Alta., Can.	C1	68
Grande Comore, i., Com.	D8	44
Grande de Matagalpa, stm., Nic.	H5	64
Grande de Santiago, Río, stm., Mex.	G7	62
Grande do Gurupá, Ilha, i., Braz.	D8	54
Grand-Entrée, Que., Can.	B8	71
Grande Prairie, Alta., Can.	B1	68
Grand Erg de Bilma, des., Niger	E8	42
Grand Erg Occidental, des., Alg.	B6	42
Grand Erg Oriental, des., Alg.	B7	42
Grande rivière de la Baleine, stm., Que., Can.	g11	74
Grande Ronde, stm., U.S.	C8	124
Grandes, Salinas, pl., Arg.	B4	56
Grandes-Bergeronnes, Que., Can.	A8	74
Grande-Terre, i., Guad.	F17	64
Grand Falls (Grand-Sault), N.B., Can.	B2	71
Grand Falls, wtfl, Me., U.S.	C5	96

Name | Map Ref | Page
Grand Falls [-Windsor], Newf., Can. D4 72
Grandfather Mountain, mtn., N.C., U.S. A1 110
Grandfield, Ok., U.S. C3 113
Grand Forks, B.C., Can. E8 69
Grand Forks, N.D., U.S. B8 111
Grand Forks, co., N.D., U.S. B8 111
Grand Forks Air Force Base, mil., N.D., U.S. B8 111
Grand-Fougeray, Fr. E5 10
Grand Harbour, N.B., Can. E3 71
Grand Haven, Mi., U.S. E4 99
Grand Island, Ne., U.S. D7 104
Grand Island, i., La., U.S. D6 95
Grand Island, i., Mi., U.S. B4 99
Grand Isle, La., U.S. E6 95
Grand Isle, co., Vt., U.S. B2 122
Grand Isle, i., La., U.S. E6 95
Grand Junction, Co., U.S. B2 83
Grand Junction, Ia., U.S. B3 92
Grand Lake, l., N.B., Can. D3 71
Grand Lake, l., Newf., Can. D3 72
Grand Lake, l., La., U.S. E6 95
Grand Lake, l., La., U.S. E3 95
Grand Lake, l., Mi., U.S. C7 99
Grand Lake, l., Oh., U.S. B1 112
Grand Lake Matagamon, l., Me., U.S. B4 96
Grand Lake Seboeis, l., Me., U.S. B4 96
Grand Ledge, Mi., U.S. F6 99
Grand Manan Island, i., N.B., Can. E3 71
Grand Marais, Mn., U.S. k9 100
Grand Meadow, Mn., U.S. G6 100
Grand-Mère, Que., Can. C5 74
Grand Mound, Ia., U.S. C7 92
Grand Portage Indian Reservation, Mn., U.S. k10 100
Grand Portage National Monument, Mn., U.S. h10 100
Grand Prairie, Tx., U.S. n10 120
Grand Rapids, Mi., U.S. F5 99
Grand Rapids, Mn., U.S. C5 100
Grand Rapids, Oh., U.S. f6 112
Grand Rivière de la Baleine, stm., Que., Can. E17 66
Grand-Saint-Bernard, Tunnel du, Eur. G14 10
Grand Saline, Tx., U.S. C5 120
Grand Terre Islands, is., La., U.S. E6 95
Grand Teton, mtn., Wy., U.S. C2 127
Grand Teton National Park, Wy., U.S. C2 127
Grand Tower, Il., U.S. F4 90
Grand Traverse, co., Mi., U.S. D5 99
Grand Traverse Bay, b., Mi., U.S. C5 99
Grand Turk, T./C. Is. D12 64
Grand Valley, Ont., Can. D4 73
Grandview, Man., Can. D1 70
Grandview, In., U.S. I4 91
Grandview, Mo., U.S. C3 102
Grandview, Wa., U.S. C6 124
Grandview Heights, Oh., U.S. m10 112
Grandville, Mi., U.S. F5 99
Grandy, N.C., U.S. A7 110
Granger, In., U.S. A5 91
Granger, Ia., U.S. C4 92
Granger, Tx., U.S. D4 120
Granger, Wa., U.S. C5 124
Grangeville, Id., U.S. D2 89
Granisle, B.C., Can. B4 69
Granite, Ok., U.S. C2 113
Granite, co., Mt., U.S. D3 103
Granite City, Il., U.S. E3 90
Granite Falls, Mn., U.S. F3 100
Granite Falls, N.C., U.S. B1 110
Granite Falls, Wa., U.S. A4 124
Granite Lake, res., Newf., Can. D3 72
Granite Mountain, mtn., Ak., U.S. B7 79
Granite Mountains, mts., Az., U.S. E2 80
Granite Mountains, mts., Wy., U.S. D5 127
Granite Pass, Wy., U.S. B5 127
Granite Peak, mtn., Mt., U.S. E7 103
Granite Peak, mtn., Nv., U.S. C2 105
Granite Peak, mtn., Nv., U.S. B4 105
Granite Peak, mtn., Ut., U.S. C2 121
Granite Peak, mtn., Ut., U.S. E3 121
Granite Peak, mtn., Wy., U.S. D4 127
Granite Quarry, N.C., U.S. B2 110
Granite Range, mts., Nv., U.S. C2 105
Graniteville, S.C., U.S. D4 117
Graniteville, Vt., U.S. C4 122
Granollers, Spain D14 12
Grant, Al., U.S. A3 78
Grant, Mi., U.S. E5 99
Grant, Ne., U.S. D4 104
Grant, co., Ar., U.S. C3 81
Grant, co., In., U.S. D6 91
Grant, co., Ks., U.S. E2 93
Grant, co., Ky., U.S. B5 94
Grant, co., La., U.S. C3 95
Grant, co., Mn., U.S. E2 100
Grant, co., Ne., U.S. C4 104
Grant, co., N.M., U.S. E1 108
Grant, co., N.D., U.S. C4 111
Grant, co., Ok., U.S. A4 113
Grant, co., Or., U.S. C7 114
Grant, co., S.D., U.S. B8 118
Grant, co., Wa., U.S. B6 124
Grant, co., W.V., U.S. B5 125
Grant, co., Wi., U.S. F3 126
Grant, Mount, mtn., Nv., U.S. E3 105
Grant City, Mo., U.S. A3 102
Grantham, Eng., U.K. I12 7
Grant Park, Il., U.S. B6 90
Grant Range, mts., Nv., U.S. E6 105
Grants, N.M., U.S. B2 108
Grantsburg, Wi., U.S. C1 126
Grants Pass, Or., U.S. E3 114
Grantsville, Ut., U.S. C3 121
Grantsville, W.V., U.S. C3 125
Grant Town, W.V., U.S. B4 125
Grantville, Ga., U.S. C2 87
Granville, Fr. D5 10
Granville, Il., U.S. B4 90
Granville, N.Y., U.S. B7 109
Granville, Oh., U.S. B3 112
Granville, W.V., U.S. h11 125
Granville, co., N.C., U.S. A4 110
Granville Lake, l., Man., Can. A1 70
Granvin, Nor. F6 6
Grapeland, Tx., U.S. D5 120
Grapeview, Wa., U.S. B3 124
Grapevine, Tx., U.S. C4 120
Grapevine Lake, res., Tx., U.S. n9 120
Grapevine Peak, mtn., Nv., U.S. G4 105
Gras, Lac de, l., N.W. Ter., Can. D10 66
Grasonville, Md., U.S. C5 97
Grass, stm., Man., Can. B2 70
Grass, stm., N.Y., U.S. f9 109
Grasse, Fr. I13 10
Grass Lake, Il., U.S. h8 90
Grass Lake, Mi., U.S. F6 99
Grass Lake, l., Il., U.S. h8 90
Grass Valley, Ca., U.S. C3 82
Grassy Brook, stm., Vt., U.S. E3 122
Grassy Lake, l., La., U.S. k9 95
Grates Point, c., Newf., Can. D5 72
Gratiot, co., Mi., U.S. E6 99
Gratis, Oh., U.S. C1 112
Grave Creek, stm., W.V., U.S. g8 125
Gravelly Branch, stm., De., U.S. F4 85
Gravelly Range, mts., Mt., U.S. E4 103
Gravenhurst, Ont., Can. C5 73
Grave Peak, mtn., Id., U.S. C4 89
Graves, co., Ky., U.S. f9 94
Gravette, Ar., U.S. A1 81
Gravina in Puglia, Italy I11 14
Gray, Fr. E12 10
Gray, Ga., U.S. C3 87
Gray, Ky., U.S. D5 94
Gray, La., U.S. k10 95
Gray, Me., U.S. g7 96
Gray, co., Ks., U.S. E3 93
Gray, co., Tx., U.S. B2 120
Grayback Mountain, mtn., Or., U.S. E3 114
Gray Court, S.C., U.S. B3 117
Grayland, Wa., U.S. C1 124
Grayling, Mi., U.S. D6 99
Graylyn Crest, De., U.S. A3 85
Grays Harbor, co., Wa., U.S. B2 124
Grays Harbor, b., Wa., U.S. C1 124
Grayslake, Il., U.S. A5 90
Grays Lake, sw., Id., U.S. F7 89
Grayson, Ky., U.S. B7 94
Grayson, co., Ky., U.S. C3 94
Grayson, co., Tx., U.S. C4 120
Grayson, co., Va., U.S. D1 123
Grayson Lake, res., Ky., U.S. B7 94
Grays Peak, mtn., Co., U.S. B5 83
Gray Summit, Mo., U.S. g12 102
Graysville, Al., U.S. f7 78
Graysville, Tn., U.S. D8 119
Grayville, Il., U.S. E5 90
Graz, Aus. H15 8
Gr'azi, Russia I22 18
Great Abaco, i., Bah. A9 64
Great Artesian Basin, Austl. D8 50
Great Australian Bight, Austl. F5 50
Great Averill Pond, l., Vt., U.S. B5 122
Great Barrier Reef, rf., Austl. C9 50
Great Barrington, Ma., U.S. B1 98
Great Basin National Park, Nv., U.S. E7 105
Great Bay, b., N.H., U.S. D5 106
Great Bay, b., N.J., U.S. D4 107
Great Bear Lake, l., N.W. Ter., Can. C9 66
Great Bend, Ks., U.S. D5 93
Great Captain Island, i., Ct., U.S. F1 84
Great Channel, strt., Asia K3 34
Great Dismal Swamp, sw., U.S. D6 123
Great Divide Basin, Wy., U.S. E4 127
Great Dividing Range, mts., Austl. D9 50
Great East Lake, l., U.S. C5 106
Great Egg Harbor, stm., N.J., U.S. D3 107
Greater Antilles, is., N.A. D10 64
Greater Sunda Islands, is., Asia F4 32
Great Exuma, i., Bah. C10 64
Great Falls, Mt., U.S. C5 103
Great Falls, S.C., U.S. B6 117
Great Falls, wtfl, Md., U.S. B3 97
Great Falls Dam, Tn., U.S. D6 119
Great Guana Cay, i., Bah. B9 64
Great Himalaya Range, mts., Asia F10 38
Greathouse Peak, mtn., Mt., U.S. D7 103
Great Inagua, i., Bah. D11 64
Great Indian Desert (Thar Desert), des., Asia G4 38
Great Island, spit, Ma., U.S. C7 98
Great Island, i., N.C., U.S. B6 110
Great Karroo, plat., S. Afr. H4 44
Great Lakes Naval Training Center, mil., Il., U.S. h9 90
Great Miami, stm., U.S. C1 112
Great Misery Island, i., Ma., U.S. f12 98
Great Moose Lake, l., Me., U.S. D3 96
Great Neck, N.Y., U.S. h13 109
Great Nicobar, i., India K2 34
Great Pee Dee, stm., U.S. D9 117
Great Plain of the Koukdjuak, pl., N.W. Ter., Can. C18 66
Great Plains, pl., N.A. E10 61
Great Point, c., Ma., U.S. D7 98
Great Ruaha, stm., Tan. C7 44
Great Sacandaga Lake, l., N.Y., U.S. C6 109
Great Salt Lake, l., Ut., U.S. B3 121
Great Salt Lake Desert, des., Ut., U.S. C2 121
Great Salt Plains Lake, res., Ok., U.S. A3 113
Great Salt Pond, b., R.I., U.S. h7 116
Great Sand Dunes National Monument, Co., U.S. D5 83
Great Sandy Desert, des., Austl. D4 50
Great Slave Lake, l., N.W. Ter., Can. D10 66
Great Smoky Mountains, mts., U.S. B8 119
Great Smoky Mountains National Park, U.S. B8 119
Great Swamp, sw., R.I., U.S. F3 116
Great Victoria Desert, des., Austl. E5 50
Great Village, N.S., Can. D6 71
Great Wass Island, i., Me., U.S. D5 96
Great Yarmouth, Eng., U.K. I14 7
Greece, N.Y., U.S. B3 109
Greece, ctry., Eur. H12 4
Greeley, Co., U.S. A6 83
Greeley, Pa., U.S. D12 115
Greeley, co., Ks., U.S. D2 93
Greeley, co., Ne., U.S. C7 104
Green, Or., U.S. D3 114
Green, co., Ky., U.S. C4 94
Green, co., Wi., U.S. F4 126
Green, stm., N.A. D5 76
Green, stm., U.S. A1 83
Green, stm., U.S. F3 122
Green, stm., Il., U.S. B4 90
Green, stm., Ky., U.S. C2 94
Green, stm., Wa., U.S. B3 124
Green Acres, De., U.S. h8 85
Greenacres, Wa., U.S. B8 124
Greenacres City, Fl., U.S. F6 86
Greenback, Tn., U.S. D9 119
Green Bay, Wi., U.S. D6 126
Green Bay, b., U.S. D3 99
Greenbelt, Md., U.S. C4 97
Greenbriar, Va., U.S. g12 123
Greenbrier, Ar., U.S. B3 81
Green Brier, Tn., U.S. A5 119
Greenbrier, co., W.V., U.S. D4 125
Greenbrier, stm., W.V., U.S. D4 125
Greenbush, Mn., U.S. B2 100
Greencastle, In., U.S. E4 91
Greencastle, Pa., U.S. G6 115
Green City, Mo., U.S. A5 102
Green Cove Springs, Fl., U.S. C5 86
Greendale, In., U.S. F8 91
Greendale, Wi., U.S. F6 126
Greene, Ia., U.S. B5 92
Greene, N.Y., U.S. C5 109
Greene, co., Al., U.S. C1 78
Greene, co., Ar., U.S. A5 81
Greene, co., Ga., U.S. C3 87
Greene, co., Il., U.S. D3 90
Greene, co., In., U.S. F4 91
Greene, co., Ia., U.S. B3 92
Greene, co., Ms., U.S. D5 101
Greene, co., Mo., U.S. D4 102
Greene, co., N.Y., U.S. C6 109
Greene, co., N.C., U.S. B5 110
Greene, co., Oh., U.S. C2 112
Greene, co., Pa., U.S. G1 115
Greene, co., Tn., U.S. C11 119
Greene, co., Va., U.S. B4 123
Greeneville, Tn., U.S. C11 119
Green Fall, stm., U.S. F1 116
Greenfield, Ca., U.S. D3 82
Greenfield, Il., U.S. D3 90
Greenfield, In., U.S. E6 91
Greenfield, Ia., U.S. C3 92
Greenfield, Ma., U.S. A2 98
Greenfield, Mo., U.S. D4 102
Greenfield, N.H., U.S. E3 106
Greenfield, Oh., U.S. C2 112
Greenfield, Tn., U.S. A3 119
Greenfield, Wi., U.S. n12 126
Greenfield Plaza, Ia., U.S. e8 92
Green Forest, Ar., U.S. A2 81
Green Harbor, Ma., U.S. B6 98
Green Hill Pond, l., R.I., U.S. G3 116
Greenhills, Oh., U.S. n12 112
Green Lake, Wi., U.S. E5 126
Green Lake, co., Wi., U.S. E4 126
Green Lake, l., Me., U.S. D4 96
Green Lake, l., Wi., U.S. E5 126
Greenland, Ar., U.S. B1 81
Greenland, N.H., U.S. D5 106
Greenland, dep., N.A. B16 61
Greenland Sea B13 128
Greenlee, co., Az., U.S. D6 80
Green Lookout Mountain, mtn., Wa., U.S. D3 124
Green Mountain, mtn., Wy., U.S. D5 127
Green Mountain Reservoir, res., Co., U.S. B4 83
Green Mountains, mts., Vt., U.S. F2 122
Greenock, Scot., U.K. F8 7
Greenock, Pa., U.S. F2 115
Green Peter Lake, res., Or., U.S. C4 114
Green Pond, Al., U.S. B2 78
Green Pond, l., N.J., U.S. A4 107
Greenport, N.Y., U.S. m16 109
Green River, Ut., U.S. E5 121
Green River, Wy., U.S. E3 127
Green River Lake, res., Ky., U.S. C4 94
Green River Lock and Dam, U.S. I2 91
Green River Reservoir, res., Vt., U.S. B3 122
Green Rock, Il., U.S. B3 90
Greensboro, Al., U.S. C2 78
Greensboro, Ga., U.S. C3 87
Greensboro, Md., U.S. C6 97
Greensboro, N.C., U.S. A3 110
Greensburg, In., U.S. F7 91
Greensburg, Ks., U.S. E4 93
Greensburg, Ky., U.S. C4 94
Greensburg, Pa., U.S. F2 115
Greens Peak, mtn., Az., U.S. C6 80
Green Springs, Oh., U.S. A2 112
Greensville, co., Va., U.S. D5 123
Green Swamp, sw., N.C., U.S. C4 110
Greentown, In., U.S. D6 91
Greenup, Il., U.S. D5 90
Greenup, Ky., U.S. B7 94
Greenup, co., Ky., U.S. B7 94
Green Valley, Az., U.S. F5 80
Greenview, Il., U.S. C4 90
Greenville, Lib. G4 42
Greenville, Al., U.S. D3 78
Greenville, Ca., U.S. B3 82
Greenville, De., U.S. A3 85
Greenville, Ga., U.S. C2 87
Greenville, Il., U.S. E4 90
Greenville, Ky., U.S. C2 94
Greenville, Me., U.S. C3 96
Greenville, Mi., U.S. E5 99
Greenville, Ms., U.S. B2 101
Greenville, N.H., U.S. E3 106
Greenville, N.C., U.S. B5 110
Greenville, Oh., U.S. B1 112
Greenville, Pa., U.S. D1 115
Greenville, R.I., U.S. C3 116
Greenville, S.C., U.S. B3 117
Greenville, Tx., U.S. C4 120
Greenville, co., S.C., U.S. B3 117
Greenville Creek, stm., Oh., U.S. B1 112
Greenville Junction, Me., U.S. C3 96
Greenwich, Ct., U.S. E1 84
Greenwich, N.Y., U.S. B7 109
Greenwich, Oh., U.S. A3 112
Greenwich Bay, b., R.I., U.S. D4 116
Greenwich Point, c., Ct., U.S. E1 84
Greenwood, B.C., Can. E8 69
Greenwood, Ar., U.S. B1 81
Greenwood, De., U.S. E3 85
Greenwood, In., U.S. E5 91
Greenwood, La., U.S. B2 95
Greenwood, Ms., U.S. B3 101
Greenwood, Mo., U.S. k11 102
Greenwood, Pa., U.S. E5 115
Greenwood, S.C., U.S. C3 117
Greenwood, Wi., U.S. D3 126
Greenwood, co., Ks., U.S. E7 93
Greenwood, co., S.C., U.S. C3 117
Greenwood, Lake, res., In., U.S. G4 91
Greenwood, Lake, res., S.C., U.S. C4 117
Greenwood Lake, N.Y., U.S. D6 109
Greenwood Lake, l., U.S. A4 107
Greenwood Lake, l., Mn., U.S. C7 100
Greer, S.C., U.S. B3 117
Greer, co., Ok., U.S. C2 113
Greers Ferry Lake, res., Ar., U.S. B3 81
Greeson, Lake, res., Ar., U.S. C2 81
Gregg, co., Tx., U.S. C5 120
Gregory, S.D., U.S. D6 118
Gregory, co., S.D., U.S. D6 118
Greifswald, Ger. A13 8
Greilickville, Mi., U.S. D5 99
Greiz, Ger. E12 8
Grenada, Ms., U.S. B4 101
Grenada, co., Ms., U.S. B4 101
Grenada, ctry., N.A. H17 64
Grenada Lake, res., Ms., U.S. B4 101
Grenadine Islands, is., N.A. H17 64
Grenchen, Switz. E14 10
Grenoble, Fr. G12 10
Grenville, Que., Can. D3 74
Grenville, Cape, c., Austl. B8 50
Grenville Point, c., Wa., U.S. B1 124
Gresham, Or., U.S. B4 114
Gresik, Indon. m16 33a
Gretna, Man., Can. E3 70
Gretna, Fl., U.S. B2 86
Gretna, La., U.S. E5 95
Gretna, Ne., U.S. C9 104
Gretna, Va., U.S. D3 123
Greven, Ger. C7 8
Grevená, Grc. I5 16
Grevesmühlen, Ger. B11 8
Grey, stm., Newf., Can. E3 72
Greybull, Wy., U.S. B4 127
Greybull, stm., Wy., U.S. B4 127
Greylock, Mount, mtn., Ma., U.S. A1 98
Greymouth, N.Z. E3 52
Greys, stm., Wy., U.S. C2 127
Gridley, Ca., U.S. C3 82
Gridley, Il., U.S. C5 90
Griffin, Ga., U.S. C2 87
Griffiss Air Force Base, mil., N.Y., U.S. B5 109
Griffith, Austl. F9 50
Griffith, In., U.S. A3 91
Grifton, N.C., U.S. B5 110
Griggs, co., N.D., U.S. B7 111
Griggsville, Il., U.S. D3 90
Grik, Malay. L6 34
Grimes, Ia., U.S. C4 92
Grimes, co., Tx., U.S. D4 120
Grimmen, Ger. A13 8
Grimsby, Ont., Can. D5 73
Grimsby, Eng., U.K. H12 7
Grimselpass, Switz. F15 10
Grimshaw, Alta., Can. A2 68
Grimsley, Tn., U.S. C9 119
Grimstad, Nor. G7 6
Grindall Creek, Va., U.S. n18 123
Grinnell, Ia., U.S. C5 92
Grinnell Peninsula, pen., N.W. Ter., Can. A14 66
Gris-Nez, Cap, c., Fr. B8 10
Grissom Air Force Base, mil., In., U.S. C5 91
Griswold, Ia., U.S. C2 92
Grizzly Mountain, mtn., Id., U.S. B2 89
Grizzly Mountain, mtn., Or., U.S. C6 114
Grizzly Mountain, mtn., Wa., U.S. A7 124
Groais Island, i., Newf., Can. C4 72
Grodno, Bela. H6 18
Groesbeck, Tx., U.S. D4 120
Grombalia, Tun. M5 14
Gronau, Ger. C6 8
Grong, Nor. D9 6
Groningen, Neth. B6 8
Groom Lake, l., Nv., U.S. F6 105
Groom Range, mts., Nv., U.S. F6 105
Groote Eylandt, i., Austl. B7 50
Grootfontein, Nmb. E3 44
Gros Morne National Park, Newf., Can. D3 72
Grosse Isle Naval Air Station, mil., Mi., U.S. p15 99
Grossenhain, Ger. D13 8
Grosse Pointe, Mi., U.S. *p16 99
Grosse Pointe Park, Mi., U.S. p16 99
Grosse Pointe Woods, Mi., U.S. p16 99
Grosseto, Italy G6 14
Grossglockner, mtn., Aus. H12 8
Grossmont, Ca., U.S. o16 82
Gros Ventre, stm., Wy., U.S. C2 127
Gros Ventre Range, mts., Wy., U.S. C2 127
Groswater Bay, b., Newf., Can. F21 66
Groton, Ct., U.S. D7 84
Groton, N.Y., U.S. C4 109
Groton, S.D., U.S. B7 118
Groton Long Point, Ct., U.S. D7 84
Grottaglie, Italy I12 14
Grottaminarda, Italy H10 14
Grottoes, Va., U.S. B4 123
Grouse Creek, stm., Ut., U.S. B2 121
Grouse Creek Mountain, mtn., Id., U.S. E5 89
Grove, Ok., U.S. A7 113
Grove City, Fl., U.S. F4 86
Grove City, Oh., U.S. C2 112
Grove City, Pa., U.S. D1 115
Grove Hill, Al., U.S. D2 78
Groveland, Fl., U.S. D5 86
Groveland, Ma., U.S. A5 98
Grove Point, c., Md., U.S. B5 97
Groveport, Oh., U.S. C3 112
Grover City, Ca., U.S. E3 82
Groves, Tx., U.S. E6 120
Groveton, N.H., U.S. A3 106
Groveton, Tx., U.S. D5 120
Groveton, Va., U.S. g12 123
Groveton Gardens, Va., U.S. *B5 123
Grovetown, Ga., U.S. C4 87
Groveville, N.J., U.S. C3 107
Growler Peak, mtn., Az., U.S. E2 80
Groznyj, Russia I7 22
Grudziądz, Pol. B18 8
Gruetli-Laager, Tn., U.S. D8 119
Grulla, Tx., U.S. F3 120
Grundy, Va., U.S. e9 123
Grundy, co., Il., U.S. B5 90
Grundy, co., Ia., U.S. B5 92
Grundy, co., Mo., U.S. A4 102
Grundy, co., Tn., U.S. D8 119
Grundy Center, Ia., U.S. B5 92
Grunthal, Man., Can. E3 70
Gruver, Tx., U.S. A2 120
Guacanayabo, Golfo de, b., Cuba D9 64
Guachochic, Mex. D6 62
Guadalajara, Mex. G8 62
Guadalajara, Spain E8 12
Guadalcanal, i., Sol.Is. A11 50
Guadalquivir, stm., Spain H6 12
Guadalupe, Mex. E9 62
Guadalupe, Az., U.S. m9 80
Guadalupe, Ca., U.S. E3 82
Guadalupe, co., N.M., U.S. C5 108
Guadalupe, co., Tx., U.S. E4 120
Guadalupe Garzarón, Mex. E9 62
Guadalupe Mountains, mts., U.S. E5 108
Guadalupe Mountains National Park, Tx., U.S. o12 120
Guadalupe Peak, mtn., Tx., U.S. o12 120
Guadeloupe, dep., N.A. F17 64
Guadeloupe Passage, strt., N.A. F17 64
Guadiana, stm., Eur. H4 12
Guadix, Spain H8 12
Guafo, Isla, i., Chile E2 56
Guajará Mirim, Braz. F5 54
Gualeguaychú, Arg. C5 56
Gualicho, Salina, pl., Arg. E3 56
Guam, dep., Oc. F22 2
Guaminí, Arg. D4 56
Guamo, Col. E5 58
Guampí, Sierra de, mts., Ven. B5 54
Guanaja, Isla de, i., Hond. F5 64
Guanajuato, Mex. G9 62
Guanambi, Braz. C7 57
Guanare, Ven. C8 58
Guanarito, Ven. C8 58
Guanay, Cerro, mtn., Ven. E9 58
Guane, Cuba C5 64
Guang'an, China E8 26
Guangdong, prov., China G9 26
Guanghua, China E9 26
Guangxi Zhuang Zizhiqu, prov., China G8 26
Guangyuan, China E8 26
Guangzhou (Canton), China L2 28
Guano Lake, l., Or., U.S. E7 114
Guantánamo, Cuba D10 64
Guanxian, China E7 26
Guápiles, C.R. I6 64
Guaporé (Iténez), stm., S.A. F6 54
Guaqui, Bol. G5 54
Guarabira, Braz. E11 54
Guaranda, Ec. H3 58
Guarapuava, Braz. B6 56
Guaratinguetá, Braz. G6 57
Guarda, Port. E4 12
Guardo, Spain C7 12
Guárico, Embalse del, res., Ven. C9 58
Guarulhos, Braz. G5 57
Guarus, Braz. F8 57
Guasave, Mex. E5 62
Guasdualito, Ven. D7 58
Guatemala, Guat. G2 64
Guatemala, ctry., N.A. G2 64
Guaviare, stm., Col. F8 58
Guaxupé, Braz. F5 57
Guayama, P.R. F14 64
Guayaquil, Ec. I3 58
Guayaquil, Golfo de, b., S.A. I2 58
Guaymallén, Arg. C3 56
Guaymas, Mex. D4 62
Gubbio, Italy F7 14
Guben, Ger. D14 8
Guchengzi, China D7 26
Güdalūr, India G4 37
Gudiyāttam, India F5 37
Güdūr, India E5 37
Guebwiller, Fr. E14 10
Guelma, Alg. A7 42
Guelph, Ont., Can. D4 73
Guérande, Fr. E4 10
Guéret, Fr. F8 10
Guernsey, Wy., U.S. D8 127
Guernsey, co., Oh., U.S. B4 112
Guernsey, dep., Eur. C4 10
Gueydan, La., U.S. D3 95
Guga, Russia G21 24
Guibes, Nmb. G3 44
Güicán, Col. D6 58
Guichen, Fr. E5 10
Guiding, China A9 34
Guijuelo, Spain E6 12
Guilford, Ct., U.S. D5 84
Guilford, Me., U.S. C3 96
Guilford, co., N.C., U.S. A3 110
Guilin (Kweilin), China B11 34
Guillaumes, Fr. H13 10
Guimarães, Port. D3 12

Name	Map Ref	Page
Guin, Al., U.S.	B2	78
Guinea, ctry., Afr.	F3	42
Guinea, Gulf of, b., Afr.	H6	42
Guinea-Bissau, ctry., Afr.	F2	42
Güines, Cuba	C6	64
Guingamp, Fr.	D3	10
Güira de Melena, Cuba	C6	64
Guiratinga, Braz.	G8	54
Güiria, Ven.	B11	58
Guixian, China	C10	34
Guiyang (Kweiyang), China	A9	34
Guizhou, prov., China	F8	26
Gujarat, state, India	I4	38
Gujar Khān, Pak.	D5	38
Gujrānwāla, Pak.	D6	38
Gujrāt, Pak.	D6	38
Gulbarga, India	D4	37
Guledagudda, India	D3	37
Gulf, co., Fl., U.S.	C1	86
Gulf Gate Estates, Fl., U.S.	E4	86
Gulf Islands National Seashore, U.S.	E5	101
Gulfport, Fl., U.S.	E4	86
Gulfport, Ms., U.S.	E4	101
Gulf Shores, Al., U.S.	E2	78
Gull Island, i., N.C., U.S.	B7	110
Gullivan Bay, b., Fl., U.S.	G5	86
Gull Lake, l., Alta., Can.	C4	68
Gull Lake, l., Mn., U.S.	D4	100
Güllük, Tur.	L11	16
Gülpınar, Tur.	J10	16
Gulu, Ug.	H12	42
Gumal (Gowmal), stm., Asia	D3	38
Gumboro, De., U.S.	G4	85
Gummersbach, Ger.	D7	8
Guna, India	H7	38
Gunisao, stm., Man., Can.	C3	70
Gunnarn, Swe.	D11	6
Gunnison, Co., U.S.	C4	83
Gunnison, Ms., U.S.	B3	101
Gunnison, Ut., U.S.	D4	121
Gunnison, co., Co., U.S.	C3	83
Gunnison, stm., Co., U.S.	C2	83
Gunnison, Mount, mtn., Co., U.S.	C3	83
Gunpowder Neck, c., Md., U.S.	B5	97
Gunpowder River, b., Md., U.S.	B5	97
Guntakal, India	E4	37
Gunter Air Force Base, mil., Al., U.S.	C3	78
Guntersville, Al., U.S.	A3	78
Guntersville Lake, res., Al., U.S.	A3	78
Guntown, Ms., U.S.	A5	101
Guntūr, India	D6	37
Gunungsitoli, Indon.	N4	34
Günzburg, Ger.	G10	8
Gunzenhausen, Ger.	F10	8
Gurdāspur, India	D6	38
Gurdon, Ar., U.S.	D2	81
Guri, Embalse, res., Ven.	D11	58
Gurley, Al., U.S.	A3	78
Gurnee, Il., U.S.	h9	90
Gurnet Point, c., Ma., U.S.	B6	98
Gurupi, Braz.	F9	54
Gurupi, stm., Braz.	D9	54
Gusau, Nig.	F7	42
Gus'-Chrustal'nyj, Russia	F23	18
Gusev, Russia	G5	18
Gushi, China	C4	28
Gushikawa, Japan	y27	31b
Gusinoozersk, Russia	G15	24
Guspini, Italy	J3	14
Gustav Holm, Kap, c., Grnld.	C26	66
Gustine, Ca., U.S.	D3	82
Güstrow, Ger.	B12	8
Gütersloh, Ger.	D8	8
Guthrie, Ky., U.S.	D2	94
Guthrie, Ok., U.S.	B4	113
Guthrie, W.V., U.S.	m12	125
Guthrie, co., Ia., U.S.	C3	92
Guthrie Center, Ia., U.S.	C3	92
Guttenberg, Ia., U.S.	B6	92
Guttenberg, N.J., U.S.	h8	107
Guyana, ctry., S.A.	B7	54
Guyandotte, stm., W.V., U.S.	C2	125
Guymon, Ok., U.S.	e9	113
Guysborough, N.S., Can.	D8	71
Guyton, Ga., U.S.	D5	87
Güzelyurt Körfezi, b., N. Cyp.	B3	40
Gwādar, Pak.	D1	36
Gwai, Zimb.	E5	44
Gwalior, India	G8	38
Gwanda, Zimb.	F5	44
Gweru, Zimb.	E5	44
Gwinhurst, De., U.S.	h8	85
Gwinn, Mi., U.S.	B3	99
Gwinner, N.D., U.S.	C8	111
Gwinnett, co., Ga., U.S.	C2	87
Gwydyr Bay, b., Ak., U.S.	A10	79
Gwynns Falls, stm., Md., U.S.	g10	97
Gympie, Austl.	E10	50
Gyöngyös, Hung.	H19	8
Győr, Hung.	H17	8
Gypsum, Co., U.S.	B4	83

H

Name	Map Ref	Page
Haakon, co., S.D., U.S.	C4	118
Haapajärvi, Fin.	E15	6
Haapamäki, Fin.	E15	6
Haar, Ger.	G11	8
Haarlem, Neth.	C4	8
Haast, N.Z.	E2	52
Habersham, co., Ga., U.S.	B3	87
Habiganj, Bngl.	H14	38
Hachijō-jima, i., Japan	E14	26
Hachinohe, Japan	B14	30
Hachiōji, Japan	G12	30
Hackberry, La., U.S.	E2	95
Hackensack, N.J., U.S.	B4	107
Hackensack, stm., N.J., U.S.	h8	107
Hackettstown, N.J., U.S.	B3	107
Hackleburg, Al., U.S.	A2	78
Hadd, Ra's al-, c., Oman	D6	46
Haddam, Ct., U.S.	D5	84
Haddock, Ga., U.S.	C3	87
Haddonfield, N.J., U.S.	D2	107
Haddon Heights, N.J., U.S.	D2	107
Hadejia, stm., Nig.	F8	42
Ḥadera, Isr.	C4	40
Haderslev, Den.	I7	6
Hadīyah, Sau. Ar.	C2	46
Hadjeb el Aïoun, Tun.	N4	14
Hadley Bay, b., N.W. Ter., Can.	B11	66
Hadley Lake, l., Me., U.S.	D5	96
Hadlock, Wa., U.S.	A3	124
Ha Dong, Viet.	D8	34
Ḥaḍramawt, reg., Yemen	E4	46
Haeju, N. Kor.	D12	26
Hāfizābād, Pak.	D5	38
Hafun, Ras, c., Som.	F5	46
Hagan, Ga., U.S.	D5	87
Hagemeister Island, i., Ak., U.S.	D7	79
Hagen, Ger.	D7	8
Hagerman, Id., U.S.	G4	89
Hagerman, N.M., U.S.	D5	108
Hagerstown, In., U.S.	E7	91
Hagerstown, Md., U.S.	A2	97
Hagfors, Swe.	F9	6
Haggin, Mount, mtn., Mt., U.S.	D3	103
Hagi, Japan	H4	30
Ha Giang, Viet.	C8	34
Hague, Sask., Can.	E2	75
Hague, Cap de la, c., Fr.	C5	10
Haguenau, Fr.	D14	10
Hagues Peak, mtn., Co., U.S.	A5	83
Ha!Ha!, Baie des, b., Que., Can.	C2	72
Hahira, Ga., U.S.	F3	87
Hahnville, La., U.S.	E5	95
Haian, China	C9	28
Haicheng, China	C11	26
Hai Duong, Viet.	D9	34
Haifa see Ḥefa, Isr.	C4	40
Haikou, China	D11	34
Haiku, Hi., U.S.	C5	88
Ḥā'il, Sau. Ar.	C3	46
Hailaer, China	B10	26
Hailey, Id., U.S.	F4	89
Haileybury, Ont., Can.	p20	73
Haileyville, Ok., U.S.	C6	113
Haimen, China	G10	28
Haimen, China	L5	28
Hainan, China	H8	26
Hainan Dao, i., China	E10	34
Haines, Ak., U.S.	D12	79
Haines City, Fl., U.S.	D5	86
Haines Junction, Yukon, Can.	D5	66
Hainfeld, Aus.	G15	8
Haining, China	E9	28
Hai Phong, Viet.	D9	34
Haiti (Haïti), ctry., N.A.	E11	64
Haizhou, China	A8	28
Hakodate, Japan	r18	30a
Hāla, Pak.	H3	38
Ḥalab (Aleppo), Syria	A5	40
Ḥalā'ib, Sudan	D13	42
Halawa, Cape, c., Hi., U.S.	B5	88
Halawa Heights, Hi., U.S.	g10	88
Ḥalbā, Leb.	B5	40
Halberstadt, Ger.	D11	8
Halden, Nor.	G8	6
Haldensleben, Ger.	C11	8
Haldimand, Ont., Can.	E5	73
Haldwāni, India	F8	38
Hale, co., Al., U.S.	C2	78
Hale, co., Tx., U.S.	B2	120
Haleakala Crater, crat., Hi., U.S.	C5	88
Haleakala National Park, Hi., U.S.	C6	88
Hale Center, Tx., U.S.	B2	120
Haleiwa, Hi., U.S.	B3	88
Hales Corners, Wi., U.S.	n11	126
Halethorpe, Md., U.S.	B4	97
Haleyville, Al., U.S.	A2	78
Half Moon Bay, Ca., U.S.	k8	82
Halfway, Md., U.S.	A2	97
Haliburton, Ont., Can.	B6	73
Halibut Point, c., Ma., U.S.	A6	98
Halifax, N.S., Can.	E6	71
Halifax, Va., U.S.	D4	123
Halifax, co., N.C., U.S.	A5	110
Halifax, co., Va., U.S.	D4	123
Halifax Bay, b., Austl.	C9	50
Haliimaile, Hi., U.S.	C5	88
Halkirk, Scot., U.K.	C9	7
Hall, co., Ga., U.S.	B3	87
Hall, co., Ne., U.S.	D7	104
Hall, co., Tx., U.S.	B2	120
Hallam Peak, mtn., B.C., Can.	C8	69
Hallandale, Fl., U.S.	G6	86
Halla-san, mtn., S. Kor.	E12	26
Halle, Ger.	D11	8
Hällefors, Swe.	G10	6
Hallein, Aus.	H13	8
Hallettsville, Tx., U.S.	E4	120
Hallie, Wi., U.S.	D2	126
Hall Island, i., Ak., U.S.	C5	79
Hall Meadow Brook Reservoir, res., Ct., U.S.	B3	84
Hall Mountain, mtn., Wa., U.S.	A8	124
Hällnäs, Swe.	D12	6
Hallock, Mn., U.S.	B2	100
Hallowell, Me., U.S.	D3	96
Hall Peninsula, pen., N.W. Ter., Can.	D19	66
Halls, Tn., U.S.	B2	119
Hallsberg, Swe.	G10	6
Halls Creek, Austl.	C5	50
Halls Creek, stm., Ut., U.S.	F5	121
Halls Crossroads, Tn., U.S.	m14	119
Halls Stream, stm., N.H., U.S.	f7	106
Hallstavik, Swe.	F12	6
Hallstead, Pa., U.S.	C10	115
Hallsville, Mo., U.S.	B5	102
Hallsville, Tx., U.S.	C5	120
Halmahera, i., Indon.	E8	32
Halmahera, Laut, Indon.	F8	32
Halmstad, Swe.	H9	6
Halsey, Or., U.S.	C3	114
Hälsingborg see Helsingborg, Swe.	H9	6
Halstad, Mn., U.S.	C2	100
Halstead, Ks., U.S.	E6	93
Haltern, Ger.	D7	8
Haltiatunturi, mtn., Eur.	B13	6
Halton Hills, Ont., Can.	D5	73
Hamada, Japan	H5	30
Hamadān, Iran	B4	46
Ḥamāh, Syria	B5	40
Hamamatsu, Japan	H10	30
Hamar, Nor.	F8	6
Hamblen, co., Tn., U.S.	C10	119
Hamburg, Ger.	B9	8
Hamburg, Ar., U.S.	D4	81
Hamburg, Ia., U.S.	D2	92
Hamburg, N.Y., U.S.	C2	109
Hamburg, Pa., U.S.	E10	115
Hamden, Ct., U.S.	D4	84
Hamden, Oh., U.S.	C3	112
Hämeenlinna, Fin.	F15	6
Hamel, Mn., U.S.	m11	100
Hameln, Ger.	C9	8
Hamersley Range, mts., Austl.	D3	50
Hamhŭng, N. Kor.	D12	26
Hami, China	C5	26
Hamilton, Ber.	E14	76
Hamilton, Ont., Can.	D5	73
Hamilton, N.Z.	B5	52
Hamilton, Scot., U.K.	F8	7
Hamilton, Al., U.S.	A2	78
Hamilton, Il., U.S.	C2	90
Hamilton, In., U.S.	A8	91
Hamilton, Mi., U.S.	F4	99
Hamilton, Ms., U.S.	B5	101
Hamilton, Mo., U.S.	B3	102
Hamilton, Mt., U.S.	D2	103
Hamilton, N.Y., U.S.	C5	109
Hamilton, Oh., U.S.	C1	112
Hamilton, Tx., U.S.	D3	120
Hamilton, Va., U.S.	A5	123
Hamilton, co., Fl., U.S.	B3	86
Hamilton, co., Il., U.S.	E5	90
Hamilton, co., In., U.S.	D5	91
Hamilton, co., Ia., U.S.	B4	92
Hamilton, co., Ks., U.S.	E2	93
Hamilton, co., Ne., U.S.	D7	104
Hamilton, co., N.Y., U.S.	B6	109
Hamilton, co., Oh., U.S.	C1	112
Hamilton, co., Tn., U.S.	D8	119
Hamilton, co., Tx., U.S.	D3	120
Hamilton, Lake, res., Ar., U.S.	C2	81
Hamilton, Mount, mtn., Ak., U.S.	C8	79
Hamilton, Mount, mtn., Ca., U.S.	k9	82
Hamilton, Mount, mtn., Nv., U.S.	D6	105
Hamilton Inlet, b., Newf., Can.	A2	72
Hamilton Reservoir, res., Ma., U.S.	B3	98
Hamilton Sound, strt., Newf., Can.	D4	72
Hamilton Square, N.J., U.S.	C3	107
Hamiota, Man., Can.	D1	70
Hamlet, In., U.S.	B4	91
Hamlet, N.C., U.S.	C3	110
Hamlet, Mount, mtn., Ak., U.S.	B6	79
Hamlin, Pa., U.S.	D11	115
Hamlin, Tx., U.S.	C2	120
Hamlin, W.V., U.S.	C2	125
Hamlin, co., S.D., U.S.	C8	118
Hamlin Lake, l., Mi., U.S.	D4	99
Hamm, Ger.	D7	8
Hammamet, Tun.	M5	14
Hammam Lif, Tun.	M5	14
Hammerdal, Swe.	E10	6
Hammon, Ok., U.S.	B2	113
Hammonasset, stm., Ct., U.S.	D5	84
Hammonasset Point, c., Ct., U.S.	E5	84
Hammond, In., U.S.	A2	91
Hammond, La., U.S.	D5	95
Hammond, Wi., U.S.	D1	126
Hammond Bay, b., Mi., U.S.	C6	99
Hammonton, N.J., U.S.	D3	107
Hampden, Newf., Can.	D3	72
Hampden, Me., U.S.	D4	96
Hampden, co., Ma., U.S.	B2	98
Hampden Highlands, Me., U.S.	D4	96
Hampshire, Il., U.S.	A5	90
Hampshire, co., Ma., U.S.	B2	98
Hampshire, co., W.V., U.S.	B6	125
Hampstead, Md., U.S.	A4	97
Hampstead, N.C., U.S.	C5	110
Hampton, N.B., Can.	D4	71
Hampton, Ar., U.S.	D3	81
Hampton, Ga., U.S.	C2	87
Hampton, Ia., U.S.	B4	92
Hampton, N.H., U.S.	E5	106
Hampton, S.C., U.S.	F5	117
Hampton, Tn., U.S.	C11	119
Hampton, Va., U.S.	C6	123
Hampton, co., S.C., U.S.	F5	117
Hampton Bays, N.Y., U.S.	n16	109
Hampton Beach, N.H., U.S.	E5	106
Hampton Butte, mtn., Or., U.S.	D6	114
Hampton Roads, Va., U.S.	k15	123
Hampton Roads Bridge-Tunnel, Va., U.S.	k15	123
Hams Fork, stm., Wy., U.S.	E2	127
Hamtramck, Mi., U.S.	p15	99
Hana, Hi., U.S.	C6	88
Hanahan, S.C., U.S.	F7	117
Hanalei Bay, b., Hi., U.S.	A2	88
Hanamaki, Japan	C14	30
Hanamaulu, Hi., U.S.	B2	88
Hanapepe, Hi., U.S.	B2	88
Hanau, Ger.	E8	8
Hanceville, Al., U.S.	A3	78
Hancock, Md., U.S.	A1	97
Hancock, Mi., U.S.	A2	99
Hancock, Mn., U.S.	E3	100
Hancock, co., Ga., U.S.	C3	87
Hancock, co., Il., U.S.	C2	90
Hancock, co., In., U.S.	E6	91
Hancock, co., Ia., U.S.	A4	92
Hancock, co., Ky., U.S.	C3	94
Hancock, co., Me., U.S.	D4	96
Hancock, co., Ms., U.S.	E4	101
Hancock, co., Oh., U.S.	A2	112
Hancock, co., Tn., U.S.	C10	119
Hancock, co., W.V., U.S.	A4	125
Hand, co., S.D., U.S.	C6	118
Handa, Japan	H9	30
Handan, China	D9	26
Hando, Som.	F5	46
HaNegev, reg., Isr.	D4	40
Hanford, Ca., U.S.	D4	82
Hangchow see Hangzhou, China	E9	28
Hangman Creek, stm., Wa., U.S.	B8	124
Hangö (Hanko), Fin.	G14	6
Hangzhou (Hangchow), China	E9	28
Hangzhou Wan, b., China	E9	28
Ḥanīsh, Jazā'ir, is., Yemen	F3	46
Hanjiang, China	J8	28
Hankinson, N.D., U.S.	C9	111
Hanna, Alta., Can.	D5	68
Hanna, Wy., U.S.	E6	127
Hanna City, Il., U.S.	C4	90
Hannahville Indian Reservation, Mi., U.S.	C3	99
Hannibal, Mo., U.S.	B6	102
Hannover, Ger.	C9	8
Ha Noi, Viet.	D8	34
Hanover, Ont., Can.	C3	73
Hanover, Il., U.S.	A3	90
Hanover, In., U.S.	G7	91
Hanover, Ks., U.S.	C7	93
Hanover, Ma., U.S.	B6	98
Hanover, Mn., U.S.	m11	100
Hanover, N.H., U.S.	C2	106
Hanover, Pa., U.S.	G8	115
Hanover, co., Va., U.S.	C5	123
Hanover Park, Il., U.S.	k8	90
Hansen, Id., U.S.	G4	89
Hansford, co., Tx., U.S.	A2	120
Hanson, Ma., U.S.	B6	98
Hanson, co., S.D., U.S.	D8	118
Hantsport, N.S., Can.	D5	71
Hanzhong, China	E8	26
Haparanda, Swe.	D15	6
Hapeville, Ga., U.S.	C2	87
Happy Valley, N.M., U.S.	E5	108
Happy Valley-Goose Bay, Newf., Can.	B1	72
Harahan, La., U.S.	k11	95
Haralson, co., Ga., U.S.	C1	87
Harare, Zimb.	E6	44
Ḥarash, Bi'r al-, well, Libya	C10	42
Harbeson, De., U.S.	F4	85
Harbin, China	B12	26
Harbor, Or., U.S.	E2	114
Harbor Beach, Mi., U.S.	E8	99
Harborcreek, Pa., U.S.	B2	115
Harbor Springs, Mi., U.S.	C6	99
Harbour Breton, Newf., Can.	E4	72
Harbour Grace, Newf., Can.	E5	72
Harcuvar Mountains, mts., Az., U.S.	D2	80
Harda, India	I7	38
Hardangerfjorden, Nor.	F5	6
Hardee, co., Fl., U.S.	E5	86
Hardeeville, S.C., U.S.	G5	117
Hardeman, co., Tn., U.S.	B2	119
Hardeman, co., Tx., U.S.	B3	120
Hardin, Il., U.S.	D3	90
Hardin, Mt., U.S.	E9	103
Hardin, co., Il., U.S.	F5	90
Hardin, co., Ia., U.S.	B4	92
Hardin, co., Ky., U.S.	C4	94
Hardin, co., Oh., U.S.	B2	112
Hardin, co., Tn., U.S.	B3	119
Hardin, co., Tx., U.S.	D5	120
Harding, co., N.M., U.S.	B5	108
Harding, co., S.D., U.S.	B2	118
Harding, Lake, res., U.S.	C4	78
Hardinsburg, Ky., U.S.	C3	94
Hardisty, Alta., Can.	C5	68
Hardwār, India	F8	38
Hardwick, Ga., U.S.	C3	87
Hardwick, Vt., U.S.	B4	122
Hardwood Ridge, mtn., Pa., U.S.	D11	115
Hardy, co., W.V., U.S.	B6	125
Hardy Lake, res., In., U.S.	G6	91
Hare Bay, Newf., Can.	D4	72
Hare Bay, b., Newf., Can.	C4	72
Harer, Eth.	G3	46
Harford, co., Md., U.S.	A5	97
Hargeysa, Som.	G3	46
Harihar, India	E3	37
Harīrūd (Tedžen), stm., Asia	J10	22
Harkers Island, N.C., U.S.	C6	110
Harlan, In., U.S.	B8	91
Harlan, Ia., U.S.	C2	92
Harlan, Ky., U.S.	D6	94
Harlan, co., Ky., U.S.	D6	94
Harlan, co., Ne., U.S.	D6	104
Harlan County Lake, res., Ne., U.S.	E6	104
Harlem, Fl., U.S.	F6	86
Harlem, Ga., U.S.	C4	87
Harlem, Mt., U.S.	B8	103
Harleyville, S.C., U.S.	E7	117
Harlingen, Neth.	B5	8
Harlingen, Tx., U.S.	F4	120
Harlow, Eng., U.K.	J13	7
Harlowton, Mt., U.S.	D7	103
Harmon, co., Ok., U.S.	C2	113
Harmon Creek, stm., W.V., U.S.	f8	125
Harmony, In., U.S.	E3	91
Harmony, Mn., U.S.	G6	100
Harmony, Pa., U.S.	E1	115
Harmony, R.I., U.S.	B3	116
Harnett, co., N.C., U.S.	B4	110
Harney, co., Or., U.S.	D7	114
Harney Lake, l., Fl., U.S.	D5	86
Harney Lake, l., Or., U.S.	D7	114
Harney Peak, mtn., S.D., U.S.	D2	118
Härnösand, Swe.	E11	6
Haro, Spain	C9	12
Haro Strait, strt., Wa., U.S.	A2	124
Harper, Lib.	H4	42
Harper, Ks., U.S.	E5	93
Harper, co., Ks., U.S.	E5	93
Harper, co., Ok., U.S.	A2	113
Harper, Mount, mtn., Ak., U.S.	C11	79
Harpers Ferry, W.V., U.S.	B7	125
Harpers Ferry National Historical Park, W.V., U.S.	B7	125
Harpersville, Al., U.S.	B3	78
Harpeth, stm., Tn., U.S.	A5	119
Harquahala Mountain, mtn., Az., U.S.	D2	80
Harquahala Mountains, mts., Az., U.S.	D2	80
Harrah, Ok., U.S.	B4	113
Harricana, stm., Can.	F17	66
Harriman, Tn., U.S.	D9	119
Harriman Reservoir, res., Vt., U.S.	F3	122
Harrington, De., U.S.	E3	85
Harrington Park, N.J., U.S.	h9	107
Harris, Mn., U.S.	E6	100
Harris, R.I., U.S.	D3	116
Harris, co., Ga., U.S.	D2	87
Harris, co., Tx., U.S.	E5	120
Harris, Lake, l., Fl., U.S.	D5	86
Harrisburg, Ar., U.S.	B5	81
Harrisburg, Il., U.S.	F5	90
Harrisburg, Or., U.S.	C3	114
Harrisburg, Pa., U.S.	F8	115
Harrisburg, S.D., U.S.	D9	118
Harrison, Ar., U.S.	A2	81
Harrison, Mi., U.S.	D6	99
Harrison, N.J., U.S.	k8	107
Harrison, N.Y., U.S.	h13	109
Harrison, Oh., U.S.	C1	112
Harrison, Tn., U.S.	h11	119
Harrison, co., In., U.S.	H5	91
Harrison, co., Ia., U.S.	C2	92
Harrison, co., Ky., U.S.	B5	94
Harrison, co., Ms., U.S.	E4	101
Harrison, co., Mo., U.S.	A3	102
Harrison, co., Oh., U.S.	B4	112
Harrison, co., Tx., U.S.	C5	120
Harrison, co., W.V., U.S.	B4	125
Harrison, Cape, c., Newf., Can.	g10	72
Harrison Bay, b., Ak., U.S.	A9	79
Harrisonburg, Va., U.S.	B4	123
Harrison Hot Springs, B.C., Can.	f14	69
Harrison Lake, l., B.C., Can.	E7	69
Harrisonville, Mo., U.S.	C3	102
Harriston, Ont., Can.	D4	73
Harristown, Il., U.S.	D4	90
Harrisville, R.I., U.S.	B2	116
Harrisville, Ut., U.S.	B4	121
Harrisville, W.V., U.S.	B3	125
Harrodsburg, Ky., U.S.	C5	94
Harrogate, Eng., U.K.	G11	7
Harrow, Ont., Can.	E2	73
Harry S. Truman Reservoir, res., Mo., U.S.	C4	102
Harry Strunk Lake, res., Ne., U.S.	D5	104
Harstad, Nor.	B11	6
Hart, Mi., U.S.	E4	99
Hart, Tx., U.S.	B1	120
Hart, co., Ga., U.S.	B4	87
Hart, co., Ky., U.S.	C4	94
Hart, Lake, l., Fl., U.S.	D5	86
Hartford, Al., U.S.	D4	78
Hartford, Ar., U.S.	B1	81
Hartford, Ct., U.S.	B5	84
Hartford, Il., U.S.	E3	90
Hartford, Ia., U.S.	C4	92
Hartford, Ky., U.S.	C3	94
Hartford, Mi., U.S.	F4	99
Hartford, S.D., U.S.	D9	118
Hartford, Vt., U.S.	D4	122
Hartford, Wi., U.S.	E5	126
Hartford, co., Ct., U.S.	B4	84
Hartford City, In., U.S.	D7	91
Hartington, Ne., U.S.	B8	104
Hart Lake, l., Or., U.S.	E7	114
Hartland, N.B., Can.	C2	71
Hartland, Me., U.S.	D3	96
Hartland, Wi., U.S.	E5	126
Hartland Point, c., Eng., U.K.	J8	7
Hartlepool, Eng., U.K.	G11	7
Hartley, Ia., U.S.	A2	92
Hartley, co., Tx., U.S.	B1	120
Hartney, Man., Can.	E1	70
Hartselle, Al., U.S.	A3	78
Hartshorne, Ok., U.S.	C6	113
Hartsville, S.C., U.S.	C7	117
Hartsville, Tn., U.S.	A5	119
Hartville, Oh., U.S.	B4	112
Hartwell, Ga., U.S.	B4	87
Hartwell Lake, res., U.S.	B1	117
Hārūnābād, Pak.	F5	38
Hārūt, stm., Afg.	C1	36
Harvard, Il., U.S.	A5	90
Harvard, Ne., U.S.	D7	104
Harvard, Mount, mtn., Co., U.S.	C4	83
Harvey, Il., U.S.	B6	90
Harvey, La., U.S.	E5	95
Harvey, Mi., U.S.	B3	99
Harvey, N.D., U.S.	B6	111
Harvey, co., Ks., U.S.	D6	93
Harvey Lake, res., Pa., U.S.	m16	115
Harveys Creek, stm., Pa., U.S.	n16	115
Harwich, Eng., U.K.	J14	7
Harwich Port, Ma., U.S.	C7	98
Harwinton, Ct., U.S.	B3	84
Haryana, state, India	F7	38
Harz, mts., Ger.	D10	8
Hasbrouck Heights, N.J., U.S.	h8	107
Haskell, Ar., U.S.	C3	81
Haskell, Ok., U.S.	B6	113
Haskell, Tx., U.S.	C3	120
Haskell, co., Ks., U.S.	E3	93
Haskell, co., Ok., U.S.	B6	113
Haskell, co., Tx., U.S.	C3	120
Haskovo, Bul.	H9	16
Hassan, India	F4	37
Hassayampa, stm., Az., U.S.	D3	80
Hasselt, Bel.	E5	8
Hassfurt, Ger.	E10	8
Hässleholm, Swe.	H9	6
Hastings, Ont., Can.	C7	73
Hastings, N.Z.	C6	52
Hastings, Eng., U.K.	K13	7
Hastings, Mi., U.S.	F5	99
Hastings, Mn., U.S.	F6	100
Hastings, Ne., U.S.	D7	104
Hastings, Pa., U.S.	E4	115
Hastings-on-Hudson, N.Y., U.S.	h13	109
Hatch, N.M., U.S.	E2	108
Hatchet Lake, N.S., Can.	E6	71
Hatchie, stm., Tn., U.S.	B2	119
Hatchineha, Lake, l., Fl., U.S.	D5	86
Hat Creek, stm., S.D., U.S.	E2	118
Hatfield, In., U.S.	I3	91
Hatfield, Pa., U.S.	F11	115
Hāthras, India	G8	38
Ha Tinh, Viet.	E8	34
Hat Mountain, mtn., Az., U.S.	E3	80
Hatteras, N.C., U.S.	B7	110

Name	Map Ref	Page
Hatteras, Cape, c., N.C., U.S.	B7	110
Hatteras Inlet, b., N.C., U.S.	B7	110
Hattiesburg, Ms., U.S.	D4	101
Hatton, N.D., U.S.	B8	111
Hat Yai, Thai.	K6	34
Haubstadt, In., U.S.	H2	91
Haugesund, Nor.	G5	6
Haughton, La., U.S.	B2	95
Haukivuori, Fin.	E16	6
Hauser, Or., U.S.	D2	114
Haut, Isle au, i., Me., U.S.	D4	96
Haut Atlas, mts., Mor.	B4	42
Hauula, Hi., U.S.	B4	88
Havana, Fl., U.S.	B2	86
Havana, Il., U.S.	C3	90
Havana see La Habana, Cuba	C6	64
Havant, Eng., U.K.	K12	7
Havasu, Lake, res., U.S.	C1	80
Havasupai Indian Reservation, Az., U.S.	A3	80
Havelberg, Ger.	C12	8
Havelock, Ont., Can.	C7	73
Havelock, N.C., U.S.	C6	110
Haven, Ks., U.S.	E6	93
Haverford [Township], Pa., U.S.	o20	115
Haverhill, Ma., U.S.	A5	98
Hāveri, India	E3	37
Haverstraw, N.Y., U.S.	D7	109
Haviland, Ks., U.S.	E4	93
Havířov, Czech.	F18	8
Havre, Mt., U.S.	B7	103
Havre de Grace, Md., U.S.	A5	97
Havre North, Mt., U.S.	B7	103
Haw, stm., N.C., U.S.	B3	110
Hawaii, co., Hi., U.S.	D6	88
Hawaii, state, U.S.	C5	88
Hawaii, i., Hi., U.S.	D6	88
Hawaiian Islands, is., Hi., U.S.	m14	88
Hawaii Volcanoes National Park, Hi., U.S.	D6	88
Hawarden, Ia., U.S.	A1	92
Hawesville, Ky., U.S.	C3	94
Hawi, Hi., U.S.	C6	88
Hawick, Scot., U.K.	F10	7
Hawke Bay, b., N.Z.	C6	52
Hawkesbury, Ont., Can.	B10	73
Hawkesbury Island, i., B.C., Can.	C3	69
Hawkins, co., Tn., U.S.	C11	119
Hawkinsville, Ga., U.S.	D3	87
Hawley, Mn., U.S.	D2	100
Hawley, Pa., U.S.	D11	115
Haworth, N.J., U.S.	h9	107
Haw River, N.C., U.S.	A3	110
Hawthorne, Ca., U.S.	n12	82
Hawthorne, Fl., U.S.	C4	86
Hawthorne, Nv., U.S.	E3	105
Hawthorne, N.J., U.S.	B4	107
Hawthorne, N.Y., U.S.	g13	109
Haxtun, Co., U.S.	A8	83
Hay, Austl.	F8	50
Hay, stm., Austl.	D7	50
Hay, stm., Can.	E9	66
Hay, Cape, c., N.W. Ter., Can.	B10	66
Hayange, Fr.	C13	10
Hayden, Az., U.S.	E5	80
Hayden, Co., U.S.	A3	83
Hayden Lake, l., Id., U.S.	B2	89
Hayes, La., U.S.	D3	95
Hayes, co., Ne., U.S.	D4	104
Hayes, stm., Man., Can.	B5	70
Hayes, Mount, mtn., Ak., U.S.	C10	79
Hayfield, Mn., U.S.	G6	100
Hayford Peak, mtn., Nv., U.S.	G6	105
Haymock Lake, l., Me., U.S.	B3	96
Haynesville, La., U.S.	B2	95
Hayneville, Al., U.S.	C3	78
Hayrabolu, Tur.	H11	16
Hay River, N.W. Ter., Can.	D9	66
Hays, Ks., U.S.	D4	93
Hays, N.C., U.S.	A1	110
Hays, co., Tx., U.S.	D3	120
Hays Canyon Peak, mtn., Nv., U.S.	B2	105
Hay Springs, Ne., U.S.	B3	104
Haystack Mountain, mtn., Nv., U.S.	B6	105
Haysville, Ks., U.S.	g12	93
Hayti, Mo., U.S.	E8	102
Hayti Heights, Mo., U.S.	E8	102
Hayward, Ca., U.S.	h8	82
Hayward, Wi., U.S.	B2	126
Haywood, co., N.C., U.S.	f9	110
Haywood, co., Tn., U.S.	B2	119
Hazard, Ky., U.S.	C6	94
Hazardville, Ct., U.S.	B5	84
Hazārībāgh, India	I11	38
Hazel Crest, Il., U.S.	k9	90
Hazel Dell, Wa., U.S.	D3	124
Hazel Green, Al., U.S.	A3	78
Hazel Green, Wi., U.S.	F3	126
Hazel Park, Mi., U.S.	p15	99
Hazelton Pyramid, mtn., Wy., U.S.	B5	127
Hazelwood, N.C., U.S.	f10	110
Hazen, Ar., U.S.	C4	81
Hazen, N.D., U.S.	B4	111
Hazen Bay, b., Ak., U.S.	C6	79
Hazlehurst, Ga., U.S.	E4	87
Hazlehurst, Ms., U.S.	D3	101
Hazlet, N.J., U.S.	C4	107
Hazleton, Ia., U.S.	B6	92
Hazleton, Pa., U.S.	E10	115
Head Harbor Island, i., Me., U.S.	D5	96
Headland, Al., U.S.	D4	78
Headley, Mount, mtn., Mt., U.S.	C1	103
Healdsburg, Ca., U.S.	C2	82
Healdton, Ok., U.S.	C4	113
Healy, Ak., U.S.	C10	79
Heard, co., Ga., U.S.	C1	87
Hearne, Tx., U.S.	D4	120
Hearst, Ont., Can.	o19	73
Heart, stm., N.D., U.S.	C3	111
Heart Butte Dam, N.D., U.S.	C4	111
Heart Lake, l., Wy., U.S.	B2	127
Heart's Content, Newf., Can.	E5	72
Heath, Oh., U.S.	B3	112
Heath Springs, S.C., U.S.	B6	117
Heavener, Ok., U.S.	C7	113
Hebbronville, Tx., U.S.	F3	120
Hebei, prov., China	D10	26
Heber, Az., U.S.	C5	80
Heber City, Ut., U.S.	C4	121
Heber Springs, Ar., U.S.	B3	81
Hébertville, Que., Can.	A6	74
Hebgen Lake, res., Mt., U.S.	F5	103
Hebrides, is., Scot., U.K.	D6	4
Hebron, N.S., Can.	F3	71
Hebron, Il., U.S.	A5	90
Hebron, In., U.S.	B3	91
Hebron, Ky., U.S.	h13	94
Hebron, Md., U.S.	D6	97
Hebron, Ne., U.S.	D8	104
Hebron, N.D., U.S.	C3	111
Hebron, Oh., U.S.	C3	112
Hebron see Al-Khalīl, Jord.	D4	40
Hecate Strait, strt., B.C., Can.	C2	69
Heceta Island, i., Ak., U.S.	n23	79
Hechi, China	B9	34
Hechingen, Ger.	G8	8
Hechuan, China	E8	26
Hecla Island, i., Man., Can.	D3	70
Hector, Mn., U.S.	F4	100
Hedemora, Swe.	F10	6
He Devil, mtn., Id., U.S.	D2	89
Hedrick, Ia., U.S.	C5	92
Heerenveen, Neth.	C5	8
Heerlen, Neth.	E5	8
Ḥefa (Haifa), Isr.	C4	40
Hefei, China	D6	28
Heflin, Al., U.S.	B4	78
Hefner, Lake, res., Ok., U.S.	B4	113
Hegang, China	B13	26
Hegins, Pa., U.S.	E9	115
Heide, Ger.	A9	8
Heidelberg, Ger.	F8	8
Heidelberg, Ms., U.S.	D5	101
Heidenheim, Ger.	F10	8
Heidenreichstein, Aus.	G15	8
Heidrick, Ky., U.S.	D6	94
Heihe (Naquka), China	E14	38
Heilbron, S. Afr.	G5	44
Heilbronn, Ger.	F9	8
Heiligenstadt, Ger.	D10	8
Heilongjiang, prov., China	B12	26
Heilongjiang (Amur), stm., Asia	G19	24
Heinola, Fin.	F16	6
Hejaz see Al-Ḥijāz, reg., Sau. Ar.	C2	46
Hekla, vol., Ice.	C4	4
Hekou, China	C7	34
Helena, Al., U.S.	B3	78
Helena, Ar., U.S.	C5	81
Helena, Ga., U.S.	D4	87
Helena, Mt., U.S.	D4	103
Helena, Ok., U.S.	A3	113
Helensburgh, Scot., U.K.	E8	7
Helgoland, i., Ger.	A7	8
Helgoländer Bucht, b., Ger.	A8	8
Hellam, Pa., U.S.	G8	115
Hellertown, Pa., U.S.	E11	115
Hellesylt, Nor.	E6	6
Hellín, Spain	G10	12
Hells Canyon, val., U.S.	B10	114
Hells Canyon National Recreation Area, U.S.	B10	114
Hell-Ville, Madag.	D9	44
Helmand, stm., Asia	C2	36
Helmond, Neth.	D5	8
Helmsdale, Scot., U.K.	C9	7
Helmstedt, Ger.	C10	8
Helotes, Tx., U.S.	h7	120
Helper, Ut., U.S.	D5	121
Helsingborg, Swe.	H9	6
Helsingfors see Helsinki, Fin.	F15	6
Helsingør (Elsinore), Den.	H9	6
Helsinki (Helsingfors), Fin.	F15	6
Hematite, Mo., U.S.	C7	102
Hemet, Ca., U.S.	F5	82
Hemingford, Ne., U.S.	B2	104
Hemingway, S.C., U.S.	D9	117
Hemlock, Mi., U.S.	E6	99
Hemlock Reservoir, res., Ct., U.S.	E2	84
Hemmingford, Que., Can.	D4	74
Hemphill, Tx., U.S.	D6	120
Hemphill, co., Tx., U.S.	B2	120
Hempstead, N.Y., U.S.	n15	109
Hempstead, Tx., U.S.	D4	120
Hempstead, co., Ar., U.S.	D2	81
Hemse, Swe.	H12	6
Henagar, Al., U.S.	A4	78
Henan, prov., China	E9	26
Henderson, Ky., U.S.	C2	94
Henderson, La., U.S.	D4	95
Henderson, Mn., U.S.	F5	100
Henderson, Ne., U.S.	D8	104
Henderson, Nv., U.S.	G7	105
Henderson, N.C., U.S.	A4	110
Henderson, Tn., U.S.	B3	119
Henderson, Tx., U.S.	C5	120
Henderson, co., Il., U.S.	C3	90
Henderson, co., Ky., U.S.	C2	94
Henderson, co., N.C., U.S.	f10	110
Henderson, co., Tn., U.S.	B3	119
Henderson, co., Tx., U.S.	C5	120
Henderson's Point, Ms., U.S.	g7	101
Hendersonville, N.C., U.S.	f10	110
Hendersonville, Tn., U.S.	A5	119
Hendricks, Mn., U.S.	F2	100
Hendricks, co., In., U.S.	E4	91
Hendry, co., Fl., U.S.	F5	86
Hengelo, Neth.	C6	8
Hengshan, China	H1	28
Hengyang, China	F9	26
Henlawson, W.V., U.S.	n12	125
Henlopen, Cape, c., De., U.S.	E5	85
Hennef, Ger.	E7	8
Hennepin, co., Mn., U.S.	E5	100
Hennessey, Ok., U.S.	A4	113
Henniker, N.H., U.S.	D3	106
Henning, Mn., U.S.	D3	100
Henning, Tn., U.S.	B2	119
Henrico, co., Va., U.S.	C5	123
Henrietta, N.C., U.S.	B1	110
Henrietta, Tx., U.S.	C3	120
Henrietta Maria, Cape, c., Ont., Can.	n19	73
Henry, Il., U.S.	B4	90
Henry, co., Al., U.S.	D4	78
Henry, co., Ga., U.S.	C2	87
Henry, co., Il., U.S.	B3	90
Henry, co., In., U.S.	E7	91
Henry, co., Ia., U.S.	C6	92
Henry, co., Ky., U.S.	B4	94
Henry, co., Mo., U.S.	C4	102
Henry, co., Oh., U.S.	A1	112
Henry, co., Tn., U.S.	A3	119
Henry, co., Va., U.S.	D3	123
Henry, Mount, mtn., Mt., U.S.	B1	103
Henryetta, Ok., U.S.	B6	113
Henry Kater, Cape, c., N.W. Ter., Can.	C19	66
Henrys Fork, stm., U.S.	E2	127
Henryville, Que., Can.	D4	74
Henryville, In., U.S.	G6	91
Hensall, Ont., Can.	D3	73
Henzada, Mya.	F3	34
Hephzibah, Ga., U.S.	C4	87
Heppner, Or., U.S.	B7	114
Hepu (Lianzhou), China	D10	34
Herāt, Afg.	C1	36
Herbes, Isle aux, i., Al., U.S.	E1	78
Herbignac, Fr.	E4	10
Herculaneum, Mo., U.S.	C7	102
Hereford, Eng., U.K.	I10	7
Hereford, Md., U.S.	A4	97
Hereford, Tx., U.S.	B1	120
Hereford Inlet, b., N.J., U.S.	E3	107
Herford, Ger.	C8	8
Herington, Ks., U.S.	D7	93
Herkimer, N.Y., U.S.	B6	109
Herkimer, co., N.Y., U.S.	B5	109
Hermann, Mo., U.S.	C6	102
Hermano Peak, mtn., Co., U.S.	D2	83
Hermantown, Mn., U.S.	D6	100
Hermanus, S. Afr.	H3	44
Herminie, Pa., U.S.	F2	115
Hermiston, Or., U.S.	B7	114
Hermitage, Newf., Can.	E4	72
Hermitage, Ar., U.S.	D3	81
Hermitage Bay, b., Newf., Can.	E3	72
Hermosillo, Mex.	C4	62
Hernando, Fl., U.S.	D4	86
Hernando, Ms., U.S.	A4	101
Hernando, co., Fl., U.S.	D4	86
Herndon, Va., U.S.	B5	123
Herning, Den.	H7	6
Heron Lake, Mn., U.S.	G3	100
Herrera del Duque, Spain	F6	12
Herrera de Pisuerga, Spain	C7	12
Herrin, Il., U.S.	F4	90
Herring Bay, b., Md., U.S.	C4	97
Herring Cove, N.S., Can.	E6	71
Herrington Lake, res., Ky., U.S.	C5	94
Herscher, Il., U.S.	B5	90
Hershey, Pa., U.S.	F8	115
Hertford, N.C., U.S.	A6	110
Hertford, co., N.C., U.S.	A5	110
Hervás, Spain	E6	12
Hesdin, Fr.	B9	10
Hesperia, Ca., U.S.	E5	82
Hesperia, Mi., U.S.	E4	99
Hesperus Mountain, mtn., Co., U.S.	D2	83
Hesston, Ks., U.S.	D6	93
Hetian, China	B8	38
Hettinger, N.D., U.S.	D3	111
Hettinger, co., N.D., U.S.	C3	111
Heyburn, Id., U.S.	G5	89
Heyworth, Il., U.S.	C5	90
Hialeah, Fl., U.S.	G6	86
Hiawatha, Ia., U.S.	B6	92
Hiawatha, Ks., U.S.	C8	93
Hibbing, Mn., U.S.	C6	100
Hickam Air Force Base, mil., Hi., U.S.	g10	88
Hickman, Ky., U.S.	f8	94
Hickman, Ne., U.S.	D9	104
Hickman, co., Ky., U.S.	f8	94
Hickman, co., Tn., U.S.	B4	119
Hickory, N.C., U.S.	B1	110
Hickory, co., Mo., U.S.	D4	102
Hicksville, N.Y., U.S.	E7	109
Hicksville, Oh., U.S.	A1	112
Hico, Tx., U.S.	D3	120
Hico, W.V., U.S.	C3	125
Hidaka-sammyaku, mts., Japan	q20	30a
Hidalgo, Mex.	E10	62
Hidalgo, Tx., U.S.	F3	120
Hidalgo, co., N.M., U.S.	F1	108
Hidalgo, co., Tx., U.S.	F3	120
Hidalgo del Parral, Mex.	D7	62
Hiddenite, N.C., U.S.	B1	110
Hieroglyphic Mountains, mts., Az., U.S.	k8	80
Hierro, i., Spain	C2	42
Higashiōsaka, Japan	H8	30
Higbee, Mo., U.S.	B5	102
Higganum, Ct., U.S.	D5	84
Higgins Lake, l., Mi., U.S.	D6	99
Higgins Millpond, res., Md., U.S.	C6	97
Higginsville, Mo., U.S.	B4	102
High Bridge, N.J., U.S.	B3	107
High Falls Reservoir, res., Wi., U.S.	C5	126
High Island, i., Mi., U.S.	C5	99
Highland, Il., U.S.	E4	90
Highland, In., U.S.	A3	91
Highland, Ks., U.S.	C8	93
Highland, Mi., U.S.	o14	99
Highland, N.Y., U.S.	D7	109
Highland, Wi., U.S.	E3	126
Highland, co., Oh., U.S.	C2	112
Highland, co., Va., U.S.	B3	123
Highland Lake, l., Me., U.S.	g7	96
Highland Lakes, N.J., U.S.	A4	107
Highland Park, Il., U.S.	A6	90
Highland Park, Mi., U.S.	p15	99
Highland Park, Tx., U.S.	n10	120
Highland Peak, mtn., Ca., U.S.	C4	82
Highland Point, c., Fl., U.S.	G5	86
Highlands, N.J., U.S.	C5	107
Highlands, N.C., U.S.	f9	110
Highlands, Tx., U.S.	r14	120
Highlands, co., Fl., U.S.	E5	86
Highland Springs, Va., U.S.	C5	123
High Level, Alta., Can.	F7	68
Highmore, S.D., U.S.	C6	118
High Point, N.C., U.S.	B2	110
High Prairie, Alta., Can.	B2	68
High Ridge, Mo., U.S.	g12	102
High River, Alta., Can.	D4	68
Highrock Lake, l., Man., Can.	B1	70
High Rock Lake, res., N.C., U.S.	B2	110
High Spire, Pa., U.S.	F8	115
High Springs, Fl., U.S.	C4	86
Hightstown, N.J., U.S.	C3	107
Highwood, Il., U.S.	A6	90
Highwood Baldy, mtn., Mt., U.S.	C6	103
Highwood Mountains, mts., Mt., U.S.	C6	103
Higuerote, Ven.	B9	58
Higüey, Dom. Rep.	E13	64
Híjar, Spain	D11	12
Hikari, Japan	I4	30
Hikone, Japan	G9	30
Hiko Range, mts., Nv., U.S.	F6	105
Hilbert, Wi., U.S.	D5	126
Hildale, Ut., U.S.	F3	121
Hilden, N.S., Can.	D6	71
Hildesheim, Ger.	C9	8
Hill, co., Mt., U.S.	B6	103
Hill, co., Tx., U.S.	D4	120
Hill City, Ks., U.S.	C4	93
Hill City, S.D., U.S.	D2	118
Hillcrest, Il., U.S.	B4	90
Hillcrest Heights, Md., U.S.	C4	97
Hilliard, Fl., U.S.	B5	86
Hilliard, Oh., U.S.	k10	112
Hill Island Lake, l., N.W. Ter., Can.	D11	66
Hill Lake, l., Ar., U.S.	h10	81
Hills, Ia., U.S.	C6	92
Hills, Mn., U.S.	G2	100
Hillsboro, Il., U.S.	D4	90
Hillsboro, Ks., U.S.	D6	93
Hillsboro, Mo., U.S.	C7	102
Hillsboro, N.H., U.S.	D3	106
Hillsboro, N.D., U.S.	B8	111
Hillsboro, Oh., U.S.	C2	112
Hillsboro, Or., U.S.	B4	114
Hillsboro, Tx., U.S.	C4	120
Hillsboro, Wi., U.S.	E3	126
Hillsboro Canal, Fl., U.S.	F6	86
Hillsborough, N.B., Can.	D5	71
Hillsborough, N.C., U.S.	A3	110
Hillsborough, co., Fl., U.S.	E4	86
Hillsborough, co., N.H., U.S.	E3	106
Hillsborough Bay, b., P.E.I., Can.	C6	71
Hillsburgh, Ont., Can.	D4	73
Hills Creek Lake, res., Or., U.S.	D4	114
Hillsdale, Mi., U.S.	G6	99
Hillsdale, N.J., U.S.	g8	107
Hillsdale, co., Mi., U.S.	G6	99
Hillside, N.J., U.S.	k8	107
Hillsville, Pa., U.S.	D1	115
Hillsville, Va., U.S.	D2	123
Hilo, Hi., U.S.	D6	88
Hilo Bay, b., Hi., U.S.	D6	88
Hilton, N.Y., U.S.	B3	109
Hilton Head Island, S.C., U.S.	G6	117
Hilton Head Island, i., S.C., U.S.	G6	117
Hilversum, Neth.	C5	8
Himachal Pradesh, ter., India	E7	38
Himalayas, mts., Asia	F10	38
Himeji, Japan	H7	30
Himi, Japan	F9	30
Hims (Homs), Syria	B5	40
Hinchinbrook Island, i., Austl.	C9	50
Hinchinbrook Island, i., Ak., U.S.	g18	79
Hinckley, Il., U.S.	B5	90
Hinckley, Mn., U.S.	D6	100
Hinckley, Ut., U.S.	D3	121
Hinckley Reservoir, res., N.Y., U.S.	B5	109
Hindaun, India	G7	38
Hindman, Ky., U.S.	C7	94
Hinds, co., Ms., U.S.	C3	101
Hindu Kush, mts., Asia	B4	38
Hindupur, India	F4	37
Hines, Or., U.S.	D7	114
Hinesville, Ga., U.S.	E5	87
Hinganghāt, India	B5	37
Hingham, Ma., U.S.	B6	98
Hingham Bay, b., Ma., U.S.	g12	98
Hingoli, India	C4	37
Hinojosa del Duque, Spain	G6	12
Hinsdale, Il., U.S.	k9	90
Hinsdale, N.H., U.S.	E2	106
Hinsdale, co., Co., U.S.	D3	83
Hinton, Alta., Can.	C2	68
Hinton, Ia., U.S.	B1	92
Hinton, Ok., U.S.	B3	113
Hinton, W.V., U.S.	D4	125
Hirado, Japan	I2	30
Hīrākud, res., India	J10	38
Hiram, Ga., U.S.	C2	87
Hiram, Oh., U.S.	A4	112
Hirara, Japan	G12	26
Hiratsuka, Japan	G12	30
Hirosaki, Japan	B13	30
Hiroshima, Japan	H5	30
Hirson, Fr.	C11	10
Hisār, India	F6	38
Hispaniola, i., N.A.	E12	64
Hita, Japan	I3	30
Hitachi, Japan	F13	30
Hitchcock, Tx., U.S.	r14	120
Hitchcock, co., Ne., U.S.	D4	104
Hitchcock Lake, Ct., U.S.	C4	84
Hitoyoshi, Japan	J3	30
Hitra, i., Nor.	E7	6
Hiwassee, stm., Tn., U.S.	D9	119
Hiwassee Lake, res., N.C., U.S.	f8	110
Hjørring, Den.	H7	6
Ho, Ghana	G6	42
Hoa Binh, Viet.	D8	34
Hoagland, In., U.S.	C8	91
Hoback, stm., Wy., U.S.	C2	127
Hobart, Austl.	H9	50
Hobart, In., U.S.	A3	91
Hobart, Ok., U.S.	B2	113
Hobbs, N.M., U.S.	E6	108
Hobe Sound, Fl., U.S.	E6	86
Hobo, Col.	F5	58
Hoboken, N.J., U.S.	k8	107
Höchstadt an der Aisch, Ger.	F10	8
Hockessin, De., U.S.	A3	85
Hocking, co., Oh., U.S.	C3	112
Hocking, stm., Oh., U.S.	C3	112
Hockley, co., Tx., U.S.	C1	120
Hodgeman, co., Ks., U.S.	D4	93
Hodgenville, Ky., U.S.	C4	94
Hodges Village Reservoir, res., Ma., U.S.	B4	98
Hódmezővásárhely, Hung.	I20	8
Hodna, Chott el, l., Alg.	J16	12
Hodonín, Czech.	G17	8
Hof, Ger.	E11	8
Hoffman Estates, Il., U.S.	h8	90
Hofgeismar, Ger.	D9	8
Hofheim in Unterfranken, Ger.	E10	8
Hofors, Swe.	F11	6
Hōfu, Japan	H4	30
Hogansville, Ga., U.S.	C2	87
Hogback Mountain, mtn., Mt., U.S.	F4	103
Hog Island, i., Fl., U.S.	C3	86
Hog Island, i., Mi., U.S.	C5	99
Hog Island, i., N.C., U.S.	B6	110
Hog Island, i., R.I., U.S.	D5	116
Hog Island, i., Va., U.S.	C7	123
Hoh, stm., Wa., U.S.	B1	124
Hohenau an der March, Aus.	G16	8
Hohenwald, Tn., U.S.	B4	119
Hohe Tauern, mts., Aus.	H12	8
Hoh Head, c., Wa., U.S.	B1	124
Hohhot, China	C9	26
Hohoe, Ghana	G5	42
Hōhoku, Japan	H3	30
Ho-Ho-Kus, N.J., U.S.	h8	107
Hoh Xil Shan, mts., China	C13	38
Hoi An, Viet.	G10	34
Hoisington, Ks., U.S.	D5	93
Hokah, Mn., U.S.	G7	100
Hoke, co., N.C., U.S.	B3	110
Hokes Bluff, Al., U.S.	B4	78
Hokitika, N.Z.	E3	52
Hokkaidō, i., Japan	p20	30a
Holbrook, Az., U.S.	C5	80
Holbrook, Ma., U.S.	B5	98
Holcomb, Ks., U.S.	E3	93
Holden, Ma., U.S.	B4	98
Holden, Mo., U.S.	C4	102
Holden, W.V., U.S.	D2	125
Holdenville, Ok., U.S.	B5	113
Holdrege, Ne., U.S.	D6	104
Hole in the Mountain Peak, mtn., Nv., U.S.	C6	105
Holgate, Oh., U.S.	A1	112
Holguín, Cuba	D9	64
Höljes, Swe.	F9	6
Hollabrunn, Aus.	G16	8
Holladay, Ut., U.S.	C4	121
Holland, In., U.S.	H3	91
Holland, Mi., U.S.	F4	99
Holland, Oh., U.S.	A2	112
Holland, Tx., U.S.	D4	120
Hollandale, Ms., U.S.	B3	101
Holland Island, i., Md., U.S.	D5	97
Holland see Netherlands, ctry., Eur.	E9	4
Holland Point, c., Md., U.S.	C4	97
Holland Straits, strt., Md., U.S.	D5	97
Holley, N.Y., U.S.	B2	109
Holliday, Tx., U.S.	C3	120
Hollidaysburg, Pa., U.S.	F5	115
Hollins, Va., U.S.	C3	123
Hollis, Ok., U.S.	C2	113
Hollister, Ca., U.S.	D3	82
Hollister, Mo., U.S.	E4	102
Holliston, Ma., U.S.	B5	98
Holloman Air Force Base, mil., N.M., U.S.	E3	108
Hollow Rock, Tn., U.S.	A3	119
Hollowtop Mountain, mtn., Mt., U.S.	E4	103
Holly, Co., U.S.	C8	83
Holly, Mi., U.S.	F7	99
Holly Grove, Ar., U.S.	C4	81
Holly Hill, Fl., U.S.	C5	86
Holly Hill, S.C., U.S.	E7	117
Holly Pond, Al., U.S.	A3	78
Holly Ridge, N.C., U.S.	C5	110
Holly Shelter Swamp, sw., N.C., U.S.	C5	110
Holly Springs, Ga., U.S.	B2	87
Holly Springs, Ms., U.S.	A4	101
Holly Springs, N.C., U.S.	B4	110
Hollywood, Al., U.S.	A4	78
Hollywood, Fl., U.S.	F6	86
Hollywood, Md., U.S.	D4	97
Hollywood, S.C., U.S.	k11	117
Hollywood Indian Reservation, Fl., U.S.	r3	86
Holman Island, N.W. Ter., Can.	B9	66
Holmen, Wi., U.S.	E2	126
Holmes, co., Fl., U.S.	u16	86
Holmes, co., Ms., U.S.	B3	101
Holmes, co., Oh., U.S.	B4	112
Holmes, Mount, mtn., Wy., U.S.	B2	127
Holmes Reefs, rf., Austl.	C9	50
Holstebro, Den.	H7	6
Holstein, Ia., U.S.	B2	92
Holsteinsborg, Grnld.	C22	66
Holston, stm., Tn., U.S.	C11	119
Holston, Middle Fork, stm., Va., U.S.	f10	123
Holston High Knob, mtn., Tn., U.S.	C11	119
Holsworthy, Eng., U.K.	K8	7
Holt, Al., U.S.	B2	78
Holt, Mi., U.S.	F6	99
Holt, co., Mo., U.S.	A2	102
Holt, co., Ne., U.S.	B7	104
Holt Lake, res., Al., U.S.	B2	78
Holton, Ks., U.S.	C8	93
Holtville, Ca., U.S.	F6	82
Holualoa, Hi., U.S.	D6	88
Holy Cross, Mountain of the, mtn., Co., U.S.	B4	83
Holyhead, Wales, U.K.	H8	7
Holyoke, Co., U.S.	A8	83
Holyoke, Ma., U.S.	B2	98
Holyoke Range, hills, Ma., U.S.	B2	98

Name	Map Ref	Page
Holzminden, Ger.	D9	8
Hombori Tondo, mtn., Mali	E5	42
Homburg, Ger.	F7	8
Home Bay, b., N.W. Ter., Can.	C19	66
Homecroft, In., U.S.	m10	91
Homedale, Id., U.S.	F2	89
Home Hill, Austl.	C9	50
Homeland, Ga., U.S.	F4	87
Home Place, In., U.S.	E5	91
Homer, Ak., U.S.	D9	79
Homer, Ga., U.S.	B3	87
Homer, Il., U.S.	C6	90
Homer, La., U.S.	B2	95
Homer, Mi., U.S.	F6	99
Homer, N.Y., U.S.	C4	109
Homer City, Pa., U.S.	E3	115
Homerville, Ga., U.S.	E4	87
Homer Youngs Peak, mtn., Mt., U.S.	E3	103
Homestead, Fl., U.S.	G6	86
Homestead, Pa., U.S.	k14	115
Homestead Air Force Base, mil., Fl., U.S.	G6	86
Homestead National Monument of America, Ne., U.S.	D9	104
Homewood, Al., U.S.	g7	78
Homewood, Il., U.S.	B6	90
Homewood, Oh., U.S.	C1	112
Hominy, Ok., U.S.	A5	113
Hominy Creek, stm., Ok., U.S.	A5	113
Homme Dam, N.D., U.S.	A8	111
Homochitto, stm., Ms., U.S.	D2	101
Homosassa, Fl., U.S.	D4	86
Homs see Ḥimṣ, Syria	B5	40
Honaker, Va., U.S.	e10	123
Honaunau, Hi., U.S.	D6	88
Honda, Col.	E5	58
Hondo, Japan	J3	30
Hondo, Tx., U.S.	E3	120
Hondo, stm., N.A.	H15	62
Hondo, Rio, stm., N.M., U.S.	D4	108
Honduras, ctry., N.A.	G4	64
Honduras, Gulf of, b., N.A.	F4	64
Honea Path, S.C., U.S.	C3	117
Hønefoss, Nor.	F8	6
Honeoye Falls, N.Y., U.S.	C3	109
Honesdale, Pa., U.S.	C11	115
Honey Brook, Pa., U.S.	F10	115
Honey Grove, Tx., U.S.	C5	120
Honey Lake, l., Ca., U.S.	B3	82
Honeypot Glen, Ct., U.S.	C4	84
Honeyville, Ut., U.S.	B3	121
Hon Gai, Viet.	D9	34
Honga River, b., Md., U.S.	D5	97
Hongdong, China	D9	26
Honghu, China	F2	28
Hong Kong, dep., Asia	M3	28
Hongliuyuan, China	C6	26
Honguedo, Détroit d', strt., Que., Can.	G20	66
Hongze Hu, l., China	B7	28
Honiara, Sol.Is.	A11	50
Honjō, Japan	F12	30
Honningsvåg, Nor.	A15	6
Honokaa, Hi., U.S.	C6	88
Honolulu, Hi., U.S.	B4	88
Honolulu, co., Hi., U.S.	B3	88
Honolulu International Airport, Hi., U.S.	g10	88
Honomu, Hi., U.S.	D6	88
Honouliuli, Hi., U.S.	g9	88
Honshū, i., Japan	F10	30
Honuapo Bay, b., Hi., U.S.	D6	88
Hood, co., Tx., U.S.	C4	120
Hood, Mount, mtn., Or., U.S.	B5	114
Hood Canal, b., Wa., U.S.	B2	124
Hoodoo Peak, mtn., Wa., U.S.	A5	124
Hood River, Or., U.S.	B5	114
Hood River, co., Or., U.S.	B5	114
Hoodsport, Wa., U.S.	B2	124
Hoogeveen, Neth.	C6	8
Hooker, Ok., U.S.	e9	113
Hooker, co., Ne., U.S.	C4	104
Hook Head, c., Ire.	I6	7
Hooksett, N.H., U.S.	D4	106
Hoonah, Ak., U.S.	D12	79
Hoopa Valley Indian Reservation, Ca., U.S.	B2	82
Hooper, Ne., U.S.	C9	104
Hooper Bay, Ak., U.S.	C6	79
Hooper Islands, is., Md., U.S.	D5	97
Hooper Strait, strt., Md., U.S.	D5	97
Hoopes Reservoir, res., De., U.S.	A3	85
Hoopeston, Il., U.S.	C6	90
Hoorn, Neth.	C5	8
Hoosac Range, mts., U.S.	A1	98
Hoosic, stm., U.S.	C7	109
Hoosick Falls, N.Y., U.S.	C7	109
Hoover Dam, U.S.	G7	105
Hoover Reservoir, res., Oh., U.S.	B3	112
Hooverson Heights, W.V., U.S.	f8	125
Hopatcong, N.J., U.S.	B3	107
Hopatcong, Lake, l., N.J., U.S.	A3	107
Hope, B.C., Can.	E7	69
Hope, Ar., U.S.	D2	81
Hope, In., U.S.	F6	91
Hope, R.I., U.S.	D3	116
Hope, Ben, mtn., Scot., U.K.	C8	7
Hope, Point, c., Ak., U.S.	B6	79
Hopedale, Il., U.S.	C4	90
Hopedale, Ma., U.S.	B4	98
Hope Island, i., R.I., U.S.	E5	116
Hope Mills, N.C., U.S.	C4	110
Hopes Advance, Cap, c., Que., Can.	f13	74
Hopetown, S. Afr.	G4	44
Hope Valley, R.I., U.S.	E2	116
Hopewell, Va., U.S.	C5	123
Hopewell Junction, N.Y., U.S.	D7	109
Hopi Indian Reservation, Az., U.S.	A5	80
Hopkins, Mn., U.S.	n12	100
Hopkins, S.C., U.S.	D6	117
Hopkins, co., Ky., U.S.	C2	94
Hopkins, co., Tx., U.S.	C5	120
Hopkinsville, Ky., U.S.	D2	94
Hopkinton, Ia., U.S.	B6	92
Hopkinton, Ma., U.S.	B4	98
Hopkinton, R.I., U.S.	F1	116
Hopkinton Lake, res., N.H., U.S.	D3	106
Hopwood, Pa., U.S.	G2	115
Hoquiam, Wa., U.S.	C2	124
Horace, N.D., U.S.	C9	111
Horace Mountain, mtn., Ak., U.S.	B10	79
Horatio, Ar., U.S.	D1	81
Horgen, Switz.	E15	10
Horicon, Wi., U.S.	E5	126
Horine, Mo., U.S.	C7	102
Horlivka, Ukr.	H5	22
Hormuz, Strait of, strt., Asia	C6	46
Horn, Aus.	G15	8
Horn, Cape see Hornos, Cabo de, c., Chile	H3	56
Hornell, N.Y., U.S.	C3	109
Hornersville, Mo., U.S.	E7	102
Horn Island, i., Ms., U.S.	E5	101
Horn Island Pass, strt., Ms., U.S.	g8	101
Horn Lake, Ms., U.S.	A3	101
Hornos, Cabo de (Cape Horn), c., Chile	H3	56
Horn Plateau, plat., N.W. Ter., Can.	D9	66
Horqin Youyi Qianqi, China	B11	26
Horry, co., S.C., U.S.	D10	117
Horse, stm., Ct., U.S.	C6	84
Horse Cave, Ky., U.S.	C4	94
Horse Creek, stm., U.S.	E8	127
Horse Creek Reservoir, res., Co., U.S.	C7	83
Horsehead Lake, l., N.D., U.S.	B6	111
Horseheads, N.Y., U.S.	C4	109
Horse Heaven Hills, hills, Wa., U.S.	C6	124
Horsens, Den.	I7	6
Horse Peak, mtn., N.M., U.S.	D1	108
Horseshoe Bend, Id., U.S.	F2	89
Horseshoe Bend National Military Park, Al., U.S.	C4	78
Horseshoe Cove, b., Fl., U.S.	C3	86
Horseshoe Point, c., Fl., U.S.	C3	86
Horseshoe Reservoir, res., Az., U.S.	C4	80
Horsham, Austl.	G8	50
Horten, Nor.	G8	6
Horton, Ks., U.S.	C8	93
Hortonia, Lake, l., Vt., U.S.	D2	122
Hortonville, Wi., U.S.	D5	126
Hoschton, Ga., U.S.	B3	87
Hoshangābād, India	I7	38
Hoshiārpur, India	E6	38
Hospers, Ia., U.S.	A2	92
Hospet, India	E4	37
Hospitalet, Spain	D14	12
Hosta Butte, mtn., N.M., U.S.	B1	108
Hoste, Isla, i., Chile	H3	56
Hotchkiss, Co., U.S.	C3	83
Hot Creek Range, mts., Nv., U.S.	E5	105
Hot Creek Valley, val., Nv., U.S.	E5	105
Hoting, Swe.	D11	6
Hot Spring, co., Ar., U.S.	C2	81
Hot Springs, S.D., U.S.	D2	118
Hot Springs, co., Wy., U.S.	C4	127
Hot Springs National Park, Ar., U.S.	C2	81
Hot Springs National Park, Ar., U.S.	C2	81
Hot Springs Peak, mtn., Ca., U.S.	B3	82
Hot Springs Peak, mtn., Nv., U.S.	B4	105
Hottah Lake, l., N.W. Ter., Can.	C9	66
Houghton, Mi., U.S.	A2	99
Houghton, N.Y., U.S.	C2	109
Houghton, co., Mi., U.S.	B2	99
Houghton Lake, Mi., U.S.	D6	99
Houghton Lake, l., Mi., U.S.	D6	99
Houghton Lake Heights, Mi., U.S.	D6	99
Houlton, Me., U.S.	B5	96
Houma, China	D9	26
Houma, La., U.S.	E5	95
Housatonic, stm., U.S.	D3	84
House Springs, Mo., U.S.	g12	102
Houston, De., U.S.	E3	85
Houston, Mn., U.S.	G7	100
Houston, Ms., U.S.	B4	101
Houston, Mo., U.S.	D6	102
Houston, Pa., U.S.	F1	115
Houston, Tx., U.S.	E5	120
Houston, co., Al., U.S.	D4	78
Houston, co., Ga., U.S.	D3	87
Houston, co., Mn., U.S.	G7	100
Houston, co., Tn., U.S.	A4	119
Houston, co., Tx., U.S.	D5	120
Houston, stm., La., U.S.	D2	95
Houston, Lake, res., Tx., U.S.	r14	120
Houston Intercontinental Airport, Tx., U.S.	r14	120
Houtman Rocks, Austl.	E2	50
Houtzdale, Pa., U.S.	E5	115
Hovenweep National Monument, Ut., U.S.	F6	121
Hovmantorp, Swe.	H10	6
Howard, Ks., U.S.	E7	93
Howard, S.D., U.S.	C8	118
Howard, Wi., U.S.	D5	126
Howard, co., Ar., U.S.	C2	81
Howard, co., In., U.S.	C5	91
Howard, co., Ia., U.S.	A5	92
Howard, co., Md., U.S.	B4	97
Howard, co., Mo., U.S.	B5	102
Howard, co., Ne., U.S.	C7	104
Howard, co., Tx., U.S.	C2	120
Howard City, Mi., U.S.	E5	99
Howard Hanson Reservoir, res., Wa., U.S.	B4	124
Howard Lake, Mn., U.S.	E4	100
Howard Prairie Lake, res., Or., U.S.	E4	114
Howards Grove-Millersville, Wi., U.S.	E6	126
Howell, Mi., U.S.	F7	99
Howell, co., Mo., U.S.	E6	102
Howells, Ne., U.S.	C8	104
Howe Sound, strt., B.C., Can.	E6	69
Howick, Que., Can.	D4	74
Howland, Me., U.S.	C4	96
Howrah, India	I13	38
Hoxie, Ar., U.S.	A5	81
Hoxie, Ks., U.S.	C3	93
Höxter, Ger.	D9	8
Hoy, i., Scot., U.K.	C9	7
Høyanger, Nor.	F6	6
Hoyerswerda, Ger.	D14	8
Hoyos, Spain	E5	12
Hoyt Lakes, Mn., U.S.	C6	100
Hradec Králové, Czech.	E15	8
Hsilo, Tai.	L9	28
Hsinchu, Tai.	K9	28
Hsüehchia, Tai.	L9	28
Huacho, Peru	F3	54
Huachuca City, Az., U.S.	F5	80
Hua Hin, Thai.	H5	34
Huahua, stm., Nic.	G6	64
Huaian, China	B8	28
Huainan, China	C6	28
Huaiyang, China	B3	28
Huaiyin, China	B8	28
Huaiyuan, China	C6	28
Hualalai, vol., Hi., U.S.	D6	88
Hualapai Indian Reservation, Az., U.S.	B2	80
Hualapai Mountains, mts., Az., U.S.	C2	80
Hualapai Peak, mtn., Az., U.S.	B2	80
Hualien, Tai.	L10	28
Huallaga, stm., Peru	E3	54
Huallanca, Peru	E3	54
Huamachuco, Peru	E3	54
Huambo, Ang.	D3	44
Huancayo, Peru	F3	54
Huang (Yellow), stm., China	D10	26
Huangchuan, China	C4	28
Huangling, China	D8	26
Huangshi, China	E4	28
Huangyan, China	G10	28
Huánuco, Peru	E3	54
Huaraz, Peru	E3	54
Huascarán, Nevado, mtn., Peru	E3	54
Huasco, Chile	B2	56
Huatabampo, Mex.	D5	62
Huauchinango, Mex.	G10	62
Hubbard, Ia., U.S.	B4	92
Hubbard, Oh., U.S.	A5	112
Hubbard, Or., U.S.	B4	114
Hubbard, Tx., U.S.	D4	120
Hubbard, co., Mn., U.S.	C4	100
Hubbard Creek Lake, res., Tx., U.S.	C3	120
Hubbard Lake, l., Mi., U.S.	D7	99
Hubbardton, stm., Vt., U.S.	D2	122
Hubbell, Mi., U.S.	A2	99
Hubei, prov., China	E9	26
Hubli, India	E3	37
Huckleberry Mountain, mtn., Or., U.S.	D4	114
Huddersfield, Eng., U.K.	H11	7
Huddinge, Swe.	G11	6
Hudiksvall, Swe.	F11	6
Hudson, Que., Can.	D3	74
Hudson, Co., U.S.	A6	83
Hudson, Fl., U.S.	D4	86
Hudson, Il., U.S.	C5	90
Hudson, Ia., U.S.	B5	92
Hudson, Ma., U.S.	B4	98
Hudson, Mi., U.S.	G6	99
Hudson, N.H., U.S.	E4	106
Hudson, N.Y., U.S.	C7	109
Hudson, N.C., U.S.	B1	110
Hudson, Oh., U.S.	A4	112
Hudson, Wi., U.S.	D1	126
Hudson, Wy., U.S.	D4	127
Hudson, co., N.J., U.S.	B4	107
Hudson, stm., U.S.	E7	109
Hudson, Lake, res., Ok., U.S.	A6	113
Hudson Bay, b., Can.	D15	66
Hudson Falls, N.Y., U.S.	B7	109
Hudson Hope, B.C., Can.	A6	69
Hudson Lake, In., U.S.	A4	91
Hudson Strait, strt., Can.	D18	66
Hudsonville, Mi., U.S.	F5	99
Hudspeth, co., Tx., U.S.	o12	120
Hue, Viet.	F9	34
Huehuetenango, Guat.	G2	64
Huelma, Spain	H8	12
Huelva, Spain	H5	12
Huércal-Overa, Spain	H10	12
Huerfano, co., Co., U.S.	D5	83
Huerfano, stm., Co., U.S.	D6	83
Huerfano Mountain, mtn., N.M., U.S.	A2	108
Huesca, Spain	C11	12
Hueytown, Al., U.S.	g6	78
Huffakers, Nv., U.S.	D2	105
Hugh Butler Lake, res., Ne., U.S.	D5	104
Hughenden, Austl.	D8	50
Hughes, Ar., U.S.	C5	81
Hughes, co., Ok., U.S.	B5	113
Hughes, co., S.D., U.S.	C5	118
Hughes, North Fork, stm., W.V., U.S.	B3	125
Hughes, South Fork, stm., W.V., U.S.	B3	125
Hughesville, Md., U.S.	C4	97
Hughesville, Pa., U.S.	D8	115
Hugo, Co., U.S.	B7	83
Hugo, Mn., U.S.	m13	100
Hugo, Ok., U.S.	C6	113
Hugo Lake, res., Ok., U.S.	C6	113
Hugoton, Ks., U.S.	E2	93
Huidong, China	A7	34
Huila, Nevado del, mtn., Col.	F4	58
Huili, China	A7	34
Huinan, China	C12	26
Huittinen (Lauttakylä), Fin.	F14	6
Huitzuco [de los Figueroa], Mex.	H10	62
Huixtla, Mex.	J13	62
Huiyang (Huizhou), China	L3	28
Hulah Lake, res., Ok., U.S.	A5	113
Hulan, China	B12	26
Hulett, Wy., U.S.	B8	127
Hull, Que., Can.	D2	74
Hull, Ia., U.S.	A1	92
Hull, Ma., U.S.	B6	98
Hultsfred, Swe.	H10	6
Hulun Nur, l., China	B10	26
Humaitá, Braz.	E6	54
Humansville, Mo., U.S.	D4	102
Humber, stm., Eng., U.K.	H12	7
Humble, Tx., U.S.	E5	120
Humboldt, Az., U.S.	C3	80
Humboldt, Ia., U.S.	B3	92
Humboldt, Ks., U.S.	E8	93
Humboldt, Ne., U.S.	D10	104
Humboldt, Tn., U.S.	B3	119
Humboldt, co., Ca., U.S.	B2	82
Humboldt, co., Ia., U.S.	B3	92
Humboldt, co., Nv., U.S.	B3	105
Humboldt, stm., Nv., U.S.	C3	105
Humboldt Range, mts., Nv., U.S.	C3	105
Hummels Wharf, Pa., U.S.	E8	115
Humphrey, Ar., U.S.	C4	81
Humphrey, Ne., U.S.	C8	104
Humphreys, co., Ms., U.S.	B3	101
Humphreys, co., Tn., U.S.	A4	119
Humphreys, Mount, mtn., Ca., U.S.	D4	82
Humphreys Peak, mtn., Az., U.S.	B4	80
Hunan, prov., China	F9	26
Hundred Acre Pond, l., R.I., U.S.	E3	116
Hunedoara, Rom.	D6	16
Hünfeld, Ger.	E9	8
Hungary, ctry., Eur.	F11	4
Hungf'ou Hsü, i., Tai.	M10	28
Hŭngnam, N. Kor.	D12	26
Hungry Horse, Mt., U.S.	B2	103
Hungry Horse Reservoir, res., Mt., U.S.	B3	103
Hunsrück, mts., Ger.	F6	8
Hunt, co., Tx., U.S.	C4	120
Hunt, stm., R.I., U.S.	D4	116
Hunterdon, co., N.J., U.S.	B3	107
Hunter Island, i., Austl.	H8	50
Hunter Island, i., B.C., Can.	D3	69
Huntertown, In., U.S.	B7	91
Huntingburg, In., U.S.	H4	91
Huntingdon, Que., Can.	D3	74
Huntingdon, Pa., U.S.	F6	115
Huntingdon, Tn., U.S.	A3	119
Huntingdon, co., Pa., U.S.	F5	115
Hunting Island, i., S.C., U.S.	G7	117
Huntington, Ar., U.S.	B1	81
Huntington, In., U.S.	C7	91
Huntington, N.Y., U.S.	E7	109
Huntington, Tx., U.S.	D5	120
Huntington, Ut., U.S.	D5	121
Huntington, W.V., U.S.	C2	125
Huntington, co., In., U.S.	C6	91
Huntington Beach, Ca., U.S.	F4	82
Huntington Lake, res., In., U.S.	C7	91
Huntington Woods, Mi., U.S.	p15	99
Huntingtown, Md., U.S.	C4	97
Huntland, Tn., U.S.	B5	119
Huntley, Il., U.S.	A5	90
Hunt Mountain, mtn., Wy., U.S.	B5	127
Huntsville, Ont., Can.	B5	73
Huntsville, Al., U.S.	A3	78
Huntsville, Ar., U.S.	A2	81
Huntsville, Mo., U.S.	B5	102
Huntsville, Tn., U.S.	C9	119
Huntsville, Tx., U.S.	D5	120
Huon Gulf, b., Pap. N. Gui.	m16	50a
Hurao, China	B13	26
Hurd, Cape, c., Ont., Can.	B3	73
Hurley, Ms., U.S.	E5	101
Hurley, N.M., U.S.	E1	108
Hurley, N.Y., U.S.	D6	109
Hurley, Wi., U.S.	B3	126
Hurlock, Md., U.S.	C6	97
Huron, Oh., U.S.	A3	112
Huron, S.D., U.S.	C7	118
Huron, co., Mi., U.S.	E7	99
Huron, co., Oh., U.S.	A3	112
Huron, stm., Mi., U.S.	p14	99
Huron, Lake, l., N.A.	C10	76
Huron Mountains, hills, Mi., U.S.	B3	99
Hurricane, Ut., U.S.	F2	121
Hurricane, W.V., U.S.	C2	125
Hurst, Il., U.S.	F4	90
Hurt, Va., U.S.	C3	123
Hurtsboro, Al., U.S.	C4	78
Húsavík, Ice.	B4	4
Huskvarna, Swe.	H10	6
Hustisford, Wi., U.S.	E5	126
Husum, Ger.	A9	8
Hutchins, Tx., U.S.	n10	120
Hutchinson, Ks., U.S.	D6	93
Hutchinson, Mn., U.S.	F4	100
Hutchinson, co., S.D., U.S.	D8	118
Hutchinson, co., Tx., U.S.	B2	120
Hutchinson Island, i., Fl., U.S.	E6	86
Hutchinson Island, i., S.C., U.S.	k11	117
Hutch Mountain, mtn., Az., U.S.	C4	80
Hüttental, Ger.	E8	8
Huttig, Ar., U.S.	D3	81
Huwei, Tai.	L9	28
Huxley, Ia., U.S.	C4	92
Huy, Bel.	E5	8
Huzhou, China	E9	28
Hvannadalshnúkur, mtn., Ice.	C4	4
Hvar, Cro.	F11	14
Hwange, Zimb.	E5	44
Hwang Ho see Huang, stm., China	D10	26
Hyannis, Ma., U.S.	C7	98
Hyannis Port, Ma., U.S.	C7	98
Hyattsville, Md., U.S.	C4	97
Hybla Valley, Va., U.S.	g12	123
Hyco, stm., Va., U.S.	D3	123
Hyco Lake, res., N.C., U.S.	A3	110
Hydaburg, Ak., U.S.	D13	79
Hyde, Pa., U.S.	D5	115
Hyde, co., N.C., U.S.	B6	110
Hyde, co., S.D., U.S.	C6	118
Hyde Park, Guy.	D13	58
Hyde Park, N.Y., U.S.	D7	109
Hyde Park, Ut., U.S.	B4	121
Hyder, Ak., U.S.	D13	79
Hyderābād, India	D5	37
Hyderābād, Pak.	H3	38
Hydeville, Vt., U.S.	D2	122
Hydro, Ok., U.S.	B3	113
Hyères, Fr.	I13	10
Hyesan, N. Kor.	C12	26
Hymera, In., U.S.	F3	91
Hyndman, Pa., U.S.	G4	115
Hyndman Peak, mtn., Id., U.S.	F4	89
Hyrum, Ut., U.S.	B4	121
Hythe, Alta., Can.	B1	68
Hyūga, Japan	J4	30
Hyūga-nada, Japan	J4	30
Hyvinkää, Fin.	F15	6

I

Name	Map Ref	Page
Iamonia, Lake, l., Fl., U.S.	B2	86
Iași, Rom.	B11	16
Iatt, Lake, res., La., U.S.	C3	95
Ibadan, Nig.	G6	42
Ibagué, Col.	E5	58
Ibapah Peak, mtn., Ut., U.S.	D2	121
Ibarra, Ec.	G3	58
Ibb, Yemen	F3	46
Iberia, Mo., U.S.	C5	102
Iberia, co., La., U.S.	E4	95
Iberville, Que., Can.	D4	74
Iberville, co., La., U.S.	D4	95
Iberville, Mont d' (Mount Caubvick), mtn., Can.	g14	74
Ibiá, Braz.	E5	57
Ibicaraí, Braz.	C9	57
Ibiza, Spain	G13	12
Ibiza, i., Spain	G13	12
Ibo, Moz.	D8	44
Ica, Peru	F3	54
Içá (Putumayo), stm., S.A.	I8	58
Içana, Braz.	C5	54
Içana, stm., S.A.	C5	54
Ice Harbor Dam, Wa., U.S.	C7	124
İçel, Tur.	H14	4
Iceland, ctry., Eur.	B4	4
Ichalkaranji, India	D3	37
Ich Bogd Uul, mts., Mong.	C7	26
Ichinomiya, Japan	G9	30
Ichinoseki, Japan	D14	30
Icicle Creek, stm., Wa., U.S.	B5	124
Icó, Braz.	E11	54
Icy Cape, c., Ak., U.S.	A7	79
Icy Strait, strt., Ak., U.S.	k22	79
Ida, Mi., U.S.	G7	99
Ida, co., Ia., U.S.	B2	92
Ida, Lake, l., Mn., U.S.	D3	100
Idabel, Ok., U.S.	D7	113
Ida Grove, Ia., U.S.	B2	92
Idaho, co., Id., U.S.	D3	89
Idaho, state, U.S.	E3	89
Idaho Falls, Id., U.S.	F6	89
Idaho Springs, Co., U.S.	B5	83
Idalou, Tx., U.S.	C2	120
Idamay, W.V., U.S.	k10	125
Idanha-a-Nova, Port.	F4	12
Idāppādi, India	G4	37
Idar-Oberstein, Ger.	F7	8
Idaville, In., U.S.	C4	91
Ider, Al., U.S.	A4	78
Idfū, Egypt	D12	42
Idlib, Syria	B5	40
Ídolo, Isla del, i., Mex.	G11	62
Ieper, Bel.	E2	8
Ierápetra, Grc.	N9	16
Iesi, Italy	F8	14
Ife, Nig.	G6	42
Iferouâne, Niger	E7	42
Ifôras, Adrar des, mts., Afr.	D6	42
Iglesias, Italy	J3	14
Igloolik, N.W. Ter., Can.	C16	66
Ignacio, Co., U.S.	D3	83
Iguaçu, Saltos do (Iguassu Falls), wtfl, S.A.	B6	56
Iguala, Mex.	H10	62
Igualada, Spain	D13	12
Iguape, Braz.	A7	56
Iguatu, Braz.	E11	54
Iguéla, Gabon	B1	44
Iguidi, Erg, dunes, Afr.	C4	42
Ihosy, Madag.	F9	44
Iida, Japan	G10	30
Iisalmi, Fin.	E16	6
Iizuka, Japan	I3	30
IJmuiden, Neth.	C4	8
IJsselmeer (Zuiderzee), Neth.	C5	8
Ika, Russia	F15	24
Ikela, Zaire	B4	44
Ikerre, Nig.	G7	42
Ila, Nig.	G6	42
Ilagan, Phil.	B7	32
Ilan, Tai.	K10	28
Ilbenge, Russia	E18	24
Île-à-la-Crosse, Lac, l., Sask., Can.	B2	75
Ilebo, Zaire	B4	44
Île-de-France, hist. reg., Fr.	C9	10
Île-Perrot, Que., Can.	q19	74
Ilhéus, Braz.	C9	57
Ili, stm., Asia	I13	22
Iliamna Lake, l., Ak., U.S.	D8	79
Iliamna Volcano, vol., Ak., U.S.	C9	79
Ilion, N.Y., U.S.	B5	109
Ilio Point, c., Hi., U.S.	B4	88
Ilirska Bistrica, Slo.	D9	14
Iljinskij, Russia	H22	24
Ilkal, India	E4	37
Illampu, Nevado, mtn., Bol.	G5	54
Illapel, Chile	C2	56
Illescas, Mex.	F8	62
Illiers, Fr.	D8	10
Illimani, Nevado, mtn., Bol.	G5	54
Illinois, state, U.S.	C4	90
Illinois, stm., U.S.	A7	113
Illinois, stm., Il., U.S.	B5	90
Illinois, stm., Or., U.S.	E3	114
Illinois Peak, mtn., Id., U.S.	B3	89
Illiopolis, Il., U.S.	D4	90
Illizi, Alg.	C7	42
Illmo, Mo., U.S.	D8	102
Il'men', Ozero, l., Russia	C14	18
Ilo, Peru	G4	54
Iloilo, Phil.	C7	32
Ilomantsi, Fin.	E18	6
Ilorin, Nig.	G6	42
Il'pyrskij, Russia	F26	24
Ilwaco, Wa., U.S.	C1	124
Imabari, Japan	H6	30
Iman, Russia	H20	24

Name — Map Ref — Page

Imari, Japan I2 30
Imatra, Fin. F17 6
Imboden, Ar., U.S. A4 81
Imlay, Nv., U.S. C3 105
Imlay City, Mi., U.S. E7 99
Immenstadt, Ger. H10 8
Immokalee, Fl., U.S. F5 86
Imnaha, stm., Or., U.S. B10 114
Imola, Italy E6 14
Imperatriz, Braz. E9 54
Imperia, Italy F3 14
Imperial, Ca., U.S. F6 82
Imperial, Mo., U.S. C7 102
Imperial, Ne., U.S. D4 104
Imperial, Pa., U.S. k13 115
Imperial, co., Ca., U.S. F6 82
Imperial Beach, Ca., U.S. o15 82
Imperial Dam, U.S. E1 80
Imperial Reservoir, res., U.S. E1 80
Imperial Valley, val., Ca., U.S. F6 82
Impfondo, Congo A3 44
Imphāl, India H15 38
Imst, Aus. H10 8
Imuris, Mex. B4 62
Ina, Japan G10 30
Inari, Fin. B16 6
Inca, Spain F14 12
İncekum Burnu, c., Tur. A3 40
Inch'ŏn, S. Kor. D12 26
Incline Village, Nv., U.S. D2 105
Independence, Ia., U.S. B6 92
Independence, Ks., U.S. E8 93
Independence, Ky., U.S. B5 94
Independence, La., U.S. D5 95
Independence, Mo., U.S. B3 102
Independence, Or., U.S. C3 114
Independence, Va., U.S. D1 123
Independence, Wi., U.S. D2 126
Independence, co., Ar., U.S. B4 81
Independence, stm., N.Y., U.S. B5 109
Independence Mountains, mts., Nv., U.S. C5 105
Independence National Historical Park, Pa., U.S. p21 115
Independence Rock, mtn., Wy., U.S. D5 127
India, ctry., Asia E4 36
Indian, stm., Ont., Can. B7 73
Indian, stm., De., U.S. F4 85
Indian, stm., Mi., U.S. B4 99
Indian, stm., N.Y., U.S. A5 109
Indiana, Pa., U.S. E3 115
Indiana, co., Pa., U.S. E3 115
Indiana, state, U.S. E5 91
Indiana Dunes National Lakeshore, In., U.S. A3 91
Indianapolis, In., U.S. E5 91
Indian Bay, b., Fl., U.S. D4 86
Indian Cedar Swamp, sw., R.I., U.S. F2 116
Indian Creek, stm., Oh., U.S. C1 112
Indian Creek, stm., S.D., U.S. B2 118
Indian Creek, stm., Tn., U.S. B3 119
Indian Creek, stm., W.V., U.S. k9 125
Indian Creek, stm., W.V., U.S. D4 125
Indian Head, Md., U.S. C3 97
Indian Island, i., N.C., U.S. B6 110
Indian Lake, l., Mi., U.S. C4 99
Indian Lake, l., N.Y., U.S. B6 109
Indian Lake, l., Oh., U.S. B2 112
Indian Lake, l., R.I., U.S. F4 116
Indian Neck, Ct., U.S. D4 84
Indian Ocean G17 2
Indianola, Ia., U.S. C4 92
Indianola, Ms., U.S. B3 101
Indianola, Ne., U.S. D5 104
Indian Peak, mtn., Ut., U.S. E2 121
Indian Peak, mtn., Wy., U.S. B3 127
Indian Prairie Canal, Fl., U.S. E5 86
Indian River, co., Fl., U.S. E6 86
Indian River, b., Fl., U.S. D6 86
Indian River Bay, b., De., U.S. F5 85
Indian Rock, mtn., Wa., U.S. D5 124
Indian Rocks Beach, Fl., U.S. p10 86
Indian Springs, Nv., U.S. G6 105
Indian Stream, stm., N.H., U.S. f7 106
Indiantown, Fl., U.S. E6 86
Indian Trail, N.C., U.S. B2 110
Indigirka, stm., Russia C23 24
Indio, Ca., U.S. F5 82
Indispensable Reefs, rf., Sol.Is. B12 50
Indonesia, ctry., Asia F6 32
Indore, India I6 38
Indoukâl-n-Taghès, mtn., Niger E7 42
Indramayu, Indon. m14 33a
Indrāvati, stm., India C6 37
Indus, stm., Asia H2 38
İnegöl, Tur. I13 16
Infiernillo, Presa del, res., Mex. H9 62
I-n-Gall, Niger E7 42
Ingalls, In., U.S. E6 91
Ingalls Park, Il., U.S. B5 90
Ingersoll, Ont., Can. D4 73
Ingham, Austl. C9 50
Ingham, co., Mi., U.S. F6 99
Ingleside, Tx., U.S. F4 120
Inglewood, Ca., U.S. n12 82
Ingolstadt, Ger. G11 8
Ingraham, Lake, l., Fl., U.S. G5 86
Ingram, Pa., U.S. k13 115
In Guezzam, Alg. E7 42
Inhambane, Moz. F7 44
Inhambupe, Braz. F11 54
Inhaminga, Moz. E6 44
Inharrime, Moz. F7 44
Inírida, stm., Col. F8 58
Inkerman, N.B., Can. B5 71
Inkom, Id., U.S. G6 89
Inkster, Mi., U.S. p15 99
Inland Sea see Seto-naikai, Japan H6 30
Inle Lake, l., Mya. D4 34
Inman, Ks., U.S. D6 93
Inman, S.C., U.S. A3 117
Inn (En), stm., Eur. G13 8
Innamincka, Austl. E8 50
Inner Hebrides, is., Scot., U.K. E6 7
Innisfail, Alta., Can. C4 68
Innsbruck, Aus. H11 8
Inola, Ok., U.S. A6 113
Inongo, Zaire B3 44
Inowrocław, Pol. C18 8
In Salah, Alg. C6 42
Inscription House Ruin, hist., Az., U.S. A5 80
Insein, Mya. F4 34
Institute, W.V., U.S. m12 125
Interlachen, Fl., U.S. C5 86
Interlaken, Switz. F14 10
International Falls, Mn., U.S. B5 100
Inthanon, Doi, mtn., Thai. E5 34
Intiyaco, Arg. B4 56
Intracoastal Waterway, U.S. E4 95
Inukjuak, Que., Can. g11 74
Inveraray, Scot., U.K. E7 7
Invercargill, N.Z. G2 52
Inverell, Austl. E10 50
Inver Grove Heights, Mn., U.S. n12 100
Invermere, B.C., Can. D9 69
Inverness, Scot., U.K. D8 7
Inverness, Ca., U.S. C2 82
Inverness, Fl., U.S. D4 86
Inverness, Ms., U.S. B3 101
Inverurie, Scot., U.K. D10 7
Investigator Group, is., Austl. F6 50
Investigator Strait, strt., Austl. G7 50
Invisible Mountain, mtn., Id., U.S. F5 89
Inwood, Ia., U.S. A1 92
Inwood, N.Y., U.S. k13 109
Inwood, W.V., U.S. B6 125
Inyangani, mtn., Zimb. E6 44
Inyan Kara Creek, stm., Wy., U.S. B8 127
Inyan Kara Mountain, mtn., Wy., U.S. B8 127
Inyo, co., Ca., U.S. D5 82
Inyo, Mount, mtn., Ca., U.S. D5 82
Inyo Mountains, mts., Ca., U.S. D4 82
Ioánnina, Grc. J4 16
Iola, Ks., U.S. E8 93
Iola, Wi., U.S. D4 126
Iona, Id., U.S. F7 89
Ione, Ca., U.S. C3 82
Ionia, Mi., U.S. F5 99
Ionia, co., Mi., U.S. F5 99
Ionian Islands see Iónioi Nísoi, is., Grc. K4 16
Ionian Sea, Eur. H11 4
Iónioi Nísoi, is., Grc. K4 16
Iosco, co., Mi., U.S. D7 99
Iota, La., U.S. D3 95
Iowa, La., U.S. D2 95
Iowa, co., Ia., U.S. C5 92
Iowa, co., Wi., U.S. E3 126
Iowa, state, U.S. C4 92
Iowa, stm., Ia., U.S. C6 92
Iowa, West Branch, stm., Ia., U.S. B4 92
Iowa City, Ia., U.S. C6 92
Iowa Falls, Ia., U.S. B4 92
Iowa Indian Reservation, U.S. C8 93
Iowa Lake, l., U.S. A3 92
Iowa Park, Tx., U.S. C3 120
Ipameri, Braz. D4 57
Iphigenia Bay, b., Ak., U.S. n22 79
Ipiales, Col. G4 58
Ipiaú, Braz. C9 57
Ipoh, Malay. L6 34
Ipswich, Austl. E10 50
Ipswich, Eng., U.K. I14 7
Ipswich, Ma., U.S. A6 98
Ipswich, S.D., U.S. B6 118
Ipswich, stm., Ma., U.S. A5 98
Ipu, Braz. D10 54
Iqaluit, N.W. Ter., Can. D19 66
Iquique, Chile H4 54
Iquitos, Peru D4 54
Iraan, Tx., U.S. D2 120
Iráklion, Grc. N9 16
Iran, ctry., Asia B5 46
Iran Mountains, mts., Asia E5 32
Īrānshahr, Iran C7 46
Irapa, Ven. B11 58
Irapuato, Mex. G9 62
Iraq, ctry., Asia B3 46
Irazú, Volcán, vol., C.R. J6 64
Irbid, Jord. C4 40
Irbīl, Iraq A3 46
Iredell, co., N.C., U.S. B2 110
Ireland, ctry., Eur. E6 4
Iriga, Phil. r20 32
Iringa, Tan. C7 44
Irion, co., Tx., U.S. D2 120
Iriri, stm., Braz. D8 54
Irish, Mount, mtn., Nv., U.S. F6 105
Irish Sea, Eur. H8 7
Irkutsk, Russia G14 24
Irmo, S.C., U.S. C5 117
Iron, co., Mi., U.S. B2 99
Iron, co., Mo., U.S. D7 102
Iron, co., Ut., U.S. F2 121
Iron, co., Wi., U.S. B3 126
Irondale, Al., U.S. f7 78
Irondequoit, N.Y., U.S. B3 109
Iron Gate, val., Eur. E6 16
Iron Gate Reservoir, res., Eur. E5 16
Iron Gate Reservoir, res., Ca., U.S. B2 82
Iron Mountain, Mi., U.S. C2 99
Iron Mountain, mtn., Az., U.S. D4 80
Iron Mountains, mts., U.S. D1 123
Iron Ridge, Wi., U.S. E5 126
Iron River, Mi., U.S. B2 99
Iron River, Wi., U.S. B2 126
Ironton, Mo., U.S. D7 102
Ironton, Oh., U.S. D3 112
Ironwood, Mi., U.S. n11 99
Iroquois, Ont., Can. C9 73
Iroquois, co., Il., U.S. C6 90
Iroquois, stm., U.S. C6 90
Iroquois, Lake, l., Vt., U.S. B2 122
Iroquois Falls, Ont., Can. o19 73
Irrawaddy see Ayeyarwady, stm., Mya. G3 34
Irricana, Alta., Can. D4 68
Irrigon, Or., U.S. B7 114
Irtyš (Ertix), stm., Asia F11 22
Irumu, Zaire A5 44
Irún, Spain B10 12
Irurzun, Spain C10 12
Irú Tepuy, mtn., Ven. E12 58
Irvine, Scot., U.K. F8 7
Irvine, Ca., U.S. n13 82
Irvine, Ky., U.S. C6 94
Irving, Tx., U.S. n10 120
Irvington, Al., U.S. E1 78
Irvington, Il., U.S. E4 90
Irvington, Ky., U.S. C3 94
Irvington, N.J., U.S. k8 107
Irvington, N.Y., U.S. g13 109
Irwin, Pa., U.S. F2 115
Irwin, co., Ga., U.S. E3 87
Irwinton, Ga., U.S. D3 87
Isabel, Mount, mtn., Wy., U.S. D2 127
Isabella, co., Mi., U.S. E6 99
Isabella, Cordillera, mts., Nic. G5 64
Isabella Indian Reservation, Mi., U.S. E6 99
Isabella Lake, l., Mn., U.S. C7 100
Ísafjördur, Ice. B3 4
Isahaya, Japan J3 30
Isanti, Mn., U.S. E5 100
Isanti, co., Mn., U.S. E5 100
Isar, stm., Eur. G11 8
Ischia, Italy I8 14
Ise, Japan H9 30
Isernia, Italy H9 14
Isesaki, Japan F12 30
Ise-wan, b., Japan H9 30
Isherton, Guy. F13 58
Ishikari-wan, b., Japan p18 30a
Ishinomaki, Japan D14 30
Ishpeming, Mi., U.S. B3 99
Isinglass, stm., N.H., U.S. D4 106
Isiolo, Kenya A7 44
Isiro, Zaire H11 42
İskele, N. Cyp. B3 40
İskenderun, Tur. H15 4
İskenderun Körfezi, b., Tur. A4 40
Iskitim, Russia G10 24
İslâhiye, Tur. A5 40
Islāmābād, Pak. D5 38
Islamorada, Fl., U.S. H6 86
Isla Mujeres, Mex. G16 62
Island, co., Wa., U.S. A3 124
Island Beach, N.J., U.S. D4 107
Island City, Or., U.S. B8 114
Island Falls, Me., U.S. B4 96
Island Lake, l., Man., Can. C4 70
Island Park, R.I., U.S. E6 116
Island Park Reservoir, res., Id., U.S. E7 89
Island Pond, Vt., U.S. B5 122
Island Pond, l., N.H., U.S. E4 106
Islands, Bay of, b., Newf., Can. D2 72
Isla Vista, Ca., U.S. E4 82
Islay, i., Scot., U.K. F6 7
Isle-aux-Morts, Newf., Can. E2 72
Isle of Man, dep., Eur. E7 4
Isle of Palms, S.C., U.S. k12 117
Isle of Wight, co., Va., U.S. D6 123
Isle of Wight Bay, b., Md., U.S. D7 97
Isle Royale National Park, Mi., U.S. h9 99
Islesboro Island, i., Me., U.S. D4 96
Isleta, N.M., U.S. C3 108
Isleta Indian Reservation, N.M., U.S. C3 108
Islington, Ma., U.S. h11 98
Isola, Ms., U.S. B3 101
Isola della Scala, Italy D5 14
Ispica, Italy M9 14
Israel (Yisra'el), ctry., Asia D4 40
Israel, stm., N.H., U.S. B3 106
Issano, Guy. E13 58
Issaquah, Wa., U.S. B3 124
Issaquena, co., Ms., U.S. C2 101
Issoire, Fr. G10 10
Issoudun, Fr. F8 10
Is-sur-Tille, Fr. E12 10
Issyk-Kul', Kyrg. I13 22
İstanbul, Tur. G13 4
İstanbul Boğazı (Bosporus), strt., Tur. H13 16
Isto, Mount, mtn., Ak., U.S. B11 79
Istokpoga, Lake, l., Fl., U.S. E5 86
Itabaiana, Braz. F11 54
Itaberaí, Braz. G9 54
Itabira, Braz. E7 57
Itabuna, Braz. C9 57
Itacoatiara, Braz. D7 54
Itagüí, Col. D5 58
Itaituba, Braz. D7 54
Itajaí, Braz. B7 56
Itajubá, Braz. G6 57
Italy, Tx., U.S. C4 120
Italy, ctry., Eur. G10 4
Itaperuna, Braz. F8 57
Itapetinga, Braz. C8 57
Itapetininga, Braz. G4 57
Itapeva, Braz. G4 57
Itapicuru, stm., Braz. D10 54
Itapira, Braz. G5 57
Itaquari, Braz. F8 57
Itararé, Braz. H4 57
Itārsi, India I7 38
Itasca, Il., U.S. k8 90
Itasca, Tx., U.S. C4 120
Itasca, co., Mn., U.S. C5 100
Itasca, Lake, l., Mn., U.S. C3 100
Itawamba, co., Ms., U.S. A5 101
Ithaca, Mi., U.S. E6 99
Ithaca, N.Y., U.S. C4 109
Itō, Japan H12 30
Itta Bena, Ms., U.S. B3 101
Ittiri, Italy I3 14
Ituberá, Braz. B9 57
Ituiutaba, Braz. E4 57
Itumbiara, Braz. E4 57
Ituni, Guy. E13 58
Ituri, stm., Zaire A5 44
Iturup, Ostrov (Etorofu-tō), i., Russia I23 24
Ituverava, Braz. F5 57
Ituxi, stm., Braz. E5 54
Itzehoe, Ger. B9 8
Iuka, Ms., U.S. A5 101
Iva, S.C., U.S. C2 117
Ivalo, Fin. B16 6
Ivanhoe, Mn., U.S. F2 100
Ivanić Grad, Cro. D11 14
Ivano-Frankivs'k, Ukr. H2 22
Ivanovo, Russia D23 18
Ivigtut, Grnld. D23 66
Ivinheima, stm., Braz. G2 57
Ivins, Ut., U.S. F2 121
Ivory Coast, ctry., Afr. G4 42
Ivoryton, Ct., U.S. D6 84
Ivrea, Italy D2 14
Iwaki (Taira), Japan E13 30
Iwakuni, Japan H5 30
Iwanai, Japan q18 30a
Iwanuma, Japan D13 30
Iwo, Nig. G6 42
Ixtacihuatl, vol., Mex. H10 62
Iyo-nada, Japan I5 30
Izabal, Lago de, l., Guat. G3 64
Izard, co., Ar., U.S. A4 81
Izegem, Bel. E3 8
Iževsk, Russia F8 22
İzmir, Tur. H13 4
İzmit, Tur. G13 4
Iznalloz, Spain H8 12
İznik Gölü, l., Tur. I13 16
Izozog, Bañados de, sw., Bol. G6 54
Izúcar de Matamoros, Mex. H10 62
Izuhara, Japan H2 30
Izumo, Japan G5 30
Izu-shotō, is., Japan H12 30
Izvestij CIK, Ostrova, is., Russia B10 24

J

Jabalpur, India I8 38
Jabbūl, Sabkhat al-, l., Syria A5 40
Jablah, Syria B4 40
Jablonec nad Nisou, Czech. E15 8
Jaboatão, Braz. E11 54
Jabrīn, well, Sau. Ar. D4 46
Jaca, Spain C11 12
Jacarèzinho, Braz. G4 57
Jáchal, Arg. C3 56
Jacinto City, Tx., U.S. r14 120
Jack, co., Tx., U.S. C3 120
Jackfish Lake, l., Sask., Can. D1 75
Jackman, Me., U.S. C2 96
Jackman Station, Me., U.S. C2 96
Jack Mountain, mtn., Mt., U.S. D4 103
Jack Mountain, mtn., Wa., U.S. A5 124
Jackpot, Nv., U.S. B7 105
Jacksboro, Tn., U.S. C9 119
Jacksboro, Tx., U.S. C3 120
Jacks Mountain, mtn., Pa., U.S. E6 115
Jackson, Al., U.S. D2 78
Jackson, Ca., U.S. C3 82
Jackson, Ga., U.S. C3 87
Jackson, Ky., U.S. C6 94
Jackson, La., U.S. D4 95
Jackson, Mi., U.S. F6 99
Jackson, Mn., U.S. G4 100
Jackson, Ms., U.S. C3 101
Jackson, Mo., U.S. D8 102
Jackson, Oh., U.S. C3 112
Jackson, S.C., U.S. E4 117
Jackson, Tn., U.S. B3 119
Jackson, Wi., U.S. E5 126
Jackson, Wy., U.S. C2 127
Jackson, co., Al., U.S. A3 78
Jackson, co., Ar., U.S. B4 81
Jackson, co., Co., U.S. A4 83
Jackson, co., Fl., U.S. B1 86
Jackson, co., Ga., U.S. B3 87
Jackson, co., Il., U.S. F4 90
Jackson, co., In., U.S. G5 91
Jackson, co., Ia., U.S. B7 92
Jackson, co., Ks., U.S. C8 93
Jackson, co., Ky., U.S. C5 94
Jackson, co., La., U.S. B3 95
Jackson, co., Mi., U.S. F6 99
Jackson, co., Mn., U.S. G3 100
Jackson, co., Ms., U.S. E5 101
Jackson, co., Mo., U.S. B3 102
Jackson, co., N.C., U.S. f9 110
Jackson, co., Oh., U.S. C3 112
Jackson, co., Ok., U.S. C2 113
Jackson, co., Or., U.S. E4 114
Jackson, co., S.D., U.S. D4 118
Jackson, co., Tn., U.S. C8 119
Jackson, co., Tx., U.S. E4 120
Jackson, co., W.V., U.S. C3 125
Jackson, co., Wi., U.S. D3 126
Jackson, stm., Va., U.S. C3 123
Jackson, Lake, l., Fl., U.S. E5 86
Jackson, Lake, l., Fl., U.S. B2 86
Jackson, Mount, mtn., N.H., U.S. B4 106
Jackson Center, Oh., U.S. B1 112
Jackson Lake, res., Wy., U.S. C2 127
Jackson Mountains, mts., Nv., U.S. B3 105
Jackson's Arm, Newf., Can. D3 72
Jacksons Gap, Al., U.S. C4 78
Jacksonville, Al., U.S. B4 78
Jacksonville, Ar., U.S. C3 81
Jacksonville, Fl., U.S. B5 86
Jacksonville, Il., U.S. D3 90
Jacksonville, N.C., U.S. C5 110
Jacksonville, Or., U.S. E4 114
Jacksonville, Tx., U.S. D5 120
Jacksonville Beach, Fl., U.S. B5 86
Jacksonville Naval Air Station, mil., Fl., U.S. B5 86
Jacks Peak, mtn., Ut., U.S. E3 121
Jacmel, Haiti E11 64
Jacobābād, Pak. F3 38
Jacques-Cartier, stm., Que., Can. B6 74
Jacques-Cartier, Détroit de, strt., Que., Can. h8 72
Jacquet River, N.B., Can. B4 71
Jadraque, Spain E9 12
Jaén, Peru E3 54
Jaén, Spain H8 12
Jaffna, Sri L. H6 37
Jaffrey, N.H., U.S. E2 106
Jafr, Qā' al-, depr., Jord. D5 40
Jagādhri, India E7 38
Jagdalpur, India C7 37
Jagersfontein, S. Afr. G5 44
Jagodnoje, Russia E23 24
Jagtiāl, India C5 37
Jaguarão, Braz. C6 56
Jahrom, Iran C5 46
Jaidak, Afg. E2 38
Jaipur, India G6 38
Jajce, Bos. E12 14
Jakarta, Indon. m13 32
Jakobshavn, Grnld. C22 66
Jakobstad (Pietarsaari), Fin. E14 6
Jakutsk, Russia E19 24
Jal, N.M., U.S. E6 108
Jalālābād, Afg. C4 38
Jalapa, Guat. G3 64
Jalapa Enríquez, Mex. H11 62
Jālgaon, India B3 37
Jālna, India C3 37
Jalostotitlán, Mex. G8 62
Jalpaiguri, India G13 38
Jaltepec, stm., Mex. I12 62
Jamaica, ctry., N.A. E9 64
Jamaica Bay, b., N.Y., U.S. k13 109
Jamaica Channel, strt., N.A. E10 64
Jamālpur, Bngl. H13 38
Jamālpur, India H12 38
Jamame, Som. A8 44
Jambi, Indon. F3 32
Jambol, Bul. G10 16
James, stm., U.S. C7 76
James, stm., Mo., U.S. E4 102
James, stm., Va., U.S. C5 123
James, Lake, l., In., U.S. A7 91
James, Lake, res., N.C., U.S. B1 110
James Bay, b., Can. F16 66
James Branch, stm., De., U.S. F3 85
Jamesburg, N.J., U.S. C4 107
James City, N.C., U.S. B5 110
James City, co., Va., U.S. C6 123
James Island, S.C., U.S. k12 117
James Island, i., Md., U.S. C5 97
James Island, i., S.C., U.S. F8 117
James River Bridge, Va., U.S. k15 123
Jamestown, In., U.S. E4 91
Jamestown, Ky., U.S. D4 94
Jamestown, N.Y., U.S. C1 109
Jamestown, N.C., U.S. B3 110
Jamestown, N.D., U.S. C7 111
Jamestown, Oh., U.S. C2 112
Jamestown, R.I., U.S. F5 116
Jamestown, Tn., U.S. C9 119
James Town, Wy., U.S. E3 127
Jamestown Dam, N.D., U.S. C7 111
Jamestown Reservoir, res., N.D., U.S. C7 111
Jamiltepec, Mex. I11 62
Jamkhandi, India D3 37
Jammu, India D6 38
Jammu and Kashmir, dep., Asia C6 38
Jāmnagar, India I4 38
Jāmpur, Pak. F4 38
Jämsä, Fin. F15 6
Jamshedpur, India I12 38
Jamsk, Russia F24 24
Jamūi, India H12 38
Jamuna, stm., Bngl. H13 38
Jana, stm., Russia C21 24
Janaucu, Ilha, i., Braz. C8 54
Janesville, Ca., U.S. B3 82
Janesville, Ia., U.S. B5 92
Janesville, Mn., U.S. F5 100
Janesville, Wi., U.S. F4 126
Jangipur, India H13 38
Janīn, W. Bank C4 40
Janskij, Russia D20 24
Janskij Zaliv, b., Russia C21 24
Januária, Braz. C6 57
Jaora, India I6 38
Japan, ctry., Asia D14 26
Japan, Sea of, Asia D13 26
Japurá (Caquetá), stm., S.A. D5 54
Jaqué, Pan. K8 64
Jarābulus, Syria A6 40
Jaraiz de la Vera, Spain E6 12
Jarash, Jord. C4 40
Jarcevo, Russia F15 18
Jardines de la Reina, is., Cuba D8 64
Jari, stm., Braz. D8 54
Jaridih, India I12 38
Jaroslavl', Russia D22 18
Jarosław, Pol. E22 8
Jarrettsville, Md., U.S. A5 97
Järvenpää, Fin. F15 6
Järvsö, Swe. F11 6
Jask, Iran C6 46
Jasmine Estates, Fl., U.S. D4 86
Jasnyj, Russia G19 24
Jasonville, In., U.S. F3 91
Jasper, Al., U.S. B2 78
Jasper, Fl., U.S. B4 86
Jasper, Ga., U.S. B2 87
Jasper, In., U.S. H4 91
Jasper, Mo., U.S. D3 102
Jasper, Tn., U.S. D8 119
Jasper, Tx., U.S. D6 120
Jasper, co., Ga., U.S. C3 87
Jasper, co., Il., U.S. D5 90
Jasper, co., In., U.S. B3 91
Jasper, co., Ia., U.S. C4 92
Jasper, co., Ms., U.S. C4 101
Jasper, co., Mo., U.S. D3 102
Jasper, co., S.C., U.S. G5 117
Jasper, co., Tx., U.S. D5 120
Jasper National Park, Alta., Can. C1 68
Jataí, Braz. D3 57
Játiva, Spain G11 12
Jatni, India J11 38
Jaú, Braz. G4 57
Jauaperi, stm., Braz. C6 54
Jauja, Peru F3 54
Jaunpur, India H10 38
Java see Jawa, i., Indon. G4 32
Javari (Yavarí), stm., S.A. D4 54

Name — Map Ref — Page

Java Sea see Jawa, Laut, Indon. G4 32
Jävre, Swe. D13 6
Jawa, i., Indon. G4 32
Jawa, Laut (Java Sea), Indon. G4 32
Jaworzno, Pol. E19 8
Jay, Ok., U.S. A7 113
Jay, co., In., U.S. D7 91
Jaya, Puncak, mtn., Indon. F10 32
Jayapura, Indon. F11 32
Jayb, Wādī al-, val., Asia D4 40
J. B. Thomas, Lake, res., Tx., U.S. C2 120
Jean, Nv., U.S. H6 105
Jeanerette, La., U.S. E4 95
Jean Lafitte National Historical Park, La., U.S. k12 95
Jeannette, Pa., U.S. F2 115
Jebba, Nig. G6 42
Jeddore Lake, res., Newf., Can. D3 72
Jeff Davis, co., Ga., U.S. E4 87
Jeff Davis, co., Tx., U.S. o12 120
Jefferson, Ga., U.S. B3 87
Jefferson, Ia., U.S. B3 92
Jefferson, La., U.S. k11 95
Jefferson, N.C., U.S. A1 110
Jefferson, Oh., U.S. A5 112
Jefferson, Or., U.S. C3 114
Jefferson, S.C., U.S. B7 117
Jefferson, Tx., U.S. C5 120
Jefferson, Wi., U.S. E5 126
Jefferson, co., Al., U.S. B3 78
Jefferson, co., Ar., U.S. C3 81
Jefferson, co., Co., U.S. B5 83
Jefferson, co., Fl., U.S. B3 86
Jefferson, co., Ga., U.S. C4 87
Jefferson, co., Id., U.S. F6 89
Jefferson, co., Il., U.S. E5 90
Jefferson, co., In., U.S. G6 91
Jefferson, co., Ia., U.S. C5 92
Jefferson, co., Ks., U.S. C8 93
Jefferson, co., Ky., U.S. B4 94
Jefferson, co., La., U.S. E5 95
Jefferson, co., Ms., U.S. D2 101
Jefferson, co., Mo., U.S. C7 102
Jefferson, co., Mt., U.S. D4 103
Jefferson, co., Ne., U.S. D8 104
Jefferson, co., N.Y., U.S. A5 109
Jefferson, co., Oh., U.S. B5 112
Jefferson, co., Ok., U.S. C4 113
Jefferson, co., Or., U.S. C5 114
Jefferson, co., Pa., U.S. D3 115
Jefferson, co., Tn., U.S. C10 119
Jefferson, co., Tx., U.S. E5 120
Jefferson, co., Wa., U.S. B1 124
Jefferson, co., W.V., U.S. B7 125
Jefferson, co., Wi., U.S. E5 126
Jefferson, stm., Mt., U.S. E5 103
Jefferson, Mount, mtn., Id., U.S. E7 89
Jefferson, Mount, mtn., Nv., U.S. E5 105
Jefferson, Mount, mtn., Or., U.S. C5 114
Jefferson City, Mo., U.S. C5 102
Jefferson City, Tn., U.S. C10 119
Jefferson Davis, co., La., U.S. D3 95
Jefferson Davis, co., Ms., U.S. D4 101
Jefferson Farms, De., U.S. i7 85
Jefferson Proving Ground, mil., In., U.S. G7 91
Jeffersontown, Ky., U.S. B4 94
Jeffersonville, Ga., U.S. D3 87
Jeffersonville, In., U.S. H6 91
Jeffersonville, Ky., U.S. C6 94
Jeffersonville, Oh., U.S. C2 112
Jeffrey, W.V., U.S. D3 125
Jeffrey City, Wy., U.S. D5 127
Jeffries Creek, stm., S.C., U.S. C8 117
Jefremov, Russia H21 18
Jegorjevsk, Russia F22 18
Jehossee Island, i., S.C., U.S. k11 117
Jejsk, Russia H5 22
Jekaterinburg, Russia F10 22
Jekyll Island, i., Ga., U.S. E5 87
Jelec, Russia I21 18
Jelenia Góra (Hirschberg), Pol. E15 8
Jelgava, Lat. E6 18
Jellico, Tn., U.S. C9 119
Jelm Mountain, mtn., Wy., U.S. E7 127
Jeloguj, stm., Russia E11 24
Jember, Indon. n16 32
Jemez, stm., N.M., U.S. k7 108
Jemez Canyon Dam, N.M., U.S. k7 108
Jemez Indian Reservation, N.M., U.S. h7 108
Jemez Pueblo, N.M., U.S. B3 108
Jemison, Al., U.S. C3 78
Jena, Ger. E11 8
Jena, La., U.S. C3 95
Jenašimskij Polkan, Gora, mtn., Russia F12 24
Jendouba (Souk el Arba), Tun. M3 14
Jenisej, stm., Russia D11 24
Jenisejsk, Russia F12 24
Jenisejskij Zaliv, b., Russia C10 24
Jenkins, Ky., U.S. C7 94
Jenkins, co., Ga., U.S. D5 87
Jenkintown, Pa., U.S. o21 115
Jenks, Ok., U.S. A6 113
Jennings, La., U.S. D3 95
Jennings, Mo., U.S. f13 102
Jennings, co., In., U.S. G6 91
Jensen Beach, Fl., U.S. E6 86
Jepara, Indon. m15 33a
Jequié, Braz. B8 57
Jequitinhonha, stm., Braz. D9 57
Jerada, Mor. B5 42
Jerauld, co., S.D., U.S. C7 118
Jérémie, Haiti E10 64
Jeremoabo, Braz. F11 54
Jerevan, Arm. I6 22
Jerez de García Salinas, Mex. F8 62
Jerez de la Frontera, Spain I5 12
Jerez de los Caballeros, Spain G5 12
Jericho, Vt., U.S. B3 122
Jericho see Arīḥā, W. Bank D4 40
Jerimoth Hill, hill, R.I., U.S. C1 116
Jermyn, Pa., U.S. C10 115
Jerofej Pavlovič, Russia G18 24
Jerome, Id., U.S. G4 89
Jerome, Pa., U.S. F4 115
Jerome, co., Id., U.S. G4 89
Jeropol, Russia D27 24
Jersey, co., Il., U.S. D3 90
Jersey, dep., Eur. C4 10
Jersey City, N.J., U.S. B4 107
Jersey Mountain, mtn., Id., U.S. E3 89
Jersey Shore, Pa., U.S. D7 115
Jerseyville, Il., U.S. D3 90
Jerusalem see Yerushalayim, Isr. D4 40
Jervis Inlet, b., B.C., Can. D6 69
Jesenice, Slo. C9 14
Jessamine, co., Ky., U.S. C5 94
Jessore, Bngl. I13 38
Jessup, Md., U.S. B4 97
Jessup, Pa., U.S. m18 115
Jesup, Ga., U.S. E5 87
Jesup, Ia., U.S. B5 92
Jesup, Lake, l., Fl., U.S. D5 86
Jésus, Île, i., Que., Can. p19 74
Jesús Carranza, Mex. I12 62
Jetmore, Ks., U.S. D4 93
Jeumont, Fr. B11 10
Jever, Ger. B7 8
Jewel Cave National Monument, S.D., U.S. D2 118
Jewell, Ia., U.S. B4 92
Jewell, co., Ks., U.S. C5 93
Jewett City, Ct., U.S. C8 84
Jeypore, India C7 37
Jhang Maghiāna, Pak. E5 38
Jhānsi, India H8 38
Jharia, India I12 38
Jhelum, Pak. D5 38
Jhelum, stm., Asia E5 38
Jiading, China D10 28
Jiaganj, India H13 38
Jiamusi, China B13 26
Jian, China H3 28
Jianchuan, China A5 34
Jiangmen, China M2 28
Jiangsu, prov., China E10 26
Jiangxi, prov., China F10 26
Jiangyin, China D9 28
Jiangzi, China F13 38
Jianou, China H7 28
Jianshui, China C7 34
Jiaoxian, China D10 26
Jiaozuo, China D9 26
Jiashan, China C6 28
Jiawang, China A6 28
Jiaxian, China A2 28
Jiaxing, China E9 28
Jiazi, China M5 28
Jicarilla Apache Indian Reservation, N.M., U.S. A2 108
Jiddah, Sau. Ar. D2 46
Jieshou, China B4 28
Jieyang, China L5 28
Jihlava, Czech. F15 8
Jijiga, Eth. G3 46
Jijona, Spain G11 12
Jilemutu, China A11 26
Jilin, China C12 26
Jilin, prov., China C12 26
Jill, Kediet ej, mtn., Maur. D3 42
Jima, Eth. G2 46
Jimena de la Frontera, Spain I6 12
Jim Hogg, co., Tx., U.S. F3 120
Jim Lake, res., N.D., U.S. B7 111
Jim Thorpe, Pa., U.S. E10 115
Jim Wells, co., Tx., U.S. F3 120
Jinan (Tsinan), China D10 26
Jīnd, India F7 38
Jingdezhen (Kingtechen), China F6 28
Jingjiang, China C9 28
Jingxi, China C9 34
Jinhua, China F8 28
Jining, China C6 26
Jining, China D10 26
Jinja, Ug. A6 44
Jinning (Jiukunyang), China B7 34
Jinotega, Nic. H4 64
Jinshi, China F9 26
Jinxian, China D11 26
Jinzhou, China C11 26
Jiparaná, stm., Braz. E6 54
Jipijapa, Ec. H2 58
Jirjā, Egypt C12 42
Jisr ash-Shughūr, Syria B5 40
Jiujiang, China F4 28
Jiuling Shan, mts., China G3 28
Jiumangya, China B14 38
Jiuquan, China D6 26
Jixi, China B13 26
Joaçaba, Braz. B6 56
Joanna, S.C., U.S. C4 117
João Pessoa, Braz. E12 54
Joaquín V. González, Arg. B4 56
Job Peak, mtn., Nv., U.S. D3 105
Jobson (Vera), Arg. B4 56
Jocassee, Lake, res., U.S. B1 117
Jódar, Spain H8 12
Jo Daviess, co., Il., U.S. A3 90
Jodhpur, India G5 38
Joe Batt's Arm [-Barr'd Islands-Shoal Bay], Newf., Can. D4 72
Joensuu, Fin. E17 6
Joes Brook, stm., Vt., U.S. C4 122
Joes Creek, stm., W.V., U.S. m12 125
Joffre, Mount, mtn., Can. D3 68
Jogjakarta see Yogyakarta, Indon. G5 32
Johannesburg, S. Afr. G5 44
Johar, Som. H4 46
John, Cape, c., N.S., Can. D6 71
John Day, Or., U.S. C8 114
John Day, stm., Or., U.S. B6 114
John Day Dam, U.S. D5 124
John Day Fossil Beds National Monument, Or., U.S. C6 114
John F. Kennedy Space Center, sci., Fl., U.S. D6 86
John H. Kerr Dam, Va., U.S. D4 123
John H. Kerr Reservoir, res., U.S. D4 123
John Martin Reservoir, res., Co., U.S. C7 83
John Muir National Historical Site, hist., Ca., U.S. h8 82
John o' Groats, Scot., U.K. C9 7
John Redmond Reservoir, res., Ks., U.S. D8 93
John Sevier, Tn., U.S. m14 119
Johns Island, i., S.C., U.S. F7 117
Johnson, Ks., U.S. E2 93
Johnson, Vt., U.S. B3 122
Johnson, co., Ar., U.S. B2 81
Johnson, co., Ga., U.S. D4 87
Johnson, co., Il., U.S. F5 90
Johnson, co., In., U.S. F5 91
Johnson, co., Ia., U.S. C6 92
Johnson, co., Ks., U.S. D9 93
Johnson, co., Ky., U.S. C7 94
Johnson, co., Mo., U.S. C4 102
Johnson, co., Ne., U.S. D9 104
Johnson, co., Tn., U.S. C12 119
Johnson, co., Tx., U.S. C4 120
Johnson, co., Wy., U.S. B6 127
Johnsonburg, Pa., U.S. D4 115
Johnson City, N.Y., U.S. C5 109
Johnson City, Tn., U.S. C11 119
Johnson City, Tx., U.S. D3 120
Johnson Creek, Wi., U.S. E5 126
Johnsonville, S.C., U.S. D9 117
Johns Pass, strt., Fl., U.S. p10 86
Johnston, Ia., U.S. e8 92
Johnston, R.I., U.S. C4 116
Johnston, S.C., U.S. D4 117
Johnston, co., N.C., U.S. B4 110
Johnston, co., Ok., U.S. C5 113
Johnston City, Il., U.S. F5 90
Johnston Key, i., Fl., U.S. H5 86
Johnstown, Co., U.S. A6 83
Johnstown, N.Y., U.S. B6 109
Johnstown, Oh., U.S. B3 112
Johnstown, Pa., U.S. F4 115
John W. Flannagan Reservoir, res., Va., U.S. e9 123
Johor Baharu, Malay. N7 34
Joigny, Fr. E10 10
Joiner, Ar., U.S. B5 81
Joinvile, Braz. B7 56
Joinville, Fr. D12 10
Jokkmokk, Swe. C12 6
Joliet, Il., U.S. B5 90
Joliette, Que., Can. C4 74
Jolo Island, i., Phil. D7 32
Jombang, Indon. m16 33a
Jones, Ok., U.S. B4 113
Jones, co., Ga., U.S. C3 87
Jones, co., Ia., U.S. B6 92
Jones, co., Ms., U.S. D4 101
Jones, co., N.C., U.S. B5 110
Jones, co., S.D., U.S. D5 118
Jones, co., Tx., U.S. C3 120
Jonesboro, Ar., U.S. B5 81
Jonesboro, Ga., U.S. C2 87
Jonesboro, Il., U.S. F4 90
Jonesboro, In., U.S. D6 91
Jonesboro, La., U.S. B3 95
Jonesborough, Tn., U.S. C11 119
Jonesburg, Mo., U.S. C6 102
Jones Creek, Tx., U.S. s14 120
Jones Mill, Ar., U.S. C3 81
Jonesport, Me., U.S. D5 96
Jones Sound, strt., N.W. Ter., Can. A15 66
Jonestown, Ms., U.S. A3 101
Jonesville, La., U.S. C4 95
Jonesville, Mi., U.S. G6 99
Jonesville, N.C., U.S. A2 110
Jonesville, S.C., U.S. B4 117
Jonesville, Va., U.S. f8 123
Jongkha, China F11 38
Jönköping, Swe. H10 6
Jonquière, Que., Can. A6 74
Jonzac, Fr. G6 10
Joplin, Mo., U.S. D3 102
Joppatowne, Md., U.S. B5 97
Jordan, Mn., U.S. F5 100
Jordan, ctry., Asia D5 40
Jordan, stm., Asia C4 40
Jordan, stm., Ut., U.S. C4 121
Jordan Creek, stm., U.S. E9 114
Jordan Lake, res., Al., U.S. C3 78
Jorhāt, India G16 38
Jörn, Swe. D13 6
Jornado del Muerto, des., N.M., U.S. D3 108
Jos, Nig. G7 42
José Battle y Ordóñez, Ur. C5 56
Joseph, Or., U.S. B9 114
Joseph, Lac, l., Newf., Can. h8 72
Joseph Bonaparte Gulf, b., Austl. B5 50
Joseph City, Az., U.S. C5 80
Josephine, co., Or., U.S. E3 114
Joshua, Tx., U.S. n9 120
Joshua Tree, Ca., U.S. E5 82
Joshua Tree National Monument, Ca., U.S. F6 82
Joškar-Ola, Russia F7 22
Jourdanton, Tx., U.S. E3 120
Joutsijärvi, Fin. C16 6
Jovellanos, Cuba C7 64
J. Percy Priest Lake, res., Tn., U.S. A5 119
Juab, co., Ut., U.S. D2 121
Juan Aldama, Mex. E8 62
Juan de Fuca, Strait of, strt., N.A. G8 66
Juan de Nova, Île, i., Reu. E8 44
Juárez, Arg. D5 56
Juàzeiro, Braz. E10 54
Juàzeiro do Norte, Braz. E11 54
Jūbā, Sudan H12 42
Juba (Genale), stm., Afr. H3 46
Juchitán [de Zaragoza], Mex. I12 62
Judenburg, Aus. H14 8
Judith, stm., Mt., U.S. C7 103
Judith, Point, c., R.I., U.S. G4 85
Judith Basin, co., Mt., U.S. C6 103
Judith Island, i., N.C., U.S. B6 110
Judith Mountains, mts., Mt., U.S. C7 103
Judith Peak, mtn., Mt., U.S. C7 103
Judoma, stm., Russia F21 24
Judsonia, Ar., U.S. B4 81
Juigalpa, Nic. H5 64
Juiz de Fora, Braz. F7 57
Jukagirskoje Ploskogorje, plat., Russia D24 24
Jukte, Russia E15 24
Julesburg, Co., U.S. A8 83
Juliaca, Peru G4 54
Julian, Ca., U.S. F5 82
Julian, W.V., U.S. C3 125
Julian Alps, mts., Eur. C8 14
Juliana Top, mtn., Sur. C7 54
Julianehåb, Grnld. D23 66
Jülich, Ger. E6 8
Jullundur, India E6 38
Jumbo Peak, mtn., Nv., U.S. G7 105
Jumentos Cays, is., Bah. C10 64
Jumet, Bel. E4 8
Jumilla, Spain G10 12
Jump, stm., Wi., U.S. C3 126
Junāgadh, India J4 38
Junction, Tx., U.S. D3 120
Junction City, Ar., U.S. D3 81
Junction City, Ks., U.S. C7 93
Junction City, Ky., U.S. C5 94
Junction City, La., U.S. A3 95
Junction City, Or., U.S. C3 114
Jundiaí, Braz. G5 57
Juneau, Ak., U.S. D13 79
Juneau, Wi., U.S. E5 126
Juneau, co., Wi., U.S. E3 126
June in Winter, Lake, l., Fl., U.S. E5 86
Jungfrau, mtn., Switz. F14 10
Junggar Pendi, China B4 26
Juniata, Ne., U.S. D7 104
Juniata, co., Pa., U.S. F7 115
Juniata, stm., Pa., U.S. F7 115
Junín, Arg. C4 56
Junín, Lago de, l., Peru F3 54
Junín de los Andes, Arg. D2 56
Junior Lake, l., Me., U.S. C4 96
Juniper Mountains, mts., Az., U.S. B2 80
Junipero Serra Peak, mtn., Ca., U.S. D3 82
Junsele, Swe. E11 6
Jupiter, Fl., U.S. F6 86
Jupiter Inlet, b., Fl., U.S. F6 86
Jupiter Island, i., Fl., U.S. E6 86
Jura, mts., Eur. F13 10
Jura, i., Scot., U.K. F7 7
Jurga, Russia F10 24
Jūrmala, Lat. E6 18
Juruá, stm., S.A. D5 54
Juruena, stm., Braz. E7 54
Justin, Tx., U.S. C4 120
Justo Daract, Arg. C3 56
Jutaí, stm., Braz. D5 54
Jüterbog, Ger. D13 8
Jutiapa, Guat. G3 64
Juticalpa, Hond. G4 64
Jutland see Jylland, pen., Den. H7 6
Juventud, Isla de la (Isle of Pines), i., Cuba D6 64
Juwara, Oman E6 46
Juža, Russia E25 18
Južno-Sachalinsk, Russia H22 24
Južnyj, Mys, c., Russia F25 24
Jwayyā, Leb. C4 40
Jylland, pen., Den. H7 6
Jyväskylä, Fin. E15 6

K

K2 (Qogir Feng), mtn., Asia C7 38
Kaaawa, Hi., U.S. f10 88
Kaala, mtn., Hi., U.S. f9 88
Kaala Djerda, Tun. N3 14
Kaalualu Bay, b., Hi., U.S. E6 88
Kaaumakua, Puu, mtn., Hi., U.S. f10 88
Kabale, Ug. B5 44
Kabalo, Zaire C5 44
Kabambare, Zaire B5 44
Kåbdalis, Swe. C12 6
Kabetogama Lake, l., Mn., U.S. B5 100
Kabīr Kūh, mts., Iran B4 46
Kābol, Afg. C3 38
Kabompo, stm., Zam. D4 44
Kabongo, Zaire C5 44
Kābul, stm., Asia C4 38
Kabwe (Broken Hill), Zam. D5 44
Kachess Lake, res., Wa., U.S. B4 124
K'achta, Russia G15 24
Kačug, Russia G15 24
Kadan Kyun, i., Mya. H5 34
Kadiri, India E5 37
Kadoka, S.D., U.S. D4 118
Kaduna, Nig. F7 42
Kāduqlī, Sudan F11 42
Kadykčan, Russia E23 24
Kaédi, Maur. E3 42
Kaena Point, c., Hi., U.S. B3 88
Kaesŏng, N. Kor. D12 26
Kafia Kingi, Sudan G10 42
Kafue, stm., Zam. D5 44
Kaga, Japan F9 30
Kagamigahara, Japan G9 30
Kagaznagar, India C5 37
Kagoshima, Japan K3 30
Kahaluu, Hi., U.S. D6 88
Kahaluu, Hi., U.S. g10 88
Kahana Bay, b., Hi., U.S. f10 88
Kahemba, Zaire C3 44
Kahoka, Mo., U.S. A6 102
Kahoolawe, i., Hi., U.S. C5 88
Kahramanmaraş, Tur. H15 4
Kahuku, Hi., U.S. B4 88
Kahuku Point, c., Hi., U.S. B4 88
Kahului, Hi., U.S. C5 88
Kahului Bay, b., Hi., U.S. C5 88
Kai, Kepulauan, is., Indon. G9 32
Kaibab Indian Reservation, Az., U.S. A3 80
Kaieteur Fall, wtfl, Guy. E13 58
Kaifeng, China E9 26
Kaikoura, N.Z. E4 52
Kaili, China A10 34
Kailua, Hi., U.S. B4 88
Kailua Bay, b., Hi., U.S. g11 88
Kailua Kona, Hi., U.S. D6 88
Kaimana, Indon. F9 32
Kaimanawa Mountains, mts., N.Z. C5 52
Kainan, Japan H8 30
Kaiserslautern, Ger. F7 8
Kaitangata, N.Z. G2 52
Kaiwi Channel, strt., Hi., U.S. B4 88
Kajaani, Fin. D16 6
Kajakī, Band-e, res., Afg. D1 38
Kajan, stm., Indon. E6 32
Kajang, Malay. M6 34
Kakamas, S. Afr. G4 44
Kaka Point, c., Hi., U.S. C5 88
Kake, Ak., U.S. D13 79
Kakegawa, Japan H11 30
Kakie, Bots. F4 44
Kākināda, India D7 37
Kakogawa, Japan H7 30
Kaladan, stm., Asia D2 34
Ka Lae, c., Hi., U.S. E6 88
Kalahari Desert, des., Afr. F4 44
Kālahasti, India F5 37
Kalaheo, Hi., U.S. B2 88
Kalajoki, Fin. D14 6
Kalakan, Russia F17 24
Kalām, Pak. C5 38
Kalama, Wa., U.S. C3 124
Kalámai, Grc. L6 16
Kalamazoo, Mi., U.S. F5 99
Kalamazoo, co., Mi., U.S. F5 99
Kalamazoo, stm., Mi., U.S. F5 99
Kalasin, Thai. F7 34
Kalāt, Pak. F2 38
Kalaupapa Peninsula, pen., Hi., U.S. B5 88
Kalawao, co., Hi., U.S. B5 88
Kalb, Ra's al-, c., Yemen F4 46
Kale, Tur. L12 16
Kaleden, B.C., Can. E8 69
Kalemie (Albertville), Zaire C5 44
Kalena, Puu, mtn., Hi., U.S. g9 88
Kalgin Island, i., Ak., U.S. g16 79
Kalgoorlie, Austl. F4 50
Kalima, Zaire B5 44
Kálimnos, Grc. M10 16
Kaliningrad (Königsberg), Russia G3 18
Kalinkoviči, Bela. I12 18
Kalispel Indian Reservation, Wa., U.S. A8 124
Kalispell, Mt., U.S. B2 103
Kalisz, Pol. D18 8
Kalkaska, Mi., U.S. D5 99
Kalkaska, co., Mi., U.S. D5 99
Kalmar, Swe. H11 6
Kalohi Channel, strt., Hi., U.S. C4 88
Kālol, India I5 38
Kaloli Point, c., Hi., U.S. D7 88
Kalona, Ia., U.S. C6 92
Kalone Peak, mtn., B.C., Can. C4 69
Kaluga, Russia G19 18
Kalutara, Sri L. I5 37
Kamaishi, Japan C14 30
Kamakou, mtn., Hi., U.S. B5 88
Kamakura, Japan G12 30
Kamālia, Pak. E5 38
Kamarān, i., Yemen E3 46
Kamas, Ut., U.S. C4 121
Kamba, China F13 38
Kambam, India H4 37
Kambar, Pak. G2 38
Kamčatka, stm., Russia F25 24
Kamčatka, Poluostrov, pen., Russia F25 24
Kamčatskij Zaliv, b., Russia F26 24
Kamen', Gora, mtn., Russia D12 24
Kamen'-na-Obi, Russia G10 24
Kamenz, Ger. D14 8
Kamiah, Id., U.S. C2 89
Kamiak Butte, mtn., Wa., U.S. C8 124
Kamienna Góra, Pol. E16 8
Kamilukuak Lake, l., N.W. Ter., Can. D12 66
Kamina, Zaire C5 44
Kaminak Lake, l., N.W. Ter., Can. D13 66
Kaminuriak Lake, l., N.W. Ter., Can. D13 66
Kamitsushima, Japan H2 30
Kamloops, B.C., Can. D7 69
Kamo, Japan E12 30
Kāmoke, Pak. E6 38
Kampala, Ug. A6 44
Kampar, Malay. L6 34
Kampen, Neth. C5 8
Kampeska, Lake, l., S.D., U.S. C8 118
Kâmpóng Cham, Camb. H8 34
Kâmpóng Chhnăng, Camb. H8 34
Kâmpóng Saôm, Camb. I7 34
Kâmpóng Saôm, Chhâk, b., Camb. I7 34
Kâmpóng Thum, Camb. H8 34
Kâmpôt, Camb. I8 34
Kāmthi, India B5 37
Kamuela (Waimea), Hi., U.S. C6 88
Kamui-misaki, c., Japan p18 30a
Kan, stm., Asia H9 34
Kanab, Ut., U.S. F3 121
Kanab Creek, stm., U.S. A3 80
Kanabec, co., Mn., U.S. E5 100
Kanaga Island, i., Ak., U.S. E4 79
Kanairiktok, stm., Newf., Can. g9 72
Kananga (Luluabourg), Zaire C4 44
Kanapou Bay, b., Hi., U.S. C5 88
Kanata, Ont., Can. B9 73
Kanawha, Ia., U.S. B4 92
Kanawha, co., W.V., U.S. C3 125
Kanawha, stm., W.V., U.S. C3 125
Kanazawa, Japan F9 30
Kanchanaburi, Thai. G5 34

Name	Map Ref	Page
Kānchenjunga, mtn., Asia	G13	38
Kānchipuram, India	F5	37
Kandhkot, Pak.	F3	38
Kāndi, India	I13	38
Kandiyohi, co., Mn., U.S.	E3	100
Kandy, Sri L.	I6	37
Kane, Pa., U.S.	C4	115
Kane, co., Il., U.S.	B5	90
Kane, co., Ut., U.S.	F3	121
Kaneohe, Hi., U.S.	B4	88
Kaneohe Bay, b., Hi., U.S.	g10	88
Kaneohe Bay Marine Corps Air Station, mil., Hi., U.S.	g10	88
Kangar, Malay.	K6	34
Kangaroo Island, i., Austl.	G7	50
Kangean, Kepulauan, is., Indon.	G6	32
Kangnŭng, S. Kor.	D12	26
Kango, Gabon	A2	44
Kangto, mtn., Asia	G15	38
Kaniama, Zaire	C4	44
Kankakee, Il., U.S.	B6	90
Kankakee, co., Il., U.S.	B6	90
Kankakee, stm., U.S.	B5	90
Kankan, Gui.	F4	42
Kanmaw Kyun, i., Mya.	I5	34
Kannapolis, N.C., U.S.	B2	110
Kannauj, India	G8	38
Kannonkoski, Fin.	E15	6
Kannus, Fin.	E14	6
Kano, Nig.	F7	42
Kanonji, Japan	H6	30
Kanopolis, Ks., U.S.	D5	93
Kanopolis Lake, res., Ks., U.S.	D5	93
Kanoya, Japan	K3	30
Kānpur, India	G9	38
Kansas, Il., U.S.	D6	90
Kansas, state, U.S.	D5	93
Kansas, stm., Ks., U.S.	C7	93
Kansas City, Ks., U.S.	C9	93
Kansas City, Mo., U.S.	B3	102
Kansk, Russia	F13	24
Kantō-sammyaku, mts., Japan	F11	30
Kanuma, Japan	F12	30
Kanye, Bots.	F5	44
Kaohsiung, Tai.	M9	28
Kaohsiunghsien, Tai.	M9	28
Kaokoveld, plat., Nmb.	E2	44
Kaolack, Sen.	F2	42
Kapaa, Hi., U.S.	A2	88
Kapaau, Hi., U.S.	C6	88
Kapadvanj, India	I5	38
Kapanga, Zaire	C4	44
Kapapa Island, i., Hi., U.S.	g10	88
Kapfenberg, Aus.	H15	8
Kaplan, La., U.S.	D3	95
Kaposvár, Hung.	I17	8
Kaptai, Bngl.	I15	38
Kapuas, stm., Indon.	F4	32
Kapūrthala, India	E6	38
Kapuskasing, Ont., Can.	o19	73
Karabük, Tur.	G14	4
Karacabey, Tur.	I12	16
Karacaköy, Tur.	H12	16
Karāchi, Pak.	H2	38
Karād, India	D3	37
Karaganda, Kaz.	H8	24
Karaginskij, Ostrov, i., Russia	F26	24
Karaginskij Zaliv, b., Russia	F26	24
Karagoš, Gora, mtn., Russia	G11	24
Kāraikkudi, India	G5	37
Karakelong, Pulau, i., Indon.	E8	32
Karakoram Range, mts., Asia	C7	38
Karakumskij kanal, Turk.	J10	22
Karaman, Tur.	H14	4
Karaman, Tur.	L13	16
Karamay, China	B3	26
Karamürsel, Tur.	I13	16
Kāranja, India	B4	37
Karasburg, Nmb.	G3	44
Karasjok, Nor.	B15	6
Karatsu, Japan	I2	30
Karaul, Russia	C10	24
Karauli, India	G7	38
Karawang, Indon.	m13	33a
Karawanken, mts., Eur.	C9	14
Karbalā', Iraq	B3	46
Kårböle, Swe.	F10	6
Karcag, Hung.	H20	8
Kardeljevo, Cro.	F12	14
Kardhítsa, Grc.	J5	16
Kărdžali, Bul.	H9	16
Kargasok, Russia	F10	24
Karhula, Fin.	F16	6
Kariba, Zimb.	E5	44
Kariba, Lake, res., Afr.	E5	44
Karibib, Nmb.	F3	44
Karigasniemi, Fin.	B15	6
Karimata, Kepulauan, is., Indon.	F4	32
Karimata, Selat (Karimata Strait), strt., Indon.	F4	32
Karīmganj, India	H15	38
Karīmnagar, India	C5	37
Karin, Som.	F4	46
Karis (Karjaa), Fin.	F14	6
Kariya, Japan	H9	30
Karkabet, Erit.	E2	46
Karlovac, Cro.	D10	14
Karlovo, Bul.	G8	16
Karlovy Vary, Czech.	E12	8
Karlshamn, Swe.	H10	6
Karlskoga, Swe.	G10	6
Karlskrona, Swe.	H10	6
Karlsruhe, Ger.	F8	8
Karlstad, Swe.	G9	6
Karlstad, Mn., U.S.	B2	100
Karnāl, India	F7	38
Karnaphuli Reservoir, res., Bngl.	I15	38
Karnataka, state, India	E3	37
Karnes, co., Tx., U.S.	E4	120
Karnes City, Tx., U.S.	E4	120
Karns, Tn., U.S.	n13	119
Karonga, Mwi.	C6	44
Kárpathos, i., Grc.	N11	16
Karpenísion, Grc.	K5	16
Kars, Tur.	G16	4
Kärsämäki, Fin.	E15	6
Karši, Uzb.	J11	22
Kartal, Tur.	I13	16
Karufa, Indon.	F9	32
Karungi, Swe.	C14	6
Karūr, India	G5	37
Karviná, Czech.	F18	8
Kārwār, India	E3	37
Kasai (Cassai), stm., Afr.	B3	44
Kasaji, Zaire	D4	44
Kasama, Zam.	D6	44
Kasanga, Tan.	C6	44
Kasaoka, Japan	H6	30
Kāsaragod, India	F3	37
Kasba Lake, l., N.W. Ter., Can.	D12	66
Kaseda, Japan	K3	30
Kasempa, Zam.	D5	44
Kasenga, Zaire	D5	44
Kasese, Zaire	B5	44
Kāsganj, India	G8	38
Kāshān, Iran	B5	46
Kashi, China	D2	26
Kashima-nada, Japan	F13	30
Kashīpur, India	F8	38
Kashiwa, Japan	G12	30
Kashiwazaki, Japan	E11	30
Kashmir see Jammu and Kashmir, dep., Asia	C6	38
Kasimov, Russia	G24	18
Kašin, Russia	D20	18
Kašira, Russia	G21	18
Kaskaskia, stm., Il., U.S.	D5	90
Kaskö (Kaskinen), Fin.	E13	6
Kaslo, B.C., Can.	E9	69
Kasongo, Zaire	B5	44
Kasota, Mn., U.S.	F5	100
Kasr, Ra's, c., Sudan	E13	42
Kassalā, Sudan	E13	42
Kassel, Ger.	D9	8
Kasson, Mn., U.S.	F6	100
Kastoría, Grc.	I5	16
Kasugai, Japan	G9	30
Kasūr, Pak.	E6	38
Katahdin, Mount, mtn., Me., U.S.	C4	96
Katanga Plateau, plat., Zaire	D5	44
Katchall Island, i., India	K2	34
Kateríni, Grc.	I6	16
Kates Needle, mtn., Ak., U.S.	m24	79
Katherine, Austl.	B6	50
Kāthiāwār, pen., India	I4	38
Kathleen, Fl., U.S.	D4	86
Kāthmāndau, Nepal	G11	38
Katihār, India	H12	38
Katiola, C. Iv.	G4	42
Katmai, Mount, mtn., Ak., U.S.	D9	79
Katmai National Park, Ak., U.S.	D9	79
Katmandu see Kāthmāndau, Nepal	G11	38
Katowice, Pol.	E19	8
Kātrīnā, Jabal, mtn., Egypt	C12	42
Katrineholm, Swe.	G11	6
Katsina, Nig.	F7	42
Katsuta, Japan	F13	30
Kattegat, strt., Eur.	H8	6
Katy, Tx., U.S.	r14	120
Kauai, co., Hi., U.S.	B1	88
Kauai, i., Hi., U.S.	A2	88
Kauai Channel, strt., Hi., U.S.	B3	88
Kau Desert, des., Hi., U.S.	D6	88
Kaufbeuren, Ger.	H10	8
Kaufman, Tx., U.S.	C4	120
Kaufman, co., Tx., U.S.	C4	120
Kauiki Head, c., Hi., U.S.	C6	88
Kaukauna, Wi., U.S.	D5	126
Kaukauveld, mts., Afr.	F3	44
Kaula Island, i., Hi., U.S.	m15	88
Kaulakahi Channel, strt., Hi., U.S.	A2	88
Kaumakani, Hi., U.S.	B2	88
Kaunakakai, Hi., U.S.	B4	88
Kauna Point, c., Hi., U.S.	D6	88
Kaunas, Lith.	G6	18
Kaura Namoda, Nig.	F7	42
Kaustinen, Fin.	E14	6
Kavača, Russia	E27	24
Kavacık, Tur.	J12	16
Kavalerovo, Russia	I21	24
Kavála, Grc.	I8	16
Kavaratti, India	G2	37
Kavieng, Pap. N. Gui.	k17	50a
Kawagoe, Japan	G12	30
Kawaguchi, Japan	G12	30
Kawaihoa Point, c., Hi., U.S.	B1	88
Kawaikini, mtn., Hi., U.S.	A2	88
Kawambwa, Zam.	C5	44
Kawanoe, Japan	H6	30
Kawasaki, Japan	G12	30
Kawich Peak, mtn., Nv., U.S.	F5	105
Kawich Range, mts., Nv., U.S.	F5	105
Kaw Lake, res., Ok., U.S.	A5	113
Kawm Umbū, Egypt	D12	42
Kay, co., Ok., U.S.	A4	113
Kayankulam, India	H4	37
Kaycee, Wy., U.S.	C6	127
Kayenta, Az., U.S.	A5	80
Kayes, Mali	F3	42
Kayseri, Tur.	H15	4
Kaysville, Ut., U.S.	B4	121
Kažačinskoje, Russia	F12	24
Kazačje, Russia	C21	24
Kazakhstan, ctry., Asia	H11	22
Kazan', Russia	F7	22
Kazanlăk, Bul.	G9	16
Kāzerūn, Iran	C5	46
Keaau, Hi., U.S.	D6	88
Keahiakahoe, Puu, mtn., Hi., U.S.	g10	88
Keahole Point, c., Hi., U.S.	D5	88
Kealaikahiki Channel, strt., Hi., U.S.	C5	88
Kealaikahiki Point, c., Hi., U.S.	C5	88
Kealakekua, Hi., U.S.	D6	88
Kealia, Hi., U.S.	A2	88
Keams Canyon, Az., U.S.	B5	80
Keanapapa Point, c., Hi., U.S.	C4	88
Keansburg, N.J., U.S.	C4	107
Kearney, Mo., U.S.	B3	102
Kearney, Ne., U.S.	D6	104
Kearney, co., Ne., U.S.	D7	104
Kearns, Ut., U.S.	C4	121
Kearny, Az., U.S.	D5	80
Kearny, N.J., U.S.	h8	107
Kearny, co., Ks., U.S.	D2	93
Kebri Dehar, Eth.	G3	46
Kechika, stm., B.C., Can.	E7	66
Kecskemét, Hung.	I19	8
Kedges Straits, strt., Md., U.S.	D5	97
Kedgwick, N.B., Can.	B2	71
Kediri, Indon.	m16	32
Kedon, Russia	E25	24
Kédougou, Sen.	F3	42
Kędzierzyn, Pol.	E18	8
Keego Harbor, Mi., U.S.	o15	99
Keele Peak, mtn., Yukon, Can.	D6	66
Keelung see Chilung, Tai.	J10	28
Keene, N.H., U.S.	E2	106
Keene, Tx., U.S.	n9	120
Keeper Hill, hill, Ire.	I4	7
Keeseville, N.Y., U.S.	f11	109
Keesler Air Force Base, mil., Ms., U.S.	E5	101
Keetmanshoop, Nmb.	G3	44
Keet Seel Ruin, hist., Az., U.S.	A5	80
Keewatin, Ont., Can.	E4	70
Keewatin, Mn., U.S.	C5	100
Kefallinía, i., Grc.	K4	16
Keffi, Nig.	G7	42
Keflavík, Ice.	C3	4
Ke Ga, Mui, c., Viet.	H10	34
Kegonsa, Lake, l., Wi., U.S.	F4	126
Keiser, Ar., U.S.	B5	81
Keith, Scot., U.K.	D10	7
Keith, co., Ne., U.S.	C4	104
Keizer, Or., U.S.	C3	114
Kejimkujik National Park, N.S., Can.	E4	71
Kekaha, Hi., U.S.	B2	88
Kelafo, Eth.	G3	46
Kelang, Malay.	M6	34
Kelheim, Ger.	G11	8
Kelibia, Tun.	M6	14
Keller, Tx., U.S.	n9	120
Kellett, Cape, c., N.W. Ter., Can.	B7	66
Kelleys Island, i., Oh., U.S.	A3	112
Kellogg, Id., U.S.	B2	89
Kellogg, Ia., U.S.	C5	92
Kelloselkä, Fin.	C17	6
Kelly Air Force Base, mil., Tx., U.S.	k7	120
Kelly Island, i., De., U.S.	D4	85
Kellyville, Ok., U.S.	B5	113
Kélo, Chad	G9	42
Kelottijärvi, Fin.	B14	6
Kelowna, B.C., Can.	E8	69
Kelso, Wa., U.S.	C3	124
Keluang, Malay.	M7	34
Kemerovo, Russia	F11	24
Kemi, Fin.	D15	6
Kemijärvi, Fin.	C16	6
Kemijoki, stm., Fin.	C15	6
Kemmerer, Wy., U.S.	E2	127
Kemp, Tx., U.S.	C4	120
Kemp, Lake, res., Tx., U.S.	C3	120
Kemper, co., Ms., U.S.	C5	101
Kemps Bay, Bah.	B9	64
Kempt, Lac, l., Que., Can.	G18	66
Kempten [Allgäu], Ger.	H10	8
Kemptville, Ont., Can.	B9	73
Kemul, Kong, mtn., Indon.	E6	32
Kenai, Ak., U.S.	C9	79
Kenai Fjords National Park, Ak., U.S.	D10	79
Kenai Mountains, mts., Ak., U.S.	h16	79
Kenai Peninsula, pen., Ak., U.S.	h16	79
Kenansville, N.C., U.S.	C5	110
Kenbridge, Va., U.S.	D4	123
Kendall, Fl., U.S.	s13	86
Kendall, co., Il., U.S.	B5	90
Kendall, co., Tx., U.S.	E3	120
Kendall, Cape, c., N.W. Ter., Can.	D15	66
Kendall Park, N.J., U.S.	C3	107
Kendallville, In., U.S.	B7	91
Kendari, Indon.	F7	32
Kenedy, Tx., U.S.	E4	120
Kenedy, co., Tx., U.S.	F4	120
Kenema, S.L.	G3	42
Kenesaw, Ne., U.S.	D7	104
Kēng Tung, Mya.	D5	34
Kenhardt, S. Afr.	G4	44
Kenilworth, Il., U.S.	h9	90
Kenitra, Mor.	B4	42
Kenly, N.C., U.S.	B4	110
Kenmare, N.D., U.S.	A3	111
Kenmore, N.Y., U.S.	C2	109
Kennaday Peak, mtn., Wy., U.S.	E6	127
Kennebago Lake, l., Me., U.S.	C2	96
Kennebec, co., Me., U.S.	D3	96
Kennebec, stm., Me., U.S.	D3	96
Kennebunk, Me., U.S.	E2	96
Kennebunkport, Me., U.S.	E2	96
Kennedy Entrance, strt., Ak., U.S.	D9	79
Kennedy Peak, mtn., Mya.	C2	34
Kenner, La., U.S.	E5	95
Kennesaw, Ga., U.S.	B2	87
Kennesaw Mountain, mtn., Ga., U.S.	C2	87
Kennett, Mo., U.S.	E7	102
Kennett Square, Pa., U.S.	G10	115
Kennewick, Wa., U.S.	C6	124
Kenn Reefs, rf., Austl.	D11	50
Kennydale, Wa., U.S.	e11	124
Keno, Or., U.S.	E5	114
Kénogami, Lac, l., Que., Can.	A6	74
Kenora, Ont., Can.	o16	73
Kenosha, Wi., U.S.	F6	126
Kenosha, co., Wi., U.S.	F5	126
Kenova, W.V., U.S.	C2	125
Kensett, Ar., U.S.	B4	81
Kensico Reservoir, res., N.Y., U.S.	g13	109
Kensington, P.E.I., Can.	C6	71
Kensington, Ct., U.S.	C4	84
Kensington, Md., U.S.	B3	97
Kent, Oh., U.S.	A4	112
Kent, Wa., U.S.	B3	124
Kent, co., De., U.S.	D3	85
Kent, co., Md., U.S.	B5	97
Kent, co., Mi., U.S.	E5	99
Kent, co., R.I., U.S.	D2	116
Kent, co., Tx., U.S.	C2	120
Kent City, Mi., U.S.	E5	99
Kent Island, i., De., U.S.	D4	85
Kent Island, i., Md., U.S.	C5	97
Kentland, In., U.S.	C3	91
Kenton, De., U.S.	D3	85
Kenton, Oh., U.S.	B2	112
Kenton, Tn., U.S.	A2	119
Kenton, co., Ky., U.S.	B5	94
Kent Peninsula, pen., N.W. Ter., Can.	C11	66
Kent Point, c., Md., U.S.	C5	97
Kentucky, state, U.S.	C4	94
Kentucky, stm., Ky., U.S.	B5	94
Kentwood, La., U.S.	D5	95
Kentwood, Mi., U.S.	F5	99
Kenvil, N.J., U.S.	B3	107
Kenvir, Ky., U.S.	D6	94
Kenya, ctry., Afr.	B7	44
Kenya, Mount see Kirinyaga, mtn., Kenya	B7	44
Kenyon, Mn., U.S.	F6	100
Kenyon, R.I., U.S.	F2	116
Keokea, Hi., U.S.	C5	88
Keokuk, Ia., U.S.	D6	92
Keokuk, co., Ia., U.S.	C5	92
Keokuk Lock and Dam, U.S.	D6	92
Keosauqua, Ia., U.S.	D6	92
Keota, Ia., U.S.	C6	92
Keota, Ok., U.S.	B7	113
Keowee, Lake, res., S.C., U.S.	B2	117
Kepi, Indon.	G10	32
Kerala, state, India	G4	37
Kerch, Ukr.	H5	22
Keremeos, B.C., Can.	E8	69
Keren, Erit.	E2	46
Kerens, Tx., U.S.	C4	120
Kerguélen, Îles, is., F.S.A.T.	J17	2
Kerhonkson, N.Y., U.S.	D6	109
Kericho, Kenya	B7	44
Kerinci, Gunung, mtn., Indon.	F3	32
Kerkhoven, Mn., U.S.	E3	100
Kérkira (Corfu), Grc.	J3	16
Kérkira, i., Grc.	J3	16
Kermān, Iran	B6	46
Kerme Körfezi, b., Tur.	M11	16
Kermit, Tx., U.S.	D1	120
Kermode, Mount, mtn., B.C., Can.	C2	69
Kern, co., Ca., U.S.	E4	82
Kern, stm., Ca., U.S.	E4	82
Kernersville, N.C., U.S.	A2	110
Kernville, Ca., U.S.	E4	82
Kerr, co., Tx., U.S.	D3	120
Kerr, Lake, l., Fl., U.S.	C5	86
Kerrville, Tx., U.S.	D3	120
Kerry Head, c., Ire.	I3	7
Kersey, Co., U.S.	A6	83
Kershaw, S.C., U.S.	B6	117
Kershaw, co., S.C., U.S.	C6	117
Kerulen (Cherlen), stm., Asia	B9	26
Kesagami Lake, l., Ont., Can.	F16	66
Keşan, Tur.	I10	16
Kesennuma, Japan	D14	30
Keshena, Wi., U.S.	D5	126
Ket', stm., Russia	F11	24
Keta, Ozero, l., Russia	D11	24
Ketchikan, Ak., U.S.	D13	79
Ketchum, Id., U.S.	F4	89
Kettering, Eng., U.K.	I12	7
Kettering, Oh., U.S.	C1	112
Kettle, stm., Mn., U.S.	D6	100
Kettle Creek, stm., Pa., U.S.	D6	115
Kettle Creek Lake, res., Pa., U.S.	D6	115
Kettle Falls, Wa., U.S.	A7	124
Keuka Lake, l., N.Y., U.S.	C3	109
Kew, T./C. Is.	D11	64
Kewanee, Il., U.S.	B4	90
Kewaskum, Wi., U.S.	E5	126
Kewaunee, Wi., U.S.	D6	126
Kewaunee, co., Wi., U.S.	D6	126
Keweenaw, co., Mi., U.S.	A2	99
Keweenaw Bay, b., Mi., U.S.	B2	99
Keweenaw Peninsula, pen., Mi., U.S.	A3	99
Keweenaw Point, c., Mi., U.S.	A3	99
Keya Paha, co., Ne., U.S.	B6	104
Keya Paha, stm., U.S.	A5	104
Keyhole Reservoir, res., Wy., U.S.	B8	127
Key Largo, Fl., U.S.	G6	86
Keyport, N.J., U.S.	C4	107
Keyser, W.V., U.S.	B6	125
Keystone, W.V., U.S.	D3	125
Keystone Heights, Fl., U.S.	C4	86
Keystone Lake, res., Ok., U.S.	A5	113
Keystone Peak, mtn., Az., U.S.	F4	80
Keysville, Va., U.S.	C4	123
Key West, Fl., U.S.	H5	86
Key West Naval Air Station, mil., Fl., U.S.	H5	86
Kezar Falls, Me., U.S.	E2	96
Kezar Lake, l., Me., U.S.	D2	96
Kežma, Russia	F14	24
Khadki (Kirkee), India	C2	37
Khairpur, Pak.	G3	38
Khalkís, Grc.	K7	16
Khambhāliya, India	I3	38
Khambhāt, Gulf of, b., India	B2	37
Khāmgaon, India	B4	37
Khammam, India	D6	37
Khānābād, Afg.	B3	38
Khānaqīn, Iraq	B4	46
Khandwa, India	B4	37
Khānewāl, Pak.	E4	38
Khaniá, Grc.	N8	16
Khanna, India	E7	38
Khānpur, Pak.	F4	38
Khān Yūnus, Isr. Occ.	D4	40
Kharagpur, India	I12	38
Khargon, India	J6	38
Kharkiv, Ukr.	G5	22
Khartoum see Al-Kharṭūm, Sudan	E12	42
Kherson, Ukr.	H4	22
Khíos, Grc.	K10	16
Kholm, Afg.	B2	38
Khong, Laos	G8	34
Khong Sédone, Laos	G8	34
Khon Kaen, Thai.	F7	34
Khóra Sfakíon, Grc.	N8	16
Khorramābād, Iran	B4	46
Khorramshahr, Iran	B4	46
Khouribga, Mor.	B4	42
Khowst, Afg.	D3	38
Khulna, Bngl.	I13	38
Khunjerab Pass, Asia	B6	38
Khurja, India	F7	38
Khūryān Mūryān (Kuria Muria Isls, is., Oman	E6	46
Khushāb, Pak.	D5	38
Khvājeh Moḥammad, Kūh-e, mts., Afg.	B4	38
Khvoy, Iran	J6	22
Khyber Pass, Asia	C4	38
Kiamichi, stm., Ok., U.S.	C6	113
Kiamika, stm., Que., Can.	C2	74
Kiana, Ak., U.S.	B7	79
Kiawah Island, i., S.C., U.S.	F7	117
Kibangou, Congo	B2	44
Kibombo, Zaire	B5	44
Kibre Mengist, Eth.	G2	46
Kičevo, Mac.	H4	16
Kichčik, Russia	G25	24
Kickamuit, stm., R.I., U.S.	D5	116
Kickapoo, stm., Wi., U.S.	E3	126
Kickapoo, Lake, res., Tx., U.S.	C3	120
Kickapoo Indian Reservation, Ks., U.S.	C8	93
Kicking Horse Pass, Can.	D2	68
Kidal, Mali	E6	42
Kidder, co., N.D., U.S.	C6	111
Kidira, Sen.	F3	42
Kiefer, Ok., U.S.	B5	113
Kiel, Ger.	A10	8
Kiel, Wi., U.S.	E5	126
Kielce, Pol.	E20	8
Kieler Bucht, b., Ger.	A10	8
Kiester, Mn., U.S.	G5	100
Kiev see Kyyiv, Ukr.	G4	22
Kiffa, Maur.	E3	42
Kigali, Rw.	B6	44
Kigoma, Tan.	B5	44
Kihei, Hi., U.S.	C5	88
Kihniö, Fin.	E14	6
Kiholo Bay, b., Hi., U.S.	D5	88
Kii-suidō, strt., Japan	I7	30
Kikinda, Yugo.	D4	16
Kikládhes, is., Grc.	L8	16
Kikwit, Zaire	C3	44
Kilauea, Hi., U.S.	A2	88
Kilauea Crater, crat., Hi., U.S.	D6	88
Kilauea Point, c., Hi., U.S.	A2	88
Kilgore, Tx., U.S.	C5	120
Kilimanjaro, mtn., Tan.	B7	44
Kilis, Tur.	A5	40
Kilkee, Ire.	I3	7
Kilkenny, Ire.	I5	7
Kilkís, Grc.	H6	16
Killala, Ire.	G3	7
Killaloe Station, Ont., Can.	B7	73
Killam, Alta., Can.	C5	68
Killarney, Man., Can.	E2	70
Killarney, Ire.	I3	7
Killarney Provincial Park, Ont., Can.	A3	73
Killdeer, N.D., U.S.	B3	111
Killeen, Tx., U.S.	D4	120
Killen, Al., U.S.	A2	78
Killian, La., U.S.	h10	95
Killik, stm., Ak., U.S.	B9	79
Killona, La., U.S.	h11	95
Killorglin, Ire.	I3	7
Kilmarnock, Scot., U.K.	F8	7
Kilmarnock, Va., U.S.	C6	123
Kilmichael, Ms., U.S.	B4	101
Kiln, Ms., U.S.	E4	101
Kilombero, stm., Tan.	C7	44
Kilosa, Tan.	C7	44
Kilpisjärvi, Fin.	B13	6
Kilwa, Zaire	C5	44
Kilwa Kivinje, Tan.	C7	44
Kimball, Mn., U.S.	E4	100
Kimball, Ne., U.S.	C2	104
Kimball, S.D., U.S.	D7	118
Kimball, co., Ne., U.S.	C2	104
Kimball, Mount, mtn., Ak., U.S.	C11	79
Kimberley, B.C., Can.	E9	69
Kimberley, S. Afr.	G4	44
Kimberley Plateau, plat., Austl.	C5	50
Kimberlin Heights, Tn., U.S.	n14	119
Kimberly, Al., U.S.	B3	78
Kimberly, Id., U.S.	G4	89
Kimberly, W.V., U.S.	m13	125
Kimberly, Wi., U.S.	h9	126
Kimble, co., Tx., U.S.	D3	120
Kimch'aek, N. Kor.	C12	26
Kimovsk, Russia	H21	18
Kimry, Russia	E20	18
Kinabalu, Gunong, mtn., Malay.	D6	32
Kinbasket Lake, res., B.C., Can.	D8	69
Kincaid, Il., U.S.	D4	90
Kincaid, W.V., U.S.	m13	125
Kincaid, Lake, res., Il., U.S.	D4	90
Kincardine, Ont., Can.	C3	73
Kincheloe Air Force Base, mil., Mi., U.S.	B6	99
Kinder, La., U.S.	D3	95
Kindia, Gui.	F3	42
Kindu, Zaire	B5	44
Kinešma, Russia	D25	18
King, N.C., U.S.	A2	110
King, Wi., U.S.	D4	126
King, co., Tx., U.S.	C2	120
King, co., Wa., U.S.	B3	124
King and Queen, co., Va., U.S.	C6	123
Kingaroy, Austl.	E10	50
King City, Ca., U.S.	D3	82
King City, Mo., U.S.	A3	102

Name — Map Ref — Page

King Cove, Ak., U.S. E7 79
Kingfield, Me., U.S. D2 96
Kingfisher, Ok., U.S. B4 113
Kingfisher, co., Ok., U.S. B3 113
King George, co., Va., U.S. B5 123
King Island, i., Austl. G8 50
King Island, i., B.C., Can. C4 69
King Lear Peak, mtn., Nv., U.S. B3 105
King Leopold Ranges, mts., Austl. C5 50
Kingman, Az., U.S. B1 80
Kingman, Ks., U.S. E5 93
Kingman, co., Ks., U.S. E5 93
King Mountain, mtn., Or., U.S. E3 114
King Mountain, mtn., Or., U.S. D8 114
King Peak, mtn., Ca., U.S. B1 82
Kings, Ms., U.S. C3 101
Kings, co., Ca., U.S. D4 82
Kings, co., N.Y., U.S. E7 109
Kings, stm., Ar., U.S. A2 81
Kings, stm., Ca., U.S. D4 82
Kings, stm., Nv., U.S. B3 105
King Salmon, Ak., U.S. D8 79
Kingsburg, Ca., U.S. D4 82
Kingsbury, co., S.D., U.S. C8 118
Kings Canyon National Park, Ca., U.S. D4 82
Kingsey-Falls, Que., Can. D5 74
Kingsford, Mi., U.S. C2 99
Kingsland, Ga., U.S. F5 87
Kingsland, Tx., U.S. D3 120
Kingsley, Ia., U.S. B2 92
Kingsley, Mi., U.S. D5 99
King's Lynn, Eng., U.K. I13 7
Kings Mountain, N.C., U.S. B1 110
King Sound, strt., Austl. C4 50
Kings Park West, Va., U.S. *B5 123
Kings Peak, mtn., Ut., U.S. C5 121
King's Point, Newf., Can. D3 72
Kingsport, Tn., U.S. C11 119
Kingston, Ont., Can. C8 73
Kingston, Jam. E9 64
Kingston, Ga., U.S. B2 87
Kingston, Id., U.S. B2 89
Kingston, Ma., U.S. C6 98
Kingston, N.H., U.S. E4 106
Kingston, N.Y., U.S. D6 109
Kingston, Oh., U.S. C3 112
Kingston, Ok., U.S. D5 113
Kingston, Pa., U.S. D10 115
Kingston, R.I., U.S. F3 116
Kingston, Tn., U.S. D9 119
Kingston Springs, Tn., U.S. A4 119
Kingston upon Hull, Eng., U.K. H12 7
Kingstown, St. Vin. H17 64
Kingstown, Md., U.S. B5 97
Kingstree, S.C., U.S. D8 117
Kingsville, Ont., Can. E2 73
Kingsville, Md., U.S. B5 97
Kingsville (North Kingsville), Oh., U.S. A5 112
Kingsville, Tx., U.S. F4 120
Kingsville Naval Air Station, mil., Tx., U.S. F4 120
King William, co., Va., U.S. C5 123
King William Island, i., N.W. Ter., Can. C13 66
King William's Town, S. Afr. H5 44
Kingwood, W.V., U.S. B5 125
Kinistino, Sask., Can. E3 75
Kinkaid Lake, res., Il., U.S. F4 90
Kinloch, Mo., U.S. f13 102
Kinmundy, Il., U.S. E5 90
Kinna, Swe. H9 6
Kinnairds Head, c., Scot., U.K. D10 7
Kinnelon, N.J., U.S. B4 107
Kinneret, Yam, l., Isr. C4 40
Kinney, co., Tx., U.S. E2 120
Kinross, Scot., U.K. E9 7
Kinsale, Ire. J4 7
Kinsarvik, Nor. F6 6
Kinsey, Al., U.S. D4 78
Kinshasa (Léopoldville), Zaire B3 44
Kinsley, Ks., U.S. E4 93
Kinston, N.C., U.S. B5 110
Kintyre, pen., Scot., U.K. F7 7
Kintyre, Mull of, c., Scot., U.K. F7 7
Kinyeti, mtn., Sudan H12 42
Kiowa, Ks., U.S. E5 93
Kiowa, Ok., U.S. C6 113
Kiowa, co., Co., U.S. C8 83
Kiowa, co., Ks., U.S. E4 93
Kiowa, co., Ok., U.S. C2 113
Kiowa Creek, stm., Ok., U.S. A1 113
Kipembawe, Tan. C6 44
Kipili, Tan. C6 44
Kipnuk, Ak., U.S. C7 79
Kipushi, Zaire D5 44
Kirbyville, Tx., U.S. D6 120
Kirchdorf an der Krems, Aus. H14 8
Kirenga, stm., Russia F15 24
Kirensk, Russia F15 24
Kirghizia see Kyrgyzstan, state, Asia I12 22
Kiribati, ctry., Oc. G24 2
Kırıkhan, Tur. A5 40
Kırıkkale, Tur. H14 4
Kirin see Jilin, China C12 26
Kirinyaga (Mount Kenya), mtn., Kenya B7 44
Kırkağaç, Tur. J11 16
Kirkcaldy, Scot., U.K. E9 7
Kirkcudbright, Scot., U.K. G8 7
Kirkenes, Nor. B18 6
Kirkland, Il., U.S. A5 90
Kirkland, Wa., U.S. B3 124
Kirkland Lake, Ont., Can. o19 73
Kırklareli, Tur. H11 16
Kirklin, In., U.S. D5 91
Kirksville, Mo., U.S. A5 102
Kirkūk, Iraq A3 46
Kirkwall, Scot., U.K. C10 7
Kirkwood, De., U.S. B3 85
Kirkwood, Il., U.S. C3 90
Kirkwood, Mo., U.S. f13 102
Kirov, Russia G17 18
Kirov, Russia F7 22
Kirovohrad, Ukr. H4 22
Kirovskij, Russia G25 24
Kırşehir, Tur. H14 4
Kīrthar Range, mts., Pak. G2 38
Kirtland, N.M., U.S. A1 108
Kirtland Air Force Base, mil., N.M., U.S. k7 108
Kiruna, Swe. C13 6
Kirwin Reservoir, res., Ks., U.S. C4 93
Kiryū, Japan F12 30
Kisa, Swe. H10 6
Kisangani (Stanleyville), Zaire A5 44
Kisarazu, Japan G12 30
K.I. Sawyer Air Force Base, mil., Mi., U.S. B3 99
Kisel'ovsk, Russia G11 24
Kishanganj, India G12 38
Kishangarh, India G6 38
Kishinev see Chişinău, Mol. H3 22
Kishiwada, Japan H8 30
Kishorganj, Bngl. H14 38
Kishwaukee, stm., Il., U.S. A5 90
Kiska Island, i., Ak., U.S. E3 79
Kiskunfélegyháza, Hung. I19 8
Kiskunhalas, Hung. I19 8
Kislovodsk, Russia I6 22
Kismayu, Som. B8 44
Kissidougou, Gui. G3 42
Kissimmee, Fl., U.S. D5 86
Kissimmee, stm., Fl., U.S. E5 86
Kissimmee, Lake, l., Fl., U.S. E5 86
Kississing Lake, l., Man., Can. B1 70
Kistanje, Cro. F10 14
Kistler, W.V., U.S. D3 125
Kisumu, Kenya B6 44
Kitaibaraki, Japan F13 30
Kitakami, stm., Japan C14 30
Kitakami-sanchi, mts., Japan C14 30
Kitakyūshū, Japan I3 30
Kitale, Kenya A6 44
Kitami, Japan p21 30a
Kitami-sanchi, mts., Japan o20 30a
Kit Carson, co., Co., U.S. B8 83
Kitchener, Ont., Can. D4 73
Kíthira, i., Grc. M6 16
Kitimat, B.C., Can. B3 69
Kitsap, co., Wa., U.S. B3 124
Kitscoty, Alta., Can. C5 68
Kittanning, Pa., U.S. E2 115
Kittatinny Mountain, mtn., U.S. B2 107
Kittery, Me., U.S. E2 96
Kittery Point, Me., U.S. E2 96
Kittilä, Fin. C15 6
Kittitas, Wa., U.S. C5 124
Kittitas, co., Wa., U.S. B4 124
Kitts, Ky., U.S. D6 94
Kittson, co., Mn., U.S. B2 100
Kitty Hawk, N.C., U.S. A7 110
Kitty Hawk Bay, b., N.C., U.S. A7 110
Kitwe, Zam. D5 44
Kitzbühel, Aus. H12 8
Kitzingen, Ger. F10 8
Kivu, Lac, l., Afr. B5 44
Kızıl, stm., Tur. G14 4
Kjustendil, Bul. G6 16
Kladno, Czech. E14 8
Klagenfurt, Aus. I14 8
Klaipėda (Memel), Lith. F4 18
Klamath, co., Or., U.S. E5 114
Klamath, stm., U.S. B2 82
Klamath Falls, Or., U.S. E5 114
Klamath Mountains, mts., U.S. E2 114
Klangenan, Indon. m14 33a
Klarälven, stm., Eur. F9 6
Klawock, Ak., U.S. D13 79
Kleberg, co., Tx., U.S. F4 120
Klerksdorp, S. Afr. G5 44
Kleve, Ger. D6 8
Klickitat, Wa., U.S. D4 124
Klickitat, co., Wa., U.S. D4 124
Klickitat, stm., Wa., U.S. C4 124
Klimovsk, Russia F20 18
Klin, Russia E19 18
Klincy, Russia I15 18
Kłodzko, Pol. E16 8
Klondike, hist. reg., Yukon, Can. D5 66
Klondike Gold Rush National Historical Park, Ak., U.S. k22 79
Klosterneuburg, Aus. G16 8
Kluane Lake, l., Yukon, Can. D5 66
Klutina Lake, l., Ak., U.S. g19 79
Knapp Creek, stm., W.V., U.S. C5 125
Knee Lake, l., Man., Can. B4 70
Kneža, Bul. F8 16
Knife, stm., N.D., U.S. B3 111
Knightdale, N.C., U.S. B4 110
Knight Inlet, b., B.C., Can. D5 69
Knight Island, i., Ak., U.S. g18 79
Knightstown, In., U.S. E6 91
Knightsville, In., U.S. E3 91
Knightville Reservoir, res., Ma., U.S. B2 98
Knin, Cro. E11 14
Knittelfeld, Aus. H14 8
Knob Noster, Mo., U.S. C4 102
Knokke, Bel. D3 8
Knollwood, W.V., U.S. m12 125
Knott, co., Ky., U.S. C6 94
Knox, In., U.S. B4 91
Knox, Pa., U.S. D2 115
Knox, co., Il., U.S. B3 90
Knox, co., In., U.S. G3 91
Knox, co., Ky., U.S. D6 94
Knox, co., Me., U.S. D4 96
Knox, co., Mo., U.S. A5 102
Knox, co., Ne., U.S. B8 104
Knox, co., Oh., U.S. B3 112
Knox, co., Tn., U.S. C10 119
Knox, co., Tx., U.S. C3 120
Knox, Cape, c., B.C., Can. B1 69
Knox City, Tx., U.S. C3 120
Knoxville, Il., U.S. C3 90
Knoxville, Ia., U.S. C4 92
Knoxville, Tn., U.S. D10 119
Knysna, S. Afr. H4 44
Kōbe, Japan H8 30
København (Copenhagen), Den. I9 6
Koblenz, Ger. E7 8
Kobrin, Bela. I7 18
Kobuk, stm., Ak., U.S. B8 79
Kobuk Valley National Park, Ak., U.S. B8 79
Kočani, Mac. H6 16
Kočevje, Slo. D9 14
Kōchi, Japan I6 30
Koch Peak, mtn., Mt., U.S. E5 103
Kodiak, Ak., U.S. D9 79
Kodiak Island, i., Ak., U.S. D9 79
Koes, Nmb. G3 44
Kofa Mountains, mts., Az., U.S. D2 80
Köflach, Aus. H15 8
Kōfu, Japan G11 30
Koga, Japan F12 30
Kogaluc, Baie, b., Que., Can. E17 66
Kogaluk, stm., Newf., Can. g9 72
Køge Bugt, b., Grnld. D24 66
Kohala Mountains, mts., Hi., U.S. C6 88
Kohāt, Pak. D4 38
Kohīma, India H16 38
Kohler, Wi., U.S. E6 126
Kohtla-Järve, Est. B10 18
Kokand, Uzb. I12 22
Kokanee Glacier Provincial Park, B.C., Can. E9 69
Kokemäki, Fin. F14 6
Kokkola (Gamlakarleby), Fin. E14 6
Koko Head, c., Hi., U.S. B4 88
Kokolik, stm., Ak., U.S. B7 79
Kokomo, In., U.S. D5 91
Kokonau, Indon. F10 32
Kokopo, Pap. N. Gui. k17 50a
Kokosing, stm., Oh., U.S. B3 112
Koksoak, stm., Que., Can. E19 66
Kokstad, S. Afr. H5 44
Kolaka, Indon. F7 32
Kola Peninsula see Kol'skij poluostrov, pen., Russia D5 22
Kolār, India F5 37
Kolār Gold Fields, India F5 37
Kol'čugino, Russia E22 18
Kolda, Sen. F3 42
Kolding, Den. I7 6
Kolhāpur, India D3 37
Kolín, Czech. E15 8
Kollegāl, India F4 37
Köln (Cologne), Ger. E6 8
Koloa, Hi., U.S. B2 88
Kołobrzeg, Pol. A15 8
Kolomna, Russia F21 18
Kolpaševo, Russia F10 24
Kolpino, Russia B13 18
Kol'skij poluostrov (Kola Peninsula), pen., Russia D5 22
Kolwezi, Zaire D5 44
Kolyma, stm., Russia D25 24
Kolymskaja Nizmennost', pl., Russia D24 24
Komárno, Slov. H18 8
Komatsu, Japan F9 30
Komló, Hung. I18 8
Kommunizma, pik, mtn., Taj. J12 22
Komoé, stm., Afr. G5 42
Komotini, Grc. H9 16
Komsomolec, Ostrov, i., Russia A12 24
Komsomol'sk-na-Amure, Russia G21 24
Komsomol'skoj Pravdy, Ostrova, is., Russia B15 24
Konahuanui, Puu, mtn., Hi., U.S. g10 88
Konakovo, Russia E19 18
Konawa, Ok., U.S. C5 113
Konch, India H8 38
Kondrovo, Russia G18 18
Kŏng, Kaôh, i., Camb. I7 34
Kongolo, Zaire C5 44
Kongsberg, Nor. G7 6
Kongsvinger, Nor. F8 6
Kongsvoll, Nor. E7 6
Kongur Shan, mtn., China A6 38
Königs Wusterhausen, Ger. C13 8
Konin, Pol. C18 8
Konjic, Bos. F12 14
Konomoc, Lake, res., Ct., U.S. D7 84
Konqi, stm., China C4 26
Konstanz, Ger. H9 8
Kontagora, Nig. F7 42
Kontiomäki, Fin. D17 6
Kon Tum, Viet. G10 34
Konya, Tur. H14 4
Konza, Kenya B7 44
Koochiching, co., Mn., U.S. B4 100
Koolau Range, mts., Hi., U.S. f10 88
Koontz Lake, In., U.S. B5 91
Kooskia, Id., U.S. C3 89
Kootenai, co., Id., U.S. B2 89
Kootenay Lake, l., B.C., Can. E9 69
Kootenay National Park, B.C., Can. D9 69
Kopargaon, India C3 37
Koper, Slo. D8 14
Kopetdag, chrebet, mts., Asia J9 22
Köping, Swe. G10 6
Koppal, India E4 37
Koppang, Nor. F8 6
Koppel, Pa., U.S. E1 115
Koprivnica, Cro. C11 14
Kor'akskoje Nagorje, mts., Russia E27 24
Korba, India I10 38
Korbach, Ger. D8 8
Korçë, Alb. I4 16
Korčula, Cro. G12 14
Korea, North, ctry., Asia C12 26
Korea, South, ctry., Asia D12 26
Korea Bay, b., Asia D11 26
Korea Strait, strt., Asia E12 26
Korf, Russia E27 24
Korhogo, C. Iv. G4 42
Korinthiakós Kólpos, b., Grc. K6 16
Kórinthos (Corinth), Grc. L6 16
Kōriyama, Japan E13 30
Korliki, Russia E10 24
Korogwe, Tan. C7 44
Koronis, Lake, l., Mn., U.S. E4 100
Koro Toro, Chad E9 42
Korovin Volcano, vol., Ak., U.S. E5 79
Korsakov, Russia H22 24
Korsnäs, Fin. E13 6
Korso, Fin. F15 6
Kortrijk (Courtrai), Bel. E3 8
Koruçam Burnu, c., N. Cyp. B3 40
Koš-Agač, Russia G11 24
Kosciusko, Ms., U.S. B4 101
Kosciusko, co., In., U.S. B6 91
Kosciusko, Mount, mtn., Austl. G9 50
Koshkonong, Lake, l., Wi., U.S. F5 126
Košice, Slov. G21 8
Kosovska Mitrovica, Yugo. G4 16
Kossuth, co., Ia., U.S. A3 92
Kostroma, Russia D23 18
Koszalin (Köslin), Pol. A16 8
Kota, India H6 38
Kota Baharu, Malay. K7 34
Kotabumi, Indon. F3 32
Kot Addu, Pak. E4 38
Kota Kinabalu (Jesselton), Malay. D6 32
Kotel'nyj, Ostrov, i., Russia B21 24
Köthen, Ger. D11 8
Kotka, Fin. F16 6
Kot Kapūra, India E6 38
Kotlas, Russia E7 22
Kotlik, Ak., U.S. C7 79
Kotor Varoš, Bos. E12 14
Kotovsk, Russia I24 18
Kotri, Pak. H3 38
Kötschach [-Mauthen], Aus. I12 8
Kottagūdem, India D6 37
Kottayam, India H4 37
Kotte, Sri L. I5 37
Kotto, stm., Cen. Afr. Rep. G10 42
Kotuj, stm., Russia C14 24
Kotzebue, Ak., U.S. B7 79
Kotzebue Sound, strt., Ak., U.S. B7 79
Kouchibouguac National Park, N.B., Can. C5 71
Koudougou, Burkina F5 42
Koula-Moutou, Gabon B2 44
Koumra, Chad G9 42
Kountze, Tx., U.S. D5 120
Koussi, Emi, mtn., Chad E9 42
Koutiala, Mali F4 42
Kouts, In., U.S. B3 91
Kouvola, Fin. F16 6
Kovrov, Russia E24 18
Kowkcheh, stm., Afg. B4 38
Kowloon (Jiulong), H.K. M3 28
Kowt-e 'Ashrow, Afg. C3 38
Koyukuk, stm., Ak., U.S. B8 79
Koza, Japan y27 31b
Kozáni, Grc. I5 16
Kra, Isthmus of, Asia I5 34
Krâchéh, Camb. H9 34
Kragerø, Nor. G7 6
Kragujevac, Yugo. E4 16
Kraków, Pol. E19 8
Kraljevica, Cro. D9 14
Kraljevo, Yugo. F4 16
Kramfors, Swe. E11 6
Krångede, Swe. E11 6
Kranj, Slo. C9 14
Krasneno, Russia E28 24
Krasnodar, Russia H5 22
Krasnogorsk, Russia F20 18
Krasnojarsk, Russia F12 24
Krasnoje, Ozero, l., Russia E28 24
Krasnosel'kup, Russia D10 24
Krasnozavodsk, Russia E21 18
Krebs, Ok., U.S. C6 113
Kremenchuk, Ukr. H4 22
Kremmling, Co., U.S. A4 83
Krems an der Donau, Aus. G15 8
Kresta, Zaliv, b., Russia D30 24
Kribi, Cam. H7 42
Kričov, Bela. H14 18
Krishna, stm., India D5 37
Krishnanagar, India I13 38
Kristiansand, Nor. G7 6
Kristianstad, Swe. H10 6
Kristiansund, Nor. E6 6
Kristinehamn, Swe. G10 6
Kríti, i., Grc. N8 16
Kritikón Pélagos, Grc. N8 16
Krivoy Rog see Kryvyy Rih, Ukr. H4 22
Krnov, Czech. E17 8
Kroken, Nor. D10 6
Kroměříž, Czech. F17 8
Kronach, Ger. E11 8
Krŏng Khémôreăh Phumint, Camb. I7 34
Kronockij Zaliv, b., Russia G26 24
Kronoki, Russia G26 24
Kronštadt, Russia B12 18
Kroonstad, S. Afr. G5 44
Kropotkin, Russia F17 24
Krosno, Pol. F21 8
Krotz Springs, La., U.S. D4 95
Krško, Slo. D10 14
Kr'ukovo, Russia D25 24
Krung Thep (Bangkok), Thai. H6 34
Kruševac, Yugo. F5 16
Krušné hory (Erzgebirge), mts., Eur. E12 8
Kruzenšterna, Proliv, strt., Russia H24 24
Kruzof Island, i., Ak., U.S. m21 79
Kryms'kyy pivostriv (Crimea), pen., Ukr. H4 22
Kryvyy Rih, Ukr. H4 22
Ksenjevka, Russia G17 24
Ksour Essaf, Tun. N5 14
Kuala Kangsar, Malay. L6 34
Kualakapuas, Indon. F5 32
Kuala Krai, Malay. L7 34
Kuala Kubu Baharu, Malay. M6 34
Kuala Lumpur, Malay. M6 34
Kuala Nerang, Malay. K6 34
Kuala Pilah, Malay. M7 34
Kuala Terengganu, Malay. L7 34
Kuantan, Malay. M7 34
Kubokawa, Japan I6 30
Kuche, China C3 26
Kuching, Malay. E5 32
Kudat, Malay. D6 32
Kudus, Indon. m15 32
Kuee Ruins, hist., Hi., U.S. D6 88
Kufstein, Aus. H12 8
Kuhmo, Fin. D17 6
Kuito, Ang. D3 44
Kuiu Island, i., Ak., U.S. m23 79
Kuivaniemi, Fin. D15 6
Kukawa, Nig. F8 42
Kula, Tur. K12 16
Kula, Hi., U.S. C5 88
Kul'ab, Taj. B3 38
Kula Kangri, mtn., Bhu. F14 38
Kulebaki, Russia F25 18
Kulen Vakuf, Bos. E11 14
Kulim, Malay. L6 34
Kulmbach, Ger. E11 8
Kulpmont, Pa., U.S. E9 115
Kulunqi, China C11 26
Kumagaya, Japan F12 30
Kumajri, Arm. I6 22
Kumamoto, Japan J3 30
Kumano, Japan I9 30
Kumano-nada, Japan I9 30
Kumanovo, Mac. G5 16
Kumasi, Ghana G5 42
Kumbakonam, India G5 37
Kume-shima, i., Japan y26 31b
Kumo, Nig. F8 42
Kumon Range, mts., Mya. B4 34
Kumukahi, Cape, c., Hi., U.S. D7 88
Kuna, Id., U.S. F2 89
Kunašir, Ostrov (Kunashiri-tō), i., Russia I23 24
Kundiān, Pak. D4 38
Kundla, India J4 38
Kunes, Nor. A16 6
Kunghit Island, i., B.C., Can. C2 69
Kuningan, Indon. m14 33a
Kunlun Shan, mts., China B12 38
Kunming, China B7 34
Kunsan, S. Kor. D12 26
Kunshan, China D9 28
Kuopio, Fin. E16 6
Kupang, Indon. H7 32
Kupreanof Island, i., Ak., U.S. m23 79
Kupres, Bos. E12 14
Kura, stm., Asia I7 22
Kurashiki, Japan H6 30
Kurayoshi, Japan G6 30
Kure, Japan H5 30
Kure Island, i., Hi., U.S. k12 88
Kurejka, stm., Russia D11 24
Kurenalus, Fin. D16 6
Kurgan-T'ube, Taj. B3 38
Kurikka, Fin. E14 6
Kuril'sk, Russia H23 24
Kuril'skije Ostrova (Kuril Islands), is., Russia H23 24
Kurmuk, Sudan F12 42
Kurnool, India E5 37
Kurow, N.Z. F3 52
Kursk, Russia G5 22
Kurtistown, Hi., U.S. D6 88
Kuruman, S. Afr. G4 44
Kurume, Japan I3 30
Kurumkan, Russia G16 24
Kurunegala, Sri L. I6 37
Kuşadası Körfezi, b., Tur. L11 16
Kuş Gölü, l., Tur. I11 16
Kushima, Japan K4 30
Kushiro, Japan q22 30a
Kushtia, Bngl. I13 38
Kushui, China C5 26
Kuskokwim, stm., Ak., U.S. C8 79
Kuskokwim Bay, b., Ak., U.S. D7 79
Kuskokwim Mountains, mts., Ak., U.S. C8 79
Kūstī, Sudan F12 42
K'us'ur, Russia C19 24
Kut, Ko, i., Thai. I7 34
Kutaisi, Geor. I6 22
Kūt al-Imāra, Iraq B4 46
Kutch, Gulf of, b., India I3 38
Kutina, Cro. D11 14
Kutno, Pol. C19 8
Kutu, Zaire B3 44
Kutztown, Pa., U.S. E10 115
Kuujjuaq, Que., Can. g13 74
Kuusamo, Fin. D17 6
Kuusankoski, Fin. F16 6
Kuvango, Ang. D3 44
Kuwait, ctry., Asia C4 46
Kuwait see Al-Kuwayt, Kuw. C4 46
Kuwana, Japan G9 30
Kuybyshev see Samara, Russia G8 22
Kuzneck, Russia G7 22
Kvikkjokk, Swe. C11 6
Kwando (Cuando), stm., Afr. E4 44
Kwangchow see Guangzhou, China L2 28
Kwangju, S. Kor. D12 26
Kwango (Cuango), stm., Afr. B3 44
Kwekwe, Zimb. E5 44
Kwethluk, Ak., U.S. C7 79
Kwidzyn, Pol. B18 8
Kwigillingok, Ak., U.S. D7 79
Kwilu (Cuilo), stm., Afr. B3 44
Kyaiklat, Mya. F3 34
Kyaikto, Mya. F4 34
Kyle, Tx., U.S. E4 120
Kyle of Lochalsh, Scot., U.K. D7 7
Kyoga, Lake, l., Ug. A6 44
Kyōto, Japan G8 30
Kyrgyzstan, ctry., Asia I12 22
Kyuquot Sound, strt., B.C., Can. E4 69
Kyūshū, i., Japan I3 30
Kyūshū-sanchi, mts., Japan J4 30
Kyyiv, Ukr. G4 22
Kyyjärvi, Fin. E15 6
Kyzyl, Russia G12 24

Name	Map Ref	Page
Kzyl-Orda, Kaz.	I11	22

L

Laa an der Thaya, Aus. G16 8
La Almunia de Doña Godina, Spain D10 12
La Asunción, Ven. B11 58
Laau Point, c., Hi., U.S. B4 88
L'Abacou, Pointe, c., Haiti E11 64
Labadieville, La., U.S. E5 95
La Bañeza, Spain C6 12
La Barca, Mex. G8 62
La Barge, Wy., U.S. D2 127
La Barge Creek, stm., Wy., U.S. D2 127
La Baule, Fr. E4 10
Labé, Gui. F3 42
Labe (Elbe), stm., Eur. E14 8
La Belle, Fl., U.S. F5 86
La Belle, Mo., U.S. A6 102
Labette, co., Ks., U.S. E8 93
Labin, Cro. D9 14
La Bisbal, Spain D15 12
Labouheyre, Fr. H6 10
Labrador, reg., Newf., Can. g9 72
Labrador City, Newf., Can. h8 72
Labrador Sea, N.A. E22 66
Lábrea, Braz. E6 54
Labutta, Mya. F3 34
La Canada Flintridge, Ca., U.S. m12 82
Lacanau, Fr. H5 10
La Cañiza, Spain C3 12
La Canourgue, Fr. H10 10
La Carolina, Spain G8 12
Lacaune, Fr. I9 10
Lac-Bouchette, Que., Can. A5 74
Lac-Brome, Que., Can. D5 74
Laccadive Sea, Asia H3 37
Lac-Carré, Que., Can. C3 74
Lac Courte Oreilles Indian Reservation, Wi., U.S. C2 126
Lac du Bonnet, Man., Can. D3 70
Lac du Flambeau, Wi., U.S. B4 126
Lac du Flambeau Indian Reservation, Wi., U.S. C3 126
La Ceiba, Hond. G4 64
La Ceiba, Ven. C7 58
La Center, Ky., U.S. e9 94
Lac-Etchemin, Que., Can. C7 74
Lacey, Wa., U.S. B3 124
La Charité [-sur-Loire], Fr. E10 10
La Châtre, Fr. F8 10
La Chaux-de-Fonds, Switz. E13 10
Lachine, Que., Can. D4 74
La Chorrera, Col. H6 58
La Chorrera, Pan. J8 64
Lachute, Que., Can. D3 74
La Ciotat, Fr. I12 10
Lackawanna, N.Y., U.S. C2 109
Lackawanna, co., Pa., U.S. D10 115
Lackland Air Force Base, mil., Tx., U.S. k7 120
Lac La Biche, Alta., Can. B5 68
Lac la Hache, B.C., Can. D7 69
Laclede, co., Mo., U.S. D5 102
Lac-Mégantic, Que., Can. D7 74
Lacolle, Que., Can. D4 74
Lacombe, Alta., Can. C4 68
Lacombe, La., U.S. D6 95
Lacon, Il., U.S. B4 90
Laconia, N.H., U.S. C4 106
La Conner, Wa., U.S. A3 124
Lacoochee, Fl., U.S. D4 86
La Coruña, Spain B3 12
Lac qui Parle, co., Mn., U.S. F2 100
Lac qui Parle, stm., Mn., U.S. F2 100
La Creek Lake, l., S.D., U.S. D4 118
La Crescent, Mn., U.S. G7 100
La Crete, Alta., Can. f7 68
La Crosse, In., U.S. B4 91
La Crosse, Ks., U.S. D4 93
La Crosse, Wi., U.S. E2 126
La Crosse, co., Wi., U.S. E2 126
La Crosse, stm., Wi., U.S. E3 126
La Cruz, Nic. H5 64
La Cygne, Ks., U.S. D9 93
Ladd, Il., U.S. B4 90
Ladies Island, i., S.C., U.S. G6 117
Lādīz, Iran C7 46
Lādnun, India G6 38
Ladoga, In., U.S. E4 91
Ladoga, Lake see Ladožskoje Ozero, l., Russia F18 6
La Dorada, Col. E5 58
Ladožskoje Ozero (Lake Ladoga), l., Russia F18 6
Ladson, S.C., U.S. F7 117
Lady Lake, Fl., U.S. D5 86
Lady Laurier, Mount, mtn., B.C., Can. A6 69
Ladysmith, B.C., Can. E6 69
Ladysmith, S. Afr. G5 44
Ladysmith, Wi., U.S. C2 126
Lae, Pap. N. Gui. m16 50a
La Encantada, Cerro de, mtn., Mex. B2 62
La Esmeralda, Ven. F10 58
La Esperanza, Hond. G3 64
La Estrada, Spain C3 12
La Farge, Wi., U.S. E3 126
Lafayette, Al., U.S. C4 78
Lafayette, Co., U.S. B5 83
Lafayette, Ga., U.S. B1 87
Lafayette, In., U.S. D4 91
Lafayette, La., U.S. D3 95
Lafayette, N.C., U.S. B3 110
Lafayette, Or., U.S. B3 114
La Fayette, R.I., U.S. E4 116
Lafayette, Tn., U.S. A5 119
Lafayette, co., Ar., U.S. D2 81
Lafayette, co., Fl., U.S. C3 86
Lafayette, co., La., U.S. D3 95
Lafayette, co., Ms., U.S. A4 101
Lafayette, co., Mo., U.S. B4 102
Lafayette, co., Wi., U.S. F3 126
Lafayette, Mount, mtn., N.H., U.S. B3 106
La Feria, Tx., U.S. F4 120
La Ferté-Bernard, Fr. D7 10
La Ferté-Macé, Fr. D6 10
La Ferté-Saint-Aubin, Fr. E8 10
Lafia, Nig. G7 42
Lafitte, La., U.S. k11 95
La Flèche, Fr. E6 10
La Follette, Tn., U.S. C9 119
La Fontaine, In., U.S. C6 91
La Fortuna, C.R. I5 64
Lafourche, La., U.S. E5 95
Lafourche, co., La., U.S. E5 95
La France, S.C., U.S. B2 117
La Fregeneda, Spain E5 12
La Fría, Ven. C6 58
La Fuente de San Esteban, Spain E5 12
Lågen, stm., Nor. F8 6
Laghouat, Alg. B6 42
Lago, Mount, mtn., Wa., U.S. A5 124
Lagonegro, Italy I10 14
Lagos, Nig. G6 42
Lagos de Moreno, Mex. G9 62
La Goulette, Tun. M5 14
La Grand'Combe, Fr. H11 10
La Grande, Or., U.S. B8 114
La Grande, stm., Que., Can. h11 74
La Grande Deux, Réservoir, res., Que., Can. h11 74
La Grange, Austl. C4 50
La Grange, Ga., U.S. C1 87
La Grange, Il., U.S. B6 90
Lagrange, In., U.S. A7 91
La Grange, Ky., U.S. B4 94
La Grange, Mo., U.S. A6 102
La Grange, N.C., U.S. B5 110
Lagrange, Oh., U.S. A3 112
La Grange, Tx., U.S. E4 120
Lagrange, co., In., U.S. A7 91
La Grange Park, Il., U.S. k9 90
La Gran Sabana, pl., Ven. E12 58
La Grita, Ven. C7 58
La Guadeloupe (Saint-Evariste), Que., Can. D7 74
La Guaira, Ven. B9 58
La Guajira, Península de, pen., S.A. A7 58
Laguardia, Spain C9 12
La Guardia, Spain D3 12
La Guerche-de-Bretagne, Fr. E5 10
La Guerche-sur-l'aubois, Fr. F9 10
Laguiole, Fr. H9 10
Laguna, N.M., U.S. B2 108
Laguna Beach, Ca., U.S. F5 82
Laguna Dam, U.S. E1 80
Laguna Indian Reservation, N.M., U.S. C2 108
Lagunillas, Bol. G6 54
La Habana (Havana), Cuba C6 64
La Habra, Ca., U.S. n13 82
Lahaina, Hi., U.S. C5 88
La Harpe, Il., U.S. C3 90
La Harpe, Ks., U.S. E8 93
Lahat, Indon. F3 32
La Have, stm., N.S., Can. E5 71
La Haye-du-Puits, Fr. C5 10
Lahij, Yemen F3 46
Laholm, Swe. H9 6
Lahoma, Ok., U.S. A3 113
Lahontan Reservoir, res., Nv., U.S. D2 105
Lahore, Pak. E6 38
Lahr, Ger. G7 8
Lahti, Fin. F15 6
Laie, Hi., U.S. B4 88
L'Aigle, Fr. D7 10
Laignes, Fr. E11 10
Laihia, Fin. E14 6
Laingsburg, S. Afr. H4 44
Laingsburg, Mi., U.S. F6 99
Lairg, Scot., U.K. C8 7
Laissac, Fr. H9 10
Laiyang, China D11 26
La Jara, Co., U.S. D5 83
Lajes, Braz. E11 54
La Jolla, Point, c., Ca., U.S. o15 82
La Joya, Mex. A2 62
La Junta, Mex. C6 62
La Junta, Co., U.S. D7 83
Lake, co., Ca., U.S. C2 82
Lake, co., Co., U.S. B4 83
Lake, co., Fl., U.S. D5 86
Lake, co., Il., U.S. A6 90
Lake, co., In., U.S. B3 91
Lake, co., Mi., U.S. E5 99
Lake, co., Mn., U.S. C7 100
Lake, co., Mt., U.S. C2 103
Lake, co., Oh., U.S. A4 112
Lake, co., Or., U.S. E6 114
Lake, co., S.D., U.S. C8 118
Lake, co., Tn., U.S. A2 119
Lake Alfred, Fl., U.S. D5 86
Lake Andes, S.D., U.S. D7 118
Lake Ariel, Pa., U.S. D11 115
Lake Arrowhead, Ca., U.S. E5 82
Lake Arthur, La., U.S. D3 95
Lake Barcroft, Va., U.S. *B5 123
Lake Benton, Mn., U.S. F2 100
Lake Bluff, Il., U.S. A6 90
Lake Butler, Fl., U.S. B4 86
Lake Charles, La., U.S. D2 95
Lake Chelan National Recreation Area, Wa., U.S. A5 124
Lake City, Ar., U.S. B5 81
Lake City, Fl., U.S. B4 86
Lake City, Ia., U.S. B3 92
Lake City, Mi., U.S. D5 99
Lake City, Mn., U.S. F6 100
Lake City, Pa., U.S. B1 115
Lake City, S.C., U.S. D8 117
Lake City, Tn., U.S. C9 119
Lake Clark National Park, Ak., U.S. C9 79
Lake Cowichan, B.C., Can. g11 69
Lake Creek, stm., Wa., U.S. B7 124
Lake Crystal, Mn., U.S. F4 100
Lake Delta, N.Y., U.S. B5 109
Lake Delton, Wi., U.S. E4 126
Lake District National Park, Eng., U.K. G9 7
Lake Elsinore, Ca., U.S. F5 82
Lake Erie Beach, N.Y., U.S. C1 109
Lakefield, Ont., Can. C6 73
Lakefield, Mn., U.S. G3 100
Lake Forest, Il., U.S. A6 90
Lake Fork, stm., Ut., U.S. C5 121
Lake Geneva, Wi., U.S. F5 126
Lake Hamilton, Ar., U.S. g7 81
Lake Harbour, N.W. Ter., Can. D19 66
Lake Havasu City, Az., U.S. C1 80
Lake Helen, Fl., U.S. D5 86
Lakehurst, N.J., U.S. C4 107
Lakehurst Naval Air Station, mil., N.J., U.S. C4 107
Lake in the Hills, Il., U.S. h8 90
Lake Jackson, Tx., U.S. r14 120
Lake Katrine, N.Y., U.S. D7 109
Lakeland, Fl., U.S. D5 86
Lakeland, Ga., U.S. E3 87
Lake Linden, Mi., U.S. A2 99
Lake Louise, Alta., Can. D2 68
Lake Magdalene, Fl., U.S. o11 86
Lake Mary, Fl., U.S. D5 86
Lake Mead National Recreation Area, U.S. H7 105
Lake Meredith National Recreation Area, Tx., U.S. B2 120
Lake Mills, Ia., U.S. A4 92
Lake Mills, Wi., U.S. E5 126
Lakemore, Oh., U.S. A4 112
Lake Mountain, mtn., Wy., U.S. E6 127
Lake Nebagamon, Wi., U.S. B2 126
Lake Odessa, Mi., U.S. F5 99
Lake of the Woods, co., Mn., U.S. B4 100
Lake Orion, Mi., U.S. F7 99
Lake Oswego, Or., U.S. B4 114
Lake Ozark, Mo., U.S. C5 102
Lake Park, Fl., U.S. F6 86
Lake Park, Ia., U.S. A2 92
Lake Park, Mn., U.S. D2 100
Lake Placid, Fl., U.S. E5 86
Lake Placid, N.Y., U.S. A7 109
Lake Pontchartrain Causeway, La., U.S. h11 95
Lakeport, Ca., U.S. C2 82
Lake Preston, S.D., U.S. C8 118
Lake Providence, La., U.S. B4 95
Lake Range, mts., Nv., U.S. C2 105
Lake Ridge, Va., U.S. *B5 123
Lake Shore, Md., U.S. B5 97
Lakeshore, Ms., U.S. E4 101
Lakeside, Az., U.S. C6 80
Lakeside, Ca., U.S. F5 82
Lakeside, Ct., U.S. D3 84
Lakeside, Mt., U.S. B2 103
Lakeside, Oh., U.S. A3 112
Lakeside, Or., U.S. D2 114
Lakeside Park, Ky., U.S. h13 94
Lake Station, In., U.S. A3 91
Lake Station, Ok., U.S. A5 113
Lake Stevens, Wa., U.S. A3 124
Lake Superior Provincial Park, Ont., Can. p18 73
Lake Swamp, stm., S.C., U.S. D8 117
Lake Tansi Village, Tn., U.S. D8 119
Lake Valley, val., Nv., U.S. E7 105
Lake View, Ia., U.S. B2 92
Lakeview, Mi., U.S. E5 99
Lakeview, Oh., U.S. B2 112
Lakeview, Or., U.S. E6 114
Lake View, S.C., U.S. C9 117
Lake Villa, Il., U.S. h8 90
Lake Village, Ar., U.S. D4 81
Lake Village, In., U.S. B3 91
Lakeville, Ct., U.S. B2 84
Lakeville, In., U.S. A5 91
Lakeville, Ma., U.S. C6 98
Lakeville, Mn., U.S. F5 100
Lake Waccamaw, N.C., U.S. C4 110
Lake Wales, Fl., U.S. E5 86
Lakewood, Ca., U.S. n12 82
Lakewood, Co., U.S. B5 83
Lakewood, Il., U.S. D5 90
Lakewood, Ia., U.S. f8 92
Lakewood, N.J., U.S. C4 107
Lakewood, N.Y., U.S. C1 109
Lakewood, Oh., U.S. A4 112
Lakewood Center, Wa., U.S. B3 124
Lake Worth, Fl., U.S. F6 86
Lake Worth Inlet, b., Fl., U.S. F7 86
Lake Zurich, Il., U.S. h8 90
Lakhīmpur, India G9 38
Lakin, Ks., U.S. E2 93
Lakota, N.D., U.S. A7 111
Lakselv, Nor. A15 6
Lakshadweep, state, India H3 37
Lakshadweep, is., India H2 37
Lalbenque, Fr. H8 10
La Libertad, Guat. F2 64
La Libertad, Mex. C3 62
Lalinde, Fr. H7 10
La Línea, Spain I6 12
Lalitpur, India H8 38
Lalitpur, Nepal G11 38
La Loupe, Fr. D8 10
La Luz, N.M., U.S. E4 108
Lama, Ozero, l., Russia D12 24
La Maddalena, Italy H4 14
La Madrid, Arg. B3 56
La Malbaie, Que., Can. B7 74
La Mancha, Mex. E8 62
La Mancha, reg., Spain G8 12
Lamar, Ar., U.S. B2 81
Lamar, Co., U.S. C8 83
Lamar, Mo., U.S. D3 102
Lamar, Pa., U.S. D7 115
Lamar, S.C., U.S. C7 117
Lamar, co., Al., U.S. B1 78
Lamar, co., Ga., U.S. C2 87
Lamar, co., Ms., U.S. D4 101
Lamar, co., Tx., U.S. C5 120
Lamar, stm., Wy., U.S. B2 127
Lamarche, Fr. D12 10
La Mauricie, Parc National de, Que., Can. C5 74
Lamb, co., Tx., U.S. B1 120
Lamballe, Fr. D4 10
Lambaréné, Gabon B2 44
Lambert, Ms., U.S. A3 101
Lambert Glacier, Ant. B19 47
Lamberton, Mn., U.S. F3 100
Lambert's Bay, S. Afr. H3 44
Lambertville, Mi., U.S. G7 99
Lambertville, N.J., U.S. C3 107
Lambton, Cape, c., N.W. Ter., Can. B8 66
Lame Deer, Mt., U.S. E10 103
Lamego, Port. D4 12
Lamèque, N.B., Can. B5 71
Lamèque, Île, i., N.B., Can. B5 71
La Mesa, Ca., U.S. F5 82
La Mesa, N.M., U.S. E3 108
Lamesa, Tx., U.S. C2 120
Lamía, Grc. K6 16
Lamoille, Nv., U.S. C6 105
Lamoille, co., Vt., U.S. B3 122
Lamoille, stm., Vt., U.S. B3 122
La Moine, stm., Il., U.S. C3 90
Lamoni, Ia., U.S. D4 92
Lamont, Alta., Can. C4 68
Lamont, Ca., U.S. E4 82
La Monte, Mo., U.S. C4 102
La Motte, Isle, i., Vt., U.S. B2 122
Lamotte-Beuvron, Fr. E9 10
La Moure, N.D., U.S. C7 111
La Moure, co., N.D., U.S. C7 111
Lampang, Thai. E5 34
Lampasas, Tx., U.S. D3 120
Lampasas, co., Tx., U.S. D3 120
Lampedusa, Isola di, i., Italy N7 14
Lampertheim, Ger. F8 8
Lampman, Sask., Can. H4 75
Lamprey, stm., N.H., U.S. D4 106
Lamu, Kenya B8 44
La Mure, Fr. H12 10
Lanai, i., Hi., U.S. C4 88
Lanai City, Hi., U.S. C5 88
Lanaihale, mtn., Hi., U.S. C5 88
Lanark, Ont., Can. C8 73
Lanark, Il., U.S. A4 90
Lanark, W.V., U.S. D3 125
Lanbi Kyun, i., Mya. I5 34
Lancaster, Ont., Can. B10 73
Lancaster, Eng., U.K. G10 7
Lancaster, Ca., U.S. E4 82
Lancaster, Ky., U.S. C5 94
Lancaster, Mo., U.S. A5 102
Lancaster, N.H., U.S. B3 106
Lancaster, N.Y., U.S. C2 109
Lancaster, Oh., U.S. C3 112
Lancaster, Pa., U.S. F9 115
Lancaster, S.C., U.S. B6 117
Lancaster, Tx., U.S. n10 120
Lancaster, Wi., U.S. F3 126
Lancaster, co., Ne., U.S. D9 104
Lancaster, co., Pa., U.S. G9 115
Lancaster, co., S.C., U.S. B6 117
Lancaster, co., Va., U.S. C6 123
Lancaster Sound, strt., N.W. Ter., Can. B16 66
Lance Creek, stm., Wy., U.S. C8 127
Lanciano, Italy G9 14
Landau, Ger. F8 8
Landau an der Isar, Ger. G12 8
Land Between the Lakes, U.S. f9 94
Lander, Wy., U.S. D4 127
Lander, co., Nv., U.S. C4 105
Landerneau, Fr. D2 10
Landess, In., U.S. C6 91
Landete, Spain F10 12
Landis, N.C., U.S. B2 110
Lando, S.C., U.S. B5 117
Landquart, Switz. F16 10
Landrum, S.C., U.S. A3 117
Land's End, c., Eng., U.K. K7 7
Lands End, c., R.I., U.S. F5 116
Landshut, Ger. G12 8
Landskrona, Swe. I9 6
Lane, co., Ks., U.S. D3 93
Lane, co., Or., U.S. C4 114
Lanesboro, Mn., U.S. G7 100
Lanett, Al., U.S. C4 78
Langar, Afg. B5 38
Långban, Swe. G10 6
Langdon, N.D., U.S. A7 111
Langeac, Fr. G10 10
Langeais, Fr. E7 10
Langeloth, Pa., U.S. F1 115
Langenhagen, Ger. C9 8
Langenthal, Switz. E14 10
Langholm, Scot., U.K. F9 7
Langhorne, Pa., U.S. F12 115
Langlade, co., Wi., U.S. C4 126
Langley, B.C., Can. f13 69
Langley, S.C., U.S. E4 117
Langley, Wa., U.S. A3 124
Langley Air Force Base, mil., Va., U.S. h15 123
Langley Park, Md., U.S. f9 97
Langnau, Switz. F14 10
Langogne, Fr. H10 10
Langon, Fr. H6 10
Langres, Fr. E1 10
Langsa, Indon. E2 32
Lang Son, Viet. D9 34
Langston, Ok., U.S. B4 113
Languedoc, hist. reg., Fr. I9 10
L'Anguille, stm., Ar., U.S. B5 81
Langzhong, China E8 26
Lanham, Md., U.S. C4 97
Lanier, co., Ga., U.S. E3 87
Lannemezan, Fr. I7 10
Lannilis, Fr. D2 10
Lannion, Fr. D3 10
Lannon, Wi., U.S. m11 126
L'Annonciation, Que., Can. C3 74
Lansdale, Pa., U.S. F11 115
Lansdowne, Md., U.S. B4 97
L'Anse, Mi., U.S. B2 99
L'Anse-au-Loup, Newf., Can. C3 72
L'Anse Indian Reservation, Mi., U.S. B2 99
Lansford, Pa., U.S. E10 115
Lansing, Il., U.S. B6 90
Lansing, Ia., U.S. A6 92
Lansing, Ks., U.S. C9 93
Lansing, Mi., U.S. F6 99
Lantana, Fl., U.S. F6 86
Lantau Island, i., H.K. M2 28
Lanusei, Italy J4 14
Lanxi, China F8 28
Lanzarote, i., Spain p27 13b
Lanzhou, China D7 26
Laoag, Phil. B7 32
Lao Cai, Viet. C7 34
Laon, Fr. C10 10
La Oroya, Peru F3 54
Laos, ctry., Asia B3 32
Lapalisse, Fr. F10 10
La Palma, Col. E5 58
La Palma, Pan. J8 64
La Palma, i., Spain p23 13b
La Paragua, Ven. D11 58
La Paz, Arg. C5 56
La Paz, Arg. C3 56
La Paz, Bol. G5 54
La Paz, Mex. E4 62
La Paz, co., Az., U.S. D2 80
La Paz, Bahía de, b., Mex. E4 62
Lapeer, Mi., U.S. E7 99
Lapeer, co., Mi., U.S. E7 99
Lapel, In., U.S. D6 91
La Perouse Strait, strt., Asia B15 26
La Piedad [Cavadas], Mex. G8 62
La Pine, Or., U.S. D5 114
Lapinlahti, Fin. E16 6
La Place, La., U.S. h11 95
Lapland, reg., Eur. C14 6
La Plata, Arg. C5 56
La Plata, Md., U.S. C4 97
La Plata, Mo., U.S. A5 102
La Plata, co., Co., U.S. D3 83
La Plata Mountains, mts., Co., U.S. D3 83
La Plata Peak, mtn., Co., U.S. B4 83
La Platte, stm., Vt., U.S. C2 122
La Pocatière, Que., Can. B7 74
Laporte, Co., U.S. A5 83
La Porte, In., U.S. A4 91
La Porte, Tx., U.S. r14 120
La Porte, co., In., U.S. A4 91
La Porte City, Ia., U.S. B5 92
Lappeenranta, Fin. F17 6
La Prairie, Que., Can. D4 74
La Pryor, Tx., U.S. E3 120
Laptevych, More (Laptev Sea), Russia B19 24
Lapua, Fin. E14 6
La Puebla, Spain F15 12
La Puebla de Montalbán, Spain F7 12
La Push, Wa., U.S. B1 124
Lapwai, Id., U.S. C2 89
La Quiaca, Arg. A3 56
L'Aquila, Italy G8 14
Lār, Iran C5 46
Larache, Mor. A4 42
Laramie, Wy., U.S. E7 127
Laramie, co., Wy., U.S. E8 127
Laramie, stm., U.S. E7 127
Laramie Mountains, mts., Wy., U.S. D7 127
Laramie Peak, mtn., Wy., U.S. D7 127
Larantuka, Indon. G7 32
L'Arbresle, Fr. G11 10
Lärbro, Swe. H12 6
Larche, Col de, Eur. H13 10
Larchmont, N.Y., U.S. h13 109
Larchwood, Ia., U.S. A1 92
Laredo, Tx., U.S. F3 120
La Réole, Fr. H6 10
Largeau, Chad E9 42
L'argentière-la-Bessée, Fr. H13 10
Lar Gerd, Afg. C2 38
Largo, Fl., U.S. E4 86
Largo, Cañon, val., N.M., U.S. A2 108
Largo, Key, i., Fl., U.S. G6 86
Largs, Scot., U.K. F8 7
Larimer, co., Co., U.S. A5 83
Larimore, N.D., U.S. B8 111
La Rioja, Arg. B3 56
Lárisa, Grc. J6 16
Larjak, Russia E10 24
Lārkāna, Pak. G3 38
Lark Harbour, Newf., Can. D2 72
Larkspur, Ca., U.S. h7 82
Larksville, Pa., U.S. n17 115
Lárnax (Larnaca), Cyp. B3 40
Larne, N. Ire., U.K. G7 7
Larned, Ks., U.S. D4 93
La Robla, Spain C6 12
La Roca de la Sierra, Spain F5 12
La Rochefoucauld, Fr. G7 10
La Rochelle, Fr. F5 10
La Roche-sur-Yon, Fr. F5 10
La Roda, Spain F9 12
La Romana, Dom. Rep. E13 64
Laroquebrou, Fr. H9 10
Larose, La., U.S. E5 95
La Rubia, Arg. C4 56
Larue, co., Ky., U.S. C4 94
Laruns, Fr. J6 10
Larvik, Nor. G7 6
LaSalle, Que., Can. q19 74
La Salle, Co., U.S. A6 83
La Salle, Il., U.S. B4 90
La Salle, co., Il., U.S. B4 90
La Salle, co., La., U.S. C3 95
La Salle, co., Tx., U.S. E3 120
Las Animas, Co., U.S. C7 83
Las Animas, co., Co., U.S. D6 83
Las Anod, Som. G4 46

Name — Map Ref — Page

La Sarre, Que., Can. k11 74
Las Casitas, Cerro, mtn., Mex. F5 62
Las Choapas, Mex. I12 62
La Scie, Newf., Can. D4 72
Las Colimas, Mex. E10 62
Las Cruces, N.M., U.S. E3 108
Las Delicias, Mex. J14 62
La Selle, Pic, mtn., Haiti E11 64
La Serena, Chile B2 56
Las Escobas, Mex. B2 62
La Seyne, Fr. I12 10
Las Flores, Arg. D5 56
Lashio, Mya. C4 34
Laško, Slo. C10 14
Las Lomitas, Arg. A4 56
Las Minas, Cerro, mtn., Hond. G3 64
La Solana, Spain G8 12
Las Palmas de Gran Canaria, Spain p25 13b
La Spezia, Italy E4 14
Las Piedras, Ur. C5 56
Las Plumas, Arg. E3 56
Lassen, co., Ca., U.S. B3 82
Lassen Peak, vol., Ca., U.S. B3 82
Lassen Volcanic National Park, Ca., U.S. B3 82
L'Assomption, Que., Can. D4 74
Las Termas, Arg. B4 56
Last Mountain Lake, l., Sask., Can. F3 75
Las Tórtolas, Cerro, mtn., S.A. B3 56
Las Varas, Mex. C5 62
Las Vegas, Nv., U.S. G6 105
Las Vegas, N.M., U.S. B4 108
Latacunga, Ec. H3 58
Latah, co., Id., U.S. C2 89
Latakia see Al-Lādhiqīyah, Syria B4 40
La Teste-de-Buch, Fr. H5 10
Lathrop, Mo., U.S. B3 102
Lathrop Wells, Nv., U.S. G5 105
Latimer, co., Ok., U.S. C6 113
Latina, Italy H7 14
Laton, Ca., U.S. D4 82
La Tortuga, Isla, i., Ven. B10 58
Latour Peak, mtn., Id., U.S. B2 89
Latrobe, Pa., U.S. F3 115
Latta, S.C., U.S. C9 117
La Tuque, Que., Can. B5 74
Lātūr, India C4 37
Latvia, ctry., Eur. E7 18
Lauchhammer, Ger. D13 8
Lauderdale, Ms., U.S. C5 101
Lauderdale, co., Al., U.S. A2 78
Lauderdale, co., Ms., U.S. C5 101
Lauderdale, co., Tn., U.S. B2 119
Lauderdale Lakes, Fl., U.S. r13 86
Lauenburg, Ger. B10 8
Laughlin, Nv., U.S. H7 105
Laughlin Air Force Base, mil., Tx., U.S. E2 120
Laughlin Peak, mtn., N.M., U.S. A5 108
Laughlintown, Pa., U.S. F3 115
Launceston, Austl. H9 50
Launceston, Eng., U.K. K8 7
Launching Point, c., P.E.I., Can. C7 71
La Union, El Sal. H4 64
La Unión, Spain H11 12
La Unión, Ven. C9 58
La Urbana, Ven. D9 58
Laurel, De., U.S. F3 85
Laurel, Fl., U.S. E4 86
Laurel, Md., U.S. B4 97
Laurel, Ms., U.S. D4 101
Laurel, Mt., U.S. E8 103
Laurel, Ne., U.S. B8 104
Laurel, Va., U.S. C5 123
Laurel, co., Ky., U.S. C5 94
Laurel, stm., Ky., U.S. D5 94
Laurel Bay, S.C., U.S. G6 117
Laurel Creek, stm., W.V., U.S. n14 125
Laurel Creek, stm., W.V., U.S. m12 125
Laureldale, Pa., U.S. F10 115
Laurel Fork, stm., W.V., U.S. C5 125
Laurel Hill, N.C., U.S. C3 110
Laurel River Lake, res., Ky., U.S. D5 94
Laurence G. Hanscom Air Force Base, mil., Ma., U.S. g10 98
Laurence Harbor, N.J., U.S. C4 107
Laurens, Ia., U.S. B3 92
Laurens, S.C., U.S. C3 117
Laurens, co., Ga., U.S. D4 87
Laurens, co., S.C., U.S. C4 117
Laurentides, Que., Can. D4 74
Laurentides, Parc Provincial des, Que., Can. B6 74
Laurier, Que., Can. C6 74
Laurière, Fr. F8 10
Laurierville, Que., Can. C6 74
Laurinburg, N.C., U.S. C3 110
Laurium, Mi., U.S. A2 99
Lausanne, Switz. F13 10
Laut, Pulau, i., Indon. F6 32
Laut, Pulau, i., Indon. L9 34
Lautaro, Chile D2 56
Lauterbach, Ger. E9 8
Laut Kecil, Kepulauan, is., Indon. F6 32
Lauzon (part of Lévis-Lauzon), Que., Can. C6 74
Lava Beds National Monument, Ca., U.S. B3 82
Lavaca, Ar., U.S. B1 81
Lavaca, co., Tx., U.S. E4 120
Lavagh More, mtn., Ire. G4 7
Laval, Que., Can. D4 74
Laval, Fr. D6 10
La Vale, Md., U.S. k13 97
Lavaltrie, Que., Can. D4 74
Lavapié, Punta, c., Chile D2 56
Laveen, Az., U.S. m8 80
La Vega, Dom. Rep. E12 64
La Vela, Cabo de, c., Col. A6 58
Lavello, Italy H10 14
L'Avenir, Que., Can. D5 74
La Vergne, Tn., U.S. A5 119
La Verkin, Ut., U.S. F2 121
La Verne, Ca., U.S. m13 82
Laverne, Ok., U.S. A2 113
La Veta, Co., U.S. D5 83
Lavia, Fin. F14 6
La Vista, Ga., U.S. *h8 87
La Vista, Ne., U.S. g12 104
Lavonia, Ga., U.S. B3 87
Lavon Lake, res., Tx., U.S. m10 120
La Voulte-sur-Rhône, Fr. H11 10
Lavras, Braz. F6 57
Lawai, Hi., U.S. B2 88
Lawang, Indon. m16 33a
Lawers, Ben, mtn., Scot., U.K. E8 7
Lawn, Newf., Can. E4 72
Lawrence, In., U.S. E5 91
Lawrence, Ks., U.S. D8 93
Lawrence, Ma., U.S. A5 98
Lawrence, Mi., U.S. F4 99
Lawrence, N.Y., U.S. k13 109
Lawrence, co., Al., U.S. A2 78
Lawrence, co., Ar., U.S. A4 81
Lawrence, co., Il., U.S. E6 90
Lawrence, co., In., U.S. G4 91
Lawrence, co., Ky., U.S. B7 94
Lawrence, co., Ms., U.S. D3 101
Lawrence, co., Mo., U.S. D4 102
Lawrence, co., Oh., U.S. D3 112
Lawrence, co., Pa., U.S. E1 115
Lawrence, co., Tn., U.S. B4 119
Lawrenceburg, In., U.S. F8 91
Lawrenceburg, Ky., U.S. B5 94
Lawrenceburg, Tn., U.S. B4 119
Lawrence Park, Pa., U.S. B1 115
Lawrenceville, Ga., U.S. C3 87
Lawrenceville, Il., U.S. E6 90
Lawrenceville, Va., U.S. D5 123
Lawson, Mo., U.S. B3 102
Lawsonia, Md., U.S. E6 97
Lawtell, La., U.S. D3 95
Lawton, Mi., U.S. F5 99
Lawton, Ok., U.S. C3 113
Lawz, Jabal al-, mtn., Sau. Ar. C2 46
Lay Lake, res., Al., U.S. B3 78
Laysan Island, i., Hi., U.S. k13 88
Layton, Ut., U.S. B4 121
La Zarca, Mex. E7 62
Lazarev, Russia G22 24
Lazi, China F12 38
Lea, co., N.M., U.S. D6 108
Leachville, Ar., U.S. B5 81
Lead, S.D., U.S. C2 118
Leadbetter Point, c., Wa., U.S. C1 124
Leadville, Co., U.S. B4 83
Leadwood, Mo., U.S. D7 102
Leaf, stm., Ms., U.S. D5 101
Leaf Rapids, Man., Can. A1 70
Leake, co., Ms., U.S. C4 101
Leakesville, Ms., U.S. D5 101
Lealman, Fl., U.S. p10 86
Leamington, Ont., Can. E2 73
Leary, Ga., U.S. E2 87
Leatherman Peak, mtn., Id., U.S. E5 89
Leavenworth, Ks., U.S. C9 93
Leavenworth, Wa., U.S. B5 124
Leavenworth, co., Ks., U.S. C8 93
Leavittsburg, Oh., U.S. A5 112
Leawood, Ks., U.S. D9 93
Lebanon, De., U.S. D4 85
Lebanon, Il., U.S. E4 90
Lebanon, In., U.S. D5 91
Lebanon, Ky., U.S. C4 94
Lebanon, Mo., U.S. D5 102
Lebanon, N.H., U.S. C2 106
Lebanon, Oh., U.S. C1 112
Lebanon, Or., U.S. C4 114
Lebanon, Pa., U.S. F9 115
Lebanon, Tn., U.S. A5 119
Lebanon, Va., U.S. f9 123
Lebanon, co., Pa., U.S. F8 115
Lebanon, ctry., Asia C4 40
Lebanon Junction, Ky., U.S. C4 94
Le Blanc, Fr. F8 10
Lebo, Ks., U.S. D8 93
Lębork, Pol. A17 8
Lebrija, Spain I5 12
Lecce, Italy I13 14
Lecco, Italy D4 14
Le Center, Mn., U.S. F5 100
Le Cheylard, Fr. H11 10
Le Claire, Ia., U.S. C7 92
Lecompte, La., U.S. C3 95
Lecompton, Ks., U.S. C8 93
Le Creusot, Fr. F11 10
Le Dorat, Fr. F8 10
Leduc, Alta., Can. C4 68
Lee, Ma., U.S. B1 98
Lee, co., Al., U.S. C4 78
Lee, co., Ar., U.S. C5 81
Lee, co., Fl., U.S. F5 86
Lee, co., Ga., U.S. E2 87
Lee, co., Il., U.S. B4 90
Lee, co., Ia., U.S. D6 92
Lee, co., Ky., U.S. C6 94
Lee, co., Ms., U.S. A5 101
Lee, co., N.C., U.S. B3 110
Lee, co., S.C., U.S. C7 117
Lee, co., Tx., U.S. D4 120
Lee, co., Va., U.S. f8 123
Lee, Lake, l., Ms., U.S. B3 101
Leechburg, Pa., U.S. E2 115
Leech Lake, l., Mn., U.S. C4 100
Leech Lake Indian Reservation, Mn., U.S. C4 100
Lee Creek, stm., U.S. B1 81
Leeds, Eng., U.K. H11 7
Leeds, Al., U.S. B3 78
Leelanau, co., Mi., U.S. D5 99
Leelanau, Lake, l., Mi., U.S. C5 99
Lee Park, Pa., U.S. n17 115
Leer, Ger. B7 8
Leesburg, Fl., U.S. D5 86
Leesburg, Ga., U.S. E2 87
Leesburg, Oh., U.S. C2 112
Leesburg, Va., U.S. A5 123
Lees Summit, Mo., U.S. C3 102
Leesville, La., U.S. C2 95
Leesville, S.C., U.S. D4 117
Leesville Lake, res., Va., U.S. C3 123
Leeton, Mo., U.S. C4 102
Leetonia, Oh., U.S. B5 112
Leetsdale, Pa., U.S. h13 115
Leeuwarden, Neth. B5 8
Leeuwin, Cape, c., Austl. F3 50
Leeward Islands, is., N.A. F17 64
Leflore, co., Ms., U.S. B3 101
Le Flore, co., Ok., U.S. C7 113
Legal, Alta., Can. C4 68
Legazpi, Phil. r20 33b
Leghorn see Livorno, Italy F5 14
Legnago, Italy D6 14
Legnano, Italy D3 14
Legnica (Liegnitz), Pol. D16 8
Le Grand, Ca., U.S. D3 82
Le Grand, Ia., U.S. B5 92
Le Havre, Fr. C7 10
Lehi, Ut., U.S. C4 121
Lehigh, co., Pa., U.S. E10 115
Lehigh, stm., Pa., U.S. E10 115
Lehigh Acres, Fl., U.S. F5 86
Lehighton, Pa., U.S. E10 115
Lehua Island, i., Hi., U.S. A1 88
Lehututu, Bots. F4 44
Leiah, Pak. E4 38
Leibnitz, Aus. I15 8
Leicester, Eng., U.K. I11 7
Leicester, Ma., U.S. B4 98
Leichhardt, stm., Austl. C7 50
Leiden, Neth. C4 8
Leighton, Al., U.S. A2 78
Leikanger, Nor. F6 6
Leinster, hist. reg., Ire. H5 7
Leinster, Mount, mtn., Ire. I6 7
Leipsic, De., U.S. D3 85
Leipsic, Oh., U.S. A2 112
Leipsic, stm., De., U.S. C3 85
Leipzig, Ger. D12 8
Leiria, Port. F3 12
Leisler, Mount, mtn., Austl. D5 50
Leisure City, Fl., U.S. s13 86
Leitchfield, Ky., U.S. C3 94
Leitrim, Ire. G4 7
Leiyang, China I1 28
Leizhou Bandao, pen., China D11 34
Leland, Il., U.S. B5 90
Leland, Ms., U.S. B3 101
Leleiwi Point, c., Hi., U.S. D7 88
Leleque, Arg. E2 56
Le Lion-d'Angers, Fr. E6 10
Leli Shan, mtn., China D9 38
Le Locle, Switz. E13 10
Le Lude, Fr. E7 10
Le Maire, Estrecho de, strt., Arg. G4 56
Le Mans, Fr. D7 10
Le Mars, Ia., U.S. B1 92
Leme, Braz. G5 57
Lemesós (Limassol), Cyp. B3 40
Lemgo, Ger. C8 8
Lemhi, co., Id., U.S. E4 89
Lemhi, stm., Id., U.S. E5 89
Lemhi Pass, Id., U.S. E5 89
Lemhi Range, mts., Id., U.S. E5 89
Lemmon, S.D., U.S. B3 118
Lemmon, Mount, mtn., Az., U.S. E5 80
Lemmon Valley, Nv., U.S. D2 105
Lemon, Lake, l., In., U.S. F5 91
Lemon Fair, stm., Vt., U.S. C2 122
Lemon Grove, Ca., U.S. o15 82
Lemon Island, i., S.C., U.S. G6 117
Lemont, Il., U.S. B5 90
Lemont, Pa., U.S. E6 115
Lemonweir, stm., Wi., U.S. D3 126
Lemoore, Ca., U.S. D4 82
Lemoore Naval Air Station, mil., Ca., U.S. D4 82
Lempa, stm., N.A. H3 64
Lem Peak, mtn., Id., U.S. E5 89
Lena, Il., U.S. A4 90
Lena, stm., Russia C19 24
Lenawee, co., Mi., U.S. G6 99
Lencloître, Fr. F7 10
Lenexa, Ks., U.S. D9 93
Lenghu, China D5 26
Leninabad, Taj. I11 22
Leningrad see Sankt-Peterburg, Russia B13 18
Leninogorsk, Kaz. G10 24
Leninsk-Kuzneckij, Russia G11 24
Leninskoje, Russia H20 24
Lennox, S.D., U.S. D9 118
Lennoxville, Que., Can. D6 74
Lenoir, N.C., U.S. B1 110
Lenoir, co., N.C., U.S. B5 110
Lenoir City, Tn., U.S. D9 119
Lenore Lake, l., Sask., Can. E3 75
Lenore Lake, l., Wa., U.S. B6 124
Lenox, Ga., U.S. E3 87
Lenox, Ia., U.S. D3 92
Lenox, Ma., U.S. B1 98
Lens, Fr. B9 10
Lensk, Russia E16 24
Lentini, Italy L10 14
Leo, In., U.S. B7 91
Leoben, Aus. H15 8
Leominster, Eng., U.K. I10 7
Leominster, Ma., U.S. A4 98
León, Nic. H4 64
León, Spain C6 12
Leon, Ia., U.S. D4 92
Leon, Ks., U.S. E7 93
Leon, co., Fl., U.S. B2 86
Leon, co., Tx., U.S. D5 120
Leonard, Tx., U.S. C4 120
Leonardo, N.J., U.S. C4 107
Leonardtown, Md., U.S. D4 97
Leonberg, Ger. G9 8
León [de los Aldamas], Mex. G9 62
Leonia, N.J., U.S. h9 107
Leonora, Austl. E4 50
Leonville, La., U.S. D4 95
Léopold II, Lac see Mai-Ndombe, Lac, l., Zaire B3 44
Leopoldina, Braz. F7 57
Léopoldville see Kinshasa, Zaire B3 44
Leoti, Ks., U.S. D2 93
Le Palais, Fr. E3 10
Lepanto, Ar., U.S. B5 81
Lepe, Spain H4 12
Leping, China G6 28
L'Épiphanie, Que., Can. D4 74
Lepontine, Alpi, mts., Eur. F15 10
Le Puy, Fr. G10 10
Lercara Friddi, Italy L8 14
Lerici, Italy E4 14
Lérida, Col. G7 58
Lérida, Spain D12 12
Lerma, Spain C8 12
Le Roy, Il., U.S. C5 90
Le Roy, Mn., U.S. G6 100
Le Roy, N.Y., U.S. C3 109
Lerwick, Scot., U.K. A11 7
Léry, Que., Can. q19 74
Lery, Lake, l., La., U.S. k12 95
Les Andelys, Fr. C8 10
Lesbos see Lésvos, i., Grc. J10 16
Les Cayes, Haiti E11 64
Les Échelles, Fr. G12 10
Les Herbiers, Fr. F5 10
Leskovac, Yugo. G5 16
Leslie, Mi., U.S. F6 99
Leslie, S.C., U.S. B6 117
Leslie, co., Ky., U.S. C6 94
Lesotho, ctry., Afr. G5 44
Lesozavodsk, Russia H20 24
Les Sables-d'Olonne, Fr. F5 10
Lesser Antilles, is. G17 64
Lesser Slave Lake, l., Alta., Can. B3 68
Lesser Sunda Islands, is., Indon. G6 32
Lester Prairie, Mn., U.S. F4 100
Le Sueur, Mn., U.S. F5 100
Le Sueur, co., Mn., U.S. F5 100
Lésvos (Lesbos), i., Grc. J10 16
Leszno, Pol. D16 8
Letcher, co., Ky., U.S. C7 94
Lethbridge, Alta., Can. E4 68
Lethbridge, Newf., Can. D5 72
Lethem, Guy. F13 58
Le Thillot, Fr. E13 10
Leti, Kepulauan, is., Indon. G8 32
Leticia, Col. J8 58
Le Tréport, Fr. B8 10
Letsôk-Aw Kyun, i., Mya. I5 34
Letterkenny, Ire. G5 7
Leutkirch, Ger. H10 8
Leuven, Bel. E4 8
Levádhia, Grc. K6 16
Levante, Riviera di, Italy E4 14
Levelland, Tx., U.S. C1 120
Leveque, Cape, c., Austl. C4 50
Leverkusen, Ger. D6 8
Le Vigan, Fr. I10 10
Levisa Fork, stm., U.S. C7 94
Lévis [-Lauzon], Que., Can. C6 74
Levittown, N.Y., U.S. E7 109
Levittown, Pa., U.S. F12 115
Levy, co., Fl., U.S. C4 86
Levy Lake, l., Fl., U.S. C4 86
Lewes, Eng., U.K. K13 7
Lewes, De., U.S. E5 85
Lewes and Rehoboth Canal, De., U.S. F5 85
Lewis, co., Id., U.S. C2 89
Lewis, co., Ky., U.S. B6 94
Lewis, co., Mo., U.S. A6 102
Lewis, co., N.Y., U.S. B5 109
Lewis, co., Tn., U.S. B4 119
Lewis, co., Wa., U.S. C3 124
Lewis, co., W.V., U.S. C4 125
Lewis, stm., Wa., U.S. C4 124
Lewis, stm., Wy., U.S. B2 127
Lewis, Isle of, i., Scot., U.K. C6 7
Lewis, Mount, mtn., Nv., U.S. C5 105
Lewis and Clark, co., Mt., U.S. C4 103
Lewis and Clark Cavern, Mt., U.S. D5 103
Lewis and Clark Lake, res., U.S. E8 118
Lewisburg, Ky., U.S. D3 94
Lewisburg, Oh., U.S. C1 112
Lewisburg, Pa., U.S. E8 115
Lewisburg, Tn., U.S. B5 119
Lewisburg, W.V., U.S. D4 125
Lewis Creek, stm., Vt., U.S. C2 122
Lewis Lake, l., Wy., U.S. B2 127
Lewisport, Ky., U.S. C3 94
Lewisporte, Newf., Can. D4 72
Lewis Smith Lake, res., Al., U.S. B2 78
Lewiston, Id., U.S. C1 89
Lewiston, Me., U.S. D2 96
Lewiston, Mn., U.S. G7 100
Lewiston, N.Y., U.S. B1 109
Lewiston, Ut., U.S. B4 121
Lewiston Peak, mtn., Ut., U.S. C3 121
Lewiston Woodville, N.C., U.S. A5 110
Lewistown, Il., U.S. C3 90
Lewistown, Mt., U.S. C7 103
Lewistown, Pa., U.S. E6 115
Lewisville, Ar., U.S. D2 81
Lewisville, Tx., U.S. C4 120
Lewisville Lake, res., Tx., U.S. C4 120
Lexington, Al., U.S. A2 78
Lexington, Il., U.S. C5 90
Lexington, Ky., U.S. B5 94
Lexington, Ma., U.S. B5 98
Lexington, Mi., U.S. E8 99
Lexington, Ms., U.S. B3 101
Lexington, Mo., U.S. B4 102
Lexington, Ne., U.S. D6 104
Lexington, N.C., U.S. B2 110
Lexington, Oh., U.S. B3 112
Lexington, Ok., U.S. B4 113
Lexington, S.C., U.S. D5 117
Lexington, Tn., U.S. B3 119
Lexington, Va., U.S. C3 123
Lexington, co., S.C., U.S. D5 117
Lexington Park, Md., U.S. D5 97
Leyte, i., Phil. C7 32
Leyte Gulf, b., Phil. C8 32
Lhasa, China F14 38
Lhokseumawe, Indon. D2 32
Lianhua Shan, mts., China L4 28
Lianxian, China G9 26
Lianyungang, China E10 26
Liao, stm., China C11 26
Liaocheng, China D10 26
Liaodong Wan, b., China C11 26
Liaoning, prov., China C11 26
Liaotung, Gulf of see Liaodong Wan, b., China C11 26
Liaoyang, China C11 26
Liaoyuan, China C12 26
Liard, stm., Can. E8 66
Libby, Mt., U.S. B1 103
Libenge, Zaire H9 42
Liberal, Ks., U.S. E3 93
Liberal, Mo., U.S. D3 102
Liberec, Czech. E15 8
Liberia, C.R. I5 64
Liberia, ctry., Afr. G4 42
Libertad, Ven. C8 58
Liberty, In., U.S. E8 91
Liberty, Ky., U.S. C5 94
Liberty, Ms., U.S. D3 101
Liberty, Mo., U.S. B3 102
Liberty, N.Y., U.S. D6 109
Liberty, N.C., U.S. B3 110
Liberty, S.C., U.S. B2 117
Liberty, Tx., U.S. D5 120
Liberty, co., Fl., U.S. B2 86
Liberty, co., Ga., U.S. E5 87
Liberty, co., Mt., U.S. B5 103
Liberty, co., Tx., U.S. D5 120
Liberty Center, Oh., U.S. A1 112
Liberty Lake, Wa., U.S. g14 124
Liberty Lake, res., Md., U.S. B4 97
Libertyville, Il., U.S. A6 90
Lībīyah, Aṣ-Ṣaḥrā' al- (Libyan Desert), des., Afr. D11 42
Libourne, Fr. H6 10
Libreville, Gabon A1 44
Libuse, La., U.S. C3 95
Libya, ctry., Afr. C9 42
Libyan Desert see Lībīyah, Aṣ-Ṣaḥrā' al-, des., Afr. D11 42
Licata, Italy L8 14
Lichinga, Moz. D7 44
Lichtenfels, Ger. E11 8
Lick Creek, stm., Tn., U.S. C11 119
Licking, Mo., U.S. D6 102
Licking, co., Oh., U.S. B3 112
Licking, stm., Ky., U.S. B6 94
Lida, Bela. H8 18
Lida, Lake, l., Mn., U.S. D3 100
Lidgerwood, N.D., U.S. C8 111
Lidköping, Swe. G9 6
Lido di Ostia, Italy H7 14
Liechtenstein, ctry., Eur. F9 4
Liège, Bel. E5 8
Lieksa, Fin. E18 6
Lienz, Aus. I12 8
Liepāja, Lat. E4 18
Lier, Bel. D4 8
Liestal, Switz. E14 10
Liévin, Fr. B9 10
Lièvre, Rivière du, stm., Que., Can. D2 74
Liezen, Aus. H14 8
Lifford, Ire. G5 7
Ligao, Phil. r20 33b
Lighthouse Inlet, b., S.C., U.S. k12 117
Lighthouse Point, c., Fl., U.S. C2 86
Lighthouse Point, c., La., U.S. E3 95
Lighthouse Point, c., Mi., U.S. C5 99
Lightning Creek, stm., Wy., U.S. C8 127
Ligny-en-Barrois, Fr. D12 10
Ligonier, In., U.S. B6 91
Ligonier, Pa., U.S. F3 115
Ligurian Sea, Eur. F3 14
Lihou Reefs, rf., Austl. C10 50
Lihue, Hi., U.S. B2 88
Lijiang, China F7 26
Likasi (Jadotville), Zaire D5 44
Likino-Dulevo, Russia F22 18
Likneš, Nor. G6 6
Likouala, stm., Congo B3 44
Lilbourn, Mo., U.S. E8 102
Lilburn, Ga., U.S. h8 87
Liling, China H2 28
Lille, Fr. B10 10
Lillehammer, Nor. F8 6
Lillestrøm, Nor. G8 6
Lillian, Al., U.S. E2 78
Lillington, N.C., U.S. B4 110
Lillinonah, Lake, l., Ct., U.S. C2 84
Lillo, Spain F8 12
Lillooet, B.C., Can. D7 69
Lillooet, stm., B.C., Can. D6 69
Lilly, Pa., U.S. F4 115
Lilly Fork, stm., W.V., U.S. m13 125
Lilly Grove, W.V., U.S. D3 125
Lilongwe, Mwi. D6 44
Lily, Ky., U.S. C5 94
Lima, Peru F3 54
Lima, N.Y., U.S. C3 109
Lima, Oh., U.S. B1 112
Lima Reservoir, res., Mt., U.S. F4 103
Limassol see Lemesós, Cyp. B3 40
Limbdi, India I4 38
Limburg an der Lahn, Ger. E8 8
Limeira, Braz. G5 57
Limerick, Ire. I4 7
Limestone, Me., U.S. B5 96
Limestone, co., Al., U.S. A2 78
Limestone, co., Tx., U.S. D4 120
Limestone Point, pen., Man., Can. C2 70
Liminka, Fin. D15 6
Limmen Bight, Austl. B7 50
Límnos, i., Grc. J9 16
Limoges, Ont., Can. B9 73
Limoges, Fr. G8 10
Limón, C.R. I6 64
Limón, Hond. G5 64
Limon, Co., U.S. B7 83
Limousins, Plateau du, plat., Fr. G8 10

Name	Map Ref	Page
Limoux, Fr.	I9	10
Limpopo, stm., Afr.	F6	44
Linares, Chile	D2	56
Linares, Col.	G4	58
Linares, Mex.	E10	62
Linares, Spain	G8	12
Lincoln, Arg.	C4	56
Lincoln, Ont., Can.	D5	73
Lincoln, Eng., U.K.	H12	7
Lincoln, Al., U.S.	B3	78
Lincoln, Ar., U.S.	B1	81
Lincoln, Ca., U.S.	C3	82
Lincoln, De., U.S.	E4	85
Lincoln, Id., U.S.	F6	89
Lincoln, Il., U.S.	C4	90
Lincoln, Ks., U.S.	C5	93
Lincoln, Me., U.S.	C4	96
Lincoln, Ma., U.S.	g10	98
Lincoln, Mo., U.S.	C4	102
Lincoln, Ne., U.S.	D9	104
Lincoln, N.H., U.S.	B3	106
Lincoln, co., Ar., U.S.	D4	81
Lincoln, co., Co., U.S.	C7	83
Lincoln, co., Ga., U.S.	C4	87
Lincoln, co., Id., U.S.	G4	89
Lincoln, co., Ks., U.S.	C5	93
Lincoln, co., Ky., U.S.	C5	94
Lincoln, co., La., U.S.	B3	95
Lincoln, co., Me., U.S.	D3	96
Lincoln, co., Mn., U.S.	F2	100
Lincoln, co., Ms., U.S.	D3	101
Lincoln, co., Mo., U.S.	B7	102
Lincoln, co., Mt., U.S.	B1	103
Lincoln, co., Ne., U.S.	D5	104
Lincoln, co., Nv., U.S.	F6	105
Lincoln, co., N.M., U.S.	D4	108
Lincoln, co., N.C., U.S.	B1	110
Lincoln, co., Ok., U.S.	B5	113
Lincoln, co., Or., U.S.	C3	114
Lincoln, co., S.D., U.S.	D9	118
Lincoln, co., Tn., U.S.	B5	119
Lincoln, co., Wa., U.S.	B7	124
Lincoln, co., W.V., U.S.	C2	125
Lincoln, co., Wi., U.S.	C4	126
Lincoln, co., Wy., U.S.	D2	127
Lincoln, Mount, mtn., Co., U.S.	B4	83
Lincoln Acres, Ca., U.S.	o15	82
Lincoln City, Or., U.S.	C3	114
Lincoln Heights, Oh., U.S.	o13	112
Lincoln Park, Co., U.S.	C5	83
Lincoln Park, Ga., U.S.	D2	87
Lincoln Park, Mi., U.S.	p15	99
Lincoln Park, N.J., U.S.	B4	107
Lincolnshire, Il., U.S.	h9	90
Lincoln Tomb State Memorial, hist., Il., U.S.	D4	90
Lincolnton, Ga., U.S.	C4	87
Lincolnton, N.C., U.S.	B1	110
Lincolnville, S.C., U.S.	h11	117
Lincolnwood, Il., U.S.	h9	90
Lincroft, N.J., U.S.	C4	107
Lindale, Ga., U.S.	B1	87
Lindale, Tx., U.S.	C5	120
Lindau, Ger.	H9	8
Linden, Al., U.S.	C2	78
Linden, In., U.S.	D4	91
Linden, Mi., U.S.	F7	99
Linden, N.J., U.S.	k8	107
Linden, Tn., U.S.	B4	119
Linden, Tx., U.S.	C5	120
Lindenhurst, Il., U.S.	h8	90
Lindenhurst, N.Y., U.S.	n15	109
Lindenwold, N.J., U.S.	D3	107
Lindesnes, c., Nor.	G6	6
Lindi, Tan.	C7	44
Lindon, Ut., U.S.	C4	121
Lindsay, Ont., Can.	C6	73
Lindsay, Ca., U.S.	D4	82
Lindsay, Ok., U.S.	C4	113
Lindsborg, Ks., U.S.	D6	93
Lindstrom, Mn., U.S.	E6	100
Linesville, Pa., U.S.	C1	115
Lineville, Al., U.S.	B4	78
Lingao, China	D10	34
Lingayen, Phil.	B7	32
Lingen, Ger.	C7	8
Lingga, Kepulauan, is., Indon.	F3	32
Lingle, Wy., U.S.	D8	127
Linglestown, Pa., U.S.	F8	115
Lingling, China	A11	34
Linh, Ngoc, mtn., Viet.	G9	34
Linhai, China	G10	28
Linière, Que., Can.	C7	74
Linjiang, China	C12	26
Linköping, Swe.	G10	6
Linkou, China	B13	26
Linn, Mo., U.S.	C6	102
Linn, co., Ia., U.S.	B6	92
Linn, co., Ks., U.S.	D9	93
Linn, co., Mo., U.S.	B4	102
Linn, co., Or., U.S.	C4	114
Lino Lakes, Mn., U.S.	m12	100
Linqing, China	D10	26
Linru, China	A1	28
Lins, Braz.	F4	57
Lintao, China	D7	26
Linthicum Heights, Md., U.S.	B4	97
Linton, In., U.S.	F3	91
Linton, N.D., U.S.	C5	111
Linwood, N.J., U.S.	E3	107
Linxi, China	C10	26
Linxia, China	D7	26
Linyi, China	D10	26
Linz, Aus.	G14	8
Lion, Golfe du, b., Fr.	I11	10
Lipa, Phil.	r19	33b
Lipeck, Russia	I22	18
Lippstadt, Ger.	D8	8
Lipscomb, Al., U.S.	B3	78
Lipscomb, co., Tx., U.S.	A2	120
Lira, Ug.	H12	42
Liria, Spain	F11	12
Lisala, Zaire	A4	44
Lisboa (Lisbon), Port.	G2	12
Lisbon, Ia., U.S.	C6	92
Lisbon, Me., U.S.	D2	96
Lisbon, Md., U.S.	B3	97
Lisbon, N.H., U.S.	B3	106
Lisbon, N.D., U.S.	C8	111
Lisbon, Oh., U.S.	B5	112
Lisbon Center, Me., U.S.	f7	96
Lisbon Falls, Me., U.S.	E2	96
Lisbon see Lisboa, Port.	G2	12
Lisburne, Cape, c., Ak., U.S.	B6	79
Lishui, China	G8	28
Lisianski Island, i., Hi., U.S.	k13	88
Lisieux, Fr.	C7	10
Lisle, Il., U.S.	k8	90
L'Isle Jourdain, Fr.	F7	10
L'Isle-Jourdain, Fr.	I8	10
L'Islet-sur-Mer, Que., Can.	B7	74
L'Isle-Verte, Que., Can.	A8	74
Lismore, Austl.	E10	50
Listowel, Ont., Can.	D4	73
Listowel, Ire.	I3	7
Lit, Swe.	E10	6
Litang, China	G8	26
Litchfield, Ct., U.S.	C3	84
Litchfield, Il., U.S.	D4	90
Litchfield, Mi., U.S.	F6	99
Litchfield, Mn., U.S.	E4	100
Litchfield, co., Ct., U.S.	B2	84
Litchfield Park, Az., U.S.	m8	80
Lithia Springs, Ga., U.S.	h7	87
Lithonia, Ga., U.S.	C2	87
Lithuania, ctry., Eur.	F6	18
Litija, Slo.	C9	14
Lititz, Pa., U.S.	F9	115
Litovko, Russia	H21	24
Little, stm., U.S.	B5	81
Little, stm., U.S.	D7	113
Little, stm., Ct., U.S.	C7	84
Little, stm., Ky., U.S.	D2	94
Little, stm., La., U.S.	C3	95
Little, stm., N.C., U.S.	B3	110
Little, stm., Ok., U.S.	B5	113
Little, stm., S.C., U.S.	C2	117
Little, stm., Tn., U.S.	n14	119
Little, stm., Vt., U.S.	C3	122
Little, stm., Va., U.S.	D2	123
Little Abaco Island, i., Bah.	A9	64
Little Acres, Az., U.S.	D5	80
Little Andaman, i., India	I2	34
Little Arkansas, stm., Ks., U.S.	D6	93
Little Belt Mountains, mts., Mt., U.S.	D6	103
Little Bighorn, stm., U.S.	E9	103
Little Black, stm., Me., U.S.	A3	96
Little Blue, stm., U.S.	C6	93
Little Blue, stm., In., U.S.	H5	91
Little Bow, stm., Alta., Can.	D4	68
Little Cacapon, stm., W.V., U.S.	B6	125
Little Catalina, Newf., Can.	D5	72
Little Cayman, i., Cay. Is.	E7	64
Little Cedar, stm., Ia., U.S.	A5	92
Little Churchill, stm., Man., Can.	A4	70
Little Chute, Wi., U.S.	D5	126
Little Coal, stm., W.V., U.S.	C3	125
Little Colorado, stm., Az., U.S.	B4	80
Little Compton, R.I., U.S.	E6	116
Little Creek, De., U.S.	D4	85
Little Creek Naval Amphibious Base, mil., Va., U.S.	k15	123
Little Creek Peak, mtn., Ut., U.S.	F3	121
Little Current, Ont., Can.	B3	73
Little Diomede Island, i., Ak., U.S.	B6	79
Little Egg Harbor, b., N.J., U.S.	D4	107
Little Egg Inlet, b., N.J., U.S.	E4	107
Little Falls, Mn., U.S.	E4	100
Little Falls, N.J., U.S.	B4	107
Little Falls, N.Y., U.S.	B6	109
Little Ferry, N.J., U.S.	h8	107
Littlefield, Tx., U.S.	C1	120
Little Fishing Creek, stm., W.V., U.S.	h9	125
Littlefork, Mn., U.S.	B5	100
Little Fork, stm., Mn., U.S.	B5	100
Little Goose Creek, stm., Wy., U.S.	B6	127
Little Gunpowder Falls, stm., Md., U.S.	A4	97
Little Humboldt, stm., Nv., U.S.	B4	105
Little Inagua, i., Bah.	D11	64
Little Kanawha, stm., W.V., U.S.	C4	125
Little Lake, Mi., U.S.	B3	99
Little Lake, l., La., U.S.	E5	95
Little Lynches, stm., S.C., U.S.	C7	117
Little Manatee, stm., Fl., U.S.	p11	86
Little Mecatina, stm., Can.	h9	72
Little Miami, stm., Oh., U.S.	C1	112
Little Minch, strt., Scot., U.K.	D6	7
Little Missouri, stm., U.S.	B6	76
Little Missouri, stm., Ar., U.S.	D2	81
Little Muddy, stm., Il., U.S.	E4	90
Little Muddy, stm., N.D., U.S.	A2	111
Little Nicobar, i., India	K2	34
Little Osage, stm., U.S.	E9	93
Little Otter Creek, stm., Vt., U.S.	C2	122
Little Owyhee, stm., U.S.	B5	105
Little Pee Dee, stm., S.C., U.S.	C9	117
Little Powder, stm., U.S.	F11	103
Little Red, stm., Ar., U.S.	B4	81
Little River, co., Ar., U.S.	D1	81
Little River Inlet, b., S.C., U.S.	D10	117
Little Rock, Ar., U.S.	C3	81
Little Rock, stm., U.S.	A1	92
Little Rock Air Force Base, mil., Ar., U.S.	C3	81
Little Sable Point, c., Mi., U.S.	E4	99
Little Salt Lake, l., Ut., U.S.	F3	121
Little Sandy, stm., Ky., U.S.	B6	94
Little Sandy Creek, stm., Wy., U.S.	D3	127
Little Sebago Lake, l., Me., U.S.	g7	96
Little Silver, N.J., U.S.	C4	107
Little Sioux, stm., U.S.	B2	92
Little Sioux, West Fork, stm., Ia., U.S.	B2	92
Little Smoky, stm., Alta., Can.	B2	68
Little Snake, stm., U.S.	A2	83
Little Spokane, stm., Wa., U.S.	B8	124
Littlestown, Pa., U.S.	G7	115
Little Tallapoosa, stm., U.S.	B4	78
Little Tenmile Creek, stm., W.V., U.S.	k10	125
Little Tennessee, stm., U.S.	D9	119
Littleton, Co., U.S.	B6	83
Littleton, Me., U.S.	B5	96
Littleton, Ma., U.S.	f10	98
Littleton, N.H., U.S.	B3	106
Littleton, N.C., U.S.	A5	110
Littleville, Al., U.S.	A2	78
Little Wabash, stm., Il., U.S.	E5	90
Little Walnut, stm., Ks., U.S.	g13	93
Little White, stm., S.D., U.S.	D5	118
Little Wolf, stm., Wi., U.S.	D4	126
Little Wood, stm., Id., U.S.	F4	89
Liuan, China	D5	28
Liuhe, China	C7	28
Liuzhou, China	B10	34
Live Oak, Ca., U.S.	C3	82
Live Oak, Fl., U.S.	B4	86
Live Oak, co., Tx., U.S.	E3	120
Livermore, Ca., U.S.	h9	82
Livermore, Ky., U.S.	C2	94
Livermore, Mount, mtn., Tx., U.S.	o12	120
Livermore Falls, Me., U.S.	D2	96
Liverpool, Eng., U.K.	H10	7
Liverpool, Cape, c., N.W. Ter., Can.	B17	66
Livingston, Al., U.S.	C1	78
Livingston, Ca., U.S.	D3	82
Livingston, Il., U.S.	E4	90
Livingston, La., U.S.	D5	95
Livingston, Mt., U.S.	E6	103
Livingston, N.J., U.S.	B4	107
Livingston, Tn., U.S.	C8	119
Livingston, Tx., U.S.	D5	120
Livingston, co., Il., U.S.	C5	90
Livingston, co., Ky., U.S.	e9	94
Livingston, co., La., U.S.	D5	95
Livingston, co., Mi., U.S.	F7	99
Livingston, co., Mo., U.S.	B4	102
Livingston, co., N.Y., U.S.	C3	109
Livingston, Lake, res., Tx., U.S.	D5	120
Livingstone, Zam.	E5	44
Livingstonia, Mwi.	D6	44
Livno, Bos.	F12	14
Livny, Russia	I20	18
Livonia, La., U.S.	D4	95
Livonia, Mi., U.S.	F7	99
Livorno (Leghorn), Italy	F5	14
Liyang, China	D8	28
Lizard Head Pass, Co., U.S.	D3	83
Lizard Head Peak, mtn., Wy., U.S.	D3	127
Lizard Point, c., Eng., U.K.	L7	7
Lizella, Ga., U.S.	D3	87
Ljubljana, Slo.	C9	14
Ljungby, Swe.	H9	6
Ljusdal, Swe.	F11	6
Llandudno, Wales, U.K.	H9	7
Llanelli, Wales, U.K.	J8	7
Llanes, Spain	B7	12
Llanidloes, Wales, U.K.	I9	7
Llano, Tx., U.S.	D3	120
Llano, co., Tx., U.S.	D3	120
Llano, stm., Tx., U.S.	D3	120
Llanos, pl., S.A.	E7	58
Llanwrtyd Wells, Wales, U.K.	I9	7
Llera, Mex.	F10	62
Llerena, Spain	G5	12
Lloyd, Ky., U.S.	B7	94
Lloydminster, Alta., Can.	C5	68
Lloyds, stm., Newf., Can.	D3	72
Lluchmayor, Spain	F14	12
Llullaillaco, Volcán, vol., S.A.	A3	56
Lo, stm., Viet.	C8	34
Loami, Il., U.S.	D4	90
Loange, stm., Afr.	C3	44
Löbau, Ger.	D14	8
Lobaye, stm., Cen. Afr. Rep.	G9	42
Lobelville, Tn., U.S.	B4	119
Lobito, Ang.	D2	44
Lobos de Afuera, Islas, is., Peru	E2	54
Lobos de Tierra, Isla, i., Peru	E2	54
Lobster Lake, l., Me., U.S.	C3	96
Locarno, Switz.	F15	10
Lochaline, Scot., U.K.	E7	7
Lochboisdale, Scot., U.K.	D5	7
Loches, Fr.	E7	10
Lochgilphead, Scot., U.K.	E7	7
Loch Lomond, Va., U.S.	*B5	123
Loch Raven Reservoir, res., Md., U.S.	B4	97
Lochsa, stm., Id., U.S.	C3	89
Lockeport, N.S., Can.	F4	71
Lockesburg, Ar., U.S.	D1	81
Lockhart, Tx., U.S.	E4	120
Lock Haven, Pa., U.S.	D7	115
Lockland, Oh., U.S.	o13	112
Lockney, Tx., U.S.	B2	120
Lockport, Il., U.S.	B5	90
Lockport, La., U.S.	E5	95
Lockport, N.Y., U.S.	B2	109
Lockwood, Mo., U.S.	D4	102
Lockwood, Mt., U.S.	E8	103
Loc Ninh, Viet.	I9	34
Locust, N.C., U.S.	B2	110
Locust Fork, stm., Al., U.S.	B3	78
Locust Grove, Ga., U.S.	C2	87
Locust Grove, Ok., U.S.	A6	113
Lod, Isr.	D4	40
Lodejnoje Polje, Russia	A16	18
Lodève, Fr.	I10	10
Lodgepole Creek, stm., U.S.	C3	104
Lodi, Italy	D4	14
Lodi, Ca., U.S.	C3	82
Lodi, N.J., U.S.	h8	107
Lodi, Oh., U.S.	A3	112
Lodi, Wi., U.S.	E4	126
Lodja, Zaire	B4	44
Lodore, Canyon of, val., Co., U.S.	A2	83
Lodwar, Kenya	H2	46
Łódź, Pol.	D19	8
Loffa, stm., Afr.	G3	42
Logan, Ia., U.S.	C2	92
Logan, Ks., U.S.	C4	93
Logan, N.M., U.S.	B6	108
Logan, Oh., U.S.	C3	112
Logan, Ut., U.S.	B4	121
Logan, W.V., U.S.	D3	125
Logan, co., Ar., U.S.	B2	81
Logan, co., Co., U.S.	A7	83
Logan, co., Il., U.S.	C4	90
Logan, co., Ks., U.S.	D2	93
Logan, co., Ky., U.S.	D3	94
Logan, co., Ne., U.S.	C5	104
Logan, co., N.D., U.S.	C6	111
Logan, co., Oh., U.S.	B2	112
Logan, co., Ok., U.S.	B4	113
Logan, co., W.V., U.S.	D3	125
Logan, Mount, mtn., Yukon, Can.	D4	66
Logan, Mount, mtn., Wa., U.S.	A5	124
Logandale, Nv., U.S.	G7	105
Logan Lake, B.C., Can.	D7	69
Logan Martin Lake, res., Al., U.S.	B3	78
Logan Pass, Mt., U.S.	B2	103
Logansport, In., U.S.	C5	91
Logansport, La., U.S.	C2	95
Loganville, Ga., U.S.	C3	87
Loganville, Pa., U.S.	G8	115
Loggieville, N.B., Can.	B4	71
Log Lane Village, Co., U.S.	A7	83
Logone, stm., Afr.	F9	42
Logroño, Spain	C9	12
Logrosán, Spain	F6	12
Lohr, Ger.	E9	8
Loi-Kaw, Mya.	E4	34
Loimaa, Fin.	F14	6
Loire, stm., Fr.	E5	10
Loja, Ec.	J3	58
Loja, Spain	H7	12
Lokolama, Zaire	B3	44
Lol, stm., Sudan	G11	42
Lola, Mount, mtn., Ca., U.S.	C3	82
Lolo, Mt., U.S.	D2	103
Lolo Pass, U.S.	C4	89
Lomami, stm., Zaire	B4	44
Lombard, Il., U.S.	k8	90
Lomblen, Pulau, i., Indon.	G7	32
Lombok, i., Indon.	G6	32
Lomé, Togo	G6	42
Lomela, Zaire	B4	44
Lomela, stm., Zaire	B4	44
Lomira, Wi., U.S.	E5	126
Lomond, Loch, l., Scot., U.K.	E8	7
Lomonosov, Russia	B12	18
Lompoc, Ca., U.S.	E3	82
Łomża, Pol.	B22	8
Lonaconing, Md., U.S.	k13	97
Lonāvale, India	C2	37
Loncoche, Chile	D2	56
London, Ont., Can.	E3	73
London, Eng., U.K.	J12	7
London, Ar., U.S.	B2	81
London, Ky., U.S.	C5	94
London, Oh., U.S.	C2	112
Londonderry, N. Ire., U.K.	G5	7
Londonderry, N.H., U.S.	E4	106
Londonderry, Cape, c., Austl.	B5	50
Londonderry, Isla, i., Chile	H2	56
Londontown, Md., U.S.	C4	97
Londrina, Braz.	G3	57
Lone Grove, Ok., U.S.	C4	113
Lone Mountain, mtn., Nv., U.S.	E4	105
Lone Pine, Ca., U.S.	D4	82
Lone Tree, Ia., U.S.	C6	92
Long, co., Ga., U.S.	E5	87
Longa, Proliv, strt., Russia	C29	24
Longarone, Italy	C7	14
Long Bar Harbor, Md., U.S.	B5	97
Long Beach, Ca., U.S.	F4	82
Long Beach, In., U.S.	A4	91
Long Beach, Md., U.S.	D5	97
Long Beach, Ms., U.S.	g7	101
Long Beach, N.Y., U.S.	E7	109
Long Beach, Wa., U.S.	C1	124
Long Beach Naval Shipyard, mil., Ca., U.S.	n12	82
Longboat Key, Fl., U.S.	q10	86
Longboat Key, i., Fl., U.S.	E4	86
Longboat Pass, strt., Fl., U.S.	q10	86
Long Branch, N.J., U.S.	C5	107
Longbranch, Wa., U.S.	B3	124
Long Creek Mountain, mtn., Wy., U.S.	D5	127
Longeau, Fr.	E12	10
Long Grove, Ia., U.S.	C7	92
Long Harbour [-Mount Arlington Heights], Newf., Can.	E5	72
Long Island, i., Bah.	C10	64
Long Island, i., N.S., Can.	E3	71
Long Island, i., Me., U.S.	g7	96
Long Island, i., Ma., U.S.	g12	98
Long Island, i., N.Y., U.S.	E7	109
Long Island Sound, strt., U.S.	E7	109
Longjiang, China	B11	26
Long Key, i., Fl., U.S.	H6	86
Long Lake, Il., U.S.	h8	90
Long Lake, l., Me., U.S.	A4	96
Long Lake, l., Me., U.S.	D2	96
Long Lake, l., Mi., U.S.	D5	99
Long Lake, l., Mi., U.S.	C7	99
Long Lake, l., Mn., U.S.	D4	100
Long Lake, l., N.Y., U.S.	B6	109
Long Lake, l., N.D., U.S.	C6	111
Long Lake, l., Wa., U.S.	f10	124
Long Lake, l., Wi., U.S.	C2	126
Longli, China	A9	34
Longmeadow, Ma., U.S.	B2	98
Longmont, Co., U.S.	A5	83
Long Point, c., Man., Can.	C2	70
Long Point, pen., Ont., Can.	E4	73
Long Pond, res., Fl., U.S.	C4	86
Long Prairie, Mn., U.S.	E4	100
Long Range Mountains, mts., Newf., Can.	D3	72
Longreach, Austl.	D8	50
Longsheng, China	B11	34
Longs Peak, mtn., Co., U.S.	A5	83
Longué, Fr.	E6	10
Longueuil, Que., Can.	D4	74
Longuyon, Fr.	C12	10
Long View, N.C., U.S.	B1	110
Longview, Tx., U.S.	C5	120
Longview, Wa., U.S.	C3	124
Longwy, Fr.	C12	10
Long Xuyen, Viet.	I8	34
Lonigo, Italy	D6	14
Löningen, Ger.	C7	8
Lonoke, Ar., U.S.	C4	81
Lonoke, co., Ar., U.S.	C4	81
Lønsdal, Nor.	C10	6
Lonsdale, Mn., U.S.	F5	100
Lonsdale, R.I., U.S.	B4	116
Lons-le-Saunier, Fr.	F12	10
Loogootee, In., U.S.	G4	91
Lookout, Ky., U.S.	C7	94
Lookout, Cape, c., N.C., U.S.	C6	110
Lookout, Point, c., Mi., U.S.	d7	99
Lookout Mountain, Tn., U.S.	h11	119
Lookout Mountain, mtn., U.S.	D8	119
Lookout Mountain, mtn., Or., U.S.	C6	114
Lookout Pass, U.S.	B3	89
Lookout Point Lake, res., Or., U.S.	D4	114
Loon Lake, Wa., U.S.	A8	124
Loon Lake, l., Me., U.S.	B3	96
Loop Creek, stm., W.V., U.S.	m13	125
Loop Head, c., Ire.	I3	7
Loosahatchie, stm., Tn., U.S.	B2	119
Lopatina, Gora, mtn., Russia	G22	24
Lopatka, Mys, c., Russia	G25	24
Lop Buri, Thai.	G6	34
Lopez, Cap, c., Gabon	B1	44
López Collada, Mex.	B3	62
Lopez Island, i., Wa., U.S.	A3	124
Lop Nur, l., China	C5	26
Lora del Río, Spain	H6	12
Lorain, Oh., U.S.	A3	112
Lorain, co., Oh., U.S.	A3	112
Loramie, Lake, res., Oh., U.S.	B1	112
Lorca, Spain	H10	12
Lord Howe Island, i., Austl.	F11	50
Lordsburg, N.M., U.S.	E1	108
Loreauville, La., U.S.	D4	95
Lorena, Braz.	G6	57
Lorenzo, Tx., U.S.	C2	120
Loreto, Braz.	E9	54
Loreto, Col.	I7	58
Loreto, Mex.	F9	62
Lorette, Man., Can.	E3	70
Loretteville, Que., Can.	C6	74
Loretto, Ky., U.S.	C4	94
Loretto, Pa., U.S.	F4	115
Loretto, Tn., U.S.	B4	119
Lorica, Col.	C5	58
Lorient, Fr.	E3	10
L'Orignal, Ont., Can.	B10	73
Loring Air Force Base, mil., Me., U.S.	B5	96
Loriol [-du-Comtat], Fr.	H11	10
Loris, S.C., U.S.	C10	117
Lorne, N.B., Can.	B3	71
Lörrach, Ger.	H7	8
Lorraine, hist. reg., Fr.	D13	10
Los Alamos, N.M., U.S.	B3	108
Los Alamos, co., N.M., U.S.	B3	108
Los Aldamas, Mex.	D10	62
Los Altos, Ca., U.S.	k8	82
Los Ángeles, Chile	D2	56
Los Angeles, Ca., U.S.	E4	82
Los Angeles, co., Ca., U.S.	E4	82
Los Angeles Aqueduct, Ca., U.S.	E4	82
Los Banos, Ca., U.S.	D3	82
Los Blancos, Arg.	A4	56
Los Fresnos, Tx., U.S.	F4	120
Los Gatos, Ca., U.S.	D2	82
Los Lagos, Chile	D2	56
Los Lunas, N.M., U.S.	C3	108
Los Mochis, Mex.	E5	62
Los Palacios y Villafranca, Spain	H6	12
Los Pinos, stm., Co., U.S.	D3	83
Los Ranchos de Albuquerque, N.M., U.S.	B3	108
Los Roques, Islas, is., Ven.	B9	58
Lost, stm., In., U.S.	G4	91
Lost, stm., Wa., U.S.	A5	124
Lost, stm., W.V., U.S.	B6	125
Lost Creek, stm., Wy., U.S.	D4	127
Los Teques, Ven.	B9	58
Los Testigos, Islas, is., Ven.	B11	58
Lost Peak, mtn., Ut., U.S.	F2	121
Lost Ranger Peak, mtn., Co., U.S.	A4	83
Lost River Glacial Caverns, N.H., U.S.	B3	106
Lost River Range, mts., Id., U.S.	E5	89
Lost Trail Pass, U.S.	D5	89
Los Vilos, Chile	C2	56
Los Yébenes, Spain	F8	12
Lota, Chile	D2	56
Lotawana, Lake, res., Mo., U.S.	k11	102
Lotbinière, Que., Can.	C6	74
Louang Namtha, Laos	D6	34
Louangphrabang, Laos	E7	34
Loudéac, Fr.	D4	10
Loudon, Tn., U.S.	D9	119
Loudon, co., Tn., U.S.	D9	119
Loudonville, Oh., U.S.	B3	112
Loudoun, co., Va., U.S.	A5	123
Loudun, Fr.	E7	10
Louga, Sen.	E2	42
Loughrea, Ire.	H4	7
Louhans, Fr.	F12	10
Louisa, Ky., U.S.	B7	94
Louisa, Va., U.S.	B4	123
Louisa, co., Ia., U.S.	C6	92
Louisa, co., Va., U.S.	C5	123
Louisa, Lake, l., Fl., U.S.	D5	86
Louisbourg, N.S., Can.	D10	71
Louisburg, Ks., U.S.	D9	93
Louisburg, N.C., U.S.	A4	110
Louisdale, N.S., Can.	D8	71
Louise, Lake, l., Ak., U.S.	f18	79
Louise Island, i., B.C., Can.	C2	69
Louiseville, Que., Can.	C5	74

Name — Map Ref — Page

Louisiade Archipelago, is., Pap. N. Gui. B10 50
Louisiana, Mo., U.S. B6 102
Louisiana, state, U.S. C3 95
Louisiana Point, c., La., U.S. E2 95
Louis Trichardt, S. Afr. F5 44
Louisville, Al., U.S. D4 78
Louisville, Co., U.S. B5 83
Louisville, Ga., U.S. C4 87
Louisville, Il., U.S. E5 90
Louisville, Ky., U.S. B4 94
Louisville, Ms., U.S. B4 101
Louisville, Ne., U.S. D9 104
Louisville, Oh., U.S. B4 112
Louis-XIV, Pointe, c., Que., Can. h11 74
Loulé, Port. H3 12
Loup, co., Ne., U.S. C6 104
Loup, stm., Ne., U.S. C8 104
Loup City, Ne., U.S. C7 104
Lourdes, Newf., Can. D2 72
Lourdes, Fr. I6 10
Lourenço Marques see Maputo, Moz. G6 44
Louth, Eng., U.K. H12 7
Louviers, Fr. C8 10
Louviers, Co., U.S. B6 83
Love, co., Ok., U.S. D4 113
Loveč, Bul. F8 16
Loveland, Co., U.S. A5 83
Loveland, Oh., U.S. n13 112
Loveland Park, Oh., U.S. C1 112
Loveland Pass, Co., U.S. B5 83
Lovell, Wy., U.S. B4 127
Lovelock, Nv., U.S. C3 105
Lovely, Ky., U.S. C7 94
Lovenia, Mount, mtn., Ut., U.S. C5 121
Love Point, c., Md., U.S. B5 97
Lovere, Italy D5 14
Loves Park, Il., U.S. A4 90
Lovettsville, Va., U.S. A5 123
Loving, N.M., U.S. E5 108
Loving, co., Tx., U.S. D1 120
Lovington, Il., U.S. D5 90
Lovington, Ia., U.S. e8 92
Lovington, N.M., U.S. E6 108
Lövstabruk, Swe. F11 6
Low, Cape, c., N.W. Ter., Can. D15 66
Lowden, Ia., U.S. C7 92
Lowell, Ar., U.S. A1 81
Lowell, In., U.S. B3 91
Lowell, Ma., U.S. A5 98
Lowell, Mi., U.S. F5 99
Lowell, N.C., U.S. B1 110
Lowell, Or., U.S. D4 114
Lowell, Lake, res., Id., U.S. F2 89
Lowellville, Oh., U.S. A5 112
Lower Arrow Lake, res., B.C., Can. E8 69
Lower Brule Indian Reservation, S.D., U.S. C6 118
Lower California see Baja California, pen., Mex. D3 62
Lower Hutt, N.Z. D5 52
Lower Klamath Lake, l., Ca., U.S. B3 82
Lower Matecumbe Key, i., Fl., U.S. H6 86
Lower Monumental Lake, res., Wa., U.S. C7 124
Lower New York Bay, b., N.J., U.S. B4 107
Lower Otay Lake, res., Ca., U.S. o16 82
Lower Paia, Hi., U.S. C5 88
Lower Red Lake, l., Mn., U.S. C3 100
Lower Rice Lake, l., Mn., U.S. C3 100
Lower Salmon Dam, Id., U.S. G4 89
Lower West Pubnico, N.S., Can. F4 71
Lowestoft, Eng., U.K. I14 7
Lowndes, co., Al., U.S. C3 78
Lowndes, co., Ga., U.S. F3 87
Lowndes, co., Ms., U.S. B5 101
Lowry Air Force Base, mil., Co., U.S. B6 83
Lowry City, Mo., U.S. C4 102
Lowville, N.Y., U.S. B5 109
Loxley, Al., U.S. E2 78
Loyal, Wi., U.S. D3 126
Loyall, Ky., U.S. D6 94
Loyalsock Creek, stm., Pa., U.S. D8 115
Loznica, Yugo. E3 16
Lozoyuela, Spain E8 12
Lua, stm., Zaire H9 42
Lualaba, stm., Zaire B5 44
Lua Makika, crat., Hi., U.S. C5 88
Luanda, Ang. C2 44
Luang Praban Range, mts., Asia E6 34
Luanguinga, stm., Afr. D4 44
Luangwa, stm., Afr. D6 44
Luanshya, Zam. D5 44
Luarca, Spain B5 12
Luau, Ang. D4 44
Lubang Island, i., Phil. C7 32
Lubango, Ang. D2 44
Lübben, Ger. D13 8
Lübbenau, Ger. D13 8
Lubbock, Tx., U.S. C2 120
Lubbock, co., Tx., U.S. C2 120
Lubec, Me., U.S. D6 96
Lübeck, Ger. B10 8
Lübecker Bucht, b., Ger. A11 8
L'ubercy, Russia F20 18
Lubilash, stm., Zaire C4 44
Lubin, Pol. D16 8
Lublin, Pol. D22 8
Lubudi, Zaire C4 44
Lubuksikaping, Indon. N6 34
Lubumbashi (Élisabethville), Zaire D5 44
Lubutu, Zaire B5 44
Lucama, N.C., U.S. B4 110
Lucan, Ont., Can. D3 73
Lucania, Mount, mtn., Yukon, Can. D4 66
Lucas, co., Ia., U.S. C4 92
Lucas, co., Oh., U.S. A2 112
Lucasville, Oh., U.S. D3 112
Lucca, Italy F5 14
Luce, co., Mi., U.S. B5 99
Luce Bay, b., Scot., U.K. G8 7
Lucedale, Ms., U.S. E5 101
Lucena, Phil. r19 33b
Lucena, Spain H7 12
Lucena del Cid, Spain E11 12
Luc-en-Diois, Fr. H12 10
Lucera, Italy H10 14
Lucerne, Ca., U.S. C2 82
Lucerne see Luzern, Switz. E15 10
Lucernemines, Pa., U.S. E3 115
Lucerne Valley, Ca., U.S. E5 82
Luceville, Que., Can. A9 74
Luchiang, Tai. K9 28
Lüchow, Ger. C11 8
Lucira, Ang. D2 44
Luck, Wi., U.S. C1 126
Luckeesarai, India H12 38
Luckenwalde, Ger. C13 8
Lucknow, Ont., Can. D3 73
Lucknow, India G9 38
Lucky Peak Lake, res., Id., U.S. F3 89
Luçon, Fr. F5 10
Lüderitz, Nmb. G3 44
Ludhiāna, India E6 38
Ludington, Mi., U.S. E4 99
L'udinovo, Russia H17 18
Ludlow, Ky., U.S. h13 94
Ludlow, Ma., U.S. B3 98
Ludlow, Vt., U.S. E3 122
Ludowici, Ga., U.S. E5 87
Ludvika, Swe. F10 6
Ludwigsburg, Ger. G9 8
Ludwigsfelde, Ger. C13 8
Ludwigshafen, Ger. F8 8
Luena, stm., Ang. D4 44
Luene, Ang. D3 44
Lufeng, China M4 28
Lufkin, Tx., U.S. D5 120
Luga, Russia C12 18
Lugano, Switz. F15 10
Lugenda, stm., Moz. D7 44
Lugh Ganane, Som. H3 46
Lugnaquillia Mountain, mtn., Ire. I6 7
Lugo, Italy E6 14
Lugo, Spain B4 12
Lugoff, S.C., U.S. C6 117
Lugoj, Rom. D5 16
Luhans'k, Ukr. H5 22
Luhit, stm., Asia G16 38
Luilaka, stm., Zaire B4 44
Luino, Italy C3 14
Lukachukai, Az., U.S. A6 80
Luke Air Force Base, mil., Az., U.S. D3 80
Lukulu, Zam. D4 44
Lula, Ga., U.S. B3 87
Luleå, Swe. D14 6
Lüleburgaz, Tur. H11 16
Luling, La., U.S. k11 95
Luling, Tx., U.S. E4 120
Lulonga, stm., Zaire A3 44
Lumajang, Indon. n16 33a
Lumber, stm., U.S. C9 117
Lumber City, Ga., U.S. E4 87
Lumberport, W.V., U.S. B4 125
Lumberton, Ms., U.S. D4 101
Lumberton, N.C., U.S. C3 110
Lumbrales, Spain E5 12
Lumby, B.C., Can. D8 69
Lumding, India H15 38
Lummi Indian Reservation, Wa., U.S. A3 124
Lumpkin, Ga., U.S. D2 87
Lumpkin, co., Ga., U.S. B2 87
Lumsden, Newf., Can. D5 72
Luna, co., N.M., U.S. E2 108
Luna Pier, Mi., U.S. G7 99
Lund, Swe. I9 6
Lund, Nv., U.S. E6 105
Lundar, Man., Can. D2 70
Lundazi, Zam. D6 44
Lüneburg, Ger. B10 8
Lüneburger Heide, reg., Ger. B10 8
Lunel, Fr. I11 10
Lunenburg, Ma., U.S. A4 98
Lunenburg, co., Va., U.S. D4 123
Lunéville, Fr. D13 10
Lunga, stm., Zam. D5 44
Luohe, China B3 28
Luolong, China E17 38
Luopu, China B9 38
Luoyang, China E9 26
Lūrah, stm., Afg. D2 38
Luray, Va., U.S. B4 123
Lure, Fr. E13 10
Lure, Lake, res., N.C., U.S. f10 110
Lurgan, N. Ire., U.K. G6 7
Lúrio, stm., Moz. D7 44
Lusaka, Zam. E5 44
Lusambo, Zaire B4 44
Lusby, Md., U.S. D5 97
Luseland, Sask., Can. E1 75
Lushan, China B1 28
Lushnje, Alb. I3 16
Lushoto, Tan. B7 44
Lüshun (Port Arthur), China D11 26
Lusk, Wy., U.S. D8 127
Lussac-les-Châteaux, Fr. F7 10
Lūt, Dasht-e, des., Iran B6 46
Lutcher, La., U.S. D5 95
Luther, Ok., U.S. B4 113
Luthersville, Ga., U.S. C2 87
Lutherville-Timonium, Md., U.S. B4 97
Luton, Eng., U.K. J12 7
Luts'k, Ukr. G3 22
Luttrell, Tn., U.S. C10 119
Lutz, Fl., U.S. D4 86
Luverne, Al., U.S. D3 78
Luverne, Mn., U.S. G2 100
Luwegu, stm., Tan. C7 44
Luxapallila Creek, stm., U.S. B5 101
Luxembourg, Lux. F6 8
Luxembourg, ctry., Eur. F9 4
Luxemburg, Wi., U.S. D6 126
Luxomni, Ga., U.S. h8 87
Luxora, Ar., U.S. B6 81
Luzern, Switz. E15 10
Luzerne, Pa., U.S. n17 115
Luzerne, co., Pa., U.S. D9 115
Luzhou, China F8 26
Luzon, i., Phil. B7 32
Luzon Strait, strt., Asia G11 26
Luzy, Fr. F10 10
L'viv, Ukr. H2 22
Lycksele, Swe. D12 6
Lycoming, co., Pa., U.S. D7 115
Lycoming Creek, stm., Pa., U.S. D7 115
Lydenburg, S. Afr. G6 44
Lyell, Mount, mtn., Can. D2 68
Lyford, Tx., U.S. F4 120
Lykens, Pa., U.S. E8 115
Lyle, Wa., U.S. D4 124
Lyman, S.C., U.S. B3 117
Lyman, Wy., U.S. E2 127
Lyman, co., S.D., U.S. D6 118
Lyman Lake, res., Az., U.S. C6 80
Lynch, Ky., U.S. D7 94
Lynchburg, Oh., U.S. C2 112
Lynchburg, Tn., U.S. B5 119
Lynchburg, Va., U.S. C3 123
Lynches, stm., S.C., U.S. D8 117
Lynden, Wa., U.S. A3 124
Lynde Point, c., Ct., U.S. D6 84
Lyndhurst, N.J., U.S. h8 107
Lyndhurst, Oh., U.S. g9 112
Lyndon, Ks., U.S. D8 93
Lyndon, Ky., U.S. g11 94
Lyndon B. Johnson National Historical Site, hist., Tx., U.S. D3 120
Lyndon B. Johnson Space Center, sci., Tx., U.S. r14 120
Lyndonville, Vt., U.S. B4 122
Lyndora, Pa., U.S. E2 115
Lynher Reef, rf., Austl. C4 50
Lynn, Al., U.S. A2 78
Lynn, In., U.S. D8 91
Lynn, Ma., U.S. B6 98
Lynn, co., Tx., U.S. C2 120
Lynn, Lake, res., W.V., U.S. B5 125
Lynn Canal, b., Ak., U.S. k22 79
Lynne Acres, Md., U.S. *B4 97
Lynnfield, Ma., U.S. f11 98
Lynn Garden, Tn., U.S. C11 119
Lynn Garden, Tn., U.S. A9 119
Lynn Haven, Fl., U.S. u16 86
Lynnhaven Roads, b., Va., U.S. k15 123
Lynnville, In., U.S. H3 91
Lynnwood, Wa., U.S. B3 124
Lynton, Eng., U.K. J9 7
Lynwood, Ca., U.S. n12 82
Lyon, Fr. G11 10
Lyon, co., Ia., U.S. A1 92
Lyon, co., Ks., U.S. D7 93
Lyon, co., Ky., U.S. C1 94
Lyon, co., Mn., U.S. F3 100
Lyon, co., Nv., U.S. D2 105
Lyons, Co., U.S. A5 83
Lyons, Ga., U.S. D4 87
Lyons, Il., U.S. k9 90
Lyons, In., U.S. G3 91
Lyons, Ks., U.S. D5 93
Lyons, Mi., U.S. F6 99
Lyons, Ne., U.S. C9 104
Lyons, N.Y., U.S. B3 109
Lyons, Or., U.S. C4 114
Lyster Station, Que., Can. C6 74
Lysychans'k, Ukr. H5 22
Lytle, Tx., U.S. E3 120

M

Ma, stm., Asia D8 34
Maalaea Bay, b., Hi., U.S. C5 88
Ma'ān, Jord. D4 40
Maanshan, China D7 28
Ma'arrat an-Nu'mān, Syria B5 40
Maas (Meuse), stm., Eur. D5 8
Maastricht, Neth. E5 8
Mabank, Tx., U.S. C4 120
Mabaruma, Guy. C13 58
Mabel, Mn., U.S. G7 100
Maben, Ms., U.S. B4 101
Mableton, Ga., U.S. h7 87
Mabscott, W.V., U.S. D3 125
Mabton, Wa., U.S. C5 124
Mača, Russia F17 24
Macaé, Braz. G8 57
Macão, Port. F3 12
Macao see Macau, dep., Asia M2 28
Macapá, Braz. C8 54
Macará, Ec. J3 58
Macarani, Braz. C8 57
Macas, Ec. I3 58
Macau, Braz. E11 54
Macau (Aomen), Macao M2 28
Macau (Aomen), dep., Asia M2 28
MacClenny, Fl., U.S. B4 86
MacDill Air Force Base, mil., Fl., U.S. E4 86
Macdonnell Ranges, mts., Austl. D6 50
MacDowell Reservoir, res., N.H., U.S. E2 106
Macduff, Scot., U.K. D10 7
Macdui, Ben, mtn., Scot., U.K. D9 7
Macedo de Cavaleiros, Port. D5 12
Macedonia, Oh., U.S. A4 112
Macedonia, hist. reg., Eur. H6 16
Macedonia, ctry., Eur. H5 16
Maceió, Braz. E11 54
Macerata, Italy F8 14
Maces Bay, b., N.B., Can. D3 71
MacGregor, Man., Can. E2 70
Machačkala, Russia I7 22
Machagai, Arg. B4 56
Machala, Ec. I3 58
Machecoul, Fr. E5 10
Machias, Me., U.S. D5 96
Machias, stm., Me., U.S. B4 96
Machias, stm., Me., U.S. D5 96
Machias Bay, b., Me., U.S. D5 96
Machias Lakes, l., Me., U.S. C5 96
Machilīpatnam (Bandar), India D6 37
Machiques, Ven. B6 58
Macho, Arroyo del, val., N.M., U.S. C4 108
Machupicchu, Peru F4 54
Macina, reg., Mali F4 42
Mackay, Austl. D9 50
Mackay, Lake, l., Austl. D5 50
MacKenzie, B.C., Can. B6 69
Mackenzie, stm., N.W. Ter., Can. C6 66
Mackenzie Bay, b., Can. C5 66
Mackenzie Mountains, mts., Can. D7 66
Mackinac, co., Mi., U.S. B5 99
Mackinac, Straits of, strt., Mi., U.S. C6 99
Mackinac Bridge, Mi., U.S. C6 99
Mackinac Island, i., Mi., U.S. C6 99
Mackinaw, Il., U.S. C4 90
Mackinaw, stm., Il., U.S. C4 90
Mackinaw City, Mi., U.S. C6 99
Maclear, S. Afr. H5 44
Macmillan, stm., Yukon, Can. D6 66
Macomb, Il., U.S. C3 90
Macomb, co., Mi., U.S. F8 99
Macomer, Italy I3 14
Mâcon, Fr. F11 10
Macon, Ga., U.S. D3 87
Macon, Il., U.S. D5 90
Macon, Ms., U.S. B5 101
Macon, Mo., U.S. B5 102
Macon, co., Al., U.S. C4 78
Macon, co., Ga., U.S. D2 87
Macon, co., Il., U.S. D4 90
Macon, co., Mo., U.S. B5 102
Macon, co., N.C., U.S. f9 110
Macon, co., Tn., U.S. A5 119
Macon, Bayou, stm., U.S. B4 95
Macoupin, co., Il., U.S. D4 90
MacTier, Ont., Can. B5 73
Macungie, Pa., U.S. E10 115
Mad, stm., Ca., U.S. B2 82
Mad, stm., Ct., U.S. B3 84
Mad, stm., N.H., U.S. C3 106
Mad, stm., Oh., U.S. C2 112
Mad, stm., Vt., U.S. C3 122
Ma'dabā, Jord. D4 40
Madagascar, ctry., Afr. E9 44
Madame, Isle, i., N.S., Can. D9 71
Madanapalle, India F5 37
Madang, Pap. N. Gui. m16 50a
Mādārīpur, Bngl. I14 38
Madawaska, Me., U.S. A4 96
Madawaska, stm., Can. B9 74
Madawaska, stm., Ont., Can. B7 73
Madawaska Lake, l., Me., U.S. A4 96
Maddaloni, Italy H9 14
Madeira, Oh., U.S. o13 112
Madeira, i., Port. B2 42
Madeira, stm., S.A. E6 54
Madeira, Arquipélago da (Madeira Islands), is., Port. m20 13a
Mädelegabel, mtn., Eur. E17 10
Madeleine, Îles de la, is., Que., Can. B8 71
Madelia, Mn., U.S. F4 100
Madeline Island, i., Wi., U.S. B3 126
Madera, Ca., U.S. D3 82
Madera, co., Ca., U.S. D4 82
Madhubani, India G12 38
Madhya Pradesh, state, India I8 38
Madill, Ok., U.S. C5 113
Madīnat ash-Sha'b, Yemen F3 46
Madingou, Congo B2 44
Madison, Al., U.S. A3 78
Madison, Ar., U.S. B5 81
Madison, Ct., U.S. D5 84
Madison, Fl., U.S. B3 86
Madison, Ga., U.S. C3 87
Madison, Il., U.S. E3 90
Madison, In., U.S. G7 91
Madison, Ks., U.S. D7 93
Madison, Me., U.S. D3 96
Madison, Mn., U.S. E2 100
Madison, Ms., U.S. C3 101
Madison, Ne., U.S. C8 104
Madison, N.J., U.S. B4 107
Madison, N.C., U.S. A3 110
Madison, Oh., U.S. A4 112
Madison, S.D., U.S. D8 118
Madison, W.V., U.S. C3 125
Madison, Wi., U.S. E4 126
Madison, co., Al., U.S. A3 78
Madison, co., Ar., U.S. B2 81
Madison, co., Fl., U.S. B3 86
Madison, co., Ga., U.S. B3 87
Madison, co., Id., U.S. F7 89
Madison, co., Il., U.S. E4 90
Madison, co., In., U.S. D6 91
Madison, co., Ia., U.S. C3 92
Madison, co., Ky., U.S. C5 94
Madison, co., La., U.S. B4 95
Madison, co., Ms., U.S. C4 101
Madison, co., Mo., U.S. D7 102
Madison, co., Mt., U.S. E5 103
Madison, co., Ne., U.S. C8 104
Madison, co., N.Y., U.S. C5 109
Madison, co., N.C., U.S. f10 110
Madison, co., Oh., U.S. C2 112
Madison, co., Tn., U.S. B3 119
Madison, co., Tx., U.S. D5 120
Madison, co., Va., U.S. B4 123
Madison, stm., Mt., U.S. E5 103
Madison Heights, Mi., U.S. o15 99
Madison Heights, Va., U.S. C3 123
Madison Lake, Mn., U.S. F5 100
Madison Range, mts., Mt., U.S. E5 103
Madisonville, Ky., U.S. C2 94
Madisonville, La., U.S. D5 95
Madisonville, Tn., U.S. D9 119
Madisonville, Tx., U.S. D5 120
Madiun, Indon. m15 32
Madoc, Ont., Can. C7 73
Mado Gashi, Kenya B7 44
Madras, India F6 37
Madras, Or., U.S. C5 114
Madre, Laguna, b., Mex. E11 62
Madre, Laguna, b., Tx., U.S. F4 120
Madre, Sierra, mts., N.A. J14 62
Madre, Sierra, mts., Phil. B7 32
Madre de Dios, stm., S.A. F5 54
Madre de Dios, Isla, i., Chile G1 56
Madre del Sur, Sierra, mts., Mex. I10 62
Madre Occidental, Sierra, mts., Mex. E6 62
Madre Oriental, Sierra, mts., Mex. F9 62
Madrid, Spain E8 12
Madrid, Ia., U.S. C4 92
Madridejos, Spain F8 12
Maduo, China E6 26
Madura, i., Indon. G5 32
Madurai, India H5 37
Maebashi, Japan F12 30
Mae Hong Son, Thai. E4 34
Maeser, Ut., U.S. C6 121
Mae Sot, Thai. F5 34
Maestra, Sierra, mts., Cuba D9 64
Maevatanana, Madag. E9 44
Mafia Island, i., Tan. C7 44
Mafikeng, S. Afr. G5 44
Mafra, Braz. B7 56
Magadan, Russia F24 24
Magadi, Kenya B7 44
Magallanes, Estrecho de (Strait of Magellan), strt., S.A. G2 56
Magangué, Col. C5 58
Magazine, Ar., U.S. B2 81
Magazine Mountain, mtn., Ar., U.S. B2 81
Magdagači, Russia G19 24
Magdalena, Bol. F6 54
Magdalena, Mex. B4 62
Magdalena, N.M., U.S. C2 108
Magdalena, stm., Col. B5 58
Magdalena, Bahía, b., Mex. E3 62
Magdalena, Isla, i., Chile E2 56
Magdalena Mountains, mts., N.M., U.S. D2 108
Magdeburg, Ger. C11 8
Magee, Ms., U.S. D4 101
Magelang, Indon. m15 33a
Magellan, Strait of see Magallanes, Estrecho de, strt., S.A. G2 56
Magenta, Italy D3 14
Maggie Creek, stm., Nv., U.S. C5 105
Maggiore, Lago, l., Eur. C3 14
Magic Reservoir, res., Id., U.S. F4 89
Magione, Italy F7 14
Magna, Ut., U.S. C3 121
Magnetawan, stm., Ont., Can. B4 73
Magnitogorsk, Russia G9 22
Magnolia, Ar., U.S. D2 81
Magnolia, Ky., U.S. C4 94
Magnolia, Ms., U.S. D3 101
Magnolia, N.C., U.S. C4 110
Magnolia, Oh., U.S. B4 112
Magoffin, co., Ky., U.S. C6 94
Magog, Que., Can. D5 74
Magothy River, b., Md., U.S. B4 97
Magpie, Lac, l., Que., Can. F20 66
Magrath, Alta., Can. E4 68
Magruder Mountain, mtn., Nv., U.S. F4 105
Maguarinho, Cabo, c., Braz. D9 54
Magway, Mya. D3 34
Mahābād, Iran J7 22
Mahābhārat Range, mts., Nepal F10 38
Mahaicony Village, Guy. D14 58
Mahajamba, Baie de la, b., Madag. E9 44
Mahajanga, Madag. E9 44
Mahakam, stm., Indon. E6 32
Mahānadi, stm., India J11 38
Mahanoro, Madag. E9 44
Mahanoy City, Pa., U.S. E9 115
Mahārāshtra, state, India C3 37
Maha Sarakham, Thai. F7 34
Mahaska, co., Ia., U.S. C5 92
Maḥaṭṭat al-Qaṭrānah, Jord. D5 40
Maḥaṭṭat Ḥaraḍ, Sau. Ar. D4 46
Mahbūbnagar, India D4 37
Mahé Island, i., Sey. B11 44
Mahenge, Tan. C7 44
Mahi, stm., India I5 38
Mahmūd-e 'Erāqī, Afg. C3 38
Mahnomen, Mn., U.S. C3 100
Mahnomen, co., Mn., U.S. C3 100
Mahoba, India H8 38
Mahogany Mountain, mtn., Or., U.S. D9 114
Mahomet, Il., U.S. C5 90
Mahón, Spain F16 12
Mahone Bay, N.S., Can. E5 71
Mahoning, co., Oh., U.S. B5 112
Mahoning, stm., U.S. A5 112
Mahopac, N.Y., U.S. D7 109
Mahuva, India J4 38
Mahwah, N.J., U.S. A4 107
Maiden, N.C., U.S. B1 110
Maidstone, Eng., U.K. J13 7
Maidstone Lake, l., Vt., U.S. B5 122
Maiduguri, Nig. F8 42
Maili, Hi., U.S. g9 88
Maili Point, c., Hi., U.S. g9 88
Maillezais, Fr. F6 10
Main, stm., Ger. F9 8
Mainburg, Ger. G11 8
Main Channel, strt., Ont., Can. B3 73
Mai-Ndombe, Lac, l., Zaire B3 44
Maine, state, U.S. C3 96
Mainland, i., Scot., U.K. B9 7
Mainland, i., Scot., U.K. A11 7
Main Pass, strt., La., U.S. E6 95
Mainz, Ger. E8 8
Maipo, Volcán, vol., S.A. C3 56
Maipú, Arg. D5 56
Maiquetía, Ven. B9 58
Maisonnette, N.B., Can. B4 71
Maitland, Austl. F10 50

Name	Map Ref	Page
Maitland, Ont., Can.	C9	73
Maize, Ks., U.S.	g12	93
Maizuru, Japan	G8	30
Maja, stm., Russia	F20	24
Majene, Indon.	F6	32
Maji, Eth.	G2	46
Majkop, Russia	I6	22
Majno-Pyl'gino, Russia	E29	24
Major, co., Ok., U.S.	A3	113
Majorca see Mallorca, i., Spain	F15	12
Makaha, Hi., U.S.	g9	88
Makaha Point, c., Hi., U.S.	A2	88
Makah Indian Reservation, Wa., U.S.	A1	124
Makahuena Point, c., Hi., U.S.	B2	88
Makakilo City, Hi., U.S.	g9	88
Makale, Indon.	F6	32
Makapuu Head, c., Hi., U.S.	B4	88
Makarska, Cro.	F12	14
Makasar, Selat (Makassar Strait), strt., Indon.	F6	32
Makasar see Ujungpandang, Indon.	G6	32
Makawao, Hi., U.S.	C5	88
Makaweli, Hi., U.S.	B2	88
Makeni, S.L.	G3	42
Makgadikgadi Pans, pl., Bots.	F5	44
Makhachkala see Machačkala, Russia	I7	22
Makindu, Kenya	B7	44
M'akit, Russia	E24	24
Makkah (Mecca), Sau. Ar.	D2	46
Maklakovo, Russia	F12	24
Makó, Hung.	I20	8
Makokou, Gabon	A2	44
Makthar, Tun.	N4	14
Makumbi, Zaire	C4	44
Makurazaki, Japan	K3	30
Makurdi, Nig.	G7	42
Makushin Volcano, vol., Ak., U.S.	E6	79
Malabar, Fl., U.S.	D6	86
Malabar Coast, India	G4	37
Malabo, Eq. Gui.	H7	42
Malacca, Strait of, strt., Asia	M6	34
Malad City, Id., U.S.	G6	89
Málaga, Col.	D6	58
Málaga, Spain	I7	12
Malagón, Spain	F8	12
Malaimbandy, Madag.	F9	44
Malaja Kuril'skaja Gr'ada (Habomai-shotō), is., Russia	p24	30a
Malakāl, Sudan	G12	42
Malakoff, Tx., U.S.	C4	120
Malang, Indon.	m16	32
Malanje, Ang.	C3	44
Malanville, Benin	F6	42
Mälaren, l., Swe.	G11	6
Malargüe, Arg.	D3	56
Malartic, Que., Can.	k11	74
Malaspina Glacier, Ak., U.S.	D11	79
Malatya, Tur.	H15	4
Malawi, ctry., Afr.	D6	44
Malaya, reg., Malay.	M7	34
Malay Peninsula, pen., Asia	K6	34
Malaysia, ctry., Asia	E3	32
Malbaie, stm., Que., Can.	B7	74
Malbork, Pol.	A19	8
Malcolm, Austl.	E4	50
Malden, Ma., U.S.	B5	98
Malden, Mo., U.S.	E8	102
Malden, W.V., U.S.	m12	125
Maldives, ctry., Asia	I2	37
Maldonado, Ur.	C6	56
Mālegaon, India	B3	37
Malek Dīn, Afg.	D3	38
Malha Wells, Sudan	E11	42
Malheur, co., Or., U.S.	D9	114
Malheur, stm., Or., U.S.	D9	114
Malheur Lake, l., Or., U.S.	D8	114
Mali, ctry., Afr.	E5	42
Malibu, Ca., U.S.	m11	82
Malik, Wādī al-, val., Sudan	E11	42
Malin, Or., U.S.	E5	114
Malindi, Kenya	B8	44
Malino, Bukit, mtn., Indon.	E7	32
Malka, Russia	G25	24
Malkāpur, India	B4	37
Malkara, Tur.	I10	16
Mallaig, Scot., U.K.	D7	7
Mallawī, Egypt	C12	42
Malletts Bay, b., Vt., U.S.	B2	122
Mallnitz, Aus.	I13	8
Mallorca, i., Spain	F14	12
Mallow, Ire.	I4	7
Malmberget, Swe.	C13	6
Malmédy, Bel.	E6	8
Malmesbury, S. Afr.	H3	44
Malmö, Swe.	I9	6
Malmstrom Air Force Base, mil., Mt., U.S.	C5	103
Malolos, Phil.	q19	33b
Malone, N.Y., U.S.	f10	109
Maloney Reservoir, res., Ne., U.S.	C5	104
Måløy, Nor.	F5	6
Malpaso, Presa de, res., Mex.	I13	62
Malpelo, Isla de, i., Col.	C2	54
Malpeque Bay, b., P.E.I., Can.	C6	71
Malta, Il., U.S.	B5	90
Malta, Mt., U.S.	B9	103
Malta, ctry., Eur.	H10	4
Malta Channel, strt., Eur.	M9	14
Maltahöhe, Nmb.	F3	44
Maluku (Moluccas), is., Indon.	F8	32
Maluku, Laut (Molucca Sea), Indon.	F7	32
Malung, Swe.	F9	6
Malvern, Ar., U.S.	C3	81
Malvern, Ia., U.S.	D2	92
Malvern, Oh., U.S.	B4	112
Malvern, Pa., U.S.	o19	115
Malverne, N.Y., U.S.	k13	109
Malyj An'uj, stm., Russia	D26	24
Malyj Tajmyr, Ostrov, i., Russia	B15	24
Mama, Russia	F16	24
Mamala Bay, b., Hi., U.S.	g10	88
Mamaroneck, N.Y., U.S.	h13	109
Mamberamo, stm., Indon.	F10	32
Mamers, Fr.	D7	10
Mamfe, Cam.	G7	42
Mammoth, Az., U.S.	E5	80
Mammoth Cave National Park, Ky., U.S.	C4	94
Mammoth Lakes, Ca., U.S.	D4	82
Mammoth Spring, Ar., U.S.	A4	81
Mamoré, stm., S.A.	F5	54
Mamou, Gui.	F3	42
Mamou, La., U.S.	D3	95
Man, C. Iv.	G4	42
Man, W.V., U.S.	D3	125
Manacapuru, Braz.	D6	54
Manacor, Spain	F15	12
Manado, Indon.	E7	32
Managua, Nic.	H4	64
Managua, Lago de, l., Nic.	H4	64
Manakara, Madag.	F9	44
Manama see Al-Manāmah, Bahr.	C5	46
Manana Island, i., Hi., U.S.	g11	88
Mananara, Madag.	E9	44
Mananjary, Madag.	F9	44
Manantico Creek, stm., N.J., U.S.	E3	107
Mana Point, c., Hi., U.S.	A2	88
Manas, China	C4	26
Manasquan, N.J., U.S.	C4	107
Manasquan, stm., N.J., U.S.	C4	107
Manassa, Co., U.S.	D5	83
Manassas, Va., U.S.	B5	123
Manassas National Battlefield Park, Va., U.S.	g11	123
Manassas Park, Va., U.S.	B5	123
Manatee, co., Fl., U.S.	E4	86
Manatee, stm., Fl., U.S.	E4	86
Manaus, Braz.	D6	54
Manawa, Wi., U.S.	D5	126
Manbij, Syria	A5	40
Mancelona, Mi., U.S.	D5	99
Mancha Real, Spain	H8	12
Manchester, Eng., U.K.	H10	7
Manchester, Ct., U.S.	B5	84
Manchester, Ga., U.S.	D2	87
Manchester, Ia., U.S.	B6	92
Manchester, Ky., U.S.	C6	94
Manchester, Me., U.S.	D3	96
Manchester, Md., U.S.	A4	97
Manchester, Ma., U.S.	A6	98
Manchester, Mi., U.S.	F6	99
Manchester, Mo., U.S.	f12	102
Manchester, N.H., U.S.	E4	106
Manchester, N.Y., U.S.	C3	109
Manchester, Oh., U.S.	D2	112
Manchester, Pa., U.S.	F8	115
Manchester, Tn., U.S.	B5	119
Manchester, Vt., U.S.	E2	122
Manchester Center, Vt., U.S.	E2	122
Manchuria, reg., China	B12	26
Manciano, Italy	G6	14
Mancos, Co., U.S.	D2	83
Mancos, stm., U.S.	D2	83
Mand, stm., Iran	C5	46
Manda, Tan.	D6	44
Mandal, Nor.	G6	6
Mandalay, Mya.	C4	34
Mandalgov', Mong.	B8	26
Mandan, N.D., U.S.	C5	111
Mandas, Italy	J4	14
Mandasor, India	H6	38
Mandeb, Bāb el-, strt.	F3	46
Mandeville, Ar., U.S.	D2	81
Mandeville, La., U.S.	D5	95
Mandi Bahāuddīn, Pak.	D5	38
Mandimba, Moz.	D7	44
Mandla, India	I9	38
Manduria, Italy	I12	14
Māndvi, India	I3	38
Mandya, India	F4	37
Manerbio, Italy	D5	14
Manfredonia, Italy	H10	14
Mangabeiras, Chapada das, hills, Braz.	F9	54
Mangalore, India	F3	37
Mangkalihat, Tanjung, c., Indon.	E6	32
Manglares, Cabo, c., Col.	G3	58
Mangoche, Mwi.	D7	44
Mangoky, stm., Madag.	F8	44
Mangole, Pulau, i., Indon.	F8	32
Māngrol, India	J4	38
Mangrove Cay, i., Bah.	B9	64
Mangualde, Port.	E4	12
Mangum, Ok., U.S.	C2	113
Mangya, China	D5	26
Manhattan, Ks., U.S.	C7	93
Manhattan, Mt., U.S.	E5	103
Manhattan Beach, Ca., U.S.	n12	82
Manhattan Island, i., N.Y., U.S.	h13	109
Manheim, Pa., U.S.	F9	115
Manhuaçu, Braz.	F7	57
Manicoré, Braz.	E6	54
Manicouagan, stm., Que., Can.	F19	66
Manicouagan, Réservoir, res., Que., Can.	h13	74
Manila, Phil.	q19	32
Manila, Ar., U.S.	B5	81
Manila Bay, b., Phil.	C7	32
Manilla, Ia., U.S.	C2	92
Manipur, ter., India	H15	38
Manisa, Tur.	K11	16
Manistee, Mi., U.S.	D4	99
Manistee, co., Mi., U.S.	D4	99
Manistee, stm., Mi., U.S.	D5	99
Manistique, Mi., U.S.	C4	99
Manistique, stm., Mi., U.S.	B4	99
Manistique Lake, l., Mi., U.S.	B5	99
Manito, Il., U.S.	C4	90
Manitoba, prov., Can.	C3	70
Manitoba, Lake, l., Man., Can.	D2	70
Manitou, Man., Can.	E2	70
Manitou, Lake, l., Ont., Can.	B3	73
Manitou Island, i., Mi., U.S.	A3	99
Manitou Lake, l., Sask., Can.	E1	75
Manitoulin Island, i., Ont., Can.	B2	73
Manitou Springs, Co., U.S.	C6	83
Manitowoc, Wi., U.S.	D6	126
Manitowoc, co., Wi., U.S.	D6	126
Manitowoc, stm., Wi., U.S.	h10	126
Maniwaki, Que., Can.	C2	74
Manizales, Col.	E5	58
Manjacaze, Moz.	F6	44
Mānjra, stm., India	C4	37
Mankato, Ks., U.S.	C5	93
Mankato, Mn., U.S.	F5	100
Mankoya, Zam.	D4	44
Manlius, N.Y., U.S.	C5	109
Manlléu, Spain	C14	12
Manly, Ia., U.S.	A4	92
Manmād, India	B3	37
Mannar, Gulf of, b., Asia	H5	37
Mannārgudi, India	G5	37
Mannar Island, i., Sri L.	H5	37
Mannford, Ok., U.S.	A5	113
Mannheim, Ger.	F8	8
Manning, Alta., Can.	A2	68
Manning, Ia., U.S.	C2	92
Manning, S.C., U.S.	D7	117
Mannington, W.V., U.S.	B4	125
Manns Creek, stm., W.V., U.S.	n14	125
Mannville, Alta., Can.	C5	68
Manokin, stm., Md., U.S.	D6	97
Manokotak, Ak., U.S.	D8	79
Manokwari, Indon.	F9	32
Manomet, Ma., U.S.	C6	98
Manomet Point, c., Ma., U.S.	C6	98
Manono, Zaire	C5	44
Manor, Tx., U.S.	D4	120
Manosque, Fr.	I12	10
Manouane, Lac, l., Que., Can.	h12	74
Manresa, Spain	D13	12
Mānsa, India	F6	38
Mansa, Zam.	D5	44
Manseau, Que., Can.	C5	74
Mansel Island, i., N.W. Ter., Can.	D17	66
Mansfield, Eng., U.K.	H11	7
Mansfield, Ar., U.S.	B1	81
Mansfield, Il., U.S.	C5	90
Mansfield, La., U.S.	B2	95
Mansfield, Ma., U.S.	B5	98
Mansfield, Mo., U.S.	D5	102
Mansfield, Oh., U.S.	B3	112
Mansfield, Pa., U.S.	C7	115
Mansfield, Tx., U.S.	n9	120
Mansfield, Mount, mtn., Vt., U.S.	B3	122
Mansfield Center, Ct., U.S.	B7	84
Mansfield Hollow Lake, res., Ct., U.S.	B7	84
Manson, Ia., U.S.	B3	92
Manson, Wa., U.S.	B5	124
Mansonville, Que., Can.	D5	74
Mansura, La., U.S.	C3	95
Manta, Ec.	H2	58
Mantachie, Ms., U.S.	A5	101
Manteca, Ca., U.S.	D3	82
Manteno, Il., U.S.	B6	90
Manteo, N.C., U.S.	B7	110
Mantes-la-Jolie, Fr.	D8	10
Manti, Ut., U.S.	D4	121
Mantiqueira, Serra da, mts., Braz.	F6	57
Manton, Mi., U.S.	D5	99
Mantorville, Mn., U.S.	F6	100
Mantova, Italy	D5	14
Mantua, Oh., U.S.	A4	112
Mantua, Ut., U.S.	B4	121
Manturovo, Russia	C27	18
Manukau Harbour, b., N.Z.	B5	52
Manumuskin, stm., N.J., U.S.	E3	107
Manus Island, i., Pap. N. Gui.	k16	50a
Manvel, Tx., U.S.	r14	120
Manville, N.J., U.S.	B3	107
Manville, R.I., U.S.	B4	116
Many, La., U.S.	C2	95
Many Farms, Az., U.S.	A6	80
Manzanares, Spain	F8	12
Manzanillo, Cuba	D9	64
Manzanillo, Mex.	H7	62
Manzano Mountains, mts., N.M., U.S.	C3	108
Manzano Peak, mtn., N.M., U.S.	C3	108
Manzhouli, China	B10	26
Mao, Chad	F9	42
Maoke, Pegunungan, mts., Indon.	F10	32
Mapastepec, Mex.	J13	62
Mapi, Indon.	G10	32
Mapia, Kepulauan, is., Indon.	E9	32
Mapimí, Mex.	E8	62
Mapimí, Bolsón de, des., Mex.	D8	62
Mapire, Ven.	D10	58
Maple, stm., U.S.	A7	118
Maple, stm., Ia., U.S.	B2	92
Maple, stm., N.D., U.S.	C8	111
Maple Bluff, Wi., U.S.	E4	126
Maple Grove, Mn., U.S.	m12	100
Maple Heights, Oh., U.S.	h9	112
Maple Lake, Mn., U.S.	E5	100
Maple Plain, Mn., U.S.	m11	100
Maple Shade, N.J., U.S.	D2	107
Maplesville, Al., U.S.	C3	78
Mapleton, Ia., U.S.	B2	92
Mapleton, Mn., U.S.	G5	100
Mapleton, N.D., U.S.	C8	111
Mapleton, Or., U.S.	C3	114
Mapleton, Ut., U.S.	C4	121
Maple Valley, Wa., U.S.	f11	124
Mapleville, R.I., U.S.	B2	116
Maplewood, Mn., U.S.	n12	100
Maplewood, Mo., U.S.	f13	102
Maplewood, N.J., U.S.	B4	107
Mapuera, stm., Braz.	D7	54
Maputo (Lourenço Marques), Moz.	G6	44
Maqueda, Spain	E7	12
Maquela do Zombo, Ang.	C3	44
Maquinchao, Arg.	E3	56
Maquoketa, Ia., U.S.	B7	92
Maquoketa, stm., Ia., U.S.	B6	92
Maquoketa, North Fork, stm., Ia., U.S.	B7	92
Mar, Serra do, clf, Braz.	A7	56
Marabá, Braz.	E9	54
Maracá, Ilha de, i., Braz.	C8	54
Maracaibo, Ven.	B7	58
Maracaibo, Lago de, l., Ven.	C7	58
Maracay, Ven.	B9	58
Marādah, Libya	C9	42
Maradi, Niger	F7	42
Marāgheh, Iran	J7	22
Maragogipe, Braz.	B9	57
Marahuaca, Cerro, mtn., Ven.	F10	58
Marais des Cygnes, stm., U.S.	D8	93
Marajó, Baía de, b., Braz.	D9	54
Marajó, Ilha de, i., Braz.	D9	54
Maralal, Kenya	A7	44
Marambaia, Ilha da, i., Braz.	G7	57
Marana, Az., U.S.	E4	80
Marang, Malay.	L7	34
Marañón, stm., Peru	D3	54
Marans, Fr.	F5	10
Marapanim, Braz.	D9	54
Marathon, Fl., U.S.	H5	86
Marathon, Wi., U.S.	D4	126
Marathon, co., Wi., U.S.	D4	126
Marawī, Sudan	E1	46
Marble, Mn., U.S.	C5	100
Marble, N.C., U.S.	f9	110
Marble Bar, Austl.	D3	50
Marble Canyon, val., Az., U.S.	A4	80
Marble Falls, Tx., U.S.	D3	120
Marblehead, Ma., U.S.	B6	98
Marble Hill, Mo., U.S.	D8	102
Marbleton, Wy., U.S.	D2	127
Marburg an der Lahn, Ger.	E8	8
Marbury, Md., U.S.	C3	97
Marcaria, Italy	D5	14
Marceline, Mo., U.S.	B5	102
Marcellus, Mi., U.S.	F5	99
March (Morava), stm., Eur.	G16	8
Marcha, Russia	E18	24
March Air Force Base, mil., Ca., U.S.	F5	82
Marche-en-Famenne, Bel.	E5	8
Marchena, Spain	H6	12
Mar Chiquita, Laguna, l., Arg.	C4	56
Marco, Fl., U.S.	G5	86
Marcus, Ia., U.S.	B2	92
Marcus Baker, Mount, mtn., Ak., U.S.	g18	79
Marcus Hook, Pa., U.S.	G11	115
Marcy, Mount, mtn., N.Y., U.S.	A7	109
Mardān, Pak.	C5	38
Mar del Plata, Arg.	D5	56
Mardin, Tur.	H16	4
Mareeba, Austl.	C9	50
Mareg, Som.	H4	46
Marengo, Il., U.S.	A5	90
Marengo, In., U.S.	H5	91
Marengo, Ia., U.S.	C5	92
Marengo, co., Al., U.S.	C2	78
Marennes, Fr.	G5	10
Marfa, Tx., U.S.	o12	120
Margaret, Al., U.S.	B3	78
Margarita, Isla de, i., Ven.	B10	58
Margate, Fl., U.S.	F6	86
Margate City, N.J., U.S.	E3	107
Margherita Peak, mtn., Afr.	A5	44
Marghī, Afg.	C2	38
Margrethe, Lake, l., Mi., U.S.	D6	99
María Cleofas, Isla, i., Mex.	G6	62
María Madre, Isla, i., Mex.	G6	62
María Magdalena, Isla, i., Mex.	G6	62
Marian, Lake, l., Fl., U.S.	E5	86
Marianao, Cuba	C6	64
Marianna, Ar., U.S.	C5	81
Marianna, Fl., U.S.	B1	86
Marias, stm., Mt., U.S.	B4	103
Marías, Islas, is., Mex.	G6	62
Marias Pass, Mt., U.S.	B3	103
Mariato, Punta, c., Pan.	K7	64
Mariazell, Aus.	H15	8
Maribor, Slo.	C10	14
Marica (Évros) (Meriç), stm., Eur.	G9	16
Maricopa, Az., U.S.	E3	80
Maricopa, Ca., U.S.	E4	82
Maricopa, co., Az., U.S.	D3	80
Maricopa Mountains, mts., Az., U.S.	m7	80
Marie-Galante, i., Guad.	G17	64
Mariehamn, Fin.	F12	6
Mariemont, Oh., U.S.	o13	112
Mariental, Nmb.	F3	44
Marienville, Pa., U.S.	D3	115
Maries, co., Mo., U.S.	C6	102
Mariestad, Swe.	G9	6
Marietta, Ga., U.S.	C2	87
Marietta, Oh., U.S.	C4	112
Marietta, Ok., U.S.	D4	113
Marietta, S.C., U.S.	A2	117
Marieville, Que., Can.	D4	74
Marília, Braz.	G4	57
Marimba, Ang.	C3	44
Marín, Spain	C3	12
Marin, co., Ca., U.S.	C2	82
Marinduque Island, i., Phil.	C7	32
Marine, Il., U.S.	E4	90
Marine City, Mi., U.S.	F8	99
Marine On St. Croix, Mn., U.S.	E6	100
Marinette, Wi., U.S.	C6	126
Marinette, co., Wi., U.S.	C5	126
Maringá, Braz.	G3	57
Maringouin, La., U.S.	D4	95
Marinha Grande, Port.	F3	12
Marion, Al., U.S.	C2	78
Marion, Ar., U.S.	B5	81
Marion, Il., U.S.	F5	90
Marion, In., U.S.	C6	91
Marion, Ia., U.S.	B6	92
Marion, Ks., U.S.	D6	93
Marion, Ky., U.S.	e9	94
Marion, La., U.S.	B3	95
Marion, Mi., U.S.	D5	99
Marion, Ms., U.S.	C5	101
Marion, N.C., U.S.	B1	110
Marion, Oh., U.S.	B2	112
Marion, Pa., U.S.	G6	115
Marion, S.C., U.S.	C9	117
Marion, S.D., U.S.	D8	118
Marion, Va., U.S.	f10	123
Marion, Wi., U.S.	D5	126
Marion, co., Al., U.S.	A2	78
Marion, co., Ar., U.S.	A3	81
Marion, co., Fl., U.S.	C4	86
Marion, co., Ga., U.S.	D2	87
Marion, co., Il., U.S.	E4	90
Marion, co., In., U.S.	E5	91
Marion, co., Ia., U.S.	C4	92
Marion, co., Ks., U.S.	D6	93
Marion, co., Ky., U.S.	C4	94
Marion, co., Ms., U.S.	D4	101
Marion, co., Mo., U.S.	B6	102
Marion, co., Oh., U.S.	B2	112
Marion, co., Or., U.S.	C4	114
Marion, co., S.C., U.S.	C9	117
Marion, co., Tn., U.S.	D8	119
Marion, co., Tx., U.S.	C5	120
Marion, co., W.V., U.S.	B4	125
Marion, Lake, res., S.C., U.S.	E7	117
Marion Station, Md., U.S.	D6	97
Marionville, Mo., U.S.	D4	102
Maripa, Ven.	D10	58
Mariposa, co., Ca., U.S.	D3	82
Mariscal Estigarribia, Para.	A4	56
Marissa, Il., U.S.	E4	90
Maritime Alps, mts., Eur.	H14	10
Mariupol' (Ždanov), Ukr.	H5	22
Marka, Som.	H3	46
Markaryd, Swe.	H9	6
Markdale, Ont., Can.	C4	73
Marked Tree, Ar., U.S.	B5	81
Markesan, Wi., U.S.	E5	126
Markham, Ont., Can.	D5	73
Markham, Il., U.S.	k9	90
Markham, Tx., U.S.	E4	120
Markham, Mount, mtn., Ant.	A29	47
Markland Lock and Dam, U.S.	B5	94
Markle, In., U.S.	C7	91
Markovo, Russia	E28	24
Marks, Ms., U.S.	A3	101
Marksville, La., U.S.	C3	95
Marktredwitz, Ger.	E12	8
Mark Twain Lake, res., Mo., U.S.	B6	102
Marlboro, N.Y., U.S.	D6	109
Marlboro, Va., U.S.	n17	123
Marlboro, co., S.C., U.S.	B8	117
Marlborough, Ct., U.S.	C6	84
Marlborough, Ma., U.S.	B4	98
Marlborough, N.H., U.S.	E2	106
Marle, Fr.	C10	10
Marlette, Mi., U.S.	E7	99
Marley, Md., U.S.	B4	97
Marlin, Tx., U.S.	D4	120
Marlinton, W.V., U.S.	C4	125
Marlow, Ok., U.S.	C4	113
Marlowe, W.V., U.S.	B7	125
Marlton, N.J., U.S.	D3	107
Marmaduke, Ar., U.S.	A5	81
Marmande, Fr.	H7	10
Marmara Adası, i., Tur.	I11	16
Marmara Denizi (Sea of Marmara), Tur.	I12	16
Marmaris, Tur.	M12	16
Marmet, W.V., U.S.	C3	125
Marmora, Ont., Can.	C7	73
Marne, stm., Fr.	C10	10
Maroa, Il., U.S.	C5	90
Maroa, Ven.	F9	58
Maroantsetra, Madag.	E9	44
Maromokotro, mtn., Madag.	D9	44
Marondera, Zimb.	E6	44
Maros (Mureş), stm., Eur.	C4	16
Maroua, Cam.	F8	42
Marovoay, Madag.	E9	44
Marquesas Keys, is., Fl., U.S.	H4	86
Marquette, Mi., U.S.	B3	99
Marquette, co., Mi., U.S.	B3	99
Marquette, co., Wi., U.S.	E4	126
Marquette Heights, Il., U.S.	C4	90
Marquise, Fr.	B8	10
Marrah, Jabal, mtn., Sudan	F10	42
Marrakech, Mor.	B4	42
Marrero, La., U.S.	E5	95
Mars, Pa., U.S.	E1	115
Marsabit, Kenya	H2	46
Marsala, Italy	L7	14
Marsā Maṭrūḥ, Egypt	B11	42
Marseille, Fr.	J12	10
Marseille-en-Beauvaisis, Fr.	C8	10
Marseilles, Il., U.S.	B5	90
Marshall, Sask., Can.	D1	75
Marshall, Ar., U.S.	B3	81
Marshall, Il., U.S.	D6	90
Marshall, Mi., U.S.	F6	99
Marshall, Mn., U.S.	F3	100
Marshall, Mo., U.S.	B4	102
Marshall, N.C., U.S.	f10	110
Marshall, Tx., U.S.	C5	120
Marshall, Va., U.S.	B5	123
Marshall, Wi., U.S.	E4	126
Marshall, co., Al., U.S.	A3	78
Marshall, co., Il., U.S.	B4	90
Marshall, co., In., U.S.	B5	91
Marshall, co., Ia., U.S.	C4	92
Marshall, co., Ks., U.S.	C7	93
Marshall, co., Ky., U.S.	f9	94
Marshall, co., Mn., U.S.	B2	100
Marshall, co., Ms., U.S.	A4	101
Marshall, co., Ok., U.S.	C5	113
Marshall, co., S.D., U.S.	B8	118
Marshall, co., Tn., U.S.	B5	119
Marshall, co., W.V., U.S.	B4	125
Marshallton, De., U.S.	B3	85
Marshalltown, Ia., U.S.	B5	92
Marshallville, Ga., U.S.	D3	87
Marshes Siding, Ky., U.S.	D5	94
Marshfield, Ma., U.S.	B6	98
Marshfield, Mo., U.S.	D5	102
Marshfield, Wi., U.S.	D3	126
Marshfield Hills, Ma., U.S.	B6	98
Marsh Fork, stm., W.V., U.S.	n13	125
Marsh Harbour, Bah.	A9	64
Mars Hill, Me., U.S.	B5	96
Mars Hill, N.C., U.S.	f10	110
Marsh Island, i., La., U.S.	E4	95

Name	Map Ref	Page
Marsh Lake, res., Mn., U.S.	E2	100
Marsh Peak, mtn., Ut., U.S.	C6	121
Marshville, N.C., U.S.	C2	110
Marsing, Id., U.S.	F2	89
Märsta, Swe.	G11	6
Marston, Mo., U.S.	E8	102
Mart, Tx., U.S.	D4	120
Martaban, Gulf of, b., Mya.	F4	34
Marthasville, Mo., U.S.	C6	102
Martha's Vineyard, i., Ma., U.S.	D6	98
Martigny, Switz.	F14	10
Martigues, Fr.	I12	10
Martin, Slov.	F18	8
Martin, Ky., U.S.	C7	94
Martin, S.D., U.S.	D4	118
Martin, Tn., U.S.	A3	119
Martin, co., Fl., U.S.	E6	86
Martin, co., In., U.S.	G4	91
Martin, co., Ky., U.S.	C7	94
Martin, co., Mn., U.S.	G4	100
Martin, co., N.C., U.S.	B5	110
Martin, co., Tx., U.S.	C2	120
Martina Franca, Italy	I12	14
Martinez, Ca., U.S.	C2	82
Martinez, Ga., U.S.	C4	87
Martínez de la Torre, Mex.	G11	62
Martinique, dep., N.A.	G17	64
Martin Lake, res., Al., U.S.	C4	78
Martin Point, c., Ak., U.S.	A11	79
Martinsberg, Aus.	G15	8
Martinsburg, Pa., U.S.	F5	115
Martinsburg, W.V., U.S.	B7	125
Martins Ferry, Oh., U.S.	B5	112
Martinsville, Il., U.S.	D6	90
Martinsville, In., U.S.	F5	91
Martinsville, Va., U.S.	D3	123
Martos, Spain	H8	12
Martre, Lac la, l., N.W. Ter., Can.	D9	66
Martti, Fin.	C17	6
Marugame, Japan	H6	30
Ma'rūt, Afg.	E2	38
Marvejols, Fr.	H10	10
Marvell, Ar., U.S.	C5	81
Marvine, Mount, mtn., Ut., U.S.	E4	121
Mary, Turk.	J10	22
Mary, Lake, l., Mn., U.S.	E3	100
Mary, Lake, l., Ms., U.S.	D2	101
Maryborough, Austl.	E10	50
Maryland, state, U.S.	B4	97
Maryland City, Md., U.S.	B4	97
Maryland Heights, Mo., U.S.	f13	102
Maryland Point, c., Md., U.S.	D3	97
Maryport, Eng., U.K.	G9	7
Marys, stm., Nv., U.S.	B6	105
Marys Peak, mtn., Or., U.S.	C3	114
Marystown, Newf., Can.	E4	72
Marysville, Ca., U.S.	C3	82
Marysville, Ks., U.S.	C7	93
Marysville, Mi., U.S.	F8	99
Marysville, Oh., U.S.	B2	112
Marysville, Pa., U.S.	F8	115
Marysville, Wa., U.S.	A3	124
Maryville, Mo., U.S.	A3	102
Maryville, Tn., U.S.	D10	119
Marzūq, Libya	C8	42
Marzūq, Idehan, reg., Libya	C8	42
Masai Steppe, plat., Tan.	B7	44
Masaka, Ug.	B6	44
Masan, S. Kor.	D12	26
Masasi, Tan.	D7	44
Masaya, Nic.	I4	64
Masbate Island, i., Phil.	C7	32
Mascarene Islands, is., Afr.	F11	44
Mascoma, stm., N.H., U.S.	C2	106
Mascoma Lake, l., N.H., U.S.	C2	106
Mascot, Tn., U.S.	C10	119
Mascota, Mex.	G7	62
Mascouche, Que., Can.	D4	74
Mascoutah, Il., U.S.	E4	90
Maseru, Leso.	G5	44
Mashābih, i., Sau. Ar.	C2	46
Mashapaug Pond, l., Ct., U.S.	A7	84
Masherbrum, mtn., Pak.	C7	38
Mashhad, Iran	J9	22
Masi Manimba, Zaire	B3	44
Masindi, Ug.	H12	42
Masjed Soleymān, Iran	B4	46
Mask, Lough, l., Ire.	H3	7
Maskanah, Syria	A6	40
Maskinongé, Que., Can.	C4	74
Mason, Mi., U.S.	F6	99
Mason, Nv., U.S.	E2	105
Mason, Oh., U.S.	C1	112
Mason, Tx., U.S.	D3	120
Mason, W.V., U.S.	B2	125
Mason, co., Il., U.S.	C4	90
Mason, co., Ky., U.S.	B6	94
Mason, co., Mi., U.S.	D4	99
Mason, co., Tx., U.S.	D3	120
Mason, co., Wa., U.S.	B2	124
Mason, co., W.V., U.S.	C3	125
Mason City, Il., U.S.	C4	90
Mason City, Ia., U.S.	A4	92
Masontown, Pa., U.S.	G2	115
Masontown, W.V., U.S.	B5	125
Masqaṭ (Muscat), Oman	D6	46
Massa, Italy	E5	14
Massabesic Lake, l., N.H., U.S.	E4	106
Massac, co., Il., U.S.	F5	90
Massachusetts, state, U.S.	B4	98
Massachusetts Bay, b., Ma., U.S.	B6	98
Massacre Lake, l., Nv., U.S.	B2	105
Massafra, Italy	I12	14
Massa Marittima, Italy	F5	14
Massangena, Moz.	F6	44
Massapoag Lake, l., Ma., U.S.	h11	98
Massarosa, Italy	F5	14
Massasecum, Lake, l., N.H., U.S.	D3	106
Massena, N.Y., U.S.	f10	109
Massenya, Chad	F9	42
Masset, B.C., Can.	C1	69
Massey, Ont., Can.	A2	73
Massif Central see Central, Massif, mts., Fr.	G10	10
Massillon, Oh., U.S.	B4	112
Massive, Mount, mtn., Co., U.S.	B4	83
Masterton, N.Z.	D5	52
Mastic Beach, N.Y., U.S.	n16	109
Mastung, Pak.	F2	38
Masuda, Japan	H4	30
Masury, Oh., U.S.	A5	112
Matadi, Zaire	C2	44
Matagalpa, Nic.	H5	64
Matagorda, co., Tx., U.S.	E5	120
Matagorda Bay, b., Tx., U.S.	E4	120
Matagorda Island, i., Tx., U.S.	E4	120
Matagorda Peninsula, pen., Tx., U.S.	E5	120
Matale, Sri L.	I6	37
Matamoras, Pa., U.S.	D12	115
Matamoros, Mex.	E11	62
Matamoros de la Laguna, Mex.	E8	62
Matandu, stm., Tan.	C7	44
Matane, Que., Can.	k13	74
Matanuska, stm., Ak., U.S.	g18	79
Matanzas, Cuba	C7	64
Matanzas Inlet, b., Fl., U.S.	C5	86
Matara, Sri L.	J6	37
Mataró, Spain	D14	12
Matatiele, S. Afr.	H5	44
Matawan, N.J., U.S.	C4	107
Matehuala, Mex.	F9	62
Mateira, Braz.	E3	57
Matelica, Italy	F7	14
Matera, Italy	I11	14
Mateur, Tun.	L4	14
Matewan, W.V., U.S.	D2	125
Mather, Pa., U.S.	G1	115
Mather Air Force Base, mil., Ca., U.S.	C3	82
Mather Peaks, mts., Wy., U.S.	B5	127
Mathews, La., U.S.	E5	95
Mathews, Va., U.S.	C6	123
Mathews, co., Va., U.S.	C6	123
Mathews, Lake, l., Ca., U.S.	n14	82
Mathis, Tx., U.S.	E4	120
Mathiston, Ms., U.S.	B4	101
Mathura, India	G7	38
Matías Romero, Mex.	I12	62
Matinicus Island, i., Me., U.S.	E3	96
Mātli, Pak.	H3	38
Mato, Cerro, mtn., Ven.	D10	58
Matoaca, Va., U.S.	n18	123
Mato Grosso, Braz.	F7	54
Mato Grosso, Planalto do, plat., Braz.	G7	54
Matosinhos, Port.	D3	12
Matou, Tai.	L9	28
Maṭraḥ, Oman	D6	46
Matsqui, B.C., Can.	f13	69
Matsudo, Japan	G12	30
Matsue, Japan	G6	30
Matsumae, Japan	r18	30a
Matsumoto, Japan	F10	30
Matsusaka, Japan	H9	30
Matsu Tao, i., Tai.	I8	28
Matsuyama, Japan	I5	30
Mattagami, stm., Ont., Can.	F16	66
Mattamiscontis Lake, l., Me., U.S.	C4	96
Mattamuskeet, Lake, l., N.C., U.S.	B6	110
Mattāncheri, India	H4	37
Mattapoisett, Ma., U.S.	C6	98
Mattaponi, stm., Va., U.S.	C5	123
Mattawa, Ont., Can.	A6	73
Mattawamkeag, Me., U.S.	C4	96
Mattawamkeag, stm., Me., U.S.	C4	96
Mattawamkeag Lake, l., Me., U.S.	C4	96
Matterhorn, mtn., Eur.	G14	10
Matterhorn, mtn., Nv., U.S.	B6	105
Matteson, Il., U.S.	k9	90
Matthews, Mo., U.S.	E8	102
Matthews, N.C., U.S.	B2	110
Matthews Ridge, Guy.	D12	58
Matthew Town, Bah.	D11	64
Mattighofen, Aus.	G13	8
Mattituck, N.Y., U.S.	n16	109
Mattoon, Il., U.S.	D5	90
Mattoon, Lake, res., Il., U.S.	D5	90
Mattydale, N.Y., U.S.	B4	109
Matunuck, R.I., U.S.	G3	116
Maturín, Ven.	C11	58
Maúa, Moz.	D7	44
Maubeuge, Fr.	B10	10
Maud, Ok., U.S.	B5	113
Maugansville, Md., U.S.	A2	97
Maui, co., Hi., U.S.	B5	88
Maui, i., Hi., U.S.	C6	88
Mauldin, S.C., U.S.	B3	117
Mauléon-Licharre, Fr.	I6	10
Maulvi Bāzār, Bngl.	H14	38
Maumee, Oh., U.S.	A2	112
Maumee, stm., U.S.	A2	112
Maumee Bay, b., U.S.	G7	99
Maumelle, Lake, res., Ar., U.S.	C3	81
Maun, Bots.	E4	44
Mauna Kea, vol., Hi., U.S.	D6	88
Maunaloa, Hi., U.S.	B4	88
Mauna Loa, vol., Hi., U.S.	D6	88
Maunalua Bay, b., Hi., U.S.	g10	88
Maunath Bhanjan, India	H10	38
Maunawili, Hi., U.S.	g10	88
Mau Rānīpur, India	H8	38
Maurepas, Lake, l., La., U.S.	D5	95
Mauriac, Fr.	G9	10
Maurice, Ia., U.S.	B1	92
Maurice, stm., N.J., U.S.	E2	107
Mauritania, ctry., Afr.	D3	42
Mauritius, ctry., Afr.	F11	44
Maurs, Fr.	H9	10
Maury, co., Tn., U.S.	B4	119
Maury City, Tn., U.S.	B2	119
Maury Island, i., Wa., U.S.	f11	124
Mauston, Wi., U.S.	E3	126
Mauterndorf, Aus.	H13	8
Mauthausen, Aus.	G14	8
Maverick, co., Tx., U.S.	E2	120
Maw-Daung Pass, Asia	I5	34
Mawlaik, Mya.	C3	34
Mawlamyine (Moulmein), Mya.	F4	34
Maw Taung, mtn., Asia	I5	34
Maxinkuckee, Lake, l., In., U.S.	B5	91
Max Meadows, Va., U.S.	D2	123
Maxton, N.C., U.S.	C3	110
Maxville, Ont., Can.	B10	73
Maxwell, Ia., U.S.	C4	92
Maxwell Acres, W.V., U.S.	g8	125
Maxwell Air Force Base, mil., Al., U.S.	C3	78
Mayaguana, i., Bah.	C11	64
Mayaguana Passage, strt., Bah.	C11	64
Mayagüez, P.R.	E14	64
Maya Mountains, mts., N.A.	F3	64
Maybole, Scot., U.K.	F8	7
Mayen, Ger.	E7	8
Mayenne, Fr.	D6	10
Mayer, Az., U.S.	C3	80
Mayerthorpe, Alta., Can.	C3	68
Mayes, co., Ok., U.S.	A6	113
Mayesville, S.C., U.S.	D7	117
Mayfield, Ky., U.S.	f9	94
Mayfield, Pa., U.S.	C10	115
Mayfield Heights, Oh., U.S.	A4	112
Mayfield Lake, res., Wa., U.S.	C3	124
Mayflower, Ar., U.S.	C3	81
Mayking, Ky., U.S.	C7	94
Maykop see Majkop, Russia	I6	22
Maymyo, Mya.	C4	34
Maynard, Ma., U.S.	B5	98
Maynardville, Tn., U.S.	C10	119
Mayne, B.C., Can.	g12	69
Mayo, Yukon, Can.	D5	66
Mayo, Md., U.S.	C4	97
Mayo, S.C., U.S.	A4	117
Mayodan, N.C., U.S.	A3	110
Mayotte, ter., Afr.	D9	44
Mayotte, i., May.	D9	44
May Park, Or., U.S.	B8	114
Mayport Naval Station, mil., Fl., U.S.	B5	86
Maysville, Ga., U.S.	B3	87
Maysville, Ky., U.S.	B6	94
Maysville, Mo., U.S.	B3	102
Maysville, N.C., U.S.	C5	110
Maysville, Ok., U.S.	C4	113
Mayumba, Gabon	B2	44
Māyūram, India	G5	37
Mayville, Mi., U.S.	E7	99
Mayville, N.Y., U.S.	C1	109
Mayville, N.D., U.S.	B8	111
Mayville, Wi., U.S.	E5	126
Maywood, Il., U.S.	k9	90
Maywood, N.J., U.S.	h8	107
Maywood Park, Or., U.S.	*B4	114
Mazabuka, Zam.	E5	44
Mazamet, Fr.	I9	10
Mazara del Vallo, Italy	L7	14
Mazār-e Sharīf, Afg.	B2	38
Mazaruni, stm., Guy.	E13	58
Mazatenango, Guat.	G2	64
Mazatlán, Mex.	F6	62
Mazatzal Mountains, mts., Az., U.S.	C4	80
Mazatzal Peak, mtn., Az., U.S.	C4	80
Mazeppa, Mn., U.S.	F6	100
Mazoe, stm., Afr.	E6	44
Mazomanie, Wi., U.S.	E4	126
Mazon, Il., U.S.	B5	90
Mbabane, Swaz.	G6	44
Mbaiki, Cen. Afr. Rep.	H9	42
Mbala, Zam.	C6	44
Mbale, Ug.	A6	44
Mbandaka (Coquilhatville), Zaire	A3	44
Mbanza-Ngungu, Zaire	C2	44
M'banz Congo, Ang.	C2	44
Mbeya, Tan.	C6	44
Mbomou (Bomu), stm., Afr.	H10	42
Mbout, Maur.	E3	42
Mbuji-Mayi (Bakwanga), Zaire	C4	44
McAdam, N.B., Can.	D2	71
McAdoo, Pa., U.S.	E9	115
McAfee Peak, mtn., Nv., U.S.	B6	105
McAlester, Ok., U.S.	C6	113
McAlester, Lake, res., Ok., U.S.	B6	113
McAllen, Tx., U.S.	F3	120
McAlmont, Ar., U.S.	h10	81
McAlpine, Md., U.S.	B4	97
McAlpine Lock and Dam, U.S.	H6	91
McArthur, Oh., U.S.	C3	112
McBee, S.C., U.S.	C7	117
McCall, Id., U.S.	E2	89
McCalla, Al., U.S.	g6	78
McCamey, Tx., U.S.	D1	120
McCammon, Id., U.S.	G6	89
McCandless, Pa., U.S.	h13	115
McCartney Mountain, mtn., Mt., U.S.	E4	103
McCaysville, Ga., U.S.	B2	87
McChord Air Force Base, mil., Wa., U.S.	f11	124
McClain, co., Ok., U.S.	C4	113
McCleary, Wa., U.S.	B2	124
McClellan Air Force Base, mil., Ca., U.S.	C3	82
McClintock, Mount, mtn., Ant.	A28	47
McCloud, Ca., U.S.	B2	82
McClure, Pa., U.S.	E7	115
McColl, S.C., U.S.	B8	117
McComas, W.V., U.S.	D3	125
McComb, Ms., U.S.	D3	101
McComb, Oh., U.S.	A2	112
McCone, co., Mt., U.S.	C11	103
McConnell Air Force Base, mil., Ks., U.S.	g12	93
McConnellsburg, Pa., U.S.	G6	115
McConnelsville, Oh., U.S.	C4	112
McCook, Ne., U.S.	D5	104
McCook, co., S.D., U.S.	D8	118
McCordsville, In., U.S.	E6	91
McCormick, S.C., U.S.	D3	117
McCormick, co., S.C., U.S.	D3	117
McCracken, co., Ky., U.S.	e9	94
McCreary, Man., Can.	D2	70
McCreary, co., Ky., U.S.	D5	94
McCrory, Ar., U.S.	B4	81
McCulloch, co., Tx., U.S.	D3	120
McCullough Mountain, mtn., Nv., U.S.	H6	105
McCurtain, co., Ok., U.S.	C7	113
McDermitt, Nv., U.S.	B4	105
McDonald, co., Mo., U.S.	E3	102
McDonough, Ga., U.S.	C2	87
McDonough, co., Il., U.S.	C3	90
McDougall, Mount, mtn., Wy., U.S.	D2	127
McDowell, Ky., U.S.	C7	94
McDowell, co., N.C., U.S.	f10	110
McDowell, co., W.V., U.S.	D3	125
McDowell Mountains, mts., Az., U.S.	k9	80
McDowell Peak, mtn., Az., U.S.	k9	80
McDuffie, co., Ga., U.S.	C4	87
McElroy Creek, stm., W.V., U.S.	k9	125
Mcensk, Russia	H19	18
McEwen, Tn., U.S.	A4	119
McFarland, Ca., U.S.	E4	82
McFarland, Wi., U.S.	E4	126
McGehee, Ar., U.S.	D4	81
McGill, Nv., U.S.	D7	105
McGrath, Ak., U.S.	C8	79
McGregor, Ia., U.S.	A6	92
McGregor, Tx., U.S.	D4	120
McGregor, stm., B.C., Can.	B7	69
McGregor Lake, l., Alta., Can.	D4	68
McGuire, Mount, mtn., Id., U.S.	D4	89
McGuire Air Force Base, mil., N.J., U.S.	C3	107
McHenry, Il., U.S.	A5	90
McHenry, Md., U.S.	k12	97
McHenry, co., Il., U.S.	A5	90
McHenry, co., N.D., U.S.	A5	111
McIntosh, Mn., U.S.	C3	100
McIntosh, co., Ga., U.S.	E5	87
McIntosh, co., N.D., U.S.	C6	111
McIntosh, co., Ok., U.S.	B6	113
McKean, co., Pa., U.S.	C4	115
McKee, Ky., U.S.	C6	94
McKeesport, Pa., U.S.	F2	115
McKees Rocks, Pa., U.S.	F1	115
McKenzie, Tn., U.S.	A3	119
McKenzie, co., N.D., U.S.	B2	111
McKenzie, stm., Or., U.S.	C4	114
McKinley, co., N.M., U.S.	B1	108
McKinley, Mount, mtn., Ak., U.S.	C9	79
McKinleyville, Ca., U.S.	B1	82
McKinney, Tx., U.S.	C4	120
McKinney, Lake, l., Ks., U.S.	E2	93
McKittrick Summit, mtn., Ca., U.S.	E4	82
McLaughlin, S.D., U.S.	B5	118
McLean, Il., U.S.	C4	90
McLean, Va., U.S.	g12	123
McLean, co., Il., U.S.	C4	90
McLean, co., Ky., U.S.	C2	94
McLean, co., N.D., U.S.	B4	111
McLeansboro, Il., U.S.	E5	90
McLennan, Alta., Can.	B2	68
McLennan, co., Tx., U.S.	D4	120
McLeod, co., Mn., U.S.	F4	100
McLeod, Lake, l., Austl.	D2	50
M'Clintock Channel, strt., N.W. Ter., Can.	B12	66
McLoud, Ok., U.S.	B4	113
McLoughlin, Mount, mtn., Or., U.S.	D4	114
McLouth, Ks., U.S.	C8	93
McMechen, W.V., U.S.	B4	125
McMillan, Lake, res., N.M., U.S.	E5	108
McMinn, co., Tn., U.S.	D9	119
McMinnville, Or., U.S.	B3	114
McMinnville, Tn., U.S.	D8	119
McMullen, co., Tx., U.S.	E3	120
McNairy, co., Tn., U.S.	B3	119
McNary, Az., U.S.	C6	80
McNary Dam, U.S.	B7	114
McNeil, Ar., U.S.	D2	81
McNeil, Mount, mtn., B.C., Can.	B2	69
McNeil Island, i., Wa., U.S.	f10	124
McNeill, Ms., U.S.	E4	101
McPherson, Ks., U.S.	D6	93
McPherson, co., Ks., U.S.	D6	93
McPherson, co., Ne., U.S.	C4	104
McPherson, co., S.D., U.S.	B6	118
McQueeney, Tx., U.S.	h7	120
McRae, Ar., U.S.	B4	81
McRae, Ga., U.S.	D4	87
McRoberts, Ky., U.S.	C7	94
McSherrystown, Pa., U.S.	G7	115
Mead, Wa., U.S.	B8	124
Mead, Lake, res., U.S.	A1	80
Meade, Ks., U.S.	E3	93
Meade, co., Ks., U.S.	E3	93
Meade, co., Ky., U.S.	C3	94
Meade, co., S.D., U.S.	C3	118
Meade, stm., Ak., U.S.	B8	79
Meaden Peak, mtn., Co., U.S.	A3	83
Meade Peak, mtn., Id., U.S.	G7	89
Meadow, stm., W.V., U.S.	C4	125
Meadow Creek, stm., W.V., U.S.	n14	125
Meadow Lands, Pa., U.S.	F1	115
Meadow Valley Wash, val., Nv., U.S.	F7	105
Meadowview, Va., U.S.	f10	123
Meadville, Pa., U.S.	C1	115
Meaford, Ont., Can.	C4	73
Meagher, co., Mt., U.S.	D6	103
Mealhada, Port.	E3	12
Meander Creek Reservoir, res., Oh., U.S.	A5	112
Meath, hist. reg., Ire.	H5	7
Meaux, Fr.	D9	10
Mebane, N.C., U.S.	A3	110
Mecca, Ca., U.S.	F5	82
Mecca see Makkah, Sau. Ar.	D2	46
Mechanic Falls, Me., U.S.	D2	96
Mechanicsburg, Oh., U.S.	B2	112
Mechanicsburg, Pa., U.S.	F7	115
Mechanicsville, Ia., U.S.	C6	92
Mechanicsville, Md., U.S.	D4	97
Mechanicsville, Va., U.S.	C5	123
Mechanicville, N.Y., U.S.	C7	109
Mechant, Lake, l., La., U.S.	E4	95
Mechelen, Bel.	D4	8
Mecklenburg, co., N.C., U.S.	B2	110
Mecklenburg, co., Va., U.S.	D4	123
Mecklenburg, hist. reg., Ger.	B12	8
Mecklenburger Bucht, b., Ger.	A11	8
Mecosta, co., Mi., U.S.	E5	99
Medan, Indon.	E2	32
Medanosa, Punta, c., Arg.	F3	56
Medaryville, In., U.S.	B4	91
Meddybumps Lake, l., Me., U.S.	C5	96
Medeiros Neto, Braz.	D8	57
Medellín, Col.	D5	58
Médenine, Tun.	B8	42
Medfield, Ma., U.S.	h10	98
Medford, Ma., U.S.	B5	98
Medford, Mn., U.S.	F5	100
Medford, Ok., U.S.	A4	113
Medford, Or., U.S.	E4	114
Medford, Wi., U.S.	C3	126
Medford Lakes, N.J., U.S.	D3	107
Medgidia, Rom.	E12	16
Media, Pa., U.S.	G11	115
Mediapolis, Ia., U.S.	C6	92
Mediaș, Rom.	C8	16
Medical Lake, Wa., U.S.	B8	124
Medicine Bow, Wy., U.S.	E6	127
Medicine Bow, stm., Wy., U.S.	E6	127
Medicine Bow Mountains, mts., U.S.	E6	127
Medicine Bow Peak, mtn., Wy., U.S.	E6	127
Medicine Hat, Alta., Can.	D5	68
Medicine Lodge, Ks., U.S.	E5	93
Medicine Lodge, stm., U.S.	E4	93
Medina, N.Y., U.S.	B2	109
Medina, Oh., U.S.	A4	112
Medina, Tn., U.S.	B3	119
Medina, Wa., U.S.	e11	124
Medina, co., Oh., U.S.	A4	112
Medina, co., Tx., U.S.	E3	120
Medina, stm., Tx., U.S.	k7	120
Medina see Al-Madīnah, Sau. Ar.	D2	46
Medinaceli, Spain	D9	12
Medina del Campo, Spain	D7	12
Medina de Ríoseco, Spain	D6	12
Mediterranean Sea	D14	2
Medjez el Bab, Tun.	M4	14
Médoc, reg., Fr.	G5	10
Medora, In., U.S.	G5	91
Médouneu, Gabon	A2	44
Medway, Me., U.S.	C4	96
Medway, Ma., U.S.	B5	98
Medway, stm., N.S., Can.	E5	71
Meekatharra, Austl.	E3	50
Meeker, Co., U.S.	A3	83
Meeker, Ok., U.S.	B5	113
Meeker, co., Mn., U.S.	E4	100
Meelpaeg Lake, res., Newf., Can.	D3	72
Meerut, India	F7	38
Meeteetse, Wy., U.S.	B4	127
Mega, Eth.	H2	46
Mégantic, Lac, l., Que., Can.	D7	74
Mégantic, Mont, mtn., Que., Can.	D6	74
Mégara, Grc.	K7	16
Meggett, S.C., U.S.	F7	117
Meghalaya, state, India	H14	38
Meherrin, stm., U.S.	A4	110
Mehlville, Mo., U.S.	f13	102
Mehsāna, India	I5	38
Mehtar Lām, Afg.	C4	38
Mehun-sur-Yèvre, Fr.	E9	10
Meigs, Ga., U.S.	E2	87
Meigs, co., Oh., U.S.	C3	112
Meigs, co., Tn., U.S.	D9	119
Meiktila, Mya.	D3	34
Meiningen, Ger.	E10	8
Meissen, Ger.	D13	8
Meixian, China	K5	28
Mekambo, Gabon	A2	44
Mekele, Eth.	F2	46
Meknès, Mor.	B4	42
Mekong, stm., Asia	H8	34
Melaka, Malay.	M7	34
Melanesia, is., Oc.	G23	2
Melbourne, Austl.	G8	50
Melbourne, Ar., U.S.	A4	81
Melbourne, Fl., U.S.	D6	86
Melbourne, Ia., U.S.	C4	92
Melbourne, Ky., U.S.	h14	94
Melbourne Beach, Fl., U.S.	D6	86
Melcher, Ia., U.S.	C4	92
Meldorf, Ger.	A9	8
Mélèzes, Rivière aux, stm., Que., Can.	g12	74
Melfi, Chad	F9	42
Melfi, Italy	I10	14
Melgaço, Port.	C3	12
Melhus, Nor.	E8	6
Melilla, Sp. N. Afr.	A5	42
Melita, Man., Can.	E1	70
Melito di Porto Salvo, Italy	L10	14
Melitopol', Ukr.	H5	22
Melk, Aus.	G15	8
Mellansel, Swe.	E12	6
Melle, Fr.	F6	10
Mellen, Wi., U.S.	B3	126
Mellerud, Swe.	G9	6
Mellette, co., S.D., U.S.	D5	118
Mellish Reef, atoll, Austl.	C11	50
Melo, Ur.	C6	56
Melocheville, Que., Can.	q19	74
Melrhir, Chott, l., Alg.	B7	42
Melrose, Fl., U.S.	C4	86
Melrose, Ma., U.S.	B5	98
Melrose, Mn., U.S.	E4	100
Melrose, N.M., U.S.	C6	108
Meltaus, Fin.	C15	6
Melton Hill Lake, res., Tn., U.S.	D9	119
Melton Mowbray, Eng., U.K.	I12	7
Melun, Fr.	D9	10
Melvern Lake, res., Ks., U.S.	D8	93
Melville, Sask., Can.	G4	75
Melville, La., U.S.	D4	95
Melville, Lake, l., Newf., Can.	B2	72
Melville Hills, hills, N.W. Ter., Can.	C8	66
Melville Island, i., Austl.	B6	50
Melville Island, i., N.W. Ter., Can.	A10	66

Name	Map Ref	Page
Melville Peninsula, pen., N.W. Ter., Can.	C16	66
Melvin, Ky., U.S.	C7	94
Memmingen, Ger.	H10	8
Memphis, Fl., U.S.	p10	86
Memphis, Mi., U.S.	F8	99
Memphis, Mo., U.S.	A5	102
Memphis, Tn., U.S.	B1	119
Memphis, Tx., U.S.	B2	120
Memphis Naval Air Station, mil., Tn., U.S.	B2	119
Mena, Ar., U.S.	C1	81
Menahga, Mn., U.S.	D3	100
Ménaka, Mali	E6	42
Menan, Id., U.S.	F7	89
Menands, N.Y., U.S.	C7	109
Menard, Tx., U.S.	D3	120
Menard, co., Il., U.S.	C4	90
Menard, co., Tx., U.S.	D3	120
Menasha, Wi., U.S.	D5	126
Mendawai, stm., Indon.	F5	32
Mende, Fr.	H10	10
Mendenhall, Ms., U.S.	D4	101
Méndez, Ec.	I3	58
Mendham, N.J., U.S.	B3	107
Mendi, Eth.	G2	46
Mendip Hills, hills, Eng., U.K.	J10	7
Mendocino, co., Ca., U.S.	C2	82
Mendon, Il., U.S.	C2	90
Mendon, Mi., U.S.	F5	99
Mendon, Ut., U.S.	B4	121
Mendota, Ca., U.S.	D3	82
Mendota, Il., U.S.	B4	90
Mendota, Lake, l., Wi., U.S.	E4	126
Mendoza, Arg.	C3	56
Mene de Mauroa, Ven.	B7	58
Mene Grande, Ven.	C7	58
Menemen, Tur.	K11	16
Menfi, Italy	L7	14
Mengzhi, China	C7	34
Mengzi, China	B5	34
Menifee, co., Ky., U.S.	C6	94
Menlo Park, Ca., U.S.	k8	82
Menno, S.D., U.S.	D8	118
Menominee, Mi., U.S.	C3	99
Menominee, co., Mi., U.S.	C3	99
Menominee, co., Wi., U.S.	C5	126
Menominee, stm., U.S.	C6	126
Menominee Indian Reservation, Wi., U.S.	C5	126
Menomonee, stm., Wi., U.S.	m11	126
Menomonee Falls, Wi., U.S.	E5	126
Menomonie, Wi., U.S.	D2	126
Menongue, Ang.	D3	44
Menorca, i., Spain	F16	12
Mentawai, Kepulauan, is., Indon.	F2	32
Menton, Fr.	I14	10
Mentone, In., U.S.	B5	91
Mentor, Oh., U.S.	A4	112
Mentor-on-the-Lake, Oh., U.S.	A4	112
Menzel Bourguiba, Tun.	L4	14
Meoqui, Mex.	C7	62
Meppel, Neth.	C6	8
Meppen, Ger.	C7	8
Mequon, Wi., U.S.	E6	126
Mer, Fr.	E8	10
Meramec, stm., Mo., U.S.	C7	102
Merano (Meran), Italy	C6	14
Merasheen Island, i., Newf., Can.	E4	72
Merauke, Indon.	G11	32
Meraux, La., U.S.	k12	95
Mercaderes, Col.	G4	58
Merced, Ca., U.S.	D3	82
Merced, co., Ca., U.S.	D3	82
Merced, stm., Ca., U.S.	D3	82
Mercedes, Arg.	B5	56
Mercedes, Arg.	C3	56
Mercedes, Tx., U.S.	F4	120
Mercedes, Ur.	C5	56
Mercer, Pa., U.S.	D1	115
Mercer, Wi., U.S.	B3	126
Mercer, co., Il., U.S.	B3	90
Mercer, co., Ky., U.S.	C5	94
Mercer, co., Mo., U.S.	A4	102
Mercer, co., N.J., U.S.	C3	107
Mercer, co., N.D., U.S.	B4	111
Mercer, co., Oh., U.S.	B1	112
Mercer, co., Pa., U.S.	D1	115
Mercer, co., W.V., U.S.	D3	125
Mercer Island, Wa., U.S.	B3	124
Mercer Island, i., Wa., U.S.	e11	124
Mercersburg, Pa., U.S.	G6	115
Mercerville, N.J., U.S.	C3	107
Mercier, Que., Can.	D4	74
Meredith, N.H., U.S.	C3	106
Meredith, Lake, l., Co., U.S.	C7	83
Meredith, Lake, res., Tx., U.S.	B2	120
Meredosia, Il., U.S.	D3	90
Meredosia Lake, l., Il., U.S.	D3	90
Mergui (Myeik), Mya.	H5	34
Mergui Archipelago, is., Mya.	H4	34
Meriç (Marica) (évros), stm., Eur.	H10	16
Mérida, Mex.	G15	62
Mérida, Spain	G5	12
Mérida, Ven.	C7	58
Meriden, Ct., U.S.	C4	84
Meriden, Ks., U.S.	C8	93
Meridian, Id., U.S.	F2	89
Meridian, Ms., U.S.	C5	101
Meridian, Pa., U.S.	E2	115
Meridian, Tx., U.S.	D4	120
Meridian Hills, In., U.S.	k10	91
Meridian Naval Air Station, mil., Ms., U.S.	C5	101
Meridianville, Al., U.S.	A3	78
Mérignac, Fr.	H6	10
Merikarvia, Fin.	F13	6
Meriwether, co., Ga., U.S.	C2	87
Merkel, Tx., U.S.	C2	120
Merlin, Ont., Can.	E2	73
Mermentau, La., U.S.	D3	95
Mermentau, stm., La., U.S.	E3	95
Meron, Hare, mtn., Isr.	C4	40
Merriam, Ks., U.S.	k16	93
Merrick, co., Ne., U.S.	C7	104
Merrickville, Ont., Can.	C9	73
Merrill, Ia., U.S.	B1	92
Merrill, Mi., U.S.	E6	99
Merrill, Or., U.S.	E5	114
Merrill, Wi., U.S.	C4	126
Merrillville, In., U.S.	B3	91
Merrimac, Ma., U.S.	A5	98
Merrimack, N.H., U.S.	E4	106
Merrimack, co., N.H., U.S.	D3	106
Merrimack, stm., U.S.	A5	98
Merritt, B.C., Can.	D7	69
Merritt Island, Fl., U.S.	D6	86
Merritt Reservoir, res., Ne., U.S.	B5	104
Merrymeeting Lake, l., N.H., U.S.	D4	106
Merryville, La., U.S.	D2	95
Merseburg, Ger.	D11	8
Merthyr Tydfil, Wales, U.K.	J9	7
Mértola, Port.	H4	12
Merton, Wi., U.S.	m11	126
Méru, Fr.	C9	10
Merwin Lake, res., Wa., U.S.	C3	124
Merzig, Ger.	F6	8
Mesa, Az., U.S.	D4	80
Mesa, co., Co., U.S.	C2	83
Mesabi Range, hills, Mn., U.S.	C6	100
Mesagne, Italy	I12	14
Mesa Mountain, mtn., Co., U.S.	D4	83
Mesa Verde National Park, Co., U.S.	D2	83
Mescalero, N.M., U.S.	D4	108
Mescalero Indian Reservation, N.M., U.S.	D4	108
Mesilla, N.M., U.S.	E3	108
Mesolóngion, Grc.	K5	16
Mesopotamia, reg., Asia	B3	46
Mesquite, Nv., U.S.	G7	105
Mesquite, N.M., U.S.	E3	108
Mesquite, Tx., U.S.	n10	120
Messalo, stm., Moz.	D7	44
Messalonskee Lake, l., Me., U.S.	D3	96
Messina, Italy	K10	14
Messina, S. Afr.	F5	44
Messina, Stretto di, strt., Italy	K10	14
Mesta (Néstos), stm., Eur.	H7	16
Mestre, Italy	D7	14
Meta, stm., S.A.	D9	58
Métabetchouan, Que., Can.	A6	74
Métabetchouane, stm., Que., Can.	A5	74
Metairie, La., U.S.	k11	95
Metamora, Il., U.S.	C4	90
Metán, Arg.	B3	56
Metcalfe, Ont., Can.	B9	73
Metcalfe, Ms., U.S.	B2	101
Metcalfe, co., Ky., U.S.	C4	94
Metedeconk, North Branch, stm., N.J., U.S.	C4	107
Metedeconk, South Branch, stm., N.J., U.S.	C3	107
Meteghan, N.S., Can.	E3	71
Meteghan River, N.S., Can.	E3	71
Meteor Crater, crat., Az., U.S.	C4	80
Methow, stm., Wa., U.S.	A5	124
Methuen, Ma., U.S.	A5	98
Metković, Cro.	F12	14
Metlakatla, Ak., U.S.	D13	79
Metlatonoc, Mex.	I10	62
Metlika, Slo.	D10	14
Metonga, Lake, l., Wi., U.S.	C5	126
Metro, Indon.	k12	33a
Metropolis, Il., U.S.	F5	90
Mettawee, stm., U.S.	E2	122
Metter, Ga., U.S.	D4	87
Mettūr, India	G4	37
Metuchen, N.J., U.S.	B4	107
Metz, Fr.	C13	10
Metzger, Or., U.S.	h12	114
Meuse (Maas), stm., Eur.	E5	8
Mexia, Tx., U.S.	D4	120
Mexia, Lake, res., Tx., U.S.	D4	120
Mexiana, Ilha, i., Braz.	D9	54
Mexicali, Mex.	A2	62
Mexico, In., U.S.	C5	91
Mexico, Me., U.S.	D2	96
Mexico, Mo., U.S.	B6	102
Mexico (México), ctry., N.A.	F8	62
Mexico, Gulf of, b., N.A.	F9	76
Mexico City see Ciudad de México, Mex.	H10	62
Meximieux, Fr.	G12	10
Meycauayan, Phil.	q19	33b
Meyersdale, Pa., U.S.	G3	115
Meymaneh, Afg.	C1	38
Meyrueis, Fr.	H10	10
Meždurečensk, Russia	G11	24
Mèze, Fr.	I10	10
Mezőtúr, Hung.	H20	8
Mezquital, Mex.	F7	62
Mezzolombardo, Italy	C6	14
Mhow, India	I6	38
Miami, Az., U.S.	D5	80
Miami, Fl., U.S.	G6	86
Miami, Ok., U.S.	A7	113
Miami, co., In., U.S.	C5	91
Miami, co., Ks., U.S.	D9	93
Miami, co., Oh., U.S.	B1	112
Miami Beach, Fl., U.S.	G6	86
Miami Canal, Fl., U.S.	F6	86
Miami International Airport, Fl., U.S.	G6	86
Miamisburg, Oh., U.S.	C1	112
Miami Shores, Fl., U.S.	G6	86
Miami Springs, Fl., U.S.	G6	86
Miandrivazo, Madag.	E9	44
Mīāneh, Iran	J7	22
Miānwāli, Pak.	D4	38
Mica Mountain, mtn., Az., U.S.	E5	80
Micco, Fl., U.S.	E6	86
Miccosukee, Lake, res., Fl., U.S.	B2	86
Michelson, Mount, mtn., Ak., U.S.	B11	79
Michie, Tn., U.S.	B3	119
Michigamme, Lake, l., Mi., U.S.	B2	99
Michigamme Reservoir, res., Mi., U.S.	B2	99
Michigan, state, U.S.	E6	99
Michigan, stm., Co., U.S.	A4	83
Michigan, Lake, l., U.S.	C9	76
Michigan Center, Mi., U.S.	F6	99
Michigan City, In., U.S.	A4	91
Michigan Island, i., Wi., U.S.	B3	126
Michikamau Lake, l., Newf., Can.	F20	66
Michipicoten Island, i., Ont., Can.	G15	66
Micronesia, is., Oc.	F23	2
Mičurinsk, Russia	I23	18
Middelburg, Neth.	D3	8
Middelburg, S. Afr.	H4	44
Middelharnis, Neth.	D4	8
Middle, stm., Ia., U.S.	C3	92
Middle, stm., Mn., U.S.	B2	100
Middle Andaman, i., India	H2	34
Middleboro (Middleborough Center), Ma., U.S.	C6	98
Middlebourne, W.V., U.S.	B4	125
Middleburg, Fl., U.S.	B5	86
Middleburg, Pa., U.S.	E7	115
Middleburg Heights, Oh., U.S.	h9	112
Middlebury, Ct., U.S.	C3	84
Middlebury, In., U.S.	A6	91
Middlebury, Vt., U.S.	C2	122
Middlefield, Ct., U.S.	C5	84
Middlefield, Oh., U.S.	A4	112
Middle Island Creek, stm., W.V., U.S.	B3	125
Middle Nodaway, stm., Ia., U.S.	C3	92
Middle Park, val., Co., U.S.	A4	83
Middle Patuxent, stm., Md., U.S.	B4	97
Middleport, N.Y., U.S.	B2	109
Middleport, Oh., U.S.	C3	112
Middle Raccoon, stm., Ia., U.S.	C3	92
Middle River, Md., U.S.	B5	97
Middlesboro, Ky., U.S.	D6	94
Middlesex, N.J., U.S.	B4	107
Middlesex, N.C., U.S.	B4	110
Middlesex, co., Ct., U.S.	D5	84
Middlesex, co., Ma., U.S.	A5	98
Middlesex, co., N.J., U.S.	C4	107
Middlesex, co., Va., U.S.	C6	123
Middlesex Fells Reservation, Ma., U.S.	g11	98
Middleton, N.S., Can.	E4	71
Middleton, Id., U.S.	F2	89
Middleton, Ma., U.S.	A5	98
Middleton, Wi., U.S.	E4	126
Middleton Reef, atoll, Austl.	E11	50
Middletown, Ca., U.S.	C2	82
Middletown, Ct., U.S.	C5	84
Middletown, De., U.S.	C3	85
Middletown, In., U.S.	D6	91
Middletown, Ky., U.S.	g11	94
Middletown, Md., U.S.	B2	97
Middletown, N.J., U.S.	C4	107
Middletown, N.Y., U.S.	D6	109
Middletown, Oh., U.S.	C1	112
Middletown, Pa., U.S.	F8	115
Middletown, R.I., U.S.	E5	116
Middletown, Va., U.S.	A4	123
Middleville, Mi., U.S.	F5	99
Midfield, Al., U.S.	g7	78
Midland, Ont., Can.	C5	73
Midland, Mi., U.S.	E6	99
Midland, N.C., U.S.	B2	110
Midland, Pa., U.S.	E1	115
Midland, Tx., U.S.	D1	120
Midland, co., Mi., U.S.	E6	99
Midland, co., Tx., U.S.	D1	120
Midland City, Al., U.S.	D4	78
Midland Park, Ks., U.S.	g12	93
Midland Park, N.J., U.S.	B4	107
Midland Park, S.C., U.S.	k11	117
Midleton, Ire.	J4	7
Midlothian, Il., U.S.	k9	90
Midlothian, Tx., U.S.	C4	120
Midnapore, India	I12	38
Midongy Sud, Madag.	F9	44
Midvale, Ut., U.S.	C4	121
Midville, Ga., U.S.	D4	87
Midway, B.C., Can.	E8	69
Midway, De., U.S.	F5	85
Midway, Ky., U.S.	B5	94
Midway, Pa., U.S.	G7	115
Midway, Ut., U.S.	C4	121
Midway Islands, dep., Oc.	E1	2
Midwest, Wy., U.S.	C6	127
Midwest City, Ok., U.S.	B4	113
Mielec, Pol.	E21	8
Mieres, Spain	B6	12
Miesbach, Ger.	H11	8
Mifflin, co., Pa., U.S.	E6	115
Mifflinburg, Pa., U.S.	E7	115
Mifflinville, Pa., U.S.	D9	115
Miguel Alemán, Presa, res., Mex.	H11	62
Miguel Auza, Mex.	E8	62
Mihajlovgrad, Bul.	F7	16
Mihara, Japan	H6	30
Mikasa, Japan	p19	30a
Mikkeli, Fin.	F16	6
Mikumi, Tan.	C7	44
Milaca, Mn., U.S.	E5	100
Milagro, Arg.	C3	56
Milagro, Ec.	I3	58
Milam, co., Tx., U.S.	D4	120
Milan, Ga., U.S.	D3	87
Milan, Il., U.S.	B3	90
Milan, In., U.S.	F7	91
Milan, Mi., U.S.	F7	99
Milan, Mo., U.S.	A4	102
Milan, N.M., U.S.	B2	108
Milan, Oh., U.S.	A3	112
Milan, Tn., U.S.	B3	119
Milan see Milano, Italy	D4	14
Milano (Milan), Italy	D4	14
Milâs, Tur.	L11	16
Milazzo, Italy	K10	14
Milbank, S.D., U.S.	B9	118
Mildmay, Ont., Can.	C3	73
Mildura, Austl.	F8	50
Milesburg, Pa., U.S.	E6	115
Miles City, Mt., U.S.	D11	103
Milestone, Sask., Can.	G3	75
Milford, Ct., U.S.	E3	84
Milford, De., U.S.	E4	85
Milford, Il., U.S.	C6	90
Milford, In., U.S.	B6	91
Milford, Ia., U.S.	A2	92
Milford, Me., U.S.	D4	96
Milford, Ma., U.S.	B4	98
Milford, Mi., U.S.	F7	99
Milford, Ne., U.S.	D8	104
Milford, N.H., U.S.	E3	106
Milford, Oh., U.S.	C1	112
Milford, Pa., U.S.	D12	115
Milford, Ut., U.S.	E2	121
Milford Haven, Wales, U.K.	J7	7
Milford Lake, res., Ks., U.S.	C6	93
Milford Station, N.S., Can.	D6	71
Mililani Town, Hi., U.S.	g9	88
Mil'kovo, Russia	G25	24
Milk River, Alta., Can.	E4	68
Mill, stm., Ma., U.S.	h9	98
Millard, co., Ut., U.S.	D2	121
Millau, Fr.	H10	10
Millbrae, Ca., U.S.	h8	82
Millbrook, Ont., Can.	C6	73
Millbrook, Al., U.S.	C3	78
Mill Brook, stm., Vt., U.S.	B5	122
Millburn, N.J., U.S.	B4	107
Millbury, Ma., U.S.	B4	98
Millbury, Oh., U.S.	e7	112
Mill City, Or., U.S.	C4	114
Millcreek, Ut., U.S.	C4	121
Mill Creek, W.V., U.S.	C5	125
Mill Creek, stm., N.J., U.S.	D4	107
Mill Creek, stm., Oh., U.S.	B2	112
Mill Creek, stm., Tn., U.S.	g10	119
Mill Creek, stm., W.V., U.S.	m13	125
Mill Creek, stm., W.V., U.S.	C3	125
Millcreek Township, Pa., U.S.	B1	115
Milledgeville, Ga., U.S.	C3	87
Milledgeville, Il., U.S.	B4	90
Mille Îles, Rivière des, stm., Que., Can.	p19	74
Mille Lacs, co., Mn., U.S.	E5	100
Mille Lacs, Lac des, l., Ont., Can.	G14	66
Mille Lacs Indian Reservation, Mn., U.S.	D5	100
Mille Lacs Lake, l., Mn., U.S.	D5	100
Millen, Ga., U.S.	D5	87
Miller, S.D., U.S.	C7	118
Miller, co., Ar., U.S.	D2	81
Miller, co., Ga., U.S.	E2	87
Miller, co., Mo., U.S.	C5	102
Miller, Mount, mtn., Ak., U.S.	C11	79
Miller Peak, mtn., Az., U.S.	F5	80
Miller Run, stm., Vt., U.S.	B4	122
Millers, stm., Ma., U.S.	A3	98
Millersburg, In., U.S.	A6	91
Millersburg, Ky., U.S.	B5	94
Millersburg, Oh., U.S.	B4	112
Millersburg, Pa., U.S.	E8	115
Millersport, Oh., U.S.	C3	112
Millersville, Pa., U.S.	F9	115
Millet, Alta., Can.	C4	68
Mill Hall, Pa., U.S.	D7	115
Milliken, Co., U.S.	A6	83
Millington, Mi., U.S.	E7	99
Millington, Tn., U.S.	B2	119
Millinocket, Me., U.S.	C4	96
Millinocket Lake, l., Me., U.S.	C4	96
Millinocket Lake, l., Me., U.S.	B4	96
Millis, Ma., U.S.	B5	98
Millport, Al., U.S.	B1	78
Millry, Al., U.S.	D1	78
Mills, Wy., U.S.	D6	127
Mills, co., Ia., U.S.	C2	92
Mills, co., Tx., U.S.	D3	120
Millsboro, De., U.S.	F4	85
Millsboro, Pa., U.S.	G1	115
Millstadt, Il., U.S.	E3	90
Millstone, stm., N.J., U.S.	C4	107
Milltown, In., U.S.	H5	91
Milltown, N.J., U.S.	C4	107
Milltown, Wi., U.S.	C1	126
Milltown [-Head of Bay d'Espoir], Newf., Can.	E4	72
Milltown Malbay, Ire.	I3	7
Millvale, Pa., U.S.	k14	115
Mill Valley, Ca., U.S.	D2	82
Millville, Ma., U.S.	B4	98
Millville, N.J., U.S.	E2	107
Millville, Pa., U.S.	D9	115
Millville, Ut., U.S.	B4	121
Millville Lake, N.H., U.S.	E4	106
Millwood, Wa., U.S.	g14	124
Millwood Lake, res., Ar., U.S.	D1	81
Milner Dam, Id., U.S.	G5	89
Milnor, N.D., U.S.	C8	111
Milo, Ia., U.S.	C4	92
Milo, Me., U.S.	C4	96
Milparinka, Austl.	E8	50
Milroy, In., U.S.	F7	91
Milroy, Pa., U.S.	E6	115
Milstead, Ga., U.S.	C3	87
Milton, Ont., Can.	D5	73
Milton, De., U.S.	E4	85
Milton, Fl., U.S.	u14	86
Milton, In., U.S.	E7	91
Milton, Ma., U.S.	B5	98
Milton, N.H., U.S.	D5	106
Milton, Pa., U.S.	D8	115
Milton, Vt., U.S.	B2	122
Milton, Wa., U.S.	f11	124
Milton, W.V., U.S.	C2	125
Milton, Wi., U.S.	F5	126
Milton, Lake, l., Oh., U.S.	A4	112
Miltona, Lake, l., Mn., U.S.	D3	100
Milton-Freewater, Or., U.S.	B8	114
Milton Reservoir, res., Co., U.S.	A6	83
Milverton, Ont., Can.	D4	73
Milwaukee, Wi., U.S.	E6	126
Milwaukee, co., Wi., U.S.	E6	126
Milwaukee, stm., Wi., U.S.	m12	126
Milwaukie, Or., U.S.	B4	114
Mimizan, Fr.	H5	10
Mims, Fl., U.S.	D6	86
Min, stm., China	I7	28
Mina, Nv., U.S.	E3	105
Minahasa, pen., Indon.	E7	32
Minamata, Japan	J3	30
Minas, Ur.	C5	56
Minas, Sierra de las, mts., Guat.	G3	64
Minas Basin, b., N.S., Can.	D5	71
Minas Channel, strt., N.S., Can.	D5	71
Minas de Barroterán, Mex.	D9	62
Minas Novas, Braz.	D7	57
Minatare, Ne., U.S.	C2	104
Minatitlán, Mex.	I12	62
Minco, Ok., U.S.	B4	113
Mindanao, i., Phil.	D7	32
Mindanao, stm., Phil.	D7	32
Mindanao Sea, Phil.	D7	32
Mindelheim, Ger.	G10	8
Minden, Ger.	C8	8
Minden, La., U.S.	B2	95
Minden, Ne., U.S.	D7	104
Minden, Nv., U.S.	E2	105
Minden, W.V., U.S.	D3	125
Mindoro, i., Phil.	C7	32
Mindoro Strait, strt., Phil.	C7	32
Mine Hill, N.J., U.S.	B3	107
Mineiros, Braz.	D2	57
Mineola, N.Y., U.S.	E7	109
Mineola, Tx., U.S.	C5	120
Miner, Mo., U.S.	E8	102
Miner, co., S.D., U.S.	D8	118
Mineral, co., Co., U.S.	D4	83
Mineral, co., Mt., U.S.	C1	103
Mineral, co., Nv., U.S.	E3	105
Mineral, co., W.V., U.S.	B6	125
Mineral Point, Wi., U.S.	F3	126
Mineral Springs, Ar., U.S.	D2	81
Mineral Wells, Tx., U.S.	C3	120
Minersville, Pa., U.S.	E9	115
Minersville, Ut., U.S.	E3	121
Minerva, Oh., U.S.	B4	112
Minervino Murge, Italy	H11	14
Minetto, N.Y., U.S.	B4	109
Mingo, co., W.V., U.S.	D2	125
Mingo Junction, Oh., U.S.	B5	112
Minho (Miño), stm., Eur.	D3	12
Minidoka, co., Id., U.S.	G5	89
Minidoka Dam, Id., U.S.	G5	89
Minier, Il., U.S.	C4	90
Minisink Island, i., N.J., U.S.	A3	107
Minitonas, Man., Can.	C1	70
Minna, Nig.	G7	42
Minneapolis, Ks., U.S.	C6	93
Minneapolis, Mn., U.S.	F5	100
Minnedosa, Man., Can.	D2	70
Minnedosa, stm., Man., Can.	D1	70
Minnehaha, co., S.D., U.S.	D9	118
Minneola, Ks., U.S.	E3	93
Minneota, Mn., U.S.	F3	100
Minnesota, state, U.S.	E4	100
Minnesota, stm., Mn., U.S.	F2	100
Minnesota Lake, Mn., U.S.	G5	100
Minnetonka, Mn., U.S.	n12	100
Minnetonka, Lake, l., Mn., U.S.	n11	100
Minnewaska, Lake, l., Mn., U.S.	E3	100
Miño (Minho), stm., Eur.	D3	12
Minocqua, Wi., U.S.	C4	126
Minonk, Il., U.S.	C4	90
Minooka, Il., U.S.	B5	90
Minot, N.D., U.S.	A4	111
Minot Air Force Base, mil., N.D., U.S.	A4	111
Minquadale, De., U.S.	i7	85
Minsk, Bela.	H10	18
Mińsk Mazowiecki, Pol.	C21	8
Minster, Oh., U.S.	B1	112
Mint Hill, N.C., U.S.	B2	110
Minto, N.B., Can.	C3	71
Minto Inlet, b., N.W. Ter., Can.	B9	66
Minturn, Co., U.S.	B4	83
Minturno, Italy	H8	14
Minusinsk, Russia	G12	24
Minute Man National Historical Park, Ma., U.S.	g10	98
Minxian, China	E7	26
Mio, Mi., U.S.	D6	99
Mira, Italy	D7	14
Mirabel, Que., Can.	D3	74
Miraflores, Col.	E6	58
Miraflores, Col.	G6	58
Miraj, India	D3	37
Miramar, Fl., U.S.	s13	86
Miramar Naval Air Station, mil., Ca., U.S.	F5	82
Miramas, Fr.	I11	10
Mirambeau, Fr.	G6	10
Miramichi Bay, b., N.B., Can.	B5	71
Miranda de Ebro, Spain	C9	12
Miranda do Douro, Port.	D5	12
Mirande, Fr.	I7	10
Mirandela, Port.	D4	12
Mirandola, Italy	E6	14
Mirbāṭ, Oman	E5	46
Mirebeau-sur-Bèze, Fr.	E12	10
Miri, Malay.	E5	32
Mirnyj, Russia	E16	24
Mīrpur Khās, Pak.	H3	38
Mirror Lake, l., N.H., U.S.	C4	106
Mirzāpur, India	H10	38
Misawa, Japan	B14	30
Miscouche, P.E.I., Can.	C6	71
Miscou Island, i., N.B., Can.	B5	71
Miscou Point, c., N.B., Can.	A5	71
Misenheimer, N.C., U.S.	B2	110
Mishawaka, In., U.S.	A5	91
Misheguk Mountain, mtn., Ak., U.S.	B7	79
Mishicot, Wi., U.S.	D6	126
Mishmi Hills, hills, Asia	F16	38
Misima Island, i., Pap. N. Gui.	B10	50
Miskitos, Cayos, is., Nic.	G6	64
Miskolc, Hung.	G20	8
Misool, Pulau, i., Indon.	F9	32
Mispillion, stm., De., U.S.	E4	85
Misrātah, Libya	B9	42
Missaukee, co., Mi., U.S.	D5	99
Missaukee, Lake, l., Mi., U.S.	D5	99
Mission, Ks., U.S.	m16	93
Mission, S.D., U.S.	D5	118

Name — Map Ref — Page

Mission, Tx., U.S. F3 120
Mission Range, mts., Mt., U.S. C3 103
Mission Viejo, Ca., U.S. n13 82
Missisquoi, stm., Vt., U.S. B3 122
Missisquoi Bay, b., Vt., U.S. A2 122
Mississauga, Ont., Can. D5 73
Mississinewa, stm., U.S. D7 91
Mississinewa Lake, res., In., U.S. C6 91
Mississippi, co., Ar., U.S. B5 81
Mississippi, co., Mo., U.S. E8 102
Mississippi, state, U.S. C4 101
Mississippi, stm., U.S. E8 76
Mississippi Delta, La., U.S. E6 95
Mississippi Sound, strt., U.S. E5 101
Mississippi State, Ms., U.S. B5 101
Missoula, Mt., U.S. D2 103
Missoula, co., Mt., U.S. D2 103
Missouri, state, U.S. C5 102
Missouri, stm., U.S. C7 76
Missouri City, Tx., U.S. r14 120
Missouri Valley, Ia., U.S. C2 92
Mistassini, Que., Can. h12 74
Mistassini, Lac, l., Que., Can. h12 74
Misti, Volcán, vol., Peru G4 54
Mistretta, Italy L9 14
Mita, Punta de, c., Mex. G7 62
Mitchell, Austl. E9 50
Mitchell, Ont., Can. D3 73
Mitchell, Il., U.S. E3 90
Mitchell, In., U.S. G5 91
Mitchell, Ne., U.S. C2 104
Mitchell, S.D., U.S. D7 118
Mitchell, co., Ga., U.S. E2 87
Mitchell, co., Ia., U.S. A5 92
Mitchell, co., Ks., U.S. C5 93
Mitchell, co., N.C., U.S. e10 110
Mitchell, co., Tx., U.S. C2 120
Mitchell, stm., Austl. C8 50
Mitchell, Lake, l., Mi., U.S. D5 99
Mitchell, Lake, res., Al., U.S. C3 78
Mitchell, Mount, mtn., N.C., U.S. f10 110
Mitchell Island, i., La., U.S. E6 95
Mitchellville, Ia., U.S. C4 92
Mitilíni, Grc. J10 16
Mitkof Island, i., Ak., U.S. m23 79
Mito, Japan F13 30
Mitsiwa, Erit. E2 46
Mitsuke, Japan E11 30
Mittenwald, Ger. H11 8
Mittweida, Ger. E12 8
Mitú, Col. G7 58
Mitumba, Monts, mts., Zaire C5 44
Mitwaba, Zaire C5 44
Mitzic, Gabon A2 44
Miura, Japan G12 30
Mixian, China A2 28
Miyako, Japan C14 30
Miyako-jima, i., Japan G12 26
Miyakonojō, Japan K4 30
Miyazaki, Japan K4 30
Miyoshi, Japan H5 30
Miyun, China C10 26
Mizdah, Libya B8 42
Mizen Head, c., Ire. J3 7
Mizoram, ter., India I15 38
Mizpe Ramon, Isr. D4 40
Mizque, Bol. G5 54
Mjölby, Swe. G10 6
Mjøsa, l., Nor. F8 6
Mkalama, Tan. B6 44
Mladá Boleslav, Czech. E14 8
Mława, Pol. B20 8
Mo, Nor. C10 6
Moab, Ut., U.S. E6 121
Moanda, Gabon B2 44
Moapa River Indian Reservation, Nv., U.S. G7 105
Moate, Ire. H5 7
Mobara, Japan G13 30
Mobaye, Cen. Afr. Rep. H10 42
Moberly, Mo., U.S. B5 102
Mobile, Al., U.S. E1 78
Mobile, co., Al., U.S. E1 78
Mobile, stm., Al., U.S. E1 78
Mobile Bay, b., Al., U.S. E1 83
Mobridge, S.D., U.S. B5 118
Moçambique, Moz. E8 44
Mocanaqua, Pa., U.S. D9 115
Mocha, Isla, i., Chile D2 56
Mochudi, Bots. F5 44
Mocksville, N.C., U.S. B2 110
Moclips, Wa., U.S. B1 124
Môco, Serra do, mtn., Ang. D3 44
Mocoa, Col. G4 58
Mococa, Braz. F5 57
Moctezuma, Mex. C5 62
Mocuba, Moz. E7 44
Modane, Fr. G13 10
Model Reservoir, res., Co., U.S. D6 83
Modena, Italy E5 14
Modesto, Ca., U.S. D3 82
Modica, Italy M9 14
Mödling, Aus. G16 8
Modoc, co., Ca., U.S. B3 82
Modowi, Indon. F9 32
Moengo, Sur. B8 54
Moenkopi, Az., U.S. A4 80
Moffat, Scot., U.K. F9 7
Moffat, co., Co., U.S. A2 83
Moffat Tunnel, Co., U.S. B5 83
Moffett Field Naval Air Station, mil., Ca., U.S. k8 82
Moga, India E6 38
Mogadisho see Muqdisho, Som. H4 46
Mogadore, Oh., U.S. A4 112
Mogadouro, Port. D5 12
Mogaung, Mya. B4 34
Mogi das Cruzes, Braz. G5 57
Mogil'ov, Bela. H13 18
Mogi-Mirim, Braz. G5 57
Mogincual, Moz. E8 44
Mogoča, Russia G17 24
Mogočin, Russia F10 24
Mogok, Mya. C4 34
Mogollon Mountains, mts., N.M., U.S. D1 108
Mogollon Rim, clf, Az., U.S. C5 80
Mogotón, Pico, mtn., N.A. H4 64
Mohall, N.D., U.S. A4 111
Mohave, co., Az., U.S. B1 80
Mohave, Lake, res., U.S. H7 105
Mohave Mountains, mts., Az., U.S. C1 80
Mohave Valley, Az., U.S. C1 80
Mohawk, N.Y., U.S. C5 109
Mohawk, stm., N.H., U.S. g7 106
Mohawk, stm., N.Y., U.S. C6 109
Mohawk Lake, l., N.J., U.S. A3 107
Mohawk Mountains, mts., Az., U.S. E2 80
Moheli, i., Com. D8 44
Mohican, stm., Oh., U.S. B3 112
Mohinora, Cerro, mtn., Mex. D6 62
Mohnton, Pa., U.S. F10 115
Moi, Nor. G6 6
Moisie, Que., Can. h8 72
Moisie, stm., Que., Can. F19 66
Moissac, Fr. H8 10
Mojave, Ca., U.S. E4 82
Mojave, stm., Ca., U.S. E5 82
Mojave Desert, des., Ca., U.S. E5 82
Mojjero, stm., Russia D14 24
Mojo, Eth. G2 46
Mokapu Peninsula, pen., Hi., U.S. g10 88
Mokapu Point, c., Hi., U.S. g11 88
Mokelumne, stm., Ca., U.S. C3 82
Mokena, Il., U.S. k9 90
Mokp'o, S. Kor. E12 26
Moku Manu, i., Hi., U.S. g11 88
Mol, Bel. D5 8
Molalla, Or., U.S. B4 114
Moldau see Vltava, stm., Czech. F14 8
Moldavia see Moldova, ctry., Eur. H3 22
Molde, Nor. E6 6
Moldova, ctry., Eur. H3 22
Molepolole, Bots. F5 44
Molfetta, Italy H11 14
Molina de Aragón, Spain E10 12
Molina de Segura, Spain G10 12
Moline, Il., U.S. B3 90
Moline, Mi., U.S. F5 99
Molino, Fl., U.S. u14 86
Molins de Rey, Spain D14 12
Mollendo, Peru G4 54
Mölln, Ger. B10 8
Mölndal, Swe. H9 6
Molodečno, Bela. G9 18
Molokai, i., Hi., U.S. B5 88
Molokini, i., Hi., U.S. C5 88
Molson Lake, l., Man., Can. B3 70
Molucca Sea see Maluku, Laut, Indon. F7 32
Moluccas see Maluku, is., Indon. F8 32
Moma, Moz. E7 44
Moma, stm., Russia D22 24
Mombasa, Kenya B7 44
Mombetsu, Japan o21 30a
Momence, Il., U.S. B6 90
Momotombo, Volcán, vol., Nic. H4 64
Mon, stm., Mya. D3 34
Mona, Canal de la, strt., N.A. E14 64
Mona, Isla, i., P.R. E14 64
Monaca, Pa., U.S. E1 115
Monaco, ctry., Eur. G9 4
Monadhliath Mountains, mts., Scot., U.K. D8 7
Monadnock, Mount, mtn., N.H., U.S. E2 106
Monadnock Mountain, mtn., Vt., U.S. B5 122
Monahans, Tx., U.S. D1 120
Monarch Mills, S.C., U.S. B4 117
Monarch Pass, Co., U.S. C4 83
Monashee Mountains, mts., B.C., Can. D8 69
Monastir, Tun. N5 14
Moncalieri, Italy D2 14
Monção, Braz. D9 54
Mönchengladbach, Ger. D6 8
Monchique, Port. H3 12
Moncks Corner, S.C., U.S. E7 117
Monclova, Mex. D9 62
Moncton, N.B., Can. C5 71
Mondoñedo, Spain B4 12
Mondovì, Italy E2 14
Mondovi, Wi., U.S. D2 126
Mondragone, Italy H8 14
Monee, Il., U.S. B6 90
Monessen, Pa., U.S. F2 115
Monett, Mo., U.S. E4 102
Monette, Ar., U.S. B5 81
Monfalcone, Italy D8 14
Monforte de Lemos, Spain C4 12
Monfort Heights, Oh., U.S. *o12 112
Mong Cai, Viet. D9 34
Möng Hsat, Mya. D5 34
Monghyr, India H12 38
Mongo, Chad F9 42
Mongol Altajn Nuruu, mts., Asia B5 26
Mongolia, ctry., Asia B7 26
Mongu, Zam. E4 44
Monhegan Island, i., Me., U.S. E3 96
Monida Pass, U.S. E6 89
Moniteau, co., Mo., U.S. C5 102
Monitor Range, mts., Nv., U.S. E5 105
Monitor Valley, val., Nv., U.S. D5 105
Monmouth, Il., U.S. C3 90
Monmouth, Or., U.S. C3 114
Monmouth, co., N.J., U.S. C4 107
Monmouth Beach, N.J., U.S. C5 107
Monmouth Mountain, mtn., B.C., Can. D6 69
Mono, co., Ca., U.S. D4 82
Monocacy, stm., Md., U.S. B3 97
Mono Lake, l., Ca., U.S. D4 82
Monomonac, Lake, l., U.S. E3 106
Monomoy Island, i., Ma., U.S. C7 98
Monomoy Point, c., Ma., U.S. C7 98
Monon, In., U.S. C4 91
Monona, Ia., U.S. A6 92
Monona, Wi., U.S. E4 126
Monona, co., Ia., U.S. B1 92
Monona, Lake, l., Wi., U.S. E4 126
Monongah, W.V., U.S. B4 125
Monongahela, Pa., U.S. F2 115
Monongahela, stm., U.S. G2 115
Monongalia, co., W.V., U.S. B4 125
Monopoli, Italy I12 14
Monóvar, Spain G11 12
Monreal del Campo, Spain E10 12
Monroe, Ga., U.S. C3 87
Monroe, In., U.S. C8 91
Monroe, Ia., U.S. C4 92
Monroe, La., U.S. B3 95
Monroe, Mi., U.S. G7 99
Monroe, N.Y., U.S. D6 109
Monroe, N.C., U.S. C2 110
Monroe, Oh., U.S. C1 112
Monroe, Ut., U.S. E3 121
Monroe, Wa., U.S. B4 124
Monroe, Wi., U.S. F4 126
Monroe, co., Al., U.S. D2 78
Monroe, co., Ar., U.S. C4 81
Monroe, co., Fl., U.S. G5 86
Monroe, co., Ga., U.S. D3 87
Monroe, co., Il., U.S. E3 90
Monroe, co., In., U.S. F4 91
Monroe, co., Ia., U.S. D5 92
Monroe, co., Ky., U.S. D4 94
Monroe, co., Mi., U.S. G7 99
Monroe, co., Ms., U.S. B5 101
Monroe, co., Mo., U.S. B5 102
Monroe, co., N.Y., U.S. B3 109
Monroe, co., Oh., U.S. C4 112
Monroe, co., Pa., U.S. D11 115
Monroe, co., Tn., U.S. D9 119
Monroe, co., W.V., U.S. D4 125
Monroe, co., Wi., U.S. E3 126
Monroe Center, Ct., U.S. D3 84
Monroe City, Mo., U.S. B6 102
Monroe Lake, res., In., U.S. F5 91
Monroe Park, De., U.S. h7 85
Monroeville, Al., U.S. D2 78
Monroeville, In., U.S. C8 91
Monroeville, Oh., U.S. A3 112
Monroeville, Pa., U.S. k14 115
Monrovia, Lib. G3 42
Monrovia, Ca., U.S. m13 82
Monrovia, In., U.S. E5 91
Mons, Bel. E3 8
Monson, Ma., U.S. B3 98
Montague, P.E.I., Can. C7 71
Montague, Ca., U.S. B2 82
Montague, Mi., U.S. E4 99
Montague, co., Tx., U.S. C4 120
Montague, Isla, i., Mex. B2 62
Montague Island, i., Ak., U.S. D10 79
Montague Peak, mtn., Ak., U.S. g18 79
Montague Strait, strt., Ak., U.S. h18 79
Montaigu, Fr. F5 10
Montalbán, Spain E11 12
Montalcino, Italy F6 14
Montalegre, Port. D4 12
Mont Alto, Pa., U.S. G6 115
Montana, state, U.S. D7 103
Montánchez, Spain F5 12
Montargis, Fr. D9 10
Montauban, Fr. H8 10
Montauk, N.Y., U.S. m17 109
Montbard, Fr. E11 10
Montbéliard, Fr. E13 10
Mont Belvieu, Tx., U.S. E5 120
Montblanch, Spain D13 12
Montbrison, Fr. G11 10
Montcalm, co., Mi., U.S. E5 99
Montchanin, De., U.S. h7 85
Montclair, Ca., U.S. m13 82
Montclair, N.J., U.S. B4 107
Mont Clare, Pa., U.S. o19 115
Mont-de-Marsan, Fr. I6 10
Montdidier, Fr. C9 10
Monteagle, Tn., U.S. D8 119
Monteagudo, Bol. G6 54
Monte Azul, Braz. C7 57
Montebello, Que., Can. D3 74
Montebello, Ca., U.S. m12 82
Monte Caseros, Arg. C5 56
Montecatini Terme, Italy F5 14
Monte Comán, Arg. C3 56
Montecristi, Dom. Rep. E12 64
Montecristi, Ec. H2 58
Montefiascone, Italy G7 14
Montego Bay, Jam. E9 64
Montegut, La., U.S. E5 95
Montélimar, Fr. H11 10
Montello, Nv., U.S. B7 105
Montello, Wi., U.S. E4 126
Montemorelos, Mex. E10 62
Montemor-o-Novo, Port. G3 12
Montendre, Fr. G6 10
Montenero di Bisaccia, Italy H9 14
Montepuez, Moz. D8 44
Montepulciano, Italy F6 14
Monte Quemado, Arg. B4 56
Montereau-faut-Yonne, Fr. D9 10
Monterey, Ca., U.S. D3 82
Monterey, Tn., U.S. C8 119
Monterey, co., Ca., U.S. D3 82
Monterey Bay, b., Ca., U.S. D2 82
Monterey Park, Ca., U.S. m12 82
Montería, Col. C5 58
Monterotondo, Italy G7 14
Monterrey, Mex. E9 62
Montesano, Wa., U.S. C2 124
Monte Sant'Angelo, Italy H10 14
Montes Claros, Braz. D7 57
Montevallo, Al., U.S. B3 78
Montevarchi, Italy F6 14
Montevideo, Mn., U.S. F3 100
Montevideo, Ur. C5 56
Monte Vista, Co., U.S. D4 83
Montezuma, Ga., U.S. D2 87
Montezuma, In., U.S. E3 91
Montezuma, Ia., U.S. C5 92
Montezuma, Ks., U.S. E3 93
Montezuma, co., Co., U.S. D2 83
Montezuma Castle National Monument, Az., U.S. C4 80
Montezuma Peak, mtn., Az., U.S. D3 80
Montgomery, Al., U.S. C3 78
Montgomery, Il., U.S. B5 90
Montgomery, La., U.S. C3 95
Montgomery, Mn., U.S. F5 100
Montgomery, N.Y., U.S. D6 109
Montgomery, Oh., U.S. o13 112
Montgomery, Pa., U.S. D8 115
Montgomery, W.V., U.S. C3 125
Montgomery, co., Al., U.S. C3 78
Montgomery, co., Ar., U.S. C2 81
Montgomery, co., Ga., U.S. D4 87
Montgomery, co., Il., U.S. D4 90
Montgomery, co., In., U.S. D4 91
Montgomery, co., Ia., U.S. C2 92
Montgomery, co., Ks., U.S. E8 93
Montgomery, co., Ky., U.S. B6 94
Montgomery, co., Md., U.S. B3 97
Montgomery, co., Ms., U.S. B4 101
Montgomery, co., Mo., U.S. C6 102
Montgomery, co., N.Y., U.S. C6 109
Montgomery, co., N.C., U.S. B3 110
Montgomery, co., Oh., U.S. C1 112
Montgomery, co., Pa., U.S. F11 115
Montgomery, co., Tn., U.S. A4 119
Montgomery, co., Tx., U.S. D5 120
Montgomery, co., Va., U.S. C2 123
Montgomery City, Mo., U.S. C6 102
Monthey, Switz. F13 10
Monticello, Ar., U.S. D4 81
Monticello, Fl., U.S. B3 86
Monticello, Ga., U.S. C3 87
Monticello, Il., U.S. C5 90
Monticello, In., U.S. C4 91
Monticello, Ia., U.S. B6 92
Monticello, Ky., U.S. D5 94
Monticello, Mn., U.S. E5 100
Monticello, Ms., U.S. D3 101
Monticello, N.Y., U.S. D6 109
Monticello, Ut., U.S. F6 121
Monticello, Wi., U.S. F4 126
Montichiari, Italy D5 14
Montignac, Fr. G8 10
Montijo, Port. G3 12
Montijo, Spain G5 12
Montilla, Spain H7 12
Montivilliers, Fr. C7 10
Mont-Joli, Que., Can. A9 74
Mont-Laurier, Que., Can. C2 74
Mont-Louis, Fr. J9 10
Montluçon, Fr. F9 10
Montmagny, Que., Can. C7 74
Montmorenci, S.C., U.S. D4 117
Montmorency, co., Mi., U.S. C6 99
Montmorillon, Fr. F7 10
Montmort, Fr. D10 10
Montoro, Spain G7 12
Montour, co., Pa., U.S. D8 115
Montour Falls, N.Y., U.S. C4 109
Montoursville, Pa., U.S. D8 115
Montpelier, Id., U.S. G7 89
Montpelier, In., U.S. C7 91
Montpelier, Oh., U.S. A1 112
Montpelier, Vt., U.S. C3 122
Montpellier, Fr. I10 10
Montréal, Que., Can. D4 74
Montreal, Wi., U.S. B3 126
Montréal, Île de, i., Que., Can. q19 74
Montreal Lake, l., Sask., Can. C3 75
Montréal-Nord, Que., Can. p19 74
Montreat, N.C., U.S. f10 110
Montreuil-Bellay, Fr. E6 10
Montreux, Switz. F13 10
Mont-Rolland, Que., Can. D3 74
Montrose, B.C., Can. E9 69
Montrose, Scot., U.K. E10 7
Montrose, Al., U.S. E2 78
Montrose, Co., U.S. C3 83
Montrose, Ia., U.S. D6 92
Montrose, Mi., U.S. E7 99
Montrose, Pa., U.S. C10 115
Montrose, Va., U.S. m18 123
Montrose, co., Co., U.S. C2 83
Mont-Royal, Que., Can. p19 74
Montserrat, dep., N.A. F16 64
Mont-Tremblant, Parc Provincial du, Que., Can. C3 74
Montvale, N.J., U.S. A4 107
Montville, Ct., U.S. D7 84
Monument, Co., U.S. B6 83
Monument Beach, Ma., U.S. C6 98
Monument Peak, mtn., Co., U.S. B3 83
Monument Peak, mtn., Id., U.S. G4 89
Monument Valley, val., Az., U.S. A5 80
Monywa, Mya. C3 34
Monza, Italy D4 14
Monzón, Spain D12 12
Moodus, Ct., U.S. D6 84
Moodus Reservoir, res., Ct., U.S. C6 84
Moody, Tx., U.S. D4 120
Moody, co., S.D., U.S. C9 118
Moon Lake, l., Ms., U.S. A3 101
Moora, Austl. F3 50
Moorcroft, Wy., U.S. B8 127
Moore, Ok., U.S. B4 113
Moore, co., N.C., U.S. B3 110
Moore, co., Tn., U.S. B5 119
Moore, co., Tx., U.S. B2 120
Moore Dam, U.S. B3 106
Moorefield, W.V., U.S. B6 125
Moore Haven, Fl., U.S. F5 86
Mooreland, Ok., U.S. A2 113
Moore Reservoir, res., U.S. B3 106
Moores Creek National Military Park, N.C., U.S. C4 110
Moores Hill, In., U.S. F7 91
Moorestown, N.J., U.S. D3 107
Mooresville, In., U.S. E5 91
Mooresville, N.C., U.S. B2 110
Moorhead, Mn., U.S. D2 100
Moorhead, Ms., U.S. B3 101
Mooringsport, La., U.S. B2 95
Moose, stm., N.H., U.S. B4 106
Moose, stm., N.Y., U.S. B5 109
Moose, stm., Vt., U.S. B5 122
Moosehead Lake, l., Me., U.S. C3 96
Moose Jaw, stm., Sask., Can. G3 75
Moose Lake, Man., Can. C1 70
Moose Lake, Mn., U.S. D6 100
Moose Lake, l., Wi., U.S. B2 126
Mooseleuk Stream, stm., Me., U.S. B4 96
Mooselookmeguntic Lake, l., Me., U.S. D2 96
Moose Mountain Creek, stm., Sask., Can. H4 75
Moose Mountain Provincial Park, Sask., Can. H4 75
Moosic, Pa., U.S. m18 115
Moosup, Ct., U.S. C8 84
Moosup, stm., U.S. C1 116
Mopang Lake, l., Me., U.S. D5 96
Mopti, Mali F5 42
Moquegua, Peru G4 54
Mora, Port. G3 12
Mora, Spain F8 12
Mora, Swe. F10 6
Mora, Mn., U.S. E5 100
Mora, N.M., U.S. B4 108
Mora, co., N.M., U.S. A5 108
Mora, stm., N.M., U.S. B5 108
Morādābād, India F8 38
Morada Nova de Minas, Braz. E6 57
Morafenobe, Madag. E8 44
Moraleda, Canal, strt., Chile E2 56
Morant Cays, is., Jam. F9 64
Mor'arovskij Zaton, Russia F10 24
Moratuwa, Sri L. I5 37
Morava, hist. reg., Czech. F17 8
Morava (March), stm., Eur. G16 8
Moravia, Ia., U.S. D5 92
Moravia see Morava, hist. reg., Czech. F17 8
Morawhanna, Guy. C13 58
Moray Firth, est., Scot., U.K. D9 7
Morden, Man., Can. E2 70
More, Ben, mtn., Scot., U.K. E8 7
More Assynt, Ben, mtn., Scot., U.K. C8 7
Moreau, stm., S.D., U.S. B3 118
Moreauville, La., U.S. C4 95
Morecambe, Eng., U.K. G10 7
Moree, Austl. E9 50
Morehead, Ky., U.S. B6 94
Morehead City, N.C., U.S. C6 110
Morehouse, Mo., U.S. E8 102
Morehouse, co., La., U.S. B4 95
Morelia, Mex. H9 62
Morella, Spain E11 12
Morena, India G8 38
Morenci, Az., U.S. D6 80
Morenci, Mi., U.S. G6 99
Moresby Island, i., B.C., Can. C2 69
Moreuil, Fr. C9 10
Morey, Lake, l., Vt., U.S. D4 122
Morey Peak, mtn., Nv., U.S. E5 105
Morgan, Mn., U.S. F4 100
Morgan, Ut., U.S. B4 121
Morgan, co., Al., U.S. A3 78
Morgan, co., Co., U.S. A7 83
Morgan, co., Ga., U.S. C3 87
Morgan, co., Il., U.S. D3 90
Morgan, co., In., U.S. F5 91
Morgan, co., Ky., U.S. C6 94
Morgan, co., Mo., U.S. C5 102
Morgan, co., Oh., U.S. C4 112
Morgan, co., Tn., U.S. C9 119
Morgan, co., Ut., U.S. B4 121
Morgan, co., W.V., U.S. B6 125
Morgan City, La., U.S. E4 95
Morganfield, Ky., U.S. C2 94
Morgan Hill, Ca., U.S. D3 82
Morgan Island, i., S.C., U.S. G6 117
Morgan Point, c., Ct., U.S. E4 84
Morganton, N.C., U.S. B1 110
Morgantown, In., U.S. F5 91
Morgantown, Ky., U.S. C3 94
Morgantown, Ms., U.S. D2 101
Morgantown, Tn., U.S. D8 119
Morgantown, W.V., U.S. B5 125
Morganza, La., U.S. D4 95
Mori, Japan q18 30a
Moriah, Mount, mtn., Nv., U.S. D7 105
Moriarty, N.M., U.S. C3 108
Morinville, Alta., Can. C4 68
Morioka, Japan C14 30
Morkoka, stm., Russia D16 24
Morlaix, Fr. D3 10
Morley, Mo., U.S. D8 102
Mormon Peak, mtn., Nv., U.S. G7 105
Morning Sun, Ia., U.S. C6 92
Mornington Island, i., Austl. C7 50
Morobe, Pap. N. Gui. m16 50a
Morocco, In., U.S. C3 91
Morocco, ctry., Afr. B4 42
Morogoro, Tan. C7 44
Moro Gulf, b., Phil. D7 32
Morombe, Madag. F8 44
Morón, Cuba C8 64
Morondava, Madag. F8 44
Morón de la Frontera, Spain H6 12
Moroni, Com. D8 44
Moroni, Ut., U.S. D4 121
Morošečnoje, Russia F25 24
Morotai, i., Indon. E8 32
Morrill, Ne., U.S. C2 104
Morrill, co., Ne., U.S. C2 104
Morrilton, Ar., U.S. B3 81
Morrinhos, Braz. D4 57
Morris, Man., Can. E3 70
Morris, Al., U.S. B3 78
Morris, Il., U.S. B5 90
Morris, Mn., U.S. E3 100
Morris, Ok., U.S. B6 113
Morris, co., Ks., U.S. D7 93
Morris, co., N.J., U.S. B3 107
Morris, co., Tx., U.S. C5 120
Morrisburg, Ont., Can. C9 73
Morris Island, i., S.C., U.S. F8 117

Name — Map Ref — Page

Morrison, Il., U.S. B4 90
Morrison, Ok., U.S. A4 113
Morrison, co., Mn., U.S. D4 100
Morrison City, Tn., U.S. C11 119
Morrisonville, Il., U.S. D4 90
Morrisonville, N.Y., U.S. f11 109
Morris Plains, N.J., U.S. B4 107
Morristown, In., U.S. E6 91
Morristown, Mn., U.S. F5 100
Morristown, N.J., U.S. B4 107
Morristown, Tn., U.S. C10 119
Morristown National Historical Park, N.J., U.S. B3 107
Morrisville, N.Y., U.S. C5 109
Morrisville, Pa., U.S. F12 115
Morrisville, Vt., U.S. B3 122
Morro, Ec. I2 58
Morro, Punta, c., Chile B2 56
Morro Bay, Ca., U.S. E3 82
Morro do Chapéu, Braz. F10 54
Morrow, Ga., U.S. C2 87
Morrow, Oh., U.S. C1 112
Morrow, co., Oh., U.S. B3 112
Morrow, co., Or., U.S. B7 114
Moršansk, Russia H24 18
Morse, La., U.S. D3 95
Morse Reservoir, res., In., U.S. D5 91
Morses Creek, stm., N.J., U.S. k8 107
Mortagne, Fr. D7 10
Mortagne-sur-Sèvre, Fr. E6 10
Mortara, Italy D3 14
Mortes, Rio das, stm., Braz. G8 54
Morton, Il., U.S. C4 90
Morton, Ms., U.S. C4 101
Morton, Tx., U.S. C1 120
Morton, Wa., U.S. C3 124
Morton, co., Ks., U.S. E2 93
Morton, co., N.D., U.S. C4 111
Morton Grove, Il., U.S. h9 90
Morton Pass, Wy., U.S. E7 127
Mortons Gap, Ky., U.S. C2 94
Morven, mtn., Scot., U.K. C9 7
Morvi, India I4 38
Morwell, Austl. G9 50
Mosbach, Ger. F9 8
Moscos Islands, is., Mya. G4 34
Moscow, Id., U.S. C2 89
Moscow, Pa., U.S. m18 115
Moscow Mills, Mo., U.S. C7 102
Moscow see Moskva, Russia F20 18
Mosel (Moselle), stm., Eur. F6 8
Moselle, Ms., U.S. D4 101
Moselle (Mosel), stm., Eur. F6 8
Moses Coulee, val., Wa., U.S. B6 124
Moses Lake, Wa., U.S. B6 124
Moses Lake, l., Wa., U.S. B6 124
Mosheim, Tn., U.S. C11 119
Moshi, Tan. B7 44
Mosinee, Wi., U.S. D4 126
Mosjøen, Nor. D9 6
Moskva (Moscow), Russia F20 18
Mosquera, Col. F3 58
Mosquito Creek Lake, res., Oh., U.S. A5 112
Mosquito Lagoon, b., Fl., U.S. D6 86
Mosquitos, Golfo de los, b., Pan. J7 64
Moss, Nor. G8 6
Mossaka, Congo B3 44
Moss Bluff, La., U.S. D2 95
Mosselbaai, S. Afr. H4 44
Mossendjo, Congo B2 44
Mossoró, Braz. E11 54
Moss Point, Ms., U.S. E5 101
Most, Czech. E13 8
Mostaganem, Alg. A6 42
Mostar, Bos. F12 14
Mostardas, Braz. C6 56
Møsting, Kap, c., Grnld. D24 66
Moswansicut Pond, l., R.I., U.S. C3 116
Mota del Marqués, Spain D6 12
Motala, Swe. G10 6
Motherwell, Scot., U.K. F8 7
Motīhāri, India G11 38
Motilla del Palancar, Spain F10 12
Motley, co., Tx., U.S. B2 120
Motril, Spain I8 12
Mott, N.D., U.S. C3 111
Motueka, N.Z. D4 52
Motul de Felipe Carrillo Puerto, Mex. G15 62
Motygino, Russia F12 24
Mouchoir Passage, strt., N.A. D12 64
Moudjéria, Maur. E3 42
Mouila, Gabon B2 44
Moulamein Creek, stm., Austl. G8 50
Moulins, Fr. F10 10
Moulmeingyun, Mya. F3 34
Moulouya, Oued, stm., Mor. B5 42
Moulton, Al., U.S. A2 78
Moulton, Ia., U.S. D5 92
Moultrie, Ga., U.S. E3 87
Moultrie, co., Il., U.S. D5 90
Moultrie, Lake, res., S.C., U.S. E7 117
Mound, Mn., U.S. n11 100
Mound Bayou, Ms., U.S. B3 101
Mound City, Il., U.S. F4 90
Mound City, Ks., U.S. D9 93
Mound City, Mo., U.S. A2 102
Mound City Group National Monument, Oh., U.S. C2 112
Moundou, Chad G9 42
Moundridge, Ks., U.S. D6 93
Mounds, Il., U.S. F4 90
Mounds, Ok., U.S. B5 113
Mounds View, Mn., U.S. m12 100
Moundsville, W.V., U.S. B4 125
Moundville, Al., U.S. C2 78
Mountainair, N.M., U.S. C3 108
Mountainaire, Az., U.S. B4 80
Mountain Brook, Al., U.S. g7 78
Mountain City, Ga., U.S. B3 87
Mountain City, Nv., U.S. B6 105
Mountain City, Tn., U.S. C12 119
Mountain Fork, stm., U.S. C7 113
Mountain Grove, Mo., U.S. D5 102
Mountain Home, Ar., U.S. A3 81
Mountain Home, Id., U.S. F3 89
Mountain Home Air Force Base, mil., Id., U.S. F3 89
Mountain Iron, Mn., U.S. C6 100
Mountain Lake, Mn., U.S. G4 100
Mountain Lake Park, Md., U.S. m12 97
Mountain Nile (Bahr al-Jabal), stm., Sudan G12 42
Mountain Pine, Ar., U.S. C2 81
Mountainside, N.J., U.S. B4 107
Mountain View, Ar., U.S. B3 81
Mountain View, Ca., U.S. k8 82
Mountain View, Mo., U.S. D6 102
Mountain View, N.M., U.S. C3 108
Mountain View, Ok., U.S. B3 113
Mountain View, Wy., U.S. E2 127
Mountain Village, Ak., U.S. C7 79
Mount Airy, Md., U.S. B3 97
Mount Airy, N.C., U.S. A2 110
Mount Albert, Ont., Can. C5 73
Mount Angel, Or., U.S. B4 114
Mount Arlington, N.J., U.S. B3 107
Mount Ayr, Ia., U.S. D3 92
Mount Carmel, Il., U.S. E6 90
Mount Carmel, Oh., U.S. o13 112
Mount Carmel, Pa., U.S. E9 115
Mount Carmel [-Mitchell's Brook-Saint Catherine's], Newf., Can. E5 72
Mount Carroll, Il., U.S. A4 90
Mount Clare, W.V., U.S. B4 125
Mount Clemens, Mi., U.S. F8 99
Mount Desert Island, i., Me., U.S. D4 96
Mount Dora, Fl., U.S. D5 86
Mount Forest, Ont., Can. D4 73
Mount Gambier, Austl. G8 50
Mount Gay, W.V., U.S. D2 125
Mount Gilead, N.C., U.S. B3 110
Mount Gilead, Oh., U.S. B3 112
Mount Healthy, Oh., U.S. o12 112
Mount Holly, N.J., U.S. D3 107
Mount Holly, N.C., U.S. B1 110
Mount Holly Springs, Pa., U.S. F7 115
Mount Hope, Austl. F7 50
Mount Hope, Ks., U.S. E6 93
Mount Hope, W.V., U.S. D3 125
Mount Hope, stm., Ct., U.S. B7 84
Mount Hope Bay, b., U.S. D6 116
Mount Horeb, Wi., U.S. E4 126
Mount Ida, Ar., U.S. C2 81
Mount Isa, Austl. D7 50
Mount Jackson, Va., U.S. B4 123
Mount Jewett, Pa., U.S. C4 115
Mount Joy, Pa., U.S. F9 115
Mount Juliet, Tn., U.S. A5 119
Mount Kisco, N.Y., U.S. D7 109
Mount Lebanon, Pa., U.S. F1 115
Mount Magnet, Austl. E3 50
Mount Morris, Il., U.S. A4 90
Mount Morris, Mi., U.S. E7 99
Mount Morris, N.Y., U.S. C3 109
Mount Olive, Al., U.S. B3 78
Mount Olive, Il., U.S. D4 90
Mount Olive, Ms., U.S. D4 101
Mount Olive, N.C., U.S. B4 110
Mount Olive, Tn., U.S. n14 119
Mount Orab, Oh., U.S. C2 112
Mount Pearl, Newf., Can. E5 72
Mount Penn, Pa., U.S. F10 115
Mount Pleasant, Ia., U.S. D6 92
Mount Pleasant, Mi., U.S. E6 99
Mount Pleasant, N.C., U.S. B2 110
Mount Pleasant, Pa., U.S. F2 115
Mount Pleasant, S.C., U.S. F8 117
Mount Pleasant, Tn., U.S. B4 119
Mount Pleasant, Tx., U.S. C5 120
Mount Pleasant, Ut., U.S. D4 121
Mount Pocono, Pa., U.S. D11 115
Mount Prospect, Il., U.S. A6 90
Mount Pulaski, Il., U.S. C4 90
Mountrail, co., N.D., U.S. A3 111
Mount Rainier, Md., U.S. f9 97
Mount Rainier National Park, Wa., U.S. C4 124
Mount Revelstoke National Park, B.C., Can. D8 69
Mount Rogers National Recreation Area, Va., U.S. D1 123
Mount Rushmore National Memorial, hist., S.D., U.S. D2 118
Mount Savage, Md., U.S. k13 97
Mount Shasta, Ca., U.S. B2 82
Mount Sterling, Il., U.S. D3 90
Mount Sterling, Ky., U.S. B6 94
Mount Sterling, Oh., U.S. C2 112
Mount Uniacke, N.S., Can. E6 71
Mount Union, Pa., U.S. F6 115
Mount Vernon, Al., U.S. D1 78
Mount Vernon, Ga., U.S. D4 87
Mount Vernon, Il., U.S. E5 90
Mount Vernon, In., U.S. I2 91
Mount Vernon, Ia., U.S. C6 92
Mount Vernon, Ky., U.S. C5 94
Mount Vernon, Mo., U.S. D4 102
Mount Vernon, N.Y., U.S. h13 109
Mount Vernon, Oh., U.S. B3 112
Mount Vernon, Tx., U.S. C5 120
Mount Vernon, Wa., U.S. A3 124
Mount View, R.I., U.S. D4 116
Mount Washington, Ky., U.S. B4 94
Mount Wolf, Pa., U.S. F8 115
Mount Zion, Il., U.S. D5 90
Moura, Braz. D6 54
Moura, Port. G4 12
Mourne Mountains, mts., N. Ire., U.K. G6 7
Moussoro, Chad F9 42
Moutong, Indon. E7 32
Moville, Ia., U.S. B1 92
Moweaqua, Il., U.S. D4 90
Mower, co., Mn., U.S. G6 100
Moxee City, Wa., U.S. C5 124
Moxos, Llanos de, pl., Bol. G6 54
Moyahua, Mex. G8 62
Moyale, Kenya H2 46
Moyen Atlas, mts., Mor. B5 42
Moyeuvre-Grande, Fr. C13 10
Moyock, N.C., U.S. A6 110
Moyu, China B8 38
Možajsk, Russia F19 18
Mozambique, ctry., Afr. E6 44
Mozambique Channel, strt., Afr. E8 44
Mozyr', Bela. G3 22
Mpanda, Tan. C6 44
Mpika, Zam. D6 44
Mrkonjić Grad, Bos. E12 14
Msaken, Tun. N5 14
Mtwara, Tan. D8 44
Muang Khammouan, Laos F8 34
Muang Pakxan, Laos E7 34
Muar, Malay. M7 34
Muaratewe, Indon. F5 32
Muāri, Rās, c., Pak. H2 38
Mücheln, Ger. D11 8
Muchinga Mountains, mts., Zam. D6 44
Muckleshoot Indian Reservation, Wa., U.S. f11 124
Mud, stm., Ky., U.S. C3 94
Mud, stm., Mn., U.S. B3 100
Mud, stm., W.V., U.S. C2 125
Mudanjiang, China C12 26
Mud Creek, stm., Ok., U.S. C4 113
Muddy Boggy Creek, stm., Ok., U.S. C6 113
Muddy Creek, stm., Ut., U.S. E4 121
Muddy Creek, stm., Wy., U.S. E2 127
Muddy Creek, stm., Wy., U.S. E5 127
Muddy Creek, stm., Wy., U.S. D6 127
Muddy Creek, stm., Wy., U.S. C4 127
Muddy Mountains, mts., Nv., U.S. G7 105
Muddy Peak, mtn., Nv., U.S. G7 105
Mud Lake, l., Me., U.S. A4 96
Mud Lake, l., Nv., U.S. F4 105
Mudon, Mya. F4 34
Muenster, Tx., U.S. C4 120
Mufulira, Zam. D5 44
Mu Gia, Deo (Mu Gia Pass), Asia F8 34
Muğla, Tur. H13 4
Mühldorf, Ger. G12 8
Muhlenberg, co., Ky., U.S. C2 94
Mühlhausen, Ger. D10 8
Mühlviertel, reg., Aus. G14 8
Muhola, Fin. E15 6
Muirkirk, Md., U.S. B4 97
Muiron Islands, is., Austl. D2 50
Muir Woods National Monument, Ca., U.S. h7 82
Mukden see Shenyang, China C11 26
Mukilteo, Wa., U.S. B3 124
Mukwonago, Wi., U.S. F5 126
Mula, Spain G10 12
Mulanje, Mwi. E7 44
Mulberry, Ar., U.S. B1 81
Mulberry, Fl., U.S. E4 86
Mulberry, In., U.S. D4 91
Mulberry, N.C., U.S. A1 110
Mulberry, stm., Ar., U.S. B1 81
Mulberry Fork, stm., Al., U.S. B3 78
Muldraugh, Ky., U.S. C4 94
Muldrow, Ok., U.S. B7 113
Muleshoe, Tx., U.S. B1 120
Mulgrave, N.S., Can. D8 71
Mulhacén, mtn., Spain H8 12
Mulhouse, Fr. E14 10
Mull, Island of, i., Scot., U.K. E6 7
Mullan, Id., U.S. B3 89
Mullan Pass, Mt., U.S. D4 103
Mullens, W.V., U.S. D3 125
Muller, Pegunungan, mts., Indon. E5 32
Mullet Key, i., Fl., U.S. p10 86
Mullett Lake, l., Mi., U.S. C6 99
Mullewa, Austl. E3 50
Mullica, stm., N.J., U.S. D3 107
Mullins, S.C., U.S. C9 117
Multān, Pak. E4 38
Multnomah, co., Or., U.S. B4 114
Mulvane, Ks., U.S. E6 93
Mumbwa, Zam. D5 44
Mummy Range, mts., Co., U.S. A5 83
Muna, Pulau, i., Indon. F7 32
Muncar, Indon. n17 33a
München (Munich), Ger. G11 8
Muncie, In., U.S. D7 91
Muncy, Pa., U.S. D8 115
Munday, Tx., U.S. C3 120
Mundelein, Il., U.S. A5 90
Münden, Ger. D9 8
Munford, Al., U.S. B4 78
Munford, Tn., U.S. B2 119
Munfordville, Ky., U.S. C4 94
Mungbere, Zaire H11 42
Munhall, Pa., U.S. k14 115
Munhango, Ang. D3 44
Munich see München, Ger. G11 8
Munising, Mi., U.S. B4 99
Munster, Ger. C10 8
Münster, Ger. D7 8
Munster, In., U.S. A2 91
Munster, hist. reg., Ire. I4 7
Munsungan Lake, l., Me., U.S. B3 96
Munuscong Lake, l., Mi., U.S. B6 99
Muong Sing, Laos D6 34
Muqayshit, i., U.A.E. D5 46
Muqdisho, Som. H4 46
Mur (Mura), stm., Eur. I15 8
Mura (Mur), stm., Eur. I16 8
Murat, Fr. G9 10
Murat, stm., Tur. H16 4
Murau, Aus. H14 8
Muravera, Italy J4 14
Murça, Port. D4 12
Murchison, stm., Austl. E3 50
Murcia, Spain H10 12
Murderkill, stm., De., U.S. D4 85
Murdo, S.D., U.S. D5 118
Mureș (Maros), stm., Eur. C5 16
Muret, Fr. I8 10
Murfreesboro, Ar., U.S. C2 81
Murfreesboro, N.C., U.S. A5 110
Murfreesboro, Tn., U.S. B5 119
Mūrīān, Hāmūn-e, l., Iran C6 46
Murmansk, Russia D4 22
Murom, Russia F25 18
Muroran, Japan q18 30a
Muros, Spain C2 12
Muroto, Japan I7 30
Muroto-zaki, c., Japan I7 30
Murphy, Mo., U.S. g13 102
Murphy, N.C., U.S. f8 110
Murphy Island, i., S.C., U.S. E9 117
Murphysboro, Il., U.S. F4 90
Murray, Ia., U.S. C4 92
Murray, Ky., U.S. f9 94
Murray, Ut., U.S. C4 121
Murray, co., Ga., U.S. B2 87
Murray, co., Mn., U.S. F3 100
Murray, co., Ok., U.S. C4 113
Murray, stm., Austl. F7 50
Murray, Lake, res., Ok., U.S. C4 113
Murray, Lake, res., S.C., U.S. C5 117
Murray Head, c., P.E.I., Can. C7 71
Murraysburg, S. Afr. H4 44
Murrayville, Ga., U.S. B3 87
Murrells Inlet, S.C., U.S. D9 117
Murrells Inlet, b., S.C., U.S. D10 117
Murten, Switz. F14 10
Murukta, Russia D14 24
Murwāra, India I9 38
Murwillumbah, Austl. E10 50
Mürzzuschlag, Aus. H15 8
Muş, Tur. H16 4
Musay'īd, Qatar D5 46
Muscat and Oman see Oman, ctry., Asia D6 46
Muscatatuck, stm., In., U.S. G5 91
Muscatine, Ia., U.S. C6 92
Muscatine, co., Ia., U.S. C6 92
Muscat see Masqaṭ, Oman D6 46
Mus-Chaja, Gora, mtn., Russia E22 24
Muscle Shoals, Al., U.S. A2 78
Musclow, Mount, mtn., B.C., Can. C4 69
Muscoda, Wi., U.S. E3 126
Muscogee, co., Ga., U.S. D2 87
Musconetcong, stm., N.J., U.S. B4 107
Muscooten Bay, l., Il., U.S. C3 90
Muse, Pa., U.S. F1 115
Musgrave, Austl. B8 50
Musgrave Harbour, Newf., Can. D5 72
Musgrave Ranges, mts., Austl. E6 50
Musgravetown, Newf., Can. D5 72
Mushin, Nig. G6 42
Muskeg Bay, b., Mn., U.S. B3 100
Muskeget Island, i., Ma., U.S. D7 98
Muskego, Wi., U.S. F5 126
Muskego Lake, l., Wi., U.S. n11 126
Muskegon, Mi., U.S. E4 99
Muskegon, co., Mi., U.S. E4 99
Muskegon, stm., Mi., U.S. E4 99
Muskegon Heights, Mi., U.S. E4 99
Muskegon Lake, l., Mi., U.S. E4 99
Muskingum, co., Oh., U.S. B4 112
Muskingum, stm., Oh., U.S. C4 112
Muskogee, Ok., U.S. B6 113
Muskogee, co., Ok., U.S. B6 113
Musoma, Tan. B6 44
Musquacook Lakes, l., Me., U.S. B3 96
Musquodoboit Harbour, N.S., Can. E6 71
Musselshell, co., Mt., U.S. D8 103
Musselshell, stm., Mt., U.S. D9 103
Mussidan, Fr. G7 10
Mussuma, Ang. D4 44
Mustafakemalpaşa, Tur. I12 16
Mustang, Ok., U.S. B4 113
Mustinka, stm., Mn., U.S. E2 100
Mut, Tur. A3 40
Mutare, Zimb. E6 44
Mutoraj, Russia E14 24
Mutsu, Japan A14 30
Mutsu-wan, b., Japan A13 30
Mutton Mountains, mts., Or., U.S. C5 114
Muzaffarābād, Pak. C5 38
Muzaffarnagar, India F7 38
Muzaffarpur, India G11 38
Muzon, Cape, c., Ak., U.S. n23 79
Muztag, mtn., China B9 38
Muztag, mtn., China B12 38
Mvuma, Zimb. E6 44
Mwanza, Tan. B6 44
Mweelrea, mtn., Ire. H3 7
Mweka, Zaire B4 44
Mwenezi, Zimb. F6 44
Mweru, Lake, l., Afr. C5 44
Mwinilunga, Zam. D4 44
Myakka, stm., Fl., U.S. E4 86
Myanaung, Mya. E3 34
Myaungmya, Mya. F3 34
Myerstown, Pa., U.S. F9 115
Myingyan, Mya. D3 34
Myitkyinā, Mya. B4 34
Mykolayiv, Ukr. H4 22
Myllymäki, Fin. E15 6
Mymensingh, Bngl. H14 38
Mynämäki, Fin. F13 6
Myrskylä (Mörskom), Fin. F15 6
Myrtle Beach, S.C., U.S. D10 117
Myrtle Beach Air Force Base, mil., S.C., U.S. D10 117
Myrtle Grove, Fl., U.S. u14 86
Myrtle Point, Or., U.S. D2 114
Mysen, Nor. G8 6
Mysore, India F4 37
Mys Šmidta, Russia D30 24
Mystic, Ct., U.S. D8 84
Mystic Lakes, l., Ma., U.S. g11 98
My Tho, Viet. I9 34
Mytišči, Russia F20 18
Mzimba, Mwi. D6 44
Mzuzu, Mwi. D6 44

N

Naalehu, Hi., U.S. D6 88
Naas, Ire. H6 7
Nabadwīp, India I13 38
Naberežnyje Čelny, Russia F8 22
Nabeul, Tun. M5 14
Nabī Shu'ayb, Jabal an-, mtn., Yemen E3 46
Nabnasset, Ma., U.S. A5 98
Nābulus, W. Bank C4 40
Nacala-Velha, Moz. D8 44
Naches, stm., Wa., U.S. C5 124
Nachingwea, Tan. D7 44
Nachodka, Russia I20 24
Nacimiento, Lake, res., Ca., U.S. E3 82
Naco, Mex. B5 62
Naco, Az., U.S. F6 80
Nacogdoches, Tx., U.S. D5 120
Nacogdoches, co., Tx., U.S. D5 120
Nadiād, India I5 38
Nadym, stm., Russia E8 24
Næstved, Den. I8 6
Naga, Phil. r20 32
Nagahama, Japan G9 30
Nagaland, state, India H16 38
Nagano, Japan F11 30
Nagaoka, Japan E11 30
Nāgappattinam, India G5 37
Nagasaki, Japan J2 30
Nāgaur, India G5 38
Nāgda, India I6 38
Nāgercoil, India H4 37
Nago, Japan y27 31b
Nagornyj, Russia F18 24
Nagoya, Japan G9 30
Nāgpur, India B5 37
Nags Head, N.C., U.S. B7 110
Nagykanizsa, Hung. I16 8
Nagykőrös, Hung. H19 8
Naha, Japan y27 31b
Nahant, Ma., U.S. g12 98
Nahariya, Isr. C4 40
Nahmakanta Lake, l., Me., U.S. C3 96
Nahunta, Ga., U.S. E5 87
Naidong, China F14 38
Nain, Newf., Can. g9 72
Nā'īn, Iran B5 46
Nairn, Scot., U.K. D9 7
Nairobi, Kenya B7 44
Najafābād, Iran B5 46
Nájera, Spain C9 12
Najin, N. Kor. C13 26
Nakaminato, Japan F13 30
Nakatsu, Japan I4 30
Nakatsugawa, Japan G10 30
Nakhon Pathom, Thai. H6 34
Nakhon Phanom, Thai. F8 34
Nakhon Ratchasima, Thai. G7 34
Nakhon Sawan, Thai. G6 34
Nakhon Si Thammarat, Thai. J5 34
Nakina, Ont., Can. o18 73
Naknek, Ak., U.S. D8 79
Naknek Lake, l., Ak., U.S. D8 79
Nakskov, Den. I8 6
Nakuru, Kenya B7 44
Nakusp, B.C., Can. D9 69
Nalchik see Nal'čik, Russia I6 22
Nal'čik, Russia I6 22
Nalgonda, India D5 37
Nālūt, Libya B8 42
Namak, Daryācheh-ye, l., Iran K8 22
Namangan, Uzb. I12 22
Namanock Island, i., N.J., U.S. A3 107
Namapa, Moz. D7 44
Namatanai, Pap. N. Gui. k17 50a
Nambour, Austl. E10 50
Namcha Barwa see Namjagbarwa Feng, mtn., China F16 38
Nam Co, l., China E14 38
Nam Dinh, Viet. D9 34
Namekagon, stm., Wi., U.S. B2 126
Namekagon Lake, l., Wi., U.S. B2 126
Namhkam, Mya. C4 34
Namib Desert, des., Nmb. F2 44
Namibe, Ang. E2 44
Namibia, ctry., Afr. F3 44
Namjagbarwa Feng, mtn., China F16 38
Namlea, Indon. F8 32
Nampa, Id., U.S. F2 89
Namp'o, N. Kor. D12 26
Nampula, Moz. E7 44
Namsos, Nor. D8 6
Namur, Bel. E4 8
Nanaimo, B.C., Can. E5 69
Nanakuli, Hi., U.S. B3 88
Nanao, Japan E9 30
Nance, co., Ne., U.S. C7 104
Nanchang, China G4 28
Nanchong, China E8 26
Nancy, Fr. D13 10
Nanda Devi, mtn., India E8 38
Nānded, India C4 37
Nandurbār, India B3 37
Nandyāl, India E5 37
Nānga Parbat, mtn., Pak. C6 38
Nangqian (Xiangda), China D17 38
Nanjing (Nanking), China C7 28
Nanking see Nanjing, China C7 28
Nankoku, Japan I6 30
Nankou, China C10 26
Nan Ling, mts., China F9 26
Nanning, China C10 34
Nanping, China I7 28
Nansei-shotō (Ryukyu Islands), is., Japan F12 26
Nansemond, stm., Va., U.S. k14 123
Nantes, Fr. E5 10
Nanticoke, Ont., Can. E4 73
Nanticoke, Pa., U.S. D10 115
Nanticoke, stm., U.S. D6 97
Nanton, Alta., Can. D4 68
Nantong, China C9 28
Nant'ou, Tai. L9 28
Nantua, Fr. F12 10
Nantucket, Ma., U.S. D7 98
Nantucket, co., Ma., U.S. D7 98
Nantucket Island, i., Ma., U.S. D7 98
Nantucket Sound, strt., Ma., U.S. C7 98
Nantuxent Point, c., N.J., U.S. E2 107
Nanty Glo, Pa., U.S. F4 115

Name	Map Ref	Page
Nanuet, N.Y., U.S.	g12	109
Nanuque, Braz.	D8	57
Nanxiang, China	D10	28
Nanxiong, China	J3	28
Nanyang, China	B1	28
Naoetsu, Japan	E11	30
Naoma, W.V., U.S.	n13	125
Naomi Peak, mtn., Ut., U.S.	B4	121
Náousa, Grc.	I6	16
Napa, Ca., U.S.	C2	82
Napa, co., Ca., U.S.	C2	82
Napanee, Ont., Can.	C8	73
Napatree Point, c., R.I., U.S.	G1	116
Napavine, Wa., U.S.	C3	124
Naperville, Il., U.S.	B5	90
Napier, N.Z.	C6	52
Napierville, Que., Can.	D4	74
Naples, Fl., U.S.	F5	86
Naples, Tx., U.S.	C5	120
Naples, Ut., U.S.	C6	121
Naples see Napoli, Italy	I9	14
Napo, stm., S.A.	I6	58
Napoleon, N.D., U.S.	C6	111
Napoleon, Oh., U.S.	A1	112
Napoleonville, La., U.S.	E4	95
Napoli (Naples), Italy	I9	14
Nappanee, In., U.S.	B5	91
Nara, Japan	H8	30
Nara, Mali	E4	42
Naracoorte, Austl.	G8	50
Naramata, B.C., Can.	E8	69
Naranja, Fl., U.S.	G6	86
Narasapur, India	D6	37
Narasaraopet, India	D6	37
Narathiwat, Thai.	K6	34
Nārāyanganj, Bngl.	I14	38
Narberth, Pa., U.S.	p20	115
Narbonne, Fr.	I9	10
Nardò, Italy	I13	14
Narew, stm., Eur.	C21	8
Nārīn Ghar, Afg.	B3	38
Narita, Japan	G13	30
Narmada, stm., India	J5	38
Nārnaul, India	F7	38
Narni, Italy	G7	14
Naro-Fominsk, Russia	F19	18
Narragansett, R.I., U.S.	F4	116
Narragansett Bay, b., R.I., U.S.	E5	116
Narraguagus, stm., Me., U.S.	D5	96
Narrows, Va., U.S.	C2	123
Narsimhapur, India	I8	38
Narssag, Grnld.	D23	66
Naruto, Japan	H7	30
Narva, Est.	B11	18
Narvik, Nor.	B11	6
Naselle, Wa., U.S.	C2	124
Nash, Tx., U.S.	C5	120
Nash, co., N.C., U.S.	A4	110
Nashawena Island, i., Ma., U.S.	D6	98
Nash Stream, stm., N.H., U.S.	A4	106
Nashua, Ia., U.S.	B5	92
Nashua, N.H., U.S.	E4	106
Nashua, stm., U.S.	E3	106
Nashville, Ar., U.S.	D2	81
Nashville, Ga., U.S.	E3	87
Nashville, Il., U.S.	E4	90
Nashville, In., U.S.	F5	91
Nashville, Mi., U.S.	F5	99
Nashville, N.C., U.S.	B5	110
Nashville, Tn., U.S.	A5	119
Nashwauk, Mn., U.S.	C5	100
Nāsik, India	C2	37
Nāsir, Sudan	G12	42
Naskaupi, stm., Newf., Can.	g9	72
Nassau, Bah.	B9	64
Nassau, co., Fl., U.S.	B5	86
Nassau, co., N.Y., U.S.	E7	109
Nassau, stm., Fl., U.S.	k8	86
Nassau Sound, b., Fl., U.S.	B5	86
Nasser, Lake, res., Afr.	D12	42
Nässjö, Swe.	H10	6
Nasukoin Mountain, mtn., Mt., U.S.	B2	103
Natal, Braz.	E11	54
Natalbany, La., U.S.	D5	95
Natalia, Tx., U.S.	E3	120
Natashquan, stm., Can.	h9	72
Natchaug, stm., Ct., U.S.	B7	84
Natchez, Ms., U.S.	D2	101
Natchitoches, La., U.S.	C2	95
Natchitoches, co., La., U.S.	C2	95
Nāthdwāra, India	H5	38
Natick, Ma., U.S.	B5	98
National City, Ca., U.S.	F5	82
Natron, Lake, l., Afr.	B7	44
Natrona, co., Wy., U.S.	D5	127
Natrona Heights, Pa., U.S.	E2	115
Nattaung, mtn., Mya.	E4	34
Natuna Besar, i., Indon.	M10	34
Natuna Besar, Kepulauan, is., Indon.	M10	34
Natuna Selatan, Kepulauan, is., Indon.	M10	34
Natural Bridge, Ut., U.S.	F3	121
Natural Bridge, Va., U.S.	C3	123
Natural Bridges National Monument, Ut., U.S.	F6	121
Naturaliste, Cape, c., Austl.	F3	50
Nauen, Ger.	C12	8
Naugatuck, Ct., U.S.	D3	84
Naugatuck, stm., Ct., U.S.	D3	84
Naumburg, Ger.	D11	8
Naushon Island, i., Ma., U.S.	D6	98
Nautilus Park, Ct., U.S.	D7	84
Nauvoo, Il., U.S.	C2	90
Nava del Rey, Spain	D6	12
Navahermosa, Spain	F7	12
Navajo, co., Az., U.S.	B5	80
Navajo Dam, N.M., U.S.	A2	108
Navajo Indian Reservation, U.S.	A4	80
Navajo Mountain, mtn., Ut., U.S.	F5	121
Navajo National Monument, Az., U.S.	A5	80
Navajo Reservoir, res., U.S.	A2	108
Navalcarnero, Spain	E7	12
Navalmoral de la Mata, Spain	F6	12
Navalvillar de Pela, Spain	F6	12
Navan, Ont., Can.	B9	73
Navan, Ire.	H6	7
Navarin, Mys, c., Russia	E29	24
Navarino, Isla, i., Chile	H3	56
Navarre, Oh., U.S.	B4	112
Navarro, co., Tx., U.S.	D4	120
Navasota, Tx., U.S.	D4	120
Navassa Island, i., N.A.	E10	64
Navoi, Uzb.	I11	22
Navojoa, Mex.	D5	62
Navolato, Mex.	E6	62
Navsāri, India	B2	37
Nawābganj, Bngl.	H13	38
Nawābganj, India	G9	38
Nawābshāh, Pak.	G3	38
Nāwah, Afg.	D2	38
Nawalgarh, India	G6	38
Nawiliwili Bay, b., Hi., U.S.	B2	88
Náxos, i., Grc.	L9	16
Nayak, Afg.	C2	38
Naylor, Mo., U.S.	E7	102
Nayoro, Japan	o20	30a
Nazaré, Braz.	B9	57
Nazaré, Port.	F2	12
Nazareth, Pa., U.S.	E11	115
Nazca, Peru	F4	54
Naze, Japan	w29	31b
Nazilli, Tur.	L12	16
Nazko, stm., B.C., Can.	C6	69
Ndélé, Cen. Afr. Rep.	G10	42
N'Djamena (Fort-Lamy), Chad	F9	42
Ndola, Zam.	D5	44
Neagh, Lough, l., N. Ire., U.K.	G6	7
Neah Bay, Wa., U.S.	A1	124
Néa Páfos (Paphos), Cyp.	B3	40
Neápolis, Grc.	M7	16
Near Islands, is., Ak., U.S.	E2	79
Nebo, Mount, mtn., Ut., U.S.	D4	121
Nebraska, state, U.S.	C6	104
Nebraska City, Ne., U.S.	D10	104
Nechako, stm., B.C., Can.	C5	69
Neches, stm., Tx., U.S.	D5	120
Nechí, Col.	C5	58
Neckar, stm., Ger.	F9	8
Necker Island, i., Hi., U.S.	m15	88
Necochea, Arg.	D5	56
Nederland, Co., U.S.	B5	83
Nederland, Tx., U.S.	E6	120
Nedrow, N.Y., U.S.	C4	109
Needham, Ma., U.S.	g11	98
Needle Mountain, mtn., Wy., U.S.	B3	127
Needles, Ca., U.S.	E6	82
Needville, Tx., U.S.	r14	120
Neenah, Wi., U.S.	D5	126
Neepawa, Man., Can.	D2	70
Neffs, Oh., U.S.	B5	112
Neffsville, Pa., U.S.	F9	115
Negage, Ang.	C3	44
Negaunee, Mi., U.S.	B3	99
Negele, Eth.	G2	46
Negev Desert see Hanegev, reg., Isr.	D4	40
Negley, Oh., U.S.	B5	112
Negombo, Sri L.	I5	37
Negra, Punta, c., Peru	E2	54
Negro, stm., Arg.	E4	56
Negro, stm., S.A.	H12	58
Negros, i., Phil.	C7	32
Neguac, N.B., Can.	B4	71
Nehalem, stm., Or., U.S.	A3	114
Nehbandān, Iran	B7	46
Neheim-Hüsten, Ger.	D7	8
Neiba, Bahía de, b., Dom. Rep.	E12	64
Neijiang, China	F8	26
Neill Point, c., Wa., U.S.	f11	124
Neillsville, Wi., U.S.	D3	126
Nei Monggol Zizhiqu (Inner Mongolia), prov., China	C10	26
Neisse (Nysa Łużycka), stm., Eur.	D14	8
Neiva, Col.	F5	58
Neja, Russia	C26	18
Nekemte, Eth.	G2	46
Nekoosa, Wi., U.S.	D4	126
Nelidovo, Russia	E15	18
Neligh, Ne., U.S.	B7	104
Nel'kan, Russia	F21	24
Nellikuppam, India	G5	37
Nellis Air Force Base, mil., Nv., U.S.	G6	105
Nellore, India	E5	37
Nelson, B.C., Can.	E9	69
Nelson, N.Z.	D4	52
Nelson, Ne., U.S.	D7	104
Nelson, co., Ky., U.S.	C4	94
Nelson, co., N.D., U.S.	B7	111
Nelson, co., Va., U.S.	C4	123
Nelson, stm., Man., Can.	A4	70
Nelsonville, Oh., U.S.	C3	112
Néma, Maur.	E4	42
Nemacolin, Pa., U.S.	G2	115
Nemadji, stm., U.S.	B1	126
Nemaha, co., Ks., U.S.	C7	93
Nemaha, co., Ne., U.S.	D10	104
Nemours, Fr.	D9	10
Nemuro, Japan	p23	30a
Nemuro Strait, strt., Asia	o23	30a
Nenagh, Ire.	I4	7
Nenana, Ak., U.S.	C10	79
Neodesha, Ks., U.S.	E8	93
Neoga, Il., U.S.	D5	90
Neola, Ia., U.S.	C2	92
Neola, Ut., U.S.	C5	121
Neopit, Wi., U.S.	D5	126
Neosho, Mo., U.S.	E3	102
Neosho, co., Ks., U.S.	E8	93
Neosho, stm., Ok., U.S.	A6	113
Nepal (Nepāl), ctry., Asia	D5	36
Nepālganj, Nepal	F9	38
Nepaug Reservoir, res., Ct., U.S.	B3	84
Nepean, Ont., Can.	h12	73
Nepewassi Lake, l., Ont., Can.	A4	73
Nephi, Ut., U.S.	D4	121
Nepisiguit, stm., N.B., Can.	B3	71
Nepisiguit Bay, b., N.B., Can.	B4	71
Neponset, stm., Ma., U.S.	h11	98
Neptune, N.J., U.S.	C4	107
Neptune Beach, Fl., U.S.	B5	86
Neptune City, N.J., U.S.	C4	107
Nérac, Fr.	H7	10
Nerastro, Sarīr, des., Libya	D10	42
Nerčinskij Zavod, Russia	G17	24
Nerechta, Russia	D23	18
Neriquinha, Ang.	E4	44
Nerva, Spain	H5	12
Nesbyen, Nor.	F7	6
Nescopeck, Pa., U.S.	D9	115
Neshanic, stm., N.J., U.S.	C3	107
Neshoba, co., Ms., U.S.	C4	101
Neskaupstaður, Ice.	B5	4
Nesna, Nor.	C9	6
Nesowadnehunk, l., Me., U.S.	B3	96
Nesquehoning, Pa., U.S.	E10	115
Ness, co., Ks., U.S.	D4	93
Ness, Loch, l., Scot., U.K.	D8	7
Ness City, Ks., U.S.	D4	93
Néstos (Mesta), stm., Eur.	H8	16
Netanya, Isr.	C4	40
Netcong, N.J., U.S.	B3	107
Netherlands, ctry., Eur.	E9	4
Netherlands Antilles (Nederlandse Antillen), dep., N.A.	H13	64
Netrakona, Bngl.	H14	38
Nettie, W.V., U.S.	C4	125
Nettilling Lake, l., N.W. Ter., Can.	C18	66
Nett Lake, l., Mn., U.S.	B5	100
Nett Lake Indian Reservation, Mn., U.S.	B6	100
Nettleton, Ms., U.S.	A5	101
Nettuno, Italy	H7	14
Neubrandenburg, Ger.	B13	8
Neuburg an der Donau, Ger.	G11	8
Neuchâtel, Switz.	F13	10
Neuchâtel, Lac de, l., Switz.	F13	10
Neufchâteau, Bel.	F5	8
Neufchâteau, Fr.	D12	10
Neufchâtel-en-Bray, Fr.	C8	10
Neuillé-Pont-Pierre, Fr.	E7	10
Neumarkt in der Oberpfalz, Ger.	F11	8
Neumünster, Ger.	A9	8
Neunkirchen, Aus.	H16	8
Neunkirchen/Saar, Ger.	F7	8
Neuquén, Arg.	D3	56
Neuruppin, Ger.	C12	8
Neuse, stm., N.C., U.S.	B6	110
Neusiedler See, l., Eur.	H16	8
Neuss, Ger.	D6	8
Neustadt Jan der Aisch—, Ger.	F10	8
Neustadt an der Weinstrasse, Ger.	F8	8
Neustadt in Holstein, Ger.	A10	8
Neustrelitz, Ger.	B13	8
Neu-Ulm, Ger.	G10	8
Neuville, Que., Can.	C6	74
Neuville-de-Poitou, Fr.	F7	10
Neuwied, Ger.	E7	8
Nevada, Ia., U.S.	B4	92
Nevada, Mo., U.S.	D3	102
Nevada, co., Ar., U.S.	D2	81
Nevada, co., Ca., U.S.	C3	82
Nevada, state, U.S.	D5	105
Nevada, Sierra, mts., Spain	H8	12
Nevada, Sierra, mts., Ca., U.S.	D4	82
Nevada City, Ca., U.S.	C3	82
Nevado, Cerro, mtn., Arg.	D3	56
Nevado, Cerro, mtn., Col.	F5	58
Never, Russia	G18	24
Nevers, Fr.	E10	10
Neversink, stm., N.Y., U.S.	D6	109
Nevis, i., St. K./N.	F16	64
Nevis, Ben, mtn., Scot., U.K.	E7	7
New, stm., U.S.	C3	125
New, stm., Az., U.S.	k8	80
New, stm., N.C., U.S.	C5	110
New Albany, In., U.S.	H6	91
New Albany, Ms., U.S.	A4	101
New Albany, Oh., U.S.	k11	112
New Amsterdam, Guy.	D14	58
Newark, Ar., U.S.	B4	81
Newark, Ca., U.S.	h8	82
Newark, De., U.S.	B3	85
Newark, Il., U.S.	B5	90
Newark, N.J., U.S.	B4	107
Newark, N.Y., U.S.	B3	109
Newark, Oh., U.S.	B3	112
Newark Bay, b., N.J., U.S.	k8	107
Newark Lake, l., Nv., U.S.	D6	105
New Athens, Il., U.S.	E4	90
New Augusta, Ms., U.S.	D4	101
Newaygo, Mi., U.S.	E5	99
Newaygo, co., Mi., U.S.	E5	99
New Baden, Il., U.S.	E4	90
New Baltimore, Mi., U.S.	F8	99
New Bedford, Ma., U.S.	C6	98
New Bedford, Pa., U.S.	D1	115
Newberg, Or., U.S.	B4	114
New Berlin, Il., U.S.	D4	90
New Berlin, Wi., U.S.	n11	126
New Bern, N.C., U.S.	B5	110
Newbern, Tn., U.S.	A2	119
Newberry, Fl., U.S.	C4	86
Newberry, Mi., U.S.	B5	99
Newberry, S.C., U.S.	C4	117
Newberry, co., S.C., U.S.	C4	117
New Bethlehem, Pa., U.S.	D3	115
New Bloomfield, Pa., U.S.	F7	115
New Boston, Mi., U.S.	p15	99
New Boston, Oh., U.S.	D3	112
New Boston, Tx., U.S.	C5	120
New Braunfels, Tx., U.S.	E3	120
New Bremen, Oh., U.S.	B1	112
New Brighton, Mn., U.S.	m12	100
New Brighton, Pa., U.S.	E1	115
New Britain, Ct., U.S.	C4	84
New Britain, i., Pap. N. Gui.	m16	50a
New Brockton, Al., U.S.	D4	78
New Brunswick, N.J., U.S.	C4	107
New Brunswick, prov., Can.	C3	71
New Buffalo, Mi., U.S.	G4	99
Newburg, Wi., U.S.	E5	126
Newburgh, Ont., Can.	C8	73
Newburgh, In., U.S.	I3	91
Newburgh, N.Y., U.S.	D6	109
Newburgh Heights, Oh., U.S.	h9	112
Newburyport, Ma., U.S.	A6	98
New Caledonia, dep., Oc.	H24	2
New Canaan, Ct., U.S.	E2	84
New Carlisle, In., U.S.	A4	91
New Carlisle, Oh., U.S.	C1	112
Newcastle, Austl.	F10	50
Newcastle, N.B., Can.	C4	71
Newcastle, Ont., Can.	D6	73
Newcastle, S. Afr.	G5	44
Newcastle, N. Ire., U.K.	G7	7
New Castle, Al., U.S.	B3	78
New Castle, Co., U.S.	B3	83
New Castle, De., U.S.	B3	85
New Castle, In., U.S.	E7	91
New Castle, Ky., U.S.	B4	94
Newcastle, Ok., U.S.	B4	113
New Castle, Pa., U.S.	D1	115
Newcastle, Wy., U.S.	C8	127
New Castle, co., De., U.S.	B3	85
Newcastle upon Tyne, Eng., U.K.	G11	7
Newcastle Waters, Austl.	C6	50
New City, N.Y., U.S.	D6	109
Newcomerstown, Oh., U.S.	B4	112
New Concord, Oh., U.S.	C4	112
New Cumberland, Pa., U.S.	F8	115
New Cumberland, W.V., U.S.	A4	125
Newdegate, Austl.	F3	50
New Delhi, India	F7	38
Newell, Ia., U.S.	B2	92
Newell, S.D., U.S.	C2	118
Newell, W.V., U.S.	A4	125
New Ellenton, S.C., U.S.	E4	117
Newellton, La., U.S.	B4	95
New England, N.D., U.S.	C3	111
Newenham, Cape, c., Ak., U.S.	D7	79
New Fairfield, Ct., U.S.	D2	84
Newfane, N.Y., U.S.	B2	109
Newfields, N.H., U.S.	D5	106
New Florence, Mo., U.S.	C6	102
Newfound Gap, U.S.	f9	110
Newfound Lake, l., N.H., U.S.	C3	106
Newfoundland, prov., Can.	D4	72
Newfoundland, i., Newf., Can.	D3	72
New Franklin, Mo., U.S.	B5	102
New Freedom, Pa., U.S.	G8	115
New Georgia, i., Sol.Is.	A11	50
New Germany, N.S., Can.	E5	71
New Glarus, Wi., U.S.	F4	126
New Guinea, i.	m14	50a
Newhall, Ia., U.S.	C6	92
New Hampshire, state, U.S.	C3	106
New Hampton, Ia., U.S.	A5	92
New Hanover, co., N.C., U.S.	C5	110
New Hanover, i., Pap. N. Gui.	k17	50a
New Harbour, Newf., Can.	E5	72
New Harmony, In., U.S.	H2	91
New Hartford, Ct., U.S.	B4	84
New Hartford, Ia., U.S.	B5	92
New Haven, Ct., U.S.	D4	84
New Haven, In., U.S.	B7	91
New Haven, Ky., U.S.	C4	94
New Haven, Mi., U.S.	F8	99
New Haven, Mo., U.S.	C6	102
New Haven, W.V., U.S.	C3	125
New Haven, co., Ct., U.S.	D4	84
New Haven, stm., Vt., U.S.	C2	122
New Haven Harbor, b., Ct., U.S.	E4	84
New Hazelton, B.C., Can.	B4	69
New Hebrides see Vanuatu, ctry., Oc.	H24	2
New Holland, Ga., U.S.	B3	87
New Holland, Pa., U.S.	F9	115
New Holstein, Wi., U.S.	E5	126
New Hope, Al., U.S.	A3	78
New Hope, Ky., U.S.	C4	94
New Hope, Mn., U.S.	m12	100
New Hope, Pa., U.S.	F12	115
New Hudson, Mi., U.S.	o14	99
New Iberia, La., U.S.	D4	95
Newington, Ct., U.S.	C5	84
New Inlet, b., N.C., U.S.	D5	110
New Ireland, i., Pap. N. Gui.	k17	50a
New Jersey, state, U.S.	C4	107
New Johnsonville, Tn., U.S.	A4	119
New Kensington, Pa., U.S.	E2	115
New Kent, co., Va., U.S.	C5	123
Newkirk, Ok., U.S.	A4	113
New Laguna, N.M., U.S.	B2	108
New Lake, l., N.C., U.S.	B6	110
New Lenox, Il., U.S.	B6	90
New Lexington, Oh., U.S.	C3	112
New Lisbon, Wi., U.S.	E3	126
New Liskeard, Ont., Can.	p20	73
Newllano, La., U.S.	C2	95
New London, Ct., U.S.	D7	84
New London, Ia., U.S.	D6	92
New London, Mn., U.S.	E4	100
New London, Mo., U.S.	B6	102
New London, N.H., U.S.	D3	106
New London, Oh., U.S.	A3	112
New London, Wi., U.S.	D5	126
New London, co., Ct., U.S.	C7	84
New London Submarine Base, mil., Ct., U.S.	D7	84
New Madison, Oh., U.S.	C1	112
New Madrid, Mo., U.S.	E8	102
New Madrid, co., Mo., U.S.	E8	102
Newman, Ca., U.S.	D3	82
Newman, Il., U.S.	D6	90
New Manchester, W.V., U.S.	e8	125
Newman Grove, Ne., U.S.	C8	104
Newman Lake, l., Wa., U.S.	B8	124
Newmanstown, Pa., U.S.	F9	115
Newmarket, Ont., Can.	C5	73
New Market, Al., U.S.	A3	78
New Market, In., U.S.	E4	91
Newmarket, N.H., U.S.	D5	106
New Market, Tn., U.S.	C10	119
New Market, Va., U.S.	B4	123
New Martinsville, W.V., U.S.	B4	125
New Matamoras, Oh., U.S.	C4	112
New Mexico, state, U.S.	C3	108
New Miami, Oh., U.S.	C1	112
New Milford, Ct., U.S.	C2	84
New Milford, N.J., U.S.	h8	107
New Milford, Pa., U.S.	C10	115
Newnan, Ga., U.S.	C2	87
Newnans Lake, l., Fl., U.S.	C4	86
New Norfolk, Austl.	H9	50
New Orleans, La., U.S.	E5	95
New Orleans Naval Air Station, mil., La., U.S.	k11	95
New Oxford, Pa., U.S.	G7	115
New Palestine, In., U.S.	E6	91
New Paltz, N.Y., U.S.	D6	109
New Paris, In., U.S.	B6	91
New Paris, Oh., U.S.	C1	112
New Philadelphia, Oh., U.S.	B4	112
New Philadelphia, Pa., U.S.	E9	115
New Plymouth, N.Z.	C5	52
New Plymouth, Id., U.S.	F2	89
New Point Comfort, c., Va., U.S.	C6	123
Newport, Eng., U.K.	K11	7
Newport, Wales, U.K.	J9	7
Newport, Ar., U.S.	B4	81
Newport, De., U.S.	B3	85
Newport, In., U.S.	E3	91
Newport, Ky., U.S.	A5	94
Newport, Me., U.S.	D3	96
Newport, Mi., U.S.	G7	99
Newport, Mn., U.S.	n13	100
Newport, N.H., U.S.	D2	106
Newport, N.C., U.S.	C6	110
Newport, Oh., U.S.	C4	112
Newport, Or., U.S.	C2	114
Newport, Pa., U.S.	F7	115
Newport, R.I., U.S.	F5	116
Newport, Tn., U.S.	D10	119
Newport, Vt., U.S.	B4	122
Newport, Wa., U.S.	A8	124
Newport, co., R.I., U.S.	E5	116
Newport Beach, Ca., U.S.	n13	82
Newport News, Va., U.S.	D6	123
New Port Richey, Fl., U.S.	D4	86
New Prague, Mn., U.S.	F5	100
New Preston, Ct., U.S.	C2	84
New Providence, N.J., U.S.	B4	107
New Providence, i., Bah.	B9	64
Newquay, Eng., U.K.	K7	7
New Richland, Mn., U.S.	G5	100
New Richmond, Que., Can.	A4	71
New Richmond, Oh., U.S.	D1	112
New Richmond, Wi., U.S.	C1	126
New River Inlet, b., N.C., U.S.	C5	110
New Roads, La., U.S.	D4	95
New Rochelle, N.Y., U.S.	E7	109
New Rockford, N.D., U.S.	B6	111
New Ross, Ire.	I6	7
Newry, N. Ire., U.K.	G6	7
New Salem, N.D., U.S.	C4	111
New Sarpy, La., U.S.	k11	95
New Sharon, Ia., U.S.	C5	92
New Site, Al., U.S.	B4	78
New Smyrna Beach, Fl., U.S.	C6	86
New South Wales, state, Austl.	F9	50
New Straitsville, Oh., U.S.	C3	112
New Tazewell, Tn., U.S.	C10	119
Newton, Al., U.S.	D4	78
Newton, Ga., U.S.	E2	87
Newton, Il., U.S.	E5	90
Newton, Ia., U.S.	C4	92
Newton, Ks., U.S.	D6	93
Newton, Ma., U.S.	B5	98
Newton, Ms., U.S.	C4	101
Newton, N.J., U.S.	A3	107
Newton, N.C., U.S.	B1	110
Newton, Tx., U.S.	D6	120
Newton, Ut., U.S.	B4	121
Newton, co., Ar., U.S.	B2	81
Newton, co., Ga., U.S.	C3	87
Newton, co., In., U.S.	B3	91
Newton, co., Ms., U.S.	C4	101
Newton, co., Mo., U.S.	E3	102
Newton, co., Tx., U.S.	D6	120
Newton Falls, Oh., U.S.	A5	112
Newton Lake, res., Il., U.S.	E5	90
Newton Stewart, Scot., U.K.	G8	7
Newtown, Ct., U.S.	D2	84
New Town, N.D., U.S.	B3	111
Newtown, Oh., U.S.	C1	112
Newtownabbey, N. Ire., U.K.	G7	7
Newtownards, N. Ire., U.K.	G7	7
Newtown Square, Pa., U.S.	p20	115
New Ulm, Mn., U.S.	F4	100
New Vienna, Oh., U.S.	C2	112
Newville, Pa., U.S.	F7	115
New Washington, In., U.S.	G6	91
New Washington, Oh., U.S.	B3	112
New Waterford, Oh., U.S.	B5	112
New Westminster, B.C., Can.	E6	69
New Whiteland, In., U.S.	E5	91
New Wilmington, Pa., U.S.	D1	115
New Windsor, Il., U.S.	B3	90
New Windsor, Md., U.S.	A3	97
New Windsor, N.Y., U.S.	D6	109
New World Island, i., Newf., Can.	D4	72
New York, N.Y., U.S.	E7	109
New York, co., N.Y., U.S.	k13	109
New York, state, U.S.	C6	109
New York Mills, Mn., U.S.	D3	100
New Zealand, ctry., Oc.	D4	52
Nez Perce, co., Id., U.S.	C2	89
Nez Perce Indian Reservation, Id., U.S.	C2	89
Ngami, Lake, l., Bots.	F4	44
Nganglong Kangri, mts., China	D10	38
Nganjuk, Indon.	m15	33a
Ngaoundéré, Cam.	G8	42
Nguigmi, Niger	F8	42
Nguru, Nig.	F8	42
Nha Trang, Viet.	H10	34
Niafounké, Mali	E5	42
Niagara, Wi., U.S.	C6	126
Niagara, co., N.Y., U.S.	B2	109
Niagara Falls, Ont., Can.	D5	73
Niagara Falls, N.Y., U.S.	B1	109
Niagara-on-the-Lake, Ont., Can.	D5	73

Name — Map Ref — Page

Niamey, Niger F6 42
Niangara, Zaire H11 42
Niangua, stm., Mo., U.S. D5 102
Niantic, Ct., U.S. D7 84
Nias, Pulau, i., Indon. N4 34
Nibley, Ut., U.S. B4 121
Nicaragua, ctry., N.A. H5 64
Nicaragua, Lago de, l., Nic. I5 64
Nicastro (Lamezia Terme), Italy K11 14
Nicatous Lake, l., Me., U.S. C4 96
Nice, Fr. I14 10
Niceville, Fl., U.S. u15 86
Nichinan, Japan K4 30
Nicholas, co., Ky., U.S. B6 94
Nicholas, co., W.V., U.S. C4 125
Nicholas Channel, strt., N.A. C7 64
Nicholasville, Ky., U.S. C5 94
Nicholls, Ga., U.S. E4 87
Nichols Hills, Ok., U.S. B4 113
Nicholson, Ms., U.S. E4 101
Nickajack Lake, res., Tn., U.S. D8 119
Nickel Centre, Ont., Can. p19 73
Nickerson, Ks., U.S. D5 93
Nicobar Islands, is., India J2 34
Nicolet, Que., Can. C5 74
Nicolet, stm., Que., Can. C5 74
Nicolet, Lake, l., Mi., U.S. B6 99
Nicollet, Mn., U.S. F4 100
Nicollet, co., Mn., U.S. F4 100
Nicolls Town, Bah. B8 64
Nicoma Park, Ok., U.S. B4 113
Nicosia, Cyp. B3 40
Nicosia, N. Cyp. B3 40
Nicosia, Italy L9 14
Nicoya, Golfo de, b., C.R. J5 64
Nicoya, Península de, pen., C.R. I5 64
Niebüll, Ger. A8 8
Nienburg, Ger. C9 8
Nieuw Nickerie, Sur. B7 54
Nieves, Mex. E8 62
Nigadoo, N.B., Can. B4 71
Niger, ctry., Afr. E7 42
Niger, stm., Afr. G7 42
Nigeria, ctry., Afr. F7 42
Nigríta, Grc. I7 16
Nihoa, i., Hi., U.S. m15 88
Niigata, Japan E12 30
Niihama, Japan I6 30
Niihau, i., Hi., U.S. B1 88
Niinisalo, Fin. F14 6
Niitsu, Japan E12 30
Níjar, Spain I9 12
Nijmegen, Neth. D5 8
Nikishka, Ak., U.S. g16 79
Nikkō, Japan F12 30
Nikolajevsk-na-Amure, Russia G22 24
Nikšić, Yugo. G2 16
Niland, Ca., U.S. F6 82
Nile (Nahr an-Nīl), stm., Afr. C12 42
Niles, Il., U.S. h9 90
Niles, Mi., U.S. G4 99
Niles, Oh., U.S. A5 112
Nileshwar, India F3 37
Nīmach, India H6 38
Nimba, Mont, mtn., Afr. G4 42
Nîmes, Fr. I11 10
Nimrod Lake, res., Ar., U.S. C2 81
Nine Degree Channel, strt., India H2 37
Nine Mile Creek, stm., Ut., U.S. D5 121
Ninemile Point, c., Mi., U.S. C6 99
Ninety Six, S.C., U.S. C3 117
Ningbo, China F10 28
Ningming, China C9 34
Ningxia Huizu Zizhiqu, prov., China D8 26
Ninh Binh, Viet. D8 34
Ninigret Pond, l., R.I., U.S. G2 116
Ninilchik, Ak., U.S. C9 79
Ninnescah, stm., Ks., U.S. E6 93
Niobrara, co., Wy., U.S. C8 127
Niobrara, stm., U.S. B7 104
Niono, Mali F4 42
Nioro du Sahel, Mali E4 42
Niort, Fr. F6 10
Niota, Tn., U.S. D9 119
Nipāni, India D3 37
Nipigon, Lake, l., Ont., Can. o17 73
Nipissing, Lake, l., Ont., Can. A5 73
Nipomo, Ca., U.S. E3 82
Nipple Mountain, mtn., Co., U.S. D2 83
Nirmal, India C5 37
Niš, Yugo. F5 16
Nisa, Port. F4 12
Nishinoomote, Japan u30 31b
Nishiwaki, Japan H7 30
Niskayuna, N.Y., U.S. C7 109
Nisqually, stm., Wa., U.S. C3 124
Nisswa, Mn., U.S. D4 100
Niterói, Braz. G7 57
Nitra, Slov. G18 8
Nitro, W.V., U.S. C3 125
Niue, dep., Oc. H1 2
Nivelles, Bel. E4 8
Niverville, Man., Can. E3 70
Niwot, Co., U.S. A5 83
Nixa, Mo., U.S. D4 102
Nixon, Nv., U.S. D2 105
Nixon, Tx., U.S. E4 120
Nizāmābād, India C5 37
Nizip, Tur. A5 40
Nižn'aja Pojma, Russia F13 24
Nižn'aja Tunguska, stm., Russia E12 24
Nižneangarsk, Russia F15 24
Nižneilimsk, Russia F14 24
Nižneudinsk, Russia G13 24
Nižnij Novgorod (Gorki), Russia E27 18
Nizza Monferrato, Italy E3 14
Njombe, Tan. C6 44
Nkhota Kota, Mwi. D6 44
Nkongsamba, Cam. H7 42
Noākhāli, Bngl. I14 38
Noank, Ct., U.S. D8 84
Noatak, Ak., U.S. B7 79
Noatak, stm., Ak., U.S. B7 79
Nobel, Ont., Can. B4 73
Nobeoka, Japan J4 30
Noble, Ok., U.S. B4 113
Noble, co., In., U.S. B7 91
Noble, co., Oh., U.S. C4 112
Noble, co., Ok., U.S. A4 113
Nobles, co., Mn., U.S. G3 100
Noblesville, In., U.S. D6 91
Noboribetsu, Japan q19 30a
Nocatee, Fl., U.S. E5 86
Nocera [Inferiore], Italy I9 14
Nochixtlán, Mex. I11 62
Nocona, Tx., U.S. C4 120
Nodaway, co., Mo., U.S. A3 102
Nodaway, stm., U.S. A2 102
Noel, Mo., U.S. E3 102
Nogales, Mex. B4 62
Nogales, Az., U.S. F5 80
Nōgata, Japan I3 30
Nogent-le-Rotrou, Fr. D7 10
Noginsk, Russia F21 18
Nogoyá, Arg. C5 56
Noirmoutier, Fr. E4 10
Nojima-zaki, c., Japan H12 30
Nokia, Fin. F14 6
Nokomis, Fl., U.S. E4 86
Nokomis, Il., U.S. D4 90
Nokomis, Lake, res., Wi., U.S. C4 126
Nolan, co., Tx., U.S. C2 120
Nolichucky, stm., Tn., U.S. C10 119
Nolin, stm., Ky., U.S. C3 94
Nolin Lake, res., Ky., U.S. C3 94
Nomans Land, i., Ma., U.S. D6 98
Nombre de Dios, Mex. F7 62
Nome, Ak., U.S. C6 79
Nominingue, Que., Can. C2 74
Nonacho Lake, l., N.W. Ter., Can. D11 66
Nonesuch, stm., Me., U.S. g7 96
Nong'an, China C12 26
Nong Khai, Thai. F7 34
Nonquit Pond, l., R.I., U.S. E6 116
Nontron, Fr. G7 10
Nooksack, North Fork, stm., Wa., U.S. A4 124
Nooksack, South Fork, stm., Wa., U.S. A3 124
Noordoost Polder, reg., Neth. C5 8
Noorvik, Ak., U.S. B7 79
Nootka Island, i., B.C., Can. G7 66
Nootka Sound, strt., B.C., Can. E4 69
No Point, Point, c., Md., U.S. D5 97
Noquebay, Lake, l., Wi., U.S. C6 126
Noranda (part of Rouyn [-Noranda]), Que., Can. k11 74
Nora Springs, Ia., U.S. A5 92
Norborne, Mo., U.S. B4 102
Norco, La., U.S. E5 95
Norcross, Ga., U.S. C2 87
Norden, Ger. B7 8
Nordenham, Ger. B8 8
Nordenšel'da, Archipelag, is., Russia B13 24
Norderney, i., Ger. B7 8
Nordfjordeid, Nor. F5 6
Nordfold, Nor. C10 6
Nordhausen, Ger. D10 8
Nordhorn, Ger. C7 8
Nordkapp, c., Nor. A15 6
Nordkjosbotn, Nor. B12 6
Nördlingen, Ger. G10 8
Nordmaling, Swe. E12 6
Nordreisa, Nor. B13 6
Nordre Strømfjord, Grnld. C22 66
Nordvik, Russia C16 24
Norfolk, Ct., U.S. B3 84
Norfolk, Ne., U.S. B8 104
Norfolk, N.Y., U.S. f9 109
Norfolk, Va., U.S. D6 123
Norfolk, co., Ma., U.S. B5 98
Norfolk Naval Base, mil., Va., U.S. k15 123
Norfolk Naval Shipyard, mil., Va., U.S. k15 123
Norfork Dam, Ar., U.S. A3 81
Norfork Lake, res., U.S. A3 81
Noril'sk, Russia D11 24
Norland, Fl., U.S. s13 86
Norlina, N.C., U.S. A4 110
Normal, Il., U.S. C5 90
Norman, Ok., U.S. B4 113
Norman, co., Mn., U.S. C2 100
Norman, Lake, res., N.C., U.S. B2 110
Normandie, hist. reg., Fr. D6 10
Normandy, Mo., U.S. f13 102
Normandy see Normandie, hist. reg., Fr. D6 10
Norman Park, Ga., U.S. E3 87
Normanton, Austl. C8 50
Norman Wells, N.W. Ter., Can. C7 66
Norphlet, Ar., U.S. D3 81
Ñorquincó, Arg. E2 56
Norridge, Il., U.S. k9 90
Norridgewock, Me., U.S. D3 96
Norris, S.C., U.S. B2 117
Norris, Tn., U.S. C9 119
Norris Arm, Newf., Can. D4 72
Norris City, Il., U.S. F5 90
Norris Dam, Tn., U.S. C9 119
Norris Lake, res., Tn., U.S. C10 119
Norris Point, Newf., Can. D3 72
Norristown, Pa., U.S. F11 115
Norrköping, Swe. G11 6
Norrtälje, Swe. G12 6
Norseman, Austl. F4 50
Norsk, Russia G19 24
Norte, Serra do, plat., Braz. F7 54
North, S.C., U.S. D5 117
North, stm., Al., U.S. B2 78
North, stm., Ia., U.S. f8 92
North, stm., Ma., U.S. h12 98
North, stm., W.V., U.S. B6 125
North, Cape, c., N.S., Can. B9 71
North Adams, Ma., U.S. A1 98
North Albany, Or., U.S. k11 114
Northam, Austl. F3 50
North America E10 61
North Amherst, Ma., U.S. B2 98
Northampton, Eng., U.K. I12 7
Northampton, Ma., U.S. B2 98
Northampton, Pa., U.S. E11 115
Northampton, co., N.C., U.S. A5 110
Northampton, co., Pa., U.S. E11 115
Northampton, co., Va., U.S. C7 123
North Andaman, i., India H2 34
North Andover, Ma., U.S. A5 98
North Andrews Gardens, Fl., U.S. *r13 86
North Anna, stm., Va., U.S. B5 123
North Anson, Me., U.S. D3 96
North Apollo, Pa., U.S. E2 115
North Arapaho Peak, mtn., Co., U.S. A5 83
North Arlington, N.J., U.S. h8 107
North Atlanta, Ga., U.S. h8 87
North Attleboro, Ma., U.S. C5 98
North Augusta, S.C., U.S. D4 117
North Aurora, Il., U.S. k8 90
North Baltimore, Oh., U.S. A2 112
North Bay, Ont., Can. A5 73
North Beach, Md., U.S. C4 97
North Belmont, N.C., U.S. B1 110
North Bend, Ne., U.S. C9 104
North Bend, Or., U.S. D2 114
North Bend, Wa., U.S. B4 124
North Bennington, Vt., U.S. F2 122
North Bergen, N.J., U.S. h8 107
North Berwick, Me., U.S. E2 96
North Billerica, Ma., U.S. A5 98
Northborough, Ma., U.S. B4 98
North Branch, Mi., U.S. E7 99
North Branch, Mn., U.S. E6 100
North Branch, N.H., U.S. D3 106
North Branch, N.J., U.S. B3 107
North Branford, Ct., U.S. D4 84
Northbridge, Ma., U.S. B4 98
Northbrook, Il., U.S. h9 90
North Brookfield, Ma., U.S. B3 98
North Brunswick, N.J., U.S. C4 107
North Caldwell, N.J., U.S. B4 107
North Canadian, stm., Ok., U.S. A5 113
North Canton, Ga., U.S. B2 87
North Canton, Oh., U.S. B4 112
North Cape, c., P.E.I., Can. B6 71
North Cape May, N.J., U.S. F3 107
North Cape see Nordkapp, c., Nor. A15 6
North Caribou Lake, l., Ont., Can. F14 66
North Carolina, state, U.S. B3 110
North Cascades National Park, Wa., U.S. A4 124
North Channel, strt., Ont., Can. A2 73
North Channel, strt., U.K. F7 7
North Charleston, S.C., U.S. F8 117
North Chicago, Il., U.S. A6 90
North Clarendon, Vt., U.S. D3 122
North College Hill, Oh., U.S. o12 112
North Conway, N.H., U.S. B4 106
North Corbin, Ky., U.S. D5 94
North Crossett, Ar., U.S. D4 81
North Cyprus, ctry., Asia B3 40
North Dakota, state, U.S. B5 111
North Dartmouth, Ma., U.S. C6 98
North Druid Hills, Ga., U.S. *h8 87
North Eagle Butte, S.D., U.S. B4 118
North East, Md., U.S. A6 97
North East, Pa., U.S. B2 115
Northeast, stm., Md., U.S. A6 97
Northeast Cape, c., Ak., U.S. C6 79
Northeast Cape Fear, stm., N.C., U.S. C5 110
Northeast Harbor, Me., U.S. D4 96
Northeast Henrietta, N.Y., U.S. *B3 109
North Easton, Ma., U.S. B5 98
Northeast Pond, l., N.H., U.S. D5 106
Northeast Providence Channel, strt., Bah. B9 64
North Edisto, stm., S.C., U.S. k11 117
Northeim, Ger. D9 8
North English, Ia., U.S. C5 92
North English, stm., Ia., U.S. C5 92
North Enid, Ok., U.S. A4 113
Northern Cheyenne Indian Reservation, Mt., U.S. E10 103
Northern Indian Lake, l., Man., Can. A3 70
Northern Ireland, ter., U.K. G6 7
Northern Territory, ter., Austl. C6 50
North Falmouth, Ma., U.S. C6 98
Northfield, Mn., U.S. F5 100
Northfield, N.H., U.S. D3 106
Northfield, N.J., U.S. E3 107
Northfield, Oh., U.S. h9 112
Northfield, Vt., U.S. C3 122
Northfield Falls, Vt., U.S. C3 122
North Flinders Ranges, mts., Austl. F7 50
North Fond du Lac, Wi., U.S. E5 126
Northford, Ct., U.S. D4 84
North Fork Reservoir, res., Or., U.S. B4 114
North Fort Myers, Fl., U.S. F5 86
North Fox Island, i., Mi., U.S. C5 99
North Frisian Islands, is., Eur. A8 8
Northglenn, Co., U.S. B6 83
North Gower, Ont., Can. B9 73
North Grafton, Ma., U.S. B4 98
North Grosvenordale, Ct., U.S. B8 84
North Gulfport, Ms., U.S. E4 101
North Haledon, N.J., U.S. B4 107
North Hampton, N.H., U.S. E5 106
North Hartland Reservoir, res., Vt., U.S. D4 122
North Hatley, Que., Can. D6 74
North Haven, Ct., U.S. D4 84
North Head, N.B., Can. E3 71
North Hero Island, i., Vt., U.S. B2 122
North Horn Lake, l., Tn., U.S. e8 119
North Industry, Oh., U.S. B4 112
North Inlet, b., S.C., U.S. E9 117
North Island, i., N.Z. C5 52
North Island, i., S.C., U.S. E9 117
North Island Naval Air Station, mil., Ca., U.S. o15 82
North Islands, is., La., U.S. E7 95
North Judson, In., U.S. B4 91
North Kansas City, Mo., U.S. h10 102
North Kingstown, R.I., U.S. E4 116
North Kingsville, Oh., U.S. A5 112
North La Junta, Co., U.S. C7 83
Northlake, Il., U.S. k9 90
North Laramie, stm., Wy., U.S. D7 127
North Las Vegas, Nv., U.S. G6 105
North La Veta Pass, Co., U.S. D5 83
North Lewisburg, Oh., U.S. B2 112
North Liberty, In., U.S. A5 91
North Liberty, Ia., U.S. C6 92
North Lima, Oh., U.S. B5 112
North Little Rock, Ar., U.S. C3 81
North Logan, Ut., U.S. B4 121
North Loon Mountain, mtn., Id., U.S. D3 89
North Magnetic Pole B22 128
North Mamm Peak, mtn., Co., U.S. B3 83
North Manchester, In., U.S. C6 91
North Manitou Island, i., Mi., U.S. C4 99
North Mankato, Mn., U.S. F4 100
North Merrydale, La., U.S. *D4 95
North Miami, Fl., U.S. G6 86
North Miami Beach, Fl., U.S. s13 86
North Middletown, Ky., U.S. B5 94
North Moose Lake, l., Man., Can. B1 70
North Mountain, mtn., Pa., U.S. D9 115
North Muskegon, Mi., U.S. E4 99
North Myrtle Beach, S.C., U.S. D10 117
North Naples, Fl., U.S. F5 86
North New River Canal, Fl., U.S. F6 86
North Ogden, Ut., U.S. B4 121
North Olmsted, Oh., U.S. h9 112
North Palisade, mtn., Ca., U.S. D4 82
North Park, Il., U.S. A4 90
North Park, val., Co., U.S. A4 83
North Pass, strt., La., U.S. E7 95
North Pembroke, Ma., U.S. B6 98
North Plainfield, N.J., U.S. B4 107
North Plains, Or., U.S. B4 114
North Plains, pl., N.M., U.S. C1 108
North Platte, Ne., U.S. C5 104
North Platte, stm., U.S. C6 76
North Point, c., Md., U.S. B5 97
North Point, c., Mi., U.S. C7 99
North Pole A12 128
Northport, Al., U.S. B2 78
North Prairie, Wi., U.S. F5 126
North Providence, R.I., U.S. C4 116
North Raccoon, stm., Ia., U.S. C3 92
North Reading, Ma., U.S. f11 98
North Richland Hills, Tx., U.S. n9 120
Northridge, Oh., U.S. C2 112
North Ridgeville, Oh., U.S. A3 112
North Royalton, Oh., U.S. h9 112
North Rustico, P.E.I., Can. C6 71
North Salem, N.H., U.S. E4 106
North Salt Lake, Ut., U.S. C4 121
North Santee, stm., S.C., U.S. E9 117
North Saskatchewan, stm., Can. F10 66
North Schell Peak, mtn., Nv., U.S. D7 105
North Scituate, Ma., U.S. h12 98
North Sea, Eur. D8 4
North Shoshone Peak, mtn., Nv., U.S. D4 105
North Sioux City, S.D., U.S. E9 118
North Skunk, stm., Ia., U.S. C5 92
North Springfield, Vt., U.S. E3 122
North Springfield Reservoir, res., Vt., U.S. E4 122
North Star, De., U.S. A3 85
North St. Paul, Mn., U.S. m13 100
North Stratford, N.H., U.S. A3 106
North Sudbury, Ma., U.S. g10 98
North Swanzey, N.H., U.S. E2 106
North Syracuse, N.Y., U.S. B4 109
North Tarrytown, N.Y., U.S. D7 109
North Terre Haute, In., U.S. E3 91
North Thompson, stm., B.C., Can. D8 69
North Tonawanda, N.Y., U.S. B2 109
North Troy, Vt., U.S. B4 122
North Tunica, Ms., U.S. A3 101
North Twin Lake, l., Wi., U.S. B4 126
Northumberland, Pa., U.S. E8 115
Northumberland, co., Pa., U.S. D8 115
Northumberland, co., Va., U.S. C6 123
Northumberland National Park, Eng., U.K. F10 7
Northumberland Strait, strt., Can. C6 71
North Umpqua, stm., Or., U.S. D3 114
North Uxbridge, Ma., U.S. B4 98
Northvale, N.J., U.S. g9 107
North Vancouver, B.C., Can. E6 69
North Vassalboro, Me., U.S. D3 96
North Vernon, In., U.S. F6 91
Northville, Mi., U.S. p15 99
North Wales, Pa., U.S. F11 115
North Walpole, N.H., U.S. D2 106
North Warren, Pa., U.S. C3 115
North Webster, In., U.S. B6 91
North West Cape, c., Austl. D2 50
Northwest Miramichi, stm., N.B., Can. B3 71
Northwest Providence Channel, strt., Bah. A8 64
Northwest Territories, prov., Can. C13 66
North Wildwood, N.J., U.S. E3 107
North Wilkesboro, N.C., U.S. A1 110
North Windham, Ct., U.S. C7 84
North Windham, Me., U.S. E2 96
Northwood, Ia., U.S. A4 92
Northwood, N.D., U.S. B8 111
North Woodstock, N.H., U.S. B3 106
North York, Ont., Can. D5 73
North York, Pa., U.S. G8 115
North York Moors National Park, Eng., U.K. G12 7
Norton, N.B., Can. D4 71
Norton, Ks., U.S. C4 93
Norton, Ma., U.S. C5 98
Norton, Oh., U.S. A4 112
Norton, Va., U.S. f9 123
Norton, co., Ks., U.S. C4 93
Norton Air Force Base, mil., Ca., U.S. E5 82
Norton Bay, b., Ak., U.S. C7 79
Norton Pond, l., Vt., U.S. B5 122
Norton Reservoir, res., Ks., U.S. C3 93
Norton Shores, Mi., U.S. E4 99
Norton Sound, strt., Ak., U.S. C6 79
Nortonville, Ks., U.S. C8 93
Nortonville, Ky., U.S. C2 94
Norwalk, Ca., U.S. n12 82
Norwalk, Ct., U.S. E2 84
Norwalk, Ia., U.S. C4 92
Norwalk, Oh., U.S. A3 112
Norwalk, stm., Ct., U.S. E2 84
Norwalk Islands, is., Ct., U.S. E2 84
Norway, Me., U.S. D2 96
Norway, Mi., U.S. C3 99
Norway, ctry., Eur. C9 4
Norway Bay, b., N.W. Ter., Can. B12 66
Norway House, Man., Can. C3 70
Norway Lake, l., Mn., U.S. E3 100
Norwegian Sea, Eur. C12 128
Norwich, Eng., U.K. I14 7
Norwich, Ct., U.S. C7 84
Norwich, N.Y., U.S. C5 109
Norwich, Vt., U.S. D4 122
Norwood, Ont., Can. C7 73
Norwood, Ma., U.S. B5 98
Norwood, Mn., U.S. F5 100
Norwood, N.J., U.S. h9 107
Norwood, N.Y., U.S. f10 109
Norwood, N.C., U.S. B2 110
Norwood, Oh., U.S. o13 112
Norwood, Pa., U.S. p20 115
Norwoodville, Ia., U.S. e8 92
Noshiro, Japan B13 30
Notasulga, Al., U.S. C4 78
Notch Peak, mtn., Ut., U.S. D2 121
Noto, Italy M10 14
Notodden, Nor. G7 6
Notre Dame, Monts, mts., Que., Can. k13 74
Notre Dame Bay, b., Newf., Can. D4 72
Notre Dame de Lourdes, Man., Can. E2 70
Notre-Dame-du-Lac, Que., Can. B9 74
Nottawasaga Bay, b., Ont., Can. C4 73
Nottaway, stm., Que., Can. h11 74
Nottingham, Eng., U.K. I11 7
Nottingham Island, i., N.W. Ter., Can. D17 66
Nottoway, co., Va., U.S. C4 123
Nottoway, stm., Va., U.S. D5 123
Nouadhibou, Maur. D2 42
Nouakchott, Maur. E2 42
Nouamrhar, Maur. E2 42
Noupoort, S. Afr. H4 44
Nouveau-Québec, Cratère du, crat., Que., Can. D18 66
Nova América, Braz. C4 57
Nova Cruz, Braz. E11 54
Nova Freixo, Moz. D7 44
Nova Friburgo, Braz. G7 57
Nova Gaia, Ang. D3 44
Nova Gradiška, Cro. D12 14
Nova Iguaçu, Braz. G7 57
Novaja Sibir', Ostrov, i., Russia B23 24
Novaja Zemľa, is., Russia C5 24
Nova Lima, Braz. E7 57
Nova Lisboa see Huambo, Ang. D3 44
Nova Mambone, Moz. F7 44
Novara, Italy D3 14
Nova Scotia, prov., Can. D6 71
Nova Sofala, Moz. F6 44
Novato, Ca., U.S. C2 82
Novelda, Spain G11 12
Nové Zámky, Slov. H18 8
Novgorod, Russia C14 18
Novi, Mi., U.S. p15 99
Novi Ligure, Italy E3 14
Novi Pazar, Bul. F11 16
Novi Pazar, Yugo. F4 16
Novi Sad, Yugo. D3 16
Novoaltajsk, Russia G10 24
Novo Aripuanã, Braz. E6 54
Novogrudok, Bela. H8 18
Novokuzneck, Russia G11 24
Novo Mesto, Slo. D10 14
Novo Redondo, Ang. D2 44
Novorossijsk, Russia I5 22
Novorybnoje, Russia C15 24
Novosibirsk, Russia D4 128
Novosibirskije Ostrova, is., Russia B22 24
Novosibirskoje Vodochranilišče, res., Russia G10 24
Novotroick, Russia G9 22
Novozybkov, Russia I14 18
Novska, Cro. D11 14
Nowa Sól (Neusalz), Pol. D15 8
Nowata, Ok., U.S. A6 113
Nowata, co., Ok., U.S. A6 113
Nowgong, India G15 38
Nowood, stm., Wy., U.S. B5 127
Nowshāk, mtn., Asia B4 38
Nowshera, Pak. C4 38
Nowy Sącz, Pol. F20 8
Nowy Targ, Pol. F20 8
Noxon Reservoir, res., Mt., U.S. C1 103
Noxontown Lake, res., De., U.S. C3 85
Noxubee, co., Ms., U.S. B5 101
Noxubee, stm., U.S. B5 101
Noyes Island, i., Ak., U.S. n22 79
Noyon, Fr. C9 10
Nozay, Fr. E5 10
Nsanje, Mwi. E7 44
Nsawam, Ghana G5 42
Nubanusit Lake, l., N.H., U.S. E2 106
Nubian Desert, des., Sudan D12 42
Nuckolls, co., Ne., U.S. D7 104
Nucla, Co., U.S. C2 83
Nueces, co., Tx., U.S. F4 120
Nueces, stm., Tx., U.S. E3 120
Nueltin Lake, l., Can. E13 66
Nueva Casas Grandes, Mex. B6 62
Nueva Rosita, Mex. D9 62
Nueva San Salvador, El Sal. H3 64

Index

Name	Map Ref	Page
Nueve de Julio, Arg.	D4	56
Nuevitas, Cuba	D9	64
Nuevo, Golfo, b., Arg.	E4	56
Nuevo Laredo, Mex.	D10	62
Nuevo Rocafuerte, Ec.	H5	58
Nuits-Saint-Georges, Fr.	E11	10
Nukus, Uzb.	I9	22
Nulato, Ak., U.S.	C8	79
Nulhegan, stm., Vt., U.S.	B5	122
Nullagine, Austl.	D4	50
Nullarbor Plain, pl., Austl.	F5	50
Numata, Japan	F12	30
Numazu, Japan	G11	30
Numfoor, Pulau, i., Indon.	F9	32
Nun, stm., China	A12	26
Nunivak Island, i., Ak., U.S.	D6	79
Nunjiang, China	B12	26
Nuoro, Italy	I4	14
N'urba, Russia	E17	24
Nuremberg, Pa., U.S.	E9	115
Nuremberg see Nürnberg, Ger.	F11	8
Nürnberg, Ger.	F11	8
Nurri, Italy	J4	14
Nutley, N.J., U.S.	B4	107
Nutter Fort, W.V., U.S.	k10	125
Nutting Lake, Ma., U.S.	f10	98
Nuuanu Pali, Hi., U.S.	g10	88
Nyack, N.Y., U.S.	D7	109
Nyainqêntanglha Shan, mts., China	E13	38
Nyala, Sudan	F10	42
Nyanda, Zimb.	F6	44
Nyasa, Lake, l., Afr.	D6	44
Nyaunglebin, Mya.	F4	34
Nybro, Swe.	H10	6
Nye, co., Nv., U.S.	E5	105
Nyenyam, China	F11	38
Nyeri, Kenya	B7	44
Nyíregyháza, Hung.	H21	8
Nykøbing, Den.	I8	6
Nyköping, Swe.	G11	6
Nylstroom, S. Afr.	F5	44
Nynäshamn, Swe.	G11	6
Nyngan, Austl.	F9	50
Nyon, Switz.	F13	10
Nyons, Fr.	H12	10
Nysa, Pol.	E17	8
Nysa Łużycka (Neisse) (Nisa), stm., Eur.	D14	8
Nyssa, Or., U.S.	D9	114
Nzérékoré, Gui.	G4	42
N'zeto, Ang.	C2	44

O

Name	Map Ref	Page
Oahe, Lake, res., U.S.	B6	76
Oahe Dam, S.D., U.S.	C5	118
Oahu, i., Hi., U.S.	B4	88
Oak Bay, B.C., Can.	h12	69
Oak Bluffs, Ma., U.S.	D6	98
Oak Creek, Co., U.S.	A4	83
Oak Creek, Wi., U.S.	n12	126
Oakdale, Ca., U.S.	D3	82
Oakdale, Ga., U.S.	h8	87
Oakdale, La., U.S.	D3	95
Oakdale, Pa., U.S.	k13	115
Oakes, N.D., U.S.	C7	111
Oakfield, N.Y., U.S.	B2	109
Oakfield, Wi., U.S.	E5	126
Oak Forest, Il., U.S.	k9	90
Oak Grove, Ky., U.S.	D2	94
Oak Grove, La., U.S.	B4	95
Oak Grove, Or., U.S.	B4	114
Oak Harbor, Oh., U.S.	A2	112
Oak Harbor, Wa., U.S.	A3	124
Oak Hill, Mi., U.S.	D4	99
Oak Hill, Oh., U.S.	D3	112
Oak Hill, W.V., U.S.	D3	125
Oak Hill, mtn., Ma., U.S.	f9	98
Oakhurst, Ok., U.S.	A5	113
Oak Island, i., Wi., U.S.	B3	126
Oak Lake, l., Man., Can.	E1	70
Oakland, Ca., U.S.	D2	82
Oakland, Il., U.S.	D5	90
Oakland, Ia., U.S.	C2	92
Oakland, Me., U.S.	D3	96
Oakland, Md., U.S.	m12	97
Oakland, Ne., U.S.	C9	104
Oakland, N.J., U.S.	A4	107
Oakland, Ok., U.S.	C5	113
Oakland, Or., U.S.	D3	114
Oakland, R.I., U.S.	B2	116
Oakland, co., Mi., U.S.	F7	99
Oakland City, In., U.S.	H3	91
Oakland Park, Fl., U.S.	r13	86
Oak Lawn, Il., U.S.	B6	90
Oaklawn, Ks., U.S.	g12	93
Oakley, Id., U.S.	G5	89
Oakley, Ks., U.S.	C3	93
Oakman, Al., U.S.	B2	78
Oakmont, Pa., U.S.	E2	115
Oak Mountain, mtn., Ga., U.S.	D2	87
Oak Orchard, De., U.S.	F5	85
Oak Park, Il., U.S.	B6	90
Oak Park, Mi., U.S.	p15	99
Oak Ridge, N.C., U.S.	A3	110
Oakridge, Or., U.S.	D4	114
Oak Ridge, Tn., U.S.	C9	119
Oak Ridge Reservoir, res., N.J., U.S.	A3	107
Oakton, Va., U.S.	g12	123
Oaktown, In., U.S.	G3	91
Oak Valley, N.J., U.S.	D2	107
Oakville, Ont., Can.	D5	73
Oakville, Ct., U.S.	C3	84
Oakville, Mo., U.S.	g13	102
Oakwood, Ga., U.S.	B3	87
Oakwood, Il., U.S.	C6	90
Oakwood, Oh., U.S.	C1	112
Oamaru, N.Z.	F3	52
Oaxaca [de Juárez], Mex.	I11	62
Ob', stm., Russia	D7	24
Oban, Scot., U.K.	E7	7
Obbia, Som.	G4	46
Obed, stm., Tn., U.S.	C9	119
Oberlin, Ks., U.S.	C3	93
Oberlin, La., U.S.	D3	95
Oberlin, Oh., U.S.	A3	112
Oberwart, Aus.	H16	8
Obetz, Oh., U.S.	C3	112
Obi, Kepulauan, is., Indon.	F8	32
Obi, Pulau, i., Indon.	F8	32
Óbidos, Braz.	D7	54
Obihiro, Japan	q21	30a
Obion, Tn., U.S.	A2	119
Obion, co., Tn., U.S.	A2	119
Obion, stm., Tn., U.S.	A2	119
Oblong, Il., U.S.	D6	90
Obluč'e, Russia	H20	24
Obninsk, Russia	F19	18
Obock, Dji.	F3	46
O'Brien, co., Ia., U.S.	A2	92
Obrovac, Cro.	E10	14
Observation Peak, mtn., Ca., U.S.	B3	82
Observatoire, Caye de l', i., N. Cal.	D11	50
Obuasi, Ghana	G5	42
Ocala, Fl., U.S.	C4	86
Ocaña, Col.	C6	58
Ocaña, Spain	F8	12
Occidental, Cordillera, mts., Col.	E4	58
Occidental, Cordillera, mts., Peru	F4	54
Ocean, co., N.J., U.S.	D4	107
Oceana, W.V., U.S.	D3	125
Oceana, co., Mi., U.S.	E4	99
Oceana Naval Air Station, mil., Va., U.S.	k15	123
Ocean Bluff, Ma., U.S.	B6	98
Ocean City, Fl., U.S.	u15	86
Ocean City, Md., U.S.	D7	97
Ocean City, N.J., U.S.	E3	107
Ocean Grove, Ma., U.S.	C5	98
Ocean Park, Wa., U.S.	C1	124
Oceanport, N.J., U.S.	C4	107
Oceanside, Ca., U.S.	F5	82
Ocean Springs, Ms., U.S.	E5	101
Ocean [Township], N.J., U.S.	C4	107
Ocean View, De., U.S.	F5	85
Ocha, Russia	G22	24
Ocheda Lake, l., Mn., U.S.	G3	100
Ocheyedan, stm., Ia., U.S.	A2	92
Ochiltree, co., Tx., U.S.	A2	120
Ochlockonee, stm., Fl., U.S.	B2	86
Ochoco Lake, res., Or., U.S.	C6	114
Ocho Rios, Jam.	E9	64
Ochota, stm., Russia	F22	24
Ochotsk, Russia	F22	24
Ochsenfurt, Ger.	F10	8
Ocilla, Ga., U.S.	E3	87
Ockelbo, Swe.	F11	6
Ocmulgee, stm., Ga., U.S.	D3	87
Ocoee, Fl., U.S.	D5	86
Ocoee, Lake, res., Tn., U.S.	D9	119
Oconee, co., Ga., U.S.	C3	87
Oconee, co., S.C., U.S.	B1	117
Oconee, stm., Ga., U.S.	C3	87
Oconee, Lake, res., Ga., U.S.	C3	87
Oconomowoc, Wi., U.S.	E5	126
Oconto, Wi., U.S.	D6	126
Oconto, co., Wi., U.S.	D5	126
Oconto, stm., Wi., U.S.	D5	126
Oconto Falls, Wi., U.S.	D5	126
Ocotal, Nic.	H4	64
Ocotlán, Mex.	G8	62
Ocracoke Inlet, b., N.C., U.S.	B6	110
Ocracoke Island, i., N.C., U.S.	B7	110
Octoraro Creek, stm., U.S.	A5	97
Ocumare del Tuy, Ven.	B9	58
Ocussi, Indon.	G7	32
Oda, Ghana	G5	42
Oda, Jabal, mtn., Sudan	D13	42
Ōdate, Japan	B13	30
Odawara, Japan	G12	30
Odda, Nor.	F6	6
Odebolt, Ia., U.S.	B2	92
Odell, Il., U.S.	B5	90
Odell, Or., U.S.	B5	114
Odell Lake, l., Or., U.S.	E5	114
Odem, Tx., U.S.	F4	120
Odemira, Port.	H3	12
Ödemiş, Tur.	K11	16
Odense, Den.	I8	6
Odenton, Md., U.S.	B4	97
Odenville, Al., U.S.	B3	78
Oder (Odra), stm., Eur.	C14	8
Oderberg, Ger.	C14	8
Odesa, Ukr.	H4	22
Odessa, Ont., Can.	C8	73
Odessa, De., U.S.	C3	85
Odessa, Mo., U.S.	C4	102
Odessa, Tx., U.S.	D1	120
Odessa, Wa., U.S.	B7	124
Odienné, C. Iv.	G4	42
Odin, Il., U.S.	E4	90
Odincovo, Russia	F20	18
Odon, In., U.S.	G4	91
O'Donnell, Tx., U.S.	C2	120
Odra (Oder), stm., Eur.	C14	8
Oelsnitz, Ger.	E12	8
Oelwein, Ia., U.S.	B6	92
O'Fallon, Il., U.S.	E4	90
O'Fallon, Mo., U.S.	f12	102
Offenbach, Ger.	E8	8
Offenburg, Ger.	G7	8
Offutt Air Force Base, mil., Ne., U.S.	g3	104
Ōfunato, Japan	C14	30
Ōgaki, Japan	G9	30
Ogallala, Ne., U.S.	C4	104
Ogbomosho, Nig.	G6	42
Ogden, Ia., U.S.	B3	92
Ogden, Ks., U.S.	C7	93
Ogden, Ut., U.S.	B4	121
Ogden, Mount, mtn., N.A.	k23	79
Ogdensburg, N.J., U.S.	A3	107
Ogdensburg, N.Y., U.S.	f9	109
Ogeechee, stm., Ga., U.S.	D5	87
Ogemaw, co., Mi., U.S.	D6	99
Ogilvie Mountains, mts., Yukon, Can.	D5	66
Ogle, co., Il., U.S.	A4	90
Oglesby, Il., U.S.	B4	90
Oglethorpe, Ga., U.S.	D2	87
Oglethorpe, co., Ga., U.S.	C3	87
Oglethorpe, Mount, mtn., Ga., U.S.	B2	87
Ogooué, stm., Afr.	B2	44
Ogulin, Cro.	D10	14
Ogunquit, Me., U.S.	E2	96
Oğuzeli, Tur.	A5	40
Ohanet, Alg.	C7	42
Ōhata, Japan	A14	30
Ohatchee, Al., U.S.	B3	78
O'Higgins, Lago (Lago San Martín), l., S.A.	F2	56
Ohio, co., In., U.S.	G7	91
Ohio, co., Ky., U.S.	C3	94
Ohio, co., W.V., U.S.	A4	125
Ohio, state, U.S.	B3	112
Ohio, stm., U.S.	D9	76
Ohio Brush Creek, stm., Oh., U.S.	D2	112
Ohio City, Oh., U.S.	B1	112
Ohio Peak, mtn., Co., U.S.	C3	83
Ohioville, Pa., U.S.	E1	115
Ohoopee, stm., Ga., U.S.	D4	87
Ohrid, Lake, l., Eur.	H4	16
Öhringen, Ger.	F9	8
Oiapoque, Braz.	C8	54
Oil City, La., U.S.	B2	95
Oil City, Pa., U.S.	D2	115
Oil Creek, stm., Pa., U.S.	C2	115
Oildale, Ca., U.S.	E4	82
Oil Springs, Ont., Can.	E2	73
Oilton, Ok., U.S.	A5	113
Ōita, Japan	I4	30
Ojai, Ca., U.S.	E4	82
Ojinaga, Mex.	C7	62
Ojm'akon, Russia	E22	24
Ojo de Liebre, Laguna, b., Mex.	D2	62
Ojos del Salado, Cerro, mtn., S.A.	B3	56
Oka, stm., Russia	F25	18
Oka, stm., Russia	G14	24
Okaba, Indon.	G10	32
Okahandja, Nmb.	F3	44
Okaloosa, co., Fl., U.S.	u15	86
Okamanpeedan Lake, l., U.S.	A3	92
Okanagan Falls, B.C., Can.	E8	69
Okanagan Lake, l., B.C., Can.	D8	69
Okanagan Landing, B.C., Can.	D8	69
Okanogan, Wa., U.S.	A6	124
Okanogan, co., Wa., U.S.	A5	124
Okāra, Pak.	E5	38
Okarche, Ok., U.S.	B4	113
Okatibbee Reservoir, res., Ms., U.S.	C5	101
Okauchee Lake, Wi., U.S.	*E5	126
Okavango (Cubango), stm., Afr.	E3	44
Okavango Swamp, sw., Bots.	E4	44
Ōkawa, Japan	I3	30
Okawville, Il., U.S.	E4	90
Okaya, Japan	F11	30
Okayama, Japan	H6	30
Okazaki, Japan	H10	30
Okeechobee, Fl., U.S.	E6	86
Okeechobee, co., Fl., U.S.	E6	86
Okeechobee, Lake, l., Fl., U.S.	F6	86
Okeene, Ok., U.S.	A3	113
Okefenokee Swamp, sw., U.S.	F4	87
Okemah, Ok., U.S.	B5	113
Okfuskee, co., Ok., U.S.	B5	113
Okhotsk, Sea of (Ochotskoje More), Asia	G23	24
Oki-guntō, is., Japan	F6	30
Okinawa-jima, i., Japan	y27	31b
Okinoerabu-shima, i., Japan	x28	31b
Okino-Tori-shima, i., Japan	G14	26
Oklahoma, co., Ok., U.S.	B4	113
Oklahoma, state, U.S.	B4	113
Oklahoma City, Ok., U.S.	B4	113
Oklawaha, Fl., U.S.	C5	86
Oklawaha, stm., Fl., U.S.	C5	86
Oklawaha, Lake, res., Fl., U.S.	C5	86
Okmulgee, Ok., U.S.	B6	113
Okmulgee, co., Ok., U.S.	B5	113
Okoboji, Ia., U.S.	A2	92
Okobojo Creek, stm., S.D., U.S.	C5	118
Okolona, Ky., U.S.	g11	94
Okolona, Ms., U.S.	B5	101
Okotoks, Alta., Can.	D4	68
Okt'abr'skoj Revol'ucii, Ostrov, i., Russia	B13	24
Oktibbeha, co., Ms., U.S.	B5	101
Ola, Ar., U.S.	B2	81
Olancha Peak, mtn., Ca., U.S.	D4	82
Olanchito, Hond.	G4	64
Öland, i., Swe.	H11	6
Olanta, S.C., U.S.	D8	117
Olathe, Co., U.S.	C3	83
Olathe, Ks., U.S.	D9	93
Olavarría, Arg.	D4	56
Olbia, Italy	I4	14
Ol'chon, Ostrov, i., Russia	G15	24
Olcott, N.Y., U.S.	B2	109
Old Bahama Channel, strt., N.A.	C8	64
Old Bridge, N.J., U.S.	C4	107
Oldenburg, Ger.	B8	8
Oldenburg, In., U.S.	F7	91
Oldenburg [in Holstein], Ger.	A10	8
Old Faithful Geyser, Wy., U.S.	B2	127
Old Forge, Pa., U.S.	D10	115
Old Fort, N.C., U.S.	f10	110
Oldham, co., Ky., U.S.	B4	94
Oldham, co., Tx., U.S.	B1	120
Old Harbor, Ak., U.S.	D9	79
Old Head of Kinsale, c., Ire.	J4	7
Old Hickory Lake, res., Tn., U.S.	A5	119
Oldman, stm., Alta., Can.	E4	68
Old Man of the Mountain, N.H., U.S.	B3	106
Oldmans Creek, stm., N.J., U.S.	D2	107
Old Orchard Beach, Me., U.S.	E2	96
Old Perlican, Newf., Can.	D5	72
Old Point Comfort, c., Va., U.S.	h15	123
Old Rhodes Key, i., Fl., U.S.	G6	86
Old River Lake, l., Ar., U.S.	k10	81
Olds, Alta., Can.	D3	68
Old Saybrook, Ct., U.S.	D6	84
Oldsmar, Fl., U.S.	o10	86
Old Tampa Bay, b., Fl., U.S.	p10	86
Old Tappan, N.J., U.S.	g9	107
Old Topsail Inlet, b., N.C., U.S.	C5	110
Old Town, Me., U.S.	D4	96
Old Wives Lake, l., Sask., Can.	G2	75
Olean, N.Y., U.S.	C2	109
O'Leary, P.E.I., Can.	C5	71
Ølen, Nor.	G5	6
Olenij, Ostrov, i., Russia	C9	24
Olen'ok, Russia	D16	24
Olen'ok, stm., Russia	C18	24
Olen'okskij Zaliv, b., Russia	C18	24
Olentangy, stm., Oh., U.S.	B3	112
Oleśnica, Pol.	D17	8
Ol'ga, Russia	I21	24
Olga, Mount, mtn., Austl.	E6	50
Olhão, Port.	H3	12
Ólimbos, mtn., Cyp.	B3	40
Ólimbos, Óros, mtn., Grc.	I6	16
Olímpia, Braz.	F4	57
Olin, Ia., U.S.	B6	92
Olinda, Braz.	E12	54
Olite, Spain	C10	12
Oliva, Arg.	C4	56
Oliva, Spain	G11	12
Oliva de la Frontera, Spain	G5	12
Olive Branch, Ms., U.S.	A4	101
Olive Hill, Ky., U.S.	B6	94
Olivehurst, Ca., U.S.	C3	82
Oliveira, Braz.	F6	57
Olivenza, Spain	G4	12
Oliver, B.C., Can.	E8	69
Oliver, Pa., U.S.	G2	115
Oliver, co., N.D., U.S.	B4	111
Oliver Dam, U.S.	C5	78
Oliver Springs, Tn., U.S.	C9	119
Olivet, Mi., U.S.	F6	99
Olivia, Mn., U.S.	F4	100
Olla, La., U.S.	C3	95
Ollagüe, Chile	A3	56
Olmedo, Spain	D7	12
Olmito, Tx., U.S.	F4	120
Olmos, Peru	E3	54
Olmos Park, Tx., U.S.	k7	120
Olmsted, co., Mn., U.S.	G6	100
Olmsted Falls, Oh., U.S.	h9	112
Olney, Il., U.S.	E5	90
Olney, Md., U.S.	B3	97
Olney, Tx., U.S.	C3	120
Oloj, stm., Russia	D26	24
Ol'okma, stm., Russia	F18	24
Ol'okminsk, Russia	E18	24
Olomouc, Czech.	F17	8
Olongapo, Phil.	q19	33b
Oloron-Sainte-Marie, Fr.	I6	10
Olot, Spain	C14	12
Olov'annaja, Russia	G17	24
Olsztyn (Allenstein), Pol.	B20	8
Olten, Switz.	E14	10
Olton, Tx., U.S.	B1	120
Oluan Pi, c., Tai.	N9	28
Olustee, Ok., U.S.	C2	113
Ol'utorskij, Mys, c., Russia	F28	24
Olympia, Wa., U.S.	B3	124
Olympic Mountains, mts., Wa., U.S.	B2	124
Olympic National Park, Wa., U.S.	B2	124
Olympus, Mount, mtn., Wa., U.S.	B2	124
Olympus, Mount see Ólimbos, Óros, mtn., Grc.	I6	16
Olyphant, Pa., U.S.	D10	115
Ōmae-zaki, c., Japan	H11	30
Omagh, N. Ire., U.K.	G5	7
Omaha, Ne., U.S.	C10	104
Omaha Indian Reservation, Ne., U.S.	B9	104
Omak, Wa., U.S.	A6	124
Omak Lake, l., Wa., U.S.	A6	124
Oman, ctry., Asia	D6	46
Oman, Gulf of, b., Asia	D6	46
Omar, W.V., U.S.	D3	125
Ōma-zaki, c., Japan	A13	30
Omčak, Russia	E23	24
Omega, Ga., U.S.	E3	87
Omegna, Italy	D3	14
Omemee, Ont., Can.	C6	73
Omerville, Que., Can.	D5	74
Ometepe, Isla de, i., Nic.	I5	64
Ometepec, Mex.	I10	62
Omineca, stm., B.C., Can.	B5	69
Omineca Mountains, mts., B.C., Can.	A4	69
Ōmiya, Japan	G12	30
Ommaney, Cape, c., Ak., U.S.	D12	79
Ommanney Bay, b., N.W. Ter., Can.	B12	66
Ommen, Neth.	C6	8
Omo, stm., Eth.	G2	46
Omolon, stm., Russia	D25	24
Ompompanoosuc, stm., Vt., U.S.	D4	122
Omro, Wi., U.S.	D5	126
Omsk, Russia	F8	24
Omsukčan, Russia	E25	24
Ōmura, Japan	J2	30
Ōmuta, Japan	I3	30
Onaga, Ks., U.S.	C7	93
Onalaska, Wa., U.S.	C3	124
Onalaska, Wi., U.S.	E2	126
Onamia, Mn., U.S.	D5	100
Onancock, Va., U.S.	C7	123
Onarga, Il., U.S.	C6	90
Onawa, Ia., U.S.	B1	92
Onawa, Lake, l., Me., U.S.	C3	96
Onaway, Mi., U.S.	C6	99
Onda, Spain	F11	12
Ondangua, Nmb.	E3	44
Ondjiva, Ang.	E3	44
Öndörchaan, Mong.	B9	26
Oneco, Fl., U.S.	E4	86
Onega, Lake see Onežskoje ozero, l., Russia	E5	22
One Hundred Fifty Mile House, B.C., Can.	C7	69
One Hundred Mile House, B.C., Can.	D7	69
Oneida, Ky., U.S.	C6	94
Oneida, N.Y., U.S.	B5	109
Oneida, Oh., U.S.	C1	112
Oneida, Tn., U.S.	C9	119
Oneida, co., Id., U.S.	G6	89
Oneida, co., N.Y., U.S.	B5	109
Oneida, co., Wi., U.S.	C4	126
Oneida Lake, l., N.Y., U.S.	B5	109
O'Neill, Ne., U.S.	B7	104
Onekotan, Ostrov, i., Russia	H24	24
Oneonta, Al., U.S.	B3	78
Oneonta, N.Y., U.S.	C5	109
Onești, Rom.	C10	16
Onežskoje ozero, l., Russia	E5	22
Ongole, India	E6	37
Onida, S.D., U.S.	C5	118
Onitsha, Nig.	G7	42
Onoda, Japan	I4	30
Onomichi, Japan	H6	30
Onondaga, co., N.Y., U.S.	C4	109
Onondaga Indian Reservation, N.Y., U.S.	C4	109
Onota Lake, l., Ma., U.S.	B1	98
Onoway, Alta., Can.	C3	68
Onset, Ma., U.S.	C6	98
Onslow, Austl.	D3	50
Onslow, co., N.C., U.S.	C5	110
Onslow Bay, b., N.C., U.S.	C5	110
Onsted, Mi., U.S.	F6	99
Ontario, Ca., U.S.	E5	82
Ontario, Oh., U.S.	B3	112
Ontario, Or., U.S.	C10	114
Ontario, co., N.Y., U.S.	C3	109
Ontario, prov., Can.	C6	73
Ontario, Lake, l., N.A.	C11	76
Onteniente, Spain	G11	12
Ontonagon, Mi., U.S.	m12	99
Ontonagon, co., Mi., U.S.	m12	99
Ontonagon Indian Reservation, Mi., U.S.	B1	99
Onverwacht, Sur.	B7	54
Oodnadatta, Austl.	E7	50
Ooldea, Austl.	F6	50
Oolitic, In., U.S.	G4	91
Oologah, Ok., U.S.	A6	113
Oologah Lake, res., Ok., U.S.	A6	113
Ooltewah, Tn., U.S.	D8	119
Oostburg, Wi., U.S.	E6	126
Oostende (Ostende), Bel.	D2	8
Oosterhout, Neth.	D4	8
Ootacamund, India	G4	37
Ootsa Lake, l., B.C., Can.	C4	69
Opala, Zaire	B4	44
Opa-Locka, Fl., U.S.	s13	86
Opatija, Cro.	D9	14
Opava, Czech.	F17	8
Opelika, Al., U.S.	C4	78
Opelousas, La., U.S.	D3	95
Opequon Creek, stm., W.V., U.S.	B6	125
Opiscotéo, Lac, l., Que., Can.	F19	66
Opole (Oppeln), Pol.	E17	8
Opotiki, N.Z.	C6	52
Opp, Al., U.S.	D3	78
Oppdal, Nor.	E7	6
Oppelo, Ar., U.S.	B3	81
Opportunity, Wa., U.S.	B8	124
Optima Reservoir, res., Ok., U.S.	e9	113
Oquawka, Il., U.S.	C3	90
Ora, Italy	C6	14
Oracle, Az., U.S.	E5	80
Oradea, Rom.	B5	16
Oradell, N.J., U.S.	h8	107
Oradell Reservoir, res., N.J., U.S.	h9	107
Orai, India	H8	38
Oraibi, Az., U.S.	B5	80
Oran (Wahran), Alg.	A5	42
Oran, Mo., U.S.	D8	102
Orange, Austl.	F9	50
Orange, Fr.	H11	10
Orange, Ca., U.S.	n13	82
Orange, Ct., U.S.	D3	84
Orange, Ma., U.S.	A3	98
Orange, N.J., U.S.	B4	107
Orange, Tx., U.S.	D6	120
Orange, Va., U.S.	B4	123
Orange, co., Ca., U.S.	F5	82
Orange, co., Fl., U.S.	D5	86
Orange, co., In., U.S.	G4	91
Orange, co., N.Y., U.S.	D6	109
Orange, co., N.C., U.S.	A3	110
Orange, co., Tx., U.S.	D6	120
Orange, co., Vt., U.S.	D3	122
Orange, co., Va., U.S.	B4	123
Orange (Oranje), stm., Afr.	G3	44
Orange, Cabo, c., Braz.	C8	54
Orange Beach, Al., U.S.	E2	78
Orangeburg, S.C., U.S.	E6	117
Orangeburg, co., S.C., U.S.	E6	117
Orange City, Fl., U.S.	D5	86
Orange City, Ia., U.S.	B1	92
Orange Grove, Ms., U.S.	E5	101
Orange Grove, Tx., U.S.	F4	120
Orange Lake, l., Fl., U.S.	C4	86
Orange Park, Fl., U.S.	B5	86
Orangeville, Ont., Can.	D4	73
Orangeville, Ut., U.S.	D4	121
Orange Walk, Belize	E3	64
Orani, Phil.	q19	33b
Oranienburg, Ger.	C13	8
Oranjestad, Aruba	H12	64
Orbetello, Italy	G6	14
Orbost, Austl.	G9	50
Örbyhus, Swe.	F11	6
Orcas Island, i., Wa., U.S.	A3	124
Orcera, Spain	G9	12
Orchard City, Co., U.S.	C3	83
Orchard Homes, Mt., U.S.	D2	103
Orchard Park, N.Y., U.S.	C2	109
Orchards, Wa., U.S.	D3	124
Orchard Valley, Wy., U.S.	E8	127
Orchila, Isla, i., Ven.	B9	58
Orchon, stm., Mong.	B7	26

Name	Map Ref	Page
Orcutt, Ca., U.S.	E3	82
Ord, Ne., U.S.	C7	104
Ord, Mount, mtn., Austl.	C5	50
Ordenes, Spain	B3	12
Ordway, Co., U.S.	C7	83
Ordzhonikidze see Vladikavkaz, Russia	I6	22
Oreana, Il., U.S.	D5	90
Örebro, Swe.	G10	6
Orechovo-Zujevo, Russia	F21	18
Oregon, Il., U.S.	A4	90
Oregon, Mo., U.S.	B2	102
Oregon, Oh., U.S.	A2	112
Oregon, Wi., U.S.	F4	126
Oregon, co., Mo., U.S.	E6	102
Oregon, state, U.S.	C6	114
Oregon Caves National Monument, Or., U.S.	E2	114
Oregon City, Or., U.S.	B4	114
Oregon Inlet, b., N.C., U.S.	B7	110
Orel, Russia	I19	18
Orem, Ut., U.S.	C4	121
Orenburg, Russia	G9	22
Orense, Spain	C4	12
Orestiás, Grc.	H10	16
Orfordville, Wi., U.S.	F4	126
Organ Mountains, mts., N.M., U.S.	E3	108
Organ Pipe Cactus National Monument, Az., U.S.	E3	80
Orgūn, Afg.	D3	38
Oriental, N.C., U.S.	B6	110
Oriental, Cordillera, mts., Col.	E6	58
Oriental, Cordillera, mts., Peru	F4	54
Orihuela, Spain	G11	12
Orillia, Ont., Can.	C5	73
Orinoco, stm., S.A.	C11	58
Orinoco, Delta del, Ven.	C12	58
Orion, Il., U.S.	B3	90
Oripää, Fin.	F14	6
Orissa, state, India	J11	38
Oristano, Italy	I3	14
Orivesi, Fin.	F15	6
Orizaba, Mex.	H11	62
Orizaba, Pico de (Volcán Citlaltépetl), vol., Mex.	H11	62
Orkney Islands, is., Scot., U.K.	B9	7
Orland, Ca., U.S.	C2	82
Orlando, Fl., U.S.	D5	86
Orland Park, Il., U.S.	k9	90
Orléans, Fr.	E8	10
Orleans, Ma., U.S.	C7	98
Orleans, Vt., U.S.	B4	122
Orleans, co., La., U.S.	E6	95
Orleans, co., N.Y., U.S.	B2	109
Orleans, co., Vt., U.S.	B4	122
Orléans, Île d', i., Que., Can.	C6	74
Orman Dam, S.D., U.S.	C2	118
Ormond Beach, Fl., U.S.	C5	86
Ormož, Slo.	C11	14
Ormstown, Que., Can.	D3	74
Ornans, Fr.	E13	10
Örnsköldsvik, Swe.	E12	6
Orocué, Col.	E7	58
Orofino, Id., U.S.	C2	89
Oromocto, N.B., Can.	D3	71
Oromocto Lake, l., N.B., Can.	D2	71
Orono, Me., U.S.	D4	96
Oronoco, Mn., U.S.	F6	100
Oroville, Ca., U.S.	C3	82
Oroville, Wa., U.S.	A6	124
Oroville, Lake, res., Ca., U.S.	C3	82
Orrick, Mo., U.S.	B3	102
Orrville, Oh., U.S.	B4	112
Orsk, Russia	G9	22
Orta Nova, Italy	H10	14
Ortegal, Cabo, c., Spain	B4	12
Orting, Wa., U.S.	B3	124
Ortiz, Ven.	C9	58
Ortona, Italy	G9	14
Ortonville, Mi., U.S.	F7	99
Ortonville, Mn., U.S.	E2	100
Orūmīyeh (Reẓā'īyeh), Iran	J7	22
Orūmīyeh, Daryācheh-ye, l., Iran	J7	22
Oruro, Bol.	G5	54
Orūzgān (Qala-I-Hazār Qadam), Afg.	D2	38
Orvieto, Italy	G7	14
Orwell, Oh., U.S.	A5	112
Orwigsburg, Pa., U.S.	E9	115
Oš, Kyrg.	I12	22
Osa, Península de, pen., C.R.	J6	64
Osage, Ia., U.S.	A5	92
Osage, Wy., U.S.	C8	127
Osage, co., Ks., U.S.	D8	93
Osage, co., Mo., U.S.	C6	102
Osage, co., Ok., U.S.	A5	113
Osage, stm., Mo., U.S.	C3	102
Osage Beach, Mo., U.S.	C5	102
Osage City, Ks., U.S.	D8	93
Ōsaka, Japan	H8	30
Ōsaka-wan, b., Japan	H8	30
Osakis, Mn., U.S.	E3	100
Osakis, Lake, l., Mn., U.S.	E3	100
Osawatomie, Ks., U.S.	D9	93
Osborne, Ks., U.S.	C5	93
Osborne, co., Ks., U.S.	C5	93
Osburn, Id., U.S.	B3	89
Osceola, Ar., U.S.	B6	81
Osceola, In., U.S.	A5	91
Osceola, Ia., U.S.	C4	92
Osceola, Mo., U.S.	C4	102
Osceola, Ne., U.S.	C8	104
Osceola, Wi., U.S.	C1	126
Osceola, co., Fl., U.S.	E5	86
Osceola, co., Ia., U.S.	A2	92
Osceola, co., Mi., U.S.	E5	99
Osceola Mills, Pa., U.S.	E5	115
Oschersleben, Ger.	C11	8
Oscoda, Mi., U.S.	D7	99
Oscoda, co., Mi., U.S.	D6	99
Oscura Mountains, mts., N.M., U.S.	D3	108
Osen, Nor.	D8	6
Osgood, In., U.S.	F7	91
Oshawa, Ont., Can.	D6	73
Oshima-hantō, pen., Japan	q18	30a
Oshkosh, Ne., U.S.	C3	104
Oshkosh, Wi., U.S.	D5	126
Oshogbo, Nig.	G6	42
Osh see Oš, Kyrg.	I12	22
Oshwe, Zaire	B3	44
Osijek, Cro.	D2	16
Osimo, Italy	F8	14
Osinniki, Russia	G11	24
Osipoviči, Bela.	H11	18
Oskaloosa, Ia., U.S.	C5	92
Oskaloosa, Ks., U.S.	C8	93
Oskarshamn, Swe.	H11	6
Oslo, Nor.	G8	6
Osmānābād, India	C4	37
Osmaniye, Tur.	A5	40
Osmond, Ne., U.S.	B8	104
Osnabrück, Ger.	C8	8
Osorno, Chile	E2	56
Osorno, Spain	C7	12
Osoyoos, B.C., Can.	E8	69
Osoyoos Lake, l., Wa., U.S.	A6	124
Ospino, Ven.	C8	58
Osprey, Fl., U.S.	E4	86
Osprey Reef, rf., Austl.	B9	50
Ossa, Mount, mtn., Austl.	H9	50
Ossabaw Island, i., Ga., U.S.	E5	87
Osseo, Mn., U.S.	m12	100
Osseo, Wi., U.S.	D2	126
Ossian, In., U.S.	C7	91
Ossian, Ia., U.S.	A6	92
Ossining, N.Y., U.S.	D7	109
Ossipee, stm., U.S.	C5	106
Ossipee Lake, l., N.H., U.S.	C4	106
Ostaškov, Russia	D16	18
Osterholz-Scharmbeck, Ger.	B8	8
Osterode, Ger.	D10	8
Östersund, Swe.	E10	6
Osterville, Ma., U.S.	C7	98
Ostrava, Czech.	F18	8
Ostrołęka, Pol.	B21	8
Ostrov, Russia	D11	18
Ostrowiec Świętokrzyski, Pol.	E21	8
Ostrów Wielkopolski, Pol.	D17	8
Ostuni, Italy	I12	14
Ōsumi-kaikyō, strt., Japan	L3	30
Ōsumi-shotō, is., Japan	u30	31b
Osuna, Spain	H6	12
Osvaldo Cruz, Braz.	F3	57
Oswegatchie, stm., N.Y., U.S.	f9	109
Oswego, Il., U.S.	B5	90
Oswego, Ks., U.S.	E8	93
Oswego, N.Y., U.S.	B4	109
Oswego, co., N.Y., U.S.	B4	109
Oswego, stm., N.J., U.S.	D4	107
Oswego, stm., N.Y., U.S.	B4	109
Oswestry, Eng., U.K.	I9	7
Oświęcim, Pol.	E19	8
Ōta, Japan	F12	30
Otaki, N.Z.	D5	52
Otaru, Japan	p18	30a
Otavi, Nmb.	E3	44
Oteen, N.C., U.S.	f10	110
Otero, co., Co., U.S.	D7	83
Otero, co., N.M., U.S.	E3	108
Othello, Wa., U.S.	C6	124
Oti, stm., Afr.	G6	42
Otish, Monts, mts., Que., Can.	F18	66
Otis Orchards, Wa., U.S.	g14	124
Otis Reservoir, res., Ma., U.S.	B1	98
Otisville, Mi., U.S.	E7	99
Otjiwarongo, Nmb.	F3	44
Otočac, Cro.	E10	14
Otoe, co., Ne., U.S.	D9	104
Otranto, Italy	I13	14
Otranto, Strait of, mth., Eur.	I2	16
Otsego, Mi., U.S.	F5	99
Otsego, co., Mi., U.S.	C6	99
Otsego, co., N.Y., U.S.	C5	109
Otsego Lake, l., N.Y., U.S.	C6	109
Ōtsu, Japan	G8	30
Otta, Nor.	F7	6
Ottauquechee, stm., Vt., U.S.	D4	122
Ottawa, Ont., Can.	B9	73
Ottawa, Il., U.S.	B5	90
Ottawa, Ks., U.S.	D8	93
Ottawa, Oh., U.S.	A1	112
Ottawa, co., Ks., U.S.	C6	93
Ottawa, co., Mi., U.S.	F4	99
Ottawa, co., Oh., U.S.	A2	112
Ottawa, co., Ok., U.S.	A7	113
Ottawa, stm., Can.	G17	66
Ottawa, stm., Oh., U.S.	e6	112
Ottawa Hills, Oh., U.S.	e6	112
Ottawa Islands, is., N.W. Ter., Can.	E16	66
Ottenby, Swe.	H11	6
Otterbein, In., U.S.	D3	91
Otter Brook, stm., N.H., U.S.	E2	106
Otter Brook Lake, res., N.H., U.S.	E2	106
Otter Creek, stm., Ut., U.S.	E4	121
Otter Creek, stm., Vt., U.S.	C2	122
Otter Creek Reservoir, res., Ut., U.S.	E4	121
Otter Islands, is., S.C., U.S.	m11	117
Otter Tail, co., Mn., U.S.	D3	100
Otter Tail, stm., Mn., U.S.	D2	100
Otter Tail Lake, l., Mn., U.S.	D3	100
Otterville, Ont., Can.	E4	73
Ottumwa, Ia., U.S.	C5	92
Otwock, Pol.	C21	8
Ötztaler Alpen, mts., Eur.	C5	14
Ouachita, co., Ar., U.S.	D3	81
Ouachita, co., La., U.S.	B3	95
Ouachita, Lake, res., Ar., U.S.	C2	81
Ouachita Mountains, mts., U.S.	E8	76
Ouadda, Cen. Afr. Rep.	G10	42
Ouagadougou, Burkina	F5	42
Ouahigouya, Burkina	F5	42
Oualâta, Maur.	E4	42
Ouallene, Alg.	D6	42
Ouanda Djallé, Cen. Afr. Rep.	G10	42
Ouarane, reg., Maur.	D3	42
Ouargla, Alg.	B7	42
Ouarzazate, Mor.	B4	42
Oubangui, stm., Afr.	A3	44
Oudtshoorn, S. Afr.	H4	44
Oued Meliz, Tun.	M3	14
Oued Zarga, Tun.	M4	14
Ouémé, stm., Benin	G6	42
Ouesso, Congo	A3	44
Ouezzane, Mor.	B4	42
Oujda, Mor.	B5	42
Oulu, Fin.	D15	6
Oulujärvi, l., Fin.	D16	6
Oum Chalouba, Chad	E10	42
Ounianga Kébir, Chad	E10	42
Ouray, Co., U.S.	C3	83
Ouray, co., Co., U.S.	C3	83
Ouray, Mount, mtn., Co., U.S.	C4	83
Ourinhos, Braz.	G4	57
Ourique, Port.	H3	12
Ouro Prêto, Braz.	F7	57
Ōu-sammyaku, mts., Japan	D13	30
Outagamie, co., Wi., U.S.	D5	126
Outardes Quatre, Réservoir, res., Que., Can.	h13	74
Outer Hebrides, is., Scot., U.K.	D5	7
Outer Island, i., Wi., U.S.	A3	126
Outer Santa Barbara Passage, strt., Ca., U.S.	F4	82
Outpost Mountain, mtn., Ak., U.S.	B9	79
Outremont, Que., Can.	p19	74
Ovalle, Chile	C2	56
Ovamboland, hist. reg., Nmb.	E3	44
Ovana, Cerro, mtn., Ven.	E9	58
Ovar, Port.	E3	12
Overbrook, Ks., U.S.	D8	93
Overgaard, Az., U.S.	C5	80
Overland, Mo., U.S.	f13	102
Overland Park, Ks., U.S.	m16	93
Overlea, Md., U.S.	B4	97
Overton, Nv., U.S.	G7	105
Overton, Tx., U.S.	C5	120
Overton, co., Tn., U.S.	C8	119
Övertorneå, Swe.	C14	6
Ovett, Ms., U.S.	D4	101
Ovid, Mi., U.S.	E6	99
Oviedo, Spain	B6	12
Owando, Congo	B3	44
Owasco Lake, l., N.Y., U.S.	C4	109
Owase, Japan	H9	30
Owasso, Ok., U.S.	A6	113
Owatonna, Mn., U.S.	F5	100
Owego, N.Y., U.S.	C4	109
Owen, Wi., U.S.	D3	126
Owen, co., In., U.S.	F4	91
Owen, co., Ky., U.S.	B5	94
Owen, Lake, l., Wi., U.S.	B2	126
Owen, Mount, mtn., Co., U.S.	C3	83
Owens, stm., Ca., U.S.	D4	82
Owensboro, Ky., U.S.	C2	94
Owens Cross Roads, Al., U.S.	A3	78
Owens Lake, l., Ca., U.S.	D5	82
Owen Sound, Ont., Can.	C4	73
Owen Sound, b., Ont., Can.	C4	73
Owen Stanley Range, mts., Pap. N. Gui.	m16	50a
Owensville, In., U.S.	H2	91
Owensville, Mo., U.S.	C6	102
Owensville, Oh., U.S.	C1	112
Owenton, Ky., U.S.	B5	94
Owings Mills, Md., U.S.	B4	97
Owingsville, Ky., U.S.	B6	94
Owl Creek, stm., Wy., U.S.	C4	127
Owl Creek Mountains, mts., Wy., U.S.	C4	127
Owo, Nig.	G7	42
Owosso, Mi., U.S.	E6	99
Owsley, co., Ky., U.S.	C6	94
Owyhee, Nv., U.S.	B5	105
Owyhee, co., Id., U.S.	G2	89
Owyhee, stm., U.S.	E9	114
Owyhee, Lake, res., Or., U.S.	D9	114
Owyhee Dam, Or., U.S.	D9	114
Owyhee Mountains, mts., U.S.	G2	89
Oxbow Dam, U.S.	E2	89
Oxelösund, Swe.	G11	6
Oxford, N.S., Can.	D6	71
Oxford, N.Z.	E4	52
Oxford, Eng., U.K.	J11	7
Oxford, Al., U.S.	B4	78
Oxford, Ct., U.S.	D3	84
Oxford, Ga., U.S.	C3	87
Oxford, In., U.S.	C3	91
Oxford, Ia., U.S.	C6	92
Oxford, Ks., U.S.	E6	93
Oxford, Me., U.S.	D2	96
Oxford, Md., U.S.	C5	97
Oxford, Ma., U.S.	B4	98
Oxford, Mi., U.S.	F7	99
Oxford, Ms., U.S.	A4	101
Oxford, Ne., U.S.	D6	104
Oxford, N.Y., U.S.	C5	109
Oxford, N.C., U.S.	A4	110
Oxford, Oh., U.S.	C1	112
Oxford, Pa., U.S.	G10	115
Oxford, co., Me., U.S.	D2	96
Oxford Lake, l., Man., Can.	B4	70
Oxford Peak, mtn., Id., U.S.	G6	89
Oxnard, Ca., U.S.	E4	82
Oxon Hill, Md., U.S.	f9	97
Oxus see Amu Darya, stm., Asia	I10	22
Oyama, B.C., Can.	D8	69
Oyama, Japan	F12	30
Oyem, Gabon	A2	44
Oyen, Alta., Can.	D5	68
Oyonnax, Fr.	F12	10
Oyster Bay, N.Y., U.S.	E7	109
Oyster Keys, is., Fl., U.S.	G6	86
Ozamiz, Phil.	D7	32
Ozark, Al., U.S.	D4	78
Ozark, Ar., U.S.	B2	81
Ozark, Mo., U.S.	D4	102
Ozark, co., Mo., U.S.	E5	102
Ozark Plateau, plat., U.S.	D8	76
Ozark Reservoir, res., Ar., U.S.	B1	81
Ozarks, Lake of the, res., Mo., U.S.	C5	102
Ozaukee, co., Wi., U.S.	E6	126
Ózd, Hung.	G20	8
Ozernovskij, Russia	G25	24
Ozette Lake, l., Wa., U.S.	A1	124
Ozieri, Italy	I3	14
Ožogino, Ozero, l., Russia	D23	24
Ozona, Fl., U.S.	o10	86
Ozona, Tx., U.S.	D2	120
Ōzu, Japan	I5	30
P		
Paarl, S. Afr.	H3	44
Paauilo, Hi., U.S.	C6	88
Pabianice, Pol.	D19	8
Pābna, Bngl.	H13	38
Pacasmayo, Peru	E3	54
Pace, Fl., U.S.	u14	86
Pachaug Pond, l., Ct., U.S.	C8	84
Pachino, Italy	M10	14
Pachuca [de Soto], Mex.	G10	62
Pacific, Mo., U.S.	C7	102
Pacific, Wa., U.S.	f11	124
Pacific, co., Wa., U.S.	C2	124
Pacifica, Ca., U.S.	h8	82
Pacific Beach, Wa., U.S.	B1	124
Pacific City, Or., U.S.	B3	114
Pacific Creek, stm., Wy., U.S.	D3	127
Pacific Grove, Ca., U.S.	D3	82
Pacific Ocean	F2	2
Pacific Palisades, Hi., U.S.	g10	88
Pacific Ranges, mts., B.C., Can.	D4	69
Pacific Rim National Park, B.C., Can.	E5	69
Pack Monadnock Mountain, mtn., N.H., U.S.	E3	106
Packwood, Wa., U.S.	C4	124
Pacolet, S.C., U.S.	B4	117
Pacolet, stm., S.C., U.S.	A4	117
Pacolet Mills, S.C., U.S.	B4	117
Pactola Reservoir, res., S.D., U.S.	C2	118
Padang, Indon.	F3	32
Padangpanjang, Indon.	O6	34
Padangsidempuan, Indon.	N5	34
Paddock Lake, Wi., U.S.	n11	126
Paden City, W.V., U.S.	B4	125
Paderborn, Ger.	D8	8
Padova, Italy	D6	14
Padre Island, i., Tx., U.S.	F4	120
Padre Island National Seashore, Tx., U.S.	F4	120
Padrón, Spain	C3	12
Padstow, Eng., U.K.	K8	7
Padua see Padova, Italy	D6	14
Paducah, Ky., U.S.	e9	94
Paducah, Tx., U.S.	B2	120
Paektu-san, mtn., Asia	C12	26
Pafúri, Moz.	F6	44
Pag, Cro.	E10	14
Pagai Selatan, Pulau, i., Indon.	F3	32
Page, Az., U.S.	A4	80
Page, W.V., U.S.	C3	125
Page, co., Ia., U.S.	D2	92
Page, co., Va., U.S.	B4	123
Pageland, S.C., U.S.	B7	117
Pagoda Peak, mtn., Co., U.S.	A3	83
Pagoda Point, c., Mya.	G3	34
Pagosa Springs, Co., U.S.	D3	83
Paguate, N.M., U.S.	B2	108
Pahala, Hi., U.S.	D6	88
Pahang, stm., Malay.	M7	34
Pahoa, Hi., U.S.	D7	88
Pahokee, Fl., U.S.	F6	86
Pahrump, Nv., U.S.	G6	105
Pahute Mesa, mtn., Nv., U.S.	F5	105
Paia, Hi., U.S.	C5	88
Päijänne, l., Fin.	F15	6
Pailolo Channel, strt., Hi., U.S.	B5	88
Paimpol, Fr.	D3	10
Paincourtville, La., U.S.	k9	95
Painesville, Oh., U.S.	A4	112
Paint, stm., Mi., U.S.	B2	99
Paint Creek, stm., Oh., U.S.	C2	112
Paint Creek, stm., W.V., U.S.	m13	125
Paint Creek, North Fork, stm., Oh., U.S.	C2	112
Paint Creek Lake, res., Oh., U.S.	C2	112
Painted Desert, des., Az., U.S.	B4	80
Painted Post, N.Y., U.S.	C3	109
Painted Rock Reservoir, res., Az., U.S.	D3	80
Paintsville, Ky., U.S.	C7	94
Paisley, Ont., Can.	C3	73
Paisley, Scot., U.K.	F8	7
Paita, Peru	E2	54
Pajala, Swe.	C14	6
Paján, Ec.	H2	58
Pakanbaru, Indon.	E3	32
Pakaraima Mountains, mts., S.A.	E12	58
Pakistan (Pākistān), ctry., Asia	D2	36
Pakistan, East see Bangladesh, ctry., Asia	E6	36
Pakokku, Mya.	D3	34
Pakowki Lake, l., Alta., Can.	E5	68
P'akupur, stm., Russia	E9	24
Pakxé, Laos	G8	34
Pala, Chad	G8	42
Palacios, Tx., U.S.	E4	120
Palamós, Spain	D15	12
Palana, Russia	F25	24
Pālanpur, India	H5	38
Palaoa Point, c., Hi., U.S.	C4	88
Palapye, Bots.	F5	44
Palatine, Il., U.S.	A5	90
Palatka, Russia	E24	24
Palatka, Fl., U.S.	C5	86
Palau, ctry, Oc.	D9	32
Palawan, i., Phil.	D6	32
Pālayankottai, India	H4	37
Palembang, Indon.	F3	32
Palencia, Spain	C7	12
Palermo, Italy	K8	14
Palestine, Ar., U.S.	C5	81
Palestine, Il., U.S.	D6	90
Palestine, Tx., U.S.	D5	120
Palestine, ctry., Asia	C4	40
Palestine, Lake, res., Tx., U.S.	C5	120
Paletwa, Mya.	D2	34
Pālghāt, India	G4	37
Pāli, India	H5	38
Palikea, mtn., Hi., U.S.	g9	88
Palisade, Co., U.S.	B2	83
Palisades Park, N.J., U.S.	h8	107
Palisades Reservoir, res., U.S.	F7	89
Pālitāna, India	J4	38
Palk Strait, strt., Asia	H5	37
Pallastunturi, mtn., Fin.	B14	6
Palma, Moz.	D8	44
Palma del Río, Spain	H6	12
Palma [de Mallorca], Spain	F14	12
Palma di Montechiaro, Italy	L8	14
Palmanova, Italy	D8	14
Palmarito, Ven.	D7	58
Palmas, Cape, c., Lib.	H4	42
Palma Soriano, Cuba	D9	64
Palm Bay, Fl., U.S.	D6	86
Palm Beach, Fl., U.S.	F6	86
Palm Beach, co., Fl., U.S.	F6	86
Palm Beach Gardens, Fl., U.S.	*F6	86
Palmdale, Ca., U.S.	E4	82
Palmelo, Braz.	D4	57
Palmer, Ak., U.S.	C10	79
Palmer, Ma., U.S.	B3	98
Palmer, Mi., U.S.	B3	99
Palmer, Ms., U.S.	D4	101
Palmer, Ne., U.S.	C7	104
Palmer, Tn., U.S.	D8	119
Palmer, Tx., U.S.	n10	120
Palmer Lake, Co., U.S.	B6	83
Palmerston, Ont., Can.	D4	73
Palmerston, Cape, c., Austl.	D9	50
Palmerston North, N.Z.	D5	52
Palmerton, Pa., U.S.	E10	115
Palmetto, Fl., U.S.	E4	86
Palmetto, Ga., U.S.	C2	87
Palm Harbor, Fl., U.S.	o10	86
Palmi, Italy	K10	14
Palmira, Col.	F4	58
Palmira, Ec.	I3	58
Palms, Isle of, i., S.C., U.S.	F8	117
Palm Springs, Ca., U.S.	F5	82
Palm Springs, Fl., U.S.	*F6	86
Palmyra, In., U.S.	H5	91
Palmyra, Mo., U.S.	B6	102
Palmyra, N.J., U.S.	C2	107
Palmyra, N.Y., U.S.	B3	109
Palmyra, Pa., U.S.	F8	115
Palmyra, Wi., U.S.	F5	126
Palni, India	G4	37
Palo Alto, Ca., U.S.	D2	82
Palo Alto, co., Ia., U.S.	A3	92
Paloich, Sudan	F12	42
Palomar Mountain, mtn., Ca., U.S.	F5	82
Palomas Mountains, mts., Az., U.S.	D2	80
Palo Pinto, co., Tx., U.S.	C3	120
Palos Park, Il., U.S.	k9	90
Palos Verdes Estates, Ca., U.S.	n12	82
Palourde, Lake, l., La., U.S.	k9	95
Palouse, Wa., U.S.	C8	124
Palouse, stm., Wa., U.S.	C7	124
Palu, Indon.	F6	32
Palwal, India	F7	38
Pamekasan, Indon.	m16	33a
Pamiers, Fr.	I8	10
Pamir, mts., Asia	B3	36
Pamlico, co., N.C., U.S.	B6	110
Pamlico, stm., N.C., U.S.	B6	110
Pamlico Sound, strt., N.C., U.S.	B6	110
Pampa, Tx., U.S.	B2	120
Pampas, reg., Arg.	C4	56
Pamplico, S.C., U.S.	D8	117
Pamplona, Col.	D6	58
Pamplona, Spain	C10	12
Pamunkey, stm., Va., U.S.	C5	123
Pana, Il., U.S.	D4	90
Panaca, Nv., U.S.	F7	105
Panache, Lake, l., Ont., Can.	A3	73
Panaji (Panjim), India	E2	37
Panamá, Pan.	J8	64
Panama, Ok., U.S.	B7	113
Panama, ctry., N.A.	J7	64
Panama, Gulf of, b., Pan.	J8	64
Panama, Isthmus of, Pan.	J8	64
Panama Canal, Pan.	J8	64
Panama City, Fl., U.S.	u16	86
Panama City Beach, Fl., U.S.	u16	86
Panamint Range, mts., Ca., U.S.	D5	82
Panay, i., Phil.	C7	32
Pancake Range, mts., Nv., U.S.	E6	105
Pandharpur, India	D3	37
Pandora, Oh., U.S.	B2	112
P'andž (Panj), stm., Asia	A4	38
Panevėžys, Lith.	F7	18
Pangala, Congo	B2	44
Pangburn, Ar., U.S.	B4	81
Pangkalanbuun, Indon.	F5	32
Pangkalpinang, Indon.	F4	32
Pangnirtung, N.W. Ter., Can.	C19	66
Panguitch, Ut., U.S.	F3	121
Pangutaran Group, is., Phil.	D7	32
Panhandle, Tx., U.S.	B2	120
Paniau, mtn., Hi., U.S.	B1	88
Pānīpat, India	F7	38
Panj (P'andž), stm., Asia	B4	38
Panjāb, Afg.	C2	38
Panjgūr, Pak.	D1	36
Panola, co., Ms., U.S.	A3	101
Panola, co., Tx., U.S.	C5	120
Panora, Ia., U.S.	C3	92
Pantelleria, Italy	M6	14
Panvel, India	C2	37
Panxian, China	B8	34
Panyam, Nig.	G7	42
Panyu, China	M2	28
Paola, Italy	J11	14
Paola, Ks., U.S.	D9	93
Paoli, In., U.S.	G5	91
Paoli, Pa., U.S.	o20	115
Paonia, Co., U.S.	C3	83
Pápa, Hung.	H17	8

Name | Map Ref | Page

Papago Indian Reservation, Az., U.S. E3 80
Papaikou, Hi., U.S. D6 88
Papantla [de Olarte], Mex. G11 62
Papawai Point, c., Hi., U.S. C5 88
Papenburg, Ger. B7 8
Papillion, Ne., U.S. C9 104
Papineauville, Que., Can. D2 74
Papua, Gulf of, b., Pap. N. Gui. m15 50a
Papua New Guinea, ctry., Oc. m15 50a
Pará, stm., Braz. D9 54
Paracatu, Braz. D5 57
Paracatu, stm., Braz. D6 57
Paracel Islands, is., Asia B5 32
Parachute, Co., U.S. B2 83
Paradis, La., U.S. k11 95
Paradise, Ca., U.S. C3 82
Paradise, Nv., U.S. G6 105
Paradise, stm., Newf., Can. B3 72
Paradise Hills, N.M., U.S. B3 108
Paradise Valley, Az., U.S. k9 80
Paradise Valley, Nv., U.S. B4 105
Paragould, Ar., U.S. A5 81
Paraguaçu Paulista, Braz. G3 57
Paraguaipoa, Ven. B7 58
Paraguaná, Península de, pen., Ven. B7 58
Paraguarí, Para. B5 56
Paraguay, ctry., S.A. A5 56
Paraguay, stm., S.A. B5 56
Paraíba do Sul, stm., Braz. F7 57
Parakou, Benin G6 42
Paramagudi, India H5 37
Paramaribo, Sur. B7 54
Paramirim, Braz. B7 57
Paramount, Md., U.S. A2 97
Paramus, N.J., U.S. h8 107
Paramušir, Ostrov, i., Russia G25 24
Paraná, Arg. C4 56
Paranã, Braz. B5 57
Paranã, stm., Braz. B5 57
Paraná, stm., S.A. C5 56
Paranaguá, Braz. B7 56
Paranaíba, Braz. E3 57
Paranaíba, stm., Braz. E3 57
Paranapanema, stm., Braz. G3 57
Paranavaí, Braz. G2 57
Parangaba, Braz. D11 54
Paratinga, Braz. B7 57
Paraúna, Braz. D3 57
Paray-le-Monial, Fr. F11 10
Pārbati, stm., India H7 38
Parbhani, India C4 37
Parchim, Ger. B11 8
Parchment, Mi., U.S. F5 99
Pardeeville, Wi., U.S. E4 126
Pardo, stm., Braz. F5 57
Pardubice, Czech. E15 8
Parece Vela see Okino-Tori-shima, i., Japan G14 26
Parecis, Serra dos, mts., Braz. F7 54
Paredes de Nava, Spain C7 12
Paren', Russia E26 24
Parepare, Indon. F6 32
Pargas (Parainen), Fin. F14 6
Paria, stm., U.S. A4 80
Paria, Gulf of, b. I16 64
Pariaguán, Ven. C10 58
Pariaman, Indon. O6 34
Parícutin, vol., Mex. H8 62
Parikkala, Fin. F17 6
Parima, Sierra, mts., S.A. F10 58
Pariñas, Punta, c., Peru D2 54
Parintins, Braz. D7 54
Paris, Ont., Can. D4 73
Paris, Fr. D9 10
Paris, Ar., U.S. B2 81
Paris, Il., U.S. D6 90
Paris, Ky., U.S. B5 94
Paris, Mo., U.S. B5 102
Paris, Tn., U.S. A3 119
Paris, Tx., U.S. C5 120
Paris Peak, mtn., Id., U.S. G7 89
Parit Buntar, Malay. L6 34
Park, co., Co., U.S. B5 83
Park, co., Mt., U.S. E6 103
Park, co., Wy., U.S. B3 127
Park, stm., N.D., U.S. A8 111
Parkano, Fin. E14 6
Park City, Ks., U.S. g12 93
Park City, Ut., U.S. C4 121
Parkdale, P.E.I., Can. C6 71
Parke, co., In., U.S. E3 91
Parker, Az., U.S. C1 80
Parker, Co., U.S. B6 83
Parker, Fl., U.S. u16 86
Parker, S.D., U.S. D8 118
Parker, co., Tx., U.S. C4 120
Parker, Cape, c., N.W. Ter., Can. A17 66
Parker City, In., U.S. D7 91
Parker Dam, U.S. C1 80
Parkersburg, Ia., U.S. B5 92
Parkersburg, W.V., U.S. B3 125
Parkers Prairie, Mn., U.S. D3 100
Parkesburg, Pa., U.S. G10 115
Park Falls, Wi., U.S. C3 126
Park Forest, Il., U.S. B6 90
Park Hall, Md., U.S. D5 97
Parkhill, Ont., Can. D3 73
Park Hills, Ky., U.S. h13 94
Parkin, Ar., U.S. B5 81
Parkland, Wa., U.S. f11 124
Park Layne, Oh., U.S. C1 112
Park Range, mts., Co., U.S. A4 83
Park Rapids, Mn., U.S. D3 100
Park Ridge, Il., U.S. B6 90
Park Ridge, N.J., U.S. g8 107
Park River, N.D., U.S. A8 111
Parkrose, Or., U.S. B4 114
Parksley, Va., U.S. C7 123
Parkston, S.D., U.S. D8 118
Parksville, B.C., Can. E5 69
Parkville, Md., U.S. B4 97
Parkville, Mo., U.S. B3 102
Parkwater, Wa., U.S. g14 124
Parkwood, N.C., U.S. B4 110
Parlākimidi, India C8 37
Parle, Lac qui, l., Mn., U.S. E3 100
Parlier, Ca., U.S. D4 82
Parma, Italy E5 14
Parma, Id., U.S. F2 89
Parma, Mi., U.S. F6 99
Parma, Mo., U.S. E8 102
Parma, Oh., U.S. A4 112
Parmachenee Lake, l., Me., U.S. C2 96
Parma Heights, Oh., U.S. h9 112
Parmer, co., Tx., U.S. B1 120
Parnaíba, Braz. D10 54
Parnaíba, stm., Braz. D10 54
Pärnu, Est. C7 18
Paro, Bhu. G13 38
Parowan, Ut., U.S. F3 121
Par Pond, res., S.C., U.S. D5 117
Parral, Chile D2 56
Parramore Island, i., Va., U.S. C7 123
Parras de la Fuente, Mex. E8 62
Parrish, Al., U.S. B2 78
Parrsboro, N.S., Can. D5 71
Parry, Cape, c., N.W. Ter., Can. B8 66
Parry, Mount, mtn., B.C., Can. C3 69
Parry Bay, b., N.W. Ter., Can. C16 66
Parry Sound, Ont., Can. B4 73
Parshall, N.D., U.S. B3 111
Parsons, Ks., U.S. E8 93
Parsons, Tn., U.S. B3 119
Parsons, W.V., U.S. B5 125
Parsonsburg, Md., U.S. D7 97
Parthenay, Fr. F6 10
Partinico, Italy K8 14
Partridge Point, c., Newf., Can. C3 72
Paru, stm., Braz. D8 54
Pārvatīpuram, India C7 37
Parys, S. Afr. G5 44
Pasadena, Newf., Can. D3 72
Pasadena, Ca., U.S. E4 82
Pasadena, Md., U.S. B4 97
Pasadena, Tx., U.S. r14 120
Pascagoula, Ms., U.S. E5 101
Pascagoula, stm., Ms., U.S. E5 101
Pascagoula Bay, b., Ms., U.S. f8 101
Pasco, Wa., U.S. C6 124
Pasco, co., Fl., U.S. D4 86
Pascoag, R.I., U.S. B2 116
Pascoag Reservoir, res., R.I., U.S. B2 116
Pascua, Isla de (Easter Island), i., Chile H5 2
Pasewalk, Ger. B13 8
Pasig, Phil. q19 33b
P'asina, stm., Russia C11 24
P'asino, Ozero, l., Russia D11 24
P'asinskij Zaliv, b., Russia C10 24
Pasirpengarajan, Indon. N6 34
Pasir Puteh, Malay. L7 34
Pasni, Pak. D1 36
Paso de Indios, Arg. E3 56
Paso de los Libres, Arg. B5 56
Paso Robles, Ca., U.S. E3 82
Pasque Island, i., Ma., U.S. D6 98
Pasquotank, co., N.C., U.S. A6 110
Passagem, Braz. B7 57
Passaic, N.J., U.S. B4 107
Passaic, co., N.J., U.S. A4 107
Passaic, stm., N.J., U.S. h8 107
Passamaquoddy Bay, b., Me., U.S. C6 96
Passau, Ger. G13 8
Pass Christian, Ms., U.S. E4 101
Passo Fundo, Braz. B6 56
Passos, Braz. F5 57
Passumpsic, stm., Vt., U.S. C4 122
Pasto, Col. G4 58
Pastora Peak, mtn., Az., U.S. A6 80
Pastrana, Spain E9 12
Pasuruan, Indon. m16 33a
Patagonia, Az., U.S. F5 80
Patagonia, reg., Arg. E3 56
Pātan, India I5 38
Patapsco, stm., Md., U.S. B4 97
Pataskala, Oh., U.S. C3 112
Patchet Brook Reservoir, res., R.I., U.S. E6 116
Patchogue, N.Y., U.S. n15 109
Pate Island, i., Kenya B8 44
Paternò, Italy L9 14
Paterson, N.J., U.S. B4 107
Pathānkot, India D6 38
Pathein, Mya. F3 34
Pathfinder Reservoir, res., Wy., U.S. D6 127
Pati, Indon. m15 33a
Patiāla, India E7 38
Patience Island, i., R.I., U.S. D5 116
P'atigorsk, Russia I6 22
Pātkai Range, mts., Asia G16 38
Patman, Lake, res., Tx., U.S. C5 120
Patna, India H11 38
Patoka, In., U.S. H2 91
Patoka, stm., In., U.S. H2 91
Patoka Lake, res., In., U.S. H4 91
Patos, Braz. E11 54
Patos, Lagoa dos, b., Braz. C6 56
Patos de Minas, Braz. E5 57
Patquía, Arg. C3 56
Pátrai, Grc. K5 16
Patricio Lynch, Isla, i., Chile F1 56
Patrick, co., Va., U.S. D2 123
Patrick Air Force Base, mil., Fl., U.S. D6 86
Patrocínio, Braz. E5 57
Pattani, Thai. K6 34
Patten, Me., U.S. C4 96
Patterson, Ga., U.S. E4 87
Patterson, La., U.S. E4 95
Patterson Creek, stm., W.V., U.S. B5 125
Pattoki, Pak. E5 38
Patton, Pa., U.S. E4 115
Patuākhāli, Bngl. I14 38
Patuca, stm., Hond. G5 64
Patuxent, stm., Md., U.S. D4 97
Patuxent Naval Air Test Center, mil., Md., U.S. D5 97
Pátzcuaro, Mex. H9 62
Pau, Fr. I6 10
Paul, Id., U.S. G5 89
Paulding, Oh., U.S. A1 112
Paulding, co., Ga., U.S. C2 87
Paulding, co., Oh., U.S. A1 112
Paulina, La., U.S. h10 95
Paulina Mountains, mts., Or., U.S. D5 114
Paulina Peak, mtn., Or., U.S. E5 114
Paulins Kill, stm., N.J., U.S. A3 107
Paulistana, Braz. E10 54
Paulistas, Braz. E7 57
Paullina, Ia., U.S. B2 92
Paulo Afonso, Braz. E11 54
Paulsboro, N.J., U.S. D2 107
Paul Stream, stm., Vt., U.S. B5 122
Pauls Valley, Ok., U.S. C4 113
Paungde, Mya. E3 34
Pavia, Italy D4 14
Pavilion Key, i., Fl., U.S. G5 86
Pavlodar, Kaz. G9 24
Pavlof Volcano, vol., Ak., U.S. D7 79
Pavlovo, Russia F26 18
Pavlovsk, Russia G7 24
Pavlovskij Posad, Russia F21 18
Pavo, Ga., U.S. F3 87
Pavón, Col. F6 58
Pavullo nel Frignano, Italy E5 14
Pawcatuck, Ct., U.S. D8 84
Pawcatuck, stm., R.I., U.S. G1 116
Paw Creek, N.C., U.S. B2 110
Pawhuska, Ok., U.S. A5 113
Pawling, N.Y., U.S. D7 109
Pawnee, Il., U.S. D4 90
Pawnee, Ok., U.S. A5 113
Pawnee, co., Ks., U.S. D4 93
Pawnee, co., Ne., U.S. D9 104
Pawnee, co., Ok., U.S. A5 113
Pawnee, stm., Ks., U.S. D3 93
Pawnee City, Ne., U.S. D9 104
Pawpaw, Il., U.S. B5 90
Paw Paw, Mi., U.S. F5 99
Paw Paw, stm., Mi., U.S. F4 99
Pawpaw Creek, stm., W.V., U.S. h10 125
Pawtuckaway Pond, l., N.H., U.S. D4 106
Pawtucket, R.I., U.S. C4 116
Pawtuxet, stm., R.I., U.S. C4 116
Paxton, Il., U.S. C5 90
Paxton, Ma., U.S. B4 98
Payakumbuh, Indon. O6 34
Payette, Id., U.S. E2 89
Payette, co., Id., U.S. E2 89
Payette, North Fork, stm., Id., U.S. E2 89
Payette, South Fork, stm., Id., U.S. E3 89
Payette Lake, res., Id., U.S. E3 89
Payne, Oh., U.S. A1 112
Payne, co., Ok., U.S. A4 113
Paynesville, Mn., U.S. E4 100
Paysandú, Ur. C5 56
Payson, Az., U.S. C4 80
Payson, Il., U.S. D2 90
Payson, Ut., U.S. C4 121
Pazardžik, Bul. G8 16
Pazarköy, Tur. J11 16
Paz de Río, Col. E6 58
Pazin, Cro. D8 14
Pea, stm., Al., U.S. D3 78
Peabody, Ks., U.S. D6 93
Peabody, Ma., U.S. A6 98
Peabody, stm., N.H., U.S. B4 106
Peace, stm., Can. E9 66
Peace, stm., Fl., U.S. E5 86
Peace Dale, R.I., U.S. F3 116
Peace River, Alta., Can. A2 68
Peach, co., Ga., U.S. D3 87
Peacham Pond, res., Vt., U.S. C4 122
Peach Point, c., Ma., U.S. f12 98
Peach Springs, Az., U.S. B2 80
Peak District National Park, Eng., U.K. H11 7
Peaks Island, i., Me., U.S. g7 96
Peale, Mount, mtn., Ut., U.S. E6 121
Pea Patch Island, i., De., U.S. B3 85
Pea Ridge, Ar., U.S. A1 81
Pea Ridge National Military Park, Ar., U.S. A1 81
Pearisburg, Va., U.S. C2 123
Pearl, Ms., U.S. C3 101
Pearl, stm., U.S. D3 101
Pearland, Tx., U.S. r14 120
Pearl and Hermes Reef, rf., Hi., U.S. k12 88
Pearl City, Hi., U.S. B4 88
Pearl Harbor, b., Hi., U.S. B3 88
Pearl Harbor Naval Station, mil., Hi., U.S. g10 88
Pearlington, Ms., U.S. E4 101
Pearl River, La., U.S. D6 95
Pearl River, N.Y., U.S. g12 109
Pearl River, co., Ms., U.S. E4 101
Pearsall, Tx., U.S. E3 120
Pearsoll Peak, mtn., Or., U.S. E3 114
Pearson, Ga., U.S. E4 87
Peary Land, reg., Grnld. A16 128
Pease, stm., Tx., U.S. B3 120
Pease Air Force Base, mil., N.H., U.S. D5 106
Pebane, Moz. E7 44
Peć, Yugo. G4 16
Pecatonica, Il., U.S. A4 90
Pecatonica, stm., U.S. A4 90
Pecatonica, East Branch, stm., Wi., U.S. F4 126
Peckerwood Lake, res., Ar., U.S. C4 81
Pečora, stm., Russia D5 24
Pecos, N.M., U.S. B4 108
Pecos, Tx., U.S. D1 120
Pecos, co., Tx., U.S. D1 120
Pecos, stm., U.S. E6 76
Pecos National Monument, N.M., U.S. B4 108
Pécs, Hung. I18 8
Peculiar, Mo., U.S. C3 102
Peddocks Island, i., Ma., U.S. g12 98
Pedernales, Ven. C11 58
Pedregal, Ven. B7 58
Pedro, Point, c., Sri L. H6 37
Pedro de Valdivia, Chile A3 56
Pedro Juan Caballero, Para. G1 57
Peebles, Oh., U.S. D2 112
Peekskill, N.Y., U.S. D7 109
Peel, I. of Man G8 7
Peel, stm., Can. C5 66
Peel Point, c., N.W. Ter., Can. B10 66
Peel Sound, strt., N.W. Ter., Can. B13 66
Pegram, Tn., U.S. A4 119
Pehuajó, Arg. D4 56
Peikang, Tai. L9 28
Peine, Ger. C10 8
Pekalongan, Indon. m14 32
Pekin, Il., U.S. C4 90
Pekin, In., U.S. G5 91
Peking see Beijing, China D10 26
Pelagie, Isole, is., Italy N7 14
Pelahatchie, Ms., U.S. C4 101
Pelée, Montagne, mtn., Mart. G17 64
Pelee Island, i., Ont., Can. F2 73
Peleng, Pulau, i., Indon. F7 32
Pelham, Ont., Can. D5 73
Pelham, Al., U.S. B3 78
Pelham, Ga., U.S. E2 87
Pelham, N.H., U.S. E4 106
Pelham Manor, N.Y., U.S. h13 109
Pelican Bay, b., Man., Can. C1 70
Pelican Lake, l., Man., Can. C1 70
Pelican Lake, l., Mn., U.S. D4 100
Pelican Lake, l., Mn., U.S. D3 100
Pelican Lake, l., Mn., U.S. B6 100
Pelican Lake, l., Mn., U.S. E5 100
Pelican Lake, l., Wi., U.S. C4 126
Pelican Mountain, mtn., Alta., Can. B4 68
Pelican Rapids, Mn., U.S. D2 100
Pella, Ia., U.S. C5 92
Pell City, Al., U.S. B3 78
Pell Lake, Wi., U.S. n11 126
Pello, Fin. C14 6
Pelly Mountains, mts., Yukon, Can. D6 66
Pelopónnisos, reg., Grc. L5 16
Pelotas, Braz. C6 56
Pelton, Lake, l., La., U.S. E5 95
Pemadumcook Lake, l., Me., U.S. C3 96
Pemalang, Indon. m14 33a
Pematangsiantar, Indon. E2 32
Pemba, Moz. D8 44
Pemba Island, i., Tan. C7 44
Pemberton, Austl. F3 50
Pemberville, Oh., U.S. A2 112
Pembina, N.D., U.S. A8 111
Pembina, co., N.D., U.S. A8 111
Pembina, stm., Alta., Can. C3 68
Pembroke, Ont., Can. B7 73
Pembroke, Wales, U.K. J8 7
Pembroke, Ga., U.S. D5 87
Pembroke, Ky., U.S. D2 94
Pembroke, Ma., U.S. B6 98
Pembroke, N.C., U.S. C3 110
Pembroke, Va., U.S. C2 123
Pembroke Pines, Fl., U.S. r13 86
Pemigewasset, stm., N.H., U.S. C3 106
Pemiscot, co., Mo., U.S. E8 102
Peñafiel, Spain D7 12
Penápolis, Braz. F3 57
Peñaranda de Bracamonte, Spain E6 12
Pen Argyl, Pa., U.S. E11 115
Peñarroya-Pueblonuevo, Spain G6 12
Penas, Golfo de, b., Chile F1 56
Penasco, N.M., U.S. A4 108
Peñasco, Rio, stm., N.M., U.S. E4 108
Penbrook, Pa., U.S. F8 115
Pender, Ne., U.S. B9 104
Pender, co., N.C., U.S. C4 110
Pendleton, In., U.S. E6 91
Pendleton, Or., U.S. B8 114
Pendleton, S.C., U.S. B2 117
Pendleton, co., Ky., U.S. B5 94
Pendleton, co., W.V., U.S. C5 125
Pendley Hills, Ga., U.S. *h8 87
Pend Oreille, co., Wa., U.S. A8 124
Pend Oreille, Lake, l., Id., U.S. A2 89
Pend Oreille, Mount, mtn., Id., U.S. A2 89
Penetanguishene, Ont., Can. C5 73
P'enghu Liehtao, is., Tai. L8 28
Penglai, China D11 26
Penhold, Alta., Can. C4 68
Peniche, Port. F2 12
Penjamo, Mex. G9 62
Pennant Point, c., N.S., Can. E6 71
Pennask Mountain, mtn., B.C., Can. E7 69
Penne, Italy G8 14
Pennell, Mount, mtn., Ut., U.S. F5 121
Penner, stm., India E5 37
Penn Hills, Pa., U.S. k14 115
Pennines, mts., Eng., U.K. G10 7
Pennines, Alpes, mts., Eur. F14 10
Pennington, co., Mn., U.S. B2 100
Pennington, co., S.D., U.S. D2 118
Pennington Gap, Va., U.S. f8 123
Pennsauken, N.J., U.S. D2 107
Pennsboro, W.V., U.S. B4 125
Pennsburg, Pa., U.S. F11 115
Penns Grove, N.J., U.S. D2 107
Pennsville, N.J., U.S. D1 107
Pennsylvania, state, U.S. E7 115
Pennville, In., U.S. D7 91
Penn Yan, N.Y., U.S. C3 109
Penobscot, co., Me., U.S. C4 96
Penobscot, stm., Me., U.S. C4 96
Penobscot Bay, b., Me., U.S. D3 96
Penobscot Lake, l., Me., U.S. C2 96
Penonomé, Pan. J7 64
Penrith, Eng., U.K. G10 7
Pensacola, Fl., U.S. u14 86
Pensacola Bay, b., Fl., U.S. u14 86
Pensacola Dam, Ok., U.S. A6 113
Pensacola Naval Air Station, mil., Fl., U.S. u14 86
Pentagon Mountain, mtn., Mt., U.S. C3 103
Penticton, B.C., Can. E8 69
Pentland Firth, strt., Scot., U.K. C9 7
Pentwater, Mi., U.S. E4 99
Penyu, Kepulauan, is., Indon. G8 32
Penza, Russia G7 22
Penzance, Eng., U.K. K7 7
Penžina, stm., Russia E27 24
Penžinskaja Guba, b., Russia E26 24
Penžinskij Chrebet, mts., Russia E27 24
Peonan Point, c., Man., Can. D2 70
Peoria, Az., U.S. D3 80
Peoria, Il., U.S. C4 90
Peoria, co., Il., U.S. C4 90
Peoria Heights, Il., U.S. C4 90
Peotone, Il., U.S. B6 90
Pepacton Reservoir, res., N.Y., U.S. C6 109
Pepeekeo, Hi., U.S. D6 88
Pepin, Wi., U.S. D1 126
Pepin, co., Wi., U.S. D2 126
Pepin, Lake, l., U.S. D1 126
Pepperell, Ma., U.S. A4 98
Pequannock, N.J., U.S. B4 107
Pequest, stm., N.J., U.S. B2 107
Pequop Mountains, mts., Nv., U.S. C7 105
Pequot Lakes, Mn., U.S. D4 100
Perabumulih, Indon. F3 32
Percy, Il., U.S. E4 90
Perdido, Al., U.S. D2 78
Perdido, stm., U.S. E2 78
Perdido Bay, b., Al., U.S. E2 78
Pereira, Col. E5 58
Pere Marquette, stm., Mi., U.S. E4 99
Pereslavl'-Zalesskij, Russia E21 18
Pergamino, Arg. C4 56
Pergine Valsugana, Italy C6 14
Perham, Mn., U.S. D3 100
Péribonca, stm., Que., Can. G18 66
Peridot, Az., U.S. D5 80
Périgueux, Fr. G7 10
Perijá, Sierra de, mts., S.A. B6 58
Perkasie, Pa., U.S. F11 115
Perkins, Ok., U.S. B4 113
Perkins, co., Ne., U.S. D4 104
Perkins, co., S.D., U.S. B3 118
Perkinston, Ms., U.S. E4 101
Perlas, Archipiélago de las, is., Pan. J8 64
Perlas, Laguna de, b., Nic. H6 64
Perleberg, Ger. B11 8
Perm', Russia F9 22
Pernik, Bul. G7 16
Péronne, Fr. C9 10
Perpignan, Fr. J9 10
Perquimans, co., N.C., U.S. A6 110
Perrine, Fl., U.S. G6 86
Perris, Ca., U.S. F5 82
Perro, Laguna del, l., N.M., U.S. C4 108
Perros-Guirec, Fr. D3 10
Perrot, Île, i., Que., Can. q19 74
Perry, Fl., U.S. B3 86
Perry, Ga., U.S. D3 87
Perry, Ia., U.S. C3 92
Perry, Ks., U.S. C8 93
Perry, Mi., U.S. F6 99
Perry, Mo., U.S. B6 102
Perry, N.Y., U.S. C2 109
Perry, Oh., U.S. A4 112
Perry, Ok., U.S. A4 113
Perry, Ut., U.S. B3 121
Perry, co., Al., U.S. C2 78
Perry, co., Ar., U.S. C3 81
Perry, co., Il., U.S. E4 90
Perry, co., In., U.S. H4 91
Perry, co., Ky., U.S. C6 94
Perry, co., Ms., U.S. D4 101
Perry, co., Mo., U.S. D8 102
Perry, co., Oh., U.S. C3 112
Perry, co., Pa., U.S. F7 115
Perry, co., Tn., U.S. B4 119
Perry Hall, Md., U.S. B5 97
Perry Lake, res., Ks., U.S. C8 93
Perryman, Md., U.S. B5 97
Perrysburg, Oh., U.S. A2 112
Perry Stream, stm., N.H., U.S. f7 106
Perry's Victory and International Peace Memorial, hist., Oh., U.S. A2 112
Perryton, Tx., U.S. A2 120
Perryville, Ar., U.S. B3 81
Perryville, Ky., U.S. C5 94
Perryville, Md., U.S. A5 97
Perryville, Mo., U.S. D8 102
Pershing, co., Nv., U.S. C3 105
Persia see Iran, ctry., Asia B5 46
Persian Gulf, b., Asia C5 46
Person, co., N.C., U.S. A3 110
Perth, Austl. F3 50
Perth, Ont., Can. C8 73
Perth, Scot., U.K. E9 7
Perth Amboy, N.J., U.S. B4 107
Perth-Andover, N.B., Can. D10 71
Pertuis, Fr. I12 10
Peru, Il., U.S. B4 90
Peru, In., U.S. C5 91
Peru, Ne., U.S. D10 104
Peru, N.Y., U.S. f11 109
Peru (Perú), ctry., S.A. E3 54
Perugia, Italy F7 14
Perušić, Cro. E10 14
Pesaro, Italy F7 14
Pescadores see P'enghu Liehtao, is., Tai. L8 28
Pescara, Italy G9 14
Pescia, Italy F5 14
Peshastin, Wa., U.S. B5 124
Peshāwar, Pak. C4 38
Peshtigo, Wi., U.S. C6 126
Peshtigo, stm., Wi., U.S. C5 126
Pesqueira, Braz. E11 54
Pessac, Fr. H6 10
Petaḥ Tiqwa, Isr. C4 40

Name	Map Ref	Page
Petal, Ms., U.S.	D4	101
Petaluma, Ca., U.S.	C2	82
Petatlán, Mex.	I9	62
Petawawa, Ont., Can.	B7	73
Petawawa, stm., Ont., Can.	A6	73
Petenwell Lake, res., Wi., U.S.	D4	126
Peterborough, Austl.	F7	50
Peterborough, Ont., Can.	C6	73
Peterborough, Eng., U.K.	I12	7
Peterborough, N.H., U.S.	E3	106
Peterhead, Scot., U.K.	D11	7
Peter Pond Lake, l., Sask., Can.	m7	75
Petersburg, Ak., U.S.	D13	79
Petersburg, Il., U.S.	C4	90
Petersburg, In., U.S.	H3	91
Petersburg, Mi., U.S.	G7	99
Petersburg, Oh., U.S.	B5	112
Petersburg, Tx., U.S.	C2	120
Petersburg, Va., U.S.	C5	123
Petersburg, W.V., U.S.	B5	125
Peters Creek, stm., W.V., U.S.	m14	125
Peterson, Al., U.S.	B2	78
Peterson Field, mil., Co., U.S.	C6	83
Petersville, Al., U.S.	A2	78
Petit Bois Island, i., Ms., U.S.	E5	101
Petitcodiac, N.B., Can.	D4	71
Petitcodiac, stm., N.B., Can.	C5	71
Petite Amite, stm., La., U.S.	h10	95
Petit Jean, stm., Ar., U.S.	B2	81
Petit Lac Des Allemands, l., La., U.S.	k11	95
Petit Lake, l., La., U.S.	k12	95
Petitot, stm., Can.	E8	66
Petit-Rocher, N.B., Can.	B4	71
Petitsikapau Lake, l., Newf., Can.	g8	72
Petlād, India	I5	38
Petone, N.Z.	D5	52
Petoskey, Mi., U.S.	C6	99
Petrified Forest National Park, Az., U.S.	B6	80
Petrila, Rom.	D7	16
Petrinja, Cro.	D11	14
Petroleum, co., Mt., U.S.	C8	103
Petrolia, Ont., Can.	E2	73
Petrolina, Braz.	E10	54
Petropavlovsk-Kamčatskij, Russia	G25	24
Petrópolis, Braz.	G7	57
Petros, Tn., U.S.	C9	119
Petroşani, Rom.	D7	16
Petrovsk-Zabajkal'skij, Russia	G15	24
Petrozavodsk, Russia	E4	22
Pettaquamscutt Lake Shores, R.I., U.S.	F4	116
Pettingell Peak, mtn., Co., U.S.	B5	83
Pettis, co., Mo., U.S.	C4	102
Pevek, Russia	D28	24
Pevely, Mo., U.S.	g13	102
Pewaukee, Wi., U.S.	E5	126
Pewaukee Lake, l., Wi., U.S.	m11	126
Pewee Valley, Ky., U.S.	B4	94
Pézenas, Fr.	I10	10
Pforzheim, Ger.	G8	8
Pfungstadt, Ger.	F8	8
Pha-an, Mya.	F4	34
Phagwāra, India	E6	38
Phalsbourg, Fr.	D14	10
Phaltan, India	D3	37
Phangan, Ko, i., Thai.	J6	34
Phangnga, Thai.	J5	34
Phanom Dongrak, Thiu Khao, mts., Asia	G7	34
Phan Rang, Viet.	I10	34
Phan Si Pan, mtn., Viet.	C7	34
Phan Thiet, Viet.	I10	34
Pharr, Tx., U.S.	F3	120
Phatthalung, Thai.	K6	34
Phayao, Thai.	E5	34
Phelps, Ky., U.S.	C7	94
Phelps, N.Y., U.S.	C3	109
Phelps, Wi., U.S.	B4	126
Phelps, co., Mo., U.S.	D6	102
Phelps, co., Ne., U.S.	D6	104
Phelps Lake, l., N.C., U.S.	B6	110
Phenix City, Al., U.S.	C4	78
Phetchaburi, Thai.	H5	34
Philadelphia, Ms., U.S.	C4	101
Philadelphia, Pa., U.S.	G11	115
Philadelphia, co., Pa., U.S.	G12	115
Philadelphia Naval Shipyard, mil., Pa., U.S.	P21	115
Phil Campbell, Al., U.S.	A2	78
Philip, S.D., U.S.	C4	118
Philippeville, Bel.	E4	8
Philippi, W.V., U.S.	B4	125
Philippines, ctry., Asia	C7	32
Philippine Sea	E21	2
Philipsburg, Mt., U.S.	D3	103
Philipsburg, Pa., U.S.	E5	115
Philleo Lake, l., Wa., U.S.	h14	124
Phillips, Me., U.S.	D2	96
Phillips, Tx., U.S.	B2	120
Phillips, Wi., U.S.	C3	126
Phillips, co., Ar., U.S.	C5	81
Phillips, co., Co., U.S.	A8	83
Phillips, co., Ks., U.S.	C4	93
Phillips, co., Mt., U.S.	B8	103
Phillips Brook, stm., N.H., U.S.	A4	106
Phillipsburg, Ks., U.S.	C4	93
Phillipsburg, N.J., U.S.	B2	107
Philmont, N.Y., U.S.	C7	109
Philo, Il., U.S.	C5	90
Philomath, Or., U.S.	C3	114
Philpots Island, i., N.W. Ter., Can.	B17	66
Philpott Reservoir, res., Va., U.S.	D2	123
Phitsanulok, Thai.	F6	34
Phnom Penh see Phnum Pénh, Camb.	I8	34
Phnum Pénh (Phnom Penh), Camb.	I8	34
Phoenix, Az., U.S.	D3	80
Phoenix, Il., U.S.	k9	90
Phoenix, N.Y., U.S.	B4	109
Phoenix, Or., U.S.	E4	114
Phoenixville, Pa., U.S.	F10	115
Phôngsali, Laos	D7	34
Phrae, Thai.	E6	34
Phra Nakhon Si Ayutthaya, Thai.	G6	34
Phuket, Thai.	K5	34
Phuket, Ko, i., Thai.	K5	34
Phu Ly, Viet.	D8	34
Phumĭ Béng, Camb.	H8	34
Phumĭ Kâmpóng Trâbêk, Camb.	H8	34
Phu Quoc, Dao, i., Viet.	I7	34
Phu Tho, Viet.	D8	34
Piacenza, Italy	D4	14
Piatra-Neamţ, Rom.	C10	16
Piatt, co., Il., U.S.	D5	90
Piazza Armerina, Italy	L9	14
Pibor Post, Sudan	G12	42
Picacho, Az., U.S.	E4	80
Picardie, hist. reg., Fr.	C9	10
Picayune, Ms., U.S.	E4	101
Piccadilly, Newf., Can.	D2	72
Pichanal, Arg.	A4	56
Picher, Ok., U.S.	A7	113
Pickaway, co., Oh., U.S.	C2	112
Pickens, Ms., U.S.	C4	101
Pickens, S.C., U.S.	B2	117
Pickens, co., Al., U.S.	B1	78
Pickens, co., Ga., U.S.	B2	87
Pickens, co., S.C., U.S.	B2	117
Pickerel Lake, l., Wi., U.S.	C5	126
Pickering, Ont., Can.	D5	73
Pickerington, Oh., U.S.	C3	112
Pickett, co., Tn., U.S.	C8	119
Pickwick Lake, res., U.S.	A6	101
Pickworth Point, c., Ma., U.S.	f12	98
Pico Rivera, Ca., U.S.	n12	82
Picos, Braz.	E10	54
Picquigny, Fr.	C9	10
Picton, Ont., Can.	D7	73
Pictou Island, i., N.S., Can.	D7	71
Picture Butte, Alta., Can.	E4	68
Pictured Rocks National Lakeshore, Mi., U.S.	B4	99
Pidálion, Akrotírion, c., Cyp.	B4	40
Pidurutalagala, mtn., Sri L.	I6	37
Piedmont, Al., U.S.	B4	78
Piedmont, Ca., U.S.	h8	82
Piedmont, Mo., U.S.	D7	102
Piedmont, Ok., U.S.	B4	113
Piedmont, S.C., U.S.	B3	117
Piedmont, W.V., U.S.	B5	125
Piedmont Lake, res., Oh., U.S.	B4	112
Piedra, stm., Co., U.S.	D3	83
Piedrabuena, Spain	F7	12
Piedrahita, Spain	E6	12
Piedras Blancas, Point, c., Ca., U.S.	E3	82
Piedras Negras, Guat.	F2	64
Piedras Negras, Mex.	C9	62
Pieksämäki, Fin.	E16	6
Pierce, Co., U.S.	A6	83
Pierce, Id., U.S.	C3	89
Pierce, Ne., U.S.	B8	104
Pierce, co., Ga., U.S.	E4	87
Pierce, co., Ne., U.S.	B8	104
Pierce, co., N.D., U.S.	A5	111
Pierce, co., Wa., U.S.	C3	124
Pierce, co., Wi., U.S.	D1	126
Pierce, Lake, l., Fl., U.S.	E5	86
Pierce City, Mo., U.S.	E3	102
Pierceton, In., U.S.	B6	91
Pierre, S.D., U.S.	C5	118
Pierre-Buffière, Fr.	G8	10
Pierrefonds, Que., Can.	q19	74
Pierre Part, La., U.S.	k9	95
Pierreville, Que., Can.	C5	74
Pierson, Fl., U.S.	C5	86
Pierz, Mn., U.S.	E4	100
Pietermaritzburg, S. Afr.	G6	44
Pietersburg, S. Afr.	F5	44
Pietrasanta, Italy	F5	14
Piet Retief, S. Afr.	G6	44
Pigeon, Mi., U.S.	E7	99
Pigeon, stm., U.S.	f9	110
Pigeon, stm., In., U.S.	A6	91
Pigeon, stm., Mn., U.S.	h10	100
Pigeon, stm., Wi., U.S.	k10	126
Pigeon Cove, Ma., U.S.	A6	98
Pigeon Forge, Tn., U.S.	D10	119
Pigeon Point, c., Mn., U.S.	h10	100
Pigg, stm., Va., U.S.	D3	123
Piggott, Ar., U.S.	A5	81
Pihlajavesi, l., Fin.	F17	6
Pihtipudas, Fin.	E15	6
Pijijiapan, Mex.	J13	62
Pikal'ovo, Russia	B17	18
Pike, co., Al., U.S.	D4	78
Pike, co., Ar., U.S.	C2	81
Pike, co., Ga., U.S.	C2	87
Pike, co., Il., U.S.	D2	90
Pike, co., In., U.S.	H3	91
Pike, co., Ky., U.S.	C7	94
Pike, co., Ms., U.S.	D3	101
Pike, co., Mo., U.S.	B6	102
Pike, co., Oh., U.S.	C2	112
Pike, co., Pa., U.S.	D11	115
Pike, stm., Wi., U.S.	C6	126
Pike Island Dam, U.S.	f8	125
Pike Lake, Mn., U.S.	D6	100
Pikes Peak, mtn., Co., U.S.	C5	83
Pikesville, Md., U.S.	B4	97
Piketberg, S. Afr.	H3	44
Piketon, Oh., U.S.	C2	112
Pikeville, Ky., U.S.	C7	94
Pikeville, Tn., U.S.	D8	119
Piła (Schneidemühl), Pol.	B16	8
Pilar do Sul, Braz.	G5	57
Pilcomayo, stm., S.A.	A4	56
Pīlībhīt, India	F8	38
Pillar Point, c., Ca., U.S.	k7	82
Pilot Grove, Mo., U.S.	C5	102
Pilot Knob, Mo., U.S.	D7	102
Pilot Knob, mtn., Id., U.S.	D3	89
Pilot Mound, Man., Can.	E2	70
Pilot Mountain, N.C., U.S.	A2	110
Pilot Peak, mtn., Nv., U.S.	B7	105
Pilot Peak, mtn., Nv., U.S.	E4	105
Pilot Peak, mtn., Wy., U.S.	B3	127
Pilot Point, Tx., U.S.	C4	120
Pilot Range, mts., Nv., U.S.	B7	105
Pilot Rock, Or., U.S.	B8	114
Pilot Station, Ak., U.S.	C7	79
Pima, Az., U.S.	E6	80
Pima, co., Az., U.S.	E3	80
Pimentel, Peru	E3	54
Pimmit Hills, Va., U.S.	g12	123
Pina, Spain	D11	12
Pinal, co., Az., U.S.	E4	80
Pinaleno Mountains, mts., Az., U.S.	E5	80
Pinal Mountains, mts., Az., U.S.	D5	80
Pinang see George Town, Malay.	L6	34
Pinar del Río, Cuba	C6	64
Pinardville, N.H., U.S.	E3	106
Pincher Creek, Alta., Can.	E4	68
Pinckard, Al., U.S.	D4	78
Pinckney, Mi., U.S.	F7	99
Pinckney Island, i., S.C., U.S.	G6	117
Pinckneyville, Il., U.S.	E4	90
Pinconning, Mi., U.S.	E7	99
Píndhos Óros, mts., Grc.	J5	16
Pindi Gheb, Pak.	D5	38
Pindus Mountains see Píndhos Óros, mts., Grc.	J5	16
Pine, Az., U.S.	C4	80
Pine, co., Mn., U.S.	D6	100
Pine, stm., Mi., U.S.	D7	99
Pine, stm., Mi., U.S.	D5	99
Pine, stm., N.H., U.S.	C4	106
Pine, stm., Wi., U.S.	C5	126
Pine, stm., Wi., U.S.	C4	126
Pine Barrens, reg., N.J., U.S.	D3	107
Pine Bluff, Ar., U.S.	C3	81
Pinebluff, N.C., U.S.	B3	110
Pine Bluffs, Wy., U.S.	E8	127
Pine Bridge, Ct., U.S.	D3	84
Pine Castle, Fl., U.S.	D5	86
Pine City, Mn., U.S.	E6	100
Pine Creek, stm., Nv., U.S.	C5	105
Pine Creek, stm., Pa., U.S.	C6	115
Pine Creek, stm., Wa., U.S.	B8	124
Pine Creek Lake, res., Ok., U.S.	C6	113
Pinedale, Wy., U.S.	D3	127
Pine Falls, Man., Can.	D3	70
Pine Forest Range, mts., Nv., U.S.	B3	105
Pine Grove, Pa., U.S.	E9	115
Pine Grove Mills, Pa., U.S.	E6	115
Pine Hill, N.J., U.S.	D3	107
Pine Hills, Fl., U.S.	D5	86
Pinehouse Lake, Sask., Can.	B2	75
Pinehouse Lake, l., Sask., Can.	B2	75
Pinehurst, Ma., U.S.	f11	98
Pinehurst, N.C., U.S.	B3	110
Pine Island, Mn., U.S.	F6	100
Pine Island, i., Fl., U.S.	F4	86
Pine Island Sound, strt., Fl., U.S.	F4	86
Pine Key, i., Fl., U.S.	p10	86
Pine Knot, Ky., U.S.	D5	94
Pine Lake, Ga., U.S.	h8	87
Pine Lake, l., In., U.S.	A4	91
Pine Lake, l., Wi., U.S.	C5	126
Pine Lawn, Mo., U.S.	f13	102
Pine Level, N.C., U.S.	B4	110
Pinellas, co., Fl., U.S.	D4	86
Pinellas, Point, c., Fl., U.S.	p10	86
Pinellas Park, Fl., U.S.	E4	86
Pine Mountain, Ga., U.S.	D2	87
Pine Mountain, mtn., Or., U.S.	D6	114
Pine Mountain, mtn., Wy., U.S.	E3	127
Pine Point, N.W. Ter., Can.	D10	66
Pine Point, Me., U.S.	E2	96
Pine Prairie, La., U.S.	D3	95
Pine Ridge, S.D., U.S.	D3	118
Pine Ridge Indian Reservation, S.D., U.S.	D3	118
Pine River, Mn., U.S.	D4	100
Pinerolo, Italy	E2	14
Pines, Lake O' the, res., Tx., U.S.	C5	120
Pinesdale, Mt., U.S.	D2	103
Pinetops, N.C., U.S.	B5	110
Pine Valley, val., Ut., U.S.	E2	121
Pineville, Ky., U.S.	D6	94
Pineville, La., U.S.	C3	95
Pineville, N.C., U.S.	B2	110
Pineville, W.V., U.S.	D3	125
Pinewood, S.C., U.S.	D7	117
Piney Creek, stm., W.V., U.S.	n13	125
Piney Fork, stm., W.V., U.S.	h9	125
Piney Point, Md., U.S.	D4	97
Piney View, W.V., U.S.	n13	125
Ping, stm., Thai.	F5	34
Pingdingshan, China	E9	26
Pinghu, China	E10	28
Pingliang, China	D8	26
Pingtan Dao, i., China	J8	28
P'ingtung, Tai.	M9	28
Pingxiang, China	H2	28
Pingyao, China	D9	26
Pinhel, Port.	E4	12
Pinnacles National Monument, Ca., U.S.	D3	82
Pinneberg, Ger.	B9	8
Pinole, Ca., U.S.	h8	82
Pinopolis Dam, S.C., U.S.	E8	117
Pinos, Mount, mtn., Ca., U.S.	E4	82
Pins, Pointe aux, c., Ont., Can.	E3	73
Pinsk, Bela.	I9	18
Pinson, Al., U.S.	f7	78
Pinta, Sierra, mts., Az., U.S.	E2	80
Pintwater Range, mts., Nv., U.S.	G6	105
Pioche, Nv., U.S.	F7	105
Piombino, Italy	G5	14
Pioneer, Oh., U.S.	A1	112
Pioneer Mountains, mts., Id., U.S.	F5	89
Pioneer Mountains, mts., Mt., U.S.	E3	103
Pioner, Ostrov, i., Russia	B12	24
Piotrków Trybunalski, Pol.	D19	8
Pipe Spring National Monument, Az., U.S.	A3	80
Pipestem Creek, stm., N.D., U.S.	B6	111
Pipestone, Mn., U.S.	G2	100
Pipestone, co., Mn., U.S.	F2	100
Pipestone, stm., Ont., Can.	F14	66
Pipestone National Monument, Mn., U.S.	G2	100
Pipestone Pass, Mt., U.S.	E4	103
Pipmuacan, Réservoir, res., Que., Can.	k12	74
Piqua, Oh., U.S.	B1	112
Piracicaba, Braz.	G5	57
Piraeus see Piraiévs, Grc.	L7	16
Piraí do Sul, Braz.	A7	56
Piraiévs (Piraeus), Grc.	L7	16
Piraju, Braz.	G4	57
Piran, Slo.	D8	14
Pirané, Arg.	B5	56
Pirapora, Braz.	D6	57
Pires do Rio, Braz.	D4	57
Pírgos, Grc.	L5	16
Pirmasens, Ger.	F7	8
Pirna, Ger.	E13	8
Pirtleville, Az., U.S.	F6	80
Piru, Indon.	F8	32
Pisa, Italy	F5	14
Pisagua, Chile	G4	54
Piscataqua, stm., N.H., U.S.	D5	106
Piscataquis, co., Me., U.S.	C3	96
Piscataquis, stm., Me., U.S.	C3	96
Piscataquog, stm., N.H., U.S.	D3	106
Piscataway, N.J., U.S.	B4	107
Pisco, Peru	F3	54
Piseco Lake, l., N.Y., U.S.	B6	109
Písek, Czech.	F14	8
Pisgah, Al., U.S.	A4	78
Pisgah, Oh., U.S.	n13	112
Pisgah, Mount, mtn., Wy., U.S.	B8	127
Pisgah Forest, N.C., U.S.	f10	110
Pishan, China	B8	38
Pismo Beach, Ca., U.S.	E3	82
Pisticci, Italy	I11	14
Pistoia, Italy	F5	14
Pistolet Bay, b., Newf., Can.	C4	72
Pit, stm., Ca., U.S.	B3	82
Pitalito, Col.	G4	58
Pitcairn, Pa., U.S.	k14	115
Pitcairn, dep., Oc.	H4	2
Piteå, Swe.	D13	6
Piteşti, Rom.	E8	16
Pithāpuram, India	D7	37
Pithiviers, Fr.	D9	10
Pitiquito, Mex.	B3	62
Pitkin, co., Co., U.S.	B4	83
Pitlochry, Scot., U.K.	E9	7
Pitman, N.J., U.S.	D2	107
Pitt, co., N.C., U.S.	B5	110
Pitt Island, i., B.C., Can.	C3	69
Pittsboro, In., U.S.	E5	91
Pittsboro, N.C., U.S.	B3	110
Pittsburg, Ca., U.S.	g9	82
Pittsburg, Ks., U.S.	E9	93
Pittsburg, Ky., U.S.	C5	94
Pittsburg, Tx., U.S.	C5	120
Pittsburg, co., Ok., U.S.	C6	113
Pittsburgh, Pa., U.S.	F1	115
Pittsfield, Il., U.S.	D3	90
Pittsfield, Me., U.S.	D3	96
Pittsfield, Ma., U.S.	B1	98
Pittsfield, N.H., U.S.	D4	106
Pittsford, Vt., U.S.	D2	122
Pittston, Pa., U.S.	D10	115
Pittsville, Md., U.S.	D7	97
Pittsville, Wi., U.S.	D3	126
Pittsylvania, co., Va., U.S.	D3	123
Piu, Cerro, mtn., Nic.	H5	64
Piura, Peru	E2	54
Piute, co., Ut., U.S.	E3	121
Piute Peak, mtn., Ca., U.S.	E4	82
Piute Reservoir, res., Ut., U.S.	E3	121
Pivdennyy Buh, stm., Ukr.	H3	22
Pixley, Ca., U.S.	E4	82
Pizzo, Italy	K11	14
Placentia, Newf., Can.	E5	72
Placentia Bay, b., Newf., Can.	E4	72
Placer, co., Ca., U.S.	C3	82
PLacer Mountain, mtn., N.M., U.S.	k8	108
Placerville, Ca., U.S.	C3	82
Placetas, Cuba	C8	64
Placid, Lake, l., Fl., U.S.	E5	86
Placid, Lake, l., N.Y., U.S.	f11	109
Placitas, N.M., U.S.	B3	108
Plain City, Oh., U.S.	B2	112
Plain City, Ut., U.S.	B3	121
Plain Dealing, La., U.S.	B2	95
Plainfield, Ct., U.S.	C8	84
Plainfield, Il., U.S.	B5	90
Plainfield, In., U.S.	E5	91
Plainfield, N.J., U.S.	B4	107
Plainfield, Vt., U.S.	C4	122
Plainfield, Wi., U.S.	D4	126
Plainfield Heights, Mi., U.S.	*E5	99
Plains, Ga., U.S.	D2	87
Plains, Ks., U.S.	E3	93
Plains, Mt., U.S.	C2	103
Plains, Pa., U.S.	n17	115
Plains, Tx., U.S.	C1	120
Plainview, Ar., U.S.	C2	81
Plainview, Mn., U.S.	F6	100
Plainview, Ne., U.S.	B8	104
Plainview, Tx., U.S.	B2	120
Plainville, Ct., U.S.	C4	84
Plainville, Ks., U.S.	C4	93
Plainville, Ma., U.S.	B5	98
Plainwell, Mi., U.S.	F5	99
Plaistow, N.H., U.S.	E4	106
Plankinton, S.D., U.S.	D7	118
Plano, Il., U.S.	B5	90
Plano, Tx., U.S.	C4	120
Plantagenet, Ont., Can.	B9	73
Plantation, Fl., U.S.	r13	86
Plant City, Fl., U.S.	D4	86
Plantersville, Al., U.S.	C3	78
Plantersville, Ms., U.S.	A5	101
Plantsite, Az., U.S.	D6	80
Plantsville, Ct., U.S.	C4	84
Plaquemine, La., U.S.	D4	95
Plaquemines, co., La., U.S.	E6	95
Plasencia, Spain	E5	12
Plaški, Cro.	D10	14
Plaster Rock, N.B., Can.	C2	71
Plata, Río de la, est., S.A.	D5	56
Platte, S.D., U.S.	D7	118
Platte, co., Mo., U.S.	B3	102
Platte, co., Ne., U.S.	C8	104
Platte, co., Wy., U.S.	D7	127
Platte, stm., U.S.	B3	102
Platte, stm., Mn., U.S.	E4	100
Platte, stm., Ne., U.S.	D6	104
Platte City, Mo., U.S.	B3	102
Platte Island, i., Sey.	C11	44
Platteville, Co., U.S.	A6	83
Platteville, Wi., U.S.	F3	126
Plattling, Ger.	G12	8
Plattsburg, Mo., U.S.	B3	102
Plattsburgh, N.Y., U.S.	f11	109
Plattsburgh Air Force Base, mil., N.Y., U.S.	f11	109
Plattsmouth, Ne., U.S.	D10	104
Plau, Ger.	B12	8
Plauen, Ger.	E12	8
Playas Lake, l., N.M., U.S.	F2	108
Play Cu, Viet.	H9	34
Playgreen Lake, l., Man., Can.	B2	70
Pleasant, stm., Me., U.S.	C3	96
Pleasant, Lake, res., Az., U.S.	D3	80
Pleasant Gap, Pa., U.S.	E6	115
Pleasant Garden, N.C., U.S.	B3	110
Pleasant Grove, Al., U.S.	g7	78
Pleasant Grove, Ut., U.S.	C4	121
Pleasant Hill, Ca., U.S.	h8	82
Pleasant Hill, Il., U.S.	D3	90
Pleasant Hill, Ia., U.S.	e8	92
Pleasant Hill, La., U.S.	C2	95
Pleasant Hill, Mo., U.S.	C3	102
Pleasant Hill, Oh., U.S.	B1	112
Pleasant Lake, In., U.S.	A7	91
Pleasant Lake, l., Me., U.S.	C5	96
Pleasant Lake, l., N.H., U.S.	D4	106
Pleasanton, Ca., U.S.	h9	82
Pleasanton, Ks., U.S.	D9	93
Pleasanton, Tx., U.S.	E3	120
Pleasant Prairie, Wi., U.S.	n12	126
Pleasants, co., W.V., U.S.	B3	125
Pleasant Valley, Ia., U.S.	g11	92
Pleasant Valley, Mo., U.S.	h11	102
Pleasant View, Ut., U.S.	B3	121
Pleasantville, Ia., U.S.	C4	92
Pleasantville, N.J., U.S.	E3	107
Pleasantville, N.Y., U.S.	D7	109
Pleasantville, Oh., U.S.	C3	112
Pleasure Beach, Ct., U.S.	D7	84
Pleasure Ridge Park, Ky., U.S.	g11	94
Pleasureville, Ky., U.S.	B4	94
Pleiku see Play Cu, Viet.	H9	34
Pléneuf, Fr.	D4	10
Plenty, Bay of, b., N.Z.	B6	52
Plentywood, Mt., U.S.	B12	103
Plessisville, Que., Can.	C6	74
Pleternica, Cro.	D12	14
Plétipi, Lac, l., Que., Can.	F18	66
Pleven, Bul.	F8	16
Pljevlja, Yugo.	F3	16
Płock, Pol.	C19	8
Ploërmel, Fr.	E4	10
Ploieşti, Rom.	E10	16
Plomosa Mountains, mts., Az., U.S.	D1	80
Plonge, Lac la, l., Sask., Can.	B2	75
Plouguenast, Fr.	D4	10
Plovdiv, Bul.	G8	16
Plover, Wi., U.S.	D4	126
Plover, stm., Wi., U.S.	D4	126
Plum, Pa., U.S.	k14	115
Plumas, co., Ca., U.S.	B3	82
Plum Coulee, Man., Can.	E3	70
Plumerville, Ar., U.S.	B3	81
Plum Island, i., Ma., U.S.	A6	98
Plummer, Id., U.S.	B2	89
Plumsteadville, Pa., U.S.	F11	115
Plumtree, Zimb.	F5	44
Plymouth, Monts.	F16	64
Plymouth, Eng., U.K.	K8	7
Plymouth, Ct., U.S.	C3	84
Plymouth, Fl., U.S.	D5	86
Plymouth, In., U.S.	B5	91
Plymouth, Ma., U.S.	C6	98
Plymouth, Mi., U.S.	p15	99
Plymouth, Mn., U.S.	m12	100
Plymouth, N.H., U.S.	C3	106
Plymouth, N.C., U.S.	B6	110
Plymouth, Oh., U.S.	A3	112
Plymouth, Pa., U.S.	D10	115
Plymouth, Wi., U.S.	E6	126
Plymouth, co., Ia., U.S.	B1	92
Plymouth, co., Ma., U.S.	C6	98
Plymouth Bay, b., Ma., U.S.	C6	98
Plzeň, Czech.	F13	8
Po, stm., Italy	E7	14
Po, stm., Va., U.S.	B5	123
Pobeda, Gora, mtn., Russia	D23	24
Pocahontas, Ar., U.S.	A5	81
Pocahontas, Il., U.S.	E4	90
Pocahontas, Ia., U.S.	B3	92
Pocahontas, co., Ia., U.S.	B3	92
Pocahontas, co., W.V., U.S.	C4	125
Pocasset, Ma., U.S.	C6	98
Pocatalico, W.V., U.S.	C3	125
Pocatalico, stm., W.V., U.S.	C3	125
Pocatello, Id., U.S.	G6	89
Počep, Russia	I16	18
Pochutla, Mex.	J11	62
Poções, Braz.	C8	57
Pocola, Ok., U.S.	B7	113
Pocomoke, stm., Md., U.S.	D7	97
Pocomoke City, Md., U.S.	D6	97
Pocomoke Sound, strt., Md., U.S.	E6	97
Pocono Mountains, hills, Pa., U.S.	E11	115
Pocono Pines, Pa., U.S.	D11	115
Poços de Caldas, Braz.	F5	57
Pocotopaug Lake, res., Ct., U.S.	C6	84
Podensac, Fr.	H6	10
Podgorica, Yugo.	G3	16
Podkamennaja Tunguska, Russia	E12	24

Name	Map Ref	Page
Podkamennaja Tunguska, stm., Russia	E13	24
Podol'sk, Russia	F20	18
Podor, Sen.	E3	42
Podravska Slatina, Cro.	D12	14
Pofadder, S. Afr.	G3	44
Poge, Cape, c., Ma., U.S.	D7	98
Poggibonsi, Italy	F6	14
P'ohang, S. Kor.	D12	26
Pohénégamook, Que., Can.	B8	74
Pohue Bay, b., Hi., U.S.	E6	88
Poinsett, co., Ar., U.S.	B5	81
Poinsett, Lake, l., Fl., U.S.	D6	86
Poinsett, Lake, l., S.D., U.S.	C8	118
Point Clear, Al., U.S.	E2	78
Pointe a la Hache, La., U.S.	E6	95
Pointe-à-Pitre, Guad.	F17	64
Pointe-au-Pic, Que., Can.	B7	74
Pointe-Calumet, Que., Can.	p19	74
Pointe-Claire, Que., Can.	D4	74
Pointe Coupee, co., La., U.S.	D4	95
Pointe-des-Cascades, Que., Can.	q19	74
Point Edward, Ont., Can.	D2	73
Pointe-Noire, Congo	B2	44
Pointe-Verte, N.B., Can.	B4	71
Point Fortin, Trin.	I17	64
Point Hope, Ak., U.S.	B6	79
Point Imperial, mtn., Az., U.S.	A4	80
Point Judith Pond, l., R.I., U.S.	F4	116
Point Lake, l., N.W. Ter., Can.	C10	66
Point Leamington, Newf., Can.	D4	72
Point Marion, Pa., U.S.	G2	115
Point Mugu Naval Air Station, mil., Ca., U.S.	E4	82
Point of Rocks, Md., U.S.	B2	97
Point Pelee National Park, Ont., Can.	F2	73
Point Pleasant, N.J., U.S.	C4	107
Point Pleasant, W.V., U.S.	C2	125
Point Pleasant Beach, N.J., U.S.	C4	107
Point Reyes National Seashore, Ca., U.S.	C2	82
Point Roberts, Wa., U.S.	A2	124
Poipu, Hi., U.S.	B2	88
Poison Creek, stm., Wy., U.S.	C5	127
Poisson Blanc, Lac du, res., Que., Can.	C2	74
Poitiers, Fr.	F7	10
Poitou, reg., Fr.	F6	10
Poix, Fr.	C8	10
Pokegama Lake, l., Mn., U.S.	C5	100
Pokegama Lake, l., Wi., U.S.	C2	126
Polacca, Az., U.S.	B5	80
Poland, ctry., Eur.	E11	4
Polar Bear Provincial Park, Ont., Can.	n18	73
Polecat Creek, stm., Ok., U.S.	B5	113
Pol-e Khomrī, Afg.	C3	38
Polesje, reg., Eur.	I10	18
Pólis, Cyp.	B3	40
Polistena, Italy	K11	14
Polk, Pa., U.S.	D2	115
Polk, co., Ar., U.S.	C1	81
Polk, co., Fl., U.S.	E5	86
Polk, co., Ga., U.S.	C1	87
Polk, co., Ia., U.S.	C4	92
Polk, co., Mn., U.S.	C2	100
Polk, co., Mo., U.S.	D4	102
Polk, co., Ne., U.S.	C8	104
Polk, co., N.C., U.S.	f10	110
Polk, co., Or., U.S.	C3	114
Polk, co., Tn., U.S.	D9	119
Polk, co., Tx., U.S.	D5	120
Polk, co., Wi., U.S.	C1	126
Polk City, Fl., U.S.	D5	86
Polk City, Ia., U.S.	C4	92
Pol'kino, Russia	C13	24
Pollāchi, India	G4	37
Polo, Il., U.S.	B4	90
Polock, Bela.	F11	18
Polson, Mt., U.S.	C2	103
Poltava, Ukr.	H4	22
Polynesia, is., Oc.	G2	2
Pomabamba, Peru	E3	54
Pomaro, Mex.	H8	62
Pombal, Port.	F3	12
Pomerania, hist. reg., Pol.	A16	8
Pomeranian Bay, b., Eur.	A14	8
Pomeroy, Ia., U.S.	B3	92
Pomeroy, Oh., U.S.	C3	112
Pomeroy, Wa., U.S.	C8	124
Pomme de Terre, stm., Mn., U.S.	E3	100
Pomme de Terre, stm., Mo., U.S.	D4	102
Pomme de Terre Lake, res., Mo., U.S.	D4	102
Pomona, Ca., U.S.	E5	82
Pomona, Ks., U.S.	D8	93
Pomona Lake, res., Ks., U.S.	D7	93
Pompano Beach, Fl., U.S.	F6	86
Pompton Lakes, N.J., U.S.	A4	107
Ponaganset, stm., R.I., U.S.	C2	116
Ponaganset Reservoir, res., R.I., U.S.	B2	116
Ponca, Ne., U.S.	B9	104
Ponca City, Ok., U.S.	A4	113
Ponca Creek, stm., U.S.	A6	104
Ponca Indian Reservation, Ne., U.S.	B7	104
Ponce, P.R.	E14	64
Ponce de Leon Bay, b., Fl., U.S.	G5	86
Ponce de Leon Inlet, b., Fl., U.S.	C6	86
Poncha Pass, Co., U.S.	C4	83
Ponchatoula, La., U.S.	D5	95
Pond, stm., Ky., U.S.	C2	94
Pond Creek, Ok., U.S.	A3	113
Pondera, co., Mt., U.S.	B4	103
Pond Fork, stm., W.V., U.S.	D3	125
Pondicherry, India	G5	37
Pondicherry, ter., India	G5	37
Pond Inlet, N.W. Ter., Can.	B17	66
Pone Island, i., Md., U.S.	D5	97
Ponferrada, Spain	C5	12
Ponoka, Alta., Can.	C4	68
Ponorogo, Indon.	m15	33a
Pons, Fr.	G6	10
Ponta Grossa, Braz.	B6	56
Pont-à-Mousson, Fr.	D13	10
Ponta Porã, Braz.	G1	57
Pontarlier, Fr.	F13	10
Pontassieve, Italy	F6	14
Pont-Audemer, Fr.	C7	10
Pontchartrain, Lake, l., La., U.S.	D5	95
Pontchâteau, Fr.	E4	10
Pont de Suert, Spain	C12	12
Ponte Branca, Braz.	D2	57
Ponte da Barca, Port.	D3	12
Pontedera, Italy	F5	14
Ponte de Sor, Port.	F3	12
Ponteix, Sask., Can.	H2	75
Ponte Nova, Braz.	F7	57
Pontevedra, Spain	C3	12
Ponte Vedra Beach, Fl., U.S.	B5	86
Pontgibaud, Fr.	F9	10
Pontiac, Il., U.S.	C5	90
Pontiac, Mi., U.S.	F7	99
Pontianak, Indon.	F4	32
Pontivy, Fr.	D4	10
Pont-l'Abbé, Fr.	E2	10
Pontoise, Fr.	C9	10
Pontoosuc Lake, l., Ma., U.S.	B1	98
Pontorson, Fr.	D5	10
Pontotoc, Ms., U.S.	A4	101
Pontotoc, co., Ms., U.S.	A4	101
Pontotoc, co., Ok., U.S.	C5	113
Pont-Rouge, Que., Can.	C6	74
Pontypool, Ont., Can.	C6	73
Pontypool, Wales, U.K.	J9	7
Poole, Eng., U.K.	K11	7
Pooler, Ga., U.S.	D5	87
Pooles Island, i., Md., U.S.	B5	97
Poolesville, Md., U.S.	B3	97
Poopó, Lago de, l., Bol.	G5	54
Popayán, Col.	F4	58
Pope, co., Ar., U.S.	B2	81
Pope, co., Il., U.S.	F5	90
Pope, co., Mn., U.S.	E3	100
Pope Air Force Base, mil., N.C., U.S.	B3	110
Poplar, Mt., U.S.	B11	103
Poplar, stm., Can.	C3	70
Poplar, stm., Mn., U.S.	C2	100
Poplar Bluff, Mo., U.S.	E7	102
Poplar Island, i., Md., U.S.	C5	97
Poplarville, Ms., U.S.	E4	101
Popocatépetl, Volcán, vol., Mex.	H10	62
Popokabaka, Zaire	C3	44
Popomanasiu, Mount, mtn., Sol.Is.	A11	50
Popondetta, Pap. N. Gui.	m16	50a
Popple, stm., Wi., U.S.	C5	126
Poquonock, Ct., U.S.	B5	84
Poquonock Bridge, Ct., U.S.	D7	84
Poquoson, Va., U.S.	C6	123
Porangatu, Braz.	F9	54
Porbandar, India	J3	38
Porcher Island, i., B.C., Can.	C2	69
Porcupine Mountains, mts., Mi., U.S.	m12	99
Pordenone, Italy	D7	14
Poreč, Cro.	D8	14
Pori, Fin.	F13	6
Porkkala, Fin.	G15	6
Porlamar, Ven.	B11	58
Poronajsk, Russia	H22	24
Porsgrunn, Nor.	G7	6
Portadown, N. Ire., U.K.	G6	7
Portage, In., U.S.	A3	91
Portage, Mi., U.S.	F5	99
Portage, Pa., U.S.	F4	115
Portage, Wi., U.S.	E4	126
Portage, co., Oh., U.S.	A4	112
Portage, co., Wi., U.S.	D4	126
Portage, stm., Oh., U.S.	B2	112
Portage Bay, b., Man., Can.	D2	70
Portage Head, c., Wa., U.S.	A1	124
Portage Lake, l., Me., U.S.	B4	96
Portage Lakes, Oh., U.S.	B4	112
Portage la Prairie, Man., Can.	E2	70
Portageville, Mo., U.S.	E8	102
Port Alberni, B.C., Can.	E5	69
Portalegre, Port.	F4	12
Portales, N.M., U.S.	C6	108
Port Alice, B.C., Can.	D4	69
Port Allegany, Pa., U.S.	C5	115
Port Allen, La., U.S.	D4	95
Port Angeles, Wa., U.S.	A2	124
Port Antonio, Jam.	E9	64
Port Aransas, Tx., U.S.	F4	120
Port Arthur, Tx., U.S.	E6	120
Port Arthur see Lüshun, China	D11	26
Port Augusta, Austl.	F7	50
Port au Port Bay, b., Newf., Can.	D2	72
Port au Port [West-Aguathuna-Felix Cove], Newf., Can.	D2	72
Port-au-Prince, Haiti	E11	64
Port au Prince Peninsula, pen., Newf., Can.	D2	72
Port Austin, Mi., U.S.	D7	99
Port Barre, La., U.S.	D4	95
Port-Bergé, Madag.	E9	44
Port Blair, India	I2	34
Port Blandford, Newf., Can.	D4	72
Port Bolivar, Tx., U.S.	E5	120
Port Burwell, Ont., Can.	E4	73
Port Byron, Il., U.S.	B3	90
Port Carbon, Pa., U.S.	E9	115
Port Carling, Ont., Can.	B5	73
Port-Cartier-Ouest, Que., Can.	k13	74
Port Chalmers, N.Z.	F3	52
Port Charlotte, Fl., U.S.	F4	86
Port Chester, N.Y., U.S.	E7	109
Port Clinton, Oh., U.S.	A3	112
Port Colborne, Ont., Can.	E5	73
Port Coquitlam, B.C., Can.	E6	69
Port Deposit, Md., U.S.	A5	97
Port Dickinson, N.Y., U.S.	C5	109
Port Dickson, Malay.	M6	34
Port Edward, B.C., Can.	B2	69
Port Edwards, Wi., U.S.	D4	126
Portel, Braz.	D8	54
Portel, Port.	G4	12
Port Elgin, Ont., Can.	C3	73
Port Elizabeth, S. Afr.	H5	44
Port Ellen, Scot., U.K.	F6	7
Porter, In., U.S.	A3	91
Porter, Tx., U.S.	D5	120
Porter, co., In., U.S.	B3	91
Porter Creek, stm., W.V., U.S.	m13	125
Porterdale, Ga., U.S.	C3	87
Porterville, Ca., U.S.	D4	82
Port Ewen, N.Y., U.S.	D7	109
Port Gamble Indian Reservation, Wa., U.S.	B3	124
Port-Gentil, Gabon	B1	44
Port Gibson, Ms., U.S.	D3	101
Port Harcourt, Nig.	H7	42
Port Hedland, Austl.	D3	50
Port Hood, N.S., Can.	C8	71
Port Hope, Ont., Can.	D6	73
Port Hope Simpson, Newf., Can.	B3	72
Port Hueneme, Ca., U.S.	E4	82
Port Huron, Mi., U.S.	F8	99
Portimão, Port.	H3	12
Port Isabel, Tx., U.S.	F4	120
Port Jefferson, N.Y., U.S.	n15	109
Port Jervis, N.Y., U.S.	D6	109
Portland, Austl.	G8	50
Portland, Ct., U.S.	C5	84
Portland, In., U.S.	D8	91
Portland, Me., U.S.	E2	96
Portland, Mi., U.S.	F6	99
Portland, N.D., U.S.	B8	111
Portland, Or., U.S.	B4	114
Portland, Tn., U.S.	A5	119
Portland, Tx., U.S.	F4	120
Portland, Bill of, c., Eng., U.K.	K10	7
Portland Inlet, b., B.C., Can.	B2	69
Portland Point, c., Jam.	F9	64
Port Lavaca, Tx., U.S.	E4	120
Port Lincoln, Austl.	F7	50
Port Loko, S.L.	G3	42
Port Louis, Mrts.	F11	44
Port Ludlow, Wa., U.S.	B3	124
Port-Lyautey see Kenitra, Mor.	B4	42
Port Macquarie, Austl.	F10	50
Port Madison Indian Reservation, Wa., U.S.	B3	124
Port McNeil, B.C., Can.	D4	69
Port McNicoll, Ont., Can.	C5	73
Port Monmouth, N.J., U.S.	C4	107
Port Moresby, Pap. N. Gui.	m16	50a
Port Morien, N.S., Can.	C10	71
Port Neches, Tx., U.S.	E6	120
Portneuf, Que., Can.	C6	74
Port Nolloth, S. Afr.	G3	44
Porto, Port.	D3	12
Porto Alegre, Braz.	C6	56
Porto Amboim, Ang.	D2	44
Portobelo, Pan.	J8	64
Porto de Moz, Braz.	D8	54
Porto Esperança, Braz.	G7	54
Porto Esperidião, Braz.	G7	54
Pôrto Feliz, Braz.	G5	57
Portoferraio, Italy	G5	14
Pôrto Ferreira, Braz.	F5	57
Port of Spain, Trin.	I17	64
Portogruaro, Italy	D7	14
Portola, Ca., U.S.	C3	82
Porto Murtinho, Braz.	H7	54
Porto Nacional, Braz.	F9	54
Porto-Novo, Benin	G6	42
Port Orange, Fl., U.S.	C6	86
Port Orchard, Wa., U.S.	B3	124
Port Orford, Or., U.S.	E2	114
Porto San Giorgio, Italy	F8	14
Porto Santo Stefano, Italy	G6	14
Pôrto São José, Braz.	G2	57
Pôrto Seguro, Braz.	D9	57
Porto Torres, Italy	I3	14
Porto União, Braz.	B6	56
Porto Velho, Braz.	E6	54
Portoviejo, Ec.	H2	58
Port Penn, De., U.S.	B3	85
Port Pirie, Austl.	F7	50
Port Richey, Fl., U.S.	D4	86
Port Rowan, Ont., Can.	E4	73
Port Royal, S.C., U.S.	G6	117
Port Royal Island, i., S.C., U.S.	G6	117
Port Royal Sound, strt., S.C., U.S.	G6	117
Port Said see Būr Saʻīd, Egypt	B12	42
Port-Sainte-Marie, Fr.	H7	10
Port Saint Joe, Fl., U.S.	C1	86
Port Saint Johns, S. Afr.	H5	44
Port Saint Lucie, Fl., U.S.	E6	86
Port Salerno, Fl., U.S.	E6	86
Port Saunders, Newf., Can.	C3	72
Port Shepstone, S. Afr.	H6	44
Portsmouth, Eng., U.K.	K11	7
Portsmouth, N.H., U.S.	D5	106
Portsmouth, Oh., U.S.	D3	112
Portsmouth, R.I., U.S.	E6	116
Portsmouth, Va., U.S.	D6	123
Portsmouth Naval Shipyard, mil., Me., U.S.	D5	106
Port Stanley, Ont., Can.	E3	73
Port Sulphur, La., U.S.	E6	95
Port Talbot, Wales, U.K.	J9	7
Port Townsend, Wa., U.S.	A3	124
Portugal, ctry., Eur.	H6	4
Portugalete, Spain	B8	12
Portuguese Guinea see Guinea-Bissau, ctry., Afr.	F2	42
Portumna, Ire.	H4	7
Port Union, Newf., Can.	D5	72
Port-Vendres, Fr.	J10	10
Port Washington, N.Y., U.S.	h13	109
Port Washington, Wi., U.S.	E6	126
Port Wentworth, Ga., U.S.	D5	87
Porum, Ok., U.S.	B6	113
Porz, Ger.	E7	8
Porzuna, Spain	F7	12
Posadas, Arg.	B5	56
Poschiavo, Switz.	F17	10
Posen, Il., U.S.	k9	90
Posey, co., In., U.S.	H2	91
Poseyville, In., U.S.	H2	91
Poso, Indon.	F7	32
Posse, Braz.	C5	57
Pössneck, Ger.	E11	8
Post, Tx., U.S.	C2	120
Post Falls, Id., U.S.	B2	89
Post Maurice Cortier (Bidon Cinq), Alg.	D6	42
Postojna, Slo.	D9	14
P'ostraja Dresva, Russia	E25	24
Postville, Ia., U.S.	A6	92
Potawatomi Indian Reservation, Ks., U.S.	C8	93
Potchefstroom, S. Afr.	G5	44
Poté, Braz.	D8	57
Poteau, Ok., U.S.	B7	113
Poteau, stm., U.S.	B7	113
Poteet, Tx., U.S.	E3	120
Potenza, Italy	I10	14
Potes, Spain	B7	12
Potgietersrus, S. Afr.	F5	44
Poth, Tx., U.S.	E3	120
Potholes Reservoir, res., Wa., U.S.	B6	124
Potiraguá, Braz.	C9	57
Potiskum, Nig.	F8	42
Potlatch, Id., U.S.	C2	89
Potomac, Md., U.S.	B3	97
Potomac, stm., U.S.	D4	97
Potomac Heights, Md., U.S.	C3	97
Potomac Park, Md., U.S.	k13	97
Potosí, Bol.	G5	54
Potosi, Mo., U.S.	D7	102
Potosí, Cerro, mtn., Mex.	E9	62
Potsdam, Ger.	C13	8
Potsdam, N.Y., U.S.	f10	109
Pottawatomie, co., Ks., U.S.	C7	93
Pottawatomie, co., Ok., U.S.	B4	113
Pottawattamie, co., Ia., U.S.	C2	92
Potter, co., Pa., U.S.	C6	115
Potter, co., S.D., U.S.	B6	118
Potter, co., Tx., U.S.	B2	120
Potter Valley, Ca., U.S.	C2	82
Potts Creek, stm., U.S.	C2	123
Pottstown, Pa., U.S.	F10	115
Pottsville, Ar., U.S.	B2	81
Pottsville, Pa., U.S.	E9	115
P'otzu, Tai.	L9	28
Pouce Coupe, B.C., Can.	B7	69
Pouch Cove, Newf., Can.	E5	72
Poughkeepsie, N.Y., U.S.	D7	109
Poulan, Ga., U.S.	E3	87
Poulsbo, Wa., U.S.	B3	124
Poultney, Vt., U.S.	D2	122
Poultney, stm., Vt., U.S.	D2	122
Pound, Va., U.S.	e9	123
Pound Gap, U.S.	C7	94
Pouso Alegre, Braz.	G6	57
Poŭthĭsăt, Camb.	H7	34
Pouzauges, Fr.	F6	10
Póvoa de Varzim, Port.	D3	12
Povungnituk, Que., Can.	f11	74
Powassan, Ont., Can.	A5	73
Poway, Ca., U.S.	F5	82
Powder, stm., U.S.	B5	76
Powder, stm., Or., U.S.	C9	114
Powder, Middle Fork, stm., Wy., U.S.	C6	127
Powder, North Fork, stm., Wy., U.S.	C6	127
Powder, South Fork, stm., Wy., U.S.	C6	127
Powder River, co., Mt., U.S.	E11	103
Powder River Pass, Wy., U.S.	B5	127
Powder Springs, Ga., U.S.	h8	87
Powell, Oh., U.S.	B2	112
Powell, Tn., U.S.	m13	119
Powell, Wy., U.S.	B4	127
Powell, co., Ky., U.S.	C6	94
Powell, co., Mt., U.S.	D4	103
Powell, stm., U.S.	C10	119
Powell, Lake, res., U.S.	F5	121
Powell, Mount, mtn., Co., U.S.	B4	83
Powell, Mount, mtn., N.M., U.S.	B1	108
Powell Butte, Or., U.S.	C5	114
Powell Park, reg., Co., U.S.	A2	83
Powell River, B.C., Can.	E5	69
Powellton, W.V., U.S.	C3	125
Power, co., Id., U.S.	G5	89
Powers, Or., U.S.	E2	114
Powerview, Man., Can.	D3	70
Poweshiek, co., Ia., U.S.	C5	92
Powhatan, Va., U.S.	C5	123
Powhatan, co., Va., U.S.	C5	123
Powhatan Point, Oh., U.S.	C5	112
Poxoreu, Braz.	C1	57
Poyang, China	G5	28
Poyang Hu, l., China	F5	28
Poygan, Lake, l., Wi., U.S.	D5	126
Poynette, Wi., U.S.	E4	126
Poza Rica de Hidalgo, Mex.	G11	62
Poznań, Pol.	C16	8
Pozo Alcón, Spain	H9	12
Pozoblanco, Spain	G7	12
Pozo Redondo Mountains, mts., Az., U.S.	E3	80
Pozuelo de Alarcón, Spain	E8	12
Pozzuoli, Italy	I9	14
Prachin Buri, Thai.	G6	34
Prachuap Khiri Khan, Thai.	I5	34
Prague, Ok., U.S.	B5	113
Prague see Praha, Czech.	E14	8
Praha (Prague), Czech.	E14	8
Prainha, Braz.	E6	54
Prairie, co., Ar., U.S.	C4	81
Prairie, co., Mt., U.S.	D11	103
Prairie, stm., Mn., U.S.	C5	100
Prairie, stm., Wi., U.S.	C4	126
Prairie City, Ia., U.S.	C4	92
Prairie City, Or., U.S.	C8	114
Prairie Creek Reservoir, res., In., U.S.	D7	91
Prairie Dog Creek, stm., U.S.	C3	93
Prairie du Chien, Wi., U.S.	E2	126
Prairie du Sac, Wi., U.S.	E4	126
Prairie Grove, Ar., U.S.	B1	81
Prairies, Rivière des, stm., Que., Can.	p19	74
Prairie View, Tx., U.S.	D5	120
Prairie Village, Ks., U.S.	m16	93
Praslin Island, i., Sey.	B11	44
Pratas Islands see Tungsha Tao, is., Tai.	G10	26
Prat de Llobregat, Spain	D14	12
Prater Mountain, mtn., Wy., U.S.	C2	127
Prato, Italy	F6	14
Pratt, Ks., U.S.	E5	93
Pratt, co., Ks., U.S.	E5	93
Prattville, Al., U.S.	C3	78
Pravia, Spain	B5	12
Preble, co., Oh., U.S.	C1	112
Predazzo, Italy	C6	14
Predlitz [-Turrach], Aus.	H13	8
Pré-en-Pail, Fr.	D6	10
Preetz, Ger.	A10	8
Premont, Tx., U.S.	F3	120
Prentiss, Ms., U.S.	D4	101
Prentiss, co., Ms., U.S.	A5	101
Prenzlau, Ger.	B13	8
Preparis Island, i., Mya.	G2	34
Preparis North Channel, strt., Mya.	G2	34
Preparis South Channel, strt., Mya.	G2	34
Přerov, Czech.	F17	8
Prescott, Ont., Can.	C9	73
Prescott, Az., U.S.	C3	80
Prescott, Ar., U.S.	D2	81
Prescott, Wi., U.S.	D1	126
Presho, S.D., U.S.	D5	118
Presidencia Roca, Arg.	B5	56
Presidente Epitácio, Braz.	F2	57
Presidente Prudente, Braz.	G3	57
Presidential Range, mts., N.H., U.S.	B4	106
Presidio, Tx., U.S.	p12	120
Presidio, co., Tx., U.S.	o12	120
Presidio of San Francisco, mil., Ca., U.S.	h8	82
Prešov, Slov.	F21	8
Prespa, Lake, l., Eur.	I4	16
Presque Isle, Me., U.S.	B5	96
Presque Isle, co., Mi., U.S.	C6	99
Preston, Eng., U.K.	H10	7
Preston, Id., U.S.	G7	89
Preston, Ia., U.S.	B7	92
Preston, Mn., U.S.	G6	100
Preston, co., W.V., U.S.	B5	125
Preston Peak, mtn., Ca., U.S.	B2	82
Prestonsburg, Ky., U.S.	C7	94
Presumpscot, stm., Me., U.S.	g7	96
Pretoria, S. Afr.	G5	44
Prettyboy Reservoir, res., Md., U.S.	A4	97
Pretty Prairie, Ks., U.S.	E5	93
Préveza, Grc.	K4	16
Prewitt Reservoir, res., Co., U.S.	A7	83
Prey Vêng, Camb.	I8	34
Pribilof Islands, is., Ak., U.S.	D5	79
Příbram, Czech.	F14	8
Price, Ut., U.S.	D5	121
Price, co., Wi., U.S.	C3	126
Price, stm., Ut., U.S.	D5	121
Price Inlet, b., S.C., U.S.	k12	117
Prichard, Al., U.S.	E1	78
Priego, Spain	E9	12
Priego de Córdoba, Spain	H7	12
Prien, Ger.	H12	8
Prieska, S. Afr.	G4	44
Priest Lake, l., Id., U.S.	A2	89
Priest Rapids Dam, Wa., U.S.	C6	124
Priest Rapids Lake, res., Wa., U.S.	C6	124
Priest River, Id., U.S.	A2	89
Prievidza, Slov.	G18	8
Prijedor, Bos.	E11	14
Prilep, Mac.	H5	16
Prim, Point, c., P.E.I., Can.	C6	71
Primghar, Ia., U.S.	A2	92
Primrose, R.I., U.S.	B3	116
Primrose Lake, l., Can.	F11	66
Prince, Lake, res., Va., U.S.	k14	123
Prince Albert National Park, Sask., Can.	C2	75
Prince Albert Sound, strt., N.W. Ter., Can.	B9	66
Prince Charles Island, i., N.W. Ter., Can.	C17	66
Prince-de-Galles, Cap du, c., Que., Can.	D18	66
Prince Edward, co., Va., U.S.	C4	123
Prince Edward Island, prov., Can.	C6	71
Prince Edward Island National Park, P.E.I., Can.	C6	71
Prince Frederick, Md., U.S.	C4	97
Prince George, B.C., Can.	C6	69
Prince George, co., Va., U.S.	C5	123
Prince Georges, co., Md., U.S.	C4	97
Prince of Wales, Cape, c., Ak., U.S.	B6	79
Prince of Wales Island, i., Austl.	B8	50
Prince of Wales Island, i., N.W. Ter., Can.	B13	66
Prince of Wales Island, i., Ak., U.S.	n23	79
Prince of Wales Strait, strt., N.W. Ter., Can.	B9	66
Prince Regent Inlet, b., N.W. Ter., Can.	B14	66
Prince Rupert, B.C., Can.	B2	69
Princes Lakes, In., U.S.	F5	91
Princess Anne, Md., U.S.	D6	97
Princess Royal Channel, strt., B.C., Can.	C3	69
Princess Royal Island, i., B.C., Can.	C3	69
Princeton, B.C., Can.	E7	69
Princeton, Fl., U.S.	G6	86
Princeton, Il., U.S.	B4	90
Princeton, In., U.S.	H2	91
Princeton, Ia., U.S.	C7	92
Princeton, Ky., U.S.	C2	94

Name	Map Ref	Page
Princeton, Me., U.S.	**C5**	96
Princeton, Mn., U.S.	**E5**	100
Princeton, Mo., U.S.	**A4**	102
Princeton, N.J., U.S.	**C3**	107
Princeton, N.C., U.S.	**B4**	110
Princeton, W.V., U.S.	**D3**	125
Princeton, Wi., U.S.	**E4**	126
Princeton, Mount, mtn., Co., U.S.	**C4**	83
Princeville, Que., Can.	**C6**	74
Princeville, Il., U.S.	**C4**	90
Princeville, N.C., U.S.	**B5**	110
Prince William, co., Va., U.S.	**B5**	123
Prince William Sound, strt., Ak., U.S.	**g18**	79
Príncipe, i., S. Tom./P.	**A1**	44
Principe Channel, strt., B.C., Can.	**C3**	69
Príncipe da Beira, Braz.	**F6**	54
Prineville, Or., U.S.	**C6**	114
Prineville Reservoir, res., Or., U.S.	**C6**	114
Pringsewu, Indon.	**k12**	33a
Prinzapolca, Nic.	**H6**	64
Prior Lake, Mn., U.S.	**F5**	100
Priština, Yugo.	**G5**	16
Pritchards Island, i., S.C., U.S.	**G6**	117
Pritzwalk, Ger.	**B12**	8
Privas, Fr.	**H11**	10
Privolžsk, Russia	**D24**	18
Probolinggo, Indon.	**m16**	33a
Proctor, Mn., U.S.	**D6**	100
Proctor, Vt., U.S.	**D2**	122
Proctor Lake, res., Tx., U.S.	**C3**	120
Proctorsville, Vt., U.S.	**E3**	122
Proddatūr, India	**E5**	37
Professor Dr. Ir. W.J. van Blommestein Meer, res., Sur.	**C7**	54
Progreso, Mex.	**G15**	62
Prokopjevsk, Russia	**G11**	24
Prokuplje, Yugo.	**F5**	16
Promontory Mountains, mts., Ut., U.S.	**B3**	121
Prophetstown, Il., U.S.	**B4**	90
Propriá, Braz.	**F11**	54
Prospect, Ct., U.S.	**C4**	84
Prospect, Ky., U.S.	**g11**	94
Prospect, Oh., U.S.	**B2**	112
Prospect, Or., U.S.	**E4**	114
Prospect, Pa., U.S.	**E1**	115
Prospect Hill, mtn., Or., U.S.	**k11**	114
Prospect Park, N.J., U.S.	**B4**	107
Prospect Park, Pa., U.S.	**p20**	115
Prosperity, S.C., U.S.	**C4**	117
Prosperity, W.V., U.S.	**n13**	125
Prosser, Wa., U.S.	**C6**	124
Prostějov, Czech.	**F17**	8
Protection, Ks., U.S.	**E4**	93
Protville, Tun.	**M5**	14
Provence, hist. reg., Fr.	**I13**	10
Providence, Ky., U.S.	**C2**	94
Providence, R.I., U.S.	**C4**	116
Providence, Ut., U.S.	**B4**	121
Providence, co., R.I., U.S.	**C2**	116
Providence, stm., R.I., U.S.	**C5**	116
Providence Island, i., Sey.	**C10**	44
Providence Point, c., R.I., U.S.	**D5**	116
Providencia, Isla de, i., Col.	**H7**	64
Providenija, Russia	**E31**	24
Province Lake, l., N.H., U.S.	**C5**	106
Provincetown, Ma., U.S.	**B7**	98
Provins, Fr.	**D10**	10
Provo, Ut., U.S.	**C4**	121
Provo, stm., Ut., U.S.	**C4**	121
Provost, Alta., Can.	**C5**	68
Prowers, co., Co., U.S.	**D8**	83
Prozor, Bos.	**F12**	14
Prudence Island, i., R.I., U.S.	**E5**	116
Prudenville, Mi., U.S.	**D6**	99
Prudhoe Bay, Ak., U.S.	**A10**	79
Prudhoe Bay, b., Ak., U.S.	**A10**	79
Prüm, Ger.	**E6**	8
Pruszków, Pol.	**C20**	8
Prut, stm., Eur.	**D12**	16
Pryor, Mt., U.S.	**E8**	103
Pryor, Ok., U.S.	**A6**	113
Pryor Mountains, mts., Mt., U.S.	**E8**	103
Przemyśl, Pol.	**F22**	8
Pskov, Russia	**D11**	18
Ptolemaís, Grc.	**I5**	16
Ptuj, Slo.	**C10**	14
Pucallpa, Peru	**E4**	54
Pucheng, China	**H7**	28
Puckaway Lake, l., Wi., U.S.	**E4**	126
Pudukkottai, India	**G5**	37
Puebla de Sanabria, Spain	**C5**	12
Puebla de Trives, Spain	**C4**	12
Puebla [de Zaragoza], Mex.	**H10**	62
Pueblo, Co., U.S.	**C6**	83
Pueblo, co., Co., U.S.	**C6**	83
Pueblo Hundido, Chile	**B2**	56
Pueblo Mountain, mtn., Or., U.S.	**E8**	114
Pueblo Mountains, mts., Or., U.S.	**E8**	114
Pueblo Reservoir, res., Co., U.S.	**C6**	83
Puentedeume, Spain	**B3**	12
Puente-Genil, Spain	**H7**	12
Pueo Point, c., Hi., U.S.	**B1**	88
Puerco, stm., U.S.	**C6**	80
Puerco, Rio, stm., N.M., U.S.	**B2**	108
Puerto Aisén, Chile	**F2**	56
Puerto Alfonso, Col.	**I7**	58
Puerto Ángel, Mex.	**J11**	62
Puerto Armuelles, Pan.	**J6**	64
Puerto Asís, Col.	**G4**	58
Puerto Ayacucho, Ven.	**E9**	58
Puerto Barrios, Guat.	**G3**	64
Puerto Berrío, Col.	**D5**	58
Puerto Boyacá, Col.	**E5**	58
Puerto Cabello, Ven.	**B8**	58
Puerto Cabezas, Nic.	**G6**	64
Puerto Carreño, Col.	**D9**	58
Puerto Casado, Para.	**A5**	56
Puerto Chicama, Peru	**E3**	54
Puerto Cortés, C.R.	**J6**	64
Puerto Cortés, Hond.	**G4**	64
Puerto Cumarebo, Ven.	**B8**	58
Puerto de Pollensa, Spain	**F15**	12
Puerto de San José, Guat.	**H2**	64
Puerto Deseado, Arg.	**F3**	56
Puerto Escondido, Mex.	**J11**	62
Puerto Francisco de Orellana, Ec.	**H4**	58
Puerto Inírida, Col.	**F9**	58
Puerto Juárez, Mex.	**G16**	62
Puerto la Cruz, Ven.	**B10**	58
Puerto Leguízamo, Col.	**H5**	58
Puerto Limón, Col.	**F6**	58
Puertollano, Spain	**G7**	12
Puerto Lobos, Arg.	**E3**	56
Puerto Madryn, Arg.	**E3**	56
Puerto Maldonado, Peru	**F5**	54
Puerto Montt, Chile	**E2**	56
Puerto Morelos, Mex.	**G16**	62
Puerto Nariño, Col.	**E9**	58
Puerto Natales, Chile	**G2**	56
Puerto Padre, Cuba	**D9**	64
Puerto Peñasco, Mex.	**B3**	62
Puerto Plata, Dom. Rep.	**E12**	64
Puerto Princesa, Phil.	**D6**	32
Puerto Real, Spain	**I5**	12
Puerto Rico, dep., N.A.	**E14**	64
Puerto Rondón, Col.	**D7**	58
Puerto Suárez, Bol.	**G7**	54
Puerto Tejada, Col.	**F4**	58
Puerto Vallarta, Mex.	**G7**	62
Puerto Wilches, Col.	**D6**	58
Puget Sound, strt., Wa., U.S.	**B3**	124
Puget Sound Naval Shipyard, mil., Wa., U.S.	**e10**	124
Pugwash, N.S., Can.	**D6**	71
Puhi, Hi., U.S.	**B2**	88
Puigcerdá, Spain	**C13**	12
Pukalani, Hi., U.S.	**C5**	88
Pukaskwa National Park, Ont., Can.	**o18**	73
Pukch'ŏng, N. Kor.	**C12**	26
Pukë, Alb.	**G3**	16
Pukeashun Mountain, mtn., B.C., Can.	**D8**	69
Pukekohe, N.Z.	**B5**	52
Pukou, China	**C7**	28
Pula, Cro.	**E8**	14
Pulacayo, Bol.	**H5**	54
Pulaski, N.Y., U.S.	**B4**	109
Pulaski, Tn., U.S.	**B4**	119
Pulaski, Va., U.S.	**C2**	123
Pulaski, Wi., U.S.	**D5**	126
Pulaski, co., Ar., U.S.	**C3**	81
Pulaski, co., Ga., U.S.	**D3**	87
Pulaski, co., Il., U.S.	**F4**	90
Pulaski, co., In., U.S.	**B4**	91
Pulaski, co., Ky., U.S.	**C5**	94
Pulaski, co., Mo., U.S.	**D5**	102
Pulaski, co., Va., U.S.	**C2**	123
Puli, Tai.	**L9**	28
Puliyangudi, India	**H4**	37
Pulkkila, Fin.	**D15**	6
Pullman, Wa., U.S.	**C8**	124
Pulog, Mount, mtn., Phil.	**B7**	32
Pumphrey, Md., U.S.	**h11**	97
Puná, Isla, i., Ec.	**I2**	58
Punakha, Bhu.	**G13**	38
Pūnch, India	**D6**	38
Pune (Poona), India	**C2**	37
Pungo Lake, l., N.C., U.S.	**B6**	110
Punjab, state, India	**E6**	38
Puno, Peru	**G4**	54
Punta, Cerro de, mtn., P.R.	**E14**	64
Punta Alta, Arg.	**D4**	56
Punta Arenas, Chile	**G2**	56
Punta Delgada, Arg.	**E4**	56
Punta de Mata, Ven.	**C11**	58
Punta Gorda, Belize	**F3**	64
Punta Gorda, Nic.	**I6**	64
Punta Gorda, Fl., U.S.	**F4**	86
Puntarenas, C.R.	**J5**	64
Punto Fijo, Ven.	**B7**	58
Punxsutawney, Pa., U.S.	**E4**	115
Puolanka, Fin.	**D16**	6
Purcell, Ok., U.S.	**B4**	113
Purcellville, Va., U.S.	**A5**	123
Purdy, Mo., U.S.	**E4**	102
Purgatoire, stm., Co., U.S.	**D7**	83
Purgatoire Peak, mtn., Co., U.S.	**D5**	83
Puri, India	**K11**	38
Purli, India	**C4**	37
Purnea, India	**H12**	38
Purūlia, India	**I12**	38
Purus (Purús), stm., S.A.	**D6**	54
Purvis, Ms., U.S.	**D4**	101
Purwakarta, Indon.	**m13**	33a
Purwokerto, Indon.	**m14**	32
Purworejo, Indon.	**m15**	33a
Pusan, S. Kor.	**D12**	26
Pushaw Lake, l., Me., U.S.	**D4**	96
Pushmataha, co., Ok., U.S.	**C6**	113
Puškin, Russia	**B13**	18
Puškino, Russia	**E20**	18
Putao, Mya.	**F6**	26
Putian, China	**J8**	28
Puting, Tanjung, c., Indon.	**F5**	32
Putnam, Ct., U.S.	**B8**	84
Putnam, co., Fl., U.S.	**C5**	86
Putnam, co., Ga., U.S.	**C3**	87
Putnam, co., Il., U.S.	**B4**	90
Putnam, co., In., U.S.	**E4**	91
Putnam, co., Mo., U.S.	**A4**	102
Putnam, co., N.Y., U.S.	**D7**	109
Putnam, co., Oh., U.S.	**B1**	112
Putnam, co., Tn., U.S.	**C8**	119
Putnam, co., W.V., U.S.	**C3**	125
Putney, Ga., U.S.	**E2**	87
Putney, Vt., U.S.	**F3**	122
Putorana, Plato, plat., Russia	**D12**	24
Puttalam, Sri L.	**H5**	37
Puttgarden, Ger.	**A11**	8
Putumayo (Içá), stm., S.A.	**I7**	58
Putuo, China	**F11**	28
Puukohola Heiau National Historic Site, hist., Hi., U.S.	**D6**	88
Puxico, Mo., U.S.	**E7**	102
Puyallup, Wa., U.S.	**B3**	124
Puyallup, stm., Wa., U.S.	**C3**	124
Puy de Dôme, mtn., Fr.	**G9**	10
Puy de Sancy, mtn., Fr.	**G9**	10
Puylaurens, Fr.	**I9**	10
Puyo, Ec.	**H4**	58
Pweto, Zaire	**C5**	44
Pwllheli, Wales, U.K.	**I8**	7
Pyapon, Mya.	**F3**	34
Pyatigorsk see P'atigorsk, Russia	**I6**	22
Pyè (Prome), Mya.	**E3**	34
Pyhäjoki, Fin.	**D15**	6
Pyhäselkä, Fin.	**E17**	6
Pyinmana, Mya.	**E4**	34
Pyles Fork, stm., W.V., U.S.	**h10**	125
Pymatuning Reservoir, res., U.S.	**C1**	115
P'yŏngyang, N. Kor.	**D12**	26
Pyramid Lake, l., Nv., U.S.	**C2**	105
Pyramid Lake Indian Reservation, Nv., U.S.	**D2**	105
Pyramid Mountains, mts., N.M., U.S.	**E1**	108
Pyramid Peak, mtn., N.M., U.S.	**E1**	108
Pyramid Peak, mtn., Wy., U.S.	**C2**	127
Pyrenees, mts., Eur.	**C12**	12
Pyskowice, Pol.	**E18**	8
Pyu, Mya.	**E4**	34

Q

Name	Map Ref	Page
Qaidam Pendi, China	**B16**	38
Qalāt, Afg.	**D2**	38
Qal'at Bīshah, Sau. Ar.	**E3**	46
Qal'eh-ye Kānsī, Afg.	**C2**	36
Qal'eh-ye Sarkārī, Afg.	**C2**	38
Qallābāt, Sudan	**F13**	42
Qamar, Ghubbat al-, b., Yemen	**E5**	46
Qamdo, China	**E6**	26
Qandahār, Afg.	**E1**	38
Qandala, Som.	**F4**	46
Qarqan, stm., China	**B11**	38
Qarqīn, Afg.	**B2**	38
Qaṣr al-Burayqah, Libya	**B9**	42
Qaṣr al-Farāfirah, Egypt	**C11**	42
Qaṭanā, Syria	**C5**	40
Qatar, ctry., Asia	**C5**	46
Qazvīn, Iran	**J8**	22
Qeshm, i., Iran	**C6**	46
Qeyṣār, Afg.	**C1**	38
Qeẕi'ot, Isr.	**D4**	40
Qiemo, China	**A11**	38
Qijiang, China	**F8**	26
Qinā, Egypt	**C12**	42
Qingdao (Tsingtao), China	**D11**	26
Qinghai, prov., China	**D6**	26
Qinghai Hu, l., China	**D7**	26
Qingjiang, China	**G4**	28
Qinglong, China	**B8**	34
Qingyang, China	**D8**	26
Qingyuan, China	**G8**	26
Qingyuan, China	**L2**	28
Qinhuangdao, China	**D10**	26
Qin Ling, mts., China	**E8**	26
Qinzhou, China	**D10**	34
Qiongzhou Haixia, strt., China	**D11**	34
Qiqihar, China	**B11**	26
Qiryat Shemona, Isr.	**C4**	40
Qitai, China	**C4**	26
Qīzān, Sau. Ar.	**E3**	46
Qom, Iran	**B5**	46
Qomsheh, Iran	**B5**	46
Qondūz, Afg.	**B3**	38
Qondūz, stm., Afg.	**C3**	38
Quabbin Reservoir, res., Ma., U.S.	**B3**	98
Quaddick Reservoir, res., Ct., U.S.	**B8**	84
Quail Oaks, Va., U.S.	**n18**	123
Quaker Hill, Ct., U.S.	**D7**	84
Quakertown, Pa., U.S.	**F11**	115
Qualicum Beach, B.C., Can.	**E5**	69
Quanah, Tx., U.S.	**B3**	120
Quang Ngai, Viet.	**G10**	34
Quannapowitt, Lake, l., Ma., U.S.	**f11**	98
Quantico, Va., U.S.	**B5**	123
Quantico Marine Corps Air Station, mil., Va., U.S.	**B5**	123
Quanzhou, China	**K7**	28
Quapaw, Ok., U.S.	**A7**	113
Qu'Appelle, Sask., Can.	**G4**	75
Qu'Appelle, stm., Can.	**G4**	75
Quarryville, Pa., U.S.	**G9**	115
Quartu Sant'Elena, Italy	**J4**	14
Quartz Lake, l., N.W. Ter., Can.	**B16**	66
Quartz Mountain, mtn., Or., U.S.	**D4**	114
Quartzsite, Az., U.S.	**D1**	80
Quassapaug, Lake, l., Ct., U.S.	**C3**	84
Quatsino Sound, strt., B.C., Can.	**D3**	69
Quay, co., N.M., U.S.	**C6**	108
Qūchān, Iran	**J9**	22
Québec, Que., Can.	**C6**	74
Quebec, prov., Can.	**C5**	74
Quechee, Vt., U.S.	**D4**	122
Quedlinburg, Ger.	**D11**	8
Queen, stm., R.I., U.S.	**E3**	116
Queen Annes, co., Md., U.S.	**B5**	97
Queen Bess, Mount, mtn., B.C., Can.	**D5**	69
Queen Charlotte, B.C., Can.	**C1**	69
Queen Charlotte Islands, is., B.C., Can.	**C1**	69
Queen Charlotte Mountains, mts., B.C., Can.	**C1**	69
Queen Charlotte Sound, strt., B.C., Can.	**n17**	69
Queen Charlotte Strait, strt., B.C., Can.	**D4**	69
Queen City, Mo., U.S.	**A5**	102
Queen City, Tx., U.S.	**C5**	120
Queen Creek, Az., U.S.	**m9**	80
Queen Maud Gulf, b., N.W. Ter., Can.	**C12**	66
Queen Maud Land, reg., Ant.	**B14**	47
Queens, co., N.Y., U.S.	**E7**	109
Queens Channel, strt., N.W. Ter., Can.	**A13**	66
Queensland, state, Austl.	**D8**	50
Queenstown, N.Z.	**F2**	52
Queenstown, S. Afr.	**H5**	44
Quelimane, Moz.	**E7**	44
Quemoy see Chinmen Tao, i., Tai.	**K7**	28
Querétaro, Mex.	**G9**	62
Querobabi, Mex.	**B4**	62
Quesnel, B.C., Can.	**C6**	69
Quesnel, stm., B.C., Can.	**C6**	69
Quesnel Lake, l., B.C., Can.	**C7**	69
Questa, N.M., U.S.	**A4**	108
Questembert, Fr.	**E4**	10
Quetico Provincial Park, Ont., Can.	**o17**	73
Quetta, Pak.	**E2**	38
Quevedo, Ec.	**H3**	58
Quevedo, stm., Ec.	**H3**	58
Quezaltenango, Guat.	**G2**	64
Quezon City, Phil.	**q19**	32
Qufu, China	**D10**	26
Quibdó, Col.	**E4**	58
Quiberon, Fr.	**E3**	10
Quicksand Pond, l., R.I., U.S.	**E6**	116
Quidnessett, R.I., U.S.	**E4**	116
Quidnick, R.I., U.S.	**D3**	116
Quidnick Reservoir, res., R.I., U.S.	**D2**	116
Quilá, Mex.	**E6**	62
Quilcene, Wa., U.S.	**B3**	124
Quileute Indian Reservation, Wa., U.S.	**B1**	124
Quillan, Fr.	**J9**	10
Quilon, India	**H4**	37
Quilpie, Austl.	**E8**	50
Quimilí, Arg.	**B4**	56
Quimper, Fr.	**D2**	10
Quimperlé, Fr.	**E3**	10
Quinault, stm., Wa., U.S.	**B1**	124
Quinault, Lake, l., Wa., U.S.	**B2**	124
Quinault Indian Reservation, Wa., U.S.	**B1**	124
Quincemil, Peru	**F4**	54
Quincy, Ca., U.S.	**C3**	82
Quincy, Fl., U.S.	**B2**	86
Quincy, Il., U.S.	**D2**	90
Quincy, Ma., U.S.	**B5**	98
Quincy, Mi., U.S.	**G6**	99
Quincy, Wa., U.S.	**B6**	124
Quincy Bay, b., Ma., U.S.	**g12**	98
Quinebaug, Ct., U.S.	**A8**	84
Quinebaug, stm., Ct., U.S.	**C8**	84
Quinhagak, Ak., U.S.	**D7**	79
Qui Nhon, Viet.	**H10**	34
Quinlan, Tx., U.S.	**C4**	120
Quinn, stm., Nv., U.S.	**B3**	105
Quinn Canyon Range, mts., Nv., U.S.	**F6**	105
Quinnesec, Mi., U.S.	**C3**	99
Quinnipiac, stm., Ct., U.S.	**D4**	84
Quintanar de la Orden, Spain	**F8**	12
Quinter, Ks., U.S.	**C3**	93
Quinton, Ok., U.S.	**B6**	113
Quiroga, Spain	**C4**	12
Quitman, Ar., U.S.	**B3**	81
Quitman, Ga., U.S.	**F3**	87
Quitman, Ms., U.S.	**C5**	101
Quitman, Tx., U.S.	**C5**	120
Quitman, co., Ga., U.S.	**E1**	87
Quitman, co., Ms., U.S.	**A3**	101
Quito, Ec.	**H3**	58
Quixadá, Braz.	**D11**	54
Qujing, China	**B7**	34
Qumalai (Sewugou), China	**C16**	38
Quoich, stm., N.W. Ter., Can.	**D14**	66
Quonnipaug Lake, l., Ct., U.S.	**D5**	84
Quonochontaug, R.I., U.S.	**G2**	116
Quonochontaug Pond, l., R.I., U.S.	**G2**	116
Quonset Point, c., R.I., U.S.	**E4**	116
Qutdligssat, Grnld.	**B22**	66
Quthing, Leso.	**H5**	44
Quxian, China	**G7**	28

R

Name	Map Ref	Page
Raalte, Neth.	**C6**	8
Rab, Cro.	**E9**	14
Raba, Indon.	**G6**	32
Rába (Raab), stm., Eur.	**H17**	8
Rábade, Spain	**B4**	12
Rabat (Victoria), Malta	**M9**	14
Rabat, Mor.	**B4**	42
Rabaul, Pap. N. Gui.	**k17**	50a
Rabbit Creek, stm., S.D., U.S.	**B3**	118
Rabbit Ears Pass, Co., U.S.	**A4**	83
Rābigh, Sau. Ar.	**D2**	46
Rabun, co., Ga., U.S.	**B3**	87
Rabun Bald, mtn., Ga., U.S.	**B3**	87
Raccoon Creek, stm., Oh., U.S.	**D3**	112
Raccourci Island, i., La., U.S.	**D4**	95
Race, Cape, c., Newf., Can.	**E5**	72
Raceland, Ky., U.S.	**B7**	94
Raceland, La., U.S.	**E5**	95
Race Point, c., Ma., U.S.	**B7**	98
Rach Gia, Viet.	**I8**	34
Racibórz (Ratibor), Pol.	**E18**	8
Racine, W.V., U.S.	**C3**	125
Racine, Wi., U.S.	**F6**	126
Racine, co., Wi., U.S.	**F5**	126
Racine Dam, U.S.	**C3**	125
Radcliff, Ky., U.S.	**C4**	94
Radeberg, Ger.	**D13**	8
Radebeul, Ger.	**D13**	8
Radeče, Slo.	**C10**	14
Radford, Va., U.S.	**C2**	123
Radolfzell, Ger.	**H8**	8
Radom, Pol.	**D21**	8
Radomsko, Pol.	**D19**	8
Rae, N.W. Ter., Can.	**D9**	66
Rāe Bareli, India	**G9**	38
Raeford, N.C., U.S.	**C3**	110
Rae Isthmus, N.W. Ter., Can.	**C15**	66
Rae Strait, strt., N.W. Ter., Can.	**C13**	66
Raetihi, N.Z.	**C5**	52
Rafaela, Arg.	**C4**	56
Rafah, Gaza Strip	**D4**	40
Rafḥā', Sau. Ar.	**C3**	46
Rafsanjān, Iran	**K9**	22
Rafsanjān, Iran	**B6**	46
Raft, stm., Id., U.S.	**G5**	89
Raft River Mountains, mts., Ut., U.S.	**B2**	121
Raga, Sudan	**G11**	42
Ragged Island, i., Me., U.S.	**E4**	96
Ragged Lake, l., Me., U.S.	**C3**	96
Ragged Top Mountain, mtn., Wy., U.S.	**E7**	127
Ragland, Al., U.S.	**B3**	78
Ragusa, Italy	**M9**	14
Ragusa see Dubrovnik, Cro.	**G13**	14
Rahīmyār Khān, Pak.	**F4**	38
Rahway, N.J., U.S.	**B4**	107
Rahway, stm., N.J., U.S.	**k7**	107
Rāichūr, India	**D4**	37
Raigarh, India	**B7**	37
Railroad Valley, val., Nv., U.S.	**E6**	105
Rainbow Bridge National Monument, Ut., U.S.	**F5**	121
Rainbow Falls, wtfl, Tn., U.S.	**D10**	119
Rainbow Flowage, res., Wi., U.S.	**C4**	126
Rainbow Lake, l., Me., U.S.	**C3**	96
Rainelle, W.V., U.S.	**D4**	125
Rainier, Or., U.S.	**A4**	114
Rainier, Wa., U.S.	**C3**	124
Rainier, Mount, mtn., Wa., U.S.	**C4**	124
Rains, co., Tx., U.S.	**C5**	120
Rainsville, Al., U.S.	**A4**	78
Rainy Lake, l., N.A.	**G14**	66
Rainy Lake, l., Mn., U.S.	**B5**	100
Rainy River, Ont., Can.	**o16**	73
Raipur, India	**B6**	37
Rājahmundry, India	**D6**	37
Raja-Jooseppi, Fin.	**B17**	6
Rājapālaiyam, India	**H4**	37
Rājasthān, prov., India	**G5**	38
Rājasthān Canal, India	**F5**	38
Rajčichinsk, Russia	**H19**	24
Rājkot, India	**I4**	38
Rāj-Nāndgaon, India	**B6**	37
Rājpīpla, India	**J5**	38
Rājshāhi, Bngl.	**H13**	38
Rakaposhi, mtn., Pak.	**B6**	38
Rakata, Pulau, i., Indon.	**m12**	33a
Råkvåg, Nor.	**E8**	6
Raleigh, Ms., U.S.	**C4**	101
Raleigh, N.C., U.S.	**B4**	110
Raleigh, W.V., U.S.	**n13**	125
Raleigh, co., W.V., U.S.	**D3**	125
Raleigh Bay, b., N.C., U.S.	**C6**	110
Ralls, Tx., U.S.	**C2**	120
Ralls, co., Mo., U.S.	**B6**	102
Ralston, Ne., U.S.	**g12**	104
Ralston Valley, val., Nv., U.S.	**E4**	105
Rama, Nic.	**H5**	64
Ramah, N.M., U.S.	**B1**	108
Ramah Indian Reservation, N.M., U.S.	**C1**	108
Rām Allāh, W. Bank	**D4**	40
Ramapo, stm., N.J., U.S.	**A4**	107
Ramblewood, N.J., U.S.	**D3**	107
Rambouillet, Fr.	**D8**	10
Ramea, Newf., Can.	**E3**	72
Ramenskoje, Russia	**F21**	18
Rāmeswaram, India	**H5**	37
Rāmgarh, Bngl.	**I14**	38
Ramla, Isr.	**D4**	40
Ramlo, mtn., Erit.	**F3**	46
Ramona, Ca., U.S.	**F5**	82
Rampart Range, mts., Co., U.S.	**B5**	83
Rāmpur, India	**F8**	38
Ramree Island, i., Mya.	**E2**	34
Ramsay, Mi., U.S.	**n12**	99
Ramseur, N.C., U.S.	**B3**	110
Ramsey, I. of Man	**G8**	7
Ramsey, Il., U.S.	**D4**	90
Ramsey, Mn., U.S.	***E5**	100
Ramsey, N.J., U.S.	**A4**	107
Ramsey, co., Mn., U.S.	**E5**	100
Ramsey, co., N.D., U.S.	**A7**	111
Ramsgate, Eng., U.K.	**J14**	7
Ramshorn Peak, mtn., Mt., U.S.	**E5**	103
Ramshorn Peak, mtn., Wy., U.S.	**C3**	127
Rāmu, Bngl.	**J15**	38
Ramu, stm., Pap. N. Gui.	**m16**	50a
Rancagua, Chile	**C2**	56
Rancharia, Braz.	**G3**	57
Rancheria Rock, mtn., Or., U.S.	**C6**	114
Ranchester, Wy., U.S.	**B5**	127
Rānchī, India	**I11**	38
Rancho Palos Verdes, Ca., U.S.	***n12**	82
Ranchos de Taos, N.M., U.S.	**A4**	108
Rancocas Creek, stm., N.J., U.S.	**C3**	107
Rand, W.V., U.S.	**C3**	125
Randall, co., Tx., U.S.	**B2**	120
Randallstown, Md., U.S.	**B4**	97
Randazzo, Italy	**L9**	14
Randers, Den.	**H8**	6
Randle, Wa., U.S.	**C4**	124
Randleman, N.C., U.S.	**B3**	110
Randolph, Me., U.S.	**D3**	96
Randolph, Ma., U.S.	**B5**	98
Randolph, Ne., U.S.	**B8**	104
Randolph, Vt., U.S.	**D3**	122
Randolph, Wi., U.S.	**E5**	126
Randolph, co., Al., U.S.	**B4**	78
Randolph, co., Ar., U.S.	**A4**	81
Randolph, co., Ga., U.S.	**E2**	87
Randolph, co., Il., U.S.	**E4**	90
Randolph, co., In., U.S.	**D7**	91
Randolph, co., Mo., U.S.	**B5**	102
Randolph, co., N.C., U.S.	**B3**	110
Randolph, co., W.V., U.S.	**C5**	125
Randolph Air Force Base, mil., Tx., U.S.	**h7**	120
Randolph Hills, Md., U.S.	**B3**	97
Random Island, i., Newf., Can.	**D5**	72
Random Lake, Wi., U.S.	**E6**	126
Rangeley, Me., U.S.	**D2**	96
Rangeley Lake, l., Me., U.S.	**D2**	96
Rangely, Co., U.S.	**A2**	83
Ranger, Tx., U.S.	**C3**	120
Ranger Lake, l., N.M., U.S.	**D6**	108
Rangoon see Yangon, Mya.	**B2**	32
Rangpur, Bngl.	**H13**	38

Name Map Ref Page

Rankin, Pa., U.S. k14 115
Rankin, co., Ms., U.S. C4 101
Rankin Inlet, N.W. Ter., Can. D14 66
Rann of Kutch, pl., Asia H3 38
Ransom, co., N.D., U.S. C8 111
Ranson, W.V., U.S. B7 125
Rantauprapat, Indon. E2 32
Rantekombola, Bulu, mtn., Indon. F7 32
Rantoul, Il., U.S. C5 90
Raoping, China L6 28
Raoul, Ga., U.S. B3 87
Rapallo, Italy E4 14
Rapid, stm., Mn., U.S. B4 100
Rapid City, S.D., U.S. C2 118
Rapides, co., La., U.S. C3 95
Rapid River, Mi., U.S. C4 99
Rapids City, Il., U.S. B3 90
Rappahannock, co., Va., U.S. B4 123
Rappahannock, stm., Va., U.S. B5 123
Raquette, stm., N.Y., U.S. f10 109
Raquette Lake, l., N.Y., U.S. B6 109
Raritan, N.J., U.S. B3 107
Raritan, stm., N.J., U.S. C4 107
Raritan Bay, b., N.J., U.S. C4 107
Ra's al-'Ayn, Syria A7 40
Ra's an-Naqb, Jord. D4 40
Ras Dashen, mtn., Eth. F2 46
Ras Djebel, Tun. L5 14
Rasht, Iran J7 22
Rāsipuram, India G5 37
Rasskazovo, Russia I24 18
Rastatt, Ger. G8 8
Ratangarh, India F6 38
Rätansbyn, Swe. E10 6
Rathbun Lake, res., Ia., U.S. D5 92
Rathdrum, Id., U.S. B2 89
Rathenow, Ger. C12 8
Rathkeale, Ire. I4 7
Rathlin Island, i., N. Ire., U.K. F6 7
Rat Islands, is., Ak., U.S. E3 79
Ratlām, India I6 38
Ratnāgiri, India D2 37
Ratnapura, Sri L. I6 37
Raton, N.M., U.S. A5 108
Raton Pass, N.M., U.S. A5 108
Rattlesnake Creek, stm., Oh., U.S. C2 112
Rattlesnake Creek, stm., Wa., U.S. C6 124
Rättvik, Swe. F10 6
Ratz, Mount, mtn., B.C., Can. E6 66
Ratzeburg, Ger. B10 8
Raub, Malay. M6 34
Rauch, Arg. D5 56
Rauma, Fin. F13 6
Raurkela, India I11 38
Ravalli, co., Mt., U.S. D2 103
Raven, Va., U.S. e10 123
Ravena, N.Y., U.S. C7 109
Ravenel, S.C., U.S. k11 117
Ravenna, Italy E7 14
Ravenna, Ky., U.S. C6 94
Ravenna, Mi., U.S. E5 99
Ravenna, Ne., U.S. C7 104
Ravenna, Oh., U.S. A4 112
Raven Park, reg., Co., U.S. A2 83
Ravensburg, Ger. H9 8
Ravenshoe, Austl. C9 50
Ravensthorpe, Austl. F3 50
Ravenswood, W.V., U.S. C3 125
Rāwalpindi, Pak. D5 38
Rawdon, Que., Can. C4 74
Rawhide Creek, stm., Wy., U.S. D8 127
Rawlings, Md., U.S. k13 97
Rawlinna, Austl. F5 50
Rawlins, Wy., U.S. E5 127
Rawlins, co., Ks., U.S. C2 93
Rawson, Arg. E3 56
Ray, N.D., U.S. A2 111
Ray, co., Mo., U.S. B3 102
Ray, Cape, c., Newf., Can. E2 72
Raya, Bukit, mtn., Indon. F5 32
Rāyadrug, India E4 37
Ray City, Ga., U.S. E3 87
Raymond, Alta., Can. E4 68
Raymond, Il., U.S. D4 90
Raymond, Mn., U.S. E3 100
Raymond, Ms., U.S. C3 101
Raymond, N.H., U.S. D4 106
Raymond, Wa., U.S. C2 124
Raymondville, Tx., U.S. F4 120
Raymore, Sask., Can. F3 75
Raymore, Mo., U.S. C3 102
Rayne, La., U.S. D3 95
Raynham, Ma., U.S. C5 98
Raynham Center, Ma., U.S. C5 98
Raytown, Mo., U.S. h11 102
Rayville, La., U.S. B4 95
R'azan', Russia G22 18
Razgrad, Bul. F10 16
R'ažsk, Russia H23 18
Reader, W.V., U.S. B4 125
Reading, Eng., U.K. J12 7
Reading, Ma., U.S. A5 98
Reading, Mi., U.S. G6 99
Reading, Oh., U.S. C1 112
Reading, Pa., U.S. F10 115
Readlyn, Ia., U.S. B5 92
Reagan, co., Tx., U.S. D2 120
Real, co., Tx., U.S. E3 120
Realicó, Arg. D4 56
Réalmont, Fr. I9 10
Reamstown, Pa., U.S. F9 115
Recanati, Italy F8 14
Recherche, Archipelago of the, is., Austl. F4 50
Rečica, Bela. I13 18
Recife, Braz. E12 54
Recklinghausen, Ger. D7 8
Recreo, Arg. B3 56
Rector, Ar., U.S. A5 81
Red (Hong) (Yuan), stm., Asia C8 34
Red, stm., N.A. B7 76
Red, stm., U.S. E8 76
Red, stm., Ky., U.S. C6 94
Red, stm., Tn., U.S. A4 119
Red Bank, N.J., U.S. C4 107
Red Bank, Tn., U.S. D8 119
Red Bay, Al., U.S. A1 78
Redberry Lake, l., Sask., Can. E2 75
Redbird, Oh., U.S. A4 112
Red Bird, stm., Ky., U.S. C6 94
Red Bluff, Ca., U.S. B2 82
Red Bluff Lake, res., U.S. o12 120
Red Boiling Springs, Tn., U.S. C8 119
Red Bud, Il., U.S. E4 90
Red Butte, mtn., Ut., U.S. B2 121
Red Cedar, stm., Wi., U.S. C2 126
Red Cedar Lake, l., Wi., U.S. C2 126
Redcliff, Alta., Can. D5 68
Redcliffe, Mount, mtn., Austl. E4 50
Red Cliff Indian Reservation, Wi., U.S. B2 126
Red Cloud, Ne., U.S. D7 104
Redcloud Peak, mtn., Co., U.S. D3 83
Red Deer, Alta., Can. C4 68
Red Deer, stm., Can. D4 68
Red Deer, stm., Can. E4 75
Redding, Ca., U.S. B2 82
Redding, Ct., U.S. D2 84
Redeye, stm., Mn., U.S. D3 100
Redfield, Ar., U.S. C3 81
Redfield, Ia., U.S. C3 92
Redfield, S.D., U.S. C7 118
Redford, Mi., U.S. F7 99
Redgranite, Wi., U.S. D4 126
Red Hook, N.Y., U.S. C7 109
Red Indian Lake, l., Newf., Can. D3 72
Red Jacket, W.V., U.S. D2 125
Redkey, In., U.S. D7 91
Redlake, Mn., U.S. C3 100
Red Lake, co., Mn., U.S. C2 100
Red Lake, l., Az., U.S. B1 80
Red Lake, stm., Mn., U.S. C2 100
Red Lake Falls, Mn., U.S. C2 100
Red Lake Indian Reservation, Mn., U.S. B3 100
Redlands, Ca., U.S. E5 82
Red Lion, Pa., U.S. G8 115
Red Lodge, Mt., U.S. E7 103
Red Mill Pond, l., De., U.S. E5 85
Redmond, Or., U.S. C5 114
Redmond, Ut., U.S. E4 121
Redmond, Wa., U.S. e11 124
Red Mountain, mtn., Ca., U.S. B2 82
Red Mountain, mtn., Mt., U.S. C4 103
Red Mountain Pass, Co., U.S. D3 83
Red Oak, Ga., U.S. h7 87
Red Oak, Ia., U.S. D2 92
Red Oak, Ok., U.S. C6 113
Red Oak, Tx., U.S. n10 120
Red Oaks, La., U.S. h9 95
Redon, Fr. E4 10
Redondela, Spain C3 12
Redondo, Port. G4 12
Redondo, Wa., U.S. f11 124
Redondo Beach, Ca., U.S. n12 82
Redoubt Volcano, vol., Ak., U.S. g15 79
Red Peak, mtn., Co., U.S. B4 83
Red River, co., La., U.S. B2 95
Red River, co., Tx., U.S. C5 120
Red Rock, stm., Mt., U.S. F4 103
Red Rock, Lake, res., Ia., U.S. C4 92
Red Sea D2 46
Red Springs, N.C., U.S. C3 110
Red Table Mountain, mts., Co., U.S. B4 83
Redwater, Alta., Can. C4 68
Redwater, stm., Mt., U.S. C11 103
Red Willow, co., Ne., U.S. D5 104
Redwillow, stm., Can. B7 69
Red Wing, Mn., U.S. F6 100
Redwood, co., Mn., U.S. F3 100
Redwood, stm., Mn., U.S. F3 100
Redwood City, Ca., U.S. D2 82
Redwood Falls, Mn., U.S. F3 100
Redwood National Park, Ca., U.S. B2 82
Redwood Valley, Ca., U.S. C2 82
Ree, Lough, l., Ire. H4 7
Reed City, Mi., U.S. E5 99
Reedley, Ca., U.S. D4 82
Reedsburg, Wi., U.S. E3 126
Reeds Peak, mtn., N.M., U.S. D2 108
Reedsport, Or., U.S. D2 114
Reedsville, Pa., U.S. E6 115
Reedsville, Wi., U.S. D6 126
Reedy, stm., S.C., U.S. C3 117
Reedy Lake, l., Fl., U.S. E5 86
Reelfoot Lake, l., Tn., U.S. A2 119
Reese, Mi., U.S. E7 99
Reese, stm., Nv., U.S. C4 105
Reese Air Force Base, mil., Tx., U.S. C1 120
Reeves, co., Tx., U.S. o13 120
Reform, Al., U.S. B1 78
Refugio, Tx., U.S. E4 120
Refugio, co., Tx., U.S. E4 120
Regen, Ger. G13 8
Regencia, Braz. E9 57
Regensburg, Ger. F12 8
Reggane, Alg. C6 42
Reggio di Calabria, Italy K10 14
Reggio nell'Emilia, Italy E5 14
Regina, Sask., Can. G3 75
Regina Beach, Sask., Can. G3 75
Rehoboth, Nmb. E3 44
Rehoboth Bay, b., De., U.S. F5 85
Rehoboth Beach, De., U.S. F5 85
Reḥovot, Isr. D4 40
Reichenbach, Ger. E12 8
Reid, Mount, mtn., Ak., U.S. n24 79
Reidland, Ky., U.S. e9 94
Reidsville, Ga., U.S. D4 87
Reidsville, N.C., U.S. A3 110
Reims, Fr. C11 10
Reina Adelaida, Archipiélago, is., Chile G2 56
Reinbeck, Ia., U.S. B5 92
Reindeer Island, i., Man., Can. C3 70
Reindeer Lake, l., Can. m8 75
Reinosa, Spain B7 12
Reisterstown, Md., U.S. B4 97
Reliance, Wy., U.S. E3 127
Remada, Tun. B8 42
Remanso, Braz. E10 54
Rembang, Indon. m15 33a
Remington, In., U.S. C3 91
Remiremont, Fr. D13 10
Remmel Dam, Ar., U.S. g8 81
Remscheid, Ger. D7 8
Remsen, Ia., U.S. B2 92
Rend Lake, res., Il., U.S. E5 90
Rendova, i., Sol.Is. A11 50
Rendsburg, Ger. A9 8
Renforth, N.B., Can. D4 71
Renfrew, Ont., Can. B8 73
Rengat, Indon. O7 34
Rennell Island, i., Sol.Is. B12 50
Rennes, Fr. D5 10
Reno, Nv., U.S. D2 105
Reno, co., Ks., U.S. E5 93
Reno, Lake, l., Mn., U.S. E3 100
Reno Hill, mtn., Wy., U.S. D6 127
Renovo, Pa., U.S. D6 115
Rensselaer, In., U.S. C3 91
Rensselaer, N.Y., U.S. C7 109
Rensselaer, co., N.Y., U.S. C7 109
Renton, Wa., U.S. B3 124
Renville, Mn., U.S. F3 100
Renville, co., Mn., U.S. F4 100
Renville, co., N.D., U.S. A4 111
Reo, Indon. G7 32
Repentigny, Que., Can. D4 74
Republic, Mi., U.S. B3 99
Republic, Mo., U.S. D4 102
Republic, Pa., U.S. G2 115
Republic, Wa., U.S. A7 124
Republic, co., Ks., U.S. C6 93
Republican, stm., U.S. C6 93
Repulse Bay, N.W. Ter., Can. C15 66
Repvåg, Nor. A15 6
Réquista, Fr. H9 10
Reschenpass, Eur. C5 14
Reserve, La., U.S. h10 95
Resistencia, Arg. B5 56
Reşiţa, Rom. D5 16
Resolute, N.W. Ter., Can. B14 66
Resolution Island, i., N.W. Ter., Can. D20 66
Reston, Man., Can. E1 70
Reston, Va., U.S. B5 123
Resülhnzır, c., Tur. A4 40
Retalhuleu, Guat. G2 64
Rethel, Fr. C11 10
Réthimnon, Grc. N8 16
Reunion (Réunion), dep., Afr. F11 44
Reus, Spain D13 12
Reutlingen, Ger. G9 8
Revelo, Ky., U.S. D5 94
Revelstoke, B.C., Can. D8 69
Revelstoke, Lake, res., B.C., Can. D8 69
Revere, Ma., U.S. g11 98
Revillagigedo, Islas de, is., Mex. H4 62
Revillagigedo Island, i., Ak., U.S. n24 79
Revin, Fr. C11 10
Rewa, India H9 38
Rewāri, India F7 38
Rex, Ga., U.S. h8 87
Rexburg, Id., U.S. F7 89
Rexton, N.B., Can. C5 71
Rey, Iran J8 22
Rey, Isla del, i., Pan. J8 64
Reyes, Bol. F5 54
Reyes, Point, c., Ca., U.S. C2 82
Reyhanlı, Tur. A5 40
Reykjavík, Ice. C3 4
Reynolds, Ga., U.S. D2 87
Reynolds, co., Mo., U.S. D6 102
Reynoldsburg, Oh., U.S. C3 112
Reynoldsville, Pa., U.S. D4 115
Reynosa, Mex. D10 62
Rēzekne, Lat. E10 18
Rhaetian Alps, mts., Eur. F16 10
Rhea, co., Tn., U.S. D9 119
Rheine, Ger. C7 8
Rheydt, Ger. D6 8
Rhine (Rhein) (Rhin), stm., Eur. D6 8
Rhinebeck, N.Y., U.S. D7 109
Rhinelander, Wi., U.S. C4 126
Rho, Italy D4 14
Rhode Island, state, U.S. D3 116
Rhode Island, i., R.I., U.S. E5 116
Rhode Island Sound, strt., U.S. F5 116
Rhodesia see Zimbabwe, ctry., Afr. E5 44
Rhodes Peak, mtn., Id., U.S. C4 89
Rhodes see Ródhos, Grc. M12 16
Rhodope Mountains, mts., Eur. H8 16
Rhondda, Wales, U.K. J9 7
Rhône, stm., Eur. H11 10
Rialto, Ca., U.S. m14 82
Riau, Kepulauan, is., Indon. N8 34
Riaza, Spain D8 12
Ribadeo, Spain B4 12
Ribadesella, Spain B6 12
Ribeirão Prêto, Braz. F5 57
Ribera, Italy L8 14
Riberalta, Bol. F5 54
Rib Lake, Wi., U.S. C3 126
Ribnitz-Damgarten, Ger. A12 8
Riccione, Italy F7 14
Rice, Mn., U.S. E4 100
Rice, co., Ks., U.S. D5 93
Rice, co., Mn., U.S. F5 100
Riceboro, Ga., U.S. E5 87
Rice Lake, Wi., U.S. C2 126
Rice Lake, l., Ont., Can. C6 73
Rice Lake, l., Mn., U.S. D5 100
Riceville, Ia., U.S. A5 92
Rich, co., Ut., U.S. B4 121
Rich, Cape, c., Ont., Can. C4 73
Richards-Gebaur Air Force Base, mil., Mo., U.S. C3 102
Richards Island, i., N.W. Ter., Can. C6 66
Richardson, Tx., U.S. n10 120
Richardson, co., Ne., U.S. D10 104
Richardson Lakes, l., Me., U.S. D2 96
Richardson Mountains, mts., Can. C5 66
Richardton, N.D., U.S. C3 111
Rich Creek, Va., U.S. C2 123
Riche, Pointe, c., Newf., Can. C3 72
Richfield, Mn., U.S. F5 100
Richfield, Ut., U.S. E3 121
Richford, Vt., U.S. B3 122
Rich Hill, Mo., U.S. C3 102
Richibucto, N.B., Can. C5 71
Richland, Ga., U.S. D2 87
Richland, Mo., U.S. D5 102
Richland, Wa., U.S. C6 124
Richland, co., Il., U.S. E5 90
Richland, co., La., U.S. B4 95
Richland, co., Mt., U.S. C12 103
Richland, co., N.D., U.S. C8 111
Richland, co., Oh., U.S. B3 112
Richland, co., S.C., U.S. D6 117
Richland, co., Wi., U.S. E3 126
Richland Balsam, mtn., N.C., U.S. f10 110
Richland Center, Wi., U.S. E3 126
Richland Creek, stm., Tn., U.S. B5 119
Richlands, N.C., U.S. C5 110
Richlands, Va., U.S. e10 123
Richlandtown, Pa., U.S. F11 115
Richmond, Austl. D8 50
Richmond, B.C., Can. E6 69
Richmond, Que., Can. D5 74
Richmond, Ca., U.S. D2 82
Richmond, Il., U.S. A5 90
Richmond, In., U.S. E8 91
Richmond, Ky., U.S. C5 94
Richmond, Me., U.S. D3 96
Richmond, Mi., U.S. F8 99
Richmond, Mn., U.S. E4 100
Richmond, Mo., U.S. B4 102
Richmond, Tx., U.S. E5 120
Richmond, Ut., U.S. B4 121
Richmond, Vt., U.S. C3 122
Richmond, Va., U.S. C5 123
Richmond, co., Ga., U.S. C4 87
Richmond, co., N.Y., U.S. E6 109
Richmond, co., N.C., U.S. B3 110
Richmond, co., Va., U.S. C6 123
Richmond Beach, Wa., U.S. B3 124
Richmond Heights, Fl., U.S. s13 86
Richmond Heights, Mo., U.S. f13 102
Richmond Highlands, Wa., U.S. B3 124
Richmond Hill, Ont., Can. D5 73
Richmond Hill, Ga., U.S. E5 87
Richmond National Battlefield Park, Va., U.S. n18 123
Rich Square, N.C., U.S. A5 110
Richthofen, Mount, mtn., Co., U.S. A5 83
Richton, Ms., U.S. D5 101
Richwood, Oh., U.S. B2 112
Richwood, W.V., U.S. C4 125
Rickenbacker Air Force Base, mil., Oh., U.S. m11 112
Rickman, Tn., U.S. C8 119
Riddle, Or., U.S. E3 114
Riddle Mountain, mtn., Or., U.S. D8 114
Rideau, stm., Ont., Can. B9 73
Ridgecrest, Ca., U.S. E5 82
Ridge Farm, Il., U.S. D6 90
Ridgefield, Ct., U.S. D2 84
Ridgefield, N.J., U.S. h8 107
Ridgefield, Wa., U.S. D3 124
Ridgefield Park, N.J., U.S. B4 107
Ridgeland, Ms., U.S. C3 101
Ridgeland, S.C., U.S. G6 117
Ridgeley, W.V., U.S. B6 125
Ridgely, Md., U.S. C6 97
Ridgely, Tn., U.S. A2 119
Ridge Spring, S.C., U.S. D4 117
Ridgetop, Tn., U.S. A5 119
Ridgetown, Ont., Can. E3 73
Ridgeview, W.V., U.S. C3 125
Ridgeville, In., U.S. D7 91
Ridgeville, S.C., U.S. E7 117
Ridgeway, Va., U.S. D3 123
Ridgewood, N.J., U.S. B4 107
Ridgway, Il., U.S. F5 90
Ridgway, Pa., U.S. D4 115
Riding Mountain National Park, Man., Can. D1 70
Ridley Park, Pa., U.S. p20 115
Ried im Innkreis, Aus. G13 8
Riesa, Ger. D13 8
Riesi, Italy L9 14
Rieti, Italy G7 14
Rif, mts., Mor. A5 42
Riffe Lake, res., Wa., U.S. C3 124
Rifle, Co., U.S. B3 83
Rifle, stm., Mi., U.S. D6 99
Rift Valley, val., Afr. B5 44
Riga, Lat. E7 18
Riga, Gulf of, b., Eur. D6 18
Rigaud, Que., Can. D3 74
Rigby, Id., U.S. F7 89
Rīgestān, reg., Afg. C1 36
Riihimäki, Fin. F15 6
Rijeka, Cro. D9 14
Riley, Ks., U.S. C7 93
Riley, co., Ks., U.S. C7 93
Riley, Mount, mtn., N.M., U.S. F2 108
Rimbey, Alta., Can. C3 68
Rimersburg, Pa., U.S. D3 115
Rimini, Italy E7 14
Rimouski, Que., Can. A9 74
Rimouski, stm., Que., Can. A9 74
Rimouski-Est, Que., Can. A9 74
Rimrock Lake, res., Wa., U.S. C4 124
Rincon, Ga., U.S. D5 87
Rincon Mountains, mts., Az., U.S. E5 80
Rindal, Nor. E7 6
Ringebu, Nor. F8 6
Ringgold, Ga., U.S. B1 87
Ringgold, La., U.S. B2 95
Ringgold, co., Ia., U.S. D3 92
Ringling, Ok., U.S. C4 113
Ringwood, N.J., U.S. A4 107
Rio, Fl., U.S. E6 86
Rio, Wi., U.S. E4 126
Rio Arriba, co., N.M., U.S. A2 108
Riobamba, Ec. H3 58
Rio Benito, Eq. Gui. H7 42
Rio Blanco, co., Co., U.S. B2 83
Rio Branco, Braz. E5 54
Rio Claro, Braz. G5 57
Río Colorado, Arg. D4 56
Río Cuarto, Arg. C4 56
Rio de Janeiro, Braz. G7 57
Rio Dell, Ca., U.S. B1 82
Rio do Sul, Braz. B7 56
Río Gallegos, Arg. G3 56
Río Grande, Arg. G3 56
Rio Grande, Braz. C6 56
Río Grande, Mex. F8 62
Río Grande, Nic. H6 64
Rio Grande, Oh., U.S. D3 112
Rio Grande, co., Co., U.S. D4 83
Rio Grande City, Tx., U.S. F3 120
Rio Grande Reservoir, res., Co., U.S. D3 83
Ríohacha, Col. B6 58
Rio Hondo, Tx., U.S. F4 120
Rioja, Peru E3 54
Riom, Fr. G10 10
Río Mayo, Arg. F2 56
Río Negro, Embalse del, res., Ur. C5 56
Rio Negro, Pantanal do, sw., Braz. G7 54
Rionero in Vulture, Italy I10 14
Rio Pardo, Braz. B6 56
Rio Pardo de Minas, Braz. G10 54
Rio Rancho, N.M., U.S. B3 108
Río Sucio, Col. E5 58
Rio Verde, Braz. D3 57
Ríoverde, Mex. G10 62
Rio Vista, Ca., U.S. C3 82
Rioz, Fr. E13 10
Ripley, Ms., U.S. A5 101
Ripley, Oh., U.S. D2 112
Ripley, Tn., U.S. B2 119
Ripley, W.V., U.S. C3 125
Ripley, co., In., U.S. F7 91
Ripley, co., Mo., U.S. E7 102
Ripoll, Spain C14 12
Ripon, Eng., U.K. G11 7
Ripon, Wi., U.S. E5 126
Rippowam, stm., Ct., U.S. E1 84
Ririe Lake, res., Id., U.S. F7 89
Rishon leZiyyon, Isr. D4 40
Rising Sun, De., U.S. D3 85
Rising Sun, In., U.S. G8 91
Rising Sun, Md., U.S. A5 97
Rison, Ar., U.S. D3 81
Ritchie, co., W.V., U.S. B3 125
Ritter, Mount, mtn., Ca., U.S. D4 82
Rittman, Oh., U.S. B4 112
Ritzville, Wa., U.S. B7 124
Riva, Italy D5 14
Rivanna, stm., Va., U.S. C4 123
Rivas, Nic. I5 64
Rivera, Ur. C5 56
Riverbank, Ca., U.S. D3 82
River Bourgeois, N.S., Can. D9 71
Riverdale, Ca., U.S. D4 82
Riverdale, Il., U.S. k9 90
Riverdale, Md., U.S. C4 97
River Edge, N.J., U.S. h8 107
River Falls, Al., U.S. D3 78
River Falls, Wi., U.S. D1 126
River Forest, Il., U.S. k9 90
River Grove, Il., U.S. k9 90
Riverhead, N.Y., U.S. n16 109
River Hebert, N.S., Can. D5 71
River Heights, Ut., U.S. B4 121
River Hills, Wi., U.S. m12 126
River Pines, Ma., U.S. f10 98
River Ridge, La., U.S. k11 95
River Road, Or., U.S. C3 114
River Rouge, Mi., U.S. p15 99
Rivers, Man., Can. D1 70
Riverside, Al., U.S. B3 78
Riverside, Ca., U.S. F5 82
Riverside, Il., U.S. k9 90
Riverside, Ia., U.S. C6 92
Riverside, N.J., U.S. C3 107
Riverside, Pa., U.S. E8 115
Riverside, co., Ca., U.S. F5 82
Riverside Reservoir, res., Co., U.S. A6 83
Riverton, Man., Can. D3 70
Riverton, Il., U.S. D4 90
Riverton, Ks., U.S. E9 93
Riverton, N.J., U.S. C3 107
Riverton, Ut., U.S. C4 121
Riverton, Vt., U.S. C3 122
Riverton, Wy., U.S. C4 127
Riverton Heights, Wa., U.S. f11 124
River Vale, N.J., U.S. h8 107
Riverview, Fl., U.S. p11 86
Riverview, Mi., U.S. p15 99
Rivesaltes, Fr. J9 10
Rivesville, W.V., U.S. B4 125
Riviera Beach, Fl., U.S. F6 86
Riviera Beach, Md., U.S. B4 97
Rivière-du-Loup, Que., Can. B8 74
Rivière-Verte, N.B., Can. B1 71
Rivne, Ukr. G3 22
Rivoli, Italy D2 14
Riyadh see Ar-Riyāḍ, Sau. Ar. D4 46
Rize, Tur. G16 4
Roa, Spain D8 12
Roachdale, In., U.S. E4 91
Roane, co., Tn., U.S. D9 119
Roane, co., W.V., U.S. C3 125
Roan Mountain, Tn., U.S. C11 119
Roanne, Fr. F11 10
Roanoke, Al., U.S. B4 78
Roanoke, Il., U.S. C4 90
Roanoke, In., U.S. C7 91
Roanoke, La., U.S. D3 95
Roanoke, Tx., U.S. m9 120
Roanoke, Va., U.S. C3 123
Roanoke, co., Va., U.S. C2 123

Name	Map Ref	Page
Roanoke, stm., U.S.	A5	110
Roanoke Island, i., N.C., U.S.	B7	110
Roanoke Rapids, N.C., U.S.	A5	110
Roanoke Rapids Lake, res., U.S.	A5	110
Roaring Fork, stm., Co., U.S.	C4	83
Roaring Spring, Pa., U.S.	F5	115
Roatán, Isla de, i., Hond.	F4	64
Robbins, Il., U.S.	k9	90
Robbins, N.C., U.S.	B3	110
Robbinsdale, Mn., U.S.	m12	100
Robbinsville, N.C., U.S.	f9	110
Röbel, Ger.	B12	8
Robersonville, N.C., U.S.	B5	110
Roberta, Ga., U.S.	D2	87
Robert Lee, Tx., U.S.	D2	120
Roberts, Wi., U.S.	C1	126
Roberts, co., S.D., U.S.	B8	118
Roberts, co., Tx., U.S.	B2	120
Roberts, Point, c., Wa., U.S.	A2	124
Robert's Arm, Newf., Can.	D4	72
Roberts Creek Mountain, mtn., Nv., U.S.	D5	105
Robertsdale, Al., U.S.	E2	78
Robertsfors, Swe.	D13	6
Robert S. Kerr Reservoir, res., Ok., U.S.	B6	113
Roberts Mountain, mtn., Ak., U.S.	C6	79
Roberts Mountain, mtn., Wy., U.S.	D3	127
Robertson, co., Ky., U.S.	B5	94
Robertson, co., Tn., U.S.	A5	119
Robertson, co., Tx., U.S.	D4	120
Robertsonville, Que., Can.	C6	74
Roberts Peak, mtn., B.C., Can.	F8	66
Robertsport, Lib.	G3	42
Robertville, N.B., Can.	B4	71
Roberval, Que., Can.	A5	74
Robeson, co., N.C., U.S.	C3	110
Robins, Ia., U.S.	B6	92
Robinson, Il., U.S.	D6	90
Robinson Fork, stm., W.V., U.S.	m14	125
Robinson Fork, stm., W.V., U.S.	k9	125
Roblin, Man., Can.	D1	70
Roboré, Bol.	G7	54
Robson, Mount, mtn., B.C., Can.	C8	69
Robstown, Tx., U.S.	F4	120
Roca Partida, Isla, i., Mex.	H3	62
Roca Partida, Punta, c., Mex.	H12	62
Rocas, Atol das, atoll, Braz.	D12	54
Roccastrada, Italy	F6	14
Rocha, Ur.	C6	56
Rochefort, Fr.	G6	10
Rochelle, Ga., U.S.	E3	87
Rochelle, Il., U.S.	B4	90
Rochelle Park, N.J., U.S.	h8	107
Rochester, Il., U.S.	D4	90
Rochester, In., U.S.	B5	91
Rochester, Mi., U.S.	F7	99
Rochester, Mn., U.S.	F6	100
Rochester, N.H., U.S.	D5	106
Rochester, N.Y., U.S.	B3	109
Rochester, Pa., U.S.	E1	115
Rochester, Vt., U.S.	D3	122
Rochester, Wa., U.S.	C2	124
Rochester, Wi., U.S.	n11	126
Rock, co., Mn., U.S.	G2	100
Rock, co., Ne., U.S.	B6	104
Rock, co., Wi., U.S.	F4	126
Rock, stm., U.S.	B3	90
Rock, stm., U.S.	A1	92
Rockall, i., Scot., U.K.	D5	4
Rockaway, N.J., U.S.	B3	107
Rockaway, Or., U.S.	B3	114
Rockbridge, co., Va., U.S.	C3	123
Rockcastle, co., Ky., U.S.	C5	94
Rockcastle, stm., Ky., U.S.	C5	94
Rockcliffe Park, Ont., Can.	h12	73
Rock Creek, Mn., U.S.	E6	100
Rock Creek, stm., U.S.	B3	91
Rock Creek, stm., U.S.	h14	124
Rock Creek, stm., Nv., U.S.	C5	105
Rock Creek, stm., Or., U.S.	B6	114
Rock Creek, stm., Wa., U.S.	D5	124
Rock Creek, stm., Wa., U.S.	B8	124
Rock Creek, stm., Wy., U.S.	E6	127
Rock Creek Butte, mtn., Or., U.S.	C8	114
Rockdale, Il., U.S.	B5	90
Rockdale, Md., U.S.	B4	97
Rockdale, Tx., U.S.	D4	120
Rockdale, co., Ga., U.S.	C3	87
Rockfall, Ct., U.S.	C5	84
Rock Falls, Il., U.S.	B4	90
Rockford, Il., U.S.	A4	90
Rockford, Ia., U.S.	A5	92
Rockford, Mi., U.S.	E5	99
Rockford, Mn., U.S.	E5	100
Rockford, Oh., U.S.	B1	112
Rockford, Tn., U.S.	D10	119
Rock Hall, Md., U.S.	B5	97
Rockhampton, Austl.	D10	50
Rock Hill, S.C., U.S.	B5	117
Rockingham, N.C., U.S.	C3	110
Rockingham, co., N.H., U.S.	D4	106
Rockingham, co., N.C., U.S.	A3	110
Rockingham, co., Va., U.S.	B4	123
Rock Island, Que., Can.	D5	74
Rock Island, Il., U.S.	B3	90
Rock Island, co., Il., U.S.	B3	90
Rock Island, i., Fl., U.S.	C3	86
Rock Island, i., Wi., U.S.	C7	126
Rock Lake, l., Wa., U.S.	B8	124
Rockland, Ont., Can.	B9	73
Rockland, Me., U.S.	D3	96
Rockland, Ma., U.S.	B6	98
Rockland, co., N.Y., U.S.	D6	109
Rockledge, Fl., U.S.	D6	86
Rockledge, Pa., U.S.	o20	115
Rocklin, Ca., U.S.	C3	82
Rockmart, Ga., U.S.	B1	87
Rock Mountain, mtn., Co., U.S.	D3	83
Rockport, In., U.S.	I3	91
Rockport, Me., U.S.	D3	96
Rockport, Ma., U.S.	A6	98
Rock Port, Mo., U.S.	A2	102
Rockport, Tx., U.S.	F4	120
Rock Rapids, Ia., U.S.	A1	92
Rock River, Wy., U.S.	E7	127
Rock Sound, Bah.	B9	64
Rocksprings, Tx., U.S.	D2	120
Rock Springs, Wy., U.S.	E3	127
Rockstone, Guy.	E13	58
Rockton, Il., U.S.	A4	90
Rock Valley, Ia., U.S.	A1	92
Rockville, In., U.S.	E3	91
Rockville, Md., U.S.	B3	97
Rockville Centre, N.Y., U.S.	n15	109
Rockwall, Tx., U.S.	C4	120
Rockwall, co., Tx., U.S.	C4	120
Rockwell, Ia., U.S.	B4	92
Rockwell, N.C., U.S.	B2	110
Rockwell City, Ia., U.S.	B3	92
Rockwell Park, N.C., U.S.	B2	110
Rockwood, Mi., U.S.	F7	99
Rockwood, Pa., U.S.	G3	115
Rockwood, Tn., U.S.	D9	119
Rocky, stm., N.C., U.S.	B2	110
Rocky, stm., S.C., U.S.	C2	117
Rocky, East Branch, stm., Oh., U.S.	h9	112
Rocky, West Branch, stm., Oh., U.S.	h9	112
Rocky Boys Indian Reservation, Mt., U.S.	B7	103
Rocky Ford, Co., U.S.	C7	83
Rocky Fork Lake, l., Oh., U.S.	C2	112
Rocky Harbour, Newf., Can.	D3	72
Rocky Hill, Ct., U.S.	C5	84
Rocky Lake, l., Me., U.S.	D5	96
Rocky Mount, N.C., U.S.	B5	110
Rocky Mount, Va., U.S.	D3	123
Rocky Mountain, mtn., Mt., U.S.	C4	103
Rocky Mountain House, Alta., Can.	C3	68
Rocky Mountain National Park, Co., U.S.	A5	83
Rocky Mountains, mts., N.A.	E9	61
Rocky Ripple, In., U.S.	k10	91
Rocky River, Oh., U.S.	A4	112
Rocky Top, mtn., Or., U.S.	C4	114
Roddickton, Newf., Can.	C3	72
Roderfield, W.V., U.S.	D3	125
Rodez, Fr.	H9	10
Ródhos (Rhodes), Grc.	M12	16
Ródhos, i., Grc.	M11	16
Rodney, Ont., Can.	E3	73
Rodney, Cape, c., Ak., U.S.	C6	79
Rodney Village, De., U.S.	D3	85
Rodniki, Russia	D24	18
Roebourne, Austl.	D3	50
Roebuck, S.C., U.S.	B4	117
Roeland Park, Ks., U.S.	k16	93
Roeselare, Bel.	E3	8
Roes Welcome Sound, strt., N.W. Ter., Can.	D15	66
Roff, Ok., U.S.	C5	113
Rogagua, Lago, l., Bol.	F5	54
Roger Mills, co., Ok., U.S.	B2	113
Rogers, Ar., U.S.	A1	81
Rogers, Mn., U.S.	E5	100
Rogers, Tx., U.S.	D4	120
Rogers, co., Ok., U.S.	A6	113
Rogers, Mount, mtn., Va., U.S.	f10	123
Rogers City, Mi., U.S.	C7	99
Rogers Lake, res., Ct., U.S.	D6	84
Rogers Pass, Mt., U.S.	C4	103
Rogersville, N.B., Can.	C4	71
Rogersville, Al., U.S.	A2	78
Rogersville, Mo., U.S.	D4	102
Rogersville, Tn., U.S.	C10	119
Roggiano Gravina, Italy	J11	14
Rogue, stm., Or., U.S.	E2	114
Rogue River, Or., U.S.	E3	114
Rohtak, India	F7	38
Roi Et, Thai.	F7	34
Rojo, Cabo, c., Mex.	G11	62
Roland, Ia., U.S.	B4	92
Roland, Ok., U.S.	B7	113
Roland, Lake, res., Md., U.S.	g11	97
Rolândia, Braz.	G3	57
Røldal, Nor.	G6	6
Rolette, N.D., U.S.	A6	111
Rolette, co., N.D., U.S.	A6	111
Rolfe, Ia., U.S.	B3	92
Rolla, Mo., U.S.	D6	102
Rolla, N.D., U.S.	A6	111
Rollingbay, Wa., U.S.	e10	124
Rolling Fork, Ms., U.S.	C3	101
Rolling Fork, stm., Ar., U.S.	C1	81
Rolling Fork, stm., Ky., U.S.	C4	94
Rolling Meadows, Il., U.S.	h8	90
Rollingstone, Mn., U.S.	F7	100
Rollinsford, N.H., U.S.	D5	106
Roma (Rome), Italy	H7	14
Roma, Tx., U.S.	F3	120
Romain, Cape, c., S.C., U.S.	F9	117
Roman, Rom.	C10	16
Romania, ctry., Eur.	F13	4
Roman Nose Mountain, mtn., Or., U.S.	D3	114
Romano, Cape, c., Fl., U.S.	G5	86
Romano, Cayo, i., Cuba	C8	64
Romans [-sur-Isère], Fr.	G12	10
Romanzof, Cape, c., Ak., U.S.	C6	79
Romanzof Mountains, mts., Ak., U.S.	B11	79
Rome, Ga., U.S.	B1	87
Rome, Il., U.S.	C4	90
Rome, N.Y., U.S.	B5	109
Rome City, In., U.S.	B7	91
Romeo, Mi., U.S.	F7	99
Romeoville, Il., U.S.	k8	90
Rome see Roma, Italy	H7	14
Romilly-sur-Seine, Fr.	D10	10
Romney, W.V., U.S.	B6	125
Romorantin-Lanthenay, Fr.	E8	10
Romulus, Mi., U.S.	p15	99
Ron, Mui, c., Viet.	E9	34
Ronan, Mt., U.S.	C2	103
Roncador, Serra do, plat., Braz.	F8	54
Roncesvalles, Spain	B10	12
Ronceverte, W.V., U.S.	D4	125
Ronda, Spain	I6	12
Rondônia, Braz.	F6	54
Rondonópolis, Braz.	D1	57
Ronge, Lac la, l., Sask., Can.	B3	75
Rønne, Den.	I10	6
Ronneby, Swe.	H10	6
Ronne Ice Shelf, Ant.	B6	47
Ronse, Bel.	E3	8
Roodhouse, Il., U.S.	D3	90
Rooks, co., Ks., U.S.	C4	93
Roorkee, India	F7	38
Roosendaal, Neth.	D4	8
Roosevelt, Ut., U.S.	C5	121
Roosevelt, co., Mt., U.S.	B11	103
Roosevelt, co., N.M., U.S.	C6	108
Roosevelt, stm., Braz.	E6	54
Roosevelt Park, Mi., U.S.	E4	99
Root, stm., Mn., U.S.	G7	100
Root, stm., Wi., U.S.	n12	126
Roper, N.C., U.S.	B6	110
Roquefort, Fr.	H6	10
Roraima, Mount, mtn., S.A.	E12	58
Røros, Nor.	E8	6
Rorschach, Switz.	E16	10
Rørvik, Nor.	D8	6
Rošal', Russia	F22	18
Rosamond, Ca., U.S.	E4	82
Rosamorada, Mex.	F7	62
Rosario, Arg.	C4	56
Rosário, Braz.	D10	54
Rosario, Mex.	F7	62
Rosario, Mex.	B2	62
Rosario, Ven.	B6	58
Rosário Oeste, Braz.	F7	54
Rosarno, Italy	K10	14
Rosas, Golfo de, b., Spain	C15	12
Roscoe, Il., U.S.	A5	90
Roscoe, Tx., U.S.	C2	120
Roscommon, Ire.	H4	7
Roscommon, Mi., U.S.	D6	99
Roscommon, co., Mi., U.S.	D6	99
Roscrea, Ire.	I5	7
Rose, Mount, mtn., Nv., U.S.	D2	105
Roseau, Dom.	G17	64
Roseau, Mn., U.S.	B3	100
Roseau, co., Mn., U.S.	B3	100
Roseau, South Fork, stm., Mn., U.S.	B3	100
Rose-Blanche [-Harbour le Cou], Newf., Can.	E2	72
Roseboro, N.C., U.S.	C4	110
Rosebud, S.D., U.S.	D5	118
Rosebud, Tx., U.S.	D4	120
Rosebud, co., Mt., U.S.	D10	103
Rosebud Indian Reservation, S.D., U.S.	D5	118
Roseburg, Or., U.S.	D3	114
Rosedale, In., U.S.	E3	91
Rosedale, Md., U.S.	g11	97
Rosedale, Ms., U.S.	B2	101
Rose Hill, Ks., U.S.	E6	93
Rose Hill, N.C., U.S.	C4	110
Rose Hill, Va., U.S.	f8	123
Roseland, Fl., U.S.	E6	86
Roseland, In., U.S.	A5	91
Roseland, La., U.S.	D5	95
Roseland, Oh., U.S.	B3	112
Roselle, Il., U.S.	k8	90
Roselle, N.J., U.S.	k7	107
Roselle Park, N.J., U.S.	k7	107
Rosemère, Que., Can.	p19	74
Rosemount, Mn., U.S.	F5	100
Rosenberg, Tx., U.S.	E5	120
Rosendale, Wi., U.S.	E5	126
Rosenheim, Ger.	H12	8
Rose Peak, mtn., Az., U.S.	D6	80
Rosepine, La., U.S.	D2	95
Rose Point, c., B.C., Can.	B2	69
Roseto, Pa., U.S.	E11	115
Roseville, Ca., U.S.	C3	82
Roseville, Il., U.S.	C3	90
Roseville, Mi., U.S.	o16	99
Roseville, Mn., U.S.	m12	100
Roseville, Oh., U.S.	C3	112
Rosewood Heights, Il., U.S.	E3	90
Rosiclare, Il., U.S.	F5	90
Rosignano Marittimo, Italy	F5	14
Roskilde, Den.	I9	6
Roslags-Näsby, Swe.	G12	6
Roslavl', Russia	H15	18
Roslyn, Wa., U.S.	B4	124
Roslyn Heights, N.Y., U.S.	h13	109
Ross, Oh., U.S.	C1	112
Ross, co., Oh., U.S.	C2	112
Rossano, Italy	J11	14
Rossan Point, c., Ire.	G4	7
Ross Barnett Reservoir, res., Ms., U.S.	C3	101
Rossburn, Man., Can.	D1	70
Ross Dam, Wa., U.S.	A4	124
Rossel Island, i., Pap. N. Gui.	B10	50
Rossford, Oh., U.S.	A2	112
Ross Ice Shelf, Ant.	A31	47
Rossignol, Lake, l., N.S., Can.	E4	71
Ross Island, i., Man., Can.	B3	70
Ross Lake National Recreation Area, Wa., U.S.	A5	124
Rossland, B.C., Can.	E9	69
Rosslare, Ire.	I6	7
Rosso, Maur.	E2	42
Ross River, Yukon, Can.	D6	66
Ross Sea, Ant.	B31	47
Rossville, Ga., U.S.	B1	87
Rossville, Il., U.S.	C6	90
Rossville, In., U.S.	D4	91
Rossville, Ks., U.S.	C8	93
Rostock, Ger.	A12	8
Rostov, Russia	D22	18
Rostov-na-Donu, Russia	H5	22
Roswell, Ga., U.S.	B2	87
Roswell, N.M., U.S.	D5	108
Rotan, Tx., U.S.	C2	120
Rotenburg, Ger.	B9	8
Rothaargebirge, mts., Ger.	D8	8
Rothenburg ob der Tauber, Ger.	F10	8
Rothesay, N.B., Can.	D4	71
Rothschild, Wi., U.S.	D4	126
Rothsville, Pa., U.S.	F9	115
Roti, Pulau, i., Indon.	H7	32
Rotondella, Italy	I11	14
Rotorua, N.Z.	C6	52
Rotterdam, Neth.	D4	8
Rotterdam, N.Y., U.S.	C6	109
Rottweil, Ger.	G8	8
Roubaix, Fr.	B10	10
Rouen, Fr.	C8	10
Rouge, stm., Que., Can.	D3	74
Rough, stm., Ky., U.S.	C3	94
Rough River Lake, res., Ky., U.S.	C3	94
Roulette, Pa., U.S.	C5	115
Round Island, i., Ms., U.S.	g8	101
Round Lake, Il., U.S.	h8	90
Round Lake Beach, Il., U.S.	h8	90
Round Mountain, Nv., U.S.	E4	105
Round Rock, Tx., U.S.	D4	120
Roundup, Mt., U.S.	D8	103
Round Valley Indian Reservation, Ca., U.S.	C2	82
Round Valley Reservoir, res., N.J., U.S.	B3	107
Rouses Point, N.Y., U.S.	f11	109
Roussillon, hist. reg., Fr.	J9	10
Routt, co., Co., U.S.	A3	83
Rouyn [-Noranda], Que., Can.	k11	74
Rouzerville, Pa., U.S.	G6	115
Rovaniemi, Fin.	C15	6
Rovato, Italy	D4	14
Rovereto, Italy	D6	14
Rovigo, Italy	D6	14
Rovinj, Cro.	D8	14
Rowan, co., Ky., U.S.	B6	94
Rowan, co., N.C., U.S.	B2	110
Rowland, N.C., U.S.	C3	110
Rowlesburg, W.V., U.S.	B5	125
Rowley Island, i., N.W. Ter., Can.	C17	66
Rowley Shoals, rf., Austl.	C3	50
Roxboro, N.C., U.S.	A4	110
Roxton Falls, Que., Can.	D5	74
Roxton Pond, Que., Can.	D5	74
Roy, Ut., U.S.	B3	121
Royal, stm., Me., U.S.	g7	96
Royal Canal, Ire.	H5	7
Royal Center, In., U.S.	C4	91
Royale, Isle, i., Mi., U.S.	h9	99
Royal Gorge, val., Co., U.S.	C5	83
Royal Oak, Mi., U.S.	F7	99
Royal Pines, N.C., U.S.	f10	110
Royalton, Il., U.S.	F4	90
Royalton, Mn., U.S.	E4	100
Royan, Fr.	G5	10
Royersford, Pa., U.S.	F10	115
Royerton, In., U.S.	D7	91
Royse City, Tx., U.S.	C4	120
Royston, B.C., Can.	E5	69
Royston, Ga., U.S.	B3	87
Rubbestadneset, Nor.	G5	6
Rubcovsk, Russia	G10	24
Rubidoux, Ca., U.S.	n14	82
Rubio, Ven.	D6	58
Ruby Dome, mtn., Nv., U.S.	C6	105
Ruby Lake, l., Nv., U.S.	C6	105
Ruby Mountains, mts., Nv., U.S.	C6	105
Ruby Range, mts., Co., U.S.	C3	83
Ruby Range, mts., Mt., U.S.	E4	103
Rudolf, Lake, l., Afr.	H2	46
Rudolstadt, Ger.	E11	8
Rudyard, Mi., U.S.	B6	99
Rue, Fr.	B8	10
Rufā'ah, Sudan	F12	42
Ruffec, Fr.	F7	10
Rufino, Arg.	C4	56
Rufus Woods Lake, res., Wa., U.S.	A6	124
Rugao, China	C9	28
Rugby, Eng., U.K.	I11	7
Rugby, N.D., U.S.	A6	111
Ruian, China	H9	28
Ruidoso, N.M., U.S.	D4	108
Ruidoso Downs, N.M., U.S.	D4	108
Ruijin, China	F10	26
Ruijin, China	J4	28
Rukwa, Lake, l., Tan.	C6	44
Ruleville, Ms., U.S.	B3	101
Rum, stm., Mn., U.S.	D5	100
Ruma, Yugo.	D3	16
Rumbek, Sudan	G11	42
Rum Cay, i., Bah.	C10	64
Rum Creek, stm., W.V., U.S.	n12	125
Rumford, Me., U.S.	D2	96
Rumia, Pol.	A18	8
Rum Jungle, Austl.	B6	50
Rumoi, Japan	p19	30a
Rumson, N.J., U.S.	C4	107
Rumstick Point, c., R.I., U.S.	D5	116
Ru'nan, China	B3	28
Runanga, N.Z.	E3	52
Runge, Tx., U.S.	E4	120
Rungwa, Tan.	C6	44
Runnels, co., Tx., U.S.	D3	120
Runnemede, N.J., U.S.	D2	107
Ruoqiang, China	D4	26
Rupert, Id., U.S.	G5	89
Rupert, W.V., U.S.	D4	125
Rupert, Rivière de, stm., Que., Can.	h11	74
Rural Hall, N.C., U.S.	A2	110
Rural Retreat, Va., U.S.	D1	123
Rusagonis, N.B., Can.	D3	71
Ruse, Bul.	F9	16
Rush, co., In., U.S.	E6	91
Rush, co., Ks., U.S.	D4	93
Rush, stm., Mn., U.S.	F4	100
Rush, stm., Wi., U.S.	D1	126
Rush City, Mn., U.S.	E6	100
Rush Creek, stm., Oh., U.S.	B2	112
Rush Creek, stm., Ok., U.S.	C4	113
Rushford, Mn., U.S.	G7	100
Rush Lake, l., Mn., U.S.	E5	100
Rush Lake, l., Mn., U.S.	D3	100
Rush Lake, l., Wi., U.S.	E5	126
Rushmere, Va., U.S.	h14	123
Rush Springs, Ok., U.S.	C4	113
Rushville, Il., U.S.	C3	90
Rushville, In., U.S.	E7	91
Rushville, Ne., U.S.	B3	104
Rusk, Tx., U.S.	D5	120
Rusk, co., Tx., U.S.	C5	120
Rusk, co., Wi., U.S.	C2	126
Ruskin, Fl., U.S.	E4	86
Russas, Braz.	D11	54
Russell, Man., Can.	D1	70
Russell, Ont., Can.	B9	73
Russell, Ks., U.S.	D5	93
Russell, Ky., U.S.	B7	94
Russell, Pa., U.S.	C3	115
Russell, co., Al., U.S.	C4	78
Russell, co., Ks., U.S.	D5	93
Russell, co., Ky., U.S.	D4	94
Russell, co., Va., U.S.	f9	123
Russell, Mount, mtn., Ak., U.S.	f16	79
Russell Cave National Monument, Al., U.S.	A4	78
Russell Fork, stm., U.S.	C7	94
Russell Island, i., N.W. Ter., Can.	B13	66
Russell Springs, Ky., U.S.	C4	94
Russellville, Al., U.S.	A2	78
Russellville, Ar., U.S.	B2	81
Russellville, Ky., U.S.	D3	94
Russellville, Mo., U.S.	C5	102
Russellville, Tn., U.S.	C10	119
Rüsselsheim, Ger.	E8	8
Russia, ctry., Eur.	E15	22
Russian, stm., Ca., U.S.	C2	82
Russiaville, In., U.S.	D5	91
Rustavi, Geor.	I7	22
Rustburg, Va., U.S.	C3	123
Rustenburg, S. Afr.	G5	44
Ruston, La., U.S.	B3	95
Ruston, Wa., U.S.	B3	124
Ruth, Nv., U.S.	D6	105
Rutherford, N.J., U.S.	B4	107
Rutherford, Tn., U.S.	A3	119
Rutherford, co., N.C., U.S.	B1	110
Rutherford, co., Tn., U.S.	B5	119
Rutherfordton, N.C., U.S.	B1	110
Ruthven, Ia., U.S.	A3	92
Rutland, Ma., U.S.	B4	98
Rutland, Vt., U.S.	D3	122
Rutland, co., Vt., U.S.	D2	122
Rutledge, Ga., U.S.	C3	87
Rutledge, Tn., U.S.	C10	119
Ruukki, Fin.	D15	6
Ruvuma (Rovuma), stm., Afr.	D7	44
Ružomberok, Slov.	F19	8
Rwanda, ctry., Afr.	B5	44
Ryan, Ok., U.S.	C4	113
Ryan Peak, mtn., Id., U.S.	F4	89
Rybinsk, Russia	C21	18
Rybinskoje Vodochranilišče, res., Russia	C21	18
Rybnik, Pol.	E18	8
Rycroft, Alta., Can.	B1	68
Ryde, Eng., U.K.	K11	7
Rye, N.H., U.S.	D5	106
Rye, N.Y., U.S.	h13	109
Rye Beach, N.H., U.S.	E5	106
Rye Patch Dam, Nv., U.S.	C3	105
Rye Patch Reservoir, res., Nv., U.S.	C3	105
Ryfoss, Nor.	F7	6
Ryōtsu, Japan	D11	30
Rysy, mtn., Eur.	F20	8
Ryukyu Islands see Nansei-shotō, is., Japan	F12	26
Rzeszów, Pol.	E21	8
Ržev, Russia	E17	18

S

Name	Map Ref	Page
Saalfeld, Ger.	E11	8
Saarbrücken, Ger.	F6	8
Saaremaa, i., Est.	C5	18
Saarijärvi, Fin.	E15	6
Saarlouis, Ger.	F6	8
Sab, Tônlé, l., Camb.	H7	34
Saba, i., Neth. Ant.	F16	64
Sabadell, Spain	D14	12
Sabae, Japan	G9	30
Sabana, Archipiélago de, is., Cuba	C8	64
Sabanagrande, Hond.	H4	64
Sabanalarga, Col.	B5	58
Sabang, Indon.	E6	32
Sabanilla, Mex.	E9	62
Sabará, Braz.	E7	57
Sabattus, Me., U.S.	D2	96
Sabetha, Ks., U.S.	C8	93
Sabhah, Libya	C8	42
Sabi (Save), stm., Afr.	F6	44
Sabillasville, Md., U.S.	A3	97
Sabina, Oh., U.S.	C2	112
Sabinal, Tx., U.S.	E3	120
Sabiñánigo, Spain	C11	12
Sabinas, Mex.	D9	62
Sabinas Hidalgo, Mex.	D9	62
Sabine, co., La., U.S.	C2	95
Sabine, co., Tx., U.S.	D6	120
Sabine, stm., U.S.	D6	120
Sabine Lake, l., U.S.	E2	95
Sabine Pass, strt., U.S.	E2	95
Sable, Cape, c., N.S., Can.	H19	66
Sable, Cape, c., Fl., U.S.	G5	86
Sable, Îles de, i., N. Cal.	C11	50
Sable Island, i., N.S., Can.	F10	71
Sabula, Ia., U.S.	B7	92
Sabzevār, Iran	J9	22
Sac, co., Ia., U.S.	B2	92
Sac, stm., Mo., U.S.	D4	102
Sacajawea, Lake, res., Wa., U.S.	C7	124
Sacajawea Peak, mtn., Or., U.S.	B9	114
Sacandaga Lake, l., N.Y., U.S.	B6	109
Sac and Fox Indian Reservation, Ia., U.S.	C5	92
Sacaton, Az., U.S.	D4	80
Sac City, Ia., U.S.	B2	92
Sacedón, Spain	E9	12

Name	Map Ref	Page
Sachalin, Ostrov (Sakhalin), i., Russia	G22	24
Sachalinskij Zaliv, b., Russia	G22	24
Sachigo, stm., Ont., Can.	F14	66
Sachse, Tx., U.S.	n10	120
Sachs Harbour, N.W. Ter., Can.	B8	66
Šachty, Russia	H6	22
Sachuest Point, c., R.I., U.S.	F6	116
Sackville, N.B., Can.	D5	71
Saco, Me., U.S.	E2	96
Saco, stm., U.S.	E2	96
Saco, East Branch, stm., N.H., U.S.	B4	106
Sacramento, Ca., U.S.	C3	82
Sacramento, co., Ca., U.S.	C3	82
Sacramento, stm., Ca., U.S.	C3	82
Sacramento, stm., N.M., U.S.	E4	108
Sacramento Mountains, mts., N.M., U.S.	E4	108
Sacramento Valley, val., Ca., U.S.	C2	82
Sacré-Coeur-Saguenay, Que., Can.	A8	74
Sacred Heart, Mn., U.S.	F3	100
Sádaba, Spain	C10	12
Ṣa'dah, Yemen	E3	46
Saddle, stm., N.J., U.S.	h8	107
Saddleback Mountain, mtn., Az., U.S.	k8	80
Saddle Brook, N.J., U.S.	h8	107
Saddlebunch Keys, is., Fl., U.S.	H5	86
Saddle Mountain, mtn., Or., U.S.	B3	114
Saddle Mountains, mts., Wa., U.S.	C5	124
Saddle River, N.J., U.S.	A4	107
Sa Dec, Viet.	I8	34
Sādiqābad, Pak.	F4	38
Sado, i., Japan	D11	30
Sado-kaikyō, strt., Japan	E11	30
Saegertown, Pa., U.S.	C1	115
Safety Harbor, Fl., U.S.	E4	86
Säffle, Swe.	G9	6
Safford, Az., U.S.	E6	80
Safi, Mor.	B4	42
Safīd, stm., Afg.	B1	38
Safīd Kūh, Selseleh-ye, mts., Afg.	C1	36
Safonovo, Russia	F16	18
Saga, Japan	I3	30
Sagadahoc, co., Me., U.S.	E3	96
Sagaing, Mya.	D3	34
Sagamihara, Japan	G12	30
Sagami-nada, b., Japan	G12	30
Sagamore Hills, Oh., U.S.	h9	112
Saganaga Lake, l., Mn., U.S.	B7	100
Sāgar, India	E3	37
Sāgar, India	I8	38
Sag Harbor, N.Y., U.S.	m16	109
Saginaw, Mi., U.S.	E7	99
Saginaw, Tx., U.S.	n9	120
Saginaw, co., Mi., U.S.	E6	99
Saginaw Bay, b., Mi., U.S.	E7	99
Saglek Bay, b., Newf., Can.	f9	72
Sagres, Port.	H3	12
Saguache, co., Co., U.S.	C4	83
Sagua de Tánamo, Cuba	D10	64
Sagua la Grande, Cuba	C7	64
Saguaro Lake, res., Az., U.S.	k10	80
Saguaro National Monument, Az., U.S.	E5	80
Saguaro National Monument (Tucson Mountain Section), Az., U.S.	E4	80
Saguenay, stm., Que., Can.	A7	74
Sagunto, Spain	F11	12
Sahagún, Col.	C5	58
Sahagún, Spain	C6	12
Sahara, des., Afr.	D6	42
Sahāranpur, India	F7	38
Sāhīwāl (Montgomery), Pak.	E5	38
Sahuaripa, Mex.	C5	62
Sahuarita, Az., U.S.	F5	80
Sahuayo, Mex.	G8	62
Saibai, i., Austl.	A8	50
Saïda, Alg.	B6	42
Saidpur, Bngl.	H13	38
Saidu, Pak.	C5	38
Saigō, Japan	F6	30
Saigon see Thanh Pho Ho Chi Minh, Viet.	I9	34
Saijō, Japan	I6	30
Saimaa, l., Fin.	F16	6
Saint Abb's Head, c., Scot., U.K.	F10	7
Saint Adolphe, Man., Can.	E3	70
Saint-Affrique, Fr.	I9	10
Sainte-Agathe, Que., Can.	C6	74
Sainte-Agathe-des-Monts, Que., Can.	C3	74
Saint-Aimé (Massueville), Que., Can.	D5	74
Saint-Alban, Que., Can.	C5	74
Saint Alban's, Newf., Can.	E4	72
Saint Albans, Eng., U.K.	J12	7
Saint Albans, Vt., U.S.	B2	122
Saint Albans, W.V., U.S.	C3	125
Saint Albans Bay, b., Vt., U.S.	B2	122
Saint Albert, Alta., Can.	C4	68
Saint-Amand-Mont-Rond, Fr.	F9	10
Saint-Ambroise, Que., Can.	A6	74
Saint-Ambroix, Fr.	H11	10
Saint-André, Cap, c., Madag.	E8	44
Saint-André-Avellin, Que., Can.	D2	74
Saint-André-Est, Que., Can.	D3	74
Saint-André-les-Alpes, Fr.	I13	10
Saint Andrew Bay, b., Fl., U.S.	u16	86
Saint Andrews, N.B., Can.	D2	71
Saint Andrews, Scot., U.K.	E10	7
Saint Andrews, S.C., U.S.	F7	117
Saint Andrews, S.C., U.S.	C5	117
Saint Anne, Il., U.S.	B6	90
Sainte-Anne-de-Beaupré, Que., Can.	B7	74
Sainte-Anne [-de-Bellevue], Que., Can.	q19	74
Sainte Anne-de-Madawaska, N.B., Can.	B1	71
Sainte Anne-des-Chênes, Man., Can.	E3	70
Saint-Anselme, Que., Can.	C7	74
Saint Ansgar, Ia., U.S.	A5	92
Saint Anthony, Newf., Can.	C4	72
Saint Anthony, Id., U.S.	F7	89
Saint Antoine, N.B., Can.	C5	71
Saint-Apollinaire, Que., Can.	C6	74
Saint Arthur, N.B., Can.	B3	71
Saint-Astier, Fr.	G7	10
Saint-Aubert, Que., Can.	B7	74
Saint Augustin, stm., Can.	C2	72
Saint Augustine, Fl., U.S.	C5	86
Saint Austell, Eng., U.K.	K8	7
Saint-Avold, Fr.	C13	10
Saint-Barthélemy, i., Guad.	F16	64
Saint Basile, N.B., Can.	B1	71
Saint-Basile [-Sud], Que., Can.	C6	74
Saint-Benoît-du-Sault, Fr.	F8	10
Saint-Bernard, Que., Can.	C6	74
Saint Bernard, Al., U.S.	A3	78
Saint Bernard, La., U.S.	E6	95
Saint Bernard, Oh., U.S.	o13	112
Saint Bernard, co., La., U.S.	E6	95
Saint Bernice, In., U.S.	E2	91
Saint Bride, Mount, mtn., Alta., Can.	D3	68
Saint Bride's, Newf., Can.	E4	72
Saint-Brieuc, Fr.	D4	10
Saint-Bruno, Que., Can.	A6	74
Saint-Calais, Fr.	E7	10
Saint-Casimir, Que., Can.	C5	74
Saint Catharines, Ont., Can.	D5	73
Saint Catherine, Lake, l., Vt., U.S.	E2	122
Saint Catherines Island, i., Ga., U.S.	E5	87
Saint-Célestin (Annaville), Que., Can.	C5	74
Saint-Céré, Fr.	H8	10
Saint-Césaire, Que., Can.	D4	74
Saint-Chamond, Fr.	G11	10
Saint-Charles, Que., Can.	C7	74
Saint Charles, Il., U.S.	B5	90
Saint Charles, Mi., U.S.	E6	99
Saint Charles, Mn., U.S.	G6	100
Saint Charles, Mo., U.S.	C7	102
Saint Charles, co., La., U.S.	E5	95
Saint Charles, co., Mo., U.S.	C7	102
Saint-Chély-d'Apcher, Fr.	H10	10
Saint Christopher (Saint Kitts), i., St. K./N.	F16	64
Saint Christopher-Nevis see Saint Kitts and Nevis, ctry., N.A.	F16	64
Saint-Chrysostome, Que., Can.	D4	74
Saint Clair, Mi., U.S.	F8	99
Saint Clair, Mn., U.S.	F5	100
Saint Clair, Mo., U.S.	C6	102
Saint Clair, Pa., U.S.	E9	115
Saint Clair, co., Al., U.S.	B3	78
Saint Clair, co., Il., U.S.	E3	90
Saint Clair, co., Mi., U.S.	F8	99
Saint Clair, co., Mo., U.S.	C4	102
Saint Clair Shores, Mi., U.S.	p16	99
Saint Clairsville, Oh., U.S.	B5	112
Saint Claude, Man., Can.	E2	70
Saint-Claude, Fr.	F12	10
Saint Cloud, Fl., U.S.	D5	86
Saint Cloud, Mn., U.S.	E4	100
Saint-Coeur-de-Marie, Que., Can.	A6	74
Saint-Constant, Que., Can.	q19	74
Sainte-Croix, Que., Can.	C6	74
Saint Croix, co., Wi., U.S.	C1	126
Saint Croix, i., V.I.U.S.	F15	64
Saint Croix, stm., U.S.	C1	126
Saint Croix, Lake, l., U.S.	D1	126
Saint Croix Falls, Wi., U.S.	C1	126
Saint Croix Stream, stm., Me., U.S.	B4	96
Saint-Damase, Que., Can.	D4	74
Saint David, Az., U.S.	F5	80
Saint-David-de-l'Auberivière, Que., Can.	n17	74
Saint David's, Wales, U.K.	J7	7
Saint-Denis, Que., Can.	D4	74
Saint-Denis, Fr.	D9	10
Saint-Denis, Reu.	F11	44
Saint-Dié, Fr.	D13	10
Saint-Dizier, Fr.	D11	10
Saint-Dominique, Que., Can.	D5	74
Saint Edward, Ne., U.S.	C8	104
Saint Eleanor's, P.E.I., Can.	C6	71
Saint Elias, Cape, c., Ak., U.S.	D11	79
Saint Elmo, Al., U.S.	E1	78
Saint Elmo, Il., U.S.	D5	90
Saint-Éphrem [-de-Tring], Que., Can.	C7	74
Saint Étienne, Fr.	G11	10
Saint-Eustache, Que., Can.	D4	74
Saint-Félicien, Que., Can.	A5	74
Saint-Félix-de-Valois, Que., Can.	C4	74
Saint-Ferdinand (Bernierville), Que., Can.	C6	74
Saint-Ferréol [-les-Neiges], Que., Can.	B7	74
Saint-Flavien, Que., Can.	C6	74
Saint-Florentin, Fr.	D10	10
Saint-Florent-sur-Cher, Fr.	F9	10
Saint-Flour, Fr.	G10	10
Sainte-Foy, Que., Can.	n17	74
Sainte-Foy-la-Grande, Fr.	H7	10
Saint Francis, Ks., U.S.	C2	93
Saint Francis, Mn., U.S.	E5	100
Saint Francis, S.D., U.S.	D5	118
Saint Francis, Wi., U.S.	n12	126
Saint Francis, co., Ar., U.S.	B5	81
Saint Francis, stm., U.S.	A5	81
Saint Francis, Cape, c., Newf., Can.	E5	72
Saint Francisville, Il., U.S.	E6	90
Saint Francisville, La., U.S.	D4	95
Saint Francois, co., Mo., U.S.	D7	102
Saint-François, stm., Que., Can.	D5	74
Saint-François, Lac, l., Que., Can.	D6	74
Saint Francois Mountains, hills, Mo., U.S.	D7	102
Saint Froid Lake, l., Me., U.S.	B4	96
Saint-Fulgence, Que., Can.	A7	74
Saint-Gabriel, Que., Can.	C4	74
Saint-Gaudens, Fr.	I7	10
Saint-Gédéon, Que., Can.	D7	74
Sainte Genevieve, Mo., U.S.	D7	102
Sainte Genevieve, co., Mo., U.S.	D7	102
Saint George, Austl.	E9	50
Saint George, N.B., Can.	D3	71
Saint George, Ont., Can.	D4	73
Saint George, S.C., U.S.	E6	117
Saint George, Ut., U.S.	F2	121
Saint George, Cape, c., Newf., Can.	D2	72
Saint George, Cape, c., Fl., U.S.	C1	86
Saint George Island, i., Ak., U.S.	D6	79
Saint George Island, i., Fl., U.S.	C2	86
Saint George's, Newf., Can.	D2	72
Saint-Georges, Que., Can.	C5	74
Saint-Georges, Fr. Gu.	C8	54
Saint George's, Gren.	H17	64
Saint Georges, De., U.S.	B3	85
Saint George's Bay, b., Newf., Can.	D2	72
Saint Georges Bay, b., N.S., Can.	D8	71
Saint George's Channel, strt., Eur.	J6	7
Saint-Georges-Ouest (part of Ville-Saint-Georges), Que., Can.	C7	74
Saint-Germain, Fr.	D9	10
Saint-Gervais, Que., Can.	C7	74
Saint-Gilles, Que., Can.	C6	74
Saint-Gilles-Croix-de-Vie, Fr.	F5	10
Saint-Girons, Fr.	J8	10
Saint-Grégoire (Larochelle), Que., Can.	C5	74
Saint-Guénolé, Fr.	E2	10
Saint-Guillaume-d'Upton, Que., Can.	D5	74
Saint Helen, Lake, l., Mi., U.S.	D6	99
Saint Helena, Ca., U.S.	C2	82
Saint Helena, co., La., U.S.	D5	95
Saint Helena Bay, b., S. Afr.	H3	44
Saint Helena Island, i., S.C., U.S.	G6	117
Saint Helena Sound, strt., S.C., U.S.	G7	117
Saint Helens, Or., U.S.	B4	114
Saint Helens, Mount, vol., Wa., U.S.	C3	124
Saint Helier, Jersey	C4	10
Saint Henry, Oh., U.S.	B1	112
Saint-Hippolyte, Fr.	E13	10
Saint-Honoré, Que., Can.	D7	74
Saint-Hubert, Que., Can.	q20	74
Saint-Hubert-de-Témiscouata, Que., Can.	B8	74
Saint-Hyacinthe, Que., Can.	D5	74
Saint Ignace, Mi., U.S.	C6	99
Saint Ignace Island, i., Ont., Can.	G15	66
Saint Ignatius, Mt., U.S.	C2	103
Saint Isidore de Prescott, Ont., Can.	B10	73
Saint Jacobs, Ont., Can.	D4	73
Saint Jacques, N.B., Can.	B1	71
Saint-Jacques, Que., Can.	D4	74
Saint James, Mn., U.S.	G4	100
Saint James, Mo., U.S.	D6	102
Saint James, co., La., U.S.	D5	95
Saint James, Cape, c., B.C., Can.	D2	69
Saint James City, Fl., U.S.	F4	86
Saint-Jean, stm., Que., Can.	A7	74
Saint-Jean, Lac, l., Que., Can.	A5	74
Saint Jean Baptiste, Man., Can.	E3	70
Saint-Jean-Chrysostome, Que., Can.	o17	74
Saint-Jean-d'Angély, Fr.	G6	10
Saint-Jean-de-Luz, Fr.	I5	10
Saint-Jean-de-Maurienne, Fr.	G13	10
Saint-Jean-de-Monts, Fr.	F4	10
Saint-Jean-Pied-de-Port, Fr.	I5	10
Saint-Jean-sur-Richelieu, Que., Can.	D4	74
Saint-Jérôme, Que., Can.	D3	74
Saint Jo, Tx., U.S.	C4	120
Saint-Joachim, Que., Can.	B7	74
Saint Joe, stm., Id., U.S.	B3	89
Saint John, N.B., Can.	D3	71
Saint John, In., U.S.	B3	91
Saint John, Ks., U.S.	E5	93
Saint John, i., V.I.U.S.	E15	64
Saint John, stm., N.A.	G19	66
Saint John, Cape, c., Newf., Can.	D4	72
Saint John Bay, b., Newf., Can.	C3	72
Saint Johns, Antig.	F17	64
Saint John's, Newf., Can.	E5	72
Saint Johns, Az., U.S.	C6	80
Saint Johns, Mi., U.S.	F6	99
Saint Johns, co., Fl., U.S.	C5	86
Saint Johns, stm., Fl., U.S.	B5	86
Saint Johnsbury, Vt., U.S.	C4	122
Saint Johnsville, N.Y., U.S.	B6	109
Saint John the Baptist, co., La., U.S.	D5	95
Saint Jones, stm., De., U.S.	D4	85
Saint Joseph, N.B., Can.	D5	71
Saint Joseph, Il., U.S.	C5	90
Saint Joseph, La., U.S.	C4	95
Saint Joseph, Mi., U.S.	F4	99
Saint Joseph, Mn., U.S.	E4	100
Saint Joseph, Mo., U.S.	B3	102
Saint Joseph, Tn., U.S.	B4	119
Saint Joseph, co., In., U.S.	A5	91
Saint Joseph, co., Mi., U.S.	G5	99
Saint Joseph, stm., U.S.	F5	99
Saint-Joseph, Lac, l., Que., Can.	n16	74
Saint Joseph, Lake, l., Ont., Can.	o17	73
Saint Joseph Bay, b., Fl., U.S.	C1	86
Saint-Joseph-de-Beauce, Que., Can.	C7	74
Saint Joseph Point, c., Fl., U.S.	v16	86
Saint Joseph Sound, strt., Fl., U.S.	o10	86
Saint-Jovite, Que., Can.	C3	74
Saint-Julien-en-Born, Fr.	H5	10
Saint-Junien, Fr.	G7	10
Saint-Just-en-Chaussée, Fr.	C9	10
Saint Kilda, i., Scot., U.K.	D4	7
Saint Kitts-Nevis, ctry., N.A.	F16	64
Saint-Lambert, Que., Can.	p19	74
Saint Landry, co., La., U.S.	D3	95
Saint-Laurent, Que., Can.	p19	74
Saint Lawrence, Newf., Can.	E4	72
Saint Lawrence, co., N.Y., U.S.	A5	109
Saint Lawrence, stm., N.A.	G19	66
Saint Lawrence, Cape, c., N.S., Can.	B9	71
Saint Lawrence, Gulf of, b., Can.	G20	66
Saint Lawrence Island, i., Ak., U.S.	C5	79
Saint Lawrence Islands National Park, Ont., Can.	C9	73
Saint Léonard, N.B., Can.	B2	71
Saint-Léonard [-d'Aston], Que., Can.	C5	74
Saint-Liboire, Que., Can.	D5	74
Saint-Lô, Fr.	C5	10
Saint-Louis, Sen.	E2	42
Saint Louis, Mi., U.S.	E6	99
Saint Louis, Mo., U.S.	C7	102
Saint Louis, co., Mn., U.S.	C6	100
Saint Louis, co., Mo., U.S.	C7	102
Saint Louis, stm., U.S.	D6	100
Saint-Louis, Lac, l., Que., Can.	q19	74
Saint Louis Bay, b., Ms., U.S.	f7	101
Saint-Louis-de-Gonzague, Que., Can.	D3	74
Saint-Louis-de-Kent, N.B., Can.	C5	71
Saint-Louis-du-Ha! Ha!, Que., Can.	B8	74
Saint Louis Park, Mn., U.S.	n12	100
Saint-Luc, Que., Can.	D4	74
Saint Lucia, ctry., N.A.	H17	64
Saint Lucia Channel, strt., N.A.	G17	64
Saint Lucie, co., Fl., U.S.	E6	86
Saint Lucie Canal, Fl., U.S.	F6	86
Saint Lucie Inlet, b., Fl., U.S.	E6	86
Sainte-Madeleine, Que., Can.	D4	74
Saint Malo, Man., Can.	E3	70
Saint-Malo, Fr.	D4	10
Saint-Malo, Golfe de, b., Fr.	D4	10
Saint-Marc, Haiti	E11	64
Saint-Marc [-des-Carrières], Que., Can.	C5	74
Saint-Marcellin, Fr.	G12	10
Saint Margaret Bay, b., Newf., Can.	C3	72
Sainte-Marguerite, stm., Que., Can.	A7	74
Sainte-Marie, Que., Can.	C6	74
Sainte-Marie, Cap, c., Madag.	G9	44
Saint Maries, Id., U.S.	B2	89
Sainte-Marthe, Que., Can.	D3	74
Saint Martin, co., La., U.S.	D4	95
Saint-Martin (Sint Maarten), i., N.A.	E16	64
Saint Martin, Lake, l., Man., Can.	D2	70
Saint Martin Island, i., Mi., U.S.	C4	99
Saint Martinville, La., U.S.	D4	95
Saint Mary, co., La., U.S.	E4	95
Saint Mary-of-the-Woods, In., U.S.	E3	91
Saint Mary Peak, mtn., Austl.	F7	50
Saint Marys, Austl.	H9	50
Saint Mary's, Newf., Can.	E5	72
Saint Mary's, Ont., Can.	D3	73
Saint Marys, Ak., U.S.	C7	79
Saint Marys, Ga., U.S.	F5	87
Saint Marys, In., U.S.	A5	91
Saint Marys, Ks., U.S.	C7	93
Saint Marys, Oh., U.S.	B1	112
Saint Marys, Pa., U.S.	D4	115
Saint Marys, W.V., U.S.	B3	125
Saint Marys, co., Md., U.S.	D4	97
Saint Marys, stm., N.S., Can.	D8	71
Saint Marys, stm., U.S.	F5	87
Saint Marys, stm., U.S.	C8	91
Saint Marys, stm., Md., U.S.	D5	97
Saint Mary's, Cape, c., Newf., Can.	E4	72
Saint Mary's Bay, b., Newf., Can.	E5	72
Saint Marys Bay, b., N.S., Can.	E3	71
Saint Marys City, Md., U.S.	D5	97
Saint-Mathieu, Pointe de, c., Fr.	D2	10
Saint Matthew Island, i., Ak., U.S.	C5	79
Saint Matthews, Ky., U.S.	B4	94
Saint Matthews, S.C., U.S.	D6	117
Sainte-Maure-du-Touraine, Fr.	E7	10
Saint-Maurice, stm., Que., Can.	C5	74
Sainte-Maxime, Fr.	I13	10
Saint-Méen-le-Grand, Fr.	D4	10
Sainte-Menehould, Fr.	C11	10
Sainte-Mère-Église, Fr.	C5	10
Saint Michael, Mn., U.S.	E5	100
Saint Michaels, Md., U.S.	C5	97
Saint-Michel [-de-Bellechasse], Que., Can.	C7	74
Saint-Mihiel, Fr.	D12	10
Saint-Moritz see Sankt Moritz, Switz.	F16	10
Saint-Nazaire, Fr.	E4	10
Saint-Nicolas, Que., Can.	o17	74
Saint-Odilon, Que., Can.	C7	74
Saint-Omer, Fr.	B9	10
Saint-Ours, Que., Can.	D4	74
Saint-Pacôme, Que., Can.	B8	74
Saint-Pamphile, Que., Can.	C8	74
Saint Paris, Oh., U.S.	B2	112
Saint-Pascal, Que., Can.	B8	74
Saint Paul, Alta., Can.	B5	68
Saint Paul, Ak., U.S.	D5	79
Saint Paul, In., U.S.	F6	91
Saint Paul, Ks., U.S.	E8	93
Saint Paul, Mn., U.S.	F5	100
Saint Paul, Mo., U.S.	f12	102
Saint Paul, Ne., U.S.	C7	104
Saint Paul, Va., U.S.	f9	123
Saint Paul Island, i., Ak., U.S.	D5	79
Saint Paul Park, Mn., U.S.	n12	100
Saint Pauls, N.C., U.S.	C4	110
Sainte-Perpétue-de-L'Islet, Que., Can.	B8	74
Saint Peter, Mn., U.S.	F5	100
Saint Peter Port, Guernsey	C4	10
Saint Peters, N.S., Can.	D9	71
Saint Peters, Mo., U.S.	C7	102
Saint Petersburg, Fl., U.S.	E4	86
Saint Petersburg Beach, Fl., U.S.	p10	86
Saint Petersburg see Sankt-Peterburg, Russia	B13	18
Saint Phillips Island, i., S.C., U.S.	G6	117
Saint-Pie, Que., Can.	D5	74
Saint-Pierre, Reu.	F11	44
Saint-Pierre, St. P./M.	E3	72
Saint-Pierre, Lac, l., Que., Can.	C5	74
Saint Pierre and Miquelon, dep., N.A.	G21	66
Saint Pierre Island, i., Sey.	C10	44
Saint Pierre-Jolys, Man., Can.	E3	70
Saint-Pierre-le-Moûtier, Fr.	F10	10
Saint-Pol-de-Léon, Fr.	D3	10
Saint-Pons, Fr.	I9	10
Saint-Pourçain-sur-Sioule, Fr.	F10	10
Saint-Prime, Que., Can.	A5	74
Saint Quentin, N.B., Can.	B2	71
Saint-Quentin, Fr.	C10	10
Saint-Raphaël, Que., Can.	C7	74
Saint-Raphaël, Fr.	I13	10
Saint-Raymond, Que., Can.	C6	74
Saint-Rédempteur, Que., Can.	o17	74
Saint Regis, Mt., U.S.	C1	103
Saint Regis, West Branch, stm., N.Y., U.S.	f10	109
Saint-Rémi, Que., Can.	D4	74
Saint-Romuald, Que., Can.	C6	74
Saint Rose, La., U.S.	k11	95
Sainte Rose du Lac, Man., Can.	D2	70
Saintes, Fr.	G6	10
Saint Sauveur, N.B., Can.	B4	71
Saint-Sauveur-des-Monts, Que., Can.	D3	74
Saint-Sébastien, Cap, c., Madag.	D9	44
Saint-Siméon, Que., Can.	B8	74
Saint Simons Island, Ga., U.S.	E5	87
Saint Simons Island, i., Ga., U.S.	E5	87
Saint Stephen, N.B., Can.	D2	71
Saint Stephen, S.C., U.S.	E8	117
Saint Tammany, co., La., U.S.	D5	95
Sainte-Thècle, Que., Can.	C5	74
Sainte-Thérèse, Que., Can.	D4	74
Saint Thomas, Ont., Can.	E3	73
Saint Thomas, i., V.I.U.S.	E15	64
Saint Timothée, Que., Can.	q18	74
Saint-Tite, Que., Can.	C5	74
Saint-Tropez, Fr.	I13	10
Saint-Valéry-en-Caux, Fr.	C7	10
Saint-Varent, Fr.	F6	10
Sainte-Véronique, Que., Can.	C3	74
Saint-Victor, Que., Can.	C7	74
Saint-Vincent, Cap, c., Madag.	F8	44
Saint Vincent, Gulf, b., Austl.	F7	50
Saint Vincent and the Grenadines, ctry., N.A.	H17	64
Saint Vincent Island, i., Fl., U.S.	C1	86
Saint Vincent Passage, strt., N.A.	H17	64
Saint Vincent's [-Saint Stephens-Peter's River], Newf., Can.	E5	72
Saint-Vith, Bel.	E6	8
Saint Walburg, Sask., Can.	D1	75
Saint-Zacharie, Que., Can.	C7	74
Sairecábur, Cerro, mtn., S.A.	A3	56
Saito, Japan	J4	30
Saitula, China	B8	38
Sajama, Nevado, mtn., Bol.	G5	54
Sajia, China	F13	38
Sajnšand, Mong.	C9	26
Sakai, Japan	H8	30
Sakaide, Japan	H6	30
Sakai-minato, Japan	G6	30
Sakakawea, Lake, res., N.D., U.S.	B3	111
Sakami, Lac, l., Que., Can.	F17	66
Sakata, Japan	D12	30
Sakhalin see Sachalin, Ostrov, i., Russia	G22	24
Sākhar, Afg.	D1	38
Sakishima-shotō, is., Japan	G11	26
Sakon Nakhon, Thai.	F8	34
Sakonnet, stm., R.I., U.S.	E6	116
Sakonnet Point, c., R.I., U.S.	F6	116
Saku, Japan	F11	30
Sakurai, Japan	H8	30
Sal, Point, c., Ca., U.S.	E3	82
Sala, Swe.	G11	6
Salaberry-de-Valleyfield, Que., Can.	D3	74
Sala Consilina, Italy	I10	14
Salado, stm., Arg.	C4	56
Salado, Rio, stm., N.M., U.S.	C2	108
Ṣalālah, Oman	E5	46
Salamanca, Mex.	G9	62
Salamanca, Spain	E6	12
Salamanca, N.Y., U.S.	C2	109
Salamina, Col.	E5	58
Salamonie, stm., In., U.S.	C6	91
Salamonie Lake, res., In., U.S.	C6	91
Salatiga, Indon.	m15	33a
Salavat, Russia	G9	22
Salawati, i., Indon.	F9	32
Saldanha, S. Afr.	H3	44
Sale, Austl.	G9	50
Sale Creek, Tn., U.S.	D8	119
Salem, India	G5	37
Salem, Ar., U.S.	A4	81
Salem, Il., U.S.	E5	90
Salem, In., U.S.	G5	91
Salem, Ky., U.S.	e9	94
Salem, Ma., U.S.	A6	98
Salem, Mo., U.S.	D6	102
Salem, N.H., U.S.	E4	106
Salem, N.J., U.S.	D2	107
Salem, Oh., U.S.	B5	112
Salem, Or., U.S.	C4	114
Salem, S.D., U.S.	D8	118
Salem, Ut., U.S.	C4	121
Salem, Va., U.S.	C2	123
Salem, W.V., U.S.	B4	125
Salem, Wi., U.S.	n11	126
Salem, co., N.J., U.S.	D2	107
Salem, stm., N.J., U.S.	D2	107

Name	Map Ref	Page
Salem, Lake, l., Vt., U.S.	B4	122
Salemi, Italy	L7	14
Sälen, Swe.	F9	6
Salerno, Italy	I9	14
Salford, Eng., U.K.	H10	7
Salgótarján, Hung.	G19	8
Sali, Cro.	F10	14
Salida, Co., U.S.	C5	83
Salies-de-Béarn, Fr.	I6	10
Salihli, Tur.	K12	16
Salina, Ks., U.S.	D6	93
Salina, Ok., U.S.	A6	113
Salina, Ut., U.S.	E4	121
Salina Cruz, Mex.	I12	62
Salinas, Braz.	D7	57
Salinas, Ca., U.S.	D3	82
Salinas, stm., Ca., U.S.	D3	82
Salinas de Hidalgo, Mex.	F9	62
Salinas Peak, mtn., N.M., U.S.	D3	108
Salinas Pueblo Missions National Monument, N.M., U.S.	C3	108
Saline, Mi., U.S.	F7	99
Saline, co., Ar., U.S.	C3	81
Saline, co., Il., U.S.	F5	90
Saline, co., Ks., U.S.	D6	93
Saline, co., Mo., U.S.	B4	102
Saline, co., Ne., U.S.	D8	104
Saline, stm., Ar., U.S.	C1	81
Saline, stm., Ar., U.S.	D4	81
Saline, stm., Ks., U.S.	C3	93
Saline, North Fork, stm., Il., U.S.	F5	90
Saline Lake, res., La., U.S.	C3	95
Salineville, Oh., U.S.	B5	112
Salisbury, N.B., Can.	C4	71
Salisbury, Eng., U.K.	J11	7
Salisbury, Ct., U.S.	B2	84
Salisbury, Md., U.S.	D6	97
Salisbury, Ma., U.S.	A6	98
Salisbury, Mo., U.S.	B5	102
Salisbury, N.C., U.S.	B2	110
Salisbury see Harare, Zimb.	E6	44
Salisbury Island, i., N.W. Ter., Can.	D17	66
Salisbury Plain, pl., Eng., U.K.	J11	7
Salish Mountains, mts., Mt., U.S.	B2	103
Salkehatchie, stm., S.C., U.S.	E5	117
Şalkhad, Syria	C5	40
Salles-Curan, Fr.	H9	10
Sallisaw, Ok., U.S.	B7	113
Salluit, Que., Can.	f11	74
Salmo, B.C., Can.	E9	69
Salmon, Id., U.S.	D5	89
Salmon, stm., N.B., Can.	C4	71
Salmon, stm., Id., U.S.	D3	89
Salmon Creek, Wa., U.S.	D3	124
Salmon Creek Reservoir, res., Id., U.S.	G4	89
Salmon Falls, stm., U.S.	D5	106
Salmon Falls Creek, stm., U.S.	G4	89
Salmon Mountains, mts., Ca., U.S.	B2	82
Salmon Point, c., Ont., Can.	D7	73
Salmon River Mountains, mts., Id., U.S.	E3	89
Salmon River Reservoir, res., N.Y., U.S.	B5	109
Salo, Fin.	F14	6
Salome, Az., U.S.	D2	80
Salon-De-Provence, Fr.	I12	10
Salonika see Thessaloníki, Grc.	I6	16
Salsomaggiore Terme, Italy	E4	14
Salt, stm., Az., U.S.	D4	80
Salt, stm., Ky., U.S.	C4	94
Salt, stm., Mo., U.S.	B6	102
Salta, Arg.	A3	56
Salt Creek, stm., N.M., U.S.	D5	108
Salt Creek, stm., Oh., U.S.	C3	112
Salt Creek, stm., Wy., U.S.	C6	127
Salter Path, N.C., U.S.	C6	110
Salt Fork Lake, res., Oh., U.S.	B4	112
Saltillo, Mex.	E9	62
Saltillo, Ms., U.S.	A5	101
Salt Lake, co., Ut., U.S.	C3	121
Salt Lake, l., Hi., U.S.	g10	88
Salt Lake, l., N.M., U.S.	E6	108
Salt Lake City, Ut., U.S.	C4	121
Salto, Ur.	C5	56
Salton Sea, l., Ca., U.S.	F5	82
Saltonstall, Lake, l., Ct., U.S.	D4	84
Salt Point, c., Ca., U.S.	C2	82
Salt River Indian Reservation, Az., U.S.	k9	80
Salt River Range, mts., Wy., U.S.	D2	127
Saltsburg, Pa., U.S.	F3	115
Salt Springs, Fl., U.S.	C5	86
Saltville, Va., U.S.	f10	123
Salt Wells Creek, stm., Wy., U.S.	E4	127
Saluda, S.C., U.S.	C4	117
Saluda, co., S.C., U.S.	C4	117
Saluda, stm., S.C., U.S.	C4	117
Saluda Dam, S.C., U.S.	C5	117
Sālūr, India	C7	37
Saluzzo, Italy	E2	14
Salvador, Braz.	B9	57
Salvador, Lake, l., La., U.S.	E5	95
Salvatierra, Mex.	G9	62
Salween (Nu) (Thanlwin), stm., Asia	D5	34
Salyersville, Ky., U.S.	C6	94
Salzburg, Aus.	H13	8
Salzgitter, Ger.	C10	8
Salzwedel, Ger.	C11	8
Sama [de Langreo], Spain	B6	12
Samaná, Bahía de, b., Dom. Rep.	E13	64
Samana Cay, i., Bah.	C11	64
Samandağı, Tur.	A4	40
Samar, i., Phil.	C8	32
Samara, Russia	G8	22
Samarai, Pap. N. Gui.	n17	50a
Samariapo, Ven.	E9	58
Samarinda, Indon.	F6	32
Samarkand, Uzb.	J11	22
Sāmarrā', Iraq	B3	46
Samāstipur, India	H11	38
Sambalpur, India	J10	38
Sambas, Indon.	E4	32
Sambava, Madag.	D10	44
Sambhal, India	F8	38
Sāmbhar, India	G6	38
Samborondón, Ec.	H3	58
Sammamish Lake, l., Wa., U.S.	e11	124
Samneua, Laos	D8	34
Samobor, Cro.	D10	14
Sámos, i., Grc.	L10	16
Samoset, Fl., U.S.	q10	86
Sampit, Indon.	F5	32
Sampit, stm., S.C., U.S.	E9	117
Sampson, co., N.C., U.S.	B4	110
Sam Rayburn Reservoir, res., Tx., U.S.	D5	120
Samson, Al., U.S.	D3	78
Samsun, Tur.	G15	4
Samuels, Id., U.S.	A2	89
Samui, Ko, i., Thai.	J6	34
Samut Prakan, Thai.	H6	34
Samut Sakhon, Thai.	H6	34
San, Mali	F5	42
San, stm., Eur.	E22	8
Şan'ā', Yemen	E3	46
Sanaga, stm., Cam.	H7	42
San Agustín, Col.	G4	58
San Agustin, Cape, c., Phil.	D8	32
San Agustin, Plains of, pl., N.M., U.S.	C2	108
Sanak Islands, is., Ak., U.S.	E7	79
Sanana, Pulau, i., Indon.	F8	32
Sanandaj, Iran	A4	46
San Andreas, Ca., U.S.	C3	82
San Andrés, Isla de, i., Col.	H7	64
San Andres Mountains, mts., N.M., U.S.	E3	108
San Andres Peak, mtn., N.M., U.S.	E3	108
San Andrés Tuxtla, Mex.	H12	62
San Angelo, Tx., U.S.	D2	120
San Anselmo, Ca., U.S.	h7	82
San Antonio, Tx., U.S.	E3	120
San Antonio, Cabo, c., Arg.	D5	56
San Antonio, Cabo, c., Cuba	D5	64
San Antonio Abad, Spain	G13	12
San Antonio Bay, b., Tx., U.S.	E4	120
San Antonio de Bravo, Mex.	B7	62
San Antonio de los Cobres, Arg.	A3	56
San Antonio del Táchira, Ven.	D6	58
San Antonio Mountain, mtn., N.M., U.S.	A3	108
San Antonio Oeste, Arg.	E4	56
San Augustine, Tx., U.S.	D5	120
San Augustine, co., Tx., U.S.	D5	120
San Benedetto del Tronto, Italy	G8	14
San Benedicto, Isla, i., Mex.	H4	62
San Benito, Guat.	F3	64
San Benito, Tx., U.S.	F4	120
San Benito, co., Ca., U.S.	D3	82
San Benito Mountain, mtn., Ca., U.S.	D3	82
San Bernardino, Ca., U.S.	E5	82
San Bernardino, co., Ca., U.S.	E5	82
San Bernardo, Chile	C2	56
San Blas, Mex.	G7	62
San Blas, Mex.	D5	62
San Blas, Cape, c., Fl., U.S.	v16	86
San Borja, Bol.	F5	54
Sanborn, Ia., U.S.	A2	92
Sanborn, co., S.D., U.S.	D7	118
Sanbornville, N.H., U.S.	C4	106
San Bruno, Ca., U.S.	D2	82
San Carlos, Nic.	I5	64
San Carlos, Az., U.S.	D5	80
San Carlos, Ca., U.S.	k8	82
San Carlos, Ven.	C8	58
San Carlos de Bariloche, Arg.	E2	56
San Carlos de Guaroa, Col.	F6	58
San Carlos de la Rápita, Spain	E12	12
San Carlos del Zulia, Ven.	C7	58
San Carlos de Río Negro, Ven.	G9	58
San Carlos Indian Reservation, Az., U.S.	D5	80
San Carlos Lake, res., Az., U.S.	D5	80
San Cataldo, Italy	L9	14
Sancerre, Fr.	E9	10
Sánchez, Mex.	D10	62
San Clemente, Ca., U.S.	F5	82
San Clemente Island, i., Ca., U.S.	F4	82
Sancoins, Fr.	F9	10
San Cristóbal, Arg.	C4	56
San Cristóbal, Ven.	D6	58
San Cristóbal, Volcán, vol., Nic.	H4	64
San Cristóbal las Casas, Mex.	I13	62
Sancti-Spíritus, Cuba	D8	64
Sand, Nor.	G6	6
Sandakan, Malay.	D6	32
Sanday, i., Scot., U.K.	B10	7
Sand Creek, stm., Wy., U.S.	C7	127
Sanders, Az., U.S.	B6	80
Sanders, co., Mt., U.S.	C1	103
Sanderson, Tx., U.S.	D1	120
Sandersville, Ga., U.S.	D4	87
Sandersville, Ms., U.S.	D4	101
Sand Hill, Ma., U.S.	h13	98
Sand Hill, stm., Mn., U.S.	C2	100
Sandia, Peru	F5	54
Sandia Crest, mtn., N.M., U.S.	k8	108
Sandia Indian Reservation, N.M., U.S.	k7	108
Sandia Mountains, mts., N.M., U.S.	k8	108
San Diego, Ca., U.S.	F5	82
San Diego, Tx., U.S.	F3	120
San Diego, co., Ca., U.S.	F5	82
San Diego, stm., Ca., U.S.	o15	82
San Diego Naval Station, mil., Ca., U.S.	o15	82
San Diego Naval Training Center, mil., Ca., U.S.	o15	82
Sand Island, i., Hi., U.S.	g10	88
Sand Island, i., Wi., U.S.	B3	126
Sand Key, i., Fl., U.S.	E4	86
Sandlick Creek, stm., W.V., U.S.	n13	125
Sandnes, Nor.	G5	6
Sandoa, Zaire	C4	44
San Donà di Piave, Italy	D7	14
Sandoval, Il., U.S.	E4	90
Sandoval, co., N.M., U.S.	B2	108
Sandoway, Mya.	E3	34
Sand Point, Ak., U.S.	D7	79
Sandpoint, Id., U.S.	A2	89
Sands Key, i., Fl., U.S.	s3	86
Sand Springs, Ok., U.S.	A5	113
Sandston, Va., U.S.	m18	123
Sandstone, Austl.	E3	50
Sandstone, Mn., U.S.	D6	100
Sandusky, Mi., U.S.	E8	99
Sandusky, Oh., U.S.	A3	112
Sandusky, co., Oh., U.S.	A2	112
Sandusky, stm., Oh., U.S.	B2	112
Sandviken, Swe.	F11	6
Sandwich, Il., U.S.	B5	90
Sandwich, Ma., U.S.	C7	98
Sandwich Bay, b., Newf., Can.	B3	72
Sandy, Or., U.S.	B4	114
Sandy, Ut., U.S.	C4	121
Sandy, stm., Me., U.S.	D2	96
Sandy Creek, stm., Oh., U.S.	B4	112
Sandy Creek, stm., Ok., U.S.	C2	113
Sandy Hook, Ct., U.S.	D2	84
Sandy Hook, spit, N.J., U.S.	C5	107
Sandy Island, i., S.C., U.S.	D9	117
Sandy Lake, l., Newf., Can.	D3	72
Sandy Lake, l., Ont., Can.	n16	73
Sandy Neck, pen., Ma., U.S.	C7	98
Sandy Point, c., R.I., U.S.	h7	116
Sandy Springs, Ga., U.S.	h8	87
Sandy Springs, S.C., U.S.	B2	117
Sandyville, Md., U.S.	A4	97
San Felipe, Ven.	B8	58
San Felipe Indian Reservation, N.M., U.S.	k8	108
San Felipe Pueblo, N.M., U.S.	B3	108
San Feliu de Guixols, Spain	D15	12
San Fernando, Chile	C2	56
San Fernando, Mex.	E10	62
San Fernando, Phil.	B7	32
San Fernando, Phil.	q19	32
San Fernando, Spain	I5	12
San Fernando, Trin.	I17	64
San Fernando, Ca., U.S.	m12	82
San Fernando de Apure, Ven.	D9	58
San Fernando de Atabapo, Ven.	E9	58
Sanford, Co., U.S.	D5	83
Sanford, Fl., U.S.	D5	86
Sanford, Me., U.S.	E2	96
Sanford, Mi., U.S.	E6	99
Sanford, N.C., U.S.	B3	110
Sanford, Mount, mtn., Ak., U.S.	C11	79
San Francisco, Arg.	C4	56
San Francisco, Ca., U.S.	D2	82
San Francisco, co., Ca., U.S.	D2	82
San Francisco, stm., U.S.	D6	80
San Francisco Bay, b., Ca., U.S.	h8	82
San Francisco de Borja, Mex.	D6	62
San Francisco del Oro, Mex.	D7	62
San Francisco del Rincón, Mex.	G9	62
San Francisco de Macorís, Dom. Rep.	E12	64
San Fratello, Italy	K9	14
San Gabriel, Ec.	G4	58
San Gabriel, Ca., U.S.	*m12	82
San Gabriel Mountains, mts., Ca., U.S.	m12	82
Sangamner, India	C3	37
Sangamon, co., Il., U.S.	D4	90
Sangamon, stm., Il., U.S.	C3	90
San Gavino Monreale, Italy	J3	14
Sangay, Volcán, vol., Ec.	H3	58
Sang-e Māsheh, Afg.	D2	38
Sanger, Ca., U.S.	D4	82
Sanger, Tx., U.S.	C4	120
Sangerhausen, Ger.	D11	8
Sangha, stm., Afr.	B3	44
Sanghar, Pak.	G3	38
Sangihe, Kepulauan, is., Indon.	E8	32
Sangihe, Pulau, i., Indon.	E8	32
San Gil, Col.	D6	58
San Giovanni in Fiore, Italy	J11	14
San Giovanni in Persiceto, Italy	E6	14
San Giovanni Valdarno, Italy	F6	14
Sāngli, India	D3	37
Sangolquí, Ec.	H3	58
San Gorgonio Mountain, mtn., Ca., U.S.	E5	82
San Gregorio, Ur.	C5	56
Sangrūr, India	E6	38
Sangüesa, Spain	C10	12
Sanibel, Fl., U.S.	F4	86
Sanibel Island, i., Fl., U.S.	F4	86
San Ignacio, Arg.	B5	56
San Ignacio, Hond.	G4	64
Sanilac, co., Mi., U.S.	E8	99
San Isidro, Arg.	C5	56
San Isidro, C.R.	J6	64
San Jacinto, Col.	C5	58
San Jacinto, Ca., U.S.	F5	82
San Jacinto, co., Tx., U.S.	D5	120
San Jacinto, stm., Tx., U.S.	r14	120
Sanjō, Japan	E11	30
San Joaquin, co., Ca., U.S.	D3	82
San Joaquin, stm., Ca., U.S.	D3	82
San Joaquin Valley, val., Ca., U.S.	D3	82
San Jorge, Golfo, b., Arg.	F3	56
San Jorge, Golfo de, b., Spain	E12	12
San José, C.R.	J5	64
San Jose, Ca., U.S.	D3	82
San José, Isla, i., Mex.	E4	62
San José de Chiquitos, Bol.	G6	54
San José de Guanipa, Ven.	C10	58
San José del Cabo, Mex.	F5	62
San José del Guaviare, Col.	F6	58
San José de Mayo, Ur.	C5	56
San José de Ocuné, Col.	E7	58
San José de Raíces, Mex.	E9	62
San Jose Island, i., Tx., U.S.	E4	120
San Juan, Arg.	C3	56
San Juan, Mex.	D8	62
San Juan, P.R.	E14	64
San Juan, Tx., U.S.	F3	120
San Juan, co., Co., U.S.	D3	83
San Juan, co., N.M., U.S.	A1	108
San Juan, co., Ut., U.S.	F5	121
San Juan, co., Wa., U.S.	A2	124
San Juan, stm., N.A.	I6	64
San Juan Capistrano, Ca., U.S.	F5	82
San Juan de Colón, Ven.	C6	58
San Juan [de la Maguana], Dom. Rep.	E12	64
San Juan del Norte, Nic.	I6	64
San Juan de los Cayos, Ven.	B8	58
San Juan de los Morros, Ven.	C9	58
San Juan del Río, Mex.	G9	62
San Juan del Sur, Nic.	I5	64
San Juan Island, i., Wa., U.S.	A2	124
San Juan Mountains, mts., Co., U.S.	D3	83
San Julián, Arg.	F3	56
San Justo, Arg.	C4	56
Sankt Gallen, Aus.	H14	8
Sankt Gallen, Switz.	E16	10
Sankt Johann im Pongau, Aus.	H13	8
Sankt Moritz, Switz.	F16	10
Sankt Peter, Ger.	A8	8
Sankt-Peterburg (Saint Petersburg), Russia	B13	18
Sankt Pölten, Aus.	G15	8
Sankt Veit an der Glan, Aus.	I14	8
Sankt Wendel, Ger.	F7	8
Sankuru, stm., Zaire	B4	44
San Lázaro, Cabo, c., Mex.	E3	62
San Leandro, Ca., U.S.	h8	82
Şanlıurfa, Tur.	H15	4
San Lope, Col.	D7	58
San Lorenzo, Arg.	C4	56
San Lorenzo, Ec.	G3	58
San Lorenzo, Isla, i., Peru	F3	54
San Lorenzo de El Escorial, Spain	E7	12
San Lorenzo de la Parrilla, Spain	F9	12
Sanlúcar de Barrameda, Spain	I5	12
San Lucas, Ec.	I3	58
San Lucas, Cabo, c., Mex.	F5	62
San Luis, Arg.	C3	56
San Luis, Cuba	D10	64
San Luis, Guat.	F3	64
San Luis, Az., U.S.	E1	80
San Luis, Co., U.S.	D5	83
San Luis, Ven.	B8	58
San Luis, Lago de, l., Bol.	F6	54
San Luis, Point, c., Ca., U.S.	E3	82
San Luis de la Paz, Mex.	G9	62
San Luis Obispo, Ca., U.S.	E3	82
San Luis Obispo, co., Ca., U.S.	E3	82
San Luis Pass, strt., Tx., U.S.	r14	120
San Luis Peak, mtn., Co., U.S.	D4	83
San Luis Potosí, Mex.	F9	62
San Luis Río Colorado, Mex.	A2	62
San Luis Valley, val., Co., U.S.	D4	83
San Manuel, Az., U.S.	E5	80
San Marcos, Col.	C5	58
San Marcos, Mex.	D8	62
San Marcos, Mex.	I10	62
San Marcos, Tx., U.S.	E4	120
San Marcos, stm., Tx., U.S.	h8	120
San Marino, Ca., U.S.	m12	82
San Marino, ctry., Eur.	G10	4
San Martín de Valdeiglesias, Spain	E7	12
San Mateo, Spain	E12	12
San Mateo, Ca., U.S.	D2	82
San Mateo, co., Ca., U.S.	D2	82
San Mateo Mountains, mts., N.M., U.S.	B2	108
San Mateo Mountains, mts., N.M., U.S.	D2	108
San Matías, Golfo, b., Arg.	E4	56
San Miguel, El Sal.	H3	64
San Miguel, co., Co., U.S.	D2	83
San Miguel, co., N.M., U.S.	B5	108
San Miguel, stm., Bol.	F6	54
San Miguel, stm., Co., U.S.	C2	83
San Miguel de Allende, Mex.	G9	62
San Miguel del Monte, Arg.	D5	56
San Miguel de Tucumán, Arg.	B3	56
San Miguel el Alto, Mex.	G8	62
San Miguel Island, i., Ca., U.S.	E3	82
San Miguel Mountains, mts., Co., U.S.	D2	83
Sannār, Sudan	F12	42
Sannicandro Garganico, Italy	H10	14
San Nicolas, Phil.	o19	33b
San Nicolás de los Arroyos, Arg.	C4	56
San Nicolas Island, i., Ca., U.S.	F4	82
Sannikova, Proliv, strt., Russia	C21	24
Sanniquellie, Lib.	G4	42
Sano, Japan	F12	30
Sanok, Pol.	F22	8
San Onofre, Col.	C5	58
San Pablo, Col.	G4	58
San Pablo, Phil.	q19	32
San Pablo Balleza, Mex.	D6	62
San Pablo Bay, b., Ca., U.S.	g8	82
San Patricio, co., Tx., U.S.	E4	120
San Pedro, stm., Az., U.S.	E5	80
San Pedro, Punta, c., Chile	B2	56
San Pedro, Volcán, vol., Chile	A3	56
San Pedro Bay, b., Ca., U.S.	n12	82
San Pedro Carchá, Guat.	G2	64
San Pedro de las Colonias, Mex.	E8	62
San Pedro de Macorís, Dom. Rep.	E13	64
San Pedro Mártir, Sierra, mts., Mex.	B2	62
San Pedro Peaks, mts., N.M., U.S.	A3	108
San Pedro Sula, Hond.	G4	64
Sanpete, co., Ut., U.S.	D4	121
Sanpoil, stm., Wa., U.S.	A7	124
San Quintín, Cabo, c., Mex.	B1	62
San Rafael, Arg.	C3	56
San Rafael, Mex.	E9	62
San Rafael, Ca., U.S.	D2	82
San Rafael, N.M., U.S.	B2	108
San Rafael, stm., Ut., U.S.	D5	121
San Rafael Knob, mtn., Ut., U.S.	E5	121
San Rafael Mountains, mts., Ca., U.S.	E4	82
San Ramón, Nic.	G5	64
San Ramon, Ca., U.S.	h9	82
San Remo, Italy	F2	14
San Saba, Tx., U.S.	D3	120
San Saba, co., Tx., U.S.	D3	120
San Salvador, El Sal.	H3	64
San Salvador (Watling Island), i., Bah.	B10	64
San Salvador de Jujuy, Arg.	A3	56
Sansanné-Mango, Togo	F6	42
San Sebastián, Spain	B10	12
Sansepolcro, Italy	F7	14
San Severo, Italy	H10	14
San Simon, stm., Az., U.S.	E6	80
Sanski Most, Bos.	E11	14
Santa Ana, Bol.	G5	54
Santa Ana, Bol.	F5	54
Santa Ana, El Sal.	H3	64
Santa Ana, Mex.	E9	62
Santa Ana, Mex.	B4	62
Santa Ana, Ca., U.S.	F5	82
Santa Ana, stm., Ca., U.S.	n13	82
Santa Ana Indian Reservation, N.M., U.S.	h7	108
Santa Ana Mountains, mts., Ca., U.S.	n13	82
Santa Anna, Tx., U.S.	D3	120
Santa Bárbara, Mex.	D7	62
Santa Barbara, Ca., U.S.	E4	82
Santa Barbara, co., Ca., U.S.	E3	82
Santa Barbara Channel, strt., Ca., U.S.	E3	82
Santa Barbara Island, i., Ca., U.S.	F4	82
Santa Catalina, Gulf of, b., Ca., U.S.	F5	82
Santa Catalina Island, i., Ca., U.S.	F4	82
Santa Catalina Mountains, mts., Az., U.S.	E5	80
Santa Catarina, Ilha de, i., Braz.	B7	56
Santa Clara, Cuba	C8	64
Santa Clara, Ca., U.S.	D2	82
Santa Clara, Ut., U.S.	F2	121
Santa Clara, co., Ca., U.S.	D3	82
Santa Clara, stm., Ca., U.S.	E4	82
Santa Claus, In., U.S.	H4	91
Santa Coloma de Farnés, Spain	D14	12
Santa Comba Dão, Port.	E3	12
Santa Cruz, Arg.	F3	56
Santa Cruz, Bol.	G6	54
Santa Cruz, C.R.	I5	64
Santa Cruz, Phil.	q19	33b
Santa Cruz, Ca., U.S.	D2	82
Santa Cruz, N.M., U.S.	B3	108
Santa Cruz, co., Az., U.S.	F5	80
Santa Cruz, co., Ca., U.S.	D2	82
Santa Cruz, stm., Az., U.S.	E4	80
Santa Cruz del Quiché, Guat.	G2	64
Santa Cruz de Tenerife, Spain	p24	13b
Santa Cruz do Rio Pardo, Braz.	G4	57
Santa Cruz Island, i., Ca., U.S.	F4	82
Santa Elena, Ec.	I2	58
Santa Elena, Punta, c., Ec.	I2	58
Santa Eugenia, Spain	C2	12
Santa Eulalia, Spain	E10	12
Santa Eulalia del Río, Spain	G13	12
Santa Fe, Arg.	C4	56
Santa Fé, Braz.	C3	57
Santa Fé, Cuba	D6	64
Santa Fe, Spain	H8	12
Santa Fe, N.M., U.S.	B4	108
Santa Fe, Tx., U.S.	r14	120
Santa Fe, co., N.M., U.S.	B3	108
Santa Fe, stm., N.M., U.S.	h8	108
Santa Fe Baldy, mtn., N.M., U.S.	B4	108
Santa Fe de Bogotá, Col.	E5	58
Santa Inés, Isla, i., Chile	G2	56
Santa Isabel, Ec.	I3	58
Santa Isabel, i., Sol.Is.	A11	50
Santa Isabel see Malabo, Eq. Gui.	H7	42
Santa Lucia Range, mts., Ca., U.S.	E3	82
Santa Magdalena, Isla, i., Mex.	E3	62
Santa Margarita, Ca., U.S.	E3	82
Santa Margarita, Isla de, i., Mex.	E4	62
Santa Maria, Braz.	B6	56
Santa Maria, Ca., U.S.	E3	82
Santa Maria, stm., Az., U.S.	C2	80
Santa Maria, Cabo de, c., Ang.	D2	44
Santa Maria do Suaçuí, Braz.	E7	57
Santa Maria Mountains, mts., Az., U.S.	C3	80
Santa Marta, Col.	B5	58
Santa Monica, Ca., U.S.	m12	82
Santana do Livramento, Braz.	C5	56
Santander, Col.	F4	58
Santander, Spain	B8	12
Sant' Antioco, Italy	J3	14
Santa Paula, Ca., U.S.	E4	82
Santaquin, Ut., U.S.	D4	121
Sant'Arcangelo, Italy	I11	14
Santarém, Braz.	D8	54
Santarém, Port.	F3	12
Santa Rita, Col.	G6	58
Santa Rita, Hond.	G4	64
Santa Rosa, Arg.	D4	56
Santa Rosa, Arg.	C3	56
Santa Rosa, Ec.	I3	58
Santa Rosa, Ca., U.S.	C2	82
Santa Rosa, N.M., U.S.	C5	108
Santa Rosa, co., Fl., U.S.	u14	86
Santa Rosa de Cabal, Col.	E5	58
Santa Rosa [de Copán], Hond.	G3	64
Santa Rosa Island, i., Ca., U.S.	F3	82
Santa Rosa Island, i., Fl., U.S.	u14	86
Santa Rosa Range, mts., Nv., U.S.	B4	105
Šantarskije Ostrova, is., Russia	F21	24
Santa Teresa Gallura, Italy	H4	14
Santa Vitória do Palmar, Braz.	C6	56
Santa Ynez, Ca., U.S.	E3	82
Santee, Ca., U.S.	o16	82
Santee, stm., S.C., U.S.	E8	117
Santee Dam, S.C., U.S.	E7	117

Name	Map Ref	Page
Santee Indian Reservation, Ne., U.S.	**B8**	104
Santhià, Italy	**D3**	14
Santiago, Chile	**C2**	56
Santiago, Dom. Rep.	**E12**	64
Santiago, Pan.	**J7**	64
Santiago de Compostela, Spain	**C3**	12
Santiago de Cuba, Cuba	**D10**	64
Santiago del Estero, Arg.	**B4**	56
Santiago do Cacém, Port.	**G3**	12
Santiago Ixcuintla, Mex.	**G7**	62
Santiago Papasquiaro, Mex.	**E7**	62
Santiago Peak, mtn., Ca., U.S.	**n13**	82
Santiago Reservoir, res., Ca., U.S.	**n13**	82
Santiaguillo, Laguna de, l., Mex.	**E7**	62
Santiam Pass, Or., U.S.	**C4**	114
Sāntipur, India	**I13**	38
Santisteban del Puerto, Spain	**G8**	12
Santo Amaro, Braz.	**B9**	57
Santo Anastácio, Braz.	**F3**	57
Santo André, Braz.	**G5**	57
Santo Ângelo, Braz.	**B6**	56
Santo Antônio de Jesus, Braz.	**B9**	57
Santo Antônio do Içá, Braz.	**D5**	54
Santo Domingo, Dom. Rep.	**E13**	64
Santo Domingo, Nic.	**H5**	64
Santo Domingo de la Calzada, Spain	**C9**	12
Santo Domingo de los Colorados, Ec.	**H3**	58
Santo Domingo Indian Reservation, N.M., U.S.	**h8**	108
Santo Domingo Pueblo, N.M., U.S.	**B3**	108
Santoña, Spain	**B8**	12
Santos, Braz.	**G5**	57
Santos Dumont, Braz.	**F7**	57
Santo Tomás, Mex.	**B1**	62
Santo Tomé, Arg.	**B5**	56
San Valentín, Monte, mtn., Chile	**F2**	56
San Vicente, El Sal.	**H3**	64
San Vicente, Mex.	**B1**	62
San Vicente de Baracaldo, Spain	**B9**	12
San Vicente de la Barquera, Spain	**B7**	12
San Vicente del Caguán, Col.	**F5**	58
San Vicente Reservoir, res., Ca., U.S.	**o16**	82
San Xavier Indian Reservation, Az., U.S.	**E4**	80
Sanzao Dao, i., China	**M2**	28
Sanza Pombo, Ang.	**C3**	44
São Bento, Braz.	**D10**	54
São Borja, Braz.	**B5**	56
São Caetano do Sul, Braz.	**G5**	57
São Carlos, Braz.	**G5**	57
São Domingos, Braz.	**B5**	57
São Francisco, stm., Braz.	**E11**	54
São Francisco do Sul, Braz.	**B7**	56
São Gabriel, Braz.	**E8**	57
São João da Boa Vista, Braz.	**F5**	57
São João da Madeira, Port.	**E3**	12
São João del Rei, Braz.	**F6**	57
São Joaquim da Barra, Braz.	**F5**	57
São José do Rio Prêto, Braz.	**F4**	57
São José dos Campos, Braz.	**G6**	57
São Leopoldo, Braz.	**B6**	56
São Lourenço, Braz.	**G6**	57
São Lourenço, Pantanal de, sw., Braz.	**G7**	54
São Luís, Braz.	**D10**	54
São Manuel, Braz.	**G4**	57
São Mateus, Braz.	**E9**	57
Saona, Isla, i., Dom. Rep.	**E13**	64
Saône, stm., Fr.	**F11**	10
São Paulo, Braz.	**G5**	57
São Pedro do Ivaí, Braz.	**G3**	57
São Pedro do Sul, Port.	**E3**	12
São Romão, Braz.	**D6**	57
São Roque, Cabo de, c., Braz.	**E11**	54
São Sebastião, Ponta, c., Moz.	**F7**	44
São Sebastião do Paraíso, Braz.	**F5**	57
São Tomé, S. Tom./P.	**A1**	44
São Tomé, i., S. Tom./P.	**A1**	44
São Tomé, Cabo de, c., Braz.	**F8**	57
Sao Tome and Principe, ctry., Afr.	**A1**	44
São Vicente, Braz.	**G5**	57
São Vicente, Cabo de, c., Port.	**H2**	12
Sapé, Braz.	**E11**	54
Sapele, Nig.	**G7**	42
Sapelo Island, i., Ga., U.S.	**E5**	87
Sapitwa, mtn., Mwi.	**E7**	44
Sappa Creek, stm., U.S.	**E5**	104
Sapphire Mountains, mts., Mt., U.S.	**D3**	103
Sappington, Mo., U.S.	**f13**	102
Sapporo, Japan	**p19**	30a
Sapri, Italy	**I10**	14
Sapulpa, Ok., U.S.	**B5**	113
Sara Buri, Thai.	**G6**	34
Sarajevo, Bos.	**F2**	16
Saraland, Al., U.S.	**E1**	78
Saranac, Mi., U.S.	**F5**	99
Saranac, stm., N.Y., U.S.	**F11**	109
Saranac Lake, N.Y., U.S.	**f10**	109
Saranac Lakes, l., N.Y., U.S.	**f10**	109
Sarangani Islands, is., Phil.	**D8**	32
Saransk, Russia	**G7**	22
Sarapul, Russia	**F8**	22
Sarasota, Fl., U.S.	**E4**	86
Sarasota, co., Fl., U.S.	**E4**	86
Sarasota Bay, b., Fl., U.S.	**E4**	86
Saratoga, Ca., U.S.	**k8**	82
Saratoga, Tx., U.S.	**D5**	120
Saratoga, Wy., U.S.	**E6**	127
Saratoga, co., N.Y., U.S.	**B7**	109
Saratoga Lake, l., N.Y., U.S.	**C7**	109
Saratoga National Historical Park, N.Y., U.S.	**B7**	109
Saratoga Springs, N.Y., U.S.	**B7**	109
Saratov, Russia	**G7**	22
Saravane, Laos	**G9**	34
Sarcoxie, Mo., U.S.	**D3**	102
Sardalas, Libya	**C8**	42
Sardārshahr, India	**F6**	38
Sardegna, i., Italy	**I3**	14
Sardinia see Sardegna, i., Italy	**I3**	14
Sardis, Ga., U.S.	**D5**	87
Sardis, Ms., U.S.	**A4**	101
Sardis Lake, res., Ms., U.S.	**A4**	101
Sar-e Pol, Afg.	**B1**	38
Sarepta, La., U.S.	**B2**	95
Sarera, Teluk, b., Indon.	**F10**	32
Sargent, Ga., U.S.	**C2**	87
Sargent, Ne., U.S.	**C6**	104
Sargent, co., N.D., U.S.	**C8**	111
Sargodha, Pak.	**D5**	38
Sarh, Chad	**G9**	42
Sariñena, Spain	**D11**	12
Şarköy, Tur.	**I11**	16
Sarlat-la-Canéda, Fr.	**H8**	10
Sarmi, Indon.	**F10**	32
Sarmiento, Arg.	**F3**	56
Särna, Swe.	**F9**	6
Sarnia, Ont., Can.	**E2**	73
Sarpy, co., Ne., U.S.	**C9**	104
Sarralbe, Fr.	**C14**	10
Sarrebourg, Fr.	**D14**	10
Sarreguemines, Fr.	**C14**	10
Sarria, Spain	**C4**	12
Sartang, stm., Russia	**D20**	24
Sartell, Mn., U.S.	**E4**	100
Sarthe, stm., Fr.	**E6**	10
Sarufutsu, Japan	**n20**	30a
Sarzeau, Fr.	**E4**	10
Sasarām, India	**H11**	38
Sasebo, Japan	**I2**	30
Saskatchewan, prov., Can.	**E3**	75
Saskatchewan, stm., Can.	**F12**	66
Saskylach, Russia	**C16**	24
Sasovo, Russia	**G24**	18
Sassafras, stm., Md., U.S.	**B5**	97
Sassafras Mountain, mtn., U.S.	**A2**	117
Sassandra, C. Iv.	**H4**	42
Sassandra, stm., C. Iv.	**G4**	42
Sassari, Italy	**I3**	14
Sassnitz, Ger.	**A13**	8
Sassuolo, Italy	**E5**	14
Sastown, Lib.	**H4**	42
Satah Mountain, mtn., B.C., Can.	**C5**	69
Sata-misaki, c., Japan	**L3**	30
Satanta, Ks., U.S.	**E3**	93
Sātāra, India	**D2**	37
Satilla, stm., Ga., U.S.	**E5**	87
Satkānia, Bngl.	**I15**	38
Satna, India	**H9**	38
Sātpura Range, mts., India	**B4**	37
Satsuma, Al., U.S.	**E1**	78
Satsunan-shotō, is., Japan	**v29**	31b
Satu Mare, Rom.	**B6**	16
Satura, Russia	**F22**	18
Satus Creek, stm., Wa., U.S.	**C5**	124
Sauceda Mountains, mts., Az., U.S.	**E3**	80
Sauda, Nor.	**G6**	6
Saudi Arabia, ctry., Asia	**D4**	46
Saufley Field Naval Air Station, mil., Fl., U.S.	**u14**	86
Saugatuck, Mi., U.S.	**F4**	99
Saugatuck, stm., Ct., U.S.	**D2**	84
Saugatucket, stm., R.I., U.S.	**F4**	116
Saugatuck Reservoir, res., Ct., U.S.	**D2**	84
Saugerties, N.Y., U.S.	**C7**	109
Saugus, Ma., U.S.	**B5**	98
Saugus, stm., Ma., U.S.	**g11**	98
Sauk, co., Wi., U.S.	**E4**	126
Sauk, stm., Mn., U.S.	**E4**	100
Sauk, stm., Wa., U.S.	**A4**	124
Sauk Centre, Mn., U.S.	**E4**	100
Sauk City, Wi., U.S.	**E4**	126
Sauk Rapids, Mn., U.S.	**E4**	100
Saukville, Wi., U.S.	**E6**	126
Saulgau, Ger.	**G9**	8
Saulnierville, N.S., Can.	**E3**	71
Sault-au-Mouton, Que., Can.	**A8**	74
Sault Sainte Marie, Ont., Can.	**p18**	73
Sault Sainte Marie, Mi., U.S.	**B6**	99
Saumarez Reef, rf., Austl.	**D10**	50
Saumur, Fr.	**E6**	10
Saunders, co., Ne., U.S.	**C9**	104
Saunderstown, R.I., U.S.	**E4**	116
Saurimo, Ang.	**C4**	44
Sausalito, Ca., U.S.	**D2**	82
Sava, Italy	**I12**	14
Sava, stm., Eur.	**E3**	16
Savage, Md., U.S.	**B4**	97
Savage, stm., Md., U.S.	**k12**	97
Savage River Reservoir, res., Md., U.S.	**k12**	97
Savanna, Il., U.S.	**A3**	90
Savanna, Ok., U.S.	**C6**	113
Savannah, Ga., U.S.	**D5**	87
Savannah, Mo., U.S.	**B3**	102
Savannah, Tn., U.S.	**B3**	119
Savannah, stm., U.S.	**F5**	117
Savannah River Plant, sci., S.C., U.S.	**E4**	117
Savannakhet, Laos	**F8**	34
Savanna Lake, l., Md., U.S.	**D6**	97
Savanna-la-Mar, Jam.	**E8**	64
Savaştepe, Tur.	**J11**	16
Save (Sabi), stm., Afr.	**F6**	44
Savenay, Fr.	**E5**	10
Saverdun, Fr.	**I8**	10
Saverne, Fr.	**D14**	10
Savigliano, Italy	**E2**	14
Saville Dam, Ct., U.S.	**B4**	84
Savona, Italy	**E3**	14
Savonlinna, Fin.	**F17**	6
Savonranta, Fin.	**E17**	6
Savoonga, Ak., U.S.	**C5**	79
Savoy, Il., U.S.	**C5**	90
Savu Sea see Sawu, Laut, Indon.	**G7**	32
Sawai Mādhopur, India	**G7**	38
Sawākin, Sudan	**E13**	42
Sawang, Indon.	**N7**	34
Sawatch Range, mts., Co., U.S.	**B4**	83
Sawdā', Qurnat as-, mtn., Leb.	**B5**	40
Sawel Mountain, mtn., N. Ire., U.K.	**G5**	7
Sawhāj, Egypt	**C12**	42
Sawknah, Libya	**C9**	42
Sawnee Mountain, mtn., Ga., U.S.	**B2**	87
Sawtooth Mountains, mts., Id., U.S.	**F4**	89
Sawtooth National Recreation Area, Id., U.S.	**E3**	89
Sawu, Laut (Savu Sea), Indon.	**G7**	32
Sawu, Pulau, i., Indon.	**H7**	32
Şawwān, Arḍ aṣ-, pl., Jord.	**D5**	40
Sawyer, co., Wi., U.S.	**C2**	126
Sawyerville, Que., Can.	**D6**	74
Saxmundham, Eng., U.K.	**I14**	7
Saxonburg, Pa., U.S.	**E2**	115
Saxtons, stm., Vt., U.S.	**E3**	122
Saxtons River, Vt., U.S.	**E3**	122
Sayabouri, Laos	**E6**	34
Sayan Mountains (Sajany), mts., Asia	**G12**	24
Sayaxché, Guat.	**F2**	64
Saybrook, Il., U.S.	**C5**	90
Saybrook Manor, Ct., U.S.	**D6**	84
Şaydā (Sidon), Leb.	**C4**	40
Saydel, Ia., U.S.	**e8**	92
Sayḥūt, Yemen	**E5**	46
Saylesville, R.I., U.S.	**B4**	116
Saylorsburg, Pa., U.S.	**E11**	115
Saylorville, Ia., U.S.	**e8**	92
Saylorville Lake, res., Ia., U.S.	**C4**	92
Sayre, Al., U.S.	**B3**	78
Sayre, Ok., U.S.	**B2**	113
Sayre, Pa., U.S.	**C8**	115
Sayreville, N.J., U.S.	**C4**	107
Sayula, Mex.	**H8**	62
Say'ūn, Yemen	**E4**	46
Sayville, N.Y., U.S.	**n15**	109
Scafell Pikes, mtn., Eng., U.K.	**G9**	7
Scalp Level, Pa., U.S.	**F4**	115
Scanlon, Mn., U.S.	**D6**	100
Scapegoat Mountain, mtn., Mt., U.S.	**C3**	103
Ščapino, Russia	**F25**	24
Scappoose, Or., U.S.	**B4**	114
Scarborough, Ont., Can.	**m15**	73
Scarborough, Trin.	**I17**	64
Scarborough, Me., U.S.	**E2**	96
Scarbro, W.V., U.S.	**n13**	125
Scarsdale, N.Y., U.S.	**h13**	109
Ščelkovo, Russia	**F21**	18
Ščerbakovo, Russia	**D26**	24
Schaefferstown, Pa., U.S.	**F9**	115
Schaffhausen, Switz.	**E15**	10
Schaller, Ia., U.S.	**B2**	92
Schaumburg, Il., U.S.	**h8**	90
Schell Creek Range, mts., Nv., U.S.	**D7**	105
Schenectady, N.Y., U.S.	**C7**	109
Schenectady, co., N.Y., U.S.	**C6**	109
Schererville, In., U.S.	**B3**	91
Schertz, Tx., U.S.	**h7**	120
Schiller Park, Il., U.S.	**k9**	90
Schio, Italy	**D6**	14
Schladming, Aus.	**H13**	8
Schleicher, co., Tx., U.S.	**D2**	120
Schleiden, Ger.	**E6**	8
Schleswig, Ger.	**A9**	8
Schleswig, Ia., U.S.	**B2**	92
Schley, co., Ga., U.S.	**D2**	87
Schneverdingen, Ger.	**B9**	8
Schofield, Wi., U.S.	**D4**	126
Schofield Barracks, mil., Hi., U.S.	**g9**	88
Schoharie, co., N.Y., U.S.	**C6**	109
Schoharie Creek, stm., N.Y., U.S.	**C6**	109
Schönebeck, Ger.	**B13**	8
Schongau, Ger.	**H10**	8
Schoodic Lake, l., Me., U.S.	**C4**	96
Schoolcraft, Mi., U.S.	**F5**	99
Schoolcraft, co., Mi., U.S.	**B4**	99
Schramberg, Ger.	**G8**	8
Schrobenhausen, Ger.	**G11**	8
Schroon Lake, l., N.Y., U.S.	**B7**	109
Schulenburg, Tx., U.S.	**E4**	120
Schulter, Ok., U.S.	**B6**	113
Schurz, Nv., U.S.	**E3**	105
Schuyler, Ne., U.S.	**C8**	104
Schuyler, co., Il., U.S.	**C3**	90
Schuyler, co., Mo., U.S.	**A5**	102
Schuyler, co., N.Y., U.S.	**C4**	109
Schuylkill, co., Pa., U.S.	**E9**	115
Schuylkill, stm., Pa., U.S.	**F10**	115
Schuylkill Haven, Pa., U.S.	**E9**	115
Schwabach, Ger.	**F11**	8
Schwaben, hist. reg., Ger.	**G10**	8
Schwäbische Alb, mts., Ger.	**G9**	8
Schwäbisch Gmünd, Ger.	**G9**	8
Schwäbisch Hall, Ger.	**F9**	8
Schwandorf in Bayern, Ger.	**F12**	8
Schwaner, Pegunungan, mts., Indon.	**F5**	32
Schwarzwald, mts., Ger.	**G8**	8
Schwaz, Aus.	**H11**	8
Schwechat, Aus.	**G16**	8
Schwedt, Ger.	**B14**	8
Schweinfurt, Ger.	**E10**	8
Schwerin, Ger.	**B11**	8
Schwyz, Switz.	**E15**	10
Sciacca, Italy	**L8**	14
Scicli, Italy	**M9**	14
Science Hill, Ky., U.S.	**C5**	94
Scilly, Isles of, is., Eng., U.K.	**L6**	7
Scio, Or., U.S.	**C4**	114
Scioto, co., Oh., U.S.	**D3**	112
Scioto, stm., Oh., U.S.	**B2**	112
Scituate, Ma., U.S.	**B6**	98
Scituate Reservoir, res., R.I., U.S.	**C3**	116
Scobey, Mt., U.S.	**B11**	103
Scofield Reservoir, res., Ut., U.S.	**D4**	121
Ščokino, Russia	**G20**	18
Scotch Plains, N.J., U.S.	**B4**	107
Scotia, Ca., U.S.	**B1**	82
Scotia, N.Y., U.S.	**C7**	109
Scotland, Ont., Can.	**D4**	73
Scotland, S.D., U.S.	**D8**	118
Scotland, co., Mo., U.S.	**A5**	102
Scotland, co., N.C., U.S.	**C3**	110
Scotland, ter., U.K.	**D8**	7
Scotland Neck, N.C., U.S.	**A5**	110
Scotlandville, La., U.S.	**D4**	95
Scotrun, Pa., U.S.	**D11**	115
Scotstown, Que., Can.	**D6**	74
Scott, La., U.S.	**D3**	95
Scott, co., Ar., U.S.	**C1**	81
Scott, co., Il., U.S.	**D3**	90
Scott, co., In., U.S.	**G6**	91
Scott, co., Ia., U.S.	**C7**	92
Scott, co., Ks., U.S.	**D3**	93
Scott, co., Ky., U.S.	**B5**	94
Scott, co., Mn., U.S.	**F5**	100
Scott, co., Ms., U.S.	**C4**	101
Scott, co., Mo., U.S.	**D8**	102
Scott, co., Tn., U.S.	**C9**	119
Scott, co., Va., U.S.	**f9**	123
Scott, Cape, c., B.C., Can.	**D3**	69
Scott, Mount, mtn., Or., U.S.	**E4**	114
Scott Air Force Base, mil., Il., U.S.	**E4**	90
Scott City, Ks., U.S.	**D3**	93
Scott City, Mo., U.S.	**D8**	102
Scottdale, Ga., U.S.	**h8**	87
Scottdale, Pa., U.S.	**F2**	115
Scott Islands, is., B.C., Can.	**F7**	66
Scott Mountain, mtn., Id., U.S.	**E3**	89
Scott Peak, mtn., Id., U.S.	**E6**	89
Scott Reef, rf., Austl.	**B4**	50
Scott Reservoir, res., N.C., U.S.	**A1**	110
Scottsbluff, Ne., U.S.	**C2**	104
Scotts Bluff, co., Ne., U.S.	**C2**	104
Scotts Bluff National Monument, Ne., U.S.	**C2**	104
Scottsboro, Al., U.S.	**A3**	78
Scottsburg, In., U.S.	**G6**	91
Scottsdale, Austl.	**H9**	50
Scottsdale, Az., U.S.	**D4**	80
Scottsville, Ky., U.S.	**D3**	94
Scottsville, N.Y., U.S.	**B3**	109
Scottville, Mi., U.S.	**E4**	99
Scourie, Scot., U.K.	**C7**	7
Scraggly Lake, l., Me., U.S.	**B4**	96
Scranton, Ks., U.S.	**D8**	93
Scranton, Pa., U.S.	**D10**	115
Scranton, S.C., U.S.	**D8**	117
Screven, Ga., U.S.	**E4**	87
Screven, co., Ga., U.S.	**D5**	87
Scribner, Ne., U.S.	**C9**	104
Scugog, Lake, l., Ont., Can.	**C6**	73
Scurry, co., Tx., U.S.	**C2**	120
Scutari, Lake, l., Eur.	**G3**	16
Seaboard, N.C., U.S.	**A5**	110
Seabreeze, De., U.S.	**F5**	85
Seabrook, N.H., U.S.	**E5**	106
Seabrook, Tx., U.S.	**r14**	120
Seabrook Island, i., S.C., U.S.	**F7**	117
Seadrift, Tx., U.S.	**E4**	120
Seaford, De., U.S.	**F3**	85
Seaford, Va., U.S.	**h15**	123
Seaforth, Ont., Can.	**D3**	73
Seagoville, Tx., U.S.	**n10**	120
Seagraves, Tx., U.S.	**C1**	120
Seaham, Eng., U.K.	**G11**	7
Sea Isle City, N.J., U.S.	**E3**	107
Seal, stm., Man., Can.	**E13**	66
Seal Cove, Newf., Can.	**D3**	72
Seal Point, c., P.E.I., Can.	**C5**	71
Seal Rock, Or., U.S.	**C2**	114
Sealy, Tx., U.S.	**E4**	120
Seaman, Oh., U.S.	**D2**	112
Seaman Range, mts., Nv., U.S.	**F6**	105
Searchlight, Nv., U.S.	**H7**	105
Searcy, Ar., U.S.	**B4**	81
Searcy, co., Ar., U.S.	**B3**	81
Searles Lake, l., Ca., U.S.	**E5**	82
Searsport, Me., U.S.	**D4**	96
Seaside, Or., U.S.	**B3**	114
Seat Pleasant, Md., U.S.	**C4**	97
Seattle, Wa., U.S.	**B3**	124
Seattle-Tacoma International Airport, Wa., U.S.	**f11**	124
Seaview, Wa., U.S.	**C1**	124
Sebago Lake, Me., U.S.	**E2**	96
Šebalino, Russia	**G11**	24
Sebastian, Fl., U.S.	**E6**	86
Sebastian, co., Ar., U.S.	**B1**	81
Sebastian, Cape, c., Or., U.S.	**E2**	114
Sebastian Inlet, b., Fl., U.S.	**E6**	86
Sebastián Vizcaíno, Bahía, b., Mex.	**C2**	62
Sebasticook Lake, l., Me., U.S.	**D3**	96
Sebec Lake, l., Me., U.S.	**C3**	96
Sebeka, Mn., U.S.	**D3**	100
Sebewaing, Mi., U.S.	**E7**	99
Seboeis, stm., Me., U.S.	**B4**	96
Seboeis Lake, l., Me., U.S.	**C4**	96
Seboomook Lake, l., Me., U.S.	**C3**	96
Sebree, Ky., U.S.	**C2**	94
Sebring, Fl., U.S.	**E5**	86
Sebring, Oh., U.S.	**B4**	112
Secaucus, N.J., U.S.	**h8**	107
Sechelt, B.C., Can.	**E6**	69
Second Lake, l., N.H., U.S.	**f7**	106
Second Mesa, Az., U.S.	**B5**	80
Secret Lake, l., R.I., U.S.	**E4**	116
Section, Al., U.S.	**A4**	78
Security, Co., U.S.	**C6**	83
Sedalia, Mo., U.S.	**C4**	102
Sedan, Fr.	**C11**	10
Sedan, Ks., U.S.	**E7**	93
Sedano, Spain	**C8**	12
Sedgewick, Alta., Can.	**C5**	68
Sedgewick, Mount, mtn., N.M., U.S.	**B1**	108
Sedgwick, Ks., U.S.	**E6**	93
Sedgwick, co., Co., U.S.	**A8**	83
Sedgwick, co., Ks., U.S.	**E6**	93
Sedley, Va., U.S.	**D6**	123
Sedona, Az., U.S.	**C4**	80
Sedro Woolley, Wa., U.S.	**A3**	124
Seeheim, Nmb.	**G3**	44
Seekonk, Ma., U.S.	**C5**	98
Seekonk, stm., R.I., U.S.	**C4**	116
Seeley, Ca., U.S.	**F6**	82
Seeley Lake, Mt., U.S.	**C3**	103
Seelyville, In., U.S.	**F3**	91
Sées, Fr.	**D7**	10
Segamat, Malay.	**M7**	34
Ségou, Mali	**F4**	42
Segovia, Col.	**D5**	58
Segovia, Spain	**E7**	12
Segré, Fr.	**E6**	10
Seguam Island, i., Ak., U.S.	**E5**	79
Seguam Pass, strt., Ak., U.S.	**E5**	79
Séguédine, Niger	**D8**	42
Seguin, Tx., U.S.	**E4**	120
Sehore, India	**I7**	38
Seia, Port.	**E4**	12
Seiling, Ok., U.S.	**A3**	113
Seinäjoki, Fin.	**E14**	6
Seine, stm., Fr.	**C7**	10
Seki, Tur.	**M13**	16
Sekiu, Wa., U.S.	**A1**	124
Sekondi-Takoradi, Ghana	**H5**	42
Šelagskij, Mys, c., Russia	**C28**	24
Selah, Wa., U.S.	**C5**	124
Selaru, Pulau, i., Indon.	**G9**	32
Selatan, Tanjung, c., Indon.	**F5**	32
Selawik, Ak., U.S.	**B7**	79
Selawik Lake, l., Ak., U.S.	**B7**	79
Selayar, Pulau, i., Indon.	**G7**	32
Selb, Ger.	**E12**	8
Selby, S.D., U.S.	**B5**	118
Selbyville, De., U.S.	**G5**	85
Selçuk, Tur.	**L11**	16
Seldovia, Ak., U.S.	**D9**	79
Selemdža, stm., Russia	**G20**	24
Selenn'ach, stm., Russia	**D21**	24
Sélestat, Fr.	**D14**	10
Sélibaby, Maur.	**E3**	42
Šelichova, Zaliv, b., Russia	**E25**	24
Seligman, Az., U.S.	**B3**	80
Selinsgrove, Pa., U.S.	**E8**	115
Selkirk, Man., Can.	**D3**	70
Selkirk, Scot., U.K.	**F10**	7
Selkirk Mountains, mts., N.A.	**F9**	66
Sellersburg, In., U.S.	**H6**	91
Sellersville, Pa., U.S.	**F11**	115
Selles-sur-Cher, Fr.	**E8**	10
Sells, Az., U.S.	**F4**	80
Selma, Al., U.S.	**C2**	78
Selma, Ca., U.S.	**D4**	82
Selma, In., U.S.	**D7**	91
Selma, N.C., U.S.	**B4**	110
Selmer, Tn., U.S.	**B3**	119
Selva, Arg.	**B4**	56
Selvas, for., Braz.	**E6**	54
Selway, stm., Id., U.S.	**C3**	89
Selwyn Mountains, mts., Can.	**D6**	66
Semara, W. Sah.	**C3**	42
Semarang, Indon.	**m15**	32
Semeru, Gunung, vol., Indon.	**n16**	33a
Seminoe Mountains, mts., Wy., U.S.	**D6**	127
Seminoe Reservoir, res., Wy., U.S.	**D6**	127
Seminole, Ok., U.S.	**B5**	113
Seminole, Tx., U.S.	**C1**	120
Seminole, co., Fl., U.S.	**D5**	86
Seminole, co., Ga., U.S.	**F2**	87
Seminole, co., Ok., U.S.	**B5**	113
Seminole, Lake, res., U.S.	**F2**	87
Semipalatinsk, Kaz.	**G10**	24
Semisopochnoi Island, i., Ak., U.S.	**E3**	79
Semmes, Al., U.S.	**E1**	78
Šemonaicha, Kaz.	**G10**	24
Semur-en-Auxois, Fr.	**E11**	10
Sên, stm., Camb.	**H8**	34
Sena, Moz.	**E6**	44
Senachwine Lake, l., Il., U.S.	**B4**	90
Senador Pompeu, Braz.	**E11**	54
Sena Madureira, Braz.	**E5**	54
Senanga, Zam.	**E4**	44
Senath, Mo., U.S.	**E7**	102
Senatobia, Ms., U.S.	**A4**	101
Sendai, Japan	**K3**	30
Sendai, Japan	**D13**	30
Seneca, Il., U.S.	**B5**	90
Seneca, Ks., U.S.	**C7**	93
Seneca, Mo., U.S.	**E3**	102
Seneca, Pa., U.S.	**D2**	115
Seneca, S.C., U.S.	**B2**	117
Seneca, co., N.Y., U.S.	**C4**	109
Seneca, co., Oh., U.S.	**A2**	112
Seneca Falls, N.Y., U.S.	**C4**	109
Seneca Lake, l., N.Y., U.S.	**C4**	109
Senecaville Lake, res., Oh., U.S.	**C4**	112
Senegal (Sénégal), ctry., Afr.	**F3**	42
Sénégal, stm., Afr.	**E3**	42
Senekal, S. Afr.	**G5**	44
Senftenberg, Ger.	**D13**	8
Senigallia, Italy	**F8**	14
Senise, Italy	**I11**	14
Senmonorom, Camb.	**H9**	34
Senneterre, Que., Can.	**k11**	74
Sennori, Italy	**I3**	14
Senoia, Ga., U.S.	**C2**	87
Sens, Fr.	**D10**	10
Senta, Yugo.	**D4**	16
Sentinel, Ok., U.S.	**B2**	113
Seo de Urgel, Spain	**C13**	12
Seoni, India	**I8**	38
Seoul see Sŏul, S. Kor.	**D12**	26
Sept-Îles (Seven Islands), Que., Can.	**h13**	74
Sepulga, stm., Al., U.S.	**D3**	78
Sepúlveda, Spain	**D8**	12
Sequatchie, co., Tn., U.S.	**D8**	119
Sequatchie, stm., Tn., U.S.	**D8**	119
Sequim, Wa., U.S.	**A2**	124
Sequoia National Park, Ca., U.S.	**D4**	82
Sequoyah, co., Ok., U.S.	**B7**	113
Seraing, Bel.	**E5**	8
Seram, i., Indon.	**F8**	32
Seram, Laut (Ceram Sea), Indon.	**F8**	32
Serang, Indon.	**m13**	33a
Seremban, Malay.	**M6**	34
Serengeti Plain, pl., Tan.	**B6**	44
Serenje, Zam.	**D6**	44
Sergeant Bluff, Ia., U.S.	**B1**	92

Name	Map Ref	Page
Sergeja Kirova, Ostrova, is., Russia	B11	24
Sergijev Podad, Russia	E21	18
Serowe, Bots.	F5	44
Serpa, Port.	H4	12
Serpuchov, Russia	G20	18
Sérrai, Grc.	H7	16
Serra San Bruno, Italy	K11	14
Serra Talhada, Braz.	E11	54
Serres, Fr.	H12	10
Serrezuela, Arg.	C3	56
Serri, Italy	J4	14
Serrinha, Braz.	F11	54
Sertã, Port.	F3	12
Sesfontein, Nmb.	E2	44
Sesheke, Zam.	E4	44
Sessa Aurunca, Italy	H8	14
Sesser, Il., U.S.	E4	90
Sestri Levante, Italy	E4	14
Sète, Fr.	I10	10
Sete Lagoas, Braz.	E6	57
Seth, W.V., U.S.	C3	125
Sétif, Alg.	A7	42
Seto, Japan	G10	30
Seto-naikai, Japan	H6	30
Setúbal, Port.	G3	12
Seul, Lac, l., Ont., Can.	o16	73
Seul Choix Point, c., Mi., U.S.	C5	99
Sevan, ozero, l., Arm.	I7	22
Sevastopol', Ukr.	I4	22
Seven Devils Lake, res., Ar., U.S.	D4	81
Seven Devils Mountains, mts., Id., U.S.	D2	89
Seven Hills, Oh., U.S.	h9	112
Seven Mile Beach, N.J., U.S.	E3	107
Sévérac-le-Château, Fr.	H10	10
Severn, Md., U.S.	B4	97
Severn, stm., Ont., Can.	n17	73
Severn, stm., Eng., U.K.	J10	7
Severnaja Dvina, stm., Russia	E6	22
Severnaja Zemľa, is., Russia	B13	24
Severna Park, Md., U.S.	B4	97
Severn River, b., Md., U.S.	B4	97
Severodvinsk, Russia	E5	22
Severo-Kuril'sk, Russia	G25	24
Severo-Sibirskaja Nizmennost', pl., Russia	C13	24
Severo-Zadonsk, Russia	G21	18
Sevettijärvi, Fin.	B17	6
Sevier, co., Ar., U.S.	D1	81
Sevier, co., Tn., U.S.	D10	119
Sevier, co., Ut., U.S.	E4	121
Sevier, stm., Ut., U.S.	D3	121
Sevier Bridge Reservoir, res., Ut., U.S.	D4	121
Sevier Lake, l., Ut., U.S.	E2	121
Sevierville, Tn., U.S.	D10	119
Sevilla, Col.	E5	58
Sevilla, Spain	H6	12
Seville, Oh., U.S.	A4	112
Seville see Sevilla, Spain	H6	12
Sewanee, Tn., U.S.	D8	119
Seward, Ak., U.S.	C10	79
Seward, Ne., U.S.	D8	104
Seward, co., Ks., U.S.	E3	93
Seward, co., Ne., U.S.	D8	104
Seward Peninsula, pen., Ak., U.S.	B7	79
Sewickley, Pa., U.S.	E1	115
Sexsmith, Alta., Can.	B1	68
Seychelles, ctry., Afr.	B11	44
Seydisfjördur, Ice.	B5	4
Seymour, Ct., U.S.	D3	84
Seymour, In., U.S.	G6	91
Seymour, Ia., U.S.	D4	92
Seymour, Mo., U.S.	D5	102
Seymour, Tx., U.S.	C3	120
Seymour, Wi., U.S.	D5	126
Seymour Inlet, b., B.C., Can.	D4	69
Seymour Johnson Air Force Base, mil., N.C., U.S.	B5	110
Seymour Lake, l., Vt., U.S.	B4	122
Seymourville, La., U.S.	h9	95
Seyne, Fr.	H13	10
Seyssel, Fr.	G12	10
Sézanne, Fr.	D10	10
Sezze, Italy	H8	14
Sfax, Tun.	B8	42
's-Gravenhage (The Hague), Neth.	C4	8
Shabbona, Il., U.S.	B5	90
Shache, China	A7	38
Shackelford, co., Tx., U.S.	C3	120
Shackleton Ice Shelf, Ant.	C22	47
Shaddādī, Syria	A7	40
Shadehill Dam, S.D., U.S.	B3	118
Shadehill Reservoir, res., S.D., U.S.	B3	118
Shadow Mountain National Recreation Area, Co., U.S.	A4	83
Shady Cove, Or., U.S.	E4	114
Shady Side, Md., U.S.	C4	97
Shadyside, Oh., U.S.	C5	112
Shady Spring, W.V., U.S.	D3	125
Shafer, Lake, l., In., U.S.	C4	91
Shafer Butte, mtn., Id., U.S.	F2	89
Shafter, Ca., U.S.	E4	82
Shaftsbury, Vt., U.S.	E2	122
Shāhdādkot, Pak.	G2	38
Shahdol, India	I9	38
Shāhjahānpur, India	G8	38
Shāh Jūy, Afg.	D2	38
Shahrak, Afg.	C1	38
Shājāpur, India	I7	38
Shakawe, Bots.	E4	44
Shaker Heights, Oh., U.S.	A4	112
Shakhty see Šachty, Russia	H6	22
Shaki, Nig.	G6	42
Shakopee, Mn., U.S.	F5	100
Shaler Mountains, mts., N.W. Ter., Can.	B10	66
Shallotte, N.C., U.S.	D4	110
Shallotte Inlet, b., N.C., U.S.	D4	110
Shallowater, Tx., U.S.	C2	120
Shām, Bādiyat ash-, des., Asia	C6	40
Shām, Jabal ash-, mtn., Oman	D6	46
Shamokin, Pa., U.S.	E8	115
Shamokin Dam, Pa., U.S.	E8	115
Shamrock, Tx., U.S.	B2	120
Shandī, Sudan	E12	42
Shandong, prov., China	D10	26
Shandong Bandao, pen., China	D11	26
Shanghai, China	D10	28
Shanghai Shih, China	E11	26
Shangqiu, China	A4	28
Shangrao, China	G6	28
Shangshui, China	B3	28
Shangzhi, China	B12	26
Shannock, R.I., U.S.	F2	116
Shannon, Ga., U.S.	B1	87
Shannon, Il., U.S.	A4	90
Shannon, Ms., U.S.	A5	101
Shannon, co., Mo., U.S.	D6	102
Shannon, co., S.D., U.S.	D3	118
Shannon, stm., Ire.	I3	7
Shannon, Lake, l., Wa., U.S.	A4	124
Shannontown, S.C., U.S.	D7	117
Shantou (Swatow), China	L5	28
Shantung Peninsula see Shandong Bandao, pen., China	D11	26
Shănxī, prov., China	D8	26
Shānxī, prov., China	D9	26
Shanyin, China	D9	26
Shaoguan, China	K2	28
Shaowu, China	H6	28
Shaoxing, China	E9	28
Shaoyang, China	F9	26
Shark Bay, b., Austl.	E2	50
Sharkey, co., Ms., U.S.	C3	101
Shark Point, c., Fl., U.S.	H5	86
Sharktooth Mountain, mtn., B.C., Can.	E7	66
Sharon, Ct., U.S.	B2	84
Sharon, Ma., U.S.	B5	98
Sharon, Pa., U.S.	D1	115
Sharon, Tn., U.S.	A3	119
Sharon, Wi., U.S.	F5	126
Sharon Hill, Pa., U.S.	p20	115
Sharon Park, Oh., U.S.	n12	112
Sharon Springs, Ks., U.S.	D2	93
Sharonville, Oh., U.S.	n13	112
Sharp, co., Ar., U.S.	A4	81
Sharpe, Lake, res., S.D., U.S.	C6	118
Sharpes, Fl., U.S.	D6	86
Sharpley, De., U.S.	h7	85
Sharpsburg, Md., U.S.	B2	97
Sharpsburg, N.C., U.S.	B5	110
Sharpsburg, Pa., U.S.	k14	115
Sharpsville, In., U.S.	D5	91
Sharpsville, Pa., U.S.	D1	115
Sharptown, Md., U.S.	C6	97
Sharqīyah, Aş-Şaḥrā' ash- (Arabian Desert), des., Egypt	C12	42
Shashi, China	E9	26
Shashi, stm., Afr.	F5	44
Shasta, co., Ca., U.S.	B3	82
Shasta, Mount, vol., Ca., U.S.	B2	82
Shasta Lake, res., Ca., U.S.	B2	82
Shattuck, Ok., U.S.	A2	113
Shaw, Ms., U.S.	B3	101
Shaw Air Force Base, mil., S.C., U.S.	D7	117
Shawano, Wi., U.S.	D5	126
Shawano, co., Wi., U.S.	D5	126
Shawano Lake, l., Wi., U.S.	D5	126
Shawinigan, Que., Can.	C5	74
Shawinigan-Sud, Que., Can.	C5	74
Shawnee, Ks., U.S.	k16	93
Shawnee, Ok., U.S.	B5	113
Shawnee, co., Ks., U.S.	D8	93
Shawneetown, Il., U.S.	F5	90
Shawsheen, stm., Ma., U.S.	f11	98
Shaybārā, i., Sau. Ar.	C2	46
Shaykh, Jabal ash-, mtn., Asia	C4	40
Shebele (Shebelle), stm., Afr.	G3	46
Sheberghān, Afg.	B1	38
Sheboygan, Wi., U.S.	E6	126
Sheboygan, co., Wi., U.S.	E6	126
Sheboygan, stm., Wi., U.S.	k10	126
Sheboygan Falls, Wi., U.S.	E6	126
Shediac, N.B., Can.	C5	71
Sheenjek, stm., Ak., U.S.	B11	79
Sheep Mountain, mtn., Az., U.S.	E1	80
Sheep Mountain, mtn., Wy., U.S.	B5	127
Sheep Mountain, mtn., Wy., U.S.	C2	127
Sheep Peak, mtn., Nv., U.S.	G6	105
Sheep Range, mts., Nv., U.S.	G6	105
Sheet Harbour, N.S., Can.	E7	71
Sheffield, Eng., U.K.	H11	7
Sheffield, Al., U.S.	A2	78
Sheffield, Il., U.S.	B4	90
Sheffield, Ia., U.S.	B4	92
Sheffield, Pa., U.S.	C3	115
Sheffield Lake, Oh., U.S.	A3	112
Sheila, N.B., Can.	B5	71
Shekhābād, Afg.	C3	38
Shekhūpura, Pak.	E5	38
Shelagyote Peak, mtn., B.C., Can.	B4	69
Shelbiana, Ky., U.S.	C7	94
Shelbina, Mo., U.S.	B5	102
Shelburn, In., U.S.	F3	91
Shelburne, Ont., Can.	C4	73
Shelburne Falls, Ma., U.S.	A2	98
Shelburne Pond, l., Vt., U.S.	C2	122
Shelby, Al., U.S.	B3	78
Shelby, In., U.S.	B3	91
Shelby, Ia., U.S.	C2	92
Shelby, Mi., U.S.	E4	99
Shelby, Ms., U.S.	B3	101
Shelby, Mt., U.S.	B5	103
Shelby, Ne., U.S.	C8	104
Shelby, N.C., U.S.	B1	110
Shelby, Oh., U.S.	B3	112
Shelby, co., Al., U.S.	B3	78
Shelby, co., Il., U.S.	D5	90
Shelby, co., In., U.S.	E6	91
Shelby, co., Ia., U.S.	C2	92
Shelby, co., Ky., U.S.	B4	94
Shelby, co., Mo., U.S.	B5	102
Shelby, co., Oh., U.S.	B1	112
Shelby, co., Tn., U.S.	B2	119
Shelby, co., Tx., U.S.	D5	120
Shelbyville, Il., U.S.	D5	90
Shelbyville, In., U.S.	F6	91
Shelbyville, Ky., U.S.	B4	94
Shelbyville, Tn., U.S.	B5	119
Shelbyville, Lake, res., Il., U.S.	D5	90
Sheldon, Il., U.S.	C6	90
Sheldon, Ia., U.S.	A2	92
Sheldon, Tx., U.S.	r14	120
Shelikof Strait, strt., Ak., U.S.	D9	79
Shell Creek, stm., U.S.	A2	83
Shell Creek, stm., Wy., U.S.	B5	127
Shelley, Id., U.S.	F6	89
Shell Lake, Wi., U.S.	C2	126
Shell Lake, l., Mn., U.S.	D3	100
Shell Lake, l., Wi., U.S.	C2	126
Shellman, Ga., U.S.	E2	87
Shell Rock, Ia., U.S.	B5	92
Shell Rock, stm., Ia., U.S.	B5	92
Shellsburg, Ia., U.S.	B6	92
Shelly Mountain, mtn., Id., U.S.	F5	89
Shelter Island, N.Y., U.S.	m16	109
Shelton, Ct., U.S.	D3	84
Shelton, Ne., U.S.	D7	104
Shelton, Wa., U.S.	B2	124
Shemya Air Force Base, mil., Ak., U.S.	E2	79
Shenandoah, Ia., U.S.	D2	92
Shenandoah, Pa., U.S.	E9	115
Shenandoah, Va., U.S.	B4	123
Shenandoah, co., Va., U.S.	B4	123
Shenandoah, stm., U.S.	A5	123
Shenandoah, North Fork, stm., Va., U.S.	B4	123
Shenandoah, South Fork, stm., Va., U.S.	B4	123
Shenandoah Mountain, mtn., U.S.	B3	123
Shenandoah National Park, Va., U.S.	B4	123
Shenango River Lake, res., U.S.	D1	115
Shengfang, China	D10	26
Shengze, China	E9	28
Shenipsit Lake, l., Ct., U.S.	B6	84
Shenyang (Mukden), China	C11	26
Shenzha, China	E13	38
Shepaug, stm., Ct., U.S.	C2	84
Shepaug Dam, Ct., U.S.	D2	84
Shepaug Reservoir, res., Ct., U.S.	C2	84
Shepherd, Mi., U.S.	E6	99
Shepherd, Tx., U.S.	D5	120
Shepherdstown, W.V., U.S.	B7	125
Shepherdsville, Ky., U.S.	C4	94
Sheppard Air Force Base, mil., Tx., U.S.	C3	120
Shepparton, Austl.	G9	50
Sherborn, Ma., U.S.	h10	98
Sherbro Island, i., S.L.	G3	42
Sherbrooke, Que., Can.	D6	74
Sherburn, Mn., U.S.	G4	100
Sherburne, co., Mn., U.S.	E5	100
Sheridan, Ar., U.S.	C3	81
Sheridan, Il., U.S.	B5	90
Sheridan, In., U.S.	D5	91
Sheridan, Mi., U.S.	E5	99
Sheridan, Mt., U.S.	E4	103
Sheridan, Or., U.S.	B3	114
Sheridan, Wy., U.S.	B6	127
Sheridan, co., Ks., U.S.	C3	93
Sheridan, co., Mt., U.S.	B12	103
Sheridan, co., Ne., U.S.	B3	104
Sheridan, co., N.D., U.S.	B5	111
Sheridan, co., Wy., U.S.	B5	127
Sheridan, Mount, mtn., Wy., U.S.	B2	127
Sheringham Cromer, Eng., U.K.	I14	7
Sherman, Tx., U.S.	C4	120
Sherman, co., Ks., U.S.	C2	93
Sherman, co., Ne., U.S.	C6	104
Sherman, co., Or., U.S.	B6	114
Sherman, co., Tx., U.S.	A2	120
Sherman Reservoir, res., Ne., U.S.	C7	104
Sherrelwood, Co., U.S.	*B6	83
Sherrill, N.Y., U.S.	B5	109
's-Hertogenbosch, Neth.	D5	8
Sherwood, P.E.I., Can.	C6	71
Sherwood, Ar., U.S.	C3	81
Sherwood, Or., U.S.	h12	114
Sherwood, Wi., U.S.	h9	126
Sherwood Manor, Ct., U.S.	A5	84
Sherwood Park, De., U.S.	i7	85
Shetek, Lake, l., Mn., U.S.	G3	100
Shetland Islands, is., Scot., U.K.	A11	7
Shetucket, stm., Ct., U.S.	C7	84
Sheyenne, stm., N.D., U.S.	C8	111
Sheyenne Lake, res., N.D., U.S.	B5	111
Shiawassee, co., Mi., U.S.	F6	99
Shibata, Japan	E12	30
Shibetsu, Japan	p23	30a
Shibukawa, Japan	F11	30
Shickshinny, Pa., U.S.	D9	115
Shijiazhuang, China	D9	26
Shijushan, China	D8	26
Shikārpur, Pak.	G3	38
Shikohābād, India	G8	38
Shikoku, i., Japan	I6	30
Shikoku-sanchi, mts., Japan	I6	30
Shikotsu-ko, l., Japan	q19	30a
Shillington, Pa., U.S.	F10	115
Shillong, India	H14	38
Shiloh National Military Park, Tn., U.S.	B3	119
Shilong, China	L2	28
Shimabara, Japan	J3	30
Shimada, Japan	H11	30
Shimbiris, mtn., Som.	F4	46
Shimizu, Japan	G11	30
Shimminato, Japan	F10	30
Shimodate, Japan	F12	30
Shimoga, India	F3	37
Shimonoseki, Japan	I3	30
Shinano, stm., Japan	E11	30
Shīndand, Afg.	C1	36
Shiner, Tx., U.S.	E4	120
Shinglehouse, Pa., U.S.	C5	115
Shingū, Japan	I8	30
Shinjō, Japan	D13	30
Shinnston, W.V., U.S.	B4	125
Shinshār, Syria	B5	40
Shinyanga, Tan.	B6	44
Shiocton, Wi., U.S.	D5	126
Shiogama, Japan	D14	30
Shiojiri, Japan	F10	30
Shiping, China	C7	34
Ship Island, i., Ms., U.S.	E5	101
Ship Island Pass, strt., Ms., U.S.	g7	101
Shippegan, N.B., Can.	B5	71
Shippensburg, Pa., U.S.	F6	115
Shiprock, N.M., U.S.	A1	108
Ship Rock, mtn., N.M., U.S.	A1	108
Shirakawa, Japan	E13	30
Shīrāz, Iran	C5	46
Shire, stm., Afr.	E6	44
Shiretoko-misaki, c., Japan	o23	30a
Shirley, In., U.S.	E6	91
Shirley, Ma., U.S.	A4	98
Shirley Mountains, mts., Wy., U.S.	D6	127
Shirpur, India	B3	37
Shishaldin Volcano, vol., Ak., U.S.	E7	79
Shishmaref, Ak., U.S.	B6	79
Shively, Ky., U.S.	B4	94
Shivpuri, India	H7	38
Shizuoka, Japan	H11	30
Shkodër, Alb.	G3	16
Shoal Creek, stm., U.S.	B4	119
Shoal Harbour, Newf., Can.	D4	72
Shoal Lake, Man., Can.	D1	70
Shoals, In., U.S.	G4	91
Shoals, Isles of, is., Me., U.S.	E2	96
Shoalwater, Cape, c., Wa., U.S.	C1	124
Shōdo-shima, i., Japan	H7	30
Shoemakersville, Pa., U.S.	F10	115
Sholāpur, India	D3	37
Shongopovi, Az., U.S.	B5	80
Shonto, Az., U.S.	A5	80
Shoreham, Mi., U.S.	F4	99
Shores Acres, R.I., U.S.	E4	116
Shoreview, Mn., U.S.	m12	100
Shorewood, Il., U.S.	k8	90
Shorewood, Mn., U.S.	n11	100
Shorewood, Wi., U.S.	E6	126
Short Beach, Ct., U.S.	D4	84
Shoshone, Id., U.S.	G4	89
Shoshone, co., Id., U.S.	B2	89
Shoshone, stm., Wy., U.S.	B4	127
Shoshone Falls, wtfl, Id., U.S.	G4	89
Shoshone Lake, l., Wy., U.S.	B2	127
Shoshone Mountains, mts., Nv., U.S.	E4	105
Shoshone Peak, mtn., Nv., U.S.	G5	105
Shoshone Range, mts., Nv., U.S.	C5	105
Shoshong, Bots.	F5	44
Shoshoni, Wy., U.S.	C4	127
Shoup, Id., U.S.	D4	89
Shouxian, China	C5	28
Show Low, Az., U.S.	C5	80
Shreve, Oh., U.S.	B3	112
Shreveport, La., U.S.	B2	95
Shrewsbury, Eng., U.K.	I10	7
Shrewsbury, Ma., U.S.	B4	98
Shrewsbury, N.J., U.S.	C4	107
Shrewsbury, Pa., U.S.	G8	115
Shuajingsi, China	E7	26
Shuangcheng, China	B12	26
Shuangyashan, China	B13	26
Shubenacadie, N.S., Can.	D6	71
Shuksan, Mount, mtn., Wa., U.S.	A4	124
Shullsburg, Wi., U.S.	F3	126
Shumagin Islands, is., Ak., U.S.	E7	79
Shunde, China	M2	28
Shungnak, Ak., U.S.	B8	79
Shuqrā', Yemen	F4	46
Shūshtar, Iran	B4	46
Shuswap Lake, l., B.C., Can.	D8	69
Shwebo, Mya.	C3	34
Siaksriinderapura, Indon.	N7	34
Siālkot, Pak.	D6	38
Siam, Gulf of see Thailand, Gulf of, b., Asia	J6	34
Sian see Xi'an, China	E8	26
Siargao Island, i., Phil.	D8	32
Šiaškotan, Ostrov, i., Russia	H24	24
Šiauliai, Lith.	F6	18
Šibenik, Cro.	F10	14
Siberia see Sibir', reg., Russia	D16	24
Siberut, Pulau, i., Indon.	F2	32
Sibi, Pak.	F2	38
Sibir' (Siberia), reg., Russia	D16	24
Sibir'akova, Ostrov, i., Russia	C9	24
Sibiti, Congo	B2	44
Sibiu, Rom.	D8	16
Sibley, Ia., U.S.	A2	92
Sibley, La., U.S.	B2	95
Sibley, co., Mn., U.S.	F4	100
Sibolga, Indon.	E2	32
Sibsāgar, India	G16	38
Sibu, Malay.	E5	32
Sibutu Island, i., Phil.	E6	32
Sibuyan Island, i., Phil.	C7	32
Sibuyan Sea, Phil.	C7	32
Sicamous, B.C., Can.	D8	69
Sichote-Alin', mts., Russia	H21	24
Sichuan, prov., China	E7	26
Sicié, Cap, c., Fr.	I12	10
Sicilia, i., Italy	L9	14
Sicily, Strait of, strt.	L7	14
Sicily see Sicilia, i., Italy	L9	14
Sico, stm., Hond.	G5	64
Sicuani, Peru	F4	54
Siddipet, India	C5	37
Siderno, Italy	K11	14
Sidhpur, India	I5	38
Sidi bel Abbès, Alg.	A5	42
Sidi Ifni, Mor.	C3	42
Sidmouth, Eng., U.K.	K9	7
Sidney, B.C., Can.	E6	69
Sidney, Il., U.S.	C5	90
Sidney, Ia., U.S.	D2	92
Sidney, Mt., U.S.	C12	103
Sidney, Ne., U.S.	C3	104
Sidney, N.Y., U.S.	C5	109
Sidney, Oh., U.S.	B1	112
Sidney Lanier, Lake, res., Ga., U.S.	B2	87
Sidon see Şaydā, Leb.	C4	40
Sidra, Gulf of see Surt, Khalīj, b., Libya	B9	42
Siedlce, Pol.	C22	8
Siegburg, Ger.	E7	8
Siegen, Ger.	E8	8
Siĕmréab, Camb.	H7	34
Siena, Italy	F6	14
Sierra, co., Ca., U.S.	C3	82
Sierra, co., N.M., U.S.	D2	108
Sierra Blanca Peak, mtn., N.M., U.S.	D4	108
Sierra Colorada, Arg.	E3	56
Sierra Estrella, mts., Az., U.S.	m8	80
Sierra Leone, ctry., Afr.	G3	42
Sierra Madre, Ca., U.S.	m12	82
Sierra Vista, Az., U.S.	F5	80
Sierre, Switz.	F14	10
Siesta Key, i., Fl., U.S.	E4	86
Sighetul Marmaţiei, Rom.	B7	16
Sighişoara, Rom.	C8	16
Siglufjördur, Ice.	B4	4
Signal Mountain, Tn., U.S.	D8	119
Signal Peak, mtn., Az., U.S.	D1	80
Signal Peak, mtn., Ut., U.S.	F2	121
Signy-l'Abbaye, Fr.	C11	10
Sigourney, Ia., U.S.	C5	92
Sigüenza, Spain	D9	12
Sigües, Spain	C10	12
Siguiri, Gui.	F4	42
Siilinjärvi, Fin.	E16	6
Si-Kacha, Thai.	H6	34
Sīkar, India	G6	38
Sikasso, Mali	F4	42
Sikeston, Mo., U.S.	E8	102
Sikiá, Grc.	I7	16
Síkinos, Grc.	M9	16
Sikkim, state, India	G13	38
Šikotan, Ostrov (Shikotan-tō), i., Russia	I23	24
Sikt'ach, Russia	D19	24
Silandro, Italy	C5	14
Silao, Mex.	G9	62
Silay, Phil.	C7	32
Silba, Cro.	E9	14
Silchar, India	H15	38
Siler City, N.C., U.S.	B3	110
Silesia, hist. reg., Pol.	E16	8
Siletz, Or., U.S.	C3	114
Silifke, Tur.	A3	40
Silīguri, India	G13	38
Siling Co, l., China	E13	38
Silistra, Bul.	E11	16
Šilka, Russia	G18	24
Šilka, stm., Russia	G17	24
Silkeborg, Den.	H7	6
Sillamäe, Est.	B10	18
Sillé-le-Guillaume, Fr.	D6	10
Sillery, Que., Can.	n17	74
Sillon de Talbert, pen., Fr.	D3	10
Siloam Springs, Ar., U.S.	A1	81
Silsbee, Tx., U.S.	D5	120
Silt, Co., U.S.	B3	83
Silvânia, Braz.	G9	54
Silvassa, India	B2	37
Silver Bay, Mn., U.S.	C7	100
Silver Bow, co., Mt., U.S.	E4	103
Silver City, Nv., U.S.	D2	105
Silver City, N.M., U.S.	E1	108
Silver Creek, Ne., U.S.	C8	104
Silver Creek, N.Y., U.S.	C1	109
Silver Creek, stm., Or., U.S.	D7	114
Silverdale, Wa., U.S.	B3	124
Silver Grove, Ky., U.S.	h14	94
Silver Hill, Md., U.S.	f9	97
Silver Lake, Ks., U.S.	C8	93
Silver Lake, Ma., U.S.	f11	98
Silver Lake, Mn., U.S.	F4	100
Silver Lake, Wi., U.S.	F5	126
Silver Lake, l., De., U.S.	D3	85
Silver Lake, l., Ia., U.S.	A3	92
Silver Lake, l., Me., U.S.	C3	96
Silver Lake, l., N.H., U.S.	E2	106
Silver Lake, l., N.H., U.S.	C4	106
Silver Lake, l., Or., U.S.	D7	114
Silver Lake, l., Wa., U.S.	g13	124
Silverpeak, Nv., U.S.	F4	105
Silver Peak Range, mts., Nv., U.S.	F4	105
Silver Spring, Md., U.S.	C3	97
Silver Springs, Nv., U.S.	D2	105
Silver Star Mountain, mtn., Wa., U.S.	A5	124
Silverthrone Mountain, mtn., B.C., Can.	D4	69
Silvertip Mountain, mtn., Mt., U.S.	C3	103
Silverton, Co., U.S.	D3	83
Silverton, Id., U.S.	B3	89
Silverton, N.J., U.S.	C4	107
Silverton, Oh., U.S.	o13	112
Silverton, Or., U.S.	C4	114
Silvi, Italy	G9	14
Silvies, stm., Or., U.S.	D7	114
Silview, De., U.S.	B3	85
Silvis, Il., U.S.	B3	90
Simanggang, Malay.	E5	32
Simanovsk, Russia	G19	24
Simav, Tur.	J12	16
Simcoe, Ont., Can.	E4	73
Simcoe, Lake, l., Ont., Can.	C5	73
Simeulue, Pulau, i., Indon.	M3	34
Simferopol', Ukr.	I4	22
Simi Valley, Ca., U.S.	E4	82
Simla, India	E7	38
Simmesport, La., U.S.	D4	95
Simms Stream, stm., N.H., U.S.	g7	106
Simojovel [de Allende], Mex.	I13	62
Simonette, stm., Alta., Can.	B1	68
Simplon Pass, Switz.	F15	10
Simpson, Pa., U.S.	C11	115
Simpson, co., Ky., U.S.	D3	94
Simpson, co., Ms., U.S.	D4	101
Simpson Creek, stm., W.V., U.S.	k10	125
Simpson Desert, des., Austl.	D7	50

Name	Map Ref	Page
Simpson Peninsula, pen., N.W. Ter., Can.	C15	66
Simpsonville, Ky., U.S.	B4	94
Simpsonville, S.C., U.S.	B3	117
Simsboro, La., U.S.	B3	95
Simsbury, Ct., U.S.	B4	84
Simušir, Ostrov, i., Russia	H24	24
Sīnā', Shibh Jazīrat (Sinai Peninsula), pen., Egypt	C12	42
Sinabang, Indon.	M4	34
Sinai Peninsula see Sīnā', Shibh Jazīrat, pen., Egypt	C12	42
Sin'aja, stm., Russia	E18	24
Sinaloa, stm., Mex.	E5	62
Sīnāwan, Libya	B8	42
Sincé, Col.	C5	58
Sincé, Col.	J10	64
Sincelejo, Col.	C5	58
Sinclair, Wy., U.S.	E5	127
Sindri, India	I12	38
Sines, Port.	H3	12
Sinfães, Port.	D3	12
Singānallūr, India	G4	37
Singapore, Sing.	N7	34
Singapore, ctry., Asia	E3	32
Singapore Strait, strt., Asia	N7	34
Singen [Hohentwiel], Ger.	H8	8
Singida, Tan.	B6	44
Singkang, Indon.	F7	32
Singkawang, Indon.	E4	32
Siniscola, Italy	I4	14
Sinj, Cro.	F11	14
Sinjah, Sudan	F12	42
Sinkāt, Sudan	E13	42
Sinnamary, Fr. Gu.	B8	54
Sinnemahoning Creek, stm., Pa., U.S.	D5	115
Sinop, Tur.	G15	4
Sinskoje, Russia	E19	24
Sintang, Indon.	E5	32
Sint Eustatius, i., Neth. Ant.	F16	64
Sint Marten (Saint-Martin), i., N.A.	E16	64
Sint-Niklaas, Bel.	D4	8
Sinton, Tx., U.S.	E4	120
Sintra, Port.	G2	12
Sinŭiju, N. Kor.	C11	26
Sion, Switz.	F14	10
Sioux, co., Ia., U.S.	A1	92
Sioux, co., Ne., U.S.	B2	104
Sioux, co., N.D., U.S.	C4	111
Sioux Center, Ia., U.S.	A1	92
Sioux City, Ia., U.S.	B1	92
Sioux Falls, S.D., U.S.	D9	118
Sioux Lookout, Ont., Can.	o17	73
Sioux Rapids, Ia., U.S.	B2	92
Siping, China	C11	26
Sipiwesk Lake, l., Man., Can.	B3	70
Sipsey, stm., Al., U.S.	B2	78
Sipsey Fork, stm., Al., U.S.	A2	78
Siracusa, Italy	L10	14
Sirājganj, Bngl.	H13	38
Sir Douglas, Mount, mtn., Can.	D3	68
Sir Edward Pellew Group, is., Austl.	C7	50
Siren, Wi., U.S.	C1	126
Siret, stm., Eur.	C11	16
Sirevåg, Nor.	G5	6
Sir James MacBrien, Mount, mtn., N.W. Ter., Can.	D7	66
Sirohi, India	H5	38
Sirsa, India	F6	38
Sir Sandford, Mount, mtn., B.C., Can.	D9	69
Sirsi, India	E3	37
Sir Wilfrid Laurier, Mount, mtn., B.C., Can.	C8	69
Sisak, Cro.	D11	14
Siskiyou, co., Ca., U.S.	B2	82
Siskiyou Mountains, mts., U.S.	F3	114
Siskiyou Pass, Or., U.S.	E4	114
Sisseton, S.D., U.S.	B8	118
Sisseton Indian Reservation, U.S.	B8	118
Sissiboo, stm., N.S., Can.	E4	71
Sisson Branch Reservoir, res., N.B., Can.	B2	71
Sissonville, W.V., U.S.	C3	125
Sisteron, Fr.	H12	10
Sisters, Or., U.S.	C5	114
Sistersville, W.V., U.S.	B4	125
Sītāpur, India	G9	38
Sitka, Ak., U.S.	D12	79
Sitka National Historical Park, Ak., U.S.	m22	79
Sitka Sound, strt., Ak., U.S.	m22	79
Sittard, Neth.	D5	8
Sittoung, stm., Mya.	E4	34
Sittwe (Akyab), Mya.	D2	34
Situbondo, Indon.	m16	33a
Sivas, Tur.	H15	4
Sīwah, Egypt	C11	42
Siwān, India	G11	38
Sjælland, i., Den.	I8	6
Skagen, Den.	H8	6
Skagerrak, strt., Eur.	H7	6
Skagit, co., Wa., U.S.	A4	124
Skagway, Ak., U.S.	D12	79
Skaidi, Nor.	A15	6
Skamania, co., Wa., U.S.	D3	124
Skaneateles, N.Y., U.S.	C4	109
Skaneateles Lake, l., N.Y., U.S.	C4	109
Skārdu, Pak.	C6	38
Skarżysko-Kamienna, Pol.	D20	8
Skeena Mountains, mts., B.C., Can.	E7	66
Skegness, Eng., U.K.	H13	7
Skeleton Lake, l., Ont., Can.	B5	73
Skellefteå, Swe.	D13	6
Skelleftehamn, Swe.	D13	6
Skiatook, Ok., U.S.	A5	113
Skiatook Reservoir, res., Ok., U.S.	A5	113
Skibotn, Nor.	B13	6
Skiddaw, mtn., Eng., U.K.	G9	7
Skien, Nor.	G7	6
Skierniewice, Pol.	D20	8
Skihist Mountain, mtn., B.C., Can.	D7	69
Skikda, Alg.	A7	42
Skillet Fork, stm., Il., U.S.	E5	90
Skillingaryd, Swe.	H10	6
Sklad, Russia	C18	24
Škofja Loka, Slo.	C9	14
Skokie, Il., U.S.	A6	90
Skokomish Indian Reservation, Wa., U.S.	B2	124
Skopje, Mac.	H5	16
Skövde, Swe.	G9	6
Skovorodino, Russia	G18	24
Skowhegan, Me., U.S.	D3	96
Skull Valley, val., Ut., U.S.	C3	121
Skull Valley Indian Reservation, Ut., U.S.	C3	121
Skuna, stm., Ms., U.S.	B4	101
Skunk, stm., Ia., U.S.	D6	92
Skwentna, stm., Ak., U.S.	g15	79
Skye, Island of, i., Scot., U.K.	D6	7
Skykomish, stm., Wa., U.S.	B4	124
Skyland, Nv., U.S.	D2	105
Skyland, N.C., U.S.	f10	110
Skyline, Al., U.S.	A3	78
Slagnäs, Swe.	D12	6
Slamet, Gunung, vol., Indon.	m14	33a
Slancy, Russia	B11	18
Slano, Cro.	G12	14
Slater, Ia., U.S.	C4	92
Slater, Mo., U.S.	B4	102
Slater, S.C., U.S.	A3	117
Slatersville, R.I., U.S.	A3	116
Slatersville Reservoir, res., R.I., U.S.	B3	116
Slatington, Pa., U.S.	E10	115
Slaton, Tx., U.S.	C2	120
Slaughter, La., U.S.	D4	95
Slave, stm., Can.	D10	66
Slave Lake, Alta., Can.	B3	68
Slavonia see Slavonija, reg., Cro.	D12	14
Slavonija, reg., Cro.	D12	14
Slavonska Požega, Cro.	D12	14
Slavonski Brod, Cro.	D2	16
Slayton, Mn., U.S.	G3	100
Sleeping Bear Dunes National Lakeshore, Mi., U.S.	D4	99
Sleeping Bear Point, c., Mi., U.S.	D4	99
Sleepy Eye, Mn., U.S.	F4	100
Slickville, Pa., U.S.	F2	115
Slidell, La., U.S.	D6	95
Sliderock Mountain, mtn., Mt., U.S.	D3	103
Sligo, Ire.	G4	7
Slinger, Wi., U.S.	E5	126
Slippery Rock, Pa., U.S.	D1	115
Sliven, Bul.	G10	16
Sloan, Ia., U.S.	B1	92
Sloan, N.Y., U.S.	C2	109
Slocomb, Al., U.S.	D4	78
Slonim, Bela.	H8	18
Slope, co., N.D., U.S.	C2	111
Slovakia, ctry., Eur.	G19	8
Slovenia, ctry., Eur.	C9	14
Slovenjgradec, Slo.	C10	14
Slovenska Bistrica, Slo.	C10	14
Sluck, Bela.	H10	18
Sl'ud'anka, Russia	G14	24
Słupsk (Stolp), Pol.	A17	8
Smackover, Ar., U.S.	D3	81
Small Point, c., Me., U.S.	g8	96
Smallwood Reservoir, res., Newf., Can.	g8	72
Smederevo, Yugo.	E4	16
Smethport, Pa., U.S.	C5	115
Šmidovič, Russia	H20	24
Šmidta, Ostrov, i., Russia	A12	24
Smith, co., Ks., U.S.	C5	93
Smith, co., Ms., U.S.	C4	101
Smith, co., Tn., U.S.	A5	119
Smith, co., Tx., U.S.	C5	120
Smith, stm., U.S.	D3	123
Smith, stm., Mt., U.S.	D5	103
Smith and Sayles Reservoir, res., R.I., U.S.	B2	116
Smith Bay, b., Ak., U.S.	A9	79
Smith Canyon, val., Co., U.S.	D7	83
Smith Center, Ks., U.S.	C5	93
Smithers, B.C., Can.	B4	69
Smithers, W.V., U.S.	C3	125
Smithfield, N.C., U.S.	B4	110
Smithfield, Pa., U.S.	G2	115
Smithfield, Ut., U.S.	B4	121
Smithfield, Va., U.S.	D6	123
Smith Island, i., U.S.	D5	97
Smith Island, i., Va., U.S.	C7	123
Smith Mountain Lake, res., Va., U.S.	C3	123
Smith Peak, mtn., Id., U.S.	A2	89
Smith Point, c., Ma., U.S.	D7	98
Smith Point, c., Va., U.S.	C6	123
Smiths, Al., U.S.	C4	78
Smithsburg, Md., U.S.	A2	97
Smiths Falls, Ont., Can.	C8	73
Smiths Grove, Ky., U.S.	C3	94
Smithton, Austl.	H9	50
Smithton, Il., U.S.	E4	90
Smithtown, N.Y., U.S.	n15	109
Smithville, Ga., U.S.	E2	87
Smithville, Ms., U.S.	A5	101
Smithville, Mo., U.S.	B3	102
Smithville, Oh., U.S.	B4	112
Smithville, Tn., U.S.	D8	119
Smithville, Tx., U.S.	D4	120
Smithville Lake, res., Mo., U.S.	B3	102
Smoke Creek Desert, des., Nv., U.S.	C2	105
Smokey, Cape, c., N.S., Can.	C9	71
Smokey Dome, mtn., Id., U.S.	F4	89
Smoky, stm., Alta., Can.	B1	68
Smoky Hill, stm., U.S.	D5	93
Smoky Lake, Alta., Can.	B4	68
Smoky Mountains, mts., Id., U.S.	F4	89
Smolensk, Russia	G15	18
Smooth Rock Falls, Ont., Can.	o19	73
Smoothstone Lake, l., Sask., Can.	C2	75
Smyrna, De., U.S.	C3	85
Smyrna, Ga., U.S.	C2	87
Smyrna, Tn., U.S.	B5	119
Smyrna, stm., De., U.S.	C3	85
Smyth, co., Va., U.S.	f10	123
Smythe, Mount, mtn., B.C., Can.	E8	66
Snake, stm., U.S.	D5	100
Snake, stm., Mn., U.S.	B1	100
Snake, stm., Ne., U.S.	B4	104
Snake Range, mts., Nv., U.S.	E7	105
Snake River Plain, pl., Id., U.S.	F2	89
Snake River Range, mts., U.S.	C2	127
Sneads, Fl., U.S.	B2	86
Sneedville, Tn., U.S.	C10	119
Sneek, Neth.	B5	8
Snipe Keys, is., Fl., U.S.	H5	86
Snohomish, Wa., U.S.	B3	124
Snohomish, co., Wa., U.S.	A4	124
Snoqualmie, Wa., U.S.	B4	124
Snoqualmie, stm., Wa., U.S.	B4	124
Snoqualmie Pass, Wa., U.S.	B4	124
Snowbank Lake, l., Mn., U.S.	B7	100
Snowdon, mtn., Wales, U.K.	H8	7
Snowdonia National Park, Wales, U.K.	I9	7
Snowdrift, N.W. Ter., Can.	D10	66
Snowflake, Az., U.S.	C5	80
Snow Hill, Md., U.S.	D7	97
Snow Hill, N.C., U.S.	B5	110
Snowking Mountain, mtn., Wa., U.S.	A4	124
Snow Lake, Man., Can.	B1	70
Snowmass Mountain, mtn., Co., U.S.	B3	83
Snow Peak, mtn., Wa., U.S.	A7	124
Snowshoe Lake, l., Me., U.S.	B4	96
Snowshoe Peak, mtn., Mt., U.S.	B1	103
Snow Water Lake, l., Nv., U.S.	C7	105
Snowyside Peak, mtn., Id., U.S.	F4	89
Snyder, Ok., U.S.	C3	113
Snyder, Tx., U.S.	C2	120
Snyder, co., Pa., U.S.	E7	115
Soacha, Col.	E5	58
Soalala, Madag.	E9	44
Soap Lake, Wa., U.S.	B6	124
Sobat, stm., Sudan	G12	42
Sobinka, Russia	F23	18
Sobral, Braz.	D10	54
Socastee, S.C., U.S.	D9	117
Sochi see Soči, Russia	I5	22
Soči, Russia	I5	22
Social Circle, Ga., U.S.	C3	87
Society Hill, S.C., U.S.	B8	117
Socorro, Col.	D6	58
Socorro, N.M., U.S.	C3	108
Socorro, co., N.M., U.S.	D2	108
Socorro, Isla, i., Mex.	H4	62
Socotra see Suquṭrā, i., Yemen	F5	46
Soc Trang, Viet.	J8	34
Socuéllamos, Spain	F9	12
Sodankylä, Fin.	C16	6
Soda Springs, Id., U.S.	G7	89
Soddy-Daisy, Tn., U.S.	D8	119
Söderhamn, Swe.	F11	6
Södertälje, Swe.	G11	6
Sodo, Eth.	G2	46
Sodus, N.Y., U.S.	B3	109
Soest, Ger.	D8	8
Sofia, stm., Madag.	E9	44
Sofia see Sofija, Bul.	G7	16
Sofija (Sofia), Bul.	G7	16
Sogamoso, Col.	E6	58
Sognafjorden, Nor.	F5	6
Søgne, Nor.	G6	6
Soignies, Bel.	E4	8
Sointula, B.C., Can.	D4	69
Soissons, Fr.	C10	10
Šokal'skogo, Proliv, strt., Russia	B14	24
Söke, Tur.	L11	16
Sokodé, Togo	G6	42
Sokol, Russia	B23	18
Sokol, Russia	C19	24
Sokoto, Nig.	F7	42
Sol, Costa del, Spain	I7	12
Solana, Fl., U.S.	F5	86
Solano, Phil.	p19	33b
Solano, co., Ca., U.S.	C3	82
Solbad Hall in Tirol, Aus.	H11	8
Soldier, stm., Ia., U.S.	C2	92
Soldier Key, i., Fl., U.S.	s3	86
Soldotna, Ak., U.S.	g16	79
Soledad, Col.	B5	58
Soledad, Ca., U.S.	D3	82
Soledad, Ven.	C11	58
Soleduck, stm., Wa., U.S.	B1	124
Solingen, Ger.	D7	8
Sollefteå, Swe.	E11	6
Sollentuna, Swe.	G11	6
Sóller, Spain	F14	12
Solnečnogorsk, Russia	E19	18
Sologoncy, Russia	D16	24
Solok, Indon.	O6	34
Solomon, Ks., U.S.	D6	93
Solomon, stm., Ks., U.S.	C6	93
Solomon Islands, ctry., Oc.	G23	2
Solomons, Md., U.S.	D5	97
Solomon Sea, Oc.	A10	50
Solon, Ia., U.S.	C6	92
Solon, Oh., U.S.	A4	112
Solothurn, Switz.	E14	10
Solsona, Spain	D13	12
Soltau, Ger.	C9	8
Solvay, N.Y., U.S.	B4	109
Solwezi, Zam.	D5	44
Soma, Tur.	J11	16
Somalia, ctry., Afr.	G4	46
Sombor, Yugo.	D3	16
Sombrerete, Mex.	F8	62
Somerdale, N.J., U.S.	D2	107
Somers, Ct., U.S.	B6	84
Somers, Mt., U.S.	B2	103
Somerset, Man., Can.	E2	70
Somerset, Ky., U.S.	C5	94
Somerset, Ma., U.S.	C5	98
Somerset, N.J., U.S.	B3	107
Somerset, Oh., U.S.	C3	112
Somerset, Pa., U.S.	F3	115
Somerset, Tx., U.S.	k7	120
Somerset, Wi., U.S.	C1	126
Somerset, co., Me., U.S.	C2	96
Somerset, co., Md., U.S.	D6	97
Somerset, co., N.J., U.S.	B3	107
Somerset, co., Pa., U.S.	G3	115
Somerset Island, i., N.W. Ter., Can.	B14	66
Somerset Reservoir, res., Vt., U.S.	E3	122
Somers Point, N.J., U.S.	E3	107
Somersville, Ct., U.S.	B6	84
Somersworth, N.H., U.S.	D5	106
Somerton, Az., U.S.	E1	80
Somervell, co., Tx., U.S.	C4	120
Somerville, Ma., U.S.	B5	98
Somerville, N.J., U.S.	B3	107
Somerville, Tn., U.S.	B2	119
Somerville, Tx., U.S.	D4	120
Somerville Lake, res., Tx., U.S.	D4	120
Someș (Szamos), stm., Eur.	B6	16
Sömmerda, Ger.	D11	8
Somonauk, Il., U.S.	B5	90
Somoto, Nic.	H4	64
Son, stm., India	H10	38
Sønderborg, Den.	I7	6
Sondershausen, Ger.	D10	8
Søndre Strømfjord, Grnld.	C22	66
Sondrio, Italy	C4	14
Song Cau, Viet.	H10	34
Songea, Tan.	D7	44
Songhua, stm., China	B12	26
Songjiang, China	D10	28
Songkhla, Thai.	K6	34
Songnim, N. Kor.	D12	26
Sonīpat, India	F7	38
Son La, Viet.	D7	34
Sonmiāni Bay, b., Pak.	H2	38
Sonneberg, Ger.	E11	8
Sonoita, Mex.	B3	62
Sonoma, Ca., U.S.	C2	82
Sonoma, co., Ca., U.S.	C2	82
Sonoma Peak, mtn., Nv., U.S.	C4	105
Sonoma Range, mts., Nv., U.S.	C4	105
Sonora, Ca., U.S.	D3	82
Sonora, Tx., U.S.	D2	120
Sonora, stm., Mex.	C4	62
Sonseca, Spain	F8	12
Sonsón, Col.	E5	58
Sonsonate, El Sal.	H3	64
Sonsorol Islands, is., Palau	D9	32
Son Tay, Viet.	D8	34
Sonthofen, Ger.	H10	8
Soochow see Suzhou, China	D9	28
Soperton, Ga., U.S.	D4	87
Sophia, W.V., U.S.	D3	125
Sopot, Pol.	A18	8
Sopron, Hung.	H16	8
Sopur, India	C6	38
Sora, Italy	H8	14
Sore, Fr.	H6	10
Sorel, Que., Can.	C4	74
Sorgono, Italy	I4	14
Sorgues, Fr.	H11	10
Soria, Spain	D9	12
Sorocaba, Braz.	G5	57
Sorong, Indon.	F9	32
Soroti, Ug.	H12	42
Sorrento, Italy	I9	14
Sorrento, La., U.S.	D5	95
Sorsele, Swe.	D11	6
Sorsogon, Phil.	C7	32
Sort, Spain	C13	12
Sorūbī, Afg.	C3	38
Sos del Rey Católico, Spain	C10	12
Sosnovo-Oz'orskoje, Russia	G16	24
Sosnowiec, Pol.	E19	8
Šoštanj, Slo.	C10	14
Sotkamo, Fin.	D17	6
Soto la Marina, Mex.	F10	62
Sotteville, Fr.	C8	10
Soucook, stm., N.H., U.S.	D4	106
Soudan, Mn., U.S.	C6	100
Souderton, Pa., U.S.	F11	115
Souhegan, stm., N.H., U.S.	E3	106
Souillac, Fr.	H8	10
Sŏul (Seoul), S. Kor.	D12	26
Soulac-sur-Mer, Fr.	G5	10
Souris, Man., Can.	E1	70
Souris, P.E.I., Can.	C7	71
Sousa, Braz.	E11	54
Sousse, Tun.	N5	14
South, stm., Ia., U.S.	C4	92
South, stm., N.C., U.S.	C4	110
South Acton, Ma., U.S.	g10	98
South Africa, ctry., Afr.	G5	44
South Amboy, N.J., U.S.	C4	107
South America	E4	53
South Amherst, Ma., U.S.	B2	98
South Amherst, Oh., U.S.	A3	112
Southampton, Ont., Can.	C3	73
Southampton, Eng., U.K.	K11	7
Southampton, N.Y., U.S.	n16	109
Southampton, co., Va., U.S.	D5	123
Southampton Island, i., N.W. Ter., Can.	D16	66
South Andaman, i., India	I2	34
South Anna, stm., Va., U.S.	C5	123
South Aulatsivik Island, i., Newf., Can.	E20	66
South Australia, state, Austl.	F7	50
Southaven, Ms., U.S.	A3	101
South Bald Mountain, mtn., Co., U.S.	A5	83
South Baldy, mtn., N.M., U.S.	D2	108
South Barre, Vt., U.S.	C3	122
South Bay, Fl., U.S.	F6	86
South Beloit, Il., U.S.	A4	90
South Bend, In., U.S.	A5	91
South Bend, Wa., U.S.	C2	124
South Berwick, Me., U.S.	E2	96
South Bloomfield, Oh., U.S.	C3	112
South Boston, Va., U.S.	D4	123
South Bound Brook, N.J., U.S.	B3	107
South Branch Lake, l., Me., U.S.	C4	96
Southbridge, Ma., U.S.	B3	98
South Bristol, Me., U.S.	E3	96
South Britain, Ct., U.S.	D3	84
South Broadway, Wa., U.S.	C5	124
South Bruny, i., Austl.	H9	50
South Burlington, Vt., U.S.	C2	122
Southbury, Ct., U.S.	D3	84
South Carolina, state, U.S.	D6	117
South Charleston, Oh., U.S.	C2	112
South Charleston, W.V., U.S.	C3	125
South Chicago Heights, Il., U.S.	m9	90
South China Sea, Asia	C5	32
South Coffeyville, Ok., U.S.	A6	113
South Congaree, S.C., U.S.	D5	117
South Connellsville, Pa., U.S.	G2	115
South Dakota, state, U.S.	C5	118
South Dartmouth, Ma., U.S.	C6	98
South Daytona, Fl., U.S.	C5	86
South Deerfield, Ma., U.S.	B2	98
South Dennis, Ma., U.S.	C7	98
South Duxbury, Ma., U.S.	B6	98
South East Cape, c., Austl.	H9	50
Southeast Cape, c., Ak., U.S.	C6	79
South Easton, Ma., U.S.	B5	98
Southeast Pass, strt., La., U.S.	E7	95
Southeast Point, c., R.I., U.S.	h7	116
South Elgin, Il., U.S.	B5	90
Southend-on-Sea, Eng., U.K.	J13	7
Southern Alps, mts., N.Z.	E3	52
Southern Cross, Austl.	F3	50
Southern Indian Lake, l., Man., Can.	f8	70
Southern Pines, N.C., U.S.	B3	110
Southern Ute Indian Reservation, Co., U.S.	D2	83
South Euclid, Oh., U.S.	g9	112
Southey, Sask., Can.	G3	75
South Fabius, stm., Mo., U.S.	A5	102
South Fallsburg, N.Y., U.S.	D6	109
Southfield, Mi., U.S.	o15	99
South Fork, Pa., U.S.	F4	115
South Fox Island, i., Mi., U.S.	C5	99
South Fulton, Tn., U.S.	A3	119
South Gastonia, N.C., U.S.	B1	110
South Gate, Ca., U.S.	n12	82
Southgate, Ky., U.S.	h14	94
Southgate, Mi., U.S.	p15	99
South Georgia, i., Falk. Is.	G9	56
South Glastonbury, Ct., U.S.	C5	84
South Glens Falls, N.Y., U.S.	B7	109
South Grafton, Ma., U.S.	B4	98
South Grand, stm., Mo., U.S.	C3	102
South Hadley, Ma., U.S.	B2	98
South Hadley Falls, Ma., U.S.	B2	98
South Hamilton, Ma., U.S.	A6	98
South Haven, In., U.S.	A3	91
South Haven, Mi., U.S.	F4	99
South Henik Lake, l., N.W. Ter., Can.	D13	66
South Hero Island, i., Vt., U.S.	B2	122
South Hill, Va., U.S.	D4	123
South Hingham, Ma., U.S.	h12	98
South Holland, Il., U.S.	k9	90
South Holston Lake, res., U.S.	A9	119
South Hooksett, N.H., U.S.	D4	106
South Hopkinton, R.I., U.S.	F1	116
South Houston, Tx., U.S.	r14	120
South Hutchinson, Ks., U.S.	f11	93
South Indian Lake, Man., Can.	A2	70
Southington, Ct., U.S.	C4	84
South International Falls, Mn., U.S.	B5	100
South Island, i., N.Z.	E3	52
South Island, i., S.C., U.S.	E9	117
South Jacksonville, Il., U.S.	D3	90
South Jordan, Ut., U.S.	C3	121
South Kenosha, Wi., U.S.	F6	126
South Lake Tahoe, Ca., U.S.	C4	82
South Lancaster, Ma., U.S.	B4	98
South Laurel, Md., U.S.	*B4	97
South Lebanon, Oh., U.S.	C1	112
South Lyon, Mi., U.S.	F7	99
South Magnetic Pole	C26	47
South Manitou Island, i., Mi., U.S.	C4	99
South Marsh Island, i., Md., U.S.	D5	97
South Miami, Fl., U.S.	G6	86
South Miami Heights, Fl., U.S.	s13	86
South Mills, N.C., U.S.	A6	110
South Milwaukee, Wi., U.S.	F6	126
Southmont, N.C., U.S.	B2	110
South Moose Lake, l., Man., Can.	C1	70
South Mountain, mtn., Id., U.S.	G2	89
South Mountain, mtn., N.M., U.S.	k8	108
South Mountains, mts., Az., U.S.	m8	80
South Mountains, mts., N.C., U.S.	B1	110
South Nahanni, stm., N.W. Ter., Can.	D7	66
South New River Canal, Fl., U.S.	r3	86
South Ogden, Ut., U.S.	B4	121
Southold, N.Y., U.S.	m16	109
South Orange, N.J., U.S.	B4	107
South Orkney Islands, is., B.A.T.	C8	47
South Paris, Me., U.S.	D2	96
South Park, val., Co., U.S.	B5	83
South Pass, Wy., U.S.	D4	127
South Pass, strt., La., U.S.	F6	95
South Patrick Shores, Fl., U.S.	D6	86
South Pekin, Il., U.S.	C4	90
South Pittsburg, Tn., U.S.	D8	119
South Plainfield, N.J., U.S.	B4	107
South Platte, stm., U.S.	C6	76
South Point, c., Mi., U.S.	D7	99
South Pole, Ant.	A12	47
Southport, Eng., U.K.	H9	7
Southport, Fl., U.S.	u16	86
Southport, In., U.S.	E5	91
Southport, N.Y., U.S.	C4	109
Southport, N.C., U.S.	D4	110
South Portland, Me., U.S.	E2	96
South Portsmouth, Ky., U.S.	B6	94
South Range, Mi., U.S.	A2	99
South River, Ont., Can.	B5	73
South River, N.J., U.S.	C4	107
South River, b., Md., U.S.	C4	97
South Ronaldsay, i., Scot., U.K.	C10	7

Name	Map Ref	Page
South Royalton, Vt., U.S.	D3	122
South Saint Paul, Mn., U.S.	n12	100
South Sandwich Islands, is., Falk. Is.	D10	47
South San Francisco, Ca., U.S.	h8	82
South Saskatchewan, stm., Can.	F11	66
South Shetland Islands, is., B.A.T.	C7	47
South Shields, Eng., U.K.	F11	7
Southside, Al., U.S.	B3	78
Southside Place, Tx., U.S.	r14	120
South Sioux City, Ne., U.S.	B9	104
South Skunk, stm., Ia., U.S.	C4	92
South Stony Brook, N.Y., U.S.	*n15	109
South Streator, Il., U.S.	B5	90
South Toms River, N.J., U.S.	D4	107
South Torrington, Wy., U.S.	D8	127
South Tucson, Az., U.S.	E5	80
South Valley Stream, N.Y., U.S.	*n15	109
South Venice, Fl., U.S.	E4	86
South Ventana Cone, vol., Ca., U.S.	D3	82
South Waverly, Pa., U.S.	C8	115
South Wellfleet, Ma., U.S.	C8	98
South Wellington, B.C., Can.	f12	69
South West Africa see Namibia, ctry., Afr.	F3	44
South Westbury, N.Y., U.S.	*n15	109
South West Cape, c., Austl.	H9	50
Southwest Channel, strt., Fl., U.S.	E4	86
South West City, Mo., U.S.	E3	102
Southwest Harbor, Me., U.S.	D4	96
Southwest Head, c., N.B., Can.	E3	71
Southwest Miramichi, stm., N.B., Can.	C3	71
Southwest Pass, strt., La., U.S.	E3	95
Southwest Pass, strt., La., U.S.	F6	95
Southwest Point, c., R.I., U.S.	h7	116
South Weymouth Naval Air Station, mil., Ma., U.S.	h12	98
South Whitley, In., U.S.	B6	91
South Williamson, Ky., U.S.	C7	94
South Williamsport, Pa., U.S.	D7	115
South Windham, Ct., U.S.	C7	84
South Windham, Me., U.S.	E2	96
South Windsor, Ct., U.S.	B5	84
Southwood, Co., U.S.	*B6	83
Southwood Acres, Ct., U.S.	A5	84
South Woodstock, Ct., U.S.	B8	84
South Yarmouth, Ma., U.S.	C7	98
South Zanesville, Oh., U.S.	C3	112
Sovetsk (Tilsit), Russia	F4	18
Sovetskaja Gavan', Russia	H22	24
Spa, Bel.	E5	8
Spain, ctry., Eur.	G7	4
Spalding, co., Ga., U.S.	C2	87
Spanaway, Wa., U.S.	B3	124
Spangler, Pa., U.S.	E4	115
Spaniard's Bay, Newf., Can.	E5	72
Spanish Fork, Ut., U.S.	C4	121
Spanish Fort, Al., U.S.	E2	78
Spanish Lake, Mo., U.S.	f13	102
Spanish North Africa, dep., Afr.	A4	42
Spanish Peak, mtn., Or., U.S.	C7	114
Spanish Sahara see Western Sahara, dep., Afr.	D3	42
Spanish Town, Jam.	E9	64
Sparks, Ga., U.S.	E3	87
Sparks, Nv., U.S.	D2	105
Sparta, Ga., U.S.	C4	87
Sparta, Il., U.S.	E4	90
Sparta, Mi., U.S.	E5	99
Sparta, Mo., U.S.	D4	102
Sparta (Lake Mohawk), N.J., U.S.	A3	107
Sparta, N.C., U.S.	A1	110
Sparta, Tn., U.S.	D8	119
Sparta, Wi., U.S.	E3	126
Spartanburg, S.C., U.S.	B4	117
Spartanburg, co., S.C., U.S.	B3	117
Sparta see Spárti, Grc.	L6	16
Spartel, Cap, c., Mor.	J6	12
Spárti (Sparta), Grc.	L6	16
Spartivento, Capo, c., Italy	K3	14
Sparwood, B.C., Can.	E10	69
Spassk-Dal'nij, Russia	I20	24
Spavinaw Creek, stm., Ok., U.S.	A7	113
Spear, Cape, c., Newf., Can.	E5	72
Spearfish, S.D., U.S.	C2	118
Spearman, Tx., U.S.	A2	120
Spearville, Ks., U.S.	E4	93
Speed, In., U.S.	H6	91
Speedway, In., U.S.	E5	91
Spence Bay, N.W. Ter., Can.	C14	66
Spencer, In., U.S.	F4	91
Spencer, Ia., U.S.	A2	92
Spencer, Ma., U.S.	B4	98
Spencer, N.C., U.S.	B2	110
Spencer, Tn., U.S.	D8	119
Spencer, W.V., U.S.	C3	125
Spencer, Wi., U.S.	D3	126
Spencer, co., In., U.S.	H4	91
Spencer, co., Ky., U.S.	B4	94
Spencer, Cape, c., Ak., U.S.	k21	79
Spencer Gulf, b., Austl.	F7	50
Spencer Lake, l., Me., U.S.	C2	96
Spencerport, N.Y., U.S.	B3	109
Spencerville, Md., U.S.	B4	97
Spencerville, Oh., U.S.	B1	112
Sperry, Ok., U.S.	A6	113
Spesutie Island, i., Md., U.S.	B5	97
Spey, stm., Scot., U.K.	D9	7
Speyer, Ger.	F8	8
Spiceland, In., U.S.	E7	91
Spicer, Mn., U.S.	E4	100
Spider Lake, l., Wi., U.S.	B2	126
Spindale, N.C., U.S.	B1	110
Spink, co., S.D., U.S.	C7	118
Spirit Lake, Id., U.S.	B2	89
Spirit Lake, Ia., U.S.	A2	92
Spirit Lake, l., Ia., U.S.	A2	92
Spirit Lake, l., Wa., U.S.	C3	124
Spirit River, Alta., Can.	B1	68
Spirit River Flowage, res., Wi., U.S.	C4	126
Spiro, Ok., U.S.	B7	113
Spittal an der Drau, Aus.	I13	8
Spitz, Aus.	G15	8
Split, Cro.	F11	14
Split, Cape, c., N.S., Can.	D5	71
Split Lake, l., Man., Can.	A4	70
Split Rock Creek, stm., U.S.	G2	100
Splügen, Switz.	F16	10
Spofford Lake, l., N.H., U.S.	E2	106
Spokane, Wa., U.S.	B8	124
Spokane, co., Wa., U.S.	B8	124
Spokane, stm., U.S.	B8	124
Spokane, Mount, mtn., Wa., U.S.	B8	124
Spokane Indian Reservation, Wa., U.S.	B8	124
Spoleto, Italy	G7	14
Spoon, stm., Il., U.S.	C3	90
Spooner, Wi., U.S.	C2	126
Spooner Lake, l., Wi., U.S.	C2	126
Spornoje, Russia	E24	24
Spotswood, N.J., U.S.	C4	107
Spotsylvania, co., Va., U.S.	B5	123
Sprague, W.V., U.S.	n13	125
Sprague, stm., Or., U.S.	E5	114
Sprague Lake, l., Wa., U.S.	B7	124
Spratly Island, i., Asia	D5	32
Spremberg, Ger.	D14	8
Spring, stm., Ar., U.S.	A4	81
Spring Arbor, Mi., U.S.	F6	99
Spring Bay, b., Ut., U.S.	B3	121
Springbok, S. Afr.	G3	44
Springboro, Oh., U.S.	C1	112
Spring Brook, stm., Pa., U.S.	n18	115
Spring City, Pa., U.S.	F10	115
Spring City, Tn., U.S.	D9	119
Spring City, Ut., U.S.	D4	121
Spring Creek, stm., U.S.	D4	104
Spring Creek, stm., Nv., U.S.	C4	105
Spring Creek, stm., N.D., U.S.	B3	111
Springdale, Newf., Can.	D3	72
Springdale, Ar., U.S.	A1	81
Springdale, Oh., U.S.	n13	112
Springdale, Pa., U.S.	E2	115
Springdale, S.C., U.S.	D5	117
Springer, N.M., U.S.	A5	108
Springerville, Az., U.S.	C6	80
Springfield, Co., U.S.	D8	83
Springfield, Fl., U.S.	u16	86
Springfield, Ga., U.S.	D5	87
Springfield, Il., U.S.	D4	90
Springfield, Ky., U.S.	C4	94
Springfield, Ma., U.S.	B2	98
Springfield, Mn., U.S.	F4	100
Springfield, Mo., U.S.	D4	102
Springfield, Ne., U.S.	C9	104
Springfield, N.J., U.S.	B4	107
Springfield, Oh., U.S.	C2	112
Springfield, Or., U.S.	C4	114
Springfield, Pa., U.S.	p20	115
Springfield, S.D., U.S.	E8	118
Springfield, Tn., U.S.	A5	119
Springfield, Vt., U.S.	E4	122
Springfield, Va., U.S.	g12	123
Springfield, Lake, res., Il., U.S.	D4	90
Springfontein, S. Afr.	H5	44
Spring Garden, Guy.	D13	58
Spring Glen, Ut., U.S.	D5	121
Spring Green, Wi., U.S.	E3	126
Spring Grove, Il., U.S.	h8	90
Spring Grove, Mn., U.S.	G7	100
Spring Grove, Pa., U.S.	G8	115
Spring Hill, Fl., U.S.	D4	86
Spring Hill, Ks., U.S.	D9	93
Springhill, La., U.S.	A2	95
Spring Hill, Tn., U.S.	B5	119
Spring Hope, N.C., U.S.	B4	110
Spring Island, i., S.C., U.S.	G6	117
Spring Lake, Mi., U.S.	E4	99
Spring Lake, N.J., U.S.	C4	107
Spring Lake, N.C., U.S.	B4	110
Spring Lake, l., Me., U.S.	C2	96
Spring Lake, res., U.S.	B3	90
Spring Lake Heights, N.J., U.S.	C4	107
Spring Mountains, mts., Nv., U.S.	G6	105
Springport, Mi., U.S.	F6	99
Springs, S. Afr.	G5	44
Springside, Sask., Can.	F4	75
Springvale, Me., U.S.	E2	96
Spring Valley, Ca., U.S.	o16	82
Spring Valley, Il., U.S.	B4	90
Spring Valley, Mn., U.S.	G6	100
Spring Valley, N.Y., U.S.	g12	109
Spring Valley, Wi., U.S.	D1	126
Springville, Al., U.S.	B3	78
Springville, Ia., U.S.	B6	92
Springville, N.Y., U.S.	C2	109
Springville, Ut., U.S.	C4	121
Spruce Fork, stm., W.V., U.S.	m12	125
Spruce Grove, Alta., Can.	C4	68
Spruce Knob, mtn., W.V., U.S.	C6	125
Spruce Knob-Seneca Rocks National Recreation Area, W.V., U.S.	C5	125
Spruce Mountain, mtn., Az., U.S.	C3	80
Spruce Mountain, mtn., Nv., U.S.	C7	105
Spruce Pine, N.C., U.S.	f10	110
Spruce Run Reservoir, res., N.J., U.S.	B3	107
Spur, Tx., U.S.	C2	120
Spurr, Mount, mtn., Ak., U.S.	g15	79
Squam Lake, l., N.H., U.S.	C4	106
Squapan Lake, l., Me., U.S.	B4	96
Square Lake, l., Me., U.S.	A4	96
Squatec, Que., Can.	B9	74
Squaw Cap Mountain, mtn., N.B., Can.	B3	71
Squaw Hill, mtn., Wy., U.S.	E7	127
Squaw Peak, mtn., Mt., U.S.	C2	103
Squibnocket Point, c., Ma., U.S.	D6	98
Squinzano, Italy	I13	14
Squire, W.V., U.S.	D3	125
Sragen, Indon.	m15	33a
Sredinnyj Chrebet, mts., Russia	F26	24
Srednekolymsk, Russia	D24	24
Srednerusskaja Vozvyšennost', plat., Russia	H20	18
Srednesibirskoje Ploskogorje, plat., Russia	D14	24
Sremska Mitrovica, Yugo.	E3	16
Sri Gangānagar, India	F5	38
Srīkākulam, India	C7	37
Sri Lanka, ctry., Asia	H5	36
Srīnagar, India	C6	38
Srīrampur, India	C3	37
Stack Reservoir, res., R.I., U.S.	C3	116
Stade, Ger.	B9	8
Stadthagen, Ger.	C9	8
Stafford, Eng., U.K.	I10	7
Stafford, Ks., U.S.	E5	93
Stafford, Va., U.S.	B5	123
Stafford, co., Ks., U.S.	D5	93
Stafford, co., Va., U.S.	B5	123
Stafford Pond, l., R.I., U.S.	D6	116
Stafford Springs, Ct., U.S.	B6	84
Staked Plain see Estacado, Llano, pl., U.S.	E6	76
Stalheim, Nor.	F6	6
Stalingrad see Volgograd, Russia	H6	22
Stalowa Wola, Pol.	E22	8
Stambaugh, Mi., U.S.	B2	99
Stamford, Ct., U.S.	E1	84
Stamford, Tx., U.S.	C3	120
Stamford, Vt., U.S.	F2	122
Stamford, Lake, res., Tx., U.S.	C3	120
Stamping Ground, Ky., U.S.	B5	94
Stamps, Ar., U.S.	D2	81
Stanaford, W.V., U.S.	D3	125
Stanberry, Mo., U.S.	A3	102
Standerton, S. Afr.	G5	44
Standing Rock Indian Reservation, U.S.	B4	118
Standish, Mi., U.S.	E7	99
Stanfield, Az., U.S.	E3	80
Stanfield, Or., U.S.	B7	114
Stanford, Ky., U.S.	C5	94
Stanhope, N.J., U.S.	B3	107
Stanislaus, co., Ca., U.S.	D3	82
Stanke Dimitrov, Bul.	G7	16
Stanley, Falk. Is.	G5	56
Stanley, N.C., U.S.	B1	110
Stanley, N.D., U.S.	A3	111
Stanley, Va., U.S.	B4	123
Stanley, Wi., U.S.	D3	126
Stanley, co., S.D., U.S.	C5	118
Stanley Falls, wtfl, Zaire	A5	44
Stanleytown, Va., U.S.	D3	123
Stanleyville, N.C., U.S.	A2	110
Stanleyville see Kisangani, Zaire	A5	44
Stanly, co., N.C., U.S.	B2	110
Stann Creek, Belize	F3	64
Stanovoj Chrebet, mts., Russia	F19	24
Stanovoje Nagorje (Stanovoy Mountains), mts., Russia	F16	24
Stanstead, Que., Can.	D5	74
Stanton, Ia., U.S.	D2	92
Stanton, Ky., U.S.	C6	94
Stanton, Mi., U.S.	E5	99
Stanton, Ne., U.S.	C8	104
Stanton, Tx., U.S.	C2	120
Stanton, co., Ks., U.S.	E2	93
Stanton, co., Ne., U.S.	C8	104
Stantonsburg, N.C., U.S.	B5	110
Stanwood, Ia., U.S.	C6	92
Stanwood, Wa., U.S.	A3	124
Staples, Mn., U.S.	D4	100
Stapleton, Al., U.S.	E2	78
Star, Id., U.S.	F2	89
Star, N.C., U.S.	B3	110
Starachowice, Pol.	D21	8
Staraja Russa, Russia	C14	18
Stara Planina (Balkan Mountains), mts., Eur.	G8	16
Stara Zagora, Bul.	G9	16
Starbuck, Mn., U.S.	E3	100
Star City, Ar., U.S.	D4	81
Star City, W.V., U.S.	B5	125
Stargard Szczeciński (Stargard in Pommern), Pol.	B15	8
Stargo, Az., U.S.	D6	80
Stark, co., Il., U.S.	B4	90
Stark, co., N.D., U.S.	C3	111
Stark, co., Oh., U.S.	B4	112
Starke, Fl., U.S.	C4	86
Starke, co., In., U.S.	B4	91
Starks, La., U.S.	D2	95
Starkville, Ms., U.S.	B5	101
Star Lake, l., Mn., U.S.	D3	100
Starnberg, Ger.	G11	8
Starogard Gdański, Pol.	B18	8
Star Peak, mtn., Nv., U.S.	C3	105
Starr, co., Tx., U.S.	F3	120
Startex, S.C., U.S.	B3	117
Start Point, c., Eng., U.K.	K9	7
Startup, Wa., U.S.	B4	124
State Center, Ia., U.S.	B4	92
State College, Pa., U.S.	E6	115
Stateline, Nv., U.S.	E2	105
State Line, Pa., U.S.	G6	115
Staten Island, i., N.Y., U.S.	k12	109
Statenville, Ga., U.S.	F4	87
Statesboro, Ga., U.S.	D5	87
Statesville, N.C., U.S.	B2	110
Statham, Ga., U.S.	C3	87
Statue of Liberty National Monument, N.J., U.S.	k8	107
Staunton, Il., U.S.	D4	90
Staunton, Va., U.S.	B3	123
Stavanger, Nor.	G5	6
Stavropol', Russia	H6	22
Stayner, Ont., Can.	C4	73
Stayton, Or., U.S.	C4	114
Steamboat, Nv., U.S.	D2	105
Steamboat Mountain, mtn., Mt., U.S.	C4	103
Steamboat Mountain, mtn., Wy., U.S.	E4	127
Steamboat Springs, Co., U.S.	A4	83
Stearns, Ky., U.S.	D5	94
Stearns, co., Mn., U.S.	E4	100
Stearns Brook, stm., N.H., U.S.	A4	106
Stebbins, Ak., U.S.	C7	79
Steele, Al., U.S.	B3	78
Steele, Mo., U.S.	E8	102
Steele, N.D., U.S.	C6	111
Steele, co., Mn., U.S.	F5	100
Steele, co., N.D., U.S.	B8	111
Steele, Mount, mtn., Wy., U.S.	E6	127
Steeleville, Il., U.S.	E4	90
Steelton, Pa., U.S.	F8	115
Steelville, Mo., U.S.	D6	102
Steenkool, Indon.	F9	32
Steens Mountain, mts., Or., U.S.	E8	114
Stefansson Island, i., N.W. Ter., Can.	B11	66
Steger, Il., U.S.	B6	90
Steilacoom, Wa., U.S.	f10	124
Steinbach, Man., Can.	E3	70
Steinhatchee, stm., Fl., U.S.	C3	86
Steinkjer, Nor.	D8	6
Stellenbosch, S. Afr.	H3	44
Stenay, Fr.	C12	10
Stendal, Ger.	C11	8
Stephen, Mn., U.S.	B2	100
Stephens, Ar., U.S.	D2	81
Stephens, co., Ga., U.S.	B3	87
Stephens, co., Ok., U.S.	C4	113
Stephens, co., Tx., U.S.	C3	120
Stephens City, Va., U.S.	A4	123
Stephens Lake, res., Man., Can.	A4	70
Stephenson, Mi., U.S.	C3	99
Stephenson, co., Il., U.S.	A4	90
Stephens Passage, strt., Ak., U.S.	m23	79
Stephenville, Newf., Can.	D2	72
Stephenville, Tx., U.S.	C3	120
Stephenville Crossing, Newf., Can.	D2	72
Sterling, Ak., U.S.	g16	79
Sterling, Co., U.S.	A7	83
Sterling, Il., U.S.	B4	90
Sterling, Ks., U.S.	D5	93
Sterling, Ok., U.S.	C3	113
Sterling, Va., U.S.	A5	123
Sterling, co., Tx., U.S.	D2	120
Sterling City, Tx., U.S.	D2	120
Sterling Heights, Mi., U.S.	o15	99
Sterling Reservoir, res., Co., U.S.	A7	83
Sterlington, La., U.S.	B3	95
Sterlitamak, Russia	G9	22
Stettin see Szczecin, Pol.	B14	8
Stettler, Alta., Can.	C4	68
Steuben, co., In., U.S.	A7	91
Steuben, co., N.Y., U.S.	C3	109
Steubenville, Oh., U.S.	B5	112
Stevenage, Eng., U.K.	J12	7
Stevens, co., Ks., U.S.	E2	93
Stevens, co., Mn., U.S.	E3	100
Stevens, co., Wa., U.S.	A7	124
Stevens Creek Dam, U.S.	C4	87
Stevenson, Al., U.S.	A4	78
Stevenson, Ct., U.S.	D3	84
Stevenson, Wa., U.S.	D4	124
Stevenson Lake, l., Man., Can.	C4	70
Stevens Pass, Wa., U.S.	B4	124
Stevens Peak, mtn., Id., U.S.	B3	89
Stevens Point, Wi., U.S.	D4	126
Stevensville, Md., U.S.	C5	97
Stevensville, Mi., U.S.	F4	99
Stevensville, Mt., U.S.	D2	103
Stewart, co., Ga., U.S.	D2	87
Stewart, co., Tn., U.S.	A4	119
Stewart Island, i., N.Z.	G1	52
Stewart Mountain, mtn., Az., U.S.	k9	80
Stewartstown, Pa., U.S.	G8	115
Stewartsville, Mo., U.S.	B3	102
Stewartville, Mn., U.S.	G6	100
Stewiacke, N.S., Can.	D6	71
Steyr, Aus.	G14	8
Stigler, Ok., U.S.	B6	113
Stigliano, Italy	I11	14
Stikine, stm., B.C., Can.	E7	66
Stikine, stm., Ak., U.S.	D13	79
Stikine Ranges, mts., B.C., Can.	E6	66
Still, stm., Ct., U.S.	B3	84
Stillaguamish, North Fork, stm., Wa., U.S.	A4	124
Stillaguamish, South Fork, stm., Wa., U.S.	A4	124
Stillhouse Hollow Lake, res., Tx., U.S.	D4	120
Stillman Valley, Il., U.S.	A4	90
Stillmore, Ga., U.S.	D4	87
Stillwater, Mn., U.S.	E6	100
Stillwater, Ok., U.S.	A4	113
Stillwater, co., Mt., U.S.	E7	103
Stillwater Range, mts., Nv., U.S.	D3	105
Stillwater Reservoir, res., N.Y., U.S.	B5	109
Stillwater Reservoir, res., R.I., U.S.	B3	116
Stilwell, Ok., U.S.	B7	113
Stimson, Mount, mtn., Mt., U.S.	B3	103
Stine Mountain, mtn., Mt., U.S.	E3	103
Stinking Lake, l., N.M., U.S.	A3	108
Stinnett, Tx., U.S.	B2	120
Štip, Mac.	H6	16
Stirling, Alta., Can.	E4	68
Stirling, Ont., Can.	C7	73
Stirling, Scot., U.K.	E9	7
Stjørdalshalsen, Nor.	E8	6
Stockbridge, Ga., U.S.	C2	87
Stockbridge, Mi., U.S.	F6	99
Stockbridge-Munsee Indian Reservation, Wi., U.S.	D5	126
Stockdale, Tx., U.S.	E4	120
Stockerau, Aus.	G16	8
Stockholm, Swe.	G12	6
Stockton, Ca., U.S.	D3	82
Stockton, Il., U.S.	A3	90
Stockton, Ks., U.S.	C4	93
Stockton, Md., U.S.	D7	97
Stockton, Mo., U.S.	D4	102
Stockton Island, i., Wi., U.S.	B3	126
Stockton Lake, res., Mo., U.S.	D4	102
Stoddard, Wi., U.S.	E2	126
Stoddard, co., Mo., U.S.	E8	102
Stoke-on-Trent, Eng., U.K.	H10	7
Stokes, co., N.C., U.S.	A2	110
Stokesdale, N.C., U.S.	A3	110
Stolbovoj, Ostrov, i., Russia	C21	24
Stollings, W.V., U.S.	n12	125
Ston, Cro.	G12	14
Stone, co., Ar., U.S.	B3	81
Stone, co., Ms., U.S.	E4	101
Stone, co., Mo., U.S.	E4	102
Stoneboro, Pa., U.S.	D1	115
Stone Corral Lake, l., Or., U.S.	E7	114
Stoneham, Ma., U.S.	g11	98
Stonehaven, Scot., U.K.	E10	7
Stone Mountain, Ga., U.S.	C2	87
Stone Mountain, mtn., Ga., U.S.	C2	87
Stones River National Battlefield, hist., Tn., U.S.	B4	119
Stoneville, N.C., U.S.	A3	110
Stonewall, Man., Can.	D3	70
Stonewall, La., U.S.	B2	95
Stonewall, Ms., U.S.	C5	101
Stonewall, co., Tx., U.S.	C2	120
Stonewood, W.V., U.S.	k10	125
Stoney Creek, Ont., Can.	D5	73
Stonington, Ct., U.S.	D8	84
Stonington, Il., U.S.	D4	90
Stonington, Me., U.S.	D4	96
Stono, stm., S.C., U.S.	k11	117
Stono Inlet, b., S.C., U.S.	F8	117
Stony Brook, N.Y., U.S.	n15	109
Stony Brook, stm., N.J., U.S.	C3	107
Stony Creek, stm., Va., U.S.	C5	123
Stony Island, i., N.Y., U.S.	B4	109
Stony Plain, Alta., Can.	C3	68
Stony Point, N.C., U.S.	B1	110
Storby, Fin.	F12	6
Støren, Nor.	E8	6
Storey, co., Nv., U.S.	D2	105
Storfors, Swe.	G10	6
Storkerson Peninsula, pen., N.W. Ter., Can.	B11	66
Storlien, Swe.	E9	6
Storm Lake, Ia., U.S.	B2	92
Storm Lake, l., Ia., U.S.	B2	92
Storm Mountain, mtn., Ak., U.S.	h16	79
Stornoway, Scot., U.K.	C6	7
Storrs, Ct., U.S.	B7	84
Storuman, Swe.	D11	6
Storvreta, Swe.	G11	6
Story, Wy., U.S.	B6	127
Story, co., Ia., U.S.	B4	92
Story City, Ia., U.S.	B4	92
Stoughton, Sask., Can.	H4	75
Stoughton, Ma., U.S.	B5	98
Stoughton, Wi., U.S.	F4	126
Stover, Mo., U.S.	C5	102
Stow, Oh., U.S.	A4	112
Stow Creek, stm., N.J., U.S.	E2	107
Stowe, Pa., U.S.	F10	115
Stowe, Vt., U.S.	C3	122
Stoyoma Mountain, mtn., B.C., Can.	E7	69
Strabane, Pa., U.S.	F1	115
Strafford, Mo., U.S.	D4	102
Strafford, co., N.H., U.S.	D4	106
Straffordville, Ont., Can.	E4	73
Strahan, Austl.	H9	50
Strakonice, Czech.	F13	8
Stralsund, Ger.	A13	8
Stranraer, Scot., U.K.	G7	7
Strasbourg, Fr.	D14	10
Strasburg, Co., U.S.	B6	83
Strasburg, Oh., U.S.	B4	112
Strasburg, Pa., U.S.	G9	115
Strasburg, Va., U.S.	B4	123
Stratford, Ont., Can.	D3	73
Stratford, Ct., U.S.	E3	84
Stratford, Ia., U.S.	B4	92
Stratford, N.J., U.S.	D2	107
Stratford, Ok., U.S.	C5	113
Stratford, Tx., U.S.	A1	120
Stratford, Wi., U.S.	D3	126
Stratford Point, c., Ct., U.S.	E3	84
Stratford-upon-Avon, Eng., U.K.	I11	7
Stratham, N.H., U.S.	D5	106
Strathmore, Alta., Can.	D4	68
Strathmore, Ca., U.S.	D4	82
Strathroy, Ont., Can.	E3	73
Stratton, Co., U.S.	B8	83
Straubing, Ger.	G12	8
Strausberg, Ger.	C13	8
Strawberry, stm., Ar., U.S.	A4	81
Strawberry, stm., Ut., U.S.	C5	121
Strawberry Mountain, mtn., Or., U.S.	C8	114
Strawberry Point, Ia., U.S.	B6	92
Strawberry Point, c., Ma., U.S.	B6	98
Strawberry Range, mts., Or., U.S.	C8	114
Strawberry Reservoir, res., Ut., U.S.	C4	121
Streator, Il., U.S.	B5	90
Stretensk, Russia	G17	24
Strickland, stm., Pap. N. Gui.	m15	50a
Strimón (Struma), stm., Eur.	I7	16
Stromness, Scot., U.K.	C9	7
Stromsburg, Ne., U.S.	C8	104
Strömstad, Swe.	G8	6
Strömsund, Swe.	E10	6
Strong, Ar., U.S.	D3	81
Strong, Me., U.S.	D2	96
Strong, stm., Ms., U.S.	C4	101
Strong City, Ks., U.S.	D7	93
Stronghurst, Il., U.S.	C3	90
Strongsville, Oh., U.S.	A4	112
Stronsay, i., Scot., U.K.	B10	7
Stroud, Ok., U.S.	B5	113
Stroudsburg, Pa., U.S.	E11	115
Stroudwater, stm., Me., U.S.	g7	96
Strum, Wi., U.S.	D2	126
Struma (Strimón), stm., Eur.	H7	16
Strumble Head, c., Wales, U.K.	I7	7
Strumica, Mac.	H6	16
Strunino, Russia	E21	18
Struthers, Oh., U.S.	A5	112
Stryker, Oh., U.S.	A1	112
Stuart, Fl., U.S.	E6	86
Stuart, Ia., U.S.	C3	92
Stuart, Ne., U.S.	B6	104
Stuart, Va., U.S.	D2	123

Name	Map Ref	Page
Stuart, Mount, mtn., Wa., U.S.	B5	124
Stuart Lake, l., B.C., Can.	B5	69
Stuarts Draft, Va., U.S.	B3	123
Stull, stm., Can.	B5	70
Stump Lake, l., N.D., U.S.	B7	111
Stump Pond, res., R.I., U.S.	D2	116
Stung Treng, Camb.	H8	34
Stupino, Russia	G21	18
Sturbridge, Ma., U.S.	B3	98
Sturgeon, Mo., U.S.	B5	102
Sturgeon, stm., Mi., U.S.	B4	99
Sturgeon Bay, Wi., U.S.	D6	126
Sturgeon Bay, b., Man., Can.	C3	70
Sturgeon Falls, Ont., Can.	A5	73
Sturgeon Lake, l., Ont., Can.	C6	73
Sturgis, Sask., Can.	F4	75
Sturgis, Ky., U.S.	e10	94
Sturgis, Mi., U.S.	G5	99
Sturgis, S.D., U.S.	C2	118
Sturtevant, Wi., U.S.	F6	126
Stutsman, co., N.D., U.S.	B6	111
Stuttgart, Ger.	G9	8
Stuttgart, Ar., U.S.	C4	81
Suaita, Col.	D6	58
Subang, Indon.	m13	33a
Subansiri, stm., Asia	G16	38
Subiaco, Italy	H8	14
Sublette, Ks., U.S.	E3	93
Sublette, co., Wy., U.S.	D2	127
Sublett Range, mts., Id., U.S.	G6	89
Sublimity, Or., U.S.	C4	114
Subotica, Yugo.	C3	16
Sučan, Russia	I20	24
Sucarnoochee, stm., Al., U.S.	C1	78
Succasunna, N.J., U.S.	B3	107
Suceava, Rom.	B10	16
Süchbaatar, Mong.	A8	26
Suchumi, Geor.	I6	22
Sucre, Bol.	G5	54
Sucuaro, Col.	E8	58
Sudan, ctry., Afr.	F12	42
Sudan, reg., Afr.	F7	42
Sudbury, Ont., Can.	A4	73
Sudbury, Ma., U.S.	B5	98
Sudbury, stm., Ma., U.S.	B5	98
Sudbury Center, Ma., U.S.	g10	98
Sudbury Reservoir, res., Ma., U.S.	g10	98
Sudeten see Sudety, mts., Eur.	E15	8
Sudety, mts., Eur.	E15	8
Sue, stm., Sudan	G11	42
Sueca, Spain	F11	12
Suez see As-Suways, Egypt	C12	42
Suez Canal see Suways, Qanāt as-, Egypt	D3	40
Suffern, N.Y., U.S.	D6	109
Suffield, Ct., U.S.	B5	84
Suffolk, Va., U.S.	D6	123
Suffolk, co., Ma., U.S.	B5	98
Suffolk, co., N.Y., U.S.	n15	109
Sugar, stm., U.S.	F4	126
Sugar, stm., N.H., U.S.	D2	106
Sugar City, Id., U.S.	F7	89
Sugar Creek, Mo., U.S.	h11	102
Sugarcreek, Pa., U.S.	D2	115
Sugar Creek, stm., Oh., U.S.	C2	112
Sugar Creek, stm., Pa., U.S.	C8	115
Sugar Grove, Va., U.S.	D1	123
Sugar Hill, Ga., U.S.	B2	87
Sugar Island, i., Mi., U.S.	B6	99
Sugar Land, Tx., U.S.	E5	120
Sugarland Run, Va., U.S.	*A5	123
Sugar Loaf, Va., U.S.	C3	123
Sugarloaf Mountain, mtn., Mt., U.S.	C4	103
Sugar Notch, Pa., U.S.	n17	115
Suggi Lake, l., Sask., Can.	C4	75
Sugoj, stm., Russia	E25	24
Şuḩār, Oman	D6	46
Suhl, Ger.	E10	8
Suiattle, stm., Wa., U.S.	A4	124
Suide, China	D9	26
Suihua, China	B12	26
Suining, China	E8	26
Suiping, China	B2	28
Suitland, Md., U.S.	C4	97
Suizhong, China	C11	26
Suja, Russia	E24	18
Sukabumi, Indon.	m13	32
Sukagawa, Japan	E13	30
Sukhumi see Suchumi, Geor.	I6	22
Sukkertoppen, Grnld.	C22	66
Sukkur, Pak.	G3	38
Sukumo, Japan	J5	30
Sula, Kepulauan, is., Indon.	F8	32
Sulaimān Range, mts., Pak.	F3	38
Sulawesi (Celebes), i., Indon.	F7	32
Sullana, Peru	D2	54
Sulligent, Al., U.S.	B1	78
Sullivan, Il., U.S.	D5	90
Sullivan, In., U.S.	F3	91
Sullivan, Mo., U.S.	C6	102
Sullivan, co., In., U.S.	F3	91
Sullivan, co., Mo., U.S.	A4	102
Sullivan, co., N.H., U.S.	D2	106
Sullivan, co., N.Y., U.S.	D6	109
Sullivan, co., Pa., U.S.	D9	115
Sullivan, co., Tn., U.S.	C11	119
Sullivan Lake, l., Alta., Can.	D5	68
Sullivans Island, S.C., U.S.	k12	117
Sully, Fr.	E9	10
Sully, Ia., U.S.	C5	92
Sully, co., S.D., U.S.	C5	118
Sulmona, Italy	G8	14
Sulphur, La., U.S.	D2	95
Sulphur, Ok., U.S.	C5	113
Sulphur, stm., U.S.	D2	81
Sulphur Spring Range, mts., Nv., U.S.	C5	105
Sulphur Springs, Tx., U.S.	C5	120
Sultan, Wa., U.S.	B4	124
Sultānpur, India	G10	38
Sulu Archipelago, is., Phil.	D7	32
Sulu Sea, Asia	D6	32
Sulzbach-Rosenberg, Ger.	F11	8
Sumas, Wa., U.S.	A3	124
Sumatera (Sumatra), i., Indon.	F3	32
Sumatra see Sumatera, i., Indon.	F3	32
Sumba, i., Indon.	G7	32
Sumbawa, i., Indon.	G6	32
Sumbawanga, Tan.	C6	44
Sumedang, Indon.	m13	33a
Šumen, Bul.	F10	16
Sumenep, Indon.	m16	33a
Sumgait, Azer.	I7	22
Sumiton, Al., U.S.	B2	78
Summerfield, N.C., U.S.	A3	110
Summerford, Newf., Can.	D4	72
Summer Island, i., Mi., U.S.	C4	99
Summer Lake, l., Or., U.S.	E6	114
Summerland, B.C., Can.	E8	69
Summers, co., W.V., U.S.	D4	125
Summerside, P.E.I., Can.	C6	71
Summersville, W.V., U.S.	C4	125
Summersville Lake, res., W.V., U.S.	C4	125
Summerton, S.C., U.S.	D7	117
Summertown, Tn., U.S.	B4	119
Summerville, Ga., U.S.	B1	87
Summerville, S.C., U.S.	E7	117
Summit, Il., U.S.	k9	90
Summit, Ms., U.S.	D3	101
Summit, N.J., U.S.	B4	107
Summit, Tn., U.S.	h11	119
Summit, co., Co., U.S.	B4	83
Summit, co., Oh., U.S.	A4	112
Summit, co., Ut., U.S.	C5	121
Summit Hill, Pa., U.S.	E10	115
Summit Lake, l., Ia., U.S.	C3	92
Summit Lake Indian Reservation, Nv., U.S.	B2	105
Summit Mountain, mtn., Nv., U.S.	D5	105
Summit Peak, mtn., Co., U.S.	D4	83
Summitville, In., U.S.	D6	91
Sumner, Il., U.S.	E6	90
Sumner, Ia., U.S.	B5	92
Sumner, Wa., U.S.	B3	124
Sumner, co., Ks., U.S.	E6	93
Sumner, co., Tn., U.S.	A5	119
Sumner, Lake, res., N.M., U.S.	C5	108
Sumner Dam, N.M., U.S.	C5	108
Sumner Strait, strt., Ak., U.S.	m23	79
Sumoto, Japan	H7	30
Šumperk, Czech.	F16	8
Sumrall, Ms., U.S.	D4	101
Šumšu, Ostrov, i., Russia	G25	24
Sumter, S.C., U.S.	D7	117
Sumter, co., Al., U.S.	C1	78
Sumter, co., Fl., U.S.	D4	86
Sumter, co., Ga., U.S.	D2	87
Sumter, co., S.C., U.S.	D7	117
Sumy, Ukr.	G4	22
Sun, stm., Mt., U.S.	C4	103
Sunagawa, Japan	p19	30a
Sunapee, N.H., U.S.	D2	106
Sunapee Lake, l., N.H., U.S.	D2	106
Sunbright, Tn., U.S.	C9	119
Sunbury, Oh., U.S.	B3	112
Sunbury, Pa., U.S.	E8	115
Sunchales, Arg.	C4	56
Sun City, Az., U.S.	k8	80
Suncook, N.H., U.S.	D4	106
Suncook, stm., N.H., U.S.	D4	106
Suncook Lakes, l., N.H., U.S.	D4	106
Sunda, Selat, strt., Indon.	G4	32
Sundance, Wy., U.S.	B8	127
Sundance Mountain, mtn., Wy., U.S.	B8	127
Sundarbans, reg., Asia	J13	38
Sunderland, Ont., Can.	C5	73
Sunderland, Eng., U.K.	G11	7
Sundown, Tx., U.S.	C1	120
Sundre, Alta., Can.	D3	68
Sundridge, Ont., Can.	B5	73
Sundsvall, Swe.	E11	6
Sunflower, Ms., U.S.	B3	101
Sunflower, co., Ms., U.S.	B3	101
Sunflower, Mount, mtn., Ks., U.S.	C2	93
Sungaidareh, Indon.	O6	34
Sungei Patani, Malay.	L6	34
Suniteyouqi, China	C9	26
Sunland Park, N.M., U.S.	F3	108
Sunlight Creek, stm., Wy., U.S.	B3	127
Sunman, In., U.S.	F7	91
Sunndalsøra, Nor.	E7	6
Sunnyside, Newf., Can.	E5	72
Sunnyside, Wa., U.S.	C5	124
Sunnyvale, Ca., U.S.	k8	82
Sun Prairie, Wi., U.S.	E4	126
Sunray, Tx., U.S.	A2	120
Sunrise Manor, Nv., U.S.	*G6	105
Sunset, La., U.S.	D3	95
Sunset, Ut., U.S.	B4	121
Sunset Beach, Hi., U.S.	f9	88
Sunset Crater National Monument, Az., U.S.	B4	80
Sunset Lake, l., Vt., U.S.	D2	122
Suntar, Russia	E17	24
Suntar-Chajata, Chrebet, mts., Russia	E22	24
Suntaug Lake, l., Ma., U.S.	f11	98
Sun Valley, Id., U.S.	F4	89
Sun Valley, Nv., U.S.	D2	105
Sunyani, Ghana	G5	42
Suō-nada, Japan	I4	30
Suonenjoki, Fin.	E16	6
Suordach, Russia	D20	24
Superior, Az., U.S.	D4	80
Superior, Mt., U.S.	C2	103
Superior, Ne., U.S.	D7	104
Superior, Wi., U.S.	B1	126
Superior, Wy., U.S.	E4	127
Superior, Lake, l., N.A.	B9	76
Superstition Mountains, mts., Az., U.S.	m10	80
Supetar, Cro.	F11	14
Suphan Buri, Thai.	G6	34
Suqian, China	B7	28
Suquamish, Wa., U.S.	B3	124
Suquṭrā (Socotra), i., Yemen	F5	46
Ṣūr (Tyre), Leb.	C4	40
Şūr, Oman	D6	46
Sur, Point, c., Ca., U.S.	D3	82
Surabaya, Indon.	m16	32
Surakarta, Indon.	m15	32
Şūrān, Syria	B5	40
Surat, India	B2	37
Surat Thani (Ban Don), Thai.	J5	34
Surendranagar, India	I4	38
Surfside, Fl., U.S.	s13	86
Surfside Beach, S.C., U.S.	D10	117
Surgoinsville, Tn., U.S.	C11	119
Sūri, India	I12	38
Surigao, Phil.	D8	32
Surin, Thai.	G7	34
Suriname, ctry., S.A.	C7	54
Sūrmaq, Iran	B5	46
Surprise, Az., U.S.	k8	80
Surrey, N.D., U.S.	A4	111
Surry, co., N.C., U.S.	A2	110
Surry, co., Va., U.S.	C6	123
Surry Mountain Lake, res., N.H., U.S.	D2	106
Surt, Libya	B9	42
Surt, Khalīj, b., Libya	B9	42
Sürüç, Tur.	A6	40
Suruga-wan, b., Japan	H11	30
Susa, Italy	D2	14
Susanville, Ca., U.S.	B3	82
Susitna, stm., Ak., U.S.	C10	79
Susquehanna, Pa., U.S.	C10	115
Susquehanna, co., Pa., U.S.	C10	115
Susquehanna, stm., U.S.	A5	97
Susquehanna, West Branch, stm., Pa., U.S.	D5	115
Sussex, N.B., Can.	D4	71
Sussex, N.J., U.S.	A3	107
Sussex, Wi., U.S.	m11	126
Sussex, co., De., U.S.	F4	85
Sussex, co., N.J., U.S.	A3	107
Sussex, co., Va., U.S.	D5	123
Susurluk, Tur.	J12	16
Sutherland, S. Afr.	H4	44
Sutherland, Ia., U.S.	B2	92
Sutherland, Ne., U.S.	C4	104
Sutherlin, Or., U.S.	D3	114
Sutlej (Satluj) (Langqên), stm., Asia	F4	38
Sutter, co., Ca., U.S.	C3	82
Sutter Creek, Ca., U.S.	C3	82
Sutton, Que., Can.	D5	74
Sutton, Ne., U.S.	D8	104
Sutton, W.V., U.S.	C4	125
Sutton, co., Tx., U.S.	D2	120
Sutton Lake, res., W.V., U.S.	C4	125
Sutwik Island, i., Ak., U.S.	D8	79
Suur Munamägi, hill, Est.	D10	18
Suwa, Japan	F11	30
Suwałki, Pol.	A22	8
Suwanee, Ga., U.S.	B2	87
Suwannee, co., Fl., U.S.	B3	86
Suwannee, stm., U.S.	C4	86
Suwannee Sound, strt., Fl., U.S.	C3	86
Suways, Qanāt as- (Suez Canal), Egypt	D3	40
Suwŏn, S. Kor.	D12	26
Suxian, China	B5	28
Suzaka, Japan	F11	30
Suzhou (Soochow), China	D9	28
Suzuka, Japan	H9	30
Suzu-misaki, c., Japan	E10	30
Suzzara, Italy	D5	14
Svappavaara, Swe.	C13	6
Svartenhuk, pen., Grnld.	B22	66
Sv'atoj Nos, Mys, c., Russia	C22	24
Sveg, Swe.	E10	6
Svenljunga, Swe.	H9	6
Svensen, Or., U.S.	A3	114
Sverdlovsk see Jekaterinburg, Russia	F10	22
Svetlaja, Russia	H21	24
Svetlyj, Russia	F17	24
Svištov, Bul.	F9	16
Svobodnyj, Russia	G19	24
Svolvær, Nor.	B10	6
Swain, co., N.C., U.S.	f9	110
Swainsboro, Ga., U.S.	D4	87
Swakopmund, Nmb.	F2	44
Swampscott, Ma., U.S.	B6	98
Swan, stm., Can.	C1	70
Swan Creek, stm., Oh., U.S.	e6	112
Swan Falls, wtfl, Id., U.S.	F2	89
Swan Hill, Austl.	G8	50
Swan Hills, Alta., Can.	B3	68
Swan Islands, is., Hond.	F6	64
Swan Lake, l., Man., Can.	C1	70
Swan Lake, l., Me., U.S.	D4	96
Swan Lake, l., Ne., U.S.	C3	104
Swannanoa, N.C., U.S.	f10	110
Swan Peak, mtn., Mt., U.S.	C3	103
Swan Range, mts., Mt., U.S.	C3	103
Swan River, Man., Can.	C1	70
Swansboro, N.C., U.S.	C5	110
Swansea, Wales, U.K.	J9	7
Swansea, Il., U.S.	E4	90
Swanson Lake, res., Ne., U.S.	D4	104
Swanton, Oh., U.S.	A2	112
Swanton, Vt., U.S.	B2	122
Swanzey Center, N.H., U.S.	E2	106
Swarthmore, Pa., U.S.	p20	115
Swartswood Lake, l., N.J., U.S.	A3	107
Swartz Creek, Mi., U.S.	F7	99
Swayzee, In., U.S.	C6	91
Swaziland, ctry., Afr.	G6	44
Swea City, Ia., U.S.	A3	92
Sweden, ctry., Eur.	C10	4
Sweeny, Tx., U.S.	r14	120
Sweet Grass, co., Mt., U.S.	E7	103
Sweet Home, Or., U.S.	C4	114
Sweetser, In., U.S.	C6	91
Sweet Springs, Mo., U.S.	C4	102
Sweetwater, Tn., U.S.	D9	119
Sweetwater, Tx., U.S.	C2	120
Sweetwater, co., Wy., U.S.	E3	127
Sweetwater, stm., Wy., U.S.	D4	127
Sweetwater Creek, Fl., U.S.	p10	86
Sweetwater Creek, stm., Ok., U.S.	B1	113
Swellendam, S. Afr.	H4	44
Swepsonville, N.C., U.S.	A3	110
Świdnica (Schweidnitz), Pol.	E16	8
Swift, co., Mn., U.S.	E3	100
Swift, stm., N.H., U.S.	B4	106
Swift Creek, stm., N.C., U.S.	B5	110
Swift Creek, stm., Va., U.S.	n17	123
Swift Creek Reservoir, res., Wa., U.S.	C3	124
Swift Diamond, stm., N.H., U.S.	g7	106
Swifton, Ar., U.S.	B4	81
Swinburne, Cape, c., N.W. Ter., Can.	B13	66
Swindon, Eng., U.K.	J11	7
Swinford, Ire.	H4	7
Swinomish Indian Reservation, Wa., U.S.	A3	124
Świnoujście (Swinemünde), Pol.	B14	8
Swisher, Ia., U.S.	C6	92
Swisher, co., Tx., U.S.	B2	120
Swissvale, Pa., U.S.	k14	115
Switzer, W.V., U.S.	D3	125
Switzerland, Fl., U.S.	m8	86
Switzerland, co., In., U.S.	G7	91
Switzerland, ctry., Eur.	F9	4
Swoyerville, Pa., U.S.	D10	115
Syalach, Russia	D18	24
Sycamore, Al., U.S.	B3	78
Sycamore, Il., U.S.	B5	90
Sycamore, Oh., U.S.	B2	112
Sycamore Creek, stm., W.V., U.S.	m13	125
Sydenham, Ont., Can.	C8	73
Sydney, Austl.	F10	50
Syke, Ger.	C8	8
Sykesville, Md., U.S.	B4	97
Sykesville, Pa., U.S.	D4	115
Sykkylven, Nor.	E6	6
Syktyvkar, Russia	E8	22
Sylacauga, Al., U.S.	B3	78
Sylhet, Bngl.	H14	38
Sylva, N.C., U.S.	f9	110
Sylvania, Al., U.S.	A4	78
Sylvania, Ga., U.S.	D5	87
Sylvania, Oh., U.S.	A2	112
Sylvan Lake, Alta., Can.	C3	68
Sylvan Lake, Mi., U.S.	o15	99
Sylvan Lake, l., In., U.S.	B7	91
Sylvan Pass, Wy., U.S.	B2	127
Sylvester, Ga., U.S.	E3	87
Sym, Russia	E11	24
Symmes Creek, stm., Oh., U.S.	D3	112
Symsonia, Ky., U.S.	f9	94
Syracuse, In., U.S.	B6	91
Syracuse, Ks., U.S.	E2	93
Syracuse, Ne., U.S.	D9	104
Syracuse, N.Y., U.S.	B4	109
Syracuse, Ut., U.S.	B3	121
Syrdarja (Syr Darya), stm., Asia	I11	22
Syria, ctry., Asia	B5	40
Syriam, Mya.	F4	34
Syrian Desert see Shām, Bādiyat ash-, des., Asia	C6	40
Sysladobsis Lake, l., Me., U.S.	C4	96
Syzran', Russia	G7	22
Szamos (Someş), stm., Eur.	B6	16
Szczecin (Stettin), Pol.	B14	8
Szczecinek (Neustettin), Pol.	B16	8
Szeged, Hung.	I20	8
Székesfehérvár, Hung.	H18	8
Szentes, Hung.	I20	8
Szolnok, Hung.	H20	8
Szombathely, Hung.	H16	8

T

Name	Map Ref	Page
Taal, Lake, l., Phil.	r19	33b
Tabaco, Phil.	r20	33b
Tabarka, Tun.	M3	14
Tabatinga, Serra da, hills, Braz.	F10	54
Tabbys Peak, mtn., Ut., U.S.	C3	121
Tabelbala, Alg.	C5	42
Taber, Alta., Can.	E4	68
Tabernes de Valldigna, Spain	F11	12
Tablas Island, i., Phil.	C7	32
Table Head, c., Newf., Can.	B4	72
Table Mountain, mtn., Az., U.S.	E5	80
Table Rock Lake, res., U.S.	E4	102
Table Top, mtn., Az., U.S.	E3	80
Tabor, Russia	C24	24
Tabor, Ia., U.S.	D2	92
Tabora, Tan.	C6	44
Tabor City, N.C., U.S.	C4	110
Tabou, C. Iv.	H4	42
Tabrīz, Iran	J7	22
Tabūk, Sau. Ar.	C2	46
Tacámbaro de Codallos, Mex.	H9	62
Tachikawa, Japan	G12	30
Tacna, Peru	G4	54
Tacoma, Wa., U.S.	B3	124
Taconic Range, mts., U.S.	A1	98
Tacuarembó, Ur.	C5	56
Tacubaya, Mex.	C7	62
Tadjerouine, Tun.	N3	14
Tadoule Lake, l., Man., Can.	E13	66
Tadoussac, Que., Can.	A8	74
Tādpatri, India	E5	37
Taegu, S. Kor.	D12	26
Taejŏn, S. Kor.	D12	26
Tafalla, Spain	C10	12
Taft, Ca., U.S.	E4	82
Taft, Tx., U.S.	F4	120
Tagajō, Japan	D13	30
Taganrog, Russia	H5	22
Taglio di Po, Italy	D7	14
Taguatinga, Braz.	B5	57
Taguke, China	D11	38
Tagula Island, i., Pap. N. Gui.	B10	50
Tagus (Tejo) (Tajo), stm., Eur.	F3	12
Tahan, Gunong, mtn., Malay.	L7	34
Tahat, mtn., Alg.	D7	42
Tahlequah, Ok., U.S.	B7	113
Tahoe, Lake, l., U.S.	E1	105
Tahoe City, Ca., U.S.	C3	82
Tahoka, Tx., U.S.	C2	120
Taholah, Wa., U.S.	B1	124
Tahoua, Niger	F7	42
Tahquamenon, stm., Mi., U.S.	B5	99
Tahsis, B.C., Can.	E4	69
Tahtsa Peak, mtn., B.C., Can.	C4	69
T'aichung, Tai.	K9	28
T'aichunghsien, Tai.	K9	28
Taihape, N.Z.	C5	52
Tai Hu, l., China	D9	28
Tailai, China	B11	26
Tain, Scot., U.K.	D8	7
T'ainan, Tai.	L9	28
T'aipei, Tai.	J10	28
T'aipeihsien, Tai.	J10	28
Taiping, Malay.	L6	34
Taishun, China	H8	28
Taitao, Península de, pen., Chile	F2	56
T'aitung, Tai.	M10	28
Taivalkoski, Fin.	D17	6
Taiwan (T'aiwan), ctry., Asia	G11	26
Taiwan Strait, strt., Asia	K8	28
Taixian, China	C9	28
Taixing, China	C9	28
Taiyuan, China	D9	26
Taizhou, China	C8	28
Ta'izz, Yemen	F3	46
Tajikistan, ctry., Asia	J12	22
Tajitos, Mex.	B3	62
Tajmyr, Ozero, l., Russia	C14	24
Tajmyr, Poluostrov, pen., Russia	B14	24
Tajšet, Russia	F13	24
Tajumulco, Volcań, vol., Guat.	G2	64
Tak, Thai.	F5	34
Takada, Japan	E11	30
Takalar, Indon.	G6	32
Takamatsu, Japan	H7	30
Takaoka, Japan	F10	30
Takapuna, N.Z.	B5	52
Takasaki, Japan	F12	30
Takatsuki, Japan	H8	30
Takawa, Japan	I3	30
Takayama, Japan	F10	30
Takefu, Japan	G9	30
Takêv, Camb.	I8	34
Takijuq Lake, l., N.W. Ter., Can.	C10	66
Takikawa, Japan	p19	30a
Takla Lake, l., B.C., Can.	B5	69
Taklimakan Shamo, des., China	D3	26
Takoma Park, Md., U.S.	f8	97
Taku Glacier, Ak., U.S.	k22	79
Tala, Mex.	G8	62
Talagang, Pak.	D5	38
Talaimannar, Sri L.	H5	37
Talara, Peru	D2	54
Talarrubias, Spain	F6	12
Talasea, Pap. N. Gui.	m17	50a
Talaud, Kepulauan, is., Indon.	E8	32
Talavera de la Reina, Spain	F7	12
Talawdī, Sudan	F12	42
Talbot, co., Ga., U.S.	D2	87
Talbot, co., Md., U.S.	C5	97
Talbot Island, i., Fl., U.S.	B5	86
Talbot Lake, l., Man., Can.	B2	70
Talbotton, Ga., U.S.	D2	87
Talca, Chile	D2	56
Talcahuano, Chile	D2	56
Talent, Or., U.S.	E4	114
Taliabu, Pulau, i., Indon.	F7	32
Taliaferro, co., Ga., U.S.	C4	87
Talihina, Ok., U.S.	C6	113
Talkeetna, Ak., U.S.	C10	79
Talkeetna Mountains, mts., Ak., U.S.	f17	79
Talladega, Al., U.S.	B3	78
Talladega, co., Al., U.S.	B3	78
Tallahassee, Fl., U.S.	B2	86
Tallahatchie, co., Ms., U.S.	B3	101
Tallahatchie, stm., Ms., U.S.	B3	101
Tallapoosa, Ga., U.S.	C1	87
Tallapoosa, co., Al., U.S.	C4	78
Tallapoosa, stm., Al., U.S.	C3	78
Tallassee, Al., U.S.	C4	78
Talleyville, De., U.S.	A3	85
Tallinn, Est.	B7	18
Tall Kalakh, Syria	B5	40
Tallmadge, Oh., U.S.	A4	112
Tall Tamir, Syria	A7	40
Tallulah, La., U.S.	B4	95
Tal'menka, Russia	G10	24
Talo, mtn., Eth.	F2	46
Tāloqān, Afg.	B3	38
Talquin, Lake, res., Fl., U.S.	B2	86
Talu, Indon.	N5	34
Taluk, Indon.	O6	34
Tama, Ia., U.S.	C5	92
Tama, co., Ia., U.S.	B5	92
Tamale, Ghana	G5	42
Tamalpais, Mount, mtn., Ca., U.S.	h7	82
Tamana, Japan	J3	30
Tamanrasset, Alg.	D7	42
Tamaqua, Pa., U.S.	E10	115
Tamaroa, Il., U.S.	E4	90
Tamazula de Gordiano, Mex.	H8	62
Tamazunchale, Mex.	G10	62
Tambacounda, Sen.	F3	42
Tambohorano, Madag.	E8	44
Tambov, Russia	I24	18
Tambura, Sudan	G11	42
Tamchaket, Maur.	E3	42
Tamel Aike, Arg.	F2	56
Tamiahua, Laguna de, b., Mex.	G11	62
Tamiami Canal, Fl., U.S.	G6	86
Tamil Nadu, state, India	G5	37
Tam Ky, Viet.	G10	34
Tampa, Fl., U.S.	E4	86
Tampa Bay, b., Fl., U.S.	E4	86
Tampere, Fin.	F14	6
Tampico, Mex.	F11	62
Tampico, Il., U.S.	B4	90
Tamrida, Yemen	F5	46
Tamsagbulag, Mong.	B10	26
Tamworth, Austl.	F10	50
Tana, Nor.	A17	6
Tana, stm., Eur.	A16	6
Tana, stm., Kenya	B7	44

Name	Map Ref	Page
Tana, Lake, l., Eth.	F2	46
Tanabe, Japan	I8	30
Tanaga Island, i., Ak., U.S.	E4	79
Tanahjampea, Pulau, i., Indon.	G7	32
Tanami Desert, des., Austl.	C5	50
Tanana, Ak., U.S.	B9	79
Tanana, stm., Ak., U.S.	C10	79
Tananarive see Antananarivo, Madag.	E9	44
Tānda, India	G10	38
Tandil, Arg.	D5	56
Tando Ādam, Pak.	H3	38
Tando Muhammad Khān, Pak.	H3	38
Tanega-shima, i., Japan	u30	31b
Taney, co., Mo., U.S.	E4	102
Taneycomo, Lake, res., Mo., U.S.	E4	102
Taneytown, Md., U.S.	A3	97
Tanezrouft, des., Afr.	D5	42
Tanga, Tan.	C7	44
Tangail, Bngl.	H13	38
Tanganyika, Lake, l., Afr.	C5	44
Tanger (Tangier), Mor.	A4	42
Tangerang, Indon.	m13	33a
Tangermünde, Ger.	C11	8
Tanggula Shan, mts., China	D13	38
Tangier, Va., U.S.	C7	123
Tangier Island, i., Va., U.S.	C6	123
Tangier Sound, strt., Md., U.S.	D6	97
Tangier see Tanger, Mor.	A4	42
Tangipahoa, co., La., U.S.	D5	95
Tangipahoa, stm., La., U.S.	D5	95
Tangra Yumco, l., China	E12	38
Tangshan, China	D10	26
Tanimbar, Kepulauan, is., Indon.	G9	32
Tanjungbalai, Indon.	M5	34
Tanjungkarang-Telukbetung, Indon.	k12	32
Tanjungpinang, Indon.	N8	34
Tanjungselor, Indon.	E6	32
Tānk, Pak.	D4	38
Tännäs, Swe.	E9	6
Tanner, Al., U.S.	A3	78
Tânout, Niger	F7	42
Tanshui, Tai.	J10	28
Ṭanṭā, Egypt	B12	42
Tanuku, India	D6	37
Tanzania, ctry., Afr.	C6	44
Taos, Mo., U.S.	C5	102
Taos, N.M., U.S.	A4	108
Taos, co., N.M., U.S.	A4	108
Taos Pueblo, N.M., U.S.	A4	108
Taoudenni, Mali	D5	42
Tapachula, Mex.	J13	62
Tapah, Malay.	L6	34
Tapajós, stm., Braz.	E7	54
Taphan Hin, Thai.	F6	34
Tāpi, stm., India	B2	37
Tappahannock, Va., U.S.	C6	123
Tappan, N.Y., U.S.	g13	109
Tappan, Lake, res., N.J., U.S.	g9	107
Tappan Lake, res., Oh., U.S.	B4	112
Taqāṭu' Hayyā, Sudan	E13	42
Taquaritinga, Braz.	F4	57
Tar, stm., N.C., U.S.	B5	110
Tara, Ont., Can.	C3	73
Ṭarābulus (Tripoli), Leb.	B4	40
Ṭarābulus (Tripoli), Libya	B8	42
Ṭarābulus (Tripolitania), reg., Libya	B8	42
Tarakan, Indon.	E6	32
Tarancón, Spain	E8	12
Taranto, Italy	I12	14
Taranto, Golfo di, b., Italy	I12	14
Tarapacá, Col.	I8	58
Tarare, Fr.	G11	10
Tarascon, Fr.	J8	10
Tarata, Bol.	G5	54
Tarazona, Spain	D10	12
Tarazona de la Mancha, Spain	F10	12
Tarbert, Scot., U.K.	F7	7
Tarbert, Scot., U.K.	D6	7
Tarbes, Fr.	I7	10
Tarboro, N.C., U.S.	B5	110
Tarcento, Italy	C8	14
Taree, Austl.	F10	50
Tareja, Russia	C12	24
Tarentum, Pa., U.S.	E2	115
Tarfaya, Mor.	C3	42
Targhee Pass, U.S.	E7	89
Tarifa, Punta de, c., Spain	I6	12
Tariffville, Ct., U.S.	B4	84
Tarija, Bol.	H6	54
Tarim, stm., China	C3	26
Tarīn Kowt, Afg.	D1	38
Tarkio, Mo., U.S.	A2	102
Tarkwa, Ghana	G5	42
Tarlac, Phil.	q19	32
Tarn, stm., Fr.	I8	10
Tärnaby, Swe.	D10	6
Tarnak, stm., Afg.	D2	38
Tarnów, Pol.	E20	8
Tarnowskie Góry, Pol.	E18	8
Tarpey, Ca., U.S.	D4	82
Tarpon, Lake, l., Fl., U.S.	o10	86
Tarpon Springs, Fl., U.S.	D4	86
Tarquinia, Italy	G6	14
Tarragona, Spain	D13	12
Tarrant, Al., U.S.	B3	78
Tarrant, co., Tx., U.S.	C4	120
Tarrasa, Spain	D14	12
Tarryall Mountains, mts., Co., U.S.	B5	83
Tarrytown, N.Y., U.S.	D7	109
Tarsus, Tur.	A4	40
Tartagal, Arg.	A4	56
Tartas, Fr.	I6	10
Tartu, Est.	C9	18
Ṭarṭūs, Syria	B4	40
Tarutung, Indon.	M5	34
Tašauz, Turk.	I9	22
Tasejeva, stm., Russia	F12	24
Tasejevo, Russia	F12	24
Taseko Mountain, mtn., B.C., Can.	D6	69
Tashi Gang Dzong, Bhu.	G14	38
Tashkent see Taškent, Uzb.	I11	22
Tasikmalaya, Indon.	m14	32
Taškent, Uzb.	I11	22
Tasmania, state, Austl.	H9	50
Tasman Sea, Oc.	G11	50
Tasso, Tn., U.S.	D9	119
Taštagol, Russia	G11	24
Tatabánya, Hung.	H18	8
Tatarskij Proliv, strt., Russia	H22	24
Tate, Ga., U.S.	B2	87
Tate, co., Ms., U.S.	A4	101
Tateville, Ky., U.S.	D5	94
Tateyama, Japan	H12	30
Tathlina Lake, l., N.W. Ter., Can.	D9	66
Tatnam, Cape, c., Man., Can.	f9	70
Tatta, Pak.	H2	38
Tattnall, co., Ga., U.S.	D4	87
Tatum, N.M., U.S.	D6	108
Tatvan, Tur.	H16	4
Tau, Nor.	G5	6
Taubaté, Braz.	G6	57
Tauberbischofsheim, Ger.	F9	8
Taujskaja Guba, b., Russia	F24	24
Taumarunui, N.Z.	C5	52
Taum Sauk Mountain, mtn., Mo., U.S.	D6	102
Taungdwingyi, Mya.	D3	34
Taunggyi, Mya.	D4	34
Taungup Pass, Mya.	E3	34
Taunton, Eng., U.K.	J9	7
Taunton, Ma., U.S.	C5	98
Taunton, stm., Ma., U.S.	C5	98
Taupo, Lake, l., N.Z.	C5	52
Tauranga, N.Z.	B6	52
Taureau, Réservoir, res., Que., Can.	C4	74
Taurus Mountains see Toros Dağları, mts., Tur.	H14	4
Tauste, Spain	D10	12
Tavares, Fl., U.S.	D5	86
Tavernier, Fl., U.S.	G6	86
Tavira, Port.	H4	12
Tavoy Point, c., Mya.	H5	34
Tavşanlı, Tur.	J13	16
Tawakoni, Lake, res., Tx., U.S.	C4	120
Tawas City, Mi., U.S.	D7	99
Tawas Lake, l., Mi., U.S.	D7	99
Tawau, Malay.	E6	32
Tawitawi Island, i., Phil.	D6	32
Ṭawkar, Sudan	E13	42
Taxco de Alarcón, Mex.	H10	62
Tay, Loch, l., Scot., U.K.	E8	7
Taylor, B.C., Can.	A7	69
Taylor, Az., U.S.	C5	80
Taylor, Ar., U.S.	D2	81
Taylor, Mi., U.S.	p15	99
Taylor, Pa., U.S.	D10	115
Taylor, Tx., U.S.	D4	120
Taylor, co., Fl., U.S.	B3	86
Taylor, co., Ga., U.S.	D2	87
Taylor, co., Ia., U.S.	D3	92
Taylor, co., Ky., U.S.	C4	94
Taylor, co., Tx., U.S.	C3	120
Taylor, co., W.V., U.S.	B4	125
Taylor, co., Wi., U.S.	C3	126
Taylor, stm., Co., U.S.	C4	83
Taylor, Mount, mtn., N.M., U.S.	B2	108
Taylor Mill, Ky., U.S.	k14	94
Taylor Mountain, mtn., Id., U.S.	E4	89
Taylor Park Reservoir, res., Co., U.S.	C4	83
Taylors, S.C., U.S.	B3	117
Taylors Falls, Mn., U.S.	E6	100
Taylors Island, i., Md., U.S.	D5	97
Taylorsville, In., U.S.	F6	91
Taylorsville, Ky., U.S.	B4	94
Taylorsville, Ms., U.S.	D4	101
Taylorsville, N.C., U.S.	B1	110
Taylorville, Il., U.S.	D4	90
Taymā', Sau. Ar.	C2	46
Tay Ninh, Viet.	I9	34
Tayoltita, Mex.	E7	62
Taytay, Phil.	C6	32
Taz, stm., Russia	D10	24
Taza, Mor.	B5	42
Tazewell, Tn., U.S.	C10	119
Tazewell, Va., U.S.	e10	123
Tazewell, co., Il., U.S.	C4	90
Tazewell, co., Va., U.S.	e10	123
Tazin Lake, l., Sask., Can.	E11	66
Tbessa, Alg.	A7	42
Tbilisi, Geor.	I6	22
Tbong, Camb.	H8	34
Tchefuncta, stm., La., U.S.	D5	95
Tchibanga, Gabon	B2	44
Tchien, Lib.	G4	42
Tchula, Ms., U.S.	B3	101
Tczew, Pol.	A18	8
Tea, S.D., U.S.	D9	118
Teacapán, Mex.	F7	62
Teague, Tx., U.S.	D4	120
Teakean Butte, mtn., Id., U.S.	C2	89
Te Anau, Lake, l., N.Z.	F1	52
Teaneck, N.J., U.S.	h8	107
Teano, Italy	H9	14
Teaticket, Ma., U.S.	C6	98
Tebingtinggi, Indon.	M5	34
Téboursouk, Tun.	M4	14
Tecate, Mex.	A1	62
Tecolotlan, Mex.	G7	62
Tecomán, Mex.	H8	62
Tecpan de Galeana, Mex.	I9	62
Tecuala, Mex.	F7	62
Tecuci, Rom.	D11	16
Tecumseh, Ont., Can.	E2	73
Tecumseh, Ks., U.S.	k14	93
Tecumseh, Mi., U.S.	G7	99
Tecumseh, Ne., U.S.	D9	104
Tecumseh, Ok., U.S.	B5	113
Tedžen (Harīrūd), stm., Asia	J10	22
Teeswater, Ont., Can.	C3	73
Tefé, Braz.	D6	54
Tegal, Indon.	m14	32
Tegucigalpa, Hond.	G4	64
Tehachapi, Ca., U.S.	E4	82
Tehachapi Mountains, mts., Ca., U.S.	E4	82
Tehama, co., Ca., U.S.	B2	82
Tehrān, Iran	J8	22
Tehuacán, Mex.	H11	62
Tehuantepec, Mex.	I12	62
Tehuantepec, Golfo de, b., Mex.	J12	62
Tehuantepec, Istmo de, Mex.	I12	62
Teide, Pico de, mtn., Spain	p24	13b
Tejamén, Mex.	E7	62
Tejkovo, Russia	E23	18
Tejupan, Punta, c., Mex.	H8	62
Tekamah, Ne., U.S.	C9	104
Tekirdağ, Tur.	I11	16
Tekoa, Wa., U.S.	B8	124
Tekonsha, Mi., U.S.	F5	99
Tela, Hond.	G4	64
Telavåg, Nor.	F5	6
Tel Aviv-Yafo, Isr.	C4	40
Teleckoje, Ozero, l., Russia	G11	24
Telén, Arg.	D3	56
Telescope Peak, mtn., Ca., U.S.	D5	82
Teles Pires, stm., Braz.	E7	54
Telfair, co., Ga., U.S.	E4	87
Telford, Pa., U.S.	F11	115
Telfs, Aus.	H11	8
Teli, Russia	G12	24
Telkwa, B.C., Can.	B4	69
Tell City, In., U.S.	I4	91
Teller, co., Co., U.S.	C5	83
Tellicherry, India	G3	37
Tellico Plains, Tn., U.S.	D9	119
Telluride, Co., U.S.	D3	83
Telok Anson, Malay.	L6	34
Telos Lake, l., Me., U.S.	B3	96
Temagami, Lake, l., Ont., Can.	G16	66
Tembeling, stm., Malay.	L7	34
Tembenči, stm., Russia	D13	24
Temecula, Ca., U.S.	F5	82
Temerloh, Malay.	M7	34
Teminabuan, Indon.	F9	32
Témiscouata, Lac, l., Que., Can.	B9	74
Te-Moak Indian Reservation, Nv., U.S.	C6	105
Temósachic, Mex.	C6	62
Tempe, Az., U.S.	D4	80
Temperance, Mi., U.S.	G7	99
Temperance, stm., Mn., U.S.	C8	100
Tempio Pausania, Italy	I4	14
Temple, Ga., U.S.	C1	87
Temple, Ok., U.S.	C3	113
Temple, Pa., U.S.	F10	115
Temple, Tx., U.S.	D4	120
Temple Terrace, Fl., U.S.	o11	86
Templin, Ger.	B13	8
Temuco, Chile	D2	56
Tena, Ec.	H4	58
Tenafly, N.J., U.S.	B5	107
Tenaha, Tx., U.S.	D5	120
Tenāli, India	D6	37
Tendaho, Eth.	F3	46
Tende, Col de, Eur.	H14	10
Ten Degree Channel, strt., India	J2	34
Ténéré, des., Niger	E8	42
Tenerife, i., Spain	p24	13b
Tengchong, China	B5	34
Tenino, Wa., U.S.	C3	124
Tenkāsi, India	H4	37
Tenkiller Ferry Lake, res., Ok., U.S.	B6	113
Tenkodogo, Burkina	F5	42
Tenmile, stm., U.S.	B5	116
Tenmile Creek, stm., W.V., U.S.	k10	125
Tenmile Lake, l., Mn., U.S.	D4	100
Tennant Creek, Austl.	C6	50
Tennessee, state, U.S.	B5	119
Tennessee, stm., U.S.	D9	76
Tennessee Pass, Co., U.S.	B4	83
Tennessee Ridge, Tn., U.S.	A4	119
Tennille, Ga., U.S.	D4	87
Tenom, Malay.	D6	32
Tenryū, stm., Japan	G10	30
Tensas, co., La., U.S.	B4	95
Tensas, stm., La., U.S.	B4	95
Tensaw, stm., Al., U.S.	E2	78
Ten Sleep, Wy., U.S.	B5	127
Tenterfield, Austl.	E10	50
Ten Thousand Islands, is., Fl., U.S.	G5	86
Teocaltiche, Mex.	G8	62
Teófilo Otoni, Braz.	D8	57
Tepa, Indon.	G8	32
Tepatitlán [de Morelos], Mex.	G8	62
Tepic, Mex.	G7	62
Teplice, Czech.	E13	8
Teramo, Italy	G8	14
Teresina, Braz.	E10	54
Teresópolis, Braz.	G7	57
Termez, Uzb.	B2	38
Termini Imerese, Italy	L8	14
Términos, Laguna de, b., Mex.	H14	62
Termoli, Italy	G9	14
Ternej, Russia	H21	24
Terni, Italy	G7	14
Ternopil', Ukr.	H3	22
Terpenija, Mys, c., Russia	H22	24
Terpenija, Zaliv, b., Russia	H22	24
Terra Alta, W.V., U.S.	B5	125
Terrace, B.C., Can.	B3	69
Terracina, Italy	H8	14
Terralba, Italy	J3	14
Terra Nova National Park, Newf., Can.	D4	72
Terrebonne, Que., Can.	D4	74
Terrebonne, Or., U.S.	C5	114
Terrebonne, co., La., U.S.	E5	95
Terrebonne Bay, b., La., U.S.	E5	95
Terre Haute, In., U.S.	F3	91
Terre Hill, Pa., U.S.	F9	115
Terrell, Tx., U.S.	C4	120
Terrell, co., Ga., U.S.	E2	87
Terrell, co., Tx., U.S.	D1	120
Terrell Hills, Tx., U.S.	k7	120
Terrenceville, Newf., Can.	E4	72
Terry, Ms., U.S.	C3	101
Terry, Mt., U.S.	D11	103
Terry, co., Tx., U.S.	C1	120
Terrytown, Ne., U.S.	C2	104
Terryville, Ct., U.S.	C3	84
Teruel, Spain	E10	12
Tervola, Fin.	C15	6
Teseney, Erit.	E2	46
Teshekpuk Lake, l., Ak., U.S.	A9	79
Teshio, Japan	o19	30a
Teslin, Yukon, Can.	D6	66
Teslin, stm., Can.	D6	66
Tesouro, Braz.	D2	57
Tessalit, Mali	D6	42
Tesuque, N.M., U.S.	B4	108
Tete, Moz.	E6	44
Teterow, Ger.	B12	8
Teton, co., Id., U.S.	F7	89
Teton, co., Mt., U.S.	C4	103
Teton, co., Wy., U.S.	C2	127
Teton, stm., Mt., U.S.	C5	103
Teton Pass, Wy., U.S.	C2	127
Teton Range, mts., Wy., U.S.	C2	127
Teton Village, Wy., U.S.	C2	127
Tétouan, Mor.	A4	42
Tetovo, Mac.	G4	16
Tet'uche, Russia	I21	24
Teulada, Italy	K3	14
Teulon, Man., Can.	D3	70
Teutopolis, Il., U.S.	D5	90
Teuva, Fin.	E13	6
Tevere (Tiber), stm., Italy	G7	14
Teverya, Isr.	C4	40
Tewksbury, Ma., U.S.	A5	98
Texada Island, i., B.C., Can.	E5	69
Texarkana, Ar., U.S.	D1	81
Texarkana, Tx., U.S.	C5	120
Texas, co., Mo., U.S.	D5	102
Texas, co., Ok., U.S.	e9	113
Texas, state, U.S.	D3	120
Texas City, Tx., U.S.	E5	120
Texhoma, Ok., U.S.	e9	113
Texico, N.M., U.S.	C6	108
Texoma, Lake, res., U.S.	D5	113
Teyvareh, Afg.	D1	38
Teziutlán, Mex.	H11	62
Tezpur, India	G15	38
Thabazimbi, S. Afr.	F5	44
Thai Binh, Viet.	D9	34
Thailand, ctry., Asia	B3	32
Thailand, Gulf of, b., Asia	J6	34
Thai Nguyen, Viet.	D8	34
Thal, Pak.	D4	38
Thames, stm., Ont., Can.	E3	73
Thames, stm., Eng., U.K.	J14	7
Thames, stm., Ct., U.S.	D7	84
Thamesville, Ont., Can.	E3	73
Thāna, India	C2	37
Thanh Hoa, Viet.	E8	34
Thanh Pho Ho Chi Minh (Saigon), Viet.	I9	34
Thanjāvūr, India	G5	37
Thar Desert (Great Indian Desert), des., Asia	G3	38
Thargomindah, Austl.	E8	50
Thatcher, Az., U.S.	E6	80
Thaton, Mya.	F4	34
Thayer, Mo., U.S.	E6	102
Thayer, co., Ne., U.S.	D8	104
Thayetmyo, Mya.	E3	34
Thayne, Wy., U.S.	D1	127
Thealka, Ky., U.S.	C7	94
The Barrens, plat., Tn., U.S.	B5	119
The Bight, Bah.	B10	64
The Cheviot, mtn., Eng., U.K.	F10	7
The Colony, Tx., U.S.	*C4	120
The Dalles, Or., U.S.	B5	114
The Dells, val., Wi., U.S.	E4	126
Thedford, Ont., Can.	D3	73
The English Company's Islands, is., Austl.	B7	50
The Everglades, sw., Fl., U.S.	G6	86
The Fens, sw., Eng., U.K.	I12	7
The Flat Tops, mts., Co., U.S.	B3	83
The Flume, wtfl, N.H., U.S.	B3	106
The Graves, is., Ma., U.S.	g12	98
The Hague see 's-Gravenhage, Neth.	C4	8
The Heads, c., Or., U.S.	E2	114
Thelon, stm., N.W. Ter., Can.	D12	66
The Narrows, strt., Wa., U.S.	f10	124
Theodore, Austl.	D10	50
Theodore, Al., U.S.	E1	78
Theodore Roosevelt Lake, res., Az., U.S.	D4	80
Theodore Roosevelt National Park (South Unit), N.D., U.S.	C2	111
Theodore Roosevelt National Park (North Unit), N.D., U.S.	B2	111
The Pas, Man., Can.	C1	70
The Plains, Oh., U.S.	C3	112
Theresa, Wi., U.S.	E5	126
Thermopolis, Wy., U.S.	C4	127
The Rockies, mts., Wa., U.S.	C3	124
Thessalon, Ont., Can.	p19	73
Thessaloníki (Salonika), Grc.	I6	16
Thetford Mines, Que., Can.	C6	74
The Thimbles, is., Ct., U.S.	E5	84
The Village, Ok., U.S.	B4	113
The Warburton, stm., Austl.	E7	50
The Wash, b., Eng., U.K.	I13	7
The Weald, reg., Eng., U.K.	J13	7
Thibodaux, La., U.S.	E5	95
Thief, stm., Mn., U.S.	B2	100
Thief Lake, l., Mn., U.S.	B3	100
Thief River Falls, Mn., U.S.	B2	100
Thielsen, Mount, mtn., Or., U.S.	D4	114
Thiene, Italy	D6	14
Thiensville, Wi., U.S.	E6	126
Thiers, Fr.	G10	10
Thiès, Sen.	F2	42
Thika, Kenya	B7	44
Thimphu, Bhu.	G13	38
Thingangyun, Mya.	F4	34
Thionville, Fr.	C13	10
Thíra, i., Grc.	M9	16
Third Lake, l., N.H., U.S.	f7	106
Thirsk, Eng., U.K.	G11	7
Thisted, Den.	H7	6
Thívai (Thebes), Grc.	K7	16
Thiviers, Fr.	G7	10
Thomas, Ok., U.S.	B3	113
Thomas, co., Ga., U.S.	F3	87
Thomas, co., Ks., U.S.	C2	93
Thomas, co., Ne., U.S.	C5	104
Thomasboro, Il., U.S.	C5	90
Thomaston, Ct., U.S.	C3	84
Thomaston, Ga., U.S.	D2	87
Thomaston, Me., U.S.	D3	96
Thomaston Reservoir, res., Ct., U.S.	C3	84
Thomastown, Ire.	I5	7
Thomasville, Al., U.S.	D2	78
Thomasville, Ga., U.S.	F3	87
Thomasville, N.C., U.S.	B2	110
Thompson, Man., Can.	B3	70
Thompson, Ct., U.S.	B8	84
Thompson, N.D., U.S.	B8	111
Thompson, stm., U.S.	A4	102
Thompson Falls, Mt., U.S.	C1	103
Thompson Island, i., Ma., U.S.	g11	98
Thompson Lake, l., U.S.	D2	96
Thompson Peak, mtn., Ca., U.S.	B2	82
Thompson Peak, mtn., N.M., U.S.	h9	108
Thompson Reservoir, res., Or., U.S.	E5	114
Thomsen, stm., N.W. Ter., Can.	B9	66
Thomson, Ga., U.S.	C4	87
Thon Buri, Thai.	H6	34
Thongwa, Mya.	F4	34
Thonon-les-Bains, Fr.	F13	10
Thonotosassa, Fl., U.S.	D4	86
Thonze, Mya.	F3	34
Thorburn, N.S., Can.	D7	71
Thoreau, N.M., U.S.	B1	108
Thornbury, Ont., Can.	C4	73
Thorndale, Tx., U.S.	D4	120
Thornton, Ont., Can.	C5	73
Thorntown, In., U.S.	D4	91
Thorold, Ont., Can.	D5	73
Thorp, Wi., U.S.	D3	126
Thorsby, Al., U.S.	C3	78
Thouars, Fr.	F6	10
Thousand Islands, is., N.Y., U.S.	A4	109
Thousand Lake Mountain, mtn., Ut., U.S.	E4	121
Thousand Springs Creek, stm., U.S.	B7	105
Thrace, hist. reg., Eur.	G13	4
Thrakikón Pélagos, Grc.	I8	16
Three Fingered Jack, mtn., Or., U.S.	C5	114
Three Forks, Mt., U.S.	E5	103
Three Hills, Alta., Can.	D4	68
Three Lakes, Wi., U.S.	C4	126
Three Mile Plains, N.S., Can.	E5	71
Three Oaks, Mi., U.S.	G4	99
Three Pagodas Pass, Asia	G5	34
Three Points, Cape, c., Ghana	H5	42
Three Rivers, Ma., U.S.	B3	98
Three Rivers, Mi., U.S.	G5	99
Three Rivers, Tx., U.S.	E3	120
Three Sisters, mtn., Or., U.S.	C5	114
Three Springs, Austl.	E3	50
Throckmorton, co., Tx., U.S.	C3	120
Throop, Pa., U.S.	m18	115
Throssell Range, mts., Austl.	D4	50
Thu Dao Mot, Viet.	I9	34
Thule, Grnld.	B19	128
Thun, Switz.	F14	10
Thunder Bay, Ont., Can.	o17	73
Thunder Bay, b., Mi., U.S.	D7	99
Thunder Bay, stm., Mi., U.S.	D6	99
Thunderbird, Lake, res., Ok., U.S.	B4	113
Thunderbolt, Ga., U.S.	D5	87
Thunder Butte Creek, stm., S.D., U.S.	B3	118
Thunersee, l., Switz.	F14	10
Thüringen, hist. reg., Ger.	D11	8
Thurles, Ire.	I5	7
Thurmont, Md., U.S.	A3	97
Thurso, Que., Can.	D2	74
Thurso, Scot., U.K.	C9	7
Thurston, co., Ne., U.S.	B9	104
Thurston, co., Wa., U.S.	C2	124
Tiancang, China	C7	26
Tiandong, China	C9	34
Tianjin (Tientsin), China	D10	26
Tianjun, China	D6	26
Tianmen, China	E2	28
Tianshui, China	E8	26
Tiaret, Alg.	A6	42
Tibagi, Braz.	A6	56
Tibasti, Sarīr, des., Libya	D9	42
Tiber see Tevere, stm., Italy	G7	14
Tibesti, mts., Chad	D9	42
Tibet, hist. reg., China	E12	38
Tiburón, Isla, i., Mex.	C3	62
Tice, Fl., U.S.	F5	86
Tichît, Maur.	E4	42
Tichvin, Russia	B16	18
Tickfaw, stm., La., U.S.	C5	95
Ticonderoga, N.Y., U.S.	B7	109
Ticul, Mex.	G15	62
Tide Head, N.B., Can.	B3	71
Tidjikdja, Maur.	E3	42
Tieling, China	C11	26
Tienen, Bel.	E4	8
Tien Shan, mts., Asia	C2	26
Tientsin see Tianjin, China	D10	26
Tierra Amarilla, N.M., U.S.	A3	108
Tierra Blanca, Mex.	H11	62
Tierra del Fuego, Isla Grande de, i., S.A.	G3	56
Tierralta, Col.	C4	58
Tietê, stm., Braz.	F3	57
Tieton, Wa., U.S.	C5	124
Tieton, stm., Wa., U.S.	C4	124
Tieton Dam, Wa., U.S.	C4	124
Tiffany Mountain, mtn., Wa., U.S.	A6	124
Tiffin, Oh., U.S.	A2	112
Tiffin, stm., Oh., U.S.	A1	112
Tift, co., Ga., U.S.	E3	87
Tifton, Ga., U.S.	E3	87

Index

Name — Map Ref — Page

Tigard, Or., U.S. h12 114
Tigerton, Wi., U.S. D4 126
Tigil', Russia F25 24
Tignall, Ga., U.S. C4 87
Tignish, P.E.I., Can. C5 71
Tigre, stm., Peru D3 54
Tigris (Dijlah), stm., Asia A3 46
Tiguentourine, Alg. C7 42
Tijesno, Cro. F10 14
Tijuana, Mex. A1 62
Tikamgarh, India H8 38
Tikrīt, Iraq B3 46
Tilburg, Neth. D5 8
Tilbury, Ont., Can. E2 73
Tilden, Il., U.S. E4 90
Tilden, Ne., U.S. B8 104
Tilghman, Md., U.S. C5 97
Tilghman Island, i., Md., U.S. C5 97
Tilhar, India G8 38
Tillabéry, Niger F6 42
Tillamook, Or., U.S. B3 114
Tillamook, co., Or., U.S. B3 114
Tillanchong Island, i., India J2 34
Tillery, Lake, res., N.C., U.S. B2 110
Tillman, co., Ok., U.S. C2 113
Tillmans Corner, Al., U.S. E1 78
Tillsonburg, Ont., Can. E4 73
Tilton, Il., U.S. C6 90
Tilton, N.H., U.S. D3 106
Tiltonsville, Oh., U.S. B5 112
Timaru, N.Z. F3 52
Timbalier Island, i., La., U.S. E5 95
Timberlake, Va., U.S. C3 123
Timberville, Va., U.S. B4 123
Timbuktu see Tombouctou, Mali E5 42
Timimoun, Alg. C6 42
Timiris, Cap, c., Maur. E2 42
Timişoara, Rom. D5 16
Timmins, Ont., Can. o19 73
Timmonsville, S.C., U.S. C8 117
Timms Hill, hill, Wi., U.S. C3 126
Timor, i., Indon. G8 32
Timor Sea B5 50
Timotes, Ven. C7 58
Timpanogos Cave National Monument, Ut., U.S. C4 121
Timpton, stm., Russia F19 24
Tims Ford Lake, res., Tn., U.S. B5 119
Tinaquillo, Ven. C8 58
Tindivanam, India F5 37
Tindouf, Alg. C4 42
Tingmerkpuk Mountain, mtn., Ak., U.S. B7 79
Tingo María, Peru E3 54
Tingvoll, Nor. E7 6
Tinharé, Ilha de, i., Braz. F11 54
Tinker Air Force Base, mil., Ok., U.S. B4 113
Tinley Park, Il., U.S. k9 90
Tinniswood, Mount, mtn., B.C., Can. D6 69
Tinogasta, Arg. B3 56
Tinsukia, India G16 38
Tinton Falls, N.J., U.S. C4 107
Tioga, La., U.S. C3 95
Tioga, N.D., U.S. A3 111
Tioga, co., N.Y., U.S. C4 109
Tioga, co., Pa., U.S. C7 115
Tioga, stm., Pa., U.S. B7 115
Tiogue Lake, res., R.I., U.S. D3 116
Tioman, Pulau, i., Malay. M8 34
Tionesta Creek, stm., Pa., U.S. C3 115
Tionesta Lake, res., Pa., U.S. D3 115
Tioughnioga, stm., N.Y., U.S. C4 109
Tippah, co., Ms., U.S. A5 101
Tippah, stm., Ms., U.S. A4 101
Tipp City, Oh., U.S. C1 112
Tippecanoe, co., In., U.S. D4 91
Tippecanoe, stm., In., U.S. C4 91
Tipperary, Ire. I4 7
Tipton, Ca., U.S. D4 82
Tipton, In., U.S. D5 91
Tipton, Ia., U.S. C6 92
Tipton, Mo., U.S. C5 102
Tipton, Ok., U.S. C2 113
Tipton, co., In., U.S. D5 91
Tipton, co., Tn., U.S. B2 119
Tipton, Mount, mtn., Az., U.S. B1 80
Tiptonville, Tn., U.S. A2 119
Tiquisate, Guat. G2 64
Tiracambu, Serra do, plat., Braz. D9 54
Tīrān, Maḍīq, strt. F4 40
Tiran, Strait of see Tīrān, Maḍīq, strt. F4 40
Tiranë, Alb. H3 16
Tirano, Italy C5 14
Tiraspol, Mol. H3 22
Tirat Karmel, Isr. C4 40
Tire, Tur. K11 16
Tiree, i., Scot., U.K. E6 7
Tîrgovişte, Rom. E9 16
Tîrgu-Jiu, Rom. D7 16
Tîrgu Mureş, Rom. C8 16
Tîrgu-Ocna, Rom. C10 16
Tírnavos, Grc. J6 16
Tirschenreuth, Ger. F12 8
Tiruchchirāppalli, India G5 37
Tirunelveli, India H4 37
Tirupati, India F5 37
Tiruppattūr, India F5 37
Tiruppur, India G4 37
Tiruvannāmalai, India F5 37
Tishomingo, Ok., U.S. C5 113
Tishomingo, co., Ms., U.S. A5 101
Tiskilwa, Il., U.S. B4 90
Tisza (Tisa), stm., Eur. C4 16
Tit-Ary, Russia C19 24
Titicaca, Lago, l., S.A. G5 54
Titonka, Ia., U.S. A3 92
Titov Veles, Mac. H5 16
Titule, Zaire H11 42
Titus, co., Tx., U.S. C5 120
Titusville, Fl., U.S. D6 86
Titusville, Pa., U.S. C2 115
Tiverton, Ont., Can. C3 73
Tiverton, Eng., U.K. K9 7
Tiverton, R.I., U.S. D6 116
Tivoli, Italy H7 14
Tizimín, Mex. G15 62
Tizi-Ouzou, Alg. A6 42
Tlahualilo de Zaragoza, Mex. D8 62
Tlaltenango de Sánchez Román, Mex. G8 62
Tlaxiaco, Mex. I11 62
Tlemcen, Alg. B5 42
Tlētē Ouāte Gharbī, Jabal, mtn., Syria B6 40
Toamasina, Madag. E9 44
Toano, Va., U.S. C6 123
Toano Range, mts., Nv., U.S. C7 105
Toast, N.C., U.S. A2 110
Toba, Japan H9 30
Toba, Danau, l., Indon. M5 34
Tobacco Root Mountains, mts., Mt., U.S. E5 103
Tobago, i., Trin. I17 64
Toba Inlet, b., B.C., Can. D5 69
Toba Kākar Range, mts., Pak. E2 38
Tobarra, Spain G10 12
Tobermory, Scot., U.K. E6 7
Tobin, Mount, mtn., Nv., U.S. C4 105
Tobin Lake, l., Sask., Can. D4 75
Tobin Range, mts., Nv., U.S. C4 105
Tobique, stm., N.B., Can. B2 71
Tobruk see Ṭubruq, Libya B10 42
Tobyhanna, Pa., U.S. D11 115
Tocantínia, Braz. E9 54
Tocantinópolis, Braz. E9 54
Tocantins, stm., Braz. D9 54
Toccoa, Ga., U.S. B3 87
Toccoa, stm., Ga., U.S. B2 87
Toccoa Falls, Ga., U.S. B3 87
Tochigi, Japan F12 30
Töcksfors, Swe. G8 6
Toco, Chile A3 56
Tocopilla, Chile A2 56
Todd, co., Ky., U.S. D2 94
Todd, co., Mn., U.S. D4 100
Todd, co., S.D., U.S. D5 118
Todi, Italy G7 14
Todos Santos, Mex. F4 62
Todtnau, Ger. H7 8
Tofield, Alta., Can. C4 68
Tofino, B.C., Can. E5 69
Togiak, Ak., U.S. D7 79
Togian, Kepulauan, is., Indon. F7 32
Togo, ctry., Afr. G6 42
Togwotee Pass, Wy., U.S. C2 127
Tohakum Peak, mtn., Nv., U.S. C2 105
Tohatchi, N.M., U.S. B1 108
Tohopekaliga, Lake, l., Fl., U.S. D5 86
Toiyabe Range, mts., Nv., U.S. D4 105
Tok, Ak., U.S. C11 79
Tōkamachi, Japan E11 30
Tokara-kaikyō, strt., Japan u30 31b
Tokara-rettō, is., Japan v29 31b
Tokat, Tur. G15 4
Tokelau Islands, dep., Oc. G1 2
Toki, Japan G10 30
Tokuno-shima, i., Japan x28 31b
Tokushima, Japan H7 30
Tokuyama, Japan H4 30
Tōkyō, Japan G12 30
Tokzār, Afg. C2 38
Toleak Point, c., Wa., U.S. B1 124
Toledo, Spain F7 12
Toledo, Il., U.S. D5 90
Toledo, Ia., U.S. B5 92
Toledo, Oh., U.S. A2 112
Toledo, Or., U.S. C3 114
Toledo Bend Reservoir, res., U.S. C2 95
Tolentino, Italy F8 14
Toler, Ky., U.S. C7 94
Toliara, Madag. F8 44
Toljatti, Russia G7 22
Tol'ka, Russia E10 24
Tolland, Ct., U.S. B6 84
Tolland, co., Ct., U.S. B6 84
Tollesboro, Ky., U.S. B6 94
Tolleson, Az., U.S. m8 80
Tolmezzo, Italy C8 14
Tolmin, Slo. C8 14
Tolo, Teluk, b., Indon. F7 32
Tolono, Il., U.S. D5 90
Tolosa, Spain B9 12
Tolstoj, Mys, c., Russia F25 24
Tolt Reservoir, res., Wa., U.S. B4 124
Toluca, Il., U.S. C4 90
Toluca, Nevado de, vol., Mex. H10 62
Toluca [de Lerdo], Mex. H10 62
Tom', stm., Russia F11 24
Tomah, Wi., U.S. E3 126
Tomahawk, Wi., U.S. C4 126
Tomahawk Lake, l., Wi., U.S. C4 126
Tomakomai, Japan q19 30a
Tomar, Port. F3 12
Tomaszów Mazowiecki, Pol. D20 8
Tomatlán, Mex. H7 62
Tombador, Serra do, plat., Braz. F7 54
Tomball, Tx., U.S. D5 120
Tombigbee, stm., U.S. D1 78
Tombouctou (Timbuktu), Mali E5 42
Tombstone, Az., U.S. F5 80
Tombua, Ang. E2 44
Tomelloso, Spain F9 12
Tom Green, co., Tx., U.S. D2 120
Tomini, Teluk, b., Indon. F7 32
Tommot, Russia F19 24
Tom Nevers Head, c., Ma., U.S. D8 98
Tomo, stm., Col. E8 58
Tompkins, co., N.Y., U.S. C4 109
Tompkinsville, Ky., U.S. D4 94
Tomptokan, Russia F20 24
Tomra, Nor. E6 6
Toms, stm., N.J., U.S. C4 107
Tomsk, Russia F10 24
Toms River, N.J., U.S. D4 107
Tonalá, Mex. I13 62
Tonasket, Wa., U.S. A6 124
Tonawanda Indian Reservation, N.Y., U.S. B2 109
Tondabayashi, Japan H8 30
Tone, stm., Japan F12 30
Tonga, ctry., Oc. H1 2
Tonganoxie, Ks., U.S. C8 93
Tongbai, China C2 28
Tongchuan, China D8 26
Tongeren, Bel. E5 8
Tongguan, China E9 26
Tonghai, China B7 34
Tonghua, China C12 26
Tongliao, China C11 26
Tongling, China E6 28
Tongsa Dzong, Bhu. G14 38
Tongtianheyan, China D15 38
Tongue, Scot., U.K. C8 7
Tongue, stm., Mt., U.S. E10 103
Tongue, stm., Tx., U.S. p13 120
Tongzi, China F8 26
Tonk, India G6 38
Tonkawa, Ok., U.S. A4 113
Tonkin, Gulf of, b., Asia E9 34
Tonle Sap see Sab, Tônlé, l., Camb. H7 34
Tonneins, Fr. H7 10
Tonnerre, Fr. E10 10
Tonopah, Nv., U.S. E4 105
Tønsberg, Nor. G8 6
Tonstad, Nor. G6 6
Tonto National Monument, Az., U.S. D4 80
Tonto Natural Bridge, Az., U.S. C4 80
Tooele, Ut., U.S. C3 121
Tooele, co., Ut., U.S. C2 121
Toole, co., Mt., U.S. B5 103
Toombs, co., Ga., U.S. D4 87
Toomsboro, Ga., U.S. D3 87
Toowoomba, Austl. E10 50
Topeka, In., U.S. A6 91
Topeka, Ks., U.S. C8 93
Topia, Mex. E6 62
Topock, Az., U.S. C1 80
Toppenish, Wa., U.S. C5 124
Topsfield, Ma., U.S. A6 98
Topsham, Me., U.S. E3 96
Topton, Pa., U.S. F10 115
Toquima Range, mts., Nv., U.S. E5 105
Torbay, Newf., Can. E5 72
Torbert, Mount, mtn., Ak., U.S. g15 79
Torch Lake, l., Mi., U.S. D5 99
Tordesillas, Spain D6 12
Töre, Swe. D14 6
Torgau, Ger. D12 8
Torhout, Bel. D3 8
Torino (Turin), Italy D2 14
Torit, Sudan H12 42
Torkestān, Band-e, mts., Afg. C2 38
Torneälven, stm., Eur. B12 4
Torngat Mountains, mts., Can. f8 72
Toro, Spain D6 12
Toronto, Ont., Can. D5 73
Toronto, Oh., U.S. B5 112
Toronto Lake, res., Ks., U.S. E7 93
Toro Peak, mtn., Ca., U.S. F5 82
Tororo, Ug. A6 44
Toros Dağları, mts., Tur. H14 4
Torquay (Torbay), Eng., U.K. K9 7
Torquemada, Spain C7 12
Torrance, Ca., U.S. n12 82
Torrance, co., N.M., U.S. C3 108
Torrão, Port. G3 12
Torre Annunziata, Italy I9 14
Torre Baja, Spain E10 12
Torreblanca, Spain E12 12
Torrecilla en Cameros, Spain C9 12
Torre de Moncorvo, Port. D4 12
Torredonjimeno, Spain H8 12
Torrelaguna, Spain E8 12
Torrelavega, Spain B7 12
Torremaggiore, Italy H10 14
Torremolinos, Spain I7 12
Torrens, Lake, l., Austl. F7 50
Torrente, Spain F11 12
Torreón, Mex. E8 62
Torres Novas, Port. F3 12
Torres Strait, strt., Oc. B8 50
Torres Vedras, Port. F2 12
Torrevieja, Spain H11 12
Torridon, Scot., U.K. D7 7
Torriglia, Italy E4 14
Torrijos, Spain F7 12
Torrington, Ct., U.S. B3 84
Torrington, Wy., U.S. D8 127
Torrox, Spain I8 12
Torsby, Swe. F9 6
Tórshavn, Faer. Is. C6 4
Tortola, i., Br. Vir. Is. E15 64
Tortoli, Italy J4 14
Tortona, Italy E3 14
Tortosa, Spain E12 12
Tortue, Île de la, i., Haiti D11 64
Toruń, Pol. B18 8
Toržok, Russia D17 18
Tosa-shimizu, Japan J5 30
Tosa-wan, b., Japan I6 30
Tostado, Arg. B4 56
Totagatic, stm., Wi., U.S. B2 126
Totana, Spain H10 12
Toteng, Bots. F4 44
Tôtes, Fr. C8 10
Tot'ma, Russia B25 18
Totowa, N.J., U.S. B4 107
Totson Mountain, mtn., Ak., U.S. C8 79
Tottenham (part of Alliston Beeton Tecumseth and Tottenham), Ont., Can. C5 73
Tottori, Japan G7 30
Toubkal, Jbel, mtn., Mor. B4 42
Touchet, stm., Wa., U.S. C7 124
Touggourt, Alg. B7 42
Touisset, Ma., U.S. C5 98
Toul, Fr. D12 10
Toulon, Fr. I12 10
Toulon, Il., U.S. B4 90
Toulouse, Fr. I8 10
Tounan, Tai. L9 28
Toungoo, Mya. E4 34
Tourcoing, Fr. B10 10
Tournai, Bel. E3 8
Tournon, Fr. G11 10
Tournus, Fr. F11 10
Tours, Fr. E7 10
Touside, Pic, mtn., Chad D9 42
Toussaint Creek, stm., Oh., U.S. f7 112
Toutle, North Fork, stm., Wa., U.S. C3 124
Tovar, Ven. C7 58
Towanda, Il., U.S. C5 90
Towanda, Ks., U.S. E7 93
Towanda, Pa., U.S. C9 115
Towanda Creek, stm., Pa., U.S. C8 115
Tower City, Pa., U.S. E8 115
Town Creek, Al., U.S. A2 78
Towner, N.D., U.S. A5 111
Towner, co., N.D., U.S. A6 111
Towns, co., Ga., U.S. B3 87
Townsend, De., U.S. C3 85
Townsend, Mt., U.S. D5 103
Townshend Reservoir, res., Vt., U.S. E3 122
Townsville, Austl. C9 50
Towson, Md., U.S. B4 97
Toyama, Japan F10 30
Toyohashi, Japan H10 30
Toyokawa, Japan H10 30
Toyonaka, Japan H8 30
Toyooka, Japan G7 30
Toyota, Japan G10 30
Tozeur, Tun. B7 42
Trabzon, Tur. G15 4
Tracadie, N.B., Can. B5 71
Tracy, N.B., Can. D3 71
Tracy, Que., Can. C4 74
Tracy, Ca., U.S. D3 82
Tracy, Mn., U.S. F3 100
Tracy City, Tn., U.S. D8 119
Tracyton, Wa., U.S. e10 124
Tradewater, stm., Ky., U.S. C2 94
Traer, Ia., U.S. B5 92
Trafford, Pa., U.S. k14 115
Trafford, Lake, l., Fl., U.S. F5 86
Trail, B.C., Can. E9 69
Trail Creek, In., U.S. A4 91
Traill, co., N.D., U.S. B8 111
Trail Ridge, mtn., U.S. F4 87
Tralee, Ire. I3 7
Tranås, Swe. G10 6
Trancas, Arg. B3 56
Trang, Thai. K5 34
Trangan, Pulau, i., Indon. G9 32
Trani, Italy H11 14
Transylvania, co., N.C., U.S. f10 110
Transylvania, hist. reg., Rom. C7 16
Transylvanian Alps see Carpaţii Meridionali, mts., Rom. D8 16
Trapani, Italy K7 14
Trappe, Md., U.S. C5 97
Trapper Peak, mtn., Mt., U.S. E2 103
Traun, Aus. G14 8
Traunstein, Ger. H12 8
Travelers Rest, S.C., U.S. B3 117
Traverse, co., Mn., U.S. E2 100
Traverse, Lake, l., U.S. B9 118
Traverse City, Mi., U.S. D5 99
Tra Vinh, Viet. J9 34
Travis, co., Tx., U.S. D4 120
Travis Air Force Base, mil., Ca., U.S. C2 82
Travnik, Bos. E12 14
Tray Mountain, mtn., Ga., U.S. B3 87
Treasure, co., Mt., U.S. D9 103
Treasure Island Naval Station, mil., Ca., U.S. h8 82
Trecate, Italy D3 14
Trego, co., Ks., U.S. D4 93
Tregosse Islets, is., Austl. C10 50
Tréguier, Fr. D3 10
Treherne, Man., Can. E2 70
Treinta y Tres, Ur. C6 56
Trélazé, Fr. E6 10
Trelew, Arg. E3 56
Trelleborg, Swe. I9 6
Tremblant, Mont, mtn., Que., Can. C3 74
Tremont, Il., U.S. C4 90
Tremont, Pa., U.S. E9 115
Tremonton, Ut., U.S. B3 121
Tremp, Spain C12 12
Trempealeau, Wi., U.S. D2 126
Trempealeau, co., Wi., U.S. D2 126
Trempealeau, stm., Wi., U.S. D2 126
Trenche, stm., Que., Can. B5 74
Trenčín, Slov. G18 8
Trenque Lauquen, Arg. D4 56
Trent, stm., N.C., U.S. B5 110
Trente et un Milles, Lac des, l., Que., Can. C2 74
Trento, Italy C6 14
Trenton, Ont., Can. C7 73
Trenton, Fl., U.S. C4 86
Trenton, Ga., U.S. B1 87
Trenton, Il., U.S. E4 90
Trenton, Mi., U.S. F7 99
Trenton, Mo., U.S. A4 102
Trenton, Ne., U.S. D4 104
Trenton, N.J., U.S. C3 107
Trenton, Oh., U.S. C1 112
Trenton, Tn., U.S. B3 119
Trepassey, Newf., Can. E5 72
Trepassey Bay, b., Newf., Can. E5 72
Tres Arroyos, Arg. D4 56
Tresckow, Pa., U.S. E10 115
Três Corações, Braz. F6 57
Tres Esquinas, Col. G5 58
Três Lagoas, Braz. F3 57
Três Marias, Represa, res., Braz. E6 57
Tres Picos, Cerro, mtn., Arg. D4 56
Três Pontas, Braz. F6 57
Tres Puntas, Cabo, c., Arg. F3 56
Três Rios, Braz. G7 57
Treutlen, co., Ga., U.S. D4 87
Treviglio, Italy D4 14
Treviso, Italy D7 14
Trevor, Wi., U.S. n11 126
Trevorton, Pa., U.S. E8 115
Treynor, Ia., U.S. C2 92
Trezevant, Tn., U.S. A3 119
Triadelphia, W.V., U.S. A4 125
Triadelphia Reservoir, res., Md., U.S. B3 97
Triangle, Va., U.S. B5 123
Tribune, Ks., U.S. D2 93
Trichūr, India G4 37
Tri City, Or., U.S. E3 114
Trident Peak, mtn., Nv., U.S. B3 105
Trieben, Aus. H14 8
Trier, Ger. F6 8
Trieste, Italy D8 14
Trigg, co., Ky., U.S. D2 94
Triglav, mtn., Slo. C8 14
Trigo Mountains, mts., Az., U.S. D1 80
Tríkala, Grc. J5 16
Trikora, Puncak, mtn., Indon. F10 32
Tri Lakes, In., U.S. B7 91
Trim, Ire. H6 7
Trimble, Tn., U.S. A2 119
Trimble, co., Ky., U.S. B4 94
Trimont, Mn., U.S. G4 100
Trincheras, Mex. B4 62
Trincomalee, Sri L. H6 37
Třinec, Czech. F18 8
Tring Jonction, Que., Can. C6 74
Trinidad, Bol. F6 54
Trinidad, Col. E7 58
Trinidad, Cuba D8 64
Trinidad, Co., U.S. D6 83
Trinidad, Tx., U.S. C4 120
Trinidad, i., Trin. I17 64
Trinidad and Tobago, ctry., N.A. I17 64
Trinidad Head, c., Ca., U.S. B1 82
Trinity, Al., U.S. A2 78
Trinity, Tx., U.S. D5 120
Trinity, co., Ca., U.S. B2 82
Trinity, co., Tx., U.S. D5 120
Trinity, stm., Ca., U.S. B2 82
Trinity, stm., Tx., U.S. D5 120
Trinity Bay, b., Newf., Can. D5 72
Trinity Islands, is., Ak., U.S. D9 79
Trinity Mountain, mtn., Id., U.S. F3 89
Trinity Mountains, mts., Ca., U.S. B2 82
Trinity Peak, mtn., Nv., U.S. C3 105
Trinity Range, mts., Nv., U.S. C3 105
Trion, Ga., U.S. B1 87
Tripoli, Ia., U.S. B5 92
Trípolis, Grc. L6 16
Tripoli see Ṭarābulus, Leb. B4 40
Tripoli see Ṭarābulus, Libya B8 42
Tripp, S.D., U.S. D8 118
Tripp, co., S.D., U.S. D6 118
Triumph, La., U.S. E6 95
Trivandrum, India H4 37
Trnava, Slov. G17 8
Troarn, Fr. C6 10
Trobriand Islands, is., Pap. N. Gui. A10 50
Trochu, Alta., Can. D4 68
Trogir, Cro. F11 14
Trois-Pistoles, Que., Can. A8 74
Trois-Rivières, Que., Can. C5 74
Trois-Rivières-Ouest, Que., Can. C5 74
Trojan, Bul. G8 16
Trollhättan, Swe. G9 6
Trombetas, stm., Braz. C7 54
Tromelin, i., Afr. E10 44
Tromsø, Nor. B12 6
Trona, Ca., U.S. E5 82
Tronador, Monte, mtn., S.A. E2 56
Trondheim, Nor. E8 6
Trondheimsfjorden, Nor. E8 6
Tropea, Italy K10 14
Trophy Mountain, mtn., B.C., Can. D8 69
Trotwood, Oh., U.S. C1 112
Troup, co., Ga., U.S. C1 87
Trousdale, co., Tn., U.S. A5 119
Trout, stm., Fl., U.S. m8 86
Trout, stm., Vt., U.S. B3 122
Trout Creek, Ont., Can. B5 73
Trout Creek Pass, Co., U.S. C5 83
Trout Lake, Wa., U.S. D4 124
Trout Lake, l., N.W. Ter., Can. D8 66
Trout Lake, l., Ont., Can. o16 73
Trout Lake, l., Mn., U.S. B6 100
Trout Lake, l., Wi., U.S. B4 126
Troutman, N.C., U.S. B2 110
Trout Peak, mtn., Wy., U.S. B3 127
Trout River, Newf., Can. D2 72
Trouville [-sur-Mer], Fr. C7 10
Troy, Al., U.S. D4 78
Troy, Id., U.S. C2 89
Troy, Il., U.S. E4 90
Troy, Ks., U.S. C8 93
Troy, Mi., U.S. o15 99
Troy, Mo., U.S. C7 102
Troy, Mt., U.S. B1 103
Troy, N.H., U.S. E2 106
Troy, N.Y., U.S. C7 109
Troy, N.C., U.S. B3 110
Troy, Oh., U.S. B1 112
Troy, Pa., U.S. C8 115
Troy, Tn., U.S. A2 119
Troyes, Fr. D11 10
Troy Peak, mtn., Nv., U.S. E6 105
Truchas Peak, mtn., N.M., U.S. B4 108
Trucial States see United Arab Emirates, ctry., Asia D5 46
Truckee, Ca., U.S. C3 82
Truckee, stm., U.S. D2 105
Trujillo, Hond. G4 64
Trujillo, Peru E3 54
Trujillo, Spain F6 12
Trujillo, Ven. C7 58
Truman, Mn., U.S. G4 100
Trumann, Ar., U.S. B5 81
Trumansburg, N.Y., U.S. C4 109
Trumbull, Ct., U.S. E3 84
Trumbull, co., Oh., U.S. A5 112
Trumbull, Mount, mtn., Az., U.S. A2 80
Truro, Eng., U.K. K7 7
Trussville, Al., U.S. B3 78

Name	Map Ref	Page
Trustom Pond, l., R.I., U.S.	G3	116
Truth or Consequences (Hot Springs), N.M., U.S.	D2	108
Trutnov, Czech.	E15	8
Tryon, N.C., U.S.	f10	110
Tržič, Slo.	C9	14
Tsala Apopka Lake, l., Fl., U.S.	D4	86
Tsaratanana, Madag.	E9	44
Tsaratanana, Massif du, mts., Madag.	D9	44
Tschida, Lake, res., N.D., U.S.	C4	111
Tshabong, Bots.	G4	44
Tshangalele, Lac, l., Zaire	D5	44
Tshikapa, Zaire	C4	44
Tshofa, Zaire	C5	44
Tshuapa, stm., Zaire	B4	44
Tsoying, Tai.	M9	28
Tsu, Japan	H9	30
Tsubame, Japan	E11	30
Tsuchiura, Japan	F13	30
Tsugaru-kaikyō, strt., Japan	A13	30
Tsukumi, Japan	I4	30
Tsukushi-sanchi, mts., Japan	I3	30
Tsumeb, Nmb.	E3	44
Tsuruga, Japan	G9	30
Tsuruoka, Japan	D12	30
Tsushima, is., Japan	H2	30
Tsushima-kaikyō, strt., Japan	I2	30
Tsuyama, Japan	G7	30
Tual, Indon.	G9	32
Tualatin, stm., Or., U.S.	h11	114
Tuba City, Az., U.S.	A4	80
Tuban, Indon.	m16	33a
Tubarão, Braz.	B7	56
Tubruq, Libya	B10	42
Tucannon, stm., Wa., U.S.	C8	124
Tucano, Braz.	F11	54
Tuckahoe, N.Y., U.S.	h13	109
Tuckahoe, stm., N.J., U.S.	E3	107
Tucker, Ga., U.S.	h8	87
Tucker, co., W.V., U.S.	B5	125
Tucker Island, i., N.J., U.S.	E4	107
Tuckerman, Ar., U.S.	B4	81
Tuckernuck Island, i., Ma., U.S.	D7	98
Tuckerton, N.J., U.S.	D4	107
Tucson, Az., U.S.	E5	80
Tucumcari, N.M., U.S.	B6	108
Tucumcari Mountain, mtn., N.M., U.S.	B6	108
Tucupita, Ven.	C11	58
Tucuruí, Braz.	D9	54
Tudela, Spain	C10	12
Tudmur (Palmyra), Syria	B6	40
Tugaloo Lake, res., U.S.	B1	117
Tug Fork, stm., U.S.	C2	125
Tuguegarao, Phil.	p19	32
Tugur, Russia	G21	24
Tukangbesi, Kepulauan, is., Indon.	G7	32
Tuktoyaktuk, N.W. Ter., Can.	C6	66
Tukwila, Wa., U.S.	f11	124
Tula, Mex.	F10	62
Tula, Russia	G20	18
Tulalip Indian Reservation, Wa., U.S.	A3	124
Tulancingo, Mex.	G10	62
Tulare, Ca., U.S.	D4	82
Tulare, co., Ca., U.S.	D4	82
Tulare Lake, l., Ca., U.S.	D4	82
Tularosa, N.M., U.S.	D3	108
Tularosa Mountains, mts., N.M., U.S.	D1	108
Tularosa Valley, val., N.M., U.S.	E3	108
Tulcán, Ec.	G4	58
Tulcea, Rom.	D12	16
Tule Lake, sw., Ca., U.S.	B3	82
Tule River Indian Reservation, Ca., U.S.	E4	82
Tule Valley, val., Ut., U.S.	D2	121
Tulia, Tx., U.S.	B2	120
Tūlkarm, W. Bank	C4	40
Tullahoma, Tn., U.S.	B5	119
Tullamore, Ire.	H5	7
Tulle, Fr.	G8	10
Tullins, Fr.	G12	10
Tulsa, Ok., U.S.	A6	113
Tulsa, co., Ok., U.S.	B6	113
Tuluá, Col.	E4	58
Tulum, Mex.	G16	62
Tulun, Russia	G14	24
Tulungagung, Indon.	n15	33a
Tuma, stm., Nic.	H5	64
Tumacacori National Monument, Az., U.S.	F4	80
Tumaco, Col.	G3	58
Tuman-gang, stm., Asia	C12	26
Tumany, Russia	E25	24
Tumatumari, Guy.	E13	58
Tumba, Lac, l., Zaire	B3	44
Tumbes, Peru	D2	54
Tumble Mountain, mtn., Mt., U.S.	E7	103
Tumbler Ridge, B.C., Can.	B7	69
Tumen, China	C12	26
Tumiritinga, Braz.	E8	57
Tumkūr, India	F4	37
Tummo, Libya	D8	42
Tumsar, India	B5	37
Tumuc-Humac Mountains, mts., S.A.	C8	54
Tumwater, Wa., U.S.	B3	124
Tunbridge Wells, Eng., U.K.	J13	7
Tunduru, Tan.	D7	44
Tundža, stm., Eur.	G10	16
T'ung, stm., Russia	D17	24
Tungabhadra, stm., India	E4	37
Tungabhadra Reservoir, res., India	E4	37
Tungchiang, Tai.	M9	28
Tungsha Tao (Pratas Islands), is., Tai.	G10	26
Tungshih, Tai.	K9	28
Tunica, Ms., U.S.	A3	101
Tunica, co., Ms., U.S.	A3	101
Tunis, Tun.	M5	14
Tunisia, ctry., Afr.	B7	42
Tunja, Col.	E6	58
Tunkhannock, Pa., U.S.	C10	115
Tunk Lake, l., Me., U.S.	D4	96
Tunnel Hill, Ga., U.S.	B1	87
Tunp Range, mts., Wy., U.S.	D2	127
Tununak, Ak., U.S.	C6	79
Tunxi, China	F7	28
Tuobuja, Russia	E18	24
Tuolumne, Ca., U.S.	D3	82
Tuolumne, co., Ca., U.S.	C4	82
Tuolumne, stm., Ca., U.S.	D3	82
Tupã, Braz.	F3	57
Tupaciguara, Braz.	E4	57
Tupanciretã, Braz.	B6	56
Tupelo, Ms., U.S.	A5	101
Tupiza, Bol.	H5	54
Tupper Lake, N.Y., U.S.	A6	109
Tupper Lake, l., N.Y., U.S.	A6	109
Túquerres, Col.	G4	58
Tura, India	H14	38
Tura, Russia	E14	24
Turan, Russia	G12	24
Turbat, Pak.	D1	36
Turbeville, S.C., U.S.	D7	117
Turbo, Col.	C4	58
Turda, Rom.	C7	16
Turgutlu, Tur.	K11	16
Turimiquire, Cerro, mtn., Ven.	B11	58
Turin see Torino, Italy	D2	14
Turkey, ctry., Asia	H14	4
Turkey, stm., Ia., U.S.	B6	92
Turkey Creek, stm., Ok., U.S.	A3	113
Turkey Point, c., Md., U.S.	B5	97
Turkmenistan, ctry., Asia	I9	22
Turks and Caicos Islands, dep., N.A.	D12	64
Turks Islands, is., T./C. Is.	D12	64
Turku (Åbo), Fin.	F14	6
Turley, Ok., U.S.	A6	113
Turlock, Ca., U.S.	D3	82
Turnbull, Mount, mtn., Az., U.S.	D5	80
Turneffe Islands, is., Belize	F4	64
Turner, Or., U.S.	C4	114
Turner, co., Ga., U.S.	E3	87
Turner, co., S.D., U.S.	D8	118
Turners Falls, Ma., U.S.	A2	98
Turner Valley, Alta., Can.	D3	68
Turnhout, Bel.	D4	8
Turnor Lake, l., Sask., Can.	m7	75
Turnu-Măgurele, Rom.	F8	16
Turpan, China	C4	26
Turquino, Pico, mtn., Cuba	E9	64
Turrell, Ar., U.S.	B5	81
Turret Peak, mtn., Az., U.S.	C4	80
Turtle Creek, Pa., U.S.	k14	115
Turtle Flambeau Flowage, res., Wi., U.S.	B3	126
Turtle Lake, N.D., U.S.	B5	111
Turtle Lake, Wi., U.S.	C1	126
Turtle Lake, l., Sask., Can.	D1	75
Turtle Mountain Indian Reservation, N.D., U.S.	A6	111
Turu, stm., Russia	D14	24
Turuchan, stm., Russia	D11	24
Turuchansk, Russia	D11	24
Tuscaloosa, Al., U.S.	B2	78
Tuscaloosa, co., Al., U.S.	B2	78
Tuscarawas, co., Oh., U.S.	B4	112
Tuscarawas, stm., Oh., U.S.	B4	112
Tuscarora Indian Reservation, N.Y., U.S.	B2	109
Tuscarora Mountain, mtn., Pa., U.S.	F6	115
Tuscarora Mountains, mts., Nv., U.S.	B5	105
Tuscola, Il., U.S.	D5	90
Tuscola, co., Mi., U.S.	E7	99
Tuscumbia, Al., U.S.	A2	78
Tuskegee, Al., U.S.	C4	78
Tusket, stm., N.S., Can.	E4	71
Tustumena Lake, l., Ak., U.S.	g16	79
Tuticorin, India	H5	37
Tutóia, Braz.	D10	54
Tuttle, Ok., U.S.	B4	113
Tuttle Creek Lake, res., Ks., U.S.	C7	93
Tututalak Mountain, mtn., Ak., U.S.	B7	79
Tutwiler, Ms., U.S.	A3	101
Tuvalu, ctry., Oc.	G24	2
Tuwayq, Jabal, mts., Sau. Ar.	D4	46
Tuxedo, N.C., U.S.	f10	110
Tuxedo Park, De., U.S.	i7	85
Tuxpan, Mex.	G7	62
Tuxpan de Rodríguez Cano, Mex.	G11	62
Tuxtla Gutiérrez, Mex.	I13	62
Túy, Spain	C3	12
Tuy Hoa, Viet.	H10	34
Tuz Gölü, l., Tur.	H14	4
Tuzigoot National Monument, Az., U.S.	C4	80
Tuzla, Bos.	E2	16
Tveitsund, Nor.	G7	6
Tver', Russia	E18	18
Tweed, Ont., Can.	C7	73
Tweedsmuir Provincial Park, B.C., Can.	C4	69
Tweedy Mountain, mtn., Mt., U.S.	E4	103
Twelvepole Creek, stm., W.V., U.S.	C2	125
Twentymile Creek, stm., W.V., U.S.	C3	125
Twentynine Palms, Ca., U.S.	E5	82
Twentynine Palms Marine Corps Base, mil., Ca., U.S.	E5	82
Twiggs, co., Ga., U.S.	D3	87
Twillingate, Newf., Can.	D4	72
Twin Buttes, mtn., Or., U.S.	C4	114
Twin Buttes Reservoir, res., Tx., U.S.	D2	120
Twin City, Ga., U.S.	D4	87
Twin Creek, stm., Oh., U.S.	C1	112
Twin Falls, Id., U.S.	G4	89
Twin Falls, co., Id., U.S.	G4	89
Twin Knolls, Az., U.S.	m9	80
Twin Lakes, Ga., U.S.	F3	87
Twin Lakes, Wi., U.S.	F5	126
Twin Lakes, l., Ct., U.S.	A2	84
Twin Lakes, l., Ia., U.S.	B3	92
Twin Lakes, l., Me., U.S.	C4	96
Twin Mountains, mtn., Wy., U.S.	E7	127
Twin Peaks, mts., Id., U.S.	E4	89
Twin Rivers, N.J., U.S.	C4	107
Twinsburg, Oh., U.S.	A4	112
Twin Valley, Mn., U.S.	C2	100
Twisp, Wa., U.S.	A5	124
Two Harbors, Mn., U.S.	C7	100
Two Hills, Alta., Can.	C5	68
Two Mile Beach, N.J., U.S.	F3	107
Two Rivers, Wi., U.S.	D6	126
Two Rivers, North Branch, stm., Mn., U.S.	B2	100
Two Rivers, South Branch, stm., Mn., U.S.	B2	100
Tybee Island, Ga., U.S.	D6	87
Tychy, Pol.	E18	8
Tygart Lake, res., W.V., U.S.	B5	125
Tygart River, Falls of the, wtfl, W.V., U.S.	k10	125
Tygart Valley, stm., W.V., U.S.	B4	125
Tyger, stm., S.C., U.S.	B4	117
Tyler, Mn., U.S.	F2	100
Tyler, Tx., U.S.	C5	120
Tyler, co., Tx., U.S.	D5	120
Tyler, co., W.V., U.S.	B4	125
Tyler, Lake, res., Tx., U.S.	C5	120
Tyler Branch, stm., Vt., U.S.	B3	122
Tyler Heights, W.V., U.S.	C3	125
Tylertown, Ms., U.S.	D3	101
Tymochtee Creek, stm., Oh., U.S.	B2	112
Tyndall, S.D., U.S.	E8	118
Tyndall Air Force Base, mil., Fl., U.S.	u16	86
Tyonek, Ak., U.S.	C9	79
Tyre see Şūr, Leb.	C4	40
Tyrma, Russia	G20	24
Tyrone, N.M., U.S.	E1	108
Tyrone, Ok., U.S.	e9	113
Tyrone, Pa., U.S.	E5	115
Tyronza, Ar., U.S.	B5	81
Tyrrell, co., N.C., U.S.	B6	110
Tyrrhenian Sea (Mare Tirreno), Eur.	I6	14
Tysse, Nor.	F5	6
Tzaneen, S. Afr.	F6	44

U

Name	Map Ref	Page
Uatumã, stm., Braz.	D7	54
Uaupés, Braz.	D5	54
Ubá, Braz.	F7	57
Ubangi (Oubangui), stm., Afr.	H9	42
Ube, Japan	I4	30
Úbeda, Spain	G8	12
Uberaba, Braz.	E5	57
Uberlândia, Braz.	E4	57
Ubly, Mi., U.S.	E8	99
Ubon Ratchathani, Thai.	G8	34
Ubundi, Zaire	B5	44
Učami, Russia	E13	24
Ucayali, stm., Peru	E4	54
Uchiura-wan, b., Japan	q18	30a
Ucluelet, B.C., Can.	E5	69
Ucon, Id., U.S.	F7	89
Uda, stm., Russia	G13	24
Uda, stm., Russia	G20	24
Udaipur, India	H5	38
Udall, Ks., U.S.	E6	93
Uddevalla, Swe.	G8	6
Udgīr, India	C4	37
Udine, Italy	C8	14
Udipi, India	F3	37
Udon Thani, Thai.	F7	34
Udskaja Guba, b., Russia	G21	24
Udža, Russia	C17	24
Ueckermünde, Ger.	B14	8
Ueda, Japan	F11	30
Uele, stm., Zaire	H10	42
Uelen, Russia	D31	24
Uelzen, Ger.	C10	8
Ueno, Japan	H9	30
Uere, stm., Zaire	H11	42
Ufa, Russia	G9	22
Uganda, ctry., Afr.	A6	44
Ugashik Lakes, l., Ak., U.S.	D8	79
Ugine, Fr.	G13	10
Uglegorsk, Russia	H22	24
Uglič, Russia	D21	18
Uhrichsville, Oh., U.S.	B4	112
Uige, Ang.	C3	44
Uinta, co., Wy., U.S.	E2	127
Uinta, stm., Ut., U.S.	C5	121
Uintah, co., Ut., U.S.	D6	121
Uintah and Ouray Indian Reservation, Ut., U.S.	C5	121
Uinta Mountains, mts., Ut., U.S.	C5	121
Uitenhage, S. Afr.	H5	44
Uivak, Cape, c., Newf., Can.	f9	72
Ujandina, stm., Russia	D22	24
Uji, Japan	H8	30
Ujiji, Tan.	B5	44
Ujjain, India	I6	38
Ujungpandang, Indon.	G6	32
Uka, Russia	F26	24
Ukiah, Ca., U.S.	C2	82
Ukraine, ctry., Eur.	H4	22
Ulaanbaatar (Ulan Bator), Mong.	B8	26
Ulaangom, Mong.	B5	26
Ulak Island, i., Ak., U.S.	E4	79
Ulan Bator see Ulaanbaatar, Mong.	B8	26
Ulan-Ude, Russia	G15	24
Ulhāsnagar, India	C2	37
Uliastaj, Mong.	B6	26
Ulindi, stm., Zaire	B5	44
Ulja, Russia	F22	24
Uljanovsk, Russia	G7	22
Ullapool, Scot., U.K.	D7	7
Ullŭng-do, i., S. Kor.	D13	26
Ulm, Ger.	G10	8
Ulsan, S. Kor.	D12	26
Ulster, co., N.Y., U.S.	D6	109
Ulster, hist. reg., Eur.	G5	7
Ulu, Russia	E19	24
Ulubat Gölü, l., Tur.	I12	16
Ulungur Hu, l., China	B4	26
Ulysses, Ks., U.S.	E2	93
Umag, Cro.	D8	14
Uman', Ukr.	H4	22
Umanak, Grnld.	B22	66
Umanak Fjord, Grnld.	B22	66
Umatilla, Fl., U.S.	D5	86
Umatilla, Or., U.S.	B7	114
Umatilla, co., Or., U.S.	B8	114
Umatilla, stm., Or., U.S.	B7	114
Umatilla Indian Reservation, Or., U.S.	B8	114
Umbagog Lake, l., U.S.	A4	106
Umcolcus Lake, l., Me., U.S.	B4	96
Umeå, Swe.	E13	6
Umm Durmān (Omdurman), Sudan	E12	42
Umnak Island, i., Ak., U.S.	E6	79
Umnäs, Swe.	D11	6
Umpqua, stm., Or., U.S.	D3	114
Umsaskis Lake, l., Me., U.S.	B3	96
Umtata, S. Afr.	H5	44
Umzinto, S. Afr.	H6	44
Unadilla, Ga., U.S.	D3	87
Unadilla, stm., N.Y., U.S.	C5	109
Unalakleet, Ak., U.S.	C7	79
Unalaska Island, i., Ak., U.S.	E6	79
'Unayzah, Sau. Ar.	C3	46
Uncasville, Ct., U.S.	D7	84
Uncompahgre, stm., Co., U.S.	C3	83
Uncompahgre Mountains, mts., Co., U.S.	C3	83
Uncompahgre Peak, mtn., Co., U.S.	C3	83
Underwood, Al., U.S.	B3	78
Underwood, N.D., U.S.	B4	111
Ungava, Péninsule d', pen., Que., Can.	g12	74
Ungava Bay, b., Can.	E19	66
União dos Palmares, Braz.	E11	54
Unicoi, Tn., U.S.	C11	119
Unicoi, co., Tn., U.S.	C11	119
Unicoi Mountains, mts., U.S.	D9	119
Unimak Island, i., Ak., U.S.	D7	79
Unimak Pass, strt., Ak., U.S.	E6	79
Union, Ky., U.S.	k13	94
Union, Ms., U.S.	C4	101
Union, Mo., U.S.	C6	102
Union, Or., U.S.	B9	114
Union, S.C., U.S.	B4	117
Union, Wa., U.S.	B2	124
Union, co., Ar., U.S.	D3	81
Union, co., Fl., U.S.	B4	86
Union, co., Ga., U.S.	B2	87
Union, co., Il., U.S.	F4	90
Union, co., In., U.S.	E8	91
Union, co., Ia., U.S.	C3	92
Union, co., Ky., U.S.	C2	94
Union, co., La., U.S.	B3	95
Union, co., Ms., U.S.	A4	101
Union, co., N.J., U.S.	B4	107
Union, co., N.M., U.S.	A6	108
Union, co., N.C., U.S.	B2	110
Union, co., Oh., U.S.	B2	112
Union, co., Or., U.S.	B8	114
Union, co., Pa., U.S.	E7	115
Union, co., S.C., U.S.	B4	117
Union, co., S.D., U.S.	E9	118
Union, co., Tn., U.S.	C10	119
Union, West Branch, stm., Me., U.S.	D4	96
Union Beach, N.J., U.S.	C4	107
Union Bridge, Md., U.S.	A3	97
Union City, Ca., U.S.	h8	82
Union City, Ga., U.S.	C2	87
Union City, In., U.S.	D8	91
Union City, Mi., U.S.	F5	99
Union City, N.J., U.S.	h8	107
Union City, Oh., U.S.	B1	112
Union City, Ok., U.S.	B4	113
Union City, Pa., U.S.	C2	115
Union City, Tn., U.S.	A2	119
Union Flat Creek, stm., Wa., U.S.	C8	124
Union Gap, Wa., U.S.	C5	124
Union Grove, Wi., U.S.	F5	126
Union Lake, l., N.J., U.S.	E2	107
Union Pier, Mi., U.S.	G4	99
Union Point, Ga., U.S.	C3	87
Union Springs, Al., U.S.	C4	78
Uniontown, Al., U.S.	C2	78
Uniontown, Ky., U.S.	C2	94
Uniontown, Oh., U.S.	B4	112
Uniontown, Pa., U.S.	G2	115
Union Village, R.I., U.S.	B3	116
Union Village Reservoir, res., Vt., U.S.	D4	122
Unionville, Ct., U.S.	B4	84
Unionville, Mo., U.S.	A4	102
United Arab Emirates, ctry., Asia	D5	46
United Kingdom, ctry., Eur.	E7	4
United Nations Headquarters, N.Y., U.S.	h12	109
United States, ctry., N.A.	D7	76
United States Air Force Academy, mil., Co., U.S.	B6	83
United States Military Academy, mil., N.Y., U.S.	C6	109
United States Naval Academy, mil., Md., U.S.	C4	97
Unity Reservoir, res., Or., U.S.	C8	114
University City, Mo., U.S.	C7	102
University Heights, Ia., U.S.	C6	92
University Heights, Oh., U.S.	h9	112
University Park, Ia., U.S.	C5	92
University Park, N.M., U.S.	E3	108
University Park, Tx., U.S.	n10	120
University Place, Wa., U.S.	f10	124
Unnāo, India	G9	38
Uozu, Japan	F10	30
Upata, Ven.	C11	58
Upemba, Lac, l., Zaire	C5	44
Upernavik, Grnld.	B21	66
Upington, S. Afr.	G4	44
Upland, Ca., U.S.	E5	82
Upland, In., U.S.	D7	91
Upleta, India	J4	38
Upolu Point, c., Hi., U.S.	C6	88
Upper Ammonoosuc, stm., N.H., U.S.	A4	106
Upper Arlington, Oh., U.S.	B2	112
Upper Arrow Lake, l., B.C., Can.	F9	66
Upper Arrow Lake, res., B.C., Can.	D9	69
Upperco, Md., U.S.	A4	97
Upper Darby, Pa., U.S.	G11	115
Upper Greenwood Lake, N.J., U.S.	A4	107
Upper Humber, stm., Newf., Can.	D3	72
Upper Iowa, stm., Ia., U.S.	A5	92
Upper Island Cove, Newf., Can.	E5	72
Upper Kapuas Mountains, mts., Asia	E5	32
Upper Klamath Lake, l., Or., U.S.	E4	114
Upper Marlboro, Md., U.S.	C4	97
Upper New York Bay, b., U.S.	k8	107
Upper Red Lake, l., Mn., U.S.	B4	100
Upper Saddle River, N.J., U.S.	A4	107
Upper Sandusky, Oh., U.S.	B2	112
Upper Sheila [Haut Sheila], N.B., Can.	B5	71
Upper Volta see Burkina Faso, ctry., Afr.	F5	42
Uppsala, Swe.	G11	6
Upright, Cape, c., Ak., U.S.	C5	79
Upshur, co., Tx., U.S.	C5	120
Upshur, co., W.V., U.S.	C4	125
Upson, co., Ga., U.S.	D2	87
Upton, Que., Can.	D5	74
Upton, Ky., U.S.	C4	94
Upton, Ma., U.S.	B4	98
Upton, Wy., U.S.	B8	127
Upton, co., Tx., U.S.	D2	120
Uquía, Cerro, mtn., Ven.	E11	58
Urabá, Golfo de, b., Col.	C4	58
Ural, stm., Asia	H8	22
Ural Mountains see Ural'skije gory, mts., Russia	F9	22
Ural'sk, Kaz.	G8	22
Ural'skije gory (Ural Mountains), mts., Russia	F9	22
Urania, La., U.S.	C3	95
Urbana, Il., U.S.	C5	90
Urbana, Oh., U.S.	B2	112
Urbancrest, Oh., U.S.	m10	112
Urbandale, Ia., U.S.	C4	92
Urbino, Italy	F7	14
Urgenč, Uzb.	I10	22
Uribe, Col.	F5	58
Uribia, Col.	B6	58
Urla, Tur.	K10	16
Uruaçu, Braz.	C4	57
Uruapan [del Progreso], Mex.	H8	62
Urubamba, stm., Peru	F4	54
Urucuia, stm., Braz.	D6	57
Uruguaiana, Braz.	B5	56
Uruguay, ctry., S.A.	C5	56
Uruguay (Uruguai), stm., S.A.	C5	56
Ürümqi, China	C4	26
Ur'ung-Chaja, Russia	C16	24
Urun-Islāmpur, India	D3	37
Urup, Ostrov, i., Russia	H23	24
Usa, Japan	I4	30
Uşak, Tur.	K13	16
Usedom, i., Eur.	B14	8
Ushibuka, Japan	J3	30
Ushuaia, Arg.	G3	56
Usolje-Sibirskoje, Russia	G14	24
Usquepaug, R.I., U.S.	F3	116
Ussel, Fr.	G9	10
Ussuri (Wusuli), stm., Asia	B14	26
Ussurijsk, Russia	I20	24
Ust'-Barguzin, Russia	G15	24
Ust'-Belaja, Russia	D28	24
Ust'Čaun, Russia	D28	24
Ústí nad Labem, Czech.	E14	8
Ust'-Kamčatsk, Russia	F26	24
Ust'-Kamenogorsk, Kaz.	H10	24
Ust'-Kut, Russia	F15	24
Ust'-Maja, Russia	E20	24
Ust'-Nera, Russia	E22	24
Usu, China	C3	26
Usuki, Japan	I4	30
Usulután, El Sal.	H3	64
Usumacinta, stm., N.A.	I14	62
Utah, co., Ut., U.S.	C4	121
Utah, state, U.S.	D4	121
Utah Lake, l., Ut., U.S.	C4	121
Utashinai, Japan	p20	30a
Ute Creek, stm., N.M., U.S.	A6	108
Ute Mountain Indian Reservation, U.S.	D2	83
Ute Reservoir, res., N.M., U.S.	B6	108
Utete, Tan.	C7	44
Uthai Thani, Thai.	G6	34
Utiariti, Braz.	F7	54
Utica, Il., U.S.	B5	90
Utica, Mi., U.S.	F7	99
Utica, Ms., U.S.	C3	101
Utica, Ne., U.S.	D8	104
Utica, N.Y., U.S.	B5	109
Utica, Oh., U.S.	B3	112
Utiel, Spain	F10	12
Utikuma Lake, l., Alta., Can.	B3	68
Utrecht, Neth.	C5	8
Utrera, Spain	H6	12
Utsunomiya, Japan	F12	30
Uttar Pradesh, state, India	G8	38
Uusikaupunki (Nystad), Fin.	F13	6
Uvá, stm., Col.	F8	58
Uvalde, Tx., U.S.	E3	120
Uvalde, co., Tx., U.S.	E3	120
Uvdal, Nor.	F7	6
Uvinza, Tan.	C6	44
Uvs Nuur, l., Asia	A5	26
Uwajima, Japan	I5	30
'Uwaynāt, Jabal al-, mtn., Afr.	D10	42
Uwharrie, stm., N.C., U.S.	B3	110
Uxbridge, Ma., U.S.	B4	98
Uyuni, Bol.	H5	54
Uyuni, Salar de, pl., Bol.	H5	54

Name — Map Ref — Page

Uzbekistan, state, Asia I10 22
Uzerche, Fr. G8 10
Uzès, Fr. H11 10
Užice, Yugo. F3 16
Uzlovaja, Russia H21 18
Uzunköprü, Tur. H10 16
Užur, Russia F11 24

V

Vaala, Fin. D16 6
Vaasa (Vasa), Fin. E13 6
Vác, Hung. H19 8
Vaca Key, i., Fl., U.S. H5 86
Vacaville, Ca., U.S. C3 82
Vaccarès, Étang de, b., Fr. I11 10
Vach, stm., Russia E9 24
Vacherie, La., U.S. h10 95
Vadsø, Nor. A17 6
Vaduz, Liech. H9 8
Váh, stm., Slov. G18 8
Vaiden, Ms., U.S. B4 101
Vail, Co., U.S. B4 83
Vākhān, stm., Afg. B5 38
Vākhān, reg., Afg. B5 38
Vålådalen, Swe. E9 6
Val-Bélair, Que., Can. n17 74
Valcheta, Arg. E3 56
Valcourt, Que., Can. D5 74
Valdagno, Italy D6 14
Val-David, Que., Can. C3 74
Valdecañas, Embalse de, res., Spain F6 12
Valdemarsvik, Swe. G11 6
Valdepeñas, Spain G8 12
Valderrobres, Spain E12 12
Valders, Wi., U.S. D6 126
Valdés, Península, pen., Arg. E4 56
Valdese, N.C., U.S. B1 110
Valdez, Ak., U.S. C10 79
Val-d'Isère, Fr. G13 10
Valdivia, Chile D2 56
Valdivia, Col. D5 58
Val-d'Or, Que., Can. k11 74
Valdosta, Ga., U.S. F3 87
Vale, Or., U.S. D9 114
Valemount, B.C., Can. C8 69
Valença, Braz. B9 57
Valença, Port. C3 12
Valençay, Fr. E8 10
Valence, Fr. H11 10
Valencia, Spain F11 12
Valencia, Az., U.S. m7 80
Valencia, Ven. C8 58
Valencia, co., N.M., U.S. C3 108
Valencia, Golfo de, b., Spain F12 12
Valencia de Alcántara, Spain F4 12
Valencia de Don Juan, Spain C6 12
Valencia Heights, S.C., U.S. D6 117
Valenciennes, Fr. B10 10
Valentine, Ne., U.S. B5 104
Valenza, Italy D3 14
Valera, Ven. C7 58
Valga, Est. D9 18
Valhalla, N.Y., U.S. D7 109
Valhermoso Springs, Al., U.S. A3 78
Valjevo, Yugo. E3 16
Valkeakoski, Fin. F15 6
Valkenswaard, Neth. D5 8
Valladolid, Mex. G15 62
Valladolid, Spain D7 12
Vall de Uxó, Spain F11 12
Vallecito Reservoir, res., Co., U.S. D3 83
Valle de Guanape, Ven. C10 58
Valle de la Pascua, Ven. C9 58
Valle de Santiago, Mex. G9 62
Valle de Zaragoza, Mex. D7 62
Valledupar, Col. B6 58
Vallée-Jonction, Que., Can. C7 74
Valle Hermoso, Mex. E11 62
Vallejo, Ca., U.S. C2 82
Vallelunga Pratameno, Italy L8 14
Vallenar, Chile B2 56
Valletta, Malta N9 14
Valley, Ne., U.S. C9 104
Valley, co., Id., U.S. E3 89
Valley, co., Mt., U.S. B10 103
Valley, co., Ne., U.S. C6 104
Valley, stm., Man., Can. D1 70
Valley Center, Ks., U.S. E6 93
Valley City, N.D., U.S. C8 111
Valley Cottage, N.Y., U.S. g13 109
Valley East, Ont., Can. p19 73
Valley Falls, Ks., U.S. C8 93
Valley Falls, R.I., U.S. B4 116
Valley Forge, Pa., U.S. o20 115
Valley Mills, Tx., U.S. D4 120
Valley Park, Mo., U.S. f12 102
Valley Springs, S.D., U.S. D9 118
Valley Station, Ky., U.S. g11 94
Valley Stream, N.Y., U.S. n15 109
Valleyview, Alta., Can. B2 68
Valley View, Pa., U.S. E8 115
Valliant, Ok., U.S. D6 113
Vallo della Lucania, Italy I10 14
Valls, Spain D13 12
Vallscreek, W.V., U.S. D3 125
Valmeyer, Il., U.S. E3 90
Valognes, Fr. C5 10
Valparai, India G4 37
Valparaíso, Chile C2 56
Valparaíso, Mex. F8 62
Valparaiso, Fl., U.S. u15 86
Valparaiso, In., U.S. B3 91
Valréas, Fr. H11 10
Vals, Tanjung, c., Indon. G10 32
Valtimo, Fin. E17 6
Val Verda, Ut., U.S. C4 121
Valverde, Dom. Rep. E12 64
Val Verde, co., Tx., U.S. E2 120
Valverde del Camino, Spain H5 12
Van, Tur. H16 4
Van, Tx., U.S. C5 120
Van, W.V., U.S. n12 125
Van Alstyne, Tx., U.S. C4 120
Vanavara, Russia E14 24
Van Buren, Ar., U.S. B1 81
Van Buren, In., U.S. C6 91
Van Buren, Me., U.S. A5 96
Van Buren, Mo., U.S. E6 102
Van Buren, co., Ar., U.S. B3 81
Van Buren, co., Ia., U.S. D6 92
Van Buren, co., Mi., U.S. F4 99
Van Buren, co., Tn., U.S. D8 119
Vance, co., N.C., U.S. A4 110
Vance Air Force Base, mil., Ok., U.S. A3 113
Vanceboro, N.C., U.S. B5 110
Vanceburg, Ky., U.S. B6 94
Vancleave, Ms., U.S. E5 101
Vancouver, B.C., Can. E6 69
Vancouver, Wa., U.S. D3 124
Vancouver, Cape, c., Austl. G3 50
Vancouver Island, i., B.C., Can. E4 69
Vancouver Island Ranges, mts., B.C., Can. D4 69
Vandalia, Il., U.S. E4 90
Vandalia, Mo., U.S. B6 102
Vandenberg Air Force Base, mil., Ca., U.S. E3 82
Vander, N.C., U.S. B4 110
Vanderbilt Peak, mtn., N.M., U.S. E1 108
Vanderburgh, co., In., U.S. H2 91
Vandergrift, Pa., U.S. E2 115
Vanderhoof, B.C., Can. C5 69
Van Diemen Gulf, b., Austl. B6 50
Vänern, l., Swe. G9 6
Vänersborg, Swe. G9 6
Vangaindrano, Madag. F9 44
Van Gölü, l., Tur. H16 4
Vangunu, i., Sol.Is. A11 50
Van Horn, Tx., U.S. o12 120
Van Horne, Ia., U.S. B5 92
Vanier, Ont., Can. h12 73
Vāniyambādi, India F5 37
Vankarem, Russia D30 24
Vankleek Hill, Ont., Can. B10 73
Van Kull, Kill, stm., N.J., U.S. k8 107
Van Lear, Ky., U.S. C7 94
Van Meter, Ia., U.S. C4 92
Vännäs, Swe. E12 6
Vannes, Fr. E4 10
Van Rees, Pegunungan, mts., Indon. F10 32
Vanrhynsdorp, S. Afr. H3 44
Vansant, Va., U.S. e9 123
Vansbro, Swe. F10 6
Vansittart Island, i., N.W. Ter., Can. C16 66
Vanuatu, ctry., Oc. H24 2
Van Vleck, Tx., U.S. r14 120
Van Wert, Oh., U.S. B1 112
Van Wert, co., Oh., U.S. B1 112
Van Zandt, co., Tx., U.S. C5 120
Varades, Fr. E5 10
Vārānasi (Benares), India H10 38
Varaždin, Cro. C11 14
Varazze, Italy E3 14
Varberg, Swe. H9 6
Vardaman, Ms., U.S. B4 101
Vardar (Axiós), stm., Eur. H6 16
Vardø, Nor. A18 6
Varennes, Que., Can. D4 74
Varennes-sur-Allier, Fr. F10 10
Varese, Italy D3 14
Varginha, Braz. F6 57
Varina, Va., U.S. C5 123
Varkaus, Fin. E16 6
Varkhān, stm., Afg. D1 38
Varna, Bul. F11 16
Värnamo, Swe. H10 6
Varnville, S.C., U.S. F5 117
Varzy, Fr. E10 10
Vasai (Bassein), India C2 37
Vashon, Point, c., Wa., U.S. e11 124
Vashon Island, i., Wa., U.S. f11 124
Vass, N.C., U.S. B3 110
Vassar, Mi., U.S. E7 99
Västerås, Swe. G11 6
Västervik, Swe. H11 6
Vasto, Italy G9 14
Vas'ugan, stm., Russia F9 24
Vatican City (Città del Vaticano), ctry., Eur. H7 14
Vatnajökull, Ice. C4 4
Vättern, l., Swe. G10 6
Vaucouleurs, Fr. D12 10
Vaudreuil, Que., Can. D3 74
Vaughan, Ont., Can. D5 73
Vaughn, Mt., U.S. C5 103
Vaughn, N.M., U.S. C4 108
Vaupés (Uaupés), stm., S.A. G7 58
Vauxhall, Alta., Can. D4 68
Växjö, Swe. H10 6
Vazante, Braz. D5 57
V'azemskij, Russia H20 24
V'az'ma, Russia F17 18
V'azniki, Russia E25 18
Veazie, Me., U.S. D4 96
Vechta, Ger. C8 8
Veedersburg, In., U.S. D3 91
Veendam, Neth. B6 8
Vegreville, Alta., Can. C4 68
Vejer de la Frontera, Spain I6 12
Vejle, Den. I7 6
Vela Luka, Cro. G11 14
Velda Rose Estates, Az., U.S. *D4 80
Velenje, Slo. C10 14
Vélez-Málaga, Spain I7 12
Vélez Rubio, Spain H9 12
Velhas, Rio das, stm., Braz. D6 57
Velike Lašče, Slo. D9 14
Velikije Luki, Russia E13 18
Veliko Tărnovo, Bul. F9 16
Vella Lavella, i., Sol.Is. A11 50
Velletri, Italy H7 14
Vellore, India F5 37
Velma, Ok., U.S. C4 113
Velva, N.D., U.S. A5 111
Venado Tuerto, Arg. C4 56
Venango, co., Pa., U.S. D2 115
Venda Nova, Braz. E7 57
Vendeuvre-sur-Barse, Fr. D11 10
Vendôme, Fr. E8 10
Veneta, Or., U.S. C3 114
Venezia (Venice), Italy D7 14
Venezuela, ctry., S.A. B5 54
Venezuela, Golfo de, b., S.A. B7 58
Veniaminof, Mount, mtn., Ak., U.S. D8 79
Venice, Fl., U.S. E4 86
Venice, Il., U.S. E3 90
Venice, Gulf of, b., Eur. D7 14
Venice see Venezia, Italy D7 14
Vénissieux, Fr. G11 10
Venlo, Neth. D6 8
Venosa, Italy I10 14
Ventanas, Ec. H3 58
Ventnor City, N.J., U.S. E4 107
Ventspils, Lat. D4 18
Ventuari, stm., Ven. E9 58
Ventura (San Buenaventura), Ca., U.S. E4 82
Ventura, co., Ca., U.S. E4 82
Venustiano Carranza, Mex. I13 62
Vera, Spain H10 12
Veracruz [Llave], Mex. H11 62
Verāval, India J4 38
Verbania, Italy D3 14
Vercelli, Italy D3 14
Verchères, Que., Can. D4 74
Verchn'aja Amga, Russia F19 24
Verchneimbatskoje, Russia E11 24
Verchojansk, Russia D20 24
Verchojanskij Chrebet, mts., Russia D19 24
Verda, Ky., U.S. D6 94
Verde, stm., Az., U.S. C4 80
Verden, Ger. C9 8
Verdi, Nv., U.S. D2 105
Verdigre, Ne., U.S. B7 104
Verdigris, Ok., U.S. A6 113
Verdigris, stm., U.S. A6 113
Verdi Peak, mtn., Nv., U.S. C6 105
Verdun, Que., Can. q19 74
Verdun, Fr. C12 10
Vereeniging, S. Afr. G5 44
Vergara, Spain B9 12
Vergennes, Vt., U.S. C2 122
Veríssimo, Braz. E4 57
Vermilion, Alta., Can. C5 68
Vermilion, Oh., U.S. A3 112
Vermilion, co., Il., U.S. C6 90
Vermilion, co., La., U.S. E3 95
Vermilion, stm., Alta., Can. C5 68
Vermilion, stm., Il., U.S. C5 90
Vermilion, stm., La., U.S. E3 95
Vermilion, stm., Mn., U.S. B6 100
Vermilion, stm., Oh., U.S. A3 112
Vermilion Bay, b., La., U.S. E3 95
Vermilion Lake, l., Mn., U.S. C6 100
Vermilion Pass, Can. D2 68
Vermillion, S.D., U.S. E9 118
Vermillion, co., In., U.S. E2 91
Vermillion, East Fork, stm., S.D., U.S. D8 118
Vermillion, stm., Que., Can. B4 74
Vermont, Il., U.S. C3 90
Vermont, state, U.S. D3 122
Vermontville, Mi., U.S. F5 99
Vernal, Ut., U.S. C6 121
Verneuil-sur-Avre, Fr. D7 10
Vernon, B.C., Can. D8 69
Vernon, Fr. C8 10
Vernon, Al., U.S. B1 78
Vernon, Tx., U.S. B3 120
Vernon, co., La., U.S. C2 95
Vernon, co., Mo., U.S. D3 102
Vernon, co., Wi., U.S. E3 126
Vernon Hills, Il., U.S. h9 90
Vernonia, Or., U.S. B3 114
Vero Beach, Fl., U.S. E6 86
Véroia, Grc. I6 16
Verona, Ont., Can. C8 73
Verona, Italy D6 14
Verona, Ms., U.S. A5 101
Verona, N.J., U.S. B4 107
Verona, Pa., U.S. k14 115
Verona, Wi., U.S. E4 126
Verret, Lake, l., La., U.S. E4 95
Versailles, Fr. D9 10
Versailles, In., U.S. F7 91
Versailles, Ky., U.S. B5 94
Versailles, Mo., U.S. C5 102
Versailles, Oh., U.S. B1 112
Vert, Cap, c., Sen. F2 42
Vertientes, Cuba D8 64
Vertou, Fr. E5 10
Verviers, Bel. E5 8
Vesoul, Fr. E13 10
Vestal, N.Y., U.S. C4 109
Vestavia Hills, Al., U.S. g7 78
Vestmannaeyjar, Ice. C3 4
Vesuvio, vol., Italy I9 14
Vesuvius see Vesuvio, vol., Italy I9 14
Veszprém, Hung. H17 8
Vetlanda, Swe. H10 6
Vevay, In., U.S. G7 91
Vevey, Switz. F13 10
Veynes, Fr. H12 10
Viadana, Italy E5 14
Vian, Ok., U.S. B7 113
Viana del Bollo, Spain C4 12
Viana do Alentejo, Port. G3 12
Viana do Castelo, Port. D3 12
Viangchan, Laos F7 34
Viareggio, Italy F5 14
Viborg, Den. H7 6
Viborg, S.D., U.S. D8 118
Vibo Valentia, Italy K11 14
Viburnum, Mo., U.S. D6 102
Vic-en-Bigorre, Fr. I7 10
Vicente, Point, c., Ca., U.S. n12 82
Vicenza, Italy D6 14
Vich, Spain D14 12
Vichada, stm., Col. E8 58
Vichy, Fr. F10 10
Vici, Ok., U.S. A2 113
Vicksburg, Mi., U.S. F5 99
Vicksburg, Ms., U.S. C3 101
Vicksburg National Military Park, Ms., U.S. C3 101
Viçosa, Braz. F7 57
Victor, Ia., U.S. C5 92
Victor, N.Y., U.S. C3 109
Victoria, B.C., Can. E6 69
Victoria, Newf., Can. E5 72
Victoria (Xianggang), H.K. M3 28
Victoria, Sey. B11 44
Victoria, Ks., U.S. D4 93
Victoria, Tx., U.S. E4 120
Victoria, Va., U.S. *C4 123
Victoria, state, Austl. G9 50
Victoria, co., Tx., U.S. E4 120
Victoria, Lake, l., Afr. B6 44
Victoria, Mount, mtn., Mya. D2 34
Victoria de las Tunas, Cuba D9 64
Victoria Falls, wtfl, Afr. E5 44
Victoria Harbour, Ont., Can. C5 73
Victoria Island, i., N.W. Ter., Can. B10 66
Victoria Lake, res., Newf., Can. D3 72
Victoria Land, reg., Ant. B28 47
Victoria Nile, stm., Ug. H12 42
Victoria Peak, mtn., Belize F3 64
Victoria Strait, strt., N.W. Ter., Can. C12 66
Victoriaville, Que., Can. C6 74
Victoria West, S. Afr. H4 44
Victorville, Ca., U.S. E5 82
Vičuga, Russia D24 18
Vidalia, Ga., U.S. D4 87
Vidalia, La., U.S. C4 95
Vidisha, India I7 38
Vidor, Tx., U.S. D5 120
Viechtach, Ger. F12 8
Viedma, Arg. E4 56
Viedma, Lago, l., Arg. F2 56
Viella, Spain C12 12
Vienna, Ga., U.S. D3 87
Vienna, Il., U.S. F5 90
Vienna, Mo., U.S. C6 102
Vienna, Va., U.S. B5 123
Vienna, W.V., U.S. B3 125
Vienna see Wien, Aus. G16 8
Vienne, Fr. G11 10
Vientiane see Viangchan, Laos F7 34
Vieques, Isla de, i., P.R. E15 64
Vieremä, Fin. E16 6
Vierwaldstätter See, l., Switz. F15 10
Vierzon, Fr. E9 10
Vieste, Italy H11 14
Vietnam, ctry., Asia B4 32
Vieux Desert, Lac, l., Wi., U.S. B4 126
Vigan, Phil. p19 33b
Vigevano, Italy D3 14
Vignola, Italy E5 14
Vigo, Spain C3 12
Vigo, co., In., U.S. F3 91
Vihti, Fin. F15 6
Vijayawāda, India D6 37
Vijosë (Aóös), stm., Eur. I3 16
Vikajärvi, Fin. C16 6
Viking, Alta., Can. C5 68
Vila Coutinho, Moz. D6 44
Vila do Conde, Port. D3 12
Vila Fontes, Moz. E7 44
Vilafranca del Panadés, Spain D13 12
Vila Franca de Xira, Port. G3 12
Vilanculos, Moz. F7 44
Vila Nova de Famalicão, Port. D3 12
Vila Nova de Foz Côa, Port. D4 12
Vila Nova de Gaia, Port. D3 12
Vila Pery, Moz. E6 44
Vila Real, Port. D4 12
Vilas, co., Wi., U.S. B4 126
Vila Velha, Braz. F8 57
Vila Velha de Ródão, Port. F4 12
Vilhelmina, Swe. D11 6
Vilhena, Braz. F6 54
Vil'kickogo, Proliv, strt., Russia B14 24
Villa Ahumada, Mex. B6 62
Villa Bella, Bol. F5 54
Villablino, Spain C5 12
Villa Bruzual, Ven. C8 58
Villacañas, Spain F8 12
Villacarriedo, Spain B8 12
Villacarrillo, Spain G8 12
Villach, Aus. I13 8
Villacidro, Italy J3 14
Villa Colón (Caucete), Arg. C3 56
Villa del Rosario, Ven. I11 64
Villa de Méndez, Mex. E10 62
Villadiego, Spain C7 12
Villafranca del Bierzo, Spain C5 12
Villafranca de los Barros, Spain G5 12
Villafranca di Verona, Italy D5 14
Villa Frontera, Mex. D9 62
Villagaracía, Spain C3 12
Villa Grove, Il., U.S. D5 90
Villaguay, Arg. C5 56
Villa Hayes, Para. B5 56
Villahermosa, Mex. I13 62
Villajoyosa, Spain G11 12
Villalón de Campos, Spain C6 12
Villalonga, Arg. D4 56
Villalpando, Spain D6 12
Villa María, Arg. C4 56
Villamartín, Spain I6 12
Villa Montes, Bol. H6 54
Villanova Monteleone, Italy I3 14
Villanueva, Col. B6 58
Villanueva de Córdoba, Spain G7 12
Villanueva de la Serena, Spain G6 12
Villanueva de los Infantes, Spain G9 12
Villanueva del Río y Minas, Spain H6 12
Villanueva y Geltrú, Spain D13 12
Villa Park, Il., U.S. k8 90
Villa Pedro Montoya, Mex. G10 62
Villarcayo, Spain C8 12
Villa Rica, Ga., U.S. C2 87
Villarreal, Spain F11 12
Villarrica, Chile D2 56
Villarrobledo, Spain F9 12
Villas, N.J., U.S. E3 107
Villa San Giovanni, Italy K10 14
Villasayas, Spain D9 12
Villa Unión, Arg. B4 56
Villavicencio, Col. E6 58
Villaviciosa de Córdoba, Spain G6 12
Villedieu, Fr. D5 10
Villefort, Fr. H10 10
Villefranche, Fr. G11 10
Villefranche-de-Rouergue, Fr. H9 10
Villena, Spain G11 12
Villeneuve-de-Berg, Fr. H11 10
Villeneuve-Saint-Georges, Fr. D9 10
Villeneuve-sur-Lot, Fr. H7 10
Ville Platte, La., U.S. D3 95
Villers-Bocage, Fr. C6 10
Villers-Cotterêts, Fr. C10 10
Ville Saint-Georges, Que., Can. C7 74
Villeurbanne, Fr. G11 10
Villingen-Schwenningen, Ger. G8 8
Villisca, Ia., U.S. D3 92
Villupuram, India G5 37
Vilnius, Lith. G8 18
Vilonia, Ar., U.S. B3 81
Vilsbiburg, Ger. G12 8
Vil'uj, stm., Russia E18 24
Vil'ujsk, Russia E18 24
Vimianzo, Spain B2 12
Vimoutiers, Fr. D7 10
Vina, stm., Cam. G8 42
Viña del Mar, Chile C2 56
Vinalhaven, Me., U.S. D4 96
Vinalhaven Island, i., Me., U.S. D4 96
Vinaroz, Spain E12 12
Vincennes, In., U.S. G2 91
Vincent, Al., U.S. B3 78
Vinces, Ec. H3 58
Vindeln, Swe. D12 6
Vindhya Range, mts., India I7 38
Vine Brook, stm., Ma., U.S. g11 98
Vinegar Hill, mtn., Or., U.S. C8 114
Vine Grove, Ky., U.S. C4 94
Vineland, N.J., U.S. E2 107
Vineyard Haven, Ma., U.S. D6 98
Vineyard Sound, strt., Ma., U.S. D6 98
Vinh, Viet. E8 34
Vinhais, Port. D4 12
Vinh Long, Viet. I8 34
Vinita, Ok., U.S. A6 113
Vinkovci, Cro. D2 16
Vinnytsya, Ukr. H3 22
Vinson Massif, mtn., Ant. B4 47
Vinton, Ia., U.S. B5 92
Vinton, La., U.S. D2 95
Vinton, Va., U.S. C3 123
Vinton, co., Oh., U.S. C3 112
Viola, Il., U.S. B3 90
Violet, La., U.S. k12 95
Vipava, Slo. D8 14
Vipiteno, Italy C6 14
Virac, Phil. C7 32
Viramgām, India I5 38
Viranşehir, Tur. A6 40
Virden, Man., Can. E1 70
Virden, Il., U.S. D4 90
Vire, Fr. D6 10
Virgin, stm., U.S. G8 105
Virginia, S. Afr. G5 44
Virginia, Al., U.S. g6 78
Virginia, Il., U.S. D3 90
Virginia, Mn., U.S. C6 100
Virginia, state, U.S. C4 123
Virginia Beach, Va., U.S. D7 123
Virginia City, Nv., U.S. D2 105
Virginia Peak, mtn., Nv., U.S. D2 105
Virgin Islands, dep., N.A. E15 64
Virje, Cro. C11 14
Virkie, Scot., U.K. B11 7
Viroqua, Wi., U.S. E3 126
Virovitica, Cro. D12 14
Virtaniemi, Fin. B17 6
Virudunagar, India H4 37
Vis, Cro. F11 14
Visalia, Ca., U.S. D4 82
Visby, Swe. H12 6
Viscount Melville Sound, strt., N.W. Ter., Can. B10 66
Viseu, Port. E4 12
Vishākhapatnam, India D7 37
Vislinskij Zaliv, b., Eur. A19 8
Visnagar, India I5 38
Vista, Ca., U.S. F5 82
Vistula see Wisła, stm., Pol. A18 8
Vitarte, Peru F3 54
Vitebsk, Bela. F13 18
Viterbo, Italy G7 14
Vitigudino, Spain D5 12
Vitim, Russia F16 24
Vitim, stm., Russia F16 24
Vitória, Braz. F8 57
Vitoria, Spain C9 12
Vitória da Conquista, Braz. C8 57
Vitré, Fr. D5 10
Vitry-le-François, Fr. D11 10
Vitteaux, Fr. E11 10
Vittel, Fr. D12 10
Vittoria, Italy M9 14
Vittorio Veneto, Italy D7 14
Viver, Spain F11 12
Vivero, Spain B4 12
Vivian, La., U.S. B2 95
Viviers, Fr. H11 10
Vivonne, Fr. F7 10
Vizcachas, Meseta de las, plat., Arg. G2 56
Vizcaíno, Desierto de, des., Mex. D3 62
Vizianagaram, India C7 37
Vizille, Fr. G12 10
Vlaardingen, Neth. D4 8
Vladikavkaz, Russia I6 22
Vladimir, Russia E23 18
Vladivostok, Russia E35 128
Vlissingen (Flushing), Neth. D3 8

Name	Map Ref	Page
Vlorë, Alb.	I3	16
Vltava, stm., Czech.	F14	8
Vöcklabruck, Aus.	G13	8
Vodnjan, Cro.	E8	14
Vogelsberg, mts., Ger.	E9	8
Voghera, Italy	E4	14
Vohenstrauss, Ger.	F12	8
Vohibinany, Madag.	E9	44
Vohimarina, Madag.	D10	44
Voi, Kenya	B7	44
Voinjama, Lib.	G4	42
Voiron, Fr.	G12	10
Voitsberg, Aus.	H15	8
Volcano, Hi., U.S.	D6	88
Volchov, Russia	B15	18
Volda, Nor.	E6	6
Volga, S.D., U.S.	C9	118
Volga, stm., Russia	H7	22
Volgograd (Stalingrad), Russia	H6	22
Volkovysk, Bela.	H7	18
Voločanka, Russia	C12	24
Vologda, Russia	B22	18
Volokolamsk, Russia	E18	18
Vólos, Grc.	J6	16
Volta, Lake, res., Ghana	G5	42
Volta Blanche (White Volta), stm., Afr.	F5	42
Volta Noire (Black Volta), stm., Afr.	F6	42
Volta Redonda, Braz.	G6	57
Volterra, Italy	F5	14
Volusia, co., Fl., U.S.	C5	86
Volžskij, Russia	H6	22
Von Frank Mountain, mtn., Ak., U.S.	C9	79
Vonore, Tn., U.S.	D9	119
Voríai Sporádhes, is., Grc.	J7	16
Voronež, Russia	G5	22
Voronezh see Voronež, Russia	G5	22
Vosges, mts., Fr.	D14	10
Voskresensk, Russia	F21	18
Voss, Nor.	F6	6
Vostočno-Sibirskoje More (East Siberian Sea), Russia	C25	24
Vostočnyj Sajan, mts., Russia	G13	24
Votkinsk, Russia	F8	22
Votuporanga, Braz.	F4	57
Vouziers, Fr.	C11	10
Voyageurs National Park, Mn., U.S.	B5	100
Vraca, Bul.	F7	16
Vrangel'a, Ostrov, i., Russia	C29	24
Vranje, Yugo.	G5	16
Vrhnika, Slo.	D9	14
Vryburg, S. Afr.	G4	44
Vryheid, S. Afr.	G6	44
Vsevidof, Mount, mtn., Ak., U.S.	E6	79
Vsevoložsk, Russia	A13	18
Vukovar, Cro.	D2	16
Vulcan, Alta., Can.	D4	68
Vung Tau (Cap-St.-Jacques), Viet.	I9	34
Vuoggatjålme, Swe.	C11	6
Vuokseniska, Fin.	F17	6
Vyborg, Russia	A11	18
Vyška, Russia	D18	18
Vyšnij Voloček, Russia	D17	18
Vysokogornyj, Russia	G21	24

W

Name	Map Ref	Page
Wa, Ghana	F5	42
Waawaa, Puu, mtn., Hi., U.S.	D6	88
Wabana (Bell Island), Newf., Can.	E5	72
Wabasca, Alta., Can.	B4	68
Wabasca, stm., Alta., Can.	f1	68
Wabash, In., U.S.	C6	91
Wabash, co., Il., U.S.	E6	90
Wabash, co., In., U.S.	C6	91
Wabash, stm., U.S.	H2	91
Wabasha, Mn., U.S.	F6	100
Wabasha, co., Mn., U.S.	F6	100
Wabasso, Fl., U.S.	E6	86
Wabasso, Mn., U.S.	F3	100
Wabaunsee, co., Ks., U.S.	D7	93
Wabeno, Wi., U.S.	C5	126
Wabowden, Man., Can.	B2	70
Wabush, Newf., Can.	h8	72
Waccamaw, stm., U.S.	D9	117
Waccamaw, Lake, l., N.C., U.S.	C4	110
Waccasassa Bay, b., Fl., U.S.	C4	86
Wachusett Mountain, mtn., Ma., U.S.	B4	98
Wachusett Reservoir, res., Ma., U.S.	B4	98
Waco, Tx., U.S.	D4	120
Waco Lake, res., Tx., U.S.	D4	120
Waconda Lake, res., Ks., U.S.	C5	93
Waconia, Mn., U.S.	F5	100
Waddeneilanden, is., Neth.	B5	8
Waddenzee, Neth.	B5	8
Waddi, Chappal, mtn., Nig.	G8	42
Waddington, Mount, mtn., B.C., Can.	D5	69
Wadena, Mn., U.S.	D3	100
Wadena, co., Mn., U.S.	D4	100
Wädenswil, Switz.	E15	10
Wadesboro, N.C., U.S.	C2	110
Wādī Halfā', Sudan	D12	42
Wading, stm., N.J., U.S.	D3	107
Wadley, Ga., U.S.	D4	87
Wad Madanī, Sudan	F12	42
Wadmalaw Island, i., S.C., U.S.	F7	117
Wadsworth, Il., U.S.	h9	90
Wadsworth, Nv., U.S.	D2	105
Wadsworth, Oh., U.S.	A4	112
Wagener, S.C., U.S.	D5	117
Wageningen, Neth.	D5	8
Wager Bay, b., N.W. Ter., Can.	C15	66
Wagga Wagga, Austl.	G9	50
Wagin, Austl.	F3	50
Wagner, S.D., U.S.	D7	118
Wagoner, Ok., U.S.	B6	113
Wagoner, co., Ok., U.S.	B6	113
Wagontire Mountain, mtn., Or., U.S.	D7	114
Wągrowiec, Pol.	C17	8
Wah, Pak.	D5	38
Waha, Libya	C9	42
Wahiawa, Hi., U.S.	B3	88
Wahiawa Reservoir, res., Hi., U.S.	g9	88
Wahkiakum, co., Wa., U.S.	C2	124
Wahoo, Ne., U.S.	C9	104
Wahpeton, N.D., U.S.	C9	111
Wahweap Creek, stm., Ut., U.S.	F4	121
Waialua, Hi., U.S.	B3	88
Waialua Bay, b., Hi., U.S.	B3	88
Waianae, Hi., U.S.	B3	88
Waianae Range, mts., Hi., U.S.	f9	88
Waidhofen an der Ybbs, Aus.	H14	8
Waigeo, Pulau, i., Indon.	F9	32
Waihi, N.Z.	B5	52
Waikapu, Hi., U.S.	C5	88
Waikiki Beach, Hi., U.S.	g10	88
Wailua, Hi., U.S.	A2	88
Wailuku, Hi., U.S.	C5	88
Waimanalo, Hi., U.S.	B4	88
Waimanalo Bay, b., Hi., U.S.	g11	88
Waimea, Hi., U.S.	f9	88
Waimea, Hi., U.S.	B2	88
Wainwright, Alta., Can.	C5	68
Wainwright, Ak., U.S.	A8	79
Waipahu, Hi., U.S.	B3	88
Waipio Acres, Hi., U.S.	g9	88
Waipio Peninsula, pen., Hi., U.S.	g10	88
Waipukurau, N.Z.	D6	52
Waite Park, Mn., U.S.	E4	100
Waits, stm., Vt., U.S.	C4	122
Waitsburg, Wa., U.S.	C7	124
Wajir, Kenya	H3	46
Wakarusa, In., U.S.	A5	91
Wakarusa, stm., Ks., U.S.	D8	93
Wakasa-wan, b., Japan	G8	30
Wakatomika Creek, stm., Oh., U.S.	B3	112
Wakayama, Japan	H8	30
Wake, co., N.C., U.S.	B4	110
WaKeeney, Ks., U.S.	C4	93
Wakefield, Que., Can.	D2	74
Wakefield, Ks., U.S.	C6	93
Wakefield, Ma., U.S.	B5	98
Wakefield, Mi., U.S.	n12	99
Wakefield, Ne., U.S.	B9	104
Wakefield, R.I., U.S.	F3	116
Wakefield, Va., U.S.	D6	123
Wake Forest, N.C., U.S.	B4	110
Wake Island, dep., Oc.	E24	2
Wakema, Mya.	F3	34
Wakeman, Oh., U.S.	A3	112
Wakkanai, Japan	n19	30a
Wakulla, co., Fl., U.S.	B2	86
Walbridge, Oh., U.S.	e6	112
Wałbrzych (Waldenburg), Pol.	E16	8
Walcott, Ia., U.S.	C7	92
Walcott, Lake, res., Id., U.S.	G5	89
Walden, Ont., Can.	A3	73
Walden, Co., U.S.	A4	83
Walden, N.Y., U.S.	D6	109
Walden Ridge, mtn., Tn., U.S.	D8	119
Waldheim, Sask., Can.	E2	75
Waldo, Ar., U.S.	D2	81
Waldo, co., Me., U.S.	D3	96
Waldoboro, Me., U.S.	D3	96
Waldo Lake, l., Ma., U.S.	h11	98
Waldo Lake, l., Or., U.S.	D4	114
Waldport, Or., U.S.	C2	114
Waldron, Ar., U.S.	C1	81
Waldron, In., U.S.	F6	91
Waldshut, Ger.	H8	8
Waldwick, N.J., U.S.	A4	107
Wales, ter., U.K.	I9	7
Wales Island, i., N.W. Ter., Can.	C15	66
Waleska, Ga., U.S.	B2	87
Walgett, Austl.	E9	50
Walhalla, N.D., U.S.	A8	111
Walhalla, S.C., U.S.	B1	117
Walhonding, stm., Oh., U.S.	B3	112
Walker, Ia., U.S.	B6	92
Walker, La., U.S.	g10	95
Walker, Mi., U.S.	E5	99
Walker, Mn., U.S.	C4	100
Walker, co., Al., U.S.	B2	78
Walker, co., Ga., U.S.	B1	87
Walker, co., Tx., U.S.	D5	120
Walker, stm., Nv., U.S.	D3	105
Walker Lake, l., Nv., U.S.	E3	105
Walker River Indian Reservation, Nv., U.S.	D3	105
Walkersville, Md., U.S.	B3	97
Walkerton, Ont., Can.	C3	73
Walkerton, In., U.S.	B5	91
Walkertown, N.C., U.S.	A2	110
Walkerville, Mt., U.S.	D4	103
Wall, S.D., U.S.	D3	118
Wallace, Id., U.S.	B3	89
Wallace, N.C., U.S.	B4	110
Wallace, co., Ks., U.S.	D2	93
Wallaceburg, Ont., Can.	E2	73
Wallace Lake, res., La., U.S.	B2	95
Walla Walla, Wa., U.S.	C7	124
Walla Walla, co., Wa., U.S.	C7	124
Walla Walla, stm., U.S.	C7	124
Walled Lake, Mi., U.S.	o15	99
Wallen, In., U.S.	B7	91
Wallenpaupack, Lake, l., Pa., U.S.	D11	115
Waller, Tx., U.S.	q14	120
Waller, co., Tx., U.S.	E4	120
Wallingford, Ct., U.S.	D4	84
Wallingford, Vt., U.S.	E3	122
Wallington, N.J., U.S.	h8	107
Wallis and Futuna, dep., Oc.	G1	2
Wallkill, N.Y., U.S.	D6	109
Wallkill, stm., N.Y., U.S.	D6	109
Wall Lake, Ia., U.S.	B2	92
Wall Lake, l., Ia., U.S.	B4	92
Walloomsac, stm., U.S.	F2	122
Walloon Lake, l., Mi., U.S.	C6	99
Wallowa, Or., U.S.	B9	114
Wallowa, co., Or., U.S.	B9	114
Wallowa Mountains, mts., Or., U.S.	B9	114
Wallula, Lake, res., U.S.	C7	124
Wallum Lake, l., U.S.	A1	116
Walnut, Il., U.S.	B4	90
Walnut, Ia., U.S.	C2	92
Walnut, stm., Ks., U.S.	E6	93
Walnut Canyon National Monument, Az., U.S.	B4	80
Walnut Cove, N.C., U.S.	A2	110
Walnut Creek, Ca., U.S.	h8	82
Walnut Creek, stm., Ks., U.S.	D4	93
Walnut Grove, Al., U.S.	A3	78
Walnut Grove, Mn., U.S.	F3	100
Walnutport, Pa., U.S.	E10	115
Walnut Ridge, Ar., U.S.	A5	81
Walpole, Ma., U.S.	B5	98
Walpole, N.H., U.S.	D2	106
Walsall, Eng., U.K.	I11	7
Walsenburg, Co., U.S.	D6	83
Walsh, Co., U.S.	D8	83
Walsh, co., N.D., U.S.	A8	111
Walsrode, Ger.	C9	8
Walterboro, S.C., U.S.	F6	117
Walter F. George Dam, U.S.	D4	78
Walter F. George Lake, res., U.S.	D4	78
Walters, Ok., U.S.	C3	113
Walthall, co., Ms., U.S.	D3	101
Waltham, Ma., U.S.	B5	98
Walthill, Ne., U.S.	B9	104
Walthourville, Ga., U.S.	E5	87
Walton, In., U.S.	C5	91
Walton, Ky., U.S.	B5	94
Walton, N.Y., U.S.	C5	109
Walton, co., Fl., U.S.	u15	86
Walton, co., Ga., U.S.	C3	87
Walvis Bay, Nam.	F2	44
Walworth, Wi., U.S.	F5	126
Walworth, co., S.D., U.S.	B5	118
Walworth, co., Wi., U.S.	F5	126
Wamac, Il., U.S.	E4	90
Wamba, stm., Afr.	C3	44
Wamego, Ks., U.S.	C7	93
Wamesit, Ma., U.S.	A5	98
Wamsutter, Wy., U.S.	E5	127
Wanaka, N.Z.	F2	52
Wanamingo, Mn., U.S.	F6	100
Wanapum Dam, Wa., U.S.	C6	124
Wanapum Lake, res., Wa., U.S.	B6	124
Wanaque, N.J., U.S.	A4	107
Wanaque Reservoir, res., N.J., U.S.	A4	107
Wanatah, In., U.S.	B4	91
Wanchese, N.C., U.S.	B7	110
Wando, stm., S.C., U.S.	F8	117
Wando Woods, S.C., U.S.	k11	117
Wanganui, N.Z.	C5	52
Wanganui, stm., N.Z.	C5	52
Wangaratta, Austl.	G9	50
Wangen [im Allgäu], Ger.	H9	8
Wangpan Yang, b., China	E10	28
Wānkāner, India	I4	38
Wanxian, China	E8	26
Wapakoneta, Oh., U.S.	B1	112
Wapato, Wa., U.S.	C5	124
Wapawekka Lake, l., Sask., Can.	C3	75
Wapello, Ia., U.S.	C6	92
Wapello, co., Ia., U.S.	C5	92
Wapiti, stm., Can.	B1	68
Wappapello, Lake, res., Mo., U.S.	D7	102
Wappingers Falls, N.Y., U.S.	D7	109
Wapsipinicon, stm., Ia., U.S.	B6	92
War, W.V., U.S.	D3	125
Waramaug, Lake, l., Ct., U.S.	C2	84
Warangal, India	C5	37
Ward, Ar., U.S.	B4	81
Ward, co., N.D., U.S.	A4	111
Ward, co., Tx., U.S.	D1	120
Warden, Wa., U.S.	C6	124
Wardha, India	B5	37
Ward Mountain, mtn., Mt., U.S.	D2	103
Ware, Ma., U.S.	B3	98
Ware, co., Ga., U.S.	E4	87
Ware, stm., Ma., U.S.	B3	98
War Eagle Mountain, mtn., Id., U.S.	G2	89
Wareham, Ma., U.S.	C6	98
Warehouse Point, Ct., U.S.	B5	84
Waren, Ger.	B12	8
Warendorf, Ger.	D7	8
Ware Shoals, S.C., U.S.	C3	117
Warfield, B.C., Can.	E9	69
Warminster, Eng., U.K.	J10	7
Warminster, Pa., U.S.	F11	115
Warm Springs Indian Reservation, Or., U.S.	C5	114
Warm Springs Reservoir, res., Or., U.S.	D8	114
Warnemünde, Ger.	A12	8
Warner, N.H., U.S.	D3	106
Warner, Ok., U.S.	B6	113
Warner, stm., N.H., U.S.	D3	106
Warner Mountains, mts., Ca., U.S.	B3	82
Warner Peak, mtn., Or., U.S.	E7	114
Warner Robins, Ga., U.S.	D3	87
Warr Acres, Ok., U.S.	B4	113
Warren, Ar., U.S.	D3	81
Warren, Il., U.S.	A4	90
Warren, In., U.S.	C7	91
Warren, Ma., U.S.	B3	98
Warren, Mi., U.S.	F7	99
Warren, Mn., U.S.	B2	100
Warren, Oh., U.S.	A5	112
Warren, Or., U.S.	B4	114
Warren, Pa., U.S.	C3	115
Warren, R.I., U.S.	D5	116
Warren, Vt., U.S.	C3	122
Warren, co., Ga., U.S.	C4	87
Warren, co., Il., U.S.	C3	90
Warren, co., In., U.S.	D3	91
Warren, co., Ia., U.S.	C4	92
Warren, co., Ky., U.S.	C3	94
Warren, co., Ms., U.S.	C3	101
Warren, co., Mo., U.S.	C6	102
Warren, co., N.J., U.S.	B3	107
Warren, co., N.Y., U.S.	B7	109
Warren, co., N.C., U.S.	A4	110
Warren, co., Oh., U.S.	C1	112
Warren, co., Pa., U.S.	C3	115
Warren, co., Tn., U.S.	D8	119
Warren, co., Va., U.S.	B4	123
Warren, stm., U.S.	D5	116
Warren Park, In., U.S.	k10	91
Warren Peaks, mts., Wy., U.S.	B8	127
Warrensburg, Il., U.S.	D4	90
Warrensburg, Mo., U.S.	C4	102
Warrensburg, N.Y., U.S.	B7	109
Warrensville Heights, Oh., U.S.	h9	112
Warrenton, S. Afr.	G4	44
Warrenton, Ga., U.S.	C4	87
Warrenton, Mo., U.S.	C6	102
Warrenton, N.C., U.S.	A4	110
Warrenton, Or., U.S.	A3	114
Warrenton, Va., U.S.	B5	123
Warrenville, Il., U.S.	k8	90
Warrenville, S.C., U.S.	D4	117
Warri, Nig.	G7	42
Warrick, co., In., U.S.	H3	91
Warrina, Austl.	E7	50
Warrington, Eng., U.K.	H10	7
Warrington, Fl., U.S.	u14	86
Warrior, Al., U.S.	B3	78
Warrior Lake, res., Al., U.S.	C2	78
Warrnambool, Austl.	G8	50
Warroad, Mn., U.S.	B3	100
Warsaw, Il., U.S.	C2	90
Warsaw, In., U.S.	B6	91
Warsaw, Ky., U.S.	B5	94
Warsaw, Mo., U.S.	C4	102
Warsaw, N.Y., U.S.	C2	109
Warsaw, N.C., U.S.	B4	110
Warsaw, Va., U.S.	C6	123
Warsaw see Warszawa, Pol.	C21	8
Warszawa (Warsaw), Pol.	C21	8
Warta, stm., Pol.	C15	8
Wartburg, Tn., U.S.	C9	119
Warthe see Warta, stm., Pol.	C15	8
Warwick, Austl.	E10	50
Warwick, Que., Can.	D6	74
Warwick, Eng., U.K.	I11	7
Warwick, Md., U.S.	B6	97
Warwick, N.Y., U.S.	D6	109
Warwick, R.I., U.S.	D4	116
Wasaga Beach, Ont., Can.	C4	73
Wasatch, co., Ut., U.S.	C4	121
Wasco, Ca., U.S.	E4	82
Wasco, co., Or., U.S.	B5	114
Waseca, Mn., U.S.	F5	100
Waseca, co., Mn., U.S.	F5	100
Washakie, co., Wy., U.S.	C5	127
Washakie Needles, mts., Wy., U.S.	C3	127
Washburn, Il., U.S.	C4	90
Washburn, Ia., U.S.	B5	92
Washburn, Me., U.S.	B4	96
Washburn, N.D., U.S.	B5	111
Washburn, Wi., U.S.	B3	126
Washburn, co., Wi., U.S.	C2	126
Washburn, Mount, mtn., Wy., U.S.	B2	127
Washington, D.C., U.S.	C3	97
Washington, Ga., U.S.	C4	87
Washington, Il., U.S.	C4	90
Washington, In., U.S.	G3	91
Washington, Ia., U.S.	C6	92
Washington, Ks., U.S.	C6	93
Washington, Ky., U.S.	B6	94
Washington, La., U.S.	D3	95
Washington, Ms., U.S.	D2	101
Washington, Mo., U.S.	C6	102
Washington, N.J., U.S.	B3	107
Washington, N.C., U.S.	B5	110
Washington, Pa., U.S.	F1	115
Washington, Ut., U.S.	F2	121
Washington, co., Al., U.S.	D1	78
Washington, co., Ar., U.S.	A1	81
Washington, co., Co., U.S.	B7	83
Washington, co., Fl., U.S.	u16	86
Washington, co., Ga., U.S.	C4	87
Washington, co., Id., U.S.	E2	89
Washington, co., Il., U.S.	E4	90
Washington, co., In., U.S.	G5	91
Washington, co., Ia., U.S.	C6	92
Washington, co., Ks., U.S.	C6	93
Washington, co., Ky., U.S.	C4	94
Washington, co., La., U.S.	D5	95
Washington, co., Me., U.S.	D5	96
Washington, co., Md., U.S.	A2	97
Washington, co., Mn., U.S.	E6	100
Washington, co., Ms., U.S.	B3	101
Washington, co., Mo., U.S.	D7	102
Washington, co., Ne., U.S.	C9	104
Washington, co., N.Y., U.S.	B7	109
Washington, co., N.C., U.S.	B6	110
Washington, co., Oh., U.S.	C4	112
Washington, co., Ok., U.S.	A6	113
Washington, co., Or., U.S.	B3	114
Washington, co., Pa., U.S.	F1	115
Washington, co., R.I., U.S.	E2	116
Washington, co., Tn., U.S.	C11	119
Washington, co., Tx., U.S.	D4	120
Washington, co., Ut., U.S.	F2	121
Washington, co., Vt., U.S.	C3	122
Washington, co., Va., U.S.	f9	123
Washington, co., Wi., U.S.	E5	126
Washington, state, U.S.	B5	124
Washington, Lake, l., Fl., U.S.	D6	86
Washington, Lake, l., Mn., U.S.	E4	100
Washington, Lake, l., Ms., U.S.	B3	101
Washington, Lake, l., Wa., U.S.	e11	124
Washington, Mount, mtn., N.H., U.S.	B4	106
Washington Court House, Oh., U.S.	C2	112
Washington Island, i., Wi., U.S.	C7	126
Washington Park, Il., U.S.	E3	90
Washington Terrace, Ut., U.S.	B4	121
Washita, co., Ok., U.S.	B2	113
Washita, stm., Ok., U.S.	C4	113
Washoe, co., Nv., U.S.	C2	105
Washoe City, Nv., U.S.	D2	105
Washougal, Wa., U.S.	D3	124
Washow Bay, b., Man., Can.	D3	70
Washtenaw, co., Mi., U.S.	F7	99
Wasilla, Ak., U.S.	C10	79
Wasior, Indon.	F9	32
Waskom, Tx., U.S.	C5	120
Waspán, Nic.	G5	64
Wasque Point, c., Ma., U.S.	D7	98
Wassen, Switz.	F15	10
Wassookeag, Lake, l., Me., U.S.	C3	96
Wassuk Range, mts., Nv., U.S.	E3	105
Wataga, Il., U.S.	B3	90
Watauga, co., N.C., U.S.	A1	110
Watauga, stm., Tn., U.S.	C12	119
Watauga Lake, res., Tn., U.S.	C12	119
Watchaug Pond, l., R.I., U.S.	F2	116
Watch Hill Point, c., R.I., U.S.	G1	116
Watchung, N.J., U.S.	B4	107
Waterbury, Ct., U.S.	C3	84
Waterbury, Vt., U.S.	C3	122
Waterbury Center, Vt., U.S.	C3	122
Waterbury Reservoir, res., Vt., U.S.	C3	122
Wateree, stm., S.C., U.S.	D6	117
Wateree Lake, res., S.C., U.S.	C6	117
Waterford, Ire.	I5	7
Waterford, Ct., U.S.	D7	84
Waterford, N.Y., U.S.	C7	109
Waterford, Pa., U.S.	C2	115
Waterford, Wi., U.S.	F5	126
Waterhen Lake, l., Man., Can.	C2	70
Waterloo, Bel.	E4	8
Waterloo, Ont., Can.	D4	73
Waterloo, Que., Can.	D5	74
Waterloo, Il., U.S.	E3	90
Waterloo, In., U.S.	B7	91
Waterloo, Ia., U.S.	B5	92
Waterloo, N.Y., U.S.	C4	109
Waterloo, Wi., U.S.	E5	126
Waterman, Il., U.S.	B5	90
Waterman Reservoir, res., R.I., U.S.	B3	116
Waterproof, La., U.S.	C4	95
Watersmeet, Mi., U.S.	n12	99
Waterton Lakes National Park, Alta., Can.	E3	68
Watertown, Ct., U.S.	C3	84
Watertown, Ma., U.S.	g11	98
Watertown, N.Y., U.S.	B5	109
Watertown, S.D., U.S.	C8	118
Watertown, Tn., U.S.	A5	119
Watertown, Wi., U.S.	E5	126
Water Valley, Ms., U.S.	A4	101
Waterville, Ks., U.S.	C7	93
Waterville, Me., U.S.	D3	96
Waterville, Mn., U.S.	F5	100
Waterville, N.Y., U.S.	C5	109
Waterville, Oh., U.S.	A2	112
Waterville, Wa., U.S.	B5	124
Watervliet, Mi., U.S.	F4	99
Watervliet, N.Y., U.S.	C7	109
Watford, Ont., Can.	E3	73
Watford City, N.D., U.S.	B2	111
Wathena, Ks., U.S.	C9	93
Watkins, Mn., U.S.	E4	100
Watkins Glen, N.Y., U.S.	C4	109
Watkinsville, Ga., U.S.	C3	87
Watonga, Ok., U.S.	B3	113
Watonwan, co., Mn., U.S.	F4	100
Watonwan, stm., Mn., U.S.	G4	100
Watseka, Il., U.S.	C6	90
Watson Lake, Yukon, Can.	D7	66
Watsontown, Pa., U.S.	D8	115
Watsonville, Ca., U.S.	D3	82
Watts Bar Dam, Tn., U.S.	D9	119
Watts Bar Lake, res., Tn., U.S.	D9	119
Wattsville, S.C., U.S.	B4	117
Wattwil, Switz.	E16	10
Watubela, Kepulauan, is., Indon.	F9	32
Waubaushene, Ont., Can.	C5	73
Waubay, S.D., U.S.	B8	118
Waubay Lake, l., S.D., U.S.	B8	118
Wauchula, Fl., U.S.	E5	86
Wauconda, Il., U.S.	h8	90
Waugh Mountain, mtn., Id., U.S.	D4	89
Waukee, Ia., U.S.	C4	92
Waukegan, Il., U.S.	A6	90
Waukesha, Wi., U.S.	F5	126
Waukesha, co., Wi., U.S.	E5	126
Waukewan, Lake, l., N.H., U.S.	C3	106
Waukomis, Ok., U.S.	A4	113
Waukon, Ia., U.S.	A6	92
Waunakee, Wi., U.S.	E4	126
Wauneta, Ne., U.S.	D4	104
Waungumbaug Lake, l., Ct., U.S.	B6	84
Waupaca, Wi., U.S.	D4	126
Waupaca, co., Wi., U.S.	D5	126
Waupun, Wi., U.S.	E5	126
Wauregan, Ct., U.S.	C8	84
Waurika, Ok., U.S.	C4	113
Waurika Lake, res., Ok., U.S.	C3	113
Wausau, Wi., U.S.	D4	126
Wausau, Lake, res., Wi., U.S.	D4	126
Wauseon, Oh., U.S.	A1	112
Waushara, co., Wi., U.S.	D4	126
Wautoma, Wi., U.S.	D4	126
Wauwatosa, Wi., U.S.	m12	126
Wave Hill, Austl.	C6	50
Waveland, Ms., U.S.	E4	101
Waverley, N.S., Can.	E6	71
Waverly, Il., U.S.	D4	90
Waverly, Ia., U.S.	B5	92
Waverly, Ks., U.S.	D8	93
Waverly, Mn., U.S.	E5	100
Waverly, Mo., U.S.	B4	102
Waverly, Ne., U.S.	D9	104
Waverly, N.Y., U.S.	C4	109
Waverly, Oh., U.S.	C3	112
Waverly, Tn., U.S.	A4	119
Waverly, Va., U.S.	C5	123
Waverly, W.V., U.S.	B3	125
Waverly Hall, Ga., U.S.	D2	87
Wāw, Sudan	G11	42
Wawanesa, Man., Can.	E2	70
Wawasee, Lake, l., In., U.S.	B6	91
Wawayanda Lake, l., N.J., U.S.	A4	107
Wawota, Sask., Can.	H4	75
Waxahachie, Tx., U.S.	C4	120

Name — Map Ref — Page

Waxhaw, N.C., U.S. C2 110
Waycross, Ga., U.S. E4 87
Wayland, Ia., U.S. C6 92
Wayland, Ma., U.S. g10 98
Wayland, Mi., U.S. F5 99
Wayland, N.Y., U.S. C3 109
Waylyn, S.C., U.S. k12 117
Waymart, Pa., U.S. C11 115
Wayne, Mi., U.S. p15 99
Wayne, Ne., U.S. B8 104
Wayne, N.J., U.S. B4 107
Wayne, W.V., U.S. C2 125
Wayne, co., Ga., U.S. E5 87
Wayne, co., Il., U.S. E5 90
Wayne, co., In., U.S. E7 91
Wayne, co., Ia., U.S. D4 92
Wayne, co., Ky., U.S. D5 94
Wayne, co., Mi., U.S. F7 99
Wayne, co., Ms., U.S. D5 101
Wayne, co., Mo., U.S. D7 102
Wayne, co., Ne., U.S. B8 104
Wayne, co., N.Y., U.S. B3 109
Wayne, co., N.C., U.S. B4 110
Wayne, co., Oh., U.S. B4 112
Wayne, co., Pa., U.S. C11 115
Wayne, co., Tn., U.S. B4 119
Wayne, co., Ut., U.S. E4 121
Wayne, co., W.V., U.S. C2 125
Wayne City, Il., U.S. E5 90
Waynesboro, Ga., U.S. C4 87
Waynesboro, Ms., U.S. D5 101
Waynesboro, Pa., U.S. G6 115
Waynesboro, Tn., U.S. B4 119
Waynesboro, Va., U.S. B4 123
Waynesburg, Oh., U.S. B4 112
Waynesburg, Pa., U.S. G1 115
Waynesville, Mo., U.S. D5 102
Waynesville, N.C., U.S. f10 110
Waynesville, Oh., U.S. C1 112
Waynetown, In., U.S. D3 91
Waynewood, Va., U.S. g12 123
Waynoka, Ok., U.S. A3 113
Wayzata, Mn., U.S. n11 100
Wazīrābād, Pak. D6 38
Weakley, co., Tn., U.S. A3 119
Weatherford, Ok., U.S. B3 113
Weatherford, Tx., U.S. C4 120
Weatherly, Pa., U.S. E10 115
Weatogue, Ct., U.S. B4 84
Weaver, Al., U.S. B4 78
Weaver Mountains, mts., Az., U.S. C3 80
Weaverville, Ca., U.S. B2 82
Weaverville, N.C., U.S. f10 110
Webb, Al., U.S. D4 78
Webb, Ms., U.S. B3 101
Webb, co., Tx., U.S. F3 120
Webb City, Mo., U.S. D3 102
Webbers Falls, Ok., U.S. B6 113
Webberville, Mi., U.S. F6 99
Webb Lake, l., Me., U.S. D2 96
Weber, co., Ut., U.S. B4 121
Weber City, Va., U.S. f9 123
Webster, Ma., U.S. B4 98
Webster, N.Y., U.S. B3 109
Webster, Pa., U.S. F2 115
Webster, S.D., U.S. B8 118
Webster, co., Ga., U.S. D2 87
Webster, co., Ia., U.S. B3 92
Webster, co., Ky., U.S. C2 94
Webster, co., La., U.S. B2 95
Webster, co., Ms., U.S. B4 101
Webster, co., Mo., U.S. D5 102
Webster, co., Ne., U.S. D7 104
Webster, co., W.V., U.S. C4 125
Webster City, Ia., U.S. B4 92
Webster Groves, Mo., U.S. f13 102
Webster Reservoir, res., Ks., U.S. C4 93
Webster Springs, W.V., U.S. C4 125
Websterville, Vt., U.S. C4 122
Weddell Sea, Ant. B8 47
Wedgeport, N.S., Can. F4 71
Wedgewood, Mo., U.S. f13 102
Wedowee, Al., U.S. B4 78
Weed, Ca., U.S. B2 82
Weed Heights, Nv., U.S. E2 105
Weedon, Que., Can. D6 74
Weedsport, N.Y., U.S. B4 109
Weedville, Pa., U.S. D5 115
Weehawken, N.J., U.S. h8 107
Weeksbury, Ky., U.S. C7 94
Weeping Water, Ne., U.S. D9 104
Wegscheid, Ger. G13 8
Weiden in der Oberpfalz, Ger. F12 8
Weifang, China D10 26
Weihai, China D11 26
Weilburg, Ger. E8 8
Weilheim, Ger. H11 8
Weimar, Ger. E11 8
Weimar, Tx., U.S. E4 120
Weiner, Ar., U.S. B5 81
Weinheim, Ger. F8 8
Weipa, Austl. B8 50
Weippe, Id., U.S. C3 89
Weir, Ks., U.S. E9 93
Weir, Lake, l., Fl., U.S. C5 86
Weirsdale, Fl., U.S. D5 86
Weirton, W.V., U.S. A4 125
Weiser, Id., U.S. E2 89
Weiser, stm., Id., U.S. E2 89
Weishi, China A3 28
Weissenburg in Bayern, Ger. F10 8
Weissenfels, Ger. D11 8
Weiss Lake, res., U.S. A4 78
Weisswasser, Ger. D14 8
Weiz, Aus. H15 8
Wejherowo, Pol. A18 8
Welch, W.V., U.S. D3 125
Welcome, Mn., U.S. G4 100
Welcome, S.C., U.S. B3 117
Weld, co., Co., U.S. A6 83
Weldon, N.C., U.S. A5 110
Weldon Spring, Mo., U.S. f12 102
Weleetka, Ok., U.S. B5 113
Welkom, S. Afr. G5 44
Welland, Ont., Can. E5 73
Wellesley, Ont., Can. D4 73
Wellesley, Ma., U.S. B5 98
Wellesley Islands, is., Austl. C7 50
Wellford, S.C., U.S. B3 117
Wellington, Ont., Can. D7 73
Wellington, N.Z. D5 52
Wellington, Co., U.S. A5 83
Wellington, Ks., U.S. E6 93
Wellington, Mo., U.S. B4 102
Wellington, Nv., U.S. E2 105
Wellington, Oh., U.S. A3 112
Wellington, Tx., U.S. B2 120
Wellington, Ut., U.S. D5 121
Wellington, Isla, i., Chile F2 56
Wellington Channel, strt., N.W. Ter., Can. A14 66
Wellman, Ia., U.S. C6 92
Wells, Me., U.S. E2 96
Wells, Mi., U.S. C3 99
Wells, Mn., U.S. G5 100
Wells, Nv., U.S. B7 105
Wells, co., In., U.S. C7 91
Wells, co., N.D., U.S. B6 111
Wells, stm., Vt., U.S. C4 122
Wellsboro, Pa., U.S. C7 115
Wellsburg, Ia., U.S. B5 92
Wellsburg, W.V., U.S. A4 125
Wellston, Oh., U.S. C3 112
Wellston, Ok., U.S. B4 113
Wellsville, Ks., U.S. D8 93
Wellsville, Mo., U.S. B6 102
Wellsville, N.Y., U.S. C3 109
Wellsville, Oh., U.S. B5 112
Wellsville, Ut., U.S. B4 121
Wellton, Az., U.S. E1 80
Wels, Aus. G14 8
Welsh, La., U.S. D3 95
Welshpool, Wales, U.K. I9 7
Wembley, Alta., Can. B1 68
Wenatchee, Wa., U.S. B5 124
Wenatchee, stm., Wa., U.S. B5 124
Wenatchee Lake, l., Wa., U.S. B5 124
Wenatchee Mountains, mts., Wa., U.S. B5 124
Wendell, Id., U.S. G4 89
Wendell, N.C., U.S. B4 110
Wendover, Ut., U.S. C1 121
Wenham, Ma., U.S. A6 98
Wenham Lake, l., Ma., U.S. f12 98
Wenona, Il., U.S. B4 90
Wenshan, China C8 34
Wentworth, Lake, l., N.H., U.S. C4 106
Wentzville, Mo., U.S. C7 102
Wenzhou, China G9 28
Weohyakapka, Lake, l., Fl., U.S. E5 86
Wernigerode, Ger. D10 8
Wertheim, Ger. F9 8
Wesel, Ger. D6 8
Weser, stm., Ger. B8 8
Weslaco, Tx., U.S. F4 120
Wesleyville, Newf., Can. D5 72
Wesleyville, Pa., U.S. B2 115
Wessel Islands, is., Austl. B7 50
Wesserunsett Lake, l., Me., U.S. D3 96
Wessington Springs, S.D., U.S. C7 118
Wesson, Ms., U.S. D3 101
West, Tx., U.S. D4 120
West, stm., Ct., U.S. D5 84
West, stm., Ma., U.S. h9 98
West, stm., Vt., U.S. E3 122
West Acton, Ma., U.S. g10 98
West Alexandria, Oh., U.S. C1 112
West Allis, Wi., U.S. m11 126
West Alton, Mo., U.S. f13 102
West Andover, Ma., U.S. A5 98
West Baden Springs, In., U.S. G4 91
West Baton Rouge, co., La., U.S. D4 95
West Bay, b., Fl., U.S. u16 86
West Bay, b., N.C., U.S. B6 110
West Bay, b., Tx., U.S. r15 120
West Bend, Ia., U.S. B3 92
West Bend, Wi., U.S. E5 126
West Bengal, state, India I12 38
West Berlin, N.J., U.S. D3 107
West Billerica, Ma., U.S. f10 98
West Blocton, Al., U.S. B2 78
Westborough, Ma., U.S. B4 98
West Bountiful, Ut., U.S. C4 121
West Boylston, Ma., U.S. B4 98
West Branch, Ia., U.S. C6 92
West Branch, Mi., U.S. D6 99
West Branch Reservoir, res., Ct., U.S. B3 84
West Bridgewater, Ma., U.S. B5 98
Westbrook, Ct., U.S. D6 84
Westbrook, Me., U.S. E2 96
Westbrook, Mn., U.S. F3 100
West Burlington, Ia., U.S. D6 92
West Butte, mtn., Mt., U.S. B5 103
Westby, Wi., U.S. E3 126
West Cache Creek, stm., Ok., U.S. C3 113
West Caldwell, N.J., U.S. B4 107
West Canada Creek, stm., N.Y., U.S. B6 109
West Carroll, co., La., U.S. B4 95
West Carrollton, Oh., U.S. C1 112
West Carthage, N.Y., U.S. B5 109
Westchester, Il., U.S. k9 90
West Chester, Pa., U.S. G10 115
Westchester, co., N.Y., U.S. D7 109
West Chicago, Il., U.S. k8 90
West Chop, c., Ma., U.S. D6 98
West College Corner, In., U.S. E8 91
West Columbia, S.C., U.S. D5 117
West Columbia, Tx., U.S. E5 120
West Concord, Ma., U.S. B5 98
West Concord, Mn., U.S. F6 100
West Concord, N.C., U.S. B2 110
Westconnaug Reservoir, res., R.I., U.S. C2 116
West Cote Blanche Bay, b., La., U.S. E4 95
West Covina, Ca., U.S. m13 82
West Crossett, Ar., U.S. D4 81
West Cumberland, Me., U.S. E2 96
West Dennis, Ma., U.S. C7 98
West Des Moines, Ia., U.S. C4 92
West Elk Mountains, mts., Co., U.S. C3 83
West Elk Peak, mtn., Co., U.S. C3 83
Westerly, R.I., U.S. F1 116
Western Australia, state, Austl. D4 50
Western Desert see Gharbīyah, Aṣ-Ṣaḥrā' al-, des., Egypt C11 42
Western Ghāts, mts., India E3 37
Westernport, Md., U.S. m12 97
Western Sahara, dep., Afr. D3 42
Western Samoa, ctry., Oc. G1 2
Western Springs, Il., U.S. k9 90
Westerstede, Ger. B7 8
Westerville, Oh., U.S. B3 112
West Falkland, i., Falk. Is. G4 56
West Falmouth, Ma., U.S. C6 98
West Fargo, N.D., U.S. C9 111
West Feliciana, co., La., U.S. D4 95
Westfield, N.B., Can. D3 71
Westfield, In., U.S. D5 91
Westfield, Ma., U.S. B2 98
Westfield, N.J., U.S. B4 107
Westfield, N.Y., U.S. C1 109
Westfield, Pa., U.S. C6 115
Westfield, Wi., U.S. E4 126
Westfield, stm., Ma., U.S. B2 98
West Fork, Ar., U.S. B1 81
West Fork, stm., W.V., U.S. B4 125
West Frankfort, Il., U.S. F5 90
West Freehold, N.J., U.S. C4 107
West Friendship, Md., U.S. B4 97
Westgate, Fl., U.S. F6 86
West Grand Lake, l., Me., U.S. C5 96
West Grove, Pa., U.S. G10 115
West Hanover, Ma., U.S. h12 98
West Hartford, Ct., U.S. B4 84
West Haven, Ct., U.S. D4 84
West Hazleton, Pa., U.S. E9 115
West Helena, Ar., U.S. C5 81
West Hill Reservoir, res., Ma., U.S. B4 98
Westhope, N.D., U.S. A4 111
West Indies, is. E12 64
West Island, i., Ma., U.S. C6 98
West Jefferson, N.C., U.S. A1 110
West Jefferson, Oh., U.S. C2 112
West Jordan, Ut., U.S. C3 121
West Kingston, R.I., U.S. F3 116
West Lafayette, In., U.S. D4 91
West Lafayette, Oh., U.S. B4 112
Westlake, La., U.S. D2 95
Westlake, Oh., U.S. h9 112
West Lake, l., Me., U.S. C4 96
Westland, Mi., U.S. F7 99
West Laramie, Wy., U.S. E7 127
West Lawn, Pa., U.S. F10 115
West Lebanon, In., U.S. D3 91
West Liberty, Ia., U.S. C6 92
West Liberty, Ky., U.S. C6 94
West Liberty, Oh., U.S. B2 112
West Liberty, W.V., U.S. f8 125
West Linn, Or., U.S. B4 114
Westlock, Alta., Can. B4 68
West Long Branch, N.J., U.S. C4 107
West Lorne, Ont., Can. E3 73
West Marion, N.C., U.S. f10 110
West Medway, Ma., U.S. B5 98
West Memphis, Ar., U.S. B5 81
West Miami, Fl., U.S. s13 86
West Middlesex, Pa., U.S. D1 115
West Mifflin, Pa., U.S. F2 115
West Milton, Oh., U.S. C1 112
West Milwaukee, Wi., U.S. m12 126
Westminster, Ca., U.S. n12 82
Westminster, Co., U.S. B5 83
Westminster, Md., U.S. A4 97
Westminster, S.C., U.S. B1 117
West Monroe, La., U.S. B3 95
Westmont, Ca., U.S. *n12 82
Westmont, Il., U.S. k9 90
Westmont, N.J., U.S. D2 107
Westmont, Pa., U.S. F4 115
Westmoreland, Tn., U.S. A5 119
Westmoreland, co., Pa., U.S. F2 115
Westmoreland, co., Va., U.S. B6 123
Westmorland, Ca., U.S. F6 82
West Musquash Lake, l., Me., U.S. C5 96
West Mystic, Ct., U.S. D8 84
West Newton, Pa., U.S. F2 115
West New York, N.J., U.S. h8 107
West Nishnabotna, stm., Ia., U.S. C2 92
West Norriton, Pa., U.S. o20 115
Weston, Ct., U.S. E2 84
Weston, Ma., U.S. g10 98
Weston, Mo., U.S. B3 102
Weston, Oh., U.S. A2 112
Weston, Or., U.S. B8 114
Weston, W.V., U.S. B4 125
Weston, Wi., U.S. *D4 126
Weston, co., Wy., U.S. C8 127
Weston-super-Mare, Eng., U.K. J10 7
West Orange, N.J., U.S. B4 107
Westover, Md., U.S. D6 97
Westover, W.V., U.S. B5 125
Westover Air Force Base, mil., Ma., U.S. B2 98
West Palm Beach, Fl., U.S. F6 86
West Pawlet, Vt., U.S. E2 122
West Pearl, stm., La., U.S. D6 95
West Pelzer, S.C., U.S. B3 117
West Pensacola, Fl., U.S. u14 86
West Peoria, Il., U.S. C4 90
Westphalia, Mi., U.S. F6 99
West Pittsburg, Pa., U.S. E1 115
West Pittston, Pa., U.S. m17 115
West Plains, Mo., U.S. E6 102
West Point, Ca., U.S. C3 82
West Point, Ga., U.S. D1 87
West Point, Ia., U.S. D6 92
West Point, Ky., U.S. C4 94
West Point, Ms., U.S. B5 101
West Point, Ne., U.S. C9 104
West Point, N.Y., U.S. D7 109
West Point, Va., U.S. C6 123
West Point, mtn., Ak., U.S. C11 79
West Point Lake, res., U.S. C1 87
Westport, Ont., Can. C8 73
Westport, N.Z. D3 52
Westport, Ct., U.S. E2 84
Westport, In., U.S. F6 91
Westport, Wa., U.S. C1 124
West Portsmouth, Oh., U.S. D2 112
West Quoddy Head, c., Me., U.S. D6 96
Westray, i., Scot., U.K. B10 7
Westray Firth, strt., Scot., U.K. B9 7
West Reading, Pa., U.S. F10 115
West Rutland, Vt., U.S. D2 122
West Saint Paul, Mn., U.S. n12 100
West Salem, Il., U.S. E5 90
West Salem, Oh., U.S. B3 112
West Salem, Wi., U.S. E2 126
West Scarborough, Me., U.S. E2 96
West Seneca, N.Y., U.S. C2 109
West Simsbury, Ct., U.S. B4 84
West Slope, Or., U.S. g12 114
West Spanish Peak, mtn., Co., U.S. D6 83
West Springfield, Ma., U.S. B2 98
West Springfield, Va., U.S. g12 123
West Swanzey, N.H., U.S. E2 106
West Terre Haute, In., U.S. F3 91
West Thompson Lake, res., Ct., U.S. B8 84
West Union, Ia., U.S. B6 92
West Union, Oh., U.S. D2 112
West Union, W.V., U.S. B4 125
West Unity, Oh., U.S. A1 112
West University Place, Tx., U.S. r14 120
West Valley City, Ut., U.S. C4 121
West Vancouver, B.C., Can. f12 69
West Van Lear, Ky., U.S. C7 94
West View, Pa., U.S. h13 115
Westville, Il., U.S. C6 90
Westville, In., U.S. A4 91
Westville, N.H., U.S. E4 106
Westville, N.J., U.S. D2 107
Westville, Ok., U.S. A7 113
Westville Lake, res., Ma., U.S. B3 98
West Virginia, state, U.S. C4 125
West Walker, stm., U.S. E2 105
West Wareham, Ma., U.S. C6 98
West Warwick, R.I., U.S. D3 116
Westwego, La., U.S. k11 95
Westwood, Ca., U.S. B3 82
Westwood, Ks., U.S. k16 93
Westwood, Ky., U.S. B7 94
Westwood, Ma., U.S. B5 98
Westwood, N.J., U.S. B4 107
Westwood Lakes, Fl., U.S. s13 86
West Wyoming, Pa., U.S. n17 115
West Yarmouth, Ma., U.S. C7 98
West Yellowstone, Mt., U.S. F5 103
West York, Pa., U.S. G8 115
Wetar, Pulau, i., Indon. G8 32
Wetaskiwin, Alta., Can. C4 68
Wethersfield, Ct., U.S. C5 84
Wet Mountains, mts., Co., U.S. C5 83
Wetumka, Ok., U.S. B5 113
Wetumpka, Al., U.S. C3 78
Wetzel, co., W.V., U.S. B4 125
Wetzlar, Ger. E8 8
Wewahitchka, Fl., U.S. B1 86
Wewak, Pap. N. Gui. k15 50a
Wewoka, Ok., U.S. B5 113
Wexford, Ire. I6 7
Wexford, co., Mi., U.S. D5 99
Weyauwega, Wi., U.S. D5 126
Weymouth, Eng., U.K. K10 7
Weymouth, Ma., U.S. B6 98
Whaleysville, Md., U.S. D7 97
Whalsay, i., Scot., U.K. A12 7
Whangarei, N.Z. A5 52
Wharton, N.J., U.S. B3 107
Wharton, Tx., U.S. E4 120
Wharton, co., Tx., U.S. E4 120
What Cheer, Ia., U.S. C5 92
Whatcom, co., Wa., U.S. A4 124
Whatcom, Lake, l., Wa., U.S. A3 124
Wheatfield, In., U.S. B3 91
Wheatland, Ca., U.S. C3 82
Wheatland, Ia., U.S. C7 92
Wheatland, Wy., U.S. D8 127
Wheatland, co., Mt., U.S. D7 103
Wheatland Reservoir, res., Wy., U.S. E7 127
Wheatley, Ont., Can. E2 73
Wheaton, Il., U.S. B5 90
Wheaton, Md., U.S. B3 97
Wheaton, Mn., U.S. E2 100
Wheaton, Mo., U.S. E3 102
Wheat Ridge, Co., U.S. B5 83
Wheelbarrow Peak, mtn., Nv., U.S. F5 105
Wheeler, Ms., U.S. A5 101
Wheeler, Tx., U.S. B2 120
Wheeler, co., Ga., U.S. D4 87
Wheeler, co., Ne., U.S. C7 104
Wheeler, co., Or., U.S. C6 114
Wheeler, co., Tx., U.S. B2 120
Wheeler Air Force Base, mil., Hi., U.S. g9 88
Wheeler Lake, res., Al., U.S. A2 78
Wheeler Peak, mtn., Ca., U.S. C4 82
Wheeler Peak, mtn., Nv., U.S. E7 105
Wheeler Peak, mtn., N.M., U.S. A4 108
Wheelersburg, Oh., U.S. D3 112
Wheeling, Il., U.S. h9 90
Wheeling, W.V., U.S. A4 125
Wheeling Creek, stm., W.V., U.S. f8 125
Wheelwright, Ky., U.S. C7 94
Whetstone, stm., U.S. E2 100
Whidbey Island, i., Wa., U.S. A3 124
Whidbey Island Naval Air Station, mil., Wa., U.S. A3 124
Whigham, Ga., U.S. F2 87
Whiskey Peak, mtn., Wy., U.S. D5 127
Whiskeytown-Shasta-Trinity National Recreation Area, Ca., U.S. B2 82
Whistler, B.C., Can. D6 69
Whitacres, Ct., U.S. A5 84
Whitakers, N.C., U.S. A5 110
Whitbourne, Newf., Can. E5 72
Whitby, Ont., Can. D6 73
Whitchurch-Stouffville, Ont., Can. D5 73
White, co., Ar., U.S. B4 81
White, co., Ga., U.S. B3 87
White, co., Il., U.S. E5 90
White, co., In., U.S. C4 91
White, co., Tn., U.S. D8 119
White, stm., N.A. D4 66
White, stm., U.S. C4 81
White, stm., U.S. D5 118
White, stm., U.S. C7 121
White, stm., Az., U.S. D5 80
White, stm., In., U.S. H2 91
White, stm., Mi., U.S. E4 99
White, stm., Nv., U.S. E6 105
White, stm., Tx., U.S. C2 120
White, stm., Vt., U.S. D4 122
White, stm., Wa., U.S. B4 124
White, stm., Wa., U.S. B5 124
White, Lake, l., Austl. D5 50
White Bay, b., Newf., Can. D3 72
White Bear, stm., Newf., Can. E3 72
White Bear Lake, Mn., U.S. E5 100
White Bluff, Tn., U.S. A4 119
White Butte, mtn., N.D., U.S. C2 111
White Castle, La., U.S. D4 95
White Center, Wa., U.S. e11 124
White City, Or., U.S. E4 114
White Clay Creek, stm., U.S. A3 104
White Cloud, Mi., U.S. E5 99
Whitecourt, Alta., Can. B3 68
White Creek, stm., U.S. E2 122
Whiteday, stm., W.V., U.S. h10 125
White Deer, Tx., U.S. B2 120
White Earth Indian Reservation, Mn., U.S. C3 100
White Earth Lake, l., Mn., U.S. C3 100
Whiteface, stm., Mn., U.S. C6 100
Whiteface Mountain, mtn., N.Y., U.S. f11 109
Whitefield, N.H., U.S. B3 106
Whitefish, Mt., U.S. B2 103
Whitefish Bay, Wi., U.S. m12 126
Whitefish Bay, b., Mi., U.S. B6 99
Whitefish Lake, l., Mn., U.S. D4 100
Whitefish Range, mts., Mt., U.S. B2 103
Whiteford, Md., U.S. A5 97
White Hall, Al., U.S. C3 78
White Hall, Ar., U.S. C3 81
White Hall, Il., U.S. D3 90
Whitehall, Mi., U.S. E4 99
Whitehall, Mt., U.S. E4 103
Whitehall, N.Y., U.S. B7 109
Whitehall, Oh., U.S. m11 112
Whitehall, Wi., U.S. D2 126
Whitehall Reservoir, res., Ma., U.S. h9 98
Whitehaven, Eng., U.K. G9 7
White Haven, Pa., U.S. D10 115
Whitehorn, Point, c., Wa., U.S. A3 124
Whitehorse, Yukon, Can. D5 66
White Horse, N.J., U.S. C3 107
Whitehouse, Oh., U.S. A2 112
White House, Tn., U.S. A5 119
White Island Shores, Ma., U.S. C6 98
White Knob Mountains, mts., Id., U.S. F5 89
White Lake, l., La., U.S. E3 95
Whiteman Air Force Base, mil., Mo., U.S. C4 102
White Meadow Lake, N.J., U.S. *B3 107
White Mesa Natural Bridge, Az., U.S. A4 80
White Mountain Peak, mtn., Ca., U.S. D4 82
White Mountains, mts., U.S. D4 82
White Mountains, mts., N.H., U.S. B3 106
Whitemouth, stm., Man., Can. E4 70
Whitemouth Lake, l., Man., Can. E4 70
White Nile (Al-Bahr al-Abyad), stm., Sudan F12 42
White Oak, Oh., U.S. o12 112
White Oak Creek, stm., Oh., U.S. D2 112
Whiteoak Creek, stm., Tn., U.S. A4 119
White Oak Lake, res., Ar., U.S. D2 81
White Pigeon, Mi., U.S. G5 99
White Pine, Mi., U.S. m12 99
White Pine, Tn., U.S. C10 119
White Pine, co., Nv., U.S. D6 105
White Plains, Md., U.S. C4 97
White Plains, N.Y., U.S. D7 109
Whiteriver, Az., U.S. D6 80
White River Junction, Vt., U.S. D4 122
White Rock, B.C., Can. E6 69
White Russia see Belarus, ctry., Eur. G3 18
White Salmon, Wa., U.S. D4 124
White Salmon, stm., Wa., U.S. D4 124
White Sands Missile Range, mil., N.M., U.S. E3 108
White Sands National Monument, N.M., U.S. E3 108
Whitesboro, N.Y., U.S. B5 109
Whitesboro, Tx., U.S. C4 120
Whitesburg, Ga., U.S. C2 87
Whitesburg, Ky., U.S. C7 94
Whites Creek, stm., Tn., U.S. g10 119
White Sea see Beloje more, Russia D5 22
Whiteside, co., Il., U.S. B3 90
White Sulphur Springs, Mt., U.S. D6 103
White Sulphur Springs, W.V., U.S. D4 125
Whitesville, Ky., U.S. C3 94
White Swan, Wa., U.S. C5 124
White Tank Mountains, mts., Az., U.S. k7 80
Whiteville, N.C., U.S. C4 110
Whiteville, Tn., U.S. B2 119

Name Map Ref Page
White Volta (Volta Blanche), stm., Afr. F5 42
Whitewater, Ks., U.S. E6 93
Whitewater, Wi., U.S. F5 126
Whitewater, stm., U.S. F7 91
Whitewater, stm., Ks., U.S. E6 93
Whitewater Baldy, mtn., N.M., U.S. D1 108
Whitewater Bay, b., Fl., U.S. G6 86
Whitewood, S.D., U.S. C2 118
Whitewright, Tx., U.S. C4 120
Whitfield, co., Ga., U.S. B2 87
Whitfield Estates, Fl., U.S. q10 86
Whiting, In., U.S. A3 91
Whiting, Ia., U.S. B1 92
Whiting, Wi., U.S. D4 126
Whiting Field Naval Air Station, mil., Fl., U.S. u14 86
Whitinsville, Ma., U.S. B4 98
Whitley, co., In., U.S. B6 91
Whitley, co., Ky., U.S. D5 94
Whitley City, Ky., U.S. D5 94
Whitman, Ma., U.S. B6 98
Whitman, W.V., U.S. D2 125
Whitman, co., Wa., U.S. B8 124
Whitman Square, N.J., U.S. D2 107
Whitmire, S.C., U.S. B4 117
Whitmore Lake, Mi., U.S. p14 99
Whitmore Village, Hi., U.S. f9 88
Whitney, S.C., U.S. B4 117
Whitney, Tx., U.S. D4 120
Whitney, Lake, res., Tx., U.S. D4 120
Whitney, Mount, mtn., Ca., U.S. D4 82
Whitney Point Lake, res., N.Y., U.S. C5 109
Whittier, Ak., U.S. C10 79
Whittier, Ca., U.S. F4 82
Whitwell, Tn., U.S. D8 119
Wholdaia Lake, l., N.W. Ter., Can. D12 66
Whyalla, Austl. F7 50
Wiarton, Ont., Can. C3 73
Wibaux, Mt., U.S. D12 103
Wibaux, co., Mt., U.S. D12 103
Wichita, Ks., U.S. E6 93
Wichita, co., Ks., U.S. D2 93
Wichita, co., Tx., U.S. B3 120
Wichita Falls, Tx., U.S. C3 120
Wichita Mountains, mts., Ok., U.S. C3 113
Wick, Scot., U.K. C9 7
Wickenburg, Az., U.S. D3 80
Wickiup Reservoir, res., Or., U.S. E5 114
Wickliffe, Ky., U.S. f8 94
Wickliffe, Oh., U.S. A4 112
Wicklow, Ire. I6 7
Wicklow Head, c., Ire. I6 7
Wicklow Mountains, mts., Ire. H6 7
Wicomico, co., Md., U.S. D6 97
Wicomico, stm., Md., U.S. D6 97
Wiconisco, Pa., U.S. E8 115
Widefield, Co., U.S. C6 83
Wielkopolska, reg., Pol. D17 8
Wien (Vienna), Aus. G16 8
Wiener Neustadt, Aus. H16 8
Wiesbaden, Ger. E8 8
Wiesloch, Ger. F8 8
Wiggins, Ms., U.S. E4 101
Wiggins Peak, mtn., Wy., U.S. C3 127
Wikwemikong, Ont., Can. B3 73
Wilbarger, co., Tx., U.S. B3 120
Wilber, Ne., U.S. D9 104
Wilberforce, Oh., U.S. C2 112
Wilbraham, Ma., U.S. B3 98
Wilbur, Wa., U.S. B7 124
Wilburton, Ok., U.S. C6 113
Wilcannia, Austl. F8 50
Wilcox, Pa., U.S. C4 115
Wilcox, co., Al., U.S. D2 78
Wilcox, co., Ga., U.S. E3 87
Wild, stm., U.S. B4 106
Wild Ammonoosuc, stm., N.H., U.S. B3 106
Wild Branch, stm., Vt., U.S. B4 122
Wilder, Id., U.S. F2 89
Wilder, Vt., U.S. D4 122
Wilder Dam, U.S. C2 106
Wildhorse Creek, stm., Ok., U.S. C4 113
Wild Horse Reservoir, res., Nv., U.S. B6 105
Wildorado, Tx., U.S. B1 120
Wild Rice, stm., Mn., U.S. C2 100
Wild Rice, stm., N.D., U.S. C8 111
Wildwood, Fl., U.S. D4 86
Wildwood, N.J., U.S. F3 107
Wildwood Crest, N.J., U.S. F3 107
Wilhelm, Mount, mtn., Pap. N. Gui. m16 50a
Wilhelmina Gebergte, mts., Sur. C7 54
Wilhelmina Peak see Trikora, Puntjak, mtn., Indon. F10 32
Wilhelmshaven, Ger. B8 8
Wilkes, co., Ga., U.S. C4 87
Wilkes, co., N.C., U.S. A1 110
Wilkes-Barre, Pa., U.S. D10 115
Wilkesboro, N.C., U.S. A1 110
Wilkes Land, reg., Ant. C24 47
Wilkin, co., Mn., U.S. D2 100
Wilkinsburg, Pa., U.S. F2 115
Wilkinson, W.V., U.S. D3 125
Wilkinson, co., Ga., U.S. D3 87
Wilkinson, co., Ms., U.S. D2 101
Will, co., Il., U.S. B6 90
Willacoochee, Ga., U.S. E3 87
Willacy, co., Tx., U.S. F4 120
Willamette, stm., Or., U.S. C3 114
Willamette Pass, Or., U.S. D4 114
Willamina, Or., U.S. B3 114
Willapa Bay, b., Wa., U.S. C1 124
Willard, Mo., U.S. D4 102
Willard, Oh., U.S. A3 112
Willard, Ut., U.S. B3 121
Willard Bay, b., Ut., U.S. B3 121
Willards, Md., U.S. D7 97
Willard Stream, stm., Vt., U.S. B5 122
Willcox, Az., U.S. E6 80
Willcox Playa, l., Az., U.S. E5 80
Willemstad, Neth. Ant. H13 64
William Bill Dannelly Reservoir, res., Al., U.S. C2 78
Williams, Az., U.S. B3 80
Williams, Ca., U.S. C2 82
Williams, co., N.D., U.S. A2 111
Williams, co., Oh., U.S. A1 112
Williams, stm., Vt., U.S. E3 122
Williams, stm., W.V., U.S. C4 125
Williams Air Force Base, mil., Az., U.S. D4 80
Williams Bay, Wi., U.S. F5 126
Williamsburg, In., U.S. E8 91
Williamsburg, Ia., U.S. C5 92
Williamsburg, Ky., U.S. D5 94
Williamsburg, Oh., U.S. C1 112
Williamsburg, Pa., U.S. F5 115
Williamsburg, Va., U.S. C6 123
Williamsburg, co., S.C., U.S. D8 117
Williams Fork, stm., Co., U.S. A3 83
Williams Lake, B.C., Can. C6 69
Williamson, N.Y., U.S. B3 109
Williamson, W.V., U.S. D2 125
Williamson, co., Il., U.S. F4 90
Williamson, co., Tn., U.S. B5 119
Williamson, co., Tx., U.S. D4 120
Williamsport, In., U.S. D3 91
Williamsport, Md., U.S. A2 97
Williamsport, Pa., U.S. D7 115
Williamston, Mi., U.S. F6 99
Williamston, N.C., U.S. B5 110
Williamston, S.C., U.S. B3 117
Williamstown, Ky., U.S. B5 94
Williamstown, Ma., U.S. A1 98
Williamstown, N.J., U.S. D3 107
Williamstown, Pa., U.S. E8 115
Williamstown, Vt., U.S. C3 122
Williamstown, W.V., U.S. B3 125
Williamsville, Il., U.S. D4 90
Williamsville, N.Y., U.S. C2 109
Willimantic, Ct., U.S. C7 84
Willimantic, stm., Ct., U.S. B6 84
Willimantic Reservoir, res., Ct., U.S. C7 84
Willingboro, N.J., U.S. C3 107
Willis, Tx., U.S. D5 120
Willis Islets, is., Austl. C9 50
Williston, Fl., U.S. C4 86
Williston, N.D., U.S. A2 111
Williston, S.C., U.S. E5 117
Williston Lake, res., B.C., Can. B6 69
Willits, Ca., U.S. C2 82
Willmar, Mn., U.S. E3 100
Willoughby, Oh., U.S. A4 112
Willoughby, Lake, l., Vt., U.S. B4 122
Willoughby Hills, Oh., U.S. A4 112
Willow, Ak., U.S. g17 79
Willow Creek, stm., Nv., U.S. E5 105
Willow Creek, stm., Ut., U.S. D6 121
Willow Creek, stm., Wy., U.S. C6 127
Willow Grove Naval Air Station, mil., Pa., U.S. F11 115
Willowick, Oh., U.S. A4 112
Willowmore, S. Afr. H4 44
Willow Reservoir, res., Wi., U.S. C3 126
Willow Run, De., U.S. i7 85
Willow Run, Mi., U.S. p14 99
Willows, Ca., U.S. C2 82
Willow Springs, Il., U.S. k9 90
Willow Springs, Mo., U.S. E6 102
Willston, Va., U.S. *B5 123
Wilmar, Ar., U.S. D4 81
Wilmerding, Pa., U.S. k14 115
Wilmette, Il., U.S. A6 90
Wilmington, De., U.S. B3 85
Wilmington, Il., U.S. B5 90
Wilmington, Ma., U.S. A5 98
Wilmington, N.C., U.S. C5 110
Wilmington, Oh., U.S. C2 112
Wilmington, Vt., U.S. F3 122
Wilmington Manor, De., U.S. i7 85
Wilmore, Ky., U.S. C5 94
Wilmot, Ar., U.S. D4 81
Wilson, Ar., U.S. B5 81
Wilson, Ks., U.S. D5 93
Wilson, La., U.S. D4 95
Wilson, N.C., U.S. B5 110
Wilson, Ok., U.S. C4 113
Wilson, Pa., U.S. E11 115
Wilson, Wy., U.S. C2 127
Wilson, co., Ks., U.S. E8 93
Wilson, co., N.C., U.S. B5 110
Wilson, co., Tn., U.S. A5 119
Wilson, co., Tx., U.S. E3 120
Wilson, Cape, c., N.W. Ter., Can. C16 66
Wilson, Mount, mtn., Az., U.S. B1 80
Wilson, Mount, mtn., Ca., U.S. m12 82
Wilson, Mount, mtn., Co., U.S. D2 83
Wilson, Mount, mtn., Nv., U.S. E7 105
Wilson, Mount, mtn., Or., U.S. B5 114
Wilson Creek, stm., Wa., U.S. B6 124
Wilson Creek, stm., Wa., U.S. B5 124
Wilson Lake, res., Al., U.S. A2 78
Wilson Lake, res., Ks., U.S. D4 93
Wilsons Beach, N.B., Can. E3 71
Wilsonville, Al., U.S. B3 78
Wilsonville, Or., U.S. h12 114
Wilton, Al., U.S. B3 78
Wilton, Ct., U.S. E2 84
Wilton, Ia., U.S. C6 92
Wilton, Me., U.S. D2 96
Wilton, N.H., U.S. E3 106
Wilton, N.D., U.S. B5 111
Wiluna, Austl. E4 50
Wimauma, Fl., U.S. E4 86
Wimico, Lake, l., Fl., U.S. C1 86
Winamac, In., U.S. B4 91
Wincheck Pond, l., R.I., U.S. E1 116
Winchendon, Ma., U.S. A3 98
Winchester, Ont., Can. B9 73
Winchester, Eng., U.K. J11 7
Winchester, Il., U.S. D3 90
Winchester, In., U.S. D8 91
Winchester, Ks., U.S. k15 93
Winchester, Ky., U.S. C5 94
Winchester, Ma., U.S. g11 98
Winchester, Nv., U.S. G6 105
Winchester, N.H., U.S. E2 106
Winchester, Oh., U.S. D2 112
Winchester, Tn., U.S. B5 119
Winchester, Va., U.S. A4 123
Winchester Bay, Or., U.S. D2 114
Wind, stm., Wa., U.S. D4 124
Wind, stm., Wy., U.S. C4 127
Windber, Pa., U.S. F4 115
Wind Cave National Park, S.D., U.S. D2 118
Winder, Ga., U.S. C3 87
Windermere, Eng., U.K. G10 7
Windfall, In., U.S. D6 91
Windgap, Pa., U.S. E11 115
Windham, Ct., U.S. C7 84
Windham, Oh., U.S. A4 112
Windham, co., Ct., U.S. B7 84
Windham, co., Vt., U.S. F3 122
Windhoek, Nmb. F3 44
Wind Lake, Wi., U.S. F5 126
Wind Lake, l., Wi., U.S. n11 126
Windmill Point, c., Va., U.S. C6 123
Windom, Mn., U.S. G3 100
Windom Peak, mtn., Co., U.S. D3 83
Windorah, Austl. E8 50
Window Rock, Az., U.S. B6 80
Wind Point, Wi., U.S. n12 126
Wind River Indian Reservation, Wy., U.S. C4 127
Wind River Peak, mtn., Wy., U.S. D3 127
Wind River Range, mts., Wy., U.S. C3 127
Windsor (part of Grand Falls-Windsor), Newf., Can. D4 72
Windsor, Ont., Can. E1 73
Windsor, Que., Can. D5 74
Windsor, Eng., U.K. J12 7
Windsor, Co., U.S. A6 83
Windsor, Ct., U.S. B5 84
Windsor, Il., U.S. D5 90
Windsor, Mo., U.S. C4 102
Windsor, N.C., U.S. A6 110
Windsor, Pa., U.S. G8 115
Windsor, Vt., U.S. E4 122
Windsor, Va., U.S. D6 123
Windsor, co., Vt., U.S. D3 122
Windsor Heights, Ia., U.S. e8 92
Windsor Locks, Ct., U.S. B5 84
Windward Islands, is., N.A. H17 64
Windward Passage, strt., N.A. E10 64
Windy Hill, S.C., U.S. C8 117
Windy Peak, mtn., Wa., U.S. A6 124
Winefred Lake, l., Alta., Can. B5 68
Winfield, Al., U.S. B2 78
Winfield, Ia., U.S. C6 92
Winfield, Ks., U.S. E7 93
Winfield, Mo., U.S. C7 102
Winfield, W.V., U.S. C3 125
Wing, stm., Mn., U.S. D3 100
Wingate, N.C., U.S. C2 110
Wingham, Ont., Can. D3 73
Winifrede, W.V., U.S. m12 125
Winisk, stm., Ont., Can. n18 73
Winisk Lake, l., Ont., Can. F15 66
Wink, Tx., U.S. D1 120
Winkelman, Az., U.S. E5 80
Winkler, Man., Can. E3 70
Winkler, co., Tx., U.S. D1 120
Winlock, Wa., U.S. C3 124
Winn, co., La., U.S. C3 95
Winnebago, Il., U.S. A4 90
Winnebago, Mn., U.S. G4 100
Winnebago, Ne., U.S. B9 104
Winnebago, Wi., U.S. h8 126
Winnebago, co., Il., U.S. A4 90
Winnebago, co., Ia., U.S. A4 92
Winnebago, co., Wi., U.S. D5 126
Winnebago, stm., Ia., U.S. A4 92
Winnebago, Lake, l., Wi., U.S. E5 126
Winnebago Indian Reservation, Ne., U.S. B9 104
Winneconne, Wi., U.S. D5 126
Winnemucca, Nv., U.S. C4 105
Winnemucca Lake, l., Nv., U.S. C2 105
Winner, S.D., U.S. D6 118
Winneshiek, co., Ia., U.S. A6 92
Winnetka, Il., U.S. A6 90
Winnfield, La., U.S. C3 95
Winnibigoshish, Lake, l., Mn., U.S. C4 100
Winnipeg, Man., Can. E3 70
Winnipeg, stm., Can. D4 70
Winnipeg, Lake, l., Man., Can. C3 70
Winnipeg Beach, Man., Can. D3 70
Winnipegosis, Man., Can. D2 70
Winnipegosis, Lake, l., Man., Can. C2 70
Winnipesaukee, Lake, l., N.H., U.S. C4 106
Winnisquam, N.H., U.S. C3 106
Winnisquam Lake, l., N.H., U.S. C3 106
Winnsboro, La., U.S. B4 95
Winnsboro, S.C., U.S. C5 117
Winnsboro, Tx., U.S. C5 120
Winnsboro Mills, S.C., U.S. C5 117
Winona, Mn., U.S. F7 100
Winona, Ms., U.S. B4 101
Winona, Mo., U.S. D6 102
Winona, co., Mn., U.S. F7 100
Winona Lake, In., U.S. B6 91
Winona Lake, l., Vt., U.S. C2 122
Winooski, Vt., U.S. C2 122
Winooski, stm., Vt., U.S. C3 122
Winslow, Az., U.S. C5 80
Winslow, In., U.S. H3 91
Winslow, Me., U.S. D3 96
Winsted, Ct., U.S. B3 84
Winsted, Mn., U.S. F4 100
Winston, Fl., U.S. D4 86
Winston, Or., U.S. D3 114
Winston, co., Al., U.S. A2 78
Winston, co., Ms., U.S. B4 101
Winston-Salem, N.C., U.S. A2 110
Winter Garden, Fl., U.S. D5 86
Winter Harbor, Me., U.S. D4 96
Winter Haven, Fl., U.S. D5 86
Winter Park, Fl., U.S. D5 86
Winter Park, N.C., U.S. C5 110
Winterport, Me., U.S. D4 96
Winter Ridge, mtn., Or., U.S. E6 114
Winters, Ca., U.S. C2 82
Winters, Tx., U.S. D3 120
Winterset, Ia., U.S. C4 92
Wintersville, Oh., U.S. B5 112
Winterswijk, Neth. D6 8
Winterthur, Switz. E15 10
Winterton, Newf., Can. E5 72
Winterville, Ga., U.S. C3 87
Winterville, N.C., U.S. B5 110
Winthrop, Ia., U.S. B6 92
Winthrop, Me., U.S. D3 96
Winthrop, Ma., U.S. B6 98
Winthrop, Mn., U.S. F4 100
Winthrop, Lake, l., Ma., U.S. h10 98
Winthrop Harbor, Il., U.S. A6 90
Winton, Austl. D8 50
Winton, N.C., U.S. A6 110
Winton Lake, res., Oh., U.S. o12 113
Winyah Bay, b., S.C., U.S. E9 117
Wirt, co., W.V., U.S. B3 125
Wiscasset, Me., U.S. D3 96
Wisconsin, state, U.S. D4 126
Wisconsin, stm., Wi., U.S. E3 126
Wisconsin, Lake, res., Wi., U.S. E4 126
Wisconsin Dells, Wi., U.S. E4 126
Wisconsin Rapids, Wi., U.S. D4 126
Wise, Va., U.S. f9 123
Wise, co., Tx., U.S. C4 120
Wise, co., Va., U.S. e9 123
Wishek, N.D., U.S. C6 111
Wishram, Wa., U.S. D4 124
Wisła, stm., Pol. A18 8
Wismar, Ger. B11 8
Wisner, La., U.S. C4 95
Wisner, Ne., U.S. C9 104
Wissota, Lake, res., Wi., U.S. D2 126
Wister, Ok., U.S. C7 113
Wister Lake, res., Ok., U.S. C7 113
Witbank, S. Afr. G5 44
Withamsville, Oh., U.S. C1 112
Witherspoon, Mount, mtn., Ak., U.S. g18 79
Withlacoochee, stm., U.S. B3 86
Withlacoochee, stm., Fl., U.S. C4 86
Witless Bay, Newf., Can. E5 72
Witt, Il., U.S. D4 90
Wittenberg, Ger. D12 8
Wittenberg, Wi., U.S. D4 126
Wittenberge, Ger. B11 8
Wittlich, Ger. F6 8
Wittman, Md., U.S. C5 97
Wittmann, Az., U.S. D3 80
Wittstock, Ger. B12 8
Wixom, Mi., U.S. o14 99
Wixom Lake, res., Mi., U.S. E6 99
Włocławek, Pol. C19 8
Woburn, Ma., U.S. B5 98
Wokam, Pulau, i., Indon. G9 32
Woking, Eng., U.K. J12 7
Wolcott, Ct., U.S. C4 84
Wolcott, In., U.S. C3 91
Wolcottville, In., U.S. A7 91
Wolf, stm., Ms., U.S. E4 101
Wolf, stm., Tn., U.S. e9 119
Wolf, stm., Wi., U.S. C5 126
Wolf Creek, Or., U.S. E3 114
Wolf Creek, stm., U.S. A2 113
Wolf Creek, stm., W.V., U.S. m13 125
Wolf Creek Pass, Co., U.S. D3 83
Wolfe, co., Ky., U.S. C6 94
Wolfeboro, N.H., U.S. C4 106
Wolfeboro Falls, N.H., U.S. C4 106
Wolfe City, Tx., U.S. C4 120
Wolfen, Ger. D12 8
Wolfenbüttel, Ger. C10 8
Wolf Lake, Mi., U.S. E4 99
Wolf Lake, l., Il., U.S. k9 90
Wolf Mountain, mtn., Ak., U.S. B9 79
Wolf Point, Mt., U.S. B11 103
Wolfsberg, Aus. I14 8
Wolfsburg, Ger. C10 8
Wolf Swamp, sw., N.C., U.S. C5 110
Wolgast, Ger. A13 8
Wollaston, Cape, c., N.W. Ter., Can. B9 66
Wollaston, Islas, is., Chile H3 56
Wollaston Lake, l., Sask., Can. m8 75
Wollaston Peninsula, pen., N.W. Ter., Can. C10 66
Wollongong, Austl. F10 50
Wolverhampton, Eng., U.K. I10 7
Woman Lake, l., Mn., U.S. D4 100
Womelsdorf, Pa., U.S. F9 115
Wonder Lake, Il., U.S. A5 90
Wonewoc, Wi., U.S. E3 126
Wŏnsan, N. Kor. D12 26
Wood, co., Oh., U.S. A2 112
Wood, co., Tx., U.S. C5 120
Wood, co., W.V., U.S. B3 125
Wood, co., Wi., U.S. D3 126
Wood, stm., Sask., Can. H2 75
Wood, stm., R.I., U.S. F2 116
Wood, stm., Wy., U.S. C3 127
Wood, Mount, mtn., Mt., U.S. E7 103
Woodall Mountain, mtn., Ms., U.S. A5 101
Woodbine, Ga., U.S. F5 87
Woodbine, Ia., U.S. C2 92
Woodbine, Ky., U.S. D5 94
Woodbine, N.J., U.S. E3 107
Woodbridge, Ct., U.S. D3 84
Woodbridge, Va., U.S. B5 123
Woodbridge [Township], N.J., U.S. B4 107
Woodburn, In., U.S. B8 91
Woodburn, Or., U.S. B4 114
Woodbury, Ct., U.S. C3 84
Woodbury, Ga., U.S. D2 87
Woodbury, Mn., U.S. F6 100
Woodbury, N.J., U.S. D2 107
Woodbury, Tn., U.S. B5 119
Woodbury, co., Ia., U.S. B1 92
Woodcliff Lake, N.J., U.S. g8 107
Woodcliff Lake, l., N.J., U.S. g8 107
Wood Dale, Il., U.S. k9 90
Wood End, spit, Ma., U.S. B7 98
Woodfield, S.C., U.S. C6 117
Woodford, co., Il., U.S. C4 90
Woodford, co., Ky., U.S. B5 94
Woodhull, Il., U.S. B3 90
Woodlake, Ca., U.S. D4 82
Woodland, Ca., U.S. C3 82
Woodland, Me., U.S. C5 96
Woodland, N.C., U.S. A5 110
Woodland, Wa., U.S. D3 124
Woodland Acres, Co., U.S. D6 83
Woodland Park, Co., U.S. C5 83
Woodlark Island, i., Pap. N. Gui. A10 50
Woodlawn, Ky., U.S. e9 94
Woodlawn, Md., U.S. g10 97
Woodlawn, Oh., U.S. n13 112
Woodlawn, Va., U.S. D2 123
Woodmont, Ct., U.S. E4 84
Woodmoor, Md., U.S. B4 97
Woodridge, Il., U.S. k8 90
Wood-Ridge, N.J., U.S. h8 107
Wood River, Il., U.S. E3 90
Wood River, Ne., U.S. D7 104
Woodroffe, Mount, mtn., Austl. E6 50
Woodruff, S.C., U.S. B3 117
Woodruff, Wi., U.S. C4 126
Woodruff, co., Ar., U.S. B4 81
Woods, co., Ok., U.S. A3 113
Woods, Lake, res., Tn., U.S. B5 119
Woods, Lake of the, l., N.A. G14 66
Woodsboro, Tx., U.S. E4 120
Woods Cross, Ut., U.S. C4 121
Woodsfield, Oh., U.S. C4 112
Woods Hole, Ma., U.S. C6 98
Woodson, Ar., U.S. C3 81
Woodson, co., Ks., U.S. E8 93
Woodstock, N.B., Can. C2 71
Woodstock, Ont., Can. D4 73
Woodstock, Ga., U.S. B2 87
Woodstock, Il., U.S. A5 90
Woodstock, Md., U.S. B4 97
Woodstock, N.Y., U.S. C6 109
Woodstock, Vt., U.S. D3 122
Woodstock, Va., U.S. B4 123
Woodstown, N.J., U.S. D2 107
Woodsville, N.H., U.S. B2 106
Woodville, N.Z. D5 52
Woodville, Fl., U.S. B2 86
Woodville, Ms., U.S. D2 101
Woodville, Oh., U.S. A2 112
Woodville, Tx., U.S. D5 120
Woodville, Wi., U.S. D1 126
Woodward, Ia., U.S. C4 92
Woodward, Ok., U.S. A2 113
Woodward, co., Ok., U.S. A2 113
Woodworth, La., U.S. C3 95
Woolmarket, Ms., U.S. E5 101
Woolrich, Pa., U.S. D7 115
Woolsey Peak, mtn., Az., U.S. D3 80
Woomera, Austl. F7 50
Woonsocket, R.I., U.S. A3 116
Woonsocket, S.D., U.S. C7 118
Woonsocket Reservoir Number Three, res., R.I., U.S. B3 116
Wooramel, Austl. E2 50
Wooster, Oh., U.S. B4 112
Worcester, S. Afr. H3 44
Worcester, Eng., U.K. I10 7
Worcester, Ma., U.S. B4 98
Worcester, co., Md., U.S. D7 97
Worcester, co., Ma., U.S. A3 98
Worden, Il., U.S. E4 90
Worden Pond, l., R.I., U.S. F3 116
Workington, Eng., U.K. G9 7
Worland, Wy., U.S. B5 127
Worms, Ger. F8 8
Worth, Il., U.S. k9 90
Worth, co., Ga., U.S. E3 87
Worth, co., Ia., U.S. A4 92
Worth, co., Mo., U.S. A3 102
Worthing, Eng., U.K. K12 7
Worthington, In., U.S. F4 91
Worthington, Ky., U.S. B7 94
Worthington, Mn., U.S. G3 100
Worthington, Oh., U.S. B2 112
Worthington Peak, mtn., Nv., U.S. F6 105
Wowoni, Pulau, i., Indon. F7 32
Wrangell, Ak., U.S. D13 79
Wrangell, Cape, c., Ak., U.S. E2 79
Wrangell, Mount, mtn., Ak., U.S. f19 79
Wrangell Island, i., Ak., U.S. m24 79
Wrangell Mountains, mts., Ak., U.S. C11 79
Wrangell-Saint Elias National Park, Ak., U.S. C11 79
Wrath, Cape, c., Scot., U.K. C7 7
Wray, Co., U.S. A8 83
Wreck Reefs, rf., Austl. D11 50
Wrens, Ga., U.S. C4 87
Wrentham, Ma., U.S. B5 98
Wrexham, Wales, U.K. H9 7
Wright, co., Ia., U.S. B4 92
Wright, co., Mn., U.S. E4 100
Wright, co., Mo., U.S. D5 102
Wright, Mount, mtn., Mt., U.S. C4 103
Wright Brothers National Memorial, hist., N.C., U.S. A7 110
Wright City, Mo., U.S. C8 102
Wright City, Ok., U.S. C6 113
Wright-Patterson Air Force Base, mil., Oh., U.S. C1 112
Wrightson, Mount, mtn., Az., U.S. F5 80
Wrightstown, N.J., U.S. C3 107
Wrightstown, Wi., U.S. D5 126
Wrightsville, Ar., U.S. C3 81
Wrightsville, Ga., U.S. D4 87
Wrightsville, Pa., U.S. F8 115
Wrightsville Beach, N.C., U.S. C5 110
Wrightsville Reservoir, res., Vt., U.S. C3 122
Wrigley, N.W. Ter., Can. D8 66
Wrocław (Breslau), Pol. D17 8

Name — Map Ref — Page

Wuchuan, China D11 34
Wudu, China E7 26
Wugang, China F9 26
Wuhan, China E3 28
Wuhu, China D7 28
Wunstorf, Ger. C9 8
Wupatki National Monument, Az., U.S. B4 80
Wuppertal, Ger. D7 8
Wurtsmith Air Force Base, mil., Mi., U.S. D7 99
Würzburg, Ger. F9 8
Wurzen, Ger. D12 8
Wushan, China E8 26
Wushenqi, China D8 26
Wusong, China D10 28
Wutongqiao, China F7 26
Wuwei, China D7 26
Wuwei, China D6 28
Wuxi (Wuhsi), China D9 28
Wuyi Shan, mts., China I5 28
Wuyuan, China C8 26
Wuzhong, China D8 26
Wuzhou (Wuchow), China C11 34
Wyaconda, stm., Mo., U.S. A6 102
Wyandot, co., Oh., U.S. B2 112
Wyandotte, Mi., U.S. F7 99
Wyandotte, co., Ks., U.S. C9 93
Wyanet, Il., U.S. B4 90
Wyk, Ger. A8 8
Wylie, Lake, res., U.S. A5 117
Wyman Lake, res., Me., U.S. C3 96
Wymore, Ne., U.S. D9 104
Wyndham, Austl. C5 50
Wynndel, B.C., Can. E9 69
Wynne, Ar., U.S. B5 81
Wynnewood, Ok., U.S. C4 113
Wynoochee, stm., Wa., U.S. B2 124
Wyoming, Ont., Can. E2 73
Wyoming, De., U.S. D3 85
Wyoming, Il., U.S. B4 90
Wyoming, Ia., U.S. B6 92
Wyoming, Mi., U.S. F5 99
Wyoming, Mn., U.S. E6 100
Wyoming, Oh., U.S. o13 112
Wyoming, Pa., U.S. n17 115
Wyoming, R.I., U.S. E2 116
Wyoming, co., N.Y., U.S. C2 109
Wyoming, co., Pa., U.S. D9 115
Wyoming, co., W.V., U.S. D3 125
Wyoming, state, U.S. C5 127
Wyoming Peak, mtn., Wy., U.S. D2 127
Wyoming Range, mts., Wy., U.S. D2 127
Wyomissing, Pa., U.S. F10 115
Wysocking Bay, b., N.C., U.S. B7 110
Wythe, co., Va., U.S. D1 123
Wytheville, Va., U.S. D1 123

X

Xai-Xai, Moz. G6 44
Xangongo, Ang. E3 44
Xánthi, Grc. H8 16
Xapuri, Braz. F5 54
Xenia, Oh., U.S. C2 112
Xertigny, Fr. D13 10
Xi, stm., China G9 26
Xiaguan, China E9 26
Xiahe, China D7 26
Xiamen (Amoy), China K7 28
Xi'an (Sian), China E8 26
Xiangcheng, China B2 28
Xiangfan, China E9 26
Xiangkhoang, Laos E7 34
Xiangride, China D6 26
Xiangtan, China H1 28
Xianyou, China J7 28
Xiaogan, China E2 28
Xiaolan, China M2 28
Xiashi, China E9 28
Xichang, China F7 26
Xiegeer, China F12 38
Xigazê, China F13 38
Xihua, China B3 28
Xilinhaote, China C10 26
Xinavane, Moz. G6 44
Xingtai, China D9 26
Xingu, stm., Braz. D8 54
Xingyi, China B8 34
Xinhui, China M2 28
Xining, China D7 26
Xinjiang Uygur Zizhiqu, prov., China B9 38
Xinxiang, China D9 26
Xinyang, China C3 28
Xiping, China B3 28
Xique-Xique, Braz. F10 54
Xizang Zizhiqu, prov., China D12 38
Xuancheng, China E7 28
Xuanhua, China C10 26
Xuchang, China A2 28
Xuwen, China D11 34
Xuyong, China F8 26
Xuzhou (Süchow), China A6 28

Y

Yaan, China E7 26
Yacolt, Wa., U.S. D3 124
Yacuiba, Bol. H6 54
Yādgīr, India D4 37
Yadkin, co., N.C., U.S. A2 110
Yadkin, stm., N.C., U.S. B2 110
Yadkinville, N.C., U.S. A2 110
Yainax Butte, mtn., Or., U.S. E5 114
Yaizu, Japan H11 30
Yakima, Wa., U.S. C5 124
Yakima, co., Wa., U.S. C4 124
Yakima, stm., Wa., U.S. C6 124
Yakima Indian Reservation, Wa., U.S. C5 124
Yakobi Island, i., Ak., U.S. m21 79
Yakumo, Japan q18 30a
Yaku-shima, i., Japan u30 31b
Yakutat, Ak., U.S. D12 79
Yakutat Bay, b., Ak., U.S. D11 79
Yala, Thai. K6 34
Yale, Mi., U.S. E8 99
Yale, Ok., U.S. A5 113
Yale, Mount, mtn., Co., U.S. C5 83
Yale Lake, res., Wa., U.S. D3 124
Yalobusha, co., Ms., U.S. A4 101
Yalobusha, stm., Ms., U.S. B4 101
Yalta, Ukr. I4 22
Yalu (Amnok-kang), stm., Asia C12 26
Yamachiche, Que., Can. C5 74
Yamagata, Japan D13 30
Yamaguchi, Japan H4 30
Yamato-takada, Japan H8 30
Yambio, Sudan H11 42
Yamdena, Pulau, i., Indon. G9 32
Yamethin, Mya. D4 34
Yamhill, Or., U.S. h11 114
Yamhill, co., Or., U.S. B3 114
Yamoussoukro, C. Iv. G4 42
Yampa, stm., Co., U.S. A2 83
Yamsay Mountain, mtn., Or., U.S. E5 114
Yamuna, stm., India H9 38
Yanbu', Sau. Ar. D2 46
Yancey, co., N.C., U.S. f10 110
Yanceyville, N.C., U.S. A3 110
Yanchang, China D9 26
Yancheng, China B9 28
Yandoon, Mya. F3 34
Yangjiang, China G9 26
Yangon (Rangoon), Mya. B2 32
Yangquan, China D9 26
Yangtze see Chang, stm., China E10 26
Yangzhou, China C8 28
Yanji, China C12 26
Yankton, S.D., U.S. E8 118
Yankton, co., S.D., U.S. D8 118
Yanqi, China C4 26
Yantai (Chefoo), China D11 26
Yantic, stm., Ct., U.S. C7 84
Yaoundé, Cam. H8 42
Yapen, Pulau, i., Indon. F10 32
Yaqui, stm., Mex. C5 62
Yaraka, Austl. D8 50
Yardley, Pa., U.S. F12 115
Yardville, N.J., U.S. C3 107
Yaritagua, Ven. B8 58
Yarmouth, Me., U.S. E2 96
Yarnell, Az., U.S. C3 80
Yarumal, Col. D5 58
Yashiro-jima, i., Japan I5 30
Yates, co., N.Y., U.S. C3 109
Yates Center, Ks., U.S. E8 93
Yates City, Il., U.S. C3 90
Yathkyed Lake, l., N.W. Ter., Can. D13 66
Yatsushiro, Japan J3 30
Yatta Plateau, plat., Kenya B7 44
Yaupi, Ec. I4 58
Yavapai, co., Az., U.S. C3 80
Yavarí (Javari), stm., S.A. D4 54
Yavatmāl, India B5 37
Yaví, Cerro, mtn., Ven. E10 58
Yaviza, Pan. J9 64
Yawatahama, Japan I5 30
Yawgoog Pond, l., R.I., U.S. E1 116
Yaxian, China E10 34
Yazd, Iran B5 46
Yazoo, co., Ms., U.S. C3 101
Yazoo, stm., Ms., U.S. C3 101
Yazoo City, Ms., U.S. C3 101
Ye, Mya. G4 34
Yeadon, Pa., U.S. p21 115
Yeagertown, Pa., U.S. E6 115
Yecheng, China B7 38
Yecla, Spain G10 12
Yei, stm., Sudan G12 42
Yekaterinburg see Jekaterinburg, Russia F10 22
Yell, co., Ar., U.S. B2 81
Yell, i., Scot., U.K. A11 7
Yellow, stm., U.S. u15 86
Yellow, stm., In., U.S. B4 91
Yellow, stm., Wi., U.S. D3 126
Yellow, stm., Wi., U.S. C3 126
Yellow Creek, stm., Tn., U.S. A4 119
Yellowhead Pass, Can. C1 68
Yellow see Huang, stm., China D10 26
Yellowjacket Mountains, mts., Id., U.S. D4 89
Yellowknife, N.W. Ter., Can. D10 66
Yellow Lake, l., Wi., U.S. C1 126
Yellow Medicine, co., Mn., U.S. F2 100
Yellow Sea, Asia D11 26
Yellow Springs, Oh., U.S. C2 112
Yellowstone, co., Mt., U.S. D8 103
Yellowstone, stm., U.S. D10 103
Yellowstone Lake, l., Wy., U.S. B2 127
Yellowstone National Park, co., Mt., U.S. E6 103
Yellowstone National Park, U.S. B2 127
Yellville, Ar., U.S. A3 81
Yelm, Wa., U.S. C3 124
Yemassee, S.C., U.S. F6 117
Yemen, ctry., Asia E4 46
Yenangyaung, Mya. D3 34
Yen Bai, Viet. D8 34
Yendéré, Burkina F5 42
Yendi, Ghana G5 42
Yenisey see Jenisej, stm., Russia D11 24
Yenshui, Tai. L9 28
Yentna, stm., Ak., U.S. f16 79
Yeovil, Eng., U.K. K10 7
Yerevan see Jerevan, Arm. I6 22
Yerington, Nv., U.S. E2 105
Yerington Indian Reservation, Nv., U.S. D2 105
Yermasóyia, Cyp. B3 40
Yermo, Ca., U.S. E5 82
Yerupajá, Nevado, mtn., Peru F3 54
Yerushalayim (Jerusalem), Isr. D4 40
Yeste, Spain G9 12
Yevpatoriya, Ukr. H4 22
Yexian, China B2 28
Yiannitsá, Grc. I6 16
Yibin, China F7 26
Yichang, China E9 26
Yichun, China B12 26
Yichun, China H3 28
Yilan, China B12 26
Yiliang, China B7 34
Yinchuan, China D8 26
Yingde, China K2 28
Yingkou, China C11 26
Yining, China C3 26
Yirga Alem, Eth. G2 46
Yishan, China B10 34
Yíthion, Grc. M6 16
Yitulihe, China A11 26
Yiyang, China F9 26
Ylivieska, Fin. D15 6
Ynykčanskij, Russia E21 24
Yoakum, Tx., U.S. E4 120
Yoakum, co., Tx., U.S. C1 120
Yockanookany, stm., Ms., U.S. C4 101
Yocona, stm., Ms., U.S. A4 101
Yogyakarta, Indon. m15 32
Yoho National Park, B.C., Can. D9 69
Yokkaichi, Japan H9 30
Yokohama, Japan G12 30
Yokosuka, Japan G12 30
Yokote, Japan C13 30
Yola, Nig. G8 42
Yolo, co., Ca., U.S. C2 82
Yolombó, Col. D5 58
Yomba Indian Reservation, Nv., U.S. D4 105
Yonago, Japan G6 30
Yoncalla, Or., U.S. D3 114
Yonezawa, Japan E13 30
Yongdeng, China D7 26
Yongdingzhen, China A6 34
Yongfeng, China H4 28
Yonkers, N.Y., U.S. E7 109
Yopal, Col. E6 58
York, Ont., Can. D5 73
York, Eng., U.K. H11 7
York, Al., U.S. C1 78
York, Me., U.S. E2 96
York, Ne., U.S. D8 104
York, Pa., U.S. G8 115
York, S.C., U.S. B5 117
York, co., Me., U.S. E2 96
York, co., Ne., U.S. D8 104
York, co., Pa., U.S. G8 115
York, co., S.C., U.S. A5 117
York, co., Va., U.S. C6 123
York, stm., Ont., Can. B7 73
York, stm., Va., U.S. C6 123
York, Cape, c., Austl. B8 50
York Beach, Me., U.S. E2 96
York Harbor, Me., U.S. E2 96
Yorklyn, De., U.S. A3 85
Yorktown, In., U.S. D7 91
Yorktown, Tx., U.S. E4 120
Yorktown, Va., U.S. C6 123
Yorktown Manor, R.I., U.S. E4 116
Yorkville, Il., U.S. B5 90
Yorkville, N.Y., U.S. B5 109
Yorkville, Oh., U.S. B5 112
Yoro, Hond. G4 64
Yoron-jima, i., Japan x28 31b
Yosemite National Park, Ca., U.S. D4 82
Yŏsu, S. Kor. E12 26
Youbou, B.C., Can. g11 69
Youghal, Ire. J5 7
Youghiogheny, stm., U.S. F2 115
Youghiogheny River Lake, res., U.S. G3 115
Young, Az., U.S. C5 80
Young, co., Tx., U.S. C3 120
Young Harris, Ga., U.S. B3 87
Youngs, Lake, l., Wa., U.S. f11 124
Youngstown, N.Y., U.S. B1 109
Youngstown, Oh., U.S. A5 112
Youngsville, La., U.S. D3 95
Youngsville, Pa., U.S. C3 115
Youngtown, Az., U.S. k8 80
Youngwood, Pa., U.S. F2 115
Youyang, China F8 26
Ypres see Ieper, Bel. E2 8
Ypsilanti, Mi., U.S. F7 99
Yreka, Ca., U.S. B2 82
Yssingeaux, Fr. G11 10
Ystad, Swe. I9 6
Yu, stm., China C10 34
Yuanling, China F9 26
Yuba, co., Ca., U.S. C3 82
Yuba, stm., Ca., U.S. C3 82
Yuba City, Ca., U.S. C3 82
Yūbari, Japan p19 30a
Yucatan Channel, strt., N.A. C4 64
Yucatan Peninsula, pen., N.A. H15 62
Yucca Lake, l., Nv., U.S. F5 105
Yucca Mountain, mtn., Nv., U.S. G5 105
Yuci, China D9 26
Yueyang, China F2 28
Yugoslavia, ctry., Eur. G11 4
Yukon, Ok., U.S. B4 113
Yukon, prov., Can. D6 66
Yukon, stm., N.A. m19 76a
Yukuhashi, Japan I3 30
Yulee, Fl., U.S. B5 86
Yulin, China D8 26
Yulin, China C11 34
Yuma, Az., U.S. E1 80
Yuma, Co., U.S. A8 83
Yuma, co., Az., U.S. E1 80
Yuma, co., Co., U.S. A8 83
Yuma Marine Corps Air Station, mil., Az., U.S. E1 80
Yumen, China D6 26
Yuncheng, China D9 26
Yunnan, prov., China F7 26
Yurimaguas, Peru E3 54
Yuriria, Mex. G9 62
Yü Shan, mtn., Tai. L9 28
Yushu, China E6 26
Yutan, Ne., U.S. C9 104
Yutian, China B9 38
Yuty, Para. B5 56
Yuxian, China A2 28
Yuyao, China E10 28
Yverdon, Switz. F13 10
Yvetot, Fr. C7 10

Z

Zaandam, Neth. C4 8
Zabīd, Yemen F3 46
Zabrze, Pol. E18 8
Zacapa, Guat. G3 64
Zacapu, Mex. H9 62
Zacatecas, Mex. F8 62
Zachary, La., U.S. D4 95
Zacualtipán, Mex. G10 62
Zadar, Cro. E10 14
Zadetkyi Kyun, i., Mya. J5 34
Zafer Burnu, c., N. Cyp. B4 40
Zafra, Spain G5 12
Zagreb, Cro. D10 14
Zāgros, Kūhhā-ye, mts., Iran B5 46
Zāhedān, Iran C7 46
Zahlah, Leb. C4 40
Zaire, ctry., Afr. B4 44
Zajsan, Kaz. H10 24
Zajsan, Ozero, l., Kaz. H10 24
Zákinthos, i., Grc. L4 16
Zakopane, Pol. F19 8
Zalaegerszeg, Hung. I16 8
Zambezi (Zambeze), stm., Afr. E6 44
Zambia, ctry., Afr. D5 44
Zamboanga, Phil. D7 32
Zamfara, stm., Nig. F7 42
Zamora, Ec. J3 58
Zamora, Spain D6 12
Zamora de Hidalgo, Mex. H8 62
Zamość, Pol. E23 8
Zanesville, Oh., U.S. C4 112
Zanjān, Iran J7 22
Zanzibar, Tan. C7 44
Zanzibar, i., Tan. C7 44
Zaouia el Kahla, Alg. C7 42
Zaouiet el Mgaïz, Tun. M5 14
Zaoz'ornyj, Russia F12 24
Zapadnyj Sajan, mts., Russia G12 24
Zapala, Arg. D2 56
Zapata, Tx., U.S. F3 120
Zapata, co., Tx., U.S. F3 120
Zapata, Península de, pen., Cuba C7 64
Zaporizhzhya, Ukr. H5 22
Zaragoza, Spain D11 12
Zarajsk, Russia G21 18
Zárate, Arg. C5 56
Zaraza, Ven. C10 58
Zard Kūh, mtn., Iran B5 46
Zarembo Island, i., Ak., U.S. m23 79
Zarghūn Shahr, Afg. D3 38
Zaria, Nig. F7 42
Żary (Sorau), Pol. D15 8
Zarzal, Col. E4 58
Zāskār, stm., India D7 38
Zāskār Mountains, mts., Asia C4 36
Zavala, co., Tx., U.S. E3 120
Zavolžje, Russia E26 18
Zavolžsk, Russia D25 18
Zawiercie, Pol. E19 8
Zduńska Wola, Pol. D18 8
Zearing, Ia., U.S. B4 92
Zebulon, Ga., U.S. C2 87
Zebulon, N.C., U.S. B4 110
Zeehan, Austl. H9 50
Zeeland, Mi., U.S. F5 99
Zeerust, S. Afr. G5 44
Zehdenick, Ger. C13 8
Zeigler, Il., U.S. F4 90
Zeila, Som. F3 46
Zeitz, Ger. D12 8
Zeja, Russia G19 24
Zeja, stm., Russia G19 24
Železnogorsk-Ilimskij, Russia F14 24
Zelienople, Pa., U.S. E1 115
Zelina, Cro. D11 14
Zell, Ger. E7 8
Zell am See, Aus. H12 8
Zemio, Cen. Afr. Rep. G11 42
Zenica, Bos. E12 14
Zenith, Wa., U.S. f11 124
Zenobia Peak, mtn., Co., U.S. A2 83
Zephyr Cove, Nv., U.S. E2 105
Zephyrhills, Fl., U.S. D4 86
Zerbst, Ger. D12 8
Zereh, Gowd-e, l., Afg. D1 36
Zermatt, Switz. F14 10
Zeytindağ, Tur. K11 16
Zgierz, Pol. D19 8
Zhalutegi, China C11 26
Zhangjiakou (Kalgan), China C9 26
Zhangzhou (Longxi), China K6 28
Zhanjiang, China D11 34
Zhaoan, China L6 28
Zhaotong, China F7 26
Zhaxigang, China D8 38
Zhejiang, prov., China F10 26
Zhengzhou, China E9 26
Zhenjiang, China C8 28
Zhenyuan, China F8 26
Zhob, stm., Pak. E3 38
Zhongba, China F10 38
Zhongshan, China M2 28
Zhoushan Dao, i., China E11 28
Zhoushan Qundao, is., China E10 28
Zhujiangkou, stm., Asia M2 28
Zhumadian, China C3 28
Zhungeerqi, China D9 26
Zhuoxian, China D10 26
Zhuzhou, China H2 28
Zhytomyr, Ukr. G3 22
Zia Indian Reservation, N.M., U.S. h7 108
Zibo, China D10 26
Ziebach, co., S.D., U.S. C4 118
Ziel, Mount, mtn., Austl. D6 50
Zielona Góra (Grünberg), Pol. D15 8
Žigalovo, Russia G15 24
Žigansk, Russia D18 24
Zigong, China F7 26
Ziguinchor, Sen. F2 42
Zihuatanejo, Mex. I9 62
Žilina, Slov. F18 8
Zillah, Wa., U.S. C5 124
Zillertaler Alpen, mts., Eur. B6 14
Zilwaukee, Mi., U.S. E7 99
Zima, Russia G14 24
Zimbabwe, ctry., Afr. E5 44
Zimmerman, Mn., U.S. E5 100
Zinder, Niger F7 42
Zion, Il., U.S. A6 90
Zion National Park, Ut., U.S. F3 121
Zion Reservoir, res., Az., U.S. C6 80
Zionsville, In., U.S. E5 91
Zipaquirá, Col. E5 58
Zirkel, Mount, mtn., Co., U.S. A4 83
Ziro, India G15 38
Zitácuaro, Mex. H9 62
Zittau, Ger. E14 8
Ziway, Lake, l., Eth. G2 46
Žižickoje, Ozero, l., Russia E14 18
Zlarin, Cro. F10 14
Zlín, Czech. F17 8
Žlobin, Bela. I13 18
Zmeinogorsk, Russia G10 24
Znojmo, Czech. G16 8
Zolfo Springs, Fl., U.S. E5 86
Zomba, Mwi. E7 44
Zonguldak, Tur. G14 4
Zorita, Spain F6 12
Zouar, Chad D9 42
Zrenjanin, Yugo. D4 16
Zuckerhütl, mtn., Aus. I11 8
Zudañez, Bol. G6 54
Zuera, Spain D11 12
Zug, Switz. E15 10
Zugspitze, mtn., Eur. H10 8
Zuiderzee see IJsselmeer, Neth. C5 8
Zumba, Ec. J3 58
Zumbo, Moz. E6 44
Zumbro, stm., Mn., U.S. F6 100
Zumbrota, Mn., U.S. F6 100
Zuni (Zuni Pueblo), N.M., U.S. B1 108
Zuni, stm., U.S. C6 80
Zuni Indian Reservation, N.M., U.S. B1 108
Zuni Mountains, mts., N.M., U.S. B1 108
Zunyi, China F8 26
Zuqar, Jazīrat, i., Yemen F3 46
Zurich, Ont., Can. D3 73
Zürich, Switz. E15 10
Zürichsee, l., Switz. E15 10
Zutphen, Neth. C6 8
Zvishavane, Zimb. F6 44
Zvolen, Slov. G19 8
Zwettl, Aus. G15 8
Zwickau, Ger. E12 8
Zwolle, Neth. C6 8
Zwolle, La., U.S. C2 95
Zyr'anka, Russia D24 24
Żyrardów, Pol. C20 8

World Political Information

This table lists the area, population, population density, form of government, political status, and capital for every country in the world.

The populations are estimates for January 1, 1995 made by Rand McNally on the basis of official data, United Nations estimates, and other available information. Area figures include inland water.

The political units listed in the table are categorized by political status, as follows:

A–independent countries; B–internally independent political entities which are under the protection of other countries in matters of defense and foreign affairs; C–colonies and other dependent political units; D–the major administrative subdivisions of Australia, Canada, China, the United Kingdom, and the United States. For comparison, the table also includes the continents and the world.

All footnotes to this table appear on page 196.

Country, Division or Region English (Conventional)	Area in sq. mi.	Area in sq. km.	Estimated Population 1/1/95	Pop. per sq. mi.	Pop. per sq. km.	Form of Government and Political Status	Capital
† Afghanistan	251,826	652,225	19,715,000	78	30	Islamic republic .... A	Kābol (Kabul)
Africa	11,700,000	30,300,000	697,600,000	60	23		
Alabama	52,423	135,775	4,254,000	81	31	State (U.S.) .... D	Montgomery
Alaska	656,424	1,700,139	614,000	0.9	0.4	State (U.S.) .... D	Juneau
† Albania	11,100	28,748	3,394,000	306	118	Republic .... A	Tiranë
Alberta	255,287	661,190	2,632,000	10	4.0	Province (Canada) .... D	Edmonton
† Algeria	919,595	2,381,741	27,965,000	30	12	Provisional military government ... A	Alger (Algiers)
American Samoa	77	199	56,000	727	281	Unincorporated territory (U.S.) ... C	Pago Pago
† Andorra	175	453	59,000	337	130	Parliamentary co-principality (Spanish and French protection) ..... B	Andorra
† Angola	481,354	1,246,700	10,690,000	22	8.6	Republic .... A	Luanda
Anguilla	35	91	7,100	203	78	Dependent territory (U.K. protection) .... B	The Valley
Anhui	53,668	139,000	59,490,000	1,108	428	Province (China) .... D	Hefei
Antarctica	5,400,000	14,000,000	(1)	—	—		
† Antigua and Barbuda	171	442	67,000	392	152	Parliamentary state .... A	St. Johns
† Argentina	1,073,519	2,780,400	34,083,000	32	12	Republic .... A	Buenos Aires and Viedma (4)
Arizona	114,006	295,276	4,070,000	36	14	State (U.S.) .... D	Phoenix
Arkansas	53,182	137,742	2,468,000	46	18	State (U.S.) .... D	Little Rock
† Armenia	11,506	29,800	3,794,000	330	127	Republic .... A	Jerevan
Aruba	75	193	67,000	893	347	Self-governing territory (Netherlands protection) ..... B	Oranjestad
Asia	17,300,000	44,900,000	3,422,700,000	198	76		
† Australia	2,966,155	7,682,300	18,205,000	6.1	2.4	Federal parliamentary state ...... A	Canberra
Australian Capital Territory	927	2,400	309,000	333	129	Territory (Australia) .... D	Canberra
† Austria	32,377	83,856	7,932,000	245	95	Federal republic .... A	Wien (Vienna)
† Azerbaijan	33,436	86,600	7,491,000	224	87	Republic .... A	Baku
† Bahamas	5,382	13,939	275,000	51	20	Parliamentary state .... A	Nassau
† Bahrain	267	691	563,000	2,109	815	Monarchy .... A	Al-Manāmah
† Bangladesh	55,598	143,998	119,370,000	2,147	829	Republic .... A	Dhaka (Dacca)
† Barbados	166	430	261,000	1,572	607	Parliamentary state .... A	Bridgetown
Beijing Shi	6,487	16,800	11,490,000	1,771	684	Autonomous city (China) .... D	Beijing (Peking)
† Belarus	80,155	207,600	10,425,000	130	50	Republic .... A	Minsk
† Belgium	11,783	30,518	10,075,000	855	330	Constitutional monarchy .... A	Bruxelles (Brussels)
† Belize	8,866	22,963	212,000	24	9.2	Parliamentary state .... A	Belmopan
† Benin	43,475	112,600	5,433,000	125	48	Republic .... A	Porto-Novo and Cotonou
Bermuda	21	54	61,000	2,905	1,130	Dependent territory (U.K.) C	Hamilton
† Bhutan	17,954	46,500	1,758,000	98	38	Monarchy (Indian protection) .... B	Thimphu
† Bolivia	424,165	1,098,581	6,790,000	16	6.2	Republic .... A	La Paz and Sucre
† Bosnia and Herzegovina	19,741	51,129	4,481,000	227	88	Republic .... A	Sarajevo
† Botswana	224,711	582,000	1,438,000	6.4	2.5	Republic .... A	Gaborone
† Brazil	3,286,500	8,511,996	159,690,000	49	19	Federal republic .... A	Brasília
British Columbia	365,948	947,800	3,395,000	9.3	3.6	Province (Canada) .... D	Victoria
British Indian Ocean Territory	23	60	(1)	—	—	Dependent territory (U.K.) C	
† Brunei	2,226	5,765	289,000	130	50	Monarchy .... A	Bandar Seri Begawan
† Bulgaria	42,855	110,994	8,787,000	205	79	Republic .... A	Sofija (Sofia)
† Burkina Faso	105,792	274,000	10,275,000	97	38	Republic .... A	Ouagadougou
Burma, see Myanmar			—	—	—		
† Burundi	10,745	27,830	6,192,000	576	222	Republic .... A	Bujumbura
California	163,707	424,002	32,090,000	196	76	State (U.S.) .... D	Sacramento
† Cambodia	69,898	181,035	9,713,000	139	54	Constitutional monarchy .... A	Phnum Pénh (Phnom Penh)
† Cameroon	183,568	475,440	13,330,000	73	28	Republic .... A	Yaoundé
† Canada	3,849,674	9,970,610	28,285,000	7.3	2.8	Federal parliamentary state ...... A	Ottawa
† Cape Verde	1,557	4,033	429,000	276	106	Republic .... A	Praia
Cayman Islands	100	259	33,000	330	127	Dependent territory (U.K.) C	Georgetown
† Central African Republic	240,535	622,984	3,177,000	13	5.1	Republic .... A	Bangui
† Chad	495,755	1,284,000	6,396,000	13	5.0	Republic .... A	N'Djamena
† Chile	292,135	756,626	14,050,000	48	19	Republic .... A	Santiago
† China (excl. Taiwan)	3,689,631	9,556,100	1,196,980,000	324	125	Socialist republic .... A	Beijing (Peking)
Christmas Island	52	135	1,000	19	7.4	External territory (Australia) C	
Cocos (Keeling) Islands	5.4	14	600	111	43	Territory (Australia) C	
† Colombia	440,831	1,141,748	34,870,000	79	31	Republic .... A	Santa Fe de Bogotá
Colorado	104,100	269,620	3,649,000	35	14	State (U.S.) .... D	Denver
† Comoros (excl. Mayotte)	863	2,235	540,000	626	242	Federal Islamic republic .... A	Moroni
† Congo	132,047	342,000	2,474,000	19	7.2	Republic .... A	Brazzaville
Connecticut	5,544	14,358	3,266,000	589	227	State (U.S.) .... D	Hartford
Cook Islands	91	236	19,000	209	81	Self-governing territory (New Zealand protection) ..... B	Avarua
† Costa Rica	19,730	51,100	3,379,000	171	66	Republic .... A	San José
† Cote d'Ivoire	124,518	322,500	14,540,000	117	45	Republic .... A	Abidjan and Yamoussoukro (4)
† Croatia	21,829	56,538	4,801,000	220	85	Republic .... A	Zagreb
† Cuba	42,804	110,861	11,560,000	270	104	Socialist republic .... A	La Habana (Havana)
† Cyprus (excl. North Cyprus)	2,276	5,896	551,000	242	93	Republic .... A	Nicosia (Levkosía)
Cyprus, North (2)	1,295	3,355	182,000	141	54	Republic .... A	Nicosia (Lefkoşa)
† Czech Republic	30,450	78,864	10,430,000	343	132	Republic .... A	Praha (Prague)
Delaware	2,489	6,447	709,000	285	110	State (U.S.) .... D	Dover
† Denmark	16,639	43,094	5,207,000	313	121	Constitutional monarchy .... A	København (Copenhagen)
District of Columbia	68	177	575,000	8,456	3,249	Federal district (U.S.) .... D	Washington
† Djibouti	8,958	23,200	557,000	62	24	Republic .... A	Djibouti
† Dominica	305	790	89,000	292	113	Republic .... A	Roseau
† Dominican Republic	18,704	48,442	7,896,000	422	163	Republic .... A	Santo Domingo
† Ecuador	105,037	272,045	11,015,000	105	40	Republic .... A	Quito
† Egypt	386,662	1,001,449	58,100,000	150	58	Socialist republic .... A	Al-Qāhirah (Cairo)
† El Salvador	8,124	21,041	5,280,000	650	251	Republic .... A	San Salvador
England	50,352	130,410	48,730,000	968	374	Administrative division (U.K.) ... D	London
† Equatorial Guinea	10,831	28,051	394,000	36	14	Republic .... A	Malabo
† Eritrea	36,170	93,679	3,458,000	96	37	Republic .... A	Asmera
† Estonia	17,413	45,100	1,515,000	87	34	Republic .... A	Tallinn
† Ethiopia	446,953	1,157,603	55,070,000	123	48	Provisional military government ... A	Adis Abeba
Europe	3,800,000	9,900,000	712,100,000	187	72		
Faeroe Islands	540	1,399	49,000	91	35	Self-governing territory (Danish protection) .... B	Tórshavn
Falkland Islands (3)	4,700	12,173	2,100	0.4	0.2	Dependent territory (U.K.) C	Stanley

World Political Information

Country, Division or Region English (Conventional)	Area in sq. mi.	Area in sq. km.	Estimated Population 1/1/95	Pop. per sq. mi.	Pop. per sq. km.	Form of Government and Political Status		Capital
† Fiji	7,056	18,274	775,000	110	42	Republic	A	Suva
† Finland	130,559	338,145	5,098,000	39	15	Republic	A	Helsinki (Helsingfors)
Florida	65,758	170,313	13,995,000	213	82	State (U.S.)	D	Tallahassee
† France (excl. Overseas Departments)	211,208	547,026	58,000	275	106	Republic	A	Paris
French Guiana	35,135	91,000	138,000	3.9	1.5	Overseas department (France)	C	Cayenne
French Polynesia	1,359	3,521	217,000	160	62	Overseas territory (France)	C	Papeete
Fujian	46,332	120,000	31,720,000	685	264	Province (China)	D	Fuzhou
† Gabon	103,347	267,667	1,035,000	10	3.9	Republic	A	Libreville
† Gambia	4,127	10,689	1,082,000	262	101	Provisional military government	A	Banjul
Gansu	173,746	450,000	23,700,000	136	53	Province (China)	D	Lanzhou
Gaza Strip	146	378	774,000	5,301	2,048	Israeli territory with limited self-government		
Georgia	59,441	153,953	7,065,000	119	46	State (U.S.)	D	Atlanta
† Georgia	26,911	69,700	5,704,000	212	82	Republic	A	Tbilisi
† Germany	137,822	356,955	81,710,000	593	229	Federal republic	A	Berlin and Bonn
† Ghana	92,098	238,533	17,210,000	187	72	Republic	A	Accra
Gibraltar	2.3	6.0	32,000	13,913	5,333	Dependent territory (U.K.)	C	Gibraltar
Golan Heights	454	1,176	29,000	64	25	Occupied by Israel		
† Greece	50,949	131,957	10,475,000	206	79	Republic	A	Athínai (Athens)
Greenland	840,004	2,175,600	57,000	0.1	—	Self-governing territory (Danish protection)	B	Godthåb (Nuuk)
† Grenada	133	344	92,000	692	267	Parliamentary state	A	St. George's
Guadeloupe (incl. Dependencies)	687	1,780	432,000	629	243	Overseas department (France)	C	Basse-Terre
Guam	209	541	152,000	727	281	Unincorporated territory (U.S.)	C	Agana
Guangdong	68,726	178,000	66,550,000	968	374	Province (China)	D	Guangzhou (Canton)
† Guatemala	42,042	108,889	10,420,000	248	96	Republic	A	Guatemala
Guernsey (incl. Dependencies)	30	78	64,000	2,133	821	Crown dependency (U.K. protection)	B	St. Peter Port
† Guinea	94,926	245,857	6,469,000	68	26	Provisional military government	A	Conakry
† Guinea-Bissau	13,948	36,125	1,111,000	80	31	Republic	A	Bissau
Guizhou	65,637	170,000	34,355,000	523	202	Province (China)	D	Guiyang
† Guyana	83,000	214,969	726,000	8.7	3.4	Republic	A	Georgetown
Hainan	13,127	34,000	6,945,000	529	204	Province (China)	D	Haikou
† Haiti	10,714	27,750	7,069,000	660	255	Provisional military government	A	Port-au-Prince
Hawaii	10,932	28,313	1,181,000	108	42	State (U.S.)	D	Honolulu
Hebei	73,359	190,000	64,640,000	881	340	Province (China)	D	Shijiazhuang
Heilongjiang	181,082	469,000	37,345,000	206	80	Province (China)	D	Harbin
Henan	64,479	167,000	90,495,000	1,403	542	Province (China)	D	Zhengzhou
† Honduras	43,277	112,088	5,822,000	135	52	Republic	A	Tegucigalpa
Hong Kong	414	1,072	5,927,000	14,316	5,529	Chinese territory under British administration	C	Victoria (Xianggang)
Hubei	72,356	187,400	57,100,000	789	305	Province (China)	D	Wuhan
Hunan	81,081	210,000	64,280,000	793	306	Province (China)	D	Changsha
† Hungary	35,919	93,030	10,270,000	286	110	Republic	A	Budapest
† Iceland	39,769	103,000	265,000	6.7	2.6	Republic	A	Reykjavik
Idaho	83,574	216,456	1,129,000	14	5.2	State (U.S.)	D	Boise
Illinois	57,918	150,007	11,870,000	205	79	State (U.S.)	D	Springfield
† India (incl. part of Jammu and Kashmir)	1,237,062	3,203,975	909,150,000	735	284	Federal republic	A	New Delhi
Indiana	36,420	94,328	5,805,000	159	62	State (U.S.)	D	Indianapolis
† Indonesia	752,410	1,948,732	193,680,000	257	99	Republic	A	Jakarta
Inner Mongolia (Nei Mongol Zizhiqu)	456,759	1,183,000	22,745,000	50	19	Autonomous region (China)	D	Hohhot
Iowa	56,276	145,754	2,862,000	51	20	State (U.S.)	D	Des Moines
† Iran	632,457	1,638,057	63,810,000	101	39	Islamic republic	A	Tehrän
† Iraq	169,235	438,317	20,250,000	120	46	Republic	A	Baghdäd
† Ireland	27,137	70,285	3,546,000	131	50	Republic	A	Dublin (Baile Átha Cliath)
Isle of Man	221	572	72,000	326	126	Crown dependency (U.K. protection)	B	Douglas
† Israel	8,019	20,770	5,059,000	631	244	Republic	A	Yerushalayim (Jerusalem)
† Italy	116,324	301,277	57,330,000	493	190	Republic	A	Roma (Rome)
† Jamaica	4,244	10,991	2,568,000	605	234	Parliamentary state	A	Kingston
† Japan	145,870	377,801	125,360,000	859	332	Constitutional monarchy	A	Tōkyō
Jersey	45	116	86,000	1,911	741	Crown dependency (U.K. protection)	B	St. Helier
Jiangsu	39,614	102,600	70,980,000	1,792	692	Province (China)	D	Nanjing
Jiangxi	64,325	166,600	39,980,000	622	240	Province (China)	D	Nanchang
Jilin	72,201	187,000	26,095,000	361	140	Province (China)	D	Changchun
† Jordan	35,135	91,000	4,028,000	115	44	Constitutional monarchy	A	'Ammän
Kansas	82,282	213,110	2,575,000	31	12	State (U.S.)	D	Topeka
† Kazakhstan	1,049,156	2,717,300	17,025,000	16	6.3	Republic	A	Alma-Ata and Akmola [4]
Kentucky	40,411	104,665	3,835,000	95	37	State (U.S.)	D	Frankfort
† Kenya	224,961	582,646	28,380,000	126	49	Republic	A	Nairobi
Kiribati	313	811	79,000	252	97	Republic	A	Bairiki
† Korea, North	46,540	120,538	23,265,000	500	193	Socialist republic	A	P'yŏngyang
† Korea, South	38,230	99,016	44,655,000	1,168	451	Republic	A	Sŏul (Seoul)
† Kuwait	6,880	17,818	1,866,000	271	105	Constitutional monarchy	A	Al-Kuwayt (Kuwait)
Kwangsi Chuang (Guangxi Zhuang Zizhiqu)	91,236	236,300	44,765,000	491	189	Autonomous region (China)	D	Nanning
† Kyrgyzstan	76,641	198,500	4,541,000	59	23	Republic	A	Biškek
† Laos	91,429	236,800	4,768,000	52	20	Socialist republic	A	Viangchan (Vientiane)
† Latvia	24,595	63,700	2,532,000	103	40	Republic	A	Rïga
† Lebanon	4,015	10,400	3,660,000	912	352	Republic	A	Bayrüt (Beirut)
† Lesotho	11,720	30,355	1,967,000	168	65	Constitutional monarchy under military rule	A	Maseru
Liaoning	56,255	145,700	41,775,000	743	287	Province (China)	D	Shenyang (Mukden)
† Liberia	38,250	99,067	2,771,000	72	28	Republic	A	Monrovia
† Libya	679,362	1,759,540	5,148,000	7.6	2.9	Socialist republic	A	Taräbulus (Tripoli)
† Liechtenstein	62	160	30,000	484	188	Constitutional monarchy	A	Vaduz
† Lithuania	25,212	65,300	3,757,000	149	58	Republic	A	Vilnius
Louisiana	51,843	134,275	4,360,000	84	32	State (U.S.)	D	Baton Rouge
† Luxembourg	998	2,586	396,000	397	153	Constitutional monarchy	A	Luxembourg
Macau	7.0	18	396,000	56,571	22,000	Chinese territory under Portuguese administration	C	Macau
† Macedonia	9,928	25,713	2,102,000	212	82	Republic	A	Skopje
† Madagascar	226,658	587,041	13,645,000	60	23	Republic	A	Antananarivo
Maine	35,387	91,653	1,260,000	36	14	State (U.S.)	D	Augusta
† Malawi	45,747	118,484	8,984,000	196	76	Republic	A	Lilongwe
† Malaysia	127,320	329,758	19,505,000	153	59	Federal constitutional monarchy	A	Kuala Lumpur
† Maldives	115	298	251,000	2,183	842	Republic	A	Male
† Mali	482,077	1,248,574	9,585,000	20	7.7	Republic	A	Bamako
† Malta	122	316	368,000	3,016	1,165	Republic	A	Valletta
Manitoba	250,947	649,950	1,131,000	4.5	1.7	Province (Canada)	D	Winnipeg
† Marshall Islands	70	181	55,000	786	304	Republic (U.S. protection)	A	Majuro (island)

Country, Division or Region English (Conventional)	Area in sq. mi.	Area in sq. km.	Estimated Population 1/1/95	Pop. per sq. mi.	Pop. per sq. km.	Form of Government and Political Status		Capital
Martinique	425	1,100	384,000	904	349	Overseas department (France)	C	Fort-de-France
Maryland	12,407	32,135	5,045,000	407	157	State (U.S.)	D	Annapolis
Massachusetts	10,555	27,337	6,117,000	580	224	State (U.S.)	D	Boston
† Mauritania	395,956	1,025,520	2,228,000	5.6	2.2	Republic	A	Nouakchott
† Mauritius (incl. Dependencies)	788	2,040	1,121,000	1,423	550	Republic	A	Port Louis
Mayotte (5)	144	374	95,000	660	254	Territorial collectivity (France)	C	Dzaoudzi and Mamoudzou (4)
† Mexico	759,534	1,967,183	93,860,000	124	48	Federal republic	A	Ciudad de México (Mexico City)
Michigan	96,810	250,738	9,615,000	99	38	State (U.S.)	D	Lansing
† Micronesia, Federated States of	271	702	122,000	450	174	Republic (U.S. protection)	A	Kolonia and Paliker (4)
Midway Islands	2.0	5.2	500	250	96	Unincorporated territory (U.S.)	C	
Minnesota	86,943	225,182	4,595,000	53	20	State (U.S.)	D	St. Paul
Mississippi	48,434	125,443	2,678,000	55	21	State (U.S.)	D	Jackson
Missouri	69,709	180,546	5,330,000	76	30	State (U.S.)	D	Jefferson City
† Moldova	13,012	33,700	4,377,000	336	130	Republic	A	Chişinău (Kishinev)
† Monaco	0.7	1.9	31,000	44,286	16,316	Constitutional monarchy	A	Monaco
† Mongolia	604,829	1,566,500	2,462,000	4.1	1.6	Republic	A	Ulaanbaatar (Ulan Bator)
Montana	147,046	380,850	840,000	5.7	2.2	State (U.S.)	D	Helena
Montserrat	39	102	13,000	333	127	Dependent territory (U.K.)	C	Plymouth
† Morocco (excl. Western Sahara)	172,414	446,550	26,890,000	156	60	Constitutional monarchy	A	Rabat
† Mozambique	308,642	799,380	17,860,000	58	22	Republic	A	Maputo
† Myanmar	261,228	676,577	44,675,000	171	66	Provisional military government	A	Yangon (Rangoon)
† Namibia	318,253	824,272	1,623,000	5.1	2.0	Republic	A	Windhoek
Nauru	8.1	21	10,000	1,235	476	Republic	A	Yaren District
Nebraska	77,358	200,358	1,628,000	21	8.1	State (U.S.)	D	Lincoln
† Nepal	56,827	147,181	21,295,000	375	145	Constitutional monarchy	A	Kātmāndāū (Kathmandu)
† Netherlands	16,164	41,864	15,425,000	954	368	Constitutional monarchy	A	Amsterdam and 's-Gravenhage (The Hague)
Netherlands Antilles	309	800	187,000	605	234	Self-governing territory (Netherlands protection)	B	Willemstad
Nevada	110,567	286,368	1,444,000	13	5.0	State (U.S.)	D	Carson City
New Brunswick	28,355	73,440	764,000	27	10	Province (Canada)	D	Fredericton
New Caledonia	7,358	19,058	183,000	25	9.6	Overseas territory (France)	C	Nouméa
Newfoundland	156,649	405,720	594,000	3.8	1.5	Province (Canada)	D	St. John's
New Hampshire	9,351	24,219	1,100,000	118	45	State (U.S.)	D	Concord
New Jersey	8,722	22,590	7,985,000	916	353	State (U.S.)	D	Trenton
New Mexico	121,598	314,939	1,655,000	14	5.3	State (U.S.)	D	Santa Fe
New South Wales	309,500	801,600	6,171,000	20	7.7	State (Australia)	D	Sydney
New York	54,475	141,089	18,460,000	339	131	State (U.S.)	D	Albany
† New Zealand	104,454	270,534	3,558,000	34	13	Parliamentary state	A	Wellington
† Nicaragua	50,054	129,640	4,438,000	89	34	Republic	A	Managua
† Niger	489,191	1,267,000	9,125,000	19	7.2	Provisional military government	A	Niamey
† Nigeria	356,669	923,768	97,300,000	273	105	Provisional military government	A	Lagos and Abuja
Ningsia Hui (Ningxia Huizu Zizhiqu)	25,637	66,400	4,908,000	191	74	Autonomous region (China)	D	Yinchuan
Niue	100	259	1,900	19	7.3	Self-governing territory (New Zealand protection)	B	Alofi
Norfolk Island	14	36	2,700	193	75	External territory (Australia)	C	Kingston
North America	9,500,000	24,700,000	453,300,000	48	18			
North Carolina	53,821	139,397	7,065,000	131	51	State (U.S.)	D	Raleigh
North Dakota	70,704	183,123	656,000	9.3	3.6	State (U.S.)	D	Bismarck
Northern Ireland	5,461	14,144	1,636,000	300	116	Administrative division (U.K.)	D	Belfast
Northern Mariana Islands	184	477	51,000	277	107	Commonwealth (U.S. protection)	B	Saipan (island)
Northern Territory	519,771	1,346,200	182,000	0.4	0.1	Territory (Australia)	D	Darwin
Northwest Territories	1,322,910	3,426,320	57,000	—	—	Territory (Canada)	D	Yellowknife
† Norway (incl. Svalbard and Jan Mayen)	149,412	386,975	4,339,000	29	11	Constitutional monarchy	A	Oslo
Nova Scotia	21,425	55,490	933,000	44	17	Province (Canada)	D	Halifax
Oceania (incl. Australia)	3,300,000	8,500,000	28,400,000	8.6	3.3			
Ohio	44,828	116,103	11,270,000	251	97	State (U.S.)	D	Columbus
Oklahoma	69,903	181,049	3,282,000	47	18	State (U.S.)	D	Oklahoma City
† Oman	82,030	212,457	2,089,000	25	9.8	Monarchy	A	Masqat (Muscat)
Ontario	412,581	1,068,580	10,435,000	25	9.8	Province (Canada)	D	Toronto
Oregon	98,386	254,819	3,098,000	31	12	State (U.S.)	D	Salem
† Pakistan (incl. part of Jammu and Kashmir)	339,732	879,902	129,630,000	382	147	Federal Islamic republic	A	Islāmābād
† Palau (Belau)	196	508	17,000	87	33	Republic	A	Koror and Melekeok (4)
† Panama	29,157	75,517	2,654,000	91	35	Republic	A	Panamá
† Papua New Guinea	178,704	462,840	4,057,000	23	8.8	Parliamentary state	A	Port Moresby
† Paraguay	157,048	406,752	4,400,000	28	11	Republic	A	Asunción
Pennsylvania	46,058	119,291	12,215,000	265	102	State (U.S.)	D	Harrisburg
† Peru	496,225	1,285,216	23,095,000	47	18	Republic	A	Lima
† Philippines	115,831	300,000	67,910,000	586	226	Republic	A	Manila
Pitcairn (incl. Dependencies)	19	49	100	5.3	2.0	Dependent territory (U.K.)	C	Adamstown
† Poland	121,196	313,895	38,730,000	320	123	Republic	A	Warszawa (Warsaw)
† Portugal	35,516	91,985	9,907,000	279	108	Republic	A	Lisboa (Lisbon)
Prince Edward Island	2,185	5,660	141,000	65	25	Province (Canada)	D	Charlottetown
Puerto Rico	3,515	9,104	3,625,000	1,031	398	Commonwealth (U.S. protection)	B	San Juan
† Qatar	4,412	11,427	519,000	118	45	Monarchy	A	Ad-Dawḥah (Doha)
Qinghai	277,994	720,000	4,670,000	17	6.5	Province (China)	D	Xining
Quebec	594,860	1,540,680	7,157,000	12	4.6	Province (Canada)	D	Québec
Queensland	666,876	1,727,200	3,259,000	4.9	1.9	State (Australia)	D	Brisbane
Reunion	969	2,510	660,000	681	263	Overseas department (France)	C	Saint-Denis
Rhode Island	1,545	4,002	1,024,000	663	256	State (U.S.)	D	Providence
† Romania	91,699	237,500	22,745,000	248	96	Republic	A	Bucureşti (Bucharest)
† Russia	6,592,849	17,075,400	150,500,000	23	8.8	Federal republic	A	Moskva (Moscow)
† Rwanda	10,169	26,338	7,343,000	722	279	Republic	A	Kigali
St. Helena (incl. Dependencies)	121	314	7,000	58	22	Dependent territory (U.K.)	C	Jamestown
† St. Kitts and Nevis	104	269	42,000	404	156	Parliamentary state	A	Basseterre
† St. Lucia	238	616	138,000	580	224	Parliamentary state	A	Castries
St. Pierre and Miquelon	93	242	6,700	72	28	Territorial collectivity (France)	C	Saint-Pierre
† St. Vincent and the Grenadines	150	388	110,000	733	284	Parliamentary state	A	Kingstown
† San Marino	24	61	24,000	1,000	393	Republic	A	San Marino
† Sao Tome and Principe	372	964	127,000	341	132	Republic	A	São Tomé
Saskatchewan	251,866	652,330	1,018,000	4.0	1.6	Province (Canada)	D	Regina
† Saudi Arabia	830,000	2,149,690	18,190,000	22	8.5	Monarchy	A	Ar-Riyāḍ (Riyadh)
Scotland	30,421	78,789	5,142,000	169	65	Administrative division (U.K.)	D	Edinburgh
† Senegal	75,951	196,712	8,862,000	117	45	Republic	A	Dakar
† Serbia	34,116	88,361	10,095,000	296	114	Republic (Yugoslavia)	D	Beograd (Belgrade)
† Seychelles	175	453	75,000	429	166	Republic	A	Victoria

World Political Information

Country, Division or Region English (Conventional)	Area in sq. mi.	Area in sq. km.	Estimated Population 1/1/95	Pop. per sq. mi.	Pop. per sq. km.	Form of Government and Political Status		Capital
Shandong	59,074	153,000	89,400,000	1,513	584	Province (China)	D	Jinan
Shanghai Shi	2,394	6,200	14,125,000	5,900	2,278	Autonomous city (China)	D	Shanghai
Shansi (Shǎnxī)	60,232	156,000	30,405,000	505	195	Province (China)	D	Taiyuan
Shensi (Shǎnxī)	79,151	205,000	34,830,000	440	170	Province (China)	D	Xi'an (Sian)
Sichuan	220,078	570,000	113,470,000	516	199	Province (China)	D	Chengdu
† Sierra Leone	27,925	72,325	4,690,000	168	65	Transitional military government	A	Freetown
† Singapore	246	636	2,921,000	11,874	4,593	Republic	A	Singapore
Sinkiang (Xinjiang Uygur Zizhiqu)	617,764	1,600,000	16,040,000	26	10	Autonomous region (China)	D	Ürümqi
† Slovakia	18,933	49,035	5,353,000	283	109	Republic	A	Bratislava
† Slovenia	7,820	20,253	1,993,000	255	98	Republic	A	Ljubljana
† Solomon Islands	10,954	28,370	393,000	36	14	Parliamentary state	A	Honiara
† Somalia	246,201	637,657	7,187,000	29	11	None	A	Muqdisho (Mogadishu)
† South Africa	471,010	1,219,909	44,500,000	94	36	Republic	A	Pretoria, Cape Town, and Bloemfontein
South America	6,900,000	17,800,000	313,900,000	45	18			
South Australia	379,925	984,000	1,493,000	3.9	1.5	State (Australia)	D	Adelaide
South Carolina	32,007	82,898	3,702,000	116	45	State (U.S.)	D	Columbia
South Dakota	77,121	199,745	735,000	9.5	3.7	State (U.S.)	D	Pierre
South Georgia (incl. Dependencies)	1,450	3,755	(1)	—	—	Dependent territory (U.K.)	C	
† Spain	194,885	504,750	39,260,000	201	78	Constitutional monarchy	A	Madrid
Spanish North Africa (6)	12	32	146,000	12,167	4,563	Five possessions (Spain)		
† Sri Lanka	24,962	64,652	18,240,000	731	282	Socialist republic	A	Colombo and Kotte
† Sudan	967,500	2,505,813	25,840,000	27	10	Provisional military government	A	Al-Khartūm (Khartoum)
† Suriname	63,251	163,820	426,000	6.7	2.6	Republic	A	Paramaribo
† Swaziland	6,704	17,364	889,000	133	51	Monarchy	A	Mbabane and Lobamba
† Sweden	173,732	449,964	8,981,000	52	20	Constitutional monarchy	A	Stockholm
Switzerland	15,943	41,293	7,244,000	454	175	Federal republic	A	Bern (Berne)
† Syria	71,498	185,180	14,100,000	197	76	Socialist republic	A	Dimashq (Damascus)
Taiwan	13,900	36,002	21,150,000	1,522	587	Republic	A	T'aipei
† Tajikistan	55,251	143,100	6,073,000	110	42	Republic	A	Dušanbe
† Tanzania	341,217	883,749	28,350,000	83	32	Republic	A	Dar es Salaam and Dodoma
Tasmania	26,178	67,800	492,000	19	7.3	State (Australia)	D	Hobart
Tennessee	42,146	109,158	5,175,000	123	47	State (U.S.)	D	Nashville
Texas	268,601	695,676	18,330,000	68	26	State (U.S.)	D	Austin
† Thailand	198,115	513,115	59,870,000	302	117	Constitutional monarchy	A	Krung Thep (Bangkok)
Tianjin Shi	4,363	11,300	9,337,000	2,140	826	Autonomous city (China)	D	Tianjin (Tientsin)
Tibet (Xizang Zizhiqu)	471,045	1,220,000	2,275,000	4.8	1.9	Autonomous region (China)	D	Lhasa
† Togo	21,925	56,785	4,332,000	198	76	Provisional military government	A	Lomé
Tokelau Islands	4.6	12	1,500	326	125	Island territory (New Zealand)	C	
Tonga	288	747	110,000	382	147	Constitutional monarchy	A	Nuku'alofa
† Trinidad and Tobago	1,980	5,128	1,281,000	647	250	Republic	A	Port of Spain
† Tunisia	63,170	163,610	8,806,000	139	54	Republic	A	Tunis
† Turkey	300,948	779,452	62,030,000	206	80	Republic	A	Ankara
† Turkmenistan	188,456	488,100	4,035,000	21	8.3	Republic	A	Ašchabad
Turks and Caicos Islands	193	500	14,000	73	28	Dependent territory (U.K.)	C	Grand Turk
† Tuvalu	10	26	10,000	1,000	385	Parliamentary state	A	Funafuti
† Uganda	93,104	241,139	18,270,000	196	76	Republic	A	Kampala
† Ukraine	233,090	603,700	52,140,000	224	86	Republic	A	Kyyiv (Kiev)
† United Arab Emirates	32,278	83,600	2,855,000	88	34	Federation of monarchs	A	Abū Zaby (Abu Dhabi)
† United Kingdom	94,249	244,101	58,430,000	620	239	Parliamentary monarchy	A	London
† United States	3,787,425	9,809,431	262,530,000	69	27	Federal republic	A	Washington
† Uruguay	68,500	177,414	3,317,000	48	19	Republic	A	Montevideo
Utah	84,904	219,902	1,890,000	22	8.6	State (U.S.)	D	Salt Lake City
† Uzbekistan	172,742	447,400	22,860,000	132	51	Republic	A	Taškent
† Vanuatu	4,707	12,190	161,000	34	13	Republic	A	Port Vila
Vatican City	0.2	0.4	1,000	5,000	2,500	Monarchical-sacerdotal state	A	Città del Vaticano (Vatican City)
† Venezuela	352,145	912,050	21,395,000	61	23	Federal republic	A	Caracas
Vermont	9,615	24,903	578,000	60	23	State (U.S.)	D	Montpelier
Victoria	87,877	227,600	4,570,000	52	20	State (Australia)	D	Melbourne
† Vietnam	127,428	330,036	73,760,000	579	223	Socialist republic	A	Ha Noi
Virginia	42,769	110,771	6,595,000	154	60	State (U.S.)	D	Richmond
Virgin Islands (U.S.)	133	344	97,000	729	282	Unincorporated territory (U.S.)	C	Charlotte Amalie
Virgin Islands, British	59	153	13,000	220	85	Dependent territory (U.K.)	C	Road Town
Wake Island	3.0	7.8	300	100	38	Unincorporated territory (U.S.)	C	
Wales	8,015	20,758	2,922,000	365	141	Administrative division (U.K.)	D	Cardiff
Wallis and Futuna	98	255	14,000	143	55	Overseas territory (France)	D	Mata-Utu
Washington	71,303	184,674	5,360,000	75	29	State (U.S.)	D	Olympia
West Bank (incl. East Jerusalem and Jericho)	2,347	6,078	1,717,000	732	282	Israeli territory with limited self-government		
Western Australia	975,101	2,525,500	1,729,000	1.8	0.7	State (Australia)	D	Perth
Western Sahara	102,703	266,000	215,000	2.1	0.8	Occupied by Morocco	C	
† Western Samoa	1,093	2,831	172,000	157	61	Constitutional monarchy	A	Apia
West Virginia	24,231	62,759	1,838,000	76	29	State (U.S.)	D	Charleston
Wisconsin	65,503	169,653	5,120,000	78	30	State (U.S.)	D	Madison
Wyoming	97,818	253,349	473,000	4.8	1.9	State (U.S.)	D	Cheyenne
† Yemen	203,850	527,968	12,910,000	63	24	Republic	A	San'ā'
Yugoslavia	39,449	102,173	10,765,000	273	105	Republic	A	Beograd (Belgrade)
Yukon Territory	186,661	483,450	28,000	0.2	0.1	Territory (Canada)	D	Whitehorse
Yunnan	152,124	394,000	39,140,000	257	99	Province (China)	D	Kunming
† Zaire	905,355	2,344,858	43,365,000	48	18	Republic	A	Kinshasa
† Zambia	290,587	752,618	8,809,000	30	12	Republic	A	Lusaka
Zhejiang	39,305	101,800	43,930,000	1,118	432	Province (China)	D	Hangzhou
† Zimbabwe	150,872	390,757	11,075,000	73	28	Republic	A	Harare
WORLD	57,900,000	150,100,000	5,628,000,000	97	37			

† Member of the United Nations (1993).
(1) No permanent population.
(2) North Cyprus unilaterally declared its independence from Cyprus in 1983.
(3) Claimed by Argentina.
(4) Future capital.
(5) Claimed by Comoros.
(6) Comprises Ceuta, Melilla, and several small islands.

World Geographical Information

General

MOVEMENTS OF THE EARTH

The earth makes one complete revolution around the sun every 365 days, 5 hours, 48 minutes, and 46 seconds.

The earth makes one complete rotation on its axis in 23 hours, 56 minutes and 4 seconds.

The earth revolves in its orbit around the sun at a speed of 66,700 miles per hour (107,343 kilometers per hour).

The earth rotates on its axis at an equatorial speed of more than 1,000 miles per hour (1,600 kilometers per hour).

MEASUREMENTS OF THE EARTH

Estimated age of the earth, at least 4.6 billion years.

Equatorial diameter of the earth, 7,926.38 miles (12,756.27 kilometers).

Polar diameter of the earth, 7,899.80 miles (12,713.50 kilometers).

Mean diameter of the earth, 7,917.52 miles (12,742.01 kilometers).

Equatorial circumference of the earth, 24,901.46 miles (40,075.02 kilometers).

Polar circumference of the earth, 24,855.34 miles (40,000.79 kilometers).

Difference between equatorial and polar circumferences of the earth, 46.12 miles (74.23 kilometers).

Weight of the earth, 6,600,000,000,000,000,000,000 tons, or 6,600 billion billion tons (6,000 billion billion metric tons).

THE EARTH'S SURFACE

Total area of the earth, 197,000,000 square miles (510,000,000 square kilometers).

Total land area of the earth (including inland water and Antarctica), 57,900,000 square miles (150,100,000 square kilometers).

Highest point on the earth's surface, Mt. Everest, Asia, 29,028 feet (8,848 meters).

Lowest point on the earth's land surface, shores of the Dead Sea, Asia, 1,299 feet (396 meters) below sea level.

Greatest known depth of the ocean, the Mariana Trench, southwest of Guam, Pacific Ocean, 35,810 feet (10,915 meters).

THE EARTH'S INHABITANTS

Population of the earth is estimated to be 5,477,000,000 (January 1, 1993).

Estimated population density of the earth, 95 per square mile (36 per square kilometer).

EXTREMES OF TEMPERATURE AND RAINFALL OF THE EARTH

Highest temperature ever recorded, 136° F. (58° C.) at Al-'Azīzīyah, Libya, Africa, on September 13, 1922.

Lowest temperature ever recorded, -129° F. (-89° C.) at Vostok, Antarctica on July 21, 1983.

Highest mean annual temperature, 94° F. (34° C.) at Dallol, Ethiopia.

Lowest mean annual temperature, -70° F. (-50° C.) at Plateau Station, Antarctica.

The greatest local average annual rainfall is at Mt. Waialeale, Kauai, Hawaii, 460 inches (11,680 millimeters).

The greatest 24-hour rainfall, 74 inches (1,880 millimeters), is at Cilaos, Reunion Island, March 15-16, 1952.

The lowest local average annual rainfall is at Arica, Chile, .03 inches (8 millimeters).

The longest dry period, over 14 years, is at Arica, Chile, October 1903 to January 1918.

The Continents

CONTINENT	Area (sq. mi.) (sq. km.)	Estimated Population Jan. 1, 1993	Population per sq. mi. (sq. km.)	Mean Elevation (feet) (M.)	Highest Elevation (feet) (m.)	Lowest Elevation (feet) (m.)	Highest Recorded Temperature	Lowest Recorded Temperature
North America	9,500,000 (24,700,000)	438,200,000	46 (18)	2,000 (610)	Mt. McKinley, Alaska, United States 20,320 (6,194)	Death Valley, California, United States 282 (84) below sea level	Death Valley, California 134° F (57° C)	Northice, Greenland -87° F (-66° C)
South America	6,900,000 (17,800,000)	310,700,000	45 (17)	1,800 (550)	Cerro Aconcagua, Argentina 22,831 (6,959)	Salinas Chicas, Argentina 138 (42) below sea level	Rivadavia, Argentina 120° F (49° C)	Sarmiento, Argentina -27° F (-33° C)
Europe	3,800,000 (9,900,000)	694,700,000	183 (70)	980 (300)	Gora El'brus, Russia 18,510 (5,642)	Caspian Sea, Asia-Europe 92 (28) below sea level	Sevilla, Spain 122° F (50° C)	Ust' Ščugor, Russia -67° F (-55° C)
Asia	17,300,000 (44,900,000)	3,337,800,000	193 (74)	3,000 (910)	Mt. Everest, China-Nepal 29,028 (8,848)	Dead Sea, Israel-Jordan 1,299 (396) below sea level	Tirat Zevi, Israel 129° F (54° C)	Ojm'akon and Verchojansk, Russia -90° F (-68° C)
Africa	11,700,000 (30,300,000)	668,700,000	57 (22)	1,900 (580)	Kilimanjaro, Tanzania 19,340 (5,895)	Lac Assal, Djibouti 502 (153) below sea level	Al-'Azīzīyah, Libya 136° F (58° C)	Ifrane, Morocco -11° F (-24° C)
Oceania, incl. Australia	3,300,000 (8,500,000)	26,700,000	8.1 (3.1)	....	Mt. Wilhelm, Papua New Guinea 14,793 (4,509)	Lake Eyre, South Australia, Australia 52 (16) below sea level	Cloncurry, Queensland, Australia 128° F (53° C)	Charlotte Pass, New South Wales, Australia -8° F (-22° C)
Australia	2,966,155 (7,682,300)	16,965,000	5.7 (2.2)	1,000 (300)	Mt. Kosciusko, New South Wales 7,316 (2,230)	Lake Eyre, South Australia 52 (16) below sea level	Cloncurry, Queensland 128° F (53° C)	Charlotte Pass, New South Wales -8° F (-22° C)
Antarctica	5,400,000 (14,000,000)	....	....	6,000 (1830)	Vinson Massif 16,066 (4,897)	sea level	Vanda Station 59° F (15° C)	Vostok -129° F (-89° C)
World	57,900,000 (150,100,000)	5,477,000,000	95 (36)	....	Mt. Everest, China-Nepal 29,028 (8,848)	Dead Sea, Israel-Jordan 1,299 (396) below sea level	Al-'Azīzīyah, Libya 136° F (58° C)	Vostok, Antarctica -129° F (-89° C)

Historical Populations *

AREA	1650	1750	1800	1850	1900	1920	1950	1970	1980	1990
North America	5,000,000	5,000,000	13,000,000	39,000,000	106,000,000	147,000,000	219,000,000	316,600,000	365,000,000	423,600,000
South America	8,000,000	7,000,000	12,000,000	20,000,000	38,000,000	61,000,000	111,000,000	187,400,000	239,000,000	293,700,000
Europe	100,000,000	140,000,000	190,000,000	265,000,000	400,000,000	453,000,000	530,000,000	623,700,000	660,300,000	688,000,000
Asia	335,000,000	476,000,000	593,000,000	754,000,000	932,000,000	1,000,000,000	1,418,000,000	2,086,200,000	2,581,000,000	3,156,100,000
Africa	100,000,000	95,000,000	90,000,000	95,000,000	118,000,000	140,000,000	199,000,000	346,900,000	463,800,000	648,300,000
Oceania, incl. Australia	2,000,000	2,000,000	2,000,000	2,000,000	6,000,000	9,000,000	13,000,000	19,200,000	22,700,000	26,300,000
Australia	*	*	*	*	4,000,000	6,000,000	8,000,000	12,460,000	14,510,000	16,950,000
World	550,000,000	725,000,000	900,000,000	1,175,000,000	1,600,000,000	1,810,000,000	2,490,000,000	3,580,000,000	4,332,000,000	5,236,000,000

* Figures prior to 1970 are rounded to the nearest million.   Figures in italics represent very rough estimates.

Largest Countries : Population

		Population 1/1/93				Population 1/1/93
1	China	1,179,030,000	16	Turkey		58,620,000
2	India	873,850,000	17	Thailand		58,030,000
3	United States	256,420,000	18	United Kingdom		57,890,000
4	Indonesia	186,180,000	19	France		57,570,000
5	Brazil	159,630,000	20	Egypt		57,050,000
6	Russia	150,500,000	21	Italy		56,550,000
7	Japan	124,710,000	22	Ukraine		51,990,000
8	Pakistan	123,490,000	23	Ethiopia		51,715,000
9	Bangladesh	120,850,000	24	South Korea		43,660,000
10	Nigeria	91,700,000	25	Myanmar		43,070,000
11	Mexico	86,170,000	26	Zaire		39,750,000
12	Germany	80,590,000	27	Spain		39,155,000
13	Vietnam	69,650,000	28	Poland		38,330,000
14	Philippines	65,500,000	29	Colombia		34,640,000
15	Iran	60,500,000	30	South Africa		33,017,000

Largest Countries : Area

		Area (sq. mi.)	Area (sq. km.)			Area (sq. mi.)	Area (sq. km.)
1	Russia	6,592,849	17,075,400	16	Indonesia	752,410	1,948,732
2	Canada	3,849,674	9,970,610	17	Libya	679,362	1,759,540
3	United States	3,787,425	9,809,431	18	Iran	632,457	1,638,057
4	China	3,689,631	9,556,100	19	Mongolia	604,829	1,566,500
5	Brazil	3,286,500	8,511,996	20	Peru	496,225	1,285,216
6	Australia	2,966,155	7,682,300	21	Chad	495,755	1,284,000
7	India	1,237,062	3,203,975	22	Niger	489,191	1,267,000
8	Argentina	1,073,519	2,780,400	23	Mali	482,077	1,248,574
9	Kazakhstan	1,049,156	2,717,300	24	Angola	481,354	1,246,700
10	Sudan	967,500	2,505,813	25	Ethiopia	446,953	1,157,603
11	Algeria	919,595	2,381,741	26	Colombia	440,831	1,141,748
12	Zaire	905,446	2,345,095	27	South Africa	433,246	1,122,102
13	Greenland	840,004	2,175,600	28	Bolivia	424,165	1,098,581
14	Saudi Arabia	830,000	2,149,690	29	Mauritania	395,956	1,025,520
15	Mexico	759,534	1,967,183	30	Egypt	386,662	1,001,449

World Geographical Information

Principal Mountains

NORTH AMERICA

	Height (feet)	Height (meters)
McKinley, Mt., ▲ Alaska (▲ United States; ▲ North America)	20,320	*6,194*
Logan, Mt., ▲ Canada (▲ Yukon; ▲ St. Elias Mts.)	19,524	*5,951*
Orizaba, Pico de, ▲ Mexico	18,406	*5,610*
St. Elias, Mt., Alaska-Canada	18,008	*5,489*
Popocatépetl, Volcán, Mexico	17,930	*5,465*
Foraker, Mt., Alaska	17,400	*5,304*
Ixtacihuatl, Mexico	17,159	*5,230*
Lucania, Mt., Canada	17,147	*5,226*
Fairweather, Mt., Alaska-Canada (▲ British Columbia)	15,300	*4,663*
Whitney, Mt., ▲ California,	14,494	*4,418*
Elbert, Mt., ▲ Colorado (▲ Rocky Mts.)	14,433	*4,399*
Massive, Mt., Colorado	14,421	*4,396*
Harvard, Mt., Colorado	14,420	*4,395*
Rainier, Mt., ▲ Washington (▲ Cascade Range)	14,410	*4,392*
Williamson, Mt., California	14,375	*4,382*
Blanca Pk., Colorado (▲ Sangre de Cristo Mts.)	14,345	*4,372*
La Plata Pk., Colorado	14,336	*4,370*
Uncompahgre Pk., Colorado (▲ San Juan Mts.)	14,309	*4,361*
Grays Pk., Colorado (▲ Front Range)	14,270	*4,349*
Evans, Mt., Colorado	14,264	*4,348*
Longs Pk., Colorado	14,255	*4,345*
Wrangell, Mt., Alaska	14,163	*4,317*
Shasta, Mt., California	14,162	*4,317*
Pikes Pk., Colorado	14,110	*4,301*
Colima, Nevado de, Mexico	13,993	*4,265*
Tajumulco, Volcán, ▲ Guatemala (▲ Central America)	13,845	*4,220*
Gannett Pk., ▲ Wyoming	13,804	*4,207*
Mauna Kea, ▲ Hawaii	13,796	*4,205*
Grand Teton, Wyoming	13,770	*4,197*
Mauna Loa, Hawaii	13,679	*4,169*
Kings Pk., ▲ Utah	13,528	*4,123*
Cloud Pk., Wyoming (▲ Bighorn Mts.)	13,167	*4,013*
Wheeler Pk., ▲ New Mexico	13,161	*4,011*
Boundary Pk., ▲ Nevada	13,143	*4,006*
Waddington, Mt., Canada (▲ Coast Mts.)	13,104	*3,994*
Robson, Mt., Canada (▲ Canadian Rockies)	12,972	*3,954*
Granite Pk., ▲ Montana	12,799	*3,901*
Borah Pk., ▲ Idaho	12,662	*3,859*
Humphreys Pk., ▲ Arizona	12,633	*3,851*
Chirripó, Cerro, ▲ Costa Rica	12,530	*3,819*
Columbia, Mt., Canada (▲ Alberta)	12,294	*3,747*
Adams, Mt., Washington	12,276	*3,742*
Gunnbjørn Mtn., ▲ Greenland	12,139	*3,700*
San Gorgonio Mtn., California	11,499	*3,505*
Barú, Volcán, ▲ Panama	11,411	*3,475*
Hood, Mt., ▲ Oregon	11,239	*3,426*
Lassen Pk., California	10,457	*3,187*
Duarte, Pico, ▲ Dominican Rep. (▲ West Indies)	10,417	*3,175*
Haleakala Crater, Hawaii (▲ Maui)	10,023	*3,055*
Paricutín, Mexico	9,213	*2,808*
El Pital, Cerro, ▲ El Salvador-Honduras	8,957	*2,730*
La Selle, Pic, ▲ Haiti	8,773	*2,674*
Guadalupe Pk., ▲ Texas	8,749	*2,667*
Olympus, Mt., Washington (▲ Olympic Mts.)	7,965	*2,428*
Blue Mountain Pk., ▲ Jamaica	7,402	*2,256*
Harney Pk., ▲ South Dakota (▲ Black Hills)	7,242	*2,207*
Mitchell, Mt., ▲ North Carolina (▲ Appalachian Mts.)	6,684	*2,037*
Clingmans Dome, North Carolina-▲ Tennessee (▲ Great Smoky Mts.)	6,643	*2,025*
Turquino, Pico, ▲ Cuba	6,470	*1,972*
Washington, Mt., ▲ New Hampshire (▲ White Mts.)	6,288	*1,917*
Rogers, Mt., ▲ Virginia	5,729	*1,746*
Marcy, Mt., ▲ New York (▲ Adirondack Mts.)	5,344	*1,629*
Katahdin, Mt., ▲ Maine	5,268	*1,606*
Kawaikini, Hawaii (▲ Kauai)	5,243	*1,598*
Spruce Knob, ▲ West Virginia	4,862	*1,482*
Pelée, Montagne, ▲ Martinique	4,583	*1,397*
Mansfield, Mt., ▲ Vermont (▲ Green Mts.)	4,393	*1,339*
Punta, Cerro de, ▲ Puerto Rico	4,389	*1,338*
Black Mtn., ▲ Kentucky-Virginia	4,145	*1,263*
Kaala, Hawaii (▲ Oahu)	4,040	*1,231*

SOUTH AMERICA

Aconcagua, Cerro, ▲ Argentina; ▲ Andes; (▲ South America)	22,831	*6,959*
Ojos del Salado, Nevado, Argentina-▲ Chile	22,615	*6,893*
Illimani, Nevado, ▲ Bolivia	22,579	*6,882*
Bonete, Cerro, Argentina	22,546	*6,872*
Huascarán, Nevado, ▲ Peru	22,133	*6,746*
Llullaillaco, Volcán, Argentina-Chile	22,057	*6,723*
Yerupaja, Nevado, Peru	21,765	*6,634*
Tupungato, Cerro, Argentina-Chile	21,555	*6,570*
Sajama, Nevado, Bolivia	21,463	*6,542*
Illampu, Nevado, Bolivia	20,873	*6,362*
Chimborazo, ▲ Ecuador	20,702	*6,310*
Antofalla, Volcán, Argentina	20,013	*6,100*
Cotopaxi, Ecuador	19,347	*5,897*
Misti, Volcán, Peru	19,101	*5,822*
Huila, Nevado del, Colombia (▲ Cordillera Central)	16,896	*5,150*
Bolívar, Pico, ▲ Venezuela	16,427	*5,007*
Fitzroy, Monte (Cerro Chaltel), Argentina-Chile	11,073	*3,375*
Neblina, Pico da, ▲ Brazil-Venezuela	9,888	*3,014*

EUROPE

El'brus, gora, ▲ Russia (▲ Caucasus; ▲ Europe)	18,510	*5,642*
Dykh-Tau, Mt., Russia	17,073	*5,204*
Shkhara, Mt., ▲ Georgia-Russia	16,627	*5,068*
Blanc, Mont (Monte Bianco), ▲ France-▲ Italy (▲ Alps)	15,771	*4,807*
Dufourspitze, Italy-▲ Switzerland	15,203	*4,634*
Weisshorn, Switzerland	14,783	*4,506*
Matterhorn, Italy-Switzerland	14,692	*4,478*
Finsteraarhorn, Switzerland	14,022	*4,274*
Jungfrau, Switzerland	13,642	*4,158*
Écrins, Barre des, France	13,458	*4,102*
Viso, Monte, Italy (▲ Alpes Cottiennes)	12,602	*3,841*
Grossglockner, ▲ Austria	12,457	*3,797*
Teide, Pico de, ▲ Spain (▲ Canary Is.)	12,188	*3,715*
Mulhacén, ▲ Spain (continental)	11,410	*3,478*
Aneto, Pico de, Spain (▲ Pyrenees)	11,168	*3,404*
Perdido, Monte, Spain	11,007	*3,355*
Etna, Monte, Italy (▲ Sicily)	10,902	*3,323*
Zugspitze, Austria-▲ Germany	9,721	*2,963*
Musala, ▲ Bulgaria	9,596	*2,925*
Olympus, Mount (Óros Ólimbos), ▲ Greece	9,570	*2,917*
Corno Grande, Italy (▲ Apennines)	9,554	*2,912*
Triglav, ▲ Slovenia	9,393	*2,863*
Korabit, Maja e ▲ Albania-Macedonia	9,035	*2,754*
Cinto, Monte, France (▲ Corsica)	8,878	*2,706*
Gerlachovský Štít, ▲ Slovakia (▲ Carpathian Mts.)	8,711	*2,655*
Moldoveanu, ▲ Romania	8,346	*2,544*
Rysy, Czechoslovakia-▲ Poland	8,199	*2,499*
Glittertinden, ▲ Norway (▲ Scandinavia)	8,110	*2,472*
Parnassos, Greece	8,061	*2,457*
Ídhi, Óros, Greece (▲ Crete)	8,057	*2,456*
Pico, Ponta do, ▲ Portugal (▲ Azores Is.)	7,713	*2,351*
Hvannadalshnúkur, ▲ Iceland	6,952	*2,119*
Kebnekaise, ▲ Sweden	6,926	*2,111*
Estrela, ▲ Portugal (continental)	6,539	*1,993*
Narodnaja, gora, Russia (▲ Ural Mts.)	6,217	*1,895*
Sancy, Puy de, France (▲ Massif Central)	6,184	*1,885*
Marmora, Punta la, Italy (▲ Sardinia)	6,017	*1,834*
Hekla, Iceland	4,892	*1,491*
Nevis, Ben, ▲ United Kingdom (▲ Scotland)	4,406	*1,343*
Haltiatunturi, ▲ Finland-Norway	4,357	*1,328*
Vesuvio, Italy	4,190	*1,277*
Snowdon, United Kingdom (▲ Wales)	3,560	*1,085*
Carrauntoohil, ▲ Ireland	3,406	*1,038*
Kékes, ▲ Hungary	3,330	*1,015*
Scafell Pikes, United Kingdom (▲ England)	3,210	*978*

ASIA

Everest, Mount, ▲ China-▲ Nepal (▲ Tibet; ▲ Himalayas; ▲ Asia; ▲ World)	29,028	*8,848*
K2 (Qogir Feng), China-▲ Pakistan (▲ Kashmir; ▲ Karakoram Range)	28,250	*8,611*
Kānchenjunga, ▲ India-Nepal	28,208	*8,598*
Makālu, China-Nepal	27,825	*8,481*
Dhawlagiri, Nepal	26,810	*8,172*
Nānga Parbat, Pakistan	26,660	*8,126*
Annapurna, Nepal	26,504	*8,078*
Gasherbrum, China-Pakistan	26,470	*8,068*
Xixabangma Feng, China	26,286	*8,012*
Nanda Devi, India	25,645	*7,817*
Kamet, China-India	25,447	*7,756*
Namjagbarwa Feng, China	25,442	*7,755*
Muztag, China (▲ Kunlun Shan)	25,338	*7,723*
Tirich Mir, Pakistan (▲ Hindu Kush)	25,230	*7,690*
Gongga Shan, China	24,790	*7,556*
Kula Kangri, ▲ Bhutan	24,784	*7,554*
Kommunizma, pik, ▲ Tajikistan (▲ Pamir)	24,590	*7,495*
Nowshāk, ▲ Afghanistan-Pakistan	24,557	*7,485*
Pobedy, pik, China-Russia	24,406	*7,439*
Chomo Lhari, Bhutan-China	23,997	*7,314*
Muztag, China	23,891	*7,282*
Lenin, pik, ▲ Kyrgyzstan-Tajikistan	23,406	*7,134*
Api, Nepal	23,399	*7,132*
Kangrinboqê Feng, China	22,028	*6,714*
Hkakabo Razi, ▲ Myanmar	19,296	*5,881*
Damāvend, Qollah-ye, ▲ Iran	18,386	*5,604*
Ağrı Dağı, ▲ Turkey	16,804	*5,122*
Jaya, Puncak, ▲ Indonesia (▲ New Guinea)	16,503	*5,030*
Fūlādī, Kūh-e, Afghanistan	16,243	*4,951*
Kl'učevskaja Sopka, vulkan, Russia (▲ Poluostrov Kamčatka)	15,584	*4,750*
Trikora, Puncak, Indonesia	15,584	*4,750*
Belucha, gora, Russia-Kazakhstan	14,783	*4,506*
Munch Chajrchan Ula, Mongolia	14,311	*4,362*
Kinabalu, Gunong, ▲ Malaysia (▲ Borneo)	13,455	*4,101*
Yü Shan, ▲ Taiwan	13,114	*3,997*
Erciyes Dağı, Turkey	12,851	*3,917*
Kerinci, Gunung, Indonesia (▲ Sumatra)	12,467	*3,800*
Fuji-san, ▲ Japan (▲ Honshu)	12,388	*3,776*
Rinjani, Indonesia (▲ Lombok)	12,224	*3,726*
Semeru, Indonesia (▲ Java)	12,060	*3,676*
Nabī Shu'ayb, Jabal an-, ▲ Yemen (▲ Arabian Peninsula)	12,008	*3,660*
Rantekombola, Bulu, Indonesia (▲ Celebes)	11,335	*3,455*
Slamet, Indonesia	11,247	*3,428*
Phan Si Pan, ▲ Vietnam	10,312	*3,143*
Shām, Jabal ash-, ▲ Oman	9,957	*3,035*
Apo, Mount, ▲ Philippines (▲ Mindanao)	9,692	*2,954*
Pulog, Mount, Philippines (▲ Luzon)	9,626	*2,934*
Bia, Phou, ▲ Laos	9,249	*2,819*
Shaykh, Jabal ash-, Lebanon-▲ Syria	9,232	*2,814*
Paektu-san, ▲ North Korea-China	9,003	*2,744*
Inthanon, Doi, ▲ Thailand	8,530	*2,600*
Pidurutalagala, ▲ Sri Lanka	8,281	*2,524*
Mayon Volcano, Philippines	8,077	*2,462*
Asahi-dake, Japan (▲ Hokkaidō)	7,513	*2,290*
Tahan, Gunong, Malaysia (▲ Malaya)	7,174	*2,187*
Ólimbos, ▲ Cyprus	6,401	*1,951*
Halla-san, ▲ South Korea	6,398	*1,950*
Aôral, Phnum, ▲ Cambodia	5,948	*1,813*
Kujū-san, Japan (▲ Kyūshū)	5,863	*1,787*
Ramm, Jabal, ▲ Jordan	5,755	*1,754*
Meron, Hare, ▲ Israel	3,963	*1,208*
Carmel, Mt., Israel	1,791	*546*

AFRICA

Kilimanjaro, ▲ Tanzania (▲ Africa)	19,340	*5,895*
Kirinyaga (Mount Kenya), ▲ Kenya	17,058	*5,199*
Margherita Peak, ▲ Uganda-▲ Zaire	16,763	*5,109*
Ras Dashen Terara, ▲ Ethiopia	15,158	*4,620*
Meru, Mount, Tanzania	14,978	*4,565*
Karisimbi, Volcan, ▲ Rwanda-Zaire	14,787	*4,507*
Elgon, Mount, Kenya-Uganda	14,178	*4,321*
Toubkal, Jbel, ▲ Morocco (▲ Atlas Mts.)	13,665	*4,165*
Cameroon Mountain, ▲ Cameroon	13,451	*4,100*
Ntlenyana, Thabana, ▲ Lesotho	11,425	*3,482*
eNjesuthi, ▲ South Africa	11,306	*3,446*
Koussi, Emi, ▲ Chad (▲ Tibesti)	11,204	*3,415*
Kinyeti, ▲ Sudan	10,456	*3,187*
Santa Isabel, Pico de, ▲ Equatorial Guinea (▲ Bioko)	9,869	*3,008*
Tahat, ▲ Algeria (▲ Ahaggar)	9,541	*2,908*
Maromokotro, ▲ Madagascar	9,436	*2,876*
Kātrīnā, Jabal, ▲ Egypt	8,668	*2,642*
Sao Tome, Pico de, ▲ Sao Tome	6,640	*2,024*

OCEANIA

Wilhelm, Mount, ▲ Papua New Guinea	14,793	*4,509*
Giluwe, Mount, Papua New Guinea	14,330	*4,368*
Bangeta, Mt., Papua New Guinea	13,520	*4,121*
Victoria, Mount, Papua New Guinea (▲ Owen Stanley Range)	13,238	*4,035*
Cook, Mount, ▲ New Zealand (▲ South Island)	12,349	*3,764*
Ruapehu, New Zealand (▲ North Island)	9,177	*2,797*
Balbi, Papua New Guinea (▲ Solomon Is.)	9,000	*2,743*
Egmont, Mount, New Zealand	8,260	*2,518*
Orohena, Mont, ▲ French Polynesia (▲ Tahiti)	7,352	*2,241*
Kosciusko, Mount, ▲ Australia (▲ New South Wales)	7,316	*2,230*
Silisili, Mount, ▲ Western Samoa	6,096	*1,858*
Panié, Mont, ▲ New Caledonia	5,341	*1,628*
Bartle Frere, Australia (▲ Queensland)	5,322	*1,622*
Ossa, Mount, Australia (▲ Tasmania)	5,305	*1,617*
Woodroffe, Mount, Australia (▲ South Australia)	4,724	*1,440*
Sinewit, Mt., Papua New Guinea (▲ Bismarck Archipelago)	4,462	*1,360*
Tomanivi, ▲ Fiji (▲ Viti Levu)	4,341	*1,323*
Meharry, Mt., Australia (▲ Western Australia)	4,104	*1,251*
Ayers Rock, Australia	2,844	*867*

ANTARCTICA

Vinson Massif, ▲ Antarctica	16,066	*4,897*
Kirkpatrick, Mount, Antarctica	14,856	*4,528*
Markham, Mount, Antarctica	14,049	*4,282*
Jackson, Mount, Antarctica	13,747	*4,190*
Sidley, Mount, Antarctica	13,717	*4,181*
Wade, Mount, Antarctica	13,399	*4,084*

▲ Highest mountain in state, country, range, or region named.

Oceans, Seas and Gulfs

	Area (sq. mi.)	Area (sq. km.)		Area (sq. mi.)	Area (sq. km.)		Area (sq. mi.)	Area (sq. km.)
Pacific Ocean	63,800,000	165,200,000	South China Sea	1,331,000	3,447,000	Okhotsk, Sea of	619,000	1,603,000
Atlantic Ocean	31,800,000	82,400,000	Caribbean Sea	1,063,000	2,753,000	Norwegian Sea	597,000	1,546,000
Indian Ocean	28,900,000	74,900,000	Mediterranean Sea	967,000	2,505,000	Mexico, Gulf of	596,000	1,544,000
Arctic Ocean	5,400,000	14,000,000	Bering Sea	876,000	2,269,000	Hudson Bay	475,000	1,230,000
Arabian Sea	1,492,000	3,864,000	Bengal, Bay of	839,000	2,173,000	Greenland Sea	465,000	1,204,000

Principal Lakes

	Area (sq. mi.)	Area (sq. km.)		Area (sq. mi.)	Area (sq. km.)		Area (sq. mi.)	Area (sq. km.)
Caspian Sea, Asia—Europe (Salt)	143,240	370,990	Ontario, Lake, Canada—U.S.	7,540	19,529	Issyk-Kul', ozero, Kyrgyzstan (Salt)	2,425	6,280
Superior, Lake, Canada—U.S.	31,700	82,100	Balchaš, ozero, Kazakhstan	Δ 7,100	18,300	Torrens, Lake, Australia (Salt)	2,300	5,900
Victoria, Lake, Kenya—Tanzania—Uganda	26,820	69,463	Ladožskoje ozero, Russia	6,833	17,700	Albert, Lake, Uganda—Zaire	2,160	5,594
Aral Sea, Asia (Salt)	24,700	64,100	Chad, Lake (Lac Tchad), Cameroon—			Vänern, Sweden	2,156	5,584
Huron, Lake, Canada—U.S.	23,000	60,000	Chad—Nigeria	6,300	16,300	Nettilling Lake, Canada	2,140	5,542
Michigan, Lake, U.S.	22,300	57,800	Onežskoje ozero, Russia	3,753	9,720	Winnipegosis, Lake, Canada	2,075	5,374
Tanganyika, Lake, Africa	12,350	31,986	Eyre, Lake, Australia (Salt)	Δ 3,700	9,500	Bangweulu, Lake, Zambia	1,930	4,999
Bajkal, ozero, Russia	12,200	31,500	Titicaca, Lago, Bolivia—Peru	3,200	8,300	Nipigon, Lake, Canada	1,872	4,848
Great Bear Lake, Canada	12,095	31,326	Nicaragua, Lago de, Nicaragua	3,150	8,158	Orūmīyeh, Daryācheh-ye, Iran (Salt)	Δ 1,815	4,701
Malawi, Lake (Lake Nyasa), Malawi—			Mai—Ndombe, Lac, Zaire	Δ 3,100	8,000	Manitoba, Lake, Canada	1,785	4,624
Mozambique—Tanzania	11,150	28,878	Athabasca, Lake, Canada	3,064	7,935	Woods, Lake of the, Canada—U.S.	1,727	4,472
Great Slave Lake, Canada	11,030	28,568	Reindeer Lake, Canada	2,568	6,650	Kyoga, Lake, Uganda	1,710	4,429
Erie, Lake, Canada—U.S.	9,910	25,667	Tônlé Sab, Cambodia	Δ 2,500	6,500	Gairdner, Lake, Australia (Salt)	Δ 1,700	4,300
Winnipeg, Lake, Canada	9,416	24,387	Rudolf, Lake, Ethiopia—Kenya (Salt)	2,473	6,405	Great Salt Lake, U.S. (Salt)	1,680	4,351

Δ *Due to seasonal fluctuations in water level, areas of these lakes vary considerably.*

Principal Rivers

	Length (miles)	Length (km.)		Length (miles)	Length (km.)		Length (miles)	Length (km.)
Nile, Africa	4,145	6,671	Euphrates, Asia	1,510	2,430	Canadian, North America	906	1,458
Amazon-Ucayali, South America	4,000	6,400	Ural, Asia	1,509	2,428	Brazos, North America	900	1,400
Yangtze (Chang), Asia	3,900	6,300	Arkansas, North America	1,459	2,348	Salado, South America	900	1,400
Mississippi-Missouri, North America	3,740	6,019	Colorado, North America (U.S.-Mexico)	1,450	2,334	Darling, Australia	864	1,390
Huang (Yellow), Asia	3,395	5,464	Aldan, Asia	1,412	2,273	Fraser, North America	851	1,370
Ob'-Irtyš, Asia	3,362	5,410	Syrdarja, Asia	1,370	2,205	Parnaíba, South America	850	1,368
Río de la Plata-Paraná, South America	3,030	4,876	Dnieper, Europe	1,400	2,200	Colorado, North America (Texas)	840	1,352
Congo (Zaïre), Africa	2,900	4,700	Araguaia, South America	1,400	2,200	Dniester, Europe	840	1,352
Paraná, South America	2,800	4,500	Kasai (Cassai), Africa	1,338	2,153	Rhine, Europe	820	1,320
Amur-Argun', Asia	2,761	4,444	Tarim, Asia	1,328	2,137	Narmada, Asia	800	1,300
Amur (Heilong), Asia	2,744	4,416	Kolyma, Asia	1,323	2,129	St. Lawrence, North America	800	1,300
Lena, Asia	2,700	4,400	Orange, Africa	1,300	2,100	Ottawa, North America	790	1,271
Mackenzie, North America	2,635	4,241	Negro, South America	1,300	2,100	Athabasca, North America	765	1,231
Mekong, Asia	2,600	4,200	Ayeyarwady, Asia	1,300	2,100	Pecos, North America	735	1,183
Niger, Africa	2,600	4,200	Red, North America	1,270	2,044	Severskij Donec, Europe	735	1,183
Jenisej, Asia	2,543	4,092	Juruá, South America	1,250	2,012	Green, North America	730	1,175
Missouri-Red Rock, North America	2,533	4,076	Columbia, North America	1,200	2,000	White, North America (Ar.-Mo.)	720	1,159
Mississippi, North America	2,348	3,779	Xingu, South America	1,230	1,979	Cumberland, North America	720	1,159
Murray-Darling, Australia	2,330	3,750	Ucayali, South America	1,220	1,963	Elbe (Labe), Europe	720	1,159
Missouri, North America	2,315	3,726	Saskatchewan-Bow, North America	1,205	1,939	James, North America (N./S. Dakota)	710	1,143
Volga, Europe	2,194	3,531	Peace North America,	1,195	1,923	Gambia, Africa	680	1,094
Madeira, South America	2,013	3,240	Tigris, Asia	1,180	1,899	Yellowstone, North America	671	1,080
São Francisco, South America	1,988	3,199	Don, Europe	1,162	1,870	Tennessee, North America	652	1,049
Grande, Rio (Río Bravo), North America	1,885	3,034	Songhua, Asia	1,140	1,835	Gila, North America	630	1,014
Purús, South America	1,860	2,993	Pečora, Europe	1,124	1,809	Wisła (Vistula), Europe	630	1,014
Indus, Asia	1,800	2,900	Kama, Europe	1,122	1,805	Tagus (Tejo) (Tajo), Europe	625	1,006
Danube, Europe	1,776	2,858	Limpopo, Africa	1,100	1,800	Loire, Europe	625	1,006
Brahmaputra, Asia	1,770	2,849	Angara, Asia	1,105	1,779	Cimarron, North America	600	1,000
Yukon, North America	1,770	2,849	Snake, North America	1,038	1,670	North Platte, North America	618	995
Salween (Nu), Asia	1,750	2,816	Uruguay, South America	1,025	1,650	Albany, North America	610	982
Zambezi, Africa	1,700	2,700	Churchill, North America	1,000	1,600	Tisza (Tisa), Europe	607	977
Vil'uj, Asia	1,647	2,650	Marañón, South America	1,000	1,600	Back, North America	605	974
Tocantins, South America	1,640	2,639	Tobol, Asia	989	1,591	Ouachita, North America	605	974
Orinoco South America	1,600	2,600	Ohio, North America	981	1,579	Sava, Europe	585	941
Paraguay, South America	1,610	2,591	Magdalena, South America	950	1,529	Nemunas (Neman), Europe	582	937
Amu Darya, Asia	1,578	2,540	Roosevelt, South America	950	1,529	Branco, South America	580	933
Murray, Australia	1,566	2,520	Oka, Europe	900	1,500	Meuse (Maas), Europe	575	925
Ganges, Asia	1,560	2,511	Xiang, Asia	930	1,497	Oder (Odra), Europe	565	909
Pilcomayo, South America	1,550	2,494	Godāvari, Asia	930	1,497	Rhône, Europe	500	800

Principal Islands

	Area (sq. mi.)	Area (sq. km.)		Area (sq. mi.)	Area (sq. km.)		Area (sq. mi.)	Area (sq. km.)
Grønland (Greenland), North America	840,000	2,175,600	Hispaniola, North America	29,400	76,200	New Caledonia, Oceania	6,252	16,192
New Guinea, Asia—Oceania	309,000	800,000	Banks Island, Canada	27,038	70,028	Timor, Indonesia	5,743	14,874
Borneo (Kalimantan), Asia	287,300	744,100	Tasmania, Australia	26,200	67,800	Flores, Indonesia	5,502	14,250
Madagascar, Africa	226,500	587,000	Sri Lanka, Asia	24,900	64,600	Samar, Philippines	5,100	13,080
Baffin Island, Canada	195,928	507,451	Devon Island, Canada	21,331	55,247	Negros, Philippines	4,907	12,710
Sumatera (Sumatra), Indonesia	182,860	473,606	Tierra del Fuego, Isla Grande de, South			Palawan, Philippines	4,550	11,785
Honshū, Japan	89,176	230,966	America	18,600	48,200	Panay, Philippines	4,446	11,515
Great Britain, United Kingdom	88,795	229,978	Kyūshū, Japan	17,129	44,363	Jamaica, North America	4,200	11,000
Victoria Island, Canada	83,897	217,291	Melville Island, Canada	16,274	42,149	Hawaii, United States	4,034	10,448
Ellesmere Island, Canada	75,767	196,236	Southampton Island, Canada	15,913	41,214	Cape Breton Island, Canada	3,981	10,311
Sulawesi (Celebes), Indonesia	73,057	189,216	Spitsbergen, Norway	15,260	39,523	Mindoro, Philippines	3,759	9,735
South Island, New Zealand	57,708	149,463	New Britain, Papua New Guinea	14,093	36,500	Kodiak Island, United States	3,670	9,505
Jawa (Java), Indonesia	51,038	132,187	T'aiwan, Asia	13,900	36,000	Bougainville, Papua New Guinea	3,600	9,300
North Island, New Zealand	44,332	114,821	Hainan Dao, China	13,100	34,000	Cyprus, Asia	3,572	9,251
Cuba, North America	42,800	110,800	Prince of Wales Island, Canada	12,872	33,339	Puerto Rico, North America	3,500	9,100
Newfoundland, Canada	42,031	108,860	Vancouver Island, Canada	12,079	31,285	New Ireland, Papua New Guinea	3,500	9,000
Luzon, Philippines	40,420	104,688	Sicilia (Sicily), Italy	9,926	25,709	Corse (Corsica), France	3,367	8,720
Ísland (Iceland), Europe	39,800	103,000	Somerset Island, Canada	9,570	24,786	Kríti (Crete), Greece	3,189	8,259
Mindanao, Philippines	36,537	94,630	Sardegna (Sardinia), Italy	9,301	24,090	Vrangel'a, ostrov (Wrangel Island),		
Ireland, Europe	32,600	84,400	Shikoku, Japan	7,258	18,799	Russia	2,800	7,300
Hokkaidō, Japan	32,245	83,515	Seram (Ceram)	7,191	18,625	Leyte, Philippines	2,785	7,214
Novaja Zeml'a (Novaya Zemlya), Russia	31,900	82,600	Nordaustlandet (North East Land),			Guadalcanal, Solomon Islands	2,060	5,336
Sachalin, ostrov (Sakhalin), Russia	29,500	76,400	Norway	6,350	16,446	Long Island, United States	1,377	3,566

World Populations

This table includes every urban center of 50,000 or more population in the world, as well as many other important or well-known cities and towns.

The population figures are all from recent censuses (designated C) or official estimates (designated E), except for a few cities for which only unofficial estimates are available (designated U). The date of the census or estimate is specified for each country. Individual exceptions are dated in parentheses.

For many cities, a second population figure is given accompanied by a star (★). The starred population refers to the city's entire metropolitan area, including suburbs. These metropolitan areas have been defined by Rand McNally, following consistent rules to facilitate comparisons among the urban centers of various countries. Where a place is part of the metropolitan area of another city, that city's name is specified in parentheses preceded by a (★). Some important places that are considered to be secondary central cities of their areas are designated by (★ ★) preceding the name of the metropolitan area's main city. A population preceded by a triangle (▲) refers to an entire municipality, commune, or other district, which includes rural areas in addition to the urban center itself. The names of capital cities appear in CAPITALS; the largest city in each country is designated by the symbol (•).

For more recent population totals for countries, see the Rand McNally population estimates in the World Political Information table.

AFGHANISTAN / Afghānestān

1988 E 15,513,000

Cities and Towns

Herāt 177,300
Jalālābād (1982 E) 58,000
• KĀBOL 1,424,400
Mazār-e Sharīf 130,600
Qandahār 225,500
Qondūz (1982 E) 57,000

ALBANIA / Shqipëri

1987 E 3,084,000

Cities and Towns

Durrës 78,700
Elbasan 78,300
Korçë 61,500
Shkodër 76,300
• TIRANË 255,700
Vlorë 67,700

ALGERIA / Algérie / Djazaïr

1987 C 23,038,942

Cities and Towns

Aïn el Beïda 61,997
Aïn Oussera 44,270
Aïn Témouchent 47,479
• ALGER (ALGIERS) (★ 2,547,983) 1,507,241
Annaba (Bône) 305,526
Bab Ezzouar (★ Alger) 55,211
Barika 56,488
Batna 181,601
Béchar 107,311
Bejaïa (Bougie) 114,534
Biskra 128,281
Blida 170,935
Bordj Bou Arreridj 84,264
Bordj el Kiffan (★ Alger) 61,035
Bou Saada 66,688
Constantine 440,842
El Asnam 129,976
El Djelfa 84,207
El Eulma 67,933
El Wad 70,073
Ghardaïa 89,415
Ghilizane 80,091
Guelma 77,821
Jijel 62,793
Khemis 55,335
Khenchla 69,743
Laghouat 67,214
Lemdiyya 85,195
Maghniyya 52,275
Mostaganem 114,037
Mouaskar 64,691
M'Sila 65,805
Oran 628,558
Saïda 80,825
Sidi bel Abbès 152,778
Skikda 128,747
Souq Ahras 83,015
Stif 170,182
Tébessa 107,559
Tihert 95,821
Tizi-Ouzou 61,163
Tlemcen 126,882
Touggourt 70,645
Wargla 81,721

AMERICAN SAMOA / Amerika Samoa

1980 C 32,279

Cities and Towns

• PAGO PAGO 3,075

ANDORRA

1986 C 46,976

Cities and Towns

• ANDORRA 18,463

ANGOLA

1989 E 9,739,100

Cities and Towns

Benguela (1983 E) 155,000
Huambo (Nova Lisboa) (1983 E) 203,000
Lobito (1983 E) 150,000
• LUANDA 1,459,900
Lubango (1984 E) 95,915
Namibe (1981 E) 100,000

ANGUILLA

1984 C 6,680

Cities and Towns

• THE VALLEY 1,042

ANTIGUA AND BARBUDA

1977 E 72,000

Cities and Towns

• SAINT JOHNS 24,359

ARGENTINA

1980 C 27,947,446

Cities and Towns

Almirante Brown (★ Buenos Aires) 331,919
Avellaneda (★ Buenos Aires) 334,145
Bahía Blanca 223,818
Berazategui (★ Buenos Aires) 201,862
Berisso (★ Buenos Aires) 66,152
• BUENOS AIRES (★ 10,750,000) 2,922,829
Campana (★ Buenos Aires) 54,832
Caseros (Tres de Febrero) (★ Buenos Aires) 345,424
Catamarca (★ 90,000) 78,799
Comodoro Rivadavia 96,817
Concordia 94,222
Córdoba (★ 1,070,000) 993,055
Corrientes 180,612
Esteban Echeverría (★ Buenos Aires) 188,923
Florencio Varela (★ Buenos Aires) 173,452
Formosa 93,603
General San Martín (★ Buenos Aires) 385,625
General Sarmiento (San Miguel) (★ Buenos Aires) 502,926
Godoy Cruz (★ Mendoza) 142,408
Gualeguaychú 51,400
Junín 62,458
Lanús (★ Buenos Aires) 466,980
La Plata (★ ★ Buenos Aires) 477,175
La Rioja 67,043
Las Heras (★ Mendoza) 101,579
Lomas de Zamora (★ Buenos Aires) 510,130
Mar del Plata 414,696
Mendoza (★ 650,000) 119,088
Mercedes 50,992
Merlo (★ Buenos Aires) 292,587
Moreno (★ Buenos Aires) 194,440
Morón (★ Buenos Aires) 598,420
Necochea 51,069
Neuquén 90,089
Olavarría 64,097
Paraná 161,638
Pergamino 68,612
Pilar (★ Buenos Aires) 84,429
Posadas 143,889
Presidencia Roque Sáenz Peña 49,341
Punta Alta 56,620
Quilmes (★ Buenos Aires) 446,587
Rafaela 53,273
Resistencia 220,104
Río Cuarto 110,254
Rosario (★ 1,045,000) 938,120
Salta 260,744
San Carlos de Bariloche 48,980
San Fernando (★ Buenos Aires) 133,624
San Francisco (★ 58,536) 51,932
San Isidro (★ Buenos Aires) 289,170
San Juan (★ 300,000) 118,046
San Justo (★ Buenos Aires) 949,566
San Lorenzo (★ Rosario) 96,891
San Luis 70,999
San Miguel de Tucumán (★ 525,000) 392,888
San Nicolás de los Arroyos 98,495
San Rafael 70,959
San Salvador de Jujuy 124,950
Santa Fe 292,165
Santiago del Estero (★ 200,000) 148,758
San Vicente (★ Buenos Aires) 55,803
Tandil 79,429
Tigre (★ Buenos Aires) 206,349
Trelew 52,372
Vicente López (★ Buenos Aires) 291,072
Villa Krause (★ San Juan) 66,693
Villa María 67,560
Villa Nueva (★ Mendoza) 164,670
Zárate 67,143

ARMENIA / Hayastan

1989 C 3,283,000

Cities and Towns

Abovjan (1987 E) 53,000
Čardžou 161,000
Ečmiadzin (★ Jerevan) (1987 E) 53,000
• JEREVAN (★ 1,315,000) 1,199,000
Kirovakan (1987 E) 169,000
Kumajri 120,000
Razdan (1987 E) 56,000

ARUBA

1987 E 64,763

Cities and Towns

• ORANJESTAD 19,800

AUSTRALIA

1989 E 16,833,100

Cities and Towns

Adelaide (★ 1,036,747) 12,340
Albury (★ 66,530) 40,730
Auburn (★ Sydney) 49,950
Ballarat (★ 80,090) 36,680
Bankstown (★ Sydney) 158,750
Bendigo (★ 67,920) 32,050
Berwick (★ Melbourne) 64,100
Blacktown (★ Sydney) 210,900
Blue Mountains (★ Sydney) 70,800
Brisbane (★ 1,273,511) 744,828
Broadmeadows (★ Melbourne) 105,500
Cairns (★ 80,875) 42,839
Camberwell (★ Melbourne) 87,700
Campbelltown (★ Sydney) 139,500
CANBERRA (★ 271,362) (1986 C) 247,194
Canning (★ Perth) 69,104
Canterbury (★ Sydney) 135,200
Caulfield (★ Melbourne) 70,100
Coburg (★ Melbourne) 54,500
Cockburn (★ Perth) 49,802
Dandenong (★ Melbourne) 59,400
Darwin (★ 72,937) 63,900
Doncaster (★ Melbourne) 107,300
Enfield (★ Adelaide) 64,058
Essendon (★ Melbourne) 55,300
Fairfield (★ Sydney) 176,350
Footscray (★ Melbourne) 48,700
Frankston (★ Melbourne) 90,500
Geelong (★ 148,980) 13,190
Gosford 126,600
Gosnells (★ Perth) 71,862
Heidelberg (★ Melbourne) 63,500
Hobart (★ 181,210) 47,280
Holroyd (★ Sydney) 82,500
Hurstville (★ Sydney) 66,350
Ipswich (★ Brisbane) 75,283
Keilor (★ Melbourne) 103,700
Knox (★ Melbourne) 121,300
Lake Macquarie (★ Newcastle) 161,700
Launceston (★ 92,350) 32,150
Leichhardt (★ Sydney) 58,950
Liverpool (★ Sydney) 99,750
Logan (★ Brisbane) 142,222
Mackay (★ 50,885) 22,583
Marion (★ Adelaide) 74,631
Marrickville (★ Sydney) 84,650
Melbourne (★ 3,039,100) 55,300
Melville (★ Perth) 85,590
Mitcham (★ Adelaide) 63,301
Moorabbin (★ Melbourne) 98,900
Newcastle (★ 425,610) 130,940
Noarlunga (★ Adelaide) 77,352
Northcote (★ Melbourne) 49,100
North Sydney (★ Sydney) 53,400
Nunawading (★ Melbourne) 96,400
Oakleigh (★ Melbourne) 57,600
Parramatta (★ Sydney) 134,600
Penrith (★ Sydney) 152,650
Perth (★ 1,158,387) 82,413
Preston (★ Melbourne) 82,000
Randwick (★ Sydney) 119,200
Redcliffe (★ Brisbane) 48,123
Rockdale (★ Sydney) 88,200
Rockhampton (★ 61,694) 58,890
Ryde (★ Sydney) 94,400
Salisbury (★ Adelaide) 106,129
Shoalhaven 64,070
Southport (★ 254,861) 135,408
South Sydney (★ Sydney) 74,100
Springvale (★ Melbourne) 88,700
Stirling (★ Perth) 181,556
Sunshine (★ Melbourne) 97,700
• Sydney (★ 3,623,550) 9,800
Tea Tree Gully (★ Adelaide) 82,324
Toowoomba 81,071
Townsville (★ 111,972) 83,339
Wagga Wagga 52,180
Wanneroo (★ Perth) 163,324
Waverley (★ Melbourne) 126,300
Waverley (★ Sydney) 61,850
Willoughby (★ Sydney) 53,950
Wollongong (★ 236,690) 174,770
Woodville (★ Adelaide) 82,590
Woollahra (★ Sydney) 53,850

AUSTRIA / Österreich

1981 C 7,555,338

Cities and Towns

Graz (★ 325,000) 243,166
Innsbruck (★ 185,000) 117,287
Klagenfurt (★ 115,000) 87,321
Linz (★ 335,000) 199,910
Salzburg (★ 220,000) 139,426
Sankt Pölten (★ 67,000) 50,419
Villach (★ 65,000) 52,692
Wels (★ 76,000) 51,060
• WIEN (VIENNA) (★ 1,875,000) (1988 E) 1,482,800

AZERBAIJAN / Azärbayjan

1989 C 7,029,000

Cities and Towns

Ali-Bajramly (1987 E) 51,000
• BAKU (★ 2,020,000) 1,150,000
Chudžand 160,000
Gjandža 278,000
Kurgan-T'ube (1987 E) 55,000
Mingečaur (1987 E) 78,000
Nachičevan' (1987 E) 51,000
Šeki (Nucha) (1987 E) 54,000
Sumgait (★ Baku) 231,000

BAHAMAS

1982 E 218,000

Cities and Towns

• NASSAU 135,000

BAHRAIN / Al-Baḥrayn

1981 C 350,798

Cities and Towns

• AL-MANĀMAH (★ 224,643) 115,054
Al-Muharraq (★ Al-Manāmah) 57,688

BANGLADESH

1981 C 87,119,965

Cities and Towns

Barisāl 172,905
Begamganj 69,623
Bhairab Bāzār 63,563
Bogra 68,749
Brāhmanbāria 87,570
Chāndpur 85,656
Chittagong (★ 1,391,877) 980,000
Chuādanga 76,000
Comilla 184,132
• DHAKA (DACCA) (★ 3,430,312) 2,365,695
Dinājpur 96,718
Farīdpur 66,579
Gulshan (★ Dhaka) 215,444
Jamālpur 91,815
Jessore 148,927
Khulna 648,359
Kishorganj 52,302
Kushtia 74,892
Mādārīpur 63,917
Mīrpur (★ Dhaka) 349,031
Mymensingh 190,991
Naogaon 52,975
Nārāyanganj (★ ★ Dhaka) 405,562
Narsinghdi 76,841
Nawābganj 87,724
Noākhāli 59,065
Pābna 109,065
Patuākhāli 48,121
Rājshāhi 253,740
Rangpur 153,174
Saidpur 126,608
Sātkhira 52,156
Sherpur 48,214
Sirājganj 106,774
Sītākunda (★ Chittagong) 237,520
Sylhet 168,371
Tangail 77,518
Tongi (★ Dhaka) 94,580

BARBADOS

1980 C 244,228

Cities and Towns

• BRIDGETOWN (★ 115,000) 7,466

BELARUS / Byelarus'

1989 C 10,200,000

Cities and Towns

Baranoviči 159,000
Bobrujsk 223,000
Borisov 144,000
Brest 258,000
Gomel' 500,000
Grodno 270,000
Lida (1987 E) 81,000
• MINSK (★ 1,650,000) 1,589,000
Mogil'ov 356,000
Molodečno (1987 E) 87,000
Mozyr' 101,000
Novopolock (1987 E) 90,000
Orša 123,000
Pinsk 119,000
Polock (1987 E) 80,000
Rečica (1987 E) 71,000
Sluck (1987 E) 55,000
Soligorsk (1987 E) 92,000
Svetlogorsk (1987 E) 68,000
Vitebsk 350,000
Žlobin (1987 E) 52,000
Žodino (1987 E) 51,000

BELGIUM / België / Belgique

1987 E 9,864,751

Cities and Towns

Aalst (Alost) (★ Bruxelles) 77,113
Anderlecht (★ Bruxelles) 88,849
Antwerpen (★ 1,100,000) 479,748
Brugge (Bruges) (★ 223,000) 117,755
• BRUXELLES (BRUSSEL) (★ 2,385,000) 136,920
Charleroi (★ 480,000) 209,395
Forest (★ Bruxelles) 48,266
Genk (★ ★ Hasselt) 61,391
Gent (Gand) (★ 465,000) 233,856
Hasselt (★ 290,000) 65,563
Ixelles (★ Bruxelles) 76,241
Kortrijk (Courtrai) (★ 202,000) 76,216
La Louvière (★ 147,000) 76,340
Leuven (Louvain) (★ 173,000) 84,583
Liège (Luik) (★ 750,000) 200,891
Mechelen (Malines) (★ 121,000) 75,808
Molenbeek-St.-Jean (★ Bruxelles) 69,764
Mons (Bergen) (★ 242,000) 89,697
Mouscron (★ Lille, France) 53,713
Namur (★ 147,000) 102,670
Oostende (Ostende) (★ 122,000) 68,318

C Census. E Official estimate. U Unofficial estimate.
• Largest city in country.

★ Population or designation of metropolitan area, including suburbs (see headnote).
▲ Population of an entire municipality, commune, or district, including rural area.

Roeselare (Roulers) 51,963
Schaerbeek (★ Bruxelles) 104,919
Seraing (★ Liège) 61,731
Sint-Niklaas (Saint-Nicolas) 68,082
Tournai (Doornik) (▲ 66,998) 44,900
Uccle (★ Bruxelles) 75,876
Verviers (★ 101,000) 53,498

BELIZE
1985 E 166,400

Cities and Towns

• Belize City 47,000
BELMOPAN 4,500

BENIN / Bénin
1984 E 3,825,000

Cities and Towns

Abomey 53,000
• COTONOU 478,000
Natitingou (1975 E) 51,000
Ouidah (1979 E) 53,000
Parakou 92,000
PORTO-NOVO 164,000

BERMUDA
1985 E 56,000

Cities and Towns

• HAMILTON (★ 15,000) 1,676

BHUTAN / Druk-Yul
1982 E 1,333,000

Cities and Towns

• THIMPHU 12,000

BOLIVIA
1985 E 6,429,226

Cities and Towns

Cochabamba 317,251
• LA PAZ 992,592
Oruro 178,393
Potosí 113,380
Santa Cruz 441,717
SUCRE 86,609
Tarija 60,621

BOSNIA AND HERZEGOVINA / Bosna i Hercegovina
1987 E 4,400,464

Cities and Towns

Banja Luka (▲ 193,890) 130,900
• SARAJEVO (▲ 479,688) 341,200
Tuzla (▲ 129,967) 67,300
Zenica (▲ 144,869) 67,500

BOTSWANA
1987 E 1,169,000

Cities and Towns

Francistown (1986 E) 43,837
• GABORONE 107,677
Selebi Phikwe (1986 E) 41,382

BRAZIL / Brasil
1985 E 135,564,395

Cities and Towns

Alagoinhas (▲ 116,959) 87,500
Alegrete (▲ 71,898) 56,700
Alvorada 105,730
Americana 156,030
Anápolis 225,840
Apucarana (▲ 92,812) 73,700
Aracaju 360,013
Araçatuba 129,304
Araguari (▲ 96,035) 84,300
Arapiraca (▲ 147,879) 91,400
Araraquara (▲ 145,042) 87,500
Araras (▲ 71,652) 59,900
Araxá 61,418
Assis (▲ 74,238) 63,100
Bagé (▲ 106,155) 70,800
Barbacena (▲ 99,337) 80,200
Barra do Piraí (▲ 78,189) 55,700
Barra Mansa (★ Volta Redonda) 149,200
Barretos 80,202
Bauru 220,105
Bayeux (★ João Pessoa) 67,182
Belém (★ 1,200,000) 1,116,578
Belford Roxo (★ Rio de Janeiro) 340,700
Belo Horizonte (★ 2,950,000) 2,114,429
Betim (★ Belo Horizonte) 96,810
Blumenau 192,074
Boa Vista 66,028
Botucatu (▲ 71,139) 62,600
Bragança Paulista (▲ 105,099) 76,300
BRASÍLIA 1,567,709
Caçapava (▲ 64,213) 56,600
Cachoeira do Sul (▲ 91,492) 58,900
Cachoeirinha (★ Porto Alegre) 73,117
Cachoeiro de Itapemirim (▲ 138,156) 95,000
Campina Grande 279,929
Campinas (★ 1,125,000) 841,016
Campo Grande 384,398
Campos (▲ 366,716) 187,900
Campos Elyseos (★ Rio de Janeiro) 188,200
Canoas (★ Porto Alegre) 261,222
Carapicuíba (★ São Paulo) 265,856
Carazinho (▲ 62,108) 48,500
Cariacica (★ Vitória) 74,300
Caruaru (▲ 190,794) 152,100
Cascavel (▲ 200,485) 123,100
Castanhal (▲ 89,703) 71,200
Catanduva (▲ 80,309) 71,400
Caucaia (★ Fortaleza) 78,500
Cavaleiro (★ Recife) 106,600
Caxias (▲ 148,230) 66,300
Caxias do Sul 266,809
Chapecó (▲ 100,997) 64,200
Coelho da Rocha (★ Rio de Janeiro) 164,400
Colatina (▲ 106,260) 58,600
Colombo (★ Curitiba) 65,900
Conselheiro Lafaiete 77,958
Contagem (★ Belo Horizonte) 152,700
Corumbá (▲ 80,666) 65,800
Crato (▲ 86,371) 52,700
Criciúma (▲ 128,410) 85,900
Cruz Alta (▲ 71,817) 58,300
Cruzeiro 63,918
Cubatão (★ Santos) 98,322
Cuiabá (▲ 279,651) 220,400
Curitiba (★ 1,700,000) 1,279,205
Diadema (★ São Paulo) 320,187
Divinópolis 139,940
Dourados (▲ 123,757) 89,200
Duque de Caxias (★ Rio de Janeiro) 353,200
Embu (★ São Paulo) 119,791
Erechim (▲ 70,709) 54,300
Esteio (★ Porto Alegre) 58,964
Feira de Santana (▲ 355,201) 278,600
Ferraz de Vasconcelos (★ São Paulo) 68,831
Florianópolis (★ 365,000) 178,400
Fortaleza (★ 1,825,000) 1,582,414
Foz do Iguaçu (▲ 182,101) 124,900
Franca 182,820
Garanhuns 73,100
Goiânia (★ 990,000) 923,333
Governador Valadares (▲ 216,957) 192,300
Guaratinguetá (▲ 93,534) 80,400
Guarujá (★ Santos) 83,500
Guarulhos (★ São Paulo) 571,700
Ijuí (▲ 82,064) 64,400
Ilhéus (▲ 145,810) 79,400
Imperatriz (▲ 235,453) 119,500
Ipatinga (★ 270,000) 149,100
Ipiiba (★ Rio de Janeiro) 116,200
Itabira (▲ 81,771) 66,300
Itabuna (▲ 167,543) 142,200
Itajaí 104,232
Itajubá (▲ 69,675) 61,500
Itapecerica da Serra (★ São Paulo) 65,500
Itapetininga (▲ 105,512) 76,700
Itapevi (★ São Paulo) 66,825
Itaquaquecetuba (★ São Paulo) 91,366
Itaquari (★ Vitória) 163,900
Itaúna 61,446
Itu (▲ 92,786) 77,900
Ituiutaba (▲ 85,365) 74,900
Itumbiara (▲ 78,844) 57,200
Jaboatão (★ Recife) 82,900
Jacareí 149,061
Jaú (▲ 92,547) 74,500
Jequié (▲ 127,070) 92,100
João Pessoa (★ 550,000) 348,500
Joinvile 302,877
Juàzeiro (★ Petrolina) 78,600
Juàzeiro do Norte 159,806
Juiz de Fora 349,720
Jundiaí (▲ 313,652) 268,900
Lajes (▲ 143,246) 103,600
Lavras 52,100
Limeira 186,986
Linhares (▲ 122,453) 53,400
Londrina (▲ 346,676) 296,400
Lorena 63,230
Luziânia (▲ 98,408) 71,400
Macapá (▲ 168,839) 109,400
Maceió 482,195
Manaus 809,914
Marabá (▲ 133,559) 92,700
Marília (▲ 136,187) 116,100
Maringá 196,871
Mauá (★ São Paulo) 269,321
Mesquita (★ Rio de Janeiro) 161,300
Mogi das Cruzes (★ São Paulo) 144,800
Mogi-Guaçu (▲ 91,994) 81,800
Mogi-Mirim (▲ 63,313) 52,300
Monjolo (★ Rio de Janeiro) 113,900
Montes Claros (▲ 214,472) 183,500
Mossoró (▲ 158,723) 128,300
Muriaé (▲ 80,466) 57,600
Muribeca dos Guararapes (★ Recife) 171,200
Natal 510,106
Neves (★ Rio de Janeiro) 163,600
Nilópolis (★ Rio de Janeiro) 112,800
Niterói (★ Rio de Janeiro) 441,684
Nova Friburgo (▲ 143,529) 103,500
Nova Iguaçu (★ Rio de Janeiro) 592,800
Novo Hamburgo (★ Porto Alegre) 167,744
Olinda (★ Recife) 316,600
Osasco (★ São Paulo) 591,568
Ourinhos (▲ 65,841) 58,100
Paranaguá (▲ 94,809) 82,300
Paranavaí (▲ 75,511) 60,900
Parnaíba (▲ 116,206) 90,200
Parque Industrial (★ Belo Horizonte) 228,400
Passo Fundo (▲ 137,843) 117,500
Passos (▲ 79,393) 65,500
Patos 74,298
Patos de Minas (▲ 99,027) 69,000
Paulo Afonso (▲ 86,182) 75,300
Pelotas (▲ 277,730) 210,300
Petrolina (★ 225,000) 92,100
Petrópolis (★ Rio de Janeiro) 170,300
Pindamonhangaba (▲ 86,990) 64,100
Pinheirinho (★ Curitiba) 51,600
Piracicaba (▲ 252,079) 211,000
Poá (★ São Paulo) 66,006
Poços de Caldas 100,004
Ponta Grossa 223,154
Porto Alegre (★ 2,600,000) 1,272,121
Porto Velho (▲ 202,011) 152,700
Pouso Alegre (▲ 65,958) 58,300
Praia Grande (★ Santos) 67,800
Presidente Prudente 155,883
Queimados (★ Rio de Janeiro) 113,700
Recife (★ 2,625,000) 1,287,623
Ribeirão Prêto 383,125
Rio Branco (▲ 145,486) 109,800
Rio Claro 129,859
Rio de Janeiro (★ 10,150,000) 5,603,388
Rio Grande 164,221
Rio Verde (▲ 92,954) 59,400
Rondonópolis (▲ 101,642) 65,500
Salvador (★ 2,050,000) 1,804,438
Santa Bárbara d'Oeste 95,818
Santa Cruz do Sul (▲ 115,288) 60,300
Santa Maria (▲ 196,827) 163,900
Santana do Livramento (▲ 70,489) 60,100
Santarém (▲ 226,618) 120,800
Santa Rita (★ João Pessoa) 60,100
Santo André (★ São Paulo) 635,129
Santo Ângelo (▲ 107,559) 57,700
Santos (★ 1,065,000) 460,100
São Bernardo do Campo (★ São Paulo) 562,485
São Caetano do Sul (★ São Paulo) 171,005
São Carlos 140,383
São Gonçalo (★ Rio de Janeiro) 262,400
São João da Boa Vista (▲ 61,653) 50,400
São João del Rei (▲ 74,385) 61,400
São João de Meriti (★ Rio de Janeiro) 241,700
São José do Rio Prêto 229,221
São José dos Campos 372,578
São José dos Pinhais (★ Curitiba) 64,100
São Leopoldo (★ Porto Alegre) 114,065
São Lourenco da Mata (★ Recife) 65,936
São Luís (★ 600,000) 227,900
• São Paulo (★ 15,175,000) 10,063,110
São Vicente (★ Santos) 239,778
Sapucaia do Sul (★ Porto Alegre) 91,820
Sete Lagoas 121,418
Sete Pontes (★ Rio de Janeiro) 72,300
Sobral (▲ 112,275) 69,400
Sorocaba 327,468
Suzano (★ São Paulo) 128,924
Taboão da Serra (★ São Paulo) 122,112
Tatuí (▲ 69,358) 56,000
Taubaté 205,120
Teófilo Otoni (▲ 126,265) 82,700
Teresina (★ 525,000) 425,300
Teresópolis (▲ 115,859) 92,600
Timon (★ Teresina) 68,300
Tubarão (▲ 82,082) 70,400
Uberaba 244,875
Uberlândia 312,024
Uruguaiana (▲ 105,862) 91,500
Varginha 74,630
Vicente de Carvalho (★ Santos) 102,700
Vila Velha (★ Vitória) 91,900
Vitória (★ 735,000) 201,500
Vitória da Conquista (▲ 198,150) 145,800
Vitória de Santo Antão (▲ 100,450) 67,800
Volta Redonda (★ 375,000) 219,267

BRITISH VIRGIN ISLANDS
1980 C 12,034

Cities and Towns

• ROAD TOWN 2,479

BRUNEI
1981 C 192,832

Cities and Towns

• BANDAR SERI BEGAWAN (★ 64,000) 22,777

BULGARIA / Bâlgarija
1986 E 9,913,000

Cities and Towns

Blagoevgrad 67,766
Burgas 186,369
Dimitrovgrad 54,898
Dobrič 110,471
Gabrovo 81,688
Haskovo 89,273
Jambol 92,321
Kârdžali 56,906
Kazanlâk 61,780
Kjustendil 54,773
Loveč (1985 E) 48,862
Mihajlovgrad 53,529
Pazardžik 79,198
Pernik 96,277
Pleven 132,206
Plovdiv 349,148
Razgrad 51,277
Ruse 186,428
Silistra 54,627
Sliven 104,345
• SOFIJA (SOFIA) (★ 1,205,000) 1,119,152
Stara Zagora 153,538
Šumen 102,886
Varna 303,071
Veliko Târnovo 70,610
Vidin 63,813
Vraca 77,934

BURKINA FASO
1985 C 7,964,705

Cities and Towns

Bobo Dioulasso 228,668
Koudougou 51,926
• OUAGADOUGOU 441,514

BURUNDI
1986 E 4,782,000

Cities and Towns

• BUJUMBURA 273,000
Gitega 95,000

CAMBODIA / Kâmpŭchéa
1986 E 7,492,000

Cities and Towns

Kâmpóng Saôm (1981 E) 53,000
• PHNUM PÉNH 700,000

CAMEROON / Cameroun
1986 E 10,446,409

Cities and Towns

Bafoussam (1985 E) 89,000
Bamenda (1985 E) 72,000
• Douala 1,029,731
Foumban (1985 E) 50,000
Garoua (1985 E) 96,000
Kumba (1985 E) 67,000
Maroua 103,653
Ngaoundéré (1985 E) 61,000
Nkongsamba 123,149
YAOUNDÉ 653,670

CANADA
1986 C 25,354,064

CANADA: ALBERTA
1986 C 2,375,278

Cities and Towns

Calgary (★ 671,326) 636,104
Edmonton (★ 785,465) 573,982
Fort McMurray (★ 48,497) 34,949
Lethbridge 58,841
Medicine Hat (★ 50,734) 41,804
Red Deer 54,425

CANADA: BRITISH COLUMBIA
1986 C 2,889,207

Cities and Towns

Burnaby (★ Vancouver) 145,161
Chilliwack (★ 50,288) 41,337
Kamloops 61,773
Kelowna (★ 89,730) 61,213
Matsqui (★ 88,420) 51,449
Nanaimo (★ 60,420) 49,029
Prince George 67,621
Richmond (★ Vancouver) 108,492
Vancouver (★ 1,380,729) 431,147
Victoria (★ 255,547) 66,303

CANADA: MANITOBA
1986 C 1,071,232

Cities and Towns

Brandon 38,708
Portage la Prairie 13,198
Winnipeg (★ 625,304) 594,551

CANADA: NEW BRUNSWICK
1986 C 710,422

Cities and Towns

Fredericton (★ 65,768) 44,352
Moncton (★ 102,084) 55,468
Saint John (★ 121,265) 76,381

CANADA: NEWFOUNDLAND
1986 C 568,349

Cities and Towns

Corner Brook (★ 33,730) 22,719
Gander 10,207
Saint John's (★ 161,901) 96,216

CANADA: NORTHWEST TERRITORIES
1986 C 52,238

Cities and Towns

Inuvik 3,389
Yellowknife 11,753

CANADA: NOVA SCOTIA
1986 C 873,199

Cities and Towns

Dartmouth (★ Halifax) 65,243
Halifax (★ 295,990) 113,577
Sydney (★ 119,470) 27,754

CANADA: ONTARIO
1986 C 9,113,515

Cities and Towns

Barrie (★ 67,703) 48,287
Brampton (★ Toronto) 188,498
Brantford (★ 90,521) 76,146
Burlington (★ Hamilton) 116,675
Cambridge (Galt) (★ ★ Kitchener) 79,920
East York (★ Toronto) 101,085
Etobicoke (★ Toronto) 302,973
Gloucester (★ Ottawa) 89,810
Guelph (★ 85,962) 78,235
Hamilton (★ 557,029) 306,728
Kingston (★ 122,350) 55,050
Kitchener (★ 311,195) 150,604
London (★ 342,302) 269,140
Markham (★ Toronto) 114,597
Mississauga (★ Toronto) 374,005
Nepean (★ Ottawa) 95,490
Niagara Falls (★ ★ Saint Catharines) 72,107
North Bay (★ 57,422) 50,623
North York (★ Toronto) 556,297
Oakville (★ Toronto) 87,107
Oshawa (★ 203,543) 123,651
OTTAWA (★ 819,263) 300,763
Peterborough (★ 87,083) 61,049
Saint Catharines (★ 343,258) 123,455
Sarnia (★ 85,700) 49,033
Sault Sainte Marie (★ 84,617) 80,905

C Census. E Official estimate. U Unofficial estimate.
• Largest city in country.
★ Population or designation of metropolitan area, including suburbs (see headnote).
▲ Population of an entire municipality, commune, or district, including rural area.

Scarborough (★ Toronto) 484,676
Sudbury (★ 148,877) 88,717
Thunder Bay (★ 122,217) 112,272
• Toronto (★ 3,427,168) 612,289
Vaughan (★ Toronto) 65,058
Waterloo (★ Kitchener) 58,718
Windsor (★ 253,988) 193,111
York (★ Toronto) 135,401

CANADA: PRINCE EDWARD ISLAND

1986 C 126,646

Cities and Towns

Charlottetown (★ 53,868) 15,776
Summerside (★ 15,614) 8,020

CANADA: QUÉBEC

1986 C 6,540,276

Cities and Towns

Beauport (★ Québec) 62,869
Brossard (★ Montréal) 57,441
Charlesbourg (★ Québec) 68,996
Chicoutimi (★ 158,468) 61,083
Gatineau (★ Ottawa) 81,244
Hull (★ Ottawa) 58,722
Jonquière (★ ★ Chicoutimi) 58,467
LaSalle (★ Montréal) 75,621
Laval (★ Montréal) 284,164
Longueuil (★ Montréal) 125,441
Montréal (★ 2,921,357) 1,015,420
Montréal-Nord (★ Montréal) 90,303
Québec (★ 603,267) 164,580
Sainte-Foy (★ Québec) 69,615
Saint-Hubert (★ Montréal) 66,218
Saint-Laurent (★ Montréal) 67,002
Saint-Léonard (★ Montréal) 75,947
Sherbrooke (★ 129,960) 74,438
Trois-Rivières (★ 128,888) 50,122
Verdun (★ Montréal) 60,246

CANADA: SASKATCHEWAN

1986 C 1,010,198

Cities and Towns

Moose Jaw (★ 37,219) 35,073
Prince Albert (★ 40,841) 33,686
Regina (★ 186,521) 175,064
Saskatoon (★ 200,665) 177,641

CANADA: YUKON

1986 C 23,504

Cities and Towns

Dawson 896
Whitehorse 15,199

CAPE VERDE / Cabo Verde

1990 C 336,798

Cities and Towns

• PRAIA 61,797

CAYMAN ISLANDS

1988 E 25,900

Cities and Towns

• GEORGETOWN 13,700

CENTRAL AFRICAN REPUBLIC / République centrafricaine

1984 E 2,517,000

Cities and Towns

• BANGUI 473,817
Bouar (1982 E) 48,000

CHAD / Tchad

1979 E 4,405,000

Cities and Towns

Abéché 54,000
Moundou 66,000
• N'DJAMENA 303,000
Sarh 65,000

CHILE

1982 C 11,329,736

Cities and Towns

Antofagasta 185,486
Apoquindo (★ Santiago) 175,735
Arica 139,320
Calama 81,684
Cerrillos (★ Santiago) 67,013
Cerro Navia (★ Santiago) 137,777
Chillán 118,163
Concepción (★ 675,000) 267,891
Conchalí (★ Santiago) 157,884
Copiapó 69,045
Coquimbo 62,186
Coronel (★ Concepción) 65,918
Curicó 60,550
El Bosque (★ Santiago) 143,717
Huechuraba (★ Santiago) 56,313
Independencia (★ Santiago) 86,724
Iquique 110,153
La Cisterna (★ Santiago) 95,863
La Florida (★ Santiago) 191,883
La Granja (★ Santiago) 109,168
La Pintana (★ Santiago) 73,932
La Reina (★ Santiago) 80,452
La Serena 83,283
Las Rejas (★ Santiago) 147,918
Lo Espejo (★ Santiago) 124,462
Lo Prado (★ Santiago) 103,575
Los Angeles 70,529
Macul (★ Santiago) 113,100
Maipú (★ Santiago) 114,117
Ñuñoa (★ Santiago) 168,919
Osorno 95,286
Pedro Aguirre Cerda (★ Santiago) 145,207
Peñalolén (★ Santiago) 137,298
Providencia (★ Santiago) 115,449
Pudahuel (★ Santiago) 97,578
Puente Alto (★ Santiago) 109,239
Puerto Montt 84,410
Punta Arenas 95,332
Quilpué (★ Valparaíso) 84,136
Quinta Normal (★ Santiago) 128,989
Rancagua 139,925
Recoleta (★ Santiago) 164,292
Renca (★ Santiago) 93,928
San Antonio 61,486
San Bernardo (★ Santiago) 117,132
San Joaquín (★ Santiago) 123,904
San Miguel (★ Santiago) 88,764
San Ramón (★ Santiago) 99,410
• SANTIAGO (★ 4,100,000) 232,667
Talca 128,544
Talcahuano (★ ★ Concepción) 202,368
Temuco 157,297
Valdivia 100,046
Valparaíso (★ 675,000) 265,355
Villa Alemana (★ Valparaíso) 55,766
Viña del Mar (★ Valparaíso) 244,899
Vitacura (★ Santiago) 72,038

CHINA / Zhongguo

1988 E 1,103,983,000

Cities and Towns

Abagnar Qi (▲ 100,700) (1986 E) 71,700
Acheng (1985 E) 100,304
Aihui (▲ 135,000) (1986 E) 76,700
Akesu (▲ 345,900) (1986 E) 143,100
Altay (▲ 141,700) (1986 E) 62,800
Anci (Langfang) (▲ 522,800) (1986 E) 122,100
Anda (▲ 425,500) (1986 E) 130,200
Andong (1986 E) 579,800
Ankang (1985 E) 89,188
Anqing (▲ 433,900) (1986 E) 213,200
Anshan 1,330,000
Anshun (▲ 214,700) (1986 E) 128,800
Anyang (▲ 541,900) (1986 E) 361,200
Baicheng (▲ 282,000) (1986 E) 198,600
Baiquan (1985 E) 50,996
Baiyin (▲ 301,900) (1986 E) 157,100
Baoding (▲ 535,100) (1986 E) 423,200
Baoji (▲ 359,500) (1986 E) 286,200
Baoshan (▲ 688,400) (1986 E) 52,300
Baotou (Paotow) 1,130,000
Baoying (1985 E) 50,479
Bei'an (▲ 440,500) (1986 E) 199,500
Beihai (▲ 175,900) (1986 E) 119,000
BEIJING (PEKING) (★ 6,450,000) 6,710,000
Beipiao (▲ 603,700) (1986 E) 180,900
Bengbu (▲ 612,600) (1986 E) 403,900
Benxi (Penhsi) 860,000
Bijie (1985 E) 54,871
Binxian (▲ 177,900) (1986 E) 86,700
Binxian (1982 C) 127,326
Boli (1985 E) 61,990
Bose (▲ 271,400) (1986 E) 82,000
Boshan (1975 U) 100,000
Boxian (1985 E) 63,222
Boxing (1982 C) 57,554
Boyang (1985 E) 60,688
Butha Qi (Zalantun) (▲ 389,500) (1986 E) 111,300
Cangshan (Bianzhuang) (1982 C) 79,334
Cangzhou (▲ 293,600) (1986 E) 196,700
Changchun (▲ 2,000,000) 1,822,000
Changde (▲ 220,800) (1986 E) 178,200
Changge (1982 C) 67,002
Changji (▲ 233,400) (1986 E) 110,500
Changqing (1982 C) 65,094
Changsha 1,230,000
Changshou (1985 E) 51,923
Changshu (▲ 998,000) (1986 E) 281,300
Changtu (1985 E) 49,937
Changyi (1982 C) 64,513
Changzhi (▲ 463,400) (1986 E) 273,000
Changzhou (Changchow) (1986 E) 522,700
Chaoan (▲ 1,214,500) (1986 E) 265,400
Chaoxian (▲ 739,500) (1986 E) 116,800
Chaoyang, Guangdong prov. (1985 E) 85,968
Chaoyang, Liaoning prov. (▲ 318,900) (1986 E) 180,300
Chengde (▲ 330,400) (1986 E) 226,600
Chengdu (Chengtu) (▲ 2,960,000) 1,884,000
Chenghai (1985 E) 50,631
Chenxian (▲ 191,900) (1986 E) 143,500
Chifeng (Ulanhad) (▲ 882,900) (1986 E) 299,000
Chongqing (Chungking) (▲ 2,890,000) 2,502,000
Chuxian (▲ 365,000) (1986 E) 113,300
Chuxiong (▲ 379,400) (1986 E) 67,700
Da'an (1985 E) 70,552
Dachangzhen (1975 U) 50,000
Dalian (Dairen) 2,280,000
Danyang (1985 E) 48,449
Daqing (▲ 880,000) 640,000
Dashiqiao (1985 E) 68,898
Datong (1985 E) 55,529
Datong (▲ 1,040,000) 810,000
Dawa (1985 E) 142,581
Daxian (▲ 209,400) (1986 E) 142,000
Dehui (1985 E) 60,247
Dengfeng (1982 C) 49,746
Deqing (1982 C) 48,726
Deyang (▲ 753,400) (1986 E) 184,800
Dezhou (▲ 276,200) (1986 E) 161,300
Didao (1975 U) 50,000
Dinghai (1985 E) 50,161
Dongchuan (Xincun) (▲ 275,100) (1986 E) 67,400
Dongguan (▲ 1,208,500) (1986 E) 254,900
Dongsheng (▲ 121,300) (1986 E) 57,500
Dongtai (1985 E) 65,788
Dongying (▲ 514,400) (1986 E) 178,100
Dukou (▲ 551,200) (1986 E) 380,200
Dunhua (▲ 448,000) (1986 E) 217,100
Duyun (▲ 386,600) (1986 E) 123,800
Echeng (▲ 938,000) (1986 E) 217,400
Enshi (▲ 679,000) (1986 E) 84,300
Ergun Zuoqi (1985 E) 55,970
Feixian (1982 C) 73,246
Fengcheng (1985 E) 66,745
Foshan (▲ 312,700) (1986 E) 243,500
Fujin (1985 E) 60,948
Fuling (▲ 973,500) (1986 E) 166,300
Fushun (Funan) 1,290,000
Fuxian (Wafangdian) (▲ 960,700) (1986 E) 246,200
Fuxinshi 700,000
Fuyang (▲ 195,200) (1986 E) 143,400
Fuyu, Heilongjiang prov. (1985 E) 48,670
Fuyu, Jilin prov. (1985 E) 98,373
Fuzhou, Fujian prov. (▲ 1,240,000) 910,000
Fuzhou, Jiangxi prov. (▲ 171,800) (1986 E) 106,700
Gaixian (1985 E) 67,587
Ganhe (1985 E) 48,128
Ganzhou (▲ 346,000) (1986 E) 191,600
Gaoqing (Tianzhen) (1982 C) 70,411
Gaoyou (1985 E) 57,844
Gejiu (Kokiu) (▲ 341,700) (1986 E) 193,600
Golmud (1986 E) 60,300
Gongchangling (1982 C) 49,281
Guanghua (▲ 420,000) (1986 E) 104,400
Guangyuan (▲ 805,500) (1986 E) 162,200
Guangzhou (Canton) (▲ 3,420,000) 3,100,000
Guanxian, Shandong prov. (1982 C) 49,782
Guanxian, Sichuan prov. (1985 E) 65,039
Guilin (Kweilin) (▲ 457,500) (1986 E) 324,200
Guixian (1985 E) 61,970
Guiyang (Kweiyang) (▲ 1,430,000) 1,030,000
Haicheng (▲ 984,800) (1986 E) 210,700
Haifeng (1985 E) 50,401
Haikou (▲ 289,600) (1986 E) 209,200
Hailaer (1986 E) 180,000
Hailin (1985 E) 58,909
Hailong (Meihekou) (▲ 534,200) (1986 E) 117,500
Hailun (1985 E) 83,448
Haiyang (Dongcun) (1982 C) 77,098
Hami (Kumul) (▲ 270,300) (1986 E) 146,400
Hancheng (▲ 304,200) (1986 E) 66,600
Handan (▲ 1,030,000) 870,000
Hangu (1975 U) 100,000
Hangzhou (Hangchow) 1,290,000
Hanzhong (▲ 415,000) (1986 E) 151,700
Harbin 2,710,000
Hebi (▲ 321,600) (1986 E) 158,500
Hechi (▲ 266,800) (1986 E) 74,400
Hechuan (1985 E) 65,237
Hefei (▲ 930,000) 740,000
Hegang (1986 E) 588,300
Helong (1985 E) 62,665
Hengshui (▲ 286,500) (1986 E) 83,100
Hengyang (▲ 601,300) (1986 E) 419,200
Heze (Caozhou) (▲ 1,001,500) (1986 E) 115,400
Hohhot (▲ 830,000) 670,000
Hongjiang (▲ 67,000) (1986 E) 54,300
Horqin Youyi Qianqi (Ulan Hot) (▲ 192,100) (1986 E) 129,100
Hotan (▲ 122,800) (1986 E) 71,700
Houma (▲ 158,500) (1986 E) 67,000
Huadian (1985 E) 75,183
Huaian (1985 E) 65,673
Huaibei (▲ 447,200) (1986 E) 252,100
Huaide (▲ 899,400) (1986 E) 187,600
Huaihua (▲ 427,100) (1986 E) 102,000
Huainan (▲ 1,110,000) 700,000
Huaiyin (Wangying) (▲ 382,500) (1986 E) 201,700
Huanan (1985 E) 66,596
Huanggang (1982 C) 65,961
Huangshi (1986 E) 451,900
Huayun (Huarong) (▲ 313,500) (1986 E) 81,000
Huinan (Chaoyang) (1985 E) 52,429
Huizhou (▲ 182,100) (1986 E) 117,000
Hulan (1985 E) 74,989
Hunjiang (Badaojiang) (▲ 687,700) (1986 E) 442,600
Huzhou (▲ 964,400) (1986 E) 208,500
Jiading (1985 E) 60,718
Jiamusi (Kiamusze) (▲ 557,700) (1986 E) 429,800
Jian (▲ 184,300) (1986 E) 132,200
Jiangling (1985 E) 77,887
Jiangmen (▲ 231,700) (1986 E) 168,800
Jiangyin (1985 E) 66,476
Jiangyou (1985 E) 72,663
Jianou (1985 E) 55,180
Jiaohe (1985 E) 51,504
Jiaojiang (▲ 385,200) (1986 E) 82,300
Jiaoxian (1985 E) 51,869
Jiaozuo (▲ 509,900) (1986 E) 335,400
Jiawang (1975 U) 50,000
Jiaxing (▲ 686,500) (1986 E) 210,200
Jiayuguan (▲ 102,100) (1986 E) 73,800
Jiexiu (1985 E) 51,300
Jieyang (1985 E) 98,531
Jilin (Kirin) 1,200,000
Jinan (Tsinan) (▲ 2,140,000) 1,546,000
Jinchang (Baijiazui) (▲ 136,000) (1986 E) 90,500
Jincheng (▲ 612,700) (1986 E) 99,900
Jingdezhen (Kingtechen) (▲ 569,700) (1986 E) 304,000
Jingmen (▲ 946,500) (1986 E) 227,000
Jinhua (▲ 799,900) (1986 E) 147,800
Jining, Nei Monggol prov. (1986 E) 163,300
Jining, Shandong prov. (▲ 765,700) (1986 E) 222,600
Jinshi (▲ 219,700) (1986 E) 73,700
Jinxi (▲ 634,300) (1986 E) 223,100
Jinxian (1985 E) 95,761
Jinzhou (Chinchou) (▲ 810,000) 710,000
Jishou (▲ 194,500) (1986 E) 59,500
Jishu (1985 E) 75,587
Jiujiang (▲ 382,300) (1986 E) 248,500
Jiuquan (Suzhou) (▲ 269,900) (1986 E) 56,300
Jiutai (1985 E) 63,021
Jixi (▲ 820,000) 700,000
Jixian (1985 E) 59,725
Juancheng (1982 C) 54,110
Junan (Shizilu) (1982 C) 90,222
Junxian (▲ 423,400) (1986 E) 97,000
Juxian (1982 C) 51,666
Kaifeng (▲ 629,100) (1986 E) 458,800
Kaili (▲ 342,100) (1986 E) 96,600
Kaiping (1985 E) 54,145
Kaiyuan (▲ 342,100) (1986 E) 96,600
Kaiyuan (1985 E) 85,762
Karamay (1986 E) 185,300
Kashi (▲ 194,500) (1986 E) 146,300
Keshan (1985 E) 65,088
Korla (▲ 219,000) (1986 E) 129,400
Kunming (▲ 1,550,000) 1,310,000
Kuqa (1985 E) 63,847
Kuytun (1986 E) 60,200
Laiwu (▲ 1,041,800) (1986 E) 143,500
Langxiang (1985 E) 64,658
Lanxi (1985 E) 53,236
Lanxi (▲ 606,800) (1986 E) 70,500
Lanzhou (Lanchow) (▲ 1,420,000) 1,297,000
Lechang (1986 E) 56,913
Lengshuijiang (▲ 277,600) (1986 E) 101,700
Lengshuitan (▲ 362,000) (1986 E) 60,900
Leshan (▲ 972,300) (1986 E) 307,300
Lhasa (▲ 107,700) (1986 E) 84,400
Lianyungang (Xinpu) (▲ 459,400) (1986 E) 288,000
Liaocheng (▲ 724,300) (1986 E) 119,000
Liaoyang (▲ 576,900) (1986 E) 442,600
Liaoyuan (1986 E) 370,400
Liling (▲ 856,300) (1986 E) 107,100
Linfen (▲ 530,100) (1986 E) 157,600
Lingling (▲ 515,300) (1986 E) 72,700
Lingyuan (1985 E) 66,825
Linhai (1985 E) 52,653
Linhe (▲ 365,900) (1986 E) 99,800
Linkou (1985 E) 52,936
Linqing (▲ 603,000) (1986 E) 87,000
Linqu (1982 C) 84,196
Linxia (▲ 150,200) (1986 E) 72,900
Linyi (▲ 1,365,000) (1986 E) 190,000
Liuzhou 680,000
Longjiang (1985 E) 51,156
Longyan (▲ 378,500) (1986 E) 114,500
Loudi (▲ 254,300) (1986 E) 84,200
Lu'an (▲ 163,400) (1986 E) 122,600
Lufeng (1985 E) 53,015
Luohe (▲ 159,100) (1986 E) 102,300
Luoyang (Loyang) (▲ 1,090,000) 760,000
Luzhou (▲ 360,300) (1986 E) 237,800

C Census. E Official estimate. U Unofficial estimate.
• Largest city in country.
★ Population or designation of metropolitan area, including suburbs (see headnote).
▲ Population of an entire municipality, commune, or district, including rural area.

Maanshan (▲ 367,000) (1986 E) ... 258,900
Manzhouli (1986 E) ... 116,600
Maoming (▲ 434,900) (1986 E) ... 118,600
Meixian (▲ 740,600) (1986 E) ... 169,100
Mengxian ... 55,000
Mengyin (1982 C) ... 70,602
Mianyang, Sichuan prov. (▲ 848,500) (1986 E) ... 233,900
Minhang (1975 U) ... 60,000
Mishan (1985 E) ... 54,919
Mixian (1982 C) ... 64,776
Mudanjiang ... 650,000
Nahe (1985 E) ... 49,725
N'aizishen (1985 E) ... 51,982
Nancha (1975 U) ... 50,000
Nanchang (▲ 1,260,000) ... 1,090,000
Nanchong (▲ 238,100) (1986 E) ... 158,000
Nanjing (Nanking) ... 2,390,000
Nanning (▲ 1,000,000) ... 720,000
Nanpiao (1982 C) ... 67,274
Nanping (▲ 420,800) (1986 E) ... 157,100
Nantong (▲ 411,000) (1986 E) ... 308,800
Nanyang (▲ 294,800) (1986 E) ... 199,400
Neihuang (1982 C) ... 56,039
Neijiang (▲ 298,500) (1986 E) ... 191,100
Ning'an (1985 E) ... 49,334
Ningbo (▲ 1,050,000) ... 570,000
Ningyang (1982 C) ... 55,424
Nong'an (1985 E) ... 55,966
Nunjiang (1985 E) ... 59,276
Orogen Zizhiqi (1985 E) ... 48,042
Panshan (▲ 343,100) (1986 E) ... 248,100
Panshi (1985 E) ... 59,270
Pingdingshan (▲ 819,900) (1986 E) ... 363,200
Pingliang (▲ 362,500) (1986 E) ... 85,400
Pingxiang (▲ 1,286,700) (1986 E) ... 368,700
Pingyi (1982 C) ... 89,373
Pingyin (1982 C) ... 62,827
Potou (▲ 456,100) (1986 E) ... 59,000
Puqi (1985 E) ... 65,239
Putian (▲ 265,400) (1986 E) ... 64,600
Putuo (1985 E) ... 50,962
Puyang (▲ 1,086,100) (1986 E) ... 131,000
Qian Gorlos (1985 E) ... 79,494
Qingdao (Tsingtao) ... 1,300,000
Qingjiang (▲ 246,617) (1982 C) ... 150,000
Qingyuan (1985 E) ... 51,756
Qinhuangdao (Chinwangtao) (★ 436,000) (1986 E) ... 307,500
Qinzhou (▲ 923,400) (1986 E) ... 97,100
Qiqihar (Tsitsihar) (▲ 1,330,000) ... 1,180,000
Qitaihe (▲ 309,900) (1986 E) ... 166,400
Qixia (1982 C) ... 54,158
Qixian (1982 C) ... 53,041
Quanzhou (Chuanchou) (▲ 436,000) (1986 E) ... 157,000
Qujing (▲ 758,000) (1986 E) ... 135,000
Quxian (▲ 704,800) (1986 E) ... 124,000
Raoping (1985 E) ... 54,831
Rizhao (▲ 970,300) (1986 E) ... 93,300
Rongcheng (1982 C) ... 52,878
Rugao (1985 E) ... 50,643
Ruian (1985 E) ... 57,993
Sanmenxia (Shanxian) (▲ 150,000) (1986 E) ... 79,000
Sanming (▲ 214,300) (1986 E) ... 144,900
• Shanghai (★ 9,300,000) ... 7,220,000
Shangqiu (Zhuji) (▲ 199,400) (1986 E) ... 135,400
Shangrao (▲ 142,500) (1986 E) ... 113,000
Shangshui (1982 C) ... 50,191
Shantou (Swatow) (▲ 790,000) ... 560,000
Shanwei (1985 E) ... 61,234
Shaoguan (1986 E) ... 363,100
Shaowu (▲ 266,700) (1986 E) ... 81,400
Shaoxing (▲ 250,900) (1986 E) ... 167,100
Shaoyang (▲ 465,900) (1986 E) ... 218,600
Shashi (1986 E) ... 253,700
Shenxian (1982 C) ... 50,208
Shenyang (Mukden) (▲ 4,370,000) ... 3,910,000
Shenzhen (▲ 231,900) (1986 E) ... 189,600
Shiguaigou (1975 U) ... 50,000
Shihezi (▲ 549,300) (1987 E) ... 304,700
Shijiazhuang ... 1,220,000
Shiyan (▲ 332,600) (1986 E) ... 227,300
Shizuishan (▲ 317,400) (1986 E) ... 225,500
Shouguang (1982 C) ... 83,400
Shuangcheng (1985 E) ... 91,163
Shuangliao (1985 E) ... 67,326
Shuangyashan (1986 E) ... 427,300
Shuicheng (▲ 2,216,500) (1986 E) ... 363,500
Shulan (1986 E) ... 50,582
Shunde (1985 E) ... 50,262
Siping (▲ 357,800) (1986 E) ... 280,100
Sishui (1982 C) ... 82,990
Songjiang (1985 E) ... 71,864
Songjianghe (1985 E) ... 53,023
Suihua (▲ 732,100) (1986 E) ... 200,400
Suileng (1985 E) ... 68,399
Suining (▲ 1,174,900) (1986 E) ... 118,500
Suixian (▲ 1,281,600) (1986 E) ... 187,700
Suqian (1985 E) ... 50,742
Suxian (▲ 218,600) (1986 E) ... 123,300
Suzhou (Soochow) ... 740,000
Tai'an (▲ 1,325,400) (1986 E) ... 215,900
Taiyuan (▲ 1,980,000) ... 1,700,000
Taizhou (▲ 210,800) (1987 E) ... 143,200
Tancheng (1982 C) ... 61,857
Tangshan (▲ 1,440,000) ... 1,080,000
Tao'an (1985 E) ... 76,269
Tengxian (1985 E) ... 53,254
Tianjin (Tientsin) (▲ 5,540,000) ... 4,950,000
Tianshui (▲ 953,200) (1986 E) ... 209,500
Tiefa (▲ 146,367) (1982 C) ... 60,000
Tieli (1985 E) ... 102,527
Tieling (▲ 454,100) (1986 E) ... 326,100
Tongchuan (▲ 393,200) (1986 E) ... 268,900
Tonghua (▲ 367,400) (1986 E) ... 290,200
Tongliao (▲ 253,100) (1986 E) ... 190,100
Tongling (▲ 216,400) (1986 E) ... 182,900
Tongren (1985 E) ... 50,307
Tongxian (1985 E) ... 97,168
Tumen (▲ 99,700) (1986 E) ... 77,600
Tunxi (▲ 104,500) (1986 E) ... 61,800
Turpan (▲ 196,800) (1986 E) ... 52,300
Ürümqi ... 1,060,000
Wangkui (1985 E) ... 52,021
Wangqing (1985 E) ... 61,237
Wanxian (▲ 280,800) (1986 E) ... 138,700
Weifang (▲ 1,042,200) (1986 E) ... 312,500
Weihai (▲ 220,800) (1986 E) ... 83,000
Weinan (▲ 699,400) (1986 E) ... 111,300
Weishan (Xiazhen) (1982 C) ... 57,932
Weixian (Hanting) (1982 C) ... 50,180
Wenzhou (▲ 530,600) (1986 E) ... 372,200
Wuchang (1985 E) ... 64,403
Wuhai (1986 E) ... 266,000
Wuhan ... 3,570,000
Wuhu (▲ 502,200) (1986 E) ... 396,000
Wulian (Hongning) (1982 C) ... 51,718
Wusong (1982 C) ... 64,017
Wuwei (Liangzhou) (▲ 804,000) (1986 E) ... 115,500
Wuxi (Wuhsi) ... 880,000
Wuzhong (▲ 402,400) (1986 E) ... 48,600
Wuzhou (Wuchow) (▲ 261,500) (1986 E) ... 194,800
Xiaguan (▲ 395,800) (1986 E) ... 112,100
Xiamen (Amoy) (▲ 546,400) (1986 E) ... 343,700
Xi'an (Sian) (▲ 2,580,000) ... 2,210,000
Xiangfan (▲ 421,200) (1986 E) ... 314,900
Xiangtan (▲ 511,100) (1986 E) ... 389,500
Xianning (▲ 402,200) (1986 E) ... 122,200
Xianyang (▲ 641,800) (1986 E) ... 285,900
Xiaogan (▲ 1,204,400) (1986 E) ... 125,500
Xiaoshan (1985 E) ... 63,074
Xichang (▲ 161,000) (1986 E) ... 105,000
Xinghua (1985 E) ... 75,573
Xinglongzhen (1982 C) ... 52,961
Xingtai (▲ 350,800) (1986 E) ... 265,600
Xinhui (1985 E) ... 77,381
Xining (Sining) ... 620,000
Xinmin (1985 E) ... 47,900
Xintai (▲ 1,157,300) (1986 E) ... 171,400
Xinwen (Suncun) (1975 U) ... 50,000
Xinxian (▲ 398,600) (1986 E) ... 74,200
Xinxiang (▲ 540,500) (1986 E) ... 411,000
Xinyang (▲ 234,200) (1986 E) ... 169,100
Xinyu (▲ 610,600) (1986 E) ... 140,200
Xuancheng (1985 E) ... 52,387
Xuanhua (1975 U) ... 140,000
Xuanwei (1982 C) ... 70,081
Xuchang (▲ 247,200) (1986 E) ... 167,800
Xuguit Qi (Yakeshi) (1986 E) ... 390,000
Xuzhou (Süchow) ... 860,000
Yaan (▲ 277,600) (1986 E) ... 89,200
Yan'an (▲ 259,800) (1986 E) ... 86,700
Yancheng (▲ 1,251,400) (1986 E) ... 258,400
Yangcheng (1982 C) ... 57,255
Yangjiang (1986 E) ... 91,433
Yangquan (▲ 478,900) (1986 E) ... 295,100
Yangzhou (▲ 417,300) (1986 E) ... 321,500
Yanji (▲ 216,900) (1986 E) ... 175,000
Yanji (Longjing) (1985 E) ... 55,035
Yanling (1982 C) ... 52,679
Yantai (Chefoo) (▲ 717,300) (1986 E) ... 327,000
Yanzhou (1985 E) ... 48,972
Yaxian (Sanya) (▲ 321,700) (1986 E) ... 70,500
Yi'an (1986 E) ... 54,253
Yibin (Ipin) (▲ 636,500) (1986 E) ... 218,800
Yichang (Ichang) (1986 E) ... 410,500
Yichuan (1982 C) ... 58,914
Yichun, Heilongjiang prov. ... 840,000
Yichun, Jiangxi prov. (▲ 770,200) (1986 E) ... 132,600
Yidu (1985 E) ... 54,838
Yilan (1985 E) ... 50,436
Yima (▲ 84,800) (1986 E) ... 53,700
Yinan (Jiehu) (1982 C) ... 67,803
Yinchuan (▲ 396,900) (1986 E) ... 268,200
Yingchengzi (1985 E) ... 59,072
Yingkou (▲ 480,000) (1986 E) ... 366,900
Yingtan (▲ 116,200) (1986 E) ... 64,500
Yining (Kuldja) (▲ 232,000) (1986 E) ... 153,200
Yiyang (▲ 365,000) (1986 E) ... 155,300
Yiyuan (Nanma) (1982 C) ... 53,800
Yongan (▲ 269,000) (1986 E) ... 105,100
Yongchuan (1985 E) ... 70,444
Yuci (▲ 420,700) (1986 E) ... 171,000
Yueyang (▲ 411,300) (1986 E) ... 239,500
Yulin, Guangxi Zhuangzu prov. (▲ 1,228,800) (1986 E) ... 115,600
Yulin, Shaanxi prov. (1985 E) ... 51,610
Yumen (Laojunmiao) (▲ 160,100) (1986 E) ... 84,300
Yuncheng, Shandong prov. (1982 C) ... 54,262
Yuncheng, Shansi prov. (▲ 434,900) (1986 E) ... 87,000
Yunyang (1982 C) ... 54,903
Yushu (1985 E) ... 57,222
Yuyao (▲ 772,700) (1986 E) ... 169,700
Zaozhuang (▲ 1,592,000) (1986 E) ... 292,200
Zhangjiakou (Kalgan) (▲ 640,000) ... 500,000
Zhangye (▲ 394,200) (1986 E) ... 73,000
Zhangzhou (Longxi) (▲ 310,400) (1986 E) ... 159,400
Zhanhua (Fuguo) (1982 C) ... 48,193
Zhanjiang (▲ 920,900) (1986 E) ... 335,500
Zhaodong (1985 E) ... 99,836
Zhaoqing (Gaoyao) (▲ 187,600) (1986 E) ... 145,700
Zhaotong (▲ 546,600) (1986 E) ... 77,500
Zhaoyuan (1982 C) ... 56,389
Zhengzhou (Chengchow) (▲ 1,580,000) ... 1,150,000
Zhenjiang (1986 E) ... 412,400
Zhongshan (Shiqizhen) (▲ 1,059,700) (1986 E) ... 238,700
Zhoucun (1975 U) ... 50,000
Zhoukouzhen (▲ 220,400) (1986 E) ... 110,500
Zhuhai (▲ 155,000) (1986 E) ... 88,800
Zhumadian (▲ 149,500) (1986 E) ... 99,400
Zhuoxian (1985 E) ... 54,523
Zhuzhou (Chuchow) (▲ 499,600) (1986 E) ... 344,800
Zibo (Zhangdian) (▲ 2,370,000) ... 840,000
Zigong (Tzukung) (▲ 909,300) (1986 E) ... 361,700
Zixing (▲ 334,300) (1986 E) ... 97,100
Ziyang (1985 E) ... 57,349
Zouping (1982 C) ... 49,274
Zouxian (1985 E) ... 61,578
Zunyi (▲ 347,600) (1986 E) ... 236,600

COLOMBIA

1985 C ... 27,867,326

Cities and Towns

Armenia ... 187,130
Barrancabermeja ... 137,406
Barranquilla (★ 1,140,000) ... 899,781
Bello (★ Medellín) ... 212,861
Bucaramanga (★ 550,000) ... 352,326
Buenaventura ... 160,342
Buga ... 82,992
Cali (★ 1,400,000) ... 1,350,565
Cartagena ... 531,426
Cartago ... 97,791
Ciénaga ... 56,860
Cúcuta (★ 445,000) ... 379,478
Dos Quebradas (★ Pereira) ... 101,480
Duitama ... 56,390
Envigado (★ Medellín) ... 91,391
Florencia ... 66,430
Floridablanca (★ Bucaramanga) ... 143,824
Girardot ... 70,078
Ibagué ... 292,965
Itagüí (★ Medellín) ... 137,623
Magangué ... 49,160
Malambo (★ Barranquilla) ... 52,584
Manizales (★ 330,000) ... 299,352
Medellín (★ 2,095,000) ... 1,468,089
Montería ... 157,466
Neiva ... 194,556
Ocaña ... 51,443
Palmira ... 175,186
Pasto ... 197,407
Pereira (★ 390,000) ... 233,271
Popayán ... 141,964
• SANTA FE DE BOGOTÁ (★ 4,260,000) ... 3,982,941
Santa Marta ... 177,922
Sincelejo ... 120,537
Soacha (★ Santa Fe de Bogotá) ... 109,051
Sogamoso ... 64,437
Soledad (★ Barranquilla) ... 165,791
Tuluá ... 99,721
Tunja ... 93,792
Valledupar ... 142,771
Villa Rosario (★ Cúcuta) ... 63,615
Villavicencio ... 178,685

COMOROS / Al-Qumur / Comores

1990 E ... 452,742

Cities and Towns

• MORONI ... 23,432

CONGO

1984 C ... 1,912,429

Cities and Towns

• BRAZZAVILLE ... 585,812
Dolisie ... 49,134
Pointe-Noire ... 294,203

COOK ISLANDS

1986 C ... 18,155

Cities and Towns

• AVARUA ... 9,678

COSTA RICA

1988 E ... 2,851,000

Cities and Towns

Limón (▲ 62,600) ... 40,400
• SAN JOSÉ (★ 670,000) ... 278,600

COTE D'IVOIRE / Côte d' Ivoire

1983 E ... 9,300,000

Cities and Towns

• ABIDJAN ... 1,950,000
Bouaké ... 275,000
Daloa ... 70,000
Korhogo ... 125,000
Man ... 55,000
YAMOUSSOUKRO ... 80,000

CROATIA / Hrvatska

1987 E ... 4,673,517

Cities and Towns

Osijek (▲ 162,490) ... 106,800
Rijeka (▲ 199,282) ... 166,400
Split ... 197,074
• ZAGREB ... 697,925

CUBA

1987 E ... 10,288,000

Cities and Towns

Bayamo ... 108,716
Camagüey ... 265,588
Cárdenas (1981 C) ... 59,352
Cienfuegos ... 112,225
Guantánamo ... 179,091
Holguín ... 199,861
• LA HABANA (HAVANA) (★ 2,125,000) ... 2,036,800
Manzanillo (1981 C) ... 87,830
Matanzas ... 106,954
Palma Soriano (1981 C) ... 55,851
Pinar del Río ... 108,109
Santa Clara ... 182,349
Santiago de Cuba ... 364,554
Victoria de las Tunas (1985 E) ... 91,400

CYPRUS / Kıbrıs / Kípros

1982 C ... 512,097

Cities and Towns

Lemesós (Limassol) (★ 107,161) ... 74,782
• NICOSIA (LEVKOSÍA) (★ 185,000) ... 48,221

CYPRUS, NORTH / Kuzey Kıbrıs

1985 E ... 160,287

Cities and Towns

• NICOSIA (LEFKOŞA) ... 37,400

CZECH REPUBLIC / Česká Republika

1990 E ... 10,362,553

Cities and Towns

Brno (★ 450,000) ... 392,285
České Budějovice (★ 114,000) ... 99,428
Chomutov (★ 80,000) ... 55,735
Děčín (★ 72,000) ... 56,034
Frýdek-Místek (★ Ostrava) ... 66,791
Havířov (★ Ostrava) ... 92,037
Hradec Králové (★ 113,000) ... 101,302
Jihlava ... 54,855
Karlovy Vary (Carlsbad) ... 58,039
Karviná (★ ★ Ostrava) ... 69,521
Kladno (★ 88,500) ... 73,347
Liberec (★ 175,000) ... 104,256
Mladá Boleslav ... 49,195
Most (★ 135,000) ... 71,360
Olomouc (★ 126,000) ... 107,044
Opava (★ 77,500) ... 63,440
Ostrava (★ 760,000) ... 331,557
Pardubice ... 95,909
Plzeň (★ 210,000) ... 175,038
• PRAHA (PRAGUE) (★ 1,325,000) ... 1,215,656
Přerov ... 51,996
Prostějov ... 52,074
Teplice (★ 94,000) ... 55,287
Ústí nad Labem (★ 115,000) ... 106,499
Zlín (★ 124,000) ... 87,189

DENMARK / Danmark

1990 E ... 5,135,409

Cities and Towns

Ålborg (▲ 155,019) ... 114,000
Århus (▲ 261,437) ... 202,300
Esbjerg (▲ 81,504) ... 71,900
Frederiksberg (★ København) ... 85,611
Gentofte (★ København) ... 65,303
Gladsakse (★ København) ... 60,882
Helsingør (Elsinore) (★ København) ... 56,701
• KØBENHAVN (★ 1,685,000) ... 466,723
Kongens Lyngby (★ København) ... 49,317
Odense (▲ 176,133) ... 140,100
Randers ... 61,020

DJIBOUTI

1976 E ... 226,000

Cities and Towns

• DJIBOUTI ... 120,000

C Census. E Official estimate. U Unofficial estimate.
• Largest city in country.
★ Population or designation of metropolitan area, including suburbs (see headnote).
▲ Population of an entire municipality, commune, or district, including rural area.

DOMINICA

1984 E 77,000

Cities and Towns

• ROSEAU 9,348

DOMINICAN REPUBLIC / República Dominicana

1981 C 5,647,977

Cities and Towns

Barahona 49,334
La Romana 91,571
San Cristóbal 58,520
San Francisco de Macorís 64,906
San Juan [de la Maguana] 49,764
San Pedro de Macorís 78,562
Santiago [de los Caballeros] 278,638
• SANTO DOMINGO 1,313,172

ECUADOR

1987 E 9,923,000

Cities and Towns

Alfaro (★ Guayaquil) (1982 C) 51,023
Ambato 126,067
Cuenca 201,490
Esmeraldas 120,387
• Guayaquil (★ 1,580,000) 1,572,615
Ibarra (1982 C) 53,428
Loja (1982 C) 71,652
Machala 144,396
Manta 135,990
Milagro 102,884
Portoviejo 141,568
Quevedo (1982 C) 67,023
QUITO (★ 1,300,000) 1,137,705
Riobamba (1982 C) 75,455
Santo Domingo de los Colorados 104,059

EGYPT / Miṣr

1986 C 48,205,049

Cities and Towns

Abū Kabīr 69,509
Akhmīm 70,602
Al-'Arīsh 67,638
Al-Fayyūm 212,523
Al-Hawāmidīyah (★ Al-Qāhirah) 73,060
Al-Iskandarīyah (Alexandria) (★ 3,350,000) 2,917,327
Al-Ismā'īlīyah (★ 235,000) 212,567
Al-Jīzah (Giza) (★ Al-Qāhirah) 1,870,508
Al-Maḥallah al-Kubrā 358,844
Al-Manṣūrah (★ 375,000) 316,870
Al-Manzilah 55,090
Al-Maṭarīyah 74,554
Al-Minyā 179,136
• AL-QĀHIRAH (CAIRO) (★ 9,300,000) 6,052,836
Al-Uqṣur (Luxor) 125,404
Armant 54,650
Ashmūn 54,450
As-Sinbillāwayn 60,285
As-Suways (Suez) 326,820
Aswān 191,461
Asyūṭ 273,191
Az-Zaqāzīq 245,496
Bahtīm (★ Al-Qāhirah) 275,807
Banhā 115,571
Banī Suwayf 151,813
Bilbays 96,540
Bilqās Qism Awwal 73,162
Būlāq ad-Dakrūr (★ Al-Qāhirah) 148,787
Būr Sa'īd (Port Said) 399,793
Būsh 54,482
Damanhūr 190,840
Disūq 78,119
Dumyāṭ (Damietta) 89,498
Hawsh 'Īsā (1980 C) 53,619
Idkū 70,729
Jirjā 70,899
Kafr ad-Dawwār (★ Al-Iskandarīyah) 195,102
Kafr ash-Shaykh 102,910
Kafr az-Zayyāt 58,061
Kawm Umbū 52,131
Maghāghah 50,807
Mallawī 99,062
Manfalūṭ 52,644
Minūf 69,883
Mīt Ghamr (★ 100,000) 92,253
Qalyūb 86,684
Qinā 119,794
Rashīd (Rosetta) 52,014
Rummānah 50,014
Samālūṭ 62,404
Sāqiyat Makkī 51,062
Sawhāj 132,965
Shibīn al-Kawm 132,751
Shubrā al-Khaymah (★ Al-Qāhirah) 710,794
Sinnūris 55,323
Ṭahṭā 58,516
Ṭalkhā (★ Al-Manṣūrah) 55,757
Ṭanṭā 334,505
Warrāq al-'Arab (★ Al-Qāhirah) 127,108
Ziftā (★ ★ Mīt Ghamr) 69,050

EL SALVADOR

1985 E 5,337,896

Cities and Towns

Delgado (★ San Salvador) 67,684
Mejicanos (★ San Salvador) 91,465
Nueva San Salvador (★ San Salvador) 53,688
San Miguel 88,520
• SAN SALVADOR (★ 920,000) 462,652
Santa Ana 137,879
Soyapango (★ San Salvador) 60,000

EQUATORIAL GUINEA / Guinea Ecuatorial

1983 C 300,000

Cities and Towns

• MALABO 31,630

ERITREA

1987 E 2,951,100

Cities and Towns

• ASMERA (1988 E) 319,353
Mitsiwa (1984 C) 15,441

ESTONIA / Eesti

1989 C 1,573,000

Cities and Towns

Kohtla-Järve (1987 E) 78,000
Narva (1987 E) 81,000
Pärnu (1987 E) 53,000
• TALLINN 482,000
Tartu 114,000

ETHIOPIA / Ityopiya

1987 E 43,004,600

Cities and Towns

• ADIS ABEBA (★ 1,500,000) (1988 E) 1,686,300
Akaki Beseka (★ Adis Abeba) 54,146
Bahir Dar 54,800
Debre Zeyit 51,143
Dese 68,848
Dire Dawa (1988 E) 117,042
Gonder 68,958
Harer 62,160
Jima 60,992
Mekele 61,583
Nazret 76,284

FAEROE ISLANDS / Føroyar

1990 E 47,946

Cities and Towns

• TÓRSHAVN 14,767

FALKLAND ISLANDS

1986 C 1,916

Cities and Towns

• STANLEY 1,200

FIJI

1986 C 715,375

Cities and Towns

Lautoka (★ 39,057) 28,728
• SUVA (★ 141,273) 69,665

FINLAND / Suomi

1988 E 4,938,602

Cities and Towns

Espoo (Esbo) (★ Helsinki) 164,569
Hämeenlinna 42,486
• HELSINKI (HELSINGFORS) (★ 1,040,000) 490,034
Joensuu 47,099
Jyväskylä (★ 93,000) 65,719
Kotka 57,745
Kouvola (★ 53,821) 31,933
Kuopio 78,916
Lahti (★ 108,000) 74,300
Lappeenranta (▲ 53,780) 47,400
Oulu (★ 121,000) 98,582
Pori 77,395
Tampere (★ 241,000) 170,533
Turku (Åbo) (★ 228,000) 160,456
Vaasa (Vasa) 53,737
Vantaa (Vanda) (★ Helsinki) 149,063

FRANCE

1982 C 54,334,871

Cities and Towns

Aix-en-Provence (★ 126,552) 121,327
Ajaccio 54,089
Albi (★ 60,181) 45,947
Alès (★ 70,180) 43,268
Amiens (★ 154,498) 131,332
Angers (★ 195,859) 136,038
Angoulême (★ 103,552) 46,197
Annecy (★ 112,632) 49,965
Antibes (★ ★ Cannes) 62,859
Antony (★ Paris) 54,610
Argenteuil (★ Paris) 95,347
Arras (★ 80,477) 41,736
Asnières [-sur-Seine] (★ Paris) 71,077
Aubervilliers (★ Paris) 67,719
Aulnay-sous-Bois (★ Paris) 75,996
Avignon (★ 174,264) 89,132
Bayonne (★ 127,477) 41,381
Beauvais (★ 55,817) 52,365
Belfort (★ 76,221) 51,206
Besançon (★ 120,772) 113,283
Béthune (★ 258,383) 25,508
Béziers (★ 81,347) 76,647
Bordeaux (★ 640,012) 208,159
Boulogne-Billancourt (★ Paris) 102,582
Boulogne-sur-Mer (★ 98,566) 47,653
Bourges (★ 92,202) 76,432
Brest (★ 201,145) 156,060
Brive-la-Gaillarde (★ 64,301) 51,511
Caen (★ 183,526) 114,068
Calais (★ 100,823) 76,527
Cannes (★ 295,525) 72,259
Châlons-sur-Marne (★ 63,061) 51,137
Chalon-sur-Saône (★ 78,064) 56,194
Chambéry (★ 96,163) 53,427
Champigny-sur-Marne (★ Paris) 76,176
Charleville-Mézières (★ 67,694) 58,667
Châteauroux (★ 66,851) 51,942
Cherbourg (★ 85,485) 28,442
Cholet 55,524
Clermont-Ferrand (★ 256,189) 147,361
Colmar (★ 82,468) 62,483
Colombes (★ Paris) 78,777
Courbevoie (★ Paris) 59,830
Créteil (★ Paris) 71,693
Dieppe (★ 41,812) 35,957
Dijon (★ 215,865) 140,942
Douai (★ 202,366) 42,576
Drancy (★ Paris) 60,183
Dunkerque (★ 195,705) 73,120
Épinay-sur-Seine (★ Paris) 50,314
Fontenay-sous-Bois (★ Paris) 52,627
Forbach (★ 99,606) 27,187
Grenoble (★ 392,021) 156,637
Hagondange (★ 119,669) 9,091
Ivry-sur-Seine (★ Paris) 55,699
La Rochelle (★ 102,143) 75,840
La Seyne [-sur-Mer] (★ Toulon) 57,659
Laval (★ 55,984) 50,360
Le Havre (★ 254,595) 199,388
Le Mans (★ 191,080) 147,697
Levallois-Perret (★ Paris) 53,500
Lille (★ 1,020,000) 168,424
Limoges (★ 171,689) 140,400
Lorient (★ 104,025) 62,554
Lyon (★ 1,275,000) 413,095
Maisons-Alfort (★ Paris) 51,065
Mantes-la-Jolie (★ 170,265) 43,564
Marseille (★ 1,225,000) 874,436
Maubeuge (★ 105,714) 36,061
Melun (★ 82,479) 35,005
Mérignac (★ Bordeaux) 51,306
Metz (★ 186,437) 114,232
Montbéliard (★ 128,194) 31,836
Montluçon (★ 67,963) 49,912
Montpellier (★ 221,307) 197,231
Montreuil-sous-Bois (★ Paris) 93,368
Mulhouse (Mülhausen) (★ 220,613) 112,157
Nancy (★ 306,982) 96,317
Nanterre (★ Paris) 88,578
Nantes (★ 464,857) 240,539
Neuilly-sur-Seine (★ Paris) 64,170
Nice (★ 449,496) 337,085
Nîmes (★ 132,343) 124,220
Niort (★ 61,959) 58,203
Orléans (★ 220,478) 102,710
• PARIS (★ 9,775,000) (1987 E) 2,078,900
Pau (★ 131,265) 83,790
Perpignan (★ 137,915) 111,669
Pessac (★ Bordeaux) 50,267
Poitiers (★ 103,204) 79,350
Quimper 56,907
Reims (★ 199,388) 194,656
Rennes (★ 234,418) 117,234
Roanne (★ 81,786) 48,705
Roubaix (★ ★ Lille) 101,602
Rouen (★ 379,879) 101,945
Rueil-Malmaison (★ Paris) 63,412
Saint-Brieuc (★ 83,900) 48,563
Saint-Chamond (★ 82,059) 40,267
Saint-Denis (★ Paris) 90,829
Saint-Étienne (★ 317,228) 204,955
Saint-Maur-des-Fossés (★ Paris) 80,811
Saint-Nazaire (★ 130,271) 68,348
Saint-Quentin (★ 71,887) 63,567
Sarcelles (★ Paris) 53,630
Strasbourg (★ 400,000) 248,712
Tarbes (★ 78,056) 51,422
Thionville (★ 138,034) 40,573
Toulon (★ 410,393) 179,423
Toulouse (★ 541,271) 347,995
Tourcoing (★ ★ Lille) 96,908
Tours (★ 262,786) 132,209
Troyes (★ 125,240) 63,581
Valence (★ 106,041) 66,356
Valenciennes (★ 349,505) 40,275
Vénissieux (★ Lyon) 64,804
Versailles (★ Paris) 91,494
Villejuif (★ Paris) 52,448
Villeneuve-d'Ascq (★ Lille) 59,527
Villeurbanne (★ Lyon) 115,960
Vitry-sur-Seine (★ Paris) 85,263

FRENCH GUIANA / Guyane française

1982 C 73,022

Cities and Towns

• CAYENNE 38,091

FRENCH POLYNESIA / Polynésie française

1988 C 188,814

Cities and Towns

• PAPEETE (★ 80,000) 23,555

GABON

1985 E 1,312,000

Cities and Towns

Franceville 58,800
Lambaréné 49,500
• LIBREVILLE 235,700
Port Gentil 124,400

GAMBIA

1983 C 696,000

Cities and Towns

• BANJUL (★ 95,000) 44,536

GEORGIA / Sakartvelo

1989 C 5,449,000

Cities and Towns

Batumi 136,000
Gori (1987 E) 62,000
Kutaisi 235,000
Poti (1977 E) 54,000
Rustavi (★ Tbilisi) 159,000
Suchumi 121,000
• TBILISI (★ 1,460,000) 1,260,000

GERMANY / Deutschland

1989 E 78,389,735

Cities and Towns

Aachen (★ 535,000) 233,255
Aalen (★ 80,000) 62,812
Ahlen 52,836
Altenburg 53,288
Arnsberg 73,912
Aschaffenburg (★ 145,000) 62,048
Augsburg (★ 405,000) 247,731
Baden-Baden 50,761
Bad Homburg (★ Frankfurt am Main) 51,035
Bad Salzuflen (★ ★ Herford) 50,875
Bamberg (★ 120,000) 69,809
Bautzen 52,394
Bayreuth (★ 90,000) 70,933
Bergheim (★ Köln) 55,997
Bergisch Gladbach (★ Köln) 101,983
Bergkamen (★ Essen) 48,489
BERLIN (★ 3,825,000) 3,352,848
Bielefeld (★ 515,000) 311,946
Bitterfeld (★ 105,000) 20,513
Bocholt 67,565
Bochum (★ ★ Essen) 389,087
BONN (★ 570,000) 282,190
Bottrop (★ Essen) 116,363
Brandenburg 94,872
Braunschweig (★ 330,000) 253,794
Bremen (★ 800,000) 535,058
Bremerhaven (★ 190,000) 126,934
Castrop-Rauxel (★ Essen) 77,660
Celle 71,050
Chemnitz (★ 450,000) 311,765
Cottbus 128,639
Cuxhaven 55,249
Darmstadt (★ 305,000) 136,067
Delmenhorst (★ ★ Bremen) 72,901
Dessau (★ 140,000) 103,867
Detmold 66,809
Dinslaken (★ Essen) 63,246
Dormagen (★ Köln) 55,935
Dorsten (★ Essen) 75,518
Dortmund (★ ★ Essen) 587,328
Dresden (★ 670,000) 518,057
Duisburg (★ ★ Essen) 527,447
Düren (★ 110,000) 83,120
Düsseldorf (★ 1,190,000) 569,641
Eberswalde 54,822
Eisenhüttenstadt 53,048
Emden 49,803
Erfurt 220,016
Erlangen (★ ★ Nürnberg) 100,583
Eschweiler (★ ★ Aachen) 53,516
• Essen (★ 4,950,000) 620,594
Esslingen (★ Stuttgart) 90,537
Flensburg (★ 103,000) 85,830
Frankfurt am Main (★ 1,855,000) 625,258
Frankfurt an der Oder 87,863
Freiberg 51,341
Freiburg [im Breisgau] (★ 225,000) 183,979
Friedrichshafen 52,295
Fulda (★ 79,000) 54,320
Fürth (★ ★ Nürnberg) 98,832
Garbsen (★ Hannover) 59,225
Garmisch-Partenkirchen 25,908
Gelsenkirchen (★ ★ Essen) 287,255
Gera 134,834
Giessen (★ 160,000) 71,751
Gladbeck (★ Essen) 79,187
Göppingen (★ 155,000) 52,873
Görlitz 77,609
Goslar (★ 84,000) 45,614
Gotha 57,365
Göttingen 118,073
Greifswald 68,597
Grevenbroich (★ Düsseldorf) 59,204
Gummersbach 49,017
Gütersloh (★ ★ Bielefeld) 83,407
Hagen (★ ★ Essen) 210,640
Halle (★ 475,000) 236,044
Halle-Neustadt (★ Halle) 93,446
Hamburg (★ 2,225,000) 1,603,070
Hameln (★ 72,000) 57,642
Hamm 173,611
Hanau (★ ★ Frankfurt am Main) 84,300
Hannover (★ 1,000,000) 498,495
Hattingen (★ Essen) 56,242
Heidelberg (★ ★ Mannheim) 131,429
Heidenheim (★ 89,000) 48,497
Heilbronn (★ 230,000) 112,278
Herford (★ 120,000) 61,700
Herne (★ Essen) 174,664
Herten (★ Essen) 68,111
Hilden (★ Düsseldorf) 53,725
Hildesheim (★ 140,000) 103,512
Hof 50,938
Hoyerswerda 69,361
Hürth (★ Köln) 49,094
Ingolstadt (★ 138,000) 97,702
Iserlohn 93,337
Jena 108,010
Kaiserslautern (★ 138,000) 96,990
Karlsruhe (★ 485,000) 265,100
Kassel (★ 360,000) 189,156
Kempten (Allgäu) 60,052
Kerpen (★ Köln) 54,699
Kiel (★ 335,000) 240,675
Kleve 44,416
Koblenz (★ 180,000) 107,286
Köln (Cologne) (★ 1,760,000) 937,482
Konstanz 72,862
Krefeld (★ ★ Essen) 235,423
Landshut 57,194
Langenfeld (★ Düsseldorf) 50,777
Leipzig (★ 700,000) 545,307
Leverkusen (★ Köln) 157,358
Lippstadt 60,396
Lübeck (★ 260,000) 210,681
Lüdenscheid 76,118
Ludwigsburg (★ Stuttgart) 79,342
Ludwigshafen (★ ★ Mannheim) 158,478
Lüneburg 60,053
Lünen (★ Essen) 85,584
Magdeburg (★ 400,000) 290,579
Mainz (★ ★ Wiesbaden) 174,828
Mannheim (★ 1,400,000) 300,468
Marburg an der Lahn 70,905
Marl (★ Essen) 89,651

C Census. E Official estimate. U Unofficial estimate.
• Largest city in country.
★ Population or designation of metropolitan area, including suburbs (see headnote).
▲ Population of an entire municipality, commune, or district, including rural area.

Meerbusch (★ Düsseldorf) ... 50,452
Menden ... 54,899
Minden (★ 125,000) ... 75,169
Moers (★ Essen) ... 101,809
Mönchengladbach (★ 410,000) ... 252,910
Mülheim an der Ruhr (★ Essen) ... 175,454
München (Munich) (★ 1,955,000) ... 1,211,617
Münster ... 248,919
Neubrandenburg ... 90,471
Neumünster ... 79,574
Neunkirchen (★ 135,000) ... 50,784
Neuss (★ Düsseldorf) ... 143,976
Neustadt an der Weinstrasse ... 50,453
Neuwied (★ 150,000) ... 60,665
Norderstedt (★ Hamburg) ... 66,747
Nürnberg (★ 1,030,000) ... 480,078
Oberhausen (★ ★ Essen) ... 221,017
Offenbach (★ Frankfurt am Main) ... 112,450
Offenburg ... 51,730
Oldenburg ... 140,785
Osnabrück (★ 270,000) ... 154,594
Paderborn ... 114,148
Passau ... 49,137
Pforzheim (★ 220,000) ... 108,887
Plauen ... 77,593
Potsdam (★ Berlin) ... 142,862
Ratingen (★ Düsseldorf) ... 89,880
Ravensburg (★ 75,000) ... 44,146
Recklinghausen (★ Essen) ... 121,666
Regensburg (★ 205,000) ... 119,078
Remscheid (★ ★ Wuppertal) ... 120,979
Reutlingen (★ 160,000) ... 100,400
Rheine ... 69,324
Rosenheim ... 54,304
Rostock ... 253,990
Rüsselsheim (★ ★ Wiesbaden) ... 58,426
Saarbrücken (★ 385,000) ... 188,467
Saarlouis (★ 115,000) ... 37,662
Salzgitter ... 111,674
Sankt Augustin (★ Bonn) ... 50,230
Schwäbisch Gmünd ... 57,861
Schwedt ... 52,419
Schweinfurt (★ 110,000) ... 52,818
Schwerin ... 130,685
Schwerte (★ Essen) ... 49,017
Siegburg (★ 170,000) ... 34,402
Siegen (★ 200,000) ... 106,160
Sindelfingen (★ Stuttgart) ... 57,524
Solingen (★ ★ Wuppertal) ... 160,824
Stendal ... 49,906
Stolberg (★ ★ Aachen) ... 56,182
Stralsund ... 75,498
Stuttgart (★ 1,925,000) ... 562,658
Suhl ... 56,345
Trier (★ 125,000) ... 95,692
Troisdorf (★ ★ Siegburg) ... 62,011
Tübingen ... 76,046
Ulm (★ 210,000) ... 106,508
Unna (★ Essen) ... 61,989
Velbert (★ Essen) ... 88,058
Viersen (★ ★ Mönchengladbach) ... 76,163
Villingen-Schwenningen ... 76,258
Weimar ... 63,412
Wesel ... 57,986
Wetzlar (★ 105,000) ... 50,299
Wiesbaden (★ 795,000) ... 254,209
Wilhelmshaven (★ 135,000) ... 89,892
Wismar ... 58,058
Witten (★ Essen) ... 109,637
Wittenberg ... 53,358
Wolfenbüttel (★ ★ Braunschweig) ... 50,960
Wolfsburg ... 125,831
Worms (★ ★ Mannheim) ... 74,809
Wuppertal (★ 830,000) ... 371,283
Würzburg (★ 210,000) ... 125,589
Zweibrücken (★ 105,000) ... 33,377
Zwickau (★ 165,000) ... 121,749

GHANA

1984 C ... 12,205,574

Cities and Towns

• ACCRA (★ 1,250,000) ... 859,640
Ashiaman (★ Accra) ... 49,427
Cape Coast ... 86,620
Koforidua ... 54,400
Kumasi (★ 600,000) ... 348,880
Obuasi ... 60,146
Sekondi-Takoradi (★ 175,352) ... 93,882
Tafo (★ Kumasi) ... 50,432
Tamale (★ 168,091) ... 136,828
Tema (★ ★ Accra) ... 99,608
Teshie (★ Accra) ... 62,954

GIBRALTAR

1988 E ... 30,077

Cities and Towns

• GIBRALTAR ... 30,077

GREECE / Ellás

1981 C ... 9,740,417

Cities and Towns

Aiyáleo (★ Athínai) ... 81,906
• ATHÍNAI (ATHENS) (★ 3,027,331) ... 885,737
Áyios Dhimítrios (★ Athínai) ... 51,421
Galátsion (★ Athínai) ... 50,096
Ilioúpolis (★ Athínai) ... 69,560
Iráklion (★ 110,958) ... 102,398
Kalamariá (★ Thessaloníki) ... 51,676
Kallithéa (★ Athínai) ... 117,319
Kavála ... 56,375
Keratsínion (★ Athínai) ... 74,179
Khalándrion (★ Athínai) ... 54,320
Khaniá (★ 61,976) ... 47,451
Khíos (★ 29,742) ... 24,070
Koridhallós (★ Athínai) ... 61,313
Lárisa ... 102,048
Néa Ionía (★ Athínai) ... 59,202
Néa Liósia (★ Athínai) ... 72,427
Néa Smírni (★ Athínai) ... 67,408
Níkaia (★ Athínai) ... 90,368
Palaión Fáliron (★ Athínai) ... 53,273
Pátrai (★ 154,596) ... 142,163
Peristérion (★ Athínai) ... 140,858
Piraiévs (Piraeus) (★ ★ Athínai) ... 196,389
Spárti (Sparta) (★ 14,388) ... 12,975
Thessaloníki (Salonika) (★ 706,180) ... 406,413
Víron (★ Athínai) ... 57,880
Vólos (★ 107,407) ... 71,378
Zográfos (★ Athínai) ... 84,548

GREENLAND / Grønland / Kalaallit Nunaat

1990 E ... 55,558

Cities and Towns

• GODTHÅB (NUUK) ... 12,217

GRENADA

1981 C ... 89,088

Cities and Towns

• SAINT GEORGE'S (★ 25,000) ... 4,788

GUADELOUPE

1982 C ... 328,400

Cities and Towns

BASSE-TERRE (★ 26,600) ... 13,656
Les Abymes (★ Pointe-à-Pitre) ... 56,165
• Pointe-à-Pitre (★ 83,000) ... 25,310

GUAM

1980 C ... 105,979

Cities and Towns

• AGANA (★ 44,000) ... 896

GUATEMALA

1989 E ... 8,935,395

Cities and Towns

Escuintla ... 60,673
• GUATEMALA (★ 1,400,000) ... 1,057,210
Quetzaltenango ... 88,769

GUERNSEY

1986 C ... 55,482

Cities and Towns

• SAINT PETER PORT (★ 36,000) ... 16,085

GUINEA / Guinée

1986 E ... 6,225,000

Cities and Towns

• CONAKRY ... 800,000
Kankan ... 100,000
Kindia ... 80,000
Labé ... 110,000
Nzérékoré (1983 C) ... 55,356

GUINEA-BISSAU / Guiné-Bissau

1988 E ... 945,000

Cities and Towns

• BISSAU ... 125,000

GUYANA

1983 E ... 918,000

Cities and Towns

• GEORGETOWN (★ 188,000) ... 78,500

HAITI / Haïti

1987 E ... 5,531,802

Cities and Towns

Cap-Haïtien ... 72,161
• PORT-AU-PRINCE (★ 880,000) ... 797,000

HONDURAS

1988 C ... 4,376,839

Cities and Towns

Choluteca ... 53,799
El Progreso ... 55,523
La Ceiba ... 68,289
San Pedro Sula ... 279,356
• TEGUCIGALPA ... 551,606

HONG KONG

1986 C ... 5,395,997

Cities and Towns

Kowloon (Jiulong) (★ ★ Victoria) ... 774,781
Kwai Chung (★ Victoria) ... 131,362
New Kowloon (Xinjiulong) (★ ★ Victoria) ... 1,526,910
Sha Tin (★ Victoria) ... 355,810
Sheung Shui ... 87,206
Tai Po ... 119,679
Tsuen Wan (Quanwan) (★ Victoria) ... 514,241
Tuen Mun (★ Victoria) ... 262,458
• VICTORIA (★ 4,770,000) ... 1,175,860
Yuen Long ... 75,740

HUNGARY / Magyarország

1990 C ... 10,375,000

Cities and Towns

Békéscsaba (▲ 67,621) ... 58,800
• BUDAPEST (★ 2,565,000) ... 2,016,132
Debrecen ... 212,247
Dunaújváros ... 59,049
Eger ... 61,908
Győr ... 129,356
Kaposvár ... 71,793
Kecskemét (▲ 102,528) ... 81,200
Miskolc ... 196,449
Nagykanizsa ... 54,059
Nyíregyháza (▲ 114,166) ... 88,500
Pécs ... 170,119
Sopron ... 55,088
Szeged ... 175,338
Székesfehérvár ... 108,990
Szolnok ... 78,333
Szombathely ... 85,418
Tatabánya ... 74,271
Veszprém ... 63,902
Zalaegerszeg ... 62,221

ICELAND / Ísland

1987 E ... 247,357

Cities and Towns

• REYKJAVÍK (★ 137,941) ... 93,425

INDIA / Bharat

1981 C ... 685,184,692

Cities and Towns

Abohar ... 86,334
Achalpur ... 81,186
Ādilābād ... 53,482
Ādityapur (★ Jamshedpur) ... 53,421
Ādoni ... 108,939
Agartala ... 132,186
Āgra (★ 747,318) ... 694,191
Ahmadābād (★ 2,400,000) ... 2,059,725
Ahmadnagar (★ 181,210) ... 143,937
Ajmer ... 375,593
Akola ... 225,412
Akot ... 51,936
Alandur (★ Madras) ... 97,449
Alīgarh ... 320,861
Alijal ... 74,493
Allahābād (★ 650,070) ... 616,051
Alleppey ... 169,940
Alwar ... 145,795
Amalner ... 67,516
Amarnāth (★ Bombay) ... 96,347
Ambāla (★ 233,110) ... 104,565
Ambāla Sadar (★ Ambāla) ... 80,741
Ambattur (★ Madras) ... 115,901
Āmbūr ... 66,042
Amrāvati ... 261,404
Amreli (★ 58,241) ... 56,598
Amritsar ... 594,844
Amroha ... 112,682
Anakāpalle ... 73,179
Ānand ... 83,936
Anantapur ... 119,531
Arcot (★ 94,363) ... 38,836
Arkonam ... 59,405
Arni ... 49,365
Arrah ... 125,111
Aruppukkottai ... 72,245
Asansol (★ 1,050,000) ... 183,375
Ashoknagar-Kalyangarh (★ Hābra) ... 55,176
Āttūr ... 50,517
Aurangābād (★ 316,421) ... 284,607
Avadi (★ Madras) ... 124,701
Azamgarh ... 66,523
Badagara ... 64,174
Bāgalkot ... 67,858
Baharampur (★ 102,311) ... 92,889
Bahraich ... 99,889
Baidyabāti (★ Calcutta) ... 70,573
Bālāghāt (★ 53,183) ... 49,564
Balāngīr ... 54,943
Balasore ... 65,779
Ballālpur ... 61,398
Ballia ... 61,704
Bally (★ Calcutta) ... 147,735
Bally (★ Calcutta) ... 54,859
Bālurghāt (★ 112,621) ... 104,646
Bānda ... 72,379
Bangalore (★ 2,950,000) ... 2,476,355
Bangaon ... 69,885
Bānkura ... 94,954
Bansberia (★ Calcutta) ... 77,020
Bāpatla ... 55,347
Bārākpur (★ Calcutta) ... 115,253
Baranagar (★ Calcutta) ... 170,343
Bārāsat (★ Calcutta) ... 66,504
Bareilly (★ 449,425) ... 386,734
Barmer ... 55,554
Baroda (★ 744,881) ... 734,473
Bārsi ... 72,537
Bāruni ... 56,366
Basīrhāt ... 81,040
Basti ... 69,357
Batala (★ 101,966) ... 87,135
Beāwar ... 89,998
Begusarai (★ 68,305) ... 56,633
Behāla (South Suburban) (★ Calcutta) ... 378,765
Bela ... 49,932
Belgaum (★ 300,372) ... 274,430
Bellary ... 201,579
Berhampur ... 162,550
Bettiah ... 72,167
Bhadrakh ... 60,600
Bhadrāvati (★ 130,606) ... 53,551
Bhadrāvati New Town (★ ★ Bhadrāvati) ... 77,055
Bhadreswar (★ Calcutta) ... 58,858
Bhāgalpur ... 225,062
Bhandāra ... 56,025
Bharatpur ... 105,274
Bhathinda ... 124,453
Bhātpāra (★ Calcutta) ... 260,761
Bhaunagar (★ 308,642) ... 307,121
Bhilai (★ 490,214) ... 290,090
Bhīlwāra ... 122,625
Bhīmavaram ... 101,894
Bhind ... 74,515
Bhiwandi (★ Bombay) ... 115,298
Bhiwāni ... 101,277
Bhopāl ... 671,018
Bhubaneswar ... 219,211
Bhuj (★ 70,211) ... 69,693
Bhusāwal (★ 132,142) ... 123,133
Bīdar ... 78,856
Bihār ... 151,343
Bijāpur ... 147,313
Bijnor ... 56,713
Bīkaner (★ 287,712) ... 253,174
Bilāspur (★ 187,104) ... 147,218
Bīr ... 80,287
Bodhan ... 50,807
Bodināyakkanūr ... 59,168
Bokāro Steel City (★ 264,480) ... 224,099
Bombay (★ 9,950,000) ... 8,243,405
Botād ... 50,274
Brajrajnagar ... 54,033
Broach (★ 120,524) ... 110,070
Budaun ... 93,004
Budge Budge (★ Calcutta) ... 66,424
Bulandshahr ... 103,436
Bulsār (★ Bombay) ... 54,017
Burdwān ... 167,364
Burhānpur ... 140,896
• Calcutta (★ 11,100,000) ... 3,305,006
Calicut (★ 546,058) ... 394,447
Cambay ... 68,791
Cannanore (★ 157,797) ... 60,904
Chākdaha ... 59,308
Chakradharpur (★ 44,532) ... 29,272
Chālisgaon ... 59,342
Champdāni (★ Calcutta) ... 76,138
Chandannagar (★ Calcutta) ... 101,925
Chandausi ... 66,970
Chandīgarh (★ 422,841) ... 373,789
Chandrapur ... 115,777
Changanācheri ... 51,955
Channapatna ... 50,725
Chāpra ... 111,564
Chhatarpur ... 51,959
Chhindwāra ... 75,178
Chidambaram (★ 62,543) ... 55,920
Chikmagalūr ... 60,582
Chilakalurupet ... 61,645
Chīrāla ... 72,040
Chitradurga ... 74,580
Chittaranjan (★ 61,045) ... 50,748
Chittoor ... 86,230
Churu (★ 62,070) ... 61,811
Cochin (★ 685,836) ... 513,249
Coimbatore (★ 965,000) ... 704,514
Cooch Behār (★ 80,101) ... 62,127
Coonoor (★ 92,242) ... 44,750
Cuddalore ... 127,625
Cuddapah ... 103,125
Cuttack (★ 327,412) ... 269,950
Dabgram ... 76,402
Dāhod (★ 82,256) ... 55,256
Dāltonganj ... 51,952
Damoh (★ 76,758) ... 75,573
Dānāpur (★ Patna) ... 58,684
Darbhanga ... 176,301
Darjiling ... 57,603
Datia ... 49,386
Dāvangere ... 196,621
Dehra Dūn (★ 293,010) ... 211,416
Dehri ... 90,409
Delhi (★ 7,200,000) ... 4,884,234
Delhi Cantonment (★ Delhi) ... 85,166
Deoband ... 51,270
Deoghar (★ 59,120) ... 52,904
Deolāli (★ ★ Nāsik) ... 77,666
Deolāli Cantonment (★ Nāsik) ... 57,745
Deoria ... 55,720
Dewās ... 83,465
Dhamtari ... 55,797
Dhānbād (★ 825,000) ... 120,221
Dharmapuri ... 51,223
Dharmavaram ... 50,969
Dhorāji (★ 77,716) ... 76,556
Dhrāngadhra ... 51,280
Dhule ... 210,759
Dibrugarh (1971 C) ... 80,348
Dindigul ... 164,103
Dombivli (★ Bombay) ... 103,222
Durg (★ ★ Bhilai) ... 114,637
Durgāpur ... 311,798
Elūru ... 168,154
English Bāzār ... 79,010
Erode (★ 275,999) ... 142,252
Etah ... 53,784
Etāwah ... 112,174
Faizābād (★ 143,167) ... 101,873
Farīdābād New Township (★ Delhi) ... 330,864
Farrukhābād (★ 160,796) ... 145,793
Fatehpur, Rājasthān state ... 51,084
Fatehpur, Uttar Pradesh state ... 84,831
Fīrozābād ... 202,338
Fīrozpur (★ 105,840) ... 61,162
Gadag ... 117,368
Gandhidham (★ 61,489) ... 61,415
Gandhinagar ... 62,443
Gangāwati ... 58,735
Garden Reach (★ Calcutta) ... 191,107
Gārulia (★ Calcutta) ... 57,061
Gauhāti (★ 200,377) (1971 C) ... 123,783
Gaya ... 247,075
Ghāziābād (★ 287,170) ... 271,730
Ghāzīpur ... 60,725
Giridih ... 65,444
Godhra (★ 86,228) ... 85,784
Gonda ... 70,847
Gondal (★ 66,818) ... 66,096
Gondia ... 100,423
Gorakhpur (★ 307,501) ... 290,814
Gudivāda ... 80,198
Gudiyāttam (★ 80,674) ... 75,044
Gulbarga ... 221,325
Guna (★ 64,659) ... 60,255
Guntakal ... 84,599
Guntūr ... 367,699
Gurgaon (★ 100,877) ... 89,115
Gwalior (★ 555,862) ... 539,015
Hābra (★ 129,610) ... 74,434
Hājīpur ... 62,520
Haldwāni ... 77,300
Hālisahar (★ Calcutta) ... 95,579
Hānsi ... 50,365
Hanumāngarh ... 60,071
Hāpur ... 102,837
Hardoi ... 67,259
Hardwār (★ 145,946) ... 114,180
Harihar ... 52,334
Hassan ... 71,534
Hāthras ... 92,962
Hazāribāgh ... 80,155
Hindupur ... 55,901
Hinganghāt ... 59,075
Hisār (★ 137,369) ... 131,309
Hoshiārpur ... 85,648
Hospet (★ 115,351) ... 90,572
Howrah (★ Calcutta) ... 744,429
Hubli-Dhārwār ... 527,108
Hugli-Chinsurah (★ Calcutta) ... 125,193
Hyderābād (★ 2,750,000) ... 2,187,262
Ichalkaranji ... 133,751
Imphāl ... 156,622
Indore (★ 850,000) ... 829,327

C Census. E Official estimate. U Unofficial estimate.
• Largest city in country.
★ Population or designation of metropolitan area, including suburbs (see headnote).
▲ Population of an entire municipality, commune, or district, including rural area.

Itārsi (★ 69,619) 62,499
Jabalpur (★ 757,303) 614,162
Jabalpur Cantonment
(★ Jabalpur) 61,026
Jādabpur (★ Calcutta) 251,968
Jagdalpur (★ 63,632) 51,286
Jagtiāl 53,213
Jaipur (★ 1,025,000) 977,165
Jālgaon 145,335
Jālna 122,276
Jalpaiguri 61,743
Jamālpur 78,356
Jammu (★ 223,361) 206,135
Jāmnagar (★ 317,362) 277,615
Jamshedpur
(★ 669,580) 438,385
Jangoon 70,727
Jaridih (★ 101,946) 46,477
Jaunpur 105,140
Jetpur (★ 63,074) 62,806
Jeypore 53,981
Jhānsi (★ 284,141) 246,172
Jharia (★ ★ Dhānbād) 57,496
Jhārsuguda 54,859
Jīnd 56,748
Jodhpur 506,345
Jotacamund 78,277
Jullundur (★ 441,552) 408,186
Junāgadh (★ 120,416) 118,646
Kadaiyanallūr 60,306
Kadiri 52,774
Kaithal 58,385
Kākināda 226,409
Kālahasti 51,306
Kālol (★ Ahmadābād) 69,946
Kalyān (★ Bombay) 136,052
Kāmārhāti (★ Calcutta) 234,951
Kambam 50,340
Kāmthi (★ Nāgpur) 67,364
Kānchipuram
(★ 145,254) 130,926
Kānchrāpāra
(★ Calcutta) 88,798
Kānpur (★ 1,875,000) .. 1,481,789
Kānpur Cantonment
(★ Kānpur) 90,311
Kapūrthala 50,300
Karād 54,364
Kāraikkudi (★ 100,141) 66,993
Karīmnagar 86,125
Karnāl 132,107
Karūr (★ 93,810) 72,692
Kāsganj 61,402
Kashīpur 51,773
Katihār (★ 122,005) 104,781
Kayankulam 61,327
Kerkend (★ Dhānbād) 75,186
Khadki Cantonment
(★ Pune) 80,835
Khāmgaon 61,992
Khammam 98,757
Khandwa 114,725
Khanna 53,761
Kharagpur (★ 232,575) 150,475
Kharagpur Railway
Settlement
(★ Kharagpur) 82,100
Khargon 52,749
Khurja 67,119
Kishanganj 51,790
Kishangarh 62,032
Kolār 65,834
Kolār Gold Fields
(★ 144,385) 77,679
Kolhāpur (★ 351,392) 340,625
Konnagar (★ Calcutta) 51,211
Korba 83,387
Kota 358,241
Kottagūdem 94,894
Kottayam 64,431
Kovilpatti 63,964
Krishnanagar 98,141
Kumbakonam
(★ 141,794) 132,832
Kundla (★ 51,431) 49,740
Kurnool 206,362
Lakhīmpur 61,003
Lalitpur 55,756
Lātūr 111,986
Lucknow (★ 1,060,000) 895,721
Lucknow Cantonment
(★ Lucknow) 59,614
Ludhiāna 607,052
Machilīpatnam (Bandar) 138,530
Madanapalle 54,938
Madgaon (Margao)
(★ 64,858) 53,076
Madras (★ 4,475,000) .. 3,276,622
Madurai (★ 960,000) 820,891
Mahbūbnagar 87,503
Mahuva (★ 56,072) 53,625
Mainpuri 58,928
Mālegaon 245,883
Māler Kotla 65,756
Malkajgiri
(★ Hyderābād) 65,776
Mandasor 77,603
Mandya 100,285
Mangalore (★ 306,078) 172,252
Mango (★ Jamshedpur) 67,284
Manjeri 53,959
Manmād 51,439
Mannārgudi 51,738
Mathura (★ 160,995) 147,493
Maunath Bhanjan 86,326
Māyūram 67,675
Meerut (★ 536,615) 417,395
Meerut Cantonment
(★ Meerut) 94,210
Mehsāna (★ 73,024) 72,872

Melappālaiyam
(★ Tirunelveli) 57,683
Mettuppālaiyam 59,537
Mhow (★ 76,037) 70,130
Midnapore 86,118
Miraj (★ ★ Sāngli) 105,455
Mirzāpur 127,787
Modinagar (★ 87,665) 78,243
Moga 80,272
Mokāma 51,047
Monghyr 129,260
Morādābād (★ 345,350) 330,051
Morena 69,864
Mormugao 69,684
Morvi 73,327
Motihāri (★ 63,212) 57,911
Muktsar 50,941
Murwāra (★ 123,017) 77,862
Muzaffarnagar 171,816
Muzaffarpur 190,416
Mysore (★ 479,081) 441,754
Nabadwip (★ 129,800) 109,108
Nadiād 142,689
Nāgappattinam
(★ 90,650) 82,828
Nāgda 56,602
Nāgercoil 171,648
Nagīna 50,405
Nāgpur (★ 1,302,066) .. 1,219,461
Naihāti (★ Calcutta) 114,607
Najībābād 55,109
Nalgonda 62,458
Nānded 191,269
Nandurbār 65,394
Nandyāl 88,185
Nangi (★ Calcutta) 54,035
Narasaraopet 67,032
Nāsik (★ 429,034) 262,428
Navsāri (★ 129,266) 106,793
Nawābganj (★ 62,216) 51,518
Neemuch (★ 68,853) 65,860
Nellore 237,065
NEW DELHI (★ ★ Delhi) 273,036
Neyveli (★ 98,866) 88,000
Nizāmābād 183,061
North Bārākpur
(★ Calcutta) 81,758
North Dum Dum
(★ Calcutta) 96,418
Nowgong (1971 C) 56,537
Ongole 85,302
Orai 66,397
Outer Burnpur
(★ Asansol) 86,803
Pālanpur 61,262
Pālayankottai
(★ ★ Tirunelveli) 87,302
Pālghāt (★ 117,986) 111,245
Pāli 91,568
Pallavaram (★ Madras) 83,901
Palni (★ 68,389) 64,444
Pānchur (★ Calcutta) 51,223
Pandharpur 64,380
Pānihāti (★ Calcutta) 205,718
Pānīpat 137,927
Paramagudi 61,149
Parbhani 109,364
Pātan 79,196
Pathānkot 110,039
Patiāla (★ 206,254) 205,141
Patna (★ 1,025,000) 776,371
Pattukkottai 49,484
Phagwāra (★ 75,961) 72,499
Pīlībhīt 88,548
Pimpri-Chinchwad
(★ Pune) 220,966
Pollāchi (★ 114,971) 82,354
Pondicherry
(★ 251,420) 162,636
Ponmalai
(★ Tiruchchirāppalli) 55,995
Ponnūru Nidubrolu 50,206
Porbandar (★ 133,307) 115,182
Port Blair 49,634
Proddatūr 107,070
Pudukkottai 87,952
Pune (Poona)
(★ 1,775,000) 1,203,351
Pune Cantonment
(★ Pune) 85,986
Puri 100,942
Purnea (★ 109,875) 91,144
Purūlia 73,904
Quilon (★ 167,598) 137,943
Rabkavi Banhatti 51,693
Rāe Bareli 89,697
Rāichūr 124,762
Raiganj (★ 66,705) 60,343
Raigarh (★ 69,791) 68,060
Raipur 338,245
Rājahmundry
(★ 268,370) 203,358
Rājapālaiyam 101,640
Rajhara-Jharandalli 55,307
Rājkot 445,076
Rāj-Nāndgaon 86,367
Rājpura 58,645
Rāmpur 204,610
Rānāghāt (★ 83,744) 58,356
Rānchī (★ 502,771) 489,626
Rānībennur 58,118
Rānīganj (★ 119,101) 48,702
Ratlām (★ 155,578) 142,319
Raurkela (★ 322,610) 206,821
Raurkela Civil Township
(★ Raurkela) 96,000
Rewa 100,641
Rewāri 51,562
Rishra (★ Calcutta) 81,001

Robertson Pet (★ Kolār
Gold Fields) 61,099
Rohtak 166,767
Roorkee (★ 79,076) 61,851
Sāgar (★ 207,479) 160,392
Sahāranpur 295,355
Saharsa 57,580
Sahijpur Bogha
(★ Ahmadābād) 65,327
Salem (★ 518,615) 361,394
Sambalpur (★ 162,214) 110,282
Sambhal 108,232
Sāngli (★ 268,988) 152,339
Sāntipur 82,980
Sardarnagar
(★ Ahmadābād) 50,128
Sardārshahr (★ 56,388) 55,473
Sasarām 73,457
Sātāra 83,336
Satna (★ 96,667) 90,476
Saunda (★ 99,990) 70,780
Secunderābād
Cantonment
(★ Hyderābād) 135,994
Sehore 52,190
Seoni 54,017
Serampore (★ Calcutta) 127,304
Shāhjahānpur
(★ 205,095) 185,396
Shāmli 51,850
Shillong (★ 174,703) 109,244
Shimoga 151,783
Shivpuri 75,738
Sholāpur (★ 514,860) 511,103
Shrirampur 55,491
Sidhpur (★ 52,706) 51,953
Sīkar 102,970
Silchar (1971 C) 52,596
Silīguri 154,378
Simla 70,604
Sindri (★ ★ Dhānbād) 70,645
Sirsa 89,068
Sītāpur 101,210
Sivakāsi (★ 83,072) 59,827
Siwān 51,284
Sonīpat 109,369
South Dum Dum
(★ Calcutta) 230,266
Sri Gangānagar 123,692
Srīkākulam 68,145
Srīnagar (★ 606,002) 594,775
Srīrangam
(★ Tiruchchirāppalli) 64,241
Srīvilliputtūr 61,458
Sujāngarh 55,546
Surat (★ 913,806) 776,583
Surendranagar
(★ 130,602) 89,619
Tādepallegūdem 62,574
Tādpatri 53,920
Tāmbaram (★ Madras) 86,923
Tānda 54,474
Tanuku 53,618
Tellicherry (★ 98,704) 75,561
Tenāli 119,257
Tenkāsi 49,214
Thāna (★ Bombay) 309,897
Thānesar 49,052
Thanjāvūr 184,015
Theni-Allinagaram 53,018
Tindivanam 56,520
Tinsukia (1971 C) 54,911
Tiruchchirāppalli
(★ 609,548) 362,045
Tiruchengodu 53,941
Tirunelveli (★ 323,344) 128,850
Tirupati 115,292
Tiruppattūr 52,422
Tiruppur (★ 215,859) 165,223
Tiruvannāmalai 89,462
Tirūvottiyūr (★ Madras) 134,014
Titāgarh (★ Calcutta) 104,534
Tonk 77,653
Trichūr (★ 170,122) 77,923
Trivandrum (★ 520,125) 483,086
Tumkūr 108,670
Tuticorin (★ 250,677) 192,949
Udaipur 232,588
Udamalpet 54,852
Udgīr 50,564
Ujjain (★ 282,203) 278,454
Ulhāsnagar (★ Bombay) 273,668
Unnāo 75,983
Upleta 54,907
Uttarpara-Kotrung
(★ Calcutta) 79,598
Valparai 115,452
Vāniyambādi (★ 75,042) 59,107
Vārānasi (Benares)
(★ 925,000) 708,647
Vellore (★ 274,041) 174,247
Verāval (★ 105,307) 85,048
Vidisha 65,521
Vijayawāda (★ 543,008) 454,577
Vikramasingapuram 49,319
Villupuram 77,091
Virudunagar 68,047
Vishākhapatnam
(★ 603,630) 565,321
Vizianagaram 114,806
Warangal 335,150
Wardha 88,495
Yamunānagar
(★ 160,424) 109,304
Yavatmāl 89,071
Yemmiganur 50,701

INDONESIA

1980 C 147,490,298

Cities and Towns

Ambon (▲ 207,702) 111,914
Balikpapan (▲ 279,852) 208,040
Banda Aceh (Kuturaja) 71,868
Bandung (★ 1,800,000)
(1985 C) 1,633,000
Banjarmasin (1983 E) 424,000
Banyuwangi 90,378
Batang 49,328
Bekasi (★ Jakarta) 144,290
Binjai 71,444
Blitar (★ 100,000) 78,503
Bogor (★ 560,000) 246,946
Bojonegoro 57,483
Bukittinggi (▲ 70,691) 55,577
Cianjur 105,655
Cibinong 87,580
Cilacap 127,017
Cimahi (★ Bandung)
(1971 C) 72,367
Ciparay 66,854
Cirebon (★ 275,000) 223,504
Denpasar 159,233
Depok (★ Jakarta) 126,693
Garut 145,624
Genteng 59,481
Gorontalo (▲ 97,610) 63,554
Gresik 86,418
• JAKARTA
(★ 1,000,000)
(1989 E) 9,200,000
Jambi (▲ 230,046) 155,761
Jayapura (Sukarnapura) 60,641
Jember 171,284
Jombang 58,800
Karawang 72,195
Kediri (▲ 221,830) 176,261
Kisaran 58,129
Klangenang 64,013
Klaten 117,560
Kudus 154,478
Kupang 84,587
Lumajang 58,495
Madiun (★ 180,000) 150,562
Magelang (★ 160,000) 123,358
Majalaya 87,474
Malang (1983 E) 547,000
Manado 217,091
Mataram 210,485
Medan (1985 E) 2,110,000
Mojokerto 68,849
Padang (▲ 657,000)
(1983 E) 405,600
Padangsidempuan 56,984
Palangkaraya
(▲ 60,447) 51,686
Palembang (1983 E) 874,000
Pangkalpinang 90,078
Parepare (▲ 86,360) 62,865
Pasuruan (★ 125,000) 95,864
Pati 50,159
Pekalongan
(★ 260,000) 132,413
Pekanbaru 186,199
Pemalang 72,663
Pematangsiantar
(★ 175,000) 150,296
Ponorogo 55,523
Pontianak (1983 E) 343,000
Pringsewu 56,115
Probolinggo 100,296
Purwakarta 61,995
Purwokerto 143,787
Salatiga 85,740
Samarinda (▲ 264,012) 182,473
Semarang (1983 E) 1,206,000
Serang 78,209
Sibolga 59,466
Sidoarjo 56,090
Singaraja 53,368
Singkawang 58,693
Situbondo 58,299
Sorong 52,041
Subang 52,041
Sukabumi (★ 225,000) 109,898
Surabaya (1985 E) 2,345,000
Surakarta (★ 575,000)
(1983 E) 491,000
Taman 64,358
Tangerang 97,091
Tanjungkarang-
Telukbetung
(★ 375,000) 284,167
Tasikmalaya 192,267
Tebingtinggi (▲ 92,068) 69,569
Tegal (★ 340,000) 131,440
Tembilahan 52,140
Tulungagung 91,585
Ujungpandang
(Makasar) (1983 E) 841,000
Yogyakarta (★ 510,000)
(1983 E) 421,000

IRAN / Īrān

1986 C 49,445,010

Cities and Towns

Ābādān (1976 C) 296,081
Āghā Jārī (1982 E) 64,000
Ahar (1982 E) 52,000
Ahvāz 579,826
Āmol 118,242
Andīmeshk (1982 E) 53,000
Arāk 265,349
Ardabīl 281,973
Bābol 115,320
Bakhtarān
(Kermānshāh) 560,514
Bandar-e 'Abbās 201,642
Bandar-e Anzalī
(Bandar-e Pahlavī)
(1982 E) 83,000
Bandar-e Būshehr 120,787
Bandar-e Māh Shahr
(1982 E) 88,000
Behbahān (1982 E) 84,000
Bīrjand (1982 E) 68,000
Bojnūrd (1982 E) 82,000
Borāzjān (1982 E) 53,000
Borūjerd 183,879
Dezfūl 151,420
Do Rūd (1982 E) 52,000
Emāmshahr (Shāhrūd)
(1982 E) 68,000
Eṣfahān (★ 1,175,000) 986,753
Eslāmābād (1982 E) 71,000
Eslāmshahr (★ Tehrān) 215,129
Fasā (1982 E) 67,000
Gonbad-e Qābūs
(1982 E) 75,000
Gorgān 139,430
Hamadān 272,499
Īlām (1982 E) 75,000
Jahrom (1982 E) 68,000
Karaj (★ Tehrān) 275,100
Kāshān 138,599
Kāzerūn (1982 E) 63,000
Kermān 257,284
Khomeynīshahr
(★ Eṣfahān) 104,647
Khorramābād 208,592
Khorramshahr (1976 C) 146,709
Khvoy 115,343
Mahābād (1982 E) 63,000
Malāyer 103,640
Marāgheh 100,679
Marand (1982 E) 59,000
Marv Dasht (1982 E) 72,000
Mashhad 1,463,508
Masjed Soleymān 104,787
Mīāndoāb (1982 E) 52,000
Mīāneh (1982 E) 57,000
Najafābād 129,058
Neyshābūr 109,258
Orūmīyeh (Reẓā'īyeh) 300,746
Qā'emshahr 109,288
Qazvīn 248,591
Qom 543,139
Qomsheh (1982 E) 67,000
Qūchān (1982 E) 61,000
Rafsanjān (1982 E) 61,000
Rāmhormoz (1982 E) 53,000
Rasht 290,897
Sabzevār 129,103
Sanandaj 204,537
Saqqez (1982 E) 76,000
Sārī 141,020
Semnān (1982 E) 54,000
Shahr-e Kord (1982 E) 63,000
Shīrāz 848,289
Sīrjān (1982 E) 67,000
Tabrīz 971,482
• TEHRĀN
(★ 7,500,000) 6,042,584
Torbat-e Heydarīyeh
(1982 E) 62,000
Varāmīn (1982 E) 51,000
Yazd 230,483
Zābol (1982 E) 58,000
Zāhedān 281,923
Zanjān 215,261
Zarrīn Shahr (1982 E) 69,000

IRAQ / Al 'Irāq

1985 E 15,584,987

Cities and Towns

Ad-Dīwānīyah (1970 E) 62,300
Al-'Amārah 131,758
Al-Baṣrah 616,700
Al-Ḥillah 215,249
Al-Kūt 73,022
Al-Mawṣil 570,926
An-Najaf 242,603
An-Nāṣirīyah 138,842
Ar-Ramādī 137,388
As-Samāwah 75,293
As-Sulaymānīyah 279,424
• BAGHDĀD (1987 C) 3,841,268
Ba'qūbah 114,516
Irbīl 333,903
Karbalā' 184,574
Kirkūk (1970 E) 207,900

IRELAND / Éire

1986 C 3,540,643

Cities and Towns

Cork (★ 173,694) 133,271
• DUBLIN (BAILE ÁTHA
CLIATH)
(★ 1,140,000) 502,749
Dún Laoghaire
(★ Dublin) 54,715
Galway 47,104
Limerick (★ 76,557) 56,279
Waterford (★ 41,054) 39,529

ISLE OF MAN

1986 C 64,282

Cities and Towns

• DOUGLAS (★ 28,500) 20,368

C Census. E Official estimate. U Unofficial estimate.
• Largest city in country.

★ Population or designation of metropolitan area, including suburbs (see headnote).
▲ Population of an entire municipality, commune, or district, including rural area.

ISRAEL / Isrā'īl / Yisra'el

1989 E	4,386,000
Cities and Towns	
Al-Khalīl (Hebron) (1971 E)	43,000
Ashdod	74,700
Ashqelon	56,300
Bat Yam (★ Tel Aviv-Yafo)	133,100
Bayt Lahm (Bethlehem) (1971 E)	25,000
Be'ér Sheva (Beersheba)	113,200
Bene Beraq (★ Tel Aviv-Yafo)	109,400
Elat	24,700
Giv'atayim (★ Tel Aviv-Yafo)	45,600
Hefa (★ 435,000)	222,600
Herzliyya (★ Tel Aviv-Yafo)	71,600
Holon (★ Tel Aviv-Yafo)	146,100
Kefar Sava (★ Tel Aviv-Yafo)	54,800
Lod (Lydda) (★ Tel Aviv-Yafo)	41,300
Nābulus (1971 E)	64,000
Nazerat (Nazareth) (★ 77,000)	50,600
Netanya (★ Tel Aviv-Yafo)	117,800
Petah Tiqwa (★ Tel Aviv-Yafo)	133,600
Ra'ananna (★ Tel Aviv-Yafo)	49,400
Ramat Gan (★ Tel Aviv-Yafo)	115,700
Rehovot (★ Tel Aviv-Yafo)	72,500
Rishon leZiyyon (★ Tel Aviv-Yafo)	123,800
• Tel Aviv-Yafo (★ 1,735,000)	317,800
YERUSHALAYIM (AL-QUDS) (JERUSALEM) (★ 530,000)	493,500

ITALY / Italia

1987 E	57,290,519
Cities and Towns	
Afragola (★ Napoli)	59,397
Alessandria (▲ 96,014)	76,100
Altamura	54,784
Ancona	104,409
Andria	88,348
Arezzo (▲ 91,681)	74,200
Asti (▲ 75,459)	63,600
Avellino	56,407
Aversa (★ Napoli)	57,827
Bari (★ 475,000)	362,524
Barletta	86,954
Benevento (▲ 65,661)	54,400
Bergamo (★ 345,000)	118,959
Biella	51,788
Bitonto	51,962
Bologna (★ 525,000)	432,406
Bolzano	101,515
Brescia	199,286
Brindisi	92,280
Busto Arsizio (★ Milano)	78,056
Cagliari (★ 305,000)	220,574
Caltanissetta	62,352
Carpi (▲ 60,614)	49,500
Carrara (★ ★ Massa)	69,229
Caserta	65,974
Casoria (★ Napoli)	54,100
Castellammare [di Stabia] (★ Napoli)	68,491
Catania (★ 550,000)	372,486
Catanzaro	102,558
Cava de'Tirreni (★ Salerno)	52,028
Cerignola	53,463
Cesena (▲ 90,012)	72,600
Chieti	55,827
Cinisello Balsamo (★ Milano)	78,917
Civitavecchia	50,806
Collegno (★ Torino)	49,334
Cologno Monzese (★ Milano)	52,554
Como (★ 165,000)	91,738
Cosenza (★ 150,000)	106,026
Cremona	76,979
Crotone (▲ 61,005)	53,600
Ercolano (★ Napoli)	62,783
Ferrara (▲ 143,950)	113,300
Firenze (★ 640,000)	425,835
Foggia	155,051
Forlì (▲ 110,482)	91,200
Gela	79,378
Genova (Genoa) (★ 805,000)	727,427
Giugliano in Campania (★ Napoli)	51,187
Grosseto (▲ 70,592)	56,400
La Spezia (★ 185,000)	108,937
Latina (▲ 98,479)	67,800
Lecce	100,981
Livorno	174,065
Lucca	88,024
Manfredonia	57,707
Mantova (▲ 56,817)	49,000
Marsala	80,468
Massa (★ 145,000)	66,872
Matera	52,819
Messina	268,896
Mestre (★ Venezia)	189,700
• Milano (Milan) (★ 3,750,000)	1,495,260
Modena	176,880
Molfetta	64,519
Moncalieri (★ Torino)	62,306
Monza (★ Milano)	122,064
Napoli (Naples) (★ 2,875,000)	1,204,211
Nicastro (▲ 67,562)	52,100
Novara	102,742
Padova (★ 270,000)	225,769
Palermo	723,732
Parma	175,842
Pavia	82,065
Perugia (▲ 146,713)	106,700
Pesaro (▲ 90,336)	78,700
Pescara	131,027
Piacenza	105,626
Pisa	104,384
Pistoia (▲ 90,689)	76,800
Pordenone	50,825
Portici (★ Napoli)	76,302
Potenza (▲ 67,114)	57,600
Pozzuoli (★ Napoli)	65,000
Prato (★ 215,000)	164,595
Quartu Sant'Elena	52,838
Ragusa	67,748
Ravenna (▲ 136,016)	86,500
Reggio di Calabria	178,821
Reggio nell'Emilia (▲ 130,086)	107,300
Rho (★ Milano)	50,876
Rimini (▲ 130,698)	114,600
Rivoli (★ Torino)	50,786
ROMA (ROME) (★ 3,175,000)	2,815,457
Salerno (★ 250,000)	154,848
San Giorgio a Cremano (★ Napoli)	63,656
San Remo	60,797
San Severo	55,239
Sassari	120,152
Savona (★ 112,000)	62,300
Scandicci (★ Firenze)	54,367
Sesto San Giovanni (★ Milano)	91,624
Siena	59,712
Siracusa	122,857
Taranto	244,997
Terni (▲ 111,157)	94,500
Torino (★ 1,550,000)	1,035,565
Torre Annunziata (★ Napoli)	57,508
Torre del Greco (★ Napoli)	105,066
Trapani (▲ 73,083)	63,000
Trento (▲ 100,202)	81,500
Treviso	85,083
Trieste (Triest)	239,031
Udine (★ 126,000)	100,211
Varese	88,353
Venezia (Venice) (★ 420,000)	88,700
Vercelli	51,008
Verona	259,151
Viareggio (▲ 59,146)	50,300
Vicenza	110,449
Vigevano	62,671
Vittoria	54,795

JAMAICA

1982 C	2,190,357
Cities and Towns	
• KINGSTON (★ 770,000) (1987 E)	646,400
Montego Bay	70,265
Portmore (★ Kingston)	73,426
Spanish Town (★ Kingston)	89,097

JAPAN / Nihon

1985 C	121,048,923
Cities and Towns	
Abiko (★ Tōkyō)	111,659
Ageo (★ Tōkyō)	178,587
Aizu-wakamatsu	118,140
Akashi (★ Ōsaka)	263,363
Akishima (★ Tōkyō)	97,543
Akita	296,400
Akō	52,374
Amagasaki (★ Ōsaka)	509,115
Anjō	133,059
Aomori	294,045
Arao (★ Ōmuta)	62,570
Asahikawa	363,631
Asaka (★ Tōkyō)	94,431
Ashikaga	167,656
Ashiya (★ Ōsaka)	87,127
Atami	49,374
Atsugi (★ Tōkyō)	175,600
Ayase (★ Tōkyō)	71,152
Beppu	134,775
Bisai (★ Nagoya)	56,234
Chiba (★ Tōkyō)	788,930
Chichibu	61,013
Chigasaki (★ Tōkyō)	185,030
Chikushino (★ Fukuoka)	63,242
Chiryū (★ Nagoya)	50,506
Chita (★ Nagoya)	70,013
Chitose	73,610
Chōfu (★ Tōkyō)	191,071
Chōshi	87,883
Daitō (★ Ōsaka)	122,441
Dazaifu (★ Fukuoka)	57,737
Ebetsu (★ Sapporo)	90,328
Ebina (★ Tōkyō)	93,159
Fuchū (★ Tōkyō)	201,972
Fuji (★ 370,000)	214,448
Fujieda (★ Shizuoka)	111,985
Fujiidera (★ Ōsaka)	65,252
Fujimi (★ Tōkyō)	85,697
Fujinomiya (★ ★ Fuji)	112,642
Fujisawa (★ Tōkyō)	328,387
Fuji-yoshida	54,796
Fukaya (▲ 89,121)	71,600
Fukuchiyama (▲ 65,995)	56,200
Fukui	250,261
Fukuoka (★ 1,750,000)	1,160,440
Fukushima	270,762
Fukuyama	360,261
Funabashi (★ Tōkyō)	506,966
Fussa (★ Tōkyō)	51,478
Gamagōri	85,580
Gifu	411,743
Ginowan	69,206
Gotemba	74,882
Gushikawa	51,351
Gyōda	79,359
Habikino (★ Ōsaka)	111,394
Hachinohe	241,430
Hachiōji (★ Tōkyō)	426,654
Hadano (★ Tōkyō)	141,803
Hagi	52,740
Hakodate	319,194
Hamada	51,071
Hamakita	77,228
Hamamatsu	514,118
Hanamaki (▲ 69,886)	54,500
Handa (★ Nagoya)	92,883
Hannō (★ Tōkyō)	66,550
Hashima	59,760
Hasuda (★ Tōkyō)	53,991
Hatogaya (★ Tōkyō)	55,424
Hatsukaichi (★ Hiroshima)	52,020
Hekinan	63,778
Higashihiroshima (★ Hiroshima)	84,717
Higashikurume (★ Tōkyō)	110,079
Higashimatsuyama	70,426
Higashimurayama (★ Tōkyō)	123,798
Higashiōsaka (★ Ōsaka)	522,805
Higashiyamato (★ Tōkyō)	69,881
Hikari (★ Tokuyama)	49,246
Hikone	94,204
Himeji (★ 660,000)	452,917
Himi (▲ 62,112)	52,300
Hino (★ Tōkyō)	156,031
Hirakata (★ Ōsaka)	382,257
Hiratsuka (★ Tōkyō)	229,990
Hirosaki (▲ 176,082)	134,800
Hiroshima (★ 1,575,000)	1,044,118
Hita (▲ 65,730)	57,900
Hitachi	206,074
Hōfu	118,067
Honjō	56,495
Hōya (★ Tōkyō)	91,568
Hyūga	59,163
Ibaraki (★ Ōsaka)	250,463
Ichihara (★ Tōkyō)	237,617
Ichikawa (★ Tōkyō)	397,822
Ichinomiya (★ ★ Nagoya)	257,388
Ichinoseki (▲ 60,941)	49,200
Iida (▲ 92,401)	65,000
Iizuka (★ 110,000)	81,868
Ikeda (★ Ōsaka)	101,683
Ikoma (★ Ōsaka)	86,293
Imabari	125,115
Imari (▲ 62,044)	50,700
Inagi (★ Tōkyō)	50,766
Inazawa (★ Nagoya)	94,479
Inuyama (★ Nagoya)	68,723
Iruma (★ Tōkyō)	118,603
Isahaya	88,376
Ise (Uji-yamada)	105,455
Isesaki	112,459
Ishinomaki	122,674
Itami (★ Ōsaka)	182,731
Itō	70,197
Iwaki (Taira)	350,569
Iwakuni	111,833
Iwamizawa	81,664
Iwata	80,810
Iwatsuki (★ Tōkyō)	100,903
Izumi (★ Ōsaka)	137,641
Izumi (★ Sendai)	124,216
Izumi-ōtsu (★ Ōsaka)	67,755
Izumi-sano (★ Ōsaka)	91,563
Izumo (▲ 80,749)	68,000
Jōyō (★ Ōsaka)	81,850
Kadoma (★ Ōsaka)	140,590
Kaga	68,630
Kagoshima	530,502
Kainan (★ Wakayama)	50,779
Kaizuka (★ Ōsaka)	79,591
Kakamigahara	124,464
Kakegawa (▲ 68,724)	55,600
Kakogawa (★ Ōsaka)	227,311
Kamagaya (★ Tōkyō)	85,705
Kamaishi	60,007
Kamakura (★ Tōkyō)	175,495
Kameoka	76,207
Kamifukuoka (★ Tōkyō)	57,638
Kanazawa	430,481
Kani (★ Nagoya)	69,630
Kanoya (▲ 76,029)	60,200
Kanuma (▲ 88,078)	73,200
Karatsu (▲ 78,744)	70,100
Kariya (★ Nagoya)	112,403
Kasai	52,107
Kasaoka (▲ 60,598)	53,500
Kashihara (★ Ōsaka)	112,888
Kashiwa (★ Tōkyō)	273,128
Kashiwara (★ Ōsaka)	73,252
Kashiwazaki (▲ 86,020)	73,350
Kasuga (★ Fukuoka)	75,555
Kasugai (★ Nagoya)	256,990
Kasukabe (★ Tōkyō)	171,890
Katano (★ Ōsaka)	64,205
Katsuta	102,763
Kawachi-nagano (★ Ōsaka)	91,313
Kawagoe (★ Tōkyō)	285,437
Kawaguchi (★ Tōkyō)	403,015
Kawanishi (★ Ōsaka)	136,376
Kawasaki (★ Tōkyō)	1,088,624
Kesennuma	68,137
Kimitsu (▲ 84,310)	71,900
Kiryū	131,267
Kisarazu	120,201
Kishiwada (★ Ōsaka)	185,731
Kitaibaraki	51,035
Kitakyūshū (★ 1,525,000)	1,056,402
Kitami	107,281
Kitamoto (★ Tōkyō)	58,114
Kiyose (★ Tōkyō)	65,066
Kōbe (★ ★ Ōsaka)	1,410,834
Kōchi	312,241
Kodaira (★ Tōkyō)	158,673
Kōfu	202,405
Koga (★ Tōkyō)	57,541
Koganei (★ Tōkyō)	104,642
Kokubunji (★ Tōkyō)	95,467
Komae (★ Tōkyō)	73,784
Komaki (★ Nagoya)	113,284
Komatsu	106,041
Kōnan (★ Nagoya)	92,049
Kōnosu (★ Tōkyō)	60,565
Kōriyama	301,673
Koshigaya (★ Tōkyō)	253,479
Kudamatsu (★ ★ Tokuyama)	54,445
Kuki (★ Tōkyō)	58,636
Kumagaya	143,496
Kumamoto	555,719
Kunitachi (★ Tōkyō)	64,881
Kurashiki	413,632
Kure (★ ★ Hiroshima)	226,488
Kurume	222,847
Kusatsu (★ Ōsaka)	87,542
Kushiro	214,541
Kuwana (★ Nagoya)	94,731
Kyōto (★ ★ Ōsaka)	1,479,218
Machida (★ Tōkyō)	321,188
Maebashi	277,319
Maizuru	98,775
Marugame	74,272
Matsubara (★ Ōsaka)	136,455
Matsudo (★ Tōkyō)	427,473
Matsue	140,005
Matsumoto	197,340
Matsusaka	116,886
Matsuyama	426,658
Mihara	85,975
Miki (★ Ōsaka)	74,527
Minō (★ Ōsaka)	114,770
Misato (★ Tōkyō)	107,964
Mishima (★ ★ Numazu)	99,600
Mitaka (★ Tōkyō)	166,252
Mito	228,985
Miura (★ Tōkyō)	50,471
Miyako	61,654
Miyakonojō (▲ 132,098)	107,600
Miyazaki	279,114
Mobara	76,929
Moriguchi (★ Ōsaka)	159,400
Morioka	235,469
Moriyama	53,052
Mukō (★ Ōsaka)	52,216
Munakata	60,971
Muroran (★ 195,000)	136,208
Musashimurayama (★ Tōkyō)	60,930
Musashino (★ Tōkyō)	138,783
Mutsu	49,292
Nabari	56,474
Nagahama	55,531
Nagano	336,973
Nagaoka	183,756
Nagaokakyō (★ Ōsaka)	75,242
Nagareyama (★ Tōkyō)	124,682
Nagasaki	449,382
Nagoya (★ 4,800,000)	2,116,381
Naha	303,674
Nakama (★ Kitakyūshū)	50,294
Nakatsu	66,260
Nakatsugawa	53,277
Nanao	50,582
Nara (★ Ōsaka)	327,702
Narashino (★ Tōkyō)	136,365
Narita	77,181
Naruto	64,329
Naze	49,765
Neyagawa (★ Ōsaka)	258,228
Niigata	475,630
Niihama	132,184
Niitsu (▲ 63,846)	55,600
Niiza (★ Tōkyō)	129,287
Nishinomiya (★ Ōsaka)	421,267
Nishio	91,930
Nobeoka	136,381
Noboribetsu (★ Muroran)	58,370
Noda (★ Tōkyō)	105,937
Nōgata	64,479
Noshiro (▲ 59,170)	50,400
Numazu (★ 495,000)	210,490
Obihiro	162,932
Ōbu (★ Nagoya)	66,696
Ōdate (▲ 71,794)	60,900
Odawara	185,941
Ōgaki	145,910
Ōita	390,096
Okaya	61,747
Okayama	572,479
Okazaki	284,996
Okegawa (★ Tōkyō)	61,499
Okinawa	101,210
Ōme (★ Tōkyō)	110,828
Ōmi-hachiman (★ Ōsaka)	63,791
Ōmiya (★ Tōkyō)	373,022
Ōmura	69,472
Ōmuta (★ 225,000)	159,424
Ōnojō (★ Fukuoka)	69,435
Onomichi	100,640
Ōsaka (★ 16,450,000)	2,636,249
Ōta	133,670
Otaru (★ ★ Sapporo)	172,486
Ōtsu (★ Ōsaka)	234,551
Owariashi (★ Nagoya)	57,415
Oyama (▲ 134,242)	113,100
Sabae	61,452
Saeki	54,706
Saga	168,252
Sagamihara (★ Tōkyō)	482,778
Saijō	56,516
Sakado (★ Tōkyō)	87,586
Sakai (★ Ōsaka)	818,271
Sakaide	66,087
Sakata	101,392
Sakura (★ Tōkyō)	121,213
Sakurai	58,894
Sanjō	86,325
Sano	80,753
Sapporo (★ 1,900,000)	1,542,979
Sasebo	250,633
Satte	51,462
Sayama (★ Tōkyō)	144,366
Sayama (★ Ōsaka)	50,246
Seki	64,149
Sendai, Kagoshima pref. (▲ 71,444)	57,800
Sendai, Miyagi pref. (★ 1,175,000)	700,254
Sennan (★ Ōsaka)	60,059
Seto	124,623
Settsu (★ Ōsaka)	86,332
Shibata (▲ 77,219)	62,800
Shijōnawate (★ Ōsaka)	50,352
Shiki (★ Tōkyō)	58,935
Shimada (▲ 72,388)	63,200
Shimizu (★ ★ Shizuoka)	242,166
Shimodate (▲ 63,958)	52,400
Shimonoseki (★ ★ Kitakyūshū)	269,169
Shiogama (★ Sendai)	61,825
Shizuoka (★ 975,000)	468,362
Sōka (★ Tōkyō)	194,205
Suita (★ Ōsaka)	348,948
Suwa	52,329
Suzuka	164,936
Tachikawa (★ Tōkyō)	146,523
Tagajō (★ Sendai)	54,436
Tagawa	59,727
Tajimi (★ Nagoya)	84,829
Takada	130,659
Takaishi (★ Ōsaka)	66,974
Takamatsu	326,999
Takaoka (★ 220,000)	175,780
Takarazuka (★ Ōsaka)	194,273
Takasago (★ Ōsaka)	91,434
Takasaki	231,766
Takatsuki (★ Ōsaka)	348,784
Takayama	65,033
Takefu	69,148
Takikawa	52,004
Tama (★ Tōkyō)	122,135
Tamano	76,954
Tanabe (▲ 70,835)	59,800
Tanashi (★ Tōkyō)	71,331
Tatebayashi	75,141
Tenri	69,129
Tochigi	86,290
Toda (★ Tōkyō)	76,960
Tōkai (★ Nagoya)	95,278
Toki	65,308
Tokoname (★ Nagoya)	53,077
Tokorozawa (★ Tōkyō)	275,168
Tokushima	257,884
Tokuyama (★ 250,000)	112,638
• TŌKYŌ (★ 27,700,000)	8,354,615
Tomakomai	158,061
Tondabayashi (★ Ōsaka)	102,619
Toride (★ Tōkyō)	78,608
Tosu	55,791
Tottori	137,060
Toyama	314,111
Toyoake (★ Nagoya)	57,969
Toyohashi	322,142

C Census. E Official estimate. U Unofficial estimate.
• Largest city in country.
★ Population or designation of metropolitan area, including suburbs (see headnote).
▲ Population of an entire municipality, commune, or district, including rural area.

Toyokawa 107,430
Toyonaka (★ Ōsaka) 413,213
Toyota 308,111
Tsu 150,690
Tsuchiura 120,175
Tsuruga 65,670
Tsuruoka 100,200
Tsushima (★ Nagoya) 58,735
Tsuyama 86,837
Ube (★ 230,000) 174,855
Ueda 116,178
Ueno (▲ 60,812) 51,800
Uji (★ Ōsaka) 165,411
Uozu 49,825
Urasoe 81,611
Urawa (★ Tōkyō) 377,235
Urayasu (★ Tōkyō) 93,756
Ushiku 51,926
Utsunomiya 405,375
Uwajima 71,381
Wakayama (★ 495,000) 401,352
Wakkanai 51,854
Wakō (★ Tōkyō) 55,212
Warabi (★ Tōkyō) 70,408
Yachiyo (★ Tōkyō) 142,184
Yaizu (★ Shizuoka) 108,558
Yamagata 245,158
Yamaguchi 124,213
Yamato (★ Tōkyō) 177,669
Yamato-kōriyama (★ Ōsaka) 89,624
Yamato-takada (★ Ōsaka) 65,223
Yao (★ Ōsaka) 276,394
Yashio (★ Tōkyō) 67,635
Yatsushiro (▲ 108,790) 88,700
Yawata (★ Ōsaka) 72,356
Yokkaichi 263,001
Yokohama (★ ★ Tōkyō) 2,992,926
Yokosuka (★ Tōkyō) 427,116
Yonago 131,792
Yonezawa 93,721
Yono (★ Tōkyō) 71,597
Yotsukaidō (★ Tōkyō) 67,008
Yukuhashi 65,527
Zama (★ Tōkyō) 100,000
Zushi (★ Tōkyō) 57,656

JERSEY

1986 C 80,212

Cities and Towns

• SAINT HELIER (★ 46,500) 27,083

JORDAN / Al-Urdun

1989 E 3,111,000

Cities and Towns

Al-Baq'ah (★ 'Ammān) (1989 E) 63,985
• 'AMMĀN (★ 1,450,000) 936,300
Ar-Ruṣayfah (★ 'Ammān) 72,580
Az-Zarqā' (★ ★ 'Ammān) 318,055
Irbid 167,785

KAZAKHSTAN

1989 C 16,538,000

Cities and Towns

Aktau 159,000
Akt'ubinsk 253,000
• ALMA-ATA (★ 1,190,000) 1,128,000
Arkalyk (1987 E) 71,000
Aterau 149,000
Balchaš (1987 E) 84,000
Çelinograd 277,000
Čimkent 393,000
Džambul 307,000
Džezkazgan 109,000
Ekibastuz 135,000
Karaganda 614,000
Kentau (1987 E) 60,000
Kokčetav 137,000
Kustanaj 224,000
Kzyl-Orda 153,000
Leninogorsk (1987 E) 69,000
Pavlodar 331,000
Petropavlovsk 241,000
Rudnyj 124,000
Šachtinsk (1987 E) 62,000
Saptajev (1987 E) 64,000
Šaran' (1987 E) 64,000
Ščučinsk (1987 E) 53,000
Semipalatinsk 334,000
Taldy-Kurgan 119,000
Temirtau 212,000
Turkestan (1987 E) 77,000
Ural'sk 200,000
Ust'-Kamenogorsk 324,000
Žanatas (1987 E) 53,000
Zyr'anovsk (1987 E) 55,000

KENYA

1990 E 24,870,000

Cities and Towns

Eldoret (1979 C) 50,503
Kisumu (1984 E) 167,100
Machakos (1983 E) 92,300
Meru (1979 C) 72,049
Mombasa 537,000
• NAIROBI 1,505,000
Nakuru (1984 E) 101,700

KIRIBATI

1988 E 68,207

Cities and Towns

BAIRIKI 2,230
• Bikenibeu 4,580

KOREA, NORTH / Chosŏn-minjujuŭi-inmīn-konghwaguk

1981 E 18,317,000

Cities and Towns

Ch'ŏngjin 490,000
Haeju (1983 E) 213,000
Hamhŭng (1970 E) 150,000
Hŭngnam (1976 E) 260,000
Kaesŏng 259,000
Kanggye (1967 E) 130,000
Kimch'aek (Sŏngjin) (1967 E) 265,000
Namp'o 241,000
• P'YŎNGYANG (★ 1,600,000) 1,283,000
Sinŭiju 305,000
Songnim (1944 C) 53,035
Wŏnsan (1981 E) 398,000

KOREA, SOUTH / Taehan-min'guk

1985 C 40,448,486

Cities and Towns

Andong 114,216
Anyang (★ Sŏul) 361,577
Bucheon (★ Sŏul) 456,292
Changwŏn (★ Masan) 173,508
Chech'on 102,274
Cheju 202,911
Chinhae 121,341
Chinju 227,309
Ch'ŏnan 170,196
Ch'ŏngju 350,256
Chŏnju 79,323
Chŏnju, Chŏlla Pukdo prov. 426,473
Ch'unch'ŏn 162,988
Ch'ungju 113,331
Ch'ungmu 87,459
Inch'ŏn (★ ★ Sŏul) (1989 E) 1,628,000
Iri 192,269
Kangnŭng 132,897
Kimch'ŏn 77,254
Kimhae 77,903
Kumi 142,094
Kŭmsŏng 58,897
Kunsan 185,649
Kwangju (1989 E) 1,165,000
Kwangmyŏng (★ Sŏul) 219,611
Kyŏngju 127,544
Masan (★ 625,000) 448,746
Mokp'o 236,085
Namwŏn 61,447
P'ohang 260,691
Pusan (★ 3,800,000) (1989 E) 3,773,000
P'yŏngt'aek (▲ 180,513) 63,400
Samch'ŏnp'o 62,466
Sŏgwipo 82,311
Sokch'o 69,501
Sŏngnam (★ Sŏul) 447,692
Songtan 66,357
• SŎUL (★ 15,850,000) (1989 E) 10,522,000
Sunch'ŏn (▲ 116,323) 121,958
Suwŏn (★ Sŏul) 430,752
T'aebaek 113,997
Taegu (1989 C) 2,207,000
Taejŏn (1989 E) 1,041,000
Tongduchŏn 68,633
Tonghae 91,691
Ŭijŏngbu (★ Sŏul) 162,700
Ulsan 551,014
Wŏnju 151,165
Yŏngch'ŏn 52,811
Yŏngju 84,742
Yŏsu 171,933

KUWAIT / Al-Kuwayt

1985 C 1,697,301

Cities and Towns

Al-Aḥmadī (★ 285,000) 26,899
Al-Farwānīyah (★ Al-Kuwayt) 68,701
Al-Fuḥayḥīl (★ Al-Aḥmadī) 50,081
Al-Jahrah (★ Al-Kuwayt) 111,222
• AL-KUWAYT (★ 1,375,000) 44,335
As-Sālimīyah (★ Al-Kuwayt) 153,359
Aṣ-Ṣulaybīyah (★ Al-Kuwayt) 51,314
Ḥawallī (★ Al-Kuwayt) 145,126
Qalīb ash-Shuyūkh (★ Al-Kuwayt) 114,771
South Khīṭān (★ Al-Kuwayt) 69,256
Subahiya (★ Al-Aḥmadī) 60,787

KYRGYZSTAN

1989 C 4,291,000

Cities and Towns

• BIŠKEK 616,000
Džalal-Abad (1987 E) 74,000
Kara-Balta (1987 E) 55,000
Oš 213,000
Prževal'sk (1987 E) 64,000
Tokmak (1987 E) 71,000

LAOS / Lao

1985 C 3,584,803

Cities and Towns

Savannakhet (1975 E) 53,000
Viangchan (Vientiane) 377,409

LATVIA / Latvija

1989 C 2,681,000

Cities and Towns

Daugavpils 127,000
Jelgava (1987 E) 72,000
Jūrmala (★ Rīga) (1987 E) 65,000
Liepāja 114,000
• RĪGA (★ 1,005,000) 915,000
Ventspils (1987 E) 52,000

LEBANON / Lubnān

1982 U 2,637,000

Cities and Towns

• BAYRŪT (★ 1,675,000) 509,000
Ṣaydā 105,000
Ṭarābulus (Tripoli) 198,000

LESOTHO

1986 C 1,577,536

Cities and Towns

• MASERU 109,382

LIBERIA

1986 E 2,221,000

Cities and Towns

• MONROVIA 465,000

LIBYA / Lībiyā

1984 C 3,637,488

Cities and Towns

Banghāzī 435,886
Darnah 62,179
Misrātah 131,031
• ṬARĀBULUS (TRIPOLI) 990,697
Ṭubruq (Tobruk) 75,282
Zāwiyat al-Baydā' 67,120

LIECHTENSTEIN

1990 E 28,452

Cities and Towns

• VADUZ 4,874

LITHUANIA / Lietuva

1989 C 3,690,000

Cities and Towns

Alytus (1987 E) 71,000
Kaunas 423,000
Klaipėda (Memel) 204,000
Panevėžys 126,000
Šiauliai 145,000
• VILNIUS 582,000

LUXEMBOURG

1985 E 366,000

Cities and Towns

• LUXEMBOURG (★ 136,000) 76,130

MACAU

1987 E 429,000

Cities and Towns

• MACAU 429,000

MACEDONIA / Makedonija

1987 E 2,064,581

Cities and Towns

Bitola (▲ 143,090) 76,200
• SKOPJE (▲ 547,214) 444,900

MADAGASCAR / Madagasikara

1984 E 9,731,000

Cities and Towns

• ANTANANARIVO (1985 E) 663,000
Antsirabe (▲ 95,000) 50,100
Antsiranana 100,000
Fianarantsoa 130,000
Mahajanga 85,000
Toamasina 100,000
Toliara 55,000

MALAWI / Malaŵi

1987 C 7,982,607

Cities and Towns

• Blantyre 331,588
LILONGWE 233,973

MALAYSIA

1980 C 13,136,109

Cities and Towns

Alor Setar 69,435
Batu Pahat 64,727
Butterworth (★ ★ George Town) 77,982
George Town (Pinang) (★ 495,000) 248,241
Ipoh 293,849
Johor Baharu (★ Singapore, Sing.) 246,395
Kelang 192,080
Keluang 50,315
Kota Baharu 167,872
Kota Kinabalu (Jesselton) 55,997
• KUALA LUMPUR (★ 1,475,000) 919,610
Kuala Terengganu 180,296
Kuantan 131,547
Kuching 72,555
Melaka 87,494
Miri 52,125
Muar (Bandar Maharani) 65,151
Petaling Jaya (★ Kuala Lumpur) 207,805
Sandakan 70,420
Seremban 132,911
Sibu 85,231
Taiping 146,000
Telok Anson 49,148

MALDIVES

1985 C 181,453

Cities and Towns

• MALE 46,334

MALI

1987 C 7,620,225

Cities and Towns

• BAMAKO 646,163
Gao 54,874
Mopti 73,979
Ségou 88,877
Sikasso 73,050
Tombouctou (Timbuktu) 31,925

MALTA

1989 E 349,014

Cities and Towns

• VALLETTA (★ 215,000) 9,210

MARSHALL ISLANDS

1980 C 30,873

Cities and Towns

• Jarej-Uliga-Delap 8,583

MARTINIQUE

1982 C 328,566

Cities and Towns

• FORT-DE-FRANCE (★ 116,017) 99,844

MAURITANIA / Mauritanie / Mūrītāniyā

1987 E 2,007,000

Cities and Towns

• NOUAKCHOTT 285,000

MAURITIUS

1987 E 1,008,864

Cities and Towns

Beau Bassin-Rose Hill (★ Port Louis) 93,125
Curepipe (★ Port Louis) 64,243
• PORT LOUIS (★ 420,000) 139,730
Quatre Bornes (★ Port Louis) 65,480
Vacoas-Phoenix (★ Port Louis) 55,667

MAYOTTE

1985 E 67,205

Cities and Towns

• DZAOUDZI (★ 6,979) 5,865

MEXICO / México

1980 C 67,395,826

Cities and Towns

Acapulco [de Juárez] 301,902
Aguascalientes 293,152
Atlixco 53,207
Campeche 128,434
Cancún 33,273
Celaya 141,675
Chihuahua 385,603
Chilpancingo [de los Bravo] 67,498
Ciudad Chetumal 56,709
Ciudad del Carmen 72,489
• CIUDAD DE MÉXICO (MEXICO CITY) (★ 14,100,000) 8,831,079
Ciudad de Valles 65,609
Ciudad Guzmán 60,938
Ciudad Juárez 544,496
Ciudad Madero (★ Tampico) 132,444
Ciudad Mante 70,647
Ciudad Obregón 165,572
Ciudad Victoria 140,161
Coatzacoalcos 127,170
Colima 86,044
Córdoba 99,972
Cuernavaca 192,770
Culiacán 304,826
Delicias 65,504
Durango 257,915
Ecatepec (★ Ciudad de México) 741,821
Ensenada 120,483
Fresnillo 56,066
Garza García (★ Monterrey) 81,974
Gómez Palacio (★ ★ Torreón) 116,967
Guadalajara (★ 2,325,000) 1,626,152
Guadalupe (★ Monterrey) 370,524
Guaymas 54,826
Hermosillo 297,175
Hidalgo del Parral 75,590
Iguala 66,005
Irapuato 170,138
Jalapa Enríquez 204,594
La Paz 91,453
León [de los Aldamas] 593,002
Los Mochis 122,531
Matamoros 188,745
Mazatlán 199,830
Mérida 400,142
Mexicali (★ 365,000) 341,559
Minatitlán 106,765
Monclova 115,786
Monterrey (★ 2,015,000) 1,090,009
Morelia 297,544
Naucalpan de Juárez (★ Ciudad de México) 723,723
Navojoa 62,901
Nezahualcóyotl (★ Ciudad de México) 1,341,230
Nogales 65,603
Nuevo Laredo 201,731
Oaxaca [de Juárez] 154,223
Orizaba (★ 215,000) 114,848
Pachuca [de Soto] 110,351
Piedras Negras 67,455
Poza Rica de Hidalgo 166,799
Puebla [de Zaragoza] (★ 1,055,000) 835,759
Puerto Vallarta 38,645
Querétaro 215,976
Reynosa 194,693
Río Bravo 55,236
Salamanca 96,703
Saltillo 284,937
San Luis Potosí (★ 470,000) 362,371
San Luis Río Colorado 76,684
San Nicolás de los Garza (★ Monterrey) 280,696
Santa Catarina (★ Monterrey) 87,673
Soledad Díez Gutiérrez (★ San Luis Potosí) 49,173
Tampico (★ 435,000) 267,957
Tapachula 85,766
Tehuacán 79,547
Tepic 145,741
Tijuana 429,500
Tlalnepantla (★ Ciudad de México) 778,173
Tlaquepaque (★ Guadalajara) 133,500
Toluca [de Lerdo] 199,778
Torreón (★ 575,000) 328,086
Tulancingo 53,400
Tuxpan de Rodríguez Cano 56,037
Tuxtla Gutiérrez 131,096
Uruapan [del Progreso] 122,828
Veracruz [Llave] (★ 385,000) 284,822
Villahermosa 158,216
Zacatecas 80,088
Zamora de Hidalgo 86,998
Zapopan (★ Guadalajara) 345,390

MICRONESIA, FEDERATED STATES OF

C Census. E Official estimate. U Unofficial estimate.
• Largest city in country.
★ Population or designation of metropolitan area, including suburbs (see headnote).
▲ Population of an entire municipality, commune, or district, including rural area.

1985 E ... 94,534

Cities and Towns

• KOLONIA ... 6,306

MOLDOVA

1989 C ... 4,341,000

Cities and Towns

Bălţi ... 159,000
• CHIŞINĂU ... 665,000
Râbniţa (1987 E) ... 58,000
Tighina ... 130,000
Tiraspol ... 182,000

MONACO

1982 C ... 27,063

Cities and Towns

• MONACO (★ 87,000) ... 27,063

MONGOLIA / Mongol Ard Uls

1989 E ... 2,040,000

Cities and Towns

Darchan (1985 E) ... 69,800
• ULAANBAATAR ... 548,400

MONTSERRAT

1980 C ... 11,606

Cities and Towns

• PLYMOUTH ... 1,568

MOROCCO / Al-Magreb

1982 C ... 20,419,555

Cities and Towns

Agadir ... 110,479
Beni-Mellal ... 95,003
Berkane ... 60,490
• Casablanca (Dar-el-Beida) (★ 2,475,000) ... 2,139,204
El-Jadida (Mazagan) ... 81,455
Fès (★ 535,000) ... 448,823
Kenitra ... 188,194
Khemisset ... 58,925
Khouribga ... 127,181
Ksar-el-Kebir ... 73,541
Larache ... 63,893
Marrakech (★ 535,000) ... 439,728
Meknès (★ 375,000) ... 319,783
Mohammedia (Fedala) (★ Casablanca) ... 105,120
Nador ... 62,040
Oued-Zem ... 58,744
Oujda ... 260,082
RABAT (★ 980,000) ... 518,616
Safi ... 197,309
Salé (★ ★ Rabat) ... 289,391
Settat ... 65,203
Sidi Kacem ... 55,833
Sidi Slimane ... 50,457
Tanger (Tangier) (★ 370,000) ... 266,346
Taza ... 77,216
Tétouan ... 199,615

MOZAMBIQUE / Moçambique

1989 E ... 15,326,476

Cities and Towns

Beira ... 291,604
Chimoio (1986 E) ... 86,928
Inhambane (1986 E) ... 64,274
• MAPUTO ... 1,069,727
Nacala-Velha ... 101,615
Nampula ... 197,379
Pemba (1986 E) ... 50,215
Quelimane ... 78,520
Tete (1986 E) ... 56,178
Xai-Xai (1986 E) ... 51,620

MYANMAR

1983 C ... 34,124,908

Cities and Towns

Bago (Pegu) ... 150,528
Chauk ... 51,437
Dawei (Tavoy) ... 69,882
Henzada ... 82,005
Kale ... 52,628
Lashio ... 88,590
Magway ... 54,881
Mandalay ... 532,949
Mawlamyine (Moulmein) ... 219,961
Maymyo ... 63,782
Meiktila ... 96,496
Mergui (Myeik) ... 88,600
Mogok ... 49,392
Monywa ... 106,843
Myingyan ... 77,060
Myitkyinā ... 56,427
Pakokku ... 71,860
Pathein (Bassein) ... 144,096
Pyè (Prome) ... 83,332
Pyinmana ... 52,962
Shwebo ... 52,185
Sittwe (Akyab) ... 107,621
Taunggyi ... 108,231
Thaton ... 61,790
Toungoo ... 65,861
• YANGON (RANGOON) (★ 2,800,000) ... 2,705,039
Yenangyaung ... 62,582

NAMIBIA

1988 E ... 1,760,000

Cities and Towns

• WINDHOEK ... 114,500

NAURU / Naoero

1987 E ... 8,000

Cities and Towns

NEPAL / Nepāl

1981 C ... 15,022,839

Cities and Towns

Birātnagar ... 93,544
• KĀTHMĀNDAU (★ 320,000) ... 235,160

NETHERLANDS / Nederland

1989 E ... 14,880,000

Cities and Towns

Alkmaar (★ 121,000) (1987 E) ... 87,034
Almelo (1986 E) ... 62,421
Alphen aan den Rijn (1986 E) ... 55,812
Amersfoort (★ 130,158) (1986 E) ... 89,596
Amstelveen (★ Amsterdam) (1986 E) ... 68,090
• AMSTERDAM (★ 1,860,000) ... 696,500
Apeldoorn ... 147,300
Arnhem (★ 296,362) ... 129,000
Breda (★ 155,613) ... 121,400
Delft (★ ★ 's-Gravenhage) (1986 E) ... 87,440
Den Helder (1986 E) ... 63,231
Deventer (1986 E) ... 64,806
Dordrecht (★ 202,126) ... 108,300
Eindhoven (★ 379,377) ... 190,700
Enschede (★ 288,000) ... 145,200
Gouda (1986 E) ... 60,927
Groningen (★ 206,781) ... 167,800
Haarlem (★ Amsterdam) ... 149,200
Heerlen (★ 266,617) (1986 E) ... 93,871
Helmond (1987 E) ... 63,909
Hengelo (★ ★ Enschede) (1986 E) ... 76,694
Hilversum (★ Amsterdam) (1986 E) ... 86,125
Hoorn (1987 E) ... 53,788
IJmuiden (★ Amsterdam) (1986 E) ... 57,157
Kerkrade (★ Heerlen) (1986 E) ... 52,885
Leeuwarden (1986 E) ... 84,966
Leiden (★ 182,244) ... 109,200
Maastricht (★ 160,026) ... 116,400
Nieuwegein (★ Utrecht) (1987 E) ... 56,719
Nijmegen (★ 240,085) ... 145,400
Oss (1986 E) ... 50,343
Purmerend (★ Amsterdam) (1987 E) ... 52,257
Roosendaal (1986 E) ... 57,385
Rotterdam (★ 1,110,000) ... 576,300
Schiedam (★ Rotterdam) (1986 E) ... 69,078
'S-GRAVENHAGE (THE HAGUE) (★ 770,000) ... 443,900
's-Hertogenbosch (★ 189,067) (1986 E) ... 89,039
Spijkenisse (★ Rotterdam) (1987 E) ... 62,394
Tilburg (★ 224,934) ... 155,100
Utrecht (★ 518,779) ... 230,700
Venlo (★ 87,000) (1986 E) ... 63,475
Vlaardingen (★ Rotterdam) (1986 E) ... 75,536
Zaandam (★ Amsterdam) ... 129,600
Zeist (★ Utrecht) (1986 E) ... 59,743
Zoetermeer (★ 's-Gravenhage) (1987 E) ... 85,349
Zwolle (1986 E) ... 88,438

NETHERLANDS ANTILLES / Nederlandse Antillen

1990 E ... 189,687

Cities and Towns

• WILLEMSTAD (★ 130,000) (1981 C) ... 31,883

NEW CALEDONIA / Nouvelle-Calédonie

1989 C ... 164,173

Cities and Towns

• NOUMÉA (★ 88,000) ... 65,110

NEW ZEALAND

1986 C ... 3,307,084

Cities and Towns

• Auckland (★ 850,000) ... 149,046
Christchurch (★ 320,000) ... 168,200
Dunedin (★ 109,000) ... 76,964
Hamilton (★ 101,814) ... 94,511
Lower Hutt (★ Wellington) ... 63,862
Manukau (★ Auckland) ... 177,248
Napier (★ 107,060) ... 49,428
Palmerston North (★ 67,405) ... 60,503
Takapuna (★ Auckland) ... 69,419
Waitemata (★ Auckland) ... 96,365
WELLINGTON (★ 350,000) ... 137,495

NICARAGUA

1985 E ... 3,272,100

Cities and Towns

Chinandega ... 75,000
Granada (1981 E) ... 64,642
León ... 101,000
• MANAGUA ... 682,000
Masaya ... 75,000
Matagalpa ... 68,000

NIGER

1988 C ... 7,250,383

Cities and Towns

Agadez ... 50,164
Maradi ... 112,965
• NIAMEY ... 398,265
Tahoua ... 51,607
Zinder ... 120,892

NIGERIA

1987 E ... 101,907,000

Cities and Towns

Aba ... 239,800
Abakaliki ... 56,800
Abeokuta ... 341,300
ABUJA (1993 U) ... 250,000
Ado-Ekiti ... 287,000
Afikpo ... 65,790
Agege ... 83,810
Akure ... 129,600
Amaigbo ... 53,690
Apomu ... 49,570
Awka ... 88,800
Azare ... 50,020
Bauchi ... 68,840
Benin City ... 183,200
Bida ... 100,200
Calabar ... 139,800
Deba ... 110,600
Duku ... 52,880
Ede ... 245,200
Effon-Alaiye ... 122,300
Ejigbo ... 84,570
Emure-Ekiti ... 58,750
Enugu ... 252,500
Epe ... 80,560
Erin-Oshogbo ... 59,940
Eruwa ... 49,140
Fiditi ... 49,440
Gboko ... 49,390
Gbongan ... 53,990
Gombe ... 86,120
Gusau ... 126,200
Ibadan ... 1,144,000
Idah ... 50,550
Idanre ... 56,080
Ife ... 237,000
Ifon-Oshogbo ... 65,980
Igboho ... 85,230
Igbo-Ora ... 68,060
Igede-Ekiti ... 56,570
Ihiala ... 73,240
Ijebu-Igbo ... 78,680
Ijebu-Ode ... 124,900
Ijero-Ekiti ... 76,420
Ikare ... 112,500
Ikerre ... 195,400
Ikire ... 94,450
Ikirun ... 144,900
Ikole ... 71,860
Ikorodu ... 147,700
Ikot Ekpene ... 69,440
Ila ... 210,800
Ilawe-Ekiti ... 147,300
Ilesha ... 302,100
Ilobu ... 159,000
Ilorin ... 380,000
Inisa ... 95,630
Ipoti-Ekiti ... 53,220
Ise-Ekiti ... 82,580
Iseyin ... 173,500
Iwo ... 289,100
Jimeta ... 66,130
Jos ... 164,700
Kaduna ... 273,200
Kano ... 538,300
Katsina ... 165,000
Kaura Namoda ... 52,910
Keffi ... 57,790
Kishi ... 77,210
Kumo ... 118,200
Lafia ... 97,810
Lafiagi ... 57,580
• LAGOS (★ 3,800,000) ... 1,213,000
Lalupon ... 56,130
Lere ... 49,670
Maiduguri ... 255,100
Makurdi ... 98,350
Minna ... 109,300
Mubi ... 51,190
Mushin (★ Lagos) ... 266,100
Nguru ... 78,770
Offa ... 157,500
Ogbomosho ... 582,900
Oka ... 114,400
Oke-Mesi ... 55,040
Okwe ... 52,550
Olupona ... 65,720
Ondo ... 135,300
Onitsha ... 298,200
Opobo ... 64,620
Oron ... 62,260
Oshogbo ... 380,800
Owo ... 146,600
Oyan ... 50,930
Oyo ... 204,700
Pindiga ... 64,130
Port Harcourt ... 327,300
Potiskum ... 56,490
Sapele ... 111,200
Shagamu ... 93,610
Shaki ... 139,000
Shomolu (★ Lagos) ... 120,700
Sokoto ... 163,700
Ugep ... 81,910
Umuahia ... 52,550
Uyo ... 60,500
Warri ... 100,700
Zaria ... 302,800

NIUE

1986 C ... 2,531

Cities and Towns

• ALOFI ... 811

NORTHERN MARIANA ISLANDS

1980 C ... 16,780

Cities and Towns

• Chalan Kanoa ... 2,678

NORWAY / Norge

1987 E ... 4,190,000

Cities and Towns

Bærum (★ Oslo) (1985 E) ... 83,000
Bergen (★ 239,000) ... 209,320
Drammen (★ 73,000) (1985 E) ... 50,700
Fredrikstad (★ 52,000) (1983 E) ... 27,618
Hammerfest (1983 E) ... 7,208
Kristiansand (1985 E) ... 62,200
• OSLO (★ 720,000) ... 452,415
Stavanger (★ 132,000) (1985 E) ... 94,200
Tromsø (1985 E) ... 47,800
Trondheim ... 135,010

OMAN / 'Umān

1981 E ... 919,000

Cities and Towns

• MASQAT (MUSCAT) ... 50,000
Şūr (1980 E) ... 30,000

PAKISTAN / Pākistān

1981 C ... 84,253,644

Cities and Towns

Ahmadpur East ... 56,979
Bahāwalnagar ... 74,533
Bahāwalpur (★ 180,263) ... 152,009
Chārsadda ... 62,530
Chīchāwatni ... 50,241
Chiniot ... 105,559
Chishtiān Mandi ... 61,959
Daska ... 55,555
Dera Ghāzi Khān ... 102,007
Dera Ismāīl Khān (★ 68,145) ... 64,358
Drigh Road Cantonment (★ Karāchi) ... 56,742
Faisalabad (Lyallpur) ... 1,104,209
Gojra ... 68,000
Gujrānwāla (★ 658,753) ... 600,993
Gujrānwāla Cantonment (★ Gujrānwāla) ... 57,760
Gujrāt ... 155,058
Hāfizābād ... 83,464
Hyderābād (★ 800,000) ... 702,539
ISLĀMĀBĀD (★ ★ Rāwalpindi) ... 204,364
Jacobābād ... 79,365
Jarānwāla ... 69,459
Jhang Maghiāna ... 195,558
Jhelum (★ 106,462) ... 92,646
Kamālia ... 61,107
Kāmoke ... 71,097
• Karāchi (★ 5,300,000) ... 4,901,627
Karāchi Cantonment (★ Karāchi) ... 181,981
Kasūr ... 155,523
Khairpur ... 61,447
Khānewāl ... 89,090
Khānpur ... 70,589
Khushāb ... 56,274
Kohāt (★ 77,604) ... 55,832
Lahore (★ 3,025,000) ... 2,707,215
Lahore Cantonment (★ Lahore) ... 245,474
Lārkāna ... 123,890
Leiah ... 51,482
Mandi Būrewāla ... 86,311
Mardān (★ 147,977) ... 141,842
Miānwāli ... 59,159
Mingāora ... 88,078
Mīrpur Khās ... 124,371
Multān (★ 732,070) ... 696,316
Muzaffargarh ... 53,000
Nawābshāh ... 102,139
Okāra (★ 153,483) ... 127,455
Pākpattan ... 69,820
Peshāwar (★ 566,248) ... 506,896
Peshāwar Cantonment (★ Peshāwar) ... 59,352
Quetta (★ 285,719) ... 244,842
Rahīmyār Khān (★ 132,635) ... 119,036
Rāwalpindi (★ 1,040,000) ... 457,091
Rāwalpindi Cantonment (★ Rāwalpindi) ... 337,752
Sādiqābād ... 63,935
Sāhīwal ... 150,954
Sargodha (★ 291,362) ... 231,895
Sargodha Cantonment (★ Sargodha) ... 59,467
Shekhūpura ... 141,168
Shikārpur ... 88,138
Siālkot (★ 302,009) ... 258,147
Sukkur ... 190,551
Tando Ādam ... 62,744
Turbat ... 52,337
Vihāri ... 53,799
Wāh ... 122,335
Wazīrābād ... 62,725

PALAU / Belau

1986 C ... 13,873

Cities and Towns

• KOROR ... 8,629

PANAMA / Panamá

1990 C ... 2,315,047

Cities and Towns

Colón (★ 96,000) ... 54,469
David ... 65,635
• PANAMÁ (★ 770,000) ... 411,549
San Miguelito (★ Panamá) ... 242,529

PAPUA NEW GUINEA

1987 E ... 3,479,400

Cities and Towns

Lae ... 79,600
• PORT MORESBY ... 152,100
Rabaul (1980 C) ... 14,954

PARAGUAY

1985 E ... 3,279,000

Cities and Towns

• ASUNCIÓN (★ 700,000) ... 477,100
Fernando de la Mora (★ Asunción) ... 80,000
Lambaré (★ Asunción) ... 84,000
Puerto Presidente Stroessner ... 64,000
San Lorenzo (★ Asunción) (1982 C) ... 74,632

PERU / Perú

1981 C ... 17,031,221

Cities and Towns

Arequipa (★ 446,942) ... 108,023
Ayacucho (★ 69,533) ... 57,432
Breña (★ Lima) ... 112,398
Cajamarca ... 62,259
Callao (★ Lima) ... 264,133
Cerro de Pasco (★ 66,373) ... 55,597
Chiclayo (★ 279,527) ... 213,095
Chimbote ... 223,341
Chorrillos (★ Lima) ... 141,881
Chosica ... 65,139
Cuzco (★ 184,550) ... 89,563
Huancayo (★ 164,954) ... 84,845
Huánuco ... 61,812
Ica ... 114,786
Iquitos ... 178,738
Jesús María (★ Lima) ... 83,179
Juliaca ... 87,651
La Victoria (★ Lima) ... 270,778
• LIMA (★ 4,608,010) ... 371,122
Lince (★ Lima) ... 80,456
Magdalena (★ Lima) ... 55,535
Miraflores (★ Lima) ... 103,453
Pisco ... 55,604
Piura (★ 207,934) ... 144,609

C Census. E Official estimate. U Unofficial estimate.
• Largest city in country.
★ Population or designation of metropolitan area, including suburbs (see headnote).
▲ Population of an entire municipality, commune, or district, including rural area.

Pucallpa 112,263
Pueblo Libre (★ Lima) 83,985
Puno 67,397
Rímac (★ Lima) 184,484
San Isidro (★ Lima) 71,203
San Martin de Porras (★ Lima) 404,856
Santiago de Surco (★ Lima) 146,636
Sullana 89,037
Surquillo (★ Lima) 134,158
Tacna 97,173
Talara 57,351
Trujillo (★ 354,301) 202,469
Vitarte (★ Lima) 145,504

PHILIPPINES / Pilipinas

1990 C 60,477,000

Cities and Towns

Angeles 236,000
Antipolo (▲ 68,912) (1980 C) 54,117
Bacolod 364,000
Bacoor (★ Manila) (1980 C) 90,364
Baguio 183,000
Baliuag (1980 C) 70,555
Biñan (★ Manila) (1980 C) 83,684
Binangonan (1980 C) 80,980
Bocaue (1980 C) 49,693
Butuan (▲ 228,000) 99,000
Cabanatuan (▲ 173,000) 75,700
Cagayan de Oro (▲ 340,000) 255,000
Cainta (★ Manila) (1980 C) 59,025
Calamba (▲ 121,175) (1980 C) 72,359
Caloocan (★ Manila) 746,000
Carmona (★ Manila) (1980 C) 65,014
Cavite (★ 175,000) 92,000
Cebu (★ 720,000) 610,000
Cotabato 127,000
Dagupan 122,000
Davao (▲ 850,000) 569,300
Dumaguete 80,000
General Santos (Dadiangas) (▲ 250,000) 157,600
Guagua (1980 C) 72,609
Iloilo 311,000
Isabela (Basilan) (▲ 49,891) (1980 C) 11,491
Jolo (1980 C) 52,429
Lapu-Lapu (Opon) 146,000
Las Piñas (★ Manila) (1984 E) 190,364
Legaspi (▲ 121,000) 63,000
Lucena 151,000
Mabalacat (▲ 80,966) (1980 C) 54,988
Makati (★ Manila) (1984 E) 408,991
Malabon (★ Manila) (1984 E) 212,930
Malolos (1980 C) 95,699
Mandaluyong (★ Manila) (1984 E) 226,670
Mandaue (★ Cebu) 180,000
Mangaldan (1980 C) 50,434
• MANILA (★ 6,800,000) 1,587,000
Marawi 92,000
Marikina (★ Manila) (1984 E) 248,183
Meycauayan (★ Manila) (1980 C) 83,579
Muntinglupa (★ Manila) (1984 E) 172,421
Naga 115,000
Navotas (★ Manila) (1984 E) 146,899
Olongapo 192,000
Pagadian (▲ 107,000) 52,400
Parañaque (★ Manila) (1984 E) 252,791
Pasay (★ Manila) 354,000
Pasig (★ Manila) (1984 E) 318,853
Puerto Princesa (▲ 92,000) 52,000
Quezon City (★ Manila) 1,632,000
San Fernando (1980 C) 110,891
San Juan del Monte (★ Manila) (1984 E) 139,126
San Pablo (▲ 161,000) 83,900
San Pedro (1980 C) 74,556
Santa Cruz (1980 C) 60,620
Santa Rosa (★ Manila) (1980 C) 64,325
Tacloban 138,000
Tagbilaran 56,000
Tagig (★ Manila) (1984 E) 130,719
Taytay (★ Manila) (1980 C) 75,328
Valenzuela (★ Manila) (1984 E) 275,725
Zamboanga (▲ 444,000) 107,000

PITCAIRN

1988 C 59

Cities and Towns

• ADAMSTOWN 59

POLAND / Polska

1989 E 37,775,100

Cities and Towns

Będzin (★ Katowice) 77,300
Bełchatów 53,600
Biała Podlaska 50,900
Białystok 263,900
Bielsko-Biała 179,600
Bydgoszcz 377,900
Bytom (Beuthen) (★ ★ Katowice) 228,000
Chełm 63,300
Chorzów (★ ★ Katowice) 133,300
Częstochowa 254,600
Dąbrowa Górnicza (★ Katowice) 133,200
Elbląg (Elbing) 124,600
Ełk 49,600
Gdańsk (Danzig) (★ 909,000) 461,500
Gdynia (★ ★ Gdańsk) 250,200
Gliwice (Gleiwitz) (★ ★ Katowice) 222,500
Głogów 70,100
Gniezno 68,900
Gorzów Wielkopolski (Landsberg an der Warthe) 121,500
Grudziądz 99,900
Inowrocław 75,100
Jastrzębie-Zdrój 102,200
Jaworzno (★ Katowice) 97,400
Jelenia Góra (Hirschberg) 92,700
Kalisz 105,600
• Katowice (★ 2,778,000) 365,800
Kędzierzyn Kozle 71,600
Kielce 211,100
Konin 78,500
Koszalin (Köslin) 105,600
Kraków (★ 828,000) 743,700
Legionowo (★ Warszawa) 50,000
Legnica (Liegnitz) 102,800
Leszno 56,700
Łódź (★ 1,061,000) 851,500
Łomża 56,300
Lubin 78,800
Lublin (★ 389,000) 339,500
Mielec 58,600
Mysłowice (★ Katowice) 91,200
Nowy Sącz 75,100
Olsztyn (Allenstein) 158,800
Opole (Oppeln) 125,800
Ostrowiec Świętokrzyski 76,300
Ostrów Wielkopolski 71,200
Pabianice (★ Łódź) 74,400
Piekary Śląskie (★ Katowice) 68,200
Piła (Schneidemühl) (1988 E) 70,000
Piotrków Trybunalski 80,100
Płock 119,300
Poznań (★ 672,000) 586,500
Pruszków (★ Warszawa) 52,700
Przemyśl 67,300
Puławy 52,200
Racibórz (Ratibor) 61,700
Radom 223,600
Radomsko 49,700
Ruda Śląska (★ Katowice) 167,700
Rybnik 140,000
Rzeszów 148,600
Siedlce 69,200
Siemianowice Śląskie (★ Katowice) 79,200
Skarżysko-Kamienna 50,200
Słupsk (Stolp) 98,500
Sosnowiec (★ ★ Katowice) 258,700
Stalowa Wola 67,600
Starachowice 55,400
Stargard Szczeciński (Stargard in Pommern) 68,400
Suwałki 57,900
Świdnica (Schweidnitz) 61,800
Świętochłowice (★ Katowice) 58,700
Szczecin (Stettin) (★ 449,000) 409,500
Tarnów 119,100
Tarnowskie Góry (★ Katowice) 72,700
Tczew 58,400
Tomaszów Mazowiecki 69,200
Toruń 199,600
Tychy (★ Katowice) 187,600
Wałbrzych (Waldenburg) (★ 207,000) 141,400
WARSZAWA (★ 2,323,000) 1,651,200
Włocławek 119,500
Wodzisław Śląski 109,800
Wrocław (Breslau) 637,400
Zabrze (Hindenburg) (★ ★ Katowice) 201,400
Zamość 59,000
Zawiercie 55,700
Zgierz (★ Łódź) 58,500
Zielona Góra (Grünberg) 111,800
Żory 65,300

PORTUGAL

1981 C 9,833,014

Cities and Towns

Amadora (★ Lisboa) 95,518
Barreiro (★ Lisboa) 50,863
Braga 63,033
Coimbra 74,616
• LISBOA (LISBON) (★ 2,250,000) 807,167
Porto (★ 1,225,000) 327,368
Setúbal 77,885
Vila Nova de Gaia (★ Porto) 62,469

PUERTO RICO

1980 C 3,196,520

Cities and Towns

Aguadilla (★ 152,793) 22,039
Arecibo (★ 160,336) 48,779
Bayamón (★ San Juan) 185,087
Caguas (★ San Juan) 87,214
Carolina (★ San Juan) 147,835
Guaynabo (★ San Juan) 65,075
Mayagüez (★ 200,464) 82,968
Ponce (★ 232,551) 161,739
• SAN JUAN (★ 1,775,260) 424,600

QATAR / Qaṭar

1986 C 369,079

Cities and Towns

• AD-DAWHAH (DOHA) (★ 310,000) 217,294
Ar-Rayyān (★ Ad-Dawḥah) 91,996

REUNION / Réunion

1982 C 515,814

Cities and Towns

• SAINT-DENIS (▲ 109,072) 84,400

ROMANIA / România

1986 E 22,823,479

Cities and Towns

Alba-Iulia 66,100
Alexandria 52,802
Arad 187,744
Bacău 179,877
Baia Mare 139,704
Bârlad 70,365
Bistriţa 77,267
Botoşani 108,775
Brăila 235,620
Braşov 351,493
• BUCUREŞTI (BUCHAREST) (★ 2,275,000) 1,989,823
Buzău 136,080
Călăraşi 69,350
Cluj-Napoca 310,017
Constanţa 327,676
Craiova 281,044
Deva 77,976
Drobeta-Turnu Severin 99,366
Focşani 86,411
Galaţi 295,372
Giurgiu 68,002
Hunedoara 88,514
Iaşi 313,060
Lugoj 53,665
Medgidia 48,409
Mediaş 72,816
Oneşti 52,329
Oradea 213,846
Petroşani (★ 76,000) 49,131
Piatra-Neamţ 109,393
Piteşti 157,190
Ploieşti (★ 310,000) 234,886
Râmnicu Vâlcea 96,051
Reşiţa 105,914
Roman 72,415
Satu Mare 130,082
Sfântu Gheorghe 67,587
Sibiu 177,511
Slatina 76,714
Suceava 96,317
Târgovişte 91,990
Târgu Jiu 87,693
Târgu Mureş 158,998
Timişoara 325,272
Tulcea 86,336
Turda 61,594
Vaslui 65,070
Zalău 57,283

RUSSIA / Rossija

1989 C 147,386,000

Cities and Towns

Abakan 154,000
Achtubinsk (1987 E) 53,000
Ačinsk 122,000
Alapajevsk (1987 E) 51,000
Aleksandrov (1987 E) 66,000
Aleksin (1987 E) 72,000
Al'metjevsk 129,000
Amursk (1987 E) 54,000
Angarsk 266,000
Anžero-Sudžensk 108,000
Apatity (1987 E) 80,000
Archangel'sk 416,000
Armavir 161,000
Arsenjev (1987 E) 67,000
Art'om (1987 E) 73,000
Arzamas 109,000
Asbest (1987 E) 83,000
Astrachan' 509,000
Azov (1987 E) 81,000
Balakovo 198,000
Balašicha (★ Moskva) 136,000
Balašov (1987 E) 99,000
Barnaul (★ 665,000) 602,000
Batajsk (★ Rostov-na-Donu) (1987 E) 98,000
Belebej (1987 E) 51,000
Belgorod 300,000
Belogorsk (1987 E) 71,000
Beloreck (1987 E) 75,000
Belovo (1987 E) 118,000
Berdsk (★ Novosibirsk) (1987 E) 77,000
Berezniki 201,000
Ber'ozovskij (1987 E) 51,000
Bijsk 233,000
Birobidžan (1987 E) 82,000
Blagoveščensk 206,000
Bor (★ Nižnij Novgorod) (1987 E) 65,000
Borisoglebsk (1987 E) 69,000
Boroviči (1987 E) 64,000
Br'ansk 452,000
Bratsk 255,000
Bud'onnovsk (1987 E) 54,000
Bugul'ma (1987 E) 88,000
Buguruslan (1987 E) 53,000
Bujnaksk (1987 E) 53,000
Buzuluk (1987 E) 82,000
Čajkovskij (1987 E) 83,000
Čapajevsk (1987 E) 87,000
Čeboksary 420,000
Čechov (1987 E) 57,000
Čel'abinsk (★ 1,325,000) 1,143,000
Čeremchovo (1987 E) 73,000
Čerepovec 310,000
Čerkessk 113,000
Černogorsk (1987 E) 80,000
Chabarovsk 601,000
Chasav'urt (1987 E) 74,000
Chimki (★ Moskva) 133,000
Cholmsk (1987 E) 50,000
Čistopol' (1987 E) 65,000
Čita 366,000
Čusovoj (1987 E) 59,000
Derbent (1987 E) 83,000
Dimitrovgrad 124,000
Dmitrov (1987 E) 64,000
Dolgoprudnyj (★ Moskva) (1987 E) 71,000
Domodedovo (★ Moskva) (1987 E) 51,000
Dubna (1987 E) 64,000
Dzeržinsk (★ Nižnij Novgorod) 285,000
Elektrostal' 153,000
Elista (1987 E) 85,000
Engel's (★ ★ Saratov) 182,000
Fr'azino (★ Moskva) (1987 E) 52,000
Gatčina (★ Sankt-Peterburg) (1987 E) 81,000
Georgijevsk (1987 E) 62,000
Glazov 104,000
Groznyj 401,000
Gubkin (1987 E) 75,000
Gukovo (1987 E) 72,000
Gus'-Chrustal'nyj (1987 E) 75,000
Inta (1987 E) 58,000
Irbit (1987 E) 53,000
Irkutsk 626,000
Išim (1987 E) 65,000
Išimbaj (1987 E) 67,000
Iskitim (1987 E) 69,000
Ivanovo 481,000
Ivantejevka (★ Moskva) (1987 E) 53,000
Iževsk 635,000
Jakutsk 187,000
Jaroslavl' 633,000
Jefremov (1987 E) 58,000
Jegorjevsk (1987 E) 73,000
Jejsk (1987 E) 77,000
Jekaterinburg (Sverdlovsk) (★ 1,620,000) 1,367,000
Jelec 120,000
Jermolajevo (1987 E) 62,000
Jessentuki (1987 E) 84,000
Joškar-Ola 242,000
Jurga (1987 E) 92,000
Južno-Sachalinsk 157,000
Kaliningrad (Königsberg) 401,000
Kaliningrad (★ Moskva) 160,000
Kaluga 312,000
Kamensk-Šachtinskij (1987 E) 75,000
Kamensk-Ural'skij 209,000
Kamyšin 122,000
Kanaš (1987 E) 53,000
Kansk 110,000
Kaspijsk (1987 E) 61,000
Kazan' (★ 1,140,000) 1,094,000
Kemerovo 520,000
Kimry (1987 E) 61,000
Kinel' (1979 C) 40,873
Kinešma 105,000
Kiriši (1987 E) 51,000
Kirov 441,000
Kirovo-Čepeck (1987 E) 89,000
Kisel'ovsk (★ ★ Prokopjevsk) 128,000
Kislovodsk 114,000
Kizel (1979 C) 40,157
Klimovsk (★ Moskva) (1987 E) 57,000
Klin (1987 E) 95,000
Klincy (1987 E) 72,000
Kol'čugino (1979 C) 43,686
Kolomna 162,000
Kolpino (★ Sankt-Peterburg) 142,000
Komsomol'sk-na-Amure 315,000
Kopejsk (★ Čel'abinsk) (1987 E) 99,000
Korkino (1981 E) 63,000
Korsakov (1979 C) 43,348
Kostroma 278,000
Kotlas (1987 E) 69,000
Kovrov 160,000
Krasnodar 620,000
Krasnogorsk (★ Moskva) (1987 E) 89,000
Krasnojarsk 912,000
Krasnokamensk (1987 E) 70,000
Krasnokamsk (1987 E) 58,000
Krasnoturjinsk (1987 E) 66,000
Krasnoufimsk (1979 C) 40,027
Krasnoural'sk (1979 C) 38,212
Krasnyj Sulin (1979 C) 42,281
Kropotkin (1987 E) 73,000
Krymsk (1983 E) 50,000
Kstovo (★ Nižnij Novgorod) (1987 E) 64,000
Kujbyšev (1987 E) 51,000
Kulebaki (1979 C) 48,302
Kungur (1987 E) 83,000
Kurgan 356,000
Kursk 424,000
Kušva (1979 C) 43,089
Kuzneck (1987 E) 98,000
Kyzyl (1987 E) 80,000
Labinsk (1987 E) 58,000
Leninogorsk (1987 E) 61,000
Leninsk-Kuzneckij 165,000
Lipeck 450,000
Liski (1987 E) 54,000
Livny (1987 E) 51,000
Lobn'a (★ Moskva) (1987 E) 59,000
L'ubercy (★ Moskva) 165,000
Lys'va (1987 E) 77,000
Lytkarino (★ Moskva) (1987 E) 51,000
Machačkala 315,000
Magadan 152,000
Magnitogorsk 440,000
Majkop 149,000
Meždurečensk 107,000
Miass 168,000
Michajlovka (1987 E) 58,000
Mičurinsk 109,000
Mineral'nyje Vody (1987 E) 75,000
Minusinsk (1987 E) 72,000
Mončegorsk (1987 E) 65,000
Moršansk (1987 E) 51,000
• MOSKVA (MOSCOW) (★ 13,100,000) 8,769,000
Murmansk 468,000
Murom 124,000
Mytišči (★ Moskva) 154,000
Naberežnyje Čelny 501,000
Nachodka 165,000
Nal'čik 235,000
Naro-Fominsk (1987 E) 60,000
Nazarovo (1987 E) 63,000
Neftejugansk (1987 E) 86,000
Ner'ungri (1987 E) 68,000
Nevinnomyssk 121,000
Nikolo-Berjozovka 107,000
Nižnekamsk 191,000
Nižnevartovsk 242,000
Nižnij Novgorod (★ 2,025,000) 1,438,000
Nižnij Tagil 440,000
Noginsk 123,000
Nojabr'sk (1987 E) 77,000
Noril'sk 174,000
Novgorod 229,000
Novoaltajsk (★ Barnaul) (1987 E) 51,000
Novočeboksarsk 115,000
Novočerkassk 187,000
Novodvinsk (1987 E) 50,000
Novokujbyševsk (★ Kujbyšev) 113,000
Novokuzneck 600,000
Novomoskovsk (★ 365,000) 146,000
Novorossijsk 186,000
Novošachtinsk 106,000
Novosibirsk (★ 1,600,000) 1,436,000
Novotroick 106,000
Novyj Urengoj (1987 E) 79,000
Obninsk 100,000
Odincovo (★ Moskva) 125,000
Okt'abr'skij 105,000
Omsk (★ 1,175,000) 1,148,000

C Census. E Official estimate. U Unofficial estimate.
• Largest city in country.

★ Population or designation of metropolitan area, including suburbs (see headnote).
▲ Population of an entire municipality, commune, or district, including rural area.

Orechovo-Zujevo (★ 205,000) 137,000
Orel 337,208
Orenburg 547,000
Orsk 271,000
Osinniki (1987 E) 63,000
Partizansk (1979 C) 45,628
P'atigorsk 129,000
Pavlovo (1987 E) 72,000
Pavlovskij Posad (1987 E) 71,000
Pečora (1987 E) 64,000
Penza 543,000
Perm' (★ 1,160,000) 1,091,000
Pervoural'sk 142,000
Petrodvorec (★ Sankt-Peterburg) (1987 E) 77,000
Petropavlovsk-Kamčatskij 269,000
Petrozavodsk 270,000
Podol'sk (★ Moskva) 210,000
Polevskoj (1987 E) 71,000
Prochladnyj (1987 E) 53,000
Prokopjevsk (★ 410,000) 274,000
Pskov 204,000
Puškin (★ Sankt-Peterburg) (1987 E) 97,000
Puškino (1987 E) 74,000
Ramenskoje (1987 E) 86,000
R'azan' 515,000
Reutov (★ Moskva) (1987 E) 68,000
Revda (1987 E) 66,000
Roslavl' (1987 E) 61,000
Rossoš' (1987 E) 55,000
Rostov-na-Donu (★ 1,165,000) 1,020,000
Rubcovsk 172,000
Ruzajevka (1987 E) 53,000
Rybinsk 252,000
Ržev (1987 E) 70,000
Šachty 224,000
Šadrinsk (1987 E) 87,000
Safonovo (1987 E) 56,000
Salavat 150,000
Sal'sk (1987 E) 62,000
Samara (★ 1,505,000) 1,257,000
Sankt-Peterburg (Saint Petersburg) (★ 5,825,000) 4,456,000
Saransk 312,000
Sarapul 111,000
Saratov (★ 1,155,000) 905,000
Ščelkovo (★ Moskva) 109,000
Ščokino (1987 E) 70,000
Sergijev Posad 115,000
Serov 104,000
Serpuchov 144,000
Severodvinsk 249,000
Severomorsk (1987 E) 55,000
Slav'ansk-Na-Kubani (1987 E) 57,000
Smolensk 341,000
Soči 337,000
Sokol (1979 C) 45,424
Solikamsk 110,000
Solncevo (★ Moskva) (1984 E) 62,000
Solnečnogorsk (★ Moskva) (1987 E) 53,000
Sosnovyj Bor (1987 E) 56,000
Spassk-Dal'nij (1987 E) 60,000
Staryj Oskol 174,000
Stavropol' 318,000
Sterlitamak 248,000
Stupino (1987 E) 73,000
Šuja (1987 E) 72,000
Surgut 248,000
Svobodnyj (1987 E) 78,000
Syktyvkar 233,000
Syzran' 174,000
Taganrog 291,000
Talnach (1987 E) 54,000
Tambov 305,000
Tichoreck (1987 E) 67,000
Tichvin (1987 E) 70,000
Tobol'sk (1987 E) 82,000
Toljatti 630,000
Tomsk 502,000
Toržok (1987 E) 51,000
Troick (1987 E) 91,000
Tuapse (1987 E) 64,000
Tujmazy (1987 E) 54,000
Tula (★ 640,000) 540,000
Tulun (1987 E) 56,000
T'umen' 477,000
Tver' 451,000
Tyndinskij (1987 E) 61,000
Uchta 111,000
Ufa (★ 1,100,000) 1,083,000
Uglič (1979 C) 39,872
Ulan-Ude 353,000
Uljanovsk 625,000
Usolje-Sibirskoje 107,000
Ussurijsk 162,000
Ust'-Ilimsk 109,000
Ust'-Kut (1987 E) 58,000
Uzlovaja (★ Novomoskovsk) (1987 E) 63,000
V'az'ma (1987 E) 57,000
Velikije Luki 114,000
Verchn'aja Salda (1987 E) 56,000
Vičuga (1987 E) 51,000
Vladikavkaz 300,000
Vladimir 350,000
Vladivostok 648,000
Volchov (1987 E) 51,000
Volgodonsk 176,000
Volgograd (Stalingrad) (★ 1,360,000) 999,000
Vologda 283,000
Vol'sk (1987 E) 66,000
Volžsk (1987 E) 60,000
Volžskij (★ Volgograd) 269,000
Vorkuta 116,000
Voronež 887,000
Voskresensk (1987 E) 80,000
Votkinsk 103,000
Vyborg (1987 E) 81,000
Vyksa (1987 E) 60,000
Vyšnij Voločok (1987 E) 70,000
Zelenograd (★ Moskva) 158,000
Železnodorožnyj (★ Moskva) (1987 E) 90,000
Železnogorsk (1987 E) 81,000
Zel'onodol'sk (1987 E) 93,000
Žigulevsk (1977 E) 50,000
Zima (1987 E) 51,000
Zlatoust 208,000
Žukovskij 101,000

RWANDA

1983 E 5,762,000

Cities and Towns

Butare 30,000
• KIGALI 181,600

SAINT HELENA

1987 C 5,644

Cities and Towns

• JAMESTOWN 1,413

SAINT KITTS AND NEVIS

1980 C 44,404

Cities and Towns

• BASSETERRE 14,725
Charlestown 1,771

SAINT LUCIA

1987 E 142,342

Cities and Towns

• CASTRIES 53,933

SAINT PIERRE AND MIQUELON / Saint-Pierre-et-Miquelon

1982 C 6,041

Cities and Towns

• SAINT-PIERRE 5,371

SAINT VINCENT AND THE GRENADINES

1987 E 112,589

Cities and Towns

• KINGSTOWN (★ 28,936) 19,028

SAN MARINO

1988 E 22,304

Cities and Towns

• SAN MARINO 2,777

SAO TOME AND PRINCIPE / São Tomé e Príncipe

1970 C 73,631

Cities and Towns

• SÃO TOMÉ 17,380

SAUDI ARABIA / Al-'Arabīyah as-Su'ūdīyah

1980 E 9,229,000

Cities and Towns

Abhā (1974 C) 30,150
Ad-Dammām 200,000
Al-Hufūf (1974 C) 101,271
Al-Khubar (1974 C) 48,817
Al-Madīnah (Medina) 290,000
Al-Mubarraz (1974 C) 54,325
AR-RIYĀḌ (RIYADH) 1,250,000
Aṭ-Ṭā'if 300,000
Buraydah (1974 C) 69,940
Hā'il (1974 C) 40,502
• Jiddah 1,300,000
Makkah (Mecca) 550,000
Najran (1974 C) 47,501
Tabūk (1974 C) 74,825

SENEGAL / Sénégal

1988 C 6,881,919

Cities and Towns

• DAKAR 1,447,642
Diourbel 77,548
Kaolack 152,007
Louga 52,763
Saint-Louis 160,689
Thiès 184,902
Ziguinchor 124,283

SEYCHELLES

1984 E 64,718

Cities and Towns

• VICTORIA 23,000

SIERRA LEONE

1985 C 3,515,812

Cities and Towns

Bo 59,768
• FREETOWN (★ 525,000) 469,776
Kenema 52,473
Koidu 82,474
Makeni 49,038

SINGAPORE

1989 E 2,685,400

Cities and Towns

• SINGAPORE (★ 3,025,000) 2,685,400

SLOVAKIA / Slovenská Republika

1990 E 5,287,000

Cities and Towns

Banská Bystrica 87,834
• BRATISLAVA 442,999
Košice 237,099
Martin 66,678
Nitra 91,297
Poprad 53,039
Prešov 90,121
Prievidza 52,624
Trenčín 57,813
Trnava 72,866
Žilina 97,508

SLOVENIA / Slovenija

1987 E 1,936,606

Cities and Towns

• LJUBLJANA (▲ 316,607) 233,200
Maribor (▲ 187,651) 107,400

SOLOMON ISLANDS

1986 C 285,176

Cities and Towns

• HONIARA 30,413

SOMALIA / Somaliya

1984 E 5,423,000

Cities and Towns

Berbera 65,000
Hargeysa 70,000
Kismayu 70,000
Marka 60,000
• MUQDISHO 600,000

SOUTH AFRICA / Suid-Afrika

1985 C 23,385,645

Cities and Towns

Alberton (★ Johannesburg) 66,155
Alexandra (★ Johannesburg) 67,276
Atteridgeville (★ Pretoria) 73,439
Bellville (★ Cape Town) 68,915
Benoni (★ Johannesburg) 94,926
Bloemfontein (★ 235,000) 104,381
Boksburg (★ Johannesburg) 110,832
Botshabelo (★ Bloemfontein) 95,625
CAPE TOWN (KAAPSTAD) (★ 1,790,000) 776,617
Carletonville (★ 120,499) 97,874
Daveyton (★ Johannesburg) 99,056
Diepmeadow (★ Johannesburg) 192,682
Durban (★ 1,550,000) 634,301
East London (Oos-Londen) (★ 320,000) 85,699
Elsies River (★ Cape Town) 70,067
Evaton (★ Vereeniging) 52,559
Galeshewe (★ Kimberley) 63,238
Germiston (★ ★ Johannesburg) 116,718
Grassy Park (★ Cape Town) 50,193
Guguleto (★ Cape Town) 63,893
• Johannesburg (★ 3,650,000) 632,369
Kagiso (★ Johannesburg) 50,647
Katlehong (★ Johannesburg) 137,745
Kayamnandi (★ Port Elizabeth) 220,548
Kempton Park (★ Johannesburg) 87,721
Kimberley (★ 145,000) 74,061
Klerksdorp (★ 205,000) 48,947
Kroonstad (★ 65,165) 22,886
Krugersdorp (★ Johannesburg) 73,767
Kwa Makuta (★ Durban) 71,378
Kwa Mashu (★ Durban) 111,593
Kwanobuhle (★ Port Elizabeth) 52,376
Kwa-Thema (★ Johannesburg) 78,640
Ladysmith (★ 31,670) 25,102
Lekoa (Shapeville) (★ Vereeniging) 218,392
Madadeni (★ Newcastle) 65,832
Mamelodi (★ Pretoria) 127,033
Mangaung (★ Bloemfontein) 79,851
Newcastle (★ 155,000) 34,931
Ntuzuma (★ Durban) 61,834
Nyanga (★ Cape Town) 148,882
Ozisweni (★ Newcastle) 51,934
Paarl (★ ★ Cape Town) 63,671
Parow (★ Cape Town) 60,294
Pietermaritzburg (★ 230,000) 133,809
Pinetown (★ Durban) 55,770
Port Elizabeth (★ 690,000) 272,844
PRETORIA (★ 960,000) 443,059
Randburg (★ Johannesburg) 74,347
Roodepoort-Maraisburg (★ Johannesburg) 141,764
Sandton (★ Johannesburg) 86,089
Soshanguve (★ Pretoria) 68,598
Soweto (★ Johannesburg) 521,948
Springs (★ Johannesburg) 68,235
Tembisa (★ Johannesburg) 149,282
Uitenhage (★ ★ Port Elizabeth) 54,987
Umlazi (★ Durban) 194,933
Vanderbijlpark (★ ★ Vereeniging) 59,865
Vereeniging (★ 525,000) 60,584
Verwoerdburg (★ Pretoria) 49,891
Vosloosrus (★ Johannesburg) 52,061
Welkom (★ 215,000) 54,488
Witbank (★ 77,171) 41,784

SPAIN / España

1988 E 39,217,804

Cities and Towns

Albacete 125,997
Alcalá de Guadaira 50,935
Alcalá de Henares (★ Madrid) 150,021
Alcobendas (★ Madrid) 73,455
Alcorcón (★ Madrid) 139,796
Alcoy 66,074
Algeciras 99,528
Alicante 261,051
Almería 157,644
Avilés (★ 131,000) 87,811
Badajoz (▲ 122,407) 106,400
Badalona (★ Barcelona) 225,229
Baracaldo (★ Bilbao) 113,502
Barcelona (★ 4,040,000) 1,714,355
Bilbao (★ 985,000) 384,733
Burgos 160,561
Cáceres 71,598
Cádiz (★ 240,000) 156,591
Cartagena (▲ 172,710) 70,000
Castelló de la Plana 131,809
Ciudad Real 56,300
Córdoba 302,301
Cornella (★ Barcelona) 86,866
Coslada (★ Madrid) 68,765
Dos Hermanas (▲ 68,456) 60,600
Elche (▲ 180,256) 158,300
Elda 56,756
El Ferrol del Caudillo (★ 129,000) 86,503
El Puerto de Santa María (▲ 62,285) 49,900
Fuenlabrada (★ Madrid) 128,872
Getafe (★ Madrid) 135,367
Gijón 262,156
Granada 263,334
Granollers (★ Barcelona) 49,045
Guadalajara 61,309
Hospitalet (★ Barcelona) 278,449
Huelva 137,826
Irún 54,886
Jaén 106,435
Jerez de la Frontera (▲ 183,007) 156,200
La Coruña 248,862
La Línea 60,956
Las Palmas de Gran Canaria (▲ 366,347) 319,000
Leganés (★ Madrid) 168,403
León (★ 159,000) 136,558
Lérida (▲ 109,795) 91,500
Linares 58,622
Logroño 119,038
Lugo (▲ 78,795) 68,700
• MADRID (★ 4,650,000) 3,102,846
Málaga 574,456
Manresa 65,607
Mataró 100,817
Mérida 52,368
Móstoles (★ Madrid) 181,648
Murcia (▲ 314,124) 149,800
Orense 106,042
Oviedo (▲ 190,073) 168,900
Palencia 76,692
Palma [de Mallorca] (▲ 314,608) 249,000
Parla (★ Madrid) 66,253
Portugalete (★ Bilbao) 57,813
Prat del Llobregat (★ Barcelona) 64,193
Puertollano 52,284
Reus 83,800
Sabadell (★ Barcelona) 189,489
Salamanca 159,342
San Baudilio de Llobregat (★ Barcelona) 77,502
San Fernando (★ ★ Cádiz) 81,975
San Sebastián (★ 285,000) 177,622
San Sebastián de los Reyes (★ Madrid) 51,653
Santa Coloma de Gramanet (★ Barcelona) 136,042
Santa Cruz de Tenerife 215,228
Santander (▲ 190,795) 166,800
Santiago de Compostela (▲ 88,110) 68,800
Santurce-Antiguo (★ Bilbao) 52,334
Segovia 54,402
Sevilla (★ 945,000) 663,132
Talavera de la Reina 68,158
Tarragona (▲ 109,586) 63,500
Tarrasa (★ Barcelona) 161,410
Toledo 59,551
Torrejón de Ardoz (★ Madrid) 83,267
Torrente (★ València) 55,751
Valencia (★ 1,270,000) 743,933
Valladolid 331,461
Vigo (▲ 271,128) 179,500
Vitoria (Gasteiz) 204,264
Zamora 62,047
Zaragoza 582,239

SPANISH NORTH AFRICA / Plazas de Soberanía en el Norte de África

1988 E 122,905

Cities and Towns

• Ceuta 67,188
Melilla 55,717

SRI LANKA

1986 E 16,117,000

Cities and Towns

Battaramulla (★ Colombo) (1981 C) 56,535
• COLOMBO (★ 2,050,000) 683,000
Dehiwala-Mount Lavinia (★ Colombo) 191,000
Galle 109,000
Jaffna 143,000
Kandy 130,000
KOTTE (★ Colombo) 104,000
Maharagama (★ Colombo) (1981 C) 49,765
Matale (1985 E) 57,000
Matara (1985 E) 57,000
Moratuwa (★ Colombo) 138,000
Negombo (1985 E) 76,000
Ratnapura (1985 E) 51,000
Trincomalee (1985 E) 51,000

SUDAN / As-Sūdān

1983 C 20,564,364

Cities and Towns

Al-Fāshir (1973 C) 51,932
• AL-KHARṬŪM (★ 1,450,000) 476,218
Al-Kharṭūm Baḥrī (★ Al-Kharṭūm) 341,146
Al-Qaḍārif (1973 C) 66,465
Al-Ubayyiḍ 140,000
Atbarah 73,000
Būr Sūdān (Port Sudan) 206,727
Jūbā (1980 E) 116,000
Kassalā 143,000
Kūstī (1973 C) 65,257
Nyala (1973 C) 59,852

C Census. E Official estimate. U Unofficial estimate.
• Largest city in country.
★ Population or designation of metropolitan area, including suburbs (see headnote).
▲ Population of an entire municipality, commune, or district, including rural area.

Umm Durmān (Omdurman) (★ ★ Al-Kharṭūm) ... 526,287
Wad Madanī ... 141,000
Wāw (1980 E) ... 116,000

SURINAME

1988 E ... 392,000

Cities and Towns

• PARAMARIBO (★ 296,000) ... 241,000

SWAZILAND

1986 C ... 712,131

Cities and Towns

LOBAMBA ... 0
Manzini (★ 30,000) ... 18,084
• MBABANE ... 38,290

SWEDEN / Sverige

1990 E ... 8,527,036

Cities and Towns

Borås ... 101,231
Borlänge ... 46,424
Eskilstuna ... 89,460
Gävle (▲ 88,081) ... 67,500
Göteborg (★ 710,894) ... 431,840
Halmstad (▲ 79,362) ... 50,900
Helsingborg ... 108,359
Huddinge (★ Stockholm) ... 73,107
Järfälla (★ Stockholm) ... 56,386
Jönköping ... 110,860
Karlstad ... 76,120
Linköping ... 120,562
Luleå ... 67,903
Lund (★ ★ Malm320) ... 86,412
Malmö (★ 445,000) ... 232,908
Mölndal (★ Göteborg) ... 51,767
Nacka (★ Stockholm) ... 63,114
Norrköping ... 119,921
Örebro ... 120,353
Södertälje (★ Stockholm) ... 81,460
Sollentuna (★ Stockholm) ... 50,606
Solna (★ Stockholm) ... 51,427
• STOCKHOLM (★ 1,449,972) ... 672,187
Sundsvall (▲ 93,404) ... 50,600
Täby (★ Stockholm) ... 56,553
Trollhättan ... 50,602
Tumba (★ Stockholm) ... 68,255
Umeå (▲ 90,004) ... 58,700
Uppsala ... 164,754
Västerås ... 118,386
Växjö (▲ 68,849) ... 45,500

SWITZERLAND / Schweiz / Suisse / Svizzera

1990 E ... 6,673,850

Cities and Towns

Arbon (★ 41,100) ... 12,284
Baden (★ 70,700) ... 14,545
Basel (Bâle) (★ 575,000) ... 169,587
BERN (BERNE) (★ 298,800) ... 134,393
Biel (Bienne) (★ 81,900) ... 52,023
Fribourg (Freiburg) (★ 56,800) ... 33,962
Genève (Geneva) (★ 460,000) ... 165,404
Lausanne (★ 259,900) ... 122,600
Locarno (★ 42,350) ... 14,149
Lugano (★ 94,800) ... 26,055
Luzern (★ 159,500) ... 59,115
Sankt Gallen (★ 125,000) ... 73,191
Sankt Moritz (1987 E) ... 5,335
Solothurn (★ 56,800) ... 15,429
Thun (★ 77,200) ... 37,707
Winterthur (★ 107,400) ... 85,174
• Zürich (★ 860,000) ... 342,861

SYRIA / Sūrīyah

1988 E ... 11,338,000

Cities and Towns

Al-Ḥasakah (1981 C) ... 73,426
Al-Lādhiqīyah (Latakia) ... 249,000
Al-Qāmishlī ... 126,236
As-Suwaydā' ... 46,844
Dar'ā (1981 C) ... 49,534
Dārayyā ... 53,204
Dayr az-Zawr ... 112,000
• DIMASHQ (DAMASCUS) (★ 1,950,000) ... 1,326,000
Dūmā (★ Dimashq) ... 66,130
Ḥalab (Aleppo) (★ 1,275,000) ... 1,261,000
Ḥamāh ... 222,000
Ḥimṣ ... 447,000
Idlib (1981 C) ... 51,682
Jaramānah (★ Dimashq) ... 96,681
Madīnat ath Thawrah ... 58,151
Ṭarṭūs (1981 C) ... 52,589

TAIWAN / T'aiwan

1988 E ... 19,672,612

Cities and Towns

Changhua (▲ 206,603) ... 158,400
Chiai ... 254,875
Chilung ... 348,541
Chungho (★ T'aipei) ... 343,389
Chungli ... 247,639
Chutung ... 104,797
Fangshan (★ Kaohsiung) ... 276,259
Fengyüan (▲ 144,434) ... 115,300
Hsichih (★ T'aipei) (1980 C) ... 70,031
Hsinchu ... 309,899
Hsinchuang (★ T'aipei) ... 259,001
Hsintien (★ T'aipei) ... 205,094
Hualien ... 106,658
Ilan (▲ 81,751) (1980 C) ... 70,900
Kangshan (1980 C) ... 78,049
Kaohsiung (★ 1,845,000) ... 1,342,797
Lotung (1980 C) ... 57,925
Lukang (1980 C) ... 72,019
Miaoli (1980 C) ... 81,500
Nant'ou (1980 C) ... 84,038
P'ingchen (★ T'aipei) ... 134,925
P'ingtung (▲ 204,990) ... 167,600
Sanchung (★ T'aipei) ... 362,171
Shulin (★ T'aipei) (1980 C) ... 75,700
Tach'i (1980 C) ... 67,209
T'aichung ... 715,107
T'ainan ... 656,927
• T'AIPEI (★ 6,130,000) ... 2,637,100
T'aipeihsien (★ T'aipei) ... 506,220
T'aitung (▲ 109,358) ... 79,800
Taoyüan ... 220,255
T'oufen (1980 C) ... 66,536
T'uch'eng (★ T'aipei) ... 70,500
Yangmei (1980 C) ... 84,353
Yüanlin (▲ 116,936) ... 51,300
Yungho (★ T'aipei) ... 242,252
Yungkang (▲ 114,904) ... 59,600

TAJIKISTAN

1989 C ... 5,112,000

Cities and Towns

Chudžand ... 160,000
• DUŠANBE ... 595,000
Kul'ab (1987 E) ... 71,000

TANZANIA

1984 E ... 21,062,000

Cities and Towns

Arusha ... 69,000
• DAR ES SALAAM ... 1,300,000
DODOMA ... 54,000
Iringa ... 67,000
Kigoma (1978 C) ... 50,044
Mbeya ... 93,000
Morogoro ... 72,000
Moshi ... 62,000
Mtwara (1978 C) ... 48,510
Mwanza (1978 C) ... 110,611
Tabora ... 87,000
Tanga ... 121,000
Zanzibar (1985 E) ... 133,000

THAILAND / Prathet Thai

1988 E ... 54,960,917

Cities and Towns

Chiang Mai ... 164,030
Hat Yai ... 138,046
Khon Kaen ... 131,340
• KRUNG THEP (BANGKOK) (★ 6,450,000) ... 5,716,779
Nakhon Ratchasima ... 204,982
Nakhon Sawan ... 105,220
Nakhon Si Thammarat ... 72,407
Nonthaburi (★ Krung Thep) ... 218,354
Pattaya ... 56,402
Phitsanulok ... 77,675
Phra Nakhon Si Ayutthaya ... 60,847
Samut Prakan (★ Krung Thep) ... 73,327
Samut Sakhon ... 53,984
Saraburi ... 61,206
Songkhla ... 84,433
Ubon Ratchathani ... 100,374
Udon Thani ... 81,202
Yala ... 67,383

TOGO

1981 C ... 2,702,945

Cities and Towns

• LOMÉ (1984 E) ... 400,000
Sokodé ... 48,098

TOKELAU

1986 C ... 1,690

TONGA

1986 C ... 94,535

Cities and Towns

• NUKU'ALOFA ... 21,265

TRINIDAD AND TOBAGO

1990 C ... 1,234,388

Cities and Towns

• PORT OF SPAIN (★ 370,000) ... 50,878
San Fernando (★ 75,000) ... 30,092

TUNISIA / Tunis / Tunisie

1984 C ... 6,975,450

Cities and Towns

Ariana (★ Tunis) ... 98,655
Bardo (★ Tunis) ... 65,669
Béja ... 46,708
Ben Arous (★ Tunis) ... 52,105
Binzert ... 94,509
Gabès ... 92,258
Gafsa ... 60,970
Hammam Lif (★ Tunis) ... 47,009
Houmt Essouk ... 92,269
Kairouan ... 72,254
Kasserine ... 47,606
La Goulette (★ Tunis) ... 61,609
Menzel Bourguiba ... 51,399
Nabeul (★ 75,000) ... 39,531
Sfax (★ 310,000) ... 231,911
Sousse (★ 160,000) ... 83,509
• TUNIS (★ 1,225,000) ... 596,654
Zarzis ... 49,063

TURKEY / Türkiye

1990 C ... 56,969,109

Cities and Towns

Adana ... 931,555
Adapazarı ... 174,353
Adıyaman ... 101,306
Afyon ... 98,618
Ağrı ... 57,837
Akhisar ... 74,002
Aksaray ... 92,038
Akşehir ... 51,669
Amasya ... 55,602
ANKARA (★ 2,650,000) ... 2,553,209
Antakya (Antioch) ... 124,443
Antalya ... 378,726
Aydın ... 106,603
Bafra ... 66,209
Balıkesir ... 171,967
Bandırma ... 77,211
Batman ... 148,121
Bolu ... 60,600
Burdur ... 56,095
Bursa ... 838,323
Çanakkale ... 53,887
Ceyhan ... 85,000
Çorlu ... 77,025
Çorum ... 116,260
Denizli ... 203,130
Diyarbakır ... 375,767
Dörtyol ... 48,030
Düzce ... 62,606
Edirne ... 102,325
Elazığ ... 211,720
Elbistan ... 55,114
Ereğli, Konya prov. ... 74,332
Ereğli, Zonguldak prov. ... 63,776
Erzincan ... 90,799
Erzurum ... 241,344
Eskişehir ... 413,305
Gaziantep ... 627,584
Gebze (★ İstanbul) ... 156,594
Gemlik ... 50,212
Giresun ... 67,536
Gölcük ... 65,000
İçel (Mersin) ... 420,750
İnegöl ... 71,095
İskenderun ... 156,198
Isparta ... 111,706
• İstanbul (★ 7,550,000) ... 6,748,435
İzmir (★ 1,900,000) ... 1,762,849
İzmit ... 254,768
Kadirli ... 55,193
Kahramanmaraş ... 229,066
Karabük ... 104,869
Karaman ... 76,682
Kars ... 79,496
Kastamonu ... 52,363
Kayseri ... 416,276
Kilis ... 81,469
Kırıkhan ... 69,323
Kırıkkale ... 203,666
Kırşehir ... 74,546
Kızıltepe ... 60,445
Konya ... 509,208
Kozan ... 54,934
Kütahya ... 131,286
Lüleburgaz ... 51,978
Malatya ... 276,666
Manisa ... 158,283
Mardin ... 52,994
Nazilli ... 80,209
Nevşehir ... 52,514
Niğde ... 54,822
Nizip ... 58,259
Nusaybin ... 50,605
Ödemiş ... 511,110
Ordu ... 101,306
Osmaniye ... 122,315
Polatlı ... 61,026
Rize ... 51,586
Salihli ... 71,035
Samsun ... 301,412
Şanlıurfa ... 276,528
Siirt ... 66,607
Silvan (Miyafarkin) ... 59,959
Sincan (★ Ankara) ... 92,262
Sivas ... 219,122
Siverek ... 63,366
Söke ... 50,598
Soma ... 50,165
Tarsus ... 191,333
Tatvan ... 52,404
Tekirdağ ... 80,207
Tokat ... 83,174
Trabzon ... 144,805
Turgutlu ... 73,734
Turhal ... 71,406
Uşak ... 104,980
Van ... 153,525
Viranşehir ... 58,394
Yalova ... 72,874
Yarımca (1985 C) ... 48,420
Yozgat ... 51,360
Zonguldak (★ 220,000) ... 120,300

TURKMENISTAN

1989 C ... 3,534,000

Cities and Towns

• AŠCHADAD ... 398,000
Krasnovodsk (1987 E) ... 59,000
Mary (1987 E) ... 89,000
Nebit-Dag (1987 E) ... 85,000
Tašauz ... 112,000

TURKS AND CAICOS ISLANDS

1990 C ... 12,350

Cities and Towns

• GRAND TURK ... 3,761

TUVALU

1979 C ... 7,349

Cities and Towns

• FUNAFUTI ... 2,191

UGANDA

1990 E ... 17,213,407

Cities and Towns

Jinja (1982 E) ... 55,000
• KAMPALA ... 1,008,707

UKRAINE / Ukrayina

1989 C ... 51,704,000

Cities and Towns

Alchevs'k (★ Stakhanov) ... 126,000
Antratsyt (★ ★ Krasnyy Luch) (1987 E) ... 70,000
Artemivs'k (1987 E) ... 91,000
Berdyans'k ... 132,000
Berdychiv (1987 E) ... 89,000
Bila Tserkva ... 197,000
Bilhorod-Dnistrovs'kyy (1987 E) ... 54,000
Brovary (★ Kyyiv) (1987 E) ... 73,000
Bryanka (Stakhanov) (1987 E) ... 65,000
Cherkasy ... 290,000
Chernihiv ... 296,000
Chernivtsi ... 257,000
Chervonohrad (1987 E) ... 71,000
Dniprodzerzhyns'k (★ ★ Dnipropetrovs'k) ... 282,000
Dnipropetrovs'k (★ 1,600,000) ... 1,179,000
Donets'k (★ 2,200,000) ... 1,110,000
Drohobych (1987 E) ... 76,000
Druzhkivka (★ Kramatorsk) (1987 E) ... 70,000
Dymytrov (★ ★ Krasnoarmiys'k) (1987 E) ... 62,000
Dzhankoy (1987 E) ... 51,000
Fastiv (1987 E) ... 55,000
Feodosiya (1987 E) ... 83,000
Horlivka (★ 710,000) ... 337,000
Illichivs'k (★ Odesa) (1987 E) ... 52,000
Ivano-Frankivs'k ... 214,000
Izmayil (1987 E) ... 90,000
Izyum (1987 E) ... 63,000
Kalush (1987 E) ... 67,000
Kam'yanets-Podil's'kyy ... 102,000
Kerch ... 174,000
Kharkiv (★ 1,940,000) ... 1,611,000
Khartsyz'k (★ Donets'k) (1987 E) ... 69,000
Kherson ... 355,000
Khmel'nyts'kyy ... 237,000
Kirovohrad ... 269,000
Kolymyya (1987 E) ... 63,000
Konotop (1987 E) ... 93,000
Korosten' (1987 E) ... 72,000
Kostyantynivka ... 108,000
Kovel' (1987 E) ... 66,000
Kramatorsk (★ 465,000) ... 198,000
Krasnoarmiys'k (★ 175,000) (1987 E) ... 70,000
Krasnodon (1987 E) ... 52,000
Krasnyy Luch (★ 250,000) ... 113,000
Kremenchuk ... 236,000
Kryvyy Rih ... 713,000
• KYYIV (KIEV) (★ 2,900,000) ... 2,587,000
Lozova (1987 E) ... 68,000
Lubny (1987 E) ... 58,000
Luhans'k ... 497,000
Luts'k ... 198,000
L'viv ... 790,000
Lysychans'k (★ 410,000) ... 127,000
Makiyivka (★ ★ Donets'k) ... 430,000
Marhanets' (1987 E) ... 55,000
Mariupol' (Ždanov) ... 517,000
Melitopol' ... 174,000
Mukacheve (1987 E) ... 88,000
Mykolayiv ... 503,000
Nizhyn (1987 E) ... 81,000
Nikopol' ... 158,000
Nova Kakhovka (1987 E) ... 53,000
Novohrad-Volyns'kyy (1987 E) ... 52,000
Novomoskovsk (1987 E) ... 76,000
Novovolynsk (1987 E) ... 54,000
Odesa (★ 1,185,000) ... 1,115,000
Oleksandriya ... 103,000
Pavlohrad ... 131,000
Pervomays'k (1987 E) ... 79,000
Poltava ... 315,000
Pryluky (1987 E) ... 73,000
Rivne ... 228,000
Romny (1987 E) ... 53,000
Roven'ky (1987 E) ... 68,000
Rubizhne (★ ★ Lysychans'k) (1987 E) ... 72,000
Sevastopol' ... 356,000
Severodonets'k (★ ★ Lysychans'k) ... 131,000
Shakhtars'k (★ ★ Torez) (1987 E) ... 73,000
Shostka (1987 E) ... 87,000
Simferopol' ... 344,000
Slov'yans'k (★ ★ Kramatorsk) ... 135,000
Smila (1987 E) ... 76,000
Snizhne (★ Torez) (1987 E) ... 68,000
Stakhanov (★ 610,000) ... 112,000
Stryy (1987 E) ... 63,000
Sumy ... 291,000
Sverdlovsk (1987 E) ... 84,000
Svitlovods'k (1987 E) ... 55,000
Ternopil ... 205,000
Torez (★ 290,000) (1987 E) ... 88,000
Uman' (1987 E) ... 89,000
Uzhhorod ... 117,000
Vinnytsya ... 374,000
Yalta (1987 E) ... 89,000
Yenakiyeve (★ ★ Horlivka) ... 121,000
Yevpatoriya ... 108,000
Zaporizhzhya ... 884,000
Zhovti Zody (1987 E) ... 61,000
Zhytomyr ... 292,000

UNITED ARAB EMIRATES / Al-Imārāt al-'Arabīyah al-Muttaḥidah

1980 C ... 980,000

Cities and Towns

ABŪ ẒABY (ABU DHABI) ... 242,975
Al-'Ayn ... 101,663
Ash-Shāriqah ... 125,149
• Dubayy ... 265,702

UNITED KINGDOM

1981 C ... 55,678,079

UNITED KINGDOM: ENGLAND

1981 C ... 46,220,955

Cities and Towns

Aldershot (★ London) ... 53,665
Aylesbury ... 51,999
Barnsley ... 76,783
Barrow-in-Furness ... 50,174
Basildon (★ London) ... 94,800
Basingstoke ... 73,027
Bath ... 84,283
Bebington (★ Liverpool) ... 62,618
Bedford ... 75,632
Beeston and Stapleford (★ Nottingham) ... 64,785
Benfleet (★ London) ... 50,783
Birkenhead (★ Liverpool) ... 99,075
Birmingham (★ 2,675,000) ... 1,013,995
Blackburn (★ 221,900) ... 109,564
Blackpool (★ 280,000) ... 146,297
Bognor Regis ... 50,323
Bolton (★ ★ Manchester) ... 143,960
Bootle ... 70,860
Bournemouth (★ 315,000) ... 142,829
Bracknell (★ London) ... 52,257
Bradford (★ ★ Leeds) ... 293,336
Brentwood (★ London) ... 51,212
Brighton (★ 420,000) ... 134,581
Bristol (★ 630,000) ... 413,861
Burnley (★ 160,000) ... 76,365

C Census. E Official estimate. U Unofficial estimate.
• Largest city in country.

★ Population or designation of metropolitan area, including suburbs (see headnote).
▲ Population of an entire municipality, commune, or district, including rural area.

Burton [upon Trent] ... 59,040
Bury (★ Manchester) ... 61,785
Cambridge ... 87,111
Cannock
(★ Birmingham) ... 54,503
Canterbury ... 34,546
Carlisle ... 72,206
Chatham (★ London) ... 65,835
Cheadle and Gatley
(★ Manchester) ... 59,478
Chelmsford (★ London) ... 91,109
Cheltenham ... 87,188
Cheshunt (★ London) ... 49,616
Chester ... 80,154
Chesterfield
(★ 127,000) ... 73,352
Colchester ... 87,476
Corby ... 48,704
Coventry (★ 645,000) ... 318,718
Crawley (★ London) ... 80,113
Crewe ... 59,097
Crosby (★ Liverpool) ... 54,103
Darlington ... 85,519
Dartford (★ London) ... 62,032
Derby (★ 275,000) ... 218,026
Dewsbury (★ ★ Leeds) ... 49,612
Doncaster ... 74,727
Dover ... 33,461
Dudley
(★ ★ Birmingham) ... 186,513
Eastbourne ... 86,715
Eastleigh
(★ Southampton) ... 58,585
Ellesmere Port
(★ Liverpool) ... 65,829
Epsom and Ewell
(★ London) ... 65,830
Exeter ... 88,235
Fareham / Portchester
(★ Portsmouth) ... 55,563
Farnborough
(★ London) ... 48,063
Gateshead
(★ Newcastle upon Tyne) ... 91,429
Gillingham (★ London) ... 92,531
Gloucester (★ 115,000) ... 106,526
Gosport (★ Portsmouth) ... 69,664
Gravesend (★ London) ... 53,450
Greasby / Moreton
(★ Liverpool) ... 56,410
Great Yarmouth ... 54,777
Grimsby (★ 145,000) ... 91,532
Guildford (★ London) ... 61,509
Halesowen
(★ Birmingham) ... 57,533
Halifax ... 76,675
Harlow (★ London) ... 79,150
Harrogate ... 63,637
Hartlepool
(★ ★ Teesside) ... 91,749
Hastings ... 74,979
Havant (★ Portsmouth) ... 50,098
Hemel Hempstead
(★ London) ... 80,110
Hereford ... 48,277
High Wycombe
(▲ 156,800) ... 69,575
Hove (★ Brighton) ... 65,587
Huddersfield
(▲ 377,400) ... 147,825
Huyton-with-Roby
(★ Liverpool) ... 62,011
Ipswich ... 129,661
Keighley (★ Leeds) ... 49,188
Kidderminster ... 50,385
Kingston upon Hull
(★ 350,000) ... 322,144
Kingswood (★ Bristol) ... 54,736
Kirkby (★ Liverpool) ... 52,825
Leeds (★ 1,540,000) ... 445,242
Leicester (★ 495,000) ... 324,394
Lincoln ... 79,980
Littlehampton ... 46,028
Liverpool (★ 1,525,000) ... 538,809
• LONDON
(★ 11,100,000) ... 6,574,009
Lowestoft ... 59,430
Luton (★ 220,000) ... 163,209
Macclesfield ... 47,525
Maidenhead (★ London) ... 59,809
Maidstone ... 86,067
Manchester
(★ 2,775,000) ... 437,612
Mansfield (★ 198,000) ... 71,325
Margate ... 53,137
Middleton
(★ Manchester) ... 51,373
Milton Keynes ... 36,886
Newcastle-under-Lyme
(★ ★ Stoke-on-Trent) ... 73,208
Newcastle upon Tyne
(★ 1,300,000) ... 199,064
Northampton ... 154,172
Norwich (★ 230,000) ... 169,814
Nottingham (★ 655,000) ... 273,300
Nuneaton
(★ ★ Coventry) ... 60,337
Oldbury / Smethwick
(★ Birmingham) ... 153,268
Oldham
(★ ★ Manchester) ... 107,095
Oxford (★ 230,000) ... 113,847
Penzance ... 18,501
Peterborough ... 113,404
Plymouth (★ 290,000) ... 238,583
Poole
(★ ★ Bournemouth) ... 122,815
Portsmouth
(★ 485,000) ... 174,218
Preston (★ 250,000) ... 166,675
Ramsgate ... 36,678
Reading (★ 200,000) ... 194,727
Redditch
(★ Birmingham) ... 61,639
Rochdale
(★ ★ Manchester) ... 97,292
Rotherham
(★ ★ Sheffield) ... 122,374
Royal Leamington Spa
(★ ★ Coventry) ... 56,552
Rugby ... 59,039
Runcorn (★ Liverpool) ... 63,995
Saint Albans
(★ London) ... 76,709
Saint Helens ... 114,397
Sale (★ Manchester) ... 57,872
Salford (★ Manchester) ... 96,525
Scunthorpe ... 79,043
Sheffield (★ 710,000) ... 470,685
Shrewsbury ... 57,731
Slough (★ London) ... 106,341
Solihull (★ Birmingham) ... 93,940
Southampton
(★ 415,000) ... 211,321
Southend-on-Sea
(★ London) ... 155,720
Southport
(★ ★ Liverpool) ... 88,596
South Shields
(★ ★ Newcastle upon Tyne) ... 86,488
Stafford ... 60,915
Staines (★ London) ... 51,949
Stevenage ... 74,757
Stockport
(★ Manchester) ... 135,489
Stoke-on-Trent
(★ 440,000) ... 272,446
Stourbridge
(★ Birmingham) ... 55,136
Stratford-upon-Avon ... 20,941
Stretford
(★ Manchester) ... 47,522
Sunderland
(★ ★ Newcastle upon Tyne) ... 195,064
Sutton Coldfield
(★ Birmingham) ... 102,572
Swindon ... 127,348
Tamworth ... 63,260
Taunton ... 47,793
Teesside (★ 580,000) ... 245,215
Torquay (★ 112,400) ... 54,430
Tunbridge Wells ... 57,699
Wakefield (★ ★ Leeds) ... 74,764
Wallasey (★ Liverpool) ... 62,465
Walsall
(★ ★ Birmingham) ... 177,923
Walton and Weybridge
(★ London) ... 50,031
Warrington ... 81,366
Waterlooville
(★ Portsmouth) ... 57,296
Watford (★ London) ... 109,503
West Bromwich
(★ Birmingham) ... 153,725
Weston-super-Mare ... 60,821
Widnes ... 55,973
Wigan
(★ ★ Manchester) ... 88,725
Winchester ... 34,127
Windsor (★ London) ... 30,832
Woking (★ London) ... 92,667
Wolverhampton
(★ ★ Birmingham) ... 263,501
Worcester ... 75,466
Worthing
(★ ★ Brighton) ... 90,687
York (★ 145,000) ... 123,126

UNITED KINGDOM: NORTHERN IRELAND

1987 E ... 1,575,200

Cities and Towns

Antrim (1981 C) ... 22,342
Ballymena (1981 C) ... 28,166
Bangor (★ Belfast) ... 70,700
Belfast (★ 685,000) ... 303,800
Castlereagh (★ Belfast) ... 57,900
Londonderry (★ 97,200) ... 97,500
Lurgan (★ 63,000)
(1981 C) ... 20,991
Newtownabbey
(★ Belfast) ... 72,300

UNITED KINGDOM: SCOTLAND

1989 E ... 5,090,700

Cities and Towns

Aberdeen ... 210,700
Ayr (★ 100,000)
(1981 C) ... 48,493
Clydebank (★ Glasgow)
(1981 C) ... 51,832
Coatbridge (1981 C) ... 50,831
Cumbernauld
(★ Glasgow) ... 50,300
Dundee ... 172,540
Dunfermline
(★ 125,817) (1981 C) ... 52,105
East Kilbride
(★ Glasgow) ... 69,500
Edinburgh (★ 630,000) ... 433,200
Glasgow (★ 1,800,000) ... 695,630
Greenock (★ 101,000)
(1981 C) ... 58,436
Hamilton (★ Glasgow)
(1981 C) ... 51,666
Irvine (★ 94,000) ... 55,900
Kilmarnock (★ 84,000)
(1981 C) ... 51,799
Kirkcaldy (★ 148,171)
(1981 C) ... 46,356
Paisley (★ Glasgow)
(1981 C) ... 84,330
Stirling (★ 61,000)
(1981 C) ... 36,640

UNITED KINGDOM: WALES

1981 C ... 2,790,462

Cities and Towns

Barry (★ Cardiff) ... 44,443
Cardiff (★ 625,000) ... 262,313
Cwmbran (★ Newport) ... 44,592
Llanelli ... 45,336
Neath (★ ★ Swansea) ... 48,687
Newport (★ 310,000) ... 115,896
Port Talbot (★ 130,000) ... 40,078
Rhondda (★ ★ Cardiff) ... 70,980
Swansea (★ 275,000) ... 172,433

UNITED STATES

1990 C ... 248,709,873

UNITED STATES: ALABAMA

1990 C ... 4,040,587

Cities and Towns

Birmingham ... 265,968
Decatur ... 48,761
Dothan ... 53,589
Florence ... 36,426
Gadsden ... 42,523
Huntsville ... 159,789
Mobile ... 196,278
Montgomery ... 187,106
Tuscaloosa ... 77,759

UNITED STATES: ALASKA

1990 C ... 550,043

Cities and Towns

Anchorage ... 226,338
Fairbanks ... 30,843
Juneau ... 26,751

UNITED STATES: ARIZONA

1990 C ... 3,665,228

Cities and Towns

Chandler ... 90,533
Flagstaff ... 45,857
Glendale ... 148,134
Mesa ... 288,091
Peoria ... 50,618
Phoenix ... 900,013
Scottsdale ... 130,069
Sun City ... 57,000
Tempe ... 141,865
Tucson ... 405,390
Yuma ... 54,923

UNITED STATES: ARKANSAS

1990 C ... 2,350,725

Cities and Towns

Fort Smith ... 72,798
Little Rock ... 175,795
North Little Rock ... 61,741
Pine Bluff ... 57,140

UNITED STATES: CALIFORNIA

1990 C ... 29,760,021

Cities and Towns

Alameda ... 76,459
Alhambra ... 82,106
Anaheim ... 266,406
Antioch ... 62,195
Bakersfield ... 174,820
Baldwin Park ... 69,330
Bellflower ... 61,815
Berkeley ... 102,724
Beverly Hills ... 31,971
Buena Park ... 68,784
Burbank ... 93,643
Camarillo ... 52,303
Carlsbad ... 63,126
Carson ... 83,995
Cerritos ... 53,240
Chino ... 59,682
Chula Vista ... 135,163
Citrus Heights ... 107,439
Clovis ... 50,323
Compton ... 90,454
Concord ... 111,348
Corona ... 76,095
Costa Mesa ... 96,357
Cucamonga ... 101,409
Daly City ... 92,311
Diamond Bar ... 53,672
Downey ... 91,444
East Los Angeles ... 126,379
El Cajon ... 88,693
El Monte ... 106,209
Encinitas ... 55,386
Escondido ... 108,635
Fairfield ... 77,211
Fontana ... 87,535
Fountain Valley ... 53,691
Fremont ... 173,339
Fresno ... 354,202
Fullerton ... 114,144
Gardena ... 49,847
Garden Grove ... 143,050
Glendale ... 180,038
Hacienda Heights ... 52,354
Hawthorne ... 71,349
Hayward ... 111,498
Hesperia ... 50,418
Huntington Beach ... 181,519
Huntington Park ... 56,065
Inglewood ... 109,602
Irvine ... 110,330
La Habra ... 51,266
Lakewood ... 73,557
La Mesa ... 52,931
Lancaster ... 97,291
Livermore ... 56,741
Lodi ... 51,874
Long Beach ... 429,433
Los Angeles ... 3,485,398
Lynwood ... 61,945
Merced ... 56,216
Milpitas ... 50,686
Mission Viejo ... 72,820
Modesto ... 164,730
Montebello ... 59,564
Monterey Park ... 60,738
Moreno Valley ... 118,779
Mountain View ... 67,460
Napa ... 61,842
National City ... 54,249
Newport Beach ... 66,643
Norwalk ... 94,279
Oakland ... 372,242
Oceanside ... 128,398
Ontario ... 133,179
Orange ... 110,658
Oxnard ... 142,216
Palmdale ... 68,842
Palm Springs ... 40,181
Palo Alto ... 55,900
Pasadena ... 131,591
Pico Rivera ... 59,177
Pleasanton ... 50,553
Pomona ... 131,723
Redding ... 66,462
Redlands ... 60,394
Redondo Beach ... 60,167
Redwood City ... 66,072
Rialto ... 72,388
Richmond ... 87,425
Riverside ... 226,505
Rosemead ... 51,638
Sacramento ... 369,365
Salinas ... 108,777
San Bernardino ... 164,164
San Diego ... 1,110,549
San Francisco ... 723,959
San Jose ... 782,248
San Leandro ... 68,223
San Mateo ... 85,486
Santa Ana ... 293,742
Santa Barbara ... 85,571
Santa Clara ... 93,613
Santa Clarita ... 110,642
Santa Cruz ... 49,040
Santa Maria ... 61,284
Santa Monica ... 86,905
Santa Rosa ... 113,313
Santee ... 52,902
Simi Valley ... 100,217
South Gate ... 86,284
South San Francisco ... 54,312
Stockton ... 210,943
Sunnyvale ... 117,229
Thousand Oaks ... 104,352
Torrance ... 133,107
Tustin ... 50,689
Union City ... 53,762
Upland ... 63,374
Vacaville ... 71,479
Vallejo ... 109,199
Ventura (San Buenaventura) ... 92,575
Visalia ... 75,636
Vista ... 71,872
Walnut Creek ... 60,569
West Covina ... 96,086
Westminster ... 78,118
Whittier ... 77,671
Yorba Linda ... 52,422

UNITED STATES: COLORADO

1990 C ... 3,294,394

Cities and Towns

Arvada ... 89,235
Aurora ... 222,103
Boulder ... 83,312
Colorado Springs ... 281,140
Denver ... 467,610
Fort Collins ... 87,758
Greeley ... 60,536
Lakewood ... 126,481
Longmont ... 51,555
Pueblo ... 98,640
Thornton ... 55,031
Westminster ... 74,625

UNITED STATES: CONNECTICUT

1990 C ... 3,287,116

Cities and Towns

Bridgeport ... 141,686
Bristol ... 60,640
Danbury ... 65,585
East Hartford ... 50,452
Fairfield ... 52,400
Greenwich ... 58,000
Hamden ... 53,100
Hartford ... 139,739
Manchester ... 51,000
Meriden ... 59,479
Milford ... 48,168
New Britain ... 75,491
New Haven ... 130,474
Norwalk ... 78,331
Stamford ... 108,056
Stratford ... 50,400
Waterbury ... 108,961
West Hartford ... 59,100
West Haven ... 54,021

UNITED STATES: DELAWARE

1990 C ... 666,168

Cities and Towns

Dover ... 27,630
Newark ... 25,098
Wilmington ... 71,529

UNITED STATES: DISTRICT OF COLUMBIA

1990 C ... 606,900

Cities and Towns

WASHINGTON ... 606,900

UNITED STATES: FLORIDA

1990 C ... 12,937,926

Cities and Towns

Boca Raton ... 61,492
Cape Coral ... 74,991
Carol City ... 52,800
City of Sunrise ... 64,407
Clearwater ... 98,784
Corol Springs ... 79,443
Daytona Beach ... 61,921
Delray Beach ... 47,181
Fort Lauderdale ... 149,377
Gainesville ... 84,770
Hialeah ... 188,004
Hollywood ... 121,697
Jacksonville ... 635,230
Kendall ... 53,100
Lakeland ... 70,576
Largo ... 65,674
Lauderhill ... 49,708
Melbourne ... 59,646
Miami ... 358,548
Miami Beach ... 92,639
North Miami ... 49,998
Orlando ... 164,693
Palm Bay ... 62,632
Pembroke Pines ... 65,452
Pensacola ... 58,165
Plantation ... 66,692
Pompano Beach ... 72,411
Port Saint Lucie ... 55,866
Saint Petersburg ... 238,629
Sarasota ... 50,961
Tallahassee ... 124,773
Tampa ... 280,015
West Palm Beach ... 67,643

UNITED STATES: GEORGIA

1990 C ... 6,478,216

Cities and Towns

Albany ... 78,122
Athens ... 45,734
Atlanta ... 394,017
Columbus ... 178,681
Macon ... 106,612
Savannah ... 137,560

UNITED STATES: HAWAII

1990 C ... 1,108,229

Cities and Towns

Hilo ... 37,808
Honolulu ... 365,272
Pearl City ... 30,993

UNITED STATES: IDAHO

1990 C ... 1,006,749

Cities and Towns

Boise ... 125,738
Idaho Falls ... 43,929
Pocatello ... 46,080

UNITED STATES: ILLINOIS

1990 C ... 11,430,602

Cities and Towns

Arlington Heights ... 75,460
Aurora ... 99,581
Bloomington ... 51,972
Champaign ... 63,502
Chicago ... 2,783,726
Cicero ... 67,436
Decatur ... 83,885
Des Plaines ... 53,223
Elgin ... 77,010
Evanston ... 73,233
Joliet ... 76,836

C Census. E Official estimate. U Unofficial estimate.
• Largest city in country.
★ Population or designation of metropolitan area, including suburbs (see headnote).
▲ Population of an entire municipality, commune, or district, including rural area.

Mount Prospect	53,170
Naperville	85,351
Oak Lawn	56,182
Oak Park	53,648
Peoria	113,504
Rockford	139,426
Schaumburg	68,586
Skokie	59,432
Springfield	105,227
Waukegan	69,392
Wheaton	51,464

UNITED STATES: INDIANA

1990 C 5,544,159

Cities and Towns

Anderson	59,459
Bloomington	60,633
Evansville	126,272
Fort Wayne	173,072
Gary	116,646
Hammond	84,236
Indianapolis	731,327
Kokomo	44,962
Lafayette	43,764
Michigan City	33,822
Muncie	71,035
South Bend	105,511
Terre Haute	57,483

UNITED STATES: IOWA

1990 C 2,776,755

Cities and Towns

Ames	47,198
Cedar Rapids	108,751
Council Bluffs	54,315
Davenport	95,333
Des Moines	193,187
Dubuque	57,546
Iowa City	59,738
Sioux City	80,505
Waterloo	66,467

UNITED STATES: KANSAS

1990 C 2,477,574

Cities and Towns

Kansas City	149,767
Lawrence	65,608
Olathe	63,352
Overland Park	111,790
Topeka	119,883
Wichita	304,011

UNITED STATES: KENTUCKY

1990 C 3,685,296

Cities and Towns

Frankfort	25,968
Lexington	225,366
Louisville	269,063
Owensboro	53,549

UNITED STATES: LOUISIANA

1990 C 4,219,973

Cities and Towns

Alexandria	49,188
Baton Rouge	219,531
Bossier City	52,721
Houma	96,982
Kenner	72,033
Lafayette	94,440
Lake Charles	70,580
Metairie	149,428
Monroe	54,909
New Orleans	496,938
Shreveport	198,525

UNITED STATES: MAINE

1990 C 1,227,928

Cities and Towns

Augusta	21,325
Bangor	33,181
Lewiston	39,757
Portland	64,358

UNITED STATES: MARYLAND

1990 C 4,781,468

Cities and Towns

Annapolis	33,187
Baltimore	736,014
Bethesda	62,936
Columbia	75,883
Dundalk	65,800
Rockville	44,835
Silver Spring	76,200
Towson	49,445
Wheaton	58,300

UNITED STATES: MASSACHUSETTS

1990 C 6,016,425

Cities and Towns

Boston	574,283
Brockton	92,788
Brookline	54,718
Cambridge	95,802
Chicopee	56,632
Fall River	92,703
Framingham	64,989
Haverhill	51,418
Holyoke	43,704
Lawrence	70,207
Lowell	103,439
Lynn	81,245
Malden	53,884
Medford	57,407
New Bedford	99,922
Newton	82,585
Peabody	47,039
Pittsfield	48,622
Quincy	84,985
Salem	38,091
Somerville	76,210
Springfield	156,983
Taunton	49,832
Waltham	57,878
Weymouth	54,063
Worcester	169,759

UNITED STATES: MICHIGAN

1990 C 9,295,297

Cities and Towns

Ann Arbor	109,592
Battle Creek	53,540
Clinton	85,866
Dearborn	89,286
Dearborn Heights	60,838
Detroit	1,027,974
East Lansing	50,677
Farmington Hills	74,652
Flint	140,761
Grand Rapids	189,126
Kalamazoo	80,277
Lansing	127,321
Livonia	100,850
Pontiac	71,166
Redford	54,387
Rochester Hills	61,766
Roseville	51,412
Royal Oak	65,410
Saginaw	69,512
Saint Clair Shores	68,107
Southfield	75,728
Sterling Heights	117,810
Taylor	70,811
Troy	72,884
Warren	144,864
Westland	84,724
Wyoming	63,891

UNITED STATES: MINNESOTA

1990 C 4,375,099

Cities and Towns

Bloomington	86,335
Brooklyn Park	56,381
Burnsville	51,288
Coon Rapids	52,978
Duluth	85,493
Minneapolis	368,383
Minnetonka	48,370
Plymouth	50,889
Rochester	70,745
Saint Cloud	48,812
Saint Paul	272,235

UNITED STATES: MISSISSIPPI

1990 C 2,573,216

Cities and Towns

Biloxi	46,319
Hattiesburg	41,882
Jackson	196,637

UNITED STATES: MISSOURI

1990 C 5,117,073

Cities and Towns

Columbia	69,101
Florissant	51,206
Independence	112,301
Jefferson City	35,481
Kansas City	435,146
Saint Charles	54,555
Saint Joseph	71,852
Saint Louis	396,685
Springfield	140,494

UNITED STATES: MONTANA

1990 C 799,065

Cities and Towns

Billings	81,151
Great Falls	55,097
Helena	24,569

UNITED STATES: NEBRASKA

1990 C 1,578,385

Cities and Towns

Grand Island	39,386
Lincoln	191,972
Omaha	335,795

UNITED STATES: NEVADA

1990 C 1,201,833

Cities and Towns

Carson City	40,443
Henderson	64,942
Las Vegas	258,295
Paradise	124,682
Reno	133,850
Sparks	53,367
Sunrise Manor	95,362

UNITED STATES: NEW HAMPSHIRE

1990 C 1,109,252

Cities and Towns

Concord	36,006
Manchester	99,567
Nashua	79,662

UNITED STATES: NEW JERSEY

1990 C 7,730,188

Cities and Towns

Atlantic City	37,986
Bayonne	61,444
Brick [Township]	64,800
Camden	87,492
Cherry Hill	69,319
Clifton	71,742
East Orange	73,552
Edison	88,680
Elizabeth	110,002
Irvington	59,774
Jersey City	228,537
Newark	275,221
Passaic	58,041
Paterson	140,891
Trenton	88,675
Union	50,024
Union City	58,012
Vineland	54,780
Woodbridge [Township] (1986 U)	95,100

UNITED STATES: NEW MEXICO

1990 C 1,515,069

Cities and Towns

Albuquerque	384,736
Las Cruces	62,126
Roswell	44,654
Santa Fe	55,859

UNITED STATES: NEW YORK

1990 C 17,990,455

Cities and Towns

Albany	101,082
Binghamton	53,008
Buffalo	328,123
Cheektowaga	84,387
Greece	64,600
Irondequoit	52,322
Levittown	53,286
Mount Vernon	67,153
New Rochelle	67,265
• New York	7,322,564
Niagara Falls	61,840
Rochester	231,636
Schenectady	65,566
Syracuse	163,860
Tonawanda	65,284
Troy	54,269
Utica	68,637
Yonkers	188,082

UNITED STATES: NORTH CAROLINA

1990 C 6,628,637

Cities and Towns

Asheville	61,607
Charlotte	395,934
Durham	136,611
Fayetteville	75,695
Gastonia	54,732
Greensboro	183,521
High Point	69,496
Raleigh	207,951
Rocky Mount	48,997
Wilmington	55,530
Winston-Salem	143,485

UNITED STATES: NORTH DAKOTA

1990 C 638,800

Cities and Towns

Bismarck	49,256
Fargo	74,111
Grand Forks	49,425

UNITED STATES: OHIO

1990 C 10,847,115

Cities and Towns

Akron	223,019
Canton	84,161
Cincinnati	364,040
Cleveland	505,616
Cleveland Heights	54,052
Columbus	632,910
Dayton	182,044
Elyria	56,746
Euclid	54,875
Hamilton	61,368
Kettering	60,569
Lakewood	59,718
Lorain	71,245
Mansfield	50,627
Parma	87,876
Springfield	70,487
Toledo	332,943
Warren	50,793
Youngstown	95,732

UNITED STATES: OKLAHOMA

1990 C 3,145,585

Cities and Towns

Broken Arrow	58,043
Edmond	52,315
Lawton	80,561
Midwest City	52,267
Norman	80,071
Oklahoma City	444,719
Tulsa	367,302

UNITED STATES: OREGON

1990 C 2,842,321

Cities and Towns

Beaverton	53,310
Eugene	112,669
Gresham	68,235
Portland	437,319
Salem	107,786

UNITED STATES: PENNSYLVANIA

1990 C 11,881,643

Cities and Towns

Abington Township	59,300
Allentown	105,090
Altoona	51,881
Bensalem	56,788
Bethlehem	71,428
Bristol	57,129
Erie	108,718
Harrisburg	52,376
Haverford Township	51,800
Lancaster	55,551
Lower Merion	58,003
Penn Hills	51,430
Philadelphia	1,585,577
Pittsburgh	369,879
Reading	78,380
Scranton	81,805
Upper Darby	86,100

UNITED STATES: RHODE ISLAND

1990 C 1,003,464

Cities and Towns

Cranston	76,060
East Providence	50,380
Pawtucket	72,644
Providence	160,728
Warwick	85,427

UNITED STATES: SOUTH CAROLINA

1990 C 3,486,703

Cities and Towns

Charleston	80,414
Columbia	98,052
Greenville	58,282
North Charleston	70,218

UNITED STATES: SOUTH DAKOTA

1990 C 696,004

Cities and Towns

Pierre	12,906
Rapid City	54,523
Sioux Falls	100,814

UNITED STATES: TENNESSEE

1990 C 4,877,185

Cities and Towns

Chattanooga	152,466
Clarksville	75,494
Jackson	48,949
Knoxville	165,121
Memphis	610,337
Nashville	487,969

UNITED STATES: TEXAS

1990 C 16,986,510

Cities and Towns

Abilene	106,654
Amarillo	157,615
Arlington	261,721
Austin	465,622
Baytown	63,850
Beaumont	114,323
Brownsville	98,962
Bryan	55,002
Carrollton	82,169
College Station	52,456
Corpus Christi	257,453
Dallas	1,006,877
Denton	66,270
El Paso	515,342
Fort Worth	447,619
Galveston	59,070
Garland	180,650
Grand Prairie	99,616
Houston	1,630,553
Irving	155,037
Killeen	63,535
Laredo	122,899
Longview	70,311
Lubbock	186,206
McAllen	84,021
Mesquite	101,484
Midland	89,443
Odessa	89,699
Pasadena	119,363
Plano	128,713
Port Arthur	58,724
Richardson	74,840
San Angelo	84,474
San Antonio	935,933
Tyler	75,450
Victoria	55,076
Waco	103,590
Wichita Falls	96,259

UNITED STATES: UTAH

1990 C 1,722,850

Cities and Towns

Ogden	63,909
Orem	67,561
Provo	86,835
Salt Lake City	159,936
Sandy	75,058
West Valley City	86,976

UNITED STATES: VERMONT

1990 C 562,758

Cities and Towns

Burlington	39,127
Montpelier	8,247
Rutland	18,230

UNITED STATES: VIRGINIA

1990 C 6,187,358

Cities and Towns

Alexandria	111,183
Arlington	170,936
Chesapeake	151,976
Danville	53,056
Hampton	133,793
Lynchburg	66,049
Newport News	170,045
Norfolk	261,229
Petersburg	38,386
Portsmouth	103,907
Richmond	203,056
Roanoke	96,397
Suffolk	52,141
Virginia Beach	393,069

UNITED STATES: WASHINGTON

1990 C 4,866,692

Cities and Towns

Bellevue	86,874
Bellingham	52,179
Everett	69,961
Lakewood Center	62,000
Olympia	33,840
Seattle	516,259
Spokane	177,196
Tacoma	176,664
Yakima	54,827

UNITED STATES: WEST VIRGINIA

1990 C 1,793,477

Cities and Towns

Charleston	57,287
Huntington	54,844
Parkersburg	33,862
Wheeling	34,882

UNITED STATES: WISCONSIN

1990 C 4,891,769

Cities and Towns

Appleton	65,695
Eau Claire	56,856
Fond du Lac	37,757
Green Bay	96,466
Janesville	52,133
Kenosha	80,352
La Crosse	51,003
Madison	191,262
Milwaukee	628,088
Oshkosh	55,006
Racine	84,298
Sheboygan	49,676
Waukesha	56,958
Wausau	37,060
Wauwatosa	49,366
West Allis	63,221

UNITED STATES: WYOMING

1990 C 453,588

Cities and Towns

Casper	46,742
Cheyenne	50,008
Laramie	26,687

C Census. E Official estimate. U Unofficial estimate.
• Largest city in country.

★ Population or designation of metropolitan area, including suburbs (see headnote).
▲ Population of an entire municipality, commune, or district, including rural area.

URUGUAY

1985 C.................2,955,241

Cities and Towns

Las Piedras
(★ Montevideo)..........58,288
• MONTEVIDEO
(★ 1,550,000).........1,251,647
Paysandú.................76,191
Rivera...................57,316
Salto....................80,823

UZBEKISTAN / Ŭzbekiston

1989 C..............19,906,000

Cities and Towns

Almalyk.................114,000
Andižan.................293,000
Angren..................131,000
Bekabad (1987 E)........80,000
Buchara.................224,000
Chodžejli (1987 E).......55,000
Čirčik (★ Taškent)......156,000
Denau (1987 E)..........53,000
Džizak..................102,000
Fergana.................200,000
Gulistan (1987 E).......51,000
Jangijul' (1987 E)......71,000
Karši...................156,000
Kattakurgan (1987 E)....63,000
Kokand..................182,000
Margilan................125,000
Namangan................308,000
Navoi...................107,000
Nukus...................169,000
Samarkand...............366,000
• TAŠKENT
(★ 2,325,000).........2,073,000
Termez (1987 E).........72,000
Urgenč..................128,000

VANUATU

1989 C..................142,419

Cities and Towns

• PORT VILA (★ 23,000).....18,905

VATICAN CITY / Città del Vaticano

1988 E.......................766

VENEZUELA

1981 C..............14,516,735

Cities and Towns

Acarigua.................91,662

Barcelona...............156,461
Barinas.................110,462
Barquisimeto............497,635
Baruta (★ Caracas)......200,063
Cabimas.................140,435
Cagua...................53,704
Calabozo................61,995
• CARACAS
(★ 3,600,000).........1,816,901
Carora..................58,694
Carúpano................64,579
Catia La Mar
(★ Caracas)...........87,916
Chacao (★ Caracas)......72,703
Ciudad Bolívar..........182,941
Ciudad Guayana..........314,497
Ciudad Ojeda
(Lagunillas)..........83,565
Coro....................96,339
Cumaná..................179,814
El Limón................65,122
El Tigre................73,595
Guacara.................72,727
Guanare.................64,025
Guarenas (★ Caracas)....101,742
La Victoria.............70,828
Los Dos Caminos
(★ Caracas)...........63,346
Los Teques
(★ Caracas)...........112,857
Maiquetía (★ Caracas)....66,056
Maracaibo...............890,643
Maracay.................322,560
Maturín.................154,976
Mérida..................143,209
Petare (★ Caracas)......395,715
Porlamar................51,079
Pozuelos................80,342
Puerto Cabello..........71,759
Puerto la Cruz..........53,881
Punto Fijo..............71,114
San Cristóbal...........198,793
San Felipe..............57,526
San Fernando de Apure.....57,308
San Juan de los
Morros................57,219
Turmero.................111,186
Valencia................616,224
Valera..................102,068
Valle de la Pascua........55,761

VIETNAM / Viet Nam

1979 C..............52,741,766

Cities and Towns

Bac Giang...............54,506
Bien Hoa................187,254

Buon Me Thuot...........71,815
Ca Mau..................67,484
Cam Pha.................76,697
Cam Ranh (1973 E)......118,111
Can Tho................182,856
Da Lat..................87,136
Da Nang................318,653
Hai Duong...............54,579
Hai Phong
(▲ 1,279,067)
(1989 C)............456,000
HÀ NOI (★ 1,500,000)
(1989 C)..........1,089,000
Hoa Binh................51,187
Hon Gai................114,573
Hue....................165,710
Long Xuyen.............112,485
Minh Hai................72,517
My Tho.................101,493
Nam Dinh...............160,179
Nha Trang..............172,663
Phan Thiet..............75,241
Play Cu.................58,088
Qui Nhon...............127,211
Rach Gia................81,075
Sa Dec..................73,104
Soc Trang...............74,967
Thai Binh...............79,566
Thai Nguyen............138,023
Thanh Hoa...............72,646
• Thanh Pho Ho Chi Minh
(Saigon)
(★ 3,100,000)
(1989 C)..........3,169,000
Tra Vinh................44,020
Tuy Hoa.................46,617
Viet Tri................72,108
Vinh...................159,753
Vinh Long...............71,505
Vung Tau................81,694

VIRGIN ISLANDS OF THE UNITED STATES

1980 C..................96,569

Cities and Towns

• CHARLOTTE AMALIE
(★ 32,000)..............11,842

WALLIS AND FUTUNA / Wallis et Futuna

1983 E..................12,408

Cities and Towns

• MATA-UTU.................815

WESTERN SAHARA

1982 E.................142,000

Cities and Towns

• EL AAIÚN...............93,875

WESTERN SAMOA / Samoa i Sisifo

1981 C.................156,349

Cities and Towns

• APIA..................33,170

YEMEN / Al-Yaman

1990 E..............11,282,000

Cities and Towns

'Adan (★ 318,000)
(1984 E).............176,100
Al-Hudaydah (1986 C)....155,110
Al-Mukallā (1984 E).....58,000
• SAN'Ā' (1986 C)........427,150
Ta'izz (1986 C).........178,043

YUGOSLAVIA / Jugoslavija

1987 E..............10,342,020

Cities and Towns

• BEOGRAD
(★ 1,400,000).........1,130,000
Kragujevac (▲ 171,609).....94,800
Niš (▲ 240,219)........168,400
Novi Sad (▲ 266,772)...176,000
Pančevo (★ Beograd).....62,700
Podgorica (▲ 145,163)....82,500
Priština (▲ 244,830)...125,400
Subotica (▲ 153,306)...100,500
Zrenjanin (▲ 140,009)...65,400

ZAIRE / Zaïre

1984 C..............29,671,407

Cities and Towns

Bandundu................63,189
Beni....................73,319
Boma....................88,556
Bukavu.................171,064
Butembo.................78,633
Gandajika...............60,263
Gemena..................62,641

Goma....................76,745
Ilebo (Port-Francqui)....48,831
Isiro...................78,871
Kabinda.................81,752
Kalemie (Albertville)....70,694
Kananga (Luluabourg)....290,898
Kikwit.................146,784
Kindu...................68,044
• KINSHASA
(LÉOPOLDVILLE)
(1986 E)...........3,000,000
Kisangani (Stanleyville)....282,650
Kolwezi................201,382
Likasi (Jadotville)....194,465
Lubumbashi
(Élisabethville).....543,268
Manono..................51,755
Matadi.................144,742
Mbandaka
(Coquilhatville).....125,263
Mbuji-Mayi (Bakwanga)....423,363
Mwene-Ditu..............72,567
Tshikapa...............105,484
Yangambi................53,726

ZAMBIA

1980 C...............5,661,801

Cities and Towns

Chililabombwe
(Bancroft) (★ 56,582).....25,900
Chingola...............130,872
Kabwe (Broken Hill)....127,420
Kalulushi...............53,383
Kitwe (★ 283,962)......207,500
Livingstone.............61,296
Luanshya (★ 113,422)....61,600
• LUSAKA................535,830
Mufulira (★ 138,824)....77,100
Ndola..................250,490

ZIMBABWE

1983 E...............7,740,000

Cities and Towns

Bulawayo...............429,000
Chitungwiza (★ Harare)...202,000
Gweru (1982 C)..........78,940
• HARARE (★ 890,000).....681,000
Kwekwe (1982 C).........47,976
Mutare (1982 C).........75,358

C Census.   E Official estimate.   U Unofficial estimate.   ★ Population or designation of metropolitan area, including suburbs (see headnote).
• Largest city in country.   ▲ Population of an entire municipality, commune, or district, including rural area.

United States General Information

Geographical Facts

ELEVATION

The highest elevation in the United States is Mount McKinley, Alaska, 20,320 feet.

The lowest elevation in the United States is in Death Valley, California, 282 feet below sea level.

The average elevation of the United States is 2,500 feet.

EXTREMITIES

Direction	Location	Latitude	Longitude
North	Point Barrow, Ak.	71° 23'N.	156° 29'W.
South	Ka Lae (point) Hi.	18° 56'N.	155° 41'W.
East	West Quoddy Head, Me.	44° 49'N.	66° 57'W.
West	Cape Wrangell, Ak.	52° 55'N.	172° 27'E.

LENGTH OF BOUNDARIES

The total length of the Canadian boundary of the United States is 5,525 miles.

The total length of the Mexican boundary of the United States is 1,933 miles.

The total length of the Atlantic coastline of the United States is 2,069 miles.

The total length of the Pacific and Arctic coastline of the United States is 8,683 miles.

The total length of the Gulf of Mexico coastline of the United States is 1,631 miles.

The total length of all coastlines and land boundaries of the United States is 19,841 miles.

The total length of the tidal shoreline and land boundaries of the United States is 96,091 miles.

GEOGRAPHIC CENTERS

The geographic center of the United States (including Alaska and Hawaii) is in Butte County, South Dakota at 44° 58'N., 103° 46'W.

The geographic center of North America is in North Dakota, a few miles west of Devils Lake, at 48° 10'N., 100° 10'W.

EXTREMES OF TEMPERATURE

The highest temperature ever recorded in the United States was 134° F., at Greenland Ranch, Death Valley, California, on July 10, 1913.

The lowest temperature ever recorded in the United States was -80° F., at Prospect Creek, Alaska, on January 23, 1971.

Historical Facts

TERRITORIAL ACQUISITIONS

Accession	Date	Area (sq. mi.)	Cost in Dollars
Original territory of the Thirteen States	1790	888,685	
Purchase of Louisiana Territory, from France	1803	827,192	$11,250,000
By treaty with Spain: Florida	1819	58,560	5,000,000
Other areas	1819	13,443	
Annexation of Texas	1845	390,144	
Oregon Territory, by treaty with Great Britain	1846	285,580	
Mexican Cession	1848	529,017	$15,000,000
Gadsden Purchase, from Mexico	1853	29,640	$10,000,000
Purchase of Alaska, from Russia	1867	586,412	7,200,000
Annexation of Hawaiian Islands	1898	6,450	
Puerto Rico, by treaty with Spain	1899	3,435	
Guam, by treaty with Spain	1899	212	
American Samoa, by treaty with Great Britain and Germany	1900	76	
Virgin Islands, by purchase from Denmark	1917	133	$25,000,000

Note: The Philippines, ceded by Spain in 1898 for $20,000,000 were a territorial possession of the United States from 1898 to 1946. On July 4, 1946 they became the independent Republic of the Philippines.

Note: The Canal Zone, ceded by Panama in 1903 for $10,000,000 was a territory of the United States from 1903 to 1979. As a result of treaties signed in 1977, sovereignty over the Canal Zone reverted to Panama in 1979.

WESTWARD MOVEMENT OF CENTER OF POPULATION

Year	U.S.Population Total at Census	Approximate Location
1790	3,929,214	23 miles east of Baltimore, Md.
1800	5,308,483	18 miles west of Baltimore, Md.
1810	7,239,881	40 miles northwest of Washington, D.C.
1820	9,638,453	16 miles east of Moorefield, W. Va.
1830	12,866,020	19 miles southwest of Moorefield, W. Va.
1840	17,069,453	16 miles south of Clarksburg, W. Va.
1850	23,191,876	23 miles southeast of Parkersburg, W. Va.
1860	31,443,321	20 miles southeast of Chillicothe, Ohio
1870	39,818,449	48 miles northeast of Cincinnati, Ohio
1880	50,155,783	8 miles southwest of Cincinnati, Ohio
1890	62,947,714	20 miles east of Columbus, Ind.
1900	75,994,575	6 miles southeast of Columbus, Ind.
1910	91,972,266	Bloomington, Ind.
1920	105,710,620	8 miles southwest of Spencer, Ind.
1930	122,775,046	3 miles northeast of Linton, Ind.
1940	131,669,275	2 miles southeast of Carlisle, Ind.
1950	150,697,361	8 miles northwest of Olney, Ill.
1960	179,323,175	6 miles northwest of Centralia, Ill.
1970	204,816,296	5 miles southeast of Mascoutah, Ill.
1980	226,549,010	1/4 mile west of DeSoto, Mo.
1990	248,709,873	10 miles southeast of Steelville, Mo.

State Areas and Populations

STATE	Land Area* square miles	Water Area* square miles	Total Area* square miles	Area Rank land area	1990 Population	1990 Population per square mile	1980 Population	1970 Population	1960 Population	Population Rank 1990	Population Rank 1980	Population Rank 1970
Alabama	50,750	1,673	52,423	28	4,040,587	80	3,894,046	3,444,354	3,266,740	22	22	21
Alaska	570,374	86,051	656,424	1	550,043	1.0	401,851	302,583	226,167	49	50	50
Arizona	113,642	364	114,006	6	3,665,228	32	2,716,756	1,775,399	1,302,161	24	29	33
Arkansas	52,075	1,107	53,182	27	2,350,725	45	2,286,357	1,923,322	1,786,272	33	33	32
California	155,973	7,734	163,707	3	29,760,021	191	23,667,372	19,971,069	15,717,204	1	1	1
Colorado	103,730	371	104,100	8	3,294,394	32	2,889,735	2,209,596	1,753,947	26	28	30
Connecticut	4,845	698	5,544	48	3,287,116	678	3,107,576	3,032,217	2,535,234	27	25	24
Delaware	1,955	535	2,489	49	666,168	341	594,317	548,104	446,292	46	47	41
District of Columbia	61	7	68	.....	606,900	9,949	638,432	756,668	763,956	.....	.....	.....
Florida	53,997	11,761	65,758	26	12,937,926	240	9,747,015	6,791,418	4,951,560	4	7	9
Georgia	57,919	1,522	59,441	21	6,478,216	112	5,462,982	4,587,930	3,943,116	11	13	15
Hawaii	6,423	4,508	10,932	47	1,108,229	173	964,691	769,913	632,772	41	39	40
Idaho	82,751	823	83,574	11	1,006,749	12	944,127	713,015	667,191	42	41	43
Illinois	55,593	2,325	57,918	24	11,430,602	206	11,427,414	11,110,285	10,081,158	6	5	5
Indiana	35,870	550	36,420	38	5,544,159	155	5,490,212	5,195,392	4,662,498	14	12	11
Iowa	55,875	401	56,276	23	2,776,755	50	2,913,808	2,825,368	2,757,537	30	27	25
Kansas	81,823	459	82,282	13	2,477,574	30	2,364,236	2,249,071	2,178,611	32	32	28
Kentucky	39,732	679	40,411	36	3,685,296	93	3,660,324	3,220,711	3,038,156	23	23	23
Louisiana	43,566	8,277	51,843	33	4,219,973	97	4,206,098	3,644,637	3,257,022	21	19	20
Maine	30,865	4,523	35,387	39	1,227,928	40	1,125,043	993,722	969,265	38	38	38
Maryland	9,775	2,633	12,407	42	4,781,468	489	4,216,933	3,923,897	3,100,689	19	18	18
Massachusetts	7,838	2,717	10,555	45	6,016,425	768	5,737,093	5,689,170	5,148,578	13	11	10
Michigan	56,809	40,001	96,810	22	9,295,297	164	9,262,044	8,881,826	7,823,194	8	8	7
Minnesota	79,617	7,326	86,943	14	4,375,099	55	4,075,970	3,806,103	3,413,864	20	21	19
Mississippi	46,914	1,520	48,434	31	2,573,216	55	2,520,698	2,216,994	2,178,141	31	31	29
Missouri	68,898	811	69,709	18	5,117,073	74	4,916,759	4,677,623	4,319,813	15	15	13
Montana	145,556	1,490	147,046	4	799,065	5.5	786,690	694,409	674,767	44	44	44
Nebraska	76,878	481	77,358	15	1,578,385	21	1,569,825	1,485,333	1,411,330	36	35	35
Nevada	109,806	761	110,567	7	1,201,833	11	800,508	488,738	285,278	39	43	47
New Hampshire	8,969	382	9,351	44	1,109,252	124	920,610	737,681	606,921	40	42	42
New Jersey	7,419	1,303	8,722	46	7,730,188	1,042	7,365,011	7,171,112	6,066,782	9	9	8
New Mexico	121,365	234	121,598	5	1,515,069	12	1,303,542	1,017,055	951,023	37	37	37
New York	47,224	7,251	54,475	30	17,990,455	381	17,558,165	18,241,391	16,782,304	2	2	2
North Carolina	48,718	5,103	53,821	29	6,628,637	136	5,880,415	5,084,411	4,556,155	10	10	12
North Dakota	68,994	1,710	70,704	17	638,800	9.3	652,717	617,792	632,446	47	46	46
Ohio	40,953	3,875	44,828	35	10,847,115	265	10,797,603	10,657,423	9,706,397	7	6	6
Oklahoma	68,679	1,224	69,903	19	3,145,585	46	3,025,487	2,559,463	2,328,284	28	26	27
Oregon	96,003	2,383	98,386	10	2,842,321	30	2,633,156	2,091,533	1,768,687	29	30	31
Pennsylvania	44,820	1,239	46,058	32	11,881,643	265	11,864,751	11,800,766	11,319,366	5	4	3
Rhode Island	1,045	500	1,545	50	1,003,464	960	947,154	949,723	859,488	43	40	39
South Carolina	30,111	1,896	32,007	40	3,486,703	116	3,120,730	2,590,713	2,382,594	25	24	26
South Dakota	75,898	1,224	77,121	16	696,004	9.2	690,768	666,257	680,514	45	45	45
Tennessee	41,220	926	42,146	34	4,877,185	118	4,591,023	3,926,018	3,567,089	17	17	17
Texas	261,914	6,687	268,601	2	16,986,510	65	14,225,288	11,198,655	9,579,677	3	3	4
Utah	82,168	2,736	84,904	12	1,722,850	21	1,461,037	1,059,273	890,627	35	36	36
Vermont	9,249	366	9,615	43	562,758	61	511,456	444,732	389,881	48	48	48
Virginia	39,598	3,171	42,769	37	6,187,358	156	5,346,797	4,651,448	3,966,949	12	14	14
Washington	66,582	4,721	71,303	20	4,866,692	73	4,132,353	3,413,244	2,853,214	18	20	22
West Virginia	24,087	145	24,231	41	1,793,477	74	1,950,186	1,744,237	1,860,421	34	34	34
Wisconsin	54,314	11,190	65,503	25	4,891,769	90	4,705,642	4,417,821	3,951,777	16	16	16
Wyoming	97,105	714	97,818	9	453,588	4.7	469,557	332,416	330,066	50	49	49
United States	3,536,342	251,083	3,787,425	.....	248,709,873	70	226,542,360	203,302,031	179,323,175	.....	.....	.....

*Area figures for all states does not equal U.S. total due to rounding.

United States Populations and Zip Codes

The following alphabetical list shows populations for all counties and over 15,000 selected cities and towns in the United States. ZIP codes are shown for all of the cities listed in the table. The state abbreviation following each name is that used by the United States Postal Service.

ZIP codes are listed for cities and towns after the state abbreviations. For each city with more than one ZIP code, the range of numbers assigned to the city is shown: For example, the ZIP code range for Chicago is 60601–99, and this indicates that the numbers between 60601 and 60699 are valid Chicago ZIP codes. ZIP codes are not listed for counties.

Populations for cities and towns appear as *italics* after the ZIP codes, and populations for counties appear after the state abbreviations. These populations are either 1990 census figures or, where census data are not available, estimates created by Rand McNally. City populations are for central cities, not metropolitan areas. For New England, 1990 census populations are given for incorporated cities. Estimates are used for unincorporated places that are not treated separately by the census. 'Town' (or 'township') populations are not included unless the town is considered to be primarily urban and contains only one commonly used placename.

Counties are identified by a square symbol (□).

Abbreviations for State Names

AK	Alaska	**IA**	Iowa	**MS**	Mississippi	**PA**	Pennsylvania
AL	Alabama	**ID**	Idaho	**MT**	Montana	**RI**	Rhode Island
AR	Arkansas	**IL**	Illinois	**NC**	North Carolina	**SC**	South Carolina
AZ	Arizona	**IN**	Indiana	**ND**	North Dakota	**SD**	South Dakota
CA	California	**KS**	Kansas	**NE**	Nebraska	**TN**	Tennessee
CO	Colorado	**KY**	Kentucky	**NH**	New Hampshire	**TX**	Texas
CT	Connecticut	**LA**	Louisiana	**NJ**	New Jersey	**UT**	Utah
DC	District of Columbia	**MA**	Massachusetts	**NM**	New Mexico	**VA**	Virginia
		MD	Maryland	**NV**	Nevada	**VT**	Vermont
DE	Delaware	**ME**	Maine	**NY**	New York	**WA**	Washington
FL	Florida	**MI**	Michigan	**OH**	Ohio	**WI**	Wisconsin
GA	Georgia	**MN**	Minnesota	**OK**	Oklahoma	**WV**	West Virginia
HI	Hawaii	**MO**	Missouri	**OR**	Oregon	**WY**	Wyoming

A

Abbeville, AL 36310 • 3,173
Abbeville, LA 70510–11 • 11,187
Abbeville, SC 29620 • 5,778
Abbeville □, SC • 23,862
Abbotsford, WI 54405 • 1,916
Abbott Run Valley, RI 02864 • 1,050
Aberdeen, ID 83210 • 1,406
Aberdeen, MD 21001 • 13,087
Aberdeen, MS 39730 • 6,837
Aberdeen, NC 28315 • 2,700
Aberdeen, OH 45101 • 1,329
Aberdeen, SD 57401–02 • 24,927
Aberdeen, WA 98520 • 16,565
Abernathy, TX 79311 • 2,720
Abilene, KS 67410 • 6,242
Abilene, TX 79601–08 • 106,654
Abingdon, IL 61410 • 3,597
Abingdon, VA 24210 • 7,003
Abington, MA 02351 • 13,817
Abington [Township], PA 19001 • 59,084
Abita Springs, LA 70420 • 1,296
Absarokee, MT 59001 • 1,067
Absecon, NJ 08201 • 7,298
Academia, OH 43050 • 1,447
Acadia □, LA • 55,882
Accomack □, VA • 31,703
Ackerman, MS 39735 • 1,573
Ackley, IA 50601 • 1,696
Acton, CA 93510 • 1,471
Acton, MA 01720 • 2,300
Acushnet, MA 02743 • 6,030
Acworth, GA 30101 • 4,519
Ada, MN 56510 • 1,708
Ada, OH 45810 • 5,413
Ada, OK 74820–21 • 15,820
Ada □, ID • 205,775
Adair □, IA • 8,409
Adair □, KY • 15,360
Adair □, MO • 24,577
Adair □, OK • 18,421
Adairsville, GA 30103 • 2,131
Adams, CO 80022 • 2,200
Adams, MA 01220 • 6,356
Adams, NY 13605 • 1,753
Adams, WI 53910 • 1,715
Adams □, CO • 265,038
Adams □, ID • 3,254
Adams □, IL • 66,090
Adams □, IN • 31,095
Adams □, IA • 4,866
Adams □, MS • 35,356
Adams □, NE • 29,625
Adams □, ND • 3,174
Adams □, OH • 25,371
Adams □, PA • 78,274
Adams □, WA • 13,603
Adams □, WI • 15,682
Adams Center, NY 13606 • 1,675
Adamstown, PA 19501 • 1,108
Adamsville, AL 35005 • 4,161
Adamsville, RI 02801 • 600
Adamsville, TN 38310 • 1,745
Addis, LA 70710 • 1,222
Addison, CT 06033 • 2,460
Addison, IL 60101 • 32,058
Addison, NY 14801 • 1,842
Addison, TX 75001 • 8,783
Addison □, VT • 32,953
Addyston, OH 45001 • 1,198
Adel, GA 31620 • 5,093
Adel, IA 50003 • 3,304
Adelanto, CA 92301 • 8,517
Adelphi, MD 20783 • 13,524
Adobe Acres, NM 87105 • 2,400
Adrian, MI 49221 • 22,097
Adrian, MN 56110 • 1,141
Adrian, MO 64720 • 1,582
Advance, MO 63730 • 1,139
Affton, MO 63123 • 21,106
Afton, DE 19810 • 1,200
Afton, MN 55001 • 2,645
Afton, WY 83110 • 1,394
Agawam, MA 01001 • 10,190
Agoura Hills, CA 91301 • 20,390
Ahoskie, NC 27910 • 4,391
Aiea, HI 96701 • 8,906
Aiken, SC 29801–03 • 19,872
Aiken □, SC • 120,940
Ainsworth, NE 69210 • 1,870
Air Park West, NE 68524 • 3,100
Aitkin, MN 56431 • 1,698
Aitkin □, MN • 12,425
Ajo, AZ 85321 • 2,919
Akiachak, AK 99551 • 400
Akron, CO 80720 • 1,599
Akron, IA 51001 • 1,450
Akron, NY 14001 • 2,906
Akron, OH 44301–98 • 223,019
Akron, PA 17501 • 3,869
Alabaster, AL 35007 • 14,732
Alachua, FL 32615 • 4,529
Alachua □, FL • 181,596
Alakanuk, AK 99554 • 544
Alamance □, NC • 108,213
Alameda, CA 94501 • 76,459
Alameda, NM 87114 • 5,900
Alameda □, CA • 1,279,182
Alamo, CA 94507 • 12,277
Alamo, NV 89001 • 400
Alamo, TN 38001 • 2,426
Alamo, TX 78516 • 8,210
Alamogordo, NM 88310–11 • 27,596
Alamo Heights, TX 78208 • 6,502
Alamosa, CO 81101–02 • 7,579
Alamosa □, CO • 13,617
Alamosa East, CO 81101 • 1,389
Albany, CA 94706 • 16,327
Albany, GA 31701–07 • 78,122
Albany, IN 47320 • 2,357
Albany, KY 42602 • 2,062
Albany, MN 56307 • 1,548
Albany, MO 64402 • 1,958
Albany, NY 12201–60 • 101,082
Albany, OR 97321 • 29,462
Albany, TX 76430 • 1,962
Albany, WI 53502 • 1,140
Albany □, NY • 292,594
Albany □, WY • 30,797
Albemarle, NC 28001–02 • 14,939
Albemarle □, VA • 68,040
Albert Lea, MN 56007 • 18,310
Albertson, NY 11507 • 5,166
Albertville, AL 35950 • 14,507
Albertville, MN 55301 • 1,251
Albia, IA 52531 • 3,870
Albion, IL 62806 • 2,116
Albion, IN 46701 • 1,823
Albion, MI 49224 • 10,066
Albion, NE 68620 • 1,916
Albion, NY 14411 • 5,863
Albion, PA 16401 • 1,575
Albion, RI 02802 • 1,600
Albuquerque, NM 87101–99 • 384,736
Alburtis, PA 18011 • 1,415
Alcester, SD 57001 • 843
Alcoa, TN 37701 • 6,400
Alcona □, MI • 10,145
Alcorn □, MS • 31,722
Alden, NY 14004 • 2,457
Alderson, WV 24910 • 1,152
Alderwood Manor, WA 98011 • 16,524
Aledo, IL 61231 • 3,681
Alexander □, IL • 10,626
Alexander □, NC • 27,544
Alexander City, AL 35010 • 14,917
Alexandria, IN 46001 • 5,709
Alexandria, KY 41001 • 5,592
Alexandria, LA 71301–15 • 49,188
Alexandria, MN 56308 • 7,838
Alexandria, VA 22301–20 • 111,183
Alexandria Bay, NY 13607 • 1,194
Alfalfa □, OK • 6,416
Alfred, NY 14802 • 4,559
Alger □, MI • 8,972
Algoma, WI 54201 • 3,353
Algona, IA 50511 • 6,015
Algona, WA 98001 • 1,694
Algonac, MI 48001 • 4,551
Algonquin, IL 60102 • 11,663
Algood, TN 38501 • 2,399
Alhambra, CA 91801–99 • 82,106
Alice, TX 78332–33 • 19,788
Aliceville, AL 35442 • 3,009
Aliquippa, PA 15001 • 13,374
Allamakee □, IA • 13,855
Allegan, MI 49010 • 4,547
Allegan □, MI • 90,509
Allegany, NY 14706 • 1,980
Allegany □, MD • 74,946
Allegany □, NY • 50,470
Alleghany □, NC • 9,590
Alleghany □, VA • 13,176
Allegheny □, PA • 1,336,449
Allen, TX 75002 • 18,309
Allen, TX 75002 • 18,309
Allen □, IN • 300,836
Allen □, KS • 14,638
Allen □, KY • 14,628
Allen □, LA • 21,226
Allen □, OH • 109,755
Allendale, NJ 07401 • 5,900
Allendale, SC 29810 • 4,410
Allendale □, SC • 11,722
Allen Park, MI 48101 • 31,092
Allenton, RI 02852 • 600
Allentown, NJ 08501 • 1,828
Allentown, PA 18101–95 • 105,090
Alliance, NE 69301 • 9,765
Alliance, OH 44601 • 23,376
Allison, IA 50602 • 1,000
Allison Park, PA 15101 • 5,600
Allouez, WI 54301 • 14,431
Alloway, NJ 08001 • 1,371
Allyn, WA 98524 • 1,100
Alma, AR 72921 • 2,959
Alma, GA 31510 • 3,663
Alma, MI 48801 • 9,034
Alma, NE 68920 • 1,226
Almont, MI 48003 • 2,354
Aloha, OR 97006 • 34,284
Alondra Park, CA 90249 • 12,215
Alpena, MI 49707 • 11,354
Alpena □, MI • 30,605
Alpha, NJ 08865 • 2,530
Alpharetta, GA 30201–02 • 13,002
Alpine, CA 91901 • 9,695
Alpine, NJ 07620 • 1,716
Alpine, TX 79830–31 • 5,637
Alpine, UT 84003 • 3,492
Alpine □, CA • 1,113
Alsip, IL 60658 • 18,227
Alta, IA 51002 • 1,820
Altadena, CA 91001–02 • 42,658
Altamont, IL 62411 • 2,296
Altamont, KS 67330 • 1,048
Altamont, NY 12009 • 1,519
Altamont, OR 97601 • 18,591
Altamonte Springs, FL 32701 • 34,879
Alta Sierra, CA 95949 • 5,709
Altavista, VA 24517 • 3,686
Alto, TX 75925 • 1,027
Alton, IL 62002 • 32,905
Alton, IA 51003 • 1,063
Alton, NH 03809 • 975
Alton Bay, NH 03810 • 1,000
Altoona, FL 32702 • 1,300
Altoona, IA 50009 • 7,191
Altoona, PA 16601–03 • 51,881
Altoona, WI 54720 • 5,889
Alturas, CA 96101 • 3,231
Altus, OK 73521–23 • 21,910
Alva, FL 33920 • 1,200
Alva, OK 73717 • 5,495
Alvarado, TX 76009 • 2,918
Alvin, TX 77511–12 • 19,220
Amador □, CA • 30,039
Amagansett, NY 11930 • 2,188
Amana, IA 52203 • 540
Amarillo, TX 79101–76 • 157,615
Ambler, PA 19002 • 6,609
Amboy, IL 61310 • 2,377
Ambridge, PA 15003 • 8,133
Amelia, LA 70340 • 2,447
Amelia, OH 45102 • 1,837
Amelia □, VA • 8,787
Amenia, NY 12501 • 1,057
American Canyon, CA 94589 • 7,706
American Falls, ID 83211 • 3,757
American Fork, UT 84003–04 • 15,696
Americus, GA 31709 • 16,512
Amery, WI 54001 • 2,657
Ames, IA 50010 • 47,198
Amesbury, MA 01913 • 12,109
Amherst, MA 01002–04 • 17,824
Amherst, NH 03031 • 850
Amherst, NY 14226 • 45,600
Amherst, OH 44001 • 10,332
Amherst, VA 24521 • 1,060
Amherst □, VA • 28,578
Amherstdale, WV 25607 • 1,200
Amite, LA 70422 • 4,236
Amite □, MS • 13,328
Amity, OR 97101 • 1,175
Amityville, NY 11701 • 9,286
Ammon, ID 83401 • 5,002
Amory, MS 38821 • 7,093
Amsterdam, NY 12010 • 20,714
Anaconda, MT 59711 • 10,278
Anacortes, WA 98221 • 11,451
Anadarko, OK 73005 • 6,586
Anaheim, CA 92801–25 • 266,406
Anahola, HI 96703 • 1,181
Anahuac, TX 77514 • 1,993
Anamosa, IA 52205 • 5,100
Anandale, LA 71301 • 2,000
Anchorage, AK 99501–40 • 226,338
Anchorage, KY 40223 • 2,082
Andalusia, AL 36420 • 9,269
Anderson, AK 99744 • 628
Anderson, CA 96007 • 8,239
Anderson, IN 46011–18 • 59,459
Anderson, MO 64831 • 1,432
Anderson, SC 29621–25 • 26,184
Anderson □, KS • 7,803
Anderson □, KY • 14,571
Anderson □, SC • 145,196
Anderson □, TN • 68,250
Anderson □, TX • 48,024
Andover, KS 67002 • 4,047
Andover, MA 01810 • 8,242
Andover, MN 55304 • 15,216
Andover, NY 14806 • 1,125
Andover, OH 44003 • 1,216
Andrew □, MO • 14,632
Andrews, IN 46702 • 1,118
Andrews, NC 28901 • 2,551
Andrews, SC 29510 • 3,050
Andrews, TX 79714 • 10,678
Andrews □, TX • 14,338
Androscoggin □, ME • 105,259
Angelina □, TX • 69,884
Angels Camp, CA 95222 • 2,409
Angier, NC 27501 • 2,235
Angle Lake, WA 98188 • 5,000
Angleton, TX 77515–16 • 17,140
Angola, IN 46703 • 5,824
Angola, NY 14006 • 2,231
Angoon, AK 99820 • 638
Aniak, AK 99557 • 540
Anita, IA 50020 • 1,068
Ankeny, IA 50021 • 18,482
Anna, IL 62906 • 4,805
Anna, OH 45302 • 1,164
Annalee Heights, VA 22042 • 1,750
Anna Maria, FL 34216 • 1,744
Annandale, MN 55302 • 2,054
Annandale, VA 22003 • 50,975
Annapolis, MD 21401–05 • 33,187
Ann Arbor, MI 48103–08 • 109,592
Anne Arundel □, MD • 427,239
Anniston, AL 36201–06 • 26,623
Annville, PA 17003 • 4,294
Anoka, MN 55303–04 • 17,192
Anoka □, MN • 243,641
Anson, TX 79501 • 2,644
Anson □, NC • 23,474
Ansonia, CT 06401 • 18,403
Ansonia, OH 45303 • 1,279
Ansted, WV 25812 • 1,643
Antelope □, NE • 7,965
Anthony, FL 32617 • 1,200
Anthony, KS 67003 • 2,516
Anthony, NM 88021 • 5,160
Anthony, RI 02816 • 2,980
Anthony, TX 88021 • 3,328
Antigo, WI 54409 • 8,276
Antioch, CA 94509 • 62,195
Antioch, IL 60002 • 6,105
Antlers, OK 74523 • 2,524
Anton, TX 79313 • 1,212
Antrim, NH 03440 • 1,325
Antrim □, MI • 18,185
Antwerp, OH 45813 • 1,677
Apache, OK 73006 • 1,591
Apache □, AZ • 61,591
Apache Junction, AZ 85217–20 • 18,100
Apalachicola, FL 32320 • 2,602
Apalachin, NY 13732 • 1,208
Apex, NC 27502 • 4,968
Aplington, IA 50604 • 1,034
Apollo, PA 15613 • 1,895
Apollo Beach, FL 33572 • 6,025
Apopka, FL 32703–04 • 13,512
Appalachia, VA 24216 • 1,994
Appanoose □, IA • 13,743
Appleton, MN 56208 • 1,552
Appleton, WI 54911–15 • 65,695
Appleton City, MO 64724 • 1,280
Apple Valley, CA 92307–08 • 46,079
Apple Valley, MN 55124 • 34,598
Applewood, CO 80401 • 11,069
Appleyard, WA 98801 • 1,207
Appling □, GA • 15,744
Appomattox, VA 24522 • 1,707
Appomattox □, VA • 12,298
Aptos, CA 95003 • 9,061
Aquia Harbour, VA 22554 • 6,308
Arab, AL 35016 • 6,321
Arabi, LA 70032 • 8,787
Aransas □, TX • 17,892
Aransas Pass, TX 78336 • 7,180
Arapahoe, NE 68922 • 1,001
Arapahoe □, CO • 391,511
Arbuckle, CA 95912 • 1,912
Arcade, CA 95821 • 47,900
Arcade, NY 14009 • 2,081
Arcadia, CA 91006–07 • 48,290
Arcadia, FL 33821 • 6,488
Arcadia, IN 46030 • 1,468
Arcadia, LA 71001 • 3,079
Arcadia, SC 29320 • 2,088
Arcadia, WI 54612 • 2,166
Arcanum, OH 45304 • 1,953
Arcata, CA 95521 • 15,197
Archbald, PA 18403 • 6,291
Archbold, OH 43502 • 3,440
Archdale, NC 27263 • 6,913
Archer, FL 32618 • 1,372
Archer □, TX • 7,973
Archer City, TX 76351 • 1,748
Archuleta □, CO • 5,345
Arco, ID 83213 • 1,016
Arcola, IL 61910 • 2,678
Arden, CA 95825 • 62,900
Arden Hills, MN 55112 • 9,199
Ardmore, AL 35739 • 1,090
Ardmore, IN 46628 • 2,250
Ardmore, OK 73401–03 • 23,079
Ardsley, NY 10502 • 4,272
Arenac □, MI • 14,931
Argos, IN 46501 • 1,642
Arizona Sunsites, AZ 85625 • 1,100
Arkadelphia, AR 71923 • 10,014
Arkansas □, AR • 21,653
Arkansas City, KS 67005 • 12,762
Arkoma, OK 74901 • 2,393
Arlington, GA 31713 • 1,513
Arlington, MA 02174 • 44,630
Arlington, MN 55307 • 1,886
Arlington, NE 68002 • 1,178
Arlington, NY 12603 • 11,948
Arlington, OH 45814 • 1,267
Arlington, SD 57212 • 908
Arlington, TN 38002 • 1,541
Arlington, TX 76010–18 • 261,721
Arlington, VT 05250 • 1,311
Arlington, VA 22201–19 • 170,936
Arlington, WA 98223 • 4,037
Arlington □, VA • 170,936
Arlington Heights, IL 60004–07 • 75,460
Arma, KS 66712 • 1,542
Armada, MI 48005 • 1,548
Armijo, NM 87105 • 14,600
Armonk, NY 10504 • 2,745
Armour, SD 57313 • 854
Armstrong, IA 50514 • 1,025
Armstrong □, PA • 73,478
Armstrong □, TX • 2,021
Arnaudville, LA 70512 • 1,444
Arnold, MD 21012 • 20,261
Arnold, MN 55803 • 1,500
Arnold, MO 63010 • 18,828
Arnold, PA 15068 • 6,113
Arnold Mills, RI 02864 • 600
Aroostook □, ME • 86,936
Arroyo Grande, CA 93420–21 • 14,378
Artesia, CA 90701–03 • 15,464
Artesia, NM 88210–11 • 10,610
Arthur, IL 61911 • 2,112
Arthur □, NE • 462
Arundel Village, MD 21225 • 3,370
Arvada, CO 80001–06 • 89,235
Arvin, CA 93203 • 9,286
Asbury Park, NJ 07712 • 16,799
Ascension □, LA • 58,214
Ashaway, RI 02804 • 1,584
Ashburn, GA 31714 • 4,827
Ashburnham, MA 01430 • 1,300
Ashdown, AR 71822 • 5,150
Ashe □, NC • 22,209
Asheboro, NC 27203 • 16,362
Asherton, TX 78827 • 1,608
Asheville, NC 28801–16 • 61,607
Ashford, AL 36312 • 1,926
Ash Grove, MO 65604 • 1,128
Ashland, AL 36251 • 2,034
Ashland, CA 94541 • 16,590
Ashland, IL 62612 • 1,257
Ashland, KS 67831 • 1,032
Ashland, KY 41101–05 • 23,622
Ashland, MA 01721 • 9,165
Ashland, MO 65010 • 1,252
Ashland, NE 68003 • 2,136
Ashland, NH 03217 • 1,915
Ashland, OH 44805 • 20,079
Ashland, OR 97520 • 16,234
Ashland, PA 17921 • 3,859
Ashland, VA 23005 • 5,864
Ashland, WI 54806 • 8,695
Ashland □, OH • 47,507
Ashland □, WI • 16,307
Ashland City, TN 37015 • 2,552
Ashley, ND 58413 • 1,052
Ashley, OH 43003 • 1,059
Ashley, PA 18706 • 3,291
Ashley □, AR • 24,319
Ashtabula, OH 44004 • 21,633
Ashtabula □, OH • 99,821
Ashton, ID 83420 • 1,114
Ashton, IL 61006 • 1,042
Ashton, MD 20861 • 1,800
Ashton, RI 02864 • 820
Ashville, AL 35953 • 1,494
Ashville, OH 43103 • 2,254
Ashwaubenon, WI 54304 • 16,376
Asotin □, WA • 17,605
Aspen, CO 81611–15 • 5,049
Aspen Hill, MD 20906 • 45,494
Aspermont, TX 79502 • 1,214
Aspinwall, PA 15215 • 2,880
Assinippi, MA 02339 • 1,400
Assonet, MA 02702 • 1,200
Assumption, IL 62510 • 1,244
Assumption □, LA • 22,753
Astoria, IL 61501 • 1,205
Astoria, OR 97103 • 10,069
Atascadero, CA 93422–23 • 23,138
Atascosa □, TX • 30,533
Atchison, KS 66002 • 10,656
Atchison □, KS • 16,932
Atchison □, MO • 7,457
Atco, NJ 08004 • 2,020
Athens, AL 35611 • 16,901
Athens, GA 30601–13 • 45,734
Athens, IL 62613 • 1,404
Athens, NY 12015 • 1,708
Athens, OH 45701 • 21,265
Athens, PA 18810 • 3,468
Athens, TN 37303 • 12,054
Athens, TX 75751 • 10,967
Athens □, OH • 59,549
Atherton, CA 94027 • 7,163
Athol, MA 01331 • 8,732
Atkins, AR 72823 • 2,834
Atkins, VA 24311 • 1,130
Atkinson, NE 68713 • 1,380
Atkinson □, GA • 613
Atlanta, GA 30301–83 • 394,017
Atlanta, IL 61723 • 1,616
Atlanta, TX 75551 • 6,118
Atlantic, IA 50022 • 7,432
Atlantic □, NJ • 224,327
Atlantic Beach, FL 32233 • 11,636
Atlantic City, NJ 08401–06 • 37,986
Atlantic Highlands, NJ 07716 • 4,629
Atmore, AL 36502 • 8,046
Atoka, OK 74525 • 3,298
Atoka □, OK • 12,778
Attala □, MS • 18,481
Attalla, AL 35954 • 6,859
Attica, IN 47918 • 3,457
Attica, NY 14011 • 2,630
Attleboro, MA 02703 • 38,383
Atwater, CA 95301 • 22,282
Atwater, MN 56209 • 1,053
Atwood, IL 61913 • 1,253
Atwood, KS 67730 • 1,388
Atwood, TN 38220 • 1,066
Auberry, CA 93602 • 1,866
Auburn, AL 36830–49 • 33,830
Auburn, CA 95603–04 • 10,592

United States Populations and ZIP Codes

Auburn, GA 30203 • 3,139
Auburn, IL 62615 • 3,724
Auburn, IN 46706 • 9,379
Auburn, KY 42206 • 1,273
Auburn, ME 04210–12 • 24,309
Auburn, MA 01501 • 14,845
Auburn, MI 48611 • 1,855
Auburn, NE 68305 • 3,443
Auburn, NY 13021–24 • 31,258
Auburn, WA 98001–02 • 33,102
Auburndale, FL 33823 • 8,858
Auburn Heights, MI 48321 • 17,076
Audrain □, MO • 23,599
Audubon, IA 50025 • 2,524
Audubon, NJ 08106 • 9,205
Audubon, PA 19407 • 6,328
Audubon □, IA • 7,334
Auglaize □, OH • 44,585
August, CA 95201 • 6,376
Augusta, AR 72006 • 2,759
Augusta, GA 30901–19 • 44,639
Augusta, KS 67010 • 7,876
Augusta, KY 41002 • 1,336
Augusta, ME 04330–38 • 21,325
Augusta, WI 54722 • 1,510
Augusta □, VA • 54,677
Aulander, NC 27805 • 1,209
Ault, CO 80610 • 1,107
Aumsville, OR 97325 • 1,650
Aurora, CO 80010–19 • 222,103
Aurora, IL 60504–07 • 99,581
Aurora, IN 47001 • 3,825
Aurora, MN 55705 • 1,965
Aurora, MO 65605 • 6,459
Aurora, NE 68818 • 3,810
Aurora, OH 44202 • 9,192
Aurora □, SD • 3,135
Au Sable, MI 48750 • 1,542
Au Sable Forks, NY 12912 • 2,100
Austell, GA 30001 • 4,173
Austin, IN 47102 • 4,310
Austin, MN 55912 • 21,907
Austin, NV 89310 • 370
Austin, TX 78701–89 • 465,622
Austin □, TX • 19,832
Austintown, OH 44512 • 32,371
Autauga □, AL • 34,222
Ava, MO 65608 • 2,938
Avalon, CA 90704 • 2,918
Avalon, NJ 08202 • 1,809
Avalon, PA 15202 • 5,784
Avella, PA 15312 • 1,200
Avenal, CA 93204 • 9,770
Avenel, MD • 5,600
Avenel, NJ 07001 • 15,504
Aventura, FL 33180 • 14,914
Averill Park, NY 12018 • 1,656
Avery □, NC • 14,867
Avilla, IN 46710 • 1,366
Avis, PA 17721 • 1,506
Avoca, IA 51521 • 1,497
Avoca, NY 14809 • 1,033
Avoca, PA 18641 • 2,897
Avocado Heights, CA 91746 • 14,232
Avon, CT 06001 • 13,937
Avon, MA 02322 • 5,026
Avon, NY 14414 • 2,995
Avon, OH 44011 • 7,337
Avon by the Sea, NJ 07717 • 2,165
Avondale, AZ 85323 • 16,169
Avondale, LA 70094 • 5,813
Avondale, OH 45404 • 5,000
Avondale Estates, GA 30002 • 2,209
Avon Lake, OH 44012 • 15,066
Avonmore, PA 15618 • 1,089
Avon Park, FL 33825 • 8,042
Avoyelles □, LA • 39,159
Ayden, NC 28513 • 4,740
Ayer, MA 01432 • 2,889
Azalea Park, FL 32807 • 8,926
Azle, TX 76020 • 8,868
Aztec, NM 87410 • 5,479
Azusa, CA 91702 • 41,333

B

Babbitt, MN 55706 • 1,562
Babbitt, NV • 1,800
Babylon, NY 11702–04 • 12,249
Baca □, CO • 4,556
Bacliff, TX 77518 • 5,549
Bacon □, GA • 9,566
Bad Axe, MI 48413 • 3,484
Baden, PA 15005 • 5,074
Badin, NC 28009 • 1,481
Bagdad, AZ 86321 • 1,858
Bagdad, FL 32530 • 1,457
Baggs, WY 82321 • 272
Bagley, MN 56621 • 1,388
Bailey □, TX • 7,064
Baileys Crossroads, VA 22041 • 19,507
Bainbridge, GA 31717 • 10,712
Bainbridge, NY 13733 • 1,550
Baird, TX 79504 • 1,658
Bairdford, PA 15006 • 1,200
Baker, LA 70714 • 13,233
Baker, MT 59313 • 1,818
Baker, OR 97814 • 9,140
Baker □, FL • 18,486
Baker □, GA • 3,615
Baker □, OR • 15,317
Bakersfield, CA 93301–89 • 174,820
Balch Springs, TX 75180 • 17,406
Bald Knob, AR 72010 • 2,653
Baldwin, FL 32234 • 1,450
Baldwin, GA 30511 • 1,439
Baldwin, LA 70514 • 2,379
Baldwin, NY 11510 • 22,719
Baldwin, PA 15234 • 21,923
Baldwin, WI 54002 • 2,022
Baldwin □, AL • 98,280
Baldwin □, GA • 39,530
Baldwin City, KS 66006 • 2,961
Baldwin Park, CA 91706 • 69,330
Baldwinsville, NY 13027 • 6,591
Baldwinville, MA 01436 • 1,795
Baldwyn, MS 38824 • 3,204
Balfour, NC 28706 • 1,118
Ball, LA 71405 • 3,305
Ballard □, KY • 7,902
Ballardvale, MA 01810 • 1,270
Ballinger, TX 76821 • 3,975
Ballston Spa, NY 12020 • 4,937
Ballwin, MO 63011 • 21,816
Balmville, NY 12550 • 2,963
Baltic, CT 06330 • 2,000
Baltimore, MD 21201–99 • 736,014
Baltimore, OH 43105 • 2,971
Baltimore □, MD • 692,134
Baltimore Highlands, MD 21227 • 7,300
Bamberg, SC 29003 • 3,843
Bamberg □, SC • 16,902
Bandera □, TX • 10,562
Bandon, OR 97411 • 2,215
Bangor, ME 04401–02 • 33,181
Bangor, MI 49013 • 1,922
Bangor, PA 18013 • 5,383
Bangor, WI 54614 • 1,076
Bangor Township, MI 48706 • 17,494
Bangs, TX 76823 • 1,555
Banks □, GA • 10,308
Banner □, NE • 852
Banning, CA 92220 • 20,570
Bannock □, ID • 66,026
Baraboo, WI 53913 • 9,203
Baraga, MI 49908 • 1,231
Baraga □, MI • 7,954
Barataria, LA 70036 • 1,160
Barber □, KS • 5,874
Barberton, OH 44203 • 27,623
Barbour □, AL • 25,417
Barbour □, WV • 15,699
Barboursville, WV 25504 • 2,774
Barbourville, KY 40906 • 3,658
Bardstown, KY 40004 • 6,801
Bargersville, IN 46106 • 1,681
Bar Harbor, ME 04609 • 2,768
Barker Heights, NC 28739 • 1,137
Barling, AR 72923 • 4,078
Barnegat, NJ 08005 • 1,160
Barnes □, ND • 12,545
Barnesboro, PA 15714 • 2,530
Barnesville, GA 30204 • 4,747
Barnesville, MN 56514 • 2,066
Barnesville, OH 43713 • 4,326
Barnsdall, OK 74002 • 1,316
Barnstable, MA 02630 • 2,790
Barnstable □, MA • 186,605
Barnwell, SC 29812 • 5,255
Barnwell □, SC • 20,293
Barrackville, WV 26559 • 1,443
Barre, MA 01005 • 1,094
Barre, VT 05641 • 9,482
Barren □, KY • 34,001
Barrington, IL 60010–11 • 9,504
Barrington, NJ 08007 • 6,774
Barrington, RI 02806 • 15,849
Barron, WI 54812 • 2,986
Barron □, WI • 40,750
Barron Lake, MI 49120 • 1,600
Barrow, AK 99723 • 3,469
Barrow □, GA • 29,721
Barry, IL 62312 • 1,391
Barry □, MI • 50,057
Barry □, MO • 27,547
Barstow, CA 92310–12 • 21,472
Bartholomew □, IN • 63,657
Bartlesville, OK 74003–06 • 34,256
Bartlett, IL 60103 • 19,373
Bartlett, TN 38134 • 26,989
Bartlett, TX 76511 • 1,439
Barton, OH 43905 • 1,039
Barton, VT 05822 • 908
Barton □, KS • 29,382
Barton □, MO • 11,312
Bartonville, IL 61607 • 5,643
Bartow, FL 33830 • 14,716
Bartow □, GA • 55,911
Barview, OR 97420 • 1,402
Basalt, CO 81621 • 1,128
Basehor, KS 66007 • 1,591
Basile, LA 70515 • 1,808
Basin, WY 82410 • 1,180
Basking Ridge, NJ 07920 • 3,060
Bassett, VA 24055 • 1,579
Bass Lake, IN 46534 • 1,500
Bastrop, LA 71220–21 • 13,916
Bastrop, TX 78602 • 4,044
Bastrop □, TX • 38,263
Batavia, IL 60510 • 17,076
Batavia, NY 14020–21 • 16,310
Batavia, OH 45103 • 1,700
Bates □, MO • 15,025
Batesburg, SC 29006 • 4,082
Batesville, AR 72501–03 • 9,187
Batesville, IN 47006 • 4,720
Batesville, MS 38606 • 6,403
Bath, ME 04530 • 9,799
Bath, NY 14810 • 5,801
Bath, PA 18014 • 2,358
Bath, SC 29816 • 2,242
Bath □, KY • 9,692
Bath □, VA • 4,799
Baton Rouge, LA 70801–98 • 219,531
Battle Creek, MI 49015–17 • 53,540
Battle Ground, WA 98604 • 3,758
Battle Mountain, NV 89820 • 3,542
Baudette, MN 56623 • 1,146
Bawcomville, LA 71291 • 2,250
Baxley, GA 31513 • 3,841
Baxter, MN 56425 • 3,695
Baxter, TN 38544 • 1,289
Baxter □, AR • 31,186
Baxter Springs, KS 66713 • 4,351
Bay, AR 72411 • 1,660
Bay □, FL • 126,994
Bay □, MI • 111,723
Bayard, NE 69334 • 1,196
Bayard, NM 88023 • 2,598
Bayberry, NY 13088 • 6,710
Bay City, MI 48706–08 • 38,936
Bay City, OR 97107 • 1,027
Bay City, TX 77414 • 18,170
Bayfield, CO 81122 • 1,090
Bayfield □, WI • 14,008
Bay Head, NJ 08742 • 1,226
Baylor □, TX • 4,385
Bay Minette, AL 36507 • 7,168
Bayonet Point, FL 34667 • 21,860
Bayonne, NJ 07002 • 61,444
Bayou Cane, LA 70359 • 15,876
Bayou George, FL 32401 • 1,500
Bayou La Batre, AL 36509 • 2,456
Bay Pines, FL 33504 • 4,171
Bayport, MN 55003 • 3,200
Bayport, NY 11705 • 7,702
Bay Ridge, MD 21403 • 1,989
Bay Saint Louis, MS 39520–21 • 8,063
Bay Shore, NY 11706 • 21,279
Bayshore Gardens, FL 34207 • 17,062
Bayside, WI 53217 • 4,789
Bay Springs, MS 39422 • 1,729
Baytown, TX 77520–22 • 63,850
Bay Village, OH 44140 • 17,000
Bayville, NY 11709 • 7,193
Beach, IL 60085 • 9,513
Beach, ND 58621 • 1,205
Beach Haven, NJ 08008 • 1,475
Beachwood, NJ 08722 • 9,324
Beachwood, OH 44122 • 10,677
Beacon, NY 12508 • 13,243
Beacon Falls, CT 06403 • 1,285
Beacon Square, FL 34652 • 6,265
Beadle □, SD • 18,253
Bear, DE 19701 • 1,200
Bearden, AR 71720 • 1,021
Beardstown, IL 62618 • 5,270
Bear Lake □, ID • 6,084
Bear Town, MS 39648 • 1,277
Beatrice, NE 68310 • 12,354
Beatty, NV 89003 • 1,623
Beattyville, KY 41311 • 1,131
Beaufort, NC 28516 • 3,808
Beaufort, SC 29901–03 • 9,576
Beaufort □, NC • 42,283
Beaufort □, SC • 86,425
Beaumont, CA 92223 • 9,685
Beaumont, MS 39423 • 1,054
Beaumont, TX 77701–26 • 114,323
Beauregard □, LA • 30,083
Beaver, OK 73932 • 1,584
Beaver, PA 15009 • 5,028
Beaver, UT 84713 • 1,998
Beaver, WV 25813 • 1,244
Beaver □, OK • 6,023
Beaver □, PA • 186,093
Beaver □, UT • 4,765
Beavercreek, OH 45385 • 33,626
Beaverdale, PA 15921 • 1,000
Beaver Dam, KY 42320 • 2,904
Beaver Dam, WI 53916 • 14,196
Beaver Falls, PA 15010 • 10,687
Beaverhead □, MT • 8,424
Beaverton, MI 48612 • 1,150
Beaverton, OR 97005–07 • 53,310
Beckemeyer, IL 62219 • 1,070
Becker □, MN • 27,881
Beckham □, OK • 18,812
Beckley, WV 25801–02 • 18,296
Bedford, IN 47421 • 13,817
Bedford, IA 50833 • 1,528
Bedford, MA 01730 • 13,067
Bedford, NH 03102 • 1,400
Bedford, OH 44146 • 14,822
Bedford, PA 15522 • 3,137
Bedford, TX 76021–22 • 43,762
Bedford, VA 24523 • 6,073
Bedford □, PA • 47,919
Bedford □, TN • 30,411
Bedford □, VA • 45,656
Bedford Heights, OH 44146 • 12,131
Bedford Hills, NY 10507 • 3,140
Bee □, TX • 25,135
Beebe, AR 72012 • 4,455
Beecher, IL 60401 • 2,032
Beecher, MI 48458 • 14,465
Beech Grove, IN 46107 • 13,383
Beech Island, SC 29842 • 1,500
Bee Ridge, FL 34233 • 6,406
Beeville, TX 78102–04 • 13,547
Beggs, OK 74421 • 1,150
Bel Air, MD 21014 • 8,860
Bel Aire, KS 67220 • 3,695
Belchertown, MA 01007 • 2,339
Belcourt, ND 58316 • 2,458
Belding, MI 48809 • 5,969
Belen, NM 87002 • 6,547
Belfast, ME 04915 • 6,355
Belfast, NY 14711 • 1,100
Belfield, ND 58622 • 887
Belford, NJ 07718 • 6,300
Belgrade, MT 59714 • 3,411
Belhaven, NC 27810 • 2,269
Belington, WV 26250 • 1,850
Belknap □, NH • 49,216
Bell, CA 90201 • 34,365
Bell □, KY • 31,506
Bell □, TX • 191,088
Bellair, FL 32073 • 5,200
Bellaire, MI 49615 • 1,104
Bellaire, OH 43906 • 6,028
Bellaire, TX 77401–02 • 13,842
Bella Vista, AR 72712 • 9,083
Bellbrook, OH 45305 • 6,511
Belle, MO 65013 • 1,218
Belle, WV 25015 • 1,421
Belleair, FL 34616 • 3,968
Belle Chasse, LA 70037 • 8,512
Bellefontaine, OH 43311 • 12,142
Bellefontaine Neighbors, MO 63137 • 10,922
Bellefonte, DE 19809 • 1,243
Bellefonte, PA 16823 • 6,358
Belle Fourche, SD 57717 • 4,335
Belle Glade, FL 33430 • 16,177
Belle Isle, FL 32809 • 5,272
Belle Meade, TN 37205 • 2,839
Bellemoor, DE 19802 • 1,040
Belle Plaine, IA 52208 • 2,834
Belle Plaine, KS 67013 • 1,649
Belle Plaine, MN 56011 • 3,149
Belle Vernon, PA 15012 • 1,213
Belleview, FL 32506 • 8,000
Belleview, FL 32620 • 2,666
Belle View, VA 22307 • 3,500
Belleville, IL 62220–25 • 42,785
Belleville, KS 66935 • 2,517
Belleville, MI 48111–12 • 3,270
Belleville, NJ 07109 • 34,213
Belleville, PA 17004 • 1,589
Belleville, WI 53508 • 1,456
Bellevue, ID 83313 • 1,275
Bellevue, IA 52031 • 2,239
Bellevue, KY 41073 • 6,997
Bellevue, MI 49021 • 1,401
Bellevue, NE 68005 • 30,982
Bellevue, OH 44811 • 8,146
Bellevue, PA 15202 • 9,126
Bellevue, WA 98004–09 • 86,874
Bellflower, CA 90706–07 • 61,815
Bell Gardens, CA 90201 • 42,355
Bellingham, MA 02019 • 4,535
Bellingham, WA 98225–27 • 52,179
Bellmawr, NJ 08031 • 12,603
Bellmead, TX 76705 • 8,336
Bellmore, NY 11710 • 16,438
Bellows Falls, VT 05101 • 3,313
Bellport, NY 11713 • 2,572
Bells, TN 38006 • 1,643
Bellville, OH 44813 • 1,568
Bellville, TX 77418 • 3,378
Bellwood, IL 60104 • 20,241
Bellwood, PA 16617 • 1,976
Bellwood, VA 23234 • 6,178
Belmar, NJ 07719 • 5,877
Belmond, IA 50421 • 2,500
Belmont, CA 94002 • 24,127
Belmont, MA 02178 • 24,720
Belmont, MS 38827 • 1,554
Belmont, NY 14813 • 1,006
Belmont, NC 28012 • 8,434
Belmont □, OH • 71,074
Bel-Nor, MO 63133 • 2,935
Beloit, KS 67420 • 4,066
Beloit, OH 44609 • 1,037
Beloit, WI 53511–12 • 35,573
Beloit North, WI 53511 • 5,457
Belpre, OH 45714 • 6,796
Belt, MT 59412 • 571
Belton, MO 64012 • 18,150
Belton, SC 29627 • 4,646
Belton, TX 76513 • 12,476
Beltrami □, MN • 34,384
Beltsville, MD 20705 • 14,476
Belvedere, GA 30032 • 6,100
Belvedere, SC 29841 • 6,133
Belvedere Park, GA 30032 • 18,089
Belvidere, IL 61008 • 15,958
Belvidere, NJ 07823 • 2,669
Belzoni, MS 39038 • 2,536
Bement, IL 61813 • 1,668
Bemidji, MN 56601–19 • 11,245
Benavides, TX 78341 • 1,788
Benbrook, TX 76126 • 19,564
Bend, OR 97701–09 • 20,469
Benewah □, ID • 7,937
Ben Hill □, GA • 16,245
Benicia, CA 94510 • 24,437
Benkelman, NE 69021 • 1,193
Benld, IL 62009 • 1,604
Ben Lomond, CA 95005 • 7,884
Bennett, CO 80102 • 1,757
Bennett □, SD • 3,206
Bennettsville, SC 29512 • 9,345
Bennington, VT 05201 • 9,532
Bennington □, VT • 35,845
Bennion, UT 84118 • 9,575
Bensalem, PA 19020–21 • 52,368
Bensenville, IL 60106 • 17,767
Bensley, VA 23234 • 5,093
Benson, AZ 85602 • 3,824
Benson, MN 56215 • 3,235
Benson, NC 27504 • 2,810
Benson □, ND • 7,198
Bent □, CO • 5,048
Bentleyville, PA 15314 • 2,673
Benton, AR 72015 • 18,177
Benton, IL 62812 • 7,216
Benton, KY 42025 • 3,899
Benton, LA 71006 • 2,047
Benton □, AR • 97,499
Benton □, IN • 9,441
Benton □, IA • 22,429
Benton □, MN • 30,185
Benton □, MS • 8,046
Benton □, MO • 13,859
Benton □, OR • 70,811
Benton □, TN • 14,524
Benton □, WA • 112,560
Benton City, WA 99320 • 1,806
Benton Harbor, MI 49022–23 • 12,818
Benton Heights, MI 49022 • 5,465
Bentonville, AR 72712–14 • 11,257
Benwood, WV 26031 • 1,669
Benzie □, MI • 12,200
Beowawe, NV 89821 • 250
Berea, KY 40403 • 9,126
Berea, OH 44017 • 19,051
Berea, SC 29611 • 13,535
Beresford, SD 57004 • 1,849
Bergen, NY 14416 • 1,103
Bergen □, NJ • 825,380
Bergenfield, NJ 07621 • 24,458
Berkeley, CA 94701–10 • 102,724
Berkeley, IL 60163 • 5,137
Berkeley, MO 63134 • 12,450
Berkeley, RI 02864 • 830
Berkeley □, SC • 128,776
Berkeley □, WV • 59,253
Berkeley Heights, NJ 07922 • 11,980
Berkley, MI 48072 • 16,960
Berks □, PA • 336,523
Berkshire □, MA • 139,352
Berlin, CT 06037 • 1,040
Berlin, MD 21811 • 2,616
Berlin, NH 03570 • 11,824
Berlin, NJ 08009 • 5,672
Berlin, NY 12022 • 1,200
Berlin, PA 15530 • 2,064
Berlin, WI 54923 • 5,371
Bernalillo, NM 87004 • 5,960
Bernalillo □, NM • 480,577
Bernardsville, NJ 07924 • 6,597
Berne, IN 46711 • 3,559
Bernice, LA 71222 • 1,543
Bernie, MO 63822 • 1,847
Berrien □, GA • 14,153
Berrien □, MI • 161,378
Berrien Springs, MI 49103 • 1,927
Berry, AL 35546 • 1,218
Berryville, AR 72616 • 3,212
Berryville, VA 22611 • 3,097
Berthoud, CO 80513 • 2,990
Bertie □, NC • 20,388
Bertrand, MI 49120 • 5,500
Berwick, LA 70342 • 4,375
Berwick, ME 03901 • 2,378
Berwick, PA 18603 • 10,976
Berwyn, IL 60402 • 45,426
Berwyn, PA 19312 • 8,150
Bessemer, AL 35020–23 • 33,497
Bessemer, MI 49911 • 2,272
Bessemer, PA 16112 • 1,196
Bessemer City, NC 28016 • 4,698
Bethalto, IL 62010 • 9,507
Bethany, CT 06525 • 1,170
Bethany, IL 61914 • 1,369
Bethany, MO 64424 • 3,005
Bethany, OK 73008 • 20,075
Bethany, WV 26032 • 1,139
Bethany Beach, DE 19930 • 326
Bethel, AK 99559 • 4,674
Bethel, CT 06801 • 8,835
Bethel, ME 04217 • 1,225
Bethel, NC 27812 • 1,842
Bethel, OH 45106 • 2,407
Bethel, VT 05032 • 1,866
Bethel Acres, OK 74801 • 2,505
Bethel Park, PA 15102 • 33,823
Bethesda, MD 20813–17 • 62,936
Bethesda, OH 43719 • 1,161
Bethlehem, CT 06751 • 1,976
Bethlehem, PA 18015–18 • 71,428
Bethpage, NY 11714 • 15,761
Bettendorf, IA 52722 • 28,132
Beulah, ND 58523 • 3,363
Beverly, MA 01915 • 38,195
Beverly, NJ 08010 • 2,973
Beverly, OH 45715 • 1,444
Beverly Hills, CA 90209–13 • 31,971
Beverly Hills, FL 32665 • 6,163
Beverly Hills, MI 48009 • 10,610
Bexar □, TX • 1,185,394
Bexley, OH 43209 • 13,088
Bibb □, AL • 16,576
Bibb □, GA • 149,967
Bicknell, IN 47512 • 3,357
Biddeford, ME 04005 • 20,710
Bienville □, LA • 15,979
Big Bear City, CA 92314 • 3,500
Big Bend, WI 53103 • 1,299
Big Delta, AK 99737 • 400
Big Flats, NY 14814 • 2,658
Bigfork, MT 59911 • 1,080
Biggs, CA 95917 • 1,581
Big Horn □, MT • 11,337
Big Horn □, WY • 10,525
Big Lake, MN 55309 • 3,113
Big Lake, TX 76932 • 3,672
Big Pine, CA 93513 • 1,158
Big Piney, WY 83113 • 454
Big Rapids, MI 49307 • 12,603
Big Sandy, MT 59520 • 740
Big Sandy, TX 75755 • 1,185
Big Spring, TX 79720–21 • 23,093
Big Stone □, MN • 6,285
Big Stone Gap, VA 24219 • 4,748
Big Timber, MT 59011 • 1,557
Billerica, MA 01821–22 • 6,840
Billings, MT 59101–08 • 81,151
Billings □, ND • 1,108
Billings Heights, MT 59105 • 8,480
Biloxi, MS 39530–35 • 46,319
Biltmore Forest, NC 28803 • 1,327
Bingham, ME 04920 • 1,071
Bingham □, ID • 37,583
Binghamton, NY 13901–05 • 53,008
Birchwood City, MD 20745 • 4,870
Birchwood Park, DE 19711 • 2,250
Bird Island, MN 55310 • 1,326
Birdsboro, PA 19508 • 4,222
Birmingham, AL 35201–61 • 265,968
Birmingham, MI 48009–12 • 19,997
Bisbee, AZ 85603 • 6,288
Biscayne Gardens, FL 33168 • 13,000
Biscayne Park, FL 33161 • 3,068
Biscoe, NC 27209 • 1,484
Bishop, CA 93514–15 • 3,475
Bishop, TX 78343 • 3,337
Bishopville, SC 29010 • 3,560
Bismarck, MO 63624 • 1,579
Bismarck, ND 58501–07 • 49,256
Biwabik, MN 55708 • 1,097
Bixby, OK 74008 • 9,502
Black Canyon City, AZ 85324 • 1,811
Black Creek, WI 54106 • 1,152
Black Diamond, WA 98010 • 1,422
Black Earth, WI 53515 • 1,248
Blackfoot, ID 83221 • 9,646
Blackford □, IN • 14,067
Black Forest, CO 80908 • 8,143
Black Hawk, SD 57718 • 1,955
Black Hawk □, IA • 123,798
Black Jack, MO 63031 • 6,128
Black Lick, PA 15716 • 1,100
Blacklick Estates, OH 43227 • 10,080
Black Mountain, NC 28711 • 5,418
Black Point Beach Club, CT 06357 • 1,200
Black River, NY 13612 • 1,349
Black River Falls, WI 54615 • 3,490
Blacksburg, SC 29702 • 1,907
Blacksburg, VA 24060–63 • 34,590
Blackshear, GA 31516 • 3,263
Blackstone, MA 01504 • 4,460
Blackstone, VA 23824 • 3,497
Blackville, SC 29817 • 2,688
Blackwell, OK 74631 • 7,538
Blackwood, NJ 08012 • 5,120
Bladen □, NC • 28,663
Bladenboro, NC 28320 • 1,821
Bladensburg, MD 20710 • 8,064
Blades, DE 19973 • 834
Blaine, MN 55433 • 38,975
Blaine, TN 37709 • 1,326
Blaine, WA 98230 • 2,489
Blaine □, ID • 13,552
Blaine □, MT • 6,728
Blaine □, NE • 675
Blaine □, OK • 11,470
Blair, NE 68008 • 6,860
Blair, WI 54616 • 1,126
Blair □, PA • 130,542
Blairsville, PA 15717 • 3,595
Blakely, GA 31723 • 5,595
Blakely, PA 18447 • 7,222
Blanchard, LA 71009 • 1,175
Blanchard, OK 73010 • 1,922
Blanchester, OH 45107 • 4,206
Blanco, TX 78606 • 1,238
Blanco □, TX • 5,972
Bland □, VA • 6,514
Blanding, UT 84511 • 3,162
Blasdell, NY 14219 • 2,900

Blauvelt, NY 10913 • *4,470*
Blawnox, PA 15238 • *1,626*
Bleckley □, GA • *10,430*
Bledsoe □, TN • *9,669*
Blende, CO 81006 • *1,330*
Blennerhassett, WV 26101 • *2,924*
Blissfield, MI 49228 • *3,172*
Block Island, RI 02807 • *620*
Bloomer, WI 54724 • *3,085*
Bloomfield, CT 06002 • *7,120*
Bloomfield, IN 47424 • *2,592*
Bloomfield, IA 52537 • *2,580*
Bloomfield, MO 63825 • *1,800*
Bloomfield, NE 68718 • *1,181*
Bloomfield, NJ 07003 • *45,061*
Bloomfield, NM 87413 • *5,214*
Bloomfield Hills, MI 48302–04 • *4,288*
Bloomfield Township, MI 48302 • *42,137*
Bloomingdale, GA 31302 • *2,271*
Bloomingdale, IL 60108 • *16,614*
Bloomingdale, NJ 07403 • *7,530*
Bloomingdale, TN 37660 • *10,953*
Blooming Prairie, MN 55917 • *2,043*
Bloomington, CA 92316 • *15,116*
Bloomington, IL 61701–04 • *51,972*
Bloomington, IN 47401–08 • *60,633*
Bloomington, MN 55420 • *86,335*
Bloomington, TX 77951 • *1,888*
Bloomsburg, PA 17815 • *12,439*
Blossburg, PA 16912 • *1,571*
Blossom, TX 75416 • *1,440*
Blount □, AL • *39,248*
Blount □, TN • *85,969*
Blountstown, FL 32424 • *2,404*
Blountsville, AL 35031 • *1,527*
Blountville, TN 37617 • *2,605*
Blowing Rock, NC 28605 • *1,257*
Blue Ash, OH 45242 • *11,860*
Blue Diamond, NV 89004 • *420*
Blue Earth, MN 56013 • *3,745*
Blue Earth □, MN • *54,044*
Bluefield, VA 24605 • *5,363*
Bluefield, WV 24701 • *12,756*
Blue Grass, IA 52726 • *1,214*
Blue Hills, CT 06002 • *3,206*
Blue Island, IL 60406 • *21,203*
Blue Lake, CA 95525 • *1,235*
Blue Mound, IL 62513 • *1,161*
Blue Rapids, KS 66411 • *1,131*
Blue Ridge, GA 30513 • *1,336*
Blue Ridge, VA 24064 • *2,840*
Blue Ridge Summit, PA 17214 • *1,800*
Blue Springs, MO 64014–15 • *40,153*
Bluewell, WV 24701 • *2,752*
Bluff City, TN 37618 • *1,390*
Bluffdale, UT 84065 • *2,152*
Bluff Park, AL 35226 • *8,000*
Bluffton, IN 46714 • *9,020*
Bluffton, OH 45817 • *3,367*
Blythe, CA 92225–26 • *8,428*
Blytheville, AR 72315–19 • *22,906*
Boalsburg, PA 16827 • *2,206*
Boardman, OH 44512 • *38,596*
Boardman, OR 97818 • *1,387*
Boaz, AL 35957 • *6,928*
Boca Grande, FL 33921 • *1,200*
Boca Raton, FL 33431–34 • *61,492*
Boerne, TX 78006 • *4,274*
Bogalusa, LA 70427–29 • *14,280*
Bogart, GA 30622 • *1,018*
Bogata, TX 75417 • *1,421*
Boger City, NC 28092 • *1,373*
Bogota, NJ 07603 • *7,824*
Bohemia, NY 11716 • *9,556*
Boiling Springs, NC 28017 • *2,445*
Boiling Springs, PA 17007 • *1,978*
Boise, ID 83701–15 • *125,738*
Boise □, ID • *3,509*
Boise City, OK 73933 • *1,509*
Bolingbrook, IL 60440 • *40,843*
Bolivar, MO 65613 • *6,845*
Bolivar, NY 14715 • *1,261*
Bolivar, TN 38008 • *5,969*
Bolivar □, MS • *41,875*
Bollinger □, MO • *10,619*
Bolton Landing, NY 12814 • *1,600*
Bon Air, VA 23235 • *16,413*
Bonaventure, FL 33317 • *6,000*
Bond □, IL • *14,991*
Bondsville, MA 01009 • *1,992*
Bonduel, WI 54107 • *1,210*
Bondurant, IA 50035 • *1,584*
Bonham, TX 75418 • *6,686*
Bon Homme □, SD • *7,089*
Bonifay, FL 32425 • *2,612*
Bonita, CA 91903 • *12,542*
Bonita Springs, FL 33923 • *13,600*
Bonneauville, PA 17325 • *1,282*
Bonner □, ID • *26,622*
Bonners Ferry, ID 83805 • *2,193*
Bonner Springs, KS 66012 • *6,413*
Bonne Terre, MO 63628 • *3,871*
Bonneville □, ID • *72,207*
Bonney Lake, WA 98390 • *7,494*
Bonnie Doone, NC 28303 • *3,893*
Bono, AR 72416 • *1,220*
Booker, TX 79005 • *1,236*
Boomer, WV 25031 • *1,051*
Boone, IA 50036 • *12,392*
Boone, NC 28607 • *12,915*
Boone □, AR • *28,297*
Boone □, IL • *30,806*
Boone □, IN • *38,147*
Boone □, IA • *25,186*
Boone □, KY • *57,589*
Boone □, MO • *112,379*
Boone □, NE • *6,667*
Boone □, WV • *25,870*
Booneville, AR 72927 • *3,804*
Booneville, MS 38829 • *7,955*
Boonsboro, MD 21713 • *2,445*
Boonton, NJ 07005 • *8,343*
Boonville, CA 95415 • *1,000*
Boonville, IN 47601 • *6,724*
Boonville, MO 65233 • *7,095*
Boonville, NY 13309 • *2,220*
Boonville, NC 27011 • *1,009*
Boothbay Harbor, ME 04538 • *1,267*
Borden □, TX • *799*
Bordentown, NJ 08505 • *4,341*
Borger, TX 79007–08 • *15,675*
Boron, CA 93516 • *2,101*
Borrego Springs, CA 92004 • *2,244*
Boscobel, WI 53805 • *2,706*
Bosque □, TX • *15,125*
Bossert Estates, NJ 08505 • *1,830*
Bossier □, LA • *86,088*
Bossier City, LA 71111–13 • *52,721*
Boston, GA 31626 • *1,395*
Boston, MA 02101–99 • *574,283*
Boswell, PA 15531 • *1,485*
Botetourt □, VA • *24,992*
Bothell, WA 98011–12 • *12,345*
Botkins, OH 45306 • *1,340*
Bottineau, ND 58318 • *2,598*
Bottineau □, ND • *8,011*
Boulder, CO 80301–08 • *83,312*
Boulder, MT 59632 • *1,316*
Boulder □, CO • *225,339*
Boulder City, NV 89005–06 • *12,567*
Boulder Creek, CA 95006 • *6,725*
Boulder Hill, IL 60538 • *8,894*
Boulevard Heights, MD 20743 • *1,820*
Boundary □, ID • *8,332*
Bound Brook, NJ 08805 • *9,487*
Bountiful, UT 84010–11 • *36,659*
Bourbon, IN 46504 • *1,672*
Bourbon, MO 65441 • *1,188*
Bourbon □, KS • *14,966*
Bourbon □, KY • *19,236*
Bourbonnais, IL 60914 • *13,934*
Bourg, LA 70343 • *2,073*
Bourne, MA 02532 • *1,284*
Boutte, LA 70039 • *1,200*
Bovina, TX 79009 • *1,549*
Bowdon, GA 30108 • *1,981*
Bowie, MD 20715–21 • *37,589*
Bowie, TX 76230 • *4,990*
Bowie □, TX • *81,665*
Bowling Green, FL 33834 • *1,836*
Bowling Green, KY 42101–04 • *40,641*
Bowling Green, MO 63334 • *2,976*
Bowling Green, OH 43402 • *28,176*
Bowman, ND 58623 • *1,741*
Bowman, SC 29018 • *1,063*
Bowman □, ND • *3,596*
Box Butte □, NE • *13,130*
Box Elder, SD 57719 • *2,680*
Box Elder □, UT • *36,485*
Boxford, MA 01921 • *2,072*
Boyce, LA 71409 • *1,361*
Boyd □, KY • *51,150*
Boyd □, NE • *2,835*
Boyertown, PA 19512 • *3,759*
Boyes Hot Springs, CA 95416 • *5,973*
Boyle □, KY • *25,641*
Boyne City, MI 49712 • *3,478*
Boynton Beach, FL 33435–37 • *46,194*
Bozeman, MT 59715 • *22,660*
Bracken □, KY • *7,766*
Brackenridge, PA 15014 • *3,784*
Brackettville, TX 78832 • *1,740*
Braddock, PA 15104 • *4,682*
Braddock Heights, MD 21714 • *4,778*
Bradenton, FL 34201–10 • *43,779*
Bradenville, PA 15620 • *1,100*
Bradford, OH 45308 • *2,005*
Bradford, PA 16701 • *9,625*
Bradford, RI 02808 • *1,604*
Bradford, TN 38316 • *1,154*
Bradford, VT 05033 • *672*
Bradford □, FL • *22,515*
Bradford □, PA • *60,967*
Bradfordwoods, PA 15015 • *1,329*
Bradley, FL 33835 • *1,108*
Bradley, IL 60915 • *10,792*
Bradley, WV 25818 • *2,144*
Bradley □, AR • *11,793*
Bradley □, TN • *73,712*
Bradley Beach, NJ 07720 • *4,475*
Bradner, OH 43406 • *1,093*
Brady, TX 76825 • *5,946*
Braham, MN 55006 • *1,139*
Braidwood, IL 60408 • *3,584*
Brainerd, MN 56401 • *12,353*
Braintree, MA 02184 • *33,836*
Branch □, MI • *41,502*
Branch Village, RI 02895 • *400*
Branchville, SC 29432 • *1,107*
Brandenburg, KY 40108 • *1,857*
Brandon, FL 33511 • *57,985*
Brandon, MS 39042–43 • *11,077*
Brandon, SC 29611 • *2,170*
Brandon, SD 57005 • *3,543*
Brandon, VT 05733 • *1,902*
Brandywine, MD 20613 • *1,406*
Branford, CT 06405 • *27,603*
Branford Hills, CT 06405 • *3,460*
Branson, MO 65616 • *3,706*
Brantley, AL 36009 • *1,015*
Brantley □, GA • *11,077*
Brant Rock, MA 02020 • *1,850*
Bratenahl, OH 44108 • *1,356*
Brattleboro, VT 05301–04 • *8,612*
Brawley, CA 92227 • *18,923*
Braxton □, WV • *12,998*
Brazil, IN 47834 • *7,640*
Brazoria, TX 77422 • *2,717*
Brazoria □, TX • *191,707*
Brazos □, TX • *121,862*
Brea, CA 92621–22 • *32,873*
Breathitt □, KY • *15,703*
Breaux Bridge, LA 70517 • *6,515*
Breckenridge, CO 80424 • *1,285*
Breckenridge, MI 48615 • *1,301*
Breckenridge, MN 56520 • *3,708*
Breckenridge, TX 76024 • *5,665*
Breckenridge Hills, MO 63114 • *5,404*
Breckinridge □, KY • *16,312*
Brecksville, OH 44141 • *11,818*
Breese, IL 62230 • *3,567*
Bremen, GA 30110 • *4,356*
Bremen, IN 46506 • *4,725*
Bremen, OH 43107 • *1,386*
Bremer □, IA • *22,813*
Bremerton, WA 98310–15 • *38,142*
Bremond, TX 76629 • *1,110*
Brenham, TX 77833–34 • *11,952*
Brent, AL 35034 • *2,776*
Brent, FL 32503 • *21,624*
Brentwood, CA 94513 • *7,563*
Brentwood, MD 20722 • *3,005*
Brentwood, MO 63144 • *8,150*
Brentwood, NY 11717 • *45,218*
Brentwood, NY • *45,218*
Brentwood, OH 45231 • *3,568*
Brentwood, PA 15227 • *10,823*
Brentwood, SC 29405 • *2,000*
Brentwood, TN 37027 • *16,392*
Brevard, NC 28712 • *5,388*
Brevard □, FL • *398,978*
Brewer, ME 04412 • *9,021*
Brewster, MA 02631 • *1,818*
Brewster, NY 10509 • *1,566*
Brewster, OH 44613 • *2,307*
Brewster, WA 98812 • *1,633*
Brewster □, TX • *8,681*
Brewton, AL 36426–27 • *5,885*
Briarcliff Manor, NY 10510 • *7,070*
Brick [Township], NJ 08723 • *55,473*
Bridge City, LA 70094 • *8,327*
Bridge City, TX 77611 • *8,034*
Bridgehampton, NY 11932 • *1,997*
Bridgeport, AL 35740 • *2,936*
Bridgeport, CT 06601–50 • *141,686*
Bridgeport, IL 62417 • *2,118*
Bridgeport, MI 48722 • *8,569*
Bridgeport, NE 69336 • *1,581*
Bridgeport, OH 43912 • *2,318*
Bridgeport, PA 19405 • *4,292*
Bridgeport, TX 76026 • *3,581*
Bridgeport, WA 98813 • *1,498*
Bridgeport, WV 26330 • *6,739*
Bridger, MT 59014 • *692*
Bridgeton, MO 63044 • *17,779*
Bridgeton, NJ 08302 • *18,942*
Bridgetown, OH 45211 • *11,460*
Bridgeview, IL 60455 • *14,402*
Bridgeville, DE 19933 • *1,210*
Bridgeville, PA 15017 • *5,445*
Bridgewater, MA 02324 • *7,242*
Bridgewater, NJ 08807 • *5,630*
Bridgewater, VA 22812 • *3,918*
Bridgman, MI 49106 • *2,140*
Bridgton, ME 04009 • *2,195*
Brielle, NJ 08730 • *4,406*
Brigantine, NJ 08203 • *11,354*
Brigham City, UT 84302 • *15,644*
Brighton, AL 35020 • *4,518*
Brighton, CO 80601 • *14,203*
Brighton, IL 62012 • *2,270*
Brighton, MI 48116 • *5,686*
Brighton, NY 14610 • *34,455*
Brilliant, OH 43913 • *1,672*
Brillion, WI 54110 • *2,840*
Brinkley, AR 72021 • *4,234*
Briscoe □, TX • *1,971*
Bristol, CT 06010–11 • *60,640*
Bristol, IN 46507 • *1,133*
Bristol, NH 03222 • *1,483*
Bristol, RI 02809 • *21,625*
Bristol, TN 37620–25 • *23,421*
Bristol, VT 05443 • *1,801*
Bristol, VA 24201–03 • *18,426*
Bristol □, MA • *506,325*
Bristol □, RI • *48,859*
Bristol [Township], PA 19007 • *58,773*
Bristow, OK 74010 • *4,062*
Britt, IA 50423 • *2,133*
Britton, SD 57430 • *1,394*
Broadalbin, NY 12025 • *1,397*
Broad Brook, CT 06016 • *1,280*
Broadkill Beach, DE 19968 • *390*
Broadus, MT 59317 • *572*
Broadview, IL 60153 • *8,713*
Broadview Heights, OH 44141 • *12,219*
Broadview Park, FL 33314 • *6,109*
Broadwater □, MT • *3,318*
Broadway, VA 22815 • *1,209*
Brockport, NY 14420 • *8,749*
Brockton, MA 02401–05 • *92,788*
Brockway, PA 15824 • *2,207*
Brocton, NY 14716 • *1,387*
Brodhead, KY 40409 • *1,140*
Brodhead, WI 53520 • *3,165*
Brodheadsville, PA 18322 • *1,500*
Broken Arrow, OK 74011–14 • *58,043*
Broken Bow, NE 68822 • *3,778*
Broken Bow, OK 74728 • *3,961*
Bronson, MI 49028 • *2,342*
Bronx □, NY • *1,203,789*
Bronxville, NY 10708 • *6,028*
Brooke □, WV • *26,992*
Brookfield, CT 06804 • *1,500*
Brookfield, IL 60513 • *18,876*
Brookfield, MA 01506 • *2,968*
Brookfield, MO 64628 • *4,888*
Brookfield, VA 22021 • *2,100*
Brookfield, WI 53005 • *35,184*
Brookfield Center, CT 06804 • *1,400*
Brookhaven, MS 39601 • *10,243*
Brookhaven, PA 19015 • *8,567*
Brookhaven, WV 26505 • *3,836*
Brookings, OR 97415 • *4,400*
Brookings, SD 57006 • *16,270*
Brookings □, SD • *25,207*
Brooklawn, NJ 08030 • *1,805*
Brookline, MA 02146 • *54,718*
Brooklyn, CT 06234 • *1,400*
Brooklyn, IN 46111 • *1,162*
Brooklyn, IA 52211 • *1,439*
Brooklyn, OH 44144 • *11,706*
Brooklyn, SC 29720 • *1,650*
Brooklyn Center, MN 55429 • *28,887*
Brooklyn Park, MD 21225 • *10,987*
Brooklyn Park, MN 55443 • *56,381*
Brookneal, VA 24528 • *1,344*
Brook Park, OH 44142 • *22,865*
Brookport, IL 62910 • *1,070*
Brooks, KY 40109 • *2,464*
Brooks □, GA • *15,398*
Brooks □, TX • *8,204*
Brookshire, TX 77423 • *2,922*
Brookside, AL 35036 • *1,365*
Brookside, DE 19713 • *15,307*
Brookston, IN 47923 • *1,804*
Brooksville, FL 34601–14 • *7,440*
Brooksville, MS 39739 • *1,098*
Brookville, IN 47012 • *2,529*
Brookville, NY 11545 • *3,716*
Brookville, OH 45309 • *4,621*
Brookville, PA 15825 • *4,184*
Brookwood, NJ 08527 • *5,500*
Broomall, PA 19008 • *10,930*
Broome □, NY • *212,160*
Broomfield, CO 80020–21 • *24,638*
Broussard, LA 70518 • *3,213*
Broward □, FL • *1,255,488*
Browardale, FL 33311 • *6,257*
Brown □, IL • *5,836*
Brown □, IN • *14,080*
Brown □, KS • *11,128*
Brown □, MN • *26,984*
Brown □, NE • *3,657*
Brown □, OH • *34,966*
Brown □, SD • *35,580*
Brown □, TX • *34,371*
Brown □, WI • *194,594*
Brown City, MI 48416 • *1,244*
Brown Deer, WI 53209 • *12,236*
Brownfield, TX 79316 • *9,560*
Brownfields, LA 70811 • *5,229*
Browning, MT 59417 • *1,170*
Brownsburg, IN 46112 • *7,628*
Browns Mills, NJ 08015 • *11,429*
Brownstown, IN 47220 • *2,872*
Brownsville, FL 33142 • *15,607*
Brownsville, OR 97327 • *1,281*
Brownsville, PA 15417 • *3,164*
Brownsville, TN 38012 • *10,019*
Brownsville, TX 78520–26 • *98,962*
Brownville, LA 71291 • *1,700*
Brownville, NY 13615 • *1,138*
Brownwood, TX 76803–04 • *18,387*
Broxton, GA 31519 • *1,211*
Broyhill Park, VA 22042 • *3,600*
Bruce, MS 38915 • *2,127*
Bruceton, TN 38317 • *1,586*
Brule □, SD • *5,485*
Brundidge, AL 36010 • *2,472*
Brunswick, GA 31520–22 • *16,433*
Brunswick, ME 04011 • *14,683*
Brunswick, MD 21716 • *5,117*
Brunswick, MO 65236 • *1,074*
Brunswick, OH 44212 • *28,230*
Brunswick □, NC • *50,985*
Brunswick □, VA • *15,987*
Brush, CO 80723 • *4,165*
Brusly, LA 70719 • *1,824*
Bryan, OH 43506 • *8,348*
Bryan, TX 77801–06 • *55,002*
Bryan □, GA • *15,438*
Bryan □, OK • *32,089*
Bryans Road, MD 20616 • *3,809*
Bryant, AR 72022 • *5,269*
Bryantville, MA 02327 • *1,800*
Bryn Mawr, WA 98178 • *1,500*
Bryson City, NC 28713 • *1,145*
Buchanan, GA 30113 • *1,009*
Buchanan, MI 49107 • *4,992*
Buchanan, VA 24066 • *1,222*
Buchanan □, IA • *20,844*
Buchanan □, MO • *83,083*
Buchanan □, VA • *31,333*
Buckeye, AZ 85326 • *5,038*
Buckeye Lake, OH 43008 • *2,986*
Buckhannon, WV 26201 • *5,909*
Buckingham □, VA • *12,873*
Buckley, WA 98321 • *3,516*
Bucknell Manor, VA 22307 • *2,300*
Buckner, MO 64016 • *2,873*
Bucks □, PA • *541,174*
Bucksport, ME 04416 • *2,989*
Bucksport, SC 29527 • *1,022*
Bucyrus, OH 44820 • *13,496*
Buda, TX 78610 • *1,795*
Budd Lake 0L, NJ • *7,272*
Buechel, KY 40218 • *7,081*
Buena, NJ 08310 • *4,441*
Buena Park, CA 90620–24 • *68,784*
Buena Vista, CO 81211 • *1,752*
Buena Vista, FL 34691 • *3,000*
Buena Vista, GA 31803 • *1,472*
Buena Vista, VA 24416 • *6,406*
Buena Vista □, IA • *19,965*
Buffalo, IA 52728 • *1,260*
Buffalo, MN 55313 • *6,856*
Buffalo, MO 65622 • *2,414*
Buffalo, NY 14201–40 • *328,123*
Buffalo, OK 73834 • *1,312*
Buffalo, SC 29321 • *1,569*
Buffalo, TX 75831 • *1,555*
Buffalo, WY 82834 • *3,302*
Buffalo □, NE • *37,447*
Buffalo □, SD • *1,759*
Buffalo □, WI • *13,584*
Buffalo Center, IA 50424 • *1,081*
Buffalo Grove, IL 60089 • *36,427*
Buford, GA 30518 • *8,771*
Buhl, ID 83316 • *3,516*
Buhler, KS 67522 • *1,277*
Buies Creek, NC 27506 • *2,085*
Bullhead City, AZ 86430 • *21,951*
Bullitt □, KY • *47,567*
Bulloch □, GA • *43,125*
Bullock □, AL • *11,042*
Bull Shoals, AR 72619 • *1,534*
Buna, TX 77612 • *1,900*
Bunche Park, FL 33054 • *4,000*
Buncombe □, NC • *174,821*
Bunker Hill, IL 62014 • *1,722*
Bunker Hill, OR 97420 • *1,242*
Bunkerville, NV 89007 • *300*
Bunkie, LA 71322 • *5,044*
Bunnell, FL 32110 • *1,873*
Buras, LA 70041 • *1,850*
Burbank, CA 91501–10 • *93,643*
Burbank, IL 60459 • *27,600*
Burdickville, RI 02808 • *500*
Bureau □, IL • *35,688*
Burgaw, NC 28425 • *1,807*
Burgettstown, PA 15021 • *1,634*
Burgin, KY 40310 • *1,009*
Burien, WA 98062 • *25,089*
Burkburnett, TX 76354 • *10,145*
Burke, SD 57523 • *756*
Burke, VA 22015 • *57,734*
Burke □, GA • *20,579*
Burke □, NC • *75,744*
Burke □, ND • *3,002*
Burkesville, KY 42717 • *1,815*
Burleigh □, ND • *60,131*
Burleson, TX 76028 • *16,113*
Burleson □, TX • *13,625*
Burley, ID 83318 • *8,702*
Burlingame, CA 94010–11 • *26,801*
Burlingame, KS 66413 • *1,074*
Burlington, CO 80807 • *2,941*
Burlington, IA 52601 • *27,208*
Burlington, KS 66839 • *2,735*
Burlington, KY 41005 • *6,070*
Burlington, MA 01803 • *23,302*
Burlington, NJ 08016 • *9,835*
Burlington, NC 27215–17 • *39,498*
Burlington, ND 58722 • *995*
Burlington, VT 05401–04 • *39,127*
Burlington, WA 98233 • *4,349*
Burlington, WI 53105 • *8,855*
Burlington □, NJ • *395,066*
Burnet, TX 78611 • *3,423*
Burnet □, TX • *22,677*
Burnett □, WI • *13,084*
Burney, CA 96013 • *3,423*
Burnham, PA 17009 • *2,197*
Burns, OR 97720 • *2,913*
Burns, TN 37029 • *1,127*
Burns, WY 82053 • *254*
Burns Flat, OK 73624 • *1,027*
Burnsville, MN 55337 • *51,288*
Burnsville, NC 28714 • *1,482*
Burnt Hills, NY 12027 • *1,550*
Burr Ridge, IL 60521 • *7,669*
Burt □, NE • *7,868*
Burton, MI 48509 • *27,617*
Burton, OH 44021 • *1,349*
Burton, SC 29902 • *6,917*
Burtonsville, MD 20866 • *5,853*
Burwell, NE 68823 • *1,278*
Bushnell, FL 33513 • *1,998*
Bushnell, IL 61422 • *3,288*
Butler, AL 36904 • *1,872*
Butler, GA 31006 • *1,673*
Butler, IN 46721 • *2,601*
Butler, MO 64730 • *4,099*
Butler, NJ 07405 • *7,392*
Butler, PA 16001–03 • *15,714*
Butler, WI 53007 • *2,079*
Butler □, AL • *21,892*
Butler □, IA • *15,731*
Butler □, KS • *50,580*
Butler □, KY • *11,245*
Butler □, MO • *38,765*
Butler □, NE • *8,601*
Butler □, OH • *291,479*
Butler □, PA • *152,013*
Butner, NC 27509 • *4,679*
Butte, MT 59701–03 • *33,336*
Butte □, CA • *182,120*
Butte □, ID • *2,918*
Butte □, SD • *7,914*
Buttonwillow, CA 93206 • *1,301*
Butts □, GA • *15,326*
Buxton, NC 27920 • *1,300*
Buzzards Bay, MA 02532 • *3,250*
Byers, CO 80103 • *1,065*
Byesville, OH 43723 • *2,435*
Byfield, MA 01922 • *1,200*
Bylas, AZ 85530 • *1,219*
Byron, GA 31008 • *2,276*
Byron, IL 61010 • *2,284*
Byron, MN 55920 • *2,441*
Byron, WY 82412 • *470*

C

Cabarrus □, NC • *98,935*
Cabell □, WV • *96,827*
Cabin Creek, WV 25035 • *1,300*
Cabin John, MD 20818 • *1,690*
Cabool, MO 65689 • *2,006*
Cabot, AR 72023 • *8,319*
Cache, OK 73527 • *2,251*
Cache □, UT • *70,183*
Caddo □, LA • *248,253*
Caddo □, OK • *29,550*
Cadillac, MI 49601 • *10,104*
Cadiz, KY 42211 • *2,148*
Cadiz, OH 43907 • *3,439*
Cadott, WI 54727 • *1,328*
Cahaba Heights, AL 35243 • *4,778*
Cahokia, IL 62206 • *17,550*
Cairnbrook, PA 15924 • *1,081*
Cairo, GA 31728 • *9,035*
Cairo, IL 62914 • *4,846*
Cairo, NY 12413 • *1,273*
Calais, ME 04619 • *3,963*
Calaveras □, CA • *31,998*
Calavo Gardens, CA 91941 • *6,100*
Calcasieu □, LA • *168,134*
Calcutta, OH 43920 • *1,212*
Caldwell, ID 83605–06 • *18,400*
Caldwell, KS 67022 • *1,351*
Caldwell, NJ 07006 • *7,549*
Caldwell, OH 43724 • *1,786*
Caldwell, TX 77836 • *3,181*
Caldwell □, KY • *13,232*
Caldwell □, LA • *9,810*
Caldwell □, MO • *8,380*
Caldwell □, NC • *70,709*
Caldwell □, TX • *26,392*
Caledonia, MN 55921 • *2,846*
Caledonia, NY 14423 • *2,262*
Caledonia □, VT • *27,846*
Calera, AL 35040 • *2,136*
Calera, OK 74730 • *1,536*
Calexico, CA 92231–32 • *18,633*
Calhoun, GA 30701 • *7,135*
Calhoun □, AL • *116,034*
Calhoun □, AR • *5,826*
Calhoun □, FL • *11,011*
Calhoun □, GA • *5,013*
Calhoun □, IL • *5,322*
Calhoun □, IA • *11,508*
Calhoun □, MI • *135,982*
Calhoun □, MS • *14,908*
Calhoun □, SC • *12,753*
Calhoun □, TX • *19,053*
Calhoun □, WV • *7,885*
Calhoun City, MS 38916 • *1,838*
Calhoun Falls, SC 29628 • *2,328*
Caliente, NV 89008 • *1,111*
Califon, NJ 07830 • *1,073*
California, MD 20619 • *7,626*
California, MO 65018 • *3,465*
California, PA 15419 • *5,748*
Calipatria, CA 92233 • *2,690*
Calistoga, CA 94515 • *4,468*
Callahan □, TX • *11,859*
Callaway, FL 32401 • *12,253*
Callaway □, MO • *32,809*
Calloway □, KY • *30,735*
Calmar, IA 52132 • *1,026*
Calumet □, WI • *34,291*

United States Populations and ZIP Codes

Calumet City, IL 60409 • *37,840*
Calumet Park, IL 60643 • *8,418*
Calvert, TX 77837 • *1,536*
Calvert □, MD • *51,372*
Calvert City, KY 42029 • *2,531*
Calverton, MD 20705 • *12,046*
Calverton Park, MO 63136 • *1,404*
Camanche, IA 52730 • *4,436*
Camarillo, CA 93010–11 • *52,303*
Camas, WA 98607 • *6,442*
Camas □, ID • *727*
Cambria, CA 93428 • *5,382*
Cambria □, PA • *163,029*
Cambrian Park, CA 95124 • *2,998*
Cambridge, IL 61238 • *2,124*
Cambridge, MD 21613 • *11,514*
Cambridge, MA 02138 • *95,802*
Cambridge, MN 55008 • *5,094*
Cambridge, NE 69022 • *1,107*
Cambridge, NY 12816 • *1,906*
Cambridge, OH 43725 • *11,748*
Cambridge City, IN 47327 • *2,091*
Cambridge Springs, PA 16403 • *1,837*
Camden, AL 36726 • *2,414*
Camden, AR 71701 • *14,380*
Camden, DE 19934 • *1,899*
Camden, ME 04843 • *4,022*
Camden, NJ 08101–10 • *87,492*
Camden, NY 13316 • *2,552*
Camden, OH 45311 • *2,210*
Camden, SC 29020 • *6,696*
Camden, TN 38320 • *3,643*
Camden □, GA • *30,167*
Camden □, MO • *27,495*
Camden □, NJ • *502,824*
Camden □, NC • *5,904*
Camdenton, MO 65020 • *2,561*
Camelot, WA 98002 • *4,900*
Cameron, LA 70631 • *2,041*
Cameron, MO 64429 • *4,831*
Cameron, TX 76520 • *5,580*
Cameron, WV 26033 • *1,177*
Cameron, WI 54822 • *1,273*
Cameron □, LA • *9,260*
Cameron □, PA • *5,913*
Cameron □, TX • *260,120*
Cameron Park, CA 95682 • *11,897*
Camilla, GA 31730 • *5,008*
Camino, CA 95709 • *1,500*
Camp □, TX • *9,904*
Campbell, CA 95008–09 • *36,048*
Campbell, FL 34746 • *3,884*
Campbell, MO 63933 • *2,165*
Campbell, OH 44405 • *10,038*
Campbell □, KY • *83,866*
Campbell □, SD • *1,965*
Campbell □, TN • *35,079*
Campbell □, VA • *47,572*
Campbell □, WY • *29,370*
Campbellsport, WI 53010 • *1,732*
Campbellsville, KY 42718–19 • *9,577*
Camp Hill, AL 36850 • *1,415*
Camp Hill, PA 17011 • *7,831*
Camp Point, IL 62320 • *1,230*
Camp Springs, MD 20748 • *16,392*
Camp Verde, AZ 86322 • *6,243*
Canaan, CT 06018 • *1,194*
Canadensis, PA 18325 • *1,200*
Canadian, TX 79014 • *2,417*
Canadian □, OK • *74,409*
Canajoharie, NY 13317 • *2,278*
Canal Fulton, OH 44614 • *4,157*
Canal Winchester, OH 43110 • *2,617*
Canandaigua, NY 14424–25 • *10,725*
Canastota, NY 13032 • *4,673*
Canby, MN 56220 • *1,826*
Canby, OR 97013 • *8,983*
Candler □, GA • *7,744*
Candlewood Isle, CT 06812 • *1,100*
Candlewood Shores, CT 06804 • *1,620*
Cando, ND 58324 • *1,564*
Caney, KS 67333 • *2,062*
Canfield, OH 44406 • *5,409*
Canisteo, NY 14823 • *2,421*
Cannelton, IN 47520 • *1,786*
Cannon □, TN • *10,467*
Cannon Beach, OR 97110 • *1,221*
Cannondale, CT 06897 • *1,500*
Cannon Falls, MN 55009 • *3,232*
Canon City, CO 81212 • *12,687*
Canonsburg, PA 15317 • *9,200*
Canterbury, DE 19943 • *500*
Canton, CT 06019 • *1,563*
Canton, GA 30114 • *4,817*
Canton, IL 61520 • *13,922*
Canton, MA 02021 • *18,182*
Canton, MI 48187 • *57,047*
Canton, MS 39046 • *10,062*
Canton, MO 63435 • *2,623*
Canton, NY 13617 • *6,379*
Canton, NC 28716 • *3,790*
Canton, OH 44701–99 • *84,161*
Canton, PA 17724 • *1,966*
Canton, SD 57013 • *2,787*
Canton, TX 75103 • *2,949*
Cantonment, FL 32533 • *3,200*
Canutillo, TX 79835 • *4,500*
Canyon, TX 79015 • *11,365*
Canyon □, ID • *90,076*
Canyon Lake, CA 92380 • *7,938*
Canyon Lake, TX 78130 • *9,975*
Canyonville, OR 97417 • *1,219*
Capac, MI 48014 • *1,583*
Cape Canaveral, FL 32920 • *8,014*
Cape Charles, VA 23310 • *1,398*
Cape Coral, FL 33904 • *74,991*
Cape Elizabeth, ME 04107 • *8,854*
Cape Girardeau, MO 63701–02 • *34,438*
Cape Girardeau □, MO • *61,633*
Cape May, NJ 08204 • *4,668*
Cape May □, NJ • *95,089*
Cape May Court House, NJ 08210 • *4,426*
Cape Saint Claire, MD 21401 • *7,878*
Capitola, CA 95010 • *10,171*
Capitol Heights, MD 20743 • *3,633*
Capitol View, SC 29209 • *10,456*
Captain Cook, HI 96704 • *2,595*
Captiva, FL 33924 • *1,200*
Caraway, AR 72419 • *1,178*
Carbon □, MT • *8,080*
Carbon □, PA • *56,846*
Carbon □, UT • *20,228*
Carbon □, WY • *16,659*
Carbondale, CO 81623 • *3,004*
Carbondale, IL 62901–03 • *27,033*
Carbondale, KS 66414 • *1,526*
Carbondale, PA 18407 • *10,664*
Carbon Hill, AL 35549 • *2,115*
Cardington, OH 43315 • *1,770*
Carencro, LA 70520 • *5,429*
Carey, OH 43316 • *3,684*
Caribou, ME 04736 • *9,415*
Caribou □, ID • *6,963*
Carle Place, NY 11514 • *5,107*
Carleton, MI 48117 • *2,770*
Carlin, NV 89822 • *2,220*
Carlinville, IL 62626 • *5,416*
Carlisle, AR 72024 • *2,253*
Carlisle, IA 50047 • *3,241*
Carlisle, KY 40311 • *1,639*
Carlisle, OH 45005 • *4,872*
Carlisle, PA 17013 • *18,419*
Carlisle □, KY • *5,238*
Carl Junction, MO 64834 • *4,123*
Carlsbad, CA 92008–09 • *63,126*
Carlsbad, NM 88220–21 • *24,952*
Carlstadt, NJ 07072 • *5,510*
Carlton, OR 97111 • *1,289*
Carlton □, MN • *29,259*
Carlyle, IL 62231 • *3,474*
Carmel, CA 93921–23 • *4,239*
Carmel, IN 46032 • *25,380*
Carmel, NY 10512 • *3,395*
Carmi, IL 62821 • *5,564*
Carmichael, CA 95608–09 • *48,702*
Carnation, WA 98014 • *1,243*
Carnegie, OK 73015 • *1,593*
Carnegie, PA 15106 • *9,278*
Carney, MD 21234 • *25,578*
Carneys Point, NJ 08069 • *7,686*
Carnot, PA 15108 • *4,750*
Caro, MI 48723 • *4,054*
Carol City, FL 33055 • *53,331*
Caroleen, NC 28019 • *1,100*
Carolina Beach, NC 28428 • *3,630*
Caroline □, MD • *27,035*
Caroline □, VA • *19,217*
Carol Stream, IL 60188 • *31,716*
Carpentersville, IL 60110 • *23,049*
Carpinteria, CA 93013–14 • *13,747*
Carrabelle, FL 32322 • *1,200*
Carrboro, NC 27510 • *11,553*
Carrier Mills, IL 62917 • *1,991*
Carrington, ND 58421 • *2,267*
Carrizo Springs, TX 78834 • *5,745*
Carrizozo, NM 88301 • *1,075*
Carroll, IA 51401 • *9,579*
Carroll □, AR • *18,654*
Carroll □, GA • *71,422*
Carroll □, IL • *16,805*
Carroll □, IN • *18,809*
Carroll □, IA • *21,423*
Carroll □, KY • *9,292*
Carroll □, MD • *123,372*
Carroll □, MS • *9,237*
Carroll □, MO • *10,748*
Carroll □, NH • *35,410*
Carroll □, OH • *26,521*
Carroll □, TN • *27,514*
Carroll □, VA • *26,594*
Carrollton, AL 35447 • *1,170*
Carrollton, GA 30117 • *16,029*
Carrollton, IL 62016 • *2,507*
Carrollton, KY 41008 • *3,715*
Carrollton, MI 48724 • *6,521*
Carrollton, MO 64633 • *4,406*
Carrollton, OH 44615 • *3,042*
Carrollton, TX 75006–08 • *82,169*
Carrolltown, PA 15722 • *1,286*
Carrollwood, FL 33618 • *11,400*
Carson, CA 90749 • *83,995*
Carson □, TX • *6,576*
Carson City, MI 48811 • *1,158*
Carson City, NV 89701–21 • *40,443*
Carter □, KY • *24,340*
Carter □, MO • *5,515*
Carter □, MT • *1,503*
Carter □, OK • *42,919*
Carter □, TN • *51,505*
Carteret, NJ 07008 • *19,025*
Carteret □, NC • *52,556*
Carter Lake, IA 51510 • *3,200*
Cartersville, GA 30120 • *12,035*
Carterville, IL 62918 • *3,630*
Carterville, MO 64835 • *2,013*
Carthage, IL 62321 • *2,657*
Carthage, MS 39051 • *3,819*
Carthage, MO 64836 • *10,747*
Carthage, NY 13619 • *4,344*
Carthage, TN 37030 • *2,386*
Carthage, TX 75633 • *6,496*
Caruthersville, MO 63830 • *7,389*
Carver, MA 02330 • *1,500*
Carver □, MN • *47,915*
Carver Ranch Estates, FL 33023 • *5,600*
Carville, LA 70721 • *1,108*
Cary, IL 60013 • *10,043*
Cary, NC 27511 • *43,858*
Caryville, TN 37714 • *1,751*
Casa de Oro, CA 92077 • *9,500*
Casa Grande, AZ 85222 • *19,082*
Casas Adobes, AZ 85704 • *12,155*
Cascade, CO 80809 • *1,000*
Cascade, ID 83611 • *877*
Cascade, IA 52033 • *1,812*
Cascade, MT 59421 • *729*
Cascade □, MT • *77,691*
Cascade Vista, WA 98058 • *7,800*
Casey, IL 62420 • *2,914*
Casey □, KY • *14,211*
Cashion, AZ 85329 • *3,014*
Cashmere, WA 98815 • *2,544*
Casper, WY 82601–15 • *46,742*
Caspian, MI 49915 • *1,031*
Cass □, IL • *13,437*
Cass □, IN • *38,413*
Cass □, IA • *15,128*
Cass □, MI • *49,477*
Cass □, MN • *21,791*
Cass □, MO • *63,808*
Cass □, NE • *21,318*
Cass □, ND • *102,874*
Cass □, TX • *29,982*
Cass City, MI 48726 • *2,276*
Casselberry, FL 32707–08 • *18,911*
Casselton, ND 58012 • *1,601*
Cassia □, ID • *19,532*
Cassopolis, MI 49031 • *1,822*
Cassville, MO 65625 • *2,371*
Cassville, WI 53806 • *1,144*
Castanea, PA 17726 • *1,123*
Castile, NY 14427 • *1,078*
Castle Dale, UT 84513 • *1,704*
Castle Hayne, NC 28429 • *1,182*
Castle Hills, DE 19810 • *1,475*
Castle Park, CA 92011 • *6,300*
Castle Point, MO 63136 • *7,800*
Castle Rock, CO 80104 • *8,708*
Castle Rock, WA 98611 • *2,067*
Castle Shannon, PA 15234 • *9,135*
Castleton, VT 05735 • *600*
Castleton on Hudson, NY 12033 • *1,491*
Castlewood, VA 24224 • *2,110*
Castro □, TX • *9,070*
Castro Valley, CA 94546 • *48,619*
Castroville, TX 78009 • *2,159*
Caswell □, NC • *20,693*
Catahoula □, LA • *11,065*
Catalina Foothills, AZ 85718 • *1,470*
Catasauqua, PA 18032 • *6,662*
Cataumet, MA 02534 • *1,500*
Catawba □, NC • *118,412*
Catawissa, PA 17820 • *1,683*
Cathedral City, CA 92234–35 • *30,085*
Catlettsburg, KY 41129 • *2,231*
Catlin, IL 61817 • *2,173*
Catonsville, MD 21228 • *35,233*
Catoosa, OK 74015 • *2,954*
Catoosa □, GA • *42,464*
Catron □, NM • *2,563*
Catskill, NY 12414 • *4,690*
Cattaraugus, NY 14719 • *1,100*
Cattaraugus □, NY • *84,234*
Cavalier, ND 58220 • *1,508*
Cavalier □, ND • *6,064*
Cave City, AR 72521 • *1,503*
Cave City, KY 42127 • *1,953*
Cave Creek, AZ 85331 • *2,925*
Cave Junction, OR 97523 • *1,126*
Cave Spring, VA 24018 • *24,053*
Cavetown, MD 21720 • *1,533*
Cayce, SC 29033 • *11,163*
Cayuga, IN 47928 • *1,083*
Cayuga □, NY • *82,313*
Cayuga Heights, NY 14850 • *3,457*
Cazenovia, NY 13035 • *3,007*
Cecil □, MD • *71,347*
Cedar □, IA • *17,381*
Cedar □, MO • *12,093*
Cedar □, NE • *10,131*
Cedar Bluff, AL 35959 • *1,174*
Cedar Bluff Two, TN 37722 • *2,000*
Cedarburg, WI 53012 • *9,895*
Cedar City, UT 84720–22 • *13,443*
Cedar Crest, NM 87008 • *1,200*
Cedaredge, CO 81413 • *1,380*
Cedar Falls, IA 50613 • *34,298*
Cedar Grove, NJ 07009 • *12,053*
Cedar Grove, WV 25039 • *1,213*
Cedar Grove, WI 53013 • *1,521*
Cedar Hill, MO 63016 • *1,966*
Cedar Hill, TX 75104 • *19,976*
Cedar Hills, OR 97005 • *9,294*
Cedarhurst, NY 11516 • *5,716*
Cedar Lake, IN 46303 • *8,885*
Cedar Rapids, IA 52401–10 • *108,751*
Cedar Springs, MI 49319 • *2,600*
Cedartown, GA 30125 • *7,978*
Cedarville, NJ 08311 • *1,100*
Cedarville, OH 45314 • *3,210*
Celina, OH 45822 • *9,650*
Celina, TN 38551 • *1,493*
Celina, TX 75009 • *1,737*
Celoron, NY 14720 • *1,232*
Cementon, PA 18052 • *1,050*
Center, CO 81125 • *1,963*
Center, ND 58530 • *826*
Center, TX 75935 • *4,950*
Centerburg, OH 43011 • *1,323*
Centereach, NY 11720 • *26,720*
Center Line, MI 48015 • *9,026*
Center Moriches, NY 11934 • *5,987*
Center Point, AL 35215 • *22,657*
Center Point, IA 52213 • *1,693*
Centerville, IN 47330 • *2,398*
Centerville, IA 52544 • *5,936*
Centerville, MA 02632 • *9,190*
Centerville, OH 45459 • *21,082*
Centerville, PA 15417 • *3,842*
Centerville, SD 57014 • *887*
Centerville, TN 37033 • *3,616*
Centerville, UT 84014 • *11,500*
Central, NM 88026 • *1,835*
Central, SC 29630 • *2,438*
Central City, CO 80427 • *335*
Central City, IL 62801 • *1,390*
Central City, IA 52214 • *1,063*
Central City, KY 42330 • *4,979*
Central City, NE 68826 • *2,868*
Central City, PA 15926 • *1,246*
Central Falls, RI 02863 • *17,637*
Central Heights, AZ 85501 • *1,500*
Centralia, IL 62801 • *14,274*
Centralia, MO 65240 • *3,414*
Centralia, WA 98531 • *12,101*
Central Islip, NY 11722 • *26,028*
Central Park, WA 98520 • *2,669*
Central Point, OR 97502 • *7,509*
Central Square, NY 13036 • *1,671*
Central Valley, CA 96019 • *4,340*
Central Valley, NY 10917 • *1,929*
Central Village, CT 06332 • *1,600*
Centre, AL 35960 • *2,893*
Centre □, PA • *123,786*
Centre City, NJ 08051 • *2,070*
Centre Hall, PA 16828 • *1,203*
Centreville, AL 35042 • *2,508*
Centreville, IL 62207 • *7,489*
Centreville, MD 21617 • *2,097*
Centreville, MI 49032 • *1,516*
Centreville, MS 39631 • *1,771*
Centreville, VA 22020 • *26,585*
Century, FL 32535 • *1,989*
Century Village, FL 33409 • *8,363*
Ceredo, WV 25507 • *1,916*
Ceres, CA 95307 • *26,314*
Cerritos, CA 90703 • *53,240*
Cerro Gordo, IL 61818 • *1,436*
Cerro Gordo □, IA • *46,733*
Chadbourn, NC 28431 • *2,005*
Chadds Ford, PA 19317 • *1,200*
Chadron, NE 69337 • *5,588*
Chadwicks, NY 13319 • *2,000*
Chaffee, MO 63740 • *3,059*
Chaffee □, CO • *12,684*
Chaffin, MA 01520 • *3,980*
Chagrin Falls, OH 44022 • *4,146*
Chalfonte, DE 19810 • *1,740*
Challis, ID 83226 • *1,073*
Chalmette, LA 70043–44 • *31,860*
Chama, NM 87520 • *1,048*
Chamberlain, SD 57325 • *2,347*
Chambers □, AL • *36,876*
Chambers □, TX • *20,088*
Chambersburg, PA 17201 • *16,647*
Chamblee, GA 30341 • *7,668*
Champaign, IL 61820–21 • *63,502*
Champaign □, IL • *173,025*
Champaign □, OH • *36,019*
Champion, OH 44481 • *5,270*
Champlain, NY 12919 • *1,273*
Champlin, MN 55316 • *16,849*
Chandler, AZ 85224–27 • *90,533*
Chandler, IN 47610 • *3,099*
Chandler, OK 74834 • *2,596*
Chandler, TX 75758 • *1,630*
Chandler Heights, AZ 85227 • *1,000*
Chanhassen, MN 55317 • *11,732*
Channahon, IL 60410 • *4,266*
Channel Lake, IL 60002 • *1,660*
Channelview, TX 77530 • *25,564*
Chantilly, VA 22021–22 • *29,337*
Chanute, KS 66720 • *9,488*
Chapel Hill, NC 27514–16 • *38,719*
Chapel Square, VA 22003 • *2,400*
Chapman, KS 67431 • *1,264*
Chapmanville, WV 25508 • *1,110*
Chappaqua, NY 10514 • *6,380*
Chardon, OH 44024 • *4,446*
Chariton, IA 50049 • *4,616*
Chariton □, MO • *9,202*
Charleroi, PA 15022 • *5,014*
Charles □, MD • *101,154*
Charles City, IA 50616 • *7,878*
Charles City □, VA • *6,282*
Charles Mix □, SD • *9,131*
Charleston, AR 72933 • *2,128*
Charleston, IL 61920 • *20,398*
Charleston, MS 38921 • *2,328*
Charleston, MO 63834 • *5,085*
Charleston, SC 29401–22 • *80,414*
Charleston, WV 25301–75 • *57,287*
Charleston □, SC • *295,039*
Charlestown, IN 47111 • *5,889*
Charlestown, NH 03603 • *1,173*
Charlestown, RI 02813 • *1,500*
Charles Town, WV 25414 • *3,122*
Charlevoix, MI 49720 • *3,116*
Charlevoix □, MI • *21,468*
Charlotte, MI 48813 • *8,083*
Charlotte, NC 28201–41 • *395,934*
Charlotte, TX 78011 • *1,475*
Charlotte □, FL • *110,975*
Charlotte □, VA • *11,688*
Charlotte Hall, MD 20622 • *1,992*
Charlotte Harbor, FL 33980 • *3,327*
Charlottesville, VA 22901–08 • *40,341*
Charlton □, GA • *8,496*
Charlton City, MA 01508 • *1,400*
Charter Oak, CA 91724 • *8,858*
Chase □, KS • *3,021*
Chase □, NE • *4,381*
Chase City, VA 23924 • *2,442*
Chaska, MN 55318 • *11,339*
Chatfield, MN 55923 • *2,226*
Chatham, IL 62629 • *6,074*
Chatham, MA 02633 • *1,916*
Chatham, NJ 07928 • *8,007*
Chatham, NY 12037 • *1,920*
Chatham, VA 24531 • *1,354*
Chatham □, GA • *216,935*
Chatham □, NC • *38,759*
Chatom, AL 36518 • *1,094*
Chatsworth, GA 30705 • *2,865*
Chatsworth, IL 60921 • *1,186*
Chattahoochee, FL 32324 • *4,382*
Chattahoochee □, GA • *16,934*
Chattanooga, TN 37401–22 • *152,466*
Chattaroy, WV 25667 • *1,182*
Chattooga □, GA • *22,242*
Chautauqua □, KS • *4,407*
Chautauqua □, NY • *141,895*
Chauvin, LA 70344 • *3,375*
Chaves □, NM • *57,849*
Chazy, NY 12921 • *1,000*
Cheatham □, TN • *27,140*
Cheboygan, MI 49721 • *4,999*
Cheboygan □, MI • *21,398*
Checotah, OK 74426 • *3,290*
Cheektowaga, NY 14225 • *84,387*
Chehalis, WA 98532 • *6,527*
Chelan, WA 98816 • *2,969*
Chelan □, WA • *52,250*
Chelmsford, MA 01824 • *32,388*
Chelsea, MA 02150 • *28,710*
Chelsea, MI 48118 • *3,772*
Chelsea, OK 74016 • *1,620*
Chelsea Estates, DE 19720 • *1,320*
Cheltenham Township, PA 19012 • *35,509*
Chemung □, NY • *95,195*
Chenango □, NY • *51,768*
Chenango Bridge, NY 13745 • *2,890*
Cheney, KS 67025 • *1,560*
Cheney, WA 99004 • *7,723*
Cheneyville, LA 71325 • *1,005*
Chenoa, IL 61726 • *1,732*
Chenoweth, OR 97058 • *3,246*
Chepachet, RI 02814 • *900*
Cheraw, SC 29520 • *5,505*
Cherokee, AL 35616 • *1,479*
Cherokee, IA 51012 • *6,026*
Cherokee, OK 73728 • *1,787*
Cherokee □, AL • *19,543*
Cherokee □, GA • *90,204*
Cherokee □, IA • *14,098*
Cherokee □, KS • *21,374*
Cherokee □, NC • *20,170*
Cherokee □, OK • *34,049*
Cherokee □, SC • *44,506*
Cherokee □, TX • *41,049*
Cherokee Village, AR 72525 • *3,200*
Cherry □, NE • *6,307*
Cherry Hill, NJ 08002–03 • *69,319*
Cherry Hills Village, CO 80110 • *5,245*
Cherryland, CA 94541 • *11,088*
Cherryvale, KS 67335 • *2,464*
Cherry Valley, CA 92223 • *5,945*
Cherry Valley, IL 61016 • *1,615*
Cherry Valley, MA 01611 • *1,120*
Cherryville, NC 28021 • *4,756*
Chesaning, MI 48616 • *2,567*
Chesapeake, OH 45619 • *1,073*
Chesapeake, VA 23320–28 • *151,976*
Chesapeake, WV 25315 • *1,896*
Chesapeake Beach, MD 20732 • *2,403*
Cheshire, CT 06410 • *25,684*
Cheshire, MA 01225 • *1,100*
Cheshire □, NH • *70,121*
Chesilhurst, NJ 08089 • *1,526*
Chesnee, SC 29323 • *1,280*
Chester, CA 96020 • *2,082*
Chester, CT 06412 • *1,563*
Chester, IL 62233 • *8,194*
Chester, MT 59522 • *942*
Chester, NJ 07930 • *1,214*
Chester, NY 10918 • *3,270*
Chester, PA 19013–16 • *41,856*
Chester, SC 29706 • *7,158*
Chester, VT 05143 • *550*
Chester, VA 23831 • *14,896*
Chester, WV 26034 • *2,905*
Chester □, PA • *376,396*
Chester □, SC • *32,170*
Chester □, TN • *12,819*
Chester Depot, VT 05144 • *500*
Chesterfield, IN 46017 • *2,730*
Chesterfield, SC 29709 • *1,373*
Chesterfield □, SC • *38,577*
Chesterfield □, VA • *209,274*
Chesterton, IN 46304 • *9,124*
Chestertown, MD 21620 • *4,005*
Chester Township, PA 19013 • *5,399*
Chestnut Hill Estates, DE 19713 • *1,730*
Chestnut Ridge, NY 10952 • *7,517*
Cheswick, PA 15024 • *1,971*
Cheswold, DE 19936 • *321*
Chetek, WI 54728 • *1,953*
Chetopa, KS 67336 • *1,357*
Chevak, AK 99563 • *598*
Cheverly, MD 20785 • *6,023*
Cheviot, OH 45211 • *9,616*
Chevy Chase, MD 20815 • *8,559*
Chewelah, WA 99109 • *1,945*
Cheyenne, WY 82001–09 • *50,008*
Cheyenne □, CO • *2,397*
Cheyenne □, KS • *3,243*
Cheyenne □, NE • *9,494*
Cheyenne Wells, CO 80810 • *1,128*
Chicago, IL 60601–66 • *2,783,726*
Chicago Heights, IL 60411 • *33,072*
Chicago Ridge, IL 60415 • *13,643*
Chickamauga, GA 30707 • *2,149*
Chickasaw, AL 36611 • *6,649*
Chickasaw □, IA • *13,295*
Chickasaw □, MS • *18,085*
Chickasha, OK 73018 • *14,988*
Chico, CA 95926–28 • *40,079*
Chicopee, MA 01013–22 • *56,632*
Chicora, PA 16025 • *1,058*
Chiefland, FL 32626 • *1,917*
Childersburg, AL 35044 • *4,579*
Childress, TX 79201 • *5,055*
Childress □, TX • *5,953*
Chilhowie, VA 24319 • *1,971*
Chili Center, NY 14624 • *4,360*
Chillicothe, IL 61523 • *5,959*
Chillicothe, MO 64601 • *8,804*
Chillicothe, OH 45601 • *21,923*
Chillum, MD 20783 • *31,309*
Chilton, WI 53014 • *3,240*
Chilton □, AL • *32,458*
Chimayo, NM 87522 • *2,789*
China Grove, NC 28023 • *2,732*
Chincoteague, VA 23336 • *3,572*
Chinle, AZ 86503 • *5,059*
Chino, CA 91708–10 • *59,682*
Chinook, MT 59523 • *1,512*
Chino Valley, AZ 86323 • *4,837*
Chipley, FL 32428 • *3,866*
Chippewa □, MI • *34,604*
Chippewa □, MN • *13,228*
Chippewa □, WI • *52,360*
Chippewa Falls, WI 54729 • *12,727*
Chisago □, MN • *30,521*
Chisago City, MN 55013 • *2,009*
Chisholm, ME 04239 • *1,653*
Chisholm, MN 55719 • *5,290*
Chittenango, NY 13037 • *4,734*
Chittenden □, VT • *131,761*
Choctaw, OK 73020 • *8,545*
Choctaw □, AL • *16,018*
Choctaw □, MS • *9,071*
Choctaw □, OK • *15,302*
Choteau, MT 59422 • *1,741*
Chouteau, OK 74337 • *1,771*
Chouteau □, MT • *5,452*
Chowan □, NC • *13,506*
Chowchilla, CA 93610 • *5,930*
Chrisman, IL 61924 • *1,136*
Christian □, IL • *34,418*
Christian □, KY • *68,941*
Christian □, MO • *32,644*
Christiana, DE 19702 • *500*
Christiana, PA 17509 • *1,045*
Christiansburg, VA 24073 • *15,004*
Christmas, FL 32709 • *1,200*
Christopher, IL 62822 • *2,774*
Chubbuck, ID 83202 • *7,791*
Chugwater, WY 82210 • *192*
Chula Vista, CA 91909–15 • *135,163*
Church Hill, TN 37642 • *4,834*
Churchill, OH 44505 • *7,700*
Churchill □, NV • *17,938*
Church Point, LA 70525 • *4,677*
Churchville, NY 14428 • *1,731*
Churubusco, IN 46723 • *1,781*
Cibola □, NM • *23,794*
Cicero, IL 60650 • *67,436*
Cicero, IN 46034 • *3,268*
Cimarron, KS 67835 • *1,626*
Cimarron □, OK • *3,301*
Cimarron Hills, CO 80906 • *11,160*
Cincinnati, OH 45201–75 • *364,040*
Cinnaminson, NJ 08077 • *14,583*
Circle, MT 59215 • *805*

Circle Pines, MN 55014 • 4,704
Circleville, OH 43113 • 11,666
Cisco, TX 76437 • 3,813
Citra, FL 32113 • 1,500
Citronelle, AL 36522 • 3,671
Citrus, CA 91702 • 9,481
Citrus □, FL • 93,515
Citrus Heights, CA 95610–11 • 107,439
City Of Sunrise, FL 33313 • 64,407
City View, SC 29611 • 1,490
Clackamas, OR 97015 • 2,578
Clackamas □, OR • 278,850
Claiborne, LA 71291 • 8,300
Claiborne □, LA • 17,405
Claiborne □, MS • 11,370
Claiborne □, TN • 26,137
Clair-Mel City, FL 33619 • 7,000
Clairton, PA 15025 • 9,656
Clallam □, WA • 56,464
Clanton, AL 35045 • 7,669
Clara City, MN 56222 • 1,307
Clare, MI 48617 • 3,021
Clare □, MI • 24,952
Claremont, CA 91711 • 32,503
Claremont, NH 03743 • 13,902
Claremore, OK 74017–18 • 13,280
Clarence, MO 63437 • 1,026
Clarendon, AR 72029 • 2,072
Clarendon, TX 79226 • 2,067
Clarendon □, SC • 28,450
Clarendon Hills, IL 60514 • 6,994
Claridge, PA 15623 • 1,200
Clarinda, IA 51632 • 5,104
Clarion, IA 50525 • 2,703
Clarion, PA 16214 • 6,457
Clarion □, PA • 41,699
Clark, NJ 07066 • 14,629
Clark, SD 57225 • 1,292
Clark □, AR • 21,437
Clark □, ID • 762
Clark □, IL • 15,921
Clark □, IN • 87,777
Clark □, KS • 2,418
Clark □, KY • 29,496
Clark □, MO • 7,547
Clark □, NV • 741,459
Clark □, OH • 147,548
Clark □, SD • 4,403
Clark □, WA • 238,053
Clark □, WI • 31,647
Clarkdale, AZ 86324 • 2,144
Clarke □, AL • 27,240
Clarke □, GA • 87,594
Clarke □, IA • 8,287
Clarke □, MS • 17,313
Clarke □, VA • 12,101
Clarkesville, GA 30523 • 1,151
Clarksburg, WV 26301–02 • 18,059
Clarksdale, MS 38614 • 19,717
Clarks Summit, PA 18411 • 5,433
Clarkston, GA 30021 • 5,385
Clarkston, MI 48346–48 • 1,005
Clarkston, WA 99403 • 6,753
Clarksville, AR 72830 • 5,833
Clarksville, DE 19970 • 500
Clarksville, IN 47129 • 19,833
Clarksville, IA 50619 • 1,382
Clarksville, TN 37040–43 • 75,494
Clarksville, TX 75426 • 4,311
Clarksville, VA 23927 • 1,243
Clarkton, MO 63837 • 1,113
Clatskanie, OR 97016 • 1,629
Clatsop □, OR • 33,301
Claude, TX 79019 • 1,199
Clawson, MI 48017 • 13,874
Claxton, GA 30417 • 2,464
Clay, KY 42404 • 1,173
Clay □, AL • 13,252
Clay □, AR • 18,107
Clay □, FL • 105,986
Clay □, GA • 3,364
Clay □, IL • 14,460
Clay □, IN • 24,705
Clay □, IA • 17,585
Clay □, KS • 9,158
Clay □, KY • 21,746
Clay □, MN • 50,422
Clay □, MS • 21,120
Clay □, MO • 153,411
Clay □, NE • 7,123
Clay □, NC • 7,155
Clay □, SD • 13,186
Clay □, TN • 7,238
Clay □, TX • 10,024
Clay □, WV • 9,983
Clay Center, KS 67432 • 4,613
Clay City, KY 40312 • 1,258
Claymont, DE 19702 • 9,800
Claypool, AZ 85532 • 1,942
Claysburg, PA 16625 • 1,399
Clayton, AL 36016 • 1,564
Clayton, DE 19938 • 1,163
Clayton, GA 30525 • 1,613
Clayton, MO 63105 • 13,874
Clayton, NJ 08312 • 6,155
Clayton, NM 88415 • 2,484
Clayton, NY 13624 • 2,160
Clayton, NC 27520 • 4,756
Clayton □, GA • 182,052
Clayton □, IA • 19,054
Clear Creek □, CO • 7,619
Clearfield, KY 40313 • 1,250
Clearfield, PA 16830 • 6,633
Clearfield, UT 84015 • 21,435
Clearfield □, PA • 78,097
Clearlake, CA 95422 • 11,804
Clear Lake, IA 50428 • 8,183
Clear Lake, SD 57226 • 1,247
Clearlake, WA 98235 • 1,100
Clear Lake Shores, TX 77565 • 1,096
Clearwater, FL 34615–30 • 98,784
Clearwater, KS 67026 • 1,875
Clearwater, SC 29822 • 4,731
Clearwater □, ID • 8,505
Clearwater □, MN • 8,309
Cleburne, TX 76031–33 • 22,205
Cleburne □, AL • 12,730
Cleburne □, AR • 19,411
Cle Elum, WA 98922 • 1,778
Cleland Heights, DE 19805 • 1,120
Clementon, NJ 08021 • 5,601
Clemmons, NC 27012 • 6,020
Clemson, SC 29631–33 • 11,096

Clendenin, WV 25045 • 1,203
Cleona, PA 17042 • 2,322
Clermont, FL 34711–12 • 6,910
Clermont □, OH • 150,187
Cleveland, GA 30528 • 1,653
Cleveland, MS 38732–33 • 15,384
Cleveland, OH 44101–99 • 505,616
Cleveland, OK 74020 • 3,156
Cleveland, TN 37311–12 • 30,354
Cleveland, TX 77327–28 • 7,124
Cleveland, WI 53015 • 1,398
Cleveland □, AR • 7,781
Cleveland □, NC • 84,714
Cleveland □, OK • 174,253
Cleveland Heights, OH 44118 • 54,052
Cleves, OH 45002 • 2,208
Clewiston, FL 33440 • 6,085
Cliffside Park, NJ 07010 • 20,393
Clifton, AZ 85533 • 2,840
Clifton, CO 81520 • 12,671
Clifton, IL 60927 • 1,347
Clifton, NJ 07011–15 • 71,742
Clifton, TX 76634 • 3,195
Clifton Forge, VA 24422 • 4,679
Clifton Heights, PA 19018 • 7,111
Clifton Knolls, NY 12065 • 5,636
Clifton Springs, NY 14432 • 2,175
Clinch □, GA • 6,160
Clint, TX 79836 • 1,035
Clinton, AR 72031 • 2,213
Clinton, CT 06413 • 3,439
Clinton, IL 61727 • 7,437
Clinton, IN 47842 • 5,040
Clinton, IA 52732–33 • 29,201
Clinton, KY 42031 • 1,547
Clinton, LA 70722 • 1,904
Clinton, ME 04927 • 1,485
Clinton, MD 20735 • 19,987
Clinton, MA 01510 • 7,943
Clinton, MI 49236 • 2,475
Clinton, MS 39056 • 21,847
Clinton, MO 64735 • 8,703
Clinton, NJ 08809 • 2,054
Clinton, NY 13323 • 2,238
Clinton, NC 28328 • 8,204
Clinton, OK 73601 • 9,298
Clinton, SC 29325 • 7,987
Clinton, TN 37716 • 8,972
Clinton, UT 84015 • 7,945
Clinton, WA 98236 • 2,000
Clinton, WI 53525 • 1,849
Clinton □, IL • 33,944
Clinton □, IN • 30,974
Clinton □, IA • 51,040
Clinton □, KY • 9,135
Clinton □, MI • 57,883
Clinton □, MO • 16,595
Clinton □, NY • 85,969
Clinton □, OH • 35,415
Clinton □, PA • 37,182
Clinton Township, MI 48043 • 85,866
Clintonville, WI 54929 • 4,351
Clintwood, VA 24228 • 1,542
Clio, AL 36017 • 1,365
Clio, MI 48420 • 2,629
Clive, IA 50322 • 7,462
Cloquet, MN 55720 • 10,885
Closter, NJ 07624 • 8,094
Cloud □, KS • 11,023
Clover, SC 29710 • 3,422
Cloverdale, CA 95425 • 4,924
Cloverdale, IN 46120 • 1,681
Cloverleaf, TX 77015 • 18,230
Cloverport, KY 40111 • 1,207
Clovis, CA 93612–13 • 50,323
Clovis, NM 88101–03 • 30,954
Clute, TX 77531 • 8,910
Clyde, NY 14433 • 2,409
Clyde, NC 28721 • 1,041
Clyde, OH 43410 • 5,776
Clyde, TX 79510 • 3,002
Clymer, PA 15728 • 1,499
Coachella, CA 92236 • 16,896
Coahoma, TX 79511 • 1,133
Coahoma □, MS • 31,665
Coal □, OK • 5,780
Coal City, IL 60416 • 3,907
Coal Fork, WV 25306 • 2,100
Coalgate, OK 74538 • 1,895
Coal Grove, OH 45638 • 2,251
Coalinga, CA 93210 • 8,212
Coalville, UT 84017 • 1,065
Coatesville, PA 19320 • 11,038
Coats, NC 27521 • 1,493
Cobb □, GA • 447,745
Cobden, IL 62920 • 1,090
Cobleskill, NY 12043 • 5,268
Cochise □, AZ • 97,624
Cochituate, MA 01778 • 6,046
Cochran, GA 31014 • 4,390
Cochran □, TX • 4,377
Cochranton, PA 16314 • 1,174
Cocke □, TN • 29,141
Cockeysville, MD 21030 • 18,668
Cockrell Hill, TX 75211 • 3,746
Cocoa, FL 32922–27 • 17,722
Cocoa Beach, FL 32931–32 • 12,123
Coconino □, AZ • 96,591
Coconut Creek, FL 33060 • 27,485
Codington □, SD • 22,698
Cody, WY 82414 • 7,897
Coeburn, VA 24230 • 2,165
Coeur d'Alene, ID 83814 • 24,563
Coffee □, AL • 40,240
Coffee □, GA • 29,592
Coffee □, TN • 40,339
Coffey □, KS • 8,404
Coffeyville, KS 67337 • 12,917
Cohasset, MA 02025 • 6,800
Cohoes, NY 12047 • 16,825
Cokato, MN 55321 • 2,180
Coke □, TX • 3,424
Cokeville, WY 83114 • 493
Colbert, OK 74733 • 1,043
Colbert □, AL • 51,666
Colby, KS 67701 • 5,396
Colby, WI 54421 • 1,532
Colchester, CT 06415 • 3,212
Colchester, IL 62326 • 1,645
Cold Bay, AK 99571 • 148
Cold Spring, KY 41076 • 2,880
Cold Spring, MN 56320 • 2,459
Cold Spring Harbor, NY 11724 • 4,789

Coldwater, MI 49036 • 9,607
Coldwater, MS 38618 • 1,502
Coldwater, OH 45828 • 4,335
Cole □, MO • 63,579
Colebrook, NH 03576 • 2,444
Cole Camp, MO 65325 • 1,054
Coleman, MI 48618 • 1,237
Coleman, TX 76834 • 5,410
Coleman □, TX • 9,710
Coleraine, MN 55722 • 1,041
Coles □, IL • 51,644
Colfax, CA 95713 • 1,306
Colfax, IA 50054 • 2,462
Colfax, LA 71417 • 1,696
Colfax, WA 99111 • 2,713
Colfax, WI 54730 • 1,110
Colfax □, NE • 9,139
Colfax □, NM • 12,925
College, AK 99701 • 11,249
Collegedale, TN 37315 • 5,048
College Park, GA 30337 • 20,457
College Park, MD 20740–41 • 21,927
College Place, WA 99324 • 6,308
College Station, AR 72053 • 3,800
College Station, TX 77840–45 • 52,456
Collegeville, PA 19426 • 4,227
Colleton □, SC • 34,377
Colleyville, TX 76034 • 12,724
Collier □, FL • 152,099
Collierville, TN 38017 • 14,427
Collin □, TX • 264,036
Collingdale, PA 19023 • 9,175
Collingswood, NJ 08108 • 15,289
Collingsworth □, TX • 3,573
Collins, MS 39428 • 2,541
Collins Park, DE 19720 • 2,100
Collinsville, AL 35961 • 1,429
Collinsville, CT 06022 • 2,591
Collinsville, IL 62234 • 22,446
Collinsville, OK 74021 • 3,612
Collinsville, VA 24078 • 7,280
Collinwood, TN 38450 • 1,014
Colmar Manor, MD 20722 • 1,249
Coloma, MI 49038 • 1,679
Colon, MI 49040 • 1,224
Colonia, NJ 07067 • 18,238
Colonial Beach, VA 22443 • 3,132
Colonial Heights, TN 37663 • 6,716
Colonial Heights, VA 23834 • 16,064
Colonial Park, PA 17109 • 13,777
Colonie, NY 12212 • 8,019
Colorado □, TX • 18,383
Colorado City, AZ 86021 • 2,426
Colorado City, CO 81019 • 1,149
Colorado City, TX 79512 • 4,749
Colorado Springs, CO 80901–99 • 281,140
Colquitt, GA 31737 • 1,991
Colquitt □, GA • 36,645
Colstrip, MT 59323 • 3,035
Colton, CA 92324 • 40,213
Columbia, CA 95310 • 1,799
Columbia, IL 62236 • 5,524
Columbia, KY 42728 • 3,845
Columbia, MD 21044–46 • 75,883
Columbia, MS 39429 • 6,815
Columbia, MO 65201–05 • 69,101
Columbia, PA 17512 • 10,701
Columbia, SC 29201–92 • 98,052
Columbia, TN 38401–02 • 28,583
Columbia □, AR • 25,691
Columbia □, FL • 42,613
Columbia □, GA • 66,031
Columbia □, NY • 62,982
Columbia □, OR • 37,557
Columbia □, PA • 63,202
Columbia □, WA • 4,024
Columbia □, WI • 45,088
Columbia City, IN 46725 • 5,706
Columbia City, OR 97018 • 1,003
Columbia Falls, MT 59912 • 2,942
Columbia Heights, MN 55421 • 18,910
Columbiana, AL 35051 • 2,968
Columbiana, OH 44408 • 4,961
Columbiana □, OH • 108,276
Columbine, CO 80123 • 23,969
Columbus, GA 31901–09 • 178,681
Columbus, IN 47201–03 • 31,802
Columbus, KS 66725 • 3,268
Columbus, MS 39701–05 • 23,799
Columbus, MT 59019 • 1,573
Columbus, NE 68601 • 19,480
Columbus, OH 43201–91 • 632,910
Columbus, TX 78934 • 3,367
Columbus, WI 53925 • 4,093
Columbus □, NC • 49,587
Columbus Grove, OH 45830 • 2,231
Columbus Junction, IA 52738 • 1,616
Colusa, CA 95932 • 4,934
Colusa □, CA • 16,275
Colver, PA 15927 • 1,024
Colville, WA 99114 • 4,360
Colwich, KS 67030 • 1,091
Comal □, TX • 51,832
Comanche, OK 73529 • 1,695
Comanche, TX 76442 • 4,087
Comanche □, KS • 2,313
Comanche □, OK • 111,486
Comanche □, TX • 13,381
Combee Settlement, FL 33801 • 5,463
Combined Locks, WI 54113 • 2,190
Comfort, TX 78013 • 1,477
Commack, NY 11725 • 36,124
Commerce, CA 90040 • 12,135
Commerce, GA 30529 • 4,108
Commerce, OK 74339 • 2,426
Commerce, TX 75428 • 6,825
Commerce City, CO 80022 • 16,466
Common Fence Point, RI 02871 • 860
Como, MS 38619 • 1,387
Compton, CA 90220–24 • 90,454
Comstock, MI 49041 • 5,600
Comstock Park, MI 49321 • 6,530
Concho □, TX • 3,044
Concord, CA 94518–24 • 111,348
Concord, MA 01742 • 4,680
Concord, MO 63128 • 19,859
Concord, NH 03301–03 • 36,006
Concord, NC 28025–27 • 27,347
Concord, TN 37901 • 3,420
Concordia, KS 66901 • 6,167
Concordia, MO 64020 • 2,160
Concordia □, LA • 20,828

Conecuh □, AL • 14,054
Conejos □, CO • 7,453
Conemaugh, PA 15909 • 1,470
Congers, NY 10920 • 8,003
Conklin, NY 13748 • 1,800
Conley, GA 30027 • 5,528
Conneaut, OH 44030 • 13,241
Connell, WA 99326 • 2,005
Connellsville, PA 15425 • 9,229
Connersville, IN 47331 • 15,550
Conover, NC 28613 • 5,465
Conrad, MT 59425 • 2,891
Conroe, TX 77301–05 • 27,610
Conshohocken, PA 19428 • 8,064
Constantia, NY 13044 • 1,140
Constantine, MI 49042 • 2,032
Continental, OH 45831 • 1,214
Contoocook, NH 03229 • 1,334
Contra Costa □, CA • 803,732
Converse, IN 46919 • 1,144
Converse, SC 29329 • 1,173
Converse, TX 78109 • 8,887
Converse □, WY • 11,128
Convoy, OH 45832 • 1,200
Conway, AR 72032 • 26,481
Conway, FL 32809 • 13,159
Conway, NH 03818 • 1,604
Conway, PA 15027 • 2,424
Conway, SC 29526–27 • 9,819
Conway □, AR • 19,151
Conway Springs, KS 67031 • 1,384
Conyers, GA 30207–08 • 7,380
Cook □, GA • 13,456
Cook □, IL • 5,105,067
Cook □, MN • 3,868
Cooke □, TX • 30,777
Cookeville, TN 38501–02 • 21,744
Coolidge, AZ 85228 • 6,927
Coon Rapids, IA 50058 • 1,266
Coon Rapids, MN 55433 • 52,978
Cooper, TX 75432 • 2,153
Cooper □, MO • 14,835
Cooper City, FL 33328 • 20,791
Cooper Road, LA 71107 • 11,050
Coopersburg, PA 18036 • 2,599
Cooperstown, NY 13326 • 2,180
Cooperstown, ND 58425 • 1,247
Coopersville, MI 49404 • 3,421
Coos □, NH • 34,828
Coos □, OR • 60,273
Coosa □, AL • 11,063
Coos Bay, OR 97420 • 15,076
Copake, NY 12516 • 1,200
Copiague, NY 11726 • 20,769
Copiah □, MS • 27,592
Coplay, PA 18037 • 3,267
Copperas Cove, TX 76522 • 24,079
Coquille, OR 97423 • 4,121
Coral Gables, FL 33134 • 40,091
Coral Hills, MD 20743 • 11,032
Coral Springs, FL 33065 • 79,443
Coral Terrace, FL 33157 • 23,255
Coralville, IA 52241 • 10,347
Coral Way Village, FL 33155 • 9,000
Coram, NY 11727 • 30,111
Coraopolis, PA 15108 • 6,747
Corbin, KY 40701–02 • 7,419
Corcoran, CA 93212 • 13,364
Corcoran, MN 55340 • 5,199
Cordaville, MA 01772 • 1,530
Cordele, GA 31015 • 10,321
Cordell, OK 73632 • 2,903
Cordova, AL 35550 • 2,623
Cordova, AK 99574 • 2,110
Cordova, NC 28330 • 1,200
Corinth, MS 38834 • 11,820
Corinth, NY 12822 • 2,760
Cornelia, GA 30531 • 3,219
Cornelius, NC 28031 • 2,581
Cornelius, OR 97113 • 6,148
Cornell, WI 54732 • 1,541
Corning, AR 72422 • 3,323
Corning, CA 96021 • 5,870
Corning, IA 50841 • 1,806
Corning, NY 14830 • 11,938
Cornville, AZ 86325 • 1,200
Cornwall, PA 17016 • 3,231
Cornwall on Hudson, NY 12520 • 3,093
Corona, CA 91718–20 • 76,095
Coronado, CA 92118 • 26,540
Coronado, CO 80229 • 6,890
Corpus Christi, TX 78401–82 • 257,453
Corrigan, TX 75939 • 1,764
Corriganville, MD 21524 • 1,020
Corry, PA 16407 • 7,216
Corsicana, TX 75110 • 22,911
Corson □, SD • 4,195
Corte Madera, CA 94925 • 8,272
Cortez, CO 81321 • 7,284
Cortez, FL 34215 • 4,509
Cortland, NY 13045 • 19,801
Cortland, OH 44410 • 5,666
Cortland □, NY • 48,963
Corunna, MI 48817 • 3,091
Corvallis, OR 97330–33 • 44,757
Corydon, IN 47112 • 2,661
Corydon, IA 50060 • 1,675
Coryell □, TX • 64,213
Coshocton, OH 43812 • 12,193
Coshocton □, OH • 35,427
Cosmopolis, WA 98537 • 1,372
Costa Mesa, CA 92626–28 • 96,357
Costilla □, CO • 3,190
Cottage Grove, MN 55016 • 22,935
Cottage Grove, OR 97424 • 7,402
Cottle □, TX • 2,247
Cottleville, MO 63338 • 2,936
Cotton □, OK • 6,651
Cottondale, AL 35453 • 1,960
Cotton Plant, AR 72036 • 1,150
Cottonport, LA 71327 • 2,600
Cotton Valley, LA 71018 • 1,130
Cottonwood, AL 36320 • 1,385
Cottonwood, AZ 86326 • 5,918
Cottonwood, CA 96022 • 1,747
Cottonwood, ID 83522 • 822
Cottonwood, UT 84121 • 11,554
Cottonwood □, MN • 12,694
Cottonwood Heights, UT 84121 • 28,766
Cotuit, MA 02635 • 1,750
Cotulla, TX 78014 • 3,694
Coudersport, PA 16915 • 2,854
Coulee Dam, WA 99116 • 1,087

Council, ID 83612 • 831
Council Bluffs, IA 51501–03 • 54,315
Council Grove, KS 66846 • 2,228
Country Club Hills, IL 60478 • 15,431
Country Homes, WA 99218 • 5,126
Countryside, IL 60525 • 5,716
Coupeville, WA 98239 • 1,377
Coushatta, LA 71019 • 1,845
Covedale, OH 45238 • 6,669
Covelo, CA 95428 • 1,057
Coventry, CT 06238 • 10,063
Coventry, DE 19720 • 1,165
Coventry, RI 02816 • 6,980
Covina, CA 91722–24 • 43,207
Covington, GA 30209 • 10,026
Covington, IN 47932 • 2,747
Covington, KY 41011–18 • 43,264
Covington, LA 70433–34 • 7,691
Covington, OH 45318 • 2,603
Covington, TN 38019 • 7,487
Covington, VA 24426 • 6,991
Covington □, AL • 36,478
Covington □, MS • 16,527
Cowan, TN 37318 • 1,738
Cowarts, AL 36321 • 1,400
Coweta, OK 74429 • 6,159
Coweta □, GA • 53,853
Cowley, WY 82420 • 477
Cowley □, KS • 36,915
Cowlitz □, WA • 82,119
Cowpens, SC 29330 • 2,176
Coxsackie, NY 12051 • 2,789
Cozad, NE 69130 • 3,823
Crab Orchard, WV 25827 • 2,919
Crabtree, PA 15624 • 1,000
Crafton, PA 15205 • 7,188
Craig, AK 99921 • 1,260
Craig, CO 81625–26 • 8,091
Craig □, OK • 14,104
Craig □, VA • 4,372
Craighead □, AR • 68,956
Craigsville, WV 26205 • 1,955
Cramerton, NC 28032 • 2,371
Cranbury, NJ 08512 • 1,255
Crandall, TX 75114 • 1,652
Crandon, WI 54520 • 1,958
Crane, AZ 85365 • 2,650
Crane, MO 65633 • 1,218
Crane, TX 79731 • 3,533
Crane □, TX • 4,652
Cranford, NJ 07016 • 22,624
Cranston, RI 02910 • 76,060
Craven □, NC • 81,613
Crawford, NE 69339 • 1,115
Crawford □, AR • 42,493
Crawford □, GA • 8,991
Crawford □, IL • 19,464
Crawford □, IN • 9,914
Crawford □, IA • 16,775
Crawford □, KS • 35,568
Crawford □, MI • 12,260
Crawford □, MO • 19,173
Crawford □, OH • 47,870
Crawford □, PA • 86,169
Crawford □, WI • 15,940
Crawfordsville, IN 47933 • 13,584
Crawfordville, FL 32327 • 1,110
Creedmoor, NC 27522 • 1,504
Creek □, OK • 60,915
Creighton, NE 68729 • 1,223
Creighton, PA 15030 • 1,658
Crenshaw □, AL • 13,635
Creola, AL 36525 • 1,896
Cresaptown, MD 21502 • 4,645
Crescent, OK 73028 • 1,236
Crescent City, CA 95531 • 4,380
Crescent City, FL 32112 • 1,859
Crescent Springs, KY 41016 • 2,179
Cresco, IA 52136 • 3,669
Cresskill, NJ 07626 • 7,558
Cresson, PA 16630 • 1,784
Cressona, PA 17929 • 1,694
Cresthaven, FL 33064 • 2,400
Crest Hill, IL 60435 • 10,643
Crestline, CA 92325 • 8,594
Crestline, OH 44827 • 4,934
Creston, IA 50801 • 7,911
Creston, OH 44217 • 1,848
Crestview, FL 32536 • 9,886
Crestview, HI 96797 • 1,000
Crestwood, IL 60445 • 10,823
Crestwood, KY 40014 • 1,435
Crestwood, MO 63126 • 11,234
Crestwood Village, NJ 08759 • 8,030
Creswell, OR 97426 • 2,431
Crete, IL 60417 • 6,773
Crete, NE 68333 • 4,841
Creve Coeur, IL 61611 • 5,938
Creve Coeur, MO 63141 • 12,304
Crewe, VA 23930 • 2,276
Cricket, NC 28659 • 2,015
Cridersville, OH 45806 • 1,885
Crisfield, MD 21817 • 2,880
Crisp □, GA • 20,011
Crittenden □, AR • 49,939
Crittenden □, KY • 9,196
Crocker, MO 65452 • 1,077
Crockett, CA 94525 • 3,228
Crockett, TX 75835 • 7,024
Crockett □, TN • 13,378
Crockett □, TX • 4,078
Crofton, MD 21114 • 12,781
Cromwell, CT 06416 • 1,100
Crook □, OR • 14,111
Crook □, WY • 5,294
Crookston, MN 56716 • 8,119
Crooksville, OH 43731 • 2,601
Crosby, MN 56441 • 2,073
Crosby, ND 58730 • 1,312
Crosby, TX 77532 • 1,811
Crosby □, TX • 7,304
Crosbyton, TX 79322 • 2,026
Cross □, AR • 19,225
Cross City, FL 32628 • 2,041
Crossett, AR 71635 • 6,282
Crosslake, MN 56442 • 1,132
Cross Lanes, WV 25313 • 10,878
Cross Plains, TN 37049 • 1,025
Cross Plains, TX 76443 • 1,063
Cross Plains, WI 53528 • 2,098
Crossville, AL 35962 • 1,350
Crossville, TN 38555 • 6,930
Croswell, MI 48422 • 2,174

Crothersville, IN 47229 • 1,687
Croton-on-Hudson, NY 10520 • 7,018
Crow Agency, MT 59022 • 1,446
Crowell, TX 79227 • 1,230
Crowley, LA 70526–27 • 13,983
Crowley, TX 76036 • 6,974
Crowley □, CO • 3,946
Crown Point, IN 46307 • 17,728
Crownpoint, NM 87313 • 2,108
Crow Wing □, MN • 44,249
Crozet, VA 22932 • 2,256
Crystal, MN 55428 • 23,788
Crystal Bay, NV 89402 • 1,200
Crystal Beach, FL 34681 • 1,450
Crystal City, MO 63019 • 4,088
Crystal City, TX 78839 • 8,263
Crystal Falls, MI 49920 • 1,922
Crystal Lake, CT 06029 • 1,200
Crystal Lake, FL 33803 • 5,300
Crystal Lake, IL 60014 • 24,512
Crystal Lawns, IL 60435 • 1,660
Crystal River, FL 32629 • 4,044
Crystal Springs, MS 39059 • 5,643
Cuba, IL 61427 • 1,440
Cuba, MO 65453 • 2,537
Cuba, NY 14727 • 1,690
Cuba City, WI 53807 • 2,024
Cucamonga, CA 91730 • 101,409
Cudahy, CA 90201 • 22,817
Cudahy, WI 53110 • 18,659
Cuero, TX 77954 • 6,700
Culberson □, TX • 3,407
Culbertson, MT 59218 • 796
Cullen, LA 71021 • 1,642
Cullman, AL 35055–56 • 13,367
Cullman □, AL • 67,613
Culloden, WV 25510 • 2,907
Cullowhee, NC 28723 • 1,200
Culpeper, VA 22701 • 8,581
Culpeper □, VA • 27,791
Culver, IN 46511 • 1,404
Culver City, CA 90230–33 • 38,793
Cumberland, KY 40823 • 3,112
Cumberland, MD 21501–05 • 23,706
Cumberland, WI 54829 • 2,163
Cumberland □, IL • 10,670
Cumberland □, KY • 6,784
Cumberland □, ME • 243,135
Cumberland □, NJ • 138,053
Cumberland □, NC • 274,566
Cumberland □, PA • 195,257
Cumberland □, TN • 34,736
Cumberland □, VA • 7,825
Cumberland Center, ME 04021 • 1,890
Cumberland Foreside, ME 04110 • 1,000
Cumberland Hill, RI 02864 • 6,379
Cuming □, NE • 10,117
Cumming, GA 30130 • 2,828
Cupertino, CA 95014–16 • 40,263
Currituck □, NC • 13,736
Curry □, NM • 42,207
Curry □, OR • 19,327
Curtisville, PA 15032 • 1,285
Curwensville, PA 16833 • 2,924
Cushing, OK 74023 • 7,218
Cusseta, GA 31805 • 1,107
Custer, SD 57730 • 1,741
Custer □, CO • 1,926
Custer □, ID • 4,133
Custer □, MT • 11,697
Custer □, NE • 12,270
Custer □, OK • 26,897
Custer □, SD • 6,179
Cut Bank, MT 59427 • 3,329
Cutchogue, NY 11935 • 1,730
Cuthbert, GA 31740 • 3,730
Cutler, FL 33157 • 16,201
Cutler Ridge, FL 33157 • 21,268
Cutlerville, MI 49508 • 11,228
Cut Off, LA 70345 • 5,325
Cuyahoga □, OH • 1,412,140
Cuyahoga Falls, OH 44221–24 • 48,950
Cynthiana, KY 41031 • 6,497
Cypress, CA 90630 • 42,655
Cypress Lake, FL 33919 • 10,491
Cypress Quarters, FL 34972 • 1,343
Cyril, OK 73029 • 1,072

D

Dacono, CO 80514 • 2,228
Dacula, GA 30211 • 2,217
Dade □, FL • 1,937,094
Dade □, GA • 13,147
Dade □, MO • 7,449
Dade City, FL 33525–26 • 5,633
Dadeville, AL 36853 • 3,276
Daggett □, UT • 690
Dagsboro, DE 19939 • 398
Dahlonega, GA 30533 • 3,086
Daingerfield, TX 75638 • 2,572
Dakota □, MN • 275,227
Dakota □, NE • 16,742
Dakota City, IA 50529 • 1,024
Dakota City, NE 68731 • 1,470
Dale, IN 47523 • 1,553
Dale □, AL • 49,633
Dale City, VA 22193 • 47,170
Daleville, AL 36322 • 5,117
Daleville, IN 47334 • 1,681
Dalhart, TX 79022 • 6,246
Dallam □, TX • 5,461
Dallas, GA 30132 • 2,810
Dallas, NC 28034 • 3,012
Dallas, OR 97338 • 9,422
Dallas, PA 18612 • 2,567
Dallas, TX 75201–99 • 1,006,877
Dallas □, AL • 48,130
Dallas □, AR • 9,614
Dallas □, IA • 29,755
Dallas □, MO • 12,646
Dallas □, TX • 1,852,810
Dallas Center, IA 50063 • 1,454
Dallas City, IL 62330 • 1,037
Dallastown, PA 17313 • 3,974
Dalton, GA 30720–22 • 21,761
Dalton, MA 01226–27 • 6,797
Dalton, OH 44618 • 1,377
Dalton, PA 18414 • 1,369
Dalton Gardens, ID 83814 • 1,951
Daly City, CA 94014–17 • 92,311
Damascus, MD 20872 • 9,817
Dana Point, CA 92629 • 31,896
Danbury, CT 06810–13 • 65,585
Danbury, TX 77534 • 1,447
Dandridge, TN 37725 • 1,540
Dane □, WI • 367,085
Dania, FL 33004 • 13,024
Daniels □, MT • 2,266
Danielson, CT 06239 • 4,441
Dannemora, NY 12929 • 4,005
Dansville, NY 14437 • 5,002
Dante, VA 24237 • 1,083
Danvers, MA 01923 • 24,174
Danville, AR 72833 • 1,585
Danville, CA 94526 • 31,306
Danville, IL 61832–34 • 33,828
Danville, IN 46122 • 4,345
Danville, KY 40422–23 • 12,420
Danville, OH 43014 • 1,001
Danville, PA 17821 • 5,165
Danville, VA 24540–43 • 53,056
Daphne, AL 36526 • 11,290
Darby, PA 19023 • 11,140
Darby Township, PA 19036 • 10,955
Dardanelle, AR 72834 • 3,722
Dare □, NC • 22,746
Darien, CT 06820 • 18,130
Darien, GA 31305 • 1,783
Darien, IL 60559 • 18,341
Darien, WI 53114 • 1,158
Darke □, OH • 53,619
Darley Woods, DE 19810 • 1,220
Darlington, SC 29532 • 7,311
Darlington, WI 53530 • 2,235
Darlington □, SC • 61,851
Darrington, WA 98241 • 1,042
Dartmouth Woods, DE 19810 • 1,970
Dassel, MN 55325 • 1,082
Dauphin □, PA • 237,813
Davenport, FL 33837 • 1,529
Davenport, IA 52801–09 • 95,333
Davenport, WA 99122 • 1,502
David City, NE 68632 • 2,522
Davidson, NC 28036 • 4,046
Davidson □, NC • 126,677
Davidson □, TN • 510,784
Davidsville, PA 15928 • 1,167
Davie, FL 33328 • 47,217
Davie □, NC • 27,859
Daviess □, IN • 27,533
Daviess □, KY • 87,189
Daviess □, MO • 7,865
Davis, CA 95616–17 • 46,209
Davis, OK 73030 • 2,543
Davis □, IA • 8,312
Davis □, UT • 187,941
Davison, MI 48423 • 5,693
Davison □, SD • 17,503
Davisville, RI 02852 • 500
Dawes □, NE • 9,021
Dawson, GA 31742 • 5,295
Dawson, MN 56232 • 1,626
Dawson □, GA • 9,429
Dawson □, MT • 9,505
Dawson □, NE • 19,940
Dawson □, TX • 14,349
Dawson Springs, KY 42408 • 3,129
Day □, SD • 6,978
Dayton, KY 41074 • 6,576
Dayton, MN 55327 • 4,443
Dayton, NV 89403 • 2,217
Dayton, NJ 08810 • 1,200
Dayton, OH 45401–90 • 182,044
Dayton, OR 97114 • 1,526
Dayton, TN 37321 • 5,671
Dayton, TX 77535 • 5,151
Dayton, WA 99328 • 2,468
Dayton, WY 82836 • 565
Daytona Beach, FL 32114–25 • 61,921
Dayville, CT 06241 • 1,500
Deadwood, SD 57732 • 1,830
Deaf Smith □, TX • 19,153
Deal, NJ 07723 • 1,179
Deale, MD 20751 • 4,151
Dearborn, MI 48120–26 • 89,286
Dearborn □, IN • 38,835
Dearborn Heights, MI 48127 • 60,838
De Baca □, NM • 2,252
De Bary, FL 32713 • 7,176
Decatur, AL 35601–03 • 48,761
Decatur, GA 30030–37 • 17,336
Decatur, IL 62521–26 • 83,885
Decatur, IN 46733 • 8,644
Decatur, MI 49045 • 1,760
Decatur, MS 39327 • 1,248
Decatur, TN 37322 • 1,361
Decatur, TX 76234 • 4,252
Decatur □, GA • 25,511
Decatur □, IN • 23,645
Decatur □, IA • 8,338
Decatur □, KS • 4,021
Decatur □, TN • 10,472
Decherd, TN 37324 • 2,196
Deckerville, MI 48427 • 1,015
Decorah, IA 52101 • 8,063
Dedham, MA 02026 • 23,782
Deep River, CT 06417 • 2,520
Deerfield, IL 60015 • 17,327
Deerfield, WI 53531 • 1,617
Deerfield Beach, FL 33441–43 • 46,325
Deer Lodge, MT 59722 • 3,378
Deer Lodge □, MT • 10,278
Deer Park, NY 11729 • 28,840
Deer Park, OH 45236 • 6,181
Deer Park, TX 77536 • 27,652
Deer Park, WA 99006 • 2,278
Defiance, OH 43512 • 16,768
Defiance □, OH • 39,350
De Forest, WI 53532 • 4,882
De Funiak Springs, FL 32433 • 5,120
De Graff, OH 43318 • 1,331
De Kalb, IL 60115 • 34,925
De Kalb, MS 39328 • 1,073
De Kalb, TX 75559 • 1,976
De Kalb □, AL • 54,651
De Kalb □, GA • 545,837
De Kalb □, IL • 77,932
De Kalb □, IN • 35,324
De Kalb □, MO • 9,967
De Kalb □, TN • 14,360
Delafield, WI 53018 • 5,347
Del Aire, CA 90250 • 8,040
Delanco, NJ 08075 • 3,316
De Land, FL 32720–24 • 16,491
Delano, CA 93215–16 • 22,762
Delano, MN 55328 • 2,709
Delavan, IL 61734 • 1,642
Delavan, WI 53115 • 6,073
Delavan Lake, WI 53115 • 2,177
Delaware, OH 43015 • 20,030
Delaware □, IN • 119,659
Delaware □, IA • 18,035
Delaware □, NY • 47,225
Delaware □, OH • 66,929
Delaware □, OK • 28,070
Delaware □, PA • 547,651
Delaware City, DE 19706 • 1,682
Delcambre, LA 70528 • 1,978
Del City, OK 73115 • 23,928
De Leon, TX 76444 • 2,190
De Leon Springs, FL 32130 • 1,481
Delevan, NY 14042 • 1,214
Delhi, LA 71232 • 3,169
Delhi, NY 13753 • 3,064
Delhi Hills, OH 45238 • 27,647
Dell Rapids, SD 57022 • 2,484
Dellwood, MO 63136 • 5,245
Del Mar, CA 92014 • 4,860
Delmar, DE 19940 • 962
Delmar, MD 21875 • 1,430
Delmar, NY 12054 • 8,360
Del Norte, CO 81132 • 1,674
Del Norte □, CA • 23,460
Del Park Manor, DE 19808 • 1,550
Delphi, IN 46923 • 2,531
Delphos, OH 45833 • 7,093
Delran, NJ 08075 • 14,811
Delray Beach, FL 33444–47 • 47,181
Del Rio, FL 33617 • 8,248
Del Rio, TX 78840–42 • 30,705
Delta, CO 81416 • 3,789
Delta, OH 43515 • 2,849
Delta, UT 84624 • 2,998
Delta □, CO • 20,980
Delta □, MI • 37,780
Delta □, TX • 4,857
Delta Junction, AK 99737 • 652
Deltaville, VA 23043 • 1,082
Deltona, FL 32725 • 50,828
Demarest, NJ 07627 • 4,800
Deming, NM 88030–31 • 10,970
Demopolis, AL 36732 • 7,512
Demorest, GA 30535 • 1,088
Demotte, IN 46310 • 2,482
Denham Springs, LA 70726–27 • 8,381
Denison, IA 51442 • 6,604
Denison, TX 75020–21 • 21,505
Denmark, SC 29042 • 3,762
Denmark, WI 54208 • 1,612
Dennis, MA 02638 • 2,500
Dennison, OH 44621 • 3,282
Dennis Port, MA 02639 • 2,775
Denny Terrace, SC 29203 • 1,885
Dent □, MO • 13,702
Denton, MD 21629 • 2,977
Denton, NC 27239 • 1,292
Denton, TX 76201–06 • 66,270
Denton □, TX • 273,525
Dentsville, SC 29204 • 11,839
Denver, CO 80201–95 • 467,610
Denver, IA 50622 • 1,600
Denver, PA 17517 • 2,861
Denver □, CO • 467,610
Denver City, TX 79323 • 5,145
Denville, NJ 07834 • 14,380
De Pere, WI 54115 • 16,569
Depew, NY 14043 • 17,673
Deposit, NY 13754 • 1,936
Depue, IL 61322 • 1,729
De Queen, AR 71832 • 4,633
De Quincy, LA 70633 • 3,474
Derby, CT 06418 • 12,199
Derby, KS 67037 • 14,699
Derby, NY 14047 • 1,200
Derby Line, VT 05830 • 855
De Ridder, LA 70634 • 9,868
Dermott, AR 71638 • 4,715
Derry, NH 03038 • 20,446
Derry, PA 15627 • 2,950
Derwood, MD 20855 • 1,500
Des Allemands, LA 70030 • 2,504
Des Arc, AR 72040 • 2,001
Deschutes □, OR • 74,958
Desert Hot Springs, CA 92240 • 11,668
Desha □, AR • 16,798
Deshler, OH 43516 • 1,876
Desloge, MO 63601 • 4,150
De Smet, SD 57231 • 1,172
Des Moines, IA 50301–95 • 193,187
Des Moines, WA 98188 • 17,283
Des Moines □, IA • 42,614
De Soto, IL 62924 • 1,500
De Soto, IA 50069 • 1,033
De Soto, KS 66018 • 2,291
De Soto, MO 63020 • 5,993
De Soto, TX 75115 • 30,544
De Soto □, FL • 23,865
De Soto □, LA • 25,346
De Soto □, MS • 67,910
Despard, WV 26301 • 1,018
Des Peres, MO 63131 • 8,395
Des Plaines, IL 60016–19 • 53,223
Destin, FL 32540–41 • 8,080
Destrehan, LA 70047 • 8,031
Detroit, MI 48201–44 • 1,027,974
Detroit Lakes, MN 56501–02 • 6,635
Deuel □, NE • 2,237
Deuel □, SD • 4,522
Devils Lake, ND 58301 • 7,782
Devine, TX 78016 • 3,928
Devola, OH 45750 • 2,736
Devon, PA 19333 • 6,620
Devonshire, DE 19810 • 2,120
Dewey, OK 74029 • 3,326
Dewey □, OK • 5,551
Dewey □, SD • 5,523
Dewey Beach, DE 19971 • 204
Deweyville, TX 77614 • 1,218
De Witt, AR 72042 • 3,553
De Witt, IA 52742 • 4,514
De Witt, MI 48820 • 3,964
De Witt, NY 13214 • 8,244
De Witt □, IL • 16,516
De Witt □, TX • 18,840
Dexter, ME 04930 • 2,650
Dexter, MI 48130 • 1,497
Dexter, MO 63841 • 7,559
Dexter, NY 13634 • 1,030
Diamond Bar, CA 91765 • 53,672
Diamond Hill, RI 02864 • 810
Diamond Lake, IL 60060 • 1,500
Diamond Springs, CA 95619 • 2,872
Diamondville, WY 83116 • 864
Diaz, AR 72043 • 1,363
D'Iberville, MS 39532 • 6,566
Diboll, TX 75941 • 4,341
Dickens □, TX • 2,571
Dickenson □, VA • 17,620
Dickey □, ND • 6,107
Dickinson, ND 58601–02 • 16,097
Dickinson, TX 77539 • 9,497
Dickinson □, IA • 14,909
Dickinson □, KS • 18,958
Dickinson □, MI • 26,831
Dickson, TN 37055 • 8,791
Dickson □, TN • 35,061
Dickson City, PA 18519 • 6,276
Dierks, AR 71833 • 1,263
Dighton, KS 67839 • 1,361
Dighton, MA 02715 • 1,100
Dillard, OR 97432 • 1,000
Dilley, TX 78017 • 2,632
Dillingham, AK 99576 • 2,017
Dillon, MT 59725 • 3,991
Dillon, SC 29536 • 6,829
Dillon □, SC • 29,114
Dillsboro, IN 47018 • 1,200
Dillsburg, PA 17019 • 1,925
Dilworth, MN 56529 • 2,562
Dimmit □, TX • 10,433
Dimmitt, TX 79027 • 4,408
Dimondale, MI 48821 • 1,247
Dingmans Ferry, PA 18328 • 1,200
Dinuba, CA 93618 • 12,743
Dinwiddie □, VA • 20,960
Dishman, WA 99213 • 9,671
District Heights-Forestville, MD 20747 • 6,704
District of Columbia 0T15, DC •
Divernon, IL 62530 • 1,178
Divide □, ND • 2,899
Dixfield, ME 04224 • 1,300
Dix Hills, NY 11746 • 25,849
Dixie □, FL • 10,585
Dixon, CA 95620 • 10,401
Dixon, IL 61021 • 15,144
Dixon, MO 65459 • 1,585
Dixon □, NE • 6,143
Dixonville, PA 15734 • 1,000
Dobbs Ferry, NY 10522 • 9,940
Dobson, NC 27017 • 1,195
Docena, AL 35060 • 1,000
Dock Junction, GA 31520 • 7,094
Doddridge □, WV • 6,994
Dodge □, GA • 17,607
Dodge □, MN • 15,731
Dodge □, NE • 34,500
Dodge □, WI • 76,559
Dodge Center, MN 55927 • 1,954
Dodge City, KS 67801 • 21,129
Dodge Park, MD 20785 • 4,842
Dodgeville, WI 53533 • 3,882
Dolgeville, NY 13329 • 2,452
Dolomite, AL 35061 • 2,590
Dolores □, CO • 1,504
Dolton, IL 60419 • 23,930
Dona Ana, NM 88032 • 950
Dona Ana □, NM • 135,510
Donaldsonville, LA 70346 • 7,949
Donalsonville, GA 31745 • 2,761
Doneraile, SC 29532 • 1,276
Doniphan, MO 63935 • 1,713
Doniphan □, KS • 8,134
Donley □, TX • 3,696
Donna, TX 78537 • 12,652
Donora, PA 15033 • 5,928
Dooly □, GA • 9,901
Door □, WI • 25,690
Dora, AL 35062 • 2,214
Doraville, GA 30340 • 7,626
Dorchester □, MD • 30,236
Dorchester □, SC • 83,060
Dormont, PA 15216 • 9,772
Dorothy Pond, MA 01527 • 1,670
Dorr, MI 49323 • 1,450
Dorset, VT 05251 • 550
Dorsey, MD 21227 • 1,186
Dothan, AL 36301–04 • 53,589
Double Springs, AL 35553 • 1,138
Dougherty □, GA • 96,311
Douglas, AZ 85607–08 • 12,822
Douglas, GA 31533 • 10,464
Douglas, MI 49406 • 1,040
Douglas, WY 82633 • 5,076
Douglas □, CO • 60,391
Douglas □, GA • 71,120
Douglas □, IL • 19,464
Douglas □, KS • 81,798
Douglas □, MN • 28,674
Douglas □, MO • 11,876
Douglas □, NE • 416,444
Douglas □, NV • 27,637
Douglas □, OR • 94,649
Douglas □, SD • 3,746
Douglas □, WA • 26,205
Douglas □, WI • 41,758
Douglass, KS 67039 • 1,722
Douglasville, GA 30133–35 • 11,635
Dousman, WI 53118 • 1,277
Dover, AR 72837 • 1,055
Dover, DE 19901–03 • 27,630
Dover, FL 33527 • 2,606
Dover, MA 02030 • 2,163
Dover, NH 03820 • 25,042
Dover, NJ 07801 • 15,115
Dover, OH 44622 • 11,329
Dover, PA 17315 • 1,884
Dover, TN 37058 • 1,341
Dover-Foxcroft, ME 04426 • 3,077
Dover Plains, NY 12522 • 1,847
Dowagiac, MI 49047 • 6,409
Downers Grove, IL 60515–17 • 46,858
Downey, CA 90239–42 • 91,444
Downingtown, PA 19335 • 7,749
Downs, KS 67437 • 1,119
Downsville, NY 13755 • 1,100
Doylestown, OH 44230 • 2,668
Doylestown, PA 18901 • 8,575
Dracut, MA 01826 • 25,594
Drain, OR 97435 • 1,011
Draper, UT 84020 • 7,257
Drayton, ND 58225 • 961
Drayton, SC 29333 • 1,443
Drayton Plains, MI 48330 • 18,000
Dreamland Villa, AZ 85205 • 3,400
Dresden, OH 43821 • 1,581
Dresden, TN 38225 • 2,488
Dresslerville, NV 89410 • 180
Drew, MS 38737 • 2,349
Drew □, AR • 17,369
Drexel, NC 28619 • 1,746
Drexel, OH 45427 • 5,143
Drexel Hill, PA 19026 • 29,744
Dripping Springs, TX 78620 • 1,033
Druid Hills, GA 30333 • 12,174
Drumright, OK 74030 • 2,799
Dryden, NY 13053 • 1,908
Dry Ridge, KY 41035 • 1,601
Duarte, CA 91010 • 20,688
Dublin, CA 94568 • 23,229
Dublin, GA 31021 • 16,312
Dublin, OH 43017 • 16,366
Dublin, PA 18917 • 1,985
Dublin, TX 76446 • 3,190
Dublin, VA 24084 • 2,012
Du Bois, PA 15801 • 8,286
Dubois, WY 82513 • 895
Dubois □, IN • 36,616
Duboistown, PA 17701 • 1,201
Dubuque, IA 52001–04 • 57,546
Dubuque □, IA • 86,403
Duchesne, UT 84021 • 1,308
Duchesne □, UT • 12,645
Dudley, MA 01570–71 • 3,700
Due West, SC 29639 • 1,220
Dukes □, MA • 11,639
Dulce, NM 87528 • 2,438
Duluth, GA 30136 • 9,029
Duluth, MN 55801–16 • 85,493
Dumas, AR 71639 • 5,520
Dumas, TX 79029 • 12,871
Dumfries, VA 22026 • 4,282
Dumont, NJ 07628 • 17,187
Dunaire, GA 30032 • 7,170
Dunbar, PA 15431 • 1,213
Dunbar, WV 25064 • 8,697
Duncan, OK 73533–34 • 21,732
Duncan, SC 29334 • 2,152
Duncan Falls, OH 43734 • 1,200
Duncannon, PA 17020 • 1,450
Duncansville, PA 16635 • 1,309
Duncanville, TX 75116 • 35,748
Dundalk, MD 21222 • 65,800
Dundee, FL 33838 • 2,335
Dundee, IL 60118 • 3,728
Dundee, MI 48131 • 2,664
Dundee, NY 14837 • 1,588
Dundee, OR 97115 • 1,663
Dundy □, NE • 2,582
Dunedin, FL 34697–98 • 34,012
Dunellen, NJ 08812 • 6,528
Dunkirk, IN 47336 • 2,739
Dunkirk, NY 14048 • 13,989
Dunklin □, MO • 33,112
Dunlap, IN 46514 • 5,705
Dunlap, IA 51529 • 1,251
Dunlap, TN 37327 • 3,731
Dunleith, DE 19801 • 2,600
Dunmore, PA 18512 • 15,403
Dunn, NC 28334–35 • 8,336
Dunn □, ND • 4,005
Dunn □, WI • 35,909
Dunnellon, FL 32630 • 1,624
Dunn Loring Woods, VA 22180 • 2,800
Dunseith, ND 58329 • 723
Dunsmuir, CA 96025 • 2,129
Dunwoody, GA 30338 • 26,302
Du Page □, IL • 781,666
Duplin □, NC • 39,995
Dupont, CO 80024 • 5,200
Dupont, PA 18641 • 2,984
Dupont Manor, DE 19901 • 1,059
Duquesne, PA 15110 • 8,525
Du Quoin, IL 62832 • 6,697
Durand, IL 61024 • 1,100
Durand, MI 48429 • 4,283
Durand, WI 54736 • 2,003
Durango, CO 81301–02 • 12,430
Durant, IA 52747 • 1,549
Durant, MS 39063 • 2,838
Durant, OK 74701–02 • 12,823
Durham, CA 95938 • 1,500
Durham, CT 06422 • 2,650
Durham, NH 03824 • 9,236
Durham, NC 27701–22 • 136,611
Durham □, NC • 181,835
Duryea, PA 18642 • 4,869
Duson, LA 70529 • 1,465
Dutchess □, NY • 259,462
Duval □, FL • 672,971
Duval □, TX • 12,918
Duxbury, MA 02331–32 • 1,637
Dwight, IL 60420 • 4,230
Dyer, IN 46311 • 10,923
Dyer, TN 38330 • 2,204
Dyer □, TN • 34,854
Dyersburg, TN 38024–25 • 16,317
Dyersville, IA 52040 • 3,703
Dysart, IA 52224 • 1,230

E

Eagan, MN 55121 • 47,409
Eagar, AZ 85925 • 4,025
Eagle, CO 81631 • 1,580
Eagle, ID 83616 • 3,327
Eagle, NE 68347 • 1,047
Eagle, WI 53119 • 1,182
Eagle □, CO • 21,928
Eagle Grove, IA 50533 • 3,671
Eagle Lake, MN 56024 • 1,703
Eagle Lake, TX 77434 • 3,551
Eagle Lake, WI 53139 • 1,000
Eagle Pass, TX 78852–53 • 20,651
Eagle Point, OR 97524 • 3,008
Eagle River, WI 54521 • 1,374
Eagleton Village, TN 37801 • 5,331
Earle, AR 72331 • 3,393
Earlham, IA 50072 • 1,157
Earlimart, CA 93219 • 5,881

Earlington, KY 42410 • 1,833
Earlville, IL 60518 • 1,435
Early □, GA • 11,854
Earth, TX 79031 • 1,228
Easley, SC 29640-42 • 15,195
East Alton, IL 62024 • 7,063
East Arlington, VT 05252 • 600
East Aurora, NY 14052 • 6,647
East Bangor, PA 18013 • 1,006
East Barre, VT 05649 • 700
East Baton Rouge □, LA • 380,105
East Berlin, PA 17316 • 1,175
East Bernard, TX 77435 • 1,544
East Bethel, MN 55005 • 8,050
East Billerica, MA 01821 • 3,830
East Brady, PA 16028 • 1,047
East Brewton, AL 36426 • 2,579
East Bridgewater, MA 02333 • 3,270
East Brookfield, MA 01515 • 1,396
East Brooklyn, CT 06239 • 1,481
East Brunswick, NJ 08816 • 43,548
East Carbon, UT 84520 • 1,270
East Carroll □, LA • 9,709
Eastchester, NY 10709 • 18,537
East Chicago, IN 46312 • 33,892
East Cleveland, OH 44112 • 33,096
East Compton, CA 90221 • 7,967
East Dennis, MA 02641 • 1,500
East Detroit, MI 48021 • 35,283
East Douglas, MA 01516 • 1,945
East Dubuque, IL 61025 • 1,914
East Falmouth, MA 02536 • 5,577
East Farmingdale, NY 11735 • 4,510
East Feliciana □, LA • 19,211
East Flat Rock, NC 28726 • 3,218
East Gaffney, SC 29340 • 3,278
Eastgate, WA 98007 • 4,434
East Glenville, NY 12302 • 6,518
East Granby, CT 06026 • 1,200
East Grand Forks, MN 56721 • 8,658
East Grand Rapids, MI 49506 • 10,807
East Greenville, PA 18041 • 3,117
East Greenwich, RI 02818 • 11,865
East Half Hollow Hills, NY 11746 • 7,010
Eastham, MA 02642 • 1,150
East Hampton, CT 06424 • 2,167
Easthampton, MA 01027 • 15,580
East Hampton, NY 11937 • 1,402
East Hanover, NJ • 9,926
East Hartford, CT 06128 • 50,452
East Haven, CT 06512 • 26,144
East Helena, MT 59635 • 1,538
East Hemet, CA 92343 • 17,611
East Hills, NY 11576 • 6,746
East Islip, NY 11730 • 14,325
East Jordan, MI 49727 • 2,240
Eastlake, OH 44094 • 21,161
East La Mirada, CA 90638 • 9,367
Eastland, TX 76448 • 3,690
Eastland □, TX • 18,488
East Lansing, MI 48823-26 • 50,677
East Las Vegas, NV 89112 • 11,087
East Liverpool, OH 43920 • 13,654
East Longmeadow, MA 01028 • 12,905
East Los Angeles, CA 90022 • 126,379
East Lyme, CT 06333 • 1,200
Eastman, GA 31023 • 5,153
East Marietta, GA 30062 • 11,900
East Marion, NY 11939 • 1,500
East Matunuck, RI 02879 • 500
East Meadow, NY 11554 • 36,609
East Middlebury, VT 05740 • 500
East Midvale, UT 84047 • 3,800
East Millinocket, ME 04430 • 2,075
East Moline, IL 61244 • 20,147
East Montpelier, VT 05651 • 600
East Naples, FL 33962 • 22,951
East Newark, NJ 07029 • 2,157
East Newnan, GA 30263 • 1,173
East Norriton, PA 19401 • 13,324
East Northport, NY 11731 • 20,411
Easton, MD 21601 • 9,372
Easton, PA 18042-44 • 26,276
East Orange, NJ 07017-19 • 73,552
East Orleans, MA 02643 • 1,850
Eastover, SC 29044 • 1,044
East Palatka, FL 32131 • 1,989
East Palestine, OH 44413 • 5,168
East Palo Alto, CA 94303 • 23,451
East Patchogue, NY 11772 • 20,195
East Pea Ridge, WV 25705 • 4,980
East Peoria, IL 61611 • 21,378
East Pepperell, MA 01463 • 2,296
East Petersburg, PA 17520 • 4,197
East Pittsburgh, PA 15112 • 2,160
Eastpoint, FL 32328 • 1,577
East Point, GA 30344 • 34,402
Eastport, ME 04631 • 1,965
Eastport, NY 11941 • 1,500
East Porterville, CA 93257 • 5,790
East Port Orchard, WA 98366 • 5,409
East Prairie, MO 63845 • 3,416
East Providence, RI 02914 • 50,380
East Quogue, NY 11942 • 4,372
East Richmond, CA 94805 • 5,100
East Ridge, TN 37412 • 21,101
East River, CT 06443 • 3,440
East Rochester, NY 14445 • 6,932
East Rockaway, NY 11518 • 10,152
East Rockingham, NC 28379 • 4,158
East Rutherford, NJ 07073 • 7,902
East Saint Louis, IL 62201-08 • 40,944
Eastsound, WA 98245 • 1,100
East Spencer, NC 28039 • 2,055
East Stroudsburg, PA 18301 • 8,781
East Tawas, MI 48730 • 2,887
East Templeton, MA 01438 • 1,300
East Troy, WI 53120 • 2,664
East Tustin, CA 92705 • 10,000
East Vestal, NY 13902 • 6,310
East View, WV 26301 • 1,222
East Walpole, MA 02032 • 3,760
East Wareham, MA 02538 • 1,500
East Washington, PA 15301 • 2,126
East Wenatchee, WA 98802 • 2,701
East Windsor, NJ 08520 • 15,000
Eastwood, MI 49001 • 6,340
Eastwood Hills, UT 84106 • 1,200
Eaton, CO 80615 • 1,959
Eaton, IN 47338 • 1,614
Eaton, OH 45320 • 7,396
Eaton □, MI • 92,879
Eaton Rapids, MI 48827 • 4,695
Eatonton, GA 31024 • 4,737
Eatontown, NJ 07724 • 13,800
Eatonville, WA 98328 • 1,374
Eau Claire, WI 54701-03 • 56,856
Eau Claire □, WI • 85,183
Ebensburg, PA 15931 • 3,872
Eccles, WV 25836 • 1,162
Echo Bay, NV 89040 • 120
Echols □, GA • 2,334
Eckhart Mines, MD 21528 • 1,333
Eclectic, AL 36024 • 1,087
Economy, PA 15005 • 9,519
Ecorse, MI 48229 • 12,180
Ector □, TX • 118,934
Edcouch, TX 78538 • 2,878
Eddy □, NM • 48,605
Eddy □, ND • 2,951
Eddystone, PA 19013 • 2,446
Eddyville, IA 52553 • 1,010
Eddyville, KY 42038 • 1,889
Eden, NY 14057 • 3,088
Eden, NC 27288 • 15,238
Eden, TX 76837 • 1,567
Eden Prairie, MN 55344 • 39,311
Edenton, NC 27932 • 5,268
Edgar, WI 54426 • 1,318
Edgar □, IL • 19,595
Edgartown, MA 02539 • 3,062
Edgecombe □, NC • 56,558
Edgefield, SC 29824 • 2,563
Edgefield □, SC • 18,375
Edgeley, ND 58433 • 680
Edgemere, MD 21221 • 9,226
Edgemont, SD 57735 • 906
Edgemoor, DE 19802 • 5,853
Edgerton, KS 66021 • 1,244
Edgerton, MN 56128 • 1,106
Edgerton, OH 43517 • 1,896
Edgerton, WI 53534 • 4,254
Edgerton, WY 82635 • 247
Edgewater, AL 35224 • 1,120
Edgewater, CO 80214 • 4,613
Edgewater, FL 32132 • 15,337
Edgewater, MD 21037 • 1,600
Edgewater, NJ 07020 • 5,001
Edgewater Park, NJ 08010 • 8,388
Edgewood, IN 46011 • 2,057
Edgewood, KY 41017 • 8,143
Edgewood, MD • 3,470
Edgewood, MD 21040 • 23,903
Edgewood, OH 44004 • 5,189
Edgewood, PA 15218 • 3,581
Edgewood, WA 98372 • 2,650
Edgeworth, PA 15143 • 1,670
Edina, MN 55410 • 46,070
Edina, MO 63537 • 1,283
Edinboro, PA 16412 • 7,736
Edinburg, TX 78539-40 • 29,885
Edinburgh, IN 46124 • 4,536
Edison, GA 31746 • 1,182
Edison, NJ 08817-20 • 88,680
Edmond, OK 73034 • 52,315
Edmonds, WA 98020 • 30,744
Edmondson Heights, MD 21207 • 4,750
Edmonson □, KY • 10,357
Edmonton, KY 42129 • 1,477
Edmore, MI 48829 • 1,126
Edmunds □, SD • 4,356
Edna, TX 77957 • 5,343
Edwards, MS 39066 • 1,279
Edwards □, IL • 7,440
Edwards □, KS • 3,787
Edwards □, TX • 2,266
Edwardsburg, MI 49112 • 1,142
Edwardsville, IL 62025 • 14,579
Edwardsville, KS 66113 • 3,979
Edwardsville, PA 18704 • 5,399
Effingham, IL 62401 • 11,851
Effingham □, GA • 25,687
Effingham □, IL • 31,704
Egg Harbor City, NJ 08215 • 4,583
Egypt, MA 02066 • 1,100
Egypt Lake, FL 33614 • 14,580
Ehrenberg, AZ 85334 • 1,500
Elba, AL 36323 • 4,011
Elbert □, CO • 9,646
Elbert □, GA • 18,949
Elberta, GA 31093 • 1,559
Elberton, GA 30635 • 5,682
Elbow Lake, MN 56531 • 1,186
Elburn, IL 60119 • 1,275
El Cajon, CA 92019-22 • 88,693
El Campo, TX 77437 • 10,511
El Centro, CA 92243-44 • 31,384
El Cerrito, CA 94530 • 22,869
Eldersburg, MD 21784 • 9,720
Eldon, IA 52554 • 1,070
Eldon, MO 65026 • 4,419
Eldora, IA 50627 • 3,038
El Dorado, AR 71730-31 • 23,146
Eldorado, IL 62930 • 4,536
El Dorado, KS 67042 • 11,504
Eldorado, TX 76936 • 2,019
El Dorado □, CA • 125,995
El Dorado Hills, CA 95630 • 6,395
El Dorado Springs, MO 64744 • 3,830
Eldridge, IA 52748 • 3,378
Eleanor, WV 25070 • 1,256
Electra, TX 76360 • 3,113
Eleele, HI 96705 • 1,489
El Encanto Heights, CA 93117 • 7,700
Elfers, FL 34680 • 12,356
Elgin, IL 60120-23 • 77,010
Elgin, ND 58533 • 765
Elgin, OR 97827 • 1,586
Elgin, TX 78621 • 4,846
Elida, OH 45807 • 1,486
Elizabeth, NJ 07201-08 • 110,002
Elizabeth City, NC 27906-09 • 14,292
Elizabethton, TN 37643-44 • 11,931
Elizabethtown, KY 42701-02 • 18,167
Elizabethtown, NC 28337 • 3,704
Elizabethtown, PA 17022 • 9,952
Elizabethville, PA 17023 • 1,467
Elk □, KS • 3,327
Elk □, PA • 34,878
Elkader, IA 52043 • 1,510
Elk City, OK 73644 • 10,428
Elk Grove, CA 95624 • 17,483
Elk Grove Village, IL 60009 • 33,429
Elkhart, IN 46514-17 • 43,627
Elkhart, KS 67950 • 2,318
Elkhart, TX 75839 • 1,076
Elkhart □, IN • 156,198
Elkhart Lake, WI 53020 • 1,019
Elkhorn, NE 68022 • 1,398
Elkhorn, WI 53121 • 5,337
Elkin, NC 28621 • 3,790
Elkins, WV 26241 • 7,420
Elkland, PA 16920 • 1,849
Elk Mountain, WY 82324 • 174
Elko, NV 89801-02 • 14,736
Elko □, NV • 33,530
Elk Point, SD 57025 • 1,423
Elk Rapids, MI 49629 • 1,626
Elkridge, MD 21227 • 12,953
Elk River, MN 55330 • 11,143
Elkton, KY 42220 • 1,789
Elkton, MD 21921-22 • 9,073
Elkton, VA 22827 • 1,935
Elkview, WV 25071 • 1,047
Ellaville, GA 31806 • 1,724
Ellendale, DE 19941 • 313
Ellendale, ND 58436 • 1,798
Ellensburg, WA 98926 • 12,361
Ellenton, FL 34222 • 2,573
Ellenville, NY 12428 • 4,243
Ellerbe, NC 28338 • 1,132
Ellerslie, MD 21529 • 1,500
Ellettsville, IN 47429 • 3,275
Ellicott City, MD 21043 • 41,396
Ellijay, GA 30540 • 1,178
Ellington, CT 06029 • 1,500
Ellinwood, KS 67526 • 2,329
Elliott □, KY • 6,455
Ellis, KS 67637 • 1,814
Ellis □, KS • 26,004
Ellis □, OK • 4,497
Ellis □, TX • 85,167
Ellisville, MS 39437 • 3,634
Ellisville, MO 63011 • 7,545
Ellport, PA 16117 • 1,243
Ellsworth, KS 67439 • 2,294
Ellsworth, ME 04605 • 5,975
Ellsworth, PA 15331 • 1,048
Ellsworth, WI 54011 • 2,706
Ellsworth □, KS • 6,586
Ellwood City, PA 16117 • 8,894
Elma, WA 98541 • 3,011
Elm City, NC 27822 • 1,624
Elmer, NJ 08318 • 1,571
Elm Grove, WI 53122 • 6,261
Elmhurst, IL 60126 • 42,029
Elmira, NY 14901-05 • 33,724
El Mirage, AZ 85335 • 5,001
Elmira Heights, NY 14903 • 4,359
Elmont, NY 11003 • 28,612
El Monte, CA 91731-34 • 106,209
Elmora, PA 15737 • 1,500
Elmore, OH 43416 • 1,334
Elmore □, AL • 49,210
Elmore □, ID • 21,205
Elmwood, IL 61529 • 1,841
Elmwood Park, IL 60635 • 23,206
Elmwood Park, NJ 07407 • 17,623
Elmwood Place, OH 45216 • 2,937
Eloise, FL 33880 • 1,408
Elon College, NC 27244 • 4,394
Eloy, AZ 85231 • 7,211
El Paso, IL 61738 • 2,499
El Paso, TX 79901-99 • 515,342
El Paso □, CO • 397,014
El Paso □, TX • 591,610
El Portal, FL 33138 • 2,457
El Reno, OK 73036 • 15,414
Elroy, WI 53929 • 1,533
Elsa, TX 78543 • 5,242
Elsberry, MO 63343 • 1,898
El Segundo, CA 90245 • 15,223
Elsmere, DE 19805 • 5,935
Elsmere, KY 41018 • 6,847
Elsmere, NY 12054 • 4,180
El Sobrante, CA 94803 • 9,852
Elton, LA 70532 • 1,277
El Toro, CA 92630 • 62,685
Elvins, MO 63601 • 1,391
Elwood, IN 46036 • 9,494
Elwood, KS 66024 • 1,079
Elwood, NJ 08217 • 1,400
Elwood, NY 11731 • 10,916
Ely, MN 55731 • 3,968
Ely, NV 89301 • 4,756
Elyria, OH 44035-39 • 56,746
Elysburg, PA 17824 • 1,890
Emanuel □, GA • 20,546
Emerson, GA 30137 • 1,201
Emerson, NJ 07630 • 6,930
Emery □, UT • 10,332
Eminence, KY 40019 • 2,055
Emmaus, PA 18049 • 11,157
Emmet □, IA • 11,569
Emmet □, MI • 25,040
Emmetsburg, IA 50536 • 3,940
Emmett, ID 83617 • 4,601
Emmitsburg, MD 21727 • 1,688
Emmonak, AK 99581 • 642
Emmons □, ND • 4,830
Empire, NV 89405 • 300
Emporia, KS 66801 • 25,512
Emporia, VA 23847 • 5,306
Emporium, PA 15834 • 2,513
Emsworth, PA 15202 • 2,892
Encampment, WY 82325 • 490
Encinitas, CA 92023-24 • 55,386
Enderlin, ND 58027 • 997
Endicott, NY 13760 • 13,531
Endwell, NY 13760 • 12,602
Enfield (Thompsonville), CT 06082-83 • 8,458
Enfield, NH 03748 • 1,560
Enfield, NC 27823 • 3,082
England, AR 72046 • 3,351
Engleside, VA 22309 • 24,058
Englewood, CO 80110-12 • 29,387
Englewood, FL 34223-24 • 15,025
Englewood, NJ 07631-32 • 24,850
Englewood, OH 45322 • 11,432
Englewood, TN 37329 • 1,611
Englewood Cliffs, NJ 07632 • 5,634
Englishtown, NJ 07726 • 1,268
Enid, OK 73701-06 • 45,309
Enka, NC 28728 • 5,567
Ennis, MT 59729 • 773
Ennis, TX 75119-20 • 13,883
Enoch, UT 84720 • 1,947
Enola, PA 17025 • 5,961
Enon, OH 45323 • 2,605
Enoree, SC 29335 • 1,107
Enosburg Falls, VT 05450 • 1,350
Ensley, FL 32504 • 16,362
Enterprise, AL 36330-31 • 20,123
Enterprise, OR 97828 • 1,905
Enterprise, WV 26568 • 1,058
Enumclaw, WA 98022 • 7,227
Ephraim, UT 84627 • 3,363
Ephrata, PA 17522 • 12,133
Ephrata, WA 98823 • 5,349
Epping, NH 03042 • 1,384
Epworth, IA 52045 • 1,297
Erath, LA 70533 • 2,428
Erath □, TX • 27,991
Erial, NJ 08081 • 2,500
Erick, OK 73645 • 1,083
Erie, CO 80516 • 1,258
Erie, IL 61250 • 1,572
Erie, KS 66733 • 1,276
Erie, PA 16501-65 • 108,718
Erie □, NY • 968,532
Erie □, OH • 76,779
Erie □, PA • 275,572
Erin, TN 37061 • 1,586
Erlanger, KY 41018 • 15,979
Erma, NJ 08204 • 2,045
Errol Heights, OR 97266 • 10,487
Erwin, NC 28339 • 4,061
Erwin, TN 37650 • 5,015
Escalon, CA 95320 • 4,437
Escambia □, AL • 35,518
Escambia □, FL • 262,798
Escanaba, MI 49829 • 13,659
Escatawpa, MS 39552 • 3,902
Escondido, CA 92025-27 • 108,635
Esmeralda □, NV • 1,344
Esmond, RI 02917 • 4,320
Espanola, NM 87532 • 8,389
Esparto, CA 95627 • 1,487
Esperance, WA 98043 • 11,236
Espy, PA 17815 • 1,430
Essex, CT 06426 • 2,500
Essex, MD 21221 • 40,872
Essex, MA 01929 • 1,507
Essex, VT 05451 • 800
Essex □, MA • 670,080
Essex □, NJ • 778,206
Essex □, NY • 37,152
Essex □, VT • 6,405
Essex □, VA • 8,689
Essex Fells, NJ 07021 • 2,363
Essex Junction, VT 05452-53 • 8,396
Essexville, MI 48732 • 4,088
Estacada, OR 97023 • 2,016
Estelle, LA 70072 • 14,091
Estell Manor, NJ 08319 • 1,404
Estes Park, CO 80517 • 3,184
Estherville, IA 51334 • 6,720
Estill, SC 29918 • 2,387
Estill □, KY • 14,614
Estill Springs, TN 37330 • 1,408
Etna, PA 15223 • 4,200
Etowah, TN 37331 • 3,815
Etowah □, AL • 99,840
Ettrick, VA 23803 • 5,290
Euclid, OH 44117 • 54,875
Eudora, AR 71640 • 3,155
Eudora, KS 66025 • 3,006
Eufaula, AL 36027 • 13,220
Eufaula, OK 74432 • 2,652
Eugene, OR 97401-05 • 112,669
Euless, TX 76039-40 • 38,149
Eunice, LA 70535 • 11,162
Eunice, NM 88231 • 2,676
Eupora, MS 39744 • 2,145
Eureka, CA 95501-02 • 27,025
Eureka, IL 61530 • 4,435
Eureka, KS 67045 • 2,974
Eureka, MO 63025 • 4,683
Eureka, MT 59917 • 1,043
Eureka, NV 89316 • 650
Eureka, SC 29706 • 1,738
Eureka, SD 57437 • 1,197
Eureka □, NV • 1,547
Eureka Springs, AR 72632 • 1,900
Eustis, FL 32726-27 • 12,967
Eutaw, AL 35462 • 2,281
Evangeline □, LA • 33,274
Evans, CO 80620 • 5,877
Evans, GA 30809 • 2,000
Evans □, GA • 8,724
Evans City, PA 16033 • 2,054
Evansdale, IA 50707 • 4,638
Evanston, IL 60201-04 • 73,233
Evanston, WY 82930-31 • 10,903
Evansville, IN 47701-37 • 126,272
Evansville, WI 53536 • 3,174
Evansville, WY 82636 • 1,403
Evart, MI 49631 • 1,744
Evarts, KY 40828 • 1,063
Eveleth, MN 55734 • 4,064
Everett, MA 02149 • 35,701
Everett, PA 15537 • 1,777
Everett, WA 98201-08 • 69,961
Evergreen, AL 36401 • 3,911
Evergreen, CO 80439 • 7,582
Evergreen Park, IL 60642 • 20,874
Everman, TX 76140 • 5,672
Everson, WA 98247 • 1,490
Ewa, HI 96706 • 3,780
Ewa Beach, HI 96706-07 • 14,315
Ewing Township, NJ 08618 • 34,185
Excelsior Springs, MO 64024 • 10,354
Exeter, CA 93221 • 7,276
Exeter, NH 03833 • 9,556
Exeter, PA 18643 • 5,691
Exmore, VA 23350 • 1,115
Experiment, GA 30223 • 3,762
Eyota, MN 55934 • 1,448

F

Fabens, TX 79838 • 5,599
Factoryville, PA 18419 • 1,310
Fairbank, IA 50629 • 1,018
Fairbanks, AK 99701 • 30,843
Fair Bluff, NC 28439 • 1,068
Fairborn, OH 45324 • 31,300
Fairburn, GA 30213 • 4,013
Fairbury, IL 61739 • 3,643
Fairbury, NE 68352 • 4,335
Fairchance, PA 15436 • 1,918
Fairdale, KY 40118 • 6,563
Fairfax, CA 94930 • 6,931
Fairfax, DE 19803 • 2,075
Fairfax, MN 55332 • 1,276
Fairfax, OK 74637 • 1,749
Fairfax, SC 29827 • 2,317
Fairfax, VA 22030-39 • 19,622
Fairfax □, VA • 818,584
Fairfield, AL 35064 • 12,200
Fairfield, CA 94533 • 77,211
Fairfield, CT 06430-32 • 53,418
Fairfield, IL 62837 • 5,439
Fairfield, IA 52556 • 9,768
Fairfield, ME 04937 • 2,794
Fairfield, NJ 07004 • 7,615
Fairfield, OH 45014 • 39,729
Fairfield, TX 75840 • 3,234
Fairfield □, CT • 827,645
Fairfield □, OH • 103,461
Fairfield □, SC • 22,295
Fairfield Bay, AR 72088 • 2,332
Fair Grove, NC 27360 • 1,500
Fairhaven, MA 02719 • 15,759
Fair Haven, NJ 07704 • 5,270
Fair Haven, VT 05743 • 2,432
Fairhope, AL 36532-33 • 8,485
Fair Lawn, NJ 07410 • 30,548
Fairlawn, OH 44313 • 5,779
Fairlawn, VA 24141 • 2,399
Fairlea, WV 24902 • 1,743
Fairless Hills, PA 19030 • 9,026
Fairmont, IL 60441 • 2,260
Fairmont, MN 56031 • 11,265
Fairmont, NC 28340 • 2,489
Fairmont, WV 26554-55 • 20,210
Fairmount, IN 46928 • 3,130
Fairmount, NY 13031 • 12,266
Fairmount Heights, MD 20743 • 1,238
Fair Oaks, CA 95628 • 26,867
Fair Oaks, GA 30060 • 6,996
Fairoaks, PA 15003 • 1,854
Fair Plain, MI 49022 • 8,051
Fairport, NY 14450 • 5,943
Fairport Harbor, OH 44077 • 2,978
Fairton, NJ 08320 • 1,359
Fairview, MT 59221 • 869
Fairview, NJ 07022 • 10,733
Fairview, OK 73737 • 2,936
Fairview, OR 97024 • 2,391
Fairview, PA 16415 • 1,988
Fairview, TN 37062 • 4,210
Fairview Heights, IL 62208 • 14,351
Fairview Park, IN 47842 • 1,446
Fairview Park, OH 44126 • 18,028
Fairview Shores, FL 32804 • 13,192
Fairway, KS 66205 • 4,173
Fairwood, WA 98058 • 2,000
Fairwood, WA 99218 • 5,807
Falconer, NY 14733 • 2,653
Falcon Heights, MN 55113 • 5,380
Falfurrias, TX 78355 • 5,788
Falkville, AL 35622 • 1,337
Fall Branch, TN 37656 • 1,203
Fallbrook, CA 92028 • 22,095
Fall City, WA 98024 • 1,582
Fall Creek, WI 54742 • 1,034
Fallon, NV 89406 • 6,438
Fallon □, MT • 3,103
Fall River, MA 02720-26 • 92,703
Fall River □, SD • 7,353
Falls □, TX • 17,712
Falls Church, VA 22040-46 • 9,578
Falls City, NE 68355 • 4,769
Falls Creek, PA 15840 • 1,087
Fallston, MD 21047 • 5,730
Falls Township, PA 19054 • 36,083
Falmouth, KY 41040 • 2,378
Falmouth, ME 04105 • 7,610
Falmouth, MA 02540 • 4,047
Falmouth, VA 22405 • 3,541
Fannin □, GA • 15,992
Fannin □, TX • 24,804
Fanwood, NJ 07023 • 7,115
Fargo, ND 58102-09 • 74,111
Faribault, MN 55021 • 17,085
Faribault □, MN • 16,937
Farley, IA 52046 • 1,354
Farmer City, IL 61842 • 2,114
Farmers Branch, TX 75234 • 24,250
Farmersburg, IN 47850 • 1,159
Farmersville, CA 93223 • 6,235
Farmerville, LA 71241 • 3,334
Farmingdale, ME 04345 • 2,070
Farmingdale, NJ 07727 • 1,462
Farmingdale, NY 11735 • 8,022
Farmington, AR 72730 • 1,322
Farmington, CT 06032 • 2,500
Farmington, IL 61531 • 2,535
Farmington, ME 04938 • 4,197
Farmington, MI 48335-36 • 10,132
Farmington, MN 55024 • 5,940
Farmington, MO 63640 • 11,598
Farmington, NH 03835 • 3,567
Farmington, NM 87401-02 • 33,997
Farmington, UT 84025 • 9,028
Farmington Hills, MI 48331-34 • 74,652
Farmingville, NY 11738 • 14,842
Farmland, IN 47340 • 1,412
Farmville, NC 27828 • 4,392
Farmville, VA 23901 • 6,046
Farragut, TN 37922 • 12,793
Farrell, PA 16121 • 6,841
Farwell, TX 79325 • 1,373
Faulk □, SD • 2,744
Faulkland Heights, DE 19808 • 1,300
Faulkner □, AR • 60,006
Faulkton, SD 57438 • 809
Fauquier □, VA • 48,741
Fayette, AL 35555 • 4,909
Fayette, IA 52142 • 1,317
Fayette, MS 39069 • 1,853
Fayette, MO 65248 • 2,888
Fayette, OH 43521 • 1,248
Fayette □, AL • 17,962
Fayette □, GA • 62,415
Fayette □, IL • 20,893
Fayette □, IN • 26,015
Fayette □, IA • 21,843
Fayette □, KY • 225,366
Fayette □, OH • 27,466
Fayette □, PA • 145,351

Fayette □, TN • 25,559
Fayette □, TX • 20,095
Fayette □, WV • 47,952
Fayetteville, AR 72701–03 • 42,099
Fayetteville, GA 30214 • 5,827
Fayetteville, NC 28301–14 • 75,695
Fayetteville, PA 17222 • 3,033
Fayetteville, TN 37334 • 6,921
Fayetteville, WV 25840 • 2,182
Fayville, MA 01745 • 1,000
Federal Heights, CO 80221 • 9,342
Federalsburg, MD 21632 • 2,365
Federal Way, WA 98003 • 67,554
Feeding Hills, MA 01030 • 5,470
Fellowship, NJ 08057 • 4,250
Fellsmere, FL 32948 • 2,179
Felton, CA 95041 • 5,350
Felton, DE 19943 • 683
Fennimore, WI 53809 • 2,378
Fennville, MI 49408 • 1,023
Fenton, MI 48430 • 8,444
Fentress □, TN • 14,669
Ferdinand, IN 47532 • 2,318
Fergus □, MT • 12,083
Fergus Falls, MN 56537–38 • 12,362
Ferguson, MO 63135 • 22,286
Fernandina Beach, FL 32034 • 8,765
Fern Creek, KY 40291 • 16,406
Ferndale, CA 95536 • 1,331
Ferndale, MD 21061 • 16,355
Ferndale, MI 48220 • 25,084
Ferndale, PA 15905 • 2,020
Ferndale, WA 98248 • 5,398
Fernley, NV 89408 • 5,164
Fern Park, FL 32730 • 8,294
Fernway, PA 16063 • 9,072
Ferriday, LA 71334 • 4,111
Ferris, TX 75125 • 2,212
Ferron, UT 84523 • 1,606
Ferry □, WA • 6,295
Ferry Farms, VA 22405 • 1,600
Fessenden, ND 58438 • 655
Festus, MO 63028 • 8,105
Fieldale, VA 24089 • 1,018
Fig Garden, CA 93704 • 9,000
Filer, ID 83328 • 1,511
Fillmore, CA 93015–16 • 11,992
Fillmore, UT 84631 • 1,956
Fillmore □, MN • 20,777
Fillmore □, NE • 7,103
Findlay, OH 45839–40 • 35,703
Finley, TN 38030 • 1,014
Finney □, KS • 33,070
Fircrest, WA 98466 • 5,258
Firebaugh, CA 93622 • 4,429
Firestone, CO 80520 • 1,358
Fisher, IL 61843 • 1,526
Fisher □, TX • 4,842
Fishers, IN 46038 • 7,508
Fishkill, NY 12524 • 1,957
Fiskdale, MA 01518 • 2,189
Fitchburg, MA 01420 • 41,194
Fitzgerald, GA 31750 • 8,612
Five Points, NM 87105 • 4,200
Flagler □, FL • 28,701
Flagler Beach, FL 32136 • 3,820
Flagstaff, AZ 86001–16 • 45,857
Flanders, NJ 07836 • 3,040
Flandreau, SD 57028 • 2,311
Flathead □, MT • 59,218
Flatonia, TX 78941 • 1,295
Flat River, MO 63601 • 4,823
Flat Rock, MI 48134 • 7,290
Flat Rock, NC 28731 • 1,200
Flatwoods, KY 41139 • 7,799
Fleetwood, PA 19522 • 3,478
Fleming □, KY • 12,292
Flemingsburg, KY 41041 • 3,071
Flemington, NJ 08822 • 4,047
Flemington, PA 17745 • 1,321
Fletcher, NC 28732 • 2,787
Fletcher, OK 73541 • 1,002
Flint, MI 48501–32 • 140,761
Flint City, AL 35601 • 1,033
Flippin, AR 72634 • 1,006
Flomaton, AL 36441 • 1,811
Flora, IL 62839 • 5,054
Flora, IN 46929 • 2,179
Flora, MS 39071 • 1,482
Florala, AL 36442 • 2,075
Floral City, FL 32636 • 2,609
Floral Park, NY 11001–05 • 15,947
Florence, AL 35630–33 • 36,426
Florence, AZ 85232 • 7,510
Florence, CA 90001 • 43,900
Florence, CO 81226 • 2,990
Florence, KY 41042 • 18,624
Florence, MS 39073 • 1,831
Florence, NJ 08518 • 4,203
Florence, OR 97439 • 5,162
Florence, SC 29501–06 • 29,813
Florence □, SC • 114,344
Florence □, WI • 4,590
Floresville, TX 78114 • 5,247
Florham Park, NJ 07932 • 8,521
Florida, NY 10921 • 2,497
Florida City, FL 33034 • 5,806
Florida Ridge, FL 32960 • 12,218
Florin, CA 95828 • 24,330
Florissant, MO 63031–34 • 51,206
Flossmoor, IL 60422 • 8,651
Flower Hill, NY 11050 • 4,490
Flowery Branch, GA 30542 • 1,251
Flowood, MS 39208 • 2,860
Floyd □, GA • 81,251
Floyd □, IN • 64,404
Floyd □, IA • 17,058
Floyd □, KY • 43,586
Floyd □, TX • 8,497
Floyd □, VA • 12,005
Floydada, TX 79235 • 3,896
Flushing, MI 48433 • 8,542
Flushing, OH 43977 • 1,042
Fluvanna □, VA • 12,429
Foard □, TX • 1,794
Folcroft, PA 19032 • 7,506
Foley, AL 36535–36 • 4,937
Foley, MN 56329 • 1,854
Folkston, GA 31537 • 2,285
Follansbee, WV 26037 • 3,339
Folly Beach, SC 29439 • 1,398
Folsom, CA 95630 • 29,802
Folsom, NJ 08037 • 2,181
Fonda, NY 12068 • 1,007
Fond du Lac, WI 54935–36 • 37,757
Fond du Lac □, WI • 90,083
Fontana, CA 92334–36 • 87,535
Fontana, WI 53125 • 1,635
Foothill Farms, CA 95841 • 17,135
Ford □, IL • 14,275
Ford □, KS • 27,463
Ford City, CA 93268 • 3,781
Ford City, PA 16226 • 3,413
Ford Heights, IL 60411 • 4,259
Fords, NJ 08863 • 14,392
Fords Prairie, WA 98531 • 2,480
Fordyce, AR 71742 • 4,729
Foreman, AR 71836 • 1,267
Forest, MS 39074 • 5,060
Forest, OH 45843 • 1,594
Forest □, PA • 4,802
Forest □, WI • 8,776
Forest Acres, SC 29206 • 7,197
Forest City, IA 50436 • 4,430
Forest City, NC 28043 • 7,475
Forest City, PA 18421 • 1,846
Forestdale, AL 35214 • 10,395
Forestdale, RI 02824 • 530
Forest Dale, VT 05745 • 350
Forest Grove, OR 97116 • 13,559
Forest Hill, TX 76119 • 11,482
Forest Hills, PA 15221 • 7,335
Forest Knolls, CA 94933 • 2,000
Forest Lake, MN 55025 • 5,833
Forest Park, GA 30050–51 • 16,925
Forest Park, IL 60130 • 14,918
Forest Park, LA 71291 • 1,400
Forest Park, OH 45240 • 18,609
Forked River, NJ 08731 • 1,950
Forks, WA 98331 • 2,862
Forney, TX 75126 • 4,070
Forrest, IL 61741 • 1,124
Forrest □, MS • 68,314
Forrest City, AR 72335 • 13,364
Forreston, IL 61030 • 1,361
Forsyth, GA 31029 • 4,268
Forsyth, IL 62535 • 1,275
Forsyth, MO 65653 • 1,175
Forsyth, MT 59327 • 2,178
Forsyth □, GA • 44,083
Forsyth □, NC • 265,878
Fort Ashby, WV 26719 • 1,288
Fort Atkinson, WI 53538 • 10,227
Fort Bend □, TX • 225,421
Fort Benton, MT 59442 • 1,660
Fort Bragg, CA 95437 • 6,078
Fort Branch, IN 47648 • 2,447
Fort Collins, CO 80521–26 • 87,758
Fort Covington, NY 12937 • 1,200
Fort Davis, TX 79734 • 1,100
Fort Defiance, AZ 86504 • 4,489
Fort Deposit, AL 36032 • 1,240
Fort Dodge, IA 50501 • 25,894
Fort Edward, NY 12828 • 3,561
Fort Fairfield, ME 04742 • 1,729
Fort Gaines, GA 31751 • 1,248
Fort Gibson, OK 74434 • 3,359
Fort Hall, ID 83203 • 2,681
Fort Kent, ME 04743 • 2,123
Fort Laramie, WY 82212 • 243
Fort Lauderdale, FL 33301–51 • 149,377
Fort Lee, NJ 07024 • 31,997
Fort Loramie, OH 45845 • 1,042
Fort Loudon, PA 17224 • 1,200
Fort Lupton, CO 80621 • 5,159
Fort Madison, IA 52627 • 11,618
Fort McKinley, OH 45426 • 9,740
Fort Meade, FL 33841 • 4,976
Fort Mill, SC 29715 • 4,930
Fort Mitchell, KY 41017 • 7,438
Fort Morgan, CO 80701 • 9,068
Fort Myers, FL 33901–19 • 45,206
Fort Myers Beach, FL 33931–32 • 9,284
Fort Myers Shores, FL 33905 • 5,460
Fort Oglethorpe, GA 30742 • 5,880
Fort Payne, AL 35967 • 11,838
Fort Pierce, FL 34945–54 • 36,830
Fort Pierre, SD 57532 • 1,854
Fort Plain, NY 13339 • 2,416
Fort Recovery, OH 45846 • 1,313
Fort Scott, KS 66701 • 8,362
Fort Shawnee, OH 45806 • 4,128
Fort Smith, AR 72901–17 • 72,798
Fort Stockton, TX 79735 • 8,524
Fort Sumner, NM 88119 • 1,269
Fort Thomas, KY 41075 • 16,032
Fortuna, CA 95540 • 8,788
Fort Valley, GA 31030 • 8,198
Fortville, IN 46040 • 2,690
Fort Walton Beach, FL 32547–48 • 21,471
Fort Washington Forest, MD 20744 • 1,010
Fort Wayne, IN 46801–99 • 173,072
Fort Wingate, NM 87316 • 950
Fort Worth, TX 76101–85 • 447,619
Fort Wright, KY 41011 • 6,570
Forty Fort, PA 18704 • 5,049
Fort Yukon, AK 99740 • 580
Fosston, MN 56542 • 1,529
Foster □, ND • 3,983
Foster City, CA 94404 • 28,176
Foster Village, HI 96818 • 3,700
Fostoria, OH 44830 • 14,983
Fountain, CO 80817 • 9,984
Fountain □, IN • 17,808
Fountain Hill, PA 18015 • 4,637
Fountain Inn, SC 29644 • 4,388
Fountain Place, LA • 9,200
Fountain Valley, CA 92708 • 53,691
Four Corners, OR 97301 • 12,156
Four Oaks, NC 27524 • 1,308
Fowler, CA 93625 • 3,208
Fowler, CO 81039 • 1,154
Fowler, IN 47944 • 2,333
Fowlerville, MI 48836 • 2,648
Foxboro, MA 02035 • 5,706
Fox Chapel, PA 15238 • 5,319
Fox Lake, IL 60020 • 7,478
Fox Lake, WI 53933 • 1,269
Fox Point, WI 53217 • 7,238
Fox River Grove, IL 60021 • 3,551
Frackville, PA 17931 • 4,700
Framingham, MA 01701 • 64,994
Franconia, VA 22310 • 19,882
Frankenmuth, MI 48734 • 4,408
Frankford, DE 19945 • 591
Frankfort, IL 60423 • 7,180
Frankfort, IN 46041 • 14,754
Frankfort, KY 40601–22 • 25,968
Frankfort, MI 49635 • 1,546
Frankfort, NY 13340 • 2,693
Frankfort, OH 45628 • 1,065
Franklin, IN 46131 • 12,907
Franklin, KY 42134–35 • 7,607
Franklin, LA 70538 • 9,004
Franklin, MA 02038 • 9,965
Franklin, NE 68939 • 1,112
Franklin, NH 03235 • 8,304
Franklin, NJ 07416 • 4,977
Franklin, NC 28734 • 2,873
Franklin, OH 45005 • 11,026
Franklin, PA 16323 • 7,329
Franklin, TN 37064–65 • 20,098
Franklin, TX 77856 • 1,336
Franklin, VA 23851 • 7,864
Franklin, WI 53132 • 21,855
Franklin □, AL • 27,814
Franklin □, AR • 14,897
Franklin □, FL • 8,967
Franklin □, GA • 16,650
Franklin □, ID • 9,232
Franklin □, IL • 40,319
Franklin □, IN • 19,580
Franklin □, IA • 11,364
Franklin □, KS • 21,994
Franklin □, KY • 43,781
Franklin □, LA • 22,387
Franklin □, ME • 29,008
Franklin □, MA • 70,092
Franklin □, MS • 8,377
Franklin □, MO • 80,603
Franklin □, NE • 3,938
Franklin □, NY • 46,540
Franklin □, NC • 36,414
Franklin □, OH • 961,437
Franklin □, PA • 121,082
Franklin □, TN • 34,725
Franklin □, TX • 7,802
Franklin □, VT • 39,980
Franklin □, VA • 39,549
Franklin □, WA • 37,473
Franklin Lakes, NJ 07417 • 9,873
Franklin Park, IL 60131 • 18,485
Franklin Park, PA 15143 • 10,109
Franklin Square, NY 11010 • 28,205
Franklinton, LA 70438 • 4,007
Franklinton, NC 27525 • 1,615
Franklinville, NJ 08322 • 1,020
Franklinville, NY 14737 • 1,739
Frankston, TX 75763 • 1,127
Frankton, IN 46044 • 1,736
Fraser, MI 48026 • 13,899
Frazee, MN 56544 • 1,176
Frazeysburg, OH 43822 • 1,165
Frazier Park, CA 93225 • 2,201
Frederic, WI 54837 • 1,124
Frederica, DE 19946 • 761
Frederick, MD 21701–02 • 40,148
Frederick, OK 73542 • 5,221
Frederick □, MD • 150,208
Frederick □, VA • 45,723
Fredericksburg, IA 50630 • 1,011
Fredericksburg, TX 78624 • 6,934
Fredericksburg, VA 22401–08 • 19,027
Fredericktown, MO 63645 • 3,950
Fredericktown, OH 43019 • 2,443
Fredericktown, PA 15333 • 1,052
Fredonia, AZ 86022 • 1,207
Fredonia, KS 66736 • 2,599
Fredonia, NY 14063 • 10,436
Fredonia, WI 53021 • 1,558
Freeborn □, MN • 33,060
Freeburg, IL 62243 • 3,115
Freedom, CA 95019 • 8,361
Freedom, PA 15042 • 1,897
Freedom, WY 83120 • 450
Freehold, NJ 07728 • 10,742
Freeland, MI 48623 • 1,421
Freeland, PA 18224 • 3,909
Freeman, SD 57029 • 1,293
Freemansburg, PA 18017 • 1,946
Freeport, IL 61032 • 25,840
Freeport, ME 04032 • 1,829
Freeport, NY 11520 • 39,894
Freeport, PA 16229 • 1,983
Freeport, TX 77541 • 11,389
Freer, TX 78357 • 3,271
Freestone □, TX • 15,818
Fremont, CA 94536–39 • 173,339
Fremont, IN 46737 • 1,407
Fremont, MI 49412 • 3,875
Fremont, NE 68025 • 23,680
Fremont, NC 27830 • 1,710
Fremont, OH 43420 • 17,648
Fremont □, CO • 32,273
Fremont □, ID • 10,937
Fremont □, IA • 8,226
Fremont □, WY • 33,662
French Island, WI 54601 • 4,478
French Lick, IN 47432 • 2,087
Frenchtown, NJ 08825 • 1,528
Fresno, CA 93701–94 • 354,202
Fresno □, CA • 667,490
Frewsburg, NY 14738 • 1,817
Friars Point, MS 38631 • 1,334
Friday Harbor, WA 98250 • 1,492
Fridley, MN 55432 • 28,335
Friend, NE 68359 • 1,111
Friendship, NY 14739 • 1,423
Friendswood, TX 77546 • 22,814
Frio □, TX • 13,472
Friona, TX 79035 • 3,688
Frisco, CO 80443 • 1,601
Frisco City, AL 36445 • 1,581
Fritch, TX 79036 • 2,335
Frontenac, KS 66762 • 2,588
Frontier □, NE • 3,101
Front Royal, VA 22630 • 11,880
Frostburg, MD 21532 • 8,075
Frostproof, FL 33843 • 2,808
Fruita, CO 81521 • 4,045
Fruit Heights, UT 84037 • 3,900
Fruitland, ID 83619 • 2,400
Fruitland, MD 21826 • 3,511
Fruitland Park, FL 34731 • 2,754
Fruitport, MI 49415 • 1,090
Fruitvale, CO 81504 • 1,070
Fruitvale, WA 98902 • 4,125
Fruitville, FL 34232 • 9,808
Fryeburg, ME 04037 • 1,580
Fulda, MN 56131 • 1,212
Fullerton, CA 92631–35 • 114,144
Fullerton, NE 68638 • 1,452
Fulton, IL 61252 • 3,698
Fulton, KY 42041 • 3,078
Fulton, MS 38843 • 3,387
Fulton, MO 65251 • 10,033
Fulton, NY 13069 • 12,929
Fulton □, AR • 10,037
Fulton □, GA • 648,951
Fulton □, IL • 38,080
Fulton □, IN • 18,840
Fulton □, KY • 8,271
Fulton □, NY • 54,191
Fulton □, OH • 38,498
Fulton □, PA • 13,837
Fultondale, AL 35068 • 6,400
Funkstown, MD 21734 • 1,136
Fuquay-Varina, NC 27526 • 4,562
Furnas □, NE • 5,553
Fyffe, AL 35971 • 1,094

G

Gabbs, NV 89409 • 667
Gadsden, AL 35901–05 • 42,523
Gadsden □, FL • 41,105
Gaffney, SC 29340–42 • 13,145
Gage □, NE • 22,794
Gages Lake, IL 60030 • 8,349
Gahanna, OH 43230 • 27,791
Gaines □, TX • 14,123
Gainesboro, TN 38562 • 1,002
Gainesville, FL 32601–14 • 84,770
Gainesville, GA 30501–07 • 17,885
Gainesville, TX 76240 • 14,256
Gaithersburg, MD 20877–79 • 39,542
Galax, VA 24333 • 6,670
Galena, AK 99741 • 833
Galena, IL 61036 • 3,647
Galena, KS 66739 • 3,308
Galesburg, IL 61401–02 • 33,530
Galesburg, MI 49053 • 1,863
Gales Ferry, CT 06335 • 1,191
Galesville, WI 54630 • 1,278
Galeton, PA 16922 • 1,370
Galeville, NY 13088 • 4,695
Galion, OH 44833 • 11,859
Gallatin, MO 64640 • 1,864
Gallatin, TN 37066 • 18,794
Gallatin □, IL • 6,909
Gallatin □, KY • 5,393
Gallatin □, MT • 50,463
Gallia □, OH • 30,954
Galliano, LA 70354 • 4,294
Gallipolis, OH 45631 • 4,831
Gallitzin, PA 16641 • 2,003
Gallup, NM 87301–05 • 19,154
Galt, CA 95632 • 8,889
Galva, IL 61434 • 2,742
Galveston, IN 46932 • 1,609
Galveston, TX 77550–54 • 59,070
Galveston □, TX • 217,399
Gambell, AK 99742 • 525
Gambier, OH 43022 • 2,073
Gambrills, MD 21054 • 1,200
Ganado, AZ 86505 • 3,400
Ganado, TX 77962 • 1,701
Gang Mills, NY 14870 • 2,738
Gantt, SC 29605 • 13,891
Gap, PA 17527 • 1,200
Garberville, CA 95440 • 1,200
Garden □, NE • 2,460
Gardena, CA 90247–49 • 49,847
Garden City, GA 31408 • 7,410
Garden City, ID 83704 • 6,369
Garden City, KS 67846 • 24,097
Garden City, MI 48135–36 • 31,846
Garden City, MO 64747 • 1,225
Garden City, NY 11530 • 21,686
Garden City Park, NY 11040 • 7,437
Gardendale, AL 35071 • 9,251
Garden Grove, CA 92640–45 • 143,050
Garden Home, OR 97223 • 5,500
Gardiner, ME 04345 • 6,746
Gardner, IL 60424 • 1,237
Gardner, KS 66030 • 3,191
Gardner, MA 01440 • 20,125
Gardnerville, NV 89410 • 2,177
Gardnerville Ranchos, NV 89410 • 7,455
Garfield, NJ 07026 • 26,727
Garfield □, CO • 29,974
Garfield □, MT • 1,589
Garfield □, NE • 2,141
Garfield □, OK • 56,735
Garfield □, UT • 3,980
Garfield □, WA • 2,248
Garfield Heights, OH 44125 • 31,739
Garfield Park, DE 19720 • 1,415
Garland, TX 75040–48 • 180,650
Garland, UT 84312 • 1,637
Garland □, AR • 73,397
Garner, IA 50438 • 2,916
Garner, NC 27529 • 14,967
Garnett, KS 66032 • 3,210
Garrard □, KY • 11,579
Garretson, SD 57030 • 924
Garrett, IN 46738 • 5,349
Garrett □, MD • 28,138
Garrettsville, OH 44231 • 2,014
Garrison, MD 21055 • 5,045
Garrison, ND 58540 • 1,530
Garvin □, OK • 26,605
Garwood, NJ 07027 • 4,227
Gary, IN 46401–11 • 116,646
Gary, WV 24836 • 1,355
Garysburg, NC 27831 • 1,057
Garyville, LA 70051 • 3,181
Garza □, TX • 5,143
Gas City, IN 46933 • 6,296
Gasconade □, MO • 14,006
Gasport, NY 14067 • 1,336
Gassville, AR 72635 • 1,167
Gaston, NC 27832 • 1,003
Gaston □, NC • 175,093
Gastonia, NC 28051–56 • 54,732
Gate City, VA 24251 • 2,214
Gates, NY 14624 • 30,000
Gates □, NC • 9,305
Gatesville, TX 76528 • 11,492
Gatlinburg, TN 37738 • 3,417
Gautier, MS 39553 • 10,088
Gaylord, MI 49735 • 3,256
Gaylord, MN 55334 • 1,935
Gearhart, OR 97138 • 1,027
Geary, OK 73040 • 1,347
Geary □, KS • 30,453
Geauga □, OH • 81,129
Geistown, PA 15904 • 2,749
Gem □, ID • 11,844
Genesee, ID 83832 • 725
Genesee, MI 48437 • 1,400
Genesee □, MI • 430,459
Genesee □, NY • 60,060
Geneseo, IL 61254 • 5,990
Geneseo, NY 14454 • 7,187
Geneva, AL 36340 • 4,681
Geneva, IL 60134 • 12,617
Geneva, IN 46740 • 1,280
Geneva, NE 68361 • 2,310
Geneva, NY 14456 • 14,143
Geneva, OH 44041 • 6,597
Geneva □, AL • 23,647
Geneva-on-the-Lake, OH 44041 • 1,626
Genoa, IL 60135 • 3,083
Genoa, NE 68640 • 1,082
Genoa, NV 89411 • 190
Genoa, OH 43430 • 2,262
Genoa City, WI 53128 • 1,277
Gentry, AR 72734 • 1,726
Gentry □, MO • 6,848
George, IA 51237 • 1,066
George □, MS • 16,673
Georgetown, CA 95634 • 2,000
Georgetown, CT 06829 • 1,694
Georgetown, DE 19947 • 3,732
Georgetown, IL 61846 • 3,678
Georgetown, IN 47122 • 2,092
Georgetown, KY 40324 • 11,414
Georgetown, MA 01833 • 2,100
Georgetown, OH 45121 • 3,627
Georgetown, SC 29440–42 • 9,517
Georgetown, TX 78626–28 • 14,842
Georgetown □, SC • 46,302
George West, TX 78022 • 2,586
Georgiana, AL 36033 • 1,933
Gering, NE 69341 • 7,946
Gerlach, NV 89412 • 200
Germantown, IL 62245 • 1,167
Germantown, MD 20874 • 41,145
Germantown, OH 45327 • 4,916
Germantown, TN 38138 • 32,893
Germantown, WI 53022 • 13,658
Gettysburg, PA 17325 • 7,025
Gettysburg, SD 57442 • 1,510
Giants Neck, CT 06357 • 1,200
Gibbon, NE 68840 • 1,525
Gibbstown, NJ 08027 • 5,404
Gibsland, LA 71028 • 1,224
Gibson □, IN • 31,913
Gibson □, TN • 46,315
Gibsonburg, OH 43431 • 2,579
Gibson City, IL 60936 • 3,396
Gibsonia, FL 33805 • 5,168
Gibsonia, PA 15044 • 3,500
Gibsonton, FL 33534 • 7,706
Gibsonville, NC 27249 • 3,441
Giddings, TX 78942 • 4,093
Gideon, MO 63848 • 1,104
Gifford, FL 32960 • 6,278
Gig Harbor, WA 98335 • 3,236
Gila □, AZ • 40,216
Gila Bend, AZ 85337 • 1,747
Gilbert, AZ 85234 • 29,188
Gilbert, MN 55741 • 1,934
Gilbert, OR 97266 • 4,000
Gilbertsville, PA 19525 • 3,994
Gilbertville, MA 01031 • 1,029
Gilchrist □, FL • 9,667
Gilcrest, CO 80623 • 1,084
Giles □, TN • 25,741
Giles □, VA • 16,366
Gilford Park, NJ 08753 • 8,668
Gillespie, IL 62033 • 3,645
Gillespie □, TX • 17,204
Gillett, WI 54124 • 1,303
Gillette, WY 82716–17 • 17,635
Gilliam □, OR • 1,717
Gilman, IL 60938 • 1,816
Gilman, VT 05904 • 500
Gilmer, TX 75644 • 4,822
Gilmer □, GA • 13,368
Gilmer □, WV • 7,669
Gilpin □, CO • 3,070
Gilroy, CA 95020–21 • 31,487
Girard, IL 62640 • 2,164
Girard, KS 66743 • 2,794
Girard, OH 44420 • 11,304
Girard, PA 16417 • 2,879
Girardville, PA 17935 • 1,889
Glacier □, MT • 12,121
Glades □, FL • 7,591
Glade Spring, VA 24340 • 1,435
Gladeview, FL 33138 • 15,637
Gladewater, TX 75647 • 6,027
Gladstone, MI 49837 • 4,565
Gladstone, MO 64118 • 26,243
Gladstone, NJ 07934 • 2,111
Gladstone, OR 97027 • 10,152
Gladwin, MI 48624 • 2,682
Gladwin □, MI • 21,896
Glasco, NY 12432 • 1,538
Glascock □, GA • 2,357
Glasford, IL 61533 • 1,115
Glasgow, KY 42141–42 • 12,351
Glasgow, MO 65254 • 1,295
Glasgow, MT 59230 • 3,572
Glasgow, VA 24555 • 1,140
Glasgow Village, MO 63137 • 5,199
Glassboro, NJ 08028 • 15,614
Glasscock □, TX • 1,447
Glassport, PA 15045 • 5,582
Glastonbury, CT 06033 • 7,082
Gleason, TN 38229 • 1,402
Glen Allen, VA 23060 • 9,010
Glen Avon, CA • 12,663
Glenbrook, NV 89413 • 400
Glen Burnie, MD 21061 • 37,305
Glen Burnie Park, MD 21061 • 3,260
Glen Carbon, IL 62034 • 7,731
Glencoe, AL 35905 • 4,670
Glencoe, IL 60022 • 8,499
Glencoe, MN 55336 • 4,648
Glen Cove, NY 11542 • 24,149

Glendale, AZ 85301–12 • *148,134*
Glendale, CA 91201–14 • *180,038*
Glendale, CO 80222 • *2,453*
Glendale, MS 39401 • *1,329*
Glendale, MO 63122 • *5,945*
Glendale, OH 45246 • *2,445*
Glendale, RI 02826 • *700*
Glendale, SC 29346 • *1,049*
Glen Dale, WV 26038 • *1,612*
Glendale, WI 53209 • *14,088*
Glendale Heights, IL 60139 • *27,973*
Glendive, MT 59330 • *4,802*
Glendo, WY 82213 • *195*
Glendola, NJ 07719 • *2,340*
Glendora, CA 91740 • *47,828*
Glendora, NJ 08029 • *5,201*
Glen Ellyn, IL 60137–38 • *24,944*
Glen Gardner, NJ 08826 • *1,665*
Glenham, NY 12527 • *2,832*
Glen Head, NY 11545 • *6,870*
Glen Lyon, PA 18617 • *2,082*
Glenmora, LA 71433 • *1,686*
Glenn □, CA • *24,798*
Glennallen, AK 99588 • *451*
Glenn Dale, MD 20769 • *9,689*
Glenns Ferry, ID 83623 • *1,304*
Glennville, GA 30427 • *3,676*
Glenolden, PA 19036 • *7,260*
Glenpool, OK 74033 • *6,688*
Glen Raven, NC 27215 • *2,616*
Glen Ridge, NJ 07028 • *7,076*
Glen Rock, NJ 07452 • *10,883*
Glen Rock, PA 17327 • *1,688*
Glenrock, WY 82637 • *2,153*
Glen Rose, TX 76043 • *1,949*
Glens Falls, NY 12801 • *15,023*
Glenside, PA 19038 • *8,704*
Glen Ullin, ND 58631 • *927*
Glenview, IL 60025 • *37,093*
Glenville, WV 26351 • *1,923*
Glenwood, AR 71943 • *1,354*
Glenwood, IL 60425 • *9,289*
Glenwood, IA 51534 • *4,571*
Glenwood, MN 56334 • *2,573*
Glenwood, VA 24541 • *2,276*
Glenwood City, WI 54013 • *1,026*
Glenwood Farms, VA 23223 • *3,200*
Glenwood Hills, GA 30032 • *5,240*
Glenwood Springs, CO 81601–02 • *6,561*
Glidden, IA 51443 • *1,099*
Globe, AZ 85501–02 • *6,062*
Gloster, MS 39638 • *1,323*
Gloucester, MA 01930–31 • *28,716*
Gloucester, VA 23061 • *1,200*
Gloucester □, NJ • *230,082*
Gloucester □, VA • *30,131*
Gloucester City, NJ 08030 • *12,649*
Gloucester Point, VA 23062 • *8,509*
Glouster, OH 45732 • *2,001*
Gloversville, NY 12078 • *16,656*
Gloverville, SC 29828 • *2,753*
Glynn □, GA • *62,496*
Gnadenhutten, OH 44629 • *1,226*
Goddard, KS 67052 • *1,804*
Godfrey, IL 62035 • *5,436*
Goffstown, NH 03045 • *2,700*
Gogebic □, MI • *18,052*
Golconda, NV 89414 • *200*
Gold Bar, WA 98251 • *1,078*
Gold Beach, OR 97444 • *1,546*
Golden, CO 80401–03 • *13,116*
Goldendale, WA 98620 • *3,319*
Golden Gate, FL 33999 • *14,148*
Golden Glades, FL 33055 • *25,474*
Golden Meadow, LA 70357 • *2,049*
Golden Valley, MN 55427 • *20,971*
Golden Valley □, MT • *912*
Golden Valley □, ND • *2,108*
Goldfield, NV 89013 • *600*
Goldsboro, NC 27530–34 • *40,709*
Goldthwaite, TX 76844 • *1,658*
Goleta, CA 93117 • *28,600*
Golf Manor, OH 45237 • *4,154*
Goliad, TX 77963 • *1,946*
Goliad □, TX • *5,980*
Gonzales, CA 93926 • *4,660*
Gonzales, LA 70737 • *7,003*
Gonzales, TX 78629 • *6,527*
Gonzales □, TX • *17,205*
Gonzalez, FL 32560 • *7,669*
Goochland □, VA • *14,163*
Goodhue □, MN • *40,690*
Gooding, ID 83330 • *2,820*
Gooding □, ID • *11,633*
Goodland, FL 33933 • *1,000*
Goodland, IN 47948 • *1,033*
Goodland, KS 67735 • *4,983*
Goodlettsville, TN 37072 • *11,219*
Goodman, MS 39079 • *1,256*
Goodman, MO 64843 • *1,094*
Goodsprings, NV 89019 • *150*
Goodview, MN 55987 • *2,878*
Goodwater, AL 35072 • *1,840*
Goodwell, OK 73939 • *1,065*
Goodyear, AZ 85338 • *6,258*
Goose Creek, SC 29445 • *24,692*
Gordo, AL 35466 • *1,918*
Gordon, GA 31031 • *2,468*
Gordon, NE 69343 • *1,803*
Gordon □, GA • *35,072*
Gordonsville, VA 22942 • *1,351*
Gorham, ME 04038 • *3,618*
Gorham, NH 03581 • *1,910*
Gorman, TX 76454 • *1,290*
Goshen, IN 46526 • *23,797*
Goshen, NY 10924 • *5,255*
Goshen, OH 45122 • *1,400*
Goshen □, WY • *12,373*
Gosnell, AR 72319 • *3,783*
Gosper □, NE • *1,928*
Gothenburg, NE 69138 • *3,232*
Gould, AR 71643 • *1,470*
Goulding, FL 32503 • *4,159*
Goulds, FL 33170 • *7,284*
Gouverneur, NY 13642 • *4,604*
Gove □, KS • *3,231*
Gowanda, NY 14070 • *2,901*
Gower, MO 64454 • *1,249*
Gowrie, IA 50543 • *1,028*
Grace, ID 83241 • *973*
Graceville, FL 32440 • *2,675*
Gracewood, GA 30812 • *1,000*
Grady □, GA • *20,279*
Grady □, OK • *41,747*
Grafton, MA 01519 • *1,520*
Grafton, ND 58237 • *4,840*
Grafton, OH 44044 • *3,344*
Grafton, WV 26354 • *5,524*
Grafton, WI 53024 • *9,340*
Grafton □, NH • *74,929*
Graham, CA 90002 • *10,600*
Graham, NC 27253 • *10,426*
Graham, TX 76046 • *8,986*
Graham □, AZ • *26,554*
Graham □, KS • *3,543*
Graham □, NC • *7,196*
Grainger □, TN • *17,095*
Grain Valley, MO 64029 • *1,898*
Grambling, LA 71245 • *5,484*
Gramercy, LA 70052 • *2,412*
Granbury, TX 76048–49 • *4,045*
Granby, CT 06035 • *9,369*
Granby, MA 01033 • *1,327*
Granby, MO 64844 • *1,945*
Grand □, CO • *7,966*
Grand □, UT • *6,620*
Grand Bay, AL 36541 • *3,383*
Grand Blanc, MI 48439 • *7,760*
Grand Caillou, LA 70360 • *1,400*
Grand Canyon, AZ 86023 • *1,499*
Grand Coteau, LA 70541 • *1,118*
Grandfield, OK 73546 • *1,224*
Grand Forks, ND 58201–06 • *49,425*
Grand Forks □, ND • *70,683*
Grand Haven, MI 49417 • *11,951*
Grand Island, NE 68801–03 • *39,386*
Grand Isle, LA 70358 • *1,455*
Grand Isle □, VT • *5,318*
Grand Junction, CO 81501–06 • *29,034*
Grand Ledge, MI 48837 • *7,579*
Grand Marais, MN 55604 • *1,171*
Grand Prairie, TX 75050–54 • *99,616*
Grand Rapids, MI 49501–99 • *189,126*
Grand Rapids, MN 55744 • *7,976*
Grand Saline, TX 75140 • *2,630*
Grand Terrace, CA 92324 • *10,946*
Grand Traverse □, MI • *64,273*
Grandview, MO 64030 • *24,967*
Grandview, WA 98930 • *7,169*
Grandview Heights, OH 43212 • *7,010*
Grandville, MI 49418 • *15,624*
Granger, IN 46530 • *20,241*
Granger, TX 76530 • *1,190*
Granger, WA 98932 • *2,053*
Grangeville, ID 83530 • *3,226*
Granite, OK 73547 • *1,844*
Granite □, MT • *2,548*
Granite City, IL 62040 • *32,862*
Granite Falls, MN 56241 • *3,083*
Granite Falls, NC 28630 • *3,253*
Granite Falls, WA 98252 • *1,060*
Granite Quarry, NC 28072 • *1,646*
Graniteville, MA 01886 • *1,010*
Graniteville, SC 29829 • *1,158*
Graniteville, VT 05654 • *500*
Grant, NE 69140 • *1,239*
Grant □, AR • *13,948*
Grant □, IN • *74,169*
Grant □, KS • *7,159*
Grant □, KY • *15,737*
Grant □, LA • *17,526*
Grant □, MN • *6,246*
Grant □, NE • *769*
Grant □, NM • *27,676*
Grant □, ND • *3,549*
Grant □, OK • *5,689*
Grant □, OR • *7,853*
Grant □, SD • *8,372*
Grant □, WA • *54,758*
Grant □, WV • *10,428*
Grant □, WI • *49,264*
Grant Park, IL 60940 • *1,024*
Grants, NM 87020 • *8,626*
Grantsburg, WI 54840 • *1,144*
Grants Pass, OR 97526–27 • *17,488*
Grantsville, UT 84029 • *4,500*
Grantville, GA 30220 • *1,180*
Granville, IL 61326 • *1,407*
Granville, NY 12832 • *2,646*
Granville, OH 43023 • *4,353*
Granville □, NC • *38,345*
Grapeland, TX 75844 • *1,450*
Grapevine, TX 76051 • *29,202*
Grasonville, MD 21638 • *2,439*
Grass Lake, IL 60002 • *2,191*
Grass Valley, CA 95945 • *9,048*
Gratiot □, MI • *38,982*
Graves □, KY • *33,550*
Gravette, AR 72736 • *1,412*
Gray, GA 31032 • *2,189*
Gray, LA 70359 • *1,500*
Gray □, KS • *5,396*
Gray □, TX • *23,967*
Grayling, MI 49738 • *1,944*
Graylyn Crest, DE 19810 • *4,380*
Grays Harbor □, WA • *64,175*
Grayslake, IL 60030 • *7,388*
Grayson, KY 41143 • *3,510*
Grayson □, KY • *21,050*
Grayson □, TX • *95,021*
Grayson □, VA • *16,278*
Graysville, AL 35073 • *2,241*
Graysville, TN 37338 • *1,301*
Grayville, IL 62844 • *2,043*
Great Barrington, MA 01230 • *2,810*
Great Bend, KS 67530 • *15,427*
Great Falls, MT 59401–06 • *55,097*
Great Falls, SC 29055 • *2,307*
Great Falls, VA 22066 • *6,945*
Great Neck, NY 11020–27 • *8,745*
Great Neck Estates, NY 11021 • *2,790*
Greece, NY 14626 • *15,632*
Greece, NY • *15,632*
Greeley, CO 80631–34 • *60,536*
Greeley □, KS • *1,774*
Greeley □, NE • *3,006*
Green, OR 97470 • *5,076*
Green □, KY • *10,371*
Green □, WI • *30,339*
Greenacres, CA 93308 • *7,379*
Green Acres, DE 19803 • *1,140*
Greenacres, WA 99016 • *4,250*
Greenacres City, FL 33463 • *18,683*
Green Bay, WI 54301–24 • *96,466*
Greenbelt, MD 20770 • *21,096*
Greenbriar, VA 22033 • *6,200*
Greenbrier, AR 72058 • *2,130*
Green Brier, TN 37073 • *2,873*
Greenbrier □, WV • *34,693*
Green Brook, NJ 08812 • *2,380*
Greencastle, IN 46135 • *8,984*
Greencastle, PA 17225 • *3,600*
Green Cove Springs, FL 32043 • *4,497*
Greendale, IN 47025 • *3,881*
Greendale, WI 53129 • *15,128*
Greene, IA 50636 • *1,142*
Greene, NY 13778 • *1,812*
Greene □, AL • *10,153*
Greene □, AR • *31,804*
Greene □, GA • *11,793*
Greene □, IL • *15,317*
Greene □, IN • *30,410*
Greene □, IA • *10,045*
Greene □, MS • *10,220*
Greene □, MO • *207,949*
Greene □, NY • *44,739*
Greene □, NC • *15,384*
Greene □, OH • *136,731*
Greene □, PA • *39,550*
Greene □, TN • *55,853*
Greene □, VA • *10,297*
Greeneville, TN 37743–44 • *13,532*
Greenfield, CA 93927 • *7,464*
Greenfield, IL 62044 • *1,162*
Greenfield, IN 46140 • *11,657*
Greenfield, IA 50849 • *2,074*
Greenfield, MA 01301–02 • *14,016*
Greenfield, MO 65661 • *1,416*
Greenfield, OH 45123 • *5,172*
Greenfield, TN 38230 • *2,105*
Greenfield, WI 53220 • *33,403*
Greenfield Plaza, IA 50315 • *2,200*
Green Forest, AR 72638 • *2,050*
Green Harbor, MA 02041 • *1,900*
Greenhills, OH 45218 • *4,393*
Green Island, NY 12183 • *2,490*
Green Lake, WI 54941 • *1,064*
Green Lake □, WI • *18,651*
Greenlawn, NY 11740 • *13,208*
Greenlee □, AZ • *8,008*
Greenock, PA 15047 • *2,500*
Greenport, NY 11944 • *2,070*
Green River, WY 82935 • *12,711*
Green Rock, IL 61241 • *2,615*
Greensboro, AL 36744 • *3,047*
Greensboro, GA 30642 • *2,860*
Greensboro, MD 21639 • *1,441*
Greensboro, NC 27401–95 • *183,521*
Greensburg, IN 47240 • *9,286*
Greensburg, KS 67054 • *1,792*
Greensburg, KY 42743 • *1,990*
Greensburg, PA 15601 • *16,318*
Green Springs, OH 44836 • *1,446*
Greensville □, VA • *8,853*
Greentown, IN 46936 • *2,172*
Green Tree, PA 15220 • *4,905*
Greenup, IL 62428 • *1,616*
Greenup, KY 41144 • *1,158*
Greenup □, KY • *36,742*
Green Valley, AZ 85614 • *13,231*
Green Valley, MD 21771 • *9,424*
Greenview, SC 29203 • *5,515*
Greenville, AL 36037 • *7,492*
Greenville, CA 95947 • *1,396*
Greenville, DE 19807 • *800*
Greenville, GA 30222 • *1,167*
Greenville, IL 62246 • *4,806*
Greenville, KY 42345 • *4,689*
Greenville, ME 04441 • *1,601*
Greenville, MI 48838 • *8,101*
Greenville, MS 38701–04 • *45,226*
Greenville, NH 03048 • *1,135*
Greenville, NY 10583 • *9,528*
Greenville, NC 27834–36 • *44,972*
Greenville, OH 45331 • *12,863*
Greenville, PA 16125 • *6,734*
Greenville, RI 02828 • *8,303*
Greenville, SC 29601–16 • *58,282*
Greenville, TX 75401–03 • *23,071*
Greenville □, SC • *320,167*
Greenwich, CT 06830–36 • *58,441*
Greenwich, NY 12834 • *1,961*
Greenwich, OH 44837 • *1,442*
Greenwood, AR 72936 • *3,984*
Greenwood, DE 19950 • *578*
Greenwood, IN 46142 • *26,265*
Greenwood, LA 71033 • *2,092*
Greenwood, MS 38930 • *18,906*
Greenwood, MO 64034 • *1,505*
Greenwood, PA 16601 • *1,650*
Greenwood, SC 29646–49 • *20,807*
Greenwood □, KS • *7,847*
Greenwood □, SC • *59,567*
Greenwood Lake, NY 10925 • *3,208*
Greenwood Village, CO 80111 • *7,589*
Greer, SC 29650–52 • *10,322*
Greer □, OK • *6,559*
Gregg □, TX • *104,948*
Gregory, SD 57533 • *1,384*
Gregory □, SD • *5,359*
Greilickville, MI 49684 • *1,060*
Grenada, MS 38901 • *10,864*
Grenada □, MS • *21,555*
Gresham, OR 97030 • *68,235*
Gresham Park, GA 30316 • *9,000*
Gretna, FL 32332 • *1,981*
Gretna, LA 70053–54 • *17,208*
Gretna, NE 68028 • *2,249*
Gretna, VA 24557 • *1,339*
Greybull, WY 82426 • *1,789*
Gridley, CA 95948 • *4,631*
Gridley, IL 61744 • *1,304*
Griffin, GA 30223–24 • *21,347*
Griffith, IN 46319 • *17,916*
Grifton, NC 28530 • *2,393*
Griggs □, ND • *3,303*
Griggsville, IL 62340 • *1,218*
Grimes, IA 50111 • *2,653*
Grimes □, TX • *18,828*
Grindall Creek, VA 23234 • *1,710*
Grinnell, IA 50112 • *8,902*
Griswold, IA 51535 • *1,049*
Groesbeck, OH 45239 • *6,684*
Groesbeck, TX 76642 • *3,185*
Grosse Ile, MI 48138 • *9,781*
Grosse Pointe, MI 48236 • *5,681*
Grosse Pointe Farms, MI 48236 • *10,092*
Grosse Pointe Park, MI 48230 • *12,857*
Grosse Pointe Woods, MI 48225 • *17,715*
Grossmont, CA 91941 • *2,600*
Groton, CT 06340 • *9,837*
Groton, MA 01450 • *1,044*
Groton, NY 13073 • *2,398*
Groton, SD 57445 • *1,196*
Grottoes, VA 24441 • *1,455*
Grove, OK 74344 • *4,020*
Grove City, FL 34224 • *2,374*
Grove City, OH 43123 • *19,661*
Grove City, PA 16127 • *8,240*
Grove Hill, AL 36451 • *1,551*
Groveland, FL 34736 • *2,300*
Groveland, MA 01834 • *3,780*
Groveport, OH 43125 • *2,948*
Grover City, CA 93433 • *11,656*
Groves, TX 77619 • *16,513*
Groveton, NH 03582 • *1,255*
Groveton, TX 75845 • *1,071*
Groveton, VA 22303 • *19,997*
Groveton Gardens, VA 22303 • *2,600*
Grovetown, GA 30813 • *3,596*
Groveville, NJ 08620 • *2,900*
Gruetli-Laager, TN 37339 • *1,810*
Grulla, TX 78548 • *1,335*
Grundy, VA 24614 • *1,305*
Grundy □, IL • *32,337*
Grundy □, IA • *12,029*
Grundy □, MO • *10,536*
Grundy □, TN • *13,362*
Grundy Center, IA 50638 • *2,491*
Gruver, TX 79040 • *1,172*
Guadalupe, AZ 85283 • *5,458*
Guadalupe, CA 93434 • *5,479*
Guadalupe □, NM • *4,156*
Guadalupe □, TX • *64,873*
Guernsey, WY 82214 • *1,155*
Guernsey □, OH • *39,024*
Gueydan, LA 70542 • *1,611*
Guilford, CT 06437 • *2,588*
Guilford, ME 04443 • *1,082*
Guilford □, NC • *347,420*
Guin, AL 35563 • *2,464*
Gulf □, FL • *11,504*
Gulf Breeze, FL 32561 • *5,530*
Gulf Gate Estates, FL 34231 • *11,622*
Gulfport, FL 33707 • *11,727*
Gulfport, MS 39501–07 • *40,775*
Gulf Shores, AL 36542 • *3,261*
Gumboro, DE 19945 • *200*
Gunnison, CO 81230 • *4,636*
Gunnison, UT 84634 • *1,298*
Gunnison □, CO • *10,273*
Guntersville, AL 35976 • *7,038*
Gurdon, AR 71743 • *2,199*
Gurley, AL 35748 • *1,007*
Gurnee, IL 60031 • *13,701*
Gustine, CA 95322 • *3,931*
Guthrie, KY 42234 • *1,504*
Guthrie, OK 73044 • *10,518*
Guthrie □, IA • *10,935*
Guthrie Center, IA 50115 • *1,614*
Guttenberg, IA 52052 • *2,257*
Guttenberg, NJ 07093 • *8,268*
Guymon, OK 73942 • *7,803*
Gwinhurst, DE 19809 • *1,340*
Gwinn, MI 49841 • *2,370*
Gwinner, ND 58040 • *585*
Gwinnett □, GA • *352,910*
Gypsum, CO 81637 • *1,750*

H

Haakon □, SD • *2,624*
Habersham □, GA • *27,621*
Hacienda Heights, CA 91745 • *52,354*
Hackensack, NJ 07601–08 • *37,049*
Hackettstown, NJ 07840 • *8,120*
Hackleburg, AL 35564 • *1,161*
Haddam, CT 06438 • *1,200*
Haddonfield, NJ 08033 • *11,628*
Haddon Heights, NJ 08035 • *7,860*
Hadlock, WA 98339 • *1,752*
Hagerman, NM 88232 • *961*
Hagerstown, IN 47346 • *1,835*
Hagerstown, MD 21740 • *35,445*
Hahira, GA 31632 • *1,353*
Hahnville, LA 70057 • *2,599*
Hailey, ID 83333 • *3,687*
Haines, AK 99827 • *1,238*
Haines City, FL 33844 • *11,683*
Hainesport, NJ 08036 • *1,250*
Halawa Heights, HI 96701 • *7,000*
Hale □, AL • *15,498*
Hale □, TX • *34,671*
Hale Center, TX 79041 • *2,067*
Haledon, NJ 07508 • *6,951*
Haleiwa, HI 96712 • *2,442*
Hales Corners, WI 53130 • *7,623*
Halethorpe, MD 21227 • *19,750*
Haleyville, AL 35565 • *4,452*
Half Hollow Hills, NY 11746 • *5,110*
Half Moon, NC 28540 • *6,306*
Half Moon Bay, CA 94019 • *8,886*
Halfway, MD 21740 • *8,873*
Halifax □, NC • *55,516*
Halifax □, VA • *29,033*
Haliimaile, HI 96768 • *841*
Hall □, GA • *95,428*
Hall □, NE • *48,925*
Hall □, TX • *3,905*
Hallandale, FL 33009 • *30,996*
Hallettsville, TX 77964 • *2,718*
Hallie, WI 54729 • *1,300*
Hallock, MN 56728 • *1,304*
Hallowell, ME 04347 • *2,534*
Halls, TN 37918 • *6,450*
Halls, TN 38040 • *2,431*
Halls Crossroads, TN 37918 • *1,900*
Hallstead, PA 18822 • *1,274*
Hallsville, TX 75650 • *2,288*
Halstead, KS 67056 • *2,015*
Haltom City, TX 76117 • *32,856*
Hamblen □, TN • *50,480*
Hamburg, AR 71646 • *3,098*
Hamburg, IA 51640 • *1,248*
Hamburg, NJ 07419 • *2,566*
Hamburg, NY 14075 • *10,442*
Hamburg, PA 19526 • *3,987*
Hamden, CT 06514 • *52,434*
Hamel, MN 55340 • *3,096*
Hamilton, AL 35570 • *5,787*
Hamilton, IL 62341 • *3,281*
Hamilton, MA 01936 • *1,000*
Hamilton, MI 49419 • *1,000*
Hamilton, MO 64644 • *1,737*
Hamilton, MT 59840 • *2,737*
Hamilton, NY 13346 • *3,790*
Hamilton, OH 45011–18 • *61,368*
Hamilton, TX 76531 • *2,937*
Hamilton □, FL • *10,930*
Hamilton □, IL • *8,499*
Hamilton □, IN • *108,936*
Hamilton □, IA • *16,071*
Hamilton □, KS • *2,388*
Hamilton □, NE • *8,862*
Hamilton □, NY • *5,279*
Hamilton □, OH • *866,228*
Hamilton □, TN • *285,536*
Hamilton □, TX • *7,733*
Hamilton City, CA 95951 • *1,811*
Hamilton Square, NJ 08690 • *10,970*
Ham Lake, MN 55304 • *8,924*
Hamlet, NC 28345 • *6,196*
Hamlin, TX 79520 • *2,791*
Hamlin, WV 25523 • *1,030*
Hamlin □, SD • *4,974*
Hammond, IN 46320–27 • *84,236*
Hammond, LA 70401–04 • *15,871*
Hammond, WI 54015 • *1,097*
Hammonton, NJ 08037 • *12,208*
Hampden, ME 04444 • *3,895*
Hampden □, MA • *456,310*
Hampden Highlands, ME 04444 • *1,540*
Hampshire, IL 60140 • *1,843*
Hampshire □, MA • *146,568*
Hampshire □, WV • *16,498*
Hampstead, MD 21074 • *2,608*
Hampton, AR 71744 • *1,562*
Hampton, GA 30228 • *2,694*
Hampton, IA 50441 • *4,133*
Hampton, NH 03842 • *7,989*
Hampton, NJ 08827 • *1,515*
Hampton, SC 29924 • *2,997*
Hampton, TN 37658 • *2,236*
Hampton, VA 23651–70 • *133,793*
Hampton □, SC • *18,191*
Hampton Bays, NY 11946 • *7,893*
Hamtramck, MI 48212 • *18,372*
Hana, HI 96713 • *683*
Hanahan, SC 29406 • *13,176*
Hanamaulu, HI 96715 • *3,611*
Hanapepe, HI 96716 • *1,395*
Hanceville, AL 35077 • *2,246*
Hancock, MD 21750 • *1,926*
Hancock, MI 49930 • *4,547*
Hancock, NY 13783 • *1,330*
Hancock □, GA • *8,908*
Hancock □, IL • *21,373*
Hancock □, IN • *45,527*
Hancock □, IA • *12,638*
Hancock □, KY • *7,864*
Hancock □, ME • *46,948*
Hancock □, MS • *31,760*
Hancock □, OH • *65,536*
Hancock □, TN • *6,739*
Hancock □, WV • *35,233*
Hand □, SD • *4,272*
Hanford, CA 93230–32 • *30,897*
Hankinson, ND 58041 • *1,038*
Hanna, WY 82327 • *1,076*
Hanna City, IL 61536 • *1,205*
Hannibal, MO 63401 • *18,004*
Hanover, IN 47243 • *3,610*
Hanover, MA 02339 • *2,500*
Hanover, NH 03755 • *6,538*
Hanover, PA 17331 • *14,399*
Hanover □, VA • *63,306*
Hanover Center, MA 02339 • *1,000*
Hanover Park, IL 60103 • *32,895*
Hanover Township, NJ 07981 • *11,538*
Hansen, ID 83334 • *848*
Hansford □, TX • *5,848*
Hanson, MA 02341 • *2,188*
Hanson □, SD • *2,994*
Hapeville, GA 30354 • *5,483*
Happy Valley, OR 97236 • *1,519*
Harahan, LA 70123 • *9,927*
Haralson □, GA • *21,966*
Harbeson, DE 19951 • *500*
Harbor, OR 97415 • *2,143*
Harbor Beach, MI 48441 • *2,089*
Harborcreek, PA 16421 • *1,500*
Harbor Springs, MI 49740 • *1,540*
Hardee □, FL • *19,499*
Hardeeville, SC 29927 • *1,583*
Hardeman □, TN • *23,377*
Hardeman □, TX • *5,283*
Hardin, IL 62047 • *1,071*
Hardin, MT 59034 • *2,940*
Hardin □, IL • *5,189*
Hardin □, IA • *19,094*
Hardin □, KY • *89,240*
Hardin □, OH • *31,111*
Hardin □, TN • *22,633*
Hardin □, TX • *41,320*
Harding □, NM • *987*
Harding □, SD • *1,669*
Hardinsburg, KY 40143 • *1,906*
Hardwick, GA 31034 • *8,800*
Hardwick, VT 05843 • *1,400*
Hardy □, WV • *10,977*
Harford □, MD • *182,132*
Hargill, TX 78549 • *1,030*
Harker Heights, TX 76543 • *12,841*
Harkers Island, NC 28531 • *1,759*
Harlan, IN 46743 • *1,200*
Harlan, IA 51537 • *5,148*
Harlan, KY 40831 • *2,686*
Harlan □, KY • *36,574*
Harlan □, NE • *3,810*
Harlem, FL 33440 • *2,826*
Harlem, GA 30814 • *2,199*
Harlem, MT 59526 • *882*
Harleysville, PA 19438 • *7,405*
Harlingen, TX 78550–52 • *48,735*
Harlowton, MT 59036 • *1,049*
Harmon □, OK • *3,793*
Harmony, MN 55939 • *1,081*
Harmony, PA 16037 • *1,054*
Harmony, RI 02829 • *820*
Harnett □, NC • *67,822*
Harney □, OR • *7,060*
Harper, KS 67058 • *1,735*
Harper □, KS • *7,124*

Harper □, OK • *4,063*
Harpers Ferry, WV 25425 • *308*
Harper Woods, MI 48225 • *14,903*
Harrah, OK 73045 • *4,206*
Harriman, TN 37748 • *7,119*
Harrington, DE 19952 • *2,311*
Harrington Park, NJ 07640 • *4,623*
Harris, RI 02816 • *1,050*
Harris □, GA • *17,788*
Harris □, TX • *2,818,199*
Harrisburg, AR 72432 • *1,943*
Harrisburg, IL 62946 • *9,289*
Harrisburg, OR 97446 • *1,939*
Harrisburg, PA 17101–13 • *52,376*
Harris Hill, NY 14221 • *4,577*
Harrison, AR 72601–02 • *9,922*
Harrison, MI 48625 • *1,835*
Harrison, NJ 07029 • *13,425*
Harrison, NY 10528 • *23,308*
Harrison, OH 45030 • *7,518*
Harrison, TN 37341 • *7,191*
Harrison □, IN • *29,890*
Harrison □, IA • *14,730*
Harrison □, KY • *16,248*
Harrison □, MS • *165,365*
Harrison □, MO • *8,469*
Harrison □, OH • *16,085*
Harrison □, TX • *57,483*
Harrison □, WV • *69,371*
Harrisonburg, VA 22801 • *30,707*
Harrison Township, MI 48045 • *24,685*
Harrisonville, MO 64701 • *7,683*
Harristown, IL 62537 • *1,319*
Harrisville, RI 02830 • *1,654*
Harrisville, UT 84404 • *3,004*
Harrisville, WV 26362 • *1,839*
Harrodsburg, KY 40330 • *7,335*
Hart, MI 49420 • *1,942*
Hart, TX 79043 • *1,221*
Hart □, GA • *19,712*
Hart □, KY • *14,890*
Hartford, AL 36344 • *2,448*
Hartford, CT 06101–99 • *139,739*
Hartford, IL 62048 • *1,676*
Hartford, KY 42347 • *2,532*
Hartford, MI 49057 • *2,341*
Hartford, SD 57033 • *1,262*
Hartford, VT 05047 • *500*
Hartford, WI 53027 • *8,188*
Hartford □, CT • *851,783*
Hartford City, IN 47348 • *6,960*
Hartington, NE 68739 • *1,583*
Hartland, ME 04943 • *1,038*
Hartland, WI 53029 • *6,906*
Hartley, IA 51346 • *1,632*
Hartley □, TX • *3,634*
Hartsdale, NY 10530 • *9,587*
Hartselle, AL 35640 • *10,795*
Hartshorne, OK 74547 • *2,120*
Hartsville, SC 29550 • *8,372*
Hartsville, TN 37074 • *2,188*
Hartville, OH 44632 • *2,031*
Hartwell, GA 30643 • *4,555*
Harvard, IL 60033 • *5,975*
Harvard, MA 01451 • *1,200*
Harvey, IL 60426 • *29,771*
Harvey, LA 70058 • *21,222*
Harvey, MI 49855 • *1,377*
Harvey, ND 58341 • *2,263*
Harvey □, KS • *31,028*
Harwich, MA 02645 • *4,399*
Harwich Port, MA 02646 • *2,300*
Harwinton, CT 06791 • *5,228*
Harwood Heights, IL 60656 • *7,680*
Hasbrouck Heights, NJ 07604 • *11,488*
Haskell, AR 72015 • *1,342*
Haskell, OK 74436 • *2,143*
Haskell, TX 79521 • *3,362*
Haskell □, KS • *3,886*
Haskell □, OK • *10,940*
Haskell □, TX • *6,820*
Haslett, MI 48840 • *10,230*
Hastings, MI 49058 • *6,549*
Hastings, MN 55033 • *15,445*
Hastings, NE 68901–02 • *22,837*
Hastings, PA 16646 • *1,431*
Hastings-on-Hudson, NY 10706 • *8,000*
Hatboro, PA 19040 • *7,382*
Hatch, NM 87937 • *1,136*
Hatfield, MA 01038 • *1,234*
Hatfield, PA 19440 • *2,650*
Hatteras, NC 27943 • *1,000*
Hattiesburg, MS 39401–07 • *41,882*
Hatton, ND 58240 • *800*
Haubstadt, IN 47639 • *1,455*
Haughton, LA 71037 • *1,664*
Hauppauge, NY 11788 • *19,750*
Hauula, HI 96717 • *3,479*
Havana, FL 32333 • *1,654*
Havana, IL 62644 • *3,610*
Havelock, NC 28532 • *20,268*
Haven, KS 67543 • *1,198*
Haverford [Township], PA 19083 • *52,371*
Haverhill, MA 01830–35 • *51,418*
Haverstraw, NY 10927 • *9,438*
Havre, MT 59501 • *10,201*
Havre de Grace, MD 21078 • *8,952*
Havre North, MT 59501 • *1,110*
Hawaii □, HI • *120,317*
Hawaiian Gardens, CA 90716 • *13,639*
Hawarden, IA 51023 • *2,439*
Hawi, HI 96719 • *924*
Hawkins □, TN • *44,565*
Hawkinsville, GA 31036 • *3,527*
Hawley, MN 56549 • *1,655*
Hawley, PA 18428 • *1,244*
Haworth, NJ 07641 • *3,384*
Haw River, NC 27258 • *1,855*
Hawthorne, CA 90250–51 • *71,349*
Hawthorne, FL 32640 • *1,305*
Hawthorne, NV 89415–16 • *4,162*
Hawthorne, NJ 07506 • *17,084*
Hawthorne, NY 10532 • *4,764*
Hayden, CO 81639 • *1,444*
Hayden, ID 83835 • *3,744*
Hayes □, NE • *1,222*
Hayesville, OR 97303 • *14,318*
Hayfield, MN 55940 • *1,283*
Hayfield, VA 22310 • *2,300*
Hayfork, CA 96041 • *2,605*
Haynesville, LA 71038 • *2,854*
Hays, KS 67601 • *17,767*
Hays □, TX • *65,614*

Haysville, KS 67060 • *8,364*
Hayti, MO 63851 • *3,280*
Hayward, CA 94540–46 • *111,498*
Hayward, WI 54843 • *1,897*
Hayward Addition, SD 57106 • *1,000*
Haywood □, NC • *46,942*
Haywood □, TN • *19,437*
Hazard, KY 41701 • *5,416*
Hazardville, CT 06082 • *5,179*
Hazel Crest, IL 60429 • *13,334*
Hazel Dell, WA 98660 • *15,386*
Hazel Green, AL 35750 • *2,208*
Hazel Green, WI 53811 • *1,171*
Hazel Park, MI 48030 • *20,051*
Hazelwood, MO 63042–45 • *15,324*
Hazelwood, NC 28738 • *1,678*
Hazen, AR 72064 • *1,668*
Hazen, ND 58545 • *2,818*
Hazlehurst, GA 31539 • *4,202*
Hazlehurst, MS 39083 • *4,221*
Hazlet, NJ 07730 • *23,013*
Hazleton, PA 18201 • *24,730*
Headland, AL 36345 • *3,266*
Healdsburg, CA 95448 • *9,469*
Healdton, OK 73438 • *2,872*
Healy, AK 99743 • *487*
Heard □, GA • *8,628*
Hearne, TX 77859 • *5,132*
Heath, OH 43056 • *7,231*
Heavener, OK 74937 • *2,601*
Hebbronville, TX 78361 • *4,465*
Heber City, UT 84032 • *4,782*
Heber Springs, AR 72543 • *5,628*
Hebron, IN 46341 • *3,183*
Hebron, KY 41048 • *1,200*
Hebron, NE 68370 • *1,765*
Hebron, ND 58638 • *888*
Hebron, OH 43025 • *2,076*
Hector, MN 55342 • *1,145*
Heeia, HI 96744 • *5,010*
Heflin, AL 36264 • *2,906*
Hegins, PA 17938 • *1,200*
Helena, AL 35080 • *3,918*
Helena, AR 72342 • *7,491*
Helena, GA 31037 • *1,256*
Helena, MT 59601–26 • *24,569*
Helena, OK 73741 • *1,043*
Hellam, PA 17406 • *1,375*
Hellertown, PA 18055 • *5,662*
Helmetta, NJ 08828 • *1,211*
Helotes, TX 78023 • *1,535*
Helper, UT 84526 • *2,148*
Hemet, CA 92343–44 • *36,094*
Hemlock, MI 48626 • *1,601*
Hemphill, TX 75948 • *1,182*
Hemphill □, TX • *3,720*
Hempstead, NY 11550–54 • *49,453*
Hempstead, TX 77445 • *3,551*
Hempstead □, AR • *21,621*
Henagar, AL 35978 • *1,934*
Henderson, KY 42420 • *25,945*
Henderson, LA 70517 • *1,543*
Henderson, NV 89015–16 • *64,942*
Henderson, NC 27536 • *15,655*
Henderson, TN 38340 • *4,760*
Henderson, TX 75652–53 • *11,139*
Henderson □, IL • *8,096*
Henderson □, KY • *43,044*
Henderson □, NC • *69,285*
Henderson □, TN • *21,844*
Henderson □, TX • *58,543*
Henderson's Point, MS 39571 • *1,114*
Hendersonville, NC 28739 • *7,284*
Hendersonville, TN 37075 • *32,188*
Hendricks □, IN • *75,717*
Hendry □, FL • *25,773*
Hennepin □, MN • *1,032,431*
Hennessey, OK 73742 • *1,902*
Henniker, NH 03242 • *1,693*
Henrico □, VA • *217,881*
Henrietta, NY 14467 • *1,200*
Henrietta, NC 28076 • *1,412*
Henrietta, TX 76365 • *2,896*
Henry, IL 61537 • *2,591*
Henry □, AL • *15,374*
Henry □, GA • *58,741*
Henry □, IL • *51,159*
Henry □, IN • *48,139*
Henry □, IA • *19,226*
Henry □, KY • *12,823*
Henry □, MO • *20,044*
Henry □, OH • *29,108*
Henry □, TN • *27,888*
Henry □, VA • *56,942*
Henryetta, OK 74437 • *5,872*
Henryville, IN 47126 • *1,132*
Hephzibah, GA 30815 • *2,466*
Heppner, OR 97836 • *1,412*
Herculaneum, MO 63048 • *2,263*
Hercules, CA 94547 • *16,829*
Hereford, TX 79045 • *14,745*
Herington, KS 67449 • *2,685*
Heritage Village, CT 06488 • *9,700*
Herkimer, NY 13350 • *7,945*
Herkimer □, NY • *65,797*
Hermann, MO 65041 • *2,754*
Hermantown, MN 55811 • *6,761*
Herminie, PA 15637 • *2,000*
Hermiston, OR 97838 • *10,040*
Hermitage, PA 16148 • *15,300*
Hermosa Beach, CA 90254 • *18,219*
Hernando, FL 32642 • *2,103*
Hernando, MS 38632 • *3,125*
Hernando □, FL • *101,115*
Herndon, VA 22070–71 • *16,139*
Herrin, IL 62948 • *10,857*
Herscher, IL 60941 • *1,278*
Hershey, PA 17033 • *11,860*
Hertford, NC 27944 • *2,105*
Hertford □, NC • *22,523*
Hesperia, CA 92345 • *50,418*
Hesston, KS 67062 • *3,012*
Hettinger, ND 58639 • *1,574*
Hettinger □, ND • *3,445*
Hewitt, TX 76643 • *8,983*
Hewlett, NY 11557 • *6,620*
Heyburn, ID 83336 • *2,714*
Heyworth, IL 61745 • *1,627*
Hialeah, FL 33010–16 • *188,004*
Hiawatha, IA 52233 • *4,986*
Hiawatha, KS 66434 • *3,603*
Hibbing, MN 55746–47 • *18,046*
Hickman, KY 42050 • *2,689*

Hickman, NE 68372 • *1,081*
Hickman □, KY • *5,566*
Hickman □, TN • *16,754*
Hickory, NC 28601–03 • *28,301*
Hickory □, MO • *7,335*
Hickory Hills, IL 60457 • *13,021*
Hicksville, NY 11801–05 • *40,174*
Hicksville, OH 43526 • *3,664*
Hico, TX 76457 • *1,342*
Hidalgo, TX 78557 • *3,292*
Hidalgo □, NM • *5,958*
Hidalgo □, TX • *383,545*
Higganum, CT 06441 • *1,692*
Higginsville, MO 64037 • *4,693*
High Bridge, NJ 08829 • *3,886*
Highland, CA 92346 • *34,439*
Highland, IL 62249 • *7,525*
Highland, IN 46322 • *23,696*
Highland, MI 48356–57 • *750*
Highland, NY 12528 • *4,492*
Highland □, OH • *35,728*
Highland □, VA • *2,635*
Highland Falls, NY 10928 • *3,937*
Highland Heights, OH 44124 • *6,249*
Highland Lakes, NJ 07422 • *4,550*
Highland Park, IL 60035 • *30,575*
Highland Park, MI 48203 • *20,121*
Highland Park, NJ 08904 • *13,279*
Highland Park, TX 75205 • *8,739*
Highlands, NJ 07732 • *4,849*
Highlands, TX 77562 • *6,632*
Highlands □, FL • *68,432*
Highland Springs, VA 23075 • *13,823*
Highmore, SD 57345 • *835*
High Point, NC 27260–65 • *69,496*
High Ridge, MO 63049 • *2,380*
High Spire, PA 17034 • *2,668*
High Springs, FL 32643 • *3,144*
Hightstown, NJ 08520 • *5,126*
Highview, KY 40228 • *14,814*
Highwood, IL 60040 • *5,331*
Hilbert, WI 54129 • *1,211*
Hildale, UT 84784 • *1,325*
Hill □, MT • *17,654*
Hill □, TX • *27,146*
Hill City, KS 67642 • *1,835*
Hillcrest, NY 10977 • *6,447*
Hillcrest Center, CA 93306 • *26,900*
Hillcrest Heights, MD 20748 • *17,136*
Hilliard, FL 32046 • *1,751*
Hilliard, OH 43026 • *11,796*
Hillsboro, IL 62049 • *4,400*
Hillsboro, KS 67063 • *2,704*
Hillsboro, MO 63050 • *1,625*
Hillsboro, NH 03244 • *1,826*
Hillsboro, ND 58045 • *1,488*
Hillsboro, OH 45133 • *6,235*
Hillsboro, OR 97123–24 • *37,520*
Hillsboro, TX 76645 • *7,072*
Hillsboro, WI 54634 • *1,288*
Hillsborough, CA 94010 • *10,667*
Hillsborough, NC 27278 • *4,263*
Hillsborough □, FL • *834,054*
Hillsborough □, NH • *336,073*
Hillsdale, MI 49242 • *8,170*
Hillsdale, NJ 07642 • *9,750*
Hillsdale □, MI • *43,431*
Hillside, IL 60162 • *7,672*
Hillside, NJ 07205 • *21,044*
Hillside Heights, DE 19711 • *1,500*
Hillsville, VA 24343 • *2,008*
Hillview, KY 40229 • *6,119*
Hilo, HI 96720–21 • *37,808*
Hilton, NY 14468 • *5,216*
Hilton Head Island, SC 29928 • *23,694*
Hinckley, IL 60520 • *1,682*
Hinds □, MS • *254,441*
Hines, OR 97738 • *1,452*
Hinesville, GA 31313 • *21,603*
Hingham, MA 02043 • *5,454*
Hinsdale, IL 60521–22 • *16,029*
Hinsdale, NH 03451 • *1,718*
Hinsdale □, CO • *467*
Hinton, OK 73047 • *1,233*
Hinton, WV 25951 • *3,433*
Hiram, GA 30141 • *1,389*
Hiram, OH 44234 • *1,330*
Hitchcock, TX 77563 • *5,868*
Hitchcock □, NE • *3,750*
Hitchcock Lake, CT 06716 • *1,640*
Hobart, IN 46342 • *21,822*
Hobart, OK 73651 • *4,305*
Hobbs, NM 88240–41 • *29,115*
Hobe Sound, FL 33455 • *11,507*
Hoboken, NJ 07030 • *33,397*
Hockessin, DE 19707 • *2,430*
Hocking □, OH • *25,533*
Hockley □, TX • *24,199*
Hodgeman □, KS • *2,177*
Hodgenville, KY 42748 • *2,721*
Hoffman Estates, IL 60194–95 • *46,561*
Hoganville, GA 30230 • *2,976*
Hohenwald, TN 38462 • *3,760*
Ho-Ho-Kus, NJ 07423 • *3,935*
Hoisington, KS 67544 • *3,182*
Hoke □, NC • *22,856*
Hokes Bluff, AL 35903 • *3,739*
Holbrook, AZ 86025–29 • *4,686*
Holbrook, MA 02343 • *11,041*
Holbrook, NY 11741 • *25,273*
Holcomb, KS 67851 • *1,400*
Holden, MA 01520 • *4,040*
Holden, MO 64040 • *2,389*
Holden, WV 25625 • *1,246*
Holden Heights, FL 32805 • *4,387*
Holdenville, OK 74848 • *4,792*
Holdrege, NE 68949 • *5,671*
Holgate, OH 43527 • *1,290*
Holiday, FL 34690 • *19,360*
Holiday City at Berkeley, NJ 08757 • *5,750*
Holladay, UT 84117 • *22,189*
Holland, MI 49422–24 • *30,745*
Holland, NY 14080 • *1,288*
Holland, OH 43528 • *1,210*
Holland, PA 18966 • *5,250*
Holland, TX 76534 • *1,118*
Hollandale, MS 38748 • *3,576*
Holley, NY 14470 • *1,890*
Holliday, TX 76366 • *1,475*
Hollidaysburg, PA 16648 • *5,624*
Hollins, VA 24019 • *13,305*
Hollis, OK 73550 • *2,584*
Hollister, CA 95023–24 • *19,212*

Hollister, MO 65672 • *2,628*
Holliston, MA 01746 • *12,622*
Holly, MI 48442 • *5,595*
Holly Hill, FL 32117 • *11,141*
Holly Hill, SC 29059 • *1,478*
Holly Springs, GA 30142 • *2,406*
Holly Springs, MS 38634–35 • *7,261*
Hollywood, FL 33019–29 • *121,697*
Hollywood, SC 29449 • *2,094*
Holmen, WI 54636 • *3,220*
Holmes □, FL • *15,778*
Holmes □, MS • *21,604*
Holmes □, OH • *32,849*
Holstein, IA 51025 • *1,449*
Holt, AL 35404 • *4,125*
Holt, MI 48842 • *11,744*
Holt □, MO • *6,034*
Holt □, NE • *12,599*
Holton, KS 66436 • *3,196*
Holtsville, NY 11742 • *14,972*
Holtville, CA 92250 • *4,820*
Holualoa, HI 96725 • *3,834*
Holyoke, CO 80734 • *1,931*
Holyoke, MA 01040–41 • *43,704*
Homedale, ID 83628 • *1,963*
Home Gardens, CA 91720 • *7,780*
Homeland Park, SC 29621 • *6,569*
Home Place, IN 46240 • *1,300*
Homer, AK 99603 • *3,660*
Homer, IL 61849 • *1,264*
Homer, LA 71040 • *4,152*
Homer, MI 49245 • *1,758*
Homer, NY 13077 • *3,476*
Homer City, PA 15748 • *1,809*
Homerville, GA 31634 • *2,560*
Homestead, FL 33030–35 • *26,866*
Homestead, PA 15120 • *4,179*
Hometown, IL 60456 • *4,769*
Homewood, AL 35209 • *22,922*
Homewood, IL 60430 • *19,278*
Homewood, OH 45015 • *2,550*
Hominy, OK 74035 • *2,342*
Homosassa, FL 32646 • *2,113*
Hondo, TX 78861 • *6,018*
Honea Path, SC 29654 • *3,841*
Honeoye Falls, NY 14472 • *2,340*
Honesdale, PA 18431 • *4,972*
Honey Brook, PA 19344 • *1,184*
Honey Grove, TX 75446 • *1,681*
Honeypot Glen, CT 06410 • *1,200*
Honeyville, UT 84314 • *1,112*
Honokaa, HI 96727 • *2,186*
Honolulu, HI 96801–50 • *365,272*
Honolulu □, HI • *836,231*
Honomu, HI 96728 • *532*
Hood □, TX • *28,981*
Hood River, OR 97031 • *4,632*
Hood River □, OR • *16,903*
Hoodsport, WA 98548 • *1,100*
Hooker, OK 73945 • *1,551*
Hooker □, NE • *793*
Hooksett, NH 03106 • *2,573*
Hoonah, AK 99829 • *795*
Hooper Bay, AK 99604 • *845*
Hoopeston, IL 60942 • *5,871*
Hoosick Falls, NY 12090 • *3,490*
Hoover, AL 35216 • *39,788*
Hooverson Heights, WV 26037 • *3,056*
Hopatcong, NJ 07843 • *15,586*
Hope, AR 71801 • *9,643*
Hope, IN 47246 • *2,171*
Hope, RI 02831 • *270*
Hopedale, MA 01747 • *3,961*
Hope Mills, NC 28348 • *8,184*
Hope Valley, RI 02832 • *1,446*
Hopewell, NJ 08525 • *1,968*
Hopewell, VA 23860 • *23,101*
Hopewell Junction, NY 12533 • *1,786*
Hopkins, MN 55343–47 • *16,534*
Hopkins, SC 29061 • *1,600*
Hopkins □, KY • *46,126*
Hopkins □, TX • *28,833*
Hopkinsville, KY 42240–41 • *29,809*
Hopkinton, MA 01748 • *2,305*
Hopkinton, RI 02833 • *550*
Hopwood, PA 15445 • *2,021*
Hoquiam, WA 98550 • *8,972*
Horicon, WI 53032 • *3,873*
Hornell, NY 14843 • *9,877*
Horn Lake, MS 38637 • *9,069*
Horry □, SC • *144,053*
Horse Cave, KY 42749 • *2,284*
Horseheads, NY 14844–45 • *6,802*
Horsham, PA 19044 • *15,051*
Horton, KS 66439 • *1,885*
Hortonville, WI 54944 • *2,029*
Hot Spring □, AR • *26,115*
Hot Springs, SD 57747 • *4,325*
Hot Springs □, WY • *4,809*
Hot Springs National Park, AR 71901–14 • *32,462*
Hot Springs Village, AR 71901 • *6,361*
Houghton, MI 49931 • *7,498*
Houghton, NY 14744 • *1,740*
Houghton □, MI • *35,446*
Houghton Lake, MI 48629 • *3,353*
Houghton Lake Heights, MI 48630 • *2,449*
Houlton, ME 04730 • *5,627*
Houma, LA 70360–64 • *96,982*
Housatonic, MA 01236 • *1,184*
Houston, DE 19954 • *487*
Houston, MN 55943 • *1,013*
Houston, MS 38851 • *3,903*
Houston, MO 65483 • *2,118*
Houston, PA 15342 • *1,445*
Houston, TX 77001–99 • *1,630,553*
Houston □, AL • *81,331*
Houston □, GA • *89,208*
Houston □, MN • *18,497*
Houston □, TN • *7,018*
Houston □, TX • *21,375*
Houtzdale, PA 16651 • *1,204*
Howard, SD 57349 • *1,156*
Howard, WI 54303 • *9,874*
Howard □, AR • *13,569*
Howard □, IN • *80,827*
Howard □, IA • *9,809*
Howard □, MD • *187,328*
Howard □, MO • *9,631*
Howard □, NE • *6,055*
Howard □, TX • *32,343*
Howard City, MI 49329 • *1,351*
Howard Lake, MN 55349 • *1,343*

Howards Grove-Millersville, WI 53083 • *2,329*
Howell, MI 48843–44 • *8,184*
Howell □, MO • *31,447*
Howland, ME 04448 • *1,304*
Howland, OH 44484 • *6,732*
Hoxie, AR 72433 • *2,676*
Hoxie, KS 67740 • *1,342*
Hoyt Lakes, MN 55750 • *2,348*
Huachuca City, AZ 85616 • *1,782*
Hubbard, OH 44425 • *8,248*
Hubbard, OR 97032 • *1,881*
Hubbard, TX 76648 • *1,589*
Hubbard □, MN • *14,939*
Hubbell, MI 49934 • *1,174*
Huber Heights, OH 45424 • *38,696*
Huber Ridge, OH 43081 • *5,255*
Huber South, OH 45439 • *4,800*
Hudson, FL 34667 • *7,344*
Hudson, IL 61748 • *1,006*
Hudson, IA 50643 • *2,037*
Hudson, MA 01749 • *14,267*
Hudson, MI 49247 • *2,580*
Hudson, NH 03051 • *7,626*
Hudson, NY 12534 • *8,034*
Hudson, NC 28638 • *2,819*
Hudson, OH 44236 • *5,159*
Hudson, WI 54016 • *6,378*
Hudson, WY 82515 • *392*
Hudson □, NJ • *553,099*
Hudson Falls, NY 12839 • *7,651*
Hudson Lake, IN 46552 • *1,347*
Hudsonville, MI 49426 • *6,170*
Hudspeth □, TX • *2,915*
Huerfano □, CO • *6,009*
Hueytown, AL 35023 • *15,280*
Huffakers, NV 89501 • *150*
Hughes, AR 72348 • *1,810*
Hughes □, OK • *13,023*
Hughes □, SD • *14,817*
Hughesville, MD 20637 • *1,319*
Hughesville, PA 17737 • *2,049*
Hugo, MN 55038 • *4,417*
Hugo, OK 74743 • *5,978*
Hugoton, KS 67951 • *3,179*
Hulett, WY 82720 • *429*
Hull, IA 51239 • *1,724*
Hull, MA 02045 • *10,466*
Humansville, MO 65674 • *1,084*
Humble, TX 77338–39 • *12,060*
Humboldt, IA 50548 • *4,438*
Humboldt, KS 66748 • *2,178*
Humboldt, NE 68376 • *1,003*
Humboldt, TN 38343 • *9,651*
Humboldt □, CA • *119,118*
Humboldt □, IA • *10,756*
Humboldt □, NV • *12,844*
Hummels Wharf, PA 17831 • *1,069*
Humphreys □, MS • *12,134*
Humphreys □, TN • *15,795*
Hunt □, TX • *64,343*
Hunterdon □, NJ • *107,776*
Huntertown, IN 46748 • *1,330*
Huntingburg, IN 47542 • *5,242*
Huntingdon, PA 16652 • *6,843*
Huntingdon, TN 38344 • *4,180*
Huntingdon □, PA • *44,164*
Huntington, IN 46750 • *16,389*
Huntington, MA 01050 • *1,200*
Huntington, NY 11743 • *18,243*
Huntington, TX 75949 • *1,794*
Huntington, UT 84528 • *1,875*
Huntington, VA 22303 • *7,489*
Huntington, WV 25701–79 • *54,844*
Huntington □, IN • *35,427*
Huntington Bay, NY 11743 • *1,521*
Huntington Beach, CA 92646–49 • *181,519*
Huntington Park, CA 90255 • *56,065*
Huntington Station, NY 11746 • *28,247*
Huntington Woods, MI 48070 • *6,419*
Huntley, IL 60142 • *2,453*
Huntsville, AL 35801–24 • *159,789*
Huntsville, AR 72740 • *1,605*
Huntsville, MO 65259 • *1,567*
Huntsville, TX 77340–44 • *27,925*
Hurley, NM 88043 • *1,534*
Hurley, NY 12443 • *4,644*
Hurley, WI 54534 • *1,782*
Hurlock, MD 21643 • *1,706*
Huron, OH 44839 • *7,030*
Huron, SD 57350 • *12,448*
Huron □, MI • *34,951*
Huron □, OH • *56,240*
Hurricane, UT 84737 • *3,915*
Hurricane, WV 25526 • *4,461*
Hurst, TX 76053–54 • *33,574*
Hurt, VA 24563 • *1,294*
Hutchins, TX 75141 • *2,719*
Hutchinson, KS 67501–05 • *39,308*
Hutchinson, MN 55350 • *11,523*
Hutchinson □, SD • *8,262*
Hutchinson □, TX • *25,689*
Huxley, IA 50124 • *2,047*
Hyannis, MA 02601 • *14,120*
Hyannis Port, MA 02647 • *1,100*
Hyattsville, MD 20780–89 • *13,864*
Hybla Valley, VA 22306 • *15,491*
Hydaburg, AK 99922 • *384*
Hyde, PA 16843 • *1,643*
Hyde □, NC • *5,411*
Hyde □, SD • *1,696*
Hyde Park, NY 12538 • *2,550*
Hyde Park, UT 84318 • *2,190*
Hydeville, VT 05750 • *450*
Hyndman, PA 15545 • *1,019*
Hyrum, UT 84319 • *4,829*

I

Iberia □, LA • *68,297*
Iberville □, LA • *31,049*
Ida, MI 48140 • *1,000*
Ida □, IA • *8,365*
Idabel, OK 74745 • *6,957*
Ida Grove, IA 51445 • *2,357*
Idaho □, ID • *13,783*
Idaho Falls, ID 83401–15 • *43,929*
Idaho Springs, CO 80452 • *1,834*
Idalou, TX 79329 • *2,074*
Ilion, NY 13357 • *8,888*

Illmo, MO 63780 • *1,368*
Imlay, NV 89418 • *250*
Imlay City, MI 48444 • *2,921*
Immokalee, FL 33934 • *14,120*
Imperial, CA 92251 • *4,113*
Imperial, NE 69033 • *2,007*
Imperial, PA 15126 • *3,200*
Imperial □, CA • *109,303*
Imperial Beach, CA 91932–33 • *26,512*
Incline Village, NV 89450 • *4,500*
Independence, CA 93526 • *1,000*
Independence, IA 50644 • *5,972*
Independence, KS 67301 • *9,942*
Independence, KY 41051 • *10,444*
Independence, LA 70443 • *1,632*
Independence, MO 64050–58 • *112,301*
Independence, OH 44131 • *6,500*
Independence, OR 97351 • *4,425*
Independence, WI 54747 • *1,041*
Independence □, AR • *31,192*
Indiana, PA 15701 • *15,174*
Indiana □, PA • *89,994*
Indianapolis, IN 46201–90 • *731,327*
Indian Harbour Beach, FL 32937 • *6,933*
Indian Head, MD 20640 • *3,531*
Indian Heights, IN 46902 • *3,669*
Indian Hills, CO 80454 • *2,000*
Indian Neck, CT 06405 • *2,430*
Indianola, IA 50125 • *11,340*
Indianola, MS 38751 • *11,809*
Indian Ridge Estates, AZ 85715 • *1,260*
Indian River □, FL • *90,208*
Indian Rocks Beach, FL 34635 • *3,963*
Indian Springs, NV 89018 • *1,164*
Indiantown, FL 34956 • *4,794*
Indian Trail, NC 28079 • *1,942*
Indio, CA 92201–02 • *36,793*
Ingalls Park, IL 60431 • *2,730*
Ingham □, MI • *281,912*
Ingleside, TX 78362 • *5,696*
Inglewood, CA 90301–12 • *109,602*
Inglewood, TX 98011 • *6,500*
Ingram, PA 15205 • *3,901*
Inkom, ID 83245 • *769*
Inkster, MI 48141 • *30,772*
Inman, KS 67546 • *1,035*
Inman, SC 29349 • *1,742*
Inniswold, LA 70809 • *1,100*
Inola, OK 74036 • *1,444*
Institute, WV 25112 • *1,400*
Interlachen, FL 32148 • *1,160*
International Falls, MN 56649 • *8,325*
Inver Grove Heights, MN 55076–77 • *22,477*
Inverness, CA 94937 • *1,422*
Inverness, FL 32650–52 • *5,797*
Inverness, IL 60067 • *6,503*
Inverness, MS 38753 • *1,174*
Inwood, FL 33880 • *6,824*
Inwood, NY 11696 • *7,767*
Inwood, WV 25428 • *1,360*
Inyo □, CA • *18,281*
Iola, KS 66749 • *6,351*
Iola, WI 54945 • *1,125*
Iona, ID 83427 • *1,049*
Ione, CA 95640 • *6,516*
Ionia, MI 48846 • *5,935*
Ionia □, MI • *57,024*
Iosco □, MI • *30,209*
Iota, LA 70543 • *1,256*
Iowa, LA 70647 • *2,588*
Iowa □, IA • *14,630*
Iowa □, WI • *20,150*
Iowa City, IA 52240–46 • *59,738*
Iowa Falls, IA 50126 • *5,424*
Iowa Park, TX 76367 • *6,072*
Ipswich, MA 01938 • *4,132*
Ipswich, SD 57451 • *965*
Iraan, TX 79744 • *1,322*
Iredell □, NC • *92,931*
Irion □, TX • *1,629*
Irmo, SC 29063 • *11,280*
Iron □, MI • *13,175*
Iron □, MO • *10,726*
Iron □, UT • *20,789*
Iron □, WI • *6,153*
Irondale, AL 35210 • *9,454*
Irondequoit, NY 14617 • *52,322*
Ironia, NJ 07845 • *1,110*
Iron Mountain, MI 49801 • *8,525*
Iron River, MI 49935 • *2,095*
Ironton, MO 63650 • *1,539*
Ironton, OH 45638 • *12,751*
Ironwood, MI 49938 • *6,849*
Iroquois □, IL • *30,787*
Irvine, CA 92713–20 • *110,330*
Irvine, KY 40336 • *2,836*
Irving, TX 75060–63 • *155,037*
Irvington, KY 40146 • *1,180*
Irvington, NJ 07111 • *59,774*
Irvington, NY 10533 • *6,348*
Irwin, PA 15642 • *4,604*
Irwin □, GA • *8,649*
Isabella □, MI • *54,624*
Isanti, MN 55040 • *1,228*
Isanti □, MN • *25,921*
Iselin, NJ 08830 • *16,141*
Ishpeming, MI 49849 • *7,200*
Islamorada, FL 33036 • *1,220*
Island □, WA • *60,195*
Island Heights, NJ 08732 • *1,470*
Island Park, NY 11558 • *4,860*
Island Park, RI 02871 • *1,240*
Island Pond, VT 05846 • *1,222*
Isla Vista, CA 93117 • *20,395*
Isle of Palms, SC 29451 • *3,680*
Isle of Wight □, VA • *25,053*
Isleta, NM 87022 • *1,703*
Islington, MA 02090 • *4,920*
Islip, NY 11751 • *18,924*
Islip Terrace, NY 11752 • *5,530*
Issaquah, WA 98027 • *7,786*
Issaquena □, MS • *1,909*
Italy, TX 76651 • *1,699*
Itasca, IL 60143 • *6,947*
Itasca, TX 76055 • *1,523*
Itasca □, MN • *40,863*
Itawamba □, MS • *20,017*
Ithaca, MI 48847 • *3,009*
Ithaca, NY 14850–52 • *29,541*
Itta Bena, MS 38941 • *2,377*
Iuka, MS 38852 • *3,122*
Iva, SC 29655 • *1,174*
Ives Estates, FL 33162 • *13,531*
Ivins, UT 84738 • *1,630*
Ivoryton, CT 06442 • *2,200*
Izard □, AR • *11,364*

J

Jacinto City, TX 77029 • *9,343*
Jack □, TX • *6,981*
Jackpot, NV 89825 • *570*
Jacksboro, TN 37757 • *1,568*
Jacksboro, TX 76056 • *3,350*
Jackson, AL 36545 • *5,819*
Jackson, CA 95642 • *3,545*
Jackson, GA 30233 • *4,076*
Jackson, KY 41339 • *2,466*
Jackson, LA 70748 • *3,891*
Jackson, MI 49201–04 • *37,446*
Jackson, MN 56143 • *3,559*
Jackson, MS 39201–98 • *196,637*
Jackson, MO 63755 • *9,256*
Jackson, OH 45640 • *6,144*
Jackson, SC 29831 • *1,681*
Jackson, TN 38301–08 • *48,949*
Jackson, WI 53037 • *2,486*
Jackson, WY 83001–02 • *4,472*
Jackson □, AL • *47,796*
Jackson □, AR • *18,944*
Jackson □, CO • *1,605*
Jackson □, FL • *41,375*
Jackson □, GA • *30,005*
Jackson □, IL • *61,067*
Jackson □, IN • *37,730*
Jackson □, IA • *19,950*
Jackson □, KS • *11,525*
Jackson □, KY • *11,955*
Jackson □, LA • *15,705*
Jackson □, MI • *149,756*
Jackson □, MN • *11,677*
Jackson □, MS • *115,243*
Jackson □, MO • *633,232*
Jackson □, NC • *26,846*
Jackson □, OH • *30,230*
Jackson □, OK • *28,764*
Jackson □, OR • *146,389*
Jackson □, SD • *2,811*
Jackson □, TN • *9,297*
Jackson □, TX • *13,039*
Jackson □, WV • *25,938*
Jackson □, WI • *16,588*
Jackson Center, OH 45334 • *1,398*
Jacksonville, AL 36265 • *10,283*
Jacksonville, AR 72076 • *29,101*
Jacksonville, FL 32201–98 • *635,230*
Jacksonville, IL 62650–51 • *19,324*
Jacksonville, NC 28540–46 • *30,013*
Jacksonville, OR 97530 • *1,896*
Jacksonville, TX 75766 • *12,765*
Jacksonville Beach, FL 32250 • *17,839*
Jaffrey, NH 03452 • *2,558*
Jal, NM 88252 • *2,156*
Jamesburg, NJ 08831 • *5,294*
James City, NC 28560 • *4,279*
James City □, VA • *34,859*
James Island, SC 29412 • *24,124*
Jamestown, CA 95327 • *2,178*
Jamestown, KY 42629 • *1,641*
Jamestown, NY 14701–02 • *34,681*
Jamestown, NC 27282 • *2,600*
Jamestown, ND 58401–02 • *15,571*
Jamestown, OH 45335 • *1,794*
Jamestown, RI 02835 • *2,156*
Jamestown, TN 38556 • *1,862*
James Town, WY 82935 • *280*
Janesville, CA 96114 • *1,200*
Janesville, MN 56048 • *1,969*
Janesville, WI 53545–47 • *52,133*
Jarrettsville, MD 21084 • *2,148*
Jasmine Estates, FL 34668 • *17,136*
Jasonville, IN 47438 • *2,200*
Jasper, AL 35501–02 • *13,553*
Jasper, FL 32052 • *2,099*
Jasper, GA 30143 • *1,772*
Jasper, IN 47546–47 • *10,030*
Jasper, TN 37347 • *2,780*
Jasper, TX 75951 • *6,959*
Jasper □, GA • *8,453*
Jasper □, IL • *10,609*
Jasper □, IN • *24,960*
Jasper □, IA • *34,795*
Jasper □, MS • *17,114*
Jasper □, MO • *90,465*
Jasper □, SC • *15,487*
Jasper □, TX • *31,102*
Jay, OK 74346 • *2,220*
Jay □, IN • *21,512*
Jean, NV 89019 • *150*
Jeanerette, LA 70544 • *6,205*
Jeannette, PA 15644 • *11,221*
Jeff Davis □, GA • *12,032*
Jeff Davis □, TX • *1,946*
Jefferson, GA 30549 • *2,763*
Jefferson, IA 50129 • *4,292*
Jefferson, LA 70121 • *14,521*
Jefferson, NC 28640 • *1,300*
Jefferson, OH 44047 • *3,331*
Jefferson, OR 97352 • *1,805*
Jefferson, PA 15025 • *9,533*
Jefferson, TX 75657 • *2,199*
Jefferson, WI 53549 • *6,078*
Jefferson □, AL • *651,525*
Jefferson □, AR • *85,487*
Jefferson □, CO • *438,430*
Jefferson □, FL • *11,296*
Jefferson □, GA • *17,408*
Jefferson □, ID • *16,543*
Jefferson □, IL • *37,020*
Jefferson □, IN • *29,797*
Jefferson □, IA • *16,310*
Jefferson □, KS • *15,905*
Jefferson □, KY • *664,937*
Jefferson □, LA • *448,306*
Jefferson □, MS • *8,653*
Jefferson □, MO • *171,380*
Jefferson □, MT • *7,939*
Jefferson □, NE • *8,759*
Jefferson □, NY • *110,943*
Jefferson □, OH • *80,298*
Jefferson □, OK • *7,010*
Jefferson □, OR • *13,676*
Jefferson □, PA • *46,083*
Jefferson □, TN • *33,016*
Jefferson □, TX • *239,397*
Jefferson □, WA • *20,146*
Jefferson □, WV • *35,926*
Jefferson □, WI • *67,783*
Jefferson City, MO 65101–10 • *35,481*
Jefferson City, TN 37760 • *5,494*
Jefferson Davis □, LA • *30,722*
Jefferson Davis □, MS • *14,051*
Jefferson Farms, DE 19720 • *3,130*
Jefferson Manor, VA 22303 • *2,300*
Jeffersontown, KY 40299 • *23,221*
Jefferson Valley, NY 10535 • *6,420*
Jefferson Village, VA 22042 • *2,500*
Jeffersonville, GA 31044 • *1,545*
Jeffersonville, IN 47129–31 • *21,841*
Jeffersonville, KY 40337 • *1,854*
Jeffersonville, OH 43128 • *1,281*
Jeffrey City, WY 82310 • *1,882*
Jellico, TN 37762 • *2,447*
Jemez Pueblo, NM 87024 • *1,301*
Jemison, AL 35085 • *1,898*
Jena, LA 71342 • *2,626*
Jenison, MI 49428–29 • *17,882*
Jenkins, KY 41537 • *2,751*
Jenkins □, GA • *8,247*
Jenkintown, PA 19046 • *4,574*
Jenks, OK 74037 • *7,493*
Jennings, LA 70546 • *11,305*
Jennings, MO 63136 • *15,905*
Jennings □, IN • *23,661*
Jennings Lodge, OR 97222 • *11,480*
Jensen Beach, FL 34957–58 • *9,884*
Jerauld □, SD • *2,425*
Jericho, NY 11753 • *13,141*
Jericho, VT 05465 • *1,300*
Jermyn, PA 18433 • *2,263*
Jerome, ID 83338 • *6,529*
Jerome, PA 15937 • *1,074*
Jerome □, ID • *15,138*
Jersey □, IL • *20,539*
Jersey City, NJ 07301–11 • *228,537*
Jersey Shore, PA 17740 • *4,353*
Jerseyville, IL 62052 • *7,382*
Jessamine □, KY • *30,508*
Jessup, MD 20794 • *6,537*
Jessup, PA 18434 • *4,605*
Jesup, GA 31545 • *8,958*
Jesup, IA 50648 • *2,121*
Jewell, IA 50130 • *1,106*
Jewell □, KS • *4,251*
Jewett City, CT 06351 • *3,349*
Jim Hogg □, TX • *5,109*
Jim Thorpe, PA 18229 • *5,048*
Jim Wells □, TX • *37,679*
Joanna, SC 29351 • *1,735*
Jo Daviess □, IL • *21,821*
John Day, OR 97845 • *1,836*
Johnson, KS 67855 • *1,348*
Johnson, VT 05656 • *1,470*
Johnson □, AR • *18,221*
Johnson □, GA • *8,329*
Johnson □, IL • *11,347*
Johnson □, IN • *88,109*
Johnson □, IA • *96,119*
Johnson □, KS • *355,054*
Johnson □, KY • *23,248*
Johnson □, MO • *42,514*
Johnson □, NE • *4,673*
Johnson □, TN • *13,766*
Johnson □, TX • *97,165*
Johnson □, WY • *6,145*
Johnsonburg, PA 15845 • *3,350*
Johnson City, NY 13790 • *16,890*
Johnson City, TN 37601–15 • *49,381*
Johnson Creek, WI 53038 • *1,259*
Johnsonville, SC 29555 • *1,415*
Johnston, IA 50131 • *4,702*
Johnston, RI 02919 • *26,542*
Johnston, SC 29832 • *2,688*
Johnston □, NC • *81,306*
Johnston □, OK • *10,032*
Johnston City, IL 62951 • *3,706*
Johnstown, CO 80534 • *1,579*
Johnstown, NY 12095 • *9,058*
Johnstown, OH 43031 • *3,237*
Johnstown, PA 15901–09 • *28,134*
Joliet, IL 60431–36 • *76,836*
Jones, OK 73049 • *2,424*
Jones □, GA • *20,739*
Jones □, IA • *19,444*
Jones □, MS • *62,031*
Jones □, NC • *9,414*
Jones □, SD • *1,324*
Jones □, TX • *16,490*
Jonesboro, AR 72401–03 • *46,535*
Jonesboro, GA 30236–37 • *3,635*
Jonesboro, IL 62952 • *1,728*
Jonesboro, IN 46938 • *2,073*
Jonesboro, LA 71251 • *4,305*
Jonesborough, TN 37659 • *3,091*
Jones Creek, TX 77541 • *2,160*
Jonesport, ME 04649 • *1,525*
Jonestown, MS 38639 • *1,467*
Jonesville, LA 71343 • *2,720*
Jonesville, MI 49250 • *2,283*
Jonesville, NC 28642 • *1,549*
Jonesville, SC 29353 • *1,205*
Joplin, MO 64801–04 • *40,961*
Joppatowne, MD 21085 • *11,084*
Jordan, MN 55352 • *2,909*
Jordan, NY 13080 • *1,325*
Joseph, OR 97846 • *1,073*
Josephine □, OR • *62,649*
Joshua, TX 76058 • *3,828*
Joshua Tree, CA 92252 • *3,898*
Jourdanton, TX 78026 • *3,220*
Juab □, UT • *5,817*
Juanita, WA 98033 • *10,500*
Judith Basin □, MT • *2,282*
Judsonia, AR 72081 • *1,915*
Julesburg, CO 80737 • *1,295*
Julian, CA 92036 • *1,284*
Junction, TX 76849 • *2,654*
Junction City, KS 66441 • *20,604*
Junction City, KY 40440 • *1,983*
Junction City, OR 97448 • *3,670*
Juneau, AK 99801–03 • *26,751*
Juneau, WI 53039 • *2,157*
Juneau □, WI • *21,650*
Juniata □, PA • *20,625*
Jupiter, FL 33458 • *24,986*
Justice, IL 60458 • *11,137*
Justin, TX 76247 • *1,234*

K

Kaaawa, HI 96730 • *1,138*
Kadoka, SD 57543 • *736*
Kahaluu, HI 96725 • *380*
Kahaluu, HI 96744 • *3,068*
Kahoka, MO 63445 • *2,195*
Kahuku, HI 96731 • *2,063*
Kahului, HI 96732–33 • *16,889*
Kailua, HI 96734 • *36,818*
Kailua Kona, HI 96739–40 • *9,126*
Kake, AK 99830 • *700*
Kalaheo, HI 96741 • *3,592*
Kalama, WA 98625 • *1,210*
Kalamazoo, MI 49001–09 • *80,277*
Kalamazoo □, MI • *223,411*
Kalawao □, HI • *130*
Kalispell, MT 59901 • *11,917*
Kalkaska, MI 49646 • *1,952*
Kalkaska □, MI • *13,497*
Kalona, IA 52247 • *1,942*
Kamas, UT 84036 • *1,061*
Kamiah, ID 83536 • *1,157*
Kamuela (Waimea), HI 96743 • *5,972*
Kanab, UT 84741 • *3,289*
Kanabec □, MN • *12,802*
Kanawha □, WV • *207,619*
Kandiyohi □, MN • *38,761*
Kane, PA 16735 • *4,590*
Kane □, IL • *317,471*
Kane □, UT • *5,169*
Kaneohe, HI 96744 • *35,448*
Kankakee, IL 60901 • *27,575*
Kankakee □, IL • *96,255*
Kannapolis, NC 28081–83 • *29,696*
Kansas City, KS 66101–19 • *149,767*
Kansas City, MO 64101–99 • *435,146*
Kapaa, HI 96746 • *8,149*
Kapaau, HI 96755 • *1,083*
Kaplan, LA 70548 • *4,535*
Karnes □, TX • *12,455*
Karnes City, TX 78118 • *2,916*
Karns, TN 37921 • *1,458*
Kasson, MN 55944 • *3,514*
Kathleen, FL 33849 • *2,743*
Katy, TX 77449–50 • *8,005*
Kauai □, HI • *51,177*
Kaufman, TX 75142 • *5,238*
Kaufman □, TX • *52,220*
Kaukauna, WI 54130 • *11,982*
Kaumakani, HI 96747 • *803*
Kaunakakai, HI 96748 • *2,658*
Kay □, OK • *48,056*
Kaycee, WY 82639 • *256*
Kayenta, AZ 86033 • *4,372*
Kaysville, UT 84037 • *13,961*
Keaau, HI 96749 • *1,584*
Kealakekua, HI 96750 • *1,453*
Kealia, HI 96751 • *700*
Keansburg, NJ 07734 • *11,069*
Kearney, MO 64060 • *1,790*
Kearney, NE 68847–48 • *24,396*
Kearney □, NE • *6,629*
Kearns, UT 84118 • *28,374*
Kearny, AZ 85237 • *2,262*
Kearny, NJ 07031–32 • *34,874*
Kearny □, KS • *4,027*
Keego Harbor, MI 48320 • *2,932*
Keene, NH 03431 • *22,430*
Keene, TX 76059 • *3,944*
Keeseville, NY 12944 • *1,854*
Keewatin, MN 55753 • *1,118*
Keith □, NE • *8,584*
Keizer, OR 97303 • *21,884*
Kekaha, HI 96752 • *3,506*
Keller, TX 76248 • *13,683*
Kellogg, ID 83837 • *2,591*
Kelseyville, CA 95451 • *2,861*
Kelso, WA 98626 • *11,820*
Kemmerer, WY 83101 • *3,020*
Kemp, TX 75143 • *1,184*
Kemper □, MS • *10,356*
Kenai, AK 99611 • *6,327*
Kenbridge, VA 23944 • *1,264*
Ken Caryl, CO 80123 • *24,391*
Kendall, FL 33156 • *87,271*
Kendall □, IL • *39,413*
Kendall □, TX • *14,589*
Kendall Park, NJ 08824 • *7,127*
Kendallville, IN 46755 • *7,773*
Kenedy, TX 78119 • *3,763*
Kenedy □, TX • *460*
Kenilworth, IL 60043 • *2,402*
Kenilworth, NJ 07033 • *7,574*
Kenly, NC 27542 • *1,549*
Kenmare, ND 58746 • *1,214*
Kenmore, NY 14217 • *17,180*
Kenmore, WA 98028 • *8,917*
Kennebec □, ME • *115,904*
Kennebunk, ME 04043 • *4,206*
Kennebunkport, ME 04046 • *1,100*
Kennedy Heights, LA 70094 • *2,000*
Kennedy Township, PA 15108 • *7,152*
Kenner, LA 70062–65 • *72,033*
Kennesaw, GA 30144 • *8,936*
Kennett, MO 63857 • *10,941*
Kennett Square, PA 19348 • *5,218*
Kennewick, WA 99336–37 • *42,155*
Kennydale, WA 98056 • *2,000*
Kenosha, WI 53140–44 • *80,352*
Kenosha □, WI • *128,181*
Kenova, WV 25530 • *3,748*
Ken Rock, IL 61109 • *3,300*
Kensett, AR 72082 • *1,741*
Kensington, CA 94707 • *4,974*
Kensington, CT 06037 • *8,306*
Kensington, MD 20895 • *1,713*
Kent, OH 44240 • *28,835*
Kent, WA 98031–32 • *37,960*
Kent □, DE • *110,993*
Kent □, MD • *17,842*
Kent □, MI • *500,631*
Kent □, RI • *161,135*
Kent □, TX • *1,010*
Kentfield, CA 94904 • *6,030*
Kentland, IN 47951 • *1,798*
Kenton, DE 19955 • *232*
Kenton, OH 43326 • *8,356*
Kenton, TN 38233 • *1,366*
Kenton □, KY • *142,031*
Kentwood, LA 70444 • *2,468*
Kentwood, MI 49508 • *37,826*
Kenvil, NJ 07847 • *3,050*
Kenwood, OH 45236 • *7,469*
Kenyon, MN 55946 • *1,552*
Kenyon, RI 02836 • *400*
Keokea, HI 96790 • *900*
Keokuk, IA 52632 • *12,451*
Keokuk □, IA • *11,624*
Keosauqua, IA 52565 • *1,020*
Keota, IA 52248 • *1,000*
Kerens, TX 75144 • *1,702*
Kerhonkson, NY 12446 • *1,629*
Kermit, TX 79745 • *6,875*
Kern □, CA • *543,477*
Kernersville, NC 27284–85 • *10,836*
Kernville, CA 93238 • *1,656*
Kerr □, TX • *36,304*
Kerrville, TX 78028–29 • *17,384*
Kershaw, SC 29067 • *1,814*
Kershaw □, SC • *43,599*
Ketchikan, AK 99901 • *8,263*
Ketchum, ID 83340 • *2,523*
Kettering, MD 20772 • *9,901*
Kettering, OH 45429 • *60,569*
Kettle Falls, WA 99141 • *1,272*
Kewanee, IL 61443 • *12,969*
Kewaskum, WI 53040 • *2,515*
Kewaunee, WI 54216 • *2,750*
Kewaunee □, WI • *18,878*
Keweenaw □, MI • *1,701*
Keya Paha □, NE • *1,029*
Key Biscayne, FL 33149 • *8,854*
Key Largo, FL 33037 • *11,336*
Keyport, NJ 07735 • *7,586*
Keyser, WV 26726 • *5,870*
Keystone Heights, FL 32656 • *1,315*
Key West, FL 33040–41 • *24,832*
Kiana, AK 99749 • *385*
Kidder □, ND • *3,332*
Kiel, WI 53042 • *2,910*
Kihei, HI 96753 • *11,107*
Kilauea, HI 96754 • *1,685*
Kilgore, TX 75662–63 • *11,066*
Killdeer, ND 58640 • *722*
Killeen, TX 76540–47 • *63,535*
Killen, AL 35645 • *1,047*
Kilmarnock, VA 22482 • *1,109*
Kimball, NE 69145 • *2,574*
Kimball □, NE • *4,108*
Kimberly, AL 35091 • *1,096*
Kimberly, ID 83341 • *2,367*
Kimberly, WI 54136 • *5,406*
Kimble □, TX • *4,122*
Kincaid, IL 62540 • *1,353*
Kinder, LA 70648 • *2,246*
Kinderhook, NY 12106 • *1,293*
King, NC 27021 • *4,059*
King □, TX • *354*
King □, WA • *1,507,319*
King and Queen □, VA • *6,289*
King City, CA 93930 • *7,634*
King Cove, AK 99612 • *451*
Kingfisher, OK 73750 • *4,095*
Kingfisher □, OK • *13,212*
King George □, VA • *13,527*
Kingman, AZ 86401–02 • *12,722*
Kingman, KS 67068 • *3,196*
Kingman □, KS • *8,292*
King of Prussia, PA 19406 • *18,406*
Kings, MS 39180 • *1,165*
Kings □, CA • *101,469*
Kings □, NY • *2,300,664*
King Salmon, AK 99613 • *696*
Kingsburg, CA 93631 • *7,205*
Kingsbury □, SD • *5,925*
Kingsford, MI 49801 • *5,480*
Kingsgate, WA 98011 • *14,259*
Kingsland, GA 31548 • *4,699*
Kingsland, TX 78639 • *2,725*
Kingsley, IA 51028 • *1,129*
Kings Mountain, NC 28086 • *8,763*
Kings Park, NY 11754 • *17,773*
Kings Park, VA 22151 • *6,000*
Kings Park West, VA 22032 • *6,000*
Kings Point, FL 33484 • *12,422*
Kings Point, NY 11024 • *4,843*
Kingsport, TN 37660–65 • *36,365*
Kingston, ID 83839 • *1,000*
Kingston, MA 02364 • *4,774*
Kingston, NJ 08528 • *1,200*
Kingston, NY 12401 • *23,095*
Kingston, OH 45644 • *1,153*
Kingston, OK 73439 • *1,237*
Kingston, PA 18704 • *14,507*
Kingston, RI 02881 • *6,504*
Kingston, TN 37763 • *4,552*
Kingston Springs, TN 37082 • *1,529*
Kingstown, MD 21620 • *1,660*
Kingstree, SC 29556 • *3,858*
Kingsville, MD 21087 • *3,550*
Kingsville (North Kingsville), OH 44048 • *1,243*
Kingsville, TX 78363–64 • *25,276*
King William □, VA • *10,913*
Kingwood, TX 77339 • *37,397*
Kingwood, WV 26537 • *3,243*
Kinloch, MO 63140 • *2,702*
Kinnelon, NJ 07405 • *8,470*
Kinney □, TX • *3,119*
Kinsey, AL 36301 • *1,679*
Kinsley, KS 67547 • *1,875*
Kinston, NC 28501–03 • *25,295*
Kiowa, KS 67070 • *1,160*
Kiowa □, CO • *1,688*
Kiowa □, KS • *3,660*
Kiowa □, OK • *11,347*
Kipnuk, AK 99614 • *470*
Kirby, TX 78219 • *8,326*
Kirbyville, TX 75956 • *1,871*
Kirkland, IL 60146 • *1,011*
Kirkland, WA 98033–34 • *40,052*
Kirksville, MO 63501 • *17,152*
Kirkwood, DE 19708 • *350*
Kirkwood, MO 63122 • *27,291*
Kirtland, NM 87417 • *3,552*
Kirtland, OH 44094 • *5,881*
Kissimmee, FL 34741–46 • *30,050*
Kit Carson □, CO • *7,140*
Kitsap □, WA • *189,731*
Kittanning, PA 16201 • *5,120*
Kittery, ME 03904 • *5,151*

Kittery Point, ME 03905 • 1,093
Kittitas □, WA • 26,725
Kittson □, MN • 5,767
Kitty Hawk, NC 27949 • 1,937
Klamath □, OR • 57,702
Klamath Falls, OR 97601–03 • 17,737
Klawock, AK 99925 • 722
Kleberg □, TX • 30,274
Klein, TX 77379 • 12,000
Klickitat □, WA • 16,616
Knightdale, NC 27545 • 1,884
Knights Landing, CA 95645 • 1,000
Knightstown, IN 46148 • 2,048
Knob Noster, MO 65336 • 2,261
Knott □, KY • 17,906
Knox, IN 46534 • 3,705
Knox, PA 16232 • 1,182
Knox □, IL • 56,393
Knox □, IN • 39,884
Knox □, KY • 29,676
Knox □, ME • 36,310
Knox □, MO • 4,482
Knox □, NE • 9,534
Knox □, OH • 47,473
Knox □, TN • 335,749
Knox □, TX • 4,837
Knox City, TX 79529 • 1,440
Knoxville, IL 61448 • 3,243
Knoxville, IA 50138 • 8,232
Knoxville, TN 37901–50 • 165,121
Kodiak, AK 99615 • 6,365
Kohler, WI 53044 • 1,817
Kokomo, IN 46901–04 • 44,962
Koloa, HI 96756 • 1,791
Konawa, OK 74849 • 1,508
Koochiching □, MN • 16,299
Koontz Lake, IN 46574 • 1,615
Kootenai □, ID • 69,795
Koppel, PA 16136 • 1,024
Kosciusko, MS 39090 • 6,986
Kosciusko □, IN • 65,294
Kossuth □, IA • 18,591
Kotlik, AK 99620 • 461
Kotzebue, AK 99752 • 2,751
Kountze, TX 77625 • 2,056
Kouts, IN 46347 • 1,603
Krebs, OK 74554 • 1,955
Kremmling, CO 80459 • 1,166
Krotz Springs, LA 70750 • 1,285
Kula, HI 96790 • 1,300
Kulpmont, PA 17834 • 3,233
Kuna, ID 83634 • 1,955
Kurtistown, HI 96760 • 910
Kutztown, PA 19530 • 4,704
Kwethluk, AK 99621 • 558
Kwigillingok, AK 99622 • 278
Kyle, TX 78640 • 2,225

L

Labadieville, LA 70372 • 1,821
La Barge, WY 83123 • 493
La Belle, FL 33935 • 2,703
Labette □, KS • 23,693
La Canada Flintridge, CA 91011 • 19,378
Lac du Flambeau, WI 54538 • 1,180
La Center, KY 42056 • 1,040
Lacey, WA 98503 • 19,279
Lackawanna, NY 14218 • 20,585
Lackawanna □, PA • 219,039
Laclede □, MO • 27,158
Lacombe, LA 70445 • 6,523
Lacon, IL 61540 • 1,986
Laconia, NH 03246–47 • 15,743
Lacoochee, FL 33537 • 2,072
Lac qui Parle □, MN • 8,924
La Crescent, MN 55947 • 4,311
La Crescenta, CA 91214 • 12,500
La Crosse, KS 67548 • 1,427
La Crosse, WI 54601–03 • 51,003
La Crosse □, WI • 97,904
La Cygne, KS 66040 • 1,066
Ladd, IL 61329 • 1,283
Ladera Heights, CA 90045 • 6,316
Ladoga, IN 47954 • 1,124
Ladson, SC 29456 • 13,540
Ladue, MO 63124 • 8,847
Lady Lake, FL 32159 • 8,071
Ladysmith, WI 54848 • 3,938
Lafayette, AL 36862 • 3,151
Lafayette, CA 94549 • 23,501
Lafayette, CO 80026 • 14,548
Lafayette, GA 30728 • 6,313
Lafayette, IN 47901–06 • 43,764
Lafayette, LA 70501–09 • 94,440
Lafayette, NC 28304 • 3,200
Lafayette, OR 97127 • 1,292
La Fayette, RI 02852 • 640
Lafayette, TN 37083 • 3,641
Lafayette □, AR • 9,643
Lafayette □, FL • 5,578
Lafayette □, LA • 164,762
Lafayette □, MS • 31,826
Lafayette □, MO • 31,107
Lafayette □, WI • 16,076
Lafayette Southwest, LA • 5,500
La Feria, TX 78559 • 4,360
Lafitte, LA 70067 • 1,507
La Follette, TN 37766 • 7,192
Lafourche □, LA • 85,860
La Grande, OR 97850 • 11,766
La Grange, GA 30240–41 • 25,597
La Grange, IL 60525 • 15,362
Lagrange, IN 46761 • 2,382
La Grange, KY 40031 • 3,853
La Grange, MO 63448 • 1,102
La Grange, NC 28551 • 2,805
Lagrange, OH 44050 • 1,199
La Grange, TX 78945 • 3,951
Lagrange □, IN • 29,477
La Grange Highlands, IL 60525 • 3,660
La Grange Park, IL 60525 • 12,861
Laguna Beach, CA 92651–54 • 23,170
Laguna Hills, CA 92653 • 46,731
Laguna Niguel, CA 92677 • 44,400
La Habra, CA 90631–33 • 51,266
Lahaina, HI 96761 • 9,073
La Harpe, IL 61450 • 1,407
Laie, HI 96762 • 5,577
Laingsburg, MI 48848 • 1,148
La Junta, CO 81050 • 7,637
Lake □, CA • 50,631
Lake □, CO • 6,007
Lake □, FL • 152,104
Lake □, IL • 516,418
Lake □, IN • 475,594
Lake □, MI • 8,583
Lake □, MN • 10,415
Lake □, MT • 21,041
Lake □, OH • 215,499
Lake □, OR • 7,186
Lake □, SD • 10,550
Lake □, TN • 7,129
Lake Alfred, FL 33850 • 3,622
Lake Andes, SD 57356 • 846
Lake Arrowhead, CA 92317 • 6,539
Lake Arthur, LA 70549 • 3,194
Lake Barcroft, VA 22041 • 8,686
Lake Bluff, IL 60044 • 5,513
Lake Butler, FL 32054 • 2,116
Lake Carmel, NY 10512 • 8,489
Lake Charles, LA 70601–29 • 70,580
Lake City, AR 72437 • 1,833
Lake City, FL 32055–56 • 10,005
Lake City, IA 51449 • 1,841
Lake City, MN 55041 • 4,391
Lake City, PA 16423 • 2,519
Lake City, SC 29560 • 7,153
Lake City, TN 37769 • 2,166
Lake Crystal, MN 56055 • 2,084
Lake Delta, NY 13440 • 1,980
Lake Delton, WI 53940 • 1,470
Lake Elmo, MN 55042 • 5,903
Lake Elsinore, CA 92330–31 • 18,285
Lake Erie Beach, NY 14006 • 4,509
Lakefield, MN 56150 • 1,679
Lake Forest, FL 33023 • 5,400
Lake Forest, IL 60045 • 17,836
Lake Geneva, WI 53147 • 5,979
Lake Grove, NY 11755 • 9,612
Lake Hamilton, AR 71913 • 1,331
Lake Havasu City, AZ 86403–05 • 24,363
Lake Helen, FL 32744 • 2,344
Lakehurst, NJ 08733 • 3,078
Lake in the Hills, IL 60102 • 5,866
Lake Jackson, TX 77566 • 22,776
Lake Katrine, NY 12449 • 1,998
Lakeland, FL 33801–13 • 70,576
Lakeland, GA 31635 • 2,467
Lakeland Highlands, FL 33801 • 9,972
Lakeland Village, CA 92330 • 5,159
Lake Linden, MI 49945 • 1,203
Lake Lorraine, FL 32569 • 6,779
Lake Luzerne, NY 12846 • 1,160
Lake Magdalene, FL 33612 • 15,973
Lake Mary, FL 32746 • 5,929
Lake Mills, IA 50450 • 2,143
Lake Mills, WI 53551 • 4,143
Lakemore, OH 44250 • 2,684
Lake Odessa, MI 48849 • 2,256
Lake Of The Woods □, MN • 4,076
Lake Orion, MI 48360–62 • 3,057
Lake Oswego, OR 97034–35 • 30,576
Lake Park, FL 33403 • 6,704
Lake Placid, FL 33852 • 1,158
Lake Placid, NY 12946 • 2,485
Lakeport, CA 95453 • 4,390
Lake Preston, SD 57249 • 663
Lake Providence, LA 71254 • 5,380
Lake Ridge, VA 22192 • 23,862
Lake Ronkonkoma, NY 11779 • 18,997
Lake Shore, MD 21122 • 13,269
Lakeside, CA 92040 • 39,412
Lakeside, CT 06488 • 1,200
Lakeside, FL 32073 • 29,137
Lakeside, OR 97449 • 1,437
Lakeside, VA 23228 • 12,081
Lakeside Park, KY 41017 • 3,131
Lakeside-Pinetop, AZ 85935 • 2,422
Lake Station, IN 46405 • 13,899
Lake Stevens, WA 98258 • 3,380
Lake Telemark, NJ 07866 • 1,121
Lakeview, GA 30741 • 5,237
Lake View, IA 51450 • 1,303
Lakeview, MI 48850 • 1,108
Lake View, NY 14085 • 1,460
Lakeview, NY 11552 • 5,476
Lakeview, OH 43331 • 1,056
Lakeview, OR 97630 • 2,526
Lake Villa, IL 60046 • 2,857
Lake Village, AR 71653 • 2,791
Lakeville, CT 06039 • 1,800
Lakeville, MA 02346 • 1,948
Lakeville, MN 55044 • 24,854
Lakeville, NY 14480 • 1,000
Lake Wales, FL 33853 • 9,670
Lake Wissota, WI 54729 • 2,175
Lakewood, CA 90711–16 • 73,557
Lakewood, CO 80215 • 126,481
Lakewood, IL 60014 • 1,609
Lakewood, IA 50211 • 1,950
Lakewood, NJ 08701 • 26,095
Lakewood, NY 14750 • 3,564
Lakewood, OH 44107 • 59,718
Lakewood, WA 98259 • 58,412
Lakewood Center, WA 98499 • 58,412
Lakewood Park, FL 34951 • 7,211
Lake Worth, FL 33460–67 • 28,564
Lake Zurich, IL 60047 • 14,947
Lakin, KS 67860 • 2,060
Lakota, ND 58344 • 898
La Luz, NM 88337 • 1,625
Lamar, CO 81052 • 8,343
Lamar, MO 64759 • 4,168
Lamar, PA 16848 • 1,200
Lamar, SC 29069 • 1,125
Lamar □, AL • 15,715
Lamar □, GA • 13,038
Lamar □, MS • 30,424
Lamar □, TX • 43,949
La Marque, TX 77568 • 14,120
Lamb □, TX • 15,072
Lambert, MS 38643 • 1,131
Lambertville, MI 48144 • 7,860
Lambertville, NJ 08530 • 3,927
La Mesa, CA 91941–44 • 52,931
La Mesa, NM 88044 • 900
Lamesa, TX 79331 • 10,809
La Mirada, CA 90637–38 • 40,452
Lamoille, NV 89828 • 110
Lamoille □, VT • 19,735
Lamoni, IA 50140 • 2,319
Lamont, CA 93241 • 11,517
La Moure, ND 58458 • 970
La Moure □, ND • 5,383
Lampasas, TX 76550 • 6,382
Lampasas □, TX • 13,521
Lanai City, HI 96763 • 2,400
Lanark, IL 61046 • 1,382
Lancashire, DE 19810 • 1,175
Lancaster, CA 93534–39 • 97,291
Lancaster, KY 40444 • 3,421
Lancaster, NH 03584 • 1,859
Lancaster, NY 14086 • 11,940
Lancaster, OH 43130 • 34,507
Lancaster, PA 17601–05 • 55,551
Lancaster, SC 29720–21 • 8,914
Lancaster, TX 75146 • 22,117
Lancaster, WI 53813 • 4,192
Lancaster □, NE • 213,641
Lancaster □, PA • 422,822
Lancaster □, SC • 54,516
Lancaster □, VA • 10,896
Lancaster Village, DE 19805 • 1,100
Landen, OH 45040 • 9,263
Lander, WY 82520 • 7,023
Lander □, NV • 6,266
Landess, IN 46944 • 1,500
Landis, NC 28088 • 2,333
Land O' Lakes, FL 34639 • 7,892
Landover, MD 20784 • 5,052
Landrum, SC 29356 • 2,347
Lane □, KS • 2,375
Lane □, OR • 282,912
Lanesboro, MA 01237 • 1,000
Lanett, AL 36863 • 8,985
Langdon, ND 58249 • 2,241
Langeloth, PA 15054 • 1,112
Langhorne, PA 19047 • 1,361
Langlade □, WI • 19,505
Langley, SC 29834 • 1,714
Langley Park, MD 20783 • 17,474
Langston, OK 73050 • 1,471
Lanham, MD 20706 • 5,000
Lanier □, GA • 5,531
Lansdale, PA 19446 • 16,362
Lansdowne, MD 21227 • 9,430
Lansdowne, PA 19050 • 11,712
L'Anse, MI 49946 • 2,151
Lansford, PA 18232 • 4,583
Lansing, IL 60438 • 28,086
Lansing, IA 52151 • 1,007
Lansing, KS 66043 • 7,120
Lansing, MI 48901–33 • 127,321
Lantana, FL 33462 • 8,392
La Palma, CA 90623 • 15,392
La Paz □, AZ • 13,844
Lapeer, MI 48446 • 7,759
Lapeer □, MI • 74,768
Lapel, IN 46051 • 1,742
La Place, LA 70068–69 • 24,194
La Plata, MD 20646 • 5,841
La Plata, MO 63549 • 1,401
La Plata □, CO • 32,284
Laporte, CO 80535 • 1,300
La Porte, IN 46350 • 21,507
La Porte, TX 77571–72 • 27,910
La Porte □, IN • 107,066
La Porte City, IA 50651 • 2,128
La Pryor, TX 78872 • 1,343
La Puente, CA 91744–49 • 36,955
Lapwai, ID 83540 • 932
Laramie, WY 82063–71 • 26,687
Laramie □, WY • 73,142
Larchmont, NY 10538 • 6,181
Larchmont North, NY 10538 • 11,240
Laredo, TX 78040–44 • 122,899
Largo, FL 34640–49 • 65,674
Larimer □, CO • 186,136
Larimore, ND 58251 • 1,464
La Riviera, CA 95826 • 10,986
Larkspur, CA 94939 • 11,070
Larksville, PA 18704 • 4,700
Larned, KS 67550 • 4,490
Larose, LA 70373 • 5,772
Larue □, KY • 11,679
La Salle, CO 80645 • 1,783
La Salle, IL 61301 • 9,717
La Salle □, IL • 106,913
La Salle □, LA • 13,662
La Salle □, TX • 5,254
Las Animas, CO 81054 • 2,481
Las Animas □, CO • 13,765
Las Cruces, NM 88001–08 • 62,126
Lassen □, CA • 27,598
Las Vegas, NV 89101–99 • 258,295
Las Vegas, NM 87701 • 14,753
Latah □, ID • 30,617
Lathrop, MO 64465 • 1,794
Lathrop Wells, NV 89020 • 350
Latimer □, OK • 10,333
Laton, CA 93242 • 1,415
Latrobe, PA 15650 • 9,265
Latta, SC 29565 • 1,565
Lauderdale □, AL • 79,661
Lauderdale □, MS • 75,555
Lauderdale □, TN • 23,491
Lauderdale Lakes, FL 33313 • 27,341
Lauderhill, FL 33313 • 49,708
Laughlin, NV 89028–29 • 140
Laughlintown, PA 15655 • 1,000
Laurel, DE 19956 • 3,226
Laurel, FL 34272 • 8,245
Laurel, MD 20707–09 • 19,438
Laurel, MS 39440–42 • 18,827
Laurel, MT 59044 • 5,686
Laurel, VA 23060 • 13,011
Laurel □, KY • 43,438
Laurel Bay, SC 29902 • 4,972
Laureldale, PA 19605 • 3,726
Laurel Hill, NC 28351 • 2,314
Laurence Harbor, NJ 08879 • 6,361
Laurens, IA 50554 • 1,550
Laurens, SC 29360 • 9,694
Laurens □, GA • 39,988
Laurens □, SC • 58,092
Laurinburg, NC 28352–53 • 11,643
Laurium, MI 49913 • 2,268
Lavaca, AR 72941 • 1,253
Lavaca □, TX • 18,690
La Vale, MD 21502 • 5,000
Lavallette, NJ 08735 • 2,299
La Vergne, TN 37086 • 7,499
La Verkin, UT 84745 • 1,771
La Verne, CA 91750 • 30,897
Laverne, OK 73848 • 1,269
La Vista, GA 30329 • 4,900
La Vista, NE 68128 • 9,840
Lavonia, GA 30553 • 1,840
Lawai, HI 96765 • 1,787
Lawndale, CA 90260–61 • 27,331
Lawnside, NJ 08045 • 2,841
Lawrence, IN 46226 • 26,763
Lawrence, KS 66044–46 • 65,608
Lawrence, MA 01840–45 • 70,207
Lawrence, NY 11559 • 6,513
Lawrence □, AL • 31,513
Lawrence □, AR • 17,457
Lawrence □, IL • 15,972
Lawrence □, IN • 42,836
Lawrence □, KY • 13,998
Lawrence □, MS • 12,458
Lawrence □, MO • 30,236
Lawrence □, OH • 61,834
Lawrence □, PA • 96,246
Lawrence □, TN • 35,303
Lawrenceburg, IN 47025 • 4,375
Lawrenceburg, KY 40342 • 5,911
Lawrenceburg, TN 38464 • 10,412
Lawrence Park, PA 16511 • 4,310
Lawrenceville, GA 30243–46 • 16,848
Lawrenceville, IL 62439 • 4,897
Lawrenceville, NJ 08648 • 6,446
Lawrenceville, VA 23868 • 1,486
Lawson, MO 64062 • 1,876
Lawsonia, MD 21817 • 1,326
Lawtell, LA 70550 • 1,014
Lawton, MI 49065 • 1,685
Lawton, OK 73501–07 • 80,561
Layton, UT 84040–41 • 41,784
Laytonville, CA 95454 • 1,133
Lea □, NM • 55,765
Leachville, AR 72438 • 1,743
Lead, SD 57754 • 3,632
Leadville, CO 80461 • 2,629
Leadwood, MO 63653 • 1,247
League City, TX 77573–74 • 30,159
Leake □, MS • 18,436
Leakesville, MS 39451 • 1,129
Lealman, FL 33714 • 21,748
Leavenworth, KS 66048 • 38,495
Leavenworth, WA 98826 • 1,692
Leavenworth □, KS • 64,371
Leavittsburg, OH 44430 • 2,220
Leawood, KS 66206 • 19,693
Lebanon, DE 19901 • 130
Lebanon, IL 62254 • 3,688
Lebanon, IN 46052 • 12,059
Lebanon, KY 40033 • 5,695
Lebanon, MO 65536 • 9,983
Lebanon, NH 03766 • 12,183
Lebanon, NJ 08833 • 1,036
Lebanon, OH 45036 • 10,453
Lebanon, OR 97355 • 10,950
Lebanon, PA 17042 • 24,800
Lebanon, TN 37087–88 • 15,208
Lebanon, VA 24266 • 3,386
Lebanon □, PA • 113,744
Lebanon Junction, KY 40150 • 1,741
Le Center, MN 56057 • 2,006
Le Claire, IA 52753 • 2,734
Lecompte, LA 71346 • 1,592
Lee, MA 01238 • 2,020
Lee □, AL • 87,146
Lee □, AR • 13,053
Lee □, FL • 335,113
Lee □, GA • 16,250
Lee □, IL • 34,392
Lee □, IA • 38,687
Lee □, KY • 7,422
Lee □, MS • 65,581
Lee □, NC • 41,374
Lee □, SC • 18,437
Lee □, TX • 12,854
Lee □, VA • 24,496
Leechburg, PA 15656 • 2,504
Leedom Estates, DE 19720 • 1,100
Leeds, AL 35094 • 9,946
Leelanau □, MI • 16,527
Lee Park, PA 18702 • 3,800
Leesburg, FL 34748–49 • 14,903
Leesburg, GA 31763 • 1,452
Leesburg, OH 45135 • 1,063
Leesburg, VA 22075 • 16,202
Lees Summit, MO 64063–64 • 46,418
Leesville, LA 71446 • 7,638
Leesville, SC 29070 • 2,025
Leetonia, OH 44431 • 2,070
Leetsdale, PA 15056 • 1,387
Leflore □, MS • 37,341
Le Flore □, OK • 43,270
Le Grand, CA 95333 • 1,205
Lehi, UT 84043 • 8,475
Lehigh □, PA • 291,130
Lehigh Acres, FL 33936 • 13,611
Lehighton, PA 18235 • 5,914
Leicester, MA 01524 • 3,200
Leipsic, DE 19901 • 236
Leipsic, OH 45856 • 2,203
Leisure City, FL 33033 • 19,379
Leitchfield, KY 42754–55 • 4,965
Leland, MS 38756 • 6,366
Le Mars, IA 51031 • 8,454
Lemay, MO 63125 • 18,005
Lemhi □, ID • 6,899
Lemmon, SD 57638 • 1,614
Lemmon Valley, NV 89501 • 4,100
Lemon Grove, CA 91945–46 • 23,984
Lemont, IL 60439 • 7,348
Lemont, PA 16851 • 2,613
Lemoore, CA 93245 • 13,622
Lena, IL 61048 • 2,605
Lenawee □, MI • 91,476
Lenexa, KS 66215 • 34,034
Lennox, CA 90304 • 22,757
Lennox, SD 57039 • 1,767
Lenoir, NC 28645 • 14,192
Lenoir □, NC • 57,274
Lenoir City, TN 37771 • 6,147
Lenox, IA 50851 • 1,303
Lenox, MA 01240 • 1,687
Leo, IN 46765 • 1,200
Leominster, MA 01453 • 38,145
Leon, IA 50144 • 2,047
Leon □, FL • 192,493
Leon □, TX • 12,665
Leonard, TX 75452 • 1,744
Leonardo, NJ 07737 • 3,720
Leonardtown, MD 20650 • 1,475
Leonia, NJ 07605 • 8,365
Leon Valley, TX 78238 • 9,581
Leoti, KS 67861 • 1,738
Lepanto, AR 72354 • 2,033
Le Roy, IL 61752 • 2,777
Le Roy, NY 14482 • 4,974
Leslie, MI 49251 • 1,872
Leslie, SC 29730 • 1,102
Leslie □, KY • 13,642
Lester Prairie, MN 55354 • 1,180
Le Sueur, MN 56058 • 3,714
Le Sueur □, MN • 23,239
Letcher □, KY • 27,000
Levelland, TX 79336–38 • 13,986
Levittown, NY 11756 • 53,286
Levittown, PA 19058 • 55,362
Levy □, FL • 25,923
Lewes, DE 19958 • 2,295
Lewis □, ID • 3,516
Lewis □, KY • 13,029
Lewis □, MO • 10,233
Lewis □, NY • 26,796
Lewis □, TN • 9,247
Lewis □, WA • 59,358
Lewis □, WV • 17,223
Lewis and Clark □, MT • 47,495
Lewisburg, OH 45338 • 1,584
Lewisburg, PA 17837 • 5,785
Lewisburg, TN 37091 • 9,879
Lewisburg, WV 24901 • 3,598
Lewisport, KY 42351 • 1,778
Lewiston, ID 83501 • 28,082
Lewiston, ME 04240–43 • 39,757
Lewiston, MN 55952 • 1,298
Lewiston, NY 14092 • 3,048
Lewiston, UT 84320 • 1,532
Lewistown, IL 61542 • 2,572
Lewistown, MT 59457 • 6,051
Lewistown, PA 17044 • 9,341
Lewisville, AR 71845 • 1,424
Lewisville, TX 75067 • 46,521
Lexington, IL 61753 • 1,809
Lexington, KY 40501–96 • 225,366
Lexington, MA 02173 • 28,974
Lexington, MS 39095 • 2,227
Lexington, MO 64067 • 4,860
Lexington, NE 68850 • 6,601
Lexington, NC 27292–93 • 16,581
Lexington, OH 44904 • 4,124
Lexington, OK 73051 • 1,776
Lexington, SC 29071–73 • 3,289
Lexington, TN 38351 • 5,810
Lexington, VA 24450 • 6,959
Lexington □, SC • 167,611
Lexington Park, MD 20653 • 9,943
Libby, MT 59923 • 2,532
Liberal, KS 67901–05 • 16,573
Liberty, IN 47353 • 2,051
Liberty, KY 42539 • 1,937
Liberty, MO 64068 • 20,459
Liberty, NY 12754 • 4,128
Liberty, NC 27298 • 2,047
Liberty, SC 29657 • 3,228
Liberty, TX 77575 • 7,733
Liberty □, FL • 5,569
Liberty □, GA • 52,745
Liberty □, MT • 2,295
Liberty □, TX • 52,726
Liberty Acres, CA 90250 • 4,700
Liberty Center, OH 43532 • 1,084
Liberty Lake, WA 99019 • 2,015
Libertyville, IL 60048 • 19,174
Licking, MO 65542 • 1,328
Licking □, OH • 128,300
Lidgerwood, ND 58053 • 799
Lighthouse Point, FL 33064 • 10,378
Ligonier, IN 46767 • 3,443
Ligonier, PA 15658 • 1,638
Lihue, HI 96766 • 5,536
Lilbourn, MO 63862 • 1,378
Lilburn, GA 30247 • 9,301
Lillington, NC 27546 • 2,048
Lilly, PA 15938 • 1,162
Lima, NY 14485 • 2,165
Lima, OH 45801–09 • 45,549
Limestone, ME 04750–51 • 1,245
Limestone □, AL • 54,135
Limestone □, TX • 20,946
Limon, CO 80828 • 1,831
Lincoln, AL 35096 • 2,941
Lincoln, AR 72744 • 1,460
Lincoln, CA 95648 • 7,248
Lincoln, DE 19960 • 500
Lincoln, IL 62656 • 15,418
Lincoln, KS 67455 • 1,381
Lincoln, ME 04457 • 3,399
Lincoln, MA 01773 • 2,860
Lincoln, NE 68501–72 • 191,972
Lincoln □, AR • 13,690
Lincoln □, CO • 4,529
Lincoln □, GA • 7,442
Lincoln □, ID • 3,308
Lincoln □, KS • 3,653
Lincoln □, KY • 20,045
Lincoln □, LA • 41,745
Lincoln □, ME • 30,357
Lincoln □, MN • 6,890
Lincoln □, MS • 30,278
Lincoln □, MO • 28,892
Lincoln □, MT • 17,481
Lincoln □, NE • 32,508
Lincoln □, NV • 3,775
Lincoln □, NM • 12,219
Lincoln □, NC • 50,319
Lincoln □, OK • 29,216
Lincoln □, OR • 38,889
Lincoln □, SD • 15,427
Lincoln □, TN • 28,157
Lincoln □, WA • 8,864
Lincoln □, WV • 21,382
Lincoln □, WI • 26,993
Lincoln □, WY • 12,625
Lincoln Acres, CA 91947 • 1,800
Lincoln City, OR 97367 • 5,892
Lincoln Heights, OH 45215 • 4,805
Lincoln Park, CO 81212 • 3,728
Lincoln Park, GA 30286 • 1,755
Lincoln Park, MI 48146 • 41,832
Lincoln Park, NJ 07035 • 10,978
Lincolnshire, IL 60069 • 4,931
Lincolnton, GA 30817 • 1,476
Lincolnton, NC 28092 • 6,847
Lincoln Village, CA 95207 • 4,236
Lincoln Village, OH 43228 • 9,958

Lincolnwood, IL 60645 • 11,365
Lincroft, NJ 07738 • 4,740
Linda, CA 95901 • 13,033
Lindale, GA 30147 • 4,187
Lindale, TX 75771 • 2,428
Linden, AL 36748 • 2,548
Linden, MI 48451 • 2,415
Linden, NJ 07036 • 36,701
Linden, TN 37096 • 1,099
Linden, TX 75563 • 2,375
Lindenhurst, IL 60046 • 8,038
Lindenhurst, NY 11757 • 26,879
Lindenwold, NJ 08021 • 18,734
Lindgren Acres, FL 33177 • 22,290
Lindon, UT 84042 • 3,818
Lindsay, CA 93247 • 8,338
Lindsay, OK 73052 • 2,947
Lindsborg, KS 67456 • 3,076
Lindstrom, MN 55045 • 2,461
Linesville, PA 16424 • 1,166
Lineville, AL 36266 • 2,394
Lingle, WY 82223 • 473
Linglestown, PA 17112 • 3,700
Linn, MO 65051 • 1,148
Linn □, IA • 168,767
Linn □, KS • 8,254
Linn □, MO • 13,885
Linn □, OR • 91,227
Lino Lakes, MN 55014 • 8,807
Linthicum Heights, MD • 2,950
Linthicum Heights, MD 21090 • 7,547
Linton, IN 47441 • 5,814
Linton, ND 58552 • 1,410
Linwood, NJ 08221 • 6,866
Lipscomb, AL 35020 • 2,892
Lipscomb □, TX • 3,143
Lisbon, IA 52253 • 1,452
Lisbon, ME 04250 • 1,240
Lisbon, NH 03585 • 1,246
Lisbon, ND 58054 • 2,177
Lisbon, OH 44432 • 3,037
Lisbon Falls, ME 04252 • 4,674
Lisle, IL 60532 • 19,512
Litchfield, CT 06759 • 1,378
Litchfield, IL 62056 • 6,883
Litchfield, MI 49252 • 1,317
Litchfield, MN 55355 • 6,041
Litchfield □, CT • 174,092
Litchfield Park, AZ 85340 • 3,303
Lithia Springs, GA 30057 • 11,403
Lithonia, GA 30058 • 2,448
Lititz, PA 17543 • 8,280
Little Canada, MN 55110 • 8,971
Little Chute, WI 54140 • 9,207
Little Compton, RI 02837 • 500
Little Creek, DE 19961 • 167
Little Falls, MN 56345 • 7,232
Little Falls, NJ 07424 • 11,294
Little Falls, NY 13365 • 5,829
Little Ferry, NJ 07643 • 9,989
Littlefield, TX 79339 • 6,489
Little River □, AR • 13,966
Little Rock, AR 72201–31 • 175,795
Little Silver, NJ 07739 • 5,721
Littlestown, PA 17340 • 2,974
Littleton, CO 80120–27 • 33,685
Littleton, MA 01460 • 2,867
Littleton, NH 03561 • 4,633
Little Valley, NY 14755 • 1,188
Live Oak, CA 95062 • 15,212
Live Oak, CA 95953 • 4,320
Live Oak, FL 32060 • 6,332
Live Oak, TX 78233 • 10,023
Live Oak □, TX • 9,556
Live Oak Manor, LA 70094 • 2,150
Livermore, CA 94550 • 56,741
Livermore, KY 42352 • 1,534
Livermore Falls, ME 04254 • 1,935
Livingston, AL 35470 • 3,530
Livingston, CA 95334 • 7,317
Livingston, MT 59047 • 6,701
Livingston, NJ 07039 • 26,609
Livingston, TN 38570 • 3,809
Livingston, TX 77351 • 5,019
Livingston □, IL • 39,301
Livingston □, KY • 9,062
Livingston □, LA • 70,526
Livingston □, MI • 115,645
Livingston □, MO • 14,592
Livingston □, NY • 62,372
Livingston Manor, NY 12758 • 1,482
Livonia, MI 48150–54 • 100,850
Livonia, NY 14487 • 1,434
Llangollen Estates, DE 19720 • 1,070
Llano, TX 78643 • 2,962
Llano □, TX • 11,631
Lloyd Harbor, NY 11743 • 3,343
Lochearn, MD 21207 • 25,240
Loch Lomond, VA 22110 • 3,292
Lockhart, FL 32810 • 11,636
Lockhart, TX 78644 • 9,205
Lock Haven, PA 17745 • 9,230
Lockland, OH 45215 • 4,357
Lockney, TX 79241 • 2,207
Lockport, IL 60441 • 9,401
Lockport, LA 70374 • 2,503
Lockport, NY 14094 • 24,426
Lockwood, MO 65682 • 1,041
Lockwood, MT 59101 • 3,967
Locust, NC 28097 • 1,940
Locust Grove, GA 30248 • 1,681
Locust Grove, OK 74352 • 1,326
Lodi, CA 95240–42 • 51,874
Lodi, NJ 07644 • 22,355
Lodi, OH 44254 • 3,042
Lodi, WI 53555 • 2,093
Logan, IA 51546 • 1,401
Logan, OH 43138 • 6,725
Logan, UT 84321 • 32,762
Logan, WV 25601 • 2,206
Logan □, AR • 20,557
Logan □, CO • 17,567
Logan □, IL • 30,798
Logan □, KS • 3,081
Logan □, KY • 24,416
Logan □, NE • 878
Logan □, ND • 2,847
Logan □, OH • 42,310
Logan □, OK • 29,011
Logan □, WV • 43,032
Logandale, NV 89021 • 500
Logansport, IN 46947 • 16,812
Logansport, LA 71049 • 1,390
Loganville, GA 30249 • 3,180
Lolo, MT 59847 • 2,746
Loma Linda, CA 92354 • 17,400
Lombard, IL 60148 • 39,408
Lomira, WI 53048 • 1,542
Lomita, CA 90717 • 19,382
Lompoc, CA 93436 • 37,649
Lonaconing, MD 21539 • 1,122
London, KY 40741 • 5,757
London, OH 43140 • 7,807
Londonderry, NH 03053 • 10,114
Londontown, MD 21037 • 6,992
Lone Grove, OK 73443 • 4,114
Lone Pine, CA 93545 • 1,818
Long □, GA • 6,202
Long Beach, CA 90801–88 • 429,433
Long Beach, IN 46360 • 2,044
Long Beach, MS 39560 • 15,804
Long Beach, NY 11561 • 33,510
Long Beach, WA 98631 • 1,236
Longboat Key, FL 34228 • 5,937
Long Branch, NJ 07740 • 28,658
Long Lake, IL 60041 • 2,888
Longmeadow, MA 01106 • 15,467
Longmont, CO 80501–02 • 51,555
Longport, NJ 08403 • 1,224
Long Prairie, MN 56347 • 2,786
Long Valley, NJ 07853 • 1,744
Long View, NC 28601 • 3,229
Longview, TX 75601–15 • 70,311
Longview, WA 98632 • 31,499
Longwood, FL 32750 • 13,316
Lonoke, AR 72086 • 4,022
Lonoke □, AR • 39,268
Lonsdale, MN 55046 • 1,252
Lonsdale, RI 02865 • 3,850
Loogootee, IN 47553 • 2,884
Lookout Mountain, TN 37350 • 1,901
Lorain, OH 44052–55 • 71,245
Lorain □, OH • 271,126
Lordsburg, NM 88045 • 2,951
Lorenzo, TX 79343 • 1,208
Loretto, PA 15940 • 1,072
Loretto, TN 38469 • 1,515
Loris, SC 29569 • 2,067
Lorton, VA 22079 • 15,385
Los Alamitos, CA 90720–21 • 11,676
Los Alamos, NM 87544 • 11,455
Los Alamos □, NM • 18,115
Los Altos, CA 94022–24 • 26,303
Los Altos Hills, CA 94022 • 7,514
Los Angeles, CA 90001–99 • 3,485,398
Los Angeles □, CA • 8,863,164
Los Banos, CA 93635 • 14,519
Los Fresnos, TX 78566 • 2,473
Los Gatos, CA 95030–32 • 27,357
Los Lunas, NM 87031 • 6,013
Los Molinos, CA 96055 • 1,709
Los Nietos, CA 90606 • 7,100
Los Osos, CA 93402 • 8,000
Los Padillas, NM 87105 • 2,400
Los Ranchos de Albuquerque, NM 87107 • 3,955
Los Serranos, CA 91709 • 7,099
Lost Hills, CA 93249 • 1,212
Loudon, TN 37774 • 4,026
Loudon □, TN • 31,255
Loudonville, NY 12211 • 10,822
Loudonville, OH 44842 • 2,915
Loudoun □, VA • 86,129
Louisa, KY 41230 • 1,990
Louisa, VA 23093 • 1,088
Louisa □, IA • 11,592
Louisa □, VA • 20,325
Louisburg, KS 66053 • 1,964
Louisburg, NC 27549 • 3,037
Louisiana, MO 63353 • 3,967
Louisville, CO 80027 • 12,361
Louisville, GA 30434 • 2,429
Louisville, IL 62858 • 1,098
Louisville, KY 40201–99 • 269,063
Louisville, MS 39339 • 7,169
Louisville, OH 44641 • 8,087
Loup □, NE • 683
Loup City, NE 68853 • 1,104
Love □, OK • 8,157
Loveland, CO 80537–39 • 37,352
Loveland, OH 45140 • 9,990
Loveland Park, OH 45140 • 1,357
Lovell, WY 82431 • 2,131
Lovelock, NV 89419 • 2,069
Loves Park, IL 61111 • 15,462
Loving, NM 88256 • 1,243
Loving □, TX • 107
Lovington, IL 61937 • 1,143
Lovington, NM 88260 • 9,322
Lowell, AR 72745 • 1,224
Lowell, IN 46356 • 6,430
Lowell, MA 01850–54 • 103,439
Lowell, MI 49331 • 3,983
Lowell, NC 28098 • 2,704
Lowellville, OH 44436 • 1,349
Lower Burrell, PA 15068 • 12,251
Lower Merion Township, PA 19003 • 59,629
Lower Paia, HI 96779 • 1,500
Lowndes □, AL • 12,658
Lowndes □, GA • 75,981
Lowndes □, MS • 59,308
Lowville, NY 13367 • 3,632
Loxley, AL 36551 • 1,161
Loyal, WI 54446 • 1,244
Loyall, KY 40854 • 1,100
Lubbock, TX 79401–99 • 186,206
Lubbock □, TX • 222,636
Lucas □, IA • 9,070
Lucas □, OH • 462,361
Lucasville, OH 45648 • 1,575
Luce □, MI • 5,763
Lucedale, MS 39452 • 2,592
Lucerne, CA 95458 • 2,011
Lucernemines, PA 15754 • 1,074
Lucerne Valley, CA 92356 • 1,300
Luck, WI 54853 • 1,022
Ludington, MI 49431 • 8,507
Ludlow, KY 41016 • 4,736
Ludlow, MA 01056 • 18,150
Ludlow, VT 05149 • 1,123
Ludowici, GA 31316 • 1,291
Lufkin, TX 75901–03 • 30,206
Lugoff, SC 29078 • 3,211
Lula, GA 30554 • 1,018
Luling, LA 70070 • 2,803
Luling, TX 78648 • 4,661
Lumber City, GA 31549 • 1,429
Lumberport, WV 26386 • 1,014
Lumberton, MS 39455 • 2,121
Lumberton, NC 28358–59 • 18,601
Lumpkin, GA 31815 • 1,250
Lumpkin □, GA • 14,573
Luna □, NM • 18,110
Luna Pier, MI 48157 • 1,507
Lund, NV 89317 • 330
Lunenburg, MA 01462 • 1,694
Lunenburg □, VA • 11,419
Luray, VA 22835 • 4,587
Lusk, WY 82225 • 1,504
Lutcher, LA 70071 • 3,907
Luther, OK 73054 • 1,560
Lutherville-Timonium, MD 21093 • 16,442
Lutz, FL 33549 • 10,552
Luverne, AL 36049 • 2,555
Luverne, MN 56156 • 4,382
Luxemburg, WI 54217 • 1,151
Luxora, AR 72358 • 1,338
Luzerne, PA 18709 • 3,206
Luzerne □, PA • 328,149
Lycoming □, PA • 118,710
Lyford, TX 78569 • 1,674
Lykens, PA 17048 • 1,986
Lyman, SC 29365 • 2,271
Lyman, WY 82937 • 1,896
Lyman □, SD • 3,638
Lynbrook, NY 11563 • 19,208
Lynch, KY 40855 • 1,166
Lynchburg, OH 45142 • 1,212
Lynchburg, TN 37352 • 4,721
Lynchburg, VA 24501–06 • 66,049
Lyncourt, NY 13208 • 4,516
Lynden, WA 98264 • 5,709
Lyndhurst, NJ 07071 • 18,262
Lyndhurst, OH 44124 • 15,982
Lyndon, KY 40222 • 8,037
Lyndonville, VT 05851 • 1,255
Lyndora, PA 16045 • 3,000
Lynn, IN 47355 • 1,183
Lynn, MA 01901–08 • 81,245
Lynn □, TX • 6,758
Lynne Acres, MD 21207 • 5,910
Lynnfield, MA 01940 • 11,274
Lynn Garden, TN 37665 • 7,213
Lynn Garden, TN 37665 • 2,340
Lynn Haven, FL 32444 • 9,298
Lynnwood, WA 98036–37 • 28,695
Lynwood, CA 90262 • 61,945
Lyon □, IA • 11,952
Lyon □, KS • 34,732
Lyon □, KY • 6,624
Lyon □, MN • 24,789
Lyon □, NV • 20,001
Lyon Mountain, NY 12952 • 1,000
Lyons, CO 80540 • 1,227
Lyons, GA 30436 • 4,502
Lyons, IL 60534 • 9,828
Lyons, KS 67554 • 3,688
Lyons, NE 68038 • 1,144
Lyons, NY 14489 • 4,280
Lytle, TX 78052 • 2,255

M

Mabank, TX 75147 • 1,739
Mableton, GA 30059 • 25,725
Mabscott, WV 25871 • 1,543
Mabton, WA 98935 • 1,482
MacClenny, FL 32063 • 3,966
Macedon, NY 14502 • 1,400
Macedonia, OH 44056 • 7,509
Machesney Park, IL 61111 • 19,033
Machias, ME 04654 • 1,773
Mackinac □, MI • 10,674
Mackinaw, IL 61755 • 1,331
Mackinaw City, MI 49701 • 875
Macomb, IL 61455 • 19,952
Macomb □, MI • 717,400
Macon, GA 31201–95 • 106,612
Macon, IL 62544 • 1,282
Macon, MS 39341 • 2,256
Macon, MO 63552 • 5,571
Macon □, AL • 24,928
Macon □, GA • 13,114
Macon □, IL • 117,206
Macon □, MO • 15,345
Macon □, NC • 23,499
Macon □, TN • 15,906
Macoupin □, IL • 47,679
Macungie, PA 18062 • 2,597
Madawaska, ME 04756 • 3,653
Madeira, OH 45243 • 9,141
Madelia, MN 56062 • 2,237
Madera, CA 93637–39 • 29,281
Madera □, CA • 88,090
Madill, OK 73446 • 3,069
Madison, AL 35758 • 14,904
Madison, AR 72359 • 1,263
Madison, CT 06443 • 2,139
Madison, FL 32340 • 3,345
Madison, GA 30650 • 3,483
Madison, IL 62060 • 4,629
Madison, IN 47250 • 12,006
Madison, ME 04950 • 2,956
Madison, MN 56256 • 1,951
Madison, MS 39110 • 7,471
Madison, NE 68748 • 2,135
Madison, NJ 07940 • 15,850
Madison, NC 27025 • 2,371
Madison, OH 44057 • 2,477
Madison, SD 57042 • 6,257
Madison, WV 25130 • 3,051
Madison, WI 53701–19 • 191,262
Madison □, AL • 238,912
Madison □, AR • 11,618
Madison □, FL • 16,569
Madison □, GA • 21,050
Madison □, ID • 23,674
Madison □, IL • 249,238
Madison □, IN • 130,669
Madison □, IA • 12,483
Madison □, KY • 57,508
Madison □, LA • 12,463
Madison □, MS • 53,794
Madison □, MO • 11,127
Madison □, MT • 5,989
Madison □, NE • 32,655
Madison □, NY • 69,120
Madison □, NC • 16,953
Madison □, OH • 37,068
Madison □, TN • 77,982
Madison □, TX • 10,931
Madison □, VA • 11,949
Madison Heights, MI 48071 • 32,196
Madison Heights, VA 24572 • 11,700
Madisonville, KY 42431 • 16,200
Madisonville, TN 37354 • 3,033
Madisonville, TX 77864 • 3,569
Madras, OR 97741 • 3,443
Madrid, IA 50156 • 2,395
Maeser, UT 84078 • 2,598
Magalia, CA 95954 • 8,987
Magdalena, NM 87825 • 861
Magee, MS 39111 • 3,607
Magna, UT 84044 • 17,829
Magnolia, AR 71753 • 11,151
Magnolia, MS 39652 • 2,245
Magnolia, NJ 08049 • 4,861
Magoffin □, KY • 13,077
Mahanoy City, PA 17948 • 5,209
Mahaska □, IA • 21,522
Mahnomen, MN 56557 • 1,154
Mahnomen □, MN • 5,044
Mahomet, IL 61853 • 3,103
Mahoning □, OH • 264,806
Mahopac, NY 10541 • 7,755
Mahwah, NJ 07430 • 7,500
Maiden, NC 28650 • 2,574
Maili, HI 96792 • 6,059
Maine, NY 13802 • 1,110
Maitland, FL 32751 • 9,110
Maize, KS 67101 • 1,520
Major □, OK • 8,055
Makaha, HI 96792 • 7,990
Makakilo City, HI 96706 • 9,828
Makawao, HI 96768 • 5,405
Makaweli, HI 96769 • 700
Malabar, FL 32950 • 1,977
Malad City, ID 83252 • 1,946
Malaga, NJ 08328 • 2,140
Malakoff, TX 75148 • 2,038
Malden, MA 02148 • 53,884
Malden, MO 63863 • 5,123
Malheur □, OR • 26,038
Malibu, CA 90264–65 • 10,000
Malone, NY 12953 • 6,777
Malta, MT 59538 • 2,340
Malvern, AR 72104 • 9,256
Malvern, IA 51551 • 1,210
Malvern, OH 44644 • 1,112
Malvern, PA 19355 • 2,944
Malverne, NY 11565 • 9,054
Mamaroneck, NY 10543 • 17,325
Mammoth, AZ 85618 • 1,845
Mammoth Lakes, CA 93546 • 4,785
Mammoth Spring, AR 72554 • 1,097
Mamou, LA 70554 • 3,483
Manahawkin, NJ 08050 • 1,594
Manasquan, NJ 08736 • 5,369
Manassas, VA 22110–11 • 27,957
Manassas Park, VA 22111 • 6,734
Manatee □, FL • 211,707
Manawa, WI 54949 • 1,169
Mancelona, MI 49659 • 1,370
Manchaug, MA 01526 • 1,000
Manchester, CT 06040 • 51,618
Manchester, GA 31816 • 4,104
Manchester, IA 52057 • 5,137
Manchester, KY 40962 • 1,634
Manchester, MD 21102 • 2,810
Manchester, MA 01944 • 5,424
Manchester, MI 48158 • 1,753
Manchester, MO 63011 • 6,542
Manchester, NH 03101–10 • 99,567
Manchester, NY 14504 • 1,598
Manchester, OH 45144 • 2,223
Manchester, PA 17345 • 1,830
Manchester, TN 37355 • 7,709
Manchester, VT 05254 • 561
Manchester Center, VT 05255 • 1,574
Mandan, ND 58554 • 15,177
Mandeville, LA 70448 • 7,083
Mangum, OK 73554 • 3,344
Manhasset, NY 11030 • 7,718
Manhattan, KS 66502 • 37,712
Manhattan, MT 59741 • 1,034
Manhattan Beach, CA 90266 • 32,063
Manheim, PA 17545 • 5,011
Manila, AR 72442 • 2,635
Manistee, MI 49660 • 6,734
Manistee □, MI • 21,265
Manistique, MI 49854 • 3,456
Manito, IL 61546 • 1,711
Manitou Springs, CO 80829 • 4,535
Manitowoc, WI 54220–21 • 32,520
Manitowoc □, WI • 80,421
Mankato, KS 66956 • 1,037
Mankato, MN 56001–03 • 31,477
Manlius, NY 13104 • 4,764
Manly, IA 50456 • 1,349
Mannford, OK 74044 • 1,826
Manning, IA 51455 • 1,484
Manning, SC 29102 • 4,428
Mannington, WV 26582 • 2,184
Manokotak, AK 99628 • 385
Manomet, MA 02345 • 1,500
Manor, TX 78653 • 1,041
Manorhaven, NY 11050 • 5,672
Mansfield, AR 72944 • 1,018
Mansfield, LA 71052 • 5,389
Mansfield, MA 02048 • 7,170
Mansfield, MO 65704 • 1,429
Mansfield, OH 44901–07 • 50,627
Mansfield, PA 16933 • 3,538
Mansfield, TX 76063 • 15,607
Mansfield Center, CT 06250 • 1,043
Manson, IA 50563 • 1,844
Mansura, LA 71350 • 1,601
Manteca, CA 95336 • 40,773
Manteno, IL 60950 • 3,488
Manti, UT 84642 • 2,268
Manton, MI 49663 • 1,161
Mantua, NJ 08051 • 1,350
Mantua, OH 44255 • 1,178
Mantua Hills, VA 22031 • 1,600
Manvel, TX 77578 • 3,733
Manville, NJ 08835 • 10,567
Manville, RI 02838 • 3,030
Many, LA 71449 • 3,112
Many Farms, AZ 86538 • 1,294
Maple Bluff, WI 53704 • 1,352
Maple Grove, MN 55369 • 38,736
Maple Heights, OH 44137 • 27,089
Maple Lake, MN 55358 • 1,394
Maple Plain, MN 55359 • 2,005
Maple Shade, NJ 08052 • 19,211
Mapleton, IA 51034 • 1,294
Mapleton, MN 56065 • 1,526
Mapleton, UT 84663 • 3,572
Maple Valley, WA 98038 • 1,211
Mapleville, RI 02839 • 1,300
Maplewood, MN 55109 • 30,954
Maplewood, MO 63143 • 9,962
Maplewood, NJ 07040 • 21,756
Maquoketa, IA 52060 • 6,111
Marana, AZ 85653 • 2,187
Marathon, FL 33050 • 8,857
Marathon, NY 13803 • 1,107
Marathon, WI 54448 • 1,606
Marathon □, WI • 115,400
Marble Falls, TX 78654 • 4,007
Marblehead, MA 01945 • 19,971
Marble Hill, MO 63764 • 1,447
Marbleton, WY 83113 • 634
Marbury, MD 20658 • 1,244
Marceline, MO 64658 • 2,645
Marcellus, MI 49067 • 1,193
Marco, FL 33937 • 9,493
Marcus, IA 51035 • 1,171
Marcus Hook, PA 19061 • 2,546
Marengo, IL 60152 • 4,768
Marengo, IA 52301 • 2,270
Marengo □, AL • 23,084
Marfa, TX 79843 • 2,424
Margate, FL 33063 • 42,985
Margate, MD 21060 • 1,900
Margate City, NJ 08402 • 8,431
Marianna, AR 72360 • 5,910
Marianna, FL 32446 • 6,292
Maricopa, AZ 85239 • 1,600
Maricopa, CA 93252 • 1,193
Maricopa □, AZ • 2,122,101
Mariemont, OH 45227 • 3,118
Marienville, PA 16239 • 1,400
Maries □, MO • 7,976
Marietta, GA 30060–68 • 44,129
Marietta, OH 45750 • 15,026
Marietta, OK 73448 • 2,306
Marin □, CA • 230,096
Marina, CA 93933 • 26,436
Marina del Rey, CA 90292 • 7,431
Marine City, MI 48039 • 4,556
Marinette, WI 54143 • 11,843
Marinette □, WI • 40,548
Maringouin, LA 70757 • 1,149
Marion, AL 36756 • 4,211
Marion, AR 72364 • 4,391
Marion, IL 62959 • 14,545
Marion, IN 46952–53 • 32,618
Marion, IA 52302 • 20,403
Marion, KS 66861 • 1,906
Marion, KY 42064 • 3,320
Marion, MA 02738 • 1,426
Marion, MS 39342 • 1,359
Marion, NY 14505 • 1,080
Marion, NC 28752 • 4,765
Marion, OH 43301–02 • 34,075
Marion, PA 17235 • 1,000
Marion, SC 29571 • 7,658
Marion, SD 57043 • 831
Marion, VA 24354 • 6,630
Marion, WI 54950 • 1,242
Marion □, AL • 29,830
Marion □, AR • 12,001
Marion □, FL • 194,833
Marion □, GA • 5,590
Marion □, IL • 41,561
Marion □, IN • 797,159
Marion □, IA • 30,001
Marion □, KS • 12,888
Marion □, KY • 16,499
Marion □, MS • 25,544
Marion □, MO • 27,682
Marion □, OH • 64,274
Marion □, OR • 228,483
Marion □, SC • 33,899
Marion □, TN • 24,860
Marion □, TX • 9,984
Marion □, WV • 57,249
Marionville, MO 65705 • 1,920
Mariposa, CA 95338 • 1,152
Mariposa □, CA • 14,302
Marissa, IL 62257 • 2,375
Marked Tree, AR 72365 • 3,100
Markesan, WI 53946 • 1,496
Markham, IL 60426 • 13,136
Markham, TX 77456 • 1,206
Markle, IN 46770 • 1,208
Marks, MS 38646 • 1,758
Marksville, LA 71351 • 5,526
Marlboro, NY 12542 • 2,200
Marlboro □, SC • 29,361
Marlborough, CT 06447 • 5,535
Marlborough, MA 01752 • 31,813
Marlborough, NH 03455 • 1,211
Marlene Village, OR 97005 • 1,500
Marlette, MI 48453 • 1,924
Marley, MD 21060 • 7,100
Marlin, TX 76661 • 6,386
Marlinton, WV 24954 • 1,148
Marlow, OK 73055 • 4,416
Marlow Heights, MD 20748 • 5,885
Marlton, NJ 08053 • 10,228
Marmaduke, AR 72443 • 1,164
Marmet, WV 25315 • 1,879
Maroa, IL 61756 • 1,602
Marquette, MI 49855 • 21,977
Marquette □, MI • 70,887
Marquette □, WI • 12,321
Marquette Heights, IL 61554 • 3,077
Marrero, LA 70072–73 • 36,671
Mars, PA 16046 • 1,713
Marseilles, IL 61341 • 4,811
Marshall, AR 72650 • 1,318
Marshall, IL 62441 • 3,555
Marshall, MI 49068 • 6,891
Marshall, MN 56258 • 12,023
Marshall, MO 65340 • 12,711
Marshall, TX 75670–71 • 23,682
Marshall, WI 53559 • 2,329
Marshall □, AL • 70,832
Marshall □, IL • 12,846
Marshall □, IN • 42,182

United States Populations and ZIP Codes

Marshall □, IA • *38,276*
Marshall □, KS • *11,705*
Marshall □, KY • *27,205*
Marshall □, MN • *10,993*
Marshall □, MS • *30,361*
Marshall □, OK • *10,829*
Marshall □, SD • *4,844*
Marshall □, TN • *21,539*
Marshall □, WV • *37,356*
Marshallton, DE 19808 • *1,765*
Marshalltown, IA 50158 • *25,178*
Marshallville, GA 31057 • *1,457*
Marshfield, MA 02050 • *4,002*
Marshfield, MO 65706 • *4,374*
Marshfield, WI 54449 • *19,291*
Marshfield Hills, MA 02051 • *2,201*
Mars Hill, ME 04758 • *1,500*
Mars Hill, NC 28754 • *1,611*
Marshville, NC 28103 • *2,020*
Marsing, ID 83639 • *798*
Marstons Mills, MA 02648 • *8,017*
Mart, TX 76664 • *2,004*
Martha Lake, WA 98012 • *10,155*
Martin, SD 57551 • *1,151*
Martin, TN 38237 • *8,600*
Martin □, FL • *100,900*
Martin □, IN • *10,369*
Martin □, KY • *12,526*
Martin □, MN • *22,914*
Martin □, NC • *25,078*
Martin □, TX • *4,956*
Martinez, CA 94553 • *31,808*
Martinez, GA 30907 • *33,731*
Martinsburg, PA 16662 • *2,119*
Martinsburg, WV 25401 • *14,073*
Martins Ferry, OH 43935 • *7,990*
Martinsville, IL 62442 • *1,161*
Martinsville, IN 46151 • *11,677*
Martinsville, VA 24112–15 • *16,162*
Marvell, AR 72366 • *1,545*
Maryland City, MD 20724 • *6,813*
Maryland Heights, MO 63043 • *25,407*
Marysville, CA 95901 • *12,324*
Marysville, KS 66508 • *3,359*
Marysville, MI 48040 • *8,515*
Marysville, OH 43040 • *9,656*
Marysville, PA 17053 • *2,425*
Marysville, WA 98270 • *10,328*
Maryville, MO 64468 • *10,663*
Maryville, TN 37801–04 • *19,208*
Mascot, TN 37806 • *2,138*
Mascoutah, IL 62258 • *5,511*
Mason, MI 48854 • *6,768*
Mason, NV 89447 • *400*
Mason, OH 45040 • *11,452*
Mason, TX 76856 • *2,041*
Mason, WV 25260 • *1,053*
Mason □, IL • *16,269*
Mason □, KY • *16,666*
Mason □, MI • *25,537*
Mason □, TX • *3,423*
Mason □, WA • *38,341*
Mason □, WV • *25,178*
Masonboro, NC 28403 • *7,010*
Mason City, IL 62664 • *2,323*
Mason City, IA 50401 • *29,040*
Masontown, PA 15461 • *3,759*
Massac □, IL • *14,752*
Massapequa, NY 11758 • *22,018*
Massapequa Park, NY 11762 • *18,044*
Massena, NY 13662 • *11,719*
Massillon, OH 44646–48 • *31,007*
Mastic, NY 11950 • *13,778*
Mastic Beach, NY 11951 • *10,293*
Masury, OH 44438 • *1,836*
Matagorda □, TX • *36,928*
Matamoras, PA 18336 • *1,934*
Matawan, NJ 07747 • *9,270*
Mather, PA 15346 • *1,300*
Mathews □, VA • *8,348*
Mathis, TX 78368 • *5,423*
Matoaca, VA 23803 • *1,967*
Mattapoisett, MA 02739 • *2,949*
Matteson, IL 60443 • *11,378*
Matthews, NC 28105–06 • *13,651*
Mattituck, NY 11952 • *3,902*
Mattoon, IL 61938 • *18,441*
Mattydale, NY 13211 • *6,418*
Matunuck, RI 02879 • *550*
Maud, OK 74854 • *1,204*
Maugansville, MD 21767 • *1,707*
Maui □, HI • *100,374*
Mauldin, SC 29662 • *11,587*
Maumee, OH 43537 • *15,561*
Maunaloa, HI 96770 • *405*
Maunawili, HI 96734 • *4,847*
Maury □, TN • *54,812*
Mauston, WI 53948 • *3,439*
Maverick □, TX • *36,378*
Maxton, NC 28364 • *2,373*
Maxwell Acres, WV 26041 • *1,000*
Mayer, AZ 86333 • *1,800*
Mayes □, OK • *33,366*
Mayfield, KY 42066 • *9,935*
Mayfield, PA 18433 • *1,890*
Mayfield Heights, OH 44124 • *19,847*
Mayflower, AR 72106 • *1,415*
Mayflower Village, CA 91016 • *4,978*
Maynard, MA 01754 • *10,325*
Maynardville, TN 37807 • *1,298*
Mayo, MD 21106 • *2,537*
Mayodan, NC 27027 • *2,471*
Mays Landing, NJ 08330 • *2,090*
Maysville, KY 41056 • *7,169*
Maysville, MO 64469 • *1,176*
Maysville, OK 73057 • *1,203*
Mayville, MI 48744 • *1,010*
Mayville, NY 14757 • *1,636*
Mayville, ND 58257 • *2,092*
Mayville, WI 53050 • *4,374*
Maywood, CA 90270 • *27,850*
Maywood, IL 60153–54 • *27,139*
Maywood, NJ 07607 • *9,473*
Mazomanie, WI 53560 • *1,377*
McAdoo, PA 18237 • *2,459*
McAlester, OK 74501–02 • *16,370*
McAllen, TX 78501–04 • *84,021*
McAlmont, AR 72117 • *1,800*
McAlpine, MD 21043 • *2,230*
McArthur, OH 45651 • *1,541*
McCall, ID 83638 • *2,005*
McCamey, TX 79752 • *2,493*
McCandless, PA 15237 • *28,781*
McCaysville, GA 30555 • *1,065*
McClain □, OK • *22,795*
McCleary, WA 98557 • *1,235*
McCloud, CA 96057 • *1,555*
McClure, PA 17841 • *1,070*
McColl, SC 29570 • *2,685*
McComb, MS 39648 • *11,591*
McComb, OH 45858 • *1,544*
McCone □, MT • *2,276*
McConnellsburg, PA 17233 • *1,106*
McConnelsville, OH 43756 • *1,804*
McCook, NE 69001 • *8,112*
McCook □, SD • *5,688*
McCormick, SC 29835 • *1,659*
McCormick □, SC • *8,868*
McCracken □, KY • *62,879*
McCreary □, KY • *15,603*
McCrory, AR 72101 • *1,971*
McCulloch □, TX • *8,778*
McCurtain □, OK • *33,433*
McDermitt, NV 89421 • *373*
McDonald □, MO • *16,938*
McDonough, GA 30253 • *2,929*
McDonough □, IL • *35,244*
McDowell □, NC • *35,681*
McDowell □, WV • *35,233*
McDuffie □, GA • *20,119*
McEwen, TN 37101 • *1,442*
McFarland, CA 93250 • *7,005*
McFarland, WI 53558 • *5,232*
McGehee, AR 71654 • *4,997*
McGill, NV 89318 • *1,258*
McGrath, AK 99627 • *528*
McGraw, NY 13101 • *1,074*
McGregor, TX 76657 • *4,683*
McHenry, IL 60050–51 • *16,177*
McHenry □, IL • *183,241*
McHenry □, ND • *6,528*
McIntosh □, GA • *8,634*
McIntosh □, ND • *4,021*
McIntosh □, OK • *16,779*
McKean □, PA • *47,131*
McKee City, NJ 08232 • *1,200*
McKeesport, PA 15130–35 • *26,016*
McKees Rocks, PA 15136 • *7,691*
McKenzie, TN 38201 • *5,168*
McKenzie □, ND • *6,383*
McKinley □, NM • *60,686*
McKinleyville, CA 95521 • *10,749*
McKinney, TX 75069–70 • *21,283*
McLaughlin, SD 57642 • *780*
McLean, VA 22101 • *38,168*
McLean □, IL • *129,180*
McLean □, KY • *9,628*
McLean □, ND • *10,457*
McLeansboro, IL 62859 • *2,677*
McLennan □, TX • *189,123*
McLeod □, MN • *32,030*
McLoud, OK 74851 • *2,493*
McMechen, WV 26040 • *2,130*
McMinn □, TN • *42,383*
McMinnville, OR 97128 • *17,894*
McMinnville, TN 37110 • *11,194*
McMullen □, TX • *817*
McNairy □, TN • *22,422*
McPherson, KS 67460 • *12,422*
McPherson □, KS • *27,268*
McPherson □, NE • *546*
McPherson □, SD • *3,228*
McQueeney, TX 78123 • *2,063*
McRae, GA 31055 • *3,007*
McRoberts, KY 41835 • *1,101*
McSherrystown, PA 17344 • *2,769*
Mead, WA 99021 • *2,150*
Meade, KS 67864 • *1,526*
Meade □, KS • *4,247*
Meade □, KY • *24,170*
Meade □, SD • *21,878*
Meadowbrook, FL 32808 • *5,200*
Meadowood, DE 19711 • *2,100*
Meadville, PA 16335 • *14,318*
Meagher □, MT • *1,819*
Mebane, NC 27302 • *4,754*
Mecca, CA 92254 • *1,966*
Mechanic Falls, ME 04256 • *2,388*
Mechanicsburg, OH 43044 • *1,803*
Mechanicsburg, PA 17055 • *9,452*
Mechanicsville, IA 52306 • *1,012*
Mechanicsville, VA 23111 • *22,027*
Mechanicville, NY 12118 • *5,249*
Mecklenburg □, NC • *511,433*
Mecklenburg □, VA • *29,241*
Mecosta □, MI • *37,308*
Medfield, MA 02052 • *5,985*
Medford, MA 02155 • *57,407*
Medford, NJ 08055 • *1,800*
Medford, NY 11763 • *21,274*
Medford, OK 73759 • *1,172*
Medford, OR 97501–04 • *46,951*
Medford, WI 54451 • *4,283*
Medford Lakes, NJ 08055 • *4,462*
Media, PA 19063–65 • *5,957*
Mediapolis, IA 52637 • *1,637*
Medical Lake, WA 99022 • *3,664*
Medicine Bow, WY 82329 • *389*
Medicine Lodge, KS 67104 • *2,453*
Medina, NY 14103 • *6,686*
Medina, OH 44256 • *19,231*
Medina, WA 98039 • *2,981*
Medina □, OH • *122,354*
Medina □, TX • *27,312*
Medway, MA 02053 • *3,890*
Meeker, CO 81641 • *2,098*
Meeker, OK 74855 • *1,003*
Meeker □, MN • *20,846*
Meeteetse, WY 82433 • *368*
Mehlville, MO 63129 • *27,557*
Meigs, GA 31765 • *1,120*
Meigs □, OH • *22,987*
Meigs □, TN • *8,033*
Meiners Oaks, CA 93023 • *3,329*
Melbourne, AR 72556 • *1,562*
Melbourne, FL 32901–10 • *59,646*
Melbourne Beach, FL 32951 • *3,021*
Melcher, IA 50163 • *1,302*
Mellette □, SD • *2,137*
Melrose, FL 32666 • *1,700*
Melrose, MA 02176 • *28,150*
Melrose, MN 56352 • *2,561*
Melrose Park, FL 33312 • *6,477*
Melrose Park, IL 60160–63 • *20,859*
Melville, LA 71353 • *1,562*
Melville, NY 11747 • *12,586*
Melvindale, MI 48122 • *11,216*
Memphis, FL 34221 • *6,760*
Memphis, MI 48041 • *1,221*
Memphis, MO 63555 • *2,094*
Memphis, TN 38101–87 • *610,337*
Memphis, TX 79245 • *2,465*
Mena, AR 71953 • *5,475*
Menahga, MN 56464 • *1,076*
Menands, NY 12204 • *4,333*
Menard, TX 76859 • *1,606*
Menard □, IL • *11,164*
Menard □, TX • *2,252*
Menasha, WI 54952 • *14,711*
Mendenhall, MS 39114 • *2,463*
Mendham, NJ 07945 • *4,890*
Mendocino, CA 95460 • *1,008*
Mendocino □, CA • *80,345*
Mendota, CA 93640 • *6,821*
Mendota, IL 61342 • *7,018*
Mendota Heights, MN 55118 • *9,431*
Menifee □, KY • *5,092*
Menlo Park, CA 94025–28 • *28,040*
Menno, SD 57045 • *768*
Menominee, MI 49858 • *9,398*
Menominee □, MI • *24,920*
Menominee □, WI • *3,890*
Menomonee Falls, WI 53051–52 • *26,840*
Menomonie, WI 54751 • *13,547*
Mentor, OH 44060–61 • *47,358*
Mentor-on-the-Lake, OH 44060 • *8,271*
Mequon, WI 53092 • *18,885*
Meraux, LA 70075 • *8,000*
Merced, CA 95339–44 • *56,216*
Merced □, CA • *178,403*
Mercedes, TX 78570 • *12,694*
Mercer, PA 16137 • *2,444*
Mercer, WI 54547 • *1,300*
Mercer □, IL • *17,290*
Mercer □, KY • *19,148*
Mercer □, MO • *3,723*
Mercer □, NJ • *325,824*
Mercer □, ND • *9,808*
Mercer □, OH • *39,443*
Mercer □, PA • *121,003*
Mercer □, WV • *64,980*
Mercer Island, WA 98040 • *20,816*
Mercersburg, PA 17236 • *1,640*
Mercerville, NJ 08619 • *15,600*
Merchantville, NJ 08109 • *4,095*
Meredith, NH 03253 • *1,654*
Meredosia, IL 62665 • *1,134*
Meriden, CT 06450 • *59,479*
Meridian, ID 83642 • *9,596*
Meridian, MS 39301–09 • *41,036*
Meridian, PA 16001 • *3,473*
Meridian, TX 76665 • *1,390*
Meridian Hills, IN 46260 • *1,728*
Meridianville, AL 35759 • *2,852*
Meriwether □, GA • *22,411*
Merkel, TX 79536 • *2,469*
Merriam, KS 66203 • *11,821*
Merrick, NY 11566 • *23,042*
Merrick □, NE • *8,042*
Merrifield, VA 22031 • *8,399*
Merrill, WI 54452 • *9,860*
Merrillville, IN 46410 • *27,257*
Merrimac, MA 01860 • *2,050*
Merrimack, NH 03054 • *1,300*
Merrimack □, NH • *120,005*
Merritt Island, FL 32952–54 • *32,886*
Merryville, LA 70653 • *1,235*
Merton, WI 53056 • *1,199*
Mesa, AZ 85201–16 • *288,091*
Mesa □, CO • *93,145*
Mescalero, NM 88340 • *1,159*
Mesilla, NM 88046 • *1,975*
Mesquite, NV 89024 • *1,871*
Mesquite, TX 75149–50 • *101,484*
Metairie, LA 70001–11 • *149,428*
Metamora, IL 61548 • *2,520*
Metcalfe, MS 38760 • *1,092*
Metcalfe □, KY • *8,963*
Methuen, MA 01844 • *39,990*
Metlakatla, AK 99926 • *1,407*
Metropolis, IL 62960 • *6,734*
Metter, GA 30439 • *3,707*
Metuchen, NJ 08840 • *12,804*
Metzger, OR 97223 • *3,149*
Mexia, TX 76667 • *6,933*
Mexico, ME 04257 • *2,302*
Mexico, MO 65265 • *11,290*
Mexico, NY 13114 • *1,555*
Meyersdale, PA 15552 • *2,518*
Miami, AZ 85539 • *2,018*
Miami, FL 33101–99 • *358,548*
Miami, OK 74354–55 • *13,142*
Miami □, IN • *36,897*
Miami □, KS • *23,466*
Miami □, OH • *93,182*
Miami Beach, FL 33139 • *92,639*
Miami Lakes, FL 33014 • *12,750*
Miamisburg, OH 45342–43 • *17,834*
Miami Shores, FL 33138 • *10,084*
Miami Springs, FL 33166 • *13,268*
Micco, FL 32958 • *8,757*
Michigan Center, MI 49254 • *4,863*
Michigan City, IN 46360 • *33,822*
Middleboro (Middleborough Center), MA 02346 • *6,837*
Middleburg, FL 32068 • *6,223*
Middleburg, PA 17842 • *1,422*
Middleburgh, NY 12122 • *1,436*
Middleburg Heights, OH 44130 • *14,702*
Middlebury, CT 06762 • *4,140*
Middlebury, IN 46540 • *2,004*
Middlebury, VT 05753 • *6,007*
Middlefield, CT 06455 • *1,200*
Middlefield, OH 44062 • *1,898*
Middle Island, NY 11953 • *7,848*
Middleport, NY 14105 • *1,876*
Middleport, OH 45760 • *2,725*
Middle River, MD 21220 • *24,616*
Middlesboro, KY 40965 • *11,328*
Middlesex, NJ 08846 • *13,055*
Middlesex □, CT • *143,196*
Middlesex □, MA • *1,398,468*
Middlesex □, NJ • *671,780*
Middlesex □, VA • *8,653*
Middleton, ID 83644 • *1,851*
Middleton, MA 01949 • *4,135*
Middleton, WI 53562 • *13,289*
Middletown, CA 95461 • *2,000*
Middletown, CT 06457 • *42,762*
Middletown, DE 19709 • *3,834*
Middletown, IN 47356 • *2,333*
Middletown, KY 40243 • *5,016*
Middletown, MD 21769 • *1,834*
Middletown, NJ 07718 • *62,298*
Middletown, NY 10940 • *24,160*
Middletown, OH 45042–44 • *46,022*
Middletown, PA 17057 • *9,254*
Middletown, RI 02840 • *3,350*
Middletown, VA 22645 • *1,061*
Middletown Township, PA 19037 • *6,866*
Middleville, MI 49333 • *1,966*
Midfield, AL 35228 • *5,559*
Midland, MI 48640–42 • *38,053*
Midland, PA 15059 • *3,321*
Midland, TX 79701–12 • *89,443*
Midland □, MI • *75,651*
Midland □, TX • *106,611*
Midland City, AL 36350 • *1,819*
Midland Park, KS 67216 • *1,200*
Midland Park, NJ 07432 • *7,047*
Midland Park, SC 29405 • *1,300*
Midlothian, IL 60445 • *14,372*
Midlothian, TX 76065 • *5,141*
Midvale, UT 84047 • *11,886*
Midway, DE 19971 • *500*
Midway, KY 40347 • *1,290*
Midway, OR 97233 • *19,000*
Midway, PA 15060 • *1,043*
Midway, UT 84049 • *1,554*
Midwest, WY 82643 • *495*
Midwest City, OK 73110 • *52,267*
Mifflin □, PA • *46,197*
Mifflinburg, PA 17844 • *3,480*
Mifflinville, PA 18631 • *1,329*
Milaca, MN 56353 • *2,182*
Milam □, TX • *22,946*
Milan, GA 31060 • *1,056*
Milan, IL 61264 • *5,831*
Milan, IN 47031 • *1,529*
Milan, MI 48160 • *4,040*
Milan, MO 63556 • *1,767*
Milan, NM 87021 • *1,911*
Milan, OH 44846 • *1,464*
Milan, TN 38358 • *7,512*
Milbank, SD 57252 • *3,879*
Milesburg, PA 16853 • *1,144*
Miles City, MT 59301 • *8,461*
Milford, CT 06460 • *48,168*
Milford, DE 19963 • *6,040*
Milford, IL 60953 • *1,512*
Milford, IN 46542 • *1,388*
Milford, IA 51351 • *2,170*
Milford, ME 04461 • *2,228*
Milford, MA 01757 • *23,339*
Milford, MI 48380–82 • *5,511*
Milford, NE 68405 • *1,886*
Milford, NH 03055 • *8,015*
Milford, NJ 08848 • *1,273*
Milford, OH 45150 • *5,660*
Milford, PA 18337 • *1,064*
Milford, UT 84751 • *1,107*
Mililani Town, HI 96789 • *29,359*
Millard □, UT • *11,333*
Millbrae, CA 94030 • *20,412*
Millbrook, AL 36054 • *6,050*
Millbrook, NY 12545 • *1,339*
Millburn, NJ 07041 • *18,630*
Millbury, MA 01527 • *4,940*
Millbury, OH 43447 • *1,081*
Mill City, OR 97360 • *1,555*
Millcreek, UT 84109 • *32,230*
Millcreek Township, PA 16505 • *46,100*
Milledgeville, GA 31061 • *17,727*
Milledgeville, IL 61051 • *1,076*
Mille Lacs □, MN • *18,670*
Millen, GA 30442 • *3,808*
Miller, SD 57362 • *1,678*
Miller □, AR • *38,467*
Miller □, GA • *6,280*
Miller □, MO • *20,700*
Miller Place, NY 11764 • *9,315*
Millersburg, OH 44654 • *3,051*
Millersburg, PA 17061 • *2,729*
Millers Falls, MA 01349 • *1,084*
Millersport, OH 43046 • *1,010*
Millersville, PA 17551 • *8,099*
Mill Hall, PA 17751 • *1,702*
Milliken, CO 80543 • *1,605*
Millington, MI 48746 • *1,114*
Millington, TN 38053 • *17,866*
Millinocket, ME 04462 • *6,922*
Millis, MA 02054 • *3,777*
Millport, AL 35576 • *1,203*
Mills, WY 82644 • *1,574*
Mills □, IA • *13,202*
Mills □, TX • *4,531*
Millsboro, DE 19966 • *1,643*
Millstadt, IL 62260 • *2,566*
Milltown, NJ 08850 • *6,968*
Millvale, PA 15209 • *4,341*
Mill Valley, CA 94941–42 • *13,038*
Millville, MA 01529 • *1,693*
Millville, NJ 08332 • *25,992*
Millville, UT 84326 • *1,202*
Millwood, WA 99212 • *1,559*
Milnor, ND 58060 • *651*
Milo, ME 04463 • *2,129*
Milpitas, CA 95035–36 • *50,686*
Milroy, PA 17063 • *1,456*
Milstead, GA 30207 • *1,500*
Milton, DE 19968 • *1,417*
Milton, FL 32570–71 • *7,216*
Milton, MA 02186 • *25,725*
Milton, NH 03851 • *1,000*
Milton, NY 12547 • *1,140*
Milton, PA 17847 • *6,746*
Milton, VT 05468 • *1,578*
Milton, WA 98354 • *4,995*
Milton, WV 25541 • *2,242*
Milton, WI 53563 • *4,434*
Milton-Freewater, OR 97862 • *5,533*
Milwaukee, WI 53201–95 • *628,088*
Milwaukee □, WI • *959,275*
Milwaukie, OR 97222 • *18,692*
Mimosa Park, LA 70070 • *4,516*
Mims, FL 32754 • *9,412*
Mina, NV 89422 • *400*
Minco, OK 73059 • *1,411*
Minden, LA 71055 • *13,661*
Minden, NE 68959 • *2,749*
Minden, NV 89423 • *1,441*
Mine Hill, NJ 07801 • *3,250*
Mineola, NY 11501 • *18,994*
Mineola, TX 75773 • *4,321*
Miner, MO 63801 • *1,218*
Miner □, SD • *3,272*
Mineral □, CO • *558*
Mineral □, MT • *3,315*
Mineral □, NV • *6,475*
Mineral □, WV • *26,697*
Mineral Point, WI 53565 • *2,428*
Mineral Springs, AR 71851 • *1,004*
Mineral Wells, TX 76067 • *14,870*
Minersville, PA 17954 • *4,877*
Minerva, OH 44657 • *4,318*
Minetto, NY 13115 • *1,252*
Mineville, NY 12956 • *1,000*
Mingo □, WV • *33,739*
Mingo Junction, OH 43938 • *4,297*
Minidoka □, ID • *19,361*
Minier, IL 61759 • *1,155*
Minneapolis, KS 67467 • *1,983*
Minneapolis, MN 55401–80 • *368,383*
Minnehaha □, SD • *123,809*
Minneota, MN 56264 • *1,417*
Minnetonka, MN 55345 • *48,370*
Minocqua, WI 54548 • *1,280*
Minonk, IL 61760 • *1,982*
Minooka, IL 60447 • *2,561*
Minot, ND 58701–02 • *34,544*
Minquadale, DE 19720 • *790*
Minster, OH 45865 • *2,650*
Mint Hill, NC 28212 • *11,567*
Minturn, CO 81645 • *1,066*
Mio, MI 48647 • *1,500*
Mira Loma, CA 91752 • *15,786*
Miramar, FL 33023 • *40,663*
Misenheimer, NC 28109 • *1,000*
Mishawaka, IN 46544–46 • *42,608*
Mishicot, WI 54228 • *1,296*
Missaukee □, MI • *12,147*
Mission, KS 66205 • *9,504*
Mission, TX 78572 • *28,653*
Mission Hills, KS 66205 • *3,446*
Mission Viejo, CA 92691 • *72,820*
Mississippi □, AR • *57,525*
Mississippi □, MO • *14,442*
Mississippi State, MS 39762 • *12,400*
Missoula, MT 59801–07 • *42,918*
Missoula □, MT • *78,687*
Missouri City, TX 77459 • *36,176*
Missouri Valley, IA 51555 • *2,888*
Mitchell, IL 62040 • *1,320*
Mitchell, IN 47446 • *4,669*
Mitchell, NE 69357 • *1,743*
Mitchell, SD 57301 • *13,798*
Mitchell □, GA • *20,275*
Mitchell □, IA • *10,928*
Mitchell □, KS • *7,203*
Mitchell □, NC • *14,433*
Mitchell □, TX • *8,016*
Mitchellville, IA 50169 • *1,670*
Mizpah, NJ 08342 • *1,000*
Moab, UT 84532 • *3,971*
Moberly, MO 65270 • *12,839*
Mobile, AL 36601–95 • *196,278*
Mobile □, AL • *378,643*
Mobridge, SD 57601 • *3,768*
Mocanaqua, PA 18655 • *1,100*
Mocksville, NC 27028 • *3,399*
Modesto, CA 95350–56 • *164,730*
Modoc □, CA • *9,678*
Moenkopi, AZ 86045 • *1,200*
Moffat □, CO • *11,357*
Mogadore, OH 44260 • *4,008*
Mohall, ND 58761 • *931*
Mohave □, AZ • *93,497*
Mohawk, NY 13407 • *2,986*
Mohnton, PA 19540 • *2,484*
Mojave, CA 93501–02 • *3,763*
Mokena, IL 60448 • *6,128*
Molalla, OR 97038 • *3,651*
Moline, IL 61265 • *43,202*
Molino, FL 32577 • *1,207*
Momence, IL 60954 • *2,968*
Monaca, PA 15061 • *6,739*
Monahans, TX 79756 • *8,101*
Monarch Mills, SC 29379 • *2,214*
Moncks Corner, SC 29461 • *5,607*
Mondovi, WI 54755 • *2,491*
Monee, IL 60449 • *1,044*
Monessen, PA 15062 • *9,901*
Monett, MO 65708 • *6,529*
Monette, AR 72447 • *1,115*
Monfort Heights, OH 45239 • *9,745*
Moniteau □, MO • *12,298*
Monmouth, IL 61462 • *9,489*
Monmouth, OR 97361 • *6,288*
Monmouth □, NJ • *553,124*
Monmouth Beach, NJ 07750 • *3,303*
Monmouth Junction, NJ 08852 • *1,570*
Mono □, CA • *9,956*
Monon, IN 47959 • *1,585*
Monona, IA 52159 • *1,520*
Monona, WI 53716 • *8,637*
Monona □, IA • *10,034*
Monongah, WV 26554 • *1,018*
Monongahela, PA 15063 • *4,928*
Monongalia □, WV • *75,509*
Monroe, GA 30655 • *9,759*
Monroe, IA 50170 • *1,739*
Monroe, LA 71201–13 • *54,909*
Monroe, MI 48161 • *22,902*
Monroe, NY 10950 • *6,672*
Monroe, NC 28110–12 • *16,127*
Monroe, OH 45050 • *4,490*
Monroe, UT 84754 • *1,472*
Monroe, WA 98272 • *4,278*
Monroe, WI 53566 • *10,241*
Monroe □, AL • *23,968*
Monroe □, AR • *11,333*
Monroe □, FL • *78,024*
Monroe □, GA • *17,113*
Monroe □, IL • *22,422*
Monroe □, IN • *108,978*
Monroe □, IA • *8,114*
Monroe □, KY • *11,401*
Monroe □, MI • *133,600*
Monroe □, MS • *36,582*
Monroe □, MO • *9,104*
Monroe □, NY • *713,968*
Monroe □, OH • *15,497*
Monroe □, PA • *95,709*
Monroe □, TN • *30,541*
Monroe □, WV • *12,406*

Monroe □, WI • 36,633
Monroe Center, CT 06468 • 7,900
Monroe City, MO 63456 • 2,701
Monroe Park, DE 19807 • 1,000
Monroeville, AL 36460-61 • 6,993
Monroeville, IN 46773 • 1,232
Monroeville, OH 44847 • 1,381
Monroeville, PA 15146 • 29,169
Monrovia, CA 91016 • 35,761
Monsey, NY 10952 • 13,986
Monson, MA 01057 • 2,101
Montague, CA 96064 • 1,415
Montague, MI 49437 • 2,276
Montague □, TX • 17,274
Mont Alto, PA 17237 • 1,395
Montauk, NY 11954 • 3,001
Mont Belvieu, TX 77580 • 1,323
Montcalm □, MI • 53,059
Montchanin, DE 19710 • 500
Montclair, CA 91763 • 28,434
Montclair, NJ 07042-44 • 37,729
Mont Clare, PA 19453 • 1,800
Monteagle, TN 37356 • 1,138
Montebello, CA 90640 • 59,564
Montecito, CA 93108 • 9,300
Montello, NV 89830 • 200
Montello, WI 53949 • 1,329
Monterey, CA 93940 • 31,954
Monterey, TN 38574 • 2,559
Monterey □, CA • 355,660
Monterey Park, CA 91754 • 60,738
Montesano, WA 98563 • 3,064
Montevallo, AL 35115 • 4,239
Montevideo, MN 56265 • 5,499
Monte Vista, CO 81144 • 4,324
Montezuma, GA 31063 • 4,506
Montezuma, IN 47862 • 1,134
Montezuma, IA 50171 • 1,651
Montezuma □, CO • 18,672
Montgomery, AL 36101-99 • 187,106
Montgomery, IL 60538 • 4,267
Montgomery, MN 56069 • 2,399
Montgomery, NY 12549 • 2,696
Montgomery, OH 45242 • 9,753
Montgomery, PA 17752 • 1,631
Montgomery, WV 25136 • 2,449
Montgomery □, AL • 209,085
Montgomery □, AR • 7,841
Montgomery □, GA • 7,163
Montgomery □, IL • 30,728
Montgomery □, IN • 34,436
Montgomery □, IA • 12,076
Montgomery □, KS • 38,816
Montgomery □, KY • 19,561
Montgomery □, MD • 757,027
Montgomery □, MS • 12,388
Montgomery □, MO • 11,355
Montgomery □, NY • 51,981
Montgomery □, NC • 23,346
Montgomery □, OH • 573,809
Montgomery □, PA • 678,111
Montgomery □, TN • 100,498
Montgomery □, TX • 182,201
Montgomery □, VA • 73,913
Montgomery City, MO 63361 • 2,281
Montgomery Village, MD 20879 • 32,315
Monticello, AR 71655 • 8,116
Monticello, FL 32344 • 2,573
Monticello, GA 31064 • 2,289
Monticello, IL 61856 • 4,549
Monticello, IN 47960 • 5,237
Monticello, IA 52310 • 3,522
Monticello, KY 42633 • 5,357
Monticello, MN 55362 • 4,941
Monticello, MS 39654 • 1,755
Monticello, NY 12701 • 6,597
Monticello, UT 84535 • 1,806
Monticello, WI 53570 • 1,140
Montmorency □, MI • 8,936
Montour □, PA • 17,735
Montour Falls, NY 14865 • 1,845
Montoursville, PA 17754 • 4,983
Montpelier, ID 83254 • 2,656
Montpelier, IN 47359 • 1,880
Montpelier, OH 43543 • 4,299
Montpelier, VT 05601-02 • 8,247
Montrose, AL 36559 • 1,400
Montrose, CO 81401-02 • 8,854
Montrose, MI 48457 • 1,811
Montrose, PA 18801 • 1,982
Montrose, VA 23231 • 6,405
Montrose □, CO • 24,423
Montvale, NJ 07645 • 6,946
Montville, CT 06353 • 16,673
Montville, NJ 07045 • 2,600
Monument, CO 80132 • 1,020
Monument Beach, MA 02553 • 1,800
Monument Heights, VA 23226 • 2,500
Moodus, CT 06469 • 1,170
Moody, TX 76557 • 1,329
Moody □, SD • 6,507
Moonachie, NJ 07074 • 2,817
Moorcroft, WY 82721 • 768
Moore, OK 73160 • 40,318
Moore □, NC • 59,013
Moore □, TN • 4,721
Moore □, TX • 17,865
Moorefield, WV 26836 • 2,148
Moore Haven, FL 33471 • 1,432
Mooreland, OK 73852 • 1,157
Moorestown, NJ 08057 • 16,500
Mooresville, IN 46158 • 5,541
Mooresville, NC 28115 • 9,317
Moorhead, MN 56560-61 • 32,295
Moorhead, MS 38761 • 2,417
Moorpark, CA 93020-21 • 25,494
Moose Lake, MN 55767 • 1,206
Moosic, PA 18507 • 5,339
Moosup, CT 06354 • 3,289
Mora, MN 55051 • 2,905
Mora, NM 87732 • 1,200
Mora □, NM • 4,264
Moraga, CA 94556 • 15,852
Moraine, OH 45439 • 5,989
Moravia, NY 13118 • 1,559
Morehead, KY 40351 • 8,357
Morehead City, NC 28557 • 6,046
Morehouse, MO 63868 • 1,068
Morehouse □, LA • 31,938
Morenci, AZ 85540 • 1,799
Morenci, MI 49256 • 2,342
Moreno Valley, CA 92387-88 • 118,779
Morgan, UT 84050 • 2,023
Morgan □, AL • 100,043
Morgan □, CO • 21,939
Morgan □, GA • 12,883
Morgan □, IL • 36,397
Morgan □, IN • 55,920
Morgan □, KY • 11,648
Morgan □, MO • 15,574
Morgan □, OH • 14,194
Morgan □, TN • 17,300
Morgan □, UT • 5,528
Morgan □, WV • 12,128
Morgan City, LA 70380-81 • 14,531
Morganfield, KY 42437 • 3,776
Morgan Hill, CA 95037-38 • 23,928
Morganton, NC 28655 • 15,085
Morgantown, KY 42261 • 2,284
Morgantown, MS 39120 • 3,288
Morgantown, WV 26502-07 • 25,879
Moriarty, NM 87035 • 1,399
Morningdale, MA 01505 • 1,130
Morocco, IN 47963 • 1,044
Moroni, UT 84646 • 1,115
Morrill □, NE • 5,423
Morrilton, AR 72110 • 6,551
Morris, AL 35116 • 1,136
Morris, IL 60450 • 10,270
Morris, MN 56267 • 5,613
Morris, OK 74445 • 1,216
Morris □, KS • 6,198
Morris □, NJ • 421,353
Morris □, TX • 13,200
Morrison, IL 61270 • 4,363
Morrison □, MN • 29,604
Morrison City, TN 37660 • 2,032
Morrisonville, IL 62546 • 1,113
Morrisonville, NY 12962 • 1,742
Morris Plains, NJ 07950 • 5,219
Morristown, NJ 07960-63 • 16,189
Morristown, TN 37813-16 • 21,385
Morrisville, NY 13408 • 2,732
Morrisville, PA 19067 • 9,765
Morrisville, VT 05661 • 1,984
Morro Bay, CA 93442-43 • 9,664
Morrow, GA 30260 • 5,168
Morrow, OH 45152 • 1,206
Morrow □, OH • 27,749
Morrow □, OR • 7,625
Morton, IL 61550 • 13,799
Morton, MS 39117 • 3,212
Morton, TX 79346 • 2,597
Morton, WA 98356 • 1,130
Morton □, KS • 3,480
Morton □, ND • 23,700
Morton Grove, IL 60053 • 22,408
Moscow, ID 83843 • 18,519
Moscow, PA 18444 • 1,527
Moses Lake, WA 98837 • 11,235
Mosheim, TN 37818 • 1,451
Mosinee, WI 54455 • 3,820
Moss Bluff, LA 70611 • 8,039
Moss Point, MS 39563 • 17,837
Motley □, TX • 1,532
Mott, ND 58646 • 1,019
Moulton, AL 35650 • 3,248
Moultrie, GA 31768 • 14,865
Moultrie □, IL • 13,930
Mound, MN 55364 • 9,634
Mound Bayou, MS 38762 • 2,222
Mound City, MO 64470 • 1,273
Moundridge, KS 67107 • 1,531
Mounds, IL 62964 • 1,407
Mounds View, MN 55432 • 12,541
Moundsville, WV 26041 • 10,753
Moundville, AL 35474 • 1,348
Mountainair, NM 87036 • 926
Mountain Brook, AL 35223 • 19,810
Mountain City, NV 89831 • 110
Mountain City, TN 37683 • 2,169
Mountain Grove, MO 65711 • 4,182
Mountain Home, AR 72653 • 9,027
Mountain Home, ID 83647 • 7,913
Mountain Iron, MN 55768 • 3,362
Mountain Lake, MN 56159 • 1,906
Mountain Lake Park, MD 21550 • 1,938
Mountain Lakes, NJ 07046 • 3,847
Mountain Park, GA 30087 • 11,025
Mountainside, NJ 07092 • 6,657
Mountain View, AR 72560 • 2,439
Mountain View, CA 94039-43 • 67,460
Mountain View, CO 80521 • 2,100
Mountain View, MO 65548 • 2,036
Mountain View, NM 87105 • 2,300
Mountain View, OK 73062 • 1,086
Mountain View, WY 82604 • 1,200
Mountain View, WY 82939 • 1,189
Mountain Village, AK 99632 • 674
Mount Airy, MD 21771 • 3,730
Mount Airy, NC 27030 • 7,156
Mount Angel, OR 97362 • 2,778
Mount Arlington, NJ 07856 • 3,630
Mount Ayr, IA 50854 • 1,796
Mount Carmel, IL 62863 • 8,287
Mount Carmel, PA 17851 • 7,196
Mount Carroll, IL 61053 • 1,726
Mount Clemens, MI 48043-46 • 18,405
Mount Dora, FL 32757 • 7,196
Mount Ephraim, NJ 08059 • 4,517
Mount Freedom, NJ 07970 • 1,920
Mount Gay, WV 25637 • 1,200
Mount Gilead, NC 27306 • 1,336
Mount Gilead, OH 43338 • 2,846
Mount Healthy, OH 45231 • 7,580
Mount Holly, NJ 08060 • 10,639
Mount Holly, NC 28120 • 7,710
Mount Holly Springs, PA 17065 • 1,925
Mount Hope, WV 25880 • 1,573
Mount Horeb, WI 53572 • 4,182
Mount Jackson, VA 22842 • 1,583
Mount Jewett, PA 16740 • 1,029
Mount Joy, PA 17552 • 6,398
Mount Juliet, TN 37122 • 5,389
Mount Kisco, NY 10549 • 9,108
Mountlake Terrace, WA 98043 • 19,320
Mount Lebanon, PA 15228 • 33,362
Mount Morris, IL 61054 • 2,919
Mount Morris, MI 48458 • 3,292
Mount Morris, NY 14510 • 3,102
Mount Olive, AL 35117 • 2,270
Mount Olive, IL 62069 • 2,126
Mount Olive, NC 28365 • 4,582
Mount Olympus, UT 84117 • 7,413
Mount Orab, OH 45154 • 1,929
Mount Penn, PA 19606 • 2,883
Mount Pleasant, IA 52641 • 8,027
Mount Pleasant, MI 48858-59 • 23,285
Mount Pleasant, NC 28124 • 1,027
Mount Pleasant, PA 15666 • 4,787
Mount Pleasant, SC 29464-65 • 30,108
Mount Pleasant, TN 38474 • 4,278
Mount Pleasant, TX 75455 • 12,291
Mount Pleasant, UT 84647 • 2,092
Mount Pocono, PA 18344 • 1,795
Mount Prospect, IL 60056 • 53,170
Mount Pulaski, IL 62548 • 1,610
Mountrail □, ND • 7,021
Mount Rainier, MD 20712 • 7,954
Mount Savage, MD 21545 • 1,640
Mount Shasta, CA 96067 • 3,460
Mount Sinai, NY 11766 • 8,023
Mount Sterling, IL 62353 • 1,922
Mount Sterling, KY 40353 • 5,362
Mount Sterling, OH 43143 • 1,647
Mount Union, PA 17066 • 2,878
Mount Vernon, GA 30445 • 1,914
Mount Vernon, IL 62864 • 16,988
Mount Vernon, IN 47620 • 7,217
Mount Vernon, IA 52314 • 3,657
Mount Vernon, KY 40456 • 2,654
Mount Vernon, MO 65712 • 3,726
Mount Vernon, NY 10550-53 • 67,153
Mount Vernon, OH 43050 • 14,550
Mount Vernon, TX 75457 • 2,219
Mount Vernon, WA 98273 • 17,647
Mount View, RI 02852 • 610
Mount Washington, KY 40047 • 5,226
Mount Wolf, PA 17347 • 1,365
Mount Zion, IL 62549 • 4,522
Moville, IA 51039 • 1,306
Moweaqua, IL 62550 • 1,785
Mower □, MN • 37,385
Moyock, NC 27958 • 1,400
Muenster, TX 76252 • 1,387
Muhlenberg □, KY • 31,318
Mukilteo, WA 98275 • 7,007
Mukwonago, WI 53149 • 4,457
Mulberry, AR 72947 • 1,448
Mulberry, FL 33860 • 2,988
Mulberry, IN 46058 • 1,262
Mulberry, NC 28659 • 2,339
Muldraugh, KY 40155 • 1,376
Muldrow, OK 74948 • 2,889
Muleshoe, TX 79347 • 4,571
Mullan, ID 83846 • 821
Mullens, WV 25882 • 2,006
Mullica Hill, NJ 08062 • 1,117
Mullins, SC 29574 • 5,910
Multnomah □, OR • 583,887
Mulvane, KS 67110 • 4,674
Muncie, IN 47302-08 • 71,035
Muncy, PA 17756 • 2,702
Munday, TX 76371 • 1,600
Mundelein, IL 60060 • 21,215
Munford, TN 38058 • 2,326
Munfordville, KY 42765 • 1,556
Munhall, PA 15120 • 13,158
Munising, MI 49862 • 2,783
Munster, IN 46321 • 19,949
Murfreesboro, AR 71958 • 1,542
Murfreesboro, NC 27855 • 2,580
Murfreesboro, TN 37129-33 • 44,922
Murphy, MO 63026 • 9,342
Murphy, NC 28906 • 1,575
Murphys, CA 95247 • 1,517
Murphysboro, IL 62966 • 9,176
Murray, KY 42071 • 14,439
Murray, UT 84107 • 31,282
Murray □, GA • 26,147
Murray □, MN • 9,660
Murray □, OK • 12,042
Murrells Inlet, SC 29576 • 3,334
Murrysville, PA 15668 • 17,240
Muscatine, IA 52761 • 22,881
Muscatine □, IA • 39,907
Muscle Shoals, AL 35661 • 9,611
Muscoda, WI 53573 • 1,287
Muscogee □, GA • 179,278
Muscoy, CA 92405 • 7,541
Muse, PA 15350 • 1,250
Muskego, WI 53150 • 16,813
Muskegon, MI 49440-45 • 40,283
Muskegon □, MI • 158,983
Muskegon Heights, MI 49444 • 13,176
Muskingum □, OH • 82,068
Muskogee, OK 74401-03 • 37,708
Muskogee □, OK • 68,078
Musselshell □, MT • 4,106
Mustang, OK 73064 • 10,434
Myerstown, PA 17067 • 3,236
Myrtle Beach, SC 29577-78 • 24,848
Myrtle Grove, FL 32506 • 17,402
Myrtle Point, OR 97458 • 2,712
Mystic, CT 06355 • 2,618
Mystic Island, NJ 08087 • 7,400

N

Naalehu, HI 96772 • 1,027
Naamans Gardens, DE 19810 • 1,500
Nabnasset, MA 01886 • 3,600
Nacogdoches, TX 75961-63 • 30,872
Nacogdoches □, TX • 54,753
Nags Head, NC 27959 • 1,838
Nahant, MA 01908 • 3,828
Nahunta, GA 31553 • 1,049
Nampa, ID 83651-53 • 28,365
Nanakuli, HI 96792 • 9,575
Nance □, NE • 4,275
Nanticoke, PA 18634 • 12,267
Nantucket, MA 02554 • 3,069
Nantucket □, MA • 6,012
Nanty Glo, PA 15943 • 3,190
Nanuet, NY 10954 • 14,065
Napa, CA 94558-59 • 61,842
Napa □, CA • 110,765
Napanoch, NY 12458 • 1,068
Naperville, IL 60540 • 85,351
Naples, FL 33939-42 • 19,505
Naples, NY 14512 • 1,237
Naples, TX 75568 • 1,508
Naples, UT 84078 • 1,334
Naples Park, FL 33963 • 8,002
Napoleon, ND 58561 • 930
Napoleon, OH 43545 • 8,884
Nappanee, IN 46550 • 5,510
Naranja, FL 33032 • 5,790
Narberth, PA 19072 • 4,278
Narragansett, RI 02882 • 3,721
Narrows, VA 24124 • 2,082
Naselle, WA 98638 • 1,000
Nash, TX 75569 • 2,162
Nash □, NC • 76,677
Nashua, IA 50658 • 1,476
Nashua, NH 03060-63 • 79,662
Nashville, AR 71852 • 4,639
Nashville, GA 31639 • 4,782
Nashville, IL 62263 • 3,202
Nashville, MI 49073 • 1,654
Nashville, NC 27856 • 3,617
Nashville, TN 37201-35 • 487,969
Nashwauk, MN 55769 • 1,026
Nassau, NY 12123 • 1,254
Nassau □, FL • 43,941
Nassau □, NY • 1,287,348
Nassau Shores, NY 11758 • 5,110
Natalia, TX 78059 • 1,216
Natchez, MS 39120-22 • 19,460
Natchitoches, LA 71457-58 • 16,609
Natchitoches □, LA • 36,689
Natick, MA 01760 • 30,100
National City, CA 91950-51 • 54,249
National Park, NJ 08063 • 3,413
Natrona □, WY • 61,226
Natrona Heights, PA 15065 • 12,200
Naugatuck, CT 06770 • 30,625
Nautilus Park, CT 06340 • 6,500
Nauvoo, IL 62354 • 1,108
Navajo □, AZ • 77,658
Navarre, OH 44662 • 1,635
Navarro □, TX • 39,926
Navasota, TX 77868-69 • 6,296
Navesink, NJ 07752 • 1,420
Nazareth, PA 18064 • 5,713
Neah Bay, WA 98357 • 1,300
Nebraska City, NE 68410 • 6,547
Nederland, CO 80466 • 1,099
Nederland, TX 77627 • 16,192
Nedrow, NY 13120 • 2,980
Needham, MA 02192 • 27,557
Needles, CA 92363 • 5,191
Needville, TX 77461 • 2,199
Neenah, WI 54956-57 • 23,219
Neffs, OH 43940 • 1,213
Negaunee, MI 49866 • 4,741
Neillsville, WI 54456 • 2,680
Nekoosa, WI 54457 • 2,557
Neligh, NE 68756 • 1,742
Nelson □, KY • 29,710
Nelson □, ND • 4,410
Nelson □, VA • 12,778
Nelsonville, OH 45764 • 4,563
Nemacolin, PA 15351 • 1,097
Nemaha □, KS • 10,446
Nemaha □, NE • 7,980
Nenana, AK 99760 • 393
Neodesha, KS 66757 • 2,837
Neoga, IL 62447 • 1,678
Neosho, MO 64850 • 9,254
Neosho □, KS • 17,035
Nephi, UT 84648 • 3,515
Neptune, NJ 07753 • 28,366
Neptune Beach, FL 32233 • 6,816
Neptune City, NJ 07753 • 4,997
Nesconset, NY 11767 • 10,712
Nescopeck, PA 18635 • 1,651
Neshoba □, MS • 24,800
Nesquehoning, PA 18240 • 3,364
Ness □, KS • 4,033
Ness City, KS 67560 • 1,724
Netcong, NJ 07857 • 3,311
Nether Providence Township, PA 19013 • 13,229
Nettleton, MS 38858 • 2,462
Nevada, IA 50201 • 6,009
Nevada, MO 64772 • 8,597
Nevada □, AR • 10,101
Nevada □, CA • 78,510
Nevada City, CA 95959 • 2,855
New Albany, IN 47150-51 • 36,322
New Albany, MS 38652 • 6,775
New Albany, OH 43054 • 1,621
Newark, AR 72562 • 1,159
Newark, CA 94560 • 37,861
Newark, DE 19711-15 • 25,098
Newark, NJ 07101-75 • 275,221
Newark, NY 14513 • 9,849
Newark, OH 43055-58 • 44,389
Newark Valley, NY 13811 • 1,082
New Athens, IL 62264 • 2,010
Newaygo, MI 49337 • 1,336
Newaygo □, MI • 38,202
New Baden, IL 62265 • 2,602
New Baltimore, MI 48047 • 5,798
New Bedford, MA 02740-48 • 99,922
Newberg, OR 97132 • 13,086
New Berlin, NY 13411 • 1,220
New Berlin, WI 53151 • 33,592
New Bern, NC 28560-64 • 17,363
Newbern, TN 38059 • 2,515
Newberry, FL 32669 • 1,644
Newberry, MI 49868 • 1,873
Newberry, SC 29108 • 10,542
Newberry □, SC • 33,172
New Bethlehem, PA 16242 • 1,151
New Bloomfield, PA 17068 • 1,092
New Boston, MI 48164 • 1,200
New Boston, OH 45662 • 2,717
New Boston, TX 75570 • 5,057
New Braunfels, TX 78130-33 • 27,334
New Bremen, OH 45869 • 2,558
New Brighton, MN 55112 • 22,207
New Brighton, PA 15066 • 6,854
New Britain, CT 06050-53 • 75,491
New Brockton, AL 36351 • 1,184
New Brunswick, NJ 08901-06 • 41,711
New Buffalo, MI 49117 • 2,317
Newburg, KY 40218 • 21,647
Newburgh, IN 47629-30 • 2,880
Newburgh, NY 12550-53 • 26,454
Newburgh Heights, OH 44105 • 2,310
Newburyport, MA 01950-52 • 16,317
New Canaan, CT 06840 • 17,864
New Carlisle, IN 46552 • 1,446
New Carlisle, OH 45344 • 6,049
New Carrollton, MD 20784 • 12,002
New Cassel, NY 11590 • 10,257
New Castle, AL 35119 • 1,100
New Castle, DE 19720 • 4,837
New Castle, IN 47362 • 17,753
Newcastle, OK 73065 • 4,214
New Castle, PA 16101-08 • 28,334
Newcastle, WY 82701 • 3,003
New Castle □, DE • 441,946
New City, NY 10956 • 33,673
Newcomerstown, OH 43832 • 4,012
New Concord, OH 43762 • 2,086
New Cumberland, PA 17070 • 7,665
New Cumberland, WV 26047 • 1,363
New Egypt, NJ 08533 • 2,327
Newell, IA 50568 • 1,089
Newell, WV 26050 • 1,724
New Ellenton, SC 29809 • 2,515
Newellton, LA 71357 • 1,576
New England, ND 58647 • 663
New Fairfield, CT 06812 • 4,600
Newfane, NY 14108 • 3,001
Newfield, NJ 08344 • 1,592
New Franklin, MO 65274 • 1,107
New Freedom, PA 17349 • 2,920
New Glarus, WI 53574 • 1,899
New Hampton, IA 50659 • 3,660
New Hanover □, NC • 120,284
New Hartford, CT 06057 • 1,269
New Haven, CT 06501-36 • 130,474
New Haven, IN 46774 • 9,320
New Haven, MI 48048 • 2,331
New Haven, MO 63068 • 1,757
New Haven, WV 25265 • 1,632
New Haven □, CT • 804,219
New Holland, GA 30501 • 1,200
New Holland, PA 17557 • 4,484
New Holstein, WI 53061 • 3,342
New Hope, AL 35760 • 2,248
New Hope, MN 55428 • 21,853
New Hope, NC 27604 • 5,694
New Hope, PA 18938 • 1,400
New Hyde Park, NY 11040 • 9,728
New Iberia, LA 70560-62 • 31,828
Newington, CT 06131 • 29,208
Newington, VA 22122 • 17,965
New Johnsonville, TN 37134 • 1,643
New Kensington, PA 15068 • 15,894
New Kent □, VA • 10,445
Newkirk, OK 74647 • 2,168
New Lenox, IL 60451 • 9,627
New Lexington, OH 43764 • 5,117
New Lisbon, WI 53950 • 1,491
Newllano, LA 71461 • 2,660
New London, CT 06320 • 28,540
New London, IA 52645 • 1,922
New London, NH 03257 • 3,180
New London, OH 44851 • 2,642
New London, WI 54961 • 6,658
New London □, CT • 254,957
New Madrid, MO 63869 • 3,350
New Madrid □, MO • 20,928
Newman, CA 95360 • 4,151
Newmanstown, PA 17073 • 1,410
Newmarket, NH 03857 • 4,917
New Market, TN 37820 • 1,086
New Market, VA 22844 • 1,435
New Martinsville, WV 26155 • 6,705
New Matamoras, OH 45767 • 1,002
New Miami, OH 45011 • 2,555
New Milford, CT 06776 • 5,775
New Milford, NJ 07646 • 15,990
Newnan, GA 30263-65 • 12,497
New Orleans, LA 70101-95 • 496,938
New Oxford, PA 17350 • 1,617
New Paltz, NY 12561 • 5,463
New Paris, IN 46553 • 1,007
New Paris, OH 45347 • 1,801
New Philadelphia, OH 44663 • 15,698
New Philadelphia, PA 17959 • 1,283
New Plymouth, ID 83655 • 1,313
Newport, AR 72112 • 7,459
Newport, DE 19804 • 1,240
Newport, KY 41071-76 • 18,871
Newport, ME 04953 • 1,843
Newport, MI 48166 • 1,100
Newport, MN 55055 • 3,720
Newport, NH 03773 • 3,772
Newport, NC 28570 • 2,516
Newport, OR 97365 • 8,437
Newport, PA 17074 • 1,568
Newport, RI 02840 • 28,227
Newport, TN 37821 • 7,123
Newport, VT 05855 • 4,434
Newport, WA 99156 • 1,691
Newport □, RI • 87,194
Newport Beach, CA 92657-63 • 66,643
Newport East, RI 02840 • 11,080
Newport Hills, WA 98002 • 14,736
Newport News, VA 23601-09 • 170,045
New Port Richey, FL 34652-56 • 14,044
New Prague, MN 56071 • 3,569
New Preston, CT 06777 • 1,217
New Providence, NJ 07974 • 11,439
New Richland, MN 56072 • 1,237
New Richmond, OH 45157 • 2,408
New Richmond, WI 54017 • 5,106
New River Station, NC 28542 • 9,732
New Roads, LA 70760 • 5,303
New Rochelle, NY 10801-05 • 67,265
New Rockford, ND 58356 • 1,604
New Salem, ND 58563 • 909
New Sarpy, LA 70078 • 2,946
New Sharon, IA 50207 • 1,136
New Smyrna Beach, FL 32168-70 • 16,543
New Tazewell, TN 37825 • 1,864
Newton, AL 36352 • 1,580
Newton, IL 62448 • 3,154
Newton, IA 50208 • 14,789
Newton, KS 67114 • 16,700
Newton, MA 02158 • 82,585
Newton, MS 39345 • 3,701
Newton, NJ 07860 • 7,521
Newton, NC 28658 • 9,304
Newton, TX 75966 • 1,885
Newton □, AR • 7,666
Newton □, GA • 41,808
Newton □, IN • 13,551
Newton □, MS • 20,291
Newton □, MO • 44,445
Newton □, TX • 13,569
Newton Falls, OH 44444 • 4,866
Newtown, CT 06470 • 1,800
New Town, ND 58763 • 1,388
Newtown, OH 45244 • 1,589
Newtown Square, PA 19073 • 11,366

New Ulm, MN 56073 • 13,132
Newville, PA 17241 • 1,349
New Washington, OH 44854 • 1,057
New Washoe City, NV 89701 • 2,875
New Waterford, OH 44445 • 1,278
New Whiteland, IN 46184 • 4,097
New Wilmington, PA 16142 • 2,706
New Windsor, NY 12553 • 8,898
New York, NY 10001–99 • 7,322,564
New York □, NY • 1,487,536
Nez Perce □, ID • 33,754
Niagara, WI 54151 • 1,999
Niagara □, NY • 220,756
Niagara Falls, NY 14301–05 • 61,840
Niantic, CT 06357 • 3,048
Nibley, UT 84321 • 1,167
Niceville, FL 32578 • 10,507
Nicholas □, KY • 6,725
Nicholas □, WV • 26,775
Nicholasville, KY 40356 • 13,603
Nicholls, GA 31554 • 1,003
Nichols Hills, OK 73116 • 4,020
Nickerson, KS 67561 • 1,137
Nicollet □, MN • 28,076
Nicoma Park, OK 73066 • 2,353
Nikishka, AK 99635 • 1,109
Niland, CA 92257 • 1,183
Niles, IL 60648 • 28,284
Niles, MI 49120 • 12,458
Niles, OH 44446 • 21,128
Ninety Six, SC 29666 • 2,099
Ninilchik, AK 99639 • 456
Niobrara □, WY • 2,499
Nipomo, CA 93444 • 7,109
Niskayuna, NY 12309 • 4,942
Nisswa, MN 56468 • 1,391
Nitro, WV 25143 • 6,851
Niwot, CO 80544 • 2,666
Nixa, MO 65714 • 4,707
Nixon, NV 89424 • 150
Nixon, TX 78140 • 1,995
Noank, CT 06340 • 1,406
Noble, OK 73068 • 4,710
Noble □, IN • 37,877
Noble □, OH • 11,336
Noble □, OK • 11,045
Nobles □, MN • 20,098
Noblesville, IN 46060 • 17,655
Nocatee, FL 33864 • 1,300
Nocona, TX 76255 • 2,870
Nodaway □, MO • 21,709
Noel, MO 64854 • 1,169
Nogales, AZ 85621 • 19,489
Nokomis, FL 34274–75 • 3,448
Nokomis, IL 62075 • 2,534
Nolan □, TX • 16,594
Nome, AK 99762 • 3,500
Noorvik, AK 99763 • 531
Nora Springs, IA 50458 • 1,505
Norco, CA 91760 • 23,302
Norco, LA 70079 • 3,385
Norcross, GA 30071 • 5,947
Norfolk, CT 06058 • 1,500
Norfolk, NE 68701 • 21,476
Norfolk, NY 13667 • 1,412
Norfolk, VA 23501–93 • 261,229
Norfolk □, MA • 616,087
Norland, FL 33169 • 22,109
Normal, IL 61761 • 40,023
Norman, OK 73069–72 • 80,071
Norman □, MN • 7,975
Normandy, MO 63121 • 4,480
Norridge, IL 60656 • 14,459
Norridgewock, ME 04957 • 1,496
Norris, TN 37828 • 1,303
Norris City, IL 62869 • 1,341
Norristown, PA 19401–09 • 30,749
North Adams, MA 01247 • 16,797
North Albany, OR 97321 • 4,325
North Amherst, MA 01059 • 6,239
North Amityville, NY 11701 • 13,849
Northampton, MA 01060–61 • 29,289
Northampton, PA 18067 • 8,717
Northampton □, NC • 20,798
Northampton □, PA • 247,105
Northampton □, VA • 13,061
North Andover, MA 01845 • 20,129
North Andrews Gardens, FL 33308 • 9,002
North Apollo, PA 15673 • 1,391
North Arlington, NJ 07032 • 13,790
North Atlanta, GA 30319 • 27,812
North Attleboro, MA 02760–63 • 16,178
North Auburn, CA 95603 • 10,301
North Augusta, SC 29841 • 15,351
North Aurora, IL 60542 • 5,940
North Babylon, NY 11703 • 18,081
North Baltimore, OH 45872 • 3,139
North Bay Shore, NY 11706 • 12,799
North Beach, MD 20714 • 1,173
North Bellmore, NY 11710 • 19,707
North Bellport, NY 11713 • 8,182
North Belmont, NC 28012 • 10,762
North Bend, NE 68649 • 1,249
North Bend, OR 97459 • 9,614
North Bend, WA 98045 • 2,578
North Bennington, VT 05257 • 1,520
North Bergen, NJ 07047 • 48,414
North Berwick, ME 03906 • 1,568
North Billerica, MA 01862 • 5,400
Northborough, MA 01532 • 5,761
North Braddock, PA 15104 • 7,036
North Branch, MI 48461 • 1,023
North Branch, MN 55056 • 1,867
North Branch, NJ 08876 • 2,620
North Branford, CT 06471 • 6,600
Northbridge, MA 01534 • 3,570
Northbrook, IL 60062 • 32,308
Northbrook, OH 45231 • 11,471
North Brookfield, MA 01535 • 2,635
North Brunswick, NJ 08902 • 31,287
North Brunswick Township, NJ 08902 • 31,287
North Caldwell, NJ 07006 • 5,832
North Canton, OH 44720 • 14,748
North Cape May, NJ 08204 • 3,574
North Charleston, SC 29406 • 70,218
North Chicago, IL 60064 • 34,978
North City, WA 98155 • 8,200
North Cohasset, MA 02025 • 1,045
North College Hill, OH 45239 • 11,002
North Collins, NY 14111 • 1,335
North Conway, NH 03860 • 2,032
North Corbin, KY 40701 • 1,601
North Crossett, AR 71635 • 3,358
North Dartmouth, MA 02747 • 8,080
North Decatur, GA 30033 • 13,936
North Dighton, MA 02764 • 1,174
North Druid Hills, GA 30033 • 14,170
North Eagle Butte, SD 57625 • 1,423
North East, MD 21901 • 1,913
North East, PA 16428 • 4,617
North Eastham, MA 02651 • 1,570
Northeast Henrietta, NY 14534 • 10,650
North Easton, MA 02356 • 4,420
North Fair Oaks, CA 94025 • 13,912
North Falmouth, MA 02556 • 3,150
Northfield, IL 60093 • 4,635
Northfield, MA 01360 • 1,322
Northfield, MN 55057 • 14,684
Northfield, NH 03276 • 1,375
Northfield, NJ 08225 • 7,305
Northfield, OH 44067 • 3,624
Northfield, VT 05663 • 1,889
Northfield Falls, VT 05664 • 600
North Fond du Lac, WI 54935 • 4,292
Northford, CT 06472 • 3,180
North Fort Myers, FL 33903 • 30,027
Northglenn, CO 80233 • 27,195
North Grafton, MA 01536 • 3,050
North Great River, NY 11722 • 3,964
North Grosvenordale, CT 06255 • 1,705
North Gulfport, MS 39501 • 4,966
North Haledon, NJ 07508 • 7,987
North Hampton, NH 03862 • 1,000
North Haven, CT 06473 • 22,249
North Highlands, CA 95660 • 42,105
North Hill, WA 98166 • 5,706
North Houston, TX 77086 • 12,800
North Hudson, WI 54016 • 3,101
North Industry, OH 44707 • 3,250
North Judson, IN 46366 • 1,582
North Kansas City, MO 64116 • 4,130
North Kingstown, RI 02852–54 • 2,750
North Kingsville, OH 44068 • 2,672
North La Junta, CO 81050 • 1,076
Northlake, IL 60164 • 12,505
North Las Vegas, NV 89030–31 • 47,707
North Lauderdale, FL 33068 • 26,506
North Lewisburg, OH 43060 • 1,160
North Liberty, IN 46554 • 1,366
North Liberty, IA 52317 • 2,926
North Lindenhurst, NY 11757 • 10,563
North Little Rock, AR 72114–20 • 61,741
North Logan, UT 84321 • 3,768
North Madison, OH 44057 • 8,699
North Manchester, IN 46962 • 6,383
North Mankato, MN 56001 • 10,164
North Massapequa, NY 11758 • 19,365
North Merrick, NY 11566 • 12,113
North Merrydale, LA 70812 • 4,000
North Miami, FL 33161 • 49,998
North Miami Beach, FL 33162 • 35,359
North Muskegon, MI 49445 • 3,919
North Myrtle Beach, SC 29582 • 8,636
North Naples, FL 33963 • 13,422
North New Hyde Park, NY 11040 • 14,359
North Ogden, UT 84404 • 11,668
North Olmsted, OH 44070 • 34,204
North Oxford, MA 01537 • 1,250
North Palm Beach, FL 33408 • 11,343
North Park, IL 61111 • 15,806
North Patchogue, NY 11772 • 7,374
North Pembroke, MA 02358 • 2,485
North Plainfield, NJ 07060 • 18,820
North Platte, NE 69101–03 • 22,605
Northport, AL 35476 • 17,366
North Port, FL 34287 • 11,973
Northport, NY 11768 • 7,572
North Prairie, WI 53153 • 1,322
North Providence, RI 02911 • 32,090
North Reading, MA 01864 • 11,455
North Richland Hills, TX 76118 • 45,895
Northridge, OH 45502 • 5,939
Northridge, OH 45414 • 9,448
North Ridgeville, OH 44039 • 21,564
North Riverside, IL 60546 • 6,005
North Royalton, OH 44133 • 23,197
North Salt Lake, UT 84054 • 6,474
North Sarasota, FL 34234 • 6,702
North Scituate, MA 02060 • 4,891
North Sioux City, SD 57049 • 2,019
North Springfield, OR 97477 • 5,451
North Springfield, VT 05150 • 750
North Springfield, VA 22151 • 8,996
North Star, DE 19711 • 1,030
North St. Paul, MN 55109 • 12,376
North Sudbury, MA 01776 • 2,630
North Syracuse, NY 13212 • 7,363
North Tarrytown, NY 10591 • 8,152
North Terre Haute, IN 47805 • 2,000
North Tewksbury, MA 01876 • 1,030
North Tonawanda, NY 14120 • 34,989
North Troy, VT 05859 • 723
North Tunica, MS 38676 • 1,314
Northumberland, PA 17857 • 3,860
Northumberland □, PA • 96,771
Northumberland □, VA • 10,524
North Uxbridge, MA 01538 • 1,500
Northvale, NJ 07647 • 4,563
North Valley Stream, NY 11580 • 14,574
North Vernon, IN 47265 • 5,311
North Versailles, PA 15137 • 12,302
Northview, MI 49505 • 13,712
Northview, OH 45322 • 10,337
Northville, MI 48167 • 6,226
Northville, NY 12134 • 1,180
North Wales, PA 19454 • 3,802
North Wantagh, NY 11793 • 12,276
North Warren, PA 16365 • 1,232
North Wildwood, NJ 08260 • 5,017
North Wilkesboro, NC 28659 • 3,384
North Windham, ME 04062 • 4,077
Northwood, IA 50459 • 1,940
Northwood, ND 58267 • 1,166
Northwood, OH 43619 • 5,506
Northwoods, MO 63121 • 5,106
North York, PA 17404 • 1,689
Norton, KS 67654 • 3,017
Norton, MA 02766 • 1,899
Norton, OH 44203 • 11,477
Norton, VA 24273 • 4,247
Norton □, KS • 5,947
Norton Shores, MI 49441 • 21,755
Nortonville, KY 42442 • 1,209
Norwalk, CA 90650–52 • 94,279
Norwalk, CT 06850–56 • 78,331
Norwalk, IA 50211 • 5,726
Norwalk, OH 44857 • 14,731
Norway, ME 04268 • 3,023
Norway, MI 49870 • 2,910
Norwell, MA 02061 • 1,200
Norwich, CT 06360 • 37,391
Norwich, NY 13815 • 7,613
Norwich, VT 05055 • 1,000
Norwood, MA 02062 • 28,700
Norwood, MN 55368 • 1,351
Norwood, NJ 07648 • 4,858
Norwood, NY 13668 • 1,841
Norwood, NC 28128 • 1,617
Norwood, OH 45212 • 23,674
Norwood, PA 19074 • 6,162
Norwoodville, IA 50317 • 1,200
Nottoway □, VA • 14,993
Novato, CA 94947–49 • 47,585
Novi, MI 48374–77 • 32,998
Nowata, OK 74048 • 3,896
Nowata □, OK • 9,992
Noxubee □, MS • 12,604
Nuckolls □, NE • 5,786
Nueces □, TX • 291,145
Nulato, AK 99765 • 359
Nunda, NY 14517 • 1,347
Nutley, NJ 07110 • 27,099
Nutter Fort, WV 26301 • 1,819
Nutting Lake, MA 01865 • 3,180
Nyack, NY 10960 • 6,558
Nye □, NV • 17,781
Nyssa, OR 97913 • 2,629

O

Oak Bluffs, MA 02557 • 1,124
Oak Brook, IL 60521 • 9,178
Oak Creek, WI 53154 • 19,513
Oakdale, CA 95361 • 11,961
Oakdale, GA 30080 • 1,080
Oakdale, LA 71463 • 6,832
Oakdale, MN 55128 • 18,374
Oakdale, NY 11769 • 7,875
Oakdale, PA 15071 • 1,752
Oakes, ND 58474 • 1,775
Oakfield, NY 14125 • 1,818
Oakfield, WI 53065 • 1,003
Oak Forest, IL 60452 • 26,203
Oak Grove, KY 42262 • 2,863
Oak Grove, LA 71263 • 2,126
Oak Grove, OR 97267 • 12,576
Oak Grove, SC 29073 • 7,173
Oak Harbor, OH 43449 • 2,637
Oak Harbor, WA 98277 • 17,176
Oak Hill, MI 49660 • 1,000
Oak Hill, OH 45656 • 1,831
Oak Hill, WV 25901 • 6,812
Oakhurst, OK 74050 • 2,200
Oakland, CA 94601–62 • 372,242
Oakland, IA 51560 • 1,496
Oakland, ME 04963 • 3,510
Oakland, MD 21550 • 2,078
Oakland, NE 68045 • 1,279
Oakland, NJ 07436 • 11,997
Oakland, RI 02830 • 600
Oakland □, MI • 1,083,592
Oakland City, IN 47660 • 2,810
Oakland Park, FL 33334 • 26,326
Oak Lawn, IL 60453–59 • 56,182
Oaklawn, KS 67216 • 4,200
Oakley, CA 94561 • 18,374
Oakley, KS 67748 • 2,045
Oaklyn, NJ 08107 • 4,430
Oakmont, PA 15139 • 6,961
Oak Orchard, DE 19966 • 350
Oak Park, CA 91301 • 5,000
Oak Park, IL 60301–05 • 53,648
Oak Park, MI 48237 • 30,462
Oak Ridge, FL 32809 • 15,388
Oakridge, OR 97463 • 3,063
Oak Ridge, TN 37830 • 27,310
Oakton, VA 22124 • 24,610
Oak Valley, NJ 08090 • 5,400
Oakville, CT 06779 • 8,741
Oakville, MO 63129 • 31,750
Oakwood, GA 30566 • 1,464
Oakwood, IL 61858 • 1,533
Oakwood, OH 45419 • 3,392
Oberlin, KS 67749 • 2,197
Oberlin, LA 70655 • 1,808
Oberlin, OH 44074 • 8,191
Obetz, OH 43207 • 3,167
Obion, TN 38240 • 1,241
Obion □, TN • 31,717
Oblong, IL 62449 • 1,616
O'Brien □, IA • 15,444
Ocala, FL 32670–78 • 42,045
Ocean □, NJ • 433,203
Oceana, WV 24870 • 1,791
Oceana □, MI • 22,454
Ocean Bluff, MA 02065 • 2,500
Ocean City, FL 32548 • 5,422
Ocean City, MD 21842 • 5,146
Ocean City, NJ 08226 • 15,512
Ocean Gate, NJ 08740 • 2,078
Ocean Grove, MA 02777 • 4,560
Oceano, CA 93445 • 6,169
Ocean Park, WA 98640 • 1,650
Ocean Port, NJ 07757 • 6,146
Oceanside, CA 92054–56 • 128,398
Oceanside, NY 11572 • 32,423
Ocean Springs, MS 39564–65 • 14,658
Ocean [Township], NJ 07712 • 23,570
Ocean View, DE 19970 • 606
Oceanville, NJ 08231 • 1,000
Ochiltree □, TX • 9,128
Ocilla, GA 31774 • 3,182
Ocoee, FL 34761 • 12,778
Oconee □, GA • 17,618
Oconee □, SC • 57,494
Oconomowoc, WI 53066 • 10,993
Oconto, WI 54153 • 4,474
Oconto □, WI • 30,226
Oconto Falls, WI 54154 • 2,584
Odebolt, IA 51458 • 1,158
Odell, IL 60460 • 1,030
Odem, TX 78370 • 2,366
Odenton, MD 21113 • 12,833
Odessa, DE 19730 • 303
Odessa, MO 64076 • 3,695
Odessa, TX 79760–68 • 89,699
Odin, IL 62870 • 1,150
Odon, IN 47562 • 1,475
O'Donnell, TX 79351 • 1,102
Oelwein, IA 50662 • 6,493
O'Fallon, IL 62269 • 16,073
O'Fallon, MO 63366 • 18,698
Ogallala, NE 69153 • 5,095
Ogden, IA 50212 • 1,909
Ogden, KS 66517 • 1,494
Ogden, UT 84401–14 • 63,909
Ogdensburg, NJ 07439 • 2,722
Ogdensburg, NY 13669 • 13,521
Ogemaw □, MI • 18,681
Ogle □, IL • 45,957
Oglesby, IL 61348 • 3,619
Oglethorpe, GA 31068 • 1,302
Oglethorpe □, GA • 9,763
Ogunquit, ME 03907 • 1,492
Ohatchee, AL 36271 • 1,042
Ohio □, IN • 5,315
Ohio □, KY • 21,105
Ohio □, WV • 50,871
Ohioville, PA 15059 • 3,865
Oil City, LA 71061 • 1,282
Oil City, PA 16301 • 11,949
Oildale, CA 93308 • 26,553
Oilton, OK 74052 • 1,060
Ojai, CA 93023–24 • 7,613
Okaloosa □, FL • 143,776
Okanogan, WA 98840 • 2,370
Okanogan □, WA • 33,350
Okarche, OK 73762 • 1,160
Okauchee, WI 53069 • 2,300
Okauchee Lake, WI 53058 • 3,819
Okawville, IL 62271 • 1,274
Okeechobee, FL 34972–74 • 4,943
Okeechobee □, FL • 29,627
Okeene, OK 73763 • 1,343
Okemah, OK 74859 • 3,085
Okemos, MI 48864 • 20,216
Okfuskee □, OK • 11,551
Oklahoma □, OK • 599,611
Oklahoma City, OK 73101–80 • 444,719
Oklawaha, FL 32179 • 1,200
Okmulgee, OK 74447 • 13,441
Okmulgee □, OK • 36,490
Okolona, KY 40219 • 18,902
Okolona, MS 38860 • 3,267
Oktibbeha □, MS • 38,375
Ola, AR 72853 • 1,090
Olathe, CO 81425 • 1,263
Olathe, KS 66061–62 • 63,352
Olcott, NY 14126 • 1,432
Old Bethpage, NY 11804 • 5,610
Old Bridge, NJ 08857 • 22,151
Old Forge, NY 13420 • 1,061
Old Forge, PA 18518 • 8,834
Oldham □, KY • 33,263
Oldham □, TX • 2,278
Old Harbor, AK 99643 • 284
Old Orchard Beach, ME 04064 • 7,789
Old Saybrook, CT 06475 • 1,820
Oldsmar, FL 34677 • 8,361
Old Tappan, NJ 07675 • 4,254
Old Town, ME 04468 • 8,317
Olean, NY 14760 • 16,946
Olive Branch, MS 38654 • 3,567
Olive Hill, KY 41164 • 1,809
Olivehurst, CA 95961 • 9,738
Oliver, PA 15472 • 3,271
Oliver □, ND • 2,381
Oliver Springs, TN 37840 • 3,433
Olivet, MI 49076 • 1,604
Olivette, MO 63132 • 7,573
Olivia, MN 56277 • 2,623
Olla, LA 71465 • 1,410
Olmito, TX 78575 • 1,400
Olmos Park, TX 78212 • 2,161
Olmsted □, MN • 106,470
Olmsted Falls, OH 44138 • 6,741
Olney, IL 62450 • 8,664
Olney, MD 20832 • 23,019
Olney, TX 76374 • 3,519
Olton, TX 79064 • 2,116
Olympia, WA 98501–07 • 33,840
Olympia Heights, FL 33175 • 36,900
Olyphant, PA 18447 • 5,222
Omaha, NE 68101–72 • 335,795
Omak, WA 98841 • 4,117
Omro, WI 54963 • 2,836
Onalaska, WI 54650 • 11,284
Onancock, VA 23417 • 1,434
Onarga, IL 60955 • 1,281
Onawa, IA 51040 • 2,936
Onaway, MI 49765 • 1,039
Oneco, FL 34264 • 6,417
Oneida, NY 13421 • 10,850
Oneida, OH 45042 • 1,650
Oneida, TN 37841 • 3,502
Oneida □, ID • 3,492
Oneida □, NY • 250,836
Oneida □, WI • 31,679
O'Neill, NE 68763 • 3,852
Oneonta, AL 35121 • 4,844
Oneonta, NY 13820 • 13,954
Onida, SD 57564 • 761
Onondaga □, NY • 468,973
Onset, MA 02558 • 1,461
Onslow □, NC • 149,838
Ontario, CA 91761–62 • 133,179
Ontario, OH 44862 • 4,026
Ontario, OR 97914 • 9,392
Ontario □, NY • 95,101
Ontonagon, MI 49953 • 2,040
Ontonagon □, MI • 8,854
Oolitic, IN 47451 • 1,424
Ooltewah, TN 37363 • 1,200
Oostburg, WI 53070 • 1,931
Opal Cliffs, CA 95062 • 5,940
Opa-Locka, FL 33054–56 • 15,283
Opelika, AL 36801–03 • 22,122
Opelousas, LA 70570–71 • 18,151
Opp, AL 36467 • 6,985
Opportunity, WA 99206 • 22,326
Oquawka, IL 61469 • 1,442
Oracle, AZ 85623 • 3,043
Oradell, NJ 07649 • 8,024
Oran, MO 63771 • 1,164
Orange, CA 92664–69 • 110,658
Orange, CT 06477 • 12,830
Orange, MA 01364 • 3,791
Orange, NJ 07050–52 • 29,925
Orange, TX 77630–31 • 19,381
Orange, VA 22960 • 2,582
Orange □, CA • 2,410,556
Orange □, FL • 677,491
Orange □, IN • 18,409
Orange □, NY • 307,647
Orange □, NC • 93,851
Orange □, TX • 80,509
Orange □, VT • 26,149
Orange □, VA • 21,421
Orange Beach, AL 36561 • 2,253
Orangeburg, SC 29115–16 • 13,739
Orangeburg □, SC • 84,803
Orange City, FL 32763 • 5,347
Orange City, IA 51041 • 4,940
Orange Grove, MS 39503 • 15,676
Orange Grove, TX 78372 • 1,175
Orange Lake, FL 32681 • 1,000
Orange Park, FL 32073 • 9,488
Orangevale, CA 95662 • 26,266
Orangeville, UT 84537 • 1,459
Orchard City, CO 81410 • 2,218
Orchard Homes, MT 59801 • 10,317
Orchard Mesa, CO 81501 • 5,977
Orchard Park, NY 14127 • 3,280
Orchards, WA 98662 • 8,828
Orchard Valley, WY 82007 • 3,321
Orcutt, CA 93455 • 1,500
Ord, NE 68862 • 2,481
Ordway, CO 81063 • 1,025
Oregon, IL 61061 • 3,891
Oregon, OH 43616 • 18,334
Oregon, WI 53575 • 4,519
Oregon □, MO • 9,470
Oregon City, OR 97045 • 14,698
Orem, UT 84057–59 • 67,561
Orfordville, WI 53576 • 1,219
Orient, NY 11957 • 1,000
Orinda, CA 94563 • 16,642
Orion, IL 61273 • 1,821
Oriskany, NY 13424 • 1,450
Orland, CA 95963 • 5,052
Orlando, FL 32801–72 • 164,693
Orland Park, IL 60462 • 35,720
Orleans, IN 47452 • 2,083
Orleans, IN 47452 • 2,161
Orleans, MA 02653 • 1,699
Orleans, VT 05860 • 806
Orleans □, LA • 496,938
Orleans □, NY • 41,846
Orleans □, VT • 24,053
Orlovista, FL 32811 • 5,990
Ormond Beach, FL 32174–76 • 29,721
Ormond By The Sea, FL 32174 • 8,157
Orofino, ID 83544 • 2,868
Orono, ME 04473 • 9,789
Orono, MN 55323 • 7,285
Orosi, CA 93647 • 5,486
Oroville, CA 95965–66 • 11,960
Oroville, WA 98844 • 1,505
Orrville, OH 44667 • 7,712
Orting, WA 98360 • 2,106
Ortonville, MI 48462 • 1,252
Ortonville, MN 56278 • 2,205
Orwell, OH 44076 • 1,258
Orwigsburg, PA 17961 • 2,780
Osage, IA 50461 • 3,439
Osage, WY 82723 • 350
Osage □, KS • 15,248
Osage □, MO • 12,018
Osage □, OK • 41,645
Osage Beach, MO 65065 • 2,599
Osage City, KS 66523 • 2,689
Osakis, MN 56360 • 1,256
Osawatomie, KS 66064 • 4,590
Osborne, KS 67473 • 1,778
Osborne □, KS • 4,867
Osburn, ID 83849 • 1,579
Osceola, AR 72370 • 8,930
Osceola, IN 46561 • 1,999
Osceola, IA 50213 • 4,164
Osceola, WI 54020 • 2,075
Osceola □, FL • 107,728
Osceola □, IA • 7,267
Osceola □, MI • 20,146
Osceola Mills, PA 16666 • 1,310
Oscoda, MI 48750 • 1,061
Oscoda □, MI • 7,842
Osgood, IN 47037 • 1,688
Oshkosh, WI 54901–04 • 55,006
Oskaloosa, IA 52577 • 10,632
Oskaloosa, KS 66066 • 1,074
Osprey, FL 34229 • 2,597
Osseo, MN 55369 • 2,704
Osseo, WI 54758 • 1,551
Ossian, IN 46777 • 2,428
Ossining, NY 10562 • 22,582
Osterville, MA 02655 • 2,911
Oswego, IL 60543 • 3,876
Oswego, KS 67356 • 1,870
Oswego, NY 13126 • 19,195
Oswego □, NY • 121,771
Otay, CA 92010 • 6,400
Oteen, NC 28805 • 1,400
Otego, NY 13825 • 1,068
Otero □, CO • 20,185
Otero □, NM • 51,928
Othello, WA 99327 • 4,638
Otis Orchards, WA 99027 • 3,200
Otoe □, NE • 14,252
Otsego, MI 49078 • 3,937
Otsego □, MI • 17,957
Otsego □, NY • 60,517
Ottawa, IL 61350 • 17,451
Ottawa, KS 66067 • 10,667
Ottawa, OH 45875 • 3,999
Ottawa □, KS • 5,634
Ottawa □, MI • 187,768
Ottawa □, OH • 40,029
Ottawa □, OK • 30,561
Ottawa Hills, OH 43606 • 4,543
Otterbein, IN 47970 • 1,291
Otter Tail □, MN • 50,714
Ottumwa, IA 52501 • 24,488
Ouachita □, AR • 30,574
Ouachita □, LA • 142,191
Ouray, CO 81427 • 644
Ouray □, CO • 2,295
Outagamie □, WI • 140,510
Overland, MO 63114 • 17,987
Overland Park, KS 66204 • 111,790
Overlea, MD 21206 • 12,137
Overlook, OH 45431 • 6,000
Overton, NV 89040 • 1,111

Overton, TX 75684 • 2,105
Overton □, TN • 17,636
Ovid, MI 48866 • 1,442
Owasso, OK 74055 • 11,151
Owatonna, MN 55060 • 19,386
Owego, NY 13827 • 4,442
Owen □, IN • 17,281
Owen □, KY • 9,035
Owensboro, KY 42301-03 • 53,549
Owensville, IN 47665 • 1,053
Owensville, MO 65066 • 2,325
Owensville, OH 45160 • 1,019
Owenton, KY 40359 • 1,306
Owings Mills, MD 21117 • 9,474
Owingsville, KY 40360 • 1,491
Owosso, MI 48867 • 16,322
Owsley □, KY • 5,036
Owyhee, NV 89832 • 908
Owyhee □, ID • 8,392
Oxford, AL 36203 • 9,362
Oxford, CT 06483 • 1,600
Oxford, GA 30267 • 1,945
Oxford, IN 47971 • 1,273
Oxford, KS 67119 • 1,143
Oxford, MA 01540 • 5,969
Oxford, MI 48370-71 • 2,929
Oxford, MS 38655 • 9,984
Oxford, NJ 07863 • 1,767
Oxford, NY 13830 • 1,738
Oxford, NC 27565 • 7,913
Oxford, OH 45056 • 18,937
Oxford, PA 19363 • 3,769
Oxford □, ME • 52,602
Oxnard, CA 93030-35 • 142,216
Oxon Hill, MD 20745 • 36,267
Oyster Bay, NY 11771 • 6,687
Ozark, AL 36360-61 • 12,922
Ozark, AR 72949 • 3,330
Ozark, MO 65721 • 4,243
Ozark □, MO • 8,598
Ozaukee □, WI • 72,831
Ozona, FL 34660 • 1,500
Ozona, TX 76943 • 3,181

P

Paauilo, HI 96776 • 620
Pace, FL 32571 • 6,277
Pacific, MO 63069 • 4,350
Pacific, WA 98047 • 4,622
Pacific □, WA • 18,882
Pacifica, CA 94044 • 37,670
Pacific Beach, WA 98571 • 1,200
Pacific City, OR 97135 • 1,500
Pacific Grove, CA 93950 • 16,117
Pacific Palisades, HI 96782 • 10,000
Packwood, WA 98361 • 1,010
Pacolet, SC 29372 • 1,736
Paddock Lake, WI 53168 • 2,662
Paden City, WV 26159 • 2,862
Paducah, KY 42001-03 • 27,256
Paducah, TX 79248 • 1,788
Page, AZ 86040 • 6,598
Page □, IA • 16,870
Page □, VA • 21,690
Pageland, SC 29728 • 2,666
Page Manor, OH 45431 • 9,300
Pagosa Springs, CO 81147 • 1,207
Pahala, HI 96777 • 1,520
Pahoa, HI 96778 • 1,027
Pahokee, FL 33476 • 6,822
Pahrump, NV 89041 • 7,424
Paia, HI 96779 • 2,091
Paincourtville, LA 70391 • 1,550
Painesville, OH 44077 • 15,699
Painted Post, NY 14870 • 1,950
Paintsville, KY 41240 • 4,354
Pajarito, NM 87105 • 1,400
Palacios, TX 77465 • 4,418
Palatine, IL 60067 • 39,253
Palatka, FL 32177 • 10,201
Palestine, IL 62451 • 1,619
Palestine, TX 75801-02 • 18,042
Palisade, CO 81526 • 1,871
Palisades Park, NJ 07650 • 14,536
Palm Bay, FL 32905 • 62,632
Palm Beach, FL 33480 • 9,814
Palm Beach □, FL • 863,518
Palm Beach Gardens, FL 33410 • 22,965
Palm Coast, FL 32135 • 14,287
Palmdale, CA 93550-51 • 68,842
Palm Desert, CA 92260-61 • 23,252
Palmer, AK 99645 • 2,866
Palmer, MA 01069 • 4,069
Palmer, MS 39401 • 2,765
Palmer, TX 75152 • 1,659
Palmer Lake, CO 80133 • 1,480
Palmer Park, MD 20785 • 7,019
Palmerton, PA 18071 • 5,394
Palmetto, FL 34220-21 • 9,268
Palmetto, GA 30268 • 2,612
Palmetto Estates, FL 33157 • 12,293
Palm Harbor, FL 34682-85 • 50,256
Palm Springs, CA 92262-64 • 40,181
Palm Springs, FL 33460 • 9,763
Palm Springs North, FL 33015 • 5,300
Palm Valley, FL 32082 • 9,960
Palmyra, MO 63461 • 3,371
Palmyra, NJ 08065 • 7,056
Palmyra, NY 14522 • 3,566
Palmyra, PA 17078 • 6,910
Palmyra, WI 53156 • 1,539
Palo Alto, CA 94301-09 • 55,900
Palo Alto □, IA • 10,669
Palo Pinto □, TX • 25,055
Palos Heights, IL 60463 • 11,478
Palos Hills, IL 60465 • 17,803
Palos Park, IL 60464 • 4,199
Palos Verdes Estates, CA 90274 • 13,512
Pamlico □, NC • 11,372
Pampa, TX 79065-66 • 19,959
Pamplico, SC 29583 • 1,314
Pana, IL 62557 • 5,796
Panaca, NV 89042 • 700
Panama, OK 74951 • 1,528
Panama City, FL 32401-13 • 34,378
Panama City Beach, FL 32407-08 • 4,051
Pandora, OH 45877 • 1,009
Panguitch, UT 84759 • 1,444
Panhandle, TX 79068 • 2,353
Panola □, MS • 29,996
Panola □, TX • 22,035
Panora, IA 50216 • 1,100
Panthersville, GA 30032 • 9,874
Paola, KS 66071 • 4,698
Paoli, IN 47454 • 3,542
Paoli, PA 19301 • 5,603
Paonia, CO 81428 • 1,403
Papaikou, HI 96781 • 1,634
Papillion, NE 68046 • 10,372
Paradise, CA 95969 • 25,408
Paradise, NV 89109 • 124,682
Paradise Hills, NM 87114 • 5,513
Paradise Valley, AZ 85253 • 11,671
Paradise Valley, NV 89426 • 150
Paragould, AR 72450-51 • 18,540
Paramount, CA 90723 • 47,669
Paramount, MD 21740 • 1,878
Paramus, NJ 07652-53 • 25,067
Parchment, MI 49004 • 1,958
Pardeeville, WI 53954 • 1,630
Paris, AR 72855 • 3,674
Paris, IL 61944 • 8,987
Paris, KY 40361-62 • 8,730
Paris, MO 65275 • 1,486
Paris, TN 38242 • 9,332
Paris, TX 75460-61 • 24,699
Park □, CO • 7,174
Park □, MT • 14,562
Park □, WY • 23,178
Park City, KS 67219 • 5,050
Park City, UT 84060 • 4,468
Parke □, IN • 15,410
Parker, AZ 85344 • 2,897
Parker, CO 80134 • 5,450
Parker, FL 32401 • 4,598
Parker, SD 57053 • 984
Parker □, TX • 64,785
Parker City, IN 47368 • 1,323
Parkersburg, IA 50665 • 1,804
Parkersburg, WV 26101-06 • 33,862
Parkesburg, PA 19365 • 2,981
Park Falls, WI 54552 • 3,104
Park Forest, IL 60466 • 24,656
Park Hills, KY 41015 • 3,321
Parkin, AR 72373 • 1,847
Parkland, WA 98444 • 20,882
Park Layne, OH 45344 • 4,895
Park Rapids, MN 56470 • 2,863
Park Ridge, IL 60068 • 36,175
Park Ridge, NJ 07656 • 8,102
Park River, ND 58270 • 1,725
Parkrose, OR 97230 • 21,108
Parkston, SD 57366 • 1,572
Parkville, MD 21234 • 31,617
Parkville, MO 64152 • 2,402
Parkwater, WA 99211 • 4,300
Parkway, CA 95823 • 12,000
Parkwood, NC 27713 • 4,123
Parkwood, WA 98366 • 6,853
Parlier, CA 93648 • 7,938
Parma, ID 83660 • 1,597
Parma, OH 44129 • 87,876
Parma Heights, OH 44130 • 21,448
Parmer □, TX • 9,863
Parole, MD 21401 • 10,054
Parowan, UT 84761 • 1,873
Parrish, AL 35580 • 1,433
Parshall, ND 58770 • 943
Parsons, KS 67357 • 11,924
Parsons, TN 38363 • 2,033
Parsons, WV 26287 • 1,453
Pasadena, CA 91101-09 • 131,591
Pasadena, MD 21122 • 10,012
Pasadena, TX 77501-08 • 119,363
Pascagoula, MS 39567-68 • 25,899
Pasco, WA 99301-02 • 20,337
Pasco □, FL • 281,131
Pascoag, RI 02859 • 5,011
Paso Robles, CA 93446-47 • 18,583
Pasquotank □, NC • 31,298
Passaic, NJ 07055 • 58,041
Passaic □, NJ • 453,060
Pass Christian, MS 39571 • 5,557
Pataskala, OH 43062 • 3,046
Patchogue, NY 11772 • 11,060
Paterson, NJ 07501-44 • 140,891
Patrick □, VA • 17,473
Patten, ME 04765 • 1,256
Patterson, LA 70392 • 4,736
Patterson, NY 12563 • 1,200
Patton, PA 16668 • 2,206
Paul, ID 83347 • 901
Paulding, OH 45879 • 2,605
Paulding □, GA • 41,611
Paulding □, OH • 20,488
Paullina, IA 51046 • 1,134
Paulsboro, NJ 08066 • 6,577
Pauls Valley, OK 73075 • 6,150
Pawcatuck, CT 06379 • 5,289
Paw Creek, NC 28130 • 1,700
Pawhuska, OK 74056 • 3,825
Pawling, NY 12564 • 1,974
Pawnee, IL 62558 • 2,384
Pawnee, OK 74058 • 2,197
Pawnee □, KS • 7,555
Pawnee □, NE • 3,317
Pawnee □, OK • 15,575
Pawnee City, NE 68420 • 1,008
Paw Paw, MI 49079 • 3,169
Pawtucket, RI 02860-65 • 72,644
Paxton, IL 60957 • 4,289
Paxton, MA 01612 • 1,550
Payette, ID 83661 • 5,592
Payette □, ID • 16,434
Payne, OH 45880 • 1,244
Payne □, OK • 61,507
Paynesville, MN 56362 • 2,275
Payson, AZ 85541 • 8,377
Payson, IL 62360 • 1,114
Payson, UT 84651 • 9,510
Peabody, KS 66866 • 1,349
Peabody, MA 01960-61 • 47,039
Peace Dale, RI 02883 • 3,100
Peach □, GA • 21,189
Peach Orchard, GA 30906 • 13,800
Peachtree City, GA 30269 • 19,027
Pea Ridge, AR 72751 • 1,620
Pearisburg, VA 24134 • 2,064
Pearl, MS 39208 • 19,588
Pearland, TX 77581 • 18,697
Pearl City, HI 96782 • 30,993
Pearl River, LA 70452 • 1,507
Pearl River, NY 10965 • 15,314
Pearl River □, MS • 38,714
Pearsall, TX 78061 • 6,924
Pearson, GA 31642 • 1,714
Pecatonica, IL 61063 • 1,760
Pecos, NM 87552 • 1,012
Pecos, TX 79772 • 12,069
Pecos □, TX • 14,675
Peculiar, MO 64078 • 1,777
Pedricktown, NJ 08067 • 1,500
Peebles, OH 45660 • 1,782
Peekskill, NY 10566 • 19,536
Pegram, TN 37143 • 1,371
Pekin, IL 61554-55 • 32,254
Pekin, IN 47165 • 1,095
Pelahatchie, MS 39145 • 1,553
Pelham, AL 35124 • 9,765
Pelham, GA 31779 • 3,869
Pelham, NY 10803 • 6,413
Pelham Manor, NY 10803 • 5,443
Pelican Rapids, MN 56572 • 1,886
Pella, IA 50219 • 9,270
Pell City, AL 35125 • 8,118
Pell Lake, WI 53157 • 2,018
Pemberton, NJ 08068 • 1,367
Pemberville, OH 43450 • 1,279
Pembina □, ND • 9,238
Pembroke, GA 31321 • 1,503
Pembroke, MA 02359 • 2,000
Pembroke, NC 28372 • 2,241
Pembroke, VA 24136 • 1,064
Pembroke Park, FL 33009 • 4,933
Pembroke Pines, FL 33024 • 65,452
Pemiscot □, MO • 21,921
Pen Argyl, PA 18072 • 3,492
Penbrook, PA 17103 • 2,791
Pender, NE 68047 • 1,208
Pender □, NC • 28,855
Pendleton, IN 46064 • 2,309
Pendleton, OR 97801 • 15,126
Pendleton, SC 29670 • 3,314
Pendleton □, KY • 12,036
Pendleton □, WV • 8,054
Pendley Hills, GA 30032 • 5,400
Pend Oreille □, WA • 8,915
Penfield, NY 14526 • 6,260
Penn Acres, DE 19720 • 2,430
Penn Hills, PA 15235 • 51,430
Pennington, NJ 08534 • 2,537
Pennington □, MN • 13,306
Pennington □, SD • 81,343
Pennington Gap, VA 24277 • 1,922
Pennsauken, NJ 08110 • 34,733
Pennsboro, WV 26415 • 1,282
Pennsburg, PA 18073 • 2,460
Penns Grove, NJ 08069 • 5,228
Pennsville, NJ 08070 • 12,218
Penn Yan, NY 14527 • 5,248
Penobscot □, ME • 146,601
Pensacola, FL 32501-26 • 58,165
Pentwater, MI 49449 • 1,050
Peoria, AZ 85345 • 50,618
Peoria, IL 61601-56 • 113,504
Peoria □, IL • 182,827
Peoria Heights, IL 61614 • 6,930
Peotone, IL 60468 • 2,947
Pepeekeo, HI 96783 • 1,813
Pepin □, WI • 7,107
Pepperell, MA 01463 • 2,350
Pepper Pike, OH 44124 • 6,185
Pequannock, NJ 07440 • 12,844
Perdido, AL 36562 • 1,200
Perham, MN 56573 • 2,075
Perkasie, PA 18944 • 7,878
Perkins, OK 74059 • 1,925
Perkins □, NE • 3,367
Perkins □, SD • 3,932
Perquimans □, NC • 10,447
Perrine, FL 33157 • 15,576
Perris, CA 92370 • 21,460
Perry, FL 32347 • 7,151
Perry, GA 31069 • 9,452
Perry, IA 50220 • 6,652
Perry, MI 48872 • 2,163
Perry, NY 14530 • 4,219
Perry, OH 44081 • 1,012
Perry, OK 73077 • 4,978
Perry, UT 84302 • 1,211
Perry □, AL • 12,759
Perry □, AR • 7,969
Perry □, IL • 21,412
Perry □, IN • 19,107
Perry □, KY • 30,283
Perry □, MS • 10,865
Perry □, MO • 16,648
Perry □, OH • 31,557
Perry □, PA • 41,172
Perry □, TN • 6,612
Perry Hall, MD 21128 • 22,723
Perry Heights, OH 44646 • 9,055
Perryman, MD 21130 • 2,160
Perrysburg, OH 43551-52 • 12,551
Perryton, TX 79070 • 7,607
Perryville, AR 72126 • 1,141
Perryville, MD 21903 • 2,456
Perryville, MO 63775 • 6,933
Pershing □, NV • 4,336
Person □, NC • 30,180
Perth Amboy, NJ 08861-63 • 41,967
Peru, IL 61354 • 9,302
Peru, IN 46970 • 12,843
Peru, NE 68421 • 1,110
Peru, NY 12972 • 1,565
Peshtigo, WI 54157 • 3,154
Petal, MS 39465 • 7,883
Petaluma, CA 94952-55 • 43,184
Peterborough, NH 03458 • 2,685
Petersburg, AK 99833 • 3,207
Petersburg, IL 62675 • 2,261
Petersburg, IN 47567 • 2,449
Petersburg, MI 49270 • 1,201
Petersburg, TX 79250 • 1,292
Petersburg, VA 23801-05 • 38,386
Petersburg, WV 26847 • 2,360
Petersville, AL 35633 • 1,730
Petoskey, MI 49770 • 6,056
Petroleum □, MT • 519
Petros, TN 37845 • 1,286
Pettis □, MO • 35,437
Pevely, MO 63070 • 2,831
Pewaukee, WI 53072 • 4,941
Pewee Valley, KY 40056 • 1,283
Pharr, TX 78577 • 32,921
Phelps, KY 41553 • 1,120
Phelps, NY 14532 • 1,978
Phelps □, MO • 35,248
Phelps □, NE • 9,715
Phenix City, AL 36867-69 • 25,312
Philadelphia, MS 39350 • 6,758
Philadelphia, NY 13673 • 1,478
Philadelphia, PA 19101-96 • 1,585,577
Philadelphia □, PA • 1,585,577
Phil Campbell, AL 35581 • 1,317
Philip, SD 57567 • 1,077
Philippi, WV 26416 • 3,132
Philipsburg, MT 59858 • 925
Philipsburg, PA 16866 • 3,048
Phillips, TX 79007 • 1,729
Phillips, WI 54555 • 1,592
Phillips □, AR • 28,838
Phillips □, CO • 4,189
Phillips □, KS • 6,590
Phillips □, MT • 5,163
Phillipsburg, KS 67661 • 2,828
Phillipsburg, NJ 08865 • 15,757
Philmont, NY 12565 • 1,623
Philo, IL 61864 • 1,028
Philomath, OR 97370 • 2,983
Phoenix, AZ 85001-82 • 983,403
Phoenix, IL 60426 • 2,217
Phoenix, NY 13135 • 2,435
Phoenix, OR 97535 • 3,239
Phoenixville, PA 19460 • 15,066
Piatt □, IL • 15,548
Picayune, MS 39466 • 10,633
Picher, OK 74360 • 1,714
Pickaway □, OH • 48,255
Pickens, MS 39146 • 1,285
Pickens, SC 29671 • 3,042
Pickens □, AL • 20,699
Pickens □, GA • 14,432
Pickens □, SC • 93,894
Pickerington, OH 43147 • 5,668
Pickett □, TN • 4,548
Pico Rivera, CA 90660-61 • 59,177
Piedmont, AL 36272 • 5,288
Piedmont, CA 94611 • 10,602
Piedmont, MO 63957 • 2,166
Piedmont, OK 73078 • 2,522
Piedmont, SC 29673 • 4,143
Piedmont, WV 26750 • 1,094
Pierce, ID 83546 • 746
Pierce, NE 68767 • 1,615
Pierce □, GA • 13,328
Pierce □, NE • 7,827
Pierce □, ND • 5,052
Pierce □, WA • 586,203
Pierce □, WI • 32,765
Pierce City, MO 65723 • 1,382
Pierceton, IN 46562 • 1,030
Pierre, SD 57501 • 12,906
Pierre Part, LA 70339 • 3,053
Pierson, FL 32180 • 2,988
Pierz, MN 56364 • 1,014
Pigeon, MI 48755 • 1,207
Pigeon Cove, MA 01966 • 1,660
Pigeon Forge, TN 37863 • 3,027
Piggott, AR 72454 • 3,777
Pike □, AL • 27,595
Pike □, AR • 10,086
Pike □, GA • 10,224
Pike □, IL • 17,577
Pike □, IN • 12,509
Pike □, KY • 72,583
Pike □, MS • 36,882
Pike □, MO • 15,969
Pike □, OH • 24,249
Pike □, PA • 27,966
Pike Lake, MN 55811 • 1,004
Pikesville, MD 21208 • 24,815
Piketon, OH 45661 • 1,717
Pikeville, KY 41501-02 • 6,324
Pikeville, TN 37367 • 1,771
Pilot Mountain, NC 27041 • 1,181
Pilot Point, TX 76258 • 2,538
Pilot Rock, OR 97868 • 1,478
Pilot Station, AK 99650 • 463
Pima, AZ 85543 • 1,725
Pima □, AZ • 666,880
Pimmit Hills, VA 22043 • 6,019
Pinal □, AZ • 116,379
Pinardville, NH 03045 • 4,654
Pinckney, MI 48169 • 1,603
Pinckneyville, IL 62274 • 3,372
Pinconning, MI 48650 • 1,291
Pine □, MN • 21,264
Pine Bluff, AR 71601-13 • 57,140
Pine Bluffs, WY 82082 • 1,054
Pine Bridge, CT 06403 • 1,160
Pine Bush, NY 12566 • 1,445
Pine Castle, FL 32809 • 8,276
Pine City, MN 55063 • 2,613
Pinedale, WY 82941 • 1,181
Pine Grove, PA 17963 • 2,118
Pine Grove Mills, PA 16868 • 1,129
Pine Hill, NJ 08021 • 9,854
Pine Hills, FL 32808 • 35,322
Pinehurst, MA 01866 • 6,614
Pinehurst, NJ 08201 • 1,850
Pinehurst, NC 28374 • 5,103
Pine Island, MN 55963 • 2,125
Pine Island, NY 10969 • 1,200
Pine Knot, KY 42635 • 1,549
Pine Lawn, MO 63120 • 5,092
Pine Level, NC 27568 • 1,217
Pinellas □, FL • 851,659
Pinellas Park, FL 34664-66 • 43,426
Pine Plains, NY 12567 • 1,312
Pine Ridge, SD 57770 • 2,596
Pinetops, NC 27864 • 1,514
Pine Valley, CA 91962 • 1,297
Pineville, KY 40977 • 2,198
Pineville, LA 71360-61 • 12,251
Pineville, NC 28134 • 2,970
Pinewald, NJ 08721 • 1,700
Pinewood, FL 33168 • 15,518
Pinewood Park, FL 33168 • 8,300
Piney Point, MD 20674 • 1,200
Piney View, WV 25906 • 1,085
Pinole, CA 94564 • 17,460
Pinson, AL 35126 • 1,820
Pioche, NV 89043 • 830
Pioneer, OH 43554 • 1,287
Pipestone, MN 56164 • 4,554
Pipestone □, MN • 10,491
Piqua, OH 45356 • 20,612
Pirtleville, AZ 85626 • 1,364
Piscataquis □, ME • 18,653
Piscataway, NJ 08854-55 • 42,223
Pisgah, OH 45069 • 15,660
Pisgah Forest, NC 28768 • 1,899
Pismo Beach, CA 93448-49 • 7,669
Pitcairn, PA 15140 • 4,087
Pitkin □, CO • 12,661
Pitman, NJ 08071 • 9,365
Pitt □, NC • 107,924
Pittsboro, NC 27312 • 1,436
Pittsburg, CA 94565 • 47,564
Pittsburg, KS 66762 • 17,775
Pittsburg, TX 75686 • 4,007
Pittsburg □, OK • 40,581
Pittsburgh, PA 15201-90 • 369,879
Pittsfield, IL 62363 • 4,231
Pittsfield, ME 04967 • 3,222
Pittsfield, MA 01201-03 • 48,622
Pittsfield, NH 03263 • 1,717
Pittsford, VT 05763 • 650
Pittston, PA 18640-44 • 9,389
Pittsylvania □, VA • 55,655
Piute □, UT • 1,277
Pixley, CA 93256 • 2,457
Placentia, CA 92670 • 41,259
Placer □, CA • 172,796
Placerville, CA 95667 • 8,355
Plain City, OH 43064 • 2,278
Plain City, UT 84404 • 2,722
Plain Dealing, LA 71064 • 1,074
Plainedge, NY 11714 • 8,739
Plainfield, CT 06374 • 2,856
Plainfield, IL 60544 • 4,557
Plainfield, IN 46168 • 10,433
Plainfield, NJ 07059-63 • 46,567
Plainfield, VT 05667 • 600
Plainfield Heights, MI 49505 • 5,000
Plains, MT 59859 • 992
Plains, PA 18705 • 4,694
Plains, TX 79355 • 1,422
Plainsboro, NJ 08536 • 1,560
Plainview, MN 55964 • 2,768
Plainview, NE 68769 • 1,333
Plainview, NY 11803 • 26,207
Plainview, TX 79072-73 • 21,700
Plainville, CT 06062 • 17,392
Plainville, KS 67663 • 2,173
Plainville, MA 02762 • 5,857
Plainwell, MI 49080 • 4,057
Plaistow, NH 03865 • 1,850
Plano, IL 60545 • 5,104
Plano, TX 75074-75 • 128,713
Plantation, FL 33317 • 66,692
Plant City, FL 33564-67 • 22,754
Plantersville, MS 38862 • 1,046
Plantsite, AZ 85540 • 1,500
Plantsville, CT 06479 • 7,050
Plaquemine, LA 70764-65 • 7,186
Plaquemines □, LA • 25,575
Platte, SD 57369 • 1,311
Platte □, MO • 57,867
Platte □, NE • 29,820
Platte □, WY • 8,145
Platte City, MO 64079 • 2,947
Platteville, CO 80651 • 1,515
Platteville, WI 53818 • 9,708
Plattsburg, MO 64477 • 2,248
Plattsburgh, NY 12901 • 21,255
Plattsmouth, NE 68048 • 6,412
Pleasant Gap, PA 16823 • 1,699
Pleasant Garden, NC 27313 • 2,228
Pleasant Grove, AL 35127 • 8,458
Pleasant Grove, UT 84062 • 13,476
Pleasant Hill, CA 94523 • 31,585
Pleasant Hill, IL 62366 • 1,030
Pleasant Hill, IA 50301 • 3,671
Pleasant Hill, MO 64080 • 3,827
Pleasant Hill, OH 45359 • 1,066
Pleasant Hills, PA 15236 • 8,884
Pleasanton, CA 94566 • 50,553
Pleasanton, KS 66075 • 1,231
Pleasanton, TX 78064 • 7,678
Pleasant Prairie, WI 53158 • 11,961
Pleasants □, WV • 7,546
Pleasant Valley, MO 64068 • 2,731
Pleasant Valley, NY 12569 • 1,688
Pleasant View, CO 80401 • 3,460
Pleasant View, UT 84404 • 3,603
Pleasantville, IA 50225 • 1,536
Pleasantville, NJ 08232 • 16,027
Pleasantville, NY 10570-72 • 6,592
Pleasure Beach, CT 06385 • 1,356
Pleasure Ridge Park, KY 40258 • 25,131
Plentywood, MT 59254 • 2,136
Plover, WI 54467 • 8,176
Plum, PA 15239 • 25,609
Plumas □, CA • 19,739
Plumsteadville, PA 18949 • 1,200
Plymouth, CT 06782 • 1,070
Plymouth, FL 32768 • 2,700
Plymouth, IN 46563 • 8,303
Plymouth, MA 02360-61 • 7,258
Plymouth, MI 48170 • 9,560
Plymouth, MN 55441 • 50,889
Plymouth, NH 03264 • 3,967
Plymouth, NC 27962 • 4,328
Plymouth, OH 44865 • 1,942
Plymouth, PA 18651 • 7,134
Plymouth, WI 53073 • 6,769
Plymouth □, IA • 23,388
Plymouth □, MA • 435,276
Plymouth Township, PA 19401 • 17,168
Poca, WV 25159 • 1,124
Pocahontas, AR 72455 • 6,151
Pocahontas, IA 50574 • 2,085
Pocahontas □, IA • 9,525
Pocahontas □, WV • 9,008
Pocasset, MA 02559 • 2,200
Pocatalico, WV 25320 • 2,450
Pocatello, ID 83201-06 • 46,080
Pocola, OK 74902 • 3,664
Pocomoke City, MD 21851 • 3,922
Poinsett □, AR • 24,664
Point Clear, AL 36564 • 2,125
Pointe Coupee □, LA • 22,540
Point Hope, AK 99766 • 639
Point Marion, PA 15474 • 1,344
Point Pleasant, NJ 08742 • 18,177
Point Pleasant, WV 25550 • 4,996
Point Pleasant Beach, NJ 08742 • 5,112
Poipu, HI 96756 • 975
Polk, PA 16342 • 1,267
Polk □, AR • 17,347

Polk □, FL • 405,382
Polk □, GA • 33,815
Polk □, IA • 327,140
Polk □, MN • 32,498
Polk □, MO • 21,826
Polk □, NE • 5,675
Polk □, NC • 14,416
Polk □, OR • 49,541
Polk □, TN • 13,643
Polk □, TX • 30,687
Polk □, WI • 34,773
Polk City, FL 33868 • 1,439
Polk City, IA 50226 • 1,908
Polo, IL 61064 • 2,514
Polson, MT 59860 • 3,283
Pomeroy, OH 45769 • 2,259
Pomeroy, WA 99347 • 1,393
Pomona, CA 91765–69 • 131,723
Pomona, NJ 08240 • 2,624
Pompano Beach, FL 33060–69 • 72,411
Pompano Beach Highlands, FL 33060 • 17,915
Pompton Lakes, NJ 07442 • 10,539
Ponca City, OK 74601–04 • 26,359
Ponchatoula, LA 70454 • 5,425
Pondera □, MT • 6,433
Ponte Vedra Beach, FL 32082 • 1,700
Pontiac, IL 61764 • 11,428
Pontiac, MI 48340–43 • 71,166
Pontotoc, MS 38863 • 4,570
Pontotoc □, MS • 22,237
Pontotoc □, OK • 34,119
Pooler, GA 31322 • 4,453
Poolesville, MD 20837 • 3,796
Pope □, AR • 45,883
Pope □, IL • 4,373
Pope □, MN • 10,745
Poplar, MT 59255 • 881
Poplar Bluff, MO 63901 • 16,996
Poplarville, MS 39470 • 2,561
Poquonock Bridge, CT 06340 • 2,770
Poquoson, VA 23662 • 11,005
Portage, IN 46368 • 29,060
Portage, MI 49081 • 41,042
Portage, PA 15946 • 3,105
Portage, WI 53901 • 8,640
Portage □, OH • 142,585
Portage □, WI • 61,405
Portage Lakes, OH 44319 • 13,373
Portageville, MO 63873 • 3,401
Portales, NM 88130 • 10,690
Port Allegany, PA 16743 • 2,391
Port Allen, LA 70767 • 6,277
Port Angeles, WA 98362 • 17,710
Port Aransas, TX 78373 • 2,233
Port Arthur, TX 77640–43 • 58,724
Port Barre, LA 70577 • 2,144
Port Bolivar, TX 77650 • 1,600
Port Byron, IL 61275 • 1,002
Port Byron, NY 13140 • 1,359
Port Carbon, PA 17965 • 2,134
Port Charlotte, FL 33952 • 41,535
Port Chester, NY 10573 • 24,728
Port Clinton, OH 43452 • 7,106
Port Dickinson, NY 13901 • 1,785
Port Edwards, WI 54469 • 1,848
Porter, IN 46304 • 3,118
Porter, TX 77365 • 7,000
Porter □, IN • 128,932
Porterdale, GA 30270 • 1,278
Porterville, CA 93257–58 • 29,563
Port Ewen, NY 12466 • 3,444
Port Gibson, MS 39150 • 1,810
Port Henry, NY 12974 • 1,263
Port Hueneme, CA 93041–44 • 20,319
Port Huron, MI 48060–61 • 33,694
Port Isabel, TX 78578 • 4,467
Port Jefferson, NY 11777 • 7,455
Port Jefferson Station, NY 11776 • 7,232
Port Jervis, NY 12771 • 9,060
Portland, CT 06480 • 5,645
Portland, IN 47371 • 6,483
Portland, ME 04101–12 • 64,358
Portland, MI 48875 • 3,889
Portland, OR 97201–99 • 437,319
Portland, TN 37148 • 5,165
Portland, TX 78374 • 12,224
Port Lavaca, TX 77979 • 10,886
Port Monmouth, NJ 07758 • 3,800
Port Neches, TX 77651 • 12,974
Port Norris, NJ 08349 • 1,701
Port O'Connor, TX 77982 • 1,031
Portola, CA 96122 • 2,193
Port Orange, FL 32127 • 35,317
Port Orchard, WA 98366 • 4,984
Port Orford, OR 97465 • 1,025
Port Penn, DE 19731 • 300
Port Richey, FL 34667–74 • 2,523
Port Royal, SC 29935 • 2,985
Port Saint Joe, FL 32456 • 4,044
Port Saint Lucie, FL 34952 • 55,866
Port Salerno, FL 34992 • 7,786
Portsmouth, NH 03801–02 • 25,925
Portsmouth, OH 45662 • 22,676
Portsmouth, RI 02871 • 3,540
Portsmouth, VA 23701–09 • 103,907
Port St. John, FL 32922 • 8,933
Port Sulphur, LA 70083 • 3,523
Port Townsend, WA 98368 • 7,001
Portville, NY 14770 • 1,040
Port Vue, PA 15133 • 4,641
Port Washington, NY 11050 • 15,387
Port Washington, WI 53074 • 9,338
Port Wentworth, GA 31407 • 4,012
Posen, IL 60469 • 4,226
Posey □, IN • 25,968
Poseyville, IN 47633 • 1,089
Post, TX 79356 • 3,768
Post Falls, ID 83854 • 7,349
Postville, IA 52162 • 1,472
Poteau, OK 74953 • 7,210
Poteet, TX 78065 • 3,206
Poth, TX 78147 • 1,642
Potlatch, ID 83855 • 790
Potomac, MD 20851 • 45,634
Potomac Heights, MD 20640 • 1,524
Potomac Park, MD 21502 • 1,800
Potosi, MO 63664 • 2,683
Potsdam, NY 13676 • 10,251
Pottawatomie □, KS • 16,128
Pottawatomie □, OK • 58,760
Pottawattamie □, IA • 82,628
Potter □, PA • 16,717
Potter □, SD • 3,190
Potter □, TX • 97,874
Potter Valley, CA 95469 • 1,500
Pottstown, PA 19464 • 21,831
Pottsville, PA 17901 • 16,603
Poughkeepsie, NY 12601–03 • 28,844
Poulsbo, WA 98370 • 4,848
Poultney, VT 05764 • 1,731
Poway, CA 92064 • 43,516
Powder River □, MT • 2,090
Powder Springs, GA 30073 • 6,893
Powell, OH 43065 • 2,154
Powell, TN 37849 • 7,534
Powell, WY 82435 • 5,292
Powell □, KY • 11,686
Powell □, MT • 6,620
Powellhurst, OR 97236 • 28,756
Powellton, WV 25161 • 1,905
Power □, ID • 7,086
Poweshiek □, IA • 19,033
Powhatan □, VA • 15,328
Powhatan Point, OH 43942 • 1,807
Poydras, LA 70085 • 4,029
Poynette, WI 53955 • 1,662
Prague, OK 74864 • 2,308
Prairie □, AR • 9,518
Prairie □, MT • 1,383
Prairie City, IA 50228 • 1,360
Prairie City, OR 97869 • 1,117
Prairie du Chien, WI 53821 • 5,659
Prairie du Sac, WI 53578 • 2,380
Prairie Grove, AR 72753 • 1,761
Prairie View, TX 77446 • 4,004
Prairie Village, KS 66208 • 23,186
Pratt, KS 67124 • 6,687
Pratt □, KS • 9,702
Prattville, AL 36066–67 • 19,587
Preble □, OH • 40,113
Premont, TX 78375 • 2,914
Prentiss, MS 39474 • 1,487
Prentiss □, MS • 23,278
Prescott, AZ 86301–14 • 26,455
Prescott, AR 71857 • 3,673
Prescott, WI 54021 • 3,243
Presho, SD 57568 • 654
Presidio, TX 79845 • 3,072
Presidio □, TX • 6,637
Presque Isle, ME 04769 • 10,550
Presque Isle □, MI • 13,743
Preston, ID 83263 • 3,710
Preston, IA 52069 • 1,025
Preston, MN 55965 • 1,530
Preston □, WV • 29,037
Prestonsburg, KY 41653 • 3,558
Price, UT 84501 • 8,712
Price □, WI • 15,600
Prichard, AL 36610 • 34,311
Priest River, ID 83856 • 1,560
Primrose, RI 02895 • 500
Prince Edward □, VA • 17,320
Prince Frederick, MD 20678 • 1,885
Prince George □, VA • 27,394
Prince Georges □, MD • 729,268
Princes Lakes, IN 46164 • 1,055
Princess Anne, MD 21853 • 1,666
Princeton, FL 33032 • 7,073
Princeton, IL 61356 • 7,197
Princeton, IN 47670 • 8,127
Princeton, KY 42445 • 6,940
Princeton, MN 55371 • 3,719
Princeton, MO 64673 • 1,021
Princeton, NJ 08540–43 • 12,016
Princeton, NC 27569 • 1,181
Princeton, WV 24740 • 7,043
Princeton, WI 54968 • 1,458
Princeton Junction, NJ 08550 • 2,362
Princeville, IL 61559 • 1,421
Princeville, NC 27886 • 1,652
Prince William □, VA • 215,686
Prineville, OR 97754 • 5,355
Prior Lake, MN 55372 • 11,482
Proctor, MN 55810 • 2,974
Proctor, VT 05765 • 1,979
Proctorsville, VT 05153 • 480
Prophetstown, IL 61277 • 1,749
Prospect, CT 06712 • 6,807
Prospect, KY 40059 • 2,788
Prospect, OH 43342 • 1,148
Prospect, OR 97536 • 1,200
Prospect, PA 16052 • 1,122
Prospect Heights, IL 60070 • 15,239
Prospect Park, NJ 07508 • 5,053
Prospect Park, PA 19076 • 6,764
Prosperity, SC 29127 • 1,116
Prosperity, WV 25909 • 1,322
Prosser, WA 99350 • 4,476
Providence, KY 42450 • 4,123
Providence, RI 02901–40 • 160,728
Providence, UT 84332 • 3,344
Providence □, RI • 596,270
Provincetown, MA 02657 • 3,374
Provo, UT 84601–06 • 86,835
Prowers □, CO • 13,347
Prudenville, MI 48651 • 1,700
Prudhoe Bay, AK 99734 • 47
Pryor, OK 74361–62 • 8,327
Pueblo, CO 81001–19 • 98,640
Pueblo □, CO • 123,051
Puhi, HI 96766 • 1,210
Pukalani, HI 96788 • 5,879
Pulaski, NY 13142 • 2,525
Pulaski, TN 38478 • 7,895
Pulaski, VA 24301 • 9,985
Pulaski, WI 54162 • 2,200
Pulaski □, AR • 349,660
Pulaski □, GA • 8,108
Pulaski □, IL • 7,523
Pulaski □, IN • 12,643
Pulaski □, KY • 49,489
Pulaski □, MO • 41,307
Pulaski □, VA • 34,496
Pullman, WA 99163–65 • 23,478
Pumphrey, MD 21227 • 5,483
Punta Gorda, FL 33948–55 • 10,747
Punxsutawney, PA 15767 • 6,782
Purcell, OK 73080 • 4,784
Purcellville, VA 22132 • 1,744
Purvis, MS 39475 • 2,140
Pushmataha □, OK • 10,997
Putnam, CT 06260 • 6,835
Putnam □, FL • 65,070
Putnam □, GA • 14,137
Putnam □, IL • 5,730
Putnam □, IN • 30,315
Putnam □, MO • 5,079
Putnam □, NY • 83,941
Putnam □, OH • 33,819
Putnam □, TN • 51,373
Putnam □, WV • 42,835
Putney, VT 05346 • 1,100
Puyallup, WA 98371–74 • 23,875

Q

Quail Oaks, VA 23234 • 1,500
Quaker Hill, CT 06375 • 2,052
Quakertown, PA 18951 • 8,982
Quanah, TX 79252 • 3,413
Quarryville, PA 17566 • 1,642
Quartz Hill, CA 93536 • 9,626
Quartzsite, AZ 85346 • 1,876
Quay □, NM • 10,823
Quechee, VT 05059 • 550
Queen Annes □, MD • 33,953
Queen City, TX 75572 • 1,748
Queen Creek, AZ 85242 • 2,667
Queens □, NY • 1,951,598
Queensborough, WA 98021 • 4,850
Questa, NM 87556 • 1,707
Quidnessett, RI 02852 • 3,300
Quidnick, RI 02816 • 2,300
Quilcene, WA 98376 • 1,200
Quincy, CA 95971 • 2,700
Quincy, FL 32351 • 7,444
Quincy, IL 62301–06 • 39,681
Quincy, MA 02169 • 84,985
Quincy, MI 49082 • 1,680
Quincy, WA 98848 • 3,738
Quinebaug, CT 06262 • 1,031
Quinhagak, AK 99655 • 501
Quinlan, TX 75474 • 1,360
Quinton, OK 74561 • 1,133
Quitman, GA 31643 • 5,292
Quitman, MS 39355 • 2,736
Quitman, TX 75783 • 1,684
Quitman □, GA • 2,209
Quitman □, MS • 10,490
Quonochontaug, RI 02813 • 1,500

R

Rabun □, GA • 11,648
Raceland, KY 41169 • 2,256
Raceland, LA 70394 • 5,564
Racine, WI 53401–08 • 84,298
Racine □, WI • 175,034
Radcliff, KY 40159–60 • 19,772
Radford, VA 24141–43 • 15,940
Radnor Township, PA 19087 • 28,705
Raeford, NC 28376 • 3,469
Ragland, AL 35131 • 1,807
Rahway, NJ 07065–67 • 25,325
Rainbow City, AL 35901 • 7,673
Rainelle, WV 25962 • 1,681
Rainier, OR 97048 • 1,674
Rains □, TX • 6,715
Rainsville, AL 35986 • 3,875
Raleigh, MS 39153 • 1,291
Raleigh, NC 27601–61 • 207,951
Raleigh □, WV • 76,819
Raleigh Hills, OR 97225 • 6,066
Ralls, TX 79357 • 2,172
Ralls □, MO • 8,476
Ralston, NE 68127 • 6,236
Rambleton Acres, DE 19720 • 1,700
Ramblewood, NJ 08054 • 6,181
Ramona, CA 92065 • 13,040
Ramsay, MI 49959 • 1,075
Ramseur, NC 27316 • 1,186
Ramsey, MN 55303 • 12,408
Ramsey, NJ 07446 • 13,228
Ramsey □, MN • 485,765
Ramsey □, ND • 12,681
Ranchester, WY 82839 • 676
Rancho Cordova, CA 95670 • 48,731
Rancho Mirage, CA 92270 • 9,778
Rancho Palos Verdes, CA 90274 • 41,659
Rancho Rinconado, CA 95014 • 4,206
Ranchos de Taos, NM 87557 • 1,779
Rancocas Woods, NJ 08060 • 1,250
Rand, WV 25306 • 2,400
Randall □, TX • 89,673
Randallstown, MD 21133 • 26,277
Randleman, NC 27317 • 2,612
Randolph, ME 04345 • 1,949
Randolph, MA 02368 • 30,093
Randolph, NY 14772 • 1,298
Randolph, VT 05060 • 2,200
Randolph, WI 53956 • 1,729
Randolph □, AL • 19,881
Randolph □, AR • 16,558
Randolph □, GA • 8,023
Randolph □, IL • 34,583
Randolph □, IN • 27,148
Randolph □, MO • 24,370
Randolph □, NC • 106,546
Randolph □, WV • 27,803
Randolph Hills, MD 20852 • 4,180
Random Lake, WI 53075 • 1,439
Rangely, CO 81648 • 2,278
Ranger, TX 76470 • 2,803
Rankin, PA 15104 • 2,503
Rankin, TX 79778 • 1,011
Rankin □, MS • 87,161
Ransom □, ND • 5,921
Ransomville, NY 14131 • 1,542
Ranson, WV 25438 • 2,890
Rantoul, IL 61866 • 17,212
Raoul, GA 30510 • 1,400
Rapid City, SD 57701–09 • 54,523
Rapides □, LA • 131,556
Rapid Valley, SD 57701 • 5,968
Rappahannock □, VA • 6,622
Raritan, NJ 08869 • 5,798
Rathdrum, ID 83858 • 2,000
Raton, NM 87740 • 7,372
Ravalli □, MT • 25,010
Raven, VA 24639 • 2,640
Ravena, NY 12143 • 3,547
Ravenel, SC 29470 • 2,165
Ravenna, NE 68869 • 1,317
Ravenna, OH 44266 • 12,069
Ravenswood, WV 26164 • 4,189
Rawlins, WY 82301 • 9,380
Rawlins □, KS • 3,404
Ray, ND 58849 • 603
Ray □, MO • 21,971
Raymond, MS 39154 • 2,275
Raymond, NH 03077 • 2,516
Raymond, WA 98577 • 2,901
Raymondville, TX 78580 • 8,880
Raymore, MO 64083 • 5,592
Rayne, LA 70578 • 8,502
Raynham, MA 02767 • 3,709
Raynham Center, MA 02768 • 3,709
Raytown, MO 64133 • 30,601
Rayville, LA 71269 • 4,411
Reading, MA 01867 • 22,539
Reading, MI 49274 • 1,127
Reading, OH 45215 • 12,038
Reading, PA 19601–12 • 78,380
Reagan □, TX • 4,514
Real □, TX • 2,412
Reamstown, PA 17567 • 2,649
Rector, AR 72461 • 2,268
Red Bank, NJ 07701–04 • 10,636
Red Bank, SC 29073 • 6,112
Red Bank, TN 37415 • 12,322
Red Bay, AL 35582 • 3,451
Redbird, OH 44057 • 1,600
Red Bluff, CA 96080 • 12,363
Red Bud, IL 62278 • 2,918
Red Cloud, NE 68970 • 1,204
Redding, CA 96001–03 • 66,462
Redding, CT 06875 • 1,000
Redfield, AR 72132 • 1,082
Redfield, SD 57469 • 2,770
Redford, MI 48239 • 54,387
Redgranite, WI 54970 • 1,009
Red Hook, NY 12571 • 1,794
Redkey, IN 47373 • 1,383
Red Lake □, MN • 4,525
Red Lake Falls, MN 56750 • 1,481
Redlands, CA 92373–75 • 60,394
Red Lion, PA 17356 • 6,130
Red Lodge, MT 59068 • 1,958
Redmond, OR 97756 • 7,163
Redmond, WA 98052–53 • 35,800
Red Oak, GA 30272 • 2,800
Red Oak, IA 51566 • 6,264
Red Oak, TX 75154 • 3,124
Red Oaks, LA 70815 • 1,600
Red Oaks Mill, NY 12603 • 4,906
Redondo Beach, CA 90277–78 • 60,167
Red River □, LA • 9,387
Red River □, TX • 14,317
Red Springs, NC 28377 • 3,799
Red Willow □, NE • 11,705
Red Wing, MN 55066 • 15,134
Redwood, UT 84119 • 1,850
Redwood □, MN • 17,254
Redwood City, CA 94061–65 • 66,072
Redwood Falls, MN 56283 • 4,859
Redwood Valley, CA 95470 • 1,300
Reed City, MI 49677 • 2,379
Reedley, CA 93654 • 15,791
Reedsburg, WI 53959 • 5,834
Reedsport, OR 97467 • 4,796
Reedsville, PA 17084 • 1,030
Reedsville, WI 54230 • 1,182
Reedurban, OH 44710 • 6,650
Reese, MI 48757 • 1,414
Reeves □, TX • 15,852
Reform, AL 35481 • 2,105
Refugio, TX 78377 • 3,158
Refugio □, TX • 7,976
Rehoboth Beach, DE 19971 • 1,234
Reidland, KY 42001 • 4,054
Reidsville, GA 30453 • 2,469
Reidsville, NC 27320–23 • 12,183
Reinbeck, IA 50669 • 1,605
Reisterstown, MD 21136 • 19,314
Reliance, WY 82943 • 500
Remington, IN 47977 • 1,247
Remsen, IA 51050 • 1,513
Reno, NV 89501–70 • 133,850
Reno □, KS • 62,389
Renovo, PA 17764 • 1,526
Rensselaer, IN 47978 • 5,045
Rensselaer, NY 12144 • 8,255
Rensselaer □, NY • 154,429
Renton, WA 98055–59 • 41,688
Renville, MN 56284 • 1,315
Renville □, MN • 17,673
Renville □, ND • 3,160
Republic, MI 49879 • 1,100
Republic, MO 65738 • 6,292
Republic, PA 15475 • 1,400
Republic □, KS • 6,482
Reserve, LA 70084 • 8,847
Reston, VA 22090 • 48,556
Revere, MA 02151 • 42,786
Rexburg, ID 83440 • 14,302
Reynolds, GA 31076 • 1,166
Reynolds □, MO • 6,661
Reynoldsburg, OH 43068 • 25,748
Reynoldsville, PA 15851 • 2,818
Rhea □, TN • 24,344
Rhinebeck, NY 12572 • 2,725
Rhinelander, WI 54501 • 7,427
Rialto, CA 92376–77 • 72,388
Rice □, KS • 10,610
Rice □, MN • 49,183
Rice Lake, WI 54868 • 7,998
Rich □, UT • 1,725
Richardson, TX 75080–83 • 74,840
Richardson □, NE • 9,937
Richardson Park, DE 19804 • 1,100
Richardton, ND 58652 • 625
Richboro, PA 18954 • 5,332
Richfield, MN 55423 • 35,710
Richfield, UT 84701 • 5,593
Richfield Springs, NY 13439 • 1,565
Richford, VT 05476 • 1,425
Rich Hill, MO 64779 • 1,317
Richland, GA 31825 • 1,668
Richland, MO 65556 • 2,029
Richland, WA 99352 • 32,315
Richland □, IL • 16,545
Richland □, LA • 20,629
Richland □, MT • 10,716
Richland □, ND • 18,148
Richland □, OH • 126,137
Richland □, SC • 285,720
Richland □, WI • 17,521
Richland Center, WI 53581 • 5,018
Richland Hills, TX 76118 • 7,978
Richlands, VA 24641 • 4,456
Richlandtown, PA 18955 • 1,195
Richmond, CA 94801–08 • 87,425
Richmond, IL 60071 • 1,016
Richmond, IN 47374–75 • 38,705
Richmond, KY 40475–76 • 21,155
Richmond, ME 04357 • 1,775
Richmond, MI 48062 • 4,141
Richmond, MO 64085 • 5,738
Richmond, TX 77469 • 9,801
Richmond, UT 84333 • 1,955
Richmond, VT 05477 • 650
Richmond, VA 23201–94 • 203,056
Richmond □, GA • 189,719
Richmond □, NY • 378,977
Richmond □, NC • 44,518
Richmond □, VA • 7,273
Richmond Beach, WA 98160 • 5,000
Richmond Heights, FL 33156 • 8,583
Richmond Heights, MO 63117 • 10,448
Richmond Heights, OH 44143 • 9,611
Richmond Highlands, WA 98133 • 26,037
Richmond Hill, GA 31324 • 2,934
Rich Square, NC 27869 • 1,058
Richton, MS 39476 • 1,034
Richton Park, IL 60471 • 10,523
Richwood, OH 43344 • 2,186
Richwood, WV 26261 • 2,808
Riddle, OR 97469 • 1,143
Ridge, NY 11961 • 11,734
Ridgecrest, CA 93555 • 27,725
Ridgecrest, WA 98155 • 5,500
Ridgefield, CT 06877 • 6,363
Ridgefield, NJ 07657 • 9,996
Ridgefield, WA 98642 • 1,297
Ridgefield Park, NJ 07660 • 12,454
Ridgeland, MS 39157–58 • 11,714
Ridgeland, SC 29936 • 1,071
Ridgely, MD 21660 • 1,034
Ridgely, TN 38080 • 1,775
Ridgetop, TN 37152 • 1,132
Ridgeville, SC 29472 • 1,625
Ridgewood, NJ 07450–52 • 24,152
Ridgway, IL 62979 • 1,103
Ridgway, PA 15853 • 4,793
Ridley Park, PA 19078 • 7,592
Ridley Township, PA 19018 • 33,771
Rifle, CO 81650 • 4,636
Rigby, ID 83442 • 2,681
Riley □, KS • 67,139
Rimersburg, PA 16248 • 1,053
Rincon, GA 31326 • 2,697
Ringgold, GA 30736 • 1,675
Ringgold, LA 71068 • 1,856
Ringgold □, IA • 5,420
Ringling, OK 73456 • 1,250
Ringwood, NJ 07456 • 12,623
Rio, FL 34957 • 1,054
Rio Arriba □, NM • 34,365
Rio Blanco □, CO • 5,972
Rio Dell, CA 95562 • 3,012
Rio Del Mar, CA 95003 • 8,919
Rio Grande, NJ 08242 • 2,505
Rio Grande □, CO • 10,770
Rio Grande City, TX 78582 • 9,891
Rio Hondo, TX 78583 • 1,793
Rio Linda, CA 95673 • 9,481
Rio Rancho, NM 87124 • 32,505
Rio Vista, CA 94571 • 3,316
Ripley, MS 38663 • 5,371
Ripley, NY 14775 • 1,189
Ripley, OH 45167 • 1,816
Ripley, TN 38063 • 6,188
Ripley, WV 25271 • 3,023
Ripley □, IN • 24,616
Ripley □, MO • 12,303
Ripon, WI 54971 • 7,241
Rising Sun, DE 19934 • 540
Rising Sun, IN 47040 • 2,311
Rising Sun, MD 21911 • 1,263
Rison, AR 71665 • 1,258
Ritchie □, WV • 10,233
Rittman, OH 44270 • 6,147
Ritzville, WA 99169 • 1,725
Riverbank, CA 95367 • 8,547
Riverdale, CA 93656 • 1,980
Riverdale, GA 30274 • 9,359
Riverdale, IL 60627 • 13,671
Riverdale, MD 20737–38 • 5,185
Riverdale, NJ 07457 • 2,370
Riverdale, UT 84405 • 6,419
River Edge, NJ 07661 • 10,603
River Falls, WI 54022 • 10,610
River Forest, IL 60305 • 11,669
River Grove, IL 60171 • 9,961
Riverhead, NY 11901 • 8,814
River Heights, UT 84321 • 1,274
River Hills, WI 53217 • 1,612
River Oaks, TX 76114 • 6,580
River Pines, MA 01821 • 3,620
River Ridge, LA 70123 • 14,800
River Road, OR 97404 • 9,443
River Rouge, MI 48218 • 11,314
Riverside, AL 35135 • 1,004
Riverside, CA 92501–19 • 226,505
Riverside, IL 60546 • 8,774
Riverside, NJ 08075 • 7,974
Riverside, PA 17868 • 1,991
Riverside □, CA • 1,170,413
Riverton, IL 62561 • 2,638
Riverton, NJ 08077 • 2,775
Riverton, UT 84065 • 11,261
Riverton, VT 05663 • 150
Riverton, WY 82501 • 9,202
Riverton Heights, WA 98188 • 14,182
River Vale, NJ 07675 • 9,410
Riverview, FL 33569 • 6,478
Riverview, MI 48192 • 13,894
Rivesville, WV 26588 • 1,064
Riviera Beach, FL 33404 • 27,639
Riviera Beach, MD 21122 • 11,376
Roane □, TN • 47,227
Roane □, WV • 15,120
Roan Mountain, TN 37687 • 1,220
Roanoke, AL 36274 • 6,362
Roanoke, IL 61561 • 1,910
Roanoke, IN 46783 • 1,018
Roanoke, TX 76262 • 1,616
Roanoke, VA 24001–38 • 96,397
Roanoke □, VA • 79,332
Roanoke Rapids, NC 27870 • 15,722
Roaring Spring, PA 16673 • 2,615

Robbins, IL 60472 • 7,498
Robbinsdale, MN 55422 • 14,396
Robersonville, NC 27871 • 1,940
Robert Lee, TX 76945 • 1,276
Roberts, WI 54023 • 1,043
Roberts □, SD • 9,914
Roberts □, TX • 1,025
Robertsdale, AL 36567 • 2,401
Robertson □, KY • 2,124
Robertson □, TN • 41,494
Robertson □, TX • 15,511
Robertsville, NJ 07746 • 9,841
Robeson □, NC • 105,179
Robinson, IL 62454 • 6,740
Robinson, TX 76706 • 7,111
Robstown, TX 78380 • 12,849
Rochdale, MA 01542 • 1,105
Rochelle, GA 31079 • 1,510
Rochelle, IL 61068 • 8,769
Rochelle Park, NJ 07662 • 5,587
Rochester, IL 62563 • 2,676
Rochester, IN 46975 • 5,969
Rochester, MI 48306–09 • 7,130
Rochester, MN 55901–06 • 70,745
Rochester, NH 03867–68 • 26,630
Rochester, NY 14601–92 • 231,636
Rochester, PA 15074 • 4,156
Rochester, VT 05767 • 500
Rochester, WA 98579 • 1,150
Rochester Hills, MI 48309 • 61,766
Rock □, MN • 9,806
Rock □, NE • 2,019
Rock □, WI • 139,510
Rockaway, NJ 07866 • 6,243
Rockbridge □, VA • 18,350
Rockcastle □, KY • 14,803
Rock Creek, MN 55067 • 1,040
Rock Creek 0M, OR • 8,282
Rockdale, IL 60436 • 1,709
Rockdale, MD 21207 • 5,885
Rockdale, TX 76567 • 5,235
Rockdale □, GA • 54,091
Rock Falls, IL 61071 • 9,654
Rockford, IL 61101–32 • 139,426
Rockford, MI 49341 • 3,750
Rockford, MN 55373 • 2,665
Rockford, OH 45882 • 1,119
Rock Hall, MD 21661 • 1,584
Rock Hill, MO 63124 • 5,217
Rock Hill, SC 29730–32 • 41,643
Rockingham, NC 28379 • 9,399
Rockingham □, NH • 245,845
Rockingham □, NC • 86,064
Rockingham □, VA • 57,482
Rock Island, IL 61201–04 • 40,552
Rock Island □, IL • 148,723
Rockland, ME 04841 • 7,972
Rockland, MA 02370 • 15,695
Rockland □, NY • 265,475
Rockledge, FL 32955–56 • 16,023
Rockledge, PA 19111 • 2,679
Rocklin, CA 95677 • 19,033
Rockmart, GA 30153 • 3,356
Rockport, IN 47635 • 2,315
Rockport, ME 04856 • 1,100
Rockport, MA 01966 • 4,690
Rock Port, MO 64482 • 1,438
Rockport, TX 78382 • 4,753
Rock Rapids, IA 51246 • 2,601
Rock River, WY 82083 • 190
Rocksprings, TX 78880 • 1,339
Rock Springs, WY 82901–02 • 19,050
Rockton, IL 61072 • 2,928
Rock Valley, IA 51247 • 2,540
Rockville, IN 47872 • 2,706
Rockville, MD 20847–59 • 44,835
Rockville Centre, NY 11570–71 • 24,727
Rockwall, TX 75087 • 10,486
Rockwall □, TX • 25,604
Rockwell, IA 50469 • 1,008
Rockwell, NC 28138 • 1,598
Rockwell City, IA 50579 • 1,981
Rockwell Park, NC 28213 • 2,600
Rockwood, MI 48173 • 3,141
Rockwood, OR 97233 • 11,000
Rockwood, PA 15557 • 1,014
Rockwood, TN 37854 • 5,348
Rocky Creek, FL 33615 • 7,800
Rocky Ford, CO 81067 • 4,162
Rocky Hill, CT 06067 • 14,559
Rocky Mount, NC 27801–04 • 48,997
Rocky Mount, VA 24151 • 4,098
Rocky Point, NY 11778 • 8,596
Rocky River, OH 44116 • 20,410
Rodeo, CA 94572 • 7,589
Roderfield, WV 24881 • 1,200
Rodney Village, DE 19901 • 1,745
Roebling, NJ 08554 • 2,415
Roebuck, SC 29376 • 1,966
Roeland Park, KS 66203 • 7,706
Roessleville, NY 12205 • 10,753
Roger Mills □, OK • 4,147
Rogers, AR 72756–57 • 24,692
Rogers, TX 76569 • 1,131
Rogers □, OK • 55,170
Rogers City, MI 49779 • 3,642
Rogersville, AL 35652 • 1,125
Rogersville, TN 37857 • 4,149
Rogue River, OR 97537 • 1,759
Rohnert Park, CA 94927–28 • 36,326
Roland, IA 50236 • 1,035
Roland, OK 74954 • 2,481
Rolette □, ND • 12,772
Rolla, MO 65401 • 14,090
Rolla, ND 58367 • 1,286
Rolling Fork, MS 39159 • 2,444
Rolling Hills Estates, CA 90274 • 7,789
Rolling Meadows, IL 60008 • 22,591
Rollinsford, NH 03869 • 2,645
Roma, TX 78584 • 8,059
Rome, GA 30161–65 • 30,326
Rome, IL 61562 • 1,902
Rome, NY 13440 • 44,350
Rome City, IN 46784 • 1,138
Romeo, MI 48065 • 3,520
Romeoville, IL 60441 • 14,074
Romney, WV 26757 • 1,966
Romulus, MI 48174 • 22,897
Ronan, MT 59864 • 1,547
Ronceverte, WV 24970 • 1,754
Ronkonkoma, NY 11779 • 20,391
Roodhouse, IL 62082 • 2,139
Rooks □, KS • 6,039
Roosevelt, NY 11575 • 15,030
Roosevelt, UT 84066 • 3,915
Roosevelt □, MT • 10,999
Roosevelt □, NM • 16,702
Roosevelt Park, MI 49441 • 3,885
Rosamond, CA 93560 • 7,430
Roscoe, IL 61073 • 2,079
Roscoe, TX 79545 • 1,446
Roscommon □, MI • 19,776
Roseau, MN 56751 • 2,396
Roseau □, MN • 15,026
Roseboro, NC 28382 • 1,441
Rosebud, TX 76570 • 1,638
Rosebud □, MT • 10,505
Roseburg, OR 97470 • 17,032
Rosedale, MD 21237 • 18,703
Rosedale, MS 38769 • 2,595
Rose Hill, KS 67133 • 2,399
Rose Hill, NC 28458 • 1,287
Rose Hill, VA 22310 • 12,675
Roseland, CA 95407 • 8,779
Roseland, FL 32957 • 1,379
Roseland, LA 70456 • 1,093
Roseland, NJ 07068 • 4,847
Roseland, OH 44906 • 3,000
Roselle, IL 60172 • 20,819
Roselle, NJ 07203 • 20,314
Roselle Park, NJ 07204 • 12,805
Rosemead, CA 91770 • 51,638
Rosemont, CA 95826 • 22,851
Rosemount, MN 55068 • 8,622
Rosenberg, TX 77471 • 20,183
Rosepine, LA 70659 • 1,135
Roseto, PA 18013 • 1,555
Roseville, CA 95678 • 44,685
Roseville, IL 61473 • 1,151
Roseville, MI 48066 • 51,412
Roseville, MN 55113 • 33,485
Roseville, OH 43777 • 1,847
Rosewood Heights, IL 62024 • 4,821
Rosiclare, IL 62982 • 1,378
Roslyn Heights, NY 11577 • 6,405
Ross, OH 45061 • 2,124
Ross □, OH • 69,330
Rossford, OH 43460 • 5,861
Rossmoor, CA 90720 • 9,893
Ross Township, PA 15237 • 33,482
Rossville, GA 30741–42 • 3,601
Rossville, IL 60963 • 1,334
Rossville, IN 46065 • 1,175
Rossville, KS 66533 • 1,052
Roswell, GA 30075–77 • 47,923
Roswell, NM 88201–02 • 44,654
Rotan, TX 79546 • 1,913
Rothschild, WI 54474 • 3,310
Rothsville, PA 17543 • 2,097
Rotterdam, NY 12303 • 21,228
Roulette, PA 16746 • 1,500
Round Lake, IL 60073 • 3,550
Round Lake Beach, IL 60073 • 16,434
Round Mountain, NV 89045 • 210
Round Rock, TX 78664 • 30,923
Roundup, MT 59072 • 1,808
Rouses Point, NY 12979 • 2,377
Routt □, CO • 14,088
Rouzerville, PA 17250 • 1,188
Rowan □, KY • 20,353
Rowan □, NC • 110,605
Rowland, NC 28383 • 1,139
Rowland Heights, CA 91748 • 32,700
Rowlett, TX 75088 • 23,260
Rowley, MA 01969 • 1,144
Roxboro, NC 27573 • 7,332
Roy, UT 84067 • 24,603
Royal Oak, MI 48067–73 • 65,410
Royal Pines, NC 28704 • 1,600
Royalton, IL 62983 • 1,191
Royersford, PA 19468 • 4,458
Royse City, TX 75089 • 2,206
Royston, GA 30662 • 2,758
Rubidoux, CA 92509 • 24,367
Rugby, ND 58368 • 2,909
Ruidoso, NM 88345 • 4,600
Ruidoso Downs, NM 88346 • 920
Ruleville, MS 38771 • 3,245
Rumford, ME 04276 • 5,419
Rumson, NJ 07760 • 6,701
Runge, TX 78151 • 1,139
Runnels □, TX • 11,294
Runnemede, NJ 08078 • 9,042
Rupert, ID 83350 • 5,455
Rupert, WV 25984 • 1,104
Rural Hall, NC 27045 • 1,652
Rush □, IN • 18,129
Rush □, KS • 3,842
Rush City, MN 55069 • 1,497
Rushford, MN 55971 • 1,485
Rushmere, VA 23430 • 1,064
Rush Springs, OK 73082 • 1,229
Rushville, IL 62681 • 3,229
Rushville, IN 46173 • 5,533
Rushville, NE 69360 • 1,127
Rusk, TX 75785 • 4,366
Rusk □, TX • 43,735
Rusk □, WI • 15,079
Ruskin, FL 33570–73 • 6,046
Russell, KS 67665 • 4,781
Russell, KY 41169 • 4,014
Russell, PA 16345 • 1,000
Russell □, AL • 46,860
Russell □, KS • 7,835
Russell □, KY • 14,716
Russell □, VA • 28,667
Russell Springs, KY 42642 • 2,363
Russellville, AL 35653 • 7,812
Russellville, AR 72801 • 21,260
Russellville, KY 42276 • 7,454
Russellville, OR 97216 • 6,500
Russellville, TN 37860 • 1,069
Ruston, LA 71270–73 • 20,027
Ruth, NV 89319 • 550
Rutherford, NJ 07070–75 • 17,790
Rutherford, TN 38369 • 1,303
Rutherford □, NC • 56,918
Rutherford □, TN • 118,570
Rutherfordton, NC 28139 • 3,617
Rutland, MA 01543 • 2,145
Rutland, VT 05701–02 • 18,230
Rutland □, VT • 62,142
Rye, NH 03870 • 830
Rye, NY 10580 • 14,936
Rye Brook, NY 10573 • 7,765

S

Sabattus, ME 04280 • 3,696
Sabetha, KS 66534 • 2,341
Sabina, OH 45169 • 2,662
Sabinal, TX 78881 • 1,584
Sabine □, LA • 22,646
Sabine □, TX • 9,586
Sac □, IA • 12,324
Sacaton, AZ 85221 • 1,452
Sac City, IA 50583 • 2,492
Sachse, TX 75040 • 5,346
Sackets Harbor, NY 13685 • 1,313
Saco, ME 04072 • 15,181
Sacramento, CA 95801–66 • 369,365
Sacramento □, CA • 1,041,219
Saddle Brook, NJ 07662 • 13,296
Saddle River, NJ 07458 • 2,950
Saegertown, PA 16433 • 1,066
Safety Harbor, FL 34695 • 15,124
Safford, AZ 85546 • 7,359
Sagadahoc □, ME • 33,535
Sagamore, MA 02561 • 2,589
Sagamore Hills, OH 44067 • 4,700
Sag Harbor, NY 11963 • 2,134
Saginaw, MI 48601–08 • 69,512
Saginaw, TX 76179 • 8,551
Saginaw □, MI • 211,946
Saguache □, CO • 4,619
Saint Albans, VT 05478 • 7,339
Saint Albans, WV 25177 • 11,194
Saint Andrews, SC 29407 • 9,908
Saint Andrews, SC 29210 • 25,692
Saint Ann, MO 63074 • 14,489
Saint Anne, IL 60964 • 1,153
Saint Ansgar, IA 50472 • 1,063
Saint Anthony, ID 83445 • 3,010
Saint Anthony, MN 55418 • 7,727
Saint Augustine, FL 32084–86 • 11,692
Saint Bernard, OH 45217 • 5,344
Saint Bernard □, LA • 66,631
Saint Charles, IL 60174–75 • 22,501
Saint Charles, MD 20601 • 28,717
Saint Charles, MI 48655 • 2,144
Saint Charles, MN 55972 • 2,642
Saint Charles, MO 63301–03 • 54,555
Saint Charles □, LA • 42,437
Saint Charles □, MO • 212,907
Saint Charles Mesa, CO 81006 • 7,050
Saint Clair, MI 48079 • 5,116
Saint Clair, MO 63077 • 3,917
Saint Clair, PA 17970 • 3,524
Saint Clair □, AL • 50,009
Saint Clair □, IL • 262,852
Saint Clair □, MI • 145,607
Saint Clair □, MO • 8,457
Saint Clair Shores, MI 48080–82 • 68,107
Saint Clairsville, OH 43950 • 5,162
Saint Cloud, FL 34769–73 • 12,453
Saint Cloud, MN 56301–04 • 48,812
Saint Croix □, WI • 50,251
Saint Croix Falls, WI 54024 • 1,640
Saint David, AZ 85630 • 1,500
Saint Elmo, IL 62458 • 1,473
Saint Francis, KS 67756 • 1,495
Saint Francis, MN 55070 • 2,538
Saint Francis, SD 57572 • 815
Saint Francis, WI 53207 • 9,245
Saint Francis □, AR • 28,497
Saint Francisville, LA 70775 • 1,700
Saint Francois □, MO • 48,904
Sainte Genevieve, MO 63670 • 4,411
Sainte Genevieve □, MO • 16,037
Saint George, SC 29477 • 2,077
Saint George, UT 84770–71 • 28,502
Saint Georges, DE 19733 • 500
Saint Helena, CA 94574 • 4,990
Saint Helena □, LA • 9,874
Saint Helens, OR 97051 • 7,535
Saint Henry, OH 45883 • 1,907
Saint Ignace, MI 49781 • 2,568
Saint Ignatius, MT 59865 • 778
Saint James, MN 56081 • 4,364
Saint James, MO 65559 • 3,256
Saint James, NY 11780 • 12,703
Saint James □, LA • 20,879
Saint James City, FL 33956 • 1,094
Saint Jo, TX 76265 • 1,048
Saint John, IN 46373 • 4,921
Saint John, KS 67576 • 1,357
Saint Johns, AZ 85936 • 3,294
Saint Johns, MI 48879 • 7,284
Saint Johns, MO 63114 • 7,466
Saint Johns □, FL • 83,829
Saint Johnsbury, VT 05819 • 6,424
Saint Johnsville, NY 13452 • 1,825
Saint John the Baptist □, LA • 39,996
Saint Joseph, IL 61873 • 2,052
Saint Joseph, LA 71366 • 1,517
Saint Joseph, MI 49085 • 9,214
Saint Joseph, MN 56374 • 3,294
Saint Joseph, MO 64501–08 • 71,852
Saint Joseph □, IN • 247,052
Saint Joseph □, MI • 58,913
Saint Landry □, LA • 80,331
Saint Lawrence □, NY • 111,974
Saint Leo, FL 33574 • 1,009
Saint Louis, MI 48880 • 3,828
Saint Louis, MO 63101–88 • 396,685
Saint Louis □, MN • 198,213
Saint Louis □, MO • 993,529
Saint Louis Park, MN 55426 • 43,787
Saint Lucie □, FL • 150,171
Saint Maries, ID 83861 • 2,442
Saint Martin □, LA • 43,978
Saint Martinville, LA 70582 • 7,137
Saint Mary □, LA • 58,086
Saint Marys, AK 99658 • 441
Saint Marys, GA 31558 • 8,187
Saint Marys, IN 46556 • 1,800
Saint Marys, KS 66536 • 1,791
Saint Marys, OH 45885 • 8,441
Saint Marys, PA 15857 • 5,511
Saint Marys, WV 26170 • 2,148
Saint Marys □, MD • 75,974
Saint Marys City, MD 20686 • 3,200
Saint Matthews, KY 40207 • 15,800
Saint Matthews, SC 29135 • 2,345
Saint Michael, MN 55376 • 2,506
Saint Michaels, MD 21663 • 1,301
Saint Paris, OH 43072 • 1,842
Saint Paul, AK 99660 • 763
Saint Paul, IN 47272 • 1,032
Saint Paul, MN 55101–89 • 272,235
Saint Paul, MO 63366 • 1,192
Saint Paul, NE 68873 • 2,009
Saint Paul, VA 24283 • 1,007
Saint Paul Park, MN 55071 • 4,965
Saint Pauls, NC 28384 • 1,992
Saint Peter, MN 56082 • 9,421
Saint Peters, MO 63376 • 45,779
Saint Petersburg, FL 33701–84 • 238,629
Saint Petersburg Beach, FL 33706 • 9,200
Saint Rose, LA 70087 • 2,800
Saint Simons Island, GA 31522 • 12,026
Saint Stephen, SC 29479 • 1,697
Saint Stephens, NC 28601 • 8,734
Saint Tammany □, LA • 144,508
Salamanca, NY 14779 • 6,566
Sale Creek, TN 37373 • 1,050
Salem, AR 72576 • 1,474
Salem, IL 62881 • 7,470
Salem, IN 47167 • 5,619
Salem, MA 01970–71 • 38,091
Salem, MO 65560 • 4,486
Salem, NH 03079 • 12,000
Salem, NJ 08079 • 6,883
Salem, OH 44460 • 12,233
Salem, OR 97301–14 • 107,786
Salem, SD 57058 • 1,289
Salem, UT 84653 • 2,284
Salem, VA 24153 • 23,756
Salem, WV 26426 • 2,063
Salem, WI 53168 • 1,020
Salem □, NJ • 65,294
Salida, CO 81201 • 4,737
Salina, KS 67401–02 • 42,303
Salina, OK 74365 • 1,153
Salina, UT 84654 • 1,943
Salinas, CA 93901–15 • 108,777
Saline, MI 48176 • 6,660
Saline □, AR • 64,183
Saline □, IL • 26,551
Saline □, KS • 49,301
Saline □, MO • 23,523
Saline □, NE • 12,715
Salineville, OH 43945 • 1,474
Salisbury, CT 06068 • 1,600
Salisbury, MD 21801–03 • 20,592
Salisbury, MA 01952 • 3,729
Salisbury, MO 65281 • 1,881
Salisbury, NC 28144–46 • 23,087
Sallisaw, OK 74955 • 7,122
Salmon, ID 83467 • 2,941
Salmon Creek, WA 98665 • 11,989
Saltillo, MS 38866 • 1,782
Salt Lake □, UT • 725,956
Salt Lake City, UT 84101–90 • 159,936
Salt Springs, FL 32113 • 1,500
Saltville, VA 24370 • 2,300
Saltwater, WA 98188 • 2,200
Saluda, SC 29138 • 2,798
Saluda □, SC • 16,357
Salyersville, KY 41465 • 1,917
Samoset, FL 34208 • 3,119
Sampson □, NC • 47,297
Samson, AL 36477 • 2,190
Samtown, LA 71301 • 3,500
San Andreas, CA 95249 • 2,115
San Angelo, TX 76901–06 • 84,474
San Anselmo, CA 94960 • 11,743
San Antonio, TX 78201–99 • 935,933
Sanatoga, PA 19464 • 5,534
San Augustine, TX 75972 • 2,337
San Augustine □, TX • 7,999
San Benito, TX 78586 • 20,125
San Benito □, CA • 36,697
San Bernardino, CA 92401–27 • 164,164
San Bernardino □, CA • 1,418,380
Sanborn, IA 51248 • 1,345
Sanborn □, SD • 2,833
San Bruno, CA 94066 • 38,961
San Carlos, AZ 85550 • 2,918
San Carlos, CA 94070 • 26,167
San Carlos Park, FL 33912 • 11,785
San Clemente, CA 92672–74 • 41,100
Sandalfoot Cove, FL 33433 • 14,214
Sanders □, MT • 8,669
Sanderson, TX 79848 • 1,128
Sandersville, GA 31082 • 6,290
Sand Hill, MA 02066 • 1,800
Sandia, NM 87047 • 6,742
San Diego, CA 92101–99 • 1,110,549
San Diego, TX 78384 • 4,983
San Diego □, CA • 2,498,016
San Dimas, CA 91773 • 32,397
Sandoval, IL 62882 • 1,535
Sandoval □, NM • 63,319
Sand Point, AK 99661 • 878
Sandpoint, ID 83862–65 • 5,203
Sand Springs, OK 74063 • 15,346
Sandston, VA 23150 • 3,630
Sandstone, MN 55072 • 2,057
Sandusky, MI 48471 • 2,403
Sandusky, OH 44870–71 • 29,764
Sandusky □, OH • 61,963
Sandwich, IL 60548 • 5,567
Sandwich, MA 02563 • 2,998
Sandy, OR 97055 • 4,152
Sandy, UT 84070 • 75,058
Sandy Hook, CT 06482 • 1,100
Sandy Springs, GA 30328 • 67,842
Sandy Springs, SC 29677 • 1,200
San Felipe Pueblo, NM 87001 • 1,557
San Fernando, CA 91340–46 • 22,580
Sanford, FL 32771–73 • 32,387
Sanford, ME 04073 • 10,296
Sanford, NC 27330–31 • 14,475
San Francisco, CA 94101–88 • 723,959
San Francisco □, CA • 723,959
Sangamon □, IL • 178,386
Sanger, CA 93657 • 16,839
Sanger, TX 76266 • 3,508
Sanibel, FL 33957 • 5,468
Sanilac □, MI • 39,928
San Jacinto, CA 92383 • 16,210
San Jacinto □, TX • 16,372
San Joaquin □, CA • 480,628
San Jose, CA 95101–96 • 782,248
San Juan, TX 78589 • 10,815
San Juan □, CO • 745
San Juan □, NM • 91,605
San Juan □, UT • 12,621
San Juan □, WA • 10,035
San Juan Capistrano, CA 92690–93 • 26,183
San Leandro, CA 94577–79 • 68,223
San Lorenzo, CA 94580 • 19,987
San Luis, AZ 85634 • 4,212
San Luis Obispo, CA 93401–12 • 41,958
San Luis Obispo □, CA • 217,162
San Manuel, AZ 85631 • 4,009
San Marcos, CA 92069 • 38,974
San Marcos, TX 78666–67 • 28,743
San Marino, CA 91108 • 12,959
San Mateo, CA 94401–04 • 85,486
San Mateo □, CA • 649,623
San Miguel □, CO • 3,653
San Miguel □, NM • 25,743
San Pablo, CA 94806 • 25,158
San Patricio □, TX • 58,749
Sanpete □, UT • 16,259
San Rafael, CA 94901–15 • 48,404
San Ramon, CA 94583 • 35,303
San Remo, NY 11754 • 7,770
San Saba, TX 76877 • 2,626
San Saba □, TX • 5,401
Sans Souci, SC 29609 • 7,612
Santa Ana, CA 92701–08 • 293,742
Santa Anna, TX 76878 • 1,249
Santa Barbara, CA 93101–90 • 85,571
Santa Barbara □, CA • 369,608
Santa Clara, CA 95050–56 • 93,613
Santa Clara, OR 97404 • 12,834
Santa Clara, UT 84765 • 2,322
Santa Clara □, CA • 1,497,577
Santa Cruz, CA 95060–67 • 49,040
Santa Cruz, NM 87567 • 975
Santa Cruz □, AZ • 29,676
Santa Cruz □, CA • 229,734
Santa Fe, NM 87501–06 • 55,859
Santa Fe, TX 77510 • 8,429
Santa Fe □, NM • 98,928
Santa Fe Springs, CA 90670–71 • 15,520
Santa Margarita, CA 93453 • 1,200
Santa Maria, CA 93454–56 • 61,284
Santa Monica, CA 90401–11 • 86,905
Santa Paula, CA 93060–61 • 25,062
Santaquin, UT 84655 • 2,386
Santa Rosa, CA 95401–09 • 113,313
Santa Rosa, NM 88435 • 2,263
Santa Rosa □, FL • 81,608
Santa Venetia, CA 94901 • 6,000
Santa Ynez, CA 93460 • 4,200
Santee, CA 92071 • 52,902
Santo Domingo Pueblo, NM 87052 • 2,866
San Ygnacio, TX 78067 • 1,000
Sappington, MO 63126 • 10,917
Sapulpa, OK 74066–67 • 18,074
Saraland, AL 36571 • 11,751
Saranac, MI 48881 • 1,461
Saranac Lake, NY 12983 • 5,377
Sarasota, FL 34230–43 • 50,961
Sarasota □, FL • 277,776
Sarasota Springs, FL 34232 • 16,088
Saratoga, CA 95070–71 • 28,061
Saratoga, TX 77585 • 1,200
Saratoga, WY 82331 • 1,969
Saratoga □, NY • 181,276
Saratoga Springs, NY 12866 • 25,001
Sarcoxie, MO 64862 • 1,330
Sardis, GA 30456 • 1,116
Sardis, MS 38666 • 2,128
Sargent □, ND • 4,549
Sarpy □, NE • 102,583
Sartell, MN 56377 • 5,393
Satanta, KS 67870 • 1,073
Satellite Beach, FL 32937 • 9,889
Satsuma, AL 36572 • 5,194
Saugerties, NY 12477 • 3,915
Saugus, MA 01906 • 25,549
Sauk □, WI • 46,975
Sauk Centre, MN 56378 • 3,581
Sauk City, WI 53583 • 3,019
Sauk Rapids, MN 56379 • 7,825
Sauk Village, IL 60411 • 9,926
Saukville, WI 53080 • 3,695
Sault Sainte Marie, MI 49783 • 14,689
Saunders □, NE • 18,285
Saunderstown, RI 02874 • 400
Sausalito, CA 94965–66 • 7,152
Savage, MD 20763 • 2,850
Savage, MN 55378 • 9,906
Savanna, IL 61074 • 3,819
Savannah, GA 31401–20 • 137,560
Savannah, MO 64485 • 4,352
Savannah, TN 38372 • 6,547
Savoonga, AK 99769 • 519
Savoy, IL 61874 • 2,674
Sawyer □, WI • 14,181
Saxonburg, PA 16056 • 1,345
Saxtons River, VT 05154 • 541
Saybrook Manor, CT 06475 • 1,073
Saydel, IA 50313 • 3,500
Saylesville, RI 02865 • 3,510
Saylorsburg, PA 18353 • 1,500
Sayre, OK 73662 • 2,881
Sayre, PA 18840 • 5,791
Sayreville, NJ 08872 • 34,986
Sayville, NY 11782 • 16,550
Scalp Level, PA 15963 • 1,158
Scappoose, OR 97056 • 3,529
Scarborough, ME 04074 • 2,586
Scarsdale, NY 10583 • 16,987
Schaumburg, IL 60192–94 • 68,586
Schenectady, NY 12301–09 • 65,566
Schenectady □, NY • 149,285
Schererville, IN 46375 • 19,926
Schertz, TX 78154 • 10,555
Schiller Park, IL 60176 • 11,189
Schleicher □, TX • 2,990
Schley □, GA • 3,588
Schofield, WI 54476 • 2,415
Schoharie, NY 12157 • 1,045
Schoharie □, NY • 31,859
Schoolcraft, MI 49087 • 1,517
Schoolcraft □, MI • 8,302
Schroon Lake, NY 12870 • 1,100
Schulenburg, TX 78956 • 2,455
Schurz, NV 89427 • 617
Schuyler, NE 68661 • 4,052
Schuyler □, IL • 7,498
Schuyler □, MO • 4,236
Schuyler □, NY • 18,662
Schuylerville, NY 12871 • 1,364
Schuylkill □, PA • 152,585

Schuylkill Haven, PA 17972 • *5,610*
Scioto □, OH • *80,327*
Scituate, MA 02066 • *5,180*
Scobey, MT 59263 • *1,154*
Scotch Plains, NJ 07076 • *21,160*
Scotchtown, NY 10940 • *8,765*
Scotia, CA 95565 • *1,200*
Scotia, NY 12302 • *7,359*
Scotland, SD 57059 • *968*
Scotland □, MO • *4,822*
Scotland □, NC • *33,754*
Scotland Neck, NC 27874 • *2,575*
Scotlandville, LA 70807 • *15,113*
Scott, LA 70583 • *4,912*
Scott □, AR • *10,205*
Scott □, IL • *5,644*
Scott □, IN • *20,991*
Scott □, IA • *150,979*
Scott □, KS • *5,289*
Scott □, KY • *23,867*
Scott □, MN • *57,846*
Scott □, MS • *24,137*
Scott □, MO • *39,376*
Scott □, TN • *18,358*
Scott □, VA • *23,204*
Scott City, KS 67871 • *3,785*
Scott City, MO 63780 • *4,292*
Scottdale, GA 30079 • *8,636*
Scottdale, PA 15683 • *5,184*
Scott Lake, FL 33055 • *14,588*
Scottsbluff, NE 69361–63 • *13,711*
Scotts Bluff □, NE • *36,025*
Scottsboro, AL 35768 • *13,786*
Scottsburg, IN 47170 • *5,334*
Scottsdale, AZ 85250–71 • *130,069*
Scotts Valley, CA 95066–67 • *8,615*
Scottsville, KY 42164 • *4,278*
Scottsville, NY 14546 • *1,912*
Scott Township, PA 15106 • *17,118*
Scottville, MI 49454 • *1,287*
Scranton, PA 18501–19 • *81,805*
Screven □, GA • *13,842*
Scurry □, TX • *18,634*
Seabreeze, DE 19971 • *350*
Sea Bright, NJ 07760 • *1,693*
Seabrook, MD 20706 • *7,660*
Seabrook, NJ 08302 • *1,457*
Seabrook, TX 77586 • *6,685*
Sea Cliff, NY 11579 • *5,054*
Seadrift, TX 77983 • *1,277*
Seaford, DE 19973 • *5,689*
Seaford, NY 11783 • *15,597*
Seaford, VA 23696 • *2,340*
Seagate, NC 28403 • *5,444*
Sea Girt, NJ 08750 • *2,099*
Seagoville, TX 75159 • *8,969*
Seagraves, TX 79359 • *2,398*
Sea Isle City, NJ 08243 • *2,692*
Seal Beach, CA 90740 • *25,098*
Sealy, TX 77474 • *4,541*
Seaman, OH 45679 • *1,013*
Searchlight, NV 89029 • *430*
Searcy, AR 72143 • *15,180*
Searcy □, AR • *7,841*
Searsport, ME 04974 • *1,151*
Seaside, CA 93955 • *38,901*
Seaside, OR 97138 • *5,359*
Seaside Heights, NJ 08751 • *2,366*
Seaside Park, NJ 08752 • *1,871*
Seat Pleasant, MD 20743 • *5,359*
Seattle, WA 98101–99 • *516,259*
Sebastian, FL 32958 • *10,205*
Sebastian □, AR • *99,590*
Sebewaing, MI 48759 • *1,923*
Sebree, KY 42455 • *1,510*
Sebring, FL 33870–72 • *8,900*
Sebring, OH 44672 • *4,848*
Secaucus, NJ 07094 • *14,061*
Security, CO 80911 • *6,660*
Sedalia, MO 65301–02 • *19,800*
Sedan, KS 67361 • *1,306*
Sedgwick, KS 67135 • *1,438*
Sedgwick □, CO • *2,690*
Sedgwick □, KS • *403,662*
Sedona, AZ 86336 • *7,720*
Sedro Woolley, WA 98284 • *6,031*
Seekonk, MA 02771 • *12,269*
Seeley, CA 92273 • *1,228*
Seelyville, IN 47878 • *1,090*
Seguin, TX 78155–56 • *18,853*
Seiling, OK 73663 • *1,031*
Selah, WA 98942 • *5,113*
Selawik, AK 99770 • *596*
Selby, SD 57472 • *707*
Selbyville, DE 19975 • *1,335*
Selden, NY 11784 • *20,608*
Seldovia, AK 99663 • *316*
Selinsgrove, PA 17870 • *5,384*
Sellersburg, IN 47172 • *5,745*
Sellersville, PA 18960 • *4,479*
Sells, AZ 85634 • *2,750*
Selma, AL 36701–02 • *23,755*
Selma, CA 93662 • *14,757*
Selma, NC 27576 • *4,600*
Selmer, TN 38375 • *3,838*
Seminole, OK 74868 • *7,071*
Seminole, TX 79360 • *6,342*
Seminole □, FL • *287,529*
Seminole □, GA • *9,010*
Seminole □, OK • *25,412*
Seminole Park, FL 34647 • *8,000*
Semmes, AL 36575 • *2,250*
Senath, MO 63876 • *1,622*
Senatobia, MS 38668 • *4,772*
Seneca, IL 61360 • *1,878*
Seneca, KS 66538 • *2,027*
Seneca, MO 64865 • *1,885*
Seneca, PA 16346 • *1,300*
Seneca, SC 29678–79 • *7,726*
Seneca □, NY • *33,683*
Seneca □, OH • *59,733*
Seneca Falls, NY 13148 • *7,370*
Sequatchie □, TN • *8,863*
Sequim, WA 98382 • *3,616*
Sequoyah □, OK • *33,828*
Sergeant Bluff, IA 51054 • *2,772*
Sesser, IL 62884 • *2,087*
Seven Hills, OH 44131 • *12,339*
Seven Oaks, SC 29210 • *15,722*
Severn, MD 21144 • *24,499*
Severna Park, MD 21146 • *25,879*
Sevier □, AR • *13,637*
Sevier □, TN • *51,043*
Sevier □, UT • *15,431*
Sevierville, TN 37862 • *7,178*
Seville, OH 44273 • *1,810*
Sewanee, TN 37375 • *2,128*
Seward, AK 99664 • *2,699*
Seward, NE 68434 • *5,634*
Seward □, KS • *18,743*
Seward □, NE • *15,450*
Sewell, NJ 08080 • *1,870*
Sewickley, PA 15143 • *4,134*
Seymour, CT 06483 • *14,288*
Seymour, IN 47274 • *15,576*
Seymour, MO 65746 • *1,636*
Seymour, TN 37865 • *7,026*
Seymour, TX 76380 • *3,185*
Seymour, WI 54165 • *2,782*
Seymourville, LA 70764 • *2,891*
Shackelford □, TX • *3,316*
Shady Cove, OR 97539 • *1,351*
Shady Side, MD 20764 • *4,107*
Shadyside, OH 43947 • *3,934*
Shady Spring, WV 25918 • *1,929*
Shafter, CA 93263 • *8,409*
Shaftsbury, VT 05262 • *700*
Shaker Heights, OH 44120 • *30,831*
Shakopee, MN 55379 • *11,739*
Shaler Township, PA 15116 • *30,533*
Shallowater, TX 79363 • *1,708*
Shamokin, PA 17872 • *9,184*
Shamokin Dam, PA 17876 • *1,690*
Shamrock, TX 79079 • *2,286*
Shannock, RI 02875 • *950*
Shannon, GA 30172 • *1,703*
Shannon, MS 38868 • *1,419*
Shannon □, MO • *7,613*
Shannon □, SD • *9,902*
Shannontown, SC 29150 • *7,900*
Sharkey □, MS • *7,066*
Sharon, MA 02067 • *5,893*
Sharon, PA 16146 • *17,493*
Sharon, TN 38255 • *1,047*
Sharon, WI 53585 • *1,250*
Sharon Hill, PA 19079 • *5,771*
Sharonville, OH 45241 • *13,153*
Sharp □, AR • *14,109*
Sharpes, FL 32922 • *3,348*
Sharpley, DE 19803 • *1,250*
Sharpsburg, MD 21782 • *659*
Sharpsburg, NC 27878 • *1,536*
Sharpsburg, PA 15215 • *3,781*
Sharpsville, PA 16150 • *4,729*
Shasta □, CA • *147,036*
Shattuck, OK 73858 • *1,454*
Shaw, MS 38773 • *2,349*
Shawano, WI 54166 • *7,598*
Shawano □, WI • *37,157*
Shawnee, KS 66203 • *37,993*
Shawnee, OK 74801–02 • *26,017*
Shawnee □, KS • *160,976*
Shawneetown, IL 62984 • *1,575*
Sheboygan, WI 53081–83 • *49,676*
Sheboygan □, WI • *103,877*
Sheboygan Falls, WI 53085 • *5,823*
Sheffield, AL 35660–62 • *10,380*
Sheffield, IA 50475 • *1,174*
Sheffield, MA 01257 • *1,100*
Sheffield, PA 16347 • *1,294*
Sheffield Lake, OH 44054 • *9,825*
Shelbina, MO 63468 • *2,172*
Shelburn, IN 47879 • *1,147*
Shelburne Falls, MA 01370 • *1,996*
Shelby, MI 49455 • *48,655*
Shelby, MS 38774 • *2,806*
Shelby, MT 59474 • *2,763*
Shelby, NC 28150–51 • *14,669*
Shelby, OH 44875 • *9,564*
Shelby □, AL • *99,358*
Shelby □, IL • *22,261*
Shelby □, IN • *40,307*
Shelby □, IA • *13,230*
Shelby □, KY • *24,824*
Shelby □, MO • *6,942*
Shelby □, OH • *44,915*
Shelby □, TN • *826,330*
Shelby □, TX • *22,034*
Shelbyville, IL 62565 • *4,943*
Shelbyville, IN 46176 • *15,336*
Shelbyville, KY 40065 • *6,238*
Shelbyville, TN 37160 • *14,049*
Sheldon, IL 60966 • *1,109*
Sheldon, IA 51201 • *4,937*
Sheldon, TX 77028 • *1,653*
Shelley, ID 83274 • *3,536*
Shell Lake, WI 54871 • *1,161*
Shellman, GA 31786 • *1,162*
Shell Rock, IA 50670 • *1,385*
Shelter Island, NY 11964 • *1,193*
Shelton, CT 06484 • *35,418*
Shelton, WA 98584 • *7,241*
Shenandoah, IA 51601 • *5,572*
Shenandoah, PA 17976 • *6,221*
Shenandoah, VA 22849 • *2,213*
Shenandoah □, VA • *31,636*
Shepherd, MI 48883 • *1,413*
Shepherd, TX 77371 • *1,812*
Shepherdstown, WV 25443 • *1,287*
Shepherdsville, KY 40165 • *4,805*
Sherborn, MA 01770 • *1,490*
Sherburn, MN 56171 • *1,105*
Sherburne, NY 13460 • *1,531*
Sherburne □, MN • *41,945*
Sheridan, AR 72150 • *3,098*
Sheridan, CO 80110 • *4,976*
Sheridan, IL 60551 • *1,288*
Sheridan, IN 46069 • *2,046*
Sheridan, OR 97378 • *3,979*
Sheridan, WY 82801 • *13,900*
Sheridan □, KS • *3,043*
Sheridan □, MT • *4,732*
Sheridan □, NE • *6,750*
Sheridan □, ND • *2,148*
Sheridan □, WY • *23,562*
Sheridan Beach, WA 98155 • *6,518*
Sherman, TX 75090–91 • *31,601*
Sherman □, KS • *6,926*
Sherman □, NE • *3,718*
Sherman □, OR • *1,918*
Sherman □, TX • *2,858*
Sherrelwood, CO 80221 • *16,636*
Sherrill, NY 13461 • *2,864*
Sherwood, AR 72116 • *18,893*
Sherwood, OR 97140 • *3,093*
Sherwood Manor, CT 06082 • *6,357*
Sherwood Park, DE 19808 • *2,000*
Shiawassee □, MI • *69,770*
Shickshinny, PA 18655 • *1,108*
Shillington, PA 19607 • *5,062*
Shiloh, OH 44878 • *11,607*
Shiloh, PA 17404 • *8,245*
Shiner, TX 77984 • *2,074*
Shinglehouse, PA 16748 • *1,243*
Shinnston, WV 26431 • *2,543*
Ship Bottom, NJ 08008 • *1,352*
Shippensburg, PA 17257 • *5,331*
Shiprock, NM 87420 • *7,687*
Shirley, MA 01464 • *1,559*
Shirley, NY 11967 • *22,936*
Shishmaref, AK 99772 • *456*
Shively, KY 40216 • *15,535*
Shoemakersville, PA 19555 • *1,443*
Shore Acres, MA 02066 • *1,200*
Shores Acres, RI 02852 • *410*
Shoreview, MN 55112 • *24,587*
Shorewood, IL 60435 • *6,264*
Shorewood, MN 55331 • *5,917*
Shorewood, WI 53211 • *14,116*
Shorewood Hills, WI 53705 • *1,680*
Short Beach, CT 06405 • *2,500*
Shortsville, NY 14548 • *1,485*
Shoshone, ID 83352 • *1,249*
Shoshone □, ID • *13,931*
Shoshoni, WY 82649 • *497*
Show Low, AZ 85901 • *5,019*
Shreve, OH 44676 • *1,584*
Shreveport, LA 71101–10 • *198,525*
Shrewsbury, MA 01545 • *23,400*
Shrewsbury, MO 63119 • *6,416*
Shrewsbury, NJ 07702 • *3,096*
Shrewsbury, PA 17361 • *2,672*
Shullsburg, WI 53586 • *1,236*
Shungnak, AK 99773 • *223*
Sibley, IA 51249 • *2,815*
Sibley □, MN • *14,366*
Sicklerville, NJ 08081 • *1,750*
Sidney, IL 61877 • *1,027*
Sidney, IA 51652 • *1,253*
Sidney, MT 59270 • *5,217*
Sidney, NE 69162 • *5,959*
Sidney, NY 13838 • *4,720*
Sidney, OH 45365 • *18,710*
Siegle, LA 71291 • *1,600*
Sierra □, CA • *3,318*
Sierra □, NM • *9,912*
Sierra Madre, CA 91024 • *10,762*
Sierra Vista, AZ 85635–36 • *32,983*
Siesta Key, FL 34242 • *7,772*
Signal Hill, CA 90806 • *8,371*
Signal Mountain, TN 37377 • *7,034*
Sigourney, IA 52591 • *2,111*
Sikeston, MO 63801 • *17,641*
Siler City, NC 27344 • *4,808*
Siloam Springs, AR 72761 • *8,151*
Silsbee, TX 77656 • *6,368*
Silt, CO 81652 • *1,095*
Silver Bay, MN 55614 • *1,894*
Silver Bow □, MT • *33,941*
Silver City, NV 89428 • *100*
Silver City, NM 88061–62 • *10,683*
Silver Creek, NY 14136 • *2,927*
Silverdale, WA 98383 • *7,660*
Silver Grove, KY 41085 • *1,102*
Silver Hill, MD 20746 • *1,580*
Silver Lake, KS 66539 • *1,390*
Silver Lake, MA 01887 • *2,900*
Silver Lake, WI 53170 • *1,801*
Silverpeak, NV 89047 • *190*
Silver Spring, MD 20901–12 • *76,046*
Silver Springs, FL 32688 • *1,082*
Silver Springs, NV 89429 • *2,253*
Silver Springs Shores, FL 32672 • *6,421*
Silverton, NJ 08753 • *9,175*
Silverton, OH 45236 • *5,859*
Silverton, OR 97381 • *5,635*
Silview, DE 19804 • *1,500*
Silvis, IL 61282 • *6,926*
Simi Valley, CA 93062–65 • *100,217*
Simmesport, LA 71369 • *2,092*
Simpson, PA 18407 • *1,670*
Simpson □, KY • *15,145*
Simpson □, MS • *23,953*
Simpsonville, SC 29681 • *11,708*
Simsbury, CT 06070 • *5,577*
Sinclair, WY 82334 • *500*
Sinton, TX 78387 • *5,549*
Sioux □, IA • *29,903*
Sioux □, NE • *1,549*
Sioux □, ND • *3,761*
Sioux Center, IA 51250 • *5,074*
Sioux City, IA 51101–11 • *80,505*
Sioux Falls, SD 57101–18 • *100,814*
Siskiyou □, CA • *43,531*
Sisseton, SD 57262 • *2,181*
Sistersville, WV 26175 • *1,797*
Sitka, AK 99835 • *8,588*
Skagit □, WA • *79,555*
Skagway, AK 99840 • *692*
Skamania □, WA • *8,289*
Skaneateles, NY 13152 • *2,724*
Skiatook, OK 74070 • *4,910*
Skokie, IL 60076–77 • *59,432*
Skowhegan, ME 04976 • *6,990*
Sky Lake, FL 32809 • *6,202*
Skyland, NV 89448 • *660*
Skyland, NC 28776 • *1,100*
Skyway, WA 98178 • *8,500*
Slackwoods, NJ 08638 • *8,100*
Slater, IA 50244 • *1,268*
Slater, MO 65349 • *2,186*
Slater, SC 29683 • *1,000*
Slatersville, RI 02876 • *2,330*
Slatington, PA 18080 • *4,678*
Slaton, TX 79364 • *6,078*
Slayton, MN 56172 • *2,147*
Sleepy Eye, MN 56085 • *3,694*
Slickville, PA 15684 • *1,178*
Slidell, LA 70458–61 • *24,124*
Slinger, WI 53086 • *2,340*
Slippery Rock, PA 16057 • *3,008*
Sloan, NY 14225 • *3,830*
Sloatsburg, NY 10974 • *3,035*
Slocomb, AL 36375 • *1,906*
Slope □, ND • *907*
Smackover, AR 71762 • *2,232*
Smethport, PA 16749 • *1,734*
Smith □, KS • *5,078*
Smith □, MS • *14,798*
Smith □, TN • *14,143*
Smith □, TX • *151,309*
Smith Center, KS 66967 • *2,016*
Smithers, WV 25186 • *1,162*
Smithfield, NC 27577 • *7,540*
Smithfield, PA 15478 • *1,000*
Smithfield, UT 84335 • *5,566*
Smithfield, VA 23430 • *4,686*
Smith River, CA 95567 • *1,000*
Smiths, AL 36877 • *1,700*
Smithsburg, MD 21783 • *1,221*
Smithton, IL 62285 • *1,587*
Smithtown, NY 11787 • *25,638*
Smithville, MO 64089 • *2,525*
Smithville, OH 44677 • *1,354*
Smithville, TN 37166 • *3,791*
Smithville, TX 78957 • *3,196*
Smyrna, DE 19977 • *5,231*
Smyrna, GA 30080–82 • *30,981*
Smyrna, TN 37167 • *13,647*
Smyth □, VA • *32,370*
Sneads, FL 32460 • *1,746*
Sneedville, TN 37869 • *1,446*
Snellville, GA 30278 • *12,084*
Snohomish, WA 98290 • *6,499*
Snohomish □, WA • *465,642*
Snoqualmie, WA 98065 • *1,546*
Snowflake, AZ 85937 • *3,679*
Snow Hill, MD 21863 • *2,217*
Snow Hill, NC 28580 • *1,378*
Snyder, OK 73566 • *1,619*
Snyder, TX 79549 • *12,195*
Snyder □, PA • *36,680*
Soap Lake, WA 98851 • *1,149*
Socastee, SC 29577 • *10,426*
Social Circle, GA 30279 • *2,755*
Socorro, NM 87801 • *8,159*
Socorro □, NM • *14,764*
Soda Springs, ID 83276 • *3,111*
Soddy-Daisy, TN 37379 • *8,240*
Sodus, NY 14551 • *1,904*
Sodus Point, NY 14555 • *1,190*
Solana, FL 33950 • *1,128*
Solana Beach, CA 92075 • *12,962*
Solano □, CA • *340,421*
Soldotna, AK 99669 • *3,482*
Soledad, CA 93960 • *7,146*
Solomons, MD 20688 • *1,500*
Solon, IA 52333 • *1,050*
Solon, OH 44139 • *18,548*
Solvay, NY 13209 • *6,717*
Somerdale, NJ 08083 • *5,440*
Somers, CT 06071 • *9,108*
Somerset, KY 42501–02 • *10,733*
Somerset, MA 02725 • *17,655*
Somerset, NJ 08873–75 • *22,070*
Somerset, OH 43783 • *1,390*
Somerset, PA 15501 • *6,454*
Somerset, TX 78069 • *1,144*
Somerset, WI 54025 • *1,065*
Somerset □, ME • *49,767*
Somerset □, MD • *23,440*
Somerset □, NJ • *240,279*
Somerset □, PA • *78,218*
Somers Point, NJ 08244 • *11,216*
Somersville, CT 06072 • *1,200*
Somersworth, NH 03878 • *11,249*
Somerton, AZ 85350 • *5,282*
Somervell □, TX • *5,360*
Somerville, MA 02143 • *76,210*
Somerville, NJ 08876–77 • *11,632*
Somerville, TN 38068 • *2,047*
Somerville, TX 77879 • *1,542*
Somonauk, IL 60552 • *1,263*
Sonoma, CA 95476 • *8,121*
Sonoma □, CA • *388,222*
Sonora, CA 95370 • *4,153*
Sonora, TX 76950 • *2,751*
Soperton, GA 30457 • *2,797*
Sophia, WV 25921 • *1,182*
Soquel, CA 95073 • *9,188*
Sorrento, LA 70778 • *1,119*
Souderton, PA 18964 • *5,957*
Sound Beach, NY 11789 • *9,102*
South Acton, MA 01720 • *3,220*
South Amboy, NJ 08879 • *7,863*
South Amherst, MA 01002 • *5,053*
South Amherst, OH 44001 • *1,765*
Southampton, NY 11968–69 • *3,980*
Southampton □, VA • *17,550*
South Ashburnham, MA 01466 • *1,110*
Southaven, MS 38671 • *17,949*
South Barre, VT 05670 • *1,314*
South Bay, FL 33493 • *3,558*
South Belmar, NJ 07719 • *1,482*
South Beloit, IL 61080 • *4,072*
South Bend, IN 46601–80 • *105,511*
South Bend, WA 98586 • *1,551*
South Berwick, ME 03908 • *5,877*
Southborough, MA 01772 • *1,450*
South Boston, VA 24592 • *6,997*
South Bound Brook, NJ 08880 • *4,185*
South Bradenton, FL 34205 • *20,398*
Southbridge, MA 01550 • *13,631*
South Broadway, WA 98902 • *2,735*
South Burlington, VT 05403 • *12,809*
Southbury, CT 06488 • *3,000*
South Charleston, OH 45368 • *1,626*
South Charleston, WV 25303 • *13,645*
South Chicago Heights, IL 60411 • *3,597*
South Congaree, SC 29169 • *2,406*
South Connellsville, PA 15425 • *2,204*
South Dartmouth, MA 02748 • *9,850*
South Daytona, FL 32121 • *12,482*
South Decatur, GA 30034 • *19,350*
South Deerfield, MA 01373 • *1,906*
South Dennis, MA 02660 • *2,500*
South Duxbury, MA 02332 • *3,017*
South Easton, MA 02375 • *1,530*
South Elgin, IL 60177 • *7,474*
South El Monte, CA 91733 • *20,850*
Southern Pines, NC 28387–88 • *9,129*
South Euclid, OH 44121 • *23,866*
South Fallsburg, NY 12779 • *2,115*
South Farmingdale, NY 11735 • *15,377*
Southfield, MI 48034 • *75,728*
South Fork, PA 15956 • *1,197*
South Fulton, TN 38257 • *2,688*
South Gastonia, NC 28052 • *5,487*
South Gate, CA 90280 • *86,284*
Southgate, FL 34239 • *7,324*
Southgate, KY 41071 • *3,266*
South Gate, MD 21061 • *27,564*
Southgate, MI 48195 • *30,771*
South Glastonbury, CT 06073 • *1,570*
Southglenn, CO 80122 • *43,087*
South Glens Falls, NY 12801 • *3,506*
South Grafton, MA 01560 • *2,610*
South Hackensack, NJ 07606 • *2,229*
South Hadley, MA 01075 • *5,340*
South Hadley Falls, MA 01075 • *5,100*
South Hamilton, MA 01982 • *2,720*
South Haven, IN 46383 • *6,112*
South Haven, MI 49090 • *5,563*
South Hill, NY 14850 • *5,423*
South Hill, VA 23970 • *4,217*
South Hingham, MA 02043 • *4,080*
South Holland, IL 60473 • *22,105*
South Hooksett, NH 03106 • *3,638*
South Hopkinton, RI 02813 • *900*
South Houston, TX 77587 • *14,207*
South Huntington, NY 11746 • *9,624*
South Hutchinson, KS 67505 • *2,444*
Southington, CT 06489 • *38,518*
South International Falls, MN 56679 • *2,806*
South Jacksonville, IL 62650 • *3,187*
South Jordan, UT 84065 • *12,220*
South Lake Tahoe, CA 95702 • *21,586*
South Lancaster, MA 01561 • *1,772*
South Laramie, WY 82070 • *1,500*
South Laurel, MD 20708 • *18,591*
South Lebanon, OH 45065 • *2,696*
South Lockport, NY 14094 • *7,112*
South Lyon, MI 48178 • *5,857*
South Miami, FL 33143 • *10,404*
South Miami Heights, FL 33157 • *30,030*
South Milwaukee, WI 53172 • *20,958*
South Nyack, NY 10960 • *3,352*
South Ogden, UT 84403 • *12,105*
Southold, NY 11971 • *5,192*
South Orange, NJ 07079 • *16,390*
South Paris, ME 04281 • *2,320*
South Pasadena, CA 91030 • *23,936*
South Patrick Shores, FL 32937 • *10,249*
South Pekin, IL 61564 • *1,184*
South Pittsburg, TN 37380 • *3,295*
South Plainfield, NJ 07080 • *20,489*
Southport, FL 32409 • *1,992*
Southport, IN 46227 • *1,969*
Southport, NY 14904 • *7,753*
Southport, NC 28461 • *2,369*
South Portland, ME 04106 • *23,163*
South River, NJ 08882 • *13,692*
South Royalton, VT 05068 • *700*
South Saint Paul, MN 55075–77 • *20,197*
South Salt Lake, UT 84115 • *10,129*
South San Francisco, CA 94080–83 • *54,312*
South San Gabriel, CA 91770 • *7,700*
South San Jose Hills, CA 91744 • *17,814*
South Sarasota, FL 34239 • *5,298*
South Setauket, NY 11733 • *5,990*
Southside, AL 35901 • *5,580*
Southside Place, TX 77005 • *1,392*
South Sioux City, NE 68776 • *9,677*
South Stony Brook, NY 11790 • *6,120*
South Streator, IL 61364 • *2,334*
South Sumter, SC 29150 • *4,371*
South Toms River, NJ 08757 • *3,869*
South Torrington, WY 82240 • *300*
South Tucson, AZ 85713 • *5,093*
South Valley Stream, NY 11581 • *5,328*
South Venice, FL 34293 • *11,951*
South Walpole, MA 02071 • *1,300*
South Waverly, PA 14892 • *1,049*
South Wellfleet, MA 02663 • *2,300*
South Westbury, NY 11590 • *9,732*
Southwest Harbor, ME 04679 • *1,952*
South Whitley, IN 46787 • *1,482*
South Whittier, CA 90605 • *51,100*
Southwick, MA 01077 • *1,170*
South Williamsport, PA 17701 • *6,496*
South Windham, CT 06266 • *1,644*
South Windham, ME 04082 • *1,350*
South Windsor, CT 06074 • *10,800*
Southwood, CO 80120 • *2,050*
Southwood Acres, CT 06082 • *8,963*
South Woodstock, CT 06267 • *1,112*
South Yarmouth, MA 02664 • *10,358*
South Yuba City, CA 95991 • *8,816*
South Zanesville, OH 43701 • *1,969*
Spalding □, GA • *54,457*
Spanaway, WA 98387 • *15,001*
Spangler, PA 15775 • *2,068*
Spanish Fork, UT 84660 • *11,272*
Spanish Fort, AL 36527 • *3,732*
Spanish Lake, MO 63138 • *20,322*
Sparks, GA 31647 • *1,205*
Sparks, NV 89431–36 • *53,367*
Sparr, FL 32192 • *1,100*
Sparta, GA 31087 • *1,710*
Sparta, IL 62286 • *4,853*
Sparta, MI 49345 • *3,968*
Sparta (Lake Mohawk), NJ 07871 • *8,930*
Sparta, NC 28675 • *1,957*
Sparta, TN 38583 • *4,681*
Sparta, WI 54656 • *7,788*
Spartanburg, SC 29301–18 • *43,467*
Spartanburg □, SC • *226,800*
Spearfish, SD 57783 • *6,966*
Spearman, TX 79081 • *3,197*
Speedway, IN 46224 • *13,092*
Spencer, IN 47460 • *2,609*
Spencer, IA 51301 • *11,066*
Spencer, MA 01562 • *6,306*
Spencer, NC 28159 • *3,219*
Spencer, TN 38585 • *1,125*
Spencer, WV 25276 • *2,279*
Spencer, WI 54479 • *1,757*
Spencer □, IN • *19,490*
Spencer □, KY • *6,801*
Spencerport, NY 14559 • *3,606*
Spencerville, MD 20868 • *1,780*
Spencerville, OH 45887 • *2,288*
Spicer, MN 56288 • *1,020*
Spindale, NC 28160 • *4,040*
Spink □, SD • *7,981*
Spirit Lake, ID 83869 • *790*
Spirit Lake, IA 51360 • *3,871*
Spiro, OK 74959 • *2,146*
Spokane, WA 99201–28 • *177,196*
Spokane □, WA • *361,364*
Spooner, WI 54801 • *2,464*
Spotswood, NJ 08884 • *7,983*
Spotsylvania □, VA • *57,403*
Sprague, WV 25926 • *2,090*

Spring, TX 77373 • *33,111*
Spring Arbor, MI 49283 • *2,010*
Springboro, OH 45066 • *6,590*
Spring City, PA 19475 • *3,433*
Spring City, TN 37381 • *2,199*
Spring Creek 0M, NV • *5,866*
Springdale, AR 72764–66 • *29,941*
Springdale, OH 45246 • *10,621*
Springdale, PA 15144 • *3,992*
Springdale, SC 29169 • *3,226*
Springer, NM 87747 • *1,262*
Springerville, AZ 85938 • *1,802*
Springfield, CO 81073 • *1,475*
Springfield, FL 32401 • *8,715*
Springfield, GA 31329 • *1,415*
Springfield, IL 62701–94 • *105,227*
Springfield, KY 40069 • *2,875*
Springfield, MA 01101–05 • *156,983*
Springfield, MI 49015 • *5,582*
Springfield, MN 56087 • *2,173*
Springfield, MO 65801–99 • *140,494*
Springfield, NE 68059 • *1,426*
Springfield, NJ 07081 • *13,240*
Springfield, OH 45501–06 • *70,487*
Springfield, OR 97477–78 • *44,683*
Springfield, PA 19064 • *24,160*
Springfield, SD 57062 • *834*
Springfield, TN 37172 • *11,227*
Springfield, VT 05156 • *4,207*
Springfield, VA 22150 • *23,706*
Spring Garden, PA 17403 • *11,127*
Spring Green, WI 53588 • *1,283*
Spring Grove, IL 60081 • *1,066*
Spring Grove, MN 55974 • *1,153*
Spring Grove, PA 17362 • *1,863*
Spring Hill, FL 34606 • *31,117*
Spring Hill, KS 66083 • *2,191*
Springhill, LA 71075 • *5,668*
Spring Hill, TN 37174 • *1,464*
Spring Hope, NC 27882 • *1,221*
Spring Lake, MI 49456 • *2,537*
Spring Lake, NJ 07762 • *3,499*
Spring Lake, NC 28390 • *7,524*
Spring Lake Heights, NJ 07762 • *5,341*
Spring Lake Park, MN 55432 • *6,532*
Springvale, ME 04083 • *3,542*
Spring Valley, IL 61362 • *5,246*
Spring Valley, MN 55975 • *2,461*
Spring Valley, NY 10977 • *21,802*
Spring Valley, WI 54767 • *1,051*
Springville, AL 35146 • *1,910*
Springville, IA 52336 • *1,068*
Springville, NY 14141 • *4,310*
Springville, UT 84663–64 • *13,950*
Spruce Pine, NC 28777 • *2,010*
Spur, TX 79370 • *1,300*
Staatsburg, NY 12580 • *1,100*
Stafford, KS 67578 • *1,344*
Stafford □, KS • *5,365*
Stafford □, VA • *61,236*
Stafford Springs, CT 06076 • *4,100*
Stambaugh, MI 49964 • *1,281*
Stamford, CT 06901–12 • *108,056*
Stamford, NY 12167 • *1,211*
Stamford, TX 79553 • *3,817*
Stamford, VT 05352 • *400*
Stamps, AR 71860 • *2,478*
Stanaford, WV 25927 • *1,706*
Stanberry, MO 64489 • *1,310*
Standish, MI 48658 • *1,377*
Stanfield, AZ 85272 • *1,700*
Stanfield, OR 97875 • *1,568*
Stanford, CA 94305 • *18,097*
Stanford, KY 40484 • *2,686*
Stanhope, NJ 07874 • *3,393*
Stanislaus □, CA • *370,522*
Stanley, NC 28164 • *2,823*
Stanley, ND 58784 • *1,371*
Stanley, VA 22851 • *1,186*
Stanley, WI 54768 • *2,011*
Stanley □, SD • *2,453*
Stanleytown, VA 24168 • *1,563*
Stanleyville, NC 27045 • *4,779*
Stanly □, NC • *51,765*
Stanton, CA 90680 • *30,491*
Stanton, KY 40380 • *2,795*
Stanton, MI 48888 • *1,504*
Stanton, NE 68779 • *1,549*
Stanton, TX 79782 • *2,576*
Stanton □, KS • *2,333*
Stanton □, NE • *6,244*
Stanwood, WA 98292 • *1,961*
Staples, MN 56479 • *2,754*
Stapleton, AL 36578 • *1,300*
Starbuck, MN 56381 • *1,143*
Star City, AR 71667 • *2,138*
Star City, WV 26505 • *1,251*
Stargo, AZ 85540 • *1,038*
Stark □, IL • *6,534*
Stark □, ND • *22,832*
Stark □, OH • *367,585*
Starke, FL 32091 • *5,226*
Starke □, IN • *22,747*
Starkville, MS 39759 • *18,458*
Starr □, TX • *40,518*
Startex, SC 29377 • *1,162*
State Center, IA 50247 • *1,248*
State College, PA 16801–05 • *38,923*
Stateline, NV 89449 • *1,379*
State Line, PA 17263 • *1,253*
Statesboro, GA 30458 • *15,854*
Statesville, NC 28677 • *17,567*
Statham, GA 30666 • *1,360*
Staunton, IL 62088 • *4,806*
Staunton, VA 24401 • *24,461*
Stayton, OR 97383 • *5,011*
Steamboat, NV 89511 • *450*
Steamboat Springs, CO 80487 • *6,695*
Stearns, KY 42647 • *1,550*
Stearns □, MN • *118,791*
Stebbins, AK 99671 • *400*
Steele, AL 35987 • *1,046*
Steele, MO 63877 • *2,395*
Steele, ND 58482 • *762*
Steele □, MN • *30,729*
Steele □, ND • *2,420*
Steeleville, IL 62288 • *2,059*
Steelton, PA 17113 • *5,152*
Steelville, MO 65565 • *1,465*
Steger, IL 60475 • *8,584*
Steilacoom, WA 98388 • *5,728*
Stephens, AR 71764 • *1,137*
Stephens □, GA • *23,257*
Stephens □, OK • *42,299*
Stephens □, TX • *9,010*
Stephens City, VA 22655 • *1,186*
Stephenson □, IL • *48,052*
Stephenville, TX 76401 • *13,502*
Sterling, AK 99672 • *3,802*
Sterling, CO 80751 • *10,362*
Sterling, IL 61081 • *15,132*
Sterling, KS 67579 • *2,115*
Sterling, MA 01564 • *1,250*
Sterling, VA 22170 • *20,512*
Sterling □, TX • *1,438*
Sterling City, TX 76951 • *1,096*
Sterling Heights, MI 48310–14 • *117,810*
Sterlington, LA 71280 • *1,140*
Steuben □, IN • *27,446*
Steuben □, NY • *99,088*
Steubenville, OH 43952 • *22,125*
Stevens □, KS • *5,048*
Stevens □, MN • *10,634*
Stevens □, WA • *30,948*
Stevenson, AL 35772 • *2,046*
Stevenson, WA 98648 • *1,147*
Stevens Point, WI 54481 • *23,006*
Stevensville, MI 49127 • *1,230*
Stevensville, MT 59870 • *1,221*
Stewart □, GA • *5,654*
Stewart □, TN • *9,479*
Stewartstown, PA 17363 • *1,308*
Stewartville, MN 55976 • *4,520*
Stickney, IL 60402 • *5,678*
Stigler, OK 74462 • *2,574*
Stillwater, MN 55082–83 • *13,882*
Stillwater, NY 12170 • *1,531*
Stillwater, OK 74074–76 • *36,676*
Stillwater □, MT • *6,536*
Stilwell, OK 74960 • *2,663*
Stinnett, TX 79083 • *2,166*
Stirling, NJ 07980 • *1,800*
Stockbridge, GA 30281 • *3,359*
Stockbridge, MA 01262 • *2,408*
Stockbridge, MI 49285 • *1,202*
Stockdale, TX 78160 • *1,268*
Stockholm, NJ 07460 • *1,200*
Stockton, CA 95201–19 • *210,943*
Stockton, IL 61085 • *1,871*
Stockton, KS 67669 • *1,507*
Stockton, MO 65785 • *1,579*
Stoddard □, MO • *28,895*
Stokes □, NC • *37,223*
Stokesdale, NC 27357 • *2,134*
Stollings, WV 25646 • *1,200*
Stone □, AR • *9,775*
Stone □, MS • *10,750*
Stone □, MO • *19,078*
Stoneboro, PA 16153 • *1,091*
Stoneham, MA 02180 • *22,203*
Stone Harbor, NJ 08247 • *1,025*
Stone Mountain, GA 30083 • *6,494*
Stoneville, NC 27048 • *1,109*
Stonewall, LA 71078 • *1,266*
Stonewall, MS 39363 • *1,148*
Stonewall □, TX • *2,013*
Stonewood, WV 26301 • *1,996*
Stonington, CT 06378 • *1,100*
Stonington, IL 62567 • *1,006*
Stony Brook, NY 11790 • *13,726*
Stony Point, NY 10980 • *10,587*
Stony Point, NC 28678 • *1,286*
Storey □, NV • *2,526*
Storm Lake, IA 50588 • *8,769*
Storrs, CT 06268 • *12,198*
Story, WY 82842 • *700*
Story □, IA • *74,252*
Story City, IA 50248 • *2,959*
Stottville, NY 12172 • *1,369*
Stoughton, MA 02072 • *26,777*
Stoughton, WI 53589 • *8,786*
Stow, MA 01775 • *1,200*
Stow, OH 44224 • *27,702*
Stowe, PA 19464 • *3,598*
Stowe, VT 05672 • *450*
Stowe Township, PA 15136 • *7,681*
Strabane, PA 15363 • *1,200*
Strafford, MO 65757 • *1,166*
Strafford □, NH • *104,233*
Strasburg, CO 80136 • *1,005*
Strasburg, OH 44680 • *1,995*
Strasburg, PA 17579 • *2,568*
Strasburg, VA 22657 • *3,762*
Stratford, CT 06497 • *49,389*
Stratford, DE 19720 • *1,950*
Stratford, NJ 08084 • *7,614*
Stratford, OK 74872 • *1,404*
Stratford, TX 79084 • *1,781*
Stratford, WI 54484 • *1,515*
Stratford Landing, VA 22308 • *2,800*
Strathmore, CA 93267 • *2,353*
Strathmore, NJ 07747 • *7,060*
Strawberry Point, IA 52076 • *1,357*
Streamwood, IL 60103 • *30,987*
Streator, IL 61364 • *14,121*
Streetsboro, OH 44241 • *9,932*
Stromsburg, NE 68666 • *1,241*
Strongsville, OH 44136 • *35,308*
Stroud, OK 74079 • *2,666*
Stroudsburg, PA 18360 • *5,312*
Struthers, OH 44471 • *12,284*
Stryker, OH 43557 • *1,468*
Stuart, FL 34994–97 • *11,936*
Stuart, IA 50250 • *1,522*
Stuarts Draft, VA 24477 • *5,087*
Sturbridge, MA 01566 • *2,093*
Sturgeon Bay, WI 54235 • *9,176*
Sturgis, KY 42459 • *2,184*
Sturgis, MI 49091 • *10,130*
Sturgis, SD 57785 • *5,330*
Sturtevant, WI 53177 • *3,803*
Stutsman □, ND • *22,241*
Stuttgart, AR 72160 • *10,420*
Sublette, KS 67877 • *1,378*
Sublette □, WY • *4,843*
Sublimity, OR 97385 • *1,491*
Succasunna, NJ 07876 • *7,750*
Sudbury, MA 01776 • *1,860*
Sudbury Center, MA 01776 • *2,590*
Sudley, VA 22110 • *7,321*
Suffern, NY 10901 • *11,055*
Suffield, CT 06078 • *1,353*
Suffolk, VA 23432–38 • *52,141*
Suffolk □, MA • *663,906*
Suffolk □, NY • *1,321,864*
Sugar City, ID 83448 • *1,275*
Sugar Creek, MO 64054 • *3,982*
Sugarcreek, PA 16323 • *5,532*
Sugar Grove, VA 24375 • *1,027*
Sugar Hill, GA 30518 • *4,557*
Sugar Land, TX 77478–79 • *24,529*
Sugarland Run, VA 22170 • *9,357*
Sugar Loaf, VA 24018 • *2,000*
Sugar Notch, PA 18706 • *1,044*
Suisun City, CA 94585 • *22,686*
Suitland, MD 20746 • *35,400*
Sulligent, AL 35586 • *1,886*
Sullivan, IL 61951 • *4,354*
Sullivan, IN 47882 • *4,663*
Sullivan, MO 63080 • *5,661*
Sullivan □, IN • *18,993*
Sullivan □, MO • *6,326*
Sullivan □, NH • *38,592*
Sullivan □, NY • *69,277*
Sullivan □, PA • *6,104*
Sullivan □, TN • *143,596*
Sullivans Island, SC 29482 • *1,623*
Sully □, SD • *1,589*
Sulphur, LA 70663–64 • *20,125*
Sulphur, OK 73086 • *4,824*
Sulphur Springs, TX 75482 • *14,062*
Sultan, WA 98294 • *2,236*
Sumiton, AL 35148 • *2,604*
Summerfield, NC 27358 • *2,051*
Summers □, WV • *14,204*
Summersville, WV 26651 • *2,906*
Summerville, GA 30747 • *5,025*
Summerville, SC 29483–85 • *22,519*
Summit, IL 60501 • *9,971*
Summit, MS 39666 • *1,566*
Summit, NJ 07901 • *19,757*
Summit, TN 37363 • *8,307*
Summit □, CO • *12,881*
Summit □, OH • *514,990*
Summit □, UT • *15,518*
Summit Hill, PA 18250 • *3,332*
Sumner, IL 62466 • *1,083*
Sumner, IA 50674 • *2,078*
Sumner, WA 98390 • *6,281*
Sumner □, KS • *25,841*
Sumner □, TN • *103,281*
Sumter, SC 29150–54 • *41,943*
Sumter □, AL • *16,174*
Sumter □, FL • *31,577*
Sumter □, GA • *30,228*
Sumter □, SC • *102,637*
Sunbury, OH 43074 • *2,046*
Sunbury, PA 17801 • *11,591*
Sun City, AZ 85351 • *38,126*
Sun City, CA 92381 • *14,930*
Sun City Center, FL 33573 • *8,326*
Suncook, NH 03275 • *5,214*
Sundance, WY 82729 • *1,139*
Sundown, TX 79372 • *1,759*
Sunflower □, MS • *32,867*
Sunland Park, NM 88063 • *8,179*
Sunny Isles, FL 33160 • *11,772*
Sunnyside, CA 93727 • *5,000*
Sunnyside, WA 98944 • *11,238*
Sunnyvale, CA 94086–89 • *117,229*
Sun Prairie, WI 53590 • *15,333*
Sunray, TX 79086 • *1,729*
Sunrise Manor, NV 89110 • *95,362*
Sunset, FL 33143 • *15,810*
Sunset, LA 70584 • *2,201*
Sunset, UT 84015 • *5,128*
Sunset Beach, HI 96712 • *800*
Sun Valley, ID 83353–54 • *938*
Sun Valley, NV 89433 • *11,391*
Superior, AZ 85273 • *3,468*
Superior, MT 59872 • *881*
Superior, NE 68978 • *2,397*
Superior, WI 54880 • *27,134*
Superior, WY 82945 • *273*
Suquamish, WA 98392 • *3,105*
Surf City, NJ 08008 • *1,375*
Surfside, FL 33154 • *4,108*
Surfside Beach, SC 29575 • *3,845*
Surgoinsville, TN 37873 • *1,499*
Surprise, AZ 85374 • *7,122*
Surrey, ND 58785 • *856*
Surry □, NC • *61,704*
Surry □, VA • *6,145*
Susanville, CA 96130 • *7,279*
Susquehanna, PA 18847 • *1,760*
Susquehanna □, PA • *40,380*
Sussex, NJ 07461 • *2,201*
Sussex, WI 53089 • *5,039*
Sussex □, DE • *113,229*
Sussex □, NJ • *130,943*
Sussex □, VA • *10,248*
Sutherland, NE 69165 • *1,032*
Sutherlin, OR 97479 • *5,020*
Sutter □, CA • *64,415*
Sutter Creek, CA 95685 • *1,835*
Sutton, NE 68979 • *1,353*
Sutton □, TX • *4,135*
Suwanee, GA 30174 • *2,412*
Suwannee □, FL • *26,780*
Swain □, NC • *11,268*
Swainsboro, GA 30401 • *7,361*
Swampscott, MA 01907 • *13,650*
Swannanoa, NC 28778 • *3,538*
Swansboro, NC 28584 • *1,165*
Swansea, IL 62221 • *8,201*
Swanton, OH 43558 • *3,557*
Swanton, VT 05488 • *2,360*
Swanwyck Estates, DE 19720 • *1,320*
Swarthmore, PA 19081 • *6,157*
Swartz Creek, MI 48473 • *4,851*
Swatara Township, PA 17111 • *19,700*
Swayzee, IN 46986 • *1,059*
Swedesboro, NJ 08085 • *2,024*
Sweeny, TX 77480 • *3,297*
Sweet Grass □, MT • *3,154*
Sweet Home, OR 97386 • *6,850*
Sweet Springs, MO 65351 • *1,595*
Sweetwater, FL 33152 • *13,909*
Sweetwater, TN 37874 • *5,066*
Sweetwater, TX 79556 • *11,967*
Sweetwater □, WY • *38,823*
Sweetwater Creek, FL 33614 • *18,000*
Swift □, MN • *10,724*
Swisher □, TX • *8,133*
Swissvale, PA 15218 • *10,637*
Switzer, WV 25647 • *1,004*
Switzerland, FL 32043 • *2,400*
Switzerland □, IN • *7,738*
Swoyerville, PA • *5,630*
Sycamore, AL 35149 • *1,250*
Sycamore, IL 60178 • *9,708*
Sykesville, MD 21784 • *2,303*
Sykesville, PA 15865 • *1,387*
Sylacauga, AL 35150 • *12,520*
Sylva, NC 28779 • *1,809*
Sylvan Beach, NY 13157 • *1,119*
Sylvania, GA 30467 • *2,871*
Sylvania, OH 43560 • *17,301*
Sylvan Lake, MI 48320 • *1,884*
Sylvester, GA 31791 • *5,702*
Syosset, NY 11791 • *18,967*
Syracuse, IN 46567 • *2,729*
Syracuse, KS 67878 • *1,606*
Syracuse, NE 68446 • *1,646*
Syracuse, NY 13201–90 • *163,860*
Syracuse, UT 84075 • *4,658*

T

Tabor City, NC 28463 • *2,330*
Tacoma, WA 98401–99 • *176,664*
Taft, CA 93268 • *5,902*
Taft, TX 78390 • *3,222*
Tahlequah, OK 74464–65 • *10,398*
Tahoe City, CA 95730 • *1,300*
Tahoka, TX 79373 • *2,868*
Takoma Park, MD 20912 • *16,700*
Talbot □, GA • *6,524*
Talbot □, MD • *30,549*
Talbotton, GA 31827 • *1,046*
Talent, OR 97540 • *3,274*
Taliaferro □, GA • *1,915*
Talihina, OK 74571 • *1,297*
Talladega, AL 35160 • *18,175*
Talladega □, AL • *74,107*
Tallahassee, FL 32301–17 • *124,773*
Tallahatchie □, MS • *15,210*
Tallapoosa, GA 30176 • *2,805*
Tallapoosa □, AL • *38,826*
Tallassee, AL 36078 • *5,112*
Talleyville, DE 19803 • *6,346*
Tallmadge, OH 44278 • *14,870*
Tallulah, LA 71282–84 • *8,526*
Tama, IA 52339 • *2,697*
Tama □, IA • *17,419*
Tamalpais Valley, CA 94941 • *5,000*
Tamaqua, PA 18252 • *7,943*
Tamarac, FL 33321 • *44,822*
Tamiami, FL 33165 • *33,845*
Tampa, FL 33601–97 • *280,015*
Tanana, AK 99777 • *345*
Taney □, MO • *25,561*
Taneytown, MD 21787 • *3,695*
Tangipahoa □, LA • *85,709*
Taos, NM 87571 • *4,065*
Taos □, NM • *23,118*
Taos Pueblo, NM 87571 • *1,030*
Tappahannock, VA 22560 • *1,550*
Tappan, NY 10983 • *6,867*
Tara Hills, CA 94564 • *6,000*
Tarboro, NC 27886 • *11,037*
Tarentum, PA 15084 • *5,674*
Tariffville, CT 06081 • *1,477*
Tarkio, MO 64491 • *2,243*
Tarpey, CA 93727 • *4,000*
Tarpon Springs, FL 34688–91 • *17,906*
Tarrant, AL 35217 • *8,046*
Tarrant □, TX • *1,170,103*
Tarrytown, NY 10591 • *10,739*
Tate, GA 30177 • *1,000*
Tate □, MS • *21,432*
Tattnall □, GA • *17,722*
Taunton, MA 02780 • *49,832*
Tavares, FL 32778 • *7,383*
Tavernier, FL 33070 • *2,433*
Tawas City, MI 48763–64 • *2,009*
Taylor, AZ 85939 • *2,418*
Taylor, MI 48180 • *70,811*
Taylor, PA 18517 • *6,941*
Taylor, TX 76574 • *11,472*
Taylor □, FL • *17,111*
Taylor □, GA • *7,642*
Taylor □, IA • *7,114*
Taylor □, KY • *21,146*
Taylor □, TX • *119,655*
Taylor □, WV • *15,144*
Taylor □, WI • *18,901*
Taylor Mill, KY 41015 • *5,530*
Taylors, SC 29687 • *19,619*
Taylorsville, IN 47280 • *1,044*
Taylorsville, MS 39168 • *1,412*
Taylorsville, NC 28681 • *1,566*
Taylorville, IL 62568 • *11,133*
Tazewell, TN 37879 • *2,150*
Tazewell, VA 24651 • *4,176*
Tazewell □, IL • *123,692*
Tazewell □, VA • *45,960*
Tchula, MS 39169 • *2,186*
Teague, TX 75860 • *3,268*
Teaneck, NJ 07666 • *37,825*
Teaticket, MA 02536 • *2,600*
Tecumseh, MI 49286 • *7,462*
Tecumseh, NE 68450 • *1,702*
Tecumseh, OK 74873 • *5,750*
Tehachapi, CA 93561 • *5,791*
Tehama □, CA • *49,625*
Tekamah, NE 68061 • *1,852*
Telfair □, GA • *11,000*
Telford, PA 18969 • *4,238*
Tell City, IN 47586 • *8,088*
Teller □, CO • *12,468*
Telluride, CO 81435 • *1,309*
Temecula, CA 92390 • *27,099*
Tempe, AZ 85280–85 • *141,865*
Temperance, MI 48182 • *6,542*
Temple, GA 30179 • *1,870*
Temple, OK 73568 • *1,223*
Temple, PA 19560 • *1,491*
Temple, TX 76501–05 • *46,109*
Temple City, CA 91780 • *31,100*
Temple Terrace, FL 33617 • *16,444*
Templeton, MA 01468 • *1,000*
Tenafly, NJ 07670 • *13,326*
Tenaha, TX 75974 • *1,072*
Tenino, WA 98589 • *1,292*
Tennessee Ridge, TN 37178 • *1,271*
Tennille, GA 31089 • *1,552*
Tensas □, LA • *7,103*
Ten Sleep, WY 82442 • *311*
Terra Alta, WV 26764 • *1,713*
Terrebonne □, LA • *96,982*
Terre Haute, IN 47801–08 • *57,483*
Terre Hill, PA 17581 • *1,282*
Terrell, TX 75160 • *12,490*
Terrell □, GA • *10,653*
Terrell □, TX • *1,410*
Terrell Hills, TX 78209 • *4,592*
Terry, MT 59349 • *659*
Terry □, TX • *13,218*
Terrytown, LA 70053 • *23,787*
Terryville, CT 06786 • *5,426*
Terryville, NY 11776 • *7,380*
Tesuque, NM 87574 • *1,490*
Teton □, ID • *3,439*
Teton □, MT • *6,271*
Teton □, WY • *11,172*
Teton Village, WY 83025 • *250*
Teutopolis, IL 62467 • *1,417*
Tewksbury, MA 01876 • *10,540*
Texarkana, AR 75502 • *22,631*
Texarkana, TX 75501–05 • *31,656*
Texas □, MO • *21,476*
Texas □, OK • *16,419*
Texas City, TX 77590–92 • *40,822*
Texico, NM 88135 • *966*
Thatcher, AZ 85552 • *3,763*
Thayer, MO 65791 • *1,996*
Thayer □, NE • *6,635*
Thayne, WY 83127 • *267*
The Colony, TX 75056 • *22,113*
The Dalles, OR 97058 • *11,060*
Theodore, AL 36582 • *6,509*
The Plains, OH 45780 • *2,644*
Thermalito, CA 95965 • *5,646*
Thermopolis, WY 82443 • *3,247*
The Village, OK 73120 • *10,353*
The Village of Indian Hill, OH 45243 • *5,383*
The Woodlands, TX 77380 • *29,205*
Thibodaux, LA 70301–02 • *14,035*
Thief River Falls, MN 56701 • *8,010*
Thiensville, WI 53092 • *3,301*
Thomas, OK 73669 • *1,246*
Thomas □, GA • *38,986*
Thomas □, KS • *8,258*
Thomas □, NE • *851*
Thomasboro, IL 61878 • *1,250*
Thomaston, CT 06787 • *3,590*
Thomaston, GA 30286 • *9,127*
Thomaston, ME 04861 • *2,445*
Thomasville, AL 36784 • *4,301*
Thomasville, GA 31792 • *17,457*
Thomasville, NC 27360–61 • *15,915*
Thompson, ND 58278 • *930*
Thompson Falls, MT 59873 • *1,319*
Thomson, GA 30824 • *6,862*
Thonotosassa, FL 33592 • *1,500*
Thoreau, NM 87323 • *1,099*
Thorndale, TX 76577 • *1,092*
Thorndike, MA 01079 • *1,100*
Thornton, CO 80229 • *55,031*
Thorntown, IN 46071 • *1,506*
Thornwood, NY 10594 • *7,025*
Thorofare, NJ 08086 • *1,800*
Thorp, WI 54771 • *1,657*
Thorsby, AL 35171 • *1,465*
Thousand Oaks, CA 91359–62 • *104,352*
Three Forks, MT 59752 • *1,203*
Three Oaks, MI 49128 • *1,786*
Three Rivers, MA 01080 • *3,006*
Three Rivers, MI 49093 • *7,413*
Three Rivers, TX 78071 • *1,889*
Throckmorton, TX 76083 • *1,036*
Throckmorton □, TX • *1,880*
Throop, PA 18512 • *4,070*
Thunderbolt, GA 31404 • *2,786*
Thurmont, MD 21788 • *3,398*
Thurston □, NE • *6,936*
Thurston □, WA • *161,238*
Tiburon, CA 94920 • *7,532*
Tice, FL 33905 • *3,971*
Ticonderoga, NY 12883 • *2,770*
Tierra Amarilla, NM 87575 • *900*
Tiffin, OH 44883 • *18,604*
Tift □, GA • *34,998*
Tifton, GA 31793–94 • *14,215*
Tigard, OR 97223 • *29,344*
Tillamook, OR 97141 • *4,001*
Tillamook □, OR • *21,570*
Tillman □, OK • *10,384*
Tillmans Corner, AL 36619 • *17,988*
Tillson, NY 12486 • *1,688*
Tilton, IL 61833 • *2,729*
Tilton, NH 03276 • *1,380*
Tiltonsville, OH 43963 • *1,517*
Timberlake, VA 24502 • *10,314*
Timberville, VA 22853 • *1,596*
Timmonsville, SC 29161 • *2,182*
Timpson, TX 75975 • *1,029*
Tinley Park, IL 60477 • *37,121*
Tinton Falls, NJ 07724 • *12,361*
Tioga, LA 71477 • *1,200*
Tioga, ND 58852 • *1,278*
Tioga □, NY • *52,337*
Tioga □, PA • *41,126*
Tippah □, MS • *19,523*
Tipp City, OH 45371 • *6,027*
Tippecanoe □, IN • *130,598*
Tipton, CA 93272 • *1,383*
Tipton, IN 46072 • *4,751*
Tipton, IA 52772 • *2,998*
Tipton, MO 65081 • *2,026*
Tipton, OK 73570 • *1,043*
Tipton □, IN • *16,119*
Tipton □, TN • *37,568*
Tiptonville, TN 38079 • *2,149*
Tishomingo, OK 73460 • *3,116*
Tishomingo □, MS • *17,683*
Titus □, TX • *24,009*
Titusville, FL 32780–83 • *39,394*
Titusville, PA 16354 • *6,434*
Tiverton, RI 02878 • *7,259*
Tivoli, NY 12583 • *1,035*
Toast, NC 27049 • *2,125*
Tobyhanna, PA 18466 • *1,200*
Toccoa, GA 30577 • *8,266*
Todd □, KY • *10,940*
Todd □, MN • *23,363*
Todd □, SD • *8,352*
Todd Estates, DE 19713 • *2,000*
Togiak, AK 99678 • *613*
Tohatchi, NM 87325 • *661*
Tok, AK 99780 • *935*
Toledo, IL 62468 • *1,199*

Toledo, IA 52342 • *2,380*
Toledo, OH 43601–99 • *332,943*
Toledo, OR 97391 • *3,174*
Tolland, CT 06084 • *1,200*
Tolland □, CT • *128,699*
Tolleson, AZ 85353 • *4,434*
Tolono, IL 61880 • *2,605*
Toluca, IL 61369 • *1,315*
Tomah, WI 54660 • *7,570*
Tomahawk, WI 54487 • *3,328*
Tomball, TX 77375 • *6,370*
Tombstone, AZ 85638 • *1,220*
Tom Green □, TX • *98,458*
Tompkins □, NY • *94,097*
Tompkinsville, KY 42167 • *2,861*
Toms River, NJ 08753–57 • *7,524*
Tonawanda, NY 14150–51 • *17,284*
Tonawanda, NY 14223 • *65,284*
Tonganoxie, KS 66086 • *2,347*
Tonkawa, OK 74653 • *3,127*
Tonopah, NV 89049 • *3,616*
Tooele, UT 84074 • *13,887*
Tooele □, UT • *26,601*
Toole □, MT • *5,046*
Toombs □, GA • *24,072*
Topeka, KS 66601–99 • *119,883*
Toppenish, WA 98948 • *7,419*
Topsfield, MA 01983 • *2,711*
Topsham, ME 04086 • *6,147*
Topton, PA 19562 • *1,987*
Toronto, OH 43964 • *6,127*
Torrance, CA 90501–10 • *133,107*
Torrance □, NM • *10,285*
Torrington, CT 06790 • *33,687*
Torrington, WY 82240 • *5,651*
Totowa, NJ 07512 • *10,177*
Touisset, MA 02777 • *1,520*
Toulon, IL 61483 • *1,328*
Towaco, NJ 07082 • *1,020*
Towanda, KS 67144 • *1,289*
Towanda, PA 18848 • *3,242*
Tower City, PA 17980 • *1,518*
Town and Country, WA 99210 • *4,921*
Town Creek, AL 35672 • *1,379*
Towner, ND 58788 • *669*
Towner □, ND • *3,627*
Town 'n Country, FL 33615 • *60,946*
Towns □, GA • *6,754*
Townsend, DE 19734 • *322*
Townsend, MA 01469 • *1,164*
Townsend, MT 59644 • *1,635*
Towson, MD 21204 • *49,445*
Tracy, CA 95376–78 • *33,558*
Tracy, MN 56175 • *2,059*
Tracy City, TN 37387 • *1,556*
Tracyton, WA 98393 • *2,621*
Traer, IA 50675 • *1,552*
Trafford, PA 15085 • *3,345*
Trail Creek, IN 46360 • *2,463*
Traill □, ND • *8,752*
Transylvania □, NC • *25,520*
Travelers Rest, SC 29690 • *3,069*
Traverse □, MN • *4,463*
Traverse City, MI 49684 • *15,155*
Travis □, TX • *576,407*
Treasure □, MT • *874*
Treasure Island, FL 33706 • *7,266*
Trego □, KS • *3,694*
Tremont, IL 61568 • *2,088*
Tremont, PA 17981 • *1,814*
Tremonton, UT 84337 • *4,264*
Trempealeau, WI 54661 • *1,039*
Trempealeau □, WI • *25,263*
Trenton, FL 32693 • *1,287*
Trenton, GA 30752 • *1,994*
Trenton, IL 62293 • *2,481*
Trenton, MI 48183 • *20,586*
Trenton, MO 64683 • *6,129*
Trenton, NJ 08601–91 • *88,675*
Trenton, OH 45067 • *6,189*
Trenton, TN 38382 • *4,836*
Tresckow, PA 18254 • *1,033*
Treutlen □, GA • *5,994*
Trevorton, PA 17881 • *2,058*
Triangle, VA 22172 • *4,740*
Tri City, OR 97457 • *3,585*
Trigg □, KY • *10,361*
Tri Lakes, IN 46725 • *3,299*
Trimble □, KY • *6,090*
Trinidad, CO 81082 • *8,580*
Trinidad, TX 75163 • *1,056*
Trinity, AL 35673 • *1,380*
Trinity, NC 27370 • *5,469*
Trinity, TX 75862 • *2,648*
Trinity □, CA • *13,063*
Trinity □, TX • *11,445*
Trion, GA 30753 • *1,661*
Tripoli, IA 50676 • *1,188*
Tripp □, SD • *6,924*
Triumph, LA 70041 • *1,200*
Trona, CA 93562 • *1,400*
Trooper, PA 19401 • *5,137*
Trotwood, OH 45426 • *8,816*
Troup □, GA • *55,536*
Trousdale □, TN • *5,920*
Troutdale, OR 97060 • *7,852*
Troutman, NC 28166 • *1,493*
Troy, AL 36081 • *13,051*
Troy, ID 83871 • *699*
Troy, IL 62294 • *6,046*
Troy, KS 66087 • *1,073*
Troy, MI 48083–84 • *72,884*
Troy, MO 63379 • *3,811*
Troy, MT 59935 • *953*
Troy, NH 03465 • *2,097*
Troy, NY 12180–83 • *54,269*
Troy, NC 27371 • *3,404*
Troy, OH 45373 • *19,478*
Troy, PA 16947 • *1,262*
Troy, TN 38260 • *1,047*
Truckee, CA 95734 • *3,484*
Truman, MN 56088 • *1,292*
Trumann, AR 72472 • *6,304*
Trumansburg, NY 14886 • *1,611*
Trumbull, CT 06611 • *32,000*
Trumbull □, OH • *227,813*
Trussville, AL 35173 • *8,266*
Truth or Consequences (Hot Springs), NM 87901 • *6,221*
Tryon, NC 28782 • *1,680*
Tualatin, OR 97062 • *15,013*
Tuba City, AZ 86045 • *7,323*
Tuckahoe, NY 10707 • *6,302*
Tucker, GA 30084 • *25,781*
Tucker □, WV • *7,728*
Tuckerman, AR 72473 • *2,020*
Tuckerton, NJ 08087 • *3,048*
Tucson, AZ 85701–51 • *405,390*
Tucumcari, NM 88401 • *6,831*
Tukwila, WA 98188 • *11,874*
Tulare, CA 93274–75 • *33,249*
Tulare □, CA • *311,921*
Tularosa, NM 88352 • *2,615*
Tulelake, CA 96134 • *1,010*
Tulia, TX 79088 • *4,699*
Tullahoma, TN 37388 • *16,761*
Tulsa, OK 74101–94 • *367,302*
Tulsa □, OK • *503,341*
Tumwater, WA 98502 • *9,976*
Tunica, MS 38676 • *1,175*
Tunica □, MS • *8,164*
Tunkhannock, PA 18657 • *2,251*
Tununak, AK 99681 • *316*
Tuolumne, CA 95379 • *1,686*
Tuolumne □, CA • *48,456*
Tupelo, MS 38801–03 • *30,685*
Tupper Lake, NY 12986 • *4,087*
Turley, OK 74156 • *2,930*
Turlock, CA 95380–81 • *42,198*
Turner, OR 97392 • *1,281*
Turner □, GA • *8,703*
Turner □, SD • *8,576*
Turners Falls, MA 01376 • *4,731*
Turtle Creek, PA 15145 • *6,556*
Turtle Lake, ND 58575 • *681*
Tuscaloosa, AL 35401–06 • *77,759*
Tuscaloosa □, AL • *150,522*
Tuscarawas □, OH • *84,090*
Tuscola, IL 61953 • *4,155*
Tuscola □, MI • *55,498*
Tuscumbia, AL 35674 • *8,413*
Tuskegee, AL 36083 • *12,257*
Tustin, CA 92680–81 • *50,689*
Tuttle, OK 73089 • *2,807*
Tutwiler, MS 38963 • *1,391*
Tuxedo Park, DE 19804 • *1,300*
Twentynine Palms, CA 92277–78 • *11,821*
Twiggs □, GA • *9,806*
Twin City, GA 30471 • *1,466*
Twin Falls, ID 83301–03 • *27,591*
Twin Falls □, ID • *53,580*
Twin Knolls, AZ 85207 • *5,210*
Twin Lakes, CA 95060 • *5,379*
Twin Lakes, WI 53181 • *3,989*
Twin Rivers, NJ 08520 • *7,715*
Twinsburg, OH 44087 • *9,606*
Two Harbors, MN 55616 • *3,651*
Two Rivers, WI 54241 • *13,030*
Tybee Island, GA 31328 • *2,842*
Tyler, MN 56178 • *1,257*
Tyler, TX 75701–13 • *75,450*
Tyler □, TX • *16,646*
Tyler □, WV • *9,796*
Tyler Heights, WV 25312 • *4,070*
Tylertown, MS 39667 • *1,938*
Tyndall, SD 57066 • *1,201*
Tyrone, NM 88065 • *950*
Tyrone, PA 16686 • *5,743*
Tyrrell □, NC • *3,856*
Tysons Corner, VA 22102 • *13,124*

U

Ucon, ID 83454 • *895*
Uhrichsville, OH 44683 • *5,604*
Uinta □, WY • *18,705*
Uintah □, UT • *22,211*
Ukiah, CA 95482 • *14,599*
Uleta, FL 33162 • *10,000*
Ulster □, NY • *165,304*
Ulysses, KS 67880 • *5,474*
Umatilla, FL 32784 • *2,350*
Umatilla, OR 97882 • *3,046*
Umatilla □, OR • *59,249*
Unadilla, GA 31091 • *1,620*
Unadilla, NY 13849 • *1,265*
Unalakleet, AK 99684 • *714*
Unalaska, AK 99685 • *3,089*
Uncasville, CT 06382 • *1,597*
Underwood, AL 35630 • *1,950*
Underwood, ND 58576 • *976*
Unicoi □, TN • *16,549*
Union, KY 41091 • *1,001*
Union, MS 39365 • *1,875*
Union, MO 63084 • *5,909*
Union, NJ 07083 • *50,024*
Union, OH 45322 • *5,501*
Union, OR 97883 • *1,847*
Union, SC 29379 • *9,836*
Union, UT 84047 • *13,684*
Union □, AR • *46,719*
Union □, FL • *10,252*
Union □, GA • *11,993*
Union □, IL • *17,619*
Union □, IN • *6,976*
Union □, IA • *12,750*
Union □, KY • *16,557*
Union □, LA • *20,690*
Union □, MS • *22,085*
Union □, NJ • *493,819*
Union □, NM • *4,124*
Union □, NC • *84,211*
Union □, OH • *31,969*
Union □, OR • *23,598*
Union □, PA • *36,176*
Union □, SC • *30,337*
Union □, SD • *10,189*
Union □, TN • *13,694*
Union Beach, NJ 07735 • *6,156*
Union City, CA 94587 • *53,762*
Union City, GA 30291 • *8,375*
Union City, IN 47390 • *3,612*
Union City, MI 49094 • *1,767*
Union City, NJ 07087 • *58,012*
Union City, OH 45390 • *1,984*
Union City, OK 73090 • *1,000*
Union City, PA 16438 • *3,537*
Union City, TN 38261 • *10,513*
Uniondale, NY 11553 • *20,328*
Union Gap, WA 98903 • *3,120*
Union Grove, WI 53182 • *3,669*
Union Lake, MI 48386–87 • *8,500*
Union Park, FL 32817 • *6,890*
Union Pier, MI 49129 • *1,039*
Union Point, GA 30669 • *1,753*
Union Springs, AL 36089 • *3,975*
Union Springs, NY 13160 • *1,142*
Uniontown, AL 36786 • *1,730*
Uniontown, KY 42461 • *1,008*
Uniontown, OH 44685 • *1,500*
Uniontown, PA 15401 • *12,034*
Union Village, RI 02895 • *2,150*
Unionville, CT 06085 • *3,500*
Unionville, MO 63565 • *1,989*
Universal City, TX 78148 • *13,057*
University City, MO 63130 • *40,087*
University Gardens, NY 11020 • *4,600*
University Heights, IA 52240 • *1,042*
University Heights, OH 44118 • *14,790*
University Park, IL 60466 • *6,204*
University Park, NM 88003 • *4,520*
University Park, TX 75205 • *22,259*
University Place, WA 98465 • *27,701*
Upland, CA 91785–86 • *63,374*
Upland, IN 46989 • *3,295*
Upper Arlington, OH 43221 • *34,128*
Upper Darby, PA 19082–83 • *84,054*
Upper Dublin Township, PA 19002 • *22,348*
Upper Greenwood Lake, NJ 07421 • *2,734*
Upper Merion Township, PA 19406 • *26,138*
Upper Moreland Township, PA 19090 • *25,874*
Upper Providence Township, PA 19063 • *9,727*
Upper Saddle River, NJ 07458 • *7,198*
Upper Saint Clair, PA 15241 • *19,692*
Upper Sandusky, OH 43351 • *5,906*
Upshur □, TX • *31,370*
Upshur □, WV • *22,867*
Upson □, GA • *26,300*
Upton, MA 01568 • *1,500*
Upton, WY 82730 • *980*
Upton □, TX • *4,447*
Urbana, IL 61801 • *36,344*
Urbana, OH 43078 • *11,353*
Urbandale, IA 50322 • *23,500*
Usquepaug, RI 02892 • *400*
Utah □, UT • *263,590*
Utica, MI 48315–18 • *5,081*
Utica, MS 39175 • *1,033*
Utica, NY 13501–05 • *68,637*
Utica, OH 43080 • *1,997*
Uvalde, TX 78801–02 • *14,729*
Uvalde □, TX • *23,340*
Uxbridge, MA 01569 • *3,340*

V

Vacaville, CA 95687–88 • *71,479*
Vacherie, LA 70090 • *2,169*
Vadnais Heights, MN 55110 • *11,041*
Vail, CO 81657–58 • *3,659*
Valatie, NY 12184 • *1,487*
Valdese, NC 28690 • *3,914*
Valdez, AK 99686 • *4,068*
Valdosta, GA 31601–04 • *39,806*
Vale, OR 97918 • *1,491*
Valencia, AZ 85326 • *1,200*
Valencia □, NM • *45,235*
Valencia Heights, SC 29205 • *4,122*
Valentine, NE 69201 • *2,826*
Valhalla, NY 10595 • *6,200*
Valinda, CA 91744 • *18,735*
Vallejo, CA 94589–92 • *109,199*
Valle Vista, CA 92343 • *8,751*
Valley, AL 36854 • *8,173*
Valley, NE 68064 • *1,775*
Valley □, ID • *6,109*
Valley □, MT • *8,239*
Valley □, NE • *5,169*
Valley Center, KS 67147 • *3,624*
Valley City, ND 58072 • *7,163*
Valley Cottage, NY 10989 • *9,007*
Valley Falls, KS 66088 • *1,253*
Valley Falls, RI 02864 • *11,175*
Valley Forge, PA 19481–82 • *1,500*
Valley Mills, TX 76689 • *1,085*
Valley Park, MO 63088 • *4,165*
Valley Ridge, WA 98188 • *6,500*
Valley Springs, SD 57068 • *739*
Valley Station, KY 40272 • *22,840*
Valley Stream, NY 11580–82 • *33,946*
Valley View, PA 17983 • *1,749*
Valparaiso, FL 32580 • *4,672*
Valparaiso, IN 46383–84 • *24,414*
Val Verda, UT 84010 • *3,712*
Val Verde □, TX • *38,721*
Van, TX 75790 • *1,854*
Van Alstyne, TX 75095 • *2,090*
Van Buren, AR 72956 • *14,979*
Van Buren, ME 04785 • *2,759*
Van Buren □, AR • *14,008*
Van Buren □, IA • *7,676*
Van Buren □, MI • *70,060*
Van Buren □, TN • *4,846*
Vance □, NC • *38,892*
Vanceburg, KY 41179 • *1,713*
Vancleave, MS 39564 • *3,214*
Vancouver, WA 98660–68 • *46,380*
Vandalia, IL 62471 • *6,114*
Vandalia, MO 63382 • *2,683*
Vandalia, OH 45377 • *13,882*
Vandenberg Village, CA 93436 • *5,871*
Vander, NC 28301 • *1,179*
Vanderburgh □, IN • *165,058*
Vandergrift, PA 15690 • *5,904*
Van Horn, TX 79855 • *2,930*
Van Lear, KY 41265 • *1,050*
Vansant, VA 24656 • *1,187*
Van Vleck, TX 77482 • *1,534*
Van Wert, OH 45891 • *10,891*
Van Wert □, OH • *30,464*
Van Zandt □, TX • *37,944*
Varina, VA 23231 • *2,500*
Varnville, SC 29944 • *1,970*
Vassar, MI 48768 • *2,559*
Vaughn, MT 59487 • *2,270*
Veazie, ME 04401 • *1,610*
Veedersburg, IN 47987 • *2,192*
Velda Rose Estates, AZ 85205 • *2,330*
Velva, ND 58790 • *968*
Venango □, PA • *59,381*
Veneta, OR 97487 • *2,519*
Venice, FL 34292–93 • *16,922*
Venice, IL 62090 • *3,571*
Venice Gardens, FL 34293 • *7,701*
Ventnor City, NJ 08406 • *11,005*
Ventura (San Buenaventura), CA 93001–07 • *92,575*
Ventura □, CA • *669,016*
Veradale, WA 99037 • *7,836*
Verda, KY 40828 • *1,133*
Verdi, NV 89439 • *1,140*
Vergennes, VT 05491 • *2,578*
Vermilion, OH 44089 • *11,127*
Vermilion □, IL • *88,257*
Vermilion □, LA • *50,055*
Vermillion, SD 57069 • *10,034*
Vermillion □, IN • *16,773*
Vernal, UT 84078–79 • *6,644*
Vernon, AL 35592 • *2,247*
Vernon, CT 06066 • *30,200*
Vernon, TX 76384 • *12,001*
Vernon □, LA • *61,961*
Vernon □, MO • *19,041*
Vernon □, WI • *25,617*
Vernon Hills, IL 60061 • *15,319*
Vernonia, OR 97064 • *1,808*
Vero Beach, FL 32960–68 • *17,350*
Verona, MS 38879 • *2,893*
Verona, NJ 07044 • *13,597*
Verona, PA 15147 • *3,260*
Verona, WI 53593 • *5,374*
Versailles, IN 47042 • *1,791*
Versailles, KY 40383 • *7,269*
Versailles, MO 65084 • *2,365*
Versailles, OH 45380 • *2,351*
Vestal, NY 13850–51 • *5,530*
Vestavia Hills, AL 35216 • *19,749*
Vevay, IN 47043 • *1,393*
Vian, OK 74962 • *1,414*
Vicksburg, MI 49097 • *2,216*
Vicksburg, MS 39180–82 • *20,908*
Victor, NY 14564 • *2,308*
Victoria, KS 67671 • *1,157*
Victoria, TX 77901–05 • *55,076*
Victoria, VA 23974 • *1,830*
Victoria □, TX • *74,361*
Victorville, CA 92392–93 • *40,674*
Vidalia, GA 30474 • *11,078*
Vidalia, LA 71373 • *4,953*
Vidor, TX 77662 • *10,935*
Vienna, GA 31092 • *2,708*
Vienna, IL 62995 • *1,446*
Vienna, VA 22180–83 • *14,852*
Vienna, WV 26105 • *10,862*
View Park, CA 90043 • *5,900*
Vigo □, IN • *106,107*
Vilas □, WI • *17,707*
Villa Grove, IL 61956 • *2,734*
Villa Hills, KY 41016 • *7,739*
Villa Park, CA 92667 • *6,299*
Villa Park, IL 60181 • *22,253*
Villa Rica, GA 30180 • *6,542*
Villas, NJ 08251 • *8,136*
Ville Platte, LA 70586 • *9,037*
Villisca, IA 50864 • *1,332*
Vilonia, AR 72173 • *1,133*
Vincennes, IN 47591 • *19,859*
Vincent, AL 35178 • *1,767*
Vine Grove, KY 40175 • *3,586*
Vineland, NJ 08360 • *54,780*
Vineyard Haven, MA 02568 • *1,762*
Vinita, OK 74301 • *5,804*
Vinton, IA 52349 • *5,103*
Vinton, LA 70668 • *3,154*
Vinton, VA 24179 • *7,665*
Vinton □, OH • *11,098*
Viola, NY 10952 • *4,504*
Violet, LA 70092 • *8,574*
Virden, IL 62690 • *3,635*
Virginia, IL 62691 • *1,767*
Virginia, MN 55792 • *9,410*
Virginia Beach, VA 23450–67 • *393,069*
Virginia City, NV 89440 • *920*
Viroqua, WI 54665 • *3,922*
Visalia, CA 93277–79 • *75,636*
Vista, CA 92083–84 • *71,872*
Vivian, LA 71082 • *4,156*
Volcano, HI 96785 • *1,516*
Volga, SD 57071 • *1,263*
Volusia □, FL • *370,712*

W

Wabash, IN 46992 • *12,127*
Wabash □, IL • *13,111*
Wabash □, IN • *35,069*
Wabasha, MN 55981 • *2,384*
Wabasha □, MN • *19,744*
Wabasso, FL 32970 • *1,145*
Wabaunsee □, KS • *6,603*
Waco, TX 76701–16 • *103,590*
Waconia, MN 55387 • *3,498*
Wade Hampton, SC 29607 • *20,014*
Wadena, MN 56482 • *4,131*
Wadena □, MN • *13,154*
Wadesboro, NC 28170 • *3,645*
Wading River, NY 11792 • *5,317*
Wadley, GA 30477 • *2,473*
Wadsworth, IL 60083 • *1,826*
Wadsworth, NV 89442 • *640*
Wadsworth, OH 44281 • *15,718*
Wagner, SD 57380 • *1,462*
Wagoner, OK 74467 • *6,894*
Wagoner □, OK • *47,883*
Wahiawa, HI 96786 • *17,386*
Wahkiakum □, WA • *3,327*
Wahoo, NE 68066 • *3,681*
Wahpeton, ND 58074–75 • *8,751*
Waialua, HI 96791 • *3,943*
Waianae, HI 96792 • *8,758*
Waikapu, HI 96793 • *729*
Wailua, HI 96746 • *2,018*
Wailuku, HI 96793 • *10,688*
Waimanalo, HI 96795 • *3,508*
Waimea, HI 96712 • *600*
Waimea, HI 96796 • *5,972*
Wainwright, AK 99782 • *492*
Waipahu, HI 96797 • *31,435*
Waipio Acres, HI 96786 • *5,304*
Waite Park, MN 56387 • *5,020*
Wakarusa, IN 46573 • *1,667*
Wake □, NC • *423,380*
Wa Keeney, KS 67672 • *2,161*
Wakefield, MA 01880 • *24,825*
Wakefield, MI 49968 • *2,318*
Wakefield, NE 68784 • *1,082*
Wakefield, RI 02879–83 • *3,450*
Wakefield, VA 23888 • *1,070*
Wake Forest, NC 27587–88 • *5,769*
Wakulla □, FL • *14,202*
Walbridge, OH 43465 • *2,736*
Walcott, IA 52773 • *1,356*
Walden, NY 12586 • *5,836*
Waldo, AR 71770 • *1,495*
Waldo, FL 32694 • *1,017*
Waldo □, ME • *33,018*
Waldoboro, ME 04572 • *1,420*
Waldport, OR 97394 • *1,595*
Waldron, AR 72958 • *3,024*
Waldwick, NJ 07463 • *9,757*
Walhalla, ND 58282 • *1,131*
Walhalla, SC 29691 • *3,755*
Walker, LA 70785 • *3,727*
Walker, MI 49504 • *17,279*
Walker □, AL • *67,670*
Walker □, GA • *58,340*
Walker □, TX • *50,917*
Walkersville, MD 21793 • *4,145*
Walkerton, IN 46574 • *2,061*
Walkertown, NC 27051 • *1,200*
Walkerville, MT 59701 • *605*
Wall, SD 57790 • *834*
Wallace, ID 83873 • *1,010*
Wallace, NC 28466 • *2,939*
Wallace □, KS • *1,821*
Walla Walla, WA 99362 • *26,478*
Walla Walla □, WA • *48,439*
Walled Lake, MI 48390 • *6,278*
Wallen, IN 46806 • *1,000*
Waller, TX 77484 • *1,493*
Waller □, TX • *23,390*
Wallingford, CT 06492 • *17,827*
Wallingford, VT 05773 • *1,148*
Wallington, NJ 07057 • *10,828*
Wallis, TX 77485 • *1,001*
Wallkill, NY 12589 • *2,125*
Wallowa □, OR • *6,911*
Walnut, CA 91789 • *29,105*
Walnut, IL 61376 • *1,463*
Walnut Cove, NC 27052 • *1,088*
Walnut Creek, CA 94593–98 • *60,569*
Walnut Park, CA 90255 • *14,722*
Walnutport, PA 18088 • *2,055*
Walnut Ridge, AR 72476 • *4,388*
Walpole, MA 02081 • *5,495*
Walsenburg, CO 81089 • *3,300*
Walsh □, ND • *13,840*
Walterboro, SC 29488 • *5,492*
Walters, OK 73572 • *2,519*
Walthall □, MS • *14,352*
Waltham, MA 02154 • *57,878*
Walthourville, GA 31333 • *2,024*
Walton, IN 46994 • *1,053*
Walton, KY 41094 • *2,034*
Walton, NY 13856 • *3,326*
Walton □, FL • *27,760*
Walton □, GA • *38,586*
Walworth, WI 53184 • *1,614*
Walworth □, SD • *6,087*
Walworth □, WI • *75,000*
Wamac, IL 62801 • *1,501*
Wamego, KS 66547 • *3,706*
Wamesit, MA 01876 • *2,700*
Wamsutter, WY 82336 • *240*
Wanaque, NJ 07465 • *9,711*
Wanchese, NC 27981 • *1,380*
Wando Woods, SC 29405 • *5,253*
Wantagh, NY 11793 • *18,567*
Wapakoneta, OH 45895 • *9,214*
Wapato, WA 98951 • *3,795*
Wapello, IA 52653 • *2,013*
Wapello □, IA • *35,687*
Wappingers Falls, NY 12590 • *4,605*
War, WV 24892 • *1,081*
Ward, AR 72176 • *1,269*
Ward □, ND • *57,921*
Ward □, TX • *13,115*
Warden, WA 98857 • *1,639*
Ware, MA 01082 • *6,533*
Ware □, GA • *35,471*
Wareham, MA 02571 • *2,607*
Warehouse Point, CT 06088 • *1,880*
Ware Shoals, SC 29692 • *2,497*
Waretown, NJ 08758 • *1,283*
Warminster, PA 18974 • *35,463*
Warner, OK 74469 • *1,479*
Warner Robins, GA 31088 • *43,726*
Warr Acres, OK 73132 • *9,288*
Warren, AR 71671 • *6,455*
Warren, IL 61087 • *1,550*
Warren, IN 46792 • *1,185*
Warren, MA 01083 • *1,516*
Warren, MI 48089–93 • *144,864*
Warren, MN 56762 • *1,813*
Warren, OH 44481–85 • *50,793*
Warren, PA 16365 • *11,122*
Warren, RI 02885 • *11,385*
Warren, VT 05674 • *350*
Warren □, GA • *6,078*
Warren □, IL • *19,181*
Warren □, IN • *8,176*
Warren □, IA • *36,033*
Warren □, KY • *76,673*
Warren □, MS • *47,880*
Warren □, MO • *19,534*
Warren □, NJ • *91,607*
Warren □, NY • *59,209*
Warren □, NC • *17,265*
Warren □, OH • *113,909*
Warren □, PA • *45,050*
Warren □, TN • *32,992*
Warren □, VA • *26,142*
Warren Park, IN 46219 • *1,763*
Warrensburg, IL 62573 • *1,274*
Warrensburg, MO 64093 • *15,244*
Warrensburg, NY 12885 • *3,204*
Warrensville Heights, OH 44122 • *15,745*
Warrenton, GA 30828 • *2,056*
Warrenton, MO 63383 • *3,564*
Warrenton, OR 97146 • *2,681*
Warrenton, VA 22186 • *4,830*
Warrenville, IL 60555 • *11,333*
Warrenville, SC 29851 • *1,029*
Warrick □, IN • *44,920*
Warrington, FL 32507 • *16,040*
Warrington, PA 18976 • *6,980*

Warrior, AL 35180 • 3,280
Warroad, MN 56763 • 1,679
Warsaw, IL 62379 • 1,882
Warsaw, IN 46580-81 • 10,968
Warsaw, KY 41095 • 1,202
Warsaw, MO 65355 • 1,696
Warsaw, NY 14569 • 3,830
Warsaw, NC 28398 • 2,859
Warwick, NY 10990 • 5,984
Warwick, RI 02886-89 • 85,427
Wasatch □, UT • 10,089
Wasco, CA 93280 • 12,412
Wasco □, OR • 21,683
Waseca, MN 56093 • 8,385
Waseca □, MN • 18,079
Washakie □, WY • 8,388
Washburn, IL 61570 • 1,075
Washburn, IA 50706 • 1,400
Washburn, ME 04786 • 1,880
Washburn, ND 58577 • 1,506
Washburn, WI 54891 • 2,285
Washburn □, WI • 13,772
Washington, DC 20001-99 • 606,900
Washington, GA 30673 • 4,279
Washington, IL 61571 • 10,099
Washington, IN 47501 • 10,838
Washington, IA 52353 • 7,074
Washington, KS 66968 • 1,304
Washington, LA 70589 • 1,253
Washington, MO 63090 • 10,704
Washington, NJ 07882 • 6,474
Washington, NC 27889 • 9,075
Washington, PA 15301 • 15,864
Washington, UT 84780 • 4,198
Washington □, AL • 16,694
Washington □, AR • 113,409
Washington □, CO • 4,812
Washington □, FL • 16,919
Washington □, GA • 19,112
Washington □, ID • 8,550
Washington □, IL • 14,965
Washington □, IN • 23,717
Washington □, IA • 19,612
Washington □, KS • 7,073
Washington □, KY • 10,441
Washington □, LA • 43,185
Washington □, ME • 35,308
Washington □, MD • 121,393
Washington □, MN • 145,896
Washington □, MS • 67,935
Washington □, MO • 20,380
Washington □, NE • 16,607
Washington □, NY • 59,330
Washington □, NC • 13,997
Washington □, OH • 62,254
Washington □, OK • 48,066
Washington □, OR • 311,554
Washington □, PA • 204,584
Washington □, RI • 110,006
Washington □, TN • 92,315
Washington □, TX • 26,154
Washington □, UT • 48,560
Washington □, VT • 54,928
Washington □, VA • 45,887
Washington □, WI • 95,328
Washington Court House, OH 43160 • 12,983
Washington Park, FL 33314 • 6,930
Washington Park, IL 62204 • 7,431
Washington Terrace, UT 84403 • 8,189
Washington Township, NJ 07675 • 9,245
Washita □, OK • 11,441
Washoe □, NV • 254,667
Washoe City, NV 89701 • 400
Washougal, WA 98671 • 4,764
Washtenaw □, MI • 282,937
Wasilla, AK 99687 • 4,028
Waskom, TX 75692 • 1,812
Watauga, TX 76148 • 20,009
Watauga □, NC • 36,952
Watchung, NJ 07060 • 5,110
Waterbury, CT 06701-26 • 108,961
Waterbury, VT 05676 • 1,702
Waterbury Center, VT 05677 • 500
Waterford, CT 06385 • 17,930
Waterford, MI 48327-29 • 66,692
Waterford, NY 12188 • 2,370
Waterford, PA 16441 • 1,492
Waterford, WI 53185 • 2,431
Waterford Works, NJ 08089 • 1,200
Waterloo, IL 62298 • 5,072
Waterloo, IN 46793 • 2,040
Waterloo, IA 50701-07 • 66,467
Waterloo, NY 13165 • 5,116
Waterloo, WI 53594 • 2,712
Waterman, IL 60556 • 1,074
Waterproof, LA 71375 • 1,080
Watertown, CT 06795 • 20,456
Watertown, FL 32055 • 3,340
Watertown, MA 02172 • 33,284
Watertown, NY 13601-03 • 29,429
Watertown, SD 57201 • 17,592
Watertown, TN 37184 • 1,250
Watertown, WI 53094 • 19,142
Water Valley, MS 38965 • 3,610
Waterville, ME 04901-03 • 17,173
Waterville, MN 56096 • 1,771
Waterville, NY 13480 • 1,664
Waterville, OH 43566 • 4,517
Watervliet, MI 49098 • 1,867
Watervliet, NY 12189 • 11,061
Watford City, ND 58854 • 1,784
Wathena, KS 66090 • 1,160
Watkins Glen, NY 14891 • 2,207
Watkinsville, GA 30677 • 1,600
Watonga, OK 73772 • 3,408
Watonwan □, MN • 11,682
Watseka, IL 60970 • 5,424
Watsontown, PA 17777 • 2,310
Watsonville, CA 95076-77 • 31,099
Wattsville, SC 29360 • 1,324
Wauchula, FL 33873 • 3,253
Wauconda, IL 60084 • 6,294
Waukee, IA 50263 • 2,512
Waukegan, IL 60085-87 • 69,392
Waukesha, WI 53186-88 • 56,958
Waukesha □, WI • 304,715
Waukomis, OK 73773 • 1,322
Waukon, IA 52172 • 4,019
Waunakee, WI 53597 • 5,897
Waupaca, WI 54981 • 4,957
Waupaca □, WI • 46,104
Waupun, WI 53963 • 8,207
Wauregan, CT 06387 • 1,200
Waurika, OK 73573 • 2,088
Wausau, WI 54401-02 • 37,060
Wauseon, OH 43567 • 6,322
Waushara □, WI • 19,385
Wautoma, WI 54982 • 1,784
Wauwatosa, WI 53213 • 49,366
Waveland, MS 39576 • 5,369
Waverly, IL 62692 • 1,402
Waverly, IA 50677 • 8,539
Waverly, MI 48917 • 15,614
Waverly, NE 68462 • 1,869
Waverly, NY 14892 • 4,787
Waverly, OH 45690 • 4,477
Waverly, TN 37185 • 3,925
Waverly, VA 23890 • 2,223
Waxahachie, TX 75165 • 18,168
Waxhaw, NC 28173 • 1,294
Waycross, GA 31501 • 16,410
Wayland, MA 01778 • 2,550
Wayland, MI 49348 • 2,751
Wayland, NY 14572 • 1,976
Waylyn, SC 29405 • 2,400
Waymart, PA 18472 • 1,337
Wayne, MI 48184-88 • 19,899
Wayne, NE 68787 • 5,142
Wayne, NJ 07470-74 • 47,025
Wayne, WV 25570 • 1,128
Wayne □, GA • 22,356
Wayne □, IL • 17,241
Wayne □, IN • 71,951
Wayne □, IA • 7,067
Wayne □, KY • 17,468
Wayne □, MI • 2,111,687
Wayne □, MS • 19,517
Wayne □, MO • 11,543
Wayne □, NE • 9,364
Wayne □, NY • 89,123
Wayne □, NC • 104,666
Wayne □, OH • 101,461
Wayne □, PA • 39,944
Wayne □, TN • 13,935
Wayne □, UT • 2,177
Wayne □, WV • 41,636
Wayne City, IL 62895 • 1,099
Waynesboro, GA 30830 • 5,701
Waynesboro, MS 39367 • 5,143
Waynesboro, PA 17268 • 9,578
Waynesboro, TN 38485 • 1,824
Waynesboro, VA 22980 • 18,549
Waynesburg, OH 44688 • 1,068
Waynesburg, PA 15370 • 4,270
Waynesville, MO 65583 • 3,207
Waynesville, NC 28786 • 6,758
Waynesville, OH 45068 • 1,949
Waynewood, VA 22308 • 5,000
Wayzata, MN 55391 • 3,806
Weakley □, TN • 31,972
Weatherford, OK 73096 • 10,124
Weatherford, TX 76086-87 • 14,804
Weatherly, PA 18255 • 2,640
Weatogue, CT 06089 • 2,521
Weaver, AL 36277 • 2,715
Weaverville, CA 96093 • 3,370
Weaverville, NC 28787 • 2,107
Webb, AL 36376 • 1,039
Webb □, TX • 133,239
Webb City, MO 64870 • 7,449
Webberville, MI 48892 • 1,698
Weber □, UT • 158,330
Weber City, VA 24251 • 1,377
Webster, MA 01570 • 11,849
Webster, NY 14580 • 5,464
Webster, PA 15087 • 1,000
Webster, SD 57274 • 2,017
Webster □, GA • 2,263
Webster □, IA • 40,342
Webster □, KY • 13,955
Webster □, LA • 41,989
Webster □, MS • 10,222
Webster □, MO • 23,753
Webster □, NE • 4,279
Webster □, WV • 10,729
Webster City, IA 50595 • 7,894
Webster Groves, MO 63119 • 22,987
Websterville, VT 05678 • 600
Wedgewood, MO 63031 • 6,700
Weed, CA 96094 • 3,062
Weed Heights, NV 89447 • 230
Weedsport, NY 13166 • 1,996
Weehawken, NJ 07087 • 12,385
Weeping Water, NE 68463 • 1,008
Weigelstown, PA 17315 • 8,665
Weimar, TX 78962 • 2,052
Weippe, ID 83553 • 532
Weirsdale, FL 32195 • 1,500
Weirton, WV 26062 • 22,124
Weiser, ID 83672 • 4,571
Wekiva Springs, FL 32750 • 23,026
Welch, WV 24801 • 3,028
Welcome, SC 29611 • 6,560
Weld □, CO • 131,821
Weldon, NC 27890 • 1,392
Weleetka, OK 74880 • 1,112
Wellesley, MA 02181 • 26,615
Wellfleet, MA 02667 • 1,200
Wellford, SC 29385 • 2,511
Wellington, CO 80549 • 1,340
Wellington, FL 33414 • 20,670
Wellington, KS 67152 • 8,411
Wellington, NV 89444 • 280
Wellington, OH 44090 • 4,140
Wellington, TX 79095 • 2,456
Wellington, UT 84542 • 1,632
Wellman, IA 52356 • 1,085
Wells, ME 04090 • 1,200
Wells, MI 49894 • 1,150
Wells, MN 56097 • 2,465
Wells, NV 89835 • 1,256
Wells □, IN • 25,948
Wells □, ND • 5,864
Wellsboro, PA 16901 • 3,430
Wellsburg, WV 26070 • 3,385
Wellston, OH 45692 • 6,049
Wellsville, KS 66092 • 1,563
Wellsville, MO 63384 • 1,430
Wellsville, NY 14895 • 5,241
Wellsville, OH 43968 • 4,532
Wellsville, UT 84339 • 2,206
Wellton, AZ 85356 • 1,066
Welsh, LA 70591 • 3,299
Wenatchee, WA 98801-07 • 21,756
Wendell, ID 83355 • 1,963
Wendell, NC 27591 • 2,822
Wendover, UT 84083 • 1,127
Wenham, MA 01984 • 3,897
Wenonah, NJ 08090 • 2,331
Wentzville, MO 63385 • 5,088
Weslaco, TX 78596 • 21,877
Wesleyville, PA 16510 • 3,655
Wessington Springs, SD 57382 • 1,083
Wesson, MS 39191 • 1,510
West, TX 76691 • 2,515
West Acton, MA 01720 • 5,230
West Alexandria, OH 45381 • 1,460
West Allis, WI 53214 • 63,221
West Andover, MA 01810 • 1,970
West Athens, CA 90247 • 8,859
West Babylon, NY 11704 • 42,410
West Barnstable, MA 02668 • 1,000
West Baton Rouge □, LA • 19,419
West Bay Shore, NY 11706 • 4,907
West Bend, WI 53095 • 23,916
West Berlin, NJ 08091 • 2,970
West Billerica, MA 01862 • 1,920
West Blocton, AL 35184 • 1,468
Westborough, MA 01581 • 3,917
West Bountiful, UT 84087 • 4,477
West Boylston, MA 01583 • 3,130
West Bradenton, FL 34205 • 4,528
West Branch, IA 52358 • 1,908
West Branch, MI 48661 • 1,914
West Bridgewater, MA 02379 • 2,140
Westbrook, CT 06498 • 2,060
Westbrook, ME 04092 • 16,121
West Brookfield, MA 01585 • 1,419
West Burlington, IA 52655 • 3,083
Westbury, NY 11590 • 13,060
Westby, WI 54667 • 1,866
West Caldwell, NJ 07004 • 10,422
West Cape May, NJ 08204 • 1,026
West Carroll □, LA • 12,093
West Carrollton, OH 45449 • 14,403
West Carson, CA 90502 • 20,143
West Carthage, NY 13619 • 2,166
West Chatham, MA 02669 • 1,504
Westchester, FL 33136 • 29,883
Westchester, IL 60153 • 17,301
West Chester, PA 19380-82 • 18,041
Westchester □, NY • 874,866
West Chicago, IL 60185-86 • 14,796
West Columbia, SC 29169-72 • 10,588
West Columbia, TX 77486 • 4,372
West Compton, CA 90220 • 5,451
West Concord, MA 01742 • 5,761
West Concord, NC 28027 • 5,859
West Covina, CA 91790-93 • 96,086
West Crossett, AR 71635 • 2,019
West Dennis, MA 02670 • 2,307
West Des Moines, IA 50265 • 31,702
West Elmira, NY 14905 • 5,218
Westerly, RI 02891 • 16,477
Westernport, MD 21562 • 2,454
Western Springs, IL 60558 • 11,984
Westerville, OH 43081-82 • 30,269
West Fairview, PA 17025 • 1,403
West Falmouth, MA 02574 • 1,600
West Fargo, ND 58078 • 12,287
West Feliciana □, LA • 12,915
Westfield, IN 46074 • 3,304
Westfield, MA 01085-86 • 38,372
Westfield, NJ 07090-92 • 28,870
Westfield, NY 14787 • 3,451
Westfield, PA 16950 • 1,119
Westfield, WI 53964 • 1,125
Westford, MA 01886 • 1,200
West Fork, AR 72774 • 1,607
West Frankfort, IL 62896 • 8,526
West Freehold, NJ 07728 • 11,166
Westgate, FL 33401 • 2,100
West Gate, VA 22110 • 6,565
West Gate of Lomond, VA 22110 • 5,400
West Glens Falls, NY 12801 • 5,964
West Goshen, PA 19380 • 8,948
West Grove, PA 19390 • 2,128
Westham, VA 23229 • 3,200
West Hanover, MA 02339 • 1,700
West Hartford, CT 06127 • 60,110
West Haven, CT 06516 • 54,021
West Haven, OR 97225 • 3,400
West Haverstraw, NY 10993 • 9,183
West Hazleton, PA 18201 • 4,136
West Helena, AR 72390 • 9,695
West Hempstead, NY 11552 • 17,689
West Hollywood, CA 90069 • 36,118
Westhope, ND 58793 • 578
West Hyannisport, MA 02672 • 1,200
West Islip, NY 11795 • 28,419
West Jefferson, NC 28694 • 1,002
West Jefferson, OH 43162 • 4,504
West Jordan, UT 84084 • 42,892
West Kingston, RI 02892 • 1,150
West Lafayette, IN 47906-07 • 25,907
West Lafayette, OH 43845 • 2,129
Westlake, LA 70669 • 5,007
Westlake, OH 44145 • 27,018
Westlake Village, CA 91361 • 7,455
Westland, MI 48185 • 84,724
West Lawn, PA 19609 • 1,606
West Liberty, IA 52776 • 2,935
West Liberty, KY 41472 • 1,887
West Liberty, OH 43357 • 1,613
West Liberty, WV 26074 • 1,434
West Linn, OR 97068 • 16,367
West Long Branch, NJ 07764 • 7,690
West Marion, NC 28752 • 1,291
West Medway, MA 02053 • 1,940
West Melbourne, FL 32901 • 8,399
West Memphis, AR 72301 • 28,259
Westmere, NY 12203 • 6,750
West Miami, FL 33174 • 5,727
West Mifflin, PA 15122-23 • 23,644
West Milford, NJ 07480 • 25,430
West Milton, OH 45383 • 4,348
West Milwaukee, WI 53214 • 3,973
Westminster, CA 92683-84 • 78,118
Westminster, CO 80030-31 • 74,625
Westminster, MD 21157 • 13,068
Westminster, SC 29693 • 3,120
West Modesto, CA 95351 • 6,135
West Monroe, LA 71291-94 • 14,096
Westmont, CA 90044 • 31,100
Westmont, IL 60559 • 21,228
Westmont, NJ 08108 • 5,630
Westmont, PA 15905 • 5,789
Westmoreland, TN 37186 • 1,726
Westmoreland □, PA • 370,321
Westmoreland □, VA • 15,480
Westmorland, CA 92281 • 1,380
West Mystic, CT 06388 • 3,595
West Newton, PA 15089 • 3,152
West New York, NJ 07093 • 38,125
West Norriton, PA 19401 • 15,209
West Nyack, NY 10960 • 3,437
Weston, CT 06883 • 1,370
Weston, MA 02193 • 11,169
Weston, MO 64098 • 1,528
Weston, OH 43569 • 1,716
Weston, WV 26452 • 4,994
Weston, WI 54476 • 9,714
Weston □, WY • 6,518
West Orange, NJ 07052 • 39,103
Westover, WV 26505 • 4,201
West Palm Beach, FL 33401-20 • 67,643
West Pasco, WA 99301 • 7,312
West Paterson, NJ 07424 • 10,982
West Pawlet, VT 05775 • 350
West Pensacola, FL 32505 • 22,107
West Peoria, IL 61604 • 5,314
West Pittsburg, CA 94565 • 17,453
West Pittsburg, PA 16160 • 1,133
West Pittston, PA 18643 • 5,590
West Plains, MO 65775 • 8,913
West Point, CA 95255 • 1,500
West Point, GA 31833 • 3,571
West Point, IA 52656 • 1,079
West Point, KY 40177 • 1,216
West Point, MS 39773 • 8,489
West Point, NE 68788 • 3,250
West Point, NY 10996-97 • 8,024
West Point, UT 84015 • 4,258
West Point, VA 23181 • 2,938
Westport, CT 06880-83 • 24,407
Westport, IN 47283 • 1,478
Westport, WA 98595 • 1,892
West Portsmouth, OH 45662 • 3,551
West Puente Valley, CA 91744 • 20,254
West Reading, PA 19611 • 4,142
West Rutland, VT 05777 • 2,246
West Sacramento, CA 95691 • 28,898
West Saint Paul, MN 55118 • 19,248
West Salem, IL 62476 • 1,042
West Salem, OH 44287 • 1,534
West Salem, WI 54669 • 3,611
West Sayville, NY 11796 • 4,680
West Seneca, NY 14224 • 47,866
West Simsbury, CT 06092 • 2,149
West Slope, OR 97225 • 7,959
West Springfield, MA 01089-90 • 27,537
West Springfield, VA 22152 • 28,126
West Swanzey, NH 03469 • 1,055
West Terre Haute, IN 47885 • 2,495
West Union, IA 52175 • 2,490
West Union, OH 45693 • 3,096
West Unity, OH 43570 • 1,677
West University Place, TX 77005 • 12,920
West Upton, MA 01587 • 1,300
Westvale, NY 13219 • 5,952
West Valley City, UT 84120 • 86,976
Westview, FL 33168 • 9,668
West View, PA 15229 • 7,734
Westville, IL 61883 • 3,387
Westville, IN 46391 • 5,255
Westville, NJ 08093 • 4,573
Westville, OK 74965 • 1,374
West Wareham, MA 02576 • 2,059
West Warren, MA 01092 • 1,200
West Warwick, RI 02893 • 29,268
West Webster, NY 14580 • 8,690
Westwego, LA 70094-96 • 11,218
West Whittier, CA 90606 • 13,800
West Willow, MI 48198 • 4,300
Westwood, CA 96137 • 2,017
Westwood, KS 66205 • 1,772
Westwood, KY 41101 • 5,300
Westwood, MA 02090 • 6,500
Westwood, MI 49007 • 8,957
Westwood, NJ 07675 • 10,446
Westwood Lakes, FL 33165 • 11,522
West Wyoming, PA 18644 • 3,117
West Yarmouth, MA 02673 • 5,409
West Yellowstone, MT 59758 • 913
West York, PA 17404 • 4,283
Wethersfield, CT 06129 • 25,651
Wetumka, OK 74883 • 1,427
Wetumpka, AL 36092 • 4,670
Wetzel □, WV • 19,258
Wewahitchka, FL 32465 • 1,779
Wewoka, OK 74884 • 4,050
Wexford □, MI • 26,360
Weyauwega, WI 54983 • 1,665
Weymouth, MA 02188 • 54,063
Whalom, MA 01420 • 1,340
Wharton, NJ 07885 • 5,405
Wharton, TX 77488 • 9,011
Wharton □, TX • 39,955
Whatcom □, WA • 127,780
Wheatland, CA 95692 • 1,631
Wheatland, WY 82201 • 3,271
Wheatland □, MT • 2,246
Wheaton, IL 60187-89 • 51,464
Wheaton, MD 20902 • 58,300
Wheaton, MN 56296 • 1,615
Wheat Ridge, CO 80033-34 • 29,419
Wheeler, TX 79096 • 1,393
Wheeler □, GA • 4,903
Wheeler □, NE • 948
Wheeler □, OR • 1,396
Wheeler □, TX • 5,879
Wheelersburg, OH 45694 • 5,113
Wheeling, IL 60090 • 29,911
Wheeling, WV 26003 • 34,882
Whitacres, CT 06082 • 2,410
White □, AR • 54,676
White □, GA • 13,006
White □, IL • 16,522
White □, IN • 23,265
White □, TN • 20,090
White Bear Lake, MN 55110 • 24,704
White Bluff, TN 37187 • 1,988
White Castle, LA 70788 • 2,102
White Center, WA 98126 • 15,700
White City, OR 97503 • 5,891
White City, UT 84070 • 6,506
White Cloud, MI 49349 • 1,147
White Deer, TX 79097 • 1,125
Whitefield, NH 03598 • 1,041
Whitefish, MT 59937 • 4,368
Whitefish Bay, WI 53217 • 14,272
White Hall, AR 71602 • 3,849
White Hall, IL 62092 • 2,814
Whitehall, MI 49461 • 3,027
Whitehall, MT 59759 • 1,067
Whitehall, NY 12887 • 3,071
Whitehall, OH 43213 • 20,572
Whitehall, PA 15227 • 14,451
Whitehall, WI 54773 • 1,494
White Haven, PA 18661 • 1,132
White Horse, NJ 08610 • 9,397
White Horse Beach, MA 02381 • 1,200
Whitehouse, OH 43571 • 2,528
White House, TN 37188 • 2,987
White House Station, NJ 08889 • 1,400
White Island Shores, MA 02538 • 2,000
White Meadow Lake, NJ 07866 • 8,002
White Oak, MD 20901 • 18,671
White Oak, OH 45239 • 12,430
White Oak, PA 15131 • 8,761
White Pigeon, MI 49099 • 1,458
White Pine, MI 49971 • 1,142
White Pine, TN 37890 • 1,771
White Pine □, NV • 9,264
White Plains, MD 20695 • 3,560
White Plains, NY 10601-07 • 48,718
Whiteriver, AZ 85941 • 3,775
White River Junction, VT 05001 • 2,521
White Rock, NM 87544 • 6,192
White Salmon, WA 98672 • 1,861
Whitesboro, NY 13492 • 4,195
Whitesboro, TX 76273 • 3,209
Whitesburg, KY 41858 • 1,636
White Settlement, TX 76108 • 15,472
Whiteside □, IL • 60,186
White Sulphur Springs, MT 59645 • 963
White Sulphur Springs, WV 24986 • 2,779
Whiteville, NC 28472 • 5,078
Whiteville, TN 38075 • 1,050
Whitewater, WI 53190 • 12,636
Whitewood, SD 57793 • 891
Whitewright, TX 75491 • 1,713
Whitfield □, GA • 72,462
Whitfield Estates, FL 34243 • 3,152
Whiting, IN 46394 • 5,155
Whiting, WI 54481 • 1,838
Whitinsville, MA 01588 • 5,639
Whitley □, IN • 27,651
Whitley □, KY • 33,326
Whitley City, KY 42653 • 1,133
Whitman, MA 02382 • 13,534
Whitman, WV 25652 • 1,651
Whitman □, WA • 38,775
Whitman Square, NJ 08012 • 3,490
Whitmire, SC 29178 • 1,702
Whitmore Lake, MI 48189 • 3,251
Whitmore Village, HI 96786 • 3,373
Whitney, SC 29303 • 4,052
Whitney, TX 76692 • 1,626
Whitney Point, NY 13862 • 1,054
Whittier, AK 99693 • 243
Whittier, CA 90601-12 • 77,671
Whitwell, TN 37397 • 1,622
Wibaux, MT 59353 • 628
Wibaux □, MT • 1,191
Wichita, KS 67201-78 • 304,011
Wichita □, KS • 2,758
Wichita □, TX • 122,378
Wichita Falls, TX 76301-11 • 96,259
Wickenburg, AZ 85358 • 4,515
Wickliffe, OH 44092 • 14,558
Wickliffe, OH 44515 • 7,240
Wicomico □, MD • 74,339
Wiconisco, PA 17097 • 1,321
Widefield, CO 80911 • 12,112
Wiggins, MS 39577 • 3,185
Wilbarger □, TX • 15,121
Wilber, NE 68465 • 1,527
Wilberforce, OH 45384 • 2,639
Wilbraham, MA 01095 • 3,352
Wilburton, OK 74578 • 3,092
Wilcox, PA 15870 • 1,000
Wilcox □, AL • 13,568
Wilcox □, GA • 7,008
Wilder, ID 83676 • 1,232
Wilder, VT 05088 • 1,576
Wildorado, TX 79098 • 2,000
Wildwood, FL 34785 • 3,421
Wildwood, IL 60030 • 2,034
Wildwood, NJ 08260 • 4,484
Wildwood Crest, NJ 08260 • 3,631
Wilkes □, GA • 10,597
Wilkes □, NC • 59,393
Wilkes-Barre, PA 18701-73 • 47,523
Wilkesboro, NC 28697 • 2,573
Wilkin □, MN • 7,516
Wilkinsburg, PA 15221 • 21,080
Wilkinson □, GA • 10,228
Wilkinson □, MS • 9,678
Wilkins Township, PA 15145 • 7,487
Will □, IL • 357,313
Willacoochee, GA 31650 • 1,205
Willacy □, TX • 17,705
Willamina, OR 97396 • 1,717
Willard, MO 65781 • 2,177
Willard, NY 14588 • 1,339
Willard, OH 44890 • 6,210
Willard, UT 84340 • 1,298
Willcox, AZ 85643 • 3,122
Williams, AZ 86046 • 2,532
Williams, CA 95987 • 2,297
Williams □, ND • 21,129
Williams □, OH • 36,956
Williams Bay, WI 53191 • 2,108
Williamsburg, IA 52361 • 2,174
Williamsburg, KY 40769 • 5,493
Williamsburg, MA 01096 • 1,200
Williamsburg, OH 45176 • 2,322
Williamsburg, PA 16693 • 1,456
Williamsburg, VA 23185-88 • 11,530
Williamsburg □, SC • 36,815
Williamson, NY 14589 • 1,768
Williamson, WV 25661 • 4,154
Williamson □, IL • 57,733
Williamson □, TN • 81,021
Williamson □, TX • 139,551
Williamsport, IN 47993 • 1,798
Williamsport, MD 21795 • 2,103
Williamsport, PA 17701-03 • 31,933
Williamston, MI 48895 • 2,922
Williamston, NC 27892 • 5,503
Williamston, SC 29697 • 3,876
Williamstown, KY 41097 • 3,023
Williamstown, MA 01267 • 4,791

Williamstown, NJ 08094 • *10,891*
Williamstown, PA 17098 • *1,509*
Williamstown, VT 05679 • *650*
Williamstown, WV 26187 • *2,774*
Williamsville, IL 62693 • *1,140*
Williamsville, NY 14221 • *5,583*
Willimantic, CT 06226 • *14,746*
Willingboro, NJ 08046 • *36,291*
Willis, TX 77378 • *2,764*
Williston, FL 32696 • *2,179*
Williston, ND 58801-02 • *13,131*
Williston, SC 29853 • *3,099*
Williston Park, NY 11596 • *7,516*
Willits, CA 95490 • *5,027*
Wilmar, MN 56201 • *17,531*
Willoughby, OH 44094-95 • *20,510*
Willoughby Hills, OH 44092 • *8,427*
Willow Brook, CA 90222 • *32,772*
Willowbrook, IL 60521 • *8,598*
Willow Grove, PA 19090 • *16,325*
Willowick, OH 44094 • *15,269*
Willow Springs, IL 60480 • *4,509*
Willow Springs, MO 65793 • *2,038*
Williston, VA 22044 • *2,000*
Wilmette, IL 60091 • *26,690*
Wilmington, DE 19801-99 • *71,529*
Wilmington, IL 60481 • *4,743*
Wilmington, MA 01887 • *17,654*
Wilmington, NC 28401-12 • *55,530*
Wilmington, OH 45177 • *11,199*
Wilmington, VT 05363 • *550*
Wilmington Island, GA 31410 • *11,230*
Wilmington Manor, DE 19720 • *8,568*
Wilmington Manor Gardens, DE 19720 • *1,500*
Wilmore, KY 40390 • *4,215*
Wilmot, AR 71676 • *1,047*
Wilson, AR 72395 • *1,068*
Wilson, NY 14172 • *1,307*
Wilson, NC 27893-95 • *36,930*
Wilson, OK 73463 • *1,639*
Wilson, PA 18042 • *7,830*
Wilson, WY 83014 • *500*
Wilson ⬜, KS • *10,289*
Wilson ⬜, NC • *66,061*
Wilson ⬜, TN • *67,675*
Wilson ⬜, TX • *22,650*
Wilsonville, AL 35186 • *1,185*
Wilsonville, OR 97070 • *7,106*
Wilton, CT 06897 • *7,200*
Wilton, IA 52778 • *2,577*
Wilton, ME 04294 • *2,453*
Wilton, NH 03086 • *1,165*
Wilton, ND 58579 • *728*
Wilton Manors, FL 33334 • *11,804*
Wimauma, FL 33598 • *2,932*
Winamac, IN 46996 • *2,262*
Winchendon, MA 01475 • *4,316*
Winchester, IL 62694 • *1,769*
Winchester, IN 47394 • *5,095*
Winchester, KY 40391-92 • *15,799*
Winchester, MA 01890 • *20,267*
Winchester, NV 89101 • *23,365*
Winchester, NH 03470 • *1,735*
Winchester, TN 37398 • *6,305*
Winchester, VA 22601 • *21,947*
Windber, PA 15963 • *4,756*
Windcrest, TX 78239 • *5,331*
Winder, GA 30680 • *7,373*
Windgap, PA 18091 • *2,741*
Windham, CT 06280 • *1,100*
Windham, OH 44288 • *2,943*
Windham ⬜, CT • *102,525*
Windham ⬜, VT • *41,588*
Wind Lake, WI 53185 • *3,000*
Windom, MN 56101 • *4,283*
Window Rock, AZ 86515 • *3,306*
Wind Point, WI 53402 • *1,941*
Windsor, CO 80550 • *5,062*
Windsor, CT 06095 • *27,817*
Windsor, IL 61957 • *1,143*
Windsor, MO 65360 • *3,044*

Windsor, NC 27983 • *2,056*
Windsor, PA 17366 • *1,355*
Windsor, VT 05089 • *3,478*
Windsor, VA 23487 • *1,025*
Windsor ⬜, VT • *54,055*
Windsor Heights, IA 50311 • *5,190*
Windsor Hills, CA 90052 • *6,200*
Windsor Locks, CT 06096 • *12,358*
Windy Hill, SC 29506 • *1,622*
Windy Hills, DE 19711 • *1,130*
Winfield, AL 35594 • *3,689*
Winfield, IA 52659 • *1,051*
Winfield, KS 67156 • *11,931*
Winfield, NJ 07036 • *1,785*
Winfield, WV 25213 • *1,164*
Wingate, NC 28174 • *2,821*
Wink, TX 79789 • *1,189*
Winkler ⬜, TX • *8,626*
Winlock, WA 98596 • *1,027*
Winn ⬜, LA • *16,269*
Winnebago, IL 61088 • *1,840*
Winnebago, MN 56098 • *1,565*
Winnebago, WI 54985 • *1,433*
Winnebago ⬜, IL • *252,913*
Winnebago ⬜, IA • *12,122*
Winnebago ⬜, WI • *140,320*
Winneconne, WI 54986 • *2,059*
Winnemucca, NV 89445 • *6,134*
Winner, SD 57580 • *3,354*
Winneshiek ⬜, IA • *20,847*
Winnetka, IL 60093 • *12,174*
Winnfield, LA 71483 • *6,138*
Winnsboro, LA 71295 • *5,755*
Winnsboro, SC 29180 • *3,475*
Winnsboro, TX 75494 • *2,904*
Winnsboro Mills, SC 29180 • *2,275*
Winona, MN 55987 • *25,399*
Winona, MS 38967 • *5,705*
Winona, MO 65588 • *1,081*
Winona ⬜, MN • *47,828*
Winona Lake, IN 46590 • *4,053*
Winooski, VT 05404 • *6,649*
Winslow, AZ 86047 • *8,190*
Winslow, ME 04901 • *5,436*
Winsted, CT 06098 • *8,254*
Winsted, MN 55395 • *1,581*
Winston, FL 33801 • *9,118*
Winston, OR 97496 • *3,773*
Winston ⬜, AL • *22,053*
Winston ⬜, MS • *19,433*
Winston-Salem, NC 27101-27 • *143,485*
Winter Garden, FL 34787 • *9,745*
Winter Haven, FL 33880-84 • *24,725*
Winter Park, FL 32789-90 • *22,242*
Winter Park, CO 80403 • *4,504*
Winterport, ME 04496 • *1,274*
Winters, CA 95694 • *4,639*
Winters, TX 79567 • *2,905*
Winterset, IA 50273 • *4,196*
Winter Springs, FL 32708 • *22,151*
Wintersville, OH 43952 • *4,102*
Winterville, NC 28590 • *2,816*
Winthrop, ME 04364 • *2,819*
Winthrop, MA 02152 • *18,127*
Winthrop, MN 55396 • *1,279*
Winthrop Harbor, IL 60096 • *6,240*
Winton, CA 95388 • *7,559*
Wirt ⬜, WV • *5,192*
Wiscasset, ME 04578 • *1,350*
Wisconsin Dells, WI 53965 • *2,393*
Wisconsin Rapids, WI 54494-95 • *18,245*
Wise, VA 24293 • *3,193*
Wise ⬜, TX • *34,679*
Wise ⬜, VA • *39,573*
Wishek, ND 58495 • *1,171*
Wisner, LA 71378 • *1,153*
Wisner, NE 68791 • *1,253*
Withamsville, OH 45245 • *5,000*
Witherbee, NY 12998 • *1,000*
Wittenberg, WI 54499 • *1,145*
Wixom, MI 48393 • *8,550*
Woburn, MA 01801 • *35,943*
Wolcott, CT 06716 • *6,070*
Wolcott, NY 14590 • *1,544*
Wolfe ⬜, KY • *6,503*
Wolfeboro, NH 03894 • *2,783*

Wolfe City, TX 75496 • *1,505*
Wolf Lake, MI 49442 • *4,110*
Wolf Point, MT 59201 • *2,880*
Wolf Trap, VA 22182 • *13,133*
Womelsdorf, PA 19567 • *2,270*
Wonder Lake, IL 60097 • *6,664*
Wood ⬜, OH • *113,269*
Wood ⬜, TX • *29,380*
Wood ⬜, WV • *86,915*
Wood ⬜, WI • *73,605*
Woodbine, GA 31569 • *1,212*
Woodbine, IA 51579 • *1,500*
Woodbine, NJ 08270 • *2,678*
Woodbourne, NY 12788 • *1,155*
Woodbourne, OH 45459 • *6,000*
Woodbridge, CT 06525 • *7,924*
Woodbridge, NJ 07095 • *17,434*
Woodbridge, VA 22191-94 • *26,401*
Woodbridge [Township], NJ 07095 • *17,434*
Woodburn, IN 46797 • *1,321*
Woodburn, OR 97071 • *13,404*
Woodbury, CT 06798 • *1,212*
Woodbury, GA 30293 • *1,429*
Woodbury, MN 55125 • *20,075*
Woodbury, NJ 08096 • *10,904*
Woodbury, NY 11797 • *8,008*
Woodbury, TN 37190 • *2,287*
Woodbury ⬜, IA • *98,276*
Woodcliff Lake, NJ 07675 • *5,303*
Wood Dale, IL 60191 • *12,425*
Woodfield, SC 29206 • *8,862*
Woodford ⬜, IL • *32,653*
Woodford ⬜, KY • *19,955*
Woodhaven, MI 48183 • *11,631*
Woodlake, CA 93286 • *5,678*
Woodland, CA 95695 • *39,802*
Woodland, ME 04694 • *1,287*
Woodland, WA 98674 • *2,500*
Woodland Park, CO 80863 • *4,610*
Woodlawn, KY 42001 • *1,600*
Woodlawn, MD 21207 • *5,329*
Woodlawn, MD 20784 • *5,329*
Woodlawn, OH 45215 • *2,674*
Woodlawn, VA 24381 • *1,689*
Woodlynne, NJ 08107 • *2,547*
Woodmere, NY 11598 • *15,578*
Woodmont, CT 06460 • *1,770*
Woodmoor, MD 21207 • *8,630*
Woodridge, IL 60517 • *26,256*
Wood-Ridge, NJ 07075 • *7,506*
Wood River, IL 62095 • *11,490*
Wood River, NE 68883 • *1,156*
Woodruff, SC 29388 • *4,365*
Woodruff, WI 54568 • *1,500*
Woodruff ⬜, AR • *9,520*
Woods ⬜, OK • *9,103*
Woodsboro, TX 78393 • *1,731*
Woods Cross, UT 84087 • *5,384*
Woodsfield, OH 43793 • *2,832*
Woods Hole, MA 02543 • *1,080*
Woodside, CA 94062 • *5,035*
Woodson ⬜, KS • *4,116*
Woodstock, GA 30188 • *4,361*
Woodstock, IL 60098 • *14,353*
Woodstock, NY 12498 • *1,870*
Woodstock, VT 05091 • *1,037*
Woodstock, VA 22664 • *3,182*
Woodstown, NJ 08098 • *3,154*
Woodville, FL 32362 • *2,260*
Woodville, MS 39669 • *1,393*
Woodville, OH 43469 • *1,953*
Woodville, TX 75979 • *2,636*
Woodward, IA 50276 • *1,197*
Woodward, OK 73801-02 • *12,340*
Woodward ⬜, OK • *18,976*
Woodway, TX 76710 • *8,695*
Woonsocket, RI 02895 • *43,877*
Woonsocket, SD 57385 • *766*
Wooster, OH 44691 • *22,191*
Worcester, MA 01601-15 • *169,759*
Worcester ⬜, MD • *35,028*
Worcester ⬜, MA • *709,705*
Worland, WY 82401 • *5,742*

Worth, IL 60482 • *11,208*
Worth ⬜, GA • *19,745*
Worth ⬜, IA • *7,991*
Worth ⬜, MO • *2,440*
Wortham, TX 76693 • *1,020*
Worthington, IN 47471 • *1,473*
Worthington, KY 41183 • *1,751*
Worthington, MN 56187 • *9,977*
Worthington, OH 43085 • *14,869*
Wrangell, AK 99929 • *2,479*
Wray, CO 80758 • *1,998*
Wrens, GA 30833 • *2,414*
Wrentham, MA 02093 • *2,110*
Wright, FL 32548 • *18,945*
Wright ⬜, IA • *14,269*
Wright ⬜, MN • *68,710*
Wright ⬜, MO • *16,758*
Wright City, MO 63390 • *1,250*
Wrightstown, NJ 08562 • *3,843*
Wrightstown, WI 54180 • *1,262*
Wrightsville, AR 72183 • *1,062*
Wrightsville, GA 31096 • *2,331*
Wrightsville, PA 17368 • *2,396*
Wrightsville Beach, NC 28480 • *2,937*
Wrightwood, CA 92397 • *3,308*
Wurtsboro, NY 12790 • *1,048*
Wyandanch, NY 11798 • *8,950*
Wyandot ⬜, OH • *22,254*
Wyandotte, MI 48192 • *30,938*
Wyandotte ⬜, KS • *161,993*
Wyanet, IL 61379 • *1,017*
Wyckoff, NJ 07481 • *15,372*
Wymore, NE 68466 • *1,611*
Wynne, AR 72396-97 • *8,187*
Wynnewood, OK 73098 • *2,451*
Wyoming, DE 19934 • *977*
Wyoming, IL 61491 • *1,462*
Wyoming, MI 49509 • *63,891*
Wyoming, MN 55092 • *2,142*
Wyoming, OH 45215 • *8,128*
Wyoming, PA 18644 • *3,255*
Wyoming ⬜, NY • *42,507*
Wyoming ⬜, PA • *28,076*
Wyoming ⬜, WV • *28,990*
Wyomissing, PA 19610 • *7,332*
Wythe ⬜, VA • *25,466*
Wytheville, VA 24382 • *8,038*

X

Xenia, OH 45385 • *24,664*

Y

Yadkin ⬜, NC • *30,488*
Yadkinville, NC 27055 • *2,525*
Yakima, WA 98901-09 • *54,827*
Yakima ⬜, WA • *188,823*
Yakutat, AK 99689 • *534*
Yale, MI 48097 • *1,977*
Yale, OK 74085 • *1,392*
Yalobusha ⬜, MS • *12,033*
Yamhill ⬜, OR • *65,551*
Yancey ⬜, NC • *15,419*
Yanceyville, NC 27379 • *1,973*
Yankton, SD 57078 • *12,703*
Yankton ⬜, SD • *19,252*
Yaphank, NY 11980 • *5,000*
Yardley, PA 19067 • *2,288*
Yardville, NJ 08620 • *6,190*
Yarmouth, ME 04096 • *3,338*
Yarmouth, MA 02675 • *1,200*
Yarnell, AZ 85362 • *1,500*
Yates ⬜, NY • *22,810*
Yates Center, KS 66783 • *1,815*
Yavapai ⬜, AZ • *107,714*
Yazoo ⬜, MS • *25,506*
Yazoo City, MS 39194 • *12,427*
Yeadon, PA 19050 • *11,980*
Yeagertown, PA 17099 • *1,150*
Yell ⬜, AR • *17,759*
Yellow Medicine ⬜, MN • *11,684*

Yellow Springs, OH 45387 • *3,973*
Yellowstone ⬜, MT • *113,419*
Yellowstone National Park, WY 82190 • *400*
Yellowstone National Park ⬜, MT • *52*
Yellville, AR 72687 • *1,181*
Yelm, WA 98597 • *1,337*
Yerington, NV 89447 • *2,367*
Yermo, CA 92398 • *1,092*
Yoakum, TX 77995 • *5,611*
Yoakum ⬜, TX • *8,786*
Yolo ⬜, CA • *141,092*
Yonkers, NY 10701-10 • *188,082*
Yorba Linda, CA 92686 • *52,422*
York, AL 36925 • *3,160*
York, ME 03909 • *3,130*
York, NE 68467 • *7,884*
York, PA 17401-07 • *42,192*
York, SC 29745 • *6,709*
York ⬜, ME • *164,587*
York ⬜, NE • *14,428*
York ⬜, PA • *339,574*
York ⬜, SC • *131,497*
York ⬜, VA • *42,422*
Yorketown, NJ 07726 • *6,313*
York Harbor, ME 03911 • *2,555*
Yorklyn, DE 19736 • *600*
Yorkshire, NY 14173 • *1,340*
Yorktown, IN 47396 • *4,106*
Yorktown, NY 10598 • *5,270*
Yorktown, TX 78164 • *2,207*
Yorktown, VA 23690-93 • *270*
Yorktown Heights, NY 10598 • *7,690*
Yorktown Manor, RI 02852 • *2,520*
Yorkville, IL 60560 • *3,925*
Yorkville, NY 13495 • *2,972*
Yorkville, OH 43971 • *1,246*
Yosemite National Park, CA 95389 • *1,073*
Young ⬜, TX • *18,126*
Youngstown, NY 14174 • *2,075*
Youngstown, OH 44501-15 • *95,732*
Youngsville, LA 70592 • *1,195*
Youngsville, PA 16371 • *1,775*
Youngtown, AZ 85363 • *2,542*
Youngwood, PA 15697 • *3,372*
Ypsilanti, MI 48197-98 • *24,846*
Yreka, CA 96097 • *6,948*
Yuba ⬜, CA • *58,228*
Yuba City, CA 95991-92 • *27,437*
Yucaipa, CA 92399 • *20,000*
Yucca Valley, CA 92284-86 • *13,701*
Yukon, OK 73099 • *20,935*
Yulee, FL 32097 • *6,915*
Yuma, AZ 85364-69 • *54,923*
Yuma, CO 80759 • *2,719*
Yuma ⬜, AZ • *106,895*
Yuma ⬜, CO • *8,954*

Z

Zachary, LA 70791 • *9,036*
Zanesville, OH 43701-02 • *26,778*
Zapata, TX 78076 • *7,119*
Zapata ⬜, TX • *9,279*
Zavala ⬜, TX • *12,162*
Zebulon, GA 30295 • *1,035*
Zebulon, NC 27597 • *3,173*
Zeeland, MI 49464 • *5,417*
Zeigler, IL 62999 • *1,746*
Zelienople, PA 16063 • *4,158*
Zenith, WA 98188 • *1,100*
Zephyr Cove, NV 89448 • *1,700*
Zephyrhills, FL 33539-44 • *8,220*
Ziebach ⬜, SD • *2,220*
Zillah, WA 98953 • *1,911*
Zilwaukee, MI 48604 • *1,850*
Zimmerman, MN 55398 • *1,350*
Zion, IL 60099 • *19,775*
Zionsville, IN 46077 • *5,281*
Zolfo Springs, FL 33890 • *1,219*
Zumbrota, MN 55992 • *2,312*
Zuni (Zuni Pueblo), NM 87327 • *5,857*
Zwolle, LA 71486 • *1,779*